PREFACE

Language and our ideas about language change as rapidly and inevitably as the world around us. The "Information Age" we now live in has been made possible by the sophisticated technology of computers and the potential of databases for information storage and retrieval; we receive and process more information than ever before. These innovations did not exist even a generation ago. Further, the research and development of artificial intelligence systems has led to a new examination of the complex cognitive relationships human beings form between their ideas and the words they choose—how this process works, and how it can be recreated. Current lexicographical research must go beyond traditional methods and techniques to consider these new discoveries and applications in developing viable contemporary reference materials for students, linguists, and writers.

The results of recent studies on students' ability to develop reference skills show that most people learn a new word by guessing, based on context, what that word means. Combining this proven trend with the advanced theories of language gained through electronic media, I have arrived at an "onomasiological" approach to understanding American English. That is, the capability of traveling successfully from a meaning to a word instead of the only other practical method to date—the straight-forward dictionary approach of going from word to meaning. Onomasiologically, readers move from the concepts of "yellow" and "flower" to a selection of words that describe the combination, or from the notion of a "positive state of mind" to its qualities, actions, and conditions.

For the general public, we cannot believe that the printed book will go out of style within our lifetime. Indeed, its popularity is increasing. I have searched for a method of presenting this lexical theory in a format that provides diversified access within one resource. In *Roget's 21st Century Thesaurus,* the text is designed to do just that: allowing users to search both from word to meaning and from meaning to word. The dictionary format lends familiarity of use, while the Concept Index illustrates the language's semantic structure and displays links between words. The A to Z listings further amplify the resonances between words by specifying syntactic function through part-of-speech and sense division.

The result is the most complete and comprehensive selection of synonyms published in print media: *Roget's* for the 21st-century reader.

BARBARA ANN KIPFER, PH.D.

INTRODUCTION

In 1805, P. M. Roget, a British surgeon and inventor, took up a peculiar hobby: the classification of words according to ideas. His intention: to present those words in a kind of verbal catalogue that would assist writers and linguists in their search for the right manner of expression. As he worked, he perhaps had in mind the ancient Sanskrit *Amarakosha*, arguably the first arrangement of words by subject, or the French *Pasigraphie*, published in 1797, which was an attempt to order words so they could be understood universally, without translation. Roget called his own work a "thesaurus"—a Latin word meaning "treasury" or "storehouse of knowledge."

Roget's pastime became a lifelong passion and in 1852, at the age of seventy-three, Roget published his *Thesaurus of English Words and Phrases, Classified and Arranged so as to Facilitate the Expression of Ideas and Assist in Literary Composition.* This new reference book became enormously popular and a second edition appeared only a year after the first. By the time of Roget's death in 1869, there had been over twenty-five editions and printings. Today, his name is synonymous with the thesaurus.

MAKING A BETTER THESAURUS

Because Roget's thesaurus assumes contemporary users share the compiler's ideas about language, Roget's 19th-century system is a difficult one for "21st-century" readers to use to advantage. Its abstruse classifications and indexes only present modern users with an agonizing labyrinth of possibility where each route dead-ends in a disappointing and many times inappropriate selection of synonyms. Synonyms are buried in the text in a way that is arcane and nearly impenetrable. All too often, the right word remains elusive and the thesaurus remains on the shelf.

While Roget's original idea was brilliant, his eccentrically organized hierarchy of the English language is demonstrably Victorian and outdated by today's standards. For over a century, thesaurus editors have strived to redefine the nature and function of the thesaurus, and to accomplish the primary objective of combining optimum accuracy with a highly usable format. Attempts to improve Roget's thesaurus began with Roget's own son, John Lewis, who expanded the selection of synonyms. Later, Thomas Y. Crowell acquired publishing rights to the thesaurus and his 1886 edition of Roget's provided a clearer page design and format that enhanced the book's readability. Subsequent generations of Crowells have added Americanisms, foreign expressions, slang and nonstandard speech, prefixes, suffixes, and quotations. However, Roget's structure of abbreviations, categories, cross-references, and indexes has only become further complicated by an elaborately conceived type design, boldface entries, numbered paragraphs, and a decimal system that requires an explanatory diagram.

Very few successful arrangements of lexical information have been devised to access words non-alphabetically. C. O. Sylvester Mawson was the first to attempt to simplify and reorganize Roget's thesaurus in dictionary form. In 1911, he issued his own alphabetical presentation of the famous Roget system. Twentieth-century editors quickly followed his lead, eager to arrive at an easier method for frustrated thesaurus users.

But because the dictionary-style thesauri do not suggest any relationships between words beyond the simple aggregation of synonyms listed with a main entry, adoption of a strict dictionary format is but a limited improvement. Although these thesauri do offer a more straightforward presentation than the old Roget's, they neither help users organize thoughts nor do they infer broad conceptual links between ideas as expressed through language in words.

INNOVATION ON A CLASSIC THEME

Until *Roget's 21st Century Thesaurus,* no other thesaurus has been able to proficiently combine the utility of a dictionary format with the sophistication made possible by arranging words according to ideas. This revolutionary design supersedes the traditional Roget and all other thesauri as the new standard for thesaurus users. It is, simultaneously, a fast and efficient handbook for writers and a medium to facilitate the expression of ideas—both of Roget's objectives brought forward and reinterpreted for the 21st-century user.

Electronically compiled using state-of-the-art techniques, *Roget's 21st Century Thesaurus* lists 17,000 main entries or headwords in alphabetical order that generate hundreds of thousands of synonyms—more than any other thesaurus in dictionary form.

Roget's 21st Century Thesaurus is the forerunner of the latest changes in the language. The editor's final selection of main entry words and synonyms reflects modern practices of speaking and writing, and appreciates contemporary linguistic sensitivities. Dialectic and obsolete terms have been replaced by timely words and phrases recently evolved from new technologies and disciplines including computers, video equipment, biotechnology, and environmental chemistry. A nonsexist approach to language replaces outmoded epithets. Foreign words and phrases that reflect our global consciousness have been included, as well as hundreds of Americanisms. Drawing upon computer technology and recent innovations in typesetting and design, the pages are printed in a highly readable and contemporary format for ease in making skillful and effective decisions.

The synonym lists contain no superfluous cross-references, compendious usage labels, or cumbersome abbreviations to come between users and the words themselves. Like main entries, the synonym lists are arranged in alphabetical order. This is done so as not to proscribe or suggest any particular preference to the wealth of synonym choices available, and also for the user's convenience.

Synonyms that represent nonstandard usage are marked with an unobtrusive asterisk. These include both informal words and colloquial phrases and expressions common to the language.

THE CONCEPT INDEX

Thesaurus entries are enriched by directing users to related concepts in *Roget's 21st Century Thesaurus*'s Concept Index. This unique index offers users an up-to-the-minute language hierarchy that stimulates the path of thought into expression by mirroring the cognitive process of the human brain. By considering subject and concept as well as presenting an agglomeration of synonyms, *Roget's 21st Century Thesaurus*'s Concept Index actually helps writers organize their thoughts and generates possibilities for millions of word choices—far beyond the capabilities of traditional thesauri.

The Index lists over 800 individual numbered concepts to which each of the book's 17,000 headwords is referenced. The words "SEE CONCEPT(S)" appear in small caps at the end of a main entry, followed by all relevant numerical assignments of concepts for that word. When an initial search does not yield adequate results, the Concept Index automatically provides users with alternative places to look when further exploration is desired.

For example, if none of the synonyms listed with the word "scintillating" seem appropriate, the Concept Index directs the writer to concepts #401, "attributes of behavior;" #529, "cognitive qualities;" and #617, "visual brightness." Each concept gathers together scores of headwords that share the same characteristics. Persistent writers or linguists can turn back in the A to Z listing to the synonym aggregates for any of these headwords again and again to accumulate a plethora of ideas for possible word choices.

In determining concept names and classifications, the most advanced theories of communication and learning available have been applied. The word hierarchies in *Roget's 21st Century Thesaurus* have been streamlined into categories that reflect contemporary ways of thinking. There are no misunderstandings or irksome inconsistencies about what concepts mean or confusion about how they are organized. Whether performing a speedy search through concepts referenced to a main entry in the A to Z listing, or entering the index with just a vague notion in mind, users will find the Concept Index to be a fast and reliable research tool.

HOW TO USE
ROGET'S 21ST CENTURY THESAURUS

Roget's 21st Century Thesaurus's sensible format ensures swift access to the right alternatives. For quick identification, each main entry in the A to Z listing is printed in boldface; its part of speech follows in bracketed italics. Some headwords have more than one listing; separate entries are included for each different part of speech and are ordered in the following manner: noun forms, adjectives, verbs, adverbs, conjunctions, and prepositions. "Pass," for example, has 13 entries in *Roget's 21st Century Thesaurus*—four noun forms and nine verb forms. Each sense of the word "pass" is treated exclusively to help writers pinpoint the precise sense of the word desired.

Although no thesaurus is intended to replace a dictionary, concise definitions accompany main entries in order to supply users with a basic reference point and help them to evaluate synonym choices. Semicolons sometimes appear within definitions to denote fine points of sense for a word's particular usage when the discernments are too subtle to warrant a separate entry.

Remember that no two words mean *exactly* the same thing; no two words are directly interchangeable. It is the subtle nuance and flavor of particular words that give the English language its rich and various texture. While we turn to a thesaurus to find different, more expressive ways of speaking and writing, we must turn to a dictionary, a sophisticated semantic tool, to determine meaning. Always consider synonyms in their desired context and consult a dictionary if there remains any doubt about a word or phrase's application.

The Concept Index follows the alphabetical listing of headwords and begins with a reference key to its 837 concepts. The concepts appear in the index in numerical order and are divided into ten overarching categories of interest: Actions, Causes, Fields of Human Activity, Life Forms, Objects, The Planet, Qualities, Senses, States, and Weights and Measures. All main entry words grouped under a specific concept are ordered alphabetically. Headwords that denote different parts of speech appear together in these lists, allowing users to enhance their prose from more than one perspective—and to think more about the relationships between the words they choose.

TOMORROW'S CLASSIC FOR TODAY'S USER

In the minds of writers, Roget has always been the trademark of a dependable thesaurus. As we enter an era unimagined by P. M. Roget two hundred years ago, *Roget's 21st Century Thesaurus* secures that reputation. Adapting Roget's idea for his thesaurus to reflect today's concerns, this new text represents a living reference of American English.

ROGET'S
21ST CENTURY THESAURUS

A

abandon [n] *careless disregard for consequences*
disregard, freedom, impulse, licentiousness, recklessness, spontaneity, thoughtlessness, uninhibitedness, unrestraint, wantonness, wildness; SEE CONCEPTS 633,645

abandon [v1] *leave behind, relinquish*
abdicate, back out, bail out*, bow out*, chicken out*, cop out*, cut loose*, desert, discard, discontinue, ditch*, drop, drop out, duck*, dump*, dust*, flake out*, fly the coop*, give up the ship*, kiss goodbye*, leave, leg it*, let go, opt out, pull out, quit, run out on, screw*, ship out, stop, storm out*, surrender, take a powder*, take a walk*, throw over*, vacate, walk out on, wash hands of*, withdraw, yield; SEE CONCEPT 195

abandon [v2] *leave in troubled state*
back out, desert, disown, forsake, jilt, leave, leave behind, quit, reject, renounce, throw over*, walk out on; SEE CONCEPTS 7,19,195

abandoned [adj1] *left alone, deserted*
alone, cast aside, cast away, deserted, discarded, dissipated, dropped, dumped, eighty-sixed*, eliminated, empty, forgotten, forsaken, given up, godforsaken*, jilted, left, left in the cold*, left in the lurch*, neglected, on the rocks*, outcast, passed up*, pigeon-holed*, rejected, relinquished, shunned, sidelined*, side-tracked*, unoccupied, vacant, vacated; SEE CONCEPT 577

abandoned [adj2] *free from moral restraint; uninhibited*
corrupt, depraved, dissolute, immoral, incontinent, incorrigible, licentious, profligate, shameless, sinful, uncontrolled, unprincipled, unrestrained, wanton, wicked, wild; SEE CONCEPT 545

abase [v] *deprive of self-esteem, confidence*
belittle, debase, degrade, demean, diminish, disgrace, dishonor, humble, humiliate, lower, mortify, reduce, shame; SEE CONCEPTS 7,19

abashed [adj] *exhibiting mental discomfort, ill at ease*
ashamed, bewildered, bugged*, chagrined, confounded, confused, crushed, discombobulated*, disconcerted, embarrassed, fazed*, fuddled, humbled, humiliated, in a tizzy*, mortified, rattled, shamed, taken aback; SEE CONCEPT 403

abate [v] *lessen, grow or cause to grow less*
allay, chill out*, coast*, cool, cool it*, decline, decrease, diminish, dull, dwindle, ebb, go with the flow*, hang easy*, hang loose*, lay back*, let go, let it all hang out*, let up, mellow out*, moderate, quell, recede, reduce, slacken, slow, subdue, subside, take it easy*, taper, taper off, unlax*, wane; SEE CONCEPTS 240,698

abbey [n] *building that houses monks, nuns, or priests; church*
cloister, convent, friary, ministry, monastery, nunnery, priory, temple; SEE CONCEPTS 368,439

abbreviate [v1] *shorten*
abridge, abstract, boil down*, clip, compress, condense, contract, cut, cut back, cut down, cut off, cut out, digest, encapsulate, get to the meat*, pare, prune, put in a nutshell*, reduce, summarize, take out, trim; SEE CONCEPTS 236,247

abbreviate [v2] *cut short an activity*
abort, curtail, restrict, stop short, truncate; SEE CONCEPT 234

abbreviation [n] *something shortened*
abridgement, abstract, abstraction, clipping, compendium, compression, condensation, contraction, digest, outline, precis, reduction, sketch, summary, syllabus, synopsis; SEE CONCEPTS 283,652

abdicate [v] *give up a right, position, or power*
abandon, abjure, abnegate, bag it*, bail out*, cede, demit, drop, forgo, give up, leave, leave high and dry*, leave holding the bag*, leave in the lurch*, opt out*, quit, quitclaim, relinquish, renounce, resign, retire, sell out*, step down, surrender, vacate, waive, withdraw, yield; SEE CONCEPTS 133,298

abdomen [n] *the stomach and area directly below in an animate being*
bay window*, belly, bowels, breadbasket*, corporation, gut*, guts, intestines, middle, midriff, midsection, paunch, pot*, potbelly*, spare tire*, tummy, venter, viscera; SEE CONCEPT 393

abdominal [adj] *concerning the stomach and the area below it*
belly, duodenal, gastric, intestinal, stomachic, ventral, visceral; SEE CONCEPT 393

abduct [v] *take by force and without permission*
carry off, dognap*, grab, kidnap, make off with, put the snatch on*, remove, seize, shanghai*, snatch, sneeze*, spirit away*; SEE CONCEPT 139

aberrant [adj] *not normal; varying from the usual*
abnormal, atypical, bizarre, deviant, different, flaky*, mental*, nonstandard, odd, off-base, off-color, out of line*, peculiar, psycho*, strange, unusual, weird; SEE CONCEPT 547

aberration [n1] *state of abnormality*
delusion, eccentricity, oddity, peculiarity, quirk, strangeness, weirdness; SEE CONCEPT 647

aberration [n2] *different from that expected*
departure, deviation, difference, distortion, divergence, diversion, irregularity, lapse, straying, wandering; SEE CONCEPT 665

abet [v] *assist, help in wrongdoing*
advocate, back, condone, egg on*, encourage, endorse, goad, incite, instigate, prod, promote, provoke, sanction, spur, support, urge; SEE CONCEPTS 14,110

abeyance [n] *being inactive or suspended temporarily*
deferral, discontinuation, dormancy, inactivity, intermission, latency, postponement, quiescence, recess, remission, suspension, waiting; SEE CONCEPTS 681,705

abhor [v] *regard with contempt or disgust*
abominate, be allergic to*, be down on*, be grossed out by*, despise, detest, hate, have no use for*, loathe, scorn; SEE CONCEPT 29

abide [v1] *submit to, put up with*
accept, acknowledge, bear, bear with*, be big about*, concede, consent, defer, endure, hang in*, hang in there*, hang tough*, live with*, put up with*, receive, sit tight*, stand, stand for, stomach, suffer, swallow, take, tolerate, withstand; SEE CONCEPTS 23,35

abide [v2] *live in a certain place*
bide, bunk*, bunk out*, crash*, dwell, hang out*, inhabit, lodge, nest, perch, reside, room, roost, settle, squat, stay; SEE CONCEPT 226

abide [v3] *remain or continue in a state*
continue, endure, keep on, last, persevere, persist, remain, survive; SEE CONCEPTS 23,239

abide [v4] *stop temporarily and wait for*
anticipate, bide, expect, linger, pause, remain, rest, sojourn, stay, stick around*, stop, tarry, wait; SEE CONCEPTS *119,681*

abiding [adj] *continuing or existing for an indefinite time*
constant, continuing, enduring, eternal, everlasting, fast, indissoluble, lasting, permanent, perpetual, persistent, persisting, steadfast, steady; SEE CONCEPT *551*

ability [n1] *power to act, perform*
aptitude, capability, capacity, competence, competency, comprehension, dexterity, endowment, facility, faculty, intelligence, might, potentiality, qualification, resourcefulness, skill, strength, talent, understanding; SEE CONCEPT *630*

ability [n2] *natural or acquired power in a particular activity*
adeptness, adroitness, bent, capability, cleverness, command, craft, deftness, expertise, expertness, finesse, flair, genius, gift, handiness, ingenuity, knack, know-how, mastery, mind for, proficiency, savvy, skill, skillfulness, strength, talent, the goods*, the right stuff*, what it takes*; SEE CONCEPT *706*

abject [adj] *hopeless and downtrodden*
base, contemptible, degraded, dejected, deplorable, dishonorable, fawning, forlorn, groveling, hangdog, humiliated, low, miserable, outcast, pitiable, servile, submissive, worthless, wretched; SEE CONCEPT *571*

ablaze [adj1] *on fire*
afire, aflame, alight, blazing, burning, conflagrant, fiery, flaming, flaring, ignited, lighted; SEE CONCEPTS *485,605*

ablaze [adj2] *very excited*
afire, angry, aroused, enthusiastic, fervent, frenzied, fuming, furious, heated, impassioned, incensed, intense, on fire, passionate, raging, stimulated, vehement; SEE CONCEPT *550*

ablaze [adj3] *brightly illuminated*
aflame, aglow, brilliant, flashing, gleaming, glowing, incandescent, luminous, radiant, refulgent, sparkling; SEE CONCEPT *617*

able [adj1] *capable of performing; having an innate capacity*
adept, adequate, adroit, agile, alert, apt, bright, capable, competent, cunning, deft, dexterous, easy, effortless, endowed, equipped, facile, fitted, good, intelligent, knowing, powerful, ready, smart, strong, worthy; SEE CONCEPTS *402,527*

able [adj2] *able to perform well; having a proven capacity*
accomplished, adroit, agile, artful, au fait, brilliant, capable, clever, deft, dexterous, effective, effectual, efficient, equal to, experienced, expert, facile, gifted, ingenious, intelligent, keen, know backwards and forwards*, know one's onions*, know the ropes*, learned, masterful, masterly, powerful, practiced, prepared, proficient, qualified, responsible, savvy, sharp, skilled, skillful, smart, talented, there*, trained, up to it*, up to snuff*, up to speed*, with it*; SEE CONCEPTS *402,528*

able-bodied [adj] *physically strong and capable*
firm, fit, hale, hardy, healthy, hearty, lusty, powerful, robust, staunch, stout, strapping*, sturdy, vigorous; SEE CONCEPTS *314,489*

abnegation [n] *denial, renouncement of something*
abandonment, abstinence, eschewal, forbearance, giving up, nixing, refusal, rejection, relinquishment, renunciation, sacrifice, self-denial, stonewall*, surrender, temperance; SEE CONCEPTS *18,25*

abnormal [adj] *different from standard or norm*
aberrant, anomalistic, anomalous, atypical, bizarre, curious, deviant, deviate, deviating, divergent, eccentric, exceptional, extraordinary, fantastic, funny, grody*, gross, heteroclite, heterodox, heteromorphic, irregular, odd, off-base, off-color, out of line, peculiar, preternatural, queer, screwy*, spastic*, strange, uncommon, unexpected, unnatural, unorthodox, unusual, weird; SEE CONCEPT *547*

abnormality [n] *being different from standard or norm*
aberrancy, aberration, anomalism, anomaly, atypicalness, bizarreness, deformity, deviance, deviancy, deviation, eccentricity, exception, extraordinariness, flaw, irregularity, oddity, peculiarity, preternaturalness, singularity, strangeness, uncommonness, unnaturalness, unusualness, weirdness; SEE CONCEPT *647*

aboard [adj] *on or in a transportation object*
boarded, consigned, embarked, en route, in transit, loaded, on, on board, traveling; SEE CONCEPT *583*

abode [n] *building or place where one resides*
address, apartment, base, casa, condo, co-op, crash pad*, crib*, den, digs*, domicile, dwelling, flat, flop*, habitat, haunt, headquarters, hearth, hole*, home, homestead, house, joint*, lodging, pad, quarters, residence, roost*, sanctuary, seat; SEE CONCEPT *515*

abolish [v] *do away with or put an end to*
abate, abrogate, annihilate, annul, call off, cancel, destroy, disestablish, dissolve, end, eradicate, erase, expunge, extinguish, extirpate, finish, inhibit, invalidate, kill, negate, nix, nullify, obliterate, overthrow, overturn, prohibit, put an end to, put kibosh on*, put the kibosh on*, quash, repeal, repudiate, rescind, revoke, scrub*, set aside, squelch, stamp out, subvert, supersede, suppress, terminate, undo, vacate, vitiate, void, wipe out, zap*; SEE CONCEPTS *121,252,298*

abolition [n] *formal act of putting an end to, annulling*
abolishment, abrogation, annihilation, annulment, cancellation, destruction, dissolution, elimination, end, ending, eradication, extirpation, invalidation, negation, nullification, obliteration, overthrow, overturning, quashing, repeal, repudiation, rescinding, rescindment, rescission, revocation, subversion, suppression, termination, voiding, wiping out, withdrawal; SEE CONCEPTS *121,252,298*

abominable [adj] *awful, detestable*
abhorrent, atrocious, awful, bad, base, beastly, contemptible, cursed, despicable, disgusting, foul, grim, grody*, gross*, hairy*, hateful, heinous, hellish, horrible, horrid, loathsome, lousy, nauseating, obnoxious, odious, offensive, repellent, reprehensible, repugnant, repulsive, revolting, rotten, sleazy*, stinking, terrible, vile, wretched; SEE CONCEPTS *29,544,571*

abomination [n1] *object of extreme dislike, hate*
anathema, aversion, bother, curse, detestation, evil, horror, nuisance, plague, shame, torment; SEE CONCEPTS *29,666*

abomination [n2] *wrongdoing*
crime, offense, wrong; SEE CONCEPT **691**

aboriginal [adj] *belonging to one, existing in a place since prehistory*
ancient, earliest, endemic, first, indigenous, native, original, primary, primeval, primitive, primordial; SEE CONCEPT **549**

abort [v1] *stop or cancel something*
arrest, break off, call it quits*, call off, check, cut off, drop, end, fail, halt, interrupt, knock it off*, lay off*, nullify, scrap, scratch, scrub*, terminate; SEE CONCEPT **121**

abort [v2] *terminate or fail to complete pregnancy*
miscarry; SEE CONCEPTS **121,304,308**

abortion [n] *failure*
disappointment, disaster, fiasco, misadventure, premature delivery; SEE CONCEPTS **304,308,674**

abortive [adj] *failing to achieve a goal*
failed, failing, fruitless, futile, ineffective, ineffectual, miscarried, unavailing, unproductive, unsuccessful, useless, vain, worthless; SEE CONCEPT **528**

abound [v] *exist in abundance*
be alive with, be all over the place*, be knee deep in*, be no end to*, be plentiful, be thick with*, be up to one's ears in*, crawl with*, crowd, flourish, flow, have a full plate*, infest, overflow, proliferate, swarm, swell, teem, thrive; SEE CONCEPT **141**

about [adv1] *in an opposite direction*
around, back, backward, in reverse, round; SEE CONCEPT **581**

about [adv2] *lying anywhere without order, arrangement*
anyhow, any which way*, around, here and there; SEE CONCEPT **583**

about [prep1] *near an amount, quantity*
almost, approximately, in general, in the ball park*, in the neighborhood*, nearly, practically, pretty nearly, roughly; SEE CONCEPT **771**

about [prep2] *concerning, relating to*
apropos, as concerns, as respects, dealing with, in connection with, in relation to, in respect to, referring to, regarding, relative to, touching, touching on; SEE CONCEPT **532**

about [prep3] *near or close to in position*
adjacent, beside, nearby; SEE CONCEPTS **586, 778**

about [prep4] *on every side, in every direction*
around, encircling, round, surrounding, through, throughout; SEE CONCEPT **586**

about-face [n] *change in direction*
changeabout, double, doubleback, reversal, reverse, turn, turnabout, volte-face; SEE CONCEPT **697**

above [prep1] *higher in position*
aloft, atop, beyond, high, on high, on top of, over, overhead, raised, superior, upon; SEE CONCEPT **752**

above [prep2] *more, higher in amount, degree*
beyond, exceeding, greater than, larger than, over; SEE CONCEPT **793**

above [prep3] *superior to*
before, beyond, exceeding, prior to, superior to, surpassing; SEE CONCEPT **567**

aboveboard [adj] *candid*
forthright, frank, honest, open, overt, right on*, square, straight, straightforward, straight from shoulder*, true, trustworthy, truthful, up front*, veracious; SEE CONCEPT **404**

aboveboard [adv] *candidly*
frankly, honestly, on the up and up*, openly, overtly, truly, truthfully, veraciously; SEE CONCEPT **404**

abrasion [n1] *scraped area*
chafe, injury, scrape, scratch, scuff; SEE CONCEPT **309**

abrasion [n2] *scraping or wearing down by friction*
abrading, chafing, erosion, grating, rubbing, scratching, scuffing; SEE CONCEPT **186**

abrasive [adj1] *irritating in manner*
annoying, biting, caustic, cutting, galling, hard to take*, hateful, hurtful, nasty, rough, rubbing the wrong way*, sharp, spiky*, unpleasant; SEE CONCEPT **404**

abrasive [adj2] *scraping or wearing*
cutting, erosive, grinding, polishing, rough, scratching, scratchy, scuffing, sharpening, smoothing; SEE CONCEPT **606**

abreast [adv1] *next to, alongside*
beside, equal, in alignment, in line, level, opposite, shoulder to shoulder, side by side; SEE CONCEPT **586**

abreast [adv2] *up-to-date*
acquainted, au courant, au fait, contemporary, familiar, informed, in touch, knowledgeable, up*, versed; SEE CONCEPT **402**

abridge [v] *shorten*
abbreviate, abstract, blue pencil*, chop, clip, compress, concentrate, condense, contract, curtail, cut, decrease, digest, diminish, downsize, lessen, limit, narrow, put in nutshell*, reduce, restrict, slash, snip*, summarize, trim, truncate; SEE CONCEPTS **236,247**

abridgement [n] *shortening, summary*
abbreviation, abstract, brief, compendium, condensation, conspectus, contraction, curtailment, cutting, decrease, digest, diminishment, diminution, lessening, outline, precis, reducing, reduction, synopsis; SEE CONCEPTS **283,652**

abroad [adj] *in a foreign country*
away, elsewhere, in foreign lands, in foreign parts, out of the country, overseas, touring, traveling; SEE CONCEPT **583**

abrogate [v] *formally put an end to*
abate, abolish, annul, cancel, dissolve, do in*, end, finish off*, invalidate, knock out*, negate, nix, nullify, quash, reject, renege, repeal, retract, revoke, scrub*, torpedo*, undo, vacate, vitiate, void; SEE CONCEPT **121**

abrupt [adj1] *rude or brief in manner*
blunt, brusque, crude, crusty, curt, direct, discourteous, gruff, impetuous, impolite, matter-of-fact, rough, short, snappy, snippy, uncivil, ungracious; SEE CONCEPT **542**

abrupt [adj2] *happening suddenly and unexpectedly*
hasty, hurried, jerky, precipitate, precipitous, quick, rushing, sudden, surprising, unanticipated, unceremonious, unexpected, unforeseen; SEE CONCEPT **820**

abscond [v] *run away, depart secretly*
beat it*, bolt*, break, clear out*, cut and run*, decamp, disappear, dog it*, duck out, escape, fade*, flee, fly the coop*, get, go AWOL*, go south*, hightail*, jump*, leave, make a break*, make off, make scarce*, pull out, quit, run off, scram*, skedaddle*, skip out*, slip, sneak away,

split*, steal away, take off*, vamoose*, vanish; SEE CONCEPTS *102,195*

absence [*n1*] *state of not being present*
absenteeism, AWOL*, cut*, French leave*, hooky*, nonappearance, nonattendance, no show*, truancy, vacancy; SEE CONCEPT *746*

absence [*n2*] *state of lacking something needed or usual*
dearth, deficiency, drought, inadequacy, insufficiency, lack, need, omission, privation, unavailability, void, want; SEE CONCEPT *646*

absent [*adj1*] *not present*
astray, away, AWOL*, elsewhere, ghost, gone, hooky*, missing, nobody home*, no-show*, removed, vanished; SEE CONCEPT *583*

absent [*adj2*] *deficient in something needed or usual*
bare, blank, devoid, empty, hollow, lacking, minus, missing, nonexistent, omitted, unavailable, vacant, vacuous, wanting; SEE CONCEPT *546*

absentee [*adj*] *not being present*
absent, distant, oblivious, remote; SEE CONCEPTS *403,583*

absenteeism [*n*] *state of not being present*
absence, defection, desertion, skipping, truancy; SEE CONCEPT *746*

absent-minded [*adj*] *unaware of events, surroundings*
absent, absorbed, abstracted, airheaded*, bemused, daydreaming, distracted, distrait, dreaming, dreamy, engrossed, faraway, forgetful, goofing off*, heedless, inattentive, inconscient, lost, mooning*, moony*, oblivious, out to lunch*, pipe dreaming*, preoccupied, remote, removed, space cadet*, spacey*, unconscious, unheeding, unmindful, unobservant, unthinking, withdrawn, woolgathering*; SEE CONCEPT *403*

absolute [*adj1*] *without limit*
complete, consummate, downright, entire, flat out*, free, full, infinite, no catch*, no fine print*, no holds barred*, no ifs ands or buts*, no joke*, no strings attached*, outright, plenary, pure, sheer, simple, straight out, supreme, thorough, total, unabridged, unadulterated, unconditional, unlimited, unqualified, unrestricted, utter; SEE CONCEPT *554*

absolute [*adj2*] *in control or complete authority*
absolutist, arbitrary, authoritarian, autocratic, autonomous, despotic, dictatorial, full, monocratic, preeminent, sovereign, supreme, totalitarian, tyrannical, tyrannous; SEE CONCEPT *536*

absolute [*adj3*] *certain*
actual, categorical, conclusive, consummate, decided, decisive, definite, exact, factual, fixed, genuine, infallible, positive, precise, sure, unambiguous, undeniable, unequivocal, unmitigated, unquestionable; SEE CONCEPT *535*

absolute [*adj4*] *excellent, perfect*
categorical, complete, faultless, flawless, ideal, impeccable, thorough, ultimate, unblemished, unflawed, untarnished; SEE CONCEPT *574*

absolutely [*adv1*] *certainly, without question*
actually, categorically, come hell or high water*, conclusively, decidedly, decisively, definitely, doubtless, easily, exactly, for sure*, no ifs ands or buts*, no strings attached*, on the button*, on the money*, on the nose*, positively, precisely, really, right on*, straight out*, sure as can be*, sure as hell*, sure enough*, surely, sure thing*, the very thing*, truly, unambiguously, unconditionally, unquestionably; SEE CONCEPT *535*

absolutely [*adv2*] *in a complete manner, degree*
completely, consummately, entirely, fully, thoroughly, utterly, wholly; SEE CONCEPT *531*

absolve [*v*] *free from responsibility, duty*
acquit, bleach, blink at, clear, discharge, exculpate, excuse, exempt, exonerate, forgive, free, go easy on, launder*, let off*, let off easy*, let off the hook*, let up on*, liberate, lifeboat*, loose, pardon, release, relieve, sanitize*, set free, spare, spring*, vindicate, whitewash, wink at*, wipe it off*, wipe the slate clean*, write off*; SEE CONCEPTS *83,317*

absorb [*v1*] *physically take in a liquid*
blot, consume, devour, drink in, imbibe, ingest, ingurgitate, osmose, soak up, sop up*, sponge up*, suck in*, swallow, take in; SEE CONCEPT *256*

absorb [*v2*] *mentally take in information*
assimilate, comprehend, digest, follow, get, get into*, grasp, incorporate, latch onto, learn, sense, soak up, take in, understand; SEE CONCEPT *31*

absorb [*v3*] *occupy complete attention*
captivate, concern, consume, employ, engage, engross, fascinate, fill, hold, immerse, involve, monopolize, obsess, preoccupy, rivet; SEE CONCEPT *17*

absorbed [*adj*] *being completely occupied mentally*
captivated, consumed, deep in thought, engaged, engrossed, fascinated, fixed, gone*, head over heels*, held, immersed, intent, involved, lost, preoccupied, rapt, really into*, up to here*, wrapped up*; SEE CONCEPT *403*

absorbent [*adj*] *capable of physically taking in a liquid*
absorptive, bibulous, dry, imbibing, penetrable, permeable, porous, pregnable, retentive, spongy, thirsty; SEE CONCEPT *603*

absorbing [*adj*] *holding one's attention*
arresting, captivating, consuming, engrossing, enthralling, exciting, fascinating, gripping, interesting, intriguing, monopolizing, preoccupying, riveting, spellbinding; SEE CONCEPT *403*

absorption [*n1*] *assimilation, incorporation*
consumption, digestion, drinking in, exhaustion, fusion, imbibing, impregnation, ingestion, inhalation, intake, osmosis, penetration, reception, retention, saturation, soaking up, suction, taking in; SEE CONCEPTS *169,256*

absorption [*n2*] *total attention toward something*
captivation, concentration, engagement, engrossment, enthrallment, fascination, hang-up*, holding, immersion, intentness, involvement, occupation, preoccupation, raptness; SEE CONCEPT *410*

abstain [*v*] *hold back from doing*
abjure, abnegate, avoid, cease, constrain, curb, decline, deny oneself, do without, eschew, evade, fast, fence-sit*, forbear, forgo, give the go by*, give up, go on the wagon*, keep from, pass, pass up, quit, refrain, refuse, renounce, shun, sit on one's hands*, sit on the fence*, sit out, spurn, starve, stop, take the cure*, take the pledge*, withhold; SEE CONCEPTS *25,121*

abstemious [*adj*] *restraining behavior or appetite*
abstinent, ascetic, austere, continent, frugal, moderate, moderating, restrained, self-denying, self-

restrained, sober, sparing, temperate; SEE CONCEPT *401*

abstinence [n] *restraint from desires, especially physical desires*
abnegation, abstaining, abstemiousness, asceticism, avoidance, chastity, continence, fasting, forbearance, frugality, moderation, refraining, renunciation, self-control, self-denial, self-restraint, soberness, sobriety, teetotalism, temperance; SEE CONCEPT *633*

abstract [n] *short document prepared from a longer one*
abridgment, brief, compendium, condensation, conspectus, digest, outline, precis, résumé, summary, synopsis; SEE CONCEPT *283*

abstract [adj] *conceptual, theoretical*
abstruse, complex, deep, hypothetical, ideal, indefinite, intellectual, nonconcrete, philosophical, recondite, transcendent, transcendental, unreal; SEE CONCEPT *582*

abstract [v1] *take away from*
detach, disconnect, disengage, dissociate, extract, isolate, part, remove, separate, steal, take out, uncouple, withdraw; SEE CONCEPTS *135,211*

abstract [v2] *prepare short document from longer one*
abbreviate, abridge, condense, digest, outline, review, shorten, summarize; SEE CONCEPTS *79,236,247*

abstraction [n] *state of being lost in thought*
absorption, aloofness, brooding, cogitation, consideration, contemplation, daydreaming, detachment, engrossment, entrancement, musing, pensiveness, pondering, preoccupation, reflecting, reflection, remoteness, reverie, ruminating, thinking, trance; SEE CONCEPT *410*

abstruse [adj] *difficult to understand*
abstract, clear as dishwater*, complex, complicated, deep, enigmatic, esoteric, Greek to me*, heavy*, hidden, incomprehensible, intricate, involved, muddy, obscure, perplexing, profound, puzzling, recondite, subtle, unfathomable, vague; SEE CONCEPTS *402,562*

absurd [adj] *ridiculous, senseless*
batty, campy, crazy, daffy, dippy*, flaky*, fooling around, foolish, for grins*, freaky, gagged up*, goofy*, idiotic, illogical, inane, incongruous, irrational, jokey, joshing, laughable, loony, ludicrous, nonsensical, nutty, off the wall*, preposterous, sappy*, screwy*, silly, stupid, tomfool, unreasonable, wacky; SEE CONCEPTS *544,552,558*

absurdity [n] *ridiculous situation or behavior*
applesauce*, BS*, bull*, crap*, craziness, farce, flapdoodle*, folly, foolishness, hot air*, idiocy, illogicality, illogicalness, improbability, inanity, incongruity, insanity, irrationality, jazz*, jive*, ludicrousness, ridiculousness, senselessness, silliness, stupidity, unreasonableness; SEE CONCEPTS *650,656*

abundance [n] *great amount or supply*
affluence, ampleness, bounty, copiousness, fortune, myriad, opulence, plenitude, plenty, plethora, profusion, prosperity, prosperousness, riches, thriving, wealth; SEE CONCEPTS *710,767*

abundant [adj] *plentiful, large in number*
abounding, ample, bounteous, bountiful, copious, crawling with*, cup runs over with*, eco-rich, exuberant, filled, full, generous, heavy, lavish, liberal, lousy with*, luxuriant, mucho*, no end

of*, overflowing, plate is full of*, plenteous, plenty, profuse, rich, rolling in*, stinking with*, sufficient, teeming; SEE CONCEPT *781*

abuse [n1] *wrong use*
corruption, crime, debasement, delinquency, desecration, exploitation, fault, injustice, misapplication, misconduct, misdeed, mishandling, mismanage, misuse, offense, perversion, prostitution, sin, wrong, wrongdoing; SEE CONCEPT *156*

abuse [n2] *physical hurting, injuring*
crime, damage, defilement, harm, hurt, impairment, injury, malevolence, maltreatment, manhandling, misdeed, offense, pollution, violation, wrongdoing; SEE CONCEPT *246*

abuse [n3] *verbal attack*
bad-mouthing*, blame, castigation, censure, curse, curses*, defamation, derision, hosing*, insults, invective, kicking around*, knifing*, libel, obloquy, opprobrium, pushing around*, putdown, quinine*, reproach, revilement, scolding, signifying, slander, swearing, tirade, upbraiding, vilification, vituperation; SEE CONCEPT *54*

abuse [v1] *physically hurt or injure*
bang up*, beat up, bung up*, corrupt, cut up*, damage, defile, deprave, desecrate, harm, hose*, ill-treat, impair, maltreat, mar, mess up*, mishandle, mistreat, misuse, molest, oppress, persecute, pollute*, roughhouse, rough up, ruin, shake up*, spoil, taint, total*, victimize, violate, wax*; SEE CONCEPT *246*

abuse [v2] *use wrongly*
dissipate, exhaust, misemploy, mishandle, misuse, overburden, overtax, overwork, prostitute, spoil, squander, taint, waste; SEE CONCEPT *156*

abuse [v3] *attack with words*
backbite, bad-mouth, bash, belittle, berate, blow off*, calumniate, cap*, castigate, cuss out*, cut down*, cut to the quick*, decry, defame, derogate, discount, do a number on*, dump on*, give a black eye*, hurl brickbat*, insult, knock*, minimize, nag, offend, oppress, persecute, pick on, put down*, rag on*, reproach, revile, ride*, rip up*, run down*, scold, signify, slam*, slap*, sling mud*, smear*, sound*, swear at*, tear apart*, trash*, upbraid, vilify, vituperate, zing*; SEE CONCEPTS *52,54*

abuse [v4] *take advantage of*
do an injustice to, exploit, impose on, use, wrong; SEE CONCEPTS *156,384*

abusive [adj] *exhibiting unkind behavior or words*
calumniating, castigating, censorious, contumelious, defamatory, derisive, disparaging, insolent, insulting, invective, libelous, maligning, obloquious, offensive, opprobrious, reproachful, reviling, rude, sarcastic, scathing, scolding, scurrilous, sharp-tongued, slanderous, traducing, upbraiding, vilifying, vituperative; SEE CONCEPT *267*

abut [v] *touch or be next to something*
adjoin, be adjacent to, border on, butt against, join, neighbor; SEE CONCEPT *749*

abysmal [adj1] *great extent; immeasurable*
bottomless, boundless, complete, deep, endless, extreme, illimitable, incalculable, infinite, profound, thorough, unending, unfathomable, vast; SEE CONCEPTS *772,793*

abysmal [adj2] *extending deeply*
bottomless, fathomless, plumbless, plummetless; SEE CONCEPT *777*

abyss [n] *something very deep, usually a feature of land*
abysm, chasm, crevasse, depth, fissure, gorge, gulf, hole, pit, void; SEE CONCEPTS **509,514**

academic [n] *scholar or university/college teacher*
academician, lecturer, professor, pupil, scholar, scholastic, student, tutor; SEE CONCEPT **350**

academic [adj1] *relating to schooling, learning*
bookish, book-learned, college, collegiate, erudite, intellectual, learned, pedantic, scholarly, scholastic, studious, university; SEE CONCEPT **536**

academic [adj2] *relating to theories, philosophy*
abstract, closet, conjectural, formalistic, hypothetical, notional, speculative, theoretical; SEE CONCEPTS **402,529**

academy [n1] *school, especially for higher education*
boarding school, brainery*, finishing school, halls of ivy*, institute, military school, preparatory school, prep school, secondary school, seminary; SEE CONCEPT **289**

academy [n2] *society or institution interested in learning*
alliance, association, circle, council, federation, foundation, fraternity, institute, league; SEE CONCEPT **288**

accede [v] *agree or consent*
accept, acquiesce, admit, allow, assent, be game for*, cave in*, comply, concede, concur, cooperate, cry uncle*, endorse, enter into, fold, give the go-ahead*, give the green light*, go along with, grant, let, okay, permit, play ball*, roll over and play dead*, subscribe, throw in the towel*, yield; SEE CONCEPTS **8,50,82,88**

accelerate [v] *increase speed, timing*
advance, drive, dust*, expedite, fire up*, forward, further, gun*, hammer on*, hasten, hurry, impel, lay a patch*, lay rubber*, make tracks*, nail it*, open up*, peel rubber*, precipitate, put on afterburners*, put pedal to metal*, quicken, railroad*, rev, rev up, roll*, speed up, spur, step on gas*, step up, stimulate, tool*; SEE CONCEPTS **234,242**

acceleration [n] *increasing speed, timing*
dispatch, expedition, hastening, hurrying, quickening, speeding up, spurring, stepping up, stimulation; SEE CONCEPT **234**

accent [n1] *importance, emphasis*
significance, stress, weight; SEE CONCEPT **668**

accent [n2] *stress or pitch in pronunciation*
accentuation, articulation, beat, cadence, emphasis, enunciation, force, inflection, intonation, meter, modulation, pronunciation, rhythm, stroke, timbre, tonality, tone; SEE CONCEPT **77**

accent [v] *place emphasis, importance*
accentuate, draw attention to, emphasize, highlight, intensify, stress, underline, underscore; SEE CONCEPTS **69,243**

accept [v1] *receive something given physically*
acquire, gain, get, obtain, secure, take, welcome; SEE CONCEPT **124**

accept [v2] *allow into group*
admit, receive, welcome; SEE CONCEPT **384**

accept [v3] *believe the goodness, realness of something*
acknowledge, affirm, approbate, approve, buy*, countenance, fancy, favor, go for*, hold, hold with, like, recognize, relish, swallow*, take as gospel truth*, take stock in*, trust; SEE CONCEPT **12**

accept [v4] *put up with*
acknowledge, acquiesce, agree, assent, bear, bear with, bow, capitulate, defer to, don't make waves*, don't rock the boat*, endure, fit in, go along with, live with, play the game*, recognize, respect, sit still for*, stand, stand for, stomach, submit to, suffer, swallow, take, tolerate, yield to; SEE CONCEPT **23**

accept [v5] *receive by agreeing, consenting*
accede, acknowledge, acquiesce, admit, adopt, affirm, agree to, approve, assent, assume, avow, bear, buy, check out*, comply, concur with, cooperate with, give stamp of approval*, give the go-ahead*, give the green light*, give the nod*, go for*, lap up*, okay; recognize, rubber-stamp*, set store by*, sign, sign off on*, take on*, take one up on*, thumbs up*, undertake; SEE CONCEPTS **8,82**

acceptable [adj] *satisfactory, agreeable*
adequate, admissible, all right, A-OK*, average, big*, common, cooking with gas*, cool*, copacetic, decent, delightful, fair, hep*, hip*, hunky-dory*, in the swim*, kosher*, large, okay, on the ball*, on the beam*, passable, peachy keen*, pleasant, pleasing, respectable, right on*, standard, sufficient, swell*, tolerable, trendy, unexceptional, unobjectionable, up to code*, up to snuff*, welcome; SEE CONCEPTS **533,558**

acceptance [n1] *agreement, taking*
accepting, acknowledgment, acquiring, admission, approval, assent, compliance, consent, cooperation, gaining, getting, go-ahead*, green light*, nod*, obtaining, okay, permission, receipt, receiving, reception, recognition, securing, taking on, undertaking, yes; SEE CONCEPTS **8,124**

acceptance [n2] *belief in goodness of something*
accedence, accession, acknowledgment, acquiescence, admission, adoption, affirmation, agreement, approbation, approval, assent, concession, concurrence, favor, recognition, seal of approval; SEE CONCEPTS **12,32**

accepted [adj] *generally agreed upon*
accustomed, acknowledged, allowed, approved, arrived at, authorized, card-carrying*, chosen, confirmed, conventional, credited, current, customary, endorsed, established, fashionable, in vogue, kosher*, legit*, normal, okayed, orthodox, passed, popular, preferred, received, recognized, regular, sanctioned, standard, straight*, time-honored, touted, universal, unopposed, usual, welcomed; SEE CONCEPTS **547,558**

access [n] *admission, means of entry, approach*
admittance, approach, avenue, connection, contact, course, door, entrance, entree, entry, in, ingress, introduction, key, open arms*, open door*, passage, path, road, route, way; SEE CONCEPTS **501,631**

accessible [adj] *approachable; ready for use*
attainable, available, door's always open*, employable, exposed, getatable, handy, near, obtainable, open, operative, possible, practicable, public, reachable, susceptible, unrestricted, usable; SEE CONCEPT **576**

accession [n1] *something that augments, adds to*
accretion, addition, augmentation, enlargement, extension, increase, increment, raise, rise; SEE CONCEPTS **700,775**

accession [n2] *coming to power*
assumption, attainment, inauguration, induction,

investment, succession, taking on, taking over; SEE CONCEPTS **133,298**

accession [n3] *agreement*
accedence, acceptance, acquiescence, assent, concurrence, consent; SEE CONCEPTS **8,410**

accessory [n1] *ornament; accompanying item; supplementary part*
accent, addition, adjunct, adornment, appendage, appendix, appliance, appurtenance, attachment, component, decoration, extension, extra, frill, help, supplement, trim, trimming; SEE CONCEPT **834**

accessory [n2] *person peripherally involved in illegal activity*
abettor, accomplice, aid, aide, assistant, associate, co-conspirator, colleague, confederate, conspirator, helper, insider, partner, plant*, ringer*, shill*, stall*, subordinate; SEE CONCEPT **412**

accident [n1] *unexpected, undesirable event; often physically injurious*
blow, calamity, casualty, collision, crack-up*, disaster, fender-bender*, fluke*, hazard, misadventure, misfortune, mishap, pileup*, rear ender*, setback, smash*, smashup*, stack-up*, total*, wrack-up*; SEE CONCEPT **674**

accident [n2] *chance event*
adventure, circumstance, contingency, fate, fluke*, fortuity, fortune, happening, luck, occasion, occurrence, turn; SEE CONCEPT **679**

accidental [adj] *happening unexpectedly*
adventitious, casual, chance, coincidental, contingent, fluky*, fortuitous, inadvertent, incidental, random, uncalculated, unexpected, unforeseen, unintended, unintentional, unplanned; SEE CONCEPTS **530,552**

acclaim [n] *expression of approval*
acclamation, acknowledgment, applause, approbation, celebration, cheering, clapping, commendation, eulogizing, exaltation, honor, kudos, pat on the back*, pat on the head*, plaudits, PR, praise, puff, pumping up*, rave, recognition, strokes*, stroking*; SEE CONCEPT **69**

acclaim [v] *give approval*
applaud, approve, blow horn*, boost, celebrate, cheer, clap, commend, complement, eulogize, exalt, extol, give a bouquet*, give a posy*, give kudos*, hail, hand it to*, hear it for*, honor, laud, praise, puff up*, push*, rave, recommend, root, salute, stroke*; SEE CONCEPT **69**

acclamation [n] *enthusiastic expression of approval*
acclaim, adulation, applause, approbation, big hand*, cheer, cheering, cheers, hand, honor, jubilation, laudation, ovation, plaudits, salutation, standing O*, tribute; SEE CONCEPTS **69,377**

acclimate [v] *make or become adjusted, adapted*
acclimatize, accommodate, acculture, accustom, climatize, conform, get used to, habituate, harden, season, toughen; SEE CONCEPTS **202,701**

accolade [n] *strong praise, recognition of achievement*
approval, award, badge, decoration, distinction, honor, kudos*, laurels; SEE CONCEPT **69**

accommodate [v1] *make room, lodging available*
board, contain, domicile, entertain, furnish, harbor, hold, house, put up*, quarter, receive, rent, shelter, supply, take in, welcome; SEE CONCEPT **226**

accommodate [v2] *make, become suitable for something*
accord, accustom, adapt, adjust, agree, attune, bend over backwards*, comply, compose, conform, coordinate, correspond, don't make waves*, don't rock the boat*, fit, go by the book*, go with the flow*, harmonize, integrate, make consistent, modify, play the game*, proportion, reconcile, settle, shape up, suit, tailor, tailor-make, tune; SEE CONCEPTS **23,126**

accommodate [v3] *perform service*
afford, aid, arrange, assist, avail, benefit, bow, comfort, convenience, defer, favor, furnish, gratify, help, humor, indulge, oblige, pamper, please, provide, serve, settle, submit, suit, supply, support, sustain, yield; SEE CONCEPT **136**

accommodating [adj] *willing to help*
considerate, cooperative, friendly, generous, handy, helpful, hospitable, kind, neighborly, obliging, on deck*, on tap*, polite, unselfish, user friendly*; SEE CONCEPTS **542,555**

accommodation [n] *adjustment for different situation, circumstances*
adaptation, compliance, composition, compromise, conformity, fifty-fifty deal*, fitting, modification, reconciliation, settlement; SEE CONCEPT **697**

accommodations [n] *place of residence, usually temporary*
apartment, board, boardinghouse, crash pad*, crib*, digs*, hotel, house, housing, lodging, motel, pad*, quarters, roof, room and board, rooming house, rooms, shelter; SEE CONCEPT **516**

accompaniment [n1] *necessary part or embellishment*
accessory, adjunct, appendage, appurtenance, attachment, attendant, attribute, augmentation, complement, concomitant, enhancement, enrichment, supplement; SEE CONCEPTS **834,835**

accompaniment [n2] *music that supports a theme or performer in a composition*
back, background, backing, back-up, harmony, instrument, part; SEE CONCEPT **262**

accompany [v1] *go or be with something*
associate with, attend, chaperon, come along, conduct, consort, convoy, date, dog*, draft*, drag*, escort, follow, go along, guard, guide, hang around with*, hang out*, keep company, lead, look after, shadow, shlep along*, show about, show around, spook, squire, stick to*, string along*, tag along*, tailgate*, take out, usher; SEE CONCEPTS **113,224**

accompany [v2] *occur with something*
add, appear with, append, be connected, belong to, characterize, coexist, coincide with, come with, complete, co-occur, follow, go together, happen with, join with, occur with, supplement, take place with; SEE CONCEPT **643**

accomplice [n] *helper, especially in committing a crime*
abettor, accessory, aid, aide, ally, assistant, associate, co-conspirator, collaborator, colleague, confederate, conspirator, insider, partner, plant*, stall*; SEE CONCEPT **412**

accomplish [v] *succeed in doing*
achieve, arrive, attain, bring about, bring off, carry out, conclude, consummate, do, do a bang-up job*, do justice*, do one proud*, do the trick*, effect, finish, fulfill, gain, get someplace*, get there*, hit*, make hay*, make it, manage, nail

it*, perform, produce, pull off*, put it over*, rack up*, reach, realize, score*, sew up*, take care of, win; SEE CONCEPTS 91,706

accomplished [adj] skilled in activity
able, adept, brainy, consummate, cool*, cultivated, expert, gifted, hep*, hip*, masterly, polished, practiced, proficient, savvy, sharp, skillful, talented, wised up*, with it*; SEE CONCEPTS 326,528

accomplishment [n] something successfully done, completed
ability, achievement, act, art, attainment, bringing about, capability, carrying out, completion, conclusion, consummation, coup, deed, effecting, effort, execution, exploit, feat, finish, fulfillment, performance, production, proficiency, realization, skill, stroke, talent, triumph; SEE CONCEPT 706

accord [n] agreement, mutual understanding (often written)
accordance, concert, concord, concurrence, conformity, congruence, correspondence, deal, good vibes*, good vibrations*, harmony, okay, pact, rapport, reconciliation, sympathy, 10-4*, treaty, unanimity; SEE CONCEPT 684

accord [v1] give approval, grant
accede, acquiesce, admit, allow, award, bestow, concede, confer, endow, give, present, render, tender, vouchsafe; SEE CONCEPTS 50,83,88

accord [v2] come to agreement
affirm, agree, assent, be in tune, concur, conform, correspond, fit, harmonize, jibe, match, square, suit, tally; SEE CONCEPTS 8,664

accordingly [adv] in an appropriate, suitable way
appropriately, as a consequence, as a result, consequently, correspondingly, duly, equally, ergo, fitly, hence, in consequence, in respect to, in that event, properly, proportionately, respectively, resultantly, so, subsequently, suitably, then, therefore, thus, under the circumstances; SEE CONCEPT 558

accost [v] approach for conversation or solicitation
address, annoy, bother, brace*, buttonhole*, call, challenge, confront, cross, dare, entice, face, flag, greet, hail, proposition, run into, salute, welcome, whistle for*; SEE CONCEPTS 48,51

account [n1] written description of past events
ABCs*, annal, blow by blow*, bulletin, chronicle, detail, explanation, history, lowdown*, make*, narration, narrative, play by play*, recital, report, run-down, score, story, tab, take, tale, the picture*, the whole picture*; version; SEE CONCEPT 282

account [n2] record of finances, fees, or charges
bad news*, balance, bill, book, books, charge, check, computation, cuff*, grunt*, inventory, invoice, IOU*, ledger, reckoning, record, register, report, score, statement, tab, tally; SEE CONCEPTS 331,332

account [n3] basis or consideration for action
cause, ground, grounds, interest, justification, motive, rationale, rationalization, reason, regard, sake; SEE CONCEPT 229

accountable [adj] responsible for having done
answerable, charged with, culpable, liable, obligated, obliged, on the hook*; SEE CONCEPT 527

accountant [n] person who maintains financial accounts of a business
actuary, analyst, auditor, bookkeeper, calculator, cashier, clerk, comptroller, CPA, examiner, public accountant, reckoner, teller; SEE CONCEPTS 348,353

account for [v] offer reason, explanation
answer for, clarify, elucidate, explain, illuminate, justify, rationalize, resolve; SEE CONCEPT 57

accredit [v1] attribute responsibility or achievement
ascribe, assign, charge, credit, refer; SEE CONCEPTS 49,69

accredit [v2] give authorization or control
appoint, approve, authorize, certify, commission, empower, enable, endorse, entrust, guarantee, license, okay, recognize, sanction, vouch for; SEE CONCEPTS 50,88

accretion [n] gradual growth, addition
accession, accumulation, augmentation, build-up, increase, increment, raise, rise; SEE CONCEPT 780

accrue [v] increase by addition or growth, often financial
accumulate, amass, build up, collect, enlarge, flow, gather, grow, increase; SEE CONCEPTS 763,780

accumulate [v] gather or amass something
accrue, acquire, add to, agglomerate, aggregate, amalgamate, assemble, bring together, cache, clean up*, collect, collocate, compile, concentrate, cumulate, draw together, expand, gain, gather, grow, heap, heap together, hoard, incorporate, increase, load up*, lump*, make a bundle*, make a killing*, mass, pile*, pile up*, procure, profit, rack up* roll up*, round up*, scare up*, stack up, stockpile, store, store up, swell, unite; SEE CONCEPTS 236,245

accumulation [n] gathering or amassing
accession, accretion, addition, agglomeration, aggrandizement, agglutination, amassment, augmentation, build-up, chunk, collecting, collection, conglomeration, enlargement, gob, growth, heap, hoarding, hunk, increase, inflation, intensification, mass, multiplication, pile, quantity, stack, stock, store, trove, up, upping; SEE CONCEPTS 432,780

accuracy [n] precision or correctness
accurateness, carefulness, certainty, closeness, definiteness, definitiveness, definitude, efficiency, exactitude, exactness, faultlessness, incisiveness, mastery, meticulousness, preciseness, sharpness, skill, skillfulness, strictness, sureness, truthfulness, veracity, verity; SEE CONCEPTS 638,654

accurate [adj1] precise
authentic, careful, close, concrete, correct, defined, definite, deft, detailed, discriminating, discriminative, distinct, exact, explicit, factual, faithful, genuine, judicious, just, literal, matter-of-fact, methodical, meticulous, on the button*, on the money*, on the nose*, particular, proper, punctilious, punctual, regular, right, rigid, rigorous, scientific, scrupulous, severe, sharp, skillful, solid, specific, strict, systematic, true, ultraprecise, unerring, unmistakable, veracious; SEE CONCEPT 535

accurate [adj2] correct, without error
absolute, actual, authentic, authoritative, certain, conclusive, definite, definitive, errorless, exact, factual, faultless, final, flawless, genuine, infallible, irrefutable, official, perfect, right, straight, strict, true, truthful, undeniable, undisputed, unimpeachable, unquestionable, unrefuted, valid, veracious; SEE CONCEPT 557

accusation [n] *charge of wrongdoing, fault*
allegation, arraignment, attribution, beef*, blast*, bum rap*, censure, citation, complaint, denunciation, dido, exposé, gripe, impeachment, imputation, incrimination, indictment, insinuation, recrimination, roar*, rumble*, slur, squawk*, stink*; SEE CONCEPT 54

accuse [v] *place blame for wrongdoing, fault*
allege, apprehend, arraign, arrest, attack, attribute, betray, blame, blow the whistle*, brand, bring charges, censure, charge, cite, complain, criminate, denounce, file claim, finger*, frame, hang something on*, hold accountable, impeach, implicate, impute, incriminate, inculpate, indict, lay at door*, let have it*, libel, litigate, lodge complaint, name, pin on*, point finger at*, prosecute, recriminate, serve summons, slander, slur, sue, summon, tax; SEE CONCEPT 44

accustomed [adj1] *be or become prepared, used to*
acclimatized, acquainted, adapted, addicted, confirmed, disciplined, familiar, familiarized, given to, grooved*, habituated, habituated in, in the habit, inured, seasoned, settled in, trained; SEE CONCEPT 403

accustomed [adj2] *normal, usual*
accepted, chronic, common, conventional, customary, established, everyday, expected, general, habitual, ordinary, orthodox, regular, routine, set, traditional, typical; SEE CONCEPT 547

ace [n] *expert in some activity*
champion, genius, master, pro, star, virtuoso, winner, wizard; SEE CONCEPT 416

ace [adj] *exhibiting expertise in some activity*
brilliant, champion, distinguished, excellent, expert, first-rate, great, master, outstanding, superb, virtuoso; SEE CONCEPT 528

acerbity [n1] *bitterness of taste*
acidity, asperity, astringency, mordancy, sourness, tartness; SEE CONCEPTS 462,613

acerbity [n2] *harsh speech, behavior*
acrimoniousness, causticity, ill temper, irritability, rancor, rudeness, sarcasm, sarcasticness, vitriolicism; SEE CONCEPTS 267,401

ache [n] *sore feeling; dull pain*
anguish, hurt, misery, pang, pounding, smarting, soreness, spasm, suffering, throb, throbbing, throe, twinge; SEE CONCEPTS 316,410,728

ache [v] *feeling soreness or dull pain, often physical*
be sore, hurt, pain, pound, smart, suffer, throb, twinge; SEE CONCEPTS 13,17,303,308,313

achieve [v] *bring to successful conclusion; reach a goal*
accomplish, acquire, actualize, attain, bring about, bring off*, bring to pass, cap, carry out, carry through, close, complete, conclude, consummate, deliver, discharge, dispatch, do, earn, earn wings*, effect, effectuate, enact, end, execute, finish, follow through, fulfill, gain, get, get done, manage, negotiate, obtain, perfect, perform, procure, produce, rack up*, reach, realize, resolve, score, seal, see through, settle, sign, solve, win, wind up, work out; SEE CONCEPT 706

achievement [n] *something completed successfully; goal reached*
accomplishment, acquirement, acquisition, act, actualization, attainment, completion, conquest, consummation, contrivance, creation, deed, effectuation, effort, enactment, encompassment, execution, exploit, feat, fulfillment, hit, masterpiece,

performance, production, realization, stroke, success, tour de force, triumph, victory; SEE CONCEPT 706

acid [adj1] *bitter, sour in taste*
acerbic, acidulous, biting, piquant, pungent, sharp, tart, vinegarish, vinegary; SEE CONCEPT 613

acid [adj2] *having acidic, corrosive properties*
acerbic, acidulous, acrid, anti-alkaline, biting, bleaching, corroding, disintegrative, dissolvent, eating away, eroding, erosive, oxidizing, rusting; SEE CONCEPT 485

acid [adj3] *bitter in words or behavior*
acerbic, biting, caustic, cutting, dry, harsh, hateful, hurtful, mordant, nasty, offensive, sarcastic, sharp, stinging, trenchant, vitriolic; SEE CONCEPTS 267,401

acidulous [adj1] *bitter, sour*
acerb, acidulous, acetose, dry, piquant, sharp, tart; SEE CONCEPT 613

acidulous [adj2] *bitter in speech*
biting, cutting, ironical, mocking, sarcastic; SEE CONCEPT 267

acknowledge [v1] *verbally recognize authority*
accede, accept, acquiesce, agree, allow, approve, attest to, certify, defend, defer to, endorse, grant, own, ratify, recognize, subscribe to, support, take an oath, uphold, yield; SEE CONCEPTS 8,50,88

acknowledge [v2] *admit truth or reality of something*
accede, accept, acquiesce, allow, avow, come clean*, come out of closet*, concede, confess, cop a plea*, crack*, declare, fess up*, get off chest*, grant, let on*, open up*, own, profess, recognize, yield; SEE CONCEPTS 12,49

acknowledge [v3] *verbally recognize receipt of something*
address, answer, greet, hail, notice, react, remark, reply, respond, return, salute, thank; SEE CONCEPTS 38,45,51,60

acknowledgment [n1] *act of recognizing authority or truth of something*
acceptance, accession, acquiescence, admission, admitting, affirmation, allowance, allowing, assent, assertion, asseveration, avowal, compliance, conceding, concession, concurrence, confession, confirmation, corroboration, declaration, profession, ratification, realization, recognition, yielding; SEE CONCEPTS 8,50,88

acknowledgment [n2] *physical symbol of recognition*
acclamation, addressing, answer, apology, applause, appreciation, bestowal, bow, card, confession, contract, credit, gift, gratitude, greeting, guarantee, hail, hailing, letter, nod, notice, reaction, receipt, reply, response, return, salutation, salute, signature, statement, support, thanks, token; SEE CONCEPTS 595,628

acme [n] *pinnacle of achievement or physical object*
apogee, capstone, climax, culmination, height, highest point, high point, meridian, optimum, peak, summit, top, ultimate, vertex, zenith; SEE CONCEPTS 706,836

acolyte [n] *attendant, usually in a church*
aid, assistant, follower, helper; SEE CONCEPT 361

acquaint [v] *inform oneself or another about something new*
accustom, advise, apprise, bring out, clue, come out with*, disclose, divulge, enlighten, familiar-

ize, fill in, fix up*, get together*, habituate, inform, intro*, introduce, knock down*, let know, make familiar, notify, post, present, reveal, tell, warn; SEE CONCEPTS *31,60*

acquaintance [n1] *a person known informally*
associate, association, colleague, companion, contact, friend, neighbor; SEE CONCEPT *423*

acquaintance [n2] *knowledge of something through experience*
awareness, cognizance, conversance, familiarity, fellowship, grasp, intimacy, ken, relationship, understanding; SEE CONCEPT *409*

acquiesce [v] *agree with some reluctance*
accede, accept, accommodate, adapt, adjust, agree, allow, approve, bow to, buy, cave in*, come across, come around, comply, concur, conform, consent, cry uncle*, cut a deal*, ditto*, give in, give out, go along, jibe*, okay, pass, play ball*, reconcile, roll over and play dead*, say uncle*, set, shake on, submit, subscribe, yes, yield; SEE CONCEPTS *8,10,23,82*

acquiescence [n] *reluctant agreement*
acceptance, accession, approval, assent, compliance, concurrence, conformity, consent, giving in, obedience, permission, resignation, submission, submissiveness, yielding; SEE CONCEPTS *8,10*

acquire [v] *obtain or receive*
access, achieve, amass, annex, attain, bring in, buy, catch, collect, cop*, corral*, earn, gain, gather, get, get hands on, get hold of, grab, have, hustle, land, latch onto, lock up, pick up, procure, promote, rack up*, scare up*, secure, snag*, take, take possession of*, wangle*, win; SEE CONCEPTS *120,124,142*

acquisition [n1] *obtaining or receiving*
accretion, achievement, acquirement, acquiring, addition, attainment, buy, gain, gaining, learning, obtainment, possession, prize, procuration, procurement, procuring, property, purchase, pursuit, recovery, redemption, retrieval, salvage, winning; SEE CONCEPTS *120,124,142*

acquisition [n2] *something obtained, received*
accomplishment, achievement, allowance, annuity, award, benefit, bonus, commission, dividend, donation, earnings, fortune, gain, gift, grant, income, increment, inheritance, net, premium, prize, proceeds, profit, remuneration, return, reward, riches, salary, security, wages, wealth, winnings; SEE CONCEPTS *120,337,710*

acquisitive [adj] *eager to obtain knowledge or things*
avaricious, avid, covetous, demanding, desirous, grabbing, grabby, grasping, greedy, predatory, prehensile, rapacious; SEE CONCEPT *542*

acquit [v1] *announce removal of blame*
absolve, blink at*, clear, deliver, discharge, disculpate, exculpate, excuse, exonerate, free, let go, let off, let off the hook*, liberate, release, relieve, vindicate, whitewash*, wink at*, wipe off*; SEE CONCEPTS *50,83,88,317*

acquit [v2] *behave some way*
act, bear, carry, comport, conduct, deport, perform; SEE CONCEPT *633*

acquittal [n] *declaration removing blame*
absolution, acquitting, amnesty, clearance, deliverance, discharge, discharging, dismissal, dismissing, exculpation, exemption, exoneration, freeing, letting off, liberation, pardon, release, re-

leasing, relief from, reprieve, vindication; SEE CONCEPTS *127,317,318*

acre [n] *piece of land, unit of area*
acreage, bit, estate, grounds, manor, plot, property; SEE CONCEPT *792*

acrid [adj1] *bitter, sour to taste*
acid, amaroidal, astringent, biting, burning, caustic, harsh, irritating, pungent, sharp, stinging; SEE CONCEPT *613*

acrid [adj2] *nasty in behavior or words*
acrimonious, austere, biting, bitter, caustic, cutting, harsh, mordant, sarcastic, sharp, trenchant, vitriolic; SEE CONCEPTS *267,401*

acrimonious [adj] *nasty in behavior, speech*
acerbic, acid, angry, astringent, belligerent, biting, bitter, caustic, censorious, churlish, crabby, cranky, cross, cutting, indignant, irascible, irate, ireful, mad, mordant, peevish, petulant, rancorous, sarcastic, sharp, spiteful, splenetic, tart, testy, trenchant, wrathful; SEE CONCEPTS *267,401*

acrimony [n] *nasty behavior, speech*
acerbity, animosity, antipathy, asperity, astringency, belligerence, bitterness, churlishness, crankiness, harshness, ill will, irascibility, malevolence, malice, mordancy, peevishness, rancor, rudeness, sarcasm, spite, tartness, unkindness, virulence; SEE CONCEPTS *633,657*

acrobat [n] *performer who does tricks, physical feats*
aerialist, artist, athlete, balancer, clown, contortionist, dancer, funambulist, gymnast, performer, stunt person, trapezist, tumbler; SEE CONCEPT *352*

across [prep] *traversing a space, side to side*
athwart, beyond, cross, crossed, crosswise, opposite, over, transversely; SEE CONCEPT *581*

act [n1] *something done*
accomplishment, achievement, action, deed, doing, execution, exploit, feat, move, operation, performance, step, thing, undertaking; SEE CONCEPT *1*

act [n2] *legislative document*
amendment, announcement, bill, clause, code, commitment, decree, edict, enactment, judgment, law, measure, order, ordinance, resolution, statute, subpoena, summons, verdict, warrant, writ; SEE CONCEPTS *271,318*

act [n3] *part of a performance*
bit*, curtain, epilogue, gag*, introduction, number, piece, prologue, routine, scene, schtick*, show, sketch, spot, turn; SEE CONCEPT *264*

act [n4] *pretended behavior*
affectation, attitude, bit*, chaser*, dissimulation, fake, false front*, feigning, front, performance, phony, pose, posture, pretense, put-on, sham, show, shuck and jive*, simulation, soft soap*, stall, stance, stunt, sweet talk*; SEE CONCEPT *633*

act [v1] *do something*
accomplish, achieve, begin, carry on, carry out, consummate, cook, create, develop, do, do a number*, do one's thing*, enforce, execute, function, get in there*, go about, go for broke*, go for it*, go in for*, go that route*, go to town*, intrude, knock off*, labor, make progress, maneuver, move, officiate, operate, percolate*, perk*, perpetrate, persevere, persist, practice, preside, pursue, respond, serve, take effect, take part, take steps, take up, transort, undertake, work out; SEE CONCEPTS *1,4*

act [v2] *behave in a certain way*
appear, behave, carry, carry oneself, carry out,

comport, conduct, do, enact, execute, exert, function, give the appearance, go about, impress as, operate, perform, play part, react, represent oneself, seem, serve, strike, take on; SEE CONCEPT *633*

act [*v3*] *initiate by playing a role*
be on*, bring down the house*, burlesque, characterize, do a turn*, dramatize, emote, enact, feign, go on, go over, ham*, ham it up*, impersonate, lay an egg*, make debut, mime, mimic, mug, parody, perform, personate, personify, play, play act, play gig, play part, play role, portray, pretend, put it over*, rehearse, represent, say one's piece*, simulate, star, stooge*, strut*, take part, tread the boards*; SEE CONCEPT *292*

acting [*n*] *entertaining, performing*
assuming, characterization, depiction, dramatics, dramatizing, enacting, enactment, feigning, hamming*, histrionics, imitating, imitation, impersonation, improvisation, mime, mimicry, pantomime, performance, play acting, playing, portrayal, portraying, posing, posturing, pretending, pretense, putting, rendition, seeming, showing off, simulating, stagecraft, stooging*, theatre, theatricals; SEE CONCEPT *292*

acting [*adj*] *substituting in a role*
ad interim, adjutant, alternate, assistant, delegated, deputy, interim, pro tem, pro tempore, provisional, surrogate, temporary; SEE CONCEPT *560*

action [*n1*] *something done*
activity, agility, alacrity, alertness, animation, bag*, ballgame*, big idea*, bit*, business, bustle, commotion, dash, deal, energy, enterprise, flurry, force, functioning, game, going, happening, haste, hoopla*, hopper*, industry, in the works, life, liveliness, motion, movement, occupation, operation, plan, power, process, proposition, racket*, reaction, response, rush, scene, spirit, stir, stunt, trip, turmoil, vigor, vim, vitality, vivacity; SEE CONCEPT *1*

action [*n2*] *individual deed*
accomplishment, achievement, act, blow, commission, dealings, doing, effort, enterprise, execution, exercise, exertion, exploit, feat, handiwork, maneuver, manipulation, move, operation, performance, procedure, step, stroke, thrust, transaction, undertaking; SEE CONCEPTS *91,706*

action [*n3*] *a legal process*
case, cause, claim, lawsuit, litigation, proceeding, prosecution, suit; SEE CONCEPT *317*

action [*n4*] *an aggressive military deed*
battle, combat, conflict, contest, encounter, engagement, fight, fighting, fray, skirmish, warfare; SEE CONCEPT *320*

activate [*v*] *initiate something; start a function*
actify, actuate, arouse, call up, energize, impel, mobilize, motivate, move, prompt, propel, rouse, set in motion, start, stimulate, stir, switch on, take out of mothballs*, trigger, turn on; SEE CONCEPT *234*

active [*adj1*] *having movement*
alive, astir, at work, bustling, effective, efficacious, exertive, flowing, functioning, going, hasty, impelling, in force, in play, in process, mobile, movable, moving, operating, operative, progressive, pushing, rapid, restless, rolling, running, rushing, rustling, shifting, simmering, speeding, speedy, streaming, swarming, traveling, turning, walking, working; SEE CONCEPT *542*

active [*adj2*] *very involved in activity*
aggressive, agile, alert, alive, animated, assiduous, bold, brisk, bustling, busy, chipper, daring, dashing, determined, dexterous, diligent, dynamic, eager, energetic, engaged, enlivened, enterprising, enthusiastic, eventful, fireball*, forceful, forcible, fresh, frisky, hard-working, high-spirited, hyper*, industrious, intense, inventive, jumping, keen, lively, nimble, on the move, perky, persevering, purposeful, pushing, quick, rapid, ready, resolute, sharp, sprightly, spry, whiz*, zealous; SEE CONCEPTS *401,542*

activity [*n1*] *state of being active*
action, activeness, animation, bustle, enterprise, exercise, exertion, hustle, labor, life, liveliness, motion, movement; SEE CONCEPTS *1,748*

activity [*n2*] *special interest or pursuit*
act, avocation, bag*, ballgame*, bit*, deed, endeavor, enterprise, entertainment, game, hobby, job, labor, occupation, pastime, project, racket, scene*, scheme, stunt, task, trip, undertaking, venture, work, zoo*; SEE CONCEPT *32*

actor [*n*] *person who performs, entertains by role-playing*
amateur, artist, barnstormer, bit player, character, clown, comedian, entertainer, extra, foil, ham*, hambone*, headliner, idol, impersonator, ingénue, lead, mime, mimic, pantomimist, performer, play-actor, player, soubrette, stand-in, star, stooge*, straight person, thesp*, thespian, trouper, understudy, ventriloquist, villain, walkon; SEE CONCEPT *352*

actual [*adj1*] *truly existing, real*
absolute, authentic, categorical, certain, concrete, confirmed, definite, factual, for real*, genuine, hard, honest injun*, honest to God*, indisputable, indubitable, kosher*, physical, positive, realistic, substantial, substantive, sure enough*, tangible, true, truthful, undeniable, unquestionable, verified; SEE CONCEPT *582*

actual [*adj2*] *existing at the present time*
current, exact, existent, extant, live, living, original, prevailing; SEE CONCEPT *799*

actuality [*n*] *something that truly exists, is real*
achievement, actualization, attainment, brass tacks*, fact, materiality, materialization, reality, real world*, straight stuff*, substance, substantiality, truth, what it is*; SEE CONCEPT *725*

actually [*adj*] *truly real, existent*
absolutely, as a matter of fact, de facto, genuinely, indeed, in fact, in point of fact, in reality, in truth, literally, really, veritably, very; SEE CONCEPT *582*

actuate [*v*] *start a function or action, motivate*
activate, animate, arouse, cause, drive, egg on*, energize, excite, fire up*, impel, incite, induce, influence, inspire, instigate, key up*, mobilize, motivate, move, prompt, propel, put up to*, quicken, rouse, spur, stimulate, turn on*, work into lather*, work up*; SEE CONCEPTS *221,234*

acumen [*n*] *ability to understand and reason*
acuity, acuteness, astuteness, awareness, brains, brilliance, cleverness, comprehension, cunning, discernment, discrimination, farsightedness, good taste, grasp, guile, ingenuity, insight, intellect, intelligence, intuition, judgment, keenness, perception, percipience, perspicacity, perspicuity, refinement, sagacity, sensitivity, sharpness, shrewdness, smartness, smarts*, understanding, vision, wisdom, wit; SEE CONCEPT *409*

acute [adj1] *deeply perceptive*
astute, canny, clever, discerning, discriminating, incisive, ingenious, insightful, intense, intuitive, judicious, keen, observant, penetrating, perspicacious, piercing, quick-witted, sensitive, sharp, smart, subtle; SEE CONCEPT 402

acute [adj2] *very important*
afflictive, critical, crucial, dangerous, decisive, desperate, dire, essential, grave, serious, severe, sudden, urgent, vital; SEE CONCEPT 568

acute [adj3] *severe, intense*
cutting, distressing, excruciating, exquisite, fierce, keen, overpowering, overwhelming, piercing, poignant, powerful, racking, severe, sharp, shooting, stabbing, sudden, violent; SEE CONCEPT 569

acute [adj4] *having a sharp end or point*
acicular, aciculate, acuminate, acuminous, cuspate, cuspidate, knifelike, needle-shaped, peaked, piked, pointed, sharpened, spiked; SEE CONCEPT 485

adage [n] *saying or proverb*
aphorism, apothegm, axiom, byword, dictum, maxim, motto, precept, saw; SEE CONCEPT 276

adamant [adj1] *unyielding*
determined, firm, fixed, hanging tough*, hardnosed, immovable, inexorable, inflexible, insistent, intransigent, obdurate, pat*, relentless, resolute, rigid, set, set in stone*, standing pat*, stiff, stubborn, unbendable, unbending, uncompromising, unrelenting, unshakable, unswayable; SEE CONCEPT 401

adamant [adj2] *hard like rock*
adamantine, flinty, impenetrable, indestructible, rock-hard, tough, unbreakable; SEE CONCEPT 604

adapt [v] *adjust to a different situation or condition*
acclimate, accommodate, accustom, alter, change, come around, comply, conform, familiarize, fashion, fit, get act together*, get used to, grow used to, habituate, harmonize, make, match, modify, play the game*, prepare, qualify, readjust, reconcile, remodel, revise, roll with punches*, shape, shape up*, square, suit, tailor; SEE CONCEPTS 232,697

adaptable [adj] *able and usually willing to change*
AC-DC*, adjustable, all around, alterable, cando*, changeable, compliant, conformable, convertible, ductile, easy-going, flexible, hanging loose*, malleable, modifiable, moldable, plastic, pliable, pliant, resilient, supple, switch-hitting, tractable, variable, versatile; SEE CONCEPTS 550,576

adaptation [n1] *act of adapting*
adjustment, adoption, alteration, conversion, modification, refitting, remodeling, reworking, shift, transformation, variation; SEE CONCEPT 697

adaptation [n2] *condition of something resulting from change*
acclimatization, accustomedness, agreement, compliance, correspondence, familiarization, habituation, naturalization; SEE CONCEPT 697

add [v1] *simple arithmetical process of increase; accumulation*
calculate, cast, compute, count, count up, do addition, enumerate, figure, reckon, reckon up, sum, summate, tally, tot*, total, tote*, tot up*; SEE CONCEPT 764

add [v2] *adjoin, increase; make further comment*
affix, annex, ante, append, augment, beef up*,

boost, build up, charge up, continue, cue in*, figure in, flesh out*, heat up*, hike, hike up*, hitch on*, hook on*, hook up with*, include, jack up*, jazz up*, join together, pad, parlay, piggyback*, plug into*, pour it on*, reply, run up*, say further, slap on*, snowball*, soup up*, speed up, spike, step up, supplement, sweeten*, tack on*, tag; SEE CONCEPTS 51,113,236,245

addendum [n] *something conjoined, added*
addition, adjunct, appendage, appendix, attachment, augmentation, codicil, extension, extra, postscript, rider, supplement; SEE CONCEPTS 270,827

addict [n] *person who has compulsion toward activity, often injurious*
aficionado, buff, devotee, enthusiast, fan, fanatic, fiend, follower, freak*, habitué, hound*, junkie*, nut, practitioner, zealot; SEE CONCEPTS 412,423

addicted [adj] *dependent on something, compulsive*
absorbed, accustomed, attached, dependent, devoted, disposed, fanatic, fond, given over to, given to, habituated, hooked, hyped*, imbued, inclined, obsessed, predisposed, prone to, spaced out*, strung out*, under the influence, used to, wedded to; SEE CONCEPT 542

addiction [n] *a habit of activity, often injurious*
bag*, bent, craving, dependence, enslavement, fixation, hang-up*, hook, inclination, jones*, kick*, monkey*, monkey on back*, obsession, shot*, sweet tooth*, thing*; SEE CONCEPTS 20,316,709

addition [n1] *process of conjoining, adding*
accession, adding, adjoining, affixing, annexation, attachment, augmentation, enlargement, extension, inclusion, increasing; SEE CONCEPTS 236,245

addition [n2] *something conjoined to or enlargement of something*
accession, accessory, accretion, accrual, addendum, additive, adjunct, aggrandizement, annex, appendage, appendix, attachment, augmentation, bonus, boost, commission, dividend, enhancement, enlargement, expansion, extension, extra, gain, hike, increase, increment, profit, raise, reinforcement, rise, supplement, wing; SEE CONCEPTS 640,835

addition [n3] *arithmetical process of augmentation*
accretion, accruing, adding, computing, counting, enlarging, expanding, increasing, reckoning, summation, summing, tabulating, totaling, toting*; SEE CONCEPT 764

additional [adj] *extra, supplementary*
added, affixed, appended, further, increased, more, new, on the side, option, other, over-and-above, padding, perk, spare, supplementary; SEE CONCEPT 771

addled [adj] *confused*
balled up*, befuddled, bewildered, fouled up*, gone*, mixed up, out of it, punchy, rattled, shaken, shook, shook up, slap-happy, thrown, unglued*, woozy*; SEE CONCEPT 403

address [n1] *place of residence or business where one can be contacted*
abode, box number, direction, domicile, dwelling, headquarters, home, house, living quarters, location, lodging, number, place of business, place of residence, street, whereabouts, zip code; SEE CONCEPT 516

address [n2] *speech given to formal gathering*
chalk talk*, discourse, dissertation, lecture, oration, pep talk*, pitch, sermon, soapbox*, spiel*, talk; SEE CONCEPT *278*

address [v1] *write directions for delivery*
consign, dispatch, forward, inscribe, label, mark, postmark, remit, route, send, ship, superscribe, transmit; SEE CONCEPTS *60,79*

address [v2] *speak to a formal gathering*
approach, bespeak, call, deliver speech, deliver talk, discourse, discuss, get on a soapbox*, give speech, give talk, greet, hail, lecture, memorialize, orate, pitch, pontificate, root for, sermonize, spiel*, spout, stump*, take the floor, talk; SEE CONCEPTS *60,266,285*

address [v3] *devote effort to something*
apply oneself to, attend to, concentrate on, devote oneself to, dig, direct, engage in, focus on, give, go at*, go for*, hammer away*, have a go at*, have at*, knuckle down to*, peg away*, pitch into*, plug away at*, take care of, take up, throw oneself into, try, turn, turn to, undertake; SEE CONCEPT *100*

adept [adj] *very able*
accomplished, ace*, adroit, brainy, capable, clean*, crack*, crackerjack*, deft, dexterous, expert, hot*, hotshot*, know stuff*, masterful, masterly, nobody's fool*, no dummy*, no slouch*, on the ball*, on the beam*, practiced, proficient, quick, savvy, sharp, sharp as a tack*, skilled, skillful, slick, smooth, there*, up to speed*, versed, whiz*, wizard; SEE CONCEPTS *402,527*

adequacy [n] *ability, competency in some action*
capability, capacity, commensurateness, competence, enough, fairness, plenty, requisiteness, satisfactoriness, sufficiency, suitableness, tolerableness; SEE CONCEPTS *636,656*

adequate [adj] *enough, able*
acceptable, all right, capable, comfortable, commensurate, competent, decent, equal, fair, passable, requisite, satisfactory, sufficient, sufficing, suitable, tolerable, unexceptional, unobjectionable; SEE CONCEPTS *533,558*

adequately [adv] *sufficiently*
abundantly, acceptably, appropriately, capably, competently, copiously, decently, fairly well, fittingly, modestly, pleasantly enough, presentably, satisfactorily, sufficiently, suitably, to an acceptable degree, tolerably, well enough; SEE CONCEPTS *558,560*

adhere [v1] *conform to or follow rules exactly*
abide by, be attached, be constant, be devoted, be devoted to, be faithful, be loyal, be true, cleave to, comply, follow, fulfill, heed, keep, maintain, mind, obey, observe, practice, respect, stand by, support; SEE CONCEPTS *87,636*

adhere [v2] *stick or become stuck to, either physically or mentally*
attach, cement, cleave, cling like ivy*, cohere, fasten, fix, freeze to*, glue, hold fast, hold on like bulldog*, paste, stay put, stick like a barnacle*, stick like glue*, unite; SEE CONCEPTS *85,113,160*

adhesive [adj] *sticking*
adherent, adhering, agglutinant, attaching, clinging, clingy, gelatinous, glutinous, gluey, gummed, gummy, holding, hugging, mucilaginous, pasty, resinous, sticky, tenacious, viscid, viscous, waxy; SEE CONCEPTS *488,606*

adieu [n] *parting remark or action*
adios*, congé, farewell, goodbye, leave-taking, parting, so long, valediction; SEE CONCEPT *276*

ad infinitum [adj] *neverending*
ceaselessly, endlessly, forever, perpetually; SEE CONCEPT *798*

adjacent [adj] *next to, abutting*
adjoining, alongside, beside, bordering, close, close by, contiguous, near, neighboring, next door, touching; SEE CONCEPT *586*

adjective [n] *word that modifies a noun*
accessory, additional, adjunct, adnoun, attribute, attributive, dependent, descriptive, identifier, modifier, qualifier; SEE CONCEPT *275*

adjoin [v1] *be next to*
abut, approximate, be adjacent to, border, butt, communicate, connect, join, lie, lie beside, link, neighbor, touch, verge; SEE CONCEPT *747*

adjoin [v2] *attach*
add, affix, annex, append, combine, connect, couple, interconnect, join, link, unite; SEE CONCEPTS *85,113,160*

adjoining [adj] *being next to*
abutting, adjacent, approximal, bordering on, connecting, conterminous, contiguous, coterminous, impinging, interconnecting, joined, joining, juxtaposed, near, neighboring, next door, touching, verging; SEE CONCEPT *586*

adjourn [v] *stop a proceeding*
curb, defer, delay, discontinue, hold off, hold over, hold up, postpone, prorogue, put off, recess, restrain, shelve, stay, suspend; SEE CONCEPTS *121,234*

adjournment [n] *discontinuation or delay of a proceeding*
break, deferment, deferral, intermission, interruption, pause, postponement, prorogation, putting off, recess, stay, suspension; SEE CONCEPTS *121,703*

adjudicate [v] *formally judge*
adjudge, arbitrate, decide, determine, mediate, referee, settle, umpire; SEE CONCEPTS *18,317*

adjunct [n] *addition; help*
accessory, addendum, appendage, appendix, appurtenance, associate, auxiliary, complement, detail, partner, subordinate, supplement; SEE CONCEPTS *484,835*

adjust [v1] *become or make prepared, adapted*
acclimatize, accommodate, accustom, adapt, alter, arrange, compose, conform, dispose, do as Romans do*, doctor*, fiddle with*, fine-tune, fit, fix, fix up, get act together*, get it together*, grin and bear it*, habituate, harmonize, make conform, modify, order, quadrate, reconcile, rectify, redress, regulate, remodel, settle, suit, swim with the tide*, tailor, tailor-make, tune; SEE CONCEPTS *35,232,697*

adjust [v2] *mechanically alter, especially to improve*
accommodate, align, balance, bring into line, calibrate, connect, correct, fine-tune, fit, fix, focus, grind, improve, mend, overhaul, polish, put in working order, readjust, rectify, regulate, renovate, repair, service, set, sharpen, square, tighten, troubleshoot, tune up; SEE CONCEPTS *202,212*

adjust [v3] *bring into agreement or to a standard*
accord, allocate, arrange, clarify, conclude, conform, coordinate, doctor*, fiddle with*, fine-tune, fix up, grade, methodize, modify, organize, reconcile, regulate, settle, sort, standardize, straighten, systematize, tally; SEE CONCEPTS *84,117*

adjustment [n1] *adaptation*
acclimation, acclimatization, alteration, arrangement, balancing, conformance, correcting, fitting, fixing, improvement, mending, modification, ordering, organization, organizing, orientation, readjustment, redress, regulating, regulation, repairing, setting, shaping, standardization, turning; SEE CONCEPT 697

adjustment [n2] *financial retribution, payment of claim*
agreement, allotment, apportionment, benefit, compensation, compromise, pay, reconciliation, reimbursement, remuneration, settlement, share, stake, stipulation; SEE CONCEPT 332

adjutant [n] *assistant*
aide, auxiliary, helper; SEE CONCEPT 348

ad-lib [adj] *improvised*
extemporaneous, extempore, extemporized, impromptu, made-up, off-the-cuff*, spontaneous, unprepared, unrehearsed; SEE CONCEPT 267

ad-lib [v] *improvise speech*
extemporize, invent, make up, speak extemporaneously, speak impromptu, speak off the cuff*; SEE CONCEPT 266

ad-lib [adv] *in an improvised manner*
extemporaneously, extempore, impromptu, off the cuff*, off the top of one's head*, spontaneously, without preparation, without rehearsal; SEE CONCEPT 267

administer [v1] *manage an organization or effort*
administrate, be in the driver's seat*, be in the saddle*, boss*, carry out, conduct, control, crack the whip*, direct, execute, govern, head, head up*, hold the reins*, oversee, pull the strings*, pull the wires*, render, ride herd on*, run, run the show*, sit on top of*, superintend, supervise; SEE CONCEPTS 117,298

administer [v2] *dispense something needed*
apply, apportion, authorize, bring, contribute, deal, deliver, disburse, distribute, dole out, execute, extend, furnish, give, impose, inflict, issue, measure out, mete out, offer, perform, portion, proffer, provide, regulate, serve, supply, tender; SEE CONCEPTS 108,136

administration [n1] *management of an organization or effort*
administering, agency, application, authority, charge, command, conduct, conducting, control, directing, direction, dispensation, disposition, distribution, enforcement, execution, governing, government, guidance, handling, jurisdiction, legislation, order, organization, overseeing, oversight, performance, policy, power, provision, regulation, rule, running, strategy, superintendence, supervision, surveillance; SEE CONCEPTS 117,298

administration [n2] *human or group who manages effort of an organization*
admiral, advisers, board, bureau, cabinet, chair, chairperson, chargé d'affaires, command, commander, committee, consulate, department, directors, embassy, executive, executives, feds*, front office*, general, governing body, headquarters, legislature, management, ministry, officers, officials, powers, presidency, president, presidium, stewards, superintendents, supervisors, top brass*, upstairs*; SEE CONCEPT 299

administration [n3] *period during which a particular human group is in power*
dynasty, incumbency, presidency, regime, reign, stay, tenure, term; SEE CONCEPTS 298,816

administrative [adj] *involved in managing or using power*
authoritative, bureaucratic, central, commanding, controlling, deciding, decisive, departmental, directing, directive, directorial, executive, governing, governmental, in charge, in control, jurisdictional, legislative, managerial, official, organizational, policy-making, presiding, regulative, regulatory, ruling, superintending, supervising, supervisory; SEE CONCEPTS 319,536

administrator [n] *person who manages organization*
ambassador, authority, boss, bureaucrat, captain, CEO, chair, chairperson, chief, commander, consul, controller, custodian, dean, director, exec*, executive, front office*, governor, head, head honcho*, head person*, inspector, judge, leader, manager, mayor, minister, officer, official, organizer, overseer, person upstairs*, premier, president, prez*, producer, superintendent, supervisor; SEE CONCEPTS 347,354

admirable [adj] *held in great respect*
ace*, A-OK*, A-1*, attractive, best ever, cat's pajamas*, choice, commendable, cool*, copacetic*, crackerjack*, deserving, dream*, estimable, excellent, exquisite, fine, good, great, greatest, hunky dory*, keen*, laudable, meritable, meritorious, neat*, out of sight*, out of this world*, peachy*, praiseworthy, rare, solid, super, superduper*, superior, unreal*, valuable, wicked*, wonderful, worthy, zero cool*; SEE CONCEPTS 572,574

admiration [n] *great respect*
account, adoration, affection, applause, appreciation, approbation, approval, deference, delight, esteem, estimation, favor, fondness, glorification, homage, honor, idolatry, idolization, liking, love, marveling, obeisance, pleasure, praise, prizing, recognition, regard, reverence, valuing, veneration, wonder, wonderment, worship; SEE CONCEPT 32

admire [v] *hold in high regard*
adore, applaud, appreciate, approve, be crazy about*, be crazy for*, be crazy over*, be mad about*, be nuts about*, be stuck on*, be sweet on*, be wild about*, cherish, commend, credit, delight in, esteem, eulogize, extol, fall for*, get high on*, glorify, go for*, groove on*, hail, hold in respect, honor, idolize, laud, look up to, marvel at, moon over*, pay homage to, praise, prize, rate highly, respect, revere, take pleasure in, think highly of, treasure, value, venerate, wonder at, worship; SEE CONCEPT 32

admirer [n] *person who holds someone in high regard*
adherent, beau, believer, booster, boyfriend, buff, bug*, cat*, devotee, disciple, enthusiast, fan, fancier, fiend*, follower, freak*, girlfriend, groupie*, hound*, junkie*, lover, nut*, partisan, patron, rooter*, suitor, supporter, swain, sweetheart, wooer, worshiper; SEE CONCEPT 423

admissible [adj] *able or deserving of consideration; allowable*
acceptable, allowed, applicable, appropriate, concedable, fair, fitting, just, justifiable, lawful, legal, legitimate, licit, likely, logical, not impossible, not unlikely, okay, passable, permissible, permitted, pertinent, possible, probable, proper, rational, reasonable, relevant, right, suit-

able, tolerable, tolerated, warranted, worthy; SEE CONCEPT *533*

admission [*n1*] *entering or allowing entry*
acceptance, access, admittance, certification, confirmation, designation, door, entrance, entree, ingress, initiation, introduction, permission, reception, recognition, way, welcome; SEE CONCEPTS *83,159*

admission [*n2*] *confession or acknowledgment*
accession, admittance, affidavit, affirmation, allowance, assent, assertion, attestation, averment, avowal, concession, confirmation, declaration, deposition, disclosure, divulgence, profession, revelation, statement, testimonial, testimony; SEE CONCEPT *57*

admit [*v1*] *allow entry or use*
accept, be big on*, bless, buy, concede, enter, entertain, give access, give the nod*, give thumbs up*, grant, harbor, house, initiate, introduce, let, let in, lodge, okay, permit, receive, shelter, sign*, sign off on*, suffer, take, take in; SEE CONCEPT *83*

admit [*v2*] *confess, acknowledge*
accept, accord, acquiesce, adopt, affirm, agree, allow, approve, avow, bare, bring to light*, communicate, concede, concur, confide, confirm, consent, cop a plea*, credit, declare, disclose, divulge, enumerate, expose, go into details*, grant, indicate, let, let on, make known, narrate, number, open up, own, own up*, permit, proclaim, profess, recite, recognize, relate, reveal, spill*, subscribe to, talk, tell, tolerate, uncover, unveil, yield; SEE CONCEPTS *57,82*

admonish [*v*] *warn, strongly criticize*
advise, berate, call down, call on the carpet*, censure, check, chide, come down hard on*, counsel, ding*, draw the line*, enjoin, exhort, forewarn, give a going over*, give a piece of one's mind*, glue*, growl*, hoist*, jack up*, notice, rap*, rap on knuckles*, rebuke, reprimand, reprove, scold, sit on, slap on wrist*, speak to, talk to, tell a thing or two*, tell off*, upbraid, warn; SEE CONCEPTS *52,78*

adolescence [*n*] *state of puberty, preadulthood*
boyhood, girlhood, greenness, juvenility, minority, pubescence, spring, teens, youth, youthfulness; SEE CONCEPT *817*

adolescent [*n*] *person in puberty, preadulthood*
juvenile, minor, stripling, sweet sixteen*, teen, teenager, teenybopper*, youngster, youth; SEE CONCEPT *424*

adolescent [*adj*] *preadult or immature*
boyish, girlish, growing, juvenile, pubescent, puerile, teen, teenage, young, youthful; SEE CONCEPTS *401,578,797*

adopt [*v1*] *choose or take something as one's own*
accept, adapt, affiliate, affirm, appropriate, approve, assent, assume, borrow, embrace, endorse, espouse, follow, go down the line*, go in for*, imitate, maintain, mimic, opt, ratify, seize, select, support, take on, take over, take up, tap, use, utilize; SEE CONCEPT *18*

adopt [*v2*] *legally care for another's child*
choose, foster, naturalize, pick, raise, select, take in; SEE CONCEPT *317*

adoption [*n1*] *choosing or taking something as one's own*
acceptance, approbation, appropriation, approval, assumption, choice, confirmation, embracement, embracing, enactment, endorsement, espousal,

following, maintenance, ratification, selection, support, taking on, taking over, taking up; SEE CONCEPT *18*

adoption [*n2*] *legal taking of another's child*
adopting, fosterage, fostering, naturalizing, raising, taking in; SEE CONCEPT *317*

adorable [*adj*] *cute, lovable*
ambrosial, appealing, attractive, captivating, charming, cute, darling, dear, delectable, delicious, delightful, dishy*, dreamy*, fetching, heavenly, hot*, luscious, pleasing, precious, sexy, suave; SEE CONCEPTS *579,589*

adoration [*n*] *intense love*
admiration, amore, ardor, attachment, crush, devotion, esteem, estimation, exaltation, glorification, hankering, honor, idolatry, idolization, infatuation, pash*, passion, puppy love*, reverence, shine*, veneration, weakness*, worship, worshipping, yen*; SEE CONCEPT *32*

adore [*v*] *love intensely*
admire, be crazy about*, be gone on*, be mad for*, be nuts about*, be serious about*, be smitten with*, be stuck on*, be sweet on*, be wild about*, cherish, delight in, dig*, dote on, esteem, exalt, fall for, flip over*, glorify, go for*, honor, idolize, prize, revere, reverence, treasure, venerate, worship; SEE CONCEPT *32*

adorn [*v*] *decorate*
array, beautify, bedeck, deck, doll up*, dress up, embellish, enhance, enrich, fix up, furbish, garnish, grace, gussy up*, ornament, spruce up, trim; SEE CONCEPTS *162,177*

adornment [*n1*] *decorating, enhancing*
beautification, decoration, embellishment, gilding, ornamentation, trimming; SEE CONCEPTS *162,177*

adornment [*n2*] *a decoration*
accessory, dingbat, doodad, embellishment, fandangle*, floss*, frill, frippery, furbelow*, gewgaw*, jazz*, ornament, thing, trimming; SEE CONCEPTS *446,484*

adrift [*adv1*] *floating out of control*
afloat, drifting, loose, unanchored, unmoored; SEE CONCEPT *488*

adrift [*adv2*] *without purpose*
aimless, directionless, goalless, purposeless; SEE CONCEPT *542*

adrift [*adv3*] *off course*
amiss, astray, erring, wrong; SEE CONCEPT *581*

adroit [*adj*] *very able or skilled*
adept, apt, artful, clean, clever, crack*, crackerjack*, cunning, cute, deft, dexterous, expert, foxy*, good, handy, hot tamale*, ingenious, masterful, neat*, nifty*, nimble, on the ball*, on the beam*, proficient, quick on the trigger*, quick on the uptake*, quick-witted, savvy, sharp, skillful, slick, smart, up*, up to speed*, whiz*, wizard; SEE CONCEPT *527*

adulation [*n*] *overenthusiastic praise*
applause, audation, blandishment, bootlicking*, commendation, fawning, flattery, sycophancy, worship; SEE CONCEPTS *32,69*

adult [*n*] *a mature, fully grown person*
gentleperson, grownup, man, person, woman; SEE CONCEPTS *394,424*

adult [*adj*] *being mature, fully grown*
developed, grown, grown-up, of age, ripe, ripened; SEE CONCEPT *406*

adulterate [*v*] *alter or debase, often for profit*
alloy, amalgamate, attenuate, blend, cheapen,

commingle, contaminate, cook, corrupt, cut*, defile, degrade, denature, depreciate, deteriorate, devalue, dilute, dissolve, doctor*, doctor up*, falsify, impair, infiltrate, intermix, irrigate, lace*, make impure, mingle, mix, phony up*, plant*, pollute, shave*, spike*, taint, thin, transfuse, vitiate, water down*, weaken; SEE CONCEPTS 240,254

adulterated [adj] debased or dirty
attenuated, blended, contaminated, corrupt, defiled, degraded, depreciated, deteriorated, devalued, diluted, dissolved, impaired, mixed, polluted, tainted, thinned, vitiated, watered down, weakened; SEE CONCEPT 485

adulterous [adj] unfaithful
cheating, double-crossing*, extracurricular*, fast and loose*, illicit, immoral, moonlighting*, speedy*, two-faced*, two-timing*, unchaste; SEE CONCEPT 372

adultery [n] extramarital affair
affair, carrying on*, cheating, extracurricular activity*, fling, fornication, hanky-panky*, immorality, infidelity, matinee*, playing around*, relationship, thing*, two-timing*; SEE CONCEPT 633

advance [n1] forward movement
advancement, headway, impetus, motion, progress, progression; SEE CONCEPTS 152,208

advance [n2] improvement, progress in development
advancement, amelioration, betterment, boost, break*, breakthrough, buildup, development, enrichment, furtherance, gain, go-ahead*, growth, headway, increase, progress, promotion, rise, step, up, upgrade, upping; SEE CONCEPTS 700,704

advance [n3] money given beforehand
accommodation, allowance, bite*, credit, deposit, down payment, floater*, front money*, hike, increase, loan, prepayment, retainer, rise*, score, stake, take*, touch*; SEE CONCEPTS 340,344

advance(s) [n4] desirous pursuit of someone
approach, move, overture, proposal, proposition, suggestion; SEE CONCEPTS 20,384

advance [adj] ahead in position or time
beforehand, earlier, early, first, foremost, forward, in front, in the forefront, in the lead, leading, previously, prior; SEE CONCEPTS 583, 585,799

advance [v1] move something forward, often quickly
accelerate, achieve, bring forward, come forward, conquer, continue ahead, continue on, dispatch, drive, elevate, forge ahead, gain ground, get ahead, get green light*, get there*, get with it*, go ahead, go forth, go forward, go great guns*, go places*, go to town*, hasten, launch, make headway, make the scene*, march, move on, move onward, move up, press on, proceed, progress, promote, propel, push ahead, push on, quicken, send forward, skyrocket*, speed, step forward, storm; SEE CONCEPTS 152,208,704

advance [v2] promote or propose an idea
adduce, allege, ballyhoo, beat the drum for, benefit, boost, cite, encourage, foster, further, get ink for*, hype*, introduce, lay forward, make a pitch for*, offer, plug*, present, proffer, puff*, push, put forward, put on the map*, serve, set forth, splash, spot, submit, suggest, throw spotlight on*, urge; SEE CONCEPTS 49,60,68

advance [v3] give money beforehand
furnish, lend, loan, pay, provide; SEE CONCEPT 341

advance [v4] increase in amount, number, or position
boost, break the bank*, develop, elevate, enlarge, get fat*, get rich*, grade, grow, hit pay dirt*, hit the jackpot*, improve, magnify, make a killing*, make out*, multiply, pan out*, prefer, prosper, raise, strike gold*, strike it rich*, thrive, up, upgrade, uplift; SEE CONCEPTS 236,244,245

advanced [adj] ahead in position, time, manner
avant-garde, breakthrough, cutting-edge*, excellent, exceptional, extreme, first, foremost, forward, higher, late, leading, leading-edge*, liberal, precocious, progressive, radical, state-of-the-art*, unconventional; SEE CONCEPTS 574,578,585,797

advancement [n1] promotion, progress
advance, amelioration, betterment, elevation, gain, growth, headway, improvement, preference, preferment, prelation, rise, upgrading; SEE CONCEPTS 700,704

advancement [n2] forward movement
advance, anabasis, gain, headway, march, progress, progression; SEE CONCEPTS 152,208

advantage [n] benefit, favored position or circumstance
aid, ascendancy, asset, assistance, authority, avail, blessing, boon, break, choice, comfort, convenience, dominance, edge, eminence, expediency, favor, gain, good, gratification, help, hold, improvement, influence, interest, lead, leeway, leg-up*, leverage, luck, mastery, odds, position, power, precedence, pre-eminence, preference, prestige, prevalence, profit, protection, recognition, resources, return, sanction, starting, superiority, support, supremacy, upper hand*, utility, wealth; SEE CONCEPT 574

advent [n] beginning or arrival of something anticipated
appearance, approach, arrival, coming, entrance, occurrence, onset, visitation; SEE CONCEPTS 119,159

adventure [n] risky or unexpected undertaking
chance, contingency, emprise, endangerment, enterprise, experience, exploit, feat, happening, hazard, incident, jeopardy, occurrence, peril, scene, speculation, trip, undertaking, venture; SEE CONCEPTS 384,386

adventurer [n] person who takes risks
charlatan, daredevil, entrepreneur, explorer, fortune-hunter, gambler, globetrotter, hero, heroine, madcap, mercenary, opportunist, pioneer, pirate, romantic, speculator, stunt person, swashbuckler, traveler, venturer, voyager, wanderer; SEE CONCEPT 423

adventurous [adj] daring, risk-taking
adventuresome, audacious, bold, brave, courageous, dangerous, daredevil, enterprising, foolhardy, hazardous, headstrong, intrepid, rash, reckless, risky, temerarious, venturesome, venturous; SEE CONCEPTS 404,542

adverb [n] word modifying a verb
limiter, modifier, qualifier; SEE CONCEPT 275

adversary [n] opponent
antagonist, attacker, bad person, bandit, competitor, contestant, enemy, foe, match, opposer, opposite number*, oppugner, rival; SEE CONCEPT 412

adverse [adj] unfavorable, antagonistic
allergic to*, conflicting, contrary, detrimental, disadvantageous, down on*, down side*, have no use for*, inimical, injurious, inopportune, negative, opposed, opposing, opposite, oppugning, ornery*, reluctant, repugnant, stuffy*, unfortunate, unfriendly, unlucky, unpropitious, unwilling; SEE CONCEPT 570

adversity [n] bad luck, situation
affliction, bad break*, bummer*, calamity, can of worms*, catastrophe, clutch, contretemps, crunch*, difficulty, disaster, distress, downer*, drag*, evil eye*, hard knocks*, hardship, hard times, hurting, ill fortune, jam, jinx, kiss of death*, misery, misfortune, · mishap, on the skids*, pain in the neck*, poison*, reverse, sorrow, suffering, the worst*, tough luck*, trial, trouble; SEE CONCEPT 674

advertise [v] publicize for the purpose of selling or causing one to want
acquaint, advance, advise, announce, apprise, ballyhoo*, beat the drum for*, bill, blazon, boost*, build up, circularize, communicate, declare, disclose, display, divulge, drum*, endorse, exhibit, expose, flaunt, get on soapbox for*, hard sell, herald, hype*, inform, make a pitch*, make known, notify, pitch, plug, press agent*, proclaim, promote, promulgate, puff*, push, put on the map*, reveal, show, soft sell, splash*, sponsor, spot, tout, uncover, unmask; SEE CONCEPTS 60,324

advertisement [n] public notice of sale
ad, announcement, bill, blurb, broadcast, circular, classified ad, commercial, communication, declaration, display, endorsement, exhibit, exhibition, flyer, literature, notice, notification, placard, plug, poster, proclamation, promotion, promulgation, propaganda, publication, publicity, squib, throwaway, want ad; SEE CONCEPTS 270,277,278,280

advertising [n] public notice of sale; notices to increase consumer desire
announcement, announcing, ballyhoo*, billing, blasting*, broadcasting, buildup, displaying, exhibiting, exhibition, exposition, hard sell, hoopla*, hype*, pitch, plug, posting, PR, proclamation, promo*, promoting, promotion, publicity, puff*, screamer*, spread, squib; SEE CONCEPTS 97,138,324

advice [n] recommendation
admonition, advisement, advocacy, aid, bum steer*, caution, charge, consultation, counsel, directions, dissuasion, encouragement, exhortation, forewarning, guidance, help, information, injunction, input, instruction, judgment, lesson, news, opinion, persuasion, prescription, proposal, proposition, recommendation, steer, suggestion, teaching, telltale, tidings, tip, tip-off*, two cents' worth*, view, warning, word, word to the wise*; SEE CONCEPTS 75,274

advisable [adj] recommended, wise
appropriate, apt, commendable, desirable, expedient, fit, fitting, judicious, politic, prudent, seemly, sensible, sound, suggested, suitable, tactical; SEE CONCEPT 574

advise [v] offer recommendation
admonish, advocate, caution, charge, commend, counsel, direct, dissuade, encourage, enjoin, exhort, forewarn, give a pointer*, give a tip*, guide, instruct, kibitz*, level with*, move, opine, point out, preach, prepare, prescribe, prompt, put bug in ear*, put in two cents*, recommend, steer, suggest, tout, update, urge, warn; SEE CONCEPT 75

advise [v2] offer information
acquaint, apprise, clue*, clue in*, fill in, give the word*, inform, keep posted*, lay it out*, let in on*, make known, notify, post*, put next to*, put on the line*, put on to*, report, show, tell, tip off*, update, warn; SEE CONCEPT 60

advisedly [adv] with due consideration
carefully, cautiously, consciously, deliberately, discreetly, intentionally, prudently, thoughtfully; SEE CONCEPT 544

adviser/advisor [n] person who recommends, teaches, or otherwise helps
aide, attorney, authority, backseat driver*, buttinski*, clubhouse lawyer*, coach, confidant, consultant, counsel, counselor, director, doctor, Dutch uncle*, expert, friend, guide, helper, instructor, judge, kibitzer*, lawyer, mentor, monitor, partner, priest, quarterback*, referee, righthand person, second-guesser, teacher, tutor; SEE CONCEPTS 348,350

advisory [adj] able, authorized to recommend
advising, consultative, consultive, counseling, helping, recommending; SEE CONCEPT 537

advocacy [n] support for an idea or cause
advancement, aid, assistance, backing, campaigning for, championing, defense, encouragement, justification, pleading for, promotion, promulgation, propagation, proposal, recommendation, upholding, urging; SEE CONCEPT 689

advocate [n] person supporting an idea or cause publicly
apostle, attorney, backer, campaigner, champion, counsel, defender, exponent, expounder, lawyer, pleader, promoter, proponent, proposer, speaker, spokesperson, supporter, upholder; SEE CONCEPTS 359,423

advocate [v] support idea or cause publicly
advance, advise, argue for, back, be in corner*, bless, bolster, boost*, brace up*, build up, campaign for, champion, countenance, defend, encourage, favor, further, get on bandwagon*, give a leg up*, give a lift*, go for, go to bat for*, go with, hold with, justify, plead for, plug*, plump for*, press for, promote, propose, push, recommend, ride shotgun for*, root for*, run interference for*, say so*, side, speak for, spread around*, stump for*, support, tout, uphold, urge, vindicate; SEE CONCEPTS 10,49,75

aerial [adj] occurring in the air
aeriform, aeronautical, airy, atmospheric, birdlike, ethereal, flying, lofty, pneumatic, up above, vaporous; SEE CONCEPT 583

aerobics/aerobic [n/adj] exercise regime designed to increase heart and lung activity while toning muscles
aquarobics, dance workout, drill, exercise, high impact, low impact, slimnastics, step, warm-up, workout; SEE CONCEPT 363

aesthetic/esthetic [adj] beautiful or artful
artistic, creative, gorgeous, inventive; SEE CONCEPTS 485,579

afar [adv] a great distance away
distant, far away, far off, remote; SEE CONCEPT 778

affable [adj] friendly
amiable, amicable, approachable, benevolent, benign, breezy, civil, clubby*, congenial, cordial,

courteous, genial, gentle, good-humored, good-natured, gracious, kindly, mild, nice, obliging, pleasant, polite, sociable, urbane, warm; SEE CONCEPT *401*

affair [*n1*] *matter or business to be taken care of; happening*

activity, assignment, avocation, calling, case, circumstance, concern, duty, employment, episode, event, hap, happening, incident, interest, job, mission, obligation, occupation, occurrence, office function, proceeding, profession, project, province, pursuit, question, realm, responsibility, subject, task, thing*, topic, transaction, undertaking; SEE CONCEPTS *2,349,362*

affair [*n2*] *illicit sexual relationship*

affaire, amour, carrying on*, extracurricular activity*, fling, goings-on*, hanky-panky*, intimacy, intrigue, liaison, love, playing around*, relationship, rendezvous, romance, thing together*, two-timing*; SEE CONCEPTS *32,375*

affair [*n3*] *party or celebration*

do, entertainment, function, gathering, reception, shindig, soiree; SEE CONCEPTS *377,383*

affect [*v1*] *influence, affect emotionally*

act on, alter, change, disturb, impinge, impress, induce, influence, inspire, interest, involve, modify, move, overcome, perturb, prevail, regard, relate, stir, sway, touch, transform, upset; SEE CONCEPTS *7,19,22,228*

affect [*v2*] *pretend, imitate*

act, adopt, aspire to, assume, bluff, contrive, counterfeit, do a bit*, fake, feign, lay it on thick, make out like*, playact, put on, put up a front*, sham*, simulate, take on; SEE CONCEPT *59*

affectation [*n*] *pretended behavior to make an impression*

air, airs, appearance, artificiality, facade, false front*, front, going Hollywood*, imitation, insincerity, mannerism, pose, pretense, pretension, pretentiousness, put-on, putting on airs*, sham*, show, showing off, simulation; SEE CONCEPT *633*

affected [*adj1*] *deeply moved or hurt emotionally*

afflicted, altered, changed, compassionate, concerned, damaged, distressed, excited, grieved, impaired, impressed, influenced, injured, overwhelmed, overwrought, sorry, stimulated, stirred, sympathetic, tender, touched, troubled, upset; SEE CONCEPT *403*

affected [*adj2*] *changed in a bad or artificial way*

apish, artificial, assumed, awkward, campy*, chichi*, conceited, contrived, counterfeit, counterfeited, faked, false, feigned, fraud*, gone Hollywood*, ham*, hammy*, high falutin'*, hollow, imitated, insincere, melodramatic, ostentatious, overdone, pedantic, phony, playacting, pompous, precious, pretended, pretentious, put-on*, schmaltzy*, self-conscious, shallow, sham*, simulated, spurious, stiff, stilted, studied, superficial, theatrical, unnatural; SEE CONCEPTS *401,570*

affection [*n*] *strong fondness*

amore, ardor, attachment, care, case*, closeness, concern, crush, desire, devotion, emotion, endearment, feeling, friendliness, friendship, good will, hankering*, heart, inclination, itch*, kindness, liking, love, passion, predilection, propensity, puppy love*, regard, sentiment, shine*, soft spot*, solicitude, tenderness, warmth, weakness*, yen*; SEE CONCEPT *32*

affectionate [*adj*] *having or showing fondness*

all over*, attached, caring, crazy over*, dear, devoted, doting, fond, friendly, huggy*, kind, lovey-dovey*, loving, mushy*, nutty about*, partial, soft on*, sympathetic, tender, warm, warm-hearted; SEE CONCEPTS *401,403*

affective [*adj*] *concerning feelings and intuition*

emotional, emotive, feeling, intuitive, noncognitive, perceptual, visceral; SEE CONCEPT *529*

affidavit [*n*] *written legal declaration*

affirmation, oath, sworn statement, testimony; SEE CONCEPTS *271,318*

affiliate [*n*] *organization that is associated with another*

affil*, associate, branch, offshoot, partner, sibling; SEE CONCEPT *381*

affiliate [*v*] *associate or be associated with a larger organization*

ally, amalgamate, annex, associate, band together, combine, come aboard, confederate, connect, form connection, go partners*, hook up*, incorporate, join, line up*, plug into*, relate*, team up, throw in with*, tie up, unite; SEE CONCEPTS *113,114*

affiliation [*n*] *association with an organization*

alliance, amalgamation, banding together, bunch, cahoots*, clan, coalition, combination, confederation, conjunction, connection, crew, crowd, gang, hookup*, incorporation, joining, league, merging, mob, outfit, partnership, relationship, ring, syndicate, tie-in, union; SEE CONCEPT *381*

affinity [*n1*] *liking or inclination toward something*

affection, attraction, closeness, compatibility, cotton*, cup of tea*, druthers*, fondness, good vibrations*, leaning, partiality, rapport, same wavelength, simpatico, sympathy, thing*, weakness*; SEE CONCEPTS *20,32,709*

affinity [*n2*] *similarity*

alikeness, alliance, analogy, association, closeness, connection, correspondence, kinship, likeness, relation, relationship, resemblance, semblance, similitude; SEE CONCEPT *670*

affirm [*v*] *declare the truth of something*

assert, asseverate, attest, aver, avouch, avow, certify, cinch, clinch, confirm, cross heart, declare, guarantee, have a lock on*, ice*, insist, lock up*, maintain, nail down*, okay, predicate, profess, pronounce, put on ice*, ratify, repeat, rubber-stamp*, say so, set, state, swear, swear on bible*, swear up and down*, testify, vouch, witness; SEE CONCEPTS *49,50,88*

affirmation [*n*] *declaration of the truth of something*

affidavit, assertion, asseveration, attestation, averment, avouchment, avowal, certification, confirmation, declaration, green light*, oath, okay, pronouncement, ratification, stamp of approval*, statement, sworn statement, testimonial, testimony; SEE CONCEPT *49*

affirmative [*adj*] *being agreeable or assenting*

acknowledging, acquiescent, affirmatory, affirming, approving, complying, concurring, confirmative, confirmatory, confirming, consenting, corroborative, endorsing, favorable, positive, ratifying, supporting; SEE CONCEPTS *542,572*

affix [*v*] *attach or stick*

add, annex, append, bind, fasten, glue, hitch on*, join, paste, put on, rivet, slap on*, subjoin, tack, tack on*, tag, tag on*; SEE CONCEPTS *85,113,160*

afflict [v] *cause or become hurt*
agonize, annoy, beset, bother, burden, crucify, distress, grieve, harass, harrow, harry, irk, lacerate, martyr, oppress, pain, pester, plague, press, rack, smite, strike, torment, torture, trouble, try, vex, worry, wound; SEE CONCEPTS 7,19,246,313

affliction [n] *hurt condition; something that causes hurt*
adversity, anguish, calamity, cross, crux, depression, difficulty, disease, disorder, distress, grief, hardship, illness, infirmity, misery, misfortune, ordeal, pain, plague, plight, scourge, sickness, sorrow, suffering, torment, trial, tribulation, trouble, woe; SEE CONCEPTS 306,309,674,728

affluent [adj1] *wealthy*
flush*, loaded*, moneyed*, opulent, prosperous, rich, stinking rich*, upper class, upscale, well-off, well-to-do; SEE CONCEPT 334

affluent [adj2] *plentiful*
abundant, bountiful, copious, full, plenteous; SEE CONCEPT 771

afford [v1] *able to have or do; within financial means*
allow, be able to, bear, be disposed to, have enough for, have the means for, incur, manage, spare, stand, support, sustain; SEE CONCEPTS 335,713

afford [v2] *give, produce*
bestow, furnish, grant, impart, offer, provide, render, supply, yield; SEE CONCEPTS 108,143

affront [n] *an insult*
abuse, backhanded compliment*, brickbat*, dirty deed*, indignity, injury, left-handed compliment*, offense, outrage, provocation, put-down*, slap*, slap in the face*, slight, slur, vexation, wrong; SEE CONCEPTS 7,19,44,54

affront [v] *insult or involve in entanglement*
abuse, anger, annoy, confront, criticize, displease, dispraise, dump on*, encounter, face, give a zinger*, give the cold shoulder*, hit where one lives*, meet, offend, outrage, pique, provoke, put down*, slander, slight, taunt, vex; SEE CONCEPTS 7,19,44,54

afraid [adj1] *fearful*
abashed, aghast, alarmed, anxious, apprehensive, aroused, blanched, cowardly, cowed, daunted, discouraged, disheartened, dismayed, distressed, disturbed, faint-hearted, frightened, frozen, have cold feet*, horrified, in awe, intimidated, nervous, panic-stricken, perplexed, perturbed, petrified, rattled, run scared*, scared, scared stiff*, scared to death*, shocked, spooked, startled, stunned, suspicious, terrified, terror-stricken, timid, timorous, trembling, upset, worried; SEE CONCEPTS 403,690

afraid [adj2] *reluctant, regretful*
averse, backward, disinclined, hesitant, indisposed, loath, reluctant, sorry, uneager, unhappy, unwilling; SEE CONCEPT 529

afresh [adj] *new or repeated*
again, anew, de novo, lately, newly, of late, once again, once more, over, over again, recently; SEE CONCEPTS 578,799

after [adj] *following in position or time*
afterwards, back, back of, behind, below, ensuing, hind, hindmost, in the rear, later, next, posterior, postliminary, rear, subsequential, subsequently, succeeding, thereafter; SEE CONCEPTS 586,820

aftermath [n] *situation following an event, occurrence*
after-effects, causatum, chain reaction*, consequences, end, eventuality, flak*, impact, issue, outcome, payoff*, remainder, residual, residuum, results, upshot, waves*; SEE CONCEPT 230

afternoon [n] *period after 12 noon and before sunset*
cocktail hour, P.M., post meridian, siesta, tea-time; SEE CONCEPTS 801,806,810

afterthought [n] *idea that occurs after it is timely*
reconsideration, review, second thought; SEE CONCEPT 529

afterward/afterwards [adv] *following a time, event*
after, another time, at a later time, a while later, behind, by and by, ensuingly, eventually, in a while, intra, late, later, latterly, next, on the next day, soon, subsequently, then, thereafter, thereon, ultimately; SEE CONCEPT 799

again [adv1] *another time; repeated*
afresh, anew, anon, bis, come again, encore, freshly, newly, once more, one more time, over, over and over, recurrently, reiteratively, repeatedly; SEE CONCEPTS 553,799

again [adv2] *in addition*
additionally, also, besides, further, furthermore, moreover, on the contrary, on the other hand, then; SEE CONCEPT 577

age [n1] *period of animate existence*
adolescence, adulthood, boyhood, childhood, dotage, elderliness, girlhood, infancy, life, lifetime, majority, maturity, middle age, milestone, old age, senility, seniority, wear and tear*, youth; SEE CONCEPTS 816,817

age [n2] *a period of time*
aeon, blue moon*, century, date, day, duration, epoch, era, generation, interim, interval, life, lifetime, millennium, span; SEE CONCEPT 807

age [v] *become older*
decline, deteriorate, develop, get along, grow, grow feeble, grow old, grow up, mature, mellow, push, put mileage on*, ripen, wane; SEE CONCEPT 105

aged [adj] *old*
age-old, ancient, antediluvian, antiquated, antique, been around*, creaky*, elderly, getting on*, gray, moth-eaten*, oldie*, over the hill*, passé*, rusty*, senescent, senior citizen, shot*, timeworn, venerable, worn, worse for wear*; SEE CONCEPTS 578,797

ageism [n] *age-based discrimination*
age bias, generation gap; SEE CONCEPT 689

agency [n1] *organization, often business-related*
bureau, company, department, firm, office; SEE CONCEPTS 325,381,441

agency [n2] *power, instrumentality*
action, activity, auspices, channel, efficiency, force, influence, instrument, instrumentality, intercession, intervention, means, mechanism, mediation, medium, operation, organ, vehicle, work; SEE CONCEPTS 376,658

agenda [n] *list of things to do*
calendar, card, diary, docket, lineup, plan, program, schedule, timetable; SEE CONCEPT 283

agent [n1] *person representing an organization or person in business*
abettor, actor, advocate, ambassador, assignee, assistant, attorney, broker, commissioner, delegate, deputy, doer, emissary, envoy, executor,

factor, factotum, functionary, go-between, handler, intermediary, lawyer, mediary, middleperson, minister, mover, negotiator, officer, operative, operator, principal, proctor, promoter, proxy, representative, salesperson, servant, steward, substitute, surrogate, ten percenter*, worker; SEE CONCEPT 348

agent [n2] *power, instrument for achievement*
cause, channel, factor, force, means, medium, organ, power, vehicle; SEE CONCEPTS 376,658

aggrandize [v] *cause something to seem or be greater, bigger*
acclaim, applaud, augment, beef up*, boost, commend, dignify, distinguish, enlarge, ennoble, expand, extend, glorify, heighten, hike, hike up*, honor, hype, increase, intensify, jack up*, jump, magnify, multiply, parlay, praise; SEE CONCEPTS 50,69,88,236,245

aggravate [v1] *annoy*
be at*, be on the back of*, bother, bug, bum*, dog, drive up the wall*, exasperate, gall, get, get on one's nerves, get to, give a hard time, grate, hack, irk, irritate, nag, needle, nettle, peeve, pester, pick on, pique, provoke, tease, vex, wig*; SEE CONCEPTS 7,19

aggravate [v2] *cause to become worse*
complicate, deepen, enhance, exacerbate, exaggerate, heighten, increase, inflame, intensify, magnify, mount, rise, rouse, worsen; SEE CONCEPT 240

aggravation [n1] *annoyance*
affliction, aggro*, bother, botheration*, difficulty, distress, exasperation, hang-up*, headache*, irksomeness, irritation, pain, pain in the neck*, pet peeve*, provocation, teasing, vexation, worry; SEE CONCEPT 410

aggravation [n2] *worsening of a situation, condition*
deepening, exacerbation, exaggeration, heightening, increase, inflaming, inflammation, intensification, magnification, sharpening, strengthening, worsening; SEE CONCEPT 240

aggregate [n] *collection*
accumulation, agglomerate, agglomeration, all, amount, assemblage, body, bulk, combination, conglomerate, conglomeration, gross, heap, lump, mass, mixture, pile, quantity, sum, the works*, total, totality, whole, whole ball of wax*, whole enchilada*, whole schmear*, whole shooting match*; SEE CONCEPT 432

aggregate [adj] *forming a collection from separate parts*
accumulated, added, amassed, assembled, collected, collective, combined, composite, corporate, cumulative, heaped, mixed, piled, total; SEE CONCEPT 781

aggregate [v] *combine into a collection*
accumulate, add up, amass, amount, assemble, collect, combine, come, heap, mix, number, pile, sum, total; SEE CONCEPT 109

aggression [n1] *attack, often military*
assailment, assault, blitz, blitzkrieg, encroachment, injury, invasion, offense, offensive, onset, onslaught, push, raid; SEE CONCEPTS 86,320

aggression [n2] *hostile or forceful behavior, attitude*
aggressiveness, antagonism, belligerence, blitz, combativeness, destructiveness, fight, hostility, pugnacity, push; SEE CONCEPTS 29,411

aggressive [adj1] *belligerent, hostile*
advancing, antipathetic, assailing, attacking, barbaric, bellicose, combative, contentious, destructive, disruptive, disturbing, encroaching, hawkish, intruding, intrusive, invading, martial, militant, offensive, pugnacious, quarrelsome, rapacious, threatening, warlike; SEE CONCEPT 550

aggressive [adj2] *assertive*
assertory, bold, brassy*, cheeky*, cocky*, come on*, domineering, dynamic, energetic, enterprising, flip*, forceful, fresh*, get up and go*, go after, hard sell, imperious, masterful, militant, nervy*, pushing, pushy, sassy, shooting from the hip*, smart*, smart alecky*, strenuous, tough, vigorous, zealous; SEE CONCEPTS 404,542

aggrieved [adj] *very distressed*
afflicted, depressed, disturbed, grieving, harmed, hurt, injured, oppressed, pained, peeved, persecuted, saddened, unhappy, woeful, wronged; SEE CONCEPT 403

aghast [adj] *horrified; very surprised*
afraid, agape, agog, alarmed, amazed, anxious, appalled, astonished, astounded, awestruck, confounded, dismayed, dumbfounded, frightened, horror-struck, overwhelmed, shocked, startled, stunned, terrified, thunderstruck; SEE CONCEPTS 403,690

agile [adj] *physically or mentally nimble, deft*
active, acute, alert, athletic, brisk, buoyant, bustling, clever, dexterous, easy-moving, energetic, fleet, frisky, limber, lithe, lively, mercurial, prompt, quick, quick on the draw*, quick on the trigger*, quick-witted, rapid, ready, sharp, spirited, sportive, spright, sprightly, spry, stirring, supple, swift, twinkle toes*, vigorous, vivacious, winged, zippy; SEE CONCEPTS 485,527,588

agility [n] *physical or mental nimbleness, deftness*
activity, acuteness, adroitness, alacrity, alertness, briskness, celerity, cleverness, dexterity, dispatch, expedition, fleetness, friskiness, litheness, liveliness, promptitude, promptness, quickness, quick-wittedness, sharpness, sprightliness, spryness, suppleness, swiftness; SEE CONCEPTS 410,630,748

aging [n] *becoming older*
crumbling, declining, developing, fading, fermenting, getting along*, getting on*, maturing, mellowing, senescent, slumping, stale, waning, wearing out*; SEE CONCEPT 701

agitate [v1] *shake physically*
beat, churn, concuss, convulse, disturb, rock, rouse, stir, toss; SEE CONCEPT 152

agitate [v2] *disturb, trouble someone*
alarm, argue, arouse, bug*, bug up*, burn up*, confuse, craze*, debate, discompose, disconcert, discuss, dispute, disquiet, distract, disturb, egg on*, examine, excite, ferment, flurry, fluster, get to*, incite, inflame, make flip*, move, perturb, psych*, push buttons*, rouse, ruffle, spook, stimulate, stir, trouble, turn on*, unhinge*, upset, ventilate*, work up*, worry; SEE CONCEPTS 7,19,46

agitator [n] *person who disturbs, causes trouble*
adjy, advocate, agent, anarchist, champion, demagogue, disrupter, dissident, dogmatist, fighter, firebrand*, fomenter, heretic, incendiary, inciter, instigator, leftist, malcontent, mover, partisan, propagandist, provocateur, pusher, rabble-rouser, radical, reactionary, rebel, reformer, revisionist, revolutionary, ringleader, sparkplug*, troublemaker, wave maker*, zealot; SEE CONCEPT 412

agnostic [n] *person unsure that God exists*
doubter, freethinker, materialist, skeptic, unbeliever; SEE CONCEPT *361*

ago [adv] *in the past*
ages ago, back, back when, before, from way back, from year one*, gone, since, since God knows when*, time was; SEE CONCEPT *820*

agonize [v] *suffer or cause another to suffer*
afflict, bleed, carry on, crucify, distress, disturb, eat heart out*, excruciate, harrow, hurt, labor, lament, martyr, pain, rack, sing the blues*, squirm, stew over, strain, strive, struggle, take it badly*, torment, torture, try, wince, worry, writhe; SEE CONCEPTS *7,19,410*

agonizing [adj] *difficult and painful, suffering*
disturbing, excruciating, extreme, fierce, harrowing, intense, racking, struggling, tearing, tormenting, tortuous, torturing, vehement, violent; SEE CONCEPTS *403,565*

agony [n] *suffering, pain*
affliction, anguish, distress, dolor, misery, pangs, passion, throes, torment, torture, woe; SEE CONCEPTS *410,728*

agrarian [adj] *concerning land, farming*
agricultural, natural, peasant, rural, rustic, uncultivated, undomesticated; SEE CONCEPT *536*

agree [v1] *be in unison, assent with another*
accede, acknowledge, acquiesce, admit, allow, be of the same mind*, bury the hatchet*, buy into*, check, clinch the deal*, come to terms, comply, concede, concur, consent, cut a deal*, engage, give blessing*, give carte blanche*, give green light*, give the go-ahead*, go along with, grant, make a deal*, okay, pass on, permit, play ball*, recognize, see eye to eye*, set, settle, shake on*, side with, sign*, subscribe, take one up on*, yes*; SEE CONCEPTS *8,10,45,235*

agree [v2] *be similar or consistent*
accord, answer, attune, be in harmony, blend, click, cohere, coincide, concert, concord, concur, conform, consort, correspond, equal, fall in with*, fit, get along with, go hand in hand*, go together, go well with, harmonize, jibe, match, parallel, square, suit, synchronize, tally; SEE CONCEPTS *118,656,670*

agreeable [adj1] *pleasing*
acceptable, dandy, delicious, delightful, enjoyable, fair, fine, gratifying, hunky-dory*, mild, nice, peach*, peachy*, pleasant, pleasurable, pleasureful, pussycat*, ready, satisfying, spiffy*, swell*, to one's liking, to one's taste, welcome; SEE CONCEPT *572*

agreeable [adj2] *appropriate, in keeping*
befitting, compatible, congruous, consistent, consonant, fitting, proper; SEE CONCEPT *558*

agreeable [adj3] *willing to be in unison, assent*
acquiescent, amenable, approving, complying, concurring, congenial, consenting, grateful, in accord, responsive, sympathetic, well-disposed, willing; SEE CONCEPTS *401,542*

agreeably [adv] *willingly, assenting; pleasantly; in keeping*
affably, affirmatively, amiably, amicably, appropriately, benevolently, charmingly, cheerfully, convivially, favorably, genially, good-humoredly, good-naturedly, graciously, happily, kindly, mutually, obligingly, peacefully, pleasingly, politely, satisfactorily, sympathetically, well, wonderfully; SEE CONCEPTS *401,572*

agreement [n1] *concurrence*
acceding, accession, accommodation, accord, accordance, acknowledging, adjustment, affiliation, affinity, alliance, amity, approving, arbitration, arrangement, assenting, authorizing, bargaining, compatibility, compliance, complying, compromise, concert, concession, concord, concordance, concurring, conformity, congruity, consistency, correspondence, endorsing, granting, harmony, mediation, ratifying, reconciliation, similarity, suitableness, sympathy, understanding, union, unison, verification, verifying; SEE CONCEPT *684*

agreement [n2] *document of concurrence, contract*
acknowledgment, adjudication, affidavit, approval, arrangement, assent, avowal, bargain, bond, cartel, charter, codicil, compact, compromise, confirmation, covenant, deal, indenture, lease, negotiation, note, oath, okay, pact, piece of paper*, protocol, recognition, settlement, stipulation, the nod*, transaction, treaty, understanding, writ; SEE CONCEPTS *271,331*

agricultural [adj] *concerning farming, land*
aggie*, agronomical, arboricultural, floricultural, gardening, horticultural, ranch, rural, rustic; SEE CONCEPTS *536,583*

agriculture [n] *farming, crop production*
agronomics, agronomy, cultivation, culture, horticulture, husbandry, tillage; SEE CONCEPTS *205,257*

aground [adv] *on the bottom of*
ashore, beached, disabled, foundered, grounded, high and dry*, marooned, reefed, shipwrecked, stranded, stuck, swamped, wrecked; SEE CONCEPT *583*

ahead [adv] *in front or advance of*
advanced, advancing, ahead, along, ante, antecedently, at an advantage, at the head, before, beforehand, earlier, first, fore, foremost, forward, forwards, in the foreground, in the lead, leading, on, onward, onwards, precedent, precedently, preceding, previous, progressing, to the fore; SEE CONCEPTS *586,632,820*

aid [n1] *help, support*
advancement, advice, advocacy, alleviation, allowance, assist, assistance, attention, backing, backup, benefaction, benefit, benevolence, bounty, care, charity, comfort, compensation, cooperation, deliverance, encouragement, endowment, favor, furtherance, gift, giving, guidance, hand, handout, leg up*, lift, ministration, ministry, patronage, promotion, reinforcement, relief, rescue, reward, salvation, service, shot in the arm*, subsidy, sustenance, treatment; SEE CONCEPT *110*

aid/aide [n2] *person who helps*
abettor, adjutant, aide-de-camp, assistant, attendant, coadjutant, coadjutor, crew, deputy, helper, lieutenant, second, supporter; SEE CONCEPT *348*

aid [v] *help, support*
abet, alleviate, assist, bail out, befriend, benefact, encourage, favor, go to bat for*, go with*, lend a hand*, lighten, mitigate, open doors for*, promote, relieve, serve, stick up for*, straighten out*, subsidize, sustain; SEE CONCEPT *110*

ailing [adj] *not feeling well*
below par, debilitated, diseased, down, down with, enfeebled, feeble, feeling awful, ill, indisposed, rocky*, run down*, sick, sick as a dog*, sickly, under the weather*, unwell, wasting, weak; SEE CONCEPT *314*

ailment [n] *mild sickness*
ache, bug, complaint, condition, disease, disorder, dose*, flu, illness, indisposition, infirmity, malady, syndrome; SEE CONCEPTS *306,316*

aim [n] *goal*
ambition, aspiration, course, desideratum, design, desire, direction, end, intent, intention, mark, object, objective, plan, purpose, scheme, target, where one is heading*, wish; SEE CONCEPT *659*

aim [v] *point or direct at a goal*
address, angle, aspire, attempt, cast, concentrate, contemplate, covet, design, direct, endeavor, essay, fix, focus, intend, level, mean, plan, propose, purpose, set one's sights on*, sight, slant, steer, strive, target, train, try, want, wish, zero in on, zoom in; SEE CONCEPTS *20,41,201*

aimless [adj] *having no goal*
accidental, any which way*, bits-and-pieces*, blind, capricious, careless, casual, chance, desultory, directionless, drifting, erratic, fanciful, fickle, fits and starts*, flighty, fortuitous, frivolous, goalless, haphazard, heedless, hit-or-miss*, indecisive, indiscriminate, irresolute, objectless, pointless, purposeless, random, shiftless, stray, thoughtless, unavailing, undirected, unguided, unplanned, unpredictable, vagrant, wandering, wanton, wayward; SEE CONCEPTS *401,535,544*

air [n1] *gases forming the atmosphere*
blast, breath, breeze, draft, heavens, ozone, puff, sky, stratosphere, troposphere, ventilation, waft, whiff, wind, zephyr; SEE CONCEPT *437*

air [n2] *distinctive quality or character; style*
address, affectation, ambience, appearance, atmosphere, aura, bearing, comportment, demeanor, deportment, effect, feel, feeling, flavor, impression, look, manner, mannerism, mien, mood, pose, presence, property, quality, semblance, tone; SEE CONCEPTS *644,673*

air [n3] *musical tune*
aria, descant, lay, melody, song, strain, theme; SEE CONCEPTS *77,595*

air [v1] *put into the atmosphere; freshen*
aerate, aerify, air-condition, circulate, cool, eject, expel, expose, fan, open, oxygenate, purify, refresh, ventilate; SEE CONCEPT *255*

air [v2] *express opinion publicly*
broadcast, circulate, communicate, declare, disclose, display, disseminate, divulge, exhibit, expose, make known, make public, proclaim, publicize, publish, put, reveal, speak, state, tell, utter, ventilate, voice; SEE CONCEPTS *51,52*

airplane [n] *vehicle that transports cargo or passengers through the air*
aeroplane, airbus, aircraft, airliner, airship, cab*, crate*, jet, kite*, plane, ramjet*, ship*; SEE CONCEPT *504*

airport [n] *center for transportation by air*
aerodrome, airdrome, airfield, airstrip, hangar, helipad, heliport, home plate*, installation, landing strip, runway, strip; SEE CONCEPTS *325,439*

airs [n] *affectation; pretended behavior*
affectedness, arrogance, false front, front, haughtiness, hauteur, mannerism, ostentation, pomposity, pose, pretense, pretension, pretentiousness, put-on*, show, superciliousness; SEE CONCEPT *633*

airtight [adj1] *sealed*
closed, impenetrable, impermeable, shut; SEE CONCEPTS *483,490*

airtight [adj2] *certain*
incontestable, indisputable, invulnerable, irrefutable, unassailable; SEE CONCEPT *535*

airy [adj1] *open to the atmosphere*
aerial, atmospheric, blowy, breezy, drafty, exposed, fluttering, fresh, gaseous, gusty, light, lofty, out-of-doors, uncluttered, vaporous, ventilated, well-ventilated, windy; SEE CONCEPT *583*

airy [adj2] *delicate or ethereal*
dainty, diaphanous, flimsy, fragile, frail, frivolous, illusory, imaginary, immaterial, intangible, light, rare, rarefied, tenuous, thin, vaporous, visionary, volatile, weightless, wispy; SEE CONCEPTS *490,582*

airy [adj3] *buoyant, light, or lively in nature*
animated, blithe, bouncy, cheerful, cheery, effervescent, elastic, fanciful, flippant, frolicsome, gay, graceful, happy, high-spirited, jaunty, light, light-hearted, merry, nonchalant, resilient, sprightly, volatile, whimsical; SEE CONCEPTS *404,550*

aisle [n] *passageway dividing something*
alley, artery, avenue, clearing, corridor, course, egress, gangway, hallway, ingress, lane, opening, passage, path, walk, way; SEE CONCEPTS *440,513,830*

ajar [adj/adv] *slightly open*
open, unclosed, unlatched, unshut; SEE CONCEPT *586*

akin [adj] *related or connected*
affiliated, agnate, alike, allied, analogous, cognated, comparable, connate, consonant, corresponding, incident, kindred, like, parallel, similar; SEE CONCEPTS *487,563,573*

alacrity [n] *liveliness; promptness*
alertness, avidity, briskness, cheerfulness, dispatch, eagerness, enthusiasm, expedition, fervor, gaiety, hilarity, joyousness, promptitude, quickness, readiness, speed, sprightliness, willingness, zeal; SEE CONCEPTS *633,657*

alarm [n1] *feeling of sudden fear*
anxiety, apprehension, cold feet*, consternation, dismay, distress, dread, fright, horror, nervousness, panic, scare, strain, stress, tension, terror, trepidation, unease, uneasiness; SEE CONCEPTS *410,690*

alarm [n2] *warning, signaling device*
alert, bell, blast, buzzer, call, caution, clock, cry, drum, flap*, flash*, forewarning, gong, high sign*, horn, Mayday*, nod*, scramble*, scream, shout, sign, signal, siren, SOS, squeal, tip, tip off*, tocsin, trumpet, warning, whistle, wink*, yell; SEE CONCEPTS *269,463*

alarm [v] *upset*
amaze, astonish, chill, daunt, dismay, distress, frighten, give a turn*, make jump*, panic, scare, scare silly*, scare stiff*, scare to death*, spook, startle, surprise, terrify, unnerve; SEE CONCEPTS *7,14,19,42*

album [n] *blank book for collecting; holder*
anthology, collection, depository, index, memento, memory book, miscellany, notebook, portfolio, register, registry, scrapbook; SEE CONCEPTS *271,446*

alcohol [n] *intoxicating, flammable liquid*
alky*, booze*, canned heat*, cocktail, drink, ethanol, firewater*, hard stuff*, hootch*, intoxicant, liquor, methanol, moonshine*, palliative*, redeye*, rotgut*, sauce*, smoke*, spirits, tipple*, toddy*; SEE CONCEPTS *454,467*

alcoholic [adj] intoxicating
brewed, distilled, hard, inebriant, inebriating, sprituous, vinous; SEE CONCEPT 462

alcove [n] nook, secluded spot
anteroom, bay, bower, compartment, corner, cubbyhole, cubicle, niche, recess, study; SEE CONCEPTS 440,448,513

ale [n] intoxicating, fermented beverage
beer, brew, hops, malt, suds*; SEE CONCEPT 454

alert [n] warning
admonition, alarm, flap*, high sign*, Mayday*, sign, signal, siren, SOS, tip off, wink*; SEE CONCEPTS 78,278,595,628

alert [adj] attentive, lively
active, all ears*, bright, cagey*, careful, circumspect, clever, fast on the draw*, good hands*, heads up*, heedful, hip, intelligent, jazzed*, observant, on guard*, on one's toes*, on the ball*, on the job*, on the lookout*, on the qui vive*, perceptive, psyched up*, quick, ready, sharp, spirited, switched on*, vigilant, wary, watchful, wide-awake, wired*, wise, with it*; SEE CONCEPTS 402,403

alert [v] warn
alarm, flag, forewarn, give the high sign*, inform, notify, put on guard, signal, tip, tip off, wave flag*; SEE CONCEPT 78

algae [n] rootless, leafless plants living in water
dulse, kelp, scum, seaweed; SEE CONCEPT 429

alias [n] false name
AKA, anonym, assumed name, handle*, moniker, nickname, nom de guerre, nom de plume, pen name, pseudonym, stage name, summer name*; SEE CONCEPT 683

alias [adv] otherwise known as
also called, also known as, otherwise; SEE CONCEPT 582

alibi [n] defense against charges of wrongdoing; evidence of absence
account, affirmation, airtight case*, allegation, answer, assertion, assurance, avowal, case, copout*, cover, declaration, excuse, explanation, fish story*, justification, plea, pretext, profession, proof, reason, reply, retort, song and dance*, stall, statement, vindication; SEE CONCEPT 661

alien [n] foreign being
blow in*, floater*, foreigner, greenhorn*, guest, immigrant, incomer*, interloper, intruder, invader, migrant, newcomer, noncitizen, outsider, refugee, settler, squatter, stranger, visitor, weed*; SEE CONCEPT 423

alien [adj] foreign
conflicting, contrary, estranged, exotic, extraneous, extrinsic, inappropriate, incompatible, incongruous, opposed, remote, separate, unusual; SEE CONCEPT 564

alienate [v] cause unfriendliness, hostility
break off, come between, disaffect, disunite, divide, divorce, estrange, make indifferent, part, separate, set against, turn away, turn off, wean, withdraw the affections of; SEE CONCEPTS 7,19,231

alienation [n] unfriendliness
breach, breaking off, coolness, disaffection, diverting, division, divorce, estrangement, indifference, remoteness, rupture, separation, setting against, turning away, variance, withdrawal; SEE CONCEPT 410

align [v1] line up, arrange next to
adjust, allineate, coordinate, even, even up, fix,
make parallel, order, range, regulate, straighten; SEE CONCEPT 158

align [v2] join; bring to agreement
affiliate, agree, ally, associate, cooperate, enlist, follow, join sides, sympathize; SEE CONCEPTS 8,114

alike [adj] similar
akin, allied, analogous, approximate, associated, carbon copy*, cognate, comparable, concurrent, correspondent, corresponding, dead ringer*, ditto*, double, duplicate, equal, equivalent, even, facsimile, identical, indistinguishable, kindred, like, look-alike, matched, matching, mated, parallel, proportionate, related, resembling, same, same difference*, similar, spitting image*, undifferentiated, uniform, Xerox*; SEE CONCEPTS 487,566,573

alike [adv] similarly
analogously, comparably, comparatively, consonantly, correspondingly, equally, equivalently, evenly, identically, in accordance with, in common, in the same degree, in the same manner, likewise, similarly, the same way, uniformly; SEE CONCEPTS 487,566,573

alimentary [adj] digestive
comestible, dietary, digestible, nourishing, nutrient, nutritional, nutritious, nutritive, peptic, salutary, sustaining, sustentative; SEE CONCEPTS 406,485

alimony [n] money paid in support of a former spouse
keep, livelihood, living, maintenance, provision, remittance, subsistence, sustenance, upkeep; SEE CONCEPT 344

alive [adj1] being animately existent
animate, around, awake, breathing, cognizant, conscious, dynamic, existing, extant, functioning, growing, knowing, live, living, mortal, operative, running, subsisting, viable, vital, working, zoetic; SEE CONCEPT 539

alive [adj2] being active, full of life
abounding, alert, animated, awake, brisk, bustling, cheerful, dynamic, eager, energetic, lively, overflowing, quick, ready, replete, rife, sharp, spirited, sprightly, spry, stirring, swarming, teeming, vigorous, vital, vivacious, zestful; SEE CONCEPTS 401,542

alkali [n] soluble base; opposite of an acid
antacid, caustic soda, salt; SEE CONCEPT 472

alkaline [adj] being basic, not acid (chemically)
acrid, alkalescent, alkali, antacid, bitter, caustic, neutralizing, salty, soluble; SEE CONCEPT 472

all [n] whole; totality
accumulation, across the board, aggregate, aggregation, collection, ensemble, entirety, everyone, everything, gross, group, integer, jackpot*, lock stock and barrel*, mass, quantity, sum, sum total, total, unit, utmost, wall to wall*, whole ball of wax*, whole enchilada*, whole nine yards*, whole schmear*, whole shooting match*, whole show*, works; SEE CONCEPTS 787,837

all [adj1] whole quantity
complete, entire, full, greatest, gross, outright, perfect, total, utter; SEE CONCEPT 771

all [adj2] each; every one of a class
any, bar none*, barring no one, complete, each and every, entire, every, every bit of, every single, sum, total, totality, whole; SEE CONCEPT 772

all [adj3] exclusively
alone, nothing but, only, solely; SEE CONCEPT 554

all [adv] completely, without exception
all in all, altogether, entirely, exactly, fully, just, purely, quite, totally, utterly, wholly; SEE CONCEPTS 771,772

allay [v] reduce something, usually a pain or a problem
abate, alleviate, assuage, calm, compose, cool out*, decrease, ease, lessen, lighten, make nice*, mitigate, moderate, mollify, pacify, play up to*, pour oil on*, quiet, square, take the bite out*, take the sting out*; SEE CONCEPTS 7,22,244

allegation [n] assertion placing blame
accusation, affirmation, asseveration, avowal, charge, claim, declaration, deposition, overment, plea, profession, statement; SEE CONCEPT 49

allege [v] assert; claim
adduce, advance, affirm, asseverate, aver, avouch, avow, charge, cite, declare, depose, lay, maintain, offer, plead, present, profess, put forward, recite, recount, state, testify; SEE CONCEPT 49

alleged [adj] asserted, often doubtful
averred, declared, described, dubious, ostensible, pretended, professed, purported, questionable, so-called, stated, supposed, suspect, suspicious; SEE CONCEPT 552

allegiance [n] loyalty
adherence, ardor, consecration, constancy, dedication, deference, devotion, duty, faithfulness, fealty, fidelity, homage, honor, obedience, obligation, piety; SEE CONCEPT 689

allegorical [adj] symbolic
emblematic, figurative, illustrative, metaphorical, parabolic, symbolizing, typifying; SEE CONCEPT 582

allegory [n] indirect representation, storytelling
apologue, emblem, fable, figuration, moral, myth, parable, story, symbol, symbolism, symbolization, tale, typification; SEE CONCEPT 282

alleviate [v] relieve; lessen
allay, assuage, ease, lighten, mitigate, mollify, pacify, pour oil on*, soft-pedal*, take the bite out*, take the edge off*, take the sting out*; SEE CONCEPTS 7,22,110,236,247

alley [n] narrow passage
alleyway, back street, lane, passageway, path, pathway, walk; SEE CONCEPT 501

alliance [n] friendly association, agreement
accord, affiliation, affinity, betrothal, bond, coalition, coherence, collaboration, collusion, combination, communion, compact, concord, concurrence, confederacy, confederation, congruity, conjunction, connection, consanguinity, cooperation, engagement, entente, federation, fraternization, friendship, interrelation, kinship, league, marriage, matrimony, membership, mutuality, pact, participation, partnership, relation, support, tie, treaty, union; SEE CONCEPTS 301,423,684

allied [adj] friendly; united
affiliated, agnate, akin, amalgamated, associated, bound, cognate, combined, confederate, connate, connected, incident, in league, joined, joint, kindred, linked, married, related, unified, wed; SEE CONCEPTS 555,563

allocate [v] assign; divide among
admeasure, allot, apportion, appropriate, budget, cut, designate, dish out*, divvy*, earmark, give, mete, set aside, share, slice; SEE CONCEPTS 41,98,108,129

allot [v] assign; give portion
admeasure, allocate, appoint, apportion, appropriate, assign, budget, cut, cut the pie*, designate, distribute, divvy*, dole, earmark, mete, set aside, share, shell out*, slice, split up; SEE CONCEPTS 41,108

allotment [n] portion assigned or given
allocation, allowance, apportionment, appropriation, bite, chunk, cut, cut of pie*, end, grant, lot, measure, part, piece, piece of the action*, quota, rake off*, ration, share, slice, split, stint*; SEE CONCEPT 835

all-out [adj] complete
absolute, determined, entire, exhaustive, full, full-blown, full-fledged, full-scale, maximum, optimum, resolute, supreme, thorough, total, undivided, unlimited, utmost, utter; SEE CONCEPTS 531,772

allow [v1] admit; acknowledge
acquiesce, avow, concede, confess, grant, let on, own; SEE CONCEPTS 60,82

allow [v2] permit an action
accord, accredit, admit, approve, authorize, bear, be big*, be game for*, brook, certify, commission, consent, empower, endorse, endure, favor, free up*, give a blank check*, give carte blanche, give leave, give permission, give the go-ahead, give the green light*, go along with, grant permission, hear of, hold with, indulge, let, license, live with*, oblige, okay, pass, pass on, put up with, recognize, release, sanction, sit still for*, stand, suffer, support, take kindly to, tolerate, warrant; SEE CONCEPTS 83,99

allow [v3] set aside
admeasure, allocate, allot, apportion, assign, deduct, give, grant, lot, mete, provide, remit, spare; SEE CONCEPTS 41,108

allowance [n1] amount of money or other supply
aid, alimony, allocation, allotment, annuity, apportionment, bequest, bite*, bounty, commission, contribution, cut, endowment, fee, fellowship, gift, grant, honorarium, inheritance, interest, legacy, lot, measure, part, pay, pension, piece, portion, prize, quantity, quota, ration, recompense, remittance, salary, scholarship, share, slice, stint, stipend, subsidy, taste, wage; SEE CONCEPTS 337,340

allowance [n2] discount; concession
accommodation, adaptation, adjustment, admission, advantage, cut, deduction, rebate, reduction, sanction, sufferance, toleration; SEE CONCEPT 775

alloy [n] mixture, usually of two metals
admixture, adulterant, adulteration, amalgam, amalgamation, blend, combination, composite, compound, debasement, denaturant, fusion, hybrid, intermixture, reduction; SEE CONCEPTS 260,476

alloy [v1] mix metals
admix, amalgamate, blend, combine, compound, fuse, intermix, mix; SEE CONCEPTS 109,113

alloy [v2] adulterate
debase, denature, devalue, diminish, impair, reduce; SEE CONCEPT 240

all right [adj1] satisfactory
acceptable, adequate, appropriate, average, decent, fair, fit, fitting, good, hunky-dory*, okay, okey-dokey*, passable, proper, satisfying, stan-

dard, sufficient, swell*, tolerable, unexceptional, unobjectionable; SEE CONCEPTS 547,558

all right [adj2] in good condition or health
hale, healthy, safe, sound, unharmed, unhurt, unimpaired, well, whole; SEE CONCEPT 572

all right [adj3] correct; excellent
accurate, exact, good, great, precise, right; SEE CONCEPTS 557,574

all right [adv1] satisfactorily
acceptably, adequately, okay, passably, tolerably, unobjectionably, well enough; SEE CONCEPTS 547,558

all right [adv2] yes
agreed, certainly, definitely, of course, okay, positively, surely, very well, without a doubt; SEE CONCEPT 572

all-time [adj] unsurpassed and permanent
best, champion, enduring, everlasting, perpetual; SEE CONCEPTS 574,798

allude [v] hint at
advert, bring up, imply, insinuate, intimate, point, refer, suggest; SEE CONCEPTS 60,66

allure [n] appeal
attraction, bedroom eyes*, charisma, charm, come-hither look*, come-on*, enchantment, enticement, glamor, inveiglement, lure, magnetism, seductiveness, temptation, the jazz*; SEE CONCEPTS 673,720

allure [v] entice
attract, bait, beguile, bewitch, cajole, captivate, charm, coax, come on*, decoy, draw, enchant, entrap, fascinate, hook*, inveigle, lead on, lure, magnetize, persuade, pull, seduce, suck in*, sweep off feet*, tempt, turn on*, wile, win over; SEE CONCEPTS 7,22

allusion [n] indirect reference; hint
casual remark, charge, citation, connotation, denotation, figure of speech, implication, imputation, incidental mention, indication, inference, innuendo, insinuation, intimation, mention, play on words, quotation, remark, statement, suggestion; SEE CONCEPTS 60,274

ally [n] something united with another, especially by treaty
accessory, accomplice, associate, coadjutor, collaborator, colleague, confederate, co-worker, friend, helper, partner; SEE CONCEPTS 299, 322,354,359

alma mater [n] school from which one has graduated
academy, college, institution, old school, place of graduation, place of matriculation, university; SEE CONCEPTS 288,289

almanac [n] document containing information for a year
annual, calendar, chronicle, ephemeris, journal, record, register, registry, yearbook; SEE CONCEPTS 280,801,809,823

almighty [adj1] having complete power, control
absolute, all-powerful, invincible, mighty, omnipotent, puissant, supreme, unlimited; SEE CONCEPT 540

almighty [adj2] godlike
all-knowing, all-seeing, boundless, celestial, deathless, deific, divine, enduring, eternal, everlasting, godly, heavenly, illimitable, immortal, infinite, omnipotent, omnipresent, omniscient, pervading; SEE CONCEPT 539

almighty [adj3] severe
awful, desperate, enormous, excessive, extreme,

great, intense, loud, terrible; SEE CONCEPT 569

almost [adv] nearly, very nearly
about, about to, all but, approximately, around, as good as, bordering on, close to, close upon, essentially, for all practical purposes, for the greatest part, in effect, in the neighborhood of, in the vicinity of, just about, most, much, near to, nigh, not far from, not quite, on the brink of, on the edge of, on the point of, on the verge of, practically, pretty near, relatively, roughly, substantially, virtually, well-nigh, within sight of; SEE CONCEPTS 531,586,799

alone [adj1] separate; apart
abandoned, batching it*, by itself/oneself, companionless, deserted, desolate, detached, forlorn, forsaken, friendless, hermit, individual, in solitary*, isolated, lone, lonely, lonesome, me and my shadow*, me myself and I*, onliest*, only, on one's own, shag*, single, sole, solitary, solo, stag, traveling light*, unaccompanied, unaided, unassisted, unattached, unattended, unescorted, unmarried, widowed; SEE CONCEPTS 577,583

alone [adj2] to the exclusion of; unique
incomparable, matchless, peerless, singly, singular, solely, unequalled, unique, unmatched, unparalleled, unrivaled, unsurpassed; SEE CONCEPTS 556,653

along [adv1] ahead
forth, forward, on, onward; SEE CONCEPT 581

along [adv2] together with
accompanying, additionally, also, as companion, as well, at same time, besides, coupled with, furthermore, in addition to, likewise, moreover, side by side, simultaneously, too, with; SEE CONCEPT 577

along [adv3] near
adjacent, at, by; SEE CONCEPT 586

alongside [prep] close, near side of
along the side of, apace with, at the side of, beside, by, by the side of, close at hand, close by, equal with, in company with, next to, parallel to, side by side; SEE CONCEPT 586

aloof [adj] remote
above, apart, casual, chilly, cold, cold fish*, cool, detached, distant, forbidding, hard-boiled*, hardhearted, haughty, incurious, indifferent, laid back*, loner*, lone wolf*, offish*, on ice*, putting on airs*, reserved, secluded, solitary, standoffish*, stuck up*, supercilious, thick-skinned*, unapproachable, unconcerned, unfriendly, uninterested, unresponsive, unsociable, unsympathetic, uppity*, withdrawn; SEE CONCEPTS 401,542

aloud [adv] in a spoken voice, usually not softly
audibly, clearly, distinctly, intelligibly, loudly, lustily, noisily, out loud, plainly, vociferously; SEE CONCEPT 594

alphabet [n] letters of a writing system
ABCs, characters, elements, fundamentals, graphic representation, hieroglyphs, ideograph, morphemes, phonemes, pictograph, rune, signs, syllabary, symbols; SEE CONCEPT 276

alphabetical [adj] in ascending order of a writing system
A to Z, consecutive, graded, indexed, logical, ordered, progressive; SEE CONCEPT 585

alphabetize [v] place in order of a writing system
index, order, systematize; SEE CONCEPT 84

alpine [adj] mountaintop; high altitude
aerial, elevated, high, high-reaching, in the

clouds, lofty, montane, mountainous, rangy, snowcapped, soaring, towering; SEE CONCEPTS 779,836

already [adv] *before expected time*
as of now, at present, before, before now, but now, by now, by that time, by then, by the time mentioned, by this time, earlier, even now, formerly, heretofore, in the past, just now, now, once, previously, then, up to now; SEE CONCEPT 799

also [adv] *in addition to*
additionally, again, along, along with, and, as well, as well as, besides, conjointly, further, furthermore, including, in conjunction with, in like manner, likewise, more, moreover, more than that, on top of, over and above, plus, still, to boot*, together with, too, withal; SEE CONCEPT 577

altar [n] *church table, pedestal*
chantry, font, reredos, retable, shrine, tabernacle; SEE CONCEPT 443

alter [v1] *change*
adapt, adjust, amend, change, convert, cook, correct mid-course*, develop, dial back*, diversify, doctor, fine tune*, make different, metamorphose, modify, mutate, phony up*, recalibrate, recast, reconstruct, refashion, reform, remodel, renovate, reshape, revamp, revise, shift, transform, transmute, turn, vary; SEE CONCEPT 232

alter [v2] *sterilize animal*
caponize, castrate, change, desexualize, emasculate, fix, geld, mutilate, neuter, spay, unsex; SEE CONCEPTS 310,375

alteration [n] *change*
about-face, accommodation, adaptation, adjustment, amendment, conversion, correction, difference, diversification, exchange, fixing, flip-flop*, metamorphosis, mid-course correction*, modification, mutation, reformation, remodeling, reshaping, revision, shift, switch, switch-over*, transformation, transmutation, turn, variance, variation; SEE CONCEPT 701

altercation [n] *fight, often verbal*
argument, beef*, bickering, blowup*, bone of contention*, brawl*, brush*, combat, contest, controversy, dispute, embroilment, flap*, fracas*, fuss, go*, hassle, quarrel, row, rumble*, run-in*, set-to*, squabbling, tiff*, words*, wrangle; SEE CONCEPTS 46,106

altered [adj] *changed*
adapted, adjusted, amended, converted, cooked, corrected, diversified, doctored, fitted, fixed, modified, qualified, redone, refitted, reformed, remade, remodeled, renovated, reshaped, retailored, revised, spiked, transformed, turned, updated; SEE CONCEPT 564

alter ego [n] *other side to personality*
doppelganger, evil twin*, second self; SEE CONCEPTS 410,423

alternate [n] *substitute*
backup, double, equivalent, fill-in, proxy, replacement, stand-in, sub*, surrogate; SEE CONCEPT 667

alternate [adj1] *every other*
alternating, every second, intermittent, periodic, recurrent, recurring, rotating; SEE CONCEPT 553

alternate [adj2] *substitute*
alternative, another, backup, different, interchanging, makeshift, second, surrogate, temporary; SEE CONCEPT 566

alternate [v] *take turns, change back and forth*
act reciprocally, alter, blow hot and cold*, change, come and go, exchange, fill in for, fluctuate, follow, follow in turn, interchange, intersperse, oscillate, relieve, rotate, seesaw, shift, shilly-shally*, substitute, sway, vacillate, vary, waver, yo-yo*; SEE CONCEPTS 13,104,232,701

alternative [n] *possible choice*
back-up, druthers*, opportunity, option, other, other fish in sea*, other fish to fry*, pick, preference, recourse, redundancy, selection, sub*, substitute, take it or leave it*; SEE CONCEPT 529

alternative [adj] *other, alternate*
another, back-up, different, flipside, other side, second, substitute, surrogate; SEE CONCEPT 564

although [conj] *even though*
admitting, albeit, despite, despite the fact, even if, even supposing, granting, granting all this, in spite of, much as, notwithstanding, still, supposing, though, when, whereas, while; SEE CONCEPT 544

altitude [n] *height in the sky*
apex, distance, elevation, eminence, loftiness, peak, summit; SEE CONCEPTS 739,752,791

altogether [adv1] *as a whole*
all, all in all, all things considered, all told, bodily, by and large, collectively, conjointly, en masse, everything considered, everything included, for the most part, generally, in all, in sum, in toto, on the whole, taken together; SEE CONCEPT 771

altogether [adv2] *completely*
absolutely, fully, perfectly, quite, thoroughly, totally, utterly, well, wholly; SEE CONCEPT 531

altruistic [adj] *unselfish*
all heart*, benevolent, big*, big-hearted*, bleeding heart*, charitable, considerate, generous, good, good scout, human, humane, humanitarian, kind, magnanimous, openhanded, philanthropic, Robin Hood*, self-sacrificing; SEE CONCEPT 404

alumnus/alumna [n] *graduate*
alum, old grad*, postgraduate; SEE CONCEPT 350

always [adv] *forever; continually*
consistently, constantly, eternally, ever, everlastingly, evermore, forevermore, for keeps, in perpetuum, invariably, perpetually, regularly, repeatedly, till blue in the face*, till cows come home*, till hell freezes over*, unceasingly, without exception; SEE CONCEPTS 551,798

amalgam [n] *mixture*
admixture, alloy, amalgamation, blend, combination, combo*, composite, compound, fusion, mishmash*, soup; SEE CONCEPT 432

amalgamate [v] *blend*
admix, alloy, ally, coalesce, combine, come together, compound, consolidate, fuse, hook up with*, incorporate, integrate, interface, intermix, join together, meld, merge, mingle, network, pool, team up*, tie in, tie up*, unite; SEE CONCEPT 113

amass [v] *gather, accumulate*
aggregate, assemble, clean up*, collect, compile, corral*, garner, heap*, hoard, lay up*, make a killing*, make a pile*, pile, round up*, scare up*, stockpile, store; SEE CONCEPTS 109,120

amateur [n] *casual participant*
abecedarian, apprentice, aspirant, beginner, bush leaguer*, dabbler, dilettante, greenhorn, ham*, hopeful, layperson, learner, neophyte, nonprofessional, novice, probationer, putterer, recruit, Sunday driver*, tenderfoot*, tyro; SEE CONCEPT 366

amatory [*adj*] *affectionate, desirous*
admiring, amorous, aphrodisiac, ardent, attracted, devoted, doting, erotic, fervent, fond, languishing, lovesick, loving, passionate, rapturous, romantic, sentimental, tender, wooing, yearning; SEE CONCEPTS 372,403

amaze [*v*] *surprise*
affect, alarm, astonish, astound, bewilder, blow away*, blow one's mind*, bowl over*, daze, dumbfound, electrify, flabbergast*, impress, move, perplex, put one away*, shock, stagger, startle, strike, stun, stupefy, touch*; SEE CONCEPT 42

amazement [*n*] *state of surprise*
admiration, astonishment, awe, bewilderment, confoundment, confusion, marvel, one for the books*, perplexity, shock, something else*, stopper*, stunner*, stupefaction, wonder, wonderment; SEE CONCEPTS 230,410

ambassador [*n*] *representative to a foreign country*
agent, consul, deputy, diplomat, emissary, envoy, minister, plenipotentiary; SEE CONCEPT 354

amber [*n/adj*] *gold-colored*
brown, golden, tan, yellowish; SEE CONCEPT 618

ambience [*n*] *environment*
ambient, atmosphere, climate, medium, surroundings; SEE CONCEPT 673

ambiguity [*n*] *uncertainty of meaning*
double-entendre, double meaning, doubt, doubtfulness, dubiety, dubiousness, enigma, equivocacy, equivocality, equivocation, incertitude, inconclusiveness, indefiniteness, indeterminateness, obscurity, puzzle, tergiversation, uncertainty, unclearness, vagueness; SEE CONCEPTS 638,682

ambiguous [*adj*] *having more than one meaning*
clear as dishwater*, cryptic, doubtful, dubious, enigmatic, enigmatical, equivocal, inconclusive, indefinite, indeterminate, inexplicit, muddy, obscure, opaque, puzzling, questionable, tenebrous, uncertain, unclear, unintelligible, vague; SEE CONCEPTS 267,535

ambition [*n1*] *strong desire for success*
appetite, ardor, aspiration, avidity, craving, desire, drive, eagerness, earnestness, emulation, energy, enterprise, enthusiasm, fire in belly*, get up and go*, hankering*, hope, hunger, initiative, itch*, keenness, longing, love, lust, moxie*, passion, pretension, push, right stuff*, spirit, striving, thirst, vigor, yearning, zeal; SEE CONCEPT 20

ambition [*n2*] *something desired*
aim, aspiration, desire, dream, end, enterprise, goal, hope, intent, mark, objective, purpose, target, wish; SEE CONCEPT 659

ambitious [*adj1*] *desiring success*
aggressive, anxious, ardent, aspiring, avid, ball of fire*, bent upon, climbing, come on, come on strong, designing, desirous, determined, driving, eager, eager beaver*, earnest, energetic, enterprising, enthusiastic, fireball*, get up and go*, goal-oriented, go-getter*, hard ball*, high-reaching, hopeful, hungry, industrious, inspired, intent, longing, power-loving, purposeful, pushing, pushy*, resourceful, self-starting, sharp, soaring, striving, thirsty, vaulting, zealous; SEE CONCEPTS 326,542

ambitious [*adj2*] *requiring great effort, ability*
arduous, bold, challenging, demanding, difficult, elaborate, energetic, exacting, formidable, grandiose, hard, impressive, industrious, lofty, pretentious, severe, strenuous, visionary; SEE CONCEPT 538

ambivalent [*adj*] *conflicting*
clashing, contradictory, debatable, doubtful, equivocal, fluctuating, hesitant, inconclusive, irresolute, mixed, opposed, uncertain, undecided, unresolved, unsure, vacillating, warring, wavering; SEE CONCEPTS 534,564

amble [*v*] *walk casually*
ankle*, boogie*, dawdle, drift, gander*, hoof it*, loiter, meander, mosey*, percolate*, ramble, sashay*, saunter, stroll, toddle*, wander; SEE CONCEPT 151

ambulance [*n*] *emergency vehicle*
EMS, hospital wagon, rescue, transport; SEE CONCEPT 505

ambulatory [*adj*] *changing position; able to move under own power*
ambulant, itinerant, nomadic, perambulant, perambulatory, peripatetic, roving, vagabond, vagrant; SEE CONCEPT 584

ambush [*n*] *lying in wait; concealed position*
ambuscade, ambushment, camouflage, concealment, deception, hiding, hiding place, lurking, pitfall, shelter, trap, trick*, waiting, waylaying; SEE CONCEPTS 86,188

ambush [*v*] *lie in wait; attack*
ambuscade, assail, assault, box in*, bushwhack*, decoy, dry gulch*, ensnare, entrap, hem in*, hide, hook*, jap*, jump, lay for, lurk, net, set trap, surprise, surround, trap, wait, waylay; SEE CONCEPTS 86,188

ameliorate [*v*] *make, become better*
alleviate, amend, help, improve, lighten, meliorate, mitigate, relieve, step up, upgrade; SEE CONCEPT 244

amenable [*adj1*] *willing, cooperative*
acquiescent, agreeable, biddable, docile, influenceable, manageable, obedient, open, persuadable, pliable, responsive, susceptible, tractable; SEE CONCEPT 404

amenable [*adj2*] *able to be judged; responsible*
accountable, answerable, chargeable, liable, subject; SEE CONCEPT 402

amend [*v*] *improve, correct*
alter, ameliorate, better, change, elevate, enhance, fix, help, lift, make up for, mend, modify, pay one's dues*, raise, rectify, reform, remedy, repair, revise, right, square*; SEE CONCEPTS 126,244

amendment [*n1*] *correction, improvement*
alteration, amelioration, betterment, change, correction, enhancement, improvement, mending, modification, rectification, reform, reformation, remedy, repair, revision; SEE CONCEPT 700

amendment [*n2*] *addition to a document*
act, addendum, adjunct, alteration, attachment, bill, clarification, clause, codicil, measure, modification, motion, revision, rider, suggestion, supplement; SEE CONCEPT 270

amends [*n*] *compensation*
apology, atonement, expiation, indemnification, indemnity, quittance, recompense, redress, reparation, reprisal, requital, restitution, restoration, satisfaction; SEE CONCEPTS 67,104,384

amenity [*n1*] *pleasant thing*
advantage, betterment, comfort, convenience, enhancement, enrichment, excellence, extravagance, facility, frill, improvement, luxury, merit,

quality, service, superfluity, virtue; SEE CONCEPT 712

amenity [n2] *pleasing, agreeable behavior*
affability, agreeableness, amiability, attention, attractiveness, charity, charm, complaisance, cordiality, courtesy, delightfulness, enjoyableness, etiquette, gallantry, geniality, gentility, gratefulness, kindness, mildness, pleasantness, politeness, refinement, suavity, sweetness; SEE CONCEPT 633

amiable [adj] *friendly, agreeable*
affable, amicable, attractive, benign, breezy, buddy-buddy*, charming, cheerful, clubby*, complaisant, cool*, copacetic*, cordial, cozy, delightful, downright neighborly*, easy, engaging, friendly, genial, good-humored, good-natured, gracious, home cooking*, kind, kindly, lenient, lovable, mellow, mild, obliging, palsy-walsy*, pleasant, pleasing, princely*, pussycat*, responsive, right, righteous, sociable, sweet-tempered, swell*, tight*, warm, warmhearted, winning; SEE CONCEPT 401

amicable [adj] *friendly, especially regarding an agreement*
accordant, agreeing, amiable, civil, clubby*, concordant, cordial, courteous, cozy, empathic, good-humored, harmonious, kind, kindly, like-minded, mellow, neighborly, pacific, peaceable, peaceful, polite, regular, right nice*, sociable, square shooting*, sympathetic, understanding; SEE CONCEPTS 529,542

amid/amidst [prep] *in middle of; among*
amongst, between, during, in the midst of, in the thick of, mid, over, surrounded by, throughout; SEE CONCEPTS 586,820

amiss [adj] *wrong; defective*
awry, bad, confused, crooked, erring, erroneous, fallacious, false, faulty, flawed, foul, glitched up*, haywire, imperfect, improper, inaccurate, inappropriate, incorrect, mistaken, out of order, sick, unfair, unlawful, unsuitable, untoward; SEE CONCEPT 570

amiss [adv] *wrongly; defectively*
afield, afoul, badly, erringly, erroneously, faultily, improperly, inappropriately, incorrectly, mistakenly, out of turn, unfavorably, unsuitably; SEE CONCEPT 570

amity [n] *friendship*
amicableness, benevolence, comity, concord, cordiality, friendliness, good vibrations*, goodwill, harmony, hitting it off*, kindliness, neighborliness, same wavelength*, simpatico*, togetherness*; SEE CONCEPT 388

ammonia [n] *pungent gas, liquid*
alkali, salts, spirits, vapor; SEE CONCEPT 472

ammunition [n] *projectiles for weaponry*
ammo*, armament, ball, bomb, buckshot, bullet, cannonball, cartridge, charge, chemical, confetti*, explosive, fuse, grenade, gunpowder, iron rations*, materiel, missile, munition, napalm, powder, rocket, round, shell, shot, shrapnel, torpedo; SEE CONCEPTS 498,500

amnesty [n] *pardon, often by government*
absolution, condonation, dispensation, forgiveness, immunity, reprieve; SEE CONCEPTS 298,300

among [prep1] *in the middle of; between*
amid, amidst, betwixt, encompassed by, in dispersion through, in the midst of, in the thick of, mid, surrounded by, with; SEE CONCEPT 586

among [prep2] *in a group*
by all of, by the whole of, in association with, in connection with, in the class of, in the company of, mutually, out of, together with, with, with one another; SEE CONCEPT 785

amorous [adj] *loving, affectionate*
amative, amatory, aphrodisiac, ardent, attached, boy crazy*, doting, enamored, erotic, fond, girl crazy*, have a crush on*, horny*, hot, hot and heavy*, impassioned, infatuated, in love, lovesick, lovey dovey*, lustful, passionate, romantic, sexy, sweet for*, sweet on*, tender, turned on*; SEE CONCEPTS 372,403,555

amorphous [adj] *without definite shape, character*
baggy, blobby, characterless, formless, inchoate, indeterminate, irregular, nebulous, nondescript, shapeless, unformed, unshaped, unstructured, vague; SEE CONCEPTS 404,490

amount [n1] *quantity*
aplenty, bags*, bulk, bundle, chunk, expanse, extent, flock, gob*, heap, hunk, jillion*, load, lot, magnitude, mass, measure, mess*, mint*, mucho*, number, oodles*, pack, passle, peck, pile, scads*, score, slat*, slew*, supply, ton*, volume, whopper*; SEE CONCEPTS 787,837

amount [n2] *total*
addition, aggregate, all, bad news*, body, budget, cost, damage*, entirety, expense, extent, list, lot, net, outlay, output, price tag*, product, quantum, score, set-back*, sum, tab*, tidy sum*, whole; SEE CONCEPTS 329,784,787

amount [n3] *whole effect*
body, burden, core, full value, import, matter, purport, result, sense, significance, substance, thrust, upshot, value; SEE CONCEPT 676

amount [v] *equal, add up to*
aggregate, approach, approximate, become, be equivalent to, be tantamount to, check with, come to, correspond, develop into, effect, extend, grow, match, mean, number, purport, reach, rival, sum, tally, total, touch; SEE CONCEPT 667

amour [n] *romance*
affair, entanglement, liaison, love, love affair, passion, relationship; SEE CONCEPT 32

ample [adj] *more than necessary, sufficient*
abounding, abundant, big, bounteous, bountiful, broad, capacious, commodious, copious, enough, expansive, extensive, full, galore, generous, great, heavy, large, lavish, liberal, no end, plenteous, plentiful, plenty, profuse, rich, roomy, spacious, spare, substantial, unrestricted, voluminous, wide; SEE CONCEPTS 558,781

amplification [n] *increase in size or effect*
addition, augmentation, boost, boosting, buildup, deepening, development, elaboration, enlargement, exaggeration, expansion, expatiation, extension, fleshing out, heightening, intensification, lengthening, magnification, padding, raising, strengthening, stretching, supplementing, upping, widening; SEE CONCEPTS 236,245,780

amplify [v] *increase in size or effect*
add, augment, beef up*, boost, build up, deepen, develop, elaborate, enlarge, exaggerate, expand, expatiate, extend, flesh out*, heighten, hike up*, inflate, intensify, jack up*, lengthen, magnify, pad, pyramid, raise, soup up*, strengthen, stretch, supplement, swell, up, widen; SEE CONCEPTS 236,245

amply [adv] *fully, sufficiently*
abundantly, acceptably, adequately, appropri-

ately, bountifully, capaciously, completely, copiously, enough, extensively, fittingly, generously, greatly, lavishly, liberally, plenteously, plentifully, profusely, properly, richly, rightly, satisfactorily, substantially, suitably, thoroughly, well; SEE CONCEPTS 558,771

amputate [v] *remove a limb*
cut away, cut off, dismember, eliminate, excise, lop, separate, sever, truncate; SEE CONCEPTS 176,211

amuck [adv] *crazily*
berserk, destructively, ferociously, frenziedly, in a frenzy, insanely, madly, maniacally, murderously, savagely, uncontrollably, violently, wildly; SEE CONCEPT 401

amulet [n] *charm*
fetish, lucky piece, ornament, talisman; SEE CONCEPTS 260,446

amuse [v] *entertain; make laugh*
break one up*, charm, cheer, crack up*, delight, divert, fracture*, gladden, grab*, gratify, interest, kill*, knock dead*, make roll in the aisles*, occupy, panic*, please, put away*, regale, slay*, tickle, wow*; SEE CONCEPTS 9,292,384

amusement [n1] *entertaining, making someone laugh*
action, ball*, beguilement, cheer, delight, diversion, enjoyment, entertainment, field day*, fun, fun and games*, gladdening, gratification, grins*, high time*, hilarity, hoopla*, laughs*, laughter, merriment, merry go round* mirth, picnic*, play, pleasing, pleasure, regalement, whoopee*; SEE CONCEPT 292

amusement [n2] *game, pastime*
distraction, diversion, entertainment, hobby, interest, joke, lark, play, prank, recreation, sport; SEE CONCEPT 364

amusing [adj] *entertaining, funny*
agreeable, boffo*, camp, campy, charming, cheerful, cheering, comical, cut up*, delightful, diverting, droll, enchanting, engaging, enjoyable, entertaining, for grins*, fun, gladdening, gratifying, gut-busting*, humorous, interesting, jocular, jokey*, joshing*, laughable, lively, merry, pleasant, pleasing, priceless, screaming*, sidesplitting*, too funny for words*, witty; SEE CONCEPTS 267,548

anachronism [n] *error in time placement*
chronological error, metachronism, misdate, misplacement, postdate, prolepsis, solecism; SEE CONCEPT 818

analgesic [n] *pain remover*
anesthetic, anodyne, painkiller, soother; SEE CONCEPT 307

analogous [adj] *agreeing, similar*
akin, alike, comparable, consonant, convertible, correspondent, corresponding, equivalent, homologous, interchangeable, kindred, like, parallel, related, resembling, undifferentiated, uniform; SEE CONCEPTS 487,573

analogy [n] *agreement, similarity*
affinity, alikeness, comparison, correlation, correspondence, equivalence, homology, likeness, metaphor, parallel, relation, relationship, resemblance, semblance, simile, similitude; SEE CONCEPTS 278,670

analysis [n1] *examination and determination*
assay, breakdown, dissection, dissolution, division, inquiry, investigation, partition, reasoning, resolution, scrutiny, search, separation, study, subdivision, test; SEE CONCEPTS 24,103

analysis [n2] *statement of results from examination*
estimation, evaluation, finding, interpretation, judgment, opinion, outline, reasoning, report, study, summary; SEE CONCEPTS 271,274

analyst [n] *person who examines and determines; psychoanalyst*
accountant, couch doctor*, examiner, guru*, head shrinker*, inquisitor, investigator, number cruncher*, psychiatrist, psychotherapist, questioner, shrink*, therapist; SEE CONCEPTS 348,357

analytic/analytical [adj] *examining and determining*
cogent, conclusive, detailed, diagnostic, discrete, dissecting, explanatory, expository, inquiring, inquisitive, interpretive, investigative, judicious, logical, organized, penetrating, perceptive, perspicuous, precise, problem-solving, questioning, ratiocinative, rational, reasonable, scientific, searching, solid, sound, studious, subtle, systematic, testing, thorough, valid, well-grounded; SEE CONCEPT 402

analyze [v1] *examine and determine*
assay, beat a dead horse*, chew over*, confab*, consider, estimate, evaluate, figure, figure out, get down to brass tacks*, hash*, inspect, interpret, investigate, judge, kick around*, rehash, resolve, scrutinize, sort out, spell out, study, talk game*, test, think through; SEE CONCEPTS 24,37,103

analyze [v2] *break down to components*
anatomize, break up, cut up, decompose, decompound, determine, disintegrate, dissect, dissolve, divide, electrolyze, hydrolyze, lay bare, parse, part, resolve, separate, x-ray; SEE CONCEPTS 135,310

anarchist [n] *person who opposes the idea of government and laws*
agitator, insurgent, insurrectionist, malcontent, mutineer, nihilist, rebel, revolter, revolutionary, terrorist; SEE CONCEPTS 359,412

anarchy [n] *lawlessness; absence of government*
chaos, confusion, disorder, disorganization, disregard, hostility, misrule, mob rule, nihilism, nongovernment, rebellion, reign of terror, revolution, riot, turmoil, unrest; SEE CONCEPTS 29,674

anathema [n1] *something hated*
abomination, bane, bugbear, detestation, enemy, hate, pariah; SEE CONCEPT 529

anathema [n2] *denouncement*
ban, censure, commination, condemnation, curse, damnation, denunciation, excommunication, execration, imprecation, malediction, proscription, reprehension, reprobation, reproof, taboo; SEE CONCEPT 278

anatomy [n1] *study of animal, plant structure*
analysis, biology, cytology, diagnosis, dissection, division, embryology, etiology, examination, genetics, histology, inquiry, investigation, medicine, morphology, physiology, zoology; SEE CONCEPT 349

anatomy [n2] *physical structure of animals, plants*
build, composition, figure, form, frame, framework, makeup, physique, shape; SEE CONCEPT 733

ancestor [n] *predecessor in family*
antecedent, antecessor, ascendant, forebear, forefather, foregoer, foremother, forerunner, founder, precursor, primogenitor, progenitor; SEE CONCEPT 414

ancestral [adj] *related to previous family or family trait*
affiliated, born with, congenital, consanguine, consanguineous, familial, genealogical, inborn, inbred, inherited, innate, in the family, lineal, maternal, old, past, paternal, running in the family, totemic, tribal; SEE CONCEPT *549*

ancestry [n] *family predecessors; family history*
ancestor, antecedent, antecessor, blood, breed, breeding, derivation, descent, extraction, forebear, forefather, foregoer, foremother, forerunner, genealogy, heritage, house, kindred, line, lineage, origin, parentage, pedigree, precursor, primogenitor, progenitor, race, source, stock; SEE CONCEPTS *414,648*

anchor [n] *something used to hold another thing securely*
ballast, bower, comfort, defense, fastener, foothold, grapnel, grappling iron, grip, hold, hook, kedge, mainstay, mooring, mud hook, pillar, protection, safeguard, security, staff, stay, support; SEE CONCEPTS *464,502,731*

anchor [v] *hold, be held securely*
attach, berth, catch, dock, drop, fasten, fix, imbed, make port, moor, plant, secure, stay, tie, tie up; SEE CONCEPTS *85,160,190*

ancient [adj] *old, often very old*
aged, age-old, antediluvian, antiquated, antique, archaic, back number*, been around*, bygone, creaky*, early, elderly, few miles on*, fossil*, hoary, lot of mileage*, moth-eaten*, obsolete, older, old-fashioned, old goat*, oldie*, outmoded, out-of-date, primal, primeval, primordial, relic, remote, rusty, superannuated, timeworn, venerable, worse for wear*; SEE CONCEPTS *578,797*

ancillary [adj] *extra; supplementary*
accessory, accompanying, additional, adjuvant, appurtenant, attendant, attending, coincident, collateral, concomitant, contributory, incident, satellite, secondary, subordinate, subservient, subsidiary; SEE CONCEPT *835*

and [conj] *in addition to; plus*
along with, also, as a consequence, as well as, furthermore, including, moreover, together with; SEE CONCEPT *577*

anecdote [n] *interesting or amusing story*
chestnut*, episode, fairy tale*, fish story*, gag*, incident, long and short of it*, narration, narrative, old chestnut*, recital, relation, reminiscence, short story, sketch, tale, tall story*, tall tale*, yarn; SEE CONCEPT *282*

anemic [adj] *weak and pale*
bloodless, feeble, frail, infirm, pallid, sickly, wan, watery; SEE CONCEPTS *314,483,618*

anesthesia/anaesthesia [n] *induced sleep; induced absence of feeling*
analgesia, insentience, numbness, stupor, unconsciousness; SEE CONCEPTS *313,315,728*

anesthetic/anaesthetic [n] *sleep-inducing or numbing drug*
analgesic, anodyne, dope*, gas, hypnotic, inhalant, narcotic, opiate, pain-killer, shot, soporific, spinal; SEE CONCEPT *307*

anew [adj/adv] *fresh; again*
afresh, another time, come again, de novo, from scratch, from the beginning, in a different way, in a new way, lately, new, newly, once again, once more, one more time, over, over again, recently; SEE CONCEPT *820*

angel [n1] *attendant of God*
archangel, celestial being, cherub, divine messenger, God's messenger, guardian, heavenly being, holy being, seraph, spirit, spiritual being, sprite, supernatural being; SEE CONCEPTS *361,370*

angel [n2] *sweet, kind person*
beauty, darling, dear, dream, gem, ideal, jewel, paragon, saint, treasure; SEE CONCEPT *416*

angelic [adj] *sweet, kind, and usually beautiful*
adorable, archangelic, beatific, beneficent, celestial, cherubic, devout, divine, entrancing, ethereal, godly, good, heavenly, holy, humble, innocent, lovely, otherworldly, pure, radiant, rapturous, righteous, saintly, self-sacrificing, seraphic, virtuous; SEE CONCEPT *572*

anger [n] *state of being mad, annoyed*
acrimony, animosity, annoyance, antagonism, blow up*, cat fit*, chagrin, choler, conniption, dander*, disapprobation, displeasure, distemper, enmity, exasperation, fury, gall, hatred, hissy fit*, huff, ill humor, ill temper, impatience, indignation, infuriation, irascibility, ire, irritability, irritation, mad, miff, outrage, passion, peevishness, petulance, pique, rage, rankling, resentment, slow burn*, soreness, stew, storm, tantrum, temper, tiff, umbrage, vexation, violence; SEE CONCEPTS *29,410*

anger [v] *make someone mad; become mad*
acerbate, affront, aggravate, agitate, annoy, antagonize, arouse, bait, blow up*, boil*, boil over*, bristle, burn, burn up, chafe, craze*, cross, displease, egg on*, embitter, enrage, exacerbate, exasperate, excite, fret, gall, get mad, get on one's nerves*, goad, incense, inflame, infuriate, irritate, lose one's temper, madden, make sore*, miff, nettle, offend, outrage, pique, provoke, raise hell*, rankle, rant, rave, rile, ruffle, seethe, steam up*, stew, stir up*, tempt, umbrage, vex; SEE CONCEPTS *7,19*

angle [n1] *shape formed by two lines meeting at a point*
bend, corner, crook, crotch, cusp, decline, divergence, dogleg, edge, elbow, flare, flection, flexure, fork, incline, intersection, knee, nook, notch, obliquity, point, slant, turn, turning, twist, V, Y; SEE CONCEPT *436*

angle [n2] *personal approach, purpose*
aim, approach, aspect, direction, hand, intention, outlook, perspective, plan, point of view, position, side, slant, standpoint, viewpoint; SEE CONCEPTS *660,661*

angle [v] *fish*
cast, dangle a line*, drop a line*; SEE CONCEPT *363*

angle for [v] *attempt to get*
aim for, be after, cast about for, connive, conspire, contrive, fish for, hint, hunt, invite, look for, maneuver, plan, plot, scheme, seek, solicit, strive, try for; SEE CONCEPTS *20,87*

angry [adj] *being mad, often extremely mad*
affronted, annoyed, antagonized, bitter, chafed, choleric, convulsed, cross, displeased, enraged, exacerbated, exasperated, ferocious, fierce, fiery, fuming, furious, galled, hateful, heated, hot, huffy, ill-tempered, impassioned, incensed, indignant, inflamed, infuriated, irascible, irate, ireful, irritable, irritated, maddened, nettled, offended, outraged, piqued, provoked, raging, resentful, riled, sore, splenetic, storming, sulky, sullen, tu-

an
an

multous/tumultuous, turbulent, uptight, vexed, wrathful; SEE CONCEPT 403

anguish [n] *severe upset or pain*
affliction, agony, distress, dole, dolor, grief, heartache, heartbreak, hurting, misery, pang, rue, sorrow, suffering, throe, torment, torture, woe, wretchedness; SEE CONCEPT 410

angular [adj] *bent*
akimbo, bifurcate, cornered, crooked, crossing, crotched, divaricate, forked, intersecting, jagged, oblique, rambling, rectangular, skewed, slanted, staggered, V-shaped, Y-shaped, zigzag; SEE CONCEPT 486

angular [adj2] *thin, especially referring to people*
awkward, bony, gangling, gaunt, lank, lanky, lean, rangy, rawboned, scrawny, sharp, skinny, spare; SEE CONCEPT 773

animal [n] *animate being; mammal*
beast, being, brute, bum*, creature, critter, invertebrate, living thing, mutt*, pet, stray, varmint*, vertebrate, wild thing; SEE CONCEPT 394

animal [adj] *beastlike; carnal*
beastly, bestial, bodily, brute, brutish, corporeal, earthly, earthy, feral, fleshy, mammalian, muscular, natural, physical, sensual, untamed, wild, zoological; SEE CONCEPT 406

animate [adj1] *alive*
breathing, live, living, mortal, moving, viable, vital, zoetic; SEE CONCEPT 539

animate [adj2] *lively*
activated, active, alert, animated, dynamic, energized, gay, happy, spirited, vivacious; SEE CONCEPT 401

animate [v] *bring to life*
activate, arouse, cheer, embolden, encourage, energize, enliven, exalt, excite, fire, gladden, hearten, impel, incite, inform, inspire, inspirit, instigate, invigorate, kindle, liven, make alive, move, quicken, revive, revivify, rouse, spark, spur, stimulate, stir, urge, vitalize, vivify; SEE CONCEPTS 231,241

animated [adj] *lively*
activated, active, alert, animate, ardent, brisk, buoyant, dynamic, ebullient, elated, energetic, energized, enthusiastic, excited, fervent, gay, happy, passionate, peppy, quick, snappy, spirited, sprightly, vibrant, vigorous, vital, vitalized, vivacious, vivid, zealous, zestful, zingy, zippy; SEE CONCEPT 401

animation [n] *liveliness; activity*
action, ardor, bounce, brio, briskness, buoyancy, dash, dynamism, ebullience, élan, elation, energy, enthusiasm, esprit, excitement, exhilaration, fervor, gaiety, high spirits, life, oomph*, passion, pep*, sparkle, spirit, sprightliness, verve, vibrancy, vigor, vim, vitality, vivacity, zap*, zeal, zest, zing*, zip*; SEE CONCEPT 657

animosity [n] *extreme dislike, hatred*
acrimony, animus, antagonism, antipathy, bad blood, bitterness, displeasure, enmity, hate, hostility, ill will, malevolence, malice, malignity, rancor, resentment, virulence; SEE CONCEPT 29

ankle [n] *joint between leg and foot*
anklebone, astragalus, bone, talus, tarsus; SEE CONCEPTS 392,418

annal(s) [n] *history, records*
account, archive, chronicle, journal, memorial, record, register; SEE CONCEPTS 271,281

annex [n] *something added; extension*
addendum, addition, adjunct, affix, appendix, arm, attachment, ell, subsidiary, supplement, wing; SEE CONCEPTS 440,441,484

annex [v] *join or add*
adjoin, affix, append, appropriate, associate, attach, connect, fasten, hitch on*, hitch up*, hook on*, hook up*, link, slap on*, subjoin, tack on*, tag, tag on*, take on, take over, unite; SEE CONCEPTS 85,113,160

annexation [n] *adding, joining*
addition, annexing, appropriation, attachment, grab, incorporation, increase, increment, merger, takeover; SEE CONCEPTS 113,324

annihilate [v] *destroy completely*
abate, abolish, abrogate, annul, blot out*, crush*, decimate, demolish, do in*, eradicate, erase, expunge, exterminate, extinguish, extirpate, finish off, invalidate, liquidate, massacre, murder, negate, nullify, obliterate, quash, quell, raze, root out*, rub out*, ruin, slaughter, take out*, undo, vitiate, wipe out*, wrack*, wreck; SEE CONCEPT 252

anniversary [n] *yearly observance, celebration*
ceremony, commemoration, feast day, festival, holiday, jubilee, recurrence, red-letter day; SEE CONCEPTS 800,801,815,823

annotate [v] *write explanatory notes*
comment, commentate, construe, define, elucidate, explain, expound, footnote, gloss, illustrate, interpret, note, remark; SEE CONCEPTS 51,57,79

annotation [n] *explanatory note*
comment, commentary, definition, elucidation, exegesis, explanation, explication, footnote, gloss, glossary, illustration, interpretation, note, observation; SEE CONCEPTS 274,283

announce [v1] *make a proclamation*
advertise, annunciate, blast, blazon, broadcast, call, communicate, declare, disclose, disseminate, divulge, drum*, give out, impart, intimate, issue, make known, make public, pass the word*, proclaim, promulgate, propound, publicize, publish, release, report, reveal, run off at mouth*, sound off*, spread around*, state, tell, trumpet; SEE CONCEPT 49

announce [v2] *declare arrival*
augur, forebode, forecast, forerun, foreshow, foretell, harbinger, herald, indicate, portend, predict, presage, signal, signify; SEE CONCEPTS 60,70

announcement [n] *proclamation, declaration*
advertisement, advice, briefing, broadcast, broadcasting, bulletin, communication, communiqué, disclosure, dissemination, divulgence, edict, exposing, exposition, expression, intimation, message, narration, news, notice, notification, prediction, promulgation, publication, publishing, recitation, release, report, reporting, revelation, statement; SEE CONCEPTS 49,274

announcer [n] *media commentator*
anchorperson, broadcaster, communicator, deejay, disc jockey, DJ, leader of ceremonies, newscaster, reporter, rip and reader*, spieler*, talker, telecaster, veejay*, VJ; SEE CONCEPT 348

annoy [v] *irritate, upset*
abrade, agitate, ask for it*, badger, be at*, bedevil, beleaguer, be on the back of*, bore, bother, break, bug, burn up, chafe, displease, distress, disturb, egg on*, exasperate, fire up*, gall, get, gnaw, harass, harry, heat up*, henpeck, hit where one lives*, irk, madden, make waves*, miff, nag, needle, nettle, nudge, peeve, perturb, pester,

plague, provoke, push button*, ride, rile, ruffle, tease, tick off*, T-off*, trouble, turn off*, vex, work on*, worry; SEE CONCEPTS 7,19

annual [n] *book produced once a year*
annuary, report, summary, yearbook; SEE CONCEPT 271

annual [adj1] *occurring, done yearly*
anniversary, each year, every year, once a year, year end; SEE CONCEPTS 541,823

annual [adj2] *lasting for a year*
a year's worth, yearlong; SEE CONCEPT 798

annually [adv] *occurring, done yearly*
by the year, each year, every year, once a year, per annum, per year, year after year; SEE CONCEPTS 541,823

annul [v] *void an agreement*
abate, abolish, abrogate, annihilate, blot out, call off, cancel, countermand, declare, delete, discharge, dissolve, efface, erase, expunge, get off the hook*, invalidate, kill, negate, neutralize, nix, nullify, obliterate, quash, recall, render null and void, repeal, rescind, retract, reverse, revoke, scrub*, undo, vacate, vitiate, wipe out*; SEE CONCEPTS 252,297,317

annulment [n] *voiding an agreement*
abatement, abolition, abrogation, annihilation, breakup, cancellation, countermanding, dedomiciling, deletion, discharge, dissolution, erasing, going phfft*, invalidation, negation, neutralization, nullification, obliteration, recall, repeal, rescinding, rescindment, rescission, retraction, reversal, revocation, split*, split up*, undoing*, vitiation, voiding; SEE CONCEPTS 297,317,691

anoint [v] *bless, usually with oil or water*
bless, consecrate, daub, embrocate, grease, hallow, rub, sanctify, smear; SEE CONCEPT 367

anomalous [adj] *deviating from normal, usual*
aberrant, abnormal, atypical, bizarre, divergent, eccentric, exceptional, foreign, heteroclite, incongruous, inconsistent, irregular, odd, peculiar, preternatural, prodigous, rare, strange, unnatural, unorthodox, unrepresentative, untypical, unusual; SEE CONCEPT 547

anomaly [n] *deviation from normal, usual*
aberration, abnormality, departure, deviation, eccentricity, exception, incongruity, inconsistency, irregularity, oddity, peculiarity, rarity, unconformity, unorthodoxy; SEE CONCEPT 647

anonymous [adj] *unknown, usually by choice*
bearding*, incognito, innominate, Jane/John Doe*, nameless, pseudo, pseudonymous, secret, so and so*, such and such*, unacknowledged, unattested, unavowed, unclaimed, uncredited, undesignated, undisclosed, unidentified, unnamed, unsigned, unspecified, whatchamacallit*, what's his/her name*, whatsis*, X*, you know who*; SEE CONCEPT 683

another [n] *other person*
addition, a different person, one more, someone else, something else; SEE CONCEPT 423

another [prep/det] *additional, different*
added, a distinct, a further, a separate, else, farther, fresh, further, more, new, one more, other, some other, that; SEE CONCEPT 564

answer [n] *reply; reaction*
acknowledgment, antiphon, backcap*, back talk, band-aid*, close, comeback, comment, cooler*, counterclaim, crack, defense, disclosure, echo, elucidation, explanation, feedback, guff*, interpretation, justification, key, lip*, observation,

parting shot*, pay dirt*, plea, quick fix*, rebuttal, refutation, rejoinder, remark, repartee, report, resolution, response, result, retort, return, riposte, sign, solution, statement, thank-you note*, the ticket*, topper*, vindication, wisecrack; SEE CONCEPTS 274,278

answer [v1] *reply, react*
acknowledge, answer back, argue, back at you*, back talk, be in touch*, claim, comeback, contest, counterclaim, defend, deny, disprove, dispute, echo, explain, feedback, field the question*, get back at*, get back to*, give a snappy comeback*, parry, plead, rebut, refute, rejoin, remark, resolve, respond, retaliate, retort, return, sass*, say, settle, shoot back*, solve, squelch, talk back, top*; SEE CONCEPTS 45,266

answer [v2] *solve; fulfill*
clarify, conform, correlate, correspond, crack*, deal with*, do*, dope, dope out*, elucidate, fill, fit*, lick*, measure up, meet, pass, qualify, satisfy, serve, suffice, suit, unzip*, work, work through; SEE CONCEPTS 87,664

answerable [adj] *responsible*
accountable, amenable, bound, chargeable, compelled, constrained, liable, obligated, obliged, subject, to blame; SEE CONCEPT 545

antagonism [n] *causing problem; opposition*
animosity, animus, antipathy, antithesis, clashing, competition, conflict, contention, contradistinction, contrariety, difference, disagreement, discord, dissension, enmity, friction, hatred, hostility, incongruity, oppugnancy, rancor, resistance, rivalry; SEE CONCEPT 29

antagonist [n] *person causing problem*
adversary, angries*, bad person*, bandit*, competitor, contender, crip*, enemy, foe, match, opponent, opposer, opposite number*, oppugnant, rival; SEE CONCEPT 412

antagonize [v] *cause problem; oppose*
alienate, anger, annoy, counteract, estrange, insult, irritate, neutralize, offend, repel, struggle, work against; SEE CONCEPTS 7,19,231

antecedent(s) [n] *predecessor(s) in family*
ancestor, ancestry, antecessor, blood, descent, extraction, forebears, forefather/mother, genealogy, line, primogenitor, progenitor, stock; SEE CONCEPT 414

antecedent [adj] *prior*
anterior, earlier, foregoing, former, past, precedent, preceding, precursory, preliminary, previous; SEE CONCEPT 820

antedate [v] *occur or cause to occur earlier*
accelerate, anachronize, antecede, backdate, date back, forerun, misdate, pace, precede, predate; SEE CONCEPT 84

antediluvian [adj] *out-of-date; prehistoric*
age-old, ancient, antiquated, antique, archaic, hoary, obsolete, old, old-fashioned, passé, primeval, primitive, primordial, timeworn, venerable; SEE CONCEPTS 578,797,799

antenna [n] *appendages for sensing, usually on insects or electronics*
aerial, bird snapper*, bullwhip*, ears*, feelers*, rabbit ears, receiver, sky wire*, whip*, wire; SEE CONCEPT 464

anterior [adj] *beginning, prior*
antecedent, foregoing, former, past, precedent, preceding, previous; SEE CONCEPT 799

anthem [n] *song*
canticle, chant, chorus, hymn, melody, paean; SEE CONCEPTS *263,595*

anthology [n] *literary collection*
album, analect, compendium, compilation, digest, garland, omnibus, selection, treasury; SEE CONCEPTS *280,432*

anthropology [n] *study of humans and their culture*
folklore, sociology; SEE CONCEPT *349*

antic [n] *funny act*
caper, dido, frolic, joke, lark, romp, shenanigan, tomfoolery, trick; SEE CONCEPT *292*

anticipate [v1] *expect; predict*
assume, await, bargain for*, be afraid*, conjecture, count chickens*, count on, cross the bridge*, divine, entertain*, figure, forecast, foresee, foretaste, foretell, have a hunch*, hope for, jump the gun*, look for, look forward to, plan on, prepare for, prevision, prognosticate, promise oneself, prophesy, see, see coming*, see in the cards*, suppose, visualize, wait, wait for; SEE CONCEPTS *26,70*

anticipate [v2] *act in advance of*
apprehend, beat someone to it*, be early, be one step ahead of*, block, delay, forestall, hinder, hold back, intercept, precede, preclude, prepare for, prevent, provide against; SEE CONCEPTS *100,121*

anticipation [n1] *expectation*
apprehension, awaiting, contemplation, expectancy, foresight, foretaste, high hopes, hope, impatience, joy, looking forward, outlook, preconception, premonition, preoccupation, prescience, presentiment, promise, prospect, trust; SEE CONCEPTS *26,689*

anticipation [n2] *readiness; forethought*
apprehension, awareness, foreboding, forecast, foreseeing, foresight, foretaste, forethought, inkling, intuition, preconception, premonition, prescience, presentiment, prevision, prior knowledge, realization; SEE CONCEPTS *409,410*

anticlimax [n] *ineffective conclusion*
bathos, comedown, decline, descent, disappointment, drop, letdown, slump; SEE CONCEPTS *230,674*

antidote [n] *counteracting agent*
antitoxin, antivenin, corrective, counteractant, counteragent, countermeasure, counterstep, cure, medicine, negator, neutralizer, nullifier, preventive, remedy; SEE CONCEPT *307*

antipathy [n] *strong dislike, disgust*
abhorrence, allergy, animosity, animus, antagonism, aversion, avoidance, bad blood*, contrariety, distaste, dysphathy, enmity, escape, eschewal, evasion, hate, hatred, hostility, ill will, incompatibility, loathing, opposition, rancor, repellency, repugnance, repulsion; SEE CONCEPT *29*

antiquarian [adj] *old, ancient*
aged, antique, archaic, hoary, obsolete, primitive, timeworn, venerable; SEE CONCEPTS *578,797*

antiquated [adj] *obsolete*
aged, ancient, antediluvian, antique, archaic, dated, elderly, fusty*, hoary, moldy, obsolescent, old, old-fangled, old-fashioned, old hat*, outmoded, out-of-date, outworn, superannuated; SEE CONCEPTS *530,578,797*

antique [n] *old object, often of great value*
antiquity, artifact, bygone, heirloom, monument,

objet d'art, rarity, relic, ruin, vestige; SEE CONCEPTS *259,443*

antique [adj] *old*
aged, ancient, elderly, obsolescent, obsolete, outdated, out-of-date, prehistoric, superannuated; SEE CONCEPTS *578,797*

antique [adj2] *old-fashioned*
antiquarian, archaic, classic, obsolete, olden, outdated, vintage; SEE CONCEPTS *530,578,797*

antiquity [n1] *old object*
antique, relic, ruin; SEE CONCEPT *259*

antiquity [n2] *oldness*
age, ancientness, antiqueness, archaism, archaism, elderliness, hoariness, old age, venerableness; SEE CONCEPT *715*

antiquity [n3] *distant past*
ancient time(s), classical times, days of old, days of yore, former age, old days, olden days, remote time, time immemorial; SEE CONCEPT *807*

antiseptic [n] *decontaminating agent*
bactericide, detergent, disinfectant, germicide, preservative, preventative, preventive, prophylactic, purifier, sterilizer; SEE CONCEPTS *307, 472,492*

antiseptic [adj] *completely clean, uncontaminated; decontaminating*
antibacterial, antibiotic, aseptic, bactericidal, clean, disinfectant, germ-destroying, germ-free, germicidal, hygienic, medicated, prophylactic, pure, purifying, sanitary, sterile, sterilized, sterilizing, unpolluted; SEE CONCEPT *485*

antisocial [adj] *nonparticipating; avoiding company*
alienated, ascetic, asocial, austere, cold, cynical, eremetic, hermitlike, introverted, misanthropic, reclusive, remote, reserved, retiring, solitary, standoffish, uncommunicative, unfriendly, unsociable, withdrawn; SEE CONCEPT *555*

antithesis [n1] *exact opposite*
antipode, antipole, contra, contradictory, contrary, contrast, converse, counter, flip side*, inverse, other side, reverse; SEE CONCEPT *665*

antithesis [n2] *contrast, opposition*
antagonism, contradiction, contradistinction, contraposition, contrariety, inversion, opposure, reversal; SEE CONCEPTS *633,665*

antitoxin [n] *agent for negating the effect of an infection or poison*
antibiotic, antibody, antipoison, antiseptic, antiserum, antivenin, counteractant, counteragent, medicine, neutralizer, preventive, serum, vaccine; SEE CONCEPT *307*

antonym [n] *word with opposite meaning to another word*
opposite, reverse; SEE CONCEPT *275*

anxiety [n] *worry, tension*
all-overs*, angst, ants in pants*, apprehension, botheration*, butterflies*, care, cold sweat*, concern, creeps*, disquiet, disquietude, distress, doubt, downer*, drag*, dread, fidgets*, flap*, foreboding, fretfulness, fuss, goose bumps*, heebie-jeebies*, jitters, jumps*, misery, misgiving, mistrust, nail-biting*, needles*, nervousness, panic, pins and needles*, restlessness, shakes*, shivers*, solicitude, suffering, suspense, sweat*, trouble, uncertainty, unease, uneasiness, watchfulness, willies*, worriment; SEE CONCEPTS *410,532,690*

anxious [adj1] *worried, tense*
afraid, aghast, antsy*, apprehensive, basket

case*, bugged*, butterflies, careful, choked*, clutched*, concerned, disquieted, distressed, disturbed, dreading, fearful, fidgety, fretful, hacked*, hyper*, in a state*, in a tizzy*, in suspense*, jittery, jumpy, nervous, nervy, overwrought, restless, scared, shaking, shaky, shivery, shook up*, shot to pieces*, solicitous, spooked*, strung out*, sweating bullets*, taut, troubled, uneasy, unglued*, unquiet, uptight*, watchful, wired*, worried sick*, wreck*; SEE CONCEPTS 403,690

anxious [adj2] *eager*
agog, ardent, avid, breathless, desirous, enthusiastic, expectant, fervent, impatient, intent, itching*, keen, thirsty, yearning, zealous; SEE CONCEPTS 401,542

any [det] *one, some; unspecified, indiscriminate*
a bit, a little, all, each, each and every, either, in general, part of, several, whatever; SEE CONCEPT 762

anybody [n] *one, some unspecified person or people*
all, any of, anyone, anyone at all, any person, a person, each and every one, everybody, everyone, masses, one, public, whole world; SEE CONCEPT 417

anyhow [adv] *by any means*
about, anyway, any which way, around, at any rate, at random, haphazard, haphazardly, helterskelter, however, in any case, in any respect, in any way, in either way, in one way or another, in whatever way, nevertheless, random, randomly, regardless, under any circumstances, whatever happens, willy-nilly; SEE CONCEPT 544

anyone [n] *one, some unspecified person*
all, anybody, anybody at all, any of, any person, a person, each and every one, everybody, everyone, masses, one, public, whole world; SEE CONCEPT 417

anyplace [n] *unspecified area*
all over, anywhere, everywhere, in any place, in whatever place, wherever; SEE CONCEPT 198

anything [n] *unspecified object or event*
all, any one thing, anything at all, everything, whatever; SEE CONCEPTS 2,433

anytime [n] *unspecified moment, period*
at all, at any moment, at one's convenience, every-time, no matter when, whenever, when one will; SEE CONCEPTS 807,819

anyway [adv] *by any means*
anyhow, at all, at any rate, ever, however, in any case, in any event, in any manner, nevertheless, once; SEE CONCEPT 544

anywhere [n] *unspecified area*
all over, anyplace, everywhere, in any place, in whatever place, wherever; SEE CONCEPT 198

apart [adv] *separate*
afar, alone, aloof, aside, away, by itself, cut off*, disassociated, disconnected, distant, distinct, divorced, excluded, exclusively, freely, independent, independently, individually, isolated, lone wolf*, separated, separately, singly, special, to itself, to one side; SEE CONCEPTS 586,785

apartment [n] *set of rooms for rent*
accommodation, cave*, chambers, cold-water*, condo, coop, cooperative, crash pad*, den*, digs*, dump*, flat, living quarters, lodging, pad*, penthouse, rental, residence, suite, walk-up*; SEE CONCEPTS 448,516

apathetic [adj] *uncaring, disinterested*
blah*, callous, cold, cool, could care less*, couldn't care less*, don't give a damn*, draggy*, emotionless, flat, impassive, indifferent, insensible, laid-back*, languid, moony*, passive, stoic, stolid, unconcerned, unemotional, unfeeling, uninterested, unmoved, unresponsive, untouched, what the hell*, wimpy*; SEE CONCEPTS 401,403

apathy [n] *uncaring attitude, lack of interest*
aloofness, coldness, coolness, detachment, disinterest, dispassion, disregard, dullness, emotionlessness, halfheartedness, heedlessness, indifference, insensibility, insensitivity, insouciance, lassitude, lethargy, listlessness, passiveness, passivity, stoicism, unconcern, unresponsiveness; SEE CONCEPTS 410,633

ape [v] *mimic*
affect, caricature, copy, counterfeit, ditto*, do*, do like*, echo, emulate, go like*, imitate, impersonate, make like*, mirror, mock, parody, parrot, take off*, travesty; SEE CONCEPTS 111,171

aperture [n] *hole*
breach, break, chasm, chink, cleft, crack, cut, eye, fissure, gap, gash, interstice, opening, orifice, outlet, passage, perforation, pinhole, puncture, rift, rupture, slash, slit, slot, space, vent; SEE CONCEPT 757

apex [n] *top, high point*
acme, apogee, climax, crest, crown, culmination, cusp, greatest, height, max*, maximum, meridian, most*, ne plus ultra, peak, pinnacle, point, roof, spire, sublimity, summit, tip, tops, up there*, vertex, zenith; SEE CONCEPTS 706,836

aphorism [n] *saying expressing a belief, often true*
adage, apothegm, axiom, dictum, maxim, moral, precept, proverb, rule, saw, saying, truism; SEE CONCEPTS 275,278,689

aphrodisiac [n/adj] *seductive; inducing sex*
amative, amatory, amorous, erotic, love drug, popper*, Spanish fly*, turn-on*, wampole*; SEE CONCEPTS 372,537

apiece [adv] *each*
all, a pop*, aside, for each, from each, individually, one by one, per, respectively, separately, severally, singly, successively, to each; SEE CONCEPT 762

apocryphal [adj] *questionable; fake*
counterfeit, doubtful, dubious, equivocal, false, fictitious, inaccurate, mythical, spurious, unauthenticated, ungenuine, unsubstantiated, untrue, unverified, wrong; SEE CONCEPTS 570,582

apologetic [adj] *expressing remorse, regret*
atoning, attritional, compunctious, conciliatory, contrite, expiatory, explanatory, on one's knees*, penitent, penitential, propitiatory, regretful, remorseful, repentant, rueful, self-effacing, self-incriminating, sorry, supplicating; SEE CONCEPT 267

apologize [v] *express remorse, regret*
admit guilt, ask forgiveness, ask pardon, atone, beg pardon, bow to*, clear oneself, confess, cop a plea*, cop out*, crawl*, excuse oneself, get down on knees*, give satisfaction*, make amends, make reparations, make up for, make up with, offer compensation, offer excuse, purge, retract, say one is sorry, square*, withdraw; SEE CONCEPTS 48,67

apology [n] *offering of remorse, regret*
acknowledgment, admission, amends, atonement, concession, confession, defense, excuse, explana-

tion, extenuation, justification, mea culpa, mitigation, plea, redress, reparation, vindication; SEE CONCEPTS 48,67

apoplexy [n] *loss of consciousness from blockage in vein or artery*
occlusion, seizure, stroke, thrombosis; SEE CONCEPTS 316,720

apostate [n] *traitor*
backslider, defector, deserter, dissenter, heretic, nonconformist, rat*, recreant, renegade, turncoat; SEE CONCEPTS 359,412

apostle [n] *preacher; supporter*
advocate, champion, companion, converter, evangelist, follower, herald, messenger, missionary, pioneer, propagandist, proponent, proselytizer, witness; SEE CONCEPTS 359,361

appall/appal [v] *horrify*
alarm, amaze, astound, awe, consternate, daunt, disconcert, dishearten, dismay, faze, frighten, get to*, gross out*, insult, intimidate, outrage, petrify, scare, shake, shock, terrify, throw, unnerve; SEE CONCEPTS 7,19,42

appalling [adj] *horrifying*
alarming, astounding, awful, bad, daunting, dire, disheartening, dismaying, dreadful, fearful, formidable, frightening, frightful, ghastly, grim, grody*, gross*, harrowing, heavy*, hideous, horrible, horrid, horrific, intimidating, mean, petrifying, scaring, shocking, terrible, terrifying, the end*, unnerving; SEE CONCEPT 529

apparatus [n1] *equipment with a purpose*
accoutrement, appliance, black box*, contraption, device, dingbat, doodad*, doohickey*, furnishings, gaff*, gear, gimcrack*, gimmick, gizmo*, grabber*, habiliments, idiot box*, implement, jigger*, job*, machine, machinery, means, mechanism, outfit, paraphernalia, provisions, setup, stuff, supplies, tackle, thingamajig*, tools, utensils, whatchamacallit*, whatsis*, whosis*, widget*; SEE CONCEPTS 260,463,499

apparatus [n2] *organization or system*
bureaucracy, chain of command, hierarchy, network, setup, structure; SEE CONCEPTS 381,770

apparel [n] *clothing; covering*
accoutrement, array, attire, clothes, costume, drapery, dress, duds*, equipment, garb, garment, gear*, getup*, habiliment, habit, outfit, raiment, rig*, robe, suit, threads*, trapping, vestment; SEE CONCEPTS 451,473

apparent [adj1] *seeming, not proven real*
credible, illusive, illusory, likely, ostensible, outward, plausible, possible, probable, semblant, specious, superficial, supposed, supposititious; SEE CONCEPTS 552,582

apparent [adj2] *obvious*
barefaced, big as life*, clear, clear cut, conspicuous, crystal clear, discernible, distinct, evident, glaring, indubitable, make no bones*, manifest, marked, noticeable, observable, open, open and shut*, out in the open*, overt, palpable, patent, perceivable, plain, self-evident, transparent, unambiguous, under one's nose*, understandable, unequivocal, unmistakable, visible; SEE CONCEPTS 535,582

apparently [adv1] *seemingly*
allegedly, as if, as though, at a glance, at first sight, in all likelihood, intuitively, it appears that, it seems that, most likely, on the face of it, ostensibly, outwardly, plausibly, possibly, probably, professedly, reasonably, reputably, speciously,

superficially, supposedly, tangibly, to all appearances; SEE CONCEPTS 552,582

apparently [adv2] *obviously*
clearly, conspicuously, evidently, expressly, indubitably, in plain sight, manifestly, officially, openly, overtly, palpably, patently, perceptibly, plainly, transparently, unmistakably; SEE CONCEPT 535

apparition [n] *ghost*
bogeyman, bump in the night*, chimera, delusion, hallucination, haunt, illusion, phantasm, phantom, revenant, specter, spirit, spook, visitant; SEE CONCEPTS 370,689

appeal [n1] *request for help*
address, adjuration, application, bid, call, claim, demand, entreaty, imploration, importunity, invocation, overture, petition, plea, prayer, proposal, proposition, question, recourse, requisition, solicitation, submission, suit, supplication; SEE CONCEPT 48

appeal [n2] *power to attract, interest*
allure, attraction, attractiveness, beauty, charm, charmingness, engagingness, fascination, glamor, interestingness, pleasingness, seductiveness; SEE CONCEPTS 655,673

appeal [v1] *request*
address, adjure, advance, apply, ask, beg, beseech, bid, call, call upon, claim, contest, crave, demand, entreat, hit on, implore, importune, petition, plead, pray, propose, proposition, question, refer, require, resort to, solicit, strike, submit, sue, supplicate, urge; SEE CONCEPT 48

appeal [v2] *attract, interest*
allure, engage, captivate, catch the eye, charm, enchant, engage, entice, fascinate, intrigue, invite, please, tantalize, tempt; SEE CONCEPTS 7,19,22,384

appear [v1] *come into sight*
arise, arrive, attend, be present, be within view, blow in*, bob up*, break through, breeze in*, check in*, clock in*, come, come forth, come into view, come out, come to light*, crop up*, develop, drop in*, emerge, expose, issue, loom, make the scene*, materialize, occur, pop in*, pop up*, present, punch in*, punch the clock*, recur, ring in*, rise, roll in*, show, show up, spring, surface, time in*, turn out, turn up; SEE CONCEPTS 159,261

appear [v2] *seem*
have the appearance, look as if, look like, occur, resemble, sound, strike one as; SEE CONCEPTS 543,716

appear [v3] *be obvious, clear*
be apparent, be evident, be manifest, be patent, be plain; SEE CONCEPT 725

appear [v4] *be published; perform*
become available, be created, be developed, be invented, come into being, come into existence, come on, come on stage*, come out, enter, make an appearance, oblige, perform, play, play a part, present oneself, take part; SEE CONCEPTS 292,324

appearance [n1] *coming into sight*
actualization, advent, appearing, arrival, coming, debut, display, emergence, entrance, exhibition, introduction, manifestation, materialization, presence, presentation, representation, rise, showing up, turning up, unveiling; SEE CONCEPTS 159,261

appearance [n2] *outward aspect, characteristic*
air, attitude, bearing, blind, carriage, cast, character, condition, countenance, demeanor, dress,

expression, face, fashion, feature, figure, form, front, guise, image, look, looks, manner, mannerism, mien, mode, outline, pose, presence, presentation, screen, semblance, shape, stamp; SEE CONCEPTS 543,716

appearance [n3] *outward show; pretense*
aura, beard*, blind, countenance, dream, facade, front, guise, idea, illusion, image, impression, mirage, phenomenon, reflection, screen, seeming, semblance, sound, specter, vision; SEE CONCEPT 673

appease [v] *satisfy, pacify*
allay, alleviate, assuage, be enough, blunt, calm, compose, conciliate, content, diminish, do*, ease, gratify, lessen, lull, make matters up, meet halfway, mitigate, mollify, patch things up, placate, propitiate, quell, quench, quiet, serve, soften, soothe, subdue, sweeten, tranquilize; SEE CONCEPTS 7,22,126

appeasement [n] *satisfaction; pacification*
abatement, acceding, accommodation, adjustment, alleviation, amends, assuagement, blunting, compromise, concession, conciliation, easing, grant, lessening, mitigation, moderation, mollification, peace offering, placation, propitiation, quelling, quenching, quieting, reconciliation, reparation, restoration, settlement, softening, solace, soothing, tranquilization; SEE CONCEPTS 7,22,126

append [v] *add, join*
adjoin, affix, annex, attach, conjoin, fasten, fix, hang, subjoin, supplement, tack on*, tag on*; SEE CONCEPTS 85,113,160

appendage [n] *limb; accessory*
addendum, addition, adjunct, ancillary, annex, appendix, appurtenance, attachment, auxiliary, extremity, member, projection, protuberance, supplement; SEE CONCEPT 835

appendix [n] *added material at end of document*
addendum, addition, adjunct, appendage, appurtenance, attachment, codicil, excursus, index, notes, postscript, rider, sample, supplement, table, verification; SEE CONCEPT 270

appertain [v] *belong, be connected*
apply, bear, be characteristic of, be part of, be pertinent, be proper, be relevant, have to do with, pertain, refer, relate, touch upon, vest; SEE CONCEPT 532

appetite [n] *desire for food, worldly goods*
appetence, appetency, appetition, big eyes*, craving, demand, fondness, gluttony, greed, hankering, hunger, inclination, itch*, liking, longing, lust, passion, penchant, proclivity, propensity, ravenousness, relish, soft spot*, stomach, sweet tooth*, taste, thirst, urge, voracity, weakness, willingness, yearning, yen, zeal, zest; SEE CONCEPTS 20,32

appetizer [n] *snack before meal*
antipasto, aperitif, canapé, cocktail, dip, finger food, hors d'oeuvre, munchies*, relish, sample, spread, taste, tidbit; SEE CONCEPTS 457,828

appetizing [adj] *tasting very good*
aperitive, appealing, delectable, delicious, delish*, divine*, flavorsome, heavenly, inviting, luscious, mouthwatering, palatable, saporous, savory, scrumptious, succulent, sugar-coated*, sweetened, tantalizing, tasty, tempting, toothsome, yummy*; SEE CONCEPT 613

applaud [v] *clap for; express approval*
acclaim, approve, boost, cheer, commend, compliment, encourage, eulogize, extol, give a hand*, give ovation, glorify, hail, hear it for*, kudize*, laud, magnify, plug, praise, rave, recommend, root*; SEE CONCEPTS 10,69,189

applause [n] *clapping; expression of approval*
acclaim, acclamation, accolade, approbation, big hand, bring down the house*, cheering, cheers, commendation, eulogizing, hand, hand-clapping, hurrahs, kudos, laudation, ovation, plaudits, praise, rooting, round, standing ovation; SEE CONCEPTS 69,189

appliance [n] *machine, usually with domestic purpose*
apparatus, device, gadget, implement, instrument, mechanism, tool; SEE CONCEPT 463

applicable [adj] *appropriate*
applicative, applicatory, apposite, apropos, apt, associable, befitting, felicitous, fit, fitting, germane, kosher, legit*, material, on target*, on the button*, on the nose*, pertinent, relevant, right on*, suitable, suited, that's the idea*, that's the ticket*, to the point, to the purpose, useful; SEE CONCEPTS 558,563

applicant [n] *person trying for position*
appellant, aspirant, candidate, claimant, hopeful, inquirer, petitioner, postulant, seeker, suitor, suppliant; SEE CONCEPTS 348,359

application [n1] *use*
appliance, appositeness, employment, exercise, exercising, function, germaneness, operation, pertinence, play, practice, purpose, relevance, usance, utilization, value; SEE CONCEPTS 680,694

application [n2] *request*
appeal, blank, claim, demand, draft, entreaty, form, inquiry, letter, paper, petition, requisition, solicitation, suit; SEE CONCEPT 48

application [n3] *hard work*
assiduity, attention, attentiveness, busyness, commitment, concentration, consideration, dedication, deliberation, diligence, effort, industry, perseverance, study, zeal; SEE CONCEPTS 91,410

application [n4] *putting substance on another*
administering, administration, applying, creaming, dosing, oiling, rubbing, treatment; SEE CONCEPT 200

applied [adj] *used*
activated, adapted, adjusted, brought to bear, correlated, devoted, enforced, exercised, practiced, related, tested, utilized; SEE CONCEPTS 538,546

apply [v1] *put into use*
administer, assign, bring into play, bring to bear, employ, engage, execute, exercise, exploit, handle, implement, practice, utilize; SEE CONCEPT 225

apply [v2] *be appropriate, relevant*
affect, allude, appertain, be applicable, bear upon, be pertinent, concern, connect, fit, involve, pertain, refer, regard, relate, suit, touch; SEE CONCEPT 532

apply [v3] *put substance on another*
administer, affix, anoint, bestow, cover, fasten, join, lay on, massage, paint, place, put on, rub, smear, spread, touch; SEE CONCEPT 200

apply [v4] *ask, request*
appeal, claim, demand, inquire, petition, put in, put in for, requisition, solicit, sue; SEE CONCEPT 48

apply [v5] *work hard*
address, bear down, be diligent, be industrious, bend, buckle down*, commit, concentrate, dedi-

cate, devote, dig, direct, give, give all one's got*, give best shot*, give old college try*, grind, hammer away*, hit the ball*, hustle*, knuckle down*, make effort, peg away*, persevere, plug*, pour it on*, pull out all stops*, scratch, study, sweat*, throw, try, turn; SEE CONCEPTS 87,100

appoint [v1] *assign responsibility; decide*
accredit, allot, assign, choose, command, commission, decree, delegate, designate, determine, direct, elect, enjoin, establish, finger, fix, install, name, nominate, ordain, select, set, settle, tap; SEE CONCEPTS 41,50,88

appoint [v2] *furnish*
arm, equip, fit, fit out, gear, outfit, provide, rig, supply, turn out; SEE CONCEPT 140

appointment [n1] *arrangement for meeting; pre-arranged meeting*
assignation, assignment, blind date*, consultation, date, engagement, errand, gig, interview, invitation, meet, rendezvous, session, tryst, zero hour*; SEE CONCEPTS 324,384

appointment [n2] *assigning of responsibility*
allotment, approval, assigning, authorization, certification, choice, choosing, commissioning, delegation, deputation, designation, election, empowering, installation, naming, nomination, ordination, promotion, selection; SEE CONCEPTS 41,50,88

appointment [n3] *job, position of responsibility*
appointee, assignment, berth, candidate, delegate, employment, nominee, office, officeholder, place, post, representative, situation, station, work; SEE CONCEPT 349

appointment [n4] *furnishing(s)*
accoutrement, appurtenance, equipage, fitting, fixture, gear, outfit, paraphernalia, trappings; SEE CONCEPT 475

apportion [v] *divide into shares*
accord, admeasure, administer, allocate, allot, assign, bestow, cut, cut up, deal, dispense, distribute, divvy, divvy up, dole out, give, lot, measure, mete, parcel, part, partition, piece up, prorate, ration, slice, split, split up; SEE CONCEPTS 98,108

appraisal [n] *judgment, estimation*
appraisement, assessment, estimate, evaluation, opinion, pricing, rating, reckoning, stock, survey, valuation; SEE CONCEPTS 18,328,766

appraise [v] *judge, estimate*
adjudge, assay, assess, audit, calculate, check, check out*, deem, evaluate, examine, eye*, figure, figure in, figure out, gauge, guesstimate*, have one's number*, inspect, look over, peg, price, rate, read, review, set at, size, survey, take account of, valuate, value; SEE CONCEPTS 18,764

appreciable [adj] *easily noticed; considerable*
apparent, ascertainable, clear-cut, definite, detectable, discernible, distinguishable, estimable, evident, goodly, good-sized, healthy, large, manifest, marked, material, measurable, noticeable, observable, obvious, perceivable, perceptible, plain, pronounced, recognizable, sensible, significant, sizable, substantial, tangible, visible; SEE CONCEPTS 619,781

appreciate [v1] *be grateful, thankful*
acknowledge, be appreciative, be indebted, be obliged, enjoy, flip over*, freak out on*, get high on*, give thanks, groove on*, welcome; SEE CONCEPTS 12,32,76

appreciate [v2] *increase in worth*
enhance, gain, grow, improve, inflate, raise the value of, rise; SEE CONCEPT 763

appreciate [v3] *recognize worth*
acknowledge, apprehend, be aware of, be cognizant of, be conscious of, catch the drift, comprehend, dig, fathom, grasp, know, perceive, read, realize, recognize, savvy, see daylight*, sympathize with, take account of, understand; SEE CONCEPT 15

appreciate [v4] *value highly*
admire, adore, applaud, apprise, cherish, enjoy, esteem, extol, honor, like, look up to, love, praise, prize, rate highly, regard, relish, respect, savor, treasure; SEE CONCEPTS 10,32

appreciation [n1] *thankfulness*
acknowledgment, gratefulness, gratitude, indebtedness, obligation, recognition, testimonial, thanks, tribute; SEE CONCEPTS 12,32

appreciation [n2] *increase in worth*
enhancement, gain, growth, improvement, inflation, rise; SEE CONCEPTS 346,763

appreciation [n3] *recognition of worth*
admiration, aesthetic sense, affection, appraisal, assessment, attraction, awareness, cognizance, commendation, comprehension, enjoyment, esteem, estimation, grasp, high regard, knowledge, liking, love, perception, realization, recognition, regard, relish, respect, responsiveness, sensibility, sensitiveness, sensitivity, sympathy, understanding, valuation; SEE CONCEPTS 15,409

appreciative [adj1] *thankful*
beholden, grateful, indebted, obliged, responsive; SEE CONCEPT 403

appreciative [adj2] *understanding, recognizing worth*
admiring, affectionate, alive, aware, cognizant, conscious, considerate, cooperative, cordial, enlightened, enthusiastic, favorable, friendly, generous, keen, kindly, knowledgeable, magnanimous, mindful, perceptive, pleased, receptive, regardful, respectful, responsive, satisfied, sensitive, supportive, sympathetic, understanding; SEE CONCEPT 402

apprehend [v1] *catch and arrest*
bag*, bust*, capture, collar, cop*, grab, nab, nail*, place under arrest, run in, seize, take in, take into custody, take prisoner; SEE CONCEPTS 90,191,317

apprehend [v2] *understand*
absorb, accept, appreciate, believe, catch, comprehend, conceive, digest, fathom, get, get the picture*, grasp, have, imagine, know, perceive, read, realize, recognize, sense, think; SEE CONCEPT 15

apprehension [n1] *anxiety, fear*
alarm, apprehensiveness, concern, disquiet, doubt, dread, foreboding, misgiving, mistrust, premonition, presage, presentiment, suspicion, trepidation, uneasiness, worry; SEE CONCEPTS 27,690

apprehension [n2] *catching and arresting*
booking, capture, collaring, detention, seizure, taking; SEE CONCEPTS 90,317

apprehension [n3] *understanding*
awareness, comprehension, grasp, idea, intellect, intelligence, judgment, ken, knowledge, notion, perception, perspicacity, thought; SEE CONCEPT 409

apprehensive [adj] anxious, fearful
afraid, alarmed, biting nails*, butterflies*, concerned, disquieted, doubtful, feel in bones*, foreboding, frozen*, get vibes*, have a hunch*, have cold feet*, have funny feeling*, have stage fright*, hung up*, in a cold sweat*, in a dither*, in a sweat*, jellyfish*, jittery, jumpy, lily-livered*, mistrustful, running scared*, scaredy-cat*, shaky*, stiff, suspicious, troubled, uncertain, uneasy, uptight, weak, worried, worried sick*; SEE CONCEPT 403

apprentice [n] novice/learner of a trade
amateur, beginner, flunky*, greenhorn*, heel*, neophyte, newcomer, new kid on block*, novitiate, probationer, pupil, rook*, rookie*, starter, student, tenderfoot*, tyro; SEE CONCEPTS 348,423

approach [n1] way, means of arriving
access, accession, advance, advent, avenue, coming, drawing near, entrance, gate, landing, nearing, passage, path, reaching, road, way; SEE CONCEPTS 159,501

approach [n2] request, suggestion
advance, appeal, application, offer, overture, proposal, proposition; SEE CONCEPT 278

approach [n3] plan of attack, resolution
attitude, concept, course, crack, fling, go*, idea, lick, manner, means, method, mode, modus operandi, new wrinkle*, offer, procedure, program, shot, stab, style, technique, way, whack*, wrinkle*; SEE CONCEPTS 655,660

approach [v1] come nearer
advance, approximate, bear, be comparable to, be like, belly up to*, border, buzz*, catch up, close in, come, come at, come close, compare with, contact, converge, correspond to, creep up, draw near, equal, gain on, go toward, impend, loom up, match, meet, move in on, move toward, near, progress, reach, resemble, surround, take after, threaten, verge upon; SEE CONCEPTS 159,198,701

approach [v2] make request, suggestion
accost, address, advise, appeal to, apply to, beseech, confer, consult, entreat, feel, feel one out*, give a play*, give a tumble*, greet, implore, make advance, make overture, make up to, plead, propose, sound out, speak to, supplicate, take aside, talk to, thumb, tumble; SEE CONCEPTS 48,75

approach [v3] begin
commence, embark, set about, start, undertake; SEE CONCEPT 234

approachable [adj1] accessible
attainable, come-at-able*, convenient, door's always open*, getable*, obtainable, reachable; SEE CONCEPT 576

approachable [adj2] friendly
affable, agreeable, congenial, cordial, open, receptive, sociable; SEE CONCEPT 404

approbation [n] praise
admiration, approval, bells*, consent, endorsement, esteem, favor, go-ahead*, high regard, okay, permission, recognition, sanction, support, the nod*; SEE CONCEPTS 10,69

appropriate [adj] suitable
adapted, applicable, appurtenant, apropos, apt, becoming, befitting, belonging, congruous, convenient, correct, deserved, desired, due, felicitous, fit, fitting, germane, good, just, on the button*, on the nose*, opportune, pertinent, proper, relevant, right, rightful, seemly, tailor-made, true, useful, well-suited, well-timed; SEE CONCEPT 558

appropriate [v1] set aside; allocate
allot, allow, appoint, apportion, assign, budget, devote, disburse, earmark, reserve, set apart; SEE CONCEPT 135

appropriate [v2] steal
annex, borrow, clap*, confiscate, cop, embezzle, filch, get fingers on*, get hands on*, glom on to*, grab, grab hold of*, hijack, liberate, lift, misappropriate, moonlight requisition*, pilfer, pocket, secure, snatch, swipe*, take over, usurp; SEE CONCEPT 139

appropriation [n1] allocation, setting aside
allotment, allowance, apportionment, assignment, budgeting, concession, donation, earmarking, endowing, funding, giving, grant, provision, setting apart, sponsoring, stipend, stipulation, subsidy; SEE CONCEPTS 135,340

appropriation [n2] stealing
confiscation, embezzlement, expropriation, grab, misappropriation, pilfering, seizure, takeover, taking, usurpation; SEE CONCEPT 139

approval [n1] authorization
acquiescence, assent, bells*, blessing, compliance, concurrence, confirmation, consent, countenance, endorsement, go-ahead*, green light*, leave, license, mandate, okay, permission, ratification, recommendation, sanction, support, the nod*, validation; SEE CONCEPTS 10,685

approval [n2] good opinion
acclaim, admiration, applause, appreciation, approbation, commendation, esteem, favor, liking, pat on the back*, pat on the head*, PR*, praise, puff, pumping up, regard, respect, strokes, stroking, wow*; SEE CONCEPT 32

approve [v1] agree something is good
accept, acclaim, admire, applaud, appreciate, approbate, be big on*, commend, countenance, esteem, face it, favor, go along with, grin and bear it*, handle, like, live with*, praise, put up with, regard highly, respect, roll with punches*, string along with*, take up on*, think highly of; SEE CONCEPT 10

approve [v2] allow, authorize
accede, accept, accredit, acquiesce, advocate, affirm, agree, assent, authorize, back*, bless*, boost, buy, buy into*, certify, charter, concur, confirm, consent, dig*, empower, encourage, endorse, establish, get behind, give go-ahead*, go along with, groove*, hats off to*, lap up*, license, maintain, make law, make valid, mandate, okay, permit, pronounce, push for, ratify, recommend, sanction, seal, second, sign, sign off on, stump for, subscribe to, support, thumbs up*, uphold, validate; SEE CONCEPTS 50,83,88

approximate [adj1] almost accurate, exact
almost, close, comparative, exact, proximate, relative, rough; SEE CONCEPT 557

approximate [adj2] inexact
estimated, guessed, imperfect, imprecise, loose, rough, surmised, uncertain, unprecise, unscientific; SEE CONCEPT 557

approximate [adj3] similar
alike, analogous, close, comparable, like, matching, near, relative, resembling, verging on; SEE CONCEPTS 487,573

approximate [adj4] near
adjacent, bordering, close together, contiguous, nearby, neighboring; SEE CONCEPT 586

approximate [v] *come close*
approach, border on, come near, estimate, near, reach, resemble, touch, verge on; SEE CONCEPT *664*

approximately [adv] *nearly*
about, almost, around, ballpark figure*, bordering on, circa, closely, close to, comparatively, generally, in the ballpark*, in the neighborhood of, in the region of, in the vicinity of, just about, loosely, more or less, most, much, not far from, not quite, proximately, relatively, roughly, upwards of*, very close; SEE CONCEPT *566*

apropos [adj] *relevant, suitable*
applicable, apposite, appropriate, apt, befitting, belonging, correct, fit, fitting, germane, kosher*, legit*, material, on the button*, on the nose*, opportune, pertinent, proper, related, right, right on*, seemly; SEE CONCEPT *558*

apropos [adv] *relevantly, suitably*
appropriately, aptly, opportunely, pertinently, suitably, timely; SEE CONCEPT *558*

apropos [prep] *in respect of*
about, against, as for, as regards, as to, concerning, on the subject of, regarding, respecting, touching, toward, with reference to, with respect to; SEE CONCEPT *532*

apt [adj1] *suitable*
applicable, apposite, appropriate, apropos, befitting, correct, felicitous, fit, fitting, germane, happy, just, pertinent, proper, relevant, seemly, suitable, timely; SEE CONCEPT *558*

apt [adj2] *tending, inclined*
disposed, given, liable, likely, of a mind, prone, ready; SEE CONCEPT *542*

apt [adj3] *quick to learn*
able, adept, astute, bright, clever, expert, gifted, ingenious, intelligent, nobody's fool*, no dummy*, not born yesterday*, prompt, quick on the trigger*, quick on the uptake*, ready, savvy, sharp, skilled, skillful, smart, talented, teachable; SEE CONCEPT *402*

aptitude [n1] *inclination*
bent, disposition, drift, leaning, predilection, proclivity, proneness, propensity, tendency; SEE CONCEPT *657*

aptitude [n2] *quickness at learning*
ability, capability, capacity, cleverness, competence, faculty, flair, gift, giftedness, intelligence, knack, proficiency, savvy, smarts, stuff*, talent, what it takes*; SEE CONCEPT *409*

aquarium [n] *fish tank*
aquatic museum, fishbowl, marine exhibit; SEE CONCEPTS *396,438,514*

aquatic [adj] *occurring in water*
amphibian, amphibious, floating, marine, maritime, natatory, oceanic, of the sea, sea, swimming, watery; SEE CONCEPTS *396,536*

aqueduct [n] *canal*
channel, conduit, course, duct, pipeline, water passage, waterworks; SEE CONCEPT *514*

arbiter [n] *person who settles dispute*
adjudicator, arbitrator, fixer, go-between, holdout, judge, maven, mediator, middleperson, moderator, referee, umpire; SEE CONCEPT *354*

arbitrary [adj1] *whimsical, chance*
approximate, capricious, discretionary, erratic, fanciful, frivolous, inconsistent, injudicious, irrational, irresponsible, offhand, optional, random, subjective, supercilious, superficial, unaccountable, unreasonable, unscientific, wayward, willful; SEE CONCEPTS *534,542*

arbitrary [adj2] *dictatorial*
absolute, autocratic, bossy, despotic, dogmatic, domineering, downright, flat out*, high-handed, imperious, magisterial, monocratic, no ifs ands or buts*, no joke*, overbearing, peremptory, straight out*, summary, tyrannical, tyrannous; SEE CONCEPT *401*

arbitrate [v] *achieve settlement*
adjudge, adjudicate, adjust, bring to terms, come to school, come to terms, conciliate, decide, determine, hammer out a deal*, interpose, intervene, judge, make a deal, mediate, meet halfway, negotiate, parley, pass judgment, placate, play ball*, reconcile, referee, settle, smooth, soothe, step in, straighten out, strike happy medium*, trade off, umpire, work out a deal; SEE CONCEPTS *126,300*

arbitration [n] *settlement of dispute*
adjudication, adjustment, agreement, compromise, decision, determination, judgment, mediation; SEE CONCEPTS *126,300*

arbitrator [n] *settler of a dispute*
adjudicator, arbiter, fixer, go-between, holdout, judge, maven, mediator, middleperson, referee, umpire; SEE CONCEPTS *348,359*

arc [n] *curve*
arch, bend, bow, crescent, curvation, curvature, half-moon, round; SEE CONCEPT *436*

arcane [adj] *hidden, secret*
cabalistic, esoteric, impenetrable, mysterious, mystic, occult, recondite, unaccountable, unknowable; SEE CONCEPT *576*

arch [n] *curve, curved structure*
arc, archway, bend, bow, curvature, dome, semicircle, span, vault; SEE CONCEPT *436*

arch [adj1] *principal, superior*
accomplished, champion, chief, consummate, expert, finished, first, foremost, greatest, head, highest, leading, main, major, master, preeminent, premier, primary, top; SEE CONCEPT *574*

arch [adj2] *knowing, coy*
artful, frolicsome, mischievous, pert, playful, roguish, saucy, sly, waggish, wily; SEE CONCEPT *401*

arch [v] *curve*
arc, bend, bow, bridge, camber, extend, form, hook, hump, hunch, round, shape, span, stretch; SEE CONCEPT *184*

archaeologist [n] *student of the physical remains of ancient cultures or eras*
archaeologian, classicist, excavator, paleologist, paleontologist, prehistorian; SEE CONCEPT *348*

archaeology [n] *study of the physical remains of ancient cultures or eras*
antiquarianism, excavation, paleohistory, paleology, paleontology, prehistory; SEE CONCEPT *349*

archaic [adj] *very old*
ancient, antiquated, antique, bygone, obsolete, olden, old-fashioned, outmoded, out of date, passé, primitive, superannuated; SEE CONCEPTS *578,797*

archetype [n] *typical example*
classic exemplar, form, ideal, model, original, paradigm, pattern, perfect specimen, prime example, prototype, standard; SEE CONCEPTS *636,686*

architect [n] *person who designs buildings*
artist, builder, creator, designer, draftsperson, engineer, inventor, maker, master builder, originator, planner, prime mover; SEE CONCEPT *348*

architecture [n1] *design of buildings*
architectonics, building, construction, engineering, planning; SEE CONCEPTS *349,439*

architecture [n2] *design, structure of something*
composition, constitution, construction, formation, framework, make-up, style; SEE CONCEPTS *660,733*

archive [n] *collection, usually of records*
annals, chronicles, clippings, documents, excerpts, extracts, files, papers, registers, roll, scrolls, writings; SEE CONCEPTS *271,281,432*

archives [n] *place where records are stored*
athenaeum, library, museum, office, registry, repository, storage, treasury, vault; SEE CONCEPT *439*

archway [n] *curved opening*
entrance, passage; SEE CONCEPT *440*

arctic [adj] *very cold*
chill, chilly, cool, freezing, frigid, frosty, frozen, gelid, glacial, icy, nippy, polar; SEE CONCEPT *605*

ardent [adj1] *very enthusiastic*
agog, avid, blazing, burning, desirous, eager, fervent, fervid, fierce, fiery, horny*, hot*, hungry, impassioned, intense, keen, lovey-dovey*, lusty, passionate, spirited, thirsty, vehement, warm, zealous; SEE CONCEPTS *401,404*

ardent [adj2] *loyal*
allegiant, constant, devoted, faithful, resolute, steadfast, true; SEE CONCEPT *404*

ardor [n] *enthusiasm*
avidity, devotion, eagerness, earnestness, feeling, fervor, fierceness, fire, gusto, heat, intensity, jazz*, keenness, oomph*, passion, pep talk*, spirit, turn on*, vehemence, verve, warmth, weakness*, zeal, zest, zing; SEE CONCEPT *411*

arduous [adj] *difficult, hard to endure*
backbreaking, burdensome, exhausting, fatiguing, formidable, grueling, harsh, heavy, labored, laborious, murder, no picnic*, onerous, painful, punishing, rigorous, rough, severe, strenuous, taxing, tiring, toilsome, tough, troublesome, trying, uphill; SEE CONCEPT *565*

area [n1] *extent, scope of a surface*
breadth, compass, distance, expanse, field, operation, range, size, space, sphere, stretch, width; SEE CONCEPTS *651,792*

area [n2] *region, district*
belt, block, city, county, division, domain, dominion, enclosure, field, kingdom, locality, neck of the woods*, neighborhood, parcel, patch, plot, precinct, principality, quarter, section, sector, sphere, square, state, stretch, territory, township, tract, turf, vicinity, ward, zone; SEE CONCEPT *508*

arena [n1] *building or enclosure for entertainment or sports*
amphitheatre, boards*, bowl*, circus, coliseum, course, diamond, field, gridiron, ground, gym, gymnasium, hippodrome, ice, park, pit, platform, ring, rink, square, stadium, stage; SEE CONCEPT *438*

arena [n2] *area of activity*
battlefield, battleground, domain, field, province, realm, scene, sector, sphere, territory, theatre; SEE CONCEPT *198*

argue [v1] *verbally fight*
altercate, bandy, battle, bicker, break with, buck, bump heads, contend, cross, cross swords, disagree, dispute, face down, face off, feud, gang up on, get in one's face*, go one on one, hammer, hammer away, hash, hash over, hassle, have at

each other, have at it, jump, jump on, knock around, lock horns*, mix it up*, pettifog, pick an argument, put up a fight, put up a struggle, quarrel, quibble, rehash, row, sass, set to, sock it to*, squabble, stick it to, talk back, wrangle; SEE CONCEPT *46*

argue [v2] *try to convince; present support*
appeal, assert, attest, claim, contend, controvert, defend, demonstrate, denote, display, elucidate, establish, evince, exhibit, explain, hold, imply, indicate, justify, maintain, manifest, persuade, plead, present, prevail upon, reason, show, suggest, talk into, testify, vindicate, warrant, witness; SEE CONCEPT *68*

argue [v3] *discuss*
agitate, canvass, clarify, debate, dispute, expostulate, hold, maintain, question, reason, remonstrate, talk about; SEE CONCEPTS *46,56*

argument [n1] *verbal fight*
altercation, beef, bickering, blowup, bone, bone of contention, bone to pick*, brannigan*, brawl, brush, clash, controversy, crusher*, debate, difference of opinion, disagreement, dispute, donnybrook, dustup*, exchange, face-off, falling, feud, finisher*, flap, fuss, gin*, go*, hassle, knockdown*, knock down and drag out*, out, quarrel, rhubarb*, romp, row, ruckus, ruction, rumpus, run-in, scene, scrap, set-to, shindy*, spat, squabble, static*, stew*, talking heads*, tiff, words, wrangle; SEE CONCEPT *46*

argument [n2] *effort to convince; presentation of support*
argumentation, assertion, case, claim, contention, debate, defense, discussion, exchange, expostulation, grounds, line of reasoning, logic, plea, pleading, polemic, proof, questioning, reason, reasoning, remonstrance, remonstration; SEE CONCEPT *68*

argumentative [adj] *wanting to quarrel*
belligerent, combative, contentious, contrary, controversial, disputatious, factious, fire-eating, having a chip on one's shoulder*, litigious, opinionated, pugnacious, quarrelsome, salty, scrappy, spiky, touchy; SEE CONCEPT *401*

aria [n] *operatic solo*
descant, hymn, song; SEE CONCEPTS *263,595*

arid [adj1] *dry*
barren, bone-dry, desert, dry as a bone, dry as dust, dusty, moistureless, parched, thirsty, waterless; SEE CONCEPT *603*

arid [adj2] *uninterested, spiritless*
boring, colorless, drab, dreary, dry, dull, flat, insipid, lackluster, lifeless, tedious, unanimated, uninspired, vapid, wearisome; SEE CONCEPT *542*

arise [v1] *come into being; proceed*
appear, begin, come to light, commence, crop up, derive, emanate, emerge, ensue, flow, follow, happen, head, issue, occur, originate, result, rise, set in, spring, start, stem; SEE CONCEPT *105*

arise [v2] *get, stand, or go up*
ascend, climb, jump, mount, move upward, pile out*, rise, rise and shine*, roll out*, soar, stand, tower, turn out, wake up; SEE CONCEPTS *154,166*

aristocracy [n] *privileged class, government*
elite, gentility, gentry, haut monde, high society, nobility, noblesse, patricians, patriciate, peerage, society, upper class, upper crust*; SEE CONCEPTS *296,423*

aristocrat [n] *privileged person*
blueblood, gentleperson, lace curtain*, noble, pa-

trician, peer, silk stocking, swell*, upper cruster*; SEE CONCEPT 423

aristocratic [adj] privileged, elegant
aloof, blue-blooded, courtly, dignified, elegant, elite, fine, haughty, noble, patrician, polished, refined, snobbish, stylish, upper-class, well-born, well-bred; SEE CONCEPT 555

arithmetic [n] mathematics
addition, calculation, computation, division, estimation, figuring, multiplication, reckoning, subtraction; SEE CONCEPTS 349,764

arm [n1] limb, appendage
bender, bough, bow, branch, fin, flapper, flipper, handle, hook, member, offshoot, projection, prong, rod, stump, wing; SEE CONCEPTS 392,471

arm [n2] subdivision, annex
affiliate, authority, block, branch, command, department, detachment, division, ell, extension, force, offshoot, power, projection, section, sector, wing; SEE CONCEPTS 824,835

arm [n3] narrow body of water
branch, brook, channel, creek, estuary, firth, fjord, inlet, rivulet, sound, strait, stream, subdivision, tributary; SEE CONCEPT 514

arm [v] equip with weapon or power
accouter, appoint, array, deck, equalize, fortify, furnish, gear, gird, guard, heel*, heel up*, issue, load, load up, lug iron*, make ready, mobilize, outfit, pack, pack a rod*, prepare, prime, protect, provide, rig, rod up*, strengthen, supply, tote; SEE CONCEPTS 50,88,182

armada [n] group of ships or aircraft
fleet, flotilla, force, navy, squadron; SEE CONCEPTS 432,504,506

armament(s) [n] weapon(s)
ammunition, arms, defense, gun, hardware, heat*, material, materiel, munitions, ordnance, protection, security, weaponry; SEE CONCEPT 500

armistice [n] peace-establishing agreement
ceasefire, suspension, treaty, truce; SEE CONCEPTS 230,684

armor [n] protective covering, often made of metal
bulletproof vest, defense, guard, mail, plate, protection, security, sheath, shield; SEE CONCEPTS 451,476

armory [n] military building, usually for storing weapons
arsenal, center, depot, dump, factory, headquarters, magazine, plant, range; SEE CONCEPTS 321,439

arms [n1] weaponry
accoutrements, armaments, artillery, equipment, firearms, guns, munitions, ordnance, panoply, weapons; SEE CONCEPT 500

arms [n2] family crest
blazonry, coat, emblazonry, emblem, ensign, escutcheon, heraldry, insignia, shield, signet; SEE CONCEPTS 284,625

army [n1] military force, usually for land
armed force, artillery, battalion, battery, brigade, cavalry, column, command, company, corps, detail, division, flight, formation, infantry, legion, outfit, patrol unit, platoon, regiment, soldiers, soldiery, squad, troops, wing; SEE CONCEPT 322

army [n2] group resembling military force
array, cloud, company, crowd, division, flock, horde, host, legion, mob, multitude, outfit, pack, regiment, scores, swarm, throng, unit; SEE CONCEPT 417

aroma [n] distinctive smell
balm, bouquet, fragrance, incense, odor, perfume, redolence, scent, spice; SEE CONCEPT 599

aromatic [adj] distinctive smelling
ambrosial, balmy, fragrant, odoriferous, perfumed, pungent, redolent, savory, scented, spicy, sweet, sweet-smelling; SEE CONCEPT 598

around [adv1] situated on sides, circumference, or in general area
about, all over, any which way, encompassing, everywhere, in the vicinity, in this area, neighboring, over, throughout; SEE CONCEPT 581

around [adv2] close to a place
about, almost, approximately, close at hand, near, nearby; SEE CONCEPT 586

arouse [v] excite, entice
agitate, alert, animate, awaken, call, challenge, electrify, enliven, fire up, foment, foster, goad, heat up, incite, inflame, instigate, kindle, move, provoke, rally, rouse, send, spark, spur, stimulate, stir, thrill, turn on, waken, wake up, warm, whet, whip up, work up; SEE CONCEPTS 7,19,22

arraign [v] accuse
blame, charge, criminate, hang on, incriminate, inculpate, indict, lay at one's door*, pin it on*, point the finger at*, summon; SEE CONCEPTS 44,317

arrange [v1] put in an order
align, array, class, classify, clear the decks, dispose, file, fix up, form, group, line up, methodize, organize, police, police up, position, put in good shape*, put in order*, put to rights*, range, rank, regulate, sort, spruce, spruce up, systematize, tidy, whip into shape*; SEE CONCEPTS 84,158

arrange [v2] make plans, often involving agreement
adapt, adjust, agree to, blueprint, chart, come to terms, compromise, concert, construct, contrive, decide, design, determine, devise, direct, draft, establish, frame*, get act together*, get ready, hammer out a deal*, harmonize, iron out*, lay out, line up, make a connection, make ready, manage, map out, negotiate, organize, prepare, project, promote, provide, pull a wire, pull things together, quarterback*, resolve, schedule, scheme, set stage, settle, shape up, tailor, work out, work out a deal; SEE CONCEPTS 36,84

arrange [v3] prepare musical composition differently
adapt, instrument, orchestrate, score; SEE CONCEPT 292

arrangement [n1] an understanding
adjustment, agreement, compact, compromise, deal, frame-up*, game plan*, layout*, organization, package*, package deal*, plan, preparation, provision, schedule, settlement, setup, terms; SEE CONCEPT 684

arrangement [n2] something that has been ordered
alignment, array, classification, combination, composition, design, display, disposition, distribution, form, grouping, lineup, method, ordering, organization, pattern, pecking order*, ranging, rank, sequence, setup, structure, system; SEE CONCEPTS 84,727

arrangement [n3] musical adaptation
chart, composition, instrumentation, interpretation, lead sheet, orchestration, score, version; SEE CONCEPTS 262,595

array [n1] *collection, considerable group*
arrangement, batch, body, bunch, bundle, clump, cluster, design, display, disposition, exhibition, formation, host, lineup, lot, multitude, order, parade, pattern, set, show, supply, throng; SEE CONCEPTS 432,769,787

array [n2] *fine clothes*
apparel, attire, drapes*, dress, duds*, finery, full dress, garb, garments, getup*, rig*, threads*; SEE CONCEPT 451

array [v1] *arrange in collection or order*
align, display, exhibit, form, group, line up, methodize, organize, parade, range, set, show, systematize; SEE CONCEPT 84

array [v2] *dress in fine clothes*
attire, bedeck, clothe, deck, deck out, decorate, dog out*, drape, dud, dude up*, fit, fit out, garb, outfit, suit up, tog, try on, turn out, wrap; SEE CONCEPT 167

arrears [n] *debt*
back payment, balance due, claim, debit, deficiency, deficit, liability, obligation, unpaid bill; SEE CONCEPTS 332,335

arrest [n1] *taking into custody*
accommodation, apprehension, appropriation, bag*, booby trap*, bust, captivity, capture, collar, commitment, confinement, constraint, crimp*, detention, drop*, fall*, gaff*, glom*, grab*, heat*, hook*, imprisonment, incarceration, jailing, mitt*, nab*, nail*, nick*, nip*, pickle*, pick up*, pinch*, preventive custody, protective custody, pull*, pull in*, restraining, run in*, sequestering, snare, sweep*; SEE CONCEPTS 90,317

arrest [n2] *slowing or stopping*
blockage, cessation, check, checking, delay, end, halt, hindrance, inhibition, interruption, obstruction, prevention, restraining, restraint, stalling, stay, staying, stoppage, suppression, suspension; SEE CONCEPTS 121,234

arrest [v1] *take into authorized custody*
apprehend, bag*, book, brace*, bust, capture, catch, collar, detain, drop*, gaff*, get*, glom*, grab*, hook*, imprison, incarcerate, jail, kick*, nab*, nail*, net*, nick*, pick up*, pinch*, pull*, pull in*, put the arm on*, put the cuffs on*, round up*, roust*, run in*, secure*, seize*, sidetrack*, snag*, tab*, tag*, take in, take prisoner, toss in jail*; SEE CONCEPTS 90,317

arrest [v2] *stop or slow*
block, can, check, delay, drop, end, freeze, halt, hinder, hold, inhibit, interrupt, knock off, obstruct, prevent, restrain, restrict, retard, scrub*, shut down, stall, stay, suppress; SEE CONCEPTS 121,234

arrest [v3] *get someone's attention*
absorb, catch, engage, engross, fascinate, grip; SEE CONCEPTS 7,19,22

arrival [n1] *coming to a destination*
accession, advent, alighting, appearance, approach, arriving, debarkation, disembarkation, dismounting, entrance, happening, homecoming, influx, ingress, landing, meeting, occurrence, return; SEE CONCEPT 159

arrival [n2] *something that makes it to a destination*
addition, arriver, caller, cargo, comer, conferee, delegate, delivery, entrant, envoy, freight, guest, mail, newcomer, package, parcel, passenger, representative, shipment, tourist, traveler, visitant, visitor; SEE CONCEPTS 337,423,712

arrive [v1] *come to a destination*
access, alight, appear, attain, barge in, blow in, bob up*, breeze in*, bust in*, buzz*, check in*, clock in*, disembark, dismount, drop anchor, drop in, enter, fall by, fall in, get to, hit*, hit town*, land*, make it*, make the scene*, pop in*, pop up*, pull in*, punch the clock*, reach, report, roll in*, show, show up, sign in, sky in*, take place, turn up, visit, wind up at; SEE CONCEPT 159

arrive [v2] *achieve recognition*
accomplish, become famous, flourish, make good, make it, make the grade, prosper, reach the top, score, succeed, thrive; SEE CONCEPT 706

arrogance [n] *exaggerated self-opinion*
airs, aloofness, audacity, bluster, braggadocio, brass*, cheek*, chutzpah*, conceit, conceitedness, contemptuousness, crust*, disdain, disdainfulness, ego, egotism, gall, haughtiness, hauteur, high-handedness, hubris, imperiousness, insolence, loftiness, nerve, ostentation, overbearance, pomposity, pompousness, presumption, pretension, pretentiousness, pride, priggishness, scornfulness, self-importance, self-love, smugness, superciliousness, swagger, vanity; SEE CONCEPTS 411,633

arrogant [adj] *having exaggerated self-opinion*
aloof, assuming, audacious, autocratic, biggety*, bossy, bragging, cavalier, cheeky, cocky, cold-shoulder*, conceited, contemptuous, cool*, disdainful, domineering, egotistic, haughty, high and mighty*, high-handed, imperious, insolent, know-it-all*, lordly, on an ego trip*, overbearing, peremptory, pompous, presumptuous, pretentious, proud, puffed up*, scornful, self-important, smarty, smug, sniffy*, snippy*, snooty*, snotty*, stuck up*, supercilious, superior, swaggering, uppity*, vain, wise guy*; SEE CONCEPTS 401,404

arrogate [v] *claim without justification*
accroach, appropriate, assume, commandeer, confiscate, demand, expropriate, preempt, presume, seize, take, usurp; SEE CONCEPTS 142,266

arsenal [n] *storage of weapons*
armory, depository, depot, dump, factory, magazine, ordnance, plant, repository, stock, stockpile, store, storehouse, supply, warehouse; SEE CONCEPTS 432,439

arson [n] *intentional burning*
firing, incendiarism, pyromania, setting fire, torching, touching off; SEE CONCEPT 249

art [n1] *skill, creativity*
adroitness, aptitude, artistry, craft, craftsmanship, dexterity, expertise, facility, imagination, ingenuity, inventiveness, knack, know-how, knowledge, mastery, method, profession, trade, virtuosity; SEE CONCEPT 706

art [n2] *cunning*
artfulness, artifice, astuteness, canniness, craftiness, deceit, duplicity, guile, slyness, trickery, wiliness; SEE CONCEPT 411

art [n3] *creation meant to communicate or appeal to senses or mind*
abstraction, carving, description, design, illustration, imitation, modeling, molding, painting, pictorialization, portrayal, representation, sculpting, shaping, simulation, sketching, symbolization; SEE CONCEPT 349

artery [n] *channel*
avenue, boulevard, canal, conduit, corridor, course, duct, highway, line, passage, pathway,

road, route, sewer, thoroughfare, track, tube, way; SEE CONCEPT *501*

artful [adj] *skillful; cunning*
adept, adroit, clever, crafty, designing, dexterous, foxy*, ingenious, masterly, politic, proficient, resourceful, scheming, sharp, shrewd, slick*, sly, smart, smooth*, tricky, wily; SEE CONCEPTS *404,528*

article [n1] *item, object*
commodity, dojigger*, gizmo*, piece, substance, thing, thingamabob*, thingamajig*, unit; SEE CONCEPT *433*

article [n2] *piece of writing*
beat*, blurb*, column, commentary, composition, discourse, editorial, essay, exposition, feature, item, paper, piece, scoop*, spread, story, theme, think piece*, treatise, write-up; SEE CONCEPTS *270,271,280*

article [n3] *section of document*
branch, chapter, clause, detail, division, element, head, heading, item, matter, paragraph, part, passage, piece, point, portion, provision; SEE CONCEPTS *270,318*

articulate [adj] *clearly, coherently spoken*
clear, coherent, comprehensible, definite, distinct, eloquent, expressive, fluent, intelligible, lucid, meaningful, understandable, well-spoken; SEE CONCEPT *267*

articulate [v1] *say clearly, coherently*
enunciate, express, mouth, pronounce, say, sound off*, speak, state, talk, utter, verbalize, vocalize, voice; SEE CONCEPTS *47,55*

articulate [v2] *connect*
concatenate, couple, fit together, hinge, integrate, join, link; SEE CONCEPT *113*

articulation [n1] *clear, coherent speech*
delivery, diction, enunciation, expression, pronunciation, saying, speaking, statement, talking, utterance, verbalization, vocalization, voicing; SEE CONCEPT *55*

articulation [n2] *connection*
coupling, hinge, joining, joint, junction, juncture, unification, union; SEE CONCEPT *113*

artifice [n1] *hoax; clever act*
con, contrivance, device, dodge, expedient, gambit, gimmick*, machination, maneuver, play, ploy, racket*, ruse, savvy, scam*, stratagem, subterfuge, tactic, wile; SEE CONCEPT *59*

artifice [n2] *cunning; deception*
artfulness, chicanery, craftiness, dishonesty, duplicity, guile, scheming, slyness, trickery, wiliness; SEE CONCEPT *411*

artifice [n3] *skill, cleverness*
ability, adroitness, deftness, facility, finesse, ingenuity, invention, inventiveness, know-how*, skill; SEE CONCEPT *630*

artificial [adj1] *fake; imitation*
bogus, counterfeit, ersatz, fabricated, factitious, faked, false, falsie*, hyped up*, manufactured, mock, phony*, plastic, sham, simulated, specious, spurious, substitute, synthetic, unnatural, unreal; SEE CONCEPT *582*

artificial [adj2] *pretended; affected*
assumed, contrived, false, feigned, forced, hollow, insincere, labored, mannered, meretricious, phony*, put-on, spurious, theatrical, unnatural; SEE CONCEPT *401*

artillery [n] *weaponry or military unit*
arms, battery, bazooka, big guns*, cannon, cannonry, force, gunnery, heavy stuff*, munitions,

ordnance, rainmakers*, stovepipe, weapons; SEE CONCEPTS *322,500*

artist [n] *person skilled in creative activity*
artisan, artiste, authority, composer, craftsperson, creator, expert, handicrafter, inventor, painter, virtuoso, whiz*; SEE CONCEPT *352*

artistic [adj1] *beautiful, satisfying to senses*
aesthetic, creative, cultivated, cultured, decorative, dramatic, elegant, exquisite, fine, graceful, grand, harmonious, ideal, imaginative, musical, ornamental, pictorial, picturesque, pleasing, poetic, refined, rhythmical, sensitive, stimulating, stylish, sublime, tasteful; SEE CONCEPT *579*

artistic [adj2] *being skilled in creative activity*
accomplished, artful, artsy-craftsy*, arty, crafty, discriminating, gifted, imaginative, inventive, skillful, talented; SEE CONCEPT *527*

artistry [n] *great skill in creative endeavors*
ability, accomplishment, artfulness, brilliance, craftship, creativity, finesse, flair, genius, mastery, proficiency, style, talent, taste, touch, virtuosity, workmanship; SEE CONCEPTS *630,655*

artless [adj] *simple*
direct, genuine, guileless, honest, ingenuous, innocent, naive, natural, open, plain, pure, sincere, straight, straightforward, talking turkey*, true, unadorned, unaffected, uncontrived, unpretentious, unsophisticated, up front*; SEE CONCEPTS *267,562*

arty [adj] *pretended expertise in art; affected interest*
affected, deceptive, ephemeral, false, flaunting, illusory, imitative, overblown, popular, popularized, pretentious, pseudo, tasteless; SEE CONCEPT *582*

as [conj1] *while, when*
at the time that, during the time that, in the act of, in the process of, just as, on the point of; SEE CONCEPT *544*

as [conj2] *in the way that; to a degree*
acting as, being, by its nature, comparatively, equally, essentially, for instance, functioning as, in the manner that, in the same manner with, just as, just for, like, serving as, similarly, such as; SEE CONCEPT *544*

as [conj3] *because*
as long as, being, cause, considering, for, for the reason that, inasmuch as, now, seeing that, since, whereas; SEE CONCEPT *544*

as [prep] *in the character of*
being, in the character of, under the name of; SEE CONCEPT *544*

ascend [v] *go up*
arise, climb, escalate, float, fly, lift off, mount, move up, rise, scale, soar, sprout, take off, tower; SEE CONCEPTS *149,166*

ascendancy/ascendency [n] *domination*
advantage, authority, command, control, dominance, dominion, edge, influence, jump*, leg up*, mastery, on top, power, predominance, preeminence, prepotence, prevalence, reign, rule, sovereignty, superiority, supremacy, sway, upper hand*, whip hand*; SEE CONCEPTS *376,671*

ascension [n] *going up*
ascent, climbing, escalating, flying, mounting, rise, rising, scaling, soaring, towering; SEE CONCEPTS *149,166*

ascent [n1] *upward movement*
ascendance, ascending, ascension, clambering,

climb, climbing, lift, mounting, rise, rising, scaling, spring, take off; SEE CONCEPT *166*

ascent [n2] *upward slope*
acclivity, grade, gradient, incline, ramp, rise; SEE CONCEPTS *738,757*

ascertain [v] *make sure*
catch on, check, check out*, check up on*, confirm, determine, dig*, discover, divine, double-check*, establish, eye*, eyeball*, find out, fix, get down cold*, get down pat*, get hold of*, get it down*, get the hang of*, identify, learn, learn the ropes*, look-see*, make certain, make sure, peg*, pick up*, pick up on*, read, see, settle, size, size up*, tell, verify; SEE CONCEPTS *31,34,38*

ascribe [v] *assign to source*
accredit, attribute, charge, credit, hang on, impute, lay, pin on*, put down, refer, reference, set down; SEE CONCEPTS *39,49*

ash(es) [n] *remains of burning*
charcoal, cinders, dust, embers, powder, relics, remains, ruins, slag, soot; SEE CONCEPT *260*

ashamed [adj] *regretting, remorseful*
abashed, apologetic, bashful, blushing, chagrined, compunctious, conscience-stricken, contrite, crestfallen, debased, demeaned, discomfited, disconcerted, distraught, distressed, embarrassed, flustered, guilty, hesitant, humble, humbled, humiliated, meek, mortified, muddled, penitent, regretful, reluctant, repentant, shamed, shamefaced, sheepish, shy, sorry, stammering, stuttering, submissive; SEE CONCEPT *550*

ashore [adv] *toward, onto land from water*
aground, beached, on dry land, on land, on shore, shorewards; SEE CONCEPT *583*

aside [n] *confidential statement*
departure, digression, discursion, interpolation, interposition, parenthesis, tangent, throwaway*; SEE CONCEPT *51*

aside [adv] *away from; to the side*
abreast, afar, alone, alongside, apart, away, beside, by oneself, down, in isolation, in reserve, near, nearby, neck and neck, out, out of the way, privately, separately, sidewise; SEE CONCEPT *586*

ask [v1] *question*
buzz*, canvass, catechize, challenge, cross-examine, demand, direct, enjoin, examine, give the third degree*, go over, grill*, hit*, hunt for*, inquire, institute, interrogate, investigate, needle*, pick one's brains*, pop the question*, pry into, pump, put the screws to*, put through the wringer*, query, quiz, request, roast*, sweat*; SEE CONCEPT *48*

ask [v2] *request*
angle, appeal, apply, beg, beseech, bite*, bum*, call for, charge, claim, command, contend for, crave, demand, entreat, file for, hit*, hustle*, implore, impose, knock*, levy, mooch*, order, petition, plead, pray, promote*, request, requisition, seek, solicit, sue, supplicate, touch*, urge; SEE CONCEPT *53*

ask [v3] *invite*
bid, call upon, propose, suggest, summon, urge; SEE CONCEPT *75*

askew [adj] *crooked*
askance, askant, aslant, awry, bent, buckled, catawampus*, cockeyed*, crookedly, curved, knotted, lopsided, oblique, obliquely, off-center, slanted, slanting, to one side, topsy-turvey*,

turned, twisted, yaw ways*, zigzag*; SEE CONCEPT *586*

asleep [adj] *unconscious*
catching some zzz's*, comatose, conked*, crashed*, dormant, dozing, dreaming, flaked out*, getting shut-eye*, hibernating, inactive, in dreamland*, inert, in repose, napping, on the kip*, out*, out cold*, out like a light*, out of it*, reposing, resting, sacked out*, sleeping, slumbering, snoozing, snoring, somnolent, taking forty winks*; SEE CONCEPTS *210,315,681*

aspect [n1] *visible feature*
air, appearance, attitude, bearing, condition, countenance, demeanor, expression, face, facet, form, look, manner, mien; SEE CONCEPTS *434,628,673*

aspect [n2] *element to consider*
angle, bearing, direction, facet, feature, gimmick, hand, outlook, perspective, phase, point of view, position, prospect, regard, scene, side, situation, slant, switch, twist, view, vista; SEE CONCEPT *668*

asperity [n] *harshness; bad temper*
acerbity, acrimony, bitterness, churlishness, crabbiness, crossness, difficulty, disagreeableness, irascibility, irritability, meanness, moroseness, peevishness, roughness, sharpness, sourness, sullenness, tartness; SEE CONCEPT *633*

aspersion [n] *verbal exhibition of bad temper*
abuse, animadversion, backbiting, backhanded compliment, black eye*, calumny, defamation, detraction, dirty dig*, hit*, invective, knock*, libel, obloquy, put-down*, rap*, slam*, slander, smear*, vituperation; SEE CONCEPTS *52,54,58*

asphyxiate [v] *cut off air*
choke, drown, smother, stifle, strangle, strangulate, suffocate; SEE CONCEPTS *121,246*

aspiration [n] *goal, hope*
aim, ambition, ambitiousness, craving, desire, direction, dream, eagerness, endeavor, fire in the belly*, hankering, inclination, longing, object, objective, passion, pursuit, push, right stuff*, urge, vocation, wish, work, yearning; SEE CONCEPTS *20,659*

aspire [v] *aim, hope*
be ambitious, be eager, crave, desire, dream, hanker, long, pursue, seek, strive, struggle, try, want, wish, yearn; SEE CONCEPT *20*

aspiring [adj] *hopeful*
ambitious, aspirant, eager, eager beaver*, endeavoring, enthusiastic, impassioned, longing, on the make*, striving, wishful, would-be, zealous; SEE CONCEPT *403*

ass [n] *stupid person*
blockhead*, dolt, donkey*, dope, dunce, fool, idiot, imbecile, jackass*, jerk*, nitwit*, numbskull*, simpleton*, twit*; SEE CONCEPT *412*

assail [v] *attack, usually with words*
abuse, assault, bash, berate, beset, blast, blister, bust, charge, come at, criticize, encounter, have at*, impugn, invade, lambaste, lay into*, malign, maltreat, molest, revile, set upon*, trash*, vilify, work over; SEE CONCEPTS *52,86*

assailant [n] *attacker*
aggressor, antagonist, assaulter, bushwhacker*, enemy, foe, goon*, hit person, invader, mugger, opposite number*, trigger person; SEE CONCEPT *412*

assassin [n] *murderer of prominent or important person*
butcher*, clipper*, dropper*, eliminator, en-

forcer, executioner, guerrilla*, gun*, gun person, hatchet person, hit person, killer, liquidator, piece person*, plugger*, slayer, soldier, torpedo*, trigger person; SEE CONCEPT 412

assassinate [v] *murder prominent or important person*
bump off*, do in*, eliminate, execute, gun down, hit, kill, knock off*, liquidate, slaughter, slay; SEE CONCEPT 252

assault [n] *attack*
advance, aggression, charge, incursion, invasion, offensive, onset, onslaught, rape, storm, storming, strike, violation; SEE CONCEPT 86

assault [v] *attack*
abuse, advance, assail, bash, beset, blast, blitz, bushwhack, charge, come down on*, go for, haul off on*, invade, jump, jump down one's throat*, jump on one's case*, lay into, let have it*, light into*, rape, ruin, set upon, shoot down, slam, slap around, storm, strike, trash, violate, work over, zap*; SEE CONCEPTS 52,86

assay [n] *analysis*
appraisal, assessment, estimation, evaluation, examination, inspection, investigation, measurement, rating, survey, test, trial, valuation; SEE CONCEPTS 24,103,290

assay [v] *analyze*
appraise, apprise, assess, check, check out, estimate, evaluate, examine, eyeball*, inspect, investigate, measure, peg*, prove, rate, read, see, size, size up*, survey, test, try, valuate, value, weigh; SEE CONCEPTS 24,103

assemblage [v] *gathering of people*
aggregation, assembly, association, collection, company, congregation, convergence, crowd, group, throng; SEE CONCEPT 417

assemble [v1] *congregate*
accumulate, agglomerate, amass, bring together, bunch, bunch up, call, call together, capture*, collect, come together, convene, convoke, corral*, flock, gang up*, gather, group, hang around*, hang out*, huddle, lump, make the scene*, meet, meet up, mobilize, muster, rally, reunite, round up, scare up*, summon, unite; SEE CONCEPT 114

assemble [v2] *put together*
compile, connect, construct, contrive, erect, fabricate, fashion, fit, form, join, make, manufacture, model, mold, piece together, produce, set up, shape, unite, weld; SEE CONCEPT 113

assembly [n1] *congregation*
accumulation, aggregation, assemblage, association, band, body, bunch, clambake*, cluster, coffee klatch*, collection, company, conclave, confab*, conference, convocation, council, crew, crowd, faction, flock, gathering, get-together*, group, huddle, mass, meet*, meeting, multitude, rally, sit-in*, throng, turnout*; SEE CONCEPTS 381,432

assembly [n2] *putting together*
adjustment, attachment, building, collection, connecting, construction, erection, fabrication, fitting together, joining, manufacture, manufacturing, modeling, molding, piecing together, setting up, shaping, welding; SEE CONCEPT 113

assent [n] *agreement*
acceptance, accession, accord, acknowledgment, acquiescence, admission, affirmation, approval, authorization, compliance, concurrence, consent, nod, permission, sanction; SEE CONCEPTS 8,684

assent [v] *agree*
accede, accept, accord, acquiesce, adopt, allow, approve, buy, cave in*, comply, concur, conform, consent, cut a deal*, defer, ditto*, embrace, espouse, give five*, give in, go along with, grant, knuckle under*, okay*, pass on*, permit, recognize, sanction, say uncle*, shake on*, subscribe; SEE CONCEPT 8

assert [v] *insist, declare, maintain*
advance, affirm, allege, argue, asseverate, attest, aver, avouch, avow, butt in*, cite, claim, contend, defend, horn in, justify, mouth off*, pop off*, predicate, press, proclaim, profess, pronounce, protest, put forward, say, shoot off one's mouth*, shoot one's wad*, stand up for*, state, stress, swear, uphold, vindicate, warrant; SEE CONCEPT 49

assertion [n] *declaration, positive statement*
affirmation, allegation, asseveration, attestation, avowal, contention, defense, insistence, maintenance, mouthful, okay, predication, profession, pronouncement, report, say so*, stamp of approval, stressing, two cents' worth*, vindication; SEE CONCEPTS 49,278

assertive [adj] *aggressive*
absolute, assured, certain, confident, decided, decisive, demanding, dogmatic, domineering, emphatic, firm, forceful, forward, insistent, militant, overbearing, positive, pushy, self-assured, self-confident, strong-willed, sure; SEE CONCEPT 404

assess [v1] *evaluate, determine*
appraise, apprise, assay, check*, check out*, compute, determine, dig it*, estimate, figure*, fix, gauge, guess, judge, nick*, peg*, rate, reckon, set, size*, size up, survey, take measure*, valuate, value, weigh; SEE CONCEPT 24

assess [v2] *assign fee, amount*
charge, demand, evaluate, exact, fix, impose, levy, rate, tax, value; SEE CONCEPT 330

assessment [n1] *evaluation*
appraisal, computation, determination, estimate, estimation, judgment, rating, reckoning, valuation, value judgment; SEE CONCEPT 24

assessment [n2] *assignment of fee, amount*
appraisal, charge, demand, duty, estimate, fee, levy, rate, rating, tariff, tax, taxation, toll, valuation; SEE CONCEPT 332

asset [n1] *advantage*
aid, benefit, blessing, boon, credit, distinction, help, resource, service, treasure; SEE CONCEPT 661

asset(s) [n2] *property or money possessed*
ace in the hole*, ace up sleeve*, backing, bankroll, budget, capital, credit, equity, estate, funds, goods, holdings, kitty*, mattress*, means, nest egg*, nut*, possessions, rainy day*, reserve(s), resources, riches, sock*, something put aside, something put away, stake, stash*, stuff, valuables, wealth; SEE CONCEPTS 332,340,710

assiduous [adj] *hard-working*
active, attentive, busy, constant, diligent, eager beaver*, exacting, grinding, indefatigable, industrious, laborious, persevering, plugging, scrupulous, sedulous, steady, studious, unflagging, untiring, whiz, zealous; SEE CONCEPTS 538,542

assign [v1] *select and give a responsibility*
accredit, allow, appoint, ascribe, attach, attribute, authorize, cast, charge, choice, commission, commit, credit, delegate, deputize, designate, downlink, download, draft, elect, empower, enroll,

entrust, hang on*, hire, hold responsible, impute, name, nominate, ordain, pin on*, refer, reference, select, slot, tab, tag; SEE CONCEPTS 41,50,88

assign [v2] *set apart for a reason*
allocate, allot, appoint, apportion, appropriate, consign, designate, detail, determine, dish out*, distribute, divide, earmark, fix, fork out*, give, grant, hand out*, hand over, indicate, mete, prescribe, relegate, shell out*, specify, stipulate; SEE CONCEPTS 129,135

assignation [n] *clandestine meeting*
affair, appointment, date, engagement, heavy date*, illicit meeting, love nest*, one-night stand*, quickie*, rendezvous, secret meeting, tryst; SEE CONCEPTS 375,386

assignment [n1] *responsibility, task*
appointment, beat, charge, chore, commission, drill, duty, homework, job, mission, position, post, practice, stint; SEE CONCEPT 362

assignment [n2] *selecting or setting apart*
allocation, allotment, appointment, apportionment, appropriation, ascription, assignation, attribution, authorization, choice, consignment, delegation, designation, determination, distribution, giving, grant, nomination, selection, specification, stipulation; SEE CONCEPTS 41,129

assimilate [v1] *absorb mentally*
comprehend, digest, grasp, incorporate, ingest, learn, osmose, sense, soak up, take in, take up, understand; SEE CONCEPT 15

assimilate [v2] *become adjusted; adjust*
acclimatize, accommodate, acculturate, accustom, adapt, become like, become similar, blend in, conform, fit, go native*, homogenize, homologize, intermix, match, mingle, parallel, standardize; SEE CONCEPTS 232,701

assist [n] *help*
abetment, aid, assistance, backing, benefit, boost, collaboration, comfort, compensation, cooperation, facilitation, furtherance, hand, helping hand, lift, reinforcement, relief, service, support; SEE CONCEPT 110

assist [v] *help*
abet, aid, back, bail out, benefit, boost, collaborate, cooperate, do for*, expedite, facilitate, further, give a boost*, give a leg up*, give a lift*, go down the line for*, go for, go to bat for*, go with, grease the wheels*, hype*, lend a hand*, make a pitch for*, open doors*, plug*, puff*, push*, put on the map*, reinforce, relieve, ride shotgun*, root for*, run interference for*, serve, stand up for, stump*, support, sustain, take care of, thump*, work for, work with; SEE CONCEPT 110

assistance [n] *help*
abetment, aid, assist, backing, benefit, boost, collaboration, comfort, compensation, cooperation, facilitation, furtherance, hand, help, helping hand, lift, reinforcement, relief, support, sustenance; SEE CONCEPT 110

assistant [n] *helper*
abettor, accessory, accomplice, adherent, adjunct, aide, ally, appointee, apprentice, associate, attendant, auxiliary, backer, backup*, coadjutant, coadjutor, collaborator, colleague, companion, confederate, cooperator, deputy, fellow worker, flunky*, follower, friend, gofer*, help, helpmate, mate, partner, patron, peon*, representative, right-hand person, secretary, subordinate, supporter, temp*, temporary worker; SEE CONCEPTS 348,423

associate [n] *colleague*
accessory, accomplice, affiliate, aid, ally, assistant, auxiliary, branch, buddy, chum, clubber*, cohort, collaborator, companion, compatriot, comrade, confederate, consort, cooperator, co-worker, crony, fellow, friend, helper, joiner, kissing cousin, mate, offshoot, one of the folks*, pal, pard*, partner, peer, playmate, sidekick; SEE CONCEPTS 348,423

associate [v1] *connect in the mind*
affiliate, blend, bracket, combine, concord, conjoin, correlate, couple, group, identify, join, league, link, lump together, mix, pair, relate, think of together, unite, yoke; SEE CONCEPT 39

associate [v2] *befriend*
accompany, amalgamate, be friends, be in cahoots*, buddy up, bunch up, come together, confederate, consort, fraternize, gang up, get in on, get into, get in with, get together, go along with, go partners*, hang around, hang out, hang out with*, hobnob, join, join up with, line up with, mingle, mix, pal up, play footsie with*, pool, run around with, run with, string along with, swing with, take up with, team up, throw in together, tie in, tie up, truck with, work with; SEE CONCEPTS 114,384

association [n1] *group with common interest or pursuit*
affiliation, alliance, band, bunch, circle, clan, clique, club, coalition, combination, combo, company, confederacy, confederation, congress, cooperative, corporation, crew, crowd, family, federation, fellowship, fraternity, gang, guild, hookup*, league, mob, order, organization, outfit, partnership, pool, rat pack*, ring, society, sodality, sorority, syndicate, tie-in, tie-up, tribe, troops, troupe, union, zoo*; SEE CONCEPTS 323,325,387

association [n2] *friendship*
acquaintance, acquaintanceship, affiliation, agreement, assistance, camaraderie, companionship, comradeship, conjunction, cooperation, familiarity, fellowship, fraternization, frequenting, friendliness, hookup*, intimacy, membership, participation, partnership, relation, relationship; SEE CONCEPTS 387,388

association [n3] *mental connection*
bond, combination, concomitance, concordance, connotation, correlation, identification, impression, joining, juxtaposition, linkage, linking, lumping together, mixing, mixture, pairing, recollection, relation, remembrance, tie, train of thought, union; SEE CONCEPT 39

assorted [adj] *various*
different, diverse, diversified, heterogeneous, hybrid, indiscriminate, miscellaneous, mixed, motley, sundry, varied, variegated; SEE CONCEPT 564

assortment [n] *variety*
array, choice, collection, combination, combo, diversity, garbage, group, hodgepodge, jumble, kind, medley, mélange, miscellany, mishmash, mixed bag, mixture, potpourri, selection, sort; SEE CONCEPTS 432,665

assuage [v] *soothe, relieve*
allay, alleviate, appease, calm, compose, conciliate, cool*, ease, fill, lessen, lighten, lull, make nice*, mitigate, moderate, mollify, pacify, palliate, placate, pour oil on*, propitiate, quench, quiet, sate, satisfy, soften, still, surfeit, sweeten,

take the edge off*, take the sting out*, temper, tranquilize; SEE CONCEPTS 7,22,244

assume [v1] *believe, take for granted*
accept, ascertain, be afraid, be inclined to think, conclude, conjecture, consider, count upon, deduce, deem, divine, estimate, expect, fall for, fancy, find, gather, get the idea*, guess, have a hunch*, have sneaking suspicion, hypothesize, imagine, infer, judge, posit, postulate, predicate, presume, presuppose, speculate, suppose, surmise, suspect, theorize, think, understand; SEE CONCEPTS 12,26

assume [v2] *take, undertake*
accept, acquire, appropriate, arrogate, attend to, begin, confiscate, don, embark upon, embrace, enter upon, seize, set about, take on, take over, take up; SEE CONCEPTS 87,142

assume [v3] *pretend*
act, adopt, affect, bluff, counterfeit, fake, feign, imitate, impersonate, mimic, pretend, put on, simulate; SEE CONCEPT 59

assume [v4] *adopt, acquire*
annex, appropriate, arrogate, borrow, clap hands on*, commandeer, confiscate, expropriate, get fingers on*, get hands on*, glom onto*, grab, grab hold of*, hijack, kipe*, liberate, moonlight requisition*, preempt, seize, snatch, swipe, take over, usurp; SEE CONCEPTS 139,142

assumed [adj1] *pretended*
affected, artificial, bogus, counterfeit, fake, false, feigned, fictitious, imitation, made-up, make-believe, phony, pretended, put-on, sham, simulated, spurious; SEE CONCEPT 582

assumed [adj2] *expected*
accepted, conjectured, connoted, counted on, given, granted, hypothesized, hypothetical, inferred, postulated, presumed, presupposed, supposed, suppositional, surmised, tacit, taken as known, taken for granted, understood; SEE CONCEPTS 403,689

assuming [adj] *presumptuous, arrogant*
bold, conceited, disdainful, domineering, egotistic, forward, haughty, imperious, overbearing, pushy, rude; SEE CONCEPT 404

assumption [n1] *taking something for granted; something expected*
acceptance, accepting, assuming, belief, conjecture, expectation, fancy, guess, hunch, hypothesis, inference, posit, postulate, postulation, premise, presumption, presupposition, shot*, shot in the dark*, sneaking suspicion, stab, supposal, supposition, surmise, suspicion, theorization, theory; SEE CONCEPT 689

assumption [n2] *assuming possession, power*
acceptance, accepting, acquisition, adoption, appropriation, arrogation, assuming, embracing, grab, seizure, shouldering, takeover, taking, taking on, taking up, undertaking, usurpation; SEE CONCEPTS 129,142

assumption [n3] *arrogance*
brass*, chutzpah*, cockiness, conceit, imperiousness, insolence, nerve, presumption, pride, sass*, self-importance; SEE CONCEPT 411

assurance [n1] *statement to relieve doubt*
affirmation, assertion, declaration, guarantee, insurance, lock*, lock on*, oath, pledge, profession, promise, rain or shine*, security, shoo-in*, support, sure thing*, vow, warrant, warranty, word, word of honor; SEE CONCEPTS 71,278

assurance [n2] *confidence*
aggressiveness, aplomb, arrogance, assuredness, audacity, boldness, bravery, certainty, certitude, conviction, coolness, courage, effrontery, faith, firmness, impudence, nerve, poise, positiveness, presumption, security, self-confidence, self-reliance, sureness, surety, temerity, trust; SEE CONCEPT 410

assure [v1] *convince, relieve doubt*
bag*, bet on*, comfort, encourage, hearten, inspire, persuade, reassure, satisfy, sell*, sell on*, soothe; SEE CONCEPT 68

assure [v2] *promise*
affirm, attest, aver, brace up, buck up, certify, confirm, give one's word, guarantee, pledge, swear, vouch for, vow; SEE CONCEPT 71

assure [v3] *make certain*
cinch, clinch, complete, confirm, ensure, guarantee, have a lock on*, ice*, insure, lock on, lock up, make sure, nail down*, put on ice*, seal, secure, set; SEE CONCEPTS 36,91

assured [adj1] *absolutely certain*
beyond doubt, cinched, clear-cut, clinched, confirmed, decided, definite, dependable, ensured, fixed, guaranteed, indubitable, insured, in the bag*, irrefutable, made certain, nailed down*, on ice*, pronounced, racked*, sealed, secure, set, settled, sewed up*, sure, surefire, undoubted, unquestionable; SEE CONCEPT 535

assured [adj2] *confident*
assertive, audacious, bold, brazen, certain, cocksure*, collected, complacent, composed, confident, cool, gung ho*, gutsy*, high*, imperturbable, overconfident, poised, positive, puffed up*, pumped up*, pushy, rosy*, sanguine, secure, self-assured, self-confident, self-possessed, sure, unflappable, unhesitating, upbeat*; SEE CONCEPTS 401,404

astern [adv] *backward*
abaft, aft, rear, rearward; SEE CONCEPT 581

astonish [v] *surprise*
amaze, astound, bewilder, blow away*, blow one's mind*, boggle, bowl over*, confound, daze, dumbfound, flabbergast, floor*, knock over*, overwhelm, put one away*, shock, spring on, stagger, startle, stun, stupefy, take aback, throw a curve*; SEE CONCEPT 42

astonishing [adj] *surprising*
amazing, astounding, bewildering, breathtaking, extraordinary, impressive, marvelous, miraculous, spectacular, staggering, startling, striking, stunning, stupefying, stupendous, wonderful, wondrous; SEE CONCEPTS 547,572

astonishment [n] *state of surprise*
amazement, astoundment, awe, bewilderment, confusion, consternation, dumbfoundment, one for the books*, shock, something else*, stunner, stupefaction, wonder, wonderment; SEE CONCEPTS 230,410

astound [v] *amaze*
astonish, bewilder, blow away, bowl over*, confound, confuse, daze, dumbfound, flabbergast, knock over with feather*, overwhelm, shock, stagger, startle, stun, stupefy, surprise, take aback; SEE CONCEPT 42

astray [adj] *off the path or right direction*
adrift, afield, amiss, awry, gone, lost, off, off course, off the mark, roaming, straying, vanished, wandering, wrong; SEE CONCEPTS 545,581

astride [adj] with a leg on either side
astraddle, athwart, on the back of, piggyback, sitting on, straddling; SEE CONCEPT 583

astringent [adj] harsh
acetic, acrid, biting, bitter, cutting, sharp, tonic; SEE CONCEPTS 598,613

astrology [n] prophesy of the future by observation of stars and planets
astrometry, horoscope; SEE CONCEPT 70

astronaut [n] space explorer
cosmonaut, moonwalker, pilot, rocketeer, rocket scientist, space person, star person; SEE CONCEPT 348

astronomy [n] study of the stars and planets other than Earth
astrochemistry, astrography, astrolithology, astrometry, astrophysics, selenology, sky-watching, stargazing, uranology; SEE CONCEPT 349

astute [adj] perceptive
adroit, brainy, bright, calculating, canny, clever, crafty, discerning, foxy, insightful, intelligent, keen, knowing, not born yesterday*, on the ball*, perspicacious, quick on the uptake*, sagacious, savvy, sharp, sharp as a tack*, shrewd, sly; SEE CONCEPT 402

asunder [adv] apart; into pieces
disconnected, disjoined, divided, in half, loose, separated, split, torn, to shreds; SEE CONCEPT 785

asylum [n1] refuge
cover, den, harbor, haven, hideaway, hideout, hole, ivory tower*, port, preserve, refuge, retreat, safe house, safety, sanctuary, security, shelter; SEE CONCEPTS 435,515

asylum [n2] psychiatric hospital
institution, loony bin*, madhouse*, mental hospital, mental institution, sanatorium; SEE CONCEPTS 312,439,516

at [prep] about; in the direction of
appearing in, by, found in, in the vicinity of, near to, on, placed at, situated at, through, toward; SEE CONCEPTS 581,583,799

atheism [n] belief that no God exists
disbelief, doubt, freethinking, godlessness, heresy, iconoclasm, impiety, infidelity, irreligion, irreverence, nihilism, nonbelief, paganism, skepticism, unbelief; SEE CONCEPT 689

athlete [n] person involved in sports
amateur, animal, challenger, competitor, contender, contestant, games player, gorilla*, iron person*, jock, jockey, muscle person*, player, professional, shoulders, sport, sportsperson, superjock*; SEE CONCEPT 366

athletic [adj1] agile; prepared to participate in sports
able-bodied, active, brawny, energetic, fit, lusty, muscular, powerful, robust, strapping, strong, sturdy, vigorous; SEE CONCEPTS 406,489

athletic [adj2] relating to sports
competitive, contesting, exercise-related, recreational, sporting, team; SEE CONCEPT 536

athletics [n] sports
contest, drill, events, exercises, games, practice, races, recreation, workout; SEE CONCEPT 363

atmosphere [n1] gases around the earth
air, envelope, heavens, pressure, sky, substratosphere, troposphere; SEE CONCEPT 437

atmosphere [n2] general feeling or mood
air, ambience, aura, background, character, climate, color, environment, feel, feeling, flavor, impression, local color, medium, mood, place,

property, quality, scene, semblance, sense, space, spirit, surroundings, taste, tone; SEE CONCEPT 673

atom [n] smallest part of something
bit, crumb, dot, fragment, grain, iota, jot, minimum, mite, modicum, molecule, morsel, mote, ounce, particle, scintilla, scrap, shred, smidgen, speck, spot, tittle, trace, whit; SEE CONCEPT 831

atom bomb [n] nuclear weapon
A-bomb, backpack nuke*, doomsday machine*, fission bomb, H-bomb, hydrogen bomb, neutron bomb, nuclear bomb, nuke*, thermonuclear weapon; SEE CONCEPT 500

atomic [adj1] tiny
diminutive, fragmentary, granular, microscopic, minute; SEE CONCEPT 773

atomic [adj2] nuclear
atom-powered, fissionable, thermonuclear; SEE CONCEPT 485

atone [v] compensate; make amends for former misdoing
absolve, answer, apologize, appease, balance, correct, counterbalance, do penance, expiate, make amends, make redress, make reparation, make up for, offset, outweigh, pay, pay one's dues*, propitiate, recompense, reconcile, redeem, redress, repair, set off, square, take one's medicine*; SEE CONCEPTS 108,126

atonement [n] compensation
amends, expiation, indemnification, payment, penance, propitiation, recompense, redemption, redress, reparation, restitution, satisfaction; SEE CONCEPTS 126,337

atrocious [adj1] outrageous; widely condemned
awful, bad, barbaric, beastly, desperate, diabolical, fiendish, flagrant, godawful*, grody*, gross*, hairy*, heinous, lousy, monstrous, nefarious, rotten, scandalous, shocking, villainous, wicked; SEE CONCEPTS 545,571

atrocious [adj2] offensive
appalling, awful, bad, beastly, detestable, disgusting, dreadful, execrable, foul, godawful*, grody*, gross*, horrible, horrid, horrifying, icky*, loathsome, noisome, obscene, repulsive, rotten, sickening, terrible; SEE CONCEPTS 548,571

atrocity [n1] outrageous behavior
atrociousness, barbarity, barbarousness, enormity, fiendishness, heinousness, horror, monstrousness, nefariousness, shockingness, villianousness, wickedness; SEE CONCEPTS 411,657

atrocity [n2] cruelness, offensiveness; widely condemned action
abomination, barbarity, brutality, crime, enormity, evil, horror, infamy, inhumanity, iniquity, monstrosity, offense, outrage, ruthlessness, savagery, viciousness, wrong; SEE CONCEPTS 29,645

atrophy [n] wasting away, disintegration
decline, degeneracy, degeneration, deterioration, diminution, downfall, downgrade; SEE CONCEPTS 674,698

attach [v1] join, fasten
add, adhere, affix, annex, append, bind, connect, couple, fix, hitch on, hitch up, hook on, hook up, latch onto, link, make fast, prefix, rivet, secure, slap on*, stick, tag on*, tie, unite; SEE CONCEPTS 85,113,160

attach [v2] socially join
accompany, affiliate, associate, become associated with, combine, enlist, join forces with, latch

onto*, sign on with, sign up with, unite with; SEE
CONCEPT 114

attach [v3] *attribute, ascribe*
allocate, allot, appoint, assign, associate, connect,
consign, designate, detail, earmark, impute, invest with, lay, name, place, put, second, send;
SEE CONCEPTS 62,73

attachment [n1] *fastening*
adapter, bond, clamp, connection, connector, coupling, fastener, joint, junction, link, tie; SEE CON-
CEPT 471

attachment [n2] *something joined, fastened to another*
accessory, accoutrement, adapter, addition, adjunct, annex, appendage, appurtenance, auxiliary,
extension, extra, fitting, fixture, part, supplement;
SEE CONCEPT 824

attachment [n3] *affection, high regard*
affinity, amore, attraction, bond, case, crush, devotion, fidelity, fondness, friendship, hankering*,
liking, love, loyalty, partiality, possessiveness, regard, shine*, tenderness, weakness, yen*; SEE
CONCEPT 32

attack [n1] *physical assault*
advance, aggression, assailing, assailment, barrage, blitz, blitzkrieg, charge, defilement, dirty
deed*, drive, encounter, encroachment, foray, incursion, initiative, inroad, intervention, intrusion,
invasion, irruption, mugging, offense, offensive,
onrush, onset, onslaught, outbreak, push, raid,
rape, rush, skirmish, storming, strike, thrust, violation, volley; SEE CONCEPT 86

attack [n2] *verbal assault*
abuse, aggression, belligerence, blame, calumny,
censure, combativeness, criticism, denigration,
denunciation, impugnment, libel, pugnacity, slander, vilification; SEE CONCEPTS 52,54

attack [n3] *sudden dysfunction or disorder*
access, ailment, bout, breakdown, convulsion,
disease, failure, fit, illness, paroxysm, relapse,
seizure, spasm, spell, stroke, throe; SEE CONCEPT
308

attack [v1] *assault physically*
advance, aggress, ambush, assail, assault, bash,
bat, bean*, beat, beset, besiege, biff*, blast, blister, boff*, bombard, boot*, bop*, brain*, bust,
charge, chop down, clip, clock*, club, combat,
cook*, harm, hit, hurt, infiltrate, invade, jump,
kick, knock block off*, knock cold*, knock for a
loop*, larrup*, lay siege to, light into*, molest,
mug, overwhelm, pounce upon, punch, raid, rush,
set upon, slog, soak, stab, storm, strike, take the
offensive, turn on, wallop, whop*; SEE CONCEPT
86

attack [v2] *assault verbally*
abuse, berate, blame, blitz, censure, criticize, impugn, jump down one's throat*, jump on one's
case*, lay into, malign, refute, reprove, revile,
shoot down*, stretch, vilify; SEE CONCEPTS 52,54

attack [v3] *set to work*
buckle down*, deal with, dive into, plunge into,
set to, start in on, tackle, take up, tear into*; SEE
CONCEPT 112

attain [v] *achieve, accomplish*
accede, acquire, arrive, arrive at, bring off,
come through, complete, cop*, earn, effect, fulfill, gain, get*, get fat*, get hands on, get there,
glom onto*, grasp, hit, latch onto, make it, obtain, procure, promote, pull off*, rack up, reach,

realize, reap, score, secure, snag, succeed, unzip*, win; SEE CONCEPTS 120,706

attainable [adj] *within reach; achievable*
accessible, accomplishable, at hand, available,
cherry pie*, duck soup*, easy, feasible, gettable,
likely, no problem*, no sweat*, obtainable, piece
of cake*, possible, potential, practicable, probable, procurable, reachable, realizable, securable;
SEE CONCEPTS 528,552

attainment [n] *achievement, accomplishment*
acquirement, acquisition, arrival, completion,
feat, finish, fulfillment, gaining, getting, obtaining, procurement, reaching, realization, reaping,
securing, succeeding, winning; SEE CONCEPT 706

attempt [n] *try, effort*
all one's got*, attack, bid*, crack*, dry run*, endeavor, exertion, experiment, fling, go, header*,
lick*, one's all, one's darnedest*, one's level
best*, pursuit, shot, stab, striving, struggle, trial,
try, tryout, undertaking, venture, whack*, workout; SEE CONCEPT 87

attempt [v] *try, make effort*
aim, attack, do level best*, endeavor, essay, exert
oneself, experiment, give a fling*, give a whirl*,
give best shot*, give it a go*, give it a try*, give
old college try*, go the limit*, have a crack*,
have a go at*, make a run at*, pursue, push, seek,
shoot the works*, solicit, strive, tackle, take a
stab at*, take best shot*, take on, try one's hand
at*, undertake, venture; SEE CONCEPT 87

attend [v1] *be present at*
appear, be a guest, be at, be present, be there, bob
up*, catch, check in, clock in*, come to light*,
drop in, frequent, go to, haunt, make an appearance, make it*, make the scene*, pop up*, punch
in*, punch the clock*, ring in*, show, show up,
sit in on, time in, turn up, visit; SEE CONCEPT 114

attend [v2] *care for*
be in the service of, doctor, do for, look after,
mind, minister to, nurse, serve, take care of, tend,
wait upon, watch, work for; SEE CONCEPT 110

attend [v3] *pay attention; apply oneself*
catch, concentrate on, devote oneself, follow, get
a load of*, hear, hearken, heed, keep one's eye
on*, lend an ear*, listen, listen up*, look after,
look on, mark, mind, note, notice, observe, occupy oneself with, pay heed, pick up, regard, see
to, watch; SEE CONCEPTS 34,596,623

attend [v4] *accompany*
bear, be associated with, catch, be connected with,
follow, issue from, make the scene, occur with,
result from; SEE CONCEPT 714

attend [v5] *escort*
accompany, chaperon, companion, consort, convoy, escort, guard, squire, usher; SEE CONCEPTS
114,714

attendance [n1] *being present*
appearance, attending, being in evidence, being
there, participation, presence; SEE CONCEPT 388

attendance [n2] *people present at event*
assemblage, assembly, audience, box office, company, congregation, crowd, draw, gate, gathering, gross, house, observers, onlookers, patrons,
public, spectators, turnout, witnesses; SEE CON-
CEPT 417

attendant [n] *person who serves others*
aide, alarm clock*, assistant, auxiliary, baby sitter, bird dog, chaperon, companion, custodian,
domestic, escort, follower, guide, helper, lackey,

nurse, orderly, secretary, servant, understudy, usher, waitperson; SEE CONCEPT *348*

attendant [*adj*] *being present or related*
accessory, accompanying, ancillary, associated, attending, coincident, concomitant, consequent, incident; SEE CONCEPT *577*

attention [*n1*] *concentration*
absorption, application, assiduity, consideration, contemplation, debate, deliberation, diligence, engrossment, heed, heedfulness, immersion, industry, intentness, mind, scrutiny, study, thinking, thought, thoughtfulness; SEE CONCEPT *409*

attention [*n2*] *consideration, care*
awareness, big rush*, brace, concern, consciousness, looking after, ministration, notice, observation, recognition, regard, spotlight, tender loving care, TLC*, treatment; SEE CONCEPTS *32,410*

attention(s) [*n3*] *courtesy*
amenity, assiduities, care, civility, compliment, consideration, deference, gallantry, mindfulness, politeness, regard, respect, service; SEE CONCEPT *644*

attentive [*adj1*] *concentrating*
alert, all ears*, awake, aware, conscientious, enrapt, enthralled, fascinated, glued, hanging on every word*, heedful, hooked, immersed, intent, interested, listening, mindful, observant, on one's toes*, on the ball*, on the job*, on the lookout*, on the qui vive*, preoccupied, regardful, studious, vigilant, watchful; SEE CONCEPT *403*

attentive [*adj2*] *considerate*
accommodating, civil, courteous, devoted, gallant, gracious, kind, obliging, polite, respectful, solicitous, thoughtful; SEE CONCEPT *401*

attenuate [*v*] *weaken*
abate, constrict, contract, cripple, debilitate, deflate, disable, dissipate, enfeeble, extenuate, lessen, mitigate, sap, shrink, thin, undermine, vitiate; SEE CONCEPT *240*

attest [*v*] *affirm, vouch for*
adjure, announce, argue, assert, asseverate, authenticate, aver, bear out, bear witness, certify, confirm, corroborate, countersign, declare, demonstrate, display, exhibit, give evidence, indicate, prove, ratify, seal, show, substantiate, support, sustain, swear, testify, uphold, verify, warrant, witness; SEE CONCEPT *49*

attic [*n*] *space under the roof of a house*
garret, loft, sky parlor*, top floor; SEE CONCEPTS *440,448*

attire [*n*] *clothing*
accoutrements, apparel, array, bib and tucker*, clothes, costume, drapes, dress, duds*, garb, garments, gear, getup, habiliments, habit, outfit, raiment, things, threads*, togs, uniform, vestment, wear; SEE CONCEPT *451*

attire [*v*] *clothe*
accoutre, array, clad, costume, deck, deck out*, doll up*, drape, dress, dud*, dude up*, equip, fit out, outfit, suit up, tog, turn out; SEE CONCEPT *167*

attitude [*n1*] *mental outlook*
air, angle, approach, belief, bent, bias, character, demeanor, disposition, frame of mind, headset*, inclination, leaning, like it is*, mental state, mindset*, mindtrip*, mood, notion, opinion, perspective, philosophy, point of view, position, posture, predilection, prejudice, proclivity, reaction, routine, say so*, sensibility, sentiment, set, slant, stance, stand, standing, standpoint, temper, temperament, twist, view, where one is at*; SEE CONCEPTS *410,689*

attitude [*n2*] *stance*
aspect, bearing, carriage, manner, mien, pose, position, posture, stand; SEE CONCEPT *757*

attorney [*n*] *lawyer*
advocate, ambulance chaser*, barrister, counsel, counselor, DA, fixer, front, legal beagle*, legal eagle*, lip*, mouthpiece*, pleader*, proxy, spieler*; SEE CONCEPT *355*

attract [*v*] *draw attention*
allure, appeal to, bait, beckon, beguile, bewitch, bring, captivate, charm, come on*, court, drag, draw, enchant, endear, engage, enthrall, entice, entrance, exert influence, fascinate, freak out*, give the come-on*, go over big, grab, hook, induce, interest, intrigue, inveigle, invite, kill, knock dead*, knock out*, lure, magnetize, make a hit with*, mousetrap*, pull, rope in*, score, seduce, send*, slay*, solicit, spellbind, steer, suck in*, sweep off one's feet*, tempt, turn on, vamp, wile, wow*; SEE CONCEPTS *7,11,22*

attraction [*n*] *ability to draw attention; something that draws attention*
allure, allurement, appeal, attractiveness, bait, captivation, charm, chemistry, come-on*, courting, draw, drawing power, enchantment, endearment, enthrallment, enticement, fascination, gravitation, inclination, inducement, interest, invitation, it*, lure, magnetism, pull, seduction, solicitation, temptation, tendency; SEE CONCEPTS *14,676*

attractive [*adj*] *appealing, drawing attention*
adorable, agreeable, alluring, beautiful, beckoning, bewitching, captivating, charming, comely, enchanting, engaging, enthralling, enticing, fair, fascinating, fetching, glamorous, good-looking, gorgeous, handsome, hunky*, interesting, inviting, looker*, lovely, luring, magnetic, mesmeric, pleasant, pleasing, prepossessing, pretty, provocative, seductive, stunning, taking, tantalizing, teasing, tempting, winning, winsome; SEE CONCEPTS *529,579*

attribute [*n*] *feature*
aspect, character, characteristic, facet, idiosyncrasy, indication, mark, note, particularity, peculiarity, point, property, quality, quirk, sign, speciality, symbol, trait, virtue; SEE CONCEPTS *411,673,834*

attribute [*v*] *ascribe, assign to source*
account for, accredit, apply, associate, blame, charge, connect, credit, fix upon, hang on, hold responsible, impute, lay, pin on, refer, reference, trace; SEE CONCEPT *73*

attrition [*n1*] *wearing down or away*
abrasion, attenuation, debilitation, depreciation, disintegration, erosion, grinding, rubbing, thinning, weakening, wear; SEE CONCEPTS *469,776*

attrition [*n2*] *regret*
contriteness, penance, penitence, remorse, remorsefulness, repentance; SEE CONCEPTS *410,689*

attune [*v*] *adjust*
acclimatize, accommodate, accord, accustom, adapt, balance, compensate, conform, coordinate, counterbalance, familiarize, harmonize, integrate, make agree, proportion, reconcile, regulate, tune; SEE CONCEPT *232*

atypical [*adj*] *nonconforming*
aberrant, abnormal, anomalous, deviant, differ-

ent, divergent, exceptional, heteroclite, irregular, odd, peculiar, preternatural, strange, unnatural, unrepresentative; SEE CONCEPTS *547,564*

auburn [n] *reddish-brown color*
chestnut, copper, hazel, henna, nut, russet, rust, tawny, titian; SEE CONCEPT *622*

auction [n] *competitive sale; sale by bid*
bargain, jam*, sell-off; SEE CONCEPTS *324,345*

audacious [adj1] *reckless, daring*
adventurous, aweless, bold, brassy, brave, cheeky*, courageous, daredevil, dauntless, enterprising, fearless, foolhardy, gutty*, intrepid, nervy, rash, resolute, risky, smart ass*, unafraid, uncurbed, undaunted, ungoverned, valiant, venturesome; SEE CONCEPT *401*

audacious [adj2] *arrogant, presumptuous*
assuming, bantam, bold, brash, brassy, brazen, cheeky*, defiant, disrespectful, forward, impertinent, impudent, insolent, nervy, rude, saucy, shameless; SEE CONCEPTS *401,404*

audacity [n1] *recklessness, daring*
adventurousness, audaciousness, boldness, bravery, courage, dauntlessness, enterprise, fearlessness, guts, intrepidity, nerve, rashness, valor, venturesomeness; SEE CONCEPT *633*

audacity [n2] *arrogance, presumptuousness*
assurance, audaciousness, brass, cheek*, chutzpah*, cockiness*, crust, defiance, disrespectfulness, effrontery, forwardness, gall, guts*, gutsiness, hardiness, impertinence, impudence, insolence, moxie, nerve, rudeness, shamelessness, spunk, stuff*, temerity; SEE CONCEPTS *411,633*

audible [adj] *able to be heard*
aural, auricular, clear, deafening, detectable, discernible, distinct, hearable, loud, loud enough, perceptible, plain, resounding, roaring, sounding, within earshot; SEE CONCEPTS *591,594*

audience [n1] *group observing an entertainment or sporting event*
admirers, assemblage, assembly, congregation, crowd, devotees, fans, following, gallery, gathering, hearers, house, listeners, market, moviegoers, onlookers, patrons, playgoers, public, showgoers, spectators, theatergoers, turnout, viewers, witnesses; SEE CONCEPT *417*

audience [n2] *hearing*
audition, conference, consideration, consultation, conversation, discussion, interview, meeting, reception; SEE CONCEPT *266*

audit [n] *inspection of financial records*
analysis, balancing, check, checking, examination, investigation, report, review, scrutiny, survey, verification, view; SEE CONCEPT *330*

audit [v] *inspect financial records*
analyze, balance, check, examine, go over, go through, investigate, report, review, scrutinize, sit in, survey, verify; SEE CONCEPTS *103,330*

audition [n] *test of ability*
audience, demo, hearing, reading, trial, try on, tryout; SEE CONCEPT *290*

auditor [n] *person who inspects financial records*
accountant, actuary, bookkeeper, cashier; SEE CONCEPT *348*

auditorium [n] *room, building for entertainment events*
amphitheater, assembly hall, barn*, concert hall, hall, movie house, music hall, opera house, playhouse, reception hall, theater; SEE CONCEPTS *293,439,448*

augment [v] *make greater; improve*
add to, aggrandize, amplify, beef up*, boost, build, build up, compound, develop, enhance, enlarge, expand, extend, grow, heighten, increase, inflate, intensify, magnify, mount, multiply, pad, piggyback*, progress, raise, reinforce, strengthen, sweeten, swell, tag on; SEE CONCEPTS *236,244,245*

augmentation [n] *making greater; improving*
accession, accretion, addition, amplification, beefing up*, boost, buildup, development, enhancement, enlargement, enrichment, expansion, extension, fleshing out, growth, heightening, hike, increase, increment, inflation, intensification, magnification, multiplication, raise, reinforcement, rise, strengthening, swelling, up, upping; SEE CONCEPTS *244,245*

augur [n] *predictor*
diviner, forecaster, harbinger, herald, oracle, prognosticator, prophet, seer, soothsayer; SEE CONCEPT *423*

augur [v] *predict; be an omen of*
adumbrate, bespeak, bode, call it*, call the shots*, crystal-ball, figure out, forecast, foreshadow, foretell, harbinger, have a hunch, herald, portend, presage, prognosticate, promise, prophesy, psych out*, read, signify, soothsay; SEE CONCEPT *70*

augury [n1] *omen*
auspice, boding, forerunner, foretoken, forewarning, harbinger, herald, portent, precursor, presage, prognostication, promise, prophecy, sign, token, warning; SEE CONCEPT *284*

augury [n2] *prediction*
divination, prediction, prophecy, soothsaying; SEE CONCEPT *70*

august [adj] *dignified, noble*
baronial, brilliant, eminent, exalted, glorious, grand, grandiose, highfalutin'*, high-minded, high-ranking, honorable, imposing, impressive, lofty, lordly, magnificent, majestic, monumental, pompous, regal, resplendent, stately, superb, venerable; SEE CONCEPTS *404,567*

aura [n] *air, character*
ambience, appearance, aspect, atmosphere, background, emanation, feel, feeling, mood, quality, scent, semblance, suggestion, tone; SEE CONCEPT *673*

auspices [n] *protection; support*
advocacy, aegis, authority, backing, care, charge, control, countenance, guidance, influence, patronage, sponsorship, supervision; SEE CONCEPTS *94,376*

auspicious [adj] *encouraging; favorable*
advantageous, bright, favorable, felicitous, fortunate, golden, halcyon, happy, hopeful, lucky, opportune, promising, propitious, prosperous, rosy, timely, well-timed; SEE CONCEPT *572*

austere [adj1] *severe in manner*
ascetic, astringent, cold, earnest, exacting, forbidding, formal, grave, grim, hard, harsh, inexorable, inflexible, obdurate, rigid, rigorous, serious, sober, solemn, somber, stern, stiff, strict, stringent, unfeeling, unrelenting; SEE CONCEPT *550*

austere [adj2] *refraining; abstinent*
abstemious, ascetic, chaste, continent, economical, puritanical, self-denying, self-disciplined, sober, straightlaced, strict, subdued, unrelenting; SEE CONCEPT *401*

austere [adj3] *grim, barren*
bald, bare, bare-bones, bleak, clean, dour, plain,

primitive, rustic, severe, simple, spare, spartan, stark, subdued, unadorned, unembellished, vanilla*; SEE CONCEPT 485

austerity [n1] *severity*
acerbity, asperity, astringence, coldness, exactingness, exactness, formality, formalness, gravity, grimness, hardness, harshness, inclemency, inflexibility, obduracy, rigidity, rigor, seriousness, solemnity, sternness, stiffness, strictness, stringency; SEE CONCEPT 644

austerity [n2] *refraining; abstinence*
abstemiousness, asceticism, chasteness, chastity, continence, determination, economy, prudence, puritanism, self-denial, self-discipline, sobriety, stoicism, strictness, temperance; SEE CONCEPT 633

austerity [n3] *grimness, barrenness*
baldness, bareness, dourness, economy, plainness, primitiveness, rusticism, severity, simplicity, spareness, spartanism, starkness, unadornment; SEE CONCEPT 723

authentic [adj] *real, genuine*
accurate, actual, authoritative, bona fide, certain, convincing, credible, creditable, dependable, factual, faithful, for real*, legit*, legitimate, official, original, pure, reliable, sure, true, trustworthy, trusty, twenty-four carat*, valid, veritable; SEE CONCEPT 582

authenticate [v] *establish as real, genuine*
accredit, attest, authorize, bear out, certify, confirm, corroborate, endorse, guarantee, justify, prove, substantiate, validate, verify, vouch, warrant; SEE CONCEPTS 12,103

author [n] *composer of written work*
biographer, columnist, composer, creator, essayist, ghost, ghostwriter, ink slinger*, journalist, originator, playwright, poet, producer, prose writer, reporter, scribbler*, scribe, scripter, word slinger*, wordsmith, work-for-hire*, writer; SEE CONCEPT 348

authoritarian [n] *domineering person*
absolutist, autocrat, despot, dictator, disciplinarian, tyrant; SEE CONCEPTS 354,412

authoritarian [adj] *domineering*
absolute, authoritative, autocratic, despotic, dictatorial, disciplinarian, doctrinaire, dogmatic, harsh, imperious, magisterial, rigid, severe, strict, totalitarian, tyrannical, unyielding; SEE CONCEPTS 319,401

authoritative [adj1] *recognized as true, valid*
accurate, attested, authentic, authenticated, circumstantiated, confirmed, definitive, dependable, documented, factual, faithful, learned, legit*, proven, reliable, righteous, scholarly, sound, straight from horse's mouth*, supported, trustworthy, truthful, validated, verified, veritable; SEE CONCEPT 582

authoritative [adj2] *domineering*
assertive, authoritarian, autocratic, commanding, confident, decisive, dictatorial, doctrinaire, dogmatic, dominating, imperative, imperious, imposing, masterly, officious, peremptory, self-assured; SEE CONCEPT 550

authoritative [adj3] *official, authorized*
administrative, approved, bureaucratic, canonical, departmental, ex cathedra, executive, ex officio, imperial, lawful, legal, legitimate, magisterial, mandatory, ruling, sanctioned, sovereign, supreme; SEE CONCEPTS 319,536

authority [n1] *power, control*
ascendancy, authorization, beef*, charge, clout*, command, credit, domination, dominion, edge, esteem, force, goods*, government, guts*, influence, juice*, jump, jurisdiction, leg up*, license, mastery, might, might and main*, permission, permit, pizzazz*, pow*, powerhouse, prerogative, prestige, punch, right, ropes*, rule, say, say-so*, steam, strength, strong arm*, stuff*, supremacy, sway, upper hand*, warrant, weight, what it takes*, whip hand*, word, zap*; SEE CONCEPTS 376,685,688

authority [n2] *expert, animate or inanimate*
arbiter, aristocrat, bible, big cheese*, big shot*, big wig*, boss, brains*, brass*, buff*, CEO, city hall*, connoisseur, czar, egghead*, establishment*, exec*, executive, expert, feds*, front office*, governor, guru, ivory dome*, judge, kingfish*, kingpin*, law*, power elite, pro, professional, professor, pundit, scholar, specialist, textbook*, top brass*, top dog*, top hand*, upstairs*, veteran, virtuoso, whiz, wizard; SEE CONCEPTS 280,348,354

authorize [v1] *give power or control*
accredit, bless, commission, empower, enable, entitle, give authority, give the go-ahead*, give the green light*, give the word*, invest, license, okay, rubber-stamp*, say the word*, vest; SEE CONCEPTS 50,88

authorize [v2] *permit, allow*
affirm, approve, confirm, countenance, endorse, give leave, let, license, qualify, ratify, sanction, suffer, tolerate, warrant; SEE CONCEPTS 10,83

autobiography [n] *written account of one's own life*
adventures, bio, biography, confession, diary, experience, journal, letter, letters, life, life story, memoir, personal history, reminiscences, self-portrayal; SEE CONCEPT 280

autocracy [n] *government by one*
absolutism, czarism, despotism, dictatorship, monarchy, monocracy, oppression, totalitarian government, tyranny; SEE CONCEPTS 354,691

autocratic [adj] *holding power exclusively*
absolute, all-powerful, arbitrary, bossy, czarlike, despotic, dictatorial, domineering, driving, imperious, monocratic, pushing, tyrannical, tyrannous; SEE CONCEPTS 319,536

autograph [n] *handwritten signature*
endorsement, handwriting, inscription, John Hancock*, seal, token, undersignature, writing; SEE CONCEPT 284

autograph [v] *write signature*
endorse, engross, handwrite, ink, inscribe, pen, sign, signature, subscribe, write by hand; SEE CONCEPT 79

automated [adj] *made or done by a machine*
automatic, computerized, electrical, electronic, mechanical, mechanized, motorized, programmed, robotic; SEE CONCEPTS 538,549

automatic [adj1] *done or made by machine*
automated, electric, electronic, mechanical, mechanized, motorized, robotic, self-moving, self-regulating, self-starting; SEE CONCEPTS 538,549

automatic [adj2] *done by habit*
autogenetic, habitual, impulsive, instinctive, instinctual, intuitive, involuntary, knee-jerk, mechanical, natural, perfunctory, reflex, routine, spontaneous, unconscious, unforced, uninten-

tional, unmeditated, unthinking, unwilled; SEE CONCEPTS 403,538

automatic [adj3] *occurring as natural consequence*
assured, certain, inescapable, inevitable, necessary, routine, unavoidable; SEE CONCEPTS 530,535

automation [n] *machine control*
computerization, industrialization, mechanization; SEE CONCEPT 770

automobile [n] *land vehicle; car*
auto, bucket of bolts*, bug*, buggy*, bus, clunker*, compact, convertible, crate*, four-wheeler*, gas guzzler*, go-cart*, hardtop, hatchback, heap*, jalopy*, junker*, lemon*, limousine, motor car, oil burner*, passenger car, pickup truck, ride*, sedan, sports car, station wagon, subcompact, taxi, transportation, truck, tub*, van, wheels*, wreck*; SEE CONCEPT 505

autonomous [adj] *independent*
free, self-determining, self-governing, self-ruling, sovereign, uncontrolled; SEE CONCEPT 554

autonomy [n] *independence*
freedom, liberty, self-determination, self-government, self-rule, sovereignty; SEE CONCEPT 652

autopsy [n] *examination of dead body*
dissection, necropsy, pathological examination, postmortem; SEE CONCEPTS 103,310

autumn [n] *season between summer and winter*
autumnal equinox, fall, harvest; SEE CONCEPT 814

auxiliary [n] *helper*
accessory, accomplice, adjutant, ally, assistant, associate, companion, confederate, crutch*, partner, reserve, subordinate, supporter; SEE CONCEPT 423

auxiliary [adj] *supplementary*
abetting, accessory, adjuvant, ancillary, appurtenant, backup, complementary, contributory, extra, reserve, secondary, spare, subordinate, subservient, subsidiary, supporting; SEE CONCEPTS 546,824

avail [n] *use*
account, advantage, applicability, appropriateness, fitness, service, usefulness; SEE CONCEPT 680

avail [v] *be of use; use*
account, advantage, answer, be adequate, benefit, fill, fulfill, meet, profit, satisfy, serve, suffice, work; SEE CONCEPTS 91,225

available [adj] *ready for use*
accessible, achievable, applicable, at hand, at one's disposal*, attainable, come-at-able*, convenient, derivable from, feasible, free, getatable*, handy, obtainable, on deck*, on hand*, on tap*, open to, possible, prepared, procurable, purchasable, reachable, ready willing and able*, realizable, securable, serviceable, up for grabs*, usable, vacant; SEE CONCEPT 576

avalanche [n] *falling large mass; sudden rush of large quantity*
barrage, deluge, flood, inundation, landslide, landslip, snowslide, torrent; SEE CONCEPTS 509,524,787

avant-garde [adj] *unconventional, forward-looking*
beat*, experimental, head*, hip*, innovative, lead, leading-edge*, liberal, new, new wave, pioneering, progressive, radical, state-of-the-art, vanguard; SEE CONCEPTS 564,585

avarice [n] *extreme greed*
avidity, close-fistedness*, covetousness, cupidity, frugality, grabbiness, greediness, miserliness, niggardliness, parsimony, penny-pinching*, penuriousness, rapacity, stinginess, thrift; SEE CONCEPTS 335,410

avenge [v] *retaliate*
chasten, chastise, come back at, even the score, get back at, get even, payback, punish, redress, repay, requite, retribute, revenge, stick it to, take satisfaction, take vengeance, venge, vindicate; SEE CONCEPTS 122,126

avenue [n] *street; path*
access, alley, approach, boulevard, channel, course, drive, entrance, entry, exit, outlet, parkway, passage, pathway, promenade, road, route, thoroughfare, way; SEE CONCEPT 501

average [n] *normal, typical amount*
mean, median, medium, middle, midpoint, norm, par, rule, standard, usual; SEE CONCEPTS 647,787

average [adj1] *normal, typical*
boilerplate*, common, commonplace, customary, dime a dozen*, everyday, fair, fair to middling*, familiar, garden*, garden-variety*, general, humdrum*, intermediate, mainstream, mediocre, medium, middle of the road*, middling, moderate, nowhere*, ordinary, passable, plastic*, regular, run of the mill*, so-so*, standard, tolerable, undistinguished, unexceptional, usual; SEE CONCEPT 547

average [adj2] *numerical mean*
intermediate, median, medium, middle; SEE CONCEPT 762

average [v] *obtain numerical mean*
balance, equate, even out; SEE CONCEPT 764

averse [adj] *opposing*
afraid, allergic, antagonistic, antipathetic, contrary, disinclined, disliking, having no use for*, hesitant, hostile, ill-disposed, indisposed, inimical, loath, nasty, perverse, reluctant, uneager, unfavorable, unfriendly, unwilling; SEE CONCEPTS 403,564

aversion [n] *dislike; opposition*
abhorrence, abomination, allergy, animosity, antagonism, antipathy, detestation, disfavor, disgust, disinclination, disliking, displeasure, dissatisfaction, distaste, dread, hate, hatred, having no use for*, horror, hostility, indisposition, loathing, odium, reluctance, repugnance, repulsion, revulsion, unwillingness; SEE CONCEPT 29

avert [v] *thwart; avoid by turning away*
avoid, deflect, deter, divert, fend off, foil, forestall, frustrate, halt, look away, preclude, prevent, rule out, shove aside, shunt, stave off, turn, turn aside, turn away, ward off; SEE CONCEPTS 121,623

aviation [n] *flying an aircraft; study of flying aircraft*
aerodynamics, aeronautics, flight, navigation, piloting; SEE CONCEPTS 148,187,324

aviator [n] *person who flies aircraft*
ace, aeronaut, airperson, barnstormer, bird legs*, eagle*, flier, hotshot*, jockey*, navigator, pilot; SEE CONCEPTS 348,366

avid [adj] *enthusiastic*
ardent, athirst, avaricious, breathless, covetous, desirous, devoted, dying to*, eager, fanatical, fervent, gotta have*, grasping, greedy, hungry, im-

patient, insatiable, intense, keen, passionate, rapacious, ravenous, thirsty, voracious, zealous; SEE CONCEPTS 20,401,403

avocation [n] hobby
amusement, diversion, kick*, occupation, pastime, recreation, schtick*, shot*, side interest, sideline, thing*; SEE CONCEPT 364

avoid [v] refrain or stay away from; prevent
abstain, avert, bypass, circumlocute, circumvent, deflect, desist, ditch, divert, dodge, duck, elude, escape, eschew, evade, fake out*, fend off, flee, give the slip*, hide, hold off, jump, keep clear, lay low*, obviate, recoil, run for cover*, shake, shake and bake*, shake off, shirk, shrink from, shuffle off, shun, shy, sidestep, skip*, skip out on*, skip town*, skirt*, stay away, stay out, steer clear of*, step aside, turn aside, ward off, weave, withdraw; SEE CONCEPTS 102,121

avoidance [n] eluding; preventing
absention, circumvention, delay, departure, dodge, dodging, elusion, escape, escapism, eschewal, evasion, flight, forbearance, nonparticipation, parry, passive resistance, prevention, recession, recoil, restraint, retreat, run-around, self-restraint, shirking, shunning, steering clear of*; SEE CONCEPTS 102,121

avow [v] state; profess
acknowledge, admit, affirm, allow, assert, aver, avouch, concede, confess, cross one's heart*, declare, grant, maintain, own up, proclaim, swear, swear on bible*, swear up and down*; SEE CONCEPTS 49,60,71

await [v] wait with expectation
anticipate, attend, be prepared for, be ready for, cool one's heels*, count on, hang around*, hang in*, hang out*, hope, look for, look forward to, stay, sweat*, sweat it out*; SEE CONCEPT 26

awake [adj] conscious; alert
alive, aroused, attentive, awakened, aware, cognizant, excited, heedful, knowing, observant, on guard, roused, vigilant, wakeful, waking, watchful; SEE CONCEPTS 402,406

awake [v1] become alert or cause to rise from sleep
arise, awaken, call, gain consciousness, get up, roll out*, rouse, stir, wake, wake up; SEE CONCEPTS 250,315

awake [v2] become or make aware
activate, alert, animate, arouse, awaken, call forth, enliven, excite, incite, kindle, provoke, revive, stimulate, stir up, vivify; SEE CONCEPT 231

awaken [v] make conscious or alert
activate, animate, arouse, awake, call, enliven, excite, fan, incite, kindle, pile out*, provoke, rally, revive, rise and shine*, roll out*, rouse, show a leg*, stimulate, stir up, turn out*, vivify, wake; SEE CONCEPTS 7,19,22,105,231

awakening [n] making conscious or alert
activation, animating, arousal, awaking, birth, enlivening, incitement, kindling, provocation, rebirth, renewal, revival, rousing, stimulation, stirring up, vivication, waking, waking up; SEE CONCEPTS 13,105,231

award [n] prize or reward
accolade, adjudication, allotment, bestowal, citation, conferment, conferral, decision, decoration, decree, distinction, donation, endowment, feather in cap*, gift, gold, gold star*, grant, honor, order, presentation, scholarship, trophy, verdict; SEE CONCEPT 337

award [v] give prize or reward
accord, adjudge, allocate, allot, apportion, assign, bestow, concede, confer, decree, dish out*, distribute, donate, endow, fork out*, gift, grant, hand out, present, render, reward, shell out*, sweeten the kitty*; SEE CONCEPT 132

aware [adj] knowledgeable
acquainted, alert, alive, appraised, appreciative, apprehensive, apprised, attentive, au courant, awake, cognizant, conscious, cool*, enlightened, familiar, go-go*, groovy*, grounded*, heedful, hip*, informed, in the know*, in the picture*, into*, know-how, knowing, know the score*, know what's what*, latched on*, mindful, on the beam*, on to*, perceptive, plugged in*, receptive, savvy, sensible, sentient, sharp, tuned in, up on, wise, wised up*, wise to*, with it*; SEE CONCEPT 402

awareness [n] knowledge
acquaintance, acquaintanceship, alertness, aliveness, appreciation, apprehension, attention, attentiveness, cognizance, comprehension, consciousness, discernment, enlightenment, experience, familiarity, information, keenness, mindfulness, perception, realization, recognition, sensibility, sentience, understanding; SEE CONCEPT 409

away [adv1] in another direction; at a distance
abroad, absent, afar, apart, aside, beyond, distant, elsewhere, far afield, far away, far off, far remote, forth, from here, hence, not present, off, out, out of the way, over, to one side; SEE CONCEPTS 581,778

away [adv2] continuously
endlessly, forever, incessantly, interminably, on and on, relentlessly, repeatedly, tirelessly, unremittingly, without break, without end, without rest, without stopping; SEE CONCEPT 553

awe [n] amazement
admiration, apprehension, astonishment, consternation, dread, esteem, fear, fright, horror, regard, respect, reverence, shock, stupefaction, terror, veneration, wonder, wonderment, worship; SEE CONCEPTS 230,410

awe [v] amaze
alarm, appall, astonish, blow away*, cow*, daunt, dazzle, flabbergast, frighten, grandstand, horrify, hotdog*, impress, intimidate, knock socks off*, overawe, scare, showboat*, startle, strike, stun, stupefy, terrify; SEE CONCEPTS 7,19,22,42

awesome [adj] amazing
alarming, astonishing, awe-inspiring, awful, beautiful, breathtaking, daunting, dreadful, exalted, fearful, fearsome, formidable, frantic, frightening, grand, hairy*, horrible, horrifying, imposing, impressive, intimidating, magnificent, majestic, mean, mind-blowing*, moving, nervous, overwhelming, real gone*, shocking, something else*, striking, stunning, stupefying, terrible, terrifying, wonderful, wondrous, zero cool*; SEE CONCEPTS 537,572

awful [adj] very bad; terrible
abominable, alarming, appalling, atrocious, deplorable, depressing, dire, disgusting, distressing, dreadful, fearful, frightful, ghastly, grody*, gross*, gruesome, grungy*, harrowing, hideous, horrendous, horrible, horrific, horrifying, nasty, offensive, raunchy, repulsive, shocking, stinking,

synthetic, tough, ugly, unpleasant, unsightly; SEE CONCEPTS 570,571

awfully [adv1] *badly*
clumsily, disgracefully, disreputably, dreadfully, inadequately, incompletely, poorly, reprehensibly, shoddily, unforgivably, unpleasantly, wickedly, wretchedly; SEE CONCEPTS 570,571

awfully [adv2] *very*
badly, dreadfully, excessively, extremely, greatly, hugely, immensely, indeed, much, quite, terribly, truly, very much; SEE CONCEPT 569

awhile [adv] *for a short period*
briefly, for a bit, for a little while, for a moment, for a spell, for a while, for the moment, momentarily, not for long, temporarily, transiently; SEE CONCEPT 798

awkward [adj1] *clumsy, inelegant*
all thumbs*, amateurish, artless, blundering, bulky, bumbling, bungling, butterfingers*, coarse, floundering, gawky, graceless, green*, having two left feet*, having two left hands*, incompetent, inept, inexpert, klutzy*, lumbering, maladroit, oafish, rude, stiff, stumbling, uncoordinated, uncouth, unfit, ungainly, ungraceful, unhandy, unpolished, unrefined, unskilled, unskillful; SEE CONCEPTS 406,480,527

awkward [adj2] *difficult to handle*
annoying, bulky, chancy, cramped, cumbersome, dangerous, disagreeable, discommodious, hard to use, hazardous, incommodious, inconvenient, perilous, risky, troublesome, uncomfortable, unhandy, unmanageable, unwieldy; SEE CONCEPTS 558,565

awkward [adj3] *embarrassing*
compromising, delicate, difficult, embarrassed, ill at ease, inconvenient, inopportune, painful, perplexing, sticky*, thorny*, ticklish*, troublesome, trying, uncomfortable, unpleasant, untimely; SEE CONCEPT 555

awkwardness [n1] *clumsiness; inelegance*
amateurishness, artlessness, boorishness, cloddishness, coarseness, crudeness, gawkiness, gracelessness, greenness*, inaptitude, inability, incompetence, ineptitude, ineptness, inexpertness, maladroitness, oafishness, rudeness, tactlessness, uncoordination, uncouthness, ungainliness, unskillfulness; SEE CONCEPTS 405,630,717

awkwardness [n2] *difficulty*
bulkiness, chanciness, cumbersomeness, danger, hazardousness, inconvenience, peril, perilousness, risk, troublesomeness, uncomfortableness, unhandiness, unmanageability, unwieldiness; SEE CONCEPTS 656,666

awkwardness [n3] *embarrassment*
delicacy, difficulty, discomfort, inconvenience, inopportuneness, painfulness, stickiness*, thorniness*, ticklishness*, trouble, uncomfortableness, unpleasantness, untimeliness; SEE CONCEPT 388

awning [n] *canopy*
covering, door cover, marquee, protection, shade, shelter, sunshade, tent; SEE CONCEPTS 440,473

awry [adj] *off course; amiss*
afield, askance, askew, aslant, astray, badly, bent, cockeyed, crooked, curved, slanting, turned, wrong, zigzag; SEE CONCEPTS 537,581

ax/axe [n] *large cutting tool*
adz, chopper, hatchet, tomahawk; SEE CONCEPT 499

ax/axe [v1] *cut with large blade*
chop, cut, cut down, fell, hew; SEE CONCEPT 176

ax/axe [v2] *dismiss from service*
boot*, bounce*, can*, cancel, cut back, discharge, dispense with, eliminate, fire, get rid of, give a pink slip*, give the boot*, kick out, lay off, remove, sack*, terminate, throw out; SEE CONCEPT 351

axiom [n] *principle*
adage, aphorism, apothegm, device, dictum, fundamental, law, maxim, moral, postulate, precept, proposition, proverb, saying, theorem, truism, truth; SEE CONCEPTS 278,688,689

axiomatic [adj] *understood; aphoristic*
absolute, accepted, aphoristic, apothegmatic, assumed, certain, fundamental, given, indubitable, manifest, obvious, presupposed, proverbial, self-evident, unquestioned; SEE CONCEPT 529

axis [n] *point around which something revolves*
arbor, axle, hinge, pivot, pole, shaft, spindle, stalk, stem, support, turning point; SEE CONCEPT 830

axle [n] *shaft around which wheels rotate*
arbor, axis, gudgeon, mandrel, pin, pivot, pole, rod, shaft, spindle, stalk, stem, support; SEE CONCEPTS 464,830

B

babble [n] *trivial talk, often incessant*
blubbering, burble, chatter, clamor, drivel, gab, gabble, gibberish, gossip, gushing, idle talk, jabber, jabbering, jargon, murmur, muttering, prattle, ranting, tattling; SEE CONCEPTS 266,278

babble [v] *talk trivially, often incessantly*
blab, blubber, blurt, burble, cackle, chat, chatter, gibber, go on, gossip, gush, jabber, mumble, murmur, mutter, patter, prate, prattle, rant, rave, run off at the mouth*, run on, spill the beans*, squeal*, talk foolishly, talk incoherently, talk nonsensically, tattle, trivialize, yak*, yakkety yak*; SEE CONCEPTS 51,266

babe [n] *baby*
bairn, child, infant, little one, newborn, suckling; SEE CONCEPTS 414,424

baby [n] *infant*
angelface*, babe, bairn, bambino, bundle, buttercup*, button, cherub, chick, child, crawler*, deduction*, dividend*, dumpling*, kid, little angel*, little darling*, little doll*, little one*, newborn, nipper*, nursling, papoose, preemie*, suckling, tad*, toddler, tot, write-off*, youngster; SEE CONCEPTS 414,424

baby [adj] *miniature*
babyish, diminutive, dwarf, little, midget, mini*, minute, petite, small, tiny, wee, youthful; SEE CONCEPT 773

baby [v] *treat like a child*
cater to, cherish, coddle, cosset, cuddle, dandle, dote on, foster, humor, indulge, nurse, overindulge, pamper, pet, please, satisfy, serve, spoil; SEE CONCEPTS 110,295

babyhood [n] *period of infancy*
childhood, diaper days*, infanthood; SEE CONCEPT 817

av
ba

babyish [*adj*] *acting like an infant*
baby, childish, foolish, immature, infantile, juvenile, kid stuff, puerile, silly, sissy, spoiled; SEE CONCEPTS *401,550*

baby-sit [*v*] *care for a child*
guard, sit, take care, tend, watch; SEE CONCEPT *295*

bachelor [*n*] *unmarried man or woman*
available*, celibate, single*, single person, stag*, unattached; SEE CONCEPTS *415,419,423*

back [*n*] *end part*
aft, back end, backside, extremity, far end, hindpart, hindquarters, posterior, rear, reverse, stern, tail, tail end, tailpiece; SEE CONCEPTS *392, 471,827,833*

back [*adj1*] *end*
aback, abaft, aft, after, astern, back of, backward, behind, final, following, hind, hindmost, in the wake of, posterior, rear, rearmost, rearward, tail; SEE CONCEPTS *827,833*

back [*adj2*] *from earlier time*
delayed, elapsed, former, overdue, past, previous; SEE CONCEPT *820*

back [*v1*] *support*
abet, abide by, advocate, ally, angel*, assist, bankroll, boost, champion, countenance, encourage, endorse, favor, finance, give a boost, give a leg up*, give a lift*, go to bat for*, grubstake, sanction, second, side with, sponsor, stake, stand behind, stick by, stick up for, subsidize, sustain, underwrite, uphold; SEE CONCEPTS *8,50,88*

back [*v2*] *put in reverse direction*
backtrack, drive back, fall back, recede, regress, repel, repulse, retire, retract, retreat, reverse, turn tail, withdraw; SEE CONCEPTS *195,208*

backbiting [*n*] *hateful talk*
abuse, aspersion, backstabbing*, belittlement, calumniation, calumny, cattiness, defamation, denigration, depreciation, detraction, disparagement, gossip, invective, lie, malice, obloquy, scandal, slander, spite, spitefulness, tale, traducement, vilification, vituperation; SEE CONCEPTS *54,58,63*

backbone [*n1*] *strength of character*
courage, determination, firmness, fortitude, grit, guts, hardihood, heart, intestinal fortitude*, mettle, moral fiber, nerve, pluck, resolution, resolve, spunk, stamina, steadfastness, tenacity, toughness, will, willpower; SEE CONCEPT *411*

backbone [*n2*] *spinal column of vertebrate*
base, basis, foundation, spine, support, vertebrae, vertebral column; SEE CONCEPTS *420,442*

back down [*v*] *withdraw from agreement or statement*
abandon, accede, admit, back off, back out, back pedal*, backtrack, balk, beg off*, cancel, chicken out*, concede, cop out*, demur, give in, give up, go back on, hold back, recant, recoil, renege, resign, retreat, surrender, take back, withdraw, yield; SEE CONCEPTS *266,697*

backer [*n*] *supporter*
advocate, ally, angel*, benefactor, champion, endorser, follower, grubstaker, meal ticket*, money, patron, promoter, protagonist, sponsor, staker, underwriter, well-wisher; SEE CONCEPT *359*

backfire [*v*] *have an opposite effect*
backlash, boomerang, bounce back, disappoint, fail, flop, miscarry, rebound, recoil, ricochet, spring back; SEE CONCEPTS *42,701*

background [*n*] *experience or circumstances*
accomplishments, acquirement, actions, atmosphere, attainment, aura, backdrop, breeding, capacity, credentials, cultivation, culture, deeds, education, environment, framework, grounding, history, practice, preparation, qualification, rearing, seasoning, tradition, training, upbringing; SEE CONCEPTS *673,678,706*

backing [*n*] *support*
abetment, accompaniment, adherence, advocacy, aegis, aid, assistance, auspices, championing, championship, encouragement, endorsement, funds, grant, help, patronage, reinforcement, sanction, secondment, sponsorship, subsidy; SEE CONCEPTS *110,332*

backlash [*n*] *adverse reaction*
backfire, boomerang, counteraction, kickback, reaction, recoil, repercussion, resentment, resistance, response, retaliation, retroaction, tangle; SEE CONCEPT *230*

backlog [*n*] *uncompleted work; accumulation*
excess, hoard, inventory, quantity, reserve(s), reservoir, resources, stock, stockpile, store, supply; SEE CONCEPTS *432,787*

backpack [*n*] *sack carried on the back*
haversack, knapsack, pack, rucksack; SEE CONCEPT *446*

backside [*n*] *rear end*
behind, bottom, butt*, buttocks, derrière, fanny*, posterior, rear, rump*, seat*, tail*, tush*; SEE CONCEPT *392*

back talk [*n*] *nasty reply*
cheek, guff, lip, mouth, sass; SEE CONCEPTS *46,278*

backward [*adj1*] *toward the rear*
astern, behind, inverted, rearward, regressive, retrograde; SEE CONCEPT *581*

backward [*adj2*] *bashful*
afraid, averse, demure, diffident, disinclined, hesitant, hesitating, humble, indisposed, late, loath, modest, reluctant, reserved, retiring, shy, sluggish, tardy, timid, uneager, unwilling, wavering; SEE CONCEPT *401*

backward [*adj3*] *slow in growth*
arrested, behind, checked, delayed, dense, dull, feeble-minded, imbecile, late, moronic, stupid, subnormal, underdeveloped, underprivileged, undeveloped; SEE CONCEPTS *402,562*

backward [*adv*] *toward the rear*
aback, abaft, about, astern, back, behind, in reverse, inverted, rearward, turned around; SEE CONCEPT *581*

backwash [*n*] *repercussion*
aftermath, result, wake; SEE CONCEPTS *230,674*

backwoods [*n/adj*] *forests; land distant from settled area*
backcountry, boondocks*, frontier, hinterland, interior, isolation, outback, rural area, sticks*, timberland, woodland; SEE CONCEPT *509*

backyard [*n*] *expanse behind house*
courtyard, garden, grass, lawn, patio, play area, terrace, yard; SEE CONCEPT *513*

bacteria [*n*] *microorganisms*
bacilli, germs, microbes, organisms, pathogens; SEE CONCEPTS *306,393*

bad [*adj1*] *poor quality*
abominable, amiss, atrocious, awful, bad news*, beastly, blah*, bottom out, bummer*, careless, cheap, cheesy*, crappy*, cruddy*, crummy*, defective, deficient, diddly*, dissatisfactory, downer*, dreadful, erroneous, fallacious, faulty, garbage, godawful*, grody*, gross*, grungy*,

icky*, imperfect, inadequate, incorrect, inferior, junky*, lousy*, not good, off, poor, raunchy*, rough, sad, slipshod, stinking, substandard, synthetic, the pits*, unacceptable, unsatisfactory; SEE CONCEPT 571

bad [adj2] harmful
damaging, dangerous, deleterious, detrimental, hurtful, injurious, ruinous, unhealthy; SEE CONCEPTS 537,570

bad [adj3] immoral
base, corrupt, criminal, delinquent, evil, iniquitous, mean, reprobate, sinful, vicious, vile, villainous, wicked, wrong; SEE CONCEPT 545

bad [adj4] mischievous
disobedient, ill-behaved, misbehaving, naughty, unruly, wrong; SEE CONCEPT 401

bad [adj5] decayed
moldy, off, putrid, rancid, rotten, sour, spoiled; SEE CONCEPTS 485,613

bad [adj6] severe
disastrous, distressing, grave, harsh, intense, painful, serious, terrible; SEE CONCEPT 569

bad [adj7] sick
ailing, diseased, ill, in pain, unwell; SEE CONCEPT 314

bad [adj8] sorry
apologetic, conscience-stricken, contrite, crestfallen, dejected, depressed, disconsolate, down, downcast, downhearted, guilty, low, regretful, remorseful, sad, upset, woebegone; SEE CONCEPT 403

bad [adj9] distressing
adverse, disagreeable, discouraged, discouraging, displeasing, distressed, gloomy, grim, melancholy, troubled, troubling, unfavorable, unfortunate, unhappy, unpleasant; SEE CONCEPTS 403,529

badge [n] emblem worn
brand, cordon, device, identification, insignia, mark, marker, medallion, motto, pin, ribbon, scepter, shield, sign, stamp, symbol, token; SEE CONCEPTS 260,284,476

badger [v] nag, bother
annoy, bait, bug, bully, eat*, give the business*, goad, harass, harry, hassle, heckle, hound, importune, insist on, needle, nudge, pester, plague, ride, tease, torment, work on; SEE CONCEPTS 14,51

badly [adv1] inadequately
abominably, awkwardly, blunderingly, carelessly, clumsily, crudely, defectively, erroneously, faultily, feebly, haphazardly, imperfectly, incompetently, ineffectively, ineptly, maladroitly, negligently, poorly, shoddily, stupidly, unfavorably, unfortunately, unsatisfactorily, unskillfully, unsuccessfully, weakly, wrong, wrongly; SEE CONCEPT 571

badly [adv2] immorally
criminally, evilly, improperly, naughtily, shamefully, unethically, wickedly; SEE CONCEPT 545

badly [adv3] very much; desperately
acutely, deeply, exceedingly, extremely, gravely, greatly, hard, intensely, painfully, roughly, seriously, severely; SEE CONCEPT 569

baffle [v1] perplex
addle, amaze, astound, befuddle, bewilder, buffalo*, confound, confuse, daze, disconcert, dumbfound, elude, embarrass, faze, floor*, get, mix up, muddle, mystify, nonplus, puzzle, rattle,

stick*, stump*, stun, throw; SEE CONCEPTS 7,19,42

baffle [v2] hinder
beat, block, check, circumvent, dash, defeat, disappoint, foil, frustrate, impede, obstruct, prevent, ruin, thwart, upset; SEE CONCEPT 121

bag [n1] container for one's possesions
attaché, backpack, briefcase, carryall, carry-on, case, duffel, gear, handbag, haversack, holdall, kit, knapsack, pack, packet, pocket, pocketbook, poke, pouch, purse, rucksack, sac, sack, saddle-bag, satchel, suitcase, tote; SEE CONCEPTS 339,450,494

bag [n2] special interest
expertise, favorite activity, hobby, preference, speciality, thing*; SEE CONCEPTS 32,529

bag [v1] catch
acquire, apprehend, capture, collar, gain, get, hook, kill, land, nab, nail, net, seize, shoot, take, trap; SEE CONCEPT 90

bag [v2] droop
balloon, billow, bulge, flap, flop, hang, lop, sag, swell; SEE CONCEPTS 754,757

baggage [n] gear
accoutrements, bags, belongings, carry-on, effects, equipment, fortnighter, gear, impedimenta, luggage, overnighter*, paraphernalia, parcels, slough, suitcases, things, tote, tote bag, trappings, two-suiter; SEE CONCEPT 494

baggy [adj] drooping
billowing, bulging, droopy, flabby, floppy, ill-fitting, loose, oversize, roomy, sagging, slack, unshapely; SEE CONCEPTS 486,490

bail [n] money for assurance
bond, collateral, guarantee, pawn, pledge, recognizance, security, surety, warrant, warranty; SEE CONCEPTS 318,332

bail out [v1] help
aid, deliver, release, rescue, spring; SEE CONCEPT 110

bail out [v2] escape
flee, quit, retreat, withdraw; SEE CONCEPT 102

bait [n] something for luring
allurement, attraction, bribe, come-on*, drag, enticement, inducement, lure, seducement, shill, snare, temptation, trap; SEE CONCEPT 709

bait [v1] lure
allure, attract, bedevil, beguile, draw, entice, fascinate, lead on, seduce, tempt; SEE CONCEPTS 9,14

bait [v2] needle
anger, annoy, badger, bother, gall, harass, heckle, hound, irk, irritate, nag, persecute, provoke, tease, torment; SEE CONCEPTS 7,19

bake [v] cook in oven
heat, melt, scorch, simmer, stew, warm; SEE CONCEPT 170

baked [adj] cooked in oven
dried, heated, melted, scorched, simmered, stewed, warmed; SEE CONCEPT 462

baker [n] person who cooks baked goods
chef, cook, dough puncher*, pastry maker; SEE CONCEPT 348

bakery [n] cooking business where baked goods are produced
bake shop, confectionery, pastry shop, pâtisserie; SEE CONCEPTS 325,439,449

balance [n1] equilibrium
antithesis, correspondence, counterbalance, equity, equivalence, evenness, even-steven*, hang,

ba
ba

harmony, parity, proportion, stasis, symmetry, tension; SEE CONCEPTS *664,667*
balance [n2] *composure*
equanimity, poise, self-control, self-possession, stability, steadfastness; SEE CONCEPT *633*
balance [n3] *money remaining in account*
difference, dividend, excess, profit, remainder, residue, rest, surplus; SEE CONCEPT *332*
balance [v1] *make equal; cause to have equilibrium*
accord, adjust, attune, cancel, collate, come out, come out even, compensate, correspond, counteract, counterbalance, equalize, equate, even, harmonize, level, make up for, match, neutralize, nullify, offset, oppose, pair off, parallel, poise, readjust, redeem, set, square, stabilize, steady, tie, weigh; SEE CONCEPTS *197,697*
balance [v2] *compare*
assess, consider, deliberate, estimate, evaluate, weigh; SEE CONCEPT *17*
balance [v3] *make equal numerically*
adjust, audit, calculate, compute, count, enumerate, equate, estimate, figure, settle, square, sum up, tally, total; SEE CONCEPT *764*
balanced [adj1] *equalized*
counterbalanced, equitable, equivalent, evened, fair, just, offset, proportional, stabilized, symmetrical, uniform; SEE CONCEPT *566*
balanced [adj2] *settled financially*
certified, confirmed, validated; SEE CONCEPT *334*
balance sheet [n] *financial statement including gains and losses for a period*
account, annual report, assets and liabilities, budget, ledger, report; SEE CONCEPTS *271,332*
balcony [n] *porch or structure above the ground*
balustrade, box*, catwalk, gallery, mezzanine, piazza, platform, porch, portico, stoop, terrace, veranda; SEE CONCEPT *440*
bald [adj1] *having no covering*
baldheaded, bare, barren, depilated, exposed, glabrous, hairless, head*, naked, shaven, skin head*, smooth, stark, uncovered; SEE CONCEPT *485*
bald [adj2] *simple, unadorned*
austere, bare, blunt, direct, downright, forthright, outright, plain, severe, straight, straightforward, unembellished; SEE CONCEPTS *485,589*
bale [n] *bunch*
bundle, package, parcel; SEE CONCEPT *432*
baleful [adj] *menacing*
calamitous, deadly, dire, evil, foreboding, harmful, hurtful, injurious, malevolent, malignant, noxious, ominous, pernicious, ruinous, sinister, threatening, venomous, vindictive, woeful; SEE CONCEPTS *537,570*
balk [v1] *stop short*
cramp, crimp, demur, desist, dodge, evade, flinch, hesitate, recoil, refuse, resist, shirk, shrink from, shy, turn down, upset apple cart*; SEE CONCEPTS *119,121,188*
balk [v2] *thwart*
baffle, bar, beat, check, circumvent, counteract, cramp, cramp one's style*, dash, defeat, disappoint, disconcert, foil, forestall, frustrate, hinder, obstruct, prevent, ruin, stall, stop, throw a curve*, throw monkey wrench in*, upset the apple cart*; SEE CONCEPT *121*
balky [adj] *uncooperative*
averse, contrary, hesitant, immovable, indisposed, inflexible, intractable, loath, negative, negativistic, obstinate, ornery, perverse, reluctant,

stubborn, unbending, unmanageable, unpredictable, unruly; SEE CONCEPT *401*
ball [n1] *dance party*
hoedown, hoodang, hop, jump, mingle, prom, promenade, reception, shindig; SEE CONCEPT *386*
ball [n2] *globe, sphere*
apple, balloon, drop, globule, orb, pellet, pill, round, spheroid; SEE CONCEPT *436*
ballad [n] *narrative song*
carol, chant, ditty, serenade; SEE CONCEPT *595*
ballast [n] *something giving balance*
balance, brace, bracket, counterbalance, counterweight, equilibrium, sandbag, stability, stabilizer, support, weight; SEE CONCEPT *712*
ballet [n] *graceful, expressive dancing*
choreography, dance, toe dancing; SEE CONCEPT *263*
ballet dancer [n] *person who performs graceful dance*
company, coryphee, dancer, danseur, danseuse, figurant, figurante, hoofer*, prima ballerina; SEE CONCEPT *352*
balloon [n] *inflated material or vehicle*
airship, bladder, blimp, dirigible, zeppelin; SEE CONCEPTS *293,504*
balloon [v] *billow out; bloat*
belly, blow up, bulge, dilate, distend, enlarge, expand, inflate, puff out, swell; SEE CONCEPTS *208,756*
ballot [n1] *voting; recording of vote*
election, franchise, plebiscite, poll, polling, referendum, slate, tally, ticket; SEE CONCEPTS *300,301*
ballot [n2] *candidates from political party*
choice, lineup, slate, ticket; SEE CONCEPT *301*
balm [n1] *oily substance*
analgesic, application, balsam, cerate, compound, cream, demulcent, dressing, embrocation, emollient, formula, lotion, medicine, ointment, potion, poultice, preparation, prescription, salve, soother, soothing agent, unction, unguent; SEE CONCEPTS *307,466*
balm [n2] *something soothing*
alleviation, anodyne, assuagement, comfort, consolation, curative, cure, easement, mitigation, palliative, refreshment, relief, remedy, restorative, solace, soother; SEE CONCEPTS *337,529*
balmy [adj1] *comfortable with respect to weather*
mild, moderate, moist, pleasant, refreshing, summerlike, summery, temperate, tropical; SEE CONCEPTS *603,605*
balmy [adj2] *insane*
absurd, bugged out*, cracked*, crazed, crazy, daft, deranged, dotty*, foolish, harebrained*, idiotic, loony, mentally incompetent, moronic, nuts*, nutty*, odd, potty*, preposterous, silly, stupid, wacky; SEE CONCEPT *403*
bamboozle [v] *fool; cheat*
baffle, befuddle, bilk, con, confound, confuse, deceive, defraud, delude, dupe, flimflam*, hoax, hoodwink*, hornswoggle*, mystify, perplex, puzzle, stump, swindle, trick; SEE CONCEPT *59*
ban [n] *official forbiddance*
a thou-shalt-not*, boycott, censorship, don't*, embargo, injunction, interdiction, limitation, no-no*, off limits*, out of bounds*, prohibition, proscription, refusal, restriction, stoppage, suppression, taboo; SEE CONCEPTS *50,88, 121,688*
ban [v] *officially forbid*
banish, bar, blackball*, close down, close up,

curse, declare illegal, disallow, enjoin, exclude, halt, ice out*, illegalize, inhibit, interdict, outlaw, pass by, pass up, prevent, prohibit, proscribe, restrict, shut out, suppress; SEE CONCEPTS **50,88,121**

banal [adj] *commonplace*
blah*, bland, bromidic, clichéd, common, conventional, cornball*, cornfed*, corny, dull as dishwater*, dumb, everyday, flat, hackneyed, ho hum*, hokey*, humdrum*, insipid, mundane, noplace, nothing, nowhere, old hat*, ordinary, pabulum*, pedestrian, platitudinous, square, stale, stereotyped, stock, stupid, tired, tripe, trite, unimaginative, unoriginal, vapid, watery, wishywashy*, zero*; SEE CONCEPT **530**

banality [n] *common saying*
adage, boiler*, buzzword, chestnut*, cliché, corn*, dullsville*, familiar tune*, high camp*, hokum*, old chestnut*, old saw*, plate*, platitude, prosaicism, prosaism, saw*, trite phrase, trivia, triviality, truism; SEE CONCEPT **275**

band [n1] *something which encircles*
bandage, bandeau, belt, binding, bond, braid, cable, chain, circle, circuit, copula, cord, fillet, harness, hoop, ligature, line, link, manacle, ribbon, ring, rope, sash, scarf, shackle, snood, stay, strap, string, strip, tape, tie, truss; SEE CONCEPTS **470,751**

band [n2] *group of people with same interest*
assembly, association, bevy, bunch, clique, club, cluster, collection, company, corps, coterie, covey, crew, gang, gathering, horde, menagerie, outfit, party, society, troop, troupe; SEE CONCEPTS **387,391,417**

band [n3] *musical group*
combo, ensemble, orchestra, philharmonic, symphony, troupe; SEE CONCEPT **294**

band [v] *group or join group*
affiliate, ally, amalgamate, belt, coadjute, combine, conjoin, consolidate, federate, gather, league, merge, team, unite; SEE CONCEPTS **113,114**

bandage [n] *covering for wound*
cast, compress, dressing, gauze, plaster; SEE CONCEPT **311**

bandage [v] *cover a wound*
bind, dress, swathe, truss, wrap; SEE CONCEPT **310**

bandanna [n] *colorful scarf*
handkerchief, kerchief, neckerchief, silk; SEE CONCEPT **450**

bandit [n] *thief*
brigand, criminal, crook, desperado, forager, gangster, gunperson, highwayperson, hijacker, holdup person, hooligan, marauder, mobster, outlaw, pillager, pirate, plunderer, racketeer, ravager, robber, villain; SEE CONCEPT **412**

bane [n] *cause of misery*
affliction, bête noir, blight, burden, calamity, curse, despair, destruction, disaster, downfall, fatal attraction, misery, nuisance, pest, plague, poison, ruin, ruination, scourge, torment, trial, trouble, undoing, venom, woe; SEE CONCEPTS **529,674**

baneful [adj] *ruinous, injurious*
baleful, calamitous, deadly, deleterious, destructive, disastrous, evil, fatal, harmful, hurtful, malefic, noxious, pernicious, pestilent, pestilential, poisonous, venomous, wicked; SEE CONCEPTS **537,570**

bang [n1] *explosive noise*
blast, boom, burst, clang, clap, clash, crack, detonation, discharge, howl, peal, pop, report, roar, roll, rumble, salvo, shot, slam, smash, sound, thud, thump, thunder, wham; SEE CONCEPT **595**

bang [n2] *loud hit or knock*
bash, bat, belt, blow, box, bump, collide, crack, cuff, punch, slam, smack, smash, sock, stroke, wallop, whack, whop; SEE CONCEPT **189**

bang [n3] *thrilling situation*
enjoyment, excitement, kick*, pleasant feeling, smash, wallop, wow*; SEE CONCEPT **230**

bang [v1] *hit or knock loudly*
boom, burst, clang, clatter, crash, detonate, drum, echo, explode, make noise, peal, rattle, resound, sound, thump, thunder; SEE CONCEPTS **65,189**

bang [v2] *moving by hitting hard*
bash, beat, bump, clatter, collide, crash, hammer, hit, knock, pound, pummel, rap, slam, smash, strike, thump, whack; SEE CONCEPT **189**

bang [adv] *suddenly, with force*
abruptly, hard, headlong, head on, noisily, precisely, smack, straight, suddenly; SEE CONCEPT **540**

banish [v] *expel from place or situation*
ban, cast out, deport, discard, discharge, dislodge, dismiss, dispel, drive away, eject, eliminate, eradicate, evict, exclude, excommunicate, exile, expatriate, expulse, extradict, get rid of, isolate, ostracize, oust, outlaw, proscribe, relegate, remove, rusticate, sequester, shake off, shut out, transport; SEE CONCEPTS **121,217**

banister [n] *railing of stairs*
baluster, balustrade, handrail, rail, support; SEE CONCEPT **443**

bank [n1] *financial institution*
coffer, countinghouse, credit union, depository, exchequer, fund, hoard, investment firm, repository, reserve, reservoir, safe, savings, stock, stockpile, store, storehouse, thrift, treasury, trust company, vault; SEE CONCEPTS **333,339,439**

bank [n2] *ground bounding waters*
beach, cay, cliff, coast, edge, embankment, lakefront, lakeshore, lakeside, ledge, levee, oceanfront, reef, riverfront, riverside, seabank, seaboard, seafront, shore, strand, streamside, waterfront; SEE CONCEPT **509**

bank [n3] *row or tier of objects*
array, dashboard, group, line, rank, row, sequence, series, succession; SEE CONCEPT **464**

bank [v1] *collect money or advantage*
amass, deposit, heap, hill, hoard, invest, lay aside, lay away, mass, mound, pile, put by, salt away, save, sock away, speculate, squirrel, stash; SEE CONCEPTS **109,330**

bank [v2] *lean or tilt*
bend, camber, cant, incline, pitch, slant, slope; SEE CONCEPTS **148,213**

banker [n] *professional in financial institution*
broker, capitalist, croupier, dealer, financier, house, investor, manager, money-lender, officer, teller, treasurer, usurer; SEE CONCEPTS **347,348,353**

bank on [v] *depend upon*
assume, believe in, be sure about, bet on, build on, count on, gamble on, lean on, look to, reckon on, rely on, stake, trust, venture, wager; SEE CONCEPT **12**

bankrupt [adj] *unable to pay debts*
broke, depleted, destitute, exhausted, failed, im-

ba
ba

poverished, in Chapter 11*, insolvent, lacking, lost, out of business, ruined, spent, tapped out; SEE CONCEPT 334

bankruptcy [n] *inability to pay debts*
Chapter 11*, defalcation, default, destituteness, destitution, disaster, exhaustion, failure, indebtedness, indigence, insolvency, lack, liquidation, loss, nonpayment, overdraft, pauperism, privation, repudiation, ruin, ruination; SEE CONCEPT 335

banner [n] *flag, usually with message*
banderole, burgee, colors, emblem, ensign, gonfalon, heading, headline, pennant, pennon, standard, streamer; SEE CONCEPTS 270,277,278

banquet [n] *formal dinner, usually ceremonial*
feast, festivity, fete, meal, reception, regale, repast, spread, treat; SEE CONCEPTS 377,459

bantam [adj] *small*
diminutive, little, petite, tiny; SEE CONCEPTS 491,773

banter [n] *teasing*
badinage, chaff, chaffing, chitchat, derision, dissing*, exchange, fun, gossip, jeering, jesting, joking, joshing, kidding, mockery, persiflage, play, raillery, repartee, ribbing, ridicule, small talk; SEE CONCEPTS 59,278

banter [v] *tease*
chaff, deride, fool, fun, jeer, jest, jive*, joke, josh, kid, make fun of, mock, rag*, razz*, rib, ridicule, satirize, taunt; SEE CONCEPTS 59,273

baptism [n] *church rite; initiation*
ablution, baptismal, christening, debut, dedication, dunking, immersion, introduction, launching, lustration, purgation, purge, purification, rite of passage, ritual, sanctification, sprinkling; SEE CONCEPTS 367,377

baptize [v] *initiate in church rite*
admit, asperse, besprinkle, call, christen, cleanse, denominate, dip, dub, entitle, immerse, name, purify, regenerate, sprinkle, term, title; SEE CONCEPT 367

bar [n1] *rod; straight length of material*
batten, billet, boom, crossbar, crosspiece, ingot, lever, paling, pig, pole, rail, rib, rule, shaft, slab, spar, spoke, stake, stick, streak, strip, stripe, stroke; SEE CONCEPTS 470,471

bar [n2] *barrier; blockage*
barricade, blank wall, block, clog, deterrent, encumbrance, fence, hindrance, hurdle, impediment, obstacle, obstruction, pale, rail, railing, restraint, road block, snag, stop, stumbling block, traverse, wall; SEE CONCEPTS 470,652,680

bar [n3] *establishment serving alcohol*
alehouse, barroom, beer garden, bistro, canteen, cocktail lounge, drinkery, inn, lounge, pub, public house, rathskeller, saloon, tap, taproom, tavern, watering hole*; SEE CONCEPTS 325,439

bar [n4] *legal system*
attorneys, barristers, bench, counsel, counselors, court, courtroom, dock, judgment, judiciary, jurists, law, law court, law practice, lawyers, legal profession, solicitors, tribunal; SEE CONCEPTS 318,381

bar [v1] *secure, usually with a length of material*
barricade, block, blockade, bolt, caulk, clog, close, dam, deadbolt, dike, fasten, fence, jam, latch, lock, plug, seal, secure, trammel, wall; SEE CONCEPTS 121,130

bar [v2] *prohibit*
ban, boycott, circumvent, condemn, debar, deny,

disallow, discountenance, discourage, eliminate, enjoin, except, exclude, exile, forbid, freeze out, frustrate, hinder, interdict, interfere, keep out, limit, obstruct, ostracize, outlaw, override, preclude, prevent, refuse, reject, restrain, rule out, segregate, shut out, stop, suspend; SEE CONCEPTS 50,61,88

barb [n1] *point*
arrow, bristle, dart, prickle, prong, quill, shaft, spike, spur, thistle, thorn; SEE CONCEPTS 434,836

barb [n2] *pointed comment*
affront, criticism, cut, dig, gibe, insult, rebuff, sarcasm, scoff, sneer; SEE CONCEPTS 52,54

barbarian [n] *crude, savage person*
beast, bigot, boor, brute, cannibal, clod, hooligan, hun, ignoramus, lout, monster, philistine, rascal, ruffian, troglodyte, vandal; SEE CONCEPT 412

barbarian [adj] *crude, savage*
barbaric, barbarous, boorish, brutal, coarse, cruel, inhuman, lowbrow, merciless, philistine, primitive, rough, rude, uncivil, uncivilized, uncouth, uncultivated, uncultured, unsophisticated, untamed, vicious, vulgar, wild; SEE CONCEPT 401

barbaric [adj] *crude, savage*
barbarian, barbarous, boorish, brutal, coarse, cruel, fierce, graceless, inhuman, lowbrow, primitive, rough, rude, tasteless, uncivilized, uncouth, vulgar, wild; SEE CONCEPT 401

barbarism [n] *crudity, savagery, especially in speech*
atrocity, barbarity, brutality, catachresis, coarseness, corruption, cruelty, impropriety, inhumanity, localism, malapropism, misusage, misuse, primitive culture, provincialism, solecism, uncivilizedness, vernacularism, vernacularity, vulgarism; SEE CONCEPTS 275,633

barbarity [n] *crudity, savagery*
boorishness, brutality, crudeness, cruelty, inhumanity, ruthlessness, savageness, viciousness, vulgarity; SEE CONCEPT 633

barbarous [adj] *crude, savage*
atrocious, barbarian, barbaric, brutal, brutish, coarse, cruel, ferocious, heartless, ignorant, inhuman, inhumane, monstrous, primitive, rough, rude, ruthless, sadistic, truculent, uncivil, uncivilized, uncouth, uncultured, unsophisticated, vicious, vulgar, wicked, wild, wolfish; SEE CONCEPT 401

barbecue [n1] *meal cooked on grill*
bake, clam bake, cookout, party, picnic, weinie roast; SEE CONCEPT 459

barbecue [n2] *grill for cookout*
broiler, charcoal grill, fireplace, gas grill, griddle, pit of coals, roaster, spit; SEE CONCEPT 493

barbecue [v] *cook outside, usually on a grill*
broil, charcoal, fry, grill, rotisserie, sear; SEE CONCEPT 170

barber [n] *hair cutter*
beautician, coiffeur, coiffeuse, cosmetologist, hairdresser, hair stylist, shaver, tonsorial artist; SEE CONCEPT 348

bare [adj1] *without clothing*
bald, bareskinned, denuded, disrobed, divested, exposed, in one's birthday suit*, naked, nude, peeled, shorn, stripped, unclad, unclothed, uncovered, undressed, unrobed; SEE CONCEPT 485

bare [adj2] *without covering or content*
arid, barren, blank, bleak, clear, desert, desolate, empty, lacking, mean, open, poor, scanty, scarce,

stark, unfurnished, vacant, vacuous, void, wanting; SEE CONCEPT 490

bare [adj3] *simple, unadorned*
austere, bald, basic, blunt, chaste, cold, essential, hard, literal, meager, mere, modest, scant, severe, sheer, simple, spare, stark, unembellished, unornamented; SEE CONCEPT 562

bare [v] *reveal*
disclose, divulge, exhibit, expose, publish, show, uncover, unroll, unveil; SEE CONCEPTS 60,138

barefaced [adj] *shameless; open*
apparent, arrant, audacious, blatant, blunt, bold, brash, brassy, brazen, candid, clear, flagrant, frank, glaring, immodest, impudent, insolent, manifest, naked, obvious, palpable, temerarious, transparent, unabashed, unconcealed; SEE CONCEPT 401

barefoot [adj] *wearing no shoes*
barefooted, discalceate, discalced, shoeless, unshod; SEE CONCEPT 406

barely [adj] *not quite*
almost, hardly, just, only just, scantily, scarcely; SEE CONCEPT 772

bareness [n] *state of being unclothed*
dishabille, nakedness, nudity, starkness, unadornment, undress; SEE CONCEPT 453

bargain [n1] *agreement*
arrangement, bond, business, compact, contract, convention, covenant, deal, engagement, negotiation, pact, pledge, promise, stipulation, transaction, treaty, understanding; SEE CONCEPT 684

bargain [n2] *something bought at cheap price*
budget price, buy, closeout, deal, discount, giveaway, good buy, good deal, good value, low price, markdown, nominal price, reduction, steal, value; SEE CONCEPTS 332,338

bargain [v] *negotiate terms of sale or agreement*
agree, arrange, barter, buy, compromise, confer, contract, covenant, deal, dicker, do business, haggle, make terms, palter, promise, sell, stipulate, trade, traffic, transact; SEE CONCEPTS 56,330

bargain for [v] *expect*
aim for, anticipate, contemplate, count on, foresee, imagine, look for, plan on, reckon on; SEE CONCEPT 26

barge [n] *large work boat*
ark, canal boat, dory, flatboat, freight ship, lighter, raft, scow; SEE CONCEPT 506

barge in/barge into [v] *charge*
break in, burst in, collide, infringe, interrupt, intrude, muscle in, push, shove, stumble; SEE CONCEPTS 150,208

bark [n1] *plant covering*
case, casing, coat, cortex, crust, husk, peeling, rind, shell, skin; SEE CONCEPT 428

bark [n2] *animal yelp*
bay, growl, grunt, howl, roar, snarl, woof, yap, yip; SEE CONCEPT 64

bark [v1] *yelp*
arf, bay, cry, gnarl, growl, howl, snap, snarl, woof, yap, yip; SEE CONCEPT 64

bark [v2] *shout*
bawl, bellow, clamor, cry, growl, grumble, mutter, roar, snap, snarl, yell; SEE CONCEPT 77

barn [n] *animal shelter*
farm building, outbuilding, shed; SEE CONCEPTS 439,517

baroque [adj] *decorative, especially architecture*
bizarre, convoluted, elaborate, embellished, extravagant, flamboyant, florid, gilt, grotesque, ornamented, ornate, overdecorated, rich, rococo; SEE CONCEPTS 562,589

barracks [n] *shelter for military*
billet, bivouac, camp, cantonment, dormitory, encampment, enclosure, garrison, headquarters, hut, prefab, quarters, Quonset hut, tent; SEE CONCEPTS 321,516

barrage [n1] *weapon fire*
battery, blast, bombardment, broadside, cannonade, crossfire, curtain of fire, discharge, enfilade, fire, fusillade, gunfire, hail, salvo, shelling, shower, storm, volley; SEE CONCEPT 320

barrage [n2] *profusion of something*
assault, attack, blast, bombardment, burst, deluge, hail, mass, onslaught, plethora, rain, shower, storm, stream, surge, torrent; SEE CONCEPT 787

barrel [n] *cylindrical container*
butt, cask, cylinder, drum, firkin, hogshead, keg, pipe, receptacle, tub, tun, vat, vessel; SEE CONCEPT 494

barren [adj1] *unable to support growth*
arid, depleted, desert, desolate, dry, effete, empty, fallow, fruitless, impotent, impoverished, infecund, infertile, parched, sterile, unbearing, uncultivable, unfertile, unfruitful, unproductive, waste; SEE CONCEPTS 485,527

barren [adj2] *unprofitable*
dull, flat, fruitless, futile, lackluster, profitless, stale, uninspiring, unproductive, unrewarding, useless, vain, vapid; SEE CONCEPT 560

barricade [n] *blocking object*
bar, barrier, blank wall, block, blockade, bulwark, fence, obstruction, palisade, rampart, roadblock, stockade, stop, wall; SEE CONCEPT 470

barricade [v] *block, usually to protect*
bar, blockade, defend, fortify, obstruct, shut in; SEE CONCEPTS 130,201

barrier [n1] *obstruction*
bar, barricade, blank wall, blockade, bound, boundary, confines, curtain, ditch, enclosure, fence, fortification, gully, hurdle, impediment, limit, moat, obstacle, pale, palisade, railing, rampart, roadblock, stop, trench, wall; SEE CONCEPTS 435,470,513

barrier [n2] *obstruction to goal*
bar, check, difficulty, drawback, encumbrance, handicap, hindrance, hurdle, impediment, limitation, obstacle, pale, preventive, restraint, restriction, stumbling block; SEE CONCEPT 532

barter [v] *trade goods or services*
bargain, exchange, haggle, swap, trade, traffic, truck; SEE CONCEPT 104

base [n1] *foundation*
basement, basis, bed, bedrock, bottom, foot, footing, ground, groundwork, infrastructure, pedestal, rest, root, seat, seating, stand, substratum, substructure, support, underpinning; SEE CONCEPT 442

base [n2] *fundamental part*
authority, backbone, basis, chief constituent, core, essence, essential, evidence, foundation, fundamental, groundwork, heart, important part, infrastructure, key, origin, primary element, principal, principle, root, source, underpinning; SEE CONCEPT 826

base [n3] *headquarters*
camp, center, depot, dock, field, garrison, hangar, harbor, home, port, post, settlement, site, starting point, station, strip, terminal; SEE CONCEPTS 435,449

ba
ba

base [*adj*] *vulgar, low*

abject, abominable, cheap, coarse, common, contemptible, corrupt, depraved, despicable, disgraceful, dishonorable, disreputable, foul, grovelling, humble, ignoble, immoral, indelicate, loathsome, lowly, mean, menial, offensive, paltry, pitiful, plebeian, poor, scandalous, servile, shameful, shoddy, sleazy, sordid, sorry, squalid, trashy, ugly, unworthy, vile, worthless, wretched; SEE CONCEPTS *542,570*

base [*v*] *build plan or opinion on*

construct, depend, derive, establish, found, ground, hinge, locate, plant, predicate, prop, rest, set up, station, stay; SEE CONCEPT *36*

baseless [*adj*] *without substantiation*

bottomless, flimsy, foundationless, gratuitous, groundless, reasonless, unconfirmed, uncorroborated, unfounded, ungrounded, unjustifiable, unjustified, unsubstantiated, unsupported, untenable, unwarranted; SEE CONCEPT *582*

basement [*n*] *room on lower floor of building*

bottom, cellar, crypt, excavation, furnace room, storage, substructure, subterranean room, underbuilding, understructure, vault; SEE CONCEPT *440*

bashful [*adj*] *shy*

abashed, backward, blushful, blushing, chary, confused, constrained, coy, demure, diffident, embarrassed, humble, modest, nervous, overmodest, recoiling, reserved, reticent, retiring, self-conscious, self-effacing, shamefaced, sheepish, shrinking, silent, timid, timorous, unassertive; SEE CONCEPT *404*

bashing [*n*] *abuse against a group or individual based on identity or ideological beliefs*

assault, attack, beating, beating up, bias crime, censure, charge, condemnation, criticism, denigration, harassment, hate crime, hounding, jumping, offensive, persecution, strike, torment; SEE CONCEPT *86*

basic [*adj*] *elementary, fundamental*

basal, capital, central, chief, elemental, essential, indispensable, inherent, intrinsic, key, main, necessary, primary, primitive, principal, radical, substratal, underlying, vital; SEE CONCEPT *568*

basically [*adv*] *fundamentally*

at heart, at the bottom, essentially, firstly, in essence, inherently, in substance, intrinsically, mostly, primarily, radically; SEE CONCEPT *568*

basin [*n*] *container or area where water is held*

bay, bowl, concavity, depression, dip, ewer, gulf, hole, hollow, lagoon, pan, pool, pot, sag, sink, sinkage, sinkhole, tub, valley, vessel, watershed; SEE CONCEPTS *494,509,514*

basis [*n1*] *physical foundation*

base, bed, bottom, foot, footing, ground, groundwork, rest, resting place, seat, substructure, support; SEE CONCEPT *442*

basis [*n2*] *foundation for belief, action*

antecedent, assumption, authority, axiom, backbone, background, backing, base, bedrock, cause, center, chief ingredient, core, crux, data, dictum, essence, essential, evidence, explanation, footing, fundamental, hard fact, heart, infrastructure, justification, keynote, keystone, law, nexus, nucleus, postulate, premise, presumption, presupposition, principal element, principle, proof, reason, root, rudiment, sanction, security, source, substratum, support, theorem, theory, underpinning, warrant; SEE CONCEPTS *661,688,689*

bask [*v1*] *lie in sunlight*

laze, loll, lounge, relax, sun, sunbathe, swim in, toast oneself*, warm oneself; SEE CONCEPTS *162,210*

bask [*v2*] *lie in glory*

delight in, derive pleasure, enjoy, indulge, luxuriate, relish, revel, rollick, savor, take comfort, take pleasure, wallow, welter; SEE CONCEPT *32*

basket [*n*] *woven container*

bassinet, bin, box, bushel, cradle, crate, creel, hamper, nacelle, pannier; SEE CONCEPT *494*

bastard [*adj*] *illegitimate*

adulterated, baseborn, counterfeit, fake, false, imperfect, impure, inferior, irregular, misbegotten, misborn, mixed, mongrel, natural, phony, sham, spurious, supposititious, ungenuine; SEE CONCEPT *549*

bastardize [*v*] *debase*

adulterate, bestialize, brutalize, corrupt, debauch, declare illegitimate, degrade, demoralize, deprave, pervert, vitiate, warp; SEE CONCEPT *44*

baste [*v1*] *moisten during cooking*

brush with liquid, drip, grease, lard, season; SEE CONCEPT *170*

baste [*v2*] *sew temporarily*

catch, fasten, stitch, tack; SEE CONCEPT *218*

baste [*v3*] *pummel, thrash*

batter, beat, berate, blister, clobber, club, drub, lambaste, lash, maul, pelt, revile, scold, trounce, wallop, whip, whomp; SEE CONCEPTS *52,189*

bastion [*n*] *support; fortified place*

breastwork, bulwark, citadel, defense, fortification, fortress, mainstay, parapet, prop, protection, rock, stronghold, support, tower of strength; SEE CONCEPT *712*

bat [*n/v*] *a hit with a solid object*

bang, belt, blow, bop, crack, knock, rap, slam, smack, sock, strike, swat, thump, thwack, wallop, whack, whop; SEE CONCEPT *189*

batch [*n*] *group of same objects*

accumulation, aggregation, amount, array, assemblage, assortment, bunch, bundle, clump, cluster, clutch, collection, crowd, group, lot, pack, parcel, quantity, set, shipment, volume; SEE CONCEPTS *432,787*

bath [*n1*] *washing with water and, usually, soap*

ablution, cleansing, dip, douche, dousing, gargle, laving, scrubbing, shower, soak, soaking, soaping, sponging, tub, wash; SEE CONCEPTS *161,165*

bath [*n2*] *room for bathing*

bathroom, lavatory, powder room, restroom, sauna, shower, shower room, spa, steam room, toilet, washroom; SEE CONCEPT *448*

bathe [*v*] *wash with water and, usually, soap*

bath, clean, cleanse, dip, douse, dunk, flood, hose, imbathe, imbue, immerse, moisten, rinse, scour, scrub, shower, soak, soap, sponge, steep, submerge, suffuse, tub, water, wet; SEE CONCEPTS *161,165*

bathing suit [*n*] *clothing for swimming, sunning*

bathing costume, beach costume, bikini, maillot, one-piece, swimsuit, trunks, two-piece; SEE CONCEPT *451*

bathroom [*n*] *room for bathing, toilet use*

bath, lavatory, powder room, restroom, sauna, shower, shower room, spa, steam room, toilet, washroom, water closet; SEE CONCEPT *448*

baton [*n*] *stick used for conducting or for protection*

billy, billy club, blackjack, club, cudgel, mace,

nightstick, rod, staff, truncheon, wand; SEE CONCEPTS 262,470,500

battalion [n] *military division*
army, brigade, company, contingent, corps, force, horde, host, legion, multitude, regiment, squadron, throng, unit; SEE CONCEPT 322

batten [v1] *fasten securely*
board up, clamp down, cover up, fix, nail down, secure, tie, tighten; SEE CONCEPTS 85,160

batten [v2] *grow fat*
burgeon, feed on, grow, prosper, thrive, wax; SEE CONCEPT 704

batter [n] *mixture before baking*
concoction, dough, mix, mush*, paste, preparation, recipe; SEE CONCEPTS 457,466

batter [v] *strike and damage*
assault, bash, beat, break, bruise, buffet, clobber, contuse, cripple, crush, dash, deface, demolish, destroy, disable, disfigure, drub, hurt, injure, lacerate, lambaste, lame, lash, mangle, mar, maul, mutilate, pelt, pommel, pound, pummel, punish, ruin, shatter, smash, thrash, wallop, wreck; SEE CONCEPTS 189,246

battery [n1] *series of similar things*
array, batch, body, bunch, bundle, chain, clot, clump, cluster, group, lot, ring, sequence, set, suite; SEE CONCEPT 432

battery [n2] *physical abuse*
assault, attack, beating, mayhem, mugging, onslaught, thumping, violence; SEE CONCEPTS 189,246

battery [n3] *group of weapons*
artillery, cannon, cannonry, gunnery unit, guns; SEE CONCEPTS 321,500

battle [n1] *military fight*
action, assault, attack, barrage, blitzkreig, bloodshed, bombing, brush, campaign, carnage, clash, combat, conflict, contention, crusade, encounter, engagement, fighting, fray, havoc, hostility, onset, onslaught, press, ravage, scrimmage, significant contact, skirmish, sortie, strife, struggle, war, warfare; SEE CONCEPT 106

battle [n2] *struggle*
agitation, campaign, clash, conflict, contest, controversy, crusade, debate, disagreement, dispute, strife; SEE CONCEPTS 46,106

battle [v] *fight, struggle*
agitate, argue, clamor, combat, contend, contest, dispute, feud, oppugn, skirmish, strive, tug, war, wrestle; SEE CONCEPTS 46,106

battlefield [n] *location of military fights*
arena, Armageddon, battleground, combat zone, field, front, front line, salient, theater of operations, theater of war; SEE CONCEPTS 198,321

bawdy [adj] *vulgar, dirty*
blue, cheap, coarse, erotic, gross, indecent, indecorous, indelicate, lascivious, lecherous, lewd, libidinous, licentious, lustful, obscene, off-color, prurient, ribald, risqué, rude, salacious, suggestive; SEE CONCEPT 545

bawl [v1] *yell*
bark, bellow, bluster, call, cheer, clamor, holler, howl, roar, rout, scream, screech, shout, shriek, vociferate; SEE CONCEPT 77

bawl [v2] *cry*
blubber*, boohoo*, howl, shed tears, sob, squall, wail, weep, yowl; SEE CONCEPTS 77,185

bay [n1] *shoreline indentation*
anchorage, arm, basin, bayou, bight, cove, estuary, fiord, firth, gulf, harbor, inlet, lagoon, loch, mouth, narrows, sound, strait; SEE CONCEPTS 509,514

bay [n2] *alcove in wall*
bow window, compartment, niche, nook, opening, oriel, recess; SEE CONCEPT 440

bay [n3] *howl*
bark, bellow, clamor, cry, growl, howl, ululation, wail, yelp; SEE CONCEPT 64

bazaar [n] *fair; sale place*
exchange, exposition, fete, market, marketplace, mart; SEE CONCEPTS 345,438,449

be [v1] *exist*
abide, act, be alive, breathe, continue, do, endure, go on, have being, have place, hold, inhabit, last, live, move, obtain, persist, prevail, remain, rest, stand, stay, subsist, survive; SEE CONCEPT 407

be [v2] *happen*
befall, come about, come to pass, occur, take place, transpire; SEE CONCEPT 2

beach [n] *sandy area by body of water*
bank, coast, lakeshore, lakeside, littoral, margin, oceanfront, seaboard, seafront, seashore, seaside, shingle, shore, strand, waterfront; SEE CONCEPTS 509,514

beached [adj] *grounded*
abandoned, aground, ashore, deserted, high and dry, marooned, stranded, wrecked; SEE CONCEPT 583

beacon [n] *light used as signal, guide*
alarm, alert, balefire, beam, bonfire, flare, guidepost, heliograph, lamp, lantern, lighthouse, lodestar, pharos, radar, rocket, sign, signal fire, smoke signal, warning signal, watchtower; SEE CONCEPT 628

bead [n] *droplet, blob*
bean, bubble, dab, dot, driblet, drop, globule, grain, particle, pea, pellet, pill, shot, speck, spherule, stone; SEE CONCEPT 436

beads [n] *string of small, often round, objects*
chaplet, choker, necklace, necklet, pearls, pendant, rosary, wampum; SEE CONCEPTS 368,446

beak [n] *nose of animal*
bill, mandible, muzzle, neb, nib, nozzle, pecker, proboscis, projection, prow, snout; SEE CONCEPT 392

beam [n1] *length of material used as support*
axle, bail, balk, bolster, boom, brace, cantilever, column, crossbar, crosspiece, girder, jamb, joist, lath, lintel, pile, piling, pillar, plank, pole, post, prop, rafter, reach, scaffolding, scantling, shaft, sill, spar, stanchion, stay, stringer, strip, strut, stud, timber, transverse, trestle, two-by-four; SEE CONCEPTS 471,479

beam [n2] *ray of light*
bar, beacon, chink, column, dartle, emission, finger, flicker, glare, gleam, glimmer, glint, glitter, glow, laser, radiation, ray, shaft, shimmer, shoot, sparkle, streak, stream, twinkle; SEE CONCEPTS 624,628

beam [v1] *broadcast on air waves*
emit, give off, give out, glare, glimmer, glow, radiate, send, shed, shine, throw off, transmit; SEE CONCEPTS 519,624

beam [v2] *smile broadly*
gleam, glow, grin, laugh, radiate, shine, smirk; SEE CONCEPT 185

beam [v3] *shine, as a light*
burn, emit, glare, gleam, glitter, glow, radiate, yield; SEE CONCEPT 624

ba
be

beaming [*adj1*] *radiant; beautiful*
bright, brilliant, effulgent, flashing, fulgent, gleaming, glistening, glittering, glowing, incandescent, lambent, lucent, luminous, refulgent, scintillating, sparkling; SEE CONCEPT 617

beaming [*adj2*] *very happy*
animated, cheerful, genial, grinning, joyful, radiant, shining, smiling, sparkling, sunny; SEE CONCEPT 401

bear [*v1*] *bring*
buck, carry, convey, deliver, ferry, fetch, lug, move, pack, take, tote, transfer, transport; SEE CONCEPTS 108,143

bear [*v2*] *support mentally*
cherish, entertain, exhibit, harbor, have, hold, hold up, maintain, possess, shoulder, sustain, uphold, weigh upon; SEE CONCEPTS 8,12

bear [*v3*] *endure*
abide, admit, allow, brook, encounter, experience, permit, put up with, stomach, suffer, tolerate, undergo; SEE CONCEPTS 23,239

bear [*v4*] *give birth*
be delivered of, beget, breed, bring forth, create, develop, engender, form, fructify, generate, invent, make, parturiate, produce, propagate, provide, reproduce, yield; SEE CONCEPTS 173, 251,302,373

bearable [*adj*] *endurable*
acceptable, admissible, allowable, livable, manageable, passable, satisfactory, sufferable, supportable, sustainable, tolerable; SEE CONCEPT 529

beard [*n1*] *facial hair on human*
bristles, brush, five-o'clock shadow*, fuzz, goatee, imperial, muttonchops, Santa Claus*, stubble, Vandyke*; SEE CONCEPT 418

beard [*n2*] *decoy*
false face, front, mask; SEE CONCEPT 716

beard [*v*] *confront*
brave, face, oppose, stand up to; SEE CONCEPTS 46,96

bearded [*adj*] *having facial hair*
barbate, beardy, bewhiskered, bristly, bushy, goateed, hairy, hirsute, shaggy, stubbled, stubbly, unshaven, whiskered; SEE CONCEPTS 406,485

bearer [*n1*] *person who carries messages or delivery*
agent, beast of burden*, carrier, conveyor, courier, drogher, emissary, envoy, internuncio, messenger, porter, runner, servant, shipper, transporter; SEE CONCEPT 348

bearer [*n2*] *person who requests payment of bill*
beneficiary, casher, collector, consignee, payee; SEE CONCEPT 353

bearing [*n1*] *person's conduct, posture*
address, air, aspect, attitude, behavior, carriage, comportment, demeanor, deportment, display, front, look, manner, mien, poise, port, pose, presence, set, stand; SEE CONCEPTS 411,633

bearing [*n2*] *significance*
application, connection, import, meaning, pertinence, reference, relation, relevance, weight; SEE CONCEPT 668

bearing/bearings [*n3*] *position, usually of water vehicle*
aim, course, direction, location, orientation, point of compass, position, situation, track, way, whereabouts; SEE CONCEPTS 739,746

bear on/bear upon [*v*] *concern*
affect, appertain to, apply, belong to, involve, pertain to, refer to, relate to, touch upon; SEE CONCEPT 532

bear out [*v*] *substantiate*
authenticate, confirm, corroborate, endorse, justify, prove, substantiate, support, uphold, validate, verify, vindicate; SEE CONCEPTS 50,88,97

bear with [*v*] *tolerate*
be patient, endure, forbear, make allowance, put up with, suffer, wait; SEE CONCEPT 23

beast [*n*] *large wild animal; brute*
barbarian, beastie*, creature, critter*, fiend, gargoyle, glutton, lower animal, monster, monstrosity, pig, quadruped, swine, varmint*; SEE CONCEPT 394

beastly [*adv1*] *savage; vulgar*
abominable, animal, barbarous, base, bestial, boorish, brutal, brute, brutish, carnal, coarse, cruel, degraded, depraved, disgusting, feral, ferine, foul, gluttonous, gross, inhuman, irrational, loathsome, low, monstrous, obscene, piggish, prurient, repulsive, sadistic, swinish, unclean, vile; SEE CONCEPT 401

beastly [*adv2*] *offensive*
awful, disagreeable, disgusting, foul, gross, mean, nasty, revolting, rotten, terrible, unpleasant, vile; SEE CONCEPTS 537,542

beat [*n1*] *throbbing*
cadence, cadency, flow, flutter, measure, meter, oscillation, palpitation, pound, pressure, pulsation, pulse, quake, quiver, rhyme, rhythm, ripple, shake, surge, swell, swing, throb, thump, tick, undulation, vibration; SEE CONCEPTS 150,185

beat [*n2*] *blow, stroke*
hit, lash, punch, shake, slap, strike, swing, thump; SEE CONCEPT 189

beat [*n3*] *area of responsibility*
circuit, course, march, path, patrol, precinct, rounds, route, walk, way; SEE CONCEPTS 513,532

beat [*adj*] *very tired*
dog tired*, exhausted, fatigued, kaput*, wearied, weary, worn out; SEE CONCEPTS 316,720

beat [*v1*] *injure by striking*
bang, bash, bat, batter, belt, box, break, bruise, buffet, cane, castigate, clout, club, collide, crush, cudgel, drub, flagellate, flail, flog, hammer, hit, knock, lambaste*, lash, lick*, maltreat, mash, maul, pelt, pound, pummel, punch, punish, ram, rap, slap, slug, smack, spank, strike, swat, thrash, thresh, thump, thwack, trounce, wallop, whale*, whip; SEE CONCEPTS 189,246

beat [*v2*] *defeat, surpass*
best, better, be victorious, conquer, exceed, excel, outdo, outplay, outrival, outrun, outshine, outstrip, overcome, overtake, overwhelm, shoot ahead of, subdue, top, transcend, triumph, vanquish, whip; SEE CONCEPTS 95,141

beat [*v3*] *forge*
fashion, form, hammer, malleate, model, pound, shape, work; SEE CONCEPTS 137,175

beat [*v4*] *throb*
agitate, alternate, bob, bounce, buffet, flap, flicker, fluctuate, flutter, heave, jerk, jounce, oscillate, palpitate, pitch, pound, pulsate, pulse, quake, quaver, quiver, ripple, shake, shiver, swing, thrill, throb, thump, tremble, twitch, undulate, vibrate, writhe; SEE CONCEPTS 150,185

beat [*v5*] *mix*
stir, whip; SEE CONCEPT 170

beaten [*adj1*] *defeated*
baffled, bested, circumvented, conquered, cowed,

crushed, disappointed, discomfited, disheartened, frustrated, humbled, licked, mastered, overcome, overpowered, overthrown, overwhelmed, routed, ruined, subjugated, surmounted, thwarted, trounced, undone, vanquished, worsted; SEE CONCEPTS 403,674

beaten [*adj2*] *forged*
formed, hammered, milled, pounded, rolled, shaped, stamped, tamped, tramped, tramped down, trodden, worked; SEE CONCEPTS 486,490

beaten [*adj3*] *mixed*
aerated, blended, bubbly, churned, creamy, foamy, frothy, meringued, stirred, whipped, whisked; SEE CONCEPTS 491,606

beatnik [*n*] *unconventional, free-sprited person*
beat, Bohemian, demonstrator, dropout, flower child*, hippie, iconoclast, maverick, nonconformist, peacenik*, protester, radical; SEE CONCEPT 423

beau [*n*] *boyfriend*
admirer, beloved, cavalier, escort, fiancé, flame, gentleman caller, gentleman friend, honey, inamorato, love, lover, paramour, squire, steady, suitor, swain, sweetheart, true love; SEE CONCEPT 423

beautiful [*adj*] *physically attractive*
admirable, alluring, angelic, appealing, beauteous, bewitching, charming, classy, comely, cute, dazzling, delicate, delightful, divine, elegant, enticing, excellent, exquisite, fair, fascinating, fine, foxy*, good-looking, gorgeous, graceful, grand, handsome, ideal, lovely, magnificent, marvelous, nice, pleasing, pretty, pulchritudinous, radiant, ravishing, refined, resplendent, shapely, sightly, splendid, statuesque, stunning, sublime, superb, symmetrical, taking, well-formed, wonderful; SEE CONCEPTS 485,579,589

beautifully [*adv*] *in an attractive or pleasing manner*
alluringly, appealingly, attractively, bewitchingly, celestially, charmingly, cutely, delightfully, divinely, elegantly, entrancingly, excellently, exquisitely, gorgeously, gracefully, handsomely, ideally, magnificently, prettily, seductively, splendidly, sublimely, superbly, tastefully, wonderfully; SEE CONCEPT 544

beautify [*v*] *make more physically attractive*
adorn, array, bedeck, deck, decorate, dress up, embellish, enhance, garnish, gild, glamorize, grace, improve, make up, ornament, prettify, set off, trim; SEE CONCEPT 162

beauty [*n1*] *physical attractiveness*
adorableness, allure, allurement, artistry, attraction, bloom, charm, class, comeliness, delicacy, elegance, exquisiteness, fairness, fascination, glamor, good looks, grace, handsomeness, loveliness, polish, pulchritude, refinement, shapeliness, style, symmetry, winsomeness; SEE CONCEPT 718

beauty [*n2*] *good-looking person*
Adonis*, Apollo*, beaut*, charmer, dream, dreamboat*, enchanter, eyeful*, good-looker*, head turner*, looker*, ornament*, stunner*, Venus*, vision; SEE CONCEPT 424

beauty [*n3*] *advantage*
asset, attraction, benefit, blessing, boon, excellent, feature, good thing, importance, merit, value, worth; SEE CONCEPT 668

because [*conj/prep*] *on account of*
as, as a result of, as long as, as things go, being,

by cause of, by reason of, by virtue of, considering, due to, for, for the reason that, for the sake of, in as much as, in behalf of, in that, in the interest of, in view of, now that, on the grounds that, over, owing to, seeing, since, thanks to, through, whereas; SEE CONCEPT 676

beckon [*v*] *call, signal, or lure*
allure, ask, attract, bid, coax, command, demand, draw, entice, gesticulate, gesture, invite, motion, nod, pull, sign, summon, tempt, wave; SEE CONCEPTS 7,22,53,74

become [*vl*] *evolve into*
alter to, assume form of, be converted to, be reduced to, be reformed, be remodeled, be transformed into, change into, come, come to be, convert, develop into, emerge as, eventually be, grow into, incline, mature, metamorphose, pass into, ripen into, shift, turn into, turn out, wax; SEE CONCEPT 701

become [*v2*] *enhance*
accord, adorn, agree, augment, be appropriate, belong to, display, embellish, enrich, fit, flatter, garnish, go together, go with, grace, harmonize, heighten, make handsome, match, ornament, set off, suit; SEE CONCEPT 244

becoming [*adj1*] *flattering*
acceptable, agreeable, attractive, beautiful, comely, cute, effective, enhancing, excellent, fair, graceful, handsome, neat, nice, presentable, pretty, seemly, tasteful, welcome, well-chosen; SEE CONCEPTS 579,589

becoming [*adj2*] *suitable; appropriate*
befitting, comme il faut, compatible, conforming, congruous, correct, decent, decorous, fit, fitting, in keeping, nice, proper, right, seemly, worthy; SEE CONCEPT 558

bed [*n1*] *furniture for sleeping*
bassinet, bedstead, berth, bunk, chaise, cot, couch, cradle, crib, davenport, divan, mattress, pallet, platform, sack, trundle; SEE CONCEPT 443

bed [*n2*] *patch of ground for planting*
area, border, frame, garden, piece, plot, row, strip; SEE CONCEPTS 509,513

bed [*n3*] *base, foundation*
basis, bedrock, bottom, ground, groundwork, rest, seat, substratum, understructure; SEE CONCEPT 442

bed [*v*] *plant*
base, embed, establish, fix, found, implant, insert, settle, set up; SEE CONCEPTS 234,257

bedazzle [*v*] *captivate*
astound, bewilder, blind, confuse, daze, dazzle, dumbfound, enchant, overwhelm, stagger, stun; SEE CONCEPTS 7,22,42

bedding [*n*] *covering for sleeping furniture*
bedclothes, bed linen, bedspread, blanket, comforter, cover, coverlet, eiderdown, electric blanket, linen, pillow, pillowcase, quilt, sheet, spread, thermal blanket; SEE CONCEPTS 444,473

bedlam [*n*] *chaotic situation*
chaos, clamor, commotion, confusion, din, disquiet, disquietude, furor, hubbub, madhouse, maelstrom, noise, pandemonium, racket, shambles, tumult, turmoil, uproar; SEE CONCEPTS 230,674

bedraggled [*adj*] *unkempt*
decrepit, dilapidated, dirty, disheveled, disordered, dowdy, drenched, dripping, faded, messy, muddied, muddy, run-down, seedy, shabby, sloppy, slovenly, sodden, soiled, stained, sullied,

tacky, tattered, threadbare, untidy, wet; SEE CONCEPT 589

bedroom [n] *place for sleeping*
bedchamber, bunk room, chamber, cubicle, guest room; SEE CONCEPT 448

bedspread [n] *thick, often quilted, covering for bed*
bedcover, blanket, counterpane, cover, coverlet, spread; SEE CONCEPT 444

bee [n1] *honey-making, stinging insect*
bumblebee, drone, honey bee, killer bee, queen bee; SEE CONCEPT 398

bee [n2] *collective task*
communal gathering, harvest, party, social, work party; SEE CONCEPTS 362,386

beef [n1] *strong physical makeup*
arm, brawn, flesh, force, heftiness, meat, might, muscle, physique, power, robustness, sinew, steam, strength, thew, vigor; SEE CONCEPT 757

beef [n2] *complaint*
bickering, criticism, dispute, grievance, gripe, grouse, grumble, objection, protestation, quarrel, rhubarb*, squabble; SEE CONCEPT 52

beer [n] *alcoholic beverage made from malted grain*
ale, amber brew*, barley pop*, brew, brewski*, brown bottle*, chill*, cold coffee*, cold one*, hops, lager, malt, malt liquor, oil*, stout*, suds*; SEE CONCEPT 455

befall [v] *happen to; take place*
action, bechance, betide, break, chance, come down, come off, come to pass, cook*, cook up a storm*, cook with gas*, develop, ensue, fall, fall out, follow, gel, go, go down, hap*, happen, jell*, materialize, occur, shake*, smoke*, supervene, transpire; SEE CONCEPT 4

befitting [adj] *appropriate*
according to Hoyle*, apt, becoming, behooving, beseeming, comme il faut, conforming, correct, decent, decorous, felicitous, fit, fitting, happy, just, kosher*, nice, on the button*, on the nose*, proper, right, right on*, seemly, suitable, what the doctor ordered*; SEE CONCEPTS 533,558

before [adv] *earlier*
afore, aforetime, ahead, ante, antecedently, anteriorly, back, before present, ere, fore, former, formerly, forward, gone, gone by, heretofore, in advance, in days of yore, in front, in old days, in the past, past, precedently, previous, previously, since, sooner, up to now; SEE CONCEPT 820

before [prep] *earlier than*
ahead of, ante, antecedent to, anterior to, ere, in advance of, in front of, preceding, previous to, prior to, since; SEE CONCEPT 820

beforehand [adj/adv] *early*
advanced, ahead, ahead of time, already, ante, antecedently, before, before now, earlier, fore, in advance, in anticipation, precedently, precocious, previous, previously, sooner; SEE CONCEPT 820

befriend [v] *make social acquaintance; support*
advise, aid, assist, back, benefit, buddy up*, case out*, come on to*, cotton to*, encourage, favor, get chummy with, get in with*, help, hit it off*, patronize, side with, stand by, sustain, take under one's wing*, take up with, uphold, welcome; SEE CONCEPTS 110,384

befuddle [v] *confuse*
addle, baffle, ball up*, bewilder, bother, daze, disorient, distract, dumbfound, fluster, inebriate, intoxicate, make punchy*, mix up, muddle, puzzle, shake, stupefy, throw off*; SEE CONCEPTS 7,19,42

beg [v1] *request*
abjure, advocate, apply to, ask, beseech, besiege, call to, canvass, conjure, crave, desire, entreat, impetrate, implore, importune, invoke, nag, obsecrate, obtest, petition, plead, pray, press, requisition, solicit, sue, supplicate, urge, woo, worry; SEE CONCEPT 48

beg [v2] *seek charity*
ask alms, benefit, bite*, brace, bum*, burn*, buzz*, cadge*, call on, call upon, chisel*, clamor for, dime up*, ding*, freeload*, hit up*, hustle, knock, live hand to mouth*, mendicate, mooch*, nick*, nickel up*, panhandle, pass the hat*, put the bite on*, put the touch on*, score*, scrounge, solicit charity, sponge*, sponge on*, tap, touch, want; SEE CONCEPT 53

beget [v] *create, bear*
afford, breed, bring, bring about, cause, effect, engender, father, generate, get, give rise to, multiply, occasion, procreate, produce, progenerate, propagate, reproduce, result in, sire; SEE CONCEPTS 173,251,374

beggar [n1] *person asking for charity*
asker, borrower, bum, deadbeat, hobo, mendicant, panhandler, rustler, scrounger, supplicant, supplicator, tramp, vagabond; SEE CONCEPTS 412,423

beggar [n2] *person in financial trouble*
alms person, bankrupt, dependent, down-and-out*, guttersnipe*, indigent, mendicant, pauper, poor person, poverty-stricken person, street person*, suppliant, vagrant, ward of state; SEE CONCEPT 423

begin [v1] *start*
activate, actualize, break ground, break the ice*, bring about, bring to pass, cause, commence, create, do, drive, effect, embark on, enter on, enter upon, establish, eventuate, found, generate, get going, give birth to, give impulse, go ahead, go into, impel, inaugurate, induce, initiate, instigate, institute, introduce, launch, lay foundation for, lead, make, make active, motivate, mount, occasion, open, originate, plunge into, prepare, produce, set about, set in motion, set up, trigger, undertake; SEE CONCEPTS 234,241

begin [v2] *come into being; become functional*
appear, arise, be born, bud, come forth, come into existence, come out, commence, crop up, dawn, derive from, emanate, emerge, enter, germinate, get going, get show on road*, get under way, grow out of, happen, issue forth, kick off, make tick*, occur, originate, proceed from, result from, rise, sail, send off, set, spring, sprout, start, stem from, take off; SEE CONCEPTS 105,680

beginner [n] *person unskilled in something*
abecedarian, amateur, apprentice, buckwheater*, catechumen, colt, fish*, fledgling, greenhorn, greenie*, initiate, learner, neophyte, newcomer, new kid on the block*, new person, novice, noviate, probationer, recruit, starter, student, tenderfoot*, trainee, tyro; SEE CONCEPTS 423,424

beginning [n1] *start of an event or action*
alpha, basis, birth, blastoff*, commencement, creation, dawn, dawning, day one*, genesis, inauguration, inception, induction, infancy, initiation, installation, introduction, kickoff, onset, opener, opening, origin, origination, outset, point of departure, preface, prelude, presentation, rise, root,

rudiment, source, spring, square one*, starting point, takeoff, threshold, top; SEE CONCEPTS 815,833

beginning [n2] *origin, cause*
antecedent, birth, conception, egg, embryo, font, fount, fountain, fountainhead, generation, genesis, germ, heart, principle, resource, root, seed, stem, well; SEE CONCEPT 229

begrudge [v] *wish that someone did not have*
be jealous, be reluctant, be stingy, covet, eat one's heart out, envy, grudge, pinch, resent, stint; SEE CONCEPTS 17,21

beguile [v1] *fool*
betray, bluff, burn*, cheat, chisel, con, deceive, delude, double-cross, dupe, entice, exploit, finesse, flimflam*, gyp*, have, hoodwink*, impose on, jockey, juggle, lure, manipulate, mislead, play, play for a sucker*, rook*, rope in*, scam, seduce, shave*, snow*, stick*, string along, suck in*, take, take in, trick; SEE CONCEPT 59

beguile [v2] *charm*
amuse, attract, cheer, delight, distract, divert, engross, entertain, entice, knock dead, knock out, lure, occupy, seduce, send, slay, solace, sweep off one's feet, tickle, tickle pink*, tickle to death*, turn on, vamp, wow*; SEE CONCEPTS 7,19,22

behalf [n] *personal interest*
account, advantage, aid, assistance, benefit, cause, concern, countenance, defense, encouragement, favor, furtherance, good, help, part, place, profit, recommendation, representation, sake, service, side, stead, support, welfare; SEE CONCEPTS 410,532

behave [v1] *function*
act, operate, perform, react, run, take, work; SEE CONCEPTS 1,4

behave [v2] *act reasonably, properly*
act correctly, act one's age, act with decorum, be civil, be good, be nice, be on best behavior*, be orderly, comport oneself, conduct oneself properly, control, demean oneself, deport oneself, direct, discipline oneself, keep one's nose clean*, keep the peace, live up to, manage, manage oneself, mind one's manners*, mind one's p's and q's*, observe golden rule*, observe the law, play fair, shape up, toe the mark*, watch one's step*; SEE CONCEPT 633

behavior [n] *manner of conducting oneself*
act, action, air, attitude, bag*, bearing, carriage, code, comportment, conduct, convention, course, dealings, decency, decorum, deed, delivery, demeanor, deportment, ethics, etiquette, expression, form, front, guise, habits, management, mien, mode, morals, nature, observance, performance, practice, presence, propriety, ritual, role, routine, savoir-faire, seemliness, social graces, speech, style, tact, talk, taste, tenue, tone, way, way of life, ways, what's done*; SEE CONCEPTS 633,655

behead [v] *decapitate*
bring to the block, decollate, execute, guillotine, head, kill, neck; SEE CONCEPT 176

behest [n] *order; personal decree*
bidding, charge, command, commandment, demand, dictate, direction, expressed desire, injunction, instruction, mandate, order, precept, prompting, request, solicitation, wish, word; SEE CONCEPTS 20,53

behind [n] *buttocks*
backside, bottom, breech, can*, derrière, fanny*,

---

fundament, posterior, rear, rump, seat, tail, tush*; SEE CONCEPT 392

behind [adv1/prep1] *position farther back; following*
abaft, after, afterwards, at the heels of*, at the rear of, back of, bringing up the rear*, eating the dust*, in the background, in the wake, later than, next, off the pace, subsequently, trailing; SEE CONCEPTS 586,820

behind [adv2] *in debt; late*
backward, behindhand, behind schedule, behind time, belated, delayed, dilatory, have to play catch up*, in arrears, laggard, overdue, slow, sluggish, tardy; SEE CONCEPTS 334,799

behind [prep2] *being the reason for*
at the bottom of, causing, concerning the circumstances, initiating, instigating, responsible for; SEE CONCEPT 532

behind [prep3] *in support*
backing, for, in agreement, on the side of, supporting; SEE CONCEPT 388

behold [v] *regard; look at*
catch, consider, contemplate, descry, discern, distinguish, earmark, eye, eyeball*, feast one's eyes*, flash*, lay eyes on*, note, notice, observe, perceive, regard, scan, see, spot, spy, survey, view, watch, witness; SEE CONCEPTS 34,626

beholden [adj] *indebted*
bound, grateful, in hock, into, obligated, obliged, on a string*, on the arm*, on the cuff*, on the tab*, owe one, owing, responsible, under obligation; SEE CONCEPT 403

behoove [v] *be necessary, proper*
be expected, befit, be fitting, be incumbent upon, be needful, be one's obligation, be required, be requisite, be right, beseem, owe it to, suit; SEE CONCEPT 646

beige [n/adj] *light brown color*
biscuit, buff, café au lait, camel, cream, ecru, fawn, khaki, mushroom, neutral, oatmeal, off-white, sand, tan, taupe; SEE CONCEPTS 618,622

being [n1] *existence*
actuality, animation, journey, life, living, presence, reality, subsistence, vitality, world; SEE CONCEPT 407

being [n2] *essential nature*
character, entity, essence, essentia, essentiality, individuality, marrow, personality, quintessence, self, soul, spirit, substance, texture; SEE CONCEPTS 411,673

being [n3] *animate object*
animal, beast, body, conscious thing, creature, entity, human, human being, individual, living thing, mortal, organism, person, personage, soul, thing; SEE CONCEPT 389

belated [adj] *late, slow*
behindhand, behind time, delayed, long-delayed, overdue, remiss, tardy, unpunctual; SEE CONCEPT 820

belch [v] *burp; spew*
discharge, disgorge, emit, eruct, eructate, erupt, give off, gush, hiccup, irrupt, repeat, ventilate, vomit; SEE CONCEPT 185

beleaguer [v] *harass, besiege*
annoy, badger, bedevil, beset, blockade, bother, gnaw, harry, nag, persecute, pester, plague, put upon, set upon, siege, storm, tease, vex, worry; SEE CONCEPTS 7,19

belfry [n] *tower; part of tower*
bell tower, campanile, carillon, clocher, cupola,

dome, head, minaret, spire, steeple, turret; SEE CONCEPT 440

belie [v1] *disprove*
confute, contradict, contravene, controvert, deny, disaffirm, disagree, explode, gainsay, negate, negative, oppose, repudiate; SEE CONCEPTS 54,58

belie [v2] *deceive*
color, conceal, disguise, distort, falsify, garble, give the lie to, gloss over, hide, miscolor, mislead, misrepresent, misstate, pervert, trump up, twist, warp; SEE CONCEPT 63

belief [n1] *putting regard in as true*
acceptance, admission, assent, assumption, assurance, avowal, axiom, certainty, conclusion, confidence, conjecture, conviction, credence, credit, deduction, divination, expectation, faith, fancy, feeling, guess, hope, hypothesis, idea, impression, intuition, judgment, knowledge, mind, mindset, notion, opinion, persuasion, position, postulation, presumption, presupposition, profession, reliance, supposition, surmise, suspicion, theorem, theory, thesis, thinking, trust, understanding, view; SEE CONCEPTS 410,529

belief [n2] *something regarded as true, trustworthy*
assumption, concept, credence, credo, creed, doctrine, dogma, faith, fundamental, gospel, gospel truth*, hypothesis, idea, ideology, law, opinion, postulate, precept, principle, say-so*, tenet, theorem, theory; SEE CONCEPT 689

believable [adj] *trustworthy*
aboveboard, acceptable, authentic, colorable, conceivable, convincing, credential, credible, creditable, fiduciary, honest-to-God*, imaginable, impressive, likely, persuasive, plausible, possible, presumable, presumptive, probable, rational, reasonable, reliable, satisfying, straight, supposable, tenable, tried, trusty, unquestionable, up front*; SEE CONCEPTS 403,582

believe [v1] *trust, rely on*
accept, accredit, admit, affirm, attach weight to, be certain of, be convinced of, be credulous, be of the opinion, buy*, conceive, conclude, consider, count on, credit, deem, fall for*, give credence to, have, have faith in, have no doubt, hold, keep the faith, lap up*, place confidence in, posit, postulate, presume true, presuppose, reckon on, regard, rest assured, suppose, swallow*, swear by, take as gospel*, take at one's word, take for granted, take it, think, trust, understand; SEE CONCEPT 12

believe [v2] *assume or suppose*
conjecture, consider, credit, deem, expect, feel, gather, guess, hold, imagine, judge, maintain, postulate, presume, reckon, sense, speculate, suppose, suspect, take, think, understand; SEE CONCEPT 28

believer [n] *person who has trust, faith in something*
acceptor, adherent, apostle, canonist, convert, devotee, disciple, doctrinaire, dogmatist, follower, freak, orthodox, prophet, proselyte, religionist, religious person, supporter, upholder, zealot; SEE CONCEPTS 361,423

belittle [v] *detract*
bad-mouth, blister, criticize, cut down to size*, cut to the quick*, decry, deprecate, depreciate, deride, derogate, diminish, discount, discredit, disparage, dispraise, downgrade, downplay, dump on*, knock*, lower, minimize, pan, pooh pooh*, poor mouth*, put down, rip*, roast*, run down, scoff at, scorch*, scorn, shoot down*, shoot full

of holes*, slam*, smear, sneer at, sour grapes*, squash*, squelch, take a swipe at*, take down, take down a peg*, tear down*, underestimate, underrate, undervalue, write off; SEE CONCEPTS 52,54

bell [n] *signaling object or sound*
alarm, buzz, buzzer, carillon, chime, clapper, curfew, ding-dong*, dinger*, gong, peal, ringer, siren, tintinnabulum, tocsin, toll, vesper; SEE CONCEPT 595

belligerent [adj] *nasty, argumentative*
aggressive, antagonistic, ardent, at loggerheads*, battling, bellicose, cantankerous, combative, contentious, fierce, fighting, flip, have a bone to pick*, have chip on shoulder*, have it in for*, hostile, hot, hot-tempered, mean, militant, on the outs*, ornery, pugnacious, quarrelsome, scrappy, truculent, warlike; SEE CONCEPTS 401,404

bellow [v] *holler*
bark, bawl, bay, beller, blare, bluster, bray, call, clamor, cry, howl, low, roar, rout, scream, shout, shriek, wail, whoop, yawp, yell, yelp; SEE CONCEPT 77

belly [n] *stomach*
abdomen, bay window*, beer belly*, breadbasket*, corporation*, front porch*, gut, insides, intestines, paunch, pelvis, pot*, pot belly*, solar plexus, spare tire*, tank, tummy, venter; SEE CONCEPT 393

belong [v1] *be part of, be in proper place*
accord, agree, appertain, apply, associate, attach to, be a component, be a constituent, be akin to, be an adjunct of, be a part, bear, bear upon, become, be connected with, befit, be fitting, be linked with, be related, be relevant, chime, concern, correlate, correspond, exist, fit, go, go with, harmonize, have relationship to, have respect to, have to do with, inhere, match, permeate, pertain, refer, regard, reside, set, suit, touch, vest; SEE CONCEPTS 532,543

belong [v2] *be affiliated with*
be allied to, be a member, be a member of, be associated with, be classified among, be contained in, be included in, be one of, be one of the family, be part of, fit in, have a place, in, in with, owe allegiance, owe support, run with*, swing*, swing with*, take one's place with; SEE CONCEPTS 114,388

belonging [n] *sense of security in friendship*
acceptance, affinity, association, attachment, inclusion, kinship, loyalty, rapport, relationship; SEE CONCEPTS 388,410

belongings [n] *personal possessions*
accouterments, appurtenances, assets, chattels, effects, gear, goods, paraphernalia, personal property, property, stuff, things; SEE CONCEPTS 446,710

beloved [n] *someone adored*
baby*, beau, boyfriend, darling, dear, dearest, fiancé, flame, girlfriend, heartbeat*, heartthrob, honey, idol, inamorato, love, love of my life*, lover, number one*, numero uno*, object of affection, one and only, pet*, prize, rave*, significant other, steady, sugar*, sweetheart, tootsie*, treasure, true love; SEE CONCEPT 423

beloved [adj]
admired, cared for, cherished, darling, dear, dearest, doted on, endeared, esteemed, fair-haired, favorite, hallowed, highly regarded, highly valued, idolized, loved, near to one's heart*, pet*, pleas-

ing, popular, precious, prized, respected, revered, sweet, treasured, venerated, well-liked, worshiped; SEE CONCEPTS 568,572

below [adv/prep] lower
beneath, down, down from, under, underneath; SEE CONCEPTS 581,586,735

below [prep2] less than; beneath
inferior, lesser, lower, subject, subordinate, unworthy; SEE CONCEPTS 567,771

belt [n1] supporting band
cincture, cummerbund, girdle, ribbon, ring, sash, strap, string, waistband; SEE CONCEPT 450

belt [n2] strip of land with characteristic feature
area, district, layer, region, stretch, territory, tract, zone; SEE CONCEPTS 513,517

belt [v] hit hard
bash, bat, biff, blast, blow, bop, clobber, slam, slug, smack, smash, sock, strap, switch, wallop, whip, whop; SEE CONCEPT 189

bemoan [v] express sorrow
beat one's breast*, bewail, complain, cry over spilled milk*, deplore, grieve for, lament, moan over, mourn, regret, rue, sing the blues*, weep for; SEE CONCEPTS 49,51

bemuse [v] confuse
addle, amaze, bewilder, daydream, daze, gather wool*, moon, muddle, overwhelm, paralyze, perplex, pipe dream*, puzzle, stun, stupefy; SEE CONCEPTS 7,19,22

bench [n1] furniture for sitting
bank, chair, form, lawn seat, pew, seat, settee, settle, stall; SEE CONCEPT 443

bench [n2] large table
board, counter, desk, easel, ledge, shelf, trestle, workbench, work table; SEE CONCEPT 443

bench [n3] group of judges
court, courtroom, judiciary, magistrate, the bar, tribunal, your honors; SEE CONCEPTS 318,355

benchmark [n] reference point
criterion, gauge, measure, standard, touchstone, yardstick; SEE CONCEPT 688

bend [n] curve
angle, arc, bending, bow, corner, crook, curvation, curvature, deflection, deviation, flection, flexure, hook, lean, loop, round, sag, shift, tack, tilt, turn, twist, yaw, zigzag; SEE CONCEPT 436

bend [v1] form or cause a curve
angle away, angle off, arch, bow, buckle, camber, careen, circle, contort, crimp, crinkle, crook, crouch, curl, deflect, deform, detour, double, droop, flex, genuflect, hook, incline, incurvate, lean, loop, pervert, round, spiral, stoop, swerve, tilt, turn, twist, veer, verge, warp, waver, wilt, wind, yaw, zigzag; SEE CONCEPTS 149,184

bend [v2] persuade; influence
change mind, compel, direct, mold, shape, subdue, submit, sway, yield; SEE CONCEPT 68

beneath [adv] in a lower place
below, underneath; SEE CONCEPT 586

beneath [prep] inferior
below, lesser, less than, lower than, subject, subordinate, unbefitting, under, underneath, unworthy of; SEE CONCEPT 567

benediction [n] closing prayer
amen, approbation, approval, beatitude, benediction, benison, blessing, consecration, favor, grace, gratitude, invocation, laying on of hands, okay, orison, praise, sanctification, thanks, thanksgiving; SEE CONCEPT 69

benefactor [n] donor
aid, altruist, angel, assistant, backer, contributor, fairy godparent*, fan, good Samaritan, grubstaker, helper, humanitarian, mark*, patron, philanthropist, promoter, protector, Santa Claus*, sponsor, subscriber, subsidizer, supporter, wellwisher; SEE CONCEPTS 416,423

beneficial [adj] advantageous
benign, constructive, favorable, favoring, gainful, good, good for what ails you*, healthful, helpful, profitable, propitious, salubrious, salutary, serviceable, toward, useful, valuable, what the doctor ordered*, wholesome, worthy; SEE CONCEPTS 567,572

beneficiary [n] person who gains, benefits
almsperson, assignee, devisee, donee, grantee, heir, heiress, inheritor, legatee, payee, possessor, receiver, recipient, stipendiary, successor; SEE CONCEPTS 355,423

benefit [n1] advantage, profit
account, aid, asset, assistance, avail, benediction, betterment, blessing, boon, cream*, egg in one's beer*, extras, favor, gain, godsend*, good, gravy*, help, interest, perk*, profit, prosperity, use, welfare, worth; SEE CONCEPTS 337,346,661

benefit [n2] event to raise money
ball, bazaar, charitable affair, charity performance, concert, dance, dinner, exhibit, exhibition, fair, pancake breakfast, raffle; SEE CONCEPT 386

benefit [v] help, enhance
advance, advantage, aid, ameliorate, assist, avail, be good for, better, build, contribute to, do for one, do the trick, favor, fill the bill*, further, improve, make a killing*, make it*, pay, pay off*, profit, promote, relieve, serve, succor, work for; SEE CONCEPTS 110,244

benevolence [n] charity
altruism, amity, comity, compassion, feeling, friendliness, friendship, generosity, gift, goodness, good will, humanity, kindheartedness, kindness, sympathy; SEE CONCEPT 633

benevolent [adj] charitable, kind
all heart, altruistic, beneficent, benign, big, bighearted, bounteous, bountiful, caring, chivalrous, compassionate, considerate, generous, helpful, humane, humanitarian, kindhearted, liberal, magnanimous, philanthropic, tenderhearted, warmhearted, well-disposed; SEE CONCEPT 401

benign [adj1] kindly
amiable, beneficent, benevolent, benignant, complaisant, congenial, favorable, friendly, generous, genial, gentle, good, goodhearted, gracious, kind, liberal, merciful, mild, obliging, sympathetic; SEE CONCEPT 542

benign [adj2] mild, especially describing weather
auspicious, balmy, bright, favorable, fortunate, gentle, healthful, propitious, refreshing, temperate, warm; SEE CONCEPT 605

benign [adj3] advantageous
auspicious, beneficent, benevolent, bright, charitable, dexter, encouraging, favorable, fortunate, good, lucky, merciful, propitious, salutary, smiling; SEE CONCEPTS 537,572

benign [adj4] not cancerous
curable, early stage, harmless, limited, remediable, slight, superficial; SEE CONCEPT 314

bent [n] inclination; talent
ability, aim, aptitude, bag*, disposition, druthers*, facility, faculty, flair, forte, genius, gift,

be
be

head-set*, inclining, knack, leaning, mind-set*, nose, penchant, predilection, predisposition, preference, proclivity, propensity, set, tack, tendency, thing for*, tilt, turn, weakness for; SEE CONCEPTS **409,630**

bent [*adj1*] *curved*
angled, arced, arched, arciform, bowed, contorted, crooked, curvilinear, doubled over, drooping, droopy, hooked, humped, hunched, inclined, limp, looped, round, rounded, sinuous, slouchy, slumped, stooped, twined, twisted, warped, wilted; SEE CONCEPT **486**

bent [*adj2*] *determined*
bound, decided, decisive, dedicated, disposed, firm, fixed, insistent, intent, leaning, predisposed, resolute, resolved, set, settled, tending; SEE CONCEPT **403**

bequeath [*v*] *give in a will*
bestow, commit, devise, endow, entrust, grant, hand down, hand on, impart, leave, leave to, legate, pass on, transmit, will; SEE CONCEPTS **108,317**

bequest [*n*] *something given in will*
bequeathal, bequeathment, bestowal, devisal, devise, dower, endowment, estate, gift, heritage, inheritance, legacy, settlement, trust; SEE CONCEPTS **318,337**

berate [*v*] *criticize hatefully*
bawl out*, blister, call down, castigate, censure, chew*, chew out*, chide, cuss out*, eat out*, give one hell*, give what for*, jaw*, jump all over*, rail at*, rake over the coals*, rate, rebuke, reprimand, reproach, reprove, revile, scold, scorch, tell off, tongue-lash, upbraid, vituperate; SEE CONCEPT **52**

bereavement [*n*] *death; loss*
affliction, deprivation, distress, misfortune, sorrow, tribulation; SEE CONCEPTS **230,674**

bereft [*adj*] *lacking; missing*
beggared, bereaved, cut off, deprived, destitute, devoid, dispossessed, divested, fleeced, impoverished, left without, minus, naked, parted from, robbed, shorn, stripped, wanting, without; SEE CONCEPTS **546,576**

berry [*n*] *small fruit*
bean, drupe, drupelet, grain, haw, hip, kernel, pome, seed; SEE CONCEPT **426**

berth [*n1*] *harbor; bunk*
anchorage, bed, bedroom, billet, compartment, cot, dock, hammock, haven, jetty, levee, pier, port, quay, slip, wharf; SEE CONCEPTS **513,516**

berth [*n2*] *position of responsibility*
appointment, billet, capacity, connection, employment, job, living, office, place, post, profession, situation, spot; SEE CONCEPTS **362,668**

beseech [*v*] *beg*
adjure, appeal, ask, call upon, crave, entreat, implore, importune, invoke, petition, plead, pray, solicit, sue, supplicate; SEE CONCEPT **48**

beset [*v*] *plague; hem in*
aggress, assail, attack, badger, bedevil, beleaguer, besiege, bug*, circle*, compass, dog*, drive up the wall*, embarrass, encircle, enclose, encompass, entangle, environ, fall on, fall upon, girdle, give a bad time*, give a hard time*, give one the business*, give the needle*, harass, harry, hassle, infest, invade, jump on one's case*, nag, nudge, overrun, perplex, pester, pick on, put the squeeze on*, ride, ring, start in on, storm, strike, surround; SEE CONCEPTS **7,19**

beside [*adv/prep*] *next to*
abreast of, adjacent to, adjoining, alongside, aside, a step from, at one's elbow, at the edge of, at the side of, bordering on, by, cheek by jowl*, close at hand, close to, close upon, connected with, contiguous to, forrent, in juxtaposition, near, nearby, neck and neck*, neighboring, next door to, nigh, opposite, overlooking, round, side by side, verging on, with; SEE CONCEPT **586**

besides [*adv*] *in addition; as well*
added to, additionally, along with, also, and all, apart from, aside from, as well as, beyond, conjointly, else, exceeding, exclusive of, extra, further, furthermore, in conjunction with, in distinction to, in excess of, in other respects, likewise, more, moreover, more than, not counting, on the side*, on top of everything, other than, otherwise, over and above, plus, secondly, supplementary to, to boot*, together with, too, what's more*, with the exception of, yet; SEE CONCEPT **772**

besides [*prep1*] *apart from*
aside from, bar, barring, beside, but, except, excepting, excluding, exclusive of, in addition to, other than, outside of, over and above, save, without; SEE CONCEPT **772**

besides [*prep2*] *in addition to*
added to, along with, as well as, beside, beyond, in excess of, more than, on top of, other than, over and above, plus, supplementary, together with; SEE CONCEPT **772**

besiege [*v1*] *surround; assault*
assail, attack, beleaguer, beset, blockade, come at from all sides, confine, congregate, encircle, encompass, environ, hem in, invest, lay siege to, shut in, trap, work on, work over; SEE CONCEPTS **86,90**

besiege [*v2*] *bother*
badger, beleaguer, bug*, buttonhole*, harass, harry, hound*, importune, nag, pester, plague, trouble; SEE CONCEPTS **7,19**

best [*n1*] *most outstanding thing in class*
choice, cream, cream of the crop*, elite, fat, favorite, finest, first, flower, gem, model, nonpareil, paragon, pick, prime, prize, select, top; SEE CONCEPT **668**

best [*n2*] *highest personal effort*
all one's got, best shot, hardest, highest endeavor, level best*, Sunday best*, utmost; SEE CONCEPT **411**

best [*adj1*] *most excellent*
ace, A-1*, bad*, beyond compare, boss*, capital, champion, chief, choicest, cool*, culminating, finest, first, first-class, first-rate, foremost, greatest, highest, incomparable, inimitable, leading, matchless, nonpareil, number 1*, optimum, out-of-sight*, outstanding, paramount, peerless, perfect, preeminent, premium, prime, primo*, principal, sans pareil, second to none, super, superlative, supreme, 10*, terrific, tops, tough, transcendent, unequaled, unparalleled, unrivaled, unsurpassed; SEE CONCEPTS **568,572**

best [*adj2*] *correct, right*
advantageous, apt, desirable, golden, most desirable, most fitting, preferred, presentable; SEE CONCEPT **558**

best [*adj3*] *most*
biggest, bulkiest, greatest, largest; SEE CONCEPT **771**

best [v] *defeat; gain advantage*

beat, beat up*, better, blank*, blast*, bulldoze*, clobber*, conquer, cream*, deck*, drub*, exceed, excel, flax*, floor*, get the better of, knock off*, KO*, lambaste, let have it*, lick*, master, outclass, outdo, outshine, outstrip, overcome, prevail, put away, shoot down*, shut down*, surpass, take care of, take down*, tan*, thrash*, top, total, transcend, trash*, triumph, triumph over, trounce, wallop, waste*, wax*, whip*, whomp*, whop*, wipe*, wipe out, wipe the floor with*, zap*; SEE CONCEPT 95

best [adv] *most excellently*

advantageously, attractively, creditably, extremely, gloriously, greatly, honorably, illustriously, magnanimously, most deeply, most fortunately, most fully, most highly, sincerely; SEE CONCEPTS 568,572

bestow [v] *give, allot*

accord, apportion, award, bequeath, come through, commit, confer, devote, donate, entrust, favor, gift, give away, grant, hand out, honor with, impart, kick in, lavish, offer, present, put out, render to; SEE CONCEPTS 98,108

bet [n] *game of chance; money gambled*

action, ante, betting, chance, down on, hazard, long shot, lot, lottery, odds, odds on, parlay, play, pledge, plunge, pot, raffle, random shot, risk, shot, shot in the dark*, speculation, stake, sweepstakes, uncertainty, venture, wager; SEE CONCEPTS 28,293,329

bet [v] *gamble*

ante, buy in on, chance, dice, game, hazard, lay down, lay odds, play against, play for, play the ponies*, pledge, pony up*, put, put money on, risk, set, speculate, tempt fortune*, toss up, trust, venture, wager; SEE CONCEPTS 292,330

betray [v1] *be disloyal*

abandon, be unfaithful, bite the hand that feeds you*, blow the whistle*, bluff, break faith, break promise, break trust, break with, commit treason, cross, deceive, deliver up*, delude, desert, double-cross, finger*, forsake, go back on, inform against, inform on, jilt, knife*, let down, mislead, play false*, play Judas*, seduce, sell down the river*, sell out, stab in the back*, take in*, trick, turn in, turn informer, turn state's evidence, walk out on; SEE CONCEPT 384

betray [v2] *divulge, expose information*

blurt out, dime*, disclose, evince, fink on*, give away, inform, lay bare, let slip, make known, manifest, rat on*, reveal, show, sing*, snitch*, spill, squeal*, stool*, tattle, tell, tell on, turn in, uncover, unmask; SEE CONCEPTS 44,60

betrayal [n1] *exhibition of disloyalty*

deception, dishonesty, double-crossing, double-dealing, duplicity, falseness, giveaway, Judas kiss*, let-down, perfidy, sellout, treachery, treason, trickery, unfaithfulness; SEE CONCEPT 633

betrayal [n2] *divulgence of information*

blurting out, diming*, disclosure, giving away, ratting*, revelation, snitching*, spilling*, squealing*, tattling, telling; SEE CONCEPTS 44,60

betroth [v] *marry*

affiance, become engaged, bind, commit, contract, engage, espouse, give one's hand, make compact, plight faith, plight troth, promise, tie oneself to; SEE CONCEPT 297

betrothal [n] *marriage*

affiancing, betrothing, engagement, espousal,

better [adj1] *excelling, more excellent*

bigger, choice, exceeding, exceptional, finer, fitter, greater, higher quality, improved, larger, more appropriate, more desirable, more fitting, more select, more suitable, more useful, more valuable, preferable, preferred, prominent, sharpened, sophisticated, souped up*, superior, surpassing, worthier; SEE CONCEPTS 568,572

better [adj2] *improved in health*

convalescent, cured, fitter, fully recovered, healthier, improving, less ill, mending, more healthy, on the comeback trail*, on the mend, on the road to recovery*, out of the woods*, over the hump*, progressing, recovering, stronger, well; SEE CONCEPT 314

better [adj3] *larger*

bigger, greater, longer, more, preponderant, weightier; SEE CONCEPTS 771,773

better [v] *improve performance; outdo*

advance, ameliorate, amend, beat, best, cap, correct, enhance, exceed, excel, forward, further, help, meliorate, mend, outshine, outstrip, promote, raise, rectify, refine, reform, revamp, surpass, top, transcend; SEE CONCEPTS 141,244

better [adv] *in a more excellent manner*

finer, greater, in a superior way, more, more advantageously, more attractively, more competently, more completely, more effectively, more thoroughly, preferably, to a greater degree; SEE CONCEPTS 568,572

betterment [n] *improvement*

advancement, amelioration, mastery, melioration, progress, prosperity, upgrading; SEE CONCEPT 244

between [adv/prep] *middle from two points*

amid, amidst, among, at intervals, betwixt, bounded by, centrally located, enclosed by, halfway in, inserted, interpolated, intervening, in the middle, in the midst of, in the seam, in the thick of, medially, mid, midway, separating, surrounded by, 'tween, within; SEE CONCEPTS 586,820

beverage [n] *liquid refreshment*

cooler, draft, drink, drinkable, libation, liquor, potable, potation; SEE CONCEPT 454

bevy [n] *swarm*

assembly, band, bunch, cluster, collection, company, covey, crew, crowd, flight, flock, gathering, group, pack, party, troupe; SEE CONCEPT 432

bewail [v] *cry over, lament*

bemoan, deplore, eat heart out*, express sorrow, grieve for, moan, mourn, regret, repent, rue, sing the blues*, take on, wail, weep over; SEE CONCEPT 266

beware [v] *be careful*

attend, avoid, be cautious, be wary, guard against, heed, keep eyes open*, keep one's distance, keep on one's toes*, look out, mind, mind p's and q's*, notice, refrain from, shun, steer clear of*, take care, take heed, walk on eggs*, watch one's step, watch out; SEE CONCEPT 34

bewilder [v] *confuse*

addle, baffle, ball up*, befuddle, bemuse, confound, daze, disconcert, distract, floor*, fluster, mess with one's head*, mix up, muddle, mystify, perplex, puzzle, rattle, snow*, stump, stupefy, throw, upset; SEE CONCEPTS 14,42

bewildered [adj] *confused*

addled, agape, aghast, agog, appalled, astonished,

astounded, awed, awe-struck, baffled, befuddled, bowled over*, dazed, dazzled, disconcerted, dizzy, dumbfounded, dumbstruck, flabbergasted, flipped out*, floored*, flustered, giddy, in a dither*, lost, misled, muddled, mystified, perplexed, punchy*, puzzled, rattled, reeling, shocked, shook up, speechless, staggered, startled, stumped, stunned, stupefied, surprised, taken aback, thrown, thunderstruck*, uncertain, unglued*; SEE CONCEPTS 402,403

bewitch [v] *charm*

allure, attract, bedevil, beguile, captivate, capture, control, dazzle, draw, enchant, enrapture, enthrall, entrance, fascinate, hex, hypnotize, knock dead*, knock out, put horns on*, put the whammy on*, put under magic spell*, send*, slay*, spell*, spellbind, sweep off one's feet*, take, tickle*, tickle pink*, tickle to death*, trick, turn on*, vamp, voodoo, wile, wow*; SEE CONCEPTS 7,22

bewitched [adj] *charmed*

captivated, enamored, enchanted, enraptured, ensorcelled, entranced, fallen for, fascinated, gaga about*, have a bug in one's ear*, have a thing about*, head over heels*, hooked*, hung up*, mad about, mesmerized, possessed, spellbound, transformed, turned on*, under a spell; SEE CONCEPTS 32,403

beyond [adv/prep] *further; outside limits*

above, after, ahead, apart from, as well as, at a distance, away from, before, behind, besides, beyond the bounds, clear of, farther, free of, good way off, hyper, in addition to, in advance of, long way off, moreover, more remote, on the far side, on the other side, out of range, out of reach, outside, over, over and above, over there, past, remote, superior to, without, yonder; SEE CONCEPTS 554,772,778

bias [n1] *belief in one way; partiality*

bent, bigotry, chauvinism, disposition, favoritism, flash, head-set*, illiberality, inclination, intolerance, leaning, mind-set*, mind trip*, narrowmindedness, one-sidedness, penchant, preconception, predilection, predisposition, preference, prejudice, prepossession, proclivity, proneness, propensity, spin, standpoint, tendency, tilt, turn, unfairness, viewpoint; SEE CONCEPT 689

bias [n2] *diagonal weave of fabric*

angle, cant, cross, incline, oblique, slant; SEE CONCEPT 606

bias [v] *cause to favor*

distort, incline, influence, make partial, prejudice, prepossess, slant, sway, twist, warp, weight; SEE CONCEPTS 7,19

bible [n] *holy book; authoritative book*

authority, creed, doctrine, guide, guidebook, handbook, manual, sacred writ, sacred writings, scripture, testament, text, the good news; SEE CONCEPTS 280,368

bicker [v] *nastily argue*

altercate, brawl, caterwaul, cause a scene*, cavil, dig, disagree, dispute, fall out, fight, hassle, pick at, quarrel, quibble, row, scrap, scrape, spar, spat, squabble, tiff, trade zingers*, wrangle; SEE CONCEPT 46

bicycle [n] *pedal-driven recreational vehicle*

bike, cycle, tandem, two-wheeler, velocipede, wheels; SEE CONCEPTS 364,505

bid [n1] *offering of money or services*

advance, amount, declaration, feeler, hit, invitation, offer, pass, price, proffer, proposal, proposition, request, submission, suggestion, sum, summons, tender; SEE CONCEPTS 67,330

bid [n2] *endeavor*

attempt, crack, effort, essay, try, venture; SEE CONCEPT 87

bid [v1] *offer money or services*

present, proffer, propose, render, submit, tender, venture; SEE CONCEPTS 67,330

bid [v2] *say*

call, greet, tell, wish; SEE CONCEPT 266

bid [v3] *ask for; command*

call, charge, demand, desire, direct, enjoin, instruct, invite, make a pass at*, make a pitch*, make a play for*, order, proposition, request, require, solicit, summon, tell, warn; SEE CONCEPT 53

bidding [n1] *command*

behest, call, charge, demand, dictate, direction, injunction, instruction, invitation, mandate, order, request, summons, word; SEE CONCEPT 53

bidding [n2] *offering of money, services*

advance, auction, invitation, offer, proffering, proposal, proposition, request, submission, suggestion, tender; SEE CONCEPTS 67,330

bide [v] *wait*

abide, attend, await, continue, dwell, hang around, hang in*, hang out*, hold the phone*, lie in wait*, linger, live, remain, reside, sit tight*, stay, stick around, sweat it*, tarry, watch for; SEE CONCEPT 681

big [adj1] *large, great*

ample, awash, a whale of a*, brimming, bulky, bull*, burly, capacious, chock-full*, colossal, commodious, considerable, copious, crowded, enormous, extensive, fat, full, gigantic, heavyduty*, heavyweight, hefty, huge, hulking, humongous*, husky, immense, jumbo, mammoth, massive, mondo*, monster*, oversize, packed, ponderous, prodigious, roomy, sizable, spacious, strapping, stuffed, substantial, super colossal*, thundering, tremendous, vast, voluminous, walloping, whopper, whopping; SEE CONCEPTS 771,773

big [adj2] *important*

big league*, big-time*, consequential, considerable, eminent, heavy-duty*, heavyweight, influential, leading, main, major league*, material, meaningful, momentous, paramount, popular, powerful, prime, principal, prominent, serious, significant, substantial, super, super colossal*, valuable, weighty; SEE CONCEPT 568

big [adj3] *grown*

adult, elder, full-grown, grown-up, mature, tall; SEE CONCEPTS 578,797

big [adj4] *generous*

altruistic, benevolent, bighearted, chivalrous, considerate, free, gracious, greathearted, heroic, liberal, lofty, magnanimous, noble, princely, unselfish; SEE CONCEPT 404

big [adj5] *arrogant*

arty, boastful, bragging, conceited, flamboyant, haughty, high-sounding, imperious, imposing, inflated, overblown, pompous, presumptuous, pretentious, proud; SEE CONCEPT 401

bigot [n] *intolerant, prejudiced person*

chauvinist, diehard, doctrinaire, dogmatist, enthusiast, extremist, fanatic, fiend, maniac, monomaniac, opinionated person, partisan, persecutor, puritan, racist, sectarian, segregationist, sexist, stickler, superpatriot, zealot; SEE CONCEPTS *359,423*

bigoted [*adj*] *intolerant, prejudiced*
biased, chauvinistic, conservative, dogmatic, illiberal, narrow, narrow-minded, obstinate, opinionated, partial, partisan, sectarian, slanted, small-minded, twisted, unfair, warped; SEE CONCEPTS *403,555*

bigotry [*n*] *intolerance, prejudice*
bias, conservatism/conservativism, discrimination, dogmatism, fanaticism, injustice, Jim Crowism*, narrow-mindedness, partiality, provincialism, racialism, racism, sectarianism, sexism, unfairness; SEE CONCEPTS *388,410*

bilateral [*adj*] *having two sides*
mutual, reciprocal, respective, two-sided; SEE CONCEPT *562*

bilk [*v*] *cheat*
bamboozle*, beat, circumvent, con, deceive, defraud, disappoint, do*, fleece*, flimflam*, foil, frustrate, gyp*, overreach, rook*, ruin, snow*, swindle, thwart, trick; SEE CONCEPTS *59,139*

bill [*n1*] *account of charges; money owed*
bad news*, check, chit, damage*, debt, invoice, IOU, itemized account, knock*, note, reckoning, request for payment, score, statement, statement of indebtedness, tab; SEE CONCEPTS *329,332*

bill [*n2*] *list; circular*
advertisement, affiche, agenda, bulletin, card, catalogue, flyer, handbill, handout, inventory, leaflet, listing, notice, placard, playbill, poster, program, roster, schedule, syllabus; SEE CONCEPTS *280,283*

bill [*n3*] *piece of legislation*
act, draft, measure, projected law, proposal, proposed act; SEE CONCEPTS *271,318*

bill [*n4*] *piece of paper money*
bank note, buck, certificate, currency, dollar, greenback*, long green*, skin*; SEE CONCEPT *340*

bill [*n5*] *beak of animal*
mandible, neb, nib, pecker, projection; SEE CONCEPT *399*

bill [*v1*] *charge money for goods, services*
bone, chase, debit, draw upon, dun, figure, invoice, put the arm on*, put the bite on*, put the squeeze on*, reckon, record, render, solicit; SEE CONCEPTS *330,342*

bill [*v2*] *advertise*
announce, book, give advance notice, post; SEE CONCEPTS *60,292*

billow [*n*] *surging mass*
beachcomber, breaker, crest, roller, surge, swell, tide, wave; SEE CONCEPTS *437,514*

billow [*v*] *surge*
balloon, belly, bloat, bounce, bulge, ebb and flow, heave, pitch, puff up, ripple, rise and fall, rise up, rock, roll, swell, toss, undulate, wave; SEE CONCEPTS *159,208*

billowy [*adj*] *surging*
bouncing, bouncy, bulgy, distended, ebbing and flowing, heaving, puffy, rippled, rippling, rising, rising and falling, rolling, swelling, swirling, swollen, undulating, waving, wavy; SEE CONCEPTS *486,584*

bind [*n*] *predicament*
between a rock and a hard place*, crunch*, difficulty, dilemma, hot water*, no-win situation*,

nuisance, pickle*, predicament, quandary, sticky situation*, tight situation, tight spot*; SEE CONCEPTS *230,674*

bind [*v1*] *fasten, secure*
adhere, attach, bandage, border, chain, cinch, clamp, connect, constrict, cover, dress, edge, encase, enchain, enfetter, fetter, finish, fix, fold, furl, glue, hamper, handcuff, hem, hitch, hitch on, hobble, hook on, hook up, lace, lap, lash, leash, manacle, moor, muzzle, paste, peg down, pin, pin down, pinion, put together, restrain, restrict, rope, shackle, stick, strap, swathe, tack on, tether, tie, tie up, trammel, trim, truss, unite, wrap, yoke; SEE CONCEPTS *85,160*

bind [*v2*] *obligate; restrict*
compel, confine, constrain, detain, engage, enslave, force, hamper, hinder, hogtie*, indenture, lock up, necessitate, oblige, prescribe, put half nelson on*, put lock on*, require, restrain, restrict, yoke; SEE CONCEPTS *14,130*

binding [*n*] *cover; something which fastens*
adhesive, belt, fastener, jacket, tie, wrapper; SEE CONCEPT *475*

binding [*adj1*] *necessary*
bounden*, compulsory, conclusive, counted upon, essential, imperative, incumbent on, indissoluble, irrevocable, mandatory, obligatory, required, requisite, unalterable; SEE CONCEPT *546*

binding [*adj2*] *confining*
attached, enslaved, fastened, indentured, limiting, restraining, tied, tying; SEE CONCEPT *554*

binge [*n*] *spree*
affair, bender, blind*, bout*, carousal, compotation, drunk*, fling, jag*, orgy*, toot*; SEE CONCEPT *386*

biography [*n*] *account of person's life*
adventures, autobiography, bio, biog, close-up, confessions, diary, experiences, journal, letters, life, life history, life story, memoir, personal account, personal anecdote, personal narrative, personal record, picture, profile, résumé, saga, sketch, vita; SEE CONCEPTS *280,282*

bird [*n*] *flying animal*
feathered creature, fowl, game; SEE CONCEPT *395*

birth [*n1*] *becoming alive*
act of God, bearing, beginning, birthing, blessed event*, childbearing, childbirth, creation, delivery, labor, nascency, natality, nativity, parturition, producing, travail, visit from stork*; SEE CONCEPTS *302,373*

birth [*n2*] *beginning*
commencement, dawn, dawning, emergence, fountainhead, genesis, onset, opening, origin, outset, rise, source, start; SEE CONCEPT *119*

birth [*n3*] *heritage*
ancestry, background, blood, breeding, derivation, descent, extraction, forebears, genealogy, heritage, legacy, line, lineage, parentage, pedigree, position, race, rank, station, status, stock, strain; SEE CONCEPTS *296,648*

birth control [*n*] *method of preventing pregnancy*
abstinence, condom, contraception, contraceptive, diaphragm, IUD, pill, planned parenthood, rhythm method, rubber, safety*, tied tubes, vasectomy; SEE CONCEPTS *121,375*

bisect [*v*] *divide in two*
bifurcate, branch off, cleave, cross, cut across, cut in half, cut in two, dichotomize, dimidiate, divaricate, divide in two, fork, furcate, halve, he-

**be
bi**

misect, intersect, separate, split, split down the middle; SEE CONCEPTS 98,137,176

bisexual [adj] *having relations with either gender*
AC-DC*, androgynous, bi*, epicene, gynandrous, hermaphroditic, intersexual, monoclinous, swings both ways*; SEE CONCEPT 372

bit [n1] *tiny piece*
atom, butt, chicken feed*, chip, chunk, crumb, dab, dash, division, dollop, dose, dot, driblet, droplet, end, excerpt, flake, fraction, fragment, grain, iota, item, jot, lick*, lump, mite, modicum, moiety, molecule, morsel, niggle, parcel, part, particle, peanuts*, pinch, portion, sample, scale, scintilla, scrap, section, segment, shard, share, shaving, shred, slice, sliver, smidgen, snatch, snip, snippet, specimen, speck, splinter, sprinkling, stub, stump, taste, tittle, trace, trickle; SEE CONCEPTS 831,835

bit [n2] *short period of time*
instant, jiffy, little while, minute, moment, second, space, spell, stretch, tick, while; SEE CONCEPT 807

bite [n1] *injury from gripping, tearing*
chaw*, chomp*, gob*, itch*, laceration, nip, pain, pinch, prick, smarting, sting, tooth marks*, wound; SEE CONCEPT 309

bite [n2] *mouthful of food*
brunch, drop, light meal, morsel, nibble, nosh*, piece, refreshment, sample, snack, sop*, taste; SEE CONCEPTS 457,459

bite [n3] *pungency; stinging sensation*
burn, edge, guts*, kick, piquancy, punch, spice, sting, zap*, zip*; SEE CONCEPT 614

bite [n4] *allotment*
allowance, cut, lot, part, piece, portion, quota, share, slice; SEE CONCEPT 835

bite [v1] *grip or tear with teeth*
champ, chaw, chaw on, chew, chomp, clamp, crunch, crush, cut, eat, gnaw, hold, lacerate, masticate, munch, nibble, nip, pierce, pinch, rend, ruminate, seize, sever, snap, take a chunk out of*, taste, tooth, wound; SEE CONCEPTS 185,616

bite [v2] *corrode, eat away*
burn, consume, decay, decompose, deteriorate, dissolve, eat into, engrave, erode, etch, oxidize, rot, rust, scour, sear, slash, smart, sting, tingle, wear away; SEE CONCEPTS 215,250

bite [v3] *take a chance*
be victim, get hooked*, nibble, risk, volunteer; SEE CONCEPT 384

biting [adj1] *piercing, sharp*
bitter, bleak, blighting, cold, crisp, cutting, freezing, harsh, nipping, penetrating, raw; SEE CONCEPTS 569,605

biting [adj2] *sarcastic*
acerbic, acrimonious, bitter, caustic, cutting, incisive, mordant, scathing, severe, sharp, stinging, trenchant, withering; SEE CONCEPT 267

bitter [adj1] *pungent, sharp*
absinthal, absinthian, acerb, acerbic, acid, acrid, amaroidal, astringent, harsh, sour, tart, unsweetened, vinegary; SEE CONCEPT 613

bitter [adj2] *hostile, nasty*
acrimonious, alienated, antagonistic, begrudging, biting, caustic, crabby, divided, embittered, estranged, fierce, freezing, hateful, intense, irreconcilable, morose, rancorous, resentful, sardonic, severe, sore, sour, stinging, sullen, virulent, vitriolic, with chip on shoulder*; SEE CONCEPTS 267,404

bitter [adj3] *painful, distressing*
afflictive, annoying, bad, brutal, calamitous, cruel, dire, disagreeable, displeasing, distasteful, disturbing, galling, grievous, hard, harsh, heartbreaking, hurtful, inclement, intemperate, intense, merciless, offensive, poignant, provoking, rigorous, rugged, ruthless, savage, severe, sharp, stinging, unpalatable, unpleasant, vexatious, woeful; SEE CONCEPT 537

bitterness [n1] *sourness*
acerbity, acidity, acridity, astringency, brackishness, brininess, piquancy, pungency, sharpness, tartness, vinegariness; SEE CONCEPT 614

bitterness [n2] *agony*
acrimoniousness, anguish, asperity, distress, grievousness, harshness, hostility, mordancy, pain, painfulness, sarcasm, venom, virulence; SEE CONCEPTS 410,633

bizarre [adj] *strange, wild*
bugged out*, camp*, comical, curious, eccentric, extraordinary, fantastic, far-out*, freakish, grody*, grotesque, kooky, ludicrous, odd, oddball, offbeat, off the wall*, outlandish, outré, peculiar, queer, ridiculous, singular, unusual, way-out*, weird; SEE CONCEPTS 547,564

blab [v] *gossip*
babble, betray, blather, blurt out, chatter, disclose, divulge, gab, gabble, give away, go on, jabber, let out, let slip, mouth, peach*, prattle, reveal, run off at the mouth*, run on, shoot the breeze*, spill*, spill the beans*, squeal*, talk through one's hat*, tattle, tell, tell on, yak*, yakkety-yak*; SEE CONCEPTS 55,60

black [n] *African-American*
African, Afro-American, Negro.

black [adj1] *dark, inky*
atramentous, brunet, charcoal, clouded, coal, dingy, dusky, ebon, ebony, inklike, jet, livid, melanoid, murky, obsidian, onyx, piceous, pitch, pitch-dark, raven, sable, shadowy, slate, sloe, somber, sombre, sooty, starless, stygian, swart, swarthy; SEE CONCEPT 618

black [adj2] *hopeless*
atrocious, bleak, depressing, depressive, dismal, dispiriting, distressing, doleful, dreary, foreboding, funereal, gloomy, horrible, lugubrious, mournful, ominous, oppressive, sad, sinister, sombre, threatening; SEE CONCEPTS 529,570

black [adj3] *dirty*
dingy, filthy, foul, grimy, grubby, impure, nasty, soiled, sooty, spotted, squalid, stained, unclean, uncleanly; SEE CONCEPT 589

black [adj4] *angry*
enraged, fierce, furious, hostile, menacing, resentful, sour, sullen, threatening; SEE CONCEPT 403

black [adj5] *evil*
bad, diabolical, iniquitous, mean, nefarious, villainous, wicked; SEE CONCEPT 545

blacken [v1] *darken*
befoul, begrime, blot, cloud, deepen, ebonize, grow dark, grow dim, ink, make dark, shade, smudge, soil; SEE CONCEPT 250

blacken [v2] *malign; smear*
asperse, attack, bad-mouth*, blot, blotch, calumniate, decry, defame, defile, denigrate, dishonor, do a number on*, give a black eye*, knock*, libel, malign, rip*, rip up and down*, slander, slur, smudge, stain, sully, taint, tarnish, traduce, vilify; SEE CONCEPT 54

bi
bl

blacklist [v] *ban*

banish, bar, blackball, boycott, debar, exclude, expel, hit list*, ostracize, preclude, proscribe, put on hit list*, reject, repudiate, snub, thumbs down*, vote against; SEE CONCEPT 25

black magic [n] *sorcery*

diabolism, magic, necromancy, voodoo, witchcraft, wizardry; SEE CONCEPTS 370,689

blackmail [n] *intimidation for money; money to quiet informer*

bribe, bribery, exaction, extortion, hush money*, milking*, payoff, protection, ransom, slush fund*, tribute; SEE CONCEPTS 123,192

blackmail [v] *intimidating for money*

badger, bleed, coerce, compel, demand, exact, extort, force, hold to ransom, milk*, put the shake on*, ransom, shake*, shake down*, squeeze*, threaten; SEE CONCEPTS 192,342

black out [v] *delete; cover*

batten, conceal, cover up, cross out, cut off, darken, eclipse, eradicate, erase, hold back, make dark, obfuscate, rub out, shade, squash, squelch; SEE CONCEPT 250

black out [v2] *faint*

collapse, crap out*, draw a blank*, go out like a light*, lose consciousness, pass out*, slip into coma, swoon*, zone out*; SEE CONCEPT 303

blade [n] *cutting tool*

brand, cutlass, edge, épée, knife, shank, sword; SEE CONCEPTS 495,499

blah [adj] *dull, lifeless*

banausic, bland, boring, dim, dreary, humdrum, monotone, monotonous, pedestrian, plodding, yawn producing*; SEE CONCEPT 544

blame [n1] *condemnation*

accusation, animadversion, arraignment, attack, attribution, castigation, censure, charge, chiding, complaint, criticism, denunciation, depreciation, diatribe, disapprobation, disapproval, disfavor, disparagement, expostulation, exprobation, impeachment, implication, imputation, incrimination, inculpation, indictment, invective, objurgation, obloquy, opposition, rebuke, recrimination, remonstrance, reprehension, reprimand, reproach, reprobation, reproof, repudiation, slur, tirade; SEE CONCEPT 54

blame [n2] *responsibility*

accountability, answerability, burden, culpability, fault, guilt, incrimination, liability, onus, rap*; SEE CONCEPTS 639,661

blame [v] *accuse; place responsibility*

admonish, ascribe, attribute, blast, blow the whistle on*, censure, charge, chide, climb all over*, condemn, criticize, denounce, denunciate, disapprove, express disapprobation, find fault with, finger*, frame, hold responsible, impute, indict, jump all over*, jump down one's throat*, knock*, lay a bad trip on*, lay at one's door*, lay to*, let one have it*, lower the boom*, pass the buck*, point the finger*, rap, rebuke, reprehend, reproach, reprove, roast*, saddle, skin*, stick it to*, tax, upbraid; SEE CONCEPT 44

blameless [adj] *not responsible*

above suspicion, clean, clean-handed, clear, crimeless, exemplary, faultless, good, guilt-free, guiltless, immaculate, impeccable, inculpable, innocent, in the clear*, irreprehensible, irreproachable, not guilty, perfect, pure, righteous, stainless, unblemished, unimpeachable, unoffending, un-

spotted, unsullied, untarnished, upright, virtuous; SEE CONCEPT 25

blanch [v] *become afraid*

flinch, pale, recoil, shrink, start, wince; SEE CONCEPT 27

bland [adj1] *tasteless; undistinctive*

banal, blah*, boring, dull, dull as dishwater*, flat, flavorless, ho hum*, humdrum, insipid, milk-and-water*, monotonous, nerdy*, nothing, pabulum*, sapless, tame, tedious, unexciting, uninspiring, uninteresting, unstimulating, vanilla*, vapid, waterish, watery, weak, wimpy*, wishy-washy*, zero*; SEE CONCEPTS 589,613

bland [adj2] *friendly, gracious*

affable, amiable, civilized, congenial, courteous, gentle, good-natured, ingratiating, oily, pleasant, smooth, suave, unctuous, unemotional, urbane; SEE CONCEPT 401

bland [adj3] *mild, temperate*

balmy, calm, calmative, clear, lenient, mollifying, nonirritant, nonirritating, smooth, soft, soothing; SEE CONCEPTS 485,605

blank [n] *empty space*

abyss, cavity, chasm, emptiness, gap, gulf, hiatus, hole, hollow, hollowness, interstice, interval, lacuna, nihility, nothingness, nullity, omission, opening, preterition, pretermission, skip, tabula rasa, vacancy, vacuity, vacuum, void, womb; SEE CONCEPT 513

blank [adj1] *clear*

bare, barren, clean, empty, fresh, new, pale, plain, spotless, uncompleted, unfilled, unmarked, untouched, unused, vacant, vacuous, virgin, virginal, void, white; SEE CONCEPTS 485,562

blank [adj2] *expressionless*

deadpan, dull, empty, fruitless, hollow, immobile, impassive, inane, inexpressive, inscrutable, lifeless, masklike, meaningless, noncommittal, poker-faced, stiff, stupid, uncommunicative, unexpressive, vacant, vacuous, vague; SEE CONCEPT 406

blank [adj3] *dumbfounded*

at a loss, awestruck, bewildered, confounded, confused, dazed, disconcerted, muddled, nonplussed, stupefied, uncomprehending, wonderstruck; SEE CONCEPT 402

blank [adj4] *absolute, utter*

complete, downright, out-and-out, outright, perfect, regular, sheer, straight-out, thorough, total, unconditional, unqualified; SEE CONCEPT 531

blanket [n] *cover, covering*

afghan, carpet, cloak, coat, coating, comforter, covering, coverlet, envelope, film, fleece, layer, mat, puff, quilt, rug, sheath, sheet, throw, wrapper; SEE CONCEPTS 473,475

blanket [adj] *comprehensive*

absolute, across-the-board, all-inclusive, overall, powerful, sweeping, unconditional, wide-ranging; SEE CONCEPT 772

blanket [v] *cover*

bury, cloak, cloud, coat, conceal, crown, eclipse, envelop, hide, mask, obscure, overcast, overlay, overspread, suppress, surround; SEE CONCEPT 172

blare [v] *make loud noise*

bark, bellow, blast, boom, bray, clamor, clang, honk, hoot, peal, resound, roar, scream, shout, shriek, sound out, toot, trumpet; SEE CONCEPTS 65,77

blarney [n] *flattery*

adulation, a line*, baloney*, blandishment, cajolery, coaxing, compliments, exaggeration, eyewash*, fawning*, honey*, incense, ingratiation, inveiglement, oil*, overpraise, soft soap*, soft words, sweet talk*, wheedling; SEE CONCEPT 69

blasé [adj] *nonchalant*

apathetic, been around twice*, bored, cloyed, cool*, disenchanted, disentranced, done it all*, fed up*, glutted, indifferent, jaded, knowing, laid-back*, lukewarm*, mellow*, mundane, offhand, satiated, sick of, sophisticate, sophisticated, surfeited, unconcerned, unexcited, uninterested, unmoved, weary, worldly, world-weary; SEE CONCEPT 404

blasphemous [adj] *irreverent*

cursing, disrespectful, godless, impious, insulting, irreligious, profanatory, profane, sacrilegious, swearing, ungodly; SEE CONCEPT 545

blasphemy [n] *irreverence*

abuse, cursing, cussing, desecration, execration, heresy, impiety, impiousness, imprecation, indignity, lewdness, profanation, profaneness, profanity, reviling, sacrilege, scoffing, scurrility, swearing, vituperation; SEE CONCEPT 645

blast [n1/v1] *loud sound; make loud sound*

bang, blare, blow, burst, clang, clap, crack, din, honk, peal, roar, scream, slam, smash, toot, trumpet, wail, wham; SEE CONCEPTS 65,521,595

blast [n2] *explosion*

bang, blow-up, burst, crash, detonation, discharge, dynamite, eruption, outbreak, outburst, salvo, volley; SEE CONCEPTS 179,521

blast [n3] *gust of wind*

blow, draft, gale, squall, storm, strong breeze, tempest; SEE CONCEPTS 437,524

blast [n4] *fun time*

amusement, bash*, blow out*, excitement, good time, great time, party, riot*; SEE CONCEPT 386

blast [v2] *explode*

annihilate, blight, blow up, bomb, break up, burst, damage, dash, demolish, destroy, detonate, dynamite, injure, kill, ruin, shatter, shrivel, spoil, stunt, torpedo, wither, wreck; SEE CONCEPTS 86,179

blast [v3] *lambaste; defeat mentally*

attack, beat, castigate, clobber*, criticize, drub*, flay, lash out at, lick*, rail at, shellac*, whip*; SEE CONCEPT 52

blatant [adj1] *obvious; brazen*

arrant, bald, barefaced, brassy, clear, conspicuous, crying, flagrant, flashy, flaunting, garish, gaudy, glaring, glitzy, impudent, loud, meretricious, naked, obtrusive, ostentatious, outright, overbold, overt, plain, prominent, pronounced, protrusive, screaming, shameless, sheer, showy, snazzy, unabashed, unblushing, unmitigated; SEE CONCEPTS 540,569

blatant [adj2] *deafening*

boisterous, clamorous, crying, ear-splitting, harsh, loud, loudmouthed, noisy, obstreperous, obtrusive, piercing, screaming, scurrilous, strident, vociferant, vociferous, vulgar; SEE CONCEPTS 592,594

blaze [n1] *fire*

bonfire, burning, combustion, conflagration, flame, flames, holocaust, wildfire; SEE CONCEPTS 478,521

blaze [n2] *flash of light*

beam, brilliance, burst, flare, glare, gleam, glitter, glow, radiance; SEE CONCEPT 628

blaze [n3] *torrent*

blast, burst, eruption, flare-up, flash, fury, outbreak, outburst, rush, storm; SEE CONCEPT 673

blaze [v] *burn brightly*

beam, burst out, coruscate, explode, fire, flame, flare, flash, flicker, fulgurate, glare, gleam, glow, illuminate, illumine, incandesce, jet, light, radiate, scintillate, shimmer, shine, sparkle; SEE CONCEPT 249

bleach [v] *whiten*

achromatize, blanch, blench, decolor, decolorize, etiolate, fade, grow pale, lighten, make pale, peroxide, wash out; SEE CONCEPT 250

bleachers [n] *seating for watching event*

benches, boxes, grandstand, Ruthville*, seats, stands; SEE CONCEPTS 440,443

bleak [adj1] *barren*

austere, bare, blank, blighted, bombed, bulldozed, burned, chilly, cleared, cold, deforested, desert, deserted, desolate, dreary, exposed, flat, gaunt, grim, open, raw, scorched, stripped, unpopulated, unsheltered, weather-beaten, wild, windswept; SEE CONCEPT 490

bleak [adj2] *depressing*

black, cheerless, comfortless, dark, discouraging, disheartening, dismal, drear, dreary, funereal, gloomy, grim, hard, harsh, hopeless, joyless, lonely, melancholy, mournful, oppressive, sad, somber, unpromising; SEE CONCEPTS 403,537

bleed [v1] *cause blood to flow*

drain, exude, gush, hemorrhage, leech, ooze, open vein, phlebotomize, run, seep, shed, spurt, trickle, weep; SEE CONCEPT 185

bleed [v2] *extort*

blackmail, confiscate, deplete, drain, exhaust, extract, fleece, impoverish, leech*, milk*, mulct, overcharge, pauperize, put the screws to*, rook*, sap*, skin*, squeeze*, steal, stick*, strong-arm; SEE CONCEPTS 192,342

bleed [v3] *grieve*

ache, agonize, be in pain, feel for, pity, suffer, sympathize; SEE CONCEPTS 12,17

blemish [n] *flaw*

beauty spot, birthmark, blackhead, blister, bloom*, blot, blotch, blot on the landscape*, blur, brand, bruise, bug*, catch, chip, cicatrix, defacement, defect, deformity, dent, discoloration, disfigurement, disgrace, dishonor, eyesore, fault, freckle, hickey*, imperfection, impurity, lentigo, lump, macula, maculation, mark, mole, nevus, nodule, patch, pimple, pock, pockmark, scar, second, sight, smudge, snag, speck, speckle, spot, stain, stigma, taint, tarnish, vice, wart, whitehead, zit*; SEE CONCEPT 580

blemish [v] *flaw, disfigure*

blot, blotch, blur, damage, deface, distort, harm, hurt, impair, injure, maim, mangle, mar, mark, mutilate, pervert, prejudice, scar, smudge, spoil, spot, stain, sully, taint, tarnish, twist, vitiate, wrench; SEE CONCEPTS 54,246

blend [n] *composite, mix*

alloy, amalgam, amalgamation, brew, combination, commixture, composite, compound, concoction, fusion, interfusion, intermixture, mixture, synthesis, union; SEE CONCEPT 432

blend [v1] *mix*

amalgamate, cement, coalesce, combine, com-

bl
bl

mingle, commix, compound, fuse, integrate, interblend, intermix, meld, merge, mingle, synthesize, unite, weld; SEE CONCEPT **109**

blend [v2] *harmonize*
arrange, complement, fit, go well, go with, integrate, orchestrate, suit, symphonize, synthesize, unify; SEE CONCEPT **656**

bless [v1] *sanctify*
absolve, anoint, baptize, beatify, canonize, commend, confirm, consecrate, cross, dedicate, enshrine, eulogize, exalt, extol, give thanks to, glorify, hallow, honor, invoke benefits, invoke happiness, laud, magnify, make holy, offer, offer benediction, ordain, panegyrize, praise, pray for, pronounce holy, sacrifice, sign, sprinkle, thank; SEE CONCEPTS **69,367**

bless [v2] *grant, bestow*
celebrate, endow, favor, give, glorify, grace, laud, magnify, praise, provide; SEE CONCEPTS **50,88**

blessed [adj1] *sanctified*
adored, among the angels, beatified, consecrated, divine, enthroned, exalted, glorified, hallowed, holy, inviolable, redeemed, resurrected, revered, rewarded, sacred, sacrosanct, saved, spiritual, unprofane; SEE CONCEPTS **536,568**

blessed [adj2] *happy*
blissful, content, contented, endowed, favored, fortunate, glad, granted, joyful, joyous, lucky; SEE CONCEPT **404**

blessing [n1] *sanctification*
absolution, benediction, benedicite, benison, commendation, consecration, dedication, divine sanction, grace, invocation, laying on of hands, thanks, thanksgiving; SEE CONCEPT **367**

blessing [n2] *good wishes, approval*
approbation, backing, concurrence, consent, favor, Godspeed, leave, okay*, permission, regard, sanction, support, valediction; SEE CONCEPTS **10,50,88**

blessing [n3] *advantage*
asset, benediction, benefit, boon, bounty, break, favor, gain, gift, godsend, good, good fortune, good luck, help, kindness, lucky break, manna from heaven*, miracle, profit, service, stroke of luck*, windfall; SEE CONCEPTS **230,679**

blight [n] *disease; plague*
affliction, bane, blot on the landscape*, canker, contamination, corruption, curse, decay, dump, evil, eyesore, fungus, infestation, mildew, pest, pestilence, pollution, rot, scourge, sight, withering, woe; SEE CONCEPTS **306,674**

blight [v] *ruin, destroy*
annihilate, blast, crush, damage, dash, decay, disappoint, foul up*, frustrate, glitch up*, injure, mar, mess up*, nip in the bud*, nullify, shrivel, spoil, taint, trash*, wither, wreck; SEE CONCEPT **252**

blind [n] *screen, covering*
blinder, blindfold, blinker, camouflage, cloak, cover, curtain, facade, front, mask, trap, veil; SEE CONCEPT **716**

blind [adj1] *sightless*
amaurotic, blind as a bat*, dark, destitute of vision, eyeless, groping, in darkness, purblind, typhlotic, undiscerning, unseeing, unsighted, visionless; SEE CONCEPT **619**

blind [adj2] *indifferent*
careless, heedless, ignorant, imperceptive, inattentive, inconsiderate, indiscriminate, injudicious,

insensitive, myopic, nearsighted, neglectful, oblivious, thoughtless, unaware, unconscious, undiscerning, unmindful, unobservant, unperceiving, unreasoning, unseeing; SEE CONCEPT **402**

blind [adj3] *uncontrolled*
hasty, heedless, impetuous, inconsiderate, irrational, mindless, rash, reckless, senseless, shortsighted, thoughtless, unseeing, unthinking, violent, wild; SEE CONCEPT **544**

blind [adj4] *hidden or covered*
blocked, closed, closed at one end, concealed, dark, dead-end, dim, disguised, impassable, leading nowhere, obscured, obstructed, secluded, unmarked, without egress, without exit; SEE CONCEPTS **490,576**

blindly [adv1] *without direction, purpose*
aimlessly, at random, confusedly, frantically, in all directions, indiscriminately, instinctively, madly, pell-mell, purposelessly, wildly; SEE CONCEPT **542**

blindly [adv2] *carelessly*
foolishly, heedlessly, impulsively, inconsiderately, obtusely, passionately, purblindly, recklessly, regardlessly, senselessly, thoughtlessly, tumultuously, unreasonably, unreasoningly, willfully, without rhyme or reason*; SEE CONCEPT **401**

blindness [n] *sightlessness*
amaurosis, anopsia, astigmatism, cataracts, darkness, defect, myopia, presbyopia, purblindness, typhlosis; SEE CONCEPT **629**

blink [v1] *wink of eye; twinkle*
bat, flash, flicker, flutter, glimmer, glitter, nictate, nictitate, scintillate, shimmer, sparkle, squint; SEE CONCEPTS **185,624**

blink [v2] *ignore*
bypass, condone, connive, cushion, discount, disregard, fail, forget, neglect, omit, overlook, overpass, pass by, slight, turn a blind eye*; SEE CONCEPT **30**

bliss [n] *ecstasy*
beatitude, blessedness, cool*, euphoria, felicity, gladness, gone*, happiness, heaven*, joy, paradise, rapture; SEE CONCEPTS **32,230**

blissful [adj] *happy*
beatific, cool*, crazy, delighted, dreamy, ecstatic, elated, enchanted, enraptured, euphoric, floating*, flying*, gone*, heavenly, in ecstasy, in seventh heaven*, in the twilight zone*, joyful, joyous, mad*, on cloud nine*, rapturous, sent*, spaced-out*, turned-on*; SEE CONCEPT **403**

blister [n] *swelling*
abscess, blain, bleb, boil, bubble, bulla, burn, canker, carbuncle, cyst, furuncle, pimple, pustule, sac, sore, ulcer, vesication, vesicle, wale, weal, welt, wheal; SEE CONCEPT **309**

blithe [adj] *happy*
animated, buoyant, carefree, cheerful, cheery, chirpy, gay, gladsome, gleeful, jaunty, jocund, jolly, jovial, joyful, lighthearted, merry, mirthful, sprightly, sunny, vivacious; SEE CONCEPT **404**

blitz [n] *heavy attack*
assault, blitzkrieg, bombardment, bombing, lightning attack, offensive, onslaught, raid, shelling, strike; SEE CONCEPTS **86,320**

blizzard [n] *snow storm*
blast, gale, precipitation, snowfall, squall, tempest, whiteout; SEE CONCEPT **526**

bloat [v] *blow up like a balloon*
balloon, belly, bilge, billow, dilate, distend, en-

large, expand, inflate, puff up, swell; SEE CONCEPTS *184,208*

block [n1] *mass of material*
bar, brick, cake, chunk, cube, hunk, ingot, loaf, lump, oblong, piece, section, segment, slab, slice, solid, square; SEE CONCEPTS *470,471*

block [n2] *obstruction*
bar, barrier, blank wall, blockage, chunk, clog, hindrance, impediment, jam, mass, obstacle, obstruction, roadblock, snag, stop, stoppage, wall; SEE CONCEPTS *470,652*

block [v] *obstruct*
arrest, bar, barricade, blockade, block out, brake, catch, charge, check, choke, clog, close, close off, close out, congest, cut off, dam, deter, fill, halt, hang up*, hinder, hold up, impede, intercept, interfere with, occlude, plug, prevent, shut off*, shut out, stall, stonewall, stop, stopper, stop up*, stymie, tackle, take out of play*, thwart; SEE CONCEPTS *121,130*

blockade [n] *barrier*
bar, barricade, blank wall, clog, closure, embolus, encirclement, hindrance, impediment, infarct, infarction, obstacle, obstruction, restriction, roadblock, siege, snag, stop, stoppage, wall; SEE CONCEPTS *470,652*

block out [v1] *plan course*
arrange, chart, map out, outline, prepare, sketch; SEE CONCEPT *36*

block out [v2] *try to forget*
close, conceal, cover, hide, obscure, obstruct, screen, shroud, shut off, shut out; SEE CONCEPT *40*

blond/blonde [adj] *having light-colored hair*
albino, auricomous, bleached, champagne, fair, fair-haired, flaxen, golden-haired, light, pale, pearly, platinum, sallow, sandy-haired, snowy, straw, strawberry, towheaded*, washed-out, yellow-haired; SEE CONCEPT *618*

blood [n1] *red body fluid*
claret, clot, cruor, gore, hemoglobin, juice, plasma, sanguine fluid, vital fluid; SEE CONCEPTS *393,420*

blood [n2] *ancestry*
birth, consanguinity, descendants, descent, extraction, family, kindred, kinship, line, lineage, origin, pedigree, relations, stock; SEE CONCEPT *296*

bloodless [adj1] *unfeeling*
anesthetic, cold, coldhearted, dull, impassive, indolent, insensible, insensitive, languid, lazy, lifeless, listless, passionless, slow, sluggish, spiritless, torpid, unemotional, unkind; SEE CONCEPT *404*

bloodless [adj2] *pale*
anemic, ashen, cadaverous, chalky, colorless, ghostly, lifeless, pallid, pasty, sallow, sickly, wan, watery; SEE CONCEPT *618*

bloody [adj1] *bleeding*
blood-soaked, blood-spattered, bloodstained, crimson, ensanguined, gaping, gory, grisly, hematic, hemic, imbrued, open, raw, sanguinary, sanguine, unstanched, unstopped, wounded; SEE CONCEPT *485*

bloody [adj2] *hard-fought*
bloodthirsty, cruel, cutthroat, decimating, ferocious, fierce, gory, grim, heavy, homicidal, murderous, sanguinary, sanguine, savage, slaughterous; SEE CONCEPTS *540,569*

bloom [n] *flower*
blossom, blossoming, bud, efflorescence, floret, flourishing, flower, floweret, opening; SEE CONCEPT *425*

bloom [v] *flower; flourish*
bear fruit, be in flower, blossom, blow, bud, burgeon, burst, develop, effloresce, fare well, fructify, germinate, grow, open, prosper, sprout, succeed, tassel out, thrive, wax; SEE CONCEPTS *427,706*

blooper [n] *blunder*
boner*, boo-boo*, bungle, error, faux pas, fluff*, gaffe, impropriety, indecorum, lapse, mistake, slip, solecism, trip*; SEE CONCEPTS *384,674*

blossom [n] *flower*
bloom, bud, efflorescence, floret, floweret, inflorescence, posy, spike; SEE CONCEPT *425*

blossom [v1] *flower*
bloom, blow, burgeon, burst, effloresce, leaf, open, outbloom, shoot, unfold; SEE CONCEPT *427*

blossom [v2] *flourish*
batten, bloom, develop, grow, mature, progress, prosper, succeed, thrive; SEE CONCEPT *706*

blot [n] *mark; flaw*
black eye*, blemish, blotch, blur, brand, defect, discoloration, disgrace, fault, odium, onus, patch, slur, smear, smudge, speck, spot, stain, stigma, taint; SEE CONCEPTS *230,580*

blot [v1] *disgrace, disfigure*
bespatter, blemish, dirty, discolor, mark, smudge, smut, soil, spoil, spot, stain, sully, tarnish; SEE CONCEPT *240*

blot [v2] *soak up*
absorb, dry, take up; SEE CONCEPT *211*

blotch [n] *smudge*
acne, blemish, blot, breakout, eruption, mark, mottling, patch, splash, spot, stain, stigma; SEE CONCEPT *580*

blouse [n] *shirt for woman*
bodice, bodysuit, middy, pullover, shell, slipover, T-shirt, turtleneck, V-neck; SEE CONCEPT *451*

blow [n1] *blast, rush of air, wind*
draft, flurry, gale, gust, hurricane, puff, squall, strong breeze, tempest, typhoon; SEE CONCEPT *526*

blow [n2] *hard hit*
bang, bash, bat, belt, biff, blindside, bop*, buffet, bump, clip, clout, clump, collision, concussion, crack, cut, ding*, impact, jab, jar, jolt, kick, knock, knockout, knuckle sandwich*, KO*, lick, percussion, poke, pound, punch, rap, shock, slam, slap, slug, smack, smash, sock, strike, stroke, swat, swing, swipe, thrust, thump, thwack*, uppercut, wallop, whack, whomp*, zap*; SEE CONCEPT *189*

blow [n3] *catastrophe*
affliction, balk, bolt from the blue*, bombshell*, calamity, casualty, chagrin, comedown, debacle, disappointment, disaster, disgruntlement, frustration, jolt, letdown, misadventure, misfortune, mishap, reverse, setback, shock, tragedy, upset; SEE CONCEPT *674*

blow [v1] *blast, rush of air, wind*
breathe, buffet, drive, exhale, fan, flap, flow, flutter, gasp, heave, huff, inflate, pant, puff, pump, ruffle, rush, stream, swell, swirl, waft, wave, whiff, whirl, whisk, whisper, whistle; SEE CONCEPTS *185,526*

blow [v2] *make sound, usually with instrument*
blare, blast, honk, mouth, pipe, play, sound, toot, trumpet, vibrate; SEE CONCEPT 65

blow [v3] *leave suddenly*
depart, go, hit the road*, split*, take a hike*, take a powder*; SEE CONCEPT 195

blow [v4] *ruin chance*
fail, flounder, goof*, miscarry, miss; SEE CONCEPT 699

blow [v5] *use up money*
dissipate, lay out, pay out, spend, squander, waste; SEE CONCEPT 341

blowout [n1] *explosion; something exploded*
blast, bomb, burst, detonation, eruption, escape, flat tire, leak, puncture, rupture, tear; SEE CONCEPT 179

blowout [n2] *wild party*
bash, binge, feast, riot*, shindig, spree; SEE CONCEPT 383

blow up [v1] *inflate*
billow, bloat, distend, enlarge, expand, fill, inflate, puff up, pump up, swell; SEE CONCEPTS 208,236,245

blow up [v2] *explode*
blast, bomb, burst, detonate, dynamite, erupt, go off, mushroom, rupture, shatter; SEE CONCEPTS 179,320

blow up [v3] *magnify importance*
enlarge, exaggerate, heighten, overstate; SEE CONCEPTS 49,59

blow up [v4] *burst with anger*
become angry, become enraged, erupt, go off the deep end*, hit the roof*, lose control, lose temper, rage, rave; SEE CONCEPTS 29,44

blue [adj1] *sky, sea color*
azure, beryl, cerulean, cobalt, indigo, navy, royal, sapphire, teal, turquoise, ultramarine; SEE CONCEPT 618

blue [adj2] *sad*
dejected, depressed, despondent, disconsolate, dismal, dispirited, downcast, downhearted, down in the dumps*, fed up*, gloomy, glum, low, melancholy, moody, unhappy, woebegone; SEE CONCEPT 403

blue [adj3] *vulgar*
bawdy, dirty, indecent, lewd, naughty, obscene, off-color, racy, risqué, salty, shady, smutty, spicy, suggestive, wicked; SEE CONCEPT 545

blues [n] *depression*
dejection, despondency, doldrums, dumps*, gloom, gloominess, glumness, heavy heart*, low spirits, melancholy, moodiness, mournfulness, sadness, the dismals*, the mopes*, unhappiness; SEE CONCEPT 410

bluff [n1] *boast; deceit*
bluster, braggadocio, bragging, bravado, deception, delusion, facade, fake, false colors, false front, feint, fraud, front, humbug*, jiving*, lie, pretense, pretext, ruse, sham, show, snow*, stall, subterfuge, trick; SEE CONCEPTS 58,59

bluff [n2] *precipice*
bank, cliff, crag, escarpment, headland, hill, mountain, peak, promontory, ridge, rock; SEE CONCEPT 509

bluff [adj] *abrupt*
barefaced, bearish, blunt, blustering, breviloquent, brief, brusque, candid, crusty, curt, direct, downright, forthright, frank, gruff, hearty, honest, laconic, no-nonsense, open, outspoken, plain-spoken, rough, rude, short, short-spoken, sincere,

snippety, snippy, straightforward, tactless, tart, terse, unceremonious; SEE CONCEPT 267

bluff [v] *deceive*
affect, beguile, betray, bunco*, con, counterfeit, defraud, delude, double-cross, fake*, fake out*, feign, fool, humbug*, illude, jive*, juggle, lie, mislead, pretend, psych out*, put on*, sham*, shuck*, simulate, snow*, take in*, trick; SEE CONCEPTS 58,59

blunder [n] *mistake*
blooper*, boner*, boo-boo*, bungle, dumb move*, dumb thing to do*, error, fault, faux pas, flub*, flub-up*, fluff*, gaffe, goof*, howler*, impropriety, inaccuracy, indiscretion, lapse, muff*, oversight, slip, slip-up, solecism, trip*; SEE CONCEPTS 101,230

blunder [v] *make mistake*
ball up*, blow, bobble, botch, bumble, bungle, confuse, drop the ball*, err, flounder, flub*, foul up, fumble, gum up*, louse up, mess up, misjudge, screw up*, slip up, stumble; SEE CONCEPT 101

blunt [adj1] *not sharp*
dull, dulled, edgeless, insensitive, obtuse, pointless, round, rounded, unsharpened; SEE CONCEPTS 485,486

blunt [adj2] *straightforward*
abrupt, bluff, brief, brusque, candid, crusty, curt, discourteous, explicit, forthright, frank, gruff, impolite, matter-of-fact, outspoken, plain-spoken, rude, short, snappy, snippy, tactless, trenchant, unceremonious, uncivil, unpolished; SEE CONCEPT 267

blunt [v] *make dull*
attenuate, benumb, cripple, dampen, deaden, debilitate, desensitize, disable, enfeeble, numb, obtund, sap, soften, take the edge off, undermine, water down, weaken; SEE CONCEPT 240

blur [v1] *cloud, fog*
becloud, bedim, befog, blear, blind, darken, daze, dazzle, dim, glare, make hazy, make indistinct, make vague, mask, muddy, obscure, shade, soften; SEE CONCEPT 627

blur [v2] *make dirty*
besmear, blemish, blot, discolor, smear, smudge, spot, stain, taint, tarnish; SEE CONCEPT 254

blush [n] *pink coloring*
bloom, blossom, burning, color, flush, flushing, glow, glowing, mantling, pink tinge, reddening, redness, rosiness, rosy tint, ruddiness, scarlet; SEE CONCEPT 622

blush [v] *become colored, pinken*
color, crimson, flush, glow, have rosy cheeks, mantle, redden, rouge, turn red, turn scarlet; SEE CONCEPT 250

bluster [n] *bullying, intimidation*
bluff, boasting, boisterousness, bombast, braggadocio, bragging, bravado, crowing, rabidity, rampancy, swagger, swaggering; SEE CONCEPT 633

bluster [v] *bully, intimidate*
badger, bluster, brag, brazen, browbeat, bulldoze*, cow*, crow*, domineer, gloat, hector, rant, rave, ride the high horse*, roar, roister, shoot off one's mouth*, show off, storm, strut, swagger, swell, talk big*, vapor*, vaunt, yap*; SEE CONCEPTS 49,78

board [n1] *piece of wood*
lath, panel, plank, slat, strip, timber; SEE CONCEPT 479

board [n2] *meal*
daily bread*, eats*, fare, food, keep*, mess, provisions, victuals; SEE CONCEPT *459*

board [n3] *group of advisers*
advisers, advisory group, brass, cabinet, committee, conclave, council, directorate, directors, execs*, executives, executive suite, front office*,
jury, panel, trustees, upstairs*; SEE CONCEPTS
323,333,417

board [v1] *embark on vehicle*
catch, climb on, embus, emplane, enter, entrain,
get on, hop on, mount; SEE CONCEPTS *159,195*

board [v2] *provide food and sleeping quarters*
accommodate, bed, canton, care for, feed, harbor,
house, let crash*, lodge, put up, quarter, room;
SEE CONCEPT *136*

boast [n] *brag; source of pride*
avowal, bluster, bombast, braggadocio, bravado,
exaggeration, gasconade, grandiloquence, heroics, joy, pretension, pride, pride and joy, self-
satisfaction, swank, treasure, vaunt; SEE
CONCEPTS *410,710*

boast [v1] *brag*
advertise, aggrandize, attract attention, blow,
blow one's own horn*, blow smoke*, bluster,
bully, cock-a-doodle-doo*, con, congratulate oneself, crow, exaggerate, exult, fake, flatter oneself,
flaunt, flourish, gasconade, give a good account of
oneself, gloat, glory, grandstand*, hug oneself*,
jive*, lay on thick*, prate, preen, psych*, puff*,
shoot*, shovel*, showboat*, show off, shuck*,
sling*, sound off, strut, swagger, talk big*, triumph, vapor*; SEE CONCEPT *49*

boast [v2] *to have advantage*
be proud of, claim, exhibit, have in keeping, own,
possess, pride oneself on, show off; SEE CONCEPT
261

boastful [adj] *bragging*
arrogant, big, big-headed, bombastic, cocky, conceited, crowing, egotistic, egotistical, exultant,
full of hot air*, hifalutin*, hot stuff*, know-it-all,
loudmouth, on ego trip*, pompous, pretentious,
puffed-up, self-aggrandizing, self-applauding,
smart-alecky*, snooty, strutting, stuck-up, swaggering, swanky, swollen-headed, too big for one's
britches*, vainglorious, vaunting, windbag*; SEE
CONCEPTS *267,404*

boat [n] *vehicle for water travel*
ark, barge, bark, bateau, bottom, bucket, canoe,
catamaran, craft, dinghy, dory, hulk, ketch,
launch, lifeboat, pinnace, raft, sailboat, schooner,
scow, ship, skiff, sloop, steamboat, tub, yacht;
SEE CONCEPT *506*

boating [n] *travel, recreation in water*
canoeing, cruising, drifting, paddling, rowing,
sailing, sculling, trawling, yachting; SEE CON-
CEPT *363*

bob [v] *bounce up and down*
bow, duck, genuflect, hop, jerk, jounce, leap,
nod, oscillate, quaver, quiver, ricochet, seesaw,
skip, waggle, weave, wobble; SEE CONCEPT *147*

bodily [adj] *concerning animate structure*
actual, animal, carnal, corporal, corporeal,
fleshly, gross, human, material, natural, normal,
organic, physical, sensual, somatic, substantial,
tangible, unspiritual; SEE CONCEPT *406*

bodily [adv] *totally*
absolutely, altogether, as a body, as a group, collectively, completely, en masse, entirely, fully,
wholly; SEE CONCEPTS *531,772*

body [n1] *physique*
anatomy, bag of bones*, beefcake*, bod*,
boody*, build, carcass, chassis, constitution, embodiment, figure, form, frame, makeup, mortal
part, protoplasm, shaft, shape, tenement, torso,
trunk; SEE CONCEPT *405*

body [n2] *corpse*
ashes, bones, cadaver, carcass, carrion, clay, corpus delicti, dead body, deceased, dust, relic, remains, stiff*; SEE CONCEPT *390*

body [n3] *human being*
being, creature, human, individual, mortal, party,
person, personage, soul; SEE CONCEPT *389*

body [n4] *bulk; central portion*
assembly, basis, bed, box, chassis, core, corpus,
crux, essence, frame, fuselage, gist, gravamen,
groundwork, hull, main part, majority, mass, material, matter, pith, skeleton, staple, substance,
substructure, sum, tenor, total, trunk, whole; SEE
CONCEPT *829*

body [n5] *crowd*
array, batch, bunch, bundle, clump, cluster,
group, horde, lot, majority, mass, mob, multitude, parcel, party, set, society, throng; SEE CON-
CEPTS *417,432*

body [n6] *main part of written work*
argument, burden, core, discourse, dissertation,
evidence, exposition, gist, heart, material, meat,
pith, sense, substance, text, thesis, treatise, upshot; SEE CONCEPT *270*

bog [n] *swamp*
fen, lowland, marsh, marshland, mire, morass,
moss, peat, quag, quagmire, slough, sump, wet-
lands; SEE CONCEPT *509*

bog down [v] *stick; become stuck*
decelerate, delay, detain, halt, hang up, impede,
retard, set back, sink, slacken, slow down, slow
up, stall; SEE CONCEPT *121*

bogus [adj] *counterfeit*
artificial, dummy, ersatz, fake, false, fictitious,
forged, fraudulent, imitation, not what it is
cracked up to be*, phony, pretended, pseudo,
sham, simulated, spurious; SEE CONCEPT *582*

boil [n] *blister*
abscess, blain, blister, carbuncle, excrescence, furuncle, pimple, pustule, sore, tumor, ulcer; SEE
CONCEPT *309*

boil [v1] *heat to bubbling*
agitate, bubble, churn, coddle, cook, decoct, effervesce, evaporate, fizz, foam, froth, parboil,
poach, seethe, simmer, smolder, steam, steep,
stew; SEE CONCEPTS *170,255*

boil [v2] *be angry*
be indignant, blow up, bristle, burn, flare, foam at
the mouth*, fulminate, fume, rage, rave, sputter,
storm; SEE CONCEPT *29*

boiling [adj1] *very hot*
baking, blistering, broiling, burning, fiery, hot,
red-hot, roasting, scalding, scorching, sizzling,
torrid, tropical, warm; SEE CONCEPT *605*

boiling [adj2] *angered*
angry, enraged, fuming, furious, incensed, indignant, infuriated, mad, raging; SEE CONCEPT *403*

boisterous [adj] *noisy and mischievous*
bouncy, brawling, clamorous, disorderly, effervescent, impetuous, loud, obstreperous, rambunctious, raucous, riotous, rollicking, rowdy,
strident, tumultuous/tumultous, unrestrained, unruly, uproarious, vociferant, vociferous, wild;
SEE CONCEPT *401*

bold [*adj1*] *brave*
adventurous, assuming, audacious, aweless, bantam, courageous, daring, dauntless, enterprising, fearless, forward, gallant, heroic, intrepid, resolute, unafraid, undaunted, valiant, valorous; SEE CONCEPT *401*

bold [*adj2*] *brazen, insolent*
assuming, audacious, barefaced, brash, brassy, cheeky, coming on strong*, confident, forward, fresh, gritty, gutsy, immodest, impudent, insolent, nervy, pert, presumptuous, rude, sassy, saucy, shameless, smart, smart-alecky*, spunky; SEE CONCEPTS *401,404*

bold [*adj3*] *bright, striking*
clear, colorful, conspicuous, definite, evident, eye-catching, flashy, forceful, lively, loud, manifest, plain, prominent, pronounced, showy, spirited, strong, vivid; SEE CONCEPTS *589,617,618*

bolster [*v*] *help*
aid, assist, bear up, boost, brace, buck up, bulwark, buoy, buttress, carry, cushion, help, hold up, maintain, pick up, pillow, prop, reinforce, shore up, stay, strengthen, support, sustain, uphold; SEE CONCEPT *110*

bolt [*n1*] *lock; part of lock*
bar, brad, catch, coupling, dowel, fastener, lag, latch, lock, nut, padlock, peg, pin, pipe, rivet, rod, screw, skewer, sliding bar, spike, stake, staple, stud; SEE CONCEPTS *470,471,680*

bolt [*n2*] *flash; projectile*
arrow, dart, fulmination, missile, shaft, thunderbolt, thunderstroke; SEE CONCEPTS *624,687*

bolt [*n3*] *large roll of material*
coil, curl, cylinder, package, spindle, spiral, twist; SEE CONCEPT *432*

bolt [*v1*] *run quickly away*
abscond, bail out*, bound, cop out*, cut loose*, cut out*, dart, dash, ditch*, drop out*, dump*, escape, flee, flight, fly, hightail*, hotfoot*, hurtle, jump, kiss goodbye*, leap, leave flat*, leave high and dry*, leave holding the bag*, leave in the lurch*, make a break for it*, make off*, make tracks*, opt out*, run like scared rabbit*, run out on, rush, scamper, scoot, skedaddle*, skip, split*, spring, sprint, start, startle, step on it*, take flight, take off*, walk out on; SEE CONCEPTS *150,195*

bolt [*v2*] *fasten securely*
bar, deadbolt, latch, lock, secure; SEE CONCEPT *225*

bolt [*v3*] *eat very fast*
consume, cram, devour, englut, gobble, gorge, gulp, guzzle, ingurgitate, inhale, scarf*, slop, slosh, stuff, swallow whole, wolf*; SEE CONCEPT *169*

bomb [*n*] *exploding weapon*
atom bomb, bombshell, charge, device, explosive, grenade, hydrogen bomb, mine, missile, Molotov cocktail, nuclear bomb, projectile, rocket, shell, ticker*, torpedo; SEE CONCEPT *500*

bomb [*v1*] *detonate weapon*
attack, blast, blitz, blow up, bombard, cannonade, destroy, napalm, prang, raid, rain destruction*, rake, shell, strafe, torpedo, wipe out*, zero in*; SEE CONCEPTS *86,252*

bomb [*v2*] *fail miserably*
blow it*, flop, flummox, go out of business, lose, wash out*, wipe out*; SEE CONCEPT *699*

bombard [*v*] *assault, attack*
assail, barrage, batter, beset, besiege, blast, blitz, bomb, cannonade, catapult, fire upon, harass,

hound, launch, open fire, pester, pound, shell, strafe, strike; SEE CONCEPTS *7,19,86*

bombastic [*adj*] *pompous, grandiloquent*
aureate, balderdash, big-talking, declamatory, euphuistic, flowery, full of hot air*, fustian, grandiose, highfalutin*, high-flown, histrionic, inflated, loudmouthed, magniloquent, orotund, ostentatious, overblown, ranting, rhapsodic, rhetorical, sonorous, stuffed shirt*, swollen, tumid, turgid, verbose, windbag*, windy, wordy; SEE CONCEPT *267*

bond [*n1*] *binder or fastener*
band, binding, chain, connection, cord, fastening, fetter, gunk, handcuff, hookup, irons, ligature, link, linkage, manacle, network, nexus, rope, shackle, stickum*, tie, tie-in, wire; SEE CONCEPT *497*

bond [*n2*] *association, relation*
affiliation, affinity, attachment, connection, connective, friendship, hookup, interrelationship, liaison, link, marriage, network, obligation, relationship, restraint, tie, tie-in, union; SEE CONCEPT *388*

bond [*n3*] *guarantee; contract*
agreement, bargain, certificate, collateral, compact, convention, covenant, debenture, guaranty, obligation, pact, pledge, promise, security, transaction, warrant, warranty, word; SEE CONCEPTS *318,684*

bond [*v*] *fasten; stick*
bind, connect, fix, fuse, glue, gum, paste, stickum*; SEE CONCEPTS *85,160*

bondage [*n*] *slavery*
chains, enslavement, helotry, peonage, serfage, serfdom, servility, servitude, subjection, subjugation, thrall, thralldom, villenage, yoke; SEE CONCEPTS *136,652*

bone [*n*] *piece of animate skeleton*
bony process, cartilage, ossein, osseous matter; SEE CONCEPTS *393,420*

bonus [*n*] *unexpected extra*
additional compensation, benefit, bounty, commission, dividend, fringe benefit, frosting*, gift, golden parachute*, goody*, gratuity, gravy*, hand-out*, honorarium, ice*, perk*, plus*, premium, prize, reward, special compensation, tip; SEE CONCEPT *337*

book [*n1*] *published document*
album, atlas, bestseller, bible, booklet, brochure, codex, compendium, copy, dictionary, dissertation, edition, encyclopedia, essay, fiction, folio, handbook, hardcover, leaflet, lexicon, magazine, manual, monograph, nonfiction, novel, octavo, offprint, omnibus, opus, opuscule, pamphlet, paperback, periodical, portfolio, preprint, primer, publication, quarto, reader, reprint, roll, scroll, softcover, speller, text, textbook, thesaurus, tome, tract, treatise, vade mecum, volume, work, writing; SEE CONCEPT *280*

book [*n2*] *account; diary*
agenda, album, list, notebook, pad, record, register, roster; SEE CONCEPTS *271,331*

book [*v1*] *register, arrange for*
bespeak, bill, charter, engage, enroll, enter, hire, line up*, make reservation, order, organize, pencil in*, preengage, procure, program, reserve, schedule, set up, sew up*; SEE CONCEPT *36*

book [*v2*] *arrest*
accuse, charge, prefer charges, take into custody; SEE CONCEPT *317*

boom [n1] *loud sound; crash*
bang, barrage, blare, blast, blast, cannonade, clap, crack, drumfire, explosion, reverberation, roar, rumble, slam, smash, thunder, wham; SEE CONCEPTS *521,595*

boom [n2] *prosperity*
advance, boost, development, expansion, gain, growth, improvement, increase, inflation, jump, prosperousness, push, rush, spurt, upsurge, upswing, upturn; SEE CONCEPTS *230,335,700*

boom [v1] *crash; make loud sound*
bang, blast, burst, clap, crack, drum, explode, resound, reverberate, roar, roll, rumble, slam, smash, sound, thunder, wham; SEE CONCEPT *65*

boom [v2] *prosper*
appreciate, bloom, develop, enhance, expand, flourish, flower, gain, grow, increase, intensify, rise in value, spurt, strengthen, succeed, swell, thrive; SEE CONCEPTS *700,704*

boomerang [v] *backfire*
backlash, bounce back, come back, come home to roost*, kick back, react, rebound, recoil, return, reverse, ricochet; SEE CONCEPTS *242,695*

boon [n] *advantage*
benefaction, benefit, benevolence, blessing, break, compliment, donation, favor, gift, godsend, good, good fortune, grant, gratuity, help, largess, present, windfall; SEE CONCEPTS *337,661*

boor [n] *clod*
barbarian, bear, boob*, brute, buffoon, cad, churl, dork*, goon*, lout, oaf, peasant, philistine, rube*, vulgarian; SEE CONCEPT *423*

boorish [adj] *crude, awkward*
bad-mannered, barbaric, bearish, cantankerous, churlish, cloddish, clodhopping*, clownish, clumsy, coarse, countrified, gross*, gruff, illbred, ill-mannered, impolite, inurbane, loud, loutish, lowbred, oafish, ornery, out-of-line, out-of-order, provincial, rough, rude, rustic, swinish, tasteless, ugly, uncivilized, uncouth, uncultured, uneducated, ungracious, unpoised, unpolished, unrefined, vulgar; SEE CONCEPT *404*

boost [n1] *increase*
addition, advance, breakthrough, expansion, hike, improvement, increment, jump, lift, raise, rise, step-up, up, upgrade, wax; SEE CONCEPTS *700,780*

boost [n2] *encouragement*
aid, assistance, backup, buildup, goose*, hand*, handout, help, helping hand, improvement, leg*, leg up*, lift, praise, promotion, shot in the arm*, support; SEE CONCEPT *110*

boost [n3] *push, usually up*
advance, goose*, heave, hoist, lift, raise, shove, thrust; SEE CONCEPTS *196,208*

boost [v1] *further, improve*
advance, advertise, assist, encourage, foster, inspire, plug, praise, promote, push, support, sustain; SEE CONCEPT *244*

boost [v2] *push, usually up*
advance, elevate, heave, heighten, hoist, lift, raise, shove, thrust, upraise, uprear; SEE CONCEPTS *196,208*

boost [v3] *increase*
add to, aggrandize, amplify, augment, beef up*, develop, enlarge, expand, extend, heighten, hike, jack up*, jump, magnify, multiply, put up, raise, up; SEE CONCEPTS *236,245*

boot [n] *heavy, often tall, shoe*
brogan, footwear, galoshes, mukluk, oxford, snow shoes, waders, waters*; SEE CONCEPT *450*

boot [v] *kick; oust*
ax, bounce, can*, chase, chuck*, cut, discharge, dismiss, drive, dropkick*, eighty-six*, eject, evict, expel, extrude, fire, heave, kick out, knock, punt*, sack*, shove, terminate, throw out; SEE CONCEPTS *180,189*

booth [n] *small enclosure or building*
berth, box, carrel, compartment, coop, corner, cote, counter, cubbyhole, cubicle, dispensary, hut, hutch, nook, pen, pew, repository, shed, stall, stand; SEE CONCEPTS *439,440,443*

border [n1] *outermost edge, margin*
bound, boundary, bounds, brim, brink, circumference, confine, end, extremity, fringe, hem, limit, line, lip, outskirt, perimeter, periphery, rim, selvage, skirt, trim, trimming, verge; SEE CONCEPTS *484,827*

border [n2] *boundary; frontier*
beginning, borderline, door, edge, entrance, line, march, marchland, outpost, pale, perimeter, sideline, threshold; SEE CONCEPTS *484,513*

border [v] *bound on; be on the edge*
abut, adjoin, be adjacent to, bind, circumscribe, communicate, contour, decorate, define, delineate, edge, encircle, enclose, flank, frame, fringe, hem, join, line, march, margin, mark off, neighbor, outline, rim, set off, side, skirt, surround, touch, trim, verge; SEE CONCEPT *747*

borderline [adj] *inexact*
ambiguous, ambivalent, doubtful, dubitable, equivocal, indecisive, indefinite, indeterminate, marginal, open, problematic, uncertain, unclassifiable, unclear, undecided, unsettled; SEE CONCEPT *534*

border on [v] *come close to; approximate*
abut, adjoin, approach, be like, be similar to, come near, compare, connect, contact, echo, impinge, join, lie near, lie next to, march, match, near, neighbor, parallel, resemble, touch, verge on; SEE CONCEPTS *667,749*

bore [n] *nuisance*
bother, bromide, bummer*, creep*, deadhead*, downer*, drag*, drip*, dull person, flat tire*, headache, nag, nudge, pain, pain in the neck*, pest, pill*, soporific, stuffed shirt*, tedious person, tiresome person, wet blanket*, wimp*, yawn*; SEE CONCEPT *423*

bore [v1] *drill hole*
burrow, gouge out, mine, penetrate, perforate, pierce, pit, prick, punch, puncture, ream, riddle, sink, tunnel; SEE CONCEPT *178*

bore [v2] *cause weariness, disinterest*
afflict, annoy, bend one's ear*, be tedious, bother, burn out, cloy, discomfort, drag, exhaust, fatigue, irk, irritate, jade, pall, pester, put to sleep*, send to sleep*, talk one's ear off*, tire, trouble, turn one off*, vex, wear out, weary, worry; SEE CONCEPTS *7,19*

boredom [n] *disinterest; weariness*
apathy, detachment, disgust, distaste, doldrums, dullness, ennui, fatigue, flatness, incuriosity, indifference, irksomeness, jadedness, lack of interest, lassitude, lethargy, listlessness, monotony, pococurantism, sameness, taedium vitae, tediousness, tedium, tiresomeness, unconcern, worldweariness, yawn; SEE CONCEPT *410*

boring [adj] *uninteresting*
arid, bomb*, bromidic, bummer*, characterless, cloying, colorless, commonplace, dead*, drab,

drag*, drudging, dull, flat*, ho hum*, humdrum, insipid, interminable, irksome, lifeless, monotonous, moth-eaten*, mundane, nothing, nowhere, platitudinous, plebeian, prosaic, repetitious, routine, spiritless, stale, stereotyped, stodgy, stuffy, stupid, tame, tedious, threadbare, tiresome, tiring, trite, unexciting, uninteresting, unvaried, vapid, wearisome, well-worn, zero*; SEE CONCEPT 529

born [adj] *innate*
built-in, congenital, constitutional, deep-seated, essential, inborn, inbred, ingenerate, inherent, intrinsic, natural; SEE CONCEPTS 549,550

borrow [v1] *take for temporary use*
accept loan of, acquire, beg, bite, bum, cadge*, chisel*, give a note for*, hire, hit up*, lift, mooch*, negotiate, obtain, pawn, pledge, raise money, rent, run into debt, scrounge, see one's uncle*, soak, sponge, take on loan, tap, touch, use temporarily; SEE CONCEPT 89

borrow [v2] *adopt from another source; appropriate*
acquire, adopt, assume, copy, filch, imitate, make one's own, obtain, pilfer, pirate, plagiarize, simulate, steal, take, use, usurp; SEE CONCEPT 225

bosom [n1] *breast*
bust, chest, rib cage, teats; SEE CONCEPT 418

bosom [n2] *heart; core*
affections, center, circle, conscience, emotions, feelings, inside, interior, sentiments, soul, spirit, sympathies; SEE CONCEPTS 410,826

boss [n] *manager over other employees*
administrator, big cheese*, big gun*, big person*, chief, chieftain, controller, director, dominator, employer, exec*, executive, foreperson, head, head honcho*, helmer, honcho*, leader, overseer, owner, person in charge, superintendent, supervisor, taskperson, top dog*, wheel*; SEE CONCEPT 347

boss [adj] *great*
awesome*, bang-up*, capital, champion, excellent, fine, first-rate, fly*, top, whiz-bang*, wonderful; SEE CONCEPT 572

boss [v] *control; command*
administer, administrate, chaperon, direct, employ, manage, overlook, oversee, quarterback*, run, superintend, supervise, survey, take charge; SEE CONCEPT 117

botany [n] *study of plants*
anatomy, cytology, dendrology, ecology, floristics, genetics, horticulture, morphology, natural history, paleobotany, pathology, physiology, phytogeography, phytology, pomology, study of flora, study of vegetation, taxonomy; SEE CONCEPT 349

botch [v] *blunder*
blow*, bobble*, boggle*, bollix*, boot, bumble, bungle, butcher*, distort, err, fall down*, flounder, flub*, fumble, goof up*, gum up*, louse up*, mar, mend, mess, mess up*, misapply, miscalculate, miscompute, misconjecture, misconstrue, mishandle, misjudge, mismanage, muck up*, muddle, muff, mutilate, patch, pull a boner*, ruin, screw up*, spoil, stumble, wreck; SEE CONCEPT 101

both [det] *two together*
one and the other, the couple, the pair, the two, twain; SEE CONCEPT 714

bother [n] *trouble, inconvenience*
ado, aggravation, annoyance, anxiety, bellyache*, botheration, bustle, care, concern, difficulty, distress, drag*, exasperation, flurry, fuss, headache*, irritant, irritation, molestation, nudge, nuisance, pain, pain in the neck*, perplexity, pest, plague, pother*, pressure, problem, strain, to-do*, trial, trouble, vexation, worriment, worry; SEE CONCEPT 532

bother [v1] *harass, annoy; give trouble*
afflict, aggravate, agitate, alarm, badger, bedevil, bore, browbeat, carp at, concern, cross, discommode, disconcert, disgust, dismay, displease, disquiet, distress, disturb, eat, embarrass, exacerbate, exasperate, goad, grate on, grieve, harry, hinder, hurt, impede, inconvenience, insult, intrude upon, irk, irritate, molest, nag, needle, nudge, pain, perplex, perturb, pester, pick on, plague, provoke, pursue, put out, ride, scare, spite, tantalize, taunt, tease, torment, trouble, upset, vex, worry; SEE CONCEPTS 7,19

bother [v2] *take the trouble*
be concerned about, concern oneself, exert oneself, fuss over, go out of one's way*, make a fuss about*, make an effort, put oneself out*, take pains, try, worry about; SEE CONCEPT 87

bothersome [adj] *troubling*
aggravating, annoying, distressing, disturbing, exasperating, incommodious, inconvenient, irritating, rebarbative, remote, tiresome, troublesome, vexatious, vexing; SEE CONCEPT 529

bottle [n] *container, usually for liquids*
canteen, carafe, cruet, dead soldier*, decanter, ewer, flagon, flask, glass, jar, jug, phial, soldier, urn, vacuum bottle, vial; SEE CONCEPT 494

bottle up [v] *keep feeling inside oneself*
box up, check, collar, contain, coop up, corner, cramp, curb, keep back, restrain, restrict, shut in, suppress, trap; SEE CONCEPT 35

bottom [n1] *foundation*
base, basement, basis, bed, bedrock, belly, deepest part, depths, floor, foot, footing, ground, groundwork, lowest part, nadir, nether portion, pedestal, pediment, rest, seat, sole, substratum, substructure, support, terra firma, underbelly, underneath, underside; SEE CONCEPT 442

bottom [n2] *base, core*
basis, bottom line, cause, essence, essentiality, ground, heart, mainspring, marrow, origin, pith, principle, quintessence, root, soul, source, stuff, substance, virtuality; SEE CONCEPTS 648,826

bottom [n3] *rear end*
backside, behind, breech, bum*, butt*, buttocks, derriere, fanny*, fundament, posterior, rear, rump, seat, tail, tush*; SEE CONCEPT 418

bottom [adj] *lowest; fundamental*
basal, base, basement, .basic, foundational, ground, last, lowermost, lowest, meat-and-potatoes*, nethermost, primary, radical, rock-bottom, underlying, undermost; SEE CONCEPTS 585,586,735,799

bottom line [n] *conclusion*
determination, final decision, income, last word, loss, main point, net, profit; SEE CONCEPT 230

bough [n] *branch*
arm, fork, limb, offshoot, shoot, sprig, sucker; SEE CONCEPT 428

boulevard [n] *street, often lined with trees*
artery, avenue, drag, highway, passage, path, road, thoroughfare, track, way; SEE CONCEPT 501

bounce [n] *spring*
animation, bound, dynamism, elasticity, energy,

bo bo

give, go, life, liveliness, pep, rebound, recoil, resilience, springiness, vigor, vitality, vivacity, zip; SEE CONCEPTS *150,411*

bounce [v1] *spring up; rebound*
backlash, bob, boomerang, bound, buck, bump, carom, fly back, glance off, hop, hurdle, jerk up and down*, jounce, jump, kick back, leap, rebound, recoil, resile, ricochet, saltate, snap back, spring back, thump, vault; SEE CONCEPTS *150,194*

bounce [v2] *evict*
ax*, boot out*, can*, discharge, dismiss, eighty-six*, eject, fire, give one notice, give the heave ho*, heave*, kick out*, oust, sack*, terminate, throw; SEE CONCEPTS *211,351,384*

bound/bounds [n] *farthest limit*
boundary, compass, confine, edge, end, environs, extremity, fringe, limit, limitation, line, march, margin, pale, periphery, precinct, purlieus, rim, term, termination, verge; SEE CONCEPTS *484,788*

bound [adj] *obligated; destined*
apprenticed, articled, bent, bounden, certain, coerced, compelled, constrained, contracted, doomed, driven, duty-bound, enslaved, fated, firm, forced, having no alternative, impelled, indentured, intent, made, necessitated, obligated, obliged, pledged, pressed, required, restrained, sure, under compulsion, under necessity, urged; SEE CONCEPT *554*

bound [v1] *jump, bounce*
bob, caper, frisk, gambol, hop, hurdle, leap, pounce, prance, recoil, ricochet, saltate, skip, spring, vault; SEE CONCEPT *194*

bound [v2] *restrict*
circumscribe, confine, define, delimit, delimitate, demarcate, determine, encircle, enclose, hem in, limit, mark, mark out, measure, restrain, restrict, surround, terminate; SEE CONCEPT *130*

boundary [n] *outer limit*
abuttals, ambit, barrier, beginning, border, borderland, borderline, bounds, brink, circumference, circumscription, compass, confines, edge, end, environs, extent, extremity, frame, fringe, frontier, hem, horizon, limits, line, line of demarcation, march, margin, mark, mere, mete, outline, outpost, pale, perimeter, periphery, precinct, purlieus, radius, rim, side, skirt, terminal, termination, terminus, verge; SEE CONCEPTS *5,484,745*

bounded [adj] *limited, confined*
belted, bordered, boundaried, circumscribed, compassed, contiguous, defined, definite, delimited, determinate, edged, encircled, enclosed, encompassed, enveloped, fenced, finite, flanked, fringed, girdled, hedged, hog-tied*, limitary, restricted, rimmed, ringed, surrounded, walled; SEE CONCEPTS *554,772*

boundless [adj] *endless, without limit*
great, illimitable, immeasurable, immense, incalculable, indefinite, inexhaustible, infinite, limitless, measureless, no catch*, no end of, no end to, no holds barred*, no strings*, no strings attached*, tremendous, unbounded, unconfined, unending, unlimited, untold, vast, wide open; SEE CONCEPTS *554,772*

bountiful [adj] *abundant*
ample, aplenty, bounteous, copious, crawling with*, dime a dozen*, exuberant, free, galore*, generous, handsome, lavish, liberal, luxuriant, magnanimous, munificent, no end of*, plenteous,

plentiful, plenty, prolific, stink with*, unsparing; SEE CONCEPT *771*

bounty [n] *bonus; compensation*
donation, gift, grant, gratuity, largess, pay, premium, present, prize, recompense, reward; SEE CONCEPTS *337,344*

bouquet [n1] *flower arrangement*
boutonniere, buttonhole, corsage, festoon, garland, lei, nosegay, posy, pot, spray, vase, wreath; SEE CONCEPTS *425,429*

bouquet [n2] *aroma*
aura, balm, fragrance, incense, odor, perfume, redolence, savor, scent, smell, spice; SEE CONCEPT *599*

bourgeois [adj] *commonplace*
common, conservative, conventional, hidebound, illiberal, materialistic, middle-class, old-line, Philistine, traditional, Victorian; SEE CONCEPTS *530,589*

bout [n1] *period of time in which something occurs*
course, fit*, go*, round, run, session, shift, spell, stint, stretch, tear, term, tour, trick*, turn; SEE CONCEPT *807*

bout [n2] *competitive fight*
bat, battle, boxing match, competition, contest, encounter, engagement, go, match, round, set-to, struggle; SEE CONCEPTS *92,106*

bow [n1] *bend from waist*
angle, arc, arch, bend, bending, bob, curtsy, curvation, curvature, curve, flection, flexure, genuflection, inclination, kowtow*, nod, obeisance, round, salaam, turn, turning; SEE CONCEPTS *154,201*

bow [n2] *front of boat*
beak, bowsprit, fore, forepart, head, nose, prow, stem; SEE CONCEPT *502*

bow [v1] *bend over*
arch, bob, cower, crook, curtsy, curve, debase, dip, do obeisance, droop, duck, genuflect, hunch, incline, nod, round, stoop; SEE CONCEPT *213*

bow [v2] *submit, concede*
accept, acquiesce, bend, be servile, capitulate, cave, comply, defer, give in, knuckle*, knuckle under*, kowtow*, relent, succumb, surrender, yield; SEE CONCEPT *23*

bowels [n] *insides*
belly, core, deep, depths, entrails, guts, hold, innards, interior, intestines, penetralia, recesses, viscera, vitals; SEE CONCEPTS *393,830*

bowl [n] *hollow, concave container*
basin, boat, casserole, crock, deep dish, dish, porringer, pot, saucer, tureen, urn, vessel; SEE CONCEPTS *493,494*

bowl [v] *roll a ball down a lane*
fling, hurl, pitch, play duckpins, play tenpins, revolve, rotate, spin, throw, trundle, whirl; SEE CONCEPT *363*

box [n] *container, often square or rectangular*
bin, carton, case, casket, chest, coffer, crate, pack, package, portmanteau, receptacle, trunk; SEE CONCEPT *494*

box [v1] *place in square or rectangular container*
case, confine, crate, encase, pack, package, wrap; SEE CONCEPT *209*

box [v2] *punch competitively*
buffet, clout, cuff, duke*, exchange blows, hit, mix, scrap, slap, slug, sock, spar, strike, wallop, whack*; SEE CONCEPTS *106,189*

boxing [n] *punching competition*
battle, glove game*, mill*, prelim*, prizefight-

ing, pugilism, slugfest*, sparring, the ring*; SEE CONCEPTS *92,363*

boy [n] *young man*
buck, cadet, chap, child, dude*, fellow, gamin, guy, half-pint*, junior, lad, little gentleman, little guy*, little shaver*, master, punk*, puppy*, runt*, schoolboy, shaver*, small fry*, sonny*, sprout*, squirt*, stripling, tadpole*, whippersnapper*, youngster, youth; SEE CONCEPTS *419,424*

boycott [v] *ban; refrain from using*
avoid, bar, blackball, blacklist, brush off, cut off, embargo, exclude, hold aloof from, ice out*, ostracize, outlaw, pass by*, pass up*, prohibit, proscribe, refuse, reject, shut out*, snub, spurn, strike, withhold patronage; SEE CONCEPTS *25,130*

boyfriend [n] *male acquaintance or romantic companion*
admirer, beau, companion, confidant, date, escort, fiancé, flame*, follower, friend, intimate, partner, soul mate, steady, suitor, swain, sweetheart, young man; SEE CONCEPTS *419,423*

brace [n] *support*
arm, band, bar, bearing, block, bolster, boom, bracer, bracket, buttress, cantilever, clamp, girder, grip, guy, lever, mainstay, peg, prop, rafter, reinforcement, rib, shore, skid, splice, splint, staff, stanchion, stave, stay, stirrup, strengthener, strut, sustainer, truss, underpinning, vice; SEE CONCEPTS *470,475,499*

brace [v] *support*
bandage, bind, bolster, buttress, fasten, fortify, gird, hold up, prepare, prop, ready, reinforce, shove, steady, steel, strap, strengthen, support, tie, tighten, uphold; SEE CONCEPT *191*

bracelet [n] *wrist jewelry*
arm band, armlet, bangle, circlet, manacle, ornament, trinket, wristlet; SEE CONCEPT *446*

bracing [adj] *brisk; exhilarating*
animating, chilly, cool, crisp, energizing, exhilarative, fortifying, fresh, invigorating, lively, quickening, refreshing, restorative, reviving, rousing, stimulating, stimulative, tonic, vigorous; SEE CONCEPTS *537,605*

brag [v] *talk boastingly*
blow one's own horn*, bluster*, boast, crow*, exult, gasconade, gloat, grandstand*, hotdog*, jive*, mouth*, pat oneself on the back*, prate, puff*, rodomontade, showboat*, shuck*, swagger, vaunt; SEE CONCEPTS *49,51*

braggart [n] *person who talks boastingly*
bag of wind*, bigmouth, big talker*, big-timer*, blowhard*, blusterer, boaster, brag, braggadocio, bragger, egotist, exhibitionist, gasbag*, gascon*, grandstander*, hotshot*, know-it-all, peacock*, ranter, raver, show-off, strutter, swaggerer, swashbuckler*, swelled head*, trumpeter*, windbag*; SEE CONCEPTS *412,423*

braid [n] *interwoven hair style*
pigtail, plait, ponytail, queue; SEE CONCEPTS *418,716*

braid [v] *interweave*
complect, cue, entwine, interknit, interlace, intertwine, lace, mesh, pigtail, plait, ravel, twine, twist, weave; SEE CONCEPTS *184,202*

brain [n1] *very smart person*
academician, doctor, egghead*, Einstein*, genius, highbrow, intellect, intellectual, mastermind, prodigy, pundit, sage, scholar; SEE CONCEPT *350*

brain [n2] *mind, intelligence*
cerebellum, cerebrum, encephalon, gray matter*, head, intellect, medulla oblongata, mentality, upper story*, wit; SEE CONCEPTS *393,409,420*

brainwash [v] *force to believe or do things*
alter, catechize, condition, convert, convince, educate, indoctrinate, influence, instill, persuade, proselytize, teach; SEE CONCEPT *14*

brake [n] *stopping device; check*
anchor, binders, cinchers, constraint, control, curb, damper, deterrent, discouragement, hamper, hindrance, hurdle, obstacle, rein, restraint, retarding device; SEE CONCEPTS *130,463*

brake [v] *check; stop*
bar, block, dam, decelerate, halt, hinder, impede, moderate, obstruct, reduce speed, slacken, slow, slow down, stop; SEE CONCEPT *121*

bramble [n] *thorny bush*
brier, burr, catch weed, cleaver, furze, goose grass, gorse, hedge, nettle, prick, prickly shrub, shrub, spray, thistle, thistle sage, thorn; SEE CONCEPT *429*

branch [n1] *department*
annex, arm, bureau, category, chapter, classification, connection, dependency, derivative, division, extension, local, member, office, outpost, part, portion, section, subdivision, subsection, subsidiary, tributary, wing; SEE CONCEPTS *325,378*

branch [n2] *arm, limb*
bough, branchlet, bug, detour, divergence, extension, fork, growth, offshoot, prong, scion, shoot, spray, sprig, wing; SEE CONCEPTS *392,428, 471,835*

branch off/branch out [v] *extend beyond main part*
add to, develop, diverge, diversify, divide, enlarge, expand, extend, fork, grow, increase, multiply, part, proliferate, ramify, separate, spread out; SEE CONCEPT *756*

brand [n1] *type, kind*
cast, character, class, description, grade, make, quality, sort, species, variety; SEE CONCEPT *378*

brand [n2] *distinctive label, mark*
brand name, emblem, hallmark, heraldry, imprint, logo, logotype, marker, sign, stamp, symbol, trademark, welt; SEE CONCEPT *284*

brand [n3] *stigma*
bar sinister, black eye, blot, blur, disgrace, infamy, mark, mark of Cain, odium, onus, reproach, slur, smirch, spot, stain, stigma, taint; SEE CONCEPT *388*

brandish [v] *flaunt, swing around*
come on strong*, display, disport, exhibit, expose, flash, gesture, parade, raise, shake, show, show off, sport, swing, threaten, throw weight around*, trot out*, warn, wield; SEE CONCEPT *261*

brash [adj] *impulsive, brazen*
audacious, bold, brazenfaced, cheeky*, cocksure, cocky*, effervescent, flip, foolhardy, forward, hasty, headlong, heedless, hotheaded, ill-advised, impertinent, impetuous, impolitic, impudent, incautious, inconsiderate, indiscreet, insolent, madcap, maladroit, nervy, precipitate, presuming, presumptuous, pushing, rash, reckless, rude, self-asserting, self-assertive, tactless, thoughtless, undiplomatic, untactful, uppity, vivacious; SEE CONCEPTS *401,404*

bo
br

brass [n] *impulsiveness; nerve*
assumption, audacity, brashness, cheek*, chutzpah*, confidence, effrontery, gall, impertinence, impudence, insolence, presumption, rudeness; SEE CONCEPT 633

brassy [adj] *vulgar, loud to the senses*
arrant, barefaced, blaring, blatant, bold, brash, brazen, flashy, flirtatious, forward, garish, gaudy, grating, hard, harsh, impudent, insolent, jarring, jazzy, loudmouthed, noisy, obtrusive, overbold, pert, piercing, rude, saucy, shameless, showy, shrill, strident, unabashed, unblushing; SEE CONCEPTS 401,589,592,594

brat [n] *spoiled child*
devil*, enfant terrible*, holy terror*, impudent child, kid, punk*, rascal, unruly child, urchin, whippersnapper*, wild one*, youngster; SEE CONCEPT 424

bravado [n] *boastfulness*
blowing, bluff, bluster, boasting, bombast, braggadocio, bragging, bullying, crowing*, fancy talk*, fuming*, gasconade, grandiosity, guts* hot air*, pomposity, pretension, raging, railing, rant, self-glorification, storming, swaggering, swelling, talk, tall talk*; SEE CONCEPTS 49,51

brave [adj] *bold*
adventurous, audacious, chin-up*, chivalrous, confident, courageous, daring, dashing, dauntless, defiant, doughty, fearless, firm, foolhardy, forward, gallant, game, gritty, gutsy, hardy, heroic, herolike, imprudent, indomitable, intrepid, lionhearted, militant, nervy, plucky, reckless, resolute, spirited, spunky, stalwart, stout, stouthearted, strong, unabashed, unafraid, unblenching, undauntable, undaunted, undismayed, unfearful, valiant, valorous, venturesome; SEE CONCEPT 401

brave [v] *endure bad situation*
bear, beard, challenge, confront, court, dare, defy, face, face off, fly in the face of*, go through, outdare, risk, stand up to, suffer, support, take on, venture, withstand; SEE CONCEPT 23

bravery [n] *boldness*
courage, daring, dauntlessness, fearlessness, fortitude, gallantry, grit, guts, hardiness, heroism, indomitability, intrepidity, mettle, pluck, pluckiness, spirit, spunk, valor; SEE CONCEPTS 411,633

brawl [n] *nasty fight*
affray, altercation, argument, battle, battle royal*, bickering, broil, clash, disorder, dispute, donnybrook, duke out*, feud, fight, fracas, fray, free-for-all*, fuss, hassle, melee, quarrel, rhubarb*, riot, row, ruckus*, rumble*, rumpus, scrap, scuffle, squabble, tumult, uproar, wrangle; SEE CONCEPTS 46,106

brawl [v] *fight nastily*
altercate, argue, battle, bicker, buck*, caterwaul, dispute, kick up a row*, quarrel, raise Cain*, roughhouse*, row, rumble*, scrap, scuffle, spat, squabble, tussle, wrangle, wrestle; SEE CONCEPTS 46,106

brawn [n] *muscular strength and breadth*
beef, beefiness, clout, energy, flesh, kick, meat, might, moxie*, muscle, muscularity, power, punch, robustness, sinews, sock, steam, thew, vigor; SEE CONCEPTS 723,732

brawny [adj] *muscular, strong*
able-bodied, athletic, beefy, bulky, burly, fleshy, hardy, hefty, husky, powerful, robust, sinewy,

stalwart, strapping, sturdy, thewy, tough, vigorous, vital; SEE CONCEPTS 485,489

brazen [adj] *brash, unashamed*
audacious, barefaced, blatant, bold, brassy, cheeky, cocky, contumelious, defiant, flashy, flip, forward, gritty, gutsy, hotshot*, immodest, impertinent, impudent, indecent, insolent, loud, meretricious, nervy, overbold, pert, saucy, shameless, smart-alecky*, smart-ass*, spunky, tawdry, unabashed, unblushing; SEE CONCEPTS 267,401

breach [n1] *gap*
aperture, break, chasm, chip, cleft, crack, discontinuity, fissure, hole, opening, rent, rift, rupture, slit, split; SEE CONCEPT 513

breach [n2] *violation of a law*
contravention, delinquency, dereliction, disobedience, disregard, infraction, infringement, neglect, noncompliance, nonobservance, offense, transgression, trespass, violation; SEE CONCEPT 192

breach [n3] *change from friendly to unfriendly relationship*
alienation, break, difference, disaffection, disagreement, discord, disharmony, dissension, disunity, division, estrangement, falling-out, fissure, fracture, parting of the ways*, quarrel, rent, rift, rupture, schism, secession, separation, severance, split, strife, variance, withdrawal; SEE CONCEPT 388

bread [n1] *daily food*
aliment, bed and board, comestibles, diet, fare, feed, grub*, necessities, nourishment, nurture, nutriment, provender, provisions, shingle*, staff of life*, subsistence, sustenance, viands, victuals; SEE CONCEPT 457

bread [n2] *money*
cabbage*, cash, coin, dollars, dough*, finance, funds, greenbacks*, mazuma*, scratch*; SEE CONCEPT 340

breadth [n1] *width*
broadness, diameter, distance across, latitude, span, spread, wideness; SEE CONCEPT 760

breadth [n2] *extent*
amplitude, area, compass, comprehensiveness, dimension, expanse, extensiveness, fullness, gamut, greatness, inclusiveness, largeness, magnitude, measure, orbit, range, reach, scale, scope, size, space, spread, stretch, sweep, vastness; SEE CONCEPTS 651,756,788

break [n] *fissure, opening*
breach, cleft, crack, discontinuity, disjunction, division, fracture, gap, gash, hole, rent, rift, rupture, schism, split, tear; SEE CONCEPTS 230, 757

break [n2] *interruption of activity*
blow, breather, breathing space, caesura, coffee break, cutoff, downtime*, halt, hiatus, interlude, intermission, interval, lacuna, layoff*, letup*, lull, pause, recess, respite, rest, suspension, ten*, time out, time out; SEE CONCEPT 807

break [n3] *change from friendly to unfriendly relationship*
alienation, altercation, breach, clash, difference of opinion, disaffection, dispute, divergence, estrangement, fight, misunderstanding, rift, rupture, schism, separation, split, trouble; SEE CONCEPT 388

break [n4] *lucky happening*
accident, advantage, chance, favorable circumstances, fortune, good luck, luck, occasion, open-

ing, opportunity, shot, show, stroke of luck, time; SEE CONCEPT *679*

break [*v1*] *destroy; make whole into pieces*
annihilate, batter, burst, bust, bust up, crack, crash, crush, damage, demolish, disintegrate, divide, eradicate, finish off, fracture, fragment, make hash of*, make mincemeat of*, part, pull to pieces, rend, separate, sever, shatter, shiver, smash, snap, splinter, split, tear, torpedo, total, trash*; SEE CONCEPT *252*

break [*v2*] *violate law*
breach, contravene, disobey, disregard, infract, infringe, offend, renege on, transgress, violate; SEE CONCEPT *192*

break [*v3*] *weaken, cause instability*
bankrupt, bust, confound, confute, controvert, cow, cripple, declass, degrade, demerit, demoralize, demote, disconfirm, dispirit, disprove, downgrade, enervate, enfeeble, humiliate, impair, impoverish, incapacitate, pauperize, rebut, reduce, refute, ruin, subdue, tame, undermine; SEE CONCEPT *240*

break [*v4*] *stop an action*
abandon, cut, discontinue, give up, interrupt, pause, rest, suspend; SEE CONCEPT *121*

break [*v5*] *tell news*
announce, come out, communicate, convey, disclose, divulge, impart, inform, let out, make public, pass on, proclaim, reveal, tell, transmit; SEE CONCEPT *60*

break [*v6*] *better a performance*
beat, cap, exceed, excel, go beyond, outdo, outstrip, surpass, top; SEE CONCEPT *141*

break [*v7*] *emerge, happen*
appear, befall, betide, burst out, chance, come forth, come off, come to pass, develop, erupt, go, occur, transpire; SEE CONCEPT *4*

break [*v8*] *run away*
abscond, bust out*, clear out*, cut and run*, dash, decamp, escape, flee, fly, get away, get out; SEE CONCEPTS *102,195*

break [*v9*] *cushion something's effect*
diminish, lessen, lighten, moderate, reduce, soften, weaken; SEE CONCEPT *110*

breakable [*adj*] *easily hurt or destroyed*
brittle, crisp, crispy, crumbly, delicate, flimsy, fracturable, fragile, frail, frangible, friable, shatterable, shattery, splintery, vitreous, weak; SEE CONCEPTS *489,606*

breakdown [*n1*] *nervous collapse*
basket case*, crackup*, disintegration, disruption, failure, mishap, nervous prostration, neurasthenia, neurosis, psychasthenia; SEE CONCEPT *410*

breakdown [*n2*] *account of finances or other business*
analysis, categorization, classification, detailed list, diagnosis, dissection, itemization, resolution; SEE CONCEPT *283*

break in [*v1*] *intrude*
barge in, break, break and enter, burglarize, burgle, burst in*, butt in*, interfere, interject, interrupt, intervene, invade, meddle, raid, rob, steal, trespass; SEE CONCEPTS *139,192*

break in [*v2*] *train in new skill*
accustom, condition, educate, gentle, get used to, habituate, initiate, instruct, prepare, tame; SEE CONCEPT *285*

break off [*v1*] *snap off something*
detach, disassemble, divide, part, pull off, separate, sever, splinter, take apart; SEE CONCEPT *211*

break off [*v2*] *end activity*
cease, desist, discontinue, end, finish, halt, pause, stop, suspend, terminate; SEE CONCEPT *234*

break out [*v1*] *happen, emerge*
appear, arise, begin, burst forth, commence, erupt, explode, occur, set in, spring up, start; SEE CONCEPT *701*

break out [*v2*] *escape*
abscond, bolt, break loose, burst out, bust out*, depart, flee, get free, leave; SEE CONCEPTS *102,195*

breakthrough [*n*] *advance, progress*
boost, development, discovery, find, finding, gain, hike, improvement, increase, invention, leap, progress, quantum leap*, rise, step forward; SEE CONCEPT *704*

breakup [*n*] *end of relationship*
breakdown, breaking, crackup*, disintegration, dispersal, dissolution, divorce, ending, parting, rift, separation, split, splitsville*, splitting, termination, wind-up; SEE CONCEPT *385*

break up [*v*] *end relationship, activity*
adjourn, disassemble, disband, dismantle, disperse, disrupt, dissolve, divide, divorce, end, halt, part, put an end to, scatter, separate, sever, split, stop, sunder, suspend, take apart, terminate; SEE CONCEPT *234*

breast [*n1*] *front of upper body*
bosom, bust, chest, front, mammary glands, mammilla, nipple, teat, udder; SEE CONCEPT *418*

breast [*n2*] *feelings, conscience*
being, bosom, character, core, emotions, essential nature, heart, mind, psyche, seat of affections, sentiments, soul, spirit, thoughts; SEE CONCEPTS *410,529*

breath [*n1*] *respiration*
animation, breathing, eupnea, exhalation, expiration, gasp, gulp, inhalation, inspiration, insufflation, pant, wheeze; SEE CONCEPT *163*

breath [*n2*] *wind or something in the air*
aroma, faint breeze, flatus, gust, odor, puff, sigh, smell, vapor, waft, whiff, zephyr; SEE CONCEPTS *437,599*

breath [*n3*] *respite, break*
blow*, breather, breathing space*, instant, moment, pause, rest, second, ten*; SEE CONCEPT *807*

breath [*n4*] *hint, suggestion*
dash, murmur, shade, soupçon, streak, suspicion, touch, trace, undertone, whiff, whisper; SEE CONCEPTS *278,831*

breathe [*v1*] *take air in and let out*
draw in, exhale, expire, fan, gasp, gulp, inhale, insufflate, open the floodgates*, pant, puff, respire, scent, sigh, sniff, snore, snort, use lungs, wheeze; SEE CONCEPTS *163,601*

breathe [*v2*] *inspire action*
imbue, impart, infuse, inject, instill, transfuse; SEE CONCEPT *242*

breathe [*v3*] *tell information*
articulate, confide, express, murmur, say, sigh, utter, voice, whisper; SEE CONCEPT *60*

breathless [*adj1*] *unable to respire normally*
asthmatic, blown, choking, emphysematous, exhausted, gasping, gulping, out of breath, panting, short of breath, short-winded, spent, stertorous, wheezing, winded; SEE CONCEPT *406*

breathless [*adj2*] *astounded*
agog, anxious, avid, eager, excited, flabbergasted, open-mouthed, thunderstruck, with bated breath; SEE CONCEPT *403*

br
br

breathtaking [*adj*] *beautiful, awesome*
amazing, astonishing, awe-inspiring, exciting, hair-raising, heart-stirring, heart-stopping, impressive, magnificent, moving, overwhelming, spine-tingling, stunning, thrilling; SEE CONCEPT 529

breed [*n*] *kind, class*
brand, character, extraction, family, feather, genus, ilk, likes, line, lineage, lot, nature, number, pedigree, progeny, race, sort, species, stamp, stock, strain, stripe, type, variety; SEE CONCEPT 378

breed [*v1*] *generate, bring into being*
bear, beget, bring about, bring forth, cause, create, deliver, engender, give birth to, give rise to, hatch, impregnate, induce, make, multiply, originate, procreate, produce, progenerate, propagate, reproduce; SEE CONCEPTS 173,251,302,373

breed [*v2*] *raise, nurture*
bring up, cultivate, develop, discipline, educate, foster, instruct, nourish, rear; SEE CONCEPTS 285,295

breeding [*n*] *cultivation of person*
ancestry, civility, conduct, courtesy, culture, development, gentility, grace, lineage, manners, nurture, polish, raising, rearing, refinement, schooling, training, upbringing, urbanity; SEE CONCEPT 388

breeze [*n*] *light wind*
air, airflow, breath, current, draft, flurry, gust, puff, waft, whiff, zephyr; SEE CONCEPTS 437,524

breeze [*v*] *work quickly through task*
cruise, flit, glide, hurry, move, pass, sail, sally, skim, slide, slip, sweep, trip, waltz, zip; SEE CONCEPT 704

breezy [*adj1*] *windy*
airy, blowing, blowy, blusterous, blustery, drafty, fresh, gusty, squally, stormy; SEE CONCEPT 525

breezy [*adj2*] *easy, lighthearted*
airy, animated, blithe, buoyant, carefree, casual, cheerful, debonair, easy-going, effervescent, free and easy*, gay, informal, jaunty, light, lively, low-pressure, peppy, racy, relaxed, sparkling, spicy, spirited, sprightly, sunny, unconstrained, vivacious; SEE CONCEPT 544

brevity [*n*] *shortness, briefness*
conciseness, concision, condensation, crispness, curtness, economy, ephemerality, impermanence, pithiness, pointedness, succinctness, terseness, transience, transitoriness; SEE CONCEPTS 730,804

brew [*n*] *concoction*
beverage, blend, broth, compound, distillation, drink, fermentation, hash, hodgepodge*, infusion, instillation, liquor, melange, miscellany, mishmash*, mixture, potpourri, preparation; SEE CONCEPTS 260,454,457

brew [*v1*] *prepare by boiling*
boil, concoct, cook, ferment, infuse, mull, seethe, soak, steep, stew; SEE CONCEPT 170

brew [*v2*] *plan, devise*
breed, compound, concoct, contrive, develop, excite, foment, form, gather, hatch, impend, loom, mull, plot, project, scheme, start, stir up, weave; SEE CONCEPT 36

bribe [*n*] *payoff to influence illegal or wrong activity*
allurement, bait, blackmail, buyoff, compensation, contract, corrupting gift, corrupt money, enticement, envelope*, feedbag*, fringe benefit, gift, goody*, graft, gratuity, gravy*, grease*,

hush money*, ice*, incentive, inducement, influence peddling, kickback, lagniappe, lure, payola*, perk*, perquisite, present, price, protection*, remuneration, reward, sop*, sweetener*, sweetening*, take; SEE CONCEPTS 192,329

bribe [*v*] *request silence, action, or inaction for money*
approach, buy, buy back, buy off, coax, corrupt, do business*, entice, fix*, get at, get to, grease palm*, influence, instigate, lubricate, lure, make a deal, oil palm*, pay off, pervert, reward, seduce, soap*, square, suborn, sugar, sweeten the pot*, take care of, tamper, tempt, tip; SEE CONCEPTS 53,192

bridal [*adj*] *concerning marriage*
conjugal, connubial, epithalamic, espousal, hymeneal, marital, matrimonial, nubile, nuptial, pre-wedding, prothalamic, spousal; SEE CONCEPT 536

bride [*n*] *female marriage partner*
helpmate, mate, newly married woman, newly-wed, old woman*, spouse, wife; SEE CONCEPTS 296,415

bridegroom [*n*] *male marriage partner*
benedict, groom, helpmate, husband, mate, new-lywed, old man*, spouse; SEE CONCEPTS 296,419

bridge [*n*] *structure or something that makes connection*
arch, bond, branch, catwalk, connection, extension, gangplank, link, overpass, platform, pontoon, scaffold, span, tie, transit, trestle, viaduct, wing; SEE CONCEPTS 501,721

bridge [*v*] *connect, extend*
arch over, attach, bind, branch, couple, cross, cross over, go over, join, link, reach, span, subtend, traverse, unite; SEE CONCEPTS 113,756

bridle [*n*] *restraining device*
check, control, curb, deterrent, hackamore, halter, headstall, leash, rein, restraint, trammels; SEE CONCEPT 497

bridle [*v*] *check, hold back*
constrain, control, curb, govern, inhibit, keep in check, master, moderate, repress, restrain, rule, subdue, suppress, withhold; SEE CONCEPT 121

brief [*n*] *abridgment*
abstract, argument, boildown*, case, condensation, conspectus, contention, data, defense, digest, epitome, outline, précis, sketch, summary, synopsis; SEE CONCEPTS 283,318

brief [*adj1*] *short, compressed*
abrupt, bluff, blunt, boiled down*, breviloquent, brusque, compendiary, compendious, concise, crisp, curt, hasty, laconic, limited, little, pithy, sharp, short and sweet*, skimpy, small, snippy, succinct, surly, terse, to the point; SEE CONCEPTS 267,773

brief [*adj2*] *short in time*
concise, curtailed, ephemeral, fast, fleeting, hasty, instantaneous, little, meteoric, momentary, passing, quick, short-lived, short-term, swift, temporary, transient, transitory; SEE CONCEPT 798

brief [*v*] *inform of facts*
abridge, advise, apprise, edify, enlighten, epitomize, explain, fill in, give rundown*, give the lowdown*, inform, initiate, instruct, let in on*, orient, prepare, prime, recapitulate, show the lay of the land*, show the ropes*, summarize, tip off*, update; SEE CONCEPT 60

briefcase [n] *carrier for work papers*
attaché, bag, baggage, case, dispatch, folder, portfolio, valise; SEE CONCEPTS 446,494

briefing [n] *preparation by informing of facts*
background meeting, conference, directions, discussion, guidance, information, initiation, instruction, meeting, preamble, priming, rundown, update; SEE CONCEPT 60

brigade [n] *fleet of trained people*
army, band, body, company, contingent, corps, crew, detachment, force, group, organization, outfit, party, posse, squad, team, troop, unit; SEE CONCEPTS 322,381

bright [adj1] *shining, glowing in appearance*
ablaze, aglow, alight, argent, auroral, beaming, blazing, brilliant, burning, burnished, coruscating, dazzling, effulgent, fulgent, fulgid, glaring, gleaming, glistening, glittering, glossy, golden, illuminated, illumined, incandescent, intense, irradiated, lambent, light, lighted, limpid, luminous, lustrous, mirrorlike, moonlit, phosphorescent, polished, radiant, relucent, resplendent, scintillating, shimmering, shiny, silvery, sparkling, sunlit, sunny, twinkling, vivid; SEE CONCEPT 617

bright [adj2] *sunny, clear (weather)*
clement, cloudless, fair, favorable, limpid, lucid, mild, pellucid, pleasant, translucent, transparent, unclouded; SEE CONCEPT 525

bright [adj3] *intelligent*
acute, advanced, alert, astute, aware, brainy, brilliant, clear-headed, clever, discerning, egghead-ed*, Einstein*, having smarts*, ingenious, inventive, keen, knowing, precocious, quick, quick-witted, sharp, smart, whiz kid*, wide-awake; SEE CONCEPT 402

bright [adj4] *hopeful, promising*
airy, auspicious, benign, breezy, cheering, encouraging, excellent, favorable, golden, good, optimistic, palmy, propitious, prosperous, rosy; SEE CONCEPT 537

bright [adj5] *cheerful*
alert, animated, gay, genial, glad, happy, jolly, joyful, joyous, keen, lighthearted, lively, merry, optimistic, sanguine, spirited, sprightly, vivacious; SEE CONCEPT 404

bright [adj6] *famous, outstanding*
distinguished, eminent, glorious, illustrious, magnificent, prominent, remarkable, splendid; SEE CONCEPT 568

bright [adj7] *vivid in color*
brave, brilliant, clear, colored, colorful, deep, flashy, fresh, gay, glitzy*, hued, intense, psychedelic, razzle-dazzle, rich, ruddy, sharp, showy, tinged, tinted; SEE CONCEPT 618

brighten [v1] *make shine or glow*
buff up, burnish, clear up, enliven, gleam, grow sunny, illuminate, illumine, intensify, kindle, lighten, light up, polish, punch up*, spiff up*; SEE CONCEPTS 244,250

brighten [v2] *make happy, feel better*
become cheerful, buck up, buoy up, cheer, cheer up, clear up, encourage, enliven, gladden, hearten, improve, look up, perk up; SEE CONCEPTS 7,22

brilliant [adj1] *shining, glowing in appearance*
ablaze, bright, coruscating, dazzling, effulgent, flashy, fulgent, gleaming, glittering, glossy, incandescent, intense, lambent, lucent, luminous, lustrous, radiant, refulgent, resplendent, scintillat-

ing, showy, sparkling, vivid; SEE CONCEPT 617

brilliant [adj2] *famous, outstanding*
celebrated, distinguished, eminent, excellent, exceptional, glorious, illustrious, magnificent, prominent, splendid, superb; SEE CONCEPT 568

brilliant [adj3] *very intelligent*
accomplished, acute, astute, brainy, bright, clever, discerning, eggheaded*, Einstein*, expert, genius, gifted, ingenious, intellectual, inventive, knowing, knowledgeable, masterly, penetrating, profound, quick, quick-witted, sharp, smart, talented, whip, whiz kid*; SEE CONCEPT 402

brim [n] *edge of object, usually the top*
border, brink, circumference, fringe, hem, lip, margin, perimeter, periphery, rim, skirt, verge; SEE CONCEPT 836

brim [v] *flow over the top*
fill, fill up, hold no more, overflow, run over, spill, swell, teem, well over; SEE CONCEPT 740

brimming/brimful [adj] *overflowing; up to the top*
awash, chock-full, crammed, crowded, filled, flush, full, full to the top, jammed, level with, loaded, overfull, packed, running over, stuffed, topfull; SEE CONCEPTS 481,771,774

brine [n] *salt solution*
alkali, blue, brackish water, deep, drink, marinade, ocean, pickling solution, preservative, saline, salt water, sea water, sodium chloride solution, vinegar; SEE CONCEPT 514

bring [v1] *transport or accompany*
attend, back, bear, buck*, carry, chaperon, companion, conduct, consort, convey, deliver, escort, fetch, gather, guide, gun*, heel*, import, lead, lug, pack, pick up, piggyback*, ride, schlepp*, shoulder, take, take along, tote, transfer, transport, truck, usher; SEE CONCEPT 143

bring [v2] *cause; influence*
begin, compel, contribute to, convert, convince, create, dispose, effect, engender, force, induce, inflict, lead, make, move, occasion, persuade, prevail on, prevail upon, produce, prompt, result in, sway, wreak; SEE CONCEPT 242

bring [v3] *command a price*
afford, bring in, draw, earn, fetch, gross, net, produce, return, sell for, take, yield; SEE CONCEPTS 330,335

bring [v4] *file charges in court*
appeal, arraign, cite, declare, indict, initiate legal action, institute, prefer, serve, sue, summon, take to court; SEE CONCEPT 317

bring about [v] *cause success*
accomplish, achieve, beget, bring to pass, compass, create, do, draw on, effect, effectuate, engender, generate, give rise to, make happen, manage, occasion, produce, realize, secure, succeed; SEE CONCEPTS 244,706

bring around [v] *convince, induce*
argue, convert, draw, get, indoctrinate, persuade, prevail upon, prompt, prove, talk into, win over; SEE CONCEPT 68

bring down [v] *reduce or hurt*
abase, cut down, damage, drop, fell, floor, injure, knock down, KO*, lay low, level, lower, mow down, murder*, overthrow, overturn, prostrate, pull down, shoot down, slay*, throw down, tumble, undermine, upset, wound; SEE CONCEPTS 7,19,252

bring in [v] *make a profit*
accrue, acquire, bear, be worth, bring, cost, earn,

fetch, gain, get, gross, make, pay, produce, realize, return, sell, yield; SEE CONCEPTS 124,330

bring off [v] accomplish
achieve, bring home the bacon*, bring to pass,
carry off, carry out, discharge, effect, effectuate,
execute, perform, pull off, realize, succeed; SEE
CONCEPTS 704,706

bring up [v1] raise youngster
breed, cultivate, develop, discipline, educate,
feed, form, foster, nourish, nurture, provide for,
rear, school, support, teach, train; SEE CONCEPT
295

bring up [v2] initiate, mention in conversation
advance, advert, allude to, broach, discuss, introduce, moot, move, offer, point out, propose, put
forward, raise, raise a subject, refer, submit, tender, touch on, ventilate*; SEE CONCEPT 51

brink [n] edge of an object or area
border, boundary, brim, fringe, frontier, limit, lip,
margin, perimeter, periphery, point, rim, skirt,
threshold, verge; SEE CONCEPTS 484,513

brisk [adj1] fast-moving; active
adroit, agile, alert, animated, bustling, busy, energetic, lively, nimble, quick, speedy, sprightly,
spry, vigorous, vivacious, zippy; SEE CONCEPTS
542,584

brisk [adj2] chilly, refreshing (weather)
biting, bracing, crisp, exhilarating, fresh, invigorating, keen, nippy, sharp, snappy, stimulating;
SEE CONCEPT 605

bristle [n] short, prickly hair
barb, feeler, fiber, point, prickle, quill, spine,
stubble, thorn, vibrissa, whisker; SEE CONCEPT
418

bristle [v] become upset, excited
be angry, be infuriated, be maddened, blow up*,
boil, boil over, bridle, flare, flare up, fume, get
one's dander up*, rage, rise, ruffle, see red*,
seethe, spit*, stand on end*, swell; SEE CONCEPT
410

brittle [adj1] fragile
breakable, crisp, crumbling, crumbly, delicate,
frail, frangible, friable, inelastic, shatterable,
shivery, vitreous, weak; SEE CONCEPTS 488,606

brittle [adj2] tense
curt, edgy, irritable, nervous, prim, short, stiff,
stilted; SEE CONCEPT 401

broach [v1] bring up a topic
advance, approach, bring up, hint at, interject,
interpose, introduce, mention, moot, move, offer,
open up, propose, raise subject, speak of, submit,
suggest, talk of, touch on, ventilate*; SEE CON-
CEPT 51

broach [v2] open, pierce
begin, crack, decant, draw off, puncture, start,
tap, uncork; SEE CONCEPTS 142,225

broad [adj1] wide physically
ample, capacious, deep, expansive, extended, extensive, full, generous, immense, large, latitudi-
nous, outspread, outstretched, roomy, spacious,
splay, squat, thick, vast, voluminous, widespread;
SEE CONCEPTS 773,796

broad [adj2] extensive
all-embracing, all-inclusive, comprehensive, copious, encyclopedic, expansive, extended, far-
flung, far-reaching, general, inclusive,
nonspecific, scopic, sweeping, ubiquitous, undetailed, universal, unlimited, wide, wide-ranging,
widespread; SEE CONCEPT 772

broad [adj3] full, obvious
apparent, clear, explicit, open, plain, straightforward, undisguised, unequivocal; SEE CONCEPT
576

broad [adj4] liberal-minded
advanced, cultivated, experienced, open, open-
minded, permissive, progressive, radical, tolerant,
unbiased, wide; SEE CONCEPT 403

broad [adj5] vulgar
blue, coarse, dirty, gross, improper, indecent, indelicate, low-minded, off-color, purple, racy, risqué, salty, saucy, smutty, spicy, suggestive,
unrefined, unrestrained, wicked; SEE CONCEPT
545

broadcast [n] information on electronic media
advertisement, air time, announcement, newscast,
performance, program, publication, radiocast,
show, simulcast, telecast, transmission; SEE CON-
CEPTS 274,293

broadcast [v1] put forth on electronic media
air, announce, beam, be on the air, cable, circulate, colorcast, communicate, get out*, go on the
air, go on the airwaves, put on the air, radio,
radiograph, relay, send, show, simulcast, telecast,
telegraph, telephone, televise, transmit; SEE CON-
CEPTS 60,292

broadcast [v2] make public
advertise, announce, annunciate, blare, blazon,
circulate, communicate, declare, disseminate, distribute, proclaim, promulgate, publish, report,
sow, spread, strew, troll; SEE CONCEPT 60

broadcasting [n] informing via electronic media
airing, air time, announcing, auditioning, news-
casting, performing, posting online, putting on
program, radio, reporting, telecasting, television,
transmission, transmitting; SEE CONCEPTS
263,293

broaden [v] extend, supplement
augment, breadthen, develop, enlarge, expand,
fatten, grow, increase, open up, ream, spread,
stretch, swell, widen; SEE CONCEPT 239

broad-minded [adj] liberal
advanced, catholic, cosmopolitan, dispassionate,
flexible, free-thinking, indulgent, liberal, open,
open-minded, permissive, progressive, radical, receptive, receptivity, tolerant, unbiased, unbigoted, undogmatic, unprejudiced, wide; SEE
CONCEPT 403

brochure [n] short, printed document
advertisement, booklet, circular, flyer, folder,
handbill, handout, leaflet, pamphlet; SEE CON-
CEPT 280

broil [v] cook under direct heat
burn, melt, roast, scorch, sear, swelter; SEE CON-
CEPT 170

broiling [adj] very hot
baking, burning, fiery, on fire, red-hot, roasting,
scalding, scorching, sizzling, sweltering, torrid;
SEE CONCEPT 605

broke [adj] without money
bankrupt, beggared, bust*, cleaned out*, destitute, dirt poor*, flat broke*, impoverished, in
Chapter 11*, in debt, indebted, indigent, insolvent, needy, penniless, penurious, poor, ruined,
stone broke*, strapped*, tapped out; SEE CON-
CEPT 334

broken [adj1] destroyed; made into pieces from a
whole
burst, busted, collapsed, cracked, crippled, crumbled, crushed, damaged, defective, demolished,

disintegrated, dismembered, fractured, fragmentary, fragmented, hurt, injured, in pieces, mangled, mutilated, pulverized, rent, riven, ruptured, separated, severed, shattered, shredded, slivered, smashed, split; SEE CONCEPT 485

broken [adj2] discontinuous
disconnected, disturbed, erratic, fragmentary, incomplete, intermittent, interrupted, irregular, spasmodic, sporadic; SEE CONCEPT 482

broken [adj3] mentally defeated
beaten, browbeaten, crippled, crushed, defeated, demoralized, depressed, discouraged, disheartened, heartsick, humbled, oppressed, overpowered, subdued, tamed, vanquished; SEE CONCEPT 403

broken [adj4] not working
busted, coming unglued, coming unstuck, defective, disabled, down, exhausted, fallen apart, faulty, feeble, gone, gone to pieces*, gone to pot*, haywire, imperfect, in disrepair, in need of repair, inoperable, in the shop*, kaput*, not functioning, on the blink*, on the fritz*, on the shelf*, out, out of commission*, out of kilter*, out of order, out of whack*, ruined, run-down, screwed up*, shot, spent, unsatisfactory, weak, wracked*, wrecked; SEE CONCEPTS 485,560

broken [adj5] forgotten, ignored (promise)
abandoned, dishonored, disobeyed, disregarded, ignored, infringed, isolated, retracted, traduced, transgressed, violated; SEE CONCEPT 544

broken [adj6] stuttering in speech
disjointed, halting, hesitant, hesitating, imperfect, incoherent, mumbled, muttered, stammering, unintelligible, weak; SEE CONCEPT 267

brokenhearted [adj] devastated
crestfallen, crushed, desolate, despairing, despondent, disappointed, disconsolate, grief-stricken, grieved, heartbroken, heartsick, heartsore, inconsolable, miserable, mournful, prostrated, sorrowful, wretched; SEE CONCEPT 403

broker [n] financial expert
agent, business person, dealer, entrepreneur, factor, financier, go-between, interagent, interceder, intercessor, intermediary, intermediate, mediator, merchant, middleperson, negotiator, stockbroker; SEE CONCEPTS 348,353

bronze [adj] coppery-brown color
brownish, burnished, chestnut, copper, copper-colored, metallic brown, reddish-brown, reddish-tan, russet, rust, tan; SEE CONCEPT 618

brooch [n] ornamental pin
bar pin, breastpin, clip, cluster, jewelry; SEE CONCEPT 446

brood [n] cluster of children
begats, breed, chicks, clutch, descendants, family, flock, hatch, infants, issue, litter, offspring, posterity, progeniture, progeny, scions, seed, young; SEE CONCEPT 296

brood [v] agonize over
be in brown study*, bleed, chafe inwardly*, consider, daydream, deliberate, despond, dream, dwell upon, eat one's heart out*, fret, gloom, grieve, lament, languish, meditate, mope, mull over, muse, ponder, reflect, repine, ruminate, sigh, speculate, stew over*, sulk, sweat out*, sweat over*, think about, think upon, worry; SEE CONCEPT 17

brook [n] stream of water
beck, branch, burn, creek, rill, rindle, river, rivulet, run, runnel, streamlet, watercourse; SEE CONCEPT 514

brook [v] endure, accept
abide, allow, bear, be big*, countenance, go, hang in, hang in there*, hear of, live with, put up with, sit tight*, stand, stomach, suffer, support, swallow, take, tolerate, withstand; SEE CONCEPT 23

broom [n] device for cleaning floors
besom, carpet sweeper, feather duster, floor brush, mop, swab, sweeper, whisk; SEE CONCEPT 499

broth [n] soup, usually clear
borscht, bouillon, bowl, brew, chowder, concoction, consommé, decoction, dishwater*, distillation, elixir, fluid, gumbo, hodge-podge*, liquor, olio, porridge, potage, potpourri, pottage, puree, splash, stock, vichyssoise, water; SEE CONCEPTS 457,467

brothel [n] house of prostitution
bagnio, bawdy house*, bordello, call house*, cathouse*, den of iniquity*, house of assignation, house of ill repute, house with red doors*, massage parlor, red-light district, whorehouse; SEE CONCEPT 449

brother [n] male sibling
blood brother, kin, kinsperson, relation, relative, twin; SEE CONCEPTS 414,419

brow [n] forehead
countenance, eyebrow, face, frons, front, mien, temple, top; SEE CONCEPT 418

browbeat [v] castigate, nag
badger, bludgeon, bluster, bulldoze*, bully, coerce, cow, despotize, domineer, dragoon, frighten, harass, hector, intimidate, lean on*, lord it over*, oppress, overawe, overbear, put heat on*, put the chill on*, put through the wringer*, threaten, tyrannize; SEE CONCEPTS 14,52

brown [adj] dark, burnished color
amber, auburn, bay, beige, bister, brick, bronze, buff, burnt sienna, chestnut, chocolate, cinnamon, cocoa, coffee, copper, drab, dust, ecru, fawn, ginger, hazel, henna, khaki, mahogany, nut, ochre, puce, russet, rust, sepia, snuff-colored, sorrel, tan, tawny, terra-cotta, toast, umber; SEE CONCEPT 618

browse [v] look around; look through
check over, dip into*, examine cursorily, feed, flip through, get the cream*, give the once over*, glance at, graze, hit the high spots*, inspect loosely, leaf through, nibble*, once over lightly*, pass an eye over*, peruse, read, read here and there, riffle through, riff through, run through, scan, skim, skip through, survey, thumb through, wander; SEE CONCEPT 103

bruise [n] black and blue mark under skin
abrasion, black eye, black mark, blemish, boo-boo*, contusion, discoloration, injury, mark, mouse*, swelling, wale, wound; SEE CONCEPT 309

bruise [v] break blood vessel; discolor
bang up, batter, beat, black, blacken, blemish, bung up*, contuse, crush, damage, deface, do a number on*, injure, mar, mark, pound, pulverize, wound, zing*; SEE CONCEPTS 137,246,250

brunette/brunet [adj] dark hair and/or skin
bistered, brown, dusky, pigmented, swart, swarthy, tanned, tawny; SEE CONCEPTS 406,618

brunt [n] bad end of a situation
burden, force, full force, impact, pressure, shock,

strain, stress, tension, thrust, violence; SEE CON-
CEPT **674**

brush [n1] *tool with bristles for cleaning*
besom, broom, hairbrush, mop, polisher,
sweeper, toothbrush, waxer, whisk; SEE CONCEPT
499

brush [n2] *fight*
clash, conflict, confrontation, encounter, engagement, fracas, rub, run-in, scrap, set-to, skirmish,
tap, touch, tussle; SEE CONCEPT **106**

brush [n3] *scrappy bushes*
boscage, bracken, brushwood, chaparral, coppice,
copse, cover, dingle, fern, gorse, grove, hedge,
scrub, sedge, shrubbery, spinney, thicket, undergrowth, underwood; SEE CONCEPT **429**

brush [v1] *touch lightly*
caress, contact, flick, glance, graze, kiss, scrape,
shave, skim, smooth, stroke, sweep, tickle; SEE
CONCEPT **612**

brush [v2] *clean, prepare by whisking*
buff, clean, paint, polish, sweep, wash, whisk,
wipe; SEE CONCEPTS **165,202**

brush aside/brush off [v] *ignore; refuse*
boycott, cold-shoulder*, contradict, cut, deny,
disclaim, dismiss, disown, disregard, get rid of,
have no time for*, ostracize, override, rebuff, reject, repudiate, scorn, send away, slight, snub,
spurn, sweep aside; SEE CONCEPT **30**

brush up [v] *improve condition*
clean up, cram, go over, look over, polish up,
read up, refresh one's memory, refurbish, relearn,
renovate, reread, retouch, review, revise, study,
touch up; SEE CONCEPTS **202,244**

brusque [adj] *curt, surly*
abrupt, bluff, blunt, brief, crusty, discourteous,
gruff, hasty, impolite, sharp, short, snappy,
snippy, tart, terse, unmannerly; SEE CONCEPTS
267,401

brutal [adj1] *cruel, remorseless*
barbarous, bloodthirsty, callous, ferocious, gruff,
hard, harsh, heartless, impolite, inhuman, insensitive, merciless, pitiless, remorseless, rough,
rude, ruthless, savage, severe, uncivil, uncivilized, unfeeling, unmannerly, unmerciful, vicious;
SEE CONCEPT **401**

brutal [adj2] *crude, rough*
animal, bearish, beastly, bestial, brute, brutish,
carnal, coarse, feral, ferine, inhuman, inhumane,
rude, savage, swinish, unfeeling; SEE CONCEPT
544

brutality [n] *cruel treatment*
atrocity, barbarism, barbarity, bloodthirstiness,
brutishness, choke hold*, cruelty, ferocity, fierceness, grossness, inhumanity, ruthlessness, sadism,
savageness, savagery, third degree*, unfeelingness, viciousness; SEE CONCEPTS **14,86**

brutally [adv] *cruelly, without remorse*
atrociously, barbarically, barbarously, brutishly,
callously, demoniacally, diabolically, ferally, ferociously, fiercely, hardheartedly, heartlessly, in
cold blood, inexorably, inhumanely, inhumanly,
meanly, mercilessly, murderously, pitilessly, relentlessly, remorselessly, ruthlessly, savagely,
something fierce, something terrible, unkindly,
unrelentingly, viciously; SEE CONCEPT **544**

brute [n] *barbarian*
animal, beast, cannibal, creature, critter*, degenerate, devil, fiend, lout, monster, ogre, ruffian,
sadist, savage, swine, wild animal; SEE CONCEPTS
394,423

brute [adj] *very strong; animallike*
animal, beastly, bestial, bodily, carnal, feral, ferine, fleshly, instinctive, mindless, physical, senseless, swinish, unthinking; SEE CONCEPTS **489,540**

bubble [n] *globule of air*
air ball*, balloon, barm, bead, blister, blob, drop,
droplet, effervescence, foam, froth, lather, sac,
spume, vesicle; SEE CONCEPT **437**

bubble [v] *foam, froth up, especially with sound*
boil, burble, churn, eddy, effervesce, erupt, fester, fizz, gurgle, gush, issue, moil, murmur, percolate, ripple, seep, seethe, simmer, smolder,
sparkle, spume, stir, swash, trickle, well; SEE
CONCEPTS **179,469**

buck [n] *male animal*
bull, stag; SEE CONCEPTS **394,419**

buck [v] *resist, kick off*
bound, combat, contest, dislodge, dispute, duel,
fight, jerk, jump, leap, oppose, prance, repel,
start, throw, traverse, trip, unseat, vault, withstand; SEE CONCEPTS **180,222**

bucket [n] *container, often for liquids, with handle*
brazier, can, canister, cask, hod, kettle, pail, pot,
scuttle, vat; SEE CONCEPT **494**

buckle [n] *fastener with long pin*
catch, clamp, clasp, clip, fastening, fibula, harness, hasp; SEE CONCEPT **450**

buckle [v] *contort, warp*
bend, bulge, cave in, collapse, crumple, distort,
fold, twist, yield; SEE CONCEPT **702**

buckle down [v] *concentrate on*
address, apply oneself, attend to, bend, dedicate
oneself to, devote oneself to, exert oneself, give,
give oneself over to, keep close to, keep one's
mind on, launch into, occupy oneself with, pitch
in, set to, throw, turn; SEE CONCEPTS **17,87**

bud [n] *new sprout on plant*
bloom, blossom, embryo, floret, germ, incipient
flower, nucleus, shoot, spark; SEE CONCEPT **428**

bud [v] *sprout*
burgeon, burst forth, develop, grow, pullulate,
shoot; SEE CONCEPT **427**

budding [adj] *developing, flowering*
beginning, blossoming, burgeoning, bursting
forth, embryonic, fledgling, fresh, germinal, ger-
minating, growing, incipient, maturing, nascent,
opening, potential, promising, pubescent, pullulating, shooting up, sprouting, vegetating, young;
SEE CONCEPT **490**

buddy [n] *friend*
associate, chum, co-mate, companion, comrade,
confidant, co-worker, crony, intimate, mate, pal,
peer, sidekick; SEE CONCEPT **423**

budge [v] *dislodge from staid position*
bend, change, change position, convince, give
way, inch, influence, locomote, move, persuade,
propel, push, remove, roll, shift, slide, stir, sway,
yield; SEE CONCEPTS **68,147**

budget [n] *financial plan*
account, aggregate, allocation, allowance, bulk,
cost, estimated expenses, finances, fiscal estimate,
funds, means, planned disbursement, quantity,
quantum, resources, spending plan, statement, total; SEE CONCEPT **332**

budget [v] *plan money or action*
allocate, apportion, calculate, compute, cost, estimate, predict, ration; SEE CONCEPTS **36,330**

buff [n] *enthusiast*
addict, admirer, aficionado, connoisseur, devotee,

expert, fan, fiend*, freak*, habitué, hound, lover, votary; SEE CONCEPTS *352,423*

buff [*adj*] *sandy color*
bare, blonde, canary, ecru, lemon, light brown, nude, ochre, straw, tan, tawny, yellow-brown, yellowish; SEE CONCEPT *618*

buff [*v*] *polish to a shine*
brush, burnish, furbish, glaze, gloss, pumice, rub, sandpaper, scour, shine, smooth; SEE CONCEPTS *202,215*

buffer [*n*] *safeguard*
bulwark, bumper, cushion, defense, fender, intermediary, screen, shield, shock absorber; SEE CONCEPTS *484,729*

buffet [*n*] *meal set out on table for choosing*
café, cafeteria, cold table, counter, cupboard, lunch wagon, salad bar, shelf, sideboard, smorgasbord, snack bar; SEE CONCEPTS *443,459*

buffet [*v*] *hit repeatedly*
bang, batter, beat, blow, box, bump, clobber, cuff, flail, jolt, knock, pound, pummel, push, rap, shove, slap, smack, spank, strike, thrash, thump, wallop; SEE CONCEPT *189*

buffoon [*n*] *clownlike person*
antic, bozo*, clown, comedian, comic, droll, fool, harlequin, jester, joker, merry-andrew, wag, zany; SEE CONCEPT *423*

bug [*n1*] *bacterium, microorganism*
bacillus, disease, germ, infection, microbe, virus; SEE CONCEPT *306*

bug [*n2*] *insect*
ant, beetle, cootie, flea, gnat, louse, pest, vermin; SEE CONCEPT *398*

bug [*n3*] *obsession*
craze, enthusiasm, fad, mania, rage, zeal; SEE CONCEPT *532*

bug [*v1*] *bother, disturb*
abrade, annoy, badger, chafe, gall, get on someone*, harass, irk, irritate, needle, nettle, pester, plague, provoke, vex; SEE CONCEPTS *7,19*

bug [*v2*] *listen to without permission*
eavesdrop, listen in, overhear, spy, tap, wiretap; SEE CONCEPTS *192,596*

bugle [*n*] *musical horn*
clarion, cornet, misery pipe*, trumpet; SEE CONCEPT *262*

build [*n*] *physical structure, form*
body, conformation, constitution, figure, frame, habit, habitus, physique, shape; SEE CONCEPT *757*

build [*v1*] *construct structure*
assemble, bring about, carpenter, cast, compile, compose, contrive, engineer, erect, evolve, fabricate, fashion, fit together, forge, form, frame, jerry-build, knock together*, make, manufacture, model, prefabricate, produce, put together, put up, raise, rear, reconstruct, sculpture, set up, superstruct, synthesize, throw together*, throw up*; SEE CONCEPT *168*

build [*v2*] *initiate, found*
base, begin, constitute, establish, formulate, inaugurate, institute, originate, set up, start; SEE CONCEPT *234*

build [*v3*] *increase, accelerate*
aggrandize, amplify, augment, boost, compound, develop, enlarge, escalate, expand, extend, heighten, improve, intensify, magnify, mount, multiply, strengthen, swell, wax; SEE CONCEPTS *236,245*

builder [*n*] *construction worker*
architect, artisan, constructor, contractor,

craftsperson, erector, fabricator, framer, inventor, maker, manufacturer, mason, originator, producer; SEE CONCEPT *348*

building [*n*] *constructed dwelling*
architecture, construction, domicile, edifice, erection, fabric, framework, home, house, hut, pile, superstructure; SEE CONCEPTS *439,441*

buildup [*n*] *development; accumulation*
accretion, advertising, enlargement, escalation, expansion, gain, growth, heap, hype, increase, load, mass, plug, promotion, publicity, puff*, stack, stockpile, store; SEE CONCEPTS *230,704,787*

build up [*v*] *amplify, advertise*
add to, boost, develop, enhance, expand, extend, fortify, heighten, hype, increase, intensify, plug*, promote, publicize, puff*, reinforce, spotlight, strengthen; SEE CONCEPTS *236,245,266*

built-in [*adj*] *included*
congenital, constitutional, deep-seated, essential, implicit, inborn, inbred, in-built, incorporated, indwelling, ingrained, inherent, innate, inseparable, integral, part and parcel*; SEE CONCEPT *549*

bulb [*n*] *globular object*
ball, bunch, corm, corn, globe, head, knob, nodule, nub, protuberance, swelling, tube, tumor; SEE CONCEPT *436*

bulge [*n*] *swollen object*
appendage, bagginess, blob, bump, bunch, bunching, convexity, dilation, distention, excess, excrescence, gibbosity, growth, hump, intumescence, jut, lump, nodulation, nodule, outgrowth, outthrust, projection, prominence, promontory, protrusion, protuberance, sac, sagging, salience, salient, superfluity, swelling, tuberosity, tumefaction, tumor, wart; SEE CONCEPTS *436,470*

bulge [*v*] *project outward*
bag, balloon, beetle, belly, bilge, billow, bloat, blob, bug out, dilate, distend, enlarge, expand, extrude, jut, overhang, poke, pop out, pouch, protrude, protuberate, puff out, sag, stand out, stick out, swell; SEE CONCEPTS *208,780*

bulk [*n1*] *size, largeness*
aggregate, amount, amplitude, bigness, dimensions, extent, immensity, magnitude, mass, massiveness, quantity, quantum, substance, total, totality, volume, weight; SEE CONCEPT *730*

bulk [*n2*] *main part, most*
best part, better part, biggest share, body, generality, greater number, greater part, gross, lion's share*, majority, major part, mass, nearly all, plurality, predominant part, preponderance, principal part; SEE CONCEPTS *635,829*

bulky [*adj*] *huge*
awkward, beefy, big, colossal, cumbersome, cumbrous, enormous, gross, heavy, hefty, high, hulking, immense, large, long, mammoth, massive, ponderous, substantial, unhandy, unmanageable, unwieldy, voluminous, weighty; SEE CONCEPT *781*

bulldoze [*v1*] *demolish*
drive, elbow, flatten, force, jostle, level, press, propel, push, raze, shove, thrust; SEE CONCEPTS *208,252*

bulldoze [*v2*] *bully, intimidate*
bludgeon, bluster, browbeat, coerce, cow, dragoon, harass, hector; SEE CONCEPT *14*

bullet [*n*] *small missile*
ammo*, ammunition, ball, bolt, cap, cartridge, dose*, lead, love letter*, pellet, projectile, rocket,

round, shot, slug, trajectile; SEE CONCEPT *500*

bulletin [*n*] *message, notification*
account, announcement, break, calendar, communication, communiqué, dispatch, flash*, handout, hot wire*, item, list, news, news flash*, notice, program, publication, release, report, scoop*, skinny*, statement, the dope*, what's going down*, what's happening*; SEE CONCEPTS *271,274*

bully [*n*] *domineering person*
annoyer, antagonizer, browbeater, bulldozer, coercer, harrier, hector, insolent, intimidator, oppressor, persecutor, pest, rascal, rowdy, ruffian, tease, tormenter, tough; SEE CONCEPT *423*

bully [*v*] *intimidate, push around*
bludgeon, bluster, browbeat, buffalo, bulldoze, coerce, cow, despotize, domineer, dragoon, enforce, harass, hector, lean on, menace, oppress, overbear, persecute, ride roughshod*, showboat*, swagger, terrorize, threaten, torment, torture, turn on the heat*, tyrannize, walk heavy*; SEE CONCEPT *14*

bulwark [*n*] *fortification, support*
barrier, bastion, buffet, buttress, citadel, defense, embankment, fort, fortress, guard, mainstay, outwork, parapet, partition, protection, rampart, redoubt, safeguard, security, stronghold, vallation; SEE CONCEPTS *96,729*

bum [*n*] *beggar*
bindle*, black sheep*, derelict, drifter, floater, gutterpup*, guttersnipe*, hobo, stiff*, tramp, transient, vagabond, vagrant; SEE CONCEPTS *412,423*

bump [*vl*] *collide, hit, usually with sound*
bang, bounce, box, buck, bunt, butt, carom, clap, clatter, crack, crash, impinge, jar, jerk, jolt, jostle, jounce, knock, pat, plop, plunk, pound, punch, rap, rattle, thud, thump, thwack, smash into, strike, thud, thump, thunder, thwack, whack; SEE CONCEPT *189*

bump [*v*] *move over, dislodge*
budge, displace, remove, shift; SEE CONCEPT *213*

bump into [*v*] *happen upon*
chance upon, come across, encounter, hit, light, light upon, luck, meet, meet up with, run across, run into, stumble, tumble; SEE CONCEPT *114*

bun [*n*] *baked roll*
bread, cruller, Danish, doughnut, eclair, muffin, pastry, scone, sweet roll; SEE CONCEPT *457*

bunch [*n*] *collection of something*
agglomeration, assemblage, assortment, band, batch, bevy, blob, bouquet, bundle, caboodle*, chunk, clump, cluster, covey, crew, crowd, fascicle, flock, galaxy, gang, gathering, group, heap, host, hunk, knot, lot, mass, mess, mob, multitude, number, oodles*, pack, parcel, party, passel*, pile, quantity, sheaf, shebang*, shock, shooting match*, spray, stack, swarm, team, thicket, troop, tuft; SEE CONCEPT *432*

bunch [*v*] *gather in group*
assemble, bundle, cluster, collect, congregate, cram, crowd, flock, group, herd, huddle, mass, pack; SEE CONCEPT *109*

bundle [*n*] *accumulation, package of something*
array, assortment, bag, bale, batch, box, bunch, carton, clump, cluster, collection, crate, group, heap, lot, mass, pack, package, packet, pallet, parcel, pile, quantity, roll, set, stack, wad; SEE CONCEPTS *432,787*

bundle [*v*] *accumulate, package*
bale, bind, clothe, fasten, pack, palletize, tie, truss, wrap; SEE CONCEPTS *158,202*

bungle [*v*] *blunder, mess up*
ball up*, boggle, botch, butcher*, drop the ball*, err, flub, foul up*, fudge*, fumble, goof up*, gum up*, louse up*, make a mess of, mar, mess up, miscalculate, mishandle, mismanage, muff*, ruin, screw up*, spoil; SEE CONCEPT *101*

bungler [*n*] *person who blunders*
addlebrain*, blockhead*, blunderer, bonehead*, botcher*, bumbler, butcher*, butterfingers*, clod, clumsy oaf*, dolt, donkey*, duffer*, dunce, featherbrain*, fool, foul-up*, fumbler*, goofball*, goof off*, harebrain*, idiot, ignoramus, incompetent, klutz*, mismanager, muddler, muffer*, numskull*, screw up*; SEE CONCEPTS *412,423*

bunk [*nl*] *nonsense*
applesauce*, balderdash, baloney*, bilge*, claptrap, eyewash*, flimflam*, garbage*, hogwash*, hooey*, horsefeathers*, jazz*, piffle*, poppycock*, rot*, rubbish, tomfoolery*, tommyrot*, trash*, twaddle*; SEE CONCEPTS *63,278*

bunk [*n2*] *twin bed, usually placed; place to sleep*
berth, cot, doss, hay, kip, pallet, sack; SEE CONCEPT *443*

bunt [*v*] *hit half-heartedly*
butt, lay it down*, meet, sacrifice, throw, toss; SEE CONCEPTS *189,363*

buoy [*n*] *floating device*
beacon, drift, float, guide, marker, signal; SEE CONCEPT *628*

buoy (up) [*v*] *make light, encourage*
bolster, boost, buck up, cheer, cheer up, encourage, hearten, keep afloat, lift, prop, raise, support, sustain, uphold; SEE CONCEPTS *7,22*

buoyancy/buoyance [*nl*] *lightness in weight*
airiness, ethereality, floatability, levity, weightlessness; SEE CONCEPT *734*

buoyancy/buoyance [*n2*] *lightness in spirit*
animation, bounce, cheerfulness, cheeriness, ebullience, effervescence, exuberance, gaiety, good feeling, good humor, happiness, high spirits, jollity, liveliness, pep, spiritedness, sunniness, vim and vigor*, zing*, zip; SEE CONCEPTS *410,411*

buoyant [*adj1*] *light in weight*
afloat, airy, bouncy, floatable, floating, resilient, supernatant, unsinkable, weightless; SEE CONCEPT *491*

buoyant [*adj2*] *light in spirit*
animated, blithe, bouncy, breezy, bright, carefree, cheerful, debonair, effervescent, elastic, expansive, full of zip, gay, happy, invigorated, jaunty, jovial, joyful, laid back*, lighthearted, lively, peppy, resilient, sunny, supple, vivacious; SEE CONCEPTS *403,404*

burden [*n*] *mental weight; stress*
accountability, affliction, albatross*, anxiety, ball and chain*, blame, care, charge, clog, concern, deadweight, difficulty, duty, encumbrance, excess baggage*, grievance, hardship, Herculean task, hindrance, load, millstone, misfortune, mishap, obstruction, onus, punishment, responsibility, sorrow, strain, task, tax, thorn in one's side*, trial, trouble, weary load, work, worry; SEE CONCEPTS *532,690*

burden [*v*] *encumber, strain*
afflict, bear down on, bother, crush, cumber, de-

press, dish it out*, dish out*, dump on*, encumber, give it to, hamper, handicap, hinder, impede, lade, load, make heavy, obligate, oppress, overcharge, overload, overwhelm, pile, press, saddle with, snow*, snow under*, stick it to, strain, tax, trouble, try, vex, weigh down, worry; SEE CONCEPTS 7,14,19

burdensome [adj] troublesome

carking, crushing, demanding, difficult, disturbing, exacting, exigent, heavy*, irksome, onerous, oppressive, superincumbent, taxing, tough, trying, wearing, wearying, weighty; SEE CONCEPT 529

bureau [n1] branch of an organization

agency, authority, board, commission, committee, department, division, front office*, office, salt mines*, service, setup, shop, store; SEE CONCEPTS 325,441,449

bureau [n2] chest of drawers

chiffonier, commode, desk, dresser, highboy, sideboard, writing desk; SEE CONCEPT 443

bureaucracy [n] system which controls organization

administration, authority, beadledom*, city hall*, civil service, directorate, government, management, ministry, officialdom, officials, powers that be*, red tape*, regulatory commission, the Establishment*, the system*; SEE CONCEPTS 325,770

burglar [n] person who steals

cat burglar, crook, filcher*, housebreaker, midnighter*, owl*, picklock*, pilferer*, porchclimber*, prowler, robber, safecracker, sneakthief*, thief; SEE CONCEPT 412

burglary [n] stealing from residence, business

break-in, breaking and entering, caper, crime, filching, heist, housebreaking, larceny, owl job*, pilferage, prowl, robbery, safecracking, second-story work*, sting, theft, thieving; SEE CONCEPT 139

burial [n] laying in of dead body

burying, deep six*, deposition, entombment, exequies, funeral, inhumation, interment, last rites, obsequies, sepulture; SEE CONCEPT 367

burlesque [n] bawdy show; vaudeville

burly*, caricature, farce, lampoon, lampoonery, mock, mockery, parody, pastiche, peep show, revue, satire, send-up, spoof, strip, takeoff, travesty, vaudeville; SEE CONCEPT 263

burlesque [adj] farcical

caricatural, comic, ironical, ludicrous, mock, mocking, parodic, satirical, travestying; SEE CONCEPT 555

burly [adj] husky

able-bodied, athletic, beefcake*, beefy*, big, brawny, bruising, bulky, gorillalike, hefty, hulking, hulky, hunk, muscular, portly, powerful, stocky, stout, strapping, strong, sturdy, thickset, well-built; SEE CONCEPT 773

burn [v1] be on fire; set on fire

bake, be ablaze, blaze, brand, broil, calcine, cauterize, char, combust, conflagrate, cook, cremate, enkindle, flame, flare, flash, flicker, glow, heat, ignite, incinerate, kindle, light, melt, parch, reduce to ashes, rekindle, roast, scald, scorch, sear, set a match to, singe, smoke, smolder, toast, torch, wither; SEE CONCEPT 249

burn [v2] feel stinging pain

bite, hurt, pain, smart, sting, tingle; SEE CONCEPT 590

burn [v3] be excited about; yearn for

be angry, be aroused, be inflamed, be passionate, be stirred up, blaze, boil, breathe fire*, bristle, desire, eat up*, fume, lust, rage, seethe, simmer, smoulder, tingle, yearn; SEE CONCEPTS 20,29,34

burn [v4] cheat

beat, bilk, chisel, cozen, deceive, defraud, gyp, overreach, ream, swindle, take, trick, use; SEE CONCEPTS 59,142

burning [adj1] blazing, flashing

afire, aflame, alight, blistering, broiling, conflagrant, enkindled, fiery, flaming, flaring, gleaming, glowing, heated, hot, ignited, illuminated, incandescent, in flames, kindled, on fire, oxidizing, red-hot*, scorching, searing, sizzling, smoking, smouldering, torrid, white-hot*; SEE CONCEPTS 485,605

burning [adj2] fervent, excited

all-consuming, ardent, blazing, eager, earnest, fervid, feverish, frantic, frenzied, heated, hectic, impassioned, intense, passionate, red-hot*, vehement, white-hot*, zealous; SEE CONCEPT 403

burning [adj3] stinging, painful

acrid, biting, caustic, irritating, painful, piercing, prickling, pungent, reeking, sharp, smarting, tingling; SEE CONCEPTS 314,537

burning [adj4] important

acute, clamant, clamorous, compelling, critical, crucial, dire, essential, exigent, imperative, importunate, instant, pressing, significant, urgent, vital; SEE CONCEPT 568

burnish [v] polish, brighten

buff, furbish, glance, glaze, gloss, luster, patina, put on a finish, rub, sheen, shine, smooth, wax; SEE CONCEPTS 202,215

burrow [n] hole dug by animal

couch, den, hovel, lair, retreat, shelter, tunnel; SEE CONCEPT 517

burrow [v] dig a hole

delve, excavate, hollow out, scoop out, tunnel, undermine; SEE CONCEPT 178

burst [n] blow-up, blast

access, bang, barrage, blowout, bombardment, breach, break, cannonade, crack, discharge, eruption, explosion, fit, flare, fusillade, gush, gust, outbreak, outpouring, round, rupture, rush, sally, salvo, shower, spate, split, spurt, storm, surge, torrent, volley; SEE CONCEPTS 86,179,208

burst [v] blow up, break out

barge, blow, break, crack, detonate, discharge, disintegrate, erupt, explode, fly open, fracture, fragment, gush forth, perforate, pierce, pop, prick, puncture, rend asunder, run, rupture, rush, shatter, shiver, splinter, split, spout, tear apart; SEE CONCEPTS 179,252

bury [v1] lay to rest after death

consign to grave, cover up, deposit, embalm, ensepulcher, enshrine, entomb, hold last rites for*, hold services for, inearth, inhume, inter, inurn, lay out, mummify, plant*, put away*, put six feet under*, sepulcher, sepulture, tomb; SEE CONCEPT 367

bury [v2] conceal, cover

cache, cover up, ensconce, enshroud, hide, occult, plant, screen, secrete, shroud, stash, stow away; SEE CONCEPTS 172,188

bury [v3] plant in ground

drive in, embed, engulf, implant, sink, submerge; SEE CONCEPTS 172,257

bu
bu

bury [v4] *engross oneself*
absorb, concentrate, engage, immerse, interest, occupy, rivet, throw oneself into; SEE CONCEPT 24

bush [n] *shrubs; woodland*
backcountry, backwoods, boscage, bramble, briar, brush, chaparral, creeper, forest, hedge, hinterland, jungle, outback, plant, scrub, scrubland, shrubbery, the wild, thicket, vine, wilderness; SEE CONCEPT 429

bushy [adj] *shaggy, unkempt*
bristling, bristly, disordered, feathery, fluffy, fringed, full, furry, fuzzy, hairy, heavy, hirsute, leafy, luxuriant, nappy, prickly, rough, rumpled, spreading, stiff, thick, tufted, unruly, wiry, woolly; SEE CONCEPTS 406,606

busily [adv] *actively; intently*
agilely, animatedly, ardently, arduously, assiduously, briskly, carefully, diligently, eagerly, earnestly, energetically, enthusiastically, expeditiously, fervently, hastily, hurriedly, indefatigably, industriously, laboriously, like all get out*, like the devil*, like the dickens*, nimbly, painstakingly, perseveringly, persistently, purposefully, restlessly, seriously, speedily, spiritedly, strenuously, studiously, unremittingly, unweariedly, vigilantly, vigorously, vivaciously, zealously; SEE CONCEPT 544

business [n1] *job, profession*
bag*, biz*, calling, career, craft, dodge*, employment, field, function, game, line, livelihood, métier, occupation, pursuit, racket*, specialty, trade, vocation, what one is into*, work; SEE CONCEPT 360

business [n2] *company, enterprise*
cartel, concern, corporation, establishment, factory, firm, fly-by-night operation*, house, institution, market, megacorp*, mill, Mom and Pop*, monopoly, organization, outfit, partnership, setup, shoestring operation*, shop, store, syndicate, trust, venture; SEE CONCEPTS 325,449

business [n3] *commerce, trade*
affairs, bargaining, barter, buying and selling, capital and labor, commercialism, contracts, deal, dealings, exchange, free enterprise, game, industrialism, industry, manufacturing, market, merchandising, production and distribution, racket*, sales, selling, trading, traffic, transaction, undertaking; SEE CONCEPTS 325,770

business [n4] *personal concern*
affair, assignment, beeswax*, carrying on, duty, function, goings-on*, hanky-panky*, happening, interest, issue, lookout, matter, palaver, point, problem, question, responsibility, subject, task, topic; SEE CONCEPT 532

businesslike [adj] *efficient, professional*
accomplished, careful, concentrated, correct, diligent, direct, disciplined, earnest, effective, enterprising, expeditious, hardworking, industrious, intent, matter-of-fact, methodical, orderly, organized, painstaking, practical, practiced, purposeful, regular, routine, sedulous, serious, skillful, systematic, thorough, well-ordered, workaday; SEE CONCEPTS 326,544

businessperson [n] *professional working person*
baron, big-time operator*, big wheel*, capitalist, dealer, employer, entrepreneur, executive, financier, franchiser, gray flannel suit*, industrialist, manager, merchandiser, merchant, operator, organization person, small potatoes*, storekeeper,

suit*, the bacon*, tradesperson, trafficker, tycoon, wheeler-dealer*; SEE CONCEPTS 347,348

bust [n1] *chest of human*
bosom, breast, chest, front; SEE CONCEPT 392

bust [n2] *arrest for illegal action*
apprehension, arrest, capture, cop, detention, nab, pickup, pinch, raid, search, seizure; SEE CONCEPTS 298,317

bust [v1] *ruin, impoverish*
become insolvent, break, crash, fail, fold up, go bankrupt, go into Chapter 11*, pauperize; SEE CONCEPT 330

bust [v2] *arrest for illegal action*
apprehend, catch, collar, cop*, detain, nab, pick up, pinch, pull in, raid, run in, search; SEE CONCEPTS 298,317

bust [v3] *physically break*
burst, fold, fracture, rupture; SEE CONCEPT 252

bustle [n] *quick and busy activity*
ado, agitation, clamor, commotion, do*, excitement, flurry, furor, fuss, haste, hubbub, hurly-burly*, hurry, pother, rumpus, stir, to-do*, tumult, turmoil, uproar, whirl, whirlpool, whirlwind; SEE CONCEPT 386

bustle [v] *move around quickly, busily*
bestir, dash, dust, flit, flutter, fuss, hasten, hum, hurry, hustle, run, rush, scamper, scramble, scurry, scuttle, stir, tear, whirl, whisk; SEE CONCEPT 150

busy [adj1] *engaged, at work*
active, already taken*, assiduous, at it*, buried, diligent, employed, engaged, engrossed, having a full plate*, having enough on one's plate*, having fish to fry*, having many irons in the fire*, hustling, in a meeting, in conference, industrious, in someone else's possession*, in the field, in the laboratory, occupied, on assignment, on duty, on the go, overloaded, persevering, slaving, snowed*, swamped*, tied up, unavailable, up to one's ears*, with a customer, working; SEE CONCEPTS 326,544,555

busy [adj2] *active, on the go*
bustling, busy as a beaver*, energetic, full, fussy, hectic, humming*, hustling, lively, popping*, restless, strenuous, tireless, tiring; SEE CONCEPT 542

busy [adj3] *nosy, impertinent*
butting in, curious, forward, inquisitive, interfering, intrusive, meddlesome, meddling, nebby, obtrusive, officious, prying, pushy, snoopy, stirring, troublesome; SEE CONCEPT 404

busybody [n] *nosy, impertinent person*
backseat driver*, butt-in*, buttinsky*, eavesdropper, fink*, fussbudget, gossip, intermeddler, intruder, meddler, newsmonger*, nosey parker*, rubberneck*, scandalmonger*, sidewalk superintendent*, snoop, snooper, tattletale, troublemaker, yenta*; SEE CONCEPT 423

butcher [n] *meat killer, seller*
boner*, meatmarket person, meat person, processor, skinner*, slaughterer, slayer*; SEE CONCEPT 348

butcher [v1] *slay and prepare animal for meat*
beef up, carve, clean, cure, cut, cut down, dress, joint, liquidate, salt, slaughter, smoke, stick; SEE CONCEPTS 170,252

butcher [v2] *ruin*
bollix up*, botch, destroy, goof up*, louse up*, make a mess of*, mutilate, screw up*, spoil, wreck; SEE CONCEPT 101

butt [n1] *end, shaft*
base, bottom, edge, extremity, fag end, foot, fundament, haft, handle, hilt, shank, stock, stub, stump, tail, tip; SEE CONCEPT 827

butt/buttocks [n2] *animate rear end*
back end, backside, behind, bottom, bum*, derrière, fanny*, fundament, gluteus maximus, haunches, hindquarters, posterior, rear, rump, seat, tush*; SEE CONCEPT 392

butt [n3] *object of joking*
chump*, clay pigeon*, derision, dupe*, easy mark*, fall guy, fool, goat, jesteé*, joke, laughingstock, mark, patsy, pigeon*, sap, setup*, sitting duck*, softie*, subject, sucker, target, turkey, victim; SEE CONCEPT 423

butt [v1] *bang up against with head*
batter, buck, buffet, bump, bunt, collide, gore, hook, horn, jab, knock, poke, prod, punch, push, ram, run into, shove, smack, strike, thrust, toss; SEE CONCEPT 189

butt [v2] *touch, adjoin*
abut, border, bound, communicate, join, jut, meet, neighbor, project, protrude, verge; SEE CONCEPTS 113,747

buttress [n] *brace, support*
abutment, column, mainstay, pier, prop, reinforcement, shore, stanchion, stay, strut, underpinning; SEE CONCEPT 440

buttress [v] *support, bolster*
back up, beef up*, brace, build up, bulwark, carry, jack up, jazz up*, prop, reinforce, shore, step up, strengthen, sustain, uphold; SEE CONCEPT 250

buxom [adj] *bosomy*
ample, built, busty, chubby, comely, curvaceous, curvy, full-bosomed, full-figured, healthy, hearty, lusty, plump, robust, shapely, stacked*, voluptuous, well-made, well-proportioned, well-rounded, zaftig*; SEE CONCEPT 406

buy [n] *something purchased*
acquisition, bargain, closeout, deal, good deal, investment, purchase, steal, value; SEE CONCEPT 710

buy [v1] *purchase*
acquire, bargain for, barter for, contract for, get, get in exchange, go shopping, invest in, market, obtain, pay for, procure, purchase, redeem, score, secure, shop for, sign for, take; SEE CONCEPT 327

buy [v2] *bribe*
corrupt, fix, grease palm*, have, land, lubricate, oil palm*, ransom, reach, redeem, sop*, square, suborn, tamper; SEE CONCEPTS 192,341

buyer [n] *someone who purchases*
client, consumer, customer, easy make*, emptor, end user, patron, prospect, purchaser, representative, shopper, sucker*, user, vendee; SEE CONCEPT 348

buzz [n1] *droning sound*
drone, fizz, fizzle, hiss, hum, murmur, purr, ring, ringing, sibilation, whir, whisper; SEE CONCEPT 595

buzz [n2] *gossip*
comment, cry, grapevine*, hearsay, news, report, rumble*, rumor, scandal, scuttlebutt, talk, whisper; SEE CONCEPT 274

buzz [v1] *make droning sound*
bombinate, bumble, drone, fizz, fizzle, hum, murmur, reverberate, ring, sibilate, whir, whisper, whiz; SEE CONCEPT 65

buzz [v2] *gossip*
call, chatter, inform, natter, rumor, tattle; SEE CONCEPT 60

buzzword [n] *popular word or phrase*
argot, cant, doublespeak, fuzzword, jargon, lingo, mediaspeak, phraseology, policyspeak, slang; SEE CONCEPT 275

by [adv] *near*
aside, at hand, away, beyond, close, handy, in reach, over, past, through, to one side; SEE CONCEPT 586

by [prep1] *next to*
along, alongside, beside, by way of, close to, near, nearby, nigh, over, past, round, via; SEE CONCEPT 586

by [prep2] *by means of*
at the hand of, in the name of, on, over, supported by, through, through the agency of, through the medium of, under the aegis of, with, with the assistance of; SEE CONCEPT 544

bygone [adj] *in the past*
ancient, antiquated, archaic, belated, dated, dead, defunct, departed, down memory lane*, erstwhile, extinct, forgotten, former, gone, gone by, in oblivion, late, lost, of old, of yore, olden, oldfangled, old-fashioned, old-time, one-time, out-of-date, previous, quondam, sometime, vanished, water over the dam*, water under the bridge*; SEE CONCEPT 820

bypass [v] *avoid*
blink at, burke, circumnavigate, circumvent, depart from, detour, deviate from, finesse, get around, go around, go around the barn*, ignore, let go, neglect, omit, outflank, pass around, sidestep, skirt, take back road*, wink at; SEE CONCEPTS 30,102

bystander [n] *person who watches*
eyewitness, gaper*, kibitzer*, looker-on, observer, onlooker, passerby, spectator, viewer, watcher, witness; SEE CONCEPT 423

byword [n] *saying*
adage, aphorism, apophthegm, axiom, catchphrase, catchword, dictum, epithet, gnome, gnomic saying, handle, maxim, motto, nickname, precept, proverb, saw, shibboleth, slogan, standing joke; SEE CONCEPT 275

C

cab [n] *car for hire*
carriage, hack, hackney, jitney, taxi, taxicab, tourist car; SEE CONCEPT 505

cabaret [n] *nightclub with musical performances*
after-hours joint*, bar, café, disco, discothèque, dive, hideaway, hot spot*, nightery, night spot, speakeasy, supper club, tavern, watering hole*; SEE CONCEPTS 447,449

cabin [n] *tiny house; lodging*
berth, box, caboose, camp, chalet, compartment, cot, cottage, crib, deckhouse, home, hovel, hut, lodge, log house, quarters, room, shack, shanty, shed, shelter; SEE CONCEPT 516

cabinet [n1] *cupboard for storage*
case, chiffonier, closet, commode, container, depository, dresser, escritoire, locker, repository, wardrobe; SEE CONCEPTS 443,494

bu
ca

cabinet [n2] *executives serving a leader*
administration, administrators, advisers, assembly, assistants, authority, brain trust*, bureau, bureaucracy, committee, council, counselors, department heads, governing body, government, kitchen cabinet*, ministry, official family; SEE CONCEPT 299

cache [n] *hidden supply*
accumulation, assets, drop, drop joint, drop-off, fund, hideout, hiding place, hoard, kitty*, nest egg*, plant, repository, reserve, shade, stake, stash, stockpile, store, storehouse, supplies, treasure, treasury, wealth; SEE CONCEPTS 446,710

cache [v] *hide a supply of something*
accumulate, bury, conceal, cover, ditch, duck, ensconce, lay away, maintain, park, plant, put away, put in the hole*, save, screen, secrete, squirrel*, squirrel away*, stash, stash away, store; SEE CONCEPT 188

cackle [n] *a loud laugh*
chortle, chuckle, cluck, crow, gibber, giggle, gobble, guffaw, quack, snicker, snigger, titter; SEE CONCEPT 77

cackle [v] *laugh irritatingly*
babble, blather, burble, chortle, chuckle, cluck, crow, gibber, giggle, gobble, jabber, quack, snicker, snigger, titter; SEE CONCEPT 77

cacophonous [adj] *harsh sounding*
clinking, discordant, disharmonic, dissonant, grating, ill-sounding, immusical, inharmonious, jangly, jarring, noisy, raucous, sour, strident, unmusical; SEE CONCEPTS 592,594

cad [n] *sly, dastardly person*
boor, bounder*, clown, creep, cur*, dog*, heel, louse, lout, rake, rascal, rat*, rotter*, rounder*, scoundrel, stinker, worm*; SEE CONCEPT 412

cadaver [n] *dead body*
body, cage, carcass, corpse, deceased, mort*, remains, skeleton, stiff*; SEE CONCEPT 390

cadaverous [adj] *pale, corpselike*
ashen, bag of bones, blanched, bloodless, consumptive, dead, deathlike, deathly, emaciated, exsanguinous, gaunt, ghastly, ghostly, haggard, pallid, peaked, peaky, sallow, shadowy, sick, skeletal, skeletonlike, skin and bones*, spectral, thin, wan, wasted; SEE CONCEPTS 406,491,618

cadence [n] *rhythm*
accent, beat, count, inflection, intonation, lilt, measure, meter, modulation, pulse, rhythmus, swing, tempo, throb; SEE CONCEPT 65

cadre [n] *nucleus of effort*
core, force, framework, infrastructure, key group, officers, organization, personnel, staff; SEE CONCEPTS 417,432

café [n] *small, informal restaurant*
bistro, burger joint, cafeteria, cake shop, chophouse, coffee bar, coffee shop, diner, eating house, grease joint*, greasy spoon*, hash house*, luncheonette, lunchroom, noshery*, pit stop*, quick-lunch, snack bar, soup house, tearoom; SEE CONCEPT 449

cage [n] *enclosure with bars*
coop, corral, crate, enclosure, fold, jail, mew, pen, pinfold, pound; SEE CONCEPT 494

cage [v] *hold in enclosure*
close in, confine, coop up, enclose, envelop, fence in, hem, immure, impound, imprison, incarcerate, jail, lock up, mew, pen, restrain, shut in, shut up; SEE CONCEPT 191

cajole [v] *attempt to coax; flatter*
apple polish*, argue into, banter, beguile, blandish, bootlick*, brownnose*, build up, butter up*, con, crowd, deceive, decoy, delude, dupe, entice, entrap, get around, get next to*, hand a line*, induce, influence, inveigle, jolly, lay it on thick*, lure, make up to, maneuver, massage, mislead, oil*, play up to, push, rub the right way*, seduce, snow*, soap*, soften, soft-soap*, spread it on*, stroke, suck up to*, sweeten up*, sweet-talk*, tantalize, tempt, urge, wheedle, work on, work over*; SEE CONCEPTS 59,68,75

cake [n] *bar of something*
block, brick, loaf, lump, mass, slab; SEE CONCEPT 470

calamitous [adj] *disastrous; tragic*
adverse, afflictive, blighting, cataclysmic, catastrophic, deadly, deplorable, devastating, dire, fatal, grievous, harmful, heartbreaking, lamentable, messy, pernicious, regrettable, ruinous, unfavorable, unfortunate, woeful; SEE CONCEPT 537

calamity [n] *disaster; tragedy*
adversity, affliction, blue ruin*, cataclysm, catastrophe, collapse, cross, curtains, distress, downfall, hardship, holy mess*, misadventure, mischance, misfortune, mishap, reverse, ruin, scourge, the worst*, trial, tribulation, unholy mess*, visitation, waterloo*, woe, wreck, wretchedness; SEE CONCEPTS 674,675

calculable [adj] *able to be computed or estimated*
accountable, ascertainable, computable, countable, discoverable, estimable, foreseeable, measurable, predictable, reckonable; SEE CONCEPTS 402,762

calculate [v1] *compute or estimate amount*
account, add, adjust, appraise, assay, cast, cipher, consider, count, determine, divide, dope out*, enumerate, figure, forecast, foretell, gauge, guess, judge, keep tabs*, measure, multiply, number, rate, reckon, size up, subtract, sum, take account of, tally, tot, tote up*, value, weigh, work out; SEE CONCEPT 764

calculate [v2] *plan on*
aim, anticipate, assume, bank on, build, count on, depend on, design, intend, judge, plan, reckon, rely on, suppose, think likely, trust; SEE CONCEPTS 26,36

calculating [adj] *scheming to manipulate*
artful, canny, careful, cautious, chary, circumspect, considerate, contriving, crafty, cunning, designing, devious, discreet, gingerly, guarded, guileful, intelligent, Machiavellian, manipulative, politic, premeditating, safe, scheming, sharp, shrewd, sly, wary, wily; SEE CONCEPTS 401,403

calculation [n1] *computing, estimating amount*
adding, arithmetic, ciphering, computation, counting, dividing, estimate, estimation, figuring, forecast, judgment, multiplying, prediction, reckoning, subtracting, summation, totaling; SEE CONCEPTS 28,764

calculation [n2] *computed or estimated amount*
answer, computation, divination, estimate, estimation, figuring, forecast, judgment, prediction, prognosis, prognostication, reckoning, reply; SEE CONCEPT 787

calculation [n3] *forethought*
canniness, caution, circumspection, contrivance, deliberation, discretion, foresight, planning, precaution, prudence, thought; SEE CONCEPT 660

calendar [n] *schedule of events*
agenda, almanac, annal, bulletin, card, chronology, daybook, diary, docket, journal, lineup, list, log, logbook, menology, pipeline, program, record, register, sked, system of reckoning, tab, table, time, timetable; SEE CONCEPTS 274,281,809

calf [n1] *leg between knee and ankle*
foreleg, shin; SEE CONCEPT 392

calf [n2] *baby cow*
dogie, freemartin, heifer, maverick, veal, yearling, young bull, young cow; SEE CONCEPT 394

caliber [n1] *capacity; character*
ability, appetency, capability, competence, constitution, dignity, distinction, endowment, essence, faculty, force, gifts, habilitation, merit, nature, parts, power, quality, scope, stature, strength, talent, value, virtue, worth, worthiness; SEE CONCEPT 411

caliber [n2] *size of ammunition*
bore, class, diameter, gauge, grade, length, measure, measurement, quality, striking power, weight; SEE CONCEPT 730

call [n1] *yelled statement*
alarm, calling, command, cry, hail, holler*, scream, shout, signal, whoop, yawp, yell; SEE CONCEPT 278

call [n2] *demand, announcement*
appeal, bidding, command, invitation, notice, order, plea, proposal, request, solicitation, subpoena, summons, supplication, visit; SEE CONCEPT 53

call [n3] *need, cause for action*
claim, excuse, grounds, justification, necessity, obligation, occasion, reason, right, urge; SEE CONCEPT 709

call [n4] *normal sound of animal*
cheep, chirp, cry, note, peep, roar, shriek, song, tweet, twitter, warble; SEE CONCEPT 64

call [v1] *yell declaration*
announce, arouse, awaken, bawl, bellow, cry, cry out, exclaim, hail, holler*, hoot, howl, proclaim, roar, rouse, scream, screech, shout, shriek, vociferate, waken, whoop, yawp*, yoo hoo*, yowl; SEE CONCEPTS 47,266

call [v2] *arrange meeting*
ask, assemble, bid, collect, contact, convene, convoke, gather, invite, muster, phone*, rally, request, ring up, subpoena, summon, telephone; SEE CONCEPT 114

call [v3] *entitle*
address, baptize, christen, denominate, describe as, designate, dub, label, name, style, term, title; SEE CONCEPT 62

call [v4] *demand or announce action*
appeal to, appoint, ask, challenge, charge, claim, command, declare, decree, elect, entreat, exact, ordain, order, postulate, pray to, proclaim, require, requisition, set apart, solicit, summon; SEE CONCEPT 53

call [v5] *estimate, consider*
adumbrate, approximate, augur, forecast, foretell, guess, judge, make rough guess, place, portend, predict, presage, prognosticate, prophesy, put, reckon, regard, think, vaticinate; SEE CONCEPTS 28,70

call [v6] *attempt to communicate by telephone*
beep, blast*, bleep, buzz, contact, get back to*, phone, ring, telephone; SEE CONCEPTS 74,266

call [v7] *visit at residence or business*
come by, come over, crash, drop by, drop in, fall by, fall down, hit, look in on, look up, play, pop in*, run in, see, stop by, stop in, swing by; SEE CONCEPT 227

call for [v] *demand; entail*
ask for, inquire, involve, lack, necessitate, need, occasion, request, require, suggest, want; SEE CONCEPT 646

calling [n] *chosen profession*
art, business, career, craft, day gig*, do*, dodge*, employment, gig*, go*, handicraft, hang*, life's work, lifework, line, métier, mission, nine-to-five*, occupation, play, province, pursuit, racket*, rat race*, slot*, swindle*, trade, vocation, walk of life, work; SEE CONCEPT 360

callous [adj] *cruel, insensitive*
apathetic, blind to, careless, case-hardened, cold, cold-blooded, deaf to, hard, hard-bitten, hard-boiled, hardened, hardhearted, heartless, impassive, impenitent, indifferent, indurated, inflexible, insensate, insensible, insensitive, insentient, inured, obdurate, soulless, spiritless, stiff, stony, stubborn, thick-skinned, torpid, tough, toughened, unaffected, unbending, uncaring, uncompassionate, unconcerned, unfeeling, unimpressionable, unresponsive, unsusceptible, unsympathetic; SEE CONCEPT 404

callow [adj] *immature*
crude, green, guileless, inexperienced, infant, jejune, jellybean*, juvenile, kid, low tech*, naive, not dry behind ears*, puerile, raw, sophomore, tenderfoot, unbaked, unfledged, unripe, unsophisticated, untrained, untried, young; SEE CONCEPTS 578,678,797

calm [n] *quietness, composure*
calmness, dispassion, doldrums, hush, impassivity, imperturbation, lull, patience, peace, peacefulness, peace of mind, placidity, quiet, repose, rest, restraint, serenity, silence, stillness, stoicism, tranquility; SEE CONCEPTS 388,411,720

calm [adj1] *peaceful, quiet (inanimate)*
at a standstill, at peace, bland, bucolic, cool, halcyon, harmonious, hushed, inactive, in order, low-key, mild, motionless, pacific, pastoral, placid, quiescent, reposeful, reposing, restful, rural, serene, slow, smooth, soothing, still, stormless, tranquil, undisturbed, unruffled, waveless, windless; SEE CONCEPTS 544,705

calm [adj2] *composed, cool (animate)*
aloof, amiable, amicable, civil, collected, cool as cucumber*, cool-headed, detached, disinterested, dispassionate, equable, gentle, impassive, imperturbable, inscrutable, kind, laid-back*, levelheaded, listless, moderate, neutral, patient, placid, pleased, poised, relaxed, restful, satisfied, sedate, self-possessed, serene, still, temperate, unconcerned, undisturbed, unemotional, unexcitable, unexcited, unflappable, unimpressed, unmoved, unruffled, untroubled; SEE CONCEPTS 401,404

calm [v] *make composed, quiet*
allay, alleviate, appease, assuage, balm, becalm, compose, cool, cool it*, cool out*, hush, lay back*, lull, mitigate, mollify, pacify, placate, quiet, quieten, relax, relieve, sedate, settle, simmer down, soft-pedal*, soothe, steady, still, stroke, take it easy*, take the edge off*, tranquilize; SEE CONCEPT 231

ca
ca

camaraderie [n] *friendship*
cheer, companionability, companionship, comradeship, conviviality, esprit de corps, fellowship, gregariousness, intimacy, jollity, sociability, togetherness; SEE CONCEPT *388*

camouflage [n] *disguise*
beard*, blind, cloak, concealment, cover, coverup, deceit, deceptive marking, dissimulation, faking, false appearance, front, guise, mask, masking, masquerade, mimicry, paint, plain brown wrapper*, protective coloring, red herring*, screen, shade, shroud, smokescreen, veil; SEE CONCEPT *260*

camouflage [v] *disguise, cover*
beard*, becloud, befog, cloak, conceal, cover up, deceive, dim, dissemble, dissimulate, dress up, hide, mask, obfuscate, obscure, screen, throw on makeup, veil; SEE CONCEPTS *172,188*

camp [n] *site for outdoor living*
bivouac, campfire, campground, camping ground, caravansary, chalet, cottage, encampment, hut, lean-to, lodge, log cabin, shack, shanty, shed, summer home, tent, tent city, tepee, tilt, wigwam; SEE CONCEPTS *198,516*

camp [adj] *consciously affecting the unfashionable, weird, or bizarre*
affected, arch, artificial, avant-garde, Daliesque*, far out*, in*, mannered, mod, ostentatious, pop, posturing, wild; SEE CONCEPT *544*

campaign [n] *attempt to win; attack*
crusade, drive, expedition, fight, movement, offensive, operation, push, warfare; SEE CONCEPTS *87,320*

campaign [v] *attempt to win political election*
agitate, barnstorm, canvass, contend for, contest, crusade, electioneer, go to grass roots*, hit the trail*, lobby, mend fences*, muckrake, mudsling*, politick, press the flesh*, ring doorbells*, run, run for, shake hands and kiss babies*, solicit votes, stand for, stump*, tour, whistle-stop*; SEE CONCEPT *300*

can [n1] *container, usually metallic*
aluminum, bottle, bucket, canister, cannikin, gunboat*, gutbucket*, jar, package, pop top*, receptacle, tin, vessel; SEE CONCEPTS *476,494*

can [n2] *toilet*
head*, john*, johnny*, latrine, lavatory, litter box*, outhouse, pot*, potty*, privy, restroom, sandbox*, throne*, washroom, water closet; SEE CONCEPT *443*

can [n3] *buttocks*
backside, behind, butt*, derrière, fanny*, fundament, gluteus maximus, hind end, posterior, rump, seat, tush*; SEE CONCEPT *418*

can [v1] *preserve fruit, vegetable*
bottle, keep, put up; SEE CONCEPT *170*

can [v2] *be able*
be capable of, be equal to, be up to, be within one's area, be within one's control, can do*, commit, could, cut the mustard*, have it made*, lie in one's power, make it*, make out, make the grade*, manage, may, take care of; SEE CONCEPT *630*

can [v3] *fire from job*
ax*, boot*, bounce*, cashier, discharge, dismiss, expel, give the heave ho*, kick out*, let go, sack*, terminate; SEE CONCEPT *351*

canal [n] *waterway*
aqueduct, bottleneck, channel, choke point, conduit, course, cove, ditch, duct, estuary, firth, trench, water, watercourse; SEE CONCEPT *514*

cancel [v1] *call off; erase*
abolish, abort, abrogate, annul, ax, black out, blot out, break, break off, countermand, cross out, cut, deface, delete, destroy, do away with, do in, efface, eliminate, eradicate, expunge, finish off*, go back on one's word*, kill, obliterate, off*, omit, quash, remove, render invalid, repeal, repudiate, rescind, revoke, rub out, scratch out, scrub*, sink*, smash, squash, stamp across, strike out, torpedo*, total*, trash*, trim*, undo, wash out*, wipe out*, wipe slate clean*, X-out*, zap*; SEE CONCEPTS *18,211,234*

cancel [v2] *equal out*
abort, abrogate, annul, balance out, call off, compensate for, counteract, counterbalance, countercheck, countermand, counterpoise, declare invalid, discard, discharge, frustrate, ignore, invalidate, make up for, negate, neutralize, nullify, offset, overthrow, put an end to, recall, recant, redeem, redress, refute, render inert, render null and void, repeal, repudiate, rescind, retract, revoke, rule out, set aside, suppress, vacate, void; SEE CONCEPTS *232,667*

cancellation [n] *calling off; erasure*
abandoning, abandonment, abolishing, abolition, abrogation, annulment, canceling, deletion, dissolution, dissolving, elimination, invalidating, invalidation, nullification, overruling, quashing, recall, recalling, repeal, repudiation, retirement, retracting, retraction, reversal, reversing, revocation, revoking, undoing, withdrawing; SEE CONCEPT *119*

cancer [n] *malignant growth*
big C*, C*, canker, carcinoma, corruption, disease, long illness, malignancy, sickness, tumor; SEE CONCEPT *306*

candid [adj] *honest*
aboveboard, bluff, blunt, equal, equitable, fair, forthright, frank, free, frontal, genuine, guileless, impartial, ingenuous, just, objective, open, outspoken, plain, right up front*, scrupulous, sincere, straightforward, talking turkey*, telling it like it is*, truthful, unbiased, uncolored, unequivocal, unprejudiced, unpretended, up front*, upright; SEE CONCEPT *267*

candidate [n] *person desiring political office, job*
applicant, aspirant, bidder, claimant, competitor, contender, contestant, dark horse*, entrant, favorite son*, handshaker*, hopeful*, job-hunter, nominee, office-seeker, petitioner, possibility, possible choice, pothunter*, runner, seeker, solicitant, stumper*, successor, suitor, whistlestopper*, write-in*; SEE CONCEPT *359*

candlestick [n] *holder for candles*
candelabra, candelabrum, menorah, pricket, sconce, taper holder; SEE CONCEPT *444*

candor [n] *complete honesty*
artlessness, directness, fairness, forthrightness, frankness, glasnost, guilelessness, honesty, impartiality, ingenuousness, naïveté, openness, outspokenness, probity, simplicity, sincerity, straightforwardness, truthfulness, unequivocalness, uprightness, veracity; SEE CONCEPT *411*

candy [n] *confection*
bonbon, confectionery, confit, hokum*, jawbreaker*, sweet, sweetmeat; SEE CONCEPT *457*

cane [n] *stick to aid walking of disabled*
pikestaff, pole, rod, staff, vade mecum, walking stick; SEE CONCEPT *479*

canker [n] *blistered infection*
bane, blight, blister, boil, cancer, corrosion, corruption, lesion, rot, scourge, smutch, sore, ulcer; SEE CONCEPT *306*

canker [v] *blight, corrupt*
animalize, bestialize, consume, corrode, debase, debauch, demoralize, deprave, embitter, envenom, inflict, pervert, poison, pollute, rot, ruin, scourge, sore, stain, ulcer, vitiate; SEE CONCEPT *240*

cannibal [n] *beast, beastlike human*
aborigine, anthrophagite, anthropophaginian, anthropophagus, brute, bush dweller, cruel person, head-hunter, ogre, ogress, primitive, ruffian, savage; SEE CONCEPT *412*

canny [adj] *clever, artful*
able, acute, adroit, astute, cagey, careful, cautious, circumspect, cunning, dexterous, discreet, foxy*, frugal, having fancy footwork*, hep*, ingenious, intelligent, judicious, knowing, nimble-witted, perspicacious, prudent, quick, quick-witted, sagacious, shrewd, skillful, slick, slippery*, sly, smart, smooth*, street smart*, streetwise*, subtle, wary, watchful, wise, with it*, worldly-wise; SEE CONCEPT *402*

canoe [n] *light, paddled boat*
coracle, dugout, kayak, outrigger, piragua, pirogue; SEE CONCEPT *506*

canon [n1] *rule, edict*
assize, catalogue, command, commandment, criterion, declaration, decree, decretum, dictate, doctrine, dogma, formula, law, list, maxim, order, ordinance, precept, principle, regulation, roll, screed, standard, statute, table, tenet, touchstone, yardstick; SEE CONCEPTS *318,688*

canon [n2] *a body of the most important, influential or superior works in music, literature, or art*
ana, analects, anthology, chrestomathy, classics, collected works, delectus, library, miscellania, oeuvre, works; SEE CONCEPTS *280,432*

canonical [adj] *accepted, recognized*
approved, authoritative, authorized, lawful, legal, official, orthodox, received, sanctioned, sound, statutory; SEE CONCEPTS *319,535*

canonize [v] *sanctify; idolize*
apotheosize, beatify, besaint, bless, consecrate, dedicate, deify, glorify, idolatrize, love, put on a pedestal*, saint, worship; SEE CONCEPTS *32,367*

canopy [n] *overhanging covering*
awning, baldachin, cover, marquee, shade, sunshade, umbrella; SEE CONCEPTS *440,444*

cant [n1] *hypocritical speech*
affected piety, deceit, dishonesty, humbug, hypocrisy, hypocriticalness, insincerity, lip service*, pecksniffery, pharisaicalness, pious platitudes, pomposity, pretense, pretentiousness, sanctimoniousness, sanctimony, sham holiness, show; SEE CONCEPT *63*

cant [n2] *jargon*
argot, dialect, diction, idiom, language, lingo, patois, patter, phraseology, slang, vernacular, vocabulary; SEE CONCEPTS *275,278*

cant [v] *lean, slant*
angle, bevel, careen, grade, heel, incline, list, recline, rise, slope, tilt, tip; SEE CONCEPTS *154,201*

cantankerous [adj] *difficult, crabby*
bad-tempered, bearish, captious, choleric, contrary, cranky, critical, cross, crotchety*, crusty*, disagreeable, dour, grouchy*, grumpy*, huffy*, ill-humored, ill-natured, irascible, irritable, mo-

rose, obstinate, ornery*, peevish, perverse, petulant, prickly, quarrelsome, snappish, sour, stuffy*, testy, vinegarish, vinegary; SEE CONCEPT *401*

canteen [n1] *portable kitchen*
chuck wagon, mobile kitchen, snack bar, snack shop; SEE CONCEPT *449*

canteen [n2] *container for liquids, used in travels*
bota, bottle, flacon, flask, flasket, jug, thermos, water bottle; SEE CONCEPT *494*

canvas [n1] *coarse material*
awning cloth, duck, fly, sailcloth, shade, tarp, tarpaulin, tenting; SEE CONCEPT *473*

canvas [n2] *painting on coarse material*
art, artwork, oil, picture, piece, portrait, still life, watercolor; SEE CONCEPT *259*

canvass [v] *poll; discuss issues*
agitate, analyze, apply, argue, campaign, check, check over, consult, debate, dispute, electioneer, examine, inspect, investigate, review, run, scan, scrutinize, sift, solicit, study, survey, ventilate; SEE CONCEPTS *24,48,56,300*

canyon [n] *gulf in mountain area*
coulee, glen, gorge, gulch, gully, ravine, valley; SEE CONCEPTS *509,513*

cap [n] *small hat*
beanie*, beret, bonnet, dink*, fez, pillbox, skullcap, tam, tam o'shanter; SEE CONCEPT *450*

cap [v] *outdo a performance*
beat, best, better, button down*, button up*, can*, clinch*, cob*, complete, cover, crest, crown, do to a T*, eclipse, exceed, excel, finish, outshine, outstrip, pass, put the lid on*, surmount, surpass, top, top it off*, transcend, trump, wrap up*; SEE CONCEPT *141*

capability [n] *ability to perform*
adequacy, aptitude, art, capacity, competence, craft, cunning, effectiveness, efficacy, efficiency, facility, faculty, means, might, potency, potential, potentiality, power, proficiency, qualification, qualifiedness, skill, wherewithal; SEE CONCEPT *630*

capable [adj] *able to perform*
able, accomplished, adapted, adept, adequate, apt, au fait, clever, competent, dynamite, efficient, experienced, fireball*, fitted, gifted, good, green thumb*, has what it takes*, having know-how*, having the goods*, having the right stuff*, intelligent, knowing the ropes*, knowing the score*, like a one-man band*, like a pistol*, masterly, old hand*, old-timer*, on the ball*, proficient, proper, qualified, skillful, suited, talented, there*, up*, up to it*, up to snuff*, up to speed*, veteran; SEE CONCEPT *527*

capacious [adj] *ample, extensive*
abundant, broad, comfortable, commodious, comprehensive, dilatable, distensible, expandable, expansive, extended, generous, liberal, plentiful, roomy, sizable, spacious, substantial, vast, voluminous, wide; SEE CONCEPTS *481,772,773,774*

capacity [n1] *volume; limit of volume held*
accommodation, amplitude, bulk, burden, compass, contents, dimensions, expanse, extent, full, holding ability, holding power, latitude, magnitude, mass, measure, proportions, quantity, range, reach, retention, room, scope, size, space, spread, standing room only*, sufficiency, sweep; SEE CONCEPTS *481,736,774,794*

capacity [n2] *ability; competency*
adequacy, aptitude, aptness, bent, brains, caliber,

capability, cleverness, compass, competence, efficiency, facility, faculty, forte, genius, gift, inclination, intelligence, knack, might, power, qualification, readiness, skill, stature, strength, talent, the goods*, up to it*, what it takes*; SEE CONCEPTS 409,630

cape [n1] *promontory into water*
arm, beak, bill, chersonese, finger, foreland, head, headland, jetty, jutty, mole, naze, neck, ness, peninsula, point, tongue; SEE CONCEPTS 509,514

cape [n2] *sleeveless coat*
bertha, capote, cardinal, cloak, cope, dolman, fichu, gabardine, manteau, mantelletta, mantilla, mantle, overdress, paletot, pelerine, pelisse, poncho, shawl, tabard, talma, tippet, Vandyke, victorine, wrap, wrapper; SEE CONCEPT 451

caper [n] *antic, lark*
escapade, gag*, gambol, high jinks*, hop, hot foot*, jest, joke, jump, leap, mischief, monkeyshines*, practical joke, prank, put on*, revel, rib*, rollick, shenanigan*, sport, stunt, tomfoolery*, trick; SEE CONCEPT 386

caper [v] *frolic, cavort*
blow the lid off*, bounce, bound, cut capers*, cut loose*, dance, frisk, gambol, go on a tear*, hop, horse around*, jump, kick up one's heels*, leap, let loose*, play, raise hell*, rollick, romp, skip, spring, whoop it up*; SEE CONCEPT 384

capital [n1] *financial assets*
business, cash, CD, estate, finances, financing, fortune, funds, gold, interests, investment, IRA, kitty*, means, money, nest egg*, principal, property, resources, savings, stake, stock, substance, treasure, ways and means*, wealth, wherewithal; SEE CONCEPTS 332,710

capital [n2] *city of governmental seat*
control, county seat, metropolis, municipality, political front, principal city, the Hill*; SEE CONCEPTS 507,512

capital [n3] *upper case written symbol*
cap, initial, majuscule, small cap, uncial; SEE CONCEPT 284

capital [adj1] *main, essential*
basic, cardinal, central, chief, controlling, dominant, first, foremost, fundamental, important, leading, major, number one*, outstanding, overruling, paramount, predominant, preeminent, primary, prime, principal, prominent, underlying, vital; SEE CONCEPTS 546,568,829

capital [adj2] *superior*
best, champion, choice, crack, dandy, delightful, deluxe, excellent, famous, fine, first, first-class*, first-rate*, five-star*, fly, great, prime, splendid, superb, top, top-notch*, world-class*; SEE CONCEPT 574

capitalism [n] *economic system of private ownership*
commercialism, competition, democracy, free enterprise, free market, industrialism, laissez faire economics, mercantilism, private enterprise; SEE CONCEPTS 299,689,770

capitalist [n] *person engaged in private ownership of business*
backer, banker, bourgeois, businessperson, entrepreneur, financier, investor, landowner, moneybags*, one who signs the checks*, plutocrat, the boss*, the money*; SEE CONCEPT 347

capitalize [v] *benefit from situation*
avail oneself of, exploit, gain, make capital of,

obtain, profit, realize, subsidize, take advantage of; SEE CONCEPT 120

capitol [n] *building or buildings housing chief governmental offices*
Capitol Hill, center, dome, legislative hall, political scene*, seat of government, statehouse; SEE CONCEPTS 299,449

capitulate [v] *give in*
bow, buckle under, cave in, cede, come across, come to terms, concede, defer, fold, give away the store*, give out, give up, knuckle under, put out, relent, submit, succumb, surrender, yield; SEE CONCEPTS 35,83

capitulation [n] *giving in*
accedence, bowing, buckling, conceding, giving up, knuckling under, relenting, resignation, submission, succumbing, surrender, yielding; SEE CONCEPTS 83,410

caprice [n] *sudden change of behavior*
bee*, caper*, changeableness, contrariety, crotchet, fad, fancy, fickleness, fitfulness, fool notion*, freak, gag*, humor, impulse, inconsistency, inconstancy, jerk, kink, mood, notion, peculiarity, perversity, put on*, quirk, rib*, temper, thought, vagary, vein, whim, whimsy; SEE CONCEPTS 13,410

capricious [adj] *given to sudden behavior change*
any way the wind blows*, arbitrary, blowing hot and cold*, careless, changeful, contrary, crotchety, effervescent, erratic, every which way*, fanciful, fickle, fitful, flaky*, flighty, freakish, gaga*, helter-skelter*, humorous, impulsive, inconstant, kinky*, lubricious, mercurial, moody, mutable, notional, odd, picky*, punchy*, queer, quirky, temperamental, ticklish, unpredictable, unreasonable, unstable, up and down*, vagarious, variable, volatile, wayward, whimsical, yo-yo*; SEE CONCEPT 401

capsize [v] *overturn*
invert, keel over, roll, tip over, turn over, turn turtle*, upset; SEE CONCEPTS 150,152

capsule [n] *tablet, usually medicine*
bolus, cap, dose, lozenge, pellet, pill, troche; SEE CONCEPTS 260,307

capsule [adj] *shortened form*
abridged, canned, condensed, epitomized, pocket, potted, tabloid; SEE CONCEPTS 531,773

captain [n] *chief of vehicle, effort*
authority, boss, cap, CEO, CFO, chieftain, commander, director, exec*, executive, four-striper*, guide, head, head honcho*, higher up*, leader, master, mistress, number one*, officer, operator, owner, pilot, royalty, skip*, skipper*, top*, top dog*; SEE CONCEPT 347

caption [n] *heading; short description*
explanation, head, inscription, legend, rubric, subtitle, title, underline; SEE CONCEPT 283

captious [adj] *very critical*
acrimonious, cantankerous, carping, caviling, cavillous, censorious, contrary, crabby, cross, demanding, deprecating, disparaging, exacting, exceptive, fault-finding, finicky, hypercritical, irritable, nagging, nit-picking, overcritical, peevish, perverse, petulant, sarcastic, severe, testy, touchy; SEE CONCEPTS 267,404

captivate [v] *attract, enchant*
allure, beguile, bewitch, charm, dazzle, delight, draw, enamour, enrapture, enslave, ensnare, entertain, enthrall, entrance, fascinate, gratify, grip, hold, hook, hypnotize, infatuate, intrigue, lure,

magnetize, make a hit with*, mesmerize, please, rope in*, seduce, spellbind, sweep off one's feet*, take, turn one on, vamp, wile, win; SEE CONCEPTS 7,22

captive [n] *person held physically*
bondman, bondservant, bondwoman, con, convict, detainee, hostage, internee, prisoner, prisoner of war, slave; SEE CONCEPTS 412,423

captive [adj] *physically held by force*
bound, caged, confined, enslaved, ensnared, imprisoned, incarcerated, incommunicado, in custody, jailed, locked up, penned, restricted, subjugated, under lock and key*; SEE CONCEPTS 536,554

captive [adj2] *mentally enchanted, held*
beguiled, bewitched, charmed, delighted, enraptured, enthralled, fascinated, hypnotized, infatuated; SEE CONCEPTS 403

captivity [n] *physical detention by force*
bondage, committal, confinement, constraint, custody, durance, duress, enslavement, enthrallment, entombment, impoundment, imprisonment, incarceration, internment, jail, limbo, restraint, serfdom, servitude, slavery, subjection, thralldom, vassalage; SEE CONCEPTS 191,652

capture [n] *catching, forceful holding*
abduction, acquirement, acquisition, apprehension, appropriating, appropriation, arrest, bag*, bust*, catch, collar, commandeering, confiscation, drop*, ensnaring, fall, gaining, grab*, grasping, hit the jackpot*, hook*, imprisonment, knock off*, laying hold of*, nab*, nail*, obtaining, occupation, pick up*, pinch*, pull*, run in*, securing, seizing, seizure, snatching*, sweep*, taking, taking captive, taking into custody, trapping, trip, winning; SEE CONCEPT 90

capture [v] *catch and forcefully hold*
apprehend, arrest, bag*, bust*, catch, collar, conquer, cop, gain control, get, grab*, hook*, land, nab*, nail*, net, occupy, overwhelm, pick up*, pinch*, prehend, pull in, put the cuffs on*, round up*, run in*, secure, seize, snare, snatch, take captive, take into custody, take prisoner, trap, tumble; SEE CONCEPT 90

car [n] *vehicle driven on streets*
auto, automobile, bucket*, buggy*, bus, clunker*, compact, convertible, conveyance, coupe, gas guzzler*, hardtop, hatchback, heap*, jalopy*, jeep, junker*, limousine, machine, motor, motorcar, pickup, ride*, roadster, sedan, station wagon, subcompact, touring car, truck, van, wagon, wheels*, wreck*; SEE CONCEPT 505

caravan [n] *group traveling together*
band, camel train, campers, cavalcade, convoy, expedition, procession, safari, train, troop; SEE CONCEPTS 432,503

carbohydrate [n] *organic compound composed of carbon, hydrogen, and oxygen*
cellulose, dextrin, dextrose, disaccharide, fructose, galactose, glucose, glycogen, lactose, maltose, monosaccharide, polysaccharide, starch, sucrose, sugar; SEE CONCEPT 478

carcass/carcase [n] *dead body; framework, base structure*
body, cadaver, corpse, framework, hulk, mort*, remains, shell, skeleton, stiff*; SEE CONCEPTS 390,434

card [n] *piece of paper, often with purposeful writing*
agenda, badge, billet, calendar, cardboard, check,

docket, fiberboard, identification, label, pass, poster, program, schedule, sheet, square, tally, ticket, timetable, voucher; SEE CONCEPTS 260,271

cardinal [adj] *important, key*
basal, basic, central, chief, constitutive, essential, first, foremost, fundamental, greatest, highest, indispensable, leading, main, overriding, overruling, paramount, pivotal, preeminent, primary, prime, principal, ruling, vital; SEE CONCEPTS 568,574

care [n1] *personal interest, concern*
affliction, aggravation, alarm, anguish, annoyance, anxiety, apprehension, bother, burden, chagrin, charge, consternation, discomposure, dismay, disquiet, distress, disturbance, encumbrance, exasperation, fear, foreboding, fretfulness, handicap, hardship, hindrance, impediment, incubus, load, misgiving, nuisance, onus, oppression, perplexity, pressure, responsibility, solicitude, sorrow, stew, strain, stress, sweat, tribulation, trouble, uneasiness, unhappiness, vexation, woe, worry; SEE CONCEPTS 410,532

care [n2] *carefulness, attention to detail*
alertness, caution, circumspection, concentration, concern, conscientiousness, consideration, diligence, direction, discrimination, effort, enthusiasm, exactness, exertion, fastidiousness, forethought, heed, interest, management, meticulousness, nicety, pains, particularity, precaution, prudence, regard, scrupulousness, solicitude, thought, trouble, vigilance, wariness, watchfulness; SEE CONCEPT 657

care [n3] *custody of person, usually child*
administration, aegis, auspices, charge, control, direction, guardianship, keeping, management, ministration, protection, safekeeping, superintendence, supervision, trust, tutelage, ward, wardship; SEE CONCEPTS 285,295,388

care [v1] *tend to*
attend, baby sit, consider, foster, keep an eye on*, keep tabs on*, look after, mind, mind the store*, minister, mother, nurse, nurture, pay attention to, protect, provide for, ride herd on*, sit, take pains, tend, treasure, wait on, watch, watch over; SEE CONCEPTS 110,295

care [v2] *regard highly*
be crazy about*, be fond of*, cherish, desire, enjoy, find congenial, hold dear, like, love, prize, respect, take to, want; SEE CONCEPTS 20,32

careen [v] *tilt; move wildly down path*
bend, lean, lurch, pitch, sway, tilt; SEE CONCEPT 147

career [n1] *occupation*
bag*, calling, course, dodge*, employment, field, game*, job, lifework, livelihood, number*, pilgrimage, profession, pursuit, racket*, specialty, thing*, vocation, work; SEE CONCEPTS 349,360

career [n2] *course, path*
course, orbit, passage, pilgrimage, procedure, progress, race, walk; SEE CONCEPTS 501,678,692

carefree [adj] *lighthearted, untroubled*
airy, at ease, blithe, breezy, buoyant, calm, careless, cheerful, cheery, cool, easy, easy-going, feelgood*, happy, happy-go-lucky, insouciant, jaunty, jovial, laid back*, radiant, secure, sunny, unanxious, unbothered; SEE CONCEPT 404

careful [adj] *cautious; painstaking*
accurate, alert, apprehensive, assiduous, attentive, chary, choosy, circumspect, concerned, conscien-

tious, conservative, cool, deliberate, discreet, exacting, fastidious, finicky, fussy, going to great lengths*, guarded, heedful, judicious, leery, meticulous, mindful, observant, particular, playing safe*, precise, prim, protective, provident, prudent, punctilious, regardful, religious, rigorous, scrupulous, self-disciplined, shy, sober, solicitous, solid, thorough, thoughtful, vigilant, wary; SEE CONCEPTS 326,542

carefully [adv] cautiously; painstakingly
anxiously, attentively, circumspectly, concernedly, conscientiously, correctly, deliberately, delicately, dependably, discreetly, exactly, faithfully, fastidiously, fully, gingerly, guardedly, heedfully, honorably, in detail, laboriously, meticulously, particularly, precisely, providently, prudently, punctiliously, regardfully, reliably, rigorously, scrupulously, solicitously, thoroughly, thoughtfully, trustily, uprightly, vigilantly, warily, watchfully, with forethought, with reservations; SEE CONCEPT 542

careless [adj1] without sufficient attention
absent-minded, abstracted, casual, cursory, disregardful, forgetful, hasty, heedless, improvident, imprudent, inaccurate, inadvertent, incautious, inconsiderate, indifferent, indiscreet, indolent, injudicious, irresponsible, lackadaisical, lax, loose, mindless, napping, negligent, nonchalant, oblivious, offhand, perfunctory, pococurante, reckless, regardless, remiss, slipshod, sloppy, thoughtless, uncircumspect, unconcerned, unguarded, unheeding, unmindful, unobservant, unreflective, unthinking, wasteful; SEE CONCEPT 542

careless [adj2] artless
casual, modest, naive, natural, nonchalant, simple, unstudied; SEE CONCEPT 557

caress [n] loving touch
cuddle, embrace, endearment, feel, fondling, hug, kiss, pat, pet, petting, snuggle, squeeze, stroke; SEE CONCEPTS 375,590

caress [v] touch lovingly
bear hug*, brush, buss, clinch, clutch, coddle, cosset, cuddle, dandle, embrace, feel, fondle, graze, handle, hug, kiss, make love, massage, mug, neck, nestle, nuzzle, pat, pet, play around*, rub, squeeze, stroke, toy; SEE CONCEPTS 375,612

caretaker [n] person who maintains something
baby sitter, concierge, curator, custodian, housesitter, janitor, keeper, porter, sitter, super*, superintendent, supervisor, warden, watchperson; SEE CONCEPT 348

cargo [n] baggage; something to be delivered
burden, consignment, contents, freight, goods, haul, lading, load, merchandise, payload, shipload, shipment, tonnage, ware; SEE CONCEPTS 338,446

caricature [n] exaggerated description in writing, drawing
burlesque, cartoon, distortion, farce, imitation, lampoon, libel, mimicry, mockery, parody, pasquinade, pastiche, put-on*, ridicule, satire, sendup*, sham, takeoff*, travesty; SEE CONCEPTS 271,386,625

carillon [n] set of bells
angelus, chimes, glockenspiel, gong, lyra, peal, tintinnabulation, tocsin; SEE CONCEPT 595

carnage [n] massacre
annihilation, blitz, blood, blood and guts*, blood bath*, bloodshed, butchering, butchery, crime, extermination, gore, havoc, hecatomb, holocaust,

homicide, killing, liquidation, manslaughter, mass murder, murder, offing*, rapine, search and destroy*, shambles, slaughter, slaying, taking out*, warfare, wasting; SEE CONCEPT 252

carnal [adj] erotic, sensual
animal, bodily, corporal, corporeal, earthly, fleshly, genital, impure, lascivious, lecherous, lewd, libidinous, licentious, lustful, physical, prurient, salacious, sensuous, temporal, unchaste, venereal, voluptuous, vulgar, wanton, worldly; SEE CONCEPTS 372,403

carnival [n] outdoor celebration
amusement park, bacchanal, carny*, carousal, circus, conviviality, exposition, fair, feasting, festival, fete, fiesta, frolic, gala, grind show*, heyday, jamboree, jollification, jubilee, Mardi Gras, masquerade, merrymaking, orgy, ragbag*, revelry, rout, saturnalia, side show, spree, street fair; SEE CONCEPTS 377,386

carnivorous [adj] eating animal flesh
cannibal, flesh-eating, hungry, omnivorous, predatory, rapacious; SEE CONCEPT 401

carol [n] joyful hymn
ballad, canticle, canzonet, chorus, Christmas song, ditty*, lay, madrigal, noel, song, strain; SEE CONCEPTS 263,595

carouse [v] make merry, often with liquor
booze, drink, frolic, go on a spree*, have fun, imbibe, paint the town*, paint the town red*, play, quaff, raise Cain*, revel, riot, roister, wassail, whoop it up*; SEE CONCEPT 384

carp [v] nag
bother, cavil, censure, complain, criticize, find fault, fuss, grumble, hypercriticize, knock, nitpick*, objurgate, pan, peck*, pick at, quibble, reproach; SEE CONCEPT 52

carpenter [n] person who works with wood
artisan, builder, cabinetmaker, carps*, chips*, craftsperson, joiner, laborer, mason, woodworker, worker; SEE CONCEPT 348

carpet [n] nappy floor covering
carpeting, matting, rug, runner, tapestry, throw rug, wall-to-wall*; SEE CONCEPT 473

carriage [n1] delivery of freight
carrying, conveyance, conveying, delivering, freight, transit, transport, transportation; SEE CONCEPTS 148,217

carriage [n2] posture, physical and mental
air, aspect, attitude, bearing, behavior, cast, comportment, conduct, demeanor, deportment, gait, look, manner, mien, pace, positure, presence, stance, step; SEE CONCEPTS 633,720

carry [v1] transport physical object
backpack*, bear, bring, cart, channel, conduct, convey, convoy, displace, ferry, fetch, freight, funnel, give, haul, heft, hoist, import, lift, lug*, move, pack, pipe, portage, relay, relocate, remove, schlepp*, shift, shoulder*, sustain, take, tote, traject, transfer, transmit, transplant, truck, waft; SEE CONCEPTS 148,217

carry [v2] win; accomplish
affect, be victorious, capture, drive, effect, gain, get, impel, impress, influence, inspire, move, prevail, secure, spur, strike, sway, touch, urge; SEE CONCEPTS 68,706

carry [v3] broadcast electronically
air, bear, communicate, conduct, convey, display, disseminate, give, offer, pass on, publish, relay, release, send, transfer, transport; SEE CONCEPTS 217,266

carry on [v1] *continue activity*
achieve, endure, hang on, keep going, last, maintain, perpetuate, persevere, persist, proceed; SEE CONCEPT 239

carry on [v2] *manage operations*
administer, conduct, direct, engage in, keep, operate, ordain, run; SEE CONCEPT 117

carry on [v3] *lose control emotionally*
act up, be indecorous, blunder, cut up, lose it*, make a fuss*, misbehave, rage, raise Cain*; SEE CONCEPT 239

carry out [v] *complete activity*
accomplish, achieve, carry through, consummate, discharge, effect, effectuate, execute, fill, implement, meet, perform, realize; SEE CONCEPT 706

cart [n] *small attachment for transporting*
barrow, bring, convey, curricle, dolly, dray, gig, gurney, handcart, palanquin, pushcart, rickshaw, tilbury, truck, tumbrel, two-wheeler, wagon, wheelbarrow; SEE CONCEPTS 499,505

cart [v] *carry*
bear, bring, convey, ferry, haul, move, schlepp*, take, tote; SEE CONCEPTS 148,217

carte blanche [n] *full power, authority*
blank check, freedom, free hand, free rein, license, permission, power of attorney, prerogative, sanction, say, say-so, unconditional right; SEE CONCEPT 376

cartel [n] *group which shares business interest*
bunch*, chain, combine, conglomerate, consortium, corporation, crew*, crowd*, gang*, holding company, megacorp*, mob*, monopoly, multinational*, outfit*, plunderbund*, pool, ring*, syndicate, trust; SEE CONCEPTS 323,325

carton [n] *box for holding items*
bin, case, casket, chest, coffer, container, corrugated box, crate, pack, package, packet; SEE CONCEPT 494

cartoon [n] *funny drawing, often with dialogue or caption*
animation, caricature, comic strip, drawing, lampoon, parody, representation, satire, sketch, takeoff; SEE CONCEPTS 280,625

cartoonist [n] *person who draws cartoons*
artist, caricaturist, comic artist, gag person*, gagster*, illustrator, social critic; SEE CONCEPT 348

carve [v] *cut carefully with sharp instrument*
block out, chip, chisel, cleave, dissect, dissever, divide, engrave, etch, fashion, form, grave, hack, hew, incise, indent, insculpt, model, mold, mould, pattern, rough-hew, sculpt, shape, slash, slice, stipple, sunder, tool, trim, whittle; SEE CONCEPTS 137,176,184

cascade [n] *something falling, especially water*
avalanche, cataract, chute, deluge, downrush, falls, flood, force, fountain, outpouring, precipitation, rapids, shower, spout, torrent, watercourse, waterfall; SEE CONCEPTS 514,787

cascade [v] *fall in a rush*
descend, disgorge, flood, gush, heave, overflow, pitch, plunge, pour, spew, spill, spit up, surge, throw up, tumble, vomit; SEE CONCEPT 179

case [n1] *container; items in container*
bag, baggage, basket, bin, box, cabinet, caddy, caisson, canister, capsule, carton, cartridge, casing, casket, chamber, chassis, chest, coffer, compact, cover, covering, crate, crating, crib, drawer, envelope, folder, grip, holder, integument, jacket, receptacle, safe, scabbard, sheath, shell, suitcase,

tray, trunk, wallet, wrapper, wrapping; SEE CONCEPT 494

case [n2] *circumstance, conditions*
context, contingency, crisis, dilemma, event, eventuality, fact, incident, occurrence, plight, position, predicament, problem, quandary, situation, state, status; SEE CONCEPT 696

case [n3] *example*
case history, exemplification, illustration, instance, occasion, occurrence, representative, sample, sampling, specimen; SEE CONCEPT 686

case [n4] *matter brought before a court*
action, argument, cause, claim, dispute, evidence, lawsuit, litigation, petition, proceedings, process, proof, suit, trial; SEE CONCEPT 318

case [v] *check something in detail*
canvass, check out, check over, check up, examine, inspect, scrutinize, study, view; SEE CONCEPT 103

cash [n] *money; assets*
banknote, bread*, buck*, bullion, cabbage*, chicken feed*, coin, coinage, currency, dinero*, dough*, funds, green stuff*, investment, legal tender, lot, mazumah*, note, payment, pledge, principal, ready assets, refund, remuneration, reserve, resources, riches, savings, scratch*, security, skins*, stock, supply, treasure, wampum*, wherewithal; SEE CONCEPTS 340,710

cash [v] *exchange for real money*
acknowledge, break a bill*, change, discharge, draw, honor, liquidate, make change, pay, realize, redeem; SEE CONCEPT 330

cashier [n] *bank worker*
accountant, banker, bursar, clerk, collector, paymaster, purser, receiver, teller, treasurer; SEE CONCEPT 348

cashier [v] *discard, expel*
ax*, boot*, bounce, break, can*, cast off, discharge, dismiss, displace, drum out*, fire, give a pink slip*, give the heave ho*, heave*, remove, sack*, terminate; SEE CONCEPTS 211,324

casino [n] *gambling establishment*
bank, betting house, big store*, club, clubhouse, dance hall, dice joint*, dive, gambling den, hall, honky-tonk, house, joint, Monte Carlo, pool hall, roadhouse, rotunda, saloon, track; SEE CONCEPT 447

cask [n] *rounded container for liquids*
barrel, barrelet, butt, firkin, hogshead, keg, pipe, tun, vat; SEE CONCEPT 494

casket [n] *burial box*
bin, carton, case, chest, coffer, crate, funerary box, pine box, pinto, sarcophagus, wood overcoat*; SEE CONCEPTS 368,494

casserole [n] *dish consisting of a combination of cooked food*
covered dish, goulash, hash, meat pie, pot pie, pottage, stew, stroganoff; SEE CONCEPT 457

cast [n1] *a throw to the side*
casting, ejection, expulsion, fling, flinging, heave, heaving, hurl, hurling, launching, lob, lobbing, pitch, pitching, projection, propulsion, shooting, sling, slinging, thrust, thrusting, toss, tossing; SEE CONCEPT 222

cast [n2] *appearance; shade of color*
air, complexion, countenance, demeanor, embodiment, expression, face, hue, look, manner, mien, semblance, stamp, style, tinge, tint, tone, turn, visage; SEE CONCEPTS 622,716

ca
ca

cast [n3] *actors in performance*
actors, actresses, artists, characters, company, dramatis, list, parts, personae, players, roles, troupe; SEE CONCEPT 294

cast [n4] *molded structure*
conformation, copy, duplicate, embodiment, facsimile, figure, form, mold, plaster, replica, sculpture, shape; SEE CONCEPTS 470,475

cast [v1] *throw aside*
boot, bung*, chuck*, drive, drop, fire*, fling, heave, hurl, impel, launch, lob, peg, pitch, project, shed, shy, sling, thrust, toss; SEE CONCEPT 222

cast [v2] *emit, give*
aim, bestow, deposit, diffuse, direct, distribute, point, radiate, scatter, shed, spatter, spray, spread, sprinkle, strew, train; SEE CONCEPTS 108,624

cast [v3] *calculate*
add, compute, count, figure, foot, forecast, number, reckon, sum, summate, tot, total; SEE CONCEPT 764

cast [v4] *select for activity*
allot, appoint, arrange, assign, blueprint, chart, choose, decide upon, delegate, design, designate, detail, determine, devise, give parts, name, pick, plan, project; SEE CONCEPT 41

caste [n] *social class*
cultural level, degree, estate, grade, lineage, order, position, race, rank, social order, species, sphere, standing, station, status, stratum; SEE CONCEPTS 378,388

castigate [v] *criticize severely*
baste, bawl out*, beat, berate, blister, cane, censure, chasten, chastise, chew out*, come down on*, correct, criticize, discipline, drag over the coals*, dress down*, drub, excoriate, flay, flog, jump down one's throat*, lambaste, lash, lay out*, lean on*, penalize, pummel, punish, rail, rate, read the riot act*, ream, rebuke, reprimand, scarify, scathe, scold, scorch, scourge, thrash, tonguelash*, upbraid, whip; SEE CONCEPT 52

castle [n] *magnificent home, often for royalty*
acropolis, alcazar, château, citadel, donjon, estate house, fasthold, fastness, fort, fortification, fortress, hold, keep, manor, mansion, palace, peel, safehold, seat, stronghold, tower, villa; SEE CONCEPT 516

castrate [v] *remove sexual organs*
alter, asexualize, caponize, change, cut, deprive of virility, desexualize, emasculate, eunuchize, fix, geld, mutilate, neuter, spay, sterilize, unsex; SEE CONCEPT 310

casual [adj1] *chance, random*
accidental, adventitious, by chance, contingent, erratic, extemporaneous, extempore, fluky, fortuitous, impromptu, improvised, impulsive, incidental, infrequent, irregular, occasional, odd, offhand, serendipitous, spontaneous, uncertain, unexpected, unforeseen, unintentional, unplanned, unpremeditated; SEE CONCEPTS 541,544

casual [adj2] *nonchalant, relaxed in manner*
aloof, apathetic, blasé, breezy, cool*, cursory, detached, down home*, easygoing, folksy*, homey*, incurious, indifferent, informal, insouciant, lackadaisical, laid-back*, loose*, low-pressure, mellow, offhand, perfunctory, pococurante, purposeless, remote, unconcerned, unfussy, uninterested, withdrawn; SEE CONCEPTS 401,542,589

casualty [n1] *accident*
blow, calamity, catastrophe, chance, contingency, debacle, disaster, misadventure, misfortune, mishap; SEE CONCEPT 674

casualty [n2] *victim*
dead, death toll, fatality, injured, killed, loss, missing, prey, sufferer, wounded; SEE CONCEPTS 407,423

casuistry [n] *overgeneralized reasoning*
chicanery, deception, deceptiveness, delusion, equivocation, evasion, fallacy, lie, oversubtleness, sophism, sophistry, speciousness, spuriousness, trick; SEE CONCEPTS 54,63

cat [n] *feline animal, sometimes a pet*
bobcat, cheetah, cougar, grimalkin, jaguar, kitten, kitty, leopard, lion, lynx, malkin, mouser, ocelot, panther, puma, puss, pussy, tabby, tiger, tom, tomcat; SEE CONCEPTS 394,400

cataclysm [n] *disaster*
calamity, cataract, catastrophe, collapse, convulsion, crunch*, curtains*, debacle, deluge, disturbance, double trouble*, flood, flooding, holy mess*, inundation, misadventure, ruin, torrent, tragedy, unholy mess*, upheaval, waterloo*, woe; SEE CONCEPTS 674,675

catalog/catalogue [n] *written or printed matter featuring a selection of objects*
archive, brief, bulletin, calendar, cartulary, charts, classification, compendium, directory, docket, draft, enumeration, gazette, gazetteer, hit list*, index, inventory, list, prospectus, record, register, roll, roster, schedule, slate, specification, syllabus, synopsis, table; SEE CONCEPTS 271,280

catalyst [n] *something which incites activity*
adjuvant, agitator, enzyme, goad, impetus, impulse, incendiary, incentive, incitation, incitement, motivation, radical stimulus, reactant, reactionary, spark plug*, spur, stimulant, synergist, wave maker*; SEE CONCEPT 712

catapult [v] *implement for shooting weapon*
arbalest, ballista, heaver, hurler, pitcher, propeller, shooter, sling, slingshot, tosser, trebuchet; SEE CONCEPTS 463,500

catastrophe [n] *calamity; unhappy conclusion*
accident, adversity, affliction, alluvion, bad luck, bad news*, blow, calamity, casualty, cataclysm, contretemps, crash, culmination, curtains*, debacle, denouement, desolation, devastation, disaster, emergency, end, failure, fatality, fiasco, finale, grief, hardship, havoc, ill, infliction, meltdown*, misadventure, mischance, misery, misfortune, mishap, reverse, scourge, stroke, termination, the worst*, tragedy, trial, trouble, upshot, waterloo*, wreck; SEE CONCEPT 674

catch [n1] *fastener*
bolt, buckle, clamp, clasp, clip, hasp, hook, hook and eye, latch, snap; SEE CONCEPT 497

catch [n2] *trick, hidden disadvantage*
Catch-22, conundrum, deception, decoy, drawback, fly in the ointment*, hitch, joke, puzzle, puzzler, snag, stumbling block, trap; SEE CONCEPTS 674,679

catch [v1] *ensnare, apprehend*
arrest, bag, bust*, capture, clasp, claw, clench, clutch, collar, cop, corral, entangle, entrap, get one's fingers on*, glom, glove, grab, grasp, grip, hook, lasso, lay hold of, nab, nail, net, pick, pluck, pounce on, prehend, secure, seize, snag, snare, snatch, take, take hold of, trap; SEE CONCEPT 90

catch [v2] *find out, discover*
descry, detect, encounter, expose, hit upon, meet with, spot, surprise, take unawares, turn up, unmask; SEE CONCEPT *31*

catch [v3] *contract an illness*
become infected with, break out with, come down with, develop, fall ill with, fall victim to, get, incur, receive, sicken, succumb to, suffer from, take; SEE CONCEPTS *93,308*

catch [v4] *come from behind and grab*
board, climb on, come upon, cotch, get, go after, grab, hop on, jump, make, overhaul, overtake, pass, ram, reach, run down, take; SEE CONCEPT *164*

catch [v5] *hear and understand*
accept, apprehend, comprehend, discern, feel, follow, get, grasp, perceive, recognize, see, sense, take in, understand; SEE CONCEPT *15*

catching [adj] *contagious (disease)*
communicable, dangerous, endemic, epidemic, epizootic, infectious, infective, miasmatic, pandemic, pestiferous, pestilential, taking, transferable, transmittable; SEE CONCEPT *314*

catchword [n] *motto*
byword, catchphrase, household word, maxim, password, refrain, shibboleth, slogan, watchword; SEE CONCEPTS *275,278*

catchy [adj] *captivating, addictive*
fetching, haunting, having a good hook*, memorable, popular; SEE CONCEPT *544*

catechize [v] *instruct and question*
ask, cross-examine, drill, educate, examine, grill, inquire, interrogate, query, quiz, teach, train; SEE CONCEPTS *48,285*

categorical [adj] *explicit, unconditional*
absolute, all out*, certain, clear-cut, definite, definitive, direct, downright, emphatic, express, flat out*, forthright, no holds barred*, no strings attached*, positive, specific, straight out, sure, ultimate, unambiguous, unequivocal, unmitigated, unqualified, unreserved; SEE CONCEPT *535*

categorize [v] *sort by type, classification*
assort, button down*, class, classify, group, identify, peg*, pigeonhole*, put down as, rank, tab, typecast; SEE CONCEPT *39*

category [n] *classification, type*
class, department, division, grade, group, grouping, head, heading, kind, league, level, list, order, pigeonhole*, rank, section, sort, tier; SEE CONCEPT *378*

cater [v] *provide, help*
baby, coddle, cotton, furnish, gratify, humor, indulge, minister to, outfit, pamper, pander to, procure, provision, purvey, spoil, supply, victual; SEE CONCEPT *136*

caterwaul [v] *make screeching, crying noise*
bawl, bicker, howl, quarrel, scream, screech, shriek, squall, wail, yell, yowl; SEE CONCEPT *77*

catharsis [n] *purging, purification*
ablution, abreaction, cleansing, expurgation, lustration, purgation, purification, release; SEE CONCEPTS *13,165,230*

cathedral [n] *large church*
basilica, bishop's seat, chancel, holy place, house of God, house of prayer, house of worship, minster, place of worship, sanctuary, temple; SEE CONCEPTS *368,439*

catholic [adj] *all-embracing, general*
all-inclusive, broad-minded, charitable, comprehensive, cosmic, cosmopolitan, diffuse, eclectic, ecumenical, extensive, generic, global, inclusive, indeterminate, large-scale, liberal, open-minded, planetary, receptive, tolerant, unbigoted, universal, unprejudiced, unsectarian, whole, wide, world-wide; SEE CONCEPTS *557,772*

cattle [n] *bovine animals*
beasts, bovid mammals, bulls, calves, cows, dogies*, herd, livestock, longhorn*, moo cows*, oxen, shorthorns, stock, strays; SEE CONCEPT *394*

catty [adj] *nasty, malicious*
backbiting, evil, hateful, ill-natured, malevolent, mean, rancorous, spiteful, venomous, vicious, wicked; SEE CONCEPT *404*

caucus [n] *group gathered to make decision*
assembly, conclave, convention, council, gathering, get-together, meeting, parley, session; SEE CONCEPTS *301,417*

cause [n1] *agent, originator*
account, agency, aim, antecedent, author, basis, beginning, causation, consideration, creator, determinant, doer, element, end, explanation, foundation, genesis, ground, grounds, incitement, inducement, instigation, leaven, mainspring, maker, matter, motivation, motive, object, occasion, origin, prime mover, principle, producer, purpose, root, source, spring, stimulation; SEE CONCEPTS *229,661*

cause [n2] *belief; undertaking for belief*
attempt, conviction, creed, enterprise, faith, goal, ideal, intention, movement, object, objective, plan, principles, purpose; SEE CONCEPT *689*

cause [v] *bring into being; bring about*
be at the bottom of*, begin, brainstorm*, break in*, break the ice*, breed, bring to pass, come out with*, compel, cook up*, create, dream up*, effect, elicit, engender, evoke, fire up*, generate, get things rolling*, give rise to, hatch, incite, induce, introduce, kickoff*, kindle, lead to, let, make, make up, motivate, muster, occasion, open, originate, precipitate, produce, provoke, result in, revert, secure, sow the seeds, start the ball rolling*, think up, work up; SEE CONCEPTS *228,231,241*

caustic [adj1] *burning, corrosive*
abrasive, acerbic, acid, acrid, alkaline, astringent, biting, corroding, erosive, keen, mordant, pungent, tart; SEE CONCEPT *485*

caustic [adj2] *sarcastic*
acerb, acerbic, acrimonious, bitter, cutting, harsh, incisive, pithy, pungent, rough, salty, satiric, scathing, severe, sharp, stinging, trenchant, virulent; SEE CONCEPT *267*

caution [n1] *alertness, carefulness*
attention, canniness, care, circumspection, deliberation, discreetness, discretion, Fabian policy, foresight, forethought, heed, heedfulness, providence, prudence, vigilance, watchfulness; SEE CONCEPT *410*

caution [n2] *warning*
admonition, advice, bug in one's ear*, caveat, commonition, counsel, forewarning, hint, injunction, monition, notice, omen, premonition, sign, tip*, tip-off*; SEE CONCEPTS *78,274*

caution [v] *warn, advise*
admonish, alert, exhort, flag, forewarn, give the high sign*, give the lowdown on*, pull one's coat*, put one wise*, tip*, tip off*, urge, wave a red flag*, wise one up*; SEE CONCEPT *78*

cautious [adj] *careful, guarded*
alert, all ears*, cagey, calculating, chary, circum-

ca
ca

spect, considerate, discreet, forethoughtful, gingerly, hedging one's bets*, heedful, judicious, keeping on one's toes*, leery, on the lookout*, playing it cool*, playing safe*, politic, provident, prudent, pussyfoot*, safe, shrewd, taking it easy, taking it slow*, tentative, thinking twice*, vigilant, walking on eggs*, wary, watchful, watching one's step*, watching out, with one's eyes peeled*; SEE CONCEPTS 401,403

cavalcade [n] *parade*
array, drill, march-past, procession, promenade, review, spectacle, train; SEE CONCEPT 432

cavalier [adj] *arrogant*
condescending, curt, disdainful, haughty, high-and-mighty*, insolent, lofty, lordly, offhand, overbearing, proud, scornful, snooty*, snotty*, supercilious, superior; SEE CONCEPT 401

cavalry [n] *troops riding horses*
army, bowlegs*, chasseurs, cuirassiers, dragoons, horse, horse soldiers, hussars, lancers, mounted troops, Mounties, rangers, squadron, uhlans; SEE CONCEPT 322

cave [n] *hole in land formation*
cavern, cavity, den, grotto, hollow, pothole, rock shelter, subterrane, subterranean area; SEE CONCEPT 509

caveat [n] *warning*
admonition, alarm, caution, commonition, forewarning, monition, sign; SEE CONCEPTS 78,274

cavern [n] *hollow in land formation*
cave, grotto, hole, pothole, subterrane, subterranean area; SEE CONCEPT 509

cavernous [adj] *hollow and large*
alveolate, broad, chambered, chasmal, commodious, concave, curved inward, deep, deep-set, echoing, gaping, huge, resonant, reverberant, roomy, sepulchral, socketed, spacious, sunken, vast, wide, yawning; SEE CONCEPTS 490,773,796

cavity [n] *sunken or decayed area*
atrium, basin, bursa, caries, chamber, crater, decay, dent, depression, gap, hole, hollow, pit, pocket, sinus, socket, vacuity, void; SEE CONCEPT 513

cavort [v] *frolic, prance*
caper, caracole, carry on*, cut loose*, cut up*, dance, fool around*, frisk, gambol, go places and do things*, horse around*, horseplay, monkey around*, play, revel, rollick, romp, roughhouse*, sport; SEE CONCEPTS 114,384

cease [v] *stop, conclude*
back off, break off, bring to an end, call it a day*, call it quits*, close, close out, come to an end, culminate, cut it out*, desist, die, discontinue, drop, end, fail, finish, give over, halt, intermit, knock off*, leave off, pack in*, quit, quit cold turkey*, refrain, shut down, stay, surcease, terminate, wind up*; SEE CONCEPT 234

ceaseless [adj] *never-ending*
amaranthine, constant, continual, continuous, day and night*, endless, eternal, everlasting, incessant, indefatigable, interminable, nonstop, on a treadmill*, perennial, perpetual, round the clock*, unceasing, unending, uninterrupted, unremitting, untiring, world-without-end*; SEE CONCEPT 798

cede [v] *abandon, surrender*
abalienate, abdicate, accord, alien, alienate, allow, capitulate, come across with*, communicate, concede, convey, deed, drop, fold*, fork over*, give in*, give up, grant, hand over*, leave, make over, part with, relinquish, remise, renounce, re-

sign, sign over, throw in the sponge*, throw in the towel*, transfer, vouchsafe, waive, yield; SEE CONCEPTS 108,127

ceiling [n1] *top of a room*
baldachin, beam, canopy, covert, dome, fan vaulting, groin, highest point, housetop, plafond, planchement, plaster, roof, roofing, timber, topside covering; SEE CONCEPT 440

ceiling [n2] *maximum*
legal price, record, superiority, top; SEE CONCEPT 836

celebrate [v] *commemorate occasion, achievement*
beat the drum*, bless, blow off steam*, carouse, ceremonialize, commend, consecrate, dedicate, drink to, eulogize, exalt, extol, feast, fete, glorify, hallow, have a ball*, honor, jubilate, keep, kick up one's heels*, laud, let loose*, lionize, live it up*, make merry, make whoopee*, mark with a red letter*, memorialize, observe, paint the town red*, party*, perform, praise, proclaim, publicize, raise hell*, rejoice, revel, revere, ritualize, signalize, solemnize; SEE CONCEPT 377

celebrated [adj] *distinguished, famous*
acclaimed, big*, eminent, famed, glorious, great, high-powered, illustrious, immortal, important, large, laureate, lionized, notable, number one*, numero uno*, outstanding, popular, preeminent, prominent, renowned, revered, storied, up there*, well-known, w.k.*; SEE CONCEPT 568

celebration [n] *commemoration of occasion, achievement*
anniversary, bash*, birthday, blast*, blowout*, carousal, ceremony, conviviality, festival, festivity, fete, frolic, gaiety, gala, glorification, hilarity, honoring, hoopla, hullabaloo*, jollification, joviality, jubilation, jubilee, keeping, magnification, memorialization, merriment, merrymaking, observance, party, performance, recognition, remembrance, revelry, saturnalia, solemnization, spree, triumph, winging*; SEE CONCEPT 377

celebrity [n1] *dignitary*
ace, big cheese*, big deal*, big gun*, big name*, big shot*, big stuff*, bigwig*, celeb*, cynosure, famous person, figure, heavyweight, hero, hotshot*, immortal, lion*, luminary, magnate, mahatma, major leaguer*, name, notable, personage, personality, somebody, someone, star, superstar, the cheese*, VIP, worthy; SEE CONCEPT 423

celebrity [n2] *fame, notoriety*
distinction, éclat, eminence, glory, honor, notability, popularity, preeminence, prestige, prominence, renown, reputation, repute, stardom; SEE CONCEPTS 388,668

celerity [n] *swiftness*
alacrity, briskness, dispatch, expedition, expeditiousness, fleetness, gait, haste, hurry, hustle, legerity, promptness, quickness, rapidity, speed, speediness, swiftness, velocity, vivacity; SEE CONCEPT 755

celestial [adj] *heavenly*
angelic, astral, beatific, blessed, divine, elysian, empyral, empyrean, eternal, ethereal, godlike, hallowed, holy, immortal, Olympian, otherworldly, seraphic, spiritual, sublime, supernal, supernatural, transcendental, transmundane; SEE CONCEPTS 536,673

celibacy [n] *abstinence from sexual activity*
abstention, chastity, continence, frigidity, impotence, maidenhood, purity, singleness, virginity, virtue; SEE CONCEPT 388

celibate [adj] *abstaining from sexual activity*
chaste, continent, pure, virgin, virginal, virtuous;
SEE CONCEPT 372

cell [n1] *smallest living organism*
bacterium, cellule, corpuscle, egg, embryo, follicle, germ, haematid, microorganism, spore, unit,
utricle, vacuole; SEE CONCEPTS 389,478

cell [n2] *small room, container*
alcove, antechamber, apartment, bastille, booth,
burrow, cage, cavity, chamber, cloister, closet,
compartment, coop, crib, crypt, cubicle, den,
dungeon, hold, hole, keep, lockup, nook, pen,
receptacle, recess, retreat, stall, tower, vault; SEE
CONCEPTS 448,494,513

cellar [n] *underground story of building*
apartment, basement, subbasement, subterrane,
underground room, vault; SEE CONCEPTS 440,448

cement [n] *gluing, binding material*
adhesive, binder, birdlime, bond, concrete, ep-
oxy, glue, grout, gum, gunk*, lime, lute, mortar,
mucilage, mud*, paste, plaster, putty, rubber cement, sand, sealant, size, solder, stickum*, tar;
SEE CONCEPTS 475

cement [v] *attach securely, often with sticky material*
bind, blend, bond, cohere, combine, connect, fasten, fuse, glue, gum, join, merge, mortar, paste,
plaster, seal, solder, stick together, unite, weld;
SEE CONCEPTS 85,160

cemetery [n] *burial ground*
boot hill*, catacomb, charnel, charnel house,
churchyard, city of the dead*, crypt, eternal
home*, funerary grounds, garden, God's acre*,
Golgotha, grave, graveyard, marble town*, memorial park, mortuary, necropolis, ossuary, poly-
andrium, potter's field, resting place, sepulcher,
tomb, vault; SEE CONCEPTS 305,368

censor [v] *forbid; ban; selectively remove*
abridge, blacklist, black out*, bleach, bleep*,
blue-pencil*, bowdlerize, clean up, conceal, control, cork*, criticize, cut, decontaminate, delete,
drop the iron curtain*, edit, examine, excise, expurgate, exscind, inspect, launder*, narrow, oversee, prevent publication, purge, purify, put the lid
on*, refuse transmission, repress, restrain, restrict, review, revile, sanitize, scissor out*,
squelch, sterilize, strike out, supervise communications, suppress, withhold; SEE CONCEPTS
121,266

censorious [adj] *very critical*
accusatory, captious, carping, caviling, cavillous,
chiding, complaining, condemnatory, condemning, critical, culpatory, denouncing, disapproving,
disparaging, fault-finding, hypercritical, overcritical, reprehending, reproaching, severe; SEE CON-
CEPT 267

censorship [n] *forbiddance; ban*
blackout*, blue pencil*, bowdlerization, control,
forbidding, hush up*, infringing on rights, iron
curtain*, restriction, suppression, thought control*; SEE CONCEPTS 376,388

censure [n] *severe criticism*
admonishment, admonition, blame, castigation,
condemnation, disapproval, dressing down, objection, obloquy, rebuke, remonstrance, reprehension, reprimand, reproach, reproof, stricture; SEE
CONCEPTS 52,410

censure [v] *condemn; criticize severely*
abuse, admonish, animadvert, asperse, attack,
backbite, berate, blame, carp at, castigate, cavil,

chastise, chide, contemn, cut up*, denigrate, denounce, deprecate, disapprove, discipline, disparage, exprobate, find fault with, get after, impugn,
incriminate, judge, knock, lecture, look askance,
ostracize, pick apart, pull apart, read out*, rebuff,
rebuke, remonstrate, reprehend, reprimand, reproach, reprove, scold, take to task*, tear apart*,
tell off, upbraid; SEE CONCEPT 52

center [n1] *middle point*
axis, bull's-eye, centrality, centriole, centrum,
core, cynosure, equidistance, essence, focal point,
focus, gist, heart, hotbed, hub, inside, interior,
intermediacy, kernel, mainstream*, marrow, middle of the road*, midpoint, midst, nave, navel,
nucleus, omphalos, pith, pivot, place, polestar,
quick, radial point, root, seat; SEE CONCEPT 830

center [n2] *point of attraction for visitors, shop-
pers, travelers*
capital, city, club, concourse, crossroads, focal
point, focus, heart, hub, mall, market, marketplace, mart, meeting place, metropolis, nerve center, plaza, polestar, shopping center, social center,
station, town, trading center; SEE CONCEPTS
435,438,507

center [adj] *middle*
at halfway point, centermost, deepest, equidistant,
inmost, inner, innermost, inside, interior, intermediary, intermediate, internal, mean, medial,
mid, middlemost, midpoint, midway; SEE CON-
CEPTS 583,585,830

center [v] *concentrate, draw together*
attract, bring to a focus, bring together, centralize,
close on, collect, concenter, consolidate, converge
upon, focalize, focus, gather, intensify, join, me-
dialize, meet, unify; SEE CONCEPTS 35,84

central [adj] *main, principal; in the middle*
axial, basic, cardinal, center, centric, centroidal,
chief, dominant, equidistant, essential, focal,
foremost, fundamental, important, inmost, inner,
interior, intermediate, key, leading, master, mean,
median, mid, middle, middlemost, midmost, midway, nuclear, outstanding, overriding, paramount,
pivotal, predominant, primary, prime, radical, ruling, salient, significant, umbilical; SEE CONCEPTS
567,583,830

centralize [v] *concentrate, draw toward a point*
accumulate, amalgamate, assemble, compact,
concenter, condense, consolidate, converge, focus, gather, incorporate, integrate, organize, rationalize, streamline, systematize, unify; SEE
CONCEPTS 35,84

centrifugal [adj] *radiating from a central point*
deviating, diffusive, divergent, diverging, eccentric, efferent, outward, radial, spiral, spreading;
SEE CONCEPTS 581,584

ceremonial [adj] *ritual, formal*
august, conventional, imposing, liturgical, lofty,
mannered, ritualistic, solemn, stately, studied,
stylized; SEE CONCEPT 548

ceremonious [adj] *ritual, formal*
civil, courteous, courtly, decorous, deferential,
dignified, exact, grandiose, impressive, majestic,
moving, precise, proper, punctilious, seemly, solemn, starchy, stately, stiff, striking; SEE CONCEPT
548

ceremony [n] *ritual; celebratory observation*
ceremonial, commemoration, custom, formality,
function, liturgy, observance, ordinance, parade,
rite, sacrament, service, show, solemnity, tradition; SEE CONCEPT 386

ca
ce

ceremony [n2] *etiquette*
ceremonial, conformity, decorum, form, formal courtesy, formalism, formality, nicety, politeness, pomp, preciseness, prescription, propriety, protocol, strictness, usage; SEE CONCEPT 388

certain [adj1] *confident*
assertive, assured, believing, calm, cocksure, convinced, positive, questionless, sanguine, satisfied, secure, self-confident, sure, unconcerned, undisturbed, undoubtful, undoubting, unperturbed, untroubled; SEE CONCEPT 403

certain [adj2] *undoubtable, valid*
absolute, ascertained, authoritative, clear, conclusive, confirmable, definite, demonstrable, destined, determined, establishable, evident, firm, fixed, genuine, guaranteed, having down pat*, incontrovertible, indubitable, infallible, in the bag*, irrefutable, known, on ice*, plain, positive, predestined, provable, real, reliable, safe, salted away*, set, sound, supreme, sure, sure thing*, true, trustworthy, unambiguous, undeniable, undoubted, unequivocal, unerring, unmistakable, verifiable; SEE CONCEPTS 535,582

certain [adj3] *fixed*
assured, bound, certified, concluded, decided, definite, determined, ensured, established, guaranteed, insured, set, settled, stated, stipulated, sure, warranted; SEE CONCEPT 535

certain [adj4] *referring to a specifically known amount*
a couple, a few, defined, divers, express, individual, many, marked, numerous, one, particular, precise, regular, several, singular, some, special, specific, specified, sundry, upwards of, various; SEE CONCEPT 557

certainly [adv] *without doubt*
absolutely, assuredly, cert*, exactly, for a fact, of course, positively, posolutely*, right on*, surely, unquestionably, without fail; SEE CONCEPT 535

certainty [n1] *positive assurance*
all sewn up*, authoritativeness, belief, certitude, cinch, confidence, conviction, credence, definiteness, dogmatism, faith, firmness, indubitableness, inevitability, lock*, lockup*, open and shut case*, positiveness, positivism, rain or shine*, setup, shoo-in*, staunchness, steadiness, stock, store, sure bet*, surefire*, sureness, sure thing*, surety, trust, validity, wrap-up; SEE CONCEPTS 638,725

certainty [n2] *fact, resulting truth*
consequence, foregone conclusion, inevitable result, reality, sure thing*, surety; SEE CONCEPT 230

certificate [n] *authorizing document*
affidavit, affirmation, attestation, authentication, authorization, certification, coupon, credential, deed, diploma, docket, documentation, endorsement, guarantee, license, paper, pass, permit, receipt, record, sheepskin*, shingle, testament, testification, testimonial, testimony, ticket, voucher, warrant, warranty; SEE CONCEPTS 271,685

certify [v] *declare as true*
accredit, approve, ascertain, assure, attest, authenticate, authorize, aver, avow, commission, confirm, corroborate, endorse, guarantee, license, notify, okay, profess, reassure, rubber-stamp*, sanction, show, state, swear, testify, validate, verify, vouch, witness; SEE CONCEPTS 50,88

cessation [n] *ending*
abeyance, arrest, break, break-off*, breather*, cease, ceasing, close, conclusion, cutoff*, desistance, discontinuance, downtime*, end, finish, freeze*, grinding halt, halt, halting, hiatus, intermission, interruption, interval, layoff*, let-up*, pause, recess, remission, respite, rest, screaming halt*, standstill, stay, stop, stoppage, suspension, termination, time off, time-out*; SEE CONCEPT 119

chafe [v1] *rub, grind against*
abrade, bark, corrode, damage, erode, excoriate, gall, grate, graze, hurt, impair, inflame, irritate, peel, ruffle, scrape, scratch, skin, wear; SEE CONCEPT 215

chafe [v2] *annoy*
abrade, anger, annoy, bother, exasperate, exercise, fret, fume, gall, grate, harass, incense, inflame, irk, irritate, itch, offend, provoke, rage, rasp, rub, ruffle, scrape, vex, worry; SEE CONCEPTS 7,19

chaff [n] *waste*
crust, debris, dregs, husks, pod, refuse, remains, rubbish, shard, shell, trash; SEE CONCEPT 679

chaff [v] *joke, ridicule*
banter, deride, fun, jeer, jolly, josh, kid, mock, rag*, rally, razz*, rib*, scoff, taunt, tease; SEE CONCEPT 273

chagrin [n] *displeasure*
annoyance, balk, blow, crushing, discomfiture, discomposure, disgruntlement, dismay, disquiet, dissatisfaction, embarrassment, fretfulness, frustration, humiliation, ill-humor, irritation, letdown, mortification, peevishness, shame, spleen, upset, vexation; SEE CONCEPTS 410,674

chagrin [v] *cause displeasure*
abash, annoy, confuse, crush, discomfit, discompose, disconcert, disgrace, dismay, displease, disquiet, dissatisfy, embarrass, humiliate, irk, irritate, mortify, peeve, perturb, shame, upset, vex; SEE CONCEPTS 7,19

chain [n1] *succession, series*
alternation, catena, concatenation, conglomerate, consecution, continuity, group, order, progression, row, sequence, set, string, syndicate, train, trust; SEE CONCEPTS 432,727,769

chain [n2] *connected metal links; jewelry made of such links*
bond, bracelet, cable, clinker*, connection, coupling, fetter, iron, lavaliere, link, locket, manacle, pendant, shackle, trammel; SEE CONCEPTS 446,476,499

chain [v] *manacle in metal*
attach, bind, confine, connect, enslave, fetter, handcuff, hold, moor, restrain, shackle, tether, tie up, trammel; SEE CONCEPTS 85,160

chair [n1] *single-seat furniture*
armchair, bench, cathedra, recliner, rocker, sling*; SEE CONCEPT 443

chair [n2] *person in or position of authority*
captain, chairperson, director, fellowship, helm, instructorship, leader, monitor, position of control, principal, professorate, professorship, throne, tutor, tutorship; SEE CONCEPTS 348,376

chairperson [n] *person in charge of proceedings*
administrator, captain, chair, director, introducer, leader, moderator, monitor, president, presider, principal, prolocutor, speaker, spokesperson, symposiarch; SEE CONCEPTS 348,376

challenge [n] *dispute, question*
claiming, confrontation, dare, defiance, demanding, demur, interrogation, objection, protest,

provocation, remonstrance, summons to contest, test, threat, trial, ultimatum; SEE CONCEPTS *53*,*532*

challenge [*v*] *dispute, question*

accost, arouse, ask for, assert, beard, brave, call for, call out, claim, confront, cross, dare, defy, demand, denounce, exact, face down, face off, face the music*, fly in the face of*, hang in*, impeach, impose, impugn, inquire, insist upon, investigate, invite competition, make a point of, make a stand, object to, provoke, query, reclaim, require, search out, stand up to, stick it out, stimulate, summon, tax, test, throw down the gauntlet*, try, vindicate; SEE CONCEPT *53*

chamber [*n1*] *small compartment, room*

alcove, antechamber, apartment, bedchamber, bedroom, box, case, cavity, cell, chest, container, cubicle, enclosure, flat, hall, hollow, lodging, pocket, room, socket; SEE CONCEPTS *448*,*494*

chamber [*n2*] *legislative body*

assembly, council, legislature, organization, representatives; SEE CONCEPT *299*

champion [*n*] *defeater in competition; preeminent supporter*

advocate, ally, backer, challenger, champ, conqueror, defender, endorser, exponent, expounder, guardian, hero, heroine, medalist, nonpareil, number one*, numero uno*, paladin, partisan, patron, proponent, protector, supporter, sympathizer, the greatest*, titleholder, top dog*, upholder, vanquisher, victor, vindicator, warrior, winner; SEE CONCEPT *366*

champion [*adj*] *best, excellent*

blue-ribbon, boss*, capital, chief, choice, cool, dandy, distinguished, first, greatest, head, illustrious, out of sight*, out of this world*, outstanding, premier, prime, principal, prize-winning, splendid, super, superior, tip top*, top drawer*, topflight*, top-notch*, tops*, unbeaten, undefeated, world class*; SEE CONCEPT *574*

champion [*v*] *advocate, support*

back, battle, contend, defend, espouse, fight for, go to bat for*, patronize, plead for, promote, put in a good word for*, ride shotgun for*, side with, stand behind, stand up for, support, thump for, uphold; SEE CONCEPTS *10*,*69*

chance [*n1*] *possibility, probability*

break, contingency, fair shake*, fighting chance*, indications, liability, likelihood, long shot*, look-in, occasion, odds, opening, opportunity, outlook, prospect, scope, shot*, show, squeak, time, wager; SEE CONCEPT *650*

chance [*n2*] *fate, luck*

accident, advantage, adventure, bad luck, break, cast, casualty, coincidence, contingency, destination, destiny, doom, even chance, fluke, fortuity, fortune, future, gamble, good luck, hap*, haphazard, happening, hazard, heads or tails*, hit*, in the cards*, kismet, lot, lottery, luck out*, lucky break, misfortune, occurrence, odds, outcome, peradventure, peril, providence, risk, stroke of luck*, throw of the dice*, toss-up*, turn of the cards*, way the cookie crumbles*, wheel of fortune*; SEE CONCEPT *679*

chance [*n3*] *gamble, risk*

bet, craps game*, fall of the cards*, hazard, jeopardy, lottery, raffle, speculation, stake, throw of the dice*, try, venture, wager; SEE CONCEPT *363*

chance [*adj*] *accidental, unforeseeable*

adventitious, at random, casual, contingent, fluky,

fortuitous, fortunate, happy, inadvertent, incidental, lucky, odd, offhand, unforeseen, unintentional, unlooked for, unplanned; SEE CONCEPT *552*

chance [*v1*] *risk, endanger*

attempt, cast lots, draw lots, gamble, go out on a limb, have a fling at, hazard, jeopardize, play with fire*, plunge, put eggs in one basket*, put it on the line*, roll the dice*, run the risk, skate on thin ice*, speculate, stake, stick one's neck out*, take shot in the dark*, tempt fate*, tempt fortune*, toss up*, try, venture, wager, wildcat; SEE CONCEPT *87*

chance [*v2*] *happen*

arrive, befall, be one's fate, betide, blunder on, break, bump, come, come about, come off, come to pass, fall out, fall to one's lot, go, hap*, hit upon, light, light upon, luck, meet, occur, stumble, stumble on, transpire, tumble, turn up; SEE CONCEPT *4*

chancy [*adj*] *dangerous, risky*

capricious, contingent, dicey, erratic, fluctuant, fluky, hazardous, iffy*, incalculable, precarious, problematic, problematical, rocky, speculative, ticklish, touchy, tricky, uncertain, unpredictable, unsound, whimsical; SEE CONCEPTS *552*,*587*

chandelier [*n*] *light hanging from ceiling*

candelabrum, candleholder, corona, crown, electrolier, gasolier, light fixture, luster; SEE CONCEPT *444*

change [*n1*] *something made different; alteration*

about-face*, addition, adjustment, advance, break, compression, contraction, conversion, correction, development, difference, distortion, diversification, diversity, innovation, metamorphosis, modification, modulation, mutation, novelty, permutation, reconstruction, refinement, remodeling, reversal, revision, revolution, shift, surrogate, switch, tempering, transformation, transition, transmutation, turn, turnover, variance, variation, variety, vicissitude; SEE CONCEPTS *230*,*260*,*701*

change [*n2*] *substitution; replacement*

conversion, exchange, flip-flop*, interchange, swap, switch, trade, turnaround; SEE CONCEPT *128*

change [*n3*] *smaller currency in exchange for larger*

chicken feed*, coins, copper, dimes, nickels, pennies, pin money*, pocket money, quarters, silver, spending money; SEE CONCEPT *340*

change [*v1*] *make or become different*

accommodate, adapt, adjust, alter, alternate, commute, convert, diminish, diverge, diversify, evolve, fluctuate, make innovations, make over, merge, metamorphose, moderate, modify, modulate, mutate, naturalize, recondition, redo, reduce, reform, regenerate, remake, remodel, renovate, reorganize, replace, resolve, restyle, revolutionize, shape, shift, substitute, tamper with, temper, transfigure, transform, translate, transmute, transpose, turn, vacillate, vary, veer, warp; SEE CONCEPTS *228*,*232*,*235*,*701*

change [*v2*] *substitute, replace*

alternate, barter, convert, displace, exchange, interchange, invert, remove, reverse, shift, supplant, swap, switch around, trade, transmit, transpose; SEE CONCEPT *128*

changeable [*adj*] *erratic*

agitated, capricious, changeful, commutative,

convertible, fickle, fitful, flighty, fluctuating, fluid, impulsive, inconstant, indecisive, irregular, irresolute, irresponsible, kaleidoscopic, mercurial, mobile, movable, mutable, permutable, protean, restless, reversible, revocable, shifting, skittish, spasmodic, transformable, transitional, uncertain, unpredictable, unreliable, unsettled, unstable, unsteady, vacillating, vagrant, variable, variant, varying, versatile, volatile, wavering, whimsical; SEE CONCEPT 534

channel [n1] *pathway, usually containing water*
approach, aqueduct, arroyo, artery, avenue, canal, canyon, carrier, chamber, chase, conduit, course, dig, ditch, duct, fluting, furrow, gouge, groove, gully, gutter, main, means, medium, pass, passage, pipe, raceway, route, runway, sewer, slit, sound, strait, tideway, trough, tube, tunnel, vein, watercourse, way; SEE CONCEPTS 501,514

channel [n2] *means*
agency, agent, approach, avenue, course, instrument, instrumentality, instrumentation, medium, ministry, organ, route, vehicle, way; SEE CONCEPTS 6,660,770

channel [v] *direct, guide*
carry, conduct, convey, funnel, pipe, route, send, siphon, traject, transmit, transport; SEE CONCEPTS 187,217

chant [n] *chorus of song*
carol, croon, hymn, incantation, intonation, lilt, melody, psalm, shout, singing, song, trill, tune, warble; SEE CONCEPTS 263,595

chant [v] *sing simple song or song part*
cantillate, carol, chofus, croon, descant, doxologize, drone, intone, recite, shout, tune, vocalize, warble; SEE CONCEPTS 65,77

chaos [n] *utter confusion*
anarchy, ataxia, bedlam, clutter, disarray, discord, disorder, disorganization, entropy, free-for-all*, holy mess*, lawlessness, misrule, mix-up, mobocracy, muddle, pandemonium, rat's nest*, snarl, topsy-turviness*, tumult, turmoil, unruliness; SEE CONCEPTS 230,674

chaotic [adj] *utterly confused*
anarchic, deranged, disordered, disorganized, every which way*, harum-scarum*, helter-skelter*, lawless, purposeless, rampageous, riotous, topsy-turvy*, tumultuous, turbid, turbulent, uncontrolled; SEE CONCEPT 548

chaperon [n] *person who accompanies for supervision*
alarm clock*, babysitter*, bird dog*, companion, escort; SEE CONCEPT 423

chaperon [v] *accompany for supervision*
attend, carry, conduct, consort with, convoy, escort, guide, oversee, protect, safeguard, shepherd, supervise, watch over; SEE CONCEPTS 114,714

chaplain [n] *minister in church*
cleric, member of clergy, pastor, preacher, priest, rabbi, turn-around collar*; SEE CONCEPT 361

chapter [n] *section of book or group of items*
affiliate, branch, clause, division, episode, member, offshoot, part, period, phase, stage, topic, unit, wing; SEE CONCEPTS 270,382,832

char [v] *scorch, sear*
burn, carbonize, cauterize, singe; SEE CONCEPT 249

character [n1] *individuality*
appearance, aspect, attribute, badge, bent, caliber, cast, complex, complexion, constitution, cra-

sis, disposition, emotions, estimation, ethos, frame, frame of mind, genius, grain, habit, humor, kind, makeup, mettle, mood, morale, mystique, nature, personality, quality, record, reputation, repute, sense, set, shape, singularity, sort, specialty, spirit, standing, streak, style, temper, temperament, tone, trait, turn, type, vein; SEE CONCEPT 411

character [n2] *integrity*
courage, fame, honor, intelligence, mind, name, place, position, rank, rectitude, rep, report, reputation, repute, standing, station, status, uprightness; SEE CONCEPT 668

character [n3] *odd person*
card*, case*, clown, crank*, customer*, duck*, eccentric, figure, freak, nut, oddball, oddity, original*, personage, personality, queer, spook*, wack*, weirdo, zombie*; SEE CONCEPTS 412,423

character [n4] *written symbol*
cipher, device, emblem, figure, hieroglyph, letter, logo, mark, monogram, number, numeral, rune, sign, type; SEE CONCEPT 284

character [n5] *portrayal of another*
impersonation, part, personification, role; SEE CONCEPTS 263,352

characteristic [n] *typical feature, trait*
affection, aspect, attribute, badge, bag, bearing, bent, caliber, cast, complexion, component, differentia, disposition, distinction, earmark, endowment, essence, essential, faculty, flavor, frame, idiosyncrasy, inclination, individuality, lineament, mannerism, mark, mood, nature, originality, particularity, peculiarity, personality, point, property, quality, singularity, specialty, streak, stripe, style, symptom, temperament, tendency, thing, thumbprint, tinge, tone, trademark, turn, virtue; SEE CONCEPT 411

characteristic [adj] *typical; distinguishing*
appropriate, diagnostic, differentiating, discriminating, discriminative, distinctive, distinguishing, emblematic, especial, essential, exclusive, fixed, idiosyncratic, inborn, inbred, indicative, individual, individualistic, individualizing, ingrained, inherent, innate, native, normal, original, particular, peculiar, personal, private, proper, regular, representative, singular, special, specific, symbolic, symptomatic, unique; SEE CONCEPTS 542,547,550

characterize [v] *typify, distinguish*
belong to, brand, button down*, constitute, define, delineate, describe, designate, differentiate, discriminate, feature, identify, indicate, individualize, individuate, inform, make up, mark, outline, peculiarize, peg, personalize, pigeonhole*, portray, represent, signalize, singularize, stamp, style, symbolize, tab, typecast; SEE CONCEPT 644

charade [n] *pretense*
deception, disguise, fake, farce, make-believe, mimicry, pageant, pantomime, parody, pretension, pretentiousness, put-on, travesty, trick; SEE CONCEPT 59

charge [n1] *accusation*
allegation, beef*, complaint, gripe, imputation, indictment, plaint, stink*; SEE CONCEPTS 44,317

charge [n2] *attack*
assault, blitz, blitzkrieg, invasion, mugging, onset, onslaught, push, rush, sortie; SEE CONCEPT 86

charge [n3] *burden*
care, commitment, committal, concern, custody,

deadweight, duty, millstone, must, need, obligation, office, onus, ought, responsibility, rift, safekeeping, task, tax, trust, ward, weight; SEE CONCEPTS 532,709

charge [n4] *price asked for something*
amount, bad news*, bite, cost, damage, expenditure, expense, nick, outlay, payment, price, price tag, rate, squeeze, tab, tariff, tick; SEE CONCEPT 329

charge [n5] *command*
behest, bidding, dictate, direction, exhortation, injunction, instruction, mandate, order, precept, word; SEE CONCEPTS 53,274

charge [n6] *supervisory responsibility*
care, conduct, custody, handling, intendance, management, oversight, running, superintendence, superintendency, supervision, ward; SEE CONCEPT 117

charge [v1] *accuse*
arraign, blame, blow the whistle on*, censure, criminate, drag into court*, finger*, hang something on*, impeach, impugn, impute, incriminate, inculpate, indict, involve, peg, point the finger at*, reprehend, reproach, tax, turn on, whistleblow*; SEE CONCEPTS 44,317

charge [v2] *attack*
assail, assault, blindside, bolt, buck, bushwhack*, chase, dash, invade, jump on, lunge, mug, rush, smash, stampede, storm, tear; SEE CONCEPT 86

charge [v3] *load, tax*
afflict, burden, choke, clog, commit, cram, crowd, cumber, encumber, entrust, fill, heap, impregnate, instill, lade, pack, penetrate, permeate, pervade, pile, ram, saddle, saturate, suffuse, transfuse, weigh; SEE CONCEPTS 107,156,740

charge [v4] *order something done*
adjure, ask, bid, command, direct, enjoin, entrust, exhort, instruct, request, require, solicit, tell, warn; SEE CONCEPTS 53,78

charge [v5] *ask a price*
demand, fix price at, impose, levy, price, require, sell for; SEE CONCEPTS 330,345

charge [v6] *pay with credit card*
book, buy on credit, chalk up, cuff, debit, encumber, go into hock*, incur debt, nick*, paste*, put on account, put on one's card, put on the cuff, put on the tab, receive credit, run up; SEE CONCEPTS 327,330

charisma [n] *great personal charm*
allure, animal magnetism*, appeal, dazzle, drawing power, fascination, flash, glamour, it*, magnetism, pizzazz*, something*, star quality, witchcraft, witchery; SEE CONCEPT 411

charitable [adj1] *giving, generous*
accommodating, all heart, altruistic, beneficent, benevolent, benign, big*, bighearted*, bountiful, eleemosynary, good, helpful, humane, humanitarian, kind, kindly, lavish, liberal, obliging, philanthropic, sympathetic; SEE CONCEPTS 334,542

charitable [adj2] *kind, lenient*
all heart*, benevolent, big*, bighearted*, broadminded, clement, considerate, easy, favorable, forbearing, forgiving, gracious, humane, indulgent, kindly, lenient, magnanimous, merciful, sympathetic, thoughtful, tolerant, understanding; SEE CONCEPT 404

charity [n1] *generosity, gift*
alms, alms-giving, assistance, benefaction, beneficence, contribution, dole, donation, endowment, fund, gifting, hand*, hand-out, helping hand*,

largesse, oblation, offering, philanthropy, relief, write-off; SEE CONCEPTS 337,657

charity [n2] *kindness, compassion*
affection, agape, altruism, amity, attachment, benevolence, benignity, bountifulness, bounty, caritas, clemency, fellow feeling, generosity, goodness, goodwill, grace, humaneness, humanity, indulgence, kindliness, lenity, love, magnanimity, mercy, tenderheartedness; SEE CONCEPTS 32,411

charm [n1] *enchantment, allure*
agreeableness, allurement, appeal, attraction, attractiveness, beauty, bewitchery, charisma, chemistry, conjuration, delightfulness, desirability, fascination, glamour, grace, it*, lure, magic, magnetism, pizzazz*, something*, sorcery, spell, star quality, witchery; SEE CONCEPTS 411,673

charm [n2] *talisman*
amulet, fetish, good-luck piece, juju, lucky piece, madstone, mascot, phylactery, rabbit's foot, trinket, zemi; SEE CONCEPTS 284,446

charm [v] *enchant*
allure, attract, beguile, bewitch, cajole, captivate, delight, draw, enamor, enrapture, ensorcell, enthrall, entrance, fascinate, grab, hex, hypnotize, inveigle, kill*, knock dead*, knock out*, magnetize, mesmerize, please, possess, put under a spell*, send*, slay*, spell*, sweep off feet*, take*, tickle, tickle pink*, transport, turn on*, vamp, voodoo, wile, win, win over, wow*; SEE CONCEPTS 7,22

charming [adj] *captivating*
absorbing, alluring, amiable, appealing, attractive, bewitching, charismatic, choice, cute, dainty, delectable, delicate, delightful, desirable, electrifying, elegant, enamoring, engaging, engrossing, enthralling, entrancing, eye-catching, fascinating, fetching, glamorous, graceful, infatuating, inviting, irresistible, likable, lovable, lovely, magnetizing, nice, pleasant, pleasing, provocative, rapturous, ravishing, seducing, seductive, sweet, tantalizing, tempting, titillating, winning, winsome; SEE CONCEPT 404

chart [n] *map, plan*
blueprint, diagram, graph, outline, plat, plot, rough draft, scheme, sketch, table, tabulation; SEE CONCEPTS 625,660

chart [v] *plan, map out*
arrange, block out, blueprint, cast, delineate, design, devise, draft, graph, lay out, outline, plot, project, shape, sketch; SEE CONCEPTS 36,174

charter [n] *treaty, agreement*
allotment, bond, code, concession, constitution, contract, conveyance, deed, document, endowment, franchise, grant, indenture, license, pact, patent, permit, prerogative, privilege, right, settlement; SEE CONCEPTS 684,685

charter [v] *reserve, commission*
allow, authorize, borrow, contract, employ, engage, hire, lease, let, license, permit, rent, sanction; SEE CONCEPTS 48,50,88,89

chary [adj] *careful, cautious*
cagey, calculating, canny, circumspect, considerate, constrained, discreet, economical, fastidious, frugal, gingerly, guarded, heedful, hesitant, inhibited, leery, loath, miserly, particular, prudent, reluctant, restrained, safe, scrupulous, sparing, stingy, suspicious, thrifty, uneasy, wary, watchful; SEE CONCEPTS 401,587

chase [*n*] *pursuit*
hunt, hunting, quest, race, venery; SEE CONCEPT 207

chase [*v*] *run after, pursue*
bird-dog*, charge, chivy, course, drive, drive away, expel, follow, go after, hound, hunt, run down, rush, seek, shag*, speed, take off after*, tear, track, track down, trail; SEE CONCEPT 207

chasm [*n*] *gap, abyss*
abysm, alienation, arroyo, blank, breach, cavity, cleavage, cleft, clough, clove, crater, crevasse, fissure, flume, gorge, gulch, gulf, hiatus, hole, hollow, omission, opening, oversight, preterition, ravine, rent, rift, schism, skip, split, void, yawn; SEE CONCEPT 513

chaste [*adj*] *pure, incorrupt*
austere, celibate, clean, continent, controlled, decent, decorous, elegant, immaculate, impotent, inexperienced, innocent, intemerate, modest, monogamous, moral, neat, platonic, proper, prudish, quiet, refined, restrained, simple, spotless, stainless, subdued, unaffected, unblemished, uncontaminated, undefiled, unstained, unsullied, unwed, vestal, virginal, virtuous, wholesome; SEE CONCEPTS 372,404

chasten [*v*] *correct, humiliate*
abase, admonish, afflict, berate, call down, castigate, chastise, chide, cow, curb, discipline, exprobate, fulminate against, have on the carpet*, humble, objurgate, penalize, punish, rebuke, reprehend, repress, reprimand, reproach, reprove, restrain, scold, scourge, soften, subdue, take to task, tame, tongue-lash*, try, upbraid; SEE CONCEPTS 52,122

chastise [*v*] *scold, discipline*
baste, beat, berate, castigate, censure, chasten, chew out*, climb all over*, correct, ferule*, flog*, lash*, lay into*, lean on*, pummel, punish, ream, scourge, skelp, slap down*, spank, thrash, upbraid, whip; SEE CONCEPTS 52,122

chastity [*n*] *celibacy, purity*
abstemiousness, abstinence, chasteness, cleanness, continence, decency, demureness, devotion, honor, immaculacy, innocence, integrity, modesty, monogamy, morality, naïveté, restraint, singleness, sinlessness, spotlessness, temperance, uprightness, virginity, virtue; SEE CONCEPT 633

chat [*n*] *talk, often short*
babble, bull session, chatter, conversation, converse, gab*, gas*, gossip, heart-to-heart*, hot air*, jabber*, palaver, prattle*, rap*, rap session*, tête-à-tête, visit, yak*; SEE CONCEPT 278

chat [*v*] *talk, gossip*
babble, blab*, burble, cackle, chatter, chew the fat*, chew the rag*, converse, gab*, go on*, jaw*, prate, prattle*, run on*, shoot the breeze*, yap*; SEE CONCEPT 266

chatter [*n*] *constant or rapid talk*
babble, blather, chat, chitchat, gas*, gossip, jabber*, palaver, prattle*, twaddle, yakking*; SEE CONCEPTS 266,278

chatter [*v*] *speak fast and non-stop*
babble, blab*, blather, cackle, chat, chitchat, clack, gab*, gabble, gas*, gibber, go on and on, gossip, jabber, jaw*, natter, palaver, prate, prattle*, tattle, twaddle, twiddle, yak*; SEE CONCEPT 266

chatty [*adj*] *talkative*
colloquial, communicative, conversational, familiar, friendly, gabby, garrulous, gossipy, informal, intimate, loose-lipped, loquacious, multieloquent, spontaneous, talky; SEE CONCEPT 267

chauvinism [*n*] *extreme devotion to a belief or nation*
bellicism, ethnocentricity, fanatical patriotism, fanaticism, jingoism, narrowness, nationalism, zealotry; SEE CONCEPT 689

cheap [*adj1*] *inexpensive*
at a bargain, bargain, bargain-basement*, bargain-counter, bought for a song*, budget, buy, cheapo*, competitive, cost next to nothing*, cut-price, cut-rate, depreciated, dime a dozen*, easy on the pocketbook*, economical, half-priced, irregular, low-cost, lowered, low-priced, low tariff, marked down, moderate, nominal, on sale, popularly priced, real buy*, reasonable, reduced, sale, slashed, standard, steal, uncostly, undear, utility, worth the money*; SEE CONCEPT 334

cheap [*adj2*] *inferior, low in quality*
bad, base, bogus, catchpenny, cheesy, common, commonplace, crappy*, cruddy, dud, flashy, garbage, garish, glitzy*, junky*, lousy, mangy, mean, mediocre, meretricious, no bargain*, no good, ordinary, paltry, poor, ratty, raunchy, rinky-dink*, rotten, rubbishy, scroungy, second-rate, shoddy, sleazy, small-time*, tatty, tawdry, terrible, trashy, trumpery, two-bit, valueless, white elephant*, worthless; SEE CONCEPT 589

cheap [*adj3*] *low, vulgar*
abject, base, beggarly, contemptible, despicable, dirty, dishonest, mean, pitiable, scurvy, shabby, sordid, sorry, tawdry, vile; SEE CONCEPT 542

cheap [*adj4*] *concerned with saving money*
mean, mingy, miserly, penny-pinching, stingy, thrifty, tight*, tight-wad*; SEE CONCEPT 332

cheapen [*v*] *diminish worth*
abase, beat down, belittle, corrupt, damage, debase, decline, decry, degrade, demean, denigrate, depreciate, derogate, devalue, discredit, disparage, downgrade, drop, fall, lose value, lower, mar, mark down, minimize, reduce, render worthless, ruin, spoil, undervalue, write off; SEE CONCEPT 240

cheat [*n1*] *person who fools others*
bluff, charlatan, chiseler, con artist, confidence operator, conniver, cozener, crook, deceiver, decoy, defrauder, dodger, double-crosser*, double-dealer*, enticer, fake, hypocrite, impostor, inveigler, jockey, masquerader, pretender, quack, rascal, rogue, scammer*, shark, sharper, shyster, swindler, trickster; SEE CONCEPT 412

cheat [*n2*] *trick*
artifice, baloney, bamboozlement*, bill of goods*, bunco, chicanery, con, con game, cover up, cozening, deceit, deception, dirty pool*, dirty trick*, dodge, double-dealing*, fake, fast one, fast shuffle*, fix, flimflam, frame, fraud, gyp, hanky-panky*, hoax, hoaxing, humbug, hustle, imposture, jazz, jive, plant, put-on*, racket, rip-off, run around, scam, sell, shady deal, sham, shell game, snow job*, spoof, sting, stunt, swindle, trickery, whitewash, wrong; SEE CONCEPT 59

cheat [*v*] *defraud*
bamboozle*, beat, beguile, bilk, bleed, bunco, burn, caboodle, chisel, con, cozen, crib, cross, deceive, defraud, delude, diddle*, do*, do a number on*, double-cross, double-deal, dupe, fast talk, finagle, fleece, flimflam, fudge*, give bum steer*, gouge, gyp*, hoodwink, hose, jerk around, milk, mislead, pull one's leg*, ream*, rip

off*, rook*, rope in*, sandbag, scam, screw, shaft, short, shuck, skin, snow, stiff, sucker, swindle, take, take for a ride*, take in, take out, trick, trim, two-time, victimize; SEE CONCEPTS 59,139,192

cheat [v2] *frustrate, thwart*
baffle, check, defeat, deprive, foil, prevent; SEE CONCEPT 121

check [n1] *inspection, examination*
analysis, audit, checkup, control, inquiry, investigation, poll, rein, research, review, scrutiny, test; SEE CONCEPT 103

check [n2] *restraint, hindrance*
blow, constraint, control, curb, damper, disappointment, frustration, grunt, harness, holdup, impediment, inhibition, limitation, obstruction, rebuff, rejection, restrainer, reversal, reverse, setback, stoppage, trouble; SEE CONCEPTS 121,130,230

check [n3] *symbol for ticking off*
cross, dot, line, mark, score, sign, stroke, tick, X*; SEE CONCEPT 284

check [n4] *pattern of squares*
checkerboard, patchwork, plaid, quilt, tartan; SEE CONCEPT 436

check [v1] *inspect, examine*
analyze, ascertain, audit, balance account, candle, case, compare, confirm, correct, count, enquire about, eyeball*, find out, frisk, go through, investigate, keep account, look at, look over, look see*, make sure, monitor, note, overlook, probe, prove, quiz, review, scout out, scrutinize, study, take stock, tell, test, try, verify; SEE CONCEPTS 24,103

check [v2] *hinder, restrain*
arrest, baffle, bar, bit, bottleneck*, bridle, checkmate, choke, circumvent, constrain, control, counteract, curb, cut short, delay, discourage, foil, frustrate, halt, harness, hold, hold back, hold down, hold in, impede, inhibit, interrupt, keep back, limit, moderate, neutralize, nip in the bud*, obstruct, obviate, pause for time, preclude, prevent, rebuff, reduce, rein in, repress, repulse, retard, slacken pace, slow down, snub, squelch, stay, stop, suppress, tame, terminate, thwart, withhold; SEE CONCEPTS 121,130

checkered [adj] *patterned*
checky, diversified, motley, mutable, patchwork, plaid, quilted, spotted, variegated; SEE CONCEPT 486

cheek [n1] *side of human face*
chop*, choppers*, gill, jowl; SEE CONCEPT 418

cheek [n2] *audacity, boldness*
brashness, brass*, brazenness, chutzpah*, confidence, disrespect, effrontery, gall, impertinence, impudence, insolence, lip*, nerve*, presumption, rudeness, sauce*, temerity; SEE CONCEPT 633

cheep [v] *vocalize as a bird*
chip, chipper, chirp, chirrup, peek, tweedle, tweet, twitter; SEE CONCEPT 64

cheer [n1] *happiness*
animation, buoyancy, cheerfulness, cheeriness, comfort, delight, encouragement, exuberance, gaiety, geniality, gladness, glee, good cheer, hilarity, hopefulness, jauntiness, jocundity, joy, joyousness, lightheartedness, liveliness, merriment, mirth-making, mirth, optimism, solace; SEE CONCEPT 410

cheer [n2] *applause, supportive yell*
acclamation, approbation, approval, cry, encouragement, hurrah, hurray, huzzah, ovation, plaudits, roar, shout; SEE CONCEPTS 69,77

cheer [v1] *make someone feel happier*
animate, brace up, brighten, buck up*, buoy, comfort, console, elate, elevate, embolden, encourage, enliven, exhilarate, give a lift*, gladden, hearten, help, incite, inspirit, let the sun shine in*, perk up, pick up, put on cloud nine*, put on top of the world*, snap out of it*, solace, steel, strengthen, uplift, upraise, warm; SEE CONCEPTS 7,22

cheer [v2] *encourage in activity*
acclaim, applaud, clap, hail, hurrah, plug*, rise to, root, salute, sound off for, support, yell; SEE CONCEPT 69

cheerful [adj] *happy*
airy, animated, blithe, bouncy, bright, bucked, buoyant, cheery, chipper, chirpy, contented, effervescent, enlivening, enthusiastic, full of pep, gay, glad, gladsome, good-humored, good-natured, hearty, high, hilarious, hopeful, in good spirits, in high spirits, jaunty, jocund, jolly, joyful, lighthearted, lively, merry, optimistic, peppy, perky, pleasant, roseate, rosy, sanguine, snappy, sparkling, sprightly, sunny, sunny side up*, up*, upbeat, vivacious, winsome, zappy, zingy, zippy; SEE CONCEPTS 403,404

cheering [adj] *encouraging*
auspicious, bright, comforting, heartening, hopeful, promising, propitious; SEE CONCEPT 529

cheerless [adj] *depressing, unhappy*
austere, black, bleak, blue, comfortless, dark, dejected, dejecting, depressed, desolate, despondent, disconsolate, dismal, dispiriting, dolorous, drab, draggy, drearisome, dreary, dull, forlorn, funereal, gloomy, grim, in the dumps*, jarring, joyless, melancholy, miserable, mopey, mournful, oppressive, sad, somber, sorrowful, sullen, tenebrific, uncomfortable, wintry, woebegone, woeful; SEE CONCEPT 403

chemical [adj] *concerned with atom and molecule change*
actinic, alchemical, enzymatic, synthesized, synthetic, synthetical; SEE CONCEPT 536

cherish [v] *care about deeply*
admire, adore, appreciate, apprize, care for, clasp, cleave to, cling to, coddle, comfort, cosset, cultivate, defend, dote on, embrace, encourage, enshrine, entertain, fancy, fondle, foster, guard, harbor, hold dear, hold in high esteem, honor, hug, idolize, like, love, nourish, nurse, nurture, pet, preserve, prize, revere, reverence, safeguard, shelter, shield, support, sustain, treasure, value, venerate, worship; SEE CONCEPT 32

cherry [adj] *bright red color*
blooming, blushing, bright red, cerise, claret, crimson, dark red, erubescent, incarnadine, reddish, rosy, rubescent, rubicund, ruddy; SEE CONCEPT 618

chest [n1] *box for storage*
bin, bureau, cabinet, carton, case, casket, chiffonier, coffer, commode, crate, exchequer, pyxis, receptacle, reliquary, strongbox, treasury, trunk; SEE CONCEPT 494

chest [n2] *upper front of body*
bosom, breast, bust, heart, mammary glands, peritoneum, pulmonary cavity, rib cage, ribs, thorax, upper trunk; SEE CONCEPT 392

chew [v1] *grind with teeth*
bite, champ, chaw, chomp, crunch, dispatch, feast

upon, gnaw, gulp, gum, manducate, masticate, munch, nibble, rend, ruminate, scrunch; SEE CONCEPTS 169,185

chew [v2] *think about deeply*
consider, deliberate, meditate, mull, mull over, muse on, ponder, reflect upon, ruminate, weigh; SEE CONCEPT 24

chew out [v] *scold*
bawl out, carpet*, criticize, dress down, jaw, revile, tell off, tongue-lash*, vituperate, wig, yell at; SEE CONCEPT 52

chic [adj] *fashionable*
chichi*, clean*, current, dap*, dapper, dashing, elegant, exclusive, faddish, last word*, latest thing*, mod*, modern, modish, natty, sharp, smart, stylish, swank, trendy, voguish, with-it*; SEE CONCEPT 589

chicanery [n] *deception, trickery*
artifice, cheating, chicane, deviousness, dishonesty, dodge, double-crossing, double-dealing*, duplicity, feint, fourberie, fraud, furtiveness, gambit, hanky-panky*, intrigue, machination, maneuver, plot, ploy, ruse, sharp practice, skullduggery, sophistry, stratagem, subterfuge, surreptitiousness, underhandedness, wiles; SEE CONCEPTS 59,660

chicken [n1] *person afraid to try something*
coward, craven, dastard, funk, poltroon, quitter, recreant, scaredy cat*, yellow belly*; SEE CONCEPT 423

chicken [n2] *farm fowl*
banty, barnyard fowl, biddy, capon, chick, cock, cock-a-doodle-do*, cockalorum, cockerel, gump*, heeler, hen, poultry, pullet, rooster; SEE CONCEPTS 394,395

chide [v] *criticize, lecture*
admonish, berate, blame, call down*, call on the carpet*, castigate, censure, check, condemn, exprobate, find fault, flay, give a hard time*, lesson, monish, rate, rebuke, reprehend, reprimand, reproach, reprove, scold, slap on the wrist*, speak to, take down*, take down a peg*, talk to, tell off, tick off*, upbraid; SEE CONCEPT 52

chief [n] *person in charge*
big cheese*, big gun*, big wheel*, bigwig*, boss, captain, chieftain, commander, dictator, director, foreperson, general, governor, head, head honcho*, head person*, honcho*, key player*, leader, manager, monarch, overlord, overseer, president, principal, proprietor, ringleader, ruler, sovereign, superintendent, supervisor, suzerain, top brass*, top cat*; SEE CONCEPTS 347,376

chief [adj] *most important, essential*
arch, capital, cardinal, central, champion, consequential, controlling, crucial, effective, especial, first, foremost, grand, head, highest, key, leading, main, major, momentous, number one*, outstanding, paramount, potent, predominant, preeminent, premier, primal, primary, prime, principal, ruling, significant, star, stellar, superior, supreme, telling, uppermost, vital, weighty; SEE CONCEPTS 568,574,829

chiefly [adv] *most importantly*
above all, especially, essentially, in general, in the first place, in the main, largely, mainly, mostly, on the whole, overall, predominantly, primarily, principally, usually; SEE CONCEPTS 567,772

child [n] *very young person*
adolescent, anklebiter*, babe, baby, bairn, bam-

bino, brat, cherub, chick, cub, descendant, dickens*, imp, infant, innocent, issue, juvenile, kid, kiddie*, lamb*, little angel*, little darling*, little doll*, little one, minor, mite, moppet, neonate, nestling, newborn, nipper, nursling, offspring, preteen, progeny, pubescent, shaver, small fry*, sprout, squirt, stripling, suckling, tadpole, teen, teenager, teenybopper*, toddler, tot, tyke, urchin*, whippersnapper*, young one, youngster, youth; SEE CONCEPTS 414,424

childbirth [n] *giving birth*
accouchement, bearing children, blessed event*, childbed, confinement, delivering, delivery, labor, lying-in, nativity, parturience, parturition, procreation, producing, propagation, reproduction, travail, visit from the stork*; SEE CONCEPTS 302,373

childhood [n] *period of being young*
adolescence, babyhood, cradle, immaturity, infancy, juniority, juvenility, minority, nonage, nursery, puberty, pupilage, schooldays, teens, tender age, youth; SEE CONCEPTS 816,817

childish [adj] *immature, silly*
adolescent, baby, babyish, callow, childlike, foolish, frivolous, green, infantile, infantine, innocent, jejune, juvenile, kid stuff*, naive, puerile, unsophisticated, young, youthful; SEE CONCEPTS 401,402,424,578,797

childlike [adj] *innocent, naive*
artless, childish, credulous, guileless, immature, ingenuous, natural, simple, spontaneous, trustful, trusting, unaffected, unfeigned; SEE CONCEPT 404

chill [n] *cold conditions*
bite, coldness, coolness, crispness, frigidity, gelidity, iciness, nip, rawness, rigor, sharpness; SEE CONCEPT 524

chill [adj1] *cold, raw*
arctic, biting, bleak, brisk, chilly, cool, freezing, frigid, frosty, gelid, glacial, icy, nippy, sharp, wintry; SEE CONCEPT 605

chill [adj2] *unfriendly, aloof*
cool, depressing, discouraging, dismal, dispiriting, distant, emotionless, formal, frigid, glacial, hateful, hostile, icy, indifferent, reserved, solitary, standoffish, stony, uncompanionable, unemotional, ungenial, unhappy, unresponsive, unwelcoming, wintry, withdrawn; SEE CONCEPTS 401,404

chill [v1] *make cold*
air-condition, congeal, cool, freeze, frost, ice, refrigerate; SEE CONCEPTS 255,521

chill [v2] *discourage*
cloud, dampen, dash, deject, demoralize, depress, dishearten, dismay, disparage, dispirit; SEE CONCEPTS 7,19

chilly [adj1] *cold*
arctic, biting, blowy, breezy, brisk, cool, crisp, drafty, freezing, fresh, frosty, glacial, hawkish, icebox, icy, nippy, penetrating, sharp, snappy, wintry; SEE CONCEPT 605

chilly [adj2] *unfriendly, aloof*
cold, frigid, hostile, unfriendly, unresponsive, unsympathetic, unwelcoming; SEE CONCEPT 404

chime [v] *ring, peal*
bell, bong, boom, clang, dong, jingle, knell, sound, strike, tinkle, tintinnabulate, toll; SEE CONCEPT 65

chimera [n] *dream, fantasy*
bogy, bubble, delusion, fabrication, fancy, fata morgana, figment, fool's paradise*, hallucination,

ignis fatuus, illusion, mirage, monster, monstrosity, pipe dream*, rainbow*, snare, specter, virtual reality; SEE CONCEPT 529

chimney [n] smokestack for building
chase, chimney pot, chimney stack, fireplace, flue, funnel, furnace, hearth, pipe, smokeshaft, stack, vent, ventilator; SEE CONCEPT 440

chin [n] area under mouth
button, jaw, jawbone, mandible, mentum, point; SEE CONCEPT 399

china [n] dishes, often valuable
ceramics, crockery, porcelain, pottery, service, stoneware, tableware, ware; SEE CONCEPT 493

chip [n] shard, flaw
dent, flake, fragment, gobbet, nick, notch, paring, part, scrap, scratch, shaving, slice, sliver, wafer, wedge; SEE CONCEPTS 580,831

chip [v] knock a piece out of
break, chisel, chop, clip, crack, crack off, crumble, cut away, cut off, damage, flake, fragment, gash, hack, hackle, hew, incise, nick, notch, shape, shear, slash, slice, sliver, snick, snip, splinter, whack, whittle; SEE CONCEPTS 137,189,246,250

chip in [v] contribute
ante up*, break in*, chime in*, come through*, conate, go Dutch*, interpose, interrupt, pay, pitch in, subscribe; SEE CONCEPT 110

chipper [adj] happy
alert, animate, animated, bright, brisk, gay, in good spirits, keen, lively, spirited, sprightly, vivacious; SEE CONCEPT 403

chips [n] substitute for money; money
coin, currency, markers, play money, scratch; SEE CONCEPT 340

chirp [v] peep, cheep
call, chip, chipper, chirrup, lilt, pipe, purl, quaver, roll, sing, sound, trill, tweedle, tweet, twitter, warble; SEE CONCEPT 64

chisel [n] shaping tool
adze, blade, edge, gouge, knife; SEE CONCEPTS 495,500

chisel [v] cut, wear away
carve, hew, incise, roughcast, roughhew, sculpt, sculpture, shape; SEE CONCEPTS 137,176,184

chivalrous [adj] valiant
benevolent, big, bold, brave, considerate, courageous, courteous, courtly, gallant, gentlemanlike, great-hearted, heroic, high-minded, honorable, intrepid, lofty, magnanimous, manly, noble-minded, polite, quixotic, spirited, sublime, true, valorous; SEE CONCEPT 401

chivalry [n] valor, gallantry
courage, courtesy, courtliness, fairness, politeness, valiance; SEE CONCEPT 633

choice [n] power to select; selection
alternative, appraisal, choosing, cull, cup of tea*, decision, determination, discretion, discrimination, distinction, druthers*, election, evaluation, extract, favorite, finding, free will, judgment, opportunity, option, pick, preference, rating, say, substitute, variety, verdict, volition, vote, weakness; SEE CONCEPTS 41,376

choice [adj] best, superior
A-1*, elect, elite, excellent, exceptional, exclusive, exquisite, fine, first-class, hand-picked, nice, popular, precious, preferential, preferred, prime, prize, rare, select, solid gold*, special, 10*, top-drawer*, 24-karat*, uncommon, unusual, valuable, winner; SEE CONCEPT 574

choke [v] smother, block
asphyxiate, bar, check, clog, close, congest, constrict, dam, die, drown, fill, gag, garrote, gasp, gibbet, kill, noose, obstruct, occlude, overpower, retard, squeeze, stifle, stop, stopper, strangle, strangulate, stuff, stunt, suffocate, suppress, throttle, wring; SEE CONCEPTS 121,219

choose [v] pick, select
accept, adopt, appoint, call for, cast, commit oneself, co-opt, crave, cull, decide on, designate, desire, determine, discriminate between, draw lots, elect, embrace, espouse, excerpt, extract, fancy, favor, feel disposed to, finger, fix on, glean, judge, love, make choice, make decision, make up one's mind, name, opt for, predestine, prefer, see fit, separate, set aside, settle upon, sift out, single out, slot, sort, tab, tag, take, take up, tap, want, weigh, will, winnow, wish, wish for; SEE CONCEPT 41

choosy [adj] fussy, discriminating
dainty, eclectic, exacting, fastidious, finical, finicky, nice, overparticular, particular, persnickety*, picky, prissy, select, selective; SEE CONCEPT 404

chop [v] cut up with tool
axe, cleave, clip, cube, dice, divide, fell, fragment, hack, hackle, hash, hew, lop, mangle, mince, sever, shear, slash, truncate, whack; SEE CONCEPT 176

choppy [adj] wavy
inclement, ripply, rough, uneven, violent, wild; SEE CONCEPT 488

chore [n] task
assignment, burden, devoir, duty, effort, errand, grind, housework, job, KP*, routine, scutwork, stint, trial, tribulation, workout; SEE CONCEPT 362

chortle [v] laugh gleefully
cackle, chuckle, crow, giggle, guffaw, hee-haw*, snicker, sniggle, snort, teehee*, titter; SEE CONCEPT 77

chorus [n1] group of singers
carolers, choir, chorale, choristers, ensemble, glee club, singing group, vocalists, voices; SEE CONCEPT 294

chorus [n2] refrain
bob, burden, chorale, main section, melody, motif, music, recurrent verse, response, ritornelle, song, strain, theme, tune, undersong; SEE CONCEPT 264

chorus [n3] agreement
accord, concert, concord, consonance, harmony, tune, unison; SEE CONCEPTS 673,684

chosen [adj] preferred
called, conscript, elect, exclusive, got the nod*, named, pegged, pick, picked, popular, preferential, select, selected, tabbed; SEE CONCEPTS 546,567,574

christen [v] named in religious rite
asperse, baptize, bless, call, dedicate, denominate, designate, dub, entitle, godparent, immerse, sprinkle, style, term, title; SEE CONCEPTS 62,367

chronic [adj] incessant, never-ending
abiding, ceaseless, confirmed, constant, continual, continuing, continuous, deep-rooted, deep-seated, enduring, ever-present, fixed, habitual, inborn, inbred, inculcate, ineradicable, ingrained, inveterate, lasting, lifelong, lingering, long-lived, long-standing, obstinate, perennial, persistent, persisting, prolonged, protracted, recurrent, recur-

ch
ch

ring, rooted, routine, settled, stubborn, sustained, tenacious, unabating, unmitigated, unyielding, usual; SEE CONCEPTS *534,551,798*

chronicle [n] *account, narrative*
annals, archives, diary, history, journal, narration, prehistory, recital, record, recountal, register, report, story, version; SEE CONCEPTS *271,282*

chronicle [v] *report, recount*
enter, narrate, record, register, relate, set down, tell; SEE CONCEPTS *60,79*

chronological [adj] *in consecutive time order*
archival, chronographic, chronologic, chronometric, chronometrical, chronoscopic, classified, dated, historical, horological, horometrical, in due course, in due time, in order, in sequence, junctural, ordered, progressive, sequent, sequential, tabulated, temporal; SEE CONCEPTS *548,585*

chubby [adj] *slightly fat*
ample, bearish, big, butterball*, buxom, chunky, fatty, flabby, fleshy, full-figured, hefty, husky, pleasingly plump*, plump, plumpish, podgy, portly, pudgy, roly-poly*, rotund, round, stout, tubby, zaftig*; SEE CONCEPTS *491,773*

chuck [v] *throw aside, throw away, throw out*
abandon, can, cast, desert, discard, ditch, eighty-six*, eject, fire, fling, flip, forsake, give the heave ho*, heave, hurl, jettison, junk, launch, pitch, quit, reject, relinquish, renounce, scrap, shed, shy, sling, slough, toss; SEE CONCEPTS *180,222*

chuckle [v] *giggle*
cackle, chortle, crow, exult, guffaw, hee-haw*, laugh, smile, snicker, snigger, sniggle, teehee*, titter; SEE CONCEPT *77*

chum [n] *friend*
associate, bro*, buddy, co-mate, companion, comrade, crony, mate, pal, playmate, sis*; SEE CONCEPT *423*

chummy [adj] *friendly*
affectionate, buddy-buddy*, close, confidential, constant, cozy, familiar, intimate, pally*, palsy-walsy*, thick*; SEE CONCEPTS *401,555*

chunk [n] *mass, slab of something*
block, clod, dollop, glob, gob, hunk, lump, nugget, part, piece, portion, wad; SEE CONCEPT *471*

chunky [adj] *fat, plump*
beefy, chubby, dumpy, heavyset, husky, rotund, scrub, squat, stocky, stout, stubby, thick-bodied, thickset; SEE CONCEPTS *491,773*

church [n1] *religious institution, building*
abbey, basilica, bethel, cathedral, chancel, chantry, chapel, fold, house of God, house of prayer, house of worship, Lord's house, minster, mission, mosque, oratory, parish, sacellum, sanctuary, shrine, synagogue, tabernacle, temple; SEE CONCEPTS *368,449*

church [n2] *religious belief, group*
affiliation, body, chapter, communion, congregation, connection, creed, cult, denomination, doctrine, faction, faith, gathering, ism, order, persuasion, religion, schism, sect, society; SEE CONCEPTS *369,689*

churl [n] *rude and ill-bred, a boor; person overly concerned with saving money*
beast, chuff, clodhopper*, miser, mucker*, niggard*, oaf, peasant, provincial, rustic, tightwad, yokel; SEE CONCEPT *423*

churlish [adj] *crude, boorish*
base, blunt, brusque, cantankerous*, cloddish, clodhopping*, crabbed, crude, crusty, curt, cussed*, discourteous, dour, grouchy, gruff, grumpy,

harsh, ill-tempered, impolite, loutish, lowbred, mean, miserly, morose, oafish, ornery*, rude, rustic, snippy*, sullen, surly, touchy*, ugly, uncivil, uncivilized, uncultured, unmannerly, unneighborly, unpolished, unsociable, vulgar; SEE CONCEPT *404*

churn [v] *mix up, beat*
agitate, boil, bubble, convulse, ferment, foam, froth, jolt, moil, seethe, simmer, stir up, swirl, toss; SEE CONCEPTS *147,170*

chute [n] *ramp, slope*
channel, course, fall, gutter, incline, rapid, runway, slide, trough; SEE CONCEPTS *440,471*

cinder [n] *hot ash*
clinker, ember, hot coal, soot; SEE CONCEPT *260*

cinema [n] *movie industry; movie arena*
big screen*, bijou, cine, drive-in, film, flicks*, motion pictures, movie house, movie theater, moving pictures, nabes*, photoplay, pictures, picture show, playhouse, show, silver screen*; SEE CONCEPTS *293,349*

cipher [n] *zero; nothingness*
blank, diddly squat*, goose egg*, insignificancy, nada*, naught, nil, nobody, nonentity, nothing, nought, nullity, squat, zilch, zip, zippo*, zot*; SEE CONCEPTS *668,787*

cipher [v] *figure out code*
break, calculate, clear up, compute, count, decipher, estimate, figure, reckon, resolve, solve, unravel; SEE CONCEPT *37*

circa [prep] *approximately*
about, around, close on, in the region of, near, nearby, nigh, roughly; SEE CONCEPT *820*

circle [n1] *orb, loop, round figure*
amphitheater, aureole, band, belt, bowl, bracelet, circlet, circuit, circumference, circus, cirque, coil, colure, compass, cordon, corona, crown, cycle, disc, disk, ecliptic, enclosure, equator, full turn, globe, halo, hoop, horizon, lap, meridian, orbit, parallel of latitude, perimeter, periphery, record, revolution, ring, ringlet, round, sphere, stadium, tire, turn, vortex, wheel, wreath, zodiac; SEE CONCEPT *436*

circle [n2] *group of close friends, associates*
assembly, bunch, cabal, camarilla, camp, clan, class, clique, club, companions, company, comrades, coterie, crew, cronies, crowd, crush, fraternity, gang, in-group, insiders, intimates, lot, Mafia, mob, outfit, party, posse, ring, school, set, society, sorority; SEE CONCEPTS *387,417*

circle [v] *go around, circumnavigate*
begird, belt, cincture, circuit, circulate, circumduct, circumscribe, coil, compass, curve, embrace, encircle, enclose, encompass, ensphere, envelop, gird, girdle, gyrate, gyre, hem in, loop, mill around, pivot, revolve, ring, roll, rotate, round, spiral, surround, tour, wheel, whirl, wind about; SEE CONCEPT *758*

circuit [n] *revolution, track, boundary*
ambit, area, bounds, circle, circling, circulation, circumference, circumnavigation, circumscription, circumvolution, compass, course, cycle, district, gyration, gyre, journey, lap, limit, line, orbit, perambulation, perimeter, periphery, range, region, round, route, tour, tract, turn, turning, twirl, way, wheel, whirl, wind, winding, zone; SEE CONCEPTS *484,501,770*

circuitous [adj] *going around, indirect*
back road*, by way of, circular, collateral, complicated, devious, labyrinthine, long way*, long

ch
ci

way around*, meandering, oblique, rambling, roundabout, tortuous, winding around; SEE CONCEPTS 544,581

circular [n] *handbill*
advertisement, booklet, broadside, brochure, flyer, handout, insert, leaflet, literature, pamphlet, poster, publication, throwaway*; SEE CONCEPT 271

circular [adj] *going around*
annular, circling, disklike, indirect, oblique, orbicular, round, rounded, spheroid; SEE CONCEPT 486

circulate [v1] *make known*
bring out, broadcast, diffuse, disperse, disseminate, distribute, exchange, interview, issue, promulgate, propagate, publicize, publish, radiate, report, spread, strew, troll; SEE CONCEPTS 60,138

circulate [v2] *flow*
actuate, circle, fly about, get about, get around, go about, gyrate, mill around, mobilize, move around, radiate, revolve, rotate, set off, travel, wander; SEE CONCEPT 147

circulation [n1] *distribution*
apportionment, currency, dissemination, spread, transmission; SEE CONCEPTS 631,651

circulation [n2] *moving circularly*
circling, circuit, circumvolution, current, flow, flowing, gyration, gyre, motion, revolution, rotation, round, turn, twirl, wheel, whirl; SEE CONCEPTS 147,738

circumference [n] *edge, perimeter*
ambit, border, boundary, bounds, circuit, compass, confines, extremity, fringe, girth, limits, lip, margin, outline, periphery, rim, verge; SEE CONCEPT 484

circumlocution [n] *indirect speech*
beating around the bush*, circumambages, diffuseness, discursiveness, euphemism, gassiness, indirectness, periphrase, periphrasis, pleonasm, prolixity, roundabout, tautology, verbal evasion, verbality, verbiage, wordiness; SEE CONCEPTS 51,266

circumscribe [v] *mark off, delimit*
bar, bound, confine, define, delineate, demarcate, encircle, enclose, encompass, environ, girdle, hamper, hem in*, limit, nail down*, outline, prelimit, restrain, restrict, surround, trammel; SEE CONCEPTS 18,130

circumspect [adj] *cautious, discreet*
attentive, cagey, calculating, canny, careful, chary, considerate, deliberate, discriminating, gingerly, guarded, heedful, judicious, meticulous, observant, politic, prudent, punctilious, safe, sagacious, sage, scrupulous, vigilant, wary, watchful; SEE CONCEPTS 403,544

circumstance [n] *situation, condition*
accident, action, adjunct, affair, article, case, cause, coincidence, concern, contingency, crisis, destiny, detail, doom, element, episode, event, exigency, fact, factor, fate, feature, fortuity, go, happening, happenstance, incident, intervention, item, juncture, kismet, lot, matter, Moira, occasion, occurrence, particular, phase, place, point, portion, proviso, respect, scene, status, stipulation, supervention, thing, time, where it's at*; SEE CONCEPT 696

circumstances [n] *state of affairs in one's life*
assets, capital, chances, class, command, degree, dowry, financial status, footing, income, lifestyle, lot, means, net worth, outlook, position, precedence, prestige, property, prospects, prosperity, rank, rating, resources, situation, sphere, standing, state, station, status, substance, times, way of life, worldly goods; SEE CONCEPTS 335,388

circumstantial [adj] *incidental*
amplified, coincidental, concomitant, concurrent, conjectural, contingent, detailed, environmental, fortuitous, inconclusive, indirect, inferential, presumptive, provisional, uncertain; SEE CONCEPTS 556,582,653

circumvent [v] *fool, mislead*
avoid, beat, beguile, bilk, bypass, circumnavigate, cramp, crimp, deceive, detour, disappoint, dodge, dupe, elude, ensnare, entrap, escape, evade, foil, frustrate, get around, hoodwink, outflank, outwit, overreach, prevent, queer, ruin, shun, sidestep, skirt, stave off, steer clear of*, stump, stymie, thwart, trick, ward off; SEE CONCEPTS 59,102,121

circus [n] *fair with entertainment*
bazaar, big top, festival, gilly*, hippodrome, kermis, show, spectacle, three-ring*; SEE CONCEPT 293

citadel [n] *top, tower*
bastion, blockhouse, castle, fastness, fort, fortification, fortress, keep, manor, redoubt, stronghold; SEE CONCEPTS 321,836

citation [n1] *excerpt*
example, illustration, mention, passage, quotation, quote, quoting, reference, saying, source; SEE CONCEPT 283

citation [n2] *award*
bidding, charge, commendation, encomium, mention, panegyric, reward, salutation, summons, tribute; SEE CONCEPTS 69,337

cite [v1] *note, quote*
adduce, advance, allege, allude to, appeal to, enumerate, evidence, excerpt, exemplify, extract, get down to brass tacks*, give as example, illustrate with, indicate, instance, lay, mention, name, number, offer, point out, present, recite, recount, reference, refer to, rehearse, remember, reminisce, repeat, specify, spell out, tell; SEE CONCEPT 57

cite [v2] *subpoena*
arraign, call, command, name, order, summon; SEE CONCEPT 317

citizen [n] *person native of country*
aborigine, burgess, burgher, civilian, commoner, cosmopolite, denizen, dweller, freeman/woman, householder, inhabitant, John/Jane Q. Public*, member of body politic, member of community, national, native, naturalized person, occupant, resident, settler, subject, taxpayer, townsperson, urbanite, villager, voter; SEE CONCEPT 413

city [n] *large town*
apple*, boom town, borough, burg, capital, center, conurbation, downtown, megalopolis, metropolis, metropolitan area, municipality, place, polis, port, urban place, urbs*; SEE CONCEPT 507

city [adj] *metropolitan*
burghal, citified, civic, civil, interurban, intraurban, megalopolitan, municipal, urban; SEE CONCEPT 536

civic [adj] *community*
borough, civil, communal, local, metropolitan, municipal, national, public, urban; SEE CONCEPTS 536,583

civil [adj1] *civic, community*
civilian, domestic, governmental, home, interior,

local, municipal, national, political, public; SEE
CONCEPTS 536,583

civil [adj2] *obliging, kind*
accommodating, affable, civilized, complaisant,
cordial, courteous, courtly, cultivated, diplomatic,
formal, genteel, gracious, mannerly, polished, polite, politic, refined, suave, urbane, well-bred,
well-mannered; SEE CONCEPT 401

civilian [n] *nonmilitary person*
citizen, civ*, civvie*, commoner, noncombatant,
private citizen, subject; SEE CONCEPT 423

civilian [adj] *nonmilitary*
noncombatant, nonmilitary, nonmilitant, not in
armed forces, pacificist, private, unhostile; SEE
CONCEPT 555

civilization [n1] *culture, sophistication*
acculturation, advancement, breeding, civility,
cultivation, development, edification, education,
elevation, enlightenment, illumination, polish,
progress, refinement, social well-being; SEE CON-
CEPT 388

civilization [n2] *society*
civilized life, community, customs, literate society, modern humanity, mores, nation, people, polity, way of life; SEE CONCEPTS 388,417

civilize [v] *make cultured; develop*
acculturate, acquaint, advance, better, cultivate,
edify, educate, elevate, enlighten, ennoble, enrich, ethicize, foster, help forward, humanize, idealize, improve, indoctrinate, inform, instruct,
polish, promote, reclaim, refine, sophisticate,
spiritualize, tame, uplift; SEE CONCEPTS 244,385

claim [n] *property, right demanded or reserved*
affirmation, allegation, application, assertion,
birthright, call, case, counterclaim, declaration,
demand, dibs, due, entreaty, interest, lien, part,
petition, plea, postulation, prerogative, pretense,
pretension, privilege, profession, protestation,
reclamation, request, requirement, requisition,
suit, title, ultimatum; SEE CONCEPTS
278,318,376,709

claim [v] *demand, maintain property or right*
adduce, advance, allege, ask, assert, believe, call
for, challenge, collect, declare, defend, exact,
have dibs on something*, hit, hit up*, hold, hold
out for*, insist, justify, knock, lay claim to, need,
pick up, pop the question*, postulate, pretend,
profess, pronounce, require, requisition, solicit,
stake out, take, uphold, vindicate; SEE CONCEPTS
53,129

clairvoyance [n] *intuition*
acumen, discernment, ESP*, feeling, foreknowledge, insight, omen, penetration, perception, precognition, premonition, psyche, sixth sense*,
telepathy; SEE CONCEPTS 409,410

clairvoyant [n] *person who is psychic*
augur, channeller, diviner, fortune-teller, haruspex, horoscopist, medium, oracle, palm reader,
prophet, seer, sibyl, soothsayer, telepath, tele-
pathist, visionary, voodoo doctor*; SEE CONCEPT
423

clairvoyant [adj] *intuitive, psychic*
clear-sighted, discerning, extrasensory, farseeing,
far-sighted, fey, judicious, long-sighted, new
age*, oracular, penetrating, perceptive, prescient,
prophetic, second-sighted, sibylline, spiritualistic,
telepathic, vatic, visionary; SEE CONCEPTS
402,403

clam [n] *bivalve living in ocean*
cherrystone, littleneck, mollusk, quahog; SEE
CONCEPT 394

clammy [adj] *damp*
close, dank, drizzly, moist, mucid, mucous, muculent, pasty, slimy, soggy, sticky, sweating,
sweaty, wet; SEE CONCEPT 603

clamor [n] *loud cry; commotion*
agitation, babel, blare, brouhaha*, bustle, buzz,
clinker, complaint, convulsion, din, discord, exclamation, ferment, hassle, hoo-ha*, hubba-
hubba*, hubbub, hullabaloo*, hurly-burly*,
lament, noise, outcry, pandemonium, protesting,
racket, remonstrance, row, ruckus, shout, shouting, to-do, tumult, turmoil, upheaval, uproar, vociferation; SEE CONCEPTS 386,595,674

clamor [v] *cry out, make commotion*
agitate, bark, bawl, bellow, bluster, claim, debate, demand, dispute, holler, put up a howl*,
raise Cain*, raise the roof*, roar, rout, shout; SEE
CONCEPTS 77,106

clamp [n] *fastener*
bracket, catch, clasp, grip, hold, lock, nipper,
press, snap, vice; SEE CONCEPT 499

clamp [v] *fasten*
brace, clench, clinch, fix, impose, make fast, secure; SEE CONCEPTS 85,150

clan [n] *family, clique*
association, band, bunch, club, coterie, crew,
crowd, crush, faction, folks, gang, group, house,
insiders, kinfolks, mob, moiety, organization,
outfit, race, ring, sect, set, society, sodality,
stock, tribe; SEE CONCEPTS 296,387

clandestine [adj] *secret, sly*
artful, cloak-and-dagger, closet, concealed, covert, foxy, fraudulent, furtive, hidden, hush-
hush*, illegitimate, illicit, in holes and corners*,
on the Q.T.*, on the quiet, private, sneaky,
stealthy, surreptitious, undercover, underground,
underhand, under-the-counter*, under wraps*;
SEE CONCEPTS 555,576

clank [n] *metallic noise*
bang, bong, clash, clink, jangle, ring; SEE CON-
CEPT 595

clank [v] *clang, clatter*
bong, clash, clink, jangle, make noise, resound,
reverberate, ring, toll; SEE CONCEPT 65

clannish [adj] *exclusive, select*
akin, alike, associative, cliquish, close, insular,
like, narrow, related, reserved, restricting, restrictive, sectarian, unfriendly, unreceptive; SEE CON-
CEPT 555

clap [n] *loud hitting noise*
applause, bang, blast, boom, burst, crack, crash,
handclap, pat, slam, slap, smash, strike, thrust,
thunder, thunderclap, thwack, wallop, whack,
wham; SEE CONCEPTS 189,595

clap [v] *applaud; slap with approbation*
acclaim, approve, bang, cheer, give a big hand*,
give a hand*, hear it for*, pat, praise, slap, strike
gently, thwack, whack; SEE CONCEPTS 185,189

clarification [n] *explanation*
description, elucidation, exposition, illumination,
interpretation, resolution, simplification, solution,
unravelment, vivification; SEE CONCEPTS 57,274

clarify [v1] *explain, make clear*
analyze, break down, clear up, define, delineate,
draw a picture, elucidate, formulate, illuminate,
illustrate, interpret, make perfectly clear, make
plain, resolve, settle, shed light on*, simplify,

spell out*, straighten out, throw light on; SEE CONCEPT 57

clarify [v2] *purify*
clean, cleanse, depurate, distill, filter, rarefy, refine; SEE CONCEPT 165

clarion [adj] *clear, stirring sound*
blaring, definite, inspiring, loud, ringing, sharp, shrill, strident; SEE CONCEPTS 562,592,594

clarity [n] *clearness*
accuracy, articulateness, brightness, certainty, cognizability, comprehensibility, conspicuousness, decipherability, definition, directness, distinctness, evidence, exactitude, exactness, explicability, explicitness, intelligibility, legibility, limpidity, limpidness, lucidity, manifestness, obviousness, openness, overtness, palpability, penetrability, perceptibility, perspicuity, plainness, precision, prominence, purity, salience, simplicity, tangibility, transparency, unambiguity, unmistakability; SEE CONCEPTS 409,638

clash [n1] *disagreement or fight, often brief*
affray, argument, battle, brawl, break, broil, brush, bump, collision, concussion, conflict, confrontation, crash, difference of opinion, discord, discordance, disharmony, dispute, donnybrook*, embroilment, encounter, engagement, fracas, fray, have a go at each other*, impact, jam, jar, jolt, jump, melee, misunderstanding, mix up, opposition, rift, riot, row, rumpus, run-in, rupture, scrap, scrimmage, set-to, shock, showdown, skirmish, smash, wallop; SEE CONCEPTS 46,106

clash [v1] *hit with a loud noise*
bang, bump, clang, clank, clatter, collide, crash, grate, grind, jangle, jar, jolt, prang, rattle, scrap, scrimmage, shock, smash, wallop; SEE CONCEPTS 65,189

clash [v2] *fight about, often verbally*
argue, bang heads*, battle, brawl, buck, combat, conflict, contend, cross swords, differ, disagree, encounter, feud, fret, gall, grapple, grate, mix it up*, quarrel, raise Cain*, row, try, war, wrangle; SEE CONCEPTS 46,106

clash [v3] *do not match*
be dissimilar, conflict, contrast, differ, disaccord, discord, disharmonize, mismatch, not go with; SEE CONCEPTS 655,664

clasp [n] *fastener; hold on something*
brooch, buckle, catch, clamp, clench, clinch, clip, clutch, embrace, fastening, fibula, grapple, grasp, grip, hasp, hold, hook, hug, pin, safety pin, snap; SEE CONCEPTS 497,501

clasp [v] *grab tightly*
attack, bear hug*, buckle, clamp, clinch, clip, clutch, coil, concatenate, connect, embrace, enfold, fasten, glom onto*, grapple, grasp, grip, hold, hug, pin, press, seize, snatch, squeeze, take; SEE CONCEPTS 85,160,191,219

class [n1] *kind, sort, category*
branch, brand, breed, cast, caste, character, classification, collection, color, degree, denomination, department, description, designation, distinction, division, domain, estate, family, feather, frame, genre, genus, grade, grain, grouping, hierarchy, humor, ilk, kidney, league, make, mold, name, nature, order, origin, property, province, quality, range, rank, rate, school, sect, section, selection, set, source, species, sphere, standing, status, stripe, style, suit, temperament, value, variety; SEE CONCEPT 378

class [n2] *societal group, background*
ancestry, birth, bourgeoisie, breed, caliber, caste, circle, clan, clique, club, company, condition, connection, coterie, cultural level, degree, derivation, descent, estate, extraction, family, genealogy, grade, hierarchy, influence, intelligentsia, league, lineage, moiety, nobility, origin, pecking order*, pedigree, pigeonhole*, place, position, prestige, quality, sect, social rank, source, sphere, standing, state, station, status, stock, strain, stratum, the right stuff*, tier, title; SEE CONCEPTS 296,387,388,417

class [n3] *group in school*
academy, colloquium, course, course of study, division, form, grade, homeroom, lecture group, line, quiz group, recitation, room, round table, section, seminar, seminary, session, study, study group, subdivision, subject; SEE CONCEPTS 286,287,288,289

class [adj] *stylish; with panache*
chic, classy, dashing, fashionable, fine, fly*, foxy*, sharp; SEE CONCEPT 589

class [v] *categorize*
account, allot, appraise, assess, assign, assort, brand, classify, codify, consider, designate, divide, evaluate, gauge, grade, group, hold, identify, judge, mark, part, pigeonhole*, rank, rate, reckon, regard, score, separate; SEE CONCEPTS 39,135

classic [n] *model*
chef d'oeuvre, exemplar, magnum opus, paradigm, prototype, standard, tour de force; SEE CONCEPTS 259,655,686

classic/classical [adj1] *best, model*
archetypal, capital, champion, consummate, definitive, distinguished, esthetic, excellent, exemplary, famous, fine, finest, first-rate, flawless, ideal, master, masterly, paradigmatic, paramount, perfect, prime, quintessential, ranking, standard, superior, top, top-notch, vintage, well-known; SEE CONCEPT 574

classic [adj2] *characteristic, regular*
prototypal, prototypical, representative, simple, standard, time-honored, typical, usual, vintage; SEE CONCEPTS 533,547

classical [adj1] *concerning ancient culture*
academic, Attic, Augustan, belletristic, bookish, canonic, canonical, classic, classicistic, Doric, Grecian, Greek, Hellenic, Homeric, humanistic, Ionic, Latin, Roman, scholastic, Virgilian; SEE CONCEPTS 536,549

classical [adj2] *simple, chaste*
classic, elegant, harmonious, pure, refined, restrained, symmetrical, understated, well-proportioned; SEE CONCEPT 589

classicism [n] *simple style; regularity, restraint*
aesthetic principle, Atticism, balance, Ciceronianism, clarity, class, classicalism, conventional formality, dignity, elegance, excellence, finish, formality, formal style, grandeur, grand style, Hellenism, high art, lucidity, majesty, neoclassicism, nobility, objectivity, polish, proportion, propriety, pure taste, purity, rationalism, refinement, rhythm, severity, simplicity, sobriety, sublimity, symmetry; SEE CONCEPT 655

classification [n] *categorization*
allocation, alloting, allotment, analysis, apportionment, arrangement, assignment, assortment, cataloguing, categorizing, codification, collocation, consignment, coordination, denomination,

ci

cl

department, designation, disposal, disposition, distributing, distribution, division, echelon, gradation, grade, grading, graduation, group, grouping, kind, order, ordering, ordination, organization, pigeonholing*, regulation, sizing, sorting, systematization, tabulating, taxonomy, typecasting; SEE CONCEPTS 18,39,135,378

classify [v] *categorize*

allocate, allot, alphabetize, analyze, arrange, assort, brand, break down, button down*, catalogue, class, codify, collocate, coordinate, correlate, dispose, distinguish, distribute, divide, docket, embody, file, grade, group, incorporate, index, label, match, name, number, order, organize, peg*, pigeonhole*, put away, put down as, put down for, range, rank, rank out, rate, regiment, segregate, size, size up, sort, systematize, tab, tabulate, tag, take one's measure, ticket, type, typecast; SEE CONCEPTS 18,39,135

classy [adj] *stylish, having panache*

chic, dashing, elegant, exclusive, fashionable, high-class, in, in vogue, mod, modish, posh, select, sharp, superior, swank, swanky, tony, uptown; SEE CONCEPT 589

clatter [n] *loud noise*

ballyhoo*, bluster, clack, clangor, hullabaloo*, pandemonium, racket, rattle, rumpus, shattering, smashing; SEE CONCEPTS 181,189,595

clatter [v] *crash; make racket*

bang, bluster, bump, clang, clank, clash, hurtle, noise, rattle, roar, shatter, smash; SEE CONCEPTS 65,181,189

clause [n] *provision in document*

article, catch*, chapter, codicil, condition, fine print*, heading, item, joker*, kicker*, limitation, paragraph, part, passage, point, provision, proviso, requirement, rider, section, small print*, specification, stipulation, string attached to something*, ultimatum; SEE CONCEPTS 270,275

claw [n] *nail of animal; tool shaped like nail of an animal*

barb, cant hook, clapperclaw, crook, fang, fingernail, grappel, grappler, hook, manus, nail claw, nipper, paw, pincer, retractile, spur, talon, tentacle, unguis, ungula; SEE CONCEPT 392

claw [v] *using sharp nail*

break, dig, graze, hurt, itch, lacerate, mangle, maul, open, rip, scrabble, scrap, scrape, scratch, tear; SEE CONCEPTS 178,214,220

clay [n] *workable earth material*

adobe, argil, argillaceous earth, bole, brick, china material, clunch, earth, kaolin, loam, loess, marl, mud, porcelain material, pottery, slip, terra cotta, till, wacke; SEE CONCEPT 509

clean [adj1] *not dirty; uncluttered*

apple-pie order*, blank, bright, cleansed, clear, delicate, dirtless, elegant, faultless, flawless, fresh, graceful, hygienic, immaculate, laundered, neat, neat as a button*, neat as a pin*, orderly, pure, sanitary, shining, simple, snowy, sparkling, speckless, spic and span*, spotless, squeaky, stainless, taintless, tidy, trim, unblemished, unpolluted, unsmudged, unsoiled, unspotted, unstained, unsullied, untarnished, vanilla*, washed, well-kept, white; SEE CONCEPT 485

clean [adj2] *sterile*

antiseptic, aseptic, clarified, decontaminated, disinfected, hygienic, pure, purified, sanitary, sterilized, unadulterated, uncontaminated, uninfected, unpolluted, unsullied, wholesome; SEE CONCEPTS 314,485

clean [adj3] *chaste, virtuous*

blameless, crimeless, decent, exemplary, faultless, good, guiltless, honorable, inculpable, innocent, modest, moral, respectable, sinless, undefiled, unguilty, unsullied, upright, wholesome; SEE CONCEPT 404

clean [adj4] *precise, sharp*

clear, clear-cut, correct, definite, distinct, legible, neat, plain, readable, simple, trim, uncluttered; SEE CONCEPT 535

clean [adj5] *complete, thorough*

absolute, conclusive, decisive, entire, final, perfect, total, unimpaired, whole; SEE CONCEPT 531

clean [v] *make undirty, uncluttered*

absterge, bath, bathe, blot, brush, cauterize, clarify, cleanse, clear the decks*, clear up, deodorize, depurate, deterge, disinfect, do up*, dredge, dust, edulcorate, elutriate, erase, expunge, expurgate, flush, hackle, launder, lave, mop, neaten, pick, pick up, polish, purge, purify, rake, rasp, refine, rinse, rout out, sanitize, scald, scour, scrape, scrub, shake out, shampoo, soak, soap, sponge, spruce up*, sterilize, straighten up, swab, sweep, tidy up, vacuum, wash, whisk, winnow, wipe; SEE CONCEPTS 161,165

clean-cut [adj] *neat, clearly outlined*

categorical, chiseled, clear, definite, definitive, etched, explicit, express, sharp, specific, unambiguous, well-defined; SEE CONCEPTS 490,535

cleanse [v] *make undirty; wash*

absolve, clarify, clean, clear, depurate, disinfect, expurgate, launder, lustrate, purge, purify, refine, restore, rinse, sanitize, scour, scrub, sterilize; SEE CONCEPT 165

cleanser [n] *strong disinfectant, solvent*

abrasive, abstergent, antiseptic, cathartic, deodorant, detergent, fumigant, lather, polish, purgative, purifier, scourer, soap, soap powder, suds; SEE CONCEPT 492

clear [adj1] *cloudless, bright*

clarion, crystal, fair, fine, halcyon, light, luminous, pleasant, rainless, shiny, sunny, sunshiny, unclouded, undarkened, undimmed; SEE CONCEPTS 525,617,627

clear [adj2] *understandable, apparent*

apprehensible, audible, clear-cut, coherent, comprehensible, conspicuous, crystal, definite, distinct, evident, explicit, express, graspable, incontrovertible, intelligible, knowable, legible, loud enough, lucent, lucid, manifest, obvious, open and shut*, palpable, patent, perceptible, perspicuous, plain, precise, pronounced, readable, recognizable, sharp, simple, spelled out*, straightforward, transparent, transpicuous, unambiguous, unblurred, uncomplicated, unequivocal, unmistakable, unquestionable; SEE CONCEPTS 402,562

clear [adj3] *open, unhindered*

bare, empty, free, smooth, stark, unhampered, unimpeded, unlimited, unobstructed, vacant, vacuous, void; SEE CONCEPT 490

clear [adj4] *transparent*

apparent, cloudless, crystal, crystal clear, crystalline, glassy, limpid, pellucid, pure, see-through, thin, tralucent, translucent, translucid; SEE CONCEPTS 618,619

clear [adj5] *not guilty*

absolved, blameless, clean, cleared, discharged,

dismissed, exculpated, exonerated, guiltless, immaculate, innocent, pure, sinless, stainless, unblemished, uncensurable, undefiled, untarnished, untroubled; SEE CONCEPTS 319,404

clear [adj6] *certain in one's mind*
absolute, confirmed, convinced, decided, definite, positive, resolved, satisfied, sure; SEE CONCEPT 403

clear [v1] *clean, clear away*
ameliorate, break up, brighten, burn off, clarify, cleanse, disencumber, disengage, disentangle, eliminate, empty, erase, extricate, free, lighten, loosen, lose, meliorate, open, purify, refine, rid, rule out, shake off, sweep, throw off, tidy, unblock, unburden, unclog, unload, unloose, unpack, untie, vacate, void, wipe; SEE CONCEPTS 165,211

clear [v2] *liberate; free from uncertainty*
absolve, acquit, clarify, defog*, discharge, disculpate, emancipate, exculpate, exonerate, explain, find innocent, let go, let off, let off the hook*, release, relieve, set free, vindicate; SEE CONCEPTS 7,22,127

clear [v3] *pass over, often by jumping*
hurdle, leap, miss, negotiate, overleap, surmount, vault; SEE CONCEPT 194

clear [v4] *profit*
accumulate, acquire, clean up*, earn, gain, gather, get, glean, make, net, obtain, pick up, realize, reap, receive, secure, win; SEE CONCEPTS 129,342

clearance [n1] *permission for activity*
approval, authorization, consent, endorsement, go-ahead*, green light*, leave, okay, sanction, say-so*; SEE CONCEPT 376

clearance [n2] *gap above something*
allowance, assart, defoliated area, empty space, expanse, gap, headroom, margin, opening, open space; SEE CONCEPT 513

clear-cut [adj] *definite*
assured, categorical, crystalline, decided, definitive, distinct, evident, explicit, express, indubitable, lucent, lucid, obvious, plain, precise, pronounced, sharp-cut, specific, straightforward, unambiguous, undisputed, undoubted, unequivocal, unquestioned, well-defined; SEE CONCEPT 535

clearing [n] *gap in area*
allowance, assart, clearance, defoliated area, dell, empty space, expanse, gap, glade, headroom, margin, opening, open space; SEE CONCEPT 513

clearly [adv] *without any doubt*
acutely, apparently, audibly, beyond doubt, certainly, conspicuously, decidedly, definitely, discernibly, distinctly, evidently, incontestably, incontrovertibly, indubitably, lucidly, manifestly, markedly, noticeably, obviously, openly, overtly, patently, penetratingly, perceptibly, plainly, positively, precisely, prominently, purely, recognizably, seemingly, sharply, sonorously, surely, translucently, transparently, undeniably, undoubtedly, unmistakably; SEE CONCEPTS 535,552

clear out [v1] *empty something*
clean out, dispose of, eliminate, exhaust, get rid of, remove, sort, tidy up; SEE CONCEPT 211

clear out [v2] *leave, often quickly*
beat it*, begone, decamp, depart, go, hightail*, kite*, make oneself scarce*, remove oneself, retire, scram, skedaddle*, split*, take a hike*, take off, vamoose*, withdraw; SEE CONCEPT 195

clear up [v1] *explain; resolve*
answer, cipher, clarify, decipher, dissolve, elucidate, figure out, illuminate, illustrate, make plausible, make reasonable, puzzle out, resolve, solve, straighten out, tidy, unfold, unravel; SEE CONCEPTS 37,57

clear up [v2] *become improved*
become fair, become sunny, blow over, brighten, die away, die down, improve, lapse, lift, pick up, run its course*; SEE CONCEPT 700

cleavage [n] *gap*
break, chasm, cleft, discontinuity, divide, division, fracture, hole, rift, schism, separation, severance, split, valley; SEE CONCEPT 513

cleave [v1] *divide, split*
carve, chop, crack, cut, dissect, dissever, disunite, divorce, hack, hew, open, part, pierce, rend, rip, rive, separate, sever, slice, stab, sunder, tear asunder, whack; SEE CONCEPTS 98,137,176

cleave [v2] *stand by, stick together*
abide by, adhere, agree, associate, attach, be devoted to, be tight with*, be true*, cling, cohere, combine, freeze to*, hold, join, link, remain, stay put, unite; SEE CONCEPTS 8,113

cleft [n] *break, gap*
aperture, arroyo, breach, canyon, chasm, chink, cleavage, clough, clove, crack, cranny, crevasse, crevice, fissure, fracture, gorge, gulch, opening, ravine, rent, rift, rima, rimation, rime, schism, slit; SEE CONCEPT 513

cleft [adj] *separated, split*
broken, cloven, cracked, crannied, crenelated, parted, perforated, pierced, rent, riven, ruptured, separated, sundered, torn; SEE CONCEPT 490

clemency [n] *forgiveness*
caritas, charity, compassion, endurance, equitableness, fairness, forbearance, gentleness, grace, humanity, indulgence, justness, kindness, lenience, leniency, lenity, lifesaver, mercifulness, mercy, mildness, moderation, soft-heartedness, sufferance, tenderness, tolerance, toleration; SEE CONCEPTS 410,644

clement [adj1] *calm, mild (weather)*
balmy, clear, fair, fine, moderate, peaceful, temperate, warm; SEE CONCEPT 525

clement [adj2] *forgiving*
benevolent, benign, benignant, charitable, compassionate, easy, forbearing, gentle, humane, humanitarian, indulgent, kind, kind-hearted, kindly, lenient, merciful, mild, soft-hearted, sympathetic, tender, tolerant; SEE CONCEPTS 404,550

clench [v] *grasp*
clamp, clasp, clinch, clutch, constrict, contract, double up, draw together, grapple, grip, hold; SEE CONCEPT 191

clergy [n] *ministry of church*
canonicate, canonry, cardinalate, churchpersons, clerics, conclave, deaconry, diaconate, ecclesiastics, first estate, holy order, pastorate, prelacy, priesthood, rabbinate, the cloth, the desk, the pulpit; SEE CONCEPT 369

clergyperson [n] *minister of church*
abbey, archbishop, bishop, blackcoat*, cardinal, cassock, chaplain, churchperson, cleric, clerk, curate, dean*divine, ecclesiast, ecclesiastic, evangelist, father, missionary, monsignor, padre, parson, pastor, person of God, person of the cloth, pontiff, preacher, predicant, priest, primate, pulpitarian, pulpiteer, rabbi, rector, reverend, sermonizer, shepherd, vicar; SEE CONCEPT 361

cl
cl

clerical [adj1] secretarial

accounting, bookkeeping, clerkish, clerkly, office, pink collar*, scribal, stenographic, subordinate, typing, white collar*, written; SEE CONCEPT 536

clerical [adj2] concerning clergy

apostolic, canonical, churchly, cleric, ecclesiastic, ecclesiastical, episcopal, holy, ministerial, monastic, monkish, papal, parsonical, parsonish, pastoral, pontifical, prelatic, priestly, rabbinical, sacerdotal, sacred, theocratical; SEE CONCEPT 536

clerk [n] assistant

agent, amanuensis, auditor, bookkeeper, cashier, copyist, counter jumper*, counterperson, employee, notary, office helper, operator, paper pusher*, paper shuffler*, pencil pusher*, pen pusher*, receptionist, recorder, registrar, salesperson, secretary, seller, shopperson, stenographer, teller, transcriber, white collar*, worker; SEE CONCEPT 348

clever [adj] bright, ingenious

able, adept, adroit, alert, apt, astute, brainy, brilliant, cagey, canny, capable, competent, crackerjack*, cunning, deep, dexterous/dextrous, discerning, egghead*, expert, foxy*, gifted, good, handy, intelligent, inventive, keen, knowing, knowledgeable, many-sided, nimble, nobody's fool*, pretty, pro, qualified, quick, quick on trigger*, quick-witted, rational, resourceful, sagacious, savvy, sensible, sharp, shrewd, skilled, skillful, slick, sly, smart, sprightly, talented, versatile, wise, witty; SEE CONCEPT 402

cleverness [n] brightness, ingenuity

ability, adroitness, astuteness, brains, calculation, canniness, dexterity, discernment, flair, gift, gumption, intelligence, quickness, quick wit, resourcefulness, sagacity, sense, sharpness, shrewdness, skill, smartness, talent, wisdom, wit; SEE CONCEPT 409

cliché [n] overused, hackneyed phrase

adage, banality, boiler plate*, bromide, buzzword, chestnut*, commonplace, corn*, counterword, familiar tune, motto, old story*, platitude, potboiler, prosaism, proverb, rubber stamp*, saying, shibboleth, slogan, stale saying, stereotype, threadbare phrase, triteness, trite remark, triviality, truism, vapid expression; SEE CONCEPTS 275,278

click [n/v1] metallic sound

bang, beat, clack, snap, tick; SEE CONCEPTS 65,595

click [v2] fall into place

become clear, be compatible, be on same wavelength*, come off*, feel a rapport*, get on*, go, go off well*, go over, hit it off*, make a hit*, make sense, match, meet with approval, pan out*, prove out, succeed, take to each other*; SEE CONCEPT 704

client [n] customer

applicant, believer, buyer, chump, consumer, dependent, disciple, follower, front, habitué, head, mark, patient, patron, protégé, protégée, purchaser, shopper, walk-in, ward; SEE CONCEPT 348

clientele [n] customers of business

audience, business, clientage, clientry, clients, constituency, cortege, dependents, following, market, patronage, patrons, public, regulars, trade; SEE CONCEPTS 325,417

cliff [n] overhang on hill or mountain

bluff, crag, escarpment, face, precipice, rock face,

rocky height, scar, scarp, steep rock, wall; SEE CONCEPT 509

climactic/climacteric [adj] decisive

acute, climactical, critical, crucial, desperate, dire, paramount, peak; SEE CONCEPT 567

climate [n1] weather of region

altitude, aridity, atmospheric conditions, characteristic weather, clime, conditions, humidity, latitude, meteorological character, meteorologic conditions, temperature; SEE CONCEPT 524

climate [n2] mood of situation

ambience, ambient, atmosphere, disposition, environment, feeling, medium, milieu, mise-en-scène, mood, surroundings, temper, tendency, trend; SEE CONCEPT 673

climax [n] peak, culmination

acme, apex, apogee, ascendancy, capsheaf, capstone, climacteric, crest, crowning point, extremity, head, height, highlight, high spot, intensification, limit, maximum, meridian, ne plus ultra, orgasm, payoff*, pinnacle, pitch, summit, tiptop, top, turning point, utmost, zenith; SEE CONCEPTS 706,836

climax [v] come to top; culminate

accomplish, achieve, break the record*, cap, come, come to a head*, conclude, content, crown, end, finish, fulfill, hit high spot, orgasm, peak, please, reach a peak, reach the zenith, rise to crescendo*, satisfy, succeed, terminate, top, tower; SEE CONCEPTS 375,704,706

climb [v] crawl, move up

ape up*, ascend, clamber, escalade, escalate, go up, mount, rise, scale, soar, top; SEE CONCEPT 166

clinch [v1] secure a goal

assure, cap, conclude, confirm, decide, determine, seal, seize, set, settle, sew up, verify; SEE CONCEPT 706

clinch [v2] hold securely; grab

bolt, clamp, clasp, clench, clutch, cuddle, embrace, enfold, fasten, fix, grab hold of, grapple, grasp, grip, hug, lay hands on, make fast, nail, press, rivet, secure, seize, snatch, squeeze; SEE CONCEPTS 191,219

cling [v] attach to

adhere, be true to, cherish, clasp, cleave to, clutch, cohere, continue, embrace, endure, fasten, freeze to, grasp, grip, hang in, hang onto, hold fast, hug, last, linger, squeeze, stay put, stick, stick like glue*; SEE CONCEPTS 85,160,190

clinic [n] medical center

dispensary, hospital, infirmary, sick bay, surgery center; SEE CONCEPTS 312,439,449

clinical [adj] dispassionate

analytic, antiseptic, cold, detached, disinterested, emotionless, impersonal, objective, scientific, unemotional; SEE CONCEPT 404

clink [n/v] bang against, ring

chink, clang, jangle, jingle, sound, tingle, tinkle; SEE CONCEPTS 65,595

clip [v1] cut short

bob, crop, curtail, cut, cut back, decrease, dock, lower, mow, pare, prune, reduce, shave, shear, shorten, skive, slash, snip, trim, truncate; SEE CONCEPTS 137,176

clip [v2/n] punch

blow, box, clout, cuff, knock, punch, smack, sock, thump, wallop, whack; SEE CONCEPT 189

clique [n] group of friends

bunch, cabal, camarilla, camp, circle, clan, club,

coterie, crew, crowd, crush, faction, gang, in-group, insiders, lobby, Mafia, mob, organization, outfit, pack, posse, ring, set, society; SEE CONCEPTS 387,417

cloak [n] *cover; coat*
beard, blind, camouflage, cape, capote, disguise, facade, face, front, guise, manteau, mantle, mask, pretext, semblance, shawl, shield, show, veneer, wrap; SEE CONCEPTS 451,475,680

cloak [v] *disguise*
blanket, camouflage, coat, conceal, cover, curtain, dissemble, dissimulate, dress up, hide, mask, obscure, pretext, screen, shroud, veil; SEE CONCEPT 188

clobber [v] *hit, beat*
belt, blast, drub, lambaste*, lick, shellac*, slam, slug, smash, smear, smother, thrash, trim, wallop, whip; SEE CONCEPTS 189,252

clock [n] *timekeeping device*
alarm, Big Ben*, chroniker*, chronograph, chronometer, digital watch, hourglass, pendulum, stopwatch, sundial, tattler, ticker*, tick-tock*, timekeeper, timemarker, timepiece, timer, turnip*, watch; SEE CONCEPTS 463,819

clockwork [n] *being on time; precision*
accuracy, consistency, perfect timing, regularity, smoothness; SEE CONCEPT 818

clod [n] *stupid person*
blockhead*, boor, chump, clown, dimwit*, dolt, dope*, dumbbell, dummy, dunce, fool, imbecile, lame-brain*, lout, oaf, simpleton; SEE CONCEPTS 412,423

clog [n] *blockage*
bar, block, blockade, burden, cumbrance, dead weight, drag, encumbrance, hindrance, impedance, impediment, obstruction, snag; SEE CONCEPTS 121,674

clog [v] *block, hinder*
burden, choke, close, congest, curb, dam up, encumber, entrammel, fetter, fill, glut, hamper, impede, jam, leash, obstruct, occlude, plug, seal, shackle, stopper, stop up, stuff, tie, trammel; SEE CONCEPTS 121,130,190

cloister [n] *secluded religious place*
abbey, cell, chapter house, convent, friary, hermitage, house, lamasery, monastery, nunnery, order, priorate, priory, religious community, retreat, sanctuary; SEE CONCEPTS 368,516

cloistered [adj] *secluded*
cloistral, confined, hermitic, hidden, insulated, recluse, reclusive, restricted, secluse, seclusive, sequestered, sheltered, shielded, shut off, withdrawn; SEE CONCEPTS 554,583

close [n] *ending*
adjournment, cease, cessation, completion, conclusion, culmination, denouement, desistance, end, finale, finish, period, stop, termination, windup; SEE CONCEPTS 119,832

close [adj1] *near, nearby*
abutting, across the street, adjacent, adjoining, approaching, around the corner, at hand, contiguous, convenient, give or take a little*, handy, hard by, immediate, imminent, impending, in spitting distance*, in the ball park*, near-at-hand, nearest, nearly, neighboring, next, nigh, proximate, under one's nose*, warm; SEE CONCEPT 586

close [adj2] *dense, cramped*
circumscribed, close-grained, compact, confined, confining, congested, consolidated, cropped, crowded, firm, impenetrable, impermeable, jam-packed, narrow, packed, restricted, short, solid, substantial, thick, tight; SEE CONCEPTS 481,483,774

close [adj3] *accurate, precise*
conscientious, exact, faithful, lifelike, literal, resembling, similar, strict; SEE CONCEPTS 535,563

close [adj4] *intimate*
attached, buddy-buddy*, chummy, confidential, cozy with, dear, devoted, familiar, inseparable, kissing cousins*, loving, making it with*, on top of each other*, palsy-walsy*, private, related, thick*, thick as thieves*, thick with*; SEE CONCEPTS 372,555

close [adj5] *oppressive, humid*
airless, breathless, choky, confined, fusty, heavy, moldy, motionless, muggy, musty, stagnant, stale, stale-smelling, sticky, stifling, stuffy, suffocating, sultry, sweltering, sweltry, thick, tight, uncomfortable, unventilated; SEE CONCEPTS 525,605

close [adj6] *secret, reserved*
buttoning one's lip*, buttoning up*, clamming up*, close-lipped, closemouthed, hidden, hush-hush*, mum's the word*, on the Q.T.*, private, reticent, retired, secluded, secretive, silent, taciturn, tight chops*, tight-lipped*, uncommunicative, unforthcoming, zipping one's lips*; SEE CONCEPTS 267,576

close [adj7] *stingy*
chintzy*, closefisted, illiberal, mean, mingy, miserly, narrow, niggardly, parsimonious, penny-pinching, penurious, skimpy, skinflint*, tight, tight-fisted, ungenerous; SEE CONCEPTS 334,404

close [v1] *obstruct, seal*
bang, bar, block, bolt, button, caulk, choke, clap, clench, clog, confine, congest, cork, dam, exclude, fasten, fill, lock, occlude, plug, prevent passage, put to, retard flow, screen, secure, shut, shut off, shutter, slam, stopper, stop up, stuff, turn off; SEE CONCEPTS 113,121,201

close [v2] *complete, finish, stop*
button down*, button up*, call it a day*, call off, cap, cease, clear, clinch, conclude, consummate, culminate, cut loose, determine, discontinue, do, drop the curtain*, end, fold, fold up, halt, pack it in*, put a lid on*, put to bed*, sew up*, shut down, shutter, terminate, ultimate, wind down*, wind up*, wrap up*; SEE CONCEPT 234

close [v3] *join, unite*
agree, bind, chain, coalesce, come together, connect, couple, encounter, fuse, grapple, inclose, meet, put together, tie, tie up; SEE CONCEPT 113

closed [adj1] *shut, out of service*
bankrupt, dark, fastened, folded, gone fishing*, locked, not open, out of business*, out of order*, padlocked, sealed, shut down; SEE CONCEPT 576

closed [adj2] *finished, terminated*
concluded, decided, ended, final, over, resolved, settled; SEE CONCEPT 548

closed [adj3] *exclusive, independent*
restricted, self-centered, self-contained, self-sufficient, self-sufficing, self-supported, self-supporting, self-sustained, self-sustaining; SEE CONCEPT 550

closely [adv] *approximately, carefully*
by the skin of one's teeth*, exactly, firmly, hard, heedfully, in conjunction with, intently, intimately, jointly, meticulously, mindfully, minutely, nearly, punctiliously, scrupulously,

searchingly, sharply, similarly, strictly, thought-fully; SEE CONCEPTS 487,557,573

closemouthed [adj] *silent, reserved*
buttoned up*, clammed up*, close, close-lipped, dummied up, have tight chops*, hush-hush, on the Q.T.*, quiet, reticent, sedate, taciturn, tight-lipped, uncommunicative, zipped one's lips*; SEE CONCEPT 267

closet [n] *storage cupboard, usually tall*
ambry, bin, buffet, cabinet, chest of drawers, clothes room, cold storage, container, depository, locker, receptacle, recess, repository, room, safe, sideboard, vault, walk-in, wardrobe; SEE CONCEPT 440

closure [n1] *conclusion*
cease, cessation, close, closing, desistance, end, ending, finish, stop, stoppage, termination; SEE CONCEPT 119

closure [n2] *plug, seal*
blockade, bolt, bung, cap, cork, fastener, latch, lid, obstruction, occludent, occlusion, padlock, stop, stopper, stopple, tampon, tap; SEE CONCEPTS 471,680

clot [n] *blockage, mass of coagulation*
array, batch, battery, body, bulk, bunch, bundle, clotting, clump, cluster, coagulum, coalescence, conglutination, consolidation, curd, curdling, embolism, embolus, glob, gob, group, grume, lump, occlusion, precipitate, set, thickness, thrombus; SEE CONCEPTS 432,466,470

clot [v] *coagulate*
clabber, coalesce, congeal, curdle, gel, gelate, gelatinize, glop up*, jell, jellify, jelly, lopper*, lump, set, solidify, thicken; SEE CONCEPT 469

cloth [n] *fabric*
bolt, calico, cotton, dry goods, goods, material, stuff, synthetics, textiles, tissue, twill, weave, yard goods; SEE CONCEPT 473

clothe [v] *cover with apparel*
accouter, apparel, array, attire, bedizen, bedrape, breech, bundle up, caparison, cloak, coat, costume, dandify, deck, disguise, dizen, do up*, drape, dress, dress up, dud*, endow, endue, enwrap, equip, fit, fit out, garb, gown, guise, habilitate, habit, invest, jacket, livery, mantle, outfit, primp, raiment, rig, robe, spruce, suit up, swaddle, swathe, tog, turn out, vest; SEE CONCEPT 167

clothes/clothing [n] *personal attire*
accouterment, apparel, array, caparison, civvies*, costume, covering, drag*, drapery, dress, duds*, ensemble, equipment, finery, frippery, frock, full feather*, garb, garments, gear, get-up*, habiliment, habit, hand-me-downs, livery, mufti, outfit, overclothes, panoply, rags*, raiment, regalia, rigging*, sack*, sportswear, Sunday best*, tailleur, tatters*, things*, threads*, toggery*, togs, tout ensemble, trappings, trousseau, underclothes, vestment, vesture, vines*, wardrobe, wear, weeds*, zoot suit*; SEE CONCEPT 451

cloud [n1] *mass of water particles in air*
billow, brume, darkness, dimness, film, fog, fogginess, frost, gloom, haze, haziness, mare's tail*, mist, murk, nebula, nebulosity, obscurity, ol' buttermilk sky*, overcast, pea soup*, pother, puff, rack, scud, sheep, smog, smoke, smother, steam, thunderhead, vapor, veil, woolpack; SEE CONCEPTS 437,524

cloud [n2] *crowd*
army, dense mass, flock, horde, host, legion, multitude, rout, scores, shower, swarm, throng; SEE CONCEPTS 417,432

cloud [v1] *become foggy or obscured*
adumbrate, becloud, befog, blur, darken, dim, eclipse, envelop, fog, gloom, mist, obfuscate, overcast, overshadow, shade, shadow, veil; SEE CONCEPTS 469,526

cloud [v2] *confuse*
addle, becloud, befuddle, disorient, distort, distract, impair, muddle, muddy, obscure, perplex, puzzle; SEE CONCEPTS 7,19

cloudy [adj] *hazy; darkened*
blurred, confused, dark, dense, dim, dismal, dull, dusky, emulsified, foggy, gloomy, heavy, indefinite, indistinct, leaden, lowering, misty, mucky, muddy, murky, mushy, nebulous, nontranslucent, nontransparent, not clear, nubilous, obscure, opaque, overcast, somber, sullen, sunless, vaporous; SEE CONCEPT 525

clown [n1] *joking person*
antic, buffoon, comedian, comic, cut-up*, dolt, droll, farceur, fool, funnyperson, funster, gagman*, gagster*, harlequin, humorist, jester, joker, jokesmith, jokester, life of the party*, madcap, merry-andrew, merrymaker, mime, mountebank, mummer, picador, pierrot, prankster, punch, punchinello*, quipster, ribald, wag, wisecracker, wit*, zany*; SEE CONCEPT 423

clown [n2] *stupid, ignorant person*
blockhead*, boor, bucolic, buffoon, bumpkin*, chuff, churl, clodhopper*, gawk, hayseed*, hick*, hind, jake, lout, mucker*, oaf, peasant, rube, rustic, swain, yahoo*, yokel; SEE CONCEPTS 412,423

clown [v] *joke*
act crazy, act the fool*, bug out*, cut up*, fool around, have fun, jest, kid around; SEE CONCEPT 386

cloy [v] *overfill*
disgust, fill, glut, gorge, jade, nauseate, pall, sate, satiate, satisfy, sicken, stall, stodge, suffice, surfeit, weary, weary; SEE CONCEPT 740

club [n1] *bat, stick*
baton, billy*, blackjack, bludgeon, business*, conk buster*, convincer*, cosh, cudgel, hammer, hickory, mace, mallet, nightstick, persuader*, quarterstaff, rosewood, sap, shill, shillelagh, staff, swatter, truncheon, works*; SEE CONCEPTS 470,499

club [n2] *social organization*
affiliation, alliance, association, bunch, circle, clique, company, crew, faction, gang, guild, hangout*, league, lodge, meeting, mob, order, outfit, ring, set, society, sodality, stamping ground*, union; SEE CONCEPTS 387,439

club [n3] *golfing tool*
brassie, cleek, driver, iron, mashie, midiron, niblick, putter, spoon, stick, wedge, wood; SEE CONCEPT 364

club [v] *hit hard with object*
bash, baste, batter, beat, blackjack, bludgeon, clobber, clout, cosh, cudgel, fustigate, hammer, pommel, pound, pummel, strike, whack; SEE CONCEPT 189

clue [n] *hint, evidence*
cue, dead giveaway*, hot lead*, indication, inkling, intimation, key, lead, mark, notion, pointer, print, proof, sign, solution, suggestion, suspicion, telltale, tip, tip-off*, trace, track, wind; SEE CONCEPT 274

clue [v] *give information*
acquaint, advise, apprise, fill in, give the low-down*, give the skinny on*, hint, indicate, inform, intimate, lead to, leave evidence, leave trace, leave tracks, notify, point to, post, suggest, tell, warn, wise up; SEE CONCEPT *60*

clump [n1] *mass of something*
array, batch, blob, body, bunch, bundle, chunk, cluster, clutter, gob, group, hodgepodge, hunk, jumble, knot, lot, lump, nugget, parcel, set, shock, wad; SEE CONCEPTS *432,470*

clump [n2] *thumping noise*
clatter, clomp, galumph, scuff, stomp, stumble, thud; SEE CONCEPT *595*

clump [v] *make thumping noise*
barge, bumble, clatter, clomp, galumph, hobble, limp, plod, scuff, stamp, stomp, stumble, stump, thud, thump, tramp; SEE CONCEPTS *65,595*

clumsy [adj] *not agile; awkward*
all thumbs*, blundering, blunderous, bulky, bumbling, bungling, butterfingered*, clownish, crude, elephantine, gauche, gawkish, gawky, graceless, ham-handed*, heavy, heavy-handed, helpless, hulking, ill-shaped, incompetent, inelegant, inept, inexperienced, inexpert, lubberly, lumbering, lumpish, maladroit, oafish, ponderous, splay, stumbling, unable, unadept, uncoordinated, uncouth, undexterous, uneasy, ungainly, unhandy, unskillful, untactful, untalented, untoward, unwieldy, weedy; SEE CONCEPTS *401,402,584*

cluster [n] *group of something*
array, assemblage, band, batch, bevy, blob, body, bunch, bundle, chunk, clump, clutch, collection, covey, crew, gathering, hunk, knot, lot, pack, party, set; SEE CONCEPT *432*

cluster [v] *assemble, group*
accumulate, aggregate, associate, bunch, bunch up, bundle, collect, crowd around, cumulate, flock, gang around, gather, package, parcel, round up; SEE CONCEPT *109*

clutch [n] *strong hold*
clamp, clasp, clench, clinch, connection, coupling, grapple, grasp, grip, gripe, link; SEE CONCEPT *190*

clutch [v] *grab, snatch*
catch, cherish, clasp, clench, clinch, cling to, collar, embrace, fasten, glom*, grapple, grasp, grip, harbor, hold, hook, keep, nab, nail*, put the snare on*, seize, snag, snatch, take; SEE CONCEPTS *190,191*

clutches [n] *personal power*
claws, control, custody, grasp, grip, hands, keeping, possession, sway; SEE CONCEPTS *388,641,710*

clutter [n] *disarray, mess*
ataxia, chaos, confusion, derangement, disorder, hodgepodge, huddle, jumble, litter, medley, melange, muddle, rummage, scramble, shuffle, tumble, untidiness; SEE CONCEPTS *432,674*

clutter [v] *cause mess, disarray*
dirty, jumble, litter, muddle, scatter, snarl, strew; SEE CONCEPT *254*

coach [n1] *instructor, usually in recreation*
drill instructor, educator, mentor, physical education instructor, skipper, teacher, trainer, tutor; SEE CONCEPTS *350,366*

coach [n2] *carriage*
bus, car, chaise, charabanc, fourwheeler, gocart,

perambulator, stage, tallyho*, train, vehicle, victoria; SEE CONCEPT *505*

coach [v] *instruct, usually in recreation*
break in*, cram, drill, educate, home, lay it out for*, lick into shape*, prepare, pull one's coat*, put through the grind*, put through the mill*, ready, school, teach, train, tutor; SEE CONCEPTS *285,363*

coagulate [v] *clot*
clabber, coalesce, compact, concentrate, concrete, condense, congeal, consolidate, curdle, dry, gel, gelate, gelatinize, glop up*, harden, inspissate, jell, jellify, jelly, lopper*, set, solidify, thicken; SEE CONCEPT *469*

coagulation [n] *clotting*
agglomeration, caseation, concentration, concretion, condensation, congelation, consolidation, curdling, embolism, gelatination, incrassation, inspissation, jellification, thickening; SEE CONCEPT *469*

coalesce [v] *blend, come together*
adhere, amalgamate, associate, bracket, cleave, cling, cohere, combine, commingle, commix, conjoin, connect, consolidate, fuse, hook up with*, incorporate, integrate, join, join up with, link, merge, mingle, mix, relate, stick, tie in with*, unite, wed; SEE CONCEPTS *112,113*

coalition [n] *allied group, association*
affiliation, alliance, amalgam, amalgamation, anschluss, bloc, coadunation, combination, combine, compact, confederacy, confederation, conjunction, consolidation, conspiracy, faction, federation, fusion, integration, league, melding, mergence, merger, merging, party, ring, unification, union; SEE CONCEPT *381*

coarse [adj1] *not fine, rude*
base, bawdy, blue*, boorish, brutish, cheap, common, crass, crude, dirty, earthy, filthy, foul, foul-mouthed, gross, gruff, immodest, impolite, improper, impure, incult, indelicate, inelegant, loutish, low, lowbred, lowdown and dirty*, mean, nasty, obscene, off-color, offensive, raffish, raunchy, raw, ribald, rough, roughneck*, rude, scatological, smutty*, tacky, uncivil, uncouth, uncultivated, uncultured, unrefined, vulgar, vulgarian; SEE CONCEPTS *401,545*

coarse [adj2] *rough, unrefined*
chapped, coarse-grained, crude, grainy, granular, harsh, homespun, impure, inferior, loose, lumpy, mediocre, particulate, poor quality, rough-hewn, rugged, unfinished, unpolished, unprocessed, unpurified; SEE CONCEPTS *574,606*

coarseness [n] *rudeness, vulgarity*
bawdiness, boorishness, callousness, crassness, crudity, earthiness, harshness, indelicacy, offensiveness, poor taste, rawness, ribaldry, roughness, smut*, smuttiness*, uncouthness, unevenness, unrefinement; SEE CONCEPTS *633,645*

coast [n] *border by water*
bank, beach, coastline, littoral, margin, seaboard, seacoast, seashore, seaside, shore, shoreline, strand; SEE CONCEPTS *509,514*

coast [v] *glide along without much effort*
cruise, drift, float, freewheel, get by*, ride on current, sail, skate, slide, smooth along*, taxi; SEE CONCEPTS *150,704*

coastal [adj] *bordering the water*
along a coast, littoral, marginal, marshy, riverine, seaside, skirting; SEE CONCEPT *583*

cl
co

coat [n1] *animal hair*
crust, ectoderm, epidermis, felt, fleece, fur, hide, husk, integument, leather, membrane, pelage, pellicle, pelt, peltry, protective covering, rind, scale, scarfskin, shell, skin, wool; SEE CONCEPT *399*

coat [n2] *covering*
bark, coating, crust, finish, glaze, gloss, lacquer, lamination, layer, overlay, painting, plaster, priming, roughcast, set, tinge, varnish, wash, whitewashing; SEE CONCEPTS *259,475*

coat [n3] *personal outerwear*
cape, cloak, cutaway, flogger, frock, greatcoat, jacket, mackinaw, mink, overcoat, pea, raincoat, slicker, suit, tails, threads, topcoat, trench, tux, tuxedo, ulster, windbreaker, wrap; SEE CONCEPT *451*

coat [v] *cover with layer of material*
apply, cover, crust, enamel, foil, glaze, incrust, laminate, paint, plaster, plate, smear, spread, stain, surface, varnish; SEE CONCEPTS *172,202*

coating [n] *covering*
blanket, bloom, coat, crust, dusting, encrustation, film, finish, glaze, lamination, layer, membrane, patina, sheet, skin, varnish, veneer; SEE CONCEPT *475*

coax [v] *persuade*
allure, argue into, arm-twist*, barter, beguile, blandish, blarney, butter up*, cajole, come on, con, decoy, entice, flatter, get, hook, importune, induce, influence, inveigle, jawbone*, lure, pester, plague, press, prevail upon, rope in*, softsoap*, soothe, sweet-talk, talk into, tease, tempt, urge, wangle, wheedle, work on, worm; SEE CONCEPT *68*

cobweb [n] *entanglement; filament*
fiber, gossamer, labyrinth, mesh, net, network, snare, tissue, toil, web, webbing; SEE CONCEPTS *517,674*

cock [n] *rooster*
capon, chanticleer, chicken, cock-a-doodle-doo*, cockalorum, cockerel; SEE CONCEPT *394*

cock [v] *aim up toward*
erect, hump, perk up, pile, prick, raise, stack, stand erect, stand up, stick up; SEE CONCEPT *201*

cockeyed [adj] *crooked, askew*
absurd, askance, askant, asymmetrical, awry, cam, canted, crazy, crooked, cross-eyed, lopsided, ludicrous, nonsensical, preposterous, squint, strabismic; SEE CONCEPT *586*

cocky/cocksure [adj] *self-assured, full of oneself*
arrogant, brash, bumptious, certain, conceited, confident, egotistical, hotdogging*, hotshot*, hubristic, know-it-all*, lordly, nervy, overconfident, overweening, positive, presumptuous, self-confident, smart aleck*, smart guy*, smarty*, smarty pants*, sure, swaggering, swollen-headed, vain, wise guy*; SEE CONCEPTS *401,404*

cocoon [v] *protect with covering*
cushion, encase, envelop, insulate, pad, swaddle, swathe, truss, wrap; SEE CONCEPTS *130,134*

coddle [v1] *indulge, pamper*
baby, caress, cater to, cosset, cotton, favor, humor, make much of, make over, mollycoddle, nurse, pet, play up to, spoil; SEE CONCEPTS *110,295*

coddle [v2] *boil lightly, usually eggs*
brew, cook, poach, simmer, steam; SEE CONCEPT *170*

code [n1] *secret language system*
cipher, cryptograph; SEE CONCEPTS *276,284*

code [n2] *law, rule*
canon, charter, codex, constitution, convention, custom, digest, discipline, ethics, etiquette, manners, maxim, method, regulation, system; SEE CONCEPTS *318,688*

co-dependent [adj] *unhealthy psychological reliance of one person on another*
addicted, attached, hooked, interconnected, interdependent, mutually dependent, slavish trust, unhealthy confidence; SEE CONCEPTS *404,542*

codicil [n] *added part to document*
addendum, addition, appendix, postscript, rider, supplement; SEE CONCEPT *270*

codify [v] *systematize*
arrange, catalogue, classify, code, collect, condense, digest, order, organize, summarize, tabulate; SEE CONCEPTS *39,84*

coerce [v] *compel, press*
beset, browbeat, bulldoze*, bully, concuss, constrain, cow, dragoon, drive, force, high pressure*, hinder, impel, intimidate, lean on, make, make an offer they can't refuse*, menace, oblige, pressurize, push, put the squeeze on*, repress, restrict, shotgun*, strong-arm, suppress, terrorize, threaten, twist one's arm*, urge; SEE CONCEPTS *14,68*

coercion [n] *compulsion, pressure*
browbeating, bullying, constraint, duress, force, intimidation, menace, menacing, persuasion, restraint, strong-arm tactic*, threat, threatening, violence; SEE CONCEPTS *14,68*

coexistence [n] *happening or being at same time, place*
accord, coetaneousness, coevality, coincidence, concurrence, conformity, conjunction, contemporaneousness, harmony, order, peace, simultaneousness, synchronicity; SEE CONCEPT *407*

coffee [n] *hot beverage made from beans of a tree*
battery acid*, brew, café, café au lait, café noir, cappuccino, decaf, decoction, demitasse, espresso, forty weight*, hot stuff*, ink*, jamocha*, java*, joe*, mocha*, mud*, perk*, varnish remover*; SEE CONCEPT *454*

coffer [n] *large box*
case, casket, chest, exchequer, repository, strongbox, treasure chest, treasury, war chest*; SEE CONCEPT *494*

coffin [n] *box for dead person*
casket, catafalque, crate, funerary box, pall, pine box, pine drape*, sarcophagus; SEE CONCEPTS *368,479,494*

cog [n] *main part of device*
cogwheel, differential, fang, gear, pinion, prong, rack, ratchet, tine, tooth, transmission, tusk, wheel; SEE CONCEPT *464*

cogency [n] *effectiveness*
bearing, concern, connection, conviction, convincingness, force, forcefulness, pertinence, point, potency, power, punch, relevance, strength, validity, validness; SEE CONCEPTS *376,676*

cogent [adj] *effective*
apposite, apt, compelling, conclusive, consequential, convictive, convincing, fitting, forceful, forcible, inducing, influential, irresistible, justified, meaningful, momentous, persuasive, pertinent, potent, powerful, puissant, relevant, satisfactory, satisfying, significant, solid, sound, strong, suasive, telling, urgent, valid, weighty, well-grounded; SEE CONCEPT *537*

cogitate [v] *think deeply about*
brainstorm*, cerebrate, chew the cud*, conceive, consider, contemplate, deliberate, envisage, envision, figure, flash on*, imagine, kick around*, meditate, mull over, muse, noodle around*, ponder, reason, reflect, ruminate, speculate, stew over*; SEE CONCEPTS 17,24

cogitation [n] *deep thought*
brainwork, cerebration, consideration, contemplation, deliberation, meditation, reflection, rumination, speculation; SEE CONCEPT 410

cognate [adj] *alike, associated*
affiliated, agnate, akin, allied, analogous, comparable, connate, connatural, connected, consanguine, general, generic, incident, kindred, like, related, same, similar, universal; SEE CONCEPTS 487,573

cognizance/cognition [n] *understanding*
acknowledgment, apprehension, attention, awareness, comprehension, discernment, insight, intelligence, knowledge, mind, need, note, notice, observance, observation, perception, percipience, reasoning, recognition, regard; SEE CONCEPT 409

cognizant [adj] *aware*
acquainted, alive, apprehensive, au courant, awake, conscious, conversant, down with, familiar, grounded, hep to*, hip to*, informed, in on, in the know, in the picture*, judicious, knowing, knowledgeable, observant, on the beam*, on to*, perceptive, plugged in, savvy, sensible, sentient, tuned in*, up on*, versed, wise to*, with it*, witting; SEE CONCEPT 402

cohabit [v] *live together*
be roommates with, conjugate, couple, have relations, live illegally, live with, mingle, play house*, room together, shack up*, share address, take up housekeeping*; SEE CONCEPTS 226,375,384

cohere [v1] *stick to, cling*
adhere, associate, bind, blend, cleave, coalesce, combine, connect, consolidate, fuse, glue, hold, join, merge, unite; SEE CONCEPTS 85,113,160

cohere [v2] *agree, conform*
accord, be connected, be consistent, check, check out, comport, conform, correspond, dovetail, fit in go, hang together, harmonize, hold, hold water, make sense, relate, square; SEE CONCEPTS 8,636,667

coherence [n] *agreement*
adherence, attachment, bond, cementation, cling, clinging, comprehensibility, concordance, conformity, congruity, connection, consistency, consonance, construction, continuity, correspondence, inseparability, inseparableness, integrity, intelligibility, rationality, relations, solidarity, stickage, tenacity, union, unity; SEE CONCEPTS 388,684

coherent [adj] *understandable*
articulate, comprehensible, consistent, identified, intelligible, logical, lucid, meaningful, orderly, organized, rational, reasoned, sound, systematic; SEE CONCEPT 402

cohort [n] *partner in activity*
accomplice, adherent, aide, ally, assistant, associate, companion, company, comrade, confrere, consociate, contingent, disciple, follower, friend, hand, legion, mate, myrmidon, pal, partisan, regiment, satellite, sidekick, stall, supporter; SEE CONCEPT 423

coiffure [n] *hairstyle*
afro, beehive, blow dry*, braids, corn rows, crew

cut, DA*, dreadlocks, dreads, flip, fuzz cut*, hair, hair-comb, haircut, hairdo, permanent, pigtails, plait, ponytail, razor cut*, tail, tease, trim, wave; SEE CONCEPTS 418,718

coil [n] *thread that curls*
bight, braid, circle, convolution, corkscrew, curlicue, gyration, helix, involution, lap, loop, ring, roll, scroll, spiral, tendril, turn, twine, twirl, twist, whorl, wind; SEE CONCEPT 436

coil [v] *curl around, entwine*
convolute, convolve, corkscrew, fold, intertwine, intervolve, lap, loop, make serpentine, rotate, scroll, sinuate, snake, spiral, spire, turn, twine, twist, wind, wrap around, wreathe, writhe; SEE CONCEPTS 201,758

coin [n] *metallic money*
bread*, cash, change, chicken feed*, chips*, coinage, copper, currency, dough, gold, jack*, legal tender, meter money*, mintage, money, piece, scratch*, silver, small change*, specie; SEE CONCEPT 340

coin [v] *create, invent*
brainstorm*, compose, conceive, contrive, counterfeit, dream up, fabricate, forge, formulate, frame, head trip*, make up, make up off the top of one's head*, manufacture, mint, mold, originate, spark, spitball*, stamp, strike, think up, trump up*; SEE CONCEPTS 36,173

coincide [v] *go along with; coexist*
accompany, accord, acquiesce, agree, be concurrent, befall, be the same, come about, concert, concur, correspond, equal, eventuate, harmonize, identify, jibe, match, occur simultaneously, quadrate, square, sync, synchronize, tally; SEE CONCEPTS 667,714

coincidence [n1] *agreement; coexistence*
accompaniment, accord, accordance, collaboration, concomitance, concurrence, conformity, conjunction, consonance, correlation, correspondence, parallelism, synchronism, union; SEE CONCEPTS 667,684,714

coincidence [n2] *accidental happening*
accident, chance, eventuality, fate, fluke, fortuity, happening, happy accident, incident, luck, stroke of luck; SEE CONCEPTS 4,230

coincident [adj] *concurring, happening together*
ancillary, attendant, attending, coinciding, collateral, concomitant, consonant, contemporaneous, contemporary, coordinate, correspondent, incident, satellite, simultaneous, synchronous; SEE CONCEPTS 548,820

coincidental [adj] *accidental*
casual, chance, circumstantial, fluky, fortuitous, incidental, unintentional, unplanned; SEE CONCEPT 548

cold [n] *frigid conditions*
ague, algidity, algor, chill, chilliness, coldness, congelation, draft, freeze, frigidity, frost, frostbite, frostiness, frozenness, gelidity, gelidness, glaciation, goose flesh, iciness, inclemency, rawness, refrigeration, shivering, shivers, snow, wintertime, wintriness; SEE CONCEPTS 524,610

cold [adj1] *chilly, freezing*
algid, arctic, below freezing, below zero, benumbed, biting, bitter, blasting, bleak, boreal, brisk, brumal, chill, chilled, cool, crisp, cutting, frigid, frore, frosty, frozen, gelid, glacial, have goose bumps*, hawkish, hiemal, hyperborean, icebox, iced, icy, inclement, intense, keen, nipping, nippy, numbed, numbing, one-dog night*,

CO
CO

penetrating, piercing, polar, raw, rimy, severe, sharp, shivery, Siberian, sleety, snappy, snowy, stinging, two-dog night*, wintry; SEE CONCEPT 605

cold [adj2] *aloof, unresponsive*
apathetic, cold-blooded, cool, dead, distant, emotionless, frigid, frosty, glacial, icy, impersonal, imperturbable, indifferent, inhibited, inhospitable, joyless, lukewarm, matter-of-fact, passionless, phlegmatic, reserved, reticent, spiritless, standoffish, stony, unconcerned, undemonstrative, unenthusiastic, unfeeling, unimpassioned, unmoved, unresponsive, unsympathetic; SEE CONCEPT 404

cold-blooded [adj] *cruel, heartless*
barbarous, brutal, callous, cold, dispassionate, hard-boiled, hardened, hard-hearted, imperturbable, inhuman, matter-of-fact, merciless, obdurate, pitiless, relentless, ruthless, savage, steely, stony-hearted, uncompassionate, unemotional, unfeeling, unmoved; SEE CONCEPT 542

coliseum [n] *arena for events*
amphitheater, bowl, hippodrome, open-air theater, stade, stadium, theater; SEE CONCEPT 438

collaborate [v] *work together*
be in cahoots*, coact, cofunction, collude, come together, concert, concur, conspire, cooperate, co-produce, do business with, get together, glue oneself to*, go partners*, hook on, hook up*, interface, join forces, join together, join up with, participate, team up, throw in together*, throw in with*, tie in, work with; SEE CONCEPTS 100,351,384

collaborator [n] *person who works with another*
assistant, associate, colleague, confederate, co-worker, fellow traveller, helper, partner, quisling, running dog, teammate, team player*; SEE CONCEPTS 348,423

collage [n] *mixture of pictures*
abstract composition, found art, photomontage; SEE CONCEPT 259

collapse [n] *downfall, breakdown*
bankruptcy, basket case*, cataclysm, catastrophe, cave-in, conk out*, crackup*, crash, debacle, destruction, disintegration, disorganization, disruption, exhaustion, failure, faint, flop, prostration, ruination, ruining, smash, smashup, subsidence, undoing, wreck; SEE CONCEPTS 230,316,410,674

collapse [v] *fall apart, break down*
belly up*, bend, break, cave in, conk out*, crack up*, crumple, deflate, disintegrate, droop, drop, exhaust, fail, faint, fall down, flag, flake out, fold, founder, give, give in, give out, give way, go*, go to pieces*, keel over, languish, shatter, subside, succumb, tire, topple, weaken, weary, wilt, yield; SEE CONCEPTS 252,469,702

collar [n] *neck attire*
bertha, choker, dicky, Eton, fichu, fraise, frill, jabot, neckband, ruff, torque, Vandyke; SEE CONCEPTS 450,452

collar [v] *apprehend*
abduct, appropriate, arrest, bag, capture, catch, cop*, corner, get, grab, hook, lay hands on, nab, nail*, prehend, secure, seize, take, tree; SEE CONCEPTS 90,317

collate [v] *sort collection*
adduce, analogize, assemble, bracket, collect, compare, compose, contrast, examine, gather, group, match, order, relate, verify; SEE CONCEPTS 84,158

collateral [n] *monetary deposit*
assurance, bond, endorsement, guarantee, pledge, promise, security, surety, warrant, wealth; SEE CONCEPT 344

collateral [adj] *indirect, secondary*
accessory, accompanying, added, adjunctive, adjuvant, ancillary, appurtenant, attendant, auxiliary, circuitous, coincident, complementary, concomitant, concurrent, confirmatory, coordinate, corresponding, corroborative, dependent, incident, lateral, not lineal, parallel, related, roundabout, satellite, side, sub, subordinate, subservient, subsidiary, supporting, tributary, under; SEE CONCEPTS 546,567,831

colleague [n] *associate, fellow worker*
aide, ally, assistant, auxiliary, buddy, chum, coadjutor, cohort, collaborator, companion, compatriot, compeer, comrade, confederate, confrere, co-worker, crony, friend, helper, pal, partner, teammate, workmate; SEE CONCEPTS 348,423

collect [v1] *accumulate, come together*
aggregate, amass, array, assemble, cluster, compile, congregate, congress, convene, converge, convoke, corral, flock, flock together, gather, get hold of, group, heap, hoard, muster, rally, rendezvous, round up, save, scare up, stockpile; SEE CONCEPTS 109,114

collect [v2] *obtain (money)*
acquire, dig up, muster, pass the hat*, raise, requisition, secure, solicit; SEE CONCEPT 342

collected [adj] *composed, calm*
confident, cool, easy, easygoing, levelheaded, nonchalant, peaceful, placid, poised, possessed, quiet, sanguine, self-possessed, serene, still, sure, temperate, together, tranquil, unflappable, unperturbable, unperturbed, unruffled; SEE CONCEPT 401

collection [n] *group, accumulation*
accumulating, acquiring, acquisition, agglomeration, amassing, amassment, anthology, assemblage, assembling, assembly, assortment, batch, bringing together, caboodle, clump, cluster, collation, combination, company, compilation, congeries, congregation, convocation, crowd, cumulation, digest, gathering, heap, hoard, kit, levy, lot, mass, medley, mess, miscellany, mobilization, muster, number, obtaining, omnibus, pile, quantity, securing, selection, set, stack, stock, stockpile, store; SEE CONCEPTS 109,432

collective [adj] *composite*
aggregate, assembled, collated, combined, common, compiled, concentrated, concerted, conjoint, consolidated, cooperative, corporate, cumulative, gathered, grouped, heaped, hoarded, joint, massed, mutual, piled, shared, unified, united; SEE CONCEPT 585

college [n] *institution of higher education*
alma mater, association, brainery*, halls of ivy*, halls of knowledge*, institute, lyceum, organization, seminary, university; SEE CONCEPTS 287,288,289

college student [n] *person studying at institution of higher education*
first year student, grad student*, graduate student, junior, senior, sophomore, undergrad*, undergraduate student; SEE CONCEPT 350

collide [v] *slam into*
bang, beat, break up, bump, clash, conflict, crash, crunch*, disagree, fender-bend*, fragment, hit, jolt, meet head-on*, pile up*, plow into*, pulver-

ize*, scrap*, shatter, sideswipe, smash, splinter, strike, wrack up*; SEE CONCEPTS *189,248*

collision [*n*] *accident*
blow, bump, butt, concussion, contact, crash, demolishment, destruction, dilapidation, encounter, fender bender*, head-on*, hit, impact, jar, jolt, knock, percussion, pileup*, rap, ruin, shock, sideswipe, slam, smash, strike, thud, thump, wreck; SEE CONCEPTS *189,230,674*

collocate [*v*] *compile*
accumulate, assemble, collect, collimate, gather, parallel; SEE CONCEPT *84*

colloquial [*adj*] *particular, familiar to an area, informal*
chatty, common, conversational, demotic, dialectal, everyday, idiomatic, jive*, popular, street*, vernacular; SEE CONCEPT *267*

colloquy [*n*] *conversation, debate*
buzz session, chat, chinfest*, chitchat, clambake*, colloquium, confab*, confabulation, conference, converse, dialogue, discourse, discussion, flap*, gab fest*, gam*, groupthink*, huddle*, palaver, parley, powwow*, rap*, rap session*, seminar, talk, talkfest*; SEE CONCEPT *266*

collusion [*n*] *secret understanding, often with intent to defraud*
bait and switch*, bill of goods*, bunco*, cahoots*, complicity, con game*, connivance, conspiracy, craft, deceit, diddling*, dodge, doublecross, fast shuffle*, flam*, flimflam*, fraudulent artifice, graft, guilt, guiltiness, gyp, intrigue, plot, racket, scam, scheme, shell game*, skunk*, sting*, trick, whitewash; SEE CONCEPTS *114,660*

colonial [*adj*] *pioneering, relating to a nonindependent or new territory*
crude, dependent, dominion, early American, emigrant, frontier, immigrant, new, outland, pilgrim, pioneer, prerevolutionary, primitive, provincial, puritan, territorial, transplanted, uncultured, unsettled, unsophisticated, wild; SEE CONCEPTS *549,799*

colonization [*n*] *settlement of area*
clearing, establishment, expanding, expansion, founding, immigration, migration, opening up, peopling, pioneering, populating, settlement, settling, squatting, transplanting; SEE CONCEPTS *198,298*

colony [*n*] *community*
antecedents, clearing, dependency, dominion, mandate, new land, offshoot, outpost, possession, protectorate, province, satellite, settlement, subject state, swarm, tinct, territory; SEE CONCEPTS *379,512*

color [*n1*] *pigment, shade*
blush, cast, chroma, chromaticity, chromatism, chromism, colorant, coloration, coloring, complexion, dye, glow, hue, intensity, iridescence, luminosity, paint, pigmentation, polychromasia, saturation, stain, tinct, tincture, tinge, tint, undertone, value, wash; SEE CONCEPT *622*

color [*n2*] *deceptive appearance*
deception, disguise, excuse, facade, face, false show, front, guise, mask, plea, pretense, pretext, put-on, semblance, show; SEE CONCEPTS *59,716*

color [*v1*] *make pigmented; shade*
adorn, blacken, bloom, blush, burn, chalk, crayon, crimson, darken, daub, dye, embellish, emblazon, enamel, enliven, flush, fresco, gild, glaze, gloss, illuminate, imbue, infuse, lacquer, paint, pigment, pinken, redden, rouge, stain, stipple, suffuse, tinge, tint, tone, variegate, wash; SEE CONCEPTS *250,469*

color [*v2*] *distort, exaggerate*
angle*, belie, cook up*, disguise, doctor*, embroider*, fake, falsify, fudge*, garble, gloss over, magnify, misrepresent, misstate, overstate, pad*, pervert, prejudice, slant*, taint, twist*, warp*; SEE CONCEPTS *49,63*

colored [*adj1*] *not white*
dyed, flushed, glowing, hued, shaded, stained, tinged, tinted, washed; SEE CONCEPT *618*

colored [*adj2*] *distorted*
angled, biased, false, falsified, jaundiced, misrepresented, one-sided, partial, partisan, perverted, prejudiced, prepossessed, tampered with, tendentious, warped; SEE CONCEPT *582*

colorful [*adj1*] *brilliant, intensely hued*
bright, chromatic, flashy, florid, gaudy, gay, hued, intense, jazzy, kaleidoscopic, loud, motley, multicolored, picturesque, prismatic, psychedelic, rich, showy, splashy, variegated, vibrant, vivid; SEE CONCEPTS *617,618*

colorful [*adj2*] *full of life, interesting*
brave, characterful, distinctive, flaky*, gay, glamorous, graphic, jazzy, lively, picturesque, rich, stimulating, unusual, vivid; SEE CONCEPT *404*

colorless [*adj1*] *without hue*
achromatic, achromic, anemic, ashen, ashy, blanched, bleached, cadaverous, drab, drabby, dull, faded, flat, ghastly, livid, lurid, neutral, pale, sickly, uncolored, wan, washed out, waxen, white; SEE CONCEPT *618*

colorless [*adj2*] *unlively, uninteresting*
characterless, dreary, dull, insipid, lackluster, lifeless, prosaic, run-of-the-mill*, tame, unmemorable, unpassioned, vacuous, vapid; SEE CONCEPT *404*

colossal [*adj*] *very large*
barn door*, behemothic, blimp*, cyclopean, elephantine, enormous, gargantuan, giant, gigantic, huge, humongous*, immense, jumbo, mammoth, mondo*, monstrous, mountainous, super, titanic, vast; SEE CONCEPT *781*

colt [*n*] *young horse*
filly, fledgling, foal, rookie, sapling, yearling, youngling, youngster; SEE CONCEPT *394*

column [*n1*] *line, procession*
cavalcade, company, file, list, platoon, queue, rank, row, string, train; SEE CONCEPTS *432,727*

column [*n2*] *pillar*
brace, buttress, caryatid, colonnade, cylinder, mast, minaret, monolith, monument, obelisk, pedestal, peristyle, pier, pilaster, post, prop, pylon, shaft, standard, stay, stele, support, totem, tower, underpinning, upright; SEE CONCEPT *440*

coma [*n*] *deep unconsciousness*
blackout, dullness, faint, hebetude, insensibility, lethargy, oblivion, sleep, slumber, somnolence, stupor, swoon, syncope, torpidity, torpor, trance; SEE CONCEPT *315*

comatose [*adj*] *unconscious*
cold, dead, dead to the world*, dopey, drowsy, drugged, hebetudinous, inconscious, insensible, lethargic, out, out cold*, out to lunch*, senseless, sleepy, sluggish, slumberous, somnolent, soporose, stupefied, stupid, stuporous, torpid, vegged out*; SEE CONCEPT *539*

comb [*v1*] *arrange hair*
adjust, card, cleanse, curry, disentangle, dress,

CO
CO

groom, hackle, hatchel, lay smooth, rasp, scrape, separate, smooth, sort, straighten, tease, untangle; SEE CONCEPT *162*

comb [v2] *search by ransacking*
beat, beat the bushes*, examine, finecomb*, forage, go through with fine-tooth comb*, grub, hunt, inspect, investigate, leave no stone unturned*, look high and low*, probe, rake, ransack, rummage, scour, screen, scrutinize, search high heaven*, sift, sweep, turn inside out*, turn upside down*; SEE CONCEPT *216*

combat [n] *battle*
action, affray, battle royal*, brush, brush-off, conflict, contest, encounter, engagement, fight, flap, fray, jackpot*, mix-up*, run-in*, service, shoot-out*, skirmish, struggle, war, warfare; SEE CONCEPTS *86,106*

combat [v] *fight*
battle, buck, clash, contend, contest, cope, cross swords with*, defy, dispute, do battle with, duel, engage, fight, go up against, oppose, put up a fight*, repel, resist, shoot it out*, strive, struggle, traverse, war, withstand; SEE CONCEPTS *86,106*

combative [adj] *aggressive*
antagonistic, bellicose, belligerent, cantankerous, contentious, cussed, energetic, fire-eating*, gladiatorial, hawkish, militant, ornery*, pugnacious, quarrelsome, ructious, scrappy, strenuous, trigger-happy*, truculent, warlike, warring; SEE CONCEPTS *401,404*

combination [n1] *mixture, blend*
aggregate, amalgam, amalgamation, blending, brew, coalescence, combo, composite, compound, connection, consolidation, everything but kitchen sink*, fusion, junction, medley, merger, miscellany, mishmash*, mix, olio, order, sequence, solution, soup, stew, succession, synthesis, unification, union; SEE CONCEPT *432*

combination [n2] *alliance, association*
affiliation, bloc, cabal, cahoots, camarilla, cartel, circle, clique, club, coadunation, coalition, combine, compound, confederacy, confederation, conjunction, connection, consolidation, consortium, conspiracy, coterie, faction, federation, gang, guild, hookup*, mafia, melding, mergence, merger, merging, partnership, party, pool, ring, set, syndicate, tie-up*, trust, unification, union; SEE CONCEPT *381*

combine [v] *connect, integrate*
amalgamate, associate, band, bind, blend, bond, bracket, bunch up, coadjute, coalesce, commingle, compound, conjoin, cooperate, couple, dub, fuse, get together, glue oneself to, hitch on*, hook on*, incorporate, interface, join, league, link, marry, merge, mingle, mix, network, plug into, pool, put together, relate, slap on*, stand in with, synthesize, tack on*, tag on*, team up with*, throw in together*, tie up with*, unify, unite, wed; SEE CONCEPT *113*

combustible [adj] *able to be exploded*
burnable, comburent, combustive, explosive, fiery, firing, flammable, ignitable, incendiary, inflammable, kindling, volatile; SEE CONCEPTS *485,537*

combustion [n] *explosion; on fire*
agitation, candescence, disturbance, flaming, ignition, kindling, oxidization, thermogenesis, tumult, turmoil; SEE CONCEPTS *521,676,724*

come [v1] *advance, approach*
appear, arrive, attain, be accessible, be at disposal, become, be convenient, be handy, be obtainable, be ready, blow in*, bob up, breeze in*, burst, buzz*, check in*, clock in*, close in, draw near, drop in, enter, fall by, fall in, flare*, get, get in, happen, hit, hit town*, make it, make the scene*, materialize, move, move toward, near, occur, originate, pop in*, pop up*, punch in*, punch the clock*, reach, ring in*, roll in*, show, show up, sign in, sky in*, spring in, turn out, turn up, wind up at; SEE CONCEPT *159*

come [v2] *happen*
befall, betide, break, chance, come to pass, develop, fall, hap*, occur, take place, transpire, turn out; SEE CONCEPT *4*

come [v3] *extend, reach*
add up, aggregate, amount, become, come over, develop, expand, get, go, grow, join, mature, number, run, run into, spread, stretch, sum to, total, turn, wax; SEE CONCEPTS *239,701*

come about [v] *happen*
arise, befall, come to pass, occur, result, take place, transpire; SEE CONCEPT *701*

come across [v] *encounter, find*
bump into, chance upon, discover, happen upon, hit upon, light upon, meet, notice, stumble upon, uncover, unearth; SEE CONCEPTS *38,183*

come along [v] *progress, develop*
do well, get on, improve, mend, perk up, pick up, rally, recover, recuperate, show improvement; SEE CONCEPT *700*

come at [v1] *reach, attain*
accomplish, achieve, discover, feel for, find, grasp, succeed, touch, win; SEE CONCEPTS *34,706*

come at [v2] *attack*
assail, assault, charge, fall upon, fly at, go for, invade, light into*, rush; SEE CONCEPT *86*

comeback [n1] *recovery, triumph*
improvement, rally, rebound, resurgence, return, revival, victory, winning; SEE CONCEPT *706*

comeback [n2] *snappy retort*
answer back, quip, rejoinder, repartee, reply, response, retaliation, riposte; SEE CONCEPT *278*

come back [v] *return*
come again, do better, reappear, recover, recur, re-enter, remigrate, resume, triumph; SEE CONCEPT *239*

come between [v] *alienate*
divide, estrange, interfere, interpose, interrupt, intervene, meddle, part, put at odds, separate; SEE CONCEPTS *14,386*

come by [v1] *acquire*
get, lay hold of, obtain, procure, secure, take possession of, win; SEE CONCEPTS *124,129*

come by [v2] *visit someone*
call, come over, drop by, drop in, look in, look up, meet, pay a call, pop in, run in, see, step in, stop by, visit; SEE CONCEPT *227*

come clean [v] *acknowledge information*
admit, confess, explain, make clean breast*, own up, reveal; SEE CONCEPTS *49,57*

comedian [n] *funny person, often professional*
actor, banana*, card*, clown, comic, cutup, droll, entertainer, farceur, humorist, jester, joker, jokester, laugh, merry-andrew, million laughs*, quipster, stand-up comic, stooge*, top banana*, wag, wisecracker, wit*, zany*; SEE CONCEPTS *352,423*

comedown [n] *letdown, blow*
anticlimax, blow, collapse, comeuppance, crash,

cropper*, decline, defeat, deflation, demotion, descent, disappointment, discomfiture, dive, down, downfall, failure, fall, flop*, humiliation, pratfall*, reverse, ruin, setback, undoing, wreck; SEE CONCEPTS 674,699

come down [v] *worsen*
decline, decrease, degenerate, descend, deteriorate, fail, fall, go downhill, reduce, suffer; SEE CONCEPT 698

come down on [v] *criticize strongly*
attack, dress down, jump on, land on, rebuke, reprimand, scold; SEE CONCEPT 52

come down with [v] *contract illness*
be stricken with, catch, contract, fall ill, fall victim to, sicken, take, take sick; SEE CONCEPTS 93,303

comedy [n] *funny entertainment*
ball*, burlesque, camp, chaffing, comicality, comicalness, comic drama, drollery, drollness, facetiousness, farce, field day*, fun, fun and games*, funnies*, funniness, gag show, grins, high camp*, high time, hilarity, hoopla, humor, humorousness, interlude, jesting, joking, laughs, light entertainment, merry-go-round*, picnic, play on, satire, schtick*, send-up, sitcom*, slapstick, takeoff, travesty, vaudeville, wisecracking, witticism, wittiness; SEE CONCEPTS 263,293

come forward [v] *volunteer services*
appear, make proposal, offer services, present oneself, proffer oneself; SEE CONCEPT 67

come from [v] *arise, emanate*
accrue, derive from, ejaculate, emerge, end up, flow, hail from, issue, originate, proceed, result, rise, spring, stem, turn out; SEE CONCEPTS 105,179

come in [v] *enter place*
alight, appear, arrive, cross threshold, disembark, finish, immigrate, intrude, land, pass in, reach, set foot in, show up; SEE CONCEPT 159

come in for [v] *be eligible for something*
acquire, bear brunt, endure, get, receive, suffer; SEE CONCEPTS 23,124

comely [adj] *beautiful*
a ten*, attractive, beauteous, becoming, blooming, buxom, fair, fine, good-looking, gorgeous, graceful, handsome, nice, pleasing, pretty, pulchritudinous, stunning, wholesome, winsome; SEE CONCEPT 579

come off [v] *transpire*
befall, betide, break, chance, click, come about, develop, go, go off, go over, hap*, happen, occur, pan out, prove out, succeed, take place; SEE CONCEPT 4

come on [v1] *advance, progress*
develop, gain, improve, increase, make headway, proceed; SEE CONCEPT 704

come on [v2] *appear, enter*
begin, come across, come into, come upon, encounter, meet, pass in, set foot in*, take place; SEE CONCEPT 119

come out [v1] *make public*
appear, be announced, be brought out, be disclosed, be divulged, be exposed, be issued, be made known, be promulgated, be published, be released, be reported, be revealed, break*, debut, get out, leak*, out, transpire; SEE CONCEPT 60

come out [v2] *conclude*
end, result, terminate, transpire; SEE CONCEPT 119

come out with [v] *disclose information*
acknowledge, bring out, chime in*, come clean, declare, deliver, divulge, lay open, own, own up, say, state, tell, throw out, utter; SEE CONCEPT 60

come through [v1] *accomplish goal*
achieve, be successful, be victorious, carry out, chip in, contribute, kick in, pitch in, prevail, score, succeed, triumph, win; SEE CONCEPT 706

come through [v2] *survive bad situation*
endure, live through, persist, pull through, ride, ride out, survive, weather storm*, withstand; SEE CONCEPT 23

come up [v] *happen suddenly*
arise, crop up, occur, rise, spring up, turn up; SEE CONCEPT 119

come up to [v] *meet expectations*
admit of comparison with, approach, arrive, bear comparison with, come near, compare with, equal, extend, get near, match, measure up to, rank with, reach, resemble, rival, stand comparison with; SEE CONCEPT 667

come up with [v] *suggest, create*
advance, bring forth, compose, detect, discover, find, furnish, invent, offer, originate, present, produce, propose, provide, recommend, stumble upon, submit, uncover; SEE CONCEPTS 75,173

comfort [n1] *good feeling; ease*
abundance, alleviation, amenity, assuagement, bed of roses*, cheer, cheerfulness, complacency, contentment, convenience, coziness, creature comforts*, enjoyment, exhilaration, facility, gratification, happiness, luxury, opulence, peacefulness, pleasure, plenty, poise, quiet, relaxation, relief, repose, rest, restfulness, satisfaction, snugness, succor, sufficiency, warmth, well-being; SEE CONCEPTS 230,410,720

comfort [n2] *aid, help*
alleviation, assist, compassion, compensation, consolation, encouragement, hand, lift, pity, relief, secours, solace, succor, support, sympathy; SEE CONCEPTS 337,712

comfort [v] *make to feel better*
abate, aid, allay, alleviate, ameliorate, assist, assuage, bolster, buck up*, calm, cheer, commiserate with, compose, condole, confirm, console, delight, divert, ease, encourage, enliven, free, gladden, grant respite, hearten, help, inspirit, invigorate, lighten burden, make well, mitigate, nourish, put at ease, quiet fears, reanimate, reassure, refresh, relieve, remedy, revitalize, revive, salve, soften, solace, soothe, strengthen, stroke, succor, support, sustain, sympathize, uphold, upraise; SEE CONCEPTS 7,22,572

comfortable [adj1] *good feeling*
adequate, agreeable, appropriate, at rest, cared for, cheerful, complacent, contented, convenient, cozy, delightful, easy, enjoyable, enjoying, gratified, hale, happy, healthy, hearty, loose, loose-fitting, made well, pleasant, pleased, protected, relaxed, relaxing, relieved, rested, restful, restored, satisfactory, satisfying, serene, sheltered, snug, snug as a bug in a rug*, soft, soothed, strengthened, untroubled, useful, warm, well-off; SEE CONCEPT 572

comfortable [adj2] *affluent, wealthy*
ample, easy, enough, prosperous, substantial, sufficient, suitable, well-heeled*, well-off, well-to-do; SEE CONCEPT 334

comfortable [*adj3*] *more than adequate*
ample, commodious, cushy, luxurious, palatial, rich, roomy, spacious; SEE CONCEPT *485*

comforting [*adj*] *cheering*
abating, allaying, alleviating, analeptic, assuaging, consolatory, consoling, curing, encouraging, freeing, health-giving, heart-warming, inspiriting, invigorating, lightening, mitigating, reassuring, refreshing, relieving, remedying, restoring, revitalizing, revivifying, softening, solacing, soothing, succoring, sustaining, tranquilizing, upholding, warming; SEE CONCEPT *529*

comic [*n*] *funny person, often professional*
banana*, buffoon*, card*, clown, comedian, droll, humorist, jester, joker, jokester, life of the party*, million laughs*, quipster, stand-up comic, stooge*, top banana*, wag*, wit*; SEE CONCEPTS *352,423*

comic/comical [*adj*] *amusing*
absurd, batty, boffo*, camp*, comical, crazy, dippy, diverting, dizzy, droll, entertaining, facetious, farcical, flaky*, fool, foolheaded, for grins*, freaky, funny, gelastic, goofus*, goofy, gump*, horse's tail*, humorous, ironic, jerky, jocular, joking, joshing, laughable, light, loony, ludicrous, Mickey Mouse*, nutty, off the wall*, priceless, ridiculous, risible, schtick*, screwy, side-splitting, silly, wacky, waggish, whimsical, witty; SEE CONCEPTS *401,529*

coming [*n*] *arrival*
accession, advent, approach, landing, reception; SEE CONCEPTS *119,159*

coming [*adj*] *approaching, promising*
about to happen, advancing, almost on one, anticipated, aspiring, at hand, certain, close, converging, deserving, docking, drawing near, due, en route, eventual, expected, fated, foreseen, forthcoming, future, gaining upon, getting near, immediate, imminent, impending, in prospect, instant, in store, in the offing, in the wind*, in view, marked, near, nearing, next, nigh, oncoming, ordained, predestined, preparing, progressing, prospective, pursuing, running after, subsequent, to be, up-and-coming; SEE CONCEPTS *537,799*

command [*n1*] *directive, instruction*
act, adjuration, ban, behest, bidding, call, canon, caveat, charge, citation, commandment, decree, demand, devoir, dictate, dictation, dictum, direction, duty, edict, enactment, exaction, fiat, imperative, imposition, injunction, interdiction, law, mandate, notification, obligation, order, ordinance, precept, prescript, proclamation, prohibition, proscription, regulation, request, requirement, requisition, responsibility, rule, subpoena, summons, ultimatum, warrant, will, word, writ; SEE CONCEPTS *274,662*

command [*n2*] *rule, power*
ability, absolutism, aplomb, authority, authorization, charge, coercion, compulsion, constraint, control, despotism, domination, dominion, expertise, expertism, expertness, government, grasp, grip, hold, jurisdiction, know-how*, leadership, management, might, prerogative, primacy, restraint, right, royalty, skill, sovereignty, strings*, supervision, supremacy, sway, tyranny, upper hand*; SEE CONCEPT *376*

command [*v1*] *demand*
adjure, appoint, authorize, ban, bar, beckon, bid, call, call for, call on, call the signals*, call upon, charge, check, cite, compel, debar, dictate, di-

rect, enact, enjoin, exact, forbid, force upon, give directions, give orders, grant, impose, inflict, inhibit, instruct, interdict, lay down the law, mark out, oblige, ordain, order, ordinate, proclaim, prohibit, put foot down*, require, requisition, restrain, rule out, send for, set, subpoena, summon, take charge, take lead, task, tell, warn; SEE CONCEPT *53*

command [*v2*] *rule, have power*
administer, boss, charge, check, coach, coerce, compel, conduct, conquer, constrain, control, curb, determine, dictate, direct, dominate, domineer, exact, exercise power, force, govern, guide, have authority, head, hinder, hold office, influence, lead, manage, officiate, oppress, overbear, override, predominate, prescribe, preside over, prevail, push, regulate, reign, reign over, repress, restrain, run, stop, subdue, superintend, supervise, sway, take over, tyrannize, wield; SEE CONCEPTS *133,298*

commandeer [*v*] *seize, take over*
accroach, activate, annex, appropriate, arrogate, assume, confiscate, conscript, draft, enslave, expropriate, grab, hijack, liberate, moonlight requisition*, preempt, requisition, sequester, sequestrate, snatch, take, usurp; SEE CONCEPTS *90,142*

commander [*n*] *leader of military or other organization*
administrator, big cheese*, boss, captain, chief, CO*, commandant, czar, director, don, exec, guru, head, head honcho*, head person, higher up, high priest/priestess*, kingfish*, kingpin*, lead-off person*, mastermind, officer, point person*, ruler, skipper, top banana*, top brass*, top dog*; SEE CONCEPTS *347,358*

commanding [*adj*] *superior; authoritative*
advantageous, arresting, assertive, autocratic, bossy, compelling, controlling, decisive, dictatorial, dominant, dominating, forceful, imperious, imposing, impressive, in charge, lofty, peremptory, striking; SEE CONCEPTS *536,574*

commemorate [*v*] *honor, observe occasion*
admire, celebrate, immortalize, keep, memorialize, monument, monumentalize, observe, pay tribute to, perpetuate, remember, salute, solemnize; SEE CONCEPTS *69,377,384*

commemoration [*n*] *honoring, observance*
celebration, ceremony, custom, memorial service, monumentalization, recognition, remembrance, tribute; SEE CONCEPT *377*

commemorative [*adj*] *in honor of something*
celebratory, commemoratory, dedicatory, in memory, in remembrance, memorial, observing; SEE CONCEPT *555*

commence [*v*] *start action*
arise, begin, come into being, come into existence, embark on, enter upon, get cracking*, get going, get one's feet wet*, get show on road*, hit the ground running*, inaugurate, initiate, jump into, kick off*, launch, lead off, open, originate, start the ball rolling*, take up, tear into; SEE CONCEPTS *119,234*

commencement [*n*] *ceremony marking the beginning of stage*
admission, alpha, birth, bow, celebration, convocation, countdown, curtain-raiser*, dawn, dawning, genesis, graduation, initiation, kickoff*, onset, opener, opening, outset, proem, services, start, starting point, tee off*; SEE CONCEPT *377*

commend [v1] *recommend, praise*
acclaim, accredit, advocate, applaud, approve, boost, build, build up, compliment, countenance, endorse, eulogize, extol, give a posy*, gold star*, hail, hand it to*, hats off to*, hear it for*, kudize, laud, pat on the back*, puff up, sanction, speak highly of, stroke, support; SEE CONCEPTS *69,75*

commend [v2] *hand over with confidence*
assign, commit, confer, confide, consign, deliver, entrust, proffer, relegate, resign, tender, trust, turn over, yield; SEE CONCEPTS *108,132*

commendable [adj] *praiseworthy*
admirable, creditable, deserving, estimable, excellent, exemplary, laudable, meritable, meritorious, praisable, thankworthy, worthy; SEE CONCEPTS *527,572*

commendation [n] *giving of praise; acclaim*
acclamation, approbation, approval, award, bouquet, Brownie points*, credit, encomium, encouragement, good opinion, honor, panegyric, pat on the back*, pat on the head*, pay, plum, points*, posy, PR*, puff, pumping up*, rave, recommendation, shot in the arm*, stroke, stroking, tribute; SEE CONCEPTS *69,337*

commensurate [adj] *adequate, corresponding*
appropriate, coextensive, comparable, compatible, consistent, due, equal, equivalent, fit, fitting, in accord, proportionate, sufficient, symmetrical; SEE CONCEPTS *563,566*

comment [n] *statement of opinion; explanation*
animadversion, annotation, backtalk*, buzz*, comeback*, commentary, crack*, criticism, dictum, discussion, editorial, elucidation, exposition, footnote, gloss, hearsay, illustration, input, judgment, mention, mouthful, note, obiter, observation, opinion, remark, report, review, two cents' worth*, wisecrack*; SEE CONCEPTS *51,278*

comment [v] *make statement of opinion, explanation*
affirm, animadvert, annotate, assert, bring out, clarify, commentate, conclude, construe, criticize, disclose, elucidate, explain, explicate, expound, express, gloss, illustrate, interject, interpose, interpret, mention, note, notice, observe, opine, pass on, point out, pronounce, reflect, remark, say, state, touch upon; SEE CONCEPTS *51,57*

commentary [n] *analysis*
annotation, appreciation, comment, consideration, criticism, critique, description, discourse, exegesis, explanation, exposition, gloss, narration, notes, obiter dictum, observation, remark, review, treatise, voice-over; SEE CONCEPTS *51,278*

commentator [n] *reporter*
analyst, annotator, announcer, correspondent, critic, expositor, interpreter, observer, pundit, reviewer, sportscaster, writer; SEE CONCEPT *356*

commerce [n] *buying and selling*
business, dealing, dealings, economics, exchange, industry, marketing, merchandising, merchantry, retailing, trade, traffic, truck, wholesaling; SEE CONCEPTS *325,770*

commercial [adj1] *concerning business, marketing*
across the counter*, bartering, commissary, economic, exchange, financial, fiscal, for sale, in demand, in the market, market, marketable, mercantile, merchandising, monetary, pecuniary, popular, profitable, profit-making, retail, retailing, saleable, sales, supplying, trade, trading, wholesale, wholesaling; SEE CONCEPT *536*

commercial [adj2] *intended for financial gain*
exploited, for profit, investment, materialistic, mercenary, monetary, money-making, pecuniary, profitmaking, venal, Wall Street*; SEE CONCEPT *334*

commercialize [v] *prepare for saleability*
advertise, cheapen, degrade, depreciate, develop as business, lessen, lower, make bring returns, make marketable, make pay, make profitable, make saleable, market, sell; SEE CONCEPT *324*

commingle [v] *blend*
amalgamate, combine, commix, compound, inmix, integrate, intermingle, intermix, join, merge, mingle, unite; SEE CONCEPT *109*

commiserate [v] *listen to woes of another*
ache, compassionate, condole, console, feel, feel for, have mercy, pity, share sorrow, sympathize; SEE CONCEPTS *110,596*

commission [n1] *task, duty*
agency, appointment, authority, brevet, certificate, charge, consignment, delegation, deputation, diploma, embassy, employment, errand, function, instruction, legation, mandate, mission, obligation, office, permit, power of attorney, proxy, trust, warrant, work; SEE CONCEPT *362*

commission [n2] *share of a profit*
allowance, ante, bite*, bonus, brokerage, chunk, compensation, cut, cut-in*, discount, end*, factorage, fee, indemnity, juice, pay, payment, percentage, piece, piece of the action*, rake-off*, remuneration, royalty, salary, slice*, stipend, taste, vigorish; SEE CONCEPTS *329,344*

commission [n3] *group working together toward goal*
board, commissioners, committee, delegation, deputation, representative; SEE CONCEPT *381*

commission [v] *authorize or delegate task*
accredit, appoint, assign, bespeak, bid, charge, command, commit, confide to, consign, constitute, contract, crown, depute, deputize, dispatch, employ, empower, enable, engage, enlist, enroll, entrust, hire, inaugurate, induct, instruct, invest, license, name, nominate, ordain, order, select, send; SEE CONCEPTS *50,88,324,351*

commit [v1] *perform an action*
accomplish, achieve, act, carry out, complete, contravene, do, effectuate, enact, execute, go for broke*, go in for*, go out for*, offend, perpetrate, pull, pull off*, scandalize, sin, transgress, trespass, violate, wreak; SEE CONCEPTS *6,87*

commit [v2] *deliver, entrust*
allocate, allot, apportion, authorize, charge, commend, commission, confer trust, confide, consign, convey, delegate, deliver, depend upon, deposit, depute, deputize, destine, dispatch, employ, empower, engage, give, give to do, grant authority, hand over, hold, ice, imprison, institutionalize, intrust, invest, leave to, make responsible for, move, offer, ordain, promise, put away, put in the hands of, relegate, rely upon, remove, send, shift, submit, transfer, turn over to, vest; SEE CONCEPTS *108,143,217*

commitment [n] *assurance; obligation*
charge, committal, devoir, duty, engagement, guarantee, liability, must, need, ought, pledge, promise, responsibility, undertaking, vow, word; SEE CONCEPTS *71,271,274*

committee [n] *group working on project*
board, bureau, cabinet, chamber, commission, consultants, convocation, council, investigators, jury, panel, representatives, task force, trustees; SEE CONCEPT 381

commodious [adj] *ample, spacious*
big, capacious, comfortable, convenient, expansive, extensive, large, loose, roomy, wide; SEE CONCEPTS 773,781

commodity [n] *merchandise, possession*
article, asset, belonging, chattel, goods, line, material, object, produce, product, property, specialty, stock, thing, vendible, ware; SEE CONCEPTS 338,710

common [adj1] *average, ordinary*
accepted, banal, bourgeois, casual, characteristic, colloquial, comfortable, commonplace, conventional, current, customary, daily, everyday, familiar, frequent, general, habitual, hackneyed, homely, humdrum, informal, mediocre, monotonous, natural, obscure, passable, plain, prevailing, prevalent, probable, prosaic, regular, routine, run-of-the-mill*, simple, stale, standard, stereotyped, stock, trite, trivial, typical, undistinguished, universal, unvaried, usual, wearisome, workaday, worn-out; SEE CONCEPT 547

common [adj2] *generally known; held in common*
accepted, coincident, collective, communal, communistic, community, commutual, congruous, conjoint, conjunct, constant, corporate, correspondent, customary, general, generic, in common, intermutual, joint, like, mutual, popular, prevailing, prevalent, public, reciprocal, shared, social, socialistic, united, universal, usual, well-known, widespread; SEE CONCEPT 530

common [adj3] *low, coarse*
baseborn, characterless, cheap, colorless, crass, declassé, hack, hackneyed, impure, inferior, low-grade, mean, middling, nondescript, passable, pedestrian, Philistine, plebeian, poor, prosy, raffish, second-class, second-rate, shoddy, sleazy, stale, trite, undistinguished, vulgar; SEE CONCEPTS 401,545

commonly [adv] *usually*
as a rule, by ordinary, frequently, generally, more often than not, ordinarily, regularly; SEE CONCEPTS 530,541

commonplace [n] *clichéd saying or idea*
banality, bromide*, chestnut*, cliché, corn*, inanity, motto, platitude, prosaicism, prosaism, prose, rubber stamp*, shallowness, shibboleth, stereotype, tag, triteness, triusm, triviality; SEE CONCEPTS 278,689

commonplace [adj] *usual, everyday*
boiler plate*, characterless, clichéd, colorless, conventional, corny*, customary, dime-a-dozen*, familiar, familiar tune, garden variety*, hackneyed, humdrum, lowly, mainstream, matter-of-course, mediocre, middle-of-the-road*, middling, mundane, natural, normal, obvious, ordinary, pedestrian, plebeian, prevalent, prosaic, run-of-the-mill*, stale, starch, stereotyped, threadbare, trite, typical, uneventful, unexceptional, uninteresting, unnoteworthy, vanilla*, widespread, workaday, worn-out; SEE CONCEPT 530

common sense [n] *good reasoning*
acumen, cool, good sense, gumption, horse sense*, intelligence, levelheadedness, practicality, prudence, reasonableness, sense, sound judgment, soundness, wisdom, wit; SEE CONCEPT 409

common-sense [adj] *reasonable*
astute, commonsensical, cool, down-to-earth, hard-headed, judicious, levelheaded, matter-of-fact, practical, rational, realistic, sane, sensible, shrewd, sound; SEE CONCEPT 402

commonwealth [n] *political or geographic area*
body politic, citizenry, citizens, commonality, democracy, federation, nation, people, polity, republic, society; SEE CONCEPTS 301,512

commotion [n] *clamor, uproar*
ado, agitation, annoyance, backwash, ballyhoo*, bedlam, big scene*, big stink*, brouhaha, bustle, clatter, combustion, confusion, convulsion, discomposure, disquiet, dither, excitement, ferment, fermentation, flap, flurry, furor, fuss, hell broke loose*, hubbub, hurly-burly, insurgence, insurrection, lather*, mutiny, outcry, pandemonium, perturbation, pother, racket, rebellion, revolt, riot, rumpus, stew, stir, to-do, tumult, turbulence, upheaval, uprising, upset, upturn, vexation, welter, whirl; SEE CONCEPTS 388,674

communal [adj] *collective; shared*
common, communistic, community, conjoint, conjunct, cooperative, general, intermutual, joint, mutual, neighborhood, public; SEE CONCEPTS 536,708

commune [n] *group living together*
collective, commonage, commonality, community, cooperative, family, kibbutz, municipality, neighborhood, rank and file, village; SEE CONCEPT 379

commune [v] *communicate, experience with another*
confer, confide in, contemplate, converse, discourse, discuss, mediate, muse, parley, ponder, reflect; SEE CONCEPTS 17,266

communicable [adj] *able to be contracted*
catching, communicative, contagious, expansive, infectious, pandemic, taking, transferable, transmittable; SEE CONCEPT 314

communicate [v1] *give or exchange information, ideas*
acquaint, advertise, advise, announce, be in touch, betray, break, broadcast, carry, connect, contact, convey, correspond, declare, disclose, discover, disseminate, divulge, enlighten, get across, get through, hint, impart, imply, inform, interact, interface, keep in touch, let on, let out, make known, network*, pass on, phone, proclaim, publicize, publish, raise, reach out, relate, report, reveal, ring up, signify, spread, state, suggest, tell, touch base*, transfer, transmit, unfold, write; SEE CONCEPT 266

communicate [v2] *mutually exchange information*
answer, associate with, be close to, be in touch, be near, buzz, cable, chat, commune with, confabulate, confer, converse, correspond, discourse, drop a line*, drop a note*, establish contact, get on the horn*, give a call, give a ring*, have confidence of, hear from, reach, reply, talk, telephone, wire, write; SEE CONCEPTS 56,266

communication [n1] *giving, exchanging information, ideas*
advice, advisement, announcing, articulation, assertion, communion, connection, contact, conversation, converse, correspondence, corresponding, declaration, delivery, disclosing, dissemination, elucidation, expression, intelligence, interchange, intercommunication, intercourse, link, making known, mention, notifying, publication, reading,

reception, revelation, talk, talking, telling, transfer, translating, transmission, utterance, writing; SEE CONCEPT 266

communication [n2] *information transmitted*
account, advice, announcement, briefing, bulletin, communiqué, conversation, converse, declaration, directive, disclosure, dispatch, excerpt, goods*, hot story*, ideas, info*, information, inside story*, intelligence, language, lowdown, message, missive, news, note, pipeline, poop*, precis, prophecy, publicity, report, revelation, scoop*, skinny*, speech, statement, summary, tidings, translation, utterance, warning, word, work; SEE CONCEPT 274

communications [n] *systems of information exchange*
information technology, means, media, publicity, public relations, route, telecommunications, transport, travel; SEE CONCEPTS 349,770

communicative [adj] *informative*
candid, chatty, communicable, conversable, conversational, demonstrative, effusive, enlightening, expansive, forthcoming, frank, garrulous, gushing, loquacious, open, outgoing, talkative, unreserved, voluble; SEE CONCEPT 267

communion [n1] *affinity, agreement*
accord, association, closeness, close relationship, communing, concord, contact, converse, fellowship, harmony, intercommunication, intercourse, intimacy, participation, rapport, sympathy, togetherness, unity; SEE CONCEPT 684

communion [n2] *sacrament in church; body of believers sharing a sacrament*
breaking of bread, church, creed, denomination, Eucharist, faith, Lord's Supper, Mass, persuasion, religion, sacrament; SEE CONCEPT 367

communism [n] *socialist government*
Bolshevism, collectivism, Leninism, Marxism, rule of the proletariat, socialism, state ownership, totalitarianism; SEE CONCEPT 301

community [n1] *society, area of people*
association, body politic, center, colony, commonality, commonwealth, company, district, general public, hamlet, locality, nation, neck of the woods*, neighborhood, people, populace, public, residents, society, state, stomping ground*, territory, turf; SEE CONCEPTS 379,512

community [n2] *agreement, similarity*
affinity, identity, kinship, likeness, sameness, semblance; SEE CONCEPTS 664,670

commute [v1] *travel to work*
drive, go back and forth, take the bus/subway/train; SEE CONCEPT 224

commute [v2] *reduce punishment*
alleviate, curtail, decrease, mitigate, modify, remit, shorten, soften; SEE CONCEPTS 236,247,317

commute [v3] *exchange, trade*
barter, change, convert, interchange, metamorphose, substitute, switch, transfer, transfigure, transform, translate, transmogrify, transmute, transpose; SEE CONCEPTS 104,232

commuter [n] *daily traveler, usually for work*
city worker, driver, straphanger*, suburbanite, traveler; SEE CONCEPT 348

compact [n] *agreement*
alliance, arrangement, bargain, bond, concordat, contract, convention, covenant, deal, engagement, entente, indenture, pact, settlement, stipulation, transaction, treaty, understanding; SEE CONCEPTS 271,684

compact [adj1] *condensed*
appressed, bunched, close, compressed, crowded, dense, firm, hard, impenetrable, impermeable, packed, pressed, solid, thick, tight; SEE CONCEPTS 481,483,774

compact [adj2] *short, brief*
boiled down, compendious, concise, epigrammatic, in a nutshell*, laconic, make a long story short*, marrowy, meaty, pithy, pointed, short and sweet*, succinct, terse, to the point; SEE CONCEPTS 773,798

compact [v] *make condensed*
combine, compress, concentrate, condense, consolidate, contract, cram, integrate, pack, set, solidify, stuff, unify, unite; SEE CONCEPTS 137,208,250

compact disc [n] *recording of music or speech*
album, CD, cut*, cylinder, demo, digital recording, disk, laser disk, record, release, track; SEE CONCEPT 262

companion [n] *helper, friend*
accompaniment, accomplice, aide, ally, assistant, associate, attendant, buddy, chaperon, colleague, comate, complement, comrade, concomitant, confederate, consort, convoy, counterpart, cousin, co-worker, crony, cuz*, double, escort, guide, match, mate, nurse, pal, pard*, partner, playmate, protector, roomie*, safeguard, sidekick; SEE CONCEPT 423

companionable [adj] *friendly*
affable, amicable, buddy buddy*, clubby*, complacent, congenial, conversable, convivial, cordial, cozy, cozy with, familiar, genial, good-natured, gregarious, intimate, mellow, neighborly, outgoing, pally, palsy*, sociable, social, tight, tight with*; SEE CONCEPT 555

companionship [n] *friendship, accompaniment*
affiliation, alliance, amity, camaraderie, company, comradeship, conviviality, esprit de corps, rapport, society, togetherness, union; SEE CONCEPT 388

company [n1] *crowd of people*
aggregation, assemblage, assembly, association, band, body, circle, clan, clique, club, collection, community, concourse, congregation, convention, corps, cortege, coterie, crew, ensemble, gang*, gathering, group, horde, jungle*, league, mob*, muster, order, outfit, pack, party, retinue, ring, ruck, set, team, throng, troop, troupe, turnout, zoo*; SEE CONCEPT 417

company [n2] *business concern*
association, business, concern, corporation, enterprise, establishment, firm, house, megacorp*, multinational, outfit, partnership, syndicate; SEE CONCEPT 325

company [n3] *social friend, guest*
boarder, caller, companionship, cortege, party, presence, retinue, society, visitor; SEE CONCEPTS 417,423

comparable [adj1] *worthy of comparison*
a match for, as good as, commensurable, commensurate, equal, equipollent, equipotential, equivalent, in a class with, on a par, proportionate, tantamount; SEE CONCEPT 566

comparable [adj2] *corresponding, similar*
agnate, akin, alike, analogous, cognate, consonant, corresponding, like, parallel, related, relative, undifferenced, uniform; SEE CONCEPTS 487,573

co
co

comparative [adj] *approximate, close to*
allusive, analogous, approaching, by comparison, comparable, conditional, connected, contingent, contrastive, correlative, corresponding, equivalent, in proportion, like, matching, metaphorical, near, not absolute, not positive, parallel, provisional, qualified, related, relative, restricted, rivaling, similar, vying, with reservation; SEE CONCEPTS 487,566,573

compare [v1] *examine in contrast*
analyze, approach, balance, bracket, collate, confront, consider, contemplate, contrast, correlate, divide, equal, examine, hang, hold a candle to*, inspect, juxtapose, match, match up with, measure, observe, oppose, parallel, place in juxtaposition, ponder, rival, scan, scrutinize, segregate, separate, set against, set side by side, size up, stack up against*, study, touch, weigh, weigh against another; SEE CONCEPTS 24,103

compare [v2] *liken, equate*
allegorize, approach, approximate to, assimilate, balance, bear comparison, be in the same class as*, be on a par with*, bring near, come up to, compete with, connect, correlate, distinguish between, draw parallel, equal, equate, hold a candle to*, identify with, link, make like, match, notice similarities, parallel, put alongside, relate, resemble, show correspondence, stack up with*, standardize, tie up, vie; SEE CONCEPT 39

comparison [n] *contrasting; corresponding*
allegory, analogizing, analogy, analyzing, association, balancing, bringing together, collating, collation, comparability, connection, contrast, correlation, discrimination, distinguishing, dividing, estimation, example, exemplification, identification, illustration, juxtaposition, likeness, likening, measuring, metaphor, observation, opposition, paralleling, ratio, relating, relation, resemblance, segregation, separation, similarity, testing, weighing; SEE CONCEPTS 24,39,529

compartment [n] *section, subdivision*
alcove, area, bay, berth, booth, carrel, carriage, category, cell, chamber, corner, cubbyhole, cubicle, department, division, hole, locker, niche, nook, part, piece, pigeonhole, place, portion, slot, stall; SEE CONCEPT 434

compass [n] *boundary, periphery*
ambit, area, bound, circle, circuit, circumference, circumscription, confines, domain, enclosure, environs, expanse, extent, field, limit, limitation, orbit, perimeter, precinct, purlieus, purview, radius, range, reach, realm, restriction, round, scope, sphere, stretch, sweep, zone; SEE CONCEPTS 484,651,788

compass [v1] *enclose*
beset, besiege, blockade, circle, circumscribe, encircle, encompass, environ, gird, girdle, hem in, ring, round, surround; SEE CONCEPT 758

compass [v2] *achieve, get*
accomplish, annex, attain, bring about, effect, execute, fulfill, gain, have, land, obtain, perform, procure, realize, secure, win; SEE CONCEPTS 142,706

compassion [n] *tender feeling*
benevolence, charity, clemency, commiseration, compunction, condolence, consideration, empathy, fellow feeling, grace, heart, humaneness, humanity, kindness, lenity, mercy, softheartedness, softness, sorrow, sympathy, tenderheartedness, tenderness, yearning; SEE CONCEPTS 410,633

compassionate [adj] *having tender feelings*
all heart, being big*, benevolent, bleeding heart*, charitable, commiserative, forbearing, going easy on*, humane, humanitarian, indulgent, kindhearted, kindly, lenient, living with, merciful, old softie*, piteous, pitying, responsive, softhearted, soft shell*, sparing, sympathetic, tender, tenderhearted, understanding, warm, warmhearted; SEE CONCEPTS 401,403

compatibility [n] *harmony in relationship*
affinity, agreeableness, agreement, amity, congeniality, congruity, consonance, empathy, fit, likemindedness, rapport, single-mindedness, sympathy, unity; SEE CONCEPT 388

compatible [adj] *agreeable, in harmony*
accordant, adaptable, appropriate, congenial, congruent, congruous, consistent, consonant, cooperative, cotton to*, fit, fitting, getting along with, harmonious, having good vibes*, hitting it off*, in keeping, in sync with*, in the groove*, likeminded, meet, on the same wavelength*, proper, reconcilable, simpatico, suitable, sympathetic, together; SEE CONCEPT 555

compel [v] *force to act*
bulldoze*, coerce, concuss, constrain, crack down, dragoon, drive, enforce, exact, hustle, impel, make, make necessary, necessitate, oblige, put the arm on*, put the chill on*, restrain, shotgun*, squeeze, throw weight around*, turn on the heat*, urge; SEE CONCEPTS 14,384

compendious [adj] *abridged*
abbreviated, breviloquent, brief, close, compact, compendiary, comprehensive, concise, condensed, contracted, curt, inclusive, laconic, short, short and sweet*, succinct, summarized, summary, synoptic; SEE CONCEPTS 773,789

compendium [n] *abridgment*
abstract, aperçu, brief, conspectus, digest, epitome, essence, guide, handbook, manual, overview, pandect, precis, sketch, summary, survey, syllabus, sylloge; SEE CONCEPT 283

compensate [v1] *make restitution*
atone, come down with*, commit, guerdon, indemnify, make good*, pay, pay up, plank out*, pony up*, recompense, recoup, refund, reimburse, remunerate, repay, requite, reward, satisfy, shell out*, take care of, tickle the palm*; SEE CONCEPTS 108,126,341

compensate [v2] *offset, make up for*
abrogate, annul, atone for, balance, better, cancel out, counteract, counterbalance, counterpoise, countervail, fix, improve, invalidate, make amends, negate, negative, neutralize, nullify, outweigh, redress, repair, set off; SEE CONCEPTS 126,212

compensation [n] *repayment; rectification*
advantage, allowance, amends, atonement, benefit, bonus, bread*, consideration, counterclaim, coverage, damages, defrayal, deserts*, earnings, fee*, gain, honorarium, indemnification, indemnity, meet, pay, payment, payoff, premium, profit, quittance, reciprocity, reckoning, recompense, recoupment, redress, reimbursement, remittal, remittance, remuneration, reparation, reprisal, requital, restitution, reward, salary, salt, satisfaction, scale, settlement, shake, stipend, take*, take-home*, wage; SEE CONCEPTS 337,344

compete [v] *go up against in contest*
attempt, bandy, battle, be in the running*, bid, challenge, clash, collide, contend, contest, cope

with, emulate, encounter, essay, face, fence, fight, go after, go for*, go for broke*, go for the gold*, grapple, in the hunt*, jockey for position*, joust, lock horns*, match strength, match wits*, oppose, participate in, pit oneself against*, play, rival, run for, scramble for*, seek prize, spar, strive, struggle, take on, take part, tilt, try, tussle, vie, wrestle; SEE CONCEPT 92

competence [n] *ability*
adequacy, appropriateness, capability, capacity, competency, cutting it*, cutting the mustard*, expertise, fitness, hacking it*, know-how, makings, making the grade*, might, moxie, proficiency, qualification, qualifiedness, savvy, skill, suitability, the goods*, the right stuff*, what it takes*; SEE CONCEPT 630

competent [adj] *able*
adapted, adequate, all around, appropriate, au fait, being a pistol*, capable, clever, complete, crisp, decent, dynamite, efficient, endowed, enough, equal, fireball*, fit, fool, good, know ins and outs*, know one's business*, know one's stuff*, know the answers*, know the ropes*, know the score*, no slouch*, on the ball*, paid one's dues*, pertinent, polished, proficient, qualified, satisfactory, savvy, skilled, sufficient, suitable, there*, up to it, up to snuff*, up to speed*, wicked*; SEE CONCEPT 527

competition [n] *contest*
antagonism, athletic event, bout, candidacy, championship, clash, concours, contention, controversy, counteraction, dog eat dog*, do or die*, emulation, encounter, engagement, event, fight, game, go for it, go for the gold*, horse race*, jungle*, match, matchup, meeting, one on one*, one-upping, opposition, pairing off*, puzzle, quiz, race, racing, rat race*, rivalry, run, sport, strife, striving, struggle, tilt, tournament, trial, tug-of-war, warfare; SEE CONCEPTS 92,363

competitive [adj] *willing to oppose*
aggressive, ambitious, antagonistic, at odds, combative, competing, cutthroat, dog-eat-dog*, emulous, killer*, killer instinct*, opposing, rival, streetwise, vying; SEE CONCEPT 542

competitor [n] *person willing to enter contest*
adversary, antagonist, challenger, competition, contestant, corrival, dark horse*, emulator, favorite, opponent, opposition, rival; SEE CONCEPTS 366,423

compilation [n] *assemblage*
accumulating, accumulation, aggregating, anthology, assembling, assortment, collecting, collection, collocating, combining, compiling, consolidating, garner, garnering, gathering, incorporating, joining, treasury, unifying; SEE CONCEPTS 109,432

compile [v] *assemble, accumulate*
abridge, amass, anthologize, arrange, assemble, bring together, collate, collect, colligate, collocate, compose, concentrate, congregate, consolidate, cull, draw together, edit, garner, gather, get together, glean, group, heap up, marshal, muster, organize, put together, recapitulate, unite; SEE CONCEPTS 79,84,109

complacent [adj] *contented*
conceited, confident, easy-going, egoistic, egotistical, gratified, happy, obsequious, pleased, satisfied, self-assured, self-contented, self-pleased, self-possessed, self-righteous, self-satisfied, serene, smug, unconcerned; SEE CONCEPTS 401,403

complain [v] *grumble about*
accuse, ascribe, attack, beef*, bellyache*, bemoan, bewail, bitch, carp, cavil, charge, contravene, criticize, defy, demur, denounce, deplore, deprecate, differ, disagree, disapprove, dissent, expostulate, find fault, fret, fuss, gainsay, grieve, gripe, groan, grouse, growl, grumble, impute, indict, kick up a fuss*, lament, lay, look askance, make a fuss, moan, nag, object, oppose, protest, refute, remonstrate, repine, reproach, snivel, sound off, take exception to, wail, whimper, whine, yammer; SEE CONCEPT 52

complaint [n1] *statement of disagreement, discontent*
accusation, annoyance, beef*, cavil, CC*, charge, clamor, criticism, dissatisfaction, expostulation, fault-finding, grievance, gripe, grouse, grumble, guff*, jeremiad, kick, lament, moan, objection, plaint, protest, protestation, rap, remonstrance, remonstration, representation, reproach, rumble*, squawk, stink, trouble, wail, whine; SEE CONCEPTS 52,689

complaint [n2] *illness, affliction*
affection, ailment, condition, disease, disorder, ill, indisposition, infirmity, malady, sickness, syndrome, upset; SEE CONCEPTS 306,316

complaisance [n] *agreeableness*
accommodativeness, acquiescence, compliance, courtesy, deference, friendliness, kindness, obligingness, politeness, respect; SEE CONCEPT 633

complaisant [adj] *agreeable*
accommodating, amiable, compliant, conciliatory, deferential, easy, easy-going, friendly, generous, good-humored, good-natured, good-tempered, indulgent, lenient, mild, obliging, polite, solicitous, submissive; SEE CONCEPT 401

complement [n] *companion, counterpart*
accompaniment, addition, aggregate, augmentation, balance, capacity, completion, consummation, correlate, correlative, counterpart, enhancement, enrichment, entirety, filler, finishing touch, makeweight, pendant, quota, remainder, rest, rounding-off*, supplement, total, totality; SEE CONCEPTS 635,824

complement [v] *complete*
accomplish, achieve, cap, clinch, conclude, consummate, crown, finish, fulfill, integrate, perfect, round off, top off; SEE CONCEPTS 91,119,234

complementary [adj] *filling, completing*
commutual, complemental, completing, completory, conclusive, correlative, correspondent, corresponding, crowning, equivalent, fellow, integral, integrative, interconnected, interdependent, interrelated, interrelating, matched, mated, paired, parallel, reciprocal; SEE CONCEPTS 577,824

complete [adj1] *total, not lacking*
all, entire, exhaustive, faultless, full, full-dress, gross, hook line and sinker*, imperforate, intact, integral, integrated, lock stock and barrel*, organic, outright, plenary, replete, the works*, thorough, thoroughgoing, unabbreviated, unabridged, unbroken, uncondensed, uncut, undiminished, undivided, undocked, unexpurgated, unimpaired, unitary, unreduced, whole, whole enchilada*, whole-hog*, whole-length, whole nine yards*; SEE CONCEPT 531

complete [adj2] *finished*
accomplished, achieved, all-embracing, all-inclusive, all over, all over but the shouting*, at-

CO
CO

tained, compassed, concluded, consummate, done, done with, down, effected, ended, entire, executed, fini*, finished off, full, full-fledged, home free*, perfect, plenary, realized, sweeping, terminated, that's it*, through; SEE CONCEPT 528

complete [adj3] *utter, absolute*
blank, blanket, categorical, consummate, downright, dyed-in-the-wool*, flawless, impeccable, out-and-out, outright, perfect, positive, sheer, thorough, thoroughgoing, total, unblemished, unconditional, unmitigated, unqualified, whole; SEE CONCEPTS 531,535

complete [v] *carry out action*
accomplish, achieve, actualize, bring to fruition, bring to maturity, call it a day*, cap, carry off, close, conclude, consummate, crown, determine, develop, discharge, do, do thoroughly, effect, effectuate, elaborate, end, equip, execute, fill, finalize, finish, fulfill, furnish, get through, go the limit*, go through with, go whole hog*, halt, make good*, make up, perfect, perform, put to bed*, realize, refine, round off, round out, settle, sew up*, supplement, terminate, ultimate, wind up*, wrap up*; SEE CONCEPT 91

completely [adv] *entirely*
absolutely, all the way*, altogether, competently, comprehensively, conclusively, effectively, en masse, exclusively, exhaustively, extensively, finally, from A to Z*, from beginning to end*, fully, heart and soul*, hook line and sinker*, in all, in entirety, in full, in toto*, on all counts*, painstakingly, perfectly, quite, solidly, thoroughly, totally, to the end, to the limit, to the max*, to the nth degree*, ultimately, unabridged, unanimously, unconditionally, undividedly, utterly, wholly, without omission; SEE CONCEPT 531

completion [n] *accomplishment, finishing*
achievement, attainment, close, conclusion, consummation, culmination, curtains*, dispatch, end, expiration, finalization, finis, finish, fruition, fulfillment, hips*, integration, perfection, realization, swan song*, windup*, wrap-up; SEE CONCEPTS 119,706

complex [n1] *composite, aggregate*
association, compound, conglomerate, ecosystem, entanglement, group, network, organization, scheme, structure, syndrome, synthesis, system, totality; SEE CONCEPTS 432,770

complex [n2] *psychological problem*
anxiety, a thing about something*, exaggerated reaction, fear, fixation, fixed idea, hang-up*, idée fixe, insanity, mania, neurosis, obsession, phobia, preoccupation, repression; SEE CONCEPT 410

complex [adj1] *involved, intricate*
circuitous, complicated, composite, compound, compounded, confused, conglomerate, convoluted, elaborate, entangled, heterogeneous, knotty, labyrinthine, manifold, mingled, miscellaneous, mixed, mixed-up, mosaic, motley, multifarious, multiform, multiple, multiplex, tangled, tortuous, variegated; SEE CONCEPT 562

complex [adj2] *difficult to understand*
abstruse, bewildering, Byzantine, circuitous, complicated, confused, convoluted, crabbed, cryptic, Daedalean, discursive, disordered, disturbing, enigmatic, entangled, excursive, Gordian, hidden, impenetrable, inscrutable, interwoven, intricate, involved, jumbled, knotted, knotty, labyrinthine, mazy, meandering, mingled,

mixed, muddled, obscure, paradoxical, perplexing, puzzling, rambling, recondite, round-about, sinuous, snarled, sophisticated, tangled, tortuous, undecipherable, unfathomable, winding; SEE CONCEPTS 402,529

complexion [n1] *skin coloring, appearance*
cast, color, coloration, coloring, flush, front, glow, hue, looks, mug*, phiz*, pigmentation, skin, skin tone, texture, tinge, tint, tone; SEE CONCEPTS 405,622

complexion [n2] *someone's character*
appearance, aspect, cast, countenance, disposition, guise, humor, ilk, individualism, individuality, kind, light, look, make-up, nature, personality, seeming, semblance, sort, stamp, style, temper, temperament, type; SEE CONCEPT 411

complexity [n] *complicatedness*
complication, convolution, elaboration, entanglement, intricacy, involvement, multiplicity, ramification; SEE CONCEPTS 663

compliance [n] *agreement*
acquiescence, amenability, assent, complaisance, concession, concurrence, conformity, consent, deference, docility, obedience, observance, passivity, resignation, submission, submissiveness, tractibility, yielding; SEE CONCEPTS 411,684

complicate [v] *confuse, make difficult*
add fuel to fire*, bedevil, clog, combine, confound, convolute, derange, disarrange, disorder, elaborate, embroil, entangle, fold, foul up*, handicap, impede, infold, interfuse, interrelate, interweave, involve, jumble, make intricate, make waves*, mix up, muck up*, muddle, multiply, obscure, open can of worms*, perplex, ravel, render unintelligible, screw up*, snafu*, snag, snarl up*, tangle, twist, upset; SEE CONCEPTS 7,19

complicated [adj] *difficult, complex*
abstruse, arduous, Byzantine, can of worms*, convoluted, Daedalean, difficult, elaborate, entangled, fancy, gasser*, Gordian, hard, hi-tech*, interlaced, intricate, involved, knotty, labyrinthine, mega factor*, mixed, perplexing, problematic, puzzling, recondite, sophisticated, troublesome, various, wheels within wheels*; SEE CONCEPTS 562,565

complication [n] *difficult situation*
aggravation, complexity, confusion, development, difficulty, dilemma, drawback, embarrassment, entanglement, factor, intricacy, obstacle, problem, snag, web; SEE CONCEPTS 230,674

complicity [n] *conspiracy*
abetment, agreement, collaboration, collusion, complot, concurrence, confederacy, connivance, engineering, guilt, guiltiness, implication, intrigue, involvement, machination, manipulation, partnership; SEE CONCEPTS 388,660

compliment [n] *praise, flattery*
acclaim, acclamation, admiration, adulation, applause, appreciation, approval, blessing, bouquet*, buttering up*, cajolery, commendation, comp*, confirmation, congratulations, courtesy, encomium, endorsement, eulogy, favor, felicitation, good word, homage, honor, kudo, laud, laudation, laurels, notice, orchid*, ovation, panegyric, pat on the back*, posy*, regard, respects, sanction, sentiment, tribute, veneration, warm fuzzy*; SEE CONCEPTS 69,278

compliment [v] *praise, flatter*
acclaim, adulate, applaud, butter up*, cajole, cel-

ebrate, charm, cheer, commemorate, commend, congratulate, endorse, eulogize, exalt, extol, fawn upon, felicitate, give bouquet*, glorify, hail, hand it to*, honor, ingratiate oneself with, kudize*, laud, magnify, make much of, panegyrize, pat on the back*, pay respects, pay tribute to, please, puff up*, recommend, roose, salute, sanction, satisfy, sing praises of, soothe, speak highly of, take off hat to*, toast, trade last*, wish joy to, worship; SEE CONCEPT 69

complimentary [adj1] flattering

adulatory, appreciative, approbative, approbatory, approving, celebrating, commendary, congratulatory, courtly, encomiastic, encomiastical, eulogistic, fair-spoken, fawning, highly favorable, honeyed, honoring, laudatory, panegyrical, plauditory, polite, praiseful, respectful, sycophantic, unctuous, well-wishing, with highest recommendation, with high praise; SEE CONCEPT 267

complimentary [adj2] free

as a perk*, chargeless, comp, costless, courtesy, donated, free lunch*, free of charge, gratis, gratuitous, honorary, on the house*; SEE CONCEPT 334

comply [v] abide by, follow agreement or instructions

accede, accord, acquiesce, adhere to, agree to, cave in, come around, conform to, consent to, cry uncle*, defer, discharge, ditto*, don't make waves*, don't rock the boat*, fit in, fold, fulfill, give in, give out, give up, go along with, go with the flow*, keep, knuckle to*, knuckle under*, mind, obey, observe, perform, play ball*, play the game*, put out, quit, respect, roll over and play dead*, satisfy, shape up, stay in line*, straighten up, submit, throw in towel*, toss it in*, yes one*, yield; SEE CONCEPTS 8,35,91

component [n] part, element

constituent, factor, fixings, ingredient, item, making, makings, peripheral, piece, plug-in, segment, unit; SEE CONCEPTS 831,834

component [adj] constituent

basic, composing, elemental, fundamental, inherent, integral, intrinsic, part and parcel of*, part of; SEE CONCEPTS 546,567

compose [v1] be part of construction

be an adjunct, be an element of, belong to, be made of, build, compound, comprise, consist of, constitute, construct, enter in, fashion, form, go into, make, make up, merge in; SEE CONCEPTS 168,642

compose [v2] create writing, artwork, or music

author, bang out*, cast, clef*, coin a phrase, comp, conceive, contrive, cook up*, design, devise, discover, draw up, dream up, fabricate, forge, form, formulate, frame*, fudge together*, ghost*, ghostwrite, imagine, indite, invent, knock off*, knock out*, make up, note down, orchestrate, originate, pen, poetize, produce, push pencil*, put down, put pen to paper*, score, scribble, script, set type, set up, time, turn out, whip up*, write; SEE CONCEPTS 79,173,174

compose [v3] calm, bring under control

adjust, allay, appease, arrange, assuage, balm, becalm, check, collect, comfort, console, contain, control, cool, ease, ease up, hold in, lessen, let up, lull, mitigate, moderate, modulate, pacify, placate, quell, quiet, re-collect, reconcile, regulate, rein, relax, repress, resolve, restrain, settle, simmer down, slacken, smother, soften, solace,

soothe, still, suppress, temper, tranquilize, tune down; SEE CONCEPTS 7,22,117

composed [adj] calm, collected

at ease, calmed, clearheaded, commonsensical, confident, cool, cool as cucumber*, dispassioned, dispassionate, easy, easygoing, have one's act together*, imperturbable, keeping a stiff upper lip*, keeping one's shirt on*, levelheaded, nonchalant, not turn a hair*, placid, poised, possessed, quieted, relaxed, repressed, sedate, self-assured, self-possessed, sensible, serene, serious, soothed, staid, suppressed, sure of oneself, temperate, together, tranquil, unflappable, unruffled, untroubled; SEE CONCEPT 401

composite [n] combination, mixture

amalgam, amalgamation, blend, combo, commixture, complex, compost, compound, conglomerate, fusion, immixture, intermixture, medley, mix, olio, pasteup*, stew*, synthesis, union; SEE CONCEPTS 260,432

composite [adj] combined, mixed

blended, complex, compound, conglomerate, melded, synthesized; SEE CONCEPT 490

composition [n1] structure, arrangement

agreement, architecture, balance, beauty, combination, concord, configuration, consonance, constitution, content, design, distribution, form, formation, harmony, layout, make-up, placing, proportion, relation, rhythm, spacing, style, symmetry, weave; SEE CONCEPTS 733,757

composition [n2] written or musical creation

arrangement, article, chart, concerto, dissertation, drama, essay, exercise, exposition, fiction, getup*, literary work, manuscript, melody, music, novel, number, opus, paper, piece, play, poetry, rhapsody, romance, score, setup*, short story, song, stanza, study, symphony, theme, thesis, tune, verse, work, writing; SEE CONCEPTS 259,260,263,271

compost [n] organic material

admixture, blend, commixture, composition, compound, fertilizer, fusion, humus, manure, mix, mixture, mulch, ordure, pile; SEE CONCEPT 509

composure [n] calmness, collectedness

accord, aplomb, assurance, balance, calm, contentment, control, cool*, cool head*, coolheadedness, coolness, dignity, dispassion, ease, equanimity, equilibrium, evenness, even temper, fortitude, harmony, imperturbability, inexcitability, levelheadedness, moderation, nonchalance, peace of mind, placidity, poise, polish, presence of mind, quiet, quietude, repose, sang-froid, sedateness, self-assurance, self-control, self-possession, serenity, sobriety, stability, tranquility; SEE CONCEPT 410

compound [n] combination, mixture

admixture, aggregate, alloy, amalgam, amalgamation, blend, combo, commixture, composite, composition, compost, conglomerate, fusion, goulash, medley, mishmash*, soup, stew, synthesis, union; SEE CONCEPTS 260,432

compound [v1] mix, combine

admix, amalgamate, associate, blend, bracket, co-agment, coalesce, commingle, commix, concoct, connect, couple, fuse, immix, intermingle, join, link, make up, meld, mingle, synthesize, unite; SEE CONCEPTS 109,113

compound [v2] make difficult; complicate

add to, aggravate, augment, confound, confuse,

comprehend [*v1*] *understand*
appreciate, apprehend, assimilate, capiche*, catch, click, cognize, conceive, dig*, discern, envisage, envision, fathom, get*, get the picture*, gotcha*, grasp, have, know, make out*, perceive, read, savvy*, see, take in, tumble*; SEE CONCEPT 15

comprehend [*v2*] *include*
comprise, contain, embody, embrace, enclose, encompass, have, involve, subsume, take in; SEE CONCEPT 118

comprehensible [*adj*] *understandable*
apprehensible, clear, coherent, comprehendible, conceivable, explicit, fathomable, graspable, intelligible, knowable, lucid, luminous, plain; SEE CONCEPTS 402,529

comprehension [*n*] *understanding*
aha*, apperception, apprehension, awareness, capacity, cognizance, conception, discernment, double take*, grasp, intelligence, judgment, ken, knowledge, perception, prehension, realization, sense, slow take*, take*; SEE CONCEPT 409

comprehensive [*adj*] *inclusive*
absolute, across the board*, all-embracing, all-inclusive, blanket, broad, catholic, compendious, complete, comprising, containing, discursive, encircling, encyclopedic, exhaustive, expansive, extensive, far-reaching, full, general, global, in depth, infinite, lock stock and barrel*, of great scope, overall, sweeping, synoptic, the big picture*, the whole shebang*, the works*, thorough, umbrella, wall-to-wall*, whole, wide, widespread; SEE CONCEPTS 531,772

compress [*v*] *compact, condense*
abbreviate, abridge, abstract, bind, boil down, coagulate, concentrate, consolidate, constrict, contract, cram, cramp, crowd, crush, decrease, dehydrate, densen, densify, epitomize, force into space, make brief, narrow, pack, press, press together, ram, reduce, restrict, shorten, shrink, shrivel, squash, squeeze, stuff, summarize, syncopate, telescope, tighten, wedge, wrap; SEE CONCEPTS 208,236,247

comprise [*v*] *make up, consist of*
add up to, amount to, be composed of, be contained in, compass, compose, comprehend, constitute, contain, cover, embody, embrace, encircle, enclose, encompass, engross, form, hold, include, incorporate, involve, span, subsume, sum up, take in; SEE CONCEPT 643

compromise [*n*] *agreement, give-and-take*
accommodation, accord, adjustment, arrangement, bargain, compact, composition, concession, contract, copout*, covenant, deal, fifty-fifty*, half and half, half measure, happy medium*, mean, middle course, middle ground, pact, sellout, settlement, trade-off, understanding, win-win situation*; SEE CONCEPTS 230,684

compromise [*v1*] *give and take*
adjust, agree, arbitrate, compose, compound, concede, conciliate, find happy medium*, find middle ground*, go fifty-fifty*, make a deal, make concession, meet halfway, negotiate, play ball with*, settle, split the difference*, strike balance, trade off; SEE CONCEPT 8

compromise [*v2*] *put in jeopardy*
blight, cop out*, discredit, dishonor, embarrass, endanger, explode, expose, give in, hazard, imperil, implicate, jeopardize, mar, menace, peril, prejudice, put under suspicion, risk, ruin, sell out, spoil, weaken; SEE CONCEPTS 101,240

compulsion [*n*] *drive, obligation*
coercion, constraint, demand, drive, driving, duress, duty, engrossment, exigency, force, hang-up, have on the brain*, monkey*, necessity, need, obsession, preoccupation, prepossession, pressure, tiger by the tail*, urge, urgency; SEE CONCEPTS 410,532

compulsive [*adj*] *driving, obsessive*
besetting, compelling, enthusiastic, irresistible, overwhelming, passionate, uncontrollable, urgent; SEE CONCEPT 401

compulsory [*adj*] *binding*
compulsary, de rigueur, forced, imperative, imperious, mandatory, necessary, obligatory, required, requisite; SEE CONCEPT 546

compunction [*n*] *regret, sorrow*
attrition, conscience, contrition, misgiving, penitence, penitency, pity, punctiliousness, qualm, reluctance, remorse, repentance, rue, ruth, second thoughts, shame, stab of conscience, sympathy; SEE CONCEPT 410

computation [*n*] *performing arithmetic*
calculation, ciphering, computing, counting, data processing, estimating, estimation, figuring, gauge, guess, reckoning, summing, totalling; SEE CONCEPT 764

compute [*v*] *calculate, estimate*
add up, cast up, cipher, count, count heads, count noses, cut ice*, dope out*, enumerate, figure, figure out, gauge, keep tabs*, measure, rate, reckon, run down, size up, sum, take account of, take one's measure, tally, tot*, total, tote*, tote up*; SEE CONCEPT 764

computer [*n*] *calculating, data processing machine*
abacus, adding machine, analog, artificial intelligence, brain*, calculator, clone, CPU, data processor, digital, electronic brain*, laptop*, MAC, mainframe, micro*, microcomputer, mini*, minicomputer, number cruncher*, PC, personal computer, thinking machine*; SEE CONCEPTS 269,463

comrade [*n*] *ally*
associate, bosom buddy, buddy, chum, colleague, comate, companion, compatriot, compeer, confederate, confidant, confidante, co-worker, crony, friend, intimate, mate, pal, partner, sidekick; SEE CONCEPT 423

con [*n*] *trick*
bluff, cheat, crime, deception, double-cross, dupe, fraud, gold brick*, graft, mockery, swindle, take in; SEE CONCEPT 59

con [*v*] *deceive, defraud*
bamboozle*, bilk, cajole, cheat, chicane, coax, double-cross, dupe, flimflam*, fool, hoax, hoodwink, hornswoggle*, humbug, inveigle, mislead, rip off*, rook, sweet-talk*, swindle, trick, wheedle; SEE CONCEPT 59

concatenation [*n*] *connection, sequence*
chain, connecting, continuity, integration, interlocking, link, linking, nexus, series, succession, uniting; SEE CONCEPTS 721,727

concave [*adj*] *curved, depressed*
biconcave, cupped, dented, dimpled, dipped, excavated, hollow, hollowed, incurvate, incurvated, incurved, indented, round, rounded, sagging, scooped, sinking, sunken; SEE CONCEPT 486

conceal [v] *hide, disguise*
beard, burrow, bury, cache, camouflage, cloak, couch, cover, cover up, dissemble, ditch, duck, ensconce, enshroud, harbor, hole up*, keep dark, keep secret, lie low*, lurk, mask, masquerade, obscure, plant*, put in a hole*, screen, secrete, shelter, skulk, slink, sneak, stash, stay out of sight, stow, tuck away, veil, wrap; SEE CONCEPT *188*

concealed [adj] *hidden, secret*
buried, cached, camouflaged, covered, covered up, covert, enshrouded, guarded, holed up, hushed up, hush-hush*, incog*, incognito, inconspicuous, masked, obscure, obscured, on the Q.T.*, perdu, planted, privy, put in the hole*, recondite, screened, secreted, shrouded, stashed, tucked away, ulterior, under wraps*, unseen, veiled; SEE CONCEPTS *576,619*

concealment [n] *hiding, secrecy*
beard, blind, camouflage, cover, covering, coverup, curtain, disguise, dissimulation, fig leaf*, front, hideaway, hide-out, laundromat, mask, obliteration, obscuration, occultation, privacy, red herring*, secretion, smoke screen*, veil, wraps*; SEE CONCEPTS *188,631*

concede [v] *acknowledge, give in*
accept, accord, admit, allow, avow, award, bury the hatchet*, capitulate, cave in, cede, confess, cry uncle*, ditto*, fess up*, fold, give up, go along with, go with the flow*, grant, hand over, knuckle under, let on, own, own up, play ball with*, quit, relinquish, say uncle*, surrender, throw in the towel*, waive, yes one*, yield; SEE CONCEPTS *35,57,82,235*

conceit [n] *egotism*
amour-propre, arrogance, complacence, complacency, consequence, immodesty, narcissism, outrecuidance, pomposity, pride, self-admiration, self-exaltation, self-importance, self-love, self-regard, smugness, snottiness, stuffiness, swagger, swelled head*, vainglory, vainness, vanity; SEE CONCEPT *411*

conceited [adj] *egotistical*
arrogant, bigheaded*, big talking, cocky, conceity, full of hot air*, gall, ham*, hot stuff*, immodest, know-it-all, loudmouth, narcissistic, overweening, phony, puffed up*, self-important, smart-alecky*, snotty*, stuck up*, swollenheaded*, vain, vainglorious, windbag*; SEE CONCEPT *404*

conceivable [adj] *reasonable, easy to understand*
believable, convincing, credible, earthly, imaginable, likely, mortal, possible, probable, supposable, thinkable; SEE CONCEPTS *529,552*

conceive [v1] *understand*
accept, appreciate, apprehend, assume, believe, catch, compass, comprehend, deem, dig, envisage, expect, fancy, feel, follow, gather, get, grasp, imagine, judge, perceive, realize, reckon, suppose, suspect, take, twig; SEE CONCEPT *15*

conceive [v2] *create*
become pregnant, brainstorm, cogitate, consider, contrive, cook up*, depicture, design, develop, devise, dream up, envisage, envision, fancy, feature, form, formulate, head trip*, image, imagine, make up, meditate, originate, ponder, produce, project, purpose, realize, ruminate, spark, speculate, spitball, think up, trump up*, visualize; SEE CONCEPTS *35,173,251*

concentrate [v1] *think about closely*
apply, attend, be engrossed in, bring to bear, brood over, center, consider closely, contemplate, crack one's brains*, direct attention, establish, examine, fixate, fix attention, focus, focus attention, get on the beam*, give attention, hammer*, hammer away at*, head trip*, intensify, knuckle down, meditate, muse, need, occupy thoughts, peruse, ponder, pour it on*, put, put mind to, rack one's brains*, rivet, ruminate, scrutinize, set, settle, study, sweat, think hard, weigh; SEE CONCEPT *17*

concentrate [v2] *gather, collect*
accumulate, agglomerate, aggregate, amass, assemble, bunch, center, centralize, cluster, coalesce, collect, combine, compact, compress, congest, conglomerate, congregate, consolidate, constrict, contract, converge, cramp, crowd, draw together, eliminate, embody, focalize, focus, forgather, garner, get to the meat*, heap, heap up, hoard, huddle, integrate, intensify, localize, mass, muster, narrow, pile, reduce, salt away, store, strengthen, swarm, unify, zero in*; SEE CONCEPTS *84,109*

concentrated [adj1] *condensed, reduced*
boiled down, complete, crashed*, entire, evaporated, fixed, full-bodied, lusty, potent, rich, robust, straight, strong, stuffed*, telescoped*, thick, thickened, total, unadulterated, undiffused, undiluted, undivided, unmingled, unmixed, whole; SEE CONCEPTS *483,554*

concentrated [adj2] *intense*
all-out, deep, desperate, exquisite, fierce, furious, hard, intensive, terrible, vehement, vicious; SEE CONCEPTS *326,569*

concentration [n1] *consolidation of effort*
absorption, amassing, application, assembly, bringing to bear, centering, centralization, close attention, clustering, coalescing, combination, compacting, compression, concern, congregation, consolidation, convergence, converging, debate, deliberation, fixing, flocking, focusing, heed, huddling, intensification, massing, narrowing, need, single-mindedness, study, unity; SEE CONCEPT *677*

concentration [n2] *aggregation*
accumulation, army, array, audience, band, cluster, collection, company, concourse, convergence, flock, group, herd, horde, mass, miscellany, mob, party; SEE CONCEPT *432*

concept [n] *idea*
abstraction, apprehension, approach, big idea*, brainchild*, brain wave*, conceit, conception, conceptualization, consideration, fool notion*, hypothesis, image, impression, intellection, notion, perception, slant, supposition, theory, thought, twist, view, wrinkle; SEE CONCEPTS *532,689*

conception [n1] *understanding; idea*
apperception, appreciation, apprehension, clue, cogitating, cognition, communing, comprehension, conceit, concentrating, concept, consideration, considering, deliberating, design, dreaming, envisaging, explanation, exposition, fancy, fancying, image, imagining, impression, inkling, intellection, interpretation, meditating, meditation, mental grasp, musing, notion, perception, philosophizing, picture, plan, realization, representation, speculating, speculation, thought, version; SEE CONCEPTS *409,410,689*

co
co

conception [n2] *beginning, birth*
fertilization, formation, germination, impregnation, inception, initiation, insemination, invention, launching, origin, outset, start; SEE CONCEPTS *119,302,373,375*

concern [n1] *business, responsibility*
affair, burden, care, charge, company, corporation, deportment, entanglement, enterprise, establishment, field, firm, house, interest, involvement, job, jungle*, matter, megacorp*, mission, multinational, occupation, organization, outfit, shooting match*, task, thing, transaction, worry, zoo*; SEE CONCEPTS *325,362,532*

concern [n2] *interest, anxiety*
apprehension, attention, bearing, care, carefulness, concernment, consideration, disquiet, disquietude, distress, heed, heedfulness, important matter, matter, reference, regard, relation, relevance, solicitude, tender loving care, unease, worry; SEE CONCEPTS *410,690*

concern [v1] *affect personally*
apply to, bear on, become involved, be relevant to, bother, disquiet, distress, disturb, interest, involve, make anxious, make uneasy, pertain to, perturb, regard, take pains, touch, trouble, worry; SEE CONCEPTS *7,19,22*

concern [v2] *relate to, have reference to*
answer to, appertain to, apply to, be about, be applicable to, bear on, bear upon, be connected with, be dependent upon, be interdependent with, belong to, be pertinent to, be well taken, deal with, depend upon, have a bearing on, have connections with, have implications for, have relation to, have significance for, have to do with, involve, pertain to, refer to, regard; SEE CONCEPT *532*

concerned [adj1] *worried*
anxious, biting one's nails*, bothered, butterflies in stomach*, distressed, disturbed, exercised, in a stew*, on pins and needles*, perturbed, tied up in knots*, troubled, uneasy, upset, uptight, worried sick*; SEE CONCEPT *403*

concerned [adj2] *involved with*
active, affected, attentive, caring, down with, implicated, in on, interested, mixed up, privy to, solicitous; SEE CONCEPTS *401,403*

concert [n1] *musical performance*
gig, jam session, musical, musicale, recital, rockfest, selections, show; SEE CONCEPT *263*

concert [n2] *agreement, harmony*
accord, chorus, collaboration, concord, concordance, consonance, joint, league, togetherness, tune, unanimity, union, unison; SEE CONCEPTS *388,684*

concerted [adj] *coordinated*
agreed upon, collaborative, combined, joint, mutual, planned, prearranged, united; SEE CONCEPT *538*

concession [n] *yielding, adjustment*
acknowledgment, admission, allowance, assent, authorization, boon, buyback, compromise, confession, copout*, deal, giveback, giving in, grant, indulgence, permission, permit, privilege, rollback, sellout, surrender, trade-off, warrant; SEE CONCEPTS *13,50,67,88*

conciliatory [adj] *placid, yielding*
appeasing, assuaging, calm, civil, disarming, irenic, mollifying, pacific, peaceable, placating, placatory, propitiative, quiet, willing; SEE CONCEPT *401*

concise [adj] *short, to the point*
abridged, boiled down*, breviloquent, brief, compact, compendiary, compendious, compressed, condensed, curt, epigrammatic, in a nutshell*, laconic, lean, marrowy, meaty, pithy, short and sweet*, succinct, summary, synoptic, terse; SEE CONCEPTS *773,798*

conclave [n] *secret meeting*
assembly, buzz session*, cabinet*, confab*, conference, council, encounter, gathering, get-together, huddle, meet, parley, powwow*, private meeting, session; SEE CONCEPTS *324,384*

conclude [v1] *finish, come to an end*
achieve, bring down curtain*, call it a day*, cease, cinch, clinch, close, close out, complete, consummate, crown, desist, draw to close, end, halt, knock off, put the lid on*, put to bed*, round off, stop, terminate, top off, ultimate, wind up, wrap up; SEE CONCEPTS *119,234*

conclude [v2] *decide, deduce*
add up to, adjudge, analyze, assume, be afraid, boil down to*, collect, derive, draw, figure, gather, have a hunch*, infer, intuit, judge, make, make out, presume, ratiocinate, reason, reckon, sum up, suppose, surmise, the way one sees it*; SEE CONCEPTS *18,37*

conclude [v3] *settle, resolve*
accomplish, achieve, bring about, carry out, clinch, confirm, decide, determine, effect, establish, fix, pull off, rule, work out; SEE CONCEPTS *18,91,126*

conclusion [n1] *end*
cease, cessation, close, closure, completion, consequence, culmination, denouement, desistance, development, ending, end of the line*, eventuality, finale, finish, issue, outcome, payoff, period, result, stop, termination, upshot, windup, wrap; SEE CONCEPTS *119,832*

conclusion [n2] *judgment, decision*
agreement, conviction, corollary, deduction, determination, illation, inference, opinion, ratiocination, resolution, resolve, sequitur, settlement, verdict; SEE CONCEPT *689*

conclusive [adj] *definite, final*
absolute, all out*, clear, clinching, cogent, compelling, convincing, deciding, decisive, demonstrative, determinant, determinative, flat out*, incontrovertible, indisputable, irrefragable, irrefrangible, irrefutable, irrevocable, litmus test*, precise, resolving, revealing, settling, straight out, telling, ultimate, unambiguous, unanswerable, unarguable, unconditional, undeniable, unmistakable, unquestionable, what you see is what you get*; SEE CONCEPT *535*

concoct [v] *formulate, think up*
ad lib, batch*, brew*, compound, contrive, cook up, create, design, devise, discover, dream up, envisage, envision, fabricate, frame*, hatch, invent, make up, mature, originate, plan, plot, prefab*, prepare, project, scheme, slap together*, throw together*, vamp; SEE CONCEPTS *36,173,251*

concoction [n] *creation, blend*
brew, combination, compound, contrivance, intention, medley, mixture, plan, preparation, project, solution; SEE CONCEPTS *260,432,660*

concomitant [adj] *contributing, accompanying*
accessory, adjuvant, agreeing, ancillary, associated with, associative, attendant, attending, belonging, coefficient, coetaneous, coeval,

coexistent, coincident, coincidental, collateral, complementary, concordant, concurrent, conjoined, conjoined with, connected, contemporaneous, contemporary, coordinate, corollary, coterminous, coupled with, fellow, incident, in tempo, in time, isochronal, isochronous, joint, satellite, synchronal, synchronous, synergetic, synergistic; SEE CONCEPT 577

concord [n1] *unity, harmony*
accord, agreement, amity, calmness, chime, comity, concert, concordance, consensus, consonance, friendship, goodwill, peace, placidity, rapport, serenity, tranquility, tune, unanimity, understanding, unison; SEE CONCEPT 388

concord [n2] *agreement, treaty*
compact, concordat, contract, convention, entente, pact, protocol; SEE CONCEPTS 271,684

concourse [n1] *passageway*
avenue, boulevard, entrance, foyer, hall, highway, lobby, lounge, meeting place, path, rallying point*, road, street; SEE CONCEPTS 440,501

concourse [n2] *crowd, group*
assemblage, assembly, collection, concursion, confluence, convergence, crush, gang, gathering, joining, junction, linkage, meeting, mob, multitude, rout, throng; SEE CONCEPT 432

concrete [adj1] *actual, factual*
accurate, corporeal, definite, detailed, explicit, material, objective, particular, precise, real, sensible, solid, specific, substantial, tangible; SEE CONCEPTS 535,582

concrete [adj2] *hardened*
caked, calcified, cemented, compact, compressed, congealed, conglomerated, consolidated, dried, firm, indurate, monolithic, petrified, poured, precast, set, set in stone*, solid, solidified, steeled, strong, unyielding; SEE CONCEPT 604

concur [v] *agree, approve*
accede, accord, acquiesce, assent, band, be consonant with, be in harmony, coadjute, coincide, collaborate, combine, come together, consent, cooperate, cut a deal*, equal, harmonize, jibe*, join, league*, meet, okay*, pass on*, shake on*, unite; SEE CONCEPTS 8,10,82

concurrent [adj1] *simultaneous*
circumstantial, coeval, coexisting, coincident, concerted, concomitant, contemporaneous, incidental, in sync, parallel, synchronal, synchronous; SEE CONCEPT 799

concurrent [adj2] *agreeing, converging*
allied, at one, centrolineal, coinciding, compatible, concerted, confluent, consentient, consistent, convergent, cooperating, coterminous, harmonious, in agreement, in rapport, joined, likeminded, meeting, mutual, of the same mind, unified, uniting; SEE CONCEPT 563

concussion [n] *collision, shaking*
blast, blow, buffeting, bump, clash, clout, crack, crash, hit, impact, injury, jar, jarring, jolt, jolting, jounce, pounding, punch, shock, trauma; SEE CONCEPTS 189,309,521

condemn [v] *blame, convict*
adjudge, belittle, blow whistle on*, call down*, castigate, censure, chide, come down on*, criticize, damn, decry, denounce, denunciate, deprecate, depreciate, disapprove, disparage, doom, find fault with, find guilty, frame, hang something on*, judge, knock, lay at one's door*, let have it*, name, pass sentence on*, pin it on*, point finger at*, pronounce, proscribe, punish, put

away, put down, reprehend, reproach, reprobate, reprove, send up, send up the river*, sentence, skin, thumbs down on*, upbraid; SEE CONCEPTS 44,52,317

condemnation [n] *blaming, conviction*
accusation, blame, censure, damnation, denouncement, denunciation, disapproval, doom, judgment, proscription, reproach, reprobation, reproof, sentence, stricture; SEE CONCEPTS 44,52,317

condensation [n1] *abridgment*
abstract, boildown*, breviary, brief, compendium, compression, concentration, consolidation, conspectus, contraction, curtailment, digest, epitome, essence, précis, reduction, summary, synopsis; SEE CONCEPTS 283,730

condensation [n2] *water buildup*
condensate, crystallization, deliquescence, dew, distillation, liquefaction, precipitate, precipitation, rainfall; SEE CONCEPT 514

condense [v] *abridge*
abbreviate, blue pencil*, boil down*, chop, coagulate, compact, compress, concentrate, constrict, contract, curtail, cut, cut down, decoct, densen, digest, edit, encapsulate, epitomize, inventory, precipitate, précis, press together, put in a nutshell*, reduce, shorten, shrink, snip, solidify, sum, summarize, summate, synopsize, telescope, thicken, trim; SEE CONCEPTS 236,247

condescend [v] *stoop, humble oneself*
accommodate, accord, acquiesce, agree, be courteous, bend, come down off high horse*, comply, concede, degrade oneself, deign, demean oneself, descend, favor, grant, high hat*, lower oneself, oblige, see fit, submit, talk down to, toss a few crumbs*, unbend, vouchsafe, yield; SEE CONCEPT 633

condescending [adj] *snobby, lordly*
arrogant, complaisant, disdainful, egotistic, la-dee-da*, lofty, patronizing, snobbish, snooty*, snotty*, supercilious, superior, uppish, uppity*; SEE CONCEPT 401

condescension [n] *disdain, superiority*
airs, civility, deference, haughtiness, loftiness, lordliness, patronage, patronizing attitude, superciliousness, toleration; SEE CONCEPT 633

condition [n1] *circumstances*
action, ballgame*, case, estate, happening, how it goes*, how things are*, how things stack up*, lay of the land*, like it is*, mode, order, plight, position, posture, predicament, quality, rank, repair, reputation, riff, scene, shape, situation, size of it*, sphere, spot, standing, state, state of affairs, status, status quo, trim, way things are*, way things shape up*, where it's at*; SEE CONCEPTS 639,696

condition [n2] *requirement, limitation*
arrangement, article, catch, codicil, contingency, demand, essential, exception, exemption, fine print*, kicker*, modification, must, necessity, postulate, precondition, prerequisite, provision, proviso, qualification, requisite, reservation, rule, sine qua non, small print*, stipulation, strings*, terms; SEE CONCEPTS 270,688

condition [n3] *physical shape, fitness*
appearance, aspect, build, constitution, fettle, form, health, kilter, mint, order, phase, repair, state, status, tone, trim; SEE CONCEPTS 316,757

condition [n4] *illness*
affection, ailment, complaint, disease, ill, infir-

mity, malady, predicament, problem, syndrome, temper, weakness; SEE CONCEPT *306*

condition [v] *adapt, prepare*
accustom, brainwash, build up, educate, equip, habituate, inure, loosen up, make ready, modify, practice, program, ready, shape up, sharpen, tone up, toughen up, train, warm up, whip into shape*, work out, work over; SEE CONCEPTS *35,202*

conditional [adj] *dependent*
codicillary, contingent, depending on, fortuitous, granted on certain terms, guarded, iffy*, incidental, inconclusive, limited, modified, not absolute, obscure, provisional, provisory, qualified, relative, reliant, relying on, restricted, restrictive, subject to, tentative, uncertain, with grain of salt*, with reservations, with strings attached*; SEE CONCEPT *554*

condolence [n] *sympathy*
comfort, commiseration, compassion, condolement, consolation, fellow feeling, solace; SEE CONCEPT *633*

condominium [n] *tenant-owned apartment house*
apartment, condo, co-op, timeshare, townhouse; SEE CONCEPT *516*

condone [v] *make allowance for*
buy*, disregard, excuse, forget, forgive, give green light*, go along with, ignore, lap up*, let it come*, let it go by*, let pass*, look the other way*, nod at*, okay, overlook, pardon, pass over, remit, wink at*; SEE CONCEPTS *10,23*

conducive [adj] *favorable for*
accessory, calculated to produce, contributive, contributory, helpful, leading, productive of, promotive, tending, useful; SEE CONCEPT *542*

conduct [n1] *administration*
care, carrying on*, channels, charge, control, direction, execution, guidance, handling, intendance, leadership, management, manipulation, organization, oversight, plan, policy, posture, red tape*, regimen, regulation, rule, running, strategy, superintendence, supervision, tactics, transaction, treatment, wielding; SEE CONCEPT *117*

conduct [n2] *behavior*
address, attitude, bearing, carriage, comportment, demeanor, deportment, manner, manners, mien, posture, stance, tenue, ways; SEE CONCEPT *633*

conduct [v1] *administer*
accompany, attend, call the tune*, carry on*, chair, chaperon, control, convey, direct, engineer, escort, govern, guide, handle, head, keep, lead, manage, operate, ordain, order, organize, oversee, pilot, preside over, regulate, ride herd on*, rule, run, run things, shepherd, steer, supervise, trailblaze*, usher, wield baton*; SEE CONCEPT *117*

conduct [v2] *comport oneself*
acquit, act, bear, behave, carry, demean, deport, go on, quit; SEE CONCEPT *384*

conduct [v3] *transport*
accompany, attend, bring, carry, chaperon, companion, convoy, escort, guide, lead, move, pass on, pilot, nurse, send, shepherd, show, steer, transfer; SEE CONCEPT *187*

conduit [n] *passage*
aqueduct, cable, canal, channel, conductor, course, culvert, duct, flow, flume, gully, gutter, lead-in, lead-out, main, pipe, pipeline, race, sewer, spout, trough, tube, watercourse; SEE CONCEPTS *499,501*

cone [n] *circular-shaped object with pointed end*
conoid, pyramid, raceme, strobile, stroboloid; SEE CONCEPT *436*

confection [n] *sweet food*
cake, candy, dainty, jam, pastry, sweet; SEE CONCEPT *457*

confederacy [n] *coalition*
alliance, anschluss, bond, compact, confederation, conspiracy, covenant, federation, government, league, organization, union; SEE CONCEPTS *299,301*

confederate [n] *abettor*
accessory, accomplice, ally, associate, coconspirator, collaborator, colleague, conspirator, fellow, fellow traveler, partner; SEE CONCEPT *412*

confederate [adj] *allied*
amalgamated, associated, combined, corporate, federal, federated, in alliance, incorporated, leagued, organized, syndicated, unionized; SEE CONCEPT *536*

confer [v1] *discuss, deliberate*
advise, argue, bargain, blitz*, brainstorm*, breeze*, collogue, confab*, confabulate, consult, converse, deal, debate, discourse, flap*, gab*, get heads together*, give meeting*, groupthink*, huddle, jaw, kick ideas around*, negotiate, parley, pick one's brain*, powwow*, speak, talk, toss ideas around*, treat; SEE CONCEPT *56*

confer [v2] *giving honor, award*
accord, allot, award, bestow, donate, gift with, give, grant, lay on, present, provide, sweeten the kitty*, vouchsafe; SEE CONCEPT *132*

conference [n1] *convention, colloquium*
appointment, argument, chat, colloquy, confabulation, conferring, congress, consultation, conversation, convocation, deliberation, discussion, forum, gabfest*, groupthink*, huddle, interchange, interview, meeting, palaver, parley, powwow*, round robin, round table, seminar, symposium, talk, think-in*, ventilation; SEE CONCEPTS *56,324,386*

conference [n2] *league of athletic teams*
association, athletic union, circuit, league, loop, organization, ring; SEE CONCEPT *365*

confess [v] *admit, confirm*
acknowledge, affirm, allow, assert, attest, aver, avow, blow, blurt out, chirp, clue in, come clean*, come out, concede, confide, declare, disclose, divulge, dump on*, evince, finger*, fink*, grant, humble oneself, leak*, let on*, level with, make clean breast of*, manifest, narrate, open one's heart*, own, own up, post, profess, prove, rat on*, recognize, relate, reveal, sing*, snitch*, sound off*, spill the beans*, spit out*, squeal*, tip hand*, unload*, vent, weasel*; SEE CONCEPT *60*

confession [n] *admittance of information*
acknowledgment, admission, affirmation, allowance, assenting, assertion, avowal, concession, declaration, disclosing, disclosure, divulgence, enumeration, exposé, exposure, making public, narration, owning up, proclamation, profession, publication, recitation, relation, revealing, revelation, song*, squawk*, squeal*, statement, story, telling, unbosoming, utterance; SEE CONCEPTS *60,274*

confidant [n] *close friend*
acquaintance, adherent, adviser, alter ego, bosom buddy, companion, crony, familiar, intimate, mate, pal; SEE CONCEPT *423*

confide [v1] *divulge information*
admit, bend an ear*, breathe, buzz*, confess, crack to, disclose, hint, impart, insinuate, intimate, lay it on*, lay the gaff*, let in on*, reveal, spill to*, suggest, tell, unload on*, whisper; SEE CONCEPT 57

confide [v2] *entrust*
bestow, charge, commend, commit, consign, delegate, hand over, present, relegate, trust; SEE CONCEPT 108

confidence [n1] *belief in oneself*
aplomb, assurance, backbone, boldness, brashness, certainty, cool, courage, daring, dash, determination, elan, faith in oneself, fearlessness, firmness, fortitude, grit, hardihood, heart, impudence, intrepidity, mettle, morale, nerve, pluck, poise, presumption, reliance, resoluteness, resolution, self-possession, self-reliance, spirit, spunk, sureness, tenacity; SEE CONCEPT 411

confidence [n2] *belief in something*
assurance, credence, dependence, faith, hope, reliance, stock, store, sure bet*, trust; SEE CONCEPT 689

confident [adj1] *certain, assured*
bet on*, bold, brave, cocksure, convinced, counting on, courageous, dauntless, depending on, expectant, expecting, fearless, having faith in, high*, hopeful, intrepid, positive, presuming, presumptuous, puffed up*, pushy, racked, sanguine, satisfied, secure, self-assured, self-reliant, self-sufficient, sure, trusting, unafraid, undaunted, upbeat, uppity*, valiant; SEE CONCEPTS 403,404

confidential [adj] *secret*
arcane, backdoor, classified, closet, hushed, hush-hush*, inside, intimate, off the record*, private, privy; SEE CONCEPTS 267,576

confidentially [adv] *in secret*
behind closed doors*, between ourselves, between us, between you and me*, covertly, don't breathe a word*, hushedly, in confidence, in on the ground floor*, off the cuff*, off the record*, personally, privately, sub rosa; SEE CONCEPTS 267,576

confine [v] *enclose, limit*
bar, bind, bound, cage, circumscribe, constrain, cool, cool down, cramp, delimit, detain, enslave, fix, hem in, hinder, hog-tie*, hold back, ice*, immure, imprison, incarcerate, intern, jail, keep, put a lid on*, put away, put on ice*, repress, restrain, restrict, send up, shorten, shut up; SEE CONCEPTS 121,130

confined [adj] *limited, enclosed*
bedfast, bedridden, bottled up, bound, chilled, circumscribed, compassed, cooped up, cramp, cramped, detained, flattened out, grounded, hampered, held, hog-tied*, iced*, immured, imprisoned, incarcerated, in chains, incommodious, indisposed, in jail, invalided, jailed, laid up, locked up, on ice*, pent, restrained, restricted, sealed up, shut in, sick; SEE CONCEPT 554

confinement [n1] *imprisonment; restriction*
bonds, bounding, bounds, check, circumscription, coercion, constrainment, constraint, control, cramp, curb, custody, delimitation, detention, immuration, incarceration, internment, jail, keeping, limitation, repression, safekeeping, trammels; SEE CONCEPTS 90,191

confines [n] *boundaries*
borders, bounds, circumference, compass, country, dimension, edge, end, environs, extent, limits, orbit, periphery, precinct, proportions,

purlieus, purview, radius, range, reach, region, scope, sweep, term, terrain, territory; SEE CONCEPTS 484,745,788

confirm [v1] *ratify, validate, prove*
affirm, approve, attest, authenticate, back, bear out, bless, buy, certify, check, check out, circumstantiate, corroborate, debunk, double-check, endorse, establish, explain, give green light*, give high sign*, give stamp of approval*, give the go-ahead*, give the nod*, justify, lap up, make good*, make sure, okay, rubber-stamp*, sanction, settle, sign, sign off on*, size up, subscribe, substantiate, support, thumbs up*, underpin, uphold, verify, vouch, warrant, witness; SEE CONCEPTS 57,103

confirm [v2] *reinforce*
assure, buttress, clinch, establish, fix, fortify, invigorate, make firm, settle, strengthen; SEE CONCEPTS 244,250

confirmation [n] *ratification, validation, proof*
acceptance, accepting, accord, admission, affirmation, affirming, agreement, approval, assent, attestation, authenticating, authentication, authorization, authorizing, avowal, consent, corroborating, corroboration, endorsement, evidence, go ahead*, green light*, nod, okay, passage, passing, proving, recognition, sanction, sanctioning, stamp of approval*, substantiation, support, supporting, testament, testimonial, testimony, validating, verification, verifying, visa, witness; SEE CONCEPTS 661,685

confirmed [adj] *habitual; rooted*
accepted, accustomed, chronic, deep-rooted, deep-seated, dyed-in-the-wool*, entrenched, firmly established, fixed, habituated, hardened, hard-shell*, ingrained, inured, inveterate, long-established, proved, seasoned, settled, staid, valid, worn; SEE CONCEPTS 542,798

confiscate [v] *steal; seize*
accroach, annex, appropriate, arrogate, assume, commandeer, confisticate, expropriate, glom on to*, grab, hijack, impound, liberate, moonlight requisition*, possess oneself of, preempt, sequester, sequestrate, swipe, take, take over, usurp; SEE CONCEPTS 139,142

conflagration [n] *large fire*
blaze, bonfire, burning, flaming, holocaust, inferno, rapid oxidation, up in smoke*, wildfire; SEE CONCEPTS 249,478

conflict [n1] *fight, warfare*
battle, clash, collision, combat, competition, contention, contest, emulation, encounter, engagement, fracas, fray, rivalry, set-to, strife, striving, struggle, tug-of-war, war; SEE CONCEPTS 106,320

conflict [n2] *disagreement, discord*
affray, animosity, antagonism, bad blood*, brush, competition, concours, contention, contest, dance, difference, disaccord, dispute, dissension, dissent, dissidence, disunity, divided loyalties, faction, factionalism, flap, fray, friction, fuss, hassle, hostility, interference, meeting, opposition, row, ruckus, run-in, set-to, strife, variance; SEE CONCEPTS 106,388,674

conflict [v] *be at odds*
brawl, bump heads with*, clash, collide, combat, contend, contest, cross swords with*, differ, disaccord, disagree, discord, disharmonize, disturb, fight, interfere, jar, lock horns with*, mismatch, oppose, romp, run against tide*, scrap,

CO
CO

slug, square off with, strive, struggle, tangle, vary; SEE CONCEPTS *46,106*

conflicting [*adj*] *contradictory*
adverse, antagonistic, antipathetic, at odds with, clashing, contrarian, contrary, disconsonant, discordant, discrepant, dissonant, incompatible, incongruent, incongruous, inconsistent, inconsonant, opposed, opposing, paradoxical, unfavorable, unmixable; SEE CONCEPTS *542,570*

confluence [*n*] *coming together*
assemblage, assembly, concourse, concurrence, concursion, conflux, convergence, crowd, gathering, host, junction, meeting, mob, multitude, union; SEE CONCEPTS *109,114*

conform [*v*] *adjust, adapt*
accommodate, attune, be guided by, clean up act*, comply, coordinate, don't make waves*, don't rock the boat*, fall in with, fit, follow, follow beaten path*, follow the crowd, go by the book*, go with the flow*, harmonize, integrate, keep, make room, meet halfway, mind, move over, obey, observe, play the game*, proportion, quadrate, reconcile, reconciliate, roll with punches*, run with the pack*, shape up, square, straighten up, suit, tailor, tailor-make*, toe the line*, tune, yield; SEE CONCEPT *13*

conform [*v2*] *correspond, match*
accord, agree, assimilate, be regular, dovetail, fit in, fit the pattern, go, harmonize, jibe, square, suit, tally; SEE CONCEPT *664*

conformable [*adj*] *appropriate; matching*
adapted, agreeable, alike, amenable, applicable, assorted, comparable, compliant, consistent, docile, fitted, fitting, harmonious, in agreement, like, matched, obedient, orderly, proper, regular, resembling, similar, submissive, suitable, suited, tractable, unified, useable, well-regulated; SEE CONCEPTS *487,558,563,573*

conformation [*n*] *shape*
anatomy, arrangement, build, cast, configuration, figure, form, formation, frame, framework, outline, structure, symmetry, type; SEE CONCEPTS *754,757*

conformity [*n1*] *compliance*
acquiescence, allegiance, assent, consent, conventionality, docility, obedience, observance, orthodoxy, resignation, submission, willingness; SEE CONCEPTS *13,689*

conformity [*n2*] *correspondence, harmony*
accord, affinity, agreement, coherence, conformance, congruity, consistency, consonance, likeness, resemblance, similarity; SEE CONCEPT *664*

confound [*v*] *confuse*
abash, amaze, astonish, astound, baffle, befog, bewilder, blend, bug*, commingle, confute, discombobulate*, discomfit, discountenance, dumb-found, embarrass, faze, fiddle, flabbergast, jumble, metagrobolize, misidentify, mix, mix up*, mystify, nonplus, perplex, pose, puzzle, rattle, screw up*, startle, surprise, throw*; SEE CONCEPTS *16,42*

confront [*v*] *challenge*
accost, affront, beard, brave, call one's bluff*, come up against*, dare, defy, encounter, face down*, face up to*, face with*, flout, front, go one-on-one*, go up against*, make my day*, meet, meet eyeball-to-eyeball*, oppose, repel, resist, scorn, stand up to, tell off, withstand; SEE CONCEPTS *46,52,54*

confrontation [*n*] *conflict*
affray, battle, contest, crisis, dispute, encounter, fight, meeting, set-to, showdown, strife; SEE CONCEPTS *46,106*

confuse [*v1*] *bewilder someone*
abash, addle, amaze, astonish, baffle, becloud, bedevil, befuddle, bemuse, cloud, clutter, complicate, confound, darken, daze, demoralize, discomfit, discompose, disconcert, discountenance, disorient, distract, embarrass, faze, fluster, fog, frustrate, fuddle, involve, lead astray, mess up*, misinform, mislead, mortify, muddle, mystify, nonplus, obscure, perplex, perturb, puzzle, rattle, render uncertain, shame, stir up, stump, throw off, throw off balance*, trouble, unhinge, unsettle, upset, worry; SEE CONCEPT *16*

confuse [*v2*] *mix up; involve*
bedlamize, blend, clutter, confound, disarrange, disarray, discombobulate*, discreate, disorder, disorganize, embroil, encumber, entangle, intermingle, involve, jumble, litter, mess up*, mingle, mistake, muddle, muss up, rumple, snarl up, tangle, tousle, tumble; SEE CONCEPT *112*

confused [*adj*] *disoriented mentally*
abashed, addled, at a loss*, at sea*, at sixes and sevens*, baffled, befuddled, bewildered, come apart*, dazed, discombobulated*, disconcerted, disorganized, distracted, flummoxed, flustered, fouled up*, glassy-eyed*, gone*, misled, mixed up, muddled, nonplussed, not with it*, out to lunch*, perplexed, perturbed, punch-drunk*, punchy*, puzzled, screwy*, shook up*, shot to pieces*, slaphappy, spaced out*, stumped, taken aback, thrown, thrown off balance*, unglued*, unscrewed*, unzipped*; SEE CONCEPT *403*

confused [*adj2*] *mixed up, disordered*
anarchic, blurred, chaotic, disarranged, disorderly, disorganized, haywire, in a muddle, in disarray, involved, jumbled, messy, miscalculated, miscellaneous, mistaken, misunderstood, obscured, out of order, snafu*, snarled, topsy-turvy, unsettled, untidy; SEE CONCEPT *585*

confusion [*n1*] *disorientation*
abashing, abashment, addling, agitation, befuddlement, befuddling, bemusement, bewilderment, blurring, chagrin, cluttering, commotion, confounding, demoralization, disarranging, discomfiting, discomfiture, disorientation, distraction, disturbing, dither, dumbfounding, embarrassing, embarrassment, embroiling, flap, fluster, lather, mixup mystification, obscuring, perplexing, perplexity, perturbation, pother, puzzlement, stew, stirring up, tangling, tumult, turbulence, turmoil, unsettling, upsetting; SEE CONCEPT *14*

confusion [*n2*] *disoriented state*
abashment, ado, anarchy, astonishment, bustle, chaos, clutter, commotion, complexity, complication, consternation, daze, difficulty, disarray, discomposure, dislocation, disorganization, distraction, emotional upset, ferment, fog, fracas, haze, hodge-podge, imbroglio, intricacy, jumble, labyrinth, mess, mistake, muddle, mystification, pandemonium, perturbation, racket, riot, row, shambles, stir, stupefaction, surprise, tangle, trouble, tumult, turmoil, untidiness, upheaval, uproar, wilderness; SEE CONCEPTS *410,727*

confute [*v*] *disprove, refute*
blow sky high*, break, bring to naught, confound, contradict, controvert, defeat, demolish, dismay, disprove, expose, invalidate, knocks props out

from under*, negate, oppugn, overcome, overthrow, overturn, overwhelm, parry, prove false, prove wrong, put down, rebut, set aside, shut up, silence, subvert, tap, upset, vanquish; SEE CONCEPTS 46,95

congeal [v] *coagulate*

cake, clabber, clot, concrete, condense, curdle, dry, freeze, gel, gelate, gelatinate, gelatinize, glob up*, harden, indurate, jell, jellify, jelly, refrigerate, set, solidify, stiffen, thicken; SEE CONCEPTS 250,469

congenial [adj] *friendly, compatible*

adapted, affable, agreeable, amical, clubby, companionable, compatible, complaisant, congruous, consistent, consonant, conversable, convivial, cooperative, cordial, delightful, favorable, genial, good-humored, gracious, happy, harmonious, jovial, kindly, kindred, like-minded, mellow, pleasant, pleasing, regular fellow*, right neighborly, sociable, social, suitable, sympathetic, well-suited; SEE CONCEPT 555

congenital [adj] *inborn*

complete, connate, connatural, constitutional, in-bred, indigenous, indwelling, ingrained, inherent, inherited, innate, intrinsic, inveterate, latent, native, natural, thorough, unacquired, utter; SEE CONCEPTS 314,549

congested [adj] *blocked, clogged*

chock-full, choked, closed, crammed, crowded, filled, glutted, gorged, gridlocked, jam-full, jammed, jam-packed, massed, mobbed, obstructed, occluded, overcrowded, overfilled, overflowing, packed, packed like sardines*, plugged, stopped, stoppered, stuffed, stuffed-up, teeming, up to the rafters*; SEE CONCEPTS 481,483,774

congestion [n] *blockage*

bottleneck*, clogging, crowdedness, crowding, excess, jam, mass, overcrowding, overdevelopment, overpopulation, press, profusion, rubbernecking*, snarl-up*, surfeit, surplus, traffic jam; SEE CONCEPTS 230,432

conglomerate [n] *composite organization*

agglomerate, agglomeration, aggregate, aggregation, cartel, chain, combine, conglomeration, group, multinational, pool, syndicate, trust; SEE CONCEPTS 323,325

conglomerate [adj] *composite*

amassed, assorted, blended, clustered, heterogeneous, indiscriminate, massed, melded, miscellaneous, mixed, motley, multifarious, promiscuous, varied, variegated; SEE CONCEPTS 490,589

conglomeration [n] *accumulation, potpourri*

agglomeration, aggregate, aggregation, amassment, assortment, collection, combination, combo*, composite, cumulation, everything but the kitchen sink*, hoard, hodge-podge, mass, medley, miscellany, mishmash*, mixed bag*, trove; SEE CONCEPT 432

congratulate [v] *compliment on achievement, luck*

applaud, bless, boost, felicitate, give a big cigar*, give bouquet*, give regards, gold star*, hand it to*, hear it for*, laud, pat on back, praise, rejoice with, salute, stroke*, toast, wish happy returns*, wish joy to, wish one well; SEE CONCEPTS 51,69

congratulations [n] *complimentation on achievement, luck*

best wishes, compliments, felicitations, give a "hear-hear"*, good going*, good wishes, good work, greetings, hail; SEE CONCEPTS 69,278

congregate [v] *assemble, come together*

besiege, bunch up*, collect, concentrate, congress, convene, converge, convoke, corral, flock*, forgather, gang around, gang up, gather, hang out*, make the scene*, mass, meet, meet up, muster, pack, raise, rally, rendezvous, round up, swarm, teem, throng; SEE CONCEPTS 109,114

congregation [n] *assembled group, especially concerned with church-going*

aggregation, assemblage, assembly, audience, churchgoers, collection, company, confab*, crowd, disciples, flock, following, gathering, get-together, group, host, laity, meet, meeting, multitude, muster, parish, parishioners, public, sit-in, throng, turnout; SEE CONCEPTS 369,387,417

congress [n] *delegation of representatives*

assembly, association, caucus, chamber, club, committee, conclave, conference, convention, convocation, council, delegates, government, guild, league, legislative body, legislature, meeting, order, parliament, senate, society, the Hill, the house, union; SEE CONCEPTS 299,387

congruent [adj] *agreeable, harmonious*

coinciding, compatible, concurring, conforming, consistent, corresponding, identical, in agreement; SEE CONCEPT 563

congruous [adj] *corresponding, suitable*

accordant, appropriate, apt, becoming, coincidental, compatible, concordant, congruent, consistent, consonant, correspondent, fit, fitting, harmonious, meet, proper, seemly, sympathetic; SEE CONCEPTS 558,563

conical/conic [adj] *shaped cylindrically and with a point*

coned, cone-shaped, conoid, conoidal, funnel-shaped, pointed, pyramidal, sharp, strobilate, strobiloid, tapered, tapering; SEE CONCEPT 486

conjectural [adj] *speculative*

academic, assumed, doubtful, figured, guessing, guesstimated*, hypothetical, on a hunch*, on a long shot*, putative, reputed, supposed, suppositional, supposititious, suppositive, surmised, surmising, suspect, tentative, theoretical, uncertain, unresolved; SEE CONCEPT 582

conjecture [n] *speculation, assumption*

conclusion, fancy, guess, guesstimate*, guesswork, hunch, hypothesis, inference, notion, opinion, perhaps, presumption, shot in the dark*, sneaking suspicion, stab in the dark*, supposition, surmise, theorizing, theory; SEE CONCEPTS 28,274,689

conjecture [v] *speculate*

assume, believe, conceive, conclude, deem, estimate, expect, fancy, feel*, figure, gather, glean, guess, guesstimate*, hazard a guess*, hypothesize, imagine, infer, judge, presume, pretend, suppose, surmise, suspect, take a shot*, take a stab*, take for granted, theorize, think; SEE CONCEPTS 28,51

conjugal [adj] *marital*

bridal, connubial, hymeneal, married, matrimonial, nuptial, spousal, wedded; SEE CONCEPT 555

conjunction [n] *combination*

affiliation, agreement, alliance, association, cahoots, coincidence, concomitance, concurrence, congruency, conjointment, hookup*, juxtaposition, parallelism, partnership, tie-up*, union; SEE CONCEPTS 388,714

conjure [vI] *appeal to, implore*

adjure, ask, beg, beseech, brace, crave, entreat,

importune, pray, supplicate, urge; SEE CONCEPT 48

conjure [v2] *cast spell*
bewitch, call upon, charm, enchant, ensorcel, entrance, exorcise, fascinate, invoke, levitate, play tricks, raise, rouse, summon, voodoo; SEE CONCEPT 14

conjure up [v] *bring to mind*
call, contrive, create, evoke, materialize, produce as by magic, recall, recollect, remember, review, summon, urge; SEE CONCEPT 38

connect [v] *combine, link*
affix, ally, associate, attach, bridge, cohere, come aboard, conjoin, consociate, correlate, couple, equate, fasten, get into, hitch on, hook on, hook up, interface, join, join up with, marry, meld with, network with, plug into, relate, slap on, span, tack on, tag, tag on, tie in, tie in with, unite, wed, yoke; SEE CONCEPTS 85,113,160

connected [adj] *related, affiliated*
akin, allied, applicable, associated, banded together, bracketed, coherent, combined, consecutive, coupled, in on with*, joined, linked, pertinent, undivided, united; SEE CONCEPTS 482,577

connection [n1] *person who aids another in achieving goal*
acquaintance, agent, ally, associate, association, contact, friend, go-between, intermediary, kin, kindred, kinship, mentor, messenger, network, reciprocity, relation, relative, sponsor; SEE CONCEPTS 348,423

connection [n2] *something that connects, links*
affiliation, alliance, association, attachment, bond, combination, conjointment, conjunction, coupling, fastening, hookup, joining, joint, junction, juncture, link, linkage, network, partnership, seam, tie, tie-in, tie-up, union; SEE CONCEPTS 499,720

connection [n3] *something that communicates, relates*
affinity, application, association, bearing, bond, commerce, communication, correlation, correspondence, intercourse, interrelation, kinship, link, marriage, nexus, partnership, reciprocity, relation, relationship, relevance, tie-in, togetherness; SEE CONCEPTS 388,664

connive [v] *plot, scheme*
angle, be in cahoots with*, cabal, cogitate, collude, conspire, contrive, cook up, devise, diddle*, finagle, frame, frame up, intrigue, machinate, operate, promote, wangle, wire, work hand in glove*; SEE CONCEPT 36

connoisseur [n] *authority*
adept, aesthete, aficionado, appreciator, arbiter, bon vivant, buff*, cognoscente, critic, devotee, dilettante, epicure, expert, fan, freak*, gourmet, judge, maven*, nut*, one into*, savant, specialist; SEE CONCEPTS 352,376

connotation [n] *implication*
association, coloring, essence, hint, meaning, nuance, overtone, significance, suggestion, undertone; SEE CONCEPTS 682,689

connote [v] *imply*
add up to, betoken, denote, designate, evidence, express, hint at, import, indicate, insinuate, intend, intimate, involve, mean, signify, spell, suggest; SEE CONCEPTS 75,118

connubial [adj] *marital*
conjugal, hymeneal, married, matrimonial, nuptial, spousal, wedded; SEE CONCEPT 555

conquer [v1] *defeat, overcome*
beat, bring to knees*, checkmate, circumvent, clobber, control, cream*, crush, discomfit, drub, foil, frustrate, get the better of*, humble, lick, master, outwit, overmaster, overpower, override, overthrow, prevail, quell, reduce, rout, shut down, subdue, subjugate, succeed, surmount, throw, thwart, total*, trample underfoot, trash, triumph, vanquish, whip, wipe off map*, worst, zap*; SEE CONCEPT 95

conquer [v2] *win; obtain*
achieve, acquire, annex, best, master, occupy, overcome, overrun, prevail, seize, succeed, triumph; SEE CONCEPTS 90,141,706

conqueror [n] *champion*
conquistador, defeater, hero, subduer, subjugator, vanquisher, victor, winner; SEE CONCEPTS 354,358

conquest [n1] *defeat, victory*
acquisition, annexation, appropriation, big win*, clean sweep*, conquering, coup, defeating, discomfiture, grand slam*, invasion, killing*, occupation, overthrow, rout, routing, score, splash*, subdual, subjection, subjugation, success, takeover, triumph, vanquishment, win; SEE CONCEPTS 95,706

conquest [n2] *enchantment; person enchanted*
acquisition, adherent, admirer, captivation, catch, enthrallment, enticement, fan, feather in cap*, follower, prize, seduction, supporter, worshiper; SEE CONCEPTS 410,423

consanguinity [n] *family relationship*
affiliation, affinity, agnate, blood-relationship, brotherhood, cognate, connection, family tie, filiation, kin, kindred, kindredship, kinship, lineage, race, sisterhood, strain; SEE CONCEPTS 296,388

conscience [n] *moral sense*
censor, compunction, demur, duty, inner voice, morals, principles, qualms, right and wrong, scruples, shame, small voice*, squeam, still small voice*, superego; SEE CONCEPTS 645,689

conscientious [adj1] *thorough, careful*
complete, diligent, exact, exacting, faithful, fastidious, fussy, hanging in*, hanging tough*, heart and soul into*, heedful, meticulous, minding p's and q's*, painstaking, particular, playing safe, punctilious, punctual, reliable, tough, walking on eggs*; SEE CONCEPTS 531,538

conscientious [adj2] *moral, upright*
conscionable, high-minded, high-principled, honest, honorable, incorruptible, just, pious, principled, responsible, right, scrupulous, straightforward, strict, true; SEE CONCEPT 545

conscious [adj1] *alert, awake*
able to recognize, acquainted, aesthetic, alive to, apperceptive, apprised, assured, attentive, au courant, aware, certain, cognizant, conversant, discerning, felt, hep to*, informed, in on*, in right mind, keen, knowing, known, mindful, noticing, noting, observing, on to*, perceiving, percipient, recognizing, remarking, responsive, seeing, sensible, sensitive to, sentient, supraliminal, sure, understanding, vigilant, watchful, wise to*, with it*, witting; SEE CONCEPTS 402,539

conscious [adj2] *intentional*
affected, calculated, deliberate, knowing, mannered, premeditated, rational, reasoning, reflec-

tive, responsible, self-conscious, studied, willful; SEE CONCEPTS 403,535

consciousness [n] *knowledge*
alertness, apprehension, awareness, care, carefulness, cognizance, concern, heed, heedfulness, mindfulness, realization, recognition, regard, sensibility; SEE CONCEPT 409

consecrate [v] *hold in high religious regard*
anoint, beatify, bless, dedicate, devote, exalt, hallow, honor, ordain, sanctify, set apart, venerate; SEE CONCEPTS 69,367

consecutive [adj] *in sequence*
after, chronological, connected, constant, continuing, continuous, ensuing, following, going on, increasing, in order, in turn, later, logical, numerical, one after another, progressive, running, sequent, sequential, serial, serialized, seriate, seriatim, succedent, succeeding, successional, successive, understandable, uninterrupted; SEE CONCEPTS 585,799

consensus [n] *general agreement*
accord, concord, concurrence, consent, harmony, unanimity, unison, unity; SEE CONCEPTS 684,689

consent [n] *agreement; concession*
accord, acquiescence, allowance, approval, assent, authorization, blank check*, blessing, carte blanche*, compliance, concurrence, go-ahead*, green light*, leave, okay*, permission, permit, right on*, sanction, say so*, stamp of approval*, sufferance, understanding, yes; SEE CONCEPTS 684,685

consent [v] *agree*
accede, accept, acquiesce, allow, approve, assent, bless, comply, concede, concur, fold, give in, give the nod*, give up, knuckle under, let, make a deal, okay*, permit, roll over, sanction, say uncle*, say yes, sign off on*, subscribe, throw in the towel*, yes*, yield; SEE CONCEPTS 8,50,88

consequence [n1] *result, outcome of action*
aftereffect, aftermath, bottom line*, can of worms*, chain reaction*, effect, end, event, fallout, follow through, follow-up, issue, outgrowth, payback, reaction, repercussion, sequel, sequence, spin-off, upshot, waves*; SEE CONCEPT 230

consequence [n2] *importance, significance*
account, concern, exigency, fame, honor, import, interest, magnitude, moment, momentousness, need, note, pith, portent, renown, reputation, repute, signification, value, weight, weightiness; SEE CONCEPT 668

consequence [n3] *person's status*
cachet, dignity, distinction, eminence, notability, position, prestige, rank, repute, standing, state, stature, status; SEE CONCEPT 388

consequent [adj] *resultant*
consistent, ensuing, following, indirect, inferable, intelligent, logical, rational, reasonable, resulting, sensible, sequential, sound, subsequent, successive, understandable; SEE CONCEPTS 537,548

consequential [adj] *significant*
big, considerable, eventful, far-reaching, grave, important, material, meaningful, momentous, serious, substantial, weighty; SEE CONCEPT 568

conservation [n] *preservation*
attention, care, cherishing, conservancy, conserving, control, custody, directing, economy, governing, guardianship, guarding, keeping, maintenance, management, managing, preserval, preserving, protecting, protection, safeguarding,

safekeeping, salvation, saving, stewardship, storage, supervising, supervision, sustentation, upkeep; SEE CONCEPTS 134,257

conservative [n] *person who is cautious, moderate; an opponent of change*
bitter-ender*, classicist, conserver, conventionalist, diehard, hard hat*, middle-of-the-roader*, moderate, moderatist, obstructionist, old guard*, old liner*, preserver, reactionary, redneck*, right, rightist, right-winger, silk-stocking*, standpat, stick-in-the-mud*, Tory*, traditionalist, unprogressive; SEE CONCEPT 359

conservative [adj] *cautious, moderate, tending to preserve the status quo*
bourgeois, constant, controlled, conventional, diehard, fearful, firm, fogyish*, fuddy-duddy*, guarded, hard hat*, hidebound, holding to, illiberal, in a rut*, inflexible, middle-of-the-road*, not extreme, obstinate, old guard*, old line*, orthodox, quiet, reactionary, redneck*, right, right of center*, right-wing, sober, stable, steady, timid, Tory*, traditional, traditionalistic, unchangeable, unchanging, uncreative, undaring, unimaginative, unprogressive, white bread*; SEE CONCEPT 542

conservatory [n] *greenhouse*
cold frame, glasshouse, hot house, nursery; SEE CONCEPTS 439,449,517

conserve [v] *save, protect*
cut back, cut down on, go easy on*, hoard, keep, maintain, nurse, preserve, safeguard, scrimp, skimp, sock away*, squirrel*, squirrel away*, stash, steward, store up, support, sustain, take care of, use sparingly; SEE CONCEPT 134

consider [v1] *turn over in one's mind*
acknowledge, allow for, assent to, chew over*, cogitate, concede, consult, contemplate, deal with, deliberate, dream of, envisage, examine, excogitate, favor, flirt with*, grant, inspect, keep in mind, look at, meditate, mull over, muse, perpend, ponder, provide for, reason, reckon with, recognize, reflect, regard, revolve, ruminate, scan, scrutinize, see, see about, speculate, subscribe to, take into account, take under advisement, take up, think out, think over, toss around*; SEE CONCEPTS 17,24

consider [v2] *regard a certain way*
analyze, appraise, bear in mind, believe, care for, count, credit, deem, estimate, feel, hold, hold an opinion, judge, keep in view, look upon, make allowance for, reckon with, reflect, remember, respect, sense, set down, suppose, take for, take into account, think, think of, view; SEE CONCEPT 12

considerable [adj1] *abundant, large*
ample, appreciable, astronomical, big, bountiful, comfortable, commodious, extensive, goodly, great, hefty, huge, large-scale, lavish, major, marked, much, noticeable, plentiful, pretty, reasonable, respectable, sizable, substantial, tidy, tolerable; SEE CONCEPT 781

considerable [adj2] *important*
big, consequential, distinguished, doozie*, dynamite, essential, fab*, fat, influential, material, meaningful, momentous, mondo*, noteworthy, renowned, significant, solid gold*, something, something else*, substantial, super, super-duper*, to the max*, unreal*, venerable, weighty; SEE CONCEPT 568

considerably [adv] *significantly*
appreciably, far, greatly, markedly, noticeably,

quite, rather, remarkably, somewhat, substantially, very much, well; SEE CONCEPT 569

considerate [adj] respectful of others
accommodating, amiable, attentive, benevolent, big, charitable, chivalrous, circumspect, compassionate, complaisant, concerned, cool, discreet, forbearing, generous, kind, kindly, like a sport*, magnanimous, mellow, mindful, obliging, patient, polite, solicitous, sympathetic, tactful, tender, thoughtful, unselfish, warmhearted; SEE CONCEPT 401

consideration [n1] mental analysis
application, attention, cogitation, concentration, contemplation, debate, deliberation, discussion, examination, forethought, heed, reflection, regard, review, scrutiny, study, thinking, thought; SEE CONCEPT 24

consideration [n2] concern; something mentally examined
development, difficulty, emergency, estate, evidence, exigency, extent, factor, fancy, idea, incident, issue, items, judgment, magnitude, minutiae, notion, occasion, occurrence, particulars, perplexity, plan, point, problem, proposal, puzzle, scope, situation, state, thought, trouble; SEE CONCEPT 532

consideration [n3] high regard
attentiveness, awareness, concern, considerateness, esteem, estimation, favor, forbearance, friendliness, heed, heedfulness, kindliness, kindness, mercy, mindfulness, respect, solicitude, tact, thoughtfulness, tolerance; SEE CONCEPTS 32,410

consideration [n4] payment
baksheesh, commish*, commission, fee*, payback, percentage, perk, perquisite, recompense, remuneration, reward, salary, something to sweeten pot*, tip, wage; SEE CONCEPT 344

considered [adj] deliberate, thought-out
advised, aforethought, contemplated, designed, designful, examined, express, given due consideration, gone into, intentional, investigated, mediated, premeditated, prepense, studied, studious, thought-about, thought-through, treated, voluntary, weighed, well advised, well chosen, willful; SEE CONCEPTS 402,529

considering [adj] taking everything in mind
all in all, all things considered, as, as long as, because, everything being equal, for, forasmuch as, inasmuch as, in consideration of, in light of, insomuch as, in view of, now, pending, seeing, since, taking into account; SEE CONCEPT 529

consign [v] entrust, hand over for care
address, appoint, assign, authorize, commend to, commission, commit, confide, convey, delegate, deliver, deposit with, dispatch, forward, give, issue, put in charge of, relegate, remit, route, send, ship, transfer, transmit, turn over; SEE CONCEPTS 108,143,217

consignment [n1] entrusting, handing over
assignment, committal, dispatch, distribution, relegation, sending shipment, transmittal; SEE CONCEPTS 108,143,217

consignment [n2] something entrusted to another's care
batch, delivery, goods, shipment; SEE CONCEPT 338

consist [v] exist, reside
abide, be, be contained in, be expressed by, be found in, dwell, inhere, lie, repose, rest, subsist; SEE CONCEPT 539

consistency [n1] thickness
bendability, bendableness, compactness, density, elasticity, fabric, firmness, flexibility, frangibility, hardness, limberness, moldability, organization, plasticity, pliability, softness, solidity, suppleness, texture, viscidity, viscosity, viscousness; SEE CONCEPTS 611,722

consistency [n2] constancy, regularity
accord, agreement, apposition, appropriateness, aptness, coherence, cohesion, compatibility, concord, concurrence, conformability, congruity, consonance, correspondence, evenness, fitness, harmony, homogeneity, invariability, likeness, proportion, similarity, stability, steadfastness, steadiness, suitability, symmetry, uniformity, union, unity; SEE CONCEPTS 637,656,670

consistent [adj1] constant, regular
dependable, even, expected, homogeneous, invariable, logical, of a piece, persistent, rational, same, steady, true, true to type, unchanging, undeviating, unfailing, uniform, unvarying; SEE CONCEPT 534

consistent [adj2] agreeing, compatible
accordant, according to, agreeable, all of a piece, coherent, conforming with, congenial, congruous, consonant, equable, harmonious, like, logical, matching, sympathetic; SEE CONCEPT 563

consist of [v] made up of
amount to, be composed of, comprise, contain, embody, include, incorporate, involve; SEE CONCEPT 643

consolation [n] relief, comfort
alleviation, assuagement, cheer, comfort, compassion, ease, easement, encouragement, fellow feeling, help, lenity, pity, solace, succour, support, sympathy; SEE CONCEPTS 32,410

console [v] relieve, comfort
animate, assuage, buck up*, calm, cheer, condole with, encourage, express sympathy, gladden, inspirit, lift, solace, soothe, tranquilize, untrouble, upraise; SEE CONCEPTS 7,22

consolidate [v] combine; make firm
add to, amalgamate, amass, band, bind, blend, build up, bunch up, cement, centralize, compact, compound, concatenate, concentrate, condense, conjoin, connect, densen, develop, federate, fortify, fuse, harden, hitch, hitch on, hook up with, incorporate, join, league, mass, meld, mix, plug into, pool, reinforce, render solid, secure, set, slap on, solidify, stabilize, strengthen, tack on, tag on, team up with*, thicken, throw in together*, tie in, tie up with, unify; SEE CONCEPTS 109,250

consolidation [n] combination, fortification
alliance, amalgamation, association, coadunation, coalition, compression, concentration, condensation, federation, fusion, incorporation, melding, mergence, merger, merging, reinforcement, solidification, strengthening, unification; SEE CONCEPTS 109,469

consonance [n] agreement, consistency
accord, chime, chorus, concert, concord, conformity, congruence, congruity, correspondence, harmony, suitableness, tune; SEE CONCEPT 664

consonant [adj] agreeing, consistent
accordant, according, agnate, akin, alike, analogous, blending, coincident, comfortable, comparable, compatible, concordant, congenial, congruous, correspondent, corresponding, harmo-

consort [n] *associate, partner*
accompaniment, companion, concomitant, friend, husband, mate, spouse, wife; SEE CONCEPT *423*

consort [v1] *be friendly with; fraternize*
accompany, associate, attend, bear, befriend, bring, carry, chaperon, chum together*, chum with*, clique with, company, conduct, convoy, gang up with*, go around with*, hang around with*, hang out with*, hang with*, join, keep company, mingle, mix, pal, pal around with, pal with, run around with*, run with, take up with, tie up with; SEE CONCEPTS *114,384*

consort [v2] *agree*
accord, coincide, comport, concur, conform, correspond, dovetail, harmonize, march, square, tally; SEE CONCEPT *664*

conspicuous [adj1] *obvious, easily seen*
apparent, clear, discernible, distinct, evident, manifest, noticeable, open-and-shut*, patent, perceptible, plain, visible; SEE CONCEPT *619*

conspicuous [adj2] *important, prominent*
arresting, arrestive, blatant, celebrated, commanding, distinguished, eminent, famed, famous, flagrant, flashy, garish, glaring, glitzy*, illustrious, influential, jazzy, loud, marked, notable, noted, notorious, outstanding, pointed, rank, remarkable, renowned, salient, screaming, showy, signal, splashy, stick out like sore thumb*, striking, tony*, well-known; SEE CONCEPTS *542,567*

conspiracy [n] *collusion in plan*
cabal, complot, confederacy, connivance, countermine, counterplot, covin, disloyalty, fix, frame*, game, hookup*, intrigue, league, little game*, machination, perfidy, plot, practice, put-up job*, scheme, sedition, treacherousness, treachery, treason, trick, trickery; SEE CONCEPT *660*

conspire [v1] *plot, scheme with someone*
be in cahoots*, cabal, cogitate, collogue, collude, confederate, connive, contrive, cook up*, cooperate, devise, get in bed with*, hatch, intrigue, machinate, maneuver, operate, promote, put out a contract*, wangle, wire, work something out*; SEE CONCEPTS *36,192*

conspire [v2] *agree, concur*
cabal, colleague, combine, complot, conduce, consort, contribute, cooperate, join, tend, unite, work together; SEE CONCEPT *8*

constancy [n] *fixedness*
abidingness, adherence, allegiance, ardor, attachment, certainty, decision, dependability, determination, devotedness, devotion, doggedness, eagerness, earnestness, endurance, faith, fealty, fidelity, firmness, honesty, honor, integrity, love, loyalty, permanence, perseverance, principle, regularity, resolution, stability, staunchness, steadfastness, steadiness, surety, tenacity, trustiness, trustworthiness, truthfulness, unchangeableness, unfailingness, uniformity, zeal; SEE CONCEPTS *32,410,637*

constant [adj1] *fixed*
connected, consistent, continual, equable, even, firm, habitual, homogeneous, immutable, invariable, like the Rock of Gibralter*, monochrome, monophonic, monotonous, nonstop, of a piece, permanent, perpetual, regular, regularized, solid as rock*, stabile, stable, standardized, steadfast, steady, together, unalterable, unbroken, unchanging, unflappable, unfluctuating, uniform, uninterrupted, unvarying; SEE CONCEPT *534*

constant [adj2] *neverending*
abiding, ceaseless, chronic, continual, continuous, endless, enduring, eternal, everlasting, incessant, interminable, lasting, nonstop, perpetual, persistent, persisting, relentless, sustained, unending, uninterrupted, unrelenting, unremitting; SEE CONCEPTS *649,798*

constant [adj3] *loyal, determined*
allegiant, attached, dependable, devoted, dogged, faithful, fast, persevering, resolute, staunch, tried-and-true, trustworthy, trusty, unfailing, unflagging, unshaken, unwavering; SEE CONCEPT *542*

consternation [n] *dismay, distress*
alarm, amazement, anxiety, awe, bewilderment, confusion, distraction, dread, fear, fright, horror, muddle, muddlement, panic, perplexity, shock, stupefaction, terror, trepidation, trepidity, wonder; SEE CONCEPT *230*

constituency [n] *voting public*
balloters, body of voters, body politic, citizenry, city, county, district, electorate, electors, faction, nation, people, precinct, state, system, voters, voting area, ward; SEE CONCEPT *379*

constituent [n] *element*
board, component, division, essential, factor, fixins*, fraction, ingredient, makings, part, part and parcel*, plug-in*, portion, principle, unit; SEE CONCEPTS *826,834*

constituent [adj1] *component, part*
basic, combining, composing, constituting, division, elemental, essential, factor, forming, fraction, fundamental, ingredient, integral, portion; SEE CONCEPTS *826,834,835*

constituent [adj2] *voting*
balloter, citizen, electing, electoral, official, overruling; SEE CONCEPT *536*

constitute [v1] *comprise, form*
aggregate, complement, complete, compose, compound, construct, cook up*, create, develop, dream up*, embody, enact, establish, fill out, fix, flesh out*, found, frame, fudge together*, incorporate, integrate, make, make up, set up; SEE CONCEPTS *173,184,251*

constitute [v2] *authorize*
appoint, commission, decree, delegate, depute, deputize, designate, draft, empower, enact, establish, legislate, make, name, nominate, ordain, order; SEE CONCEPTS *50,88*

constitution [n1] *physical make-up and health*
architecture, build, character, composition, construction, content, contents, design, disposition, essence, form, formation, frame, habit, habitus, nature, physique, structure, temper, temperament, type, vitality; SEE CONCEPT *757*

constitution [n2] *establishment*
charter, code, composition, custom, formation, lawmaking, legislation, organization, written law; SEE CONCEPTS *271,318*

constitutional [n] *walk*
airing, ambulation, footwork, legwork, perambulation, ramble, saunter, stroll, turn, walk; SEE CONCEPT *149*

constitutional [adj1] *inherent*
built-in, congenital, deep-seated, essential, inborn, inbred, ingrained, innate, intrinsic, natural, organic, vital; SEE CONCEPT *549*

co
co

constitutional [adj2] *provided for by law*
approved, chartered, democratic, ensured, lawful, legal, representative, statutory, vested; SEE CONCEPT 319

constrain [v] *force; restrain*
ban, bar, bind, bottle up, bridle, chain, check, coerce, compel, concuss, confine, constrict, cool off*, cork, curb, deny, deprive, disallow, drive, hem in*, hog-tie*, hold back, hold down, hold in, immure, impel, imprison, incarcerate, inhibit, intern, jail, keep lid on*, make, necessitate, oblige, pressure, pressurize, put half nelson on*, shotgun*, stifle, urge, withhold; SEE CONCEPTS 14,121,130

constraint [n1] *force*
a must*, coercion, compulsion, driving, duress, goad, hang-up*, impelling, impulsion, monkey*, motive, necessity, no-no*, pressure, repression, restraint, spring, spur, suppression, violence; SEE CONCEPTS 14,121

constraint [n2] *shyness*
bashfulness, diffidence, embarrassment, hangup*, humility, inhibition, modesty, repression, reservation, reserve, restraint, timidity; SEE CONCEPT 411

constraint [n3] *restriction*
arrest, captivity, check, circumscription, confinement, constrainment, cramp, curb, damper, detention, deterrent, hindrance, limitation, restraint; SEE CONCEPTS 130,652

constrict [v] *inhibit*
astringe, choke, circumscribe, clench, compress, concentrate, condense, confine, constringe, contract, cramp, curb, draw together, limit, narrow, pinch, restrain, restrict, shrink, squeeze, strangle, strangulate, tauten, tense, tighten, tuck; SEE CONCEPTS 130,191,219

constriction [n] *blockage*
binding, choking, compression, constraint, contraction, cramp, impediment, limitation, narrowing, pressure, reduction, restriction, squeezing, stenosis, stricture, tightness; SEE CONCEPTS 130,191,219

construct [v] *assemble, build*
build up, cobble up*, compose, compound, constitute, cook up*, create, design, dream up*, elevate, engineer, envision, erect, establish, fabricate, fashion, forge, form, formulate, found, frame, fudge together*, hammer out*, hoke up*, imagine, invent, make, manufacture, organize, prefab*, produce, put out, put together, put up, raise, rear, set up, shape, throw together, throw up*, trump up*, uprear, whip up*; SEE CONCEPTS 168,173,251

construction [n1] *creation, building*
architecture, arrangement, assembly, build, cast, composition, conception, constitution, contour, cut, development, disposition, edifice, elevation, erecting, erection, fabric, fabricating, fabrication, figuration, figure, form, format, formation, foundation, improvisation, invention, makeup, making, manufacture, mold, origination, outline, plan, planning, prefab, prefabrication, putting up, raising, rearing, roadwork, shape, structure, system, systematization, turn, type; SEE CONCEPTS 168,439,757

construction [n2] *explanation*
apprehension, construal, definition, exegesis, explication, exposé, exposition, inference, interpre-

tation, reading, rendering, rendition, translation, version; SEE CONCEPT 274

constructive [adj] *helpful*
effective, positive, practical, productive, useful, valuable; SEE CONCEPT 401

construe [v] *deduce; explain*
analyze, decipher, define, explicate, expound, figure it to be*, infer, interpret, one's best guess*, parse, read, render, spell out, take, translate, understand; SEE CONCEPTS 37,57

consul [n] *representative*
delegate, emissary, envoy, lawyer, legate; SEE CONCEPTS 354,355

consulate [n] *embassy*
consular office, government office, ministry; SEE CONCEPTS 439,449

consult [v] *ask, confer*
argue, ask advice of, be closeted with, brainstorm*, call in, cogitate, collogue, commune, compare notes, confab, confabulate, consider, debate, deliberate, discuss, examine, flap*, groupthink*, huddle, interrogate, interview, kick ideas around*, negotiate, parley, pick one's brains*, powwow*, put heads together*, question, refer to, regard, respect, review, seek advice, seek opinion of, take account of, take a meeting*, take counsel, talk over, toss ideas around*, treat, turn to; SEE CONCEPTS 17,48,56

consultation [n] *asking, conference*
appointment, argument, buzz session*, clambake*, confab*, conference, council, deliberation, dialogue, discussion, examination, groupthink*, hearing, huddle, interview, meeting, powwow*, second opinion*, session; SEE CONCEPTS 48,114,324

consume [v1] *use up*
absorb, apply, avail oneself of, deplete, devour, dissipate, dominate, drain, drivel, eat up, employ, engross, exhaust, expend, finish, finish up, fritter away, frivol away, go, go through, have recourse to, lavish, lessen, monopolize, obsess, preoccupy, profit by, put away, put to use, run out of, run through, spend, squander, throw away, trifle, utilize, vanish, wash up, waste, wear out; SEE CONCEPT 225

consume [v2] *eat, drink*
absorb, bolt, chow down*, devour, down, eat up, feed, gobble*, gorge, gulp, guzzle, hoover*, ingest, ingurgitate, inhale, meal, mow*, nibble, partake, polish off*, punish, put away*, put down*, scarf*, snack, stuff one's face*, swallow, swill, take, toss down*, wolf*; SEE CONCEPT 169

consume [v3] *destroy*
annihilate, crush, decay, demolish, devastate, eat up, exhaust, expend, extinguish, lay waste, overwhelm, ravage, raze, ruin, suppress, waste, wreck; SEE CONCEPT 252

consumer [n] *person who buys merchandise, services*
buyer, customer, end user, enjoyer, purchaser, shopper, user; SEE CONCEPT 348

consummate [adj] *ultimate, best*
able, absolute, accomplished, complete, conspicuous, downright, faultless, finished, flawless, gifted, ideal, impeccable, inimitable, matchless, out-and-out*, peerless, perfect, perfected, polished, positive, practiced, ripe, skilled, superb, superlative, supreme, talented, thoroughgoing, total, trained, transcendent, unmitigated, unquali-

fied, unsurpassable, utter, virtuosic, whole; SEE
CONCEPTS 528,572

consummate [v] achieve, finish
accomplish, button down*, call a day*, can*,
carry out, clean up, clinch, close, come, come
through, compass, complete, conclude, crown,
drop curtain*, effectuate, end, fold up, get it together*, go the distance*, halt, knock off, mop
up, perfect, perform, polish off*, put away*, put
finishing touch on*, put lid on*, put to bed*, sew
up, sign, take care of, terminate, top it off, ultimate, wind up, wrap, wrap up; SEE CONCEPTS
234,704,706

consummation [n] achievement, fulfillment
cleanup, completion, culmination, doing it to a
T*, end, mop-up, payoff, perfection, realization,
to a finish, wind-up*, wrap, wrap-up*; SEE CON-
CEPT 706

consumption [n] devouring; use
burning, consuming, damage, decay, decrease,
depletion, desolation, destruction, devastation,
diminution, dispersion, dissipation, drinking, eating, exhaustion, expenditure, loss, misuse, ruin,
swallowing, using up, utilization, waste, wear and
tear; SEE CONCEPTS 156,169,225,252

contact [n1] form of communication
acquaintance, association, channel, commerce,
communion, companionship, connection, influence, intercourse, junction, meeting, network,
touch, union, unity; SEE CONCEPTS 278,388,687

contact [n2] touching
approximation, closeness, collision, connection,
contiguity, contingence, hit, impingement, junction, juxtaposition, nearness, propinquity, proximity, relation, strike, taction, touch, union; SEE
CONCEPT 747

contact [v] communicate with
approach, be in touch with, buzz*, call, check
with, connect, get, get ahold of, get in touch with,
interact, interface, network*, phone, reach, reach
out, relate, speak to, talk, telephone, touch base*,
visit, write to; SEE CONCEPT 266

contagion [n] infection
bane, contamination, corruption, illness, miasma,
pestilence, plague, poison, pollution, taint, transmission, venom, virus; SEE CONCEPT 306

contagious [adj] communicable
catching, deadly, endemic, epidemic, epizootic,
impartible, infectious, inoculable, pestiferous,
pestilential, poisonous, spreading, taking, transmissible, transmittable; SEE CONCEPT 314

contain [v1] include, hold
accommodate, be composed of, comprehend,
comprise, consist of, embody, embrace, enclose,
encompass, have, have capacity for, hold, incorporate, involve, seat, subsume, take in; SEE CON-
CEPTS 112,736,742

contain [v2] hold back, control
bottle up*, check, collect, compose, cool*, cork*,
curb, harness, hog-tie*, hold in, keep back, keep
lid on*, put half nelson on*, rein, repress, restrain, restrict, simmer down, smother, stifle,
stop; SEE CONCEPTS 94,191

container [n] holder for physical object
alembic, bag, beaker, bin, bottle, bowl, box,
bucket, bunker, caisson, can, canister, canteen,
capsule, carafe, carton, cask, casket, cauldron,
chamber, chest, churn, cistern, cradle, crate,
crock, dish, ewer, firkin, flask, hamper, hod, hopper, humidor, hutch, jar, jeroboam, jug, kettle,

magnum, package, packet, pail, pit, pod, poke,
pot, pottery, pouch, purse, receptacle, reliquary,
repository, sac, sack, scuttle, stein, storage, tank,
tub, utensil, vase, vat, vessel, vial; SEE CONCEPT
494

contaminate [v] adulterate
alloy, befoul, corrupt, debase, debauch, defile,
deprave, desecrate, dirty, harm, infect, injure,
muck up, pervert, poison, pollute, profane, radio-
activate, soil, spoil, stain, sully, taint, tarnish, vitiate; SEE CONCEPTS 252,254

contamination [n] adulteration
contagion, corruption, decay, defilement, dirtying, disease, epidemic, filth, foulness, impurity,
infection, pestilence, plague, poisoning, pollution, radioactivation, rottenness, spoliation, taint;
SEE CONCEPTS 230,306,674

contemplate [v1] think about seriously; plan
aim, aspire to, brood over, chew over, consider,
cool out*, deliberate, design, envisage, excogitate, expect, foresee, intend, kick around*, mean,
meditate on, mind, mull over, muse over, observe,
percolate, perpend, ponder, propose, purpose, reflect upon, ruminate, size up, speculate, study,
take in, think of, weigh; SEE CONCEPTS 17,36

contemplate [v2] gaze at
audit, behold, consider, examine, eye, inspect,
notice, observe, peer, penetrate, peruse, pierce,
pore over, probe, pry, regard, scan, scrutinize,
see, stare at, study, survey, view, witness; SEE
CONCEPT 623

contemplation [n1] deep thought; planning
ambition, cogitation, consideration, deliberation,
design, intention, meditation, musing, plan, pondering, purpose, reflection, reverie, rumination,
study; SEE CONCEPT 410

contemplation [n2] gazing at
examination, inspection, looking at, observation,
scrutiny, survey, viewing; SEE CONCEPT 623

contemplative [adj] deep in thought
attentive, cogitative, in brown study*, intent, introspective, lost, meditative, musing, pensive,
pondering, rapt, reflecting, reflective, ruminative,
speculative, thinking, thoughtful; SEE CONCEPTS
402,403

contemporary [adj1] modern
abreast, à la mode*, au courant, contempo*, current, existent, extant, hot off press*, in fashion,
instant, in vogue, just out*, latest, leading-edge*,
mod*, new, newfangled, now, present, present-
day, recent, red-hot*, state-of-the-art*, today's,
topical, ultramodern, up*, up-to-date, up-to-the-
minute, voguish, with it*; SEE CONCEPTS
578,589,797

contemporary [adj2] existing, occurring at same
time
accompanying, associated, attendant, coetaneous,
coeval, coexistent, coexisting, coincident, concomitant, concurrent, connected, contemporaneous, current, linked, present, related,
simultaneous, synchronal, synchronic, synchronous; SEE CONCEPT 820

contempt [n1] disdain, disrespect
antipathy, audacity, aversion, condescension,
contumely, defiance, derision, despisal, despisement, despite, disesteem, disregard, distaste, hatred, indignity, malice, mockery, neglect,
recalcitrance, repugnance, ridicule, scorn, slight,
snobbery, stubbornness; SEE CONCEPT 29

CO
CO

contempt [n2] *state of disgrace*
discredit, disesteem, disfavor, dishonor, disrepute, humiliation, ignominy, infamy, insignificancy, opprobrium, shame, stigma; SEE CONCEPTS 388,674

contemptible [adj] *despicable, shameful*
abhorrent, abject, abominable, bad, base, beggarly, cheap, crass, currish, degenerate, despisable, detestable, dirty, disgusting, hateful, heel, ignoble, ignominious, inferior, low, low-down*, lowest, mean, odious, outcast, paltry, pitiable, pitiful, poor, sad, scummy*, scurvy*, shabby, sordid, sorry*, swinish, unworthy, vile, worthless, wretched; SEE CONCEPT 550

contemptuous [adj] *arrogant, insolent*
audacious, bold, cavalier, cheeky, cold-shoulder, condescending, contumelious, cool, derisive, derisory, disdainful, disrespectful, dog it*, hard, hard-nosed, haughty, high and mighty*, high hat*, insulting, on high horse*, opprobrious, sardonic, scornful, sneering, snippy, snobbish, snooty*, snotty*, supercilious, temperamental, uppity, upstage; SEE CONCEPT 401

contend [v1] *compete, fight*
argue, battle, clash, confront, contest, controvert, cope, dispute, emulate, encounter, face, give all one's got*, give one's all*, go after, go for, go for broke*, go for it*, go for jugular*, grapple, have at*, jockey for position*, jostle, knock oneself out*, litigate, lock horns*, make play for*, meet, mix it up with*, oppose, oppugn, push, push for, resist, rival, scramble for, shoot at, shoot for, skirmish, stand, strive, struggle, tangle with, tug, vie, withstand; SEE CONCEPTS 92,106

contend [v2] *argue*
affirm, allege, assert, aver, avow, blast, charge, claim, come at, cross, debate, defend, dictate, dispute, enjoin, fly in face of*, gang up on, go at, have at*, have bone to pick*, hold, insist, jump on, justify, lace into*, lay into*, let have it*, light into*, lock horns with*, maintain, mix, mix it up*, prescribe, put up argument, report, rip*, say, set to, sock it to one*, stick it to*, take on, tell, urge, vindicate, warrant, zap*; SEE CONCEPT 46

content [n1] *comfort, happiness*
contentment, ease, gratification, peace, peace of mind, pleasure, satisfaction; SEE CONCEPT 410

content [n2] *essence, meaning*
burden, composition, constitution, gist, idea, matter, significance, subject, subject matter, substance, text, thought; SEE CONCEPT 682

content [n3] *capacity, volume*
filling, load, measure, packing, size; SEE CONCEPTS 719,740

content [adj] *happy, agreeable*
appeased, at ease, can't complain*, comfortable, complacent, contented, fat dumb and happy*, fulfilled, gratified, pleased as punch*, satisfied, smug, tickled pink*, willing; SEE CONCEPT 403

content [v] *please*
appease, bewitch, captivate, charm, delight, enrapture, gladden, gratify, humor, indulge, make happy, mollify, placate, reconcile, satisfy, suffice, thrill, tickle; SEE CONCEPTS 7,22

contented [adj] *at ease; happy*
at peace, cheerful, comfortable, complacent, content, glad, gratified, pleased, satisfied, serene, thankful; SEE CONCEPT 403

contention [n1] *competition*
altercation, argument, battle, beef*, belligerency,

bone of contention*, bone to pick*, combat, conflict, contest, controversy, difference, disaccord, discord, dispute, dissension, dissent, dissidence, disunity, enmity, feuding, fight, flak*, hassle, hostility, quarrel, rivalry, run-in, scene, scrap, set-to*, squabble, static, strife, struggle, variance, war, wrangle, wrangling; SEE CONCEPTS 92,106

contention [n2] *argument for idea*
advancement, affirmation, allegation, assertion, asseveration, avowal, belief, charge, claim, contestation, declaration, demurrer, deposition, discussion, explanation, ground, hurrah, hypothesis, idea, maintaining, opinion, plea, position, predication, profession, rumpus, stand, thesis, view; SEE CONCEPTS 46,278,689

contentment [n] *comfort, happiness*
complacency, content, contentedness, ease, equanimity, fulfillment, gladness, gratification, peace, pleasure, repletion, satisfaction, serenity; SEE CONCEPT 410

contents [n] *elements of larger object*
capacity, cargo, chapters, connotation, constituents, details, divisions, essence, filling, freight, furnishing, gist, guts, implication, ingredients, innards, inside, lading, load, meaning, nub, packing, shipment, significance, size, space, stuffing, subject matter, subjects, substance, sum, text, themes, topics, volume; SEE CONCEPT 835

contest [n1] *competition*
challenge, concours, discussion, game, match, meet, meeting, proving, rencounter, sport, testing, tournament, trial, trying; SEE CONCEPTS 92,363

contest [n2] *fight, struggle*
action, affray, altercation, battle, battle royal*, beef*, brawl, brush, combat, conflict, controversy, debate, discord, dispute, emulation, encounter, engagement, fray, go*, hassle, rivalry, row, rumble*, run-in, scrap, set-to*, shock, skirmish, static, strife, striving, tug-of-war, warfare, wrangle; SEE CONCEPTS 106,320

contest [v1] *argue, challenge*
blast, call in question, debate, dispute, doubt, give it one's all*, go for it*, go for jugular*, jockey for position*, jump on, litigate, mix it up with*, object to, oppose, push, question, scramble for, shoot for*, stand up for, tangle; SEE CONCEPT 46

contest [v2] *fight*
altercate, attack, battle, brawl, break with, buck, compete, conflict, contend, cross, defend, duel, feud, fight over, gang up on, hassle, knuckle with, lay a finger on*, lay out, put on gloves*, put up dukes*, quarrel, repel, rival, row, rumpus, scrap, scuffle, set to, sock*, square off, strike, struggle, take on, tilt, traverse, vie, withstand, wrangle; SEE CONCEPT 106

contestant [n] *competitor*
adversary, antagonist, aspirant, battler, candidate, challenger, combatant, contender, contester, dark horse*, disputant, entrant, favorite, hopeful, member, participant, player, rival, scrapper*, team member, warrior; SEE CONCEPT 366

context [n] *framework, circumstances*
ambience, background, conditions, connection, frame of reference, lexicon, relation, situation, substance, text, vocabulary; SEE CONCEPTS 682,696

contiguous [adj] *adjacent, in contact*
abutting, adjoining, approximal, beside, bordering, close, contactual, conterminous, juxtaposed,

juxtapositional, meeting, near, near-at-hand, nearby, neighboring, next, next door to, next to, touching; SEE CONCEPTS 586,778

continent [adj] chaste, pure
abstemious, abstentious, abstinent, ascetic, austere, bridled, celibate, curbed, inhibited, modest, restrained, self-restrained, sober, temperate; SEE CONCEPT 550

contingency [n] chance happening; possibility
accident, break, chance, crisis, crossroads, emergency, event, eventuality, exigency, fortuity, happening, if it's cool*, incident, juncture, likelihood, occasion, odds, opportunity, pass, pinch, predicament, probability, strait, turning point, uncertainty, zero hour*; SEE CONCEPTS 650,679,693

contingent [n] group of followers
batch, body, bunch, deputation, detachment, disciples, mission, quota, sect, section, set; SEE CONCEPT 417

contingent [adj] conditional; possible
accidental, casual, chance, controlled by, dependent, fluky, fortuitous, haphazard, incidental, likely, odd, probable, probably, random, subject to, unanticipated, uncertain, unexpected, unforeseeable, unforeseen, unpredictable; SEE CONCEPT 552

continual [adj] constant, incessant
aeonian, around-the-clock, ceaseless, connected, consecutive, continuous, dateless, endless, enduring, eternal, everlasting, frequent, interminable, oft-repeated, permanent, perpetual, persistent, persisting, recurrent, regular, relentless, repeated, repetitive, running, staying, steady, timeless, unbroken, unceasing, unchanging, unending, unfailing, unflagging, uninterrupted, unremitting, unvarying, unwaning; SEE CONCEPTS 534,798

continuance [n] duration
constancy, continuation, endurance, extension, guts*, longevity, period, permanence, perpetuation, protraction, run, survival, term, vitality; SEE CONCEPTS 637,804,807

continuation [n] addition; maintenance
assiduity, augmenting, continuance, continuing, continuity, duration, endurance, enduring, extension, furtherance, going on, increase, increasing, line, maintaining, perpetuating, perpetuation, persisting, postscript, preservation, preserving, producing, production, prolongation, prolonging, propagation, protracting, protraction, sequel, succession, supplement, sustaining, sustenance, tenacity; SEE CONCEPTS 640,651,804

continue [v1] persist, carry on
abide, advance, carry forward, draw out, endure, extend, forge ahead, get on with it*, go on, hang in*, keep at, keep on, keep on truckin'*, keep the ball rolling*, keep up, last, lengthen, linger, live on, loiter, maintain, make headway, move ahead, never cease, outlast, outlive, perdure, persevere, persist in, press on, progress, project, prolong, promote, pursue, push on, reach, remain, rest, ride, run on, stand, stay, stay on, stick at, stick to, survive, sustain, uphold; SEE CONCEPT 239

continue [v2] begin again; resume
begin over, begin where one left off, carry on, carry over, go on with, pick up, proceed, recapitulate, recommence, reestablish, reinstate, reinstitute, renew, reopen, restart, restore, return to, take up; SEE CONCEPT 234

continuity [n] progression
chain, cohesion, connection, constancy, continuance, continuousness, continuum, dovetailing, durability, duration, endurance, extension, flow, interrelationship, linking, perpetuity, persistence, prolongation, protraction, sequence, stability, stamina, succession, survival, train, uniting, unity, vitality, whole; SEE CONCEPT 721

continuous [adj] constant, unending
connected, consecutive, continued, day and night*, endless, everlasting, extended, for ever and ever, interminable, looped, no end of*, no end to, on a treadmill*, perpetual, prolonged, regular, repeated, stable, steady, timeless, unbroken, unceasing, undivided, unfaltering, uninterrupted; SEE CONCEPTS 482,798

contort [v] disfigure, distort
bend, convolute, curve, deform, gnarl, knot, misshape, torture, twist, warp, wind, wrench, writhe; SEE CONCEPTS 147,184

contortion [n] distortion, mutilation
anamorphosis, crookedness, deformation, deformity, dislocation, grimace, malformation, misproportion, misshapement, pout, twist, ugliness, unsightliness, wryness; SEE CONCEPTS 436,580

contour [n] outline, profile
curve, delineation, figuration, figure, form, lineament, lines, relief, shape, silhouette; SEE CONCEPT 436

contraband [n] black-market production
bootlegging, counterfeiting, crime, dealing, goods*, moonshine*, piracy, plunder, poaching, rum-running*, smuggling, stuff, swag, theft, trafficking, violation, wetbacking*; SEE CONCEPTS 192,338

contraband [adj] black-market; unlawful
banned, bootleg, bootlegged, disapproved, excluded, forbidden, hot*, illegal, illicit, interdicted, prohibited, proscribed, shut out, smuggled, taboo, unauthorized, verboten; SEE CONCEPTS 319,545

contraceptive [n] birth control method
armor, barrier method, coil, condom, diaphragm, foam, hormone, intrauterine device, IUD, jelly, loop, pill, planned parenthood, preventative, preventive medicine, prophylactic, rhythm method, ring, rubber, safety, shield, spermicidal cream, sponge, vaginal suppository; SEE CONCEPTS 307,446

contract [n] agreement, deal
arrangement, bargain, bond, commission, commitment, compact, concordat, convention, covenant, deposition, dicker*, engagement, evidence, guarantee, handshake*, indenture, liability, mise, obligation, pact, paper, pledge, promise, proof, record, settlement, stipulation, treaty, understanding; SEE CONCEPTS 271,684

contract [v1] condense
abate, abbreviate, abridge, become smaller, clench, compress, confine, constrict, consume, curtail, decline, decrease, deflate, draw in, dwindle, ebb, edit, epitomize, evaporate, fall away, fall off, grow less, lessen, lose, narrow, omit, purse, recede, reduce, shrink, shrivel, subside, syncopate, take in, tighten, wane, waste, weaken, wither, wrinkle; SEE CONCEPTS 169,236,247

contract [v2] come to terms
accept offer, adjust, agree, arrange, assent, bargain, become indebted, bound, buy, circumscribe, clinch, close, come around, commit, consent,

covenant, dicker*, engage, enter into, firm a deal*, give one's word, go along with*, hammer out deal*, initial*, ink*, it's a deal*, limit, make terms, negotiate, obligate, owe, pact, pledge, promise, put in writing, set, settle, shake hands on it*, sign for, sign papers, sign up, stipulate, swear to, undertake, work out details*; SEE CONCEPTS 8,50,88

contract [v3] *catch disease*
acquire, afflict, be afflicted with, become infected with, be ill with, bring on, cause, come down with, decline, derange, develop, disorder, fall, fall victim to, get, go down with, incur, indispose, induce, obtain, sicken, sink, succumb to, take, take one's death, upset, weaken; SEE CONCEPTS 93,308

contraction [n] *drawing in; shortening*
abbreviating, abbreviation, abridging, abridgment, compression, condensation, condensing, confinement, confining, constriction, curtailing, curtailment, cutting down, decrease, decreasing, deflating, deflation, diminishing, diminution, drawing together, dwindling, elision, evaporating, evaporation, lessening, lopping, narrowing, omission, omitting, receding, recession, reducing, reduction, shrinkage, shrinking, shrivelling, tensing, tightening, withdrawal, withdrawing; SEE CONCEPTS 469,776

contradict [v] *be at variance with*
belie, buck, call in question*, challenge, confront, contravene, controvert, counter, counteract, cross, dare, deny, differ, disaffirm, disclaim, disprove, dispute, fly in the face of*, gainsay, have bone to pick*, impugn, negate, negative, oppose, refuse to accept, repudiate, take on, thumbs down*, traverse; SEE CONCEPTS 46,54,665

contradiction [n] *variance to something*
bucking, conflict, confutation, contravention, defiance, denial, difference, disagreement, discrepancy, dispute, dissension, gainsaying, incongruity, inconsistency, negation, opposite, opposition; SEE CONCEPTS 46,278,665

contradictory [adj] *antagonistic*
adverse, against, agin, anti, antipodal, antipodean, antithetic, antithetical, con, conflicting, contrary, converse, counter, counteractive, diametric, discrepant, incompatible, incongruous, inconsistent, irreconcilable, negating, no go*, nullifying, opposing, opposite, ornery*, paradoxical, polar, repugnant, reverse; SEE CONCEPT 542

contrary [adj] *antagonistic; opposite*
adverse, anti, antipathetic, antipodal, antipodean, antithetical, balky, clashing, conflicting, contradictory, contrariant, contumacious, converse, counter, diametric, discordant, dissentient, dissident, froward, headstrong, hostile, inconsistent, inimical, insubordinate, intractable, negative, nonconforming, nonconformist, obstinate, opposed, ornery*, paradoxical, perverse, rebellious, recalcitrant, recusant, refractory, restive, reverse, stubborn, unruly, wayward, wrongheaded; SEE CONCEPT 401

contrast [n] *difference*
adverse, antithesis, comparison, contradiction, contradistinction, contraposition, contrariety, converse, differentiation, disagreement, disparity, dissimilarity, dissimilitude, distinction, divergence, diversity, foil, heterogeneity, incompatibility, incongruousness, inconsistency, inequality,

inverse, oppositeness, opposition, reverse, unlikeness, variance, variation; SEE CONCEPTS 561,665

contrast [v] *compare, differ*
balance, be a foil to*, be contrary to, be dissimilar, be diverse, be unlike, be variable, bracket, collate, conflict, contradict, depart, deviate, differentiate, disagree, distinguish, diverge, hang, hold a candle to*, match up, mismatch, oppose, separate, set in opposition, set off, stack up against*, stand out, vary, weigh; SEE CONCEPTS 39,561,665

contravene [v] *go against, contradict*
abjure, breach, break, combat, conflict with, counteract, cross, defy, disaffirm, disobey, encroach, exclude, fight, gainsay, hinder, impugn, infract, infringe, interfere, interpose, intrude, negate, offend, oppose, overstep, refute, reject, repudiate, resist, spurn, thwart, transgress, traverse, trespass, violate; SEE CONCEPTS 46,106,121,192

contribute [v1] *donate, provide*
accord, add, afford, ante up, assign, bequeath, bequest, bestow, chip in, come through, commit, confer, devote, dispense, dole out*, dower, endow, enrich, furnish, give, give away, go Dutch*, grant, hand out, kick in*, pitch in*, pony up*, present, proffer, sacrifice, share, subscribe, subsidize, supply, sweeten the kitty*, tender, will; SEE CONCEPTS 108,140

contribute [v2] *be partly responsible for*
add to, advance, aid, assist, augment, be conducive, be instrumental, conduce, do one's bit*, finger in the pie*, fortify, get in the act*, have a hand in*, help, lead, put in two cents*, redound, reinforce, sit in on, strengthen, supplement, support, tend, uphold; SEE CONCEPTS 83,110,244

contribution [n] *gift, offering*
addition, a hand, alms, augmentation, benefaction, beneficence, bestowal, charity, donation, do one's part*, gifting, grant, handout, helping hand, improvement, increase, input, present, significant addition, subscription, supplement, write-off*; SEE CONCEPTS 337,340

contrite [adj] *regretful*
apologetic, attritional, chastened, compunctious, conscience-stricken, humble, penitent, penitential, remorseful, repentant, sorrowful, sorry; SEE CONCEPT 403

contrition [n] *regret*
attrition, compunction, contriteness, humiliation, penance, penitence, penitency, remorse, repentance, rue, ruth, self-reproach, sorrow; SEE CONCEPT 410

contrivance [n1] *plan, fabrication*
angle, artifice, brainchild, coinage, design, dodge, expedient, formation, gimmick, intrigue, invention, inventiveness, machination, measure, plot, project, ruse, scheme, slant, stratagem, switch, trick, twist; SEE CONCEPT 660

contrivance [n2] *gadget*
apparatus, appliance, brainchild, coinage, contraption, convenience, creation, device, discovery, engine, equipment, gear, gimcrack*, harness, implement, instrument, invention, machine, material, mechanism, tackle, thingamabob*, thingamajig*, tool, utensil, whatsis*, widget*; SEE CONCEPTS 260,463,499

contrive [v1] *invent, design*
come up with, concoct, construct, cook up, create, devise, dream up*, engineer, fabricate, fashion, forge, form, formulate, frame*, handle,

hatch, improvise, make, make up*, manipulate, manufacture, move, plan, plot, project, rig*, scheme, throw together*, trump up*, vamp, wangle, whip up*; SEE CONCEPTS 36,173

contrive [v2] *bring about, succeed with difficulty*
achieve, angle, arrange, carry out, cogitate, collude, compass, concoct, connive, develop, devise, effect, elaborate, engineer, execute, finagle*, hatch, hit upon, intrigue, jockey*, machinate, manage, maneuver, manipulate, mastermind, negotiate, pass, plan, play games*, plot, project, scheme, shift, swing, work out, wrangle; SEE CONCEPTS 36,91,94

control [n] *command, mastery*
ascendancy, authority, bridle, charge, check, clout, containment, curb, determination, direction, discipline, domination, dominion, driver's seat*, force, government, guidance, inside track, juice, jurisdiction, limitation, management, manipulation, might, oversight, predomination, qualification, regimentation, regulation, restraint, restriction, ropes, rule, strings*, subjection, subordination, superintendence, supervision, supremacy, sway, upper hand*, weight, wire pulling*; SEE CONCEPT 376

control [v1] *have charge of*
administer, administrate, advise, be in saddle*, boss, bully, call, call the signals*, command, conduct, deal with, direct, discipline, dominate, domineer, govern, guide, handle, head, head up*, hold purse strings*, hold sway over*, hold the reins*, instruct, lead, manage, manipulate, overlook, oversee, pilot, predominate, push buttons*, quarterback*, regiment, regulate, reign over, rule, run*, run the show*, run things*, steer, subject, subjugate, superintend, supervise; SEE CONCEPT 117

control [v2] *curb, hold back*
adjust, awe, bridle, check, collect, compose, constrain, contain, cool, corner, cow, limit, monopolize, quell, regulate, rein in, repress, restrain, simmer down*, smother, subdue; SEE CONCEPT 130

controversial [adj] *at issue*
arguable, argumentative, contended, contentious, contestable, controvertible, debateable, disputable, disputatious, disputed, doubtable, doubtful, dubious, dubitable, in dispute, litigious, moot, open to discussion*, open to question*, polemical, questionable, suspect, uncertain, under discussion; SEE CONCEPTS 535,546

controversy [n] *debate, dispute*
altercation, argument, beef*, bickering, brush, contention, difference, discussion, disputation, dissension, embroilment, falling-out*, flak, fuss, hurrah, miff, polemic, quarrel, row, rumpus, scene, scrap, squabble, strife, tiff*, words, wrangle, wrangling; SEE CONCEPTS 46,278,665

controvert [v] *oppose, argue*
break, challenge, confound, confute, contest, contradict, counter, debate, deny, disconfirm, discuss, disprove, dispute, oppugn, question, rebut, refute, wrangle; SEE CONCEPTS 21,46

contumacious [adj] *headstrong, obstinate*
alienated, contrary, disaffected, estranged, factious, froward, haughty, inflexible, insubordinate, insurgent, intractable, intransigent, irreconcilable, mutinous, obdurate, perverse, pig-headed, rebellious, recalcitrant, refractory, seditious, stubborn, unyielding; SEE CONCEPT 401

contusion [n] *bruise, injury*
bang, bump, cut, discoloration, knock, mouse, swelling, wale, wound; SEE CONCEPT 309

conundrum [n] *puzzle*
brain-teaser, closed book*, enigma, mystery, mystification, poser*, problem, puzzlement, riddle, why*; SEE CONCEPTS 532,666,690

convalescent [adj] *improving, recuperating*
ambulatory, discharged, dismissed, gaining strength, getting better, getting over something*, getting well, healing, mending, on the mend*, past crisis, perked up*, rallying, recovering, rejuvenated, rejuvenating, released, restored, strengthening; SEE CONCEPT 314

convene [v] *bring together; meet*
assemble, call, call in, collect, come together, congregate, convoke, corral, gather, get together, hold meeting, muster, open, rally, round up, scare up*, sit, summon, unite; SEE CONCEPTS 60,114,324

convenience [n1] *availability, usefulness; useful thing*
accessibility, accessory, accommodation, advancement, advantage, agreeableness, aid, amenity, appliance, appropriateness, assistance, avail, benefit, comfort, comforts, contribution, cooperation, decency, ease, enjoyment, facility, fitness, furtherance, handiness, help, life, luxury, means, ministration, ministry, openness, opportuneness, promotion, receptiveness, relief, satisfaction, service, serviceability, succor, suitability, suitableness, support, time saver, use, utility; SEE CONCEPTS 658,712

convenience [n2] *spare time*
chance, freedom, hour, leisure, liberty, occasion, one's own sweet time*, opportunity, place, preference, spare moment*, suitable time, whenever; SEE CONCEPT 807

convenient [adj1] *appropriate, useful*
acceptable, accommodating, adaptable, adapted, advantageous, agreeable, aiding, assisting, available, beneficial, comfortable, commodious, conducive, contributive, decent, favorable, fit, fitted, good, handy, helpful, in public interest, opportune, proper, ready, roomy, seasonable, serviceable, suitable, suited, timely, time-saving, user-friendly*, well-planned*; SEE CONCEPT 560

convenient [adj2] *nearby*
accessible, adjacent, adjoining, all around, at elbows*, at fingertips*, at hand, available, central, close, close at hand, close-by, contiguous, easy to reach, handy, immediate, in neighborhood, next, next door, nigh, on deck*, on tap*, under one's nose*, within reach; SEE CONCEPT 586

convent [n] *nunnery*
abbey, cloister, monastery, religious community, retreat, school; SEE CONCEPTS 368,516

convention [n1] *conference*
assemblage, assembly, clambake, confab*, congress, convocation, council, delegates, delegation, get together, meet*, meeting, members, powwow*, rally, representatives, show; SEE CONCEPTS 114,324,417

convention [n2] *practice, tradition*
canon, code, covenance, custom, etiquette, fashion, form, formality, habit, law, percept, precept, propriety, rule, understanding, usage; SEE CONCEPT 688

convention [n3] *agreement*
bargain, bond, compact, concord, concordat, con-

CO
CO

tract, covenant, pact, protocol, stipulation, transaction, treaty; SEE CONCEPTS *271,684*

conventional [*adj1*] *common, normal*
accepted, accustomed, button-down, commonplace, correct, current, customary, decorous, everyday, expected, fashionable, formal, general, habitual, in established usage, ordinary, orthodox, plain, popular, predominant, prevailing, prevalent, proper, regular, ritual, routine, square, standard, stereotyped, straight, traditional, tralatitious, typical, usual, well-known, wonted; SEE CONCEPTS *530,547*

conventional [*adj2*] *unoriginal*
bigoted, bourgeois, commonplace, conforming, conservative, demure, doctrinal, dogmatic, drippy, hackneyed, hidebound, humdrum, illiberal, inflexible, in rut, insular, isolationist, lame, literal, moderate, moral, narrow, narrow-minded, not heretical, obstinate, parochial, pedestrian, prosaic, puritanical, rigid, routine, rube*, run-of-the-mill, sober, solemn, square, stereotyped, straight, straight-laced, strict, stuffy, uptight; SEE CONCEPT *550*

converge [*v*] *gather*
assemble, coincide, combine, come together, concenter, concentrate, concur, encounter, enter in, focalize, focus, join, meet, merge, mingle, rally, unite; SEE CONCEPTS *113,114*

conversant [*adj*] *experienced, familiar with*
abreast, acquainted, alive, apprehensive, au courant, au fait, aware, cognizant, comprehending, conscious, cool*, down with*, hep*, hip*, informed, into, kept posted, knowing, knowledgeable, learned, on the beam*, perceptive, percipient, plugged in*, practiced, proficient, sensible, sentient, skilled, up*, up-to-date, versant, versed, well-informed, witting; SEE CONCEPT *402*

conversation [*n*] *dialogue, discourse*
chat, colloquy, comment, communication, communion, confab*, confabulation, conference, consultation, converse, debate, discussion, exchange, expression, gab*, gossip, hearing, intercourse, jive*, observation, palaver, parley, pillow talk*, powwow*, questioning, remark, repartee, speech, talk, talkfest*, tête-à-tête*, ventilation*, visit, yak*; SEE CONCEPT *266*

converse [*n*] *opposite*
antipode, antipole, antithesis, contra, contrary, counter, counterpole, inverse, obverse, other side, reverse; SEE CONCEPT *665*

converse [*adj*] *opposite*
antipodal, antipodean, antithetical, contradictory, contrary, counter, counterpole, different, reverse, reversed, transposed; SEE CONCEPT *564*

converse [*v*] *talk*
chat, chew the fat*, chitchat*, commune, confer, discourse, exchange, gab*, parley, rap*, schmooze*, speak, use, yak*; SEE CONCEPT *266*

conversion [*n*] *change, adaptation*
about-face*, alteration, born again*, change of heart*, changeover, exchange, flip-flop*, flux, growth, innovation, metamorphosis, metanoia, metasis, modification, novelty, passage, passing, permutation, progress, proselytization, qualification, reclamation, reconstruction, reformation, regeneration, remodelling, reorganization, resolution, resolving, reversal, see the light*, switch, transfiguration, transformation, translation, transmogrification, transmutation, turning, turning around; SEE CONCEPTS *232,701*

convert [*n*] *new believer*
catechumen, disciple, follower, neophyte, novice, novitiate, proselyte; SEE CONCEPT *361*

convert [*v1*] *change; adapt*
alter, apply, appropriate, commute, downlink, download, interchange, make, metamorphose, modify, remodel, reorganize, restyle, revise, switch, switch over, transfigure, transform, translate, transmogrify, transmute, transpose, turn; SEE CONCEPTS *232,701*

convert [*v2*] *change belief, especially regarding religion*
actuate, alter conviction, assimilate to, baptize, be born again*, bend, bias, brainwash, bring, bring around, budge, cause to adopt, change into, change of heart*, convince, create anew, impel, incline, lead, lead to believe, make over, move, persuade, proselyte, proselytize, redeem, reform, regenerate, save, see the light*, sway, turn; SEE CONCEPTS *12,14,35*

convex [*adj*] *rounded, curving outward*
arched, bent, biconvex, bulged, bulging, bulgy, gibbous, outcurved, protuberant, raised; SEE CONCEPT *486*

convey [*v1*] *transport*
back, bear, bring, carry, channel, conduct, dispatch, ferry, fetch, forward, funnel, grant, guide, hump, lead, lug, move, pack, pipe, ride, schlepp*, send, shoulder, siphon, support, tote, traject, transfer, transmit, truck; SEE CONCEPTS *187,217*

convey [*v2*] *express message*
break, carry, communicate, conduct, disclose, impart, make known, pass on, project, put across, relate, reveal, send, tell, transmit; SEE CONCEPT *60*

conveyance [*n*] *transport*
car, carriage, carrying, communication, machine, movement, transfer, transference, transmission, transportation, vehicle; SEE CONCEPTS *143,501, 503*

convict [*n*] *criminal*
captive, con, culprit, felon, jailbird*, long-termer*, loser*, malefactor, prisoner, repeater*; SEE CONCEPT *412*

convict [*v*] *find guilty*
adjudge, attaint, bring to justice, condemn, declare guilty, doom, frame, imprison, pass sentence on, pronounce guilty, put away, put the screws to*, rap*, send up*, send up the river*, sentence, throw the book at*; SEE CONCEPTS *18,317*

conviction [*n1*] *belief, opinion*
confidence, creed, doctrine, dogma, eye, faith, feeling, judgment call, mind, persuasion, principle, reliance, say so*, sentiment, slant, tenet, view; SEE CONCEPT *689*

conviction [*n2*] *guilty sentence; assurance*
assuredness, certainty, certitude, condemnation, condemning, confidence, determining guilt, earnestness, fall, fervor, firmness, rap, reliance, sureness, surety, unfavorable verdict; SEE CONCEPTS *317,410*

convince [*v*] *gain the confidence of*
argue into, assure, brainwash, bring around, bring home to*, bring to reason*, change, demonstrate, draw, effect, establish, get, hook*, induce, make a believer*, overcome, persuade, prevail upon, prompt, prove, put across, refute, satisfy, sell*, sell one on*, sway, talk into, turn, twist one's arm*, win over; SEE CONCEPT *68*

convincing [adj] *persuasive*

acceptable, authentic, believeable, cogent, conclusive, credible, dependable, faithful, hopeful, impressive, incontrovertible, likely, moving, plausible, possible, powerful, presumable, probable, rational, reasonable, reliable, satisfactory, satisfying, solid, sound, swaying, telling, trustworthy, trusty, valid; SEE CONCEPTS 267,537,552

convivial [adj] *fun-loving*

back-slapping*, cheerful, clubby*, companionable, conversible, entertaining, festal, festive, friendly, gay, genial, glad-handering*, happy, hearty, hilarious, holiday, jocund, jolly, jovial, lively, merry, mirthful, pleasant, sociable, vivacious; SEE CONCEPTS 401,404

convocation [n] *assembly*

assemblage, conclave, concourse, confab*, conference, congregation, congress, convention, council, diet, get-together, meet, meeting, powwow*, synod, turnout; SEE CONCEPT 114

convolution [n] *loop, spiral*

coil, coiling, complexity, contortion, curlicue, flexing, gyration, helix, intricacy, involution, serpentine, sinuosity, sinuousness, snaking, swirl, tortuousness, twist, undulation, winding; SEE CONCEPT 436

convoy [n] *guard, escort*

attendance, attendant, companion, protection; SEE CONCEPT 423

convoy [v] *protect, escort*

accompany, attend, bear, bring, chaperon, companion, company, conduct, consort, defend, guard, pilot, safeguard, shepherd, shield, usher, watch; SEE CONCEPTS 96,110

convulsion [n1] *muscle spasm*

algospasm, attack, contortion, contraction, cramp, epilepsy, fit, paroxysm, seizure, throe, tremor; SEE CONCEPT 308

convulsion [n2] *disturbance*

agitation, cataclysm, clamor, commotion, disaster, ferment, furor, outcry, quaking, rocking, seism, shaking, shock, tottering, trembling, tumult, turbulence, upheaval, upturn; SEE CONCEPTS 152,748

cook [n] *person who prepares food*

baker, chef, hash slinger*, mess sergeant, servant, sous chef; SEE CONCEPT 348

cook [v] *prepare food, usually using heat*

bake, barbecue, blanch, boil, braise, brew, broil, brown, burn, coddle, curry, decoct, deep fry, devil, doctor*, escallop, fix, French fry, fricassee, fry, griddle, grill, heat, imbue, melt, microwave, mull, nuke*, panfry, parboil, parch, percolate, poach, pressure-cook, reduce, roast, ruin*, sauté, scald, scorch, sear, seethe, simmer, sizzle, spoil*, steam, steep, stew, toast, warm up; SEE CONCEPT 170

cook up [v] *devise*

arrange, concoct, contrive, dream up, fabricate, falsify, formulate, frame, hatch, improvise, invent, make up, plan, plot, prepare, scheme, vamp; SEE CONCEPTS 17,36

cool [adj1] *cold, nippy*

air-conditioned, algid, arctic, biting, chill, chilled, chilling, chilly, coldish, frigid, frore, frosty, gelid, hawkish, nipping, refreshing, refrigerated, shivery, snappy, wintry; SEE CONCEPT 605

cool [adj2] *calm, collected*

assured, composed, coolheaded, deliberate, detached, dispassionate, impassive, imperturbable, levelheaded, nonchalant, philosophical, phlegmatic, placid, quiet, relaxed, self-controlled, self-possessed, serene, stolid, together, tranquil, unagitated, unemotional, unexcited, unflappable, unruffled; SEE CONCEPT 401

cool [adj3] *aloof, disapproving*

annoyed, apathetic, distant, frigid, impertinent, impudent, incurious, indifferent, insolent, lukewarm, offended, offhand, offish, procacious, reserved, solitary, standoffish, unapproachable, uncommunicative, unenthusiastic, unfriendly, uninterested, unresponsive, unsociable, unwelcoming, withdrawn; SEE CONCEPT 404

cool [adj4] *excellent*

boss*, dandy, divine, glorious, hunky-dory*, keen, marvelous, neat, nifty, sensational, swell; SEE CONCEPT 572

cool [v1] *chill*

abate, air-condition, air-cool, ally, calm, freeze, frost, infrigidate, lessen, lose heat, mitigate, moderate, reduce, refrigerate, temper; SEE CONCEPT 255

cool [v2] *take a break; abate*

allay, assuage, calm, calm down, chill, compose, control, dampen, lessen, mitigate, moderate, quiet, reduce, rein, repress, restrain, simmer down, suppress, temper; SEE CONCEPTS 240,384

cooperate [v] *aid, assist*

abet, advance, agree, back up, band, befriend, be in cahoots*, chip in, coadjute, coincide, collaborate, combine, comply with, concert, concur, conduce, conspire, contribute, coordinate, espouse, forward, further, go along with, help, join forces, join in, league*, lend a hand*, participate, partner, pitch in*, play ball*, pool resources, pull together, second, share in, show willingness, side with, stick together, succor, take part, unite, uphold, work side by side, work together; SEE CONCEPTS 110,112

cooperation [n] *mutual effort*

aid, alliance, assistance, cahoots*, coaction, coadjuvancy, coalition, collaboration, combination, combined effort, communion, company, concert, concurrence, confederacy, confederation, confunction, conspiracy, doing business with, esprit de corps, federation, fusion, give-and-take, harmony, help, helpfulness, logrolling*, participation, partisanship, partnership, playing ball*, reciprocity, responsiveness, service, society, symbiosis, synergism, synergy, teaming, teamwork, unanimity, union, unity; SEE CONCEPTS 110,112,388,677

cooperative [adj1] *joint, unified*

agreeing, coacting, coactive, coadjuvant, coefficient, collaborating, collaborative, collective, collegial, collusive, combined, combining, common, concerted, concurring, coordinated, hand in glove*, harmonious, in league, interdependent, joining, participating, reciprocal, shared, symbiotic, synergetic, synergic, team, united, uniting; SEE CONCEPT 538

cooperative [adj2] *helpful*

accommodating, companionable, obliging, responsive, sociable, supportive, useful; SEE CONCEPTS 538,555

co-opt [v] *to assimilate in order to take over or appropriate*

absorb, accept, admit, adopt, bring in, bring into line, bring into the fold, connaturalize, convert, draw in, elect, embrace, encompass, enfold, homogenize, homologize, include, incorporate, make one's own, take in, take over; SEE CONCEPTS 232,701

coordinate [*adj*] *equivalent*
alike, coequal, correlative, correspondent, counterpart, equal, equalized, like, parallel, same, tantamount; SEE CONCEPT 566

coordinate [*v*] *match, relate*
accommodate, adjust, agree, atune, combine, conduce, conform, correlate, get it together*, get one's act together*, harmonize, integrate, mesh, organize, pool, proportion, pull together, quarterback*, reconcile, reconciliate, regulate, shape up, synchronize, systematize, team up; SEE CONCEPTS 36,84,158

cope [*v*] *manage, contend*
battle with, buffet, carry on, confront, deal, dispatch, encounter, endure, face, get a handle on*, get by, grapple, hack*, hack it*, handle, hold one's own*, live with, make go of it*, make it*, make out*, make the grade*, pit oneself against*, rise to occasion, struggle, struggle through, suffer, survive, tangle, tussle, weather, wrestle; SEE CONCEPTS 23,35

copious [*adj*] *abundant*
alive with, a mess of*, ample, aplenty, bounteous, bountiful, coming out of ears*, crawling with*, extensive, exuberant, full, galore, generous, heavy, lavish, liberal, lush, luxuriant, no end*, overflowing, plenteous, plentiful, plenty, profuse, prolix, replete, rich, superabundant, thick with, verbose, wordy; SEE CONCEPT 771

copiousness [*n*] *abundance*
affluence, amplitude, bountifulness, bounty, cornucopia, exuberance, fullness, horn of plenty*, lavishness, luxuriance, plentifulness, plenty, richness, superabundance; SEE CONCEPT 767

cop out [*v*] *abandon, quit*
back down, back off, back out, backpedal, desert, dodge, excuse, give the slip*, have alibi, rationalize, renege, renounce, revoke, skip, use pretext, welsh, withdraw; SEE CONCEPTS 121,156

copulate [*v*] *have sexual relations*
be carnal, bed, breed, cohabit, conjugate, couple, do it*, fool around*, fornicate, go all the way*, go to bed*, have coition, have relations, have sex, lay*, lie with, make it*, make love, make out*, mate, sleep together, sleep with, unite; SEE CONCEPT 375

copy [*n*] *duplicate, imitation*
archetype, carbon, carbon copy*, cast, clone, counterfeit, counterpart, ditto*, ectype, effigy, ersatz, facsimile, forgery, hard copy, image, impersonation, impression, imprint, likeness, microfiche, mimeograph, miniature, mirror, model, offprint, parallel, pattern, photocopy, photograph, photostat, portrait, print, reflection, replica, replication, representation, reprint, reproduction, rubbings, similarity, simulacrum, simulation, study, tracing, transcript, transcription, type, Xerox*; SEE CONCEPTS 269,667,716

copy [*v1*] *duplicate*
carbon, cartoon, clone, counterfeit, delineate, depict, ditto, draw, dupe, engrave, engross, fake, forge, imitate, knock off*, limn, manifold, mimeo, mirror, mold, paint, paraphrase, photocopy, photostat, picture, plagiarize, portray, reduplicate, reflect, repeat, replicate, represent, reproduce, rewrite, sculpture, simulate, sketch, stat, trace, transcribe, Xerox*; SEE CONCEPT 171

copy [*v2*] *imitate*
act like, ape, burlesque, do, do a take-off*, do like*, echo, embody, emulate, epitomize, fake, follow, follow example, follow suit, go like*, illustrate, incarnate, knock off*, make like*, mimic, mirror, mock, model, parody, parrot, personify, phony, pirate, play a role, prefigure, repeat, sham, simulate, steal, take leaf out of book*, take off*, travesty, typify; SEE CONCEPTS 59,139,242

coquet [*v*] *tease*
dally, flirt, fool, gold-dig*, lead on, make eyes at*, operate, philander, string along, titillate, toy, trifle, vamp, wanton, wink at*; SEE CONCEPTS 375,384

cord [*n*] *rope*
bond, connection, cordage, fiber, line, link, string, tendon, tie, twine; SEE CONCEPTS 470,680

cordial [*adj*] *friendly, sociable*
affable, affectionate, agreeable, amicable, buddy-buddy*, cheerful, clubby, companionable, congenial, convivial, cozy, earnest, genial, glowing, gracious, happy, heartfelt, heart-to-heart, hearty, invigorating, jovial, mellow, neighborly, palsy-walsy*, polite, red-carpet*, responsive, sincere, social, sympathetic, tender, warm, warmhearted, welcoming, wholehearted; SEE CONCEPT 401

cordiality [*n*] *friendliness, sociability*
affability, agreeability, agreeableness, amenity, amiability, approbation, approval, earnestness, enjoyableness, favor, geniality, gratefulness, heartiness, mutuality, pleasantness, reciprocity, responsiveness, sincerity, sweetness and light*, sympathy, understanding, warmth, wholeheartedness; SEE CONCEPT 633

core [*n*] *center, gist*
amount, base, basis, body, bottom line, bulk, burden, consequence, corpus, crux, essence, focus, foundation, heart, import, importance, kernel, main idea, mass, meat*, meat and potatoes*, middle, midpoint, midst, nitty gritty*, nub, nucleus, origin, pith, pivot, purport, quick, root, significance, staple, substance, thrust, upshot; SEE CONCEPTS 442,668,826

corner [*n1*] *angle*
bend, branch, cloverleaf, crook, crossing, edge, fork, intersection, joint, junction, projection, ridge, rim, shift, V*, veer, Y*; SEE CONCEPTS 436,484,513

corner [*n2*] *niche*
angle, cavity, compartment, cranny, hideaway, hide-out, hole, indentation, nook, recess, retreat; SEE CONCEPTS 440,471,513

corner [*n3*] *predicament*
box, difficulty, dilemma, distress, fix, hole, impasse, impediment, jam, knot, pickle, plight, scrape, tight spot; SEE CONCEPTS 674,675

corner [*v*] *trap*
bottle, bring to bay, capture, catch, collar*, fool, get on ropes*, have up a tree*, mousetrap*, nab, put out, seize, tree, trick, trouble; SEE CONCEPTS 59,90

corny [*adj*] *trite, clichéd*
banal, commonplace, dull, feeble, hackneyed, mawkish, melodramatic, old-fashioned, old hat*, sentimental, shopworn, stale, stereotyped, stupid, tired, warmed-over; SEE CONCEPT 550

corollary [*n*] *conclusion, deduction*
aftereffect, analogy, consequence, culmination, effect, end, end product, induction, inference, is-

sue, precipitate, result, sequel, sequence, upshot;
SEE CONCEPTS 230,410,529

corporal [adj] bodily, physical
anatomical, carnal, corporeal, fleshly, fleshy,
gross, human, material, objective, phenomenal,
sensible, somatic, substantial, tangible; SEE CON-
CEPT 542

corporation [n] business organization, usually
large
association, bunch, business, clan, company, corporate body, crew, crowd, enterprise, gang, hookup*, jungle*, legal entity, megacorp*, mob,
multinational, octopus*, outfit, partnership, ring,
shell, society, syndicate, zoo*; SEE CONCEPT 325

corporeal [adj] bodily, physical
anatomical, carnal, corporal, fleshly, fleshy, human, material, mortal, objective, phenomenal,
sensible, somatic, substantial, tangible; SEE CON-
CEPT 542

corps [n] group trained for action
band, body, brigade, company, contingent, crew,
detachment, division, outfit, party, posse, regiment, squad, squadron, team, troop, troupe; unit;
SEE CONCEPTS 294,322,417

corpse [n] dead body
body, bones*, cadaver, carcass, carrion, deceased, departed, mort*, remains, stiff*; SEE
CONCEPTS 390,417

corpulent [adj] fat, chubby
baby elephant*, beefy*, blimp*, bulky, burly,
embonpoint, fat, fleshy, gross, having a bay window*, having a spare tire*, heavy, hefty, husky,
large, lusty, obese, overblown, overweight,
plump, portly, roly-poly*, rotund, stout, tubby,
weighty, well-padded*; SEE CONCEPTS 406,491,
773

corpus [n] body of text
bulk, collection, compilation, complete works,
core, entirety, extant works, mass, oeuvre, opera
omnia, staple, substance, whole; SEE CONCEPT
271

correct [adj1] accurate, exact
according to Hoyle*, actual, amen*, appropriate,
cooking with gas*, dead on*, equitable, factual,
faithful, faultless, flawless, for sure, free of error,
impeccable, just, legitimate, nice, okay, on target*, on the ball*, on the beam*, on the button*,
on the money*, on the nose*, on track*, perfect,
precise, proper, regular, right, right as rain*, righteous, right on*, right stuff*, rigorous, stone,
strict, true, undistorted, unmistaken, veracious,
veridical; SEE CONCEPTS 542,557,574

correct [adj2] proper, appropriate
acceptable, becoming, careful, comme il faut,
conforming, conventional, decent, decorous, diplomatic, done, fitting, meticulous, nice, okay,
punctilious, right, right stuff*, scrupulous,
seemly, standard, suitable; SEE CONCEPTS
401,558

correct [v1] fix, adjust
alter, ameliorate, amend, better, change, clean up,
clean up act*, cure, debug*, doctor*, do over,
edit, emend, fiddle with, fix up, get with it*, go
over, help, improve, launder, make over, make
right, make up for, mend, pay dues*, pick up,
polish, put in order, reclaim, reconstruct, rectify,
redress, reform, regulate, remedy, remodel, reorganize, repair, retouch, review, revise, right,
scrub*, set right, set straight, shape up, straighten

out, touch up, turn around, upgrade; SEE CON-
CEPT 126

correct [v2] discipline, chastise
administer, admonish, castigate, chasten, chide,
penalize, punish, reprimand, reprove; SEE CON-
CEPTS 52,122

correction [n1] adjustment; fixing
alteration, amelioration, amending, amendment,
changing, editing, emendation, improvement, indemnification, mending, modification, rectification, redress, reexamination, remodeling, repair,
reparation, rereading, revisal, revising, righting;
SEE CONCEPTS 126,700

correction [n2] discipline
admonition, castigation, chastisement, punishment, punition, reformation, reproof, rod; SEE
CONCEPT 122

corrective [adj] healing, curing
antidotal, counteracting, curative, disciplinary,
palliative, penal, punitive, reformatory, rehabili-
tative, remedial, restorative, therapeutic; SEE
CONCEPT 537

correctly [adv] right
accurately, befittingly, decently, decorously, fitly,
fittingly, justly, nicely, perfectly, precisely, properly, rightly, to a T*, well; SEE CONCEPT 558

correctness [n1] accuracy
definiteness, definitiveness, definitude, exactitude, exactness, faultlessness, fidelity, preciseness, precision, regularity, truth; SEE CONCEPTS
638,654

correctness [n2] propriety
bon ton, civility, correctitude, decency, decorousness, decorum, fitness, good breeding, order, orderliness, properness, rightness, seemliness; SEE
CONCEPTS 633,656

correlate [v] equate, compare
associate, be on same wavelength*, connect, coordinate, correspond, have good vibes*, interact,
parallel, relate mutually, tie in*, tune in on*; SEE
CONCEPT 39

correlation [n] equating, equivalence
alternation, analogue, complement, correspondence, correspondent, counterpart, interaction, interchange, interconnection, interdependence,
interrelation, interrelationship, match, parallel,
pendant, reciprocity, relationship; SEE CONCEPTS
388,667

correspond [v1] agree, complement
accord, amount, approach, assimilate, be consistent, be identical to, be similar to, coincide, compare, conform, correlate, dovetail, equal, fit,
harmonize, lip sync, match, partake of, reciprocate, resemble, rival, square, tally, touch; SEE
CONCEPT 664

correspond [v2] communicate in writing
answer, drop a kite*, drop a line*, drop a note*,
epistolize, exchange letters, have pen pal, hear
from, keep in touch, pen, put pen to paper*, reply, scribble, send letter, send word, write; SEE
CONCEPTS 79,266

correspondence [n1] agreement
accord, analogy, coherence, coincidence, comparability, comparison, concurrence, conformity,
congruity, consistency, correlation, conformity,
fitness, harmony, likeness, match, regularity, relation, resemblance, similarity, symmetry; SEE
CONCEPT 664

CO
CO

correspondence [n2] *communication by writing*
exchange of letters, letters, mail, messages, post, reports, writing; SEE CONCEPTS 79,277,278

correspondent [n] *person communicating in writing*
contributor, epistler, epistolarian, freelancer, gazetteer, journalist, letter writer, pen pal, reporter, stringer*, writer; SEE CONCEPTS 348,423

corresponding [adj] *equivalent, matching*
agnate, akin, alike, analogous, answering, comparable, complementary, consonant, correlative, correspondent, coterminus, identical, interrelated, kin, kindred, like, parallel, reciprocal, similar, synonymous, undifferentiated; SEE CONCEPT 566

corridor [n] *hallway*
aisle, couloir, entrance hall, entranceway, foyer, hall, ingress, lobby, passage, passageway; SEE CONCEPT 440

corroborate [v] *back up information, story*
approve, authenticate, bear out, certify, check on, check out, check up, confirm, declare true, document, double check, endorse, establish, give nod*, justify, okay, prove, ratify, rubber-stamp*, strengthen, substantiate, support, sustain, validate, verify; SEE CONCEPTS 49,57

corrode [v] *wear away; eat away*
bite, canker, consume, corrupt, destroy, deteriorate, erode, gnaw, impair, oxidize, rot, rust, scour, waste; SEE CONCEPTS 156,169,186,250

corrosive [adj] *consuming, wearing; bitter*
acerb, acerbic, acrid, biting, caustic, corroding, cutting, destructive, erosive, incisive, sarcastic, strongly acid, trenchant, venomous, virulent, wasting; SEE CONCEPT 537

corrugated [adj] *ridged, grooved*
channelled, creased, crinkled, crumpled, flexed, fluted, folded, furrowed, puckered, roughened, rumpled, wrinkled; SEE CONCEPTS 485,606

corrupt [adj1] *dishonest*
base, bent, bribable, crooked, debauched, double-dealing, exploiting, extortionate, faithless, fast and loose*, fixed, foul, fraudulent, gone to the dogs*, inconstant, iniquitous, knavish, mercenary, nefarious, on the take*, open, padded*, perfidious, praetorian, profiteering, racket up*, reprobate, rotten, shady, snide, suborned, tainted, treacherous, two-faced, underhanded, unethical, unfaithful, unprincipled, unscrupulous, untrustworthy, venal, wide open*; SEE CONCEPT 545

corrupt [adj2] *debased, vicious*
abandoned, abased, baneful, boorish, degenerate, degraded, deleterious, depraved, dishonored, dissolute, evil, flagitious, infamous, loose, low, miscreant, monstrous, nefarious, perverse, profligate, rotten, villainous; SEE CONCEPTS 401,545

corrupt [adj3] *adulterated, rotten*
altered, contaminated, decayed, defiled, distorted, doctored, falsified, foul, infected, noxious, polluted, putrescent, putrid, tainted; SEE CONCEPTS 485,613

corrupt [v] *pervert; pollute*
abase, abuse, adulterate, animalize, bastardize, blemish, blight, bribe, contaminate, damage, debase, debauch, decay, decompose, deface, defile, deform, degrade, demean, demoralize, deprave, depreciate, despoil, disfigure, disgrace, dishonor, fix, grease palm*, harm, hurt, ill-treat, impair, infect, injure, lower, lure, maltreat, mar, mistreat, misuse, outrage, pull down, putrefy, ravage, reduce, rot, ruin, spoil, square, stain, suborn, sub-

vert, taint, undermine, violate, vitiate, warp, waste; SEE CONCEPTS 14,240

corruption [n1] *dishonesty*
breach of trust, bribery, bribing, crime, crookedness, demoralization, exploitation, extortion, fiddling, fraud, fraudulency, graft, jobbery, malfeasance, misrepresentation, nepotism, on the take*, payoff, payola*, profiteering, racket*, shadiness*, shady deal*, shuffle, skimming, squeeze*, unscrupulousness, venality; SEE CONCEPT 645

corruption [n2] *baseness*
atrocity, decadence, degeneration, degradation, depravity, evil, immorality, impurity, infamy, iniquity, looseness, lubricity, perversion, pravity, sinfulness, turpitude, vice, viciousness, vulgarity, wickedness; SEE CONCEPTS 633,645

corruption [n3] *adulteration*
debasement, decay, defilement, distortion, doctoring, falsification, foulness, infection, noxiousness, pollution, putrefaction, putrescence, rot, rottenness; SEE CONCEPT 723

cosmetic [adj] *beautifying; relating to appearance*
corrective, gooky*, improving, makeup, nonessential, painted, remedial, restorative, superficial, surface, touching-up; SEE CONCEPT 579

cosmic [adj] *limitless; universal*
catholic, cosmogonal, cosmogonic, cosmopolitan, ecumenical, empyrean, global, grandiose, huge, immense, infinite, measureless, planetary, vast, worldwide; SEE CONCEPT 772

cosmopolitan [adj] *worldly-wise*
catholic, cultivated, cultured, ecumenical, global, gregarious, metropolitan, planetary, polished, public, smooth, sophisticated, universal, urbane, well-travelled, worldly, worldwide; SEE CONCEPT 589

cosmos [n1] *universe*
creation, galaxy, macrocosm, macrocosmos, megacosm, nature, solar system, star system, world; SEE CONCEPTS 511,770

cosmos [n2] *ordered system*
harmony, order, organization, scheme, structure; SEE CONCEPTS 727,770

cost [n1] *expense; price paid*
amount, arm and a leg*, bad news*, bite*, bottom dollar*, bottom line*, charge, damage*, disbursement, dues, expenditure, figure, line, nick*, nut*, outlay, payment, price, price tag, rate, score*, setback*, squeeze*, tab, tariff, ticket, toll, top dollar*, value, worth; SEE CONCEPTS 328,336

cost [n2] *penalty, sacrifice*
damage, deprivation, detriment, expense, forfeit, forfeiture, harm, hurt, injury, loss, suffering; SEE CONCEPTS 676,679

cost [v1] *command a price of*
amount to, be asked, be demanded, be given, be marked at, be needed, be paid, be priced at, be received, be valued at, be worth, bring in, come to, mount up, move back, nick*, rap*, require, sell at, sell for, set back, set back, take, to the tune of*, yield; SEE CONCEPTS 328,336

cost [v2] *harm; exact a penalty*
do disservice to, expect, hurt, infuriate, lose, necessitate, obligate, require; SEE CONCEPT 246

costly [adj] *expensive*
an arm and leg*, cher*, dear, excessive, executive, exorbitant, extortionate, extravagant, fancy, high, highly priced, high-priced, inordinate, pre-

CO
CO

cious, premium, pricey, steep, stiff*, top, valuable; SEE CONCEPT 334

costly [adj2] *priceless*
gorgeous, inestimable, invaluable, lavish, luxurious, opulent, precious, rich, splendid, sumptuous, valuable; SEE CONCEPT 567

costly [adj3] *harmful, damaging*
catastrophic, deleterious, disastrous, loss-making, ruinous, sacrificial; SEE CONCEPT 537

costume [n] *set of clothes*
apparel, attire, clothing, dress, duds*, ensemble, fashion, garb, getup*, guise, livery, mode, outfit, rig*, robes*, style, suit, uniform, wardrobe; SEE CONCEPT 451

cot [n] *temporary bed*
army bed, berth, bunk, camp bed, folding bed, gurney, small bed, trundle; SEE CONCEPT 443

cottage [n] *tiny house; lodging*
box, bungalow, cabana, cabin, caboose, camp, carriage house, chalet, cot, home, hut, lean-to, lodge, ranch, shack, shanty, small house; SEE CONCEPT 516

couch [n] *sofa; long, upholstered furniture*
bed, chair, chaise longue, chesterfield, davenport, daybed, divan, lounge, love seat, ottoman, resting place, settee; SEE CONCEPT 443

couch [v] *express in particular way*
formulate, frame, phrase, put, set forth, utter, word; SEE CONCEPT 51

couch potato [n] *inactive person*
bystander, goof-off*, idler, laggard, lazy person, loafer, lotuseater*, lounger, observer, slouch, sluggard, spectator, televiewer*, TV viewer, viewer; SEE CONCEPT 423

cough [n] *expelled air with sound*
ahem, bark, cold, croup, frog in throat*, hack, hem, tickle in throat*, whoop; SEE CONCEPTS 65,316

cough [v] *expelling air with sound*
bark, choke, clear throat, convulse, expectorate, hack, hawk, hem, spit up, vomit, whoop; SEE CONCEPTS 65,308

council [n] *people assembled for purpose*
assembly, board, body, brain trust*, cabinet, chamber, clan, committee, conclave, confab*, conference, congregation, congress, convention, convocation, diet, directorate, gang, gathering, governing body, groupthink*, huddle*, kitchen cabinet*, meet, ministry, mob, official family, outfit, panel, parliament, powwow*, ring, senate, synod; SEE CONCEPTS 299,325,381

counsel [n1] *guidance*
admonition, advice, advisement, caution, consideration, consultation, deliberation, direction, forethought, information, instruction, kibitz*, recommendation, steer, suggestion, tip, tip-off*, two cents' worth*, warning, word to the wise*; SEE CONCEPTS 75,274

counsel [n2] *legal representative*
adviser, advocate, attorney, barrister, bomber*, counselor, legal adviser, legal beagle*, legal eagle*, lip*, mouthpiece*, patch*, shyster*, solicitor; SEE CONCEPT 355

counsel [v] *give advice*
admonish, advise, advocate, caution, charge, confab*, direct, enjoin, exhort, give pointer, give two cents*, guide, huddle*, inform, instruct, keep posted, kibitz*, order, prescribe, prompt, put bug in ear*, put heads together*, put on to, recommend, reprehend, show the ropes*, steer, suggest,

teach, tip, tip off*, tout, urge, warn, wise one up*; SEE CONCEPTS 75,317

counselor [n] *legal representative; adviser*
advocate, ambulance chaser*, attorney, counsel, front*, guide, instructor, legal beagle*, legal eagle*, lip*, mentor, mouthpiece*, pleader, solicitor, squeal*, teacher*; SEE CONCEPT 355

count [n] *tally; number*
calculation, computation, enumeration, numbering, outcome, poll, reckoning, result, sum, toll, total, whole; SEE CONCEPT 766

count [v1] *add, check in order*
add up, calculate, cast, cast up, cipher, compute, enumerate, estimate, figure, foot, keep tab, number, numerate, reckon, run down, score, sum, take account of, tally, tell, tick off, total, tot up; SEE CONCEPT 764

count [v2] *consider, deem*
await, esteem, expect, hope, impute, judge, look, look upon, rate, regard, think; SEE CONCEPTS 18,43

count [v3] *have importance*
carry weight, cut ice*, enter into consideration, import, matter, mean, militate, rate, signify, tell, weigh; SEE CONCEPT 668

count [v4] *include*
await, expect, hope, look, number among, take into account, take into consideration; SEE CONCEPTS 26,112

countenance [n1] *appearance, usually of the face*
aspect, biscuit*, cast, demeanor, expression, face, features, gills*, kisser*, look, looks, map*, mask, mien, mug*, phizog*, physiognomy, poker face*, potato*, puss*, visage; SEE CONCEPTS 716,718

countenance [n2] *self-control*
calmness, composure, presence of mind, self-composure; SEE CONCEPT 633

countenance [v] *approve, support*
abet, accept, advocate, aid, applaud, approbate, back, bear with, champion, commend, condone, confirm, cope, encourage, endorse, favor, get behind, give green light*, give stamp of approval*, give the nod*, go along with, go for, grin and bear it*, handle, help, hold with, invite, live with*, nod at, okay*, put John Hancock on*, put up with, sanction, sign off on*, sit still for*, smile on*, stand for, stomach something*, swallow*, thumbs up*, uphold; SEE CONCEPTS 10,50,88

counter [adj] *opposite, opposing*
adverse, against, antagonistic, anti, antipodal, antipodean, antithetical, conflicting, contradictory, contrary, contrasting, converse, diametric, hindering, impeding, obstructive, obverse, opposed, polar, reverse; SEE CONCEPTS 544,581

counter [v] *answer, respond in retaliation*
backtalk, beat, bilk, buck, circumvent, contravene, counteract, counterwork, cross, dash, disappoint, fly in the face of*, foil, frustrate, have bone to pick*, hinder, hit back, match, meet, offset, oppose, parry, pit, play off, resist, respond, retaliate, return, ruin, take on, thumbs down*, vie, ward off; SEE CONCEPTS 45,121

counter [adv] *contrary, reverse*
against, at variance with, contrarily, contrariwise, conversely, in defiance of*, opposite, versus; SEE CONCEPTS 544,581

counteract [v] *do opposing action*
annul, buck, cancel, cancel out, check, contravene, correct, counterbalance, countercheck, countervail, counterwork, cross, defeat, fix, foil,

frustrate, go against, halt, hinder, invalidate, negate, negative, neutralize, offset, oppose, prevent, rectify, redress, resist, right, thwart; SEE CONCEPTS 87,96,126

counterbalance [v] *offset an action*
amend, atone for, balance, cancel, compensate, correct, counteract, counterpoise, countervail, equalize, make up for, outweigh, rectify, redeem, set off; SEE CONCEPTS 87,96,126

counterfeit [n] *fake, forgery*
actor, bogus*, bum, copy, deceit, deception, dummy, facsimile, fraud, gyp, hoax, humbug, imitation, imposture, junque*, phony, pseudo, put-on*, reproduction, sell*, sham, simulacrum; SEE CONCEPTS 648,725

counterfeit [adj] *fake, simulated*
affected, assumed, bent, bogus*, brummagem, copied, crock, deceptive, delusive, delusory, ersatz, faked, false, feigned, fictitious, fishy*, forged, framed, fraudulent, Hollywood*, imitation, misleading, mock, not genuine, not kosher*, phony*, pirate, plant*, pretended, pretentious, pseudo, put-on*, queer, sham, snide, soft shell*, spurious, suppositious, two-faced*, won't fly*, wrong; SEE CONCEPTS 549,582

counterfeit [v] *make deceitful imitation*
act like, affect, ape, assume, bluff, carbon, cheat, circulate bad money, clone, coin, copy, defraud, delude, ditto, do, do like*, dupe, fabricate, fake, feign, forge, go like*, imitate, impersonate, knock off*, make like*, make money, mimeo, mimic, mint, phony*, phony up*, pretend, put on*, sham, simulate, stat, Xerox*; SEE CONCEPTS 59,171

countermand [v] *annul, cancel a command*
override, recall, repeal, rescind, retract, retreat, reverse, revoke; SEE CONCEPTS 50,53,88

counterpart [n] *match; identical part or thing*
analogue, carbon copy*, complement, copy, correlate, correlative, correspondent, dead ringer*, ditto*, doppelganger, duplicate, equal, equivalent, fellow, like, look alike, mate, obverse, opposite, opposite number, peas in a pod*, pendant, ringer*, spit and image*, spitting image*, supplement, tally, twin, two of a kind; SEE CONCEPTS 667,834

countless [adj] *innumerable*
bags of*, endless, gobs*, heap*, immeasurable, incalculable, infinite, innumerous, jillion*, legion, limitless, loads*, lots of, many, measureless, mess*, mint*, mucho*, multitudinous, myriad, numberless, oodles*, passel of*, peck, pile, raft*, scads*, slew*, stack*, tidy sum, umpteen*, uncountable, uncounted, untold, whole slew*, zillion*; SEE CONCEPTS 762,781

count on/count upon [v] *depend on; rely*
aim for, bank on, bargain for, believe, believe in, bet bottom dollar*, bet on, expect from, heed, lean on, pin faith on, place confidence in, plan on, reckon on, rest on, score, stake on, swear by, tab, take as gospel truth*, take for granted, take on trust, trust; SEE CONCEPTS 12,26

count out [v] *disregard, exclude*
bar, bate, debar, eliminate, except, get rid of, leave out, leave out of account, mark off, pass over, rule out, suspend; SEE CONCEPT 25

country [n1] *political territory; nation*
citizenry, citizens, commonwealth, community, constituents, electors, grass roots, homeland, inhabitants, kingdom, land, native land, patria, people, polity, populace, public, realm, region,

society, soil, sovereign state, state, terrain, voters; SEE CONCEPTS 379,508,510

country [n2] *rural area; area away from city*
back country, backwoods, boondocks*, boonies*, bush, countryside, cow country*, farmland, farms, forests, green belt*, hinterland, middle of nowhere*, outback, outdoors, province, sticks*, up country*, wide open space*, wilderness, wilds, woodlands, woods; SEE CONCEPTS 508,513

country [adj] *rural, pastoral*
agrarian, agrestic, Arcadian, bucolic, campestral, countrified, georgic, homey, out-country, outland, provincial, rustic, uncultured, unpolished, unrefined, unsophisticated; SEE CONCEPTS 401,536, 589

county [n] *province or district of area*
canton, constituency, division, shire; SEE CONCEPTS 508,513

coup [n] *achievement, often by maneuver*
accomplishment, action, coup de maître, coup d'état, deed, exploit, feat, overthrow, plot, revolution, stratagem, stroke, stroke of genius*, stunt, successful stroke, tour de force, upset; SEE CONCEPT 706

coup de grâce [n] *finishing blow*
blow, clincher*, comeuppance, deathblow, defeat, final blow, final stroke, kill, knockout, mercy stroke, mortal blow, quietus; SEE CONCEPTS 95,252

coup d'état [n] *violent seizure*
coup, overthrow, palace revolution, power play*, putsch*, rebellion, revolt, revolution, takeover; SEE CONCEPTS 86,90,320

couple [n] *pair of things*
brace, couplet, deuce*, doublet, duo, dyad, husband and wife, item, newlyweds, set, span, team, twain, twosome, yoke; SEE CONCEPTS 432,766

couple [v] *join two things*
bracket, bring together, buckle, clasp, coalesce, cohabit, come together, conjoin, conjugate, connect, copulate, harness, hitch, hook up, link, marry, match, pair, unite, wed, yoke; SEE CONCEPTS 113,114,297,375

coupon [n] *discount ticket*
advertisement, box top*, card, certificate, credit slip, detachable portion, order blank, premium certificate, ration slip, redeemable part, redemption slip, slip, token, voucher; SEE CONCEPT 331

courage [n] *boldness, braveness*
adventuresomeness, adventurousness, audacity, backbone, bravery, bravura, daring, dash, dauntlessness, determination, élan, endurance, enterprise, fearlessness, firmness, fortitude, gallantry, gameness, grit, guts, hardihood, heroism, intrepidity, lion-heartedness, mettle, nerve, pluck, power, prowess, pugnacity, rashness, recklessness, resolution, spirit, spunk, stoutheartedness, temerity, tenacity, valor, venturesomeness; SEE CONCEPTS 411,633

courageous [adj] *brave, bold*
adventuresome, adventurous, assured, audacious, cool, daredevil, daring, dauntless, doughty, fearless, fiery, fire-eating*, gallant, game, gritty*, gutsy*, hardy, heroic, high-spirited, impavid, indomitable, intrepid, lionhearted, martial, nervy, plucky*, red-blooded*, resolute, Spartan, stalwart, stand tall*, stouthearted, strong, tenacious, tough, Trojan*, unafraid, undaunted, valiant, valorous, venturesome, venturous; SEE CONCEPTS 401,404

courier [n] *messenger*

bearer, carrier, dispatcher, emissary, envoy, express, go-between, gofer*, gopher*, herald, intelligencer, internuncio, runner; SEE CONCEPT 348

course [n1] *progress, advance*

advancement, chain, channels, consecution, continuity, development, flow, furtherance, line, manner, march, movement, order, plan, policy, polity, procedure, program, progression, red tape*, row, scheme, sequel, sequence, series, string, succession, system, unfolding, way; SEE CONCEPTS 704,727

course [n2] *path, channel*

aisle, aqueduct, boards, byway, canal, circuit, conduit, direction, duct, flow, groove, itinerary, lap, line, movement, orbit, passage, range, road, route, run, rut, scope, stream, tack, track, trail, trajectory, watercourse, way; SEE CONCEPTS 501,514

course [n3] *length of action*

duration, elapsing, lapse, passage, passing, progress, sweep, term, time; SEE CONCEPT 804

course [n4] *plan of study*

class, conference, curriculum, discussion group, interest, laboratory, lecture, matriculation, meeting, method, period, preparation, procedure, program, regimen, schedule, seminar, session, speciality, subject; SEE CONCEPT 287

course [v] *flow; run*

career, chase, dart, dash, follow, gallop, gush, hasten, hunt, hurry, hustle, pursue, race, rush, scamper, scoot, scurry, speed, spring, stream, surge, tumble; SEE CONCEPTS 150,152

court [n1] *yard, garden of building*

cloister, close, compass, courtyard, curtilage, enclosure, forum, patio, piazza, plaza, quad, quadrangle, square, street; SEE CONCEPTS 509,513

court [n2] *ruler's attendants*

castle, cortege, entourage, hall, lords and ladies, palace, retinue, royal household, staff, suite, train; SEE CONCEPTS 296,348

court [n3] *judicial system*

bar, bench, court of justice, forum, judge, justice, kangaroo court*, law court, magistrate, seat of judgment, session, tribunal; SEE CONCEPTS 299,318

court [n4] *building for legal proceedings*

bar, bench, city hall, county courthouse, courthouse, courtroom, federal building, hall of justice, justice building, law court, municipal building, tribunal; SEE CONCEPTS 318,439

court [n5] *wooing*

address, attention, homage, love, respects, suit; SEE CONCEPT 32

court [v] *fawn over, pay attention to*

allure, ask in marriage, attract, beseech, bid, bootlick, captivate, charm, chase, cultivate, curry favor, date, entice, entreat, flatter, follow, gallant, go out with, go steady, go together, go with, grovel, importune, invite, keep company with, make love to, make overture, make time with*, pander to, pay addresses to, pay court to, please, pop the question*, praise, propose, pursue, run after*, seek, seek the hand of, serenade, set one's cap*, solicit, spark, spoon*, sue, sweetheart, take out, woo; SEE CONCEPTS 32,384

courteous [adj] *gentle, mannerly*

affable, attentive, ceremonious, civil, civilized, complaisant, considerate, courtly, cultivated, debonair, elegant, gallant, genteel, gracious, polished, polite, refined, respectful, soft-spoken, suave, thoughtful, urbane, well-behaved, well-bred, well-mannered, well-spoken; SEE CONCEPTS 267,401

courtesy [n1] *good manners*

address, affability, amenities, amiability, attentiveness, ceremony, chivalry, civility, comity, complaisance, consideration, cordiality, courteousness, courtliness, cultivation, culture, deference, elegance, familiarity, favor, friendliness, gallantness, gallantry, generosity, geniality, gentleness, good behavior, good breeding, graciousness, indulgence, kindness, polish, politeness, refinement, respect, reverence, solicitude, suavity, sympathy, tact, thoughtfulness, urbanity; SEE CONCEPTS 633,644

courtesy [n2] *favor, indulgence*

accommodation, benevolence, bounty, charity, chivalry, compassion, consent, consideration, dispensation, generosity, kindness, liberality, service, unselfishness; SEE CONCEPTS 337,388,633

courtly [adj] *refined manner*

adulatory, affable, aristocratic, august, ceremonious, chivalrous, civil, civilized, complimentary, conventional, cultured, decorous, dignified, elegant, flattering, formal, gallant, gracious, highbred, imposing, lofty, obliging, polished, polite, preux, prim, refined, stately, studied, urbane; SEE CONCEPT 401

courtship [n] *dating, romance*

courting, engagement, keeping company*, love, lovemaking, pursuit, suit, wooing; SEE CONCEPT 388

cove [n] *inlet, small niche*

anchorage, arm, bay, bayou, bight, cave, cavern, creek, estuary, firth, frith, gulf, harbor, hole, lagoon, nook, retreat, slough, sound, wash; SEE CONCEPT 509

covenant [n] *pact, promise*

agreement, arrangement, bargain, bond, commitment, compact, concordat, contract, convention, deal, deed, dicker*, handshake*, papers, stipulation, transaction, treaty, trust; SEE CONCEPT 684

covenant [v] *agree*

bargain, concur, contract, engage, pledge, plight, promise, stipulate, swear, undertake, vow; SEE CONCEPTS 8,71,317

cover [n1] *wrapping, cover-up*

awning, bark, binding, camouflage, canopy, canvas, cap, caparison, case, ceiling, cloak, clothing, coating, covering, coverlet, disguise, dome, dress, drop, envelope, facade, false front*, fig leaf, front, guise, hood, integument, jacket, lid, marquee, mask, masquerade, overlay, paint, parasol, polish, pretense, put-on*, roof, screen, seal, semblance, sheath, sheet, shroud, smoke screen*, spread, stopper, tarp, tarpaulin, tegument, tent, top, umbrella, varnish, veil, veneer, window-dressing, wrapper, wraps; SEE CONCEPTS 484,750

cover [n2] *hiding place*

asylum, camouflage, concealment, covert, defense, drop, front, guard, harbor, harborage, haven, port, protection, refuge, retreat, safety, sanctuary, screen, security, shelter; SEE CONCEPT 198

cover [v1] *wrap, hide*

blanket, board up, bury, bush up, cache, camouflage, canopy, cap, carpet, cloak, clothe, coat, conceal, cover up, crown, curtain, daub, disguise, do on the sly*, dress, eclipse, encase, enclose, enfold, ensconce, enshroud, envelop, hood, house, invest, layer, mantle, mask, obscure, overcast, overlay, overspread, protect, put on, screen, secrete, set on, shade, shield, shroud, superimpose, superpose, surface, veil; SEE CONCEPTS 172,188

cover [v2] *protect, guard*
bulwark, defend, fend, house, reinforce, safeguard, screen, secure, shelter, shield, watch over; SEE CONCEPT 96

cover [v3] *include, contain*
be enough, comprehend, comprise, consider, deal with, embody, embrace, encompass, examine, incorporate, involve, meet, provide for, reach, refer to, suffice, survey, take account of; SEE CONCEPT 643

cover [v4] *describe in published writing*
broadcast, detail, investigate, narrate, recount, relate, report, tell of, write up; SEE CONCEPTS 60,79

cover [v5] *fill in for, compensate*
balance, counterbalance, double for, insure, make good, make up for, offset, relieve, stand in for*, substitute, take over, take the rap for*; SEE CONCEPTS 110,126

cover [v6] *travel across area*
cross, do, journey over, pass over, pass through, range, track, traverse, trek; SEE CONCEPT 224

covert [adj] *clandestine, underhanded*
buried, camouflaged, cloaked, concealed, disguised, dissembled, furtive, hidden, hush-hush*, incog*, incognito, masked, obscured, private, privy, QT*, secret, shrouded, stealthy, sub rosa, surreptitious, ulterior, undercover, underhand, under-the-table*, under wraps*, unsuspected, veiled; SEE CONCEPTS 544,548

covertly [adv] *clandestine, underhandedly*
by stealth, clandestinely, furtively, hush-hush*, in camera, in holes and corners*, on the QT*, on the quiet, on the sly, privately, secretly, slyly, stealthily, sub rosa, surreptitiously, undercover, under wraps*, wildcat*; SEE CONCEPTS 544,548

covet [v] *desire strongly*
aspire to, begrudge, choose, crave, desiderate, envy, fancy, hanker for*, have eye on*, have hots for*, itch for*, long for, lust after, spoil for*, thirst for, want, wish for, yearn for, yen for*; SEE CONCEPT 20

covetous [adj] *greedy; very desirous*
acquisitive, avaricious, avid, close-fisted, eager, ensurient, envious, gluttonous, grabby, grasping, green-eyed*, grudging, hogging, itchy*, jealous, keen, mercenary, piggish*, prehensile, rapacious, ravenous, selfish, swinish*, voracious, yearning; SEE CONCEPT 401

cow [v] *browbeat, intimidate*
abash, appall, awe, bludgeon, bluster, buffalo, bulldoze, bully, daunt, discomfit, disconcert, dishearten, dismay, dragoon, embarrass, enforce, faze, frighten, hector, lean on*, overawe, push around*, rattle, scare, showboat*, strong-arm*, subdue, terrorize, turn on the heat*, unnerve, walk heavy*; SEE CONCEPTS 7,19,52

coward [n] *person who is scared, easily intimidated*
alarmist, baby*, caitiff, chicken*, chicken heart*, chicken liver*, craven, cur, dastard, deserter, faintheart, faint-of-heart*, fraidy-cat*, funk, gutless*, invertebrate*, jellyfish*, lily liver, malingerer, mouse*, pessimist, poltroon, quitter, rabbit*, recreant, scaredy cat*, shirk, shirker,

skulker, sneak, weakling, white liver*, wimp*, yellow*, yellow belly*; SEE CONCEPT 423

cowardly [adj] *fearful*
afraid, anxious, apprehensive, backward, base, caitiff, chicken-hearted, cowering, cowhearted, craven, dastardly, diffident, dismayed, fainthearted, frightened, gutless, having the willies*, jittery, lacking courage, lily-livered*, nervous, no guts, panicky, paper tiger*, pigeonhearted*, pusillanimous, recreant, retiring, running scared*, scared, shrinking, shy, soft*, spineless*, timid, timorous, weak, weak-kneed*, worthless, yellow*, yellow-bellied*; SEE CONCEPT 401

cower [v] *hide, hover in fear*
apple-polish*, blench, bootlick*, brownnose*, cringe, crouch, draw back, fawn, flinch, grovel, honey*, kowtow*, quail*, recoil, shrink, skulk, sneak, toady*, tremble, truckle, wince; SEE CONCEPTS 188,384

coy [adj] *very modest*
backward, bashful, blushing, coquettish, demure, diffident, evasive, flirtatious, humble, kittenish, overmodest, prudish, rabbity, reserved, retiring, self-effacing, shrinking, shy, skittish, timid, unassertive; SEE CONCEPTS 401,404

cozy [adj] *comforting, soft, warm*
comfortable, comfy, cuddled up, cushy, easeful, in clover, intimate, in velvet*, on bed of roses*, restful, safe, secure, sheltered, snug, snug as bug in rug*, snuggled down, tucked up; SEE CONCEPTS 485,605,606

crabby/crabbed [adj] *in a bad mood*
acid, acrid, acrimonious, awkward, bad-tempered, blunt, brusque, captious, choleric, churlish, cranky*, cross, crotchety, crusty*, cynical, difficult, dour, fretful, gloomy, glum, grouchy*, harsh, huffy, ill-humored, ill-tempered, irascible, irritable, misanthropic, morose, nasty-tempered, peevish, perverse, petulant, prickly, saturnine, snappish, snappy, sour, splenetic, sulky, sullen, surly, tart, testy, tough, trying, unsociable; SEE CONCEPTS 401,403

crack [n1] *break, crevice*
breach, chink, chip, cleft, cranny, crevasse, cut, discontinuity, division, fissure, fracture, gap, hole, interstice, interval, rent, rift, rima, rimation, rime, split; SEE CONCEPTS 469,513

crack [n2] *loud sound, usually from hitting*
bang, bash, belt, blast, blow, boom, buffet, burst, clap, clip, clout, crash, cuff, explosion, go, noise, pop, report, shot, slam, slap, smack, smash, snap, splintering, splitting, stab, stroke, thump, thwack, wallop, whack, wham; SEE CONCEPTS 189,595

crack [n3] *attempt to do something*
fling, go, opportunity, pop, shot, stab, try, whack, whirl; SEE CONCEPT 87

crack [n4] *joke*
dig, funny remark, gag, insult, jest, jibe, quip, remark, return, smart remark, wisecrack, witticism; SEE CONCEPT 272

crack [adj] *super, first-rate*
able, ace, adept, best, capital, choice, crackerjack*, deluxe, elite, excellent, expert, first-class, handpicked, pro*, proficient, skilled, skillful, superior, talented; SEE CONCEPTS 528,542,574

crack [v1] *break, usually into parts*
burst, chip, chop, cleave, crackle, crash, damage, detonate, explode, fracture, hurt, impair, injure, pop, ring, rive, sever, shiver, snap, splinter, split; SEE CONCEPT 248

crack [v2] *lose self-control*
become deranged, become insane, blow one's mind*, blow up, break down, bug out*, collapse, flip*, give way*, go bonkers*, go crazy, go to pieces*, lose it*, succumb, yield; SEE CONCEPT 13

crack [v3] *hit very hard*
bash, buffet, clip, clout, cuff, slap, thump, thunder, wallop, whack; SEE CONCEPT 189

crack [v4] *discover meaning, answer*
break, cryptanalyze, decipher, decode, decrypt, fathom, figure out, get answer, solve, work out; SEE CONCEPTS 37,38

cracker [n] *hard, often salted, baked wafer*
biscuit, bun, cookie, hardtack, pretzel, rusk, saltine; SEE CONCEPT 457

crack up [v] *break down mentally*
become demented, become psychotic, blow a fuse*, collapse, come apart at seams*, decline, derange, deteriorate, fail, flip out*, freak out*, go bonkers*, go crazy, go nuts, go off deep end*, go off rocker*, go out of mind*, go to pieces*, have breakdown, schizz out*, sicken; SEE CONCEPT 13

cradle [n1] *small bed for baby*
baby bed, bassinet, cot, crib, hamper, Moses basket, pannier, trundle bed; SEE CONCEPT 443

cradle [n2] *early childhood; origins*
babyhood, beginning, birthplace, fount, fountain, fountainhead, infancy, nativity, nursery, origin, source, spring, ultimate cause, wellspring; SEE CONCEPTS 648,817

cradle [v] *hold in arms; nurture*
lull, nestle, nourish, nurse, rock, support, tend, watch over; SEE CONCEPTS 190,295

craft [n1] *expertise, skill*
ability, adeptness, adroitness, aptitude, art, artistry, cleverness, competence, cunning, dexterity, expertness, ingenuity, knack, know-how*, proficiency, technique; SEE CONCEPTS 409,706

craft [n2] *deceit, scheme*
art, artfulness, artifice, cageyness, canniness, contrivance, craftiness, cunning, disingenuity, duplicity, foxiness, guile, ruse, shrewdness, slyness, stratagem, strategy, subterfuge, subtlety, trickery, wiles, wiliness; SEE CONCEPTS 645,660

craft [n3] *business, discipline*
art, calling, career, employment, handicraft, line, métier, occupation, profession, pursuit, trade, vocation, work; SEE CONCEPT 360

craft [n4] *water or air vehicle*
aircraft, airplane, air ship, barge, blimp, boat, bottom, plane, ship, shipping, spacecraft, vessel, watercraft, zeppelin; SEE CONCEPTS 504,506

craftsperson [n] *person skilled in art*
artificer, artisan, journeyperson, machinist, maker, manufacturer, mechanic, skilled worker, smith, specialist, technician, wright; SEE CONCEPT 348

crafty [adj] *clever, scheming*
adroit, artful, astute, cagey, calculating, canny, crazy like fox*, cunning, deceitful, deep, designing, devious, disingenuous, duplicitous, foxy*, fraudulent, guileful, insidious, intelligent, keen, knowing, sharp, shrewd, slick, slippery*, sly, smart, smooth, street smart*, streetwise*, subtle, tricky, vulpine, wily; SEE CONCEPT 401

craggy [adj] *jagged*
asperous, broken, cragged, harsh, precipitous, rock-bound, rocky, rough, rugged, scabrous,

scraggy, stony, uneven, unlevel, unsmooth; SEE CONCEPTS 490,606

cram [v1] *fill to overflowing; compress*
charge, chock, choke, compact, crowd, crush, devour, drive, force, gobble, gorge, guzzle, heap, ingurgitate, jam, jam-pack*, load, overcrowd, overeat, overfill, pack, pack 'em in*, pack in, pack it in*, pack like sardines*, press, ram, sardine*, satiate, shove, slop, slosh, squash, squeeze, stive, stuff, tamp*, thrust, wedge, wolf*; SEE CONCEPTS 208,740

cram [v2] *study intensely*
burn midnight oil*, heavy booking*, hit the books*, megabook*, mug up*, read, review, revise; SEE CONCEPT 17

cramp [n] *muscle spasm*
ache, charley horse*, circumscription, confinement, constipation, contraction, convulsion, crick, hindrance, impediment, kink, obstruction, pain, pang, restriction, shooting pain, stiffness, stitch, stricture, twinge; SEE CONCEPTS 308,728

cramp [v] *hinder, restrain*
bottle up*, box up*, check, circumscribe, clamp, clasp, clog, confine, constrain, coop up*, encumber, fasten, grip, hamper, hamstring, handicap, impede, inhibit, limit, object, obstruct, restrict, shackle, stymie, thwart; SEE CONCEPTS 130,191

cramped [adj] *congested, overcrowded*
awkward, circumscribed, close, closed in, confined, crabbed, crowded, hemmed in*, illegible, incommodious, indecipherable, irregular, jammed in, little, minute, narrow, packed, pent, restricted, small, squeezed, tight, tiny, tucked up, two-by-four*, uncomfortable; SEE CONCEPTS 483,773

cranky [adj] *in bad mood*
bad-humored, bearish, cantankerous, choleric, crabby, cross, crotchety, cussed, disagreeable, got up on wrong side of bed*, grouchy, grumpy, hot-tempered, ill-humored, irascible, irritable, like a bear*, mean, ornery*, out of sorts, perverse, quick-tempered, ratty, snappish, tetchy, ugly, vinegary; SEE CONCEPTS 401,403

cranny [n] *nook, opening*
breach, byplace, chink, cleft, crack, crevice, fissure, gap, hole, interstice, niche; SEE CONCEPTS 440,513

crash [n1/v1] *bang; banging sound*
blast, boom, burst, clang, clap, clash, clatter, clattering, crack, din, peal, racket, slam, smash, smashing, sound, thunder, thunderclap, wham; SEE CONCEPTS 65,521,595

crash [n2] *collision, accidental hitting*
accident, bump, collapse, concussion, crack-up*, crunch, debacle, ditch, fender bender*, fender tag*, impact, jar, jolt, percussion, pileup, ram, rear-ender*, shock, sideswipe, smash, smashup*, splashdown*, stack-up*, thud*, thump*, total*, washout*, wreck; SEE CONCEPT 189

crash [v2] *break into pieces*
bang into, crack up, crunch, dash, disintegrate, fracture, fragment, pile up, shatter, shiver, sideswipe, smash, smash up, splinter, total*, wrack up*; SEE CONCEPT 248

crash [v3] *fall*
bite the dust*, bump, collapse, collide, crashland, ditch, dive, drive into, drop, fall flat*, fall headlong, fall prostrate, give way, go in*, hurtle, lurch, meet, overbalance, overturn, pancake*, pitch, plough into*, plunge, prang, slip, smash,

splash down, sprawl, topple, tumble, upset, wash-out*; SEE CONCEPT 181

crass [adj] coarse, insensitive
asinine, blundering, boorish, bovine, churlish, dense, doltish, gross, indelicate, inelegant, loutish, lowbrow, lumpish, oafish, obtuse, Philistine, raw, rough, rude, stupid, uncouth, unrefined, vulgar, witless; SEE CONCEPT 401

crate [n] wooden container
box, cage, carton, case, chest, package; SEE CONCEPT 494

crave [v1] desire intensely
ache for, covet, cry out for, die for*, dream, eat one's heart out*, fancy, give eyeteeth for*, hunger for*, itch for*, long for, lust after, need, pine for*, require, sigh for, spoil for, suspire, thirst for*, want, yearn for, yen for*; SEE CONCEPT 20

crave [v2] beg
ask, beseech, call for, demand, entreat, implore, necessitate, petition, plead for, pray for, require, seek, solicit, supplicate, take; SEE CONCEPTS 48,53

craven [n] timid person
caitiff, chicken*, coward, dastard, fraidy cat*, nebbish, poltroon, quitter, recreant, scaredy cat*, weakling, wheyface, wimp*, wuss*, yellow belly*; SEE CONCEPT 423

craven [adj] weak, timid
chicken*, cowardly, dastardly, fearful, gutless, lily-livered*, mean-spirited, poltroonish, pusillanimous, scared, timorous, weak-kneed*, wimpish*, wimpy*, wussy*, yellow*, yellow-bellied*; SEE CONCEPTS 401,550

craving [n] strong desire
appetite, appetition, hankering, hunger, hurting, itch*, longing, lust, munchies*, need, passion, thirst, urge, yearning, yen*; SEE CONCEPTS 20,709

crawl [v1] move very slowly
clamber, creep, drag, drag oneself along, go on all fours, go on belly, grovel, hang back, inch, lag, loiter along, lollygag*, move at snail's pace*, move on hands and knees, plod, poke, pull oneself along, scrabble, slide, slither, squirm, worm, wriggle, writhe; SEE CONCEPT 151

crawl [v2] humble oneself
abase oneself, apple-polish*, brownnose*, cringe, fawn, grovel, toady, truckle; SEE CONCEPTS 35,48

craze [n] fad, strong interest
chic, cry, enthusiasm, fashion, fever, furor, infatuation, in thing*, kick*, mania, mode, monomania, newest wrinkle*, novelty, passion, preoccupation, rage, the last word*, the latest thing*, trend, vogue, wrinkle; SEE CONCEPTS 532,690

craze [v] make insane
bewilder, confuse, dement, derange, distemper, distract, drive mad, enrage, frenzy, infatuate, inflame, madden, unbalance, unhinge; SEE CONCEPTS 7,19

crazy [adj] mentally strange
ape, barmy, batty, berserk, bonkers*, cracked, crazed, cuckoo, daft, delirious, demented, deranged, dippy*, dippy*, erratic, flaky, flipped*, flipped out*, freaked out*, fruity*, idiotic, insane, kooky, lunatic, mad, maniacal, mental*, moonstruck*, nuts, nutty, nutty as fruitcake*, of unsound mind, out of one's mind, out of one's tree*, out to lunch*, potty*, psycho*, round the bend*,

schizo*, screwball*, screw loose*, screwy*, silly, touched*, unbalanced, unglued*, unhinged*, unzipped*, wacky; SEE CONCEPT 403

crazy [adj2] unrealistic, fantastic
absurd, balmy, beyond all reason, bizarre, cockeyed, derisory, eccentric, fatuous, foolhardy, foolish, goofy*, half-baked*, harebrained*, idiotic, ill-conceived, impracticable, imprudent, inane, inappropriate, insane, irresponsible, loony, ludicrous, nonsensical, odd, out of all reason, outrageous, peculiar, preposterous, puerile, quixotic, ridiculous, senseless, short-sighted, silly, strange, unworkable, weird, wild; SEE CONCEPT 529

crazy [adj3] infatuated, in love
ardent, beside oneself*, devoted, eager, enamored, fanatical, hysterical, keen, mad, passionate, smitten, wild, zealous; SEE CONCEPT 403

creak [v] grind, grate with high noise
chirr, crepitate, groan, rasp, scrape, scratch, screech, sound, squeak, squeal; SEE CONCEPTS 65,186,215

cream [n1] lotion, oil
cerate, chrism, cosmetic, demulcent, emulsion, essence, jelly, liniment, moisturizer, ointment, paste, salve, unction, unguent; SEE CONCEPTS 466,467,468

cream [n2] the best
choice, crème de la crème*, elite, fat, favorite, finest, flower, pick, pride, prime*, prize, skim*, top; SEE CONCEPT 668

creamy [adj] smooth, buttery
creamed, feathery, fluffy, gloppy*, gooey, gooky*, goopy*, greasy, gunky, luscious, lush, milky, oily, rich, soft, velvety; SEE CONCEPT 606

crease [n] fold, wrinkle
bend, bulge, cockle, corrugation, furrow, groove, line, overlap, pleat, plica, pucker, ridge, rimple, rivel, ruck, rugosity, tuck; SEE CONCEPTS 452,757

crease [v] fold, rumple
bend, cockle, corrugate, crimp, crinkle, crumple, dog-ear*, double up, plait, pleat, pucker, purse, ridge, ruck up, screw up*, wrinkle; SEE CONCEPTS 158,219

create [v] develop in mind or physically
actualize, author, beget, bring into being, bring into existence, bring to pass, build, cause to be, coin, compose, conceive, concoct, constitute, construct, contrive, design, devise, discover, dream up, effect, erect, establish, fabricate, fashion, father, forge, form, formulate, found, generate, give birth to, give life to, hatch, imagine, initiate, institute, invent, invest, make, occasion, organize, originate, parent, perform, plan, procreate, produce, rear, set up, shape, sire, spawn, start; SEE CONCEPTS 173,239,251

creation [n1] development of entity
conception, constitution, establishment, formation, formulation, foundation, generation, genesis, imagination, inception, institution, laying down, making, nascency, nativity, origination, procreation, production, setting up, siring; SEE CONCEPT 173

creation [n2] all living things
cosmos, life, living world, macrocosm, macrocosmos, megacosm, nature, totality, universe, world; SEE CONCEPTS 389,429

creation [n3] invention, concoction
achievement, brainchild, chef-d'oeuvre, concept, handiwork, magnum opus, opus, piece, pièce de

résistance, production, work, work of genius; SEE CONCEPTS 259,260

creative [adj] artistic, imaginative
clever, cool*, demiurgic, deviceful, fertile, formative, gifted, hip*, ingenious, innovational, innovative, innovatory, inspired, inventive, leading-edge*, original, originative, productive, prolific, stimulating, visionary, way out*; SEE CONCEPT 402

creator [n] inventor; God
architect, author, begetter, brain, deity, designer, founder, framer, generator, initiator, maker, originator, prime mover, producer, sire; SEE CONCEPTS 348,352,361

creature [n] being, beast
animal, body, brute, creation, critter*, fellow, individual, living being, living thing, lower animal, man, mortal, party, person, personage, quadruped, soul, varmint*, woman; SEE CONCEPT 389

credence [n] trust, acceptance
accepting, admission, admitting, assurance, belief, certainty, confidence, credit, dependence, faith, reliance, stock, store; SEE CONCEPT 689

credentials [n] references, attestation
accreditation, authorization, card, certificate, character, deed, diploma, docket, document, documentation, endorsement, letter of credence, letter of introduction, license, missive, papers, passport, proof, recommendation, sanction, testament, testimonial, title, token, voucher, warrant; SEE CONCEPTS 271,685

credibility [n] believeableness
believability, chance, integrity, likelihood, plausibility, possibility, probability, prospect, reliability, satisfactoriness, solidity, solidness, soundness, tenability, trustworthiness, validity; SEE CONCEPTS 650,725

credible [adj] believable
aboveboard, colorable, conceivable, conclusive, creditable, dependable, determinative, honest, honest to God*, imaginable, likely, plausible, possible, probable, probably, rational, reasonable, reliable, satisfactory, satisfying, seeming, sincere, solid, sound, straight, supposable, tenable, thinkable, trustworthy, trusty, up front*, valid; SEE CONCEPTS 552,582

credit [n1] recognition; trust
acclaim, acknowledgment, approval, attention, belief, Brownie points*, commendation, confidence, credence, distinction, faith, fame, glory, honor, kudos*, merit, notice, pat on the back*, points*, praise, reliance, strokes*, thanks, tribute; SEE CONCEPTS 69,410

credit [n2] reputation, status
authority, character, clout, esteem, estimation, fame, good name, influence, position, prestige, regard, renown, repute, standing, weight; SEE CONCEPT 388

credit [n3] deferred payment arrangement; assets
balance, bank, capital outlay, continuance, debenture, extension, installment buying, installment plan, lien, loan, mortgage, on account, on the arm*, on the cuff*, plastic*, respite, securities, stock, surplus cash, tab, trust, wealth; SEE CONCEPT 335

credit [v1] believe, depend on
accept, bank on, buy, consider, deem, fall for*, feel, hand it to one, have faith in, hold, pat on back, rely on, sense, swallow*, take as gospel truth*, take stock in*, think, trust; SEE CONCEPT 12

credit [v2] accredit, assign to
ascribe to, attribute to, chalk up to, charge to, defer, impute, lay, refer; SEE CONCEPT 18

creditable [adj] praiseworthy
admirable, batting a thousand*, believeable, commendable, decent, deserving, estimable, excellent, exemplary, honest, honorable, laudable, meritorious, nasty*, not too shabby*, organic, palmary, reputable, reputed, respectable, salt of the earth*, satisfactory, suitable, well-thought-of, worthy; SEE CONCEPT 542

credulous [adj] gullible, naive
accepting, believing, born yesterday*, dupable, easy mark*, falling for*, green, overtrusting, simple, swallow whole, taken in, trustful, trusting, uncritical, unquestioning, unsophisticated, unsuspecting, unsuspicious, unwary; SEE CONCEPT 404

creed [n] belief, principles
articles of faith, canon, catechism, church, confession, conviction, cult, doctrine, dogma, faith, ideology, persuasion, profession, religion, tenet, weltanschauung; SEE CONCEPTS 688,689

creek [n] stream of water
brook, brooklet, burn, crick, ditch, race, rill, rindle, river, rivulet, run, runnel, spring, streamlet, tributary, watercourse; SEE CONCEPT 514

creep [v] crawl along, usually on ground
approach unnoticed, crawl on all fours, edge, glide, grovel, gumshoe*, inch, insinuate, lurk, pussyfoot, scrabble, scramble, skulk, slink, slither, snake*, sneak, squirm, steal, tiptoe, worm, wriggle, writhe; SEE CONCEPT 151

creepy [adj] nasty, scary
awful, direful, disgusting, disturbing, dreadful, eerie, frightening, ghoulish, gruesome, hair-raising, horrible, itching, itchy, macabre, menacing, nightmarish, ominous, shuddersome, sinister, terrifying, threatening, unpleasant, weird; SEE CONCEPT 570

crescent [n] sickle-shaped object
bow, concave figure, convex figure, cresentoid, curve, demilune, half-moon, horned moon, lune, meniscus, new moon, old moon, sickle; SEE CONCEPT 436

crescent [adj] sickle-shaped
bowed, bow-shaped, concave, convex, crescentic, crescentiform, curved, falcate, semicircular; SEE CONCEPT 486

crest [n1] highest point
acme, apex, apogee, climax, crescendo, crown, culmination, fastigium, head, height, noon, peak, pinnacle, ridge, roof, summit, top, vertex; SEE CONCEPT 836

crest [n2] emblem, symbol
badge, bearings, charge, device, insignia; SEE CONCEPT 284

crest [n3] topknot on head of animal
aigrette, caruncle, chine, cockscomb, comb, crown, feather, hogback, mane, panache, plume, ridge, tassel, tuft; SEE CONCEPT 399

crestfallen [adj] disappointed
ass in a sling*, blue, cast down, chapfallen, dejected, depressed, despondent, disconsolate, discouraged, disheartened, dispirited, down, downcast, downhearted, down in the dumps*, in a funk*, inconsolable, low, sad, singing the blues*, taken down*; SEE CONCEPT 403

cr

crevice/crevasse [n] *crack, gap*
abyss, chasm, chink, cleft, crack, cranny, cut, division, fissure, fracture, hole, interstice, opening, precipice, rent, rift, slit, split; SEE CONCEPTS 509,513

crew [n] *group working together*
aggregation, assemblage, band, bevy, bunch, cluster, collection, company, complement, congregation, corps, covey, crowd, faction, gang, hands, herd, horde, lot, mob, organization, pack, party, posse, retinue, sailors, sect, set, squad, swarm, team, troop, troupe, workers, working party; SEE CONCEPTS 381,417

crib [n] *baby bed*
bassinet, bin*, box*, bunk, cot, cradle, manger, Moses basket*, rack*, stall*, trundle bed; SEE CONCEPT 443

crick [n] *muscle spasm*
ache, charley horse*, convulsion, cramp, jarring, kink, pain, stitch, twinge, wrench; SEE CONCEPTS 308,728

crime [n] *offense against the law*
abomination, antisocial behavior, atrocity, breach, break, caper, case, corruption, criminality, delict, delictum, delinquency, depravity, dereliction, enormity, evil, evil behavior, fast one*, fault, felony, hit, illegality, immorality, infraction, infringement, iniquity, job, lawlessness, malefaction, malfeasance, misconduct, misdeed, misdemeanor, mortal sin, outrage, racket, scandal, sneak, tort, transgression, trespass, unlawful act, vice, villainy, violation, wickedness, wrong, wrongdoing; SEE CONCEPT 192

criminal [n] *person who breaks the law*
bad actor*, blackmailer, black marketeer, con, convict, crook, culprit, delinquent, desperado, deuce, evildoer, ex-con, felon, fugitive, gangster, guerilla, heavy*, hood*, hoodlum, hooligan*, hustler, inside person*, jailbird, lawbreaker, malefactor, mobster, mug, muscle*, offender, outlaw, racketeer, repeater, scofflaw, sinner, slippery eel*, thug*, transgressor, trespasser, wrongdoer, yardbird*; SEE CONCEPT 412

criminal [adj] *lawless, felonious*
bent, caught, corrupt, crooked, culpable, deplorable, dirty, heavy, hung up*, illegal, illegitimate, illicit, immoral, indictable, iniquitous, nefarious, off base*, out of line*, peccant, racket, scandalous, senseless, shady*, smoking gun*, unlawful, unrighteous, vicious, villainous, wicked, wildcat*, wrong; SEE CONCEPT 545

crimp [v] *fold or curl*
coil, crease, crimple, crinkle, crisp, crumple, flow, frizz, pleat, rimple, ruck, screw, scrunch, set, swirl, undulate, wave, wrinkle; SEE CONCEPTS 137,213,250

cringe [v] *flinch, recoil from danger*
blench, cower, crawl, crouch, dodge, draw back, duck, eat dirt, grovel, kneel, quail, quiver, shrink, shy, start, stoop, tremble, wince; SEE CONCEPTS 188,195

crinkle [v] *crumple, ruffle*
cockle, coil, crackle, crease, crimp, crimple, curl, fold, hiss, pucker, ruck, rumple, rustle, scallop, screw, scrunch, seam, swish, twist, whisper, wind, wreathe, wrinkle; SEE CONCEPTS 65,137,213,250

cripple [v1] *disable; make lame*
attenuate, blunt, debilitate, disarm, dislimb, dismember, enfeeble, hamstring*, hurt, immobilize,

incapacitate, injure, lame, maim, mangle, mutilate, palsy, paralyze, prostrate, sap, sideline*, stifle, undermine, unstrengthen, weaken; SEE CONCEPT 246

cripple [v2] *hinder action, progress*
bring to standstill, cramp, damage, destroy, halt, hamstring*, impair, put out of action*, ruin, spoil, stifle, vitiate; SEE CONCEPT 121

crippled [adj] *disabled*
bedridden, broken, damaged, defective, deformed, enfeebled, game, gimp*, halt, hamstrung*, handicapped, harmed, hog-tied*, housebound, impaired, incapacitated, laid up*, lame, maimed, mangled, marred, mutilated, out of commission*, paralyzed, sidelined*; SEE CONCEPTS 314,485

crisis [n] *critical situation*
big trouble*, catastrophe, change, climacteric, climax, confrontation, contingency, corner, crossroad, crunch*, crux, culmination, deadlock, dilemma, dire straits*, disaster, embarrassment, emergency, entanglement, exigency, extremity, height, hot potato*, hour of decision*, imbroglio, impasse, juncture, mess, moment of truth*, necessity, pass, perplexity, pickle*, pinch*, plight, point of no return*, predicament, pressure, puzzle, quandary, situation, stew, strait, trauma, trial, trouble, turning point, urgency; SEE CONCEPT 674

crisp [adj1] *brittle, dry*
crispy, crumbly, crunchy, crusty, firm, fresh, friable, green, plump, ripe, short, unwilted; SEE CONCEPT 606

crisp [adj2] *fresh, chilly*
bracing, brisk, clear, cloudless, invigorating, refreshing, stimulating; SEE CONCEPTS 525,605

crisp [adj3] *short, curt in presentation*
abrupt, biting, brief, brusque, clear, clear-cut, cutting, incisive, penetrating, piquing, pithy, provoking, stimulating, succinct, tart, terse; SEE CONCEPT 267

crisp [adj4] *smart, snappy in appearance*
clean-cut, neat, orderly, spruce, tidy, well-groomed, well-pressed; SEE CONCEPT 579

criterion [n] *test, gauge for judgment*
archetype, basis, benchmark, canon, example, exemplar, fact, foundation, law, measure, model, norm, opinion, original, paradigm, pattern, point of comparison, precedent, principle, proof, prototype, rule, scale, standard, touchstone, yardstick; SEE CONCEPTS 290,688

critic [n1] *analyst, interpreter*
analyzer, annotator, arbiter, authority, caricaturist, cartoonist, commentator, connoisseur, diagnostic, evaluator, expert, expositor, judge, pundit, reviewer, sharpshooter; SEE CONCEPT 348

critic [n2] *faultfinder, detractor*
aristarch, attacker, backseat driver*, belittler, blamer, carper, caviler, censor, censurer, complainant, complainer, defamer, disapprover, disparager, disputer, doubter, fretter, hypercritic, maligner, muckraker, mud-slinger*, nagger*, nitpicker*, panner*, quibbler, reviler, scolder, sidewalk superintendent*, slanderer, vilifier, worrier, zapper*; SEE CONCEPT 412

critical [adj1] *fault-finding, detracting*
analytical, belittling, biting, calumniatory, captious, carping, caviling, cavillous, censorious, censuring, choleric, condemning, critic, cutting, cynical, demanding, demeaning, derogatory, diagnostic, disapproving, discerning, discriminat-

ing, disparaging, exacting, exceptive, finicky, fussy, hairsplitting, humbling, hypercritical, lowering, nagging, niggling, nit-picking*, overcritical, particular, penetrating, reproachful, sarcastic, satirical, scolding, severe, sharp, trenchant, withering; SEE CONCEPT 267

critical [adj2] *urgently important*
acute, all-important, climacteric, conclusive, consequential, crucial, dangerous, deciding, decisive, desperate, determinative, dire, exceptive, grave, hairy*, hazardous, high-priority, integral, momentous, perilous, pivotal, precarious, pressing, risky, serious, significant, strategic, urgent, vital, weighty; SEE CONCEPT 568

criticism [n1] *interpretation, analysis*
appraisal, appreciation, assessment, comment, commentary, critique, elucidation, essay, estimate, evaluation, examination, exposition, judgment, notice, observation, opinion, pan*, rating, rave*, review, reviewal, scorcher, sideswipe*, sleighride*, study, write-up; SEE CONCEPTS 271,277,278

criticism [n2] *verbal disapproval*
animadversion, aspersion, bad press*, blast, brickbats, Bronx cheer*, call down*, carping, cavil, caviling, censure, critical remarks, cut*, denunciation, disparagement, faultfinding, flak*, hit*, knock*, nit-picking, objection, opprobrium, pan, panning, put down, quibble, rap on knuckles*, reproof, roast*, slam*, slap*, slap on wrist*, static, stricture, swipe*, vitriol, zapper*; SEE CONCEPT 52

criticize [v1] *disapprove, judge as bad*
animadvert on, bash, blame, blast, blister, carp, castigate, censure, chastise, chide, clobber, come down on, condemn, cut down*, cut to bits*, cut up*, denounce, denunciate, disparage, do a number on*, dress down*, excoriate, find fault, flak*, fulminate against, fustigate, give bad press*, hit, jump on*, knock*, lambaste*, nag at, nit-pick, pan, pick at, rap*, reprehend, reprimand, reprobate, reprove, rip*, roast*, scathe, scorch*, skin*, skin alive*, slam*, slog*, slug*, take down*, trash*, trim*, zap*; SEE CONCEPT 52

criticize [v2] *analyze, comment*
appraise, assess, comment upon, evaluate, examine, give opinion, judge, pass judgment on, probe, review, scrutinize, study; SEE CONCEPTS 37,103

critique [n] *analysis, essay*
appraisal, assessment, comment, commentary, criticism, editorial, examination, exposition, flak*, judgment, notice, pan*, putdown*, rap*, rave*, review, reviewal, slam*, slap*, study, takedown*, write-up, zapper*; SEE CONCEPTS 51,52,271

croak [v] *make husky, squawking noise*
caw, crow, gasp, grunt, quack, squawk, utter huskily, utter throatily, wheeze; SEE CONCEPT 77

crony [n] *ally, companion*
accomplice, acquaintance, associate, bosom buddy*, buddy, chum, colleague, comate, comrade, confidant, friend, good buddy*, intimate, mate, pal, partner, sidekick*; SEE CONCEPT 423

crook [n] *criminal, thief*
cheat, filcher, knave, pilferer, purloiner, racketeer, robber, rogue, scoundrel, shark*, shyster*, swindler, villain; SEE CONCEPT 412

crook [v] *bend, angle*
bow, curve, flex, fork, hook, meander, notch,

round, slither, snake, wind, zigzag; SEE CONCEPTS 213,738

crooked [adj1] *bent, angled*
agee, anfractuous, angular, asymmetric, awry, bowed, catawampus*, circuitous, cockeyed*, contorted, crippled, curved, curving, deformed, deviating, devious, disfigured, distorted, errant, gnarled, hooked, incurving, indirect, irregular, kinky, knurly, lopsided, meandering, misshapen, not straight, oblique, out of shape, rambling, roundabout, screwy*, serpentine, sinuous, skewed, slanted, snaky, spiral, tilted, topsyturvy*, tortile, tortuous, twisted, twisting, uneven, warped, winding, zigzag; SEE CONCEPTS 486,490,581

crooked [adj2] *evil, corrupt*
crafty, criminal, deceitful, devious, dishonest, dishonorable, double-dealing, dubious, fraudulent, illegal, indirect, iniquitous, lying, nefarious, questionable, ruthless, shady, shifty, suborned, treacherous, underhand, unlawful, unprincipled, unscrupulous, untruthful; SEE CONCEPT 545

crop [n] *harvest of fruit, vegetable*
annual production, byproduct, crops, fruitage, fruits, gathering, gleaning, output, produce, product, reaping, season's growth, vintage, yield; SEE CONCEPT 429

crop [v] *cut, trim off*
chop, clip, curtail, detach, detruncate, disengage, hew, lop, mow, pare, pollard, prune, reduce, shave, shear, shorten, skive, slash, snip, top, truncate; SEE CONCEPT 176

cross [adj] *very angry; in a bad mood*
annoyed, cantankerous, captious, caviling, choleric, churlish, crabby*, cranky, crotchety*, crusty, disagreeable, faultfinding, fractious, fretful, grouchy, grumpy, ill-humored, ill-tempered, impatient, irascible, irritable, jumpy, out of humor, peeved, peevish, pettish, petulant, put out*, querulous, quick-tempered, ratty, short, snappy, splenetic, sullen, surly, testy, tetchy, touchy, vexed, waspish; SEE CONCEPTS 401,403

cross [v1] *traverse an area*
bridge, cruise, cut across, extend over, ford, go across, meet, move across, navigate, overpass, pass over, ply, sail, span, transverse, voyage, zigzag; SEE CONCEPTS 159,542

cross [v2] *intersect, lie across*
bisect, crisscross, crosscut, decussate, divide, intercross, intertwine, lace, lie athwart of, rest across; SEE CONCEPTS 738,747

cross [v3] *hybridize, mix*
blend, crossbreed, cross-fertilize, cross-mate, cross-pollinate, interbreed, intercross, mingle, mongrelize; SEE CONCEPTS 250,257

cross [v4] *betray, hinder*
backtalk, block, bollix, buck, crab, cramp, crimp, deny, double-cross, flummox, foil, foul up*, frustrate, have bone to pick*, impede, interfere, knock props out*, louse up*, obstruct, oppose, resist, sell*, sell out*, snafu*, stab in the back*, stonewall*, stump, stymie, take on, take wind out of sails*, thwart; SEE CONCEPTS 7,19,59,121

cross-examine [v] *ask pointed questions*
catechize, check, cross-question, debrief, examine, grill, interrogate, investigate, pump, put the screws to*, question, quiz, sweat, third-degree*; SEE CONCEPTS 48,53,317

crossing [n] *pathway to traverse larger path*
bridge, cloverleaf, crossroad, crosswalk, cross-

cr
cr

way, decussation, exchange, grade crossing, grating, gridiron, interchange, intersection, junction, loop, network, overpass, passage, screen, traversal, traverse, underpass; SEE CONCEPTS 501,513

crosswise/crossways [adj] *across, at an angle*
angular, aslant, athwart, at right angles, awry, contrariwise, crisscross, cross, crossing, diagonally, from side to side, horizontally, longways, on the bias, over, perpendicular, sideways, thwart, transversal, transverse, transversely, traverse, vertically; SEE CONCEPT 581

crotchety [adj] *irritable, often due to old age*
awkward, bad-tempered, bearish, cantankerous, contrary, crabby*, cranky, cross, cross-grained, crusty, curmudgeonly, difficult, disagreeable, eccentric, fractious, grouchy, grumpy, irritable, obstinate, obstreperous, odd, ornery*, peevish, queer, surly, testy, unusual, vinegary*, waspish, waspy; SEE CONCEPTS 401,403

crouch [v] *stoop low; cringe*
bend, bend down, bow, cower, dip, duck, grovel, huddle, hunch, hunker down, kneel, quail, quat, scrooch down, squat, stoop, wince; SEE CONCEPT 213

crow [v] *brag, exult*
babble, blow, bluster, boast, cackle, caw, cock-a-doodle-doo*, cry, flourish, gas, gloat, glory in, gurgle, jubilate, mouth, prate, puff, rodomontade, squawk, strut, swagger, triumph, vaunt, whoop; SEE CONCEPT 49

crowd [n1] *large assembly*
army, array, blowout, bunch, cattle, circle, clique, cloud, cluster, company, concourse, confluence, conflux, congeries, congregation, coterie, crew, crush, deluge, drove, faction, flock, flood, gaggle, great unwashed*, group, herd, horde, host, jam, legion, lot, mass, masses, meet, mob, multitude, muster, organization, pack, party, people, posse, press, rabble, rank and file*, scores, sellout, set, stream, surge, swarm, throng, troupe, tumult; SEE CONCEPTS 381,417

crowd [n2] *special group of friends*
bunch, circle, clique, coterie, faction, group, in-crowd, lot, posse, push, set; SEE CONCEPTS 387,417

crowd [v] *cram, press into area*
bear, bunch, bundle, chock, cluster, congest, congregate, crush, deluge, elbow, flock, gather, huddle, jam, jam-pack*, justle, mass, muster, overcrowd, pack, pack 'em in*, pack like sardines*, pile, push, ram, sardine*, shove, squash, squeeze, stream*, surge, swamp, swarm, throng, top off; SEE CONCEPTS 208,740

crowded [adj] *busy, congested*
awash, brimful, brimming, chock-full, clean, close, compact, crammed, cramped, crushed, dense, elbow-to-elbow*, filled to the rafters*, fit to bust*, full, full house*, full up*, huddled, jammed, jam-packed*, loaded, lousy with*, massed, mobbed, mob scene*, overflowing, packed, populous, sardined*, sold out, SRO*, standing room only*, stiff with*, stuffed, swarming, teeming, thick, thickset, thronged, topped off, up to here*, up to the hilt*, wall-to-wall*; SEE CONCEPTS 481,483,774

crown [n1] *top; best*
acme, apex, climax, crest, culmination, fastigium, head, meridian, peak, perfection, pinnacle, roof,
summit, tip, top, ultimate, vertex, zenith; SEE CONCEPTS 706,836

crown [n2] *tiara for royalty*
chaplet, circlet, coronal, coronet, diadem, garland, headband, headdress, wreath; SEE CONCEPT 452

crown [n3] *royalty*
crowned head, monarch, monarchy, potentate, ruler, sovereign, sovereignty, supreme ruler, the throne; SEE CONCEPT 422

crown [v1] *reward, dignify*
adorn, arm, authorize, commission, coronate, delegate, determine, dower, enable, endow, endue, ennoble, enthrone, erect, establish, exalt, festoon, fix, heighten, honor, inaugurate, induct, install, invest, raise, sanction, settle, set up, stabilize, strengthen; SEE CONCEPTS 50,69,88

crown [v2] *be the culmination of*
cap, climax, complete, consummate, crest, finish, fulfill, perfect, put finishing touch on, round off, surmount, terminate, top, top off; SEE CONCEPTS 234,706

crown [v3] *hit, usually on head*
biff, box, cuff, knock, punch, smite, strike; SEE CONCEPT 189

crowning [adj] *climactic*
consummate, culminating, excellent, final, paramount, principal, sovereign, supreme, ultimate; SEE CONCEPTS 531,548

crucial [adj] *critical, important*
acute, central, clamorous, climacteric, climatic, compelling, deciding, decisive, desperate, dire, essential, hanging by thread*, high-priority, imperative, insistent, momentous, necessary, on thin ice*, pivotal, pressing, searching, showdown*, touch and go*, touchy, urgent, vital; SEE CONCEPT 568

crucify [v1] *execute; torture near to death*
excruciate, hang, harrow, kill, martyr, martyrize, nail to cross, persecute, rack, torment, torture; SEE CONCEPT 252

crucify [v2] *browbeat, destroy with words*
afflict, agonize, bedevil, bother, harrow, ill-treat, lampoon, pan, ridicule, smite, tear to pieces*, torment, torture, try, wipe the floor with*; SEE CONCEPTS 7,19,52

crude [adj] *vulgar, unpolished in manner*
awkward, backward, barnyard*, boorish, cheap, cloddish, clumsy, coarse, crass, dirty, earthy, filthy, foul, grody*, gross*, ignorant, ill-bred, indecent, indelicate, inelegant, insensible, lewd, loud, loud-mouthed, loutish, lowbred, oafish, obscene, raunchy*, raw, rough, rude, savage, smutty*, tacky*, tactless, uncouth, unenlightened, ungainly, unskillful; SEE CONCEPTS 267,401

crude [adj2] *unrefined, natural*
amateurish, callow, coarse, green, harsh, homemade, homespun, immature, impure, inexpert, in the rough*, makeshift, outline, prentice, primitive, raw, rough, rough-hewn, rude, rudimentary, rustic, simple, sketchy, thick, undeveloped, unfinished, unformed, ungraded, unmatured, unmilled, unpolished, unprepared, unprocessed, unproficient, unsorted, untaught, untrained, unworked, unwrought; SEE CONCEPTS 562,578, 589,797

cruel [adj] *vicious, pitiless; causing pain*
atrocious, barbarous, bestial, bitter, bloodthirsty, brutal, brutish, callous, cold-blooded, degenerate, demoniac, depraved, evil, excruciating, ferocious,

fierce, flinty, hard, hard-hearted, harsh, hateful, heartless, hellish, implacable, inexorable, inhuman, inhumane, malevolent, merciless, monstrous, painful, pernicious, poignant, rancorous, relentless, revengeful, ruthless, sadistic, sinful, spiteful, tyrannical, unfeeling, unkind, unnatural, unrelenting, vengeful, vicious, virulent, wicked; SEE CONCEPTS *401,570*

cruelty [n] *brutality, harshness*

animality, barbarism, barbarity, bestiality, bloodthirstiness, brutishness, callousness, coarseness, coldness, depravity, despotism, ferocity, fiendishness, fierceness, hard-heartedness, heartlessness, inhumanity, insensibility, insensitiveness, malice, malignity, masochism, mercilessness, murderousness, persecution, rancor, ruthlessness, sadism, savageness, savagery, severity, spite, spitefulness, torture, truculence, unfeelingness, unkindness, venom, viciousness, wickedness; SEE CONCEPT *633*

cruise [n] *sailing expedition*

boat trip, crossing, jaunt, journey, sail, sailing, sea trip, voyage; SEE CONCEPTS *224,292,363*

cruise [v] *sail*

boat, coast, drift, fare, gad, gallivant, go, hie, jaunt, journey, keep steady pace, meander, navigate, pass, proceed, push on, repair, travel, voyage, wander about, wend; SEE CONCEPTS *147,151,159,224*

crumb [n] *tiny bit, morsel*

atom, dab, dash, dram, drop, grain, iota, jot, mite, ounce, particle, pinch, scrap, seed, shred, sliver, smidgen, snippet, soupçon, speck; SEE CONCEPT *831*

crumble [v] *break or fall into pieces*

break up, collapse, crumb, crush, decay, decompose, degenerate, deteriorate, disintegrate, dissolve, fragment, go to pieces, granulate, grind, molder, perish, powder, pulverize, putrefy, triturate, tumble; SEE CONCEPTS *181,248,469*

crumbly [adj] *brittle*

breakable, corroded, crisp, crunchy, decayed, degenerated, deteriorated, deteriorating, disintegrated, eroded, fragile, frail, frangible, friable, oxidized, perishing, powdery, pulverizable, rotted, rotten, rusted, shivery, short, soft, worn; SEE CONCEPTS *485,606*

crumple [v] *make or become wrinkled*

break down, buckle, cave in, collapse, crease, crimp, crimple, crinkle, crush, fail, fold, give way, go to pieces, pucker, rimple, ruck, rumple, screw, scrunch, shrivel, wad, wrinkle; SEE CONCEPTS *184,208,252*

crunch [n] *crucial point*

crisis, critical point, crux, difficulty, emergency, hour of decision*, moment of truth*, problem, test, trouble, trying time*; SEE CONCEPTS *388,674,675*

crunch [v] *grind, chew*

beat, bite, champ, chaw, chomp, crush, gnaw, masticate, munch, ruminate, scrunch; SEE CONCEPTS *169,186*

crusade [n] *campaign for cause*

cause, demonstration, drive, evangelism, expedition, holy war, jihad, march, movement, push; SEE CONCEPT *300*

crush [n1] *crowd of animate beings*

drove, gathering, horde, huddle, jam, multitude, party, press, push, throng, tumult; SEE CONCEPTS *417,432*

crush [n2] *infatuation*

beguin, desire, flame, love affair, passion, puppy love*, torch; SEE CONCEPT *20*

crush [v] *compress, smash*

beat, bray, break, bruise, buck, comminute, contriturate, contuse, crease, crowd, crumble, crunch, embrace, enfold, express, hug, jam, kablooey*, mash, pound, powder, press, pulverize, push, romp, rumple, squash, squeeze, squish, total*, trample, tread, triturate, wrinkle; SEE CONCEPTS *208,219,246,252*

crush [v2] *defeating soundly*

annihilate, bear down, beat, blot out*, blow away*, conquer, defeat, demolish, extinguish, force down, ice*, kill, obliterate, overcome, overpower, overwhelm, quelch, quell, reduce, ruin, squelch, stamp out*, strangle, subdue, subjugate, suppress, vanquish, wreck; SEE CONCEPTS *95,252*

crush [v3] *humiliate*

abash, browbeat, chagrin, dispose of, dump, hurt, mortify, overwhelm, put away*, put down*, quash, quell, shame, suppress; SEE CONCEPTS *7,19*

crust [n] *stiff outer layer; coating*

band, bloom, border, caking, coat, concretion, covering, edge, encrustation, film, hull, incrustation, integument, layer, outside, rind, scab, shell, skin, surface, verge; SEE CONCEPT *484*

crusty [adj1] *irritable, often due to old age*

abrupt, bluff, blunt, brief, brusque, cantankerous, captious, choleric, crabbed, crabby*, cranky, cross, curt, dour, gruff, harsh, ill-humored, irascible, peevish, prickly, sarcastic, saturnine, scornful, short, short-tempered, snappish, snarling, snippety, snippy, splenetic, surly, testy, touchy, vinegary*; SEE CONCEPT *401*

crusty [adj2] *brittle on outside*

crisp, crispy, crunchy, friable, hard, short, well-baked, well-done; SEE CONCEPTS *462,606*

crux [n] *most important part*

body, bottom line*, core, decisive point, essence, gist, heart, kernel, matter, meat*, meat and potatoes*, nitty-gritty, nub, pith, purport, substance, thrust; SEE CONCEPTS *668,826*

cry [n1] *weeping and making sad sounds*

bawl, bawling, bewailing, blubber, blubbering, howl, howling, keening, lament, lamentation, mourning, shedding tears, snivel, snivelling, sob, sobbing, sorrowing, tears, the blues*, wailing, weep, whimpering, yowl; SEE CONCEPTS *77,469*

cry [n2] *calling out; yelling*

acclamation, bark, bawl, bay, bellow, cackle, call, caw, chatter, cheer, clack, clamor, cluck, coo, crow, ejaculation, exclamation, expletive, fuss, gobble, groan, grunt, hiss, holler, hoot, howl, hullabaloo, hurrah, meow, mewling, moo, motto, nicker, note, outcry, pipe, quack, report, roar, ruckus, scream, screech, shout, shriek, song, squall, squawk, squeak, trill, uproar, vociferation, wail, whine, whinny, whistle, whoop, yammer, yawp*, yell, yelp, yoo-hoo; SEE CONCEPTS *47,77,278*

cry [v1] *weep and make sad sounds*

bawl, bemoan, bewail, blub, blubber, boohoo*, break down, burst into tears*, caterwaul, choke up, complain, crack up*, deplore, dissolve in tears*, fret, grieve, groan, howl, keen, lament, let go, let it all out*, mewl, moan, mourn, put on the weeps*, regret, ring the blues*, shed bitter tears*, shed tears, sigh, sniff, snivel, sob, sorrow, squall, turn on waterworks*, wail, weep, whimper, whine, yammer, yowl; SEE CONCEPTS 77,469

cry [v2] *call out, yell*
bark, bawl, bay, bellow, bleat, cackle, call, caw, chatter, cheer, clack, clamor, cluck, coo, croak, crow, ejaculate, exclaim, gabble, growl, grunt, hail, hiss, holler, holler out, hoot, howl, low, meow, moo, nicker, pipe, quack, roar, scream, screech, shout, shriek, sing out, snarl, squawk, trill, tweet, twitter, vociferate, whinny, whistle, whoop, yawp*, yelp; SEE CONCEPTS 47,77

cry [v3] *advertise*
announce, bark*, broadcast, build up, hawk, hype*, press-agent*, proclaim, promulgate, publicize, publish, puff*, trumpet*; SEE CONCEPT 324

crypt [n] *burial place*
catacomb, cave, cavern, cell, chamber, compartment, grave, grotto, mausoleum, room, sepulcher, tomb, undercroft, vault; SEE CONCEPT 305

cryptic [adj] *secret; obscure in meaning*
abstruse, ambiguous, apocryphal, arcane, cabbalistic, dark, Delphian, Delphic, enigmatic, equivocal, esoteric, evasive, hidden, incomprehensible, inexplicable, murky, mysterious, mystic, mystical, mystifying, occult, opaque, oracular, perplexing, puzzling, recondite, secretive, strange, tenebrous, unclear, unfathomable, uninformative, vague, veiled; SEE CONCEPTS 267,576,682

crystal [adj] *clear, transparent*
clear-cut, limpid, lucent, lucid, luminous, pellucid, translucent, transpicuous, unblurred; SEE CONCEPTS 617,618

cuddle [v] *hold fondly, closely*
bundle, burrow, caress, clasp, cosset, curl up, dandle, embrace, enfold, feel up*, fondle, huddle, hug, kiss, love, nestle, nuzzle, pet, snug, snuggle, touch; SEE CONCEPTS 190,375

cuddly [adj] *huggable, embraceable*
caressible, cuddlesome, kissable, lovable, plump, snuggly, soft, warm; SEE CONCEPT 485

cudgel [n] *baton for hitting*
bastinado, bat, billy*, billyclub, birch, blackjack, bludgeon, cane, club, cosh*, ferule, mace, nightstick, paddle, rod, sap, shill, shillelagh, spontoon, stick, switch, truncheon; SEE CONCEPT 500

cue [n] *signal to act*
catchword, clue, hint, hot lead*, idea, indication, inkling, innuendo, in the wind*, intimation, job, key, lead, mnemonic, nod, notion, prod, prompt, prompting, reminder, sign, suggestion, telltale*, tip-off, warning; SEE CONCEPTS 278,284,628

cuff [n] *beating with hands*
belt, biff, box, buffet, chop, clip, clout, hit, knock, poke, punch, rap, slap, smack, sock, thump, wallop, whack; SEE CONCEPT 189

cuff [v] *beat with hands*
bat, belt, biff, box, buffet, clap, clobber*, clout, hit, knock, pummel, punch, slap, smack, spank, thump, whack; SEE CONCEPT 189

cull [v1] *pick out for reason*
choose, discriminate, elect, extract, glean, mark, optate, opt for, pluck, prefer, select, sift, single out, take, thin, thin out, winnow; SEE CONCEPTS 41,142

cull [v2] *gather*
accumulate, amass, collect, extract, garner, glean, pick up, round up; SEE CONCEPT 109

culminate [v] *come to a climax*
cap, climax, close, come to a head*, conclude,

crown, end, end up, finish, go over the mountain*, go the route*, rise to crescendo, round off, shoot one's wad*, terminate, top off*, wind up*; SEE CONCEPT 119

culmination [n] *conclusion; climactic stage*
acme, all the way*, apex, apogee, blow off*, capper*, climax, completion, consummation, critical mass, crown, crowning touch, finale, finish, height, limit, maximum, meridian, ne plus ultra, noon, payoff, peak, perfection, pinnacle, punch line*, summit, top, zenith; SEE CONCEPTS 230,635,676

culpable [adj] *responsible for action*
amiss, answerable, at fault, blamable, blameful, blameworthy, caught, caught in the act*, caught red-handed*, censurable, demeritorious, dirty, found wanting, guilty, hung up, impeachable, indictable, in the wrong, liable, off base, out of line*, punishable, reprehensible, responsible, sinful, smoking gun*, to blame, unholy, wrong; SEE CONCEPTS 404,545

culprit [n] *person responsible for wrongdoing*
con, convict, criminal, delinquent, evildoer, ex-con, felon, fugitive, guilty party, jailbird*, malefactor, miscreant, offender, rascal, sinner, transgressor, wrongdoer, yardbird*; SEE CONCEPT 412

cult [n1] *group sharing belief*
band, body, church, clan, clique, creed, denomination, faction, faith, following, party, persuasion, religion, school, sect; SEE CONCEPTS 369,387

cult [n2] *worship; form of ceremony*
admiration, ceremony, craze, creed, cultus, devotion, faddism, faith, idolization, liturgy, persuasion, religion, reverence, rite, ritual, veneration; SEE CONCEPTS 410,689

cultivate [v1] *develop land for growing*
breed, crop, dress, farm, fertilize, garden, harvest, labor, manage, mature, plant, plow, prepare, propagate, raise, ripen, seed, tend, till, work; SEE CONCEPTS 253,257

cultivate [v2] *enrich situation; give special attention*
advance, ameliorate, better, bolster, bring on, brownnose*, butter up*, cherish, civilize, court, develop, discipline, elevate, encourage, enrich, foster, further, get in with*, get next to*, get on good side of*, improve, nourish, nurse, nurture, play up to*, polish, promote, refine, run after, seek friendship, shine up to*, suck up to*, take pains with, train; SEE CONCEPTS 244,384

cultivate [v3] *nurture, take care of*
aid, ameliorate, better, cherish, devote oneself to, educate, encourage, forward, foster, further, help, improve, instruct, nurse, patronize, promote, pursue, raise, rear, refine, support, teach, train; SEE CONCEPTS 110,295

cultivation [n1] *development of land for growing*
agrology, agronomics, agronomy, farming, gardening, horticulture, planting, plowing, tillage, tilling, working; SEE CONCEPT 257

cultivation [n2] *culture, sophistication, education*
advancement, aestheticism, breeding, civility, civilization, delicacy, discernment, discrimination, enlightenment, gentility, good taste, grounding, improvement, learning, letters, manners, polish, progress, refined taste, refinement, schooling, taste; SEE CONCEPTS 411,655,673

cultivation [n3] *nurture, help*
advancement, advocacy, development, encouragement, enhancement, fostering, furtherance, patronage, promotion, support; SEE CONCEPTS 110,657

cultural [adj] *educational, enlightening*
adorning, advancing, artistic, beautifying, beneficial, broadening, civilizing, constructive, corrective, developmental, dignifying, disciplining, edifying, educative, elevating, ennobling, enriching, expanding, glorifying, helpful, humane, humanizing, influential, inspirational, instructive, learned, liberal, liberalizing, nurturing, ornamenting, polishing, promoting, raising, refined, refining, regenerative, socializing, stimulating, uplifting, widening; SEE CONCEPTS 537,555,589

culture [n1] *breeding, education, sophistication*
ability, accomplishment, address, aestheticism, art, capacity, civilization, class, courtesy, cultivation, delicacy, dignity, discrimination, dress, elegance, elevation, enlightenment, erudition, experience, fashion, finish, gentility, good taste, grace, improvement, kindness, learning, manners, nobility, perception, polish, politeness, practice, proficiency, refinement, savoir-faire, science, skill, tact, training, urbanity; SEE CONCEPTS 388,633,678

culture [n2] *ideas, values of a people*
arts and sciences, civilization, convention, customs, development, ethnology, folklore, folkways, grounding, habit, humanism, knowledge, lifestyle, mores, society, the arts, way of life; SEE CONCEPTS 388,689

culture [n3] *development of land*
agriculture, agrology, agronomics, agronomy, cultivation, farming, gardening, raising, tending; SEE CONCEPT 257

cultured [adj] *well-bred, experienced*
able, accomplished, advanced, aesthetic, appreciative, au courant, blue-stocking*, chivalrous, civilized, courteous, cultivated, distingue, educated, elegant, enlightened, erudite, gallant, genteel, highbrow*, high-class, informed, intellectual, intelligent, knowledgeable, lettered, liberal, literary, literate, mannerly, polished, polite, refined, savant, scholarly, sensitive, sophisticated, tasteful, tolerant, traveled, understanding, up-to-date, urbane, versed, well-informed; SEE CONCEPT 550

culvert [n] *ditch for flow of water*
canal, channel, conduit, drain, duct, gutter, pipe, watercourse; SEE CONCEPT 509

cumbersome [adj] *clumsy, awkward*
bulky, burdensome, clunker, clunking, clunky, cumbrous, embarrassing, galumphing, heavy, hefty, incommodious, inconvenient, leaden, massive, oppressive, ponderous, tiresome, unhandy, unmanageable, unwieldy, wearisome, weighty; SEE CONCEPTS 544,773

cumulative [adj] *accruing; growing in size or effect*
accumulative, additive, additory, advancing, aggregate, amassed, augmenting, chain, collective, heaped, heightening, increasing, increscent, intensifying, magnifying, multiplying, snowballing*, summative; SEE CONCEPTS 540,548,786

cunning [adj1] *devious*
acute, artful, astute, cagey, canny, crafty, crazy like fox*, deep, fancy footwork*, foxy, guileful, insidious, keen, knowing, Machiavellian, sharp, shifty, shrewd, slick, slippery, sly, sly boots*, smart, smarts, smooth, street-smart*, streetwise*, subtle, tricky, wary, wily; SEE CONCEPTS 401,545

cunning [adj2] *imaginative*
able, adroit, canny, clever, crackerjack*, deft, dexterous, ingenious, intelligent, masterful, skillful, slighty, sly, smart, smooth, subtle, well-laid, well-planned; SEE CONCEPT 402

cup [n] *container for drinking*
beaker, bowl, cannikin, chalice, cupful, demitasse, draught, drink, goblet, grail, mug, potion, stein, taster, teacup, tumbler, vessel; SEE CONCEPT 494

cupboard [n] *storage cabinet*
buffet, closet, depository, facility, locker, press, repository, sideboard, storeroom, wardrobe; SEE CONCEPT 443

cupidity [n] *greed, strong desire*
acquisitiveness, avarice, avariciousness, avidity, covetousness, craving, eagerness, graspingness, greediness, hunger, infatuation, itching*, longing, lust, passion, possessiveness, rapaciousness, rapacity, voracity, yearning; SEE CONCEPTS 20,709

cur [n1] *rotten, lowly animate being*
blackguard, black sheep*, bum, cad, coward, dog*, good-for-nothing*, heel*, hound*, ne'er-do-well*, rat*, riffraff*, scoundrel, scum*, skunk*, snake*, stinker*, toad*, villain, wretch, yellow dog*; SEE CONCEPTS 389,412

cur [n2] *animal of mixed breed*
crossbreed, hybrid, mongrel, mutt; SEE CONCEPT 394

curable [adj] *able to be improved, fixed*
amenable, capable, correctable, corrigible, healable, improvable, mendable, not hopeless, not too bad, reparative, restorable, subject to cure; SEE CONCEPTS 314,485

curative [adj] *healing, health-giving*
alleviative, beneficial, corrective, curing, healthful, helpful, invigorating, medicable, medicative, medicinal, pick-me-up*, remedial, remedying, restorative, salutary, sanative, shot in the arm*, therapeutic, tonic, vulnerary, what the doctor ordered*, wholesome; SEE CONCEPTS 314,537

curb [n] *restraining device; check*
barrier, border, brake, bridle, chain, control, deterrent, edge, harness, hindrance, ledge, limitation, lip, rein, restrainer, restraint, restriction, rim; SEE CONCEPTS 376,497,652,745

curb [v] *repress, restrict*
abstain, bit, bottle up*, box in, bridle, bring to screeching halt*, check, clog, constrain, contain, control, cook*, cool down, cool off, deny, entrammel, fetter, hamper, hinder, hobble, hog-tie*, hold back, hold down, hold in, ice*, impede, inhibit, keep lid on*, keep tight rein on*, leash, manacle, moderate, muzzle, refrain, rein in, restrain, retard, scrub*, send up, shackle, subdue, suppress, tame, tie, tie up, withhold; SEE CONCEPTS 121,130

curdle [n] *sour; change into coagulated substance*
acerbate, acidify, acidulate, clabber, clot, coagulate, condense, congeal, curd, ferment, go off, spoil, thicken, turn, turn sour; SEE CONCEPT 456

cure [n] *solution to problem, often health*
aid, alleviation, antidote, assistance, catholicon, corrective, counteractant, counteragent, countermeasure, drug, elixir, elixir vitae, fix, healing, healing agent, help, medicament, medicant, medication, medicine, nostrum, panacea, pharmacon,

cr
cu

physic, placebo, proprietary, quick fix*, recovery, redress, remedy, reparation, restorative, therapeutic, treatment; SEE CONCEPTS 110,307,311

cure [v1] *heal, ease bad situation*
alleviate, ameliorate, attend, better, cold turkey*, correct, doctor, dose, dress, dry out*, help, improve, kick, kick the habit*, make better, make healthy, make whole, medicate, mend, minister to, nurse, palliate, quit cold*, rectify, redress, rehabilitate, relieve, remedy, repair, restore, restore to health, right, shake, sweat it out*, treat; SEE CONCEPTS 126,244,310

cure [v2] *cook, age food*
dry, fire, harden, keep, kipper, pickle, preserve, salt, smoke, steel, temper; SEE CONCEPT 170

curio [n] *knickknack*
antique, bauble, bibelot, bygone, collectible, collector's item, objet d'art, toy, trifle, trinket, whatnot; SEE CONCEPT 446

curiosity [n1] *intense desire to know, understand*
concern, eagerness, inquiring mind, inquiringness, inquisitiveness, interest, interestingness, intrusiveness, investigation, meddlesomeness, meddling, mental acquisitiveness, nosiness, officiousness, prying, questioning, regard, searching, snoopiness, snooping, thirst for knowledge; SEE CONCEPTS 20,410

curiosity [n2] *odd item*
anomaly, bibelot, bygone, conversation piece, curio, exoticism, freak, knickknack, marvel, monstrosity, nonesuch, objet d'art, oddity, peculiar object, prodigy, rarity, singular object, trinket, unusual object, wonder; SEE CONCEPT 260

curious [adj1] *desiring knowledge, understanding*
analytical, disquisitive, examining, impertinent, inquiring, inquisitive, inspecting, interested, interfering, intrusive, investigative, meddlesome, meddling, nosy, peeping, peering, prurient, prying, puzzled, questioning, scrutinizing, searching, snoopy*, tampering; SEE CONCEPTS 403,542

curious [adj2] *very odd*
bizarre, exotic, extraordinary, marvelous, mysterious, novel, oddball, peculiar, puzzling, quaint, queer, rare, remarkable, singular, strange, unconventional, unexpected, unique, unorthodox, unusual, weird, wonderful; SEE CONCEPTS 547,564

curl [n] *loop, ringlet, curve*
coil, crimp, crispation, curlicue, flourish, frizz, kink, quirk, spiral, swirl, twist, wave, whorl; SEE CONCEPTS 418,436

curl [v] *bend, loop*
buckle, coil, contort, convolute, corkscrew, crimp, crinkle, crisp, crook, curve, entwine, fold, form into ringlets, frizz, indent, kink, lap, meander, ringlet, ripple, roll, scallop, snake, spiral, swirl, turn, twine, twirl, twist, undulate, wave, wind, wreathe, writhe, zigzag; SEE CONCEPTS 147,184,213

curly [adj] *looping, forming ringlets*
coiled, convoluted, corkscrew, crimped, crimpy, crinkling, crinkly, crisp, curled, curling, frizzed, frizzy, fuzzy, kinky, looped, permed, spiralled, waved, waving, wavy, winding, wound; SEE CONCEPTS 406,486

currency [n] *paper and coin money of a country*
almighty dollar*, bills, bread*, cabbage*, cash, chicken feed*, coinage, coins, cold cash*, dinero*, dough*, folding money, green stuff*, legal tender, medium of exchange, moolah*, notes,

piece of change*, roll*, specie, wad*; SEE CONCEPT 340

current [n] *flow of something, usually water*
course, draught, drift, ebb and flow, flood, flux, jet, juice, progression, river, run, rush, spate, stream, tidal motion, tide; SEE CONCEPTS 514,519,738

current [adj] *contemporary; common*
accepted, accustomed, afoot, circulating, common knowledge, customary, cutting-edge*, doing, existent, extant, fad, fashionable, general, going around, hot*, in, in circulation, in progress, instant, in the mainstream, in the news, in use, in vogue, leading-edge*, mod*, modern, now*, on front burner*, ongoing, popular, present, present-day, prevailing, prevalent, rampant, regnant, rife, ruling, state-of-the-art, swinging, topical, trendy, up-to-date, widespread; SEE CONCEPTS 530,820

curse [n1] *hateful, swearing remark*
anathema, ban, bane, blaspheming, blasphemy, commination, cursing, cussing*, cuss word*, damning, denunciation, dirty name*, dirty word*, double whammy*, execration, expletive, four-letter word*, fulmination, imprecation, malediction, malison, naughty words*, no-no*, oath, objuration, obloquy, obscenity, profanation, profanity, sacrilege, swearing, swear word, vilification, whammy*; SEE CONCEPTS 54,278

curse [n2] *misfortune wished upon someone*
affliction, bane, burden, calamity, cancer, cross, disaster, evil, evil eye*, hydra, jinx, ordeal, pestilence, plague, scourge, torment, tribulation, trouble, vexation, voodoo; SEE CONCEPTS 674,675

cursed [adj1] *damned, doomed for bad ending*
accursed, bedeviled, blankety-blank*, blasted, blessed, blighted, cast out, confounded, doggone*, excommunicate, execrable, fey, foredoomed, hell fire*, ill-fated, infernal, snakebit*, star-crossed, unholy, unsanctified, villainous, voodooed*; SEE CONCEPTS 548,571

cursed [adj2] *detestable, hateful*
abominable, accursed, atrocious, damnable, devilish, disgusting, execrable, fiendish, flatitous, heinous, infamous, infernal, loathsome, odious, pernicious, pestilential, vile; SEE CONCEPTS 404,571

cursory [adj] *casual, hasty*
brief, careless, depthless, desultory, fast, half-assed*, half-baked*, haphazard, hit or miss*, hurried, offhand, passing, perfunctory, quick, random, rapid, shallow, short, sketchy, slapdash, slight, sloppy, speedy, summary, superficial, swift, uncritical; SEE CONCEPTS 562,588,589

curt [adj] *abrupt, rude*
blunt, breviloquent, brief, brusque, churlish, compendiary, compendious, concise, crusty, gruff, imperious, laconic, offhand, peremptory, pithy, sharp, short, short and sweet, snappish, snippety, snippy, succinct, summary, tart, terse, unceremonious, uncivil, ungracious; SEE CONCEPT 267

curtail [v] *cut short; abridge*
abbreviate, boil down, chop, clip, contract, cramp, cut, cut back, decrease, diminish, dock, downsize, get to meat*, halt, lessen, lop, minify, pare down, put in nutshell*, reduce, retrench, roll back, shorten, slash, trim, truncate; SEE CONCEPTS 130,236,247

curtain [n] *window covering*
blind, decoration, drape, drapery, film, hanging,

jalousie, oleo, portiere, rag, roller, screen, shade, shield, shroud, shutter, valance, veil, Venetian blind; SEE CONCEPT *444*

curvaceous [*adj*] *voluptuous, full-figured*
bosomy, buxom, curvesome, curvilinear, curvy, rounded, shapely, statuesque, well-developed, well-proportioned, well-rounded, zaftig*; SEE CONCEPTS *406,490*

curvature [*n*] *rounded part of thing, usually body part*
arc, arch, arching, bend, bow, curve, curving, curvity, deflection, flexure, incurvation, round, shape; SEE CONCEPTS *754,757*

curve [*n*] *arched, rounded line or object*
ambit, arc, arch, bend, bight, bow, camber, catenary, chord, circle, circuit, circumference, compass, concavity, contour, crook, curlicue, curvation, curvature, ellipse, festoon, flexure, hairpin, half-moon, helix, horseshoe, hyperbola, incurvation, incurvature, loop, meniscus, ogee, parabola, quirk, rondure, round, sinuosity, sweep, swerve, trajectory, turn, vault, whorl; SEE CONCEPT *436*

curve [*v*] *bending in a shape or course*
arc, arch, bend, bow, buckle, bulge, coil, concave, convex, crook, crumple, curl, deviate, divert, gyrate, hook, incurve, inflect, loop, round, skew, snake, spiral, stoop, swerve, turn, twist, veer, wind, wreathe; SEE CONCEPTS *147,184, 213,738*

curved [*adj*] *bowed, bent*
arced, arched, arciform, arrondi, biflected, circular, compass, crooked, curly, curvaceous, curvilinear, declinate, elliptical, enbowed, humped, incurvate, incurved, looped, loopy, round, rounded, serpentine, sigmoid, sinuous, skewed, snaky, S-shaped, sweeping, swirly, turned, twisted, twisting, twisty, wreathed; SEE CONCEPTS *486,490*

cushion [*n*] *pillow, pad*
beanbag, bolster, buffer, bumper, fender, hassock, headrest, mat, rest, seat, sham, squab, woolsack; SEE CONCEPTS *444,464,484*

cushion [*v*] *pad, protect from blow*
bolster, buttress, cradle, dampen, deaden, insulate, muffle, pillow, seclude, soften, stifle, support, suppress; SEE CONCEPT *680*

custodian [*n*] *caretaker, maintenance person*
baby sitter, bodyguard, cerebus, claviger, cleaner, cleaning person, concierge, curator, escort, guardian, housesitter, keeper, maintenance person, manager, overseer, protector, sitter, steward, super*, superintendent, supervisor, swamper*, warden, watchdog, watchperson; SEE CONCEPT *348*

custody [*n1*] *supervision, charge of something*
aegis, auspices, care, conservation, custodianship, guardianship, keeping, management, observation, preservation, protection, safekeeping, salvation, superintendence, trusteeship, tutelage, ward, wardship, watch; SEE CONCEPTS *117,376,710*

custody [*n2*] *confinement, jailing*
arrest, detention, duress, imprisonment, incarceration, jail, keeping; SEE CONCEPTS *90,691*

custom [*n1*] *habitual action*
addiction, beaten path*, characteristic, consuetude, daily grind*, fashion, form, grind*, groove, habit, habitude, hang-up*, into*, manner, matter of course, mode, observance, practice, praxis, precedent, procedure, proprieties, routine, rule, second nature*, shot, swim, thing, trick, usage, use, way, wont; SEE CONCEPT *633*

custom [*n2*] *ritual, traditional action*
attitude, canon, ceremony, character, convention, conventionalism, design, dictates, established way, etiquette, fashion, folkways, form, formality, inheritance, manner, matter of course, method, mode, mold, mores, observance, observation, pattern, performance, policy, practice, praxis, precedent, precept, rite, routine, rule, second nature*, style, system, taste, type, unwritten law, unwritten rule, usage, use, vogue, way; SEE CONCEPTS *644,688*

customarily [*adv*] *ordinarily; as a rule*
as a matter of course, as usual, commonly, consistently, conventionally, frequently, generally, habitually, naturally, normally, regularly, routinely, traditionally, usually, wontedly; SEE CONCEPTS *530,547*

customary [*adj*] *usual, established*
accepted, according to Hoyle*, accustomed, acknowledged, by the numbers*, chronic, common, confirmed, conventional, established, everyday, familiar, fashionable, frequent, general, habitual, household, in a rut*, in the groove*, normal, ordinary, orthodox, playing it safe*, popular, prescriptive, recognized, regular, regulation, routine, same old*, SOP*, standard, standard operating procedure*, stipulated, traditional, understood, universal, wonted; SEE CONCEPTS *530,547*

customer [*n*] *buyer of goods, services*
client, clientele, consumer, habitué, patron, prospect, purchaser, regular shopper; SEE CONCEPT *348*

cut [*n1*] *incision*
carving, chip, chop, cleavage, cleft, dissection, fissure, furrow, gash, graze, groove, intersection, kerf, laceration, mark, nick, nip, notch, opening, passage, penetration, pierce, prick, rabbet, rent, rip, scarification, sculpture, section, shave, slash, slit, slot, snip, stab, stroke, trench, trim, wound; SEE CONCEPT *309*

cut [*n2*] *reduction, diminution*
cutback, decrease, decrement, downsize, economy, fall, lessening, lowering, reduction, saving; SEE CONCEPTS *698,776*

cut [*n3*] *portion of profit*
allotment, allowance, bite, chop*, division, kickback*, lot, member, moiety, part, partage, percentage, piece, quota, section, segment, share, slice; SEE CONCEPT *344*

cut [*n4*] *style, shape of clothing*
configuration, construction, fashion, figure, form, look, mode; SEE CONCEPTS *655,754*

cut [*n5*] *insult*
abuse, hateful remark, indignity, offense; SEE CONCEPT *52*

cut [*n6*] *type, kind*
cast, description, feather, ilk, lot, mold, sort, stamp; SEE CONCEPT *378*

cut [*v1*] *sever, chop with sharp instrument; incise*
amputate, behead, bisect, bite, carve, chine, chip, chisel, cleave, clip, crop, curtail, decussate, dice, dissect, dissever, divide, facet, fell, flitch, gash, guillotine, hack, hash, hew, intersect, lacerate, lay open, lop, mince, mow, nick, notch, part, penetrate, perforate, pierce, prune, puncture, quarter, rabbet, reap, rend, rip, rive, saber, saw, scarify, scissor, score, scythe, separate, shave, shear, sickle, skive, slash, slice, slit, sliver, snip,

split, sunder, transect, truncate, whack; SEE CONCEPTS *137,176*

cut [v2] *shorten, reduce*
abbreviate, abridge, bob, clip, condense, contract, crop, curtail, cut back, cut down, decrease, delete, dock, ease up, edit out, excise, lessen, lower, mark down, mow, pare, precis, ration, reduce, shave, slash, slim, trim, truncate; SEE CONCEPTS *236,247*

cut [v3] *ignore, avoid*
cold-shoulder*, disregard, ditch*, duck, dump*, evade, freeze someone out*, grieve, hurt, insult, look straight through*, look the other way, neglect, ostracize, pain, play hooky*, play truant, shirk, skip, slam door on*, slight, snob, snub, spurn, stay away, sting, turn aside, turn one's back on, wound; SEE CONCEPTS *38,188,633*

cut [v4] *dilute*
impair, thin, undermine, weaken; SEE CONCEPT *240*

cutback [n] *reduction*
curtailment, cut, decrease, decrement, economy, lessening, retrenchment, shortening; SEE CONCEPTS *335,776*

cut back [v] *economize*
abbreviate, abridge, check, clip, curb, curtail, cut, cut down, decrease, lessen, lower, mark down, mark off, pare, prune, reduce, retrench, shave, shorten, slash, trim; SEE CONCEPTS *236,247*

cut down [v] *kill; fell*
dispatch, hew, level, lop, massacre, mow, mow down, raze, slaughter, slay; SEE CONCEPT *252*

cute [adj] *perky, attractive*
adorable, beautiful, charming, dainty, delightful, pleasant, pretty; SEE CONCEPTS *404,579*

cut in [v] *interrupt*
break in, butt in*, chisel in*, horn in*, interfere, interpose, intervene, intrude, move in, obtrude; SEE CONCEPT *234*

cut off [v1] *prevent; interrupt*
block, break in, bring to end, catch, close off, disconnect, discontinue, halt, insulate, intercept, intersect, intervene, intrude, isolate, obstruct, renounce, segregate, separate, sequester, suspend; SEE CONCEPT *234*

cut off [v2] *disinherit in will*
cut out of will, disown, renounce; SEE CONCEPT *317*

cut out [v] *excise, remove*
carve, cease, delete, displace, eliminate, exclude, exsect, extirpate, extract, give up, oust, pull out, refrain from, sever, stop, supersede, supplant, usurp; SEE CONCEPT *211*

cut out for [adj] *adapted*
adequate, competent, designed, equipped, fit, fitted, good for, qualified, suitable, suited; SEE CONCEPT *558*

cut short [v] *bring to an end; leave unfinished*
abbreviate, abort, abridge, break off, check, diminish, end, finish, halt, hinder, intercept, interrupt, postpone, quit, shorten, stop, terminate; SEE CONCEPTS *121,234*

cutting [adj] *nasty, hateful*
acerbic, acid, acrimonious, barbed, biting, bitter, caustic, clear-cut, crisp, hurtful, incisive, ingoing, malicious, penetrating, piercing, pointed, probing, raw, sarcastic, sardonic, scathing, severe, sharp, stinging, trenchant, wounding; SEE CONCEPT *267*

cut up [v1] *make fun of; criticize*
censure, condemn, crucify, denounce, give a rough time*, knock, pan*, rap, reprehend, reprobate, ridicule, skin, vilify; SEE CONCEPT *52*

cut up [v2] *be rowdy*
act up, caper, carry on*, cavort, clown, fool around, joke, misbehave, play, play jokes, romp, roughhouse, show off, whoop it up*; SEE CONCEPT *384*

cut up [v3] *chop, mince*
carve, dice, divide, slice; SEE CONCEPT *176*

cybernetics [n] *science studying brain function to design analagous mechanical systems*
artificial intelligence, automatic technology, automation, autonetics, electronic communication, radiodynamics, robotization, telemechanics; SEE CONCEPTS *274,349*

cycle [n] *era, phase*
aeon, age, alternation, chain, circle, circuit, course, eon, isochronism, loop, orbit, period, periodicity, revolution, rhythm, ring, rotation, round, run, sequel, sequence, series, succession, wheel; SEE CONCEPTS *816,817*

cynic [n] *nonbeliever*
carper, caviler, detractor, disbeliever, doubter, doubting Thomas*, egoist, egotist, flouter, misanthrope, misanthropist, misogamist, misogynist, mocker, pessimist, questioner, satirist, scoffer, skeptic, sneerer, unbeliever; SEE CONCEPTS *361,423*

cynical [adj] *nonbelieving; doubtful*
contemptuous, derisive, ironic, misanthropic, misanthropical, mocking, pessimistic, sarcastic, sardonic, scoffing, scornful, skeptical, sneering, suspicious, unbelieving, wry; SEE CONCEPTS *267,403*

cyst [n] *unusual growth*
bag, bleb, blister, injury, pouch, sac, sore, vesicle, wen; SEE CONCEPT *306*

D

dab [n] *small quantity*
bit, blob, dollop, drop, fleck, flick, pat, peck, smidgen, smudge, speck, spot, stroke, tap, touch; SEE CONCEPT *835*

dab [v] *blot up; touch lightly*
bedaub, besmear, daub, pat, peck, plaster, smear, smudge, stipple, swab, tap, wipe; SEE CONCEPT *612*

dabble [v] *play at; tinker*
amuse oneself with, be amateur, dally, dilly-dally*, fiddle with*, flirt with*, horse around*, idle, kid around*, mess around*, monkey*, monkey around*, muck around*, not be serious*, play, play around*, play games with, toy with, trifle, trifle with, work superficially; SEE CONCEPT *87*

dabbler [n] *amateur*
abecedarian, beginner, dilettante, loafer, nonprofessional, novice, potterer, pretender, smatterer, tinkerer, trifler, tyro, uninitiate; SEE CONCEPTS *348,366*

daft [adj] *stupid; crazy*
absurd, asinine, bedlamite, bonkers, cracked*,

crackers*, daffy*, demented, deranged, dopey*, flaky*, foolish, fried*, giddy, half-baked*, idiotic, inane, insane, in the ozone*, lunatic, mad, mental*, nuts, nutty*, off the wall*, out of one's gourd*, ridiculous, screwy*, silly, simple, touched, unbalanced, unhinged*, unsound, wacky, whacko*, witless; SEE CONCEPT *403*

daily [adj] *occurring every day; during the day*
circadian, common, commonplace, constantly, cyclic, day after day, day by day, day-to-day, diurnal, everyday, from day to day, often, once a day, once daily, ordinary, per diem, periodic, quotidian, regular, regularly, routine; SEE CONCEPTS *541,801*

dainty [adj1] *delicate, fragile, fine*
airy, attractive, beautiful, bonny, charming, choice, comely, cute, darling, delectable, delicious, delightful, diaphanous, elegant, ethereal, exquisite, fair, feeble, frail, graceful, lacy, light, lovely, neat, nice, palatable, petite, pleasing, precious, pretty, rare, recherché, refined, savory, select, soft, subtle, superior, sweet, tasteful, tasty, tender, thin, toothsome, trim, well-made; SEE CONCEPTS *490,491,606*

dainty [adj2] *finicky, particular*
acute, choosy, delicate, fastidious, finical, finicking, fussy, mincing, nice, perceptive, persnickety*, refined, scrupulous, tasteful; SEE CONCEPT *404*

dairy [n] *producer of milk products*
buttery, cow barn, creamery, dairy farm, factory, farm, pasteurizing plant; SEE CONCEPTS *449,517*

dalliance [n1] *dawdling*
dabbling, delay, delaying, dilly-dallying*, frittering, frivoling, idling, loafing, loitering, playing, poking*, procrastinating, procrastination, puttering, toying, trifling; SEE CONCEPTS *151,210,681*

dalliance [n2] *love affair*
affair, a little on the side*, amorous play, carrying on*, fling, fooling around*, frolicking, hanky-panky*, messing around*, relationship, seduction, toying*, working late at office*; SEE CONCEPTS *114,375,388*

dally [v] *dawdle, delay*
boondoggle*, drag, fool around, fool with, fritter away, hang about*, horse around*, idle, jerk off*, lag, linger, loiter, lollygag*, play around*, play games with*, procrastinate, put off, putter, tarry, trail, trifle with, waste time, while away; SEE CONCEPTS *151,210,681*

dally/dally with [v2] *have love affair*
be insincere with, carry on, cosset, fool around*, frivol, frolic, gambol, have a fling, lead on, play around*, rollick, romp, tamper, wanton; SEE CONCEPTS *114,375*

dam [n] *embankment, wall*
bank, barrage, barrier, dike, ditch, gate, grade, hindrance, levee, milldam, millpond, obstruction, weir; SEE CONCEPT *470*

dam [v] *hold back; block*
bar, barricade, brake, check, choke, clog, close, confine, hinder, hold in, impede, obstruct, repress, restrain, restrict, retard, slow, stop up, suppress; SEE CONCEPTS *130,191*

damage [n1] *injury, loss*
accident, adulteration, adversity, affliction, bane, blemish, blow, breakage, bruise, casualty, catastrophe, cave-in, contamination, corruption, debasement, depreciation, deprivation, destruction, deterioration, detriment, devastation, disservice,

disturbance, evil, hardship, harm, hurt, illness, impairment, infliction, knockout, marring, mischief, mishap, mutilation, outrage, pollution, ravage, reverse, ruin, ruining, spoilage, stroke, suffering, waste, wound, wreckage, wrecking, wrong; SEE CONCEPTS *309,674*

damage(s) [n2] *cost for problem*
amends, bill, charge, compensation, expense, fine, forfeit, indemnity, reimbursement, reparation, satisfaction, total; SEE CONCEPTS *123,329*

damage [v] *cause injury, loss*
abuse, bang up*, batter, bleach, blight, break, burn, contaminate, corrode, corrupt, crack, cripple, deface, defile, dirty, discolor, disfigure, disintegrate, dismantle, fade, gnaw, harm, hurt, impair, incapacitate, infect, injure, lacerate, maim, maltreat, mangle, mar, mutilate, pollute, ravage, rot, ruin, rust, scathe, scorch, scratch, smash, split, spoil, stab, stain, tamper with, tarnish, tear, undermine, vitiate, weaken, wear away, wound, wreak havoc on*, wreck, wrong; SEE CONCEPTS *246,252*

damaged [adj] *broken, not working*
beat-up, bent, blemished, busted, dinged, down, flawed, flubbed*, fouled up*, glitched*, gone, hurt, impaired, imperfect, injured, in need of repair, in poor condition, in smithereens*, kaput*, loused up*, marred, messed up*, mucked up*, no go*, on the blink*, on the fritz*, out of action*, out of kilter*, out of whack*, run-down, screwed up*, shot, snafued*, spoiled, sunk*, totaled*, unsound; SEE CONCEPTS *485,560*

damaging [adj] *hurtful to reputation*
bad, deleterious, detrimental, disadvantageous, evil, harmful, injurious, mischievous, nocent, nocuous, prejudicial, ruinous; SEE CONCEPT *537*

damn [v] *condemn, denounce*
abuse, anathematize, attack, ban, banish, blaspheme, blast, castigate, cast out, censure, complain of, confound, convict, criticize, cry down, curse, cuss*, darn, denunciate, doom, drat, excommunicate, excoriate, execrate, expel, flame, fulminate against, imprecate, inveigle against, jinx, object to, objurgate, pan*, penalize, proscribe, punish, revile, sentence, slam, swear, thunder against*; SEE CONCEPTS *52,54*

damnable [adj] *atrocious, horrible*
abhorrent, abominable, accursed, blamed, blessed, culpable, cursed, dang*, darn, depraved, despicable, detestable, dratted*, execrable, hateful, odious, offensive, outrageous, wicked; SEE CONCEPTS *545,570*

damned [adj] *hateful, unwelcome*
accursed, all-fired*, anathematized, bad, blankety-blank*, blasted, blessed*, bloody*, blooming*, condemned, confounded, cursed, cussed*, damnable, dang*, darn*, darned*, despicable, detestable, doggone*, done for*, doomed, dratted*, execrable, gone to blazes*, infamous, infernal*, loathsome, lost, lousy, reprobate, revolting, unhappy, voodooed*; SEE CONCEPTS *545,570*

damp [adj] *wet, humid*
clammy, cloudy, dank, dewy, drenched, dripping, drippy, drizzly, irriguous, misty, moist, muggy, oozy, saturated, soaked, soaking, sodden, soggy, sopping, steam bath*, steamy, sticky, vaporous, waterlogged, wettish; SEE CONCEPT *603*

dampen [v1] *make wet*
bedew, besprinkle, dabble, humidify, moisten,

cu
da

rinse, spray, sprinkle, water, wet; SEE CONCEPT 256

dampen [v2] *spoil spirits*
allay, check, chill, cloud, cool, curb, dash, deaden, deject, depress, diminish, discourage, dismay, dispirit, dull, humble, inhibit, moderate, muffle, mute, restrain, stifle; SEE CONCEPTS 7,19

dance [n1/v] *moving feet and body to music*
bob*, boogie, boogie down*, bunny hop, caper, careen, cavort, Charleston, conga, cut a rug*, disco, flit*, foot it*, foxtrot, frolic, gambol, get down*, hoof it*, hop, hustle, jig, jitter*, jitterbug, jive*, jump, leap, one-step, prance, promenade, rhumba, rock, rock 'n' roll, samba, shimmy, skip, spin, step, strut, sway, swing, tango, tap, tread, trip, trip the light fantastic*, twist, two-step, waltz, whirl; SEE CONCEPTS 292,363

dance [n2] *party for moving to music*
ball, brawl, disco, formal, hoedown, hop, jump, masquerade, mingle, prom, promenade, shindig, social, sock hop; SEE CONCEPT 383

dandle [v] *caress, cuddle*
amuse, cosset, cradle, dance, fondle, love, nuzzle, pet, play, ride on knee, rock, sport, toss, toy*, toy with*; SEE CONCEPTS 147,190

dandy [adj] *fine, excellent*
capital, cool*, exemplary, famous, first-class, first-rate, five-star*, fly*, glorious, grand, great, groovy*, hunky-dory*, keen, marvelous, model, neat, nifty, paragon, peachy*, prime, splendid, superior, swell, terrific; SEE CONCEPT 574

danger [n] *hazard, troublesome situation*
clouds, crisis, double trouble*, dynamite, emergency, endangerment, exigency, exposure, hot potato*, insecurity, instability, jeopardy, menace, peril, pitfall, possibility, precariousness, precipice, probability, risk, risky business*, slipperiness, storm, thin ice*, threat, uncertainty, venture, vulnerability; SEE CONCEPT 675

dangerous [adj] *hazardous, troubling*
alarming, bad, breakneck*, chancy, critical, dangersome, deadly, delicate, dynamite, exposed, fatal, formidable, hairy*, heavy*, hot*, impending, impregnable, insecure, jeopardous, loaded, malignant, menacing, mortal, nasty, on collision course*, parlous, perilous, portentous, precarious, pressing, queasy, risky, serious, serpentine, shaky, speculative, terrible, thorny*, threatening, ticklish*, touch-and-go*, touchy, treacherous, ugly*, unhealthy, unsafe, unstable, urgent, viperous, vulnerable, wicked; SEE CONCEPT 548

dangerously [adv] *precariously*
alarmingly, carelessly, critically, daringly, desperately, gravely, harmfully, hazardously, perilously, precariously, recklessly, riskily, seriously, severely, unsafely, unsecurely; SEE CONCEPT 548

dangle [v] *suspend*
brandish, depend, droop, entice, flap, flaunt, flourish, hang, hang down, lure, sling, sway, swing, tantalize, tempt, trail, wave; SEE CONCEPTS 153,190

dank [adj] *clammy*
chilly, close, damp, dewy, dripping, humid, moist, muggy, slimy, soggy, steamy, sticky, wet, wettish; SEE CONCEPT 603

dapper [adj] *well-groomed, neat*
bandbox, brisk, chic, chichi, classy, clean, dainty, dashing, doggy*, dressed to kill*, dressed to nines*, jaunty, natty, nice, nifty, nimble, nobby,

posh, prim, rakish, ritzy, sassy, sharp, showy, smart, snazzy*, snug, spiff, spiffy, spruce, spry, stylish, swank, swanky, swell, trim, turned out, well turned out; SEE CONCEPT 579

dappled [adj] *mottled, freckled*
brindle, brindled, checkered, discolored, flecked, motley, multicolor, multicolored, multihued, parti-colored, piebald, pied, speckled, spotted, stippled, varicolored, variegated, versicolor, versicolored; SEE CONCEPT 618

dare [n] *challenge, defiance*
cartel, defy, provocation, stump, taunt; SEE CONCEPTS 53,87

dare [v] *challenge, defy someone*
beard, brave, bully, call one's bluff, confront, cope, denounce, disregard, face, face off, front, goad, insult, knock chip off shoulder*, laugh at, make my day*, meet, mock, muster courage, oppose, outdare, provoke, resist, run the gauntlet, scorn, spurn, square off, step over the line, take one on, taunt, threaten, throw down gauntlet; SEE CONCEPTS 14,53

dare [v2] *take a risk; be courageous*
adventure, attempt, be bold, brave, endanger, endeavor, gamble, go ahead, hazard, make bold, pluck up, presume, risk, run the risk, speculate, stake, take a chance, take heart, try, try one's hand*, undertake, venture; SEE CONCEPTS 35,87

daring [adj] *adventurous*
adventuresome, audacious, bold, brassy*, brave, cheeky, cocky, courageous, crusty, fearless, fire eating*, foolhardy, forward, game, go for broke*, gritty, gutsy*, gutty*, hot shot*, impudent, impulsive, intrepid, nervy, obtrusive, out on a limb*, plucky, rash, reckless, salty*, smart, smartalecky*, spunky*, temerarious, valiant, venturesome; SEE CONCEPT 401

dark [n1] *place, time without light*
caliginosity, darkness, dead of night, dimness, dusk, duskiness, evening, gloom, midnight, murk, murkiness, night, nightfall, nighttime, obscurity, opacity, semidarkness, shade, shadows, twilight, witching hour; SEE CONCEPTS 620,810

dark [n2] *ignorance; mystery*
concealment, denseness, inscrutability, seclusion, secrecy, thickness; SEE CONCEPTS 409,410

dark [adj1] *lack of light*
aphotic, atramentous, black, blackish, caliginous, Cimmerian, clouded, cloudy, crepuscular, darkened, dim, dingy, drab, dull, dun, dusk, dusky, faint, foggy, gloomy, grimy, ill-lighted, indistinct, inky, lightless, lurid, misty, murky, nebulous, obfuscous, obscure, opaque, overcast, pitchblack, pitch-dark, pitchy, rayless, shaded, shadowy, shady, somber, sooty, stygian, sunless, tenebrous, unlighted, unlit, vague; SEE CONCEPT 617

dark [adj2] *shaded complexion, hair*
adumbral, bistered, black, brunet, brunette, dark-complexioned, dark-skinned, dusky, ebon, ebony, sable, swart, swarthy, tan; SEE CONCEPTS 406,618

dark [adj3] *hidden, secret*
abstruse, anagogic, arcane, cabalistic, complicated, concealed, cryptic, deep, Delphian, enigmatic, esoteric, intricate, knotty, mysterious, mystic, mystical, mystifying, not known, obscure, occult, puzzling, recondite; SEE CONCEPTS 402,576,582

dark [*adj4*] *grim, hopeless*
bleak, cheerless, dismal, doleful, drab, foreboding, gloomy, joyless, morbid, morose, mournful, ominous, sinister, somber, unpropitious; SEE CONCEPT 548

dark [*adj5*] *evil, satanic*
atrocious, bad, corrupt, damnable, foul, hellish, horrible, immoral, infamous, infernal, nefarious, sinful, sinister, vile, wicked; SEE CONCEPT 545

dark [*adj6*] *ignorant*
benighted, uncultivated, unenlightened, unlettered, unread; SEE CONCEPT 402

dark [*adj7*] *angry, upset*
dour, forbidding, frowning, glowering, glum, ominous, scowling, sulky, sullen, threatening; SEE CONCEPT 401

darken [*v*] *become shaded, unlit*
becloud, bedim, blacken, cloud over, cloud up, deepen, dim, eclipse, fog, gray, haze, make dim, murk, obfuscate, obscure, overcast, overshadow, shade, shadow, tone down*; SEE CONCEPTS 250,469

darkness [*n1*] *place, time that is unlit*
black, blackness, blackout, brownout, caliginosity, Cimmerian shade, cloudiness, crepuscule, dark, dimness, dusk, duskiness, eclipse, gloom, lightlessness, murk, murkiness, nightfall, obscurity, pitch darkness, shade, shadiness, shadows, smokiness, tenebrosity, twilight; SEE CONCEPT 620

darkness [*n2*] *ignorance; mystery*
blindness, concealment, denseness, inscrutability, isolation, privacy, seclusion, secrecy, unawareness; SEE CONCEPTS 409,410

darling [*n*] *sweetheart, favorite person*
angel*, apple of one's eye*, baby*, beloved, boyfriend, dear, dearest, dearie*, dear one, fair-haired boy*, flame, friend, girlfriend, heart's desire*, honeybunch, lamb*, light of my life*, love, lover, one and only*, pet*, precious, sugar*, sweetie, treasure*, truelove; SEE CONCEPT 423

dart [*v*] *race away; propel*
bound, career, cast, course, dash, flash, fling, flit, float, fly, gallop, hasten, heave, hurry, hurtle, launch, move quickly, pitch, plunge, run, rush, sail, scamper, scoot, scud, scurry, shoot, skim, speed, spring, sprint, spurt, start, tear, throw, thrust, whiz; SEE CONCEPTS 150,195,222

dash [*n1*] *fast race for short distance*
birr, bolt, dart, haste, onset, run, rush, sortie, sprint, spurt, zip; SEE CONCEPT 150

dash [*n2*] *flair, style*
animation, birr, brio, éclat, élan, energy, esprit, flourish, force, impressiveness, intensity, life, might, oomph*, panache, power, spirit, strength, vehemence, verve, vigor, vim, vivacity, zing, zip; SEE CONCEPTS 411,655,673

dash [*n3*] *small amount; suggestion*
bit, drop, few drops, flavor, grain, hint, lick, little, part, pinch, scattering, seasoning, smack, smidgen, soupçon, sprinkle, sprinkling, squirt, streak, suspicion, taste, tincture, tinge, touch, trace, trifle, zest; SEE CONCEPT 831

dash [*v1*] *run very fast for short distance*
boil, bolt, bound, career, charge, chase, course, dart, fly, gallop, get on it*, haste, hasten, hurry, lash, make a run for it*, make it snappy*, race, rush, rush at, scamper, scoot, scurry, shoot, speed, spring, sprint, tear; SEE CONCEPT 150

dash [*v2*] *break by hitting or throwing violently*
beat, bludgeon, cast, charge, crash, cudgel, destroy, fling, hit, hurl, hurtle, lunge, plunge, shatter, shiver, slam, sling, smash, splash, splatter, splinter, throw; SEE CONCEPTS 189,222,248

dash [*v3*] *discourage, frustrate*
abash, baffle, balk, beat, bilk, blast, blight, chagrin, chill, circumvent, cloud, confound, dampen, disappoint, discomfort, dismay, dispirit, foil, nip, ruin, spoil, thwart; SEE CONCEPTS 7,19,121

dashing [*adj*] *bold, flamboyant*
adventurous, alert, animated, chic, dapper, daring, dazzling, debonair, elegant, exclusive, exuberant, fashionable, fearless, gallant, gay, jaunty, keen, lively, modish, plucky, rousing, showy, smart, spirited, sporty, stylish, swank, swashbuckling, swish, vivacious; SEE CONCEPTS 404,589

data [*n*] *information in visible form*
abstracts, brass tacks*, chapter and verse*, circumstances, compilations, conclusions, details, documents, dope, dossier, evidence, experiments, facts, figures, goods, info, input, knowledge, materials, measurements, memorandums, notes, picture, proof, reports, results, scoop, score, statistics, testimony, whole story*; SEE CONCEPT 274

date [*n1*] *point in time; particular day or time*
age, century, course, day, duration, epoch, era, generation, hour, juncture, moment, period, quarter, reign, span, spell, stage, term, time, while, year; SEE CONCEPTS 800,801,802,815

date [*n2*] *social engagement*
appointment, assignation, call, interview, meeting, rendezvous, tryst, visit; SEE CONCEPTS 114,386

date [*n3*] *person accompanying another socially*
blind date, boyfriend, companion, escort, friend, girlfriend, lover, partner, steady, sweetheart; SEE CONCEPT 423

date [*v1*] *assign a date*
affix a date to, belong to, carbon-date, chronicle, come from, determine, exist from, fix, fix the date of, isolate, mark, measure, originate in, put in its place, record, register; SEE CONCEPTS 18,37

date [*v2*] *see person socially*
associate with, attend, consort with, court, deuce it*, escort, fix up, go around together*, go around with*, go out with, go steady, go together, keep company, make a date, see, step around, take out, woo; SEE CONCEPT 114

date [*v3*] *become obsolete*
antiquate, archaize, obsolesce, obsolete, outdate, show one's age; SEE CONCEPT 105

daub [*v*] *coat; make dirty*
begrime, besmear, bespray, blur, cover, dab, deface, dirty, fleck, grime, paint, plaster, slap on, smear, smirch, smudge, spatter, speckle, splatter, spot, spread, stain, sully, variegate, varnish; SEE CONCEPTS 172,250

daunt [*v*] *frighten, alarm*
appall, baffle, browbeat, bully, consternate, cow, deter, discourage, dishearten, dismay, dispirit, foil, horrify, intimidate, overawe, put off*, scare, shake, subdue, terrify, thwart; SEE CONCEPTS 7,19

dauntless [*adj*] *bold, courageous*
aweless, brave, daring, doughty, fearless, gallant, game, heroic, indomitable, intrepid, invincible, lionhearted, resolute, stouthearted, unafraid, un-

da
da

conquerable, undaunted, unfearing, unflinching, valiant, valorous; SEE CONCEPT *401*

dawdle [v] *delay; waste time*
amble, bum around*, dally, diddle-daddle*, dilly-dally*, drag, fool around*, fritter away*, get no place fast*, goof off*, hang around*, hang out*, idle, lag, laze, lazy, loaf, loiter, loll, lounge, mosey*, poke*, procrastinate, put off, saunter, scrounge around, shlep along*, sit around*, sit on one's butt*, stay, stroll, tarry, toddle, trifle, wait, warm a chair*; SEE CONCEPTS *210,681*

dawn [n1] *beginning of day*
aurora, break of day, bright, cockcrow, crack of dawn, dawning, daybreak, daylight, day peep, early bright, first blush, first light, light, morn, morning, sunrise, sunup, wee hours*; SEE CONCEPTS *810,815*

dawn [n2] *a beginning*
advent, alpha, birth, commencement, dawning, emergence, foundation, genesis, head, inception, onset, opening, origin, outset, outstart, rise, source, start, unfolding; SEE CONCEPT *832*

dawn [v] *start*
appear, begin, develop, emerge, glimmer, initiate, lighten, loom, open, originate, rise, show itself, unfold; SEE CONCEPT *119*

day [n1] *light part of every 24 hours*
astronomical day, bright, dawn-to-dark, daylight, daytime, diurnal course, early bright, light, light of day, mean solar day, nautical day, sidereal day, sunlight, sunrise-to-sunset, sunshine, working day; SEE CONCEPTS *801,803,810,821*

day [n2] *era*
age, ascendancy, cycle, epoch, generation, height, heyday, period, prime, term, time, years, zenith; SEE CONCEPTS *802,816*

daybreak [n] *beginning of light hours*
aurora, break of day, bright, cockcrow, crack of dawn, dawn, dawning, daylight, day peep, day-spring, early bright, first light, morn, morning, sunrise, sunup; SEE CONCEPTS *810,815*

daydream [n] *fantasy thought of when awake*
castle in the air*, conceiving, dream, fancy, fancying, figment of imagination, fond hope, fool's paradise*, head trip*, imagination, imagining, in a zone*, mind trip*, musing, phantasm, phantasy, pie in the sky*, pipe dream, reverie, stargazing, trip*, vision, wish, woolgathering; SEE CONCEPT *529*

daydream [v] *make up fantasy*
build castles in air*, conceive, dream, envision, fancy, fantasize, hallucinate, imagine, moon, muse, pipe dream*, stargaze, trip out*, woolgather; SEE CONCEPTS *17,36*

daylight [n1] *light part of 24 hours*
aurora, dawn, day, daybreak, daytime, during the day, light, light of day, sunlight, sunrise, sunshine; SEE CONCEPT *810*

daze [n] *confusion*
befuddlement, bewilderment, distraction, gauze, glaze, haze, lala-land*, maze, muddledness, nadaville*, narcosis, shock, stupefaction, stupor, trance; SEE CONCEPT *410*

daze [v] *confuse, shock*
addle, amaze, astonish, astound, befog, befuddle, benumb, bewilder, blind, blur, confound, dazzle, disorder, distract, dizzy, dumbfound, flabbergast, fuddle, mix up, muddle, mystify, numb, overpower, overwhelm, paralyze, perplex, petrify,

puzzle, rock, stagger, startle, stun, stupefy, surprise; SEE CONCEPTS *16,42*

dazzle [v] *confuse, amaze*
astonish, awe, bedazzle, blind, blur, bowl over*, daze, excite, fascinate, glitz*, hypnotize, impress, overawe, overpower, overwhelm, razzle-dazzle, strike dumb*, stupefy, surprise; SEE CONCEPTS *16,42*

dead [adj1] *no longer alive*
asleep, bereft of life, bloodless, bought the farm*, breathless, buried, cadaverous, checked out*, cold, cut off, deceased, defunct, departed, done for*, erased, expired, extinct, gone, gone to meet maker*, gone to reward*, inanimate, inert, late, lifeless, liquidated, mortified, no more, not existing, offed*, out of one's misery*, passed away, perished, pushing up daisies*, reposing, resting in peace, spiritless, stiff, unanimated, wasted; SEE CONCEPT *539*

dead [adj2] *indifferent, cold*
anesthetized, apathetic, asleep, boring, callous, deadened, dull, flat, frigid, glazed, inert, insensitive, insipid, lukewarm, numb, numbed, paralyzed, senseless, spiritless, stagnant, stale, still, tasteless, torpid, unfeeling, uninteresting, unresponsive, vapid, wooden; SEE CONCEPT *550*

dead [adj3] *not working*
barren, bygone, defunct, departed, exhausted, extinct, gone, inactive, inoperable, inoperative, lost, obsolete, spent, stagnant, sterile, still, tired, unemployed, unprofitable, useless, vanished, wearied, worn, worn out; SEE CONCEPT *560*

dead [adj4] *complete, total*
absolute, bloody, downright, entire, final, out-and-out*, outright, perfect, sure, thorough, unconditional, unmitigated, unqualified, utter, whole; SEE CONCEPT *531*

dead [adv] *completely, totally*
absolutely, direct, directly, due, entirely, exactly, right, straight, straightly, undeviatingly, wholly; SEE CONCEPTS *531,772*

deaden [v] *diminish, muffle, quiet*
abate, alleviate, anesthetize, benumb, blunt, check, chloroform, consume, cushion, damp, dampen, depress, deprive, desensitize, destroy, devitalize, dim, dope, drown, dull, etherize, exhaust, freeze, frustrate, gas, hush, impair, incapacitate, injure, knock out, KO*, lay out, lessen, mute, numb, paralyze, put out of order*, put to sleep, quieten, reduce, repress, retard, slow, smother, soften, stifle, stun, stupefy, suppress, tire, tone down, unnerve, weaken; SEE CONCEPTS *130,240*

deadlock [n] *stalemate, impasse*
box*, Catch-22*, cessation, checkmate, corner, dead end, dead heat, dilemma, draw, full stop, gridlock, halt, hole, pause, pickle, plight, posture, predicament, quandary, standoff, standstill, tie, wall*; SEE CONCEPT *674*

deadly [adj1] *causing end of life*
baleful, baneful, bloodthirsty, bloody, cannibalistic, carcinogenic, cruel, dangerous, death-dealing, deathly, deleterious, destroying, destructive, fatal, grim, harmful, homicidal, injurious, internecine, killing, lethal, malignant, mortal, mortiferous, murderous, noxious, pernicious, pestiferous, pestilent, pestilential, poisonous, ruthless, savage, slaying, suicidal, toxic, unrelenting, venomous, violent, virulent; SEE CONCEPT *537*

deadly [adj2] *ghostly*
ashen, corpselike, dead, deadened, deathful, deathlike, deathly, ghastly, pallid, wan, white; SEE CONCEPT *539*

deaf [adj1] *without hearing*
deafened, earless, hard of hearing, stone deaf*, unable to hear; SEE CONCEPT *591*

deaf [adj2] *unwilling to listen*
blind, bullheaded*, headstrong, indifferent, intractable, mulish*, oblivious, obstinate, pertinacious, perverse, pigheaded*, self-willed, strong-willed, stubborn, unaware, unconcerned, unhearing, unmoved; SEE CONCEPT *401*

deal [n1] *agreement, bargain*
accord, arrangement, buy, compromise, conception, contract, pact, pledge, prearrangement, transaction, understanding; SEE CONCEPT *684*

deal [n2] *amount, share*
abundance, degree, distribution, extent, plenty, plethora, portion, quantity, shake, superabundance, transaction; SEE CONCEPTS *344,787,835*

deal [n3] *distribution of playing cards*
appointment, chance, cut and shuffle*, fresh start, game, hand, opportunity, round; SEE CONCEPT *363*

deal/deal with [v1] *handle, manage*
act, approach, attend to, behave, behave toward, clear, concern, conduct oneself, consider, control, cope with, direct, discuss, get a handle on something*, hack it*, handle, have to do with, live with*, make a go of it*, make it*, oversee, play, review, rid, see to, serve, take, take care of, treat, unburden, use; SEE CONCEPTS *94,117*

deal [v2] *do business*
bargain, barter, bicker, buy and sell, dicker*, hammer out deal*, handle, horse trade*, knock down price*, negotiate, sell, stock, swap, trade, traffic, treat, work out deal; SEE CONCEPT *324*

deal [v3] *distribute*
administer, allot, apportion, assign, bestow, come across with*, deliver, disburse, dish out*, dispense, disperse, disseminate, divide, divvy*, dole out*, drop, fork out*, fork over*, give, hand out, impart, inflict, measure, mete out, partake, participate, partition, render, reward, share, strike; SEE CONCEPTS *108,140*

dealer [n] *business owner*
banker, bursar, businessperson, chandler, changer, dispenser, marketer, merchandiser, merchant, retailer, trader, tradesperson, trafficker, vendor, wholesaler; SEE CONCEPT *347*

dealings [n] *business relations*
affairs, balls in air*, business, commerce, concerns, doings, intercourse, irons in fire*, matters, proceedings, ropes*, sale, strings*, things, trade, traffic, transactions, truck, wire pulling*, wires*; SEE CONCEPT *324*

dean [n] *leader of institution*
administrator, authority, dignitary, doyen, ecclesiastic, guide, lead, legislator, pilot, president, principal, professor, senior, tack; SEE CONCEPT *350*

dear [n] *beloved person*
darling, favorite, heartthrob, honey, love, loved one, lover, pet, precious, sweetheart, treasure; SEE CONCEPT *423*

dear [adj1] *beloved, favorite*
cherished, close, darling, doll face, endeared, esteemed, familiar, intimate, loved, pet, precious,

prized, respected, treasured; SEE CONCEPTS *555,567*

dear [adj2] *very expensive*
an arm and a leg*, at a premium, cher*, costly, fancy, high, high-priced, out of sight*, over-priced, pretty penny*, pricey*, prized, steep, stiff*, valuable; SEE CONCEPT *334*

dearly [adv1] *extremely*
greatly, profoundly, to a great extent, very, very much; SEE CONCEPT *772*

dearly [adv2] *lovingly*
affectionately, devotedly, fondly, tenderly, yearningly; SEE CONCEPT *403*

dearth [n] *insufficiency, scarcity*
absence, default, defect, deficiency, exiguousness, famine, inadequacy, infrequency, lack, meagerness, miss, need, paucity, poverty, privation, rareness, scantiness, scantness, shortage, slim pickings*, sparsity, uncommonness, want; SEE CONCEPTS *646,674,709*

death [n] *end of life*
afterlife, annihilation, bereavement, casualty, cessation, curtains*, darkness, decease, demise, departure, destruction, dissolution, downfall, dying, end, ending, eradication, eternal rest, euthanasia, exit, expiration, extermination, extinction, fatality, finis*, finish, grave, grim reaper*, heaven, loss, mortality, necrosis, obliteration, oblivion, paradise, parting, passing, passing over, quietus, release, repose, ruin, ruination, silence, sleep, termination, tomb; SEE CONCEPT *304*

deathly [adj1] *suggesting end of life*
appalling, cadaverous, corpselike, deathlike, defunctive, dreadful, gaunt, ghastly, grim, gruesome, haggard, horrible, macabre, pale, pallid, wan, wasted; SEE CONCEPTS *579,618*

deathly [adj2] *fatal*
deadly, extreme, intense, lethal, mortal, mortiferous, noxious, pestilent, pestilential, terrible; SEE CONCEPT *537*

debacle [n] *catastrophe*
beating, blue ruin*, breakdown, collapse, crackup*, crash, defeasance, defeat, devastation, disaster, dissolution, downfall, drubbing, failure, fiasco, havoc, licking, overthrow, reversal, rout, ruin, ruination, shellacking*, smash, smashup, trouncing, vanquishment, washout, wreck; SEE CONCEPT *674*

debase [v1] *degrade, shame*
abase, bemean, cast down, cheapen, corrupt, cripple, debauch, debilitate, demean, demoralize, deprave, devaluate, devalue, disable, disgrace, dishonor, drag down*, dump on*, enfeeble, fluff off*, humble, humiliate, lower, put away, put down, reduce, sap, shoot down, sink, take down*, take down a peg*, undermine, weaken; SEE CONCEPTS *7,19,52,54*

debase [v2] *adulterate*
abase, animalize, bastardize, bestialize, contaminate, corrupt, damage, defile, depreciate, doctor, dope up*, impair, load, pervert, pollute, sophisticate, spoil, taint, vitiate, weight, worsen; SEE CONCEPTS *240,250*

debatable [adj] *controversial*
arguable, between rock and hard place*, between sixes and sevens*, betwixt and between*, bone of contention*, borderline, chancy*, contestable, disputable, doubtful, dubious, iffy*, in dispute, moot, mootable*, open to question, problematic, problematical, questionable, the jury's out*, touch

da
de

and go*, uncertain, undecided, unsettled, up for discussion; SEE CONCEPTS 267,535

debate [n] *discussion of issues; consideration*
agitation, altercation, argument, argumentation, blah-blah*, cogitation, contention, contest, controversy, controverting, deliberation, dialectic, disputation, dispute, forensic, hassle, match, meditation, mooting, polemic, rebutting, reflection, refuting, tiff, words, wrangle; SEE CONCEPTS 56,532

debate [v] *argue, discuss*
agitate, altercate, answer, bandy, bicker, bump heads*, canvass, chew the fat*, cogitate, confab*, confute, consider, contend, contest, controvert, cross swords*, deliberate, demonstrate, differ, discept, disprove, dispute, hammer away at*, hash over*, hassle, have at it*, kick around*, knock around*, lock horns*, moot, oppose, pettifog, pick a bone*, prove, put up argument, question, reason, rebut, refute, rehash, set to, talk back*, talk game*, thrash out*, toss around*, wrangle; SEE CONCEPTS 24,56

debauch [v] *deprave, corrupt*
abuse, bastardize, bestialize, betray, brutalize, debase, defile, deflower, demoralize, fornicate, fraternize, go bad*, go to hell*, intrigue, inveigle, lead astray*, live in the gutter*, lure, pervert, pollute, ravish, ruin, seduce, subvert, tempt, violate, vitiate, warp; SEE CONCEPTS 14,240,375

debauched [adj] *violated, corrupted*
abandoned, corrupt, debased, defiled, degenerate, degraded, depraved, deteriorated, dissipated, dissolute, fast, gone bad*, gone to the dogs*, immoral, in the gutter*, licentious, perverted, profligate, reprobate, vitiate, vitiated, wanton, wicked; SEE CONCEPT 545

debauchery [n] *immoral self-indulgence*
bender*, binge, blowout*, burning candle at both ends*, bust, carousal, depravity, dissipation, dissoluteness, drunk*, excess, fast living*, fornication, gluttony, incontinence, indulgence, intemperance, intimacy, la dolce vita*, lasciviousness, lechery, lewdness, license, licentiousness, life in fast lane*, lust, orgy, overindulgence, revel, revelry, seduction, sensuality, sybaritism, tear*; SEE CONCEPTS 633,645

debilitate [v] *incapacitate*
attenuate, blunt, cripple, devitalize, disable, enervate, enfeeble, eviscerate, exhaust, extenuate, harm, hurt, injure, mar, prostrate, relax, sap, spoil, unbrace, undermine, unstrengthen, weaken, wear out; SEE CONCEPTS 240,246

debility [n] *incapacity, weakness*
decrepitude, disease, enervation, enfeeblement, exhaustion, faintness, feebleness, frailty, infirmity, languor, malaise, sickliness, unhealthiness; SEE CONCEPT 316

debonair [adj] *charming, elegant*
affable, buoyant, casual, cheerful, courteous, dashing, detached, happy, jaunty, lighthearted, nonchalant, pleasant, refined, smooth, sprightly, suave, urbane, well-bred; SEE CONCEPT 401

debris [n] *litter, waste*
bits, crap*, detritus, dregs, dross, fragments, garbage, junk, offal, pieces, refuse, remains, riffraff, rubbish, rubble, ruins, trash, wreck, wreckage; SEE CONCEPT 260

debt [n] *money owed to others*
albatross*, arrearage, arrears, bad news*, baggage*, below the line*, bill, bite*, capital, check,

chit*, claim, commitment, credit, cuff*, damage*, dead horse*, debenture, debit, deficit, due, dues, duty, encumbrance, indebtedness, in hock*, in the hole*, in the red*, invoice, IOU, liability, manifest, mortgage, note, obligation, outstandings*, price tag*, promissory note, receipt, reckoning, red ink*, responsibility, score, tab, tally, voucher; SEE CONCEPTS 329,344

debunk [v] *disprove, ridicule*
cut down to size*, deflate, demystify, discover, disparage, expose, lampoon, mock, puncture, show up*, uncloak, unmask, unshroud; SEE CONCEPTS 49,60

debut [n] *first public appearance*
admission, appearance, beginning, bow, coming out*, coming out party*, entrance, entree, first step*, graduating, graduation, inauguration, incoming, initiation, introduction, launching, opener, presentation; SEE CONCEPT 386

decadence [n] *perversion; deterioration of morality*
corruption, debasement, decay, declension, decline, degeneracy, degeneration, degradation, devolution, dissipation, dissolution, downfall, downgrade, evil, excess, fall, gluttony, incontinence, intemperance, lasciviousness, lechery, lewdness, licentiousness, regression, sensuality, sybaritism; SEE CONCEPT 645

decadent [adj] *corrupt, self-indulgent*
debased, debauched, decaying, declining, degenerate, degraded, depraved, dissolute, effete, evil, gone bad, gone to the dogs*, immoral, lost, moribund, overripe, perverted, wanton, wicked; SEE CONCEPT 545

decay [n] *breaking down, collapse*
adulteration, appearance, blight, caries, cariosity, consumption, atrophy, corrosion, crumbling, decadence, decline, decomposition, decrease, decrepitude, degeneracy, degeneration, depreciation, deterioration, dilapidation, disintegration, disrepair, dissolution, downfall, dying, extinction, fading, failing, gangrene, impairment, mortification, perishing, putrefaction, putrescence, putridity, putridness, rot, rotting, ruin, ruination, rust, senescence, spoilage, spoilation, wasting, wasting away, withering; SEE CONCEPTS 230,674,716

decay [v] *deteriorate, crumble*
atrophy, become contaminated, be impaired, blight, break up, collapse, corrode, curdle, decline, decompose, defile, degenerate, depreciate, discolor, disintegrate, dissolve, dry-rot, dwindle, fade, fail, get worse, go bad, go to seed*, go to the dogs*, hit rock bottom*, hit the skids*, lessen, mildew, mold, molder, mortify, pejorate, perish, pollute, putrefy, putresce, reach depths, rot, sap, shrivel, sicken, sink, slump, spoil, suppurate, turn, wane, waste away, weaken, wear away, wither; SEE CONCEPTS 240,246,469

decayed [adj] *rotten, falling apart*
addled, bad, carious, carrion, corroded, decomposed, effete, gangrenous, moldered, overripe, perished, putrefied, putrescent, putrid, rank, riddled, rotted, ruined, spoiled, wasted, withered; SEE CONCEPT 485

decease [n] *death*
buying the farm*, curtains*, defunction, demise, departure, dissolution, dying, grim reaper*, passing, passing away, passing over, quietus, release, silence, sleep, taps*, the end; SEE CONCEPT 304

decease [v] *pass away; expire*
buy a one-way ticket*, call off all bets*, cease, check out*, cool off*, croak*, deep six*, depart, die, drop, go, pass, pass away, pass on, pass over, perish, succumb; SEE CONCEPT *304*

deceased [adj] *dead*
asleep, bit the dust*, cold*, defunct, departed, exanimate, expired, extinct, finished, former, gave up the ghost*, gone, inanimate, kicked the bucket*, late, lifeless, lost, passed on, pushing up daisies*; SEE CONCEPT *539*

deceit [n1] *practice of misleading*
ambidexterity, ambidextrousness, artifice, cheating, chicane, chicanery, cozening, craft, craftiness, cunning, deceitfulness, deception, defrauding, dirty dealing*, dirty pool*, dishonesty, dissemblance, dissimulation, double-dealing, duplicity, entrapping, fraud, fraudulence, guile, hypocrisy, imposition, overreaching, pretense, slyness, smoke and mirrors*, trapping, treachery, trickery, two-facedness*, two-timing*, underhandedness; SEE CONCEPTS *59,633*

deceit [n2] *particular type of trick, misleading*
artifice, blind, cheat, chicanery, crocodile tears*, deception, dirty trick*, dirty work*, duplicity, fake, feint, flimflam*, fraud, fraudulence, hoax, humbug, imposture, misrepresentation, pretense, ruse, sell, sellout, sham, shift, smoke and mirrors*, snow job*, soft soap*, spoof, stratagem, subterfuge, sweet talk*, swindle, trick, whitewash*, wile; SEE CONCEPTS *59,660*

deceitful [adj] *dishonest, insincere*
artful, astucious, astute, beguiling, clandestine, counterfeit, crafty, cunning, deceiving, deceptive, delusive, delusory, designing, disingenuous, double-dealing, duplicitous, fallacious, false, feline, foxy, fraudulent, furtive, guileful, hypocritical, illusory, impostrous, indirect, insidious, knavish, lying, mendacious, misleading, rascal, roguish, shifty, slick, sly, sneaky, stealthy, subtle, treacherous, tricky, two-faced*, underhand, underhanded, untrustworthy, untruthful, wily; SEE CONCEPT *401*

deceive [v] *mislead; be dishonest*
bamboozle*, beat, beat out of, beguile, betray, bilk, buffalo*, burn, cheat, circumvent, clip, con, cozen, cross up, defraud, delude, disappoint, double-cross, dupe, ensnare, entrap, fake, falsify, fleece, fool, gouge, gull, hoax, hoodwink, hook*, humbug, impose upon, lead on, outwit, play joke on, pull fast one*, put on, rob, scam, screw, sell, skin, suck in*, swindle, take advantage of, take for, take for ride*, take in, take to cleaners*, trick, victimize; SEE CONCEPTS *7,19,59*

decency [n] *respectable behavior*
appropriateness, ceremoniousness, civility, conventionality, correctness, courtesy, decorum, dignity, etiquette, fitness, fittingness, formality, good form, good manners, honesty, modesty, propriety, respectability, righteousness, seemliness, virtue; SEE CONCEPT *633*

decent [adj1] *respectable, appropriate*
approved, becoming, befitting, chaste, clean, comely, comme il faut, conforming, continent, correct, decorous, delicate, ethical, fit, fitting, good, honest, honorable, immaculate, mannerly, modest, moral, nice, noble, on the up and up*, polite, presentable, proper, prudent, pure, reserved, right, seemly, spotless, stainless, standard, straight, straight arrow*, straight shooting*,

suitable, trustworthy, unblemished, undefiled, untarnished, upright, virtuous, worthy; SEE CONCEPTS *401,558*

decent [adj2] *kind, generous*
accommodating, courteous, friendly, gracious, helpful, obliging, thoughtful, virtuous; SEE CONCEPTS *404,542*

decent [adj3] *sufficient, tolerable*
acceptable, adequate, all right, ample, average, comfortable, common, competent, enough, fair, fair to middling*, good, mediocre, middling, moderately good, passable, presentable, reasonable, respectable, right, satisfactory, sufficing, unexceptional, unimpeachable, unobjectionable; SEE CONCEPTS *533,558,572*

deception [n1] *misleading; being dishonest*
beguilement, betrayal, blarney*, boondoggle*, cheat, circumvention, cozenage, craftiness, cunning, deceit, deceitfulness, deceptiveness, defraudation, dirt, disinformation, dissimulation, double-dealing, dupery, duplicity, equivocation, falsehood, fast one*, flimflam*, fraud, fraudulence, guile, hokum*, hypocrisy, imposition, insincerity, juggling, legerdemain, lying, mendacity, pretense, prevarication, snow job*, sophism, treachery, treason, trickery, trickiness, trumpery, untruth; SEE CONCEPTS *7,19,59*

deception [n2] *trick*
artifice, bilk, bluff, catch, cheat, chicane, con, confidence game, con game*, cover-up, crock, decoy, device, dodge, fallacy, fast one*, fast shuffle*, feint, fib, fraud, gimmick, hoax, hogwash*, hustle, illusion, imposture, jive*, lie, malarkey*, mare's-nest*, pretext, ride*, ruse, scam, sham, shift, shuck, snare, snow job*, stall, sting, story, stratagem, subterfuge, swindle, trap, trick, whitewash*, wile, wrinkle*; SEE CONCEPTS *59,230*

deceptive [adj] *dishonest*
ambiguous, astucious, beguiling, bum*, catchy, crafty, cunning, deceitful, deceiving, deluding, delusive, delusory, designing, disingenuous, fake, fallacious, false, fishy, foxy, fraudulent, illusory, impostrous, indirect, insidious, lying, misleading, mock, oblique, off*, phony, plausible, rascal, roguish, scheming, seeming, serpentine, shifty, slick, slippery, sly, snide, specious, spurious, subtle, treacherous, tricky, two-faced*, underhand, underhanded, unreliable, wily; SEE CONCEPTS *401,582*

decide [v] *make a determination; settle an issue*
adjudge, adjudicate, agree, arrive at conclusion, award, call shots*, cast the die*, choose, cinch, clinch, come to agreement, come to conclusion, come to decision, commit oneself, conclude, conjecture, decree, determine, draw a conclusion, elect, end, establish, figure, fix upon, form opinion, gather, go down line*, guess, have final word*, judge, make a decision, make up mind, mediate, opt, pick, poll, purpose, reach decision, resolve, rule, select, set, surmise, take a stand, tap, vote, will; SEE CONCEPT *18*

decided [adj1] *certain, definite*
absolute, assured, categorical, cinched, clear, clear-cut, clinched, destined, determined, distinct, emphatic, explicit, express, fated, for sure*, indisputable, in the bag*, nailed*, on ice*, positive, prearranged, predetermined, pronounced, resolved, runaway*, settled, sure, unalterable, unambiguous, undeniable, undisputed, unequivocal, unmistakable, unquestionable; SEE CONCEPT *535*

decided [adj2] *determined, strong-willed*
assertive, bent, certain, cocksure, decisive, deliberate, earnest, emphatic, established, firm, fixed, inflexible, intent, iron-jawed*, mulish, positive, purposeful, resolute, resolved, serious, set, settled, strong-minded, sure, unbending, unfaltering, unhesitating, unwavering, unyielding; SEE CONCEPTS 401,403

decidedly [adv] *certainly*
absolutely, bloody*, by all means, clearly, decisively, determinedly, distinctly, downright, emphatically, flat out*, for a fact*, in spades*, no catch*, no holds barred*, no ifs ands or buts*, no mistake*, no strings attached*, of course, positively, powerful, real, really, right, straight out, strongly, sure, surely, terribly, terrifically, unequivocally, unmistakably; SEE CONCEPT 535

deciding [adj] *determining*
chief, conclusive, critical, crucial, decisive, important, influential, key, necessary, prime, principal, significant; SEE CONCEPTS 546,568

decipher [v] *figure out, understand*
analyze, break, break down, bring out, cipher, construe, crack, decode, deduce, disentangle, dope out, elucidate, encipher, explain, expound, find the key, interpret, make clear, make out, puzzle out, read, render, reveal, solve, spell, translate, unfold, unravel, unriddle; SEE CONCEPTS 15,31,37

decision [n1] *conclusion; resolution reached*
accommodation, accord, adjudication, adjudicature, adjustment, agreement, arbitration, arrangement, choice, compromise, declaration, determination, end, finding, judgment, opinion, outcome, prearrangement, preference, reconciliation, resolution, result, ruling, selection, sentence, settlement, showdown, the call, the nod, understanding, verdict; SEE CONCEPTS 278,689

decision [n2] *strength of mind or will*
backbone, decidedness, decisiveness, determination, doggedness, earnestness, firmness, fortitude, grit, iron will, obstinacy, obstinance, perseverance, persistence, pluck*, purpose, purposefulness, purposiveness, resoluteness, resolution, resolve, seriousness, spine, stubbornness, volition, will, will power; SEE CONCEPTS 410,411

decisive [adj] *definite*
absolute, all out*, assured, bent, certain, conclusive, crisp, critical, crucial, decided, definitive, determined, fateful, final, firm, flat out*, forceful, imperative, imperious, incisive, influential, intent, litmus test*, momentous, peremptory, positive, resolute, resolved, set, settled, significant, straight out*, strong-minded, trenchant; SEE CONCEPT 535

deck [v] *put on clothing, usually nice*
accouter, adorn, appoint, array, attire, beautify, bedeck, clothe, decorate, dress, dress up, embellish, festoon, garland, garnish, grace, gussy up*, ornament, prettify, primp, slick, trim; SEE CONCEPT 167

declaim [v] *proclaim; get on a soapbox*
attack, bloviate, blow hot air*, declare, decry, denounce, harangue, hold forth, inveigh, lecture, mouth, orate, perorate, pile it on*, proclaim, rail, rant, recite, soapbox*, speak, spiel*, spout*, talk big*; SEE CONCEPTS 49,51

declaration [n1] *assertion of belief or knowledge*
acknowledgment, admission, advertisement, affirmation, allegation, announcement, answer, attestation, averment, avowal, bomb*, broadcast, communication, deposition, disclosure, enunciation, explanation, exposition, expression, hot air*, information, notice, notification, oath, pitch, presentation, profession, promulgation, protestation, publication, remark, report, revelation, saying, say so*, spiel*, statement, story, testimony, two cents' worth*, utterance; SEE CONCEPTS 49,274,278

declaration [n2] *official proclamation*
acclamation, affidavit, allegation, announcement, article, attestation, bulletin, canon, charge, confirmation, constitution, credo, creed, denunciation, deposition, document, edict, gospel, indictment, manifesto, notice, notification, plea, proclamation, profession, promulgation, pronouncement, pronunciamento, resolution, testament, testimony, ultimatum; SEE CONCEPTS 271,274,278

declare [v1] *make known clearly or officially*
acknowledge, advance, advocate, affirm, allegate, allege, announce, argue, assert, asservate, attest, aver, avow, be positive, blaze, bring forward, certify, cite, claim, confess, confirm, contend, convey, demonstrate, disclose, enunciate, give out, inform, insist, maintain, manifest, notify, pass, proclaim, profess, promulgate, pronounce, propound, publish, put forward, reaffirm, reassert, render, repeat, reveal, set forth, show, sound, state, stress, swear, tell, testify, validate, vouch; SEE CONCEPTS 49,60

declare [v2] *claim as possession*
acknowledge, admit, avouch, avow, confess, convey, disclose, divulge, impart, indicate, manifest, notify, own, profess, represent, reveal, state, swear; SEE CONCEPTS 57,60

decline [n1] *lessening*
abatement, backsliding, comedown, cropper*, decay, decrepitude, degeneracy, degeneration, descent, deterioration, devolution, diminution, dissolution, dive, downfall, downgrade, downturn, drop, dwindling, ebb, ebbing, enfeeblement, failing, failure, fall, falling off, flop, lapse, on the skids*, pratfall, recession, relapse, senility, skids*, slump, wane, waning, weakening, worsening; SEE CONCEPTS 674,698,699

decline [n2] *downward change in value, position*
declivity, decrease, depression, descent, dip, downslide, downswing, downtrend, downturn, drop, drop-off, fall-off, hill, incline, lapse, loss, lowering, pitch, sag, slide, slip, slope, slump; SEE CONCEPTS 336,346,738

decline [v1] *say no*
abjure, abstain, avoid, balk, beg to be excused, bypass, demur, deny, desist, disapprove, dismiss, don't buy*, forbear, forgo, gainsay, nix*, not accept, not hear of, not think of, pass on*, refrain, refuse, reject, renounce, reprobate, repudiate, send regrets, shy, spurn, turn down, turn thumbs down*; SEE CONCEPTS 45,51

decline [v2] *lessen, become less*
abate, backslide, cheapen, decay, decrease, degenerate, depreciate, deteriorate, diminish, disimprove, disintegrate, droop, drop, dwindle, ebb, fade, fail, fall, fall off, flag, go downhill*, go to pot*, go to the dogs*, hit the skids*, languish, lapse, lose value, lower, pine, recede, relapse, retrograde, return, revert, rot, sag, settle, shrink, sink, slide, subside, wane, weaken, worsen; SEE CONCEPTS 240,698

decline [*v3*] *descend*

dip, droop, drop, fall, go down, lower, sag, set, settle, sink, slant, slope; SEE CONCEPTS *151,181*

decompose [*v1*] *break up*

break down, crumble, decay, disintegrate, dissolve, fall apart, fester, molder, putrefy, putresce, spoil, taint, turn; SEE CONCEPT *469*

decompose [*v2*] *analyze by taking apart*

anatomize, atomize, break down, break up, decompound, disintegrate, dissect, dissolve, distill, resolve, separate; SEE CONCEPTS *24,103*

decomposition [*n*] *rot, breakdown*

atomization, corruption, decay, disintegration, dissipation, dissolution, division, putrefaction, putrescence, putridity; SEE CONCEPTS *230,674*

deconstructionist [*n/adj*] *exposing a text's multiple meanings*

critical, debunking, demystifying, demythifying, hermeneutical, reinterpretive, revisionist; SEE CONCEPT *268*

decor [*n*] *colors, furnishings of a place*

adornment, color scheme, decoration, interior design, ornamentation; SEE CONCEPTS *622,723*

decorate [*v1*] *beautify, embellish*

add finishing touches, adorn, bedeck, bedizen, brighten, burnish, color, deck, do up*, dress out*, dress up*, enhance, enrich, festoon, finish, fix up, frill, furbish, garnish, gild, grace, gussy up*, idealize, illuminate, jazz up*, ornament, paint, perfect, prank, renovate, spruce up*, trim; SEE CONCEPTS *162,177*

decorate [*v2*] *honor and give medal*

cite, laureate, pin medal on, plume; SEE CONCEPT *132*

decoration [*n1*] *beautification, embellishment*

adornment, beautifying, bedecking, bedizenment, designing, elaboration, enhancement, enrichment, festooning, flounce, flourish, frill, furbelow, garnish, garnishing, illumination, improvement, ornament, ornamentation, redecorating, spangle, trimming; SEE CONCEPTS *162,177*

decoration [*n2*] *particular type of embellishment*

appliqué, arabesque, bauble, braid, color, curlicue, design, dingbat*, doodad*, extravagance, fandangle*, festoon, filigree, finery, flounce, flourish, fretwork, frill, frippery, furbelow, fuss, garbage*, garnish, garniture, gewgaws, gilt, gimcracks*, gingerbread, inlay, jazz*, lace, ornament, parquetry, plaque, ribbon, scroll, sequin, spangle, thing*, tinsel, tooling, trimming, trinket, wreath; SEE CONCEPTS *259,260*

decoration [*n3*] *medal of honor*

accolade, award, badge, bays, citation, colors, cross, distinction, emblem, garter, kudos, laurels, medal, mention, order, Purple Heart, ribbon, star; SEE CONCEPT *337*

decorative [*adj*] *beautifying*

adorning, cosmetic, embellishing, enhancing, fancy, florid, nonfunctional, ornamental, prettifying, pretty; SEE CONCEPT *579*

decorous [*adj*] *appropriate, suitable*

au fait, becoming, befitting, ceremonial, ceremonious, civilized, comely, comme il faut, conforming, conventional, correct, decent, demure, de rigueur, dignified, done, elegant, fit, fitting, formal, good, mannerly, meet, moral, nice, polite, prim, proper, punctilious, refined, respectable, right, seasonable, sedate, seemly, staid, well-behaved; SEE CONCEPTS *401,558*

decorum [*n*] *appropriate behavior, good manners*

breeding, civility, conduct, convenance, convention, correctitude, correctness, courtliness, decency, demeanor, deportment, dignity, etiquette, form, formality, gentility, good grace, gravity, habits, order, orderliness, politeness, politesse, properness, propriety, protocol, punctilio, respectability, seemliness, tact, usage; SEE CONCEPT *633*

decoy [*n*] *bait, trap*

allurement, attraction, beard*, blind, blow off*, booster, camouflage, catch, chicane, chicanery, come-on, deception, drawing card, ensnarement, enticement, facade, fake, front, imitation, inducement, inveiglement, lure, nark, plant, pretense, seducement, shill, sitting duck*, snare, stick, stoolie*, stool pigeon*, temptation, trick, trickery; SEE CONCEPTS *59,230,680*

decoy [*v*] *bait, entrap*

allure, come on, con, deceive, delude, egg one on*, ensnare, ensorcell, entice, fascinate, inveigle, lead on*, lead up garden path*, lure, mislead, mousetrap*, rope in*, seduce, shill, steer, suck in*, tempt, toll, tout, trap, wile; SEE CONCEPTS *16,59*

decrease [*n*] *diminishing, lessening*

abatement, compression, condensation, constriction, contraction, cutback, decline, declining, decrescence, depression, diminution, discount, downturn, dwindling, ebb, falling off, loss, reduction, shrinkage, striction, subsidence, waning; SEE CONCEPT *698*

decrease [*v*] *grow less or make less*

abate, calm down, check, contract, crumble, curb, curtail, cut down, decay, decline, degenerate, depreciate, deteriorate, devaluate, die down, diminish, droop, drop, drop off, dry up, dwindle, ease, ebb, evaporate, fade, fall off, lessen, let up, lighten, lose edge, lower, modify, narrow down, peter out, quell, quiet, reduce, restrain, run low, settle, shrink, shrivel, sink, slacken, slack off, slash, slow down, slump, soften, subside, tail off, wane, waste, weaken, wear away, wear down, wither; SEE CONCEPTS *240,698*

decree [*n*] *mandate, legal order*

act, announcement, behest, bidding, charge, charging, command, commandment, declaration, decretum, dictum, direction, directive, edict, enactment, injunction, instruction, judgment, law, order, ordinance, precept, prescript, proclamation, promulgation, pronouncement, rap*, regulation, rule, ruling, say, statute, the riot act*, the word*, ukase; SEE CONCEPTS *318,685*

decree [*v*] *order rule or action*

announce, command, compel, constrain, decide, declare, demand, determine, dictate, enact, force, impose, lay down the law*, oblige, ordain, prescribe, proclaim, pronounce, put one's foot down*, read the riot act*, require, rule, set; SEE CONCEPTS *50,53,81,88,317*

decrepit [*adj*] *deteriorated, debilitated, especially as a result of age*

aged, anile, antiquated, battered, bedraggled, broken-down, creaky, crippled, dilapidated, doddering, effete, feeble, flimsy, fragile, frail, haggard, incapacitated, infirm, insubstantial, old, quavering, ramshackle, rickety, run-down, seedy, senile, shabby, shaking, superannuated, tacky, threadbare, tired, tottering, tumble-down, unsound, used, wasted, weak, weakly, weather-beaten, worn, worn-out; SEE CONCEPTS *406,485*

de
de

decry [v] *criticize, blame*
abuse, asperse, bad-mouth*, belittle, calumniate, censure, condemn, cry down, defame, denounce, depreciate, derogate, detract, devalue, diminish, discount, discredit, disgrace, disparage, do a number on*, downgrade, dump on*, hit*, knock*, lower, malign, mark down, minimize, opprobriate, pan*, poor-mouth*, put down, rail against, rap, reprehend, reprobate, run down, slam*, take away, take swipe at*, throw stones at*, traduce, underestimate, underrate, undervalue, vilify, write off; SEE CONCEPTS 44,52

dedicate [v1] *donate, set aside for special use*
address, allot, apply, apportion, appropriate, assign, commit, consign, devote, give, give over to, inscribe, offer, pledge, restrict, surrender; SEE CONCEPTS 18,50,88,135

dedicate [v2] *sanctify*
anoint, bless, consecrate, hallow, set apart; SEE CONCEPTS 271,318

dedicated [adj] *loyal, hard-working*
committed, devoted, enthusiastic, faithful, given over to, old faithful*, purposeful, single-hearted, single-minded, sworn, true blue*, true to the end*, wholehearted, zealous; SEE CONCEPTS 404,542

dedication [n1] *faithfulness, loyalty*
adherence, allegiance, commitment, devotedness, devotion, single-mindedness, wholeheartedness; SEE CONCEPTS 411,657

dedication [n2] *speech of praise; sanctification*
address, celebration, consecration, devotion, envoy, glorification, hallowing, inscription, message; SEE CONCEPTS 69,367

deduce [v] *figure out, understand*
add up, analyze, assume, be afraid, boil down, cogitate, collect, conceive, conclude, consider, deduct, deem, derive, draw, fancy, figure, gather, glean, have a hunch*, imagine, infer, judge, make, make out, presume, presuppose, ratiocinate, read into, reason, regard, surmise, take to mean; SEE CONCEPTS 15,24

deducible [adj] *understandable*
a priori, consequent, deductive, derivable, dogmatic, following, inferable, inferential, provable, reasoned, traceable; SEE CONCEPTS 402,529

deduct [v] *take away or out; reduce*
abstract, allow, bate, cut back, decrease by, diminish, discount, dock, draw back, knock off, lessen, rebate, reduce, remove, roll back, subtract, take, take from, take off, withdraw, write off; SEE CONCEPTS 236,247,330

deduction [n1] *conclusion, understanding*
answer, assumption, cogitation, concluding, consequence, consideration, contemplation, corollary, deliberation, derivation, finding, illation, inference, inferring, judgment, meditation, mulling, musing, opinion, pondering, ratiocination, reasoning, reflection, result, rumination, sequitur, speculation, thinking, thought; SEE CONCEPTS 15,24,689

deduction [n2] *something subtracted*
abatement, abstraction, allowance, credit, cut, decrease, decrement, depreciation, diminution, discount, dockage, excision, rebate, reduction, removal, subtraction, withdrawal, write-off; SEE CONCEPTS 763,776

deed [n1] *achievement*
accomplishment, act, action, adventure, ballgame, big idea*, bit, byplay, cause, commission, crusade, do, enterprise, exploit, fact, feat, follow

through, game, happenin'*, performance, plan, quest, reality, securing, stunt, thing*, tour de force, truth, winning; SEE CONCEPTS 4,706

deed [n2] *legal paper assigning property; contract*
agreement, bargain, certificate, charter, compact, conveyance, covenant, document, indenture, instrument, lease, papers, proof, record, release, security, title, transaction, voucher, warranty; SEE CONCEPTS 271,318

deem [v] *regard, consider*
account, allow, appraise, assume, be afraid, believe, calculate, conceive, conjecture, credit, daresay, divine, esteem, estimate, expect, feel, guess, hold, imagine, judge, know, presume, reckon, sense, set store by, suppose, surmise, suspect, think, understand, view; SEE CONCEPTS 12,28

deep [n] *the sea*
blue*, brine, briny*, Davy Jones's locker*, drink*, main, middle, ocean, Poseidon's realm*, the high seas; SEE CONCEPT 514

deep [adj1] *extending very far, usually down*
abysmal, abyssal, below, beneath, bottomless, broad, buried, deep-seated, distant, downreaching, far, fathomless, immersed, inmost, low, profound, rooted, subaqueous, submarine, submerged, subterranean, sunk, underground, unfathomable, wide, yawning; SEE CONCEPTS 737,777

deep [adj2] *abstract, complicated in meaning*
abstruse, acute, arcane, complex, concealed, Delphic, difficult, discerning, esoteric, hard to understand, heavy*, hermetic, hidden, incisive, intricate, learned, mysterious, obscure, occult, Orphic, penetrating, profound, recondite, sagacious, secret, serious, Sibylline, wise; SEE CONCEPTS 402,529

deep [adj3] *scheming, devious*
acute, artful, astute, canny, contriving, crafty, cunning, designing, foxy, guileful, insidious, intriguing, keen, knowing, plotting, sharp, shrewd, sly, tricky, wily; SEE CONCEPT 404

deep [adj4] *absorbed, engrossed in activity*
abstracted, centered, concentrated, enfolded, engaged, fixed, focused, immersed, intent, into, lost, musing, preoccupied, rapt, set, wrapped, wrapped up; SEE CONCEPT 542

deep [adj5] *intense in effect on senses*
bass, booming, dark, extreme, full-toned, grave, great, hard, low, low-pitched, low-toned, profound, resonant, rich, sonorous, strong, vivid; SEE CONCEPTS 537,594,618

deepen [v1] *make depth greater*
dig, dig out, dredge, excavate, expand, extend, hollow, scoop out, scrape out; SEE CONCEPT 250

deepen [v2] *make more intense*
aggravate, develop, enhance, expand, extend, grow, heighten, increase, intensate, intensify, magnify, mount, redouble, reinforce, rise, rouse, strengthen; SEE CONCEPTS 236,245,697

deeply [adv] *completely, intensely*
acutely, affectingly, distressingly, feelingly, genuinely, gravely, intensely, mournfully, movingly, passionately, profoundly, sadly, seriously, severely, surely, thoroughly, to the quick; SEE CONCEPTS 531,772

deface [v] *mar, mutilate*
blemish, contort, damage, deform, demolish, destroy, dilapidate, disfigure, distort, harm, impair, injure, mangle, misshape, obliterate, ruin,

scratch, spoil, sully, tarnish, trash*, vandalize, wreck; SEE CONCEPTS 246,252

de facto [adv] in reality
actual, actually, existing, genuinely, in effect, in fact, real, really, tangible, truly, veritably; SEE CONCEPT 582

defamation [n] libel, slander
aspersion, backbiting, backstabbing, belittlement, black eye*, calumny, character assassination, cheap shot*, denigration, depreciation, detraction, dirt, dirty laundry*, disparagement, dump*, dynamite, hit, knock, lie, low-down dirty*, mud, obloquy, opprobrium, scorcher, slam*, slap in face*, slime, slur, smear, tale, traducement, vilification; SEE CONCEPT 54

defamatory [adj] libelous, slanderous
abusive, calumnious, contumelious, denigrating, derogatory, detracting, detractive, disparaging, injurious, insulting, maligning, opprobrious, traducing, vilifying, vituperative; SEE CONCEPTS 267,537

defame [v] inflict libel or slander
asperse, bad-mouth*, belie, besmirch, blacken, blister, calumniate, cast aspersions on, cast slur on, denigrate, detract, discredit, disgrace, dishonor, disparage, do a number on*, knock, malign, pan*, put zingers on*, roast, scandalize, scorch, slam, smear, speak evil of*, stigmatize, throw mud at*, traduce, vilify, villainize, vituperate; SEE CONCEPTS 7,19,54

default [n] failure; want
absence, blemish, blunder, dearth, defect, deficiency, delinquency, dereliction, disregard, error, fault, imperfection, inadequacy, insufficiency, lack, lapse, miss, neglect, nonpayment, offense, omission, overlooking, oversight, privation, shortcoming, slight, transgression, vice, weakness, wrongdoing; SEE CONCEPTS 335,699,709

default [v] dodge payment
bilk, defraud, dishonor, evade, fail, leave town*, meet under arch*, neglect, put on the cuff*, rat*, repudiate, run out on*, see in the alley, shirk, skate*, skip, skip out on*, stiff*, swindle, welch, welsh; SEE CONCEPTS 59,63,330

defeat [n1] overthrow, beating
ambush, annihilation, beating, blow, break, breakdown, check, collapse, conquest, count, debacle, defeasance, destruction, discomfiture, downthrow, drubbing*, embarrassment, extermination, failure, fall, insuccess, killing*, KO*, lacing, licking, loss, massacre, mastery, nonsuccess, paddling, rebuff, repulse, reverse, rout, ruin, scalping, setback, shellacking*, slaughter, subjugation, thrashing, trap, trashing, trimming, triumph, trouncing, vanquishment, waxing, whaling, whipping, whitewashing*; SEE CONCEPT 95

defeat [n2] frustration
disappointment, discomfiture, downfall, failure, foil, loss, rebuff, repulse, reversal, reverse, setback, thwarting; SEE CONCEPT 410

defeat [v1] conquer in military manner
ambush, annihilate, bar, bear down, beat, best, block, butcher, crush, decimate, demolish, discomfit, drown, entrap, finish off, halt, hinder, impede, lick, mow down, obliterate, obstruct, outflank, outmaneuver, overpower, overrun, overthrow, overwhelm, parry, prevail over, quell, reduce, repel, repress, repulse, roll back, rout, route, sack, scatter, shipwreck, sink, slaughter,

smash, subdue, subjugate, suppress, surmount, swamp, torpedo*, trample, trash, upset, vanquish, whip, wipe out; SEE CONCEPTS 95,320

defeat [v2] conquer in athletic contest
beat, bust*, clobber*, cream*, deck*, drop*, drub*, edge, flax*, flog*, floor*, knock out*, KO*, lambaste*, lick, outhit, outjump, outplay, outrun, overpower, plow under*, pommel*, pound*, powder*, pulverize*, run roughshod over*, skin*, steamroll*, take, take it all*, take to cleaners*, tan*, thrash, total, trounce, wallop*, whack*, whomp*, win, work over*, zap*; SEE CONCEPTS 95,363

defeat [v3] frustrate
baffle, balk, beat down*, beat the system*, blank, block, bury, cast down, cause setback, checkmate, circumvent, confound, contravene, cook*, counterplot, cross, disappoint, discomfit, disconcert, disprove, edge out*, foil, invalidate, neutralize, nonplus, nose out*, nullify, outwit, overturn, put end to*, puzzle, quell, reduce, refute, ruin, scuttle, shave*, shellac*, skunk*, spoil, squash, stump, subdue, subjugate, surmount, take wind out of sails*, throw for loop*, thwart, undo, victimize; SEE CONCEPTS 14,121

defect [n] blemish, imperfection
birthmark, blot, blotch, break, bug, catch, check, crack, deficiency, deformity, discoloration, drawback, error, failing, fault, flaw, foible, frailty, gap, glitch, gremlin, hole, infirmity, injury, irregularity, kink, knot, lack, mark, marring, mistake, patch, rift, rough spot, scar, scarcity, scratch, seam, second, shortage, shortcoming, sin, speck, spot, stain, taint, unsoundness, vice, want, weakness, weak point; SEE CONCEPTS 309,580,646

defect [v] break from belief, faith
abandon, abscond, apostatize, back out, break faith*, change sides, depart, desert, fall away from, forsake, go, go back on, go over, go over the fence*, lapse, leave, pull out, quit, rat*, rebel, reject, renege, renounce, revolt, run out, schism, sell out*, spurn, take a walk*, tergiversate, tergiverse, turn, turn coat*, walk out on, withdraw; SEE CONCEPTS 198,367

defection [n] abandonment
alienation, apostasy, backsliding, deficiency, dereliction, desertion, disaffection, disloyalty, disownment, divorce, estrangement, failing, failure, faithlessness, forsaking, lack, parting, rebellion, recreancy, rejection, repudiation, retreat, revolt, separation, severance, sundering, tergiversation, withdrawal; SEE CONCEPTS 195,198,367

defective [adj] broken, not working
abnormal, amiss, blemished, damaged, deficient, faulty, flawed, impaired, imperfect, inadequate, incomplete, injured, insufficient, lacking, on the bum*, out of order, poor, seconds, sick, subnormal, unfinished, unhealthy, unsound, wanting; SEE CONCEPTS 560,565

defend [v] protect
avert, battle, beat off, bulwark, care for, cherish, conserve, contend, cover, entrench, espouse, fend off, fight, fight for, fortify, foster, garrison, guard, guard against, hedge, hold, hold at bay, house, insure, keep safe, look after, maintain, mine, nourish, oppose, panoply, preserve, prevent, provide sanctuary, repel, resist, retain, safeguard, save, screen, secure, shelter, shield, stave off, sustain, take in, uphold, war, ward off, watch, watch over, withstand; SEE CONCEPTS 96,110

de
de

defend [v2] *show support for*
advocate, aid, apologize for, argue, assert, back, back up, bear one out*, befriend, champion, come to defense of, cover for, endorse, espouse, exculpate, exonerate, explain, go to bat for*, guarantee, justify, maintain, plead, prove a case, put in a good word*, rationalize, recommend, ride shotgun for*, say in defense, second, speak up for, stand by, stand up for, stick up for, stonewall*, support, sustain, thump for, uphold, vindicate, warrant; SEE CONCEPTS 10,49

defense [n1] *armament; protection system*
aegis, armor, arms, barricade, bastille, bastion, bulwark, buttress, citadel, cover, deterrence, dike, embankment, fastness, fence, fort, fortification, fortress, garrison, guard, immunity, munitions, palisade, parapet, position, protection, rampart, redoubt, resistance, safeguard, security, shelter, shield, stockade, stronghold, trench, wall, ward, warfare, weaponry, weapons; SEE CONCEPTS 321,322,500

defense [n2] *explanation, justification*
answer, apologetics, apologia, apologizing, apology, argument, cleanup, copout*, exculpation, excuse, excusing, exoneration, explaining, extenuation, fish story*, jive, off-time*, plea, rationalization, rejoinder, reply, response, retort, return, song and dance*, story, vindication, whitewash*; SEE CONCEPTS 57,278

defenseless [adj] *powerless, vulnerable*
caught, endangered, exposed, hands tied*, helpless, indefensible, in line of fire*, like a clay pigeon*, like a sitting duck*, naked*, on the line*, on the spot*, open, out on limb*, pigeon*, poor, unarmed, unguarded, unprotected, up the creek*, weak, wide open*; SEE CONCEPTS 555,576

defensible [adj] *justifiable*
condonable, defendable, excusable, fit, logical, pardonable, permissible, plausible, proper, tenable, valid, vindicable, warrantable; SEE CONCEPT 528

defensive [adj] *protective, watchful*
arresting, averting, balking, checking, conservative, coping with, defending, foiling, forestalling, frustrating, guarding, in opposition, interrupting, opposing, preservative, preventive, protecting, resistive, safeguarding, thwarting, uptight*, warding off, withstanding; SEE CONCEPTS 401,550

defer [v1] *hold off, put off*
adjourn, block, delay, detain, extend, give rain check*, hang fire*, hinder, hold up, impede, intermit, lay over, lengthen, obstruct, postpone, procrastinate, prolong, prorogue, protract, put on back burner*, put on hold*, put on ice*, remit, retard, set aside, shelve, slow, stall, stay, suspend, table, waive; SEE CONCEPTS 121,130

defer [v2] *yield*
accede, accommodate, acquiesce, adapt, adjust, admit, agree, assent, bow, buckle, capitulate, cave, comply, concede, cringe, fawn, give in to, knuckle*, knuckle under*, kowtow*, obey, submit, succumb, truckle; SEE CONCEPT 83

deference [n1] *obedience, compliance*
acquiescence, capitulation, complaisance, condescension, docility, obeisance, submission, yielding; SEE CONCEPT 633

deference [n2] *attention, homage*
acclaim, civility, consideration, courtesy, esteem, honor, obeisance, politeness, regard, respect, reverence, thoughtfulness, veneration; SEE CONCEPTS 10,410

deferential [adj] *respectful, considerate*
civil, complaisant, courteous, disarming, duteous, dutiful, ingratiating, ingratiatory, insinuating, insinuative, obedient, obeisant, obsequious, polite, regardful, reverential, saccharine, silken, silky, submissive; SEE CONCEPT 401

deferment/deferral [n] *postponement*
adjournment, delay, holdover*, moratorium, pause, putting off*, stay, suspension; SEE CONCEPTS 121,130

deferred [adj] *put off till a later time*
adjourned, assessed, charged, delayed, funded, held up, indebted, in waiting, negotiated, on hold*, on the shelf*, pigeonholed*, postponed, prolonged, protracted, remanded, renegotiated, retarded, scrubbed*, stalled, staved off, temporized; SEE CONCEPT 820

defiance [n] *disobedience, disregard*
affront, audacity, back talk*, big talk*, boldness, bravado, brazenness, call, cartel, challenge, command, confrontation, contempt, contrariness, contumacy, dare, defy, effrontery, enjoinder, factiousness, gas*, guts*, hot air*, impudence, impugnment, insolence, insubordination, insurgence, insurgency, intractableness, lip*, muster*, opposition, order, perversity, provocation, rebellion, rebelliousness, recalcitrance, revolt, sass*, spite, stump, summons, temerity, throwing of the gauntlet*, unruliness; SEE CONCEPTS 633,657

defiant [adj] *disobedient, disregardful*
aggressive, audacious, bold, challenging, contumacious, daring, gutsy*, insolent, insubmissive, insubordinate, mutinous, obstinate, provocative, rebellious, recalcitrant, reckless, refractory, resistant, resistive, sassy*, truculent; SEE CONCEPT 401

deficiency [n] *imperfection, inadequacy*
absence, bug*, dearth, defalcation, default, defect, deficit, demerit, dereliction, failing, failure, fault, flaw, frailty, glitch*, inability to hack it*, insufficience, insufficiency, lack, loss, need, neglect, paucity, privation, scantiness, scarcity, shortage, shortcoming, sin, want, weakness; SEE CONCEPTS 635,666,674

deficient [adj] *imperfect, inadequate*
amiss, bad, damaged, defective, exiguous, faulty, flawed, found wanting, impaired, incomplete, inferior, infrequent, injured, insufficient, lacking, marred, meager, not cut out for*, not enough, not make it*, not up to scratch*, outta gas*, rare, scant, scanty*, scarce, second fiddle*, second string, short, shy, sketchy, skimpy, third string*, unassembled, unequal, unfinished, unsatisfactory, wanting, weak; SEE CONCEPTS 531,565

deficit [n] *shortage of something needed, required*
arrears, dead horse*, defalcation, default, deficiency, due bill, dues, inadequacy, in hock*, insufficiency, in the hole*, in the red, lack, loss, paucity, red ink*, scantiness, shortcoming, shortfall, underage; SEE CONCEPTS 335,646

deficit spending [n] *paying out in excess of income*
debt, debt explosion, deficit financing, in the red, megadebt, negative cash flow, no assets, overspending; SEE CONCEPTS 324,330,344

defile [v] *corrupt, violate*
abuse, adulterate, befoul, besmirch, contaminate, debase, deflower, degrade, desecrate, dirty, dis-

color, disgrace, dishonor, hurt, maculate, make foul, mess up*, molest, muck up*, pollute, profane, rape, ravish, scuzz up*, seduce, shame, smear, soil, stain, sully, taint, tar, tarnish, trash, vitiate; SEE CONCEPTS 54,156,246

defiled [*adj*] *corrupted, violated*
besmirched, common, cooked, desecrated, dirty, dishonored, exposed, impure, mucked up*, polluted, profaned, ravished, spoilt, tainted, trashed*, unclean, vitiated; SEE CONCEPT 570

define [*v1*] *give specificity*
ascertain, assign, call a spade a spade*, characterize, construe, decide, delineate, denominate, denote, describe, designate, detail, determine, dub, elucidate, entitle, etch, exemplify, explain, expound, formalize, illustrate, interpret, label, lay it out*, nail it down*, name, prescribe, represent, specify, spell out, tag, translate; SEE CONCEPTS 55,57,62

define [*v2*] *delimit, outline*
belt, border, bound, circumscribe, compass, confine, curb, delineate, demarcate, distinguish, edge, encircle, enclose, encompass, envelop, establish, fence in, fix, flank, gird, girdle, limit, mark, mark out, rim, set, set bounds to, settle, stake out, surround, verge, wall in; SEE CONCEPTS 18,60,758

definite [*adj1*] *exact, clear*
audible, bold, categorical, clean-cut, clear-cut, clearly defined, complete, crisp, determinable, determined, distinct, distinguishable, downright, explicit, express, fixed, forthright, full, graphic, incisive, marked, minute, not vague, obvious, palpable, particular, plain, positive, precise, pronounced, ringing, severe, sharp, silhouetted, specific, straightforward, tangible, unambiguous, undubitable, unequivocal, unmistakable, visible, vivid, well-defined, well-grounded, well-marked; SEE CONCEPT 557

definite [*adj2*] *fixed, certain, positive*
assigned, assured, beyond doubt, circumscribed, convinced, decided, defined, determinate, determined, established, guaranteed, limited, narrow, precise, prescribed, restricted, set, settled, sure; SEE CONCEPT 535

definitely [*adv*] *certainly*
absolutely, beyond any doubt, categorically, clearly, decidedly, doubtless, doubtlessly, easily, explicitly, expressly, far and away*, finally, indubitably, no ifs ands or buts about it*, obviously, plainly, positively, specifically, surely, undeniably, unequivocally, unmistakably, unquestionably, without doubt, without fail, without question; SEE CONCEPTS 535,552

definition [*n*] *description*
analogue, annotation, answer, characterization, clarification, clue, comment, commentary, cue, delimitation, delineation, demarcation, denotation, determination, diagnosis, drift, elucidation, exemplification, explanation, explication, exposition, expounding, fixing, formalization, gloss, individuation, interpretation, key, outlining, rationale, rendering, rendition, representation, settling, signification, solution, statement of meaning, terminology, translation; SEE CONCEPTS 274,278,689

definitive [*adj*] *authoritative*
absolute, actual, categorical, clear-cut, closing, complete, completing, concluding, conclusive, decisive, definite, determining, downright*, ending, exhaustive, express, final, finishing, flat out*, last, limiting, nailed down, perfect, plain, precise, real, reliable, settling, specific, straight out, terminal, terminating, ultimate, unambiguous; SEE CONCEPTS 531,535,574

deflate [*v1*] *reduce or cause to contract*
collapse, decrease, depreciate, depress, devalue, diminish, empty, exhaust, flatten, puncture, shrink, squash, void; SEE CONCEPTS 236,247,776

deflate [*v2*] *humiliate*
chasten, cut down to size*, dash, debunk, disconcert, dispirit, humble, kick in the teeth*, knock down*, let down easy*, let wind out of sails*, mortify, puncture balloon*, put down*, shoot down*, take down*; SEE CONCEPTS 7,19

deflect [*v*] *bounce off; turn aside*
avert, bend, cover up, curve, deviate, disperse, diverge, divert, fend, glance off, hold off, hook, keep off, parry, pivot, ricochet, sheer, shy, sidetrack, slew, slip, swerve, twist, veer, volte-face, wheel, whip, whirl, wind; SEE CONCEPTS 147,189,194

deflower [*v*] *ravish; take away beauty*
assault, defile, deflorate, depredate, desecrate, despoil, devour, force, harm, have, mar, molest, outrage, possess, ravage, ravish, ruin, seduce, spoil, violate; SEE CONCEPT 375

deform [*v*] *distort, disfigure*
batter, blemish, buckle, contort, cripple, damage, deface, flaw, gnarl, grimace, impair, injure, knot, maim, malform, mangle, mar, misshape, mutilate, ruin, skew, spoil, twist, warp, wince; SEE CONCEPTS 246,250

deformed [*adj*] *disfigured, distorted*
askew, awry, bent, blemished, bowed, buckled, contorted, cramped, crippled, crooked, curved, damaged, disjointed, gnarled, grotesque, humpbacked, hunchbacked, ill-made, irregular, knotted, maimed, malformed, mangled, marred, misproportioned, misshapen, out of shape, scarred, twisted, ugly, warped; SEE CONCEPTS 485,486

deformity [*n*] *disfigurement, distortion*
aberration, abnormality, asymmetry, buckle, contortion, corruption, crookedness, damage, defacement, defect, depravity, evil, grossness, hideousness, impairment, injury, irregularity, knot, malconformation, malformation, misproportion, misshape, misshapenness, repulsiveness, ugliness, unattractiveness, unnaturalness, unsightliness, warp; SEE CONCEPT 580

defraud [*v*] *cheat, bilk*
bamboozle, beguile, burn, chouse, circumvent, clip, con, cozen, deceive, delude, do, do number on*, do out of*, dupe, embezzle, fleece, flimflam, foil, hoax, jive*, milk*, outwit, pilfer, pull fast one*, rip off*, rob, shaft*, shuck*, stick*, sucker into*, swindle, take*, take in*, take to the cleaner's*, trick, victimize; SEE CONCEPT 59

deft [*adj*] *agile, clever*
able, adept, adroit, apt, crack, crackerjack*, cute, dexterous, expert, fleet, handy, having good hands, having know-how, ingenious, neat, nimble, proficient, prompt, quick, ready, skilled, skillful; SEE CONCEPT 527

defunct [*adj*] *extinct, not functioning*
asleep, bygone, cold, dead, deceased, departed, done for*, down the drain*, exanimate, expired, gone, had it*, inanimate, inoperative, invalid, kaput*, late, lifeless, lost, nonexistent, obsolete,

de
de

out of commission*, vanished; SEE CONCEPTS **539,560**

defy [v] *challenge, frustrate*
baffle, beard, brave, confront, contemn, dare, defeat, deride, despise, disregard, elude, face, flout, fly in face of*, foil, front, gibe*, hang tough*, hurl defiance at, ignore, insult, make my day*, mock, oppose, outdare, provoke, repel, repulse, resist, ridicule, scorn, slight, spurn, stick*, stick fast*, take one on*, thwart, venture, violate, withstand; SEE CONCEPTS **78,87**

degeneracy [n1] *corruption*
abasement, decadence, degradation, depravity, dissoluteness, downfall, immorality, inferiority, meanness, poorness; SEE CONCEPT **645**

degeneracy [n2] *decay, deterioration*
atrophy, debasement, declination, decline, decrease, depravation, devolution, downfall, downgrade; SEE CONCEPTS **230,469**

degenerate [adj] *corrupt, deteriorated*
base, debased, debauched, decadent, decayed, degenerated, degraded, demeaned, depraved, dissolute, effete, failing, fallen, flatitious, immoral, infamous, low, mean, miscreant, nefarious, overripe, perverted, retrograde, retrogressive, rotten, sinking, unhealthy, vicious, villainous, vitiated, wicked, worsen; SEE CONCEPTS **545,570**

degenerate [v] *decay, deteriorate*
backslide, come apart at seams*, corrode, corrupt, decline, decrease, deprave, descend, die on vine*, disimprove, disintegrate, fall off, go downhill*, go to pieces*, go to the dogs*, lapse, lessen, regress, retrogress, return, revert, rot, sink, slip, vitiate, worsen; SEE CONCEPTS **469,698,702**

degradation [n] *depravity, shame*
abasement, debasement, decadence, decline, degeneracy, degeneration, demotion, derogation, deterioration, discredit, disgrace, dishonor, downgrading, evil, humiliation, ignominy, mortification, perversion, reduction; SEE CONCEPTS **230,410**

degrade [v] *shame, humiliate*
abase, belittle, bemean, bench, break, bump, bust, canker, cast down, cheapen, corrupt, cut down to size*, debase, debauch, declass, decry, degenerate, demean, demote, depose, deprave, derogate, deteriorate, detract, diminish, disbar, discredit, disgrace, dishonor, disparage, downgrade, humble, impair, injure, lessen, lower, mudsling*, pan*, pervert, put down, reduce, rule out, run down*, shoot down*, sink, slam, take down*, take down a peg*, tear down*, vitiate, weaken; SEE CONCEPTS **7,19,240**

degree [n1] *unit of measurement*
amount, amplitude, caliber, dimension, division, expanse, extent, gauge, gradation, grade, height, intensity, interval, length, limit, line, link, mark, notch, period, plane, point, proportion, quality, quantity, range, rate, ratio, reach, rung, scale, scope, severity, shade, size, space, stage, stair, standard, step, stint, strength, tenor, term, tier; SEE CONCEPTS **651,783,792**

degree [n2] *recognition of achievement; rank or grade of position*
approbation, approval, baccalaureate, caliber, class, compass, credentials, credit, dignification, dignity, distinction, eminence, grade, height, honor, level, magnitude, order, pitch, point, position, potency, qualification, quality, quantity, range, rank, reach, scope, sheepskin, shingle,

sort, stage, standard, standing, station, status, strength, testimonial, testimony; SEE CONCEPTS **388,706**

dehydrate [v] *take moisture out of*
cotton-mouth, desiccate, drain, dry, dry out, dry up, evaporate, exsiccate, parch, sear; SEE CONCEPTS **250,469**

deify [v] *elevate, glorify*
adore, apotheosize, consecrate, ennoble, enthrone, exalt, extol, idealize, idolize, immortalize, venerate, worship; SEE CONCEPTS **69,367**

deign [v] *lower oneself*
condescend, consent, deem worthy, patronize, see fit*, stoop, think fit*, vouchsafe; SEE CONCEPT **35**

deity [n] *god, worshiped being*
celestial, celestial being, creator, divine being, divinity, goddess, godhead, idol, immortal, supreme being; SEE CONCEPTS **368,370**

dejected [adj] *depressed, blue*
abject, all torn up*, atrabilious, black, bleak, broody, bummed out*, cast down, cheerless, clouded, crestfallen, dampened, dashed, despondent, disconsolate, discouraged, disheartened, dismal, dispirited, doleful, down, downcast, downhearted, down in the dumps*, down in the mouth*, dragged, drooping, droopy, gloomy, glum, heavyhearted, hurting*, in the pits*, low, low-spirited, melancholy, miserable, moody, mopey*, mopish*, morose, sad, sagging, shot down*, spiritless, woebegone, wretched; SEE CONCEPT **403**

delay [n] *deferment, interruption*
adjournment, bind, check, cooling-off period*, cunctation, dawdling, demurral, detention, discontinuation, downtime*, filibuster, hangup*, hindrance, holding, holding pattern*, hold-up*, impediment, interval, jam, lag, lingering, logjam*, loitering, moratorium, obstruction, postponement, problem, procrastination, prorogation, putting off*, remission, reprieve, retardation, retardment, setback, showstopper*, stall, stay, stop, stoppage, surcease, suspension, tarrying, tie-up, wait; SEE CONCEPTS **121,130,666**

delay [v] *cause stop in action*
adjourn, arrest, bar, bide time, block, check, choke, clog, confine, curb, dawdle, defer, detain, deter, dilly-dally*, discourage, drag, encumber, filibuster, gain time, hamper, hold, hold over, impede, inhibit, interfere, intermit, jam, keep, keep back, lag, lay over, linger, loiter, obstruct, postpone, prevent, procrastinate, prolong, prorogue, protract, put off, remand, repress, restrict, retard, shelve, slacken, stall, stave off, stay, suspend, table, tarry, temporize, withhold; SEE CONCEPTS **121,130,237**

delectable [adj] *delicious, enjoyable*
adorable, agreeable, ambrosial, appetizing, charming, choice, dainty, darling, delicate, delightful, delish, divine, enticing, exquisite, gratifying, heavenly, inviting, luscious, lush, palatable, pleasant, pleasurable, rare, sapid, satisfying, savory, scrumptious, tasty, toothsome, yummy; SEE CONCEPTS **574,579,613**

delegate [n] *representative, often governmental*
agent, alternate, ambassador, appointee, catchpole*, commissioner, consul, deputy, emissary, envoy, factor, front*, legate, member, member of congress, minister, mouthpiece, nominee, people's choice, pinch hitter*, plenipotentiary, proxy, regent, rep*, replacement, senator, spokesperson,

stand-in, substitute, surrogate, vicar, viceroy; SEE CONCEPT 354

delegate [v1] *give authority; empower*
accredit, appoint, assign, authorize, cast, charge, choose, commission, constitute, depute, deputize, designate, elect, give nod, invest, license, mandate, name, nominate, ordain, place trust in, select, swear in, warrant; SEE CONCEPTS 50,88

delegate [v2] *assign responsibility*
authorize, consign, devolve, entrust, give, hand over, hold responsible for, parcel out*, pass on*, relegate, send on errand, send on mission, shunt, transfer; SEE CONCEPTS 50,88,143

delegation [n1] *assignment of responsibility*
appointment, apportioning, authorization, charge, commissioning, committal, consigning, consignment, conveyance, conveying, deputation, deputization, deputizing, devolution, entrustment, giving over, installation, investiture, mandate, nomination, ordination, reference, referring, relegation, sending away, submittal, submitting, transferal, transference, transferring, trust; SEE CONCEPTS 50,88,143,685

delegation [n2] *group of representatives*
commission, contingent, deputation, embassy, envoys, gathering, legation, mission, organization; SEE CONCEPTS 299,301

delete [v] *erase, remove*
annul, black out, bleep, blot out, blue-pencil*, cancel, clean, clean up, cross out, cut, cut out, decontaminate, destroy, drop, edit, efface, eliminate, exclude, expunge, obliterate, omit, pass up, rub, rub out, rule out, sanitize, snip, squash, squelch, sterilize, strike out, trim, wipe out, X-out*; SEE CONCEPT 211

deleterious [adj] *harmful, damaging*
bad, destroying, destructive, detrimental, hurtful, injurious, mischievous, nocent, nocuous, pernicious, prejudicial, prejudicious, ruining, ruinous; SEE CONCEPTS 537,570

deliberate [adj] *intentional*
advised, aforethought, calculated, careful, cautious, cold-blooded, conscious, considered, cut-and-dried*, designed, designful, done on purpose, express, fixed, intended, judged, meticulous, planned, pondered, prearranged, predesigned, predeterminate, predetermined, premeditated, prepense, projected, provident, prudent, purposed, purposeful, purposive, reasoned, resolved, schemed, scrupulous, studied, studious, thoughtful, thought out, voluntary, wary, weighed, willful, with forethought, witting; SEE CONCEPTS 401,542

deliberate [v] *think about seriously; discuss*
argue, bat it around*, cerebrate, chew over*, cogitate, consider, consult, contemplate, debate, excogitate, hammer away at*, judge, kick around, knock around, meditate, mull over, muse, ponder, pour it on*, put on thinking cap*, rack brains*, reason, reflect, revolve, roll, ruminate, run up a flagpole*, speculate, stew over*, study, sweat over*, talk over, turn over, weigh; SEE CONCEPTS 17,24,56

deliberately [adv] *intentionally*
advisedly, after consideration, apurpose, by design, calculatingly, consciously, designed, determinedly, emphatically, freely, in cold blood, independently, knowingly, meaningfully, on purpose, pointedly, premeditatedly, prepensely, purposely, purposively, resolutely, studiously, to that

end, voluntarily, willfully, with a view to, with eyes wide open*, with malice aforethought*, without qualms, wittingly; SEE CONCEPTS 401,542

deliberation [n] *serious thought, discussion*
application, attention, brainwork, calculation, care, carefulness, caution, cerebration, circumspection, cogitation, confabulation, conference, consideration, consultation, debate, forethought, heed, meditation, prudence, purpose, rap, ratiocination, reflection, speculation, study, ventilation, wariness; SEE CONCEPTS 17,24,56

delicacy [n1] *daintiness, fineness of structure*
airiness, debility, diaphaneity, elegance, etherealness, exquisiteness, fragility, frailness, frailty, gossameriness, infirmity, lightness, slenderness, smoothness, softness, subtlety, tenderness, tenuity, translucency, transparency, weakness; SEE CONCEPTS 611,733

delicacy [n2] *delicious, gourmet food*
ambrosia, banquet, bonne bouche, dainty, delight, dessert, feast, goody, indulgence, luxury, morsel, nectar, pleasure, rarity, regale, relish, savory, special, sweet, tidbit, treat; SEE CONCEPT 457

delicate [adj1] *dainty, weak*
aerial, balmy, breakable, choice, delectable, delicious, delightful, elegant, ethereal, exquisite, faint, filmy, fine, fine-grained, finespun, flimsy, fracturable, fragile, frail, frangible, gauzy, gentle, gossamery, graceful, hairline, mild, muted, nice, pale, pastel, rare, recherché, select, shatterable, shattery, slight, soft, subdued, subtle, superior, tender; SEE CONCEPTS 490,574,606

delicate [adj2] *sickly*
ailing, debilitated, decrepit, feeble, flimsy, fragile, frail, infirm, shatterable, shattery, slender, slight, susceptible, tender, unhealthy, weak; SEE CONCEPT 314

delicate [adj3] *fussy, discriminating*
alert, careful, critical, dainty, fastidious, finical, finicking, finicky, gentle, nice, particular, persnickety, prudish, pure, refined, scrupulous, sensitive, squeamish, thin-skinned; SEE CONCEPT 404

delicate [adj4] *difficult, sticky (situation)*
critical, hair-trigger*, precarious, sensitive, ticklish, touchy, tricky, uncertain, unpredictable, volatile; SEE CONCEPT 565

delicate [adj5] *careful, tactful*
accurate, adept, cautious, considerate, deft, detailed, diplomatic, discreet, expert, foresighted, heedful, masterly, minute, politic, precise, proficient, prudent, sensitive, skilled, tactical, wary; SEE CONCEPTS 401,542

delicately [adv] *carefully*
beautifully, cautiously, daintily, deftly, elegantly, exquisitely, fastidiously, finely, gracefully, lightly, precisely, sensitively, skillfully, softly, subtly, tactfully; SEE CONCEPTS 542,544

delicious [adj] *pleasing, especially to the taste*
adorable, ambrosial, appetizing, choice, dainty, darling, delectable, delightful, delish*, distinctive, divine, enjoyable, enticing, exquisite, fit for king*, good, gratifying, heavenly, luscious, lush, mellow, mouthwatering, nectareous, nice, palatable, piquant, pleasant, rare, rich, sapid, savory, scrumptious, spicy, sweet, tasteful, tasty, tempting, titillating, toothsome, well-prepared, well-seasoned, yummy*; SEE CONCEPTS 572,613

de
de

delight [n] *enjoyment, happiness*
contentment, delectation, ecstasy, enchantment, felicity, fruition, gladness, glee, gratification, hilarity, jollity, joy, joyance, mirth, pleasure, rapture, relish, satisfaction, transport; SEE CONCEPT 410

delight [v] *make happy; experience happiness*
allure, amuse, arride, attract, be the ticket*, charm, cheer, content, delectate, divert, enchant, enrapture, entertain, exult, fascinate, freak out, gladden, glory, go over big*, gratify, groove*, hit the spot*, jubilate, knock dead*, knock out*, please, pleasure, ravish, rejoice, satisfy, score, send, slay, thrill, tickle pink*, tickle to death*, turn on, wow; SEE CONCEPTS 7,22

delighted [adj] *very happy*
captivated, charmed, ecstatic, elated, enchanted, entranced, excited, fulfilled, gladdened, gratified, joyous, jubilant, overjoyed, pleasantly surprised, pleased, thrilled; SEE CONCEPT 403

delightful [adj] *pleasant, charming*
adorable, agreeable, alluring, ambrosial, amusing, attractive, beautiful, captivating, cheery, cheerful, congenial, darling, delectable, delicious, enchanting, engaging, enjoyable, entertaining, fair, fascinating, gratifying, heavenly, ineffable, lovely, luscious, lush, pleasing, pleasurable, rapturous, ravishing, refreshing, satisfying, scrumptious, thrilling, yummy*; SEE CONCEPTS 401,404

delight in [v] *take pleasure from*
admire, adore, amuse oneself, appreciate, be content, be pleased, cherish, dig*, eat up*, enjoy, feast on, get a kick out of*, get high on*, get off on*, glory in, groove on*, indulge in, like, live a little*, live it up*, love, luxuriate in, relish, revel in, savor; SEE CONCEPTS 32,410

delinquency [n] *misconduct*
crime, default, dereliction, failure, fault, lapse, misbehavior, misdeed, misdemeanor, neglect, nonobservance, offense, oversight, weakness, wrongdoing; SEE CONCEPTS 192,645

delinquent [n] *criminal, often young*
behind, blackguard, black sheep*, culprit, dawdler, deadbeat*, deadhead*, debtor, defaulter, derelict, desperado, evader, fallen angel*, felon, hoodlum*, jailbird*, JD*, juvenile delinquent, juvie*, lawbreaker, loafer, lounger, malefactor, miscreant, neglecter, no show*, offender, outlaw, punk*, recreant, reprobate, sinner, wrongdoer, young offender; SEE CONCEPT 412

delinquent [adj] *irresponsible, defaulting*
behind, blamable, blameworthy, careless, censurable, criminal, culpable, defaultant, derelict, disregardful, faulty, guilty, lax, neglectful, negligent, offending, overdue, procrastinating, red-handed*, remiss, reprehensible, shabby, slack, tardy, unpaid; SEE CONCEPTS 401,570

delirious [adj1] *mentally imbalanced*
aberrant, bewildered, confused, crazed, crazy, demented, deranged, deviant, deviate, disarranged, disordered, distracted, disturbed, flipped*, flipped out*, hallucinatory, incoherent, insane, irrational, lightheaded, lunatic, mad, maniac, maniacal, manic, off one's head*, out of one's head*, out of one's skull*, rambling, raving, unhinged, unreasonable, unsettled, wandering; SEE CONCEPTS 402,403

delirious [adj2] *excited; very happy*
beside oneself*, carried away*, corybantic, crazy, delighted, drunk*, ecstatic, enthused, frantic, frenetic, frenzied, furious, hysterical, intoxicated, mad, overwrought, rabid*, rapturous, thrilled, transported, wild; SEE CONCEPTS 401,403

delirium [n] *madness*
aberration, ardor, dementia, derangement, ecstasy, enthusiasm, fervor, fever, frenzy, furor, fury, hallucination, hysteria, insanity, lunacy, mania, passion, rage, raving, transport, zeal; SEE CONCEPT 410

deliver [v1] *transfer, carry*
bear, bring, cart, come across with*, convey, dish out*, distribute, drop, fork over*, gimme*, give, hand, hand-carry, hand over, pass, put on, put out, remit, transport, truck; SEE CONCEPTS 108,217

deliver [v2] *relinquish possession*
abandon, cede, commit, give up, grant, hand over, let go, resign, surrender, transfer, turn over, yield; SEE CONCEPTS 116,131

deliver [v3] *free, liberate*
acquit, discharge, emancipate, loose, ransom, redeem, release, rescue, save, unshackle; SEE CONCEPT 127

deliver [v4] *announce, proclaim*
address, bring out, broach, chime in, come out with, communicate, declare, express, give, give forth, impart, present, pronounce, publish, read, say, state, tell, throw out, utter, vent, voice; SEE CONCEPTS 51,60

deliver [v5] *administer; throw*
aim, deal, direct, dispatch, fling, give, hurl, inflict, launch, pitch, send, strike, transmit; SEE CONCEPTS 217,222

deliver [v6] *discharge, give forth*
accouch, bear, birth, born, dispense, feed, find, hand, hand over, produce, provide, release, supply, turn over; SEE CONCEPTS 179,374

delivery [n1] *transfer, transmittal*
carting, commitment, consignment, conveyance, dispatch, distribution, drop, freighting, giving over, handing over, impartment, intrusting, mailing, parcel post, portage, post, rendition, shipment, surrender, transmission; SEE CONCEPTS 108,217

delivery [n2] *articulation of message*
accent, diction, elocution, emphasis, enunciation, inflection, intonation, modulation, pronunciation, speech, utterance; SEE CONCEPTS 47,595

delivery [n3] *childbirth*
accouchement, bearing, birth, birthing, bringing forth, Caesarian section, childbearing, confinement, geniture, labor, lying-in, parturition, travail; SEE CONCEPTS 302,373,374

delivery [n4] *giving of freedom*
deliverance, emancipation, escape, freeing, liberation, pardon, release, rescue, salvage, salvation; SEE CONCEPT 127

delude [v] *deceive, fool*
beguile, betray, bluff, caboodle*, cheat, con, cozen, disinform, do a number on*, double-cross, dupe*, gull*, hoax*, hoodwink*, illude, impose on, jive*, juggle*, lead up garden path*, misguide, mislead, mousetrap*, outfox, play trick on, snow*, string along, sucker*, take in, trick; SEE CONCEPT 59

deluge [n] *downpour, flood of something*
avalanche, barrage, cataclysm, cataract, drencher, flux, inundation, niagara, overflowing, overrunning, pour, rush, spate, torrent; SEE CONCEPTS 432,524,787

deluge [*v1*] *inundate with water*
douse, drench, drown, engulf, flood, flush, gush, overflow, overrun, overwhelm, pour, sluice, soak, sop, souse, stream, submerge, swamp, wet, whelm; SEE CONCEPT 256

deluge [*v2*] *overwhelm*
abound, crowd, engulf, flood, glut, inundate, overcome, overcrowd, overload, overrun, oversupply, snow*, snow under*, swamp, teem; SEE CONCEPTS 42,140

delusion [*n*] *misconception, misbelief*
apparition, blunder, casuistry, chicanery, daydream, deception, deceptiveness, dream, eidolon, error, fallacy, false impression, fancy, fantasy, figment*, fool's paradise*, ghost, hallucination, head trip*, ignis fatuus, illusion, lapse, mirage, misapprehension, mistake, optical illusion, oversight, phantasm, phantom, pipe dream*, self-deception, shade, speciousness, spuriousness, trickery, trip, vision; SEE CONCEPTS 409,410,689

delusive [*adj*] *deceptive*
apparent, beguiling, chimerical, deceiving, deluding, fallacious, false, fanciful, fantastic, illusive, illusory, imaginary, misleading, ostensible, quixotic, seeming, specious, spurious, visionary; SEE CONCEPT 582

deluxe [*adj*] *superior, plush*
choice, costly, dainty, delicate, elegant, exclusive, expensive, exquisite, first-class, grand, luscious, lush, luxuriant, luxurious, opulent, palatial, posh, rare, recherché, rich, ritzy, select, special, splendid, sumptuous, super, swank, swanky; SEE CONCEPT 574

delve [*v*] *dig into task, action*
burrow, dig, dredge, examine, excavate, explore, ferret out*, go into, gouge out, inquire, investigate, jump into, leave no stone unturned*, look into, probe, prospect, ransack, really get into*, research, rummage, scoop out, search, seek, shovel, sift, spade, trowel, turn inside out*; SEE CONCEPTS 87,103,216

demagogue [*n*] *agitating person*
agitator, fanatic, firebrand*, fomenter, haranger, hothead*, incendiary, inciter, inflamer, instigator, politician, rabble-rouser*, radical, rebel, revolutionary, soapbox orator*, troublemaker; SEE CONCEPTS 359,412

demand [*n*] *question, request*
appeal, application, arrogation, bid, bidding, call, call for, charge, claim, clamor, command, counterclaim, entreatment, entreaty, exaction, impetration, imploration, importunity, imposition, inquiry, insistence, interest, interrogation, lien, necessity, need, occasion, order, petition, plea, prayer, pursuit, requirement, requisition, rush, sale, search, solicitation, stipulation, suit, supplication, trade, ultimatum, use, vogue, want; SEE CONCEPT 662

demand [*v1*] *ask strongly for something*
abuse, appeal, apply, arrogate, badger, beg, beseech, besiege, bid, challenge, charge, cite, claim, clamor for, coerce, command, compel, constrain, counterclaim, direct, dun, enjoin, entreat, exact, expect, force, hit, hit up, impetrate, implore, importune, inquire, insist on, interrogate, knock, nag, necessitate, oblige, order, pester, petition, postulate, pray, press, question, request, require, requisition, solicit, stipulate, sue for, summon, supplicate, tax, urge, whistle for; SEE CONCEPT 53

demand [*v2*] *require*
ask, call for, command, crave, cry out for, fail, involve, lack, necessitate, need, oblige, take, want; SEE CONCEPTS 26,646

demanding [*adj*] *challenging, urgent*
ambitious, backbreaker*, bothersome, clamorous, critical, dictatorial, difficult, exacting, exhausting, exigent, fussy, grievous, hard, imperious, importunate, insistent, nagging, onerous, oppressive, pressing, querulous, strict, stringent, taxing, tough, troublesome, trying, wearing, weighty; SEE CONCEPTS 542,565

demarcation [*n*] *boundary, division*
bound, confine, delimitation, differentiation, distinction, enclosure, limit, margin, separation, split, terminus; SEE CONCEPT 745

demean [*v*] *humble, humiliate*
abase, bad-mouth*, belittle, bemean, cast down, contemn, cut down to size*, cut rate, debase, decry, degrade, derogate, descend, depress, detract, dis*, disparage, dump on*, knock down*, lower, pan*, poor-mouth*, scorn, sink, stoop*; SEE CONCEPTS 7,19,54

demeanor [*n*] *behavior, manner*
address, air, attitude, bearing, carriage, comportment, conduct, deportment, disposition, mien, poise, port, presence, set; SEE CONCEPTS 411,633

demented [*adj*] *crazy, insane*
bananas*, bemused, crackbrained*, daft, delirious, deranged, distracted, distraught, flipped out*, foolish, frenzied, fruity*, hysterical, idiotic, in the ozone*, lunatic, mad, maniac, maniacal, manic, non compos mentis, nutty as a fruitcake*, out of one's gourd*, out of one's tree*, psycho, psychopathic, psychotic, schitzy*, schizoid*, unbalanced, unglued*, unhinged*, unsound, whacko*; SEE CONCEPT 403

demise [*n*] *fate, usually death*
annihilation, collapse, curtains, decease, departure, dissolution, downfall, dying, end, ending, expiration, extinction, failure, fall, final thrill*, last out*, last roundup*, lights out*, number's up*, passing, quietus, ruin, silence, sleep, termination; SEE CONCEPTS 105,304,679

democracy [*n*] *government in which people participate*
commonwealth, egalitarianism, emancipation, equalitarianism, equality, freedom, justice, liberal government, representative government, republic, suffrage; SEE CONCEPTS 299,688,689

democratic [*adj*] *representative, self-governing*
autonomous, common, communal, constitutional, egalitarian, equal, free, friendly, individualistic, informal, just, libertarian, orderly, popular, populist, self-ruling, socialist; SEE CONCEPTS 319,536

demolish [*v*] *destroy; consume*
annihilate, break, bulldoze, burst, crack, crush, decimate, defeat, devastate, devour, dilapidate, dismantle, eat, flatten, gobble up, knock down, level, obliterate, overthrow, overturn, pulverize, put away, put in toilet!*, raze, ruin, sink, smash, take apart, take out, tear down, torpedo*, total*, trash*, undo, wax*, wipe off map*, wrack, wreck; SEE CONCEPTS 169,252

demolition [*n*] *destruction*
annihilation, bulldozing, explosion, extermination, knocking down, leveling, razing, wrecking; SEE CONCEPT 252

de
de

demon [*n*] *evil, devilish being or influence*
archfiend, beast, brute, fiend, goblin, hellion, imp, incubus, little devil*, malignant spirit, monster, rascal, rogue, Satan, succubus, vampire, villain; SEE CONCEPTS *370,412*

demonic/demoniac/demoniacal [*adj*] *evil*
aroused, crazed, devilish, diabolic, diabolical, fiendish, fired, frantic, frenetic, frenzied, hellish, impious, infernal, insane, inspired, mad, maniacal, manic, possessed, satanic, serpentine, unhallowed, violent, wicked; SEE CONCEPTS *404,545*

demonstrable [*adj*] *provable, evident*
ascertainable, attestable, axiomatic, certain, conclusive, deducible, evincible, incontrovertible, indubitable, inferable, irrefutable, obvious, palpable, positive, self-evident, undeniable, unmistakable, verifiable; SEE CONCEPTS *529,535*

demonstrate [*v1*] *display, show*
authenticate, determine, establish, evidence, evince, exhibit, expose, flaunt, indicate, make evident, make out, manifest, prove, roll out*, show and tell*, test, testify to, trot out*, try, validate; SEE CONCEPT *97*

demonstrate [*v2*] *explain, illustrate*
confirm, convey, describe, express, give for instance, make clear, ostend, proclaim, set forth, show how, teach, testify to, walk one through*; SEE CONCEPT *57*

demonstrate [*v3*] *display or take public action for a cause*
exhibit, fast, lie in, manifest, march, march on, parade, picket, protest, rally, sit in, stage walkout, strike, walkout; SEE CONCEPTS *261,300*

demonstration [*n1*] *display of proof*
affirmation, confirmation, description, evidence, exhibition, explanation, exposition, expression, illustration, induction, manifestation, presentation, proof, show, spectacle, substantiation, test, testimony, trial, validation; SEE CONCEPT *261*

demonstration [*n2*] *display of belief in cause by taking public action*
fast, lie-in*, love-in*, march, mass lobby, parade, peace march, picket, picket line, protest, rally, sit-in*, strike, teach-in*, walkout; SEE CONCEPTS *261,300*

demonstrative [*adj1*] *expressive, communicative*
affectionate, candid, effusive, emotional, evincive, expansive, explanatory, expository, frank, gushing, histrionic, illustrative, indicative, loving, open, outgoing, outpouring, outspoken, plain, profuse, symptomatic, tender, unconstrained, unreserved, unrestrained, warmhearted; SEE CONCEPTS *267,401*

demonstrative [*adj2*] *conclusive*
authenticating, certain, convincing, decisive, definite, final, proving, showing, specific, validating; SEE CONCEPTS *531,537*

demoralize [*v1*] *depress, unnerve*
abash, blow out, blow up, chill, cripple, damp, dampen, daunt, debilitate, deject, disarrange, disconcert, discountenance, discourage, dishearten, disorder, disorganize, disparage, dispirit, disturb, embarrass, enfeeble, get to*, jumble, muddle, nonplus, psych out*, rattle, sap, send up*, shake, snarl, take apart*, take steam out*, undermine, unglue*, unman, unsettle, unzip*, upset, weaken; SEE CONCEPTS *7,19*

demoralize [*v2*] *corrupt, pervert*
bastardize, bestialize, brutalize, debase, debauch, deprave, lower, vitiate, warp; SEE CONCEPT *14*

demote [*v*] *downgrade, lower in rank*
bench*, break, bump, bust, declass, degrade, demean, demerit, dismiss, disrate, hold back, kick downstairs*, lower, reduce, relegate, set back; SEE CONCEPTS *233,351*

demur [*v*] *disagree*
balk, cavil, challenge, combat, complain, deprecate, disapprove, dispute, doubt, fight, hem and haw*, hesitate, object, oppose, pause, protest, pussyfoot*, refuse, remonstrate, resist, scruple, shy, stick, stickle, strain, take exception*, vacillate, wait and see*, waver; SEE CONCEPTS *46,54*

demure [*adj*] *reserved, affected*
backward, bashful, blushing, close, coy, decorous, diffident, earnest, humble, modest, nice, prim, prissy, proper, prudish, reticent, retiring, sedate, serious, shy, silent, skittish, sober, solemn, staid, strait-laced, timid, unassertive, unassuming, unassured; SEE CONCEPTS *401,404*

den [*n1*] *cavern, hideaway*
atelier, burrow, cave, cloister, couch, cubbyhole, haunt, hideout, hole, hotbed, lair, lodge, nest, retreat, sanctuary, sanctum, shelter, snuggery, study; SEE CONCEPTS *448,513*

den [*n2*] *room for relaxation or informal entertaining*
family room, library, media room, playroom, recreation room, rec room*, rumpus room, studio, TV room; SEE CONCEPTS *440,448*

denial [*n*] *dismissal, refusal of belief in statement*
abnegation, abstaining, adjuration, brush-off, cold shoulder*, contradiction, controversion, declination, disallowance, disapproval, disavowal, disclaimer, dismissing, disproof, dissent, forswearing, gainsaying, nay, negation, negative, nix*, nonacceptance, noncommittal, no way*, prohibition, protestation, rebuff, rebuttal, refraining, refusing, refutal, refutation, rejecting, rejection, renegement, renouncement, renunciation, repudiating, repudiation, repulse, retraction, turndown, veto; SEE CONCEPTS *45,54*

denigrate [*v*] *belittle, malign*
asperse, bad mouth*, besmirch, blacken, blister, calumniate, decry, defame, dis*, disparage, give black eye*, impugn, knock*, libel, mudsling*, put down*, revile, rip up*, roast*, run down*, scandalize, slander, tear down*, traduce, vilify; SEE CONCEPTS *52,54*

denizen [*n*] *resident*
citizen, dweller, habitant, indweller, inhabitant, inhabiter, liver, national, native, occupant, resider, subject; SEE CONCEPT *413*

denomination [*n1*] *religious belief*
church, communion, connection, creed, cult, faith, group, persuasion, religion, school, sect; SEE CONCEPTS *368,689*

denomination [*n2*] *classification*
body, category, class, grade, group, size, type, unit, value; SEE CONCEPT *378*

denomination [*n3*] *name*
appellation, appellative, brand, cognomen, compellation, designation, flag, handle, identification, label, moniker, nomen, slot, style, surname, tab, tag, term, title; SEE CONCEPT *683*

denotation [*n*] *meaning, description*
designation, explanation, implication, indication, signification, specification; SEE CONCEPTS *268, 682*

denote [*v*] *designate, mean*
add up, announce, argue, bespeak, betoken, con-

note, evidence, express, finger, flash, hang sign on*, imply, import, indicate, insinuate, intend, make, mark, peg, prove, put down for, put finger on*, show, signify, spell, stand for, symbol, symbolize, tab, tag, typify; SEE CONCEPTS 55,682

denounce [v] *condemn, attack*
accuse, adjudicate, arraign, blacklist, blame, boycott, brand, castigate, censure, charge, charge with, criticize, damn, declaim, decry, denunciate, derogate, dress down, excoriate, expose, finger*, hang something on*, impeach, implicate, impugn, incriminate, indict, inveigh against, knock, ostracize, proscribe, prosecute, rap, rat*, rebuke, reprehend, reprimand, reproach, reprobate, reprove, revile, scold, show up, skin*, smear, stigmatize, take to task, threaten, upbraid, vilify, vituperate; SEE CONCEPTS 44,52

dense [adj 1] *compressed, thick*
close, close-knit, compact, condensed, crammed, crowded, heaped, heavy, impenetrable, jammed, jam-packed*, massed, opaque, packed, packed like sardines*, piled, solid, substantial, thickset; SEE CONCEPT 483

dense [adj 2] *slow, stupid*
blockheaded*, boorish, doltish, dull, dumb, fatheaded*, ignorant, imbecilic, impassive, lethargic, numskulled*, oafish, obtuse, phlegmatic, simple, slow-witted, sluggish, stolid, thick, torpid; SEE CONCEPT 402

density [n] *bulk, mass*
body, closeness, compactness, concretion, consistency, crowdedness, denseness, frequency, heaviness, impenetrability, massiveness, quantity, solidity, substantiality, thickness, tightness; SEE CONCEPT 722

dent [n] *depression, scrape, chip*
cavity, concavity, crater, crenel, cut, dimple, dint, dip, embrasure, furrow, hollow, impression, incision, indentation, nick, notch, pit, scallop, score, scratch, sink, trough; SEE CONCEPT 580

dent [v] *chip, scrape, depress*
dig, dimple, dint, furrow, gouge, hollow, imprint, indent, make concave, mark, nick, notch, perforate, pit, press in, push in, ridge, scratch; SEE CONCEPTS 176,189,208,246

denunciation [n] *condemnation, criticism*
accusation, arraignment, blame, castigation, censure, charge, cursing, damning, denouncement, derogation, dressing down*, fulmination, incrimination, indictment, invective, knock*, obloquy, rap*, reprehension, reprimand, reprobation, smearing, stigmatization, upbraidment, vilification; SEE CONCEPT 52

deny [v] *disagree, renounce, decline*
abjure, abnegate, ban, begrudge, call on, contradict, contravene, controvert, curb, disacknowledge, disallow, disavow, disbelieve, discard, disclaim, discredit, disown, disprove, doubt, enjoin from, eschew, exclude, forbid, forgo, forsake, gainsay, hold back, keep back, negate, negative, not buy, nullify, oppose, rebuff, rebut, recant, refuse, refute, reject, repudiate, restrain, revoke, sacrifice, say no to, spurn, taboo, take exception to, turn down, turn thumbs down*, veto, withhold; SEE CONCEPTS 46,49,52

deodorant [n] *something that freshens*
air freshener, antiperspirant, cleanser, cosmetic, deodorizer, disinfectant, fumigant, fumigator, smoke screen*; SEE CONCEPT 492

depart [v 1] *leave, retreat*
abandon, abdicate, absent, beat it*, blast off*, cut and run*, cut out*, decamp, desert, disappear, emigrate, escape, evacuate, exit, get away, git*, go, go away, go forth, hit the bricks*, hit the road*, hit the trail*, make a break*, march out, migrate, move on, move out, part, perish, pull out, quit, remove, retire, sally forth*, say goodbye*, scram*, secede, set forth, shove off*, slip away*, split*, start, start out, take leave, tergiversate, troop*, vacate, vanish, withdraw; SEE CONCEPT 195

depart [v 2] *diverge from normal, expected*
abandon, cast, desert, deviate, differ, digress, disagree, discard, dissent, excurse, forsake, ramble, reject, repudiate, stray, swerve, turn aside, vary, veer, wander; SEE CONCEPTS 665,697

department [n] *section of organization, area*
administration, agency, area, arena, beat, board, branch, bureau, canton, circuit, commission, commune, constituency, division, force, office, parish, precinct, quarter, range, staff, station, subdivision, territory, tract, unit, ward; SEE CONCEPTS 381,440,508

department [n 2] *area of interest, expertise*
activity, administration, assignment, avocation, bailiwick, berth, business, capacity, class, classification, domain, dominion, duty, field, function, incumbency, jurisdiction, line, niche, occupation, office, province, realm, responsibility, slot, specialty, sphere, spot, station, vocation, walk of life, wing; SEE CONCEPT 349

departure [n 1] *leaving*
abandonment, adieu, bow out*, congé, decampment, desertion, egress, egression, embarkation, emigration, escape, evacuation, exit, exodus, expatriation, farewell, flight, getaway*, going, going away, goodbye*, hegira, migration, parting, passage, powder*, quitting, recession, removal, retirement, retreat, sailing, separation, setting forth, setting out, stampede, start, takeoff, taking leave, taking off, vacation, vanishing act*, walkout, withdrawal, withdrawing; SEE CONCEPT 195

departure [n 2] *deviation from normal, expected*
aberration, branching off, branching out, change, declination, deflection, difference, digression, divergence, diversion, innovation, in thing*, last word*, latest thing*, new wrinkle*, novelty, rambling, shift, straying, turning, variance, variation, veering, wandering; SEE CONCEPTS 665,697

depend [v 1] *count on, rely upon*
bank on*, bet bottom dollar on*, bet on*, build upon, calculate on, confide in, gamble on*, lay money on*, lean on*, reckon on, trust in, turn to; SEE CONCEPT 26

depend [v 2] *be contingent on*
be at mercy of, be based on, be conditioned, be connected with, be determined by, be in control of, be in the power of, be subject to, be subordinate to, bottom, found, ground, hang, hang in suspense, hang on, hinge on, pend, rest, rest on, rest with, revolve around, revolve on, stand on, stay, trust to, turn on; SEE CONCEPT 711

dependable [adj] *reliable, responsible*
always there, carrying the load*, certain, constant, faithful, good as one's word*, loyal, rocklike*, secure, stable, staunch, steadfast, steady, sturdy, sure, to be counted on, tried, tried-and-true, true, trustworthy, trusty, unfailing; SEE CONCEPTS 542,560

de
de

dependence/dependency [n1] *confidence, reliance*
assurance, belief, credence, expectation, faith, hope, interdependence, responsibility, responsibleness, stability, steadiness, stock, trust, trustiness, trustworthiness; SEE CONCEPTS *410,689*

dependence/dependency [n2] *addiction, need*
attachment, contingency, habit, helplessness, hook, inability, security blanket, servility, subjection, subordination, subservience, vulnerability, weakness, yoke; SEE CONCEPTS *20,709*

dependent [adj1] *weak, helpless*
abased, clinging, counting on, debased, defenseless, humbled, immature, indigent, inferior, lesser, minor, poor, reliant, relying on, secondary, subordinate, tied to apron strings*, under, under thumb*, unsustaining, vulnerable; SEE CONCEPTS *404,574*

dependent [adj2] *contingent, determined by*
accessory to, ancillary, appurtenant, conditional, controlled by, counting, depending, incidental to, liable to, provisory, reckoning, regulated by, relative, reliant, relying, subject to, subordinate, subservient, susceptible, sustained by, trusting, under control of; SEE CONCEPT *546*

depict [v] *describe, render in drawing or writing*
characterize, delineate, design, detail, illustrate, image, interpret, limn, narrate, outline, paint, picture, portray, relate, report, represent, reproduce, sculpt, sketch, state; SEE CONCEPTS *79,174*

depiction [n] *description, rendering*
delineation, drawing, illustration, image, likeness, outline, picture, portraiture, portrayal, presentment, representation, sketch; SEE CONCEPTS *259,268*

deplete [v] *consume, exhaust supply*
bankrupt, bleed*, decrease, dig into, diminish, drain, draw, dry up, empty, evacuate, expend, finish, impoverish, lessen, milk*, reduce, sap, spend, squander, suck dry*, undermine, use up, wash up, waste, weaken; SEE CONCEPTS *142,169,225*

depleted [adj] *consumed, exhausted*
all in*, bare, bleary*, collapsed, decreased, depreciated, destitute, devoid of, drained, effete, emptied, far-gone*, in want, kaput*, lessened, out of, pooped out*, reduced, sapped, short of, sold, sold out, spent, sucked out*, used, used up, vacant, washed out, wasted, weakened, without resources, worn, worn out; SEE CONCEPTS *576,771*

deplorable [adj] *unfortunate, shameful*
afflicting, awful, blameworthy, bummer*, calamitous, dire, dirty, disastrous, disgraceful, dishonorable, disreputable, distressing, dolorous, downer*, dreadful, execrable, faulty, godawful*, grievous, grim, heartbreaking, heartrending, horrifying, intolerable, lamentable, lousy, melancholy, miserable, mournful, opprobrious, overwhelming, pitiable, poor, regrettable, reprehensible, rotten, sad, scandalous, sickening, stinking, terrible, tragic, unbearable, unsatisfactory, woeful, wretched; SEE CONCEPTS *529,570,574*

deplore [v] *regret; condemn*
abhor, be against, bemoan, bewail, carry on, censure, complain, cry, denounce, deprecate, disapprove of, eat one's heart out*, grieve for, hate, hurt, lament, moan, mourn, object to, repent, rue, sing the blues*, sorrow over, take on, weep; SEE CONCEPTS *21,29*

deploy [v] *redistribute, station troops or weapons*
arrange, display, dispose, expand, extend, fan

out, form front, open, position, put out patrol, set out, set up, spread out, take battle stations, unfold, use, utilize; SEE CONCEPTS *158,213,320*

deport [v] *banish*
cast out, dismiss, displace, exile, expatriate, expel, expulse, extradite, oust, relegate, ship out, transport; SEE CONCEPTS *198,211,217*

deportation [n] *banishment*
displacement, eviction, exile, expatriation, expulsion, extradition, ostracism, relegation, removal, transportation; SEE CONCEPTS *198,211,217*

deportment [n] *carriage, manner of person*
actions, address, air, appearance, aspect, bearing, behavior, cast, comportment, conduct, demeanor, mien, port, posture, set, stance; SEE CONCEPT *633*

depose [v] *oust from position*
boot out, bounce, break, can*, cashier, chuck, degrade, demote, dethrone, discrown, dismiss, displace, downgrade, drum out, eject, freeze out*, give heave-ho*, impeach, kick out*, overthrow, remove from office, ride out on rail*, run out of town*, send packing*, subvert, throw out, throw out on ear*, uncrown, unfrock, unmake, unseat, upset; SEE CONCEPTS *133,298,320*

deposit [n1] *down payment; money saved*
drop, installment, money in the bank, partial payment, pledge, retainer, security, stake, warranty; SEE CONCEPTS *340,344*

deposit [n2] *accumulation of solid*
alluvium, delta, deposition, dregs, drift, grounds, lees, precipitate, precipitation, sediment, settlings, silt; SEE CONCEPTS *432,470,471*

deposit [v] *locate, put in place for safekeeping*
accumulate, amass, bank, collect, commit, deliver, ditch, drop, entrust, garner, give in trust, hoard, install, invest, keep, lay, lay away, park, place, plant*, plop*, plunk*, plunk down*, precipitate, put aside, put by, repose, rest, salt away*, save, settle, sit down, sock away*, squirrel away*, stash, stock up, store, stow, transfer, treasure; SEE CONCEPTS *134,201,330*

deposition [n1] *dethroning, ousting*
degradation, discharge, dismissal, displacement, ejection, impeachment, overthrow, removal, unfrocking; SEE CONCEPTS *133,298,320*

deposition [n2] *attestation of truth, especially in legal matters*
affidavit, affirmation, allegation, announcement, declaration, evidence, sworn statement, testimony; SEE CONCEPTS *271,318*

depository [n] *storage place*
archive, arsenal, bank, bunker, cache, collection, depot, gallery, magazine, museum, repository, repository, safe, safe-deposit box, store, storehouse, tomb, vault, warehouse; SEE CONCEPT *435*

depot [n] *storage place; station*
annex, armory, base, depository, destination, garage, halting-place, haven, junction, loft, lot, magazine, office, repository, stopping-place, store, storehouse, storeroom, terminal, terminus, waiting room, warehouse, yard; SEE CONCEPTS *435,449*

deprave [v] *corrupt, lead astray*
bastardize, bestialize, brutalize, debase, debauch, degrade, demoralize, pervert, seduce, subvert, vitiate, warp; SEE CONCEPT *14*

depraved [adj] *corrupt, immoral*
abandoned, bad, base, debased, debauched, degenerate, degraded, dirty*, dirty-minded, dissolute, evil, fast*, filthy*, flagitious, gone to the

dogs*, kinky*, lascivious, lewd, licentious, low, mean, miscreant, nefarious, perverted, profligate, putrid, rotten, shameless, sinful, twisted, unhealthy, unnatural, vicious, vile, villainous, vitiate, vitiated, wanton, warped, wicked; SEE CONCEPT 545

depravity [n] *corruption, immorality*
abandonment, baseness, contamination, criminality, debasement, debauchery, degeneracy, degradation, depravation, evil, iniquity, lewdness, licentiousness, perversion, profligacy, sensuality, sinfulness, vice, viciousness, vitiation, wickedness; SEE CONCEPT 645

deprecate [v] *belittle, condemn*
cut down to size*, depreciate, derogate, detract, disapprove of, discommend, discountenance, disesteem, disfavor, disparage, expostulate, frown, mudsling*, not go for*, object, pooh-pooh*, poor mouth*, protest against, put down*, rip*, run down*, take dim view of, take down, take exception to; SEE CONCEPTS 7,19,52

depreciate [v1] *devalue, lose value*
abate, cheapen, decay, decrease, decry, deflate, depress, deteriorate, devalorize, diminish, downgrade, drop, dwindle, erode, fall, lessen, lower, mark down, reduce, soften, underrate, undervalue, worsen, write down, write off; SEE CONCEPTS 698,776

depreciate [v2] *belittle, ridicule*
abuse, asperse, attack, calumniate, censure, clamor against, condemn, contemn, decry, defame, denigrate, denounce, deprecate, deride, derogate, detract, discount, discountenance, discredit, disgrace, disparage, dispraise, fault, find fault with, humble, knock, look down on*, lower, malign, minimize, put down, rap, revile, roast*, run down*, scoff at, scorn, slam, slander, slight, slur, smear, sneer at, spurn, take down a peg*, traduce, underestimate, underrate, undervalue, vilify; SEE CONCEPTS 7,19,52

depredation [n] *devastation, destruction*
burglary, crime, desecration, desolation, despoiling, laying waste, marauding, pillage, plunder, ransacking, rapine, ravaging, robbery, sacking, spoliation, stealing, theft, wasting; SEE CONCEPTS 192,252

depress [v1] *deject, make despondent; exhaust*
abase, afflict, ail, bear down, beat, beat down*, bother, bug*, bum out*, cast down, chill*, cow*, damp, dampen, darken, daunt, debase, debilitate, degrade, desolate, devitalize, discourage, dishearten, dismay, dispirit, distress, disturb, drag*, drain, dull, enervate, faze, keep under, lower, mock, mortify, oppress, perturb, press, put down*, reduce, reduce to tears*, run down*, sadden, sap*, scorn, slow, throw cold water on*, torment, trouble, try, turn one off*, upset, weaken, weary, weigh down*; SEE CONCEPTS 7,19,240

depress [v2] *devalue*
cheapen, debase, depreciate, diminish, downgrade, impair, lessen, lower, reduce; SEE CONCEPTS 240,330

depress [v3] *push down*
couch, demit, dip, droop, flatten, let down, level, lower, press down, settle, sink, smoosh, squash; SEE CONCEPT 208

depressed [adj1] *discouraged*
bad, bleeding*, blue*, bummed out*, cast-down, crestfallen, crummy*, dejected, despondent, de-

stroyed, disconsolate, dispirited, down, down and out*, downcast, downhearted, down in the dumps*, down in the mouth*, dragged*, fed up*, glum, grim, hurting, in a blue funk*, in pain*, in the dumps*, in the pits*, in the toilet*, let down, low, low-down, low-spirited, lugubrious, melancholy, moody, morose, on a downer*, pessimistic, ripped, sad, sob story*, spiritless, taken down*, torn up*, unhappy, weeping, woebegone; SEE CONCEPT 403

depressed [adj2] *concave, pushed down*
hollow, indented, recessed, set back, sunken; SEE CONCEPT 490

depressed [adj3] *disadvantaged*
cheapened, depreciated, deprived, destitute, devalued, distressed, ghetto, impaired, needy, poor, poverty-stricken, run-down, shanty, skid row*, underprivileged, weakened; SEE CONCEPTS 334,555

depressing [adj] *discouraging, upsetting*
black, bleak, daunting, dejecting, disheartening, dismal, dispiriting, distressing, dreary, funereal, gloomy, heartbreaking, hopeless, joyless, melancholic, melancholy, mournful, oppressive, sad, saddening, somber; SEE CONCEPT 529

depression [n1] *low spirits; despair*
abasement, abjection, abjectness, blahs*, bleakness, blue funk*, bummer, cheerlessness, dejection, desolation, desperation, despondency, disconsolation, discouragement, dispiritedness, distress, dole, dolefulness, dolor, downheartedness, dreariness, dullness, dumps, ennui, gloom, gloominess, heaviness of heart, heavyheartedness, hopelessness, lowness, lugubriosity, melancholia, melancholy, misery, mortification, qualm, sadness, sorrow, the blues*, trouble, unhappiness, vapors*, woefulness, worry; SEE CONCEPT 410

depression [n2] *economic decline*
bad times*, bankruptcy, bear market*, big trouble*, bottom out*, bust, crash, crisis, deflation, dislocation, downturn, drop, failure, hard times*, inactivity, inflation, overproduction, panic, paralysis, rainy days*, recession, retrenchment, sag, slide, slowness, slump, stagflation, stagnation, unemployment; SEE CONCEPTS 324,330,335

depression [n3] *concavity, cavity*
basin, bowl, crater, dent, dimple, dip, excavation, hole, hollow, impression, indentation, pit, pocket, sag, scoop, sink, sinkage, sinkhole, vacuity, vacuum, valley, void; SEE CONCEPT 513

deprivation [n] *taking, keeping away; need*
denial, deprival, destitution, detriment, disadvantage, dispossession, distress, divestiture, divestment, expropriation, hardship, loss, privation, removal, seizure, want, withdrawal, withholding; SEE CONCEPTS 121,142,709

deprive [v] *keep or take away something wanted, needed*
bankrupt, bare, bereave, denude, despoil, disinherit, dismantle, dispossess, disrobe, divest, dock, expropriate, hold back, lose, oust, rob, seize, skim, stiff, strip, wrest; SEE CONCEPTS 121,142

depth [n1] *distance down or across*
base, bottom, declination, deepness, draft, drop, expanse, extent, fathomage, intensity, lower register, lowness, measure, measurement, pit, pitch, profoundness, profundity, remoteness, sounding; SEE CONCEPTS 737,790

depth [n2] *insight, wisdom*
acuity, acumen, astuteness, brain, discernment,

intellect, intelligence, keenness, penetration, profoundness, profundity, sagacity, sense, sharpness, weightiness; SEE CONCEPT 409

deputy [n] *assistant, agent*
aide, ambassador, appointee, assembly member, backup, commissioner, councilor, delegate, dogcatcher*, factor, legate, lieutenant, minister, proxy, regent, replacement, representant, representative, second-in-command, sub, subordinate, substitute, surrogate; SEE CONCEPTS 348,354

derange [v] *make crazy; confuse*
confound, craze*, dement, disarrange, disarray, discommode, discompose, disconcert, disorder, disorganize, displace, distract, disturb, drive mad, frenzy, madden, make insane, mess up*, misplace, muss*, perplex, ruffle, rummage, unbalance, unhinge*, unsettle, upset; SEE CONCEPTS 16,84

deranged [adj] *crazy, insane*
ape*, baked*, bananas*, berserk, cracked*, crazed, delirious, demented, disarranged, disconcerted, disordered, displaced, distracted, dotty*, flipped*, flipped out*, frantic, frenzied, fried*, irrational, loco*, lunatic, mad, maddened, maniac, maniacal, nuts*, perplexed, schizzo*, unbalanced, unglued*, unhinged*, unscrewed*, unsettled, unsound, unzipped*, whacko*; SEE CONCEPT 403

deregulate [v] *remove imposed controls on a system*
decontrol, denationalize, leave be, let alone, not interfere, not meddle, not tamper; SEE CONCEPTS 94,117

deregulation [n] *the removal of imposed controls on a system*
disinvolvement, free competition, free enterprise, free trade, isolationism, laissez-faire, liberalism, noninterference, nonintervention, self-regulating market; SEE CONCEPT 299

derelict [n] *destitute or down-and-out person*
beggar, bum, castaway, dawdler, drifter, floater, grifter, hobo, ne'er-do-well*, outcast, renegade, skidrow bum, stiff, stumblebum*, tramp, vagabond, vagrant; SEE CONCEPTS 412,423

derelict [adj1] *careless, negligent*
behindhand, delinquent, disregardful, irresponsible, lax, regardless, remiss, slack, undependable, unreliable, untrustworthy; SEE CONCEPT 542

derelict [adj2] *deserted, forsaken*
abandoned, castoff, desolate, dilapidated, dingy, discarded, faded, lorn, neglected, ownerless, relinquished, ruined, run-down, seedy, shabby, solitary, threadbare, uncouth; SEE CONCEPT 560

deride [v] *make fun of; insult*
banter, chaff, contemn, detract, dis*, disdain, disparage, do a number on*, dump on*, flout, gibe, jeer, jolly, kid, knock, laugh at, lout, mock, pan, pooh-pooh*, put down*, quiz, rag*, rally, razz*, rib*, ridicule, roast*, scoff, scorn, slam, sneer, taunt, twit; SEE CONCEPTS 52,54

de rigueur [adj] *proper, right*
au fait, becoming, comme il faut, conventional, correct, decent, decorous, done, fitting, necessary, required; SEE CONCEPT 558

derision [n] *insult, disrespect*
backhanded compliment*, brickbat*, Bronx cheer*, butt*, comeback, contempt, contumely, crack, dig*, disdain, disparagement, dump*, jab, jest, joke, laughingstock, laughter, mockery, object of ridicule, parting shot, pilgarlic, put-down,

raillery, ridicule, satire, scoffing, scorn, slam*, slap, sneering; SEE CONCEPTS 52,278,689

derisive [adj] *ridiculing*
cheeky*, cocky, contemptuous, crusty, disdainful, flip*, fresh, gally, insulting, jeering, mocking, nervy, out-of-line*, rude, sarcastic, sassy, scoffing, scornful, smart*, smart-alecky*, taunting; SEE CONCEPT 267

derivable [adj] *deducible*
a priori, attributable, available, determinable, dogmatic, extractable, inferable, likely, obtainable, reasoned, resultant, traceable; SEE CONCEPT 529

derivation [n] *root, source*
ancestry, basis, beginning, descent, etymology, foundation, genealogy, inception, origin, provenance, provenience, spin-off, well, wellspring, whence it came; SEE CONCEPT 648

derivative [n] *product, descendant*
by-product, offshoot, outgrowth, spin-off, wave; SEE CONCEPT 260

derivative [adj] *borrowed, transmitted from source*
acquired, ancestral, caused, cognate, coming from, connate, copied, evolved, hereditary, imitative, inferential, inferred, not original, obtained, plagiaristic, plagiarized, procured, rehashed, secondary, secondhand, subordinate, uninventive, unoriginal; SEE CONCEPT 549

derive [v] *deduce a conclusion*
acquire, arrive, assume, collect, determine, develop, draw, educe, elaborate, elicit, evolve, excogitate, extract, follow, formulate, gain, gather, get, glean, infer, judge, make, make out, obtain, procure, put together, reach, receive, trace, work out; SEE CONCEPTS 15,18

derive from [v] *come from; arise*
descend, emanate, flow, head, issue, originate, proceed, rise, spring from, stem from; SEE CONCEPT 648

derogatory [adj] *offensive, uncomplimentary*
aspersing, belittling, calumnious, censorious, contumelious, critical, damaging, decrying, defamatory, degrading, demeaning, deprecatory, depreciative, despiteful, detracting, disdainful, dishonoring, disparaging, fault-finding, humiliating, injurious, malevolent, malicious, maligning, minimizing, opprobrious, reproachful, sarcastic, scornful, slanderous, slighting, spiteful, unfavorable, unflattering, vilifying; SEE CONCEPTS 267,570

descend [v1] *move down, lower*
alight, cascade, cataract, cave in*, coast, collapse, crash, crouch, decline, deplane, detrain, dip, disembark, dismount, dive, dribble*, drop, fall, fall prostrate, get down, get off, go down, gravitate, ground, incline, light, lose balance, penetrate, pitch, plop, plummet, plunge, prolapse, set, settle, sink, slant, slide, slip, slope, slough off, slump, stoop, stumble, submerge, subside, swoop, toboggan, topple, trickle, trip, tumble, weep; SEE CONCEPTS 147,181,213

descend [v2] *condescend*
abase oneself, concede, degenerate, deteriorate, humble oneself, lower oneself, patronize, stoop; SEE CONCEPTS 23,35

descend [v3] *trace ancestry from; be passed or handed down*
arise, derive, issue, originate, proceed, spring; SEE CONCEPT 108

descendant [*n*] *person in line of ancestry*
brood, child, children, chip off old block*, get*, heir, issue, kin, offshoot, offspring, posterity, product, progeniture, progeny, scion, seed, spin-off*; SEE CONCEPTS *296,414*

descent [*n1*] *moving down; lowering*
cave-in, coast, coming down, crash, declension, declination, decline, declivity, dip, downgrade, droop, drop, drop-off*, fall, falling, grade, gradient, header, hill, inclination, incline, landslide, plummeting, plunge, plunging, precipitation, prolapse, sag, settlement, sinkage, sinking, slant, slide, slip, slope, swoop, tailspin, topple, tumble; SEE CONCEPTS *147,181,213,738*

descent [*n2*] *line of ancestry*
blood, extraction, family, family tree, genealogy, heredity, lineage, origin, parentage, pedigree, relationship; SEE CONCEPT *296*

descent [*n3*] *deterioration*
abasement, anticlimax, cadence, comedown, debasement, decadence, decline, degradation, discomfiture, down, downcome, downfall, lapse, pathos, slump; SEE CONCEPTS *230,674*

descent [*n4*] *assault, attack*
advance, foray, incursion, invasion, pounce, raid, swoop; SEE CONCEPTS *86,320*

describe [*v*] *explain in speech, writing*
call, characterize, chronicle, communicate, construe, convey image, define, delineate, depict, detail, distinguish, draw, elucidate, epitomize, exemplify, explicate, expound, express, illuminate, illustrate, image, impart, interpret, label, limn, make apparent, make clear, make sense of, make vivid, mark out, name, narrate, outline, paint, particularize, picture, portray, recite, recount, rehearse, relate, report, represent, sketch, specify, state, tell, term, trace, transmit, write up; SEE CONCEPT *55*

description [*n1*] *account in speech, writing*
ABCs*, blow by blow, brief, characterization, chronicle, confession, declaration, definition, delineation, depiction, detail, explanation, explication, fingerprint, information, make, monograph, narration, narrative, picture, portraiture, portrayal, presentment, recital, recitation, record, recountal, rehearsal, report, representation, rundown, sketch, specification, statement, story, summarization, summary, tale, version, vignette, writeup, yarn; SEE CONCEPT *268*

description [*n2*] *class, kind*
brand, breed, category, character, classification, feather, genre, genus, ilk, kidney, nature, order, sort, species, stripe, type, variety; SEE CONCEPT *378*

descriptive [*adj*] *explanatory*
anecdotic, characteristic, characterizing, circumstantial, classificatory, clear, definitive, delineative, depictive, describing, designating, detailed, eloquent, explicative, expository, expressive, extended, graphic, identifying, illuminating, illuminative, illustrative, indicative, interpretive, lifelike, narrative, particularized, pictorial, picturesque, revealing, specific, true to life, vivid; SEE CONCEPTS *267,557*

desecrate [*v*] *abuse, violate*
befoul, blaspheme, commit sacrilege, contaminate, defile, depredate, desolate, despoil, devastate, devour, dishonor, make lose face*, mess up*, pervert, pillage, pollute, profane, prostitute,

ravage, sack*, spoil, spoliate, waste; SEE CONCEPTS *246,252*

desecration [*n*] *violation, abuse*
blasphemy, debasement, defilement, impiety, irreverence, profanation, sacrilege; SEE CONCEPTS *246,252*

desert [*n*] *wasteland; dry area*
arid region, badland, barren, barren land, flats, lava bed, Sahara, sand dunes, solitude, wild, wilderness, wilds; SEE CONCEPTS *508,517*

desert [*adj*] *barren, uncultivated*
arid, bare, desolate, infertile, lonely, solitary, sterile, uninhabited, unproductive, untilled, waste, wild; SEE CONCEPT *560*

desert [*v*] *abandon, defect*
abscond, apostatize, bail out*, beach, betray, bolt, check out*, chuck, cop out*, crawl out, decamp, depart, duck*, duck out*, flee, fly, forsake, give up, go, go AWOL*, go back on, go over the hill*, go west*, jilt, leave, leave high and dry*, leave in the lurch*, leave stranded, light, maroon, opt out, play truant, pull out, quit, relinquish, renounce, resign, run out on*, sneak off*, split*, strand, take a hike*, take off, tergiversate, throw over, vacate, violate oath, walk; SEE CONCEPTS *195,297*

deserted [*adj*] *abandoned, unoccupied*
bare, barren, bereft, cast off, derelict, desolate, empty, forlorn, forsaken, godforsaken*, isolated, left, left in the lurch*, left stranded, lonely, lorn, neglected, relinquished, solitary, uncouth, uninhabited, vacant; SEE CONCEPTS *485,577*

deserter [*n*] *fugitive from responsibility*
absconder, apostate, AWOL*, backslider, betrayer, criminal, defector, delinquent, derelict, escapee, escaper, hookey player*, lawbreaker, maroon, no-show*, recreant, refugee, renegade, runaway, shirker, slacker, traitor, truant; SEE CONCEPTS *358,412,423*

desertion [*n*] *abandonment*
abrogation, absconding, apostasy, avoidance, backsliding, betrayal, castoff, defecting, departing, departure, derelict, dereliction, disaffection, disavowal, disavowing, divorce, elusion, escape, evasion, falling away, falseness, flight, forsaking, going back on*, leaving, marooning, perfidy, recreancy, rejection, relinquishment, renunciation, repudiation, resignation, retirement, retreat, running out on*, secession, tergiversation, treachery, truancy, withdrawal; SEE CONCEPTS *195,297*

deserts [*n*] *what is due one*
chastening, chastisement, comeuppance, compensation, deserving, discipline, disciplining, due, get hers*, get his*, guerdon, lumps*, meed, merit, payment, penalty, punishment, recompense, requital, retribution, return, revenge, reward, right, talion, what is coming to one*, what one is asking for*; SEE CONCEPTS *129,710*

deserve [*v*] *be entitled to*
be given one's due*, be in line for*, be worthy of, demand, earn, gain, get, get comeuppance*, get what is coming to one*, have it coming*, have the right to, justify, lay claim to, merit, procure, rate, warrant, win; SEE CONCEPT *129*

deserving [*adj*] *worthy, meritorious*
admirable, commendable, due, estimable, fitting, laudable, needy, praisable, praiseworthy, righteous, rightful, thankworthy; SEE CONCEPT *404*

desiccate [*v*] *take moisture out of*
anhydrate, dehydrate, deplete, devitalize, divest,

drain, dry, dry up, evaporate, exsiccate, parch, sear, shrivel, wither, wizen; SEE CONCEPTS 137,250

design [n1] *sketch, draft*
architecture, arrangement, blueprint, chart, comp, composition, conception, constitution, construction, delineation, depiction, diagram, doodle, drawing, dummy, form, formation, idea, layout, makeup, map, method, model, outline, paste-up, pattern, perspective, picture, plan, scheme, study, tracery, tracing, treatment; SEE CONCEPTS 268,625,660

design [n2] *artful conception*
arrangement, configuration, construction, depiction, device, doodle, drawing, figure, form, illustration, motif, motive, organization, painting, pattern, picture, portrait, shape, sketch, style; SEE CONCEPT 259

design [n3] *intention*
action, aim, angle, animus, big picture*, brainchild*, child*, conation, conspiracy, deliberation, end, enterprise, game plan*, gimmick, goal, intendment, intrigue, lay of the land*, machination, meaning, notion, object, objective, picture, pitch, plan, play, plot, point, project, proposition, purport, purpose, recipe, reflection, scenario, scene, schema, scheme, setup, story, target, thinking, thought, trick, undertaking, view, volition, what's cooking*, will; SEE CONCEPTS 410,660

design [v1] *plan, outline*
accomplish, achieve, arrange, block out, blueprint, cast, chart, construct, contrive, create, delineate, describe, devise, diagram, dope out, draft, draw, effect, execute, fashion, form, frame, fulfill, invent, lay out, perform, produce, project, set out, sketch, sketch out, trace, work out; SEE CONCEPT 36

design [v2] *create, conceive*
compose, contrive, cook up*, devise, dream up*, fabricate, fashion, form, frame, invent, make up, originate, produce, think up; SEE CONCEPTS 43,173

design [v3] *intend, mean to do*
aim, contemplate, contrive, destine, devise, make, mind, plan, prepare, project, propose, purpose, scheme, tailor; SEE CONCEPTS 35,36

designate [v1] *name, entitle*
baptize, call, christen, cognominate, denominate, dub, label, nickname, nominate, style, term, title; SEE CONCEPT 62

designate [v2] *specify as selection*
allocate, allot, appoint, apportion, appropriate, assign, authorize, button down*, characterize, charge, choose, commission, connote, constitute, define, delegate, denote, depute, deputize, describe, dictate, earmark*, elect, evidence, favor, finger*, indicate, individualize, make, mark, mete, name, nominate, opt, peg*, pick, pin down, pinpoint, prefer, put down for*, reseve, set apart, set aside, show, single, slot, stipulate, tab*, tag*, tap*; SEE CONCEPTS 41,129

designation [n1] *name, label, mark*
appellation, appellative, class, classification, cognomen, compellation, denomination, description, epithet, identification, key word, moniker, nickname, nomen, style, title; SEE CONCEPT 683

designation [n2] *delegation, selection*
appointment, classification, identification, indication, pigeonhole*, recognition, specification; SEE CONCEPT 41

designedly [adv] *intentionally*
apurpose, by design, calculatedly, deliberately, knowingly, on purpose, prepensely, purposedly, purposely, purposively, studiously, willfully, wittingly; SEE CONCEPTS 402,535

designing [adj] *plotting, crafty*
artful, astute, conniving, conspiring, crooked, cunning, deceitful, devious, heedful, intriguing, Machiavellian, observant, scheming, sharp, shrewd, sly, treacherous, tricky, unscrupulous, wily; SEE CONCEPT 542

desirable [adj1] *attractive, seductive*
adorable, alluring, beautiful*, charming, covetable, enticing, fascinating, fetching, sexy; SEE CONCEPTS 372,579

desirable [adj2] *advantageous, good*
acceptable, advisable, agreeable, beneficial, covetable, eligible, enviable, expedient, grateful, gratifying, helpful, pleasing, preferable, profitable, useful, welcome, worthwhile; SEE CONCEPTS 560,572

desire [n1] *want, longing*
admiration, ambition, appetite, ardor, aspiration, attraction, avidity, concupiscence, covetousness, craving, craze, cupidity, devotion, doting, eagerness, fancy, fascination, fervor, fondness, frenzy, greed, hankering*, hunger, inclination, infatuation, itch*, lasciviousness, lechery, libido, liking, love, lust, mania, motive, need, passion, predilection, proclivity, propensity, rapaciousness, rapture, ravenousness, relish, salacity, solicitude, thirst, urge, voracity, will, wish, yearning; SEE CONCEPTS 20,709

desire [n2] *request*
appeal, entreaty, hope, importunity, petition, solicitation, supplication, want, wish; SEE CONCEPT 662

desire [v1] *want, long for*
aim, aspire to, be smitten, be turned on by*, choose, cotton to, covet, crave, desiderate, die over*, enjoy, fall for*, fancy, give eyeteeth for*, go for*, hanker after*, have eyes for*, have the hots for*, hunger for, like, lust after, make advances to, partial to, pine, set heart on*, spoil for, sweet on*, take a liking to*, take a shine to*, take to*, thirst, wish for, yearn for; SEE CONCEPT 20

desire [v2] *ask, request*
beg, bespeak, entreat, importune, petition, seek, solicit; SEE CONCEPT 48

desirous [adj] *aspiring, hopeful*
acquisitive, ambitious, amorous, anxious, avid, covetous, craving, desiring, eager, enthusiastic, grasping, greedy, hot*, itchy*, keen, longing, lustful, passionate, prehensile, ready, stimulated, turned on*, willing, wishful, wishing, yearning; SEE CONCEPT 529

desist [v] *stop, refrain from*
abandon, abstain, avoid, break off, cease, discontinue, end, forbear, give over, give up, halt, have done with*, knock off*, leave off, no do, pause, quit, relinquish, resign, surcease, suspend, yield; SEE CONCEPTS 119,234

desktop publishing [n] *producing publications with computer software*
desktop*, electronic publishing, formatting, outputting, typesetting; SEE CONCEPT 277

desolate [adj1] *unused, barren*
abandoned, bare, bleak, derelict, desert, destroyed, dreary, empty, forsaken, godforsaken*, isolated, lonely, lonesome, lorn, ruined, solitary,

unfrequented, uninhabited, unoccupied, vacant, waste, wild; SEE CONCEPTS 485,560

desolate [adj2] *depressed, despondent*
abandoned, acheronian, bereft, black, bleak, blue, cheerless, comfortless, companionless, dejected, disconsolate, dismal, dolorous, down, downcast, forlorn, forsaken, funereal, gloomy, hurting, in a blue funk*, inconsolable, joyless, lonely, lonesome, lorn, melancholy, miserable, somber, tragic, wretched; SEE CONCEPT 403

desolate [v] *ravage, destroy*
depopulate, depredate, desecrate, despoil, devastate, devour, lay low, lay waste, pillage, plunder, ruin, sack, spoliate, waste; SEE CONCEPT 252

desolation [n1] *uninhabited area; barrenness*
bareness, bleakness, desert, devastation, dissolution, extinction, forlornness, isolation, loneliness, ruin, solitariness, solitude, waste, wildness, wreck; SEE CONCEPTS 517,710

desolation [n2] *distress, unhappiness*
anguish, dejection, despair, gloom, gloominess, loneliness, melancholy, misery, mourning, sadness, sorrow, woe, wretchedness; SEE CONCEPT 410

despair [n] *depression, hopelessness*
anguish, dashed hopes, dejection, desperation, despondency, discouragement, disheartenment, forlornness, gloom, melancholy, misery, ordeal, pain, sorrow, trial, tribulation, wretchedness; SEE CONCEPT 410

despair [v] *give up hope*
abandon, be hopeless, despond, destroy, drop, flatten, give way, have heavy heart*, let air out*, lose faith, lose heart, relinquish, renounce, resign, surrender, take down, yield; SEE CONCEPT 21

despairing [adj] *upset, despondent*
anxious, at end of one's rope*, blue, brokenhearted, can't win*, cynical, dejected, depressed, desperate, disconsolate, downcast, forlorn, frantic, grief-stricken, hopeless, inconsolable, in pain*, in the dumps*, in the pits*, in the soup*, melancholic, melancholy, miserable, not a prayer*, no-win*, oppressed, pessimistic, sad, shot down*, strabilious, suicidal, sunk*, weighed down*, wretched; SEE CONCEPT 403

desperado [n] *criminal*
bandit, convict, cutthroat, gangster, hoodlum, lawbreaker, mugger, outlaw, ruffian, thug; SEE CONCEPT 412

desperate [adj1] *reckless, outrageous*
atrocious, audacious, bold, careless, dangerous, daring, death-defying, determined, devil-may-care, foolhardy, frantic, frenzied, furious, hasty, hazardous, headlong, headstrong, heinous, impetuous, incautious, madcap, monstrous, precipitate, rash, risky, scandalous, shocking, venturesome, violent, wild; SEE CONCEPT 401

desperate [adj2] *extreme, intense*
acute, climacteric, concentrated, critical, crucial, dire, drastic, exquisite, fierce, furious, great, terrible, urgent, vehement, very grave, vicious, violent; SEE CONCEPTS 537,540,569

desperate [adj3] *hopeless*
at end of one's rope*, back to the wall*, can't win*, dead duck*, despairing, despondent, desponding, downcast, forlorn, futile, gone*, goner*, hard up*, inconsolable, in the soup*, in the toilet*, irrecoverable, irremediable, irretrievable, no-chance*, no-way*, no-win*, running out of

time*, sad, sunk*, up against it*, up the creek*, useless, vain, wretched; SEE CONCEPT 548

desperately [adv1] *severely*
badly, carelessly, dangerously, dramatically, fiercely, gravely, greatly, harmfully, hysterically, like crazy*, like mad*, perilously, seriously; SEE CONCEPT 569

desperately [adv2] *frightfully*
appallingly, fearfully, hopelessly, shockingly; SEE CONCEPT 403

desperation [n1] *hopelessness*
agony, anguish, anxiety, concern, dejection, depression, desolation, despair, despondency, discomfort, disconsolateness, distraction, distress, fear, gloom, grief, heartache, melancholy, misery, pain, pang, sorrow, torture, trouble, unhappiness, worry; SEE CONCEPT 410

desperation [n2] *rashness*
carelessness, defiance, foolhardiness, frenzy, heedlessness, impetuosity, madness, recklessness; SEE CONCEPT 633

despicable [adj] *hateful; beyond contempt*
abject, awful, base, beastly, cheap, contemptible, degrading, detestable, dirty, disgraceful, disreputable, down, ignominious, infamous, insignificant, loathsome, low, low-life*, mean, no-good*, pitiful, reprehensible, shameful, slimy*, sordid, vile, worthless, wretched; SEE CONCEPTS 404,570

despise [v] *look down on*
abhor, abominate, allergic to*, contemn, deride, detest, disdain, disregard, eschew, execrate, feel contempt for, flout, hate, have no use for*, loathe, look down nose at*, misprize, neglect, put down*, reject, renounce, repudiate, revile, scorn, shun, slight, snub, spurn, undervalue, wipe out*; SEE CONCEPT 29

despite [prep] *in spite of, regardless of*
against, although, even though, even with, in contempt of, in defiance of, in the face of, notwithstanding, undeterred by; SEE CONCEPT 544

despoil [v] *ravage, destroy*
denude, depopulate, depredate, deprive, desecrate, desolate, devastate, devour, dispossess, divest, loot, maraud, pillage, plunder, raid, rifle, rob, sack, spoil, spoliate, waste, vandalize, waste, wreak havoc, wreck; SEE CONCEPT 252

despondent [adj] *depressed*
all torn up*, blue*, bummed-out*, cast-down, dejected, despairing, disconsolate, discouraged, disheartened, dispirited, doleful, down, downcast, downhearted, forlorn, gloomy, glum, grief-stricken, grieving, hopeless, in a blue funk*, in despair, in the pits*, low, low-spirited, melancholy, miserable, morose, mourning, sad, shot down*, sorrowful, woebegone, wretched; SEE CONCEPT 403

despot [n] *dictator*
autocrat, Hitler*, monocrat, oppressor, slave-driver, tyrant; SEE CONCEPTS 354,412

destination [n] *goal; place one wants to go*
aim, ambition, design, end, harbor, haven, intention, journey's end, landing-place, object, objective, purpose, resting-place, station, stop, target, terminal, terminus; SEE CONCEPTS 198,659

destine [v] *predetermine, ordain*
allot, appoint, assign, consecrate, decide, decree, dedicate, design, determine, devote, doom, doom to, earmark*, fate, foreordain, intend, mark out, predestine, preform, preordain, purpose, reserve; SEE CONCEPT 18

de
de

destined [adj1] *bound for, fated in near future*
at hand, brewing*, certain, closed, coming, compelled, compulsory, condemned, designed, directed, doomed, foreordained, forthcoming, hanging over*, impending, ineluctable, inescapable, inevitable, inexorable, in prospect, instant, in store, intended, in the cards*, in the wind*, looming, meant, menacing, near, ordained, overhanging, predesigned, predestined, predetermined, que sera sera*, sealed, settled, stated, that is to be, that will be, threatening, to come, unavoidable, way the ball bounces*; SEE CONCEPTS 537,820

destined [adj2] *en route, on the road to*
appointed, appropriated, assigned, bent upon, booked, bound for, chosen, consigned, delegated, designated, determined, directed, entrained, heading, ordered to, prepared, routed, scheduled, specified; SEE CONCEPT 584

destiny [n] *fate*
afterlife, break*, breaks*, certainty, circumstance, conclusion, condition, constellation, course of events, cup, design, divine decree, doom, expectation, finality, foreordination, fortune, future, happenstance, hereafter, horoscope, inevitability, intent, intention, karma, kismet*, lot, luck, Moirai, objective, ordinance, portion, predestination, predetermination, prospect, serendipity, the stars*, way the ball bounces*, way the cookie crumbles*, what is written*, wheel of fortune*, world to come*; SEE CONCEPT 679

destitute [adj] *down and out; wanting*
bankrupt, beggared, bereft, busted, dead broke*, deficient, depleted, deprived of, devoid of, dirt poor*, divested, drained, empty, exhausted, flat*, flat broke*, impecunious, impoverished, indigent, in need of, insolvent, lacking, moneyless, necessitous, needy, on the breadline*, on the rocks*, penniless, penurious, pinched, played out*, poor, poverty-stricken, stony, strapped, stripped, totaled, wiped out*, without; SEE CONCEPT 334

destroy [v] *demolish, devastate*
abort, annihilate, annul, axe*, blot out, break down, butcher*, consume, cream*, crush, damage, deface, desolate, despoil, dismantle, dispatch, end, eradicate, erase, exterminate, extinguish, extirpate, gut*, impair, kill, lay waste, level, liquidate, maim, mar, maraud, mutilate, nuke*, nullify, overturn, quash, quell, ravage, ravish, raze, ruin, sabotage, shatter, slay, smash, snuff out*, spoliate, stamp out, suppress, swallow up*, tear down, torpedo*, total, trash*, vaporize, waste, wax*, wipe out, wreck, zap*; SEE CONCEPT 252

destruction [n] *demolition, devastation*
abolishing, abolition, annihilation, assassinating, bane, carnage, crashing, crushing, disintegrating, disrupting, dissolving, downfall, elimination, end, eradication, extermination, extinction, extinguishing, extirpation, havoc, invalidating, invalidation, liquidation, loss, massacre, murder, overthrow, ravaging, ruin, ruination, sacking, shattering, slaughter, slaying, subjugation, subversion, subverting, undoing, wreckage, wrecking; SEE CONCEPTS 230,252

destructive [adj1] *injurious, devastating*
annihilative, baleful, baneful, calamitous, cancerous, cataclysmic, catastrophic, consumptive, cutthroat, damaging, deadly, deleterious, detrimental, dire, disastrous, eradicative, evil, extirpative, fatal, fell, harmful, hurtful, internecine, lethal, lethiferous, mortal, noisome, noxious, pernicious, pestiferous, pestilential, ruinous, slaughterous, suicidal, toxic, venomous, wrackful, wreckful; SEE CONCEPT 537

destructive [adj2] *hurtful, disparaging*
abrasive, adverse, antagonistic, cankerous, caustic, contrary, corrosive, deleterious, derogatory, detrimental, discouraging, discrediting, erosive, hostile, injurious, invalidating, negative, offensive, opposed, troublesome, undermining, vicious; SEE CONCEPTS 267,537

detach [v] *disconnect, cut off*
abstract, disaffiliate, disassemble, disassociate, disengage, disentangle, disjoin, dismount, dissociate, disunite, divide, divorce, free, isolate, loose, loosen, part, remove, segregate, separate, sever, sunder, take apart, tear off, uncouple, unfasten, unfix, unhitch, withdraw; SEE CONCEPT 135

detached [adj1] *disconnected*
alone, apart, discrete, disjoined, divided, emancipated, free, isolate, isolated, loose, loosened, removed, separate, severed, unaccompanied, unconnected; SEE CONCEPT 490

detached [adj2] *aloof, disinterested; neutral*
abstract, apathetic, casual, cool*, dispassionate, distant, impartial, impersonal, incurious, indifferent, laid-back*, objective, out of it*, pokerfaced*, remote, removed, reserved, spaced-out, spacey*, staid, stolid, unbiased, uncommitted, unconcerned, uncurious, uninvolved, unpassioned, unprejudiced, withdrawn; SEE CONCEPTS 401,404

detachment [n1] *disconnection*
disengagement, disjoining, dissolution, disunion, division, divorce, divorcement, partition, rupture, separation, severing, split-up; SEE CONCEPTS 388,747

detachment [n2] *aloofness*
brown study*, coldness, coolness, disinterestedness, dreaminess, impartiality, incuriosity, indifference, neutrality, nonpartisanship, objectivity, preoccupation, remoteness, reverie, unconcern, woolgathering*; SEE CONCEPT 633

detachment [n3] *military troop*
army, body, detail, division, force, organization, party, patrol, special force, squad, task force, troupe, unit; SEE CONCEPT 322

detail [n1] *feature, specific aspect*
ABCs*, accessory, article, brass tacks*, chapter and verse*, circumstantiality, component, count, cue, design, dope*, element, fact, factor, fine point, fraction, item, meat and potatoes*, minor point, minutia, nicety, nitty-gritty*, nuts and bolts*, part, particular, peculiarity, plan, point, portion, respect, schedule, singularity, specialty, specification, structure, technicality, thing, trait, trivia, triviality; SEE CONCEPT 831

detail [n2] *military troop*
army, assignment, body, detachment, duty, fatigue, force, kitchen police, KP*, organization, party, special force, squad, unit; SEE CONCEPT 322

detail [v1] *specify, make clear*
analyze, catalog, circumstantiate, communicate, delineate, depict, describe, designate, elaborate, embellish, enumerate, epitomize, exhibit, fly speck*, get down to brass tacks*, individualize, itemize, lay out, narrate, particularize, portray, produce, quote chapter and verse*, recapitulate,

recite, recount, rehearse, relate, report, reveal, set forth, show, specialize, spell out, spread, stipulate, summarize, sweat details*, tell, uncover; SEE CONCEPTS 55,57,60

detail [v2] *assign specific task*
allocate, appoint, charge, commission, delegate, detach, send; SEE CONCEPTS 50,88

detailed [adj] *itemized, particularized*
abundant, accurate, all-inclusive, amplified, at length, blow-by-blow*, circumstantial, circumstantiated, clocklike, complete, complicated, comprehensive, copious, definite, described, developed, disclosed, elaborate, elaborated, enumerated, exact, exhausting, exhaustive, finicky*, full, fussy*, individual, individualized, intricate, meticulous, minute, narrow, nice, point-by-point, precise, seriatim, specific, specified, thorough, unfolded; SEE CONCEPT 557

detain [v] *hold, keep back; arrest*
apprehend, bog down*, bust*, buttonhole*, check, confine, constrain, decelerate, delay, hang up*, hinder, hold up*, ice*, impede, inhibit, intern, jail, mire, nab*, pick up, pinch*, pull in*, put away*, reserve, restrain, retard, run in, send up, set back, slow down, slow up, withhold; SEE CONCEPTS 191,317

detect [v] *discover*
ascertain, catch, descry, dig up*, disclose, distinguish, encounter, espy, expose, find, hit on*, hit upon*, identify, meet, meet with, nose out*, note, notice, observe, recognize, reveal, scent, see, smell out*, smoke out*, spot, stumble on, track down, tumble into, turn up, uncover, unmask, wise up to*; SEE CONCEPTS 38,183

detection [n] *discovery*
apprehension, disclosure, espial, exposé, exposure, ferreting out, find, revelation, strike, tracking down, uncovering, unearthing, unmasking; SEE CONCEPTS 38,183

detective [n] *investigator of crime*
agent, analyst, bird dog*, bloodhound*, bull*, constable, cop, dick*, eavesdropper, eye*, fed*, fink*, flatfoot*, gumshoe*, informer, nark*, peeper*, P.I.*, plainclothes officer, police officer, private eye, private investigator, prosecutor, reporter, roper, scout, scrounger, shadow*, shamus*, Sherlock Holmes*, shoofly*, sleuth, slewfoot*, snoop*, spy, tail*; SEE CONCEPT 348

detention [n] *confinement, imprisonment*
apprehension, arrest, arrestation, bust*, custody, delay, detainment, hindrance, holding back, holding pen*, immurement, impediment, incarceration, internment, keeping in, nab, pen*, pickup, pinch*, quarantine, restraint, retention, time up the river*, withholding; SEE CONCEPTS 191,317

deter [v] *check, inhibit from action*
act like a wet blanket*, avert, block, caution, chill, cool, damp, dampen, daunt, debar, disadvise, discourage, dissuade, divert, forestall, forfend, frighten, hinder, impede, intimidate, obstruct, obviate, preclude, prevent, prohibit, put a damper on, put off, restrain, rule out, scare, shut out, stave off, stop, talk out of, throw cold water on*, turn off, warn; SEE CONCEPT 121

deteriorate [v] *decay, degenerate*
adulterate, alloy, become worse, be worse for wear*, break, corrode, corrupt, crumble, debase, debilitate, decline, decompose, degrade, deprave, depreciate, descend, disimprove, disintegrate, ebb, fade, fail, fall apart, flag, go downhill*, go to

pieces*, go to pot*, go to the dogs*, hit the skids*, impair, injure, languish, lapse, lessen, lose it, lose quality, lower, mar, pervert, regress, retrograde, retrogress, rot, sink, skid, slide, spoil, undermine, vitiate, weaken, wear away, worsen; SEE CONCEPT 698

deterioration [n] *decay, degeneration*
abasement, adulteration, atrophy, corrosion, crumbling, debasement, decadence, decaying, declension, declination, decline, decomposition, degradation, degringolade, depreciation, descent, devaluation, dilapidation, disintegration, dislocation, disrepair, downfall, downgrade, downturn, drop, fall, lapse, lessening, perversion, retrogression, rotting, ruin, slump, spoiling, vitiation, worsening; SEE CONCEPTS 230,698

determination [n1] *perseverance*
assurance, backbone*, boldness, bravery, certainty, certitude, constancy, conviction, courage, dauntlessness, decision, dedication, doggedness, dogmatism, drive, energy, fearlessness, firmness, fortitude, grit, guts*, hardihood, heart*, independence, indomitability, intrepidity, nerve*, obstinacy, persistence, pluck*, purpose, purposefulness, resoluteness, resolution, resolve, self-confidence, single-mindedness, spine*, spunk*, steadfastness, stiff upper lip*, stubbornness, tenacity, valor, willpower; SEE CONCEPTS 411,657

determination [n2] *conclusion*
decision, judgment, measurement, opinion, perception, purpose, resolution, resolve, result, settlement, solution, verdict, visualization; SEE CONCEPTS 685,689

determine [v1] *conclude, decide*
actuate, arbitrate, call the shots*, cinch, clinch, complete, dispose, drive, end, figure, finish, fix upon, halt, impel, incline, induce, move, nail down*, opt, ordain, persuade, pin down*, predispose, regulate, resolve, rule, settle, take a decision, tap, terminate, ultimate, wind up*, wrap up*; SEE CONCEPTS 18,35,234

determine [v2] *discover, find out*
add up to*, ascertain, boil down to*, catch on, certify, check, demonstrate, detect, divine, establish, figure, figure out, have a hunch*, hear, learn, make out, see, size up, tell, tumble, unearth, verify, work out; SEE CONCEPTS 15,31

determine [v3] *choose, decide*
destine, doom, elect, establish, fate, finger*, fix, foreordain, make up mind, predestine, predetermine, preform, preordain, purpose, resolve, settle; SEE CONCEPT 18

determine [v4] *dictate, govern, regulate*
affect, bound, circumscribe, command, condition, control, decide, delimit, devise, direct, impel, impose, incline, induce, influence, invent, lead, limit, manage, mark off, measure, modify, plot, rule, shape; SEE CONCEPT 94

determined [adj] *driven, persistent*
bent, bent on, buckled down*, constant, decided, decisive, dogged, earnest, firm, fixed, hard-as-nails*, hardboiled*, intent, mean business*, obstinate, on ice*, pat, persevering, purposeful, resolute, resolved, serious, set, set on, settled, single-minded, solid, steadfast, strong-minded, strong-willed, stubborn, tenacious, unfaltering, unflinching, unhesitating, unwavering; SEE CONCEPTS 404,542

deterrent [n] *impediment, restraint*
bridle, check, curb, defense, determent, discouragement, disincentive, hindrance, leash, obstacle, preventative, preventive, rein, shackle; SEE CONCEPT **680**

detest [v] *hate; feel disgust toward*
abhor, abominate, be allergic to, despise, dislike intensely, down on, execrate, feel aversion toward, feel hostility toward, feel repugnance toward, have no use for*, loathe, recoil from, reject, repudiate; SEE CONCEPT **279**

detestable [adj] *loathsome, abominable*
abhorred, abhorrent, accursed, atrocious, awful, despicable, disgusting, execrable, godawful*, grody*, gross*, hateable, hateful, heinous, horrid, lousy, low-down, maggot, monstrous, obnoxious, odious, offensive, outrageous, repugnant, repulsive, revolting, rotten, shocking, sorry, vile; SEE CONCEPTS **529,542**

dethrone [v] *oust*
degrade, depose, discrown, dismiss, displace, uncrown, unmake; SEE CONCEPTS **298,320**

detonate [v] *set off bomb*
bang, blast, blow up, burst, discharge, explode, fulminate, kablooey*, let go, mushroom*, push the button*, shoot off, touch off, va-voom*; SEE CONCEPT **179**

detour [n] *indirect course*
alternate route, back road, branch, bypass, bypath, byway, circuit, circuitous route, circumbendibus*, circumnavigation, circumvention, crotch, deviation, divergence, diversion, fork, roundabout way, runaround, secondary highway, service road, substitute, temporary route; SEE CONCEPT **501**

detract [v] *take away a part; lessen*
backbite*, belittle, blister, cheapen, cut rate, decrease, decry, depreciate, derogate, devaluate, diminish, discount, discredit, disesteem, draw away, knock*, laugh at, lower, minimize, misprize, reduce, subtract from, underrate, undervalue, vilipend, withdraw, write off*; SEE CONCEPTS **52,54,236,247**

detraction [n] *misrepresentation; slander*
abuse, aspersion, backbiting*, backstabbing*, belittlement, calumny, damage, defamation, denigration, deprecation, derogation, disesteem, disparagement, harm, hit, hurt, injury, injustice, innuendo, insinuation, knock*, libel, libeling, lie, maligning, minimization, muckraking*, obloquy, pejorative, revilement, ridicule, running down*, scandal, scandalmongering, scurrility, slam, smear campaign*, tale, traducement, traducing, vilification, vituperation, wrong; SEE CONCEPTS **52,54,63**

detriment [n] *disadvantage*
damage, disability, disservice, drawback, handicap, harm, hurt, impairment, injury, liability, loss, marring, mischief, prejudice, spoiling; SEE CONCEPTS **309,674**

detrimental [adj] *damaging, disadvantageous*
adverse, bad, baleful, deleterious, destructive, disturbing, evil, harmful, hurtful, ill, inimical, injurious, mischievous, negative, nocuous, pernicious, prejudicial, unfavorable; SEE CONCEPTS **537,570**

devalue [v] *depreciate*
cheapen, cut rate, debase, decrease, decry, devalorize, devaluate, knock off, lower, mark down, nose dive, revalue, take down, underrate, under-value, write down, write off; SEE CONCEPTS **330,335**

devastate [v] *demolish, destroy*
depredate, desecrate, desolate, despoil, devour, do one in*, lay waste, level, pillage, plunder, raid, ravage, raze, ruin, sack, smash, spoil, spoliate, stamp out*, take apart, total*, trash*, waste, wipe off map*, wreck; SEE CONCEPTS **246,252**

devastation [n] *destruction*
confusion, defoliation, demolition, depredation, desolation, havoc, loss, pillage, plunder, ravages, ruin, ruination, spoliation, waste; SEE CONCEPT **674**

develop [v1] *cultivate, prosper*
advance, age, enroot, establish, evolve, expand, flourish, foster, grow, grow up, maturate, mature, mellow, progress, promote, ripen, thrive; SEE CONCEPTS **253,427,704**

develop [v2] *expand, work out*
actualize, advance, amplify, augment, beautify, broaden, build up, cultivate, deepen, dilate, elaborate, enlarge, enrich, evolve, exploit, extend, finish, heighten, improve, intensify, lengthen, magnify, materialize, perfect, polish, promote, realize, refine, spread, strengthen, stretch, unfold, widen; SEE CONCEPTS **700,775**

develop [v3] *begin; occur*
acquire, arise, befall, betide, break, break out, breed, chance, come about, come off, commence, contract, ensue, establish, follow, form, generate, go, happen, invest, originate, pick up, result, start, transpire; SEE CONCEPT **119**

develop [v4] *unfold; be made known*
account for, acquire, actualize, disclose, disentangle, elaborate, evolve, exhibit, explain, explicate, foretell, form, materialize, produce, reach, realize, recount, state, uncoil, uncover, unfurl, unravel, unroll, untwist, unwind; SEE CONCEPTS **60,261**

development [n1] *growth*
adding to, addition, adulthood, advance, advancement, advancing, augmentation, augmenting, boost, buildup, developing, elaborating, enlargement, evolution, evolvement, evolving, expansion, flowering, hike, improvement, increase, increasing, making progress, maturation, maturing, maturity, ongoing, perfecting, progress, progression, reinforcement, reinforcing, ripening, spread, spreading, unfolding, unraveling, upgrowth, upping; SEE CONCEPTS **700,704,775**

development [n2] *happening, incident*
change, circumstance, conclusion, denouement, event, eventuality, eventuation, issue, materialization, occurrence, outcome, phenomenon, result, situation, transpiration, turn of events, upshot; SEE CONCEPT **3**

deviant [adj] *abnormal, different*
aberrant, anomalous, atypical, bent, devious, divergent, freaky, heretical, heteroclite, irregular, kinky, off-key, perverse, perverted, preternatural, queer, twisted, unorthodox, unrepresentative, untypical, variant, varying, wandering, wayward, weird; SEE CONCEPT **564**

deviate [v] *stray from normal path*
aberrate, angle off, avert, bear off, bend, bend the rules*, break pattern, circumlocate, contrast, deflect, depart, depart from, differ, digress, divagate, diverge, drift, edge off*, err, get around, go amiss, go haywire*, go off on tangent*, go out of control*, go out of way, leave beaten path*, not

conform, part, shy, swerve, swim against stream*, take a turn, turn, turn aside, vary, veer, wander; SEE CONCEPTS *195,665,697*

deviation [n] *change, departure*
aberration, alteration, anomaly, breach, crotch, deflection, detour, difference, digression, discrepancy, disparity, divergence, diversion, fluctuation, fork, hereticism, inconsistency, irregularity, modification, shift, transgression, turning, variance, variation; SEE CONCEPTS *665,697,738*

device [n1] *instrument, tool*
accessory, agent, apparatus, appliance, arrangement, article, construction, contraption, contrivance, creation, doohickey*, equipment, expedient, gadget, gear, gimmick, implement, invention, machine, makeshift, material, means, mechanism, medium, outfit, resort, resource, rigging*, Rube Goldberg invention*, shift, tackle, thingamabob*, utensil, whatchamacallit*, whatnot*, whatsit*; SEE CONCEPTS *463,499*

device [n2] *ploy, scheme, maneuver*
artifice, cabal, chicanery, clever move, craft, craftiness, cunningness, design, dodge, evasion, expedient, fake, feint, finesse, gambit, game, gimmick, improvisation, loophole*, machination, method, pattern, plan, plot, project, proposition, purpose, racket, ruse, shift, stratagem, strategy, stunt, subterfuge, trap, trick, wile; SEE CONCEPT *660*

device [n3] *symbol, emblem*
badge, colophon, crest, design, ensign, figure, insignia, logo, motif, motto, pattern, scroll, sign, slogan, token; SEE CONCEPT *284*

devil [n] *demon*
adversary, archfiend, beast, Beelzebub, bête noire, brute, common enemy, dastard, diablo, djinn, dybbuk, enfant terrible*, evil one, fiend, genie, hellion, imp, knave, Lucifer, Mephistopheles, monster, ogre, Prince of Darkness, rogue, Satan, scamp, scoundrel, the dickens*, the Erinyes, the Furies, villain; SEE CONCEPTS *370,412*

devilish [adj] *wicked*
accursed, atrocious, bad, brutish, cloven-footed, cursed, damnable, demoniac, demonic, detestable, diabolic, diabolical, evil, execrable, fiendish, hellborn, hellish, infernal, inhuman, iniquitous, Mephistophelian, nefarious, satanic, serpentine, unhallowed, villainous; SEE CONCEPT *545*

devious [adj] *dishonest, crafty*
artful, calculating, crooked, deceitful, double-dealing, duplicitous, errant, erring, evasive, faking one out*, fishy*, foxy*, fraudulent, guileful, indirect, insidious, insincere, not straightforward, oblique, obliquitous, playing games, playing politics*, put on, roundabout, scheming, shady, shifty, shrewd, sly, sneaking, sneaky, surreptitious, treacherous, tricky, underhanded, wily; SEE CONCEPTS *401,404*

devious [adj] *crooked; indirect*
ambiguous, bending, circuitous, confounding, confusing, curving, detouring, deviating, digressing, digressory, diverting, errant, erratic, excursive, flexuous, misleading, obscure, out-of-the-way, rambling, remote, removed, roundabout, serpentine, straying, tortuous, twisting, wandering; SEE CONCEPT *581*

devise [v] *conceive, dream up*
ad-lib, arrange, blueprint*, brainstorm*, cast,

chart, cogitate, come up with, concoct, construct, contrive, cook up*, craft, create, design, discover, dope out*, fake it, forge, form, formulate, frame*, get off*, hatch, head trip*, imagine, improvise, intrigue, invent, machinate, make up, mastermind*, plan, play it by ear*, plot, prepare, project, scheme, shape, spark, think up, throw together, trump up*, vamp, whip up*, work out; SEE CONCEPTS *36,43*

devoid [adj] *empty, wanting*
bare, barren, bereft, deficient, denuded, destitute, free from, innocent, lacking, needed, sans*, unprovided with, vacant, void, without; SEE CONCEPTS *483,485*

devote [v] *commit one's energies, thoughts*
allot, apply, apportion, appropriate, assign, bestow, bless, concern oneself, confide, consecrate, consign, dedicate, donate, enshrine, entrust, give, give away, hallow, hand out, occupy oneself, pledge, present, reserve, sanctify, set apart, vow; SEE CONCEPTS *17,108,112*

devoted [adj] *committed, loyal*
adherent, affectionate, ardent, behind one, caring, concerned, consecrated, constant, crazy about*, dear, dedicated, devout, doting, dutiful, faithful, fervid, fond, gone out*, lovesome, loving, staunch, steadfast, stuck on*, thoughtful, true, true-blue*, wild about*, zealous; SEE CONCEPT *542*

devotee [n] *ardent supporter; fan*
addict, adherent, admirer, aficionado, amateur, believer, booster, buff, disciple, enthusiast, fanatic, fancier, fiend, follower, groupie, habitué, junkie, lover, rooter, supporter, votarient, votary; SEE CONCEPT *423*

devotion [n] *commitment; loyalty*
adherence, adoration, affection, allegiance, ardor, attachment, consecration, constancy, dedication, deference, devotedness, devotement, devoutness, earnestness, enthusiasm, faithfulness, fealty, fervor, fidelity, fondness, intensity, love, observance, passion, piety, reverence, sanctity, service, sincerity, spirituality, worship, zeal; SEE CONCEPTS *32,657*

devour [v] *swallow, consume*
absorb, annihilate, appreciate, be engrossed by, be preoccupied, bolt, bolt down*, chow down*, cram*, delight in, destroy, dispatch, do compulsively, do voraciously, drink in, eat, enjoy, exhaust, feast on, feed on, gloat over, gobble, gorge*, go through, gulp, guzzle, hoover*, imbibe, ingest, inhale, partake of, pig out*, polish off*, ravage, rejoice in, relish, revel in, scarf down*, spend, stuff, take, take in, use up, waste, wipe out, wolf*, wolf down*; SEE CONCEPTS *169,225*

devout [adj] *sincerely believing; devoted*
adherent, adoring, appreciate, deep, earnest, faithful, fervent, fervid, genuine, godly, goody-goody*, goody two-shoes*, heart-and-soul, heartfelt, holy, intense, orthodox, passionate, pietistic, pious, prayerful, profound, religious, reverent, revering, serious, sincere, venerating, worshiping, zealous; SEE CONCEPT *542*

dexterity [n] *aptitude, ability*
address, adroitness, aptness, art, artistry, cleverness, craft, cunning, deftness, effortlessness, expertise, expertness, facility, finesse, handiness, ingenuity, knack, know-how, mastery, neatness, nimbleness, proficiency, readiness, skill, skillful-

ness, smoothness, tact, touch; SEE CONCEPTS 409,630

dexterous [adj] ingenious, proficient
able, active, acute, adept, agile, apt, artful, canny, clever, crack*, crackerjack*, deft, effortless, expert, facile, handy, having the know-how*, masterly, neat, nimble, nimble-fingered, prompt, quick, savvy, skilled, skillful, slick, sly, smooth; SEE CONCEPTS 402,527

diabolic [adj] evil, fiendish
atrocious, cruel, damnable, demoniac, demonic, devilish, hellish, impious, infernal, Mephistophelian, monstrous, nasty, nefarious, satanic, serpentine, shocking, unhallowed, unpleasant, vicious, vile, villainous, wicked; SEE CONCEPT 545

diagnose [v] identify problem, disease
analyze, determinate, determine, diagnosticate, distinguish, interpret, investigate, pinpoint, place, pronounce, recognize, spot; SEE CONCEPTS 38,310

diagnosis [n] identification of problem, disease
analysis, conclusion, examination, interpretation, investigation, opinion, pronouncement, scrutiny, summary; SEE CONCEPTS 283,689

diagonal [adj] angled
askew, bevel, beveled, bias, biased, cater-cornered, catty-cornered, cornerways, cross, crossways, crosswise, inclining, kitty-cornered*, oblique, skewing, slanted, slanting, transversal, transverse; SEE CONCEPT 581

diagonally [adv] at an angle
askew, aslant, cater-corner, catty-corner, corner-wise, crosswise, kitty-corner*, obliquely, on a slant, on the bias, slantingways, slantways, slant-wise, slaunchways; SEE CONCEPT 581

diagram [n] drawing, sketch of form or plan
big picture*, blueprint, chart, description, design, draft, figure, floor plan, game, game plan, ground plan, layout, outline, perspective, representation, rough draft; SEE CONCEPTS 625,660

dial [v] tune to desired position
punch, ring, rotate, turn, twist, wheel, zero in on*; SEE CONCEPT 201

dialect [n] local speech
accent, argot, can, idiom, jargon, language, lingo, localism, patois, patter, pronunciation, provincialism, regionalism, slang, terminology, tongue, vernacular, vocabulary; SEE CONCEPT 276

dialectic [n] logic, reasoning
argumentation, contention, debate, deduction, discussion, disputation, forensic, logical argument, mooting, persuasion, polemics, question-and-answer method, ratiocination; SEE CONCEPT 37

dialectic [adj] logical, rational
analytic, argumentative, controversial, dialectical, persuasive, polemical, rationalistic; SEE CONCEPT 529

dialogue/dialog [n] talk, exchange of ideas
chat, colloquy, communication, confab*, confabulation, conference, conversation, converse, discourse, discussion, duologue, interlocution, lines*, parlance, parley, powwow, remarks, repartee, script, sides, small talk*; SEE CONCEPTS 56,278

diameter [n] measurement across object
bore, breadth, broadness, caliber, module, width; SEE CONCEPT 760

diametric/diametrical [adj] opposed, conflicting
adverse, antipodal, antipodean, antithetical, contradictory, contrary, contrasting, converse,

counter, facing, opposite, polar, reverse; SEE CONCEPT 564

diaphanous [adj] fine, see-through
chiffon, clear, cobweblike, delicate, filmy, flimsy, gauzy, gossamer, light, pellucid, pure, sheer, thin, translucent, transparent; SEE CONCEPTS 490,606

diary [n] recounting of activities in writing
account, agenda, appointment book, chronicle, daily record, daybook, engagement book, journal, log, minutes, notebook, record; SEE CONCEPT 283

diaspora [n] the spreading out of a group of people
disbandment, dispersal, dispersion, dissolution, escape, exodus, mass exodus, refugee flow; SEE CONCEPT 195

diatribe [n] harangue, criticism
abuse, castigation, denunciation, disputation, invective, jeremiad, objection, onslaught, philippic, reviling, screed, stricture, tirade, vituperation; SEE CONCEPT 52

dicey [adj] risky
capricious, chancy, dangerous, difficult, erratic, fluctuant, iffy*, incalculable, ticklish, tricky, uncertain, unpredictable, whimsical; SEE CONCEPTS 535,552

dicker [v] bargain; argue about
barter, buy and sell, chaffer, cut a deal*, haggle*, hammer out a deal*, huckster*, negotiate, palter, trade, work out a deal*; SEE CONCEPTS 46,330

dictate [n] command; rule
behest, bidding, code, decree, dictum, direction, edict, fiat, injunction, law, mandate, order, ordinance, precept, principle, requirement, statute, ultimatum, word; SEE CONCEPTS 274,318,688

dictate [v1] command; give instructions
bid, bulldoze*, call the play*, call the shots*, call the tune*, charge, control, decree, direct, enjoin, govern, guide, impose, instruct, lay down, lay down the law, lead, manage, ordain, order, prescribe, pronounce, put foot down*, read the riot act*, regiment, rule, set, take the reins*, walk heavy*; SEE CONCEPTS 53,60

dictate [v2] read out for the record
compose, deliver, draft correspondence, emit, formulate, give account, give forth, interview, orate, prepare draft, say, speak, talk, transmit, utter, verbalize; SEE CONCEPTS 60,324

dictator [n] absolute ruler
absolutist, adviser, authoritarian, autocrat, boss, chief, commander, despot, disciplinarian, fascist, Hitler*, leader, magnate, mogul, oligarch, oppressor, ringleader, slavedriver, totalitarian, tycoon, tyrant, usurper; SEE CONCEPT 354

dictatorial [adj] tyrannical, authoritarian
absolute, arbitrary, arrogant, autocratic, bossy, clamorous, crack-the-whip*, despotic, dictative, doctrinaire, dogmatic, domineering, egotistic, firm, haughty, imperative, imperious, iron-handed, oppressive, overbearing, peremptory, pompous, proud, stern, throwing weight around, totalitarian, unlimited, unrestricted; SEE CONCEPT 542

dictatorship [n] absolute rule
authoritarianism, autocracy, coercion, despotism, fascism, garrison state, Nazism, reign of terror*, totalitarianism, tyranny, unlimited rule; SEE CONCEPTS 133,299,641

diction [n] style of speech; articulation
command of language, delivery, elocution, eloquence, enunciation, expression, fluency, gift of

gab*, inflection, intonation, language, line, lingo, locution, oratory, parlance, phrase, phraseology, phrasing, pronunciation, rhetoric, usage, verbalism, verbiage, vocabulary, wordage, wording; SEE CONCEPTS 47,276

dictionary [n] *book of word meanings*
concordance, cyclopedia, encyclopedia, glossary, language, lexicon, palaver, promptory, reference, terminology, vocabulary; SEE CONCEPT 280

dictum [n1] *saying; proverb*
adage, aphorism, apothegm, axiom, brocard, gnome, maxim, moral, motto, precept, rule, saw, truism; SEE CONCEPTS 278,689

dictum [n2] *decree, pronouncement*
affirmation, assertion, command, declaration, dictate, edict, fiat, order; SEE CONCEPT 278

didactic [adj] *educational*
academic, advisory, donnish, edifying, enlightening, exhortative, expository, homiletic, hortative, instructive, moral, moralizing, pedagogic, pedantic, preachy, preceptive, schoolmasterist, sermonic, sermonizing, teacherish, teacherly, teachy; SEE CONCEPT 548

die [v1] *pass away; stop living*
be no more*, be taken, breathe one's last*, cease to exist, conk*, croak*, decease, demise, depart, drop, drop off, drown, expire, finish, give up the ghost*, go way of all flesh*, kick the bucket*, perish, relinquish life, rest in peace, succumb, suffocate; SEE CONCEPT 304

die [v2] *wither, dwindle*
abate, bate, break down, crumble, decay, decline, degenerate, deteriorate, dilapidate, diminish, disappear, droop, ease off, ebb, end, expire, fade, fade away, fade out, fail, fall, fizzle out*, go bad*, go downhill*, halt, lapse, let up, lose power, melt away, moderate, molder, pass, peter out*, rankle, recede, retrograde, rot, run down, run low, run out, sink, slacken, stop, subside, vanish, wane, weaken, wear away, wilt; SEE CONCEPTS 469,698

diehard [n] *overenthusiastic person*
bitter ender*, Bourbon*, dyed-in-the-wool*, extremist, fanatic, fogy, fundamentalist, intransigent, mossback*, old liner*, praetorian, pullback*, reactionary, right, rightist, rightwinger, standpat, standpatter, stick-in-the-mud*, Tory*, true blue*, ultraconservative, zealot; SEE CONCEPTS 359,423

die-hard [adj] *uncompromising*
conservative, convinced, dyed-in-the-wool*, extremist, firm, fogyish, immovable, inflexible, intransigent, old-line*, orthodox, Philistine, reactionary, right, standpat, Tory*, traditionalistic, ultraconservative, unreconstructed; SEE CONCEPTS 404,542

diet [n1] *abstinence from food*
dietary, fast, nutritional therapy, regime, regimen, restriction, starvation, weight-reduction plan; SEE CONCEPT 660

diet [n2] *daily intake of food*
aliment, bite, comestibles, commons, daily bread, edibles, fare, goodies, grubbery, menu, nourishment, nutriment, nutrition, provisions, rations, snack, subsistence, sustenance, viands, victuals; SEE CONCEPTS 457,459

diet [v] *abstain from food*
count calories*, eat sparingly, fall off, fast, go without, lose weight, reduce, skinny down*, slim, slim down, starve, tighten belt*, watch weight*; SEE CONCEPT 169

differ [v1] *be dissimilar, distinct*
alter, bear no resemblance, be distinguished from, be off the beaten path*, be unlike, clash with, conflict with, contradict, contrast, depart from, deviate from, digress, disagree, divaricate from, diverge, diversify, jar with, lack resemblance, modify, not conform, not look like, qualify, reverse, run counter to, show contrast, sing a different tune*, stand apart, take exception, turn, vary; SEE CONCEPT 665

differ [v2] *clash; hold opposing views*
bicker*, bump heads*, contend, debate, demur, disaccord, disagree, discept, discord, dispute, dissent, divide, fight, go after each other, go at it*, hit a clinker*, hit a sour note*, jar*, lock horns*, object, oppose, protest against, quarrel, squabble, take issue, vary, war; SEE CONCEPT 46

difference [n1] *dissimilarity, distinctness*
aberration, alteration, anomaly, antithesis, asymmetry, change, characteristic, contrariety, contrariness, contrast, departure, deviation, digression, discongruity, discrepancy, disparity, dissemblance, distinction, divergence, diversity, exception, heterogeneity, idiosyncrasy, inequality, irregularity, nonconformity, opposition, particularity, peculiarity, separateness, separation, singularity, unconformity, unlikeness, unorthodoxness, variance, variation, variety; SEE CONCEPT 665

difference [n2] *opposing views*
argument, beef*, blowup*, bone to pick*, brannigan, brawl, brush*, brush-off*, catamaran, clash, conflict, contention, contrariety, contretemps, controversy, debate, disaccord, disagreement, discord, discordance, dispute, dissension, dissent, dissidence, disunity, dustup*, estrangement, hassle, quarrel, row*, run-in*, scrap*, set-to*, spat*, strife, tiff*, variance, words*, wrangle; SEE CONCEPTS 46,388

different [adj1] *dissimilar, unlike*
a far cry from*, altered, antithetic, at odds, at variance, changed, clashing, colorful, contradistinct, contradistinctive, contrary, contrasting, contrastive, deviating, differential, discrepant, disparate, distant, distinct, distinctive, divergent, divers, diverse, incommensurable, incomparable, inconsistent, individual, like night and day*, mismatched, mismated, offbeat, opposed, other, otherwise, particular, peculiar, poles apart*, single, unalike, unequal, unrelated, unsimilar, variant, various; SEE CONCEPTS 487,564,573

different [adj2] *separate, distinct*
another, another story, atypical, bizarre, discrete, diverse, especial, express, extraordinary, individual, novel, original, other, out of the ordinary, particular, peculiar, rare, several, singular, something else, special, specialized, specific, startling, strange, uncommon, unconventional, unique, unusual, various; SEE CONCEPT 564

different [adj3] *miscellaneous, various*
anthologized, assorted, asymmetrical, collected, disparate, dissonant, divergent, divers, diverse, diversified, diversiform, heterogeneous, incongruous, inconsistent, indiscriminate, jarring, manifold, many, multifarious, multiform, numerous, omnifarious, omniform, several, some, sundry, varicolored, varied, variegated, varietal, variform; SEE CONCEPT 772

differentiate [v1] *make a distinction*
antithesize, characterize, comprehend, contrast,

demarcate, discern, discrepate, discriminate, extricate, individualize, individuate, know, know what's what*, mark, mark off, redline*, separate, set apart, set off, sever, severalize, split hairs*, tell apart, understand; SEE CONCEPTS 15,38

differentiate [v2] *change; make different*
adapt, alter, assort, convert, diversify, mismatch, mismate, modify, transform, variegate, vary; SEE CONCEPT 232

differently [adv] *in another way; otherwise*
abnormally, adversely, antagonistically, antithetically, asymmetrically, conflictingly, contradictorily, contrarily, contrastingly, contrastively, discordantly, disparately, dissimilarly, distinctively, divergently, diversely, hostilely, in a different manner, incompatibly, incongruously, individually, negatively, nonconformably, on the contrary, on the other hand, oppositely, poles apart, separately, uniquely, unorthodoxly, unusually, variously, vice versa; SEE CONCEPT 564

difficult [adj1] *hard on someone; hard to do*
ambitious, arduous, backbreaker*, bothersome, burdensome, challenging, crucial, demanding, difficile, easier said than done*, effortful, exacting, formidable, galling, Gargantuan*, hard-won, heavy, Herculean*, immense, intricate, irritating, labored, laborious, no picnic*, not easy, onerous, operose, painful, problem, problematic, prohibitive, rigid, severe, stiff, strenuous, titanic, toilsome, tough, troublesome, trying, unyielding, uphill, upstream, wearisome; SEE CONCEPT 538

difficult [adj2] *complicated; hard to comprehend*
abstract, abstruse, baffling, bewildering, complex, confounding, confusing, dark, deep, delicate, enigmatic, enigmatical, entangled, esoteric, formidable, hard to explain, hard to solve, hidden, inexplicable, intricate, involved, knotty, labyrinthine, loose, meandering, mysterious, mystical, mystifying, nice, obscure, obstinate, paradoxical, perplexing, problematical, profound, puzzling, rambling, subtle, tangled, thorny, ticklish, troublesome, unclear, unfathomable, unintelligible, vexing; SEE CONCEPT 529

difficult [adj3] *unmanageable socially*
argumentative, bearish, boorish, dark, demanding, fastidious, finicky, fractious, fussy, grim, hard to please, impolite, intractable, irritable, oafish, obstreperous, perverse, picky, refractory, rigid, rude, tiresome, tough, troublesome, trying, unaccommodating, unamenable; SEE CONCEPTS 404,542,555

difficulty [n1] *problem; situation requiring great effort*
adversity, arduousness, awkwardness, barricade, check, complication, crisis, crux, dead end, deadlock, deep water*, dilemma, distress, emergency, exigency, fix*, frustration, hardship, hazard, hindrance, hitch*, hot water*, impasse, knot*, labor, laboriousness, mess, misfortune, muddle, obstacle, obstruction, pain, painfulness, paradox, perplexity, pickle*, predicament, quagmire, quandary, scrape*, snag*, stew*, strain, strait, strenuousness, struggle, stumbling block*, tribulation, trouble; SEE CONCEPTS 674,677

difficulty [n2] *mental burden*
ado, aggravation, annoyance, anxiety, bafflement, bother, care, charge, complication, crisis, depression, discouragement, distress, embarrassment, emergency, exigency, frustration, grievance, hangup, harassment, imbroglio, inconvenience, irritation, jam, maze, mess, millstone*, misery, oppression, perplexity, pickle*, pinch, predicament, pressure, puzzle, quandary, ramification, responsibility, scrape*, setback, strain, strait, stress, strife, struggle, to-do*, trouble, vicissitude, weight, worry; SEE CONCEPTS 410,532,690

difficulty [n3] *argument*
altercation, beef*, bickering, controversy, dispute, falling-out*, fight, hassle, misunderstanding, quarrel, squabble, strife, trouble; SEE CONCEPT 46

diffidence [n] *hesitancy; lack of confidence*
backwardness, bashfulness, constraint, doubt, fear, hesitation, humility, insecurity, meekness, modesty, mousiness, reluctance, reserve, self-consciousness, sheepishness, shyness, timidity, timidness, timorousness, unassertiveness; SEE CONCEPT 633

diffident [adj] *hesitant; unconfident*
backward, bashful, blenching, chary, constrained, coy, demure, distrustful, doubtful, dubious, flinching, humble, insecure, meek, modest, mousy, rabbity, reluctant, reserved, retiring, self-conscious, self-effacing, sheepish, shrinking, shy, suspicious, timid, timorous, unassertive, unassuming, unassured, unobtrusive, unpoised, unsure, withdrawn; SEE CONCEPT 401

diffuse [adj1] *spread out*
broadcast, catholic, circulated, diluted, dispersed, disseminated, distributed, expanded, extended, general, prevalent, propagated, radiated, scattered, separated, strewn, thin, unconcentrated, universal, widespread; SEE CONCEPTS 530,583, 772

diffuse [adj2] *wordy*
circumlocutory, copious, diffusive, digressive, discursive, dull, exuberant, lavish, lengthy, long, long-winded, loose, meandering, palaverous, profuse, prolix, rambling, random, redundant, vague, verbose, waffling, windy; SEE CONCEPT 267

diffusion [n] *spread; wide distribution*
circulation, dispersal, dispersion, dissemination, dissipation, expansion, propagation, propagation, scattering; SEE CONCEPTS 634,651

dig [n] *insult*
crack, cut, cutting remark, gibe, innuendo, jeer, quip, slur, sneer, taunt, wisecrack; SEE CONCEPT 54

dig [v1] *delve into; hollow out*
bore, break up, bulldoze, burrow, cat, channel, clean, concave, deepen, depress, dig down, discover, dredge, drill, drive, enter, excavate, exhume, fork out, go into, gouge, grub, harvest, hoe, investigate, mine, penetrate, pierce, pit, probe, produce, quarry, root, root out, rout, sap, scoop, scoop out, search, shovel, sift, spade, till, tunnel, turn over, uncover, undermine, unearth; SEE CONCEPT 178

dig [v2] *thrust object into*
drive, gouge, jab, jog, nudge, plunge, poke, prod, punch, ram, sink, stab, stick; SEE CONCEPT 208

dig [v3] *investigate; discover*
bring to light*, come across, come up with, delve, dig down, expose, extricate, find, go into, inquire, look into, probe, prospect, research, retrieve, root, search, search high and low*, shake down*, sift*, turn inside out*, turn upside down*, uncover, unearth; SEE CONCEPTS 31,103,216

dig [v4] *enjoy, like*
appreciate, follow, go for*, groove*, love, mind, relish, understand; SEE CONCEPT 32

dig [v5] *understand*
accept, apprehend, catch, comprehend, follow, grasp, recognize, see, take, take in; SEE CONCEPT 15

digest [n] *abridgement of something written*
abstract, aperçu, brief, compendium, condensation, epitome, pandect, précis, résumé, short form, sketch, summary, survey, syllabus, sylloge, synopsis; SEE CONCEPT 271

digest [v1] *assimilate food*
absorb, chymify, consume, dissolve, eat, incorporate, macerate, swallow, take; SEE CONCEPT 169

digest [v2] *make shorter; abridge*
abbreviate, abstract, boil down, classify, codify, compress, condense, cut, cut down, cut to bone*, decrease, epitomize, get to the meat*, inventory, methodize, nutshell*, put in a nutshell*, reduce, shorten, sum, summarize, summate, sum up, survey, synopsize, systematize, tabulate, trim; SEE CONCEPTS 236,247

digest [v3] *come to understand*
absorb, analyze, assimilate, consider, contemplate, deliberate, grasp, master, meditate, ponder, study, take in, think about, think over; SEE CONCEPT 15

digest [v4] *tolerate, endure*
abide, bear, brook, go, stand, stomach, swallow, take; SEE CONCEPT 23

dig in [v] *begin with enthusiasm*
bite, burrow, chew, commence, consume, delve, eat, rise, set about, spring, start eating; SEE CONCEPTS 100,169

digit [n1] *number*
arabic, chiffer, cipher, figure, integer, notation, numeral, symbol, whole number; SEE CONCEPTS 765,784

digit [n2] *small appendage of animate being*
claw, extremity, fang, feeler, finger, fork, hook, index finger, phalange, pinkie, pointer, ring finger, thumb, toe; SEE CONCEPT 392

dignified [adj] *honorable*
aristocratic, august, courtly, decorous, distingué, distinguished, eminent, formal, grand, grave, great, highbrow*, highfalutin'*, imperial, imperious, lofty, magisterial, magnificent, nifty*, noble, proud, refined, regal, reserved, respected, solemn, somber, stately, superior, upright; SEE CONCEPTS 404,555,574

dignify [v] *make honorable; glorify*
adorn, advance, aggrandize, distinguish, elevate, ennoble, erect, exalt, grace, honor, magnify, prefer, promote, raise, sublime, uprear; SEE CONCEPTS 244,700

dignity [n] *excellence, nobility*
address, cachet, character, consequence, courtliness, culture, decency, decorum, distinction, elevation, eminence, ethics, etiquette, glory, grace, grandeur, gravity, greatness, hauteur, honor, importance, loftiness, majesty, merit, morality, nobleness, perfection, poise, prestige, propriety, quality, rank, regard, renown, respectability, seemliness, self-respect, significance, solemnity, splendor, standing, state, stateliness, station, stature, status, sublimity, virtue, worth, worthiness; SEE CONCEPTS 388,411,668

digress [v] *stray, deviate*
aberrate, beat about the bush*, be diffuse, circumlocute, depart, divagate, drift, excurse, get off the point, get off the subject, get sidetracked, go by way of*, go off on a tangent*, long way*, meander, ramble, roam, swerve, turn aside, veer, wander, wander away; SEE CONCEPTS 195,266,697

digression [n] *deviation; straying*
apostrophe, aside, deflection, departure, detour, difference, discursion, divagation, divergence, diversion, drifting, episode, excursion, excursus, footnote, incident, note, obiter dictum, parenthesis, rambling, variation, wandering; SEE CONCEPTS 278,665,697

dilapidated [adj] *falling apart; in ruins*
battered, beat-up, broken-down, crumbling, crumbly, crummy*, damaged, decayed, decaying, decrepit, derelict, dingy, dog-eared*, faded, fallen-in, impaired, in a bad way*, injured, marred, neglected, old, ramshackle, ratty*, raunchy, rickety, rinky-dink*, run-down, seedy, shabby, shaky, slummy, tacky, threadbare, tumble-down, uncared for, unimproved, unkempt, used-up, worn-out; SEE CONCEPTS 485,560

dilate [v] *stretch, widen*
amplify, augment, be profuse, be prolix, broaden, develop, distend, enlarge, expand, expatiate, expound, extend, increase, inflate, lengthen, prolong, protract, puff out, spin off, swell; SEE CONCEPTS 57,236,245

dilatory [adj] *procrastinating*
backward, behindhand, dallying, delaying, deliberate, laggard, late, lax, lazy, leisurely, lingering, loitering, moratory, neglectful, negligent, putting off, remiss, slack, slow, sluggish, snail-like*, tardy, tarrying, time-wasting, unhasty, unhurried; SEE CONCEPTS 542,799

dilemma [n] *crisis*
bind*, box*, Catch-22*, corner, difficulty, double bind*, embarrassment, fix, hole, hooker*, impasse, jam, mess, mire, perplexity, pickle*, plight, predicament, problem, puzzle, quandary, scrape, spot, strait, tight corner*; SEE CONCEPTS 674,675

dilettante [n] *amateur*
abecedarian, aesthete, connoisseur, dabbler, dallier, greenhorn*, nonprofessional, rookie, smatterer, tenderfoot*, trifler, tyro, uninitiate; SEE CONCEPT 423

dilettante [adj] *amateurish*
artsy fartsy*, dabbling, green*, half-baked*, half-cocked*, rookie, tenderfoot*, unaccomplished, ungifted, unskilled; SEE CONCEPT 527

diligence [n] *perseverance in carrying out action*
activity, alertness, application, assiduity, assiduousness, attention, attentiveness, briskness, care, carefulness, constancy, earnestness, exertion, heed, heedfulness, industry, intensity, intent, intentness, keenness, laboriousness, pertinacity, quickness, sedulousness, vigor; SEE CONCEPTS 657,677

diligent [adj] *persevering, hard-working*
active, assiduous, attentive, busy, careful, conscientious, constant, eager, eager beaver*, earnest, grind*, indefatigable, industrious, laborious, occupied, operose, painstaking, persistent, persisting, pertinacious, plugging*, sedulous, steadfast, studious, tireless, unflagging, unrelenting, untiring; SEE CONCEPTS 326,538,542

di
di

dilute [v] *make thinner; weaken*
adulterate, alter, attenuate, cook, cut, decrease, deliquesce, diffuse, diminish, doctor*, doctor up*, irrigate, lace, lessen, liquefy, mitigate, mix, moderate, modify, needle*, phony up*, plant, qualify, reduce, shave*, spike, temper, water, water down; SEE CONCEPT *250*

diluted/dilute [adj] *thinned, weakened*
adulterated, attenuated, cut, impaired, impoverished, laced, light, moderated, reduced, shaved*, spiked, tempered, washy, watered down, waterish, watery, wishy-washy*; SEE CONCEPTS *485,606*

dim [adj1] *darkish*
blah, bleary, blurred, caliginous, cloudy, dark, dingy, dreary, dull, dusk, dusky, faded, faint, flat, fuzzy, gloomy, gray, ill-defined, indistinct, lackluster, lightless, mat, monotone, monotonous, murky, muted, obscured, opaque, overcast, pale, poorly lit, shadowy, sullied, tarnished, tenebrous, unclear, unilluminated, vague, weak; SEE CONCEPT *617*

dim [adj2] *unfavorable with regard to opinion*
depressing, disapproving, discouraging, gloomy, skeptical, somber, suspicious, unpromising; SEE CONCEPT *542*

dim [adj3] *not very intelligent*
boorish, dense, dim-witted, doltish, dull, dumb, oafish, obtuse, slow, slow on uptake*, stupid, thick*, weak-minded; SEE CONCEPT *402*

dim [v] *darken; obscure*
becloud, bedim, befog, blear, blur, cloud, dull, eclipse, fade, fog, haze, lower, muddy, obfuscate, pale, tarnish, turn down; SEE CONCEPTS *250,627*

dimensions/dimension [n] *proportions; range*
admeasurement, ambit, amplitude, bigness, bulk, capacity, compass, depth, dimensionality, extension, extensity, extent, greatness, height, importance, largeness, length, magnitude, measure, measurement, reach, scale, scope, size, volume, width; SEE CONCEPTS *730,792*

diminish [v1] *become or cause to be less*
abate, abbreviate, attenuate, become smaller, close, contract, curtail, cut, decline, decrease, depreciate, die out, diminish, dwindle, ebb, extenuate, fade away, lessen, lower, minify, moderate, peter out, recede, reduce, retrench, shrink, shrivel, slacken, subside, taper, temper, wane, weaken; SEE CONCEPTS *698,776*

diminish [v2] *belittle*
abuse, bad-mouth*, cheapen, cut down to size*, decry, demean, depreciate, derogate, detract from, devalue, disparage, dump on*, give comeuppance*, knock off high horse*, minimize, pan*, poormouth*, put away*, put down*, run down*, tear down*; SEE CONCEPT *54*

diminution [n] *lessening, reduction*
abatement, alleviation, contraction, curtailment, cut, cutback, decay, decline, decrease, deduction, retrenchment, weakening; SEE CONCEPTS *698, 776*

diminutive [adj] *tiny, petite*
bantam, bitsy*, bitty*, button*, Lilliputian, little, midget, mini, miniature, minute, peewee*, pint-sized, pocket, pocket-sized, small, teensy*, teensy-weensy*, teeny*, teeny-weeny*, under-size, wee*, weeny*; SEE CONCEPT *789*

din [n] *loud, continuous noise*
babel, bedlam, boisterousness, brouhaha, buzz, clamor, clangor, clash, clatter, commotion, confusion, crash, disquiet, hoo-ha*, hubbub, hullabaloo*, hurly-burly*, jangle, music, outcry, pandemonium, percussion, racket, row, shout, sound, stridency, tintamarre*, tintinnabulation, tumult, uproar; SEE CONCEPT *595*

dine [v] *eat, often formally*
banquet, breakfast, consume, do lunch*, eat out*, fall to*, feast, feed on, lunch, sup, supper; SEE CONCEPT *169*

diner [n] *casual restaurant with varied menu*
Automat*, bistro, booth, café, canteen, chuck wagon*, coffee shop, concession, dump*, eatery*, eating house, facility, fast-food outlet, greasy spoon*, grill, hash house*, ice-cream parlor, lunch counter, lunchroom, lunch wagon, mess hall, quick-lunch, saloon, sandwich shop, snack bar, tearoom; SEE CONCEPT *449*

dingy [adj] *soiled, tacky*
bedimmed, broken-down, colorless, dark, darkish, dilapidated, dim, dirty, discolored, drab, dreary, dull, dusky, faded, gloomy, grimy, muddy, murky, obscure, run-down, seedy, shabby, smirched, somber, sullied, tarnished, threadbare, tired; SEE CONCEPTS *485,617*

dinky [adj] *tiny, small*
bush-league*, dainty, insignificant, lesser, Lilliputian, mini, miniature, minor, minor-league*, neat, petite, secondary, second rate*, small-fry*, small-time*, trim; SEE CONCEPT *789*

dinner [n] *evening meal*
banquet, blowout*, chow*, collation, din-din*, eats*, feast, feedbag*, fete, main meal, major munch*, potluck, principal meal, refection, regale, repast, ribs*, spread*, supper, table d'hôte; SEE CONCEPT *459*

dip [n1] *submersion in liquid*
bath, dive, douche, drenching, ducking, immersion, plunge, soak, soaking, swim; SEE CONCEPT *256*

dip [n2] *something for dunking*
concoction, dilution, infusion, mixture, preparation, solution, suffusion, suspension; SEE CONCEPTS *260,466*

dip [n3] *depression; decline*
basin, concavity, declivity, descent, downslide, downswing, downtrend, drop, fall, fall-off, hole, hollow, inclination, incline, lowering, pitch, sag, sink, sinkage, sinkhole, slip, slope, slump; SEE CONCEPTS *513,697,738*

dip [v1] *put into liquid*
baptize, bathe, douse, drench, duck, dunk, immerse, irrigate, lave, lower, moisten, pitch, plunge, rinse, slop, slosh, soak, souse, splash, steep, submerge, submerse, wash, water, wet; SEE CONCEPTS *201,256*

dip [v2] *lower, descend*
bend, decline, disappear, droop, drop down, fade, fall, go down, incline, nose-dive, plummet, plunge, reach, recede, sag, set, settle, sheer, sink, skew, skid, slant, slip, slope, slue, slump, spiral, subside, swoop, tilt, tumble, veer, verge; SEE CONCEPT *181*

dip [v3] *scoop, ladle*
bail, bale, bucket, decant, dish, draft off, draw, draw out, dredge, handle, lade, lift, offer, reach into, shovel, spoon, strain; SEE CONCEPTS *196,225*

dip into [v] *try, sample*
appropriate, browse, dabble, flip through, get,

glance at, glance over, leaf through, peruse, play at, rifle through*, run over, run through, scan, seize, skim, take, taste, thumb through*; SEE CONCEPTS 87,623

diploma [n] *certificate for achievement*
authority, award, charter, commission, confirmation, credentials, degree, honor, recognition, sheepskin, shingle, voucher, warrant; SEE CONCEPTS 271,337

diplomacy [n] *tact*
address, artfulness, craft, delicacy, delicatesse, discretion, expedience, finesse, negotiation, poise, politics, savoir-faire, skill, statecraft, subtlety; SEE CONCEPTS 388,633

diplomat [n] *politician, consul*
agent, ambassador, attaché, cabinet member, chargé d'affaires, conciliator, emissary, envoy, expert, go-between, legate, mediator, minister, moderator, negotiator, plenipotentiary, public relations person, representative, tactician; SEE CONCEPTS 354,359

diplomatic [adj] *politic, tactful*
adept, arch, artful, astute, bland, brainy, cagey, calculating, capable, clever, conciliatory, conniving, contriving, courteous, crafty, cunning, deft, delicate, dexterous, discreet, gracious, guileful, intriguing, opportunistic, polite, prudent, savvy, scheming, sensitive, sharp, shrewd, sly, smooth, strategic, suave, subtle, wily; SEE CONCEPTS 401,542

dire [adj1] *urgent; crucial*
acute, burning, clamant, clamorous, climacteric, critical, crying, desperate, drastic, exigent, extreme, immoderate, imperative, importunate, instant, pressing; SEE CONCEPTS 546,568,799

dire [adj2] *terrible, ominous*
afflictive, alarming, appalling, awful, black, calamitous, cataclysmic, catastrophic, cruel, deplorable, depressing, disastrous, dismal, distressing, dreadful, fearful, fierce, frightful, gloomy, grievous, grim, heartbreaking, horrible, horrid, lamentable, oppressing, portentous, redoubtable, regrettable, ruinous, scowling, shocking, terrific, ugly, unfortunate, woeful; SEE CONCEPTS 537,548,570

direct [adj1] *honest*
absolute, bald, blunt, candid, categorical, downright, explicit, express, forthright, frank, matter-of-fact, open, outspoken, person-to-person, plain, plainspoken, point-blank, sincere, straight, straightforward, straight from the shoulder*, talk turkey*, unambiguous, unconcealed, undisguised, unequivocal, unreserved; SEE CONCEPT 267

direct [adj2] *undeviating; uninterrupted*
beeline*, continuous, even, horizontal, in bee line*, in straight line, linear, nonstop, not crooked, point-blank, right, shortest, straight, straight ahead, straightaway, through, true, unbroken, unswerving; SEE CONCEPTS 482,581

direct [adj3] *face-to-face; next to*
contiguous, firsthand, head-on, immediate, lineal, next, personal, primary, prompt, proximate, resultant, succeeding; SEE CONCEPTS 585,586

direct [v1] *manage, oversee*
administer, advise, be in the driver's seat*, boss, call the shots*, carry on, conduct, control, control the affairs of, dispose, dominate, govern, guide, handle, have the say, head up*, influence, keep, lead, operate, ordain, preside over, quarterback*, regulate, rule, run, run the show*, run things*,

shepherd, superintend, supervise, take the reins*; SEE CONCEPTS 94,117

direct [v2] *give instructions; teach*
address, advise, bid, charge, command, deliver, dictate, enjoin, give directions, give orders, inform, instruct, lecture, order, read, tell, warn; SEE CONCEPTS 53,61

direct [v3] *point in a direction; guide*
address, aim, beam, cast, conduct, escort, fix, focus, head, incline, indicate, intend, lay, lead, level, mean, move in, pilot, point, point the way, present, route, see, set, shepherd, show, sight, sight on, slant, steer, target, train, turn, zero in; SEE CONCEPTS 187,201

direct [v4] *send, usually by mail system*
address, designate, inscribe, label, mail, mark, route, superscribe; SEE CONCEPT 217

direct [v5] *put all of efforts toward*
address, aim, apply, bend, buckle down, devote, endeavor, fix, give, set, settle, strive, throw, try, turn; SEE CONCEPTS 87,677

direction [n1] *management*
administration, charge, command, control, government, guidance, leadership, order, oversight, superintendence, supervision; SEE CONCEPTS 299,325

direction [n2] *course, route*
aim, angle, area, aspect, bearing, beeline*, bent, bias, current, drift, end, inclination, line, objective, orientation, outlook, path, point of compass, proclivity, range, region, road, set, side, slant, spot, standpoint, stream, tack, tendency, that-a-way*, tide, track, trajectory, trend, viewpoint, way; SEE CONCEPTS 657,738

direction(s) [n3] *instructions, guidance*
advice, advisement, assignment, briefing, directive, guidelines, indication, lowdown*, notification, plan, prescription, recommendation, regulation, sealed order, specification, specs*, steer*, summons, tip, word*; SEE CONCEPTS 271,274

directive [n] *command, instruction*
charge, communication, decree, dictate, edict, injunction, mandate, memo, memorandum, message, notice, order, ordinance, regulation, ruling, ukase, word; SEE CONCEPTS 271,274,662

directly [adv1] *the shortest route*
as a crow flies*, beeline*, dead, direct, due, exactly, plump, precisely, right, slam bang*, slap, smack, smack dab*, straight, straightly, undeviatingly, unswervingly, without deviation; SEE CONCEPTS 581,778

directly [adv2] *as soon as possible*
anon, at once, contiguously, dead*, due, first off, forthwith, immediately, in a second, instantaneously, instanter, instantly, presently, promptly, pronto*, quickly, right away, shortly, speedily, straightaway, straight off; SEE CONCEPT 820

directly [adv3] *straightforwardly*
candidly, face-to-face, honestly, in person, literally, openly, personally, plainly, point-blank, truthfully, unequivocally, verbatim, without prevarication, word for word; SEE CONCEPT 267

director [n] *manager*
administrator, big person*, boss, chair, chief, controller, exec, executive, executive officer, governor, head, head honcho*, helmer, key player*, kingpin*, leader, organizer, overseer, person upstairs*, player, principal, producer, skipper*, su-

di
di

pervisor, top dog*, top person*; SEE CONCEPTS 347,352

directory [n] *reference book; guide*
agenda, almanac, atlas, blue book, book, catalogue, charts, gazeteer, hit list*, index, laundry list*, lineup, list, little black book*, record, register, roster, scorecard, short list*, social register, syllabus, white pages*, who's who*, yellow pages*; SEE CONCEPTS 280,283

direful [adj] *fearful; horrible*
apocalyptic, appalling, awful, baleful, baneful, calamitous, dreadful, fateful, ghastly, gloomy, horrid, ill-boding, inauspicious, ominous, shocking, terrible, terrific, unlucky, unpropitious; SEE CONCEPTS 537,570

dirge [n] *sad song*
chant, coronach, cry, death march, death song, elegy, funeral song, hymn, jeremiad, keen, lament, march, monody, requiem, threnody; SEE CONCEPT 595

dirt [n1] *grime, impurity*
crud*, dreck, dregs, excrement, feculence, filth, filthiness, gook*, ground, gunk*, mire, muck, mud, rottenness, scuz*, sleaze, slime, smudge, smut, soil, stain, tarnish; SEE CONCEPT 509

dirt [n2] *obscenity; immorality*
chicanery, double-dealing, filth, fourberie, fraud, indecency, lubricity, pornography, smut; SEE CONCEPT 645

dirt [n3] *soil*
clay, dust, earth, loam, real estate, terra firma; SEE CONCEPT 509

dirty [adj1] *soiled, unclean*
bedraggled, begrimed, black, contaminated, cruddy*, crummy, defiled, disarrayed, dishabille, disheveled, dreggy, dungy, dusty, filthy, foul, fouled, greasy, grimy, grubby, grungy*, icky*, lousy, messy, mucky*, muddy, mung*, murky, nasty, pigpen*, polluted, raunchy, scummy*, scuzzy*, slatternly, slimy, sloppy, slovenly, smudged, smutty, sooty, spattered, spotted, squalid, stained, straggly, sullied, undusted, unhygienic, unkempt, unlaundered, unsanitary, unsightly, unswept, untidy, unwashed, yucky*; SEE CONCEPT 485

dirty [adj2] *obscene, pornographic*
base, blue, coarse, contemptible, despicable, filthy, immoral, impure, indecent, lewd, low, mean, nasty, off-color, ribald, risqué, salacious, scatological, scurvy, smutty, sordid, squalid, unchaste, unclean, uncleanly, vile, vulgar; SEE CONCEPTS 542,545

dirty [adj3] *violent, stormy with regard to weather*
blustering, blustery, coarse, dark, furious, gusty, lowering, raging, rainy, rough, squally, storming, tempestuous, wild; SEE CONCEPT 525

dirty [v] *cause to be soiled*
begrime, besoil, blacken, blotch, blur, botch, coat, contaminate, corrupt, debase, decay, defile, discolor, draggle, encrust, foul, grime, make dusty, make impure, mess up, mold, muddy, pollute, rot, smear, smirch, smoke, smudge, smutch, spatter, spoil, spot, stain, sully, sweat, taint, tar, tarnish; SEE CONCEPT 254

disability [n] *disadvantage, restriction*
affliction, ailment, defect, detriment, disqualification, drawback, impairment, inability, incapacity, incompetency, inexperience, infirmity, injury, invalidity, lack, unfitness, weakness; SEE CONCEPTS 309,316,410,720

disable [v] *render inoperative; cripple*
attenuate, batter, blunt, damage, debilitate, disarm, disenable, disqualify, enervate, enfeeble, exhaust, hamstring*, handicap, harm, hock*, hogtie*, hurt, immobilize, impair, incapacitate, invalidate, kibosh*, knock out*, maim, mangle, mar, mutilate, muzzle, paralyze, pinion, prostrate, put out of action*, render incapable, ruin, sabotage, sap, shatter, shoot down*, spoil, take out*, throw monkey wrench in*, total*, unbrace, undermine, unfit, unstrengthen, weaken, wreck; SEE CONCEPTS 130,246

disabled [adj] *incapacitated*
broken-down, confined, decrepit, disarmed, hamstrung*, handicapped, helpless, hurt, incapable, infirm, laid-up, lame, maimed, out-of-action*, out-of-commission*, paralyzed, powerless, rundown, sidelined, stalled, weakened, worn-out, wounded, wrecked; SEE CONCEPTS 314,527

disadvantage(s) [n1] *difficulty, trouble*
adverse circumstance, bar, blocking, burden, defect, deficiency, deprivation, detriment, disability, discommodity, drawback, failing, fault, flaw, fly in the ointment*, hamper, handicap, hardship, hindrance, impediment, imperfection, imposition, inadequacy, inconvenience, inutility, lack, liability, limitation, minus, nuisance, objection, obstacle, privation, problem, restraint, snag, stumbling block*, weakness, weak point; SEE CONCEPTS 666,674

disadvantage [n2] *hurt, loss*
damage, deprivation, detriment, disservice, harm, injury, prejudice; SEE CONCEPTS 230,309,679

disadvantageous [adj] *detrimental, inconvenient*
adverse, contrary, damaging, debit-side, deleterious, depreciative, depreciatory, derogatory, detracting, disparaging, downside, dyslogistic, harmful, hurtful, ill-timed, inexpedient, injurious, inopportune, objectionable, on the debit side, pejorative, prejudicial, slighting, uncomplimentary, unfavorable, unprofitable; SEE CONCEPTS 334, 537,555

disaffect [v] *lose affection for, estrange*
agitate, alienate, antagonize, discompose, disquiet, disturb, disunify, disunite, divide, repel, upset, wean; SEE CONCEPTS 7,19,135,384

disaffected [adj] *alienated, estranged*
antagonistic, discontented, disloyal, dissatisfied, hostile, indifferent, mutinous, rebellious, seditious, uncompliant, unfriendly, unsubmissive; SEE CONCEPTS 403,555

disaffection [n] *alienation, estrangement*
animosity, antagonism, antipathy, aversion, breach, disagreement, discontent, dislike, disloyalty, dissatisfaction, hatred, hostility, ill will, repugnance, resentment, unfriendliness; SEE CONCEPTS 388,410

disagree [v1] *be different*
be discordant, be dissimilar, clash, conflict, contradict, counter, depart, deviate, differ, discord, disharmonize, dissent, diverge, run counter to, vary, war; SEE CONCEPTS 665

disagree [v2] *argue; hold differing opinion*
altercate, battle, bicker, brawl, break with, bring action, clash, contend, contest, controversialize, controvert, debate, differ, disaccord, discept, discord, dispute, dissent, divide, fall out*, feud, fight, go for the jugular*, haggle, have words*, jump on*, lay into*, let have it, logomachize, object, oppose, palter, quarrel, quibble, rip, row,

scrap, set to, skirmish, spar, spat, sue, take issue, take on, war, wrangle, zap*; SEE CONCEPTS *12,46*

disagree [v3] *be injurious*
be distasteful, be disturbing, be sickening, be unsuitable, bother, discomfort, distress, go against the grain*, hurt, injure, make ill, nauseate, sicken, trouble, upset; SEE CONCEPT *246*

disagreeable [adj1] *bad-tempered, irritable*
bellicose, brusque, cantankerous, churlish, contentious, contrary, cross, difficult, disobliging, disputatious, eristic, grouchy, ill-natured, nasty, obnoxious, offensive, out of sorts, peevish, pettish, petulant, querulous, rude, snappy, surly, ugly, unfriendly, ungracious, unlikable, unpleasant, uptight, waspish, whiny; SEE CONCEPT *401*

disagreeable [adj2] *disgusting, offensive*
annoying, awful, bad, bothersome, displeasing, distasteful, distressing, drag, nasty, objectionable, obnoxious, pain, repellent, repugnant, repulsive, rotten, sour, unhappy, uninviting, unpalatable, unpleasant, unsavory, upsetting, woeful; SEE CONCEPTS *537,548*

disagreement [n1] *dispute, quarrel*
altercation, animosity, antagonism, argument, atmospherics, bickering, breach, break, clash, clashing, conflict, contention, contest, controversy, cross-purposes, debate, difference, discord, dissent, dissidence, disunion, disunity, division, divisiveness, falling out, feud, fight, friction, hassle, hostility, ill feeling, ill will, jarring, misunderstanding, opposition, rupture, spat, split, squabble, strife, tension, variance, vendetta, words, wrangle; SEE CONCEPTS *46,388*

disagreement [n2] *difference, unlikeness*
clash, discaccord, discordance, discrepancy, disharmonism, disharmony, disparity, dissimilarity, dissimilitude, divergence, divergency, diversity, incompatibility, incongruity, incongruousness, inconsistency, variance; SEE CONCEPT *665*

disallow [v] *reject, prohibit*
abjure, cancel, censor, debar, deny, disacknowledge, disavow, disclaim, dismiss, disown, embargo, exclude, forbid, keep back, kill, nix*, pass on, proscribe, put down, rebuff, refuse, repudiate, shut out, taboo*, veto, withhold, zing*; SEE CONCEPTS *21,25,30*

disappear [v] *vanish; cease*
abandon, abscond, be done for, be gone, be lost, be no more*, be swallowed up, cease to exist, clear, come to naught, decamp, dematerialize, depart, die, die out, disperse, dissipate, dissolve, drop out of sight*, ebb, end, end gradually, escape, evanesce, evanish, evaporate, exit, expire, fade, fade away, flee, fly, go, go south*, leave, leave no trace, melt, melt away, pass, pass away, perish, recede, retire, retreat, sink, take flight, vacate, vamoose*, wane, withdraw; SEE CONCEPTS *102,105,195*

disappearance [n] *vanishing*
ceasing to exist, decline and fall, dematerialization, departure, desertion, disappearing act, disintegration, dispersal, dissipation, dissolution, ebbing, eclipse, escape, evanescence, evaporation, exit, exodus, fading, flight, going, loss, melting, passing, receding, recession, removal, retirement, wane, wearing away, withdrawal; SEE CONCEPTS *102,105,195*

disappoint [v] *sadden, dismay; frustrate*
abort, baffle, balk, bring to naught, bungle, cast down, chagrin, circumvent, come to nothing, dash, dash hopes*, deceive, delude, disconcert, disenchant, disgruntle, dishearten, disillusion, dissatisfy, dumbfound, embitter, fail, fall down on, fall flat, fall short of, foil, founder, hamper, hinder, leave in the lurch*, let down, miscarry, mislead, not show, put out, ruin prospects, stand up, tease, thwart, torment, vex; SEE CONCEPTS *7,19,699*

disappointed [adj] *let down, saddened*
aghast, balked, beaten, chapfallen, complaining, crestfallen, defeated, depressed, despondent, disconcerted, discontented, discouraged, disenchanted, disgruntled, disillusioned, dissatisfied, distressed, down, downcast, downhearted, down in the dumps*, foiled, frustrated, hopeless, objecting, shot down, taken down, thwarted, unhappy, unsatisfied, upset, vanquished, worsted; SEE CONCEPT *403*

disappointment [n1] *saddening situation; letdown*
bitter pill*, blind alley*, blow, blunder, bringdown, bummer, bust*, calamity, defeat, disaster, discouragement, downer*, downfall, drag, dud, error, failure, false alarm*, faux pas*, fiasco, fizzle, flash in the pan*, impasse, inefficacy, lemon*, miscalculation, mischance, misfortune, mishap, mistake, obstacle, old one-two*, setback, slip, washout; SEE CONCEPTS *230,674*

disappointment [n2] *mental upset; displeasure*
adverse fate, adversity, bafflement, blow, chagrin, defeat, despondency, discontent, discouragement, disenchantment, disgruntlement, disillusion, disillusionment, dissatisfaction, distress, failure, frustration, lack of success, letdown, mortification, nonsuccess, regret, setback, the knocks*, unfulfillment; SEE CONCEPT *410*

disapproval [n] *condemnation*
blackball*, black list*, blame, boo*, boycott, brickbat, call down, castigation, catcall*, censure, criticism, denunciation, deprecation, disapprobation, discontent, disfavor, dislike, disparagement, displeasure, dissatisfaction, hiss*, nix*, objection, opprobrium, ostracism, reproach, reproof, slap on wrist*, stricture, thumbs down*, vitriol, zing*; SEE CONCEPTS *278,689*

disapprove [v] *condemn*
blame, censure, chastise, criticize, damn, decry, denounce, deplore, deprecate, detract, disallow, discommend, discountenance, disesteem, disfavor, dislike, dismiss, dispraise, expostulate, find fault with, find unacceptable, frown on, look askance at, look down on, nix*, object to, oppose, pan*, pass on, refuse, reject, remonstrate, reprehend, reprobate, reprove, set aside, slam, spurn, take dim view of, take exception to, turn down, veto, zing*; SEE CONCEPTS *18,21,52*

disarm [v1] *render defenseless*
conciliate, cripple, deactivate, debilitate, deescalate, demilitarize, demobilize, disable, disband, disqualify, incapacitate, invalidate, neutralize, occupy, pacify, paralyze, prostrate, skin, strip, subdue, subjugate, unarm, weaken; SEE CONCEPTS *142,211,320*

disarm [v2] *persuade*
allure, attract, bewitch, captivate, charm, coax, convince, enchant, fascinate, seduce, set at ease, unarm, urge, win over; SEE CONCEPTS *7,19,22,68*

disarmament [n] *reduction of weapons*
arms limitation, arms reduction, conquest, crippling, de-escalation, demilitarization, demobilization, disablement, disqualification, freeze,

di
di

neutralizing, occupation, pacification, paralyzing, rendering powerless, subjugation; SEE CONCEPTS 142,211,320

disarming [adj] charming
bewitching, convincing, deferential, ingratiating, ingratiatory, insinuating, insinuative, inveigling, irresistible, likable, persuasive, saccharine, seductive, silken, silky, winning; SEE CONCEPT 401

disarray [n] disorder, confusion, mess
anarchy, ataxia, chaos, clutter, disarrangement, discomposure, disharmony, dishevelment, disorganization, holy mess*, indiscipline, jumble, muddle, shambles*, snarl, tangle, topsy-turviness*, unholy mess*, unruliness, untidiness, upset; SEE CONCEPTS 230,727

disaster [n] accident, trouble
act of God*, adversity, affliction, bad luck, bad news*, bale, bane, blight, blow, bust, calamity, casualty, cataclysm, catastrophe, collapse, collision, crash, debacle, defeat, depression, emergency, exigency, failure, fall, fell stroke*, fiasco, flood, flop, grief, hard luck, harm, hazard, holocaust, hot water*, ill luck, misadventure, mischance, misfortune, mishap, reverse, rock, rough, ruin, ruination, setback, slip, stroke, the worst*, tragedy, undoing, upset, washout*, woe; SEE CONCEPTS 674,675

disastrous [adj] detrimental, devastating
adverse, calamitous, cataclysmal, cataclysmic, catastrophic, destructive, dire, dreadful, fatal, fateful, harmful, harmful, ill-fated, ill-starred, luckless, ruinous, terrible, tragic, unfavorable, unfortunate, unlucky, unpropitious, untoward; SEE CONCEPTS 537,548

disavow [v] reject
abjure, contradict, deny, disacknowledge, disallow, disclaim, disown, drop out, forswear, gainsay, go back on word*, impugn, negate, negative, refuse, renege, renig, repudiate, wash hands of*, weasel out of*, welsh, worm out of*; SEE CONCEPTS 18,25

disbelief [n] doubt, skepticism
atheism, distrust, dubiety, incredulity, mistrust, nihilism, rejection, repudiation, spurning, unbelief, unbelievingness, unfaith; SEE CONCEPTS 21,689

disbelieve [v] doubt
discount, discredit, distrust, eschew, give no credence to, mistrust, not accept, not buy, not credit, not swallow*, question, reject, repudiate, scoff at, scorn, scout, suspect, unbelieve; SEE CONCEPT 21

disbelieving [adj] suspicious, doubting
aporetic, cagey, cynical, incredulous, leery, mistrustful, questioning, quizzical, show-me*, skeptical, unbelieving; SEE CONCEPT 403

disburse [v] spend money
acquit, ante up*, come across, come through, come up with, contribute, cough up*, deal, defray, disperse, disperse, distribute, divide, divvy*, dole out*, expend, foot the bill*, give, lay out*, measure out, outlay, partition, pay out, pony up*, put out, shell out, use; SEE CONCEPTS 108,341

disbursement [n] payment
cost, disposal, expenditure, expense, outgoing, outlay, spending; SEE CONCEPT 344

discard [v] get rid of
abandon, abdicate, abjure, adios*, banish, can*, cancel, cashier, cast aside, chuck, deep-six*, desert, dispatch, dispense with, dispose of, dis-

possess, ditch, divorce, do away with, drop, dump, eject, eliminate, expel, forsake, free of, give up, have done with, jettison, junk*, oust, part with, protest, put by, reject, relinquish, remove, renounce, repeal, repudiate, scrap, shake off, shed, sweep away, throw away, throw out, throw overboard*, toss aside, write off; SEE CONCEPT 180

discern [v] catch sight of; recognize and understand
anticipate, apprehend, ascertain, behold, descry, detect, determine, difference, differentiate, discover, discrepate, discriminate, distinguish, divine, espy, extricate, figure out, find out, focus, foresee, get a load of*, get the picture*, get wise to, judge, know, make distinction, make out, note, notice, observe, perceive, pick out, read, remark, rubberneck*, secern, see the light*, see through, separate, severalize, spot, take in, view; SEE CONCEPTS 15,38

discernible [adj] recognizable; distinct
apparent, appreciable, audible, clear, detectable, discoverable, distinguishable, noticeable, observable, obvious, palpable, perceivable, perceptible, plain, sensible, tangible, visible; SEE CONCEPTS 535,576,619

discerning [adj] discriminating
acute, astute, bright, brilliant, clear-sighted, clever, critical, gnostic, ingenious, insighted, insightful, intelligent, judicious, knowing, knowledgeable, penetrating, perceptive, percipient, perspicacious, piercing, sagacious, sage, sensitive, sharp, shrewd, subtle, wise; SEE CONCEPT 402

discharge [n1] setting free
acquittal, clearance, disimprisonment, exoneration, liberation, pardon, parole, probation, release, remittance; SEE CONCEPT 127

discharge [n2] dismissal from responsibility
ax, bounce, bum's rush*, congé, demobilization, ejection, gate, old heave ho*, pink slip*, the boot*, the door*, walking papers*; SEE CONCEPTS 324,351

discharge [n3] detonation
barrage, blast, burst, explosion, firing, fusillade, report, salvo, shot, shower, volley; SEE CONCEPT 521

discharge [n4] pouring forth
elimination, emission, emptying, excretion, exudation, flow, ooze, pus, secretion, seepage, shower, suppuration, vent, voiding; SEE CONCEPTS 179,748

discharge [n5] unloading
disburdening, emptying, unburdening, unlading; SEE CONCEPT 211

discharge [n6] carrying out of responsibility
accomplishment, achievement, execution, fulfillment, observance, performance; SEE CONCEPT 706

discharge [n7] payment of debt
acquittal, disbursement, liquidation, satisfaction, settlement; SEE CONCEPTS 341,344

discharge [v1] set free
absolve, acquit, allow to go*, clear, disimprison, dismiss, emancipate, exonerate, expel, liberate, loose, loosen, manumit, oust, pardon, release, unbind, unchain, unshackle; SEE CONCEPT 127

discharge [v2] dismiss from responsibility
absolve, ax, boot out*, bounce, bump, bust, can*, cashier, disburden, discard, disencumber, dis-

pense, displace, eject, excuse, exempt, expel, fire, freeze out*, give one notice, kick out, lay off, let go, let off, let one go, let out, lock out*, nix*, oust, privilege from, relieve, remove, replace, ride out on rail*, run out of town*, show the door*, spare, supersede, suspend, terminate, unload; SEE CONCEPTS 324,351

discharge [v3] *detonate weapon*
blast, explode, fire, let off, set off, shoot, shoot off; SEE CONCEPT 179

discharge [v4] *pour forth*
break out, disembogue, dispense, ejaculate, emit, empty, erupt, excrete, exude, give off, gush, leak, ooze, release, send forth, spew, void, vomit; SEE CONCEPTS 152,179

discharge [v5] *unload*
carry away, disburden, empty, off-load, remove, remove cargo, send, take away, take off, unburden, unlade, unpack, unship, unstow; SEE CONCEPT 211

discharge [v6] *carry out responsibility*
accomplish, achieve, do, execute, fulfill, meet, observe, perform; SEE CONCEPT 91

discharge [v7] *pay, settle debt*
clear, honor, liquidate, meet, pay up, quit, relieve, satisfy, square up; SEE CONCEPT 341

discharge [v8] *invalidate agreement*
abrogate, annul, cancel, dissolve, quash, render void, vacate, void; SEE CONCEPT 121

disciple [n] *believer, follower*
adherent, apostle, attendant, booster, buff, bug*, catechumen, cohort, convert, devotee, enthusiast, fan, fanatic, fiend, freak, groupie, hound*, junkie*, learner, nut*, partisan, proselyte, pupil, rooter*, satellite, sectary, sectator, student, supporter, votary, witness, zealot; SEE CONCEPTS 361,423

disciplinarian [n] *person who makes others work hard*
authoritarian, bully, despot, drill sergeant, enforcer, formalist, master, sergeant, stickler, strict teacher, sundowner, teacher, trainer, tyrant; SEE CONCEPTS 350,354,423

discipline [n1] *regimen, training*
conduct, control, cultivation, curb, development, domestication, drill, drilling, education, exercise, inculcation, indoctrination, limitation, method, orderliness, practice, preparation, regulation, restraint, self-command, self-control, self-government, self-mastery, self-restraint, strictness, subordination, will, willpower; SEE CONCEPTS 94,326,410

discipline [n2] *punishment*
castigation, chastisement, comeuppance, correction, getting yours*, hell to pay*, punition, rod; SEE CONCEPTS 122,123

discipline [n3] *field of study; subject of interest*
area, branch of knowledge, course, curriculum, specialty; SEE CONCEPT 349

disclaim [v] *deny*
abandon, abjure, abnegate, belittle, contradict, contravene, criticize, decline, deprecate, disacknowledge, disaffirm, disallow, disavow, discard, disown, disparage, divorce oneself from, forswear, gainsay, minimize, negate, recant, refuse, reject, renounce, repudiate, retract, revoke, spurn, traverse, turn back on, wash hands of*; SEE CONCEPT 54

disclose [v] *reveal, make public*
acknowledge, admit, avow, bare, betray, blab, bring to light*, broadcast, come out of the closet*, communicate, confess, discover, display, divulge, exhibit, expose, give away, impart, lay bare, leak, let slip, make known, mouth*, open, own, publish, relate, reveal, show, snitch*, spill, spill the beans*, squeal*, tell, uncover, unfurl, unveil, utter; SEE CONCEPT 60

disclosure [n] *announcement, revelation*
acknowledgment, admission, advertisement, betrayal, blow-by-blow*, broadcast, confession, declaration, discovery, divulgation, divulgence, enlightenment, exposal, exposé, exposure, handout, impartance, impartation, leak, make, picture, publication, revealing, revealment, rundown, snitch*, squeal*, tip*, tip-off*, uncovering, unveilment, ventilation; SEE CONCEPT 274

discolor [v] *fading, dirtying of hue*
besmear, besmirch, blot, defile, mar, mark, rust, smear, soil, stain, streak, sully, tar, tarnish, tinge; SEE CONCEPTS 250,469

discomfit [v] *defeat, frustrate; confuse*
abash, annoy, baffle, balk, beat, bother, checkmate, confound, demoralize, discompose, disconcert, discountenance, disturb, embarrass, faze, fluster, foil, irk, outwit, overcome, perplex, perturb, prevent, rattle, ruffle, take aback, thwart, trump, unsettle, upset, vex, worry, worst; SEE CONCEPTS 7,19,95

discomfiture [n] *embarrassment, frustration*
abashment, agitation, beating, chagrin, comedown, confusion, conquest, defeasance, defeat, demoralization, descent, disappointment, discomposure, disconcertion, disconcertment, disquiet, failure, humiliation, overthrow, perturbation, rout, ruin, shame, undoing, unease, uneasiness, upset, vanquishment, vexation; SEE CONCEPTS 410,674

discomfort [n] *irritation, pain*
ache, annoyance, discomfiture, discomposure, displeasure, disquiet, distress, embarrassment, hardship, hurt, inquietude, malaise, nuisance, soreness, trouble, uneasiness, unpleasantness, upset, vexation; SEE CONCEPTS 410,728

discomfort [v] *irritate; cause pain*
discomfit, discompose, disquiet, distress, disturb, embarrass, make uncomfortable, nettle, perturb, upset, vex; SEE CONCEPTS 7,19,246,313

discommode [v] *annoy*
bother, burden, disoblige, disquiet, disturb, fluster, harass, incommode, inconvenience, irk, molest, perturb, put out, trouble, upset, vex; SEE CONCEPTS 7,19

discompose [v] *provoke, agitate*
annoy, bewilder, bother, confuse, discombobulate, discomfit, disconcert, dismay, disorganize, displease, disquiet, disturb, embarrass, faze, flurry, fluster, harass, harry, irk, irritate, nettle, perplex, perturb, pester, plague, rattle, ruffle, unhinge, unsettle, upset, vex, worry; SEE CONCEPTS 7,19

disconcert [v] *shake up; confuse*
abash, agitate, baffle, balk, bewilder, bug, confound, demoralize, disarrange, discombobulate, discomfit, discompose, discountenance, disturb, embarrass, faze, fluster, foul up, frustrate, get to, hinder, nonplus, perplex, perturb, psych out*, put off, puzzle, rattle, ruffle, take aback, throw off balance, trouble, unbalance, undo, unsettle, upset, upset apple cart*, worry; SEE CONCEPTS 7,16,19

di
di

disconcerted [adj] confused; shaken
annoyed, bewildered, caught off balance, come
apart, distracted, disturbed, embarrassed, fazed,
flustered, in botheration, messed-up, mixed-up,
nonplussed, out of countenance, perturbed,
psyched-out*, rattled, ruffled, shook-up*, spaced-
out*, taken aback, thrown, troubled, unglued, unsettled, unzipped*, upset; SEE CONCEPT 403

disconnect [v] take apart; uncouple
abstract, break it off, break it up, cut off, detach,
disassociate, disengage, disjoin, dissever, dissociate, disunite, divide, drop it, part, separate,
sever, sideline, unfix; SEE CONCEPTS 98,135

disconnected [adj] confused; discontinuous
broken, detached, disjointed, disordered, garbled,
illogical, inchoate, incoherent, incohesive, interrupted, irrational, irregular, jumbled, loose,
mixed-up, muddled, rambling, separated, uncon-
tinuous, uncoordinated, unintelligible, wandering;
SEE CONCEPTS 267,482

disconsolate [adj] depressed, unhappy
bad, black, blue, cheerless, cold, comfortless,
crestfallen, crushed, dark, dejected, desolate, despairing, destroyed, dispirited, distressed, doleful, down, downcast, downhearted, dreary,
forlorn, gloomy, grief-stricken, heartbroken,
hopeless, hurting, inconsolable, in pain*, in the
pits*, low, melancholy, miserable, ripped*, sad,
somber, sorrowful, torn-up*, woebegone, woeful,
wretched; SEE CONCEPT 403

discontent [n] dissatisfaction
depression, discontentment, displeasure, envy,
fretfulness, regret, restlessness, uneasiness, unhappiness, vexation; SEE CONCEPT 410

discontented/discontent [adj] unhappy, dissatisfied
blue, complaining, crabby, disaffected, disgruntled, displeased, disquieted, disturbed, exasperated, fed up, fretful, griping, kvetching*,
malcontent, malcontented, miserable, perturbed,
picky, restless, ungratified, upset, vexed; SEE
CONCEPT 403

discontinuance [n] stop, suspension of activity
adjournment, alternation, cease, cessation, close,
closing, desistance, desuetude, discontinuation,
disjunction, disruption, ending, finish, intermission, interruption, separation, stopping, termination; SEE CONCEPT 119

discontinue [v] prevent activity from going on
abandon, bag it*, blow off*, break off*, call it
quits, cease, close, desist, disconnect, disjoin, dissever, disunite, drop, end, finish, give over, give
up, halt, interpose, interrupt, intervene, kill,
knock off*, leave off, part, pause, put an end to,
quit, refrain from, scrub, separate, stop, surcease,
suspend, terminate; SEE CONCEPTS 121,234

discontinuous [adj] broken; intermittent
alternate, desultory, disconnected, disjointed, disordered, fitful, gaping, inchoate, incoherent, incohesive, interrupted, irregular, muddled,
spasmodic, unconnected, unorganized; SEE CON-
CEPT 482

discord [n1] conflict, disagreement
animosity, antagonism, antipathy, clash, clashing,
collision, contention, difference, disaccord, discordance, discrepancy, disharmony, dispute, dissension, dissent, dissidence, dissonance,
disunion, disunity, division, enmity, friction,
fuss, hassle, hostility, incompatibility, incongruity, inharmony, lack of concord, mischief, oppo-

sition, polarization, rancor, row, ruckus, rupture,
scene, spat, split, static, strife, variance, wrangling; SEE CONCEPT 388

discord [n2] noise
cacophony, clamor, clinker, din, disharmony, dissonance, harshness, jangle, jarring, racket, sour
note, tumult; SEE CONCEPT 595

discordant [adj] not in harmony; conflicting
antagonistic, antipathetic, at odds, cacophonous,
clashing, contradictory, contrarient, contrary, different, disagreeing, discrepant, dissonant, divergent, grating, harsh, incompatible, incongruous,
inconsistent, inconsonant, inharmonious, jangling, jarring, on a sour note*, opposite, quarrel-
ing, strident, uncongenial, unharmonious,
unmelodious, unmixable; SEE CONCEPTS
558,564,592,594

discount [n] reduction in cost
abatement, allowance, commission, concession,
cut, cut rate, decrease, deduction, depreciation,
diminution, drawback, exemption, knock-off*,
markdown, modification, percentage, premium,
qualification, rebate, remission, rollback, salvage,
something off, subtraction, tare; SEE CONCEPTS
335,763

discount [v1] lower, reduce cost
abate, allow, deduct, depreciate, diminish, hold a
sale, knock off*, make allowance for, mark down,
modify, rebate, redeem, remove, sell at discount,
strike off, subtract, take away, take off, undersell;
SEE CONCEPTS 236,247,330

discount [v2] ignore; treat as insignificant
belittle, blink at*, brush off*, depreciate, derogate, detract from, disbelieve, discredit, dispraise,
disregard, doubt, fail, forget, minimize, mistrust,
neglect, omit, overlook, overpass, pass over,
question, reject, scoff at, scout, slight; SEE CON-
CEPTS 21,30

discountenance [v1] reject, oppose
condemn, count me out*, deprecate, disapprove,
discommend, discourage, disesteem, disfavor,
dispute, frown on*, hold no brief for*, not go
for*, not stand for*, object to, put down, resist,
take a dim view of*, take exception to*; SEE CON-
CEPT 21

discountenance [v2] embarrass, disconcert
abash, chagrin, confuse, discomfit, discompose,
faze, humiliate, rattle, shame; SEE CONCEPTS
7,19,54

discourage [v1] dishearten, dispirit
abash, afflict, alarm, appall, awe, beat down,
bother, break one's heart*, bully, cast down, chill,
confuse, cow, dampen, dash, daunt, deject, demoralize, deprecate, depress, dismay, disparage,
distress, droop, frighten, intimidate, irk, overawe,
prostrate, repress, scare, throw cold water on*,
trouble, try, unnerve, vex, weigh; SEE CONCEPT
14

discourage [v2] deter, dissuade; restrain
check, chill, control, curb, deprecate, disadvise,
discountenance, disfavor, disincline, divert,
frighten, hinder, hold back, hold off, impede, indispose, inhibit, interfere, keep back, obstruct,
prevent, put off, quiet, repress, scare, shake, talk
out of, throw cold water on*, turn aside, turn off,
warn, withhold; SEE CONCEPTS 68,121

discouraged [adj] disheartened
beat, beat-down, blue, caved-in, come-apart,
crestfallen, dashed, daunted, depressed, deterred,
dismayed, dispirited, down, downbeat, downcast,

down-in-mouth*, glum*, gone to pieces*, in a funk*, in blue funk*, in the dumps*, lost momentum, pessimistic, sad; SEE CONCEPT *403*

discouragement [*n1*] *despondency*
cold feet*, dejection, depression, despair, disappointment, discomfiture, dismay, downheartedness, hopelessness, loss of confidence, low spirits, melancholy, pessimism, sadness, the blues*; SEE CONCEPT *410*

discouragement [*n2*] *restraint*
bar, constraint, curb, damper, deterrent, disincentive, hindrance, impediment, obstacle, opposition, rebuff, setback; SEE CONCEPT *674*

discouraging [*adj*] *upsetting*
black, bleak, dampening, daunting, depressing, depressive, deterring, disadvantageous, disappointing, disheartening, dismal, dismaying, dispiriting, dissuading, dreary, gloomy, hindering, inopportune, off-putting, oppressive, repressing, unfavorable, unpropitious; SEE CONCEPTS *403,529*

discourse [*n*] *dialogue; dissertation*
address, article, chat, communication, conversation, converse, descant, discussion, disquisition, essay, gabfest*, homily, huddle, lecture, memoir, monograph, monologue, oration, paper, rhetoric, sermon, speaking, speech, talk, thesis, tractate, treatise, utterance, verbalization; SEE CONCEPT *266*

discourse [*v*] *discuss, speak about*
argue, chew*, comment, commentate, confab*, confer, converse, debate, declaim, descant, develop, dilate upon, dispute, dissert, dissertate, elaborate, enlarge, expand, expatiate, explain, expound, give a meeting, harangue, hold forth, lecture, modulate, orate, perorate, remark, sermonize, talk, treat, voice; SEE CONCEPTS *51,56*

discourteous [*adj*] *rude, impolite*
abrupt, bad-mannered, boorish, brusque, cavalier, cheeky*, churlish, contumelious, crude, crusty*, curt, disrespectful, flip, fresh, ill-bred, ill-mannered, impertinent, inaffable, indelicate, insolent, inurbane, oafish, offhand, rusit, sassy, smart-alecky*, uncivil, uncouth, ungenteel, ungracious, unmannerly, unrefined; SEE CONCEPT *401*

discover [*v*] *find, uncover*
ascertain, bring to light, catch, come across, come upon, conceive, contrive, debunk, design, detect, determine, devise, dig up, discern, disclose, distinguish, elicit, espy, explore, ferret out*, get wind of*, get wise to*, glimpse, hear, identify, invent, learn, light upon, locate, look up, nose out*, notice, observe, originate, perceive, pick up on*, pioneer, realize, recognize, reveal, see, sense, smoke out*, spot, think of, turn up, unearth; SEE CONCEPTS *31,183*

discovery [*n1*] *finding, uncovering*
analysis, ascertainment, authentication, calculation, certification, detection, determination, diagnosis, discernment, disclosure, distinguishing, empiricism, encounter, espial, experimentation, exploration, exposition, exposure, feeling, hearing, identification, introduction, invention, learning, locating, location, origination, perception, revelation, sensing, sighting, strike, unearthing, verification; SEE CONCEPTS *31,183*

discovery [*n2*] *treasure; invention*
algorithm, bonanza*, breakthrough, conclusion,

contrivance, coup, data, design, device, find, finding, formula, godsend*, innovation, law, luck, luck out*, machine, method, principle, process, result, secret, theorem, way; SEE CONCEPTS *260,532*

discredit [*v1*] *blame, detract from*
blow up*, bring into disrepute, bring to naught, censure, defame, degrade, destroy, disconsider, disesteem, disfavor, disgrace, dishonor, disparage, disprove, explode, expose, frown upon*, knock bottom out of*, mudsling*, poke full of holes*, pooh-pooh*, puncture, put down, reflect on, reproach, ruin, run down, shoot, show up, slander, slur, smear, take rug out from under*, tear down*, vilify; SEE CONCEPTS *44,54*

discredit [*v2*] *doubt, question*
challenge, deny, disbelieve, discount, dispute, distrust, mistrust, put under suspicion, reject, scoff at; SEE CONCEPT *21*

discreet [*adj*] *cautious, sensible*
alert, attentive, awake, cagey, calculating, careful, chary, circumspect, civil, conservative, considerate, controlled, diplomatic, discerning, discriminating, gingerly, guarded, having foresight, heedful, intelligent, judicious, like a clam*, moderate, noncommittal, not rash, observant, on lookout*, politic, precautious, prudent, reasonable, reserved, restrained, safe, sagacious, strategic, tactful, temperate, thoughtful, vigilant, wary, watchful, wise, worldly-wise; SEE CONCEPT *401*

discrepancy [*n*] *conflict, disagreement*
alterity, contrariety, difference, discordance, disparity, dissemblance, dissimilarity, dissimilitude, dissonance, distinction, divergence, divergency, error, far cry*, incongruity, inconsistency, miscalculation, otherness, split, unlikeness, variance, variation; SEE CONCEPT *665*

discrepant [*adj*] *disagreeing*
at variance, conflicting, contradictory, contrary, different, differing, disconsonant, discordant, disparate, dissonant, divergent, diverse, incompatible, incongruent, incongruous, inconsistent, inconsonant, unmixable, varying; SEE CONCEPT *564*

discrete [*adj*] *individual*
detached, different, disconnected, discontinuous, distinct, diverse, separate, several, unattached, various; SEE CONCEPT *564*

discretion [*n*] *caution, judgment*
acumen, attention, calculation, canniness, care, carefulness, chariness, circumspection, concern, considerateness, consideration, deliberation, diplomacy, discernment, discrimination, foresight, forethought, good sense, gumption, heed, heedfulness, judiciousness, maturity, observation, perspicacity, precaution, presence of mind, providence, prudence, responsibility, sagacity, sense, shrewdness, solicitude, tact, thoughtfulness, vigilance, wariness, warning, watchfulness, wisdom; SEE CONCEPT *657*

discretionary [*adj*] *open to choice*
at the call*, elective, facultative, judge and jury, leftover, nonmandatory, nonobligatory, open, optional, unrestricted; SEE CONCEPT *546*

discriminate [*v1*] *show prejudice*
be bigot, be partial, contradistinguish, disfavor, favor, hate, incline, judge, segregate, separate, set apart, show bias, single out, treat as inferior, treat differently, victimize; SEE CONCEPTS *32,384*

di
di

discriminate [v2] *differentiate, distinguish*
assess, collate, compare, contradistinguish, contrast, difference, discern, discrepate, evaluate, extricate, judge, know, know what's what*, make out*, note, perceive, remark, segregate, separate, sever, severalize, sift, specify, split hairs*, tell apart, tell the difference; SEE CONCEPTS 15,38

discriminating [adj] *critical*
acute, astute, careful, choicy, choosy, cultivated, discerning, distinctive, eclectic, fastidious, finical, finicky, fussy, individualizing, judicious, keen, opinionated, particular, persnickety*, picky, prudent, refined, select, selective, sensitive, tasteful, wise; SEE CONCEPTS 404,542

discrimination [n1] *bias*
bigotry, favoritism, hatred, inequity, injustice, intolerance, partiality, prejudice, unfairness, wrong; SEE CONCEPTS 29,689

discrimination [n2] *particularity in taste*
acumen, acuteness, astucity, astuteness, bias, clearness, decision, difference, differentiation, discernment, distinction, judgment, keenness, penetration, perception, percipience, perspicacity, preference, refinement, sagacity, sense, separation, shrewdness, subtlety, taste, understanding; SEE CONCEPTS 32,410,655

discuss [v] *talk over with another*
altercate, argue, bounce off*, canvass, compare notes, confabulate, confer, consider, consult with, contend, contest, converse, debate, deliberate, descant, discept, discourse about, dispute, dissert, dissertate, examine, exchange views on*, explain, figure, get together, go into, groupthink*, hash over*, hold forth, jaw*, kick about*, knock around*, moot, put heads together*, reason about, review, sift, take up, thrash out*, toss around*, ventilate, weigh; SEE CONCEPT 56

discussion [n] *talk with another*
altercation, analysis, argument, argumentation, canvass, colloquy, confabulation, conference, consideration, consultation, contention, controversy, conversation, debate, deliberation, dialogue, discourse, disputation, dispute, dissertation, examination, exchange, excursus, groupthink*, huddle, interview, meet, meeting, powwow*, quarrel, review, scrutiny, symposium, ventilation, wrangling; SEE CONCEPT 56

disdain [n] *hate; indifference*
antipathy, arrogance, aversion, contempt, contumely, derision, despisal, despisement, despite, dislike, disparagement, hatred, haughtiness, hauteur, insolence, loftiness, pride, ridicule, scorn, sneering, snobbishness, superbity, superciliousness; SEE CONCEPT 29

disdain [v] *scorn*
abhor, be allergic to*, belittle, chill, contemn, deride, despise, disregard, hate, ignore, look down nose at*, look down on, misprize, pooh-pooh*, put down*, refuse, reject, scout, slight, sneer at, spurn, undervalue; SEE CONCEPTS 29,30

disdainful [adj] *scornful*
aloof, antipathetic, arrogant, averse, cavalier, contemning, contemptuous, cool, derisive, despising, egotistic, haughty, high-and-mighty*, hoity-toity*, indifferent, insolent, lordly, overbearing, proud, rejecting, repudiating, scouting, sneering, snooty*, supercilious, superior, toplofty, unsympathetic, uppity*; SEE CONCEPT 401

disease [n] *ailment, affliction*
ache, affection, attack, blight, breakdown, bug*,

cancer, canker, collapse, complaint, condition, contagion, contamination, convulsions, debility, decrepitude, defect, disorder, distemper, endemic, epidemic, feebleness, fever, fit, flu, hemorrhage, ill health, illness, indisposition, infection, infirmity, inflammation, malady, misery, pathosis, plague, seizure, sickliness, sickness, spell, stroke, syndrome, temperature, unhealthiness, unsoundness, upset, virus, visitation; SEE CONCEPT 306

diseased [adj] *unhealthy*
afflicted, ailing, indisposed, infected, infectious, infirm, rotten, sick, sickly, tainted, unsound, unwell, unwholesome; SEE CONCEPT 314

disembark [v] *get off transportation*
alight, anchor, arrive, come ashore, debark, deplane, detrain, dismount, go ashore, land, put in, step out of; SEE CONCEPT 159

disenchanted [adj] *let down*
blasé, cynical, disappointed, disenthralled, disentranced, disillusioned, embittered, indifferent, jaundiced, knowing, mondaine, out of love, sick of, sophisticate, sophisticated, soured, undeceived, worldly, worldly-wise; SEE CONCEPT 403

disengage [v] *free from connection*
abstract, back off, back out, cut loose, cut out, detach, disassociate, disconnect, disentangle, disjoin, dissociate, disunite, divide, drop out, ease, extricate, liberate, loose, loosen, opt out, pull the plug, release, separate, set free, unbind, uncouple, undo, unfasten, unfix, unloose, untie, weasel out*, withdraw; SEE CONCEPT 135

disentangle [v] *unwind, disconnect; solve*
bail one out*, clear up, detach, discumber, disembroil, disencumber, disengage, disinvolve, emancipate, expand, extricate, free, let go, let off, loose, open, part, resolve, separate, sever, simplify, sort out, sunder, unbraid, undo, unfold, unravel, unscramble, unsnarl, untangle, untie, untwine, untwist, work out; SEE CONCEPTS 127,135

disfavor [n] *dislike; disgrace*
aversion, disapprobation, disapproval, discredit, disesteem, dishonor, disinclination, displeasure, disregard, disrepute, disrespect, dissatisfaction, distaste, distrust, doghouse*, indisposition, mistrust, shame, thumbs down*, unpopularity; SEE CONCEPTS 29,388

disfigure [v] *make ugly*
blemish, damage, deface, defile, deform, disfashion, disfeature, distort, hurt, injure, maim, mangle, mar, mutilate, scar; SEE CONCEPTS 137,246,250

disgrace [n] *state of shame; bad reputation*
abasement, abuse, baseness, black eye*, blemish, blur, brand, comedown, contempt, contumely, corruption, culpability, debasement, debasing, defamation, degradation, derision, disbarment, discredit, disesteem, disfavor, dishonor, disrepute, disrespect, humbling, humiliation, ignominy, ill repute, infamy, ingloriousness, meanness, obloquy, odium, opprobrium, pollution, prostitution, put-down, reproach, scandal, scorn, slander, slight, slur, spot, stain, stigma, taint, tarnish, turpitude, venality; SEE CONCEPT 388

disgrace [v] *bring shame upon*
abase, attaint, besmirch, blot, debase, defame, defile, degrade, depress, deride, derogate, desecrate, discredit, disfavor, dishonor, disparage, disregard, disrespect, expel, give a black eye*, hum-

ble, humiliate, libel, lose face*, lower, mock, put down, reduce, reproach, ridicule, slander, slur, snub, stain, stigmatize, sully, taint, take down a peg*, tar and feather*, tarnish; SEE CONCEPTS 14,54,384

disgraceful [adj] shameful, low
blameworthy, contemptible, degrading, detestable, discreditable, dishonorable, disreputable, ignoble, ignominious, infamous, inglorious, mean, offensive, opprobrious, scandalous, shabby, shady, shocking, shoddy, unrespectable, unworthy; SEE CONCEPT 555

disgruntled [adj] unhappy; critical
annoyed, bad tempered, bellyaching*, crabbing*, crabby, cranky, disappointed, discontent, discontented, displeased, dissatisfied, griping, grouchy, grousing, grumpy, irritable, irritated, kicking, kvetching*, malcontent, malcontented, peeved, peevish, petulant, put out, sulky, sullen, testy, uncontent, ungratified, vexed; SEE CONCEPTS 401,403

disguise [n] covering, makeup for deception
beard, blind, camouflage, charade, cloak, color, coloring, concealment, costume, counterfeit, cover-up, dissimulation, dress, facade, face, faking, false front*, fig leaf*, front*, get-up, guise, illusion, make-believe, mask, masquerade, pageant, pen name, pretense, pretension, pretentiousness, pseudonym, put-on, red herring*, screen, semblance, smoke screen*, trickery, veil, veneer; SEE CONCEPTS 446,451,680

disguise [v] mask; misrepresent
affect, alter, antique, assume, beard, belie, camouflage, change, cloak, color, conceal, counterfeit, cover, cover up, deceive, dissemble, dissimulate, doctor up*, dress up, fake, falsify, feign, front, fudge*, garble, gloss over, hide, make like, make up, masquerade, muffle, obfuscate, obscure, pretend, put on a false front*, put on a front*, put on an act*, put up a front*, redo*, screen, secrete, sham, shroud, simulate, touch up, varnish, veil, wear cheaters*, whitewash*; SEE CONCEPTS 59,137,172,188,202

disguised [adj] unrecognizable
camouflaged, changed, cloaked, covered, covert, fake, false, feigned, hidden, incog, masked, pretend, undercover; SEE CONCEPTS 547,619

disgust [n] aversion; repulsion
abhorrence, abomination, antipathy, detestation, dislike, distaste, hatefulness, hatred, loathing, nausea, nauseation, nauseousness, objection, repugnance, revolt, revulsion, satiation, satiety, sickness, surfeit; SEE CONCEPTS 410,720

disgust [v] cause aversion; repel
abominate, be repulsive, bother, cloy on, disenchant, displease, disturb, fill with loathing, gross out*, insult, irk, make one sick*, nauseate, offend, offend morals of, outrage, pall, pique, put off, reluct, repulse, revolt, scandalize, shock, sicken, surfeit, turn off, turn one's stomach*, upset; SEE CONCEPTS 7,19

disgusted [adj] sickened; offended
abhorred, appalled, displeased, fastidious, fed up*, full up*, grossed out*, had bellyful*, had enough*, had it*, nauseated, nauseous, outraged, overwrought, queasy, repelled, repulsed, revolted, satiated, scandalized, sick, sick and tired of*, sick of*, squeamish, teed off*, tired, turned off*, unhappy, up to here*, weary; SEE CONCEPT 403

disgusting [adj] sickening; repulsive
abominable, awful, beastly, cloying, creepy, detestable, distasteful, foul, frightful, ghastly, grody*, gross*, gruesome, hateful, hideous, horrid, horrific, icky*, loathsome, lousy, macabre, monstrous, nasty, nauseating, nerdy*, noisome, objectionable, obnoxious, odious, offensive, outrageous, repellent, repugnant, revolting, rotten, satiating, scandalous, scuzzy*, shameless, shocking, sleazeball*, sleazy*, stinking, surfeiting, vile, vulgar, yecchy*, yucky*; SEE CONCEPTS 485,548

dish [n1] eating receptacle
bowl, casserole, ceramic, china, container, cup, mug, pitcher, plate, platter, porringer, pot, pottery, salver, saucer, tray, vessel; SEE CONCEPT 494

dish [n2] main part of meal
course, eats*, entrée, fare, food, helping, recipe, serving; SEE CONCEPTS 457,460,461

disharmony [n] conflict, discord
clash, contention, difference, disaccord, dissension, dissonance, dissonancy, friction, inharmoniousness, strife, variance; SEE CONCEPTS 388,665

dishearten [v] depress, ruin one's hopes
cast down, chill*, crush, damp, dampen, dash, daunt, deject, demoralize, deter, discourage, disincline, dismay, disparage, dispirit, get down*, humble, humiliate, indispose, put a damper on*, put down, shake, throw a pall over*; SEE CONCEPTS 7,19

disheveled [adj] wrinkled, unkempt in appearance
bagged out*, beat up*, bedraggled, blowzy*, dirty, disarranged, disarrayed, disordered, frowzy*, grubby*, messed up, messy, mussed up*, mussy, ruffled, rumpled, scuzzy, slipshod, sloppy, slovenly, tousled, unbuttoned, uncombed, unfastidious, untidy, unzipped*; SEE CONCEPTS 485,579

dishonest [adj] lying, untruthful
backbiting*, bent, bluffing, cheating, corrupt, crafty, crooked, cunning, deceitful, deceiving, deceptive, designing, disreputable, double-crossing, double-dealing, elusive, false, fraudulent, guileful, hoodwinking*, mendacious, misleading, perfidious, recreant, shady, shifty, sinister, slippery*, sneaking, sneaky, swindling, traitorous, treacherous, tricky, two-faced*, two-timing*, unctuous, underhanded, unfair, unprincipled, unscrupulous, untrustworthy, villainous, wily; SEE CONCEPT 267

dishonesty [n] lying; unwillingness to tell the truth
artifice, bunk, cheating, chicane, chicanery, corruption, craft, criminality, crookedness, cunning, deceit, double-dealing, duplicity, faithlessness, falsehood, falsity, flimflam*, fourberie, fraud, fraudulence, graft, guile, hanky-panky*, hocus-pocus*, improbity, infamy, infidelity, insidiousness, mendacity, perfidiousness, perfidy, racket, rascality, sharp practice*, slyness, stealing, swindle, treachery, trickery, trickiness, unscrupulousness, wiliness; SEE CONCEPTS 59,633,657

dishonor [n] state of shame
abasement, abuse, affront, blame, degradation, discourtesy, discredit, disesteem, disfavor, disgrace, disrepute, ignominy, indignity, infamy, insult, obloquy, odium, offense, opprobrium, outrage, reproach, scandal, slight; SEE CONCEPT 388

dishonor [v] shame, degrade
abase, attaint, blot, corrupt, debase, debauch, de-

di
di

fame, defile, disconsider, discredit, disgrace, disoblige, give a black eye*, libel, make lose face*,
reflect on, slander, sully; SEE CONCEPT 54

dishonorable [adj] shameful, corrupt
base, blackguardly, contemptible, crooked, deceitful, despicable, devious, discreditable, disgraceful, disreputable, fraudulent, ignoble,
ignominious, infamous, inglorious, low, miscreant, offensive, opprobrious, putrid, scandalous,
shabby, shady, treacherous, unprincipled, unrespectable, unscrupulous, untrustworthy; SEE CON-
CEPT 555

dish out [v] distribute
allocate, deliver, dispense, dole out*, fork over*,
furnish, give out, hand, hand out, hand over, inflict, ladle, mete out, present, produce, scoop,
serve, serve up, spoon, supply, transfer, turn over;
SEE CONCEPT 140

disillusioned [adj] disappointed
blasé, broken, brought down to earth*, debunked,
disabused, disenchanted, disenthralled, disentranced, embittered, enlightened, freed, indifferent, knowing, let-down, mondaine, out of love*,
punctured, sadder and wiser*, shattered, sophisticated, undeceived, worldly, worldly-wise*; SEE
CONCEPT 403

disinclination [n] unwillingness to do or believe
something
alienation, antipathy, aversion, demur, disfavor,
dislike, disliking, displeasure, disrelish, dissatisfaction, distaste, hatred, hesitance, indisposition,
lack of desire, lack of enthusiasm, loathness, objection, opposition, reluctance, repugnance, resistance; SEE CONCEPTS 29,410,657

disinclined [adj] unwilling
afraid, antipathetic, averse, backward, balking,
doubtful, dubious, hesitating, indisposed, loath,
not in the mood*, objecting, opposed, protesting,
reluctant, resistant, shy, shying, slow, sticking,
uneager, unsympathetic; SEE CONCEPTS 403,542

disinfect [v] make clean, pure
antisepticize, cleanse, decontaminate, deodorize,
fumigate, purify, sanitize, sterilize; SEE CONCEPT
165

disingenuous [adj] insincere
artful, crooked, cunning, deceitful, designing, dishonest, duplicitous, false, feigned, foxy, guileful,
indirect, insidious, mendacious, oblique, shifty*,
sly, tricky, two-faced*, uncandid, underhanded,
unfair, unfrank, wily; SEE CONCEPTS 401,542

disinherit [v] cut off in will of bequeathal
bereave, cut off without a cent*, deprive, disaffiliate, disown, dispossess, divest, evict, exclude,
exheridate, neglect, oust, repudiate, rob; SEE
CONCEPTS 25,317

disintegrate [v] fall apart; reduce to pieces
atomize, break apart, break down, break up, come
apart, crumble, decay, decline, decompose, degenerate, deliquesce, descend, detach, dilapidate,
disband, disconnect, disimprove, dismantle, disorganize, disperse, disunite, divide, fade away,
fall to pieces*, molder, pulverize, putrefy, rot,
separate, sever, shatter, sink, splinter, spoil, taint,
take apart, turn, turn to dust*, wash away, wash
out, wither, worsen; SEE CONCEPTS 252,469

disinterested [adj] detached, uninvolved
aloof, candid, casual, dispassionate, equitable,
even-handed, impartial, impersonal, incurious, indifferent, just watching the clock*, lackadaisical,
negative, neutral, nonpartisan, not giving a

damn*, outside, perfunctory, remote, unbiased,
unconcerned, uncurious, unprejudiced, unselfish,
withdrawn; SEE CONCEPTS 401,403

disjointed [adj] loose, disconnected
aimless, confused, cool, discontinuous, disordered, displaced, disunited, divided, far-out, fitful, fuzzy, inchoate, incoherent, incohesive,
irrational, jumbled, muddled, out-of-it*, out-to-
lunch*, rambling, separated, spaced-out*,
spacey*, spasmodic, split, unattached, unconnected, unorganized; SEE CONCEPTS 267,482,585

disk [n] round object
circle, disc, discoid, discoidal, discus, dish, flan,
plate, platter, quoit, sabot, saucer, shell; SEE CON-
CEPT 436

dislike [n] antagonism, hatred toward something
animosity, animus, antipathy, aversion, deprecation, detestation, disapprobation, disapproval, disesteem, disfavor, disgust, disinclination,
displeasure, dissatisfaction, distaste, enmity, hostility, indisposition, loathing, objection, offense,
opposition, prejudice, repugnance; SEE CONCEPT
29

dislike [v] be antagonistic toward something; hate
abhor, abominate, antipathize, avoid, be allergic
to*, bear malice toward, be averse to, be turned
off to*, condemn, contemn, deplore, despise, detest, disapprove, disesteem, disfavor, disrelish,
eschew, execrate, grossed out on*, have hard feelings*, have no stomach for*, have no taste for,
loathe, look down on, lose interest in, make faces
at*, mind, not appreciate, not care for, not endure, not feel like, not take kindly to, object to,
regret, resent, scorn, shudder at, shun; SEE CON-
CEPT 29

dislocate [v] displace
break, disarticulate, disconnect, disengage, disjoint, disorder, disrupt, disturb, disunite, divide,
jumble, misplace, mix up, move, put out of joint,
remove, rummage, separate, shift, transfer, unhinge, upset; SEE CONCEPTS 135,147,213

dislocation [n] displacement
break, confusion, disarray, disarticulation, disconnection, discontinuity, disengagement, disorder,
disorganization, disruption, disturbance, division,
luxation, misplacement, unhinging; SEE CON-
CEPTS 316,720,727

dislodge [v] knock loose
dig out, disentangle, dislocate, displace, disturb,
eject, evict, extricate, force out, oust, remove,
uproot; SEE CONCEPTS 147,213

disloyal [adj] unfaithful
alienated, apostate, cheating, disaffected, double-
crossing, estranged, faithless, false, perfidious,
recreant, seditious, snaky*, subversive, traitorous,
treacherous, treasonable, two-faced*, two-
timing*, unloyal, unpatriotic, untrue, untrustworthy, wormlike*; SEE CONCEPT 401

disloyalty [n] unfaithfulness
apostasy, bad faith, betrayal of trust, breach of
trust, breaking of faith, deceitfulness, disaffection,
double-dealing, faithlessness, falseness, falsity,
inconstancy, infidelity, perfidiousness, perfidy,
recreancy, sedition, seditiousness, subversive activity, treachery, treason, untrueness, violation;
SEE CONCEPT 633

dismal [adj] bleak, dreary, gloomy
afflictive, black, boring, cheerless, cloudy, dark,
depressed, depressing, desolate, despondent, dim,
dingy, disagreeable, discouraging, disheartening,

dispiriting, doleful, dolorous, dull, forlorn, frowning, funereal, ghastly, gruesome, hopeless, horrible, horrid, inauspicious, in the pits*, joyless, lonesome, lowering, lugubrious, melancholy, miserable, monotonous, morbid, murky, oppressive, overcast, sad, shadowy, somber, sorrowful, tedious, tenebrous, troublesome, unfortunate, unhappy; SEE CONCEPTS **525,536,548**

dismantle [v] *take apart*
annihilate, bankrupt, bare, break down, break up, decimate, demolish, denudate, denude, deprive, destroy, disassemble, dismember, dismount, disrobe, divest, fell, knock down, level, part out, pull down, raze, ruin, strike, strip, subvert, take down, take to pieces, tear down, undo, unrig, wrack, wreck; SEE CONCEPTS **135,168,252**

dismay [n] *disappointed feeling; distress*
agitation, alarm, anxiety, apprehension, blue funk*, blues*, bummer*, chagrin, cold feet*, consternation, discouragement, disheartenment, disillusionment, downer*, dread, dumps*, fear, fright, funk*, hassle, horror, letdown, panic, terror, the blahs*, trepidation, upset; SEE CONCEPTS **27,410,690**

dismay [v] *disappoint, fill with consternation*
abash, affright, agitate, alarm, appall, bewilder, bother, chill, confound, daunt, discomfit, discompose, disconcert, discourage, dishearten, disillusion, dispirit, disquiet, distress, disturb, dumbfound, embarrass, faze, flummox*, fluster, foul up*, frighten, get to, horrify, louse up*, mess up*, muck up*, mystify, nonplus, paralyze, perplex, put off, puzzle, rattle, scare, screw up*, shake, snafu*, take aback, terrify, terrorize, throw, throw into a tizzy*, unhinge*, unnerve, upset; SEE CONCEPTS **7,19**

dismember [v] *cut into pieces*
amputate, anatomize, cripple, disassemble, disjoint, dislimb, dislocate, dismantle, dismount, dissect, divide, maim, mutilate, part, rend, sever, sunder, take down; SEE CONCEPTS **98,135,176**

dismiss [v1] *send away, remove; free*
abolish, banish, boot*, brush off*, bundle, cast off*, cast out*, chase, chuck, clear, decline, deport, detach, disband, discard, dispatch, dispense with, disperse, dispose of, dissolve, divorce, do without, drive out, eject, expel, force out, have done with*, kick out, let go, let out, lock out*, outlaw, push aside, push back, reject, release, relegate, relinquish, repel, repudiate, rid, send off, send packing*, shed, show out*, slough off, supersede, sweep away*, turn out; SEE CONCEPTS **127,217**

dismiss [v2] *remove from job, responsibility*
ax*, boot*, boot out*, bounce*, bump*, can*, cashier*, defrock, depone, depose, deselect, discharge, disemploy, disfrock, displace, disqualify, drop, fire, furlough, give notice to, give the ax*, give the gate*, give the heave-ho*, give walking papers*, give warning, impeach, kick out*, lay off, let go*, let out*, oust, pension, pink-slip*, put away*, recall, retire, sack*, send packing*, shelve*, shut out*, suspend, terminate, turn away, unfrock, unseat, wash out*; SEE CONCEPTS **324,351**

dismiss [v3] *put out of one's mind*
banish, contemn, deride, despise, disdain, dispel, disregard, drop, flout, gibe, gird, jeer, kiss off*, laugh away*, lay aside, mock, pooh-pooh*, rally, reject, relegate, repudiate, repulse, ridicule, scoff, scorn, scout, set aside, shelve*, spurn, taunt, twit; SEE CONCEPT **35**

dismissal [n] *release*
adjournment, banishment, bounce, brush-off*, cold shoulder*, congé, deportation, deposal, deposition, discharge, dislodgment, displacement, dispossession, dissolution, door*, end, eviction, exile, exorcism, expatriation, expulsion, freedom, freeing, housecleaning*, kiss-off*, layoff, liberation, marching orders*, notice, old heave-ho*, ostracism, ouster, permission, pink slip*, relegation, removal, suspension; SEE CONCEPTS **127,217,351**

dismount [v] *get off something higher*
alight, debark, deplane, descend, detrain, disembark, get down, light; SEE CONCEPT **195**

disobedience [n] *misbehavior; noncompliance with rules*
defiance, dereliction, disregard, indiscipline, infraction, infringement, insubmission, insubordination, insurgence, intractableness, mutiny, neglect, nonobservance, perversity, rebellion, recalcitrance, refractoriness, revolt, revolution, riot, sabotage, sedition, strike, stubbornness, transgression, unruliness, violation, waywardness; SEE CONCEPT **633**

disobedient [adj] *defiant, mischievous*
contrary, contumacious, disorderly, fractious, froward, headstrong, insubordinate, intractable, naughty, noncompliant, nonobservant, obstreperous, perverse, recalcitrant, refractory, resistive, uncompliant, undisciplined, unruly, wayward, willful; SEE CONCEPT **401**

disobey [v] *disregard rules; refuse to conform*
balk, be remiss, break rules, contravene, counteract, dare, decline, defy, desert, differ, disagree, evade, flout, fly in face of*, go counter to, ignore, infringe, insurrect, misbehave, mutiny, neglect, not heed, not listen, not mind, object, overstep, pay no attention to, rebel, recalcitrate, resist, revolt, revolution, revolutionize, riot, rise in arms*, run riot*, set aside, shirk, strike, take law into own hands*, transgress, violate, withstand; SEE CONCEPTS **30,192,384**

disoblige [v] *displease, annoy*
affront, bother, discommode, disturb, incommode, inconvenience, insult, offend, put about, put out, slight, trouble, upset, vex; SEE CONCEPTS **7,19**

disobliging [adj] *rude, annoying*
awkward, disagreeable, discourteous, ill-disposed, ill-natured, unaccommodating, unamiable, uncivil, uncongenial, uncooperative, unhelpful, unpleasant; SEE CONCEPT **401**

disorder [n1] *chaos, clutter*
anarchy, ataxia, confusion, derangement, disarrangement, disarray, discombobulation, disorderliness, disorganization, huddle, irregularity, jumble, mess, muddle, rat's nest*, shambles, snarl, topsy-turviness*, untidiness; SEE CONCEPT **230**

disorder [n2] *social commotion; mental confusion*
agitation, anarchism, anarchy, brawl, bustle, chaos, clamor, complication, convulsion, discombobulation*, discord, disorganization, distemper, disturbance, dither, entanglement, fight, flap, fracas, fuss, hubbub, hullabaloo*, imbroglio, insurrection, lawlessness, mayhem, misrule, mob rule*, quarrel, rebellion, reign of terror*, revolution, riot, rioting, ruckus, rumpus, static, strike, terrorism, tizzy*, trouble, tumult, turbulence, tur-

moil, unrest, unruliness, uproar; SEE CONCEPTS 388,410

disorder [n3] *illness*
affliction, ailment, cachexia, complaint, disease, diseasedness, indisposition, infirmity, malady, sickness, unhealth, upset; SEE CONCEPT 306

disorder [v] *mix up, disarrange*
clutter, confound, confuse, derange, discompose, discreate, dishevel, disjoint, dislocate, disorganize, disrupt, distemper, disturb, embroil, jumble, mess up, muddle, muss up*, rummage, rumple, scatter, shuffle, tumble, unsettle, upset; SEE CONCEPTS 240,250

disordered [adj] *in a mess*
all over the place*, confused, deranged, disarranged, discombobulated, disconnected, discontinuous, disjointed, dislocated, disorganized, displaced, incoherent, in confusion, jumbled, mislaid, misplaced, molested, moved, muddled, out-of-place, removed, roiled, ruffled, rumpled, shifted, shuffled, stirred up, tampered-with, tangled, tossed, tousled, tumbled, unsettled, untidy; SEE CONCEPTS 485,535

disorderly [adj1] *messy, untidy*
all over the place*, chaotic, cluttered, confused, dislocated, disorganized, heterogeneous, indiscriminate, irregular, jumbled, mixed up, out-of-control*, out-of-line*, out-of-step*, out-of-whack*, scattered, scrambled, slovenly, topsy-turvy*, tumult, uncombed, undisciplined, unkempt, unmethodical, unrestrained, unsystematic, untrained; SEE CONCEPTS 485,535

disorderly [adj2] *causing trouble; unlawful*
boisterous, disobedient, disruptive, drunk, fractious, indisciplined, intemperate, noisy, obstreperous, off-base*, on-a-tear*, out-of-line*, out-of-order*, raucous, rebellious, refractory, riotous, rowdy, stormy, termagant, tumultuous/tumultous, turbulent, uncompliant, uncontrollable, ungovernable, unmanageable, unruly, wayward; SEE CONCEPTS 401,545

disorganization [n] *unordered situation or thing*
anarchy, chaos, confusion, derangement, disarray, disjointedness, disorder, disruption, dissolution, disunion, foul-up*, incoherence, mix-up, rat's nest*, screw-up*, unconnectedness, unholy mess*; SEE CONCEPTS 674,727

disorganize [v] *disrupt arrangement; make shambles of*
break down, break up, clutter, complicate, confound, confuse, demobilize, derange, destroy, disarrange, disarray, disband, discompose, discreate, dishevel, dislocate, disorder, disperse, disturb, embroil, jumble, litter, mess up, mislay, misplace, muddle, perturb, put out of order, scatter, scramble, shuffle, toss, turn topsy-turvy, unsettle, upset; SEE CONCEPTS 250,252,384

disorganized [adj] *unmethodical; messed up*
chaotic, confused, disordered, disorderly, haphazard, jumbled, mixed up, muddled, screwed up*, shuffled, unsystematic; SEE CONCEPTS 485,585

disoriented [adj] *confused, unstable*
adrift, all at sea*, astray, bewildered, discombobulated, lost, mixed-up, not adjusted, off-beam*, off-course, out-of-joint*, perplexed, unbalanced, unhinged, unsettled; SEE CONCEPT 403

disown [v] *refuse to acknowledge*
abandon, abjure, abnegate, cast off, deny, disacknowledge, disallow, disavow, discard, disclaim, divorce oneself from, refuse to recognize, reject,

renounce, repudiate, retract; SEE CONCEPTS 50,54,88

disparage [v] *criticize; detract from*
abuse, belittle, chill*, cry down, decry, defame, degrade, deject, demoralize, denigrate, deprecate, depreciate, deride, derogate, dis*, discourage, discredit, disdain, dishearten, dismiss, dispirit, dispraise, downcry, dump on*, lower, malign, minimize, pan*, put down, put hooks in*, rap*, ridicule, roast*, run down*, scorch, scorn, slam*, slander, smear*, sour grapes*, tear down, traduce, underestimate, underrate, undervalue, vilify, write off; SEE CONCEPTS 7,19,52,54

disparagement [n] *strong criticism; detraction*
aspersion, backbiting*, backstabbing*, belittlement, blame, calumny, censure, condemnation, contempt, contumely, debasement, degradation, denunciation, depreciation, derision, derogation, discredit, disdain, impairment, lessening, lie, prejudice, reproach, ridicule, scandal, scorn, slander, tale, underestimation; SEE CONCEPTS 52,54

disparate [adj] *at odds, different*
at variance, contrary, contrasting, discordant, discrepant, dissimilar, distant, distinct, divergent, diverse, far cry, incommensurate, incompatible, inconsistent, inconsonant, like night and day*, poles apart, separate, unalike, unequal, unequivalent, uneven, unlike, unsimilar, various; SEE CONCEPT 564

disparity [n] *difference*
alterity, discrepancy, disproportion, dissemblance, dissimilarity, dissimilitude, distinction, divergence, divergency, diverseness, gap, imbalance, imparity, incongruity, inequality, otherness, unevenness, unlikeness, variation; SEE CONCEPT 665

dispassionate [adj] *unfeeling, impartial*
abstract, aloof, calm, candid, cold-blooded, coldfish*, collected, composed, cool, cool cat*, couldn't care less*, detached, disinterested, fair, iceberg*, impersonal, imperturbable, indifferent, judicial, just, laid back, neutral, nondiscriminatory, nonpartisan, objective, pokerfaced*, quiet, serene, sober, temperate, tough, unbiased, unemotional, unexcitable, unexcited, unflappable, uninvolved, unmoved, unprejudiced, unruffled; SEE CONCEPTS 401,404

dispatch [n1] *speed in carrying out action*
alacrity, celerity, expedition, expeditiousness, haste, hurry, hustle, precipitateness, promptitude, promptness, quickness, rapidity, rustle, speediness, swiftness; SEE CONCEPTS 755,818

dispatch [n2] *communication*
account, bulletin, communiqué, document, instruction, item, letter, message, missive, news, piece, report, story; SEE CONCEPTS 271,277,278

dispatch [v1] *hurry, send fast*
accelerate, address, consign, dismiss, express, forward, hand-carry, hasten, issue, quicken, railroad*, remit, route, run with, run with ball*, ship, speed, transmit, walk through; SEE CONCEPTS 152,217

dispatch [v2] *finish; consume*
conclude, devour, discharge, dispose of, eat up, expedite, lay low, perform, polish off*, scarf down*, settle; SEE CONCEPTS 169,234

dispatch [v3] *kill*
assassinate, bump off*, butcher*, destroy, eliminate, execute, finish, finish off*, murder, put

away*, put end to, slaughter, slay, take out*; SEE CONCEPTS **238,252**

dispel [v] *drive away thought, belief*
allay, banish, beat off*, break it up*, break up*, bust up*, cancel, chase away, crumble, deploy, disband, disintegrate, dismiss, disperse, dissipate, distribute, eject, eliminate, expel, oust, repel, resolve, rout, scatter, scramble, split up*; SEE CONCEPTS **14,35**

dispensable [adj] *not necessary; able to be thrown away*
disposable, excessive, expendable, minor, needless, nonessential, removable, superfluous, trivial, unimportant, unnecessary, unrequired, useless; SEE CONCEPT **546**

dispensation [n1] *allocation of supply*
allotment, appointment, apportionment, award, bestowal, conferment, consignment, courtesy, dealing out, disbursement, distribution, dole, endowment, favor, indulgence, kindness, part, portion, quota, service, share; SEE CONCEPTS **140,337**

dispensation [n2] *management*
administration, direction, economy, plan, regulation, scheme, stewardship, system; SEE CONCEPTS **325,660,770**

dispensation [n3] *permission*
exception, exemption, immunity, indulgence, license, privilege, relaxation, relief, remission, reprieve; SEE CONCEPT **685**

dispense [v1] *dole out supply*
allocate, allot, apportion, assign, come across with, deal, deal out, disburse, dish out*, distribute, divide, divvy*, fork out*, furnish, give, give away, give with, hand out, hand over, lot, measure, mete out, partition, portion, prepare, prorate, share, shell out*; SEE CONCEPT **140**

dispense [v2] *operate, administer*
apply, carry out, command, direct, discharge, enforce, execute, handle, implement, manage, maneuver, manipulate, swing, undertake, wield; SEE CONCEPT **117**

dispense [v3] *exempt from responsibility*
absolve, discharge, except, excuse, exonerate, let off, privilege from, release, relieve, reprieve, spare; SEE CONCEPT **110**

dispense with [v] *omit; do away with*
abolish, abstain from, brush aside, cancel, dispose of, disregard, do without, forgo, get rid of, give up, ignore, pass over, relinquish, render needless, shake off, waive; SEE CONCEPT **30**

disperse [v] *distribute; scatter*
banish, besprinkle, break up, broadcast, cast forth, circulate, deal, diffuse, disappear, disband, disburse, discharge, dislodge, dismiss, dispel, disseminate, dissipate, dissolve, divvy*, dole out, eject, intersperse, measure out, partition, propagate, radiate, rout, scatter, scramble, send off, separate, shed, sow, split up, spray, spread, strew, take off in all directions*, vanish; SEE CONCEPTS **135,217**

dispirited [adj] *dejected, sad*
blue*, bummed-out*, crestfallen, depressed, despondent, disconsolate, discouraged, disheartened, down*, downbeat, downcast, downhearted, dragged*, funky*, gloomy, glum, in the doldrums, low, melancholy, morose, shot-down*, spiritless, woebegone; SEE CONCEPT **403**

displace [v1] *move, remove from normal place*
change, crowd out, derange, disarrange, disestab-lish, dislocate, dislodge, displant, dispossess, disturb, eject, evict, expel, expulse, force out, lose, mislay, misplace, relegate, shift, transpose, unsettle, uproot; SEE CONCEPTS **147,213**

displace [v2] *remove from position of responsibility*
banish, can*, cashier*, cut out*, deport, depose, dethrone, discard, discharge, discrown, disenthone, dismiss, disthrone, exile, expatriate, fire, oust, relegate, remove, replace, sack*, step into shoes of*, succeed, supersede, supplant, take over, take the place of, transport, uncrown, unmake, usurp; SEE CONCEPTS **261,300**

display [n] *public showing; spectacle*
act, affectation, arrangement, array, arrayal, blaze, bravura, dash, demonstration, example, exhibit, exhibition, expo*, exposition, exposure, fanfare, flourish, for show, frame-up*, frippery, front, grandstand play*, layout, manifestation, ostentation, ostentatiousness, pageant, panorama, parade, pedantry, pomp, presentation, pretension, pretentiousness, revelation, sample, scheme, shine, showboat*, splash, splendor, splurge, spread, unfolding, vanity; SEE CONCEPTS **261,386**

display [v] *show for public viewing, effect*
advertise, arrange, bare, betray, boast, brandish, bring to view, demonstrate, disclose, emblazon, evidence, evince, exhibit, expand, expose, extend, feature, flash, flaunt, flourish, glaze, grandstand*, illustrate, impart, lay bare*, lay out, make clear, make known, manifest, model, open, open out, parade, perform, present, promote, promulgate, publish, represent, reveal, set out, showcase, show off, spread, spread out, stretch out, trot out*, uncover, unfold, unfurl, unmask, unroll, unveil, vamp; SEE CONCEPT **261**

displease [v] *make unhappy*
aggravate, anger, annoy, antagonize, bother, cap, chagrin, cool, curdle*, cut to the quick*, disappoint, discontent, disgruntle, disgust, disoblige, dissatisfy, enrage, exasperate, fret, frustrate, gall, hurt, incense, irk, irritate, nettle, offend, perplex, pique, play dirty, provoke, put out, repel, revolt, rile, roil, sound, turn off*, upset, vex, wing*, worry, zing*; SEE CONCEPTS **7,19**

displeasure [n] *unhappiness, anger*
annoyance, aversion, disapprobation, disapproval, discontentment, disfavor, disgruntlement, disinclination, dislike, disliking, disrelish, dissatisfaction, distaste, incensement, indignation, indisposition, irritation, offense, pique, resentment, umbrage, vexation, wrath; SEE CONCEPT **410**

disposal [n1] *parting or throwing something away*
auctioning, bartering, chucking, clearance, conveyance, demolishing, demolition, destroying, destruction, discarding, dispatching, dispensation, disposition, dumping, ejection, jettison, jettisoning, junking, relegation, relinquishment, removal, riddance, sacrifice, sale, scrapping, selling, trading, transfer, transference, vending; SEE CONCEPT **180**

disposal [n2] *conclusion, settlement of situation*
action, allocation, arrangement, array, assortment, bequest, bestowal, consignment, control, conveyance, determination, dispensation, disposition, distribution, division, effectuation, end, gift, grouping, order, ordering, placing, position, provision, sequence, transfer, winding up; SEE CONCEPTS **119,230**

di
di

dispose [v] *place, order; deal with*
actuate, adapt, adjust, arrange, array, bend, bias, call the tune*, condition, determine, distribute, fix, govern, group, incline, induce, influence, lay down the law*, lead, locate, make willing, marshal, methodize, motivate, move, organize, predispose, prepare, promote, prompt, put, put one's foot down*, put to rights, range, rank, read the riot act*, regulate, ride herd on*, set, set in order, settle, shepherd, stand, sway, systematize, tailor, tempt; SEE CONCEPTS 84,117,158,180

disposed [adj] *inclined to a type of behavior*
apt, at drop of hat*, biased, fain, game*, game for, given, liable, likely, minded, of a mind to*, partial, predisposed, prone, ready, subject, tending toward, willing; SEE CONCEPTS 542,552

dispose of [v1] *throw away*
adios*, bestow, chuck*, deep six*, destroy, discard, dump, eighty-six*, eliminate, file in circular file*, get rid of, give, jettison, junk*, kiss*, kiss off*, make over, part with, relinquish, scrap, sell, transfer, unload; SEE CONCEPT 180

dispose of [v2] *settle a matter*
chop, cut, cut off, deal with, decide, determine, do the trick*, end, finish, knock off*, polish off*, put away, take care of; SEE CONCEPTS 18,234

disposition [n1] *personal temperament*
bag*, being, bent, bias, cast, character, complexion, constitution, cup of tea*, druthers*, emotions, flash, frame of mind, groove*, habit, humor, identity, inclination, individualism, individuality, leaning, make-up, mind-set*, mood, nature, penchant, personality, predilection, predisposition, proclivity, proneness, propensity, readiness, spirit, stamp, temper, tendency, tenor, thing*, tone, type, vein; SEE CONCEPT 411

disposition [n2] *arrangement, management of a situation*
adjustment, classification, control, decision, direction, disposal, distribution, grouping, method, order, ordering, organization, placement, plan, regulation, sequence; SEE CONCEPTS 6,660

disproportion [n] *imbalance*
asymmetry, difference, discrepancy, disparity, imparity, inadequacy, inequality, insufficiency, irregularity, lopsidedness, unevenness, unsuitableness; SEE CONCEPTS 665,667

disproportionate [adj] *out of balance*
asymmetric, excessive, incommensurate, inordinate, irregular, lopsided, nonsymmetrical, out of proportion, overbalanced, superfluous, too much, unequal, uneven, unreasonable, unsymmetrical; SEE CONCEPTS 564,566,771

disprove [v] *prove false*
belie, blow sky high*, blow up*, break, confound, confute, contradict, contravene, controvert, deny, disconfirm, discredit, explode, expose, find unfounded, impugn, invalidate, knock bottom out of*, knock props out*, negate, negative, overthrow, overturn, poke holes in*, puncture, rebut, refute, set aside, shoot, shoot holes in*, tear down*, throw out, traverse, weaken; SEE CONCEPT 58

disputable [adj] *debatable; open to discussion*
arguable, controversial, doubtful, dubious, moot, mootable, problematic, questionable, uncertain; SEE CONCEPTS 529,535

disputation [n] *controversy*
argumentation, debate, dialectic, dispute, dissension, forensic, mooting, polemics; SEE CONCEPTS 278,532

disputatious [adj] *argumentative*
cantankerous, captious, caviling, contentious, controversial, dissentious, litigious, polemical, pugnacious, quarrelsome; SEE CONCEPTS 401,542

dispute [n] *argument*
altercation, beef*, bickering, bone of contention*, brawl, broil, brouhaha, commotion, conflict, contention, controversy, debate, difference of opinion, disagreement, discord, discussion, dissension, disturbance, embroilment, falling-out, feud, fireworks*, flare-up, fracas, friction, fuss, hubbub, miff*, misunderstanding, polemic, quarrel, row, rumpus*, squabble, squall, strife, tiff, uproar, variance, words, wrangle; SEE CONCEPTS 46,106,278

dispute [v] *argue*
agitate, altercate, bicker, brawl, bump heads*, canvass, challenge, clash, confute, contend, contest, contradict, controvert, debate, deny, disaffirm, discept, discuss, disprove, doubt, gainsay, hassle, have at*, impugn, jump on one's case*, kick around*, lock horns*, moot, negate, pick a bone*, quarrel, question, quibble, rebut, refute, squabble, take on, thrash out, toss around*, wrangle; SEE CONCEPT 46

disqualification [n] *disability; rejection for participation*
awkwardness, clumsiness, debarment, disenablement, disentitlement, elimination, exclusion, incapacitation, incapacity, incompetence, incompetency, ineligibility, ineptitude, lack, unfitness, unproficiency; SEE CONCEPT 630

disqualify [v] *be unfit for; be ineligible*
bar, bate, debar, disable, disenable, disentitle, disfranchise, eighty-six*, except, exclude, impair, incapacitate, invalidate, nix*, not make the cut*, paralyze, preclude, prohibit, rule out, suspend, unfit, weaken; SEE CONCEPTS 121,699

disquiet [n] *worry; mental upset*
ailment, alarm, angst, anxiety, care, concern, concernment, disquietude, distress, disturbance, fear, ferment, foreboding, fretfulness, inquietude, nervousness, restiveness, restlessness, solicitude, storm, trouble, turmoil, uneasiness, unrest; SEE CONCEPTS 410,532,690

disquiet [v] *worry; make uneasy*
agitate, annoy, bother, concern, discompose, distress, disturb, fluster, fret, harass, incommode, perplex, perturb, pester, plague, trouble, unhinge, unsettle, upset, vex; SEE CONCEPTS 7,19

disquieting [adj] *upsetting*
annoying, bothersome, disconcerting, distressing, disturbing, irritating, perplexing, perturbing, troublesome, troubling, unnerving, unsettling, vexing, worrying; SEE CONCEPT 529

disregard [n] *ignoring*
apathy, brush-off*, contempt, disdain, disesteem, disfavor, disinterest, disrespect, forgetting, heedlessness, inadvertence, inattention, indifference, insouciance, lassitude, lethargy, listlessness, neglect, neglecting, negligence, oblivion, omission, omitting, overlooking, oversight, scorn, slight, slighting, the cold shoulder*, unconcern, unmindfulness; SEE CONCEPTS 30,633

disregard [v] *ignore; make light of*
blink at*, brush aside, brush away, brush off, cold-shoulder*, contemn, despise, discount, disdain, disobey, disparage, fail, forget, have no use

for*, laugh off*, leave out of account, let go, let off easy*, let pass*, live with*, look the other way*, miss, neglect, omit, overlook, overpass, pass over, pay no attention to, pay no heed to, pay no mind*, pooh-pooh*, scorn, shut eyes to*, slight, snub, take no notice of, tune out*, turn a blind eye*, turn a deaf ear*, vilipend, wink at*; SEE CONCEPT 30

disrepair [n] *state of deterioration*
collapse, decay, decrepitude, dilapidation, ruination; SEE CONCEPTS 230,674

disrepair [adj] *broken; deteriorated*
busted*, damaged, dead, decayed, decrepit, down, kaput*, not functioning, on the blink*, on the fritz*, out of commission*, out of order, worn out, wracked*; SEE CONCEPT 485

disreputable [adj] *dishonorable, lowly*
abject, bad, base, beggarly, cheap, contemptible, derogatory, despicable, discreditable, disgraceful, disorderly, dissolute, ignominious, in bad, infamous, inglorious, in low esteem, in the doghouse*, lewd, libidinous, licentious, mean, no good*, notorious, opprobrious, pitiable, scandalous, scurvy, shabby, shady, shameful, shocking, shoddy, sordid, sorry, unprincipled, vicious, vile; SEE CONCEPT 404

disrepute [n] *dishonor, shame*
blemish, blot, brand, cloud, discredit, disesteem, disfavor, disgrace, ignominy, ill fame, ill favor, ill repute, infamy, ingloriousness, notoriety, obloquy, odium, opprobrium, reproach, scandal, scar, slur, smear, spot, stain, stigma, taint, unpopularity; SEE CONCEPT 411

disrespect [n] *disregard, rudeness toward someone*
boldness, coarseness, contempt, discourtesy, dishonor, flippancy, hardihood, impertinence, impiety, impoliteness, impudence, incivility, insolence, insolency, insolentness, irreverence, lack of respect, sacrilege, unmannerliness; SEE CONCEPTS 29,633

disrespectful [adj] *insulting, rude*
aweless, bad-mannered, blasphemous, bold, cheeky*, contemptuous, discourteous, disgracious, flip*, flippant, fresh, ill-bred, ill-mannered, impertinent, impious, impolite, impudent, insolent, irreverent, misbehaved, nervy*, out-of-line*, profanatory, profane, sacrilegious, sassy*, saucy*, smart-alecky*, snippy*, uncivil, unfilial, ungracious; SEE CONCEPTS 267,401

disrobe [v] *take off one's clothes*
bare, denudate, denude, deprive, dismantle, divest, doff, husk*, peel*, remove, shed, shuck*, slip out of, strip, take it off, unbutton*, unclothe, uncover, undress; SEE CONCEPT 167

disrupt [v1] *upset, disorganize*
agitate, bollix, confuse, disarray, discombobulate, discompose, disorder, disturb, mess up, mix up, muck up*, muddle, muddy the waters*, psych out*, put off, rattle, rattle one's cage*, rummage, screw up*, shake, spoil, throw, unsettle, upset the apple cart*; SEE CONCEPTS 16,84,234

disrupt [v2] *break, interrupt*
breach, break into, break up, fracture, hole, interfere with, intrude, obstruct, open, rupture, unsettle, upset; SEE CONCEPTS 98,135

disruptive [adj] *causing trouble, confusion*
disorderly, distracting, disturbing, obstreperous, off-base*, out-of-line*, out-of-order*, rowdy,

troublemaking, troublesome, unruly, unsettling, upsetting; SEE CONCEPTS 401,537

dissatisfaction [n] *discontent, unhappiness*
annoyance, anxiety, aversion, boredom, chagrin, complaint, desolation, disapproval, discomfort, discouragement, disfavor, disgruntlement, disinclination, dislike, disliking, dismay, displeasure, disquiet, disrelish, distaste, distress, ennui, envy, exasperation, fretfulness, frustration, heartburn, hopelessness, indisposition, irritation, jealousy, lamentation, malcontent, malcontentment, oppression, querulousness, regret, resentment, trouble, uneasiness, weariness, worry; SEE CONCEPTS 29,410

dissatisfied [adj] *discontented, unhappy*
annoyed, begrudging, bothered, complaining, crabby*, critical, disaffected, disappointed, disgruntled, displeased, ennuied, envious, faultfinding, fed-up*, fretful, fretting, frustrated, griping, grudging, grumbling, grumpy*, insatiable, irked, jaundiced, jealous, kvetching*, malcontent, malcontented, not satisfied, offended, picky, plaintive, put-out*, querulous, sniveling, sulky, sullen, unappeased, unassuaged, unfulfilled, ungratified, unsated, unsatisfied, vexed; SEE CONCEPT 403

dissect [v1] *cut up; take apart*
anatomize, break up, cut, dichotomize, disjoin, disjoint, dislimb, dismember, dissever, divide, exscind, exsect, lay open, operate, part, prosect, quarter, section, sever, slice, sunder; SEE CONCEPTS 98,176

dissect [v2] *analyze*
anatomize, break down, decompose, decompound, examine, explore, inquire about, inspect, investigate, resolve, scrutinize, study; SEE CONCEPT 24

dissection [n1] *cutting up, particularly of a dead body*
anatomization, anatomy, autopsy, dismemberment, examination, necropsy, operation, postmortem, vivisection; SEE CONCEPTS 176,310

dissection [n2] *thorough analysis*
breakdown, breakup, criticism, critique, examination, inquest, inspection, investigation, resolution, review, scrutiny, study; SEE CONCEPTS 24,290

dissemble [v] *disguise, pretend*
affect, camouflage, cloak, conceal, counterfeit, cover, cover up, dissimulate, doublespeak*, double-talk*, dress up, fake, falsify, feign, four-flush*, hide, let on*, make like*, mask, pass, play possum*, pussyfoot*, put on a false front*, put on a front*, put on an act*, put up a front*, put up a smoke screen*, sham*, shroud, shuck and jive*, signify, simulate, stonewall*, whitewash*; SEE CONCEPTS 59,188,716

disseminate [v] *distribute, scatter*
advertise, announce, annunciate, blaze, blazon, broadcast, circulate, declare, diffuse, disject, disperse, dissipate, proclaim, promulgate, propagate, publicize, publish, radiate, sow, spread, strew; SEE CONCEPTS 108,140,201,222

dissemination [n] *distribution*
airing, broadcasting, circulation, diffusion, dissipation, promulgation, propagation, publication, publishing, spread; SEE CONCEPTS 651,746

dissension [n] *conflict of opinion*
altercation, argument, bad vibes*, bickering, clinker*, contention, controversy, difference, disaccord, disagreement, discord, discordance, dispute, dissent, dissidence, disunity, faction, factional-

di
di

ism, flak*, friction, fuss, quarrel, scene, sour note*, static, strife, trouble, variance, wrangle; SEE CONCEPTS 46,278,665

dissent [n] disagreement, disapproval
bone*, bone of contention*, bone to pick*, clinker*, conflict, contention, denial, difference, disaccord, discord, dissension, dissidence, disunity, far cry*, flak*, hassle, heresy, heterodoxy, misbelief, nonagreement, nonconcurrence, nonconformism, nonconformity, nope*, objection, opposition, poles apart*, protest, refusal, resistance, schism, sour note*, spat, split, strife, unorthodoxy, variance; SEE CONCEPTS 29,665,689

dissent [v] disagree
argue, balk, break with, buck, contradict, decline, demur, differ, disaccord, discord, divide, fly in the face of*, object, oppose, pettifog, protest, put up a fight*, put up an argument, refuse, say not a chance*, say nothing doing*, say no way*, shy, stickle, vary, wrangle; SEE CONCEPTS 21,46

dissertation [n] scholarly thesis
argumentation, commentary, critique, discourse, disputation, disquisition, essay, exposition, memoir, monograph, tractate, treatise; SEE CONCEPTS 271,287

disservice [n] unkindness
bad turn, detriment, disfavor, harm, hurt, injury, injustice, insult, outrage, prejudice, wrong; SEE CONCEPTS 309,645,674

dissidence [n] difference of opinion
bad vibes*, contention, discord, disagreement, discordance, disharmony, dispeace, dispute, dissension, dissent, feud, heresy, heterodoxy, misbelief, nonconformism, nonconformity, rupture, schism, sour note*, strife, unorthodoxy; SEE CONCEPTS 278,633,689

dissident [n] person who holds different belief
agitator, dissenter, heretic, misbeliever, nonconformist, protester, rebel, recusant, schismatic, schismatist, sectary, separatist; SEE CONCEPTS 359,423

dissident [adj] disagreeing, differing
discordant, dissentient, dissenting, heretical, heterodox, nonconformist, schismatic, sectarian, unorthodox; SEE CONCEPT 403

dissimilar [adj] not alike; not capable of comparison
antithetical, antonymous, contradictory, contrary, different, disparate, distant, divergent, diverse, far cry*, heterogeneous, individual, like night and day*, march to a different drummer*, mismatched, mismated, not similar, offbeat, opposite, poles apart*, unequal, unique, unlike, unrelated, unsimilar, various, weird*; SEE CONCEPT 564

dissimilarity [n] unlikeness
alterity, contrast, difference, discord, discordance, discrepancy, disparity, dissemblance, dissimilitude, distance, distinction, divarication, divergence, divergency, diversity, heterogeneity, incomparability, incongruity, inconsistency, inconsonance, nonuniformity, offset, otherness, separation, severance, unrelatedness, variance, variation; SEE CONCEPT 665

dissimulate [v] conceal, disguise
beard*, camouflage, cloak, deceive, dissemble, dress up, fake, feign, hide, make-believe, mask, present a false face*, present a false front*, pretend; SEE CONCEPTS 59,172,188

dissipate [v1] expend, spend
be wasteful with, blow*, burn up*, consume, deplete, dump*, fritter away, indulge oneself, kiss goodbye*, lavish, misspend, misuse, run through, squander, throw away, trifle away, use up, waste; SEE CONCEPTS 156,169

dissipate [v2] disappear
dispel, disperse, dissolve, drive away, evanesce, evaporate, melt away, run dry, scatter, spread, vanish; SEE CONCEPTS 105,469

dissipated [adj1] used up
blown, burnt out*, consumed, destroyed, exhausted, kaput*, played out*, scattered, spent, squandered, wasted; SEE CONCEPTS 560,576

dissipated [adj2] self-indulgent
abandoned, corrupt, debauched, dissolute, gone bad*, gone to seed*, gone to the dogs*, hellbent*, intemperate, profligate, rakish, wicked; SEE CONCEPTS 401,545

dissipation [n1] amusement, entertainment, occasionally to excess
bender*, binge, blow-out, bust*, celebration, circus, distraction, diversion, divertissement, gratification, party, recreation, self-indulgence, tear*, toot*, wingding*; SEE CONCEPTS 363,386

dissipation [n2] wantonness
abandonment, debauchery, dissoluteness, dissolution, drunkenness, evil, excess, extravagance, free-living, high-living*, indulgence, intemperance, lavishness, life in the fast lane*, prodigality, profligacy, self-gratification, squandering, to hell in handbasket*, waste; SEE CONCEPT 633

dissipation [n3] disappearance
diffusion, disintegration, dispersal, dispersion, dissemination, dissolution, distribution, emission, extravagance, improvidence, radiation, scattering, spread, vanishing, wastage, waste; SEE CONCEPTS 230,651,720

dissociate [v] part company with; separate
abstract, alienate, break off, detach, disassociate, disband, disconnect, disengage, disjoin, disperse, disrupt, distance, disunite, divide, divorce, estrange, isolate, quit, scatter, segregate, set apart, uncouple, unfix; SEE CONCEPTS 135,384

dissociation [n] detachment, separation
break, disconnection, disengagement, disjunction, distancing, disunion, division, divorce, isolation, segregation, severance; SEE CONCEPT 388

dissolute [adj] lacking restraint, indulgent
abandoned, corrupt, debauched, degenerate, depraved, dissipated, evil, fast*, fast and loose*, gone bad*, high living*, intemperate, in the fast lane*, lascivious, lax, lecherous, lewd, libertine, licentious, light, loose*, nighthawk*, night owl*, on the take*, open, player*, profligate, raffish, rakish, reprobate, slack, swift, sybaritic, unconstrained, unprincipled, unrestrained, vicious, wanton, wayward, wicked, wild; SEE CONCEPTS 401,545

dissolution [n1] separation, rupture
breaking up, detachment, disintegration, disunion, division, divorce, divorcement, parting, partition, resolution, split-up; SEE CONCEPTS 230,388

dissolution [n2] death; destruction
adjournment, conclusion, curtains, decay, decease, decomposition, defunction, demise, disappearance, disbandment, discontinuation, dismissal, dispersal, end, ending, evaporation, extinction, finish, liquefaction, melting, overthrow, passing, quietus, release, resolution, ruin, silence,

sleep, solution, suspension, termination; SEE CONCEPTS *105,304,469,703*

dissolve [*vl*] *melt from solid to liquid; mix in*
defront, deliquesce, diffuse, fluidify, flux, fuse, liquefy, liquesce, render, run, soften, thaw, waste away; SEE CONCEPTS *469,702*

dissolve [*v2*] *disappear, disintegrate*
break down, break into pieces, break up, crumble, decline, decompose, diffuse, dilapidate, disband, disperse, dissipate, dwindle, evanesce, evaporate, fade, melt away, perish, separate, unmake, vanish, waste away; SEE CONCEPTS *105,469*

dissolve [*v3*] *annul, discontinue*
abrogate, adjourn, annihilate, break up, cancel, collapse, decimate, demolish, destroy, destruct, discharge, dismiss, disorganize, disunite, divorce, do away with, end, eradicate, invalidate, loose, overthrow, postpone, put an end to, quash, render void, repeal, resolve into, ruin, separate, sever, shatter, shoot, suspend, terminate, unmake, vacate, void, wind up, wrack, wreck; SEE CONCEPTS *121,234,252*

dissonance [*nl*] *disagreement*
antagonism, conflict, contention, controversy, difference, disaccord, discord, discrepancy, disharmony, disparity, dissension, dissidence, incongruity, inconsistency, strife, variance; SEE CONCEPTS *278,665,689*

dissonance [*n2*] *noise, discord*
cacophony, harshness, jangle, jarring, unmelodiousness; SEE CONCEPT *595*

dissonant [*adj1*] *different, conflicting*
anomalous, at variance, differing, disagreeing, disconsonant, discordant, discrepant, dissentient, incompatible, incongruent, incongruous, inconsistent, inconsonant, irreconcilable, irregular, sour note*, unmixable; SEE CONCEPT *564*

dissonant [*adj2*] *unharmonious*
cacophonic, cacophonous, discordant, disharmonic, disharmonious, grating, harsh, inharmonic, inharmonious, jangling, jarring, out of tune, raucous, strident, tuneless, unmelodious, unmusical; SEE CONCEPTS *592,594*

dissuade [*v*] *talk out of*
advise against, caution against, chicken out*, counsel, cry out against, deprecate, derail, deter, disadvise, discourage, disincline, divert, exhort, expostulate, faze, hinder, lean on*, persuade not to, prevent, prick, put off, remonstrate, throw a wet blanket on*, throw cold water on*, throw off, thwart, turn off*, urge not to, warn; SEE CONCEPTS *68,73*

distance [*nl*] *interval, range*
absence, ambit, amplitude, area, bit, breadth, compass, country mile*, expanse, extension, extent, farness, far piece*, gap, good ways*, heavens, hinterland, horizon, lapse, length, objective, orbit, outpost, outskirts, provinces, purlieu, purview, radius, reach, remoteness, remove, scope, separation, size, sky, space, span, spread, stretch, sweep, way, width; SEE CONCEPTS *651,739,790*

distance [*n2*] *aloofness*
coldness, coolness, frigidity, reserve, restraint, stiffness; SEE CONCEPT *633*

distance [*v*] *dissociate oneself; leave behind*
break away from the pack, outdo, outpace, outrun, outstrip, pass, put in proportion, separate oneself; SEE CONCEPT *195*

distant [*adj1*] *faraway*
abroad, abstracted, apart, a piece, arm's length*, asunder, away, backwoods, beyond range, far, far back, far-flung, far-off, farther, further, inaccessible, indirect, in the background, in the boonies*, in the distance, in the sticks*, isolated, middle of nowhere*, not home*, obscure, outlying, out of earshot*, out of range, out of reach, out-of-the-way, remote, removed, retired, secluded, secret, separate, sequestered, telescopic, unapproachable, ways*, wide of*, yonder*; SEE CONCEPTS *576,778*

distant [*adj2*] *aloof*
arrogant, ceremonious, cold, cool, formal, haughty, insociable, laid back, modest, offish, on ice*, proud, put on airs*, remote, reserved, restrained, reticent, retiring, shy, solitary, standoff, standoffish, stiff, stuck-up*, unapproachable, uncompanionable, unconcerned, unfriendly, unsociable, uppity*, withdrawn; SEE CONCEPTS *401,404*

distaste [*n*] *dislike, hate*
abhorrence, antipathy, aversion, detestation, disfavor, disgust, disinclination, displeasure, disrelish, dissatisfaction, hatred, horror, hostility, indisposition, loathing, repugnance, repulsion, revolt, revulsion; SEE CONCEPT *29*

distasteful [*adj*] *repulsive, unpleasant*
abhorrent, abominable, afflictive, bitter, detestable, disagreeable, dislikable, displeasing, flat, flavorless, galling, grievous, grody*, gross*, hateful, icky*, insipid, loathsome, nauseous, objectionable, obnoxious, odious, offensive, painful, repellent, repugnant, savorless, tasteless, unappetizing, undesirable, uninviting, unlikable, unpalatable, unsavory, yicky*, yucky*; SEE CONCEPTS *529,589,613*

distend [*v*] *bulge, swell*
amplify, augment, balloon, bloat, dilate, distort, enlarge, expand, increase, inflate, lengthen, puff, stretch, widen; SEE CONCEPTS *157,469,780*

distill [*v*] *make pure; draw out something*
boil down, brew, clarify, concentrate, condense, cook, cut, cut down, cut to the bone*, dribble, drip, drop, evaporate, express, extract, ferment, get to the meat*, infuse, precipitate, press, press out, purify, rarefy, rectify, refine, squeeze out, steam, sublimate, trickle, trim, vaporize, volatilize; SEE CONCEPTS *165,170,211,219*

distinct [*adj1*] *apparent, obvious*
audible, categorical, clean-cut, clear, clear-cut, decided, definite, enunciated, evident, explicit, express, incisive, lucid, manifest, marked, noticeable, palatable, patent, perspicuous, plain, prescribed, recognizable, sharp, sharp-cut, specific, transparent, trenchant, unambiguous, unequivocal, unmistakable, well-defined; SEE CONCEPTS *535,591,619*

distinct [*adj2*] *different; unconnected*
detached, discrete, disparate, dissimilar, distinctive, disunited, divergent, diverse, especial, individual, offbeat, particular, peculiar, poles apart*, separate, separated, several, single, sole, special, specific, unassociated, unattached, unique, various; SEE CONCEPT *564*

distinction [*nl*] *differentiation; feature*
acumen, acuteness, alterity, analysis, characteristic, clearness, contrast, diagnosis, difference, differential, discernment, discrepancy, discreteness, discretion, discrimination, dissemblance, dissimilarity, dissimilitude, divergence, divergency, division, earmark, estimation, individuality, judg-

ment, mark, marking, nicety, otherness, particularity, peculiarity, penetration, perception, qualification, quality, refinement, sensitivity, separation, sharpness, tact, unlikeness; SEE CONCEPTS **411,665**

distinction [n2] *prominence; achievement*
accolade, account, award, badge, bays, celebrity, consequence, credit, decoration, eminence, excellence, fame, flair, greatness, illustriousness, importance, kudos, laurels, manner, merit, name, note, perfection, preeminence, prestige, quality, rank, renown, reputation, repute, style, superiority, worth; SEE CONCEPTS **388,671,706**

distinctive [adj] *different, unique*
characteristic, cool, diacritic, diagnostic, discrete, distinguishing, excellent, extraordinary, far cry, gnarly*, idiosyncratic, individual, like night and day*, offbeat, original, outstanding, peculiar, perfect, poles apart*, proper, separate, single, singular, special, superior, typical, uncommon, unreal, weird, wicked; SEE CONCEPTS **564,574**

distinguish [v1] *tell the difference*
analyze, ascertain, categorize, characterize, classify, collate, decide, demarcate, determinate, determine, diagnose, diagnosticate, differentiate, discriminate, divide, estimate, extricate, figure out, finger*, identify, individualize, individuate, judge, know, label, make out, mark, mark off, name, part, pinpoint, place, qualify, recognize, select, separate, set apart, set off, sift, signalize, single out, singularize, sort out, specify, spot, tag, tell apart, tell between, tell from; SEE CONCEPTS **15,18,38**

distinguish [v2] *discern, identify*
beam*, catch, descry, detect, dig, discover, discriminate, eye, eyeball*, flash*, focus, get a load of*, get an eyeful*, know, make out, mark, note, notice, observe, perceive, pick out, pick up on*, read, recognize, remark, see, spot, spy, take in, tell, view; SEE CONCEPTS **38,626**

distinguish [v3] *make famous*
acknowledge, admire, celebrate, dignify, honor, immortalize, pay tribute to, praise, signalize; SEE CONCEPT **69**

distinguished [adj] *famous, outstanding*
acclaimed, aristocratic, arresting, big name*, brilliant, celebrated, conspicuous, dignified, distingué, eminent, especial, esteemed, extraordinary, famed, foremost, glorious, great, highly regarded, honored, illustrious, imposing, marked, memorable, name, noble, nonpareil, notable, noted, noteworthy, peerless, prominent, remarkable, renowned, reputable, royal, salient, shining, signal, singular, special, stately, striking, superior, talked of, unforgettable, venerable, well-known; SEE CONCEPT **574**

distort [v] *deform; falsify*
alter, angle, belie, bend, bias, buckle, change, collapse, color, con, contort, crush, curve, deceive, decline, deteriorate, deviate, disfigure, doctor*, fake, fudge*, garble, gnarl, knot, lie, make out like, mangle, melt, misconstrue, misinterpret, misrepresent, misshape, pervert, phony up*, put one on*, sag, scam*, slant, slump, snow*, torture, trump up*, twist, warp, whitewash*, wind, wrench, writhe; SEE CONCEPTS **63,137,232,250**

distortion [n] *deformity; falsification*
baloney*, bend, bias, BS*, buckle, coloring, contortion, crock, crookedness, exaggeration, intorsion, jazz*, jive*, lie, line, malconformation,

malformation, misinterpretation, misrepresentation, misshape, misstatement, misuse, mutilation, perversion, slant, smoke*, story*, tall story*, torture, twist, twistedness, warp; SEE CONCEPTS **63,580**

distract [v] *divert attention; confuse*
abstract, addle, agitate, amuse, befuddle, beguile, bewilder, call away, catch flies*, confound, derange, detract, disconcert, disconcert, disturb, divert, draw away, engross, entertain, fluster, frenzy, harass, lead astray*, lead away, madden, mislead, mix up, occupy, perplex, puzzle, sidetrack, stall, throw off*, torment, trouble, turn aside, unbalance, unhinge*; SEE CONCEPTS **14,16**

distraction [n] *having one's attention drawn away*
aberration, abstraction, agitation, amusement, beguilement, bewilderment, commotion, complication, confusion, disorder, dissipation, disturbance, diversion, divertissement, engrossment, entertainment, frenzy, game, interference, interruption, pastime, perplexity, preoccupation, recreation; SEE CONCEPTS **293,410,532,690**

distraught [adj] *very upset, worked-up*
addled, agitated, anxious, beside oneself, bothered, concerned, confused, crazed*, crazy, discomposed, distracted, distrait, distressed, flustered, frantic, harassed, hysterical, in a panic, like a chicken with its head cut off*, mad, muddled, nonplussed, nuts*, out of one's mind*, overwrought, perturbed, rattled, raving, shook up, thrown*, tormented, troubled, unglued*, unscrewed*, unzipped*, wild, worried; SEE CONCEPTS **401,403,690**

distress [n1] *pain, agony*
ache, affliction, anguish, anxiety, bad news*, blues*, care, concern, cross, dejection, desolation, disappointment, discomfort, disquietude, dolor, embarrassment, grief, headache, heartache, heartbreak, irritation, malaise, misery, mortification, ordeal, pang, perplexity, sadness, shame, sorrow, stew, suffering, throe, torment, torture, trial, tribulation, trouble, twinge, unconsolability, unhappiness, vexation, visitation, woe, worriment, worry, wretchedness; SEE CONCEPTS **410,532,690,720,728**

distress [n2] *hardship, adversity*
bad luck, bummer*, calamity, can of worms*, catastrophe, crunch*, destitution, difficulty, disaster, downer*, drag*, exigency, hard knocks*, hard time*, holy mess*, hot water*, indigence, jam*, misfortune, need, pickle*, pinch*, poverty, privation, rigor, rotten luck*, scrape*, straits, throe, ticklish spot*, tough break*, tough luck*, trial, trouble, unholy mess*, vicissitude, want; SEE CONCEPT **674**

distress [v] *worry, upset*
afflict, aggrieve, agonize, ail, be on one's case*, bother, break, bug, burn up, depress, desolate, discombobulate*, disquiet, disturb, do a number on*, dog*, eat*, get*, get to*, give a hard time*, grieve, harass, harry, hound, hurt, injure, irk, irritate, make it tough for*, miff, nag, needle, nitpick, oppress, pain, peeve, perplex, pester, pick on, plague, push, push buttons*, rack, sadden, strain, strap, stress, tick off*, torment, torture, trouble, try, vex, weigh, wound; SEE CONCEPTS **7,19,313**

distressed [adj] *upset*
afflicted, agitated, all torn up*, antsy, anxious, basket case*, bothered, bugged, bummed out*,

bundle of nerves*, concerned, cut up*, discombobulated*, disconsolate, distracted, distrait, distraught, dragged, exercised, fidgety, harassed, hyper*, in a stew*, in a tizzy*, inconsolable, jittery, jumpy, miffed, peeved, perturbed, ripped*, saddened, shaky, shook*, shook up*, shot down*, spooked*, strung out*, tormented, troubled, unconsolable, unglued*, up the wall*, uptight*, wired, worried, wrecked*, wretched; SEE CONCEPT 403

distribute [vl] *allocate, deliver, spread*
administer, allot, apportion, appropriate, assign, bestow, circulate, consign, convey, cut up, deal, deal out, diffuse, disburse, dish out*, dispense, disperse, dispose, disseminate, divide, divvy up*, dole out*, donate, endow, fork out*, give, give away, hand out, issue, lot out, measure out, mete, parcel, partition, pass out, pay out, present, prorate, radiate, ration, scatter, share, shell out*, slice up, sow, strew; SEE CONCEPTS 98,140,217

distribute [v2] *classify*
arrange, assort, categorize, class, file, group, order; SEE CONCEPT 84

distribution [nl] *allocation, dispersion*
administration, alloting, allotment, apportioning, apportionment, assessment, assigning, circulating, circulation, dealing, delivery, diffusion, dispensation, dispersal, disposal, disposing, dissemination, dissipating, division, dole, handing out, handling, mailing, marketing, partition, partitioning, propagation, prorating, rationing, scattering, sharing, spreading, trading, transport, transportation; SEE CONCEPTS 98,140,217

distribution [n2] *classification*
arrangement, assortment, disposal, disposition, grouping, location, order, ordering, organization, placement, sequence; SEE CONCEPTS 109,727

district [n] *geographical area*
commune, community, department, locale, locality, neck of the woods*, neighborhood, parcel, parish, precinct, quarter, region, section, sector, stomping ground*, territory, turf*, vicinage, vicinity, ward; SEE CONCEPT 508

distrust [n] *lack of faith in something*
disbelief, doubt, misdoubt, misgiving, mistrust, qualm, question, skepticism, suspicion, wariness; SEE CONCEPTS 21,689

distrust [v] *be suspicious, skeptical of*
be wary of, disbelieve, discredit, doubt, misbelieve, mistrust, question, smell a rat*, suspect, wonder about; SEE CONCEPT 21

distrustful [adj] *disbelieving*
been hit before*, cagey, cautious, chary, cynical, doubtful, doubting, dubious, fearful, jealous, leery, mistrustful, skeptical, suspicious, uneasy, uptight, wary; SEE CONCEPTS 403,542

disturb [vl] *bother, upset*
afflict, agitate, ail, alarm, amaze, annoy, arouse, astound, badger, burn up*, complicate, confound, confuse, depress, discompose, dishearten, disrupt, distract, distress, excite, fluster, frighten, gall, grieve, harass, interfere, interrupt, intrude, irk, irritate, make uneasy, molest, muddle, outrage, pain, perplex, perturb, pester, pique, plague, provoke, puzzle, rattle, rouse, ruffle, shake, shake up*, startle, tire, trouble, unhinge*, unnerve, unsettle, vex, worry; SEE CONCEPTS 7,19

disturb [v2] *disorder; dislocate*
confuse, derange, disarrange, disarray, discompose, disorganize, displace, distort, foul up*, in-

terfere, jumble, louse up*, mess up, mix up, move, muddle, remove, replace, shift, tamper, unsettle, upset; SEE CONCEPTS 84,137,250

disturbance [n] *commotion; upset*
agitation, annoyance, big scene*, big stink*, bother, brawl, brouhaha, clamor, confusion, convulsion, derangement, disarrangement, disorder, disruption, distraction, eruption, explosion, ferment, fisticuffs, flap, fracas, fray, fuss, hindrance, hubbub, hullabaloo*, insurrection, interruption, intrusion, molestation, perturbation, quake, quarrel, racket, rampage, restlessness, riot, ruckus, rumble, shock, spasm, stink*, stir*, storm, to-do*, tremor, tumult, turmoil, upheaval, uprising, uproar, violence; SEE CONCEPTS 388,410, 674,720

ditch [n] *gulley*
canal, channel, chase, cut, dike, drain, excavation, furrow, gutter, mine, moat, trench, watercourse; SEE CONCEPTS 509,513

ditch [v] *get rid of*
abandon, desert, discard, dispose of, drop, dump*, eighty-six*, forsake, jettison, junk*, leave, reject, scrap*, throw away, throw out, throw overboard*; SEE CONCEPT 180

dive [nl] *descent, usually underwater*
belly flop*, dash, dip, duck, ducking, fall, header* headlong* jump, leap, lunge, nosedive, pitch, plunge, spring, submergence, submersion, swoop; SEE CONCEPTS 147,181,194

dive [n2] *dirty, sleazy establishment*
bar, barroom, beer garden* cabaret, dump, flea trap*, flophouse*, hangout, hole, honky-tonk*, joint, lounge, night club, pool hall, pub, saloon, taproom, tavern; SEE CONCEPT 449

dive [v] *descend, usually going underwater*
belly flop*, dip, disappear, drop, duck, fall, go headfirst, gutter, header*, jump, leap, lunge, nose-dive, pitch, plumb, plummet, plunge, spring, submerge, swoop, vanish, vault; SEE CONCEPTS 147,181,194

diverge [vl] *go in different directions*
bend, bifurcate, branch, branch off, depart, deviate, digress, divagate, divaricate, divide, excurse, fork, part, radiate, ramble, separate, split, spread, stray, swerve, veer, wander; SEE CONCEPTS 195,738

diverge [v2] *be different from; be at odds*
argue, conflict, contrast, depart, deviate, differ, digress, disagree, disapprove, dissent, oppose, stray, swerve, turn aside, vary, wander; SEE CONCEPTS 46,665

divergence [n] *branching out; difference*
aberration, alteration, alterity, crotch, deflection, departure, detour, deviation, digression, disagreeing, discrepancy, disparity, dissemblance, dissimilarity, dissimilitude, distinction, divagation, divergency, diversity, division, fork, mutation, otherness, parting, radiation, ramification, separation, turning, unlikeness, variety, varying; SEE CONCEPTS 665,738

divergent [adj] *differing*
aberrant, abnormal, anomalous, antithetical, atypical, conflicting, contradictory, contrary, deviating, different, disagreeing, disparate, dissimilar, dissonant, distant, diverging, diverse, factional, factious, irregular, off-key, opposite, poles apart*, separate, unalike, unequal, unlike, unnatural, unsimilar, untypical, variant, various; SEE CONCEPT 564

di
di

diverse [adj] different; various

assorted, contradictory, contrary, contrasted, contrasting, contrastive, differing, discrete, disparate, dissimilar, distant, distinct, divergent, diversified, diversiform, incommensurable, like night and day*, manifold, miscellaneous, mixed bag*, multifarious, opposite, separate, several, sundry, unalike, unequal, unlike, varied, varying; SEE CONCEPTS 564,772

diversify [v] spread out; branch out

alter, assort, change, expand, mix, modify, transform, variegate, vary; SEE CONCEPTS 232,697

diversion [n1] change in a course, path

aberration, alteration, deflection, departure, detour, deviation, digression, divergence, fake out*, red herring*, turning, variation; SEE CONCEPTS 501,738

diversion [n2] entertainment, recreation

amusement, ball, beguilement, delectation, delight, disport, dissipation, distraction, divertissement, enjoyment, field day*, frivolity, fun, fun and games*, game, gratification, grins*, high time*, hoopla*, laughs*, levity, merry-go-round*, pastime, picnic*, play, pleasure, relaxation, relish, sport, whoopee*; SEE CONCEPTS 292,363,386

diversity [n] variety, difference

assortment, dissimilarity, distinction, distinctiveness, divergence, diverseness, diversification, heterogeneity, medley, mixed bag*, multeity, multifariousness, multiformity, multiplicity, range, unlikeness, variance, variegation, variousness; SEE CONCEPTS 651,665

divert [v1] turn a different direction

alter, avert, change, deflect, modify, pivot, redirect, sheer, swerve, switch, turn aside, veer, volte-face, wheel, whip, whirl; SEE CONCEPTS 187,213

divert [v2] amuse, entertain

beguile, break one up*, delight, fracture one*, get one's jollies*, gladden, gratify, knock 'em dead*, make happy, panic, please, put 'em away*, recreate, regale, relax, slay, tickle, wow; SEE CONCEPT 9

divert [v3] take attention away

abstract, attract attention, bend the rules*, catch flies*, circumlocute, detach, deter, detract, disadvise, discourage, disengage, dissuade, distract, disturb, draw away, get around, lead astray, lead away, send on a wild-goose chase*, sidetrack, stall; SEE CONCEPTS 7,19,22

divest [v] dispossess; take off

bankrupt, bare, bereave, bleed, denudate, denude, deprive, despoil, disinherit, dismantle, disrobe, ditch*, doff, dump, eighty-six*, lose, milk*, oust, plunder, remove, rob, seize, spoil, strip, take from, unclothe, uncover, undress, unload; SEE CONCEPTS 139,142,211

divide [v1] separate, disconnect

abscind, bisect, branch, break, break down, carve, chop, cleave, cross, cut, cut up, demarcate, detach, dichotomize, disengage, disentangle, disjoin, dislocate, dismember, dissect, dissever, dissociate, dissolve, disunite, divorce, halve, intersect, isolate, loose, part, partition, pull away, quarter, rend, rupture, section, segment, segregate, sever, shear, split, subdivide, sunder, tear, unbind, undo; SEE CONCEPTS 98,135,137

divide [v2] distribute

allocate, allot, apportion, articulate, cut, cut in*, cut one in*, cut up, deal, deal out, disburse, dish out*, dispense, prorate, divvy up*, dole out*, factor, fork out*, go fifty-fifty*, hand out, hand over, lot out, measure out, parcel, partition, piece up, portion, prorate, quota, ration, share, shell out*, shift, slice, slice up, split up; SEE CONCEPTS 98,140

divide [v3] put in order; classify

arrange, categorize, grade, group, separate, sort; SEE CONCEPT 84

divide [v4] disagree, alienate

break up, cause to disagree, come between, differ, disaccord, dissent, disunite, estrange, part, pit against, separate, set against, set at odds*, sow dissension*, split, vary; SEE CONCEPTS 46,266

dividend [n] one's share, profit

allotment, allowance, appropriation, bonus, carrot*, check, coupon, cut*, dispensation, divvy*, extra, gain, gravy*, guerdon, interest, lagniappe*, meed, pay, portion, premium, prize, proceeds, remittance, returns, reward, surplus, taste*; SEE CONCEPTS 337,344

divine [adj] godlike, perfect

all-powerful, almighty, ambrosial, angelic, anointed, beatific, beautiful, blissful, celestial, consecrated, deific, deistic, eternal, exalted, excellent, glorious, godly, hallowed, heavenly, holy, immaculate, magnificent, marvelous, mystical, omnipotent, omnipresent, omniscient, rapturous, religious, sacramental, sacred, sacrosanct, sanctified, spiritual, splendid, superhuman, superlative, supernatural, supreme, theistic, transcendent, transcendental, transmundane, unearthly, wonderful; SEE CONCEPTS 568,574

divine [v] prophesy

anticipate, apprehend, conjecture, deduce, discern, forebode, forefeel, foreknow, foresee, foretell, go out on a limb*, guess, infer, intuit, perceive, predict, previse, prognosticate, see, see in the cards*, suppose, surmise, suspect, take a shot*, take a stab*, understand, visualize; SEE CONCEPT 28

divinity [n] absolute being; divine nature

celestial, deity, genius, god, goddess, godhead, godhood, godliness, godship, guardian spirit, higher power, holiness, lord, prime mover, sanctity, spirit; SEE CONCEPTS 368,370,689

division [n1] separation, disconnection

analysis, apportionment, autopsy, bisection, breaking, breaking down, breaking up, carving, contrasting, cutting up, demarcation, departmentalizing, detaching, detachment, diagnosis, disjuncture, dismemberment, disparting, disseverance, dissolution, distinguishing, distribution, disunion, disuniting, dividing, divorce, parceling, parting, partition, reduction, rending, rupture, segmentation, selection, separating, severance, splitting up, subdivision, vivisection; SEE CONCEPTS 98,135

division [n2] something produced from separating

affiliate, associate, border, boundary, branch, category, chunk, class, compartment, cut, degree, demarcation, department, divide, dividend, divider, dividing line, divvy*, end, fraction, fragment, grouping, head, kind, lobe, lump, member, moiety, offshoot, parcel, partition, piece, piece of action*, portion, rake-off*, ramification, section, sector, segment, share, slice, sort, split, subdivision, wedge; SEE CONCEPTS 378,382,710,835

division [n3] *breach, estrangement*
conflict, difference of opinion, difficulty, disaccord, disagreement, discord, disharmony, dispute, dissension, dissent, dissidence, dissonance, disunion, feud, rupture, split, trouble, variance, words; SEE CONCEPT 388

divorce [n] *split-up of marriage*
annulment, breach, break, breakup, decree nisi, dedomiciling, detachment, disparateness, dissociation, dissolution, disunion, division, divorcement, on the rocks*, parting of the ways*, partition, rupture, separate maintenance, separation, severance, split, splitsville*; SEE CONCEPT 297

divorce [v] *split up a marriage*
annul, break up, cancel, disconnect, disjoin, dissever, dissociate, dissolve, disunite, divide, nullify, part, put away, separate, sever, split, sunder, unmarry; SEE CONCEPT 297

divulge [v] *make known; confess*
admit, betray, blab, blow the whistle*, broadcast, communicate, cough up*, declare, disclose, discover, exhibit, expose, fess up*, give away, go public*, gossip, impart, leak, let hair down*, let slip*, mouth, open up*, own up*, proclaim, promulgate, publish, reveal, spill, spill the beans*, spring, tattle, tell, tip off*, uncover; SEE CONCEPT 60

dizzy [adj1] *light-headed, confused*
addled, befuddled, bemused, bewildered, blind, blinded, dazed, dazzled, distracted, disturbed, dumb, dumbfounded, faint, gaga*, giddy, groggy*, hazy, light, muddled, off balance*, out of control*, punch-drunk*, punchy*, puzzled, reeling, shaky, slap-happy*, staggered, staggering, swimming*, tipsy, unsteady, upset, vertiginous, weak in the knees*, weak-kneed*, whirling, wobbly, woozy; SEE CONCEPTS 314,480

dizzy [adj2] *flighty, scatterbrained*
capricious, changeable, crazy, empty-headed, fatuous, feather-brained, fickle, foolish, frivolous, giddy, harebrained, heady, inane, light-headed, silly, skittish, unstable; SEE CONCEPT 402

do [v1] *carry out*
accomplish, achieve, act, arrange, be responsible for, bring about, cause, close, complete, conclude, cook*, create, determine, discharge, do one's thing*, effect, end, engage in, execute, finish, fix, fulfill, get ready, get with it*, go for it*, look after, make, make ready, move, operate, organize, perform, prepare, produce, pull off*, see to, succeed, take care of business*, take on, transact, undertake, wind up*, work, wrap up*; SEE CONCEPT 91

do [v2] *be sufficient*
answer, avail, be adequate, be enough, be good enough for, be of use, be useful, give satisfaction*, pass muster*, satisfy, serve, suffice, suit; SEE CONCEPTS 646,656

do [v3] *figure out, solve*
adapt, decipher, decode, interpret, puzzle out, render, resolve, translate, transliterate, transpose, work out; SEE CONCEPTS 15,37

do [v4] *act, behave*
acquit oneself, appear, bear, carry, come on like*, comport, conduct, demean, deport, discourse, enact, fare, get along, get by, give, go on, impersonate, make out*, manage, muddle through*, operate, perform, personate, play, playact, portray, present, produce, put on*, quit, render the role, seem, stagger along*; SEE CONCEPT 633

do [v5] *travel, visit*
cover, explore, journey, look at, pass through, stop in, tour, track, traverse; SEE CONCEPT 224

do [v6] *cheat*
beat, bilk, chouse, con, cozen, deceive, defraud, dupe, fleece*, flimflam*, gyp*, hoax, overreach, swindle, take for a ride*, trick; SEE CONCEPT 59

do away with [v] *get rid of; destroy*
abolish, bump off*, cancel, discard, discontinue, do in*, eliminate, exterminate, finish, kill, liquidate, murder, put an end to, put to death, remove, slaughter, slay, take away, wipe out*; SEE CONCEPTS 180,252

docile [adj] *compliant, submissive*
accommodating, acquiescent, adaptable, agreeable, amenable, biddable, childlike, complacent, cool, docious, ductile, easily influenced, easy, easygoing, gentle, governable, humble, laid-back, manageable, meek, mellow, mild, obedient, obliging, orderly, pliable, pliant, quiet, resigned, soft, tame, teachable, tractable, usable, weak-kneed*, well-behaved, willing, yielding; SEE CONCEPTS 401,404

dock [n] *waterfront*
berth, embarkment, harbor, jetty, landing, landing pier, levee, lock, marina, pier, quay, slip, wharf; SEE CONCEPT 439

dock [v] *land on the waterfront*
anchor, berth, drop anchor, hook up, join, link up, moor, put in, rendezvous, tie up, unite; SEE CONCEPT 159

docket [n] *program, agenda*
calendar, card, schedule, tab, tally, ticket, timetable; SEE CONCEPT 271

doctor [n] *medical practitioner*
bones*, doc*, expert, general practitioner, healer, intern, MD, medic, medical person, medico, physician, professor*, quack*, scientist, specialist, surgeon; SEE CONCEPT 357

doctor [v1] *fix up, treat*
administer, apply medication, attend, do up, fix, give treatment, medicate, mend, overhaul, patch up*, rebuild, recondition, reconstruct, repair, revamp, supply; SEE CONCEPTS 110,310

doctor [v2] *adulterate, pervert*
add to, alter, change, cut, deacon, debase, dilute, disguise, dope up*, falsify, fudge*, gloss, load, misrepresent, mix with, sophisticate, spike*, tamper with, water down, weight; SEE CONCEPT 240

doctrinaire [adj] *dogmatic, opinionated*
authoritarian, authoritative, biased, bigoted, bull-headed*, dictative, dictatorial, dogged, fanatical, impractical, inflexible, insistent, magisterial, mulish, obstinate, one-sided, pertinacious, pigheaded*, rigid, speculative, stiff-necked*, stubborn, unrealistic; SEE CONCEPTS 267,401

doctrine [n] *opinion; principle*
article, article of faith, attitude, axiom, basic, belief, canon, concept, convention, conviction, credenda, creed, declaration, dogma, fundamental, gospel, implantation, inculcation, indoctrination, instruction, position, precept, pronouncement, propaganda, proposition, regulation, rule, statement, teaching, tenet, tradition, universal law, unwritten rule; SEE CONCEPTS 688,689

document [n] *written communication*
archive, certificate, credentials, deed, diary, evidence, form, instrument, language, pages, paper,

di
do

record, report, script, testimony, token; SEE CONCEPT 271

doddering [adj] aged, feeble
anile, decrepit, dotard, faltering, floundering, infirm, senile, shaky, tottering, trembling, unsteady, weak; SEE CONCEPTS 314,488,578,797

dodge [n] trick, feint
contrivance, device, machination, method, plan, plot, ploy, ruse, scheme, stratagem, strategy, subterfuge, wile; SEE CONCEPT 660

dodge [v] avoid
circumlocute, dark, deceive, ditch, duck, elude, equivocate, escape, evade, fence, fend off, fudge*, get around, get out of, give the slip*, hedge, juke, lurch, malinger, move to the side*, parry, pussyfoot*, put the move on*, shake, shake off*, shift, shirk, short-circuit, shuffle, sidestep, skip out on*, skirt, slide, slip, swerve, tergiversate, tergiverse, trick, turn aside, weasel*; SEE CONCEPTS 59,102

do for [v1] destroy
defeat, deprive, finish, kill, ruin, shatter, slaughter, slay; SEE CONCEPTS 238,252

do for [v2] help
abet, aid, assist, benefact, care for, help out, lend a hand*, look after, provide for, steady, support; SEE CONCEPT 110

dog [n] canine mammal
bitch, bowwow*, cur, doggy, fido*, flea bag*, hound, man's best friend*, mongrel, mutt, pooch*, pup, puppy, stray, tail-wagger*, tyke; SEE CONCEPT 400

dog [v] chase after; bother
bedog, haunt, hound, plague, pursue, shadow, tag, tail, track, trail, trouble; SEE CONCEPT 207

dogged [adj] determined, persistent
adamant, bullheaded*, firm, hanging tough*, hardheaded*, hard-nosed*, indefatigable, inexorable, inflexible, insistent, mulish, obdurate, obstinate, perseverant, perseverative, persevering, pertinacious, pigheaded*, relentless, resolute, rigid, single-minded, staunch, steadfast, steady, stubborn, tenacious, tough nut*, unbending, unflagging, unshakable, unyielding; SEE CONCEPTS 401,542

dogma [n] belief, principle
article, article of faith, canon, conviction, credenda, credo, creed, doctrine, gospel, opinion, persuasion, precept, rule, teachings, tenet, view; SEE CONCEPTS 688,689

dogmatic [adj1] dictatorial, opinionated
arbitrary, arrogant, assertive, bigoted, bullheaded*, categorical, cocksure*, confident, definite, despotic, determined, dictative, doctrinaire, domineering, downright, egotistical, emphatic, fanatical, fascistic, formal, high and mighty*, imperious, intolerant, magisterial, narrowminded, obdurate, obstinate, one-sided, overbearing, peremptory, pigheaded*, prejudiced, stiff-necked, stubborn, tenacious, tyrannical, unequivocal, wrong-headed; SEE CONCEPTS 267,542

dogmatic [adj2] based on absolute truth
a priori, as a matter of course, assertive, authoritarian, authoritative, axiomatic, by fiat, by natural law, by nature, canonical, categorical, deducible, deductive, derivable, doctrinaire, doctrinal, eternal, excathedra, formal, imperative, inevitable, on faith, oracular, orthodox, peremptory, positive, pragmatic, prophetic, reasoned, systematic, theoretical, unchangeable, unerring, unqualified; SEE CONCEPTS 570,587,582

do in [v] destroy; exhaust
assassinate, bankrupt, bump off*, butcher*, cool*, dilapidate, dispatch, do away with*, eliminate, execute, fatigue, finish, frazzle*, kill, knock out*, liquidate, murder, put away*, ruin, shatter, slaughter, slay, tire, wear out, weary, wreck; SEE CONCEPTS 137,250,252

doing [n] achievement
accomplishing, accomplishment, achieving, act, action, carrying out, deed, execution, exploit, handiwork, implementation, performance, performing, thing; SEE CONCEPT 706

doldrums [n] depression
apathy, black mood*, blahs*, blue funk*, blues*, boredom, bummer*, dejection, disinterest, dismals, downer, dullness, dumps*, ennui, funk*, gloom, inactivity, indifference, inertia, lassitude, letdown, listlessness, malaise, mopes*, slump, stagnation, stupor, tedium, torpor, yawn*; SEE CONCEPT 410

dole [n] allowance, allocation
allotment, alms, apportionment, benefit, charity, dispensation, distribution, division, donation, gift, grant, gratuity, handout, living wage, mite, modicum, parcel, pittance, portion, quota, relief, share, subsistence, trifle; SEE CONCEPTS 337,344

doleful [adj] depressing
afflicted, cast down, cheerless, crestfallen, dejected, depressed, dismal, dispirited, distressing, dolent, dolorous, down, downcast, downhearted, down in the mouth*, dreary, forlorn, funereal, gloomy, grieving, lamentable, lugubrious, melancholy, mournful, painful, piteous, pitiful, plaintive, rueful, sad, somber, sorrowful, woebegone, woeful, wretched; SEE CONCEPTS 403,529

dole out [v] allocate, distribute
administer, allot, apportion, assign, deal, deal out, dispense, disperse, divide, divvy*, give, hand out, lot, measure, mete, mete out, parcel, partition, share, share out; SEE CONCEPTS 108,140

doll [n] toy person
baby, dolly, effigy, figure, figurine, manikin, marionette, model, moppet*, puppet; SEE CONCEPT 446

dollar [n] paper money
ace*, bank note, bill, buck*, certificate, clam*, cucumber*, currency, folding money, greenback*, legal tender, note, one-spot*, single; SEE CONCEPT 340

doll up [v] beautify oneself; dress up
deck out*, fix up, gussy up*, preen, primp, put on best clothes, smarten up*, spiff*, spruce up*; SEE CONCEPTS 162,167,202

dolor [n] misery, anguish
agony, distress, grief, heartache, heartbreak, passion, ruth, sadness, sorrow, suffering; SEE CONCEPT 410

dolorous [adj] miserable, anguished
afflicted, afflictive, calamitous, deplorable, dire, distressing, doleful, dolent, dolesome, grievous, harrowing, heart-rending, lamentable, lugubrious, melancholy, mournful, painful, plaintive, regrettable, rueful, ruthful, sad, sorrowful, woebegone, woeful, wretched; SEE CONCEPTS 401,403

dolt [n] stupid person
airhead*, blockhead*, boob*, chump*, dimwit*, dodo*, dope, dork*, dumbbell*, dumdum*,

dunce, fool, goon*, idiot, ignoramus, lamebrain*, lunkhead*, meathead*, nitwit*, sap*, simpleton, stupid, yo-yo*; SEE CONCEPTS 412,423

domain [n] *area of expertise, rule*
authority, bailiwick, concern, demesne, department, discipline, district, dominion, empire, estate, field, home park*, jurisdiction, land, neck of the woods*, occupation, orbit*, power, province, quarter, realm, region, scope, slot, specialty, sphere, stomping grounds*, terrain, territory, turf, walk, wing; SEE CONCEPTS 349,518,710

dome [n] *arched part of ceiling*
arcade, arch, bubble, bulge, covering, cupola, mosque, roof, span, top, vault; SEE CONCEPT 440

domestic [adj1] *household*
calm, devoted, domiciliary, family, home, home-like, home-loving, homely, indoor, pet, private, sedentary, settled, stay-at-home, subdued, submissive, tame, trained, tranquil; SEE CONCEPT 542

domestic [adj2] *not foreign*
handcrafted, home-grown, homemade, indigenous, internal, internal, intestine, intramural, municipal, national, native; SEE CONCEPTS 536,549

domesticate [v] *tame; habituate*
acclimatize, accustom, break, break in, breed, bring up, bust, corral, domiciliate, familiarize, gentle, herd, hitch, housetrain, naturalize, raise, reclaim, round up, subdue, teach, train, yoke; SEE CONCEPTS 202,285

domestic partner [n] *live-in significant other*
beneficiary, cohabitant, companion, housemate, longtime companion, lover, partner, spouse; SEE CONCEPT 414

domicile [n] *human habitat*
abode, accommodation, apartment, castle, commorancy, condo*, condominium, co-op, crash pad*, dump, dwelling, habitation, home, house, joint, legal residence, mansion, pad*, rack*, residence, residency, roof over head*, roost*, settlement; SEE CONCEPTS 439,516

dominance [n] *supremacy*
ascendancy, authority, command, control, domination, dominion, government, influence, paramountcy, power, preeminence, preponderance, prepotence, prepotency, rule, sovereignty, sway, upper hand, whip hand; SEE CONCEPTS 376,668

dominant [adj1] *superior, controlling*
ascendant, assertive, authoritative, bossy, chief, commanding, demonstrative, despotic, domineering, effective, first, foremost, governing, imperative, imperious, leading, main, obtaining, outweighing, overbalancing, overbearing, overweighing, paramount, powerful, predominant, predominate, preeminent, preponderant, presiding, prevailing, prevalent, principal, regnant, reigning, ruling, sovereign, supreme, surpassing, transcendent; SEE CONCEPT 574

dominant [adj2] *main, primary*
capital, chief, influential, major, number one*, outstanding, paramount, predominant, preeminent, prevailing, prevalent, principal, prominent, stellar; SEE CONCEPT 568

dominate [v1] *govern, rule*
boss, call the shots*, command, control, detract from, dictate, direct, domineer, eclipse, handle, have one's way*, have upper hand*, head, hold sway over*, influence, keep under thumb*, lay down the law*, lead, lead by the nose*, manage, monopolize, outshine, overbear, overrule, over-

shadow, play first fiddle*, predominate, preponderate, prevail, prevail over, reign, rule the roost*, run, run the show*, sit on top of*, subject, subjugate, superabound, sway, tyrannize; SEE CONCEPTS 94,117,298

dominate [v2] *tower above*
bestride, bend, bluster, boss around*, browbeat, bulldoze*, bully*, call the shots*, dominate, hector, henpeck*, in the driver's seat*, intimidate, keep under thumb*, kick around*, lead by the nose*, menace, overbear, predominate, preponderate, prevail, push the buttons*, reign, rule, rule the roost*, run the show*, run things*, swagger, threaten, throw weight around*, tyrannize; SEE CONCEPTS 14,94

domineering [adj] *oppressive, authoritarian*
arrogant, autocratic, bossy, coercive, crack the whip*, despotic, dictatorial, egotistic, high-handed, imperative, imperial, imperious, in driver's seat*, insolent, iron-handed*, on high horse*, overbearing, peremptory, tyrannical; SEE CONCEPT 401

dominion [n] *area of rule; authority*
ascendancy, authorization, bailiwick, command, commission, control, country, demesne, district, domain, dominance, domination, empire, enclave, field, government, jurisdiction, management, power, preeminence, prepotence, prepotency, prerogative, privilege, property, province, realm, regency, regiment, regimentation, region, reign, rule, seniority, sovereignty, sphere, state, stomping grounds*, supremacy, sway, terrain, territory, turf, walk; SEE CONCEPTS 198,376,710

donate [v] *make a gift of*
accord, ante up*, award, bequeath, bestow, chip in*, confer, contribute, devote, dole out*, do one's part*, feed the kitty*, get in the act*, get it up*, give, give away, grant, hand out, lay on, pass the hat*, present, provide, subscribe, sweeten the pot*; SEE CONCEPT 108

donation [n] *gift*
a hand*, aid, allowance, alms, appropriation, assistance, benefaction, beneficence, bequest, boon, charity, contribution, dole, do one's part*, endowment, gifting, grant, gratuity, handout, help, helping hand* largess, lump, offering, philanthropy, pittance, present, presentation, ration, relief, subscription, subsidy, subvention, write-off*; SEE CONCEPTS 337,340

done [adj1] *accomplished, finished*
all in*, all over*, a wrap*, brought about, brought to pass, buttoned up*, compassed, complete, completed, concluded, consummated, depleted, down, drained, effected, effete, ended, executed, exhausted, fixed, fulfilled, over, perfected, performed, realized, rendered, set, spent, succeeded,

do
do

terminated, through, used up, wired, wrought;
SEE CONCEPTS *528,531*

done [*adj2*] *thoroughly cooked*
baked, boiled, brewed, broiled, browned, crisped,
fried, ready, stewed; SEE CONCEPTS *462,613*

done [*adj3*] *approved, agreed upon*
compacted, determined, okay, settled, you're on*;
SEE CONCEPT *558*

done for [*adj*] *beaten, defeated*
broken, conquered, dashed, destroyed, doomed,
finished, foiled, lost, ruined, through, undone,
vanquished, washed-up*, wrecked; SEE CON-
CEPTS *537,570*

done in [*adj*] *exhausted*
all in*, bushed*, dead, depleted, done, effete,
fagged, far-gone*, on last leg*, ready to drop*,
spent, tired, used up, washed-out*, weary, worn-
out; SEE CONCEPTS *314,485*

donkey [*n*] *small domestic horselike mammal*
ass, burro, horse, jackass, jennet, jenny, maud,
moke, mule, neddy, pony, Rocky Mountain canary*; SEE CONCEPT *394*

donor [*n*] *giver of gift*
almsgiver, altruist, angel*, backer, benefactor,
benefactress, conferrer, contributor, do-
nator, grantor, heavy hitter*, patron, philanthropist, presenter, Santa Claus*, savior, subscriber;
SEE CONCEPTS *359,423*

doom [*n*] *fate or decision, usually unpleasant*
annihilation, calamity, cataclysm, catastrophe,
circumstance, conclusion, condemnation, death,
decree, destination, destiny, destruction, disaster,
downfall, end, fixed future, foreordination, fortune, handwriting on wall*, judgment, Judgment
Day, karma, kismet, lap of the gods*, lot, Moira,
opinion, portion, predestination, predetermination, ruin, sentence, tragedy, verdict, way the ball
bounces*, way the cookie crumbles*; SEE CON-
CEPT *679*

doomed [*adj*] *condemned, hopeless*
bedeviled, bewitched, convicted, cursed, cut
down, damned, dead duck*, destroyed, done,
done for*, fated, foreordained, ill-fated, ill-
omened, in the cards*, kiss of death*, lost, luckless, menaced, overthrown, overwhelmed,
predestined, que sera sera*, reprobate, ruined,
sentenced, star-crossed, sunk, suppressed, threatened, thrown down, undone, unfortunate, unredeemed, wrecked; SEE CONCEPT *537*

door [*n*] *entrance to room, building*
aperture, egress, entry, entryway, exit, gate, gateway, hatch, hatchway, ingress, opening, portal,
postern, slammer; SEE CONCEPT *440*

do out of [*v*] *cheat*
balk, beat out of*, bilk, con, deceive, deprive,
steal, swindle, trick; SEE CONCEPTS *59,139*

dope [*n1*] *stupid person*
ass, blockhead*, dimwit*, dolt, donkey*, dunce,
fool, idiot, lame-brain*, simpleton; SEE CON-
CEPTS *412,423*

dope [*n2*] *drug*
narcotic, opiate, stimulant; SEE CONCEPT *307*

dope [*n3*] *inside news*
account, details, developments, facts, info*, information, knowledge, lowdown*, tip*; SEE CON-
CEPT *274*

dope [*v*] *drug someone*
adulterate, anesthetize, deaden, debase, inject,
knock out*, load, narcotize, put to sleep, sedate,

soak, sophisticate, stupefy; SEE CONCEPTS
156,310

dopey [*adj*] *stupid*
comatose, dense, dumb, foolish, heavy, hebetudinous, idiotic, lethargic, senseless, silly, simple,
slow, sluggish, slumberish, thick, torpid; SEE
CONCEPT *402*

dormant [*adj*] *inactive; sleeping*
abeyant, asleep, closed down, comatose, down,
fallow, hibernating, inert, inoperative, latent, lethargic, lurking, on the shelf*, out of action*,
passive, potential, prepotent, quiescent, sidelined,
slack, sluggish, slumbering, smoldering, suspended, torpid; SEE CONCEPT *539*

dose [*n*] *portion of drug or other consumable*
application, dosage, dram, draught, fill, fix*, hit*,
lot, measure, measurement, nip*, potion, prescription, quantity, share, shot*, slug*, spoonful;
SEE CONCEPTS *307,835*

dot [*n*] *tiny mark, drop*
atom, circle, dab, droplet, fleck, flyspeck, grain,
iota, jot, mite, mote, particle, period, pinpoint,
point, speck, spot, tittle; SEE CONCEPTS *284,831*

dot [*v*] *make spot(s)*
bespeckle, dab, dabble, fleck, freckle, pepper,
pimple, sprinkle, stipple, stud; SEE CONCEPTS
79,174

dotage [*n*] *feebleness, old age*
advanced age, decrepitude, elderliness, fatuity,
imbecility, infirmity, second childhood*, senectitude, senility, weakness; SEE CONCEPTS *405,715*

dote on/dote upon [*v*] *lavish affection on*
admire, adore, be fond of, be infatuated with, be
sweet on*, cherish, enjoy, fancy, hold dear, idolize, like, love, pet, prize, treasure, worship; SEE
CONCEPT *32*

doting [*adj*] *indulgent; serving*
adoring, affectionate, devoted, fascinated, fatuous, fond, foolish, lovesick, lovesome, loving,
silly, simple, struck; SEE CONCEPT *401*

double [*n*] *something which exactly resembles another*
angel, clone, companion, coordinate, copy, counterpart, dead ringer*, duplicate, image, impersonator,
lookalike*, match, mate, picture, portrait,
reciprocal, replica, ringer*, simulacrum, spitting
image*, stand-in*, twin; SEE CONCEPTS *664,716*

double [*adj*] *in a pair*
as much again, bifold, binary, binate, coupled,
dual, dualistic, duple, duplex, duplicate, duplicated, geminate, paired, repeated, second, twice,
twin, twofold, two times; SEE CONCEPT *771*

double [*v*] *make two of; make twice as large*
amplify, augment, dualize, dupe, duplicate, du-
plify, enlarge, fold, grow, increase, infold,
magnify, multiply, plait, pleat, plicate, redouble,
repeat, replicate, supplement; SEE CONCEPTS
236,245

double back [*v*] *reverse path*
backtrack, circle, dodge, loop, retrace one's steps,
return, turn; SEE CONCEPTS *224,232*

double-cross [*v*] *betray*
beguile, bluff, cheat, con, cross, deceive, defraud,
four-flush*, hoodwink*, humbug*, illude, juggle,
mislead, sell, sell out*, split, swindle, take in,
trick, two-time*; SEE CONCEPTS *7,19,59*

double-dealing [*v*] *betrayal, cheating*
bad faith, chicane, chicanery, deceit, deception,
dishonesty, duplicity, foul play*, fourberie, fraud,
hanky-panky*, hypocrisy, mendacity, perfidy,

sharp practice*, treachery, trickery, two-timing*; SEE CONCEPT 59

double-dealing [*adj*] *cheating, deceitful*
ambidextrous, crooked, dishonest, double, duplicitous, fraudulent, hypocritical, insincere, left-handed*, lying, perfidious, sneaky, swindling, treacherous, tricky, two-faced*, two-timing*, underhanded, untrustworthy, wily; SEE CONCEPT 401

double entendre [*n*] *play on words*
ambiguity, amphibiology, double meaning, equivocality, equivocation, equivoque, innuendo, joke, pun, tergiversation; SEE CONCEPTS 278,682

double-talk [*n*] *nonsense communicated*
amphibiology, balderdash, baloney*, bull*, drivel, equivocation, flimflam*, gibberish, jazz*, mumbo jumbo*, rigmarole; SEE CONCEPT 278

doubt [*n*] *lack of faith, conviction; questioning*
agnosticism, ambiguity, apprehension, confusion, demurral, difficulty, dilemma, disbelief, discredit, disquiet, distrust, dubiety, dubiousness, faithlessness, faltering, fear, hesitancy, hesitation, incertitude, incredulity, indecision, irresolution, lack of confidence, misgiving, mistrust, perplexity, problem, qualm, quandary, rejection, reluctance, scruple, skepticism, suspense, suspicion, uncertainty, vacillation, wavering; SEE CONCEPTS 21,410,689,690

doubt [*v*] *lack confidence in; question*
be apprehensive of, be curious, be dubious, be in a quandary, be puzzled, be uncertain, be undetermined, call in question, challenge, demur, disbelieve, discredit, dispute, distrust, fear, fluctuate, give no credence, harbor suspicion, have qualms, hesitate, imagine, impugn, insinuate, misdoubt, misgive, mistrust, not buy*, query, read differently, scruple, shilly-shally*, skepticize, smell a rat*, surmise, suspect, take dim view of, vacillate, waver, wonder at; SEE CONCEPT 21

doubter [*n*] *person who does not believe*
agnostic, cynic, disbeliever, headshaker*, questioner, skeptic, unbeliever, zetetic; SEE CONCEPTS 361,423

doubtful [*adj1*] *questionable, unclear*
ambiguous, borderline, chancy, clouded, contingent, debatable, dicey, disreputable, doubtable, dubious, dubitable, equivocal, far-fetched, fat chance, fishy*, hazardous, hazy, iffy*, impugnable, inconclusive, indecisive, indefinite, indeterminate, indistinct, insecure, long shot*, obscure, on thin ice*, open, pending, precarious, problematic, shady, sneaky*, speculative, suspect, suspicious, touch-and-go*, touchy, uncertain, unconfirmed, undecided, uneasy, unsettled, unstable, unsure, up for grabs*; SEE CONCEPTS 529,535

doubtful [*adj2*] *not believing*
agnostic, baffled, confused, discomposed, disconcerted, distracted, distrustful, disturbed, doubting, dubious, equivocal, faithless, faltering, flustered, hesitant, hesitating, in a quandary, in clouds*, indecisive, in dilemma, irresolute, like doubting Thomas*, lost, not following, of two minds*, perplexed, puzzled, questioning, skeptical, suspicious, tentative, theoretical, troubled, uncertain, unconvinced, undecided, unresolved, unsettled, unsure, vacillating, wavering, without belief; SEE CONCEPTS 403,542

doubtless [*adv*] *certainly; most likely*
absolutely, apparently, assuredly, clearly, easily, for sure, indisputably, no ifs ands or buts*, of course, ostensibly, positively, precisely, presumably, probably, seemingly, supposedly, surely, truly, undoubtedly, unequivocally, unquestionably, without doubt; SEE CONCEPTS 535,552

doughnut [*n*] *sweet ring-shaped fried cake*
bun, cruller, danish, dunker*, pastry, sinker*, sweet roll; SEE CONCEPTS 457,461

do up [*v*] *physically prepare; fix*
clean, doctor, enclose, finish, gift-wrap, launder, mend, overhaul, package, patch, rebuild, recondition, reconstruct, repair, revamp, wash, wrap; SEE CONCEPTS 126,165,182,202

dour [*adj*] *gloomy, grim*
bleak, crabbed, dismal, dreary, forbidding, glum, hard, harsh, morose, saturnine, severe, sour, stringent, sulky, sullen, surly, ugly, unfriendly; SEE CONCEPTS 267,404

douse [*v*] *drench, extinguish with liquid*
blow out, deluge, drown, duck, dunk, immerse, plunge, put out, quench, saturate, slop, slosh, smother, snuff, snuff out, soak, sop, souse, spatter, splash, splatter, squench, steep, submerge, submerse, wet; SEE CONCEPTS 250,256

dovetail [*v*] *link, fit together*
accord, agree, check out, coincide, conform, correspond, go, harmonize, interlock, jibe, join, match, mortise, square, sync*, sync up*, tally, tenon, unite; SEE CONCEPTS 113,664

dowdy [*adj*] *poorly dressed; old-fashioned*
antiquated, archaic, baggy, bedraggled, blowsy*, bygone, dated, dingy, drab, dull, frowzy*, frumpy*, homely, moldy, old hat*, outdated, outmoded, out-of-date, passé, plain, run-down, scrubby*, shabby, slatternly, sloppy, slovenly, stodgy, tacky, tasteless, unfashionable, unkempt, unseemly, unstylish, untidy, vintage, wrinkled; SEE CONCEPT 589

do without [*v*] *get along without*
abstain from, dispense, endure, forgo, give up; SEE CONCEPTS 23,646

down [*adj1/adv*] *below; physically lower*
bottomward, cascading, declining, depressed, descending, downgrade, downhill, downward, dropping, earthward, falling, gravitating, groundward, inferior, nether, precipitating, sagging, sinking, sliding, slipping, slumping, subjacent, to the bottom, under, underneath; SEE CONCEPTS 583,586,735

down [*adj2*] *unhappy*
bad, blue*, cast down, chapfallen, crestfallen, dejected, depressed, disheartened, dispirited, downcast, downhearted, low, miserable, off, sad, slack, sluggish; SEE CONCEPT 403

down-and-out [*adj*] *poverty-stricken*
beaten, beggared, defeated, derelict, destitute, finished, impoverished, needy, outcast, penniless, ruined, vagabond, vagrant; SEE CONCEPT 334

downcast [*adj*] *depressed, unhappy*
bad, blue, brooding, bummed out*, cast down, chapfallen, cheerless, crestfallen, daunted, dejected, despondent, disappointed, disconsolate, discouraged, disheartened, dismayed, dispirited, distressed, doleful, dour, downhearted, down in the dumps*, down-in-the-mouth*, dragged*, droopy, dull, forlorn, gloomy, glum, heartsick, in pain, listless, low, low-spirited, miserable, moody, mopey*, morose, oppressed, sad, shot down*, singing the blues*, sunk*, troubled, weighed down*, woebegone; SEE CONCEPT 403

do
do

downfall [n] *disgrace, ruin*
atrophy, bane, breakdown, cloudburst, collapse, comedown, comeuppance, debacle, decadence, declension, degeneracy, degeneration, deluge, descent, destruction, deterioration, devolution, discomfiture, down, drop, failure, fall, flood, on the rocks*, overthrow, rack and ruin*, road to ruin*, ruination, storm, the skids*, undoing; SEE CONCEPTS 674,679,699

downgrade [n] *slope*
decline, declivity, descent, dip, hill, inclination, pitch; SEE CONCEPTS 509,738

downgrade [v] *lower in opinion or rank*
abase, bench*, break*, bump*, bust*, declass, decrease, decry, degrade, demerit, demote, denigrate, depreciate, detract from, devalorize, devalue, disparage, disrate, humble, mark down, minimize, reduce, run down, set back, take down a peg*, undervalue, write off*; SEE CONCEPTS 7,19,54,240

downhearted [adj] *depressed, unhappy*
blue*, chapfallen, crestfallen, dejected, despondent, disconsolate, discouraged, disheartened, dismayed, dispirited, down, downcast, low, lowspirited, sad, sorrowful, spiritless, woebegone; SEE CONCEPT 403

downlink [n] *transmission path for data*
circuit, communications pathway, network, pathway, signal route; SEE CONCEPT 269

download [v] *to transfer data from one computer system to another*
boot up, compute, computerize, crunch numbers*, digitize, initialize, input, keyboard, key in, load, log in, log out, program, run; SEE CONCEPTS 211,217

downpour [n] *tremendous pouring of rain*
cloudburst, deluge, drencher, flood, inundation, monsoon, rainstorm, storm, torrential rain; SEE CONCEPT 526

downright [adj] *thorough, absolute*
blatant, blunt, categorical, certain, clear, complete, damned, explicit, flat, gross, honest, indubitable, open, out-and-out, outright, plain, positive, simple, sincere, straight, straightforward, sure, thoroughgoing, total, undisguised, unequivocal, unmitigated, unqualified, unquestionable, utter, whole; SEE CONCEPT 531

downside [n] *a negative aspect of a situation*
defect, disadvantage, drawback, fault, flaw, inconvenience, minus, problem, trouble; SEE CONCEPTS 666,674

downsize [v] *to decrease in size, especially of a workforce*
curtail, cut, cut back, cut down, decrease, deduct, diminish, phase down, phase out, reduce, retrench, roll back, roll down, scale back, scale down, shrink, step down, trim, trim away, tune down; SEE CONCEPTS 236,240,247

downtime [n] *time during which an activity is stopped*
break, breathing spell, freedom, free time, halt, interim, interlude, intermission, letup, lull, pause, recess, repose, respite, rest, spare time, spell, stay, suspension, time on one's hands, time out, time to burn, time to kill; SEE CONCEPT 807

down-to-earth [adj] *reasonable, practical*
common, commonsense, easy, hard, hardboiled, hardheaded, matter-of-fact, mundane, no-nonsense, plainspoken, pragmatic, rational, realistic, sane, sensible, sober, unfan-

tastic, unidealistic, unsentimental; SEE CONCEPTS 402,558

downtrodden [adj] *afflicted, abused*
abject, a slave to*, at one's beck and call*, at one's feet*, at one's mercy*, destitute, distressed, exploited, have-not, helpless, in one's clutches*, in one's pocket*, in one's power*, led by the nose*, maltreated, mistreated, needy, oppressed, overcome, persecuted, subjugated, subservient, suppressed, tyrannized, underdog*, underfoot*, under one's thumb*; SEE CONCEPT 542

downy [adj] *fluffy*
featherlike, feathery, fleecy, fuzzy, light, plumate, plumose, pubescent, silky, soft, velutinous, velvety, woolly; SEE CONCEPTS 604,606

doze [n] *light sleep*
catnap, drowse, forty winks*, nap, shut-eye*, siesta, slumber, snooze*; SEE CONCEPTS 315,681

doze [v] *take a nap*
catch a wink*, catnap, cop some z's*, drift off*, drop off*, drowse, nod off*, sleep, sleep lightly, slumber, snooze; SEE CONCEPTS 315,681

drab [adj] *dull, colorless*
arid, blah*, bleak, boring, brown, characterless, cheerless, desolate, dingy, dismal, dreary, dry, dull as dishwater*, faded, flat, gloomy, gray, grungy, lackluster, lusterless, muddy, murky, rundown, same, shabby, somber, subfuse, unchanging, uninspired, vapid, zero*; SEE CONCEPTS 536,617,618

draft [n1] *something formulated; plan*
abstract, blueprint, delineation, outline, preliminary form, rough sketch, version; SEE CONCEPTS 271,660

draft [n2] *check for paying money*
bank draft, bill, bond, cheque, coupon, debenture, IOU, letter of credit, money order, order, promissory note, receipt, warrant; SEE CONCEPTS 332,344

draft [n3] *gust of air*
breeze, current, eddy, puff, wind; SEE CONCEPT 437

draft [n4] *military conscription*
allotment, assignment, call of duty, call-up*, greetings*, impressment, induction, letter from Uncle Sam*, levy, lottery, recruiting, registration, roll call*, selection, selective service; SEE CONCEPT 321

draft [n5] *drink of beverage*
drag*, drain, drench, glass, peg*, quaff, swallow, swig*, swill*; SEE CONCEPTS 169,454

draft [v1] *formulate*
adumbrate, block out, characterize, compose, concoct, contrive, delineate, design, devise, draw, draw up, fabricate, fashion, forge, form, frame, invent, make, manufacture, outline, plan, prepare, project, rough, shape, skeleton, sketch; SEE CONCEPTS 36,79,173

draft [v2] *select for military force*
call up, choose, conscribe, conscript, dragoon, enlist, enroll, impress, induct, induce, muster, press, recruit, sign on, sign up; SEE CONCEPTS 8,320

drag [n1] *bad situation*
annoyance, bore, bother, burden, encumbrance, hang-up, hindrance, impediment, nuisance, pain, pest, pill, sway, trouble; SEE CONCEPT 674

drag [n2] *a puff while smoking*
breathing, draw, inhalation, pull, smoke; SEE CONCEPT 185

drag [v1] *haul something to a new place*
draw, hale, lug, magnetize, move, pull, schlepp*, tow, trail, transport, truck, tug, yank; SEE CONCEPTS *206,213*

drag [v2] *move very slowly*
be delayed, be quiescent, crawl, creep, dally*, dawdle*, delay, encounter difficulty*, hang*, inch*, lag, lag behind, limp along, linger, loiter, mark time*, poke*, procrastinate, put off*, sag, shamble, shuffle, slow down, stagnate, straggle, tarry, trail behind*, traipse; SEE CONCEPTS *151,681*

dragging [adj] *tiresome, monotonous*
boring, drawn-out, dull, going slowly, humdrum, lengthy, long, overlong, prolonged, protracted, tedious, wearisome; SEE CONCEPTS *482,798*

drag on/drag out [v] *extend time of action*
continue, draw out, endure, extend, go on slowly, keep going, lengthen, persist, prolong, protract, spin out, stretch out; SEE CONCEPT *239*

drain [n] *channel through which liquid runs off*
cesspool, cloaca, conduit, culvert, ditch, duct, outlet, pipe, sewer, sink, trench, watercourse; SEE CONCEPT *501*

drain [v1] *remove liquid; remove supply*
abate, bankrupt, bleed, bleed dry*, catheterize, consume, debilitate, decrease, deplete, devitalize, diminish, dissipate, divert, draft, draw off, drink up, dry, empty, evacuate, exhaust, expend, fatigue, filter off, finish, free from, get last drop*, get rid of, gulp down, impoverish, lessen, milk*, pump, pump out, quaff, reduce, sap, siphon, spend, strain, suck, suck dry*, swallow, tap, tax, tire out, use up, waste, wear, wear down, weary, withdraw; SEE CONCEPTS *142,211,225*

drain [v2] *seep, discharge liquid*
abate, decline, decrease, diminish, dwindle, effuse, exude, filter off, flow, flow out, leak, leave dry, ooze, osmose, percolate, release, run off, taper off, trickle, well; SEE CONCEPTS *179,698*

drained [adj] *used up; exhausted*
all in*, beat*, bleary, burned out*, dead, dead tired*, depleted, dragging, effete, far-gone, hacked*, pooped*, spent, washed-out, weary, wiped-out*, worn-out; SEE CONCEPTS *485,560*

drama [n1] *theatrical piece; acting*
boards*, Broadway*, climax, comedy, dramatic art, dramatization, dramaturgy, farce, footlights, histrionic art, melodrama, play, production, scene, show, show business, showmanship, stagecraft, stage show, tear-jerker*, theater, theatricals, thespian art, tragedy, vehicle*; SEE CONCEPTS *263,271,293*

drama [n2] *turmoil in real life*
climax, comedy, crisis, dramatics, emotion, excitement, farce, histrionics, melodrama, scene, spectacle, tension, theatrics, tragedy; SEE CONCEPT *674*

dramatic [adj] *exciting, moving*
affecting, breathtaking, climactic, comic, effective, electrifying, emotional, expressive, farcical, histrionic, impressive, melodramatic, powerful, sensational, startling, striking, sudden, suspenseful, tense, theatrical, thespian, thrilling, tragic, vivid; SEE CONCEPTS *537,548*

dramatize [v] *make a performance of*
act, amplify, burlesque, enact, exaggerate, execute, farcialize, give color to, ham it up*, lay it on*, make a production of, melodramatize, overdo, overstate, perform, playact, play on heart-

strings*, play to gallery, play up, present, produce, show, splash, stage, tragedize; SEE CONCEPTS *49,59,292*

drape [v] *hang over, adorn*
array, cloak, clothe, cover, dangle, display, don, dress, droop, drop, enclose, enswathe, envelop, enwrap, fold, hang, lean over, let fall, line, model, roll, sprawl, spread, spread-eagle, suspend, swathe, wrap; SEE CONCEPT *172*

drastic [adj] *severe, extreme*
desperate, dire, exorbitant, extravagant, forceful, harsh, immoderate, radical, strong; SEE CONCEPTS *537,569*

draw [n] *tie in competition*
dead end*, dead heat*, deadlock, even steven*, photo finish*, stalemate, standoff, tie; SEE CONCEPT *706*

draw [v1] *move something by pulling*
attract, bring, carry, convey, cull, draft, drag, drain, educe, elicit, evoke, extract, fetch, gather, haul, hook, jerk, lug, magnetize, pick, pluck, pump, rake, siphon, tap, tow, trail, trawl, tug, wind in, wrench, yank; SEE CONCEPT *206*

draw [v2] *create a likeness in a picture*
caricature, chart, compose, crayon, delineate, depict, describe, design, draft, engrave, etch, express, form, formulate, frame, graph, limn, map out, mark, model, outline, paint, pencil, portray, prepare, profile, sketch, trace, write; SEE CONCEPTS *79,174*

draw [v3] *deduce*
collect, conclude, derive, gather, get, infer, judge, make, make out, take; SEE CONCEPT *15*

draw [v4] *allure, influence*
argue into, attract, bewitch, bring around, bring forth, call forth, captivate, charm, convince, elicit, enchant, engage, entice, evoke, fascinate, get, induce, invite, lure, magnetize, persuade, prompt, take, wile, win over; SEE CONCEPTS *7,19,22,68*

draw [v5] *take out, extend*
attenuate, choose, drain, elongate, extort, extract, lengthen, pick, pull out, respire, select, single out, stretch, suck, take; SEE CONCEPTS *142,163,239*

drawback [n] *disadvantage*
check, defect, deficiency, detriment, difficulty, disability, evil, failing, fault, flaw, fly in the ointment*, handicap, hindrance, hitch, ill, impediment, imperfection, inconvenience, lack, nuisance, obstacle, shortcoming, snag, stumbling block*, trouble, weakness; SEE CONCEPTS *666, 674*

draw back [v] *retract from position*
deduct, discount, pull back, recede, recoil, reel in, retreat, sheathe, shrink, start back, subtract, take away, withdraw; SEE CONCEPTS *195,213*

drawing [n] *illustration*
cartoon, commercial art, comp, delineation, depiction, design, doodle, etching, graphics, layout, likeness, outline, painting, picture, portrayal, representation, sketch, storyboard, study, tracing, work of art; SEE CONCEPT *625*

drawl [v] *lengthen, draw out*
chant, drag out, drone, extend, intone, nasalize, prolong, pronounce slowly, protract, utter; SEE CONCEPTS *77,239*

drawn [adj] *tense, fatigued*
fraught, haggard, harassed, harrowed, peaked, pinched, sapped, starved, strained, stressed, taut, thin, tired, worn; SEE CONCEPT *485*

do
dr

draw on [v] *use to advantage*
effect, employ, exploit, extract, fall back on, have recourse to, make use of, rely on, require, take from; SEE CONCEPT 225

draw out [v] *prolong*
attract, continue, drag, drag out, elongate, extend, lead on, lengthen, make longer, prolongate, protract, pull, spin, spin out*, stretch, string out*, tug; SEE CONCEPTS 236,239,245

draw up [v] *draft document*
compose, formulate, frame, indite, make, prepare, write, write out; SEE CONCEPT 79

dread [n] *fear*
affright, alarm, apprehension, aversion, awe, cold feet*, consternation, creeps*, dismay, fright, funk*, goose bumps*, horror, jitters, panic, phobia, stage fright, terror, trepidation, trepidity, worriment; SEE CONCEPT 27

dread [adj] *horrible, terrifying*
alarming, awe-inspiring, awful, creepy*, dire, frightening, frightful, shuddersome, terrible; SEE CONCEPT 537

dread [v] *anticipate with horror*
apprehend, be afraid, cringe, fear, have cold feet*, misdoubt, quake, shrink from, shudder, tremble; SEE CONCEPT 27

dreadful [adj] *horrible, frightening*
abominable, alarming, appalling, atrocious, awful, bad, beastly, creepy*, dire, distressing, fearful, formidable, frightful, frozen, ghastly, godawful*, grievous, grim, grody*, gross*, hideous, horrendous, horrific, icky*, lousy, mean, monstrous, rotten, shameful, shocking, shuddersome, spooky, terrible, terrific, tragic, tremendous, wicked; SEE CONCEPTS 537,550

dream [n1] *illusion, vision*
bubble*, castle in the air*, chimera, daydream, delusion, fancy, fantasy, hallucination, head trip*, idea, image, imagination, impression, incubus, mental picture, nightmare, pie in the sky*, pipe dream*, rainbow, reverie, specter, speculation, thought, trance, vagary, wraith; SEE CONCEPT 529

dream [n2] *goal*
ambition, aspiration, design, desire, flight of fancy*, hope, notion, pipe dream*, wish; SEE CONCEPT 659

dream [v] *conjure up scenario*
be delirious, be moonstruck, be up in clouds*, brainstorm, build castles in air*, conceive, concoct, cook up*, crave, create, daydream, devise, envisage, fancy, fantasize, formulate, hallucinate, hanker*, hatch*, have a flash*, have a nightmare*, have a notion*, have a vision, hunger, idealize, imagine, invent, long, lust, make up, picture, ponder, search for pot of gold*, sigh, stargaze*, sublimate, think, think up, thirst, visualize; SEE CONCEPTS 17,529

dream up [v] *concoct plan*
contrive, cook up*, create, devise, frame, hatch*, imagine, invent, make up, spin*, think up; SEE CONCEPTS 17,36

dreamy [adj] *illusory, romantic*
abstracted, astral, calming, chimerical, daydreaming, excellent, fanciful, fantastic, gentle, idealistic, imaginary, immaterial, impractical, intangible, introspective, introverted, lulling, marvelous, misty, musing, mythical, nightmarish, otherworldly, out of this world*, pensive, phantasmagoric, phantasmagorical, preoccupied, quixotic, relaxing, shadowy, soothing, speculative,

unreal, unsubstantial, utopian, vague, visionary whimsical; SEE CONCEPT 582

dreary [adj] *gloomy, lifeless*
black, blah, bleak, boring, cheerless, colorless comfortless, damp, depressing, depressive, dingy dismal, dispiriting, doleful, downcast, drab, dull forlorn, funereal, glum, humdrum, joyless lonely, lonesome, melancholy, monotonous mournful, oppressive, pedestrian, raw, routine sad, somber, sorrowful, tedious, uneventful, uninteresting, wearisome, windy, wintry, wretched SEE CONCEPTS 525,544

drench [v] *wet thoroughly*
deluge, dip, douse, drown, duck, dunk, flood, imbrue, immerse, impregnate, inundate, pour, saturate, seethe, soak, sodden, sop, souse, steep submerge, teem; SEE CONCEPT 256

dress [n] *clothing; woman's garment*
accoutrement, apparel, attire, attirement, civvies*, costume, covering, drape, dry goods duds*, ensemble, evening clothes, frock, garb gear, gown, guise, habiliment, habit, muumuu outfit, raiment, robe, shift, skirt, smock, suit, Sunday best*, things*, threads*, tog, toga, toggery trappings, uniform, vestment, wardrobe; SEE CONCEPT 451

dress [v1] *put on clothing*
adorn, apparel, array, attire, bedeck, bundle up change, clad, clothe, costume, cover, deck, decorate, don, drape, embellish, fit out, furbish, garb ornament, outfit, primp, put on, raiment, rig robe, slip into, slip on, spruce up, suit up, trim turn out, wear; SEE CONCEPT 167

dress [v2] *physically prepare; groom*
adjust, align, arrange, comb, decorate, dispose do up, fit, make ready, ornament, set, straighten trim; SEE CONCEPT 202

dress [v3] *cover a wound*
attend, bandage, bind, cauterize, cleanse, give first aid, heal, plaster, sew up, sterilize, treat; SEE CONCEPTS 172,310

dress down [v] *scold*
bawl out, berate, carpet, castigate, censure, chew out*, lash, rail, rake over coals*, ream, rebuke reprimand, reprove, tear into*, tell off*, tongue lash*, upbraid; SEE CONCEPT 52

dress up [v] *put on one's best clothes*
array, attire, beautify, clothe, deck out*, embellish, fit out*, fix up, gussy up*, improve, overdress, preen, prettify, primp, prink, slick smarten, spiff up*, spruce up*, titivate; SEE CONCEPT 167

dressy [adj] *formal, fashionable*
chic, classy, dressed to kill*, dressed to the nines*, dressed up*, elaborate, elegant, fancy, in high feather*, looking sharp, ornate, ritzy, smart stylish; SEE CONCEPTS 579,589

dribble [v] *trickle*
distill, drip, drivel, drizzle, drool, drop, fall in drops, leak, ooze, run, salivate, seep, slaver, slobber, spout, squirt, trill, weep; SEE CONCEPTS 179,185

drift [n1] *accumulation*
alluvion, bank, batch, bunch, bundle, clump cluster, deposit, heap, hill, lot, mass, mound mountain, parcel, pile, set, shock, stack; SEE CONCEPTS 432,524

drift [n2] *meaning, significance of communication*
aim, design, direction, end, gist, implication, import, intention, object, progress, progression, pur-

port, scope, significance, tendency, tenor; SEE CONCEPT 682

drift [v] *move aimlessly*

accumulate, aim, amass, amble, be carried along, coast, dance, draw near, flicker, flit, flitter, float, flow, flutter, gad*, gallivant*, gather, go-that-a-way*, go with the tide*, gravitate, hover, kick around*, linger, malinger, meander, mosey*, muck*, ride, sail, saunter, scud, skim, slide, stray, stroll, tend, waft, wander, wash*; SEE CONCEPT 147

drill [n1] *practice, exercise*

assignment, call, conditioning, constitutional, daily dozen*, discipline, dress, drilling, dry run*, gym, homework, instruction, learning by doing, maneuvers, marching, preparation, repetition, run-through*, shakedown*, training, tryout, warm-up, workout; SEE CONCEPTS 87,290

drill [n2] *tool for boring*

auger, awl, bit, borer, corkscrew, countersink, dibble, gimlet, implement, jackhammer, punch, riveter, rotary tool, trepan, trephine, wimble; SEE CONCEPT 499

drill [v1] *train, discipline*

accustom, break, break in, exercise, get into shape, habituate, hone, instruct, lick into shape, practice, rehearse, teach, tune up, walk through, work out; SEE CONCEPTS 117,285

drill [v2] *bore hole*

dig, penetrate, perforate, pierce, prick, punch, puncture, sink in; SEE CONCEPT 220

drink [n] *beverage; alcoholic beverage*

alcohol, booze*, brew, cup, draft, glass, gulp, libation, liquid, liquor, potable, potation, potion, refreshment, shot, sip, slug*, spirits, spot*, swallow, swig, taste, thirst quencher*, toast; SEE CONCEPT 454

drink [v] *take in liquid*

absorb, belt*, booze*, consume, dissipate, down, drain, gargle, gulp, guzzle*, hit the bottle*, imbibe, indulge, inhale, irrigate, lap*, liquor up*, nip*, partake of, put away, quaff, sip, slosh, slurp, soak up, sop, sponge, suck, sup, swallow, swig, swill, tank up*, thirst, tipple*, toast, toss off*, wash down*, wet whistle*; SEE CONCEPT 169

drip [v] *drop, trickle*

dribble, drizzle, exude, filter, plop, rain, splash, sprinkle, trill, weep; SEE CONCEPT 181

drive [n1] *journey by vehicle*

airing, commute, excursion, expedition, hitch, jaunt, joyride, lift, outing, pickup, ramble, ride, run, spin, Sunday drive*, tour, trip, turn, whirl; SEE CONCEPT 224

drive [n2] *campaign for cause*

action, advance, appeal, crusade, effort, enterprise, get-up-and-go*, initiative, push, surge; SEE CONCEPTS 87,300

drive [n3] *person's will to achieve*

ambition, clout, effort, energy, enterprise, fire in belly*, get-up-and-go, goods*, gumption*, guts*, impellent, impetus, impulse, initiative, momentum, motivation, motive, moxie*, pep, pressure, punch*, push*, right stuff*, spunk*, steam*, stuff*, vigor, vitality, what it takes*, zip*; SEE CONCEPTS 411,706

drive [v1] *move or urge on*

actuate, act upon, animate, arouse, bulldoze*, chase, coerce, compel, constrain, dog*, egg on*, encourage, force, goad, goose*, harass, hasten, herd, hound*, hurl, hurry, hustle, impel, induce, inspire, instigate, kick, lean on*, make, motivate, nag, oblige, overburden, overwork, pound, press, pressure, prod, prompt, propel, provoke, push, put up to*, railroad*, ride herd on*, rouse, rush, send, shepherd, shove, spirit up, spur, steamroll*, stimulate, work on, worry; SEE CONCEPTS 68,147,208

drive [v2] *moving, controlling a vehicle*

actuate, advance, bear down, bicycle, bike, burn rubber*, burn up the road*, coast, cruise, cycle, dash, direct, drag, fire up*, floor it*, fly, guide, handle, impel, lean on the*, make sparks fly*, manage, mobilize, motor, operate, pour it on*, propel, push, ride, roll, run, send, speed, spin, start, steer, step on it*, tailgate, tool*, transport, travel, turn, vehiculate*, wheel; SEE CONCEPTS 148,187

drive [v3] *hit with heavy blow*

batter, beat, butt, dash, dig, hammer, jackhammer, knock, maul, plunge, pop, pound, ram, run, shoot, sink, smite, sock, stab, stick, strike, thrust, thump, twack*, whack*, wham*; SEE CONCEPT 189

drive at [v] *mean, suggest as meaning*

aim, allude to, contemplate, design, get at, have in mind, hint at, imply, indicate, intend, intimate, propose, refer to, signify; SEE CONCEPTS 73,682

drivel [n] *foolish talk*

babble, balderdash*, blather, bunk*, double-talk, gibberish, gobbledygook*, Greek*, hogwash*, hooey*, jabber*, nonsense, poppycock*, prating, rot*, rubbish*, tripe*, twaddle*; SEE CONCEPT 278

drivel [v1] *talk foolishly*

babble, blabber, blather, blethe, gab, gabble, prate, prattle, ramble, twaddle*, waffle*; SEE CONCEPT 266

drivel [v2] *drool*

dribble, salivate, slaver, slobber; SEE CONCEPTS 185,256

driver [n] *person who engineers vehicle*

autoist, automobilist, cabbie, chauffeur, coach person, hack*, handler, jockey, leadfoot*, motorist, operator, road hog*, trainer, whip*; SEE CONCEPT 423

driving [adj] *forceful*

active, compelling, dynamic, energetic, enterprising, galvanic, impellent, lively, propulsive, sweeping, urging, vigorous, violent; SEE CONCEPT 540

drizzle [v] *fine rain*

dribble, drip, drop, mist, mizzle, shower, spit, spray, sprinkle; SEE CONCEPT 526

droll [adj] *amusing, farcical*

absurd, camp, campy, clownish, comic, comical, crack-up, diverting, eccentric, entertaining, for grins*, funny, gagged up*, gelastic, humorous, jocular, joshing, laffer, laughable, ludicrous, odd, preposterous, quaint, queer, quizzical, ridiculous, riot, risible, waggish, whimsical; SEE CONCEPTS 267,548

drone [n1] *person who is lazy*

idler, leech, loafer, lounger, parasite, slug, sluggard, sponger*; SEE CONCEPT 412

drone [n2] *continuous noise*

buzz, hum, murmur, purr, sound, vibration, whirr; SEE CONCEPT 595

drone [v] *making noise continuously*

bombinate, buzz, chant, drawl, hum, intone, na-

dr
dr

salize, purr, sound, strum, thrum, vibrate, whirr;
SEE CONCEPTS 65,77

drool [v1] *salivate*
dribble, drivel, froth, ooze, run, slabber, slaver,
slobber, spit, water, water at the mouth; SEE CON-
CEPTS 185,256

drool [v2] *desire, lust after*
dote on, enthuse, fondle, gush, lick chops*, make
much of, pet, rave, rhapsodize, rhapsody, slobber
over*, spoil, want; SEE CONCEPT 20

droop [v] *hang down; languish*
bend, dangle, decline, depress, diminish, drop,
fade, fail, faint, fall down, flag, lean, let down,
loll, lop, sag, settle, sink, sling, slouch, slump,
subside, suspend, weaken, wilt, wither; SEE CON-
CEPTS 181,699

droopy [adj] *limp*
bent, drooping, flabby, floppy, languid, languorous, lassitudinous, pendulous, sagging, saggy,
slouchy, stooped, wilting; SEE CONCEPT 485

drop [n1] *globule*
bead, bit, bubble, crumb, dab, dash, dewdrop,
driblet, drip, droplet, iota, molecule, morsel, nip,
ounce, particle, pearl, pinch, sip, smidgen, speck,
splash, spot, taste, tear, teardrop, trace, trickle;
SEE CONCEPTS 467,468,831,835

drop [n2] *steep decline; hole*
abyss, chasm, declivity, deepness, depth, descent,
dip, fall, plunge, precipice, slope, tumble; SEE
CONCEPTS 181,509

drop [n3] *decrease*
cut, decline, descent, deterioration, dip, downfall,
downslide, downswing, downtrend, downturn,
fall, fall-off, landslide, lapse, lowering, precipitation, reduction, sag, slide, slip, slump, tumble,
upset; SEE CONCEPTS 698,776

drop [v1] *fall in globules*
bead, bleed, descend, distill, drain, dribble, drip,
emanate, hail, leak, ooze, percolate, precipitate,
seep, snow, splash, trickle, trill; SEE CONCEPT
179

drop [v2] *let go of; fall*
abandon, bring down, cave in, collapse, decline,
depress, descend, dive, duck, dump, fell, floor,
flop, give up, go down, ground, keel over*,
knock, loosen, lower, nose-dive*, pitch, plummet, plump, plunge, release, relinquish, shed,
shoot, sink, slide, slip, slump, topple, tumble,
unload; SEE CONCEPTS 181,200

drop [v3] *abandon; ignore*
abort, adios*, be alienated from, break with, call
off, cancel, cast off, cease, desert, discontinue,
dismiss, disown, ditch*, divorce, dust off*,
eighty-six*, end, forfeit, forget about, forsake,
give up, have done with*, interrupt, jilt, kick*,
leave, lose, part from, part with, quit, relinquish, remit, renounce, repudiate, resign, sacrifice, scratch*, scrub*, separate, shake, stop,
terminate, throw over, wash out*, waste one*,
wipe out*, write off*; SEE CONCEPTS 30,121,195

drop in [v] *visit*
blow in*, call, call upon, come by, come over, go
and see*, look in on, look up, pop in*, run in*,
stop, stop by, stop in, turn up; SEE CONCEPT 227

drop off [v1] *decrease*
decline, diminish, dwindle, fall away, fall off,
lessen, sag, slacken, slide, slip, slump; SEE CON-
CEPTS 698,776

drop off [v2] *deliver*
deposit, give, hand over, leave, let off, present,
set down, unload; SEE CONCEPT 108

drop off [v3] *fall asleep*
catnap, doze, doze off*, drowse, have forty
winks*, nod, nod off*, snooze; SEE CONCEPTS
210,315

drop out [v] *stop doing an activity*
abandon, back out, cease, forsake, give notice,
give up, leave, quit, renege, retreat, withdraw;
SEE CONCEPT 121

drought [n] *dryness; shortage of supply*
aridity, dearth, deficiency, dehydration, desiccation, dry spell, insufficiency, lack, need, parched-
ness, rainlessness, scarcity, want; SEE CONCEPTS
607,646

drove [n] *large gathering*
collection, company, crowd, crush, drive, flock,
herd, horde, mob, multitude, pack, press, rout,
run, swarm, throng; SEE CONCEPTS 397,432

drown [v] *submerge in liquid; submerge and die*
asphyxiate, deluge, dip, douse, drench, engulf,
flood, go down, go under, immerse, inundate,
knock over, obliterate, overcome, overflow, overpower, overwhelm, plunge, prostrate, sink, soak,
sop, souse, stifle, suffocate, swamp, whelm, wipe
out; SEE CONCEPTS 252,256

drowsy [adj] *sleepy*
comatose, dazed, dopy, dozing, dozy, dreamy,
drugged, half asleep, heavy, indolent, lackadaisical, languid, lazy, lethargic, lulling, napping,
nodding, out of it*, restful, sluggish, slumberous,
snoozy, somnolent, soothing, soporific, tired, torpid; SEE CONCEPTS 406,539

drudge [n] *slave, very hard worker*
factotum, grind*, laborer, menial, nose to grindstone*, peon*, plodder*, servant, toiler, worka-
holic, worker, workhorse; SEE CONCEPT 348

drudge [v] *work very hard*
back to the salt mines*, dig, grind*, hammer*,
keep nose to grindstone*, labor, muck*, perform,
plod, plow, plug away*, pound*, schlepp*, slave,
slog, sweat, toil, travail; SEE CONCEPTS
87,100,324

drudgery [n] *hard, tedious work*
backbreaker*, chore, daily grind*, elbow grease*,
grind*, gruntwork*, labor, menial labor, rat race,
slavery, struggle, sweat, toil, travail, workout*;
SEE CONCEPT 362

drug [n] *medication*
biologic, cure, depressant, dope, essence, medicament, medicinal, medicine, narcotic, opiate,
pharmaceutic, pharmaceutical, physic, pill, poison, potion, prescription, remedy, sedative, stimulant, tonic; SEE CONCEPT 307

drug [v] *put under influence of medication*
analgize, anesthetize, benumb, blunt, deaden, desensitize, dope*, dope up, dose, dose up*, fix,
hit, knock out*, medicate, narcotize, numb, poison, relax, sedate, stupefy, treat; SEE CONCEPT
310

drugged [adj] *under the influence of medication*
benumbed, blown away*, coked*, comatose,
dazed, doped, dopey*, floating*, flying*, high*,
junked-up*, loaded*, narcotized, on a trip*, out
of it*, ripped*, smashed*, spaced-out*, stoned*,
strung out*, stupefied, unconscious; SEE CONCEPT
314

drum [v] *beat, tap a beat*
boom*, pulsate, rap, reverberate, roar, strum, tat-

too, throb, thrum, thunder*; SEE CONCEPTS 65,189

drum into [v] *make a point strongly*
din into, drive home*, hammer away*, harp on*, instill, reiterate; SEE CONCEPTS 49,75

drum up [v] *gather support for something*
attract, bid for, canvass, discover, obtain, petition, round up, solicit, succeed in finding; SEE CONCEPTS 68,300

drunk/drunkard [n] *person who is inebriated*
alcoholic, boozer*, carouser*, dipsomaniac, drinker, guzzler*, inebriate, lush*, sot*, sponge*, wino*; SEE CONCEPT 423

drunk [adj] *intoxicated by alcohol*
bashed, befuddled, boozed up*, buzzed*, crocked*, feeling no pain*, flushed*, flying*, fuddled, glazed*, groggy, high*, inebriated, juiced*, laced*, liquored up*, lit*, lush, muddled, plastered*, potted*, seeing double*, sloshed*, stewed*, stoned*, tanked*, three sheets to the wind*, tight*, tipsy, totaled*, under the influence, under the table*, wasted*; SEE CONCEPTS 314,545

dry [adj1] *moistureless*
anhydrous, arid, athirst, baked, bald, bare, barren, dehydrated, depleted, desert, desiccant, desiccated, drained, dried-up, droughty, dusty, evaporated, exhausted, hard, impoverished, juiceless, not irrigated, parched, rainless, sapless, sapped, sear, shriveled, stale, thirsty, torrid, unmoistened, waterless; SEE CONCEPT 603

dry [adj2] *dull, uninteresting*
apathetic, blah, boring, bromidic, draggy, dreary, dull as dishwater*, dusty, ho hum*, impassive, inelaborate, insipid, matter-of-fact, modest, monotonous, naked, plain, simple, tedious, tiresome, trite, wearisome; SEE CONCEPT 529

dry [adj3] *sarcastic, sharp-tongued*
acerbic, arcane, biting, caustic, cutting, cynical, deadpan, droll, harsh, humorous, ironical, keen, low-key, restrained, salty, sardonic, satirical, sharp, sly, sour, subtle, tart; SEE CONCEPT 267

dry [v] *take moisture out of*
anhydrate, bake, blot, concentrate, condense, dehumidify, dehydrate, deplete, desiccate, drain, empty, evaporate, exhaust, exsiccate, freeze-dry, harden, kiln, mummify, parch, scorch, sear, shrivel, soak up, sponge, stale, swab, torrefy, towel, wilt, wipe, wither, wizen; SEE CONCEPTS 250,469

dual [adj] *two-fold*
bifold, binal, binary, coupled, double, double-header, duple, duplex, duplicate, matched, paired, twin; SEE CONCEPTS 762,771

dub [v] *name, label something*
baptize, bestow, call, christen, confer, denominate, designate, entitle, knight, nickname, style, tag, term, title; SEE CONCEPT 62

dubious [adj1] *doubtful*
arguable, chancy, debatable, diffident, disputable, dubitable, equivocal, far-fetched, fishy*, fly-by-night*, hesitant, iffy*, improbable, indecisive, moot, mootable, open, perplexed, problematic, questionable, reluctant, shady, skeptical, suspect, suspicious, touch and go*, trustless, unassured, uncertain, unclear, unconvinced, undecided, undependable, unlikely, unreliable, unsure, untrustworthy, untrusty, wavering; SEE CONCEPT 552

dubious [adj2] *vague, unclear*
ambiguous, debatable, disinclined, doubtful, equivocal, indefinite, indeterminate, mistrustful, obscure, open, problematic, problematical, undecided, unsettled; SEE CONCEPTS 535,576

duck [v] *drop down; avoid*
bend, bob, bow, crouch, dip, dive, dodge, double, elude, escape, evade, fence, lower, lurch, move to side, parry, plunge, shirk, shun, shy, sidestep, stoop, submerge; SEE CONCEPTS 102,154,181

duct [n] *channel, pipe*
aqueduct, canal, conduit, course, funnel, passage, tube, vessel, watercourse; SEE CONCEPT 501

ductile [adj] *pliant, flexible*
adaptable, amenable, biddable, docile, extensile, malleable, manageable, moldable, plastic, pliable, responsive, submitting, supple, tractable, yielding; SEE CONCEPTS 488,490

dud [n] *failure*
bomb, bummer, bust, debacle, flop, lemon, loser, washout; SEE CONCEPT 674

due [n] *expected reward*
be in line for*, claim, comeuppance, compensation, deserts*, entitlement, guerdon, interest, merits, need, payment, perquisite, prerogative, privilege, rate, recompense, repayment, reprisal, retaliation, retribution, revenge, right, rights, satisfaction, title, vengeance, what is coming to one*; SEE CONCEPTS 337,710

due [adj1] *unpaid; owing money*
chargeable, collectible, expected, in arrears, IOU, mature, not met, outstanding, overdue, owed, payable, receivable, scheduled, to be paid, unliquidated, unsatisfied, unsettled; SEE CONCEPT 334

due [adj2] *appropriate, proper*
becoming, coming, condign, deserved, earned, equitable, fair, fit, fitting, good, just, justified, merited, obligatory, requisite, rhadamanthine, right, rightful, suitable; SEE CONCEPT 558

due [adv] *directly*
dead, direct, exactly, right, straight, straightly, undeviatingly; SEE CONCEPTS 581,799

dues [n] *payment for membership*
ante, arrearage, assessment, charge, charges, collection, contribution, custom, debit, debt, duty, fee, kickback, levy, liability, obligation, pay, protection, rates, tax, toll; SEE CONCEPTS 344,679

dull [adj1] *unintelligent*
addled, backward, besotted, boring, brainless, daffy, daft, dense, dim, dim-witted, doltish, dumb, feeble-minded, half-baked, ignorant, imbecilic, indolent, insensate, low, moronic, not bright, numskulled, obtuse, scatterbrained, shallow, simple, simple-minded, slow, sluggish, stolid, stupid, tedious, thick, unintellectual, vacuous, wearisome, witless; SEE CONCEPT 402

dull [adj2] *insensitive*
accustomed, apathetic, blank, boring, brainless, colorless, dead, depressed, empty, even, flat, heavy, impassible, inactive, indifferent, inert, insensible, jejune, languid, lifeless, listless, lumpy, monotonous, passionless, placid, prosaic, quiet, regular, routine, slack, slow, sluggish, spiritless, stagnant, still, stolid, torpid, unexciting, unresponsive, unsympathetic, usual, vacuous; SEE CONCEPT 542

dull [adj3] *boring, uninteresting*
abused, archaic, arid, big yawn*, blah, colorless,

dr
du

common, commonplace, dead, dismal, dreary, driveling, dry, familiar, flat, hackneyed, heavy, hoary, ho hum*, humdrum*, insipid, jejune, long-winded, monotonous, oft-repeated*, ordinary, out-of-date, plain, pointless, prolix, prosaic, prosy, repetitious, repetitive, routine, run-of-the-mill*, soporific, stale, stock, stupid, tame, tedious, tired, tiresome, trite, unimaginative, uninspiring, usual, usual thing, vapid, worn-out; SEE CONCEPTS 529,530

dull [*adj4*] *not sharp*
blunt, blunted, edentate, flat, not keen, obtuse, pointless, round, square, toothless, turned, unpointed, unsharpened; SEE CONCEPT 486

dull [*adj5*] *uneventful*
accustomed, apathetic, blah, boring, dead, depressed, draggy*, even, falling off, flat, inactive, inert, languid, lifeless, listless, monotonous, placid, quiet, regular, routine, setting tight*, slack, slothful, slow, sluggish, stagnant, still, stolid, tight, torpid, unexciting, unresponsive, usual, without incident, yawn; SEE CONCEPT 548

dull [*adj6*] *drab, lackluster in effect on senses*
ashen, black, blind, cloudy, cold, colorless, dark, dead, dim, dingy, dismal, dun, dusky, faded, feeble, flat, grimy, hazy, indistinct, leaden, lifeless, low, matte, mousy, muddy, muffled, murky, muted, obscure, opaque, overcast, plain, shadowy, sober, soft, softened, somber, sooty, subdued, subfusc, toned-down, unlit; SEE CONCEPTS 594,617

duly [*adv*] *accordingly, properly*
appropriately, at the proper time, befittingly, correctly, decorously, deservedly, on time, punctually, rightfully, suitably; SEE CONCEPTS 558,799

dumb [*adj1*] *unable to speak*
at a loss for words*, inarticulate, incoherent, mousy*, mum, mute, quiet, silent, soundless, speechless, tongue-tied, uncommunicative, voiceless, wordless; SEE CONCEPT 593

dumb [*adj2*] *stupid, unintelligent*
dense, dim-witted, doltish, dull, feebleminded, foolish, moronic, simple-minded, thick*; SEE CONCEPT 402

dumbbell [*n*] *stupid person*
dodo*, dolt, dullard, dumbo*, dumdum*, dummy, dunce, idiot, ignoramus, moron, simpleton; SEE CONCEPTS 412,423

dumbfound [*v*] *astound, confuse*
amaze, astonish, bewilder, blow away*, blow one's mind*, boggle, bowl over*, confound, flabbergast, knock over with feather*, nonplus, overwhelm, puzzle, stagger, startle, stun, surprise, take aback, throw, throw into a tizzy*; SEE CONCEPTS 16,42

dumbfounded [*adj*] *astounded, confused*
agape, aghast, amazed, astonished, bamboozled*, beat, bewildered, blown away*, bowled over*, breathless, buffaloed*, confounded, dismayed, dumb, flabbergasted, floored, knocked, licked, nonplused, overcome, overwhelmed, puzzled, shocked, speechless, staggered, startled, stuck, stumped, stunned, surprised, taken aback, thrown, thunderstruck*; SEE CONCEPT 403

dummy [*n1*] *mannequin*
copy, counterfeit, duplicate, figure, form, imitation, manikin, model, ringer*, sham*, stand-in, sub, substitute; SEE CONCEPTS 436,716

dummy [*n2*] *stupid person*
blockhead*, dimwit*, dolt*, dullard*, dunce, fool, idiot, ignoramus, moron, numbskull, oaf, simpleton; SEE CONCEPTS 412,423

dump [*n1*] *junkyard*
ash heap*, cesspool, depot, dumping ground, garbage lot, junk pile*, magazine, refuse heap, rubbish pile, swamp; SEE CONCEPTS 438,449,680

dump [*n2*] *slummy establishment*
hole, hovel, joint*, mess*, pigpen*, pigsty*, shack, shanty, slum, sty; SEE CONCEPTS 449,673

dump [*v*] *drop, throw away*
cast, chuck, clear out, deep-six*, deposit, discard, discharge, dispose of, ditch, drain, eject, empty, evacuate, expel, exude, fling, fling down, get rid of, jettison, junk, leave, let fall, scrap, throw down, throw out, throw overboard*, tip, unload, unpack; SEE CONCEPTS 180,181

dunce [*n*] *stupid person*
ass, birdbrain*, blockhead*, bonehead*, buffoon, dimwit*, dolt, donkey*, dope, dork*, drip*, dullard, dunderhead*, fool, goof, goof ball*, half-wit, idiot, ignoramus, imbecile, jerk, knucklehead*, lame-brain*, lightweight*, moron, nerd*, nincompoop*, ninny*, nitwit, numskull, oaf, pinhead*, scatterbrain*, schnook*, simpleton, twit*; SEE CONCEPTS 412,423

dunk [*v*] *dip in liquid*
douse, duck, immerse, saturate, soak, sop, souse, submerge, submerse; SEE CONCEPT 256

duo [*n*] *twosome*
brace, couple, doublet, dyad, pair; SEE CONCEPT 787

dupe [*n*] *person who is fooled*
butt*, chump*, easy mark*, fish*, fool, mark*, patsy*, pigeon*, pushover*, sap*, sitting duck*, sucker, victim; SEE CONCEPT 423

dupe [*v*] *fool someone*
baffle, bamboozle*, beguile, betray, catch, cheat, chicane, circumvent, con, cozen, deceive, defraud, delude, double-cross, dust*, flimflam*, gull, hoax, hoodwink*, hornswoggle, jerk around*, kid, mislead, outwit, overreach, pull one's leg*, pull something*, rip off*, rook*, rope in*, shaft, spoof, swindle, trick, victimize; SEE CONCEPT 59

duplicate [*n*] *copy, reproduction*
analogue, carbon, carbon copy*, chip off the old block*, clone, companion, coordinate, copycat*, correlate, counterfeit, counterpart, counterscript, dead ringer*, ditto*, double, dupe*, duplication, facsimile, fake, fellow, germination, imitation, knockoff*, likeness, lookalike, match, mate, obverse, parallel, phony, photocopy, photostat, pirate, reciprocal, recurrence, repetition, replica, replication, repro*, ringer*, second, similarity, spitting image*, stat, twin, Xerox*; SEE CONCEPTS 664,667,716

duplicate [*adj*] *matching*
alike, corresponding, dualistic, duple, duplex, equal, equivalent, identic, identical, indistinguishable, same, self-same, tantamount, twin, twofold, very same; SEE CONCEPTS 563,566

duplicate [*v*] *make a copy; repeat*
act like, clone, copy, counterfeit, ditto*, do again, do a takeoff*, do like*, double, dualize, dupe, echo, fake, go like*, imitate, knock off*, make like*, make replica, make twofold, manifold, mimeo, mirror, multiply, phony, photocopy, photostat, pirate*, redo, redouble, reduplicate, re-

make, replicate, repro, reproduce, rework, stat, take off as*, trace, Xerox*; SEE CONCEPTS 91,171

duplicity [n] *deception*
artifice, chicanery, cunning, deceit, dirty dealing*, dirty pool*, dirty trick, dirty work*, dishonesty, dissemblance, dissimulation, doubledealing, dualism, duality, faithlessness, falsehood, fraud, guile, hypocrisy, Judas kiss*, one-upmanship, perfidiousness, perfidy, skullduggery, stab in back*, treacherousness, treachery, two-facedness*, twoness; SEE CONCEPTS 59,63

durability [n] *sturdiness over time*
backbone, constancy, durableness, endurance, grit, guts*, gutsiness, hard as nails*, heart*, imperishability, intestinal fortitude, lastingness, moxie*, permanence, persistence, stamina, starch*, staying power*, stick-to-itiveness*; SEE CONCEPTS 721,731,732

durable [adj] *sturdy, long-lasting*
abiding, constant, dependable, diuturnal, enduring, fast, firm, fixed, impervious, lasting, long-continued, perdurable, perduring, permanent, persistent, reliable, resistant, sound, stable, stout, strong, substantial, tenacious, tough; SEE CONCEPTS 482,488,489

duration [n] *length of action, event*
continuance, continuation, continuity, endurance, extent, period, perpetuation, persistence, prolongation, run, span, spell, stretch, term, tide, time; SEE CONCEPT 804

duress [n] *threat, hardship*
bondage, captivity, coercion, compulsion, confinement, constraint, control, detention, discipline, force, imprisonment, incarceration, pressure, restraint, violence; SEE CONCEPTS 14,674

during [prep] *concurrently with an activity, event*
all along, all the while, amid, as, at the same timeas, at the time, for the time being, in the course of, in the interim, in the meanwhile, in the middle of, in the time of, meanwhile, mid, midst, over, pending, the time between, the whole time, throughout, until, when, while; SEE CONCEPT 820

dusk [n] *early evening*
dark, dimday, dimmet, eventide, gloaming, gloom, night, nightfall, sundown, sunset, twilight; SEE CONCEPT 810

dusky [adj] *dark-hued; murky*
adusk, bistered, bleak, brunette, caliginous, cheerless, cloudy, crepuscular, dark, dark-complexioned, darkish, desolate, dim, dismal, dull, funereal, gloomy, joyless, lightless, obscure, overcast, sable, shadowy, shady, swart, swarthy, tenebrous, twilight, twilit, unilluminated, veiled; SEE CONCEPTS 617,618

dust [n] *tiny particles in the air*
ashes, cinders, dirt, dust bunnies*, earth, filth, flakes, fragments, gilings, granules, grime, grit, ground, lint, loess, powder, refuse, sand, smut, soil, soot; SEE CONCEPT 437

dust [v] *sprinkle tiny particles*
besprinkle, cover, dredge, powder, scatter, sift, spray, spread; SEE CONCEPTS 172,222

dusty [adj] *filled with or covered with powdery particles*
arenaceous, arenose, chalky, crumbly, dirty, friable, granular, grubby, sandy, sooty, unclean, undusted, unswept, untouched; SEE CONCEPT 485

dutiful [adj] *obedient*
binding, compliant, conscientious, deferential, devoted, docile, duteous, faithful, incumbent on,

obligatory, punctilious, regardful, respectful, reverential, submissive; SEE CONCEPT 542

duty [n1] *responsibility, assignment*
burden, business, calling, charge, chore, commission, commitment, committal, contract, devoir, dues, engagement, function, hook*, job, load, millstone*, minding the store*, mission, must, need, obligation, occupation, office, onus, ought*, pains, part, province, role, service, station, string*, taking care of business*, task, trouble, trust, undertaking, weight, work; SEE CONCEPTS 362,376,679

duty [n2] *tax on foreign goods*
assessment, custom, customs, due, excise, impost, levy, rate, revenue, tariff, toll; SEE CONCEPT 329

duty [n3] *moral obligation*
accountability, accountableness, allegiance, amenability, answerability, burden, call of duty, charge, conscience, deference, devoir, faithfulness, good faith, honesty, integrity, liability, loyalty, obedience, pledge, respect, reverence; SEE CONCEPT 388

dwarf [n] *very small person*
bantam, dwarfling, homunculus, Lilliputian*, midget, Tom Thumb*; SEE CONCEPT 424

dwarf [adj] *miniature, tiny*
baby, diminutive, low, petite, pocket, small, undersized; SEE CONCEPT 773

dwarf [v] *minimize*
belittle, check, detract from, dim, diminish, dominate, hinder, look down upon, lower, make small, micrify, minify, overshadow, predominate, retard, rise above, stunt, suppress, tower above, tower over; SEE CONCEPTS 7,19,698,741

dwell [v] *live in*
abide, bide, bunk*, continue, crash*, establish oneself, exist, flop*, hang one's hat*, hang out*, hole up*, inhabit, keep house, locate, lodge, make one's home, nest, occupy, park*, perch*, pitch tent*, quarter, remain, rent, reside, rest, room, roost*, settle, sojourn, squat*, stay, stop, tarry, tenant, tent; SEE CONCEPT 226

dwelling [n] *home*
abode, castle, commorancy, den, digs*, domicile, dump*, establishment, habitat, habitation, haunt, hole in the wall*, house, lodging, pad, quarters, residence, residency; SEE CONCEPT 516

dwell on/dwell upon [v] *linger over; be engrossed in*
consider, continue, elaborate, emphasize, expatiate, harp on*, involve oneself, tarry over; SEE CONCEPTS 17,239

dwindle [v] *waste away; taper off*
abate, bate, become smaller, close, contract, decay, decline, decrease, die away, die down, die out, diminish, drain, drop, ebb, fade, fall, grow less, lessen, peter out*, pine, shrink, shrivel, sink, slack off*, subside, taper, wane, weaken, wither; SEE CONCEPTS 698,776

dye [n] *coloring agent*
color, colorant, dyestuff, pigment, stain, tincture, tinge, tint; SEE CONCEPT 259

dye [v] *change color with mixture*
impregnate, pigment, stain, tincture, tinge, tint; SEE CONCEPT 250

dying [adj] *failing, expiring*
at death's door*, at end of rope*, decaying, declining, disintegrating, done for*, doomed, ebbing, fading, fated, final, giving up the ghost*,

du
dy

going, in extremis, moribund, mortal, one foot in grave*, on last leg*, passing, perishing, sinking, vanishing, withering; SEE CONCEPT *539*

dynamic [*adj*] *active, vital*
activating, aggressive, changing, charismatic, coming on strong*, compelling, driving, effective, electric, energetic, energizing, enterprising, forceful, forcible, go-ahead*, go-getter*, go-getting*, high-powered, hyped-up, influential, intense, lively, lusty, magnetic, peppy*, play for keeps*, play hard ball*, potent, powerful, productive, progressive, red-blooded*, strenuous, vehement, vigorous, vitalizing, zippy*; SEE CONCEPTS *404,540,542*

dynasty [*n*] *area of rule*
absolutism, ascendancy, dominion, empire, government, house, regime, sovereignty, sway; SEE CONCEPTS *435,508,710*

dysfunctional [*adj*] *socially impaired*
broken, debilitated, decayed, defective, deteriorated, flawed, inhibited, maladjusted, malfunctional, sick, undermined, unfit, wounded; SEE CONCEPT *314*

E

each [*adj*] *every*
all, any, exclusive, individual, one by one*, particular, personal, piece by piece*, respective, separate, several, single, specific, various, without exception; SEE CONCEPT *577*

each [*adv*] *apiece; for one*
all, a pop*, a shot*, aside, a throw*, by the, every, individually, per, per capita, per head, per person, per unit, proportionately, respectively, separately, singly, without exception; SEE CONCEPT *577*

each [*prep*] *each one*
each and every one*, each other, every last one, every one, one, one and all*, one another; SEE CONCEPT *577*

eager [*adj*] *anxious, enthusiastic*
acquisitive, agog, ambitious, antsy, appetent, ardent, athirst, avid, breathless, champing at the bit*, covetous, craving, desiring, desirous, dying to, earnest, fervent, fervid, greedy, gung ho*, hankering, heated, hot*, hot to trot*, hungry*, impatient, intent, keen, longing, pining, rarin' to go*, ready and willing*, restive, restless, self-starting, solicitous, thirsty, vehement, voracious, warmblooded*, wild, wishful, yearning, zealous; SEE CONCEPTS *326,401,542*

eagerness [*n*] *enthusiasm, anxiousness*
alacrity, ambition, anticipation, ardor, avidity, earnestness, excitement, fervor, greediness, gusto, heartiness, hunger, impatience, impetuosity, intentness, keenness, longing, promptness, quickness, solicitude, thirst, vehemence, voracity, yearning, zeal, zest, zing*; SEE CONCEPTS *20,633,657*

ear [*n*] *attention*
appreciation, consideration, discrimination, hearing, heed, mark, mind, note, notice, observance, observation, perception, regard, remark, sensitivity, taste; SEE CONCEPT *532*

early [*adj1*] *in the beginning*
a bit previous, aboriginal, ancient, antecedent, antediluvian, antiquated, brand-new, budding, early bird*, fresh, initial, new, original, preceding, premier, prevenient, previous, primal, prime, primeval, primitive, primordial, prior, pristine, proleptical, raw, recent, undeveloped, young; SEE CONCEPTS *799,828*

early [*adj2*] *sooner than expected*
advanced, ahead of time, anticipative, anticipatory, before appointed time, beforehand, direct, immature, immediate, matinal, on short notice*, on the dot*, overearly, oversoon, preceding, precipitant, precocious, preexistent, premature, previous, prompt, pronto, punctual, quick, seasonable, soon, speedy, unanticipated, unexpected, untimely; SEE CONCEPT *820*

early [*adv1*] *sooner than expected*
a bit previous, ahead of time, anon, beforehand, before long, betimes, briefly, bright and early*, directly, early bird*, ere long, far ahead, immediately, in advance, in good time*, in the bud*, in time, on short notice*, on the dot*, oversoon, prematurely, presently, previous, promptly, pronto, proximately, quick, shortly, soon, too soon, unexpectedly, with time to spare*; SEE CONCEPT *820*

early [*adv2*] *immediately*
at once, betimes, directly, first, freshly, in a jiffy*, in an instant*, in no time*, instantaneously, instantly, newly, presto, primitively, promptly, recently, right away, seasonably, soon, straightaway, summarily, thereon, thereupon, timely, without delay; SEE CONCEPTS *799,828*

earmark [*n*] *signature characteristic*
attribute, differential, distinction, feature, hallmark, label, marking, peculiarity, quality, stamp, tag, token, trademark, trait; SEE CONCEPT *644*

earmark [*v*] *reserve*
allocate, designate, keep back, label, maintain, mark out, name, set aside, slot, tab, tag; SEE CONCEPT *129*

earn [*v1*] *make money*
acquire, attain, be gainfully employed, be in line for*, bring home*, bring home the bacon*, bring home the groceries*, bring in, clean up*, clear*, collect, consummate, cop*, derive, draw, effect, gain, gather, get, gross, hustle, make, make fast buck*, make it big*, net, obtain, pay one's dues*, perform, pick up, procure, profit, pull*, pull down*, rate, realize, reap, receive, scare up*, score*, scrape together*, secure, snag*, sock*, turn, win, wrangle; SEE CONCEPTS *330,351*

earn [*v2*] *deserve a reward*
acquire, attain, bag, be entitled to, be worthy of, come by, gain, harvest, merit, net, rate, reap, score, warrant, win; SEE CONCEPTS *120,129*

earnest [*adj1*] *very enthusiastic*
ardent, busy, devoted, diligent, eager, fervent, fervid, heartfelt, impassioned, industrious, keen, passionate, perseverant, purposeful, sedulous, sincere, urgent, vehement, warm, wholehearted, zealous; SEE CONCEPTS *326,401,542*

earnest [*adj2*] *serious; very important*
close, constant, determined, firm, fixed, for real, grave, intent, mean business, meaningful, no-fooling, no-nonsense, playing hard ball*, resolute, resolved, sedate, sincere, sober, solemn, somber, stable, staid, steady, thoughtful, weighty; SEE CONCEPT *568*

earnestness [*n*] *determination; seriousness*
absorption, ardor, attentiveness, concentration, decision, deliberation, devotion, doggedness, eagerness, engrossment, enthusiasm, fervor, firmness, gravity, intensity, intentness, keenness, passion, perseverance, persistence, purposefulness, resolution, resolve, serious-mindedness, sincerity, sobriety, solemnity, stress, tenacity, urgency, vehemence, warmth, zeal; SEE CONCEPTS 633,657

earnings [*n*] *money for work performed*
balance, bottom line*, emolument, gain, gate, groceries*, income, in the black*, lucre, net, pay, payoff, piece of the pie*, proceeds, profit, receipts, remuneration, return, revenue, reward, salary, salt*, stipend, take-home*, takings, wages; SEE CONCEPT 344

Earth [*n1*] *the world*
apple*, big blue marble*, cosmos, creation, dust*, globe, macrocosm, orb, planet, sphere, star, sublunary world, terra, terra firma, terrene, terrestrial sphere, universe, vale; SEE CONCEPT 511

earth [*n2*] *ground, soil*
alluvium, clay, clod, coast, compost, deposit, dirt, dry land, dust, fill, glebe, gravel, humus, land, loam, marl, mold, muck, mud, peat moss, sand, shore, sod, subsoil, surface, terra firma, terrain, terrane, topsoil, turf; SEE CONCEPT 509

earthly [*adj1*] *physically concerning land or its inhabitants*
alluvial, carnal, corporeal, geotic, global, human, in all creation, material, mortal, mundane, nonspiritual, physical, profane, secular, substratal, sublunary, tellurian, telluric, temporal, terraqueous, terrene, terrestrial, uncelestial, under the sun*, unspiritual, worldly; SEE CONCEPT 536

earthly [*adj2*] *conceivable*
feasible, imaginable, likely, mortal, possible, potential, practical, probable; SEE CONCEPT 552

earthquake [*n*] *tremor from inside the earth*
convulsion, fault, macroseism, microseism, movement, quake, quaker*, seimicity, seism, seismism, shake, shock, slip, temblor, trembler*, undulation, upheaval; SEE CONCEPTS 144,526

earthy [*adj*] *unsophisticated*
bawdy, coarse, crude, down, down home*, down-to-earth*, dull, easygoing, folksy, funky*, hard-boiled*, home folk*, homely, homey, indelicate, lowbred, lusty, mundane, natural, pragmatic, ribald, robust, rough, simple, unidealistic, uninhibited, unrefined; SEE CONCEPT 542

ease [*n1*] *peace, quiet; lack of difficulty*
affluence, ataraxia, bed of roses*, calm, calmness, comfort, content, contentment, easiness, enjoyment, gratification, happiness, idleness, inactivity, inertia, inertness, leisure, luxury, passivity, peace of mind*, prosperity, quietness, quietude, relaxation, repose, requiescence, rest, restfulness, satisfaction, security, serenity, supinity, tranquility; SEE CONCEPTS 388,410,673

ease [*n2*] *facility, freedom*
adroitness, affability, aplomb, breeze, child's play*, cinch, cleverness, composure, dexterity, dispatch, duck soup*, easygoingness, efficiency, effortlessness, expertise, expertness, familiarity, flexibility, fluency, informality, insouciance, knack, liberty, naturalness, nonchalance, poise, pushover, quickness, readiness, relaxedness, setup, simplicity, skillfulness, smoothness,

smooth sailing*, snap, unaffectedness, unconstraint, unreservedness; SEE CONCEPTS 376, 388,630

ease [*v1*] *alleviate, help*
abate, aid, allay, ameliorate, anesthetize, appease, assist, assuage, attend to, calm, cheer, clear the way*, comfort, cure, disburden, disengage, doctor, expedite, facilitate, forward, free, further, improve, lessen, let up on, lift, lighten, make easier, meliorate, mitigate, moderate, mollify, nurse, open the door*, pacify, palliate, promote, quiet, relax, release, relent, relieve, run interference for*, simplify, slacken, smooth, soften, soothe, speed, speed up, still, tranquilize, untighten; SEE CONCEPTS 110,310

ease [*v2*] *guide, move carefully*
disentangle, edge, extricate, facilitate, handle, inch, induce, insert, join, loose, loosen, maneuver, relax, remove, right, set right, slack, slacken, slide, slip, squeeze, steer, untighten; SEE CONCEPT 187

easily [*adv1*] *without difficulty*
calmly, comfortably, competently, conveniently, coolly, dexterously, efficiently, effortlessly, evenly, facilely, fluently, freely, handily, hand over fist*, hands down*, just like that*, lightly, like nothing*, no sweat*, nothing to it*, piece of cake*, plainly, quickly, readily, regularly, simply, smoothly, steadily, surely, swimmingly, uncomplicatedly, well, with ease, with no effort, without a hitch*, without trouble; SEE CONCEPT 565

easily [*adv2*] *without a doubt*
absolutely, actually, almost certainly, assuredly, beyond question, by far, certainly, clearly, decidedly, definitely, doubtless, doubtlessly, far and away, indeed, indisputably, indubitably, no doubt, plainly, positively, probably, really, surely, truly, undeniably, undoubtedly, unequivocally, unquestionably; SEE CONCEPTS 535,552

easy [*adj1*] *not difficult*
accessible, apparent, basic, child's play*, cinch, clear, easily done, effortless, elementary, evident, facile, inconsiderable, light, little, manageable, manifest, mere, no bother*, no problem*, no sweat*, not burdensome, nothing to it*, no trouble*, obvious, painless, paltry, picnic*, piece of cake*, plain, plain sailing*, pushover*, royal, simple, simple as ABC*, slight, smooth, snap, straightforward, uncomplicated, undemanding, uninvolved, untroublesome, wieldy, yielding; SEE CONCEPT 565

easy [*adj2*] *leisurely, relaxed*
at ease, calm, carefree, comfortable, comfy, commodious, composed, content, contented, cozy, cursive, cushy, easeful, effortless, flowing, fluent, forthright, gentle, in clover*, languid, light, mild, moderate, peaceful, pleasant, prosperous, quiet, running, satisfied, secure, serene, slow, smooth, snug, soft, spontaneous, substantial, successful, temperate, thriving, tranquil, undemanding, undisturbed, unexacting, unhurried, untroubled, unworried, well-to-do; SEE CONCEPTS 542,544

easy [*adj3*] *tolerant, permissive*
accommodating, amenable, benign, biddable, charitable, clement, compassionate, compliant, condoning, deceivable, deludable, dupable, easygoing, excusing, exploitable, fleeceable, flexible, forbearing, forgiving, gentle, gullible, humoring, indulgent, kindly, lax, lenient, liberal, light, mer-

ciful, mild, moderate, mollycoddling*, naive, pampering, pardoning, soft, spoiling, submissive, susceptible, sympathetic, temperate, tractable, trusting, unburdensome, unoppressive, unsuspicious; SEE CONCEPT *401*

easy [*adj4*] *good-humored*
affable, amiable, at ease, carefree, casual, complaisant, diplomatic, familiar, friendly, gentle, good-natured, good-tempered, graceful, gracious, gregarious, informal, mild, natural, obliging, open, pleasant, polite, relaxed, secure, smooth, sociable, suave, tolerant, unaffected, unanxious, undemanding, unforced, unpretentious, urbane; SEE CONCEPT *404*

easygoing [*adj*] *complacent, permissive*
amenable, breezy, calm, carefree, casual, collected, complaisant, composed, devil-may-care*, even-tempered*, flexible, free and easy*, hangloose*, happy-go-lucky*, indolent, indulgent, informal, insouciant, laid-back*, lazy, lenient, liberal, low-pressure, mild, moderate, nonchalant, offhand, outgiving, patient, placid, poised, relaxed, self-possessed, serene, tolerant, tranquil, unconcerned, uncritical, undemanding, unhurried, uninhibited; SEE CONCEPT *404*

eat [*v1*] *consume food*
absorb, attack, banquet, bite, bolt*, break bread*, breakfast, chew, chow down*, cram*, devour, digest, dine, dispatch, dispose of, fall to, feast upon, feed, gobble up*, gorge, gormandize, graze*, have a bite*, have a meal, have for, ingest, inhale*, lunch, make pig of oneself*, masticate, munch, nibble, nosh*, partake of, peck at*, pick, pig out*, polish off*, pork out*, put away*, ruminate, scarf*, scoff, snack, sup, swallow, take food, take in, take nourishment, wolf; SEE CONCEPT *169*

eat [*v2*] *erode, wear away; use up*
bite, condense, corrode, crumble, decay, decompose, disappear, disintegrate, dissipate, dissolve, drain, exhaust, gnaw, liquefy, melt, nibble, rot, run through, rust, spill, squander, vanish, waste away; SEE CONCEPTS *225,469*

eatable [*adj*] *able to be consumed*
appetizing, comestible, culinary, delicious, delish*, dietary, digestible, edible, escutent, fit, good, harmless, kosher*, nutritious, nutritive, palatable, piquant, safe, satisfying, savory, scrumptious, succulent, tasty, tempting, wholesome, yummy*; SEE CONCEPTS *462,613*

eating disorder [*n*] *unhealthy disturbance in eating behavior*
anorexia nervosa, bingeing, bulimarexia, bulimia, compulsive eating, hyperagia, pica, psychological disorder, purging; SEE CONCEPT *316*

eavesdrop [*v*] *listen without permission*
be all ears*, bend an ear*, bug, ears into*, listen in, monitor, overhear, pry, snoop, spy, tap, tune in on*, wire, wiretap; SEE CONCEPTS *188,596*

ebb [*n*] *regression; decline*
abatement, backflow, decay, decrease, degeneration, depreciation, deterioration, diminution, drop, dwindling, fading away, flagging, going out, lessening, low tide, low water, outward flow, petering out*, recession, refluence, reflux, retreat, retrocession, retroflux, shrinkage, sinking, slackening, subsidence, sweep, wane, waning, weakening, withdrawal; SEE CONCEPTS *195,698*

ebb [*v*] *subside; decline*
abate, decay, decrease, degenerate, deteriorate,

die down, die out, diminish, drop, dwindle, ease off, fade away, fall, fall away, fall back, flag, flow back, go out, languish, lessen, let up, melt, moderate, peter out, recede, relent, retire, retreat, retrocede, shrink, sink, slacken, wane, weaken, withdraw; SEE CONCEPTS *195,698*

ebullience [*n*] *enthusiasm*
agitation, animation, buoyancy, effervescence, effusiveness, elation, excitement, exhilaration, exuberance, exuberancy, ferment, gaiety, highspiritedness, high spirits, liveliness, vitality, vivaciousness, vivacity, zest; SEE CONCEPT *633*

ebullient [*adj*] *enthusiastic*
agitated, bouncy, brash, buoyant, chipper*, chirpy*, effervescent, effusive, elated, excited, exhilarated, exuberant, frothy*, gushing, highspirited, in high spirits*, irrepressible, vivacious, zestful, zippy*; SEE CONCEPT *401*

eccentric [*n*] *person who is bizarre, unusual*
beatnik, character, freak, hippie, kook, loner, maverick, nonconformist, nut*, oddball, oddity, odd person, original, queer duck*, rare bird*, three-dollar bill*, weirdo; SEE CONCEPT *423*

eccentric [*adj*] *bizarre, unusual*
aberrant, abnormal, anomalous, beat*, bent*, bizarre, capricious, characteristic, cockeyed, crazy, curious, droll, erratic, far out*, flaky, freak, freakish, funky*, funny, idiosyncratic, irregular, kooky, nutty, odd, oddball, offbeat, off-center, off the wall*, out in left field*, outlandish, peculiar, quaint, queer, quirky, quizzical, singular, strange, uncommon, unconventional, unnatural, way out*, weird, whimsical, wild; SEE CONCEPTS *547,564*

eccentricity [*n*] *bizarreness, unusualness*
aberration, abnormality, anomaly, caprice, capriciousness, foible, freakishness, hereticism, idiocrasy, idiosyncrasy, irregularity, kink, nonconformity, oddity, oddness, outlandishness, peculiarity, queerness, quirk, singularity, strangeness, unconventionality, unorthodoxness, waywardness, weirdness, whimsicality, whimsicalness; SEE CONCEPTS *647,665*

echelon [*n*] *class, level*
degree, file, grade, line, office, place, position, queue, rank, row, string, tier; SEE CONCEPTS *378,388*

echo [*n*] *repeat, copy*
answer, imitation, mirror, mirror image, onomatopoeia, parallel, parroting, rebound, reflection, reiteration, repercussion, repetition, reply, reproduction, reverberation, ringing, rubber stamp*; SEE CONCEPTS *595,695,716*

echo [*v*] *repeat, copy*
ape, ditto*, do like*, go like*, imitate, impersonate, make like*, mimic, mirror, parallel, parrot, react, recall, redouble, reflect, reiterate, reproduce, resemble, resound, respond, reverberate, ring, rubber-stamp*, second, vibrate; SEE CONCEPTS *91,171*

eclectic [*adj*] *comprehensive, general*
all-embracing, assorted, broad, catholic, dilettantish, diverse, diversified, heterogeneous, inclusive, liberal, many-sided, mingled, mixed, multifarious, multiform, selective, universal, varied, wide-ranging; SEE CONCEPTS *537,772*

eclipse [*n*] *shadowing of the sun*
concealment, darkening, decline, diminution, dimming, extinction, extinguishment, obliterao-

tion, obscuration, occultation, penumbra, shading, shroud, veil; SEE CONCEPTS *522,624*

eclipse [*v1*] *obscure, veil*
adumbrate, becloud, bedim, blot out, cloud, darken, dim, extinguish, murk, overshadow, shadow, shroud; SEE CONCEPT *250*

eclipse [*v2*] *surpass achievement*
exceed, excel, outdo, outshine, overrun, surmount, tower above, transcend; SEE CONCEPT *141*

economic [*adj*] *business-related; financial*
bread-and-butter*, budgetary, commercial, fiscal, industrial, material, mercantile, monetary, money-making, pecuniary, productive, profitable, profit-making, remunerative, solvent, viable; SEE CONCEPTS *334,536*

economical [*adj1*] *conservative with resources; careful*
avaricious, canny, chary, circumspect, close, closefisted, cost-effective, curmudgeonly, efficient, frugal, meager, mean, methodical, miserly, money-saving, niggardly*, on the rims*, parsimonious, penny-pinching*, penny-wise*, penurious, practical, provident, prudent, prudential, saving, scrimping, skimping, spare, sparing, stingy, thrifty, tight, time-saving, unwasteful, watchful, work-saving; SEE CONCEPT *542*

economical [*adj2*] *inexpensive*
bought for a song*, cheap, cost next to nothing*, cost nothing, cut rate, dime a dozen*, dirt cheap*, dog cheap*, fair, low, low-priced, low tariff, marked down, moderate, modest, on sale, quite a buy*, reasonable, reduced, sound, steal*; SEE CONCEPT *334*

economize [*v*] *save money*
be frugal, be prudent, be sparing, conserve, cut back, cut corners*, cut down, keep within means, make ends meet*, manage, meet a budget, pay one's way*, pinch pennies*, retrench, run tight ship*, scrimp, shepherd, skimp, stint, stretch a dollar*, tighten one's belt*; SEE CONCEPT *330*

economy [*n*] *saving, frugality*
abridgement, austerity, care, carefulness, caution, curtailment, cutback, decrease, deduction, direction, discretion, husbandry, layoff, meanness, miserliness, moratorium, niggardliness, parcity, parsimony, providence, prudence, recession, reduction, regulation, restraint, retrenchment, rollback, scrimping, shrinkage, skimping, sparingness, stinginess, supervision, thrift, thriftiness; SEE CONCEPTS *117,330,335*

eco-rich [*adj*] *possessing an abundance of natural resources*
bountiful, clean, flowing, full, green, natural, plentiful, pure, rich; SEE CONCEPT *518*

ecstasy [*n*] *bliss*
beatitude, blessedness, cool*, delectation, delight, delirium, ebullience, elation, enchantment, enthusiasm, euphoria, exaltation, felicity, fervor, frenzy, gladness, happiness, heaven, inspiration, intoxication, joy, joyfulness, paradise, rapture, ravishment, rhapsody, seventh heaven*, trance, transport, twilight zone*; SEE CONCEPT *410*

ecstatic [*adj*] *very happy, blissful*
athrill, beatific, crazy, delirious, dreamy, elated, enraptured, enthusiastic, entranced, euphoric, fervent, floating, flying high*, frenzied, gone*, high*, in exaltation, in seventh heaven*, joyful, joyous, mad, on cloud nine*, out, overjoyed, pleased as punch*, rapturous, ravished, rhapsodic, sent*, sunny, thrilled, tickled pink*, tickled to

death*, transported*, turned on*, upbeat, wild; SEE CONCEPT *403*

ecumenical [*adj*] *general*
all-comprehensive, all-inclusive, all-pervading, catholic, comprehensive, cosmic, cosmopolitan, global, inclusive, planetary, unifying, universal, worldwide; SEE CONCEPTS *537,772*

edge [*n1*] *border, outline*
bend, berm, bound, boundary, brim, brink, butt, circumference, contour, corner, crook, crust, curb, end, extremity, frame, fringe, frontier, hem, hook, ledge, limb, limit, line, lip, margin, molding, mouth, outskirt, peak, perimeter, periphery, point, portal, rim, ring, shore, side, skirt, split, strand, term, threshold, tip, trimming, turn, verge; SEE CONCEPTS *484,513*

edge [*n2*] *advantage*
allowance, ascendancy, bulge, dominance, draw, handicap, head start, lead, odds, start, superiority, upper hand*, vantage; SEE CONCEPT *712*

edge [*v1*] *border, trim*
bind, bound, decorate, fringe, hem, margin, outline, rim, shape, skirt, surround, verge; SEE CONCEPTS *751,758*

edge [*v2*] *defeat narrowly*
creep, ease, inch, infiltrate, nose out*, sidle, slip by, slip past, squeeze by*, squeeze past*, steal, worm*; SEE CONCEPT *95*

edge [*v3*] *sharpen*
file, grind, hone, polish, sharpen, strop, whet; SEE CONCEPTS *137,250*

edgy [*adj*] *nervous*
anxious, critical, excitable, excited, high-strung, ill at ease, impatient, irascible, irritable, keyed up*, overstrung, restive, restless, skittish, tense, touchy, uneasy, uptight; SEE CONCEPT *401*

edible [*adj*] *able to be eaten*
comestible, digestible, eatable, esculent, fit, good, harmless, nourishing, nutritious, nutritive, palatable, savory, succulent, tasty, toothsome, wholesome; SEE CONCEPTS *462,613*

edict [*n*] *pronouncement, order*
act, canon, command, commandment, decree, decretum, dictate, dictum, directive, enactment, fiat, injunction, instrument, judgment, law, mandate, manifesto, ordinance, precept, prescript, proclamation, pronunciamento, regulation, rule, ruling, statute, ukase, writ; SEE CONCEPTS *278,662,688*

edification [*n*] *improvement, education*
betterment, elevation, elucidation, enhancement, enlightenment, guidance, illumination, information, instruction, irradiation, knowledge, learning, nurture, schooling, teaching, tuition, uplifting; SEE CONCEPTS *31,287,700*

edifice [*n*] *structure*
building, construction, erection, habitation, house, monument, pile, rockpile*, skyscraper, towers; SEE CONCEPT *439*

edit [*v*] *rewrite, refine*
adapt, alter, amplify, analyze, annotate, arrange, assemble, assign, blue-pencil*, boil down*, butcher, censor, check, choose, compile, compose, condense, correct, cut, delete, discard, doctor, draft, emend, excise, feature, fine-tune, finish, fly speck*, go over, make up, massage*, polish, prepare, prescribe, proofread, publish, put together, rearrange, recalibrate, rectify, redact, regulate, rehash, rephrase, report, revise, scrub*, select, set up, strike out, style, tighten, trim, write over; SEE CONCEPTS *79,126,203*

ea
ed

edition [n] *issue of publication*
copy, impression, imprint, number, printing, program, publication, reissue, release, reprint, reprinting, version, volume; SEE CONCEPT *280*

educate [v] *teach information, experience*
brainwash*, brief, civilize, coach, cultivate, develop, discipline, drill, drum into, edify, enlighten, exercise, explain, foster, improve, indoctrinate, inform, instruct, let in on, mature, nurture, put hip*, put through the grind*, rear, school, show the ropes*, train, tutor; SEE CONCEPTS *61,285*

educated [adj] *learned, experienced*
accomplished, acquainted with, brainy, civilized, coached, corrected, cultivated, cultured, developed, enlightened, enriched, erudite, expert, finished, fitted, formed, informed, initiated, instructed, intelligent, knowledgeable, lettered, literary, literate, nurtured, polished, prepared, professional, refined, scholarly, schooled, scientific, shaped, skilled, tasteful, taught, trained, tutored, versed in, well-informed, well-read, well-taught, well-versed; SEE CONCEPT *402*

education [n] *instruction, development of knowledge*
apprenticeship, background, book learning*, brainwashing*, breeding, catechism, civilization, coaching, cultivation, culture, direction, discipline, drilling, edification, enlightenment, erudition, finish, guidance, improvement, inculcation, indoctrination, information, learnedness, learning, literacy, nurture, pedagogy, preparation, propagandism, proselytism, reading, rearing, refinement, scholarship, schooling, science, study, teaching, training, tuition, tutelage, tutoring; SEE CONCEPTS *285,287,409*

educe [v] *bring out, elicit*
come out, conclude, deduce, derive, develop, distill, drag, draw, draw out, evince, evoke, evolve, excogitate, extort, extract, gain, get, infer, milk*, obtain, procure, pull, reason, secure, think out, wrest, wring; SEE CONCEPTS *37,142*

eerie [adj] *spooky*
awesome, bizarre, crawly, creepy, fantastic, fearful, frightening, ghostly, mysterious, scary, spectral, strange, supernatural, superstitious, uncanny, unearthly, weird; SEE CONCEPT *537*

effect [n1] *result*
aftereffect, aftermath, backlash, backwash, can of worms*, causatum, chain reaction*, conclusion, consequence, corollary, denouement, development, end, end product, event, eventuality, fallout, flak*, follow through, follow-up, fruit, issue, outcome, outgrowth, precipitate, pursuance, ramification, reaction, reflex, repercussion, response, sequel, sequence, side effect, spin-off, upshot*, waves*; SEE CONCEPT *230*

effect [n2] *impact, impression*
action, clout, drift, effectiveness, efficacy, efficiency, enforcement, essence, execution, fact, force, implementation, import, imprint, influence, mark, meaning, power, purport, purpose, reality, sense, significance, strength, tenor, use, validity, vigor, weight; SEE CONCEPT *687*

effect [v] *carry out, accomplish*
achieve, actualize, actuate, begin, bring about, bring off, bring on, buy, carry through, cause, complete, conceive, conclude, consummate, create, do a number*, do one's thing*, do the job*, do the trick*, do to a T*, draw on, effectuate,

enact, enforce, execute, fulfill, generate, get across, give rise to, implement, induce, initiate, invoke, make, make it*, make waves*, perform, procure, produce, pull it off*, put across, realize, render, secure, sell, turn out, turn the trick*, unzip*; SEE CONCEPTS *91,706*

effective [adj1] *productive, persuasive*
able, active, adequate, capable, cogent, compelling, competent, convincing, direct, effectual, efficacious, efficient, emphatic, energetic, forceful, forcible, having lead in pencil*, impressive, live, moving, on the ball*, operative, playing hardball*, potent, powerful, powerhouse*, practical, producing, resultant, serviceable, serving, sound, striking, sufficient, telling, trenchant, useful, valid, virtuous, wicked*, yielding; SEE CONCEPTS *537,540*

effective [adj2] *in use at the time*
active, actual, current, direct, dynamic, in effect, in execution, in force, in operation, operative, real; SEE CONCEPTS *560,582,799*

effectiveness [n] *influence*
capability, clout, cogency, effect, efficacy, efficiency, force, forcefulness, performance, point, potency, power, punch, strength, success, use, validity, validness, verve, vigor, weight; SEE CONCEPTS *676,687*

effectual [adj] *influential; authoritative*
accomplishing, achieving, adequate, binding, capable, conclusive, decisive, determinative, effecting, effective, efficacious, efficient, forcible, fulfilling, in force, lawful, legal, licit, potent, powerful, practicable, productive, qualified, serviceable, sound, strong, successful, telling, useful, valid, virtuous, workable; SEE CONCEPTS *319,528,537*

effeminate [adj] *having female qualities*
epicene, feminine, womanish, womanlike, womanly; SEE CONCEPTS *401,404*

effervescence [n1] *fizz, foam*
bubbles, bubbling, ebullition, ferment, fermentation, froth, frothing, sparkle; SEE CONCEPTS *437,522*

effervescence [n2] *enthusiasm, vivacity*
animation, buoyancy, ebullience, excitedness, excitement, exhilaration, exuberance, exuberancy, gaiety, happiness, high spirits, joy, liveliness, vim, vitality, volatility, zing*; SEE CONCEPTS *633,657*

effervescent [adj1] *fizzing, foaming*
airy, boiling, bouncy, bubbling, bubbly, carbonated, elastic, expansive, fermenting, frothing, frothy, resilient, sparkling, volatile; SEE CONCEPTS *462,485*

effervescent [adj2] *enthusiastic, vivacious*
animated, bouncy, brash, bubbly, buoyant, ebullient, excited, exhilarated, exuberant, gleeful, happy, high-spirited, hilarious, in high spirits*, irrepressible, jolly, joyous, lively, merry, mirthful, sprightly, vital, zingy; SEE CONCEPTS *401, 542*

effete [adj1] *spoiled, exhausted*
burnt out*, corrupt, debased, decadent, decayed, declining, decrepit, degenerate, dissipated, dissolute, drained, enervated, enfeebled, far-gone*, feeble, immoral, obsolete, overrefined, overripe, played out*, soft, spent, vitiated, washed-out*, wasted, weak, worn out; SEE CONCEPT *560*

effete [adj2] *unproductive*
barren, fruitless, impotent, infecund, infertile,

sterile, unfruitful, unprolific; SEE CONCEPT 527

efficacious [adj] *efficient, productive*

active, adequate, capable, competent, effective, effectual, energetic, influential, operative, potent, powerful, puissant, serviceable, strong, successful, useful, virtuous; SEE CONCEPTS 528,537

efficacy [n] *efficiency; productiveness*

ability, adequacy, capability, capableness, capacity, competence, effect, effectiveness, efficaciousness, energy, force, influence, performance, potency, power, strength, success, sufficiency, use, vigor, virtue, weight; SEE CONCEPTS 641,676,706

efficiency [n] *adeptness, effectiveness*

ability, abundance, adaptability, address, adequacy, capability, capableness, competence, competency, completeness, economy, effectualness, efficacy, energy, expertise, facility, faculty, know-how, performance, potency, power, powerfulness, productiveness, productivity, proficiency, prowess, quantity, readiness, resourcefulness, response, skill, skillfulness, suitability, suitableness, talent, thoroughness; SEE CONCEPTS 409,630,658

efficient [adj] *adept, effective*

able, accomplished, active, adapted, adequate, apt, businesslike, capable, clever, competent, conducive, decisive, deft, dynamic, economic, economical, effectual, efficacious, energetic, equal to, experienced, expert, familiar with, fitted, good at, good for, handy, masterly, organized, potent, powerful, practiced, productive, proficient, profitable, qualified, ready, saving, shrewd, skilled, skillful, systematic, talented, tough, useful, valuable, virtuous, well-organized; SEE CONCEPTS 402,527,560

effigy [n] *dummy*

figure, icon, idol, image, likeness, model, picture, portrait, puppet, representation, statue; SEE CONCEPT 436

effort [n] *work, exertion*

accomplishment, achievement, act, aim, application, aspiration, attempt, battle, crack*, creation, deed, discipline, drill, elbow grease*, endeavor, energy, enterprise, essay, exercise, feat, fling*, force, go*, industry, intention, job, labor, old college try*, pains, power, product, production, pull, purpose, push, resolution, shot*, spurt, stab*, strain, stress, stretch, strife, striving, struggle, sweat, tension, toil, training, travail, trial, trouble, try, tug*, undertaking, venture, whack*; SEE CONCEPTS 87,362,677,724

effortless [adj] *easy*

child's play*, cursive, duck soup*, facile, flowing, fluent, light, no problem*, no sweat*, offhand, painless, picnic*, piece of cake*, royal, running, simple, smooth, snap*, uncomplicated, undemanding, untroublesome; SEE CONCEPT 565

effrontery [n] *nerve, boldness*

arrogance, assurance, audacity, backtalk, brashness, brass*, brazenness, cheek*, cheekiness, chutzpah*, crust*, disrespect, face, gall, guff, hardihood, impertinence, impudence, incivility, insolence, lip*, presumption, rudeness, sass, sauce*, self-assurance, self-confidence, shamelessness, smart talk, temerity; SEE CONCEPTS 411,633

effulgent [adj] *glowing, luminous*

beaming, blazing, bright, brilliant, dazzling, flaming, fluorescent, incandescent, lambent, lucent, lustrous, radiant, resplendent, shining, splendid, vivid; SEE CONCEPT 617

effusion [n] *outpouring*

address, diffusion, discharge, effluence, effluvium, efflux, emanation, emission, exudate, gush, gushing, ooze, outflow, pouring, shedding, stream, verbosity, wordiness; SEE CONCEPTS 179,266

effusive [adj] *gushing, profuse*

all jaw*, big mouthed*, demonstrative, ebullient, enthusiastic, expansive, extravagant, exuberant, free-flowing, fulsome, gabby*, gushy*, lavish, outpouring, overflowing, prolix, talkative, unconstrained, unreserved, unrestrained, verbose, windbag*, windy*, wordy; SEE CONCEPTS 267,542

egg [n] *seed, cell; embryo of an animal*

bud, cackle*, cackleberry*, germ, nucleus, oospore, ovum, roe, rudiment, spawn, yellow eye*; SEE CONCEPTS 389,392

egg on [v] *push to do something*

agitate, arouse, drive, encourage, excite, exhort, goad, incite, instigate, pique, prick, prod, prompt, propel, rally, sic, spur, stimulate, stir up, urge, whip up; SEE CONCEPT 68

ego [n] *personality*

character, psyche, self, self-admiration, selfdom, self-pride; SEE CONCEPT 411

egocentric [adj] *thinking very highly of oneself*

conceited, egoistic, egoistical, egomaniacal, egotistic, egotistical, individualist, individualistic, megalomaniac, narcissistic, pompous, self-absorbed, self-centered, self-concerned, self-indulgent, self-interested, selfish, self-loving, self-serving, stuck-up, vainglorious, wrapped up in oneself; SEE CONCEPT 404

egoism/egotism [n] *self-centeredness*

arrogance, assurance, boastfulness, boasting, bragging, conceit, conceitedness, egocentricity, egomania, gasconade, haughtiness, insolence, megalomania, narcissism, ostentation, overconfidence, preoccupation with self, presumption, pride, self-absorption, self-admiration, self-confidence, self-importance, self-interest, selfishness, self-love, self-possession, self-regard, self-worship, superiority, swellheadedness, vainglory, vanity, vaunting; SEE CONCEPT 411

egotistic/egoistic [adj] *thinking very highly of oneself*

affected, aloof, autocratic, boastful, boasting, bragging, conceited, egocentric, egomaniacal, haughty, individualistic, inflated, inner-directed, intimate, intrinsic, introverted, isolated, narcissistic, obsessive, opinionated, personal, pompous, prideful, proud, puffed up*, self-absorbed, self-admiring, self-centered, self-important, snobbish, stuck on oneself*, stuck-up*, subjective, superior, swollen, vain, vainglorious; SEE CONCEPT 404

egregious [adj] *outstandingly bad; outrageous*

arrant, atrocious, capital, deplorable, extreme, flagrant, glaring, grievous, gross*, heinous, infamous, insufferable, intolerable, monstrous, nefarious, notorious, outright, preposterous, rank, scandalous, shocking, stark; SEE CONCEPTS 545,548,570

egress [n] *passage out*

departure, doorway, emanation, emergence, escape, exit, exiting, exodus, issue, opening, outlet, setting-out, vent, way out, withdrawal; SEE CONCEPTS 195,440

ed
eg

eject [v] *throw or be thrown out*
banish, bounce*, bump, cast out, debar, disbar, discharge, disgorge, dislodge, dismiss, displace, dispossess, ditch, do away with*, drive off, dump*, eighty-six*, ejaculate, eliminate, emit, eradicate, eruct, erupt, evict, exclude, expel, expulse, extrude, fire, force out, get rid of, give the boot*, heave out*, irrupt, kick out*, kiss goodbye*, oust, reject, rout, sack, send packing*, show the gate to*, spew, spit out, spout, squeeze out, throw overboard*, turn out, unloose, vomit; SEE CONCEPTS 179,222

eke out [v] *make something last*
barely exist, be economical with, be frugal with, be sparing with, economize on, get by*, stretch out; SEE CONCEPT 239

elaborate [adj] *intricate; involved*
busy, careful, complex, complicated, decorated, detailed, elegant, embellished, exact, extensive, extravagant, fancy, fussy, garnished, highly wrought, high tech*, imposing, knotty, labored, labyrinthine, luxurious, many-faceted, minute, ornamented, ornate, ostentatious, overdone, overworked, painstaking, perfected, plush, posh, precise, prodigious, refined, showy, skillful, sophisticated, studied, thorough, with all the extras*, with all the options*, with bells and whistles*; SEE CONCEPT 562

elaborate [v] *make detailed; expand*
amplify, bedeck, clarify, comment, complicate, deck, decorate, develop, devise, discuss, embellish, enhance, enlarge, evolve, expatiate, explain, expound, flesh out, garnish, improve, interpret, ornament, particularize, polish, produce, refine, specify, unfold, work out; SEE CONCEPT 57

élan [n] *vivacity*
animation, ardor, brio, dash, esprit, flair, impetuosity, impetus, life, oomph*, panache, spirit, style, verve, vigor, vim, zest, zing*; SEE CONCEPT 411

elapse [v] *go by; slip away*
expire, flow, glide by, lapse, pass, pass away, pass by, roll by, roll on, run out, transpire, vanish; SEE CONCEPTS 6,144,818

elastic [adj1] *pliant, rubbery*
adaptable, bouncy, buoyant, ductile, extendible, extensible, flexible, irrepressible, limber, lithe, malleable, moldable, plastic, pliable, resilient, rubberlike, springy, stretchable, stretchy, supple, tempered, yielding; SEE CONCEPTS 490,606

elastic [adj2] *adaptable, tolerant*
accommodating, adjustable, airy, animated, bouncy, buoyant, complaisant, compliant, ebullient, effervescent, expansive, flexible, gay, high-spirited, lively, recuperative, resilient, soaring, spirited, sprightly, supple, variable, vivacious, volatile, yielding; SEE CONCEPT 404

elated [adj] *very happy*
animated, aroused, blissful, cheered, delighted, ecstatic, elevated, enchanted, enraptured, euphoric, exalted, excited, exhilarated, exultant, fired up*, flying*, flying high*, gleeful, high, hopped up*, in heaven*, in high spirits*, in seventh heaven*, intoxicated, joyful, joyous, jubilant, looking good*, on cloud nine*, overjoyed, proud, puffed up*, roused, set up, transported, turned-on*; SEE CONCEPTS 22,403

elation [n] *extreme happiness*
bliss, buoyancy, buzz, charge, cloud nine*, delight, ecstasy, enthusiasm, euphoria, exaltation, excitement, exhilaration, exultation, glee, high, high spirits, intoxication, jollies*, joy, joyfulness, joyousness, jubilation, kick*, kicks*, rapture, stars in one's eyes*, transport, triumph, up*, upper*; SEE CONCEPT 410

elbow [n] *angular part of arm; angularly shaped item*
ancon, angle, bend, bow, corner, crazy bone*, crook, crutch, curve, fork, funny bone*, half turn, hinge, joint, turn; SEE CONCEPTS 418,436

elbow [v] *push aside*
bend, bulldoze, bump, crowd, hook, hustle, jostle, knock, nudge, press, rough and tumble*, shoulder, shove; SEE CONCEPT 208

elder [n] *older person*
ancestor, ancient, forebearer, golden ager*, matriarch, oldest, old fogey*, oldster*, patriarch, senior, senior citizen, superior, veteran; SEE CONCEPT 424

elder [adj] *born earlier*
ancient, earlier, first-born, more mature, older, senior; SEE CONCEPTS 578,797

elderly [adj] *in old age*
aged, aging, ancient, been around*, declining, gray*, hoary, long in tooth*, lot of mileage*, no spring chicken*, old, olden, on last leg*, over the hill*, retired, tired, venerable; SEE CONCEPTS 578,797

elect [v] *select as representative; choose*
accept, admit, appoint, ballot, conclude, cull, decide upon, designate, determine, go down the line, judge, mark, name, nominate, optate, opt for, pick, pick out, prefer, receive, resolve, settle, settle on, single out, take, tap, vote, vote for; SEE CONCEPTS 41,300

election [n] *choosing; voting*
alternative, appointment, ballot, balloting, choice, decision, determination, franchise, judgment, option, poll, polls, preference, primary, referendum, selection, ticket, vote-casting; SEE CONCEPTS 41,300

elective [adj] *able to be chosen*
constituent, discretionary, electoral, facultative, nonobligatory, not compulsory, optional, selective, voluntary, voting; SEE CONCEPT 535

electric/electrical [adj] *charged; energetic*
AC, DC, dynamic, electrifying, exciting, juiced*, magnetic, motor-driven, power-driven, rousing, stimulating, stirring, tense, thrilling, voltaic; SEE CONCEPT 540

electricity [n] *energized matter, power*
AC, current, DC, electromagneticism, electron, galvanism, heat, hot stuff*, ignition, juice*, light, magneticism, service, spark, tension, utilities, voltage; SEE CONCEPT 520

electrify [v] *thrill, stimulate*
amaze, animate, astonish, astound, charge, commove, disturb, dynamize, energize, enthuse, excite, fire, frenzy, galvanize, invigorate, jar, jolt, magnetize, power, provoke, rouse, send, shock, stagger, startle, stir, strike, stun, take one's breath away*, wire*; SEE CONCEPTS 7,22,42

elegance [n] *cultivated beauty, taste*
breeding, charm, class, courtliness, cultivation, culture, delicacy, dignity, discernment, distinction, exquisiteness, felicity, gentility, good taste, grace, gracefulness, grandeur, hauteur, lushness, luxury, magnificence, nicety, nobility, noblesse, ornateness, polish, politeness, poshness, propriety, purity, refinement, restraint, rhythm, sophis-

tication, splendor, style, sumptuousness, symmetry, tastefulness; SEE CONCEPTS 655,671,718

elegant [adj] beautiful, tasteful
affected, appropriate, apt, aristocratic, artistic, august, chic, choice, classic, clever, comely, courtly, cultivated, cultured, dainty, delicate, dignified, effective, exquisite, fancy, fashionable, fine, genteel, graceful, grand, handsome, ingenious, luxurious, majestic, modish, neat, nice, noble, opulent, ornamented, ornate, ostentatious, overdone, polished, rare, recherché, refined, rich, select, simple, stately, stuffy, stylish, stylized, sumptuous, superior, turgid, well-bred; SEE CONCEPTS 574,579,589

element [n1] essential feature
aspect, basic, basis, bit, component, constituent, detail, drop, facet, factor, fundamental, hint, ingredient, item, material, matter, member, part, particle, particular, piece, portion, principle, root, section, stem, subdivision, trace, unit, view; SEE CONCEPTS 668,826,829

element [n2] place where one feels comfortable
domain, environment, field, habitation, medium, milieu, sphere; SEE CONCEPTS 198,516

elementary [adj] simple, basic
ABCs, abecedarian, basal, beginning, child's play*, clear, duck soup*, easy, elemental, essential, facile, foundational, fundamental, initial, introductory, meat and potatoes*, original, plain, prefatory, preliminary, primary, primitive, primo*, rudimentary, simplest, simple, simplified, straightforward, substratal, uncomplex, uncomplicated, underlying; SEE CONCEPTS 546,562

elevate [v1] lift up
erect, fetch up*, heighten, hike up*, hoist, jack up*, levitate, poise, pump, put up, pyramid*, raise, ramp, rear, shoot up*, stilt, take up, tilt, uphold, uplift, upraise; SEE CONCEPT 196

elevate [v2] promote; augment
advance, aggrandize, appoint, boost, build up, dignify, enhance, ennoble, exalt, further, glorify, heighten, honor, increase, intensify, magnify, prefer, put up, skip, swell, upgrade; SEE CONCEPTS 69,351,700

elevate [v3] raise spirits
animate, boost, brighten, bring up, buoy up*, cheer, elate, excite, exhilarate, glorify, hearten, inspire, lift up*, perk up*, refine, rouse, sublimate, uplift; SEE CONCEPTS 7,22

elevated [adj1] highly moral or dignified
animated, big-time*, bright, elated, eloquent, eminent, ethical, exalted, exhilarated, formal, grand, grandiloquent, heavy, high, high-flown*, high-minded, honorable, inflated, lofty, noble, righteous, stately, sublime, superb, upright, upstanding, virtuous; SEE CONCEPTS 402,545,567

elevated [adj2] raised up
aerial, high, high-rise, lifted, raised, stately, tall, towering, upheaved, uplifted, upraised, uprisen; SEE CONCEPT 779

elevation [n1] height; high ground
acclivity, altitude, ascent, boost, eminence, heave, hill, hillock, hoist, levitation, mountain, platform, ridge, rise, roof, top, uplift, upthrow; SEE CONCEPTS 509,741

elevation [n2] advancement, promotion
aggrandizement, apotheosis, boost, deification, eminence, ennoblement, exaltation, exaltedness, glorification, grandeur, immortalization, lionization, loftiness, magnification, nobility, nobleness, preference, preferment, prelation, raise, sublimity, upgrading; SEE CONCEPTS 69,351,668

elf [n] small, fairytale character
brownie, elfin, fairy, fay, leprechaun, nisse, pixie; SEE CONCEPT 370

elicit [v] draw out
arm-twist*, badger, bite*, bring, bring forth, bring out, bring to light*, call forth, cause, derive, educe, evince, evoke, evolve, exact, extort, extract, fetch, give rise to, milk*, obtain, put muscle on*, put the arm on*, rattle, shake, shake down*, squeeze, wrest, wring; SEE CONCEPTS 68,142

eligible [adj] fit, worthy
acceptable, appropriate, becoming, capable of, desirable, discretionary, elective, employable, equal to, fitted, in line for*, in the running*, licensed, likely, preferable, privileged, proper, qualified, satisfactory, seemly, suitable, suited, trained, up to*, usable; SEE CONCEPTS 527,558

eliminate [v] remove, throw out
annihilate, blot out*, bump off*, cancel, cast out, count out, cut out, defeat, discard, discharge, dismiss, dispense with, dispose of, disqualify, disregard, do away with, drive out, drop, eject, eradicate, erase, evict, exclude, expel, exterminate, get rid of, ignore, invalidate, kill, knock out*, leave out, liquidate, murder, omit, oust, phase out, put out, reject, rub out*, rule out, set aside, shut the door on*, slay, stamp out*, take out, terminate, waive, waste, wipe out*; SEE CONCEPTS 30,211

elite [n] high-class persons
aristocracy, beautiful people*, best, blue blood*, carriage trade*, celebrity, choice, country club set*, cream, crème de la crème*, crowd, elect, establishment, fast lane*, fat*, flower, gentility, gentry, glitterati, high society*, in-crowd*, jet-set*, main line*, nobility, old money*, optimacy, pride, prime, prize, quality, select, society, top, upper class, upper crust*; SEE CONCEPTS 387, 388,417

elite [adj] best, first-class
aristocratic, choice, cool*, crack*, elect, exclusive, gilt-edged, greatest, noble, out of sight*, out of this world*, pick, selected, super, tip-top*, top, top drawer*, topflight, top-notch, upper-class, world-class; SEE CONCEPTS 555,574

elliptical [adj] oval-shaped
egg-shaped, ellipsoidal, oblong, ovoid; SEE CONCEPT 486

elocution [n] articulation
declamation, delivery, diction, dramatic, eloquence, enunciation, expression, locution, oratory, pronunciation, public speaking, reading, rhetoric, speech, speechcraft, speechmaking, utterance, voice culture, voice production; SEE CONCEPT 47

elongate [v] make longer
drag one's feet*, drag out, draw, draw out, extend, fill, lengthen, let out, pad*, prolong, prolongate, protract, put rubber in*, spin out, stretch; SEE CONCEPTS 137,239,250

elope [v] run away to be married
abscond, bolt, decamp, disappear, escape, flee, fly, go secretly, go to Gretna Green*, leave, run off, skip*, slip away, slip out, steal away; SEE CONCEPT 297

eloquence [n] skillful way with words
ability, appeal, articulation, command of lan-

ej
el

guage, delivery, diction, dramatic, expression, expressiveness, expressivity, facility, fervor, flow, fluency, force, forcefulness, gift of gab*, grandiloquence, loquacity, meaningfulness, mellifluousness, oration, oratory, passion, persuasiveness, poise, power, rhetoric, spirit, style, vigor, vivacity, volubility, wit, wittiness; SEE CONCEPTS 68, 278,630

eloquent [adj] having a skillful way with words
affecting, ardent, articulate, expressive, facund, fervent, fervid, fluent, forceful, glib, grandiloquent, graphic, impassioned, impressive, indicative, magniloquent, meaningful, moving, outspoken, passionate, persuasive, poignant, potent, powerful, revealing, rhetorical, sententious, significant, silver-tongued*, smooth-spoken*, stirring, suggestive, telling, touching, vivid, vocal, voluble, well-expressed; SEE CONCEPT 267

elsewhere [adv] in another place
abroad, absent, away, formerly, gone, hence, not here, not present, not under consideration, otherwhere, outside, remote, removed, somewhere, somewhere else, subsequently; SEE CONCEPT 586

elucidate [v] explain in detail
annotate, clarify, clear, clear up, decode, demonstrate, draw a picture*, enlighten, exemplify, explicate, expound, get across*, gloss, illuminate, illustrate, interpret, make perfectly clear, make plain, make see daylight*, prove, shed light on*, spell out*, throw light on*, unfold; SEE CONCEPT 57

elude [v] avoid; escape
baffle, beat around the bush*, be beyond someone*, bilk, circumvent, confound, cop out*, ditch, dodge, double, duck, eschew, evade, flee, fly, foil, frustrate, get around, get away from, give the runaround*, give the slip*, give wide berth to*, hem and haw*, not touch, outrun, outwit, pass the buck*, pass up, puzzle, run around, shirk, shuck, shun, shy, stall, stay shy of*, steer clear of*, stonewall*, stump, thwart; SEE CONCEPTS 30,38,59,102

elusive [adj] evasive, mysterious
ambiguous, baffling, cagey, deceitful, deceptive, difficult to catch, elusory, equivocal, evanescent, fallacious, fleeting, fraudulent, fugacious, fugitive, greasy, illusory, imponderable, incomprehensible, indefinable, insubstantial, intangible, misleading, occult, phantom, puzzling, shifty, shy, slippery, stonewalling*, subtle, transient, transitory, tricky, unspecific, volatile; SEE CONCEPTS 529,542

emaciated [adj] undernourished, thin
anorexic, atrophied, attenuate, attenuated, bony, cadaverous, consumptive, famished, gaunt, haggard, lank, lean, like a bag of bones*, meager, peaked, pinched, scrawny, skeletal, skeletonlike, skin-and-bones*, skinny, starved, thin as rail*, underfed, wasted, wizened; SEE CONCEPTS 490,491

emanate [v] come forth; give off
arise, birth, derive, discharge, egress, emerge, emit, exhale, exit, exude, flow, initiate, issue, originate, proceed, radiate, rise, send forth, spring, stem; SEE CONCEPTS 179,221,648

emanation [n] emergence, discharge
arising, beginning, derivation, drainage, effluence, effluent, efflux, effusion, ejaculation, emerging, emission, escape, exhalation, exudation, flow, flowing, gush, issuance, issuing, leakage, oozing, origin, origination, outflow, outpour, proceeding, radiation, springing, welling; SEE CONCEPTS 179,221,648

emancipate [v] set free
affranchise, deliver, discharge, disencumber, disenthral, enfranchise, liberate, loose, loosen, manumit, release, unbind, unchain, unfetter, unshackle; SEE CONCEPT 127

emasculate [v] weaken, deprive of force
alter, debilitate, devitalize, enervate, fix*, impoverish, vitiate; SEE CONCEPTS 240,250

embalm [v] preserve, immortalize
anoint, cherish, consecrate, conserve, enshrine, freeze, lay out, mummify, prepare, process, store, treasure, wrap; SEE CONCEPT 202

embargo [n] prohibition, restriction
ban, bar, barrier, blockage, check, hindrance, impediment, interdict, interdiction, proscription, restraint, stoppage; SEE CONCEPTS 119,130

embark [v] get on transportation object
board, commence, emplane, enter, entrain, go aboard ship, launch, leave port, plunge into, put on board, set about, set out, set sail, take on board, take ship; SEE CONCEPTS 159,195,224

embark on [v] begin undertaking, journey
broach, commence, engage, enter, get off, initiate, jump off, launch, open, plunge into, set about, set out, set to, start, take up, tee off*; SEE CONCEPTS 100,221

embarrass [v] cause mental discomfort
abash, agitate, annoy, bewilder, bother, bug, catch one short*, chagrin, confuse, discombobulate*, discomfit, discompose, disconcert, discountenance, distract, distress, disturb, dumbfound, faze, fluster, give a bad time*, give a hard time*, hang up*, irk, let down*, make a monkey of*, mortify, nonplus, perplex, perturb, plague, put in a hole*, put in a spot*, put on the spot*, put out of countenance*, puzzle, rattle, shame, show up*, stun, tease, throw, throw into a tizzy*, upset; SEE CONCEPTS 7,19,54

embarrassing [adj] humiliating, shaming
awkward, bewildering, compromising, confusing, delicate, difficult, disagreeable, discomfiting, discommoding, discommodious, disconcerting, distracting, distressing, disturbing, equivocal, exasperating, impossible, incommodious, inconvenient, inopportune, mortifying, perplexing, puzzling, rattling, sensitive, shameful, sticky, ticklish, touchy, tricky, troublesome, troubling, uncomfortable, uneasy, unpropitious, unseemly, upsetting, worrisome; SEE CONCEPTS 537,548

embarrassment [n] humiliation, shame
awkwardness, awkward situation, bashfulness, bind, boo boo*, chagrin, clumsiness, complexity, confusion, destitution, difficulty, dilemma, discomfiture, discompose, disconcertion, distress, egg on face*, faux pas, fix, hitch, hot seat*, hot water*, impecuniosity, indebtedness, indiscretion, inhibition, mess, mistake, mortification, pickle*, pinch, plight, poverty, predicament, puzzle, quandary, scrape, self-consciousness, shyness, snag, stew, strait, tangle, timidity, unease, uneasiness; SEE CONCEPTS 410,674

embassy [n] residence, offices of overseas representatives
commission, committee, consular office, consulate, delegation, diplomatic office, legation, ministry, mission; SEE CONCEPTS 439,449,516

embed [v] *sink, implant*
bury, deposit, dig in, drive in, enclose, fasten, fix, hammer in, impact, infix, ingrain, inlay, insert, install, lodge, pierce, plant, plunge, press, put into, ram in, root, set, stick in, stuff in, thrust in, tuck in; SEE CONCEPTS 178,188

embellish [v] *make beautiful; decorate*
add bells and whistles*, adorn, amplify, array, beautify, bedeck, color, deck, dress up*, elaborate, emblaze, embroider, enhance, enrich, exaggerate, festoon, fix up*, fudge*, garnish, gild, give details, grace, gussy up*, magnify, ornament, overstate, spiff up*, spruce up*, trim; SEE CONCEPTS 49,162,177,700

embellishment [n] *beautification; decorating*
adornment, coloring, decoration, doodad*, elaboration, embroidering, embroidery, enhancement, enrichment, exaggeration, fandangle*, floridity, flowery speech, frill, froufrou*, fuss*, garnish, gilding, gingerbread*, hyperbole, icing on the cake*, jazz*, ornament, ornamentation, ostentation, overstatement; SEE CONCEPTS 177,278, 700,718

embers [n] *hot ashes from fire*
ash, brand, cinders, clinkers, coals, firebrand, live coals, slag, smoking remnants, smoldering remains; SEE CONCEPTS 260,478

embezzle [v] *steal money, often from employer*
abstract, appropriate, defalcate, filch, forge, loot, misapply, misappropriate, misuse, peculate, pilfer, purloin, put hand in cookie jar*, put hand in till*, skim, thieve; SEE CONCEPT 139

embezzlement [n] *stealing money, often from employer*
abstraction, appropriation, defalcation, filching, fraud, larceny, misapplication, misappropriation, misuse, peculation, pilferage, pilfering, purloining, skimming, theft, thieving; SEE CONCEPT 139

embitter [v] *upset, alienate*
acerbate, acidulate, aggravate, anger, annoy, bitter, bother, disaffect, disillusion, envenom, exacerbate, exasperate, irritate, make bitter, make resentful, poison, sour, venom, worsen; SEE CONCEPTS 7,14,19

emblem [n] *crest*
adumbration, arms, attribute, badge, banner, brand, character, coat of arms, colophon, colors, design, device, figure, flag, hallmark, identification, image, impress, insignia, logo, mark, marker, medal, memento, miniature, monogram, motto, pennant, regalia, reminder, representation, scepter, seal, sign, standard, symbol, token, trademark, type; SEE CONCEPTS 259,284,625

embodiment [n] *representation, manifestation*
apotheosis, archetype, cast, collection, comprehension, conformation, embracement, encompassment, epitome, example, exemplar, exemplification, expression, form, formation, incarnation, inclusion, incorporation, integration, matter, organization, personification, prosopopoeia, quintessence, realization, reification, structure, symbol, systematization, type; SEE CONCEPTS 118,686

embody [v1] *represent; materialize*
actualize, complete, concretize, demonstrate, emblematize, epitomize, evince, exemplify, exhibit, express, exteriorize, externalize, hypostatize, illustrate, incarnate, incorporate, manifest, mirror, objectify, personalize, personify, realize, reify,

show, stand for, substantiate, symbolize, typify; SEE CONCEPT 118

embody [v2] *include, integrate*
absorb, amalgamate, assimilate, blend, bring together, codify, collect, combine, comprehend, comprise, concentrate, consolidate, contain, embrace, encompass, establish, fuse, have, incorporate, involve, merge, organize, subsume, systematize, take in, unify; SEE CONCEPTS 112,113

embrace [v1] *hold tightly in one's arms*
bear hug*, clasp, clinch, cling, clutch, cradle, cuddle, encircle, enfold, entwine, envelop, fold, fondle, grab, grasp, grip, hug, lock, nuzzle, press, seize, snuggle, squeeze, take in arms*, wrap; SEE CONCEPTS 190,191

embrace [v2] *include in one's beliefs; take into account*
accept, accommodate, admit, adopt, avail oneself of, comprehend, comprise, contain, cover, deal with*, embody, enclose, encompass, espouse, get into*, go in for*, grab, have, incorporate, involve, make use of, provide for, receive, seize, subsume, take advantage of, take in, take on, take up, welcome; SEE CONCEPTS 12,15,112

embroider [v1] *add fancy stitching, adornment*
beautify, bedeck, braid, color, cross-stitch, deck, decorate, embellish, fix up, garnish, gild, gussy up*, knit, ornament, pattern, quilt, spruce up*, stitch, weave pattern, work; SEE CONCEPTS 177,218

embroider [v2] *exaggerate information*
aggrandize, amplify, blow-up*, build up, color, distend, dramatize, elaborate, embellish, enhance, enlarge, expand, falsify, fudge*, heighten, hyperbolize, lie, magnify, make federal case*, make mountain out of molehill*, overdo, overelaborate, overembellish, overemphasize, overestimate, overstate, pad*, play up*, puff*, romanticize, spread on thick*, stretch, stretch the truth*, yeast*; SEE CONCEPTS 58,63

embroidery [n] *fancy stitching*
adornment, appliqué, arabesque, bargello, brocade, crewel, crochet, cross-stitch, decoration, lace, lacery, needlepoint, needlework, quilting, sampler, tapestry, tatting, tracery; SEE CONCEPTS 218,259

embroil [v] *involve in dispute; complicate*
cause trouble, compromise, confound, confuse, derange, disorder, disturb, disunite, encumber, enmesh, ensnare, entangle, implicate, incriminate, involve, mire, mix up, muddle, perplex, snarl, tangle, trouble; SEE CONCEPTS 7,19,86

emend [v] *correct*
alter, amend, better, edit, emendate, improve, polish, rectify, redact, retouch, revise, right, touch up; SEE CONCEPT 126

emerge [v] *come out, arise*
appear, arrive, become apparent, become known, become visible, come forth, come into view, come on the scene, come to light, come up, crop up, dawn, derive, develop, egress, emanate, flow, gush, issue, loom, make appearance, materialize, originate, proceed, rise, show, spring, spring up, spurt, steam, stem, surface, transpire, turn up; SEE CONCEPTS 105,118

emergency [n] *crisis, danger*
accident, climax, clutch*, compulsion, crossroad, crunch*, depression, difficulty, distress, exigency, extremity, fix, hole, impasse, juncture,

el
em

meltdown*, misadventure, necessity, pass, pinch*, plight, predicament, pressure, push, quandary, scrape, squeeze, strait, tension, turning point, urgency, vicissitude, zero hour*; SEE CONCEPTS 674,675

emergent [adj] resulting
appearing, budding, coming, developing, efflorescent, emanant, emanating, issuing forth, outgoing, rising; SEE CONCEPT 537

emigrant [n] person who leaves his or her native country
alien, colonist, departer, displaced person, émigré, evacuee, exile, expatriate, fugitive, migrant, migrator, outcast, pilgrim, refugee, traveler, wanderer, wayfarer; SEE CONCEPTS 413,423

emigrate [v] move to new country
depart, migrate, move abroad, quit, remove, transmigrate; SEE CONCEPT 198

eminence [n1] importance, fame
authority, celebrity, credit, dignity, distinction, esteem, famousness, glory, greatness, honor, illustriousness, influence, kudos, loftiness, notability, note, power, preeminence, prepotency, prestige, prominence, prominency, rank, renown, reputation, repute, significance, standing, superiority, weight; SEE CONCEPTS 388,668,671

eminence [n2] high ground
altitude, elevation, height, highland, highness, hill, hillock, knoll, loftiness, peak, project, prominence, promontory, raise, ridge, rise, summit, upland; SEE CONCEPTS 509,741

eminent [adj] very important; famous
august, big-gun*, big-league*, big-name*, big-time*, celeb*, celebrated, celebrious, conspicuous, distinguished, dominant, elevated, esteemed, exalted, famed, grand, great, high, high-ranking, illustrious, lionlike, lofty, name, noble, notable, noted, noteworthy, of note, outstanding, page-oner*, paramount, preeminent, prestigious, prominent, redoubted, renowned, star, superior, superstar, VIP*, well-known; SEE CONCEPTS 555,568

eminently [adv] exceptionally; well
conspicuously, exceedingly, extremely, greatly, highly, notably, outstandingly, prominently, remarkably, strikingly, suitably, surpassingly, very; SEE CONCEPT 574

emissary [n] deputy
agent, ambassador, bearer, carrier, consul, courier, delegate, envoy, front, go-between, herald, hired gun*, intermediary, internuncio, legate, messenger, rep*, representative, scout, spy; SEE CONCEPTS 348,423

emission [n] issuance, diffusion
discharge, ejaculation, ejection, emanation, exhalation, exudation, issue, radiation, shedding, transmission, utterance, venting; SEE CONCEPT 179

emit [v] diffuse, discharge
afford, beam, belch, breathe, cast out, disembogue, drip, eject, emanate, erupt, evacuate, excrete, exhale, expectorate, expel, expend, expire, extrude, exude, give off, give out, give vent to, gush, issue, jet, let off, loose, ooze, pass, perspire, pour, pronounce, purge, radiate, reek, secrete, send forth, send out, shed, shoot, speak, spew, spill, spit, squirt, throw out, transmit, utter, vent, voice, void, vomit, yield; SEE CONCEPTS 108,179,266

emotion [n] mental state
affect, affection, affectivity, agitation, anger, ardor, commotion, concern, desire, despair, despondency, disturbance, drive, ecstasy, elation, empathy, excitability, excitement, feeling, fervor, grief, gut reaction, happiness, inspiration, joy, love, melancholy, passion, perturbation, pride, rage, remorse, responsiveness, sadness, satisfaction, sensation, sensibility, sensitiveness, sentiment, shame, sorrow, sympathy, thrill, tremor, vehemence, vibes, warmth, zeal; SEE CONCEPT 410

emotional [adj] demonstrative about feelings
affecting, ardent, disturbed, ecstatic, emotive, enthusiastic, excitable, exciting, falling apart*, fanatical, feeling, fervent, fervid, fickle, fiery, heartwarming, heated, histrionic, hot-blooded*, hysterical, impassioned, impetuous, impulsive, irrational, moving, nervous, overwrought, passionate, pathetic, poignant, responsive, roused, sensitive, sentient, sentimental, spontaneous, stirred, stirring, susceptible, tear-jerking*, temperamental, tender, thrilling, touching, warm, zealous; SEE CONCEPTS 403,542

emotionless [adj] unfeeling, undemonstrative
blank, chill, cold, cold-blooded*, cold fish*, cool, cool cat*, deadpan, detached, dispassionate, distant, flat, frigid, glacial*, heartless, icy, immovable, impassive, impersonal, in cold blood*, indifferent, laid back*, matter-of-fact, nonemotional, nowhere*, poker face*, remote, reserved, stony-eyed*, thick-skinned*, toneless, unemotional, unimpassioned, with straight face; SEE CONCEPTS 401,403,542

empathy [n] understanding
affinity, appreciation, being on same wavelength*, being there for someone*, communion, community of interests, compassion, comprehension, concord, cottoning to*, good vibrations*, hitting it off*, insight, picking up on*, pity, rapport, recognition, responsiveness, soul, sympathy, warmth; SEE CONCEPTS 32,409,411

emphasis [n] importance, prominence
accent, accentuation, attention, decidedness, force, headline, highlight, impressiveness, insistence, intensity, moment, positiveness, power, preeminence, priority, significance, strength, stress, underlining, underscoring, weight; SEE CONCEPTS 668,682

emphasize [v] stress, give priority to
accent, accentuate, affirm, articulate, assert, bear down, charge, dramatize, dwell on, enlarge, enunciate, headline, highlight, hit*, impress, indicate, insist on, italicize, labor the point*, limelight*, maintain, make a point, make clear, make emphatic, make much of*, mark, pinpoint, play up*, point out*, point up*, press, pronounce, punctuate, put accent on*, reiterate, repeat, rub in*, spotlight*, underline, underscore, weight; SEE CONCEPTS 49,57

emphatic [adj] insistent, unequivocal
absolute, accented, assertive, assured, categorical, certain, cogent, confident, decided, definite, definitive, determined, direct, distinct, dogmatic, dynamic, earnest, energetic, explicit, express, flat, for a face*, forceful, forcible, important, impressive, marked, momentous, no mistake*, pointed, positive, potent, powerful, pronounced, resounding, significant, sober, solemn, stressed,

striking, strong, sure, telling, trenchant, unmistakable, vigorous; SEE CONCEPTS **267,535**

empire [n] *place ruled by sovereign; rule*
authority, command, commonwealth, control, domain, dominion, federation, government, people, power, realm, sovereignty, supremacy, sway, union; SEE CONCEPTS **198,299,376**

empirical /empiric [adj] *practical; based on experience*
experient, experiential, experimental, factual, observational, observed, pragmatic, provisional, speculative; SEE CONCEPTS **548,582**

employ [v1] *make use of*
apply, bestow, bring to bear*, engage, exercise, exert, exploit, fill, handle, keep busy*, manipulate, occupy, operate, put to use*, spend, take up*, use, use up*, utilize; SEE CONCEPT **225**

employ [v2] *give money in exchange for work performed*
bring on board*, come on board*, commission, contract, contract for, engage, enlist, hire, ink*, obtain, place, procure, put on*, retain, secure, sign on*, sign up*, take on, truck with*; SEE CONCEPT **351**

employed [adj] *working*
active, at it*, at work, busy, engaged, hired, in a job, in collar*, in harness*, inked*, in place, laboring, occupied, on board*, on duty*, on the job*, on the payroll*, operating, plugging away*, selected, signed*; SEE CONCEPTS **538,560**

employee [n] *person being paid for working for another or a corporation*
agent, apprentice, assistant, attendant, blue collar*, breadwinner*, clerk, cog*, company person, craftsperson, desk jockey*, domestic, hand, help, hired gun*, hired hand*, hireling, jobholder, laborer, member, operator, pink collar*, plug*, representative, sales help, salesperson, servant, slave, staff member, wage-earner, white collar*, worker, working stiff*; SEE CONCEPT **348**

employer [n] *person, business who hires workers*
big cheese*, big shot*, boss, businessperson, capitalist, CEO*, chief, CO*, company, corporation, director, entrepreneur, establishment, executive, firm, front office, head, head honcho*, juice*, kingpin*, management, manager, manufacturer, meal ticket*, organization, outfit, overseer, owner, patron, president, proprietor, slavedriver*, superintendent, supervisor; SEE CONCEPT **347**

employment [n1] *working for a living; engagement in activity*
application, assignment, avocation, awarding, business, calling, carrying, commissioning, contracting, craft, employ, engaging, enlistment, enrollment, exercise, exercising, exertion, field, function, game*, hire, hiring, job, line, métier, mission, number, occupation, occupying, office, position, post, profession, pursuit, racket*, recruitment, retaining, service, servicing, setup, signing on*, situation, taking on, thing*, trade, using, vocation, what one is into*, work; SEE CONCEPTS **349,351,360**

employment [n2] *using something*
adoption, appliance, application, disposition, exercise, exercising, exertion, exploitation, handling, operation, play, purpose, usage, usance, use, utilization; SEE CONCEPTS **225,658,694**

emporium [n] *market*
bazaar, boutique, chain, co-op, cut-rate store*, discount store, five-and-dime*, flea market, galleria, mall, mart, outlet, outlet store, shop, shopping center, shopping plaza, stand, store, supermarket, thrift shop; SEE CONCEPT **449**

empower [v] *authorize, enable*
accredit, allow, capacitate, charge, commission, delegate, entitle, entrust, grant, invest, legitimize, license, okay, permit, privilege, qualify, sanction, vest, warrant; SEE CONCEPTS **50,88**

emptiness [n] *void, bareness*
blank, blankness, chasm, depletedness, desertedness, desolation, destitution, exhaustion, gap, hollowness, inanition, vacancy, vacuity, vacuum, waste; SEE CONCEPTS **720,733**

empty [adj1] *containing nothing*
abandoned, bare, barren, blank, clear, dead, deflated, depleted, desert, deserted, desolate, despoiled, destitute, devoid, dry, evacuated, exhausted, forsaken, godforsaken*, hollow, lacking, stark, unfilled, unfurnished, uninhabited, unoccupied, vacant, vacated, vacuous, void, wanting, waste; SEE CONCEPTS **481,774,786**

empty [adj2] *fruitless, ineffective*
aimless, banal, barren, cheap, dead, deadpan, devoid, dishonest, dumb, expressionless, fatuous, flat, frivolous, futile, hollow, idle, ignorant, inane, ineffectual, inexpressive, insincere, insipid, jejune, meaningless, nugatory, otiose, paltry, petty, purposeless, senseless, silly, trivial, unintelligent, unreal, unsatisfactory, unsubstantial, vacuous, vain, valueless, vapid, worthless; SEE CONCEPTS **402,570,575**

empty [adj3] *hungry*
famished, ravenous, starving, unfed, unfilled; SEE CONCEPT **406**

empty [v] *remove contents*
clear, consume, decant, deplete, discharge, disgorge, drain, drink, dump, ebb, eject, escape, evacuate, exhaust, expel, flow out, gut, leak, leave, make void, pour out, purge, release, run out, rush out, tap, unburden, unload, use up, vacate, void; SEE CONCEPT **211**

empty-headed [adj] *flighty, scatterbrained*
brainless, dizzy, featherbrained, frivolous, giddy, harebrained, ignorant, illiterate, inane, knownothing, silly, skittish, stupid, uneducated, unschooled, untaught, vacant, vacuous; SEE CONCEPT **402**

emulate [v] *copy the actions of*
challenge, compete, compete with, contend, contend with, ditto*, do*, do like*, follow, follow in footsteps*, follow suit*, follow the example of*, go like*, imitate, make like*, mimic, mirror, outvie, pattern after*, rival, rivalize, take after*, vie with; SEE CONCEPTS **87,171**

enable [v] *allow, authorize*
accredit, approve, capacitate, commission, condition, empower, endow, facilitate, fit, give power, implement, invest, let, license, make possible, permit, prepare, provide the means*, qualify, ready, sanction, set up, warrant; SEE CONCEPTS **50,83,88,99**

enact [v1] *act out; accomplish*
achieve, appear as, depict, discourse, do, execute, go on*, perform, personate, play, playact, play the part of, portray, represent; SEE CONCEPTS **91,292**

enact [v2] *authorize, legislate*
accomplish, appoint, bring about, carry through, command, constitute, decree, determine, dictate, effect, effectuate, establish, execute, fix, formu-

em
en

late. get the floor*. institute, jam through*. make,
make into law, make laws, ordain, order, pass,
proclaim, put in force, put through, railroad*. railroad through*. ratify, sanction, set, steamroll*.
transact, vote favorably*. vote in*: SEE CONCEPTS
50,88,298,317

enactment [n1] *playacting*
achievement, acting, depiction, execution, impersonation, performance, personation, personification, playing, portrayal, representation: SEE
CONCEPTS 263,292

enactment [n2] *law; authorization*
command, commandment, decree, dictate, edict,
execution, legislation, order, ordinance, proclamation, ratification, regulation, statute: SEE CON-
CEPTS 318,685

enamel [n] *paint, often shiny*
cloisonné, coating, finish, glaze, gloss, japan, lacquer, polish, stain, topcoat, varnish, veneer: SEE
CONCEPTS 259,260,467

enamor [v] *fascinate, captivate*
attract, bewitch, charm, enchant, endear, enrapture, enthrall, entice, fall in love with*,
grab, infatuate, make hit with*. please, slay*.
sweep off feet*. turn on*: SEE CONCEPTS
7,22,375

enamored [adj] *in love*
amorous, attracted, besotted, bewitched, captivated, charmed, crazy about*. devoted, dotty, enchanted, enraptured, entranced, fascinated fond,
gone*. has a thing about*. hooked*. infatuated,
loving, nuts about*. silly about*. smitten, stuck
on*, swept off one's feet*. taken*, wild about*:
SEE CONCEPTS 32,403

enchant [v] *delight, mesmerize*
allure, beguile, bewitch, captivate, carry away*.
cast a spell on*. charm, delectate, draw, enamor,
enrapture, ensorcell, enthrall, entice, entrance,
fascinate, grab, gratify, hex, hypnotize, kill*.
knock dead*. magnetize, make a hit with*. make
happy*. please, send*. slay*. spell, spellbind,
sweep off feet*. take, thrill, turn on*. voodoo*.
wile, wow*: SEE CONCEPTS 7,22

enchanting [adj] *fascinating, delightful*
alluring, appealing, attractive, beguiling, bewitching, captivating, charming, delectable, endearing,
enthralling, entrancing, exciting, glamorous, intriguing, lovely, pleasant, pleasing, ravishing, seductive, siren, sirenic, winsome: SEE CONCEPTS
404,529

encircle [v] *circumscribe*
band, begird, cincture, circle, circuit, compass,
cover, enclose, encompass, enfold, enring, envelop, environ, gird in, girdle, halo, hem in*.
inclose, invest, ring, surround, wreathe: SEE CON-
CEPT 758

enclose [v] *put inside, surround*
blockade, block off, bound, box up, cage, circle,
circumscribe, close in, confine, coop, corral,
cover, encase, encircle, encompass, enfold, enshroud, environ, fence, fence off*. hedge, hem
in*. imbue, immure, implant, impound, imprison,
include, induct, insert, intern, jail, limit, lock in*.
lock up*. mew, mure, pen, restrict, set apart, shut
in, veil, wall in, wrap: SEE CONCEPTS
112,209,758

enclosure [n1] *area bounded by something*
asylum, aviary, bowl, building, cage, camp, cell,
close, coliseum, coop, corral, court, courtyard,
den, dungeon, garden, ghetto, hutch, jail, pale,

park, patch, pen, place, plot, pound, precinct,
prison, quad, quadrangle, region, room, stadium,
stockade, sty, vault, walk, yard, zone: SEE CON-
CEPTS 439,448,513

enclosure [n2] *something included with a letter*
check, circular, copy, document, form, information, money, printed matter, questionnaire: SEE
CONCEPT 271

encompass [v1] *surround, circumscribe*
beset, circle, compass, encircle, enclose, envelop,
environ, gird, girdle, hem in, ring: SEE CONCEPT
758

encompass [v2] *include, contain*
admit, comprehend, comprise, cover, embody,
embrace, have, hold, incorporate, involve, subsume, take in: SEE CONCEPT 112

encore [n] *another round of applause; repeat*
acclamation, cheers, number, plaudits, praise, reappearance, repeat performance, repetition, response, return: SEE CONCEPT 264

encounter [n1] *chance meeting*
appointment, brush, concurrence, confrontation,
interview, rendezvous: SEE CONCEPT 384

encounter [n2] *fight, argument*
action, battle, bout, brush, clash, collision, combat, conflict, contention, contest, dispute, engagement, flap*. fray, hassle, quarrel, rumpus*. run-
in*. scrap, set-to*. skirmish, velitation, violence:
SEE CONCEPTS 46,86,106

encounter [v1] *happen upon*
alight upon, bear, bump into, chance upon, close,
come across, come upon, confront, cross the
path*. descry, detect, espy, experience, face, fall
in with*. find, front, hit upon, meet, meet up with,
rub eyeballs*. run across, run into, run smack
into*. suffer, sustain, turn up, undergo: SEE CON-
CEPTS 38,384

encounter [v2] *fight, attack*
affront, battle, clash with, collide, combat, conflict, confront, contend, cross swords*. do battle*. engage, face, grapple, meet, strive, struggle:
SEE CONCEPTS 86,106

encourage [v1] *stimulate spiritually*
animate, applaud, boost, brighten, buck up*.
buoy, cheer, cheer up, comfort, console, embolden, energize, enhearten, enliven, excite, exhilarate, fortify, galvanize, give shot in arm*.
gladden, goad, hearten, incite, inspire, inspirit,
instigate, praise, prick, prop up*. psych up*.
push, rally, reassure, refresh, restore, revitalize,
revivify, rouse, spur, steel, stir, strengthen, sway:
SEE CONCEPTS 7,22

encourage [v2] *give support; help*
abet, advance, advocate, aid, approve, assist,
back, back up, befriend, bolster, boost, brace,
comfort, console, countenance, develop, ease,
egg on*. endorse, favor, fortify, forward, foster,
further, get behind, give a leg up*. go for*. improve, instigate, invite, pat on the back, prevail,
promote, pull for*. push, reassure, reinforce, relieve, root for*. sanction, second, serve, side
with*. smile upon*. solace, spur, strengthen, subscribe to, subsidize, succor, support, sustain, uphold: SEE CONCEPTS 8,110

encouragement [n] *help, support*
advance, advocacy, aid, animation, assistance,
backing, boost, cheer, comfort, confidence, consolation, consoling, easement, enlivening, faith,
favor, firmness, fortitude, helpfulness, hope, incentive, incitement, inspiration, inspiritment, in-

vigoration, optimism, promotion, reassurance, reassuring, refreshment, relief, relieving, reward, shot in the arm*, softening, solacing, stimulation, stimulus, succor, supporting, trust, urging; SEE CONCEPTS 7,22,110,410

encroach [v] *invade another's property, business*
appropriate, arrogate, barge in*, butt in*, crash, elbow in*, entrench, horn in*, impinge, infringe, interfere, interpose, intervene, intrude, make inroads*, meddle, muscle in*, overstep, put two cents in*, squeeze in*, stick nose into*, trench, trespass, usurp, work in, worm in*; SEE CONCEPTS 7,19,86,159

encumber [v] *bother, burden*
block, charge, clog, cramp, discommode, embarrass, hamper, handicap, hang up, hinder, hogtie*, hold up, impede, incommode, inconvenience, lade, load, make difficult, obstruct, oppress, overburden, overload, retard, saddle, saddle with*, slow down, tax, trammel, weigh down, weight; SEE CONCEPTS 121,130

encyclopedic [adj] *comprehensive*
all-embracing, all-encompassing, all-inclusive, broad, catholic, complete, discursive, exhaustive, extensive, general, thorough, thorough-going, universal, vast, wide-ranging, widespread; SEE CONCEPTS 267,772

end [n1] *extreme, limit*
borderline, bound, boundary, butt end, confine, cusp, deadline, edge, extent, extremity, foot, head, heel, limitation, neb, nib, point, prong, spire, stub, stump, tail, tail end, term, terminal, termination, terminus, tip, top, ultimate; SEE CONCEPTS 745,827,833

end [n2] *completion, stop*
accomplishment, achievement, adjournment, attainment, bottom line*, cease, cessation, close, closing, closure, conclusion, consequence, consummation, culmination, curtain, denouement, desistance, desuetude, determination, discontinuance, execution, expiration, expiry, finale, finis, finish, fulfillment, issue, last word*, omega, outcome, payoff, perfection, realization, resolution, result, retirement, sign-off*, target, termination, terminus, upshot*, windup, wrap-up*; SEE CONCEPTS 119,230,832

end [n3] *intention, aim*
aspiration, design, drift, goal, intent, mark, object, objective, point, purpose, reason, where one's heading*; SEE CONCEPT 659

end [n4] *leftover part*
bit, butt end, dregs, fragment, leaving, lees, particle, piece, portion, remainder, remnant, residue, scrap, share, side, stub, tag end; SEE CONCEPT 835

end [n5] *death, destruction*
annihilation, demise, dissolution, doom, expiration, extermination, extinction, finish, passing, ruin, ruination; SEE CONCEPT 304

end [v1] *bring to an end*
abolish, abort, accomplish, achieve, break off, break up, call it a day*, call off*, cease, close, close out, complete, conclude, consummate, crown, culminate, cut short, delay, determine, discontinue, dispose of, dissolve, drop, expire, finish, get done, give up, halt, interrupt, pack it in*, perorate, postpone, pull the plug*, put the lid on*, quit, relinquish, resolve, settle, sew up*, shut down*, stop, switch off*, terminate, top off*, ul-

timate, wind up*, wrap, wrap up*; SEE CONCEPT 234

end [v2] *die or kill*
abolish, annihilate, cease, depart, desist, destroy, die, expire, exterminate, extinguish, lapse, put to death, ruin, run out, wane; SEE CONCEPTS 252,304

endanger [v] *put in jeopardy*
be careless, chance, chance it*, expose, hazard, imperil, lay on the line*, lay open*, leave defenseless, leave in the middle*, make liable, menace, peril, play into one's hands*, put at risk, put in danger, put on the spot*, risk, stick one's neck out*, subject to loss, threaten, venture; SEE CONCEPTS 246,252,384

endear [v] *attract attention*
attach, bind, captivate, charm, cherish, engage, prize, treasure, value, win; SEE CONCEPTS 7,22,32

endeavor [n] *attempt to achieve something*
aim, all*, best shot*, crash project*, dry run*, effort, enterprise, essay, exertion, fling, full blast*, full court press*, full steam*, go, header*, labor, lick*, old college try*, one's all*, one's level best*, push, shot*, stab*, striving, struggle, toil, travail, trial, try, try-on*, undertaking, venture, whack*, whirl*, work; SEE CONCEPT 87

endeavor [v] *attempt to achieve something*
address, aim, apply, aspire, assay, bid for, buck, determine, dig, do one's best*, drive at, essay, go for*, go for broke*, grind, hammer away*, hassle, have a crack*, have a shot at*, have a swing at*, hump*, hustle, intend, labor, make an effort, make a run at*, offer, peg away*, plug, pour it on*, purpose, push, risk, scratch, seek, strain, strive, struggle, sweat, take on, take pains*, try, undertake, venture; SEE CONCEPT 87

ending [n] *conclusion*
catastrophe, cessation, close, closing, closure, completion, consummation, coup de grace, culmination, denouement, desistance, dissolution, epilogue, expiration, finale, finish, lapse, omega, outcome, period, resolution, stop, summation, swan song*, termination, terminus, upshot*, wane, windup; SEE CONCEPTS 119,230,832

endless [adj] *not stopping, not finishing*
amaranthine, boundless, ceaseless, constant, continual, continuous, countless, deathless, enduring, eternal, everlasting, illimitable, immeasurable, immortal, incalculable, incessant, indeterminate, infinite, interminable, limitless, measureless, monotonous, multitudinous, never-ending, no end of, no end to, numberless, overlong, perpetual, self-perpetuating, unbounded, unbroken, undivided, undying, unending, unfathomable, uninterrupted, unlimited, unsurpassable, untold, without end; SEE CONCEPTS 482,551,798

endorse [v1] *support, authorize*
accredit, advocate, affirm, approve, attest, authenticate, back, back up*, bless, boost, certify, champion, commend, confirm, countenance, defend, favor, give a boost to, give green light*, give one's word*, give the go-ahead*, give the nod*, go along with*, go to bat for*, go with, guarantee, lend one's name to, okay, praise, push, ratify, recommend, rubber-stamp*, sanction, second, stand behind, stand up for*, stump for*, subscribe to, sustain, underwrite, uphold, vouch for, warrant, witness; SEE CONCEPTS 10,50,69,88,300

endorse [v2] *countersign a check*
add one's name to, authenticate, autograph, co-sign, notarize, put John Hancock on*, put signature on, rubber-stamp*, say amen to*, sign, sign off on, sign on dotted line*, subscribe, superscribe, undersign, underwrite; SEE CONCEPTS *50,79,88,330*

endorsement [n] *support, authorization*
advocacy, affirmation, approbation, approval, backing, championing, commercial, confirmation, countersignature, favor, fiat, go-ahead*, green light*, hubba-hubba*, okay, pat on back*, permission, qualification, ratification, recommendation, sanction, seal of approval, signature, stroke, subscription to, superscription, the nod*, warrant; SEE CONCEPT *685*

endow [v] *give large gift*
accord, award, back, bequeath, bestow, come through with, confer, contribute, donate, empower, enable, endue, enhance, enrich, establish, favor, finance, found, fund, furnish, grant, heighten, invest, lay on*, leave, make over*, organize, promote, provide, settle on, sponsor, subscribe, subsidize, supply, support, vest in, will; SEE CONCEPTS *108,341*

endowment [n1] *large gift*
award, benefaction, benefit, bequest, bestowal, boon, bounty, dispensation, donation, fund, funding, gifting, grant, gratuity, income, inheritance, largess, legacy, nest egg, pension, presentation, property, provision, revenue, stake, stipend, subsidy, trust; SEE CONCEPTS *337,340*

endowment [n2] *personal talent, ability*
aptitude, attribute, capability, capacity, faculty, flair, genius, gift, habilitation, power, qualification, quality, turn; SEE CONCEPTS *411,630*

end up [v] *become eventually; come to a close*
arrive finally, cease, come to a halt, finish, finish as, finish up, stop, turn out to be, wind up; SEE CONCEPT *119*

endurable [adj] *tolerable*
bearable, livable, sufferable, supportable, sustainable; SEE CONCEPT *548*

endurance [n1] *bearing hardship; staying power*
ability, allowance, backbone, bearing, capacity, continuing, cool, coolness, courage, enduring, forebearance, fortitude, grit, guts, gutsiness, heart*, holding up*, intestinal fortitude, mettle, moxie*, patience, perseverance, persistence, pertinacity, pluck, resignation, resistance, resolution, restraint, spunk, stamina, standing, starch*, strength, submission, sufferance, suffering, tenacity, tolerance, toleration, undergoing, vitality, will, withstanding; SEE CONCEPTS *411,633*

endurance [n2] *continuity, lastingness*
continuance, continuation, durability, duration, immutability, longevity, permanence, persistence, stability; SEE CONCEPT *804*

endure [v1] *bear hardship*
abide, accustom, allow, bear the brunt*, be patient with, brave, brook, cope with, countenance, eat, encounter, experience, face, feel, go through, grin and bear it*, hang in*, keep up, know, live out, live through, meet with, never say die*, permit, put up with, repress feelings, resign oneself, ride out*, sit through, stand, stick, stick it out*, stomach*, subject to, submit to, suffer, support, sustain, swallow*, take, take it*, take patiently, tolerate, undergo, weather, withstand; SEE CONCEPT *23*

endure [v2] *continue; be durable*
abide, be, be left, be long lived, be timeless, bide, carry on, carry through, cling, exist, go on, hang on*, have no end, hold, hold on, hold out, keep on, last, linger, live, live on, never say die*, outlast, outlive, perdure, persist, prevail, remain, ride out*, run on, stand, stay, stay on, stick to*, superannuate, survive, sustain, wear, wear on, wear well*; SEE CONCEPTS *239,407,804*

enemy [n] *someone hated or competed against*
adversary, agent, antagonist, archenemy, asperser, assailant, assassin, attacker, backbiter, bad person*, bandit, betrayer, calumniator, competitor, contender, criminal, defamer, defiler, detractor, disputant, emulator, falsifier, fifth column*, foe, guerrilla, informer, inquisitor, invader, murderer, opponent, opposition, other side*, prosecutor, rebel, revolutionary, rival, saboteur, seditionist, slanderer, spy, terrorist, traducer, traitor, vilifier, villain; SEE CONCEPTS *322,412*

energetic [adj] *full of life; forceful*
active, aggressive, animated, ball of fire*, breezy, brisk, demoniac, driving, dynamic, enterprising, forcible, fresh, hardy, high-powered, indefatigable, industrious, kinetic, lively, lusty, peppy, potent, powerful, red-blooded*, rugged, snappy, spirited, sprightly, spry, stalwart, strenuous, strong, sturdy, tireless, tough, unflagging, untiring, vigorous, vital, vivacious, zippy*; SEE CONCEPTS *404,542*

energize [v] *activate; give more life*
actify, activize, animate, arm, build up, electrify, empower, enable, enliven, excite, fortify, goose*, innervate, inspirit, invigorate, jazz up*, juice up*, liven up, motivate, pep up, prime, pump up*, put zip into*, quicken, reinforce, start up, stimulate, strengthen, sustain, switch on, trigger, turn on, vitalize, work up, zap*; SEE CONCEPTS *7,22,231,700*

energy [n1] *person's spirit and vigor*
activity, animation, application, ardor, birr, dash, drive, effectiveness, efficacy, efficiency, élan, endurance, enterprise, exertion, fire, force, forcefulness, fortitude, get-up-and-go*, go, hardihood, initiative, intensity, juice, life, liveliness, might, moxie*, muscle, operativeness, pep, pizzazz, pluck, potency, power, puissance, punch, spirit, spontaneity, stamina, steam, strength, toughness, tuck, vehemence, verve, vim, virility, vitality, vivacity, zeal, zest, zing, zip*; SEE CONCEPT *411*

energy [n2] *generated power*
application, burn, conductivity, current, dynamism, electricity, force, friction, gravity, heat, horsepower, juice, kilowatts, magnetism, potential, pressure, radioactivity, rays, reaction, response, service, steam, strength, voltage, wattage; SEE CONCEPT *520*

enervate [v] *tire, wear out*
debilitate, devitalize, disable, enfeeble, exhaust, fatigue, incapacitate, jade, paralyze, sap, unnerve, vitiate, weaken, weary; SEE CONCEPTS *156, 225,250*

enervated [adj] *exhausted, worn out*
debilitated, deteriorated, devitalized, done in, enfeebled, fatigued, feeble, gone to seed*, incapacitated, lackadaisical, languid, languishing, languorous, limp, listless, on the ropes*, out of condition*, out of gas*, out of shape*, paralyzed, prostrate, prostrated, run-down, rusty, sapped, soft, spent, spiritless, tired, undermined, un-

nerved, vitiated, washed out, weak, weakened; SEE CONCEPTS 485,560

enfeeble [v] *make very weak*
attenuate, blunt, cripple, debilitate, deplete, devitalize, diminish, disable, exhaust, fatigue, incapacitate, sap, undermine, unhinge, unnerve, weaken, wear out; SEE CONCEPTS 240,252

enfold [v] *embrace, hug*
bear hug, cinch, clasp, clinch, clutch, cover, drape, encase, enclose, encompass, enshroud, envelop, envelope, enwrap, fold, girdle, grab, hold, invest, press, shroud, squeeze, surround, swathe, veil, wrap, wrap up; SEE CONCEPTS 191,219

enforce [v] *put a rule, plan in force*
accomplish, administer, administrate, apply, carry out, coerce, commandeer, compel, constrain, crack down, demand, dictate, discharge, dragoon, drive, effect, egg on*, emphasize, exact, execute, exert, expect, extort, force upon, fortify, fulfill, goad, hound, impel, implement, impose, incite, insist on, invoke, lash, lean on, make, necessitate, oblige, perform, press, prosecute, put into effect, put screws to*, reinforce, require, sanction, spur, strain, stress, strong-arm, support, urge, whip, wrest; SEE CONCEPTS 50,88,133,298,317

enforcement [n] *requirement to obey; implementation of rule(s)*
administration, application, carrying out, coercion, compulsion, compulsory law, constraint, duress, enforcing, exaction, execution, fulfilling, imposition, impulsion, insistence, lash, martial law, necessitation, obligation, prescription, pressure, prosecution, reinforcement, spur, whip; SEE CONCEPTS 133,298,317,685

engage [v1] *hire for job, use*
appoint, bespeak, book, bring on board*, charter, come on board*, commission, contract, employ, enlist, enroll, ink*, lease, place, prearrange, put on, reserve, retain, secure, sign on, sign up, take on, truck with*; SEE CONCEPTS 129,351

engage [v2] *occupy oneself; engross*
absorb, allure, arrest, bewitch, busy, captivate, catch, charm, draw, embark on, employ, enamor, enchant, enter into, enthrall, fascinate, give a try*, give a whirl*, go for broke*, go in for*, go out for*, grip*, have a fling at*, have a go at*, have a shot at*, imbue, immerse, interest, involve, join, keep busy, monopolize, partake, participate, pitch in, practice, preengage, preoccupy, set about, soak, tackle*, take part, tie up, try on for size*, undertake; SEE CONCEPTS 87,363

engage [v3] *promise to marry*
affiance, agree, betroth, bind, catch, commit, contract, covenant, give one's word*, guarantee, hook, obligate, oblige, pass, pledge, tie, troth, turn on*, undertake, vouch, vow; SEE CONCEPT 297

engage [v4] *start a fight; attack*
assail, assault, combat, do battle with, encounter, face, fall on, give battle to, join battle with, launch, meet, strike, take on; SEE CONCEPTS 86,106,320

engage [v5] *interconnect; bring into operation*
activate, apply, attach, dovetail, energize, fasten, get going, interact, interlace, interlock, intermesh, interplay, join, lock, mesh, switch on; SEE CONCEPTS 85,113,160,221

engaged [adj1] *promised to be married*
affianced, asked for, betrothed, bound, committed, contracted, future, given one's word*, going

steady*, hooked*, intended, matched, pinned, pledged, plighted, ringed, spoken for, steady; SEE CONCEPT 555

engaged [adj2] *operating; busy*
absorbed, at work, committed, connected with, dealing in, deep, doing, employed, engrossed, immersed, in place, intent, interested, in use, involved, occupied, performing, practicing, preoccupied, pursuing, rapt, signed, tied up, unavailable, working, wrapped up*; SEE CONCEPTS 542,555,576

engagement [n1] *pledge to marry*
assurance, betrothal, betrothing, betrothment, bond, commitment, compact, contract, espousal, match, oath, obligation, pact, plight, promise, troth, undertaking, vow, word; SEE CONCEPT 297

engagement [n2] *meeting; date*
appointment, arrangement, assignation, blind date*, commission, commitment, date, errand, get-together, gig, going out*, interview, invitation, meet, seeing one*, stint, tryst, visit; SEE CONCEPT 384

engagement [n3] *battle*
action, combat, conflict, confrontation, contest, encounter, fight, fray, skirmish; SEE CONCEPTS 106,320

engaging [adj] *charming*
agreeable, alluring, appealing, attractive, bewitching, captivating, enchanting, enticing, entrancing, fascinating, fetching, glamorous, interesting, intriguing, inviting, likable, lovable, magnetic, mesmeric, pleasant, pleasing, prepossessing, siren, sweet, winning, winsome; SEE CONCEPT 404

engender [v] *cause to happen; cause an action*
arouse, beget, breed, bring about, bring forth, create, develop, excite, foment, generate, give birth to, give rise to, hatch, incite, induce, instigate, lead to, make, muster, occasion, precipitate, procreate, produce, propagate, provoke, quicken, rouse, spawn, stimulate, stir, work up; SEE CONCEPTS 221,242

engine [n] *device that drives a machine*
agent, apparatus, appliance, barrel, contrivance, cylinder, diesel, dynamo, fan, generator, horses*, implement, instrument, means, mechanism, motor, piston, pot*, powerhouse, power plant, power train, putt-putt*, rubber band*, tool, transformer, turbine, weapon, what's under the hood*; SEE CONCEPTS 463,464

engineer [n] *person who puts together things*
architect, builder, contriver, designer, deviser, director, inventor, manager, manipulator, originator, planner, schemer, sights*, surveyor, techie*, technie*; SEE CONCEPT 348

engineer [v] *devise; bring about*
angle, arrange, cause, come up with, con, conceive, concoct, contrive, control, cook*, create, direct, doctor, effect, encompass, finagle*, jockey*, machinate, manage, maneuver, manipulate, negotiate, operate, organize, originate, plan, plant, play games*, plot, pull strings*, pull wires*, put one on*, put one over*, put over*, put through, rig*, scam, scheme, set up, superintend, supervise, swing, upstage, wangle, work; SEE CONCEPTS 36,173,251

engrave [v] *carve letters or designs into*
bite, burn, chase, chisel, crosshatch, cut, diaper, embed, enchase, etch, fix, grave, hatch, impress, imprint, infix, ingrain, initial, inscribe, instill, in-

taglio, lithograph, lodge, mezzotint, ornament, print, scratch, stipple; SEE CONCEPTS 79,174,176

engraving [n] *carving of letters or design into something*

blocking, chasing, chiselling, cutting, dry point, enchasing, etching, illustration, impression, inscribing, inscription, intaglio, lithograph, mezzotint, photoengraving, photogravure, print, rotogravure, scratch, woodcut; SEE CONCEPTS 79,174,176,625

engross [v] *hold one's attention*

absorb, apply, arrest, assimilate, attract, become lost, be hung*, bewitch, busy, captivate, consume, corner, engage, engulf, enrapture, enthrall, fascinate, fill, grip, hog*, immerse, involve, monopolize, occupy, preoccupy, sew up*, soak, take up, up on*; SEE CONCEPTS 14,17

engrossed [adj] *preoccupied; attentive to*

absorbed, all wound up*, assiduous, bugged*, busy, captivated, caught up, caught up in, consumed, deep, diligent, engaged, enthralled, fascinated, fiend for*, gone*, gripped, head over heels*, heavily into*, hooked, hung up, immersed, industrious, intent, into*, intrigued, lost, monopolized, occupied, rapt, really into*, riveted, sedulous, submerged, taken up with, tied up, turned on*, up to here in*, wrapped up*; SEE CONCEPTS 403,542

engrossing [adj] *very interesting*

absorbing, all-consuming, captivating, compelling, consuming, controlling, enthralling, exciting, fascinating, gripping, intriguing, monopolizing, obsessing, preoccupying, provoking, riveting, stimulating; SEE CONCEPT 529

engulf [v] *absorb, overwhelm*

bury, consume, deluge, drown, encompass, engross, envelop, flood, imbibe, immerse, inundate, overflow, overrun, overwhelm, plunge, submerge, swallow up, swamp, whelm; SEE CONCEPTS 169,172,256

enhance [v] *improve, embellish*

add to, adorn, aggrandize, amplify, appreciate, augment, beautify, boom, boost, build up, complement, elevate, embroider, enlarge, exaggerate, exalt, flesh out*, heighten, increase, intensify, lift, magnify, pad*, pyramid*, raise, reinforce, strengthen, swell, upgrade; SEE CONCEPTS 162, 177,244

enigma [n] *mystery*

bewilderment, cliffhanger, conundrum, crux, cryptogram, Gordian knot*, grabber*, knot*, mind-boggler*, mind-twister*, mystification, parable, perplexity, problem, puzzle, puzzlement, puzzler, question, question mark, riddle, secret, sixty-four dollar question*, sphinx*, sticker, stickler, stumper, teaser, tough nut to crack*, twister, why*; SEE CONCEPT 532

enigmatic/enigmatical [adj] *mysterious*

ambiguous, cryptic, dark, Delphian*, doubtful, equivocal, incomprehensible, indecipherable, inexplicable, inscrutable, obscure, occult, oracular, perplexing, puzzling, recondite, secret, Sibylline*, sphinxlike, stickling, stumping, teasing, uncertain, unfathomable, unintelligible; SEE CONCEPTS 529,576,582

enjoin [v1] *order, command*

adjure, admonish, advise, appoint, bid, call upon, caution, charge, counsel, decree, demand, dictate, direct, forewarn, impose, instruct, ordain, prescribe, require, rule, tell, urge, warn; SEE CONCEPTS 53,78

enjoin [v2] *forbid*

ban, bar, deny, disallow, inhibit, interdict, outlaw, place injunction on, preclude, prohibit, proscribe, restrain, taboo; SEE CONCEPTS 50,53,88,130

enjoy [v1] *take pleasure in, from something*

adore, appreciate, be entertained, be fond of, be pleased, cotton to*, delight in, dig*, dote on*, drink in*, fancy, flip over*, freak out on*, get a charge out of*, get a kick out of*, get high on*, go, have a ball*, have a good time, have fun, like, live a little*, live it up*, love, luxuriate in, mind, paint the town*, rejoice in, relish, revel in, savor, take joy in, thrill to; SEE CONCEPTS 32,384

enjoy [v2] *have the benefit or use of*

be blessed, be favored, boast, command, experience, have, hold, maintain, occupy, own, possess, process, reap the benefits*, retain, use; SEE CONCEPT 710

enjoyable [adj] *pleasing; to one's liking*

agreeable, amusing, clear sailing*, delectable, delicious, delightful, entertaining, fun, genial, gratifying, groovy*, just for grins*, just for kicks*, just for laughs*, just for the heck of it*, likable, lots of laughs*, pleasant, pleasurable, preferable, relishable, satisfying, welcome; SEE CONCEPTS 529,548

enjoyment [n1] *delight in something*

amusement, delectation, diversion, enjoying, entertainment, fruition, fun, gladness, gratification, gusto, happiness, hedonism, indulgence, joy, loving, luxury, pleasure, recreation, rejoicing, relaxation, relish, satisfaction, savor, self-indulgence, sensuality, thrill, triumph, zest; SEE CONCEPTS 32,410

enjoyment [n2] *possession; use of*

advantage, benefit, exercise, having, indulgence, ownership, spending, using; SEE CONCEPT 710

enlarge [v] *make or grow bigger; increase*

add to, aggrandize, amplify, augment, beef up*, blow up*, boost, broaden, build, bulk, develop, diffuse, dilate, distend, elaborate, elongate, embroider, exaggerate, expand, expatiate, extend, give details, grow, grow larger, heighten, inflate, jack up*, jazz up*, lengthen, magnify, make larger, mount, multiply, pad*, pyramid*, rise, slap on*, snowball*, spread, stretch, swell, upsurge, wax, widen; SEE CONCEPTS 137,236, 245,780

enlargement [n] *increase, expansion*

aggrandizement, amplification, augmentation, blow up, elongation, extension, growth, spread; SEE CONCEPT 780

enlighten [v] *explain thoroughly; make aware*

acquaint, advise, apprise, brief, catechize, cause to understand, civilize, convert, counsel, direct, disclose, divulge, edify, educate, elucidate, give faith*, give the lowdown*, give the word*, guide, illume, illuminate, illumine, imitate, improve, inculcate, indoctrinate, inform, inspirit, instruct, let in on, open up, persuade, preach, put on to*, reveal, save, school, teach, tell, train, update, uplift; SEE CONCEPTS 57,60,75

enlightened [adj] *informed, educated*

aware, broad-minded, civilized, cultivated, hip to*, instructed, in the picture*, knowing what's what*, knowledgeable, learned, liberal, literate, open-minded, plugged in*, reasonable, refined, savvy, sharp, sophisticated, tuned in*, wised up*; SEE CONCEPT *402*

enlightenment [n] *awareness, understanding*
broad-mindedness, civilization, comprehension, cultivation, culture, edification, education, information, insight, instruction, knowledge, learning, literacy, open-mindedness, refinement, sophistication, teaching, wisdom; SEE CONCEPT *409*

enlist [v] *sign up for responsibility*
admit, appoint, assign, attract, call to arms, call up, conscribe, conscript, draft, embody, employ, engage, enroll, enter, enter into, gather, get, hire, hitch, incorporate, induct, initiate, inscribe, interest, join, join up, levy, list, mobilize, muster, oblige, obtain, place, press into service, procure, record, recruit, register, reserve, secure, serve, sign on, take on, volunteer; SEE CONCEPTS *8,320*

enliven [v] *inspire, vitalize*
animate, brace up, brighten, buck up, buoy, cheer, cheer up, divert, entertain, excite, exhilarate, fire, fire up, galvanize, give a lift, give life to, gladden, hearten, inspirit, invigorate, jazz up*, juice up*, let sunshine in*, pep up*, perk up*, pick up, put pep into, quicken, recreate, refresh, rejuvenate, renew, restore, rouse, snap out of it*, spark, spice, spice up*, stimulate, vivificate, vivify, wake up, work up*, zap*; SEE CONCEPTS *7,22*

en masse [adj] *all at once*
all in all, all together, altogether, as a body, as a group, as a whole, as one, bodily, by and large*, ensemble, generally, in a body, in a group, in a mass, jointly, on the whole, together; SEE CONCEPT *577*

enmesh [v] *involve in a situation*
box in, catch, drag into*, draw in, embroil, ensnare, entangle, entrap, hook, implicate, incriminate, lay a trap for*, lay for*, make party to*, net, snare, snarl, tangle, trammel, trap; SEE CONCEPTS *59,112*

enmity [n] *hatred, animosity*
acrimony, alienation, animus, antagonism, antipathy, aversion, bad blood*, bitterness, daggers*, detestation, dislike, hate, hostility, ill will, loathing, malevolence, malice, malignancy, malignity, rancor, spite, spleen, uncordiality, unfriendliness, venom; SEE CONCEPT *29*

ennui [n] *boredom*
apathy, blahs, blues, dejection, depression, dissatisfaction, doldrums, dumps*, fatigue, ho hums*, lack of interest, languidness, languor, lassitude, listlessness, melancholy, sadness, satiety, spiritlessness, surfeit, tedium, weariness, yawn*; SEE CONCEPT *410*

enormity [n1] *horribleness*
abomination, atrociousness, atrocity, crime, depravity, disgrace, evil, evilness, flagrancy, grossness, heinousness, horror, monstrosity, monstrousness, nefariousness, outrage, outrageousness, rankness, turpitude, vice, viciousness, vileness, villainy, wickedness; SEE CONCEPTS *645,666*

enormity [n2] *extreme largeness*
bigness, bulk, enormousness, greatness, hugeness, immensity, magnitude, massiveness, size, tremendousness, vastness; SEE CONCEPT *730*

enormous [adj] *very large*
astronomic, barn door*, blimp*, colossal, excessive, gargantuan, gigantic, gross, huge, humongous, immense, jumbo*, mammoth, massive, monstrous, mountainous, prodigious, stupendous, super-colossal*, titanic*, tremendous, vast, whopping; SEE CONCEPT *773*

enough [n] *plenty*
abundance, adequacy, ampleness, ample supply, competence, plenitude, right amount, sufficiency, sufficient; SEE CONCEPTS *646,767*

enough [adj] *plenty*
abundant, acceptable, adequate, all right already*, ample, bellyful*, bounteous, bountiful, comfortable, competent, complete, copious, decent, enough already*, fed up*, full, had it*, last straw*, lavish, plenteous, plentiful, replete, satisfactory, satisfying, sick and tired of*, sufficient, sufficing, unlimited, up to here*; SEE CONCEPTS *546,771*

enough [adv] *adequately*
abundantly, acceptably, admissibly, amply, averagely, barely, commensurately, decently, fairly, moderately, passably, proportionately, rather, reasonably, satisfactorily, so-so*, sufficiently, tolerably; SEE CONCEPTS *546,558,771*

enrage [v] *make very upset*
aggravate, anger, ask for it*, exasperate, get under skin*, hack*, incense, incite, inflame, infuriate, ire, irritate, madden, make blood boil*, make see red*, needle, provoke, rile, steam up*, T-off*, umbrage, whip up*; SEE CONCEPTS *7,14,19*

enrapture [v] *captivate*
allure, attract, beguile, bewitch, charm, delight, elate, enamor, enchant, enthrall, entrance, fascinate, gladden, gratify, please, ravish, rejoice, score, send, spellbind, transport; SEE CONCEPTS *7,22*

enrich [v] *improve, embellish*
adorn, aggrandize, ameliorate, augment, beef up*, better, build, build up, cultivate, decorate, develop, endow, enhance, figure in, flesh out*, grace, hike up*, hop up*, jack up*, jazz up*, make rich, ornament, pad, parlay, pour it on*, pyramid*, refine, run up*, soup up*, spike*, step up, supplement, sweeten*, up*, upgrade; SEE CONCEPTS *177,244*

enroll [v1] *sign up for membership*
accept, admit, become student, call up, employ, engage, enlist, enter, join, join up, matriculate, muster, obtain, recruit, register, serve, sign on, subscribe, take course, take on; SEE CONCEPTS *114,129*

enroll [v2] *list, record*
affix, bill, book, catalog, chronicle, engross, enlist, enter, file, fill out, index, inscribe, insert, inventorize, mark, matriculate, note, poll, register, schedule, slate; SEE CONCEPTS *79,125*

enrollment [n] *registration for membership*
acceptance, accession, admission, conscription, engagement, enlistment, entrance, entry, induction, influx, listing, matriculation, rally, reception, record, recruitment, response, student body, students, subscription; SEE CONCEPTS *288,388,417*

en route [adj] *on the way to destination*
advancing, along the way, bound, driving, entrained, en voyage*, flying, heading toward, in passage, in transit, making headway*, midway, on the road*, pressing on, progressing, traveling; SEE CONCEPTS *577,586*

ensconce [v] *hide; tuck away*
bury, cache, conceal, cover, curl up, ditch, establish, fix, install, locate, nestle, place, plant, pro-

tect, screen, seat, secrete, set, settle, shelter, shield, situate, snuggle up, stash, station; SEE CONCEPTS *188,201*

ensemble [n1] *collection*
aggregate, assemblage, band, cast, choir, chorus, company, composite, entirety, gathering, glee club, group, octet, orchestra, organization, outfit, quartet, quintet, set, sextet, sum, total, totality, trio, troupe, whole; SEE CONCEPTS *294,432*

ensemble [n2] *clothing outfit*
coordinates, costume, garb*, get-up*, suit, togs*; SEE CONCEPT *451*

ensemble [adv] *at the same time*
all at once, altogether, as a body, as a group, as a whole, as one, at once, en masse, in concert; SEE CONCEPT *577*

enshrine [v] *hold as sacred*
apotheosize, bless, cherish, consecrate, dedicate, embalm, exalt, hallow, idolize, preserve, revere, sanctify, treasure; SEE CONCEPTS *69,367*

enslave [v] *make someone a servant*
bind, capture, chain, check, circumscribe, coerce, compel, confine, deprive, disenfranchise, disfranchise, dominate, enchain, enclose, enthrall, fetter, get hooks into*, hobble, hold, immure, imprison, incarcerate, indenture, jail, keep under thumb*, oppress, put in irons*, reduce, restrain, restrict, secure, shackle, shut in, subdue, subject, subjugate, suppress, tether, tie, yoke; SEE CONCEPTS *14,90,130,191*

ensnare [v] *trap*
bag*, bat eyes at*, capture, catch, cheat, come on, deceive, decoy, embroil, enmesh, entangle, entice, entrap, hook, inveigle, lure, mislead, net, rope in, snag, snare, snarl, suck in*, tangle, trick; SEE CONCEPTS *59,90*

ensue [v] *start to happen; come to pass*
appear, arise, attend, be consequent on, befall, be subsequent to, come after, come next, come up, derive, develop, emanate, eventualize, eventuate, flow, follow, issue, occur, proceed, result, stem, succeed, supervene, turn out, turn up; SEE CONCEPTS *119,242*

ensuing [adj] *resultant*
after, coming, coming up, consequent, consequential, following, later, next, next off, posterior, postliminary, subsequent, subsequential; SEE CONCEPTS *548,820*

ensure [v] *guarantee; make secure*
arrange, assure, certify, cinch, clinch, confirm, effect, establish, guard, insure, lock on*, lock up*, make certain, make safe, make sure, nail down*, okay, protect, provide, put on ice*, safeguard, secure, set out, warrant; SEE CONCEPTS *71,96*

entail [v] *require; result in*
bring about, call for, cause, demand, encompass, entangle, evoke, give rise to, impose, involve, lead to, necessitate, occasion, require, tangle; SEE CONCEPTS *242,646*

entangle [v] *involve, mix up*
bewilder, burden, catch, clog, come on, complicate, compromise, confuse, corner, dishevel, duke in, embarrass, embrangle, embroil, enchain, enmesh, ensnare, entrap, fetter, hamper, hook, impede, implicate, intertangle, intertwine, interweave, jumble, knot, lead on, mat, muddle, perplex, puzzle, ravel, rope in, set up, snag, snare, snarl, swindle, tangle, trammel, trap, twist, unsettle; SEE CONCEPTS *59,90,112*

entanglement [n] *complication, predicament*
affair, association, cobweb, complexity, confusion, difficulty, embarrassment, embroilment, enmeshment, ensnarement, entrapment, imbroglio, intricacy, intrigue, involvement, jumble, knot, liaison, mesh, mess, mix-up, muddle, snare, tangle, tie-up, toil, trap, web; SEE CONCEPTS *666, 674*

enter [v1] *come, put into a place*
access, arrive, barge in*, blow in*, break in, breeze in*, burst in, bust in*, butt in*, come in, crack, crawl, creep, crowd in*, drive in, drop in, fall into, gain entree, get in, go in, horn in*, immigrate, infiltrate, ingress, insert, insinuate, introduce, intrude, invade, jump in, make an entrance, make way, move in, pass into, penetrate, pierce, pile in, pop in*, probe, rush in, set foot in, slip, sneak in, work in, worm in*, wriggle; SEE CONCEPT *159*

enter [v2] *embark on; take part in*
become member, begin, commence, commit oneself, enlist, enroll, get oneself into*, inaugurate, join, join up, lead off, muster*, open, participate in, set about, set out on, set to, sign on, sign up, start, subscribe, take up, tee off*; SEE CONCEPTS *114,234*

enter [v3] *record, list*
admit, docket, inject, inscribe, insert, intercalate, interpolate, introduce, log, note, post, put in, register, set down, take down; SEE CONCEPT *125*

enterprise [n1] *adventure, undertaking*
action, activity, affair, attempt, baby*, bag*, ballgame*, biggie*, big idea*, bit*, business, campaign, cause, company, concern, crusade, deal, deed, do*, effort, endeavor, engagement, essay, establishment, firm, flier*, follow through*, game*, happening, hazard, house, move, operation, outfit, performance, pet project*, plan, plunge*, program, project, proposition, purpose, pursuit, risk, scheme, speculation, stake, striving, stunt, task, thing*, trade, try, venture, work; SEE CONCEPTS *87,324,325,362*

enterprise [n2] *resourcefulness, energy*
activity, adventurousness, alertness, ambition, audacity, boldness, courage, daring, dash, drive, eagerness, enthusiasm, force, foresight, get-up-and-go*, gumption, hustle, industry, initiative, inventiveness, pluck, push, readiness, resource, self-reliance, spirit, venturesomeness, vigor, zeal; SEE CONCEPTS *411,657*

enterprising [adj] *resourceful, energetic*
active, advancing, adventurous, aggressive, alert, ambitious, aspiring, audacious, bold, busy, coming on strong*, craving, daring, dashing, diligent, driving, eager, enthusiastic, go-ahead*, go-go*, gumptious, hard ball*, hardworking, hungry, hustling, industrious, intrepid, itching, keen, lively, lusting, peppy, progressive, pushing, ready, self-starting, snappy, spanking, spark plug*, spirited, stirring, take-over, up-and-coming*, venturesome, vigorous, yearning, zealous, zippy*; SEE CONCEPTS *326,404,542*

entertain [v1] *amuse*
absorb, beguile, captivate, charm, cheer, comfort, crack up*, delight, distract, divert, ecstasize, elate, engross, enliven, enthrall, gladden, grab, gratify, humor, indulge, inspire, inspirit, interest, knock dead*, make merry, occupy, pique, please, recreate, regale, relax, satisfy, slay, solace, stimulate, tickle; SEE CONCEPTS *9,292*

entertain [v2] *accommodate visitors*
admit, be host, board, chaperone, dine, do the honors*, feed, foster, give a party, harbor, have a do*, have a get-together*, have company, have guests, have visitors, house, invite, lodge, nourish, pick up the check*, pop for*, put up*, quarter, receive, recreate, regale, room, show hospitality, spring for*, throw a party*, treat, welcome, wine and dine*; SEE CONCEPTS 377,384

entertain [v3] *think about seriously*
cherish, cogitate on, conceive, consider, contemplate, deliberate, enslave, foster, harbor, heed, hold, imagine, keep in mind, maintain, muse over, ponder, recognize, support, think over; SEE CONCEPT 17

entertaining [adj] *amusing, pleasing*
absorbing, affecting, be a ball*, captivating, charming, cheerful, cheering, clever, compelling, delightful, diverting, droll, enchanting, engaging, engrossing, enjoyable, enthralling, enticing, entrancing, exciting, fascinating, fun, funny, gas*, gay, humorous, impressive, inspiring, interesting, lively, moving, piquant, pleasant, pleasurable, poignant, priceless, provocative, recreative, relaxing, restorative, riot, rousing, scream, side-splitting, stimulating, stirring, striking, thrilling, witty; SEE CONCEPTS 529,537

entertainment [n] *amusement, pleasure*
ball*, bash*, big time*, blast*, blow out*, celebration, cheer, clambake*, delight, dissipation, distraction, diversion, divertissement, enjoyment, feast, frolic, fun, fun and games*, gaiety, game, good time*, grins*, high time*, laughs*, leisure activity, lots of laughs*, merriment, merrymaking, party, pastime, picnic, play, recreation, regalement, relaxation, relief, revelry, satisfaction, shindig*, sport, spree, surprise, treat, winging*; SEE CONCEPTS 383,384,386,388

enthrall [v] *captivate*
absorb, beguile, bewitch, charm, enchant, engage, enrapture, enslave, entrance, fascinate, grab, grip, hold spellbound, hook, hypnotize, intrigue, mesmerize, preoccupy, rivet, spellbind, subdue, subject, subjugate; SEE CONCEPTS 7,19,22

enthusiasm [n] *keen interest, excitement*
activity, ardency, ardor, avidity, conviction, craze, dash, devotion, eagerness, earnestness, ecstasy, elan, emotion, energy, exhilaration, fad, fanaticism, feeling, fervor, fever, fieriness, fire, flame, flare, frenzy, fury, gaiety, glow, go*, heat, hilarity, hobby, impetuosity, intensity, interest, joy, joyfulness, keenness, life, mania, mirth, nerve, oomph*, orgasm, passion, pep, rapture, red heat*, relish, snap, spirit, transport, vehemence, verve, vim, vivacity, warmth, zeal, zealousness, zest; SEE CONCEPTS 633,657

enthusiast [n] *person active in interest*
addict, admirer, aficionado, believer, buff, bug*, bum*, devotee, eccentric, fan, fanatic, follower, freak, habitué, lover, maniac, monomaniac, nut*, optimist, participant, partisan, rooter, supporter, votary, worshiper, zealot; SEE CONCEPT 423

enthusiastic [adj] *interested, excited*
agog, animated, anxious, ardent, athirst, attracted, avid, bugged*, concerned, crazy about*, devoted, dying to*, eager, earnest, ebullient, exhilarated, exuberant, fanatical, fascinated, fervent, fervid, forceful, gaga*, gone on*, gung ho*, hearty, intent, keen, keyed up*, lively, nutty*, obsessed, passionate, pleased, rabid, red-hot*, rhapsodic,

spirited, tantalized, thrilled, titillated, unqualified, vehement, vigorous, wacky*, warm, whole-hearted, willing, zealous; SEE CONCEPTS 401,542

entice [v] *allure; persuade*
attract, bait, bat eyes at*, beguile, cajole, coax, decoy, draw, entrap, inveigle, lead on, lure, prevail on, seduce, tempt, toll, turn on*, wheedle; SEE CONCEPTS 7,19,22,68

enticement [n] *allurement; persuasion*
attraction, bait, blandishment, cajolery, coaxing, come hither*, come-on*, decoy, fascination, inducement, inveiglement, lure, mousetrap*, promise, seduction, snare, sweetener*, sweetening, temptation, trap; SEE CONCEPTS 7,19,22,68

entire [adj] *complete, whole*
absolute, all, choate, consolidated, continuous, full, gross, intact, integral, integrated, outright, perfect, plenary, sound, thorough, total, unbroken, undamaged, undiminished, undivided, unified, unimpaired, uninjured, unmarked, unmarred, unmitigated, unreserved, unrestricted, untouched; SEE CONCEPTS 482,531

entirely [adv] *completely*
absolutely, alone, altogether, exclusively, fully, in every respect, only, perfectly, plumb, quite, reservedly, solely, thoroughly, totally, undividedly, uniquely, utterly, well, wholly, without exception, without reservation; SEE CONCEPTS 531,535

entirety [n] *wholeness, whole*
absoluteness, aggregate, all, allness, collectiveness, collectivity, completeness, complex, comprehensiveness, ensemble, entireness, everything, fullness, gross, intactness, integrality, integrity, omneity, omnitude, oneness, perfection, plenitude, sum, sum total, the works*, total, totality, undividedness, unity, universality, whole ball of wax*, whole bit*, whole enchilada*, whole nine yards*; SEE CONCEPTS 635,837

entitle [v1] *name, label*
baptize, call, characterize, christen, denominate, designate, dub, nickname, style, subtitle, term, title; SEE CONCEPT 62

entitle [v2] *hold right to*
accredit, allow, authorize, be in line for*, confer a right, empower, enable, enfranchise, fit for, have coming*, let, license, make eligible, permit, qualify for, rate, warrant; SEE CONCEPTS 50,83,88,129

entity [n1] *object that exists*
article, being, body, creature, existence, individual, item, material, matter, organism, presence, quantity, single, singleton, something, stuff, subsistence, substance, thing; SEE CONCEPT 433

entity [n2] *nature of a being*
actuality, essence, existence, integral, integrate, quiddity, quintessence, reality, subsistence, substance, sum, system, totality; SEE CONCEPTS 411,644

entourage [n] *followers*
associates, attendants, companions, company, cortege, court, courtiers, escort, following, groupies*, hangers-on*, retainers, retinue, staff, suite, sycophants, toadies*, train; SEE CONCEPTS 387,417

entrance [n1] *a way into a place*
access, approach, archway, avenue, corridor, door, doorway, entry, entryway, gate, gateway, hall, hallway, ingress, inlet, lobby, opening, passage, passageway, path, porch, port, portal, por-

en
en

tico, staircase, threshold, vestibule, way; SEE CONCEPT **440**

entrance [n2] *coming into a place; introduction*
access, accession, adit, admission, admittance, appearance, approach, arrival, baptism, beginning, commencement, debut, enlistment, enrollment, entree, entry, immigration, import, importation, inception, incoming, ingoing, ingress, ingression, initiation, invasion, outset, passage, penetration, progress, start, trespass; SEE CONCEPTS **119,159**

entrance [v] *captivate, hypnotize*
anesthetize, attract, bewitch, charm, delight, enchant, enrapture, enthrall, fascinate, gladden, mesmerize, please, put in a trance, ravish, rejoice, spellbind, transport; SEE CONCEPTS **7,14,22**

entrant [n] *person entering competition, starting new activity*
aspirant, beginner, candidate, competitor, contestant, convert, entry, incomer, initiate, neophyte, newcomer, new member, novice, participant, petitioner, player, probationer, rival, solicitor, tenderfoot*; SEE CONCEPTS **366,423**

entrap [v] *capture, involve*
allure, bag*, beguile, benet, box in*, catch, decoy, embroil, enmesh, ensnare, entangle, entice, hook, implicate, inveigle, lay for*, lead on, lure, net, reel in*, rope in*, seduce, set up, snare, suck in*, tempt, trap, trick; SEE CONCEPTS **59,90,112**

entreat [v] *plead with*
appeal to, ask, beg, beseech, blandish, coax, conjure, crave, enjoin, exhort, implore, importune, invoke, pester, petition, plague, pray, press, request, supplicate, urge, wheedle; SEE CONCEPTS **48,53**

entreaty [n] *plea*
appeal, application, imploration, imprecation, petition, prayer, request, suit, supplication; SEE CONCEPTS **318,662**

entrée [n] *admittance*
access, adit, admission, connection, contact, debut, door, entrance, entry, importation, in, incoming, induction, ingress, introduction, open arms*, open door*, way; SEE CONCEPTS **388,685**

entrench [v1] *establish, make inroads*
anchor, confirm, define, dig in, embed, ensconce, fence, fix, fortify, found, ground, hole up, implant, infix, ingrain, install, lodge, plant, protect, root, seat, set, settle, strengthen; SEE CONCEPTS **518,710**

entrench [v2] *trespass*
break in on, encroach, impinge, infringe, interfere, interlope, intervene, intrude, invade, make inroads*, stick nose into*; SEE CONCEPT **192**

entrepreneur [n] *person who starts a business alone*
administrator, backer, businessperson, contractor, executive, founder, impressario, industrialist, manager, organizer, producer, promoter, undertaker; SEE CONCEPT **347**

entrust [v] *give custody, authority to*
allocate, allot, assign, authorize, bank, bend an ear*, charge, commend, commit, confer, confide, consign, count, delegate, deliver, depend, deposit with, hand over, impose, invest, leave with, reckon, relegate, rely, trust, turn over; SEE CONCEPTS **50,88,108**

entry [n1] *way in to a place*
access, adit, approach, avenue, door, doorway, entrance, foyer, gate, hall, ingress, ingression, inlet, lobby, opening, passage, passageway, portal, threshold, vestibule; SEE CONCEPT **440**

entry [n2] *introduction; permission to enter*
access, adit, admission, admittance, appearance, coming in, entering, entrance, entree, free passage*, ingress, initiation, introgression, way; SEE CONCEPTS **388,685**

entry [n3] *person participating in competition; effort*
attempt, candidate, competitor, contestant, entrant, participant, player, submission; SEE CONCEPT **366**

entry [n4] *listing in a record*
account, item, jotting, memo, memorandum, minute, note, registration; SEE CONCEPT **270**

entwine [v] *twist around*
braid, coil, corkscrew, curl, embrace, encircle, enmesh, entangle, interlace, interplait, intertwine, interweave, knit, lace, plait, spiral, surround, twine, weave, wind, wreathe; SEE CONCEPTS **147,201,754**

enumerate [v] *list, count*
add up, calculate, cite, compute, count noses*, detail, figure, identify, inventory, itemize, keep tabs*, mention, name, number, particularize, quote, recapitulate, recite, reckon, recount, rehearse, relate, run down, run off*, specialize, specify, spell out, sum, take account of, tally, tell, tick off*, total; SEE CONCEPTS **57,125,764**

enunciate [v] *speak clearly*
affirm, announce, articulate, declare, deliver, develop, enounce, express, intone, lay down, modulate, outline, phonate, postulate, proclaim, promulgate, pronounce, propound, publish, say, show, sound, state, submit, utter, vocalize, voice; SEE CONCEPTS **47,51**

envelop [v] *encase, hide*
blanket, cage, cloak, conceal, contain, coop, corral, cover, drape, embrace, encircle, enclose, encompass, enfold, engulf, enshroud, enwrap, fence, gird, girdle, guard, hem, immure, invest, obscure, overlay, overspread, pen, protect, roll, sheathe, shield, shroud, shut in, superimpose, surround, swaddle, swathe, veil, wrap, wrap up; SEE CONCEPTS **172,188**

envelope [n] *wrapper*
bag, box, case, casing, cloak, coat, coating, container, cover, covering, enclosure, hide, jacket, pocket, pouch, receptacle, sheath, shell, skin, vesicle, wrapping; SEE CONCEPT **494**

enviable [adj] *desired, blessed*
advantageous, covetable, desirable, excellent, favored, fortunate, good, lucky, privileged, superior, welcome; SEE CONCEPT **574**

envious [adj] *jealous, resentful*
appetent, aspiring, begrudging, coveting, covetous, craving, desiring, desirous, distrustful, fain, grasping, greedy, green-eyed*, green with envy*, grudging, hankering, invidious, jaundiced, longing for, malicious, spiteful, suspicious, umbrageous, watchful, wishful, yearning; SEE CONCEPTS **401,403**

environment [n] *surroundings, atmosphere*
ambiance, aura, backdrop, background, circumstances, climate, conditions, context, domain, element, encompassment, entourage, habitat, hood*, jungle*, locale, medium, milieu, neck of the woods*, neighborhood, purlieus, scene, scenery, setting, situation, status, stomping ground*,

surroundings, terrain, territory, turf, zoo*; SEE CONCEPTS *515,673,696*

environment [n2] *Earth's system of natural resources*
atmosphere, biosphere, ecosphere, ecosystem, environs, Gaia; SEE CONCEPTS *511,515*

environs [n] *neighborhood*
bound, boundary, compass, confine, district, fringes*, limits, locality, outskirts, precinct, purlieus, suburb, surroundings, territory, turf, vicinity; SEE CONCEPT *516*

envisage/envision [v] *picture in one's mind*
anticipate, behold, conceive, conceptualize, contemplate, externalize, fancy, feature, foresee, form mental picture of*, grasp, have a picture of*, image, imagine, look upon, materialize, objectify, predict, realize, regard, see, survey, think up, view, view in mind's eye*, vision, visualize; SEE CONCEPTS *17,43*

envoy [n] *deputy*
agent, ambassador, attaché, bearer, carrier, chargé d'affaires, consul, courier, delegate, diplomat, emissary, intermediary, internuncio, legate, medium, messenger, minister, nuncio, plenipotentiary, representative, vicar; SEE CONCEPTS *348, 354*

envy [n] *jealousy*
backbiting, coveting, covetousness, enviousness, evil eye*, green-eyed monster*, grudge, grudging, grudgingness, hatred, heartburn, ill will, invidiousness, jaundiced eye*, lusting, malevolence, malice, maliciousness, malignity, opposition, prejudice, resentfulness, resentment, rivalry, spite; SEE CONCEPT *410*

envy [v] *be jealous of another*
be envious, begrudge, covet, crave, desire, die over*, eat one's heart out*, grudge, hanker, have hard feelings*, hunger, long, lust, object to, resent, thirst, turn green*, want, yearn; SEE CONCEPTS *10,20*

ephemeral [adj] *momentary, passing*
brief, episodic, evanescent, fleeting, flitting, fugacious, fugitive, impermanent, short, short-lived, temporary, transient, transitory, unenduring, volatile; SEE CONCEPTS *798,801*

epic [n] *long story*
heroic poem, legend, narrative, saga, tale; SEE CONCEPT *282*

epicurean [n] *gourmet*
bon vivant, connoisseur, critic, epicure, gastronome, gastronomer, glutton, gourmand, hedonist, pleasure seeker, sensualist, specialist, sybarite; SEE CONCEPT *423*

epicurean [adj] *loving food and finer things*
gluttonous, gourmandizing, gourmet, hedonistic, libertine, lush, luxurious, pleasure-seeking, self-indulgent, sensual, sensuous, sybaritic, voluptuous; SEE CONCEPT *401*

epidemic [n] *widespread disease*
contagion, endemic, growth, outbreak, pest, pestilence, plague, rash, scourge, spread, upsurge, wave, what's going around*; SEE CONCEPTS *306,316*

epidemic [adj] *widespread*
catching, communicable, contagious, endemic, general, infectious, pandemic, prevailing, prevalent, rampant, rife, sweeping, wide-ranging; SEE CONCEPTS *314,537*

epigram [n] *witticism*
aphorism, bon mot, joke, motto, pithy saying, quip, quirk; SEE CONCEPT *278*

epilogue [n] *afterword*
coda, concluding speech, conclusion, ending, finale, follow-up, peroration, postlude, postscript, sequel, summation, swan song*; SEE CONCEPTS *264,270,278*

episode [n] *adventure; scene*
affair, business, chapter, circumstance, doings, event, experience, goings-on*, happening, incident, installment, interlude, matter, occasion, occurrence, part, passage, section, thing*, what's going down*; SEE CONCEPTS *3,4*

episodic [adj] *intermittent; composed of several tales*
anecdotal, digressive, disconnected, discursive, disjointed, incidental, irregular, occasional, picaresque, rambling, roundabout, segmented, soap opera*, sporadic, wandering; SEE CONCEPT *482*

epistle [n] *letter*
billet doux*, cannonball*, card, communication, dispatch, FYI*, get-well, invite, kite*, line*, love letter, memo, message, missive, note, poison pen*, postcard, scratch*, tab*, thank-you; SEE CONCEPT *271*

epitaph [n] *inscription on a gravestone*
commemoration, elegy, epigraph, eulogy, hic jacet, legend, memorial, monument, remembrance, requiscat in pacem, sentiment; SEE CONCEPT *278*

epithet [n] *nickname*
appellation, description, designation, name, sobriquet, tag, title; SEE CONCEPT *683*

epitome [n1] *perfect example*
apotheosis, archetype, embodiment, essence, exemplar, exemplification, illustration, last word*, personification, quintessence, representation, type, typification, ultimate; SEE CONCEPT *686*

epitome [n2] *abbreviation*
abridgment, abstract, brief, compendium, condensation, conspectus, contraction, digest, precis, recapitulation, résumé, summary, summation, syllabus, synopsis; SEE CONCEPT *283*

equable [adj] *steady, calm*
agreeable, composed, consistent, constant, easygoing, even, even-tempered, imperturbable, levelheaded, methodical, orderly, placid, regular, serene, smooth, stabile, stable, systematic, temperate, tranquil, unchanging, unexcitable, unflappable, unfluctuating, uniform, unruffled, unvarying; SEE CONCEPTS *401,542,544*

equal [n] *peer*
alter ego, coequal, companion, compeer, competitor, complement, copy, counterpart, double, duplicate, equivalent, like, likeness, match, mate, parallel, rival, twin; SEE CONCEPT *423*

equal [adj1] *alike*
according, balanced, break even, commensurate, comparable, coordinate, correspondent, corresponding, double, duplicate, egalitarian, equivalent, evenly matched, fifty-fifty*, homologous, identic, identical, indistinguishable, invariable, level, look-alike, matched, matching, one and the same, parallel, proportionate, same, same difference*, spit and image*, stack up with*, tantamount, to the same degree, two peas in pod*, uniform, unvarying; SEE CONCEPTS *487,566,573*

equal [adj2] *fair, unbiased*
dispassionate, egalitarian, equable, even-handed,

en
eq

impartial, just, nondiscriminatory, nonpartisan, objective, uncolored, unprejudiced, without distinction; SEE CONCEPTS **401,542**

equal [v] *make even, be even with*
agree, amount to, approach, balance, be commensurate, be identical, be level, be tantamount, break even, come up to, compare, comprise, consist of, coordinate, correspond, emulate, equalize, equate, equipoise, equiponderate, keep pace with*, level, live up to*, match, measure up, meet, parallel, partake of, rank with, reach, rise to, rival, run abreast, square with, tally, tie, touch; SEE CONCEPT **667**

equality [n] *similarity, balance; egalitarianism*
adequation, civil rights, commensurateness, coordination, correspondence, equal opportunity, equatability, equilibrium, equipoise, equivalence, evenness, fairness, fair play*, fair practice, fair shake*, homology, identity, impartiality, isonomy, likeness, par, parallelism, parity, sameness, tolerance, uniformity; SEE CONCEPTS **388,645,667**

equalize [v] *make the same; balance*
adjust, commeasure, communize, compare, coordinate, democratize, emulate, equal, equate, establish, even, even up, handicap, level, match, parallel, regularize, rival, smooth, socialize, square, standardize, trim; SEE CONCEPTS **126,232**

equanimity [n] *levelheadedness*
aplomb, assurance, ataraxia, ataraxy, calm, calmness, composure, confidence, cool, coolness, detachment, equability, imperturbability, patience, peace, phlegm, placidity, poise, presence of mind*, sangfroid, self-possession, serenity, steadiness, tranquillity; SEE CONCEPTS **410,633**

equate [v] *balance; think of together*
agree, assimilate, associate, average, be commensurate, compare, consider, correspond to, correspond with, equalize, even, hold, level, liken, make equal, match, offset, pair, paragon, parallel, regard, relate, represent, similize, square, tally, treat; SEE CONCEPTS **37,39,667**

equilibrium [n] *balance; evenness*
calm, calmness, composure, cool, coolness, counterbalance, counterpoise, equanimity, equipoise, poise, polish, rest, serenity, stability, stasis, steadiness, steadying, symmetry; SEE CONCEPTS **633,731**

equip [v] *make ready with supplies*
accouter, adorn, appoint, arm, array, attire, deck, deck out*, decorate, dress, endow, feather nest*, fit out, fix up, furnish, gear, gear up*, heel*, implement, line nest*, man, outfit, prep*, prepare, provide, qualify, ready, rig, set up, stake, stock, supply, turn out; SEE CONCEPTS **140,182**

equipment [n] *supplies, gear for activity*
accessories, accompaniments, accouterments, apparatus, appliances, appurtenances, articles, attachments, baggage, belongings, contraptions, contrivances, devices, equipage, facilities, fittings, fixtures, furnishings, furniture, gadgets, habiliments, impedimenta, kit and kaboodle*, machinery, material, materiel, miscellaneous, outfit, paraphernalia, provisioning, provisions, rig*, setup, shebang*, stock, store, stuff, tackle, things, tools, trappings, traps, utensils; SEE CONCEPTS **364,446,496**

equitable [adj] *impartial*
candid, cricket, decent, disinterested, dispassionate, due, ethical, even-handed, even-steven*, fair,

fair and square*, fair shake*, fair-to-middling*, honest, impersonal, just, level, moral, nondiscriminatory, nonpartisan, objective, proper, proportionate, reasonable, right, rightful, square, square deal*, stable, unbiased, uncolored, unprejudiced; SEE CONCEPTS **542,545**

equity [n] *impartiality*
disinterestedness, equitableness, evenhandedness, fair-mindedness, fairness, fair play, honesty, integrity, justice, justness, nonpartisanship, piece, reasonableness, rectitude, righteousness, square deal*, uprightness; SEE CONCEPTS **645,657**

equity [n2] *money invested in possession*
capital, investment, outlay; SEE CONCEPTS **332,344**

equivalence [n] *sameness, similarity*
adequation, agreement, alikeness, compatibility, conformity, correlation, correspondence, equality, evenness, exchangeability, identity, interchangeability, interchangeableness, likeness, match, par, parallel, parity, synonym, synonymity; SEE CONCEPTS **667,670**

equivalent [n] *equal, counterpart*
carbon copy*, correspondent, dead ringer*, ditto, like, match, obverse, opposite, parallel, peer, reciprocal, same difference*, spitting image*, substitute, twin; SEE CONCEPTS **667,670**

equivalent [adj] *same, similar*
agnate, akin, alike, analogous, carbon*, commensurate, comparable, convertible, copy, correlative, correspondent, corresponding, ditto*, duplicate, equal, even, homologous, identical, indistinguishable, interchangeable, like, of a kind, parallel, proportionate, reciprocal, same difference*, substitute, synonymous, tantamount; SEE CONCEPTS **487,566,573**

equivocal [adj] *doubtful, uncertain*
ambiguous, ambivalent, amphibological, borderline, clear as mud*, clouded*, disreputable, dubious, evasive, fishy*, fuzzy*, hazy*, indefinite, indeterminate, indistinct, misleading, muddled, muzzy*, oblique, obscure, open, problematic, puzzling, questionable, suspect, suspicious, tenebrous, unclear, undecided, unexplicit, unintelligible, vague, with mixed feelings*; SEE CONCEPTS **529,535**

equivocate [v] *avoid an issue*
beat around the bush*, beg the question*, blow hot and cold*, cavil, cloud the issue*, con, cop a plea*, cop out*, cover up*, dodge, double-talk, elude, escape, eschew, evade, falsify, fence, fib, flip-flop*, fudge*, give run around*, hedge, hem and haw*, jive*, lie, mince words, palter, parry, pass the buck*, prevaricate, pussyfoot, quibble, run around, shuck, shuffle, sidestep, sit on the fence*, stonewall*, tell white lie*, tergiversate, tergiverse, waffle*, weasel*; SEE CONCEPTS **63,102**

equivocation [n] *avoidance of an issue*
ambiguity, amphibology, casuistry, coloring, con, cop out, cover, cover-up, deceit, deception, deceptiveness, delusion, dissimulation, distortion, double entendre, double meaning, double talk, doubtfulness, duplicity, equivocality, evasion, fallacy, fib, fibbing, hedging, lie, line*, lying, misrepresentation, prevarication, quibbling, routine, run-around, shuffling, song*, song and dance*, sophistry, speciousness, spuriousness, stall, stone-

wall*, tergiversation, waffle*; SEE CONCEPTS *63,278*

era [n] *time period in history*
aeon, age, cycle, date, day, days, eon, epoch, generation, stage, term, time; SEE CONCEPTS *807,816*

eradicate [v] *destroy; remove*
abate, abolish, annihilate, blot out*, demolish, deracinate, do away with, efface, eliminate, erase, expunge, exterminate, extinguish, extirpate, liquidate, mow down*, obliterate, off*, purge, raze, root out*, rub out*, scratch, scrub, shoot down, squash, stamp out*, take out*, torpedo*, total, trash, unroot, uproot, wash out, waste, weed out*, wipe out*; SEE CONCEPTS *211,252*

erase [v] *remove; rub out*
abolish, annul, black out, blank, blot, blue pencil*, cancel, cross out, cut, cut out, delete, disannul, dispatch, efface, eliminate, excise, expunge, extirpate, gut, kill, launder*, negate, nullify, obliterate, scratch out*, stamp out*, strike, strike out, take out, trim, wipe out*, withdraw, X-out*; SEE CONCEPTS *211,215*

erect [adj] *straight up*
arrect, cocked, elevated, erectile, firm, perpendicular, raised, rigid, standing, stiff, upright, upstanding, vertical; SEE CONCEPTS *485,581,604*

erect [v] *build; establish*
assemble, bring about, cobble up*, cock, compose, construct, create, effect, elevate, fabricate, fashion, fit together, forge, form, found, frame, fudge together*, heighten, hoist, initiate, institute, join, knock together*, lift, make, make up, manufacture, mount, organize, pitch, plant, prefabricate*, produce, put together, put up, raise, rear, run up, set up, shape, stand, stand up, throw together*, throw up, upraise, uprear; SEE CONCEPTS *168,221*

ergo [adv] *for that reason*
accordingly, consequently, hence, in consequence, so, then, therefore, thereupon, thus, thusly; SEE CONCEPT *544*

ergonomics [n] *human engineering*
comfort design, functional design, human factors, user-friendly systems, workplace efficiency; SEE CONCEPT *349*

erode [v] *deteriorate; wear away*
abrade, bite, consume, corrode, crumble, destroy, disintegrate, eat, grind down, scour, spoil, waste, wear down; SEE CONCEPTS *252,469*

erosion [n] *deterioration; wearing away*
abrasion, attrition, consumption, corrosion, decrease, desedimentation, despoliation, destruction, disintegration, eating away, grinding down, spoiling, washing away, wear, wearing down; SEE CONCEPTS *252,257,698*

erotic [adj] *sexy*
amative, amatory, amorous, aphrodisiac, bawdy, blue*, carnal, concupiscent, earthy, erogenous, fervid, filthy, fleshly, hot*, impassioned, kinky*, lascivious, lecherous, lewd, obscene, off-color*, prurient, purple*, raunchy, raw, romantic, rousing, salacious, seductive, sensual, sexual, spicy, steamy, stimulating, suggestive, titillating, venereal, voluptuous; SEE CONCEPTS *372,545*

err [v] *make a mistake; do wrong*
be inaccurate, be incorrect, be in error, be mistaken, blow*, blunder, bollix*, boo-boo*, deviate, drop the ball*, fall, flub*, foul up*, go astray, goof*, go wrong, lapse, louse up*, make a mess

of*, mess up*, misapprehend, misbehave, miscalculate, misjudge, muff*, offend, screw up*, sin, slip up*, snafu*, snarl up, stray, stumble, transgress, trespass, wander; SEE CONCEPT *101*

errand [n] *task*
assignment, charge, commission, duty, job, message, mission; SEE CONCEPT *362*

errant [adj] *wrong; deviant*
aberrant, deviating, devious, drifting, errable, erratic, erring, fallible, heretic, meandering, misbehaving, mischievous, miscreant, naughty, offending, off straight and narrow*, rambling, ranging, roaming, roving, shifting, sinning, stray, straying, unorthodox, unreliable, wandering, wayward; SEE CONCEPTS *542,545,581*

erratic [adj] *unpredictable; wandering*
aberrant, abnormal, anomalous, arbitrary, bizarre, capricious, changeable, desultory, devious, dicey, directionless, dubious, eccentric, fitful, flaky*, fluctuant, idiosyncratic, iffy*, incalculable, inconsistent, inconstant, irregular, meandering, mercurial, nomadic, oddball*, peculiar, planetary, rambling, roving, shifting, spasmodic, strange, stray, uncertain, undirected, unnatural, unreliable, unstable, unusual, vagarious, variable, volatile, wayward, weird, whimsical; SEE CONCEPTS *535,542,581*

erroneous [adj] *wrong, incorrect*
all off*, all wet*, amiss, askew, awry, defective, fallacious, false, faulty, flawed, inaccurate, inexact, invalid, misguided, mistaken, off, specious, spurious, unfounded, unsound, untrue, way off, wrong number*; SEE CONCEPTS *267,570,582*

error [n] *mistake; wrong*
absurdity, bad job*, blunder, boner*, boo-boo*, delinquency, delusion, deviation, erratum, failure, fall, fallacy, falsehood, falsity, fault, faux pas, flaw, glitch, goof*, howler*, inaccuracy, lapse, misapprehension, misbelief, miscalculation, misconception, miscue, misdeed, misjudgment, mismanagement, miss, misstep, misunderstanding, offense, omission, oversight, screamer*, screwup*, sin, slight, slip, slipup, solecism, stumble, transgression, trespass, untruth, wrongdoing, X*; SEE CONCEPTS *101,230,674,699*

ersatz [adj] *artificial*
bogus, copied, counterfeit, fake, false, imitation, manufactured, phony, pretended, sham, simulated, spurious, substitute, synthetic; SEE CONCEPT *582*

erstwhile [adj] *former*
bygone, ex, late, old, once, one-time, past, preceding, previous, quondam, sometime; SEE CONCEPT *820*

erudite [adj] *well-educated, cultured*
brainy, cultivated, educated, highbrow, in the know, into*, knowledgeable, learned, lettered, literate, savvy, scholarly, scholastic, studious, well-read, wise up*; SEE CONCEPT *402*

erudition [n] *higher education*
bookishness, brains, cultivation, culture, enlightenment, intellectuality, knowledge, learnedness, learning, letters, literacy, lore, pedantry, refinement, savvy, scholarliness, scholarship, science, studiousness; SEE CONCEPTS *287,409*

erupt [v] *give forth, eject with force*
appear, belch, blow up, boil, break out, burst, cast out, detonate, discharge, emit, eruct, explode, extravasate, flare up*, go off*, gush, hurl, jet, pour forth, rupture, spew, spit, spout, spurt,

ec
er

throw off*, touch off*, vent, vomit; SEE CONCEPTS *179,222*

eruption [n] *ejection*
access, blast, blow-up, breakout, burst, discharge, explosion, flare-up, flow, gust, outbreak, outburst, sally, venting, vomiting; SEE CONCEPTS *179,467*

escalate [v] *increase, be increased*
amplify, ascend, broaden, climb, enlarge, expand, extend, grow, heighten, intensify, magnify, make worse, mount, raise, rise, scale, step up, widen; SEE CONCEPTS *236,245*

escapade [n] *adventure, usually lighthearted*
antic, caper, fling, folly, frolic, gag, high jinks, lark, mischief, monkeyshines*, prank, rib*, roguery, rollick, romp, scrape, shenanigans*, spree, stunt, trick, vagary; SEE CONCEPTS *384,386*

escape [n] *breaking away; getaway*
abdication, avoidance, AWOL*, beat, bolt, break, breakout, bypassing, circumvention, decampment, deliverance, departure, desertion, disappearance, dodging, ducking, elopement, elusion, elusiveness, eschewal, evasion, evasiveness, extrication, fadeout, flight, freedom, hegira, lam, leave, liberation, out, outbreak, powder, release, rescue, retreat, runaround, shunning, sidestepping, slip, spring, withdrawal; SEE CONCEPT *102*

escape [v] *break away from*
abscond, avoid, bail out*, bolt, burst out, circumvent, cut and run*, cut loose*, decamp, depart, desert, disappear, dodge, double, duck, duck out*, elope, elude, emerge, evade, flee, fly, fly the coop*, gafiate, get away with*, get off*, go scot-free*, leave, make getaway*, make off*, make oneself scarce*, pass, play hooky*, run, run away, run off*, run out on*, shun, skip, slip, slip away, steal away, take a powder*, take flight, take on the lam*, vanish, work out of, wriggle out*; SEE CONCEPTS *102*

eschew [v] *have nothing to do with*
abandon, abjure, abstain, avoid, double, duck, elude, evade, forgo, forswear, give up, have no truck with*, let well enough alone*, not touch, refrain, renounce, sacrifice, shun, shy, shy away from, steer clear of*, swear off*; SEE CONCEPTS *30,102*

escort [n] *protection; accompaniment*
alarm clock*, attendant, beau, bird dog*, bodyguard, cavalier, chaperon, companion, company, consort, convoy, convoyer, cortege, date, entourage, fellow, friend, gallant, guard, guide, partner, protector, retinue, safeguard, squire, train, warden*; SEE CONCEPTS *419,423*

escort [v] *act as a companion, guard*
accompany, attend, bear, bring, carry, chaperon, company, conduct, consort with, convoy, date, direct, drag, go with, guide, lead, partner, pilot, protect, route, see, shepherd, show, squire, steer, take out, usher; SEE CONCEPTS *114,384,714*

esoteric [adj] *mysterious, obscure*
abstruse, acroamatic, arcane, cabbalistic, cryptic, deep, Delphic, heavy, hermetic, hidden, inner, inscrutable, mystic, mystical, occult, Orphic, private, profound, recondite, secret, Sibylline; SEE CONCEPTS *529,576,582*

especial [adj] *exceptional, particular*
chief, distinguished, dominant, exclusive, express, extraordinary, individual, marked, notable, noteworthy, outstanding, paramount, peculiar, personal, predominant, preeminent, preponderant, principal, private, set, signal, singular, special, specific, supreme, surpassing, uncommon, unique, unusual; SEE CONCEPTS *535,564,574*

especially [adv] *exceptionally, particularly*
abnormally, above all, before all else, chiefly, conspicuously, curiously, eminently, exclusively, expressly, extraordinarily, in particular, in specie, mainly, markedly, notably, oddly, outstandingly, peculiarly, preeminently, primarily, principally, remarkably, signally, singularly, specially, specifically, strangely, strikingly, supremely, unaccountably, uncommonly, uncustomarily, uniquely, unusually, wonderfully; SEE CONCEPTS *535,564,574*

espouse [v1] *stand up for; support*
accept, adopt, advocate, approve, back, champion, defend, embrace, get into*, go in for*, maintain, stand behind*, take on, take up, uphold; SEE CONCEPT *10*

espouse [v2] *marry*
betroth, catch, take as spouse, unite, wed; SEE CONCEPT *297*

essay [n1] *written discourse*
article, composition, discussion, disquisition, dissertation, explication, exposition, manuscript, paper, piece, study, theme, thesis, tract, treatise; SEE CONCEPT *271*

essay [n2] *try, attempt*
aim, bid, dry run*, effort, endeavor, exertion, experiment, hassle, labor, one's all*, one's level best*, shot*, striving, struggle, test, toil, travail, trial, try on*, tryout, undertaking, venture, whack*, work; SEE CONCEPT *87*

essay [v] *try, attempt*
aim, assay, endeavor, have a crack*, have a go*, have a shot*, have at it*, labor, make a run at*, offer, put to the test*, seek, strive, struggle, take a stab at*, take a whack at*, take on, test, toil, travail, try out, undertake, venture, work; SEE CONCEPT *87*

essence [n1] *heart, significance*
aspect, attribute, backbone, base, basis, be-all and end-all*, being, bottom, bottom line*, burden, caliber, character, chief constituent, constitution, core, crux, element, entity, essentia, essentiality, fiber, form, fundamentals, germ, grain, kernel, life, lifeblood, main idea, marrow, meaning, meat*, name of game*, nature, nitty-gritty*, nub, nucleus, pith, point, principle, property, quality, quiddity, quintessence, reality, root, soul, spirit, structure, stuff, substance, timber, vein, virtuality; SEE CONCEPTS *411,461,668,688*

essence [n2] *distillate, concentrate*
balm, cologne, drug, effusion, elixir, extract, fragrance, juice, liquor, perfume, potion, scent, spirits, tincture; SEE CONCEPTS *260,467*

essential [n] *necessity, basic*
ABCs*, bottom line*, brass tacks*, condition, element, essence, fire and ice*, fundamental, groceries*, guts*, heart, meat and potatoes*, must, name of the game*, nitty-gritty*, nuts and bolts*, part and parcel*, precondition, prerequisite, principle, quintessence, requirement, requisite, rudiment, sine qua non, stuff, substance, vital part, where one's at*; SEE CONCEPTS *646,661,826*

essential [adj1] *important, vital*
capital, cardinal, chief, constitutive, crucial, foremost, fundamental, imperative, indispensable, leading, main, necessary, necessitous, needed,

needful, prerequisite, principal, required, requisite, right-hand, wanted; SEE CONCEPT 567

essential [adj2] basic, fundamental

absolute, basal, cardinal, cold, complete, congenital, connate, constitutional, deep-seated, elemental, elementary, ideal, inborn, imbred, inherent, innate, intrinsic, key, main, material, meat and potatoes*, name of the game*, nitty-gritty*, nub, perfect, primary, prime, primitive, principal, quintessential, substratal, underlying; SEE CONCEPTS 546,549

establish [v1] set up, organize

authorize, base, build, constitute, create, decree, domiciliate, enact, endow, ensconce, entrench, erect, fix, form, found, ground, implant, inaugurate, inculcate, install, institute, land, lay foundation, live, lodge, moor, originate, place, plant, practice, provide, put, ring in, rivet, root, secure, set down, settle, stabilize, start, start ball rolling*, station, stick; SEE CONCEPTS 168,173,221,251

establish [v2] authenticate; demonstrate

ascertain, authorize, base, certify, circumstantiate, confirm, constitute, corroborate, decree, determine, discover, enact, find out, formulate, learn, legislate, make, make out, predicate, prescribe, prove, ratify, rest, show, stay, substantiate, validate, verify; SEE CONCEPTS 49,50,88,97

establishment [n1] organization; creation

enactment, endowment, formation, formulation, foundation, founding, inauguration, installation, institution, setting up; SEE CONCEPTS 173,221

establishment [n2] business, institution

abode, building, company, concern, corporation, enterprise, factory, firm, foundation, house, institute, office, organization, outfit, plant, quarters, residence, setup, structure, system, workplace; SEE CONCEPTS 323,325,449

establishment [n3] ruling class; bureaucracy

authority, city hall*, conservatives, diehards*, established order, Old Guard*, powers that be*, them, the system*; SEE CONCEPTS 347,354

estate [n1] extensive manor and its property

acreage, area, country home, country place, demesne, domain, dominion, farm, finca, freehold, grounds, holdings, lands, parcel, plantation, quinta, ranch, residence, rural seat, territory, villa; SEE CONCEPT 516

estate [n2] person's possessions, property, wealth

assets, belongings, bequest, capital, chattels, devise, earthly possessions, effects, endowment, fortune, goods, heritage, inheritance, legacy, patrimony, substance; SEE CONCEPTS 340,710

estate [n3] class, rank

bracket, caste, category, classification, condition, echelon, footing, form, grade, level, lot, order, period, place, position, quality, repair, shape, situation, sphere, standing, state, station, status, stratum; SEE CONCEPTS 378,388

esteem [v1] think highly of

admire, appreciate, apprise, be fond of, cherish, consider, hold dear, honor, idolize, like, look up to*, love, prize, regard, regard highly, respect, revere, reverence, think the world of*, treasure, value, venerate, worship; SEE CONCEPT 32

esteem [v2] consider, believe

account, calculate, deem, estimate, hold, judge, rate, reckon, regard, think, view; SEE CONCEPT 12

estimable [adj] honorable, worthy

admirable, admired, appreciable, august, big

name*, big time*, commendable, decent, deserving, esteemed, excellent, good, high-powered, honored, in limelight*, laudable, major league*, meritorious, meritable, name, noble, palmary, praisable, praiseworthy, reputable, reputed, respectable, respected, sterling, valuable, valued, venerable, well-thought-of*; SEE CONCEPTS 567,572

estimate [n] approximate calculation; educated guess

appraisal, appraisement, assay, assessment, ball-park figure*, belief, conclusion, conjecture, estimation, evaluation, gauging, guess, guesstimate*, impression, judgment, measure, measurement, mensuration, opinion, point of view, projection, rating, reckoning, sizing up*, stock, surmise, survey, thought, valuation; SEE CONCEPTS 28,37,689,784

estimate [v] guess, try to value

account, appraise, assay, assess, believe, budget, calculate roughly, cast, cipher, class, classify, compute, conjecture, consider, count, decide, deduce, determine, enumerate, evaluate, examine, expect, figure, form opinion, gauge, guess, guesstimate*, judge, look into, look upon, number, outline, plan, predict, prophesy, rank, rate, reason, reckon, regard, run over*, scheme, set a figure*, size up*, sum, suppose, surmise, suspect, tax, think, think through*; SEE CONCEPTS 28,37,764

estimation [n] belief, guess

admiration, appraisal, appreciation, arithmetic, assessment, calculating, ciphering, computation, consideration, considered opinion, credit, esteem, estimate, estimating, evaluation, favor, figuring, impression, judgment, opinion, predicting, reckoning, regard, respect, stock, valuation, veneration, view; SEE CONCEPTS 28,689

estrange [v] destroy the affections of

alien, alienate, antagonize, break up, disaffect, disunify, disunite, divert, divide, divorce, drive apart, leave, make hostile, part, put on the outs*, separate, set at odds*, sever, split, sunder, turn off*, wean, withdraw, withhold; SEE CONCEPTS 7,19,297,384

estrangement [n] destruction of affections

alienation, antagonization, breach, break-up, disaffection, disassociation, disunity, division, divorce, hostility, leave, leaving, parting, removal, schism, separation, split, withdrawal, withholding; SEE CONCEPTS 297,388

et cetera [adj] and so forth

along with others, and all, and on and on, and others, and so on, and the like, and the rest, blah blah blah*, et al., whatever, whatnot; SEE CONCEPTS 267,577

etch [v] carve

compose, corrode, cut, define, delineate, depict, describe, eat into, engrave, erode, execute, furrow, grave, impress, imprint, incise, ingrain, inscribe, outline, picture, portray, reduce, represent, set forth, stamp; SEE CONCEPTS 174,176

etching [n] art created by carving

engraving, impression, imprint, inscription, mezzotint, photoengraving, photogravure, print, reproduction, rotogravure, transferring; SEE CONCEPT 259

eternal [adj] without pause; endless

abiding, ageless, always, amaranthine, boundless, ceaseless, constant, continual, continued, continuous, dateless, deathless, enduring, everlasting,

er
et

forever, illimitable, immemorial, immortal, immutable, imperishable, incessant, indefinite, indestructible, infinite, interminable, lasting, never-ending, perdurable, perennial, permanent, perpetual, persistent, relentless, termless, timeless, unbroken, unceasing, undying, unending, unfading, uninterrupted, unremitting, without end; SEE CONCEPTS 482,798

eternally [adv] endlessly
always, continually, ever, evermore, forever, forevermore, for ever so long*, for keeps, in perpetuum, perpetually, regularly, till cows come home*; SEE CONCEPT 798

eternity [n] forever
aeon, afterlife, age, ages, blue moon*, dog's age*, endlessness, endless time, everlastingness, forever and a day*, future, immortality, imperishability, infiniteness, infinitude, infinity, kingdom come*, other world*, perpetuity, timelessness, time without end, wild blue yonder*, world without end; SEE CONCEPTS 370,804,818

ethereal [adj] delicate, heavenly
aerial, airy, celestial, dainty, divine, empyreal, empyrean, exquisite, fairy, filmy, fine, gaseous, ghostly, gossamer, impalpable, insubstantial, intangible, light, rarefied, refined, spiritual, sublime, subtle, supernal, tenuous, unearthly, unsubstantial, unworldly, vaporous, vapory; SEE CONCEPTS 491,549,582,606

ethical [adj] moral, righteous
Christian, clean, conscientious, correct, decent, elevated, equitable, fair, fitting, good, high-principled, honest, honorable, humane, just, kosher*, moralistic, noble, principled, proper, respectable, right, right-minded, square, straight, true blue*, upright, upstanding, virtuous; SEE CONCEPT 545

ethics/ ethic [n] moral philosophy, values
belief, conduct, conscience, convention, conventionalities, criteria, descency, ethos, goodness, honesty, honor, ideal, imperative, integrity, moral code, morality, mores, natural law, nature, practice, principles, right and wrong, rules of conduct, standard, standards, the Golden Rule*; SEE CONCEPTS 645,688,689

ethnic [adj] racial, cultural
indigenous, national, native, traditional, tribal; SEE CONCEPT 549

etiquette [n] manners, politeness
amenities, civility, code, convention, courtesy, customs, decency, decorum, deportment, dignity, form, formalities, good behavior*, mores, politesse, proper behavior, propriety, protocol, p's and q's*, rules, seemliness, social graces, suavities, usage; SEE CONCEPT 633

eulogize [v] praise, glorify
acclaim, applaud, bless, celebrate, commend, compliment, cry up, exalt, extol, flatter, give a bouquet*, give a posy*, hymn, idolize, laud, magnify, panegyrize, pay tribute to, sing praises; SEE CONCEPT 69

eulogy [n] praise, acclamation
acclaim, accolade, adulation, applause, citation, commendation, compliment, encomium, exaltation, glorification, laudation, paean, panegyric, plaudit, salutation, tribute; SEE CONCEPTS 69,278

euphemism [n] nice way of saying something
circumlocution, delicacy, floridness, grandiloquence, inflation, pomposity, pretense, purism; SEE CONCEPTS 275,278

euphoria [n] extreme happiness
bliss, dreamland, ecstasy, elation, exaltation, exhilaration, exultation, frenzy, glee, health, high spirits, intoxication, joy, joyousness, jubilation, madness, rapture, relaxation, transport; SEE CONCEPT 410

evacuate [v] clear an area; empty
abandon, bail out*, cut out, decamp, depart, desert, discharge, displace, eject, expel, forsake, hightail, leave, move out, pack up, pull out, quit, relinquish, remove, run for the hills*, skidaddle*, vacate, withdraw; SEE CONCEPTS 179,195

evade [v] get away from
avoid, baffle, balk, beat around bush*, beg the question*, bypass, cavil, circumvent, conceal, confuse, cop out, deceive, decline, dodge, double, duck, elude, equivocate, escape, eschew, fence, fend off*, flee, fly, fudge*, get around, give the runaround*, hedge, hide, keep distance*, lay low*, lead on a merry chase*, lie, parry, pass up, pretend, prevaricate, pussyfoot, put off, shift, shirk, shuck, shuffle, shun, shy, sidestep, slip out, sneak away*, steer clear of*, tergiversate, trick, waffle*, weasel*; SEE CONCEPTS 30,102

evaluate [v] judge
appraise, assay, assess, calculate, check, check out, class, classify, criticize, decide, estimate, figure out, future, gauge, grade, guesstimate*, look over, peg*, price out, rank, rate, read, reckon, set at, size up*, survey, take account of, take measure, valuate, value, weigh; SEE CONCEPTS 18,24,103

evaluation [n] judgment
appraisal, appraisement, assessment, calculation, decision, estimate, estimation, guesstimation*, interpretation, opinion, rating, stock, take, valuation; SEE CONCEPTS 24,103,689

evaporate [v] dry up, dissolve
clear, concentrate, dehumidify, dehydrate, dematerialize, desiccate, disappear, dispel, disperse, dissipate, evanesce, evanish, fade away, melt, parch, pass, vanish, vaporize, weaken; SEE CONCEPTS 469,698

evaporation [n] drying up; dissolution
dehydration, dematerialization, desiccation, disappearance, dispelling, dispersal, dissipation, escape, evanescence, fading, melting, vanishing, vaporescence, vaporization; SEE CONCEPTS 469,607,698

evasion [n] escape, avoidance
artifice, circumvention, cop-out*, cunning, ditch*, dodge*, dodging, elusion, equivocating, equivocation, eschewal, evading, evasiveness, excuse, fancy footwork*, fudging*, jive, lie, obliqueness, pretext, prevarication, quibble, routine, run-around, ruse, shift, shirking, shuffling, shunning, slip*, sophism, sophistry, stall, stonewall*, subterfuge, trick, trickery; SEE CONCEPTS 59,63,102

evasive [adj] deceitful, tricky
ambiguous, cagey, casuistic, casuistical, cunning, deceptive, devious, dissembling, elusive, elusory, equivocating, false, fugitive, greasy, indirect, intangible, lying, misleading, oblique, prevaricating, shifty, shuffling, slippery, sly, sophistical, stonewalling*, unclear, vague; SEE CONCEPTS 267,401,542

even [adj] flat, uniform
alike, balanced, consistent, constant, continual, continuous, direct, equal, flush, homogenous,

horizontal, level, matching, metrical, parallel, planate, plane, plumb, proportional, regular, right, same, smooth, square, stabile, stable, steady, straight, surfaced, true, unbroken, unchanging, undeviating, unfluctuating, uninterrupted, unvaried, unvarying, unwavering, unwrinkled; SEE CONCEPTS 480,490

even [adj2] *calm, undisturbed*
composed, cool, equable, equanimous, eventempered, imperturbable, peaceful, placid, serene, stable, steady, tranquil, unexcitable, unruffled, well-balanced; SEE CONCEPT 401

even [adj3] *commensurate; having no advantage*
balanced, coequal, comparable, coterminous, drawn, equal, equalized, equivalent, evensteven*, exact, fifty-fifty*, horse to horse*, identical, level, matching, neck and neck*, on a par*, parallel, proportional, proportionate, same, similar, smack in the middle*, square, tied, uniform; SEE CONCEPT 566

even [adj4] *fair, impartial*
balanced, disinterested, dispassionate, equal, equitable, fair and square*, honest, just, matching, nonpartisan, square, straightforward, unbiased, unprejudiced; SEE CONCEPTS 267,542

even [v] *balance, make smooth*
align, equal, equalize, flatten, flush, grade, lay, level, match, pancake*, plane, regularize, roll, square, stabilize, steady, symmetrize, uniform; SEE CONCEPTS 231,757

even [adv] *still, yet*
all the more, despite, disregarding, indeed, in spite of, much, notwithstanding, so much as; SEE CONCEPT 544

evening [n] *latter part of a day*
black, close, dark, decline, dim, dusk, duskiness, early black*, eve, even, eventide, late afternoon, nightfall, sundown, sunset, twilight; SEE CONCEPTS 801,806,810

event [n1] *occurrence, happening*
accident, act, action, advent, adventure, affair, appearance, business, calamity, case, catastrophe, celebration, ceremony, chance, circumstance, coincidence, conjuncture, crisis, deed, development, emergency, episode, experience, exploit, fact, function, holiday, incident, juncture, marvel, matter, milestone, miracle, misfortune, mishap, mistake, occasion, occurrence, pass, phase, phenomenon, predicament, proceeding, shift, situation, story, thing*, tide, transaction, triumph, turn, wonder; SEE CONCEPT 2

event [n2] *effect, result*
aftereffect, aftermath, case, causatum, chance, conclusion, consequence, end, end result, eventuality, fortuity, hap, happenstance, issue, offshoot, outcome, outgrowth, product, resultant, sequel, sequent, termination, upshot; SEE CONCEPT 230

event [n3] *performance, competition*
bout, contest, game, match, meet, tournament; SEE CONCEPTS 263,363

eventful [adj] *significant, busy*
active, consequential, critical, crucial, decisive, exciting, fateful, full, historic, important, lively, memorable, momentous, notable, noteworthy, outstanding, remarkable, signal; SEE CONCEPT 548

eventual [adj] *future, concluding*
closing, conditional, consequent, contingent, dependent, down the pike*, down the road*, ending, endmost, ensuing, final, hindmost, indirect, inevitable, in the cards*, last, later, latter, overall, possible, prospective, resulting, secondary, succeeding, terminal, ulterior, ultimate, vicarious; SEE CONCEPTS 552,820

eventuality [n] *something that probably will happen*
aftereffect, aftermath, any case, case, chance, consequence, contingency, effect, event, godown*, goings-on*, happening, issue, likelihood, outcome, possibility, probability, result, sequel, toss-up, upshot*; SEE CONCEPTS 230,650

eventually [adv] *in the course of time*
after all, at last, at the end of the day*, finally, hereafter, in future, in the end, in the long run*, one day, someday, sometime, sooner or later*, ultimately, when all is said and done*, yet; SEE CONCEPTS 552,820

eventuate [v] *be a consequence*
be consequent, befall, come about, come to pass, end, ensue, eventualize, follow, happen, issue, occur, result, stop, take place, terminate; SEE CONCEPTS 2,242

ever [adv] *always, at any time*
anytime, at all, at all times, at any point, by any chance*, consistently, constantly, continually, endlessly, eternally, everlastingly, evermore, forever, for keeps, in any case*, incessantly, in perpetuum, invariably, on any occasion*, perpetually, relentlessly, till cows come home*, to the end of time*, unceasingly, unendingly, usually; SEE CONCEPTS 798,799

everlasting [adj] *infinite, never-ending*
abiding, amaranthine, boundless, ceaseless, constant, continual, continuous, deathless, endless, eternal, immortal, imperishable, incessant, indestructible, interminable, lasting, limitless, perdurable, permanent, perpetual, termless, timeless, unceasing, undying, unending, uninterrupted, unremitting; SEE CONCEPT 798

every [adj] *each, all*
each one, whole, without exception; SEE CONCEPT 531

everybody/everyone [n] *all involved, all human beings; the whole world*
all, all and sundry*, anybody, each one, each person, every person, generality, masses, people, populace, the public, the whole, young and old*; SEE CONCEPT 417

everyday [adj] *common*
accustomed, average, commonplace, conventional, customary, daily, dime a dozen*, dull, familiar, frequent, garden variety*, habitual, informal, lowly, mainstream, middle-of-the-road*, mundane, normal, ordinary, per diem, plain, prosaic, quotidian,, routine, run-of-the-mill*, stock, unexceptional, unimaginative, unremarkable, usual, vanilla*, whitebread*, wonted, workaday; SEE CONCEPTS 530,547

everything [n] *entirety*
aggregate, all, all in all, all that, all things, business, complex, each thing, every little thing*, fixins'*, lock stock and barrel*, lot, many things, sum, the works*, total, universe, whole, whole ball of wax*, whole caboodle*, whole enchilada*, whole lot*, whole shebang*; SEE CONCEPTS 432,837

everywhere [adv] *in all places*
all around, all over, all over creation*, all over the map*, far and wide*, here and there*, here till Sunday*, high and low*, in all quarters, in each

place, in every direction, in every place, inside and out, near and far*, omnipresent, overall, pole to pole*, the world over*, throughout, ubiquitous, ubiquitously, universally, wherever; SEE CONCEPT 583

evict [v] *throw out from residence*
boot out*, bounce*, chase, dislodge, dismiss, dispossess, eject, expel, extrude, force out, heave-ho*, kick out*, oust, out, put out, remove, send packing*, show out, show the door*, shut out, toss out on ear*, turn out; SEE CONCEPTS 122,198,211

eviction [n] *throwing out of a residence*
boot*, bounce*, bum's rush*, clearance, dislodgement, dispossession, ejection, expulsion, kicking out*, ouster, removal, rush, the gate*, walking papers*; SEE CONCEPTS 123,198,211

evidence [n] *proof*
affirmation, attestation, averment, cincher*, clincher*, clue, confirmation, corroboration, cue, data, declaration, demonstration, deposition, documentation, dope*, goods*, gospel, grabber*, grounds, index, indication, info*, information, manifestation, mark, sign, significant, smoking gun*, substantiation, symptom, testament, testimonial, testimony, token, witness; SEE CONCEPTS 274,318

evidence [v] *prove*
attest, bespeak, betoken, confirm, connote, demonstrate, denote, designate, display, evince, exhibit, expose, illustrate, indicate, manifest, mark, ostend, proclaim, reveal, show, signify, testify to, witness; SEE CONCEPTS 57,97,317

evident [adj] *apparent, clear*
axiomatic, barefaced*, clear-cut, conspicuous, crystal clear*, distinct, fact, incontestable, incontrovertible, indisputable, logical, manifest, noticeable, obvious, open-and-shut*, palpable, patent, perceptible, plain, plain as day*, reasonable, straightforward, tangible, unambiguous, unmistakable, visible; SEE CONCEPTS 529,535

evidently [adv] *apparently, clearly*
doubtless, doubtlessly, incontestably, incontrovertibly, indisputably, it seems, it would seem, manifestly, obviously, officially, ostensibly, outwardly, patently, plainly, professedly, seemingly, to all appearances*, undoubtedly, unmistakably, without question; SEE CONCEPT 535

evil [n] *badness, immorality; disaster*
affliction, baseness, blow, calamity, catastrophe, corruption, crime, criminality, curse, debauchery, depravity, devilry, diabolism, harm, hatred, heinousness, hurt, ill, impiety, indecency, infamy, iniquity, injury, knavery, lewdness, licentiousness, looseness, malevolence, malignity, meanness, mischief, misery, misfortune, obscenity, outrage, pain, perversity, ruin, sin, sinfulness, sorrow, suffering, turpitude, vice, viciousness, vileness, villainy, wickedness, woe, wrong, wrongdoing; SEE CONCEPT 645

evil [adj] *sinful, immoral*
angry, atrocious, bad, baneful, base, beastly, calamitous, corrupt, damnable, depraved, destructive, disastrous, execrable, flagitious, foul, harmful, hateful, heinous, hideous, iniquitous, injurious, loathsome, low, maleficent, malevolent, malicious, malignant, nefarious, no good, obscene, offensive, pernicious, poison, rancorous, reprobate, repugnant, repulsive, revolting, spiteful, stinking, ugly, unpleasant, unpropitious, vi-

cious, vile, villainous, wicked, wrathful, wrong; SEE CONCEPTS 545,570

evoke [v] *induce, stimulate*
arouse, awaken, call, call forth, conjure, educe, elicit, evince, evolve, excite, extort, extract, give rise to, invoke, milk*, provoke, raise, rally, recall, rouse, stir up, summon, waken; SEE CONCEPTS 228,242

evolution [n] *development, progress*
change, enlargement, evolvement, expansion, flowering, growth, increase, maturation, natural process, progression, transformation, unfolding, working out; SEE CONCEPT 704

evolve [v] *develop, progress*
advance, derive, disclose, educe, elaborate, emerge, enlarge, excogitate, expand, get, grow, increase, mature, obtain, open, result, ripen, unfold, work out; SEE CONCEPTS 236,245,704

exacerbate [v] *infuriate; make worse*
add insult to injury*, aggravate, annoy, egg on*, embitter, enrage, envenom, exasperate, excite, fan the flames*, feed the fire*, go from bad to worse*, heat up*, heighten, hit on*, increase, inflame, intensify, irritate, madden, provoke, push one's button*, rattle one's cage*, rub salt in a wound*, vex, worsen; SEE CONCEPTS 7,19

exact [adj] *accurate, precise*
bull's-eye*, careful, clear, clear-cut, correct, dead on*, definite, distinct, downright, explicit, express, faithful, faultless, identical, literal, methodical, nailed down*, nice, on target*, on the button*, on the money*, on the numbers*, orderly, particular, perfect, right, right on*, rigorous, sharp, specific, true, unequivocal, unerring, veracious, verbal, verbatim; SEE CONCEPTS 535,557

exact [adj2] *careful, painstaking*
conscientious, consciable, demanding, exacting, finicky, fussy, heedful, meticulous, punctilious, punctual, rigorous, scrupulous, severe, strict; SEE CONCEPT 542

exact [v] *demand, call for*
assess, bleed, call, challenge, claim, coerce, command, compel, constrain, extort, extract, force, gouge, impose, insist upon, lean on, levy, oblige, pinch, postulate, put on, require, requisition, shake down*, solicit, squeeze, wrench, wrest, wring; SEE CONCEPTS 53,142

exacting [adj] *demanding*
burdensome, by the book*, careful, critical, difficult, exigent, finicky, fussy, grievous, hard, harsh, hypercritical, imperious, nit-picking, onerous, oppressive, painstaking, particular, persnickety, picky, precise, rigid, rigorous, severe, stern, strict, stringent, taxing, tough, trying, unsparing, weighty; SEE CONCEPTS 401,404

exactly [adv] *accurately, particularly*
absolutely, altogether, bang*, carefully, completely, correctly, definitely, explicitly, expressly, faithfully, faultlessly, for a fact, for certain, for sure*, indeed, in every respect, just, literally, methodically, no mistake, on the dot*, on the money*, on the nail*, on the nose*, positively, precisely, quite, right, rigorously, scrupulously, severely, sharp, specifically, square, strictly, the ticket*, totally, truly, truthfully, unequivocally, unerringly, utterly, veraciously, wholly; SEE CONCEPTS 535,557

exactness [n] *accuracy, precision*
carefulness, correctness, definiteness, definitive-

ness, definitude, exactitude, faithfulness, faultlessness, nicety, orderliness, painstakingness,
preciseness, promptitude, regularity, rigor, rigor-
ousness, scrupulousness, strictness, truth, unequivocalness, veracity; SEE CONCEPTS 638,654

exaggerate [v] *overstate, embellish*
amplify, blow out of proportion*, boast, boost,
brag, build up, caricature, color, cook up*, corrupt, distort, embroider, emphasize, enlarge, exalt, expand, fabricate, falsify, fudge*, go to
extremes*, heighten, hike, hyperbolize, inflate,
intensify, lay it on thick*, lie, loud talk*, magnify, make too much of*, misquote, misreport,
misrepresent, overdo, overdraw, overemphasize,
overestimate, pad*, pretty up*, puff, put on, pyramid*, romance, romanticize, scam, stretch, up*;
SEE CONCEPT 63

exaggerated [adj] *overstated, embellished*
a bit thick*, abstract, amplified, artificial, bouncing, caricatural, distorted, embroidered, exalted,
excessive, extravagant, fabricated, fabulous,
false, fantastic, farfetched, hammy, highly colored, histrionic, hyperbolic, impossible, inflated,
magnified, melodramatic, out of proportion, overblown, overdone, overestimated, overkill, overwrought, preposterous, pretentious, schmaltzy,
sensational, spectacular, steep, strained, stylized,
tall, too much*, too-too*, unrealistic; SEE CON-
CEPTS 267,542,562

exaggeration [n] *overstatement, embellishment*
aggrandizement, amplification, baloney*, boasting, caricature, coloring, crock*, elaboration, embroidery, emphasis, enlargement, exaltation,
excess, extravagance, fabrication, falsehood,
fancy, fantasy, figure of speech, fish story*, flight
of fancy*, hogwash*, hyperbole, inflation, jazz*,
line*, magnification, misjudgment, misrepresentation, overemphasis, overestimation, pretension,
pretentiousness, rant, romance, stretch, tall story*, untruth, whopper*, yarn*; SEE CONCEPTS
63,278,663

exalt [v] *promote, praise*
acclaim, advance, aggrandize, apotheosize, applaud, bless, boost, build up*, commend, dignify,
distinguish, ennoble, erect, eulogize, extol, glorify, halo, honor, idolize, intensify, laud, magnify, pay homage to, pay tribute to, raise, revere,
set on pedestal*, sublime, transfigure, upgrade,
uprear, worship; SEE CONCEPTS 10,69

exaltation [n1] *promotion, praise*
acclaim, acclamation, advancement, aggrandizement, apotheosis, applause, blessing, dignity,
elevation, eminence, ennoblement, extolment,
glorification, glory, grandeur, high rank, homage,
honor, idolzation, laudation, lionization, loftiness,
magnification, panegyric, plaudits, prestige, reverence, rise, tribute, upgrading, uplifting, worship; SEE CONCEPTS 69,278

exaltation [n2] *great joy*
animation, bliss, delectation, delight, ecstasy, elation, elevation, euphoria, excitement, exhilaration, exultation, inspiration, intoxication,
joyousness, jubilation, rapture, stimulation, transport, uplift; SEE CONCEPTS 32,410

exalted [adj] *praised; held in high esteem*
astral, august, dignified, elevated, eminent, exaggerated, excessive, first, grand, high, highest,
highest-ranking, high-minded, high-ranking, honorable, honored, ideal, illustrious, immodest, imposing, inflated, intellectual, leading, lofty,

magnificent, noble, number one, outstanding,
overblown, pompous, prestigious, pretentious,
proud, self-important, sublime, superb, superior,
top-drawer*, top-ranking, uplifting; SEE CON-
CEPTS 404,529

examination [n1] *test, analysis*
assay, audit, battery, blue book*, breakdown,
canvass, catechism, checking, checkup, cross-
examination, diagnosis, dissection, exam, experiment, exploration, final, grilling, inquest,
inquiry, inquisition, inspection, interrogation, investigation, legwork*, make-up, observation,
once-over*, oral, perlustration, perusal, probe,
quest, questioning, questionnaire, quiz, raid, reconnaissance, research, review, scan, scrutiny,
search, study, survey, the eye*, third degree*,
trial, tryout, view, written; SEE CONCEPT 290

examination [n2] *medical checkup*
autopsy, biopsy, exam, inquiry, observation,
physical, postoperative, probe, test; SEE CON-
CEPTS 103,310

examine [v1] *analyze, test*
appraise, assay, audit, canvass, case, check,
check out, chew over*, consider, criticize, delve
into, dig into, explore, eye*, finger*, frisk, go
into, go over, go through, gun*, inquire, inspect,
investigate, look over, look see*, parse, pat down,
peruse, pick at, ponder, pore over, probe, prospect, prove, read, reconnoiter, research, review,
scan, scope, screen, scrutinate, scrutinize, search
into, sift, size up*, study, survey, sweep, take
stock of*, try, turn over*, vet, view, weigh, winnow*; SEE CONCEPTS 24,103

examine [v2] *ask questions pointedly*
catechize, check, cross-examine, experiment, give
the third*, give the third degree*, grill, inquire,
interrogate, judge, measure, pump, put through
the wringer*, query, quiz, try, try out, weigh; SEE
CONCEPT 48

example [n] *instance, model*
archetype, case, case history, case in point, citation, copy, excuse, exemplar, exemplification, for
instance, ideal, illustration, kind of thing, lesson,
object, original, paradigm, paragon, part, pattern,
precedent, prototype, quotation, representation,
sample, sampling, specimen, standard, stereotype, symbol; SEE CONCEPT 686

exasperate [v] *upset, provoke*
aggravate, agitate, anger, annoy, bug*, disturb,
drive up the wall*, embitter, enrage, exacerbate,
excite, gall, get*, get under one's skin*, incense,
inflame, infuriate, irk, irritate, madden, make
waves*, needle*, nettle, peeve, pique, rankle,
rile, roil, rouse, T-off*, try the patience of*, vex,
work up; SEE CONCEPTS 7,19

exasperation [n] *upset, provocation*
aggravation, anger, annoyance, besetment,
bother, botheration, displeasure, exacerbation,
fury, ire, irritant, irritation, nuisance, passion,
pest, pique, plague, rage, resentment, vexation,
wrath; SEE CONCEPTS 29,410

excavate [v] *dig up*
burrow, cut, delve, empty, gouge, grub, hollow,
mine, quarry, scoop, scrape, shovel, spade,
trench, tunnel, uncover, unearth; SEE CONCEPT
178

excavation [n] *site of digging; digging*
blasting, burrow, cavity, cut, cutting, dig, disin-
terring, ditch, dugout, exhuming, hole, hollow,
mine, mining, pit, quarry, removal, scooping,

ev
ex

shaft, shoveling, trench, trough, unearthing; SEE CONCEPTS *513*

exceed [v] *be superior to; surpass*
beat, best, better, break record*, cap, distance, eclipse, excel, get upper hand*, go beyond, go by, have advantage, have a jump on*, have it all over*, out-distance, outdo, outpace, outreach, outrun, outshine, outstrip, overstep, overtake, overtax, pass, rise above*, run circles around*, surmount, top, transcend; SEE CONCEPT *141*

exceedingly [adv] *very; exceptionally*
awfully, enormously, especially, excessively, extraordinarily, extremely, greatly, highly, hugely, immoderately, in a marked degree, inordinately, powerful, really, remarkably, strikingly, superlatively, surpassingly, terribly, too much, unusually, vastly, vitally; SEE CONCEPT *569*

excel [v] *be superior; surpass*
beat, be good, be master of, be proficient, be skillful, best, be talented, better, cap, come through, eclipse, exceed, go beyond, go to town*, improve upon, make it, outdo, outrival, outshine, outstrip, pass, predominate, shine, show talent, surmount, take precedence, top, transcend, wax*; SEE CONCEPTS *141,671,706*

excellence [n] *superiority*
arete, class, distinction, éclat, eminence, excellency, fineness, goodness, greatness, high quality, merit, perfection, preeminence, purity, quality, superbness, supremacy, transcendence, virtue, worth; SEE CONCEPT *671*

excellent [adj] *superior, wonderful*
accomplished, admirable, A-1*, attractive, capital, certified, champion, choice, choicest, desirable, distinctive, distinguished, estimable, exceptional, exemplary, exquisite, fine, finest, first, first-class, first-rate, good, great, high, incomparable, invaluable, magnificent, meritorious, notable, noted, outstanding, peerless, piked*, premium, priceless, prime, select, skillful, sterling, striking, superb, superlative, supreme, tiptop*, top-notch, transcendent, world-class; SEE CONCEPT *574*

except [v] *leave out*
ban, bar, bate, count out, debar, disallow, eliminate, exclude, exempt, expostulate, inveigh, object, omit, pass over, protest, reject, remonstrate, rule out, suspend, taboo; SEE CONCEPTS *25,30,211*

except [prep] *other than*
apart from, aside from, bar, barring, besides, but, excepting, excluding, exclusive of, exempting, if not, lacking, leaving out, minus, not for, omitting, outside of, rejecting, save, saving, short of, without, with the exception of; SEE CONCEPT *577*

exception [n1] *leaving out*
barring, debarment, disallowment, excepting, exclusion, excusing, expulsion, noninclusion, omission, passing over, rejection, repudiation, reservation; SEE CONCEPTS *25,30,211*

exception [n2] *special case; irregularity*
allowance, anomalism, anomaly, departure, deviation, difference, dispensation, eccentricity, exemption, freak, inconsistency, nonconformity, oddity, peculiarity, perquisitor, privilege, privileged person, quirk; SEE CONCEPTS *423,665*

exceptional [adj1] *irregular*
aberrant, abnormal, anomalous, atypical, deviant, distinct, extraordinary, inconsistent, infrequent, notable, noteworthy, odd, peculiar, phenomenal,

rare, remarkable, scarce, singular, special, strange, uncommon, uncustomary, unheard-of, unimaginable, unique, unordinary, unprecedented, unthinkable, unusual; SEE CONCEPT *564*

exceptional [adj2] *excellent, wonderful*
brainy, extraordinary, fine, first-class, first-rate, good, high, marvelous, outstanding, phenomenal, premium, prodigious, remarkable, singular, special, superior, world-class; SEE CONCEPTS *572,574*

excerpt [n] *citation; something taken from a whole*
extract, fragment, notation, note, part, passage, pericope, piece, portion, quotation, quote, saying, section, selection; SEE CONCEPTS *270,274,835*

excerpt [v] *take a part from a whole*
choose, cite, cull, extract, glean, note, pick, pick out, quote, select, single out; SEE CONCEPTS *41,142,211*

excess [n1] *overabundance of something*
balance, by-product, enough, exorbitance, exuberance, fat, fulsomeness, glut, inundation, lavishness, leavings, leftover, luxuriance, nimiety, overdose, overflow, overkill, overload, overmuch, overrun, oversupply, overweight, plenty, plethora, profusion, recrement, redundance, redundancy, refuse, remainder, residue, rest, spare, superabundance, supererogation, superfluity, surfeit, surplus, the limit, too much*, too much of a good thing*, waste, wastefulness; SEE CONCEPTS *787,824,835*

excess [n2] *overindulgence in personal desires*
debauchery, dissipation, dissoluteness, exorbitance, extravagance, extreme, extremity, immoderacy, immoderation, indulgence, inordinateness, intemperance, overdoing, prodigality, saturnalia, self-indulgence, unrestraint; SEE CONCEPTS *633,645*

excessive [adj] *too much; overdone*
boundless, disproportionate, dissipated, dizzying, enormous, exaggerated, exorbitant, extra, extravagant, extreme, immoderate, indulgent, inordinate, intemperate, limitless, more, needless, over, overboard, overkill, overmuch, plethoric, prodigal, profligate, recrementitious, redundant, self-indulgent, sky-high*, steep, stiff, stratospheric*, super, superabundant, superfluous, supernatural, too many, towering, unbounded, unconscionable, undue, unmeasurable, unreasonable, way out*; SEE CONCEPTS *560,771,781*

exchange [n1] *trade; deal*
barter, buying and selling, castling, change, commerce, commutation, conversion, correspondence, dealing, interchange, interdependence, interrelation, network, quid pro quo, rearrangement, reciprocation, reciprocity, replacement, revision, shift, shuffle, shuffling, substitution, supplanting, supplantment, swap, switch, tit for tat*, traffic, transaction, transfer, transposing, transposition, truck*; SEE CONCEPTS *104,324*

exchange [n2] *place where stocks are bought, sold*
curb, market, net, network, over the counter, stock exchange, store, the Big Board*, the Street*, Wall Street*; SEE CONCEPTS *325,449*

exchange [v] *trade*
alternate, bandy, bargain, barter, buy and sell, cash in, castle, change, change hands*, commute, contact with, convert into, correspond, deal in, displace, flip-flop*, give and take*, go over to*, hook up, horse trade, interchange, invert, link up, market, network, pass to, pay back, rearrange,

reciprocate, replace, return the compliment*, reverse, revise, seesaw, shift, shuffle, shuttle, substitute, swap, swap horses*, switch, traffic, transact, transfer, transpose, truck*, turn the tables*; SEE CONCEPT **104**

excise [n] *tax on goods*
customs, duty, import tax, levy, surcharge, tariff, toll; SEE CONCEPT **329**

excise [v] *remove, delete*
amputate, black out, blot out*, blue pencil*, cross out, cut, cut off, cut out, cut up, destroy, edit, elide, eradicate, erase, expunge, exscind, exsect, exterminate, extirpate, extract, gut, knock off*, launder*, lop off*, resect, scissor out, scratch out, slash, stamp out*, strike, trim, wipe out, X out*; SEE CONCEPT **211**

excitable [adj] *easily upset or inspired*
agitable, alarmable, demonstrative, edgy, emotional, enthusiastic, fidgety, fierce, fiery, galvanic, hasty, high-strung, hot-headed, hot-tempered, hysterical, impatient, impetuous, impulsive, inflammable, intolerant, irascible, mercurial, moody, nervous, neurotic, overzealous, passionate, peevish, quick, quick-tempered, rash, reckless, restless, sensitive, short fused, skittish, susceptible, temperamental, testy, touchy, uncontrolled, uneasy, vehement, violent, volatile, volcanic; SEE CONCEPTS **401,404**

excite [v] *inspire; upset*
accelerate, agitate, amaze, anger, animate, annoy, arouse, astound, awaken, bother, chafe, delight, discompose, disturb, electrify, elicit, energize, evoke, feed the fire*, fire, fluster, foment, galvanize, goad, incite, induce, inflame, infuriate, instigate, intensify, irritate, jar, jolt, kindle, madden, mock, move, offend, precipitate, provoke, quicken, rouse, start, stimulate, stir up, taunt, tease, thrill, titillate, touch off, vex, waken, wake up, warm, whet, work up, worry; SEE CONCEPTS **7,14,19,22**

excited [adj] *inspired; upset*
aflame, agitated, animated, annoyed, aroused, awakened, beside oneself*, charged, delighted, discomposed, disconcerted, disturbed, eager, enthusiastic, feverish, fired up*, frantic, high*, hot*, hot and bothered*, hyperactive, hysterical, in a tizzy*, inflamed, juiced up*, jumpy*, keyed up*, moved, nervous, on edge*, on fire*, overwrought, passionate, piqued, provoked, roused, ruffled, steamed up*, stimulated, stirred, thrilled, tumultous/tumultuous, wild, wired*, worked up, zipped up*; SEE CONCEPTS **401,403**

excitement [n] *enthusiasm; incitement*
action, activity, ado, adventure, agitation, animation, bother, buzz*, commotion, confusion, discomposure, disturbance, dither*, drama, elation, emotion, excitation, feeling, ferment, fever, flurry, frenzy, furor, fuss, heat*, hubbub*, hullabaloo*, hurry, hysteria, impulse, instigation, intoxication, kicks*, melodrama, motivation, motive, movement, passion, perturbation, provocation, rage, stimulation, stimulus, stir, thrill, titillation, to-do*, trepidation, tumult, turmoil, urge, warmth, wildness; SEE CONCEPTS **388,410,633**

exciting [adj] *inspiring, exhilarating*
agitative, animating, appealing, arousing, arresting, astonishing, bracing, breathtaking, commoving, dangerous, dramatic, electrifying, exhilarant, eye-popping*, far-out*, fine, flashy, groovy*, hair-raising*, heady*, hectic, impelling, impres-

sive, interesting, intoxicating, intriguing, lively, melodramatic, mind-blowing, moving, neat, overpowering, overwhelming, provocative, racy, rip-roaring*, rousing, sensational, showy, spine-tingling*, stimulating, stirring, thrilling, titillating, wild, zestful; SEE CONCEPTS **529,542,548**

exclaim [v] *shout out*
assert, bellow, blurt, burst out, call, call aloud, call out, cry, cry out, declare, ejaculate, emit, figure, holler, proclaim, rend the air*, roar, say loudly, shout, state, utter, vociferate, yawp*, yell; SEE CONCEPTS **47,49**

exclamation [n] *shout; assertion*
bellow, call, clamor, cry, ejaculation, expletive, holler, interjection, outcry, roar, utterance, vociferation, yawp*, yell; SEE CONCEPTS **49,77**

exclude [v] *expel, forbid*
ban, bar, bate, blackball*, blacklist, block, bounce, boycott, close out, count out, debar, disallow, drive out, eject, eliminate, embargo, estop, evict, except, force out, get rid of, ignore, interdict, keep out, leave out, lock out, obviate, occlude, omit, ostracize, oust, pass over, preclude, prevent, prohibit, proscribe, put out, refuse, refuse admittance, reject, remove, repudiate, rule out, set aside, shut out, shut the door on*, sideline, suspend, throw out, veto, ward off; SEE CONCEPTS **25,30,121**

exclusion [n] *expulsion; forbiddance*
ban, bar, blackball*, blockade, boycott, coventry, cut, debarment, debarring, discharge, dismissal, ejection, elimination, embargo, eviction, exception, excommunication, interdict, interdicting, interdiction, keeping out, lockout, nonadmission, occlusion, omission, ostracism, ousting, preclusion, prevention, prohibition, proscription, refusal, rejection, relegation, removal, repudiation, segregation, separation, suspension, veto; SEE CONCEPTS **25,30,121**

exclusive [adj] *unshared, restricted*
absolute, aloof, aristocratic, chic, choice, chosen, circumscribed, clannish, classy, cliquish, closed, complete, confined, country club, discriminative, elegant, entire, exclusionary, exclusory, fashionable, full, independent, licensed, limited, narrow, only, particular, peculiar, posh, preferential, private, privileged, prohibitive, restrictive, ritzy, segregated, select, selfish, single, snobbish, socially correct, sole, swank, total, undivided, unique, upper crust*, whole; SEE CONCEPTS **554,567**

exclusively [adv] *particularly*
alone, but, completely, entirely, one and only, onliest, only, singularly, solely, wholly; SEE CONCEPT **554**

exclusive of [prep] *except for*
aside from, bar, barring, bating, besides, but, debarring, excepting, excluding, leaving aside, not counting, omitting, outside of, restricting, ruling out, save; SEE CONCEPT **554**

excogitate [v] *think about seriously*
conceive, consider, contemplate, contrive, deliberate, derive, develop, devise, educe, evolve, frame, invent, mind, mull over, perpend, ponder, ruminate, study, think out, think up, weigh, work out; SEE CONCEPTS **17,24**

excommunicate [v] *banish*
anathematize, ban, cast out, curse, denounce, dismiss, eject, exclude, expel, oust, proscribe, re-

move, repudiate, unchurch; SEE CONCEPTS 317,367

excoriate [v1] *scrape layers off*
abrade, chafe, flay, fret, gall, peel, rub, scarify, scratch, skin, strip; SEE CONCEPTS 211,215

excoriate [v2] *denounce, criticize*
attack, berate, blister, castigate, censure, chastise, condemn, flay, lambaste, lash, rebuke, reproach, reprove, revile, scathe, scold, scorch, slash, tear into, upbraid, vilify; SEE CONCEPT 52

excrete [v] *discharge, usually liquified substance*
defecate, egest, ejaculate, eject, eliminate, emanate, evacuate, exhale, expel, exudate, exude, give off, leak, pass, perspire, produce, remove, secrete, sweat, throw off, urinate, void; SEE CONCEPTS 179,185

excruciating [adj] *torturous, painful*
acute, agonizing, burning, chastening, consuming, exquisite, extreme, grueling, harrowing, insufferable, intense, piercing, punishing, racking, rending, searing, severe, sharp, shooting, stabbing, tearing, tormenting, torturesome, torturing, unbearable, unendurable, violent; SEE CONCEPTS 314,548,609

exculpate [v] *forgive*
absolve, acquit, amnesty, clear, condone, discharge, disculpate, dismiss, excuse, exonerate, explain, free, justify, let off*, pardon, rationalize, release, remit, vindicate, wipe slate clean*; SEE CONCEPTS 10,127,317

excursion [n] *journey*
circuit, cruise, day trip, digression, expedition, jaunt, junket, outing, picnic, pleasure trip, ramble, round trip, safari, tour, trek, trip, walk, wandering; SEE CONCEPTS 224,384

excusable [adj] *allowable*
all right, condonable, defensible, exculpatory, explainable, fair, forgivable, justifiable, minor, moderate, not too bad*, okay, pardonable, passable, permissible, plausible, reasonable, remittable, reprievable, slight, specious, temperate, tenable, trivial, understandable, venial, vindicable, vindicatory, warrantable, within limits; SEE CONCEPT 558

excuse [n] *reason, explanation*
alibi, apology, cleanup*, cop-out*, cover*, cover story*, coverup, defense, disguise, evasion, expedient, extenuation, fish story*, grounds, jive*, justification, makeshift, mitigation, plea, pretext, rationalization, regrets, routine, semblance, shift, song*, song and dance*, stall, stopgap*, story, substitute, subterfuge, trick*, vindication, whitewash*, why and wherefore*; SEE CONCEPTS 59,661

excuse [v] *forgive, absolve; justify*
acquit, alibi, apologize for, appease, bear with, clear, condone, cover, defend, discharge, dispense from, exculpate, exempt, exempt from, exonerate, explain, extenuate, forgive, free, give absolution, grant amnesty, indulge, let off*, liberate, make allowances for, mitigate, overlook, pardon, pass over*, plead ignorance, pretext, purge, rationalize, release, relieve, remit, reprieve, shrive, shrug off*, spare, take rap for*, tolerate, vindicate, whitewash*, wink at*; SEE CONCEPTS 10,57,83

execrable [adj] *horrible, sickening*
abhorrent, abominable, accursed, atrocious, confounded, cursed, damnable, defective, deplorable, despicable, detestable, disgusting, foul, hateful,

heinous, horrific, loathsome, low, monstrous, nauseous, obnoxious, odious, offensive, repulsive, revolting, vile, wretched; SEE CONCEPT 542

execrate [v] *hate*
abhor, abominate, accurse, anathematize, censure, condemn, curse, damn, denounce, deplore, despise, detest, excoriate, imprecate, loathe, objurgate, reprehend, reprobate, reprove, revile, vilify; SEE CONCEPT 29

execration [n] *hating*
abhorrence, abomination, anathema, blasphemy, condemnation, contempt, curse, cursing, cussing, damnation, denunciation, detestation, detesting, excoriation, hatred, imprecation, loathing, malediction, odium, profanity, swearing, vilification; SEE CONCEPT 29

execute [v1] *kill*
assassinate, behead, bump off*, do in*, electrocute, eliminate, finish, gas, guillotine, hang, knock off*, liquidate, murder, purge, put away*, put to death, shoot; SEE CONCEPT 252

execute [v2] *carry out a task*
accomplish, achieve, act, administer, administrate, bring off, bring to fruition, cause, come through, complete, consummate, deal with, discharge, do, do the job*, do the trick*, do to a T*, earn wings*, effect, enact, enforce, finish, fulfill, get there*, govern, hack it*, hit*, implement, make it*, meet, percolate*, perform, play, polish off*, prosecute, pull off*, put into effect, put over*, put through, realize, render, sail through*, score*, take care of, take care of business*, transact; SEE CONCEPTS 91,706

execution [n1] *killing*
beheading, capital punishment, contract killing*, crucifixion, decapitation, electrocution, gassing, guillotining, hanging, hit, impalement, lethal injection, necktie party*, punishment, rub out*, shooting, strangling, strangulation; SEE CONCEPT 252

execution [n2] *carrying out of a task*
accomplishment, achievement, administration, completion, consummation, delivery, discharge, doing, effect, enactment, enforcement, fulfilling, implementation, nuts and bolts*, operation, performance, prosecution, realization, rendering, style; SEE CONCEPTS 91,706

executive [n] *person who manages an organization*
administration, administrator, big wheel*, boss, brass, businessperson, CEO*, chief, CO*, commander, director, directorate, entrepreneur, exec*, government, governor, head, head honcho*, head person*, heavyweight*, hierarchy, higher-up*, industrialist, key player*, leader, leadership, management, manager, officer, official, skipper*, supervisor, top brass*, tycoon, VIP*; SEE CONCEPTS 347,354

executive [adj] *administrative*
controlling, decision-making, directing, governing, managerial, managing, ruling; SEE CONCEPT 527

exemplar [n] *ideal*
archetype, copy, criterion, epitome, example, exemplification, illustration, instance, mirror, model, paradigm, paragon, pattern, prototype, specimen, standard, type; SEE CONCEPT 686

exemplary [adj] *ideal*
admirable, batting a thousand*, blameless, bueno*, characteristic, classic, classical, commendable, correct, estimable, excellent, good,

guiltless, honorable, illustrative, inculpable, innocent, irreprehensible, laudable, meritorious, model, neato*, not bad*, not too shabby*, paradigmatic, praiseworthy, prototypical, punctilious, pure, quintessential, representative, righteous, sterling, typical, virtuous, worthy; SEE CONCEPTS 404,572,574

exemplify [v] *serve as an example*
body, cite, clarify, clear up, demonstrate, depict, display, elucidate, emblematize, embody, enlighten, epitomize, evidence, exhibit, illuminate, illustrate, instance, manifest, mirror, personify, quote, represent, show, spell out, symbolize, typify; SEE CONCEPTS 97,118

exempt [adj] *freed from responsibility*
absolved, beat the rap*, clear, cleared, discharged, excepted, excluded, excused, favored, free, immune, let go*, let off*, liberated, not liable, not responsible, not subject, off the hook*, outside, privileged, released, set apart, spared, special, unbound, unchecked, unrestrained, unrestricted, unshackled, void of, walked*; SEE CONCEPTS 319,554

exempt [v] *relieve, absolve*
clear, discharge, dispense, except, excuse, exonerate, free, go easy on*, grant immunity, let off*, let off the hook*, liberate, pass by, privilege from, release, spare, wipe the slate*, write off; SEE CONCEPTS 50,83,88,127

exemption [n] *freedom from a responsibility*
absolution, discharge, dispensation, exception, exoneration, immunity, impunity, privilege, release; SEE CONCEPTS 652,685,691

exercise [n1] *work, effort*
act, action, activity, calisthenics, constitutional*, daily dozen*, discharge, discipline, drill, drilling, examination, exercising, exertion, gym, labor, lesson, movement, occupation, operation, performance, problem, pursuit, recitation, schoolwork, study, task, test, theme, toil, training, warm-up, workout; SEE CONCEPTS 87,290,362,363

exercise [n2] *accomplishment, use*
application, discharge, employment, enjoyment, exertion, fulfillment, implementation, operation, performance, practice, pursuit, utilization; SEE CONCEPTS 225,706

exercise [v1] *put to use*
apply, bestow, bring to bear, devote, drill, employ, enjoy, execute, exert, exploit, handle, operate, practice, put into practice, rehearse, sharpen, use, utilize, wield; SEE CONCEPT 225

exercise [v2] *do repeatedly, especially to improve*
break, break in, condition, cultivate, develop, discipline, drill, dry run*, exert, fix, foster, groom, habituate, hone, improve, inure, labor, lick into shape*, limber up, loosen up, maneuver, ply, practice, prepare, pump iron*, put out, put through grind*, put through mill*, rehearse, run through, set, strain, teach, train, tune up, walk through, warm up, work, work out; SEE CONCEPTS 87,363

exercise [v3] *upset, worry*
abrade, afflict, agitate, annoy, bother, burden, chafe, distress, disturb, gall, irk, occupy, pain, perturb, preoccupy, provoke, trouble, try, vex; SEE CONCEPTS 7,19

exert [v] *make use of*
apply, apply oneself, bring into play*, bring to bear*, dig*, employ, endeavor, exercise, expend, give all one's got*, give best shot*, labor, make

effort, peg away*, plug*, ply, pour it on*, push, put forth, put out, strain, strive, struggle, sweat it*, throw, toil, try hard, use, utilize, wield, work; SEE CONCEPTS 87,225

exertion [n] *hard work*
action, activity, application, attempt, effort, elbow grease*, employment, endeavor, exercise, hard pull*, industry, labor, long pull*, operation, pains, strain, stretch, striving, struggle, toil, travail, trial, trouble, use, utilization; SEE CONCEPTS 87,362,677

exhale [v] *breathe out*
breathe, discharge, eject, emanate, emit, evaporate, expel, give off, issue, let out, respire, steam, vaporize; SEE CONCEPT 163

exhaust [v1] *tire or wear out*
bankrupt, burn out*, conk out*, cripple, debilitate, disable, do in*, drain, draw, enervate, enfeeble, fag, fatigue, frazzle, impoverish, overdo, overexert, overextend, overfatigue, overtire, overwork, peter out*, poop*, poop out*, prostrate, run ragged*, sap*, suck dry*, tucker*, use up, weaken, wear down, weary; SEE CONCEPTS 250,469

exhaust [v2] *consume, use up*
bankrupt, bleed dry*, deplete, devour, dispel, disperse, dissipate, drain, draw, dry, eat, eat up*, empty, expend, finish, impoverish, run out, run through, spend, squander, strain, suck dry*, take last of, void, wash up, waste; SEE CONCEPTS 169,225

exhausted [adj1] *extremely tired*
all in*, beat*, bleary, bone-weary, bushed, crippled, dead*, dead tired*, debilitated, disabled, dog-tired*, done for*, done in*, drained, effete, enervated, frazzled, had it*, kaput*, limp, out on one's feet*, outta gas*, prostrated, ready to drop*, run-down, sapped*, short*, spent, tired out, wasted*, weak, weakened, wearied, worn, worn out; SEE CONCEPTS 406,485

exhausted [adj2] *used up*
all gone, at an end, bare, consumed, depleted, dissipated, done, drained, dry, empty, expended, finished, gone, spent, squandered, void, washed-out, wasted; SEE CONCEPTS 560,771

exhaustion [n] *tiredness*
burnout*, collapse, consumption, debilitation, debility, enervation, expenditure, fatigue, feebleness, lassitude, prostration, weariness; SEE CONCEPTS 410,720

exhaustive [adj] *all-inclusive, complete*
all-embracing, all-encompassing, all-out, catholic, comprehensive, embracive, encyclopedic, extensive, far-reaching, from A to Z*, full, full-blown, full-dress*, full-scale, in-depth, intensive, no stone unturned*, out-and-out*, profound, radical, sweeping, the word, thorough, thoroughgoing, total, whole-hog*; SEE CONCEPTS 531,772

exhibit [n] *viewing; presentation*
display, exhibition, exposition, fair, illustration, model, performance, show; SEE CONCEPTS 259,261

exhibit [v] *put on view; present*
advertise, air, brandish, demonstrate, disclose, display, disport, evidence, evince, expose, express, feature, flash, flaunt, illustrate, indicate, let it all hang out*, make clear, make plain, manifest, mark, offer, ostend, parade, parade wares*, proclaim, reveal, roll out, show, show and tell*,

exhibition [n] showing, demonstration
advertisement, airing, an act*, a scene*, carnival, display, exhibit, expo, exposition, fair, fireworks, flash*, front*, manifestation, offering, pageant, performance, presentation, representation, show, sight, spectacle; SEE CONCEPTS 261,386

exhilarate [v] make very happy
animate, boost, buoy, cheer, commove, delight, elate, enliven, exalt, excite, gladden, inspire, inspirit, invigorate, juice*, lift, pep up*, perk up*, pick up, put zip into*, quicken, rejoice, send, snap up*, stimulate, thrill, turn on*, uplift, vitalize; SEE CONCEPTS 7,22

exhilarating [adj] stimulating, cheering
animating, animative, bracing, breathtaking, electric, elevating, enlivening, exalting, exciting, exhilarant, exhilarative, exhilaratory, eye-popping*, gladdening, inspiring, inspiriting, intoxicating, invigorating, quickening, rousing, stimulative, stirring, thrilling, tonic, uplifting, vitalizing; SEE CONCEPTS 529,548

exhilaration [n] great happiness, excitement
animation, a rush*, cheerfulness, delight, elation, electrification, elevation, enlivenment, euphoria, exaltation, excitation, firing, gaiety, galvanization, gladness, gleefulness, head rush*, high spirits*, hilarity, inspiration, invigoration, joy, joyfulness, liveliness, mirth, quickening, sprightliness, stimulation, uplift, vitalization, vivacity, vivification; SEE CONCEPT 410

exhort [v] urge, warn
admonish, advise, beseech, bid, call upon, caution, counsel, egg on*, encourage, enjoin, entreat, goad, incite, insist, persuade, plead, preach, press, pressure, prick, prod, prompt, propel, spur, stimulate; SEE CONCEPTS 75,78

exhortation [n] warning, urging
admonition, advice, beseeching, bidding, caution, counsel, encouragement, enjoinder, entreaty, goading, incitement, instigation, lecture, persuasion, preaching, sermon; SEE CONCEPTS 75,78,274

exhume [v] dig up, especially the dead
disclose, disembalm, disentomb, disinhume, disinter, resurrect, reveal, unbury, uncharnel, unearth; SEE CONCEPT 178

exigency/exigence [n] difficulty; demand
acuteness, constraint, contingency, crisis, criticalness, crossroad, demandingness, dilemma, distress, duress, emergency, extremity, fix, hardship, imperativeness, jam, juncture, necessity, need, needfulness, pass, pickle*, pinch, plight, predicament, pressingness, pressure, quandary, requirement, scrape*, stress, turning point*, urgency, vicissitude, want, wont, zero hour*; SEE CONCEPTS 646,674,709

exigent [adj1] urgent, pressing
acute, burning, clamant, clamorous, constraining, critical, crucial, crying, imperative, importunate, insistent, instant, menacing, necessary, needful, threatening; SEE CONCEPTS 548,568

exigent [adj2] difficult, taxing
arduous, burdensome, demanding, exacting, grievous, hard, harsh, onerous, oppressive, rigorous, severe, stiff, strict, stringent, supincumbent, tough, weighty; SEE CONCEPTS 537,542

exiguous [adj] scanty
bare, confined, diminutive, inadequate, limited, little, meager, narrow, negligible, paltry, petty, poor, restricted, skimpy, slender, slight, small, spare, sparse, tenuous, thin, tiny; SEE CONCEPTS 771,789

exile [n1] deportation from a place
banishment, diaspora, dispersion, displacement, exclusion, expatriation, expulsion, extradition, migration, ostracism, proscription, relegation, scattering, separation; SEE CONCEPT 298

exile [n2] person deported from a place
deportee, displaced person, DP*, émigré, expatriate, expellee, fugitive, nonperson*, outcast, outlaw, person without country*, refugee; SEE CONCEPTS 354,412,423

exile [v] deport from place
banish, cast out, displace, dispossess, drive out, eject, evacuate, expatriate, expel, expulse, extradite, ostracize, oust, outlaw, proscribe, relegate, transport, turn out; SEE CONCEPTS 122,198,298

exist [v1] be living
abide, be, be extant, be latent, be present, breathe, continue, endure, happen, last, lie, live, move, obtain, occur, prevail, remain, stand, stay, subsist, survive; SEE CONCEPT 407

exist [v2] get along in life
consist, dwell, eke out a living*, endure, get by*, go on, inhere, kick*, lie, live, make it*, reside, stay alive*, subsist, survive; SEE CONCEPTS 100,226

existence [n] life
actuality, animation, being, breath, continuance, continuation, duration, endurance, entity, essence, hand one is dealt*, individuality, journey, lifing, permanence, perseverance, presence, rat race*, reality, real world*, something, subsistence, survival, the big game*, world; SEE CONCEPTS 407,639

exit [n1] way out of a place
avenue, door, egress, fire escape, gate, hole, opening, outlet, passage out, vent; SEE CONCEPT 440

exit [n2] leaving
adieu, death, demise, departure, egress, egression, evacuation, exodus, expiry, farewell, going, goodbye, leave-taking, offgoing, retirement, retreat, stampede, withdrawal; SEE CONCEPT 195

exit [v] leave a place
bid farewell, blow*, depart, do vanishing act*, flake off*, get*, get away, get off, git*, go, go away, go out, issue, move, move out, quit, retire, retreat, say goodbye, split*, take a hike*, take one's leave*, withdraw; SEE CONCEPT 195

exodus [n] leaving
departure, egress, egression, emigration, evacuation, exit, exiting, flight, going out, journey, migration, offgoing, retirement, retreat, withdrawal; SEE CONCEPT 195

exonerate [v] excuse, clear of responsibility or blame
absolve, acquit, disburden, discharge, dismiss, except, exculpate, exempt, free, justify, let off*, let off hook*, liberate, pardon, release, relieve, sanitize, vindicate, whitewash*, wipe slate clean*; SEE CONCEPTS 10,127,317

exorbitant [adj] extravagant, excessive
absonant, dear, enormous, exacting, expensive, extortionate, extreme, high, highway robbery*, immoderate, inordinate, out of sight*, outrageous, overboard, overmuch, over one's head*, prepos-

terous, pricey, steep*, stiff*, towering, unconscionable, undue, unreasonable, unwarranted, up to here*, wasteful; SEE CONCEPTS *334,547,558*

exotic [adj] *not native or usual; mysterious*
alien, alluring, avant garde, bizarre, colorful, curious, different, enticing, external, extraneous, extraordinary, extrinsic, far out*, fascinating, foreign, glamorous, imported, introduced, kinky*, outlandish, outside, peculiar, peregrine, romantic, strange, striking, unfamiliar, unusual, way out*, weird*; SEE CONCEPTS *542,549*

expand [v1] *extend, augment*
aggrandize, amplify, beef up*, bloat, blow up*, bolster, broaden, bulk up*, burgeon, detail, develop, diffuse, dilate, distend, elaborate, embellish, enlarge, explicate, fan out*, fatten, fill out, grow, heighten, hike, increase, inflate, lengthen, magnify, mount, multiply, mushroom, open, open out, outspread, pad, piggyback*, prolong, protract, puff up*, pyramid*, slap on*, soup up*, spread, spread out, stretch, stretch out, swell, tack on*, thicken, unfold, unfurl, unravel, unroll, upsurge, wax*, widen; SEE CONCEPTS *236,245*

expand [v2] *go into detail*
amplify, beef up*, build up, develop, dilate, discourse, drag out*, elaborate, embellish, enlarge, expatiate, expound, extend, flesh out*, spell out, sweeten; SEE CONCEPT *57*

expanse [n] *large space, usually open*
amplitude, area, belt, breadth, compass, distance, domain, extension, extent, field, immensity, latitude, length, margin, orbit, plain, radius, range, reach, region, remoteness, room, scope, span, sphere, spread, stretch, sweep, territory, tract, uninterrupted space, width, wilderness; SEE CONCEPTS *509,513,651,788*

expansion [n] *growth*
amplification, augmentation, breadth, development, diffusion, dilation, distance, distension, enlargement, evolution, expanse, extension, increase, inflation, magnification, maturation, multiplication, opening out, space, spread, stretch, swelling, unfolding, unfurling; SEE CONCEPTS *700,704,780*

expansive [adj1] *broad, comprehensive*
all-embracing, ample, big, dilatant, elastic, expanding, expansile, extensive, far-reaching, great, inclusive, large, scopic, scopious, stretching, thorough, unrepressed, unsuppressed, voluminous, wide, wide-ranging, widespread; SEE CONCEPT *772*

expansive [adj2] *talkative*
affable, communicative, demonstrative, easy, effervescent, effusive, extroverted, free, friendly, garrulous, generous, genial, gregarious, gushy, lavish, liberal, loquacious, open, outgoing, sociable, unconstrained, uninhibited, unreserved, unrestrained, warm; SEE CONCEPT *267*

expatriate [n] *person thrown out of a country*
departer, deportee, displaced person, emigrant, émigré, evacuee, exile, expellee, migrant, outcast, refugee; SEE CONCEPTS *354,412,423*

expatriate [v] *throw out of a country*
banish, deport, displace, exile, expel, expulse, ostracize, oust, proscribe, relegate, transport; SEE CONCEPTS *130,198,211*

expect [v1] *believe strongly; anticipate*
apprehend, assume, await, bargain for, bargain on, be afraid, calculate, conjecture, contemplate, count on, divine, envisage, feel, figure, forecast,

foreknow, foresee, gather, hope, hope for, imagine, in the cards*, look, look ahead to, look for, look forward to*, predict, presume, presuppose, reckon, see coming*, sense, suppose, surmise, suspect, take, think, trust, understand, wait for, watch for; SEE CONCEPTS *12,26*

expect [v2] *want, wish*
call for, count on, demand, exact, insist on, look for, rely upon, require; SEE CONCEPT *20*

expectancy [n] *anticipation*
assumption, assurance, belief, calculation, confidence, conjecture, expectation, hope, likelihood, looking forward, outlook, prediction, presentation, presentiment, presumption, probability, prospect, reliance, supposition, surmise, suspense, trust, view, waiting; SEE CONCEPTS *410,689*

expectant [adj1] *anticipating*
alert, anticipative, anxious, apprehensive, awaiting, breathless, eager, expecting, hopeful, hoping, in suspense, looking for, on edge*, on tenterhooks*, prepared, raring*, ready, vigilant, waiting, waiting on, watchful, with bated breath*; SEE CONCEPTS *403,406*

expectant [adj2] *preparing to give birth*
enceinte, expecting, gravid, parturient, pregnant, with child*; SEE CONCEPT *485*

expectation [n] *belief, anticipation*
apprehension, assumption, assurance, calculation, chance, confidence, conjecture, design, expectancy, fear, forecast, hope, intention, likelihood, looking forward, motive, notion, outlook, possibility, prediction, presumption, probability, promise, prospect, reliance, supposition, surmise, suspense, trust, view; SEE CONCEPTS *410,689*

expediency/expedience [n1] *appropriateness; worth*
advantage, advantageousness, advisability, appositeness, aptness, benefit, convenience, desirability, effectiveness, efficiency, fitness, helpfulness, judiciousness, meetness, opportunism, opportunity, order, policy, practicality, pragmatism, profitability, profitableness, properness, propitiousness, propriety, prudence, rightness, suitability, usefulness, utilitarianism, utility; SEE CONCEPTS *656,658*

expediency/expedience [n2] *resource*
band-aid*, contrivance, design, device, dodge, easy way out*, gimmick*, makeshift*, maneuver, means, measure, method, recourse, resort, scheme, shift, step, stopgap*, stratagem, strategy, substitute, surrogate, tactic, trick; SEE CONCEPTS *660,712*

expedient [n] *resource*
agency, contrivance, device, instrument, instrumentality, makeshift, maneuver, means, measure, medium, method, recourse, refuge, resort, scheme, shift, stopgap, stratagem, substitute; SEE CONCEPTS *660,712*

expedient [adj] *worthwhile, appropriate*
ad hoc, advantageous, advisable, beneficial, convenient, desirable, discreet, effective, feasible, fit, fitting, helpful, judicious, meet, opportune, politic, possible, practicable, practical, pragmatic, profitable, proper, prudent, seasonable, suitable, tactical, timely, useful, utilitarian, wise; SEE CONCEPTS *558,560*

expedite [v] *make happen faster*
accelerate, advance, assist, cut the red tape*, dispatch, facilitate, fast track*, forward, grease

wheels*, hand-carry, handle personally, hand-walk*, hasten, hurry, precipitate, press, promote, quicken, railroad*, run interference*, run with the ball*, rush, shoot through*, speed, speed up, urge, walk it through*; SEE CONCEPT 242

expedition [nl] *journey; people on a journey*
campaign, caravan, cavalcade, company, crew, crowd, cruise, crusade, enterprise, entrada, excursion, exploration, explorers, fleet, jaunt, junket, mission, outing, party, patrol, peregrination, picnic, posse, quest, safari, squadron, swing, team, tour, travel, travellers, trek, trip, undertaking, voyage, voyagers, wayfarers; SEE CONCEPTS 224,417

expedition [n2] *speed; speeding up*
alacrity, celerity, dispatch, expeditiousness, goodwill, haste, hurry, hustle, promptitude, promptness, punctuality, quickness, rapidity, readiness, swiftness; SEE CONCEPTS 242,755

expeditious [adj] *immediate, speedy*
active, alert, breakneck, brisk, diligent, effective, effectual, efficient, fast, fleet, hasty, instant, nimble, prompt, punctual, quick, rapid, ready, swift; SEE CONCEPTS 542,588

expel [vl] *discharge*
belch, blow out, cast out, disgorge, dislodge, drive out, ejaculate, eruct, erupt, evacuate, exhaust, exudate, exude, get rid of, irrupt, pass, remove, spew, throw out, vomit; SEE CONCEPT 179

expel [v2] *throw out, banish*
ban, bar, blackball*, bust, cast out, chase, deport, discharge, dismiss, displace, dispossess, drum out, eject, eliminate, evict, exclude, exile, expatriate, expulse, fire, give the boot*, give the hook*, give walking papers*, kick out, oust, proscribe, send packing*, show the door*, suspend, throw out on ear*, turn out; SEE CONCEPTS 122,130,198

expend [v] *exhaust; spend*
ante up*, blow*, consume, disburse, dish out*, dispense, dissipate, distribute, employ, finish, foot the bill*, fork out*, give, go through*, lay out, outlay, pay, pay out, put out*, shell out*, splurge*, spring for*, throw money at*, use up, wash up*; SEE CONCEPTS 225,341

expendable [adj] *not important*
dispensable, disposable, excess, inessential, nonessential, replaceable, superfluous, unimportant; SEE CONCEPTS 546,575

expenditure [n] *payment*
amount, application, bottom line*, cash on barrelhead*, charge, come to*, consumption, cost, disbursement, dissipation, expense, figure, investment, kickback*, outgo, outlay, output, payoff, price, rate, setback*, spending, splurge, squander, throw*, tune*, use, valuation, value, waste; SEE CONCEPT 344

expense [n] *cost, payment*
amount, assessment, bite*, bottom line*, budget, charge, consumption, debit, debt, decrement, deprivation, disbursement, duty, expenditure, forfeit, forfeiture, insurance, investment, liability, loan, loss, mortgage, obligation, outdo*, outlay, out of pocket*, output, overhead, payroll, price, price tag, rate, responsibility, risk, sacrifice, spending, sum, surcharge, tariff, toll, upkeep, use, value, worth; SEE CONCEPTS 328,329,336,344

expensive [adj] *high-priced*
an arm and a leg*, at a premium, big-ticket*,

costly, dear, excessive, exorbitant, extravagant, fancy, high, highway robbery*, holdup*, immoderate, inordinate, invaluable, lavish, out of sight*, overpriced, plush, posh, pretty penny*, pricey*, rich, ritzy*, sky-high*, steep*, stiff*, swank*, too high, uneconomical, unreasonable, upscale*, valuable; SEE CONCEPT 334

experience [nl] *knowledge*
acquaintance, action, actuality, background, caution, combat, contact, doing, empiricism, evidence, existence, exposure, familiarity, forebearance, intimacy, involvement, inwardness, judgment, know-how*, maturity, observation, participation, patience, perspicacity, practicality, practice, proof, reality, savoir-faire, seasoning, sense, skill, sophistication, strife, struggle, training, trial, understanding, wisdom, worldliness; SEE CONCEPT 409

experience [n2] *happening, occurrence*
adventure, affair, encounter, episode, event, incident, ordeal, test, trial, trip; SEE CONCEPTS 2,696

experienced [adj] *knowledgeable, knowing*
accomplished, accustomed, adept, been around*, been there*, broken in*, capable, competent, cultivated, dynamite, expert, familiar, having something on the ball*, instructed, in the know*, knowing one's stuff*, knowing the score*, matured, old, old hand*, practical, practiced, pro, professional, qualified, rounded, seasoned, skillful, sophisticated, sport, tested, the right stuff*, trained, tried, versed, vet, veteran, well-versed, wise, worldly, worldly-wise*; SEE CONCEPTS 402,527

experiment [n] *investigation, test*
agreement, analysis, assay, attempt, check, dissection, dry run*, enterprise, essay, examination, exercise, experimentation, fling*, measure, observation, operation, practice, probe, procedure, proof, quiz, R and D*, rehearsal, research, research and development, scrutiny, search, speculation, study, trial, trial and error*, trial run*, try, try-on, tryout, undertaking, venture, verification; SEE CONCEPTS 103,290

experiment [v] *investigate, test*
analyze, assay, diagnose, examine, explore, fool with*, futz around*, mess around*, play around with*, practice with, probe, prove, put to the test*, research, sample, scrutinize, search, shake down*, speculate, study, try, try on, try on for size*, try out, venture, verify, weigh; SEE CONCEPTS 24,87,103

experimental [adj] *exploratory*
beginning, developmental, empirical, experiential, first stage, laboratory, momentary, on approval, pilot, preliminary, preparatory, primary, probationary, provisional, speculative, temporary, tentative, test, trial, trial-and-error, unconcluded, under probation, unproved; SEE CONCEPT 535

expert [n] *master, specialist*
ace*, adept, artist, artiste, authority, buff, connoisseur, doyen, graduate, guru*, hot shot*, old hand*, old pro*, phenomenon, pro, professional, proficient, shark*, virtuoso, whiz*, wizard; SEE CONCEPTS 348,350,416

expert [adj] *knowledgeable, proficient*
able, adept, adroit, apt, big league*, clever, crack, crackerjack*, deft, dexterous, experienced, facile, handy, practiced, professional, qualified, savvy, schooled, sharp, skilled, skillful, slick, trained, virtuoso; SEE CONCEPTS 402,527

expertise/expertness [n] *knowledge, proficiency*
ability, ableness, adroitness, aptness, art, cleverness, command, competence, craft, cunning, deftness, dexterity, dodge*, facility, finesse, goods*, ingeniousness, judgment, knack*, know-how*, line*, makings*, oil*, one's thing*, prowess, readiness, savvy, sharpness, skill, skillfulness, stuff*; SEE CONCEPTS 409,630

expiate [v] *make amends for*
absolve, amend, appease, atone, atone for, compensate, correct, do penance, excuse, forgive, pay one's dues*, rectify, redeem, redress, remedy, square things*; SEE CONCEPTS 67,126

expiration [n] *finish, demise*
cessation, close, closing, conclusion, death, decease, departure, dying, elapsing, end, expiry, going, passing, termination, terminus; SEE CONCEPTS 119,304

expire [v1] *come to an end*
bite the dust*, buy it*, cash in chips*, cease, close, conclude, croak*, decease, depart, die, elapse, end, finish, go, kick the bucket*, lapse, pass, pass away, pass on, pass over, perish, quit, run out, stop, strike out*, terminate, up and die*; SEE CONCEPTS 119,304

expire [v2] *breathe out*
emit, exhale, expel; SEE CONCEPTS 163,185

explain [v] *make clear; give a reason for*
account for, analyze, annotate, break down, bring out, clarify, clear up, construe, decipher, define, demonstrate, describe, diagram, disclose, elucidate, excuse, explicate, expound, get across*, go into detail, illustrate, interpret, justify, make plain*, manifest, paraphrase, point out, put across, put in plain English*, rationalize, read, refine, render, resolve, reveal, set right, solve, spell out*, teach, tell, throw light upon*, translate, unfold, unravel, untangle; SEE CONCEPT 57

explanation [n] *clarification; reason*
account, annotation, answer, breakdown, brief, cause, comment, commentary, confession, definition, demonstration, description, details, display, elucidation, evidence, example, excuse, explication, exposition, expression, gloss, history, illustration, information, interpretation, justification, meaning, mitigation, motive, narration, note, recital, rendition, report, resolution, sense, showing, significance, specification, statement, story, summary, tale, talking, telling, vindication, writing; SEE CONCEPTS 271,274,661

explanatory [adj] *descriptive*
allegorical, analytical, annotative, critical, declarative, demonstrative, diagrammatic, discursive, elucidatory, enlightening, exegetic, exegetical, explicative, expositional, expository, graphic, guiding, hermeneutic, illuminative, illustrative, informative, informing, instructive, interpretive, justifying, summary, supplementary; SEE CONCEPT 267

expletive [n] *swear word; exclamation*
curse, cuss, cuss word, interjection, oath; SEE CONCEPT 275

explicate [v] *clarify, expand*
amplify, clear up, construe, demonstrate, develop, dilate, elucidate, enlarge upon, enucleate, expatiate, explain, expound, give the big picture*, illustrate, interpret, make clear, make explicit, make plain*, run down, spell out*, tell why, unfold, untangle, work out; SEE CONCEPT 57

explicit [adj] *specific, unambiguous*
absolute, accurate, categorical, certain, clean-cut, clear, clear-cut, correct, definite, definitive, direct, distinct, exact, express, frank, lucid, obvious, on the nose*, open, outspoken, patent, perspicuous, plain, positive, precise, stated, straightforward, sure, understandable, unequivocal, unqualified, unreserved; SEE CONCEPTS 267,529,535

explode [v1] *blow up*
backfire, blast, blaze, blow to kingdom come*, break out, burst, collapse, convulse, detonate, discharge, erupt, flame up, flare up, fracture, jet, kablooey*, let go*, mushroom*, rupture, set off, shatter, shiver, split, thunder; SEE CONCEPTS 179,320

explode [v2] *discredit*
belie, confute, debunk, deflate, discard, disprove, invalidate, puncture, refute, repudiate, shoot down*, shoot full of holes*; SEE CONCEPT 54

exploit [n] *achievement*
accomplishment, adventure, attainment, coup, deed, do, effort, enterprise, escapade, feat, job, maneuver, performance, stroke, stunt, tour de force, venture; SEE CONCEPT 706

exploit [v] *take advantage of; misuse*
abuse, apply, avail oneself of, bleed*, capitalize on, cash in on*, employ, exercise, finesse, fleece*, get mileage out of*, handle, impose upon, jockey*, make capital of, make use of, maneuver, manipulate, milk*, mine*, play*, play on, profit by, profit from, put to use, skin*, soak*, stick*, use, utilize, work; SEE CONCEPTS 156,225

exploration [n] *investigation; survey*
analysis, examination, expedition, inquiry, inspection, probe, reconnaissance, research, scrutiny, search, study, tour, travel, trip; SEE CONCEPTS 216,224

explore [v] *investigate; survey*
analyze, burrow, delve into, dig into, examine, go into*, have a look*, hunt, inquire into, inspect, leave no stone unturned*, look into, probe, prospect, question, reconnoitre, research, scout, scrutinize, search, seek, sift, test, tour, travel, traverse, try, turn inside out*; SEE CONCEPTS 103,216,224

explosion [n] *eruption, discharge*
access, backfire, bang, blast, blowout, blowup, burst, clap, combustion, concussion, crack, detonation, firing, fit, flare-up, fulmination, gust, ignition, outbreak, outburst, paroxysm, percussion, pop, report, roar, salvo; SEE CONCEPTS 179,320,521

explosive [n] *something that blows up*
ammunition, bomb, booby trap*, charge, detonator, dynamite, fireworks, grease*, grenade, gunpowder, mine, missile, mulligan, munition, nitroglycerin, pineapple*, powder, propellant, shell, shot, soup*, TNT*; SEE CONCEPT 500

explosive [adj] *volatile, dangerous*
at the boiling point*, bursting, charged, consequential, convulsive, detonating, detonative, ebullient, eruptive, fiery, forceful, frenzied, fulminant, fulminating, hazardous, impetuous, meteoric, overwrought, perilous, raging, rampant, stormy, tense, touchy, ugly, uncontrollable, unstable, vehement, violent, wild; SEE CONCEPT 542

exponent [n1] *person who supports, advocates*
backer, booster, champion, defender, demonstrator, expositor, expounder, interpreter, partisan,

promoter, propagandist, proponent, protagonist, second, seconder, spokesperson, supporter, upholder; SEE CONCEPT *423*

exponent [n2] *example*
denotation, exemplar, illustration, index, indication, model, representative, sample, sign, specimen, token, type; SEE CONCEPTS *284,686*

export [v] *sell or trade abroad*
consign, convey, dump, find market, find outlet, freight, send out, ship, smuggle, transport, transship; SEE CONCEPTS *217,324*

exposé [n] *disclosure*
betrayal, confession, construction, divulgence, exegesis, explanation, explication, exposal, exposition, exposure, interpretation, revelation, truth, uncovering; SEE CONCEPT *274*

expose [v1] *reveal*
advertise, air, bare, betray, brandish, bring to light*, broadcast, crack, debunk, denude, dig up*, disclose, display, disport, divulge, exhibit, feature, flash, flaunt, give away, lay bare*, lay open*, leak, let cat out of bag*, let out*, make known, manifest, open, open to view, parade, present, prove, publish, put on view, report, show, show off, smoke out*, spill, streak, tip off*, trot out*, unclothe, uncover, unearth, unfold, unmask, unshroud, unveil; SEE CONCEPTS *60,261*

expose [v2] *subject to danger*
endanger, hazard, imperil, jeopardize, lay open*, leave open*, make liable, make vulnerable, peril, put in harm's way*, risk; SEE CONCEPT *246*

exposed [adj1] *made public*
apparent, bare, bared, brought to light*, caught, clear, debunked, defined, denuded, disclosed, discovered, divulged, dug up*, evident, exhibited, for show, found out, laid bare*, made manifest, manifest, naked, on display, on the spot*, on view, open, peeled, resolved, revealed, shown, solved, stripped, unconcealed, uncovered, unhidden, unmasked, unprotected, unsealed, unsheltered, unveiled, visible; SEE CONCEPT *576*

exposed [adj2] *in danger*
accessible, in peril, laid bare*, laid open*, left open*, liable, menaced, open, prone, sensitive, subject, susceptible, threatened, unguarded, unprotected, vulnerable; SEE CONCEPTS *485,548*

exposition [n1] *written description*
account, analysis, annotation, article, comment, commentary, composition, construal, construction, critique, delineation, details, discourse, discussion, disquisition, dissertation, editorial, elucidation, enucleation, enunciation, essay, exegesis, explanation, explication, exposé, expounding, history, illustration, interpretation, monograph, paper, piece, position paper, presentation, report, review, statement, story, study, tale, text, theme, thesis, tract, tractate, treatise; SEE CONCEPTS *268,271*

exposition [n2] *fair*
bazaar, circus, county fair, demonstration, display, exhibition, expo, marketplace, mart, pageant, presentation, production, show, showing; SEE CONCEPT *386*

expository [adj] *descriptive*
critical, disquisitional, elucidative, exegetic, explanatory, explicative, explicatory, hermeneutic, illustrative, informative, interpretive; SEE CONCEPT *267*

expostulate [v] *reason with*
argue, dissuade, oppose, protest, remonstrate; SEE CONCEPT *46*

exposure [n] *uncovering; putting in view or danger*
acknowledgment, airing, baring, betrayal, confession, defenselessness, denudation, denunciation, disclosure, display, divulgence, divulging, exhibition, exposé, giveaway, hazard, introduction, jeopardy, laying open, liability, manifestation, nakedness, openness, peril, presentation, publicity, revelation, risk, showing, susceptibility, susceptiveness, susceptibility, unfolding, unmasking, unveiling, vulnerability, vulnerableness; SEE CONCEPTS *60,261*

expound [v] *talk about in great detail*
clarify, comment, construe, delineate, describe, discourse, elucidate, enucleate, exemplify, explain, explicate, express, illustrate, interpret, present, set forth, spell out, state, unfold; SEE CONCEPT *57*

express [adj1] *certain, precise*
accurate, categorical, clean-cut*, clear, clear-cut, considered, definite, definitive, deliberate, designful, direct, distinct, especial, exact, explicit, expressed, individual, intended, intentional, out-and-out*, outright, particular, plain, pointed, premeditated, set, singular, special, specific, unambiguous, unconditional, unmistakable, unqualified, uttered, voiced, voluntary, willing, witting; SEE CONCEPTS *535,556,653*

express [adj2] *direct, speedy*
accelerated, fast, high-speed, nonstop, quick, rapid, swift, velocious; SEE CONCEPTS *548,588*

express [v1] *articulate; signify, mean*
add up to*, air, assert, asseverate, bespeak, broach, circulate, communicate, connote, convey, couch, declare, denote, depict, designate, disclose, divulge, embody, enunciate, evince, exhibit, formulate, frame*, give, hint, import, indicate, insinuate, intend, intimate, make known, manifest, phrase, pop off*, proclaim, pronounce, put, put across, put into words*, represent, reveal, say, show, speak, spell, stand for, state, suggest, symbolize, tell, testify, utter, vent, ventilate, verbalize, voice, word; SEE CONCEPTS *51,682*

express [v2] *discharge by squeezing or force*
crush, dispatch, distill, expel, extract, force out, forward, press out, ship, squeeze out; SEE CONCEPT *179*

expression [n1] *verbalization*
announcement, argument, articulation, assertion, asseveration, choice of words, commentary, communication, declaration, definition, delivery, diction, elucidation, emphasis, enunciation, execution, explanation, exposition, formulation, idiom, interpretation, intonation, issue, language, locution, mention, narration, phrase, phraseology, phrasing, pronouncement, remark, rendition, set phrase, speaking, speech, statement, style, term, turn of phrase, utterance, vent, voice, voicing, word, writ; SEE CONCEPTS *47,268,276*

expression [n2] *facial appearance*
air, aspect, cast, character, contortion, countenance, face, grimace, grin, look, mien, mug*, pout*, simper, smile, smirk, sneer, visage; SEE CONCEPT *716*

expressionless [adj] *having a blank look on face*
dead*, deadpan, dull, empty, fish-eyed*, impassive, inexpressive, inscrutable, lackluster, lusterless, nobody home*, poker-faced*, stolid,

straight-faced, stupid, unexpressive, vacant, vacuous, wooden; SEE CONCEPT 406

expressive [adj] telling, revealing
alive, allusive, articulate, artistic, brilliant, colorful, demonstrative, dramatic, eloquent, emphatic, energetic, forcible, graphic, indicative, ingenious, lively, masterly, meaningful, mobile, moving, passionate, pathetic, pictorial, picturesque, poignant, pointed, pregnant, representative, responsive, revelatory, showy, significant, silver-tongued*, spirited, stimulating, stirring, striking, strong, suggestive, sympathetic, tender, thoughtful, touching, understanding, vivid, warm; SEE CONCEPTS 267,537

expressly [adv1] purposely
especially, exactly, in specie, intentionally, on purpose, particularly, precisely, specially, specifically; SEE CONCEPT 556

expressly [adv2] definitely, unambiguously
absolutely, categorically, clearly, decidedly, directly, distinctly, explicitly, in no uncertain terms*, manifestly, outright, plainly, pointedly, positively, specifically, unequivocally, unmistakably; SEE CONCEPT 535

expressway [n] large, well-travelled road
freeway, interstate, parkway, superhighway, thruway, turnpike; SEE CONCEPT 501

expropriate [v] seize
accroach, annex, appropriate, arrogate, assume, commandeer, confiscate, deprive of property, dispossess, impound, preempt, requisition, sequester, take, take over; SEE CONCEPTS 90,142

expulsion [n] banishing
banishment, boot*, bounce, debarment, deportment, discharge, dislodgment, dismissal, displacement, dispossession, driving out, ejection, eviction, exclusion, exile, expatriation, extrusion, forcing out, ostracism, ouster, ousting, proscription, purge, relegation, removal, rush, suspension; SEE CONCEPTS 130,211,298

expunge [v] destroy, obliterate
abolish, annihilate, annul, black, black out*, blot out, blue pencil*, call all bets off*, call off, cancel, cut, delete, discard, drop, efface, eradicate, erase, exclude, exterminate, extinguish, extirpate, gut, kayo*, kill, knock off*, KO*, launder*, omit, raze, remove, scrub*, strike out, take out, trim, wipe out, X out*, zap*; SEE CONCEPTS 211,252

expurgate [v] censor, cut
bleep*, bleep out*, blip*, blue pencil*, bowdlerize, cleanse, clean up, decontaminate, lustrate, purge, purify, sanitize, screen, scrub*, squash, sterilize; SEE CONCEPTS 165,232

exquisite [adj1] beautiful, excellent, finely detailed
admirable, attractive, charming, choice, comely, consummate, cultivated, dainty, delicate, delicious, discerning, discriminating, elegant, errorless, ethereal, fastidious, fine, flawless, impeccable, incomparable, irreproachable, lovely, matchless, meticulous, outstanding, peerless, perfect, pleasing, polished, precious, precise, rare, recherché, refined, select, selective, splendid, striking, subtle, superb, superior, superlative; SEE CONCEPTS 574,579,589

exquisite [adj2] intense
acute, concentrated, consummate, desperate, excruciating, extreme, fierce, furious, keen, piercing, poignant, sharp, terrible, transcending, vehement, vicious, violent; SEE CONCEPT 569

extant [adj] in existence
actual, alive, around, being, contemporary, current, existent, existing, immediate, in current use, instant, living, not lost, present, present-day, real, remaining, subsisting, surviving, undestroyed; SEE CONCEPTS 539,582

extemporaneous/extemporary [adj] unrehearsed, improvised
ad hoc, ad lib, at first glance, automatic, by ear*, casual, expedient, extempore, free, immediate, impromptu, improv*, improvisatory, improviso, informal, jamming*, made-up, makeshift, offhand, off the cuff*, off the top of head*, on impulse, on-the-spot*, snap, spontaneous, spur-of-the-moment*, taking for ride*, thought out loud*, tossed off*, tossed out*, unplanned, unpremeditated, unprepared, unstudied, winging it*; SEE CONCEPTS 267,799

extemporize [v] improvise
ad-lib, dash out, devise, do offhand*, improvisate, invent, knock off*, make up, play by ear*, toss off*; SEE CONCEPT 51

extend [v1] make larger, longer
add to, aggrandize, amplify, augment, beef up*, boost, broaden, carry on, continue, crane, develop, dilate, drag one's feet*, drag out, draw, draw out, elongate, enhance, enlarge, expand, fan out, go on, heighten, increase, last, lengthen, let out, magnify, mantle, multiply, open, pad, prolong, prolongate, protract, run on, spin out, spread, spread out, stall, stretch, string out, supplement, take, unfold, unfurl, unroll, widen; SEE CONCEPTS 236,239,245

extend [v2] offer
accord, advance, allocate, allot, award, bestow, bring forward, confer, donate, give, grant, hold out, impart, place at disposal, pose, present, proffer, put forth, put forward, reach out, stretch out, submit, tender, yield; SEE CONCEPTS 66,67

extended [adj1] lengthened
continued, drawn-out, elongate, elongated, enlarged, lengthy, long, prolonged, protracted, spread, spread out, stretched out, unfolded, unfurled, very long; SEE CONCEPTS 782,798

extended [adj2] widespread, comprehensive
broad, enlarged, expanded, expansive, extensive, far-flung, far-reaching, large-scale, outspread, scopic, scopious, spread, sweeping, thorough, wide; SEE CONCEPT 772

extension [n] enlargement, continuation
addendum, addition, adjunct, amplification, annex, appendage, appendix, arm, augmentation, branch, broadening, compass, continuing, delay, development, dilatation, distension, drawing out, elongation, expansion, extent, increase, lengthening, orbit, postponement, production, prolongation, protraction, purview, radius, reach, scope, span, spread, spreading out, stretch, stretching, supplement, sweep, widening, wing; SEE CONCEPTS 236,245,824

extensive [adj] far-reaching, thorough
across the board*, all-encompassing, all-inclusive, big, blanket*, boundless, broad, capacious, commodious, comprehensive, comprising, considerable, expanded, extended, far-flung*, general, great, hefty, huge, inclusive, indiscriminate, large, large-scale, lengthy, long, major, pervasive, prevalent, protracted, roomy, scopic, scopious, sizable, spacious, sweeping, unexclusive, universal, unrestricted, vast, voluminous,

**ex
ex**

wall to wall*, wholesale, wide, wide-ranging, widespread; SEE CONCEPTS 772,773

extent [n] *range, magnitude*
admeasurement, ambit, amount, amplitude, area, bounds, breadth, bulk, capaciousness, compass, degree, dimensions, duration, elbowroom*, expanse, expansion, extension, intensity, leeway, length, limit, mass, matter, measure, neighborhood, orbit, order, period of time, play, proliferation, proportions, purview, quantity, radius, reach, scope, size, space, spaciousness, span, sphere, stretch, sweep, term, territory, time, tract, tune, vicinity, volume, wideness, width; SEE CONCEPTS 651,730,743,745,783,788,804

extenuating [adj] *serving as an excuse*
condoning, diminishing, justifying, lessening, mitigating, moderating, palliating, qualifying, reducing, sanitizing, softening, varnishing, whitewashing; SEE CONCEPT 537

exterior [n] *visible part*
appearance, aspect, coating, cover, covering, exteriority, external, facade, face, finish, outside, polish, rind, shell, skin, superficies, superstratum, surface; SEE CONCEPT 484

exterior [adj] *outside*
exoteric, external, extraneous, extraterrestrial, extraterritorial, extrinsic, foreign, marginal, outdoor, outer, outermost, outlying, outmost, outward, over, peripheral, superficial, surface; SEE CONCEPT 583

exterminate [v] *kill*
abolish, annihilate, blot out*, decimate, destroy, do away with*, eliminate, eradicate, erase, execute, extinguish, extirpate, finish off, massacre, obliterate, put an end to*, rub out*, send to kingdom come*, slaughter, stamp out*, wipe out*; SEE CONCEPT 252

external [adj] *outside, extrinsic*
alien, apparent, exterior, extraneous, foreign, independent, out, outer, outermost, outmost, outward, over, peripheral, superficial, surface, visible; SEE CONCEPT 583

extinct [adj] *dead, obsolete*
abolished, archaic, asleep, bygone, cold*, dead and gone*, deceased, defunct, departed, disappeared, done for*, doused, ended, exanimate, exterminated, extinguished, fallen, gone, inactive, late, lifeless, lost, no longer known, out, outmoded, passé, passed on, snuffed out*, superseded, terminated, unknown, vanished, vanquished, void; SEE CONCEPT 539

extinguish [v1] *put out a fire*
blot out, blow out, choke, douse, drown, out, quench, smother, snuff out, stamp out, stifle, suffocate, trample; SEE CONCEPT 256

extinguish [v2] *kill; quash*
abate, abolish, annihilate, blot out*, check, crush, destroy, eliminate, end, eradicate, erase, expunge, exterminate, extirpate, obliterate, obscure, put down, put the lid on*, quell, remove, squash, stamp out, suppress, wipe out*; SEE CONCEPTS 95,252

extirpate [v] *destroy; uproot*
abate, abolish, annihilate, blot out*, cut out, demolish, deracinate, efface, eliminate, eradicate, erase, excise, expunge, exsect, exterminate, extinguish, kill, raze, remove, root out, wipe out*; SEE CONCEPTS 211,252

extol [v] *sing the praises of*
acclaim, applaud, bless, boost, brag about, celebrate, commend, cry up*, eulogize, exalt, give a boost to, give a bouquet*, glorify, hand it to*, hats off to*, hear it for*, hymn, laud, magnify, make much of, panegyrize, pay tribute to, praise, puff up*, push, rave, root, stroke*; SEE CONCEPT 69

extort [v] *cheat; blackmail*
bleed*, bully, clip, coerce, demand, educe, elicit, evince, exact, extract, fleece, force, get, gouge, hold up*, ice*, make pay through nose*, milk*, obtain, pinch, pull one's leg*, put screws to*, put the arm on*, secure, shake down*, skin*, soak, squeeze, stick, sting, wrench, wrest, wring; SEE CONCEPTS 53,59,139,342

extortion [n] *blackmail; cheating*
arm, badger, bite, coercion, compulsion, demand, exaction, force, fraud, oppression, payoff, payola*, pressure, protection, racket, rapacity, shake, shakedown*, squeeze, stealing, swindle, theft; SEE CONCEPTS 53,139,192,342

extra [n] *accessory*
addendum, addition, adjunct, affix, appendage, appurtenance, attachment, bonus, complement, extension, supernumerary, supplement; SEE CONCEPT 824

extra [adj] *accessory; excess*
added, additional, ancillary, another, auxiliary, beyond, button*, extraneous, extraordinary, fresh, further, fuss*, gingerbread*, gravy*, ice*, in addition, inessential, in reserve, in store, lagniappe*, leftover, more, needless, new, one more, optional, other, over and above*, perk*, plus, redundant, reserve, spare, special, superfluous, supernumerary, supplemental, supplementary, surplus, tip, unnecessary, unneeded, unused; SEE CONCEPTS 546,771

extra [adv] *particularly*
considerably, especially, exceptionally, extraordinarily, extremely, markedly, noticeably, rarely, remarkably, uncommon, uncommonly, unusually; SEE CONCEPTS 557,569

extract [n] *something condensed from whole*
abstract, citation, clipping, concentrate, cutting, decoction, distillate, distillation, elicitation, essence, excerpt, infusion, juice*, passage, quotation, selection; SEE CONCEPTS 270,835

extract [v1] *physically remove, draw out*
avulse, bring out, catheterize, cull, derive, distill, eke out, elicit, eradicate, evoke, evulse, exact, express, extirpate, extort, extricate, garner, gather, get, glean, obtain, pick up, pluck, press out, pry, pull, reap, secure, select, separate, siphon, squeeze, take, tear, uproot, weed out*, withdraw, wrest, wring, yank; SEE CONCEPTS 206,211

extract [v2] *select a quotation*
abridge, abstract, bring forth, choose, cite, condense, copy, cull, cut out, deduce, derive, educe, elicit, evolve, excerpt, glean, quote, shorten; SEE CONCEPTS 79,142,211

extraction [n1] *removal from whole; distillation*
abstraction, derivation, drawing, elicitation, eradication, evocation, evulsion, expression, extirpation, extrication, pulling, separation, taking out, uprooting, withdrawal, wrenching, wresting; SEE CONCEPT 211

extraction [n2] *ancestry, origin*
birth, blood, derivation, descent, family, lineage, parentage, pedigree, race, stock; SEE CONCEPTS 296,648

extradite [v] *send to another place by force*
abandon, apprehend, arrest, bring to justice, bring to trial, deliver, give up, release, surrender; SEE CONCEPTS 217,317

extraneous [adj] *unneeded; irrelevant*
accidental, additional, adventitious, beside the point, extra, foreign, immaterial, impertinent, inadmissible, inapplicable, inapposite, inappropriate, incidental, inessential, needless, nonessential, off the subject, peripheral, pointless, redundant, superfluous, supplementary, unconnected, unessential, unnecessary, unrelated; SEE CONCEPT 546

extraneous [adj2] *foreign*
adventitious, alien, exotic, external, extrinsic, out of place, strange; SEE CONCEPT 549

extraordinary [adj] *strange and wonderful*
amazing, bizarre, boss*, curious, exceptional, fab*, fantastic, flash*, gnarly*, heavy*, inconceivable, incredible, marvelous, odd, off beaten path*, out of the ordinary, outstanding, particular, peculiar, phenomenal, rare, remarkable, singular, special, strange, stupendous, surprising, terrific, uncommon, unfamiliar, unheard-of, unimaginable, unique, unprecedented, unthinkable, unusual, unwonted, weird, wicked*; SEE CONCEPTS 564,572

extravagance [n] *indulgence; waste*
absurdity, amenity, dissipation, exaggeration, excess, exorbitance, expenditure, folly, frill, icing on the cake*, immoderation, improvidence, lavishness, luxury, outrageousness, overdoing, overindulgence, overspending, preposterousness, prodigality, profligacy, profusion, recklessness, squander, squandering, superfluity, unreasonableness, unrestraint, unthrift, wastefulness, wildness; SEE CONCEPTS 335,337,787

extravagant [adj] *indulgent, wasteful*
absurd, bizarre, costly, crazy, exaggerated, excessive, exorbitant, expensive, extortionate, extreme, fanciful, fancy, fantastic, flamboyant, flashy, foolish, garish, gaudy, grandiose, immoderate, implausible, improvident, imprudent, inordinate, lavish, ludicrous, nonsensical, ornate, ostentatious, outrageous, overpriced, preposterous, pretentious, prodigal, profligate, reckless, ridiculous, showy, silly, spendthrift, steep, unbalanced, unconscionable, unreasonable, unrestrained; SEE CONCEPTS 334,560,773

extravaganza [n] *spectacle*
caricature, display, divertissement, flight of fancy*, pageant, parody, show, spectacular; SEE CONCEPTS 263,293

extreme [n] *ultimate; limit*
acme, apex, apogee, bitter end, boundary, ceiling, climax, consummation, crest, crown, culmination, depth, edge, end, excess, extremity, height, inordinancy, maximum, nadir, nth degree*, peak, pinnacle, pole, termination, top, utmost, uttermost, zenith; SEE CONCEPTS 484,706,745,836

extreme [adj1] *very great*
acute, consummate, high, highest, intense, maximal, maximum, severe, sovereign, supreme, top, ultimate, utmost, uttermost; SEE CONCEPTS 569,771,781

extreme [adj2] *beyond reason and convention*
absolute, desperate, dire, downright, drastic, egregious, exaggerated, exceptional, excessive, extraordinary, extravagant, fabulous, fanatical, flagrant, gross, harsh, immoderate, improper, imprudent, inordinate, intemperate, irrational, nonsensical, out-and-out*, out of proportion, outrageous, overkill, preposterous, rabid, radical, remarkable, rigid, severe, sheer, stern, strict, thorough, unbending, uncommon, uncompromising, unconventional, unreasonable, unseemly, unusual, utter, zealous; SEE CONCEPTS 547,558,569

extreme [adj3] *faraway*
far-off, farthest, final, furthermost, last, most distant, outermost, outmost, remotest, terminal, ultimate, utmost, uttermost; SEE CONCEPT 778

extremely [adv] *greatly, intensely*
acutely, almighty, awfully, drastically, exceedingly, exceptionally, excessively, exorbitantly, extraordinarily, highly, hugely, immensely, immoderately, inordinately, intensely, markedly, mortally, notably, over, overly, overmuch, parlous, plenty, powerful, prohibitively, quite, radically, rarely, remarkably, severely, strikingly, surpassingly, terribly, terrifically, to nth degree*, too, too much*, totally, ultra*, uncommonly, unduly, unusually, utterly, very*, violently, vitally; SEE CONCEPTS 569,771,781

extremist [n] *person zealous about a belief*
agitator, die-hard, fanatic, radical, revolutionary, revolutionist, ultra, ultraist, zealot; SEE CONCEPTS 359,423

extremity [n1] *ultimate; limit*
acme, acuteness, adversity, apex, apogee, border, bound, boundary, brim, brink, butt, climax, consummation, crisis, depth, dire straits, disaster, edge, end, excess, extreme, extremes, frontier, height, last, margin, maximum, nadir, outside, pinnacle, plight, pole, remote, rim, setback, terminal, termination, terminus, tip, top, trouble, verge, vertex, zenith; SEE CONCEPTS 484,706,745,836

extremity [n2] *animate being's appendage*
backside, finger, flipper, foot, hand, leg, limb, paw, posterior, toe; SEE CONCEPT 392

extricate [v] *get out of a situation; relieve of responsibility*
bail out*, clear, deliver, detach, difference, differentiate, disburden, discumber, disembarrass, disencumber, disengage, disentangle, disinvolve, extract, free, get off the hook*, get out from under*, let go, let off*, liberate, loose, loosen, pull out, release, remove, rescue, resolve, save one's neck*, separate, sever, untie, withdraw, wriggle out of*; SEE CONCEPTS 102,127

extrinsic [adj] *foreign*
acquired, alien, exotic, exterior, external, extraneous, gained, imported, outer, outside, outward, superficial; SEE CONCEPT 549

extrovert [n] *sociable person*
character*, exhibitionist, gregarious person, life of the party*, showboat*, show-off*; SEE CONCEPT 423

extrude [v] *force out*
boot*, chase, dismiss, eject, evict, expel, kick out, press, project, squeeze*, throw out, thrust; SEE CONCEPTS 208,222

exuberance [n1] *energy, enthusiasm*
abandon, animation, ardor, bounce, buoyancy, cheerfulness, eagerness, ebullience, effervescence, excitement, exhilaration, fervor, friskiness, gayness, get up and go*, high spirits, juice*, life, liveliness, pep, pepper*, spirit, sprightliness, vigor, vitality, zap*, zest*, zip*; SEE CONCEPT 633

ex
ex

exuberance [n2] *profusion*
abundance, affluence, copiousness, effusiveness, exaggeration, excessiveness, fulsomeness, lavishness, lushness, luxuriance, plenitude, plenty, prodigality, richness, superabundance, superfluity, teemingness; SEE CONCEPTS 710,767

exuberant [adj1] *energetic, enthusiastic*
animated, ardent, bouncy, brash, buoyant, cheerful, chipper, eager, ebullient, effervescent, elated, excited, exhilarated, feeling one's oats*, frolicsome, gay, high-spirited, lively, passionate, sparkling, spirited, sprightly, vigorous, vivacious, zappy*, zestful, zingy*, zippy*; SEE CONCEPT 401

exuberant [adj2] *profuse*
abundant, affluent, copious, diffuse, effusive, exaggerated, excessive, fecund, fertile, fruitful, fulsome, lavish, lush, luxuriant, opulent, overdone, overflowing, plenteous, plentiful, prodigal, prolific, rampant, rich, riotous, superabundant, superfluous, teeming; SEE CONCEPT 781

exude [v] *display, emit*
bleed, discharge, emanate, evacuate, excrete, exhibit, expel, flow out, give forth, give off, issue, leak, manifest, ooze, pass, percolate, radiate, secrete, seep, show, sweat, throw off, trickle, weep; SEE CONCEPTS 118,179

exult [v1] *be joyful*
be delighted, be elated, be happy, be in high spirits*, be jubilant, be overjoyed, celebrate, cheer, jubilate, jump for joy*, make merry*, rejoice; SEE CONCEPTS 32,266

exult [v2] *boast*
bluster, brag, bully, crow, gloat, glory, revel, show off, take delight in*, triumph, vaunt; SEE CONCEPT 49

exultant [adj] *very happy*
blown away*, delighted, ecstatic, elated, exulting, flipping, flushed, flying, gleeful, high, joyful, joyous, jubilant, overjoyed, rejoicing, revelling, transported, triumphant, turned on*, wowed*; SEE CONCEPT 403

exultation [n] *celebration, reveling*
crowing, delight, elation, glee, gloating, glory, happiness, high spirits, joy, joyousness, jubilance, jubilation, merriment, rejoicing, satisfaction, transport, triumph; SEE CONCEPTS 32,410

eye [n1] *judgment, opinion*
appreciation, belief, conviction, discernment, discrimination, eagle eye*, feeling, mind, perception, persuasion, point of view, recognition, scrutiny, sentiment, surveillance, tab, taste, view, viewpoint, watch; SEE CONCEPTS 411,689

eye [n2] *optical organ of an animate being*
baby blue*, blinder*, eyeball, headlight*, lamp*, ocular, oculus, optic, peeper*, pie*; SEE CONCEPT 392

eye [v] *gaze at, scrutinize*
check out, consider, contemplate, eyeball*, gape, give the eye*, glance at, have a look, inspect, keep eagle eye on*, leer, look at, ogle, peruse, regard, rubberneck*, scan, size up*, stare at, study, survey, take a look, take in, view, watch; SEE CONCEPTS 17,623,626

eyeful [n] *spectacular-looking person*
beauty, dazzler*, knockout*, looker, lovely, show, spectacle, stunner*, vision; SEE CONCEPT 424

eyesore [n] *mess, ugliness*
atrocity, blemish, blight, blot, blot on landscape*, deformity, disfigurement, disgrace, distortion, dump, horror, monstrosity, sight, ugly thing; SEE CONCEPTS 674,716

eyewitness [n] *person who sees an event occur*
beholder, bystander, looker-on, observer, onlooker, passer-by, spectator, viewer, watcher, witness; SEE CONCEPT 423

F

fable [n] *fantasy, story*
allegory, apologue, bestiary, bunk*, crock*, fabrication, fairy story, fairy tale, falsehood, fantasy, fib, fiction, figment, fish story*, hogwash*, invention, legend, lie, myth, old chestnut*, old saw*, one for the birds*, parable, romance, tale, tall story, untruth, white lie*, whopper*, yarn; SEE CONCEPT 282

fabled [adj] *legendary*
fabulous, famed, famous, fanciful, fictional, mythical, mythological, storied, unreal; SEE CONCEPT 568

fabric [n1] *cloth, material*
bolt, fiber, goods, stuff, textile, texture, web; SEE CONCEPT 473

fabric [n2] *structure*
building, consistency, constitution, construction, foundation, frame, framework, infrastructure, make-up, mold, organization, stamp, substance, texture; SEE CONCEPTS 733,757

fabricate [v1] *manufacture*
assemble, brainstorm, build, cobble up*, compose, concoct, construct, contrive, cook up*, create, devise, dream up, erect, fashion, fit together, form, formulate, frame, head trip*, invent, join, knock together*, make, make up, mix, organize, piece together, prefab*, produce, put together, shape, structure, think up, throw together*, throw up*, turn out, whip up*, whomp up*; SEE CONCEPTS 36,173,205,251

fabricate [v2] *falsify, make up a story*
coin, concoct, contrive, counterfeit, devise, fake, feign, fib, forge, form, fudge*, invent, jive*, lie, make like*, misrepresent, pretend, prevaricate, trump up*; SEE CONCEPTS 58,63

fabrication [n1] *lie*
artifact, concoction, deceit, fable, fairy story*, fake*, falsehood, fib, fiction, figment, forgery, hogwash*, invention, jazz*, jive*, line*, myth, opus, smoke*, song and dance*, untruth, work, yarn; SEE CONCEPTS 63,278

fabrication [n2] *something manufactured*
assemblage, assembly, building, construction, creation, erection, product, production; SEE CONCEPTS 205,260,338

fabulous [adj] *amazing, wonderful*
aces*, A-OK*, A-1*, astonishing, astounding, awesome, best, breathtaking, cool*, doozie*, extravagant, fab*, fantastic, fictitious, first-class, greatest, groovy*, immense, inconceivable, incredible, legendary, marvelous, mind-blowing*, out-of-sight*, out-of-this-world*, outrageous, peachy*, phenomenal, primo*, prodigious, rad*, remarkable, spectacular, striking, stupendous, super, superb, 10*, terrific, top drawer*, tops*, turn-

on*, unbelievable, unreal, wicked*; SEE
CONCEPTS **529,572**

facade [n] *appearance, often deceptive*
beard*, bluff, color, disguise, exterior, face, fake,
false colors*, false front*, front, frontage, guise,
look, mask, phony, pretense, put-on*, semblance,
show, veneer, window dressing*; SEE CONCEPT
716

face [nl] *front of something; expression, exterior*
air, appearance, aspect, cast, clock, countenance,
dial*, disguise, display, facet, features, finish,
frontage*, frontal, frontispiece, frown, glower,
grimace, guise, kisser*, light*, lineaments, look,
makeup, map*, mask, mug*, obverse, paint*,
physiognomy, pout, presentation, profile, scowl,
seeming, semblance, show, showing, silhouette,
simulacrum, smirk, surface, top, visage; SEE
CONCEPTS **484,716,836**

face [n2] *pretense, nerve*
air, audacity, boldness, brass*, cheek*, chutz-
pah*, cloak, confidence, cover, disguise, effrontery, facade, false front*, front, gall,
impertinence, impudence, mask, presumption,
semblance, show, veil; SEE CONCEPTS **633,657**

face [n3] *authority, status*
dignity, honor, image, prestige, reputation, self-
respect, social position, standing; SEE CONCEPT
388

face [vl] *come up against a situation*
abide, accost, affront, allow, bear, beard, be con-
fronted by, bit the bullet*, brace, brave, brook,
challenge, confront, contend, cope with, countenance, court, cross, dare, deal with, defy, encounter, endure, experience, eyeball*, fight, fly in face
of*, go up against*, grapple with, make a stand*,
meet, oppose, resist, risk, run into, square off*,
stand, stomach*, submit, suffer, sustain, swal-
low*, take, take it, take on, take the bull by the
horns*, tell off*, tolerate, venture, withstand; SEE
CONCEPTS **23,35,117**

face [v2] *be opposite; look at*
be turned toward, border, confront, front, front
onto, gaze, glare, meet, overlook, stare, watch;
SEE CONCEPTS **623,747**

face [v3] *put paint or finish on*
clad, coat, cover, decorate, dress, finish, front,
level, line, overlay, plaster, polish, redecorate,
refinish, remodel, sheathe, shingle, side, skin,
smooth, surface, veneer; SEE CONCEPTS **172,202**

facet [n] *surface; aspect*
angle, appearance, character, face, feature, front,
hand, level, obverse, part, phase, plane, side,
slant, switch, twist; SEE CONCEPT **835**

facetious [adj] *tongue-in-cheek, kidding*
amusing, blithe, capering, clever, comic, comical, droll, dry, fanciful, farcical, flip*, flippant,
frivolous, funny, gay, humorous, indecorous,
ironic, irreverent, jesting, jocose, jocular, joking,
joshing, laughable, ludicrous, merry, not serious,
playful, pleasant, pulling one's leg*, punning,
putting one on*, ridiculous, salty, sarcastic, satirical, smart, sportive, sprightly, waggish, whimsical, wisecracking, witty, wry; SEE CONCEPT **267**

facile [adj] *easy; easily mastered*
accomplished, adept, adroit, apparent, articulate,
breeze, child's play*, cursory, deft, dexterous,
easy as pie*, effortless, fast talk*, flip*, fluent,
glib, hasty, light, obvious, picnic*, practiced, proficient, pushover*, quick, ready, shallow, simple,
skillful, slick*, smooth, superficial, uncompli-

cated, untroublesome, voluble; SEE CONCEPTS
527,565

facilitate [v] *assist the progress of*
aid, ease, expedite, forward, further, grease the
wheels*, hand-carry*, help, make easy, open
doors*, promote, run interference for*, simplify,
smooth, speed, speed up, walk through*; SEE
CONCEPTS **110,242**

facility [nl] *ease; ability*
address, adroitness, aptitude, bent, child's play*,
competence, dexterity, efficiency, effortlessness,
expertness, fluency, knack, leaning, lightness,
poise, proficiency, propensity, quickness, readiness, skill, skillfulness, smoothness, smooth sail-
ing*, spontaneity, tact, turn, wit; SEE CONCEPTS
630,666

facility [n2] *convenience*
accommodation, advantage, aid, amenity, appliance, comfort, equipment, fitting, material,
means, opportunity, resource, tool; SEE CON-
CEPTS **693,712**

facsimile [n] *reproduction*
carbon, carbon copy*, chip off old block*, clone,
copy, copycat*, dead ringer*, ditto*, double,
dupe*, duplicate, knock-off*, likeness, look-
alike, mimeo, miniature, mirror, photocopy, photostat, print, reduplication, replica, replication,
repro*, ringer*, spitting image*, stat, transcript,
twin, Xerox*; SEE CONCEPTS **271,625,716**

fact [nl] *verifiable truth; reality*
actuality, appearance, authenticity, basis, bottom
line*, brass tacks*, case, certainty, certitude, concrete happening, dope*, evidence, experience,
genuineness, gospel, gospel truth*, how it is*,
intelligence, law, like it is*, matter*, naked
truth*, palpability, permanence, scene, scripture,
solidity, stability, substantiality, verity, what's
what*; SEE CONCEPTS **688,725**

fact [n2] *event; detail of action*
accomplishment, act, action, actuality, adventure,
affair, being, case, circumstance, conception,
consideration, construction, creation, data, datum,
deed, entity, episode, evidence, experience, factor, fait accompli, feature, happening, incident,
information, item, manifestation, occurrence, organism, particular, performance, phenomenon,
point, proceeding, specific, statistic, transaction,
truism; SEE CONCEPTS **2,274,433**

faction [nl] *group sharing a belief or cause*
band, bloc, bunch, cabal, camp, caucus, cell, circle, clan, clique, club, coalition, combination,
combine, combo, concern, conclave, confederacy, conspiracy, contingent, coterie, crew, crowd,
design, division, entente, gang, guild, insiders,
intrigue, junta, knot, lobby, machine, minority,
mob, network, offshoot, outfit, partnership, party,
pressure group, ring, schism, sect, section, sector,
set, side, splinter group, team, unit, wing; SEE
CONCEPTS **301,387**

faction [n2] *conflict, strife*
disagreement, discord, disharmony, dissension,
disunity, division, divisiveness, friction, infight-
ing, quarrelsomeness, rebellion, sedition, tumult,
turbulence; SEE CONCEPTS **106,684**

factious [adj] *conflicting, warring*
alienated, belligerent, contending, contentious,
contumacious, disaffected, disputatious, dissident, divisive, estranged, fighting, hostile, insubordinate, insurgent, insurrectionary, litigious,
malcontent, mutinous, partisan, quarrelsome, re-

ex
fa

bellious, refractory, rival, sectarian, seditious, troublemaking, tumultuous/tumultuous, turbulent; SEE CONCEPT *542*

factor [*n*] *determinant*
agency, agent, aid, antecedent, aspect, board, cause, circumstance, component, consideration, constituent, element, fixin's*, influence, ingredient, instrument, instrumentality, item, makin's*, means, part, part and parcel*, point, portion, thing; SEE CONCEPTS *831,835*

factory [*n*] *manufacturing plant*
branch, cooperative, firm, forge, foundry, industry, laboratory, machine shop, manufactory, mill, mint, salt mines*, shop, sweatshop*, warehouse, workroom, works, workshop; SEE CONCEPTS *439,441,449*

facts [*n*] *inside information*
bottom line*, brass tacks*, certainty, clue, cue, data, details, dope*, gospel, info*, inside dope*, like it is*, lowdown*, numbers, poop*, reality, scoop*, score*, story, whole story*; SEE CONCEPT *274*

factual [*adj*] *real, correct*
absolute, accurate, actual, authentic, card-carrying*, certain, circumstantial, close, credible, descriptive, exact, faithful, genuine, hard, kosher*, legit*, legitimate, literal, objective, on the level*, positive, precise, righteous, specific, straight from horse's mouth*, sure, sure-enough*, true, true-to-life*, unadorned, unbiased, undoubted, unquestionable, valid, veritable; SEE CONCEPTS *535,582*

faculty [*n1*] *ability, skill*
adroitness, aptitude, aptness, bent, capability, capacity, cleverness, dexterity, facility, flair, forte, genius, gift, instinct, intelligence, knack, knowing way around*, leaning, nose*, peculiarity, penchant, pistol*, power, predilection, proclivity, propensity, property, quality, readiness, reason, right stuff*, sense, strength, talent, turn, what it takes*, wits; SEE CONCEPT *630*

faculty [*n2*] *teachers in educational institution*
academics, advisers, body, clinic, college, corps, department, employees, institute, instructors, lecturers, literati, mentors, organization, pedagogues, personnel, professorate, professors, profs*, researchers, scholars, society, staff, tutors, university, workers; SEE CONCEPTS *288,350*

fad [*n*] *craze*
affectation, amusement, caprice, chic, conceit, cry, custom, dernier cri, eccentricity, fancy, fantasy, fashion, fool notion*, frivolity, furor, hobby, humor, in, innovation, in thing*, kick, kink, latest word*, mania, mode, newest wrinkle*, new look*, passing fancy*, passion, quirk, rage, sport, style, thing, trend, vagary, vogue, whim, whimsy, wrinkle; SEE CONCEPT *655*

fade [*v1*] *lose color*
achromatize, become colorless, blanch, bleach, blench, clear, decolorize, dim, disappear, discolor, dissolve, dull, etiolate, evanish, evaporate, grow dim, lose brightness, lose luster, muddy, neutralize, pale, tarnish, tone down, vanish, wash out; SEE CONCEPTS *250,469,622*

fade [*v2*] *dwindle, die out*
abate, attenuate, clear, decline, deliquesce, deteriorate, die away, die on vine*, dim, diminish, disappear, disperse, dissolve, droop, ebb, etiolate, evanesce, evanish, evaporate, fag out*, fail, fall, flag, fold, hush, languish, lessen, melt, melt

away, moderate, perish, peter out*, poop out*, quiet, rarefy, shrivel, sink, slack off*, taper, thin, tire, tucker out*, vanish, wane, waste away, weaken, wilt, wither; SEE CONCEPTS *105,698*

faded [*adj*] *bleached; used*
achromatic, ashen, bedraggled, dim, dingy, discolored, dull, etiolated, indistinct, lackluster, lusterless, murky, not shiny, pale, pallid, run-down, seedy, shabby, shopworn, tacky, tattered, threadbare, tired, wan, washed out, wasted, worn; SEE CONCEPTS *560,617,618*

fail [*v1*] *be unsuccessful*
abort, backslide, back wrong horse*, be defeated, be demoted, be found lacking*, be in vain*, be ruined, blunder, break down, come to naught, come to nothing, decline, deteriorate, fall, fall flat*, fall short*, fall through*, fizzle, flop, flounder, fold, founder, go astray*, go down*, go downhill*, go down swinging*, go up in smoke*, go wrong, hit bottom*, hit the skids*, lose control, lose out, lose status, meet with disaster, miscarry, miss, miss the boat*, play into, run aground*, slip, turn out badly; SEE CONCEPT *699*

fail [*v2*] *abandon, forsake*
abort, back out, blink, desert, disappoint, discount, disregard, fault, forget, funk, go astray, ignore, let down, miscarry, neglect, omit, overlook, overpass, slight, slip; SEE CONCEPTS *7,19*

fail [*v3*] *lose money*
be cleaned out*, become insolvent, be in arrears, be ruined, be taken to the cleaners*, break, close, close down*, close one's doors*, crash, defalcate, default, dishonor, drop, drop a bundle*, end, finish, fold, go bankrupt, go belly up*, go broke*, go bust*, go into chapter 11*, go out of business*, go to the wall*, go under*, go up*, lose big*, lose one's shirt*, overdraw, repudiate, terminate; SEE CONCEPTS *330,335*

failing [*n*] *lapse, shortcoming*
blind spot*, defect, deficiency, drawback, error, failure, fault, flaw, foible, frailty, imperfection, infirmity, miscarriage, misfortune, vice, weakness, weak point*; SEE CONCEPTS *411,674*

failing [*adj*] *not well, weak*
declining, defeated, deficient, faint, feeble, inadequate, insufficient, scant, scanty, scarce, short, shy, unavailing, unprosperous, unsuccessful, unsufficient, unthriving, vain, wanting; SEE CONCEPTS *485,489*

failure [*n1*] *lack of success*
abortion, bankruptcy, bomb, botch*, breakdown, bungle*, bust, checkmate, collapse, decay, decline, defeat, deficiency, deficit, deterioration, downfall, failing, false step*, faux pas, fiasco, flash in the pan*, flop*, frustration, implosion, inadequacy, lead balloon*, lemon*, loser, loss, mess, misadventure, miscarriage, misstep, nonperformance, nonsuccess, overthrow, rout, rupture, sinking ship*, stalemate, stoppage, total loss, turkey*, washout*, wreck; SEE CONCEPTS *699,706*

failure [*n2*] *person who does not succeed*
also-ran*, bankrupt, beat*, born loser*, bum, castaway, deadbeat, defaulter, derelict, disappointment, dud*, flop, good-for-nothing*, has-been, incompetent, insolvent, loafer, loser, lumpy*, might-have-been*, moocher*, nobody, no-good, nonperformer, prodigal, turkey*, underachiever, washout*; SEE CONCEPTS *412,423*

faint [n] *unconsciousness*

blackout, collapse, dizziness, grayout, insensibility, knockout, stupor, swoon, syncope, vertigo; SEE CONCEPTS *308,316*

faint [adj1] *having little effect on senses*

aside, bated, bland, bleached, blurred, breathless, deadened, deep, delicate, dim, distant, dull, dusty, faded, faltering, far-off, feeble, gentle, hazy, hoarse, hushed, ill-defined, imperceptible, inaudible, indistinct, lenient, light, low, low-pitched, mild, moderate, muffled, murmuring, muted, muttering, obscure, out of earshot*, padded, pale, piano, quiet, remote, shadowy, slight, smooth, soft, softened, soothing, stifled, subdued, tenuous, thin, unclear, vague, wan, weak, whispered; SEE CONCEPTS *537,594,617*

faint [adj2] *weak*

delicate, dizzy, drooping, enervated, exhausted, faltering, fatigued, feeble, fragile, languid, lethargic, lightheaded, slight, tender, unenthusiastic, woozy; SEE CONCEPTS *314,485*

faint [v] *lose consciousness*

become unconscious, be overcome, black out, collapse, drop, fade, fail, fall, flicker, go out like light*, keel over, languish, pass out, succumb, swoon, weaken; SEE CONCEPTS *303,308*

fair [n] *exposition, carnival*

bazaar, celebration, centennial, display, exhibit, exhibition, expo*, festival, fete, gala, market, observance, occasion, pageant, show, spectacle; SEE CONCEPTS *377,386*

fair [adj1] *impartial, unprejudiced*

aboveboard, benevolent, blameless, candid, civil, clean, courteous, decent, disinterested, dispassionate, equal, equitable, even-handed, frank, generous, good, honest, honorable, impartial, just, lawful, legitimate, moderate, nonpartisan, objective, on the level*, on up-and-up*, open, pious, praiseworthy, principled, proper, reasonable, respectable, righteous, scrupulous, sincere, square, straight, straightforward, temperate, trustworthy, unbiased, uncolored, uncorrupted, upright, virtuous; SEE CONCEPT *542*

fair [adj2] *light-complexioned, light-haired*

argent, blanched, bleached, blond, blonde, chalky, colorless, creamy, faded, fair-haired, fair-skinned, flaxen-haired, light, milky, neutral, pale, pale-faced, pallid, pearly, sallow, silvery, snowy, tow-haired, tow-headed, white, whitish; SEE CONCEPTS *406,618*

fair [adj3] *mediocre, satisfactory*

adequate, all right, average, common, commonplace, decent, fairish, indifferent, intermediate, mean, medium, middling, moderate, not bad*, okay, ordinary, passable, pretty good*, reasonable, respectable, satisfactory, so-so*, tolerable, up to standard*, usual; SEE CONCEPT *530*

fair [adj4] *beautiful*

attractive, beauteous, bonny, charming, chaste, comely, dainty, delicate, enchanting, exquisite, good-looking, handsome, lovely, pretty, pulchritudinous, pure; SEE CONCEPT *579*

fair [adj5] *bright, cloudless (weather)*

balmy, calm, clarion, clear, clement, dry, favorable, fine, mild, placid, pleasant, pretty, rainless, smiling, sunny, sunshiny, tranquil, unclouded, undarkened, unthreatening; SEE CONCEPT *525*

fairly [adv1] *somewhat*

adequately, averagely, enough, kind of, moderately, more or less, passably, pretty well, quite, rather, ratherish, reasonably, some, something, sort of, so-so*, tolerably; SEE CONCEPT *786*

fairly [adv2] *justly*

deservedly, equitably, honestly, honorably, impartially, objectively, properly, reasonably, without favor, without fear; SEE CONCEPT *542*

fairness [n] *justice*

candor, charitableness, charity, civility, consideration, courtesy, decency, decorum, disinterestedness, due, duty, equitableness, equity, exactitude, fair-mindedness, fair shake*, give and take*, good faith, goodness, honesty, honor, humanity, impartiality, integrity, justness, legitimacy, moderation, open-mindedness, propriety, rationality, reasonableness, right, righteousness, rightfulness, rightness, seemliness, square deal*, suitability, tolerance, truth, uprightness, veracity; SEE CONCEPTS *645,657*

fairy [n] *supernatural being*

bogie, brownie, elf, enchanter, fay, genie, gnome, goblin, gremlin, hob, imp, leprechaun, mermaid, nisse, nymph, pixie, puck, siren, spirit, sprite, sylph; SEE CONCEPT *370*

faith [n1] *trust in something*

acceptance, allegiance, assent, assurance, belief, certainty, certitude, confidence, constancy, conviction, credence, credit, credulity, dependence, faithfulness, fealty, fidelity, hope, loyalty, reliance, stock, store, sureness, surety, troth, truth, truthfulness; SEE CONCEPT *689*

faith [n2] *belief in a higher being; community of believers*

canon, church, communion, confession, connection, conviction, credo, creed, cult, denomination, doctrine, dogma, doxy, gospel, orthodoxy, persuasion, piety, piousness, principle, profession, religion, revelation, sect, teaching, tenet, theism, theology, worship; SEE CONCEPTS *368,689*

faithful [adj1] *loyal, reliable*

affectionate, allegiant, ardent, attached, behind one, circumspect, confiding, conscientious, constant, dependable, devoted, dutiful, dyed-in-the-wool*, enduring, fast, firm, genuine, hard-core*, honest, honorable, incorruptible, loving, obedient, on the level*, patriotic, resolute, scrupulous, sincere, staunch, steadfast, steady, straight, string along with*, sure, tried, tried and true*, true, true-blue*, trustworthy, trusty, truthful, unchanging, unswerving, unwavering, upright, veracious; SEE CONCEPTS *401,545*

faithful [adj2] *authentic, accurate*

close, credible, exact, just, lifelike, precise, right, similar, strict, true, trusty, undistorted, veracious, veridical; SEE CONCEPTS *487,573*

faithfulness [n] *devotion*

adherence, adhesion, allegiance, ardor, attachment, care, constancy, dependability, duty, fealty, fidelity, loyalty, piety, trustworthiness, truth; SEE CONCEPTS *633,645,689*

faithless [adj] *disloyal*

capricious, changeable, changeful, cheating, deceitful, dishonest, double-crossing*, double-dealing*, doubting, dubious, false, fickle, fluctuating, inconstant, perfidious, recreant, skeptical, traitorous, treacherous, two-faced*, two-timing*, unbelieving, unconverted, unfaithful, unloyal, unreliable, unstable, untrue, untrustworthy, untruthful, wavering; SEE CONCEPTS *401,545*

faithlessness [n] *disloyalty*

betrayal, disbelief, dishonesty, doubt, falseness,

fa
fa

 fickleness, fraud, inconstancy, infidelity, perfidiousness, perfidy, skepticism, treacherousness, treachery, treason, unfaithfulness; SEE CONCEPTS *633,645*

fake [n] *imposter, copy*
actor, bluffer, charlatan, cheat, counterfeit, deception, fabrication, faker, flimflam*, forgery, four-flusher*, fraud, gold brick*, hoax, imitation, imposition, imposture, junque, make-believe, mountebank, phony, plant*, pretender, pretense, pseudo*, put-on, reproduction, scam, sham*, sleight, spoof, swindle, trick; SEE CONCEPTS *260,412*

fake [adj] *false, imitation*
affected, artificial, assumed, bogus, concocted, counterfeit, fabricated, fictitious, forged, fraudulent, invented, make-believe, mock, phony, pretended, pseudo*, reproduction, sham, simulated, spurious; SEE CONCEPTS *401,582*

fake [v] *pretend*
act, affect, assume, bluff, copy, counterfeit, disguise, dissimulate, fabricate, feign, forge, put on, put on an act*, sham, simulate, spoof; SEE CONCEPT *59*

fall [n1] *descent; lowering*
abatement, belly flop*, cut, decline, declivity, decrease, diminution, dip, dive, downgrade, downward slope, drop, dwindling, ebb, falling off, header*, incline, lapse, lessening, nose dive*, plummet, plunge, pratfall*, recession, reduction, slant, slip, slope, slump, spill, tumble; SEE CONCEPTS *152,181,776*

fall [n2] *defeat, overthrow*
abasement, breakdown, capitulation, collapse, death, degradation, destruction, diminution, disaster, dive, downfall, drop, failure, humiliation, loss, resignation, ruin, surrender, tumble; SEE CONCEPTS *116,230,674,699*

fall [v1] *descend; become lower*
abate, backslide, be precipitated, break down, buckle, cascade, cave in, collapse, crash, decline, decrease, depreciate, diminish, dip, dive, drag, droop, drop down, dwindle, ease, ebb, flag, flop, fold up, go down, gravitate, hit the dirt*, keel over, land, lapse, lessen, nose-dive, pitch, plummet, plunge, recede, regress, relapse, settle, sink, slip, slope, slump, spin, stumble, subside, take a header*, tip over, topple, totter, trail, trip, tumble, wane; SEE CONCEPTS *152,181,776*

fall [v2] *be overthrown by an enemy; surrender*
back down, be casualty, be destroyed, be killed, be lost, bend, be taken, capitulate, defer to, die, drop, eat dirt*, fall to pieces*, give in, give up, give way, go down, go under, lie down, obey, pass into enemy hands*, perish, resign, slump, submit, succumb, yield; SEE CONCEPTS *116,699*

fall [v3] *happen*
arrive, become, befall, chance, come about, come to pass, occur, take place; SEE CONCEPT *119*

fallacious [adj] *false, wrong*
beguiling, deceiving, deceptive, deluding, delusive, delusory, erroneous, fictitious, fishy*, fraudulent, illogical, illusory, incorrect, invalid, irrational, mad, misleading, mistaken, off*, phony, reasonless, sophistic, sophistical, spurious, unfounded, ungrounded, unreal, unreasonable, unreasoned, unsound, untrue, way off*; SEE CONCEPTS *267,570,582*

fallacy [n] *illusion, misconception*
aberration, ambiguity, artifice, bias, casuistry,

cavil, deceit, deception, deceptiveness, delusion, deviation, elusion, equivocation, erratum, erroneousness, error, evasion, falsehood, faultiness, flaw, heresy, illogicality, inconsistency, inexactness, invalidity, misapprehension, miscalculation, misconstrual, misinterpretation, mistake, non sequitur, notion, paradox, perversion, preconception, prejudice, quibbling, quirk, solecism, sophism, sophistry, speciousness, subterfuge, untruth; SEE CONCEPTS *410,689,725*

fall back [v] *retreat*
back, draw back, give back, recede, recoil, retire, retrocede, retrograde, surrender, withdraw, yield; SEE CONCEPT *195*

fallen [adj1] *disgraced, ruined*
collapsed, decayed, dishonored, immoral, loose, ruinous, shaken, shamed, sinful, unchaste; SEE CONCEPTS *539,555*

fallen [adj2] *dead*
casualty, killed, lost, perished, slain, slaughtered; SEE CONCEPT *539*

fall for [v] *become infatuated with*
desire, fall in love with, flip over, go head over heels*, lose one's head over*, succumb; SEE CONCEPT *32*

fallible [adj] *able or prone to err*
careless, deceptive, errable, errant, erring, faulty, frail, heedless, human, ignorant, imperfect, in question, liable, mortal, questionable, uncertain, unreliable, untrustworthy, weak; SEE CONCEPT *542*

fall out [v1] *argue*
altercate, bicker, clash, differ, disagree, fight, quarrel, spar, squabble; SEE CONCEPT *46*

fall out [v2] *come to pass*
befall, chance, happen, occur, result, take place, turn out; SEE CONCEPT *4*

fallow [adj] *inactive*
dormant, idle, inert, neglected, quiescent, resting, slack, uncultivated, undeveloped, unplanted, unplowed, unproductive, unseeded, untilled, unused, vacant, virgin; SEE CONCEPTS *485,560*

fall to [v] *set about doing*
apply oneself to, begin, be up to, buckle down*, commence, jump in, pitch in*, start, undertake, wade into*; SEE CONCEPTS *100,221*

false [adj1] *wrong, made up*
apocryphal, beguiling, bogus, casuistic, concocted, contrary to fact, cooked-up*, counterfactual, deceitful, deceiving, delusive, dishonest, distorted, erroneous, ersatz*, fake, fallacious, fanciful, faulty, fictitious, fishy, fraudulent, illusive, imaginary, improper, inaccurate, incorrect, inexact, invalid, lying, mendacious, misleading, misrepresentative, mistaken, off the mark*, phony, sham, sophistical, specious, spurious, trumped up*, unfounded, unreal, unsound, untrue, untruthful; SEE CONCEPTS *267,570,582*

false [adj2] *dishonest, hypocritical*
apostate, base, beguiling, canting, corrupt, crooked, deceitful, deceiving, deceptive, deluding, delusive, devious, dishonorable, disloyal, double-dealing*, duplicitous, faithless, false-hearted, forsworn, foul, lying, malevolent, malicious, mean, misleading, mythomaniac, perfidious, perjured, rascally, recreant, renegade, scoundrelly, traitorous, treacherous, treasonable, two-faced*, underhanded, unfaithful, unscrupulous, untrustworthy, venal, villainous, wicked; SEE CONCEPTS *267,401*

false [adj3] *fake, counterfeit*
adulterated, alloyed, artificial, assumed, bent, bogus*, brummagem, bum*, colored, contrived, copied, crock*, deceptive, disguised, ersatz*, fabricated, factitious, feigned, fishy*, forged, framed*, hollow, imitation, made-up, make-believe, manufactured, meretricious, mock, ostensible, phony, pretended, pseudo*, seeming, shady, sham*, simulated, snide, so-called*, spurious, substitute, synthetic, unreal, wrong; SEE CONCEPT 582

falsehood [n] *lie*
canard, cover-up, deceit, deception, dishonesty, dissimulation, distortion, equivocation, erroneousness, error, fable, fabrication, fakery, fallaciousness, fallacy, falseness, falsity, feigning, fibbery, fiction, figment, fraud, half truth, hogwash*, line, mendacity, misstatement, perjury, pretense, prevarication, sham*, story, tale, tall tale*, untruism, untruth, untruthfulness, whopper*, yarn; SEE CONCEPTS 63,278

falsely [adv] *deceitfully*
basely, behind one's back*, crookedly, dishonestly, dishonorably, disloyally, faithlessly, falseheartedly, malevolently, maliciously, perfidiously, roguishly, traitorously, treacherously, underhandedly, unfaithfully, unscrupulously; SEE CONCEPTS 267,401

falsify [v] *alter, misrepresent*
adulterate, belie, change, color, con, contort, contradict, contravene, cook, counterfeit, deacon, deceive, deny, distort, doctor, dress up*, embroider, equivocate, exaggerate, fake, fake it, fib, forge, four-flush*, frame up*, garble, gloss, lie, misquote, misstate, palter, pervert, phony up*, prevaricate, promote, put on an act*, salt*, tamper with, traverse, trump up*, twist, warp; SEE CONCEPT 63

falsity [n] *dishonesty, deception*
canard, cheating, deceit, deceptiveness, disingenuousness, double-dealing, duplicity, faithlessness, error, faithlessness, fake, fallacy, falsehood, fib, fraud, fraudulence, hypocrisy, inaccuracy, infidelity, insincerity, lie, mendacity, misrepresentation, perfidiousness, perfidy, prevarication, sham*, story, tale, treachery, uncandidness, unfaithfulness, unreality, untruth; SEE CONCEPTS 278,645,725

falter [v] *stumble, stutter*
be undecided, bobble, bumble, drop the ball*, flounder, fluctuate, fluff, halt, hem and haw*, hesitate, lurch, quaver, reel, rock, roll, scruple, shake, speak haltingly, stagger, stammer, stub toe*, teeter, topple, totter, tremble, trip up, vacillate, waver, whiffle, wobble; SEE CONCEPTS 18,147,266

fame [n] *celebrity*
acclaim, acclamation, account, acknowledgment, character, credit, dignity, distinction, éclat, elevation, eminence, esteem, estimation, exaltation, favor, glory, greatness, heyday, honor, illustriousness, immortality, kudos, laurels, luster, majesty, name, nobility, note, notoriety, place, popularity, position, preeminence, prominence, public esteem, rank, recognition, regard, renown, rep*, report, reputation, repute, splendor, standing, stardom, station, superiority; SEE CONCEPT 388

familiar [adj1] *common, well-known*
accustomed, commonplace, conventional, customary, domestic, everyday, frequent, garden variety*, habitual, homespun, household, humble, informal, intimate, known, matter-of-fact, mundane, native, natural, old hat*, ordinary, plain, prosaic, proverbial, recognizable, repeated, routine, simple, stock, unceremonious, unsophisticated, usual, wonted, workaday; SEE CONCEPTS 530,547

familiar [adj2] *knowledgeable*
abreast, acquainted, apprised, at home with*, au courant, au fait, aware, cognizant, conscious, conversant, grounded*, informed, in on*, in the know*, introduced, kept posted*, mindful, no stranger to*, plugged in*, savvy, tuned in*, up*, up on*, versant, versed in, well up in*, with it*; SEE CONCEPT 402

familiar [adj3] *friendly, bold*
affable, amicable, buddy-buddy*, chummy*, close, comfortable, confidential, cordial, cozy, dear, easy, forward, free-and-easy*, fresh, genial, gracious, impudent, informal, intimate, intrusive, near, neighborly, nervy, obtrusive, officious, open, palsy, palsy-walsy*, presuming, presumptuous, relaxed, sassy*, smart, snug, sociable, thick, tight, unceremonious, unconstrained, unreserved, wise; SEE CONCEPT 555

familiarity [n1] *friendliness*
acquaintance, acquaintanceship, boldness, closeness, ease, fellowship, forwardness, freedom, freshness, friendship, informality, intimacy, liberty, naturalness, openness, presumption, sociability, unceremoniousness; SEE CONCEPT 388

familiarity [n2] *knowledgeableness*
acquaintance, awareness, cognition, comprehension, experience, feel, grasp, knowledge, sense, understanding; SEE CONCEPT 409

familiarize [v] *make or become acquainted with, knowledgeable about*
accustom, adapt, adjust, awaken to, become adept in, become aware of, break the ice*, bring into use, case*, check out, coach, come to know, condition, enlighten, gain friendship, get in, get lay of land*, get lowdown on*, get together, get to know, get with it*, habituate, inform, instruct, inure, let down hair*, let know, let next to, make conversant, make used to, mix, naturalize, popularize, post, prime, put on to*, school, season, tip off*, train, use, wont; SEE CONCEPTS 15,38

family [n] *kin, offspring; classification*
ancestors, ancestry, birth, blood, brood, children, clan, class, descendants, descent, dynasty, extraction, folk, forebears, genealogy, generations, genre, group, heirs and assigns, house, household, inheritance, in-laws, issue, kind, kindred, kith and kin, line, lineage, ménage, network, parentage, pedigree, people, progenitors, progeny, race, relations, relationship, relatives, siblings, strain, subdivision, system, tribe; SEE CONCEPTS 296,378,397

famine [n] *hunger*
dearth, destitution, drought, misery, paucity, poverty, scarcity, starvation, want; SEE CONCEPTS 674,709

famished [adj] *starving*
could eat a horse*, dog-hungry*, empty, flying light*, having the munchies*, hollow, hungering, hungry, ravening, ravenous, starved, starved to death*, voracious; SEE CONCEPTS 20,406,546

famous [adj] *legendary, notable to many*
acclaimed, applauded, august, brilliant, cele-

brated, conspicuous, distinguished, elevated, eminent, exalted, excellent, extraordinary, foremost, glorious, grand, great, honored, illustrious, important, imposing, influential, in limelight*, in spotlight*, leading, lionized, memorable, mighty, much-publicized, noble, noted, noteworthy, notorious, of note, outstanding, peerless, powerful, preeminent, prominent, recognized, remarkable, renowned, reputable, signal, splendid, talked about*, well-known; SEE CONCEPT 568

fan [n1] *blower of air*
air conditioner, blade, draft, flabellum, leaf, palm leaf, propeller, thermantidote, vane, ventilator, windmill; SEE CONCEPT 463

fan [n2] *person enthusiastic about an interest*
addict, adherent, admirer, aficionado, amateur, buff, devotee, follower, freak*, groupie*, habitué, hound, lover, rooter, supporter, votary, zealot; SEE CONCEPTS 352,366,423

fan [v1] *blow on*
acrate, air-condition, air-cool, cool, refresh, ruffle, spread, ventilate, wind, winnow; SEE CONCEPTS 199,208

fan [v2] *provoke*
add fuel, agitate, arouse, enkindle, excite, expand, extend, impassion, increase, rouse, stimulate, stir up, whip up, work up; SEE CONCEPT 14

fanatic [n] *person overenthusiastic about an interest*
activist, addict, bigot, bug*, crank*, crazy, demon, devotee, enthusiast, extremist, fiend*, fool, freak, maniac, militant, monomaniac, nut*, radical, ultraist, visionary, zealot; SEE CONCEPTS 352,359,366

fanatical [adj] *overenthusiastic*
biased, bigoted, bugged*, burning*, contumacious, credulous, devoted, dogmatic, domineering, enthusiastic, erratic, extreme, fervent, feverish, fiery, frenzied, headstrong, high on*, immoderate, impassioned, impulsive, incorrigible, infatuated, mad, monomaniacal, narrow-minded, nuts for*, obsessed, obsessive, obstinate, opinionated, partial, partisan, passionate, possessed, prejudiced, rabid, radical, raving, single-minded, stubborn, turned on*, unruly, violent, visionary, wild, willful, zealous; SEE CONCEPT 401

fanaticism [n] *overenthusiasm*
abandonment, arbitrariness, bias, bigotry, contumacy, dedication, devotion, dogma, enthusiasm, extremism, faction, frenzy, hatred, illiberality, immoderation, incorrigibility, infatuation, injustice, intolerance, madness, monomania, obsessiveness, obstinacy, partiality, partisanship, passion, prejudice, rage, single-mindedness, stubbornness, superstition, tenacity, transport, unfairness, unreasonableness, unruliness, violence, willfulness, zeal, zealotry; SEE CONCEPTS 633,689

fanciful [adj] *imaginary, romantic*
absurd, aerial, bizarre, blue sky*, capricious, castles in the air*, chimerical, curious, dreamlike, extravagant, fabulous, fairy-tale, fancied, fantastic, fantastical, fictional, fictitious, fictive, flaky*, floating, ideal, illusory, imaginative, imagined, incredible, kinky*, legendary, mythical, notional, offbeat, on cloud nine*, pie in the sky*, pipe dream*, poetic, preposterous, shadowy, supposititious, unreal, visionary, whimsical, wild; SEE CONCEPTS 529,572

fancy [n1] *impulse, urge*
caprice, conceit, conception, contrariness, creation, cup of tea*, desire, druthers*, flash, fool's paradise*, groove*, humor, idea, image, imagination, impression, inclination, irrationality, liking, mind, notion, perverseness, pleasure, thing*, thought, vagary, velleity, visualization, weakness for, whim, will; SEE CONCEPTS 20,532

fancy [n2] *liking, dream*
big eyes*, chimera, conception, daydream, delusion, envisagement, envisioning, eyes for*, fabrication, fantasy, figment, fondness, hallucination, hankering, idea, illusion, imagination, imaginativeness, inclination, invention, itch*, mirage, nightmare, notion, partiality, penchant, phantasm, picture, pie in the sky*, predilection, preference, relish, reverie, romancing, sweet tooth*, vision, yearning, yen; SEE CONCEPTS 20,32,409

fancy [adj] *extravagant, ornamental*
adorned, baroque, beautifying, chichi*, complicated, cushy, custom, decorated, decorative, deluxe, elaborate, elegant, embellished, fanciful, florid, frilly, froufrou*, garnished, gaudy, gingerbread*, intricate, lavish, ornate, ostentatious, resplendent, rich, rococo, showy, special, spiffy*, sumptuous, unusual; SEE CONCEPTS 562,579

fancy [v1] *imagine, create*
be inclined to think, believe, conceive, conjecture, dream up, envisage, envision, fantasize, feature*, guess, head trip*, image, infer, make up, make up off top of one's head*, phantom, picture, realize, reckon, spark, spitball*, suppose, surmise, think, think likely, think up, trump up*, vision, visualize; SEE CONCEPT 43

fancy [v2] *love, desire*
approve, be attracted to, be captivated by, be enamored of, be in love with, care for, crave, crazy about*, desire, dream of, endorse, fall for, favor, like, long for, lust after, mad for*, prefer, relish, sanction, set one's heart on*, take a liking to*, take to, wild for*, wish for, yearn for; SEE CONCEPTS 17,20,32

fanfare [n] *cheering*
alarum, array, ballyhoo*, demonstration, display, flourish, hullabaloo*, panoply, parade, pomp, shine, show, trump, trumpet call*; SEE CONCEPT 377

fantasize [v] *dream about desires*
build castles in air*, daydream, envision, hallucinate, head trip*, imagine, invent, live in a dream world*, moon, romance, trip out*, woolgather*; SEE CONCEPT 17

fantastic [adj1] *strange, different; imaginary*
absurd, artificial, capricious, chimerical, comical, crazy, eccentric, erratic, exotic, extravagant, extreme, fanciful, far-fetched, fictional, foolish, foreign, freakish, grotesque, hallucinatory, illusive, imaginative, implausible, incredible, insane, irrational, ludicrous, mad, misleading, nonsensical, odd, outlandish, out of sight*, peculiar, phantasmagorical, preposterous, quaint, queer, ridiculous, singular, suppositious, unbelievable, unlikely, unreal, wacky*, weird, whimsical; SEE CONCEPTS 564,582

fantastic [adj2] *enormous*
cracking, extreme, great, huge, humongous, massive, monstrous, monumental, overwhelming, prodigious, severe, stupendous, towering, tremendous; SEE CONCEPT 781

fantastic [adj3] *wonderful, excellent*
A-1*, awesome, best, best ever, cat's meow*, delicious, far out*, first-class, first-rate, great, like wow*, marvelous, out of sight*, out of this world*, primo*, sensational, superb, unreal*; SEE CONCEPTS 572,574

fantasy [n] *imagination, dream*
air castle, apparition, appearance, Atlantis*, bubble*, chimera, conceiving, creativity, daydream, delusion, envisioning, externalizing, fabrication, fairyland*, fancy, fancying, fantasia, figment*, flight, flight of imagination, fool's paradise*, hallucination, head trip*, illusion, imaginativeness, imagining, invention, mind trip*, mirage, nightmare, objectifying, originality, rainbow*, reverie, trip, Utopia, vagary, vision; SEE CONCEPTS 20,529,689

far [adj/adv1] *at a great distance*
afar, a good way, a long way, bit, deep, distant, end of rainbow*, faraway, far-flung*, far-off, far piece*, far-removed, good ways*, long, middle of nowhere*, miles, outlying, out-of-the-way*, piece, remote, removed, stone's throw*, ways*; SEE CONCEPTS 586,778

far [adv2] *considerably*
decidedly, extremely, greatly, incomparably, much, notably, quite, significantly, somewhat, very, very much, well; SEE CONCEPTS 772,781

faraway [adj] *remote, distant*
absent, abstracted, beyond the horizon, distant, dreamy, far, far-flung*, far-off, far-removed, lost, outlying, preoccupied, quite a ways*, removed, well away; SEE CONCEPTS 586,778

farce [n] *nonsense, satire*
absurdity, broad comedy, buffoonery, burlesque, camp, caricature, comedy, high camp*, horseplay*, interlude, joke, low camp*, mock, mockery, parody, play, pratfall comedy, ridiculousness, sham*, skit, slapstick, travesty; SEE CONCEPTS 263,293

farcical [adj] *absurd*
amusing, camp, campy*, comic, comical, derisory, diverting, droll, for grins*, funny, gelastic, joshing, laughable, ludicrous, nonsensical, outrageous, preposterous, ridiculous, risible, slapstick, stupid; SEE CONCEPTS 267,542

fare [n1] *amount charged for transportation*
book, charge, check, expense, passage, price, slug, tariff, ticket, token, toll; SEE CONCEPT 329

fare [n2] *food served at meals*
commons, diet, eatables, eats*, edibles, meals, menu, provision, rations, slop*, sustenance, swill*, table, victuals; SEE CONCEPTS 457,459

fare [v] *get along; turn out*
advance, do, get by, get on, go, handle, happen, hie, journey, make headway, make out, manage, muddle through, pass, proceed, progress, prosper, prove, shift, stagger; SEE CONCEPTS 100,117,704

farewell [n] *departing saying; departure*
adieu, adieus, adiós, adios, bye-bye, cheerio, ciao, goodbye, hasta la vista, have a nice day, leave-taking, parting, salutation, sendoff, so long, ta-ta, valediction; SEE CONCEPTS 195,278

far-fetched [adj] *hard to believe*
bizarre, doubtful, dubious, eccentric, fantastic, fishy*, forced, hard to swallow*, illogical, implausible, improbable, incoherent, inconsequential, incredible, labored, preposterous, queer, recondite, strained, strange, suspicious, unbeliev-able, unconvincing, unlikely, unnatural, unrealistic; SEE CONCEPTS 529,552,582

farm [n] *land for agriculture or animal breeding*
acreage, acres, arboretum, claim, demense, enclosure, estate, farmstead, field, freehold, garden, grange, grassland, holding, homestead, lawn, meadow, nursery, orchard, pasture, patch, plantation, ranch, soil, vineyard; SEE CONCEPTS 258,449,509,517

farm [v] *produce crops, raise animals*
bring under cultivation, crop, cultivate, direct, dress, garden, graze, grow, harrow, harvest, homestead, husband, landscape, look after, operate, pasture, plant, plow, ranch, reap, run, seed, sow, subdue, superintend, tend, till, till the soil, work; SEE CONCEPTS 117,253,324

farmer [n] *person who produces crops, raises animals*
agriculturalist, agriculturist, agronomist, breeder, clodhopper*, cob*, country person, cropper, cultivator, feeder, gardener, gleaner, grazer, grower, harvester, hired hand, homesteader, horticulturist, laborer, peasant, planter, plower, producer, rancher, reaper, sharecropper, sower, tender, tiller, villein; SEE CONCEPTS 347,348

farming [n] *producing crops, raising animals*
agriculture, agronomics, agronomy, breeding, crop-raising, cultivation, culture, feeding, fertilizing, gardening, geoponics, gleaning, grazing, growing, harvesting, homesteading, hydroponics, landscaping, operating, production, ranching, reaping, seeding, share-cropping, soil culture, threshing, tillage; SEE CONCEPTS 117,253,324

far-reaching [adj] *broad, widespread*
extensive, far-ranging, important, momentous, pervasive, significant, sweeping, wide; SEE CONCEPT 772

far-sighted [adj] *looking ahead wisely*
acute, canny, cautious, clairvoyant, commonsensical, cool-headed*, discerning, judicious, level-headed, perceptive, politic, prescient, provident, prudent, sagacious, sage, shrewd, well-balanced, wise; SEE CONCEPT 402

farther [adv] *at a greater distance*
beyond, further, longer, more distant, more remote, remoter, yon, yonder; SEE CONCEPTS 586,778

farthest [adv] *most distant*
extreme, farthermost, furthermost, furthest, last, lattermost, outermost, outmost, remotest, ultimate, utmost, uttermost; SEE CONCEPTS 586,778

fascinate [v] *captivate, hold spellbound*
absorb, allure, animate, arouse, attach, attract, beguile, bewitch, charm, compel, delight, draw, enamor, enchant, engage, engross, enrapture, enslave, ensnare, enthrall, entice, entrance, excite, fire, gladden, hypnotize, infatuate, interest, intoxicate, intrigue, invite, kindle, lure, mesmerize, overpower, overwhelm, pique, please, provoke, ravish, rivet, seduce, spellbind, stimulate, stir, subdue, tantalize, tempt, thrill, titillate, transfix, transport, win; SEE CONCEPTS 7,11,22

fascinated [adj] *captivated, spellbound*
absorbed, aroused, attracted, beguiled, bewitched, charmed, dazzled, delighted, enamored, enchanted, engrossed, enraptured, enthralled, enticed, entranced, excited, fond of, hypnotized, infatuated, in love with, intoxicated, mesmerized, overpowered, seduced, sent, smitten, sold on*, stuck on*, tantalized, thrilled, titillated, trans-

fa
fa

fixed, transported, under a spell*; SEE CONCEPTS *32,403*

fascinating [*adj*] *interesting, spellbinding*
alluring, appealing, attractive, bewitching, captivating, charming, compelling, delectable, delightful, enchanting, engaging, engrossing, enticing, glamorous, gripping, intriguing, irresistible, ravishing, riveting, seducing, seductive, siren; SEE CONCEPT *529*

fascination [*n*] *strong interest*
allure, appeal, attraction, bug*, charisma, charm, enchantment, enthrallment, glamour, grabber*, hang-up*, lure, magic, magnetism, obsession, piquancy, power, pull*, sorcery, spell, thing*, thing for*, trance, witchcraft, witchery; SEE CONCEPTS *20,32,532,690*

fascism [*n*] *political system of dictatorship*
absolutism, authoritarianism, autocracy, bureaucracy, despotism, Nazism, one-party system, party government, racism, regimentation, totalitarianism; SEE CONCEPTS *299,301,689*

fashion [*n1*] *latest style, prevailing taste*
appearance, bandwagon*, chic, configuration, convention, craze, cry, cultism, cultus, custom, cut, dernier cri, fad, faddism, figure, form, furor, in thing*, last word*, latest*, latest thing*, line*, look, make, mode, model, mold, newest wrinkle*, pattern, rage, shape, thing*, tone, trend, usage, vogue; SEE CONCEPT *655*

fashion [*n2*] *attitude, manner*
convention, custom, demeanor, device, etiquette, form, formality, formula, guise, method, mode, modus operandi, mores, observance, order, practice, precedent, prescription, prevalence, procedure, sort, style, system, technique, tendency, tone, trend, usage, vein, vogue, way; SEE CONCEPTS *644,657*

fashion [*v*] *adjust, design, create*
accommodate, adapt, build, carve, construct, contrive, cook up*, cut, devise, dream up*, erect, fabricate, fit, forge, form, frame*, knock together*, make, manufacture, model, mold, plan, plot, produce, sculpture, shape, suit, tailor, throw together*, turn out*, work; SEE CONCEPTS *168,173,232*

fashionable [*adj*] *stylish, up-to-date*
a go-go*, à la mode*, all the rage*, chic, chichi*, contemporary, current, customary, dashing, faddy*, favored, fly*, genteel, hot*, in style, in-thing*, in vogue, last word*, latest*, latest thing*, mod*, modern, modish*, natty*, new, newfangled, now, popular, prevailing, rakish, smart, swank, trendsetting, trendy, upscale*, up-to-the-minute*, usual, well-liked, with it*; SEE CONCEPTS *579,589*

fast [*n*] *abstention from eating*
abstinence, diet, fasting, xerophagy; SEE CONCEPT *169*

fast [*adj1*] *speedy*
accelerated, active, agile, blue streak*, breakneck*, brisk, chop-chop*, dashing, double-time*, electric, expeditious, expeditive, flashing, fleet, fleeting, flying, hairtrigger*, hasty, hot, hurried, hypersonic, in a jiffy*, in nothing flat*, lickety split*, like a bat out of hell*, like all get out*, like crazy*, like mad*, nimble, on the double*, PDQ*, posthaste, presto, pronto, quick, racing, rapid, ready, screamin'*, snap*, snappy*, speedball*, supersonic, swift, velocious, winged; SEE CONCEPTS *588,799*

fast [*adj2*] *fixed, immovable*
adherent, ardent, attached, close, constant, constrained, durable, faithful, fastened, firm, fortified, glued, held, impregnable, indelible, inextricable, lasting, loyal, permanent, resistant, resolute, secure, set, sound, stable, staunch, steadfast, stuck, sure, tenacious, tight, true, true blue*, unwavering, wedged; SEE CONCEPTS *488,542*

fast [*adj3*] *immoral, promiscuous*
bawdy, careless, debauched, depraved, devil-may-care*, dissipated, dissolute, easy, extravagant, flirtatious, frivolous, gadabout*, giddy, incontinent, indecent, intemperate, lascivious, lecherous, lewd, libertine, libidinous, licentious, light, loose, lustful, profligate, rakish, reckless, salacious, self-gratifying, self-indulgent, sportive, sporty, unchaste, wanton, wild; SEE CONCEPT *545*

fast [*v*] *go without food*
abstain, deny oneself, diet, famish, forbear, go hungry, not eat, refrain, starve; SEE CONCEPT *169*

fast [*adv1*] *speedily*
apace, chop-chop*, expeditiously, flat-out*, fleetly, full tilt*, hastily, hurriedly, in a flash*, in haste, in nothing flat*, in short order*, like a flash*, like a shot*, like greased lightning*, like wildfire*, posthaste, presto, promptly, pronto, quick, quickly, rapidly, soon, swift, swiftly; SEE CONCEPTS *588,799*

fast [*adv2*] *fixedly*
deeply, firm, firmly, hard, securely, solidly, soundly, steadfastly, tight, tightly; SEE CONCEPT *488*

fasten [*v*] *make secure; join together*
adhere, affix, anchor, attach, band, bar, batten, belt, bind, bolt, bond, brace, button, catch, cement, chain, cleave, close, cohere, connect, couple, embed, establish, fix, freeze to*, girth, glue, grip, hitch, hitch on, hold, hook, hook up, implant, infix, jam, knot, lace, leash, link, lock, lodge, make firm, moor, mortise, nail, rivet, rope, screw, seal, set, settle, solder, stay put, stick, strengthen, string, tack on, tag, tie, tighten, truss, unite, wedge, weld; SEE CONCEPTS *85,113,160*

fastidious [*adj*] *very careful, meticulous*
captious, choosy, critical, dainty, demanding, difficult, discriminating, easily disgusted, exacting, finical, finicky, fussbudgety*, fussy, hard to please*, hypercritical, nice, nit-picky, overdelicate, overnice, particular, persnickety*, picky, punctilious, queasy, squeamish, stickling; SEE CONCEPTS *542,550*

fat [*n*] *overweight, adipose tissue*
blubber, bulk, cellulite, corpulence, excess, fatness, flab, flesh, grease, lard, obesity, overabundance, overflow, paunch, plethora, suet, superfluity, surfeit, surplus, tallow; SEE CONCEPTS *723,734*

fat [*adj1*] *overweight*
beefy*, big, blimp, bovine, brawny, broad, bulging, bulky, bull, burly, butterball*, chunky*, corpulent, distended, dumpy, elephantine, fleshy, gargantuan, gross, heavy, heavyset*, hefty, husky, inflated, jelly-belly*, lard, large, meaty*, obese, oversize, paunchy, plump, plumpish, ponderous, porcine, portly, potbellied, pudgy*, roly-poly*, rotund, solid, stout, swollen, thickset*, weighty, whalelike*; SEE CONCEPT *491*

fat [adj2] *containing an oily substance*
adipose, fatlike, fatty, greasy, oleaginous, suety, unctuous; SEE CONCEPT *485*

fat [adj3] *productive, rich*
affluent, cushy, fertile, flourishing, fruitful, good, lucrative, lush, profitable, prosperous, remunerative, thriving; SEE CONCEPT *334*

fatal [adj1] *deadly, lethal*
baleful, baneful, calamitous, cataclysmic, catastrophic, deathly, destructive, disastrous, fateful, final, ill-fated, ill-starred, incurable, inevitable, killing, malefic, malignant, mortal, mortiferous, noxious, pernicious, pestilent, pestilential, poisonous, ruinous, terminal, virulent; SEE CONCEPTS *537,539*

fatal [adj2] *critical, very important*
crucial, decisive, destined, determining, doomed, fateful, final, foreordained, inevitable, predestined, unlucky; SEE CONCEPTS *531,568*

fatalism [n] *resignation to a fate*
acceptance, destinism, determinism, necessitarianism, passivity, predestinarianism, predestination, stoicism; SEE CONCEPT *689*

fatality [n] *death, loss; ability to cause such*
accident, casualty, deadliness, destructiveness, disaster, dying, inevitability, lethality, lethalness, mortality, necrosis, noxiousness, poisonousness, virulence; SEE CONCEPTS *304,675*

fate [n] *predetermined course*
break, chance, circumstance, consequence, cup*, destination, destiny, divine will*, doom, effect, end, ending, fortune, future, handwriting on the wall*, horoscope, inescapableness, issue, karma, kismet, lot, luck, Moirai, nemesis, outcome, portion, predestination, providence, stars*, termination, upshot, wheel of fortune*; SEE CONCEPT *679*

fateful [adj1] *significant*
acute, apocalyptic, conclusive, critical, crucial, decisive, determinative, direful, doomful, eventful, important, inauspicious, momentous, ominous, portentous, resultful; SEE CONCEPT *568*

fateful [adj2] *deadly*
calamitous, cataclysmic, catastrophic, destructive, disastrous, fatal, lethal, mortal, ominous, ruinous; SEE CONCEPT *537*

father [n1] *male person who begets children*
ancestor, begetter, dad, daddy*, forebearer, origin, pa, padre, papa, parent, pop*, predecessor, procreator, progenitor, sire, source; SEE CONCEPTS *394,400,414,419,423*

father/mother [n2] *founder, inventor*
administrator, architect, author, builder, creator, dean, elder, encourager, generator, initiator, introducer, leader, maker, matriarch, motor*, mover, organizer, originator, patriarch, patron, prime mover*, promoter, promulgator, publisher, sire, sponsor, supporter; SEE CONCEPTS *347,423*

father [n3] *priest*
abbé, clergyman, confessor, curé, ecclesiastic, minister, padre, parson, pastor, preacher, reverend; SEE CONCEPT *361*

fathom [v] *discern, understand*
appreciate, apprehend, catch, cognize, comprehend, dig, divine, estimate, figure out, follow, gauge, get, get to the bottom*, grasp, have, interpret, know, measure, penetrate, perceive, pierce, pinpoint, plumb, probe, recognize, savvy, sound, unravel; SEE CONCEPTS *15,38*

fatigue [n] *tiredness*
brain fag*, burnout*, debility, dullness, enerva-

tion, ennui, exhaustion, faintness, fatigation, feebleness, heaviness, languor, lassitude, lethargy, listlessness, overtiredness, weakness, weariness; SEE CONCEPTS *316,405*

fatigue [v] *tire, wear out*
bedraggle, burn out*, bush*, conk out*, debilitate, deplete, disable, drain, droop, drop, enervate, exhaust, fag, fizzle, flag, jade*, knock out*, languish, overtire, peter out*, poop*, poop out*, prostrate, sag, sink, succumb, take, tucker, weaken, wear down, weary; SEE CONCEPTS *137,225,240,250*

fatigued [adj] *tired*
all in*, beat*, bedraggled, blasé, burned out*, bushed*, dead*, dead-beat*, dead-tired*, dog-tired*, dog-weary*, done in*, droopy, dropping, enervated, exhausted, fagged out*, jaded*, languid, languorous, lassitudinous, listless, out of gas*, overtired, played out*, pooped*, prostrate, ready to drop*, spent*, tuckered*, washed out*, wasted*, weary, worn, worn-out, zonked*; SEE CONCEPT *485*

fatness [n] *overweight*
adiposity, breadth, bulkiness, corpulence, distension, flab*, flesh, fleshiness, girth, grossness, heaviness, heftiness, inflation, largeness, obesity, plumpness, portliness, protuberance, pudginess, rotundity, size, stoutness, tumidity, weight; SEE CONCEPT *734*

fatten [v] *grow or make bigger; nourish*
augment, bloat, broaden, build up, coarsen, cram, distend, expand, feed, fill, gain weight, increase, overfeed, plump, put flesh on*, put on weight, round out, spread, stuff, swell, thicken, thrive, wax; SEE CONCEPTS *236,245,250*

fatty [adj] *full of adipose tissue*
blubbery, fatlike, greasy, lardaceous, lardy, oily, oleaginous, rich, suety, unctuous; SEE CONCEPT *485*

fatuous [adj] *stupid*
absurd, asinine, birdbrained*, boneheaded*, brainless*, dense, dull, foolish, idiotic, imbecile, inane, insensate, jerky*, lamebrained*, ludicrous, lunatic, mad, mindless, moronic, puerile, sappy, silly, simple, vacuous, witless; SEE CONCEPT *402*

fault [n1] *blame, sin; mistake*
accountability, answerability, blunder, crime, culpability, defect, delinquency, dereliction, error, evil doing, failing, flaw, foible, frailty, guilt, impropriety, inaccuracy, indiscretion, infirmity, lapse, liability, loss of innocence, malfeasance, malpractice, misconduct, miscue, misdeed, misdemeanor, negligence, offense, omission, onus, oversight, peccancy, responsibility, slip, slip-up*, solecism, transgression, trespass, vice, weakness, wrong, wrongdoing; SEE CONCEPTS *101,192,699*

fault [n2] *physical defect*
blemish, debility, deficiency, demerit, imperfection, infirmity, lack, pimple, shortcoming, weakness, weak point, zit*; SEE CONCEPT *580*

faultless [adj] *having nothing wrong with it*
above reproach, accurate, blameless, classic, clean, correct, crimeless, errorless, exemplary, exquisite, faithful, flawless, foolproof, guiltless, ideal, immaculate, impeccable, inculpable, innocent, intact, irreproachable, model, on target*, perfect, pure, right on*, sinless, spotless, stainless, supreme, textbook*, unblemished, unguilty, unspotted, unsullied, whole; SEE CONCEPTS *545,572*

fa
fa

faulty [adj] *not working; incorrect*
adulterated, amiss, awry, bad, below par, blamable, blemished, botched, broken, cracked, damaged, debased, defective, deficient, distorted, erroneous, fallacious, fallible, false, flawed, frail, impaired, imperfect, imprecise, inaccurate, inadequate, incomplete, inexact, injured, insufficient, invalid, lame, leaky, lemon, maimed, malformed, malfunctioning, marred, out of order, rank, sick, tainted, unfit, unreliable, unretentive, unsound, warped, weak, wrong; SEE CONCEPTS 560,570

faux pas [n] *blunder in etiquette*
blooper*, boo-boo*, breach, break, bungle, error, flop, flub*, gaffe*, goof*, impropriety, indecorum, indiscretion, mess-up, misconduct, misjudgment, misstep, mistake, oversight, solecism; SEE CONCEPTS 101,384

favor [n] *approval, good opinion; help*
accommodation, account, admiration, aid, approbation, assistance, backing, benediction, benefit, benevolence, benignity, bias, blessing, boon, championship, compliment, consideration, cooperation, courtesy, dispensation, encouragement, esteem, estimation, friendliness, gift, good turn*, good will*, grace, indulgence, kindness, largess, obligation, okay, partiality, patronage, present, regard, respect, service, support, token; SEE CONCEPTS 10,110,689

favor [v1] *pamper, reward; help*
abet, accommodate, advance, aid, assist, befriend, be partial to, do a kindness, do right by*, esteem, facilitate, further, gratify, humor, indulge, make exception, oblige, play favorites*, promote, pull strings*, show consideration, side with, smile upon*, spare, spoil, treat well, value; SEE CONCEPT 110

favor [v2] *prefer, like*
accept, advocate, appreciate, approbate, approve, back, be in favor of, be on one's side*, buck for*, champion, choose, commend, cotton to*, countenance, encourage, endorse, esteem, eulogize, fancy, flash on*, for, go for*, hold with, honor, incline, lean toward, look up to, opt for, patronize, pick, praise, prize, regard highly, root for, sanction, single out*, support, take a liking to*, take a shine to*, take to*, think well of, tilt toward*, value; SEE CONCEPT 32

favor [v3] *look like*
be the image of*, be the picture of*, feature, resemble, simulate, take after*; SEE CONCEPT 716

favorable [adj1] *approving, friendly*
acclamatory, affirmative, agreeable, amicable, approbative, approbatory, assenting, benevolent, benign, benignant, commending, complimentary, encouraging, enthusiastic, inclined, in favor of, kind, kindly, laudatory, okay, positive, praiseful, predisposed, reassuring, recommendatory, supportive, sympathetic, understanding, welcoming, well-disposed, well-intentioned; SEE CONCEPT 401

favorable [adj2] *good, timely, advantageous*
appropriate, auspicious, benefic, beneficial, benign, bright, cheering, convenient, encouraging, fair, fit, fortunate, full of promise, gratifying, happy, healthful, helpful, hopeful, kindly, lucky, nice, opportune, pleasant, pleasing, pleasurable, pleasureful, promising, propitious, prosperous, providential, reassuring, seasonable, suitable, toward, useful, welcome, well-timed, wholesome, worthy; SEE CONCEPTS 537,558,572

favorably [adv1] *genially, in a kindly manner*
agreeably, amiably, approvingly, cordially, courteously, enthusiastically, fairly, generously, graciously, heartily, helpfully, positively, receptively, usefully, willingly, with approbation, with approval, without prejudice; SEE CONCEPT 401

favorably [adv2] *opportunely, advantageously*
auspiciously, conveniently, fortunately, happily, profitably, prosperously, satisfyingly, successfully, swimmingly, to one's advantage, well; SEE CONCEPTS 537,558,572

favored [adj] *popular*
advantaged, best-liked, blessed, chosen, elite, fair-haired*, lucky, pet*, preferred, privileged, recommended, selected, singled out, sweetheart, well-liked; SEE CONCEPTS 529,568

favorite [n] *something or someone cherished, prized*
apple of eye*, beloved, chalk*, choice, darling, dear, fave*, front-runner*, ideal, idol, love, main, minion, number one*, paramour, pet*, pick, preference, shoo-in*; teacher's pet*; SEE CONCEPTS 423,446

favorite [adj] *preferred*
admired, adored, beloved, best-loved, cherished, choice, darling, dear, dearest, desired, especial, esteemed, favored, intimate, liked, main, number one*, personal, pet*, pleasant, popular, precious, prized, revered, sweetheart*, treasured, wished-for; SEE CONCEPTS 529,568

favoritism [n] *bias, partiality*
discrimination, inclination, inequity, nepotism, one-sidedness, partisanship, preference, preferential treatment, unfairness; SEE CONCEPTS 41, 388,645

fawn [n] *baby deer*
baby buck, baby doe, yearling; SEE CONCEPTS 394,400

fawn [v] *ingratiate oneself to; serve*
abase, apple-polish*, be at beck and call*, be obsequious, be servile, blandish, bow, brownnose*, buddy up*, butter up*, cajole, cater to, cave in to*, cotton*, court, cower, crawl, creep, cringe, crouch, curry favor*, debase, defer, fall all over, fall on one's knees*, flatter, grovel, honey up*, invite, jolly, kneel, kowtow*, lay it on*, lick boots*, make up to, massage*, oil*, pander, pay court*, play up to*, scrape, slaver, snow*, stoop, stroke*, submit, toady*, truckle*, woo*, yield; SEE CONCEPTS 110,384

fawning [adj] *deferential, groveling*
abject, adulatory, bootlicking*, bowing, brownnosing*, compliant, cowering, crawling, cringing, flattering, humble, ingratiating, kowtowing*, mealy-mouthed*, obsequious, parasitic, prostrate, scraping, servile, slavish, sniveling, spineless, submissive, subservient, sycophant, sycophantic; SEE CONCEPT 401

faze [v] *embarrass*
abash, annoy, appall, bother, confound, confuse, daunt, discomfit, disconcert, discountenance, dismay, dumbfound, horrify, irritate, muddle, mystify, nonplus, perplex, puzzle, rattle, vex; SEE CONCEPTS 7,19

fear [n] *alarm, apprehension*
abhorrence, agitation, angst, anxiety, aversion, awe, bête noire, chickenheartedness*, cold feet*, cold sweat*, concern, consternation, cowardice, creeps, despair, discomposure, dismay, disquietude, distress, doubt, dread, faintheartedness,

foreboding, fright, funk*, horror, jitters, misgiving, nightmare, panic, phobia, presentiment, qualm, recreancy, reverence, revulsion, scare, suspicion, terror, timidity, trembling, tremor, trepidation, unease, uneasiness, worry; SEE CONCEPT 27

fear [v] *feel alarm; be scared of*
anticipate, apprehend, avoid, be afraid, be anxious, be apprehensive, be disquieted, be frightened, be in awe, blanch, break out in a sweat*, cower, crouch, dare not, dread, expect, falter, feel concern, flinch, foresee, fret, have butterflies*, have qualms, lose courage*, quail, quaver, shrink, shudder, shun, shy, start, suspect, tremble, wilt, worry; SEE CONCEPT 27

fearful [adj 1] *alarmed, apprehensive*
aflutter, afraid, aghast, agitated, anxious, chicken, chickenhearted*, diffident, discomposed, disquieted, disturbed, fainthearted, frightened, goosebumpy*, have cold feet*, hesitant, in a dither*, intimidated, jittery, jumpy, lily-livered*, mousy, nerveless, nervous, nervy, panicky, perturbed, phobic, pusillanimous, quivery, rabbity*, running scared*, scared, shaky, sheepish*, shrinking, shy, skittish, solicitous, spineless, tense, timid, timorous, tremulous, uneasy, unmanly, weak-kneed*, worried, yellow*; SEE CONCEPT 401

fearful [adj 2] *horrifying*
appalling, astounding, atrocious, awful, baleful, bloodcurdling, creepy, dire, distressing, dreadful, eerie, formidable, frightful, ghastly, ghoulish, grievous, grim, grisly, gruesome, hair-raising*, hideous, horrendous, horrible, horrific, lurid, macabre, monstrous, morbid, overwhelming, redoubtable, shocking, shuddersome, sinister, strange, sublime, terrible, tremendous, unearthly, unspeakable; SEE CONCEPTS 529,537,570

fearless [adj] *brave, unafraid*
assured, aweless, bodacious, bold, brassy, cheeky, chesty*, cocky, confident, cool hand*, courageous, crack*, daring, dashing, dauntless, doughty, flip*, fresh*, gallant, game, gritty, gutsy, heroic, icy*, indomitable, intrepid, lionhearted, nervy, plucky, salty*, sanguine, sassy*, smart, spunky, sure, temerarious, unabashed, undaunted, unflinching, valiant, valorous, wise; SEE CONCEPT 401

feasible [adj] *possible, doable*
achievable, advantageous, appropriate, attainable, beneficial, breeze, cinch, duck soup*, easy as pie*, expedient, fit, fitting, likely, no sweat*, performable, pie*, piece of cake*, practicable, practical, probable, profitable, pushover, realizable, reasonable, simple as ABC's*, snap, suitable, viable, workable, worthwhile; SEE CONCEPTS 528, 552,558

feast [n] *banquet and celebration*
barbecue, big feed*, blow*, blowout*, carnival, carousal, clambake, dinner, entertainment, fest, festival, festivity, fete, fiesta, gala, jollification, merrymaking, picnic, refreshment, regale, repast, spread, treat, wassail; SEE CONCEPTS 377,459

feast [v] *eat a great amount or very well*
banquet, dine, eat sumptuously, entertain, gorge, gormandize, indulge, overindulge, regale, snuff, stuff one's face*, treat, wine and dine*; SEE CONCEPT 169

feat [n] *achievement*
accomplishment, act, action, adventure, attainment, conquest, consummation, coup, deed, effort, enterprise, execution, exploit, performance, stunt, tour de force, triumph, venture, victory; SEE CONCEPTS 1,706

feather [n] *tuft of bird; plumage*
calamus, crest, down, fin, fluff, fringe, penna, pinion, pinna, plume, plumule, pompon, quill, shaft, spike, wing; SEE CONCEPT 399

feature [n 1] *characteristic*
affection, angle, article, aspect, attribute, character, component, constituent, detail, differential, earmark*, element, facet, factor, gag*, gimmick, hallmark, idiosyncrasy, individuality, ingredient, integrant, item, mark, notability, particularity, peculiarity, point, property, quality, savor, slant*, speciality, specialty, trait, twist*, unit, virtue; SEE CONCEPTS 831,834,835

feature [n 2] *highlight, special attraction*
big show*, crowd puller*, draw, drawing card*, headliner*, innovation, main item, peculiarity, prominent part, speciality, specialty; SEE CONCEPTS 386,829

feature [n 3] *special article in publication*
column, comment, item, piece, report, story; SEE CONCEPT 270

feature [v] *give prominence to*
accentuate, advertise, blaze*, call attention to, emphasize, headline*, italicize, make conspicuous, mark, play up*, point up*, present, promote, set off*, spotlight*, star, stress, underline, underscore; SEE CONCEPT 60

features [n] *facial characteristics*
appearance, countenance, face, lineaments, looks, mien, mug*, physiognomy, puss*, visage; SEE CONCEPT 418

featuring [adj] *giving prominence to*
calling attention to, displaying, drawing attention to, giving center stage to*, headlining*, highlighting, making much of*, pointing up*, presenting, promoting, pushing, recommending, showing, showing off*, starring, turning, turning the spotlight on*; SEE CONCEPT 292

febrile [adj] *feverish*
delirious, fevered, fiery, flushed, hallucinatory, hot, inflamed, pyretic; SEE CONCEPTS 314,605

feckless [adj] *without purpose*
aimless, carefree, careless, feeble, fustian, futile, good-for-nothing*, hopeless, incautious, incompetent, ineffective, ineffectual, irresponsible, meaningless, reckless, shiftless, uncareful, useless, weak, wild, worthless; SEE CONCEPTS 404,542

fecund [adj] *productive*
breeding, fertile, fructiferous, fruitful, generating, pregnant, proliferant, prolific, propagating, reproducing, rich, spawning, teeming; SEE CONCEPT 537

federation [n] *partnership, organization*
alliance, amalgamation, association, bunch, coalition, combination, confederacy, crew, crowd, entente, family, federacy, gang, league, mob, outfit, pool, ring, syndicate, syndication, tribe, union; SEE CONCEPTS 323,381,417

fed up [adj] *disgusted with*
annoyed, blasé, blue*, bored, depressed, discontented, dismal, dissatisfied, down, gloomy, glum, jaded, sated, satiated, sick and tired*, surfeited, tired, up to here*, weary; SEE CONCEPT 403

fee [n] *charge for service or privilege*
account, ante*, bill, bite*, chunk*, commission, compensation, consideration, cost, cut*, emolu-

fa
fe

ment, end*, expense, gravy*, handle, hire, honorarium, house*, juice*, pay, payment, percentage, piece*, piece of the action*, price, rake-off*, recompense, remuneration, reward, salary, share, slice*, stipend, take*, take-in*, toll, wage; SEE CONCEPTS *329,344*

feeble [*adj*] *not strong; ineffective*
aged, ailing, chicken*, debilitated, decrepit, delicate, doddering, dopey*, effete, emasculated, enervated, enfeebled, etiolated, exhausted, failing, faint, flabby*, flat, fragile, frail, gentle, helpless, impotent, inadequate, incompetent, indecisive, ineffectual, inefficient, infirm, insubstantial, insufficient, lame, languid, low, out of gas*, paltry, poor, powerless, puny, sapless, sickly, slight, strengthless, tame, thin, unconvincing, vitiated, weak, weakened, weakly, wimpy*, woozy*, zero*; SEE CONCEPTS *267,489,527*

feebleness [*n*] *lack of strength; ineffectiveness*
debility, decrepitude, delicacy, disease, effeteness, enervation, etiolation, exhaustion, flimsiness, frailness, frailty, inability, inadequacy, incapacity, incompetence, ineffectualness, infirmity, infirmness, insignificance, insufficiency, lameness, languor, lassitude, malaise, senility, sickliness, unhealthiness, weakness; SEE CONCEPTS *630,676,732*

feed [*v*] *give nourishment; augment*
banquet, bolster, cater, cram, deliver, dine, dish out*, dispense, encourage, fatten, fill, find, foster, fuel, furnish, give, gorge, hand, hand over, maintain, minister, nourish, nurse, nurture, provide, provision, regale, satisfy, stock, strengthen, stuff, supply, support, sustain, victual, wine and dine*; SEE CONCEPTS *107,140*

feed on [*v*] *consume*
devour, eat, exist on, fare, feast, graze, have a bite*, ingest, live on*, meal, munch, nibble, nurture, partake, pasture*, peck*, pig out*, prey on, scarf*, snack, sponge, subsist, take, take nourishment; SEE CONCEPT *169*

feel [*n*] *texture; air*
ambience, atmosphere, aura, feeling, finish, impression, mood, palpation, quality, semblance, sensation, sense, surface, tactility, taction, touch, vibes*; SEE CONCEPTS *611,673*

feel [*v1*] *touch, stroke*
apperceive, caress, clasp, clutch, explore, finger, fondle, frisk, fumble, grapple, grasp, grip, grope, handle, manipulate, maul, palm, palpate, paw, perceive, pinch, ply, poke, press, run hands over*, sense, squeeze, test, thumb, tickle, try, twiddle, wield; SEE CONCEPT *612*

feel [*v2*] *experience*
accept, acknowledge, appear, appreciate, be affected, be aware of, be excited, be impressed, be sensible of, be sensitive, be turned on to*, comprehend, discern, encounter, endure, enjoy, exhibit, get*, get in touch*, get vibes*, go through*, have, have a hunch*, have funny feeling*, have vibes*, know, meet, note, notice, observe, perceive, receive, remark, resemble, savor, see, seem, sense, suffer, suggest, take to heart*, taste, undergo, understand, welcome; SEE CONCEPTS *15,34,38*

feel [*v3*] *believe*
assume, be convinced, be of the opinion, conclude, conjecture, consider, credit, deduce, deem, esteem, gather, guess, have a hunch*, have the impression*, hold, infer, intuit, judge, know, presume, repute, sense, suppose, surmise, suspect, think; SEE CONCEPT *12*

feeling [*n1*] *sensation, especially of touch*
activity, awareness, consciousness, enjoyment, excitability, excitation, excitement, feel, innervation, motility, motor response, pain, perceiving, perception, pleasure, reaction, receptivity, reflex, responsiveness, sense, sensibility, sensitivity, sensuality, tactility, tangibility, titillation; SEE CONCEPT *608*

feeling [*n2*] *idea, impression*
apprehension, belief, consciousness, conviction, eye*, hunch*, inclination, inkling, instinct, mind, notion, opinion, outlook, persuasion, point of view, presentiment, reaction, sense, sentiment, suspicion, thought, view; SEE CONCEPTS *532,689,690*

feeling [*n3*] *a state of mind, often strong*
action, affection, appreciation, ardor, behavior, capacity, compassion, concern, cultivation, culture, delicacy, discernment, discrimination, emotion, empathy, faculty, fervor, fondness, heat, imagination, impression, intelligence, intensity, intuition, judgment, keenness, palpability, passion, pathos, pity, reaction, refinement, sensibility, sensitivity, sentiment, sentimentality, sharpness, spirit, sympathy, tangibility, taste, tenderness, understanding, warmth; SEE CONCEPTS *409,410*

feeling [*n4*] *ambience*
air, atmosphere, aura, impression, imprint, mood, quality, semblance; SEE CONCEPT *673*

feign [*v*] *pretend*
act, affect, assume, bluff*, counterfeit, devise, dissemble, dissimulate, do a bit*, fabricate, fake, forge, four-flush*, give appearance of, imagine, imitate, invent, make show of*, phony up*, play, play possum*, put on, put on act*, put up a front*, sham*, simulate, stonewall*; SEE CONCEPTS *59,63,292*

feigned [*adj*] *pretended*
affected, artificial, assumed, counterfeit, fabricated, fake, faked, false, fictitious, imaginary, imagined, imitation, insincere, phony, pretended, pseudo*, put-on*, sham*, simulated, spurious; SEE CONCEPTS *401,582*

feint [*n*] *pretense*
artifice, bait, blind, bluff, cheat, deceit, distraction, dodge, duck, expedient, fake, gambit, hoax, hoodwinking*, imposture, make-believe, maneuver, mock attack, play, ploy, pretension, pretext, ruse, sham*, shift, snare, stall, stratagem, subterfuge, trick, wile; SEE CONCEPTS *633,660,725*

felicitate [*v*] *congratulate*
commend, compliment, praise, recommend, rejoice with, salute, wish joy to; SEE CONCEPT *69*

felicitous [*adj*] *appropriate, suitable*
applicable, apposite, apropos, apt, convincing, fit, fitting, germane, happy, inspired, just, meet, neat, opportune, pat, pertinent, proper, propitious, relevant, seasonable, telling, timely, well-chosen, well-timed; SEE CONCEPTS *558,799*

fell [*v*] *chop down*
blow down, bowl over*, bring down, cause to fall, cleave, cut, cut down, dash, demolish, down, drop, flatten, floor*, gash, ground, hack, hew, knock down, knock over, lay low*, level, mangle, mow down*, prostrate, pull down, raze, rive, sever, shoot, shoot down*, slash, split, strike

down, sunder, throw down, tumble; SEE CONCEPTS 176,181

fellow [n2] *male or female colleague, friend*
assistant, associate, cohort, companion, compeer, comrade, concomitant, confrere, consort, coordinate, counterpart*, coworker, double, duplicate, equal, instructor, lecturer, match, mate, member, partner, peer, professor, reciprocal, twin; SEE CONCEPTS 348,423

fellowship [n] *sociability, association*
acquaintance, affability, alliance, amity, camaraderie, club, communion, companionability, companionship, company, comradeship, conviviality, familiarity, friendliness, guild, intimacy, kindliness, league, order, society, sodality, togetherness; SEE CONCEPTS 387,388

felon [n] *criminal*
con, convict, delinquent, ex-con*, jailbird*, lawbreaker, lifer*, loser*, malefactor, offender, outlaw, yardbird*; SEE CONCEPT 412

female [n] *woman*
daughter, femme, gal, gentlewoman, girl, grandmother, lady, madam, matron, Miss/Mrs./Ms., mother, she, sister; SEE CONCEPT 415

female [adj] *having the qualities or characteristics of a woman*
effeminate, fecund, feminine, fertile, maternal, muliebrous, womanish, womanly; SEE CONCEPTS 371,408

femininity/feminine [n/adj] *womanly*
effeminate, effete, fertile, gender, gynic, womanhood, womanish, womanliness; SEE CONCEPTS 371,372,408,648

fence [n] *barrier used to enclose a piece of land*
backstop, balustrade, bar, barbed wire, barricade, block, boards, chains, Cyclone, defense, dike, guard, hedge, net, paling, palisade, pickets, posts, rail, railing, rampart, roadblock, shield, stakes, stockade, stop, wall; SEE CONCEPTS 260,476,479

fence [v1] *enclose or separate an area*
bound, cage, circumscribe, confine, coop, corral, defend, encircle, fortify, girdle, guard, hedge, hem, immure, mew, mure, pen, protect, rail, restrict, secure, surround, wall; SEE CONCEPT 758

fence [v2] *dodge; beat around the bush*
avoid, baffle, cavil, duck, equivocate, evade, feint, foil, hedge, maneuver, outwit, parry, prevaricate, quibble, shift, shirk, sidestep, stonewall*, tergiversate; SEE CONCEPTS 30,59

fend [v] *defend*
bulwark, cover, dodge, guard, oppose, parry, protect, repel, resist, safeguard, screen, secure, shield; SEE CONCEPT 96

fender [n] *piece protecting part of a vehicle*
apron, buffer, bumper, cover, curb, cushion, frame, guard, mask, mudguard*, protector, screen, shield, splashboard, ward; SEE CONCEPT 502

fend for [v] *take care of*
eke out existence*, look after, make do, make provision for, provide for, stay alive*, subsist, support, survive, sustain; SEE CONCEPTS 100,117

fend off [v] *keep at bay*
avert, avoid, beat off*, deflect, drive back*, hold at bay*, keep at a distance, keep at arm's length*, keep off, parry, rebuff, rebuke, rebut, refuse, reject, repel, repulse, resist, snub, spurn, stave off, turn aside, ward off; SEE CONCEPT 96

ferment [n1] *substance causing chemicals to split into simpler substances*
bacteria, bacterium, barm, ebullition, enzyme, fermentation agent, leaven, leavening, mold, seethe, simmer, yeast; SEE CONCEPT 478

ferment [n2] *agitation, uprising*
ailment, brouhaha, clamor, commotion, convulsion, disquiet, disquietude, disruption, disturbance, excitement, fever, flap, frenzy, furor, fuss, heat, hell broke loose*, hubbub, imbroglio, outcry, restiveness, restlessness, row, rumble, scene, state of unrest, stew*, stink*, stir, storm, to-do*, tumult, turbulence, turmoil, unrest, upheaval, uproar, upturn; SEE CONCEPTS 106,674

ferment [v] *split into simpler substances; be agitated*
acidify, be violent, boil, brew, bubble, churn, concoct, dissolve, effervesce, evaporate, excite, fester, fizz, foam, foment, froth, heat, incite, inflame, leaven, moil, overflow, provoke, ripen, rise, rouse, seethe, simmer, sour, sparkle, stir up, work; SEE CONCEPTS 7,19,22,250

ferocious [adj] *violent, barbaric*
barbarous, bloodthirsty, brutal, brutish, cruel, fell, feral, fierce, frightful, grim, implacable, inhuman, inhumane, lupine, merciless, murderous, pitiless, predatory, rapacious, ravening, ravenous, relentless, ruthless, sanguinary, savage, tigerish, truculent, unmerciful, unrestrained, untamed, vehement, vicious, voracious, wild, wolfish; SEE CONCEPTS 401,542

ferret out [v] *trace, search out*
ascertain, be on to, bring to light*, chase, determine, dig up*, disclose, discover, drive out, elicit, extract, follow, get at*, hunt, learn, nose out*, penetrate, pick up on, pierce, probe, pry, pursue, quest, root out*, seek, smell out*, smoke out*, track down, trail, unearth; SEE CONCEPTS 183,216

ferry [n] *transportation boat*
barge, ferryboat, packet, packet boat, passage boat; SEE CONCEPT 506

ferry [v] *carry across*
bear, buck, carry, chauffeur, convey, lug*, move across, pack, run, schlepp*, send, ship, shuttle, tote*, transport; SEE CONCEPTS 187,217

fertile [adj] *ready to bear, produce*
abundant, arable, bearing, black, bountiful, breeding, breedy, bringing forth, childing, fecund, feracious, flowering, flowing with milk and honey*, fruitful, generative, gravid, hebetic, loamy, lush, luxuriant, plenteous, plentiful, pregnant, procreant, producing, productive, proliferant, prolific, puberal, pubescent, rank, rich, spawning, teeming, uberous, vegetative, virile, with child*, yielding; SEE CONCEPTS 372,485

fertility [n] *readiness to bear, produce*
abundance, copiousness, fecundity, feracity, fruitfulness, generative capacity, gravidity, luxuriance, plentifulness, potency, pregnancy, productiveness, productivity, prolificacy, prolificity, puberty, pubescence, richness, uberty, virility; SEE CONCEPTS 372,723

fertilize [v] *make ready to bear, produce*
beget, breed, compost, cover, dress, enrich, fecundate, feed, fructify, generate, germinate, impregnate, inseminate, lime, make fruitful, make pregnant, manure, mulch, pollinate, procreate, propagate, top-dress, treat; SEE CONCEPTS 257,374,375

fe
fe

fertilizer [n] *dressing to aid production of crops*
buffalo chips*, compost, cow chips*, dung, guano, humus, manure, maul*, mulch, peat moss, plant food, potash, top dressing*; SEE CONCEPTS 260,399,429

fervent/fervid [adj] *enthusiastic, excited*
animated, ardent, blazing, burning, devout, dying to*, eager, earnest, ecstatic, emotional, enthused, falling all over oneself*, fiery, glowing, go great guns*, heartfelt, hearty, hot*, hot-blooded*, impassioned, intense, passionate, perfervid, pious, religious, responsive, serious, sincere, unfeigned, vehement, warm, warmhearted, wholehearted, zealous; SEE CONCEPTS 401,542

fervor [n] *excitement, enthusiasm*
animation, ardency, ardor, devoutness, eagerness, earnestness, fervency, fire*, heartiness, heat*, hurrah, intensity, jazz*, love, oomph*, passion, pep talk*, piety, piousness, religiousness, seriousness, sincerity, solemnity, vehemence, warmth, weakness, wholeheartedness, zeal, zealousness; SEE CONCEPTS 633,657

fester [v] *intensify; become inflamed*
aggravate, blister, canker, chafe, decay, gall, gather, irk, maturate, putrefy, rankle, rot, smolder, suppurate, ulcer, ulcerate; SEE CONCEPTS 469,698

festival [n] *celebration*
anniversary, carnival, commemoration, competition, entertainment, fair, feast, festivities, fete, field day, fiesta, gala, holiday, jubilee, merrymaking, treat; SEE CONCEPT 377

festive [adj] *decorated, celebratory*
blithe, bouncy, carnival, cheery, chipper*, chirpy, convivial, festal, gala, gay, gleeful, go-go*, grooving, happy, hearty, holiday, jocund, jolly, jovial, joyful, joyous, jubilant, juiced up*, jumping, lighthearted, merry, mirthful, peppy*, perky, rocking*, snappy*, swinging, upbeat, zippy*; SEE CONCEPTS 403,548

festivity [n] *celebration, revelry*
amusement, bash*, blowout*, carousal*, clambake*, conviviality, do*, entertainment, festival, fun, fun and games*, gaiety, happiness, hilarity, hoopla, jamboree, jollity, joviality, joyfulness, levity, merriment, merrymaking, mirth, party, pleasure, revel, reveling, revelment, shindig*, sport, whoopee*, wingding*; SEE CONCEPTS 377,383

fetch [v] *go get, bring in*
back, bear, be sold for, bring, bring back, bring to, buck, call for, carry, conduct, convey, deliver, draw forth, earn, elicit, escort, get, give rise to, go for, gun, heel, lead, lug*, make, obtain, pack, piggyback*, produce, realize, retrieve, ride, sell, sell for, shlep*, shoulder*, tote, transport, truck*, yield; SEE CONCEPTS 90,124,131

fetching [adj] *alluring, attractive*
beautiful, captivating, charming, cute, enchanting, enticing, fascinating, intriguing, luring, pleasing, sweet, taking, tempting, winsome; SEE CONCEPTS 537,579

fete [n] *celebration, party*
ball, banquet, bazaar, do*, fair, festival, fiesta, gala; SEE CONCEPT 377

fete [v] *throw a party for someone*
celebrate, entertain, feast, festival, hold reception for, holiday, honor, lionize, make much of*, roll out the red carpet*, treat, wine and dine*; SEE CONCEPT 384

fetid [adj] *foul, rancid*
corrupt, fusty, grody*, gross*, icky*, loathsome, lousy, malodorous, mephitic, noisome, noxious, offensive, putrid, rank, reeking, repugnant, repulsive, revolting, rotten, smelly, stenchy, stinking, stinky, strong, yecchy*, yucky*; SEE CONCEPT 598

fetish [n1] *obsession*
bias, craze*, desire, fixation, golden calf*, idée fixe, leaning, luck, mania, partiality, penchant, periapt, predilection, prejudice, preoccupation, prepossession, proclivity, propensity, stimulant, thing*; SEE CONCEPTS 529,689

fetish [n2] *object believed to have supernatural powers*
amulet, charm, cult object, idol, image, juju*, mascot, phylactery, superstition, talisman, voodoo doll*, zemi; SEE CONCEPTS 446,687

fetter [v] *tie up, hold*
bind, chain, check, clog, confine, cuff, curb, drag feet, encumber, hamper, hamstring*, handcuff, hang up, hinder, hobble, hog-tie*, hold captive, leash, manacle, put straitjacket on*, repress, restrain, restrict, shackle, throw monkey wrench in*, trammel; SEE CONCEPTS 130,191

fetters [n] *bindings; bondage*
bilboes, bonds, captivity, chains, check, cuffs, curb, handcuffs, hindrance, irons, manacles, obstruction, restraint, shackles, trammels; SEE CONCEPTS 130,191,500

feud [n] *major argument; estrangement*
altercation, bad blood*, bickering, broil*, combat, conflict, contention, contest, controversy, disagreement, discord, dispute, dissension, enmity, faction, falling out*, fight, fracas, grudge, hostility, quarrel, rivalry, row, run-in*, squabble, strife, vendetta; SEE CONCEPTS 46,106,388

feud [v] *fight bitterly; fall out*
be at daggers with*, be at odds*, bicker, brawl, clash, contend, dispute, duel, quarrel, row, squabble, war; SEE CONCEPTS 46,106

fever [n] *state of high temperature or agitation*
burning up*, delirium, ecstasy, excitement, febrile disease, ferment, fervor, fire, flush, frenzy, heat, intensity, passion, pyrexia, restlessness, running a temperature*, the shakes*, turmoil, unrest; SEE CONCEPTS 410,610

feverish [adj1] *having a high temperature*
above normal*, aguey, burning, burning up*, febrile, fevered, fiery, flushed, having the shakes*, hectic, hot, inflamed, on fire, pyretic, running a temperature*; SEE CONCEPT 605

feverish [adj2] *excited, agitated*
burning, distracted, fervid, fevered, frantic, frenetic, frenzied, furious, heated, hectic, highstrung*, impatient, keyed up*, nervous, obsessive, overwrought, passionate, restless; SEE CONCEPT 401

few [adj] *hardly any*
exiguous, few and far between*, imperceptible, inconsequential, inconsiderable, infrequent, insufficient, lean, less, meager, middling, minor, minority, minute, negligible, not many, not too many*, occasional, paltry, petty, piddling, rare, scant, scanty, scarce, scarcely any, scattered, scattering, seldom, semioccasional, short, skimpy, slender, slight, slim, some, sparse, sporadic, stingy, straggling, thin, trifling, uncommon, unfrequent, widely spaced; SEE CONCEPTS 771,789

few [prep] *scarcely any*
not many, not too many*, scattering, several, slim pickings*, small number, smatter, smattering, some, spattering, sprinkling; SEE CONCEPT 787

fiancé/fiancée [n] *person engaged to marry*
affianced person, betrothed, engaged person, future*, husband-to-be, intended, prospective spouse, steady*, wife-to-be; SEE CONCEPTS 414,423

fiasco [n] *catastrophe*
abortion, blunder, botched situation, breakdown, debacle, disaster, dumb thing to do*, dumb trick*, embarrassment, error, failure, farce, flap, flop, mess, miscarriage, route, ruin, screwup*, stunt, washout*; SEE CONCEPT 674

fiat [n] *order, proclamation*
authorization, command, decree, dictate, dictum, edict, endorsement, mandate, ordinance, permission, precept, sanction, ukase, warrant; SEE CONCEPT 685

fib [n] *undetailed lie*
canard, crock*, equivocation, evasiveness, fabrication, fairy tale*, falsehood, falsity, fiction, invention, jazz*, line*, mendacity, misrepresentation, prevarication, spinach*, story, tale, untruth, untruthfulness, white lie*, whopper*, yarn*; SEE CONCEPTS 278,282

fib [v] *tell an undetailed lie*
concoct, create fiction, equivocate, fabricate, falsify, invent, jive*, make up, palter, plant, prevaricate, promote, shovel*, speak with forked tongue*, stretch the truth*, tell a little white lie*, trump up*; SEE CONCEPT 63

fiber [n1] *strand of material*
cilia, cord, fibril, filament, footlet, grain, grit, hair, shred, staple, string, strip, tendril, thread, tissue, tooth, vein, warp, web, woof; SEE CONCEPTS 392,428,611,831

fiber [n2] *texture*
essence, fabric, feel, hand, nap, nature, pile, spirit, substance; SEE CONCEPTS 411,682

fibrous [adj] *stringy*
coarse, fibroid, hairy, muscular, pulpy, ropy, sinewy, stalky, threadlike, tissued, veined, wiry, woody; SEE CONCEPT 606

fickle [adj] *vacillating, blowing hot and cold*
arbitrary, capricious, changeable, cheating, coquettish, double-crossing, faithless, fitful, flighty, frivolous, inconstant, irresolute, lubricious, mercurial, mutable, quicksilver, sneaking, temperamental, ticklish, two-timing, unfaithful, unpredictable, unstable, unsteady, untrue, variable, volatile, whimsical, yo-yo*; SEE CONCEPTS 401,534,545

fiction [n] *made-up story*
anecdote, best seller, book, cliff-hanger*, clothesline*, concoction, crock*, drama, fable, fabrication, falsehood, fancy, fantasy, fib, figment of imagination*, fish story*, hooey*, imagination, improvisation, invention, legend, lie, misrepresentation, myth, narrative, novel, potboiler*, prevarication, romance, smoke*, storytelling, tale, tall story*, terminological inexactitude, untruth, whopper*, work of imagination, yarn*; SEE CONCEPTS 63,271,280,282

fictitious [adj] *untrue, made-up*
apocryphal, artificial, assumed, bogus*, chimerical, concocted, cooked-up*, counterfeit, created, deceptive, delusive, delusory, dishonest, ersatz*, fabricated, factitious, fake, faked, false, fanciful, fantastic, fashioned, feigned, fictional, fictive, figmental, hyped up*, illusory, imaginary, imagined, improvised, invented, made, make-believe, misleading, mock, mythical, phony, queer, romantic, sham*, simulated, spurious, supposititious, suppositious, synthetic, trumped-up*, unreal; SEE CONCEPTS 267,582

fiddle [v] *mess with, tinker*
dabble, doodle, feel, fidget, finger, fool, handle, interfere, mess, mess around*, monkey*, play, potter, puddle, putter, tamper, touch, toy, trifle, twiddle; SEE CONCEPTS 87,291

fidelity [n1] *faithfulness in a relationship*
allegiance, ardor, attachment, constancy, dependability, devotedness, devotion, faith, fealty, integrity, loyalty, piety, reliability, staunchness, steadfastness, true-heartedness, trustworthiness; SEE CONCEPTS 32,388

fidelity [n2] *conformity to a standard*
accuracy, adherence, adhesion, attachment, closeness, constancy, correspondence, exactitude, exactness, faithfulness, loyalty, naturalism, preciseness, precision, realism, scrupulousness, verism; SEE CONCEPT 636

fidget [v] *move restlessly*
be antsy*, be hyper*, be nervous, be on pins and needles*, be spooked*, be wired*, bustle, chafe, fiddle, fret, fuss, hitch, jiggle, jitter, joggle, jump, play, squirm, stir, toss, trifle, twiddle, twitch, wiggle, worry; SEE CONCEPT 147

fidgety [adj] *restlessly moving*
antsy*, apprehensive, high-strung*, hyper*, impatient, jerky, jittery, jumpy, nervous, nervous wreck*, nervy, on edge*, on pins and needles*, restive, restless, spooked*, spooky*, twitchy, uneasy, unrestful, up the wall*, wired*; SEE CONCEPT 401

field [n1] *open land that can be cultivated*
acreage, cropland, enclosure, farmland, garden, glebe, grassland, green, ground, lea, mead, meadow, moorland, pasture, patch, plot, ranchland, range, terrain, territory, tillage, tract, vineyard; SEE CONCEPTS 509,517

field [n2] *persons taking part in competition*
applicants, candidates, competition, competitors, contestants, entrants, entries, nominees, participants, possibilities, runners; SEE CONCEPTS 325,365,417

field [n3] *sphere of influence, activity, interest, study*
area, avocation, bailiwick, bounds, calling, champaign, circle, compass, confines, cup of tea*, demesne, department, discipline, domain, dominion, environment, job, jurisdiction, limits, line, long suit*, margin, métier, occupation, orbit, precinct, province, purview, racket, range, reach, region, scope, speciality, specialty, sweep, terrain, territory, thing, vocation, walk, weakness, work; SEE CONCEPT 349

field [n4] *arena with special use, as athletics*
amphitheater, battlefield, circuit, course, court, diamond, fairground, golf course, green, gridiron, grounds, landing strip, lot, park, playground, playing area, racecourse, race track, range, rink, stadium, terrain, theater, track, turf; SEE CONCEPTS 364,438,449

field [v] *catch a hit or thrown object*
cover, deal with, deflect, handle, hold, occupy, patrol, pick up, play, retrieve, return, stop, turn aside; SEE CONCEPT 164

fe
fi

fiend [n1] *dastardly person*

barbarian, beast, brute, degenerate, demon, devil, diablo*, evil spirit, hellion, imp, little devil*, Mephistopheles, monster, ogre, Satan, savage, serpent, troll; SEE CONCEPT 412

fiend [n2] *person overenthusiastic about interest*

addict, aficionado, bigot, devotee, enthusiast, fan, fanatic, freak, maniac, monomaniac, nut*, votarist, votary, zealot; SEE CONCEPT 423

fierce [adj] *violent, menacing*

angry, animal, ape, awful, barbarous, bloodthirsty, blustery, boisterous, bold, brutal, brutish, cruel, cutthroat*, dangerous, enraged, fell, feral, ferocious, fiery, flipped*, frightening, furious, horrible, howling, impetuous, infuriated, intense, malevolent, malign, murderous, passionate, powerful, primitive, raging, raving, relentless, savage, stormy, strong, tempestuous, terrible, threatening, tigerish, truculent, tumultuous/tumultuous, uncontrollable, untamed, vehement, venomous, vicious, wild; SEE CONCEPTS 525, 537,540

fiercely [adv] *violently, menacingly*

angrily, awfully, boldly, brutally, ferociously, forcefully, forcibly, frantically, frenziedly, frighteningly, furiously, hard, horribly, impetuously, in a frenzy, irresistibly, like cats and dogs*, madly, maleficiently, malevolently, malignly, mightily, monstrous, no holds barred*, passionately, riotously, roughly, savagely, severely, stormily, tempestuously, terribly, threateningly, tigerishly, tooth and nail*, turbulently, uncontrollably, vehemently, venomously, viciously, wildly, with bared teeth*; SEE CONCEPTS 525,537,540

fiery [adj] *passionate; on fire*

ablaze, afire, aflame, agitable, alight, blazing, burning, choleric, combustible, conflagrant, enthusiastic, excitable, febrile, fervid, fevered, feverish, fierce, flaming, flaring, flickering, flushed, glowing, heated, hot, hot-blooded, hot-headed*, hot-tempered*, igneous, ignited, impassioned, impetuous, impulsive, inflamed, in flames, intense, irascible, irritable, madcap, peppery, perfervid, precipitate, red-hot*, spirited, unrestrained, vehement, violent; SEE CONCEPTS 401,542,605

fiesta [n] *day of rest; religious celebration*

carnival, feast, festival, holiday, holy day, saint's day, vacation; SEE CONCEPTS 377,386

fight [n1] *physical encounter*

action, affray, altercation, argument, battle, battle royal*, bout, brawl, broil, brush, clash, combat, conflict, confrontation, contention, contest, controversy, difficulty, disagreement, dispute, dissension, dogfight, duel, engagement, exchange, feud, fisticuffs*, fracas, fray, free-for-all*, fuss, hostility, joust, match, melee, quarrel, riot, rivalry, round, row, ruckus, rumble, scrap*, scrimmage, scuffle, set-to*, skirmish, sparring match, strife, struggle, tiff, to-do*, tussle, war, wrangling; SEE CONCEPT 106

fight [n2] *courage, will to resist*

aggression, aggressiveness, attack, backbone, belligerence, boldness, combativeness, gameness, hardihood, mettle, militancy, pluck, pugnacity, resistance, spirit; SEE CONCEPT 411

fight [v1] *engage in physical encounter*

altercate, assault, attack, bandy with*, battle, bear arms, bicker, box, brawl, brush with*, buck, carry on war, challenge, clash, contend, cross swords,

dispute, do battle, duel, exchange blows, feud, flare up, go to war, grapple, joust, meet, mix it up*, oppugn, ply weapons, protect, quarrel, repel, resist, rowdy, scrap, scuffle, skirmish, spar, strive, struggle, take all comers*, take the field*, take up the gauntlet*, tiff*, tilt*, traverse, tug, tussle, wage war, war, withstand, wrangle, wrestle; SEE CONCEPT 106

fight [v2] *oppose action, belief*

argue, bicker, buck*, buckle down*, carry on, combat, conduct, contest, continue, defy, dispute, effect, endure, engage in, exert oneself, fall out, force, further, hammer away*, hassle, lay into*, light into*, maintain, make a stand against*, oppose, persevere, persist, prosecute, push forward, put up an argument*, repel, resist, row, spare no effort*, squabble, stand up to*, strive, struggle, support, take on, take pains*, tangle with*, toil on, travail, traverse, uphold, wage, withstand, wrangle; SEE CONCEPTS 46,100,384

fight back/fight off [v] *defend oneself*

beat off*, bottle up*, check, contain, control, curb, fend off, hold at bay*, hold back, keep at bay*, oppose, put up fight, repel, reply, repress, repulse, resist, restrain, retaliate, stave off, ward off; SEE CONCEPTS 96,106

fighter [n] *person engaged in hostile encounter*

aggressor, antagonist, assailant, battler, belligerent, boxer, brawler, bruiser*, bully, champion, combatant, competitor, contender, contestant, disputant, duelist, GI, gladiator, heavy*, jouster, mercenary, militant, opponent, person-at-arms, pugilist, punching bag*, rival, scrapper, serviceperson, slugger, soldier, tanker*, warrior, wildcat*; SEE CONCEPTS 358,366,412

fighting [n] *battle, encounter*

argument, battle royal*, beef*, bloodshed, blowup, bout, brannigan, brawling, brush, combat, conflict, contention, dispute, donnybrook*, exchange, flap*, fracas, free-for-all*, go, hassle, hell broke loose*, hostility, joust, match, melee, mix, punch out*, riot, roughhouse*, row, rowdy, rumble, rumpus, run-in*, scramble, scrap*, scrimmage, scuffle, set-to*, spat, strife, struggle, tiff, war, warfare, words, wrangle; SEE CONCEPT 106

fighting [adj] *aggressive, warlike*

angry, argumentative, battling, bellicose, belligerent, boxing, brawling, combative, contending, contentious, determined, disputatious, disputative, fencing, ferocious, hawkish, hostile, jingoistic, jousting, martial, militant, militaristic, pugnacious, quarrelsome, ready to fight, resolute, scrappy, skirmishing, sparring, truculent, unbeatable, under arms*, up in arms*, warmongering, wrestling; SEE CONCEPT 401

figment [n] *creation in one's mind*

bubble*, castle in the air*, chimera, daydream, dream, fable, fabrication, falsehood, fancy, fantasy, fiction, illusion, improvisation, invention, lie, nightmare, production; SEE CONCEPT 529

figurative [adj] *not literal, but symbolic*

allegorical, denotative, descriptive, emblematic, emblematical, fanciful, florid, flowery, illustrative, metaphoric, metaphorical, ornate, pictorial, poetical, representative, signifying, typical; SEE CONCEPTS 267,582

figure [n1] *numeral; numeric value*

amount, character, chiffer, cipher, cost, digit, integer, number, price, quotation, rate, sum, symbol, terms, total, worth; SEE CONCEPTS 784,787

figure [n2] *form, shape; physical structure*
anatomy, appearance, attitude, bod*, body, build, carriage, cast, chassis*, configuration, conformation, constitution, delineation, development, frame, mass, measurements, outline, physique, pose, posture, proportions, shadow, silhouette, substance, torso; SEE CONCEPTS 733,754,757

figure [n3] *object with design; depiction*
cast, composition, decoration, device, diagram, drawing, effigy, embellishment, emblem, illustration, image, model, mold, motif, motive, ornamentation, pattern, piece, portrait, representation, sketch, statue; SEE CONCEPTS 259,625

figure [n4] *famous person*
celebrity, character, dignitary, force, leader, notability, notable, personage, personality, presence, somebody, worthy; SEE CONCEPTS 354,423

figure [v1] *calculate, compute*
add, cast, cipher, count, count heads*, count noses*, cut ice*, dope out*, enumerate, estimate, fix a price, foot*, guess, keep tabs*, number, reckon, run down, sum, summate, take account of, tally, tot*, total, totalize, tote*, tot up*, work out; SEE CONCEPTS 197,764

figure [v2] *understand; decide, infer*
catch on to, cipher, clear up, comprehend, conclude, crack, decipher, decode, determine, discover, disentangle, dope out*, fathom, follow, get*, make heads or tails of*, make out*, master, opine, puzzle out, reason, resolve, rule, see, settle, solve, suppose, think, think out, unfold, unravel, unriddle, unscramble, untangle; SEE CONCEPTS 15,18,37

figurehead [n] *person who is leader in name only*
cipher, front*, mouthpiece*, nominal head, nonentity, nothing, puppet*, straw boss*, straw person, titular head, token; SEE CONCEPTS 354,423

figure in [v] *contribute to*
act, appear, be conspicuous, be featured, be included, be mentioned, have a place in, play a part*; SEE CONCEPT 112

figure of speech [n] *communication that is not meant literally; stylistic device*
adumbration, allegory, alliteration, allusion, analogue, anaphora, anticlimax, antistrophe, antithesis, aposiopesis, apostrophe, asyndeton, bathos, comparison, conceit, echoism, ellipsis, euphemism, euphuism, exaggeration, hyperbole, image, imagery, irony, litotes, metaphor, metonymy, onomatopoeia, oxymoron, parable, paradox, parallel, personification, proteron, rhetoric, satire, simile, synecdoche, trope, tropology, turn of phrase, understatement; SEE CONCEPTS 275,278

filch [v] *steal*
cop*, crib*, embezzle, hustle*, lift*, misappropriate, pilfer*, pinch*, purloin, rip off*, rob, scrounge, sneak, snipe, snitch*, swipe, take, thieve, walk off with*; SEE CONCEPTS 139,142

file [n1] *system of order, placement for ease of use*
book, cabinet, case, census, charts, circular file*, data, directory, docket, documents, dossier, folder, index, information, list, notebook, pigeonhole*, portfolio, record, register, repository; SEE CONCEPTS 271,770

file [n2] *line, queue*
column, echelon, line, parade, rank, row, string, tier, troop; SEE CONCEPT 727

file [v1] *put in place, order*
alphabetize, arrange, catalog, catalogue, categorize, classify, deposit, docket, document, enter, index, list, pigeonhole*, record, register, slot, tabulate; SEE CONCEPTS 84,158

file [v2] *rub down, grind*
abrade, burnish, erode, finish, furbish, grate, level, polish, rasp, raze, refine, scrape, shape, sharpen, smooth; SEE CONCEPTS 137,186, 215,250

filibuster [n] *obstruction of progress, especially in verbal argument*
delay, hindrance, holding the floor*, interference, opposition, postponement, procrastination, stonewalling*, talkathon*; SEE CONCEPT 298

fill [n] *capacity*
all one wants, ample, enough, filler, padding, plenty, satiety, stuffing, sufficiency, sufficient; SEE CONCEPTS 719,736,794

fill [v1] *to put in and occupy the whole of*
block, blow up, brim over, bulge out, charge, choke, clog, close, congest, cram, crowd, distend, fulfill, furnish, glut, gorge, heap, impregnate, inflate, jam-pack, lade, load, meet, overflow, overspread, pack, pack like sardines*, permeate, pervade, plug, puff up*, pump up, ram, ram in*, replenish, sate, satiate, satisfy, saturate, shoal, stock, stopper*, store, stretch, stuff, supply, swell, take up, top, top off*; SEE CONCEPTS 107,209

fill [v2] *execute, fulfill*
answer, assign, carry out, discharge, dispatch, distribute, elect, engage, fix, hold, meet, name, occupy, officiate, perform, satisfy, take up; SEE CONCEPT 91

fill in [v1] *answer in writing*
advise, apprise, clue, complete, fill out, inform, insert, notify, post, sign, tell, warn, write in; SEE CONCEPTS 45,79

fill in [v2] *act as substitute*
deputize, insinuate, interject, interpose, replace, represent, stand in, substract, take the place of, understudy; SEE CONCEPT 128

filling/filler [n] *something that takes up capacity*
batting, bushing, cartridge, center, content, contents, cylinder, dressing, fill, guts*, impletion, inlay, innards, inside, layer, liner, mixture, pack, packing, pad, padding, refill, replenishment, shim, stuffing, wad, wadding; SEE CONCEPTS 826,830

film [n1] *coating, tissue; mist*
blur, brume, cloud, coat, covering, dusting, fabric, foil, fold, gauze, haze, haziness, integument, layer, leaf, membrane, mistiness, nebula, obscuration, opacity, partition, pellicle, scum*, sheet, skin, transparency, veil, web; SEE CONCEPTS 478,524

film [n2] *movie*
cinema, dailies*, flick*, footage, motion picture, moving picture, photoplay, picture, picture show, rushes, show, silent*, talkie*; SEE CONCEPT 293

film [v] *take photographs*
photograph, put in the can*, record, roll, shoot, take, turn; SEE CONCEPTS 173,205

filmy [adj1] *finespun, fragile*
chiffon, cobwebby*, dainty, delicate, diaphanous, fine, fine-grained, flimsy, floaty, gauzy, gossamer, insubstantial, see-through*, sheer, tiffany, transparent, wispy; SEE CONCEPT 606

fi
fi

filmy [adj2] *covered with mist; blurry*
bleary, blurred, cloudy, dim, hazy, membranous, milky, misty, opalescent, opaque, pearly; SEE CONCEPTS 525,603

filter [v] *separate to refine; seep through*
clarify, clean, distill, drain, dribble, escape, exude, filtrate, leak, metastasize, ooze, osmose, penetrate, percolate, permeate, purify, refine, screen, sieve, sift, soak through, strain, trickle, winnow; SEE CONCEPT 135,165

filth [n] *dirt, pollution*
carrion, contamination, corruption, crud*, defilement, dregs, dung, excrement, feces, feculence, filthiness, foul matter, foulness, garbage, grime, impurity, manure, mire, muck, mud, nastiness, ordure, putrefaction, putrescence, putridity, refuse, rottenness, sediment, sewage, silt, sleaze, slime, slop, sludge, slush, smut, trash, uncleanness; SEE CONCEPTS 260,674

filthy [adj1] *dirty, polluted*
begrimed, black, blackened, cruddy*, crummy*, disheveled, fecal, feculent, foul, grimy*, gross*, grubby*, grungy*, impure, loathsome, miry, mucky*, muddy, nasty, obscene, offensive, putrid, repulsive, revolting, scummy, sleazy, slimy, slipshod, sloppy, slovenly, smoky, soiled, soily, sooty, squalid, unclean, uncleanly, unkempt, unwashed, verminous, vile, yecchy*; SEE CONCEPTS 485,570

filthy [adj2] *vulgar, obscene*
base, bawdy, blue*, coarse, contemptible, corrupt, depraved, despicable, dirty-minded*, foul, foul-mouthed, impure, indecent, lewd, licentious, low, mean, nasty, offensive, pornographic, raunchy, scatological, scurvy, smutty, suggestive, vicious, vile; SEE CONCEPTS 267,545

final [adj1] *ending, last*
closing, concluding, crowning, end, eventual, finishing, hindmost, lag, last-minute, latest, latter, supreme, terminal, terminating, ultimate; SEE CONCEPTS 531,820

final [adj2] *conclusive, definitive*
absolute, decided, decisive, definite, determinate, determinative, finished, incontrovertible, irrefutable, irrevocable, settled, unanswerable, unappealable; SEE CONCEPT 535

finale [n] *ending of an event*
afterpiece, blow-off*, button*, cessation, chaser*, climax, close, closer*, conclusion, consummation, crowning glory*, culmination, denouement, end, end piece, epilogue, finis, finish, last act, payoff*, peroration, summation, swan song*, termination, windup*; SEE CONCEPT 832

finality [n] *definiteness, conclusiveness*
certitude, completeness, decidedness, decisiveness, entirety, finish, inevitableness, intactness, integrity, irrevocability, perfection, resolution, terminality, totality, unavoidability, wholeness; SEE CONCEPTS 635,638,832

finalize [v] *finish, complete action*
agree, clinch*, conclude, consummate, decide, settle, sew up*, tie up*, work out, wrap up; SEE CONCEPT 91

finally [adv1] *beyond any doubt*
assuredly, beyond recall*, beyond shadow of doubt*, certainly, completely, conclusively, convincingly, decisively, definitely, determinately, done with, enduringly, for all time*, for ever, for good*, in conclusion, inescapably, inexorably, irrevocably, lastly, once and for all*, past regret*,

permanently, settled, with conviction; SEE CONCEPT 535

finally [adv2] *in the end; after period of time*
after all, after a while, already, as a sequel, at last, at length, at long last*, at the end, at the last moment, belatedly, despite delay*, eventually, in conclusion, in spite of all*, in the eleventh hour*, in the long run*, lastly, someday, sometime, sooner or later*, subsequently, tardily, ultimately, yet; SEE CONCEPT 799

finance [n] *economic affairs*
accounts, banking, business, commerce, economics, financial affairs, investment, money, money management; SEE CONCEPTS 360,770

finance [v] *offer loan money; set up in business*
back, bank, bankroll, capitalize, endow, float*, fund, go for*, grubstake*, guarantee, juice*, lay on one*, loan shark*, patronize, pay for, pick up the check*, pick up the tab*, prime the pump*, promote, provide funds, provide security, put up money, raise dough*, sponsor, stake, subsidize, support, underwrite; SEE CONCEPTS 108,115,341

finances [n] *person or corporation's money, property*
affairs, assets, balance sheet, budget, capital, cash, condition, funds, net, net worth, resources, revenue, wealth, wherewithal, worth; SEE CONCEPTS 340,710

financial [adj] *having to do with money*
banking, budgeting, business, commercial, economic, fiscal, monetary, numbers*, numeric, pecuniary, pocket; SEE CONCEPT 334

financier [n] *person who lends money, advises*
backer, banker, bankroller, broker, businessperson, capitalist, entrepreneur, fat cat*, grubstaker*, manipulator*, merchant, money, moneybags*, money lender, operator*, person who writes the checks*, rich person, Santa Claus*, speculator, sponsor, staker, stockbroker, tycoon, usurer; SEE CONCEPTS 347,348,353

financing [n] *money for operating expenses*
costs, expenditure, funding, loan, matching funds, outgo, outlay, payment; SEE CONCEPTS 340,344

find [n] *discovery*
acquisition, asset, bargain, boast, bonanza, catch, gem, good buy, jewel, one in a million*, pride, treasure, treasure trove; SEE CONCEPTS 337,712

find [v1] *catch sight of, lay hands on*
arrive at, bring to light*, bump into*, chance upon, collar*, come across, come upon, come up with*, corral, descry, detect, dig up*, discern, discover, distinguish, encounter, espy, expose, fall in with*, ferret out, happen upon*, hit upon*, identify, lay fingers on, light upon*, locate, make out, meet, notice, observe, perceive, pinpoint, recognize, recover, run across, run into, scare up*, sight, smoke out*, spot, strike, stumble upon, track down, trip on*, turn up*, uncover, unearth; SEE CONCEPT 183

find [v2] *achieve, win*
acquire, attain, be one's lot*, earn, fall to the lot*, gain, get, meet, meet with, obtain, procure; SEE CONCEPTS 124,706

finding [n] *judgment, verdict*
award, conclusion, data, decision, decree, discovery, pronouncement, recommendation, sentence; SEE CONCEPT 685

find out [v] *discover, learn*
ascertain, catch, catch on, detect, determine, disclose, divine, expose, hear, identify, note, ob-

serve, perceive, realize, reveal, see, uncover, unearth, unmask; SEE CONCEPTS 31,183

fine [n] *penalty in money*
amends, amercement, assessment, damages, forfeit, mulct, punishment, reparation, rip; SEE CONCEPT 123

fine [adj1] *excellent, masterly*
accomplished, aces*, admirable, attractive, beautiful, capital, choice, cool*, crack*, dandy*, elegant, enjoyable, exceptional, expensive, exquisite, fashionable, first-class, first-rate, firststring, five-star*, gilt-edged*, gnarly*, good-looking, great, handsome, lovely, magnificent, mean, neat*, not too shabby*, ornate, outstanding, pleasant, rare, refined, select, showy, skillful, smart, solid, splendid, striking, subtle, superior, supreme, top, top-notch, unreal*, well-made, wicked*; SEE CONCEPTS 528,574,579

fine [adj2] *cloudless, sunny*
balmy, bright, clarion, clear, clement, dry, fair, pleasant, rainless, undarkened; SEE CONCEPT 525

fine [adj3] *dainty, delicate; sheer*
diaphanous, ethereal, exquisite, filmy, fine-drawn, fine-grained, fine-spun, flimsy, fragile, gauzy, gossamer, gossamery, granular, impalpable, light, lightweight, little, loose, minute, porous, powdered, powdery, pulverized, quality, slender, small, thin, threadlike, transparent; SEE CONCEPTS 491,606

fine [adj4] *discriminating, exact*
abstruse, acute, clear, critical, cryptic, delicate, distinct, enigmatic, esoteric, fastidious, fine-spun, hairline, hairsplitting, intelligent, keen, minute, nice, obscure, petty, precise, pure, quick, recondite, refined, sensitive, sharp, sterling, strict, subtle, tasteful, tenuous, trifling, unadulterated, unpolluted; SEE CONCEPT 557

fine [v] *penalize in monetary way*
alienate, amerce, confiscate, dock*, exact, extort, hit with*, levy, make pay, mulct, pay through the nose*, punish, sconce, seize, sequestrate, slap with*, tax, throw book at*; SEE CONCEPTS 122,342

finery [n] *best clothing*
apparel, bib and tucker*, caparison, decoration, fancy dress, formals, frippery*, full dress, gear, regalia, splendor, suit, Sunday best* trappings, trimmings, trinkets; SEE CONCEPT 451

finesse [n] *know-how, maneuver*
acumen, adeptness, adroitness, artfulness, artifice, big stick*, bluff, cleverness, competence, con, craft, craftiness, cunning, delicacy, diplomacy, discernment, discretion, feint, gimmick, grift, guile, polish, quickness, racket*, run-around*, ruse, savoir-faire, savvy, skill, sophistication, stratagem, subtlety, tact, trick, wile; SEE CONCEPTS 409,657

finesse [v] *maneuver, manipulate*
angle, beguile, bluff, exploit, finagle*, jockey*, operate, play, play games*, pull strings*, pull wires*, rig*, wangle; SEE CONCEPTS 36,59

finger [n] *appendage of hand*
antenna*, claw, digit, extremity, feeler*, hook*, pinky*, pointer*, ring finger, tactile member, tentacle*, thumb; SEE CONCEPT 392

finger [v1] *touch lightly*
feel, fiddle, grope, handle, manipulate, maul, meddle, palpate, paw, play with, thumb, toy with; SEE CONCEPT 612

finger [v2] *choose, designate*
appoint, determine, identify, indicate, locate, make, name, nominate, pin down*, point out, specify, tap; SEE CONCEPT 41

finicky [adj] *overparticular*
choosy, critical, dainty, difficult, fastidious, finical, finicking, fussbudget*, fussy, hard to please, nice, nit-picking, overnice, persnickety*, picky, scrupulous, squeamish, stickling; SEE CONCEPTS 401,404,556

finish [n1] *conclusion; completion*
accomplishment, achievement, acquirement, acquisition, annihilation, attainment, cease, cessation, close, closing, culmination, curtain*, curtains*, death, defeat, denouement, desistance, end, ending, end of the line*, end of the road*, finale, finis, last, last stage, ruin, stop, termination, terminus, winding-up*, wind-up, wrap, wrap-up*; SEE CONCEPTS 119,832

finish [n2] *coating; perfecting*
appearance, beauty, burnish, cultivation, culture, elaboration, glaze, grace, grain, lacquer, luster, patina, perfection, polish, refinement, shine, smoothness, surface, texture, veneer; SEE CONCEPTS 611,655

finish [v1] *bring to a conclusion; get done*
accomplish, achieve, bag it*, break up, bring to a close, carry through, cease, clinch, close, complete, conclude, crown*, culminate, deal with, determine, discharge, do, effect, end, execute, finalize, fold, fulfill, get out of the way*, halt, hang it up*, have done with*, make, make short work of*, mop up*, perfect, put finishing touches on*, round off*, round up*, scratch, scrub, settle, sew up*, shut down, shutter*, stop, terminate, top off*, ultimate, wind up*, wrap, wrap up*; SEE CONCEPTS 91,234,706

finish [v2] *consume, use up*
deplete, devour, dispatch, dispose of, drain, drink, eat, empty, exhaust, expend, go, run through*, spend, use, wash up*; SEE CONCEPTS 169,225

finish [v3] *defeat; kill*
annihilate, assassinate, best*, bring down*, carry off*, destroy, dispatch, dispose of, do in*, down, execute, exterminate, get rid of*, liquidate, overcome, overpower, put an end to, put away*, rout, rub out*, ruin, slaughter, slay, take off*, take out*, vaporize, worst*; SEE CONCEPTS 95,252

finish [v4] *put a coating on; perfect*
coat, develop, elaborate, face, gild, lacquer, polish, refine, smooth, stain, texture, veneer, wax; SEE CONCEPTS 172,202

finished [adj1] *cultivated, refined*
accomplished, all-around, classic, consummate, cultured, elegant, expert, exquisite, flawless, impeccable, many-sided, masterly, perfected, polished, professional, proficient, skilled, smooth, suave, urbane, versatile; SEE CONCEPTS 404,528

finished [adj2] *complete, done*
accomplished, achieved, brought about, ceased, closed, come to an end, compassed, concluded, consummated, decided, dispatched, disposed of, done for, done with, effected, effectuated, elaborated, ended, entire, executed, final, finalized, fulfilled, full, in the past, lapsed, made, over, over and done*, perfected, performed, put into effect*, realized, resolved, satisfied, settled, sewn up*, shut, stopped, terminated, through, tied

fi
fi

up*, worked out*, wound up*, wrapped up*; SEE CONCEPTS *528,531*

finished [*adj3*] *consumed, used up*
bankrupt, devastated, done, done for*, done in*, drained, empty, exhausted, gone, liquidated, lost, played out*, ruined, spent, through, undone, washed up*, wiped out*, wrecked*; SEE CONCEPTS *334,560*

finite [*adj*] *subject to limitations*
bound, bounded, circumscribed, conditioned, confined, definable, definite, delimited, demarcated, determinate, exact, fixed, limited, precise, restricted, specific, terminable; SEE CONCEPTS *535,554*

fire [*n1*] *burning*
blaze, bonfire, campfire, charring, coals, combustion, conflagration, devouring, element, embers, flame and smoke, flames, flare, glow, hearth, heat, holocaust, hot spot*, incandescence, inferno, luminosity, oxidation, phlogiston, pyre, rapid oxidation, scintillation, scorching, sea of flames*, searing, sparks, tinder, up in smoke*, warmth; SEE CONCEPTS *478,521*

fire [*n2*] *barrage of projectiles*
attack, bombarding, bombardment, bombing, cannonade, cannonading, crossfire, explosion, fusillade, hail, round, salvo, shelling, sniping, volley; SEE CONCEPTS *86,320*

fire [*n3*] *animation, vigor*
ardor, brio, calenture, dash, drive, eagerness, élan, energy, enthusiasm, excitement, exhilaration, fervency, fervor, force, ginger*, gusto, heartiness, heat, impetuosity, intensity, life, light, liveliness, luster, passion, pep*, punch*, radiance, red heat*, scintillation, snap*, sparkle, spirit, splendor, starch, verve, vim, virtuosity, vivacity, white heat*, zeal, zing, zip; SEE CONCEPT *411*

fire [*v1*] *cause to burn*
enkindle, ignite, kindle, light, put a match to*, set ablaze, set aflame, set alight, set fire to, set on fire, start a fire, touch off*; SEE CONCEPT *249*

fire [*v2*] *detonate or throw a weapon*
cast, discharge, eject, explode, fling, heave, hurl, launch, let off*, loose, pitch, pull trigger, set off*, shell, shoot, toss, touch off*; SEE CONCEPTS *179,222*

fire [*v3*] *excite, arouse*
animate, electrify, enliven, enthuse, exalt, galvanize, heighten, impassion, incite, inflame, inform, inspire, inspirit, intensify, intoxicate, irritate, provoke, quicken, rouse, stir, thrill; SEE CONCEPT *14*

fire [*v4*] *dismiss from responsibility*
ax*, boot*, can*, discharge, drop, eject, expel, give bum's rush*, give marching orders*, give one notice*, give pink slip*, give the sack*, hand walking papers*, kick out*, lay off, let one go*, oust, pink slip*, sack*, terminate; SEE CONCEPTS *50,88,351*

fireplace [*n*] *hearth for burning wood*
bed of coals, blaze, chimney, fireside, furnace, grate, hearthside, hob, ingle, inglenook, ingleside, settle, stove; SEE CONCEPTS *440,443*

fireproof [*adj*] *resistant to burning*
asbestos, concrete, fire-resistant, incombustible, noncandescent, noncombustible, nonflammable, noninflammable; SEE CONCEPT *485*

fireworks [*n*] *pyrotechnic display at celebrations*
bottle rockets, bursts, firecrackers, fire flowers, illuminations, rockets, Roman candles, sparklers; SEE CONCEPT *293*

firm [*n*] *business*
association, bunch, company, concern, conglomerate, corporation, crew, crowd, enterprise, gang, house, megacorp, mob, multinational, organization, outfit, partnership, ring; SEE CONCEPTS *323,325*

firm [*adj1*] *inflexible*
close, close-grained, compact, compressed, concentrated, concrete, condensed, congealed, dense, fine-grained, hard, hardened, heavy, impenetrable, impermeable, impervious, inelastic, jelled, nonporous, refractory, rigid, set, solid, solidified, stiff, sturdy, substantial, thick, tough, unyielding; SEE CONCEPTS *604,606*

firm [*adj2*] *stable, unmoving*
anchored, bolted, braced, cemented, closed, durable, embedded, fast, fastened, fixed, immobile, immovable, motionless, mounted, nailed, petrified, riveted, robust, rooted, screwed, secure, secured, set, settled, soldered, solid, sound, spiked, stationary, steady, strong, sturdy, substantial, taut, tenacious, tight, tightened, unfluctuating, unshakable, welded; SEE CONCEPT *488*

firm [*adj3*] *unalterable, definite*
abiding, adamant, bent, bound, consistent, constant, dead set on*, determined, enduring, established, exact, explicit, fixed, flat, going, hang tough*, inflexible, intent, never-failing, obdurate, persevering, persistent, prevailing, resolute, resolved, set, settled, specific, stable, stand pat*, stated, staunch, steadfast, steady, stipulated, strict, strong, sure, tenacious, true, unbending, unchangeable, undeviating, unflinching, unqualified, unshakable, unshaken, unwavering, unyielding; SEE CONCEPTS *267,403,542*

firmament [*n*] *heaven*
empyrean, lid*, sky, the blue*, the skies, vault, welkin, wild blue yonder*; SEE CONCEPT *437*

firmly [*adv1*] *immovably*
durably, enduringly, fast, fixedly, hard, inflexibly, like a rock*, motionlessly, rigidly, securely, solid, solidly, soundly, steadily, stiffly, strongly, substantially, thoroughly, tight, tightly, unflinchingly, unshakeably; SEE CONCEPTS *488,489,604*

firmly [*adv2*] *with determination*
adamantly, constantly, decisively, doggedly, indefatigably, intently, obdurately, obstinately, perseveringly, persistently, pertinaciously, purposefully, resolutely, staunchly, steadfastly, stolidly, strictly, stubbornly, tenaciously, through thick and thin*, unchangeably, unwaveringly, with heavy hand*; SEE CONCEPTS *534,542*

firmness [*n1*] *stiffness*
compactness, density, durability, fixedness, hardness, impenetrability, impermeability, imperviousness, impliability, inelasticity, inflexibility, resistance, rigidity, solidity, temper, tensile strength, toughness; SEE CONCEPTS *722,726*

firmness [*n2*] *immovability*
durability, solidity, soundness, stability, steadiness, strength, substantiality, tautness, tension, tightness; SEE CONCEPTS *731,732*

firmness [*n3*] *resolution, resolve*
constancy, decidedness, decision, determination, fixedness, fixity, inflexibility, obduracy, obstinacy, purposefulness, purposiveness, staunch-

ness, steadfastness, strength, strictness; SEE CONCEPTS 410,633

first [adj1] earliest in order

aboriginal, ahead, antecedent, anterior, basic, beginning, cardinal, early, elementary, first off*, front, fundamental, head, headmost, inaugural, inceptive, incipient, initial, in the beginning, introductory, key, leading, lead off*, least, number one*, numero uno*, opening, original, pioneer, premier, primary, prime, primeval, primitive, primogenial, primordial, pristine, right up front*, rudimentary, slightest, smallest; SEE CONCEPTS 585,632,820

first [adj2] highest in importance

advanced, A-number-1*, arch, champion, chief, dominant, eminent, first-class, first-string*, foremost, greatest, head, head of the line*, leading, main, number one*, outstanding, paramount, predominant, preeminent, premier, primary, prime, primo*, principal, ranking, ruling, sovereign, supreme, top-flight*, top of the list; SEE CONCEPT 568

first [adv] at the beginning

at the outset, before all else, beforehand, initially, in the first place, originally, to begin with, to start with; SEE CONCEPTS 585,820

first-class/first-rate [adj] superior, excellent

capital, choice, dandy, fine, first-string*, five-star*, in class by itself*, prime*, shipshape, sound, supreme, tiptop*, top, top-notch*, very good; SEE CONCEPT 574

firsthand [adj] direct

eyewitness, immediate, primary, straight, straight from the horse's mouth*; SEE CONCEPT 267

fiscal [adj] monetary

budgetary, commercial, economic, financial, money, pecuniary, pocket; SEE CONCEPT 334

fish [v] throwing bait to catch seafood

angle, bait, bait the hook*, bob, cast, cast one's hook*, cast one's net*, chum, extract, extricate, find, go fishing, haul out*, net, produce, pull out, seine, trawl, troll; SEE CONCEPT 363

fish for [v] look for; hint

angle, angle for, elicit, hope for, hunt for, invite, search for, seek, solicit, try to evoke; SEE CONCEPTS 20,75

fishy [adj] doubtful, suspicious

ambiguous, doubtable, dubious, dubitable, equivocal, far-fetched, funny, implausible, improbable, odd, problematic, queer, questionable, shady, suspect, uncertain, unlikely; SEE CONCEPT 552

fit [n] seizure; sudden emotion

access, attack, blow, bout, burst, caprice, conniption*, convulsion, epileptic attack, frenzy, humor, jumps*, mood, outbreak, outburst, paroxysm, rage, rush, spasm, spate, spell, stroke, tantrum, throe, torrent, turn, twitch, whim, whimsy; SEE CONCEPTS 13,303

fit [adj1] suitable, appropriate

able, adapted, adequate, advantageous, apposite, apt, becoming, befitting, beneficial, capable, comely, comme il faut, competent, conformable, convenient, correct, correspondent, deserving, desirable, due, equipped, equitable, expedient, favorable, feasible, felicitous, fitted, fitting, good enough, happy, just, likely, meet, opportune, practicable, preferable, prepared, proper, qualified, ready, right, rightful, seasonable, seemly, tasteful, timely, trained, well-suited, wise, worthy; SEE CONCEPT 558

fit [adj2] healthy, in good physical shape

able-bodied, competent, fit as a fiddle*, hale, in good condition, muscled, robust, slim, sound, strapping*, toned, trim, up to snuff*, well, wholesome, wrapped tight*; SEE CONCEPTS 314,485

fit [v1] belong, correspond

accord, agree, answer, apply, be apposite, be apt, become, be comfortable, be consonant, befit, be in keeping, click*, concur, conform, consist, dovetail*, go, go together, go with, harmonize, have its place, interlock, join, match, meet, parallel, relate, respond, set, suit, tally; SEE CONCEPT 664

fit [v2] equip

accommodate, accoutre, arm, fix, furnish, get, implement, kit out*, make, make up, outfit, prepare, provide, ready, rig*; SEE CONCEPT 182

fit [v3] adapt, change

adjust, alter, arrange, conform, dispose, fashion, modify, place, position, quadrate, reconcile, shape, square, suit, tailor, tailor-make*; SEE CONCEPT 232

fitful [adj] irregular, sporadic

bits and pieces*, broken, capricious, catchy*, changeable, desultory, disturbed, erratic, flickering, fluctuating, haphazard, herky-jerky*, hit-or-miss*, impulsive, inconstant, intermittent, interrupted, on-again-off-again, periodic, random, recurrent, restive, restless, shifting, spasmodic, spastic*, spotty, unstable, variable; SEE CONCEPTS 482,534

fitness [n1] good condition

fettle*, good health, health, kilter*, repair, robustness, shape, strength, trim, vigor; SEE CONCEPTS 316,723

fitness [n2] appropriateness

accommodation, accordance, adaptation, adequacy, admissibility, agreeableness, applicability, appositeness, aptitude, aptness, assimilation, auspiciousness, compatibility, competence, concurrency, congeniality, congruousness, consistency, consonance, convenience, correspondence, decency, decorum, eligibility, expediency, harmony, keeping, order, patness, pertinence, preparedness, propriety, qualification, readiness, relevancy, rightness, seasonableness, seemliness, suitability, timeliness; SEE CONCEPT 656

fitted [adj1] appropriate, right

adapted, conformable, cut out for, equipped, matched, proper, qualified, suitable, suited, tailor-made; SEE CONCEPT 558

fitted [adj2] equipped

accoutered, appointed, armed, furnished, implemented, outfitted, provided, rigged out*, set up, supplied; SEE CONCEPTS 560,589

fitting [n] accessory

accouterment, appointment, attachment, component, connection, convenience, equipment, extra, furnishing, furniture, instrument, paraphernalia, part, piece, trimming, unit; SEE CONCEPT 824

fitting [adj] appropriate, suitable

applicable, apt, becoming, comme il faut, correct, decent, decorous, desirable, due, felicitous, happy, just, just what was ordered*, meet, on the button*, on the nose*, proper, right, right on*, seemly, that's the ticket*; SEE CONCEPT 558

fix [n] difficult or ticklish situation

box*, corner*, dilemma, embarrassment, hole*, hot water*, jam*, mess*, pickle*, plight, predic-

fi
fi

ament, quandary, scrape, spot*; SEE CONCEPT *674*

fix [*v1*] *establish, make firm*
affix, anchor, attach, bind, catch, cement, congeal, connect, consolidate, couple, embed, entrench, fasten, freeze to*, glue, graft, harden, implant, inculcate, infix, ingrain, install, instill, link, locate, lodge, moor, nail down*, pin, place, plant, position, rigidify, rivet, root, secure, set, settle, solidify, stabilize, stay put, steady, stick, stiffen, thicken, tie; SEE CONCEPTS *85,113, 160,201*

fix [*v2*] *determine, decide*
agree on, appoint, arrange, arrive at, conclude, define, establish, limit, name, resolve, set, settle, solve, specify, work, work out; SEE CONCEPT *18*

fix [*v3*] *mend, repair*
adjust, amend, correct, debug, doctor, do up*, emend, face-lift*, fiddle with, overhaul, patch, put to rights*, rebuild, recondition, reconstruct, regulate, restore, retread, revamp, revise, see to*, sort, tune up; SEE CONCEPTS *126,212*

fix [*v4*] *prepare, plan ahead*
arrange, dispose, frame, prearrange, precontrive, predesign, preorder, preplan, put up, rig*, set up, stack the deck*; SEE CONCEPT *36*

fix [*v5*] *focus on*
concenter, concentrate, direct, fasten, fixate, level at, put, rivet; SEE CONCEPT *623*

fix [*v6*] *cook a meal*
fit, get, get ready, heat, make, make up, microwave, prepare, ready, warm, whip up*; SEE CONCEPT *170*

fix [*v7*] *manipulate, influence an event*
bribe, buy, buy off, corrupt, fiddle*, have, lubricate, maneuver, pull strings*, reach, square, suborn, tamper with; SEE CONCEPTS *192,232*

fix [*v8*] *wreak vengeance on*
cook someone's goose*, get*, get even, get revenge, hurt, pay back, punish, take retribution; SEE CONCEPT *86*

fixation [*n*] *obsession*
addiction, case, complex, craze, crush, fascination, fetish, hang-up*, idée fixe, infatuation, mania, preoccupation, thing; SEE CONCEPTS *532,690*

fixed [*adj1*] *permanent, steady*
anchored, attached, established, fast, firm, hitched, hooked, immobile, immotile, immovable, located, locked, made fast, nailed*, quiet, rigid, rooted, secure, set, settled, situated, solid, stable, steadfast, stiff, still, tenacious, tight; SEE CONCEPTS *488,551,583,649*

fixed [*adj2*] *intent, resolute; established*
abiding, agreed, arranged, certain, changeless, circumscribed, confirmed, decided, defined, definite, definitive, determinate, enduring, firm, inalterable, inflexible, in the bag*, inveterate, level, limited, narrow, never-failing, planned, prearranged, precise, resolved, restricted, rigged, rooted, set, settled, set-up, stated, steadfast, steady, still, stipulated, sure, unbending, unblinking, unchangeable, undeviating, unfaltering, unflinching, unmodifiable, unmovable, unqualified, unwavering; SEE CONCEPTS *535,554*

fixed [*adj3*] *repaired*
back together, going, in order, in working order, mended, put right, rebuilt, refitted, sorted, whole; SEE CONCEPT *560*

fix up [*v*] *prepare, beautify*
deck*, dress up, furnish, gussy up*, primp, provide, rehabilitate, repair, smarten, spiff*, spruce up*; SEE CONCEPTS *162,202*

fizz [*v*] *bubble*
buzz, effervesce, fizzle, froth, hiss, seethe, sibilate, simmer, sparkle, sputter, whisper, whoosh; SEE CONCEPT *469*

fizzle [*v*] *collapse, fall through*
abort, be a fiasco*, come to nothing*, die, end, end in defeat*, end in disappointment*, fail, fold, miscarry, misfire, miss the mark*, peter out*, wane; SEE CONCEPT *699*

flabbergast [*v*] *surprise*
abash, amaze, astonish, astound, blow away*, bowl over*, confound, daze, disconcert, dumbfound, make speechless, nonplus, overcome, overwhelm, put away*, shock, stagger, stun, throw, throw for a loop*; SEE CONCEPT *42*

flabby [*adj*] *baggy, fat*
drooping, enervated, flaccid, flexuous, floppy*, gone to seed*, hanging, irresilient, lax, limp, loose, out of condition*, out of shape*, pendulous, rusty, sagging, shapeless, slack, sloppy, soft, tender, toneless, unfit, yielding; SEE CONCEPTS *486,490*

flaccid [*adj*] *drooping*
debilitated, emasculated, enervated, enfeebled, flabby, flimsy, inelastic, irresilient, lax, limp, loose, nerveless, quaggy, sapped, slack, soft, weak, weakened; SEE CONCEPTS *485,604*

flag [*n*] *pennant, symbol*
banderole, banner, bannerol, burgee, colors, emblem, ensign, gonfalon, jack, pennon, standard, streamer; SEE CONCEPTS *284,473*

flag [*v1*] *decline, fall off*
abate, deteriorate, die, droop, ebb, fade, fail, faint, languish, peter out*, pine, sag, sink, slump, succumb, taper off*, wane, weaken, weary, wilt; SEE CONCEPTS *698,699*

flag [*v2*] *signal*
gesture, give a sign to, hail, indicate, motion, salute, warn, wave; SEE CONCEPT *74*

flagrant [*adj*] *flaunting, blatant; without shame*
arrant, atrocious, awful, bare-faced*, bold, brazen, capital, conspicuous, crying, disgraceful, dreadful, egregious, enormous, flagitious, flaming, flashy*, glaring, grody*, gross*, hanging out*, heinous, immodest, infamous, noticeable, notorious, obvious, open, ostentatious, out-and-out*, outrageous, rank, scandalous, shameful, shameless, shocking, stick out like sore thumb*, striking, undisguised, wicked; SEE CONCEPTS *401,545,576*

flair [*n*] *talent, style*
ability, accomplishment, aptitude, aptness, bent, chic, dash, elegance, faculty, feel, genius, gift, glamour, head, knack, mastery, panache, pizzazz*, presence, shine*, splash*, taste, turn, zip*; SEE CONCEPTS *630,706*

flak [*n*] *complaint, criticism*
abuse, bad press*, brickbat*, censure, condemnation, disapprobation, disapproval, disparagement, fault-finding, hostility, knock*, opposition, pan*, rap*, swipe*; SEE CONCEPTS *52,278*

flake [*n*] *scale, peel*
cell, disk, drop, foil, lamella, lamina, layer, leaf, membrane, pellicle, plate, scab, section, shaving, sheet, skin, slice, sliver, wafer; SEE CONCEPT *831*

flake [*v*] *peel off*
blister, chip, delaminate, desquamate, drop, ex-

foliate, pare, scab, scale, shed, slice, sliver, trim, wear away; SEE CONCEPTS 157,469

flamboyant [*adj*] *extravagant, theatrical*
baroque, bombastic, brilliant, camp, chichi*, colorful, dashing, dazzling, elaborate, exciting, flaky*, flaming, flashy, florid, gassy*, gaudy, glamorous, jazzy*, luscious, luxuriant, ornate, ostentatious, peacockish, pretentious, resplendent, rich, rococo, showy, splashy, sporty, swank*, swashbuckling*; SEE CONCEPTS 401,589

flame [*n1*] *fire*
blaze, brightness, conflagration, flare, flash, holocaust, light, rapid oxidation, wildfire; SEE CONCEPTS 478,521

flame [*n2*] *lover; passion*
affection, ardor, baby, beau, beloved, boyfriend, darling, dear, desire, enthusiasm, fervor, fire, girlfriend, heartthrob, honey, inamorata, inamorato, keenness, love, paramour, spark, steady, swain, sweetheart, sweetie, trueлove; SEE CONCEPTS 32,423

flame [*v*] *burn*
blaze, coruscate, fire, flare, flare up, flash, glare, glint, glow, ignite, kindle, light, oxidize, shine; SEE CONCEPT 249

flaming [*adj1*] *burning*
ablaze, afire, aflame, alight, blazing, brilliant, conflagrant, fiery, flaring, glowing, ignited, in flames, raging, red, red-hot*; SEE CONCEPT 485

flaming [*adj2*] *very angry, vehement*
ardent, aroused, blazing, bright, burning, fervent, frenzied, hot, hot-blooded*, impassioned, intense, passionate, raging, red-hot*, scintillating, vivid, white-hot*; SEE CONCEPTS 267,403

flammable [*adj*] *easily set afire*
burnable, combustible, ignitable, incendiary, inflammable; SEE CONCEPT 485

flank [*n*] *haunch of an animate being*
ham, hand, hip, loin, pleuron, quarter, side, thigh, wing; SEE CONCEPT 392

flap [*n1*] *winged or extended part of an object*
accessory, adjunct, appendage, apron, cover, drop, fly, fold, hanging, lapel, lobe, lug, overlap, pendant, pendulosity, ply, queue, skirt, strip, tab, tag, tail, tippet; SEE CONCEPTS 471,824

flap [*n2*] *commotion*
agitation, banging, brouhaha, confusion, dither, fluster, flutter, fuss, lather*, panic, pother*, state*, stew*, sweat*, tizzy, to-do, tumult, turbulence, turmoil, twitter*; SEE CONCEPTS 230,674

flap [*v*] *flutter*
agitate, beat, dangle, flail, flash, flop, hang, lop, shake, swing, swish, thrash, thresh, vibrate, wag, wave; SEE CONCEPT 149

flare [*v1*] *erupt, blow*
blaze, boil over, break out, burn, burn up, burst, dart, dazzle, explode, fire up, flash, flicker, flutter, fume, glare, glow, go off, lose control, rant, seethe, shimmer, shoot, waver; SEE CONCEPTS 13,179,249

flare [*v2*] *spread*
broaden, grow, splay, widen; SEE CONCEPT 469

flash [*n1*] *shimmer, flicker*
beam, bedazzlement, blaze, burst, coruscation, dazzle, flame, flare, glance, glare, gleam, glimmer, glint, glisten, glitter, glow, illumination, imprint, impulse, incandescence, luster, phosphorescence, quiver, radiation, ray, reflection, scintillation, shine, spark, sparkle, streak, stream, twinkle, twinkling, vision; SEE CONCEPTS 521,624

flash [*n2*] *instant, split second*
breathing, burst, jiffy, minute, moment, outburst, shake, show, trice, twinkling; SEE CONCEPTS 808,821

flash [*n3*] *demonstration*
burst, display, manifestation, outburst, show, sign, splash, swank; SEE CONCEPT 261

flash [*v1*] *shimmer, flicker*
beam, bedazzle, blaze, blink, coruscate, dazzle, flame, flare, glance, glare, gleam, glimmer, glint, glisten, glitter, glow, incandesce, light, phosphoresce, radiate, reflect, scintillate, shine, shoot out, spangle, spark, sparkle, twinkle; SEE CONCEPT 624

flash [*v2*] *move fast and display*
bolt, brandish, dart, dash, disport, exhibit, expose, flaunt, flit, flourish, fly, parade, race, shoot, show, show off, speed, spring, streak, sweep, trot out, whistle, zoom; SEE CONCEPTS 150,261

flashy [*adj*] *flamboyant, in poor taste*
blatant, brazen, catchpenny*, cheap, chintzy, flaunting, florid, garish, gaudy, glaring, glittering, glittery, glitzy, jazzy*, loud, meretricious, ornate, ostentatious, showy, snazzy, sparkling, tacky*, tasteless, tawdry, tinsel, vulgar; SEE CONCEPT 589

flask [*n*] *small container for liquid*
alembic, ampulla, bag, beaker, bottle, canteen, carafe, caster, chalice, crock, cruel, crystal, decanter, demijohn, ewer, fiasco, flacon, flagon, flasket, glass, goblet, gourd, horn, jar, jug, noggin, phial, retort, tumbler, urn, vial; SEE CONCEPT 494

flat [*n*] *apartment*
chambers, condo, co-op*, crash pad*, floorthrough, go-down, joint*, lodging, pad*, railroad apartment, rental, room, rooms, suite, tenement, walk-up; SEE CONCEPT 516

flat [*adj1*] *level, smooth*
collapsed, complanate, decumbent, deflated, depressed, empty, even, extended, fallen, flush, horizontal, laid low, low, oblate, outstretched, pancake*, planar, planate, plane, procumbent, prone, prostrate, punctured, reclining, recumbent, splay, spread out, supine, tabular, unbroken; SEE CONCEPTS 486,490

flat [*adj2*] *dull, lackluster to the senses*
banal, blah, bland, blind, boring, colorless, dead, dim, drab, draggy, flavorless, ho hum*, inane, innocuous, insipid, jejune, lead balloon*, lifeless, matte, monotonous, muted, pointless, prosaic, prosy, sapless, spiritless, stale, tasteless, tedious, uninteresting, unpalatable, unsavory, unseasoned, vanilla*, vapid, watery, weak, whitebread*; SEE CONCEPTS 529,537

flat [*adj3*] *absolute, positive*
categorical, direct, downright, explicit, final, fixed, indubitable, out-and-out*, peremptory, plain, straight, unconditional, unequivocal, unmistakable, unqualified, unquestionable; SEE CONCEPT 535

flatten [*v*] *level out*
abrade, beat down, compress, crush, debase, deflate, depress, even out, fell, floor, flush, grade, ground, iron out, knock down, lay, lay low, mow down, plane, plaster*, prostrate, raze, roll, smash, smooth, spread out, squash, straighten, subdue, trample; SEE CONCEPTS 137,250,469,702

fi
fl

flatter [v1] *compliment excessively*
adulate, beslaver, blandish, bootlick*, brown-nose*, build up*, butter up*, cajole, cater to, charm, con, court, fawn*, get next to*, glorify, grovel, humor, inveigle, jolly, lay it on thick*, massage, oil*, overpraise, play up to*, praise, rub the right way*, salve, sell, snow*, soften*, soft-soap*, spread it on*, stroke, suck up to*, sweeten up*, sweet-talk*, toady*, wheedle, work on*, work over*; SEE CONCEPTS *59,69*

flatter [v2] *complement, enhance*
adorn, beautify, become, decorate, do something for*, embellish, enrich, finish, go with*, grace, ornament, perfect, put in best light*, set off, show to advantage, suit; SEE CONCEPTS *162,664*

flattery [n] *false praise, compliments*
adulation, applause, approbation, blandishment, blarney*, bootlicking*, cajolery, commendation, encomium, eulogy, eyewash*, fawning*, flattering, flummery, fulsomeness, gallantry, gratification, hokum*, honeyed words, incense, ingratiation, jive*, laud, mush*, obsequiousness, palaver, plaudits, pretty speech, puffery*, servility, smoke*, snow*, snow job*, soft-soap*, soft words, stroke*, sweet talk*, sycophancy, toadyism, tribute, truckling, unctuousness; SEE CONCEPTS *59,69*

flatulent [adj] *pretentious, long-winded*
bombastic, inflated, oratorical, overblown, pompous, prolix, shallow, superficial, swollen, tedious, tumescent, tumid, turgid, windy, wordy; SEE CONCEPTS *267,404*

flaunt [v] *make an exhibition, show off*
advertise, air, boast, brandish, break out, broadcast, declare, disclose, display, disport, divulge, expose, fan it*, flash, flash about, flourish, gasconade, grandstand*, hotdog*, let it all hang out*, make a scene*, parade, proclaim, put on an act*, reveal, roll out, show and tell, showcase, show with*, sport, spring on*, streak, throw weight around*, trot out*, vaunt, wave around, whip out*; SEE CONCEPT *261*

flavor [n1] *odor and taste*
acidity, aroma, astringency, bitterness, essence, extract, gusto, hotness, piquancy, pungency, relish, saltiness, sapidity, sapor, savor, seasoning, smack, sourness, spiciness, sweetness, tang, tartness, twang, vim, wallop, zest, zing; SEE CONCEPT *614*

flavor [n2] *aura, essence*
aspect, character, feel, feeling, property, quality, soupçon, stamp, style, suggestion, tinge, tone, touch; SEE CONCEPT *673*

flavor [v] *add seasoning*
add zing, add zip, ginger, hot it up*, imbue, impart, infuse, lace, leaven, pepper, pep up*, salt, season, spice; SEE CONCEPT *170*

flavoring [n] *spice, extract added to food*
additive, condiment, distillation, essence, herb, quintessence, relish, sauce, seasoning, spirit, tincture, zest; SEE CONCEPT *428*

flaw [n] *imperfection*
blemish, bug, catch*, Catch-22*, defect, disfigurement, failing, fault, foible, glitch*, gremlin*, pitfall, slipup, speck, spot, stain, typo*, vice, wart*, weakness, weak spot; SEE CONCEPTS *580,674*

flawless [adj] *spotless, intact*
absolute, entire, faultless, immaculate, impeccable, irreproachable, perfect, sound, unblemished,

unbroken, undamaged, unimpaired, unmarred, unsullied, whole; SEE CONCEPTS *574,579*

fleck [n] *spot, pinpoint mark*
bit, dot, mite, mote, patch, pinpoint, speck, speckle, stipple, streak, stripe; SEE CONCEPTS *284,831*

fleck [v] *mark with spots*
bespeckle, besprinkle, dapple, dot, dust, maculate, mottle, speckle, stipple, streak, variegate; SEE CONCEPT *79*

fledgling [n] *beginner in activity*
apprentice, chick, colt, greenhorn*, learner, neophyte, nestling, newcomer, novice, rookie, tenderfoot*, trainee, tyro*; SEE CONCEPTS *352, 366,424*

flee [v] *run away to escape*
abscond, avoid, beat a hasty retreat*, blow*, bolt*, break, cut and run*, cut out*, decamp, depart, desert, elude, evade, fly, fly the coop*, get*, get away, get the hell out*, hotfoot*, jump, leave, make a getaway*, make off*, make oneself scarce*, make one's escape*, make quick exit*, make tracks*, retreat, scamper, scoot, scram*, skedaddle*, skip*, split*, step on it*, step on the gas*, take a hike*, take flight, take off, vamoose*, vanish; SEE CONCEPTS *102,150,195*

fleece [v] *plunder, steal*
bleed*, burn*, cheat*, clip*, con, cozen, defraud, despoil, flimflam*, gouge, hustle, jerk around*, milk*, mulct, overcharge, pluck, rifle, rip off*, rob, rook*, rope in*, run a game on*, sell a bill of goods*, shaft*, strip, swindle, take for a ride*, take to the cleaners*; SEE CONCEPTS *59,139,342*

fleecy [adj] *downy, woolly; like a lamb's coat*
floccose, flocculent, fluffy, hairy, hirsute, lanose, pileous, pilose, shaggy, soft, whiskered; SEE CONCEPT *606*

fleet [n] *group of ships*
argosy, armada, flotilla, formation, line, naval force, navy, sea power, squadron, tonnage, vessels, warships; SEE CONCEPTS *322,432,506*

fleet [adj] *quick in movement*
agile, barreling, breakneck*, brisk, expeditious, expeditive, fast, flying, hasty, in nothing flat*, like greased lightning*, lively, mercurial, meteoric, nimble, nimble-footed, on the double*, rapid, screaming, speedball*, speedy, swift, winged; SEE CONCEPTS *584,588*

fleeting [adj] *brief, transient*
cursory, ephemeral, evanescent, fading, flash in the pan*, flitting, flying, fugacious, fugitive, impermanent, meteoric, momentary, passing, short, short-lived, sudden, temporary, transitory, vanishing, volatile; SEE CONCEPTS *551,798*

flesh [n1] *body tissue, skin*
beef, brawn, cells, corpuscles, fat, fatness, flesh and blood, food, meat, muscle, plasm, plasma, protoplasm, sinews, thews, weight; SEE CONCEPT *392*

flesh [n2] *humankind*
animality, carnality, homo sapiens, humanity, human nature, human race, living creatures, mortality, people, physicality, physical nature, race, sensuality, stock, world; SEE CONCEPTS *407,417*

fleshly [adv1] *lecherous, desiring sex*
animal, animalistic, bodily, carnal, erotic, gross, lascivious, lewd, lustful, profane, sensual, venereal, voluptuous; SEE CONCEPTS *372,529,545*

fleshly [adv2] *bodily*
corporal, corporeal, earthly, human, material,

mundane, of this world, physical, secular, somatic, terrestrial, worldly; SEE CONCEPT 536

fleshy [adj] *overweight*
adipose, ample, beefy*, brawny, chubby*, chunky*, corpulent, fat, gross, heavy, hefty, husky, meaty*, obese, plump, porcine, portly, pudgy*, pulpy, sarcous, stout, tubby*, weighty, well-padded*, zaftig*; SEE CONCEPTS 406, 491,773

flex [v] *bend*
angle, contract, crook, curve, lean, mold, ply, spring, stretch, tighten, tilt, yield; SEE CONCEPTS 147,149

flexibility [n] *elasticity, adaptability*
adjustability, affability, complaisance, compliance, docility, extensibility, flaccidity, flexibleness, give, limberness, litheness, plasticity, pliability, pliancy, resilience, springiness, suppleness, tensility, tractability; SEE CONCEPTS 652,731

flexible [adj1] *pliable, bendable*
adjustable, bending, ductile, elastic, extensible, extensile, flexile, formable, formative, impressionable, like putty*, limber, lithe, malleable, moldable, plastic, pliant, soft, spongy, springy, stretch, stretchable, stretchy, supple, tensile, tractable, tractile, whippy*, willowy, yielding; SEE CONCEPTS 485,488

flexible [adj2] *adaptable, responsive*
acquiescent, adjustable, amenable, biddable, complaisant, compliant, discretionary, docile, gentle, going every which way*, hanging loose*, like putty in hands*, manageable, open, rolling with punches*, tractable, variable; SEE CONCEPTS 401,542

flicker [n] *spark, glimmer*
beam, flare, flash, gleam, oscillation, quivering, ray, scintillation, twinkle, vibration; SEE CONCEPTS 145,624,831

flicker [v] *sparkle, flutter*
blare, blaze, blink, burn, dance, flare, flash, flit, flitter, fluctuate, glance, gleam, glimmer, glint, glitter, glow, hover, oscillate, quaver, quiver, scintillate, shimmer, swing, tremble, twinkle, vibrate, waver; SEE CONCEPTS 152,624

flight [n1] *flying; journey*
aerial navigation, aeronautics, arrival, aviation, avigation, departure, gliding, hop, jump, mounting, navigation, shuttle, soaring, take-off, transport, trip, volitation, voyage, winging; SEE CONCEPT 224

flight [n2] *fleeing; departure*
beat*, break*, breakout, escape, escapement, escaping, exfiltration, exit, exodus, fugue, getaway, getaway car*, lam, out*, powder*, retreat, retreating, running away, slip*, spring*; SEE CONCEPTS 102,195

flightiness [n] *irresponsibility*
airheadedness*, capriciousness, changeability, dizziness, fickleness, flippancy, frivolity, giddiness, inconstancy, instability, levity, lightness, mercurialness, variability, volatility, whimsicality, whimsicalness; SEE CONCEPT 633

flighty [adj] *fickle, irresponsible*
airheaded*, birdbrained*, bubbleheaded*, capricious, changeable, dingbat*, dingdong*, dizzy*, effervescent, empty-headed, featherbrained*, frivolous, gaga*, giddy, harebrained*, impetuous, impulsive, inconstant, lightheaded, lively, mercurial, scatterbrained, silly, thoughtless, twit, unbal-

anced, unstable, unsteady, volatile, whimsical, wild; SEE CONCEPT 401

flimsy [adj1] *not strong; light, thin*
chiffon, cut-rate*, decrepit, defective, delicate, diaphanous, feeble, fragile, frail, gauzy, gossamer, house of cards*, inadequate, infirm, insubstantial, meager, papery, rickety, rinkydink*, shaky, shallow, sheer, slapdash*, sleazy, slight, superficial, tacky, transparent, unsound, unsubstantial, weak, wobbly; SEE CONCEPTS 489,606

flimsy [adj2] *unconvincing, implausible*
assailable, baseless, contemptible, controvertible, fallacious, false, feeble, frivolous, groundless, illogical, improbable, inadequate, inane, inconceivable, incredible, inept, lame, poor, puerile, superficial, thin, transparent, trifling, trivial, unbelievable, ungrounded, unpersuasive, unreasonable, unsatisfactory, unsubstantial, weak, weakly, wishful; SEE CONCEPT 267

flinch [v] *shy away, wince*
avoid, balk, blanch, blench, blink, cower, cringe, crouch, draw back, duck, elude, escape, eschew, evade, flee, quail, recede, recoil, retire, retreat, shirk, shrink, shun, start, swerve, withdraw; SEE CONCEPTS 102,150

fling [n1] *casual throw*
cast, chuck, firing, heave, hurl, launching, lob, peg, pitch, shot, slinging, toss; SEE CONCEPT 222

fling [n2] *unrestrained behavior*
affair, attempt, binge, celebration, crack*, essay, fun, gamble, go*, good time, indulgence, orgy, party, rampage, shot*, splurge, spree, stab*, trial, try, venture, whirl; SEE CONCEPT 386

fling [v] *throw with abandon*
cast, catapult, chuck*, dump, fire, heave, hurl, jerk, launch, let fly*, lob, peg*, pitch, precipitate, propel, send, shy*, sling, toss; SEE CONCEPT 222

flip [n/v] *throw, jump with abandon*
cast, chuck, flick, jerk, pitch, snap, spin, toss, twist; SEE CONCEPTS 194,222

flippancy [n] *irreverence*
archness, cheek, cheekiness, cockiness, disrespectfulness, flightiness, freshness, frivolity, impertinence, impishness, impudence, levity, lightness, mischievousness, pertness, playfulness, roguishness, rudeness, sauciness, volatility, waggishness; SEE CONCEPT 633

flippant [adj] *irreverent*
brassy, breezy, cheeky*, cocky, disrespectful, flighty, flip*, fresh, frivolous, glib, impertinent, impudent, insolent, lippy*, nervy*, offhand, pert, playful, rude, sassy*, smart*, smart-alecky*, superficial; SEE CONCEPT 401

flirt [n] *person who makes advances*
coquette, cruiser*, heartbreaker, operator*, philanderer, player, seducer, siren, swinger, tease, trifler, vamp, vixen, wanton, wolf*; SEE CONCEPT 423

flirt [v] *make advances toward someone*
banter, bat eyes at*, come hither*, come on*, coquet, dally, disport, eyeball*, fool, gam*, hit on*, lead on, linger with, make a move*, make a pass*, ogle, philander, pick up*, pitch*, proposition, tease, wink at*; SEE CONCEPTS 375,384

flirtation [n] *amorous advance*
amour, coquetry, courting, cruising, dalliance, flirting, intrigue, pickup*, romance, romancing, tease, teasing, toying*, trifling*; SEE CONCEPTS 32,375,384

fl
fl

flirtatious [adj] provocative, teasing
amorous, arch, come-hither*, come-on*, coquettish, coy, dallying, enticing, flirty, libidinous, spoony*, sportive; SEE CONCEPTS *401,404*

flit [v] flutter, move rapidly
dance, dart, flash, fleet, flicker, float, fly, hover, hurry, pass, run, rush, sail, scud*, skim, speed, sweep, whisk, whiz, wing, zip; SEE CONCEPT *150*

float [v] lie on the surface
be buoyant, bob, drift, glide, hang, hover, move gently, poise, rest on water, ride, sail, skim, slide, slip along, smooth along, stay afloat, swim, waft, wash; SEE CONCEPT *153*

flock [n] congregation
army, assembly, bevy, brood, cloud, collection, colony, company, convoy, crowd, crush, drift, drove, flight, gaggle, gathering, group, herd, host, legion, litter, mass, multitude, pack, progeny, rout, scores, skein, throng; SEE CONCEPTS *391,432*

flock [v] congregate
collect, converge, crowd, gather, group, herd, huddle, mass, throng, troop; SEE CONCEPTS *109,384*

flog [v] whip, lash
beat, belt, cane, castigate, chastise, ferule, flagellate, flax, flay, give the cat o'nine tails*, hide, hit, larrup, leather, leather*, paddle, scourge, spank, strike, stripe, tan one's hide*, thrash, trounce, wax*, whack, whale*, whomp*, whop*; SEE CONCEPT *189*

flood [n] overwhelming flow, quantity
abundance, alluvion, bore, bounty, cataclysm, cataract, current, deluge, downpour, drencher, drift, eager, excess, flow, flux, freshet, glut, inundation, multitude, niagara, outgushing, outpouring, overflow, plenty, pour, profusion, rush, spate, stream, superabundance, superfluity, surge, surplus, tide, torrent, tsunami, wave; SEE CONCEPTS *179,524,787*

flood [v] inundate or submerge
brim over, choke, deluge, drown, engulf, fill, flow, glut, gush, immerse, overflow, oversupply, overwhelm, pour over, rush, saturate, surge, swamp, swarm, sweep, whelm; SEE CONCEPTS *179,209,740*

floor [n] bottom of a room; level of a multistory building
basement, boards, canvas, carpet, cellar, deck, downstairs, flat, flooring, ground, landing, lowest point, mat, mezzanine, nadir, rug, stage, story, tier, upstairs; SEE CONCEPT *440*

floor [v] perplex, confound
baffle, beat, bewilder, bowl over*, bring down*, bring up short*, conquer, defeat, discomfit, disconcert, down, drop, dumbfound, fell, flatten, ground, knock down, lay low*, level, nonplus, overthrow, prostrate, puzzle, stump, throw; SEE CONCEPTS *16,95*

flop [n] miserable failure
bomb, bust, debacle, disaster, dud*, fiasco, lemon*, loser, miscarriage, nonstarter, washout*; SEE CONCEPTS *674,699*

flop [v1] fall limply, collapse
dangle, droop, drop, flag, flap, flounder, flutter, hang, jerk, lop, quiver, sag, slump, stagger, teeter, topple, toss, totter, tumble, wave, wiggle; SEE CONCEPTS *144,181*

flop [v2] fail miserably
bomb*, close, come apart*, come to nothing*,

fall flat*, fall short*, flummox, fold, founder, miscarry, misfire, wash out*; SEE CONCEPT *699*

floral [adj] decorated with flowers
blooming, blossoming, blossomy, botanic, decorative, dendritic, efflorescent, flower-patterned, flowery, herbaceous, sylvan, verdant; SEE CONCEPT *589*

florid [adj1] very elaborate
aureate, baroque, busy, decorative, embellished, euphuistic, figurative, flamboyant, flowery, fussy, garnished, grandiloquent, high-flown, luscious, magniloquent, ornamental, ornamented, ornate, overblown, pretentious, rhetorical, rich, sonorous; SEE CONCEPTS *267,589*

florid [adj2] flushed, ruddy
blowzy, flush, glowing, high-colored, pink, reddened, rubicund, sanguine; SEE CONCEPTS *406,618*

flounce [v] bounce; intermittently move
fling, jerk, mince, nancy, prance, sashay, spring, stamp, storm, strut, swish, throw, toss; SEE CONCEPT *149*

flounder [v] struggle; be in the dark
blunder, bobble, cast about, come apart at the seams*, drop the ball*, fall down, flop, flummox, foul up*, fumble, go at backwards*, go to pieces*, grope, labor, lurch, make a mess of, miss one's cue*, muddle, plunge, pratfall*, screw up*, slip up*, snafu*, strive, stub one's toe*, stumble, thrash, toil, toss, travail, trip up*, tumble, wallow, work at; SEE CONCEPTS *101,699*

flourish [n] curlicue, decoration
curl, embellishment, furbelow, garnish, ornamentation, plume, quirk, spiral, sweep, twist; SEE CONCEPTS *259,284*

flourish [v1] grow, prosper
amplify, arrive, augment, batten, bear fruit, be on top of heap*, bloom, blossom, boom, burgeon, come along, develop, do well, expand, flower, get ahead, get on*, go, go great guns*, hit it big*, increase, live high on hog*, make out*, multiply, score, succeed, thrive, wax; SEE CONCEPTS *141,704,706*

flourish [v2] wave about
brandish, display, flaunt, flutter, shake, sweep, swing, swish, twirl, vaunt, wag, wield; SEE CONCEPTS *147,152*

flourishing [adj] prospering, going well
blooming, burgeoning, doing well, expanding, exuberant, going strong, growing, in full swing*, in the pink*, in top form*, lush, luxuriant, mushrooming, profuse, prosperous, rampant, rank, rich, roaring, robust, successful, thriving, vigorous; SEE CONCEPT *528*

flout [v] show contempt for
affront, defy, deride, disregard, gibe, gird, insult, jeer, laugh at, mock, outrage, quip, repudiate, ridicule, scoff, scorn, slight, sneer, spurn, taunt, thumb nose at*; SEE CONCEPT *54*

flow [n] issue, abundance
breeze, continuance, continuation, continuity, course, current, deluge, discharge, draft, draw, dribble, drift, ebb, effusion, electricity, emanation, flood, flux, gush, juice, leakage, movement, oozing, outflow, outpouring, plenty, plethora, progress, progression, river, run, sequence, series, spate, spout, spurt, stream, succession, tide, train, wind; SEE CONCEPTS *146,179,467,787*

flow [v] issue, surge, run out
abound, arise, brim, cascade, circulate, continue,

course, deluge, discharge, disembogue, dribble, ebb, emanate, emerge, emit, exudate, exude, flood, glide, gurgle, gush, inundate, jet, leak, move, ooze, overflow, pass, percolate, pour, proceed, progress, pullulate, regurgitate, result, ripple, roll, rush, slide, sluice, smooth along, spew, spill, splash, spring, spurt, sputter, squirt, stream, sweep, swell, swirl, teem, trickle, tumble, void, well forth; SEE CONCEPTS *146,179*

flower [n1] *bloom of a plant*
annual, blossom, bud, cluster, efflorescence, floret, floweret, head, herb, inflorescence, perennial, pompon, posy, shoot, spike, spray, vine; SEE CONCEPTS *425,428*

flower [n2] *best, choicest part*
cream, elite, finest point, freshness, greatest point, height, pick, pride, prime, prize, top; SEE CONCEPTS *668,829*

flower [v] *bloom, flourish*
batten, blossom, blow, burgeon, effloresce, mature, open, outbloom, prosper, thrive, unfold; SEE CONCEPTS *253,704*

flowery [adj] *ornate, especially referring to speech or writing*
aureate, baroque, bombastic, declamatory, diffuse, embellished, euphemistic, euphuistic, fancy, figurative, florid, grandiloquent, high-flown, magniloquent, ornamented, overwrought, prolix, purple, redundant, rhetorical, rococo, sonorous, swollen, verbose, windy, wordy; SEE CONCEPTS *267,589*

flowing [adj] *gushing, abounding*
brimming, continuous, cursive, easy, falling, flooded, fluent, fluid, fluidic, full, issuing, liquefied, liquid, overrun, pouring out, prolific, rich, rippling, rolling, running, rushing, sinuous, smooth, spouting, streaming, sweeping, teeming, tidal, unbroken, uninterrupted; SEE CONCEPTS *482,584*

fluctuate [v] *vacillate, change*
alter, alternate, be undecided, blow hot and cold*, ebb and flow, flutter, go up and down*, hem and haw*, hesitate, oscillate, rise and fall*, seesaw*, shift, swing, undulate, vary, veer, vibrate, wave, waver, yo-yo*; SEE CONCEPTS *13,469,697*

fluent [adj] *articulate*
chatty, cogent, copious, cursive, declamatory, disputatious, easy, effortless, effusive, eloquent, facile, flowing, garrulous, glib, liquid, loquacious, mellifluent, mellifluous, natural, persuasive, prompt, quick, ready, running, silver-tongued*, smooth, smooth-spoken, talkative, verbose, vocal, voluble, well-versed, wordy; SEE CONCEPTS *267,584*

fluffy [adj] *soft, furry*
creamy, downy, featherlike, feathery, fleecy, flocculent, flossy, gossamer, linty, pile, silky, velutinous; SEE CONCEPT *606*

fluid [n] *liquid*
agua, broth, chaser, cooler, goo*, goop*, juice, liquor, solution, vapor; SEE CONCEPT *467*

fluid [adj1] *flowing*
aqueous, flowing, fluent, in solution, juicy, liquefied, lymphatic, melted, molten, running, runny, serous, uncongealed, watery; SEE CONCEPTS *603,757*

fluid [adj2] *adaptable, changeable*
adjustable, changeful, flexible, floating, fluctuating, indefinite, malleable, mercurial, mobile, mu-

table, protean, shifting, unsettled, unstable, unsteady, variable; SEE CONCEPTS *534,542*

fluke [n] *chance occurrence*
accident, blessing, break, contingency, fortuity, fortunate, fortune, good fortune*, good luck, incident, lucky break*, odd chance, quirk, stroke of luck*, windfall; SEE CONCEPTS *4,679,693*

fluky [adj] *chance*
accidental, casual, chancy, coincidental, contingent, fortuitous, incalculable, incidental, lucky, odd, uncertain, variable; SEE CONCEPT *552*

flurry [n] *commotion, burst*
ado, agitation, brouhaha, bustle, confusion, disturbance, excitement, ferment, flap*, flaw, fluster, flutter, furor, fuss, gust, haste, hurry, outbreak, pother, spell, spurt, squall, stir*, to-do, tumult, turbulence, turmoil, whirl, whirlwind; SEE CONCEPTS *230,524*

flurry [v] *agitate, confuse*
bewilder, bother, bustle, discombobulate*, discompose, disconcert, disquiet, distract, disturb, excite, fluster, flutter, frustrate, fuss, galvanize, hassle, hurry, hustle, perplex, perturb, provoke, quicken, rattle, ruffle, stimulate, unhinge, unsettle, upset; SEE CONCEPTS *7,19*

flush [n] *blush*
bloom, color, freshness, glow, pinkness, redness, rosiness, ruddiness; SEE CONCEPT *622*

flush [adj1] *flat*
even, horizontal, level, planate, plane, smooth, square, true; SEE CONCEPTS *486,490*

flush [adj2] *overflowing, abundant*
affluent, close, full, generous, lavish, liberal, opulent, prodigal, rich, wealthy, well-off; SEE CONCEPTS *334,771*

flush [v1] *become or make pink or red*
blush, burn, color, color up, crimson, flame, glow, go red, mantle, pink, pinken, redden, rose, rouge, suffuse; SEE CONCEPTS *250,469*

flush [v2] *inundate with liquid*
cleanse, douche, drench, eject, expel, flood, hose, rinse, swab, wash; SEE CONCEPTS *165,179*

flushed [adj] *pink, glowing*
ablaze, animated, aroused, blushing, burning, crimson, elated, embarrassed, enthused, exhilarated, feverish, florid, full-blooded, high, hot, inspired, intoxicated, red, rosy, rubicund, ruddy, sanguine, thrilled; SEE CONCEPTS *401,403,618*

fluster [n] *perturbation, upset*
agitation, brouhaha, commotion, disturbance, dither, flap*, flurry, flutter, furor, ruffle, state*, to-do*, turmoil; SEE CONCEPT *410*

fluster [v] *upset, perturb*
addle, agitate, bewilder, bother, confound, confuse, craze*, discombobulate*, discompose, disquiet, distract, disturb, excite, flip*, flurry, frustrate, fuddle*, get to*, hassle, heat*, hurry, make nervous, make waves*, muddle, mystify, nonplus, perplex, psych*, puzzle, rattle, ruffle, spook*, stir up*, throw off balance*, unhinge*, work up*; SEE CONCEPTS *7,16,19*

flutter [v] *wave rapidly, flap*
agitate, bat, beat, dance, drift, flicker, flit, flitter, flop, fluctuate, hover, lop, oscillate, palpitate, pulsate, quaver, quiver, ripple, ruffle, shake, shiver, swing, throb, tremble, vibrate, wiggle, wobble; SEE CONCEPTS *150,152*

flux [n] *state of constant change*
alteration, change, flow, fluctuation, fluidity, in-

stability, modification, motion, mutability, mutation, transition, unrest; SEE CONCEPT 697

fly [v1] *take to the air, usually employing wings*
aviate, barnstorm*, bend the throttle*, buzz*, circle, circumnavigate, climb, control, cross, dart, dash, dive, drift, flat-hat*, fleet, flit, float, flutter, glide, hop, hover, hurry, jet, jet out, jet over, maneuver, mount, operate, pilot, reach, remain aloft, rush, sail, scud*, seagull*, shoot, skim, skirt, sky out*, soar, speed, swoop, take a hop*, take flight, take off, take wing, travel, whisk*, whiz*, whoosh*, wing*, wing in*, zip*, zoom*; SEE CONCEPTS 148,150,224

fly [v2] *run or pass swiftly*
barrel, bolt, breeze, career, dart, dash, elapse, flee, flit, glide, go like the wind*, hasten, hurry, hustle, make off*, pass, race, roll, run its course*, rush, scamper, scoot, shoot, slip away*, speed, sprint, tear, whiz*, zoom*; SEE CONCEPTS 150,818

fly [v3] *escape, flee*
abscond, avoid, bolt, break, clear, clear out*, cut and run*, decamp, disappear, get away, hasten away, hide, hightail*, light out*, make a getaway*, make a quick exit*, make off, run*, run for it, run from, skedaddle*, skip, steal away, take flight, take off, withdraw; SEE CONCEPTS 102,195

fly-by-night [adj] *undependable*
brief, cowboy*, dubious, here-today-gone-tomorrow*, impermanent, questionable, shady, shifty, short-lived, slimy*, slippery*, treacherous, trustless, unreliable, unsure, untrustworthy; SEE CONCEPTS 542,551

flyer [n] *person who navigates an aircraft*
ace*, air person, aviator, flier, jet*, navigator, pilot; SEE CONCEPT 348

flying [adj] *in the air, winged*
aerial, aeronautical, airborne, avian, drifting, express, flapping, fleet, floating, fluttering, gliding, hovering, mercurial, mobile, on the wing, plumed, soaring, speedy, streaming, swooping, volant, volar, volitant, waving, winging, zooming; SEE CONCEPT 584

foam [n] *bubbles formed from a liquid*
cream, fluff, froth, head, lather, scum, spray, spume, suds, surf, yeast; SEE CONCEPT 260

foam [v] *become bubbly*
aerate, boil, burble, effervesce, ferment, fizz, froth, gurgle, hiss, lather, seethe, simmer, sparkle; SEE CONCEPTS 170,469

foamy [adj] *bubbly*
barmy, boiling, burbling, carbonated, creamy, ebullient, effervescent, fermented, fizzy, frothy, lathery, scummy*, seething, simmering, spumescent, spumous, spumy, sudsy, yeasty; SEE CONCEPT 485

focus [n] *center of attraction*
bull's eye*, center, core, cynosure, focal point, headquarters*, heart, hub, limelight*, locus, meeting place, nerve center*, point of convergence, polestar, seat, spotlight, target; SEE CONCEPTS 532,826,829

focus [v] *aim attention at*
adjust, attract, bring out, center, centralize, concenter, concentrate, convene, converge, direct, fasten, fix, fixate, get detail, home in*, home in on*, hone in*, join, key on*, knuckle down*, meet, move in, pinpoint, pour it on*, put, rivet,

sharpen, spotlight*, sweat*, zero in*, zoom in*; SEE CONCEPTS 17,623

foe [n] *person who is an opponent*
adversary, antagonist, anti*, enemy, hostile party, rival; SEE CONCEPT 412

fog [n1] *heavy mist that reduces visibility*
brume, cloud, effluvium, film, gloom, grease, ground clouds, haze, London fog, miasma, murk, murkiness, nebula, obscurity, pea soup*, smaze, smog, smoke, smother, soup*, steam, vapor, visibility zero-zero*, wisp; SEE CONCEPTS 524,627

fog [n2] *mental unclarity*
befuddlement, blindness, confusion, daze, haze, maze, mist, muddledness, muddlement, obscurity, perplexity, stupor, trance, vagueness; SEE CONCEPT 410

fog [v] *muddle, obscure*
addle, becloud, bedim, befuddle, bewilder, blind, blur, cloud, confuse, darken, daze, dim, eclipse, mist, muddy, mystify, obfuscate, perplex, puzzle, steam up, stupefy; SEE CONCEPTS 250,526

foggy [adj] *hazy, obscure*
blurred, ceiling zero*, closed in, clouded, cloudy, dark, dim, filmy, fogged in, fuzzy, gray, indistinct, misty, murky, mushy, nebulous, pea-soupy*, smazy, smoggy, socked in*, soupy*, unclear, vague, vaporous, vapory, zero-zero*; SEE CONCEPTS 403,525

foible [n] *personal imperfection*
characteristic, defect, eccentricity, failing, fault, frailty, idiosyncrasy, infirmity, kink, mannerism, oddity, peculiarity, quirk, shortcoming, singularity, vice, weakness, weak point; SEE CONCEPTS 411,644

foil [n] *contrast*
antithesis, background, complement, counterblow, defense, guard, setting; SEE CONCEPT 665

foil [v] *circumvent, nip in the bud*
baffle, balk, beat, bilk, bollix*, buffalo*, check, checkmate, counter, crab, cramp, crimp, curb, dash, defeat, disappoint, disconcert, ditch, dodge, duck, elude, faze, foul up*, frustrate, get around*, give the run-around*, give the slip*, hang up*, hinder, juke, nullify, outwit, prevent, rattle, restrain, run circles around*, run rings around*, shake, shake off, shuffle off, skip, stop, stymie, throw monkey wrench in*, thwart, upset the apple cart*; SEE CONCEPTS 121,130

fold [n] *double thickness*
bend, circumvolution, cockle, convolution, corrugation, crease, crimp, crinkle, dog's ear*, flection, flexure, furrow, gather, gathering, groove, knife-edge*, lap, lapel, layer, loop, overlap, plait, pleat, plica, plication, plicature, ply, pucker, ridge, rimple, rivel, ruche, ruck, ruffle, rumple, shirring, smocking, tuck, turn, wrinkle; SEE CONCEPT 754

fold [v1] *lay in creases*
bend, cockle, corrugate, crimp, crisp, crumple, curl, dog-ear*, double, double over, furrow, gather, groove, hem, intertwine, knit, lap, overlap, overlay, plait, pleat, plicate, pucker, purse, replicate, ridge, ruche, ruck, ruffle, telescope, tuck, turn under, wrinkle; SEE CONCEPT 184

fold [v2] *encase, enclose*
do up, enfold, entwine, envelop, involve, wrap, wrap up; SEE CONCEPT 209

fold [v3] *fail, close*
become insolvent, be ruined, break, bust, collapse, crash, crumple, give, go bankrupt, go bust,

go into Chapter 11*, go under*, impoverish, pauper, pauperize, shut down, yield; SEE CONCEPTS *324,699*

folder [n] *paper envelope for holding items*
binder, case, file, pocket, portfolio, sheath, wrapper, wrapping; SEE CONCEPT *260*

foliage [n] *leaves*
frondescence, greenness, growth, herbage, leafage, umbrage, vegetation, verdure; SEE CONCEPT *428*

folk [n] *person's relations, acquaintances*
body politic, clan, community, confederation, culture group, ethnic group, family, general public, group, house, household, inhabitants, kin, kindred, lineage, masses, ménage, nation, nationality, people, population, proletariat, public, race, settlement, society, state, stock, tribe; SEE CONCEPTS *296,379*

folklore [n] *tales from the past*
ballad, custom, fable, folk story, legend, myth, mythology, mythos, oral literature, superstition, tradition, wisdom; SEE CONCEPT *282*

follow [v1] *take the place of*
be subsequent to, chase, come after, come from, come next, displace, ensue, go after, go next, postdate, proceed from, pursue, replace, result, spring from, succeed, supersede, supervene, supplant; SEE CONCEPTS *128,242,813*

follow [v2] *trail, pursue physically*
accompany, attend, bring up the rear*, catenate, chase, come with, concatenate, convoy, dog*, dog the footsteps of*, draggle, escort, freeze, give chase, go after, go with, hound*, hunt, onto*, persecute, put a tail on*, run after, run down, schlepp along*, search, seek, shadow, shag*, spook*, stalk, stick to, string along, tag, tag after*, tag along*, tail, tailgate*, take out after, track; SEE CONCEPT *207*

follow [v3] *act in accordance with*
abide by, accord, adhere to, adopt, attend, be consistent with, be devoted to, be guided by, be in keeping, be interested in, comply, conform, copy, cultivate, do like, emulate, follow suit, give allegiance to, harmonize, heed, hold fast, imitate, keep, keep abreast of, keep an eye on, live up to, match, mimic, mind, mirror, model on, note, obey, observe, pattern oneself upon, reflect, regard, serve, string along*, support, take after, take as an example, watch; SEE CONCEPTS *8,91,171*

follow [v4] *understand*
accept, appreciate, apprehend, catch*, catch on*, comprehend, dig*, fathom, get*, get the picture*, grasp, realize, see, take in*; SEE CONCEPT *15*

follower [n] *person who believes or has great interest*
addict, adherent, admirer, advocate, apostle, attendant, backer, believer, bootlicker*, buff, client, cohort, companion, convert, copycat, devotee, disciple, fan, fancier, freak*, habitué, hanger-on*, helper, imitator, lackey*, member, minion, parasite, participant, partisan, patron, promoter, proselyte, protégé, pupil, representative, satellite, sectary, servant, sidekick, stooge*, supporter, sycophant, toady*, vassal, votary, worshiper, zealot; SEE CONCEPTS *352,366,423*

following [n] *persons of an interest or belief*
adherents, audience, circle, clientage, clientele, cortege, coterie, dependents, entourage, fans, group, groupies*, hangers-on*, patronage, pa-

trons, public, retinue, rout, suite, support, supporters, train; SEE CONCEPTS *294,387,417*

following [adj] *happening, being next or after*
after a while, afterward, attendant, a while later, back, by and by, coming, coming after, coming next, consecutive, consequent, consequential, directly after, ensuing, henceforth, hinder, in pursuit, in search of, in the wake of, later, later on, latter, next, next off*, on the scent*, posterior, presently, proximate, pursuing, rear, resulting, sequent, sequential, serial, seriate, specified, subsequent, succeeding, successive, supervenient, then, trailing, when; SEE CONCEPTS *585,811,818,820*

follow through [v] *bring to a conclusion*
complete, consummate, pursue, see through; SEE CONCEPT *91*

follow up [v] *make inquiries*
check out, find out about, investigate, look into, make sure, pursue; SEE CONCEPT *103*

folly [n] *nonsense, ridiculous idea*
absurdity, craziness, daftness, dottiness, dumb thing to do*, dumb trick*, fatuity, foolishness, idiocy, imbecility, impracticality, imprudence, inadvisability, inanity, indiscretion, irrationality, lunacy, madness, obliquity, preposterousness, rashness, recklessness, senselessness, silliness, stupidity, triviality, unsoundness, vice, witlessness; SEE CONCEPTS *410,633*

foment [v] *instigate, provoke*
abet, agitate, arouse, brew, cultivate, encourage, excite, fan the flames*, foster, goad, incite, nurse, nurture, promote, quicken, raise, set, set on, sow the seeds*, spur, start, stimulate, stir up, whip up*; SEE CONCEPTS *14,221*

fond [adj] *have a liking or taste for*
addicted, adoring, affectionate, amorous, attached, caring, devoted, doting, enamored, indulgent, keen on, lovesome, lovey-dovey*, loving, mushy*, partial, predisposed, responsive, romantic, sentimental, silly over, sympathetic, tender, warm; SEE CONCEPTS *32,542*

fondle [v] *touch lovingly*
bear hug*, caress, clutch, cosset, cuddle, dandle, embrace, feel, fool around*, grab, grope, hug, love, make love to, neck, nestle, nuzzle, pat, paw, pet, play footsie*, snuggle, squeeze, stroke; SEE CONCEPTS *190,375*

fondness [n] *liking or taste for*
affection, attachment, devotion, fancy, kindness, love, partiality, penchant, predilection, preference, soft spot, susceptibility, tenderness, weakness; SEE CONCEPT *32*

food [n] *edible material*
aliment, bite*, board, bread, cheer, chow*, comestible, cookery, cooking, cuisine, diet, drink, eatable, eats*, entrée, fare, fast food, feed, fodder*, foodstuff, goodies*, grit*, groceries*, grub*, handout*, home cooking, keep, larder, meal, meat, menu, mess*, moveable feast, nourishment, nutriment, nutrition, pabulum, provision, ration, refreshment, slop*, snack, store, subsistence, support, sustenance, table, take out, tuck, viand, victual, vittles*; SEE CONCEPTS *457,460,461*

food court [n] *public area where variety of food is sold*
cafe, counter, fast food, food festival, restaurant, smorgasbord; SEE CONCEPTS *439,448,449*

fool [n] *stupid or ridiculous person*
ass, birdbrain*, blockhead*, bonehead*, boob*,

fl
fo

bore, buffoon, clod*, clown, cretin*, dimwit*, dolt*, dope*, dumb ox*, dunce, dunderhead*, easy mark*, fair game*, fathead*, goose*, half-wit, idiot, ignoramus, illiterate, imbecile, innocent, jerk*, lamebrain*, lightweight*, loon*, moron, nerd*, nincompoop*, ninny*, nitwit, numskull*, oaf, sap*, schlemiel*, silly, simpleton, stooge*, sucker*, turkey*, twerp*, twit*, victim; SEE CONCEPTS 412,423

fool [v] *trick, mislead*
bamboozle*, bluff, cheat, chicane, con, deceive, delude, diddle, dupe, fake out*, flimflam*, fox*, gull, hoax, hoodwink*, jive*, juke*, kid, lead on, make believe, outfox, play-act*, play a trick on, pretend, put on, put one over on*, scam*, snow*, spoof*, suck in*, take in*, trifle; SEE CONCEPT 59

fool around [v] *waste time*
dawdle, hang around*, idle, kill time*, lark, mess around*, play around*; SEE CONCEPT 681

fooled [adj] *tricked*
bamboozled*, conned, deceived, deluded, duped, flimflammed*, hornswoggled*, misled, outfoxed*, snowed*, sucked in*; SEE CONCEPT 537

foolhardy [adj] *impetuous, rash*
adventuresome, adventurous, audacious, bold, breakneck*, daredevil, daring, devil-may-care*, harebrained*, headstrong, imprudent, incautious, irresponsible, madcap, off deep end*, out on limb*, precipitate, reckless, temerarious, venturesome, venturous, wide open; SEE CONCEPT 401

fooling [n] *joking, tricks*
bluffing, buffoonery, clownishness, farce, frolicking, high jinks*, horseplay, jesting, joshing, kidding, making light*, mockery, nonsense, pretense, roughhouse*, roughhousing*, rowdiness, sham*, skylarking*, spoofing, teasing, trifling; SEE CONCEPT 59

foolish [adj] *nonsensical, idiotic*
absurd, asinine, brainless, cockamamy*, crazy, daffy*, daft, dippy*, doltish*, dotty*, fantastic, fatuous, feebleminded*, half-baked*, half-witted*, harebrained*, ill-advised, ill-considered, imbecile, imprudent, incautious, indiscreet, injudicious, insane, irrational, jerky*, kooky*, loony*, ludicrous, lunatic, mad, moronic, nerdy*, nutty*, preposterous, ridiculous, senseless, short-sighted, silly, simple, stupid, unintelligent, unreasonable, unwise, wacky*, weak, witless, zany*; SEE CONCEPTS 401,542,544

foolishly [adv] *idiotic, without due consideration*
absurdly, ill-advisedly, imprudently, incautiously, indiscreetly, injudiciously, mistakenly, short-sightedly, stupidly, unwisely; SEE CONCEPTS 401,542,544

foolishness [n] *idiocy, nonsense*
absurdity, absurdness, bunk*, carrying-on*, claptrap*, craziness, dumb trick*, folly, foolery, fool trick, horse feathers*, impracticality, imprudence, inanity, indiscretion, insanity, insensibility, irrationality, irresponsibility, ludicrousness, lunacy, mistake, poppycock*, preposterousness, rubbish*, senselessness, silliness, stupidity, tommyrot*, twaddle, unreasonableness, unwiseness, weakness, witlessness; SEE CONCEPT 633

foot [n1] *extremity of an animate being*
hoof, pad, paw; SEE CONCEPT 392

foot [n2] *base of an object*
bottom, foundation, lowest point, nadir, pier; SEE CONCEPT 442

foot [n3] *twelve inches/30.48 centimeters measured*
cubic, square; SEE CONCEPTS 790,791

footing [n1] *foundation, basis*
basement, bedrock, bottom, establishment, foot, foothold, ground, groundwork, infrastructure, installation, resting place, seat, seating, settlement, substratum, substructure, underpinning, understructure, warrant; SEE CONCEPTS 442,661

footing [n2] *social status*
capacity, character, condition, grade, place, position, rank, relations, relationship, situation, standing, state, station, terms; SEE CONCEPT 388

for [conj] *in consequence of the fact that*
as, as long as, because, being, considering, inasmuch as, now, since, whereas; SEE CONCEPT 544

for [prep] *in consideration of*
after, as, beneficial to, concerning, conducive to, during, for the sake of, in contemplation of, in exchange for, in favor of, in furtherance of, in order to, in order to get, in place of, in pursuance of, in spite of, in the direction of, in the interest of, in the name of, notwithstanding, on the part of, on the side of, pro, supposing to, to, to counterbalance, to go to, to the amount of, to the extent of, toward, under the authority of, with a view to, with regard to, with respect; SEE CONCEPT 544

forage [v] *search madly for*
beat, cast about, comb, explore, fine-tooth-comb*, grub, hunt, pilfer, plunder, raid, rake, ransack, ravage, rummage, scour, scrounge, seek; SEE CONCEPT 216

foray [n] *incursion, attempt*
attack, depredation, descent, inroad, invasion, irruption, raid, reconnaissance, sally, sortie; SEE CONCEPTS 86,90,159

forbear [v] *resist the temptation to*
abstain, avoid, bridle, cease, curb, decline, desist, escape, eschew, evade, forgo, go easy*, hold back*, inhibit, keep, keep from, omit, pause, refrain, restrain, sparing, shun, stop, withhold; SEE CONCEPTS 35,121,130,681

forbearance [n] *resisting, avoidance*
abstinence, endurance, fortitude, going easy on*, living with*, longanimity, moderation, patience, patientness, refraining, resignation, restraint, self-control, temperance, tolerance; SEE CONCEPTS 410,633

forbearing [adj] *tolerant*
being big*, charitable, clement, considerate, easy, forgiving, gentle, going easy on*, going easy with*, humane, humanitarian, indulgent, lenient, living with*, longanimous, long-suffering, merciful, mild, moderate, patient, soft-shell*, thoughtful; SEE CONCEPTS 404,542

forbid [v] *outlaw, prohibit an action*
ban, block, cancel, censor, check, debar, declare illegal, deny, deprive, disallow, embargo, enjoin, exclude, forestall, forfend, freeze*, halt, hinder, hold up, impede, inhibit, interdict, lock up, nix*, obstruct, obviate, oppose, preclude, prevent, proscribe, put the chill on*, restrain, restrict, rule out, say no*, shut down*, shut out*, spike*, stop, stymie*, taboo, veto, withhold; SEE CONCEPT 121

forbidden [adj] *outlawed, prohibited*
banned, closed, closed-down*, closed-up*, contraband, no-no*, off limits, out of bounds, proscribed, refused, taboo*, verboten, vetoed; SEE CONCEPT 548

forbidding [adj] *ominous, daunting*

abhorrent, disagreeable, dour, foreboding, frightening, glowering, grim, hostile, menacing, odious, offensive, off-putting, repellent, repulsive, sinister, threatening, tough, ugly, unapproachable, unfriendly, unpleasant; SEE CONCEPTS 537,550

force [n1] *physical energy, power*

arm, brunt, clout, coercion, compulsion, conscription, constraint, draft, duress, dynamism, effort, enforcement, exaction, extortion, full head of steam*, fury, horsepower, impact, impetus, impulse, might, momentum, muscle, pains*, potency, potential, pow*, pressure, punch, push, sinew, sock*, speed, steam, stimulus, strain, strength, stress, strong arm*, stuff*, subjection, tension, trouble, velocity, vigor, violence, what it takes*; SEE CONCEPTS 641,724

force [n2] *mental power, energy*

ability, authority, bite*, capability, coercion, cogency, competence, determination, dominance, drive, duress, effect, effectiveness, efficacy, emphasis, fierceness, forcefulness, gumption, guts*, impressiveness, influence, intensity, intestinal fortitude, obligation, persistence, persuasiveness, point, pressure, puissance, punch, push, requirement, sapience, stress, validity, validness, vehemence, vigor, willpower; SEE CONCEPTS 410,677

force [n3] *military organization*

armed forces, army, battalion, body, cell, corps, crew, detachment, division, guard, horses, host, legion, patrol, regiment, reserves, shop, soldiers, squad, squadron, troop, unit; SEE CONCEPTS 322,417

force [v1] *obligate to do something*

apply, bear down, bear hard on, bind, blackmail, bring pressure to bear upon*, burden, cause, charge, choke, coerce, command, compel, concuss, conscript, constrain, contract, demand, draft, drag, dragoon*, drive, enforce, enjoin, exact, extort, fix, impel, impose, impress, inflict, insist, limit, make, move, necessitate, oblige, obtrude, occasion, order, overcome, pin down, press, pressure, pressurize, put screws to*, put squeeze on*, require, restrict, sandbag*, shotgun*, strong-arm*, urge, wrest, wring; SEE CONCEPT 14

force [v2] *use violence upon*

assault, blast, break in, break open, burst, bust open, crack open, defile, extort, jimmy*, propel, pry, push, rape, ravish, spoil, squeeze, thrust, twist, undo, violate, wrench, wrest, wring; SEE CONCEPTS 156,208

forced [adj] *compulsory, strained*

affected, artificial, begrudging, binding, bound, coerced, coercive, compelled, conscripted, constrained, contrived, enforced, factitious, false, grudging, inflexible, insincere, involuntary, labored, mandatory, obligatory, peremptory, rigid, slave, stiff, stringent, unnatural, unwilling, wooden*; SEE CONCEPTS 542,548

forceful [adj] *effective, powerful*

ball of fire*, bullish*, cogent, coming on strong, commanding, compelling, constraining, convincing, dominant, dynamic, electric, elemental, energetic, forcible, gutsy*, mighty, persuasive, pithy, potent, powerhouse, puissant, punch, punchy*, steamroller*, stringent, strong, take-charge, take-over, telling, titanic, vehement, vig-

orous, violent, virile, weighty; SEE CONCEPTS 267,401,550

forcible [adj] *powerful, aggressive*

active, armed, assertive, coercive, cogent, compelling, compulsory, drastic, effective, efficient, energetic, forceful, impressive, intense, mighty, militant, persuasive, potent, puissant, strong, telling, valid, vehement, vigorous, violent, weighty; SEE CONCEPTS 267,537

forcibly [adv] *against one's will*

by force, coercively, compulsorily, effectively, energetically, hard, mightily, powerfully, strongly, under protest, vigorously; SEE CONCEPTS 544,548

fore [adv] *in the front*

ahead, ante*, antecedently, before, beforehand, forward, in advance, near, nearest, precedently, previous; SEE CONCEPTS 585,820

forebearer [n] *family predecessor*

ancestor, antecedent, ascendant, author, begetter, forerunner, founder, materfamilias, matriarch, originator, parent, paterfamilias, patriarch, precursor, primogenitor, procreator, progenitor, relative, sire; SEE CONCEPT 414

forebode [v] *predict, warn*

augur, betoken, bode, divine, forecast, foresee, foreshadow, foretell, foretoken, forewarn, indicate, omen, portend, premonish, presage, prognosticate, promise; SEE CONCEPTS 70,78

foreboding [n] *misgiving, bad omen*

anxiety, apprehension, apprehensiveness, augury, bad vibes*, chill, dread, fear, foreshadowing, foretoken, forewarning, funny feeling*, handwriting on the wall*, portent, prediction, premonition, prenotion, presage, presentiment, prognostic, prophecy, sinking feeling*, vibes*, warning, wind change*; SEE CONCEPTS 78,689,690

forecast [n] *prediction, often of weather or business*

anticipation, augury, budget, calculation, cast, conjecture, divination, estimate, foreknowledge, foreseeing, foresight, foretelling, forethought, foretoken, guess, outlook, planning, precognition, prescience, prevision, prognosis, prognostication, projection, prophecy; SEE CONCEPTS 28,37,70,78

forecast [v] *predict, guess*

adumbrate, anticipate, augur, calculate, call the turn*, conclude, conjecture, demonstrate, determine, divine, dope out*, estimate, figure, figure out*, foresee, foretell, gather, gauge, infer, in the cards*, plan, portend, predetermine, presage, prognosticate, prophesy, reason, see it coming*, soothsay, surmise, telegraph; SEE CONCEPTS 28,37,70,78

forefront/foreground [n] *prominence*

beginning, center, cutting-edge*, focus, fore, forepart, front, lead, leading-edge*, limelight*, on the line*, spearhead*, state-of-the-art, vanguard; SEE CONCEPT 668

foregoing [adj] *come before; previous*

above, aforementioned, aforesaid, aforestated, antecedent, anterior, former, past, precedent, preceding, prior; SEE CONCEPTS 585,820

foreign [adj] *from another country, experience*

adopted, alien, alienated, antipodal, barbarian, barbaric, borrowed, derived, different, distant, estranged, exiled, exotic, expatriate, external, extralocal, extraneous, extrinsic, far, faraway, far-fetched, far-off, from abroad, immigrant, imported, inaccessible, nonnative, nonresident,

fo
fo

not domestic, not native, offshore, outlandish, outside, overseas, remote, strange, transoceanic, unaccustomed, unexplored, unfamiliar, unknown; SEE CONCEPTS 536,549

foreign [adj2] *irrelevant*
accidental, adventitious, extraneous, extrinsic, heterogeneous, immaterial, impertinent, inapposite, incompatible, incongruous, inconsistent, inconsonant, irrelative, repugnant, unassimilable, uncharacteristic, unrelated; SEE CONCEPTS 267,537

foreigner [n] *person from another country*
alien, fresh off the boat*, greenhorn*, immigrant, incomer, newcomer, outlander, outsider, stranger; SEE CONCEPT 413

foremost [adj] *first in rank, order*
A-number-1*, A-1*, arch, at the cutting edge*, at the leading edge*, champion, chief, front, head, headmost, heavy, heavy stuff*, heavyweight*, highest, hotdog*, hotshot*, hot stuff*, inaugural, initial, leading, most important, number one*, original, paramount, preeminent, premier, primary, prime, primo*, principal, supreme; SEE CONCEPTS 568,585,799

forensic [adj] *judicial, legal*
argumentative, debatable, dialectic, dialectical, disputative, juridical, juristic, moot, polemical, rhetorical; SEE CONCEPTS 267,319

foreordain [v] *doom, fate*
destinate, destine, foredoom, foreshadow, foretell, prearrange, predestine, predetermine, preform, preordain, reserve; SEE CONCEPT 70

forerunner [n1] *messenger, herald*
advertiser, advocate, ancestor, announcer, author, envoy, forebearer, foregoer, harbinger, initiator, originator, pioneer, precursor, progenitor, prognostic, prototype; SEE CONCEPTS 414,423

forerunner [n2] *example, sign*
advertisement, announcement, antecedent, antecessor, augury, exemplar, foregoer, foreshadow, foretoken, forewarning, indication, mark, model, omen, pattern, portent, precursor, predecessor, premonition, presage, prognostic, prototype, sign, token, warning; SEE CONCEPT 529

foresee [v] *anticipate, predict*
apprehend, call the turn*, crystal ball it*, discern, divine, dope out*, envisage, espy, expect, forebode, forecast, forefeel, foreknow, foretell, have a hunch*, perceive, preknow, presage, previse, prevision, prognosticate, prophesy, psych out*, see, see it coming*, understand, visualize; SEE CONCEPTS 26,70

foreshadow [v] *indicate*
adumbrate, augur, be in the wind*, betoken, bode, forebode, foretell, hint, imply, omen, portend, predict, prefigure, presage, promise, prophesy, shadow, signal, suggest, telegraph; SEE CONCEPTS 70,75,261

foresight [n] *mental preparedness*
anticipation, canniness, care, carefulness, caution, circumspection, clairvoyance, discernment, discreetness, discretion, economy, far-sightedness, foreknowledge, forethought, insight, longsightedness, perception, precaution, precognition, preconception, premeditation, premonition, prenotion, prescience, prospect, providence, provision, prudence, sagacity; SEE CONCEPTS 409,410

forest [n] *area with a large number of trees*
backwoods, brake, chase, clump, coppice, copse,

cover, covert, grove, growth, jungle, park, shelter, stand, thicket, timber, timberland, weald, wildwood, wood, woodland, woodlot, woods; SEE CONCEPTS 509,517

foretell [v] *predict, warn*
adumbrate, announce, anticipate, apprehend, augur, auspicate, betoken, bode, call, call it*, call the shot*, crystal ball it*, declare, disclose, divine, divulge, dope*, dope out*, figure, figure out*, forebode, forecast, foreknow, foreshadow, forewarn, make book*, portend, prefigure, presage, proclaim, prognosticate, prophesy, psych, read, reveal, see something coming*, signify, soothsay, tell; SEE CONCEPTS 70,78

forethought [n] *mental preparedness*
anticipation, canniness, caution, deliberation, discreetness, discretion, far-sightedness, foresight, gumption, judgment, planning, precaution, premeditation, providence, provision, prudence, sense; SEE CONCEPT 410

forever [adj1] *for all time; everlasting*
always, durably, endlessly, enduringly, eternally, evermore, everything considered*, for always, forevermore, for good*, for keeps*, for life*, immortally, infinitely, in perpetuity, in perpetuum, interminably, lastingly, now and forever*, on and on*, permanently, perpetually, till blue in the face*, till death do us part*, till Doomsday*, till the cows come home*, till the end of time*, unchangingly, world without end*; SEE CONCEPTS 551,649,798,799

forever [adj2] *not ceasing, continually*
all the time, constantly, endlessly, eternally, everlastingly, incessantly, interminably, perpetually, regularly, unendingly, unremittingly; SEE CONCEPTS 534,798

forewarn [v] *caution that something may happen*
admonish, advise, alarm, alert, apprise, dissuade, flag, forbode, give fair warning*, give the high sign*, portend, premonish, pull one's coat*, put a bug in one's ear*, put one wise*, put on guard*, telegraph, tip, tip off, wave a red flag*; SEE CONCEPT 78

foreword [n] *introduction to a document*
exordium, overture, preamble, preface, preliminary, prelude, prelusion, proem, prolegomenon, prologue; SEE CONCEPT 270

forfeit [n] *something given as sacrifice*
cost, damages, fine, loss, mulct, penalty, relinquishment; SEE CONCEPT 123

forfeit [v] *give up something in sacrifice*
abandon, be deprived of, be stripped of, drop, give over, lose, relinquish, renounce, sacrifice, surrender; SEE CONCEPT 116

forge [v1] *counterfeit*
coin, copy, design, duplicate, fabricate, fake, falsify, fashion, feign, frame, imitate, invent, make, phony up*, pirate*, produce, reproduce, scratch, trace, transcribe, trump up*; SEE CONCEPTS 59,171

forge [v2] *make something from scratch*
beat, build, construct, contrive, create, devise, fabricate, fashion, form, frame, hammer out*, invent, manufacture, mold, pound, put together, shape, turn out, work; SEE CONCEPTS 168, 173,175,205,251

forgery [n] *counterfeiting; counterfeit item*
bogus*, carbon*, carbon copy, cheat, coining, copy, fabrication, fake, faking, falsification, fraudulence, imitating, imitation, imposition, im-

posture, lookalike, phony, pseudo, sham*; twin, workalike*; SEE CONCEPTS *59,171,716*

forget [v1] *not be able to remember*
blow, clean forget*, consign to oblivion*, dismiss from mind, disremember, draw a blank*, escape one's memory*, fail to remember, let slip from memory*, lose consciousness of, lose sight of*, miscollect, obliterate, think no more of*; SEE CONCEPT *40*

forget [v2] *leave behind*
blink, discount, disregard, drop, fail, ignore, lose sight of*, neglect, omit, overlook, overpass, pass over, skip, slight, transgress, trespass; SEE CONCEPTS *30,116*

forgetful [adj] *tending to not remember*
absent, absent-minded, abstracted, airheaded*, amnemonic, amnesic, asleep on the job*, bemused, careless, distracted, dreamy, heedless, inattentive, lax, like an absent-minded professor*, looking out window*, mooning, moony*, neglectful, negligent, nirvanic, not on the job*, oblivious, out of it*, out to lunch*, pipe dreaming*, preoccupied, remiss, slack, sloppy, unmindful, unwitting, woolgathering*; SEE CONCEPTS *403, 550*

forgetfulness [n] *consistent inability to remember*
absentmindedness, abstraction, amnesia, blackout, blank, blockout, carelessness, dreaminess, fugue, heedlessness, hypomnesia, inattention, lapse of memory, laxness, lethe, limbo, loss of memory, negligence, nirvana, oblivion, obliviousness, paramnesia, repression, short memory, suppression; SEE CONCEPTS *410,644*

forgive [v] *stop blame and grant pardon*
absolve, accept apology, acquit, allow for, amnesty, bear no malice*, bear with, bury the hatchet*, clear, commute, condone, dismiss from mind, efface, exculpate, excuse, exempt, exonerate, extenuate, forget, kiss and make up*, laugh off*, let bygones be bygones*, let it go*, let off*, let off easy*, let pass*, let up on*, make allowance, overlook, palliate, pocket, purge, release, relent, remit, reprieve, respite, spring, think no more of*, turn other cheek*, wink at*, wipe slate clean*; SEE CONCEPTS *12,50,88*

forgiveness [n] *pardon; end of blame*
absolution, acquittal, amnesty, charity, clemency, compassion, condonation, dispensation, exculpation, exoneration, extenuation, grace, immunity, impunity, indemnity, justification, lenience, lenity, mercy, overlooking, palliation, purgation, quarter, quittance, remission, remittal, reprieve, respite, vindication; SEE CONCEPTS *685,689*

forgo [v] *give up, do without*
abandon, abdicate, abjure, abstain, cede, desist, eschew, forbear, forsake, give in, go on the wagon*, leave alone, leave out, pack in*, pass, pass on, pass up, quit, refrain, relinquish, renounce, resign, resist, sacrifice, sit out*, surrender, swear off*, take the cure*, take the oath*, waive, yield; SEE CONCEPTS *121,130,681*

forgotten [adj] *out of one's mind*
abandoned, blanked out*, blotted out*, blown over*, buried, bygone, clean forgot*, consigned to oblivion*, disremembered*, drew a blank*, erased, fell between the cracks*, gone, lapsed, left behind, left out, lost, obliterated, omitted, past, past recollection, repressed, slipped one's mind*, suppressed, unrecalled, unremembered; SEE CONCEPTS *402,403,529*

fork [v] *go separate ways*
angle, bifurcate, branch off, branch out, divaricate, diverge, divide, part, split; SEE CONCEPTS *98,738*

forked [adj] *going separate ways*
angled, bifid, bifurcate, bifurcated, branched, branching, dichotomous, dichotonic, divaricate, divided, furcate, furcated, pronged, split, tined, tridented, zigzag; SEE CONCEPTS *485,581*

forlorn [adj] *hopeless, inconsolable*
abandoned, alone, bereft, blue*, cheerless, comfortless, cynical, defenseless, depressed, deserted, desolate, despairing, desperate, despondent, destitute, destroyed, disconsolate, down and out*, dragging*, forgotten, forsaken, friendless, fruitless, futile, godforsaken*, helpless, homeless, in the dumps*, lonely, lonesome, lost, miserable, oppressed, pathetic, pessimistic, pitiable, pitiful, solitary, tragic, unhappy, vain, weighed down, woebegone, wretched; SEE CONCEPT *403*

form [n1] *shape; arrangement*
anatomy, appearance, articulation, cast, configuration, conformation, construction, contour, cut, design, die, embodiment, fashion, figure, formation, framework, mode, model, mold, outline, pattern, plan, profile, scheme, silhouette, skeleton, structure, style, system; SEE CONCEPTS *184,660,734,757*

form [n2] *animate body and its condition*
anatomy, being, build, condition, fettle*, figure, fitness, frame, health, object, outline, person, phenomenon, physique, shape, silhouette, thing, torso, trim*; SEE CONCEPTS *316,389,720*

form [n3] *accepted procedure; ceremony*
behavior, by the book*, by the numbers*, canon, ceremonial, channels*, conduct, convenance, convention, custom, decorum, done thing*, etiquette, fashion, formality, habit, law, layout, manner, manners, method, mode, practice, precept, proceeding, process, propriety, protocol, regulation, rite, ritual, ropes*, rule, setup, style, usage, way; SEE CONCEPT *688*

form [n4] *document that requires answers or information*
application, blank, chart, data sheet, letter, paper, questionnaire, sheet; SEE CONCEPT *271*

form [n5] *type, kind*
arrangement, character, class, description, design, grade, guise, make, manifestation, manner, method, mode, order, practice, rank, semblance, sort, species, stamp, style, system, variety, way; SEE CONCEPTS *6,378*

form [n6] *organization, arrangement*
format, framework, harmony, order, orderliness, placement, plan, proportion, scheme, structure, symmetry; SEE CONCEPT *727*

form [v1] *bring into existence; make, produce*
arrange, assemble, block out, bring about, build, cast, complete, compose, conceive, concoct, constitute, construct, consummate, contrive, cook up*, create, cultivate, cut, design, develop, devise, dream up, erect, establish, fabricate, fashion, finish, fix, forge, found, frame, hammer out*, invent, knock off*, make up, manufacture, model, mold, organize, outline, pattern, perfect, plan, plot, project, put together, scheme, set, set up, shape, structure, throw together, trace, turn out*, work; SEE CONCEPTS *168,173,205,251*

form [v2] *come into being; arise*
accumulate, acquire, appear, become a reality, be-

fo
fo

come visible, condense, crystallize, develop, eventuate, fall into place*, grow, harden, materialize, mature, rise, set, settle, shape up, show up, take on character, take shape*; SEE CONCEPTS 105,704

form [v3] *educate, discipline*
breed, bring up, give character, instruct, rear, school, teach, train; SEE CONCEPTS 285,295

form [v4] *comprise, be a part of*
act as, compose, constitute, figure in, make, make up, serve as; SEE CONCEPT 643

formal [adj1] *established, orderly*
academic, approved, ceremonial, ceremonialistic, ceremonious, confirmed, conventional, decorous, directed, explicit, express, fixed, formalistic, lawful, legal, methodical, official, precise, prescribed, pro forma, proper, punctilious, regular, rigid, ritual, ritualistic, set, solemn, stately, stereotyped, stereotypical, strict, systematic; SEE CONCEPTS 533,547

formal [adj2] *stiff, affected, correct*
aloof, by the numbers*, ceremonious, conventional, decorous, distant, exact, nominal, playing the game*, polite, precise, prim, punctilious, reserved, seemly, sententious, starched*, stilted*, straight arrow*, stuffy*, unbending; SEE CONCEPT 401

formality [n1] *convention, custom*
academism, ceremony, convenance, conventionality, form, gesture, liturgy, matter of form*, officialism, procedure, red tape*, rite, ritual, rituality, rubric, rule, service, solemnity, solemnness, stereotype, tradition; SEE CONCEPT 688

formality [n2] *etiquette, protocol*
ceremoniousness, conventionalism, correctness, decorum, formalism, honors, mummery, politesse, propriety, p's and q's*, punctiliousness; SEE CONCEPT 633

formation [n] *composition, establishment*
accumulation, architecture, arrangement, compilation, configuration, constitution, construction, creation, crystallization, deposit, design, development, dispersal, disposition, embodiment, evolution, fabrication, figure, forming, generation, genesis, grouping, induction, makeup, manufacture, order, organization, pattern, production, rank, structure, synthesis; SEE CONCEPTS 173,260

formative [adj] *influential, impressionable*
determinative, developmental, immature, impressible, malleable, moldable, pliant, sensitive, shaping, susceptible; SEE CONCEPTS 534,537

former [adj] *previous in time or order*
above, aforementioned, aforesaid, ancient, antecedent, anterior, bygone, departed, earlier, erstwhile, ex-*, first, foregoing, late, long ago*, long gone, of yore*, old, once, one-time, past, preceding, prior, quondam, sometime, whilom; SEE CONCEPTS 585,820

formerly [adv] *previously in time or order*
aforetime, already, anciently, at one time, away back, a while back, back, back when*, before, before now, before this, down memory lane*, earlier, eons ago*, erewhile, erstwhile, heretofore, in former times, in the olden days*, in the past, lately, long ago, of old, of yore, olden days*, once, once upon a time*, radically, some time ago, time was*, used to be*, water under the bridge*; SEE CONCEPTS 585,820

formidable [adj1] *horrible, terrifying*
appalling, awful, dangerous, daunting, dire, dismaying, dreadful, fearful, fierce, frightful, horrific, imposing, impregnable, intimidating, menacing, redoubtable, shocking, terrible, terrific, threatening; SEE CONCEPT 537

formidable [adj2] *difficult, overwhelming*
all-powerful, arduous, awesome, ballbuster, challenging, colossal, dismaying, effortful, great, hard, impressive, indomitable, intimidating, labored, laborious, mammoth, mighty, murder*, onerous, overpowering, powerful, puissant, rough*, rough go*, staggering, strenuous, tall order*, toilsome, tough*, tough proposition*, tremendous, uphill*; SEE CONCEPT 565

formless [adj] *disorganized, vague*
amorphous, baggy*, blobby*, chaotic, crude, inchoate, incoherent, indefinite, indeterminate, indistinct, nebulous, obscure, orderless, raw, rough, rude, shapeless, unclear, undefined, unformed, unorganized; SEE CONCEPTS 485,535,589

formula [n] *set preparation; rule, recipe*
blueprint, canon, code, credo, creed, custom, description, direction, equation, form, formulary, maxim, method, modus operandi, precept, prescription, principle, procedure, rite, ritual, rote, rubric, specifications, theorem, way; SEE CONCEPTS 268,688

formulate [v] *plan, specify systematically*
codify, coin, compose, concoct, contrive, cook up, couch, define, detail, develop, devise, draft, draw up*, dream up*, evolve, express, forge, frame, give form to, hatch, indite, invent, make, make up*, map, originate, particularize, phrase, prepare, put, set down*, systematize, vamp, work, work out; SEE CONCEPTS 36,173,202

forsake [v] *abandon, turn one's back on*
abdicate, cast off, change one's tune*, desert, disclaim, disown, drift away*, forgo, forswear, give up, have done with, jettison, jilt, kiss goodbye*, leave, leave flat*, leave high and dry*, quit, relinquish, renounce, repudiate, resign, run out on*, set aside, show the door*, spurn, surrender, take the oath*, throw over*, walk out on*, wash one's hands of*, yield; SEE CONCEPTS 30,195,384

forsaken [adj] *abandoned*
cast off, derelict, deserted, desolate, destitute, disowned, forlorn, friendless, godforsaken*, ignored, isolated, jilted, left at the altar*, left behind, left in the lurch*, lonely, lorn, marooned, outcast, solitary, thrown over*; SEE CONCEPT 555

forswear [v] *abandon, disavow*
abjure, deny, disclaim, disown, drop, forgo, forsake, give up, recall, recant, reject, renege, renounce, repudiate, retract, swear off, take back, withdraw; SEE CONCEPTS 44,54

fort/fortress [n] *stronghold*
acropolis, blockhouse, camp, castle, citadel, fastness, fortification, garrison, redoubt, station; SEE CONCEPTS 321,439

forte [n] *person's strong point*
ability, ableness, aptitude, competence, effectiveness, efficiency, eminency, faculty, gift*, long suit*, medium, métier, oyster*, speciality, strength, strong suit*, talent, thing*; SEE CONCEPTS 409,411

forth [adv] *outward*
ahead, alee, along, away, first, forward, into, into the open*, on, onward, out; SEE CONCEPT 581

forthcoming [adj] *expected, imminent*
accessible, anticipated, approaching, at hand, available, awaited, coming, destined, fated, fu-

ture, impending, inescapable, in evidence, inevitable, in preparation, in prospect, in store*, in the cards*, in the wind*, nearing, obtainable, oncoming, on tap*, open, pending, predestined, prospective, ready, resulting, upcoming; SEE CONCEPTS 548,799

forthright [adj] straightforward, honest
aboveboard, bald, blunt, call a spade a spade*, candid, categorical, direct, directly, forward, frank, from the hip*, like it is*, no lie*, open, outspoken, plain, plainspoken, real, simple, sincere, straight, undisguised, up front*; SEE CONCEPT 267

forthwith [adv] immediately
abruptly, at once, away, directly, instantly, now, quickly, right away*, right now*, straightaway, suddenly, tout de suite, without delay; SEE CONCEPTS 544,820

fortification [n] reinforced position
barricade, barrier, bastion, battlement, block, blockhouse, breastwork, buffer, bulwark, castle, citadel, consolidation, defense, earthwork, embattlement, entrenchment, fastness, fort, fortress, garrison, keep, outpost, parapet, preparation, presidio, protection, reinforcement, stockade, strengthening, stronghold, support, wall; SEE CONCEPTS 439,729

fortify [v1] make strong and secure; add to
brace, build up, bulwark, buttress, charge up, consolidate, embattle, entrench, garrison, gird, prepare, prop, protect, punch up*, ready, reinforce, secure, shore up*, soup up*, steel*, step up, strengthen, support; SEE CONCEPT 202

fortify [v2] encourage, reassure
arouse, brace, buck up*, build up, cheer, confirm, embolden, energize, enliven, hearten, invigorate, pour it on*, punch up*, rally, refresh, reinforce, renew, restore, rouse, stiffen, stir, strengthen, sustain; SEE CONCEPTS 7,22

fortitude [n] strength of mind; guts
backbone*, boldness, braveness, bravery, constancy, courage, courageousness, dauntlessness, determination, endurance, fearlessness, firmness, grit*, gutsiness, hardihood, heart, intrepidity, mettle, moxie, nerve, patience, perseverance, pith, pluck, resoluteness, resolution, spine*, spirit, spunk, stamina, starch, staying power, stick-to-itiveness*, stomach, stoutheartedness, tenacity, true grit*, valiancy, valor, valorousness, what it takes*; SEE CONCEPTS 410,411

fortuitous [adj] lucky, accidental
arbitrary, casual, chance, contingent, fluke*, fluky*, fortunate, haphazard, happy, incidental, luck in*, luck out*, lucky-dog*, odd, providential, random, serendipitous, unforeseen, unplanned; SEE CONCEPTS 548,552

fortunate [adj] having good luck
advantageous, affluent, auspicious, blessed, born with a silver spoon*, bright, charmed, convenient, encouraging, favorable, favored, felicitous, flourishing, fortuitous, gaining, get a break*, golden, happy, healthy, helpful, hopeful, in luck*, in the gravy*, lucky, on a roll*, opportune, overcoming, profitable, promising, propitious, prosperous, providential, rosy, sitting pretty, successful, sunny side*, thriving, timely, triumphant, victorious, wealthy, well-off, well-to-do; SEE CONCEPTS 404,542,572

fortunately [adv] luckily
auspiciously, by good luck, by happy chance*,

favorably, happily, in good time*, in the nick of time*, opportunely, prosperously, providentially, satisfyingly, seasonably, successfully, swimmingly, well; SEE CONCEPTS 537,544,572

fortune [n1] wealth, possessions
affluence, capital, estate, gold mine*, inheritance, opulence, portion, property, prosperity, resources, riches, substance, treasure, worth; SEE CONCEPTS 335,710

fortune [n2] fate, lot in life
accident, break*, certainty, chance, circumstances, contingency, destiny, doom, expectation, experience, fifty-fifty*, fighting chance*, fluke*, fortuity, fortuneteness, good break, hazard, history, karma*, kismet*, life, luck, lucked into*, lucked out*, luckiness, lucky break*, lucky hit*, Moirai, portion, providence, roll of the dice*, run of luck*, star, streak of luck, success, way the ball bounces*, way the cookie crumbles*, wheel of fortune*; SEE CONCEPT 679

fortune-teller [n] person attempting to tell the future
augur, clairvoyant, crystal ball gazer, diviner, medium, mind reader, oracle, palmist, palm reader, predicter, prophet, psychic, seer, soothsayer, spiritualist, tarot reader, tea-leaf reader; SEE CONCEPTS 348,423

forward [adj1] advancing, early
ahead, forth, forward-looking, in advance, leading, onward, precocious, premature, progressing, progressive, propulsive, well-developed; SEE CONCEPT 528

forward [adj2] in front, first
advance, anterior, facial, fore, foremost, front, head, leading, ventral; SEE CONCEPTS 581, 583,585

forward [adj3] brash, impertinent
aggressive, assuming, audacious, bantam, barefaced, bold, brazen, cheeky*, coming on strong*, confident, familiar, fresh, impudent, nervy*, overassertive, overweening, pert, presuming, presumptuous, pushing, pushy*, rude, sassy*, saucy*, self-assertive, smart, smart-alecky*, uppity*, wise; SEE CONCEPTS 401,404

forward [v1] aid, expedite
advance, assist, back, champion, cultivate, encourage, favor, foster, further, hasten, help, hurry, promote, serve, speed, support, uphold; SEE CONCEPTS 68,110

forward [v2] send, ship
address, consign, deliver, dispatch, express, freight, post, remit, route, transmit, transport; SEE CONCEPT 217

forward [adv] toward the front in order, time
ahead, alee, along, ante, antecedently, before, beforehand, fore, forth, in advance, into prominence, into view, on, onward, out, precedently, previous, to the fore*, vanward; SEE CONCEPTS 581,585,799

fossil [n] organic remains of a previous time
deposit, eolith, impression, neolith, paleolith, petrifaction, reconstruction, relic, skeleton, specimen, trace; SEE CONCEPTS 429,470,509

foster [v1] promote, support
advance, back, champion, cherish, cultivate, encourage, feed, foment, forward, further, harbor, nurse, nurture, serve, stimulate, uphold; SEE CONCEPT 110

foster [v2] give care or accommodation to
assist, bring up, care for, cherish, entertain, favor,

fo
fo

harbor, help, house, lodge, minister to, nourish, nurse, oblige, raise, rear, serve, shelter, sustain, take care of; SEE CONCEPTS *110,140,295*

foul [*adj1*] *disgusting, dirty*
abhorrent, abominable, base, contaminated, despicable, detestable, disgraceful, dishonorable, egregious, fetid, filthy, gross*, hateful, heinous, horrid, icky*, impure, infamous, iniquitous, loathsome, malodorous, mucky*, nasty, nauseating, nefarious, noisome, notorious, offensive, pigpen*, polluted, putrid, rank*, raunchy*, repellent, repulsive, revolting, rotten, scandalous, shameful, squalid, stinking*, sullied, tainted, unclean, vicious, vile, wicked, yecchy*, yucky*; SEE CONCEPTS *485,529*

foul [*adj2*] *vulgar, offensive*
abusive, blasphemous, blue*, coarse, dirty, filthy, foul-mouthed, gross*, indecent, lewd, low, nasty, obscene, profane, raunchy, scatological, scurrilous, smutty*; SEE CONCEPT *267*

foul [*adj3*] *corrupt, dishonest*
caitiff, crooked, dirty, fraudulent, inequitable, monstrous, shady, underhand, underhanded, unfair, unjust, unscrupulous, vicious; SEE CONCEPTS *537,548*

foul [*v*] *make or become dirty*
befoul, begrime, besmear, besmirch, block, catch, choke, clog, contaminate, defile, desecrate, discolor, ensnare, entangle, fill, jam, pollute, profane, smear, smudge, snarl, soil, spot, stain, sully, tarnish, twist; SEE CONCEPTS *250,469*

foul up [*v*] *make a mess of*
botch, bungle, confuse, jumble, mismanage, mix up*, muck up*, muddle, screw up*, snafu*, snarl, tumble; SEE CONCEPTS *16,234*

found [*v1*] *bring into being*
begin, commence, constitute, construct, create, endow, erect, establish, fashion, fix, form, get going, inaugurate, initiate, institute, launch, organize, originate, plant, raise, ring in*, settle, settle up, start, start the ball rolling*, start up; SEE CONCEPT *221*

found [*v2*] *put on a base*
bottom, build, erect, establish, ground, predicate, raise, rear, rest, root, stay, support, sustain; SEE CONCEPTS *168,221*

foundation [*n1*] *basis for something physical or mental*
ABCs*, authority, base, basics, bed, bedrock, bottom, bottom line*, brass tacks*, foot, footing, ground, groundwork, guts*, heart*, infrastructure, justification, nitty-gritty*, nub*, nuts and bolts*, prop, reason, root, stay, substratum, substructure, support, underpinning, understructure; SEE CONCEPTS *442,826*

foundation [*n2*] *established institution*
association, charity, company, corporation, endowment, establishment, guild, inauguration, institute, organization, plantation, settlement, setup, society, trusteeship; SEE CONCEPT *381*

founder [*n*] *person who establishes an institution*
architect, author, beginner, benefactor, builder, constructor, creator, designer, establisher, forebearer, framer, generator, initiator, institutor, inventor, maker, organizer, originator, patron, planner, prime mover*; SEE CONCEPTS *347,423*

founder [*v*] *go under, fail*
abort, be lost, break down, collapse, come to nothing, fall, fall through, go down, go lame, go to bottom, lurch, miscarry, misfire, sink, sprawl,

stagger, stumble, submerge, submerse, trip; SEE CONCEPTS *181,699*

fountain [*n*] *source, often of liquid*
bubbler, cause, font, fount, geyser, gush, inception, inspiration, jet, lode, mainspring, mine, origin, play, provenance, provenience, pump, reservoir, root, spout, spray, spring, stream, well, wellhead, wellspring; SEE CONCEPTS *514,648*

fountainhead [*n*] *principal source; person who originates*
administrator, architect, author, builder, creator, father, fount, fountain, generator, initiator, leader, maker, mother, originator, spring, wellspring; SEE CONCEPTS *348,350*

foxy [*adj*] *shrewd*
artful, astute, canny, crafty, cunning, deceitful, deep, devious, dishonest, experienced, guileful, insidious, intelligent, knowing, retiary, sharp, slick, sly, subtle, tricky, vulpine, wily; SEE CONCEPTS *401,404*

foyer [*n*] *receiving area*
antechamber, anteroom, entrance hall, lobby, reception, vestibule; SEE CONCEPTS *440,441,448*

fracas [*n*] *disturbance, fight*
affray, altercation, battle, battle royal*, bickering, brawl, broil*, brouhaha, dispute, donnybrook*, feud, flap*, fray, free-for-all*, hassle, knockdown-drag-out*, melee, mix up*, quarrel, riot, row, ruction, ruffle, rumpus, run-in*, scrimmage, scuffle, set-to*, squabble, stew*, trouble, tumult, uproar, words*; SEE CONCEPTS *46,106*

fraction [*n1*] *part*
bite, chunk, cut, division, end, fragment, half, piece, portion, section, share, slice; SEE CONCEPT *835*

fraction [*n2*] *incomplete number*
bit, division, fragment, part, partial, piece, portion, quotient, ratio, section, segment, slice, subdivision; SEE CONCEPT *765*

fractional [*adj*] *partial*
apportioned, compartmental, compartmented, constituent, dismembered, dispersed, divided, fragmentary, frationary, incomplete, parceled, part, piecemeal, sectional, segmented; SEE CONCEPT *785*

fractious [*adj*] *grouchy, cross*
awkward, captious, crabby*, disorderly, fretful, froward, huffy*, indocile, indomitable, intractable, irritable, mean, ornery*, peevish, perverse, pettish, petulant, querulous, recalcitrant, refractory, restive, scrappy, snappish, testy, thin-skinned, touchy, uncompliant, undisciplined, unmanageable, unruly, wayward, wild; SEE CONCEPTS *267,401*

fracture [*n*] *break, rupture*
breach, cleavage, cleft, crack, discontinuity, disjunction, displacement, fissure, fragmentation, gap, mutilation, opening, rent, rift, schism, severance, splinter, split, wound; SEE CONCEPTS *309,513*

fragile [*adj*] *breakable, dainty*
brittle, crisp, crumbly, decrepit, delicate, feeble, fine, flimsy, fracturable, frail, frangible, friable, infirm, insubstantial, shatterable, shivery, slight, unsound, weak, weakly; SEE CONCEPTS *485,489*

fragment [*n*] *part, chip*
ace, atom, bit, bite, chunk, crumb, cut, end, fraction, gob*, grain, hunk, iota, job*, lump*, minim, morsel, particle, piece, portion, remnant, scrap,

share, shiver, shred, slice, sliver, smithereens*;
SEE CONCEPT 835

fragment [v] *break into pieces*
burst, come apart, crumble, disintegrate, disunite,
divide, rend, rive, shatter, shiver, smash, splinter,
split, split up; SEE CONCEPTS 98,135,
137,246,469

fragmentary [adj] *broken, incomplete*
bitty, disconnected, discrete, disjointed, fractional, incoherent, part, partial, piecemeal, scattered, scrappy, sketchy, unsystematic; SEE
CONCEPT 785

fragrance [n] *pleasant odor*
aroma, aura, balm, bouquet, incense, perfume,
redolence, scent, smell, spice; SEE CONCEPT 600

fragrant [adj] *smelling pleasant*
ambrosial, aromal, aromatic, balmy, delectable,
delicious, delightful, odoriferous, odorous, perfumed, perfumy, redolent, savory, spicy, sweet,
sweet-scented, sweet-smelling; SEE CONCEPT 598

frail [adj] *breakable, weak*
brittle, dainty, decrepit, delicate, feeble, fishy,
flimsy, fracturable, fragile, frangible, infirm, insubstantial, puny, sad, shatterable, shattery,
sickly, slender, slight, slim, tender, tenuous, thin,
unsound, unsubstantial, vulnerable, wimpy,
wishy-washy, wispy; SEE CONCEPTS 485,489

frailty [n] *weakness, flaw*
Achilles heel*, blemish, daintiness, debility, decrepitude, defect, deficiency, delicacy, error, failing, fallibility, fault, feebleness, flimsiness,
foible, foil, imperfection, infirmity, peccability,
peccadillo, shortcoming, solecism, suscept, weak
point*; SEE CONCEPTS 101,230,411,580

frame [n] *skeleton, casing*
anatomy, architecture, body, build, cage, carcass,
construction, enclosure, fabric, flounce, form,
framework, fringe, groundwork, hem, mount,
mounting, outline, physique, scaffold, scaffolding, scheme, setting, shell, stage, structure, support, system, trim, trimming, truss, valance; SEE
CONCEPTS 442,733,757

frame [v1] *build*
assemble, back, border, constitute, construct, encase, enclose, erect, fabricate, fashion, forge,
form, institute, invent, lath, make, manufacture,
mat, model, mold, mount, panel, produce, put
together, raise, set up, shingle; SEE CONCEPTS
168,758

frame [v2] *compose, plan*
block out, conceive, concoct, contrive, cook up,
design, devise, draft, draw up, dream up*, form,
formulate, hatch, invent, invent, make, make up,
map out, outline, prepare, shape, sketch, vamp,
write; SEE CONCEPTS 36,173

framework [n] *foundation, core*
bare bones*, cage, fabric, frame, frame of reference*, groundwork, plan, schema, scheme, shell,
skeleton, structure; SEE CONCEPTS 439,479,733

franchise [n] *authority, right*
authorization, ballot, charter, exemption, freedom, immunity, patent, prerogative, privilege,
suffrage, vote; SEE CONCEPT 376

frank [adj] *completely honest*
aboveboard, apparent, artless, bare-faced*, blunt,
bold, brazen, call a spade a spade*, candid, direct, downright, easy, familiar, flat-out*, forthright, free, from the hip*, guileless, heart-to-
heart*, ingenuous, lay it on the line*, like it is*,
matter-of-fact, naive, natural, open, outright, out-

spoken, plain, plain-spoken, real, saying what one
thinks*, scrupulous, sincere, straight, straightforward, transparent, truthful, unconcealed, undisguised, uninhibited, unreserved, unrestricted, up
front*, upright; SEE CONCEPTS 267,582

frankfurter [n] *cylindrical meat sausage*
bowwow*, Coney Island*, dog*, footlong*,
frank, hot dog, link, weenie*, wiener, wiener-
wurst; SEE CONCEPTS 457,460

frankly [adv] *very honestly*
bluntly, candidly, dead level*, dead on*, directly,
forthrightly, freely, from the hip*, in truth, laid on
the line*, level, on the level*, on the line*,
openly, plainly, straight, straightforwardly, without reserve; SEE CONCEPT 267

frantic [adj] *distressed, distracted*
agitated, angry, at wits' end*, berserk, beside oneself*, corybantic, crazy, delirious, deranged, distraught, excited, flipped out*, fraught, freaked
out*, frenetic, frenzied, furious, hectic, hot and
bothered*, hot under the collar*, hyper*, in a
stew*, in a tizzy*, insane, keyed up*, mad, out of
control, overwrought, rabid, raging, raving, shook
up*, spazzed out*, unglued*, unscrewed*, unzipped*, violent, weird, weirded out*, wigged
out*, wild, wired*, worked up*, zonkers*; SEE
CONCEPTS 403,542

fraud [n1] *trickery, deception*
artifice, bamboozlement*, blackmail, cheat, chicane, chicanery, con, craft*, deceit, double-
dealing*, dupery, duping, duplicity, extortion,
fake, fast one*, fast shuffle*, flimflam*, fourberie, fraudulence, graft, guile, hanky-panky*,
hoax, hocus-pocus*, hoodwinking*, hustle*, imposture, line, misrepresentation, racket, scam,
sell, shakedown*, sham*, sharp practice*,
skunk*, smoke*, song*, song and dance*, spuriousness, sting, string, swindle, swindling, treachery; SEE CONCEPTS 59,192,645

fraud [n2] *person who is false, deceitful*
bastard, bluffer, charlatan, cheat, counterfeit,
crook, deceiver, double-dealer*, fake, forger,
four-flusher*, hoaxer, horse trader*, impostor,
mechanic*, mountebank, phony, play actor*, pretender, quack*, racketeer, sham*, shark*, swindler; SEE CONCEPT 412

fraudulent [adj] *deceptive, false*
bamboozling*, counterfeit, crafty, criminal,
crooked, deceitful, devious, dishonest, dishonorable, double-dealing*, duplicitous, fake, forged,
mock, phony, pseudo, sham*, spurious, swindling, treacherous, tricky; SEE CONCEPTS 545,582

fraught [adj] *full of*
abounding, attended, bristling, charged, filled,
heavy, laden, replete, stuffed; SEE CONCEPTS
483,771

fray [n] *fight, battle*
affray, battle royal*, brawl, broil*, brouhaha*,
clash, combat, conflict, contest, disturbance, donnybrook*, engagement, fracas, melee, quarrel,
riot, row, ruckus, rumble, rumpus, scuffle, set-
to*; SEE CONCEPTS 86,106

fray [v] *shred, come apart*
become ragged, become threadbare, chafe, erode,
frazzle, fret, ravel, rip, rub, tatter, tear, unravel,
wear, wear away, wear thin; SEE CONCEPT 214

frazzle [n] *exhaustion; something very worn*
collapse, enervation, lassitude, prostration, rag,
remnant, shred; SEE CONCEPTS 410,720

frazzle [v] *wear out*
exhaust, fray, knock out, poop*, prostrate, rip, shred, tear, tire, tucker*, wear; SEE CONCEPTS *156,186*

freak [n1] *something, someone very abnormal*
aberration, abortion, anomaly, chimera, curiosity, geek*, grotesque, malformation, miscreation, misshape, monster, monstrosity, mutant, mutation, oddity, queer, rarity, sport, weirdo*; SEE CONCEPTS *424,580*

freak [n2] *irregularity, whim*
caprice, conceit, crochet, fad, fancy, folly, humor, megrim, quirk, turn, twist, vagary, whimsy; SEE CONCEPT *679*

freak [n3] *person enthused about something*
addict, aficionado, buff, bug*, devotee, enthusiast, fan, fanatic, fiend*, maniac, nut*, zealot; SEE CONCEPTS *352,366,423*

freak [v] *become extraordinarily upset*
flip out*, go beserk, go insane, go mad, lose control, rave, unhinge*, wig out*; SEE CONCEPTS *7,19,80*

freakish [adj] *abnormal, unusual*
aberrant, arbitrary, bizarre, capricious, crazy, erratic, fantastic, far-out, freaky, grotesque, malformed, monstrous, odd, outlandish, outré, preternatural, queer, strange, unconventional, vagarious, wayward, weird, whimsical, wild; SEE CONCEPT *564*

freckle [n] *small discoloration on skin*
blemish, blotch, daisy, dot, lentigo, macula, mole, patch, pepper, pigmentation, pit, pock, pockmark, speck, speckle, sprinkle, stipple; SEE CONCEPT *392*

free [adj1] *without charge*
chargeless, comp*, complimentary, costless, for love*, for nothing*, freebie*, free of cost, free ride*, gratis, gratuitous, handout, on the cuff*, on the house*, paper*, unpaid, unrecompensed; SEE CONCEPT *334*

free [adj2] *unrestrained personally*
able, allowed, at large, at liberty, casual, clear, disengaged, easy, escaped, familiar, fancy-free*, footloose*, forward, frank, free-spirited, free-wheeling, independent, informal, lax, liberal, liberated, loose, off the hook*, on one's own*, on the loose*, open, permitted, relaxed, unattached, uncommitted, unconfined, unconstrained, unengaged, unfettered, unhampered, unimpeded, unobstructed, unregulated, unrestricted, untrammeled; SEE CONCEPTS *401,542*

free [adj3] *unrestrained politically*
at liberty, autarchic, autonomic, autonomous, democratic, emancipated, enfranchised, freed, independent, individualistic, liberated, self-directing, self-governing, self-ruling, separate, sovereign, sui juris, unconstrained, unenslaved, unregimented; SEE CONCEPTS *319,536*

free [adj4] *not busy; unoccupied*
at leisure, available, clear, empty, extra, idle, loose, not tied down*, spare, unemployed, unengaged, unhampered, unimpeded, uninhabited, unobstructed, unused, vacant; SEE CONCEPT *485*

free [adj5] *generous, unsparing*
big, big-hearted*, bounteous, bountiful, charitable, eager, handsome, hospitable, lavish, liberal, munificent, open-handed*, prodigal, unstinging, willing; SEE CONCEPT *404*

free [v] *liberate, let go*
absolve, acquit, bail, bail out*, clear, cut loose*, deliver, demobilize, discharge, disengage, disenthrall, disimprison, dismiss, emancipate, enfranchise, extricate, let loose*, let off*, let off the hook*, let out, loose, loosen, manumit, parole, put on the street*, ransom, redeem, release, relieve, reprieve, rescue, save, set free, spring*, turn loose, turn out, unbind, uncage, unchain, undo, unfetter, unfix, unleash, untie; SEE CONCEPT *127*

free [v2] *take burden from*
cast off, clear, cut loose, decontaminate, deliver, discharge, disembarrass, disencumber, disengage, disentangle, empty, excuse, exempt, extricate, put off, ransom, redeem, relieve, rescue, rid, unburden, undo, unlade, unload, unpack, unshackle; SEE CONCEPTS *110,211*

freedom [n1] *independence, license to do as one wants*
abandon, abandonment, ability, bent, carte blanche, compass, discretion, elbowroom*, exemption, facility, flexibility, free rein*, full play*, full swing*, immunity, indulgence, laissez faire, latitude, laxity, leeway, liberty, margin, opportunity, own accord*, play, plenty of rope*, power, prerogative, privilege, profligacy, rampancy, range, rein, right, rope*, scope, sweep, swing, unrestraint; SEE CONCEPT *693*

freedom [n2] *political independence*
abolition, abolitionism, autarchy, autonomy, citizenship, deliverance, delivery, democracy, discharge, disengagement, disimprisonment, emancipation, enfranchisement, exemption, extriction, franchise, home rule*, immunity, impunity, liberation, liberty, manumission, parole, prerogative, privilege, probation, redemption, release, relief, representative government, rescue, salvage, salvation, self-determination, self-government, sovereignty; SEE CONCEPT *691*

freedom [n3] *easy attitude*
abandon, boldness, brazenness, candor, directness, disrespect, ease, facility, familiarity, forthrightness, forwardness, frankness, impertinence, informality, ingenuousness, lack of reserve, lack of restraint, laxity, license, openness, overfamiliarity, presumption, readiness, spontaneity, unconstraint; SEE CONCEPT *633*

free-for-all [n] *fight*
affray, battle, brawl, broil*, brouhaha*, fracas, fray, knock-down-drag-out*, melee, riot, row, ruction; SEE CONCEPT *106*

freely [adj1] *without restriction*
advisedly, as you please*, at one's discretion, at one's pleasure, at will, candidly, deliberately, designedly, fancy-free*, frankly, intentionally, of one's own accord*, of one's own free will*, openly, plainly, purposely, spontaneously, unchallenged, unreservedly, voluntarily, willingly, without hindrance, without prompting, without reserve, without restraint, without urging; SEE CONCEPT *401*

freely [adv2] *easily, smoothly done*
abundantly, amply, as one pleases*, bountifully, cleanly, copiously, effortlessly, extravagantly, facilely, lavishly, liberally, lightly, like water*, loosely, open-handedly, readily, unhindered, unobstructedly, unstintingly, well, with a free hand*, without encumbrance*, without hindrance*, without restraint*, without stint*; SEE CONCEPT *544*

free will [n] *person's full intent and purpose*
assent, choice, consent, desire, determination, discretion, free choice, freedom, inclination, intention, mind, option, own say so*, own sweet way*, pleasure, power, say so*, velleity, volition, voluntary decision, willingness; SEE CONCEPTS 20,410

freeze [v1] *make cold enough to become solid*
benumb, bite, chill, chill to the bone*, congeal, frost, glaciate, harden, ice over, ice up, nip, pierce, refrigerate, solidify, stiffen; SEE CONCEPTS 255,521

freeze [v2] *stop*
dampen, depress, discourage, dishearten, fix, hold up, inhibit, peg, suspend; SEE CONCEPTS 14,121

freezing [adj] *very cold*
arctic, biting, bitter, chill, chilled, chilly, cutting, frigid, frost-bound, frosty, gelid, glacial, hawkish, icy, nippy, numbing, one-dog night*, penetrating, polar, raw, shivery, Siberian*, snappy*, two-dog night*, wintry; SEE CONCEPT 605

freight [n] *goods being shipped*
bales, ballast, bulk, burden, carriage, consignment, contents, conveyance, encumbrance, fardel, haul, lading, load, merchandise, pack, packages, payload, shipment, shipping, tonnage, transportation, wares, weight; SEE CONCEPT 338

frenetic [adj] *maniacal*
corybantic, agitation, delirious, demented, distraught, excited, fanatical, frantic, frenzied, furibund, furious, hyper*, in a lather*, insane, lost it*, mad, obsessive, overwrought, phrenetic, rabid, unbalanced, unscrewed*, weirded out*, wigged out*, wild, wired*; SEE CONCEPT 403

frenzied [adj] *uncontrolled*
agitated, berserk, convulsive, corybantic, delirious, distracted, distraught, excited, feverish, frantic, frenetic, furious, hysterical, mad, maniacal, nuts*, rabid, wild; SEE CONCEPTS 542,544

frenzy [n] *uncontrolled state or situation*
aberration, agitation, blow, blow a fuse*, blow one's cork*, blow one's stack*, blow one's top*, bout, burst, conniption*, convulsion, craze, delirium, derangement, distemper, distraction, dithers*, excitement, ferment, fever, fit, flap*, flip one's lid*, free-for-all*, furor, fury, fuss, hell broke loose*, hysteria, insanity, lather, lunacy, madness, mania, outburst, paroxysm, passion, rage, row, ruckus, ruction, rumble, rumpus, seizure, spasm, stew, stir, to-do*, transport, turmoil, wingding*; SEE CONCEPTS 230,410,674

frequency [n] *commonness, repetitiveness*
abundance, beat, constancy, density, frequentness, iteration, number, oscillation, periodicity, persistence, prevalence, pulsation, recurrence, regularity, reiteration, repetition, rhythm; SEE CONCEPT 634

frequent [adj] *common, repeated*
a good many*, commonplace, constant, continual, customary, everyday, expected, familiar, general, habitual, incessant, intermittent, iterated, manifold, many, monotonous, numberless, numerous, periodic, perpetual, persistent, pleonastic, profuse, recurrent, recurring, redundant, reiterated, reiterative, successive, thick, ubiquitous, usual, various; SEE CONCEPT 530

frequent [v] *be a regular customer of*
affect, attend, attend regularly, be at home in*, be found at, be often in, drop in, go to, hang about*, hang around*, hang out at*, haunt*, hit*, infest,

overrun, patronize, play*, resort, revisit, visit often; SEE CONCEPTS 227,384

frequently [adv] *commonly, repeatedly*
again and again*, as a rule*, at regular intervals, at short intervals, at times, by ordinary, customarily, every now and then*, generally, habitually, in many instances*, in quick succession, intermittently, many a time*, many times, much, not infrequently, not seldom, oft, often, oftentimes, ofttimes, ordinarily, over and over, periodically, recurrently, regularly, spasmodically, successively, thick and fast*, time and again*, usually, very often; SEE CONCEPTS 530,544,799

fresh [adj1] *new, just produced*
beginning, brand-new*, comer, contemporary, crisp, crude, current, different, gleaming, glistening, green*, hot*, hot off the press*, immature, just out*, late, latest, mint*, modern, modernistic, natural, neoteric, newborn, newfangled*, novel, now, original, radical, raw, recent, sparkling, state-of-the-art, the latest*, this season's*, unconventional, unprocessed, unseasoned, untouched, unusual, up-to-date, virginal, what's happening*, young, youthful; SEE CONCEPTS 578,797

fresh [adj2] *additional*
added, another, auxiliary, else, extra, farther, further, increased, more, new, other, renewed, supplementary; SEE CONCEPTS 546,824

fresh [adj3] *refreshing to the senses*
bracing, bright, brisk, clean, clear, colorful, cool, crisp, definite, fair, invigorating, not stale, pure, quick, sharp, spanking, sparkling, stiff, stimulating, sweet, uncontaminated, unpolluted, vivid; SEE CONCEPT 537

fresh [adj4] *energetic, healthy*
active, alert, blooming, bouncing, bright, bright-eyed, bushy-tailed*, chipper*, clear, dewy, fair, florid, glowing, good, hardy, invigorated, keen, like new, lively, refreshed, rehabilitated, relaxed, relieved, rested, restored, revived, rosy, ruddy, sprightly, spry, stimulated, undimmed, unfaded, unused, unwearied, unwithered, verdant, vigorous, vital, wholesome, young; SEE CONCEPTS 485,542

fresh [adj5] *inexperienced*
artless, callow, green*, natural, new, raw, tender-footed*, uncultivated, unpracticed, unskilled, untrained, untried, unversed, young, youthful; SEE CONCEPT 404

fresh [adj6] *sassy, brazen*
bold, cheeky*, disrespectful, familiar, flip*, flippant, forward, impertinent, impudent, insolent, nervy*, pert, presumptuous, rude, saucy*, smart*, smart-alecky*, snippy*, wise; SEE CONCEPTS 267,401

freshen [v] *make like new; revitalize*
activate, air, cleanse, enliven, invigorate, purify, refresh, restore, revive, rouse, spruce up, sweeten, titivate, ventilate; SEE CONCEPT 244

freshness [n] *newness*
bloom, brightness, callowness, cleanness, clearness, dew, dewiness, glow, greenness, inexperience, innovativeness, inventiveness, novelty, originality, rawness, shine, sparkle, vigor, viridity, youth; SEE CONCEPT 715

fret [v1] *worry, be annoyed*
affront, agonize, anguish, bleed, bother, brood, carp, carry a heavy load*, chafe, chagrin, distress oneself, eat one's heart out*, fume, fuss, get into

a dither*, grieve, lose sleep over*, mope*, pother*, stew, sweat it out*, take on, torment, upset oneself; SEE CONCEPT *410*

fret [v2] *upset someone*
abrade, agitate, bother, displease, distress, disturb, gall, get on nerves*, goad, harass, irk, irritate, nag, nettle, peeve, pique, provoke, rile, ruffle, torment, trouble, vex; SEE CONCEPTS *7,19*

fret [v3] *rub hard*
abrade, chafe, corrode, erode, excoriate, fray, gall, riffle, ripple, wear away, wear threadbare; SEE CONCEPT *215*

fretful [adj] *irritable*
captious, carping*, caviling, complaining, contrary, crabby*, cranky*, critical, cross, crotchety*, edgy, faultfinding, fractious, huffy*, mean, ornery*, out of sorts*, peevish, perverse, petulant, querulous, short-tempered, snappish*, splenetic, testy, touchy, uneasy, worried, wreck*; SEE CONCEPTS *401,403*

friction [n1] *rubbing*
abrasion, agitation, attrition, chafing, erosion, filing, fretting, grating, grinding, irritation, massage, rasping, resistance, scraping, soreness, traction, trituration, wearing away; SEE CONCEPT *215*

friction [n2] *disagreement*
animosity, antagonism, bad blood*, bad feeling*, bickering, bone to pick*, conflict, counteraction, discontent, discord, disharmony, dispute, dissension, faction, factionalism, flak*, hassle, hatred, hostility, impedance, incompatibility, interference, opposition, quarrel, resentment, resistance, rivalry, row*, ruckus*, rumpus*, set-to*, sour note*, strife, trouble, wrangling*; SEE CONCEPTS *46,106,674*

friend [n1] *confidant, companion*
acquaintance, ally, alter ego, associate, bosom buddy*, buddy, chum*, classmate, cohort, colleague, companion*, compatriot, comrade, consort, cousin, crony, familiar, intimate, mate, pal, partner, playmate, roommate, schoolmate, sidekick, soul mate*, spare*, well-wisher; SEE CONCEPT *423*

friend [n2] *benefactor*
accomplice, adherent, advocate, ally, associate, backer, partisan, patron, supporter, well-wisher; SEE CONCEPT *348*

friendless [adj] *without companionship or confidant*
abandoned, adrift, alienated, all alone*, all by one's self*, alone, cut off*, deserted, estranged, forlorn, forsaken, isolated, lonely, lonesome, marooned*, ostracized, shunned, solitary, unattached, without ties; SEE CONCEPT *555*

friendliness [n] *companionability*
affability, amiability, amity, benevolence, camaraderie, comity, comradery, congeniality, conviviality, cordiality, friendship, geniality, goodwill, kindliness, kindness, neighborliness, open arms*, sociability, warmth; SEE CONCEPT *388*

friendly [adj] *intimate, companionable*
affable, affectionate, amiable, amicable, attached, attentive, auspicious, beneficial, benevolent, benign, buddy-buddy*, chummy*, civil, close, clubby, comradely, conciliatory, confiding, convivial, cordial, faithful, familiar, favorable, fond, genial, good, helpful, kind, kindly, loving, loyal, neighborly, on good terms*, outgoing, peaceable, peaceful, propitious, receptive, sociable, solicitous, sympathetic, tender, thick, welcoming, well-disposed*; SEE CONCEPT *555*

friendship [n] *companionship*
accord, acquaintanceship, affection, affinity, agreement, alliance, amiability, amicability, amity, association, attachment, attraction, benevolence, closeness, coalition, comity, company, concord, consideration, consonance, devotion, empathy, esteem, familiarity, favor, favoritism, fondness, friendliness, fusion, good will, harmony, intimacy, league, love, pact, partiality, rapport, regard, sociability, society, sodality, solidarity, understanding; SEE CONCEPTS *388,714*

fright [n1] *extreme apprehension*
alarm, cold sweat*, consternation, dismay, dread, fear, horror, panic, quaking, scare, shiver, shock, terror, trepidation, trepidity; SEE CONCEPT *410*

fright [n2] *horrifying or unpleasant sight*
bother, eyesore*, frump*, mess, monstrosity, nuisance, scarecrow, ugliness; SEE CONCEPT *718*

frighten [v] *shock, scare*
affright, agitate, alarm, appall, astound, awe, browbeat*, bulldoze*, chill, chill to the bone*, cow, curdle the blood*, daunt, demoralize, deter, disburb, discomfit, disconcert, discourage, dishearten, dismay, disquiet, faze, horrify, intimidate, make blood run cold*, make teeth chatter*, panic, perturb, petrify, repel, scare away, scare off, scare to death*, spook, startle, stiff, strike terror into*, terrify, terrorize, unhinge*, unnerve; SEE CONCEPTS *14,42*

frightened [adj] *very scared*
abashed, affrighted, afraid, aghast, alarmed, anxious, butterflies*, chicken*, chicken-hearted*, cowed*, dismayed, fearful, frozen, have cold feet*, having kittens*, hung up*, in a cold sweat*, in a panic*, in a sweat*, jellyfish*, jittery, jumpy, lily-livered*, mousy*, numb, panicky, petrified, pushing the panic button*, rabbity*, running scared*, scared stiff*, shaky, shivery, sissy*, spooked, startled, terrified, terrorized, terror-stricken, unnerved, uptight, yellow*; SEE CONCEPTS *403,690*

frightful/frightening [adj1] *scary, shocking*
alarming, appalling, atrocious, awesome, awful, chilling, daunting, dire, direful, dismaying, disquieting, dread, dreadful, fearful, fearsome, formidable, ghastly, grabber, grim, grisly, gruesome, hair-raising, hairy, harrowing, hideous, horrendous, horrible, horrid, horrifying, inconceivable, intimidating, lurid, macabre, menacing, morbid, ominous, petrifying, portentous, repellent, spooky, terrible, terrifying, traumatic, unnerving, unspeakable; SEE CONCEPTS *529,537*

frightful [adj2] *offensive*
annoying, awful, bad, calamitous, disagreeable, dreadful, extreme, ghastly, great, hideous, horrible, insufferable, lewd, shocking, terrible, terrific, unpleasant, vile, wicked, wrong; SEE CONCEPTS *529,545*

frigid [adj1] *extremely cold*
antarctic, arctic, chill, chilly, cool, freezing, frostbound, frosty, frozen, gelid, glacial, hyperboreal, icebox*, ice-cold, icy, refrigerated, Siberian*, snappy, three-dog night*, wintry; SEE CONCEPT *605*

frigid [adj2] *unresponsive*
aloof, austere, chilly, cold, cold-hearted*, cold-shoulder*, cool, forbidding, formal, frosty, icy,

frill [n] *luxury, nice touch*
amenity, decoration, doodad*, extravagance, fandangle, flounce, foppery*, frippery*, fuss, garbage*, garnish, gathering, gimcrack*, gingerbread*, jazz*, lace, ruffle, superfluity, thing*, tuck; SEE CONCEPTS 646,655,824

fringe [n] *border, trimming*
binding, borderline, brim, brink, edge, edging, flounce, hem, limit, mane, march, margin, outside, outskirts, perimeter, periphery, rickrack, ruffle, skirt, tassel, verge; SEE CONCEPTS 484,825

frippery [n] *waste, nonsense*
adornment, bauble, decoration, fanciness, fandangle*, flashiness, frill, fussiness, gaudiness, knick-knack, meretriciousness, ornament, ostentation, pretentiousness, showiness, tawdriness, toy, trinket; SEE CONCEPTS 655,824

frisk [v1] *cavort*
bounce, caper, dance, frolic, gambol, hop, jump, lark, leap, play, prance, rollick, romp, skip, sport, trip; SEE CONCEPT 384

frisk [v2] *search*
check, fan, inspect, run over, shake down; SEE CONCEPT 216

frisky [adj] *full of spirit*
active, alive, bouncy, coltish*, dashing, feeling one's oats*, frolicsome, full of beans*, gamesome, high-spirited, in high spirits*, jumpy, kittenish*, larkish, lively, peppy, playful, prankish, rollicking, romping, spirited, sportive, wicked, zesty, zippy; SEE CONCEPTS 401,542,555

fritter [v] *waste away*
be wasteful with, blow*, cast away, consume, dally, diddle away, dissipate, frivol, go through*, idle, lavish, misspend, run through*, spend like water*, squander, throw away; SEE CONCEPTS 156,341

frivolity [n] *silliness, childishness*
coquettry, dallying, flightiness, flippancy, flirting, flummery, folly, fribble, frippery, frivolousness, fun, gaiety, game, giddiness, jest, levity, lightheartedness, lightness, nonsense, play, puerility, shallowness, sport, superficiality, toying, trifling, triviality, volatility, whimsicality, whimsy; SEE CONCEPTS 388,633

frivolous [adj] *trivial, silly*
barmy*, childish, dizzy*, empty-headed*, facetious, featherbrained*, flighty, flip, flippant, foolish, gay, giddy*, harebrained*, idiotic, idle, ill-considered, impractical, juvenile, light, light-minded, minor, niggling*, nonserious, not serious, paltry, peripheral, petty, playful, pointless, puerile, scatterbrained*, senseless, shallow, sportive, superficial, tongue-in-cheek*, unimportant, unprofound, volatile, whimsical; SEE CONCEPTS 401,402,575

frock [n] *women's garment*
apron, clothing, dress, gown, habit, muumuu, robe; SEE CONCEPT 451

frog [n] *jumping amphibian*
bullfrog, croaker*, polliwog, toad; SEE CONCEPT 394

frolic [n] *amusement, revel*
antic, drollery, escapade, fun, fun and games*, gaiety, gambol, game, high jinks*, joke, joviality, lark, merriment, monkeyshines*, play, prank, romp, shenanigan*, skylarking*, sport, spree, tomfoolery*, trick; SEE CONCEPTS 59,386

frolic [v] *have fun, make merry*
caper, carouse, cavort, cut capers, cut loose*, fool around*, frisk, gambol, go on a tear*, kick up one's heels*, lark, let go*, let loose*, play, prance, raise hell*, revel, riot, rollick, romp, sport, spree, whoop it up*; SEE CONCEPTS 384,386

frolicsome [adj] *playful*
antic, coltish, frisky, fun, gamesome, gay, gleeful, happy, impish, jocular, jovial, kittenish, lively, merry, mischievous, roguish, rollicking, sportive, sprightly; SEE CONCEPT 542

from [prep1] *outside of, separating*
against, in distinction to, out of possession of, taken away; SEE CONCEPT 583

from [prep2] *arising out of*
beginning at, coming out of, deriving out of, originating at, starting with; SEE CONCEPT 549

front [n1] *forward, beginning part of something*
anterior, bow, breast, brow, exterior, facade, face, facing, fore, foreground, forehead, forepart, frontage, frontal, frontispiece, front line, head, lead, obverse, proscenium, top, van, vanguard; SEE CONCEPTS 833,835,836

front [n2] *appearance put on for show*
air, bearing, blind, carriage, coloring, countenance, cover, cover-up*, demeanor, disguise, display, expression, exterior, facade, face, fake, figure, manner, mask, mien, phony, port, presence, pretext, put-on*, show, veil, window dressing*; SEE CONCEPT 716

front [adj] *lead, beginning*
advanced, ahead, anterior, facial, first, fore, foremost, forward, frontal, head, headmost, in the foreground, leading, obverse, topmost, vanward, ventral; SEE CONCEPTS 567,583,585,632

front [v] *look out on to*
border, confront, cover, encounter, face, look over, meet, overlook, overlook; SEE CONCEPT 746

frontier [n1] *boundary*
borderland, borderline, bound, confines, edge, limit, march, perimeter, verge; SEE CONCEPTS 513,745

frontier [n2] *unexplored, unoccupied area of land*
backcountry, backwater, backwoods, boondocks*, boonies*, bush, hinterland, outback, outskirts, sticks*, unknown*; SEE CONCEPT 509

frost [n] *extreme cold*
blight, dip, drop, freeze, hoarfrost, ice, Jack Frost*, rime; SEE CONCEPTS 524,610

frosty [adj] *very cold*
antarctic, arctic, chill, chilly, cool, frigid, frozen, gelid, glacial, hoar, ice-capped, icicled, icy, nippy*, rimy, shivery, wintry; SEE CONCEPT 605

froth [n] *lather, bubbles*
barm, ebullition, effervescence, fizz, foam, head, scud, scum, spindrift, spray, spume, suds, yeast; SEE CONCEPTS 260,467,468

frothy [adj] *bubbly*
barmy, bubbling, fermenting, fizzing, fizzy, foaming, foamy, soapy, spumescent, spumous, spumy, sudsy, with a head on*, yeasty; SEE CONCEPT 485

frown [v1] *scowl*
cloud up*, do a slow burn*, give a dirty look*, give the evil eye*, glare, gloom, glower, grimace, knit brows*, look black*, look daggers*, look stern*, lower, pout, sulk; SEE CONCEPT 185

frown [v2] *disapprove*
deprecate, discommend, discountenance, discourage, disesteem, disfavor, dislike, look askance at*, not take kindly to*, object, show displeasure, take a dim view of*; SEE CONCEPTS 21,29

frozen [adj1] *very cold*
antarctic, arctic, chilled, frigid, frosted, icebound, ice-cold, ice-covered, iced, icy, numb, Siberian*; SEE CONCEPT 605

frozen [adj2] *stopped*
fixed, pegged, petrified, rooted, stock-still, suspended, turned to stone; SEE CONCEPTS 534,584

frugal [adj] *economical*
abstemious, canny, careful, chary, conserving, discreet, meager, meticulous, mingy*, niggardly*, parsimonious, penny-pinching*, pennywise*, preserving, provident, prudent, saving, scrimping, sparing, Spartan*, stingy, thrifty, tight, tightwad*, unwasteful, wary; SEE CONCEPT 334

frugality [n] *economizing*
avarice, avariciousness, carefulness, conservation, economy, forehandedness, good management, miserliness, moderation, niggardliness, parsimoniousness, parsimony, penuriousness, providence, prudence, saving, scrimping, stinginess, thrift, thriftiness; SEE CONCEPTS 330,335

fruit [n1] *edible part of vegetative growth developed after flowering*
berry, crop, drupe, grain, harvest, nut, pome, produce, product, yield; SEE CONCEPTS 426,428

fruit [n2] *result of labor*
advantage, benefit, consequence, effect, outcome, pay, profit, result, return, reward; SEE CONCEPTS 230,337

fruitful [adj] *productive*
abounding, abundant, advantageous, beneficial, blooming, blossoming, breeding, childing, conducive, copious, effective, fecund, fertile, flourishing, flush, fructiferous, gainful, plenteous, plentiful, profitable, profuse, proliferant, prolific, propagating, reproducing, rewarding, rich, spawning, successful, useful, well-spent, worthwhile; SEE CONCEPTS 528,537,560

fruition [n] *achievement, maturation*
accomplishment, actualization, attainment, completion, consummation, enjoyment, fulfillment, gratification, materialization, maturity, perfection, pleasure, realization, ripeness, satisfaction, success; SEE CONCEPTS 704,706

fruitless [adj] *bringing no advantage, product*
abortive, barren, empty, futile, gainless, idle, ineffective, ineffectual, infertile, in vain, pointless, profitless, spinning one's wheels*, sterile, to no avail*, to no effect*, unavailable, unavailing, unfruitful, unproductive, unprofitable, unprolific, unsuccessful, useless, vain, wild goose chase*; SEE CONCEPTS 528,537,560

frustrate [v] *thwart, disappoint*
annul, arrest, baffle, balk, bar, beat, block, cancel, check, circumvent, confront, conquer, counter, counteract, cramp, cramp one's style*, crimp, dash, dash one's hope*, defeat, depress, discourage, dishearten, foil, forbid, forestall, foul up*, give the run around*, halt, hang up*, hinder, hold up, impede, inhibit, lick, negate, neutralize, nullify, obstruct, obviate, outwit, overcome, preclude, prevent, prohibit, render null and void*, ruin, stump*, stymie*, upset the applecart*; SEE CONCEPTS 7,19,121

frustrated [adj] *disappointed, thwarted*
balked*, crabbed*, cramped, crimped, defeated, discontented, discouraged, disheartened, embittered, foiled, fouled up*, hung up on*, irked, resentful, stonewalled*, stymied*, through the mill*, ungratified, unsated, unslaked, up the wall*; SEE CONCEPT 403

frustration [n] *disappointment, thwarting*
annoyance, bitter pill*, blocking, blow, bummer, chagrin, circumvention, contravention, curbing, defeat, disgruntlement, dissatisfaction, downer*, drag*, failure, fizzle, foiling, grievance, hindrance, impediment, irritation, letdown, nonfulfillment, nonsuccess, obstruction, old one-two*, resentment, setback, unfulfillment, vexation; SEE CONCEPTS 410,674

fry [v] *cook in hot oil*
brown, french fry, fricassee, frizzle, pan fry, sauté, sear, singe, sizzle; SEE CONCEPT 170

fudge [v] *fake, misrepresent*
avoid, color, cook up*, dodge, embellish, embroider, equivocate, evade, exaggerate, falsify, hedge, magnify, overstate, pad, patch, shuffle, slant, stall; SEE CONCEPTS 59,63

fuel [n] *something providing energy*
ammunition, combustible, electricity, encouragement, food, gas, incitement, juice, material, means, nourishment, propellant, provocation; SEE CONCEPTS 467,520,523,661

fuel [v] *give energy to*
charge, fan, feed, fill 'er up*, fill up, fire, gas, gas up*, incite, inflame, nourish, service, stoke up*, supply, sustain, tank up*; SEE CONCEPTS 107,140

fugitive [n] *person escaping from law or other pursuer*
bolter, derelict, deserter, displaced person, dodger, émigré, escapee, escaper, evacuee, exile, fly-by-night*, hermit, hunted person, outcast, outlaw, recluse, refugee, runagate, runaway, stray, transient, truant, vagabond, waif, walkout*; SEE CONCEPT 412

fugitive [adj] *fleeing, transient*
avoiding, brief, criminal, elusive, ephemeral, errant, erratic, escaping, evading, evanescent, fleeting, flitting, flying*, fugacious, hot*, impermanent, lamster, momentary, moving, on the lam*, passing, planetary, running away*, short*, short-lived, temporary, transitory, unstable, volatile, wandering, wanted; SEE CONCEPTS 551,584,798

fulfill [v] *bring to completion*
accomplish, achieve, answer, be just the ticket*, carry out, comply with, conclude, conform, discharge, do, effect, effectuate, execute, fill, fill the bill*, finish, hit the bull's-eye*, implement, keep, make it*, make the grade*, meet, obey, observe, perform, please, realize, render, satisfy, score*, suffice, suit; SEE CONCEPTS 7,22,91,706

fulfilled [adj] *completed*
accomplished, achieved, actualized, attained, brought about, brought to a close, carried out, compassed, concluded, consummated, crowned, delighted, dispatched, effected, effectuated, executed, finished, gratified, made good*, matured, obtained, perfected, performed, pleased, put into effect, reached, realized, satisfied; SEE CONCEPTS 403,531

fulfillment [n] *accomplishment, completion*
achievement, attainment, carrying out, carrying through, consummation, contentedness, content-

ment, crowning, discharge, discharging, effecting, end, gratification, implementation, just the ticket*, kick*, kicks* observance, perfection, realization, you got it*; SEE CONCEPTS 230,706

full [adj 1] brimming, filled

abounding, abundant, adequate, awash, big, bounteous, brimful, burdened, bursting, chockablock, chock-full, competent, complete, crammed, crowded, entire, extravagant, glutted, gorged, imbued, impregnated, intact, jammed, jammed full*, jam-packed*, laden, lavish, loaded, overflowing, packed, packed like sardines, padded, plenteous, plentiful, plethoric, profuse, replete, running over, sated, satiated, satisfied, stocked, stuffed, sufficient, suffused, surfeited, teeming, voluminous, weighted; SEE CONCEPTS 481,483, 773,774,786

full [adj2] thorough

absolute, abundant, adequate, all-inclusive, ample, blow-by-blow*, broad, choate, circumstantial, clocklike, complete, comprehensive, copious, detailed, entire, exhaustive, extensive, generous, integral, itemized, maximum, minute, particular, particularized, perfect, plenary, plenteous, plentiful, unabridged, unlimited, whole; SEE CONCEPT 531

full [adj3] deep in sound

clear, distinct, loud, resonant, rich, rounded, throaty; SEE CONCEPT 594

full [adj4] satiated in hunger

glutted, gorged, jaded, lousy with*, sated, satiate, stuffed, surfeited, up to here*; SEE CONCEPTS 406,481,774

full-bodied [adj] robust

concentrated, fruity, full-flavored, heady*, heavy, lusty, mellow, potent, redolent, rich, strong, well-matured; SEE CONCEPTS 489,613

full-grown/full-fledged [adj] developed, ripe, ready

adult, full-blown*, grown, grown-up, in one's prime*, marriageable, mature, nubile, of age, perfected, prime, ripened; SEE CONCEPTS 558,578,797

fullness [n] abundance, breadth

adequateness, ampleness, amplitude, broadness, completeness, completion, comprehensiveness, congestion, copiousness, curvaceousness, dilation, distension, enlargement, entirety, extensiveness, fill, glut, plenitude, plenty, plenum, profusion, repletion, roundness, satiation, satiety, saturation, scope, sufficiency, surfeit, swelling, totality, tumescence, vastness, voluptuousness, wealth, wholeness, wideness; SEE CONCEPTS 635,730

full-scale [adj] total, all-out

all-encompassing, comprehensive, exhaustive, extensive, full-blown*, full-dress*, full-out*, in-depth, major, proper, sweeping, thorough, thoroughgoing, total, unlimited, wide-ranging; SEE CONCEPTS 531,772

fully [adv1] completely, in all respects

absolutely, all out*, all the way*, altogether*, entirely, every inch*, from A to Z*, from soup to nuts*, heart and soul*, intimately, outright, perfectly, positively, quite, royal*, thoroughly, through and through*, totally, utterly, wholly, without exaggeration; SEE CONCEPTS 531,772

fully [adv2] sufficiently, adequately

abundantly, amply, comprehensively, enough, plentifully, satisfactorily, well; SEE CONCEPT 558

fulminate [v] criticize harshly

animadvert, berate, blow up, bluster, castigate, censure, condemn, curse, declaim, denounce, denunciate, execrate, explode, fume, intimidate, inveigh against, menace, protest, rage, rail, reprobate, swear at, thunder, upbraid, vilify, vituperate; SEE CONCEPTS 52,54

fulmination [n] tirade, condemnation

blast, curse, denunciation, diatribe, discharge, explosion, intimidation, invective, obloquy, outburst, philippic, reprobation, warning; SEE CONCEPTS 52,54,278

fulsome [adj] sickening or excessive behavior

adulatory, bombastic, buttery*, canting, cloying, coarse, extravagant, fawning, flattering, glib, grandiloquent, hypocritical, immoderate, ingratiating, inordinate, insincere, magniloquent, mealy-mouthed*, nauseating, offensive, oily*, oleaginous, overdone, saccharine, sanctimonious, slick*, slimy*, smarmy*, smooth, suave, sycophantic, unctuous, wheedling*; SEE CONCEPTS 267,401

fumble [v] bumble, mess up

bollix*, botch*, bungle*, err, feel, flounder, flub*, fluff*, goof*, grapple, grope, lose the handle*, louse up*, misfield, mishandle, mismanage, scrabble*, screw up*, spoil, stumble; SEE CONCEPTS 101,181

fume [v] get very upset about

anger, blow up*, boil, bristle, burn, chafe, chomp at the bit*, get hot*, get steamed up*, rage, rant, rave, seethe, smoke*, storm*; SEE CONCEPTS 21,29,410

fumes [n] pollution, gas in air

effluvium, exhalation, exhaust, haze, miasma, reek, smog, smoke, stench, vapor; SEE CONCEPTS 437,600

fun [n] amusement, play

absurdity, ball*, big time*, blast*, buffoonery, celebration, cheer, clowning, distraction, diversion, enjoyment, entertainment, escapade, festivity, foolery, frolic, gaiety, gambol, game*, good time*, grins*, high jinks*, holiday, horseplay*, jesting, jocularity, joke, joking, jollity, joy, junketing, laughter, living it up*, merriment, merrymaking, mirth, nonsense, pastime, picnic*, playfulness, pleasure, recreation, rejoicing, relaxation, riot, romp, romping, solace, sport, tomfoolery*, treat, whoopee*; SEE CONCEPTS 386,388

fun [adj] good, happy

amusing, boisterous, convivial, diverting, enjoyable, entertaining, lively, merry, pleasant, witty; SEE CONCEPTS 537,572

function [n1] capacity, use

action, activity, affair, behavior, business, charge, concern, duty, employment, exercise, faculty, goal, mark, mission, object, objective, occupation, office, operation, part, post, power, province, purpose, raison d'être*, responsibility, role, service, situation, target, task, use, utility, work; SEE CONCEPTS 362,659

function [n2] social occasion

affair, celebration, do*, gathering, get-together*, meeting, party, reception; SEE CONCEPT 386

function [v] perform, work

act, act the part*, behave, be in action, be in commission, be in operation, be running, cook, do, do duty*, do one's thing*, get with it*, go, go to town*, move, officialize, officiate, operate, per-

fr
fu

colate*, react, run, serve, take, take care of business*; SEE CONCEPTS 87,362

functional [adj] working
handy, occupational, operative, practicable, practical, serviceable, useful, utile, utilitarian, utility;
SEE CONCEPT 560

fund [n] repository, reserve
armamentarium, capital, endowment, foundation,
hoard, inventory, kitty*, mine, pool*, reservoir,
source, stock, store, storehouse, supply, treasury,
trust, vein; SEE CONCEPTS 332,340,710

fund [v] provide money for
back, bankroll, capitalize, endow, finance, float,
grubstake*, juice*, patronize, pay for, pick up the
check*, pick up the tab*, promote, stake, subsidize, support; SEE CONCEPTS 115,341

fundamental [n] basic, essential part
ABCs*, axiom, basis, bottom line*, brass tacks*,
coal and ice*, component, constituent, cornerstone, element, factor, foundation, guts*, heart,
law, nitty-gritty*, principium, principle, rock bottom*, rudiment, rule, sine qua non*, theorem;
SEE CONCEPTS 668,688,826,829

fundamental [adj] basic, important
axiological, axiomatic, basal, bottom, bottom-
line*, cardinal, central, constitutional, constitutive, crucial, elemental, elementary, essential,
first, foundational, grass-roots*, indispensable, integral, intrinsic, key, major, meat-and-potatoes*,
necessary, organic, original, paramount, primary,
prime, primitive, primordial, principal, radical,
requisite, rudimentary, significant, structural, substratal, substantive, supporting, sustaining, theoretical, underived, underlying, vital; SEE
CONCEPTS 546,567

funds [n] cash reserve
accounts receivable, affluence, assets, backing,
bankroll, belongings, bread*, budget, capital, collateral, currency, dough*, earnings, finance, fluid
assets, hard cash*, kitty*, lucre, means, money,
money in the bank*, money on hand*, nest egg*,
nut*, petty cash, pork barrel*, possessions, proceeds, profits, property, ready money*, resources,
revenue, savings, scratch*, securities, specie,
stakes*, store*, stuff*, substance, treasure,
wealth, wherewithal*, winnings*; SEE CONCEPTS
340,710

funeral [n] ceremony for the dead
burial, cremation, entombment, exequies, funera-
tion, inhumation, interment, last rites, obit, obsequies, planting, requiem, sepulture, services,
solemnities; SEE CONCEPTS 172,386

funereal [adj] depressing
black, bleak, dark, deathlike, dirgelike, disheartening, dismal, doleful, dreary, elegiac, gloomy,
grave, grim, lamenting, lugubrious, melancholy,
mournful, oppressive, sad, sepulchral, serious,
solemn, somber, woeful; SEE CONCEPTS
403,537,542

funk [n] fear, depression
alarm, cold sweat*, despondency, fright, gloom,
misery, panic, trembling; SEE CONCEPTS 27,410

funnel [v] direct down a path
carry, channel, conduct, convey, filter, move,
pass, pipe, pour, siphon, traject, transmit; SEE
CONCEPTS 187,217

funny [adj1] comical, humorous
absurd, amusing, antic, blithe, capricious, clever,
diverting, droll, entertaining, facetious, farcical,
for grins*, gas*, gay, gelastic, good-humored, hi-

larious, humdinger, hysterical, jocose, jocular,
joking, jolly, killing*, knee-slapper*, laughable,
ludicrous, merry, mirthful, playful, priceless,
rich, ridiculous, riot, riotous, risible, screaming,
side-splitting*, silly, slapstick, sportive, waggish,
whimsical, witty; SEE CONCEPTS 267,529,537

funny [adj2] odd, peculiar
bizarre, curious, dubious, fantastic, mysterious,
perplexing, puzzling, queer, remarkable, strange,
suspicious, unusual, weird; SEE CONCEPTS
552,564

fur [n] hair on animals
brush, coat, down, fluff, fuzz, hide, jacket, lint,
pelage, pelt, pile, skin, wool; SEE CONCEPTS 399

furbish [v] polish; renovate
brighten, buff, burnish, clean, deck out*, fix up,
glaze, gloss, gussy up*, improve, recondition, refurbish, rehabilitate, renew, restore, rub, shine,
smarten up*, spruce up*; SEE CONCEPTS
162,165,700

furious [adj1] extremely angry, very mad
bent*, bent out of shape*, beside oneself*, boiling*, browned off*, bummed out*, corybantic,
crazed, demented, desperate, enraged, fierce, fit
to be tied*, frantic, frenetic, frenzied, fuming,
hacked, hopping mad*, incensed, infuriated, insane, irrational, livid, maddened, maniac, on the
warpath*, rabid, raging, smoking*, steamed, unreasonable, up in arms*, vehement, vicious, violent, wrathful; SEE CONCEPT 403

furious [adj2] stormy, turbulent
agitated, blustering, blustery, boisterous, concentrated, excessive, exquisite, extreme, fierce, flaming, impetuous, intense, intensified, raging,
rampageous, rough, savage, tempestuous, terrible, tumultous/tumultuous, ungovernable, unrestrained, vehement, vicious, violent, wild; SEE
CONCEPTS 525,537,548

furnace [n] heating mechanism
boiler, calefactor, cinerator, cremator, forge,
Franklin stove, heater, heating system, incinera-
tor, kiln, oil burner, smithy, stove; SEE CONCEPT
463

furnish [v1] decorate, supply
accoutre, apparel, appoint, arm, array, clothe, endow, equip, feather a nest*, fit, fit out*, fix up*,
gear, line a nest*, make habitable, outfit, provide,
provision, purvey, rig, stock, store, turn out; SEE
CONCEPTS 140,177,182

furnish [v2] give, reveal information
afford, bestow, deliver, dispense, endow, feed,
grant, hand, hand over, offer, present, provide,
supply, transfer, turn over; SEE CONCEPTS
60,67,108

furniture [n] household property
appliance, appointment, bed, bookcase, buffet,
bureau, cabinet, chair, chattel, chest, commode,
couch, counter, cupboard, davenport, desk,
dresser, effect, equipment, fittings, furnishing,
goods, highboy, hutch, movables, possession,
sideboard, sofa, stool, table, thing, wardrobe; SEE
CONCEPT 443

furor [n] disturbance, excitement
ado*, agitation, big scene*, big stink*, bustle,
commotion, craze, enthusiasm, fad, ferment,
flap*, free-for-all*, frenzy, fury, fuss, hell broke
loose*, hullabaloo*, hysteria, lunacy, madness*,
mania, outburst, outcry, rage, row, ruckus, stir*,
to-do*, tumult, uproar, whirl; SEE CONCEPTS
230,388,410

furrow [n] *ditch*
channel, corrugation, crease, crinkle, crow's-foot*, dike, fluting, fold, groove, gutter, hollow, line, plica, rabbet, ridge, rimple, rivel, ruck, rut, seam, trench, wrinkle; SEE CONCEPT 513

further [adj] *additional*
added, another, else, extra, farther, fresh, in addition, more, new, other, supplementary; SEE CONCEPT 771

further [v] *advance, lend support*
aid, assist, back up, bail out*, ballyhoo*, champion, contribute, encourage, engender, expedite, facilitate, forward, foster, generate, give a boost to*, go with, hasten, help, lend a hand*, open doors*, patronize, plug, promote, propagate, push, serve, speed, succor, take care of, work for; SEE CONCEPTS 69,87,110

further [adv] *additionally*
again, also, as well as, besides, beyond, distant, farther, in addition, moreover, on top of*, over and above*, then, to boot, what's more*, yet, yonder; SEE CONCEPT 771

furtherance [n] *advancement*
advocacy, backing, boosting, carrying-out, championship, progress, progression, promotion, prosecution, pursuit; SEE CONCEPTS 110,704

furthermore [adv] *in addition*
additionally, along, as well, besides, likewise, moreover, not to mention, to boot, too, what's more*, withal, yet; SEE CONCEPTS 577,824

furthest [adj] *most distant*
extreme, farthest, most remote, outermost, outmost, remotest, ultimate, uttermost; SEE CONCEPTS 586,778

furtive [adj] *sneaky, secretive*
artful, calculating, cautious, circumspect, clandestine, cloaked, conspiratorial, covert, crafty*, creepy*, cunning, disguised, elusive, evasive, foxy, guileful, hidden, hush-hush*, insidious, masked, scheming, shifty*, skulking, slinking*, sly, stealthy, sub-rosa*, surreptitious, tricky*, undercover, underhand, underhanded, under-the-table*, under wraps*, wily; SEE CONCEPTS 548,576

fury [n] *anger, wrath*
acerbity, acrimony, asperity, boiling point*, conniption, energy, ferocity, fierceness, fire, flare-up, force, frenzy, furor, impetuosity, indignation, intensity, ire, madness, might, passion, power, rabidity, rage, rampancy, rise, savagery, severity, slow burn*, sore, stew*, storm*, tempestuousness, turbulence, vehemence, violence; SEE CONCEPTS 29,410

fuse [v] *meld, intermix*
agglutinate, amalgamate, bind, blend, cement, coalesce, combine, commingle, deliquesce, dissolve, federate, flux, integrate, interblend, interfuse, intermingle, join, liquefy, liquesce, melt, merge, mingle, run, run together, smelt, solder, thaw, unite, weld; SEE CONCEPT 113

fusion [n] *melding; mixture*
admixture, alloy, amalgam, amalgamation, blend, blending, coadunation, coalescence, coalition, commingling, commixture, compound, federation, heating, immixture, integration, intermixture, junction, liquefaction, liquification, melting, merger, merging, smelting, soldering, synthesis, unification, union, uniting, welding; SEE CONCEPTS 113,260,432

fuss [n] *disturbance, trouble*
ado, agitation, altercation, argument, bickering, bother, broil*, bustle, commotion, complaint, confusion, controversy, difficulty, display, dispute, excitement, falling-out*, fight, flap, flurry, flutter, fret, furor, hassle, kick-up*, objection, palaver, perturbation, quarrel, row, ruckus, scene, squabble, stew*, stink*, stir, storm, to-do*, turmoil, unrest, upset, winging*; SEE CONCEPTS 46,106,388,633

fussy [adj] *meticulous, particular*
careful, choosy, conscientious, consciable, dainty, difficult, discriminating, exact, exacting, fastidious, finical, finicky, fretful, fuddy-duddy*, hard to please*, heedful, nit-picking*, overfastidious, painstaking, persnickety, picky, picky-picky*, punctilious, punctual, querulous, scrupulous, squeamish, stickling; SEE CONCEPTS 401,404

futile [adj] *hopeless, pointless*
abortive, barren, bootless, delusive, empty, exhausted, forlorn, fruitless, hollow, idle, impracticable, impractical, ineffective, ineffectual, insufficient, in vain, no dice*, nugatory, on a treadmill*, otiose, out the window*, profitless, resultless, save one's breath*, sterile, to no avail*, to no effect*, to no purpose*, trifling, trivial, unavailing, unimportant, unneeded, unproductive, unprofitable, unreal, unsatisfactory, unsubstantial, unsuccessful, useless, vain, valueless, worthless; SEE CONCEPTS 528,548,560

future [n] *time to come*
aftertime, afterward, by and by*, destiny, eternity, expectation, fate, futurity, hereafter, infinity, life to come, millennium, morrow, offing, outlook, posterity, prospect, subsequent time, to be*, tomorrow, world to come*; SEE CONCEPTS 679,807,811,818

future [adj] *to come; expected*
approaching, booked, budgeted, close at hand*, coming, coming up, destined, down the line*, down the pike, down the road*, eventual, fated, final, forthcoming, from here in, from here on, from here to eternity*, from now on in*, imminent, impending, inevitable, in the cards*, in the course of time, in the offing*, just around the corner*, later, likely, looked toward, near, next, planned, prospective, scheduled, subsequent, to be*, ulterior, ultimate, unborn, unfolding, up; SEE CONCEPT 820

fuzz [n] *fluff*
down, dust ball*, dust bunnies*, fiber, floss, fur, hair, lanugo, lint, nap, pile; SEE CONCEPT 260

fuzzy [adj1] *fluffy*
down-covered, downy, flossy, frizzy, furry, hairy, linty, napped, pilate, velutinous, woolly; SEE CONCEPT 606

fuzzy [adj2] *out of focus*
bleary, blurred, dim, distorted, faint, foggy, hazy, ill-defined, indefinite, indistinct, misty, muffled, murky, obscure, shadowy, unclear, unfocused, vague; SEE CONCEPT 619

fu
ga

G

gab [n] *conversation*
blab*, blather*, chat, chitchat*, gossip, idle talk*, loquacity*, palaver*, prattle, small talk*, talk,

tête-à-tête, tongue-wagging*, yak*, yakkety-
yak*; SEE CONCEPT 278

gab [v] *talk a lot*
blabber*, blather*, buzz*, chatter, gossip, jabber*, jaw*, prate, prattle, yak*, yakkety-yak*;
SEE CONCEPT 266

gabby [adj] *talkative*
chattering, chatty, effusive, garrulous, glib, gossiping, gushing, jabbering, long-winded*, loose-
lipped*, loquacious, mouthy*, prattling, prolix,
talky, verbose, voluble, windy*, wordy; SEE CON-
CEPT 267

gad [v] *roam about*
cruise, gallivant, hit the road*, hit the trail*, jaunt,
knock about*, knock around*, maunder, mooch*,
ramble, range, rove, run around*, stray, traipse,
wander; SEE CONCEPTS 149,224

gadget [n] *device, novelty*
apparatus, appliance, business, concern, contraption, contrivance, doodad*, doohickey*, gimmick, gizmo*, invention, object, thing*,
thingamajig, tool, utensil, whatchamacallit*, widget*; SEE CONCEPTS 463,499

gaffe [n] *mistake, goof*
blooper*, blunder, boner*, boo-boo*, faux pas*,
howler*, impropriety, indecorum, indiscretion,
putting foot in mouth*, slip*, solecism; SEE CON-
CEPTS 101,230

gag [n] *practical joke*
crack, drollery, hoax, jest, quip, ruse, trick, wile,
wisecrack, witticism; SEE CONCEPT 59

gag [v1] *silence, stop up*
balk, bottle up*, choke, constrain, cork*, cork
up*, curb, deaden, demur, garrote, keep the lid
on*, muffle, muzzle, obstruct, put the lid on*,
quiet, repress, restrain, shut down, shy, squash*,
squelch, stifle, still, stumble, suppress, tape up*,
throttle*, tongue-tie*; SEE CONCEPTS 121,130

gag [v2] *vomit, choke*
be nauseated, disgorge, gasp, heave, nauseate,
pant, puke*, retch, sicken, spew, strain, struggle,
throw up; SEE CONCEPTS 179,308

gaiety [n] *happiness, celebration*
animation, blitheness, brightness, brilliance,
cheer, color, colorfulness, conviviality, effervescence, elation, entertainment, exhilaration, festivity, frolic, fun, geniality, gladness, glee, glitter,
good humor*, grins*, high spirits*, hilarity, joie
de vivre, jollity, joviality, joyousness, lighthear-
edness, liveliness, merriment, merrymaking,
mirth, pleasantness, radiance, revel, reveling, revelry, shindig*, showiness, sparkle, sport, sprightliness, vivacity, whoopee*, wingding*; SEE
CONCEPTS 377,388

gaily [adv] *happily, brightly*
blithely, brilliantly, cheerfully, colorfully, flam-
boyantly, flashily, gleefully, glowingly, joyfully,
laughingly, lightheartedly, merrily, showily, spar-
klingly, spiritedly, splendidly, vivaciously, with
élan*; SEE CONCEPTS 542,589

gain [n] *acquisition, winnings*
accretion, accrual, accumulation, achievement,
addition, advance, advancement, advantage, attainment, benefit, boost, buildup, cut, dividend,
earnings, emolument, gravy*, growth, headway*,
hike*, improvement, income, increase, increment, lucre, payoff, proceeds, produce, profit,
progress, receipts, return, rise, share, take, up*,
upping*, velvet*, yield; SEE CONCEPTS
337,344,706,710

gain [v] *acquire, win*
accomplish, achieve, advance, ameliorate, annex,
attain, augment, benefit, boost, bring in, build up,
capture, clear, collect, complete, consummate,
earn, enlarge, enlist, expand, fulfill, gather, get,
glean, grow, harvest, have, improve, increase,
land, make, make a killing*, move forward, net,
obtain, overtake, parlay, perfect, pick up, procure, produce, profit, progress, promote, rack
up*, reach, realize, reap, score*, secure, succeed,
win over; SEE CONCEPTS 120,124,129

gainful [adj] *very productive, profitable*
advantageous, beneficial, fat, fruitful, generous,
going, going concern*, good, in the black*, lucrative, lush, moneymaking, paid off, paying, remunerative, rewarding, rich, satisfying,
substantial, sweet*, useful, well-paying, worthwhile; SEE CONCEPT 334

gainsay [v] *contradict*
combat, contravene, controvert, cross, deny, disaffirm, disagree, disclaim, disprove, dispute,
fight, impugn, negate, negative, oppose, refute,
repudiate, resist, traverse, withstand; SEE CON-
CEPTS 52,54

gait [n] *way an animal or person moves, walks*
amble, bearing, canter, carriage, clip, gallop, get
along, lick, march, motion, movement, pace, run,
speed, step, stride, tread, trot, walk; SEE CON-
CEPT 149

gala [n] *festival*
affair, ball, bash, blast*, blowout*, carnival, celebration, clambake, dance, do, festivity, fete, fiesta, function, get-together*, hop, jamboree,
moveable feast, pageant, party, prom, roast, shindig*, stag, to-do*, wingding*; SEE CONCEPTS
377,383

gala [adj] *celebratory*
bright, colorful, convivial, festal, festive, gay,
happy, jovial, joyful, merry; SEE CONCEPT 548

gale [n] *violent storm*
blast, blow, burst, chinook, cyclone, hurricane,
mistral, monsoon, outbreak, outburst, squall, tempest, tornado, typhoon, wind, windstorm; SEE
CONCEPTS 524,526

gall [n] *nerve, brashness*
acrimony, animosity, arrogance, bitterness, brass,
brazenness, cheek*, chutzpah*, conceit, confidence, crust, cynicism, effrontery, guts*, haughtiness, hostility, impertinence, impudence,
insolence, malevolence, malice, overbearance,
pomposity, presumption, rancor, sauciness, self-
importance, spite, venom; SEE CONCEPTS
411,633

gall [v1] *upset, irritate*
aggravate, annoy, bedevil, bother, burn, chafe,
chide, disturb, exasperate, fret, grate, harass,
harry, inflame, irk, nag, peeve, pester, plague,
provoke, rile, roil, rub, ruffle, scrape, torment,
trouble, vex, worry; SEE CONCEPTS 7,19

gall [v2] *rub raw*
abrade, bark, burn, chafe, corrode, erode, excoriate, file, fray, frazzle, fret, grate, graze, irritate,
scrape, scratch, scuff, skin, wear; SEE CONCEPT
215

gallant [adj] *brave, splendid*
attentive, bold, considerate, courageous, courteous, courtly, daring, dashing, dauntless, dignified, doughty, fearless, fire-eating*, game*,
glorious, gracious, grand, gritty*, hairy*, heroic,
honorable, intrepid, lionhearted*, lofty, magnan-

imous, noble, plucky*, polite, quixotic, stately, stouthearted, suave, thoughtful, urbane, valiant, valorous; SEE CONCEPTS *404,542*

gallantry [*n*] *bravery, civility*
address, attentiveness, audacity, boldness, courage, courageousness, courteousness, courtesy, daring, dauntlessness, deference, derring-do*, duty, elegance, fearlessness, graciousness, honor, intrepidity, mettle, nerve, nobility, pluck*, poise, politeness, prowess, resolution, reverence, savoir-faire, spirit, tact, urbanity, valiance, valor; SEE CONCEPTS *411,657*

gallery [*n1*] *balcony*
arcade, loggia, mezzanine, patio, porch, upstairs, veranda; SEE CONCEPT *440*

gallery [*n2*] *showplace for wares*
exhibit, exhibition room, hall, museum, salon, showroom, studio, wing; SEE CONCEPTS *448,449*

gallery [*n3*] *audience, usually seated high*
attendance, onlookers, peanut gallery*, public, spectators; SEE CONCEPTS *294,417*

galling [*adj*] *very upsetting*
acid, afflictive, aggravating, annoying, bitter, bothersome, distasteful, exasperating, grievous, harassing, humiliating, irksome, irritating, nettlesome, painful, plaguing, provoking, rankling, unpalatable, vexatious, vexing; SEE CONCEPTS *7,19*

gallivant [*v*] *run around, gad about*
cruise, jaunt, meander, mooch, ramble, range, roam, rove, stray, traipse, wander; SEE CONCEPTS *149,224*

gallop [*v*] *bolt, race with slight jumping motion*
amble, canter, career, course, dart, dash, fly, hasten, hurdle, hurry, jump, leap, lope, pace, rack, run, rush, shoot, speed, spring, sprint, stride, tear along, trot, zoom; SEE CONCEPTS *150,194*

galvanize [*v*] *inspire, stimulate*
animate, arouse, astonish, awaken, commove, electrify, energize, excite, fire*, frighten, innervate, invigorate, jolt, motivate, move, pique, prime, provoke, quicken, shock, spur, startle, stir, stun, thrill, vitalize, wake, zap*; SEE CONCEPTS *7,14,22*

gambit [*n*] *plan, plot*
artifice, design, device, gimmick, jig, maneuver, play, ploy, ruse, trick; SEE CONCEPT *660*

gamble [*n*] *chance, speculation*
action, bet, fling, leap*, long shot*, lottery, outside chance*, raffle, risk, shot in the dark*, spec*, stab*, throw of the dice*, toss up*, uncertainty, venture, wager; SEE CONCEPTS *28,363*

gamble [*v*] *take a chance on winning*
back, bet, brave, buck the odds*, cast lots*, challenge, cut the cards, dare, defy, endanger, face, flip the coin*, game, go for broke*, hazard, imperil, jeopardize, lay money on*, lot, make a bet, play, plunge, put, put faith in, put trust in, risk, set, shoot the moon*, shoot the works*, speculate, stake, stick one's neck out*, take a flyer*, tempt fortune*, trust to luck, try one's luck, venture, wager; SEE CONCEPTS *28,363*

gambol [*v*] *tumble playfully*
bound, caper, carry on, cavort, cut, cut a caper*, cut loose*, fool around*, frisk, frolic, hop, horse around*, jump, kibitz around*, kick up one's heels*, lark, leap, play, prance, revel, roister, rollick, romp, skip, sport, spring, whoop it up*; SEE CONCEPTS *149,194,363*

game [*n1*] *entertainment*
adventure, amusement, athletics, business, dis-

traction, diversion, enterprise, festivity, frolic, fun, jest, joke, lark, line, merriment, merrymaking, occupation, pastime, plan, play, proceeding, pursuit, recreation, romp, scheme, sport, sports, undertaking; SEE CONCEPTS *292,363*

game [*n2*] *individual sporting event*
competition, contest, match, meeting, round, tournament; SEE CONCEPT *364*

game [*n3*] *undomesticated animals chased for food*
chase, fish, fowl, kill, meat, prey, quarry, ravin, victim, wild animals; SEE CONCEPTS *394,457,460*

game [*n4*] *plot, trick*
butt, derision, design, device, hoax, joke, object of ridicule, plan, ploy, practical joke, prank, scheme, stratagem, strategy, tactic; SEE CONCEPTS *59,660*

game [*adj1*] *brave, willing*
bold, courageous, dauntless, desirous, disposed, dogged, eager, fearless, gallant, hardy, heroic, inclined, interested, intrepid, nervy*, persevering, persistent, plucky*, prepared, ready, resolute, spirited, spunky, unafraid, unflinching, up for*, valiant, valorous; SEE CONCEPT *404*

game [*adj2*] *debilitated*
ailing, bad, crippled, deformed, disabled, incapacitated, injured, lame, maimed, weak; SEE CONCEPTS *314,485*

gamut [*n*] *range*
area, catalogue, compass, diapason, extent, field, panorama, scale, scope, series, spectrum, sweep; SEE CONCEPTS *651,788*

gang [*n*] *group, mob of people*
assemblage, band, bunch, circle, clan, clique, club, cluster, combo*, company, coterie, crew, crowd, herd, horde, knot, lot, organization, outfit, pack, party, posse, ring, set, shift, squad, syndicate, team, tribe, troop, troupe, workers, zoo*; SEE CONCEPT *387*

gangster [*n*] *person involved in illegal activities*
bandit, bruiser*, criminal, crook, dealer, desperado, goon*, hit person, hood, hoodlum, hooligan*, Mafioso*, member of the family, mobster, pusher, racketeer, robber, ruffian, soldier*, thug, tough; SEE CONCEPT *412*

gap [*n*] *break, breach*
aperture, arroyo, blank, caesura, canyon, chasm, cleft, clove, crack, cranny, crevice, cut, defile, difference, disagreement, discontinuity, disparity, divergence, divide, division, fracture, gorge, gulch, gully, hiatus, hole, hollow, inconsistency, interlude, intermission, interruption, interspace, interstice, interval, lacuna, lull, notch, opening, orifice, pause, ravine, recess, rent, respite, rest, rift, rupture, separation, slit, slot, space, vacuity, void; SEE CONCEPTS *513,665*

gape [*v1*] *gawk*
beam, bore, eye, eyeball*, focus, get a load of*, get an eyeful*, give the eye*, glare, gloat, goggle*, look, ogle, peer, rubberneck*, size up*, stare, take in*, wonder, yawp*; SEE CONCEPT *623*

gape [*v2*] *be wide open*
cleave, crack, dehisce, divide, frondesce, gap, part, split, yaw, yawn; SEE CONCEPT *135*

gaping [*adj*] *wide open*
broad, cavernous, chasmal, great, vast, yawning; SEE CONCEPTS *485,490*

garage [*n*] *storage building for vehicles, workplace*
barn, carport*, car stall*, parking lot, parking space, repair shop, shop, storage; SEE CONCEPTS *439,449*

ga
ga

garb [n] *clothing*

apparel, appearance, array, attire, clothes, costume, dress, duds*, feathers*, form, garment, gear, guise, habiliment, habit, outfit, rags*, raiment, robes*, semblance, things*, threads*, uniform, vestments, wear; SEE CONCEPT *451*

garb [v] *fit with clothes*

apparel, array, attire, clad, clothe, cover, deck, deck out*, drape, dress, dud*, fit out*, garment, raiment, rig out*, rig up*, robe, suit up*, tog*, turn out*; SEE CONCEPT *167*

garbage [n] *refuse, litter*

bits and pieces*, debris, detritus, dreck, dregs, dross, filth, junk, muck, odds and ends*, offal, rubbish, rubble, scrap, scrapings, sewage, slop*, sweepings, swill, trash, waste; SEE CONCEPT *260*

garble [v] *mix up, misrepresent*

belie, color, confuse, corrupt, distort, doctor, falsify, jumble, misinterpret, mislead, misquote, misstate, mutilate, obscure, pervert, slant, tamper with, twist, warp; SEE CONCEPTS *59,63*

garden [n] *cultivated plants, flowers*

back yard, bed, cold frame, conservatory, enclosure, field, greenhouse, hothouse, nursery, oasis, patch, patio, plot, terrace; SEE CONCEPTS *509,517*

gargantuan [adj] *very large*

big, colossal, elephantine, enormous, giant, gigantic, heavyweight, huge, humongous, immense, jumbo, leviathan, mammoth, massive, monstrous, monumental, mountainous, prodigious, super-colossal*, super-duper*, titanic, towering, tremendous, vast, whopping*; SEE CONCEPTS *491,773*

gargle [v] *rinse the mouth with liquid*

irrigate, swish, trill, use mouthwash; SEE CONCEPTS *169,308,616*

garish [adj] *flashy, tasteless*

blatant, brassy, brazen, cheap, chintzy, flaunting, gaudy, glaring, glittering, kitschy*, loud, meretricious, ornate, ostentatious, overdone, overwrought, raffish, screaming*, showy, tawdry, tinsel, vulgar; SEE CONCEPT *589*

garland [n] *strand of material, usually hung*

bays, chaplet, coronal, crown, festoon, honors, laurel, palm, wreath; SEE CONCEPTS *260,429*

garment [n] *article of clothing*

apparel, array, attire, costume, covering, drapes*, dress, duds*, feathers*, garb, gear, get-up*, habiliment, habit, outfit, raiment, robe, things*, threads*, togs*, uniform, vestments, wear, weeds*; SEE CONCEPT *451*

garner [v] *collect, accumulate*

amass, assemble, cull, cumulate, deposit, extract, gather, glean, harvest, hive, hoard, lay in*, lay up*, pick up, put by*, reap, reserve, roll up*, save, stockpile, store, stow away, treasure; SEE CONCEPTS *109,135*

garnish [n] *embellishment, improvement*

adornment, decoration, enhancement, furbelow, gingerbread*, ornament, ornamentation, tinsel, trim, trimming; SEE CONCEPT *824*

garnish [v] *embellish, improve*

adorn, beautify, bedeck, deck, decorate, dress up, enhance, fix up, grace, gussy up*, ornament, set off*, spiff up*, spruce up*, trim; SEE CONCEPT *244*

garrulous [adj] *talkative*

babbling, blabbermouth*, chattering, chatty, effusive, flap jaw*, gabby, glib, gossiping, gushing, long-winded*, loose-lipped*, loose-tongued*, loquacious, motormouth*, mouthy, prating, prattling, prolix, prosy, running on at the mouth*, verbose, voluble, wind-bag*, windy*, wordy, yakkity*, yakky*; SEE CONCEPTS *297,404*

gas [n] *something not liquid or solid*

effluvium, fumes, miasma, smoke, stream, vapor, volatile substance; SEE CONCEPT *465*

gash [n] *cut made by slicing*

cleft, furrow, gouge, incision, laceration, mark, nip, notch, rent, slash, slit, split, tear, wound; SEE CONCEPT *309*

gash [v] *cut by slicing*

carve, cleave, furrow, gouge, incise, injure, lacerate, lance, mark, nip, notch, pierce, rend, slash, slit, split, tear, wound; SEE CONCEPTS *137,176*

gasp [n] *sharply drawn breath*

blow, ejaculation, exclamation, gulp, heave, pant, puff, wheeze, whoop; SEE CONCEPTS *163,595*

gasp [v] *draw breath in sharply*

blow, catch one's breath, choke, convulse, fight for breath, gulp, heave, inhale, inspire, pant, puff, respire, sniffle, snort, wheeze, whoop; SEE CONCEPT *163*

gate [n] *movable barrier at entrance*

access, bar, conduit, door, doorway, egress, exit, gateway, issue, lock, opening, passage, port, portal, revolving door, slammer*, turnstile, way, weir; SEE CONCEPTS *440,445*

gather [v1] *come or bring together*

accumulate, aggregate, amass, assemble, associate, bunch up, capture, choose, close with, cluster, collect, concentrate, congregate, convene, converge, corral, crowd, cull, draw, draw in, flock, forgather, gang up, garner, get together, group, hang around*, hang out*, heap, herd, hoard, huddle, make the scene*, marshal, mass, meet, muster, pick, pile up, pluck, poke*, pour in, punch*, rally, reunite, round up*, scare up*, scrape together*, show up, stack up, stockpile, swarm, throng, unite; SEE CONCEPTS *109,114*

gather [v2] *be led to believe; infer*

assume, conclude, deduce, draw, expect, find, hear, imagine, judge, learn, make, presume, reckon, suppose, surmise, suspect, take, think, understand; SEE CONCEPT *15*

gather [v3] *harvest, pick out*

crop, cull, draw, extract, garner, glean, heap, ingather, mass, pick up, pile, pluck, reap, select, stack, take in; SEE CONCEPT *257*

gather [v4] *gain, increase*

build, deepen, enlarge, expand, grow, heighten, intensify, rise, swell, thicken, wax; SEE CONCEPT *780*

gathering [n] *assemblage, accumulation*

acquisition, affair, aggregate, aggregation, association, band, body, bunch, caucus, clambake*, collection, company, concentration, conclave, concourse, conference, congregation, congress, convention, convocation, crowd, crush, drove, flock, function, gain, get-together*, group, heap, herd, horde, huddle, junction, knot, levy, mass, meet, meeting, muster, parley, party, pile, powwow*, rally, roundup, social function, society, stock, stockpile, swarm, throng, turnout, union; SEE CONCEPTS *324,386,417*

gauche [adj] *tactless, unsophisticated*

awkward, bumbling, clumsy, crude, graceless, green, halting, ham-handed*, heavy-handed, ignorant, ill-bred, ill-mannered, inelegant, inept, insensitive, lacking, maladroit, oafish, uncouth, uncultured, unhappy, unpolished, wooden*; SEE CONCEPT **404**

gaudy [adj] bright and vulgar

blatant, brazen, brilliant, catchpenny*, chichi*, chintzy, coarse, crude, flashy, flaunting, florid, frou-frou*, garish, gay, glaring, gross, gussied up*, jazzy, kitschy*, loud, meretricious, obtrusive, ostentatious, pizzazz*, pretentious, putting on the ritz*, raffish, ritzy, screaming*, showy, snazzy, splashy, splendiferous, tasteless, tawdry, tinsel; SEE CONCEPTS **589,618**

gauge [n] measure, standard

barometer, basis, benchmark, bore, capacity, check, criterion, degree, depth, example, exemplar, extent, guide, guideline, height, indicator, magnitude, mark, meter, model, norm, pattern, rule, sample, scale, scope, size, span, test, thickness, touchstone*, type, width, yardstick; SEE CONCEPTS **647,680,688,792**

gauge [v] measure, judge

adjudge, appraise, ascertain, assess, calculate, calibrate, check, check out, compute, count, determine, estimate, evaluate, eye*, figure, figure in, guess, guesstimate, have one's number*, look over, meter, peg*, quantify, quantitate, rate, reckon, scale, size, size up*, take account of, tally, value, weigh; SEE CONCEPTS **37,764**

gaunt [adj] skinny

angular, anorexic, attenuated, bare, bleak, bony, cadaverous, desolate, dismal, dreary, emaciated, forbidding, forlorn, grim, haggard, harsh, lank, lean, like a bag of bones*, meager, peaked, peaky, pinched, rawboned, scraggy, scrawny, skeletal, skeleton, skin and bones*, spare, thin, wasted; SEE CONCEPTS **406,490,491**

gauzy [adj] see-through, gossamer in texture

delicate, diaphanous, filmy, flimsy, insubstantial, light, lucid, pellucid, sheer, thin, tiffany, translucent, transparent; SEE CONCEPT **606**

gawk [v] stare at in amazement

bore*, eyeball*, gape, gaze, glare, gloat, goggle*, look, ogle, peer, rubberneck*, yawp*; SEE CONCEPT **623**

gawky [adj] clumsy

awkward, bumbling, clownish, gauche, loutish*, lumbering, lumpish*, lumpy, maladroit, oafish, rude, rustic, splay, uncouth, ungainly; SEE CONCEPTS **550,584**

gay [adj] happy

alert, animate, animated, blithe, blithesome, bouncy, brash, carefree, cheerful, cheery, chipper*, chirpy, confident, convivial, devil-may-care*, festive, forward, frivolous, frolicsome, fun-loving, gamesome, glad, gleeful, hilarious, insouciant, jocund, jolly, jovial, joyful, joyous, keen, lighthearted, lively, merry, mirthful, playful, pleasure-seeking, presuming, pushy, rollicking, self-assertive, sparkling, spirited, sportive, sprightly, sunny, vivacious, wild, zippy*; SEE CONCEPTS **403,542**

gay [adj2] colorful, vivid

brave, bright, brilliant, flamboyant, flashy, fresh, garish, gaudy, intense, rich, showy; SEE CONCEPTS **589,618**

gay [adj3] homosexual

homoerotic, homophile, lesbian, Sapphic; SEE CONCEPT **372**

gaze [n] long, fixed stare

fish eye*, glaring, gun*, look, looking, ogling,

peek, peep, rubbernecking*, scrutiny, seeing, survey, watching; SEE CONCEPT **623**

gaze [v] stare at

admire, beam*, bore*, contemplate, eye, eyeball*, gape, gawk, get a load of*, get an eyeful*, glare, gloat, inspect, lamp*, look, look fixedly, moon*, observe, ogle, peek, peep, peer, pin*, pipe*, regard, rubber*, rubberneck*, scrutinize, see, size up*, survey, take in*, view, watch, wonder; SEE CONCEPTS **623,626**

gear [n1] equipment

accessory, accoutrement, adjunct, apparatus, appendage, appurtenance, baggage, belongings, contraption, effects, encumbrances, fittings, habiliment, harness, impedimenta, instrument, kit, kit and kaboodle*, luggage, machinery, material, materiel, means, outfit, paraphernalia, possessions, rigging, setup, stuff, supply, tackle, things, tools, trappings; SEE CONCEPT **496**

gear [n2] toothed part of wheel

cog, cogwheel, gearwheel, pinion, ragwheel, sprocket, spurwheel; SEE CONCEPT **464**

gear [n3] clothing

apparel, array, attire, clothes, costume, drapes*, dress, duds*, feathers*, garb, garments, habit, outfit, rags*, threads*, toggery*, togs*, wear; SEE CONCEPT **451**

gear [v] prepare, equip

accouter, adapt, adjust, appoint, arm, blend, fit, fit out*, furnish, harness, match, organize, outfit, ready, regulate, rig*, suit, tailor, turn out; SEE CONCEPTS **182,202**

gelatinous [adj] coagulated

gluey, glutinous, gummy, jelled, jellied, jellylike, mucilaginous, pudding*, sticky, thick, viscid, viscous; SEE CONCEPT **606**

gem [n] precious stone; treasure

bauble*, glass*, hardware*, jewel, jewelry, masterpiece, nonpareil, ornament, paragon, pearl, pick, prize, rock*, sparkler*, stone, trump*; SEE CONCEPTS **337,446,474**

gender [n] grammatical rules applying to nouns that connote sex or animateness

common, feminine, gender-specific, masculine, neuter; SEE CONCEPT **408**

genealogy [n] person's family tree

ancestry, blood line, derivation, descent, extraction, generation, genetics, heredity, history, line, lineage, parentage, pedigree, progeniture, stemma, stirps, stock, strain; SEE CONCEPT **296**

general [adj1] common, accepted

accustomed, broad, commonplace, conventional, customary, everyday, extensive, familiar, generic, habitual, humdrum, inclusive, matter-of-course*, natural, normal, ordinary, popular, prevailing, prevalent, public, regular, routine, run-of-the-mill*, typical, uneventful, universal, usual, wide, widespread, wonted; SEE CONCEPTS **530,547**

general [adj2] inexact, approximate

ill-defined, imprecise, inaccurate, indefinite, loose, not partial, not particular, not specific, uncertain, undetailed, unspecific, vague; SEE CONCEPT **557**

general [adj3] comprehensive

across-the-board*, all-around*, all-embracing*, all-inclusive*, ample, blanket, broad, catholic, collective, comprehending, diffuse, ecumenical, encyclopedic, endless, extensive, far-reaching, generic, global, inclusive, indiscriminate, infinite, limitless, miscellaneous, overall, panoramic,

ga
ge

sweeping, taken as a whole, total, ubiquitous, unconfined, universal, unlimited, wide, worldwide;
SEE CONCEPTS 537,772

generality [n] *vague notion*
abstraction, abstract principle, generalization,
half-truth, law, loose statement, observation, principle, sweeping statement, universality; SEE CON-
CEPTS 688,689

generalize [v] *make a sweeping assumption, statement*
be metaphysical, conclude, derive, discern, discover, establish, hypothesize, induce, observe,
philosophize, postulate, speculate, stay in the
clouds*, theorize, vapor; SEE CONCEPTS 37,49

generally [adv] *mainly, in most cases*
about, all in all, almost always, altogether, approximately, as a rule, broadly, by and large,
chiefly, commonly, conventionally, customarily,
en masse, extensively, for the most part, habitually, largely, mostly, normally, on average, on the
whole, ordinarily, overall, popularly, practically,
predominantly, primarily, principally, publicly,
regularly, roughly, roundly, thereabouts, typically, universally, usually, widely; SEE CONCEPTS
530,547,772

generate [v] *produce, create*
accomplish, achieve, bear, beget, breed, bring
about, bring to pass, cause, develop, effect, engender, form, found, get up, give birth to, give
rise to, hatch, inaugurate, induce, initiate, institute, introduce, make, multiply, muster, occasion,
originate, parent, perform, procreate, propagate,
provoke, reproduce, set up, spawn, whip up*,
work up; SEE CONCEPTS 173,205,251,374

generation [n1] *creation, production*
bearing, begetting, breeding, bringing forth, en-
genderment, formation, fructifying, genesis, multiplying, origination, procreation, propagation,
reproduction, spawning; SEE CONCEPTS
173,205,374

generation [n2] *era; age group*
aeon, breed, contemporaries, crop, day, days,
eon, epoch, peers, period, rank, span, step, time,
times; SEE CONCEPTS 807,816

generic [adj] *common, general*
all-encompassing, blanket, collective, comprehensive, inclusive, nonexclusive, sweeping, universal, wide; SEE CONCEPT 530

generosity [n] *spirit of giving*
all heart*, alms-giving, altruism, beneficence, benevolence, bounteousness, bounty, charitableness, charity, free giving, goodness, heart, high-
mindedness, hospitality, kindness, largesse,
liberality, magnanimity, munificence, nobleness,
openhandedness, philanthropy, profusion, readiness, unselfishness; SEE CONCEPTS 411,657

generous [adj1] *giving, big-hearted*
acceptable, altruistic, beneficent, benevolent, big,
bounteous, bountiful, charitable, considerate,
easy, equitable, excellent, fair, free, good, great-
hearted, helpful, high-minded, honest, honorable,
hospitable, just, kind, kindhearted, kindly, lavish,
liberal, lofty, loose, magnanimous, moderate, munificent, noble, open-handed, philanthropic, prodigal, profuse, reasonable, soft-touch*, thoughtful,
tolerant, ungrudging, unselfish, unsparing, unstinting, willing; SEE CONCEPTS 404,542

generous [adj2] *plentiful*
abundant, affluent, ample, aplenty, bounteous,
bountiful, copious, dime a dozen*, full, galore,

handsome, large, lavish, liberal, luxuriant, no
end*, no end in sight*, overflowing, plenteous,
rich, stinking with*, unstinting, wealthy; SEE
CONCEPTS 334,589,781

genesis [n] *beginning, creation*
alpha, birth, commencement, dawn, dawning, engendering, formation, generation, inception,
opening, origin, outset, propagation, provenance,
provenience, root, source, start; SEE CONCEPTS
119,832

genetic [adj] *coming from heredity*
abiogenetic, ancestral, digenetic, eugenic, genesi-
ological, genital, hereditary, historical, matricli-
nous, patrimonial, phytogenetic, sprogenous,
xenogenetic; SEE CONCEPTS 314,549

genial [adj] *extremely nice and happy*
affable, agreeable, amiable, amicable, blithe,
cheerful, cheering, cheery, chipper*, chirpy*,
congenial, convivial, cordial, easygoing, enlivening, favorable, friendly, gentle, glad, good-
natured, gracious, hearty, high, jocund, jolly,
jovial, joyous, kind, kindly, merry, neighborly,
perky, pleasant, sociable, sunny*, sunny side up*,
up*, upbeat, upper*, warm, warm-hearted; SEE
CONCEPTS 401,404

geniality [n] *extreme niceness*
affability, agreeability, agreeableness, amenity,
amiability, cheerfulness, cheeriness, congenial-
ness, conviviality, cordiality, enjoyableness,
friendliness, gladness, good cheer, good nature,
gratefulness, happiness, heartiness, jollity, joviality, joy, joyousness, kindliness, kindness, mirth,
pleasance, pleasantness, sunniness*, sweetness
and light*, warmheartedness, warmth; SEE CON-
CEPTS 411,633

genius [n] *gift of high intellect*
ability, accomplishment, acumen, acuteness,
adept, aptitude, aptness, astuteness, bent, brain,
brilliance, capability, capacity, creativity, discernment, Einstein*, endowment, expert, faculty,
flair, grasp, head, imagination, inclination, ingenuity, inspiration, intelligence, inventiveness,
knack, mature, originality, percipience, perspicacity, power, precocity, prodigy, propensity, prowess, reach, sagacity, superability, talent, turn,
understanding, virtuoso, wisdom; SEE CONCEPTS
350,409,416

genre/genus [n] *type, class*
brand, category, character, classification, fashion,
group, kind, school, sort, species, style; SEE CON-
CEPTS 378,388,655

genteel [adj] *sophisticated, cultured*
affected, aristocratic, artificial, chivalrous, civil,
confined, courteous, courtly, cultivated, distingué, elegant, fashionable, formal, graceful,
hollow, intolerant, la-di-da*, mannerly, noble, ostentatious, polished, polite, pompous, precious,
pretentious, priggish, prim, prissy, prudish, refined, respectable, straitlaced, stuffy*, stylish, urbane, well-behaved, well-bred, well-mannered;
SEE CONCEPTS 401,404

gentility [n] *sophistication, cultivation*
aristocracy, blue blood*, civility, courtesy, courtliness, culture, decorum, elegance, elite, etiquette, flower*, formality, gentle birth*,
gentlefolk, gentry, good breeding*, good family*,
good manners*, high birth*, mannerliness, nobility, optimacy, polish, politeness, propriety, quality, rank, refinement, respectability, ruling class*,

society, upper class, upper crust*, urbanity; SEE CONCEPTS *388,411*

gentle [adj1] *having a mild or kind nature*
affable, agreeable, amiable, benign, biddable, bland, compassionate, considerate, cool*, cultivated, disciplined, docile, domesticated, dovelike*, easy, genial, humane, kindly, laid back*, lenient, manageable, meek, mellow, merciful, moderate, pacific, peaceful, placid, pleasant, pleasing, pliable, quiet, soft, softhearted, sweet-tempered, sympathetic, tame, taught, temperate, tender, tractable, trained, warmhearted; SEE CONCEPTS *404,542*

gentle [adj2] *mild, temperate in effect on senses*
balmy, bland, calm, clement, delicate, easy, faint, feeble, gradual, halcyon, hushed, imperceptible, lenient, light, low, low-pitched, low-toned, mellow, mild, moderate, muted, peaceful, placid, quiet, sensitive, serene, slight, slow, smooth, soft, soothing, subdued, tender, tranquil, untroubled; SEE CONCEPTS *525,537,594*

gentle [adj3] *of noble birth*
aristocratic, blue-blooded*, Brahmin*, courteous, cultured, elegant, genteel, high-born, highbred, noble, polished, polite, refined, upper-class, well-born, well-bred; SEE CONCEPT *555*

gentleperson [n] *polite, well-mannered person*
aristocrat, brick*, good egg*, good person, nice person, noble, scholar; SEE CONCEPT *423*

genuine [adj1] *authentic, real*
18-carat*, 24-carat*, absolute, accurate, actual, authenticated, bona fide, certain, certified, demonstrable, exact, existent, factual, for real*, good, hard, honest, honest-to-goodness*, indubitable, in the flesh*, kosher*, legit, legitimate, literal, natural, official, original, palpable, plain, positive, precise, proved, pure, real stuff*, sound, sterling, sure-enough*, tested, true, unadulterated, unalloyed, undoubted, unimpeachable, unquestionable, unvarnished, valid, veritable, very, whole; SEE CONCEPT *582*

genuine [adj2] *unaffected; honest*
actual, artless, candid, earnest, frank, heartfelt, known, natural, open, positive, real, reliable, righteous, sincere, true, trustworthy, undesigning, unfeigned, unimpeachable, unpretended, unquestionable, up front*, valid, well-established; SEE CONCEPTS *267,542*

geography [n] *the earth's features; study of land*
cartography, chorography, earth science, geology, geopolitical study, geopolitics, physiographics, physiography, topography, topology; SEE CONCEPTS *349,509*

germ [n1] *microscopic organism, often causing illness*
antibody, bacterium, bug*, disease, microbe, microorganism, parasite, pathogen, plague, virus, what's going around*; SEE CONCEPTS *306,392*

germ [n2] *beginning*
bud, cause, egg, embryo, inception, nucleus, origin, ovule, ovum, root, rudiment, seed, source, spark, spore, sprig, sprout; SEE CONCEPTS *392,648,826,832*

germane [adj] *appropriate*
ad rem, akin, allied, applicable, applicative, applicatory, apposite, apropos, apt, cognate, connected, fitting, kindred, kosher*, legit*, material, on target*, on the button*, on the nose*, pertinent, proper, related, relating, relevant, right on*,

suitable, that's the ticket*, to the point, to the purpose; SEE CONCEPT *558*

germinate [v] *grow*
bud, develop, generate, live, originate, pullulate, shoot, sprout, swell, vegetate; SEE CONCEPT *427*

gestation [n] *process of early development*
evolution, fecundation, gravidity, growth, incubation, maturation, pregnancy, reproduction, ripening; SEE CONCEPTS *316,704,809*

gesture [n] *motion as communication*
action, body language, bow, curtsy, expression, genuflection, gesticulation, high sign, indication, intimation, kinesics, mime, nod, pantomime, reminder, salute, shrug, sign, signal, sign language, token, wave, wink; SEE CONCEPTS *74,185*

gesture/gesticulate [v] *make signs, motions to communicate*
act, flag, indicate, mime, pantomime, signal, signalize, use one's hands, use sign language, wave; SEE CONCEPT *74*

get [v1] *come into possession of; achieve*
access, accomplish, acquire, annex, attain, bag*, bring, bring in, build up, buy into, buy off, buy out, capture, cash in on*, chalk up*, clean up*, clear, come by, compass, cop*, draw, earn, educe, effect, elicit, evoke, extort, extract, fetch, gain, get hands on*, glean, grab, have, hustle*, inherit, land, lock up, make, make a buy, make a killing*, net, obtain, parlay, pick up, procure, pull, rack up*, realize, reap, receive, score, secure, snag*, snap up*, snowball*, succeed to, take, wangle*, win; SEE CONCEPTS *120,706,710*

get [v2] *fall victim to*
accept, be afflicted with, become infected with, be given, be smitten by, catch, come down with*, contract, get sick, receive, sicken, succumb, take; SEE CONCEPT *93*

get [v3] *seize*
apprehend, arrest, bag*, beat, capture, catch, collar*, defeat, grab, lay hold of*, lay one's hands on*, nab*, nail*, occupy, overcome, overpower, secure, take, trap; SEE CONCEPT *90*

get [v4] *come to be*
achieve, attain, become, come over, develop into, effect, go, grow, realize, run, turn, wax*; SEE CONCEPTS *697,706*

get [v5] *understand*
acquire, catch, catch on to, comprehend, fathom, figure out, follow, gain, get into one's head*, hear, know, learn, look at, memorize, notice, perceive, pick up*, receive, see, take in, work out; SEE CONCEPTS *15,31*

get [v6] *arrive*
advance, blow in*, come, come to, converge, draw near, land, make it, reach, show, show up, turn up; SEE CONCEPT *159*

get [v7] *contact for communication*
get in touch, reach; SEE CONCEPT *266*

get [v8] *arrange, manage desired goal*
adjust, contrive, dispose, dress, fit, fix, make, make up, order, prepare, ready, straighten, succeed, wangle*; SEE CONCEPT *202*

get [v9] *convince, induce*
argue into, beg, bring around, coax, compel, draw, influence, persuade, press, pressure, prevail upon, prompt, provoke, sway, talk into, urge, wheedle, win over; SEE CONCEPT *68*

get [v10] *have an effect on*
affect, amuse, arouse, bend, bias, carry, dispose, entertain, excite, gratify, impress, influence, in-

ge
ge

spire, move, predispose, prompt, satisfy, stimulate, stir, stir up, strike, sway, touch; SEE CONCEPTS 7,22

get [v11] *produce offspring*
beget, breed, generate, procreate, produce, propagate, sire; SEE CONCEPT 374

get [v12] *irritate, upset*
aggravate, annoy, bother, bug*, burn, exasperate, gall, get someone's goat*, irk, nettle, peeve, pique, provoke, put out*, rile, rub the wrong way*, try, vex; SEE CONCEPTS 7,19

get [v13] *confuse*
baffle, beat, bewilder, buffalo*, confound, discomfit, disconcert, distress, disturb, embarrass, mystify, nonplus, perplex, perturb, puzzle, stick*, stump, upset; SEE CONCEPT 16

get across [v] *communicate an idea*
bring home*, convey, get through to, impart, make clear, make understood, pass on, put over, transmit; SEE CONCEPT 60

get ahead [v] *excel, succeed*
advance, be successful, climb, do well, flourish, get on, leave behind, make good, outdo, outmaneuver, overtake, progress, prosper, surpass, thrive; SEE CONCEPTS 141,706

get along [v1] *make progress*
cope, develop, do, fare, flourish, get by*, get on*, make out, manage, muddle through*, prosper, shift, succeed, thrive; SEE CONCEPTS 117,704

get along [v2] *depart*
advance, be off, go, go away, leave, march, move, move off, move on, proceed, progress, push ahead, take a hike*; SEE CONCEPT 195

get along [v3] *be compatible*
agree, be friendly, get on*, harmonize, hit it off*; SEE CONCEPT 388

get at [v1] *attain*
access, achieve, acquire, arrive, ascertain, gain access, get hold of, reach; SEE CONCEPT 120

get at [v2] *mean, intend*
aim, hint, imply, lead up to, purpose, suggest; SEE CONCEPT 75

getaway [n] *escape*
break, breakout, decampment, flight, lam, slip; SEE CONCEPT 102

get back [v1] *regain*
reclaim, recoup, recover, repossess, retrieve, salvage; SEE CONCEPT 120

get back [v2] *return*
arrive home, come back, come home, reappear, revert, revisit, turn back; SEE CONCEPT 159

get back at [v] *settle a score*
be avenged, get even, pay back, retaliate, revenge, take vengeance; SEE CONCEPTS 14,246

get by [v] *manage, survive*
contrive, cope, do, do well enough, exist, fare, flourish, get along, get on, make ends meet*, make out, muddle through*, prosper, shift, subsist, succeed, thrive; SEE CONCEPT 117

get down [v] *dismount*
alight, bring down, climb down, come down, descend, disembark, get off, lower, step down; SEE CONCEPT 154

get in [v] *infiltrate; find a way in*
alight, appear, arrive, blow in*, come, embark, enter, gain ingress, get inside, include, insert, interpose, land, mount, penetrate, reach, show, show up, turn up; SEE CONCEPT 159

get off [v] *depart*
alight, blow*, descend, disembark, dismount, es-

cape, exit, go, go away, leave, light, pull out, quit, retire, withdraw; SEE CONCEPTS 154,195

get on [v1] *mount*
ascend, board, climb, embark, enplane, entrain, go up, scale; SEE CONCEPTS 159,166

get on [v2] *cope, progress*
advance, do, do well enough, fare, get along, get by, make out, manage, muddle through*, prosper, shift, succeed; SEE CONCEPTS 117,704

get on [v3] *be compatible*
agree, be friendly, concur, get along, harmonize, hit it off; SEE CONCEPT 388

get on [v4] *put clothing on*
assume, attire, don, draw on, dress, slip into, throw on, wear; SEE CONCEPT 167

get out [v] *escape*
alight, avoid, beat it*, begone, be off, break out, bug off*, buzz off*, clear out, decamp, depart, dodge, duck, egress, evacuate, evade, exit, extricate oneself, flee, fly, free oneself, go, hightail*, kite*, leave, make tracks*, run away, scram*, shirk, shun, skedaddle*, split, take a hike*, take off, vacate, vamoose*, withdraw; SEE CONCEPTS 102,195

get over [v] *recover*
come round, get better, mend, overcome, pull through, recuperate, shake off, survive; SEE CONCEPT 35

get together [v] *gather, accumulate*
assemble, collect, congregate, convene, converge, join, meet, muster, rally, unite; SEE CONCEPTS 109,113

get up [v] *mount; get out of bed*
arise, ascend, awake, awaken, climb, increase, move up, pile out*, rise, rise and shine*, roll out, scale, spring out, stand, turn out, uprise, upspring; SEE CONCEPT 154

ghastly [adj] *horrifying, dreadful; pale*
abhorrent, anemic, appalling, ashen, awful, bloodless, cadaverous, corpselike, deathlike, dim, disgusting, faint, frightening, frightful, funereal, ghostly, ghoulish, grim, grisly, gruesome, haggard, hideous, horrendous, horrible, horrid, livid, loathsome, lurid, macabre, mortuary, nauseating, offensive, pallid, repellent, repulsive, sepulchral, shocking, sickening, spectral, supernatural, terrible, terrifying, uncanny, unearthly, unnatural, unpleasant, wan, weak, wraithlike; SEE CONCEPTS 485,529,537

ghost [n] *spirit of the dead*
apparition, appearance, banshee, daemon, demon, devil, eidolon, ethereal being, haunt, incorporeal being, kelpie, manes, phantasm, phantom, poltergeist, revenant, shade, shadow, soul, specter, spook, vampire, vision, visitor, wraith, zombie; SEE CONCEPT 370

ghostly [adj] *spooky*
apparitional, cadaverous, corpselike, deathlike, divine, eerie, eidolic, ghastly, haunted, holy, illusory, insubstantial, pale, phantasmal, phantom, scary, shadowy, spectral, spiritual, supernatural, uncanny, unearthly, vampiric, wan, weird, wraithlike, wraithy; SEE CONCEPTS 485,537

giant [n] *extremely large person*
behemoth, bulk, colossus, cyclops, elephant*, goliath, Hercules*, hulk, jumbo*, leviathan, mammoth, monster*, mountain*, ogre, polypheme, titan, whale*, whopper*; SEE CONCEPT 424

giant [adj] *very large*
big, blimp*, brobdingnagian*, colossal, cyclo-

pean, elephantine*, enormous, gargantuan, gigantic, gross*, Herculean*, huge, hulking, humongous*, immense, jumbo*, mammoth, monstrous*, mountainous, prodigious, super-duper*, titanic, vast, whale of a*, whaling*; SEE CONCEPTS 491,773,779,781

gibberish [n] *nonsense talk*
babble, balderdash*, blah-blah*, blather, chatter, claptrap*, double talk*, drivel, gobbledygook*, hocus-pocus*, jabber*, jargon, mumbo jumbo*, palaver*, prattle, scat*, twaddle*, yammer*; SEE CONCEPT 278

gibe [n] *ridicule*
comeback, cutting remark, derision, dig*, dump*, jab, jeer, joke, mockery, parting shot*, putdown*, rank-out*, sarcasm, scoffing, slam*, sneer, swipe, taunt; SEE CONCEPT 278

gibe [v] *ridicule*
deride, dis*, disrespect, flout, jeer, make fun of*, mock, poke fun at*, scoff, scorn, sneer, taunt; SEE CONCEPTS 52,54

giddy [adj] *silly, impulsive*
bemused, brainless, bubbleheaded*, capricious, careless, changeable, changeful, ditzy*, dizzy, empty-headed*, erratic, fickle, flighty*, flustered, frivolous, gaga*, heedless, inconstant, irresolute, irresponsible, lightheaded*, punchy*, reckless, reeling, scatterbrained*, skittish*, slaphappy*, swimming*, thoughtless, unbalanced, unsettled, unstable, unsteady, vacillating, volatile, whimsical, whirling, wild, woozy*; SEE CONCEPTS 314,401

gift [n1] *something given freely, for no recompense*
allowance, alms, award, benefaction, benefit, bestowal, bonus, boon, bounty, charity, contribution, courtesy, dispensation, donation, endowment, fairing, favor, giveaway, goodie, grant, gratuity, hand, hand-me-down*, handout, honorarium, lagniappe, largesse, legacy, libation, oblation, offering, offertory, philanthropy, pittance, premium, present, presentation, provision, ration, relief, remembrance, remittance, reward, souvenir, subscription, subsidy, tip, token, tribute, write-off*; SEE CONCEPT 337

gift [n2] *talent, aptitude*
ability, accomplishment, acquirement, aptness, attainment, attribute, bent, capability, capacity, endowment, faculty, flair, forte, genius, head*, instinct, knack, leaning, nose*, numen, power, propensity, set, specialty, turn; SEE CONCEPTS 409,630,706

gifted [adj] *talented, intelligent*
able, accomplished, adroit, brilliant, capable, class act, clever, expert, got it*, have on the ball*, have smarts*, have the goods*, hot*, hotshot, ingenious, mad, masterly, phenomenal, shining at*, skilled, smart; SEE CONCEPTS 402,527,528

gigantic [adj] *very large*
blimp, brobdingnagian*, colossal, cyclopean*, elephantine, enormous, gargantuan, giant, gross*, Herculean*, huge, immense, jumbo*, mammoth, massive, Moby*, monster, monstrous, prodigious, stupendous, super-colossal*, titan, tremendous, vast, whopping*; SEE CONCEPTS 491,773,779,781

giggle [n/v] *snickering laugh*
cackle, chortle, chuckle, guffaw*, hee-haw*, snicker, snigger, teehee*, titter, twitter; SEE CONCEPT 77

gild [v] *embellish, decorate*
adorn, aureate, aurify, beautify, bedeck, begild, brighten, coat, deck, dress up, embroider, engild, enhance, enrich, garnish, glitter, grace, ornament, overlay, paint, plate, tinsel, varnish, wash, whitewash*; SEE CONCEPTS 172,177,202

gimmick [n] *contrived object; scheme*
aid, apparatus, artifice, catch, concern, counterfeit, deceit, device, dodge*, fake, feint, fixture, fun, gadget, gambit, game, gizmo*, imposture, instrument, jest, maneuver, means, method, ploy, ruse, secret, shift, sport, stratagem, stunt, trick, widget*, wile; SEE CONCEPTS 59,260,660

gingerly [adj] *careful*
calculating, cautious, chary, circumspect, considerate, dainty, delicate, discreet, fastidious, guarded, hesitant, reluctant, safe, squeamish, suspicious, timid, wary; SEE CONCEPTS 542,550

gingerly [adv] *carefully*
cautiously, charily, circumspectly, daintily, delicately, discreetly, fastidiously, guardedly, hesitantly, reluctantly, safely, squeamishly, suspiciously, timidly, warily; SEE CONCEPTS 542,550

gird [v1] *encircle; strengthen*
band, belt, bind, block, blockade, bolster, brace, buttress, cincture, circle, enclose, encompass, enfold, environ, fasten, fortify, girdle, hem in*, make ready, pen, prepare, ready, reinforce, ring, round, secure, steel, support, surround; SEE CONCEPTS 250,758

gird [v2] *make fun of*
deride, flout, fun at, gibe, jeer, jest, mock, poke, quip, ridicule, scoff, scorn, taunt; SEE CONCEPTS 52,54

girl [n] *young female person*
adolescent, damsel, daughter, lady, lassie, mademoiselle, Ms, schoolgirl, she, teenager, young lady, young woman; SEE CONCEPTS 415,424

girlfriend [n] *female acquaintance or romantic companion*
companion, confidante, date, financee, flame*, friend, intimate, partner, soul mate, steady, sweetheart; SEE CONCEPTS 415,423

gist [n] *meaning, essence*
basis, bearing, bottom line*, burden, core, drift, force, heart, idea, import, kernel*, keynote, marrow, matter, meat*, name of the game*, nature of the beast*, nitty gritty*, nuts and bolts*, pith*, point, punch line, quintessence, score, sense, short, significance, soul, spirit, stuff*, subject, substance, summary, tenor, theme, thrust, topic, upshot*; SEE CONCEPT 682

give [v1] *contribute, supply, transfer*
accord, administer, allow, ante up, award, bequeath, bestow, cede, come across, commit, confer, consign, convey, deed, deliver, dish out*, dispense, dispose of, dole out, donate, endow, entrust, fork over*, furnish, gift, grant, hand down, hand out, hand over, heap upon, lavish upon, lay upon, lease, let have, make over*, parcel out, part with, pass down, pass out, permit, pony up*, present, provide, relinquish, remit, sell, shell out*, subsidize, throw in, tip, transmit, turn over, vouchsafe, will; SEE CONCEPTS 108,223,243

give [v2] *communicate*
air, announce, be a source of, broadcast, carry, deliver, emit, express, furnish, impart, issue, notify, present, pronounce, publish, put, read, ren-

ge
gi

der, state, supply, transfer, transmit, utter, vent, ventilate; SEE CONCEPTS *60,266*

give [*v3*] *demonstrate, proffer*

administer, bestow, confer, dispense, display, evidence, extend, furnish, hold out, indicate, issue, manifest, minister, offer, pose, present, produce, provide, put on, render, return, set forth, show, tender, yield; SEE CONCEPTS *97,118*

give [*v4*] *yield, collapse*

allow, bend, bow to, break, cave, cede, concede, contract, crumble, crumple, devote, fail, fall, flex, fold, fold up, give way, go, grant, hand over, lend, open, recede, relax, relent, relinquish, retire, retreat, sag, shrink, sink, slacken, surrender, weaken; SEE CONCEPTS *13,469*

give [*v5*] *perform action*

address, apply, bend, buckle down, cause, devote, direct, do, engender, lead, make, occasion, produce, throw, turn; SEE CONCEPT *100*

give away [*v1*] *reveal*

betray, blab*, disclose, discover, divulge, expose, inform, leak, let out, let slip, mouth*, spill, tell, uncover; SEE CONCEPT *60*

give away [*v2*] *unselfishly transfer*

award, bestow, devote, donate, hand out, present; SEE CONCEPT *108*

give in/give up [*v*] *admit defeat*

abandon, back down*, bail out*, bow out*, buckle under*, capitulate, cave in*, cease, cede, chicken out*, collapse, comply, concede, cry uncle*, cut out, desist, despair, drop, drop like a hot potato*, fold, forswear, hand over, leave off, pull out, quit, relinquish, resign, stop, submit, surrender, take the oath*, throw in the towel*, waive, walk out on, wash one's hands of*, yield; SEE CONCEPTS *8,45,119,385*

given to [*adj*] *likely to*

accustomed, addicted, apt, disposed, habituated, inclined, in the habit of, inured, liable, obsessed, prone; SEE CONCEPT *542*

give off/give out [*v*] *discharge*

beam, belch, effuse, emanate, emit, exhale, exude, flow, give forth, issue, pour, produce, radiate, release, send out, smell of, throw out, vent, void; SEE CONCEPT *179*

glacial [*adj1*] *extremely cold*

antarctic, arctic, biting, bitter, chill, chilly, cool, freezing, frigid, frosty, frozen, gelid, icy, nippy, piercing, polar, raw, wintry; SEE CONCEPT *605*

glacial [*adj2*] *unfriendly*

aloof, antagonistic, chill, cold, cool, distant, emotionless, frigid, hostile, icy, inaccessible, indifferent, inimical, remote, reserved, seclusive, standoffish, unapproachable, unemotional, withdrawn; SEE CONCEPTS *401,404*

glacier [*n*] *mountain of ice, snow*

berg, floe, glacial mass, iceberg, icecap, ice field, ice floe, snow slide; SEE CONCEPT *509*

glad [*adj*] *happy, delightful*

animated, beaming, beautiful, blithesome, bright, can't complain*, cheerful, cheering, cheery, contented, exhilarated, felicitous, floating on air*, gay, genial, gleeful, gratified, gratifying, hilarious, jocund, jovial, joyful, joyous, lighthearted, merry, mirthful, overjoyed, pleasant, pleased, pleased as punch*, pleasing, radiant, rejoicing, sparkling, tickled, tickled pink*, tickled to death*, up, willing; SEE CONCEPTS *403,529*

gladly [*adv*] *happily*

acquiescently, ardently, beatifically, blissfully, blithely, cheerfully, cheerily, contentedly, cordially, delightedly, delightfully, ecstatically, enchantedly, enthusiastically, felicitously, freely, gaily, genially, gleefully, gratefully, heartily, jocundly, jovially, joyfully, joyously, lovingly, merrily, paradisaically, passionately, pleasantly, pleasingly, pleasurably, rapturously, readily, sweetly, warmly, willingly, with good grace, with pleasure, with relish, zealously, zestfully; SEE CONCEPTS *403,538,542*

gladness [*n*] *happiness*

animation, blitheness, cheer, cheerfulness, delight, felicity, gaiety, glee, high spirits*, hilarity, jollity, joy, joyousness, mirth, pleasure; SEE CONCEPT *410*

glamorous [*adj*] *sophisticated in style*

alluring, attractive, bewitching, captivating, charismatic, charming, classy, dazzling, drop-dead gorgeous*, elegant, enchanting, entrancing, exciting, fascinating, flashy, foxy*, glittering, glossy, looking like a million*, lovely, magnetic, nifty, prestigious, righteous, seductive, siren, smart; SEE CONCEPTS *579,589*

glamour [*n*] *sophisticated style*

allure, allurement, animal magnetism, appeal, attraction, beauty, bewitchment, charisma, charm, color, enchantment, fascination, interest, magnetism, prestige, ravishment, razzle-dazzle*, romance, star quality; SEE CONCEPTS *655,718*

glance [*n1*] *brief look*

eye*, eyeball*, flash*, fleeting look, gander, glimpse, lamp*, look, look-see*, peek, peep, quick look, sight, slant*, squint, swivel*, view; SEE CONCEPT *623*

glance [*n2*] *reflection of light*

coruscation, flash, gleam, glimmer, glint, glisten, shimmer, sparkle, twinkle; SEE CONCEPTS *624,628*

glance [*v1*] *look at briefly*

browse, check out, dip into*, flash*, flip through, gaze, get a load of*, glimpse, leaf through, peek, peep, peer, riffle through*, run over, run through, scan, see, skim through*, take a gander*, take in, thumb through*, view; SEE CONCEPT *623*

glance [*v2*] *reflect light*

coruscate, flash, gleam, glimmer, glint, glisten, glitter, shimmer, shine, sparkle, twinkle; SEE CONCEPT *624*

glance [*v3*] *ricochet, hit off of something*

bounce, brush, carom, contact, dart, graze, kiss*, rebound, scrape, shave*, sideswipe, skim, skip, slant, slide, strike, touch; SEE CONCEPT *189*

glare [*n1*] *very bright light, shine*

blaze, blinding light, brilliance, dazzle, flame, flare, glow; SEE CONCEPT *628*

glare [*n2*] *dirty look*

angry stare, bad eye*, black look*, evil eye*, frown, glower, lower, scowl; SEE CONCEPTS *623,716*

glare [*v1*] *give a dirty look*

bore, do a slow burn*, fix, frown, gape, gawk, gaze, glower, look daggers*, lower, menace, peer, pierce, scowl, stare, stare angrily*, stare icily*, wither; SEE CONCEPT *623*

glare [*v2*] *shine very brightly*

beam, blare, blaze, blind, blur, daze, dazzle, flame, flare, glaze, glow, radiate; SEE CONCEPT *624*

glaring [*adj1*] *obvious, unconcealed*
audacious, blatant, brazen, capital, conspicuous, crying, egregious, evident, excessive, extreme, flagrant, gross, inordinate, manifest, noticeable, obtrusive, open, outrageous, outstanding, overt, patent, protrusive, rank, visible; SEE CONCEPTS *576,619*

glaring [*adj2*] *bright, dazzling; flashy*
blatant, blazing, blinding, brazen, chintzy, florid, garish, gaudy, glowing, loud, meretricious, shining, tawdry; SEE CONCEPTS *589,617*

glass [*n1*] *object that reflects an image*
looking glass, mirror, reflector, seeing glass; SEE CONCEPTS *260,470*

glass [*n2*] *object used for drinking liquids*
beaker, bottle, chalice, cup, decanter, goblet, highball, jar, jigger, jug, mug, pilsener, pony, snifter, tumbler; SEE CONCEPT *494*

glasses [*n*] *object worn to correct vision*
bifocals, blinkers*, cheaters*, contact lenses, eyeglasses, four eyes*, frames, goggles, lorgnette, pince-nez, rims*, shades*, specs*, spectacles, trifocals; SEE CONCEPT *446*

glassy [*adj1*] *polished, smooth*
burnished, clear, glazed, glazy, glossy, hyaline, hyaloid, icy, lustrous, shiny, sleek, slick, slippery, transparent, vitreous, vitric; SEE CONCEPT *606*

glassy [*adj2*] *expressionless, especially referring to eyes*
blank, cold, dazed, dull, empty, fixed, glazed, lifeless, stupid, vacant; SEE CONCEPTS *406,619*

glaze [*n*] *varnish, lacquer*
coat, enamel, finish, glint, gloss, luster, patina, polish, sheen, shine; SEE CONCEPTS *259,475*

glaze [*v*] *varnish, lacquer*
buff, burnish, coat, cover, enamel, furbish, glance, glass, gloss, incrust, make lustrous, make vitreous, overlay, polish, rub, shine, vitrify; SEE CONCEPTS *172,202,215*

gleam [*n*] *brightness, sparkle*
beam, brilliance, coruscation, flash, flicker, glance, glim, glimmer, glint, glitz, gloss, glow, luster, ray, scintillation, sheen, shimmer, splendor, twinkle; SEE CONCEPTS *620,624*

gleam [*v*] *sparkle*
beam, burn, coruscate, flare, flash, glance, glimmer, glint, glisten, glister, glitter, glow, radiate, scintillate, shimmer, shine, twinkle; SEE CONCEPTS *620,624*

glean [*v*] *pick out, collect*
accumulate, amass, ascertain, conclude, cull, deduce, extract, garner, gather, harvest, learn, pick, reap, select, sift, winnow; SEE CONCEPTS *31,135*

glee [*n*] *extreme happiness*
blitheness, cheerfulness, delectation, delight, elation, enjoyment, exhilaration, exuberance, exultation, fun, gaiety, gladness, hilarity, jocularity, jollity, joviality, joy, joyfulness, joyousness, liveliness, merriment, mirth, pleasure, sprightliness, triumph, verve; SEE CONCEPT *410*

gleeful [*adj*] *very happy*
blithe, blithesome, boon, cheerful, delighted, elated, exalted, exuberant, exultant, frolicsome, gay, gratified, hilarious, jocund, jolly, jovial, joyful, joyous, jubilant, lighthearted, merry, mirthful, overjoyed, pleased, triumphant; SEE CONCEPT *403*

glen [*n*] *valley*
canyon, combe, dale, dell, glade, gorge, vale; SEE CONCEPT *509*

glib [*adj*] *slick, smooth-talking*
artful, articulate, easy, eloquent, facile, fast-talking*, flip, fluent, garrulous, hot-air*, insincere, loquacious, plausible, quick, ready, silver-tongued*, slippery*, smooth operator*, smooth-spoken*, smooth-tongued*, suave, talkative, urbane, vocal, vocative, voluble; SEE CONCEPTS *267,404*

glide [*v*] *move smoothly and quickly on a surface*
coast, decline, descend, drift, flit, float, flow, fly, glissade, roll, run, sail, scud, shoot, skate, skim, skip, skirr, slide, slink, slip, slither, smooth along, soar, spiral, stream, trip, waft, wing; SEE CONCEPT *150*

glimmer [*n*] *flash, sparkle*
blink, coruscation, flicker, glance, gleam, glint, glow, grain, hint, inkling, ray, scintillation, shimmer, suggestion, trace, twinkle; SEE CONCEPTS *624,831*

glimmer [*v*] *sparkle*
blink, coruscate, fade, flash, flicker, glance, gleam, glint, glisten, glister, glitter, glow, scintillate, shimmer, shine, twinkle; SEE CONCEPT *624*

glimpse [*n*] *brief look*
eye, eyeball*, flash*, gander*, glance, glom*, gun*, impression, lamp*, look-see*, peek, peep, quick look, sight, sighting, slant, squint, swivel*; SEE CONCEPT *623*

glimpse [*v*] *look briefly*
catch sight of, check out, descry, espy, eye, flash, get a load of*, get an eyeful*, peek, sight, spot, spy, take a gander*, take in*, view; SEE CONCEPT *623*

glisten [*v*] *shimmer*
coruscate, flash, flicker, glance, glare, gleam, glimmer, glint, glister, glitter, glow, scintillate, shine, sparkle, twinkle; SEE CONCEPT *624*

glitter [*n*] *brilliance, sparkle*
beam, brightness, coruscation, display, flash, gaudiness, glamour, glare, gleam, glint, glisten, glister, glitz, luster, pageantry, radiance, scintillation, sheen, shimmer, shine, show, showiness, splendor, tinsel, twinkle, zap*; SEE CONCEPTS *620,655*

glitter [*v*] *sparkle*
coruscate, flash, glance, glare, gleam, glimmer, glint, glisten, glister, glow, scintillate, shimmer, shine, spangle, twinkle; SEE CONCEPT *624*

gloat [*v*] *exclaim triumph*
celebrate, crow*, exult, glory, rejoice, relish, rub it in*, triumph, vaunt, whoop*; SEE CONCEPT *49*

global [*adj*] *worldwide, all-encompassing*
all-around, all-inclusive, all-out, blanket, catholic, comprehensive, cosmic, cosmopolitan, earthly, ecumenical, encyclopedic, exhaustive, general, grand, international, mundane, overall, pandemic, planetary, spherical, sweeping, thorough, total, unbounded, universal, unlimited, world; SEE CONCEPTS *536,772*

globe [*n*] *Earth, sphere*
apple*, ball, balloon*, big blue marble*, map, orb, planet, rondure, round, spheroid, terrene, world; SEE CONCEPTS *436,511*

gloom [*n1*] *melancholy, depression*
anguish, bitterness, blue devils*, blue funk*, blues*, catatonia, chagrin, cheerlessness, dejec-

gi
gl

tion, desolation, despair, despondency, disconsolateness, discouragement, dismals, distress, doldrums, dolor, downheartedness, dullness, dumps*, foreboding, grief, heaviness, heavyheartedness, horror, low spirits*, malaise, misery, misgiving, mopes, morbidity, mourning, oppression, pensiveness, pessimism, sadness, saturninity, sorrow, unhappiness, vexation, weariness, woe; SEE CONCEPT 410

gloom [n2] *darkness, blackness*
bleakness, cloud, cloudiness, dimness, dullness, dusk, duskiness, gloominess, murk, murkiness, obscurity, shade, shadow, twilight; SEE CONCEPTS 620,622,810

gloomy [adj1] *dark, black*
bleak, caliginous, cheerless, clouded, cloudy, crepuscular, desolate, dim, dismal, dreary, dull, dusky, forlorn, funereal, lightless, murky, obscure, overcast, overclouded, sepulchral, shadowy, somber, tenebrous, unilluminated, unlit, wintry; SEE CONCEPTS 525,617,618

gloomy [adj2] *feeling down, blue*
blue funk*, broody, chapfallen, cheerless, crabbed*, crestfallen, dejected, depressed, desolate, despondent, disconsolate, dismal, dispirited, dour, downcast, downhearted, down in the dumps*, down in the mouth*, dragged, forlorn, glum, in low spirits*, in the dumps*, joyless, low, melancholy, mirthless, miserable, moody, moping, mopish, morose, mournful, oppressed, pessimistic, sad, saturnine, solemn, sulky, sullen, surly, ugly, unhappy, weary, woebegone, woeful; SEE CONCEPT 403

gloomy [adj3] *sad, depressing*
acheronian, acherontic, bad, black, bleak, cheerless, cold, comfortless, depressive, desolate, disconsolate, discouraging, disheartening, dismal, dispiriting, drab, dreary, dull, dusky, funereal, joyless, lugubrious, morose, oppressive, saddening, somber, tenebrific; SEE CONCEPTS 537,548

glorify [v1] *praise*
acclaim, bless, boost, build up, celebrate, commend, cry up, eulogize, exalt, extol, hike, honor, hymn, laud, lionize, magnify, panegyrize, put on a pedestal*, put up, sing the praises of*; SEE CONCEPT 69

glorify [v2] *adore, idolize*
adorn, aggrandize, apotheosize, augment, beatify, bless, canonize, deify, dignify, distinguish, elevate, enhance, ennoble, enshrine, erect, exalt, halo*, honor, illuminate, immortalize, lift up, magnify, pay homage to, raise, revere, sanctify, transfigure, uprear, venerate, worship; SEE CONCEPT 12

glorious [adj] *adored, idolized; divine*
august, beautiful, bright, brilliant, celebrated, dazzling, delightful, distinguished, effulgent, elevated, eminent, enjoyable, esteemed, exalted, excellent, famed, famous, fine, gorgeous, grand, gratifying, great, heavenly, heroic, honored, illustrious, immortal, magnificent, majestic, marvelous, memorable, noble, notable, noted, pleasurable, preeminent, radiant, remarkable, renowned, resplendent, shining, splendid, sublime, superb, time-honored, triumphant, venerable, well-known, wonderful; SEE CONCEPTS 568,574,579

glory [n1] *fame, importance*
celebrity, dignity, distinction, eminence, exaltation, grandeur, greatness, honor, illustriousness,

immortality, kudos, magnificence, majesty, nobility, praise, prestige, renown, reputation, splendor, sublimity, triumph; SEE CONCEPTS 388,668

glory [n2] *great beauty*
brightness, brilliance, effulgence, fineness, gorgeousness, grandeur, luster, magnificence, majesty, pageantry, pomp, preciousness, radiance, resplendence, richness, splendor, sublimity, sumptuousness; SEE CONCEPTS 673,718

glory [v] *boast, exult*
crow, gloat, jubilate, pride oneself, relish, revel, take delight, triumph; SEE CONCEPTS 12,49

gloss [n1] *shine, sheen*
appearance, brightness, brilliance, burnish, facade, finish, front, glaze, gleam, glint, glossiness, luster, polish, shimmer, silkiness, sleekness, slickness, surface, varnish, veneer; SEE CONCEPTS 611,620

gloss [n2] *definition*
annotation, comment, commentary, elucidation, explanation, footnote, interpretation, note, translation; SEE CONCEPT 268

gloss [v1] *make shiny*
buff, burnish, finish, furbish, glance, glaze, lacquer, polish, rub, shine, varnish, veneer; SEE CONCEPTS 202,215

gloss [v2] *conceal truth*
belie, camouflage, cover up, deacon, disguise, doctor, explain, extenuate, falsify, hide, justify, mask, misrepresent, palliate, rationalize, smooth over, soft-pedal, sugarcoat*, varnish, veil, veneer, white, whiten, whitewash*; SEE CONCEPTS 49,63

gloss [v3] *define*
annotate, comment, construe, elucidate, explain, interpret, justify, translate; SEE CONCEPT 57

glossy [adj] *shiny*
bright, brilliant, burnished, glassy, glazed, gleaming, glistening, lustrous, polished, reflecting, silken, silky, sleek, slick, smooth; SEE CONCEPTS 606,617

glove [n] *hand covering for warmth, protection*
gage, gauntlet, mitt, mitten, muff; SEE CONCEPT 451

glow [n] *burning, brightness*
afterglow, bloom, blossom, blush, brilliance, effulgence, flush, glare, gleam, glimmer, glitter, gusto, heat, incandescence, intensity, lambency, light, luminosity, passion, phosphorescence, radiance, ray, splendor, vividness, warmth; SEE CONCEPTS 610,620,622,673

glow [v] *burn, radiate*
be suffused, blare, blaze, blush, brighten, color, crimson, fill, flame, flare, flush, gleam, glimmer, glisten, glitter, ignite, kindle, light, mantle, pink, pinken, redden, rose, rouge, shine, smolder, thrill, tingle, twinkle; SEE CONCEPTS 249,469,624

glower [v] *frown*
glare, gloom, look, look daggers*, lower, scowl, stare, sulk, watch; SEE CONCEPT 623

glowing [adj1] *burning, bright*
aglow, beaming, flaming, florid, flush, flushed, gleaming, lambent, luminous, lustrous, phosphorescent, red, rich, rubicund, ruddy, sanguine, suffused, vibrant, vivid, warm; SEE CONCEPTS 617,618

glowing [adj2] *very happy, enthusiastic*
adulatory, ardent, avid, blazing, burning, complimentary, desirous, eager, ecstatic, eulogistic, fervent, fervid, fierce, fiery, flaming, heated, hot-

blooded, impassioned, keen, laudatory, panegyrical, passionate, rave, rhapsodic, zealous; SEE CONCEPTS 267,401

glue [n] adhesive
cement, gum, gunk*, mucilage, paste, plaster, spit*, stickum*; SEE CONCEPT 475

glut [n] overabundance
excess, nimiety, oversupply, plenitude, saturation, superfluity, surfeit, surplus, too much*; SEE CONCEPTS 740,787

glut [v] choke; oversupply
burden, clog, cloy, congest, cram, deluge, devour, feast, fill, flood, gorge, hog*, inundate, jade, load, make a pig of*, overfeed, overload, overstock, overwhelm, pack*, pall, raven, sate, satiate, saturate, stuff, surfeit, wolf*; SEE CONCEPTS 140,169,209,740

glutton [n] person who overeats
epicure, gorger*, gormandizer, gourmand, hefty eater, hog*, pig*, sensualist, stuffer*; SEE CONCEPT 412

gnarled [adj] knotted
bent, contorted, crooked, deformed, distorted, gnarly, knurled, leathery, out of shape, rough, rugged, tortured, twisted, weather-beaten, wrinkled; SEE CONCEPTS 485,486

gnaw [v1] bite, chew
champ, chaw, chomp, consume, corrode, crunch, devour, eat, eat away, erode, gum, masticate, munch, nibble, wear; SEE CONCEPTS 169,185

gnaw [v2] be bothered, worried about
annoy, bedevil, beleaguer, distress, eat at*, fret, harass, harry, haunt, irritate, nag, pester, plague, prey on one's mind*, rankle, tease, trouble, wear down; SEE CONCEPTS 17,34

gnome [n] troll
elf, fairy; SEE CONCEPT 424

go [n1] spirit, vitality
activity, animation, bang, birr*, drive, energy, force, get-up-and-go*, hardihood, life, moxie*, oomph*, pep, potency, push, snap*, starch*, tuck*, verve, vigor, vivacity, zest; SEE CONCEPT 411

go [n2] try, attempt
bid, crack, effort, essay, fling, pop, shot, slap, stab, turn, whack, whirl; SEE CONCEPTS 87,677

go [v1] advance, proceed physically
abscond, approach, beat it*, bug out*, cruise, decamp, depart, escape, exit, fare, flee, fly, get away, get going*, get lost, get off*, hie, hightail*, hit the road*, journey, lam, leave, light out*, mosey*, move, move out, near, pass, progress, pull out, push off, push on, quit, repair, retire, run along, run away, set off, shove off*, skip out*, split*, take a hike*, take a powder*, take flight, take leave*, take off*, travel, vamoose*, wend, withdraw; SEE CONCEPTS 159,195

go [v2] operate, function
act, carry on, click*, continue, flourish, maintain, make out, move, pan out*, perform, persist, prosper, run, score, succeed, thrive, work; SEE CONCEPTS 4,239

go [v3] span, stretch
connect, cover, extend, fit, give access, lead, make, range, reach, run, spread, vary; SEE CONCEPTS 651,756

go [v4] contribute, work towards an end
avail, befall, chance, come, concur, conduce, develop, eventuate, fall out, fare, happen, incline, lead to, occur, persevere, persist, proceed, result, serve, tend, transpire, turn, turn out, wax*, work out; SEE CONCEPTS 87,704

go [v5] agree, harmonize
accord, be adapted for, be designed for, belong, blend, chime, complement, conform, correspond, dovetail*, enjoy, fit, jibe*, like, match, mesh, relish, set, square, suit; SEE CONCEPTS 8,664,714

go [v6] die, collapse
bend, break, cave, conclude, consume, crumble, decease, decline, demise, depart, deplete, devour, dissipate, drop, exhaust, expend, expire, fail, finish, fold up, fritter, give, pass away*, pass on*, perish, run through*, spend, squander, succumb, terminate, use up, waste, weaken, worsen, yield; SEE CONCEPTS 105,698,699

go [v7] elapse
be spent, expire, flow, lapse, pass, pass away, slip away, stand, transpire, waste away; SEE CONCEPT 804

go [v8] endure
abide, allow, bear, brook, consent to, let, permit, put up with*, stand, stomach, suffer, swallow*, take, tolerate; SEE CONCEPT 23

go about [v] undertake
approach, be employed, begin, devote oneself to, engage in, get busy with, occupy oneself with, set about, tackle, work at; SEE CONCEPT 100

goad [n] stimulus
catalyst, compulsion, desire, drive, impetus, impulse, impulsion, incentive, incitation, incitement, irritation, lash, lust, motivation, passion, pressure, prod, spur, urge, whip, zeal; SEE CONCEPTS 20,661

goad [v] egg on, incite
animate, annoy, arouse, bully, coerce, drive, encourage, excite, exhort, fire up*, force, goose*, harass, hound, impel, inspirit, instigate, irritate, key up*, lash, move, needle*, press, prick*, prod, prompt, propel, provoke, push, put up to*, rowel, sic*, sound, spark*, spur, stimulate, sting*, tease, thrust, trigger, turn on*, urge, whip*, work up, worry; SEE CONCEPTS 14,68

go ahead [v] proceed
advance, begin, continue, dash ahead, edge forward, go forward, go on, move on, progress, shoot ahead; SEE CONCEPTS 149,159,704

go-ahead [n] authorization
assent, consent, green light*, leave, okay, permission; SEE CONCEPT 685

go-ahead [adj] progressive
ambitious, enterprising, entrepreneurial, go-getting*, gumptious*, pioneering, up-and-coming*; SEE CONCEPTS 538,542

goal [n] aim, purpose of an action
ambition, design, destination, duty, end, ground zero*, intent, intention, limit, mark, mission, object, objective, target, use, zero*; SEE CONCEPT 659

go along/go along with [v] agree, cooperate
accompany, acquiesce, act jointly, assent, collaborate, concur, conspire, follow, share in, work together; SEE CONCEPTS 8,18

goat [n1] hollow-horned mammal
billy, buck, kid; SEE CONCEPTS 394,400

go back/go back on [v] break promise; change one's mind
abandon, betray, be unfaithful, desert, forsake, leave in the lurch*, renege, repudiate, retract, return, revert, run out on; SEE CONCEPTS 13,71

gl
go

gobble [*v*] *eat hurriedly*
cram*, devour, gorge, gulp*, guzzle, ingurgitate, scarf*, stuff*, suck up*, swallow, wolf*; SEE CONCEPT 169

go-between [*n*] *person acting as an agent*
arbitrator, attorney, broker, dealer, delegate, deputy, emissary, entrepreneur, envoy, factor, inter-agent, interceder, intercessor, intermediary, intermediate, intermediator, liaison, matchmaker, mediator, medium, messenger, negotiator, proxy, referee, representative; SEE CONCEPTS 348,423

go by [*v1*] *elapse*
exceed, flow on, make one's way, move onward, pass, proceed; SEE CONCEPT 141

go by [*v2*] *adopt, conform*
abide by, adjust to, agree, be guided by, comply, cooperate, fall in with, follow, heed, judge from, observe, take as guide; SEE CONCEPTS 8,18

god [*n*] *supernatural being worshipped by people*
Absolute Being, Allah, All Knowing, All Powerful, Almighty, Creator, daemon, deity, demigod, demon, Divine Being, divinity, Father, God, holiness, Holy Spirit, idol, Infinite Spirit, Jah, Jehovah, King of Kings, Lord, Maker, master, numen, omnipotent, power, prime mover, providence, soul, spirit, totem, tutelary, universal life force, world spirit, Yahweh; SEE CONCEPT 370

godless [*adj*] *without a god or divine faith*
adiamorphic, agnostic, atheistic, freethinking, iconoclastic, irreligious, nonbelieving, skeptical, undogmatic; SEE CONCEPT 542

godly [*adj*] *religious*
angelic, born-again, celestial, charismatic, deific, devout, divine, god-fearing, good, holy, pietistic, pious, prayerful, righteous, saintlike, saintly, virtuous; SEE CONCEPT 542

go down [*v*] *lose, fall*
be beaten, be defeated, cave in, collapse, crumple, decline, decrease, descend, droop, drop, fold, founder, go under, keel, lessen, make less, pitch, plunge, reduce, sag, set, sink, slump, submerge, submerse, submit, succumb, suffer defeat, topple, tumble; SEE CONCEPTS 181,698,699

godsend [*n*] *gift, benefit*
advantage, benediction, blessing, boon, good, manna*, stroke of luck*, windfall; SEE CONCEPTS 337,679

go far [*v*] *be successful*
achieve, advance, do well, get ahead, get on, make a name*, move up in the world*, progress, rise, succeed; SEE CONCEPTS 704,706

go for [*v1*] *reach*
clutch at, fetch, obtain, outreach, seek, stretch for; SEE CONCEPT 149

go for [*v2*] *like, choose*
accept, admire, approbate, approve, be attracted to, be fond of, care for, countenance, fancy, favor, hold with, prefer; SEE CONCEPTS 10,32

go for [*v3*] *attack*
assail, assault, launch at, run at, rush, rush upon, set upon, spring at; SEE CONCEPT 86

go into [*v1*] *begin an interest in; participate*
be absorbed in, begin, develop, engage in, enter, get involved with, take on*, take up*, take upon oneself*, undertake; SEE CONCEPT 100

go into [*v2*] *investigate*
analyze, consider, delve into, dig*, dig into*, discuss, examine, explore, inquire, look into, probe, prospect, pursue, review, scrutinize, sift, study; SEE CONCEPTS 24,103

gold/golden [*adj1*] *dark yellow*
aureate, auric, auriferous, aurous, aurulent, blond, blonde, caramel, dusty, flaxen, honeyed, mellow yellow, ochroid, straw, tan, tawny, wheat; SEE CONCEPT 618

golden [*adj2*] *beautiful, advantageous*
auspicious, best, blissful, bright, brilliant, delightful, excellent, favorable, flourishing, glorious, happy, joyful, joyous, opportune, precious, promising, propitious, prosperous, resplendent, rich, rosy, shining, successful, valuable; SEE CONCEPTS 529,574

gone [*adj*] *not present, no longer in existence*
absent, astray, away, AWOL*, burned up*, consumed, dead, decamped, deceased, defunct, departed, disappeared, disintegrated, displaced, dissipated, dissolved, done, down the drain*, dried up, elapsed, ended, extinct, finished, flown, lacking, left, lost, missing, moved, no more, non-extant, not a sign of*, not here, out the window*, over, passed, past, quit, removed, retired, run-off, shifted, spent, split, taken a powder*, taken leave*, transferred, traveling, turned to dust*, vanished, withdrawn; SEE CONCEPTS 407,586

good [*n1*] *advantage, benefit*
asset, avail, behalf, benediction, blessing, boon*, commonwealth, favor, gain, godsend, good fortune, interest, nugget*, plum*, prize, profit, prosperity, service, treasure, use, usefulness, welfare, well-being, windfall*; SEE CONCEPTS 337,658,679

good [*n2*] *morality*
class, dignity, excellence, ideal, merit, prerogative, probity, quality, rectitude, right, righteousness, straight, uprightness, value, virtue, worth; SEE CONCEPT 645

good [*adj1*] *pleasant, fine*
acceptable, ace*, admirable, agreeable, bad, boss*, bully, capital, choice, commendable, congenial, crack*, deluxe, delightful, exceptional, favorable, first-class, first-rate, gnarly*, gratifying, great, honorable, marvelous, neat*, nice, pleasing, positive, precious, prime, rad*, recherché*, reputable, satisfactory, satisfying, select, shipshape*, sound, spanking*, splendid, sterling, stupendous, super, superb, super-eminent, superexcellent, superior, tip-top*, up to snuff*, valuable, welcome, wonderful, worthy; SEE CONCEPTS 529,572

good [*adj2*] *moral, virtuous*
admirable, blameless, charitable, dutiful, estimable, ethical, exemplary, guiltless, honest, honorable, incorrupt, inculpable, innocent, irreprehensible, irreproachable, lily-white*, obedient, praiseworthy, pure, reputable, respectable, right, righteous, sound, tractable, uncorrupted, untainted, upright, well-behaved, worthy; SEE CONCEPT 545

good [*adj3*] *competent, skilled*
able, accomplished, adept, adroit, au fait, capable, clever, dexterous, efficient, expert, first-rate, proficient, proper, qualified, reliable, satisfactory, serviceable, skillful, suitable, suited, talented, thorough, trustworthy, useful; SEE CONCEPT 527

good [*adj4*] *useful, adequate*
acceptable, advantageous, all right, ample, appropriate, approving, apt, auspicious, becoming, benefic, beneficial, benignant, brave, commendatory, commending, common, conformable, congruous, convenient, decent, desirable, favorable, favoring, fit, fitting, fruitful, healthful, healthy,

helpful, hygienic, meet, needed, opportune, profitable, proper, propitious, respectable, right, salubrious, salutary, satisfying, seemly, serviceable, suitable, tolerable, toward, unobjectionable, wholesome; SEE CONCEPTS 537,558,560

good [adj5] *reliable; untainted*
dependable, eatable, fit to eat, flawless, fresh, intact, loyal, normal, perfect, safe, solid, sound, stable, trustworthy, unblemished, uncontaminated, uncorrupted, undamaged, undecayed, unhurt, unimpaired, unspoiled, vigorous, whole; SEE CONCEPT 485

good [adj6] *kind, giving*
altruistic, approving, beneficent, benevolent, charitable, considerate, friendly, gracious, humane, humanitarian, kindhearted, merciful, obliging, philanthropic, tolerant, well-disposed; SEE CONCEPTS 404,542

good [adj7] *authentic, real*
bona fide, conforming, dependable, genuine, honest, justified, kosher*, legitimate, loyal, orthodox, proper, regular, reliable, sound, strict, true, trustworthy, valid, well-founded; SEE CONCEPT 582

good [adj8] *well-behaved*
considerate, decorous, dutiful, kindly, mannerly, obedient, orderly, polite, proper, respectful, seemly, thoughtful, tolerant, tractable, well-mannered; SEE CONCEPT 401

good [adj9] *considerable*
adequate, advantageous, ample, big, complete, entire, extensive, full, great, immeasurable, large, long, lucrative, much, paying, profitable, respectable, sizable, solid, substantial, sufficient, whole, worthwhile; SEE CONCEPTS 334,771,781

goodbye [n] *farewell statement*
adieu, adios, bye-bye, cheerio, ciao, godspeed*, leave-taking, parting, so long*, swan song*, toodle-oo*; SEE CONCEPTS 195,278

good-for-nothing [n] *person who is idle, worthless*
bad lot*, black sheep*, bum, loafer, ne'er-do-well*, no-good*, profligate, rapscallion, scalawag, scamp, tramp, vagabond, waster*, wastrel; SEE CONCEPT 412

good-humored [adj] *funny, happy*
affable, amiable, buoyant, cheerful, cheery, complaisant, congenial, easy, genial, good-natured, good-tempered, lenient, merry, mild, obliging, pleasant, smiling; SEE CONCEPT 404

good-looking [adj] *handsome*
attractive, beauteous, beautiful, clean-cut, comely, fair, impressive, lovely, pretty, pulchritudinous, righteous; SEE CONCEPT 579

good-natured [adj] *easygoing, easily pleased*
acquiescent, agreeable, altruistic, amiable, benevolent, bighearted, breezy, charitable, complaisant, compliant, cordial, easy, even-tempered, friendly, good-hearted, good-humored, gracious, helpful, kind, kindly, lenient, marshmallow*, mild, moderate, nice, obliging, softie*, tolerant, warmhearted, well-disposed, willing to please; SEE CONCEPT 404

goodness [n] *decency, excellence*
advantage, beneficence, benefit, benevolence, ethicality, friendliness, generosity, good will, grace, graciousness, honesty, honor, humaneness, integrity, kindheartedness, kindliness, kindness, mercy, merit, morality, nourishment, obligingness, probity, quality, rectitude, righteousness, rightness, superiority, uprightness, value, virtue, wholesomeness, worth; SEE CONCEPTS 411,645

goods [n1] *personal possessions*
appurtenances, belongings, chattels, effects, encumbrances, equipment, furnishings, furniture, gear, impedimenta, movables, paraphernalia, property, stuff, things, trappings; SEE CONCEPT 446

goods [n2] *merchandise*
bolt, cargo, commodities, fabric, freight, line, load, materials, seconds, stock, stuff, textile, vendibles, wares; SEE CONCEPT 338

good will/goodwill [n] *kindliness*
altruism, amity, benevolence, brownie points*, charity, comity, cordiality, favor, friendliness, friendship, generosity, good deed, good side of*, helpfulness, rapport, right side of*, sympathy, tolerance; SEE CONCEPTS 411,645

gooey [adj] *sticky, gummy*
adhesive, gluey, glutinous, mucilaginous, soft, tacky, viscous; SEE CONCEPT 606

go off [v1] *explode*
befall, blow, blow up, burst, detonate, discharge, fire, happen, mushroom, occur, pass, take place; SEE CONCEPT 179

go off [v2] *leave*
decamp, depart, exit, go away, move out, part, quit; SEE CONCEPT 195

go on [v] *continue*
act, advance, bear, behave, carry on, come about, comport, conduct, deport, endure, execute, go ahead, hang on, happen, hold on, keep on, last, occur, persevere, persist, proceed, ramble, stay, take place; SEE CONCEPTS 100,239

go out [v1] *become extinguished*
become dark, burn out, cease, darken, die, die out, dim, expire, fade out, flicker, stop shining; SEE CONCEPTS 105,469

go out [v2] *leave*
decamp, depart, exit, go on strike, walk out; SEE CONCEPT 195

go over [v1] *review*
analyze, examine, inspect, investigate, look at, peruse, practice, read, rehearse, reiterate, repeat, revise, riffle through*, scan, skim, study, thumb through*; SEE CONCEPTS 24,103

go over [v2] *succeed*
be impressive, be successful, click*, come off*, go, pan out*, prove; SEE CONCEPT 706

gorge [n] *valley*
abyss, arroyo, canyon, chasm, cleft, clough, clove, crevasse, fissure, flume, gap, glen, gulch, pass, ravine; SEE CONCEPT 509

gorge [v] *eat voraciously*
blimp out*, bolt*, cloy, congest, cram, devour, eat like a horse*, feed, fill, glut, gobble, gormandize, gulp, guzzle, hoover*, jade, jam, make a pig of*, overeat, overindulge, pack, sate, satiate, stuff*, surfeit, swallow, wolf*; SEE CONCEPT 169

gorgeous [adj] *beautiful, magnificent*
attractive, beaut*, bright, brilliant, centerfold*, colorful, dazzling, delightful, dream, drop-dead*, easy on the eyes*, elegant, enjoyable, exquisite, fine, flamboyant, foxy*, gaudy, glittering, glorious, good-looking, grand, handsome, imposing, impressive, knockout*, lavish, lovely, lulu*, luxuriant, luxurious, opulent, ostentatious, pleasing, plush, pulchritudinous, ravishing, resplendent, showy, splendid, splendiferous, stunning, sublime, sumptuous, superb; SEE CONCEPTS 579,589

gory [adj] *bloody, horrible*
bleeding, blood-soaked, bloodstained, imbrued,

go
go

murderous, offensive, sanguinary, sanguine; SEE CONCEPTS *314,537*

gospel [n] *fact, doctrine*
actuality, authority, belief, certainty, credo, creed, dogma, faith, last word, scripture, testament, truism, truth, veracity, verity; SEE CONCEPT *689*

gossamer [adj] *gauzy, thin*
airy, cobweb, delicate, diaphanous, fibrous, fine, flimsy, light, sheer, silky, tiffany, translucent, transparent; SEE CONCEPT *606*

gossip [n1] *talk about others; rumor*
account, babble, back-fence talk*, blather, blether, buzz*, calumny, chatter, chitchat*, chronicle, clothesline*, conversation, cry, defamation, dirty laundry*, dirty linen*, dirty wash*, earful*, grapevine*, hearsay, idle talk, injury, malicious talk, meddling, news, prate, prattle, report, scandal, scuttlebutt*, slander, small talk*, story, tale, talk, whispering campaign*, wire*; SEE CONCEPTS *274,278*

gossip [n2] *person who talks a lot, spreads rumors*
babbler*, blabbermouth*, busybody, chatterbox, chatterer, circulator, flibbertigibbet*, gossipmonger, informer, meddler, newsmonger, parrot*, prattler, rumormonger*, scandalizer*, scandalmonger*, snoop*, talebearer, tattler, telltale; SEE CONCEPT *412*

gossip [v] *talk about others; spread rumors*
babble, bad-mouth*, bend one's ear*, blab, blather, blether, chat, chatter, cut to pieces*, cut up*, dish, hint, imply, insinuate, intimate, jaw*, prate, prattle, rattle on*, repeat, report, rumor, schmooze*, spill the beans*, spread*, suggest, talk, talk idly, tattle, tell secrets*, tell tales*, wiggle-waggle*; SEE CONCEPTS *56,60*

go through [v1] *endure*
bear, brave, experience, suffer, support, survive, swallow, tolerate, undergo, withstand; SEE CONCEPT *23*

go through [v2] *use up*
consume, deplete, exhaust, pay out, spend, squander; SEE CONCEPT *169*

go through [v3] *search*
audit, check, examine, explore, hunt, inspect, investigate, look, pass through; SEE CONCEPT *103*

go together/go with [v1] *agree, match*
accompany, accord, become, befit, be suitable, blend, complement, concur, correspond, fit, go, harmonize, make a pair*, not clash, suit; SEE CONCEPT *664*

go together/go with [v2] *accompany socially*
attend, be with, court, date, escort, go out with*, go steady with*, keep company with*; SEE CONCEPT *384*

go under [v] *fail, submerge*
bankrupt, default, die, drown, fall, fold, founder, go down, sink, submerse, submit, succumb, suffocate, surrender; SEE CONCEPTS *181,699*

gourmet [n] *person who likes, knows about food*
bon vivant, connoisseur, critic, epicure, epicurean, gastronome, gastronomer, gastronomist, gourmand; SEE CONCEPTS *348,423*

govern [v1] *take control; rule*
administer, assume command, be in power, be in the driver's seat*, call the shots*, call the signals*, captain*, carry out, command, conduct, control, dictate, direct, execute, exercise authority, guide, head, head up, hold dominion, hold office, hold sway, lay down the law*, lead, man-age, occupy throne, order, overrule, oversee, pilot, pull the strings*, regulate, reign, render, run, serve the people*, steer, superintend, supervise, sway, tyrannize, wear the crown*; SEE CONCEPT *133*

govern [v2] *influence; hold in check*
boss, bridle, check, contain, control, curb, decide, determine, direct, directionalize, discipline, dispose, dominate, get the better of*, guide, handle, incline, inhibit, manage, predispose, regulate, restrain, rule, shepherd, steer, subdue, sway, tame, underlie; SEE CONCEPTS *7,19,22,130*

government [n] *management, administration*
authority, bureaucracy, command, control, direction, domination, dominion, empire, execution, executive, governance, guidance, influence, jurisdiction, law, ministry, patronage, political practice, politics, polity, power, powers-that-be*, predominance, presidency, regency, regime, regimentation, regulation, restraint, rule, sovereignty, state, statecraft, superintendence, superiority, supervision, supremacy, sway, the feds*, union, Washington*; SEE CONCEPT *299*

governor [n] *person administrating government*
administrator, boss, chief, chief of state, commander, comptroller, controller, director, executive, gubernatorial leader, guv*, head, head honcho*, leader, manager, overseer, presiding officer, ruler, superintendent, supervisor; SEE CONCEPT *354*

go without [adj] *deny or be denied*
abstain, be deprived of, do without, fall short*, go short*, lack, need, want; SEE CONCEPT *646*

gown [n] *robe, dress*
clothes, costume, frock, garb, garment, habit; SEE CONCEPT *451*

grab [v] *latch on to*
capture, catch, catch hold of, clutch, collar*, corral*, get one's fingers on*, get one's hands on*, glom*, grapple, grasp, grip, hook, land, lay one's hands on*, nab, nail, pluck, seize, snag, snap up, snatch, take, take hold of; SEE CONCEPTS *90,190*

grace [n1] *charm, loveliness*
address, adroitness, agility, allure, attractiveness, balance, beauty, breeding, comeliness, consideration, cultivation, decency, decorum, dexterity, dignity, ease, elegance, etiquette, finesse, finish, form, gracefulness, lissomeness, lithesomeness, mannerliness, manners, nimbleness, pleasantness, pliancy, poise, polish, propriety, refinement, shapeliness, smoothness, style, suppleness, symmetry, tact, tastefulness; SEE CONCEPTS *633,655,718*

grace [n2] *mercy, forgiveness*
benefaction, beneficence, benevolence, caritas, charity, clemency, compassion, compassionateness, favor, forbearance, generosity, goodness, good will, indulgence, kindliness, kindness, leniency, lenity, love, pardon, quarter, reprieve, responsiveness, tenderness; SEE CONCEPTS *278,657,685*

grace [n3] *prayer*
benediction, blessing, invocation, petition, thanks, thanksgiving; SEE CONCEPTS *278,368*

grace [v] *beautify, embellish*
adorn, bedeck, crown, deck, decorate, dignify, distinguish, elevate, enhance, enrich, favor, garnish, glorify, honor, laureate, ornament, set off; SEE CONCEPTS *202,700*

graceful [*adj*] *agile, charming, lovely*
adroit, aesthetic, artistic, balletic, beautiful, becoming, comely, controlled, curvaceous, dainty, decorative, delicate, dexterous, easy, elastic, elegant, exquisite, fair, fine, flowing, handsome, harmonious, limber, lissome, lithe, natural, neat, nimble, pleasing, pliant, poised, practiced, pretty, refined, rhythmic, seemly, shapely, skilled, slender, smooth, springy, statuesque, supple, symmetrical, tasteful, trim, willowy; SEE CONCEPTS *579,584,589*

graceless [*adj*] *clumsy, unsophisticated*
awkward, barbarian, barbaric, barbarous, boorish, clunky*, coarse, corrupt, crude*, forced, gauche, gawky*, ill-mannered, improper, indecorous, inelegant, inept, infelicitous, klutzy*, loutish, oafish, outlandish, rough, rude, shameless, tasteless, two left feet*, uncouth, uncultured, unfortunate, ungainly, unhappy, unmannered; SEE CONCEPTS *401,584*

gracious [*adj*] *kind, giving*
accommodating, affable, amiable, amicable, approachable, beneficent, benevolent, benign, benignant, big-hearted, bland, bonhomous, charitable, chivalrous, civil, compassionate, complaisant, congenial, considerate, cordial, courteous, courtly, easy, forthcoming, friendly, gallant, genial, good-hearted, good-natured, hospitable, indulgent, lenient, loving, merciful, mild, obliging, pleasing, polite, sociable, stately, suave, tender, unctuous, urbane, well-mannered; SEE CONCEPTS *401,542*

gradation [*n*] *classification, step*
arrangement, calibration, change, degree, difference, distinction, divergence, grade, grouping, level, mark, measurement, modification, notch, nuance, ordering, place, point, position, progression, rank, scale, sequence, series, shade, sorting, stage, succession, variation; SEE CONCEPTS *378,665,727,744*

grade [*n1*] *rank, step*
brand, caliber, category, class, classification, condition, degree, division, echelon, estate, form, gradation, group, grouping, league, level, mark, notch, order, pigeonhole*, place, position, quality, rung*, size, stage, standard, station, tier; SEE CONCEPTS *286,378,665,727,744*

grade [*n2*] *incline, slope*
acclivity, ascent, bank, cant, climb, declivity, descent, downgrade, elevation, embankment, gradient, height, hill, inclination, inclined plane, lean, leaning, level, obliquity, pitch, plane, ramp, rise, slant, tangent, tilt, upgrade; SEE CONCEPTS *738,757*

grade [*v*] *evaluate, rank*
arrange, assort, brand, class, classify, group, order, range, rate, sort, value; SEE CONCEPTS *103,291*

gradient [*n*] *slope*
acclivity, angle, bank, cant, declivity, grade, hill, inclination, incline, lean, leaning, pitch, ramp, rise, slant, tilt; SEE CONCEPTS *738,757*

gradual [*adj*] *happening slowly, evenly*
bit-by-bit*, by degrees, continuous, creeping, even, gentle, graduate, moderate, piecemeal, progressive, regular, slow, steady, step-by-step*, successive, unhurried; SEE CONCEPTS *544,588,799*

gradually [*adv*] *happening slowly, evenly*
bit by bit*, by degrees, by installments, con-

stantly, continuously, deliberately, gently, imperceptibly, inch by inch*, increasingly, in small doses*, little by little*, moderately, perceptibly, piece by piece*, piecemeal, progressively, regularly, sequentially, serially, steadily, step by step*, successively, unhurriedly; SEE CONCEPTS *544,588,799*

graduate [*n*] *person who completes education, pursuit*
alum*, alumnus, baccalaureate, bachelor, collegian, diplomate, doctor, former student, grad, holder, licentiate, master, Ph.D., product, recipient; SEE CONCEPT *350*

graduate [*v1*] *complete education, pursuit*
be commissioned, certify, confer degree, earn, finish, get a degree, get out*, give sheepskin*, grant diploma, take a degree, win; SEE CONCEPT *234*

graduate [*v2*] *classify, grade*
arrange, calibrate, class, group, mark off, measure, measure out, order, proportion, range, rank, regulate, sort; SEE CONCEPTS *84,103*

graft [*n1*] *transplant*
bud*, hybridization, implant, jointure, scion, shoot, slip, splice, sprout, union; SEE CONCEPTS *113,257*

graft [*n2*] *payoff for fraud*
bribe, corruption, gain, hat*, hush money*, juice*, money, money under the table*, pay, payola*, peculation, shake*, share, skimming*, squeeze*, thievery; SEE CONCEPTS *192,344*

graft [*v*] *transplant, splice*
affix, implant, ingraft, insert, join, plant, propagate, unite; SEE CONCEPTS *113,257*

grain [*n1*] *seed, piece*
atom, bit, cereal, corn, crumb, drop, fragment, granule, grist, iota, jot, kernel, mite, modicum, molecule, morsel, mote, ounce, particle, pellet, scintilla, scrap, scruple, smidgen, spark, speck, tittle, trace, whit; SEE CONCEPTS *428,831*

grain [*n2*] *texture of fabric*
character, current, direction, fiber, make-up, nap, pattern, staple, striation, surface, tendency, tissue, tooth, warp and woof, weave, weft; SEE CONCEPT *611*

grammar [*n*] *language rules*
ABCs*, accidence, alphabet, elements, fundaments, linguistics, morphology, principles, rudiments, sentence structure, stratification, structure, syntax, tagmemics; SEE CONCEPTS *275,276,770*

grand [*adj1*] *impressive, great*
admirable, ambitious, august, awe-inspiring, dignified, dynamite, elevated, eminent, exalted, excellent, fab*, fine, first-class, first-rate, glorious, grandiose, haughty, illustrious, imposing, large, lofty, luxurious, magnificent, majestic, marvelous, monumental, noble, opulent, ostentatious, outstanding, palatial, pompous, pretentious, regal, rich, smashing, something else*, splendid, stately, striking, sublime, sumptuous, super, superb, terrific, unreal, very good; SEE CONCEPTS *574,589,773*

grand [*adj2*] *most important*
chief, dignified, elevated, exalted, grave, head, highest, leading, lofty, main, majestic, mighty, noble, preeminent, principal, regal, supreme, transcendent; SEE CONCEPT *568*

grandeur [*n*] *great importance*
amplitude, augustness, beauty, breadth, brilliance, celebrity, circumstance, dignity, distinc-

go
gr

tion, elevation, eminence, expansiveness, fame, fineness, glory, grandiosity, gravity, greatness, handsomeness, immensity, impressiveness, inclusiveness, loftiness, luxuriousness, magnificence, majesty, might, nobility, opulence, pomp, preeminence, richness, splendor, state, stateliness, sublimity, sumptuousness, superbity, sway, transcendency, vastness; SEE CONCEPT *668*

grandiloquent [adj] *pretentious, flowery (communication)*
aureate, big-talking*, bombastic, declamatory, euphistic, fustian, high-flown, histrionic, inflated, magniloquent, oratorical, orotund, overblown, pompous, purple*, rhetorical, sonorous, swollen, tall-talking*, verbose, windbag*, windy*; SEE CONCEPT *267*

grandiose [adj] *theatrical, extravagant*
affected, ambitious, august, bombastic, cosmic, egotistic, flamboyant, fustian, grand, high-falutin'*, high-flown, imposing, impressive, lofty, lordly, magnificent, majestic, monumental, noble, ostentatious, overwhelming, pompous, pretentious, purple*, royal, showy, splashy, stately, unfathomable, vast; SEE CONCEPTS *401,542,589*

grange [n] *farm*
acreage, farmstead, hacienda, manor, plantation, ranch; SEE CONCEPTS *258,516,517*

grant [n] *allowance, gift*
admission, allocation, allotment, alms, appropriation, assistance, award, benefaction, bequest, boon, bounty, charity, concession, contribution, dole, donation, endowment, fellowship, gratuity, handout, lump, present, privilege, reward, scholarship, stipend, subsidy; SEE CONCEPTS *337,344*

grant [v] *authorize, allow*
accede, accept, acknowledge, acquiesce, admit, agree to, allocate, allot, assign, assume, avow, award, bestow, bless, cede, come across, come around, come through, concede, confer, consent to, convey, donate, drop, gift with*, give, give in, give out, give the nod*, give thumbs-up*, go along with*, impart, invest, own, own up*, permit, present, profess, relinquish, shake on*, sign off on*, sign on*, stake, suppose, surrender, transfer, transmit, vouchsafe, yield; SEE CONCEPTS *8,50,82,83,88*

granted [adv] *allowed, accepted*
acknowledged, admitted, assumed, indeed, just so, yes; SEE CONCEPT *558*

granulate [v] *crush into tiny pieces*
atomize, comminute, crumble, crystallize, disintegrate, grate, grind, make coarse, make grainy, pound, powder, pulverize, triturate; SEE CONCEPT *186*

graphic [adj1] *clear, explicit*
colorful, compelling, comprehensible, concrete, convincing, definite, descriptive, detailed, distinct, eloquent, expressive, figurative, forcible, illustrative, incisive, intelligible, lively, lucid, moving, perspicuous, picturesque, precise, realistic, stirring, striking, strong, telling, unequivocal, vivid; SEE CONCEPTS *267,535,562*

graphic [adj2] *pictorial, visible*
blocked-out, delineated, depicted, descriptive, diagrammatic, drawn, engraved, etched, iconographic, illustrated, illustrational, illustrative, marked-out, outlined, painted, photographic, pictoric, pictured, portrayed, representational, seen, sketched, traced, visual; SEE CONCEPTS *576,589,619*

grapple [v] *grab, wrestle*
attack, battle, catch, clash, clasp, close, clutch, combat, confront, contend, cope, deal with, do battle*, encounter, engage, face, fasten, fight, grasp, grip, hold, hook, hug, nab, nail, scuffle, seize, snatch, struggle, tackle, take, take on*, tussle; SEE CONCEPTS *106,191*

grasp [n] *hold, grip*
butt, cinch, clamp, clasp, clench, clinch, clutches, embrace, grapple, lug, possession, purchase, tenure; SEE CONCEPTS *191,710*

grasp [n2] *understanding*
awareness, comprehension, ken, knowledge, mastery, perception, realization; SEE CONCEPT *409*

grasp [v1] *grab*
bag*, catch, clasp, clinch, clutch, collar*, corral, enclose, glom*, grapple, grip, hold, hook, land, seize, snatch, take, take hold of; SEE CONCEPTS *90,191*

grasp [v2] *understand*
accept, appreciate, apprehend, catch, catch on*, cognize, compass, comprehend, dig*, envisage, fathom, follow, get, get the drift*, get the picture*, have, know, latch on*, make, perceive, pick up*, realize, see, take, take in*; SEE CONCEPT *15*

grasping [adj] *greedy*
acquisitive, avaricious, avid, close-fisted, covetous, desirous, extorting, extortionate, grabby*, itchy*, mean, miserly, niggardly*, penny-pinching*, penurious, prehensile, rapacious, selfish, stingy*, tightfisted*, usurious, venal; SEE CONCEPTS *326,334,542*

grate [v1] *shred, grind down*
abrade, bark, bray, file, fray, gall, mince, pound, pulverize, rasp, raze, rub, scrape, scratch, scuff, skin, triturate; SEE CONCEPTS *186,215*

grate [v2] *irritate*
aggravate, annoy, burn, chafe, exasperate, fret, gall, get on one's nerves*, irk, nettle, peeve, pique, provoke, rankle, rile, rub the wrong way*, vex; SEE CONCEPTS *7,14,19*

grateful [adj1] *appreciative*
beholden, gratified, indebted, obliged, pleased, thankful; SEE CONCEPT *403*

grateful [adj2] *pleasing, nice*
acceptable, agreeable, comforting, congenial, consoling, delectable, delicious, delightful, desirable, favorable, good, gratifying, pleasant, pleasurable, pleasureful, refreshing, rejuvenating, renewing, restful, restorative, restoring, satisfactory, satisfying, solacing, welcome; SEE CONCEPTS *537,548,572*

gratification [n] *satisfaction*
delight, enjoyment, fruition, fulfillment, glee, hit, indulgence, joy, kicks*, luxury, pleasure, recompense, regalement, relish, reward, sure shock*, thrill; SEE CONCEPT *410*

gratify [v] *give pleasure; satisfy*
appease, arride, baby*, cater to, coddle, content, delectate, delight, do one proud*, do the trick*, enchant, favor, fill the bill*, fulfill*, get one's kicks*, gladden, hit the spot*, humor, indulge, make a hit*, make happy, oblige, pamper, please, recompense, requite, thrill; SEE CONCEPTS *7,22*

grating [adj] *irritating; scraping*
annoying, disagreeable, discordant, displeasing, dissonant, dry, grinding, harsh, harsh-sounding, hoarse, irksome, jarring, offensive, rasping, raucous, rough, shrill, squeaky, strident, stridulent,

gratis [adj] *free*
as a gift, chargeless, complimentary, costless, for love*, for nothing, freebie*, freely given, free of charge, free ride*, gratuitous, on someone*, on the house*, unpaid for, without charge, without recompense; SEE CONCEPT *334*

gratitude [n] *appreciation*
acknowledgment, appreciativeness, grace, gratefulness, honor, indebtedness, obligation, praise, recognition, requital, response, responsiveness, sense of obligation, thankfulness, thanks, thanksgiving; SEE CONCEPTS *32,76,278,410*

gratuitous [adj1] *free*
chargeless, complimentary, costless, for nothing, gratis, spontaneous, unasked-for, unpaid, voluntary, willing; SEE CONCEPTS *334,542*

gratuitous [adj2] *not necessary*
assumed, baseless, bottomless, causeless, groundless, indefensible, inessential, needless, reasonless, supererogatory, superfluous, uncalled-for, unessential, unfounded, unjustified, unmerited, unprovoked, unsupportable, unwarranted, wanton; SEE CONCEPT *546*

gratuity [n] *gift, tip*
alms, benefaction, bonus, boon, bounty, contribution, donation, fringe benefit, grease palm*, largesse, little something*, offering, perk*, perquisite, present, recompense, reward, salve*, sweetener*, token; SEE CONCEPTS *337,344*

grave [n] *burial place*
catacomb, crypt, final resting place*, last home*, mausoleum, mound, permanent address*, place of interment, resting place, sepulcher, shrine, six feet under*, tomb, vault; SEE CONCEPT *305*

grave [adj1] *serious; gloomy*
cold sober*, deadpan*, dignified, dour, dull, earnest, grim, grim-faced, heavy, leaden, long-faced, meaningful, muted, no-nonsense*, ponderous, quiet, sad, sage, saturnine, sedate, sober, solemn, somber, staid, strictly business*, subdued, thoughtful, unsmiling; SEE CONCEPT *401*

grave [adj2] *crucial, dangerous*
acute, afflictive, consequential, critical, deadly, destructive, exigent, fatal, fell, grievous, hazardous, heavy*, important, killing*, life-and-death*, major, momentous, of great consequence, ominous, perilous, pressing, serious, severe, significant, threatening, ugly, urgent, vital, weighty; SEE CONCEPTS *537,548,567*

graveyard [n] *burial area*
boneyard*, burial ground, cemetery, charnel house, God's acre*, memorial park, necropolis; SEE CONCEPT *305*

gravitate [v] *be drawn toward; fall to*
approach, be attracted, be influenced, be pulled, descend, drift, drop, incline, lean, move, precipitate, settle, sink, tend; SEE CONCEPTS *34,159*

gravity [n1] *force of attraction*
force, heaviness, pressure, weight; SEE CONCEPT *641*

gravity [n2] *seriousness, importance*
acuteness, concern, consequence, exigency, hazardousness, momentousness, perilousness, severity, significance, solemnity, urgency, weightiness; SEE CONCEPT *668*

gray/grey [adj] *muted silver in color*
ash, ashen, battleship*, cinereal, clouded, dingy, dove, drab, dusky, dusty, granite, heather, iron,

lead, leaden, livid, mousy, neutral, oyster, pearly, peppery, powder, sere, shaded, silvered, silvery, slate, smoky, somber, stone; SEE CONCEPT *618*

graze [v1] *touch*
abrade, brush, carom, chafe, glance off, kiss*, ricochet, rub, scrape, scratch, shave*, skim, skip; SEE CONCEPT *612*

graze [v2] *feed on*
bite, browse, champ, crop, crunch, eat, forage, gnaw, masticate, munch, nibble, pasture, ruminate, uproot; SEE CONCEPT *169*

greasy [adj] *slippery, oily*
anointed, creamy, daubed, fatty, lubricated, lubricious, oleaginous, pomaded, salved, slick, slimy*, slithery, smeared, swabbed, unctuous; SEE CONCEPT *606*

great [adj1] *very large*
abundant, ample, big, big league*, bulky, bull, colossal, considerable, decided, enormous, excessive, extended, extensive, extravagant, extreme, fat, gigantic, grievous, high, huge, humongous, husky, immense, inordinate, jumbo*, lengthy, long, major league*, mammoth, mondo*, numerous, oversize, prodigious, prolonged, pronounced, protracted, strong, stupendous, terrible, titanic*, towering, tremendous, vast, voluminous; SEE CONCEPTS *773,781*

great [adj2] *important, celebrated*
august, capital, chief, commanding, dignified, distinguished, eminent, exalted, excellent, famed, famous, fine, glorious, grand, heroic, highly regarded, high-minded, honorable, idealistic, illustrious, impressive, leading, lofty, magnanimous, main, major, noble, notable, noted, noteworthy, outstanding, paramount, primary, principal, prominent, puissant, regal, remarkable, renowned, royal, stately, sublime, superior, superlative, talented; SEE CONCEPT *568*

great [adj3] *excellent, skillful*
able, absolute, aces*, adept, admirable, adroit, awesome, bad*, best, brutal, cold*, complete, consummate, crack*, downright, dynamite, egregious, exceptional, expert, fab*, fantastic, fine, first-class*, first-rate*, good, heavy*, hellacious*, marvelous, masterly, number one*, out-and-out*, out of sight*, out of this world*, perfect, positive, proficient, super-duper*, surpassing, terrific, total, tough, transcendent, tremendous, unmitigated, unqualified, utter, wonderful; SEE CONCEPTS *527,528,574*

greatly [adv] *considerably*
abundantly, by much, conspicuously, eminently, emphatically, enormously, exceedingly, exceptionally, extremely, famously, glaringly, highly, hugely, immeasurably, immensely, incalculably, incomparably, incredibly, indeed, infinitely, in great measure, inimitably, intensely, largely, markedly, mightily, most, much, notably, on a large scale, powerfully, remarkably, strikingly, superlatively, supremely, surpassingly, tremendously, vastly, very much; SEE CONCEPTS *537,569,772*

greatness [n1] *large size*
abundance, amplitude, bigness, bulk, enormity, force, high degree, hugeness, immensity, infinity, intensity, length, magnitude, mass, might, potency, power, prodigiousness, sizableness, strength, vastness; SEE CONCEPTS *730,767*

greatness [n2] *nobleness of character; eminence*
celebrity, chivalry, dignity, distinction, fame,

gr
gr

generosity, glory, grandeur, heroism, high-mindedness, idealism, illustriousness, importance, loftiness, magnanimity, majesty, merit, morality, nobility, note, prominence, renown, stateliness, sublimity, worthiness; SEE CONCEPTS 411,645,668

greed [n] *overwhelming desire for more*
acquisitiveness, avarice, avidity, covetousness, craving, cupidity, eagerness, edacity, esurience, excess, gluttony, gormandizing, graspingness, hunger, indulgence, insatiableness, intemperance, longing, piggishness, rapacity, ravenousness, selfishness, swinishness*, the gimmies*, voracity; SEE CONCEPT 20

greedy [adj] *desiring excessively*
acquisitive, avaricious, avid, carnivorous, close, close-fisted*, covetous, craving, desirous, devouring, eager, edacious, esurient, gluttonous, gobbling, gormandizing, grabby, grasping, grudging, gulping, guzzling, hoggish*, hungry, impatient, insatiable, insatiate, intemperate, itchy*, miserly, niggardly, omnivorous, parsimonious, penny-pinching*, penurious, piggish*, prehensile, rapacious, ravening, ravenous, selfish, stingy, swinish, tight*, tight-fisted*, voracious; SEE CONCEPTS 326,403,542

green [n] *square or park in center of town*
common, field, grass, grassplot, lawn, plaza, sward, terrace, turf; SEE CONCEPTS 509,513

green [adj1] *young, new, blooming*
bosky, budding, burgeoning, callow, developing, flourishing, foliate, fresh, grassy, growing, half-formed, immature, infant, juvenile, leafy, lush, maturing, pliable, puerile, pullulating, raw, recent, sprouting, supple, tender, undecayed, undried, unfledged, ungrown, unripe, unseasoned, verdant, verduous, visculent, youthful; SEE CONCEPTS 485,578,797

green [adj2] *inexperienced*
callow, credulous, fresh, gullible, ignorant, immature, inexpert, ingenuous, innocent, naive, new, raw, tenderfoot*, unconversant, unpolished, unpracticed, unseasoned, unskillful, unsophisticated, untrained, unversed, wet behind the ears*, young, youthful; SEE CONCEPT 404

green [adj3] *emerald in color*
apple, aquamarine, beryl, chartreuse, fir, forest, grass, jade, kelly, lime, malachite, moss, olive, pea, peacock, pine, sage, sap, sea, spinach, verdigris, vert, viridian, willow; SEE CONCEPT 618

green [adj4] *referring to practices or policies that do not negatively affect the environment*
biodegradable, ecological, environmental, environmentally-safe, environment-friendly; SEE CONCEPT 485

greenhorn [n] *inexperienced person*
amateur, apprentice, babe*, beginner, colt*, hayseed*, ingénue, learner, naif, neophyte, newcomer, new hand, novice, recruit, rube*, simpleton, tenderfoot*, tyro*, virgin; SEE CONCEPT 423

greet [v] *welcome*
accost, acknowledge, address, approach, attend, bow, call to, compliment, curtsy, embrace, exchange greetings, extend one's hand, flag, hail, herald, highball*, high-five*, meet, move to, nod, pay respects, receive, recognize, roll out the red carpet*, salaam*, salute, say hello, say hi*, shake hands, shoulder, speak to, stop, tip one's hat*, usher in*, whistle for; SEE CONCEPT 51

greeting [n] *welcome; message of kindness*
accosting, acknowledgment, address, aloha*, attention, best wishes*, blow*, card*, ciao*, compellation, compliments, good wishes*, hail, hello, heralding, hi, highball*, high five*, how-do-you-do*, howdy*, letter*, not, note, notice, ovation, reception, regards, respects, rumble, salaam*, salutation, salute, speaking to, testimonial, ushering in, what's happening*; SEE CONCEPT 51

gregarious [adj] *friendly*
affable, clubby*, companionable, convivial, cordial, fun, outgoing, sociable, social; SEE CONCEPT 404

grief [n] *mental suffering*
affliction, agony, anguish, bemoaning, bereavement, bewailing, care, dejection, deploring, depression, desolation, despair, despondency, discomfort, disquiet, distress, dole, dolor, gloom, grievance, harassment, heartache, heartbreak, infelicity, lamentation, lamenting, malaise, melancholy, misery, mortification, mournfulness, mourning, pain, purgatory, regret, remorse, repining, rue, sadness, sorrow, torture, trial, tribulation, trouble, unhappiness, vexation, woe, worry, wretchedness; SEE CONCEPTS 410,728

grievance [n] *complaint, gripe*
affliction, ax to grind*, beef*, bellyache*, big stink*, blast, case, cross*, damage, distress, flack*, grief, grouse*, hardship, holler*, hoo-ha*, howl*, injury, injustice, jeremiad*, kick, knock*, objection, outrage, pain, pain in the neck*, rap*, resentment, rigor, roar, rumble, sorrow, squawk*, stink*, trial, tribulation, trouble, unhappiness, violence, wrong, yell; SEE CONCEPTS 52,278,689

grieve [v1] *mourn, feel deep distress*
ache, bear, bemoan, bewail, carry on, complain, cry, cry a river*, deplore, eat one's heart out*, endure, hang crepe*, keen, lament, regret, rue, sing the blues*, sorrow, suffer, take it hard*, wail, weep; SEE CONCEPTS 17,410

grieve [v2] *upset, distress someone*
afflict, aggrieve, agonize, break the heart of*, constrain, crush, hurt, injure, pain, sadden, wound; SEE CONCEPTS 7,19

grievous [adj] *severe, painful; serious*
afflicting, agonizing, appalling, atrocious, calamitous, damaging, deplorable, dire, dismal, disquieting, distressing, disturbing, dreadful, egregious, flagrant, glaring, grave, harmful, heart-rending, heavy*, heinous, hurtful, injurious, intolerable, lamentable, monstrous, mournful, offensive, onerous, oppressive, outrageous, pathetic, pitiful, sad, shameful, sharp, shocking, sorrowful, taxing, tough, tragic, troublesome, unbearable, upsetting, villainous, weighty*, wounding; SEE CONCEPTS 537,544,548

grill [v1] *broil food*
barbecue, burn, charcoal-broil, cook, cook over an open pit, roast, rotisserie, sear; SEE CONCEPT 170

grill [v2] *ask questions aggressively*
catechize, cross-examine, give the third degree*, go over*, inquisition, interrogate, interview, put the pressure on*, put the screws to*, question, roast*, third degree*; SEE CONCEPTS 48,53

grim [adj] *hopeless, horrible in manner, appearance*
austere, barbarous, bleak, cantankerous, churlish, crabbed*, cruel, crusty, dogged, ferocious, fierce, forbidding, foreboding, formidable, frightful, fu-

nereal, ghastly, gloomy, glowering, glum, grisly, grouchy, gruesome, grumpy*, harsh, hideous, horrid, implacable, inexorable, intractable, merciless, morose, ominous, relentless, resolute, ruthless, scowling, severe, shocking, sinister, somber, sour, splenetic, stern, stubborn, sulky, sullen, surly, terrible, truculent, unrelenting, unyielding; SEE CONCEPTS 534,544,570

grimace [n] *scowling facial expression*
face, frown, moue, mouth, mouthing, mug*, scowl, smile, smirk, sneer, wry face; SEE CONCEPT 716

grimace [v] *make a pained expression*
contort, deform, distort, frown, make a face, make a wry face, misshape, mouth, mug*, scowl, screw up one's face*, smirk, sneer; SEE CONCEPT 185

grime [n] *dirt*
crud*, dust, film, filth, gook*, gunk*, muck*, smudge, smut*, soil, soot, tarnish; SEE CONCEPT 260

grimy [adj] *dirty*
begrimed, besmirched, cruddy*, dingy*, filthy, foul, grubby*, grungy*, messy, mucky*, nasty, scuzzy*, sleazy*, smeared, smutty*, soiled, sooty, sordid, squalid, unclean; SEE CONCEPTS 485,621

grin [n/v] *smile widely*
beam, crack, simper, smirk; SEE CONCEPTS 185,716

grind [n] *tedious job*
chore, drudgery, groove*, grubwork*, hard work, labor, moil, pace, rote, routine, rut*, sweat*, task, toil, travail, treadmill*; SEE CONCEPT 362

grind [v1] *crush, pulverize*
abrade, atomize, attenuate, beat, bray, chop up, comminute, crumble, crumple, disintegrate, file, granulate, grate, kibble*, levigate, mill, pestle, pound, powder, pulverize*, rasp, reduce, roll out*, scrape, shiver, triturate; SEE CONCEPTS 186,204

grind [v2] *sharpen*
abrade, file, give an edge to, gnash, grate, grit, polish, rub, sand, scrape, smooth, whet; SEE CONCEPTS 186,215

grind [v3] *oppress*
afflict, annoy, harass, hold down, hound, persecute, plague, trouble, tyrannize, vex; SEE CONCEPTS 14,130

grip [n1] *clasp, embrace*
anchor, brace, catch, cinch, cincture, clamp, clamping, clench, clinch, clutch, coercion, constraint, crushing, duress, enclosing, enclosure, fastening, fixing, grapnel, grapple, grasp, gripe, handclasp, handgrip, handhold, handshake, hold, hook, ligature, lug, purchase, restraint, snatch, squeeze, strength, tenure, vise, wrench; SEE CONCEPT 191

grip [n2] *perception, understanding*
clutches*, comprehension, control, domination, grasp, hold, influence, keeping, ken, possession, power, tenure; SEE CONCEPT 409

grip [v1] *hold tightly*
clap a hand on, clasp, clench, clinch, clutch, get one's hands on*, grasp, latch on to*, lay hands on, nab, seize, snag, snatch, take, take hold of; SEE CONCEPT 191

grip [v2] *entrance, enchant*
catch up, compel, engross, enthrall, fascinate, hold, hypnotize, involve, mesmerize, rivet, spellbind; SEE CONCEPTS 7,11,22

gripe [n1] *complaint*
ache, aching, affliction, disorder, distress, grievance, groan, grouse, grumble, illness, indisposition, infirmity, moan, objection, pain, pang; SEE CONCEPTS 52,278,313

gripe [n2] *strong hold*
clamp, clasp, clench, clinch, clutch, crunch, grab, grapple, grasp, grip, tenure; SEE CONCEPT 191

gripe [v1] *complain*
bellyache*, blow off*, carp, crab*, fuss, groan, grouch, grouse, grumble, kvetch*, moan, murmur, mutter, nag, squawk, take on*, whine, yammer*, yawp*; SEE CONCEPTS 44,52

gripe [v2] *pain, annoy*
ache, bother, compress, cramp, disturb, hurt, irritate, pinch, press, squeeze, vex; SEE CONCEPTS 7,19,219,246

grisly [adj] *horrifying*
abominable, appalling, awful, blood-stained, bloody, disgusting, dreadful, eerie, frightful, ghastly, grim, grody*, gross*, gruesome, hideous, horrible, horrid, lurid, macabre, sanguine, shocking, sick, sickening, terrible, terrifying, yucky*; SEE CONCEPTS 537,544,570

grit [n1] *particles of dirt*
dust, foreign matter, gravel, lumps, pebbles, powder, sand; SEE CONCEPTS 260,831

grit [n2] *courage, determination*
backbone, daring, doggedness, fortitude, gameness, guts*, hardihood, intestinal fortitude*, mettle, moxie*, nerve, perseverance, pluck, resolution, spine*, spirit, spunk, steadfastness, tenacity, toughness; SEE CONCEPTS 411,633

gritty [adj1] *granular*
abrasive, branlike, calculous, crumbly, dusty, friable, grainy, gravelly, in particles, loose, lumpy, permeable, porous, powdery, pulverant, rasping, rough, sabulous, sandy, scratchy; SEE CONCEPT 606

gritty [adj2] *brave*
courageous, determined, dogged, game*, hardy, mettlesome, plucky*, resolute, spirited, steadfast, tenacious, tough; SEE CONCEPTS 401,404

groan [n] *moan, complaint*
cry, gripe, grouse, grumble, grunt, objection, sigh, sob, whine; SEE CONCEPTS 278,595

groan [v] *moan, complain*
bemoan, cry, gripe, grouse, grumble, keen, lament, mumble, murmur, object, sigh, whine; SEE CONCEPTS 44,52,77

groggy [adj] *dizzy, stunned*
befuddled, confused, dazed, dopey*, drunken, faint, hazy, out of it*, punch-drunk*, punchy*, reeling, shaky, slaphappy*, staggering, stupefied, swaying, tired, unsteady, weak, whirling, wobbly, woozy*; SEE CONCEPT 314

groom [n1] *man being married*
benedict, bridegroom, fiancé, husband, spouse, suitor; SEE CONCEPT 419

groom [n2] *stable attendant; servant*
equerry, hostler, stable person; SEE CONCEPTS 348,419

groom [v] *make ready, prepare physically*
brush, clean, coach, comb, curry, dress, drill, educate, lick into shape*, make attractive, make presentable, nurture, preen, prep*, pretty up*, prim, prime, primp, put through grind*, put through mill*, ready, refine, refresh, rub down, shape up, sleek, slick up*, smarten up*, spiff up*, spruce

gr
gr

up*, tend, tidy, train, turn out; SEE CONCEPTS 162,202,285

groove [n1] *channel, indentation*

canal, corrugation, crease, crimp, cut, cutting, depression, ditch, flute, fluting, furrow, gouge, gutter, hollow, incision, notch, pucker, rabbet, rut, scallop, score, scratch, slit, trench, valley; SEE CONCEPT 513

groove [n2] *daily routine*

daily grind*, grind, pace, rote, rut*, same old stuff*, schtick*, slot*; SEE CONCEPTS 362,677

grope [v] *feel about for*

cast about, examine, explore, feel blindly, finger*, fish*, flounder, fumble, grabble, handle, manipulate, poke, pry, root, scrabble, search, touch; SEE CONCEPTS 34,216,612

gross [n] *total, whole*

aggregate, all, entirety, sum, sum total, totality; SEE CONCEPTS 344,837

gross [adj1] *large, fat*

adipose, big, bulky, chubby*, corpulent, dense, fleshy, great, heavy, hulking, husky, lumpish, massive, obese, overweight, porcine, portly, stout, thick, unwieldy, weighty; SEE CONCEPTS 773,781

gross [adj2] *whole*

aggregate, all, before deductions, before tax, complete, entire, in sum, outright, total, whole ball of wax*, whole enchilada*, whole nine yards*, whole schmeer*, whole shebang*; SEE CONCEPT 785

gross [adj3] *crude, vulgar*

barnyard*, boorish, breezy, callous, carnal, cheap, coarse, corporeal, crass, dull, fleshly, foul, ignorant, improper, impure, indecent, indelicate, inelegant, insensitive, in the gutter*, lewd, loud-mouthed, low, low-minded, lustful, obscene, offensive, rank, raunchy, raw, ribald, rough, rude, scatological, sensual, sexual, sleazy*, smutty*, swinish*, tasteless, ugly, uncouth, uncultured, undiscriminating, unfeeling, unrefined, unseemly, unsophisticated, voluptuous; SEE CONCEPTS 267,542,545

gross [adj4] *obvious, apparent*

absolute, arrant, blatant, capital, complete, downright, egregious, excessive, exorbitant, extreme, flagrant, glaring, grievous, heinous, immoderate, inordinate, manifest, out-and-out*, outrageous, outright*, perfect, plain, rank, serious, shameful, sheer, shocking, unmitigated, unqualified, utter; SEE CONCEPTS 535,576

gross [v] *bring in as total*

earn, make, take in; SEE CONCEPTS 330,351

grotesque [adj] *ugly, misshapen*

aberrant, abnormal, absurd, antic, bizarre, deformed, distorted, eerie, extravagant, extreme, fanciful, fantastic, flamboyant, freakish, grody*, gross*, incongruous, ludicrous, malformed, monstrous, odd, outlandish, perverted, preposterous, queer, ridiculous, strange, surrealistic, uncanny, unnatural, weird, whimsical; SEE CONCEPTS 486,537,579

grouch [n] *person who complains a lot*

bear*, bellyacher*, bug*, crab*, crank, crosspatch*, curmudgeon, faultfinder, griper, grouser, growler, grumbler, grump*, kicker*, malcontent, moaner, sorehead*, sourpuss*, whiner; SEE CONCEPTS 412,423

grouch [v] *complain a lot*

bellyache*, carp, find fault, gripe, grouse, grumble, moan, murmur, mutter, scold, whine; SEE CONCEPT 52

grouchy [adj] *complaining, irritable*

cantankerous*, cross, crusty*, discontented, grumbling, grumpy*, ill-tempered, irascible, peevish, petulant, querulous, snappy, sulky, surly, testy; SEE CONCEPTS 267,401

ground [n] *earth, land*

arena, dirt, dust, field, landscape, loam, old sod, park, real estate, sand, sod, soil, terra firma, terrain, turf; SEE CONCEPT 509

ground [v1] *base, set; educate*

acquaint, bottom, coach, discipline, establish, familiarize, fit, fix, found, indoctrinate, inform, initiate, instruct, introduce, predicate, prepare, prime, qualify, rest, settle, stay, teach, train, tutor; SEE CONCEPTS 18,285

ground [v2] *restrict; drop in place*

bar, beach, bring down, dock, down, fell, floor, knock down, land, level, mow down*, prevent, strand; SEE CONCEPTS 130,181

groundless [adj] *without reason, justification*

baseless, bottomless, causeless, chimerical, empty, false, flimsy, foundationless, gratuitous, idle, illogical, illusory, imaginary, unauthorized, uncalled-for, unfounded, unjustified, unprovoked, unsupported, unwarranted; SEE CONCEPTS 267,552,582

grounds [n1] *estate, domain*

acreage, area, campus, country, district, environs, fields, gardens, habitat, holding, land, lot, premises, property, real estate, realm, sphere, spot, terrace, terrain, territory, tract, zone; SEE CONCEPTS 508,516

grounds [n2] *basis, premise*

account, antecedent, argument, base, bedrock*, call, cause, chapter and verse*, demonstration, determinant, dope*, evidence, excuse, factor, footing, foundation, goods*, groundwork, inducement, info*, information*, infrastructure, justification, motive, numbers, occasion, pretext, proof, rationale, reason, root*, seat, straight stuff*, substratum, test, testimony, trial, underpinning, wherefore, why, whyfor; SEE CONCEPTS 274,661

grounds [n3] *sediment*

deposit, dregs, grouts, leavings, lees, precipitate, precipitation, residue, settlings; SEE CONCEPT 260

groundwork [n] *basis, fundamentals*

ABCs*, background, base, bedrock*, cornerstone*, footing, foundation, ground, infrastructure, origin, preliminaries, preparation, root, substratum, underpinning, understructure; SEE CONCEPTS 274,442,660,661

group [n] *number of individuals collectively*

accumulation, aggregation, assemblage, assembly, association, assortment, band, batch, battery, bevy, body, bunch, bundle, cartel, category, chain, circle, class, clique, clot, club, clump, cluster, clutch, collection, combination, combine, company, conglomerate, congregation, coterie, covey, crew, crowd, faction, formation, gang, gathering, grade, league, lot, mess, organization, pack, parcel, party, passel, platoon, pool, posse, set, shooting match, society, sort, suite, syndicate, troop, trust; SEE CONCEPTS 391,432

group [v] *bring together*

arrange, assemble, associate, band together, bracket, bunch, bunch up*, cluster, collect, congregate, consort, corral, crowd, gang around*, gang up*, gather, get together, hang out*, harmonize, huddle, link, make the scene*, meet, organize, poke, punch*, round up*, scare up*, systematize; SEE CONCEPTS *109,114*

group [v2] *classify, sort*
arrange, assemble, associate, assort, bracket, categorize, class, dispose, file, gather, marshal, order, organize, pigeonhole*, put together, range, rank; SEE CONCEPTS *18,84,158*

grove [n] *cluster of trees*
brake, coppice, copse, covert, forest, orchard, plantation, spinney, stand, thicket, wood, woodland; SEE CONCEPTS *429,517*

grovel [v] *abase, demean oneself*
apple-polish*, beg, beg for mercy, beseech, blandish, bootlick*, bow and scrape*, brown-nose*, butter up*, cater to, court, cower, crawl, creep, cringe, crouch, eat crow*, eat dirt*, eat humble pie*, fall all over*, fawn*, flatter, humble oneself, humor, implore, kiss one's feet*, kneel, kowtow*, make much of*, make up to*, pamper, play up to*, prostrate, revere, snivel, soft-soap*, stoop, suck up to*, truckle*, wheedle, yes*; SEE CONCEPTS *384,633*

grow [v] *become larger, evolve*
abound, advance, age, amplify, arise, augment, become, branch out, breed, build, burgeon, burst forth, come, come to be, cultivate, develop, dilate, enlarge, expand, extend, fill out, flourish, gain, germinate, get bigger, get taller, heighten, increase, issue, luxuriate, mature, maturate, mount, multiply, originate, pop up*, produce, propagate, pullulate, raise, ripen, rise, shoot*, spread, spring up, sprout, stem, stretch, swell, thicken, thrive, turn, vegetate, wax*, widen; SEE CONCEPTS *427,469,704,775*

growl [n/v] *animal-like sound*
bark, bellow, gnarl, gnarr, grumble, grunt, howl, moan, roar, roll, rumble, snarl, thunder; SEE CONCEPTS *77,595*

grown-up [n] *adult*
gentleman, grown person, lady, mam, man, Miss, mister, Mr., Mrs., Ms., woman; SEE CONCEPT *424*

growth [n1] *development, progress*
advance, advancement, aggrandizement, augmentation, beefing up*, boost, buildup, crop, cultivation, enlargement, evolution, evolvement, expansion, extension, fleshing out*, flowering, gain, germination, heightening, hike, improvement, increase, maturation, maturing, multiplication, produce, production, proliferation, prosperity, rise, sprouting, stretching, success, surge, swell, thickening, unfolding, up, upping, vegetation, waxing*, widening; SEE CONCEPTS *427,469,703,704,775*

growth [n2] *tumor*
cancer, cancroid, excrescence, fibrousness, fibrous tissue, fungus, lump, mole, outgrowth, parasite, polyp, swelling, thickening, wen; SEE CONCEPT *306*

grub [n1] *larva*
caterpillar, entozoon, maggot, worm; SEE CONCEPT *398*

grub [n2] *food*
chow*, comestibles, eats*, edibles, feed, nosh*, nurture, provisions, rations, sustenance, viands, victuals, vittles*; SEE CONCEPTS *457,460*

grub [v] *dig, uncover*
beat, break, burrow, clean, clear, comb, delve, excavate, ferret, fine-tooth-comb*, forage, hunt, poke, prepare, probe, pull up, rake, ransack, root, rummage, scour, search, shovel, spade, unearth, uproot; SEE CONCEPTS *178,216*

grub [v2] *work very hard*
drudge, grind, labor, moil, plod, slave, slog, sweat, toil; SEE CONCEPT *100*

grubby [adj] *dirty, disheveled*
besmeared, black, filthy, foul, frowzy*, grimy, grungy*, impure, messy, mucky*, nasty, scruffy, scuzzy*, seedy, shabby, sloppy, slovenly, smutty*, soiled, sordid, squalid, unclean, uncleanly, unkempt, untidy, unwashed; SEE CONCEPTS *485,621*

grudge [n] *hard feelings*
animosity, animus, antipathy, aversion, bad blood*, bitterness, bone to pick*, dislike, enmity, grievance, hate, hatred, ill will, injury, injustice, malevolence, malice, maliciousness, malignancy, peeve, pet peeve*, pique, rancor, resentment, spite, spitefulness, spleen, venom; SEE CONCEPT *29*

grudge [v] *feel resentful; give unwillingly*
begrudge, be reluctant, be stingy*, complain, covet, deny, envy, hold back, mind, pinch, refuse, resent, stint; SEE CONCEPT *21*

grueling [adj] *difficult, taxing*
arduous, backbreaking, brutal, chastening, crushing, demanding, excruciating, exhausting, fatiguing, fierce, grinding, hairy*, hard, harsh, heavy*, laborious, punishing, racking, severe, stiff, strenuous, tiring, torturous, trying; SEE CONCEPT *565*

gruesome [adj] *horrible, awful*
abominable, appalling, daunting, fearful, frightful, ghastly, grim, grisly, grody*, gross*, hideous, horrendous, horrid, horrific, horrifying, loathsome, lurid, macabre, monstrous, morbid, offensive, repugnant, repulsive, shocking, sick*, spine-tingling*, terrible, terrifying, ugly, weird*; SEE CONCEPTS *485,548*

gruff [adj1] *bad-tempered, rude*
abrupt, bearish, blunt, boisterous, boorish, brusque, churlish, crabbed*, crabby*, crude, crusty*, curt, discourteous, dour, fierce, grouchy*, grumpy*, ill-natured, impolite, morose, nasty, offhand, rough, harsh, saturnine, short, snappy*, snippy*, sour, sullen, surly, truculent, uncivil, ungracious, unmannerly; SEE CONCEPTS *267,401*

gruff [adj2] *rasping in sound*
cracked, croaking, croaky, grating, guttural, harsh, hoarse, husky, low, rough, throaty; SEE CONCEPT *594*

grumble [v1] *complain*
bellyache*, carp, find fault, fuss, gripe, groan, grouch*, grouse, kick, kvetch*, moan, protest, pule, repine, scold, snivel*, squawk*, whine; SEE CONCEPTS *44,52*

grumble [v2] *murmur, rumble*
bark, croak, gnarl, gnar, growl, grunt, gurgle, mumble, mutter, roar, roll, snap, snarl, snuffle, splutter, whine; SEE CONCEPTS *65,77*

grumpy [adj] *in a bad mood*
bad-tempered, cantankerous*, crabby*, cross, crotchety, disgruntled, dissatisfied, griping, grouchy*, grumbling, irritable, peevish, pettish, petulant, querulous, sulky, sullen, surly, testy, truculent; SEE CONCEPTS *401,403*

guarantee [n] *pledge, promise*
agreement, assurance, attestation, bail, bargain, bond, certainty, certificate, certification, charter,

collateral, contract, covenant, deposit, earnest, gage, guaranty, insurance, lock, oath, pawn, pipe, recognizance, security, sure thing*, surety, testament, token, undertaking, vow, warrant, warranty, word, word of honor; SEE CONCEPTS 71,271,685

guarantee [v] *pledge, promise*
affirm, angel, answer for, assure, attest, aver, back, bankroll, be surety for, bind oneself, certify, confirm, cosign, endorse, ensure, evidence, evince, get behind*, give bond, grubstake, guaranty, insure, juice*, maintain, make bail*, make certain, make sure, mortgage, pick up the check*, pick up the tab*, protect, prove, reassure, secure, sign for, stake, stand behind*, stand up for*, support, swear, testify, vouch for, wager, warrant, witness; SEE CONCEPTS 71,110

guaranteed [adj] *made certain*
affirmed, approved, ascertained, assured, attested, bonded, certified, confirmed, endorsed, for a fact, for sure, have a lock on*, insured, on ice*, pledged, plighted, protected, sealed, secured, sure, sure enough*, sure-fire*, warranted; SEE CONCEPT 535

guard [n1] *protector*
bouncer*, chaperon, chaperone, chaser*, convoyer, custodian, defender, escort, guardian, lookout, picket, sentinel, sentry, shepherd, shield, ward, warden, watch, watchperson; SEE CONCEPT 348

guard [n2] *defense*
aegis, armament, armor, buffer, bulwark, pad, protection, rampart, safeguard, screen, security, shield, ward; SEE CONCEPT 712

guard [v] *protect, watch*
attend, baby-sit, bulwark, chaperon, chaperone, conduct, convoy, cover, cover up, defend, escort, fend, keep, keep an eye on*, keep in view, keep under surveillance, look after, lookout, mind, observe, oversee, patrol, police*, preserve, ride shotgun for*, safeguard, save, screen, secure, see after, shelter, shepherd, shield, shotgun, stonewall*, superintend, supervise, tend; SEE CONCEPTS 96,134

guarded [adj] *suspicious*
attentive, cagey, calculating, canny, careful, cautious, chary, circumspect, discreet, gingerly, leery, noncommittal, on the lookout*, overcautious, prudent, reserved, restrained, reticent, safe, vigilant, wary, watchful, with eyes peeled*; SEE CONCEPT 542

guardian [n] *keeper, protector*
angel*, attendant, baby-sitter, bird dog*, cerberus, champion, chaperon, chaperone, conservator, cop*, curator, custodian, defender, escort, guard, keeper, nurse, overseer, paladin, patrol, preserver, safeguard, sentinel, shepherd, sitter, sponsor, superintendent, supervisor, trustee, vigilante, warden, watchdog*; SEE CONCEPTS 414,423

guess [n] *belief, speculation*
assumption, ballpark figure*, conclusion, conjecture, deduction, divination, estimate, fancy, feeling, guesstimate*, guesswork, hunch*, hypothesis, induction, inference, judgment, notion, opinion, postulate, postulation, prediction, presumption, presupposition, reckoning, shot*, shot in the dark*, sneaking suspicion*, stab*, supposal, supposition, surmisal, surmise, suspicion, theory, thesis, view; SEE CONCEPT 689

guess [v] *try to figure out; imagine*
believe, calculate, chance, conjecture, dare say, deduce, deem, divine, estimate, fancy*, fathom, go out on a limb*, guesstimate*, happen upon*, hazard*, hypothesize, infer, judge, jump to a conclusion*, lump it*, opine, penetrate, pick, postulate, predicate, predict, presume, pretend, reason, reckon, select, size up*, solve, speculate, suggest, suppose, surmise, survey, suspect, take a shot at*, take a stab at*, theorize, think, think likely, venture, work out*; SEE CONCEPT 28

guest [n] *person accommodated, given hospitality*
bedfellow, boarder, caller, client, companion, company, customer, frequenter*, habitué, inmate, lodger, mate, out-of-towner*, partaker, patron, recipient, renter, roomer, sharer, sojourner, tenant, transient, vacationer, visitant, visitor; SEE CONCEPT 423

guidance [n] *counseling*
advice, auspices, conduct, conduction, control, conveyance, direction, government, help, instruction, intelligence, leadership, management, navigation, supervision, teaching; SEE CONCEPTS 75,274,278

guide [n1] *something that or someone who leads*
adviser, attendant, captain, chaperon, cicerone, conductor, controller, convoy, counselor, criterion, design, director, docent, escort, example, exemplar, exhibitor, genie, genius, guiding spirit, guru, ideal, inspiration, lead, leader, lodestar, mentor, model, monitor, paradigm, pathfinder, pattern, pilot, pioneer, rudder, scout, standard, superintendent, teacher, usher, vanguard; SEE CONCEPTS 348,423,686

guide [n2] *information, instructions*
ABCs*, beacon*, bellwether*, bible, catalog, chapter and verse*, clue, compendium, directory, enchiridion, guidebook, guiding light*, handbook, hot lead*, key, landmark, lodestar, manual, mark, marker, no-no's*, pointer, print, sign, signal, signpost, telltale, the book*, the numbers*, tip-off*, vade mecum; SEE CONCEPT 274

guide [v] *direct, lead*
accompany, advise, attend, beacon*, chaperon, command, conduct, contrive, control, convoy, counsel, coxswain, educate, engineer, escort, govern, handle, have a handle on*, influence, instruct, manage, maneuver, marshal, navigate, oversee, pilot, quarterback*, regulate, route, rule, see, shepherd, show, show the way, spearhead*, steer, superintend, supervise, sway, teach, trailblaze*, train, usher; SEE CONCEPTS 75,110,117,187

guild [n] *association, fellowship*
club, company, corporation, federation, group, interest group, league, lodge, order, organization, profession, society, sodality, trade, union; SEE CONCEPTS 381,387

guile [n] *slyness, cleverness*
artfulness, artifice, chicanery, craft, craftiness, cunning, deceit, deception, dirty dealing*, dirty pool*, dirty trick*, dirty work*, dishonesty, dissemblance, dissimulation, double-cross*, duplicity, foul play*, jive*, run-around*, ruse, sellout*, sharp practice*, stab in the back*, treachery, trickery, trickiness, wiliness; SEE CONCEPTS 645,657

guileless [adj] *honest*
aboveboard, artless, candid, frank, genuine, ingenuous, innocent, naive, natural, open, simple, simple-minded, sincere, straightforward, truthful,

guilt [n] *blame; bad conscience over responsibility*
answerability, blameworthiness, contrition, crime, criminality, culpability, delinquency, dereliction, disgrace, dishonor, error, failing, fault, indiscretion, infamy, iniquity, lapse, liability, malefaction, malfeasance, malpractice, misbehavior, misconduct, misstep, offense, onus, peccability, penitence, regret, remorse, responsibility, self-condemnation, self-reproach, shame, sin, sinfulness, slip, solecism, stigma, transgression, wickedness, wrong; SEE CONCEPTS *101,532, 645,690*

guiltless [adj] *blameless, not responsible*
clean, clear, crimeless, exemplary, faultless, free, good, immaculate, impeccable, inculpable, innocent, irreproachable, pure, righteous, sinless, spotless, unimpeachable, unsullied, untainted, untarnished, virtuous; SEE CONCEPT *545*

guilty [adj] *blameworthy; found at fault*
accusable, caught, censurable, censured, chargeable, condemned, conscience-stricken, contrite, convictable, convicted, criminal, culpable, damned, delinquent, depraved, doomed, erring, evil, felonious, hangdog*, impeached, incriminated, in error, iniquitous, in the wrong, judged, liable, licentious, offending, on one's head*, out of line*, proscribed, regretful, remorseful, reprehensible, responsible, rueful, sentenced, sheepish, sinful, sorry, wicked, wrong; SEE CONCEPT *545*

guise [n] *appearance, pretense*
air, aspect, behavior, cloak, color, cover, demeanor, disguise, disguisement, dress, facade, face, false front*, false show*, fashion, form, front, mask, mien, mode, pose, posture, role, seeming, semblance, shape, show, showing, simulacrum; SEE CONCEPTS *645,716*

gulf [n1] *sea inlet*
basin, bay, bayou, bight, cove, firth, harbor, slough, sound, whirlpool; SEE CONCEPTS *509,514*

gulf [n2] *deep, gaping hole*
abyss, breach, cave, cavity, chasm, cleft, crevasse, depth, depths, distance, expanse, gap, gulch, hiatus, hollow, opening, pit, ravine, rent, rift, separation, shaft, split, void, well, whirlpool; SEE CONCEPTS *509,513*

gullible [adj] *naive, trusting*
being a sucker*, believing, biting, credulous, easily taken in*, easy mark*, falling hook line and sinker*, foolish, green*, innocent, kidding oneself*, mark*, silly, simple, sucker, susceptible, swallowing whole*, taken in*, taking the bait*, trustful, tumbling for*, unskeptical, unsophisticated, unsuspecting, wide-eyed*; SEE CONCEPTS *402,542*

gully [n] *ravine, ditch*
channel, chase, chasm, crevasse, culvert, gutter, notch, trench, watercourse; SEE CONCEPTS *509,513*

gulp [n] *swallow*
choke, draught, gasp, mouthful, swig, swill; SEE CONCEPT *185*

gulp [v] *eat, drink fast*
belt*, choke down*, chugalug*, consume, devour, dispatch, dispose, drop*, englut, gobble*, guzzle*, imbibe, ingurgitate, inhale*, pour, quaff, scarf down*, slop*, slosh*, stuff, swallow, swig, swill, take in, toss off*, wolf*, wolf down*; SEE CONCEPTS *169,185*

gum [n] *sticky substance*
adhesive, amber, cement, cohesive substance, exudate, glue, mucilage, paste, pitch, plaster, resin, rosin, tar, wax; SEE CONCEPT *466*

gumption [n] *nerve, initiative*
ability, acumen, astuteness, cleverness, commonsense, discernment, enterprise, get-up-and-go*, good sense, horse sense*, industry, judgment, perspicaciousness, perspicacity, resourcefulness, sagaciousness, sagacity, savvy, sense, shrewdness, spirit, wisdom, wit; SEE CONCEPT *411*

gun [n] *weapon that shoots*
blaster*, cannon, difference*, equalizer*, flintlock, forty-five*, handgun, hardware*, howitzer, magnum, mortar, musket, 9 mm.*, ordnance, peashooter*, persuader*, piece*, pistol, revolver, rifle, rod*, Saturday-night special*, shotgun, thirty-eight*, Uzi*; SEE CONCEPT *500*

gurgle [n/v] *burble, murmur*
babble, bubble, crow, lap, plash, purl, ripple, slosh, splash, wash; SEE CONCEPTS *65,595*

guru [n] *mentor, guide*
authority, guiding light*, leader, master, sage, teacher, tutor; SEE CONCEPT *350*

gush [n] *outpouring*
burst, cascade, flood, flow, flush, issue, jet, run, rush, spate, spout, spring, spurt, stream, surge; SEE CONCEPTS *467,687*

gush [v1] *pour out*
burst, cascade, emanate, emerge, flood, flow, flush, issue, jet, pour, roll, run, rush, sluice, spew, spout, spring, spurt, stream, surge, well; SEE CONCEPT *179*

gush [v2] *speak with overwhelming enthusiasm*
babble*, blather, carry on about*, chatter, effervesce, effuse, enthuse, fall all over*, go on about*, jabber, make a to-do over*, overstate, prate, prattle, rave; SEE CONCEPT *49*

gust [n] *rush, eruption*
access, blast, blow, breeze, burst, explosion, fit, flare-up, flurry, gale, outburst, paroxysm, passion, puff, sally, squall, storm, surge; SEE CONCEPTS *524,787*

gusto [n] *great enthusiasm*
appetite, appreciation, ardor, brio, delectation, delight, enjoyment, exhilaration, fervor, heart, liking, palate, passion, pleasure, relish, savor, taste, verve, zeal, zest; SEE CONCEPTS *411,657*

gusty [adj] *windy*
airy, blowy, blustering, blustery, breezy, hearty, robust, squally, stormy, tempestuous; SEE CONCEPT *525*

gut [n] *stomach and abdomen*
belly, bowels, duodenum, entrails, innards, intestines, paunch, tripes, tummy*, venter, viscera; SEE CONCEPT *393*

gut [adj] *intuitive*
basic, deep-seated, emotional, heartfelt, innate, inner, instinctive, interior, internal, intimate, involuntary, natural, spontaneous, unthinking, visceral, viscerous; SEE CONCEPT *403*

gut [v] *clean out, strip*
bowel, decimate, despoil, dilapidate, disembowel, draw, dress, empty, eviscerate, exenterate, loot, pillage, plunder, ransack, ravage, rifle, sack; SEE CONCEPTS *165,211*

gutless [adj] *timid*
abject, chicken*, chicken-hearted*, coward, cowardly, craven, faint-hearted*, feeble, irresolute, lily-livered*, pusillanimous, spineless*, submis-

gu
gu

sive, weak, wimpy*, yellow*, yellow-bellied*; SEE CONCEPTS 404,542

guts [n] *nerve, boldness*
audacity, backbone*, courage, daring, dauntlessness, effrontery, forcefulness, fortitude, grit*, hardihood, heart*, intestinal fortitude*, mettle, moxie*, pluck, resolution, sand*, spine*, spirit, spunk*, willpower; SEE CONCEPTS 411,657

gutsy [adj] *bold, brave*
courageous, determined, gallant, game*, indomitable, intrepid, mettlesome, plucky, resolute, spirited, spunky*, staunch, unfearful, valiant; SEE CONCEPTS 404,542

gutter [n] *ditch*
channel, conduit, culvert, dike, drain, duct, eaves, fosse, funnel, gully, moat, pipe, runnel, sewer, sluice, spout, sulcation, trench, trough, tube, watercourse; SEE CONCEPTS 440,513

guttural [adj] *deep in sound*
glottal, grating, gravely, growling, gruff, harsh, hoarse, husky, inarticulate, low, rasping, rough, sepulchral, thick, throaty; SEE CONCEPT 594

guzzle [v] *drink down fast*
bolt*, booze*, carouse*, cram, devour, englut, gobble*, gorge, gormandize, imbibe, ingurgitate, knock back*, quaff, slop*, slosh*, soak, swig, swill, tipple; SEE CONCEPT 169

gymnasium [n] *arena for sports, recreation*
alley, amphitheater, athletic club, center, circus, coliseum, course, exercise room, field house, floor, gym, health club, hippodrome, pit, recreation center, ring, rink, spa, stadium, sweatshop*, theater; SEE CONCEPTS 364,438,439

gymnastics [n] *acrobatic exercise*
aerobatics, balance beam, bars, body-building, calisthenics, floor exercise, free exercise, gym, horse, rings, trampoline, trapeze, tumbling, vaulting, workout; SEE CONCEPT 363

gyrate [v] *revolve*
circle, circulate, circumduct, gyre, pirouette, purl, roll, rotate, spin, spiral, turn, twirl, whirl, whirligig; SEE CONCEPTS 147,149

H

habit [n1] *tendency, practice*
addiction, bent, bias, constitution, consuetude, convention, custom, dependence, disposition, fashion, fixation, fixed attitude, frame of mind*, gravitation, groove, habitude, hangup, impulsion, inclination, make-up*, manner, mannerism, mode, nature, obsession, pattern, penchant, persuasion, praxis, predisposition, proclivity, proneness, propensity, quirk, routine, rule, rut, second nature*, set, style, susceptibility, thing*, turn, usage, use, way, weakness, wont; SEE CONCEPT 644

habit [n2] *dress, clothing, often for a particular purpose*
apparel, costume, garb, garment, habiliment, riding clothes, robe, vestment; SEE CONCEPT 451

habitat/habitation [n] *place where someone resides*
abode, accommodations, address, apartment, berth, biosphere, cave, commorancy, condo, condominium, co-op, den, digs*, domicile, dwelling,

element, environment, fireside, flat, haunt*, haven, hearth, hole*, home, home plate*, homestead, house, housing, locale, locality, lodging, neck of the woods*, nest, nook, occupancy, occupation, pad*, place, quarters, range, residence, residency, roof*, roost*, seat*, settlement, site, stamping ground*, stomping ground*, surroundings, terrain, territory, turf; SEE CONCEPT 515

habitual [adj] *usual, established*
accepted, accustomed, addicted, addicting, automatic, chronic, common, confirmed, constant, continual, conventional, customary, cyclic, disciplined, familiar, fixed, frequent, hardened, ingrained, inveterate, iterated, iterative, mechanical, methodical, natural, normal, ordinary, perfunctory, permanent, perpetual, persistent, practiced, recurrent, regular, reiterative, repeated, repetitious, rooted, routine, seasoned, set, standard, steady, systematic, traditional, wonted; SEE CONCEPTS 530,547

habituate [v] *prepare, accustom*
acclimate, acclimatize, addict, adjust, break in, condition, confirm, devote, discipline, endure, familiarize, harden, inure, make used to, school, season, take to, tolerate, train; SEE CONCEPTS 35,202

hack [n1] *person who does easy work for money*
drudge*, greasy grind*, grind*, hireling, lackey*, old pro*, plodder*, servant, slave, workhorse*; SEE CONCEPT 348

hack [n2] *taxicab*
cab, carriage, coach, hackney, taxi, vehicle; SEE CONCEPT 505

hack [n3/v] *cut without care*
chop, clip, fell, gash, hackle, hew, lacerate, mangle, mutilate, notch, slash, whack; SEE CONCEPTS 137,176

hacker [n] *someone proficient at computers, especially a hobbyist*
application programmer, computer architect, computer designer, computer jock, key puncher, operator, programmer, systems analyst, systems engineer, system software specialist, systems programmer, technician; SEE CONCEPTS 360,366

hackneyed [adj] *clichéd, tired*
antiquated, banal, common, commonplace, conventional, corny*, everyday, familiar tune*, hokey*, moth-eaten*, obsolete, old, old-chestnut*, old-hat*, old-saw*, outdated, outmoded, out-of-date, overworked, pedestrian*, played-out*, quotidian, run-of-the-mill*, stale, stereotyped, stock, threadbare*, timeworn, trite, unoriginal, well-worn, worn-out*; SEE CONCEPTS 267,530

haggard [adj] *worn, weakened*
ashen, careworn, drawn, emaciated, exhausted, faded, fagged, fatigued, fretted, gaunt, ghastly, lank, lean, pale, pallid, pinched, scraggy, scrawny, shrunken, skinny, spare, starved, thin, tired, wan, wasted, weak, wearied, worn-down, wrinkled; SEE CONCEPTS 314,406,491

haggle [v] *bicker, quarrel*
argue, bargain, barter, beat down*, cavil, chaffer, deal, dicker*, dispute, hammer out a deal*, horse-trade*, make a deal*, palter, quibble, squabble, wrangle; SEE CONCEPT 46

hail [v] *torrent*
barrage, bombardment, broadside, cannonade, hailstorm, pelting, rain, salvo, shower, storm, volley; SEE CONCEPTS 189,524

hail [v1] *call to, yell for*
accost, address, flag, flag down*, greet, hello, holler*, salute, shoulder, shout, signal, sing out*, speak to, wave down, welcome, whistle down*, whistle for*, yawp*, yoo-hoo*; SEE CONCEPTS 47,74,77

hail [v2] *honor, salute*
acclaim, acknowledge, applaud, cheer, commend, compliment, exalt, glorify, greet, hear it for*, kudize, praise, recognize, recommend, root for*, welcome; SEE CONCEPT 69

hail [v3] *come from; originate*
be a native of, be born in, begin, claim as birth-place; SEE CONCEPT 648

hail [v4] *rain down on*
barrage, batter, beat down upon, bombard, pelt, shower, storm, volley; SEE CONCEPT 526

hair [n] *threadlike growth on animate being*
beard, bristle, cilium, coiffure, cowlick, cut, down, eyebrow, eyelash, feeler, fiber, filament, fluff, fringe, frizzies*, fur, grass, haircut, hair-style, lock, mane, mop*, moustache, quill, ruff, shock, sideburn, split ends, strand, thatch, tress, tuft, vibrissa, villus, whiskers, wig, wool; SEE CONCEPT 392

hairless [adj] *without growth on body part*
bald, baldheaded, beardless, clean-shaven, cue ball*, depilated, egghead*, glabrate, glabrescent, glabrous, shaved, shaven, shorn, skinhead*, smooth, smooth-faced, tonsured, whiskerless; SEE CONCEPT 406

hairstyle [n] *cut, style of a head of hair*
afro*, beehive*, blow dry*, bob*, bouffant, braid, brushcut, bubble*, bun, coiffure, crewcut, cut, do*, dreadlocks, ducktail, fade, feather cut, flat-top*, flip, haircut, hairdo, headdress, horse tail, mohawk, natural, pageboy, pigtails, pixie, pony-tail, razor cut; SEE CONCEPT 718

hairy [adj1] *having much hair*
bearded, bewhiskered, bristly, bushy, downy, fleecy, flocculent, fluffy, furry, fuzzy, hirsute, lanate, pileous, piliferous, pilose, pubescent, rough, shaggy, stubbly, tufted, unshaven, un-shorn, villous, whiskered, woolly; SEE CONCEPT 406

hairy [adj2] *dangerous*
chancy, difficult, hazardous, jeopardous, perilous, risky, scary, treacherous, uncertain, unhealthy, unsound, wicked; SEE CONCEPT 548

hale [adj] *strong and healthy*
able-bodied, alive and kicking*, blooming, fit, fit as a fiddle*, flourishing, healthy, hearty, husky, in fine fettle*, in the pink*, right, robust, sane, sound, stout, strapping, strong, trim, vigorous, well, well-conditioned, wholesome; SEE CONCEPTS 314,489

half [n] *one of two equal parts of a whole*
bisection, division, fifty percent, fraction, hemi-sphere, moiety; SEE CONCEPT 835

half [adj] *partial*
bisected, divided, even-steven*, fifty-fifty*, frac-tional, halved, incomplete, limited, moderate, partly; SEE CONCEPT 785

half-baked [adj] *stupid; not thought through*
backward, batty*, birdbrained*, blockheaded*, boneheaded*, brainless, crazy, dumb, feeble-minded, foolish, harebrained*, idiotic, ignorant, ill-conceived, imbecile, impractical, indiscreet, moronic, poorly planned, retarded, senseless, short-sighted, silly, slow, sophomoric, underde-veloped, unformed, witless; SEE CONCEPTS 403,529,548

half-breed [n] *mixed creation*
amalgam, blend, combination, conglomeration, cross, cross-breed, hodgepodge*, hybrid, medley, melange, miscegnation, mishmash*, mule, mutt*; SEE CONCEPTS 260,394

halfhearted [adj] *without enthusiasm*
apathetic, cool, impassive, indifferent, irresolute, lackluster, listless, lukewarm, neutral, passive, perfunctory, spiritless, tame, tepid, unenthusias-tic, uninterested; SEE CONCEPTS 401,542

halfway [adj] *not complete; in the middle*
betwixt and between*, center, centermost, cen-tral, equidistant, imperfect, intermediate, medial, median, mid*, middlemost, midway, moderate, part, partial, part-way, smack dab*, smack in the middle*; SEE CONCEPTS 531,586

halfway [adv] *not complete; in the middle*
comparatively, compromising, conciliatory, half the distance, imperfectly, incompletely, in part, insufficiently, medially, middling, midway, mod-erately, nearly, partially, partly, pretty*, rather, restrictedly, to a degree, to some extent, to the middle, unsatisfactorily; SEE CONCEPTS 531,586

hall [n1] *corridor*
anteroom, entrance, entranceway, entry, foyer, gallery, hallway, lobby, pass, passage, passage-way, room, rotunda, vestibule; SEE CONCEPT 440

hall [n2] *room for large affairs*
amphitheater, arena, armory, assembly room, au-ditorium, ballroom, casino, chamber, church, gal-lery, gym, gymnasium, lounge, lyceum, mart, meeting place, refectory, salon, stateroom, the-ater; SEE CONCEPTS 438,439,441,448

hallmark [n] *symbol, authentication*
badge, certification, device, emblem, endorse-ment, indication, mark, ratification, seal, sign, signet, stamp, sure sign, telltale sign, trademark; SEE CONCEPTS 284,628

hallowed [adj] *holy, revered*
anointed, beatified, blessed, consecrated, dedi-cated, divine, enshrined, holy, honored, inviola-ble, sacred, sacrosanct, sanctified, unprofane; SEE CONCEPT 568

hallucinate [v] *imagine vividly*
blow one's mind*, daydream, envision, fantasize, freak out*, have visions, head trip*, hear voices*, trip*; visualize; SEE CONCEPT 34

hallucination [n] *dream, delusion*
aberration, apparition, fantasy, figment of the imagination*, head trip*, illusion, mirage, phan-tasm, phantasmagoria, phantom, trip*, vision, wraith; SEE CONCEPTS 529,532,690

halo [n] *ring of light*
aura, aureola, aureole, aurora, corona, crown of light, glory, halation, nimbus, radiance; SEE CON-CEPTS 624,628

halt [n] *end, stoppage*
arrest, break, break-off*, close, cutoff, freeze*, grinding halt, impasse, interruption, layoff, letup, pause, screaming halt*, screeching halt*, stand, standstill, stop, termination; SEE CONCEPT 119

halt [v1] *stop, cause to stop*
adjourn, arrest, balk, bar, block, blow the whistle on*, break off*, bring to an end, bring to stand-still, call it a day*, cease, cease fire, check, close down, come to an end, cool it*, curb*, cut short, desist, deter, draw up, drop anchor*, end, frus-trate, hamper, hold at bay*, hold back, impede,

gu
ha

intermit, interrupt, obstruct, pause, pull up*, punctuate, put a cork in*, rest, stall, stand still, stay, stem, stop, suspend, terminate, wait; SEE CONCEPTS *121,234*

halt [*v2*] *hesitate, stutter*
be defective, dither, falter, hobble, limp, pause, shilly-shally*, stagger, stammer, stumble, vacillate, waver, whiffle*, wiggle-waggle*; SEE CONCEPTS *234,721,804*

halting [*adj*] *hesitant*
awkward, bumbling, clumsy, doubtful, faltering, gauche, imperfect, indecisive, inept, irresolute, labored, limping, lumbering, maladroit, slow, stammering, stumbling, stuttering, tentative, uncertain, unhandy, vacillating, vacillatory, wavering, wooden*; SEE CONCEPTS *534,550*

halve [*v*] *cut in half*
bisect, divide equally, reduce by fifty percent, share equally, split in two; SEE CONCEPT *98*

hamburger [*n*] *ground beef sandwich*
beefburger, burger, cheeseburger, chopped beefsteak, ground chuck, ground round, ground sirloin, Salisbury steak; SEE CONCEPTS *457,460*

hammer [*v*] *beat, hit*
bang, batter, bear down, clobber, defeat, drive, drub, fashion, forge, form, knock, make, pound, pummel, shape, strike, tap, thrash, trounce, wallop, whack, whomp; SEE CONCEPT *189*

hammer away/hammer into [*v*] *work hard at*
continue, drive home*, drub into*, drudge, drum into*, endeavor, grind*, grind into*, impress upon, instruct, keep on, peg away*, persevere, persist, plug away*, pound away*, repeat, stick to*, try hard, try repeatedly, work; SEE CONCEPTS *68,87,239*

hammer out [*v*] *bring to a conclusion*
accomplish, bring about, build, complete, construct, erect, establish, excogitate, fight through, finish, form, make, negotiate, produce, settle, set up, sort out, thrash out*, work out; SEE CONCEPTS *91,706*

hamper [*n*] *basket for storage*
bassinet, carton, crate, creel, laundry basket, pannier; SEE CONCEPT *494*

hamper [*v*] *impede, restrict*
baffle, balk, bar, bind, block, check, clog, cramp, cramp one's style*, cumber, curb, drag one's feet*, embarrass, encumber, entangle, fetter, foil, frustrate, get in the way*, hamstring*, handicap, hang up*, hinder, hobble, hog-tie*, hold up*, inconvenience, inhibit, interfere with, leash, obstruct, prevent, restrain, retard, shackle, slow down, stymie, thwart, tie, tie one's hands*, tie up, trammel; SEE CONCEPT *130*

hand [*n1*] *appendage at end of human arm, including fingers*
duke*, extremity, fin*, fist, grasp, grip, ham*, hold, hook, metacarpus, mitt*, palm, paw*, phalanges, shaker*; SEE CONCEPT *392*

hand [*n2*] *person who does labor*
aide, artificer, artisan, craftsperson, employee, help, helper, hired person, laborer, operative, roustabout, worker; SEE CONCEPT *348*

hand [*n3*] *help, aid*
ability, agency, assistance, control, direction, guidance, influence, instruction, knack, lift, part, participation, relief, share, skill, succor, support; SEE CONCEPTS *110,630*

hand [*n4*] *handwriting*
calligraphy, chirography, longhand, script; SEE CONCEPT *79*

hand [*n5*] *round of applause*
clap, handclapping, ovation, thunderous reception; SEE CONCEPT *189*

handbag [*n*] *person's carryall*
backpack, bag, clutch, evening bag, grip, hide, knapsack, leather, pocketbook, portmanteau, purse, reticule; SEE CONCEPT *446*

handbook [*n*] *document giving instruction, information*
bible, compendium, directory, enchiridion, encyclopedia, fundamentals, guide, guidebook, instruction book, manual, text, textbook, vade mecum; SEE CONCEPT *280*

handful [*adj*] *a small quantity*
few, scattering, small number, smattering, snow, spattering, sprinkling; SEE CONCEPT *789*

handicap [*n1*] *disadvantage*
affliction, baggage*, barrier, block, burden, detriment, disability, drawback, encumbrance, hangup*, hindrance, impairment, impediment, injury, limitation, load, millstone, obstacle, psychological baggage*, restriction, shortcoming, stumbling block*; SEE CONCEPTS *666,674*

handicap [*n2*] *advantage*
bulge, edge*, favor, head start*, odds, penalty, points*, start, upper hand*, vantage; SEE CONCEPT *693*

handicap [*v*] *give disadvantage*
burden, cripple, encumber, hamper, hamstring*, hinder, hog-tie*, hold back, impede, limit, put out of commission*, restrict, sideline*, take out*; SEE CONCEPTS *130,246*

handicraft [*n*] *artwork, skill*
achievement, art, artifact, artisanship, calling, craft, craftship, creation, design, handiwork, invention, métier, product, production, profession, result, trade, vocation; SEE CONCEPTS *259,630*

handle [*n1*] *something to grasp*
arm, bail, crank, ear, grasp, haft, handgrip, helve, hilt, hold, holder, knob, shaft, stem, stock, tiller; SEE CONCEPTS *445,502,831*

handle [*n2*] *nickname*
appellation, byname, byword, cognomen, denomination, designation, moniker, name, nomen, sobriquet, style, title; SEE CONCEPT *683*

handle [*v1*] *touch*
check, examine, feel, finger*, fondle, grasp, hold, manipulate, maul, palpate, paw*, pick up, poke, test, thumb*, try; SEE CONCEPT *612*

handle [*v2*] *manage, take care of*
administer, advise, apply, behave toward, bestow, call the signals*, command, conduct, control, cope with, cut the mustard*, deal with, direct, discuss, dispense, dominate, employ, exercise, exploit, get a handle on*, govern, guide, hack it*, make out*, make the grade*, maneuver, manipulate, operate, play, ply, run things, serve, steer, supervise, swing, take, treat, use, utilize, wield, work; SEE CONCEPTS *91,117*

handle [*v3*] *carry as merchandise*
deal in, market, offer, retail, sell, stock, trade, traffic in; SEE CONCEPT *345*

handling [*n*] *management*
administration, approach, care, charge, conduct, direction, manipulation, running, styling, superintendence, supervision, treatment; SEE CONCEPT *117*

hand out [v] *give to others*
bestow, deal out, commend, devote, disburse, dish out, dispense, disseminate, distribute, donate, give away, give out, hand over, mete, present, provide; SEE CONCEPTS 108,140

hand over [v] *give back; release*
abandon, cede, commend, commit, consign, deliver, dispense, donate, entrust, feed, find, fork out*, fork up*, give up, hand, leave, present, provide, relegate, relinquish, supply, surrender, transfer, turn over, waive, yield; SEE CONCEPTS 108,131

handsome [adj1] *attractive*
admirable, aristocratic, athletic, august, beautiful, becoming, clean-cut, comely, dapper, elegant, fair, fashionable, fine, good-looking, graceful, impressive, lovely, majestic, noble, personable, pulchritudinous, robust, sharp, smart, smooth, spruce, stately, strong, stylish, suave, virile, well-dressed, well-proportioned; SEE CONCEPT 579

handsome [adj2] *abundant*
ample, bounteous, bountiful, considerable, extensive, full, generous, gracious, large, lavish, liberal, magnanimous, munificent, openhanded, plentiful, princely, sizable, unsparing; SEE CONCEPT 781

handsomely [adv] *abundantly*
amply, bountifully, generously, lavishly, liberally, magnanimously, munificently, nobly, plentifully, richly; SEE CONCEPT 781

handwriting [n] *the way a person writes*
autography, calligraphy, chicken scratch*, chirography, ductus, griffonage, hand, hieroglyphics, longhand, manuscript, manuscription, mark, pencraft, penscript, scratching*, scrawl, scribble, script, scription, scrivenery, scrivening, style, writing; SEE CONCEPTS 284,625,628

handy [adj1] *nearby*
accessible, adjacent, at hand, available, close, close-at-hand, closeby, convenient, near, near-at-hand, on hand, ready, within reach; SEE CONCEPT 586

handy [adj2] *easy to use*
adaptable, advantageous, available, beneficial, central, convenient, functional, gainful, helpful, manageable, neat, practicable, practical, profitable, ready, serviceable, useful, utile, wieldy; SEE CONCEPT 560

handy [adj3] *adept physically*
able, adroit, clever, deft, dexterous, expert, fit, ingenious, nimble, proficient, ready, skilled, skillful; SEE CONCEPT 527

hang [v1] *suspend or be suspended*
adhere, attach, beetle, be fastened, be in mid-air, be loose, bend, be pendent, be poised, bow, cling, cover, dangle, deck, decorate, depend, drape, drift, droop, drop, fasten, fix, flap, float, flop, furnish, hold, hover, impend, incline, lean, loll, lop, lower, nail, overhang, pin, project, remain, rest, sag, stay up, stick, swing, tack, trail, wave; SEE CONCEPTS 144,201,746

hang [v2] *kill by suspension from a rope*
execute, gibbet, hoist, lynch, noose, scrag, send to the gallows, stretch*, string up*, swing*; SEE CONCEPT 252

hang [v3] *depend on future action*
await, be conditional upon, be contingent on, be dependent on, be determined by, be in limbo, be in suspense, cling, hinge, pend, rest, turn on; SEE CONCEPT 681

hang about/hang around/hang out [v] *associate with; be residing in*
abide, affect, dally, frequent, get along with, haunt, have relations with, linger, live, loiter, reside, resort, roam, spend time, stand around, swell, tarry, waste time; SEE CONCEPTS 114,226

hanger-on [n] *person who attends the powerful for status or benefit*
dependent, flunky*, follower, freeloader*, lackey*, leech*, nuisance, parasite, sponger*, sycophant, truckler*; SEE CONCEPT 423

hang on [v] *continue, endure*
be tough, carry on, cling, clutch, go on, grasp, grip, hold fast, hold on, hold out, persevere, persist, remain; SEE CONCEPTS 23,239

hangout [n] *place for socializing*
bar, den*, dive*, haunt*, home, honky-tonk*, joint*, purlieu, resort, stomping ground*, watering hole*; SEE CONCEPTS 439,447,449

hangover [n] *result of heavy drinking*
aftereffect, big head*, delirium tremens, drunkenness, DTs*, headache, morning after*, shakes*, under the weather*, willies*, withdrawal; SEE CONCEPT 316

hang-up [n] *preoccupation*
block, difficulty, dilemma, disturbance, impasse, inhibition, obsession, predicament, problem, reserve, restraint, thing; SEE CONCEPTS 532, 674,690

hanker after/hanker for [v] *desire strongly*
ache, covet, crave, hunger, itch, long, lust, partial to, pine, sigh, thirst, want, wish, yearn, yen; SEE CONCEPT 20

hankering [n] *strong desire*
ache, craving, druthers*, fire in belly*, hunger, itch*, longing, munchies*, pining, thirst, urge, want, weakness, wish, yearning, yen; SEE CONCEPTS 20,709

hanky-panky [n] *mischief*
chicane, chicanery, deception, devilry, double-dealing, fourberie, fraud, funny business*, knavery, machinations, monkey business*, sharp practice*, shenanigans*, skullduggery*, subterfuge, trickery; SEE CONCEPTS 59,384

haphazard [adj] *without plan or organization*
accidental, aimless, all over the map*, any old way*, any which way*, arbitrary, careless, casual, chance, designless, desultory, devil-may-care*, disorderly, disorganized, erratic, fluke, helter-skelter*, hit-or-miss*, incidental, indiscriminate, irregular, loose, offhand, purposeless, random, reckless, slapdash, slipshod, spontaneous, sudden, unconcerned, unconscious, unconsidered, uncoordinated, unexpected, unmethodical, unorganized, unpremeditated, unsystematic, unthinking, willy-nilly*; SEE CONCEPTS 535,581

hapless [adj] *unfortunate*
behind the eightball*, cursed, hexed, ill-fated, ill-starred, infelicitous, jinxed, jonah*, loser, luckless, miserable, poor fish*, sad sack*, snakebit*, star-crossed*, unhappy, unlucky, untoward, voodooed*, woeful, wretched; SEE CONCEPT 548

happen [v] *come to pass; occur*
appear, arise, arrive, become a fact, become known, become of, befall, be found, betide, bump, chance, come about, come after, come into being, come into existence, come off, crop up*, develop, down, ensue, eventuate, fall, follow, go on, hit, issue, light, luck, materialize, meet, pass,

ha
ha

present itself, proceed, recur, result, shake, smoke*, spring, stumble, stumble upon, supervene, take effect, take place, transpire, turn out, turn up, what goes*; SEE CONCEPT 4

happening [n] *occurrence*
accident, adventure, affair, case, chance, circumstance, episode, event, experience, go*, incident, milestone, occasion, phenomenon, proceeding, scene, thing*; SEE CONCEPT 4

happily [adv1] *with joy, pleasure*
agreeably, blissfully, blithely, brightly, buoyantly, cheerfully, contentedly, delightedly, delightfully, devotedly, elatedly, enthusiastically, exhilaratingly, exultantly, freely, gaily, gladly, gleefully, graciously, heartily, hilariously, jovially, joyfully, joyously, laughingly, lightheartedly, lightly, lovingly, merrily, optimistically, peacefully, playfully, sincerely, smilingly, sportively, vivaciously, willingly, with relish, with zeal, zestfully; SEE CONCEPTS 403,542

happily [adv2] *successfully*
appropriately, aptly, auspiciously, favorably, felicitously, fortunately, gracefully, propitiously, prosperously, providentially, satisfyingly, seasonably, swimmingly, well; SEE CONCEPT 548

happiness [n] *high spirits, satisfaction*
beatitude, blessedness, bliss, cheer, cheerfulness, cheeriness, content, contentment, delectation, delight, delirium, ecstasy, elation, enchantment, enjoyment, euphoria, exhilaration, exuberance, felicity, gaiety, geniality, gladness, glee, good cheer, good humor, good spirits, hilarity, hopefulness, joviality, joy, jubilation, laughter, lightheartedness, merriment, mirth, optimism, paradise, peace of mind, playfulness, pleasure, prosperity, rejoicing, sanctity, seventh heaven*, vivacity, well-being; SEE CONCEPT 410

happy [adj1] *in high spirits; satisfied*
blessed, blest, blissful, blithe, can't complain*, captivated, cheerful, chipper, chirpy, content, contented, convivial, delighted, ecstatic, elated, exultant, flying high*, gay, glad, gleeful, gratified, intoxicated, jolly, joyful, joyous, jubilant, laughing, light, lively, looking good*, merry, mirthful, on cloud nine*, overjoyed, peaceful, peppy, perky, playful, pleasant, pleased, sparkling, sunny, thrilled, tickled, tickled pink*, up, upbeat, walking on air*; SEE CONCEPT 403

happy [adj2] *lucky*
accidental, advantageous, appropriate, apt, auspicious, befitting, casual, convenient, correct, effective, efficacious, enviable, favorable, felicitous, fitting, fortunate, incidental, just, meet, nice, opportune, promising, proper, propitious, providential, right, satisfactory, seasonable, successful, suitable, timely, well-timed; SEE CONCEPT 558

happy-go-lucky [adj] *carefree and untroubled*
blithe, casual, cheerful, cool, devil-may-care*, easy, easygoing, feckless, free-minded, heedless, improvident, insouciant, irresponsible, lackadaisical*, lighthearted, nonchalant, reckless, unconcerned; SEE CONCEPTS 404,542

harangue [n] *long lecture*
address, chewing out*, declamation, diatribe, discourse, exhortation, hassle, jeremiad, oration, philippic, reading out*, screed, sermon, speech, spiel*, spouting, tirade; SEE CONCEPTS 51,278

harangue [v] *give a long lecture*
accost, address, apostrophize, buttonhole*, chew out*, declaim, exhort, get on a soapbox*, go on about*, hold forth, orate, perorate, rant, rave, soapbox*, spiel*, spout, stump, talk to, yell at; SEE CONCEPT 51

harass [v] *badger*
annoy, attack, bait, bedevil, beleaguer, bother, bug*, burn*, despoil, devil*, distress, disturb, eat*, exasperate, exhaust, fatigue, foray, get to*, give a bad time*, give a hard time*, gnaw*, harry, hassle, heckle, hound*, intimidate, irk, irritate, jerk around*, macerate, maraud, noodge*, pain*, perplex, persecute, pester, plague, raid, rattle one's cage*, ride, strain, stress, tease, tire, torment, trouble, try, vex, weary, work on*, worry; SEE CONCEPTS 7,14,19

harassment [n] *badgering*
aggravation, annoyance, bedevilment, bother, bothering, disturbance, exasperation, hassle, irking, irritation, molestation, nuisance, persecution, perturbation, pestering, provocation, provoking, torment, trouble, vexation, vexing; SEE CONCEPTS 14,313

harbinger [n] *indication*
augury, forerunner, foretoken, herald, messenger, omen, portent, precursor, sign, signal; SEE CONCEPTS 74,284,529

harbor [n1] *place for storing boats in the water*
anchorage, arm, bay, bight, breakwater, chuck, cove, dock, embankment, firth, gulf, haven, inlet, jetty, landing, mooring, pier, port, road, roadstead, wharf; SEE CONCEPTS 439,509,514

harbor [n2] *place for seclusion*
asylum, cover, covert, harborage, haven, port, refuge, retreat, sanctuary, sanctum, security, shelter; SEE CONCEPT 515

harbor [v1] *hide, protect*
accommodate, board, bunk, conceal, defend, domicile, entertain, guard, hold back, house, lodge, nurse, nurture, provide refuge, put up, quarter, relieve, safeguard, screen, secrete, secure, shelter, shield, suppress, withhold; SEE CONCEPTS 134,188

harbor [v2] *hold in imagination*
believe, brood over, cherish, cling to, consider, entertain, foster, hold, imagine, maintain, nurse, nurture, regard, retain; SEE CONCEPT 17

hard [adj1] *rocklike*
adamantine, callous, compact, compacted, compressed, concentrated, consolidated, dense, firm, hardened, impenetrable, indurate, indurated, inflexible, iron*, packed, rigid, rocky, set, solid, stiff, stony, strong, thick, tough, unyielding; SEE CONCEPT 604

hard [adj2] *difficult, exhausting*
arduous, backbreaking, bothersome, burdensome, complicated, demanding, difficile, distressing, effortful, exacting, exhaust, fatiguing, formidable, grinding, hairy*, heavy*, Herculean*, intricate, involved, irksome, knotty*, labored, laborious, mean, merciless, murder, onerous, rigorous, rough, rugged, scabrous, serious, severe, slavish, sticky, strenuous, terrible, tiring, toilful, toilsome, tough, troublesome, unsparing, uphill*, uphill battle*, wearing, wearisome, wearying; SEE CONCEPTS 529,538,565

hard [adj3] *cruel, ruthless*
acrimonious, angry, antagonistic, austere, bitter, bleak, brutal, callous, cold, cold-blooded*, cold fish*, dark, disagreeable, distressing, dour, exacting, grievous, grim, hard as nails*, hard-boiled*, harsh, hostile, inclement, intemperate, intolera-

ble, obdurate, painful, perverse, pitiless, rancorous, resentful, rigorous, rugged, severe, stern, strict, stringent, stubborn, thick-skinned*, tough, unfeeling, unjust, unkind, unpleasant, unrelenting, unsparing, unsympathetic, vengeful; SEE CONCEPTS 401,542

hard [adj4] *true, indisputable*
absolute, actual, bare, cold, definite, down-to-earth, genuine, plain, positive, practical, pragmatic, realistic, sure, undeniable, unvarnished, verified; SEE CONCEPTS 535,582

hard [adv1] *with great force*
actively, angrily, animatedly, boisterously, briskly, brutally, cruelly, earnestly, energetically, ferociously, fiercely, forcibly, frantically, furiously, heavily, intensely, keenly, like fury, madly, meanly, painfully, powerfully, relentlessly, rigorously, roughly, rowdily, savagely, seriously, severely, sharply, spiritedly, sprightly, stormily, strongly, tumultuously/tumultuously, turbulently, uproariously, urgently, viciously, vigorously, violently, vivaciously, wildly, with all one's might; SEE CONCEPT 540

hard [adv2] *with determination*
assiduously, closely, diligently, doggedly, earnestly, exhaustively, industriously, intensely, intensively, intently, painstakingly, persistently, searchingly, sharply, steadily, strenuously, thoroughly, unremittingly, untiringly; SEE CONCEPT 538

hard [adv3] *with difficulty*
agonizingly, arduously, awkwardly, badly, burdensomely, carefully, cumbersomely, cumbrously, distressingly, exhaustingly, gruelingly, hardly, harshly, inconveniently, laboriously, painfully, ponderously, roughly, severely, strenuously, tiredly, toilsomely, unwieldily, vigorously, with great effort; SEE CONCEPT 565

hard [adv4] *with resentment*
bitterly, hardly, keenly, rancorously, reluctantly, slowly, sorely; SEE CONCEPT 403

hard [adv5] *in a fixed manner*
close, fast, firm, firmly, solidly, steadfastly, tight, tightly; SEE CONCEPTS 488,586

hard-core [adj] *dedicated*
determined, devoted, die-hard*, dyed-in-the-wool*, explicit, extreme, faithful, intransigent, obstinate, resolute, rigid, staunch, steadfast, stubborn, uncompromising, unwavering, unyielding; SEE CONCEPTS 535,542

harden [v1] *make or become solid*
amalgamate, anneal, bake, brace, buttress, cake, calcify, callous, cement, close, clot, coagulate, compact, congeal, consolidate, contract, crystallize, curdle, densify, dry, firm, fix, fortify, fossilize, freeze, gird, indurate, jell, nerve, ossify, petrify, precipitate, press, reinforce, set, settle, solidify, starch, steel, stiffen, strengthen, temper, thicken, toughen, vitrify; SEE CONCEPTS 250,469

harden [v2] *accustom*
acclimate, acclimatize, adapt, adjust, blunt, brutalize, callous, callus, case-harden, climatize, coarsen, conform, deaden, develop, discipline, dull, embitter, habituate, indurate, inure, make callous, numb, paralyze, render insensitive, roughen, season, steel, stiffen, strengthen, stun, stupefy, teach, train; SEE CONCEPTS 35,235

hardened [adj] *unfeeling*
accustomed, benumbed, callous, case-hardened, coldhearted*, contemptuous, cruel, disdainful,

habituated, hard-as-nails*, hard-bitten*, hard-boiled*, hardhearted*, heartless, impenetrable, impious, inaccessible, indurated, inured, irreverent, obdurate, obtuse, prepared, resistant, seasoned, steeled, toughened, unashamed, unbending, uncaring, uncompassionate, unemotional, unrepenting, unsubmissive; SEE CONCEPTS 404,542

hardhearted [adj] *cold, cruel*
brutish, callous, cold-blooded*, coldhearted*, hard, hard-boiled*, heartless, indifferent, inhuman, insensitive, intolerant, merciless, obdurate, pitiless, stony, uncaring, uncompassionate, unemotional, unfeeling, unkind, unsympathetic; SEE CONCEPTS 401,404

hardly [adv] *scarcely; with difficulty*
almost inconceivably, almost not, barely, by a hair, by no means, comparatively, detectably, faintly, gradually, imperceptibly, infrequently, just, little, no more than, not a bit, not at all, not by much, not likely, not markedly, not measurably, not much, not notably, not noticeably, not often, not quite, no way, once in a blue moon*, only, only just, perceptibly, practically, pretty near, rarely, scantily, seldom, simply, slightly, somewhat, sparsely, sporadically, with trouble; SEE CONCEPTS 541,552,771

hard-nosed/hardheaded [adj] *stubborn*
astute, bullheaded*, hard*, hard-boiled*, headstrong, intractable, levelheaded, locked in*, mulish, obstinate, pertinacious, perverse, pigheaded*, practical, pragmatic, rational, realistic, resolute, sensible, shrewd, sober, stand pat, tough, toughnut*, unsentimental, unyielding, willful; SEE CONCEPTS 404,542

hardship [n] *personal burden*
accident, adversity, affliction, asperity, austerity, calamity, case, catastrophe, curse, danger, destitution, difficulty, disaster, discomfort, distress, drudgery, fatigue, grief, grievance, hard knocks*, hazard, Herculean task*, injury, labor, mischance, misery, misfortune, need, oppression, peril, persecution, privation, rainy day*, rigor, rotten luck*, sorrow, suffering, toil, torment, tough break*, tough luck*, travail, trial, tribulation, trouble, uphill battle*, vicissitude, want, worry; SEE CONCEPTS 674,675

hardware [n] *tools; fittings, especially made of metal*
accouterments, appliances, fasteners, fixtures, household furnishings, housewares, implements, ironware, kitchenware, metalware, plumbing, utensils; SEE CONCEPTS 338,499

hardy [adj] *strong, tough*
able, able-bodied, acclimatized, brawny, burly, capable, enduring, firm, fit, fresh, hale, hardened, healthy, hearty, hefty, indefatigable, in fine fettle*, in good condition, in good shape, inured, lusty, mighty, muscular, physically fit, powerful, resistant, robust, rugged, seasoned, solid, sound, stalwart, staunch, stout, sturdy, substantial, tenacious, unflagging, vigorous, well; SEE CONCEPTS 314,485,489

harebrained [adj] *stupid, unthinking*
absurd, asinine, barmy, bizarre, careless, changeable, crazy, dizzy*, empty-headed*, featherbrained*, flighty, foolish, frivolous, giddy, half-baked*, heedless, inane, irresponsible, loony*, mindless, preposterous, rash, rattlebrained, reck-

ha
ha

less, scatterbrained*, unstable, unsteady, wacky*, wild; SEE CONCEPTS *402,529*

harm [*n*] *injury, evil*

abuse, banefulness, damage, deleteriousness, detriment, disservice, foul play*, hurt, ill, immorality, impairment, infliction, iniquity, loss, marring, mischance, mischief, misfortune, misuse, noxiousness, outrage, perniciousness, prejudice, ravage, ruin, ruination, sabotage, sin, sinfulness, vandalism, vice, violence, wear and tear*, wickedness, wrong; SEE CONCEPTS *309,674,728*

harm [*v*] *injure; cause evil*

abuse, blemish, bruise, cripple, crush, damage, dilapidate, discommode, disserve, do violence to, dump on*, get, hurt, ill-treat, impair, incommode, inconvenience, louse up*, maim, maltreat, mangle, mar, mess up*, misuse, molest, muck up*, mutilate, nick, outrage, prejudice, put down*, ruin, sabotage, sap*, scathe, shatter, shock, spoil, stab, tarnish, total, trample, traumatize, tweak*, undermine, vandalize, vitiate, wing*, wound, wreck, wrench, wrong, zing*; SEE CONCEPTS *7,19, 246,313*

harmful [*adj*] *injurious, hurtful*

adverse, bad, baleful, baneful, calamitous, cataclysmic, catastrophic, consumptive, corroding, corrupting, crippling, damaging, deleterious, destructive, detrimental, dire, disadvantageous, disastrous, evil, harassing, incendiary, inimical, internecine, malefic, malicious, malignant, menacing, mischievous, murderous, nocuous, noxious, painful, pernicious, pestiferous, pestilential, risky, ruinous, sinful, sinister, subversive, toxic, undermining, unhealthy, unsafe, unwholesome, virulent; SEE CONCEPT *537*

harmless [*adj*] *not injurious or dangerous*

controllable, disarmed, gentle, guiltless, hurtless, innocent, innocuous, innoxious, inoffensive, inoperative, kind, manageable, naive, nonirritating, nontoxic, painless, paper-tiger*, powerless, pussycat*, reliable, safe, sanitary, simple, soft*, softie*, sound, sure, trustworthy, unobjectionable, unoffensive; SEE CONCEPT *537*

harmonious [*adj*] *agreeable, corresponding; friendly*

accordant, adapted, amicable, balanced, compatible, concordant, congenial, congruous, consonant, coordinated, cordial, dulcet, euphonious, harmonic, harmonizing, in accord, in chorus, in concert, in harmony, in step, in tune, in unison, like, matching, mellifluous, melodic, melodious, mix, musical, of one mind*, on same wavelength*, peaceful, rhythmical, silvery, similar, simpatico, sonorous, suitable, sweet-sounding, symmetrical, sympathetic, symphonic, symphonious, tuneful; SEE CONCEPT *563*

harmonize [*v*] *correspond, match*

accord, adapt, adjust, agree, arrange, attune, be in unison, be of one mind*, blend, carol, chime with, cohere, combine, compose, cooperate, coordinate, correlate, fit in with*, integrate, orchestrate, proportion, reconcile, reconciliate, relate, set, sing, suit, symphonize, synthesize, tune, unify, unite; SEE CONCEPTS *77,664*

harmony [*n1*] *social agreement*

accord, affinity, amicability, amity, compatibility, concord, conformity, consensus, consistency, cooperation, correspondence, empathy, friendship, good will, kinship, like-mindedness, meeting of minds*, peace, rapport, sympathy, tranquility,

unanimity, understanding, unity; SEE CONCEPT *388*

harmony [*n2*] *correspondence, balance*

accord, agreement, articulation, chime, concord, concordance, conformance, conformity, congruity, consistency, consonance, fitness, form, integration, integrity, oneness, order, parallelism, proportion, regularity, suitability, symmetry, togetherness, tune, unity; SEE CONCEPT *664*

harmony [*n3*] *musical accordance*

arrangement, attunement, blend, blending, chime, chord, chorus, composition, concentus, concert, concinnity, concurrence, consonance, diapason, euphony, harmonics, mellifluousness, melodiousness, melody, organum, overtone, piece, polyphony, richness, symphony, triad, tune, tunefulness, unison, variety; SEE CONCEPTS *65,262,595*

harness [*n*] *gear for controlling an animal*

belt, equipment, strap, tack, tackle, trappings; SEE CONCEPT *496*

harness [*v*] *rein in; control*

accouter, apply, bind, bridle, channel, check, cinch, collar, constrain, couple, curb, domesticate, employ, equip, exploit, fasten, fetter, fit, furnish, gear, govern, hitch, hold, leash, limit, make productive, mobilize, muzzle, outfit, put in harness, render useful, rig, saddle, secure, strap, tackle, tame, tie, utilize, yoke; SEE CONCEPTS *94,130,191*

harrowing [*adj*] *dangerous, frightening*

agonizing, alarming, chilling, distressing, disturbing, excruciating, heartbreaking, heart-rending, nerve-racking, painful, racking, soaring, tearing, terrifying, tormenting, torturing, torturous, traumatic; SEE CONCEPTS *529,548*

harry [*v*] *pester, annoy*

attack, badger, bedevil, beleaguer, chivy, depredate, devastate, disturb, fret, gnaw, harass, hassle, irk, irritate, lay waste, molest, persecute, perturb, pillage, plague, plunder, ravage, sack, tease, torment, trouble, upset, vex, worry; SEE CONCEPTS *7,19*

harsh [*adj1*] *rough, crude (to the senses)*

acrid, asperous, astringent, bitter, bleak, cacophonous, caterwauling, clashing, coarse, cracked, craggy, creaking, croaking, disagreeing, discordant, dissonant, disturbing, earsplitting, flat, glaring, grating, grim, guttural, hard, hoarse, incompatible, jagged, jangling, jarring, noisy, not smooth, off-key*, out-of-key*, out-of-tune*, rasping, raucous, rigid, rugged, rusty, screeching, severe, sharp, sour, strident, stridulous, tuneless, uneven, unlevel, unmelodious, unmusical, unrelenting; SEE CONCEPTS *537,569*

harsh [*adj2*] *nasty, abusive*

austere, bitter, brutal, comfortless, cruel, cussed, discourteous, dour, grim, gruff, hairy*, hard, hard-boiled, hard-nosed*, hard-shell*, mean, pitiless, punitive, relentless, rude, ruthless, severe, sharp, stern, stringent, tough, uncivil, unfeeling, ungracious, unkind, unpleasant, unrelenting, wicked; SEE CONCEPTS *267,542*

harvest [*n*] *crops; taking in of crops*

autumn, by-product, consequence, cropping, effect, fall, fruitage, fruition, gathering, gathering, harvesting, harvest-time, ingathering, intake, output, produce, reaping, repercussion, result, return, season, storing, summer, yield, yielding; SEE CONCEPTS *257,338,429*

harvest [v] *gathering of produce*
accumulate, acquire, amass, bin, cache, collect, crop, cull, cut, garner, gather, get, glean, harrow, hoard, mow, pick, pile up, plow, pluck, reap, squirrel*, stash, store, stow, strip, take in; SEE CONCEPTS *142,257*

hash [n] *mess, mix-up*
assortment, clutter, confusion, hodgepodge*, hotchpotch*, jumble, litter, medley, melange, miscellany, mishmash*, muddle*, salmagundi*, shambles*, stew*; SEE CONCEPTS *260,432*

hassle [n] *problem, fight*
altercation, argument, bickering, bother, clamor, commotion, difficulty, disagreement, dispute, inconvenience, quarrel, row, run-in*, squabble, struggle, trial, trouble, try, tumult, turmoil, tussle, uproar, upset, whirl, wrangle; SEE CONCEPTS *46,106,674*

hassle [v] *bother, harass*
annoy, argue, argufy, badger, bedevil, beleaguer, bicker, dispute, dun, harry, hound, pester, plague, quibble, squabble, worry, wrangle; SEE CONCEPTS *14,16,46*

haste [n] *extreme speed, hurry*
alacrity, briskness, bustle, carelessness, celerity, dash, dispatch, drive, expedition, expeditiousness, fleetness, flurry, foolhardiness, hastiness, heedlessness, hurry-burly*, hurriedness, hustle, hustling, impatience, impetuosity, incautiousness, nimbleness, pace, precipitancy, precipitateness, prematureness, press, promptitude, promptness, quickness, rapidity, rapidness, rashness, recklessness, rush, scamper, scramble, scurry, scuttle, swiftness, urgency, velocity; SEE CONCEPTS *755,818*

hasten [v] *speed something; hurry*
accelerate, advance, bolt, bound, burn, bustle, clip*, cover ground*, dash, dispatch, expedite, express, flee, fly, gallop, get cracking*, get the lead out*, goad, haste, hie, hustle, leap, make haste, make tracks*, move quickly, not lose a minute*, pace, plunge, precipitate, press, push, quicken, race, run, rush, scamper, scoot, scurry, scuttle, shake a leg*, skip, sprint, spurt, step on it*, step up*, take wing*, tear, trot, urge, waste no time*, whip along*; SEE CONCEPTS *150,152*

hastily [adv] *with great speed*
agilely, apace, carelessly, double-quick, expeditiously, fast, flat-out*, heedlessly, hurriedly, impetuously, impulsively, lickety-split*, nimbly, on spur of the moment*, posthaste, precipitately, prematurely, promptly, quickly, rapidly, rashly, recklessly, speedily, straightaway, subito, suddenly, swiftly, thoughtlessly, too quickly, unpremeditatedly*; SEE CONCEPTS *544,588*

hasty [adj] *speedy; without much thought*
abrupt, agile, brash, breakneck*, brief, brisk, careless, chop-chop*, cursory, eager, expeditious, fast, fiery, fleet, fleeting, foolhardy, harefooted*, headlong, heedless, hurried, ill-advised, impatient, impetuous, impulsive, incautious, inconsiderate, madcap*, on the double*, passing, PDQ*, perfunctory, precipitate, prompt, pronto*, quick, quickened, quickie, rapid, rash, reckless, rushed, short, slambang*, slapdash*, snappy*, sudden, superficial, swift, thoughtless, urgent; SEE CONCEPTS *542,588,799*

hat [n] *covering for the head*
boater, bonnet, bowler, bucket, chapeau, fedora, headgear, headpiece, helmet, lid*, millinery, Panama, sailor*, skimmer, sombrero, Stetson, stove pipe*, straw*, tam, tam o'shanter*, ten-gallon*, topper*; SEE CONCEPT *451*

hatch [v] *create, plan*
bear, brainstorm*, breed, bring forth, brood, cause, come up with, conceive, concoct, contrive, cook up*, design, devise, dream up*, engender, formulate, generate, get up, give birth, incubate, induce, invent, lay eggs, make, make up, occasion, originate, parent, plot, prepare, procreate, produce, project, provoke, scheme, set, sire, spawn, spitball*, think up*, throw together*, trump up*, whip up*, work up*; SEE CONCEPTS *36,173,251*

hate [n] *extreme dislike*
abhorrence, abomination, anathema, animosity, animus, antagonism, antipathy, aversion, bête noire*, black beast*, bother, bugbear*, detestation, disgust, enmity, execration, frost*, grievance, gripe, hatred, horror, hostility, ill will, irritant, loathing, malevolence, malignity, mislike, nasty look, no love lost*, nuisance, objection, odium, pain, rancor, rankling, repugnance, repulsion, resentment, revenge, revulsion, scorn, spite, trouble, venom; SEE CONCEPT *29*

hate [v] *dislike very strongly*
abhor, abominate, allergic to*, anathematize, bear a grudge against, be disgusted with, be hostile to, be loath, be reluctant, be repelled by, be sick of, be sorry, can't stand*, contemn, curse, deprecate, deride, despise, detest, disapprove, disdain, disfavor, disparage, down on*, execrate, feel malice to, have an aversion to*, have enough of*, have no use for*, loathe, look down on, nauseate*, not care for*, object to, recoil from, scorn, shudder at, shun, spit upon*, spurn; SEE CONCEPT *29*

hateful [adj] *nasty, obnoxious*
abhorrent, abominable, accursed, awful, bitter, blasted, catty*, confounded, cursed, cussed, damnable, damned, despicable, despiteful, detestable, disgusting, evil, execrable, forbidding, foul, gross, heinous, horrid, infamous, invidious, loathsome, malevolent, malign, mean, odious, offensive, ornery*, pesky, pestiferous, repellent, repugnant, repulsive, resentful, revolting, shuddersome, spiteful, uncool*, undesirable, vicious, vile; SEE CONCEPTS *267,404*

hatred [n] *severe dislike*
abhorrence, abomination, acrimony, alienation, allergy to*, animosity, animus, antagonism, antipathy, aversion, bitterness, coldness, contempt, detestation, disapproval, disfavor, disgust, displeasure, distaste, enmity, envy, execration, grudge, hard feelings*, hate, horror, hostility, ignominy, ill will, invidiousness, loathing, malevolence, malice, malignance, militancy, no use for*, odium, pique, prejudice, rancor, repugnance, repulsion, revenge, revulsion, scorn, spite, spleen, venom; SEE CONCEPT *29*

haughtiness [n] *air of supremacy*
aloofness, arrogance, conceit, contempt, contemptuousness, disdain, disdainfulness, hauteur, insolence, loftiness, pomposity, pride, snobbishness, superbity, superciliousness; SEE CONCEPT *633*

haughty [adj] *arrogant*
assuming, cavalier*, conceited, contemptuous, detached, disdainful, distant, egotistic, egotistical, high, high and mighty*, hoity-toity*, imperious, indifferent, lofty, on high horse*,

ha ha

overbearing, overweening, proud, reserved, scornful, sniffy*, snobbish, snooty*, snotty*, stuck-up*, supercilious, superior, uppity*; SEE CONCEPT *401*

haul [n] *something obtained or moved*
booty, burden, cargo, catch, find, freight, gain, harvest, lading, load, loot*, payload*, spoils, takings*, yield; SEE CONCEPTS *337,338*

haul [v] *move, pull to another spot*
back, boost, bring, buck, carry, cart, convey, drag, draw, elevate, gun, heave, heel, hoist, hump, jag, lift, lug, pack, piggy back*, raise, rake, remove, ride, shift, shlep*, shoulder, tote, tow, trail, transport, trawl, truck, tug; SEE CONCEPTS *147,148*

haunt [n] *place for socializing*
abode, bar, clubhouse, cubbyhole*, den, dwelling, gathering place, habitat, hangout*, headquarters, home, lair, living quarters, locality, meeting place, niche, place, purlieu, range, rendezvous, resort, retreat, site, stomping ground*, trysting place, watering hole*; SEE CONCEPTS *435,516*

haunt [v1] *visit as a spirit*
agitate, agonize, annoy, appall, appear, bedevil, be ever present, beset, besiege, come back, disquiet, dwell, float, frighten, harass, harrow, hound*, hover, infest, inhabit, irritate, madden, manifest, materialize, molest, nettle, obsess, overrun, permeate, pervade, pester, plague, possess, prey on, rack*, reappear, recur, return, rise, spook*, stay with, tease, terrify, terrorize, torment, trouble, vex, voodoo*, walk, weigh on, worry; SEE CONCEPT *14*

haunt [v2] *spend a lot of time at*
affect, frequent, habituate, hang about*, hang around*, hang out*, infest, repair, resort, tarry at, visit; SEE CONCEPT *384*

have [v1] *be in possession*
accept, acquire, admit, annex, bear, carry, chalk up, compass, corner, enjoy, gain, get, get hands on*, get hold of*, have in hand, hog*, hold, include, keep, land, latch on to*, lock up*, obtain, occupy, own, pick up, possess, procure, receive, retain, secure, sit on*, take, take in, teem with; SEE CONCEPTS *124,142,710*

have [v2] *endure, bear*
allow, become, be compelled to, be forced to, be one's duty to, be up to, consider, enjoy, entertain*, experience, fall on, feel, know, leave, let, meet with, must, need, ought, permit, put up with*, rest with, see, should, suffer, sustain, think about, tolerate, undergo; SEE CONCEPTS *23,83,646*

have [v3] *contain*
comprehend, comprise, embody, embrace, encompass, include, involve, subsume, take in; SEE CONCEPTS *642,742*

have [v4] *cheat, trick*
buy off*, deceive, dupe*, fix*, fool, outfox, outmaneuver, outsmart, outwit, overreach, swindle, take in*, tamper with, undo*; SEE CONCEPTS *59,192*

have [v5] *bring into the world*
bear, beget, bring forth, deliver, give birth; SEE CONCEPT *374*

haven [n] *refuge, port*
anchorage, asylum, cover, covert, harbor, harborage, retreat, roadstead, sanctuary, sanctum, shelter; SEE CONCEPTS *435,515*

havoc [n] *chaotic situation*
calamity, cataclysm, catastrophe, chaos, confusion, damage, desolation, despoiling, destruction, devastation, dilapidation, disorder, disruption, loss, mayhem, plunder, rack and ruin*, ravages, ruination, shambles*, vandalism, waste, wreck, wreckage; SEE CONCEPT *674*

hazard [n1] *danger*
double trouble*, dynamite, endangerment, hot potato*, imperilment, jeopardy, peril, risk, risky business*, thin ice*, threat; SEE CONCEPT *675*

hazard [n2] *luck, chance*
accident, adventure, coincidence, dynamite, fling*, fluke*, go*, hundred-to-one*, long shot, lucky break*, lucky hit*, misfortune, mishap, possibility, risk, risky business*, stroke of luck*, toss-up, venture, wager, way the ball bounces*, way the cookie crumbles*; SEE CONCEPT *693*

hazard [v] *take a chance; risk*
adventure, conjecture, dare, endanger, gamble, go for broke*, go out on limb*, guess, imperil, jeopardize, presume, proffer, skate on thin ice*, speculate, stake, submit, suppose, take a plunge*, throw out, try, venture, volunteer, wager; SEE CONCEPTS *28,87*

hazardous [adj] *dangerous, unpredictable*
chancy, dicey*, difficult, hairy*, haphazard, hot*, insecure, parlous, perilous, precarious, risky, touchy, uncertain, unhealthy, unsafe, unsound, venturesome, wicked; SEE CONCEPT *548*

haze [n] *cloudy air*
brume, cloud, dimness, film, fog, fumes, ground clouds, haziness, indistinctness, miasma, mist, murk, obscurity, smog, smokiness, smother, soup*, steam, vapor; SEE CONCEPT *524*

hazy [adj1] *cloudy*
bleared, bleary, blurred, blurry, clouded, crepuscular, dim, dull, dusky, faint, foggy, frosty, fuliginous, fumy, fuzzy, gauzy, indefinite, indistinct, misty, murky, mushy*, nebulous, obfuscated, obfuscous, obscure, opaque, overcast, rimy, screened, shadowy, smoggy, smoky, soupy*, steaming, thick, unclear, vague, vaporous, veiled; SEE CONCEPT *525*

hazy [adj2] *confused*
dazed, dizzy, dreamy, groggy, ill-defined, indefinite, indistinct, muddled, murky, nebulous, obscure, stuporous, tranced, uncertain, unclear, unintelligible, unsound, vague, whirling; SEE CONCEPTS *402,529*

head [n1] *top part of an animate body*
attic*, belfry*, brain, coconut*, cranium, crown, dome*, gray matter, noggin*, noodle*, pate, scalp, skull, thinker*, think tank*, top story*, upper story*, upstairs*; SEE CONCEPT *392*

head [n2] *leader*
boss, captain, chief, chieftain, commander, commanding officer, director, dominator, executive, honcho*, lead-off person*, manager, officer, president, principal, superintendent, supervisor, top dog*; SEE CONCEPT *347*

head [n3] *top part*
apex, banner, beak, bill, cap, cork, crest, crown, heading, headline, height, peak, pitch, point, promontory, streamer, summit, tip, vertex; SEE CONCEPT *836*

head [n4] *front, beginning*
commencement, first place, fore, forefront, fountainhead, origin, rise, source, start, van, vanguard; SEE CONCEPTS *648,727*

head [n5] *ability, intelligence*
aptitude, aptness, bent, brains, capacity, faculty, flair, genius, gift, intellect, knack, mentality, mind, talent, thought, turn, understanding; SEE CONCEPTS *409,630*

head [n6] *turning point*
acme, climax, conclusion, crisis, culmination, end; SEE CONCEPT *832*

head [adj] *most important; chief*
arch, champion, first, foremost, front, highest, leading, main, pioneer, preeminent, premier, prime, principal, stellar, supreme, topmost; SEE CONCEPTS *568,574*

head [v] *manage, oversee*
address, be first, be in charge, command, control, direct, dominate, go first, govern, guide, hold sway over*, lead, lead the way*, pioneer, precede, rule, run, supervise; SEE CONCEPT *117*

headlong [adj] *dangerous, reckless*
abrupt, brash, breakneck, daredevil, daring, foolhardy, hasty, hurried, impetuous, impulsive, inconsiderate, precipitant, precipitate, rash, rough, rushing, sudden, tempestuous, thoughtless; SEE CONCEPTS *542,588*

headstrong [adj] *stubborn*
bullheaded*, contrary, determined, foolhardy, froward, hard-core*, hard-nosed, hard-shell*, heedless, imprudent, impulsive, intractable, locked-in*, mule, mulish, murder, obstinate, perverse, pig-headed*, rash, reckless, refractory, self-willed, strong-minded, uncontrollable, ungovernable, unruly, unyielding, willful; SEE CONCEPTS *401,403*

headway [n] *progress*
advance, advancement, anabasis, ground, improvement, increase, march, proficiency, progression, promotion, way; SEE CONCEPTS *230,704*

heady [adj] *thrilling, intoxicating*
exciting, exhilarating, inebriating, overwhelming, potent, powerful, provocative, spirituous, stimulating, strong; SEE CONCEPT *529*

heal [v] *cure, recover*
alleviate, ameliorate, attend, bring around, compose, conciliate, convalesce, doctor, dress, fix, free, get well, harmonize, improve, knit, make healthy, make sound, make well, make whole, medicate, meliorate, mend, minister to, patch up, physic, put on feet again*, reanimate, rebuild, reconcile, regenerate, rehabilitate, rejuvenate, remedy, renew, renovate, repair, restore, resuscitate, revive, revivify, salve, set, settle, soothe, treat; SEE CONCEPTS *308,310*

health [n] *physical, mental wellness*
bloom*, clean bill*, complexion, constitution, energy, eupepsia, euphoria, fettle, fine feather*, fitness, form, good condition, haleness, hardihood, hardiness, healthfulness, healthiness, lustiness, pink*, prime*, robustness, salubriousness, salubrity, shape, soundness, stamina, state, strength, tone, tonicity, top form, verdure, vigor, wellbeing, wholeness; SEE CONCEPTS *316,410,720*

healthful/healthy [adj] *good for one's wellness*
advantageous, aiding, aseptic, beneficial, benign, body-building, bracing, cathartic, clean, compensatory, conducive, corrective, desirable, disease-free, energy-giving, fresh, harmless, healing, health-giving, helpful, hygienic, innocuous, invigorating, mitigative, nourishing, nutritious, nutritive, profitable, pure, restorative, salubrious, salutary, sanatory, sanitary, stimulating, sustain-

ing, tonic, unadulterated, unpolluted, untainted, useful, wholesome; SEE CONCEPT *537*

healthy [adj2] *in good condition*
able-bodied, active, all right, athletic, blooming, bright-eyed*, bushy-tailed*, chipper*, firm, fit, flourishing, fresh, full of life*, hale, hardy, healthful, hearty, husky, in fine feather*, in fine fettle*, in good shape, in the pink*, lively, lusty, muscular, normal, physically fit, potent, restored, robust, rosy-cheeked*, safe and sound*, sound, stout, strong, sturdy, tough, trim, unimpaired, vigorous, virile, well, whole; SEE CONCEPTS *314,403*

heap [n] *pile, accumulation*
abundance, agglomeration, aggregation, a lot*, amassment, assemblage, bank, batch, bulk, bunch, bundle, cargo, clump, cluster, collection, concentration, congeries, deposit, fullness, gathering, gobs*, great deal, harvest, haul, hill, hoard, jumble, load, lot, lots, lump, mass, million, mint, mound, mountain, much, ocean, oodles*, plenty, pot, profusion, quantity, scad*, stack, stock, stockpile, store, sum, thousand, ton, total, trillion, volume, whole; SEE CONCEPTS *432,787*

heap [v] *amass, collect in pile*
accumulate, add, arrange, augment, bank, bunch, concentrate, deposit, dump, fill, fill up, gather, group, hoard, increase, load, lump, mass, mound, pack, stack, stockpile, store, swell; SEE CONCEPT *109*

hear [v1] *detect by perceiving sound*
apprehend, attend, auscultate, be all ears*, become aware, catch, descry, devour, eavesdrop, get*, get an earful*, get wind of*, give an audience to*, give attention, give ears*, hark, hearken, heed, listen, make out*, overhear, pick up*, read, strain, take in*; SEE CONCEPTS *590,596*

hear [v2] *become aware of information*
apperceive, ascertain, be advised, be informed, be led to believe, be told of, catch, catch on, descry, determine, discover, find out, gather, get the picture*, get wind of*, get wise to*, glean, have on good authority*, learn, pick up*, receive, see, tumble*, understand, unearth; SEE CONCEPTS *15,31*

hearing [n1] *ability to perceive sound*
audition, auditory, auditory range, detecting, distinguishing, ear, earshot, effect, extent, faculty, hearing distance, listening, perception, range, reach, recording, sense; SEE CONCEPT *597*

hearing [n2] *opportunity to present views, knowledge, or skill*
admittance, attendance, attention, audience, audit, audition, chance, conference, congress, consultation, council, discussion, inquiry, interview, investigation, meeting, negotiation, notice, parley, performance, presentation, reception, review, test, trial, tryout; SEE CONCEPTS *48,103,317,693*

hearsay [n] *unsubstantiated information*
clothesline*, comment, cry, gossip, grapevine*, leak*, mere talk*, noise*, report, rumble*, rumor, scandal, scuttlebutt*, talk, talk of the town*, word of mouth*; SEE CONCEPTS *51,278*

heart [n1] *person's emotions*
affection, benevolence, character, compassion, concern, disposition, feeling, gusto, humanity, inclination, love, nature, palate, pity, relish, response, sensitivity, sentiment, soul, sympathy, temperament, tenderness, understanding, zest; SEE CONCEPT *410*

ha
he

heart [n2] *courage*
boldness, bravery, dauntlessness, fortitude, gallantry, guts*, mettle, mind, moxie*, nerve, pluck, purpose, resolution, soul, spirit, spunk*, will; SEE CONCEPT 411

heart [n3] *essence, central part*
basic, bosom, bottom line*, center, coal and ice*, core, crux, focal point, focus, gist, hub, kernel, marrow, middle, nitty-gritty*, nub, nucleus, pith, polestar*, quick*, quintessence, root, seat, soul; SEE CONCEPT 826

heart [n4] *blood-pumping organ in an animate being*
cardiac organ, clock*, ticker*, vascular organ; SEE CONCEPTS 393,420

heartbreak [n] *mental or emotional misery*
affliction, agony, anguish, bale, bitterness, broken heart, care, desolation, despair, distress, grief, heartache, heartsickness, heavy heart*, pain, regret, remorse, rue, sorrow, suffering, torment, torture, woe; SEE CONCEPTS 410,728

heartbreaking [adj] *disappointing*
affecting, afflictive, agonizing, bitter, calamitous, cheerless, deplorable, dire, distressing, grievous, heart-rending, joyless, lamentable, moving, pitiful, poignant, regrettable, sad, touching, tragic, unfortunate; SEE CONCEPTS 529,537

hearten [v] *raise someone's spirits*
animate, arouse, assure, buck up, buoy, cheer, comfort, console, embolden, encourage, energize, enliven, incite, inspire, inspirit, rally, reassure, revivify, rouse, steel, stimulate, stir, strengthen; SEE CONCEPTS 7,22

heartfelt [adj] *genuine*
ardent, bona fide, cordial, deep, devout, earnest, fervent, heart-to-heart, hearty, honest, profound, sincere, true, unfeigned, warm, wholehearted; SEE CONCEPTS 267,582

heartless [adj] *without feeling; cold*
brutal, callous, cold-blooded*, cold fish*, cold-hearted*, cruel, hard, hard as nails*, hard-boiled*, hard-hearted*, harsh, inhuman, insensitive, merciless, obdurate, pitiless, ruthless, savage, thick-skinned*, uncaring, uncompassionate, unemotional, unfeeling, unkind, unsympathetic; SEE CONCEPTS 401,542

hearty [adj1] *energetic, enthusiastic*
affable, animated, ardent, avid, back-slapping*, cheerful, cheery, cordial, deep, deepest, deep-felt, devout, eager, earnest, ebullient, effusive, exuberant, frank, friendly, gay, generous, genial, genuine, glad, gushing, heartfelt, honest, impassioned, intense, jolly, jovial, neighborly, passionate, profuse, real, responsive, sincere, true, unfeigned, unreserved, unrestrained, vivacious, warm, warmhearted, wholehearted, zealous; SEE CONCEPTS 401,542

hearty [adj2] *healthy, full*
active, ample, energetic, filling, glowing, good, hale, hardy, nourishing, robust, sizable, solid, sound, square, strong, substantial, vigorous, well; SEE CONCEPTS 314,773

heat [n1] *high temperature*
calefaction, calidity, dog days*, fever, fieriness, heatwave, hotness, hot spell, hot weather, incalescence, incandescence, sultriness, swelter, torridity, torridness, warmness, warmth; SEE CONCEPT 610

heat [n2] *anger, passion*
agitation, ardor, desire, earnestness, excitement,

ferocity, fervor, fever, fury, impetuosity, intensity, rage, vehemence, violence, warmth, zeal; SEE CONCEPTS 410,657

heat [v] *make or become hot*
bake, bask, blaze, boil, broil, calorify, chafe, char, enflame, enkindle, fire, flame, flush, frizzle, fry, glow, grill, grow hot, grow warm, ignite, incandesce, incinerate, inflame, kindle, melt, oxidate, oxidize, perspire, raise the temperature, reheat, roast, scald, scorch, sear, seethe, set on fire, singe, smelt, steam, sun, swelter, tepefy, thaw, toast, warm, warm up; SEE CONCEPTS 255,469

heated [adj1] *angry*
acrimonious, ardent, avid, bitter, excited, fervent, fervid, feverish, fierce, fiery, frenzied, furious, hectic, impassioned, indignant, intense, irate, ireful, mad, passionate, raging, stormy, tempestuous, vehement, violent, wrathful; SEE CONCEPT 267

heated [adj2] *warmed*
baked, baking, boiling, broiled, broiling, burned, burning, burnt, cooked, fiery, fired, fried, hot, parched, scalding, scorched, scorching, sizzling, toasted; SEE CONCEPT 605

heathen [adj] *not believing in Christian god*
agnostic, atheistic, barbarian, godless, idolatrous, infidel, irreligious, nonbeliever, pagan, profane, skeptic; SEE CONCEPT 545

heave [v1] *lift, throw with effort*
boost, cast, chuck, drag, elevate, fling, haul, heft, hoist, hurl, launch, pitch, pull, raise, send, sling, toss, tug; SEE CONCEPTS 196,222

heave [v2] *discharge with force; expel from digestive system by mouth*
billow, breathe, cast, dilate, disgorge, exhale, expand, gag, groan, huff, palpitate, pant, puff, puke*, retch, rise, sigh, sob, spew, spit up, surge, suspire, swell, throb, throw up, upchuck*, vomit; SEE CONCEPTS 163,179

heaven [n] *place where god lives; wonderful feeling*
afterworld, Arcadia, atmosphere, azure*, beyond, bliss, Canaan, dreamland, ecstasy, Elysium, empyrean, enchantment, eternal home, eternal rest, eternity, fairyland, felicity, firmament, glory, great unknown*, happiness, happy hunting ground*, harmony, heights, hereafter, immortality, kingdom, kingdom come, life everlasting, life to come, next world, nirvana, paradise, pearly gates*, promised land*, rapture, Shangri-la*, sky*, the blue*, transport, upstairs*, Utopia, wonderland*, Zion; SEE CONCEPTS 370,410,435

heavenly [adj] *very pleasant*
adorable, alluring, ambrosial, angelic, beatific, beautiful, blessed, blissful, celestial, cherubic, darling, delectable, delicious, delightful, divine, empyrean, enjoyable, entrancing, excellent, exquisite, extraterrestrial, glorious, godlike, holy, immortal, lovely, luscious, lush, paradisaical, rapturous, ravishing, scrumptious, seraphic, sublime, superhuman, supernal, supernatural, sweet, wonderful, yummy; SEE CONCEPTS 537,572

heavy [adj1] *having great weight*
abundant, ample, awkward, beefy*, big, built, bulky, burdensome, chunky*, considerable, copious, corpulent, cumbersome, cumbrous, elephantine, enceinte, excessive, expectant, fat, fleshy, gravid, gross*, hefty, huge, laden, large, lead-footed*, loaded, lumbering, massive, obese, oppressed, overweight, parturient, ponderous,

porcine, portly, pregnant, stout, substantial, top-heavy, two-ton*, unmanageable, unwieldy, weighted, weighty, zaftig*; SEE CONCEPT *491*

heavy [*adj2*] *difficult, severe*
abstruse, acroamatic, arduous, boisterous, burdensome, complex, complicated, confused, effortful, esoteric, formidable, grave, grievous, hard, harsh, intolerable, knotty*, labored, laborious, onerous, oppressive, profound, recondite, rough, serious, solemn, stormy, strenuous, tedious, tempestuous, toilsome, tough, troublesome, turbulent, vexatious, violent, wearisome, weighty, wild; SEE CONCEPTS *538,565,569*

heavy [*adj3*] *depressed, gloomy*
close, cloudy, crestfallen, damp, dark, dejected, despondent, disconsolate, dismal, downcast, dull, grieving, leaden, lowering, melancholy, oppressive, overcast, sad, sodden, soggy, sorrowful, stifling, wet; SEE CONCEPTS *403,525,548*

heavy [*adj4*] *listless, slow*
apathetic, comatose, dull, hebetudinous, indifferent, lethargic, sluggish, slumberous, torpid; SEE CONCEPT *584*

heckle [*v*] *jeer*
badger, bait, bother, bully, chivy, dis*, discomfit, disconcert, disrupt, disturb, embarrass, faze, gibe, hound*, interrupt, pester, plague, rattle, ride*, ridicule, shout at, taunt, tease, torment, worry; SEE CONCEPTS *44,47*

hectic [*adj*] *frantic, turbulent*
animated, boisterous, burning, chaotic, confused, disordered, excited, exciting, fervid, fevered, feverish, flurrying, flustering, frenetic, frenzied, furious, hassle, heated, hell broke loose*, jungle*, madhouse*, nutsy*, restless, riotous, rip-roaring, tumultuous, unsettled, wild, woolly*, zoolike*; SEE CONCEPT *548*

hedge [*n*] *boundary, obstacle, especially one made of plants*
barrier, bush, enclosure, fence, guard, hedgerow, hurdle, protection, quickset, screen, shrubbery, thicket, windbreak; SEE CONCEPTS *429,470*

hedge [*v1*] *avoid, dodge*
beat around the bush*, be noncommittal, blow hot and cold*, cop a plea*, cop out*, duck, equivocate, evade, flip-flop*, fudge*, give the run around*, hem and haw*, jive*, pass the buck*, prevaricate, pussyfoot*, quibble, run around, shilly-shally*, shuck*, shuffle, sidestep, sit on the fence*, stall, stonewall*, temporize, tergiversate, tergiverse, waffle*; SEE CONCEPTS *18,30*

hedge [*v2*] *enclose*
block, border, cage, confine, coop, corral, edge, fence, girdle, hem in, hinder, immure, obstruct, pen, restrict, ring, siege, surround; SEE CONCEPT *758*

hedonist [*n*] *person who seeks pleasure above other values*
bon vivant, debauchee, epicure, epicurean, glutton, gourmand, lecher, libertine, pleasuremonger, pleasureseeker, profligate, sensualist, sybarite, thrill-seeker, voluptuary; SEE CONCEPT *423*

heed [*n*] *care, thought*
application, attention, carefulness, caution, cognizance, concentration, concern, consideration, debate, deliberation, ear*, heedfulness, interest, listen up*, mark, mind*, note, notice, observance, observation, regard, remark, respect, spotlight*, study, tender loving care*, TLC*, watchfulness; SEE CONCEPTS *17,532*

heed [*v*] *give care, thought to*
attend, baby-sit, bear in mind, be aware, be guided by, catch, consider, dig*, do one's bidding*, follow, follow orders, get a load of*, give ear*, hark, hear, hearken, keep eye peeled*, keep tabs*, listen, mark, mind, mind the store*, note, obey, observe, pay attention, pick up, regard, ride herd on*, see, sit, spot, stay in line*, take notice of, take to heart*, toe the line*, watch, watch one's step*, watch out, watch over, watch the store*; SEE CONCEPTS *17,623*

heedless [*adj*] *careless*
asleep at the switch*, daydreaming, disregardful, fast and loose*, feckless, foolhardy, goofing off*, impetuous, imprudent, inadvertent, inattentive, incautious, inconsiderate, irreflective, neglectful, negligent, oblivious, out to lunch*, precipitate, rash, reckless, slapdash*, sloppy, thoughtless, uncaring, unmindful, unobservant, unthinking, unwary; SEE CONCEPT *401*

hefty [*adj*] *big, bulky*
ample, awkward, beefy*, brawny, burly, colossal, cumbersome, extensive, fat, forceful, heavy, hulking, husky, large, large-scale, major, massive, muscular, ponderous, powerful, robust, sizable, strapping*, strong, sturdy, substantial, thumping*, tremendous, unwieldy, vigorous, weighty; SEE CONCEPTS *491,773*

height [*n1*] *altitude, top part*
acme, apex, apogee, brow, ceiling, crest, crown, cusp, elevation, extent, highness, hill, loftiness, mountain, peak, pinnacle, pitch, prominence, rise, solstice, stature, summit, tallness, tip, tiptop, vertex, zenith; SEE CONCEPTS *741,743,791,836*

height [*n2*] *climax; importance*
acme, crest, crisis, crowning point, culmination, dignity, eminence, end, exaltation, extremity, grandeur, heyday*, high point, limit, loftiness, maximum, ne plus ultra*, prominence, sublimity, top, ultimate, utmost degree, uttermost; SEE CONCEPTS *388,668,832*

heinous [*adj*] *horrifying, monstrous*
abhorrent, abominable, accursed, atrocious, awful, bad, beastly, crying, cursed, evil, execrable, flagitious, flagrant, frightful, godawful*, grave, gross*, hateful, hideous, horrendous, infamous, iniquitous, nefarious, odious, offensive, outrageous, raunchy, revolting, scandalous, shocking, stinking*, unspeakable, vicious, villainous; SEE CONCEPTS *529,548,570*

heir [*n*] *person who inherits possessions*
beneficiary, crown prince/princess, devisee, grantee, heritor, inheritor, next in line, scion, successor; SEE CONCEPTS *355,414*

heirloom [*n*] *something inherited, often antique*
antique, bequest, birthright, gift, heritage, inheritance, legacy, patrimony, reversion; SEE CONCEPT *337*

hell [*n*] *place of the condemned; bad situation*
Abaddon*, abyss, affliction, agony, anguish, blazes*, bottomless pit*, difficulty, everlasting fire*, fire and brimstone*, Gehenna*, grave, Hades, hell-fire, infernal regions, inferno, limbo, lower world, misery, nether world, nightmare, ordeal, pandemonium, perdition, pit, place of torment, purgatory, suffering, torment, trial, underworld, wretchedness; SEE CONCEPTS *370,435,674*

help [*n1*] *assistance, relief*
advice, aid, assist, avail, balm*, benefit, comfort,

he
he

cooperation, corrective, cure, guidance, hand, helping hand*, lift*, maintenance, nourishment, remedy, service, succor, support, sustenance, use, utility; SEE CONCEPTS *658,694*

help [n2] *employee*
abettor, adjutant, aide, ally, ancilla, assistant, attendant, auxiliary, collaborator, colleague, deputy, domestic, hand, helper, helpmate, mate, partner, representative, right-hand person*, servant, subsidiary, supporter, worker; SEE CONCEPT *348*

help [v1] *aid, assist*
abet, accommodate, advocate, back, ballyhoo*, befriend, benefit, be of use, bolster, boost, buck up*, cheer, cooperate, do a favor, do a service, do one's part*, encourage, endorse, further, go to bat for*, go with, hype*, intercede, lend a hand*, maintain, open doors*, patronize, plug*, promote, prop, puff*, push, relieve, root for*, sanction, save, second, see through, serve, stand by, stick up for*, stimulate, stump for*, succor, support, sustain, take under one's wing*, uphold, work for; SEE CONCEPT *110*

help [v2] *improve*
alleviate, ameliorate, amend, attend, better, cure, doctor, ease, facilitate, heal, meliorate, mitigate, nourish, palliate, relieve, remedy, restore, revive, treat; SEE CONCEPT *244*

helpful [adj] *beneficial, beneficent*
accessible, accommodating, advantageous, applicable, benevolent, bettering, caring, conducive, considerate, constructive, contributive, convenient, cooperative, crucial, effectual, efficacious, essential, favorable, fortunate, friendly, good for, important, improving, instrumental, invaluable, kind, neighborly, operative, practical, pragmatic, productive, profitable, serendipitous, serviceable, significant, suitable, supportive, symbiotic, sympathetic, timely, usable, useful, utilitarian, valuable; SEE CONCEPTS *537,560*

helping [n] *portion of food*
allowance, course, dollop, meal, order, piece, plateful, ration, serving, share; SEE CONCEPT *457*

helpless [adj] *incapable, incompetent; vulnerable*
abandoned, basket-case*, debilitated, defenseless, dependent, destitute, disabled, exposed, feeble, forlorn, forsaken, friendless, handcuffed, impotent, inefficient, inexpert, infirm, invalid, over a barrel*, paralyzed, pinned*, powerless, prostrate, shiftless, tapped, tapped out*, unable, unfit, unprotected, up creek without paddle*, weak, with hands tied*; SEE CONCEPTS *401,542*

helter-skelter [adv] *carelessly, confused*
about, anyhow, any which way*, anywise, around, at random, cluttered, disorderly, haphazard, hastily, headlong, higgledy-piggledy*, hit-or-miss*, hotfoot*, hurriedly, impetuously, incautiously, in confusion, incontinently, irregular, jumbled, muddled, pell-mell*, random, randomly, rashly, recklessly, topsy-turvy*, tumultuous/tumultuous, unmindfully, wildly; SEE CONCEPT *544*

hem [n] *border, edge*
brim, brink, define, edging, fringe, margin, perimeter, periphery, piping, rim, selvage, skirt, skirting, trimming, verge; SEE CONCEPTS *484,513*

hem/hem in [v] *enclose, restrict*
begird, beset, border, bound, cage, circle, circumscribe, close in, confine, corral, define, edge, encircle, encompass, envelop, environ, fence,

fringe, girdle, hedge in, immure, margin, pen, rim, ring, round, shut, shut in, skirt, surround, verge; SEE CONCEPTS *130,758*

hence [adv] *for that reason; therefore*
accordingly, as a deduction, away, consequently, ergo, forward, from here, from now on, henceforth, henceforward, hereinafter, in the future, it follows that, on that account, onward, out, so, then, thence, thereupon, thus, wherefore; SEE CONCEPT *799*

herald [n] *omen, messenger*
adviser, bearer, courier, crier, forerunner, harbinger, indication, outrider, precursor, prophet, reporter, runner, sign, signal, token; SEE CONCEPTS *274,284,423*

herald [v] *bring message*
advertise, announce, ballyhoo*, broadcast, declare, forerun, foretoken, harbinger, indicate, pave the way*, portend, precede, preindicate, presage, proclaim, promise, publicize, publish, show, tout, trumpet*, usher in*; SEE CONCEPT *60*

herd [n] *large group*
assemblage, bevy, brood, clan, collection, covey, crowd, crush, drift, drove, flight, flock, gaggle, gathering, hoi polloi*, horde, lot, mass, mob, multitude, nest, pack, people, populace, press, rabble, school, swarm, throng; SEE CONCEPTS *397,432*

herd [v] *gather; shepherd*
assemble, associate, collect, congregate, corral, drive, flock, force, goad, guide, huddle, lead, muster, poke, punch, rally, round up*, run, scare up*, spur; SEE CONCEPT *109*

here [adv] *in this place*
attendant, attending, available, hereabouts, hither, hitherto, in this direction, on board, on deck, on hand, on-the-spot, on this spot, present, within reach; SEE CONCEPT *583*

hereafter [n] *life after death*
afterlife, aftertime, afterward, afterworld, by-and-by*, future, future existence, future life, heaven, hell, next world, offing, otherworld, the beyond*, to-be*, underworld, world to come*; SEE CONCEPT *370*

hereafter [adv] *from now on*
after this, eventually, hence, henceforth, henceforward, hereupon, in the course of time, in the future, ultimately; SEE CONCEPT *799*

hereditary [adj] *inherited; transmitted at birth*
ancestral, bequeathed, family, genealogical, genetic, handed down, heritable, inborn, inbred, inheritable, inherited, lineal, maternal, paternal, patrimonial, traditional, transmissible, transmitted, willed; SEE CONCEPT *549*

heredity [n] *transmission of traits from parents to offspring*
ancestry, congenital traits, constitution, eugenics, genesiology, genetic make-up, genetics, inborn character, inheritance; SEE CONCEPT *648*

heresy [n] *unorthodox opinion, especially in religious matters*
agnosticism, apostasy, atheism, blasphemy, defection, disbelief, dissent, dissidence, divergence, error, fallacy, heterodoxy, iconoclasm, impiety, infidelity, misbelief, nonconformism, nonconformity, paganism, revisionism, schism, sectarianism, secularism, sin; SEE CONCEPT *689*

heretical [adj] *unorthodox*
agnostic, apostate, atheistic, differing, disagreeing, dissenting, dissentive, dissident, freethink-

ing, heterodox, iconoclastic, idolatrous, impious, infidel, misbelieving, miscreant, nonconformist, revisionist, schismatic, sectarian, skeptical, unbelieving; SEE CONCEPTS 529,545

heritage [n] *person's background, tradition*
ancestry, bequest, birthright, convention, culture, custom, dowry, endowment, estate, fashion, heirship, heritance, inheritance, legacy, lot, patrimony, portion, right, share, tradition; SEE CONCEPTS 296,648,678

hermeneutical [adj] *interpretive*
critical, demonstrative, explanatory, explicative, expository, illustrative, investigative, revealing; SEE CONCEPT 268

hermeneutics [n] *the science of searching for hidden meaning in texts*
exegetics, exploration, interpretation, investigation, literary criticism, psychoanalytic criticism, revealing, unmasking; SEE CONCEPT 349

hermit [n] *person who chose to live alone outside of human society*
anchoret, anchorite, ascetic, eremite, misanthrope, pillarist, recluse, skeptic, solitaire, solitarian, solitary, stylite; SEE CONCEPTS 361,423

hero/heroine [n] *brave person; champion*
ace, adventurer, celebrity, combatant, conqueror, daredevil, demigod, diva, exemplar, gallant, god, goddess, great person, heavy, ideal, idol, lead, leading person*, lion, martyr, model, paladin, person of the hour*, popular figure, prima donna*, principal, protagonist, saint, star, superstar, tin god*, victor, worthy; SEE CONCEPTS 352,416

heroic [adj] *brave, champion*
bigger than life*, bold, classic, courageous, daring, dauntless, doughty, elevated, epic, exaggerated, fearless, fire-eating*, gallant, grand, grandiose, gritty, gutsy*, gutty*, high-flown, impavid, inflated, intrepid, lion-hearted, mythological, noble, stand tall*, stouthearted, unafraid, undaunted, valiant, valorous; SEE CONCEPTS 401,404

heroism [n] *bravery*
boldness, courage, courageousness, daring, doughtiness, fearlessness, fortitude, gallantry, intrepidity, nobility, prowess, spirit, strength, valiance, valiancy, valor, valorousness; SEE CONCEPTS 411,633

hesitant [adj] *uncertain, waiting*
afraid, averse, backward, dawdling, delaying, diffident, disinclined, doubtful, doubting, faltering, half-hearted, halting, hanging back, hesitating, indecisive, irresolute, lacking confidence, lazy, loath, reluctant, shy, skeptical, slow, tentative, timid, uneager, unpredictable, unsure, unwilling, vacillating, wavering; SEE CONCEPTS 534, 535,542

hesitate [v] *wait; be uncertain*
alternate, balance, balk, be irresolute, be reluctant, be unwilling, blow hot and cold*, dally, debate, defer, delay, demur, dillydally*, dither, doubt, equivocate, falter, flounder, fluctuate, fumble, hang*, hang back, hedge, hem and haw*, hold back, hold off, hover, linger, oscillate, pause, ponder, pull back, pussyfoot*, scruple, seesaw*, shift, shrink, shy away, sit on fence*, stammer, stop, straddle, stumble, stutter, swerve, tergiversate, think about, think twice*, vacillate, waffle*, waver, weigh; SEE CONCEPTS 21,121, 681

hesitation [n] *waiting; uncertainty*
averseness, dawdling, delay, delaying, demurral, doubt, dubiety, equivocation, faltering, fluctuation, fumbling, hemming and hawing*, hesitancy, indecision, indecisiveness, indisposition, irresolution, misgiving, mistrust, oscillation, pause, procrastination, qualm, reluctance, scruple, skepticism, stammering, stumbling, stuttering, unwillingness, vacillation, wavering; SEE CONCEPTS 21,121,410,681

heterogeneous [adj] *assorted, miscellaneous*
amalgamate, composite, confused, conglomerate, contrary, contrasted, different, discordant, discrepant, disparate, dissimilar, divergent, diverse, diversified, incongruous, independent, inharmonious, jumbled, mingled, mixed, mongrel, mosaic, motley, multifarious, multiplex, odd, opposed, unallied, unlike, unrelated, variant, varied, variegated; SEE CONCEPT 564

hiatus [n] *pause, interruption*
aperture, blank, breach, break, chasm, discontinuity, gap, interim, interval, lacuna, lapse, opening, rift, space; SEE CONCEPT 807

hibernate [v] *lie dormant; sleep through cold weather*
hide, hole up, immure, lie torpid, sleep, vegetate, winter; SEE CONCEPT 315

hidden [adj] *unseen, secret*
abstruse, buried, clandestine, cloaked, close, clouded, concealed, covered, covert, cryptic, dark, disguised, eclipsed, esoteric, hermetic, hermetical, imperceivable, indiscernible, in the dark, invisible, latent, masked, mysterious, mystic, mystical, obscure, occult, out of view, private, QT*, recondite, screened, secluded, sequestered, shadowy, shrouded, surreptitious, ulterior, undercover, underground, undetected, undisclosed, unexposed, unknown, unrevealed, veiled, withheld; SEE CONCEPT 576

hide [v] *conceal; remain unseen*
adumbrate, blot out, bury, cache, camouflage, cloak, cover, curtain*, disguise, dissemble, ditch, duck, eclipse, ensconce, go into hiding, go underground, harbor, hold back, hole up*, hush up, keep from, keep secret, lie low*, lock up, mask, not give away, not tell, obscure, plant, protect, put out of the way, reserve, salt away*, screen, secrete, shadow, shelter, shield, shroud, smuggle, squirrel*, stash, stifle, stow away, suppress, take cover, tuck away, veil, withhold; SEE CONCEPTS 17,188

hideous [adj] *grotesque, horrible*
abominable, animal, appalling, awful, beast, bestial, detestable, disgusting, dreadful, frightful, ghastly, grim, grisly, gross*, gruesome, hateful, horrendous, horrid, loathsome, macabre, monstrous, morbid, nasty, odious, offensive, repellent, repugnant, repulsive, revolting, shocking, sick, sickening, terrible, terrifying, ugly, uncomely, unsightly, weird; SEE CONCEPTS 537,579

high [adj1] *tall; at a great distance aloft*
aerial, alpine, altitudinous, big, colossal, elevated, eminent, flying, formidable, giant, gigantic, grand, great, high-reaching, high rise, hovering, huge, immense, large, lofty, long, sky-high, sky-scraping, soaring, steep, towering, tremendous, uplifted, upraised; SEE CONCEPTS 779,782

high [adj2] *extreme*
costly, dear, excessive, exorbitant, expensive,

he
hi

extraordinary, extravagant, grand, great, high-priced, intensified, lavish, luxurious, precious, rich, sharp, special, steep, stiff, strong, unusual; SEE CONCEPTS 334,569

high [adj3] *important*
arch, capital, chief, consequential, crucial, distinguished, eminent, essential, exalted, extreme, grave, influential, leading, necessary, noble, powerful, prominent, ruling, serious, significant, superior; SEE CONCEPT 567

high [adj4] *very happy*
boisterous, bouncy, cheerful, elated, excited, exhilarated, exuberant, joyful, lighthearted, merry, psyched*, pumped*; SEE CONCEPT 403

high [adj5] *intoxicated, drugged*
delirious, doped, drunk, euphoric, flying*, freaked out*, inebriated, on a trip*, potted*, spaced out*, stoned*, tanked*, tipsy; SEE CONCEPT 314

high [adj6] *shrill, strong (on the senses)*
acute, high-pitched, loud, malodorous, penetrating, piercing, piping, putrid, rancid, rank, reeking, sharp, smelly, soprano, strident, treble; SEE CONCEPTS 406,594,598

highlight [n] *memorable part*
best part, climax, feature, focal point, focus, high point, high spot, main feature, peak; SEE CONCEPT 832

highly [adv] *very, well*
awful, awfully, bloody*, but good*, decidedly, deeply, eminently, exceedingly, exceptionally, extraordinarily, extremely, greatly, hugely, immensely, jolly, mighty, mucho*, notably, parlous, plenty, powerful, profoundly, real, really, remarkably, right, so, so much*, strikingly, supremely, surpassingly, terribly, terrifically, too much*, tremendously, vastly, very much; SEE CONCEPTS 537,569

high-strung [adj] *nervous*
all shook up*, choked*, easily upset, edgy, excitable, fidgety, hyper*, impatient, irascible, irritable, jittery, jumpy, nervy, neurotic, on pins and needles*, on ragged edge, restless, sensitive, spooked*, stressed, taut, temperamental, tense, tight*, unrestful, uptight*, wired*, zonkers*; SEE CONCEPTS 401,404

highway [n] *heavily traveled, capacious road*
artery, avenue, boulevard, drag*, four-lane*, freeway, interstate, parking lot*, parkway, path, pike*, roadway, skyway, street, superhighway, super slab*, thoroughfare, toll road, track, turnpike; SEE CONCEPT 501

hike [n] *journey by foot*
backpack, constitutional, excursion, exploration, march, ramble, tour, traipse, tramp, trek, trip, walk, walkabout; SEE CONCEPTS 149,224,363

hike [v1] *walk for recreation*
backpack, explore, hit the road*, hoof*, leg it*, ramble, rove, stroll, stump, tour, tramp, travel, tromp; SEE CONCEPTS 149,224,363

hike [v2] *raise, increase*
advance, boost, jack, jump, lift, pull up, put up, up*, upgrade; SEE CONCEPTS 236,245

hilarious [adj] *very funny*
amusing, comical, convivial, exhilarated, frolicsome, gay, gleeful, gut-busting*, happy, humorous, jocular, jolly, jovial, joyful, joyous, laughable, lively, merry, mirthful, noisy, priceless, riot, rollicking, scream, side-splitting*, uproarious, witty; SEE CONCEPT 529

hill [n] *uprising of earth's surface; pile*
acclivity, ascent, bluff, butte, cliff, climb, down, drift, dune, elevation, eminence, esker, fell, gradient, headland, heap, height, highland, hillock, hilltop, hummock, inclination, incline, knoll, mesa, mound, mount, precipice, prominence, promontory, protuberance, range, ridge, rise, rising ground, shock, slope, stack, summit, talus, tor, upland; SEE CONCEPT 509

hinder [v] *prevent, slow down*
arrest, balk, bar, block, bottleneck, box in, burden, check, choke, clog, contravene, counteract, crab, cramp, crimp, cripple, curb, debar, delay, deter, encumber, fetter, frustrate, get in the way*, hamper, hamstring*, handicap, hog-tie*, hold back, hold up, impede, inhibit, interfere, interrupt, louse up*, muzzle, neutralize, obstruct, offset, oppose, preclude, prohibit, resist, retard, shut out, snafu*, stay, stop, stymie*, terminate, thwart, trammel; SEE CONCEPTS 121,130

hindrance [n] *obstruction, difficulty*
albatross*, baggage*, ball and chain*, bar, barrier, catch, Catch-22*, check, clog, crimp, cumbrance, deterrent, drag, drawback, encumbrance, excess baggage*, foot dragging*, glitch*, gridlock, handicap, hang-up*, hitch, impedance, impediment, interference, interruption, intervention, jam-up*, joker, limitation, lock, millstone*, monkey wrench*, obstacle, restraint, restriction, snag, stoppage, stumbling block*, trammel; SEE CONCEPTS 666,674

hinge [n] *pivot, turning point*
articulation, axis, ball-and-socket, butt, elbow, hook, joint, juncture, knee, link, pin, spring, swivel; SEE CONCEPTS 471,498

hinge [v] *be contingent on*
be subject to, be undecided, depend, hang, pend, pivot, rest, revolve around, stand on, turn, turn on; SEE CONCEPT 711

hint [n] *indication; suggestion*
adumbration, advice, allusion, announcement, clue, communication, connotation, denotation, evidence, flea in ear*, glimmering, help, idea, implication, impression, inference, information, inkling, innuendo, insinuation, intimation, iota, lead, mention, notice, notion, observation, omen, pointer, print, reference, reminder, scent, sign, signification, smattering, suspicion, symptom, taste, telltale, tinge, tip, tip-off*, token, trace, warning, whiff*, whisper, wink*, word to wise*, wrinkle*; SEE CONCEPT 274

hint [v] *suggest; indicate*
acquaint, adumbrate, advise, allude to, angle, apprise, bring up, broach, coax, connote, cue, drop, expose, fish*, foreshadow, give an inkling*, impart, imply, infer, inform, insinuate, intimate, jog memory, leak*, let it be known, let out of bag*, make*, mention, point, prefigure, press, prompt, put flea in ear*, recall, refer to, remind, say in passing, shadow, signify, solicit, spring, tip off*, tip one's hand*, touch on*, whisper, wink*; SEE CONCEPTS 60,74,75

hire [v] *commission for responsibility, use*
add to payroll, appoint, authorize, book, bring in, bring on board, carry, charter, contract for, delegate, draft, employ, empower, engage, enlist, exploit, fill a position, find help, give a break*, give job to, give work, ink*, lease, let, make use of, obtain, occupy, pick, place, pledge, procure, promise, put on*, put to work, rent, retain, se-

cure, select, sign on, sign up*, sublease, sublet, take on, truck with*, utilize; SEE CONCEPT *351*

hiss [*n*] *buzzing sound; jeer*
boo, Bronx cheer*, buzz, catcall, contempt, derision, hoot, sibilance, sibilation; SEE CONCEPTS *278,595*

hiss [*v*] *make buzzing sound; ridicule*
blow, boo, catcall, condemn, damn, decry, deride, disapprove, hoot, jeer, mock, rasp, revile, seethe, shout down, shrill, sibilate, siss, spit, wheeze, whirr, whisper, whistle, whiz; SEE CONCEPTS *52,77*

historic [*adj*] *momentous, remarkable*
celebrated, consequential, extraordinary, famous, important, memorable, notable, outstanding, red-letter*, significant, well-known; SEE CONCEPTS *548,568*

historical [*adj*] *recorded as actually having happened*
actual, ancient, archival, attested, authentic, chronicled, classical, commemorated, documented, factual, important, in truth, old, past, real, verifiable; SEE CONCEPTS *548,582,820*

history [*n1*] *past events, experiences*
ancient times, antiquity, bygone times, days of old*, days of yore*, good old days*, old days*, olden days*, past, yesterday, yesteryear; SEE CONCEPTS *678,807*

history [*n2*] *chronicle of events*
account, annals, autobiography, biography, diary, epic, journal, memoirs, narration, narrative, prehistory, recapitulation, recital, record, relation, report, saga, story, tale, version; SEE CONCEPTS *268,271*

hit [*n1*] *strike, bump*
bang, bat, bell-ringer*, belt, blow, bonk, box*, buffet, butt, chop, clash, clip, clout, collision, cuff*, fisticuff, glance, impact, knock, lick*, one-two punch*, paste*, pat, plunk, punch, rap, roundhouse*, shock, shot, slap, slog, smack, smash, sock, spank, stroke, swat, swing, swipe, tap, uppercut, wallop, whammy*, whop, zap*, zinger*; SEE CONCEPTS *189,200*

hit [*n2*] *entertainment success*
achievement, bang, click, favorite, knockout, masterstroke, sellout, sensation, smash, SRO*, triumph, winner, wow; SEE CONCEPT *706*

hit [*v1*] *strike*
bang, bash, bat, batter, beat, belt, blast, blitz, box*, brain*, buffet, bump, clap, clip, clobber, clout, club, crack, cudgel, cuff*, dab, ding*, flail, flax, flog, give a black eye*, hammer*, hook, jab, kick, knock, knock around, knock out, KO*, lace, lambaste, larrup, lather, let fly*, let have it*, lob, nail*, pellet, pelt, percuss, pop, pound, punch, rap, ride roughshod*, slap, smack, sock, stone, swat, tap, thrash, thump, thwack, trash, uppercut, wallop, whack*, whang*; SEE CONCEPTS *189,200*

hit [*v2*] *collide, bump into*
bang, bump, buffet, butt, carom, clash, crash, glance, jostle, knock, light, meet, meet head-on*, pat, rap, run into, scrape, sideswipe, smash, stumble, tap, thud, thump; SEE CONCEPTS *189,208*

hit [*v3*] *accomplish*
achieve, affect, arrive at, attain, gain, influence, leave a mark, occur, overwhelm, reach, secure, strike, touch; SEE CONCEPTS *199,706*

hitch [*n*] *problem, difficulty*
block, bug*, catch, check, delay, discontinuance, drawback, glitch*, hang-up, hindrance, hold-up,

impediment, interruption, joker, mishap, snafu*, snag, stoppage, stumbling block, tangle, trouble; SEE CONCEPTS *666,674*

hitch [*v*] *join, fasten*
attach, chain, connect, couple, harness, hook, lash, make fast, moor, strap, tether, tie, unite, yoke; SEE CONCEPTS *85,113,160*

hoard [*n*] *stockpile*
abundance, accumulation, agglomeration, aggregation, amassment, backlog, cache, collection, conglomeration, cumulation, fund, garner, heap, inventory, mass, nest egg*, pile, reserve, reservoir, riches, stock, store, supply, treasure, treasure-trove*, trove, wealth; SEE CONCEPT *712*

hoard [*v*] *put away, accumulate*
acquire, amass, buy up, cache, collect, deposit, garner, gather, hide, keep, lay away, lay up, pile up, put aside for rainy day*, put by, save, scrimp, sock away*, squirrel*, stash, stockpile, store, stow away, treasure; SEE CONCEPTS *135,710*

hoarse [*adj*] *raspy in voice*
blatant, breathy, cracked, croaking, croaky, croupy, discordant, dry, grating, gravelly, growling, gruff, guttural, harsh, husky, indistinct, jarring, piercing, ragged, raucous, rough, scratching, squawking, stertorous, strident, stridulous, thick, throaty, uneven, whispering; SEE CONCEPT *594*

hoax [*n*] *trick*
cheat, cock-and-bull story*, con*, con game*, crock*, deceit, deception, dodge, fabrication, fake, falsification, fast one*, fast shuffle*, fib, flimflam*, fraud, gimmick, gyp*, hooey*, humbug*, hustle, imposture, joke, lie, practical joke, prank, put-on, racket, ruse, scam, sell, shift, snow job*, spoof, sting, swindle, whopper*; SEE CONCEPTS *59,63*

hoax [*v*] *trick*
bamboozle, bluff, chicane, con, deceive, delude, dupe, fake out, fleece, flimflam*, fool, frame, gammon, gull, hoodwink*, Murphy*, play games with*, pull one's leg*, rook*, run a game on*, set up*, sting*, swindle, take for a ride*, take in*; SEE CONCEPT *59*

hobble [*v1*] *limp*
clump, dodder, falter, halt, hitch, scuff, shuffle, stagger, stumble, totter; SEE CONCEPT *151*

hobble [*v2*] *cripple, restrict*
clog, cramp, cramp one's style, crimp, curb, entrammel, fasten, fetter, gimp, hamper, hamstring*, hang up*, hinder, hog-tie*, leash, put a crimp in*, shackle, tie, trammel; SEE CONCEPT *130*

hobby [*n*] *pleasurable pastime*
amusement, art, avocation, bag*, craft, craze, distraction, diversion, divertissement, fad*, fancy, favorite occupation, fun, game, interest, kick*, labor of love*, leisure activity, leisure pursuit, obsession, occupation, pet topic, play, quest, relaxation, schtick*, shot, sideline, specialty, sport, thing*, vagary, weakness, whim, whimsy; SEE CONCEPTS *363,364*

hocus-pocus [*n*] *deception, magic*
abracadabra*, artifice, cant, chant, charm, cheating, chicanery, conjuring, deceit, delusion, flimflam*, fraud, gibberish, gobbledegook*, hoax, humbug, imposture, incantation, jargon, juggling, legerdemain, mumbo-jumbo*, mummery, nonsense, open-sesame*, rigmarole*, sleight of hand*, spell, swindle, trick, trickery; SEE CONCEPTS *59,278*

hi
ho

hodgepodge [*n*] *mixture, mess*
collection, combination, goulash*, hash, jumble, medley, mélange, miscellany, mishmash*, mixed bag, olio, patchwork, potpourri, salmagundi*; SEE CONCEPTS *260,432*

hogwash [*n*] *nonsense*
absurdity, balderdash*, baloney*, BS*, bull*, bunk*, debris, drivel*, foolishness, hokum, hooey*, horsefeathers*, poppycock*, refuse, ridiculousness, rot, rubbish, trash, twaddle*; SEE CONCEPT *278*

hoist [*v*] *lift*
elevate, erect, heave, pick up, raise, rear, take up, uphold, uplift, upraise, uprear; SEE CONCEPT *196*

hold [*n*] *grasp, possession*
authority, clasp, clench, clinch, clout, clutch, control, dominance, dominion, grip, influence, occupancy, occupation, ownership, pull, purchase, retention, sway, tenacity, tenure; SEE CONCEPTS *190,343,710*

hold [*v1*] *have in one's hands, possession; grasp*
adhere, arrest, bind, bottle up, carry, catch, check, cherish, clasp, cleave, clench, clinch, cling, clutch, confine, contain, cork up*, cradle, detain, embrace, enclose, enjoy, fondle, freeze to*, grip, handle, hang on, have, hug, imprison, keep, keep close, keep out, lock up, maintain, not let go, nourish, occupy, own, palm, possess, press, put a lock on, restrain, retain, secure, seize, squeeze, stay put, stick, take, trammel, vise, wield, withhold, wring; SEE CONCEPTS *190,191,200,710*

hold [*v2*] *believe*
assume, aver, bet bottom dollar*, buy*, consider, credit, cross one's heart*, deem, entertain, esteem, feel, have hunch*, have sneaking suspicion*, judge, lap up, lay money on, maintain, okay, presume, reckon, regard, sense, set store by*, swear by, swear up and down*, take as gospel truth*, take stock in*, think, view; SEE CONCEPT *12*

hold [*v3*] *continue, endure*
apply, be in effect, be in force, be the case, be valid, exist, have bearing, hold good, hold true, last, operate, persevere, persist, remain, remain true, resist, stand up, stay, stay staunch, wear; SEE CONCEPT *239*

hold [*v4*] *support*
bear, bolster, brace, buttress, carry, lock, prop, shore up, shoulder, stay, sustain, take, underpin, uphold; SEE CONCEPTS *110,190*

hold [*v5*] *have a capacity for*
accommodate, be equipped for, carry, comprise, contain, include, seat, take; SEE CONCEPTS *719,742*

hold [*v6*] *conduct meeting, function*
assemble, call, carry on, celebrate, convene, have, officiate, preside, run, solemnize; SEE CONCEPTS *324,384*

hold back/hold off [*v*] *repress*
bit, bridle, check, control, curb, defer, delay, deny, forbear, hold down, hold in, inhibit, keep, keep back, keep out, postpone, prevent, put off, refrain, refuse, restrain, stop, suppress, withhold; SEE CONCEPTS *121,130*

holdup [*n1*] *problem*
bottleneck*, delay, difficulty, gridlock*, hitch, obstruction, setback, snag, stoppage, traffic jam*, trouble, wait; SEE CONCEPTS *192,674*

holdup [*n2*] *take goods illegally by force*
burglary, crime, mugging, robbery, stickup, theft; SEE CONCEPT *192*

hold up [*v1*] *postpone*
delay, detain, hinder, hold off, impede, interfere, interrupt, pause, prorogue, retard, set back, slow down, stay, stop, suspend, waive; SEE CONCEPTS *121,130*

hold up [*v2*] *rob*
burglarize, mug, steal from, stick up, waylay; SEE CONCEPTS *139,192*

hole [*n1*] *opening in a solid object*
aperture, breach, break, burrow, cave, cavern, cavity, chamber, chasm, chink, cistern, cleft, covert, crack, cranny, crater, cut, den, dent, depression, dimple, dip, excavation, eyelet, fissure, foramen, fracture, gap, gash, gorge, hollow, hovel, keyhole, lacuna, lair, leak, mouth, nest, niche, nick, notch, orifice, outlet, passage, peephole, perforation, pit, pocket, pockmark, puncture, rent, retreat, scoop, shaft, shelter, space, split, tear, tunnel, vacuity, vent, void, window; SEE CONCEPT *513*

hole [*n2*] *predicament*
box*, corner*, difficulty, dilemma, emergency, fix, imbroglio, impasse, jam, mess, pickle*, plight, quandary, scrape, spot, tangle; SEE CONCEPT *674*

holiday [*n*] *celebratory day; time off*
anniversary, break, celebration, day of rest, feast, festival, festivity, fete, few days off*, fiesta, gala, gone fishing*, holy day, jubilee, layoff, leave, liberty, long weekend*, recess, red-letter day*, saint's day, vacation; SEE CONCEPTS *364,802*

holiness [*n*] *religiousness*
asceticism, beatitude, blessedness, consecration, devotion, devoutness, divineness, divinity, faith, godliness, grace, humility, inviolability, piety, purity, religiosity, reverence, righteousness, sacredness, saintliness, sanctity, spirituality, unction, venerableness, virtuousness, worship; SEE CONCEPTS *368,645*

hollow [*n*] *empty or dented area*
basin, bottom, bowl, cave, cavern, cavity, chamber, channel, cleft, concavity, crater, cup, dale, den, depression, dimple, dip, dish, excavation, groove, gulf, hole, indentation, notch, pit, pocket, sag, scoop, sinkage, sinkhole, socket, trough, vacuity, valley, void; SEE CONCEPTS *740,754*

hollow [*adj1*] *empty, hollowed out*
alveolate, arched, carved out, cavernous, cleft, concave, cupped, cup-shaped, curved, deep-set, depressed, dimpled, excavated, incurved, indented, infundibular, notched, not solid, pitted, striated, sunken, troughlike, unfilled, vacant, vaulted, void; SEE CONCEPTS *483,490*

hollow [*adj2*] *deep, resonant in sound*
cavernous, clangorous, dull, echoing, flat, ghostly, low, muffled, mute, muted, resounding, reverberant, ringing, roaring, rumbling, sepulchral, sounding, thunderous, toneless, vibrant, vibrating; SEE CONCEPT *594*

hollow [*adj3*] *meaningless*
empty, fruitless, futile, idle, nugatory, otiose, pointless, specious, unavailing, useless, vain, worthless; SEE CONCEPT *560*

hollow [*adj4*] *false, artificial*
cynical, deceitful, faithless, flimsy, hypocritical, insincere, treacherous, unsound, weak; SEE CONCEPT *267*

hollow [v] *empty out; make concave*

channel, chase, corrugate, dent, dig, dish, ditch, excavate, furrow, gorge, groove, indent, notch, pit, rabbet, remove, rut, scoop, shovel, trench; SEE CONCEPTS 178,211

holy [adj] *religious, sacred*

angelic, believing, blessed, chaste, clean, consecrated, dedicated, devoted, devotional, devout, divine, faithful, faultless, glorified, god-fearing, godlike, godly, good, hallowed, humble, immaculate, innocent, just, moral, perfect, pietistic, pious, prayerful, pure, revered, reverent, righteous, sacrosanct, sainted, saintlike, saintly, sanctified, seraphic, spiritual, spotless, sublime, uncorrupt, undefiled, untainted, unworldly, upright, venerable, venerated, virtuous; SEE CONCEPTS 545, 567,574

homage [n] *devotion, admiration*

adoration, adulation, allegiance, awe, deference, duty, esteem, faithfulness, fealty, fidelity, genuflection, honor, kneeling, loyalty, obeisance, praise, reverence, service, tribute, worship; SEE CONCEPTS 32,69

home [n1] *place where a human lives*

abode, address, apartment, asylum, boarding house, bungalow, cabin, castle, cave*, commorancy, condo, condominium, co-op, cottage, crash pad*, diggings*, digs*, domicile, dormitory, dump*, dwelling, farm, fireside*, flat, habitation, hangout*, haunt, hearth, hideout, hole in the wall*, home plate*, homestead, hospital, house, hut, joint*, living quarters, manor, mansion, nest*, orphanage, pad*, palace, parking place*, place, residence, resort, roof*, rooming house, roost*, shanty, shelter, trailer, turf, villa, where the hat is*; SEE CONCEPT 516

home [n2] *birthplace, environment*

abode, camping ground*, country, element, family, farm, fireside*, habitat, habitation, haunt, haven, hearth, hills, home ground, homeland, homestead, hometown, household, land, locality, neck of the woods*, neighborhood, range, roof, site, soil, stamping ground*, stomping ground*, territory; SEE CONCEPTS 510,515,648

home [adj] *domestic*

at ease, at rest, central, down home*, familiar, family, homely, homey, household, inland, in one's element*, internal, in the bosom*, local, national, native; SEE CONCEPT 536

homeless [adj] *displaced*

abandoned, banished, deported, derelict, desolate, destitute, disinherited, displaced, dispossessed, down-and-out*, estranged, exiled, forlorn, forsaken, friendless, houseless, itinerant, outcast, refugee, uncared-for, unhoused, unsettled, unwelcome, vagabond, vagrant, wandering, without a roof*; SEE CONCEPT 555

homely [adj1] *ordinary, comfortable*

comfy, cozy, domestic, everyday, familiar, friendly, homelike, homespun, homey, inelaborate, informal, modest, natural, plain, simple, snug, unaffected, unassuming, unostentatious, unpretentious, welcoming; SEE CONCEPTS 579,589

homely [adj2] *unattractive*

animal, disgusting, plain, ugly, unaesthetic, unalluring; SEE CONCEPT 579

homicide [n] *killing*

assassination, big chill*, bloodshed, bump-off*, butchery, carnage, crime, death, erase*, foul play, hit, manslaughter, murder, offing, ride, rubout*, slaying; SEE CONCEPTS

homogenous [adj] *similar, comparable*

akin, alike, analogous, cognate, consistent, homologous, identical, kindred, like, uniform, unvarying; SEE CONCEPTS 487,573

homosexual [adj] *sexually attracted to the same sex*

gay, homoerotic, homophile, lesbian; SEE CONCEPT 372

honest [adj] *truthful, candid*

above-board, authentic, bona fide*, conscientious, decent, direct, equitable, ethical, fair, fair and square*, forthright, frank, genuine, high-minded*, honorable, impartial, ingenuous, just, law-abiding*, lay it on the line*, like it is*, no lie*, on the level*, on the up and up*, open, outright, plain, proper, real, reliable, reputable, scrupulous, sincere, straight, straightforward, true, true blue*, trustworthy, trusty, undisguised, unfeigned, upfront*, upright, veracious, virtuous, what you see is what you get*; SEE CONCEPTS 267,545

honesty [n] *truthfulness, candidness*

bluntness, candor, confidence, conscientiousness, equity, evenhandedness, fairness, faithfulness, fidelity, frankness, genuineness, goodness, honor, impeccability, incorruptibility, integrity, justness, loyalty, morality, openness, outspokenness, plainness, principle, probity, rectitude, reputability, responsibility, right, scrupulousness, self-respect, sincerity, soundness, straightforwardness, straightness, trustiness, trustworthiness, uprightness, veracity, virtue; SEE CONCEPTS 633,645

honor [n1] *respect*

account, adoration, adulation, aggrandizement, apotheosis, approbation, attention, canonization, celebration, confidence, consideration, credit, deference, deification, dignity, distinction, elevation, esteem, exaltation, faith, fame, fealty, glorification, glory, greatness, high standing, homage, immortalization, laud, laurel, lionization, notice, obeisance, popularity, praise, prestige, rank, recognition, renown, reputation, repute, reverence, tribute, trust, veneration, worship, wreath; SEE CONCEPTS 668,689

honor [n2] *integrity*

character, chastity, courage, decency, fairness, goodness, honestness, honesty, incorruption, incorruptness, innocence, modesty, morality, morals, principles, probity, purity, rectitude, righteousness, trustworthiness, truthfulness, uprightness, virtue; SEE CONCEPTS 411,645

honor [n3] *praise, award*

acclaim, accolade, adoration, badge, bays, commendation, compliment, credit, decoration, deference, distinction, favor, homage, kudos, laurels, pleasure, privilege, recognition, regard, respect, reverence, source of pride, tribute, veneration; SEE CONCEPTS 278,337,689

honor [v] *recognize, treat with respect*

acclaim, admire, adore, aggrandize, appreciate, be faithful, be true, celebrate, commemorate, commend, compliment, decorate, dignify, distinguish, ennoble, erect, esteem, exalt, give glad hand*, give key to city*, glorify, hallow, keep, laud, lionize, live up to, look up to, magnify, observe, praise, prize, revere, roll out red carpet*, sanctify, sublime, uprear, value, venerate, worship; SEE CONCEPTS 10,633

ho
ho

hook [n] *curved fastener*
angle, catch, clasp, crook, curve, grapnel, grapple, hasp, holder, link, lock, peg; SEE CONCEPTS 260,498

hook [v] *grab, catch*
angle, bag, clasp, crook, curve, enmesh, ensnare, entrap, fasten, fix, hasp, lasso, net, pin, secure, snare, trap; SEE CONCEPT 190

hop [n/v] *jump on one leg*
bounce, bound, caper, dance, hurdle, leap, lop, lope, skip, skitter, spring, step, trip, vault; SEE CONCEPT 194

hope [n] *longing; dream*
achievement, ambition, anticipation, aspiration, assumption, belief, bright side*, buoyancy, castles in air*, concern, confidence, daydream, dependence, desire, endurance, expectancy, expectation, faith, fancy, fool's paradise*, fortune, gain, goal, greedy glutton*, hopefulness, light at end of tunnel*, optimism, pipe dream*, promise, promised land*, prospect, reliance, reverie, reward, rosiness, sanguineness, security, stock, thing with feathers*, Utopia, wish; SEE CONCEPTS 20,410,709

hope [v] *long for, dream about*
anticipate, aspire, assume, await, believe, be sure of, cherish, contemplate, count on, deem likely, depend on, desire, expect, feel confident, foresee, hang in*, have faith, hold, keep fingers crossed*, knock on wood*, look at sunny side*, look forward to, pray, presume, promise oneself, rely, suppose, surmise, suspect, sweat*, sweat it*, sweat it out*, take heart*, think to, trust, watch for, wish; SEE CONCEPT 20

hopeful [adj] *optimistic, expectant*
anticipating, anticipative, assured, at ease, blithe, buoyant, calm, cheerful, comfortable, confident, content, eager, elated, emboldened, enthusiastic, expecting, faithful, forward-looking*, high, hoping, inspirited, keeping the faith*, lighthearted, looking forward to, reassured, rose-colored*, rosy*, sanguine, satisfied, serene, trustful, trusting, unflagging, upbeat; SEE CONCEPT 403

hopeful [adj2] *promising, auspicious*
advantageous, arousing, beneficial, bright, cheerful, cheering, conducive, convenient, elating, encouraging, enlivening, exciting, expeditious, fair, favorable, fine, fit, flattering, fortifying, fortunate, golden, good, gracious, halcyon, heartening, helpful, inspiring, inspiriting, likely, lucky, opportune, pleasant, pleasing, probable, promiseful, propitious, providential, reasonable, reassuring, roseate, rosy*, rousing, stirring, suitable, sunny, timely, uplifting, well-timed; SEE CONCEPT 548

hopeless [adj] *futile, pessimistic*
bad, beyond recall, cynical, dejected, demoralized, despairing, desperate, despondent, disconsolate, discouraging, downhearted, fatal, forlorn, gone*, goner*, helpless, ill-fated, impossible, impracticable, incurable, in despair, irredeemable, irreparable, irreversible, irrevocable, lost, menacing, no-win, past hope, pointless, sad, shot down*, sinister, sunk, threatening, tragic, unachievable, unavailing, unfortunate, unmitigable, up the creek*, useless, vain, woebegone, worsening; SEE CONCEPTS 529,548

horde [n] *uncontrolled throng, pack*
band, crew, crowd, crush, drove, everybody, gang, gathering, host, jam, mob, multitude, press,

push, squash, swarm, troop, turnout, wall-to-wall*; SEE CONCEPTS 397,417

horizon [n] *skyline, extent*
border, boundary, compass, field of vision, ken, limit, perspective, prospect, purview, range, reach, realm, scope, sphere, stretch, vista; SEE CONCEPTS 484,509,529

horizontal [adj] *lying flat*
accumbent, aligned, even, flush, level, parallel, plane, recumbent, regular, smooth, straight, uniform; SEE CONCEPTS 581,583

horrible/horrendous/horrid [adj] *repulsive, very unpleasant*
abhorrent, abominable, appalling, awful, beastly, cruel, detestable, disagreeable, disgusting, dreadful, eerie, execrable, fearful, frightful, ghastly, grim, grisly, gross*, gruesome, heinous, hideous, loathsome, lousy, lurid, mean, nasty, obnoxious, offensive, repellent, revolting, scandalous, scary, shameful, shocking, terrible, terrifying, ungodly, unholy, unkind; SEE CONCEPTS 529,537

horrify [v] *scare*
affright, alarm, appall, chill off*, consternate, daunt, disgust, dismay, frighten, intimidate, outrage, petrify, scare to death*, shake, shock, sicken, terrify, terrorize; SEE CONCEPTS 7,14,19

horror [n] *fear, revulsion*
abhorrence, abomination, alarm, antipathy, apprehension, aversion, awe, chiller, consternation, detestation, disgust, dislike, dismay, dread, fright, hate, hatred, loathing, monstrosity, panic, repugnance, terror, trepidation; SEE CONCEPTS 27,29,532,690

hospitable [adj] *sociable, accommodating*
accessible, amenable, amicable, bountiful, charitable, companionable, convivial, cooperative, cordial, courteous, friendly, generous, genial, gracious, gregarious, kind, liberal, magnanimous, neighborly, obliging, open, open-minded, philanthropic, receptive, red-carpet treatment*, responsive, tolerant, welcoming; SEE CONCEPTS 542,555

hospital [n] *place where ill, injured are treated*
clinic, emergency room, health service, hospice, infirmary, institution, nursing home, rest home, sanatorium, sanitarium, sick bay*, surgery, ward; SEE CONCEPTS 312,439,449

hospitality [n] *neighborliness*
accommodation, affability, amiability, cheer, companionship, comradeship, consideration, conviviality, cordiality, entertainment, friendliness, generosity, geniality, good cheer, heartiness, hospitableness, obligingness, reception, sociability, warmth, welcome; SEE CONCEPTS 388,657

host [n1] *person who entertains, performs*
anchor, anchor person, emcee, entertainer, innkeeper, keeper, manager, moderator, owner, person of the house, presenter, proprietor; SEE CONCEPT 352

host [n2] *large group*
army, array, cloud, crowd, crush, drove, flock, gathering, horde, legion, multitude, myriad, rout, score, swarm, throng; SEE CONCEPTS 417,432

host [v] *entertain, accommodate*
do the honors*, introduce, pick up the check*, present, receive, spread oneself*, throw a party, treat, wine and dine*; SEE CONCEPTS 292,384

hostage [n] *person held captive until captor's demand is met*
captive, earnest, guaranty, pawn, pledge, pris-

oner, sacrificial lamb*, scapegoat*, security, surety, token, victim; SEE CONCEPTS *359,423*

hostile [*adj*] *antagonistic, mean*
adverse, alien, allergic, anti*, argumentative, bellicose, belligerent, bitter, catty*, chill*, cold*, competitive, contentious, contrary, disapproving, dour, hateful, ill-disposed, inhospitable, inimical, malevolent, malicious, malignant, militant, nasty, opposed, opposite, oppugnant, ornery*, pugnacious, rancorous, scrappy*, sour*, spiteful, surly, unfavorable, unfriendly, unkind, unpropitious, unsociable, unsympathetic, unwelcoming, viperous, virulent, vitriolic, warlike; SEE CONCEPTS *401,542*

hostility [*n*] *antagonism, meanness*
abhorrence, aggression, animosity, animus, antipathy, aversion, bad blood*, bellicosity, belligerence, bitterness, detestation, disaffection, enmity, estrangement, grudge, hatred, ill will, inimicality, malevolence, malice, opposition, rancor, resentment, spite, spleen, unfriendliness, venom, virulence, war, warpath; SEE CONCEPTS *633,657*

hot [*adj1*] *very high in temperature*
baking, blazing, blistering, boiling, broiling, burning, calescent, close, decalescent, febrile, fevered, feverish, feverous, fiery, flaming, heated, humid, igneous, incandescent, like an oven*, on fire, ovenlike, parching, piping, recalescent, red*, roasting, scalding, scorching, searing, sizzling, smoking, steaming, stuffy, sultry, summery, sweltering, sweltry, thermogenic, torrid, tropic, tropical, very warm, warm, white*; SEE CONCEPT *605*

hot [*adj2*] *spicy to taste*
acrid, biting, peppery, piquant, pungent, racy, sharp, spicy, zestful; SEE CONCEPT *613*

hot [*adj3*] *passionate, vehement*
angry, animated, ardent, aroused, distracted, eager, enthusiastic, excited, fervent, fervid, fierce, fiery, furious, ill-tempered, impassioned, impetuous, indignant, inflamed, intense, irascible, lustful, raging, stormy, temperamental, touchy, violent; SEE CONCEPTS *401,403*

hot [*adj4*] *new, in vogue*
approved, cool*, dandy, favored, fresh, glorious, groovy*, in demand, just out*, keen, latest*, marvelous, neat*, nifty*, peachy*, popular, recent, sought-after, super, trendy, up-to-the-minute*; SEE CONCEPT *589*

hot [*adj5*] *sexually excited*
aroused, carnal, concupiscent, erotic, lascivious, lewd, libidinous, lustful, passionate, prurient, salacious, sensual; SEE CONCEPTS *372,555*

hotel [*n*] *place where one pays for accommodation*
auberge, boarding house, caravansary, dump*, fleabag*, flophouse*, hospice, hostel, hostelry, house, inn, lodging, motel, motor inn, public house, resort, roadhouse, rooming house, spa, tavern; SEE CONCEPTS *439,449,516*

hound [*n*] *dog*
afghan, airedale, akita, basset, beagle, bowwow*, canine, dachshund, man's best friend*, mongrel, mutt, pointer, pooch, poodle, retriever; SEE CONCEPTS *394,400*

hound [*v*] *chase, badger*
annoy, bait, be at, beat the bushes*, be on one's back*, be on one's case*, be on one's tail*, birddog*, bother, bug, chivy, curdle, dog*, drive, give chase, goad, harass, harry, hassle, heckle, hector, hunt, hunt down, impel, leave no stone unturned*, persecute, pester, prod, provoke, pursue, rag*, rag on*, ride, scout, scratch, scratch around, search high heaven*, tail, take out after*, track down, turn inside out, turn upside down, yap at*; SEE CONCEPTS *7,19,207*

house [*n1*] *human habitat*
abode, apartment, box*, building, bullpen, castle, cave*, commoracy, condo, condominium, co-op, coop, crash pad*, crib*, cubbyhole*, den, diggings*, digs*, domicile, dump*, dwelling, edifice, flat, flophouse*, habitation, hole in the wall*, home, home plate*, homestead, joint, kennel, layout, lean-to*, mansion, pad, pied-à-terre, pigpen*, pigsty*, rack*, residence, residency, roof, roost*, setup, shack, shanty, turf*; SEE CONCEPTS *439,516*

house [*n2*] *family, ancestry*
clan, dynasty, family tree, folk, folks, household, kin, kindred, line, lineage, ménage, race, stock, tradition, tribe; SEE CONCEPTS *296*

house [*n3*] *business establishment*
company, concern, corporation, firm, organization, outfit, partnership; SEE CONCEPT *325*

house [*n4*] *government body, sometimes elected, responsible for laws*
commons, congress, council, legislative body, legislature, parliament; SEE CONCEPT *299*

household [*n*] *domestic establishment*
family, family unit, folks, home, house, ménage; SEE CONCEPTS *296,516*

household [*adj*] *domestic*
domiciliary, everyday, family, home, homely, homey, ordinary, plain; SEE CONCEPT *536*

housework [*n*] *cleaning, maintaining a home*
administration, bed-making, cooking, domestic art, domestic science, dusting, home economics, homemaking, housecraft, housekeeping, ironing, laundering, management, mopping, sewing, stewardship, sweeping, washing; SEE CONCEPTS *165,170,202*

housing [*n*] *place of accommodation*
construction, digs*, dwelling, habitation, home, house, lodgment, quarter, quarterage, residence, roof, shelter, sheltering, stopping place; SEE CONCEPTS *388,516*

hovel [*n*] *tiny unkempt house*
burrow, cabin, cottage, den, dump*, hole*, hut, hutch, lean-to, pigpen*, pigsty*, rathole*, rattrap*, shack, shanty, shed, stall, sty*; SEE CONCEPT *516*

hover [*v*] *hang, float over*
be suspended, brood over, dance, drift, flicker, flit, flitter, flutter, fly, hang about, linger, poise, wait nearby, waver; SEE CONCEPT *154*

how [*adv*] *in what way or manner*
according to what, after what precedent, by means of, by virtue of what, by what means, by what method, by whose help, from what source, through what agency, through what medium, to what degree, whence, whereby, wherewith; SEE CONCEPT *544*

however [*adv*] *still, nevertheless*
after all, all the same, anyhow, be that as it may, but, despite, for all that, howbeit, in spite of, nonetheless, notwithstanding, on the other hand, per contra, though, withal, without regard to; yet; SEE CONCEPT *544*

howl [*n/v*] *long, painful cry*
bark, bawl, bay, bellow, blubber, clamor, groan, growl, hoot, keen, lament, moan, outcry, quest, roar, scream, shout, shriek, ululate, wail, weep,

ho
ho

whimper, whine, yell, yelp, yip, yowl; SEE CONCEPTS *64,77,595*

hub [n] *center, focal point*
core, focus, heart, middle, nerve center*, pivot, polestar, seat; SEE CONCEPT *826*

hubbub [n] *commotion, disorder*
babel, bedlam, brouhaha*, clamor, confusion, din, disturbance, fuss, hassle, hell broke loose*, hue and cry*, hullabaloo*, hurly-burly*, jangle, noise, pandemonium, racket, riot, rowdydow*, ruckus, ruction, rumpus, to-do*, tumult, turmoil, uproar, whirl; SEE CONCEPTS *230,384,388*

huddle [n] *assemblage, crowd, often disorganized*
bunch, chaos, cluster, clutter, confab*, conference, confusion, disarray, discussion, disorder, gathering, group, heap, jumble, mass, meeting, mess*, muddle; SEE CONCEPTS *230,260,417,432*

huddle [v] *meet, discuss*
bunch, chase, confer, consult, converge, crouch, crowd, cuddle, curl up, draw together, flock, gather, herd, hug, hunch up*, mass, nestle, parley, powwow*, press, press close, snuggle, throng; SEE CONCEPTS *56,114,154*

hue [n] *color, shade*
aspect, cast, chroma, complexion, dye, tincture, tinge, tint, tone, value; SEE CONCEPT *622*

huff [n] *bad mood*
anger, annoyance, dudgeon, miff, offense, passion, perturbation, pet*, pique, rage, snit*, stew*, temper, tiff, umbrage; SEE CONCEPT *410*

huff [v] *sigh, breathe out forcefully*
blow, expire, gasp, heave, pant, puff; SEE CONCEPT *163*

huffy [adj] *angry, in a bad mood*
angered, annoyed, crabbed, crabby, cross, crotchety, crusty, curt, disgruntled, exasperated, fractious, grumpy, huffish, hurt, insulted, irked, irritable, miffed, moody, moping, nettled, offended, peeved, peevish, pettish, petulant, piqued, provoked, put out*, querulous, resentful, riled, short, snappish, snappy, stewed, sulky, sullen, surly, testy, touchy, vexed, waspish; SEE CONCEPTS *401,403*

hug [n] *embrace*
affection, bear hug*, bunny hug*, caress, clasp, clinch, lock, squeeze, tight grip; SEE CONCEPTS *190,375*

hug [v] *hold close, cling to*
bear hug, be near to, cherish, clasp, clinch, cradle, cuddle, embrace, enbosom, enfold, envelop, fold in arms, follow closely, grasp, hold onto, keep close, lie close, lock, love, nestle, nurse, press, receive, retain, seize, squeeze, stay near, take in one's arms, welcome; SEE CONCEPTS *190,375*

huge [adj] *extremely large*
behemothic, bulky, colossal, cyclopean, elephantine, enormous, extensive, gargantuan, giant, gigantic, great, gross*, humongous, immeasurable, immense, jumbo, leviathan, lusty, magnificent, mammoth, massive, mighty, mondo*, monster*, monstrous*, monumental, mountainous, outsize, oversize, planetary, prodigious, stupendous, titanic*, towering, tremendous, vast, walloping, whopping*; SEE CONCEPTS *771,773*

hulk [n] *large piece, lump; remains*
blob, body, bulk, chunk, clod, clump, frame, hull, hunk, mass, ruins, shambles, shell, shipwreck, skeleton, wreck; SEE CONCEPT *829*

hull [n] *skeleton, body*
bark, case, casing, cast, covering, frame, framework, husk, mold, peel, peeling, pod, rind, shell, shuck, skin, structure; SEE CONCEPTS *484,829*

hum [v] *buzz, vibrate*
bombilate, bombinate, bum, bumble, croon, drone, moan, mumble, murmur, purr, rustle, sing, sing low, sound, strum, throb, thrum, trill, warble, whir, whisper, zoom; SEE CONCEPTS *65,77*

human [n] *person, homosapien*
being, biped, body, character, child, creature, homo sapien, individual, life, mortal, personage, soul, wight; SEE CONCEPT *417*

human [adj] *characteristic of people*
animal, anthropoid, anthropological, anthropomorphic, biped, bipedal, civilized, creatural, ethnologic, ethological, fallible, fleshly, forgivable, hominal, homonid, homonine, humanistic, individual, mortal, personal, vulnerable; SEE CONCEPTS *406,549*

humane [adj] *kind, compassionate*
accommodating, altruistic, amiable, approachable, benevolent, benign, benignant, broad-minded, charitable, clement, considerate, cordial, democratic, forbearing, forgiving, friendly, generous, genial, gentle, good, good-natured, gracious, helpful, human, humanitarian, indulgent, kindhearted, kindly, lenient, liberal, magnanimous, merciful, mild, natural, obliging, open-minded, philanthropic, pitying, righteous, sympathetic, tender, tenderhearted, tolerant, understanding, unselfish, warmhearted; SEE CONCEPTS *401,542*

humanitarian [n] *person who gives generously*
altruist, benefactor, bleeding heart*, do-gooder*, Good Samaritan*, good scout*, helper, patron, philanthropist; SEE CONCEPTS *416,423*

humanitarian [adj] *giving, compassionate*
altruistic, beneficent, benevolent, charitable, eleemosynary, generous, good, humane, idealistic, kindly, philanthropic, public-spirited; SEE CONCEPT *542*

humankind [n] *the human race*
community, flesh, Homo sapiens, human beings, humanity, human species, mortality, mortals, people, populace, society; SEE CONCEPT *417*

humble [adj] *meek, unassuming*
apprehensive, backward, bashful, biddable, blushing, content, courteous, deferential, demure, diffident, docile, fearful, gentle, hesitant, lowly, manageable, mild, modest, obliging, obsequious, ordinary, polite, quiet, reserved, respectful, retiring, reverential, sedate, self-conscious, self-effacing, servile, sheepish, shy, simple, soft-spoken, standoffish, submissive, subservient, supplicatory, tentative, timid, timorous, tractable, unambitious, unobtrusive, unostentatious, unpretentious, withdrawn; SEE CONCEPTS *401,404*

humble [adj2] *poor, inferior*
base, beggarly, common, commonplace, contemptible, humdrum, ignoble, inglorious, insignificant, little, low, low-born, lowly, low-ranking, meager, mean, measly, menial, miserable, modest, obscure, ordinary, paltry, petty, pitiful, plebeian, proletarian, puny, rough, scrubby, seemly, servile, severe, shabby, simple, small, sordid, trivial, unassuming, uncouth, underprivileged, undistinguished, unfit, unimportant, unpretentious, unrefined, vulgar, wretched; SEE CONCEPTS *334,549,589*

humble [v] *shame, put down*
abase, abash, bemean, break, bring down*, cast down, chagrin, chasten, confound, confuse, crush*, cut to the quick*, debase, deflate, degrade, demean, demote, deny, discomfit, discredit, disgrace, embarrass, hide, humiliate, lower*, make eat dirt*, make one feel small*, mortify, overcome, pop one's balloon*, pull down*, put away*, put one away*, put to shame, reduce, silence, sink, snub, squash*, squelch, strike dumb, subdue, take down*, take down a peg*, upset; SEE CONCEPTS *14,16,44,52*

humdrum [adj] *boring, uneventful*
arid, banausic, blah, bromidic, common, commonplace, dim, dime a dozen*, drab, dreary, dull, everyday, garden-variety*, insipid, lifeless, monotone, monotonous, mundane, ordinary, pedestrian, plodding, prosy, repetitious, routine, tedious, tiresome, toneless, treadmill, uninteresting, unvaried, vanilla*, wearisome, white-bread*; SEE CONCEPT *548*

humid [adj] *very damp, referring to weather*
boiling, clammy, close, dank, irriguous, moist, mucky, muggy, oppressive, sodden, soggy, steamy, sticky, stifling, stuffy, sultry, sweaty, sweltering, watery, wet; SEE CONCEPTS *525,603*

humidity [n] *very damp weather*
clamminess, dampness, dankness, dew, dewiness, evaporation, fogginess, heaviness, humectation, humidness, moistness, moisture, mugginess, oppressiveness, sogginess, steam, steaminess, stickiness, sultriness, sweatiness, swelter, thickness, vaporization, wet, wetness; SEE CONCEPTS *524,607*

humiliate [v] *embarrass, put down*
abase, abash, base, bemean, blister, break, bring down*, bring low*, cast down, chagrin, chasten, confound, confuse, conquer, crush*, cut down to size*, debase, degrade, demean, denigrate, deny, depress, discomfit, discountenance, disgrace, dishonor, downplay, humble, lower, make a fool of*, make ashamed, mortify, pan, play down, put out of countenance*, put to shame, rip*, run down*, shame, shoot down*, slam*, smear, snub, squash*, subdue, take down*, take down a peg*, tear down*, vanquish, wither; SEE CONCEPTS *14,44,52*

humiliation [n] *embarrassment*
abasement, affront, chagrin, comedown*, comeuppance, condescension, confusion, degradation, discomfiture, disgrace, dishonor, humbling, ignominy, indignity, loss of face*, mental pain, mortification, put-down, resignation, self-abasement, shame, submission, submissiveness, touché*; SEE CONCEPTS *388,410*

humility [n] *humbleness, modesty*
abasement, bashfulness, demureness, diffidence, docility, fawning, inferiority complex, lack of pride, lowliness, meekness, mortification, nonresistance, obedience, obsequiousness, passiveness, reserve, resignation, self-abasement, self-abnegation, servility, sheepishness, shyness, subjection, submissiveness, subservience, timidity, timorousness, unobtrusiveness, unpretentiousness; SEE CONCEPTS *633,657*

humor [n1] *comedy, funniness*
amusement, badinage, banter, buffoonery, clowning, comicality, comicalness, drollery, facetiousness, farce, flippancy, fun, gag, gaiety, happiness, high spirits, jest, jesting, jocoseness, jocularity,

joke, joking, joyfulness, kidding, levity, lightness, playfulness, pleasantry, raillery, tomfoolery, whimsy, wisecrack, wit, witticism, wittiness; SEE CONCEPT *293*

humor [n2] *mood, temperament*
bee, bent, bias, caprice, character, complexion, conceit, disposition, fancy, frame of mind, individualism, individuality, makeup, mind, nature, notion, personality, propensity, quirk, spirits, strain, temper, tone, vagary, vein, whim; SEE CONCEPTS *9,410,411*

humorous [adj] *funny, comical*
amusing, camp*, campy*, comic, droll, entertaining, facetious, farcical, hilarious, jocose, jocular, jokey, joshing, laughable, ludicrous, merry, playful, pleasant, priceless, ribald, screaming*, side-splitting*, too funny for words*, waggish, whimsical, witty; SEE CONCEPTS *267,529*

hump [n] *swelling, projection*
bulge, bump, convexedness, convexity, dune, elevation, eminence, excrescence, gibbosity, hill, hummock, hunch, knap, knob, knurl, kyphosis, mound, prominence, protrusion, protuberance, ridge, swell, tumescence; SEE CONCEPTS *471,513*

hunch [n] *feeling, idea*
anticipation, apprehension, auguration, augury, boding, clue, expectation, feeling in one's bones*, foreboding, forecast, foreknowledge, forewarning, forewisdom, funny feeling*, glimmer, hint, impression, inkling, instinct, intuition, misgiving, notion, omination, portent, preapprehension, precognition, preconceived notion, premonition, prenotation, prenotice, presage, presagement, prescience, presentiment, qualm, suspicion, thought; SEE CONCEPT *689*

hunch [v] *cower, crouch*
arch, bend, bow, curve, draw in, draw together, huddle, hump, lean, scrooch down, squat, stoop, tense; SEE CONCEPT *154*

hunger [n] *appetite for food, other desire*
ache, appetence, appetency, appetition, a stomach for*, big eyes*, bottomless pit*, craving, desire, emptiness, esurience, eyes for*, famine, famishment, gluttony, greed, greediness, hungriness, longing, lust, mania, munchies*, ravenousness, starvation, sweet tooth*, vacancy, void, voracity, want, yearning, yen; SEE CONCEPTS *20,709*

hungry [adj] *starving; desirous*
athirst, avid, carnivorous, could eat a horse*, covetous, craving, eager, edacious, empty, esurient, famished, famishing, flying light*, got the munchies*, greedy, hankering, hoggish, hollow, hungered, insatiate, keen, omnivorous, on empty stomach*, piggish*, rapacious, ravenous, starved, unfilled, unsatisfied, voracious, yearning; SEE CONCEPTS *20,406*

hunk [n] *chunk of solid material*
a lot*, batch, bit, block, bulk, bunch, clod, glob, gob*, large piece, loads*, loaf, lump, mass, morsel, nugget, piece, pile, portion, quantity, slab, slice, wad, wedge; SEE CONCEPTS *470,471*

hunt [n] *search, chase*
coursing, exploration, field sport, following, frisking, game, hounding, hunting, inquest, inquiry, inquisition, interrogation, investigation, look-see*, meddling, probe, prosecution, prying, pursuance, pursuing, pursuit, quest, race, raid, reconnaissance, research, rummage, scrutiny, seeking, sifting, snooping, sporting, steeplechase, study, tracing, trailing; SEE CONCEPTS *207,216*

hu
hu

hunt [*v1*] *chase for killing*
beat the bushes*, bird-dog*, capture, course, dog, drag, drive, fish, follow, give chase, grouse, gun*, gun for*, hawk, heel, hound, kill, look for, poach, press, pursue, ride, run, scent, scratch, scratch around, seek, shadow, shoot, snare, stalk, start, track, trail; SEE CONCEPTS 207,216,252,363

hunt [*v2*] *look, search for*
be on the lookout*, cast about, delve, drag, examine, ferret out, fish for, forage, go after, grope, inquire, interrogate, investigate, look all over hell*, look high and low*, nose around*, probe, prowl, quest, question, ransack, rummage, run down, scour, scratch around*, search high heaven*, seek, sift, trace, trail, try to find, winnow; SEE CONCEPT 216

hurdle [*n*] *barrier, obstacle*
bar, barricade, blockade, complication, difficulty, fence, hamper, handicap, hedge, hindrance, impediment, interference, mountain, obstruction, rub, snag, stumbling block, traverse, wall; SEE CONCEPTS 470,674

hurdle [*v*] *jump over an obstacle*
bounce, bound, clear, conquer, down, hop, jump across, leap over, lick, lop, master, negotiate, over, overcome, saltate, scale, spring, surmount, vault; SEE CONCEPT 194

hurl [*v*] *throw forcefully*
bung, cast, chuck, chunk, fire, fling, gun, heave, launch, let fly, lob, peg, pitch, project, propel, send, sling, toss; SEE CONCEPT 222

hurricane [*n*] *violent windstorm*
blow, cyclone, gale, line storm, monsoon, storm, tempest, tornado, tropical cyclone, tropical storm, twister, typhoon, whirlwind; SEE CONCEPTS 524,526

hurried [*adj*] *quick, rushed*
abrupt, breakneck, brief, cursory, fast, hasty, headlong, hectic, impetuous, perfunctory, precipitant, precipitate, precipitous, rushing, short, slapdash, speedy, subitaneous, sudden, superficial, swift; SEE CONCEPTS 548,588,799

hurry [*n*] *speed in action, motion*
bustle, celerity, commotion, dash, dispatch, drive, expedition, expeditiousness, flurry, haste, precipitance, precipitateness, precipitation, promptitude, push, quickness, rush, rustle, scurry, speediness, swiftness, urgency; SEE CONCEPTS 657,748,755

hurry [*v*] *act, move speedily*
accelerate, barrel, beeline*, be quick, bestir, breeze, bullet, burst, bustle, dash, dig in, drive, expedite, fleet, flit, fly, get a move on*, goad, go like lightning*, haste, hasten, hurry up, hustle, jog, lose no time, make haste, make short work of*, make time*, make tracks*, nip, push, quicken, race, rip, rocket, roll, run, rush, sally, scoot, scurry, shake a leg*, smoke, speed, speed up, spur, step on gas*, step on it*, turn on steam*, urge, whirl, whish, whisk, whiz, zip; SEE CONCEPTS 150,234

hurt [*n*] *injury; damage*
ache, black and blue*, blow, boo-boo*, bruise, chop, detriment, disadvantage, disaster, discomfort, disservice, distress, down, gash, harm, ill, ill-treatment, loss, mark, mischief, misfortune, nick, ouch, outrage, pain, pang, persecution, prejudice, ruin, scratch, sore, soreness, suffering, wound, wrong; SEE CONCEPTS 316,728

hurt [*adj*] *physically or mentally injured*
aching, aggrieved, agonized, all torn up*, battered, bleeding, bruised, buffeted, burned, busted up*, contused, crushed, cut, damaged, disfigured, distressed, disturbed, grazed, harmed, hit, impaired, indignant, in pain, lacerated, marred, mauled, miffed, mutilated, nicked, offended, pained, piqued, put away, resentful, rueful, sad, scarred, scraped, scratched, shook, shot, sore, stricken, struck, suffering, tender, tortured, umbrageous, unhappy, warped, wounded; SEE CONCEPTS 314,403

hurt [*v1*] *cause physical pain; experience pain*
abuse, ache, afflict, ail, belt, be sore, be tender, bite, blemish, bruise, burn, cramp, cut, cut up, damage, disable, do violence, flail, flog, harm, impair, injure, kick, lacerate, lash, maltreat, mar, maul, mess up, nip, pierce, pinch, pommel, prick, pummel, punch, puncture, punish, rough up, shake up, slap, slug, smart, spank, spoil, squeeze, stab, sting, tear, throb, torment, torture, total, trouble, wax, whack, whip, wing, wound, wrack up, wring; SEE CONCEPTS 246,313

hurt [*v2*] *cause mental pain*
abuse, afflict, aggrieve, annoy, burn, chafe, constrain, cut to the quick*, discomfit, discommode, displease, distress, excruciate, faze, give no quarter*, go for jugular*, grieve, hit where one lives*, injure, lambaste, lay a bad trip on*, lean on*, martyr, martyrize, prejudice, punish, put down, put out, sadden, sting*, thumb nose at*, torment, torture, try, upset, vex, vitiate, work over*, wound, zing*; SEE CONCEPTS 7,14,19

hurtful [*adj*] *injurious, cruel*
aching, afflictive, bad, cutting, damaging, dangerous, deadly, deleterious, destructive, detrimental, disadvantageous, distressing, evil, harmful, hurting, malicious, mean, mischievous, nasty, nocuous, noxious, ominous, pernicious, poisonous, prejudicial, spiteful, unkind, upsetting, wounding; SEE CONCEPTS 537,542

hurtle [*v*] *plunge, charge*
bump, collide, fly, lunge, push, race, rush, rush headlong, scoot, scramble, shoot, speed, spurt, tear; SEE CONCEPT 150

husband [*n*] *married man*
bridegroom, companion, consort, groom, helpmate, hubby, mate, monogamist, monogynist, other half, partner, spouse; SEE CONCEPTS 414,419

hush [*n*] *quiet*
calm, lull, peace, peacefulness, quietude, silence, still, stillness, tranquility; SEE CONCEPT 65

hush [*v*] *attempt to make quiet*
burke, choke, gag, muffle, mute, muzzle, quiet, quieten, shush*, shut up, silence, stifle, still, stop, suppress; SEE CONCEPTS 65,87

hush-hush [*adj*] *secret*
clandestine, classified, closet, confidential, covert, dark, private, restricted, sub-rosa*, surreptitious, undercover, under-the-table*; SEE CONCEPT 576

hush up [*v*] *keep secret*
burke, conceal, cover, cover up, keep dark, sit on, smother, squash, stifle, suppress; SEE CONCEPT 266

husk [*n*] *covering, case*
aril, bark, case, chaff, glume, hull, outside, pod, rind, shell, shuck, skin; SEE CONCEPTS 428,484

husky [*adj1*] *deep, scratchy in sound*
croaking, croaky, growling, gruff, guttural, harsh, hoarse, loud, rasping, raucous, rough, throaty; SEE CONCEPT *594*

husky [*adj2*] *big, burly*
brawny, gigantic, hefty, Herculean*, mighty, muscular, powerful, rugged, sinewy, stalwart, stocky, stout, strapping, strong, sturdy, thickset, well-built; SEE CONCEPT *773*

hustle [*v*] *hurry; work hurriedly*
apply oneself, be conscientious, bulldoze*, bustle, elbow, fly, force, haste, hasten, hotfoot*, impel, jog, press, push, race, rush, shove, speed, thrust, use elbow grease*; SEE CONCEPTS *91,150*

hut [*n*] *tiny, often roughly built, house*
box*, bungalow, cabana, cabin, camp, chalet, cot, cottage, crib*, den, dugout, dump*, hovel*, hutch, lean-to, lodge, log house, pigeonhole*, rathole*, refuge, shack, shanty, shed, shelter, summer house, tepee, wigwam; SEE CONCEPT *516*

hybrid [*n*] *composite, mixture*
amalgam, bastard, combination, compound, cross, crossbreed, half-blood, half-breed, half-caste, incross, miscegenation, mongrel, mule, outcross; SEE CONCEPTS *260,394,414,429*

hygiene [*n*] *cleanliness*
healthful living, hygienics, preventive medicine, public health, regimen, salutariness, sanitation, wholesomeness; SEE CONCEPTS *316,405*

hygienic [*adj*] *clean*
aseptic, disinfected, germ-free, good, healthful, healthy, pure, salubrious, salutary, salutiferous, sanitary, sterile, uncontaminated, uninfected, wholesome; SEE CONCEPT *621*

hymn [*n*] *religious song*
aria, canticle, carol, chant, choral, chorale, descant, ditty, evensong, hosanna, laud, lay, lied, littany, ode, oratorio, paean, psalm, shout, song of praise, worship song; SEE CONCEPTS *262,595*

hype [*n*] *extensive publicity*
advertising, buildup*, plugging*, promotion; SEE CONCEPTS *292,324*

hyperbole [*n*] *exaggeration*
amplification, big talk*, coloring*, distortion, embellishment, embroidering, enlargement, hype*, laying it on thick*, magnification, metaphor, mountain out of molehill*, overstatement, PR*, tall talk*; SEE CONCEPT *268*

hyperinflation [*n*] *extremely high, rising economic inflation*
devaluation, overextension, run-away inflation, wheelbarrow economics; SEE CONCEPT *335*

hypermedia [*n*] *system giving access to multimedia information on a single subject*
data base, information bank, information retrieval; SEE CONCEPT *274*

hypnotic [*adj*] *spellbinding, sleep-inducing*
anesthetic, anodyne, calmative, lenitive, mesmeric, mesmerizing, narcotic, opiate, sleepy, somniferous, somnolent, soothing, soporific, soporose, trance-inducing; SEE CONCEPTS *529,537*

hypnotize [*v*] *put in trance; spellbind*
anesthetize, bring under control, captivate, charm, drug, dull the will, entrance, fascinate, hold under a spell, induce, lull to sleep, magnetize, make drowsy, make sleepy, mesmerize, narcotize, put to sleep, soothe, stupefy, subject to suggestion; SEE CONCEPT *250*

hypocrisy [*n*] *deceitfulness, pretense*
affectation, bad faith*, bigotry, cant, casuistry,

deceit, deception, dishonesty, display, dissembling, dissimulation, double-dealing, duplicity, false profession, falsity, fraud, glibness, imposture, insincerity, irreverence, lie, lip service*, mockery, pharisaicalness, pharisaism, phoniness, pietism, quackery, sanctimoniousness, sanctimony, speciousness, unctuousness; SEE CONCEPTS *63,633,657*

hypocrite [*n*] *person who pretends, is deceitful*
actor, attitudinizer, backslider*, bigot, bluffer, casuist, charlatan, cheat, con artist, crook, deceiver, decoy, dissembler, dissimulator, fake, faker, four-flusher*, fraud, hook*, humbug, impostor, informer, lip server*, malingerer, masquerader, mountebank, Pharisee, phony, playactor*, poser, pretender, quack*, smoothie*, sophist, swindler, trickster, two-face*, two-timer*, wolf in sheep's clothing*; SEE CONCEPT *412*

hypocritical [*adj*] *deceitful, pretending*
affected, artificial, assuming, bland, canting, captious, caviling, deceptive, deluding, dissembling, double, double-dealing, duplicitous, faithless, false, feigning, fishy*, fraudulent, glib, hollow, insincere, jivey, left-handed, lying, moralistic, oily, pharisaical, phony, pietistic, pious, sanctimonious, self-righteous, smooth, smooth-spoken, smooth-tongued*, snide, specious, spurious, two-faced*, unctuous, unnatural, unreliable; SEE CONCEPTS *267,401,542*

hypothesis [*n*] *theory*
antecedent, apriority, assignment, assumption, attribution, axiom, basis, belief, conclusion, condition, conjecture, data, deduction, demonstration, derivation, explanation, foundation, ground, guess, inference, interpretation, layout, lemma, philosophy, plan, position, postulate, premise, presupposition, principle, proposal, proposition, rationale, reason, scheme, shot in the dark*, speculation, starting point, suggestion, supposition, surmise, system, tentative law, term, theorem, thesis; SEE CONCEPTS *661,689*

hypothetical [*adj*] *guessed, assumed*
academic, assumptive, casual, concocted, conditional, conjectural, conjectural, contestable, contingent, debatable, disputable, doubtful, equivocal, imaginary, imagined, indefinite, indeterminate, postulated, presumptive, presupposed, pretending, problematic, provisory, putative, questionable, refutable, speculative, stochastic, supposed, suppositional, suppositious, suspect, theoretic, theoretical, uncertain, unconfirmed, vague; SEE CONCEPTS *529,552,582*

hysteria [*n*] *state of extreme upset*
agitation, delirium, excitement, feverishness, frenzy, hysterics, madness, mirth, nervousness, panic, unreason; SEE CONCEPT *410*

hysterical [*adj*] *very upset, excited*
agitated, berserk, beside oneself, blazing, carried away*, convulsive, crazed, crazy, delirious, distracted, distraught, emotional, fiery, frantic, frenzied, fuming, furious, impassioned, impetuous, in a fit, incensed, irrepressible, mad, maddened, nervous, neurotic, overwrought, panic-stricken, passionate, possessed, rabid, raging, rampant, raving, seething, spasmodic, tempestuous, turbulent, uncontrollable, uncontrolled, unnerved, unrestrained, uproarious, vehement, violent, wild, worked up*; SEE CONCEPTS *403,542*

hu
hy

ice [n] *frozen water*

chunk, crystal, cube ice, diamonds*, dry ice, floe, glacier, glaze, hail, hailstone, iceberg, ice cube, icicle, permafrost, sleet; SEE CONCEPTS 470,514

icky [adj] *not pleasant*

disgusting, horrible, loathsome, nasty, noisome, offensive, repellent, revolting, sickening, vile; SEE CONCEPT 570

icy [adj1] *frozen; slippery when frozen*

antarctic, arctic, biting, bitter, chill, chilled to the bone*, chilling, chilly, cold, freezing, frigid, frost-bound, frosty, frozen over, gelid, glacial, glaring, iced, polar, raw, refrigerated, rimy, shivering, shivery, sleeted, smooth as glass*; SEE CONCEPTS 605,606

icy [adj2] *aloof*

chill, cold, distant, emotionless, forbidding, frigid, frosty, glacial, hostile, indifferent, steely, stony, unemotional, unfriendly, unwelcoming; SEE CONCEPTS 401,404

idea [n] *something understood, planned, or believed*

abstraction, aim, approximation, belief, brainstorm*, clue, concept, conception, conclusion, conviction, design, doctrine, end, essence, estimate, fancy, feeling, flash*, form, guess, hint, hypothesis, import, impression, inkling, intention, interpretation, intimation, judgment, meaning, notion, object, objective, opinion, pattern, perception, plan, purpose, reason, scheme, sense, significance, solution, suggestion, suspicion, teaching, theory, thought, understanding, view, viewpoint; SEE CONCEPTS 529,660,661,689

ideal [n] *model*

archetype, criterion, epitome, example, exemplar, goal, idol, jewel, last word*, mirror, nonesuch, nonpareil, paradigm, paragon, pattern, perfection, prototype, standard; SEE CONCEPTS 671,686

ideal [adj1] *model, perfect*

absolute, archetypal, classic, classical, complete, consummate, excellent, exemplary, fitting, flawless, have-it-all*, indefectible, optimal, paradigmatic, pie-in-the-sky*, prototypical, quintessential, representative, Shangri-la*, supreme; SEE CONCEPTS 533,574

ideal [adj2] *conceptual; impractical*

abstract, chimerical, dreamlike, extravagant, fanciful, fictitious, high-flown, hypothetical, imaginary, intellectual, in the clouds*, ivory-tower*, mental, mercurial, notional, out-of-reach*, quixotic, theoretical, transcendent, transcendental, unattainable, unearthly, unreal, Utopian*, visionary; SEE CONCEPTS 529,552

idealist [n] *person who holds fancies in mind, who believes in perfection*

dreamer, enthusiast, escapist, optimist, Platonist, radical, romancer, romantic, romanticist, seer, stargazer, theorizer, transcendalist, Utopian, visionary; SEE CONCEPTS 359,416,423

ideals [n] *moral beliefs*

ethics, goals, principles, standards, values; SEE CONCEPTS 645,689

identical [adj] *alike, equal*

carbon copy*, corresponding, dead ringer*, ditto*, double, duplicate, equivalent, exact, identic, indistinguishable, interchangeable, like, like two peas in a pod*, look-alike, matching, same, same difference*, selfsame, spitting image*, tantamount, twin, very, very same, Xerox*; SEE CONCEPTS 487,566,573

identification [n] *labeling; means of labeling*

apperception, assimilation, badge, bracelet, cataloging, classifying, credentials, description, dog tag, establishment, ID*, identity bracelet, letter of introduction, letter of recommendation, naming, papers, passport, recognition, tag, testimony; SEE CONCEPTS 268,271

identify [v] *recognize; label*

analyze, button down*, card, catalog, classify, describe, determinate, determine, diagnose, diagnosticate, distinguish, establish, find, make out, name, peg*, pick out, pinpoint, place, put one's finger on*, select, separate, single out*, spot, tab*, tag*; SEE CONCEPTS 38,62

identify with [v] *put oneself in the place of another*

ally, associate, empathize, feel for*, put in same category*, put oneself in another's shoes*, relate to, respond to, see through someone's eyes*, sympathize, think of in connection*, understand; SEE CONCEPTS 15,39

identity [n1] *person's individuality*

character, circumstances, coherence, distinctiveness, existence, identification, integrity, ipseity, name, oneness, particularity, personality, self, selfdom, selfhood, selfness, singleness, singularity, status, uniqueness; SEE CONCEPT 411

identity [n2] *similarity, correspondence*

accord, agreement, congruence, congruity, empathy, equality, equivalence, identicalness, likeness, oneness, rapport, resemblance, sameness, self-sameness, semblance, similitude, unanimity, uniformity, unity; SEE CONCEPTS 664,670

ideology [n] *beliefs*

articles of faith*, credo, creed, culture, dogma, ideas, outlook, philosophy, principles, system, tenets, theory, view, Weltanschauung*; SEE CONCEPTS 688,689

idiocy [n] *utter stupidity*

asininity, cretinism, derangement, fatuity, fatuousness, foolishness, imbecility, inanity, insanity, insipidity, lunacy, madness, senselessness, tomfoolery; SEE CONCEPTS 409,410

idiom [n] *manner of speaking, turn of phrase*

argot, colloquialism, dialect, expression, idiosyncrasy, jargon, language, lingo*, localism, locution, parlance, patois, phrase, provincialism, set phrase, street talk*, style, talk, tongue, usage, vernacular, vernacularism, word; SEE CONCEPT 275

idiosyncrasy [n] *oddity, quirk*

affectation, bit, characteristic, distinction, eccentricity, feature, habit, mannerism, peculiarity, singularity, trait, trick; SEE CONCEPTS 411,644

idiot [n] *very stupid person*

blockhead, bonehead*, cretin, dimwit, dork, dumbbell, dunce, fool, ignoramus, imbecile, jerk, kook*, moron, nincompoop, ninny*, nitwit, out to lunch*, pinhead*, simpleton, stupid, tomfool, twit*; SEE CONCEPT 412

idiotic [adj] *very stupid*

asinine, batty*, birdbrained*, crazy, daffy*, daft, dull, dumb, fatuous, foolhardy, foolish, harebrained*, imbecile, imbecilic, inane, insane, lunatic, moronic, senseless, silly, squirrelly*, thick-witted*, unintelligent; SEE CONCEPT 402

idle [adj1] *not used; out of action*

abandoned, asleep, barren, closed down, dead,

deserted, down, dusty, empty, gathering dust*, inactive, inert, jobless, laid-off, leisured, mothballed, motionless, on the bench*, on the shelf*, out of operation, out of work*, passive, quiet, redundant, resting, rusty, sleepy, stationary, still, uncultivated, unemployed, unoccupied, untouched, unused, vacant, void, waste, workless; SEE CONCEPTS *542,560*

idle [*adj2*] *lazy*
at rest, indolent, lackadaisical, resting, shiftless, slothful, sluggish, taking it easy*; SEE CONCEPTS *401,538*

idle [*adj3*] *worthless, ineffective*
abortive, bootless, empty, frivolous, fruitless, futile, groundless, hollow, insignificant, irrelevant, not serious, nugatory, of no avail*, otiose, pointless, rambling, superficial, trivial, unavailing, unhelpful, unnecessary, unproductive, unsuccessful, useless, vain; SEE CONCEPTS *267,560*

idleness [*n*] *laziness, inaction*
dawdling, dilly-dallying*, dormancy, droning, goof-off time*, hibernation, inactivity, indolence, inertia, joblessness, laze, lazing, leisure, lethargy, loafing, loitering, otiosity, own sweet time*, pottering, shiftlessness, sloth, slothfulness, slouch, slowness, sluggishness, stupor, time on one's hands*, time to burn*, time to kill*, time-wasting, torpidity, torpor, trifling, truancy, unemployment, vegetating; SEE CONCEPTS *657,677,681*

idol [*n*] *person greatly admired*
beloved, darling, dear, deity, desire, eidolon, false god, favorite, fetish, god, goddess, golden calf*, graven image, hero, icon, image, inamorata, pagan symbol, simulacrum, superstar; SEE CONCEPTS *352,423*

idolize [*v*] *think of very highly; worship*
admire, adore, apotheosize, bow down, canonize, deify, dote on, exalt, glorify, look up to*, love, put on a pedestal*, revere, reverence, venerate; SEE CONCEPTS *10,32*

idyllic [*adj*] *perfect; extremely pleasant*
arcadian, bucolic, charming, comfortable, halcyon, heavenly, ideal, idealized, out-of-this-world*, pastoral, peaceful, picturesque, pleasing, rustic, unspoiled; SEE CONCEPTS *529,572*

iffy [*adj*] *uncertain*
capricious, chancy, conditional, dicey, doubtful, erratic, fluctuant, incalculable, in lap of gods*, problematic, undecided, unpredictable, unsettled, up in the air*, whimsical; SEE CONCEPT *552*

ignite [*v*] *set on fire*
burn, burst into flames, catch fire, enkindle, fire, flare up, inflame, kindle, light, put match to*, set alight, set fire to, start up, take fire, touch off; SEE CONCEPT *249*

ignoble [*adj*] *lowly, unworthy*
abject, base, baseborn, coarse, common, contemptible, corrupt, craven, dastardly, degenerate, degraded, despicable, disgraceful, dishonorable, heinous, humble, infamous, inferior, lewd, low, mean, menial, modest, ordinary, peasant, petty, plain, plebeian, poor, rotten, scurvy, servile, shabby, shameful, simple, sordid, unwashed, vile, vulgar, wicked, wretched, wrong; SEE CONCEPTS *542,545,549*

ignorance [*n*] *unintelligence, inexperience*
benightedness, bewilderment, blindness, callowness, crudeness, darkness, denseness, disregard, dumbness, empty-headedness*, fog*, half-knowledge, illiteracy, incapacity, incomprehen-

sion, innocence, inscience, insensitivity, lack of education, mental incapacity, naiveté, nescience, oblivion, obtuseness, philistinism, rawness, sciolism, shallowness, simplicity, unawareness, unconsciousness, uncouthness, unenlightenment, unfamiliarity, unscholarliness, vagueness; SEE CONCEPTS *409,678*

ignorant [*adj*] *unaware, unknowing*
apprenticed, benighted, birdbrained*, blind to*, cretinous, dense, green*, illiterate, imbecilic, inexperienced, innocent, insensible, in the dark*, mindless, misinformed, moronic, naive, nescient, oblivious, obtuse, shallow, thick, unconscious, unconversant, uncultivated, uncultured, uneducated, unenlightened, uninformed, uninitiated, unintellectual, unknowledgeable, unlearned, unlettered, unmindful, unread, unschooled, unsuspecting, untaught, untrained, unwitting, witless; SEE CONCEPTS *402,542*

ignore [*v*] *disregard on purpose*
avoid, be oblivious to, blink, brush off*, bury one's head in sand*, cold-shoulder*, discount, disdain, evade, fail, forget, let it go*, neglect, omit, overlook, overpass, pass over, pay no attention to, pay no mind*, pooh-pooh*, reject, scorn, shut eyes to*, slight, take no notice, tune out*, turn back on*, turn blind eye*, turn deaf ear; SEE CONCEPT *30*

ill [*n*] *misfortune*
abuse, affection, affliction, ailment, badness, complaint, condition, cruelty, damage, depravity, destruction, disease, disorder, evil, harm, hurt, illness, indisposition, infirmity, injury, insult, malady, malaise, malice, mischief, misery, pain, sickness, suffering, syndrome, trial, tribulation, trouble, unpleasantness, wickedness, woe, wrong; SEE CONCEPTS *316,674,675*

ill [*adj1*] *sick*
afflicted, ailing, a wreck*, below par*, bummed*, diseased, down, down with, feeling awful, feeling rotten, feeling terrible, got the bug*, indisposed, infirm, laid low*, off one's feet*, on sick list*, out of sorts*, peaked, poorly, queasy, rotten, run-down, running temperature, sick as a dog*, under the weather*, unhealthy, unwell, woozy*; SEE CONCEPT *314*

ill [*adj2*] *bad, evil*
acrimonious, adverse, antagonistic, cantankerous, cross, damaging, deleterious, detrimental, disrespectful, disturbing, foreboding, foul, harmful, harsh, hateful, hostile, hurtful, ill-mannered, impertinent, inauspicious, inimical, iniquitous, injurious, malevolent, malicious, nocent, nocuous, noxious, ominous, ruinous, sinister, sullen, surly, threatening, unfavorable, unfortunate, unfriendly, ungracious, unhealthy, unkind, unlucky, unpromising, unpropitious, unwholesome, vile, wicked, wrong; SEE CONCEPTS *537,545,570*

ill-advised [*adj*] *unwise, not thought out*
brash, confused, foolhardy, foolish, half-baked*, hotheaded*, ill-considered, ill-judged, impolitic, imprudent, inappropriate, incautious, inconsiderate, indiscreet, inexpedient, injudicious, madcap*, misguided, off the top of one's head*, overhasty, rash, reckless, short-sighted*, thoughtless, unseemly, wrong; SEE CONCEPTS *544,548*

ill at ease [*adj*] *uncomfortable, nervous*
anxious, awkward, discomfited, disquieted, disturbed, doubtful, edgy, faltering, fidgety, hesitant, insecure, on edge*, on pins and needles*, on ten-

ic
il

terhooks*, out of place*, restless, self-conscious, shy, suspicious, tense, uneasy, unrelaxed, unsettled, unsure; SEE CONCEPTS *401,403*

illegal [*adj*] *against the law*
actionable, banned, black-market*, bootleg*, contraband, criminal, crooked, extralegal, felonious, forbidden, heavy*, hot*, illegitimate, illicit, interdicted, irregular, lawless, not approved, not legal, outlawed, outside the law, prohibited, proscribed, prosecutable, racket, shady, smuggled, sub rosa, taboo, unauthorized, unconstitutional, under the table*, unlawful, unlicensed, unofficial, unwarrantable, unwarranted, verboten, violating, wildcat*, wrongful; SEE CONCEPTS *319,545*

illegible [*adj*] *unreadable*
cacographic, crabbed, cramped, difficult to read, faint, hard to make out*, hieroglyphic, indecipherable, indistinct, obscure, scrawled, unclear, undecipherable, unintelligible; SEE CONCEPTS *535,576*

illegitimate [*adj*] *not legal*
contraband, illegal, illicit, improper, invalid, misbegotten, spurious, supposititious, unauthorized, unconstitutional, unlawful, unsanctioned, wicked, wrong; SEE CONCEPTS *319,549*

ill-fated/ill-starred [*adj*] *doomed*
blighted, catastrophic, destroyed, disastrous, hapless, ill-omened, inauspicious, luckless, misfortunate, ruined, star-crossed*, unfortunate, unhappy, unlucky, untoward; SEE CONCEPTS *537,548*

illicit [*adj*] *not legal; forbidden*
adulterous, black-market*, bootleg*, clandestine, contraband, contrary to law, criminal, crooked, dirty*, felonious, furtive, guilty, heavy*, illegal, illegitimate, immoral, improper, in violation of law, lawless, out of line*, prohibited, racket, unauthorized, unlawful, unlicensed, wrong, wrongful; SEE CONCEPTS *319,545*

illiterate [*adj*] *unable to read well; lacking education*
benighted, catachrestic, ignorant, inerudite, solecistic, uneducated, unenlightened, ungrammatical, uninstructed, unlearned, unlettered, unread, unschooled, untaught, untutored; SEE CONCEPT *402*

ill-mannered [*adj*] *badly behaved*
bad-mannered, boorish, cheap, churlish, coarse, discourteous, disrespectful, ill-behaved, ill-bred, impertinent, impolite, insolent, loud, loud-mouthed, loutish, raunchy*, raw, rough, rough-neck*, rude, tacky*, uncivil, uncouth, ungracious, unmannerly, unrefined, vulgar; SEE CONCEPT *401*

ill-natured [*adj*] *bad-tempered*
catty, churlish, crabbed, crabby, cross, crotchety, cussed*, dirty*, disagreeable, disobliging, dyspeptic, hot-tempered, ill-humored, irritable, malevolent, malicious, mean, nasty, ornery*, perverse, petulant, spiteful, sulky, sullen, surly, temperamental, tempersome, touchy, unfriendly, unkind, unpleasant; SEE CONCEPTS *401,404*

illness [*n*] *disease; bad health*
affliction, ailing, ailment, attack, breakdown, bug*, collapse, complaint, confinement, convalescence, disability, diseasedness, disorder, disturbance, dose, failing health, fit, flu, ill health, indisposition, infirmity, malady, malaise, poor health, prostration, relapse, seizure, sickness, syndrome, unhealth, virus, what's going around*; SEE CONCEPT *306*

illogical [*adj*] *not making sense*
absurd, casuistic, cockeyed*, fallacious, false, fatuous, faulty, groundless, hollow, implausible, inconclusive, incongruous, inconsequent, inconsistent, incorrect, invalid, irrational, irrelevant, mad, meaningless, not following, nutty*, off the wall*, preposterous, screwy*, self-contradictory, senseless, sophistic, sophistical, specious, spurious, unconnected, unproved, unreasonable, unscientific, unsound, unsubstantial, untenable, wacky, without basis, without foundation; SEE CONCEPTS *267,529*

ill-timed [*adj*] *not occurring at a suitable time*
awkward, badly timed, improper, inappropriate, inconvenient, inept, inopportune, malapropos, mistimed, unbecoming, unbefitting, unfavorable, unseasonable, unseemly, unsuitable, untimely, unwelcome; SEE CONCEPT *548*

illuminate [*v1*] *make light*
brighten, fire, flash, floodlight, highlight, hit with a light*, ignite, illume, illumine, irradiate, kindle, light, lighten, light up, limelight*, spot, spotlight; SEE CONCEPT *624*

illuminate [*v2*] *make clear; educate*
better, clarify, clear up, construe, define, dramatize, edify, elucidate, enlighten, explain, expound, express, finish, give insight, gloss, illustrate, improve, instruct, interpret, perfect, polish, shed light on*, uplight; SEE CONCEPTS *57,285*

illumination [*n1*] *light; making light*
beam, brightening, brightness, brilliance, flame, flash, gleam, lighting, lights, radiance, ray; SEE CONCEPTS *620,624*

illumination [*n2*] *clear understanding*
awareness, clarification, edification, education, enlightenment, information, insight, inspiration, instruction, perception, revelation, teaching; SEE CONCEPTS *274,409*

illusion [*n*] *false appearance; false belief*
apparition, bubble*, chimera, confusion, daydream, deception, déjà vu*, delusion, error, fallacy, false impression, fancy, fantasy, figment of imagination, fool's paradise*, ghost, hallucination, head trip*, hocus-pocus*, idolism, ignus fatuus, image, invention, make-believe, mirage, misapprehension, misbelief, misconception, misimpression, mockery, myth, optical illusion, paramnesia, phantasm, pipe dream*, rainbow*, seeming, semblance, trip*, virtual reality; SEE CONCEPTS *689,716*

illusory/illusive [*adj*] *deceptive, false*
apparent, blue-sky*, chimerical, deceitful, delusive, delusory, fake, fallacious, fanciful, fantastic, fictional, fictitious, fictive, hallucinatory, ideal, imaginary, misleading, mistaken, ostensible, pseudo*, seeming, semblant, sham*, supposititious, unreal, untrue, visionary, whimsical; SEE CONCEPTS *529,552,582*

illustrate [*v1*] *demonstrate, exemplify*
allegorize, bring home*, clarify, clear, clear up, delineate, depict, disclose, draw a picture*, elucidate, emblematize, embody, emphasize, epitomize, evidence, evince, exhibit, explain, expose, expound, get across*, get over*, highlight, illuminate, imitate, instance, interpret, lay out*, limelight*, make clear, make plain, manifest, mark, mirror, ostend, personify, picture, point up*, portray, proclaim, represent, reveal, show, show and

tell*, spotlight*, symbolize, typify, vivify; SEE CONCEPTS 57,97

illustrate [v2] *explain by drawing, decorating*
adorn, delineate, depict, embellish, illuminate, limn, ornament, paint, picture, portray, represent, sketch; SEE CONCEPTS 57,174

illustration [n1] *demonstration, exemplification*
analogy, case, case history, case in point, clarification, elucidation, example, explanation, for instance, instance, interpretation, model, representative, sample, sampling, specimen; SEE CONCEPTS 268,686

illustration [n2] *drawing, artwork that assists explanation*
adornment, cartoon, decoration, depiction, design, engraving, etching, figure, frontispiece, halftone, image, line drawing, painting, photo, photograph, picture, plate, sketch, snapshot, tailpiece, vignette; SEE CONCEPT 259

illustrative [adj] *explanatory*
allegorical, clarifying, comparative, corroborative, delineative, descriptive, diagrammatic, emblematic, exemplifying, explicatory, expository, figurative, graphic, iconographic, illuminative, illustrational, illustratory, imagistic, indicative, interpretive, metaphoric, pictorial, pictoric, representative, revealing, sample, specifying, symbolic, typical; SEE CONCEPT 267

illustrious [adj] *famous, prominent*
big league*, brilliant, celeb*, celebrated, distinguished, eminent, esteemed, exalted, famed, glorious, great, heavy, lofty, monster*, name*, noble, notable, noted, outstanding, remarkable, renowned, resplendent, signal, splendid, star, sublime, superstar, well-known; SEE CONCEPT 568

ill will [n] *hatred; hard feelings*
acrimony, animosity, animus, antagonism, antipathy, aversion, bad blood*, bad will, blame, despite, dislike, enmity, envy, feud, grudge, hate, hostility, malevolence, malice, maliciousness, no love lost*, objection, rancor, resentment, spite, spitefulness, sally, unfriendliness, venom; SEE CONCEPT 29

image [n1] *representation; counterpart*
angel*, appearance, carbon*, carbon copy, carved figure, chip off old block*, copy, dead ringer*, double, drawing, effigy, equal, equivalent, facsimile, figure, form, icon, idol, illustration, likeness, match, model, photocopy, photograph, picture, portrait, reflection, replica, reproduction, similitude, simulacre, simulacrum, spitting image*, statue; SEE CONCEPTS 259,667,716

image [n2] *concept*
apprehension, conceit, conception, construct, figure, idea, impression, intellection, mental picture, notion, perception, phantasm, thought, trope, vision; SEE CONCEPTS 529,689

imaginable [adj] *believable, possible*
apprehensible, calculable, comprehensible, conceivable, conjecturable, convincing, credible, likely, plausible, sensible, supposable, thinkable, under the sun*; SEE CONCEPTS 529,552

imaginary [adj] *fictitious, invented*
abstract, apocryphal, apparitional, assumed, chimerical, deceptive, delusive, dreamed-up*, dreamlike, dreamy, fabulous, fancied, fanciful, fantastic, fictional, figmental, fool's paradise*, hallucinatory, hypothetical, ideal, illusive, illusory, imaginative, imagined, legendary, made-up, mythological, nonexistent, notional, phantasmal,

phantasmic, quixotic, shadowy, spectral, supposed, supposititious, theoretical, trumped up*, unreal, unsubstantial, visionary, whimsical; SEE CONCEPTS 529,582

imagination [n] *power to create in one's mind*
acuteness, artistry, awareness, chimera, cognition, conception, creation, creative thought, creativity, enterprise, fabrication, fancy, fantasy, flight of fancy*, idea, ideality, illusion, image, imagery, ingenuity, insight, inspiration, intelligence, invention, inventiveness, mental agility, notion, originality, perceptibility, realization, resourcefulness, sally, supposition, thought, thoughtfulness, unreality, verve, vision, visualization, wit, wittiness; SEE CONCEPTS 409,410

imaginative [adj] *creative, inventive*
artistic, avant-garde, blue-sky*, brain wave, breaking ground, clever, dreamy, enterprising, extravagant, fanciful, fantastic, fertile, fictive, high-flown*, ingenious, inspired, offbeat, original, originative, pie-in-the-sky*, poetic, poetical, productive, quixotic, romantic, utopian, visionary, vivid, way out*, whimsical; SEE CONCEPTS 529,542

imagine [v1] *dream up, conceive*
brainstorm, build castles in air*, conceptualize, conjure up, cook up*, create, depict, devise, envisage, envision, fabricate, fancy, fantasize, fantasy, feature, figure, form, frame, harbor, image, invent, make up, nurture, perceive, picture, plan, project, realize, scheme, see in one's mind*, spark, think of, think up, vision, visualize; SEE CONCEPT 43

imagine [v2] *assume, deduce*
apprehend, believe, conjecture, deem, expect, fancy, gather, guess, infer, presume, realize, reckon, suppose, surmise, suspect, take for granted, take it, think, understand; SEE CONCEPTS 12,26

imbecile [n] *very stupid person*
birdbrain, dimwit, dolt, dummy, dunce, fool, idiot, jerk, lamebrain*, moron, pinhead*, simpleton; SEE CONCEPT 412

imbecile [adj] *stupid, foolish*
asinine, backward, deranged, dim-witted, dull, fatuous, feeble-minded, idiotic, imbecilic, inane, ludicrous, moronic, simple, simple-minded, slow, thick, witless; SEE CONCEPT 402

imbibe [v] *drink, often heavily*
absorb, assimilate, belt*, consume, down, gorge, guzzle*, ingest, ingurgitate, irrigate, partake, put away*, quaff, raise a few*, sip, swallow, swig*, swill*, toss*; SEE CONCEPT 169

imbroglio [n] *misunderstanding; fight*
altercation, argument, bickering, brawl, broil*, brouhaha*, complexity, complication, dispute, embarrassment, embroilment, entanglement, falling-out*, flack*, involvement, knock-down-drag-out*, miff*, quandary, quarrel, row, run-in*, soap opera*, spat, squabble; SEE CONCEPTS 46,106

imbue [v] *infuse, saturate*
bathe, diffuse, impregnate, inculcate, infix, ingrain, inoculate, instill, invest, leaven, permeate, pervade, steep, suffuse; SEE CONCEPTS 209, 236,245

imitate [v] *pretend to be; do an impression of*
act like, affect, ape, assume, be like, borrow, burlesque, carbon*, caricature, clone, copy, counterfeit, ditto*, do like*, do likewise, duplicate, echo,

il
im

emulate, falsify, feign, follow, follow in footsteps*, follow suit*, forge, impersonate, look like, match, mime, mimic, mirror, mock, model after, parallel, parody, pattern after, personate, play a part, pretend, put on*, reduplicate, reflect, repeat, replicate, reproduce, resemble, send up*, sham, simulate, spoof, take off*, travesty, Xerox*; SEE CONCEPTS 87,111,171

imitation [n] *simulation, substitution*
apery, aping, carbon copy, clone, copy, counterfeit, counterfeiting, counterpart, ditto*, dupe*, duplicate, duplication, echoing, ersatz*, fake, forgery, image, impersonation, impression, likeness, match, matching, mime, mimicry, mirroring, mockery, parallel, paralleling, paraphrasing, parody, parroting, patterning, phony, picture, reflection, replica, representing, reproduction, resemblance, ringer, semblance, sham*, simulacrum, takeoff*, transcription, travesty, Xerox*; SEE CONCEPTS 171,260,716

imitative [adj] *simulated, unoriginal*
artful, copied, copycat, copying, counterfeit, deceptive, derivative, echoic, emulative, emulous, following, forged, mimetic, mimic, mimicking, mock, onomatopoeic, parrot*, plagiarized, pseudo*, put-on*, reflecting, reflective, secondhand, sham*, simulant; SEE CONCEPT 582

immaculate [adj1] *very clean; unspoiled*
bright, clean, errorless, exquisite, faultless, flawless, impeccable, irreproachable, neat, pure, snowy*, spick-and-span*, spotless, spruce, stainless, taintless, trim, unexceptionable, unsoiled, unsullied; SEE CONCEPT 621

immaculate [adj2] *innocent, uncorrupted*
above reproach, chaste, clean, decent, faultless, flawless, guiltless, incorrupt, modest, perfect, pure, sinless, spotless, stainless, unblemished, uncontaminated, undefiled, unpolluted, unsullied, untarnished, virtuous; SEE CONCEPTS 404,545

immaterial [adj1] *irrelevant*
extraneous, foreign, impertinent, inapplicable, inapposite, inappropriate, inconsequential, inconsiderable, inconsiderate, inessential, insignificant, irrelative, matter of indifference, meaningless, no big deal*, no never mind*, of no account*, of no consequence*, of no importance*, trifling, trivial, unimportant, unnecessary; SEE CONCEPT 575

immaterial [adj2] *not existing in physical form*
aerial, airy, apparitional, asomatous, bodiless, celestial, disbodied, discarnate, disembodied, dreamlike, dreamy, ethereal, ghostly, heavenly, impalpable, imponderable, incorporate, incorporeal, insensible, intangible, metaphysical, nonmaterial, nonphysical, psychic, shadowy, spectral, spiritlike, spiritual, subjective, supernatural, unearthly, unembodied, unfleshly, unsubstantial, unworldly, wraithlike; SEE CONCEPT 539

immature [adj] *young, inexperienced*
adolescent, baby, babyish, callow, childish, crude, green*, half-grown, imperfect, infantile, infantine, jejune, juvenile, kid, kidstuff*, premature, puerile, raw, sophomoric, tender*, tenderfoot*, underdeveloped, undergrown, undeveloped, unfinished, unfledged, unformed, unripe, unseasonable, unseasoned, unsophisticated, untimely, wet behind ears*, youthful; SEE CONCEPTS 485,578,797

immeasurable [adj] *infinite, incalculable*
alive with, bottomless, boundless, countless, crawling with, endless, extensive, illimitable, immense, indefinite, inestimable, inexhaustible, jillion*, large, limitless, measureless, no end of*, no end to*, umpteen*, unbounded, uncountable, unfathomable, unlimited, unmeasurable, unreckonable, vast, zillion*; SEE CONCEPTS 762, 773,781

immediate [adj1] *instantaneous; without delay*
actual, at once, at present time, at this moment, critical, current, existing, extant, first, hairtrigger*, instant, live, next, now, on hand*, paramount, present, pressing, prompt, up-to-date*, urgent; SEE CONCEPTS 567,585,812,820

immediate [adj2] *near, next*
adjacent, close, contiguous, direct, firsthand, near-at-hand, nearby, nearest, nigh, primary, proximal, proximate, recent; SEE CONCEPTS 586,778

immediately [adv] *at once, right away*
anon, at short notice, away, directly, double-time*, forthwith, hereupon, in a flash*, in a jiffy*, in a New York minute*, in nothing flat*, instantaneously, instanter, instantly, like now*, now, now or never*, on the dot*, on the double*, on the spot*, PDQ*, promptly, pronto*, rapidly, right now, shortly, soon, soon afterward, straight away*, straight off*, summarily, thereupon, this instant, this minute, tout de suite*, unhesitatingly, urgently, without delay, without hesitation; SEE CONCEPTS 544,820

immemorial [adj] *ancient, old*
age-old, archaic, fixed, forever, long-standing, of yore, olden, prehistoric, primeval, rooted, time-honored, traditional; SEE CONCEPTS 578,797,799

immense [adj] *extremely large*
barn door*, boundless, Brobdingnagian*, colossal, elephantine, endless, enormous, eternal, extensive, giant, gigantic, great, gross, huge, humongous, illimitable, immeasurable, infinite, interminable, jumbo*, limitless, mammoth, massive, measureless, mighty, monstrous, monumental, prodigious, stupendous, super, titanic*, tremendous, unbounded, vast; SEE CONCEPT 773

immerse [v1] *submerge in liquid*
asperse, baptize, bathe, bury, christen, dip, douse, drench, drown, duck, dunk, merge, plunge, saturate, sink, slop, soak, souse, sprinkle, steep, submerse; SEE CONCEPT 256

immerse [v2] *become deeply involved*
absorb, busy, engage, engross, interest, involve, occupy, soak, take up; SEE CONCEPTS 17,100

immersed [adj] *deeply involved with*
absorbed, bound-up*, buried*, busy, consumed, deep, eat sleep and breathe*, engaged, engrossed, intent, into*, mesmerized, occupied, preoccupied, rapt, spellbound, taken up*, tied up*, turned on*, wrapped up*; SEE CONCEPT 542

immigrant [n] *person from a foreign land*
adoptive citizen, alien, colonist, documented alien, foreigner, incomer, migrant, naturalized citizen, newcomer, outsider, pioneer, settler, undocumented alien; SEE CONCEPT 413

immigrate [v] *enter a foreign area intending to live there*
arrive, colonize, come in, go in, migrate, settle; SEE CONCEPT 159

imminent [adj] *at hand, on the way*
about to happen, approaching, brewing*, close, coming, expectant, fast-approaching, following, forthcoming, gathering, handwriting-on-the-wall*, immediate, impending, ineluctable, ines-

capable, inevasable, inevitable, in store*, in the air*, in the cards*, in the offing*, in the wind*, in view*, likely, looming, menacing, near, nearing, next, nigh, on its way, on the horizon, on the verge, overhanging, possible, probable, see it coming*, threatening, to come, unavoidable, unescapable; SEE CONCEPTS 548,820

immobile [*adj*] *motionless, fixed*
anchored, at a standstill, at rest, frozen, immobilized, immotile, immovable, nailed, nailed down, pat, quiescent, rigid, riveted, rooted, stable, stagnant, static, stationary, steadfast, stiff, still, stock-still, stolid, unmovable, unmoving; SEE CONCEPTS 488,584

immoderate [*adj*] *excessive, extreme*
dizzying, egregious, enormous, exaggerated, exorbitant, extravagant, inordinate, intemperate, overindulgent, profligate, steep, too much*, too too*, towering, unbalanced, unbridled, uncalled-for*, unconscionable, uncontrolled, undue, unjustified, unmeasurable, unreasonable, unrestrained, unwarranted, wanton; SEE CONCEPTS 544,569

immoral [*adj*] *evil, degenerate*
abandoned, bad, corrupt, debauched, depraved, dishonest, dissipated, dissolute, fast*, graceless, impure, indecent, iniquitous, lewd, licentious, loose*, nefarious, obscene, of easy virtue*, pornographic, profligate, rakish, reprobate, saturnalian, shameless, sinful, speedy, unchaste, unclean*, unethical, unprincipled, unscrupulous, vicious, vile, villainous, wicked, wrong, X-rated*; SEE CONCEPT 545

immortal [*adj1*] *death-defying, imperishable*
abiding, amaranthine, ceaseless, constant, deathless, endless, enduring, eternal, evergreen, everlasting, incorruptible, indestructible, indissoluble, interminable, lasting, never-ceasing, never-ending, perdurable, perennial, permanent, perpetual, phoenixlike, sempiternal, timeless, undying, unfading; SEE CONCEPTS 539,798

immortal [*adj2*] *famous*
celebrated, eminent, epic, genius, glorious, heroic, illustrious, laureate, paragon, storied; SEE CONCEPT 568

immovable [*adj*] *fixed, stubborn*
adamant, constant, dead set on*, dug in, fast, firm, hard-nosed, immobile, immotile, immutable, impassive, inflexible, intransigent, locked in*, motionless, obdurate, quiescent, resolute, rooted, secure, set, set in concrete*, set in stone*, solid, stable, stand pat*, stationary, steadfast, stick to guns*, stuck, tough nut*, unalterable, unchangeable, uncompromising, unmodifiable, unshakable, unwavering, unyielding; SEE CONCEPTS 404,488,534

immune [*adj*] *invulnerable*
allowed, clear, exempt, favored, free, hardened to, insusceptible, irresponsible, licensed, not affected, not liable, not subject, privileged, protected, resistant, safe, unaffected, unanswerable, unliable, unsusceptible; SEE CONCEPTS 314,552

immunity [*n*] *privilege, exemption*
amnesty, charter, exoneration, franchise, freedom, impunity, indemnity, invulnerability, liberty, license, prerogative, protection, release, resistance, right; SEE CONCEPTS 316,376,388

immutable [*adj*] *unchangeable*
abiding, ageless, changeless, constant, enduring, fixed, immovable, inflexible, invariable, permanent, perpetual, sacrosanct, stable, steadfast, unalterable, unmodifiable; SEE CONCEPT 534

imp [*n*] *mischievous child, small person*
brat, demon, devil, deviling, devilkin, elf, fiend, gamin, gnome, gremlin, hellion, minx, pixie, puck, rascal, rogue, scamp, sprite, troll, tyke, urchin, villain; SEE CONCEPT 412

impact [*n1*] *collision, force*
appulse, bang, blow, bounce, brunt, buffet, bump, clash, concussion, contact, crash, crunch, crush, encounter, hit, impingement, jar, jolt, jounce, kick, knock, meeting, percussion, pound, punch, quake, quiver, ram, rap, rock, shake, shock, slap, smash, smashup, strike, stroke, thump, tremble, tremor, wallop; SEE CONCEPTS 189,641

impact [*n2*] *effect*
brunt, burden, consequences, full force, impression, imprint, influence, mark, meaning, power, repercussion, significance, thrust, weight; SEE CONCEPT 230

impact [*v*] *hit with force*
bang into, clash, collide, crack up, crash, crush, jolt, kick, register, smash, smash up, strike, wrack up*; SEE CONCEPT 189

impair [*v*] *harm, hinder*
blemish, blunt, cheapen, damage, debase, debilitate, decrease, destroy, deteriorate, devaluate, devalue, diminish, ding*, disqualify, enervate, enfeeble, hurt, injure, invalidate, lessen, lose strength, make useless, mar, prejudice, queer, reduce, rough up*, spoil, tarnish, total, tweak, undermine, unfit, vitiate, weaken, worsen; SEE CONCEPTS 130,240,246

impaired [*adj*] *injured, faulty*
broken, busted, damaged, debilitated, defective, down*, flawed, harmed, hurt, imperfect, kaput*, marred, on the blink*, on the fritz*, spoiled, unsound; SEE CONCEPTS 485,560

impale [*v*] *stab*
lance, perforate, pierce, prick, punch, puncture, run through, skewer, skiver, spear, spike, stick, transfix; SEE CONCEPT 220

impalpable [*adj*] *intangible, unsubstantial*
airy, delicate, disembodied, fine, imperceptible, imponderable, imprecise, inappreciable, incorporeal, indiscernible, indistinct, insensible, insubstantial, nebulous, shadowy, tenuous, thin, unapparent, unobservable, unperceivable, vague; SEE CONCEPTS 485,529,619

impart [*v1*] *make known*
admit, announce, break, communicate, convey, disclose, discover, divulge, expose, inform, pass on, publish, relate, reveal, tell, transmit; SEE CONCEPT 60

impart [*v2*] *give*
accord, afford, allow, bestow, cede, confer, contribute, grant, lead, offer, part with, present, relinquish, render, yield; SEE CONCEPT 108

impartial [*adj*] *fair, unprejudiced*
candid, detached, disinterested, dispassionate, equal, equitable, evenhanded, fair-minded, impersonal, just, middle-of-the-road*, neutral, nondiscriminating, nondiscriminatory, nonpartisan, objective, on-the-fence, open-minded, unbiased, unbigoted, uncolored, unslanted, without favor; SEE CONCEPTS 403,542

impasse [*n*] *stalemate*
box*, Catch-22*, cessation, corner*, cul-de-sac*, dead end, deadlock, dilemma, fix, gridlock, jam, mire*, morass*, pause, pickle*, plight, predica-

im
im

ment, quandary, rest, scrape*, standoff, standstill;
SEE CONCEPT 674

impassioned [*adj*] *excited, vehement*
animated, ardent, blazing, burning, deep, fervent,
fervid, fierce, fiery, fired up*, flaming, furious,
glowing, heated*, hot-blooded*, inflamed, inspired, intense, melodramatic, moving, mushy,
overemotional, passionate, perfervid, powerful,
profound, red-hot*, romantic, rousing, sentimental, starry-eyed*, steamed up*, stirring, torrid, violent, vivid, warm, white-hot*, wild about,
worked up*, zealous; SEE CONCEPT 403

impassive [*adj*] *aloof, cool*
apathetic, callous, cold, cold-blooded*, collected,
composed, dispassionate, dry, emotionless, hardened, heartless, imperturbable, indifferent, indurated, inexcitable, inexpressive, inscrutable,
insensible, insusceptible, matter-of-fact, nonchalant, passionless, phlegmatic, placid, poker-
faced*, reserved, reticent, sedate, self-contained,
serene, spiritless, stoic, stoical, stolid, taciturn,
unconcerned, unemotional, unexcitable, unfeeling, unflappable, unimpressible, unmoved, unruffled, wooden; SEE CONCEPTS 404,542

impatience [*n*] *inability, unwillingness to wait*
agitation, anger, annoyance, ants in pants*,
anxiety, avidity, disquietude, eagerness, edginess,
excitement, expectancy, fretfulness, haste, hastiness, heat*, impetuosity, intolerance, irritability,
irritableness, nervousness, quick temper, rashness, restiveness, restlessness, shortness, snappi-
ness, suspense, uneasiness, vehemence, violence;
SEE CONCEPTS 633,657

impatient [*adj*] *unable, unwilling to wait*
abrupt, agog, antsy, anxious, appetent, ardent,
athirst, avid, breathless, brusque, chafing, choleric, curt, demanding, dying to*, eager, edgy,
feverish, fretful, hasty, having short fuse*, headlong, hot-tempered, hot under collar*, impetuous,
indignant, intolerant, irascible, irritable, itchy,
keen, on pins and needles*, quick-tempered, racing one's motor*, restless, ripe*, snappy, straining, sudden, testy, thirsty, unforbearing,
unindulgent, vehement, violent; SEE CONCEPTS
401,542

impeach [*v*] *denounce, censure*
accuse, arraign, blame, bring charges against, call
into question, call to account, cast aspersions on,
cast doubt on, challenge, charge, criminate, criticize, discredit, disparage, hold at fault, impugn,
incriminate, inculpate, indict, query, question,
reprehend, reprimand, reprobate, tax, try; SEE
CONCEPTS 44,52,317

impeccable [*adj*] *above suspicion; flawless*
accurate, aces, A-okay*, apple-pie*, clean, correct, errorless, exact, exquisite, faultless, fleck-
less, immaculate, incorrupt, infallible, innocent,
irreproachable, nice, note-perfect, on target*, perfect, precise, pure, right, sinless, stainless, ten*,
unblemished, unerring, unflawed, unimpeachable;
SEE CONCEPTS 535,574,621

impecunious [*adj*] *poverty-stricken*
beggared, broke*, cleaned out*, destitute, dirt
poor*, homeless, impoverished, indigent, insolvent, necessitous, needy, penniless, penurious,
poor, strapped*, unprosperous; SEE CONCEPT 334

impede [*v*] *obstruct, hinder*
bar, block, blow whistle on*, brake, check, clog,
close off, cramp one's style*, curb, cut off, dam,
delay, deter, discomfit, disconcert, disrupt, em-

barrass, faze, flag one*, freeze, hamper, hang up,
hold up, interfere, oppose, rattle, restrain, retard,
saddle with*, shut down, shut off, slow, slow
down, stonewall*, stop, stymie, thwart; SEE CON-
CEPTS 121,130

impediment [*n*] *obstruction, hindrance*
bar, barricade, barrier, block, blockage, bottleneck*, burden, catch*, Catch-22*, chain, check,
clog, cramp, curb, dead weight*, defect, delay,
deterrent, detriment, difficulty, disadvantage,
drag*, drawback, encumbrance, fault, flaw, handicap, hazard, hitch, holdup, hurdle, inhibition,
load, manacle, millstone*, obstacle, prohibition,
red tape*, restraint, restriction, retardation, retardment, road block*, rub*, setback, shackle, snag,
stoppage, stricture, stumbling block*, tie, trammel, wall; SEE CONCEPT 666

impel [*v*] *prompt, incite*
actuate, boost, compel, constrain, drive, excite,
foment, force, goad, induce, influence, inspire,
instigate, jog, lash, mobilize, motivate, move,
oblige, poke, power, press, prod, propel, push,
require, set in motion, shove, spur, start, stimulate, thrust, urge; SEE CONCEPTS 14,68,221,242

impending [*adj*] *forthcoming*
approaching, at hand, brewing, coming, gathering, handwriting-on-the-wall*, hovering, imminent, in the cards*, in the offing*, in the wind*,
looking to*, looming, menacing, near, nearing,
ominous, on the horizon*, overhanging, portend-
ing, proximate, soon, threatening, waiting to see it coming*, waiting to see it coming*,
ing to; SEE CONCEPTS 548,820

impenetrable [*adj1*] *dense*
bulletproof, close, compact, firm, hard, hermetic,
impassable, impermeable, impervious, inviolable,
solid, substantial, thick, unpierceable; SEE CON-
CEPTS 483,604

impenetrable [*adj2*] *incomprehensible*
arcane, baffling, cabalistic, dark, Delphic, enigmatic, enigmatical, hidden, incognizable, indiscernible, inexplicable, inscrutable, mysterious,
mystic, obscure, sibylline, unaccountable, unfathomable, ungraspable, unintelligible, unknowable;
SEE CONCEPTS 529,576

imperative [*adj1*] *necessary*
acute, burning, clamant, clamorous, compulsory,
critical, crucial, crying, essential, exigent, immediate, important, importunate, indispensable, inescapable, insistent, instant, no turning back*,
obligatory, pressing, urgent, vital; SEE CONCEPT
546

imperative [*adj2*] *authoritative*
aggressive, autocratic, bidding, bossy, commanding, dictatorial, dominant, domineering, harsh,
high-handed, imperial, imperious, ordering, overbearing, peremptory, powerful, stern; SEE CON-
CEPTS 267,574

imperceptible [*adj*] *hard to sense; faint*
ephemeral, evanescent, fine, gradual, impalpable,
imponderable, inappreciable, inaudible, inconsiderable, inconspicuous, indiscernible, indistinct,
indistinguishable, infinitesimal, insensible, insignificant, invisible, microscopic, minute, momentary, shadowy, slight, small, subtle, tiny, trivial,
undetectable, unnoticeable, vague; SEE CONCEPTS
406,537

imperfect [*adj*] *flawed*
amiss, below par, bottom-of-barrel*, broken,
damaged, defective, deficient, disfigured, dud*,
faulty, few bugs*, garbage*, immature, impaired,

incomplete, inexact, injured, junk*, lemon*, limited, low, marred, minus, partial, patchy, rudimentary, schlocky*, sick, sketchy, two-bit*, undeveloped, unfinished, unsound, vicious, warped; SEE CONCEPTS 570,574,579

imperfection [n] *flaw*
blemish, bug*, catch, defect, deficiency, deformity, demerit, disfigurement, failing, fallibility, fault, foible, frailty, glitch*, gremlin*, inadequacy, incompleteness, infirmity, insufficiency, peccadillo, problem, shortcoming, sin, stain, taint, weakness, weak point; SEE CONCEPTS 230,671,718

imperil [v] *cause to be in danger*
chance it, compromise, endanger, expose, hazard, jeopard, jeopardize, jeopardy, menace, peril, risk; SEE CONCEPT 240

imperious [adj] *bossy, overbearing*
arrogant, authoritative, autocratic, commanding, compulsatory, compulsory, despotic, dictatorial, domineering, exacting, haughty, high-handed, imperative, mandatory, obligatory, oppressive, overweening, peremptory, required, tyrannical, tyrannous; SEE CONCEPTS 267,574

impersonal [adj] *cold, unfriendly*
abstract, bureaucratic, businesslike, candid, cold-blooded*, cold turkey*, colorless, cool, detached, disinterested, dispassionate, emotionless, equal, equitable, fair, formal, impartial, indifferent, inhuman, neutral, nondiscriminatory, objective, poker-faced*, remote, straight, strictly business*, unbiased, uncolored, unpassioned; SEE CONCEPTS 401,542,544

impersonate [v] *pretend to be another*
act, act a part, act like, act out, ape, assume character, ditto*, do, do an impression of, double as, dress as, enact, fake, imitate, make like*, masquerade as, mimic, mirror, pass oneself off as*, perform, personate, play, playact, play a role, portray, pose as, put on an act*, represent, take the part of; SEE CONCEPTS 59,292

impertinence [n] *boldness*
assurance, audacity, backchat, back talk*, brazenness, cheek*, chutzpah*, come-back*, crust*, disrespect, disrespectfulness, effrontery, forwardness, freshness, gall, guff, hardihood, impropriety, impudence, incivility, insolence, insolency, lip*, nerve, pertness, presumption, rudeness, sass*, smart mouth*, wisecrack*, wise guy*; SEE CONCEPT 633

impertinent [adj] *bold, disrespectful*
arrogant, brash, brassy*, brazen, contumelious, discourteous, disgracious, flip*, forward, fresh, ill-mannered, impolite, impudent, inappropriate, incongruous, inquisitive, insolent, interfering, intrusive, lippy*, meddlesome, meddling, nosy*, off base*, offensive, out of line*, pert, presumptuous, procacious, prying, rude, sassy*, smart, smart alecky*, uncalled-for*, uncivil, ungracious, unmannerly, unsuitable; SEE CONCEPT 401

imperturbable [adj] *calm, collected*
assured, complacent, composed, cool, cool as cucumber*, disimpassioned, equanimous, hard as nails*, immovable, nerveless, nonchalant, roll with punches*, sedate, self-possessed, self-satisfied, smug, stiff upper lip*, stoical, thick-skinned, tranquil, unaffected, undisturbed, unexcitable, unflappable, unmoved, unruffled, untouched; SEE CONCEPT 404

impervious [adj] *unable to be penetrated*
closed to, hermetic, immune, impassable, impassive, impenetrable, impermeable, imperviable, inaccessible, invulnerable, resistant, sealed, tight, unaffected, unapproachable, unmoved, unpierceable, unreceptive, watertight; SEE CONCEPTS 485,534,604

impetuous [adj] *acting without thinking*
abrupt, ardent, eager, fervid, fierce, furious, going off deep end*, hasty, headlong, hurried, impassioned, impulsive, passionate, precipitant, precipitate, precipitous, rash, restive, rushing, spontaneous, spur-of-the-moment, subitaneous, sudden, swift, unbridled, unexpected, unplanned, unpremeditated, unreflecting, unrestrained, unthinking, vehement, violent; SEE CONCEPTS 404,542

impetus [n] *stimulus, force*
catalyst, energy, goad, impulse, impulsion, incentive, incitation, incitement, momentum, motivation, power, pressure, push, spur, stimulant, urge; SEE CONCEPTS 641,661

impinge [v] *trespass*
affect, bear upon, disturb, encroach, influence, infringe, intrude, invade, make inroads, meddle, obtrude, pry, touch, violate; SEE CONCEPTS 14,156

impious [adj] *not religious*
agnostic, apostate, atheistic, blasphemous, canting, contrary, deceitful, defiling, desecrating, desecrative, diabolic, disobedient, disrespectful, godless, hardened, hypocritical, iconoclastic, immoral, iniquitous, irreligious, irreverent, perverted, pietistical, profane, recusant, reprobate, sacrilegious, sanctimonious, satanic, scandalous, sinful, unctuous, undutiful, unethical, unfaithful, ungodly, unhallowed, unholy, unregenerate, unrighteous, unsanctified, wayward, wicked; SEE CONCEPT 545

impish [adj] *mischievous*
casual, devilish, devil-may-care*, elfin, elvish, fiendish, flippant, free and easy*, fresh, frolicsome, giddy, jaunty, naughty, offhand, pert, pixieish, playful, prankish, puckish, rascally, saucy*, sportive, waggish; SEE CONCEPT 401

implacable [adj] *merciless, cruel*
grim, inexorable, inflexible, intractable, iron-fisted, mortal, pitiless, rancorous, relentless, remorseless, ruthless, unappeasable, unbending, uncompromising, unflinching, unforgiving, unrelenting, unyielding, vindictive; SEE CONCEPT 542

implausible [adj] *not likely*
doubtful, dubious, farfetched, far out*, fishy*, flimsy, for the birds*, full of holes*, impossible, improbable, inconceivable, incredible, obscure, problematic, puzzling, reachy, suspect, thin*, too much*, unbelievable, unconvincing, unreasonable, unsubstantial, weak, won't hold water*, won't wash*; SEE CONCEPT 552

implement [n] *agent, tool*
apparatus, appliance, contraption, contrivance, device, equipment, gadget, instrument, machine, utensil; SEE CONCEPT 499

implement [v] *start, put into action*
achieve, actualize, bring about, carry out, complete, effect, enable, enforce, execute, fulfill, invoke, make good*, make possible, materialize, perform, provide the means, put into effect, realize, resolve; SEE CONCEPTS 91,99,221

im
im

implicate [v] *imply, involve*
accuse, affect, associate, blame, charge, cite, compromise, concern, connect, embroil, entangle, frame, hint, impute, include, incriminate, inculpate, insinuate, lay at one's door*, link, mean, mire, name, pin on*, point finger at*, relate, stigmatize, suggest, tangle*; SEE CONCEPTS **44,112**

implication [n] *association, suggestion*
assumption, conclusion, connection, connotation, entanglement, guess, hint, hypothesis, incrimination, indication, inference, innuendo, intimation, involvement, link, meaning, overtone, presumption, ramification, reference, significance, signification, undertone, union; SEE CONCEPTS **28,39,278**

implicit [adj] *included without question, inherent, absolute*
accurate, certain, complete, constant, constructive, contained, definite, entire, firm, fixed, full, implicative, implied, inarticulate, inevitable, inferential, inferred, latent, practical, steadfast, tacit, taken for granted, total, undeclared, understood, unexpressed, unhesitating, unqualified, unquestioned, unreserved, unsaid, unshakable, unspoken, unuttered, virtual, wholehearted; SEE CONCEPTS **267,535,549**

implied [adj] *hinted at*
adumbrated, alluded to, allusive, connoted, constructive, figured, foreshadowed, hidden, implicit, indicated, indicative, indirect, inferential, inferred, inherent, insinuated, intended, involved, latent, lurking, meant, occult, parallel, perceptible, potential, significative, signified, suggested, symbolized, tacit, tacitly assumed, undeclared, understood, unexpressed, unsaid, unspoken, uttered, wordless; SEE CONCEPTS **267,535**

implore [v] *beg*
appeal, beseech, conjure, crave, entreat, go on bended knee*, importune, plead, pray, solicit, supplicate, urge; SEE CONCEPT **48**

imply [v] *indicate, mean*
betoken, connote, denote, designate, entail, evidence, give a hint, hint, import, include, insinuate, intend, intimate, involve, mention, point to, presuppose, refer, signify, suggest; SEE CONCEPTS **75,97,682**

impolite [adj] *having bad manners*
bad-mannered, boorish, churlish, crude, discourteous, disgracious, disrespectful, ill-bred, ill-mannered, indecorous, indelicate, insolent, irritable, loutish, moody, oafish, rough, rude, sullen, uncivil, ungracious, unmannered, unmannerly, unrefined; SEE CONCEPT **401**

impolitic [adj] *unwise, careless*
brash, ill-advised, ill-judged, imprudent, inadvisable, inconsiderate, indiscreet, inexpedient, injudicious, maladroit, misguided, rash, stupid, tactless, undiplomatic, untimely; SEE CONCEPTS **401,544**

import [n1] *meaning*
acceptation, bearing, bottom line*, construction, drift*, gist*, heart*, implication, intendment, intention, interpretation, meat*, message, name of the game*, nature of beast*, nuts and bolts*, point, punch line*, purport, score*, sense, significance, significancy, signification, stuff*, thrust, understanding; SEE CONCEPT **682**

import [n2] *significance, weight*
consequence, design, emphasis, importance, intent, magnitude, moment, momentousness, object, objective, pith, purpose, signification, stress, substance, value, weightiness, worth; SEE CONCEPTS **346,668**

importance [n1] *significance, weight*
accent, attention, bearing, caliber, concern, concernment, consequence, denotation, distinction, drift*, effect, emphasis, force, gist*, gravity, import, influence, interest, materiality, moment, momentousness, notability, paramountcy, point, precedence, preponderance, preponderancy, priority, purport, relevance, sense, seriousness, signification, standing, stress, substance, tenor, usefulness, value, weightiness; SEE CONCEPTS **346,668,682**

importance [n2] *prominence, standing*
consequence, conspicuousness, distinction, eminence, esteem, fame, greatness, influence, lionization, mark, notability, note, noteworthiness, rank, reputation, salience, status, usefulness, worth; SEE CONCEPTS **388,671**

important [adj1] *valuable, substantial*
big, big-league*, chief, considerable, conspicuous, critical, crucial, decisive, determining, earnest, essential, esteemed, exceptional, exigent, extensive, far-reaching, foremost, front-page*, grave, great, heavy, imperative, importunate, influential, large, marked, material, mattering much, meaningful, momentous, necessary, of moment, of note, of substance, paramount, ponderous, pressing, primary, principal, relevant, salient, serious, signal, significant, something, standout, urgent, vital, weighty; SEE CONCEPT **567**

important [adj2] *eminent, influential, outstanding*
aristocratic, big-time*, distinctive, distinguished, effective, esteemed, extraordinary, famous, first-class*, foremost, four-star*, front-page*, grand, heavy*, high-level, high profile, high-ranking, high-up, honored, illustrious, imposing, incomparable, leading, majestic, major-league*, noble, notable, noted, noteworthy, of note, page-one*, potent, powerful, preeminent, prominent, remarkable, seminal, signal, solid, superior, talented, top-drawer*, top-notch*, upper-class, VIP*, well-known; SEE CONCEPTS **555,574**

imported [adj] *brought in from another place*
alien, carried, choice, exotic, ferried, foreign, introduced, rare, sent, shipped, transported, trucked; SEE CONCEPT **549**

importunate [adj] *demanding, insistent*
burning, clamant, clamorous, crying, disturbing, dogged, earnest, exigent, harassing, imperative, instant, overly solicitous, persevering, persistent, pertinacious, pressing, solicitous, troublesome, urgent; SEE CONCEPTS **267,401**

importune [v] *demand, insist*
appeal, ask, badger, beg, beseech, beset, besiege, con*, crave, dun, egg on*, entreat, goose*, harass, hound*, implore, invoke, nag, persuade, pester, plague, plead, pray, press, sell, solicit, supplicate, urge, work on*; SEE CONCEPT **53**

impose [v] *set, dictate*
appoint, burden, charge, command, compel, constrain, decree, demand, encroach, enforce, enjoin, establish, exact, fix, foist, force, force upon, horn in, inflict, infringe, institute, introduce, intrude, lade, lay, lay down, lay down the law, levy, move in on, oblige, obtrude, ordain, order, place, prescribe, presume, promulgate, put, put foot down*, read riot act*, require, saddle*, take advantage,

trespass, visit, wish, wreak, wreck; SEE CONCEPTS 18,53,133

imposing [adj] *impressive*
august, big, commanding, dignified, effective, exciting, grand, grandiose, imperial, magnificent, majestic, massive, mega*, mind-blowing*, monumental, moving, noble, ominous, one for the book*, overblown, overwhelming, pretentious, regal, royal, something else*, something to write home about*, stately, stirring, striking, towering; SEE CONCEPTS 537,574,773

imposition [n1] *deception*
artifice, cheating, con, craftiness, dissimulation, fraud, hoax, hocus-pocus*, hypocrisy, illusion, imposture, stratagem, trick, trickery; SEE CONCEPTS 59,645

imposition [n2] *burden*
charge, command, constraint, demand, drag, duty, encroachment, encumbrance, intrusion, levy, pain, pain in the neck*, pressure, presumption, restraint, tax; SEE CONCEPTS 14,130

impossible [adj1] *beyond the bounds of possibility*
absurd, beyond, contrary to reason, cureless, futile, hardly possible, hopeless, hundred-to-one*, impassable, impervious, impracticable, impractical, inaccessible, inconceivable, inexecutable, infeasible, insurmountable, irrealizable, irreparable, no-go*, not a prayer*, no-way*, no-win*, out of the question*, preposterous, too much, unachievable, unattainable, uncorrectable, unfeasible, unimaginable, unobtainable, unreasonable, unrecoverable, unthinkable, unworkable, useless, visionary, way out; SEE CONCEPT 552

impossible [adj2] *intolerable, ungovernable*
absurd, egregious, hopeless, improper, incongruous, ludicrous, objectionable, offensive, outrageous, preposterous, unacceptable, unanswerable, undesirable, unreasonable, unsuitable; SEE CONCEPT 401

impostor [n] *person pretending to be something else*
actor, beguiler, bluffer, charlatan, cheat, con artist, deceiver, empiric, fake, faker, four-flusher*, fraud, hypocrite, imitator, impersonator, masquerader, mimic, mocker, mountebank, pettifogger, phony, pretender, pseudo, quack, scorner, sham, sharper, shyster, trickster; SEE CONCEPT 412

imposture [n] *fraud, trick*
artifice, cheat, con, copy, counterfeit, deceit, deception, fabrication, fake, feint, fiddle, flimflam*, forgery, gambit, hoax, hocus-pocus*, illusion, imitation, impersonation, imposition, make-believe, maneuver, masquerade, phony, ploy, pretense, pretension, put-on*, quackery, ruse, sell*, sham, sleight, spoof, stratagem, swindle, wile; SEE CONCEPTS 59,192,645,674

impotent [adj] *disabled; unable to perform action*
barren, crippled, dud, effete, enervated, enfeebled, feeble, forceless, frail, gutless, helpless, inadequate, incapable, incapacitated, incompetent, ineffective, ineffectual, inept, infecund, infirm, nerveless, paper tiger*, paralyzed, powerless, prostrate, sterile, unfruitful, unproductive, weak; SEE CONCEPT 485

impoverished [adj] *poor, exhausted*
bankrupt, barren, beggared, broke, clean, depleted, destitute, distressed, drained, empty, flat*, flat broke*, have-not*, hurting, impecunious, indigent, insolvent, necessitous, needy, penurious, played out*, poverty-stricken, reduced, ruined, spent, sterile, strapped; SEE CONCEPTS 334,560

impractical/impracticable [adj] *unrealistic*
abstract, absurd, chimerical, idealistic, illogical, impossible, impracticable, improbable, inapplicable, inefficacious, infeasible, inoperable, irrealizable, ivory-tower*, no-go*, nonfunctional, nonviable, not a prayer*, otherworldly, out of the question*, quixotic, romantic, speculative, starry-eyed*, theoretical, unattainable, unbusinesslike, unfeasible, unreal, unserviceable, unusable, unwise, unworkable, useless, visionary, wild, won't fly*; SEE CONCEPT 552

impregnate [v] *infuse, fill; make pregnant*
charge, conceive, drench, fecundate, fertilize, imbrue, implant, inoculate, inseminate, leaven, overflow, percolate, permeate, pervade, procreate, produce, reproduce, saturate, seethe, soak, sodden, souse, steep, suffuse, transfuse; SEE CONCEPTS 179,375

impress [v1] *influence*
affect, arouse, awe, be conspicuous, blow away*, buffalo*, bulldoze*, carry, electrify, enforce, enthuse, excite, faze, galvanize, get*, grab, grandstand*, inspire, kill*, knock out*, make a hit*, make an impression, make splash*, move, overawe, pique, provoke, push around*, register, score, show off, slay*, stimulate, stir, strike, sway, thrill, touch*; SEE CONCEPTS 7,19,22,261

impress [v2] *press down to make design*
carve, dent, emboss, engrave, etch, imprint, indent, inscribe, mark, print, stamp; SEE CONCEPT 174

impress [v3] *emphasize*
bring home*, drive home*, establish, fix, get into head*, inculcate, instill, press, set, stress; SEE CONCEPT 49

impression [n1] *influence*
consequence, effect, feeling, impact, reaction, response, result, sway; SEE CONCEPT 230

impression [n2] *feeling, idea*
apprehension, belief, conceit, concept, conception, conjecture, conviction, fancy, feel, hunch, image, inkling, intellection, memory, notion, opinion, perception, recollection, sensation, sense, suspicion, suspicion, theory, thought, view; SEE CONCEPTS 529,689

impression [n3] *design made by pressing*
brand, cast, dent, depression, dint, fingerprint, footprint, form, hollow, impress, imprint, indentation, mark, matrix, mold, outline, pattern, print, sign, spoor, stamp, stamping, trace, track, vestige; SEE CONCEPTS 284,625

impression [n4] *pretending to be somebody*
imitation, impersonation, masquerade, parody, sendup, takeoff; SEE CONCEPT 263

impressionable [adj] *easily taught; gullible*
affectable, affected, feeling, impressible, influenceable, ingenuous, open, perceptive, plastic*, receptive, responsive, sensible, sensile, sensitive, sentient, suggestible, susceptible, susceptive, vulnerable, wax-like; SEE CONCEPTS 402,403

impressive [adj] *powerful, influential*
absorbing, affecting, arresting, august, awe-inspiring, consequential, cool*, deep*, dramatic, effective, eloquent, excited, exciting, extraordinary, forcible, grand, impassioned, important, imposing, inspiring, intense, lavish, luxurious, majestic, massive, momentous, monumental, moving, noble, notable, penetrating, prime*, pro-

found, remarkable, rousing, splendid, stately, stirring, striking, sumptuous, superb, thrilling, touching, towering, vital, well-done; SEE CONCEPTS 574,773

imprint [n] *impression; symbol*
banner, dent, design, effect, emblem, heading, impress, indentation, influence, mark, name, print, sign, signature, stamp, trace, trademark; SEE CONCEPTS 284,625

imprint [v] *stamp*
designate, engrave, establish, etch, fix, impress, inscribe, mark, offset, print; SEE CONCEPT 174

imprison [v] *confine; put in jail*
apprehend, bastille, bottle up*, cage, check, circumscribe, closet, commit, constrain, curb, detain, fence in, hold, hold captive, hold hostage, hold in custody, ice*, immure, impound, incarcerate, intern, jail, keep, keep captive, keep in custody, limit, lock in, lock up, nab*, occlude, pen, put away, put behind bars, rail in, remand, restrain, send to prison, send up*, shut in, stockade, take prisoner, trammel; SEE CONCEPTS 90,191,317

improbable [adj] *not likely*
doubtful, dubious, fanciful, far-fetched, flimsy*, hundred-to-one*, iffy*, implausible, inconceivable, not expected, outside chance*, questionable, rare, slim, slim and none*, unbelievable, uncertain, unconvincing, unheard of, unimaginable, unlikely, unsubstantial, weak; SEE CONCEPT 552

impromptu [adj/adv] *unrehearsed, improvised*
ad-lib*, dashed off, extemporaneous, extempore, extemporized, fake, faked, improv*, improviso, offhand, off the cuff*, played by ear*, shot from the hip*, spontaneous, spur-of-the-moment, thrown off*, tossed off*, unpremeditated, unprepared, unscripted, unstudied, vamped, whipped up*, winged*; SEE CONCEPT 267

improper [adj1] *not suitable*
abnormal, at odds, awkward, bad form, discordant, discrepant, erroneous, false, ill-advised, ill-timed, imprudent, inaccurate, inadmissible, inadvisable, inapplicable, inapposite, inappropriate, inapt, incongruous, incorrect, inexpedient, infelicitous, inharmonious, inopportune, irregular, ludicrous, malapropos, odd, off-base*, out-of-place*, out-of-season*, preposterous, unapt, unbefitting, uncalled-for*, uncomely, undue, unfit, unfitting, unseasonable, unsuitable, unsuited, untimely, unwarranted, wrong; SEE CONCEPT 558

improper [adj2] *vulgar, immoral*
blue*, dirty, impolite, indecent, indecorous, indelicate, lewd, malodorous, naughty, risqué, rough, salacious, suggestive, unbecoming, unconventional, unequitable, unethical, ungodly, unjust, unrighteous, unrightful, unseemly, untoward, wrong, wrongful; SEE CONCEPTS 542,545

impropriety [n] *bad taste, mistake*
barbarism, blunder, faux pas, gaffe, gaucherie, goof*, immodesty, impudence, incongruity, incorrectness, indecency, indecorum, inelegance, rudeness, slip*, solecism, unseemliness, unsuitability, vulgarism, vulgarity; SEE CONCEPTS 101,278,674

improve [v] *make or become better*
advance, ameliorate, amend, augment, better, boost, civilize, come around*, convalesce, correct, cultivate, develop, doctor up*, edit, elevate, emend, enhance, gain ground*, help, increase, lift, look up*, make strides, meliorate, mend, perk

up*, pick up*, polish, progress, promote, purify, raise, rally, recover, rectify, recuperate, refine, reform, revamp, revise, rise, set right*, shape up*, sharpen, skyrocket*, straighten out*, take off*, touch up*, turn the corner*, update, upgrade; SEE CONCEPTS 244,700

improvement [n] *bettering; something bettered*
advance, advancement, amelioration, amendment, augmentation, betterment, change, civilization, correction, cultivation, development, elevation, enhancement, enrichment, furtherance, gain, growth, increase, preferment, progress, progression, promotion, rally, reclamation, recovery, rectification, reformation, regeneration, renovation, revision, rise, upbeat, upgrade, upswing; SEE CONCEPTS 230,700

improvident [adj] *careless, spendthrift*
extravagant, heedless, imprudent, inconsiderate, lavish, negligent, prodigal, profligate, profuse, reckless, shiftless, shortsighted, thoughtless, thriftless, uneconomical, unthrifty, wasteful; SEE CONCEPTS 334,542

improvise [v] *make up*
ad-lib, brainstorm, coin, concoct, contrive, dash off*, devise, do offhand, do off top of head*, dream up, extemporize, fake, fake it, improv*, improvisate, invent, jam*, knock off*, make do*, slapdash*, spark, speak off the cuff*, throw together*, wing it*; SEE CONCEPTS 173,266

improvised [adj] *made-up*
ad-lib, autoschediastic, Band-Aid*, extemporaneous, extempore, extemporized, fly-by-night*, hit-or-miss*, impromptu, improviso, makeshift, offhand, spontaneous, spur-of-the-moment*, unprepared, unrehearsed, unstudied; SEE CONCEPTS 267,589

imprudent [adj] *without much thought*
brash, careless, foolhardy, foolish, heedless, ill-advised, ill-considered, ill-judged, impolitic, improvident, incautious, inconsiderate, indiscreet, inexpedient, injudicious, irresponsible, leaving self wide open*, off the deep end*, overhasty, playing with fire*, rash, reckless, temerarious, thoughtless, unadvisable, unthinking, unwise; SEE CONCEPTS 267,542

impudent [adj] *bold, shameless*
arrant, audacious, barefaced, blatant, boldfaced, brassy, brazen, bumptious, cheeky*, cocky*, contumelious, cool*, flip*, forward, fresh, immodest, impertinent, insolent, nervy*, off-base*, overbold, pert, presumptuous, procacious, rude, sassy*, saucy*, smart*, smart-alecky*, unabashed, unblushing, wise*; SEE CONCEPT 401

impugn [v] *criticize, challenge*
assail, attack, blast, break, call into question, cast aspersions upon, cast doubt upon, come down on*, contradict, contravene, cross, cut to shreds*, deny, disaffirm, dispute, gainsay, knock*, negate, negative, oppose, pin something on*, put down*, question, resist, run down, skin alive*, slam*, smear*, stick it to*, swipe at*, tar*, throw doubt on, throw the book at*, thumb nose at*, traduce, trash, traverse, zap*, zing*; SEE CONCEPTS 52,58

impulse [n] *drive, resolve*
actuation, appeal, bent, caprice, catalyst, desire, disposition, excitant, extemporization, fancy, feeling, flash*, goad, hunch, impellent, impulsion, incitation, incitement, inclination, influence, inspiration, instinct, itch*, lash, lust, mind, motivation, motive, notion, passion, spontaneity,

spur, thought, urge, vagary, whim, whimsy, wish, yen; SEE CONCEPTS 20,410

impulse [n2] *throb, stimulus*

augmentation, beat, bump, catalyst, drive, force, impetus, impulsion, lash, momentum, movement, pressure, propulsion, pulsation, pulse, push, rush, shock, shove, stroke, surge, thrust, vibration; SEE CONCEPT 641

impulsive [adj] *tending to act without thought*

abrupt, ad-lib*, automatic, careless, devil-may-care*, emotional, extemporaneous, flaky*, gone off deep end*, hasty, headlong, hot-and-cold*, impetuous, instinctive, intuitive, involuntary, jumping the gun*, mad, offhand, passionate, precipitate, quick, rash, spontaneous, sudden, swift, unconsidered, unexpected, unmeditated, unpredictable, unpremeditated, unprompted, up-and-down*, violent, winging it*; SEE CONCEPTS 401,542

impunity [n] *freedom*

dispensation, exception, exemption, immunity, liberty, license, nonliability, permission, privilege, security; SEE CONCEPT 376

impure [adj] *not clean mentally, physically; mixed*

admixed, adulterated, alloyed, carnal, coarse, common, contaminated, corrupt, debased, defiled, desecrated, diluted, dirty, doctored*, filthy, foul, gross*, grubby*, immodest, immoral, indecent, infected, lewd, nasty, not pure, obscene, polluted, profaned, smutty*, sullied, sullied, tainted, unchaste, unclean, unrefined, unwholesome, vile, vitiated, weighted, wicked; SEE CONCEPTS 545,621

impute [v] *attribute*

accredit, accuse, adduce, ascribe, assign, blame, brand, censure, charge, credit, hang something on*, hint, indict, insinuate, intimate, lay, pin on*, refer, reference, stigmatize; SEE CONCEPTS 44,49

inability [n] *disabling lack of talent, skill*

disqualification, failure, frailty, impotence, inadequacy, inaptitude, incapability, incapacitation, incapacity, incompetence, ineffectiveness, ineffectualness, inefficacy, inefficiency, ineptitude, ineptness, insufficiency, inutility, lack, necessity, powerlessness, shortcoming, unfitness, weakness; SEE CONCEPT 630

inaccessible [adj] *out of reach*

aloof, away, beyond, distant, elusive, far, faraway, far-off, impassable, impervious, impracticable, insurmountable, not at hand*, out-of-the-way*, remote, unachievable, unapproachable, unattainable, unavailable, unfeasible, ungettable, unobtainable, unreachable, unrealizable, unworkable; SEE CONCEPT 576

inaccuracy [n] *error, erroneousness*

blunder, corrigendum, deception, defect, erratum, exaggeration, fault, howler*, imprecision, incorrectness, inexactness, miscalculation, mistake, slip*, solecism, typo*, unfaithfulness, unreliability, wrong; SEE CONCEPTS 101,230

inaccurate [adj] *erroneous*

all wet*, careless, counterfactual, defective, discrepant, doesn't wash*, fallacious, false, faulty, imprecise, incorrect, in error, inexact, mistaken, off, off base*, out*, specious, unfaithful, unreliable, unsound, untrue, way-off*, wide*, wild*, wrong; SEE CONCEPTS 565,582

inactive [adj] *not engaged in action; inert, lazy*

abeyant, asleep, blah*, disengaged, do-nothing*, dormant, down, draggy, dull, idle, immobile, in-dolent, in holding pattern*, inoperative, jobless, latent, lax, lethargic, limp, low-key, mothballed*, motionless, on hold, ossified, out of action, out of commission*, out of service, out of work*, passive, quiescent, quiet, sedentary, slack, sleepy, slothful, slow, sluggish, somnolent, stable, static, still, torpid, unemployed, unoccupied, unused; SEE CONCEPTS 401,560,584

inadequacy [n] *shortage, defect, inability*

blemish, dearth, defalcation, defectiveness, deficiency, deficit, drawback, failing, faultiness, flaw, imperfection, inadequateness, inaptness, incapacity, incompetence, incompetency, incompleteness, ineffectiveness, ineffectualness, inefficacy, inefficiency, ineptitude, insufficiency, lack, meagerness, paucity, poverty, scantiness, shortcoming, skimpiness, underage, unfitness, unsuitableness, weakness; SEE CONCEPTS 335,674,709

inadequate [adj] *defective, insufficient, incompetent*

bare, barren, bush-league*, deficient, depleted, dry, failing, faulty, feeble, found wanting, glitch*, imperfect, impotent, inappreciable, inapt, incapable, incommensurate, incompetent, incomplete, inconsiderable, insubstantial, junk*, lacking, lame*, lemon*, lousy, low, meager, minus, miserly, niggardly, not enough, parsimonious, poor, scanty, scarce, short, shy*, sketchy*, skimpy*, small, spare, sparse, sterile, stinted, stunted*, thin*, too little, unequal, unproductive, unqualified, weak; SEE CONCEPTS 546,570,771

inadmissible [adj] *not appropriate*

exceptionable, ill-favored, ill-timed, immaterial, improper, inappropriate, inapt, incompetent, inept, irrelevant, malapropos, objectionable, unacceptable, unallowable, unbecoming, undesirable, unfit, unqualified, unreasonable, unsatisfactory, unseemly, unsuited, unwanted, unwelcome; SEE CONCEPTS 319,558

inadvertent [adj] *accidental*

careless, chance, feckless, heedless, irreflective, negligent, not on purpose, reckless, thoughtless, uncaring, unconcerned, undesigned, undevised, unheeding, unintended, unintentional, unmindful, unplanned, unpremeditated, unthinking, unthought, unwitting; SEE CONCEPTS 542,544

inadvisable [adj] *not recommended*

careless, foolhardy, foolish, harebrained*, ill-advised, impolitic, improper, imprudent, inappropriate, incautious, inconvenient, indiscreet, inexpedient, injudicious, pointless, rash, undesirable, unsensible, unsuitable, unwise, wrong; SEE CONCEPTS 529,558

inalienable [adj] *absolute, inherent*

basic, entailed, inbred, inviolable, natural, nonnegotiable, nontransferable, sacrosanct, unassailable, untransferable; SEE CONCEPT 535

inane [adj] *stupid*

absurd, asinine, daft, empty, fatuous, flat, foolish, frivolous, futile, harebrained*, idiotic, illogical, imbecilic, innocuous, insipid, jejune, laughable, meaningless, mindless, pointless, puerile, ridiculous, sappy*, senseless, silly, trifling, unintelligent, vacant, vacuous, vain, vapid, weak, wishy-washy*, worthless; SEE CONCEPTS 542, 548

inanimate [adj] *not alive, not organic*

azoic, cold, dead, defunct, dull, exanimate, extinct, idle, inactive, inert, inoperative, insensate, insentient, lifeless, mineral, motionless, nonanimal, nonvegetable, quiescent, soulless, spiritless; SEE CONCEPT *539*

inapplicable [*adj*] *not relevant*
extraneous, foreign, garbage*, immaterial, impertinent, inapposite, inappropriate, inappurtenant, inapropos, inapt, inconsistent, irrelative, irrelevant, remote, unsuitable, unsuited; SEE CONCEPTS *546,558*

inappropriate [*adj*] *not proper, suitable*
bad form, disproportionate, foot-in-mouth*, garbage*, ill-fitted, ill-suited, ill-timed, improper, inapplicable, inapropos, incongruous, inconsonant, incorrect, indecorous, inept, irrelevant, left-field*, malapropos, off*, out of line, out of place, tasteless, unbecoming, unbefitting, undue, unfit, unfitting, unmeet, unseasonable, unseemly, unsuitable, untimely, way off*, wrong, wrong-number*; SEE CONCEPT *558*

inapt [*adj*] *incompetent; not suitable*
awkward, banal, clumsy, dull, flat, gauche, ill-adapted, ill-fitted, ill-suited, improper, inadept, inapposite, inappropriate, incongruous, inept, inexperienced, inexpert, infelicitous, insipid, jejune, maladroit, malapropos, slow, stupid, unable, undexterous, unfacile, unfit, unhandy, unmeet, unproficient, unskilled, unsuitable, unsuited, untimely; SEE CONCEPTS *527,558*

inarticulate [*adj*] *unable to speak well*
blurred, dumb, faltering, halting, hesitant, hesitating, inaudible, incoherent, incomprehensible, indistinct, maundering, muffled, mumbled, mumbling, mute, obscure, reticent, silent, speechless, stammering, tongue-tied, unclear, unintelligible, unspoken, unuttered, unvocal, unvoiced, vague, voiceless, wordless; SEE CONCEPT *267*

inattentive [*adj*] *negligent, not paying attention*
absent, absentminded, apathetic, blind, bored, careless, distracted, distrait, distraught, diverted, dreamy, faraway, heedless, inadvertent, indifferent, inobservant, listless, lost*, musing, neglectful, oblivious, off-guard*, out to lunch*, preoccupied, rapt, regardless, remiss, removed, scatterbrained*, thoughtless, unconscious, undiscerning, unheeding, unmindful, unnoticing, unobservant, unobserving, unperceiving, unthinking, unwatchful, vague; SEE CONCEPTS *403,542*

inaugurate [*v*] *begin; install*
bow, break in, break the ice*, commence, commission, dedicate, get things rolling*, get under way*, induct, initiate, instate, institute, introduce, invest, jump, kick off*, launch, make up, open, ordain, originate, set in motion*, set up, start, usher in; SEE CONCEPT *221*

inauguration [*n*] *installation of newcomers*
commencement, inaugural, induction, initiation, institution, investiture, launch, launching, opening, setting up; SEE CONCEPT *386*

inauspicious [*adj*] *ominous, unpromising*
bad, baleful, baneful, black, dire, discouraging, evil, fateful, foreboding, ill-boding, ill-omened, impending, inopportune, sinister, threatening, unfavorable, unfortunate, unlucky, unpromising, unpropitious, untimely, untoward; SEE CONCEPTS *548,570*

inborn/inbred [*adj*] *coming from birth; natural*
congenital, connate, connatural, constitutional, deep-seated, essential, hereditary, inbred, indigenous, indwelling, ingenerate, ingrained, inherent,

inherited, innate, instinctive, intrinsic, intuitive, native, unacquired; SEE CONCEPTS *406,549*

incalculable [*adj*] *countless, limitless*
boundless, capricious, chancy, enormous, erratic, fluctuant, iffy*, immense, incomputable, inestimable, infinite, innumerable, jillion*, measureless, no end of*, no end to*, numberless, uncertain, uncountable, unfixed, unforeseen, unpredictable, unreckonable, untold, vast, whimsical, without number, zillion*; SEE CONCEPTS *535,773,781*

incandescent [*adj*] *glowing*
beaming, brilliant, effulgent, fulgent, intense, lambent, lucent, luminous, phosphorescent, radiant, red-hot*, refulgent, shining, white-hot*; SEE CONCEPT *617*

incantation [*n*] *spell, magic*
abracadabra*, ala kazam*, bewitchment, black magic, chant, charm, conjuration, conjuring, enchantment, formula, hex, hocus-pocus*, hoodoo*, hymn, invocation, mumbo-jumbo*, necromancy, open sesame*, rune, sorcery, voodoo*, witchcraft, wizardry; SEE CONCEPTS *370,689*

incapable [*adj*] *not adequate; helpless*
butterfingers*, disqualified, feeble, impotent, inadequate, incompetent, ineffective, ineligible, inept, inexperienced, inexpert, inproficient, insufficient, losing, naive, not equal to, not up to*, poor, powerless, unable, uncool*, unequipped, unfit, unqualified, unskilled, unskillful, unsuited, weak; SEE CONCEPT *527*

incapacitate [*v*] *put out of action*
clip wings*, cripple, damage, disable, disarm, disenable, disqualify, hamstring*, hinder, hog-tie*, hurt, immobilize, lame, lay up*, maim, paralyze, prostrate, put out of commission*, take out, undermine, weaken; SEE CONCEPTS *121,246*

incarcerate [*v*] *put in jail, confinement*
bastille, book*, cage*, commit, confine, constrain, coop up*, detain, hold, immure, impound, imprison, intern, jail, lock up, put away, put on ice*, put under lock and key*, railroad*, restrain, restrict, send up the river*, settle, slough, take away, throw book at*; SEE CONCEPTS *90,191,317*

incarnate [*adj*] *in bodily form*
embodied, exteriorized, externalized, human, in human form, in the flesh*, made flesh, manifested, materialized, personified, physical, real, substantiated, tangible, typified; SEE CONCEPTS *490,539*

incautious [*adj*] *not careful*
any old way*, bold, brash, careless, caught napping*, devil-may-care*, fast-and-loose*, foot-in-mouth*, hasty, heedless, hotheaded*, ill-advised, ill-judged, impetuous, improvident, imprudent, impulsive, inconsiderate, indiscreet, injudicious, madcap*, neglectful, negligent, off guard*, pay no mind*, playing with fire*, precipitate, rash, reckless, regardless, sticking one's neck out*, thoughtless, unalert, unguarded, unmindful, unthinking, unvigilant, unwatchful, wary, wide open*; SEE CONCEPTS *542,544*

incendiary [*n*] *person who causes fire, trouble*
agitator, arsonist, criminal, demagogue, demonstrator, firebrand*, insurgent, pyromaniac, rabble-rouser*, rebel, revolutionary, rioter; SEE CONCEPT *412*

incendiary [*adj*] *causing trouble, damage*
dangerous, demagogic, dissentious, inflamma-

tory, malevolent, provocative, rabble-rousing*, seditious, subversive, treacherous, wicked; SEE CONCEPTS 537,570

incense [n] *strongly fragrant smoke*
aroma, balm, bouquet, burnt offering, essence, flame, frankincense, fuel, myrrh, odor, perfume, punk, redolence, scent, spice; SEE CONCEPTS 599,600

incense [v] *make very angry*
anger, ask for it*, bother, disgust, egg on*, enrage, exasperate, excite, fire up*, get a rise out of*, get under one's skin*, inflame, infuriate, ire, irritate, mad, madden, make blood boil*, make see red*, provoke, rile, umbrage; SEE CONCEPT 14

incensed [adj] *very angry*
at end of one's rope*, buffaloed*, bugged*, bummed out*, burned up*, dogged, enraged, exasperated, fuming, furious, hacked, hot and bothered*, huffy*, indignant, infuriated, irate, ireful, mad, maddened, miffed, on the warpath*, peeved, riled, rousted, rubbed the wrong way*, steamed up*, up in arms*, uptight*, wrathful; SEE CONCEPT 403

incentive [n] *lure, inducement*
allurement, bait, carrot*, catalyst, come-on*, consideration, determinant, drive, encouragement, enticement, excuse, exhortation, goad, ground, impetus, impulse, incitement, influence, insistence, inspiration, instigation, motivation, motive, persuasion, provocation, purpose, rationale, reason, reason why, spring, spur, stimulant, stimulation, stimulus, temptation, urge, whip; SEE CONCEPT 661

inception [n] *beginning*
birth, commencement, dawn, derivation, fountain, inauguration, initiation, kickoff, origin, outset, provenance, provenience, rise, root, source, start, well, wellspring; SEE CONCEPTS 648,832

incessant [adj] *never-ending, persistent*
ceaseless, constant, continual, continuous, day-and-night*, endless, eternal, everlasting, interminable, interminate, monotonous, nonstop, perpetual, relentless, round-the-clock*, timeless, unbroken, unceasing, unending, unrelenting, unremitting; SEE CONCEPTS 485,578,797

inch [n] *one-twelfth of a foot/2.54 centimeters measured*
fingerbreadth, one thirty-sixth of a yard, square; SEE CONCEPTS 790,791

inchoate [adj] *undeveloped, beginning*
amorphous, elementary, embryonic, formless, immature, imperfect, inceptive, incipient, just begun, nascent, preliminary, rudimentary, shapeless, unfinished, unformed, unshaped; SEE CONCEPTS 485,578,797

incident [n] *occurrence*
adventure, circumstance, episode, event, fact, happening, matter, milestone, occasion, scene, trip; SEE CONCEPT 2

incidental [adj] *related; minor*
accidental, accompanying, adventitious, ancillary, attendant, by-the-way*, casual, chance, circumstantial, coincidental, concomitant, concurrent, contingent, contributing, contributory, fluke*, fortuitous, irregular, nonessential, occasional, odd, random, secondary, subordinate, subsidiary; SEE CONCEPTS 547,548,577

incidentally [adv] *by chance*
accidentally, as a by-product, as side effect, by the bye*, by the way, casually, fortuitously, in passing, in related manner, not by design, obiter, parenthetically, remotely, subordinately, unexpectedly; SEE CONCEPT 544

incipient [adj] *developing*
basic, beginning, commencing, elementary, embryonic, fundamental, inceptive, inchoate, initial, initiative, initiatory, introductory, nascent, originating, start; SEE CONCEPT 585

incisive [adj1] *intelligent*
acute, bright, clever, concise, keen, penetrating, perspicacious, piercing, profound, sharp, trenchant; SEE CONCEPT 402

incisive [adj2] *sarcastic*
acerb, acerbic, acid, biting, caustic, clear-cut, concise, crisp, cutting, drilling, laconic, mordant, penetrating, sardonic, satirical, scathing, severe, sharp, slashing, succinct, tart, terse, trenchant; SEE CONCEPT 267

incite [v] *encourage, provoke*
abet, activate, actuate, agitate, animate, arouse, coax, craze, drive, egg on*, encourage, excite, exhort, fan the fire*, foment, force, forward, further, get to*, goad, impel, induce, inflame, influence, inspire, inspirit, instigate, juice*, key up*, motivate, persuade, prick, promote, prompt, provoke, psych*, push, put up to*, raise, rouse, set, set off*, solicit, spur, stimulate, stir up*, talk into, taunt, trigger, urge, whip up*, work up*; SEE CONCEPTS 14,221,242

inclement [adj1] *bitter, nasty (weather)*
brutal, cold, foul, hard, harsh, intemperate, raw, rigorous, rough, rugged, severe, stormy, tempestuous, violent, wintry; SEE CONCEPT 525

inclement [adj2] *cruel, merciless*
callous, draconian, harsh, intemperate, pitiless, rigorous, ruthless, savage, severe, tyrannical unfeeling, unkind, unmerciful; SEE CONCEPT 401

inclination [n1] *tendency, bent*
affection, appetite, aptitude, aptness, attachment, attraction, bias, capability, capacity, cup of tea*, desire, disposition, drift, druthers*, fancy, fondness, groove*, idiosyncrasy, impulse, leaning, liking, mind, movement, partiality, penchant, persuasion, pleasure, predilection, predisposition, preference, prejudice, proclivity, proneness, propensity, slant*, soft spot*, stomach*, susceptibility, taste, temperament, thing*, trend, turn*, type, urge, velleity, weakness, whim, will, wish; SEE CONCEPTS 20,411,242

inclination [n2] *slant, angle*
acclivity, bank, bend, bending, bevel, bow, bowing, cant, declivity, deviation, direction, downgrade, grade, gradient, hill, incline, lean, leaning, list, pitch, ramp, slope, tilt; SEE CONCEPT 738

incline [n] *slope*
acclivity, approach, ascent, cant, declivity, descent, dip, grade, gradient, inclination, lean, leaning, plane, ramp, rise, slant, tilt; SEE CONCEPT 738

incline [v1] *tend toward*
affect, be disposed, bend, be partial, be predisposed, be willing, bias, drive, favor, govern, gravitate toward, impel, induce, influence, lean to, look, make willing, move, not mind, persuade, predispose, prefer, prejudice, prompt, sway, turn, verge; SEE CONCEPT 657

incline [v2] *bend, lean*
aim, bevel, bow, cant, cock, deviate, diverge, heel, lay, level, list, lower, nod, point, recline,

skew, slant, slope, stoop, tend, tilt, tip, train, turn, veer, yaw; SEE CONCEPT *738*

include [*v*] *contain, involve*
accommodate, add, admit, allow for, append, bear, be composed of, be made up of, build, build in, carry, combine, comprehend, comprise, consist of, constitute, count, cover, cut in on, embody, embrace, encircle, enclose, encompass, entail, enter, have, hold, implicate, incorporate, inject, insert, interject, interpolate, introduce, make allowance for, make room for, number, number among, receive, subsume, take in, take into account, teem with, work in; SEE CONCEPTS *112,532,643*

including [*adj*] *containing*
along with, among other things, as well as, containing, counting, in addition to, inclusive of, in conjunction with, made up of, not to mention, plus, together with, with; SEE CONCEPT *577*

inclusion [*n*] *addition*
admittance, composition, comprisal, embodiment, embracement, encompassment, formation, incorporation, insertion, involvement, subsumption; SEE CONCEPT *642*

inclusive [*adj*] *all-encompassing, all-embracing*
across-the-board*, all-around, all the options*, all together, ball-of-wax*, blanket*, broad, catchall*, comprehensive, encyclopedic, full, general, global, in toto*, overall, sweeping, umbrella*, wall-to-wall*, whole, without exception; SEE CONCEPT *772*

incognito [*adj*] *in disguise*
anonymous, bearded, camouflaged, concealed, disguised, hidden, incog*, isolated, masked, masquerading, obscure, under assumed name, unknown, unrecognized; SEE CONCEPTS *576,589*

incoherent [*adj*] *unintelligible*
breathless, confused, disconnected, discontinuous, discordant, disjointed, disordered, dumb, faltering, inarticulate, incohesive, incomprehensible, incongruous, inconsistent, indistinct, indistinguishable, irrational, jumbled, maundering, muddled, muffled, mumbling, mute, muttered, puzzling, rambling, stammering, stuttering, tongue-tied*, uncommunicative, unconnected, uncoordinated, uneven, unvocal, wandering, wild; SEE CONCEPT *267*

income [*n*] *money earned by work or investments*
assets, avails, benefits, bottom line*, cash, cash flow, commission, compensation, dividends, drawings, earnings, gains, gravy*, gross, harvest, honorarium, interest, in the black*, livelihood, means, net, pay, payoff, proceeds, profit, receipts, returns, revenue, royalty, salary, take home, wage; SEE CONCEPTS *340,344*

incomparable [*adj*] *superlative*
beyond compare, excellent, exceptional, ideal, inimitable, matchless, paramount, peerless, perfect, preeminent, second to none, sovereign, superior, supreme, surpassing, towering, transcendent, ultimate, unequalled, unmatchable, unmatched, unparalleled, unrivalled, unsurpassable; SEE CONCEPT *574*

incompatible [*adj*] *antagonistic, contradictory*
adverse, antipathetic, antipodal, antithetical, clashing, conflicting, contrary, counter, disagreeing, discordant, discrepant, disparate, factious, inadmissible, inappropriate, incoherent, inconformable, incongruous, inconsistent, inconsonant, inconstant, irreconcilable, jarring, marching to a

different drummer*, mismatched, night and day*, offbeat*, opposed, opposite, poles apart*, unadapted, uncongenial, unsuitable, unsuited, warring, whale of difference*; SEE CONCEPT *564*

incompetent [*adj*] *unskillful, unable*
amateur, amateurish, awkward, bungling, bushleague*, clumsy, disqualified, floundering, helpless, inadequate, incapable, ineffectual, inefficient, ineligible, inept, inexperienced, inexpert, insufficient, maladroit, not cut out for*, not equal to, not have it*, out to lunch*, raw, unadapted, unequipped, unfit, unfitted, unhandy, uninitiated, unproficient, unqualified, unskilled, untrained, useless; SEE CONCEPT *527*

incomplete [*adj*] *unfinished, wanting*
abridged, broken, crude, defective, deficient, expurgated, fractional, fragmentary, garbled, halfdone, immature, imperfect, inadequate, incoherent, insufficient, lacking, meager, part, partial, rough, rude, rudimentary, short, sketchy, unaccomplished, unconsummated, under construction, undeveloped, undone, unexecuted, unpolished; SEE CONCEPT *531*

incomprehensible [*adj*] *not understandable*
baffling, beats me*, beyond comprehension, beyond one's grasp*, clear as mud*, cryptic, Delphic*, enigmatic, fathomless, Greek*, impenetrable, incognizable, inconceivable, inscrutable, mysterious, mystifying, obscure, opaque, over one's head*, perplexing, puzzling, sibylline, unclear, unfathomable, ungraspable, unimaginable, unintelligible, unknowable; SEE CONCEPTS *402,529*

inconceivable [*adj*] *beyond reason, belief*
extraordinary, fantastic, incomprehensible, implausible, impossible, improbable, incogitable, incredible, insupposable, mind-boggling*, phony, rare, reachy, staggering, strange, thin*, unbelievable, unconvincing, unheard-of, unimaginable, unknowable, unlikely, unsubstantial, unthinkable, weak*, won't fly*, won't wash*; SEE CONCEPTS *529,552*

inconclusive [*adj*] *up in the air*
ambiguous, deficient, incomplete, indecisive, indeterminate, lacking, open, uncertain, unconvincing, undecided, uneventful, unfateful, unfinished, unsatisfactory, unsettled, vague; SEE CONCEPTS *537,548*

incongruous [*adj*] *out of place; absurd*
alien, bizarre, conflicting, contradictory, disconsonant, discordant, disparate, distorted, divergent, extraneous, fantastic, fitful, foreign, illogical, improper, inappropriate, inapropos, inapt, incoherent, incompatible, incongruent, inconsistent, irreconcilable, irregular, jumbled, lopsided, mismatched, out of keeping*, rambling, shifting, twisted, unavailing, unbalanced, unbecoming, unconnected, uncoordinated, uneven, unintelligible, unpredictable, unrelated, unsuitable, unsuited; SEE CONCEPTS *547,558*

inconsequential/inconsiderable [*adj*] *of no significance*
casual, dinky, entry-level*, exiguous, immaterial, inadequate, inappreciable, inconsequent, insignificant, insufficient, light, little, measly, minor, negligible, paltry, petty, picayune, puny, runt, scanty, shoestring*, skimpy, small, small potatoes*, small-time*, trifling, trivial, two-bit*, unconsidered, unimportant, wimpy*, worthless; SEE CONCEPT *575*

inconsiderate [*adj*] *insensitive to others*
boorish, brash, careless, discourteous, hasty, impolite, incautious, indelicate, intolerant, reckless, rude, self-centered, selfish, sharp, short, tactless, thoughtless, unceremonious, uncharitable, ungracious, unkind, unthinking; SEE CONCEPT *401*

inconsistent [*adj*] *contradictory, irregular*
at odds, at variance, capricious, changeable, conflicting, contrary, discordant, discrepant, dissonant, erratic, fickle, illogical, incoherent, incompatible, in conflict, incongruent, incongruous, inconstant, irreconcilable, lubricious, mercurial, out of step*, temperamental, uncertain, unpredictable, unstable, variable, warring; SEE CONCEPTS *534,564*

inconsolable [*adj*] *brokenhearted*
comfortless, dejected, desolate, despairing, disconsolate, discouraged, distressed, forlorn, heartbroken, heartsick, sad, unconsolable; SEE CONCEPT *403*

inconspicuous [*adj*] *hidden, unnoticeable*
camouflaged, concealed, dim, faint, hidden, indistinct, insignificant, low-key*, low-profile*, modest, muted, ordinary, plain, quiet, retiring, secretive, shy, soft-pedalled*, subtle, tenuous, unassuming, unemphatic, unobtrusive, unostentatious; SEE CONCEPTS *485,576*

incontrovertible [*adj*] *beyond dispute*
accurate, authentic, certain, established, incontestable, indisputable, indubitable, irrefutable, nailed down*, no mistake*, no two ways about it*, positive, sure, surefire*, sure thing*, uncontestable, undeniable, unequivocable, unquestionable, unshakable; SEE CONCEPT *535*

inconvenience [*n*] *bother, trouble*
aggravation, annoyance, awkwardness, bothersomeness, cumbersomeness, difficulty, disadvantage, disruption, disturbance, drawback, exasperation, fuss, hindrance, nuisance, pain*, stew*, trial, troublesomeness, uneasiness, unfitness, unhandiness, unsuitableness, untimeliness, unwieldiness, upset, vexation; SEE CONCEPT *674*

inconvenience [*v*] *bother, trouble*
aggravate, discombobulate, discommode, discompose, disoblige, disrupt, disturb, exasperate, give a hard time*, give trouble*, hang up*, interfere, irk, make it tough*, meddle, put in a spot*, put on the spot*, put to trouble*, try, upset; SEE CONCEPTS *14,242*

inconvenient [*adj*] *bothersome, troublesome*
annoying, awkward, cumbersome, detrimental, difficult, disadvantageous, discommoding, discommodious, disturbing, embarrassing, incommodious, inexpedient, inopportune, pestiferous, prejudicial, remote, tiresome, troublesome, unhandy, unmanageable, unseasonable, unsuitable, untimely, unwieldy, vexatious; SEE CONCEPTS *537,548*

incorporate [*v*] *include, combine*
absorb, add to, amalgamate, assimilate, associate, blend, charter, coalesce, consolidate, cover, dub, embody, form, fuse, gang up*, hook in*, imbibe, integrate, join, link, merge, mix, organize, pool, put together, start, subsume, tie in*, unite; SEE CONCEPTS *112,113,324*

incorrect [*adj*] *wrong*
counterfactual, erroneous, false, faulty, flawed, imprecise, improper, inaccurate, inappropriate, inexact, mistaken, not trustworthy, out*, specious, unfitting, unreliable, unseemly, unsound,

unsuitable, untrue, way off*, wide of the mark*, wrong number*; SEE CONCEPTS *558,570*

incorrigible [*adj*] *bad, hopeless*
abandoned, beastly, hardened, incurable, intractable, inveterate, irredeemable, irreparable, loser, recidivous, uncorrectable, unreformed, useless, wicked; SEE CONCEPT *570*

incorruptible [*adj*] *honest, honorable*
above suspicion, imperishable, indestructible, inextinguishable, just, loyal, moral, perpetual, persistent, pure, reliable, straight, trustworthy, unbribable, undestroyable, untouchable, upright; SEE CONCEPTS *485,545*

increase [*n*] *addition, growth*
access, accession, accretion, accrual, accumulation, aggrandizement, augmentation, boost, breakthrough, burgeoning, cumulation, development, elaboration, enlargement, escalation, exaggeration, expansion, extension, gain, hike, incorporation, increment, inflation, intensification, maximization, merger, multiplication, optimization, raise, rise, spread, step-up, surge, swell, swelling, upgrade, upsurge, upturn, waxing; SEE CONCEPTS *763,780*

increase [*v*] *add or grow*
advance, aggrandize, aggravate, amplify, annex, augment, boost, broaden, build, build up (increase), develop, dilate, distend, double, enhance, enlarge, escalate, exaggerate, expand, extend, further, heighten, inflate, intensify, lengthen, magnify, mark up, mount, multiply, pad*, progress, proliferate, prolong, protract, pullulate, raise, redouble, reinforce, rise, sharpen, slap on*, snowball*, spread, step up, strengthen, supplement, swarm, swell, tack on*, teem, thicken, triple, wax, widen; SEE CONCEPTS *236,245,780*

increasingly [*adv*] *to a greater extent*
more, more and more, progressively, with acceleration; SEE CONCEPT *772*

incredible [*adj1*] *beyond belief*
absurd, far-fetched, fishy*, flimsy*, implausible, impossible, improbable, incogitable, inconceivable, insupposable, outlandish, out of the question*, phony, preposterous, questionable, ridiculous, rings phony*, suspect, thin*, unbelievable, unconvincing, unimaginable, unsubstantial, untenable, unthinkable; SEE CONCEPT *552*

incredible [*adj2*] *marvellous*
ace*, amazing, astonishing, astounding, awe-inspiring, awesome, extraordinary, fabulous, glorious, great, prodigious, superhuman*, unreal*, wonderful; SEE CONCEPTS *529,572*

incredulous [*adj*] *unbelieving*
disbelieving, distrustful, doubtful, doubting, dubious, hesitant, mistrustful, questioning, quizzical, show-me*, skeptical, suspect, suspicious, uncertain, unconvinced, unsatisfied, wary; SEE CONCEPTS *403,529*

increment [*n*] *small step toward gain*
accession, accretion, accrual, accrument, addition, advancement, augmentation, enlargement, increase, profit, raise, rise, supplement; SEE CONCEPTS *763,780*

inculcate [*v*] *implant, infuse information*
brainwash*, break down, communicate, drill, drum into*, educate, hammer into*, impart, impress, indoctrinate, inseminate, instill, instruct, plant, program, shape up, teach, work over*; SEE CONCEPTS *14,285*

incur [v] *bring upon oneself*
acquire, arouse, be subjected to, bring down on*, catch, contract, draw, earn, expose oneself to, gain, get, induce, meet with, obtain, provoke; SEE CONCEPT *93*

incurable [adj] *unfixable, unchangeable*
cureless, deadly, fatal, hopeless, immedicable, impossible, inoperable, irrecoverable, irremediable, irreparable, nowhere to go*, out of time*, remediless, serious, terminal, uncorrectable, unrecoverable; SEE CONCEPTS *485,548*

incursion [n] *invasion*
aggression, irruption, attack, foray, infiltration, inroad, intrusion, penetration, raid; SEE CONCEPTS *86,320*

indebted [adj] *under an obligation*
accountable, answerable for, appreciative, beholden, bound, bounden, chargeable, duty-bound, grateful, honor-bound, hooked*, in debt, in hock*, liable, obligated, obliged, owed, owing, responsible, thankful; SEE CONCEPTS *334,546*

indecency [n] *obscenity, vulgarity*
bawdiness, coarseness, crudity, drunkenness, evil, foulness, grossness, immodesty, impropriety, impurity, incivility, indecorum, indelicacy, lewdness, licentiousness, offense, outrageousness, pornography, ribaldry, smuttiness, unseemliness, vileness; SEE CONCEPTS *633,645*

indecent [adj] *obscene, vulgar; offensive*
blue*, coarse, crude, dirty*, filthy, foul, foulmouthed, gross*, ill-bred, immodest, immoral, improper, impure, in bad taste, indecorous, indelicate, lewd, licentious, malodorous, off-color*, outrageous, pornographic, raunchy*, raw, ridiculous, rough, salacious, scatological, shameless, shocking, smutty*, tasteless, unbecoming, undecorous, unseemly, untoward, vile, wicked, X-rated*; SEE CONCEPT *545*

indecisive [adj] *uncertain, indefinite*
astraddle, changeable, doubtful, faltering, halting, hemming and hawing*, hesitant, hesitating, hot and cold*, inconclusive, indeterminate, irresolute, of two minds*, on the fence*, tentative, unclear, undecided, undetermined, uneventful, unsettled, unstable, vacillating, waffling, wavering, weak-kneed*, wishy-washy*; SEE CONCEPTS *534,535*

indeed [adv] *actually*
absolutely, amen*, certainly, doubtlessly, easily, even, for real, in point of fact, in truth, much, naturally, of course, positively, really, strictly, surely, sure thing*, to be sure, truly, undeniably, undoubtedly, verily, veritably, very, very much, well; SEE CONCEPT *535*

indefatigable [adj] *untiring*
active, assiduous, bound and determined*, dead set on*, determined, diligent, energetic, hell-bent*, industrious, inexhaustible, ironclad, nose to grindstone*, painstaking, patient, persevering, persistent, pertinacious, relentless, sedulous, steadfast, stop at nothing*, strenuous, tireless, unfaltering, unflagging, unflinching, unremitting, unwavering, unwearied, unwearying, vigorous; SEE CONCEPT *542*

indefensible [adj] *inexcusable*
bad, faulty, inexpiable, insupportable, unforgivable, unjustifiable, unpardonable, untenable, unwarrantable, wrong; SEE CONCEPTS *545,548*

indefinite [adj] *ambiguous, vague*
broad, confused, doubtful, dubious, equivocal, evasive, general, ill-defined, imprecise, indeterminable, indeterminate, indistinct, inexact, inexhaustible, infinite, innumerable, intangible, loose, obscure, shadowy, uncertain, unclear, undefined, undependable, undetermined, unfixed, unknown, unlimited, unsettled, unspecific, unsure, wide; SEE CONCEPT *535*

indefinitely [adv] *continually*
considerably, endlessly, forever, frequently, regularly, sine die, without end; SEE CONCEPT *798*

indelible [adj] *not able to be erased, indestructible*
enduring, ineffaceable, ineradicable, inerasable, inexpungible, inextirpable, ingrained, lasting, memorable, permanent, rememberable, stirring, unforgettable; SEE CONCEPTS *482,529*

indelicate [adj] *obscene, vulgar*
base, brash, brutish, callow, coarse, crude, earthy, embarrassing, immodest, improper, indecent, indecorous, lewd, low, lowbred, off-color*, offensive, outrageous, risqué, rude, suggestive, tasteless, unbecoming, unblushing, uncouth, unseemly, untactful, untoward; SEE CONCEPTS *544,545*

indent [v] *make a space; push in slightly*
bash, cave in, cut, dent, depress, dint, hollow, jag, mark, nick, notch, pink, pit, rabbet, rut, scallop, score, serrate; SEE CONCEPTS *158,201,208*

independence [n] *liberty, freedom*
ability, aptitude, autarchy, autonomy, home rule*, license, qualification, self-determination, self-government, self-reliance, self-rule, self-sufficiency, separation, sovereignty; SEE CONCEPTS *376,691*

independent [adj] *liberated, free*
absolute, autarchic, autarchical, autonomous, freewheeling, individualistic, nonaligned, nonpartisan, on one's own, self-contained, self-determining, self-governing, self-reliant, self-ruling, self-sufficient, self-supporting, separate, separated, sovereign, unaided, unallied, unconnected, unconstrained, uncontrolled, unregimented; SEE CONCEPT *554*

independently [adv] *alone*
all by one's self, apart, autonomously, by oneself, exclusive of, freely, individually, of one's own volition, one at a time, one by one, on one's own, separately, severally, singly, solo, unaided, unrestrictedly, unsupervised, without regard to, without support; SEE CONCEPT *554*

indescribable [adj] *beyond words*
impossible, incommunicable, indefinable, ineffable, inexpressible, nondescript, sublime, subtle, unspeakable, untellable, unutterable; SEE CONCEPT *267*

indestructible [adj] *lasting, unable to be destroyed*
abiding, deathless, durable, enduring, everlasting, immortal, immutable, imperishable, incorruptible, indelible, indissoluble, inexterminable, inextinguishable, inextirpable, irrefragable, irrefrangible, nonperishable, permanent, perpetual, unalterable, unbreakable, unchangeable, undestroyable, undying, unfading; SEE CONCEPTS *489,534*

indeterminate [adj] *uncertain, vague*
borderless, general, imprecise, inconclusive, indefinite, indistinct, inexact, undefined, undetermined, unfixed, unspecified, unstipulated; SEE CONCEPT *535*

index [n] *indication*
basis, clue, evidence, formula, guide, hand, indicant, indication, indicator, indicia, mark, model,

index [v] *arrange, order*
alphabetize, catalogue, docket, file, list, record, tabulate; SEE CONCEPT 84

indicate [v] *signify, display*
add up to, announce, argue, attest, augur, bespeak, be symptomatic, betoken, button down*, card, connote, demonstrate, denote, designate, evidence, evince, express, finger, hint, illustrate, imply, import, intimate, make, manifest, mark, mean, name, peg*, pin down*, pinpoint*, point out, point to, prove, read, record, register, reveal, show, sign, signal, slot, specify, suggest, symbolize, tab, tag, testify, witness; SEE CONCEPTS 74,118,266

indication [n] *evidence, clue*
adumbration, attestation, augury, auspice, cue, earnest, explanation, expression, forewarning, gesture, hint, implication, index, indicia, inkling, intimation, manifestation, mark, nod, note, notion, omen, pledge, portent, preamble, prefiguration, prognostic, prolegomenon, proof, reminder, show, sign, signal, significant, signifier, suggestion, symptom, telltale, token, trace, vestige, warning, wind*, wink*; SEE CONCEPTS 74,278,284

indicative [adj] *exhibitive*
apocalyptic, augural, auspicious, characteristic, connotative, demonstrative, denotative, denotive, designative, diagnostic, emblematic, evidential, evincive, expressive, inauspicious, indicatory, indicial, ominous, pointing to, prognostic, significant, significatory, suggestive, symbolic, symptomatic, testatory, testimonial; SEE CONCEPT 267

indict [v] *accuse*
arraign, censure, charge, criminate, face with charges, finger*, frame*, impeach, incriminate, inculpate, prosecute, summon, tax; SEE CONCEPTS 44,317

indictment [n] *accusation*
allegation, arraignment, bill, blame, censure, charge, citation, detention, findings, impeachment, incrimination, presentment, prosecution, statement, summons, warrant, writ; SEE CONCEPTS 44,317,318

indifference [n] *absence of feeling, interest*
alienation, aloofness, apathy, callousness, carelessness, cold-bloodedness, coldness, cold shoulder*, coolness, detachment, disdain, disinterest, disinterestedness, dispassion, disregard, equity, heedlessness, immunity, impartiality, impassiveness, impassivity, inattention, inertia, insensitivity, insouciance, isolationism, lack, lethargy, listlessness, negligence, neutrality, nonchalance, noninterference, objectivity, stoicism, torpor, unconcern, unmindfulness; SEE CONCEPTS 410,657

indifferent [adj] *unfeeling, uninterested*
aloof, apathetic, blasé, callous, cold, cool, detached, diffident, disinterested, dispassionate, distant, equitable, haughty, heartless, heedless, highbrow, impartial, impervious, inattentive, listless, neutral, nonchalant, nonpartisan, objective, passionless, phlegmatic, regardless, scornful, silent, stoical, supercilious, superior, unaroused, unbiased, uncaring, uncommunicative, unconcerned, unemotional, unimpressed, uninvolved, unmoved, unprejudiced, unresponsive, unsocial, unsympathetic; SEE CONCEPTS 403,542

indigenous [adj] *native, inborn*
aboriginal, autochthonous, chthonic, congenital, connate, domestic, endemic, homegrown, inbred, inherent, inherited, innate, natural, original, primitive, unacquired; SEE CONCEPT 549

indigent [adj] *poor*
beggared, busted, destitute, down and out*, flat broke*, hard up*, homeless, impecunious, impoverished, in want, necessitous, needy, penniless, penurious, poverty-stricken; SEE CONCEPT 334

indigestion [n] *upset stomach*
acid indigestion, acidosis, digestive upset, dyspepsia, dyspepsy, flatulence, flu, gas, gaseous stomach, heartburn, nausea, pain; SEE CONCEPT 306

indignant [adj] *angry*
acrimonious, annoyed, bent out of shape*, boiling*, bugged*, burned up*, disgruntled, displeased, exasperated, fuming, furious, heated, huffy*, in a huff*, incensed, irate, livid, mad, miffed, peeved, piqued, p.o.'d*, provoked, resentful, riled, scornful, seeing red*, up in arms*, upset, wrathful; SEE CONCEPTS 403,542

indignation [n] *anger*
animus, boiling point*, danger, displeasure, exasperation, fury, huff*, ire, mad, miff*, pique, rage, resentment, rise, scorn, slow burn*, umbrage, wrath; SEE CONCEPTS 29,657

indignity [n] *embarrassment, humiliation*
abuse, affront, backhanded compliment*, contumely, discourtesy, dishonor, disrespect, grievance, injury, injustice, insult, obloquy, opprobrium, outrage, put-down*, reproach, slap*, slight, slur, snub, take-down*, taunt; SEE CONCEPTS 278,410

indirect [adj] *roundabout; unintended*
ambiguous, ancillary, circuitous, circular, circumlocutory, collateral, complicated, contingent, crooked, devious, discursive, duplicitous, erratic, eventual, implied, incidental, long, long-drawn-out*, long way home*, long-winded*, meandering, oblique, obscure, out-of-the-way, peripheristic, rambling, secondary, serpentine*, sidelong, sinister, sinuous, snaking*, sneaking, sneaky, subsidiary, tortuous, twisting, underhand, vagrant, wandering, winding, zigzag; SEE CONCEPTS 544,581

indiscretion [n] *mistake*
bumble, crudeness, dropping the ball*, dumb move*, error, excitability, faux pas, folly, foolishness, fool mistake*, foul-up, gaffe, gaucherie, goof*, hastiness, imprudence, indiscreetness, ingenuousness, lapse, miscue, misjudgment, misspeak, naïveté, rashness, recklessness, screw-up*, simple-mindedness, slip*, slip of the tongue*, slip-up*, stumble, stupidity, tactlessness, thoughtlessness, unseemliness; SEE CONCEPTS 101,633,674

indiscriminate [adj] *random, chaotic*
aimless, assorted, broad, careless, confused, designless, desultory, extensive, general, haphazard, heterogeneous, hit-or-miss*, imperceptive, jumbled, mingled, miscellaneous, mixed, mongrel, motley*, multifarious, promiscuous, purposeless, shallow, spot, superficial, sweeping, unconsidered, uncritical, undiscriminating, unmethodical, unplanned, unselective, unsystematic, varied, variegated, wholesale*, wide; SEE CONCEPTS 403,542,585,772

indispensable [adj] necessary
basal, basic, cardinal, crucial, essential, fundamental, imperative, key, necessitous, needed, needful, prerequisite, primary, required, requisite, vital; SEE CONCEPT 546

indisposed [adj1] not well
ailing, below par, confined, down, down with*, feeling rotten*, got a bug*, ill, infirm, laid up*, on sick list*, out of action*, poorly, sick, sickly, under the weather*, unwell; SEE CONCEPT 314

indisposed [adj2] unwilling
afraid, antagonistic, antipathetic, averse, backward, disinclined, hesitant, hostile, inimical, loath, reluctant, uncaring, uneager, uninclined; SEE CONCEPT 542

indisputable [adj] beyond doubt
absolute, accurate, actual, certain, double-checked, evident, incontestable, incontrovertible, indubitable, irrefutable, no ifs ands or buts about it*, no mistake*, open and shut*, positive, real, sure, that's a fact*, true, unassailable, undeniable, undoubted, unfabled, unquestionable, veridical; SEE CONCEPTS 535,582

indistinct [adj] obscure, ambiguous
bleared, bleary, blurred, confused, dark, dim, doubtful, faint, fuzzy, hazy, ill-defined, inaudible, inconspicuous, indefinite, indeterminate, indiscernible, indistinguishable, inexact, misty, muffled, murky, out of focus, shadowy, unclear, undefined, undetermined, unheard, unintelligible, vague, weak; SEE CONCEPTS 485,535

indistinguishable [adj] alike
duplicate, equivalent, identic, identical, like, same, tantamount, twin; SEE CONCEPT 566

individual [n] singular person, thing
being, body, character, child, creature, dude*, entity, existence, human being, man, material, matter, mortal, number, party, person, personage, self, singleton, somebody, something, soul, stuff, substance, type, unit, woman; SEE CONCEPTS 389,433

individual [adj] distinctive, exclusive
alone, characteristic, definite, diacritic, diagnostic, different, discrete, distinct, especial, express, idiosyncratic, indivisible, lone, odd, only, original, own, particular, peculiar, personal, personalized, proper, reserved, respective, secluded, select, separate, several, single, singular, sole, solitary, special, specific, uncommon, unique, unitary, unusual; SEE CONCEPTS 404,564

individuality [n] personality
air, character, complexion, difference, discreteness, disposition, dissimilarity, distinction, distinctiveness, eccentricity, habit, humor, identity, idiosyncrasy, independence, individualism, ipseity, makeup, manner, nature, oddity, oneness, originality, particularity, peculiarity, rarity, seity, selfdom, selfhood, selfness, separateness, singleness, singularity, singularness, temper, temperament, uniqueness, unity, unlikeness, way; SEE CONCEPT 411

individually [adv] separately
alone, apart, by oneself, distinctively, exclusively, independently, one at a time, one by one, personally, restrictedly, severally, singly, without help; SEE CONCEPT 544

indoctrinate [v] brainwash
break down, convince, drill, ground, imbue, implant, inculcate, influence, initiate, instill, instruct, plant, program, school, teach, train, work over; SEE CONCEPTS 14,285

indolent [adj] lazy
drony, easygoing, fainéant, idle, inactive, inert, lackadaisical, languid, lax, lazy, lethargic, listless, resting, shiftless, slothful, slow, slow-going, sluggish, torpid; SEE CONCEPTS 538,542,584

indomitable [adj] steadfast, unyielding
dogged, impassable, impregnable, insuperable, insurmountable, invincible, invulnerable, obstinate, pertinacious, resolute, ruthless, staunch, stubborn, unassailable, unbeatable, unconquerable, undefeatable, unflinching, willful; SEE CONCEPTS 404,489,534

induce [v] cause to happen; encourage
abet, activate, actuate, argue into, breed, bring about, bring around, bulldoze*, cajole, cause, coax, convince, draw, draw in, effect, engender, generate, get*, get up, give rise to, goose*, impel, incite, influence, instigate, lead to, make, motivate, move, occasion, persuade, press, prevail upon, procure, produce, promote, prompt, sell one on*, set in motion, soft-soap*, squeeze, steamroll*, suck in*, sway, sweet-talk*, talk into*, twist one's arm*, urge, wheedle, win over*; SEE CONCEPTS 14,68,242

inducement [n] incentive, motive
attraction, bait, brainwash, carrot*, cause, come-on*, con*, consideration, desire, encouragement, hard sell*, hook*, impulse, incitement, influence, leader, lure, reward, snow job*, soft soap*, spur, stimulus, sweet talk*, temptation, twist, urge; SEE CONCEPTS 68,661

induct [v] take into an organization
conscript, draft, enlist, inaugurate, initiate, install, instate, introduce, invest, recruit, sign on, sign up, swear in; SEE CONCEPTS 50,88,320,384

induction [n1] taking in, initiation
consecration, draft, entrance, greetings, inaugural, inauguration, installation, instatement, institution, introduction, investiture, ordination, selection; SEE CONCEPTS 320,384,685

induction [n2] inference
conclusion, conjecture, deducement, generalization, judgment, logical reasoning, ratiocination, rationalization, reason; SEE CONCEPTS 37,689

indulge [v1] treat oneself or another to
allow, baby, cater, coddle, cosset, delight, entertain, favor, foster, give in, give rein to*, go along, go easy on*, gratify, humor, mollycoddle*, nourish, oblige, pamper, pander, pet, please, regale, satiate, satisfy, spoil, spoil rotten*, take care of*, tickle, yield; SEE CONCEPT 110

indulge [v2] luxuriate in
bask in, ego trip*, enjoy, go in for*, live it up*, look out for number one*, revel in, rollick*, take part, wallow in; SEE CONCEPT 20

indulgence [n] luxury; gratification
allowance, appeasement, attention, babying*, coddling*, courtesy, endurance, excess, extravagance, favor, favoring, fondling, fondness, forbearance, fulfillment, goodwill, gratifying, hedonism, immoderation, intemperance, intemperateness, kindness, kowtowing*, lenience, leniency, pampering, partiality, patience, permissiveness, petting, placating, pleasing, privilege, profligacy, profligateness, satiation, satisfaction, service, spoiling, toadying*, tolerance, toleration, treating, understanding; SEE CONCEPTS 337,657,712

indulgent [*adj*] *lenient, giving*
able to live with*, big*, charitable, clement, compassionate, complaisant, compliant, considerate, easy, easygoing, favorable, fond, forbearing, gentle, going along with*, going easy on*, gratifying, kind, kindly, liberal, merciful, mild, overpermissive, permissive, soft-shelled*, tender, tolerant, understanding; SEE CONCEPTS *404,542*

industrial [*adj*] *related to manufacturing*
automated, business, factory-made, industrialized, in industry, machine-made, manufactured, manufacturing, mechanical, mechanized, modern, smokestack, streamlined, technical; SEE CONCEPT *536*

industrious [*adj*] *hardworking*
active, assiduous, ball of fire*, burning, busy, conscientious, diligent, dynamic, eager, energetic, grind*, in full swing*, intent, involved, jumping, laborious, on the go*, operose, perky*, persevering, persistent, plugging, productive, psyched up on*, purposeful, sedulous, spirited, steady, tireless, zealous; SEE CONCEPT *538*

industry [*n1*] *manufacturing*
big business*, business, commerce, commercial enterprise, corporation, management, manufactory, megacorp*, mob, monopoly, multinational, outfit*, production, trade, traffic; SEE CONCEPTS *323,325*

industry [*n2*] *hard work*
activity, application, assiduity, attention, care, determination, diligence, dynamism, effort, energy, enterprise, intentness, inventiveness, labor, pains, patience, perseverance, persistence, tirelessness, toil, vigor, zeal; SEE CONCEPT *677*

inebriated [*adj*] *drunk*
blind drunk*, bombed, boozy, high*, inebriate, intoxicated, loaded*, plastered*, smashed*, tight*, tipsy, under the influence, wasted*; SEE CONCEPT *314*

ineffable [*adj*] *too great for words*
beyond words, celestial, divine, empyreal, empyrean, ethereal, heavenly, holy, ideal, impossible, incommunicable, incredible, indefinable, indescribable, inexpressible, nameless, sacred, spiritual, too sacred for words*, transcendent, transcendental, unspeakable, untellable, unutterable; SEE CONCEPTS *267,574*

ineffective/ineffectual [*adj*] *weak, useless*
abortive, anticlimactic, barren, bootless, defeasible, feckless, feeble, forceless, fruitless, futile, idle, impotent, inadequate, incompetent, indecisive, inefficacious, inefficient, inept, inferior, innocuous, inoperative, invertebrate, lame, limited, neutralized, nugatory, null, null and void*, paltry, powerless, spineless, unable, unavailing, unfruitful, unproductive, unprofitable, unsuccessful, vain, void, withered, worthless; SEE CONCEPTS *537,560*

inefficient [*adj*] *not working well; wasteful*
can't hack it*, careless, disorganized, extravagant, faulty, feeble, half-baked*, improficient, improvident, incapable, incompetent, ineffective, ineffectual, inefficacious, inept, inexpert, not cut out for*, prodigal, shooting blanks*, slack, slipshod, sloppy, slovenly, unfit, unprepared, unqualified, unskilled, unskillful, untrained, weak; SEE CONCEPTS *402,527,560*

inelegant [*adj*] *clumsy, crude*
awkward, coarse, crass, gauche, graceless, gross, indelicate, labored, oafish, raw, rough, rude, stiff*, uncouth, uncultivated, uncultured, ungainly, ungraceful, unpolished, unrefined, vulgar, wooden*; SEE CONCEPTS *267,542,555*

ineligible [*adj*] *not qualified*
disqualified, inappropriate, incompetent, objectionable, ruled out, unacceptable, unavailable, undesirable, unequipped, unfit, unqualified, unsuitable; SEE CONCEPTS *402,558*

inept [*adj*] *clumsy, unskilled; incompetent*
all thumbs*, artless, awkward, bumbling, bungling, butterfingers*, gauche, halting, inadept, incapable, incompetent, inefficient, inexpert, loser, maladroit, unapt, undexterous, unfacile, ungraceful, unhandy, unproficient, unskillful, wooden*; SEE CONCEPTS *402,527*

inept [*adj2*] *not suitable; improper*
absurd, ill-timed, inappropriate, inapt, infelicitous, malapropos, meaningless, not adapted, out of place*, pointless, ridiculous, undue, unfit, unseasonable, unseemly, unsuitable; SEE CONCEPT *558*

inequality [*n*] *prejudice; lack of balance*
asperity, bias, contrast, difference, discrimination, disparity, disproportion, dissimilarity, dissimilitude, diversity, imparity, incommensurateness, injustice, irregularity, one-sidedness, partisanship, preferentiality, roughness, unequivalence, unevenness, unfairness, unjustness, variation; SEE CONCEPT *665*

inert [*adj*] *not moving; lifeless*
apathetic, asleep, dead, dormant, down, dull, idle, immobile, impassive, impotent, inactive, inanimate, indolent, languid, languorous, lazy, leaden, listless, motionless, numb, paralyzed, passive, phlegmatic, powerless, quiescent, quiet, slack, sleepy, slothful, sluggard, sluggish, slumberous, static, still, stolid, torpid, unmoving, unreactive, unresponsive; SEE CONCEPTS *542,584*

inertia [*n*] *disinclination to move; lifelessness*
apathy, deadness, drowsiness, dullness, idleness, immobility, immobilization, inactivity, indolence, languor, lassitude, laziness, lethargy, listlessness, oscitancy, paralysis, passivity, sloth, sluggishness, stillness, stupor, torpidity, torpor, unresponsiveness; SEE CONCEPTS *657,681*

inevitable [*adj*] *certain; cannot be avoided*
all locked up*, assured, binding, compulsory, decided, decreed, destined, determined, doomed, fated, fateful, fixed, for certain, foreordained, imminent, impending, ineluctable, includible, inescapable, inexorable, inflexible, in the bag*, irresistible, irrevocable, necessary, no ifs and or buts*, obligatory, ordained, pat*, prescribed, settled, sure, unalterable, unavoidable, undeniable, unpreventable, without recourse; SEE CONCEPTS *535,552*

inexcusable [*adj*] *not forgivable*
blamable, blameworthy, censurable, criticizable, impermissible, indefensible, inexpiable, intolerable, outrageous, reprehensible, unallowable, unforgivable, unjustifiable, unpardonable, unpermissible, untenable, unwarrantable, wrong; SEE CONCEPTS *545,570*

inexorable [*adj*] *cruel, pitiless*
adamant, adamantine, bound, bound and determined*, compulsory, dead set on*, dogged, hard, harsh, hell bent on*, immobile, immovable, implacable, ineluctable, inescapable, inflexible, ironclad, like death and taxes*, locked in*, mean business*, merciless, necessary, no going back*,

obdurate, obstinate, relentless, remorseless, resolute, rigid, set in stone*, severe, single-minded, stubborn, unappeasable, unbending, uncompromising, unmovable, unrelenting, unyielding; SEE CONCEPTS 401,534

inexpensive [adj] not high priced
bargain, budget, buy, cheap, cost next to nothing*, cut-rate, dime a dozen*, dirt-cheap*, economical, for a song*, half-price, low, low-cost, low-priced, marked down, modest, nominal, popular, popularly priced, real buy*, real steal*, reasonable, reduced, steal, thrifty; SEE CONCEPT 334

inexperienced [adj] unskilled, unfamiliar
amateur, callow, fresh, green*, ignorant, immature, inept, inexpert, innocent, kid*, naive, new, prentice, raw*, rookie, rude, sophomoric, spring chicken*, tenderfoot*, unaccustomed, unacquainted, unconversant, undisciplined, unfamiliar with, unfledged, unpracticed, unschooled, unseasoned, unsophisticated, untrained, untried, unused, unversed, unworldly, verdant, wet behind ears*, young; SEE CONCEPTS 402,404,527

inexplicable [adj] beyond comprehension, explanation
baffling, enigmatic, incomprehensible, indecipherable, indescribable, inexplainable, inscrutable, insoluble, mysterious, mystifying, obscure, odd, peculiar, puzzling, strange, unaccountable, undefinable, unexplainable, unfathomable, unintelligible, unsolvable; SEE CONCEPTS 267,529

infallible [adj] unerring, dependable
acceptable, accurate, agreeable, apodictic, authoritative, certain, correct, effective, effectual, efficacious, efficient, exact, faultless, flawless, foolproof, handy, helpful, impeccable, incontrovertible, inerrable, inerrant, omniscient, perfect, positive, reliable, satisfactory, satisfying, sure, surefire, true, trustworthy, unbeatable, undeceivable, unfailing, unimpeachable, unquestionable, useful; SEE CONCEPTS 535,560,574

infamous [adj] shameful, bad in reputation
abominable, atrocious, base, caitiff, contemptible, corrupt, degenerate, despicable, detestable, disgraceful, dishonorable, disreputable, egregious, evil, flagitious, foul, hateful, heinous, ignominious, ill-famed, iniquitous, loathsome, miscreant, monstrous, nefarious, notorious, odious, offensive, opprobrious, outrageous, perverse, questionable, rotten, scandalous, scurvy, shady, shocking, sorry, unhealthy, vicious, vile, villainous, wicked; SEE CONCEPTS 404,545,570

infamy [n] shameful, bad reputation
abomination, atrocity, disapprobation, discredit, disesteem, disgrace, dishonor, disrepute, enormity, evil, ignominy, immorality, impropriety, notoriety, notoriousness, obloquy, odium, opprobrium, outrageousness, scandal, shame, stigma, villainy, wickedness; SEE CONCEPTS 411,645

infant [n] baby
babe, bairn, bambino, bantling, bundle, child, kid, little one, neonate, newborn, small child, suckling, toddler, tot; SEE CONCEPTS 414,424

infant/infantile [adj] very young
baby, babyish, callow, childish, childlike, dawning, developing, early, emergent, green*, growing, immature, infantine, initial, juvenile, kid, naive, nascent, newborn, puerile, tender, unfledged, unripe, weak, youthful; SEE CONCEPTS 542,578,797,820

infatuated [adj] in love with; obsessed
beguiled, besotted, bewitched, captivated, carried away*, charmed, crazy about*, enamored, enraptured, far gone on*, fascinated, foolish, inflamed, intoxicated, possessed, seduced, silly*, smitten, spellbound, under a spell*; SEE CONCEPTS 32,403

infect [v] pollute, contaminate
affect, blight, corrupt, defile, disease, influence, poison, spoil, spread among, spread to, taint, touch, vitiate; SEE CONCEPTS 143,246

infection [n] contamination
bug*, communicability, contagion, contagiousness, corruption, defilement, disease, epidemic, flu, germs, impurity, insanitation, poison, pollution, septicity, virus, what's going around*; SEE CONCEPTS 230,306

infectious [adj] catching, spreading
communicable, contagious, contaminating, corrupting, defiling, diseased, epidemic, infective, mephitic, miasmic, noxious, pestilent, pestilential, poisoning, polluting, toxic, transferable, transmittable, virulent, vitiating; SEE CONCEPTS 314,559

infer [v] conclude
arrive at, ascertain, assume, believe, collect, conjecture, construe, deduce, derive, draw, draw inference, figure, figure out, gather, glean, guess, induce, interpret, intuit, judge, presume, presuppose, reach conclusion, read between lines*, read into*, reason, reckon, speculate, suppose, surmise, think, understand; SEE CONCEPTS 12,15,37

inferior [n] person of lesser rank, importance
adherent, attendant, auxiliary, deputy, disciple, follower, hanger-on, hireling, junior, menial, minion, minor, peon, satellite, second banana*, subaltern, subject, subordinate, sycophant, underling; SEE CONCEPTS 348,423

inferior [adj1] less in rank, importance
back seat*, bottom, bottom-rung*, entry-level, junior, less, lesser, lower, menial, minor, minus, nether, peon, second, secondary, second-banana*, second-fiddle*, second-string*, smaller, subjacent, subordinate, subsidiary, under, underneath; SEE CONCEPT 567

inferior [adj2] poor, second-rate
average, bad, base, common, déclassé, fair, good-for-nothing*, hack*, imperfect, indifferent, junk*, lemon*, lousy, low-grade, low-rent*, mean, mediocre, middling, ordinary, paltry, poorer, sad, second-class, sorry*, substandard, tawdry, two-bit*, worse, wretched; SEE CONCEPT 574

infernal [adj] damned; underworld
accursed, blamed, blasted, chthonian, confounded, cursed, cussed, damnable, demonic, devilish, diabolical, execrable, fiendish, hellish, lower, malevolent, malicious, monstrous, nether, satanic, subterranean, sulphurous, wicked; SEE CONCEPTS 536,545

infertile [adj] not bearing fruit, young
barren, depleted, drained, effete, exhausted, impotent, impoverished, infecund, nonproductive, sterile, unbearing, unfertile, unfruitful, unproductive; SEE CONCEPTS 406,560

infest [adj] flood, overrun
abound, annoy, assail, beset, crawl, crowd, defile, fill, flock, harass, harry, infect, invade, overspread, overwhelm, pack, penetrate, pester, plague, pollute, press, ravage, swarm, teem, throng, worry; SEE CONCEPTS 14,86,179

infidelity [n] *disloyalty to an obligation*
adultery, affair, bad faith, betrayal, cheating, duplicity, extramarital relations, faithlessness, falseness, falsity, inconstancy, lewdness, perfidiousness, perfidy, treacherousness, treachery, treason, two-timing*, unfaithfulness; SEE CONCEPTS 388,645

infiltrate [v] *creep in*
access, crack*, edge in, filter through, foist, impregnate, insinuate, penetrate, percolate*, permeate, pervade, saturate, sneak in, tinge, work into, worm into*; SEE CONCEPTS 159,179

infinite [adj] *limitless, without end*
absolute, all-embracing, bottomless, boundless, enduring, enormous, eternal, everlasting, illimitable, immeasurable, immense, incalculable, incessant, inestimable, inexhaustible, interminable, measureless, million, never-ending, no end of, no end to, numberless, perdurable, perpetual, sempiternal, stupendous, supertemporal, supreme, total, unbounded, uncounted, unending, untold, vast, wide, without limit, without number; SEE CONCEPTS 762,781,798

infinitesimal [adj] *small*
atomic, imperceptible, inappreciable, inconsiderable, insignificant, little, microscopic, miniature, minuscule, minute, negligible, teeny*, tiny, unnoticeable; SEE CONCEPTS 773,789

infinity [n] *endlessness*
beyond, boundlessness, continuity, continuum, endless time, eternity, expanse, extent, immeasurability, immensity, infinitude, limitlessness, myriad, perpetuity, sempiternity, space, ubiquity, unlimited space, vastitude, vastness; SEE CONCEPTS 730,807

infirm [adj] *sick, weak*
ailing, anemic, anile, debilitated, decrepit, delicate, enfeebled, failing, faint, faltering, feeble, flimsy, fragile, frail, halting, ill, insecure, irresolute, laid low*, lame, sensile, shaky, unsound, unstable, unsubstantial, vacillating, wavering, wobbly; SEE CONCEPTS 314,485,489

infirmity [n] *weakness, sickness*
affliction, ailing, ailment, confinement, debilitation, debility, decay, decrepitude, defect, deficiency, disease, diseasedness, disorder, failing, fault, feebleness, flu, frailty, ill health, imperfection, indisposition, malady, malaise, shortcoming, sickliness, unhealth, unhealthiness, unwellness, vulnerability; SEE CONCEPTS 306,674,732

inflame [v] *anger, aggravate*
agitate, annoy, arouse, burn, disturb, embitter, enrage, exacerbate, exasperate, excite, fan, fire, fire up, foment, gall, get*, grate, heat, heat up, ignite, impassion, incense, incense, infuriate, intensify, intoxicate, irritate, kindle, light, madden, provoke, put out*, rile, roil, rouse, steam up, stimulate, vex, worsen; SEE CONCEPTS 7,14, 19,22,249

inflammable [adj] *ready to burn*
burnable, combustible, dangerous, flammable, hazardous, ignitable, incendiary, risky, unsafe; SEE CONCEPT 485

inflammatory [adj] *instigative, angering*
anarchic, demagogic, exciting, explosive, fiery, incendiary, incitive, inflaming, insurgent, intemperate, provocative, rabble-rousing*, rabid, rebellious, revolutionary, riotous, seditionary, seditious; SEE CONCEPTS 537,542

inflate [v] *blow up, increase*
aerate, aggrandize, amplify, augment, balloon*, beef up*, bloat, boost, build up, cram*, dilate, distend, enlarge, escalate, exaggerate, exalt, expand, flesh out*, magnify, maximize, overestimate, pad*, puff up*, pump up*, pyramid, raise, spread, stretch, surcharge, swell up*, widen; SEE CONCEPTS 236,245,780

inflated [adj] *exaggerated*
aggrandized, amplified, augmented, aureate, bloated, bombastic, diffuse, dilated, distended, dropsical, enlarged, euphuistic, extended, filled, flatulent, flowery, fustian, grandiloquent, grown, magnified, magniloquent, ostentatious, overblown, overestimated, pompous, pretentious, prolix, puffed, pumped up, ranting, rhapsodical, rhetorical, showy, spread, stretched, surcharged, swollen, tumescent, tumid, turgid, verbose, windy, wordy; SEE CONCEPTS 267,773

inflation [n] *increase, swelling*
aggrandizement, blowing up, boom, boost, buildup, distension, enhancement, enlargement, escalation, expansion, extension, hike, intensification, prosperity, puffiness, rise, spread, tumefaction; SEE CONCEPTS 335,763,780

inflection [n] *accent, intonation*
articulation, change, emphasis, enunciation, modulation, pitch, pronunciation, sound, timbre, tonality, tone, tone of voice, variation; SEE CONCEPTS 65,595

inflexible [adj1] *stubborn*
adamant, adamantine, determined, dogged, dyed-in-the-wool*, firm, fixed, hard, hard-and-fast*, immovable, immutable, implacable, indomitable, inexorable, intractable, iron, obdurate, obstinate, relentless, resolute, rigid, rigorous, set, set in one's ways*, single-minded, stand one's ground*, staunch, steadfast, steely, stiff, strict, stringent, unadaptable, unbending, unchangeable, uncompliant, uncompromising, unrelenting, unswayable, unyielding; SEE CONCEPT 404

inflexible [adj2] *hardened, stiff*
hard, immalleable, impliable, inelastic, nonflexible, rigid, set, starched, taut, unbending; SEE CONCEPT 604

inflict [v] *impose something*
administer, apply, bring upon, command, deal out, deliver, dispense, exact, expose, extort, force, force upon, give, give it to*, lay down the law*, levy, mete out, require, stick it to*, strike, subject, visit, wreak; SEE CONCEPTS 50,53, 88,242

influence [n] *power, authority*
access, agency, ascendancy, character, clout, command, connections, consequence, control, credit, direction, domination, dominion, drag, effect, esteem, fame, fix, force, grease*, guidance, hold, impact, importance, imprint, in, juice*, leadership, leverage, magnetism, mark, moment, money, network, notoriety, predominance, prerogative, pressure, prestige, prominence, pull, repercussion, reputation, ropes*, rule, significance, spell, supremacy, sway, weight*; SEE CONCEPT 687

influence [v] *lead to believe, do*
act upon, affect, alter, argue into, arouse, be recognized, bias, brainwash*, bribe, bring to bear, carry weight, change, channel, compel, control, count, determine, direct, dispose, form, get at*, guide, have a part in, impact on, impel, impress,

in
in

incite, incline, induce, instigate, manipulate, modify, mold, move, persuade, predispose, prejudice, prevail, prompt, pull strings*, regulate, rouse, rule, seduce, sell, shape, snow*, sway, talk into, train, turn, urge, work upon; SEE CONCEPTS 18,68,242

influential [adj] *effective, powerful*
affecting, authoritative, big-gun*, big-wheel*, controlling, dominant, efficacious, famous, forcible, governing, guiding, hot-dog*, important, impressive, inspiring, instrumental, leading, major-league*, meaningful, momentous, moving, name, persuasive, potent, prominent, significant, strong, substantial, telling, touching, weighty; SEE CONCEPTS 537,568

influx [n] *flow, rush*
arrival, coming in, convergence, entrance, incursion, inflow, inpouring, inrush, introduction, inundation, invasion, penetration; SEE CONCEPTS 159,179,786

infomercial [n] *full-length television program existing solely to market a product*
advertorial, commercial, demonstration, docutainment, infotainment, paid announcement; SEE CONCEPT 277

inform [v] *communicate knowledge, information*
acquaint, advise, apprise, betray, blab*, brief, caution, clue, edify, educate, endow, endue, enlighten, familiarize, fill in, forewarn, give a pointer, give a tip, give away, give two cents*, illuminate, inspire, instruct, invest, leak, let in on*, let know, level, make conversant with, notify, post, relate, send word, show the ropes*, snitch, squeal, tattle, teach, tell, tell on, tip, tout, update, warn, wise; SEE CONCEPT 60

informal [adj] *casual, simple*
breezy, colloquial, congenial, cool*, democratic, down home*, easy, easygoing, everyday, extempore, familiar, folksy, frank, free, free-and-easy*, homey, improv*, inconspicuous, intimate, laid back*, loose, low-pressure, mellow, mixed, motley, natural, off-the-cuff*, open, ordinary, relaxed, spontaneous, sporty, straightforward, throwaway*, unceremonious, unconstrained, unconventional, unfussy, unofficial, unrestrained, urbane, without ceremony; SEE CONCEPTS 548, 589

informant/informer [n] *person who delivers news*
accuser, adviser, announcer, betrayer, blabbermouth*, canary*, crier, deep throat*, double-crosser, herald, interviewer, journalist, messenger, newscaster/newsperson, notifier, preacher, propagandist, rat*, reporter, sneak, source, stool pigeon*, tattler, tattletale; SEE CONCEPTS 348,354,423

information [n] *facts, news*
advice, ammo*, break*, chapter and verse*, clue, confidence, counsel, cue, data, dirt*, dope*, dossier, earful*, enlightenment, erudition, illumination, info*, inside story*, instruction, intelligence, knowledge, leak, learning, lore, lowdown*, material, message, network, notice, notification, orientation, propaganda, report, science, scoop, score, tidings, tip, what's what*, whole story*, wisdom, word*; SEE CONCEPT 274

informative [adj] *educational*
advisory, chatty, communicative, descriptive, edifying, educative, elucidative, enlightening, explanatory, forthcoming, gossipy, illuminating, informational, instructional, instructive, newsy,

revealing, revelatory, significant; SEE CONCEPT 267

informed [adj] *cognizant, conversant*
abreast, acquainted, apprized, au courant*, au fait*, briefed, enlightened, erudite, expert, familiar, in the know*, into*, knowledgeable, know the score*, know what's what*, learned, on top of*, posted*, primed*, reliable, savvy*, tuned in*, up*, up on*, up-to-date, versant, versed, well-read, wise to*; SEE CONCEPT 402

infraction [n] *violation*
breach, breaking, contravention, crime, error, faux pas, infringement, lapse, offense, sin, slip*, transgression, trespass; SEE CONCEPTS 192,645

infrequent [adj] *not happening regularly*
exceptional, few, few and far between*, isolated, limited, meager, occasional, odd, rare, scant, scanty, scarce, scattered, seldom, semioccasional, sparse, spasmodic, sporadic, stray, uncommon, unusual; SEE CONCEPT 530

infringe [v] *violate*
borrow, breach, break, contravene, crash, disobey, encroach, entrench, impose, infract, intrude, invade, lift, meddle, obtrude, offend, pirate, presume, steal, transgress, trespass; SEE CONCEPTS 192,384

infuriate [v] *make angry*
aggravate, anger, enrage, exasperate, incense, ire, irritate, madden, make blood boil*, provoke, rile, T-off*, umbrage; SEE CONCEPT 14

infuse [v] *introduce; soak*
animate, breathe into, imbue, impart, implant, impregnate, inculcate, indoctrinate, ingrain, inoculate, inspire, instill, intersperse, invest, leaven, permeate, pervade, plant, saturate, steep, suffuse; SEE CONCEPTS 140,179,187

ingenious [adj] *clever; bright*
able, adroit, artistic, bright, canny, crafty, creative, cunning, deviceful, dexterous, gifted, imaginative, innovational, innovative, innovatory, intelligent, inventive, original, ready, resourceful, shrewd, skillful, sly, subtle; SEE CONCEPT 402

ingenuous [adj] *honest, trustful*
artless, candid, childlike, frank, green*, guileless, innocent, like a babe in the woods*, naive, natural, open, outspoken, plain, simple, sincere, square, straightforward, trusting, unaffected, unartful, unartificial, undisguised, unreserved, unschooled, unsophisticated, unstudied, up front*; SEE CONCEPTS 267,542,589

ingrained [adj] *deep-rooted*
built-in, chronic, confirmed, congenital, constitutional, deep-seated, fixed, fundamental, hereditary, implanted, inborn, inbred, inbuilt, indelible, indwelling, ineradicable, inherent, innate, in the blood*, intrinsic, inveterate, rooted; SEE CONCEPTS 535,549

ingratiate [v] *get on the good side of someone*
attract, blandish, brownnose*, captivate, charm, crawl, flatter, get in with*, grovel, hand a line*, insinuate oneself, kowtow*, play up to*, seek favor, truckle; SEE CONCEPTS 7,22,68

ingratiating [adj] *fawning, servile*
charming, crawling, deferential, disarming, flattering, humble, insinuating, obsequious, saccharine, serving, silken, smarmy, soft, sycophantic, toadying*, unctuous; SEE CONCEPT 401

ingredient [n] *component of concoction*
additive, constituent, element, factor, fixing, fundamental, innards, integral, integrant, making,

part, part and parcel*, piece; SEE CONCEPT 835

inhabit [v] *take up residence in*
abide, crash, dwell, indwell, live, locate, lodge, make one's home, occupy, park, people, perch, populate, possess, reside, roost, settle, squat, stay, tenant; SEE CONCEPT 226

inhabitant [n] *person who is resident of habitation*
aborigine, addressee, autochthon, boarder, citizen, colonist, denizen, dweller, householder, incumbent, indweller, inmate, lessee, lodger, native, neighbor, occupant, occupier, renter, resider, roomer, settler, squatter, suburbanite, tenant, urbanite; SEE CONCEPT 354,413

inhale [v] *breathe in*
drag, draw in, gasp, inspire, insufflate, puff, pull, respire, smell, sniff, snort, suck in; SEE CONCEPTS 163,601

inherent [adj] *basic, hereditary*
built-in, characteristic, congenital, connate, constitutional, deep-rooted, deep-seated, distinctive, elementary, essential, fixed, fundamental, genetic, immanent, implicit, inborn, inbred, inbuilt, indigenous, indispensable, individual, indwelling, ingrained, inherited, innate, inner, instinctive, integral, integrated, internal, in the grain, intimate, intrinsic, inward, latent, native, natural, original, part and parcel*, resident, running in the family*, subjective, unalienable; SEE CONCEPTS 404,549

inherit [v] *gain as possession from someone's death*
accede, acquire, be bequeathed, be granted, be left, come in for, come into, derive, fall heir, get, obtain, receive, succeed, take over; SEE CONCEPTS 124,371

inheritance [n] *possession gained through someone's death*
bequest, birthright, devise, estate, gift, heirloom, heritage, heritance, legacy, primogeniture; SEE CONCEPT 337

inhibit [v] *restrict, prevent*
arrest, avert, bar, bit, bridle, check, constrain, cramp, curb, discourage, enjoin, faze, forbid, frustrate, hang up*, hinder, hog-tie*, hold back, hold down, hold in, impede, interdict, keep in, obstruct, outlaw, prohibit, put on brakes*, repress, restrain, sandbag*, stop, stymie, suppress, taboo*, ward, withhold; SEE CONCEPTS 121,130

inhibited [adj] *shy*
bottled up*, cold, constrained, frustrated, guarded, hung up*, passionless, repressed, reserved, reticent, self-conscious, subdued, undemonstrative, unresponsive, uptight, withdrawn; SEE CONCEPTS 404,542

inhibition [n] *restriction, hindrance*
bar, barrier, blockage, check, embargo, hangup, interdict, interference, obstacle, prevention, prohibition, reserve, restraint, reticence, self-consciousness, shyness, sublimation, suppression; SEE CONCEPTS 411,657

inhospitable [adj] *unfriendly*
brusque, cold, cool, hostile, rude, short, uncongenial, unfavorable, ungenerous, unkind, unreceptive, unsociable, unwelcoming; SEE CONCEPT 401

inhuman/inhumane [adj] *animal, savage*
barbaric, barbarous, bestial, brutal, cannibalistic, cold-blooded, cruel, devilish, diabolical, fell, ferocious, fiendish, fierce, grim, hateful, heartless, implacable, malicious, malign, malignant, mean, merciless, pitiless, relentless, remorseless, ruthless, truculent, uncompassionate, unfeeling, unkind, unrelenting, unsympathetic, vicious; SEE CONCEPTS 401,545

inimical [adj] *antagonistic, contrary*
adverse, antipathetic, destructive, disaffected, harmful, hostile, hurtful, ill, ill-disposed, inimicable, injurious, noxious, opposed, oppugnant, pernicious, repugnant, unfavorable, unfriendly, unwelcoming; SEE CONCEPTS 401,537

inimitable [adj] *incomparable*
consummate, matchless, nonpareil, peerless, perfect, supreme, unequalled, unexampled, unique, unmatched, unparalleled, unrivalled, unsurpassable; SEE CONCEPT 574

iniquity [n] *sin, evil*
abomination, baseness, crime, evildoing, heinousness, immorality, infamy, injustice, miscreancy, misdeed, offense, sinfulness, unfairness, unrighteousness, wickedness, wrong, wrongdoing; SEE CONCEPT 645

initial [adj] *beginning, primary*
antecedent, basic, commencing, earliest, early, elementary, embryonic, first, foremost, fundamental, germinal, headmost, inaugural, inceptive, inchoate, incipient, infant, initiative, initiatory, introductory, leading, nascent, opening, original, pioneer, virgin; SEE CONCEPTS 585,799,828

initiate [v1] *start, introduce*
admit, begin, break the ice*, come out with, come up with, commence, dream up, enter, get ball rolling*, get feet wet*, get under way, inaugurate, induct, install, instate, institute, intro*, invest, kick off*, launch, make up, open, originate, pioneer, set in motion, set up, take in, take up, trigger, usher in; SEE CONCEPT 221

initiate [v2] *teach*
brief, coach, edify, enlighten, familiarize, indoctrinate, induct, inform, instate, instruct, introduce, invest, train; SEE CONCEPT 285

initiation [n] *start, introduction*
admission, baptism, beginning, commencement, debut, enrollment, entrance, inaugural, inauguration, inception, indoctrination, induction, installation, instatement, investiture, preliminaries; SEE CONCEPTS 221,386

initiative [n] *eagerness to do something*
action, ambition, drive, dynamism, energy, enterprise, enthusiasm, get-up-and-go*, gumption*, inventiveness, leadership, moxie*, originality, punch, push, resource, resourcefulness, spunk*, steam*, vigor; SEE CONCEPTS 411,657

inject [v1] *put in, introduce*
add, drag in, force into, imbue, implant, impregnate, include, infuse, insert, instill, interjaculate, interject, place into, squeeze in, stick in, throw in; SEE CONCEPTS 187,208,209

inject [v2] *introduce into bloodstream by use of a needle*
give a shot, inoculate, jab, mainline*, shoot, vaccinate; SEE CONCEPTS 179,310

injection [n] *introduction into bloodstream*
booster, dose, dram, enema, inoculation, needle, vaccine; SEE CONCEPT 311

injunction [n] *decree*
admonition, ban, bar, behest, bidding, charge, command, demand, dictate, embargo, enjoinder, exhortation, instruction, mandate, order, precept, prohibition, ruling, word, writ; SEE CONCEPTS 271,318

in
in

injure [*v*] *hurt, harm*
abuse, aggrieve, batter, blemish, blight, break, contort, cripple, cut up, damage, deface, deform, disable, disfigure, distort, distress, do in*, draw blood*, foul, foul up, grieve, hack up, impair, maim, maltreat, mangle, mar, mutilate, pain, pique, prejudice, ruin, shake up, spoil, sting, tarnish, torment, torture, total, undermine, vitiate, wax, weaken, wound, wrong; SEE CONCEPT 246

injurious [*adj*] *hurtful*
abusive, adverse, bad, baneful, corrupting, damaging, dangerous, deadly, deleterious, destructive, detrimental, disadvantageous, evil, harmful, iniquitous, insulting, libeling, mischievous, nocent, nocuous, noxious, opprobrious, pernicious, poisonous, prejudicial, ruinous, slanderous, unconducive, unhealthy, unjust, wrongful; SEE CONCEPTS 537,570

injury [*n*] *hurt, harm*
abrasion, abuse, affliction, affront, agony, bad, bite, blemish, boo-boo*, bruise, burn, chop, cramp, cut, damage, deformation, detriment, discomfiture, disservice, distress, evil, fracture, gash, grievance, hemorrhage, ill, impairment, indignity, injustice, insult, laceration, lesion, libel, loss, mischief, misery, mutilation, nick, ouch*, outrage, pang, ruin, scar, scratch, shock, slander, sore, sprain, stab, sting, suffering, swelling, trauma, twinge, wound, wrong; SEE CONCEPTS 309,728

injustice [*n*] *unfair treatment; bias*
abuse, breach, crime, crying shame*, damage, dirty deal*, discrimination, encroachment, favoritism, grievance, inequality, inequity, infraction, infringement, iniquity, malfeasance, malpractice, maltreatment, miscarriage, mischief, negligence, offense, onesidedness, oppression, outrage, partiality, partisanship, prejudice, railroad*, ruin, sellout*, transgression, trespass, unfairness, unjustness, unlawfulness, villainy, violation, wrong, wrongdoing; SEE CONCEPTS 192,645,674

inkling [*n*] *idea, clue*
conception, cue, faintest idea*, foggiest idea*, glimmering, hint, hot lead*, hunch*, impression, indication, innuendo, intimation, lead, notion, sneaking suspicion*, suggestion, suspicion, tip, tipoff, whisper; SEE CONCEPT 689

inlet [*n*] *arm of the sea*
basin, bay, bayou, bight, canal, channel, cove, creek, delta, entrance, estuary, firth, fjord, gulf, harbor, ingress, loch, narrows, passage, slew, slough, sound, strait; SEE CONCEPTS 509,514

inn [*n*] *accommodation for travellers*
auberge, hospice, hostel, hostelry, hotel, lodge, motel, public house, resort, roadhouse, saloon, tavern; SEE CONCEPTS 439,449,516

innate [*adj*] *inherited, native*
congenital, connate, connatural, constitutional, deep-seated, elemental, essential, hereditary, inborn, inbred, indigenous, ingrained, inherent, instinctive, intrinsic, intuitive, natural, normal, regular, standard, typical, unacquired; SEE CONCEPTS 406,549

inner [*adj1*] *central, middle physically*
close, constitutional, essential, familiar, focal, inherent, innermore, inside, interior, internal, intestinal, intimate, intrinsic, inward, nuclear; SEE CONCEPTS 826,830

inner [*adj2*] *mental, private*
central, concealed, deep-rooted, deep-seated,

emotional, esoteric, essential, focal, gut*, hidden, individual, inherent, innate, inside, interior, internal, intimate, intrinsic, intuitive, inward, personal, psychological, repressed, secret, spiritual, subconscious, unrevealed, visceral, viscerous; SEE CONCEPTS 529,576

innocence [*n1*] *blamelessness*
chastity, clean hands*, clear conscience*, guiltlessness, immaculateness, impeccability, incorruptibility, incorruption, inculpability, probity, purity, righteousness, sinlessness, stainlessness, uprightness, virtue; SEE CONCEPT 645

innocence [*n2*] *harmlessness, naïveté*
artlessness, candidness, credulousness, forthrightness, frankness, freshness, guilelessness, gullibility, ignorance, inexperience, ingenuousness, innocuousness, innoxiousness, inoffensiveness, lack, nescience, plainness, purity, simplicity, sincerity, unaffectedness, unawareness, unfamiliarity, unknowingness, unsophistication, unworldliness, virtue; SEE CONCEPTS 409,411

innocent [*adj1*] *blameless*
above suspicion, angelic, chaste, clean, cleanhanded, clear, crimeless, exemplary, faultless, free of good, guilt-free, guiltless, honest, immaculate, impeccable, impeccant, inculpable, in the clear*, irreproachable, lawful, legal, legitimate, licit, not guilty, pristine, pure, righteous, safe, sinless, spotless, stainless, unblemished, uncensurable, uncorrupt, unimpeachable, uninvolved, unoffending, unsullied, untainted, upright, virginal, virtuous; SEE CONCEPT 545

innocent [*adj2*] *harmless, naive*
artless, childlike, credulous, frank, fresh, guileless, gullible, hurtless, ignorant, inexperienced, ingenuous, innocuous, innoxious, inobnoxious, inoffensive, offenseless, open, raw, safe, simple, soft, square, unacquainted, unartificial, uncool, unfamiliar, unhurtful, uninjurious, unmalicious, unobjectionable, unoffensive, unschooled, unsophisticated, unstudied, unsuspicious, unworldly, well-intentioned, well-meant, wide-eyed, youthful; SEE CONCEPTS 404,542

innocuous [*adj*] *harmless*
banal, bland, flat, innocent, innoxious, inobnoxious, inoffensive, insipid, jejune, kind, painless, safe, sapless, unobjectionable, unoffending, weak; SEE CONCEPTS 401,572

innovation [*n*] *change, novelty*
addition, alteration, contraption, cutting edge*, departure, deviation, introduction, last word*, latest thing*, leading edge*, modernism, modernization, modification, mutation, newness, notion, permutation, shift, variation, vicissitude, wrinkle*; SEE CONCEPTS 260,529,660,665

innovative [*adj*] *creative*
avant-garde, breaking new ground*, contemporary, cutting-edge*, deviceful, ingenious, innovational, innovatory, inventive, just out*, leading-edge*, new, newfangled*, original, originative, state-of-the-art; SEE CONCEPTS 529,578,589,797

innuendo [*n*] *suggestion*
allusion, aside, aspersion, hint, implication, imputation, insinuation, intimation, overtone, reference, whisper; SEE CONCEPTS 75,278

innumerable [*adj*] *many, infinite*
alive with*, beyond number, countless, frequent, incalculable, multitudinous, myriad, numberless, numerous, uncountable, unnumbered, untold; SEE CONCEPT 762

inoffensive [adj] not obnoxious; harmless
calm, clean, friendly, humble, innocent, innocuous, innoxious, mild, neutral, nonprovocative, peaceable, pleasant, quiet, retiring, safe, unobjectionable, unobtrusive, unoffending; SEE CONCEPTS 267,542

inopportune [adj] not appropriate or suitable
contrary, disadvantageous, disturbing, ill-chosen, ill-timed, inappropriate, inauspicious, inconvenient, malapropos, mistimed, troublesome, unfavorable, unfortunate, unpropitious, unseasonable, unsuitable, untimely; SEE CONCEPT 558

inordinate [adj] excessive, extravagant
disproportionate, dizzying, exorbitant, extortionate, extreme, gratuitous, immoderate, intemperate, irrational, outrageous, overindulgent, overmuch, preposterous, supererogatory, superfluous, surplus, too much, towering, uncalled-for, unconscionable, uncurbed, undue, unmeasurable, unreasonable, unrestrained, untempered, unwarranted, wanton, wasteful; SEE CONCEPTS 570,781

inquest [n] investigation
delving, examination, hearing, inquiry, inquisition, probe, probing, quest, research, trial; SEE CONCEPTS 48,290,318

inquire [v] ask; look into
analyze, catechize, examine, explore, feel out, go over, grill, hit, hit up, inspect, interrogate, investigate, knock, probe, prospect, pry, query, question, request information, roast, scrutinize, search, seek, seek information, sift, study, test the waters*; SEE CONCEPTS 24,48

inquiring [adj] wondering, curious
analytical, catechistic, doubtful, examining, fact-finding, heuristic, inquisitive, interested, interrogative, investigative, investigatory, nosy, outward-looking, probing, prying, questioning, quizzical, searching, Socratic, speculative, studious; SEE CONCEPTS 402,542

inquiry [n] asking; looking into
analysis, audit, catechizing, check, cross-examination, delving, disquisition, examination, exploration, fishing expedition*, grilling, hearing, inquest, inquisition, inspection, interrogation, interrogatory, investigation, legwork*, poll, probe, probing, pursuit, Q and A*, query, quest, question, questioning, quizzing, request, research, scrutiny, search, study, survey, third degree*, trial balloon*; SEE CONCEPTS 24,48,290

inquisitive [adj] curious
analytical, big-eyed*, challenging, forward, impertinent, inquiring, inquisitorial, interested, intrusive, investigative, meddlesome, meddling, nosy, peering, personal, poking, presumptuous, probing, prying, questioning, scrutinizing, searching, sifting, snooping, speculative; SEE CONCEPT 402

inroad [n] advance, foray
encroachment, impingement, incursion, intrusion, invasion, irruption, onslaught, raid, trespass; SEE CONCEPTS 86,704

insane [adj] mentally ill; foolish
batty*, bizarre, cracked*, crazed, crazy, cuckoo*, daft, demented, derailed, deranged, fatuous, frenzied, idiotic, impractical, irrational, irresponsible, loony*, lunatic, mad, maniacal, mental, moonstruck*, nuts*, nutty*, off one's rocker*, of unsound mind, out of one's mind*, paranoid, preposterous, psychopathic, psychotic, rabid, raging, raving, schizophrenic, screwy, senseless,

touched, unhinged, unsettled, wild; SEE CONCEPTS 314,403,548

insanely [adv] extremely
crazily, ferociously, fiercely, furiously, idiotically, irrationally, stupidly, violently, wildly; SEE CONCEPT 569

insanity [n] mental illness; foolishness
aberration, absurdity, alienation, craziness, delirium, delusion, dementia, derangement, distraction, dotage, folly, frenzy, hallucination, hysteria, illusion, inanity, irrationality, irresponsibility, lunacy, madness, mania, mental disorder, neurosis, phobia, preposterousness, psychopathy, psychosis, senselessness, unbalance, unreasonableness, witlessness; SEE CONCEPTS 316,410

insatiable [adj] voracious, wanting
clamorous, crying, demanding, desiring, exigent, gluttonous, greedy, importunate, insatiate, insistent, intemperate, pressing, quenchless, rapacious, ravenous, unappeasable, unquenchable, unsatisfiable, unsatisfied, urgent, yearning; SEE CONCEPTS 20,403,546

inscribe [v] imprint, write
book, carve, cut, engrave, engross, etch, impress, indite, list, record, register, scribe; SEE CONCEPT 79

inscrutable [adj] hidden, mysterious; blank
ambiguous, arcane, cabalistic, deadpan*, difficult, enigmatic, impenetrable, incomprehensible, inexplicable, mysterial, mystic, poker-faced*, secret, sphinxlike, unaccountable, undiscoverable, unexplainable, unfathomable, unintelligible, unknowable, unreadable; SEE CONCEPTS 529,576

insecure [adj 1] uncertain, worried
afraid, anxious, apprehensive, choked, Delphic, diffident, hanging by thread*, hesitant, jumpy, on thin ice*, questioning, shaky, touch and go*, touchy*, troubled, unassured, unconfident, unpoised, unsure, up in the air*, uptight*, vague; SEE CONCEPTS 403,542

insecure [adj 2] dangerous, precarious
defenseless, exposed, fluctuant, frail, hazardous, immature, insubstantial, loose, open to attack*, perilous, rickety, rocky, rootless, shaky, unguarded, unprotected, unreliable, unsafe, unshielded, unsound, unstable, unsteady, vacillating, vulnerable, wavering, weak, wobbly; SEE CONCEPTS 488,570

insensitive [adj 1] indifferent, callous
aloof, bloodless*, coldhearted*, crass, feelingless, hard, hard as nails*, hard-boiled*, hardened, hardhearted*, heartless, imperceptive, incurious, obtuse, stony, tactless, thick-skinned*, tough, uncaring, unconcerned, unfeeling, unkind, unresponsive, unsusceptible; SEE CONCEPT 401

insensitive [adj 2] numb
anesthetized, asleep, benumbed, dead, deadened, immune to, impervious to, insensible, nonreactive, senseless, unfeeling; SEE CONCEPT 406

inseparable [adj] unable to be divided
as one, attached, conjoined, connected, entwined, inalienable, indissoluble, indivisible, inseverable, integral, integrated, intertwined, interwoven, molded, secure, tied up, unified, united, whole; SEE CONCEPT 531

insert [v] put, tuck in
admit, drag in, embed, enter, fill in, imbed, implant, include, infix, infuse, inject, inlay, insinuate, instill, intercalate, interject, interlope, interpolate, interpose, introduce, intrude, lug in,

obtrude, place, pop in*, root, set, shoehorn*, shove in, squeeze in, stick, work in; SEE CONCEPTS 201,209

inside [n] middle, lining
belly, bowels, breast, center, contents, gut, heart, innards, inner portion, interior, recess, soul, stuffing, womb; SEE CONCEPT 830

inside [adj 1] in the middle; interior
central, indoors, inner, innermost, internal, intramural, inward, surrounded, under a roof; SEE CONCEPTS 583,830

inside [adj 2] secret
classified, closet, confidential, esoteric, exclusive, hushed, internal, limited, private, restricted; SEE CONCEPTS 529,576

inside [adv] within
indoors, under a roof, under cover, within doors, within walls; SEE CONCEPT 583

insidious [adj] sneaky, tricky
artful, astute, corrupt, crafty, crooked, cunning, dangerous, deceitful, deceptive, deep, designing, dishonest, disingenuous, duplicitous, ensnaring, false, foxy, guileful, intriguing, like a snake in the grass*, Machiavellian, perfidious, perilous, secret, slick, sly, smooth, snaky*, sneaking, stealthy, subtle, surreptitious, treacherous, wily, wormlike*; SEE CONCEPTS 401,542,545

insight [n] intuitiveness, awareness
acumen, click*, comprehension, discernment, divination, drift*, intuition, judgment, observation, penetration, perception, perceptivity, perspicacity, sagaciousness, sagacity, sageness, sapience, shrewdness, understanding, vision, wavelength*, wisdom; SEE CONCEPTS 409,410

insignia [n] emblem
badge, coat of arms, crest, decoration, earmark, ensign, mark, paraphernalia, regalia, symbol; SEE CONCEPTS 259,284

insignificant [adj] not important; of no consequence
casual, immaterial, inappreciable, inconsequential, inconsiderable, infinitesimal, irrelevant, lesser, light, lightweight*, little, meager, meaningless, minim, minimal, minor, minuscule,' minute, negligible, nondescript, nonessential, not worth mentioning*, nugatory, paltry, petty, pointless, purportless, scanty, secondary, senseless, small, trifling, trivial, unimportant, unsubstantial; SEE CONCEPT 575

insincere [adj] dishonest, pretended
ambidextrous, backhanded, deceitful, deceptive, devious, disingenuous, dissembling, dissimulating, double, double-dealing, duplicitous, evasive, faithless, fake, false, hollow, hypocritical, lying, mendacious, perfidious, phony, pretentious, put-on*, shifty, slick, sly, snide, two-faced*, unfaithful, untrue, untruthful; SEE CONCEPTS 267, 542,545

insinuate [v1] hint, suggest
allude, ascribe, connote, imply, impute, indicate, intimate, mention, propose, purport, refer, signify; SEE CONCEPTS 49,75

insinuate [v2] force one's way into
curry favor*, edge in, fill in, foist, get in with*, horn in*, infiltrate, infuse, ingratiate, inject, insert, instill, intercalate, interject, interpose, introduce, muscle in*, slip in, wedge in, work in, worm in*; SEE CONCEPTS 159,208,384

insipid [adj 1] dull, uninteresting
anemic, arid, banal, beige, blah*, bland, charac-

terless, colorless, commonplace, dead*, drab, driveling, dry, feeble, flat, ho-hum*, inane, innocuous, jejune, lifeless, limp, mild, mundane, nebbish, nothing, ordinary, plain, pointless, prosaic, prosy, slight, soft*, spiritless, stale, stupid, subdued, tame, tedious, tenuous, thin, tired, trite, unimaginative, vapid, watery, weak, weariful, wearisome, wishy-washy*; SEE CONCEPTS 402, 404,537

insipid [adj 2] tasteless
bland, distasteful, flat, flavorless, jejune, mild, savorless, stale, unappetizing, unpalatable, unsavory, vapid, watered-down, watery; SEE CONCEPT 613

insist [v] order and expect; claim
assert, asseverate, aver, be firm, contend, demand, hold, importune, lay down the law*, maintain, persist, press, reiterate, repeat, request, require, stand firm, swear, take a stand*, urge, vow; SEE CONCEPTS 49,53

insistent [adj] demanding
assertive, burning, clamant, clamorous, continuous, crying, dire, dogged, emphatic, exigent, forceful, imperative, imperious, importunate, incessant, obstinate, peremptory, perseverant, persevering, persistent, pressing, reiterative, resolute, resounding, unrelenting, urgent; SEE CONCEPTS 267,534,540

insolence [n] boldness, disrespect
abuse, arrogance, audacity, back talk, brass*, brazenness, cheek*, chutzpah*, contempt, contemptuousness, contumely, effrontery, gall, guff*, hardihood, impertinence, impudence, incivility, insubordination, lip*, offensiveness, pertness, presumption, rudeness, sass*, sauce*, uncivility; SEE CONCEPT 633

insolent [adj] bold, disrespectful
abusive, arrogant, barefaced, brassy*, brazen, breezy, contemptuous, contumelious, dictatorial, discourteous, disdainful, flip*, fresh, imperative, impertinent, impolite, impudent, insubordinate, insulting, magisterial, nervy, off-base*, offensive, out-of-line*, overbearing, peremptory, pert, procacious, put down, rude, sassy*, saucy*, smart, smart-alecky*, uncivil, ungracious; SEE CONCEPTS 267,401

insoluble [adj] mysterious, unable to be solved or answered
baffling, difficult, impenetrable, indecipherable, inexplicable, inextricable, irresolvable, mystifying, obscure, unaccountable, unconcluded, unfathomable, unresolved, unsolvable, unsolved; SEE CONCEPTS 529,576

insolvent [adj] financially ruined
bankrupt, broke*, broken, busted*, failed, foreclosed, in Chapter 11*, in Chapter 13*, indebted, in receivership, in the red*, lost, on the rocks*, out of money, strapped*, taken to the cleaners*, unbalanced, undone, wiped out*; SEE CONCEPT 334

insomnia [n] inability to sleep soundly
indisposition, insomnolence, restlessness, sleeplessness, stress, tension, vigil, vigilance, wakefulness; SEE CONCEPT 315

insouciant [adj] easygoing, casual
airy, breezy, buoyant, carefree, careless, free and easy*, gay, happy-go-lucky*, heedless, jaunty, lighthearted, nonchalant, sunny*, thoughtless, unconcerned, untroubled, unworried; SEE CONCEPTS 404,542

inspect [v] *examine, check*
audit, canvass, case, catechize, check out, clock*, eye*, give the once-over*, go over, go through, inquire, interrogate, investigate, kick the tires*, look over, notice, observe, oversee, probe, question, review, scan, scope, scout, scrutinize, search, study, superintend, supervise, survey, vet, view, watch; SEE CONCEPTS *103,623*

inspection [n] *examination, check*
analysis, checkup, frisk, inquest, inquiry, inquisition, inventory, investigation, look-over, maneuvers, once-over*, pageant, parade, perlustration, probe, read, research, review, scan, scrutiny, search, superintendence, supervision, surveillance, survey, view; SEE CONCEPTS *103,290*

inspiration [n] *idea, stimulus*
afflatus, animus, approach, arousal, awakening, brainchild*, brainstorm*, creativity, deep think*, elevation, encouragement, enthusiasm, exaltation, fancy, flash*, genius, hunch*, illumination, impulse, incentive, inflatus, influence, insight, motivation, motive, muse, notion, revelation, rumble, spark, spur, stimulation, thought, vision, whim; SEE CONCEPTS *529,661*

inspire [v] *encourage, stimulate*
affect, animate, arouse, be responsible for, carry, cause, commove, elate, embolden, endue, enkindle, enliven, exalt, excite, exhilarate, fire up*, galvanize, get*, give impetus, give one an idea*, give rise to, hearten, imbue, impress, infect, inflame, influence, inform, infuse, inspirit, instill, invigorate, motivate, occasion, produce, provoke, quicken, reassure, set up, spark, spur, start off, stir, strike, sway, touch, trigger, urge, work up; SEE CONCEPTS *7,22,221,242*

instability [n] *imbalance, inconstancy*
alternation, anxiety, capriciousness, changeability, changeableness, disequilibrium, disquiet, fickleness, fitfulness, flightiness, fluctuation, fluidity, frailty, hesitation, immaturity, impermanence, inconsistency, inquietude, insecurity, irregularity, irresolution, mutability, oscillation, pliancy, precariousness, restlessness, shakiness, transience, uncertainty, unfixedness, unpredictability, unreliability, unsteadiness, vacillation, variability, volatility, vulnerability, wavering, weakness; SEE CONCEPTS *410,637,731*

install [v] *set up, establish*
build in, ensconce, fix, fix up, furnish, inaugurate, induct, instate, institute, introduce, invest, lay, line, lodge, place, plant, position, put in, settle, station; SEE CONCEPTS *201,221*

installation [n1] *establishment, inauguration*
accession, coronation, fitting, furnishing, inaugural, induction, installment, instatement, investiture, investment, launching, ordination, placing, positioning, setting up; SEE CONCEPTS *201,221,832*

installation [n2] *equipment*
base, establishment, fort, fortification, furnishings, lighting, machinery, plant, post, power, station, system, wiring; SEE CONCEPTS *439,463,496*

installment [n] *part, section*
chapter, division, earnest, episode, partial payment, payment, portion, repayment, token; SEE CONCEPTS *344,835*

instance [n] *case, situation*
case history, case in point, detail, example, exemplification, exponent, ground, illustration,

item, occasion, occurrence, particular, precedent, proof, reason, representative, sample, sampling, specimen, time; SEE CONCEPTS *686,696,815*

instance [v] *name*
adduce, cite, exemplify, illustrate, mention, quote, refer, show, specify; SEE CONCEPT *73*

instant [n] *moment*
bat of the eye*, breath, crack, flash, jiffy*, juncture, minute, nothing flat*, occasion, point, sec*, second, shake*, short while, split second*, tick, time, trice, twinkling*, while, wink*; SEE CONCEPTS *802,808*

instant [adj] *immediate, urgent*
burning*, clamant, contemporary, crying*, current, dire, direct, exigent, existent, extant, fast, imperative, importunate, insistent, instantaneous, on-the-spot*, present, present-day, pressing, prompt, quick, split-second*; SEE CONCEPTS *544,588,799*

instantaneous [adj] *immediate*
direct, fast, hair-trigger*, in a flash*, instant, momentary, quick, rapid, spontaneous, transitory; SEE CONCEPT *820*

instantly [adv] *right now*
at once, away, directly, double-time*, first off*, forthwith, immediately, in a flash*, instantaneously, instanter, now, on a dime*, PDQ*, pronto*, right, right away, spontaneously, straight away*, there and then*, this minute, tout de suite*, without delay; SEE CONCEPTS *544,588,799*

instead [adv] *alternatively*
alternately, alternative, as a substitute, in lieu of, in place of, in preference, on behalf of, on second thought, preferably, rather, rather than; SEE CONCEPT *560*

instigate [v] *influence, provoke*
abet, actuate, add fuel, bring about, egg on*, encourage, fire up*, foment, goad, hint, impel, incite, inflame, initiate, insinuate, kindle, make waves*, move, needle*, persuade, plan, plot, prompt, put up to, rabble-rouse*, raise, rouse, scheme, set on, spur, start, steam up, stimulate, stir up, suggest, turn on, urge, whip up*, work up; SEE CONCEPTS *7,19,22,221,242*

instill [v] *implant, introduce*
brainwash*, catechize, diffuse, disseminate, engender, engraft, force in, imbue, impart, impregnate, impress, inculcate, indoctrinate, infiltrate, infix, infuse, inject, inoculate, inseminate, insert, insinuate, inspire, interject, intermix, program, propagandize, put in head*, suffuse, transfuse; SEE CONCEPTS *285,292*

instinct [n] *gut feeling, idea*
aptitude, faculty, feeling, funny feeling*, gift, gut reaction*, hunch, impulse, inclination, intuition, knack, know-how*, nose*, predisposition, proclivity, savvy*, sense, sentiment, sixth sense*, talent, tendency, urge; SEE CONCEPTS *529,689*

instinctive [adj] *reflex, automatic*
accustomed, by seat of one's pants*, congenital, habitual, impulsive, inborn, ingrained, inherent, innate, instinctual, intrinsic, intuitional, intuitive, involuntary, knee-jerk*, mechanical, native, natural, normal, regular, rooted, second-nature*, spontaneous, typical, unlearned, unmeditated, unpremeditated, unprompted, unthinking, visceral; SEE CONCEPT *544*

in
in

institute/institution [*n1*] *organization, usually educational*
academy, association, asylum, business, clinic, college, company, conservatory, establishment, fixture, foundation, guild, hospital, orphanage, school, seminar, seminary, society, system, think tank, university; SEE CONCEPTS *288,381,439*

institute [*n2*] *law; custom*
convention, decree, decretum, doctrine, dogma, edict, establishment, fixture, habit, maxim, ordinance, practice, precedent, precept, prescript, principle, regulation, rite, ritual, rule, statute, tenet, tradition; SEE CONCEPTS *318,688*

institute [*v*] *begin; put into operation*
appoint, bow, break in, bring into being, come out with, come up with, commence, constitute, create, enact, establish, fix, found, inaugurate, induct, initiate, install, introduce, invest, launch, make up, open, open up, ordain, organize, originate, pioneer, rev*, set in motion, settle, set up, start, usher in*; SEE CONCEPTS *173,221,242*

instruct [*v1*] *inform, teach*
acquaint, advise, apprise, brainwash*, break in, break it to, brief, clue in, coach, counsel, discipline, disclose, drill, drum into*, educate, engineer, enlighten, give lessons, ground, guide, keep posted*, lead, lecture, level, notify, pilot, reveal, school, steer, tell, train, tutor, update, wise up*; SEE CONCEPTS *60,285*

instruct [*v2*] *order, command*
assign, bid, charge, define, direct, enjoin, prescribe, tell, warn; SEE CONCEPTS *53,61*

instruction [*n1*] *education*
apprenticeship, chalk talk*, coaching, direction, discipline, drilling, edification, enlightenment, grounding, guidance, information, lesson, preparation, schooling, teaching, training, tuition, tutelage; SEE CONCEPTS *274,285*

instruction [*n2*] *demand, command*
advice, briefing, direction, directive, information, injunction, mandate, order, plan, ruling; SEE CONCEPTS *274,278*

instructor [*n*] *person who educates*
adviser, coach, demonstrator, exponent, guide, lecturer, mentor, pedagogue, preceptor, professor, teacher, trainer, tutor; SEE CONCEPT *350*

instrument [*n1*] *tool, implement*
apparatus, appliance, contraption, contrivance, device, doodad*, equipment, gadget, gear, gizmo*, machine, machinery, mechanism, paraphernalia, tackle, utensil; SEE CONCEPTS *463,499*

instrument [*n2*] *means, agent*
agency, channel, factor, force, instrumentality, material, mechanism, medium, ministry, organ, vehicle, wherewithal; SEE CONCEPTS *6,687*

instrumental [*adj*] *influential, assisting*
active, auxiliary, conducive, contributory, helpful, helping, involved, of help, of service, partly responsible, serviceable, subsidiary, useful; SEE CONCEPT *560*

insubordinate [*adj*] *rebellious*
contrary, contumacious, defiant, disaffected, disobedient, disorderly, dissentious, factious, fractious, insurgent, intractable, mutinous, naughty, perverse, recalcitrant, refractory, riotous, seditious, treacherous, turbulent, uncompliant, uncomplying, undisciplined, ungovernable, unruly; SEE CONCEPT *401*

insubstantial [*adj*] *weak, imaginary*
aerial, airy, chimerical, decrepit, ephemeral,

false, fanciful, feeble, flimsy, fly-by-night*, fragile, frail, idle, illusory, immaterial, imponderable, incorporeal, infirm, intangible, metaphysical, petty, poor, puny, slender, slight, tenuous, thin, too little too late*, unreal, unsound, unsubstantial; SEE CONCEPT *485*

insufferable [*adj*] *horrible, intolerable*
detestable, distressing, dreadful, impossible, insupportable, outrageous, painful, unacceptable, unbearable, unendurable, unspeakable; SEE CONCEPTS *529,537*

insufficient [*adj*] *not enough; lacking*
bereft, defective, deficient, destitute, devoid, drained, dry, failing, faulty, imperfect, inadequate, incapable, incommensurate, incompetent, incomplete, infrequent, meager, minus, out of, poor, rare, scant, scarce, short, short of, shy, thin*, too little too late*, unample, unfinished, unfitted, unqualified, unsatisfactory, wanting; SEE CONCEPTS *546,771*

insular [*adj*] *narrow-minded*
bigoted, circumscribed, closed, confined, contracted, cut off, detached, illiberal, inward-looking, isolated, limited, narrow, parochial, petty, prejudiced, provincial, restricted, secluded, separate, separated, sequestered; SEE CONCEPTS *403,583*

insulate [*v*] *protect; close off*
coat, cocoon, cushion, cut off, inlay, island, isolate, keep apart, line, seclude, separate, sequester, set apart, shield, tape, treat, wrap; SEE CONCEPT *172*

insult [*n*] *hateful communication*
abuse, affront, aspersion, black eye*, blasphemy, cheap shot*, contempt, contumely, derision, despite, discourtesy, disdainfulness, disgrace, disrespect, ignominy, impertinence, impudence, incivility, indignity, insolence, invective, libel, mockery, obloquy, offense, opprobrium, outrage, put-down, rudeness, scorn, scurrility, shame, slam, slander, slap, slap in the face*, slight, snub, superciliousness, taunt, unpleasantry, vilification, vituperation; SEE CONCEPTS *52,54,278*

insult [*v*] *abuse, offend*
abase, affront, aggravate, annoy, blister, curse, cut to the quick*, debase, degrade, deride, dishonor, disoblige, dump on*, flout, gird, humiliate, injure, irritate, jeer, libel, mock, outrage, pan*, provoke, put down*, revile, ridicule, roast*, scoff, slam*, slander, slight, sneer, snub, step on one's toes*, taunt, tease, underestimate, vex; SEE CONCEPTS *52,54*

insurance [*n*] *protection, security*
allowance, assurance, backing, cover, coverage, guarantee, indemnification, indemnity, provision, safeguard, support, warrant, warranty; SEE CONCEPTS *318,332*

insure [*v*] *protect, secure*
assure, cinch, cover, guarantee, guard, hedge, indemnify, register, safeguard, shield, underwrite, warrant; SEE CONCEPTS *317,330*

insurgent [*n*] *rebel*
agitator, anarch, anarchist, demonstrator, frondeur, insurrectionist, malcontent, mutineer, radical, resister, revolter, revolutionary, revolutionist, rioter; SEE CONCEPTS *359,412*

insurgent [*adj*] *rebellious*
anarchical, contumacious, disobedient, factious, insubordinate, insurrectionary, mutinous, revolt-

ing, revolutionary, riotous, seditious; SEE CONCEPT **401**

insurmountable [*adj*] *impossible*

forget it, hopeless, impassable, impregnable, inaccessible, indomitable, ineluctable, insuperable, invincible, not a prayer*, no way*, no-win*, overwhelming, unbeatable, unconquerable, unmasterable; SEE CONCEPTS **552,565**

insurrection [*n*] *rebellion*

coup, disorder, insurgence, insurgency, mutiny, revolt, revolution, riot, rising, sedition, uprising; SEE CONCEPTS **86,320**

intact [*adj*] *undamaged; all in one piece*

complete, entire, flawless, imperforate, indiscrete, perfect, scatheless, sound, together, unblemished, unbroken, uncut, undefiled, unharmed, unhurt, unimpaired, uninjured, unmarred, unscathed, untouched, unviolated, whole; SEE CONCEPTS **485,531**

intangible [*adj*] *indefinite, obscured*

abstract, abstruse, airy, dim, eluding, elusive, ethereal, evading, evanescent, evasive, hypothetical, impalpable, imperceptible, imponderable, inappreciable, incorporeal, indeterminate, insensible, invisible, rare, shadowy, slender, slight, unapparent, uncertain, unobservable, unreal, unsubstantial, unsure, vague; SEE CONCEPTS **535,582**

integral [*adj1*] *necessary, basic*

component, constituent, elemental, essential, fundamental, indispensable, intrinsic, requisite; SEE CONCEPT **546**

integral [*adj2*] *complete*

aggregate, choate, elemental, entire, full, indivisible, intact, part-and-parcel*, perfect, unbroken, undivided, whole; SEE CONCEPT **531**

integrate [*v*] *mix, merge*

accommodate, amalgamate, arrange, articulate, assimilate, associate, attune, blend, coalesce, combine, come together, compact, concatenate, concentrate, conform, conjoin, consolidate, coordinate, desegregate, embody, fuse, get together, harmonize, incorporate, interface, intermix, join, knit, link, meld with, mesh, orchestrate, organize, proportion, reconcile, reconciliate, symphonize, synthesize, systematize, throw in together, tune, unify, unite, wed; SEE CONCEPTS **113,114**

integrity [*n1*] *honor, uprightness*

candor, forthrightness, goodness, honestness, honesty, honorableness, incorruptibility, incorruption, principle, probity, purity, rectitude, righteousness, sincerity, straightforwardness, virtue; SEE CONCEPT **411**

integrity [*n2*] *completeness*

absoluteness, coherence, cohesion, entireness, perfection, purity, simplicity, soundness, stability, totality, unity, wholeness; SEE CONCEPT **635**

intellect [*n*] *capability of the mind; someone with capable mind*

ability, acumen, brains*, cerebration, comprehension, egghead*, genius, intellectual, intellectuality, intelligence, intuition, judgment, mentality, mind, psyche, pundit, reason, savvy, sense, smarts, thinker, understanding, what it takes*, wits; SEE CONCEPTS **409,416**

intellectual [*n*] *very smart person*

academic, academician, avant-garde, brain*, braintruster*, doctor, egghead*, Einstein*, genius, highbrow*, intelligentsia, philosopher, pundit, sage, scholar, thinker, whiz*, wizard; SEE CONCEPTS **350,416**

intellectual [*adj*] *very smart*

bookish, brainy*, cerebral, creative, highbrow*, highbrowed*, intellective, intelligent, inventive, learned, mental, phrenic, psychological, rational, scholarly, studious, subjective, thoughtful; SEE CONCEPT **402**

intelligence [*n1*] *ability to perceive, understand*

acuity, acumen, agility, alertness, aptitude, brainpower, brains*, brightness, brilliance, capacity, cleverness, comprehension, coruscation, discernment, gray matter*, intellect, IQ*, judgment, luminosity, mentality, mind, penetration, perception, perspicacity, precocity, quickness, quotient, reason, sagacity, savvy, sense, skill, smarts, subtlety, the right stuff*, trenchancy, understanding, what it takes*, wit; SEE CONCEPT **409**

intelligence [*n2*] *secret information*

advice, clue, data, dirt, disclosure, facts, findings, hot tip*, info*, inside story*, knowledge, leak, lowdown*, news, notice, notification, picture, report, rumor, tidings, tip-off*, word*; SEE CONCEPT **274**

intelligent [*adj*] *very smart*

able, acute, alert, alive, all there*, apt, astute, brainy*, bright, brilliant, calculating, capable, clever, comprehending, creative, deep*, discerning, enlightened, exceptional, highbrow*, imaginative, ingenious, instructed, inventive, keen, knowing, knowledgeable, original, penetrating, perceptive, perspicacious, profound, quick, quick-witted, rational, ready, reasonable, resourceful, responsible, sage, sharp, smart, thinking, together*, understanding, well-informed, whiz*, wise, witty; SEE CONCEPT **402**

intelligible [*adj*] *understandable*

apprehensible, clear, comprehensible, distinct, fathomable, graspable, knowable, lucid, luminous, obvious, open, plain, unambiguous, unequivocal, unmistakable; SEE CONCEPT **529**

intend [*v*] *have in mind; determine*

add up, aim, appoint, aspire to, attempt, be determined, be resolved, connote, contemplate, decree, dedicate, denote, design, designate, destine, devote, endeavor, essay, expect, express, figure on, have in mind, hope to, import, indicate, look forward, mean, meditate, ordain, plan, plot, propose, purpose, reserve, resolve, scheme, set apart, set aside, signify, spell, strive, think, try; SEE CONCEPTS **18,36,73,129**

intended [*adj*] *engaged; destined*

accidentally on purpose*, advised, affianced, aforethought, asked for, betrothed, calculated, contemplated, contracted, designed, expected, future, intentional, meant, pinned, planned, plighted, prearranged, predestined, predetermined, promised, proposed, set, steady; SEE CONCEPT **552**

intense [*adj*] *forceful, severe; passionate*

acute, agonizing, all-consuming, ardent, biting, bitter, burning, close, concentrated, consuming, cutting, deep, diligent, eager, earnest, energetic, exaggerated, exceptional, excessive, exquisite, extraordinary, extreme, fanatical, fervent, fervid, fierce, forcible, full, great, hard, harsh, heightened, impassioned, intensified, intensive, keen, marked, piercing, powerful, profound, protracted, pungent, sharp, shrill, stinging, strained, strong,

in
in

intensify [v] *make more forceful, severe*
accent, accentuate, add fuel*, add to, aggrandize, aggravate, augment, beef up*, boost, brighten, build up, concentrate, darken, deepen, emphasize, enhance, escalate, exacerbate, exalt, heat up*, heighten, increase, intensate, lighten, magnify, point, pour it on*, quicken, raise, redouble, reinforce, rise, rouse, set off, sharpen, spike*, step up, strengthen, stress, tone up, whet; SEE CONCEPTS 233,250

intensity [n] *passion, force*
acuteness, anxiety, ardor, concentration, deepness, depth, earnestness, emotion, emphasis, energy, excess, excitement, extreme, extremity, fanaticism, ferment, ferociousness, ferocity, fervency, fervor, fierceness, fire, force, forcefulness, fury, high pitch*, intenseness, keenness, magnitude, might, nervousness, potency, power, severity, sharpness, strain, strength, tenseness, tension, vehemence, vigor, violence, volume, weightiness, wildness; SEE CONCEPTS 641,669

intensive [adj] *exhaustive*
accelerated, all-out*, complete, comprehensive, concentrated, deep, demanding, fast, hard, in-depth, out-and-out*, profound, radical, severe, speeded-up*, thorough, thoroughgoing; SEE CONCEPT 531

intent/intention [n] *aim, purpose*
acceptation, animus, bottom line*, conation, design, desire, drift, end, goal, heart, hope, idea, import, intendment, meaning, meat*, name of the game*, nature, notion, nub, nuts and bolts*, object, objective, plan, point, project, purport, scheme, score, sense, significance, significancy, signification, target, understanding, volition, will, wish; SEE CONCEPT 659

intent [adj] *determined, resolute*
absorbed, alert, attending, attentive, bent, bound, committed, concentrated, concentrating, decided, decisive, deep, eager, earnest, engaged, engrossed, enthusiastic, firm, fixed, hell-bent*, immersed, industrious, intense, minding, occupied, piercing, preoccupied, rapt, resolved, riveted*, set, settled, steadfast, steady, watchful, watching, wrapped up*; SEE CONCEPTS 403,542

intentional [adj] *deliberate*
advised, aforethought, calculated, considered, designed, designful, done on purpose, intended, meant, meditated, planned, prearranged, premeditated, proposed, purposed, studied, unforced, voluntary, willful, willing, witting; SEE CONCEPT 544

intently [adv] *with concentration*
attentively, closely, fixedly, hard, keenly, searchingly, sharply, steadily, watchfully; SEE CONCEPTS 403,544

inter [v] *bury*
cover up, entomb, inhume, inurn, lay to rest, plant, put away, sepulcher, sepulture, tomb; SEE CONCEPTS 172,178,367

interact [v] *communicate*
collaborate, combine, connect, contact, cooperate, get across*, get the message*, interface, interplay, interreact, join, keep in touch, merge, mesh, network, reach out, relate, touch, touch base*, unite; SEE CONCEPT 266

intercede [v] *mediate*
advocate, arbitrate, barge in, butt in*, intermedi-

ate, interpose, intervene, intrude, mix in, monkey with*, negotiate, plead, reconcile, speak, step in; SEE CONCEPTS 56,110

intercept [v] *head off; interrupt*
ambush, appropriate, arrest, block, catch, check, curb, cut in, cut off, deflect, head off at pass*, hijack, hinder, interlope, interpose, make off with, obstruct, prevent, seize, shortstop*, stop, take, take away; SEE CONCEPTS 121,164

interchange [n] *switch, exchange*
altering, alternation, barter, change, crossfire, give-and-take*, intersection, junction, mesh, networking, reciprocation, shift, trade, transposition, variation, varying; SEE CONCEPTS 104,697

interchange [v] *switch, exchange*
alternate, bandy, barter, commute, connect, contact, convert, interact, interface, mesh, network, reciprocate, relate, reverse, substitute, swap, trade, transpose; SEE CONCEPTS 56,104

interchangeable [adj] *identical, transposable*
changeable, commutable, compatible, converse, convertible, correspondent, equivalent, exchangeable, fungible, interconvertible, mutual, reciprocal, reciprocative, same, substitutable, synonymous, worklike; SEE CONCEPTS 487,573

intercourse [n1] *sexual act*
carnal knowledge, coition, coitus, copulation, fornication, intimacy, love-making, relations, sex, sexual relations; SEE CONCEPT 375

intercourse [n2] *communication; business exchange*
association, commerce, communion, connection, contact, converse, correspondence, dealings, give-and-take, interchange, intercommunication, mesh, networking, team play, teamwork, trade, traffic, transactions; SEE CONCEPTS 266,324

interest [n1] *attraction, curiosity*
absorption, activity, affection, attentiveness, care, case, concern, concernment, consequence, diversion, engrossment, enthusiasm, excitement, game, hobby, importance, interestedness, into, leisure activity, matter, moment, note, notice, passion, pastime, preoccupation, pursuit, racket, recreation, regard, relaxation, relevance, significance, sport, suspicion, sympathy, thing; SEE CONCEPTS 20,532,690

interest [n2] *advantage*
benefit, gain, good, profit, prosperity, welfare, well-being; SEE CONCEPT 693

interest [n3] *share, investment*
accrual, authority, bonus, claim, commitment, credit, discount, due, earnings, gain, influence, involvement, participation, percentage, piece, points, portion, premium, right, stake, title; SEE CONCEPTS 332,344,835

interest [v] *hold the attention of*
affect, amuse, appeal, appeal to, arouse, attract, be interesting to, concern, divert, engage, engross, entertain, enthrall, excite, fascinate, grab, hook, intrigue, involve, lure, move, perk up, pique, please, pull, sit up, snare, tantalize, tempt, titillate, touch, turn on; SEE CONCEPTS 7,11,22

interested [adj] *concerned, curious*
absorbed, affected, attentive, attracted, awakened, biased, caught, drawn, eat sleep and breathe*, engrossed, enticed, excited, fascinated, fired*, gone*, hooked*, implicated, impressed, inspired, inspirited, intent, into*, involved, keen, lured, moved, obsessed, occupied, on the case*, open, partial, partisan, predisposed, prejudiced, respon-

sive, roused, sold, stimulated, stirred, struck, sympathetic, taken, touched; SEE CONCEPT *403*

interesting [*adj*] *appealing, entertaining*
absorbing, affecting, alluring, amusing, arresting, attractive, beautiful, captivating, charismatic, compelling, curious, delightful, elegant, enchanting, engaging, engrossing, enthralling, entrancing, exceptional, exotic, fascinating, fine, gracious, gripping, impressive, intriguing, inviting, lovely, magnetic, pleasing, pleasurable, prepossessing, provocative, readable, refreshing, riveting, stimulating, stirring, striking, suspicious, thought-provoking, unusual, winning; SEE CONCEPTS *529,572*

interfere [*v*] *meddle, intervene*
baffle, balk, barge in, busybody*, butt in*, conflict, discommode, foil, fool with, frustrate, get in the way*, get involved, hamper, handicap, hang up*, hinder, hold up, horn in*, impede, incommode, inconvenience, inhibit, intercede, interlope, intermeddle, intermediate, intermit, interpose, intrude, jam, make*, mix in, obstruct, obtrude, oppose, poke nose in*, prevent, remit, step in, stop, suspend, tamper, thwart, trammel, trouble; SEE CONCEPTS *121,384*

interference [*n*] *meddling, impedance*
arrest, background, backseat driving*, barging in*, barring, blocking, checking, choking, clashing, clogging, conflict, hampering, hindrance, intermeddling, interposition, intervention, intrusion, meddlesomeness, obstruction, opposition, prying, resistance, retardation, tackling, tampering, trespassing; SEE CONCEPTS *121,384*

interim [*n*] *interval*
breach, break, breather, breathing spell, coffee break, cutoff, downtime*, gap, hiatus, interlude, interregnum, interruption, lacuna, layoff, letup*, meantime, meanwhile, pause, take*, ten*, time*, time-out; SEE CONCEPTS *807,822*

interim [*adj*] *temporary*
acting, ad interim, caretaker*, improvised, intervening, makeshift, pro tem, pro tempore, provisional, stopgap, thrown-together*; SEE CONCEPT *560*

interior [*n*] *center, core*
belly, bosom, contents, heart, heartland, innards, inner parts, inside, internals, intrinsicality, lining, marrow, midst, pith, pulp, soul, substance, viscera, within; SEE CONCEPTS *742,826,830*

interior [*adj*] *inside, central*
autogenous, domestic, endogenous, gut, home, in-house, inland, inner, innermost, internal, intimate, inward, private, remote, secret, visceral, viscerous, within; SEE CONCEPTS *583,826,830*

interject [*v*] *throw in; interrupt*
add, fill in, force in, implant, import, include, infiltrate, infuse, ingrain, inject, insert, insinuate, intercalate, interpolate, interpose, intersperse, introduce, intrude, parenthesize, put in, splice, squeeze in; SEE CONCEPTS *14,51*

interloper [*n*] *person who intrudes, meddles*
alien, busybody, intermeddler, intruder, meddler, obtruder, trespasser, uninvited guest, unwanted visitor; SEE CONCEPTS *412,423*

interlude [*n*] *pause, break*
breathing space*, delay, episode, halt, hiatus, idyll, interim, intermission, interregnum, interruption, interval, lull, meantime, meanwhile, parenthesis, recess, respite, rest, spell, stop, stoppage, wait; SEE CONCEPT *807*

intermediary [*n*] *person who negotiates*
agent, broker, channel, connection, cutout, delegate, emissary, entrepreneur, fixer, go-between*, influence, instrument, interagent, interceder, intercessor, intermediate, mediator, medium, middle person, negotiator, organ, vehicle; SEE CONCEPTS *348,354*

intermediate [*adj*] *middle, in-between*
average, between, center, central, common, compromising, fair, halfway, indifferent, intermediary, interposed, intervening, mean, medial, median, mediocre, medium, mid, middling, midway, moderate, neutral, so-so*, standard, transitional; SEE CONCEPTS *585,830*

interminable [*adj*] *infinite*
boring, boundless, ceaseless, constant, continuous, day-and-night*, dragged out*, dull, endless, eternal, everlasting, immeasurable, incessant, interminate, limitless, long, long-drawn-out*, long-winded, looped, never-ending, no end of*, no end to*, on a treadmill*, permanent, perpetual, protracted, spun out*, strung out*, timeless, unbound, unceasing, uninterrupted, unlimited, wearisome; SEE CONCEPT *798*

intermingle [*v*] *blend, mix*
amalgamate, associate, combine, come together, commingle, commix, fuse, immingle, interblend, interfuse, interlace, intermix, interweave, join, merge, mesh, network, pool, throw in with, throw together, wed; SEE CONCEPTS *113,114*

intermission [*n*] *break, recess*
abeyance, abeyancy, break-off, breather, breathing spell, cessation, doldrums, dormancy, downtime*, interim, interlude, interregnum, interruption, interval, latency, layoff, let-up*, lull, parenthesis, pause, quiescence, quiescency, respite, rest, spell, stop, stoppage, suspense, suspension, time, time-out, wait; SEE CONCEPT *807*

intermittent [*adj*] *irregular, sporadic*
alternate, arrested, broken, by bits and pieces*, checked, cyclic, cyclical, discontinuing, discontinuous, epochal, every other, fitful, here and there*, hit-or-miss*, infrequent, interrupted, isochronal, isochronous, iterant, iterative, metrical, now and then*, occasional, on and off*, periodic, periodical, punctuated, recurrent, recurring, rhythmic, rhythmical, seasonal, serial, shifting, spasmodic, stop-and-go*; SEE CONCEPTS *482,534,799*

internal [*adj*] *within*
centralized, circumscribed, civic, constitutional, domestic, enclosed, gut, home, indigenous, inherent, in-house, innate, inner, innermore, inside, interior, intestine, intimate, intramural, intrinsic, inward, municipal, national, native, private, subjective, visceral, viscerous; SEE CONCEPTS *536,585,826,830*

international [*adj*] *worldwide*
all-embracing, cosmopolitan, ecumenical, foreign, global, intercontinental, universal, world; SEE CONCEPTS *536,772*

interplay [*n*] *interaction*
coaction, exchange, give-and-take*, mesh, meshing, networking, reciprocation, reciprocity, team play*, teamwork, tit for tat*, transaction; SEE CONCEPT *266*

interpolate [*v*] *add*
admit, annex, append, enter, fill in, include, inject, insert, insinuate, intercalate, interjaculate, in-

in
in

terject, interlope, interpose, introduce, intrude, throw in; SEE CONCEPTS *112,201,209*

interpret [*v*] *make sense of; define*
adapt, annotate, clarify, comment, commentate, construe, decipher, decode, delineate, depict, describe, elucidate, enact, exemplify, explain, explicate, expound, gather, gloss, illustrate, image, improvise, limn, make of, mimic, paraphrase, perform, picture, play, portray, read, reenact, render, represent, solve, spell out, take*, throw light on*, translate, understand, view; SEE CONCEPTS *57,292*

interrogate [*v*] *ask pointed questions*
catechize, cross-examine, cross-question, examine, give the third degree*, go over*, grill, inquire, investigate, pump, put the screws to*, put through the wringer*, query, question, quiz, roast*, sweat out*, work over*; SEE CONCEPTS *48,53*

interrupt [*v*] *bother, interfere*
arrest, barge in, break, break, break in, break off, break train of thought*, bust in*, butt in*, check, chime in*, come between, crash, crowd in, cut, cut in on*, cut off*, cut short*, defer, delay, disconnect, discontinue, disjoin, disturb, disunite, divide, edge in, get in the way, halt, heckle, hinder, hold up, horn in, impede, in, infringe, inject, insinuate, intrude, lay aside, obstruct, prevent, punctuate, put in, separate, sever, shortstop*, stay, stop, suspend, work in; SEE CONCEPTS *51,121,384*

interruption [*n*] *break; interference*
abeyance, abeyancy, arrest, blackout, breach, break-off, cessation, check, cutoff, delay, disconnection, discontinuance, disruption, dissolution, disturbance, disuniting, division, doldrums, dormancy, gap, halt, hiatus, hindrance, hitch, impediment, interim, intermission, interval, intrusion, lacuna, latency, layoff, letup*, obstacle, obstruction, parenthesis, pause, quietus, rift, rupture, separation, severance, split, stop, stoppage, suspension; SEE CONCEPTS *807,832*

intersect [*v*] *cut across; cross at a point*
bisect, break in two, come together, converge, crisscross, cross, crosscut, cut, decussate, divide, intercross, join, meet, separate, touch, traverse; SEE CONCEPTS *113,738,749*

intersection [*n*] *crossroads*
circle, cloverleaf, crossing, crosswalk, crossway, interchange, junction, stop; SEE CONCEPT *501*

intersperse [*v*] *scatter*
bestrew, diffuse, distribute, infuse, interfuse, interlard, intermix, intersow, intersprinkle, pepper, sprinkle; SEE CONCEPTS *201,222*

interstice [*n*] *opening, crack*
aperture, chink, cleft, cranny, crevice, fissure, gap, hole, interval, slit, space; SEE CONCEPT *513*

intertwine/interweave [*v*] *twist around*
associate, braid, connect, convolute, crisscross, cross, entwine, interknit, interlace, intertwist, intervolve, interwind, interwreathe, link, mesh, network, relate, reticulate, tangle, tat, weave; SEE CONCEPTS *113,114*

interval [*n*] *break, pause*
breach, breathing space*, comma, delay, distance, downtime, five*, gap, hiatus, interim, interlude, intermission, interregnum, interruption, lacuna, layoff, letup, lull, meantime, opening, parenthesis, pausation, period, playtime, rest, season, space, spell, ten*, term, time, time-out, wait, while; SEE CONCEPTS *807,822*

intervene [*v1*] *mediate*
arbitrate, barge in, butt in*, come between, divide, horn in*, intercede, interfere, intermediate, interpose, interrupt, intrude, involve, meddle, mix in, muscle in*, negotiate, obtrude, part, put in two cents*, reconcile, separate, settle, sever, step in, take a hand*; SEE CONCEPTS *110,234,266*

intervene [*v2*] *happen*
bedevil, befall, come to pass, ensue, occur, succeed, supervene, take place; SEE CONCEPTS *4,242*

interview [*n*] *questioning and evaluation*
account, audience, call, call back, cattle call*, communication, conference, consultation, conversation, dialogue, examination, hearing, meeting, oral, parley, press conference, record, statement, talk; SEE CONCEPTS *48,351*

interview [*v*] *ask questions and evaluate*
consult, converse, examine, get for the record, get opinion, give oral examination, hold inquiry, interrogate, question, quiz, sound out, talk, talk to; SEE CONCEPTS *48,351*

intestinal/intestine [*adj*] *pertaining to digestive organs*
abdominal, alimentary, bowel, celiac, duodenal, gut, inner, inside, interior, internal, inward, rectal, stomachic, ventral, visceral; SEE CONCEPT *406*

intimacy [*n*] *closeness between people*
acquaintance, affection, affinity, close relationship, communion, confidence, confidentiality, experience, familiarity, friendship, inwardness, understanding; SEE CONCEPT *388*

intimate [*n*] *a close friend; familiar person*
associate, bosom buddy*, chum, companion, comrade, confidant, confidante, crony, familiar, family, lover, mate, pal; SEE CONCEPTS *416,423*

intimate [*adj1*] *friendly, devoted*
affectionate, bosom, buddy-buddy*, cherished, chummy*, close, clubby*, comfy, confidential, cozy, dear, dearest, faithful, fast, fond, loving, mellow, mix, near, nearest, next, nice, regular, roommate, snug, warm; SEE CONCEPT *555*

intimate [*adj2*] *private, personal*
confidential, deep, deep-seated, detailed, elemental, essential, exhaustive, experienced, firsthand, guarded, gut*, immediate, inborn, inbred, indepth, indwelling, ingrained, inherent, inmost, innate, innermost, interior, internal, intrinsic, penetrating, privy, profound, secret, special, thorough, trusted, uptight, visceral, viscerous; SEE CONCEPTS *529,549*

intimate [*v*] *suggest; tip off*
affirm, air, allude, announce, assert, aver, avouch, communicate, connote, declare, drop a hint*, expose, express, hint, impart, imply, indicate, infer, insinuate, leak, let cat out of bag*, let it be known, make known, make noise*, profess, remind, spill the beans*, spring, state, utter, vent, voice, warn; SEE CONCEPTS *49,60,75*

intimation [*n*] *clue, hint*
allusion, announcement, breath, communication, cue, declaration, implication, indication, inkling, innuendo, insinuation, notice, notion, reminder, shade, shadow, strain, streak, suggestion, suspicion, telltale, tinge, tip, trace, warning, wind; SEE CONCEPTS *274,689*

intimidate [*v*] *frighten, threaten*
alarm, appall, awe, badger, bait, bludgeon, bluster, bowl over*, browbeat*, buffalo*, bulldoze*, bully, chill, coerce, compel, constrain, cow*,

daunt, dishearten, dismay, dispirit, disquiet, dragoon, enforce, force, hound*, lean on*, oblige, overawe, push around*, ride*, ruffle, scare, showboat, spook, strong-arm, subdue, terrify, terrorize, twist someone's arm*; SEE CONCEPTS 7,14,19

intolerable [adj] *unacceptable; beyond bearing*
a bit much, enough already*, excruciating, extreme, impossible, insufferable, insupportable, last straw*, offensive, painful, unbearable, undesirable, unendurable; SEE CONCEPT 529

intolerant [adj] *impatient, prejudiced*
antipathetic, averse, biased, bigoted, chauvinistic, communist, conservative, contemptuous, dictatorial, disdainful, dogmatic, fanatical, fractious, hateful, illiberal, indignant, individualistic, inflexible, irate, irritable, jaundiced, narrow, narrow-minded, obdurate, one-sided, outraged, racialist, racist, short-fuse*, small-minded*, snappy, stuffy, tilted, uncharitable, unfair, unforbearing, unindulgent, unsympathetic, unwilling, upset, waspish, worked-up*, xenophobic; SEE CONCEPTS 403,404,542

intoxicated [adj1] *drunk*
blind*, bombed*, boozed*, buzzed*, drunken, high*, inebriated, loaded*, looped*, muddled, potted*, sloppy, smashed*, tanked*, three sheets to the wind*, tied one on*, tight*, tipsy, under the influence, unsober; SEE CONCEPT 406

intoxicated [adj2] *extremely happy*
absorbed, affected, beside oneself, captivated, concerned, delirious, dizzy, drunk, ecstatic, elated, enraptured, euphoric, excited, exhilarated, galvanized, high*, infatuated, interested, moved, piqued, quickened, sent*, stimulated, turned-on*; SEE CONCEPT 403

intoxicating [adj] *causing great happiness*
exciting, exhilarant, exhilarating, exhilarative, eye-popping, heady, inspiring, provocative, rousing, stimulating, stirring, thrilling; SEE CONCEPT 537

intractable /intransigent [adj] *difficult, stubborn*
awkward, bullheaded*, cantankerous, contrary, hang tough*, hard-line*, headstrong, immovable, incompliant, incurable, indocile, indomitable, insoluble, locked in*, mulish, obdurate, obstinate, pat, pertinacious, perverse, pigheaded*, recalcitrant, refractory, resolute, self-willed, set in stone, tenacious, tough, tough-nut*, unbending, uncompromising, uncooperative, undisciplined, ungovernable, unmanageable, unpliable, unruly, unyielding, wayward, wild, willful; SEE CONCEPTS 401,534,542

intrepid [adj] *brave, nervy*
audacious, bodacious*, bold, courageous, daring, dauntless, doughty, fearless, gallant, game, gritty, gutsy*, heroic, impavid, lionhearted, nerveless, plucky, resolute, spunky*, stalwart, unafraid, undaunted, unflinching, valiant, valorous; SEE CONCEPT 401

intricate [adj] *complicated, elaborate*
abstruse, baroque, Byzantine*, can of worms*, complex, convoluted, Daedal*, difficult, entangled, fancy, hard, high-tech*, involved, labyrinthine, obscure, perplexing, rococo, sophisticated, tangled, tortuous, tricky; SEE CONCEPT 562

intrigue [n1] *scheme*
artifice, cabal, chicanery, collusion, complication, conspiracy, contrivance, deal, design, dodge, double-dealing*, fix, frame-up*, fraud, game, graft, hookup, little game*, machination, maneuver, manipulation, plan, plot, ruse, stratagem, trickery, wile; SEE CONCEPTS 192,660

intrigue [n2] *love affair*
affair, amour, attachment, case, flirtation, infatuation, interlude, intimacy, liaison, romance; SEE CONCEPT 388

intrigue [v1] *arouse curiosity*
appeal, attract, bait, captivate, charm, con, delight, draw, enchant, entertain, excite, fascinate, grab, hook, interest, lead on*, mousetrap*, pique, please, pull, rivet, tickle, titillate, tout; SEE CONCEPTS 7,11,22

intrigue [v2] *plot*
angle, be in cahoots*, cogitate, collude, connive, conspire, contrive, cook up*, devise, finagle, frame up*, machinate, maneuver, operate, plan, promote, scheme, set up*, work hand in glove*; SEE CONCEPT 36

intrinsic [adj] *basic, inborn*
built-in, central, congenital, connate, constitutional, constitutive, deep-seated, elemental, essential, fundamental, genuine, hereditary, inbred, indwelling, inherent, inmost, innate, intimate, material, native, natural, particular, peculiar, real, true, underlying; SEE CONCEPTS 404,406,546

introduce [v1] *make known; present*
acquaint, advance, air, announce, bring out, bring up, broach, come out with, do the honors*, familiarize, fix up, get things rolling*, get together, give introduction, harbinger*, herald, kick off, knock down, lead into, lead off, moot, offer, open, open up, originate, pave the way*, precede, preface, propose, put forward, recommend, set forth, spring with, start ball rolling*, submit, suggest, usher, ventilate; SEE CONCEPTS 60,384

introduce [v2] *begin, institute*
admit, bring forward, bring in, commence, enter, establish, found, inaugurate, incept, initiate, innovate, install, invent, kick off*, launch, organize, pioneer, plan, preface, present, set up, start, unveil, usher in; SEE CONCEPT 221

introduce [v3] *add, insert*
carry, enter, fill in, freight, import, include, infix, inject, inlay, inlet, inset, insinuate, instill, intercalate, interject, interpolate, interpose, put in, send, ship, throw in, transport, work in; SEE CONCEPTS 112,113,209

introduction [n] *something new; something that begins*
addition, admittance, awakening, baptism, basic principles, basic text, beginning, commencement, debut, essentials, establishment, exordium, first acquaintance, first taste, foreword, inauguration, inception, induction, influx, ingress, initiation, insertion, installation, institution, interpolation, intro*, launch, lead, lead-in, opening, opening remarks, overture, pioneering, preamble, preface, preliminaries, prelude, presentation, primer, proem, prolegomenon, prologue, survey; SEE CONCEPTS 270,727,828

introductory [adj] *preliminary, first*
anterior, basic, beginning, early, elementary, inaugural, incipient, inductive, initial, initiatory, opening, original, precursory, prefatory, prelusive, preparative, preparatory, primary, prior, proemial, provisional, rudimentary, starting; SEE CONCEPTS 546,585

introspection [n] *self-analysis*
brooding, contemplation, deep thought, egoism,

heart-searching, introversion, meditation, reflection, rumination, scrutiny, self-absorption, self-examination, self-observation, self-questioning, soul-searching; SEE CONCEPTS 24,410

introvert [n] *person who retreats mentally*
autist, brooder, egoist, egotist, loner*, narcissist, self-observer, solitary, wallflower*; SEE CONCEPT 423

intrude [v] *trespass, interrupt*
barge in, bother, butt in*, chisel in*, cut in, disturb, encroach, entrench, go beyond, hold up, horn in*, infringe, insinuate, intercalate, interfere, interject, interlope, intermeddle, interpolate, interpose, introduce, invade, meddle, obtrude, overstep, pester, push in, thrust, violate; SEE CONCEPTS 14,159,208,266

intruder [n] *person who trespasses*
burglar, criminal, gate-crasher*, infiltrator, interferer, interloper, interrupter, invader, meddler, nuisance, obtruder, prowler, raider, snooper, squatter, thief, trespasser; SEE CONCEPTS 412,423

intuition [n] *insight*
clairvoyance, discernment, divination, ESP*, feeling*, foreknowledge, gut reaction*, hunch*, innate knowledge, inspiration, instinct, intuitiveness, nose*, penetration, perception, perceptivity, premonition, presentiment, second sight*, sixth sense*; SEE CONCEPTS 409,689

intuitive [adj] *instinctive*
automatic, direct, emotional, habitual, immediate, inherent, innate, instinctual, involuntary, natural, perceptive, spontaneous, understood, unreflecting, untaught, visceral; SEE CONCEPT 402

inundate [v] *drown, overwhelm*
deluge, dunk, engulf, flood, glut, immerse, overflow, overrun, pour down on, snow*, submerge, swamp, whelm; SEE CONCEPTS 172,179

invade [v] *attack and encroach*
access, assail, assault, breach, burglarize, burst in, crash, descend upon, entrench, fall on, foray, go in, infect, infest, infringe, inroad, interfere, loot, make inroads*, maraud, meddle, muscle in*, occupy, overrun, overspread, overswarm, penetrate, permeate, pervade, pillage, plunder, raid, ravage, storm, swarm over, trespass, violate; SEE CONCEPTS 86,159,320

invalid [n] *sick person*
consumptive, convalescent, incurable, patient, shut-in, sufferer; SEE CONCEPT 424

invalid [adj1] *worthless; unfounded*
bad, baseless, fallacious, false, ill-founded, illogical, inoperative, irrational, mad, not binding, not working, nugatory, null, null and void*, reasonless, sophistic, unreasonable, unreasoned, unscientific, unsound, untrue, void, wrong; SEE CONCEPTS 552,560

invalid [adj2] *sickly*
ailing, bedridden, below par, debilitated, disabled, down, feeble, frail, ill, infirm, laid low*, on the sick list*, out of action*, peaked, poorly, run-down, sick, weak; SEE CONCEPT 314

invalidate [v] *render null and void*
abate, abolish, abrogate, annihilate, annul, blow sky-high*, cancel, circumduct, counteract, counterbalance, disannul, discredit, disqualify, impair, negate, negative, neutralize, nix, nullify, offset, overrule, overthrow, quash, refute, revoke, shoot full of holes*, undermine, undo, unfit, weaken, X-out*; SEE CONCEPTS 121,234

invaluable [adj] *priceless*
beyond price, costly, dear, expensive, helpful, inestimable, precious, serviceable, valuable; SEE CONCEPTS 334,568

invariable [adj] *not changing*
changeless, consistent, constant, fixed, immovable, immutable, inalterable, inflexible, monotonous, perpetual, regular, rigid, same, set, static, unalterable, unchangeable, unchanging, undiversified, unfailing, uniform, unmodifiable, unrelieved, unvarying, unwavering; SEE CONCEPT 534

invasion [n] *attack, encroachment*
aggression, assault, breach, entrenchment, foray, forced entrance, incursion, infiltration, infraction, infringement, inroad, intrusion, irruption, maraud, offense, offensive, onslaught, overstepping, raid, transgression, trespass, usurpation, violation; SEE CONCEPTS 86,159,320

invective [n] *verbal abuse*
accusation, berating, billingsgate, blame, blasphemy, castigation, censure, contumely, denunciation, diatribe, epithet, jeremiad, obloquy, philippic, reproach, revilement, sarcasm, scurrility, tirade, tongue-lashing*, vilification, vituperation; SEE CONCEPTS 44,52,54,278

inveigh [v] *blame, denounce*
admonish, berate, blast, castigate, censure, condemn, crack down on*, except, expostulate, go after*, have at*, jump down one's throat*, kick, lambaste, lay into, lay out, let have it, object, protest, rail, read out*, recriminate, remonstrate, reproach, rip into, roast, scold, scorch, sound off, tongue-lash, trash*, upbraid, vituperate, work over*; SEE CONCEPTS 44,52,54

inveigle [v] *entice, manipulate*
allure, bait, bamboozle, beguile, blandish, butter*, cajole, charm, coax, con*, decoy, egg on*, ensnare, entrap, get around*, honey*, hook, influence, jolly, lay it on thick*, lead on*, lure, maneuver, massage, oil*, overdo it, persuade, play up to, rope in*, seduce, snow*, soap*, soften up*, string along*, stroke*, sweet talk*, tempt, toll, urge, wheedle, work over*; SEE CONCEPTS 11,14,59

invent [v1] *create, think up*
ad-lib, author, bear, bring into being, coin, come upon, come up with, compose, conceive, contrive, cook up*, design, devise, discover, dream up, envision, execute, fake, fashion, find, forge, form, formulate, frame, hatch, imagine, improve, improvise, inaugurate, initiate, jam*, knock off*, make, make up, mint, off-the-cuff*, originate, plan, produce, project, toss off*, turn out, wing*; SEE CONCEPTS 36,173,221

invent [v2] *fabricate*
concoct, conjure up, create out of thin air*, equivocate, fake, falsify, feign, fib, forge, lie, make believe, make up, misrepresent, misstate, pretend, prevaricate, simulate, tell a white lie*, tell untruth, think up, trump up*, vamp; SEE CONCEPTS 59,63

invention [n1] *creation, creativeness*
apparatus, black box*, brainchild*, coinage, concoction, contraption, contrivance, creativity, design, development, device, discovery, doodad*, gadget, genius, gimmick, gizmo*, imagination, ingenuity, innovation, inspiration, inventiveness, novelty, opus, original, originality, resourcefulness; SEE CONCEPTS 260,409,660

invention [n2] *fabrication, lie*
deceit, fake, falsehood, fancy, fantasy, fib, fiction, figment, forgery, prevarication, sham*, story, tall story*, untruth, yarn*; SEE CONCEPTS *63,278*

inventive [adj] *creative*
adroit, artistic, avant-garde, breaking new ground, causative, constructive, demiurgic, deviceful, fertile, forgetive, formative, fruitful, gifted, imaginative, ingenious, innovational, innovative, innovatory, inspired, original, originative, poetical, productive, resourceful, teeming; SEE CONCEPTS *402,542*

inventor [n] *person who comes up with idea*
administrator, architect, artist, author, authority, brain, brains*, director, engineer, expert, genius, intellect, philosopher, planner; SEE CONCEPTS *348,350*

inventory [n] *list of stock; stock*
account, backlog, catalogue, file, fund, hoard, index, itemization, record, register, reserve, reservoir, roll, roster, schedule, stock book, stockpile, store, summary, supply, table, tabulation; SEE CONCEPTS *283,338*

inverse [adj] *opposite*
changed, contrary, converse, flipped, inverted, reverse, reversed, reverted, transposed, turned, turned over; SEE CONCEPT *564*

invert [v] *reverse; turn upside down*
alter, backtrack, capsize, change, convert, double back, evert, flip, flip-flop*, introvert, inverse, modify, overturn, renege, revert, tip, transplace, transpose, turn, turn down, turn inside out, turn over, turn the tables*, upend, upset, upturn; SEE CONCEPTS *213,232*

invest [v1] *contribute money to make money*
advance, back, bankroll, buy into, buy stock, devote, endow, endue, get into, go in for, imbue, infuse, intrust, lay out, lend, loan, pick up the tab*, plow back into*, plunge, provide, put in, put up dough*, salt away*, sink, spend, stake, supply; SEE CONCEPTS *115,330,341*

invest [v2] *give power or authority*
adopt, authorize, bequeath, charge, consecrate, empower, endow, endue, enthrone, establish, honor, inaugurate, induct, initiate, install, instate, license, ordain, sanction, vest; SEE CONCEPTS *50,88*

investigate [v] *check into thoroughly*
be all ears*, bug, case*, check out, check over, check up, consider, delve, dig, examine, explore, eyeball*, feel out, frisk, give the once over*, go into, inquire, inquisite, inspect, interrogate, listen in, look into, look over, look-see, make inquiry, muckrake, nose around*, poke, probe, prospect, pry, put to the test*, question, read, reconnoiter, research, review, run down, scout, scrutinize, search, sift, spy, stake out, study, tap, wiretap; SEE CONCEPTS *48,103,216*

investigation [n] *thorough check*
analysis, case, delving, examination, exploration, fact-finding, gander, hearing, hustle, inquest, inquiry, inquisition, inspection, legwork, observation, observing, pike, probe, probing, quest, quiz, research, review, scrutiny, search, sounding, study, survey, surveying; SEE CONCEPTS *48,103,216,290*

investigator [n] *person who checks thoroughly*
agent, analyst, attorney, auditor, detective, examiner, gumshoe*, hound*, inquirer, inspector, plainclothes officer, police, private detective, private eye, prosecutor, researcher, reviewer, Sherlock Holmes*, sleuth, snooper, spy, tester, undercover cop; SEE CONCEPTS *348,355*

investment [n] *something given, lent for a return*
advance, ante, asset, backing, bail, contribution, endowment, expenditure, expense, finance, financing, flutter, grant, hunch, inside, interests, investing, loan, money, piece, plunge, property, purchase, smart money*, spec*, speculation, stab*, stake, transaction, venture, vested interests; SEE CONCEPTS *330,332,340*

inveterate [adj] *long-standing, established*
abiding, accustomed, addicted, chronic, confirmed, continuing, customary, deep-rooted, deep-seated, dyed-in-the-wool*, enduring, entrenched, fixed, habitual, habituated, hard-core*, hardened, inbred, incorrigible, incurable, indurated, ineradicable, ingrained, innate, lifelong, long-lasting, long-lived, obstinate, old, perennial, permanent, persistent, persisting, set, settled, stubborn, sworn, usual; SEE CONCEPTS *404,534,798*

invidious [adj] *hateful*
abominable, calumnious, defamatory, detestable, detracting, detractive, detractory, discriminatory, envious, envying, green-eyed*, jealous, libelous, maligning, obnoxious, odious, offensive, repugnant, scandalous, slanderous, slighting, undesirable, vilifying; SEE CONCEPTS *401,403*

invigorate [v] *stimulate*
activate, animate, brace, buck up, energize, enliven, excite, exhilarate, fortify, freshen, galvanize, harden, inspirit, liven up, nerve, pep up, perk up, quicken, rally, refresh, reinforce, rejuvenate, renew, restore, revitalize, rouse, snap up*, stir, strengthen, trigger, turn on*, vitalize, vivify, zap; SEE CONCEPTS *7,14,22,110*

invigorating [adj] *stimulating*
aesthetic, bracing, brisk, charged, energizing, exhilarating, exhilarative, fascinating, fresh, healthful, high*, hyper*, interesting, lively, quickening, refreshing, rejuvenating, rejuvenative, restorative, salubrious, tonic, uplifting, vitalizing; SEE CONCEPT *537*

invincible [adj] *indestructible*
bulletproof, impassable, impregnable, indomitable, insuperable, inviolable, invulnerable, irresistible, powerful, strong, unassailable, unattackable, unbeatable, unconquerable, undefeatable, unsurmountable, untouchable, unyielding; SEE CONCEPTS *489,540,551*

invisible [adj] *unable to be seen; hidden*
concealed, covert, deceptive, disguised, ethereal, gaseous, ghostly, ideal, impalpable, imperceptible, imponderable, inappreciable, inconspicuous, indiscernible, infinitesimal, insensible, intangible, masked, microscopic, not in sight, obliterated, obscured, occult, out of sight, perdu, screened, supernatural, ulterior, unapparent, undisclosed, ungraspable, unnoticeable, unobservable, unperceivable, unreal, unseeable, unseen, unviewable, vaporous, veiled, wraithlike; SEE CONCEPTS *485,582,619*

invitation [n] *proposal; asking*
allurement, appeal, attraction, begging, bid, bidding, call, challenge, compliments, coquetry, date, encouragement, enticement, feeler*, ground, hit, incitement, inducement, invite, lure, motive, offer, open door*, overture, paper, pass, petition, pressure, proffer, prompting, proposi-

tion, provocation, rain check*, reason, request, solicitation, suggestion, summons, supplication, temptation, urge; SEE CONCEPTS *48,384*

invite [v] *ask to do something socially*
allure, appeal to, attract, beg, bid, bring on, call, command, countenance, court, draw, encourage, entice, entreat, give invitation, have in, have over, include as guest, insist, inveigle, invitation, issue, lead, lure, persuade, petition, ply, pray, press, prevail on, propose, provoke, request, send invitation, solicit, suggest, summon, supplicate, tempt, urge, vamp, welcome, woo; SEE CONCEPTS *48,68,384*

inviting [adj] *alluring, captivating*
agreeable, appealing, attractive, beguiling, bewitching, charming, cordial, delightful, encouraging, engaging, enticing, fascinating, intriguing, magnetic, mouthwatering, open, persuasive, pleasing, provocative, seductive, tempting, warm, welcoming, winning, winsome; SEE CONCEPTS *404,529,537*

invocation [n] *prayer*
abracadabra*, appeal, beseeching, calling, command, conjuration, entreaty, hocus-pocus*, hoodoo*, mumbo-jumbo*, petition, rune, summons, supplication, voodoo*; SEE CONCEPTS *48, 278,368*

invoke [v1] *call upon*
adjure, appeal to, beg, beseech, call forth, conjure, crave, entreat, implore, importune, petition, plead, pray, request, send for, solicit, summon, supplicate; SEE CONCEPT *48*

invoke [v2] *put into effect*
apply, call in, effect, enforce, have recourse to, implement, initiate, resort to, use; SEE CONCEPTS *50,88*

involuntary [adj] *automatic; not done willingly*
automatic, begrudging, blind, compulsory, conditioned, forced, grudging, habitual, impulsive, instinctive, instinctual, knee-jerk*, obligatory, reflex, reflexive, reluctant, spontaneous, uncalculated, unconscious, uncontrolled, unintended, unintentional, unmeditated, unpremeditated, unprompted, unthinking, unwilling, unwitting, will-less; SEE CONCEPT *544*

involve [v] *draw in; include*
absorb, affect, argue, associate, bind, catch, commit, complicate, comprehend, comprise, compromise, concern, connect, contain, cover, denote, embrace, embroil, engage, engross, enmesh, entail, entangle, grip, hold, hook, implicate, imply, incorporate, incriminate, inculpate, link, mean, mire, mix up*, necessitate, number, point to, preoccupy, presuppose, prove, relate, require, rivet, rope in, snarl up, suggest, take in, tangle, touch, wrap up in*; SEE CONCEPT *112*

involved [adj1] *complicated*
Byzantine*, complex, confusing, convoluted, difficult, elaborate, Gordian*, high-tech*, intricate, knotty*, labyrinthine, mazy, muddled, ramified, sophisticated, tangled, tortuous, winding; SEE CONCEPT *562*

involved [adj2] *implicated in action*
affected, caught, concerned, eat sleep and breathe*, embarrassed, embroiled, enmeshed, entangled, hooked, immersed in, incriminated, interested, into, knee-deep in*, mixed up in*, mixed up with*, occupied, participating, taking part in, tangled, up to here in*, up to one's neck in*; SEE CONCEPTS *542,545*

inward [adj1] *ingoing*
entering, inbound, incoming, infiltrating, inflowing, inpouring, penetrating, through; SEE CONCEPT *581*

inward [adj2] *private*
confidential, hidden, inmost, inner, innermost, inside, intellectual, interior, internal, intimate, personal, privy, psychological, religious, secret, spiritual; SEE CONCEPT *529*

iota [n] *small bit*
atom, crumb, grain, hint, infinitesimal, jot, mite, molecule, nucleus, ounce, particle, ray, scintilla, scrap, smidgen, speck, trace, whit; SEE CONCEPT *831*

irascible [adj] *crabby*
angry, bearish, bristly, cantankerous, choleric, crabbed, cranky, cross, feisty, fractious, grouchy, hasty, hot-tempered, huffy, ireful, irritable, ogre, passionate, peevish, petulant, querulous, quick-tempered, short-tempered, snappish, surly, testy, thin-skinned*, touchy, uptight; SEE CONCEPT *401*

irate [adj] *angry*
angered, annoyed, blown a gasket*, enraged, exasperated, fuming, furious, incensed, indignant, infuriated, irritated, livid, mad, piqued, provoked, riled, steamed*, ticked off*, up in arms*, worked up*, wrathful, wroth; SEE CONCEPTS *403,542*

ire [n] *anger*
annoyance, boiling point*, conniption, conniption fit*, displeasure, exasperation, fury, indignation, more heat than light*, passion, rage, slow burn*, wrath; SEE CONCEPT *410*

iridescent [adj] *rainbow-colored*
irised, lustrous, many-colored, nacreous, opalescent, opaline, pearly, polychromatic, prismatic, rainbowlike, shimmering; SEE CONCEPT *618*

irk [v] *aggravate; rub the wrong way*
abrade, annoy, bother, bug*, discommode, disturb, eat*, fret, gall, get on nerves*, get to*, give a hard time*, harass, incommode, inconvenience, irritate, make waves*, miff, nettle, peeve, provoke, put out*, rasp, rile, ruffle, trouble, vex; SEE CONCEPTS *7,19*

iron [n1] *hard, ferrous metal*
cast, coke, pig; SEE CONCEPT *476*

iron [n2] *restraint made of metal*
bond, chain, cuffs, fetter, handcuffs, leg irons, manacles, shackles; SEE CONCEPT *476*

iron [adj] *hard, tough; inflexible*
adamant, adamantine, cruel, dense, ferric, ferrous, firm, heavy, immovable, implacable, indomitable, inexorable, insensible, obdurate, relentless, rigid, robust, steel, steely, strong, stubborn, thick, unbending, unyielding; SEE CONCEPTS *534,604*

ironic/ironical [adj] *sarcastic*
acrid, alert, arrogant, backbiting, biting, bitter, burlesque, caustic, chaffing, clever, contemptuous, contradictory, critical, cutting, cynical, defiant, derisive, disparaging, double-edged, exaggerated, implausible, incisive, incongruous, jibing, keen, mocking, mordant, paradoxical, pungent, quick-witted, ridiculous, sardonic, satiric, satirical, scathing, scoffing, sharp, sneering, spicy, trenchant, twisted, uncomplimentary, witty, wry; SEE CONCEPTS *267,548*

iron out [v] *reconcile a situation*
agree, arbitrate, clear up*, compromise, eliminate, eradicate, erase, expedite, get rid of*, harmonize, negotiate, put right*, reach agreement,

resolve, settle, settle differences, simplify, smooth over*, sort out*, straighten out*, unravel; SEE CONCEPT *126*

irony [n] *sarcasm*
banter, burlesque, contempt, contrariness, criticism, derision, humor, incongruity, jibe, mockery, mordancy, paradox, quip, raillery, repartee, reproach, ridicule, sardonicism, satire, taunt, twist, wit; SEE CONCEPTS *230,278*

irrational [adj] *illogical, senseless*
aberrant, absurd, brainless, cockamamie*, crazy, delirious, demented, disconnected, disjointed, distraught, fallacious, flaky*, foolish, freaky, incoherent, injudicious, insane, invalid, kooky*, loony*, mad, mindless, nonsensical, nutty*, off-the-wall*, preposterous, raving, reasonless, ridiculous, silly, sophistic, specious, stupid, unreasonable, unreasoning, unsound, unstable, unthinking, unwise, wacky*, wild, wrong; SEE CONCEPTS *402,403,529*

irreconcilable [adj] *hostile, conflicting*
clashing, diametrically opposed, discordant, discrepant, dissonant, hard-line, implacable, incompatible, incongruous, inconsistent, inexorable, inflexible, inharmonious, intransigent, opposed, reluctant, unappeasable, uncompromising, unfriendly; SEE CONCEPTS *401,564*

irrefutable [adj] *beyond question*
accurate, apodictic, can bet on it*, certain, double-checked, evident, final, inarguable, incontestable, incontrovertible, indisputable, indubitable, invincible, ironclad, irrebuttable, irrefragable, irresistible, no ifs ands or buts*, obvious, odds-on*, positive, proven, set, sure, unanswerable, unassailable, undeniable, unimpeachable, unquestionable; SEE CONCEPTS *529,535,582*

irregular [adj1] *random, variable*
aberrant, aimless, capricious, casual, changeable, designless, desultory, disconnected, discontinuous, eccentric, erratic, faltering, fitful, fluctuating, fragmentary, haphazard, hit-or-miss*, inconstant, indiscriminate, infrequent, intermittent, jerky, nonuniform, occasional, out of order, patchy, purposeless, recurrent, shaky, shifting, spasmodic, sporadic, uncertain, unconsidered, uneven, unmethodical, unpunctual, unreliable, unsettled, unsteady, unsystematic, up and down*, weaving; SEE CONCEPTS *534,799*

irregular [adj2] *abnormal, peculiar*
aberrant, anomalous, atypical, capricious, deviant, different, disorderly, divergent, eccentric, exceptional, extraordinary, immoderate, improper, inappropriate, inordinate, odd, off-key*, queer, quirky, singular, strange, unconventional, unique, unnatural, unofficial, unorthodox, unsuitable, unusual; SEE CONCEPT *547*

irregular [adj3] *bumpy, uneven*
aberrant, amorphous, asymmetrical, bent, broken, cockeyed*, craggy, crooked, devious, disproportionate, eccentric, elliptic, elliptical, hilly, jagged, lopsided, lumpy, meandering, notched, not uniform, off-balance, off-center, out of proportion, pitted, protuberant, rough, scarred, serrate, serrated, unaligned, unbalanced, unequal, unsymmetrical, variable, wobbly, zigzagged; SEE CONCEPTS *490,606*

irregularly [adv] *intermittently*
anyhow, any which way*, at intervals, by fits and starts*, by turns, disconnectedly, eccentrically, erratically, fitfully, haphazardly, helter-skelter*, infrequently, in snatches*, jerkily, now and again, occasionally, off and on*, out of sequence, periodically, slapdash, spasmodically, sporadically, uncertainly, uncommonly, unevenly, unmethodically, unpunctually, willy-nilly*; SEE CONCEPTS *544,548,799*

irrelevant [adj] *beside the point*
extraneous, foreign, garbage, immaterial, impertinent, inapplicable, inapposite, inappropriate, inappurtenant, inapropos, inapt, inconsequent, inconsequential, insignificant, not connected with, not germane, not pertaining to, off point, off the topic, out of order, out of place, outside, pointless, remote, trivial, unapt, unconnected, unimportant, unnecessary, unrelated, without reference; SEE CONCEPTS *560,575*

irreparable [adj] *unable to be fixed*
beyond repair, broken, cureless, destroyed, hopeless, impossible, incorrigible, incurable, irrecoverable, irredeemable, irremediable, irremedial, irreplaceable, irretrievable, irreversible, ruined, uncorrectable, unrecoverable; SEE CONCEPTS *314,485*

irrepressible [adj] *effervescent, vivacious*
boisterous, bubbling, buoyant, ebullient, enthusiastic, insuppressible, rebellious, rhapsodical, tumultous/tumultuous, unconstrained, uncontainable, uncontrollable, unmanageable, unquenchable, unrestrainable, unrestrained, unruly, unstoppable; SEE CONCEPT *401*

irreproachable [adj] *innocent*
beyond reproach, blameless, exemplary, faultless, good, guiltless, impeccable, inculpable, innocent, irreprehensible, irreprovable, perfect, pure, reproachless, righteous, unblamable, unblemished, unimpeachable, virtuous; SEE CONCEPTS *545,574*

irresistible [adj] *compelling; inescapable*
alluring, beckoning, charming, enchanting, fascinating, glamorous, imperative, indomitable, ineluctable, inevitable, inexorable, invincible, lovable, overpowering, overwhelming, potent, powerful, ravishing, scrumptious, seductive, stunning, tempting, unavoidable, unconquerable, urgent; SEE CONCEPTS *529,574,579*

irresolute [adj] *indecisive*
changing, doubtful, doubting, faltering, fearful, fickle, fluctuating, halfhearted*, halting, hesitant, hesitating, hot-and-cold*, infirm, on-the-fence*, shaky, tentative, timid, uncertain, undecided, undetermined, unsettled, unstable, unsteady, vacillating, waffling*, wavering, weak, weak-kneed*, wimpy*, wishy-washy*, wobbly; SEE CONCEPTS *403,535*

irresponsible [adj] *careless, reckless*
capricious, carefree, devil-may-care*, feckless, fickle, flighty, fly-by-night*, giddy, harebrained, ill-considered, immature, immoral, incautious, lax, loose*, no-account*, rash, scatterbrained*, shiftless, thoughtless, unaccountable, unanswerable, uncareful, undependable, unpredictable, unreliable, unstable, untrustworthy, wild; SEE CONCEPTS *404,544*

irreverence [n] *disrespect*
blasphemy, cheek, derision, discourtesy, flippancy, heresy, impertinence, impiety, impudence, insult, mockery, profanity, ridicule, rudeness, sauciness*, sin, sinfulness; SEE CONCEPT *633*

irreverent [adj] *disrespectful*
aweless, cheeky*, cocky*, contemptuous, crusty*, derisive, flip*, flippant, fresh, iconoclas-

in

ir

tic, impertinent, impious, impudent, insolent, irreverential, mocking, out-of-line*, profane, rude, sacrilegious, sassy*, saucy*, tongue-in-cheek*, ungodly, unhallowed, unholy; SEE CONCEPT 401

irrevocable [adj] fixed, unchangeable
certain, changeless, constant, doomed, established, fated, final, immutable, indelible, inevitable, invariable, irremediable, irretrievable, irreversible, lost, permanent, predestined, predetermined, settled, unalterable, unrepealable, unreversible; SEE CONCEPTS 534,551

irritable [adj] bad-tempered, crabby
annoyed, bearish, brooding, cantankerous, carping, choleric, complaining, contentious, crabbed, cross, crotchety, disputatious, dissatisfied, dyspeptic, easily offended, exasperated, fiery, fractious, fretful, fretting, gloomy, grouchy, grumbling, hasty, hot, huffy, hypercritical, illhumored, irascible, moody, morose, out of humor, oversensitive, peevish, petulant, plaintive, prickly, querulous, quick-tempered, resentful, sensitive, snappy, snarling, surly, tense, testy, touchy; SEE CONCEPT 401,403

irritate [v] upset, anger
abrade, affront, aggravate, annoy, bother, bug*, burn*, chafe, confuse, distemper, disturb, drive up the wall*, enrage, exasperate, fret, gall, get, get on nerves*, get under skin*, grate, harass, incense, inflame, infuriate, irk, madden, needle*, nettle, offend, pain, peeve, pester, pique, provoke, put out, rankle, rasp, rattle, rile, roil, rub the wrong way*, ruffle, sour, try, vex; SEE CONCEPTS 7,19

irritate [v2] hurt, chafe
aggravate, burn, erupt, fret, inflame, intensify, itch, pain, redden, rub, sensitize, sharpen, sting, swell; SEE CONCEPT 246

island [n] land surrounded by body of water
archipelago, atoll, bar, cay, enclave, haven, isle, islet, key, peninsula, reef, refuge, retreat, sanctuary, shelter; SEE CONCEPT 509

isolate [v] cut off, set apart
abstract, block off, close off, confine, detach, disconnect, disengage, divide, divorce, insulate, island, keep apart, part, quarantine, remove, seclude, segregate, separate, sequester, sever, sunder; SEE CONCEPTS 188,201

isolated [adj] unique; private
abandoned, abnormal, alone, anomalous, apart, backwoods*, confined, deserted, detached, exceptional, far-out, forsaken, hidden, incommunicado*, lonely, lonesome, off beaten track*, outlying, out-of-the-way*, random, remote, retired, screened, secluded, segregated, sequestered, single, solitary, special, stranded, unaccompanied, unfrequented, unrelated, untypical, unusual, withdrawn; SEE CONCEPTS 577,583

issue [n1] question in point
affair, argument, concern, contention, controversy, matter, matter of contention, point, point of departure, problem, puzzle, question, subject, topic; SEE CONCEPTS 278,532

issue [n2] result
causatum, conclusion, consequence, culmination, effect, end, end product, eventuality, finale, fruit, outcome, payoff, sequel, termination, upshot; SEE CONCEPT 230

issue [n3] edition of publication
copy, impression, installment, number, printing; SEE CONCEPT 280

issue [n4] distribution
circulation, delivery, dispersion, dissemination, granting, issuance, issuing, publication, sending out, supply, supplying; SEE CONCEPT 140

issue [n5] children
brood, descendants, get, heirs, offspring, posterity, progeniture, progeny, scions, seed; SEE CONCEPTS 296,414

issue [v1] distribute
air, allot, announce, assign, bring out, broadcast, circulate, consign, declare, deliver, dispatch, dispense, emit, get out, give out, promulgate, publish, put in circulation, put out, release, send, send out, transmit; SEE CONCEPTS 60,140,292

issue [v2] emit, emerge; come from
appear, arise, be a consequence, birth, come forth, derive from, emanate, exude, flow, give off, give out, ooze, originate, proceed, release, rise, send forth, spring, spurt, stem, throw off, vent, well; SEE CONCEPTS 179,648

itch [n1] scratching; tingling
crawling, creeping, irritation, itchiness, prickling, psoriasis, rawness, tickle; SEE CONCEPTS 608,728

itch [n2] strong desire
aphrodisia, appetite, appetition, concupiscence, craving, eroticism, hankering, hunger, impulse, longing, lust, lustfulness, motive, passion, prurience, restlessness, urge, yearning, yen; SEE CONCEPTS 20,529

itch [v1] scratch; tingle
crawl, creep, irritate, prick, prickle, sting, tickle, titillate; SEE CONCEPTS 185,313,612

itch [v2] desire strongly
ache, be impatient, burn, chafe, crave, hanker, have a yen for, hunger, long, lust, pant, pine, sigh, thirst, want, yearn; SEE CONCEPT 20

item [n] part, article
account, aspect, bit, blurb*, bulletin, column, component, consideration, conversation piece, detail, dispatch, element, entry, feature, incidental information, matter, minor point, minutia, news, note, notice, novelty, paragraph, particular, piece, point, report, scoop*, scrap, specific, story, thing, write-up; SEE CONCEPTS 270,831,835

itemize [v] keep detailed record
catalog, circumstantiate, cite, count, detail, document, enumerate, individualize, instance, inventory, lay out, list, mention, number, particularize, quote, recite, record, recount, rehearse, relate, set out, specify, spell out, tally; SEE CONCEPTS 57,125

itinerant [adj] roaming
afoot, ambulant, ambulatory, floating, gypsy, journeying, migratory, moving, nomadic, on foot, peripatetic, ranging, riding the rails*, roving, shifting, travelling, unsettled, vagabond, vagrant, wandering, wayfaring; SEE CONCEPTS 536,584

itinerary [n] plan of travel
beat, circuit, course, guide, guidebook, journey, line, outline, path, program, route, run, schedule, tour, way; SEE CONCEPTS 281,660

J

jab [n/v] poke
blow, buck, bump, bunt, dig, hit, jog, lunge,

nudge, prod, punch, push, stab, tap, thrust; SEE CONCEPT *189*

jabber [v] *talk incessantly and trivially*
babble, blather*, chatter, drivel, gab, go on and on*, jaw, mumble, murmur, mutter, prate, ramble, run off at mouth*, shoot the breeze*, talk, tattle, utter, yak, yap; SEE CONCEPTS *51,56*

jacket [n] *covering*
case, casing, coat, envelope, folder, fur, hide, parka, pelt, sheath, skin, threads, tunic, wrapper, wrapping; SEE CONCEPTS *451,484*

jaded [adj] *exhausted, indifferent*
been around, blah*, blasé, bored, cool*, done it all*, dulled, fagged, fatigued, fed up*, had it*, mellow, sated, satiated, sick of*, spent, surfeited, tired, tired-out*, up to here*, wearied, weary, worn, worn-down, worn-out; SEE CONCEPTS *401,406*

jagged [adj] *ragged, notched*
asperous, barbed, broken, cleft, craggy, denticulate, harsh, indented, irregular, pointed, ridged, rough, rugged, scabrous, serrated, snaggy, spiked, toothed, uneven, unlevel, unsmooth; SEE CONCEPTS *490,606*

jail [n] *place for incarceration*
bastille, black hole*, brig, bullpen*, can*, cell, clink*, cooler*, detention camp, house of correction, inside*, jailhouse, joint*, lockup, pen, penal institution, penitentiary, pound, prison, rack*, reformatory, slammer*, solitary*, stir*, stockade, up the river*; SEE CONCEPTS *439, 449,516*

jail [v] *incarcerate*
bastille, book, cage, can*, confine, constrain, detain, hold, immure, impound, imprison, lock up, prison, put away*, put behind bars*, put on ice*, railroad*, send up*, sentence, take away*, throw away the keys*, throw in dungeon, throw the book at*; SEE CONCEPT *547*

jam [n] *troublesome situation*
bind, box, corner, difficulty, dilemma, fix, hole, hot water*, pickle*, plight, predicament, problem, quandary, scrape, spot, strait, trouble; SEE CONCEPT *674*

jam [v] *squeeze in; compress*
bear, bind, block, cease, clog, congest, cram, crowd, crush, elbow, force, halt, jam-pack, jostle, obstruct, pack, press, push, ram, squash, squish, stall, stick, stuff, tamp, throng, wad, wedge; SEE CONCEPTS *121,208*

jangle [n] *cacophony of noises*
babel, clang, clangor, clash, din, dissonance, hubbub*, hullabaloo*, jar, pandemonium, racket, rattle, reverberation, roar, tumult, uproar; SEE CONCEPT *595*

jangle [v] *make clinking noises*
chime, clank, clash, clatter, conflict, disaccord, discord, disharmonize, hit a sour note*, jar, jingle, mismatch, rattle, vibrate; SEE CONCEPT *65*

janitor [n] *person who cleans and maintains*
attendant, caretaker, cleaning person, concierge, custodian, doorkeeper, doorperson, gatekeeper, house sitter, porter, sitter, super, superintendent, sweeper, watchperson; SEE CONCEPT *348*

jar [n1] *container*
basin, beaker, bottle, burette, can, chalice, crock, cruet, decanter, ewer, flagon, flask, jug, pitcher, pot, tun, urn, vase, vat, vessel; SEE CONCEPT *494*

jar [n2] *shocking hit*
bump, clash, collision, concussion, crash, impact, jolt, jounce, rock, smash, succussion, thud, thump; SEE CONCEPT *189*

jar [v1] *shock, jolt*
agitate, bang, bounce, bump, clash, convulse, crash, disturb, grate, grind, hit, irritate, jerk, jiggle, jounce, jump, offend, quake, rasp, rattle, rock, shake, slam, thump, tremor, vibrate, wiggle, wobble; SEE CONCEPTS *65,189*

jar [v2] *clash, disharmonize*
annoy, bicker, contend, disaccord, disagree, discompose, discord, grate, grind, interfere, irk, irritate, jangle, mismatch, nettle, oppose, outrage, quarrel, shock, wrangle; SEE CONCEPTS *7,19*

jargon [n] *specialized language; dialect*
abracadabra*, argot, balderdash*, banality, bombast, bunk*, buzzwords*, cant, cliché, colloquialism, commonplace term, doublespeak, drivel, fustian, gibberish, hackneyed term, idiom, insipidity, lexicon, lingo*, mumbo jumbo*, neologism, newspeak, nonsense, overused term, palaver, parlance, patois, patter, rigmarole, shoptalk, slang, slanguage*, speech, stale language, street talk*, tongue, trite language, twaddle*, usage, vernacular, vocabulary; SEE CONCEPTS *275,276*

jaundiced [adj] *tainted, prejudiced*
biased, bigoted, bitter, colored, cynical, disapproving, distorted, envious, grudging, hostile, intolerant, jealous, one-sided, opprobrious, partial, partisan, preconceived, prepossessed, resentful, skeptical, spiteful, suspicious, tendentious, unfair, unfriendly, unindifferent, warped, yellow; SEE CONCEPTS *401,403,542*

jaunt [n] *expedition*
adventure, airing, amble, beat, canter, circuit, constitutional, course, cruise, drive, excursion, frolic, gallop, hike, jog, journey, junket, march, outing, patrol, peregrination, picnic, promenade, prowl, ramble, ride, round, roundabout, run, safari, sally, saunter, stroll, tour, tramp, travel, trek, trip, turn, voyage, walk; SEE CONCEPTS *159,195,224*

jaunty [adj] *lively*
airy, animated, bold, brash, breezy, buoyant, carefree, careless, cocky, dapper, dashing, debonair, devilish, devil-may-care*, easy, exhilarated, flip*, flippant, forward, free, fresh, frisky, frolicsome, gamesome, gay, high-spirited, hilarious, impetuous, impish, impudent, jocose, joking, jolly, jovial, light, natty, nervy, perky, playful, prankish, provocative, reckless, rollicking, self-confident, showy, smart, sporty, sporty, sprightly, spruce, swaggering, trim, venturesome, vivacious; SEE CONCEPTS *401,404*

jaw [n] *bones of chin*
bone, chops*, jowl, mandible, maxilla, mouth, muzzle*, orifice; SEE CONCEPT *392*

jaw [v1] *talk a lot*
babble, chat, chatter, gab*, gossip, jabber, lecture, orate, prate, prattle, yak; SEE CONCEPTS *51,56*

jaw [v2] *criticize*
abuse, baste, berate, blame, call on the carpet*, censure, rail, rate, revile, scold, tongue-lash*, upbraid, vituperate; SEE CONCEPT *52*

jazzy [adj] *fancy*
animated, exciting, flashy, gaudy, lively, salacious, sexy, smart, snazzy*, spirited, vivacious, wild, zestful, zippy*; SEE CONCEPTS *537,589*

ir
ja

jealous [adj] *desirous; wary*
anxious, apprehensive, attentive, begrudging, covetous, demanding, doubting, emulous, envious, envying, grabby, grasping, green-eyed, grudging, guarded, intolerant, invidious, jaundiced, mistrustful, monopolizing, possessive, possessory, protective, questioning, resentful, rival, skeptical, solicitous, suspicious, vigilant, watchful, zealous; SEE CONCEPTS *403,542*

jeer [v] *heckle*
banter, comeback, contemn, deride, dig*, fleer, flout, gibe, hector, hoot, jab, jest, laugh at, make a crack*, mock, poke fun, put down, put on, quip, ridicule, scoff, sneer, snipe, taunt; SEE CONCEPT *54*

jell [v] *coagulate*
clot, cohere, come together, condense, congeal, crystallize, finalize, form, freeze, gel, gelate, gelatinize, harden, jellify, jelly, materialize, set, solidify, stick, stiffen, take shape, thicken; SEE CONCEPTS *250,469*

jeopardy [n] *danger, trouble*
accident, chance, double-trouble*, endangerment, exposure, hazard, insecurity, liability, on the line*, on the spot*, out on a limb*, peril, precariousness, risk, venture, vulnerability; SEE CONCEPT *675*

jerk [n1] *a lurching move*
bounce, bump, flick, flop, jolt, pull, quake, quiver, shiver, snag, thrust, tug, tweak, twitch, wiggle, wrench, wriggle, yank; SEE CONCEPTS *80,149,150*

jerk [n2] *stupid, bumbling person*
brute, fool, idiot, nincompoop, ninny, oaf, rascal; SEE CONCEPT *423*

jerk [v] *move with lurch*
bounce, bump, dance, flick, fling, flip, flop, grab, hook, hurtle, jolt, lug, pluck, pull, quake, quiver, seize, shiver, shrug, sling, snag, snatch, throw, thrust, tug, tweak, twitch, vellicate, whisk, wiggle, wrench, wrest, wriggle, wring, yank; SEE CONCEPTS *150,152*

jest [n] *joke*
banter, bon mot, crack, fun, funny, gag, game, hoax, jive, jolly, laugh, one-liner*, play, pleasantry, prank, quip, rib, rib-tickler*, ridicule, sally, spoof, sport, wisecrack, witticism; SEE CONCEPT *273*

jest [v] *joke*
banter, chaff, deride, flout, fool, fun*, gibe*, gird*, jeer, jive*, jolly*, josh*, kid, mock, needle*, put on, quip, rag*, razz*, rib*, roast*, scoff, sneer, spoof, tease; SEE CONCEPT *273*

jester [n] *person who jokes, plays jokes*
actor, antic, banterer, buffoon, card*, clown, comedian, comic, cutup*, droll, fool, harlequin, humorist, japer, joker, jokester, larker, life of the party*, madcap*, pantaloon, practical joker, prankster, quipster, standup comic, trickster, wag*, wisecracker*, wit; SEE CONCEPT *423*

jet [n1] *rush, gush of substance*
flow, fountain, spout, spray, spring, spritz, spurt, squirt, stream; SEE CONCEPTS *465,467*

jet [n2] *vehicle propelled by ejection of pressurized gas or liquid*
airbus, airplane, plane, supersonic, supersonic transport, turbo; SEE CONCEPTS *463,503*

jet [adj] *black*
atramentous, coal-black, dark, ebon, ebony, inky, midnight, obsidian, pitch-black, pitch-dark, raven, sable; SEE CONCEPT *618*

jet [v] *spurt, gush*
flow, fly, issue, pour, roll, rush, shoot, soar, spew, spout, spritz, squirt, stream, surge, travel, zoom; SEE CONCEPT *179*

jettison [v] *eject; throw overboard*
abandon, abdicate, cashier*, cast, cast off, deep-six*, discard, dump, expel, heave, hurl, junk*, maroon, reject, scrap*, shed, slough, throw away, unload*; SEE CONCEPTS *180,222*

jewel [n1] *precious stone*
baguette, bauble, bead, bijou, birthstone, brilliant, gem, gemstone, glass, gullion, hardware*, ornament, rock*, sparkler*, stone, trinket; SEE CONCEPTS *446,474,478*

jewel [n2] *something, someone precious*
charm, find, gem, genius, ideal, masterpiece, nonesuch, nonpareil, paragon, pearl*, phenomenon, phoenix*, prize, prodigy, rarity, specialty, treasure, wonder; SEE CONCEPT *671*

jewelry [n] *precious stones, metals worn as decoration*
adornment, anklet, band, bangle, bauble, beads, bijou, bracelet, brass, brooch, cameo, chain, charm, choker, costume, cross, crown, diamonds, earring, finery, frippery, gem, glass*, gold, ice*, jewel, junk*, knickknack, lavaliere, locket, necklace, ornament, pendant, pin, regalia, ring, rock, rosary, silver, solitaire, sparkler, stickpin, stone, tiara, tie pin, treasure, trinket; SEE CONCEPT *446*

jibe [v] *agree*
accord, conform, correspond, dovetail, fit, fit in, go, harmonize, match, resemble, square, tally; SEE CONCEPT *664*

jiffy [n] *instant*
breath, crack, flash, jiff*, minute, moment, second, shake*, split second*, trice, twinkling*; SEE CONCEPT *808*

jiggle [v] *bounce up and down*
agitate, bob, fidget, jerk, jig, jigger, jog, joggle, shake, shimmer, shimmy, twitch, vellicate, wiggle; SEE CONCEPTS *150,152*

jilt [v] *abandon, betray*
break off*, coquette, deceive, desert, disappoint, discard, ditch*, drop*, dump*, forsake, get rid of, leave, leave at the altar*, leave flat*, reject, throw over*; SEE CONCEPTS *195,297,384*

jingle [v] *make metallic clinking noise*
chime, chink, chinkle, clamor, clang, clatter, clink, ding, jangle, rattle, reverberate, ring, sound, tingle, tinkle, tintinnabulate; SEE CONCEPT *65*

jinx [n] *curse*
black magic, charm, enchantment, evil eye*, hex, hoodoo*, kiss of death*, nemesis, plague, spell, voodoo*; SEE CONCEPTS *230,679*

jinx [v] *curse*
bedevil, bewitch, cast a spell on, charm, condemn, damn*, enchant, give the evil eye*, hex; SEE CONCEPTS *14,192*

jitters [n] *nervousness*
anxiety, dither, fidgets, heebie-jeebies*, jumps, nerves, shakes, shivers, tenseness, willies*; SEE CONCEPTS *230,410,690*

job [n1] *employment*
activity, appointment, assignment, berth, billet, business, calling, capacity, career, chore, connection, craft, daily grind*, engagement, faculty, function, gig*, grind*, handicraft, line, liveli-

hood, means, métier, niche, nine-to-five*, occupation, office, opening, operation, place, position, post, posting, profession, pursuit, racket*, rat race*, situation, spot, stint, swindle*, task, trade, vocation, work; SEE CONCEPTS 351,360

job [n2] *task*

act, action, affair, assignment, burden, business, care, charge, chore, commission, concern, contribution, deed, devoir, duty, effort, enterprise, errand, function, matter, mission, obligation, office, operation, project, province, pursuit, responsibility, role, stint, task, taskwork, thing*, tour of duty, undertaking, venture, work; SEE CONCEPT 362

jocular/jocose/jocund [adj] *funny, playful*

amusing, blithe, camp, cheerful, comic, comical, crazy, daffy, droll, facetious, flaky*, frolicsome, gay, gleeful, happy, humorous, jesting, jokey, joking, jolly, joshing, jovial, joyous, laughable, lighthearted, lively, ludicrous, merry, mischievous, pleasant, roguish, sportive, teasing, wacky, waggish, whimsical, witty; SEE CONCEPTS 267,529

jog [v1] *activate, push*

agitate, arouse, bounce, dig, hit, jab, jar, jerk, jiggle, joggle, jolt, jostle, jounce, nudge, press, prod, prompt, punch, remind, rock, shake, shove, stimulate, stir, suggest, whack; SEE CONCEPTS 14,208

jog [v1] *run for recreation*

amble, canter, dash, dogtrot, lope, pace, sprint, trot; SEE CONCEPT 151

join [v1] *unite*

accompany, add, adhere, affix, agglutinate, annex, append, assemble, associate, attach, blend, bracket, cement, clamp, clasp, clip, coadunate, coalesce, combine, compound, concrete, conjoin, conjugate, connect, copulate, couple, entwine, fasten, fuse, grapple, hitch on, incorporate, interlace, intermix, juxtapose, knit, leash, link, lock, lump together, marry, mate, melt, mix, pair, put together, slap on, span, splice, stick together, tack on, tag on, tie, tie up, touch, weave, weld, yoke; SEE CONCEPT 747

join [v2] *affiliate with organization*

align, associate with, be in, come aboard*, consort, cooperate, enlist, enroll, enter, fall in with*, follow, go to, mingle with, pair with, plug into*, side with, sign on, sign up, take part in, take up with, team up with, throw in with*, tie up with; SEE CONCEPT 114

join [v3] *touch; border on*

abut, adjoin, be adjacent to, be at hand, be close to, be contiguous to, bound, butt, communicate, conjoin, extend, fringe, hem, lie beside, lie near, lie next to, line, march, meet, neighbor, open into, parallel, reach, rim, skirt, trench on, verge on; SEE CONCEPT 747

joint [n1] *intersection, juncture*

abutment, articulation, bend, bond, bracket, bridge, concourse, confluence, conjuncture, connection, copula, coupling, crux, elbow, hinge, hyphen, impingement, interconnection, junction, knot, link, meeting, nexus, node, point, seam, splice, suture, swivel, tangency, tie, union, vinculum; SEE CONCEPTS 393,830,831

joint [n2] *cheap hangout*

bar, club, dive*, hole in the wall*, honky-tonk*, juke joint*, roadhouse, tavern; SEE CONCEPTS 439,449

joint [adj] *shared, combined*

collective, common, communal, concerted, conjoint, conjunct, consolidated, cooperative, hand in hand, intermutual, joined, mutual, public, united; SEE CONCEPTS 577,708

jointly [adv] *as one*

accordingly, agreeably, alike, arm in arm*, coincidentally, collectively, combined, companionably, concomitantly, concurrently, conjointly, connectedly, cooperatively, en masse, hand in glove*, hand in hand*, harmoniously, in a group, in common, in company with, in concert, in conjunction, inextricably, in league, in partnership, inseparably, intimately, in unison, mutually, reciprocally, side by side*, similarly, simultaneously, synchronically, together, unitedly, with one another; SEE CONCEPT 577

joke [n1] *fun, quip*

antic, bon mot, buffoonery, burlesque, caper, caprice, chestnut*, clowning, drollery, epigram, escapade, farce, frolic, gag, gambol, game, ha-ha*, hoodwinking*, horseplay*, humor, jape, jest, lark, laugh, mischief, monkeyshine*, mummery, one-liner*, parody, payoff, play, pleasantry, prank, pun, put-on, quirk, raillery, repartee, revel, rib, sally, saw, shaggy-dog story*, shenanigan*, snow job*, sport, spree, stunt, tomfoolery, trick, vagary, whimsy, wisecrack, witticism, yarn; SEE CONCEPT 273

joke [n2] *person that is made fun of*

buffoon, butt, clown, derision, fool, goat, jackass, jestee, laughingstock, mockery, simpleton, sport, target; SEE CONCEPTS 412,423

joke [v] *kid, tease*

banter, chaff, deceive, deride, fool, frolic, fun, gambol, horse around*, jape, jest, jive*, jolly, josh, kid around, laugh, make merry, mock, needle, play, play the clown, play tricks, poke fun*, pull one's leg*, pun, put on, quip, rag, revel, rib, ridicule, roast*, spoof, sport, taunt, trick, wisecrack*; SEE CONCEPT 273

joker [n] *person who kids, teases*

actor, banana*, buffoon, card*, clown, comedian, comic, cutup*, droll, farceur, fool, funster*, gagster*, humorist, jester, jokesmith, jokester, josher*, kidder, life of the party*, prankster*, punster*, quipster*, second banana*, stand-up comic, stooge, straight person, top banana*, trickster*, wag, wisecracker*, wit; SEE CONCEPTS 352,423

jolly [adj] *laughing, joyful*

blithe, blithesome, bouncy, carefree, cheerful, chipper, chirpy, convivial, daffy, delightful, enjoyable, entertaining, festive, frolicsome, funny, gay, gladsome, gleeful, happy, hilarious, jocund, jokey, joshing, jovial, joyous, jubilant, larking, lighthearted, lots of laughs, merry, mirthful, playful, pleasant, sportive, sprightly, zippy*; SEE CONCEPTS 267,542,548

jolt [n] *surprise; sudden push*

blow, bombshell*, bounce, bump, clash, collision, concussion, double whammy*, impact, jar, jerk, jog, jounce, jump, kick, lurch, percussion, punch, quiver, reversal, setback, shake, shock, shot, start, surprise, thunderbolt; SEE CONCEPTS 42,208

jolt [v] *surprise; push suddenly*

astonish, bowl over*, bump, churn, convulse, discompose, disturb, floor, jar, jerk, jog, jostle, knock, knock over*, lay out*, perturb, rock,

je
jo

shake, shake up*, shock, shove, spring something on*, stagger, start, startle, stun, throw a curve*, upset; SEE CONCEPTS 42,208

jostle [v] *bump, shake*
bang into, bulldoze*, bump heads*, butt*, crash, crowd, elbow, hustle, jab, jog, joggle, jolt, nudge, press, push, push around, push aside, rough and tumble*, scramble, shoulder, shove, squeeze, thrust; SEE CONCEPTS 152,189,208

journal [n] *chronicle*
account, almanac, annals, annual, calendar, chronology, comic book, daily, daybook, diary, gazette, ledger, log, magazine, memento, memoir, minutes, monthly, newspaper, note, observation, organ, paper, periodical, publication, rag, record, register, reminder, reminiscence, review, scandal sheet*, statement, tabloid, weekly; SEE CONCEPTS 271,280,801

journalist [n] *person who writes about factual events for a living*
announcer, broadcaster, columnist, commentator, contributor, correspondent, cub, editor, hack, media person, newspaper person, newsperson, pencil pusher*, press, publicist, reporter, scribe, scrivener, stringer*, television commentator, writer; SEE CONCEPTS 348,356

journey [n] *excursion*
adventure, airing, beat, campaign, caravan, circuit, constitutional, course, crossing, drive, expedition, exploration, hike, itinerary, jaunt, junket, march, migration, odyssey, outing, passage, patrol, peregrination, pilgrimage, progress, promenade, quest, ramble, range, roaming, round, route, run, safari, sally, saunter, sojourn, stroll, survey, tour, tramp, transit, transmigration, travel, traveling, traverse, trek, trip, vagabondage, vagrancy, venture, visit, voyage, wandering, wayfaring; SEE CONCEPT 224

journey [v] *travel*
circuit, cruise, fare, fly, globe trot*, go, go places, hie, hop, jaunt, jet, junket, knock about*, pass, peregrinate, proceed, process, push on, ramble, range, repair, roam, rove, safari, take a trip, tour, traverse, trek, voyage, wander, wend; SEE CONCEPT 224

jovial [adj] *happy*
affable, airy, amiable, animated, bantering, blithe, blithesome, bouncy, buoyant, chaffing, cheery, chipper, chirpy, companionable, conversable, convivial, cordial, daffy*, delightful, dizzy*, enjoyable, facetious, festal, festive, gay, glad, gleeful, good-natured, hilarious, humorous, jocose, jocund, jokey, jolly, jollying, joshing, jubilant, larking, lighthearted, loony, lots of laughs*, merry, mirthful, nutty*, off-the-wall*, pleasant, sociable; SEE CONCEPTS 401,403

joy [n] *great happiness, pleasure*
alleviation, amusement, animation, bliss, charm, cheer, comfort, delectation, delight, diversion, ecstasy, elation, exaltation, exulting, felicity, festivity, frolic, fruition, gaiety, gem, gladness, glee, good humor, gratification, hilarity, humor, indulgence, jewel, jubilance, liveliness, luxury, merriment, mirth, pride, pride and joy, prize, rapture, ravishment, refreshment, regalement, rejoicing, revelry, satisfaction, solace, sport, transport, treasure, treat, wonder; SEE CONCEPTS 410,529

joyful/joyous [adj] *happy*
blithesome, cheerful, cheery, delighted, ecstatic, effervescent, elated, enjoyable, enraptured, ex-

pansive, festive, flying*, gay, glad, gladsome, gratified, heartening, high*, high as a kite*, jubilant, lighthearted, merry, overjoyed, pleased, pleasurable, popping*, rapturous, satisfied, sunny*, sunny-side up*, transported, upbeat; SEE CONCEPTS 403,542,548

joyless [adj] *unhappy*
black, bleak, blue, cheerless, dejected, depressant, depressed, depressing, dismal, dispirited, dispiriting, doleful, downcast, down in the mouth*, dragged, dreary, droopy, gloomy, have the blahs*, heavy*, low, melancholic, melancholy, miserable, mopey, mournful, sad, saddening, somber; SEE CONCEPTS 403,542,548

jubilant [adj] *happy*
celebrating, doing handsprings*, elated, enraptured, euphoric, excited, exuberant, exultant, exulting, flipping, flying*, glad, gleeful, joyous, overjoyed, pleased, rejoicing, rhapsodic, thrilled, tickled*, triumphal, triumphant; SEE CONCEPTS 401,403

judge [n] *person who arbitrates*
adjudicator, appraiser, arbiter, assessor, authority, bench, chancellor, conciliator, court, critic, evaluator, expert, honor, inspector, intercessor, intermediary, interpreter, judiciary, justice, justice of peace, legal official, magister, magistrate, marshal, moderator, negotiator, peacemaker, reconciler, referee, umpire, warden; SEE CONCEPT 355

judge [v] *make decision from evidence; deduce*
act on, adjudge, adjudicate, appraise, appreciate, approximate, arbitrate, arrive, ascertain, assess, check, collect, conclude, condemn, consider, criticize, decide, decree, deduct, derive, determine, discern, distinguish, doom, draw, esteem, estimate, evaluate, examine, find, gather, give a hearing, make, make out, mediate, pass sentence, place, pronounce sentence, put, rate, reckon, referee, resolve, review, rule, sentence, settle, sit, size up, suppose, test, try, umpire, value; SEE CONCEPTS 18,317

judgment [n1] *common sense*
acumen, acuteness, apprehension, astuteness, awareness, brains, capacity, comprehension, discernment, discrimination, experience, genius, grasp, incisiveness, ingenuity, intelligence, intuition, keenness, knowledge, mentality, penetration, perception, percipience, perspicacity, prudence, quickness, range, rationality, reach, readiness, reason, reasoning, sagacity, sanity, sapience, savvy, sense, sharpness, shrewdness, sophistication, soundness, taste, understanding, wisdom, wit; SEE CONCEPTS 37,409

judgment [n2] *decision about blame*
analysis, appraisal, appreciation, arbitration, assaying, assessment, award, belief, close study, conclusion, contemplation, conviction, decree, deduction, determination, estimate, estimation, evaluation, examination, exploration, finding, idea, inference, inquest, inquiry, inquisition, inspection, observation, opinion, order, probing, pursuit, quest, reconnaissance, regard, report, research, resolution, result, review, ruling, scrutiny, search, sentence, sifting, summary, verdict, view, weigh-in; SEE CONCEPTS 103,689

judgment [n3] *doom, fate*
affliction, castigation, chastisement, correction, damnation, infliction, manifestation, misfortune,

mortification, punishment, retribution, visitation; SEE CONCEPT *679*

judicial [*adj*] *legal*
administrative, authoritative, constitutional, discriminating, distinguished, equitable, forensic, impartial, judgelike, judiciary, juridical, jurisdictional, juristic, lawful, legalistic, magisterial, official, pontifical, principled, regular, statutory; SEE CONCEPT *319*

judicious [*adj*] *wise, thoughtful*
accurate, acute, astute, calculating, careful, cautious, circumspect, clear-sighted, considerate, considered, diplomatic, discerning, discreet, discriminating, efficacious, enlightened, expedient, far-sighted, informed, judicial, keen, perceptive, perspicacious, politic, profound, prudent, quick-witted, rational, reasonable, sagacious, sage, sane, sapient, seasonable, seemly, sensible, sharp, shrewd, skillful, sober, sophisticated, sound, thorough, wary, well-advised, well-judged, worldly-wise; SEE CONCEPTS *402,403,542*

jug [*n*] *container for liquid*
amphora, beaker, bottle, bucket, canteen, carafe, crock, cruet, decanter, ewer, flagon, flask, growler, hooker, jar, pitcher, pot, tub, urn, vase, vessel; SEE CONCEPT *494*

juggle [*v*] *mislead, falsify; handle several things at once*
alter, beguile, betray, bluff, change, conjure, delude, disguise, judiciary, double-cross, fix, humbug*, illude, maneuver, manipulate, misrepresent, modify, perform magic, prestidigitate, shuffle, take in, tamper with, trim; SEE CONCEPTS *59,63*

juice [*n*] *liquid squeezed from fruit, plant*
abstract, alcohol, aqua vitae, distillation, drink, essence, extract, fluid, liquor, milk, nectar, oil, sap, sauce, secretion, serum, spirit, syrup, water; SEE CONCEPTS *428,467*

juicy [*adj1*] *moist*
dank, dewy, dripping, humid, liquid, luscious, lush, mellow, oily, oozy, pulpy, sappy, saturated, sauced, slippery, slushy, soaked, sodden, succulent, syrupy, viscid, watery, wet; SEE CONCEPT *603*

juicy [*adj2*] *exciting, interesting*
colorful, fascinating, intriguing, piquant, provocative, racy, risqué, sensational, spicy, suggestive, tantalizing, vivid; SEE CONCEPTS *537,548*

jumble [*n*] *hodgepodge*
assortment, chaos, clutter, confusion, derangement, disarrangement, disarray, disorder, farrago, gallimaufry, garbage, goulash, hash*, litter, medley, mélange, mess, miscellany, mishmash, mixture, muddle, olio, pastiche, patchwork, potpourri, salmagundi, scramble, shuffle, snarl, tangle, tumble; SEE CONCEPT *432*

jumble [*v*] *mix up, confuse*
clutter, confound, derange, disarrange, disarray, dishevel, disorder, disorganize, disturb, entangle, foul up, mess up, mistake, muddle, rummage, shuffle, snarl, tangle, tumble; SEE CONCEPTS *16,84*

jumbo [*adj*] *gigantic*
colossal, cyclopean, elephantine, giant, huge, immense, large, mammoth, mighty, oversized, prodigious; SEE CONCEPT *781*

jump [*n1*] *leap*
bob, bounce, bound, buck, canter, caper, capriole, dance, dive, drop, fall, gambade, gambol,

hop, hopping, hurdle, jar, jerk, jolt, leapfrog, leapfrogging, leaping, lurch, nosedive, plummet, plunge, pounce, rise, saltation, shock, skip, skipping, spring, start, swerve, twitch, upspring, upsurge, vault, wrench; SEE CONCEPT *194*

jump [*n2*] *increase, advantage*
advance, ascent, augmentation, boost, handicap, head start, increment, inflation, rise, spurt, start, upper hand, upsurge, upturn; SEE CONCEPTS *704,763*

jump [*n3*] *obstacle*
bar, barricade, barrier, fence, hurdle, impediment, rail, stretch; SEE CONCEPTS *470,674*

jump [*v1*] *leap, spring*
bail out, barge, bob, bounce, bound, buck, canter, caper, clear, curvet, dive, drop, fall, gambol, hop, hurdle, hurtle, jerk, jiggle, jounce, lollop, lop, lunge, lurch, parachute, plummet, pop, quiver, rattle, ricochet, saltate, shake, skip, sky, somersault, surge, take, top, trip, vault, waver, wobble; SEE CONCEPT *194*

jump [*v2*] *recoil*
bob, bolt, bounce, carom, flinch, jerk, jounce, rebound, ricochet, spring, start, startle, wince; SEE CONCEPT *213*

jump [*v3*] *omit, avoid*
abandon, cancel, clear out, cover, cross out, digress, evade, leave, miss, nullify, overshoot, pass over, skip, switch; SEE CONCEPT *25*

jump [*v4*] *increase*
advance, ascend, boost, escalate, gain, hike, jack up, mount, put up, raise, rise, surge, up; SEE CONCEPTS *236,245,763*

jumpy [*adj*] *nervous*
agitated, antsy*, anxious, apprehensive, creepy*, excitable, excited, fidgety, frisky, high-strung*, jittery, on edge*, on pins and needles*, restless, sensitive, shaky, skittish, spooked, tense, timorous, unrestful; SEE CONCEPTS *401,690*

junction/juncture [*n1*] *link, connection*
alliance, annexation, articulation, assemblage, attachment, bond, coalition, coherence, collocation, combination, combine, concatenation, concourse, concursion, confluence, conjugation, consolidation, convergence, coupling, crossing, crossroads, dovetail, elbow, gathering, gore, hinge, hookup, interface, intersection, joining, joint, knee, linking, meeting, miter, mortise, node, pivot, plug-in, reunion, seam, splice, terminal, tie-in, tie-up, union, weld; SEE CONCEPTS *746,830*

juncture [*n2*] *turning point*
choice, circumstance, condition, contingency, crisis, crossroad, crux, emergency, exigency, instant, meeting point, moment, occasion, pass, pinch, plight, point, position, posture, predicament, quandary, state, status, strait, time, zero hour*; SEE CONCEPTS *388,693,815*

jungle [*n*] *wilderness full of plant and animal life*
boscage, bush, chaparral, forest, labyrinth, maze, morass, primeval forest, tangle, undergrowth, wasteland, web, wood, zoo; SEE CONCEPT *517*

junior [*adj*] *subordinate, younger*
inferior, lesser, lower, minor, second, secondary, second-string*; SEE CONCEPTS *574,578,797*

junk [*n*] *odds and ends; garbage*
clutter, collateral, debris, filth, hogwash*, litter, miscellany, offal, refuse, rubbish, rubble, rummage, salvage, scrap, trash, waste; SEE CONCEPTS *260,432*

jo
ju

jurisdiction [n] *area of authority*
administration, arbitration, area, authority, bailiwick, bounds, circuit, command, commission, compass, confines, control, discretion, district, domination, dominion, empire, extent, field, hegemony, influence, inquisition, judicature, limits, magistracy, might, orbit, power, prerogative, province, purview, range, reach, reign, right, rule, say, scope, slot, sovereignty, sphere, stomping grounds*, supervision, sway, territory, turf*, zone; SEE CONCEPTS 198,376,651

jury [n] *panel that hears legal matter*
board, judges, peers, tribunal; SEE CONCEPTS 299,318

just [adj1] *fair, impartial*
aloof, blameless, condign, conscientious, decent, dependable, dispassionate, due, equal, equitable, ethical, evenhanded, fair-minded, good, honest, honorable, lawful, nondiscriminatory, nonpartisan, objective, pure, reliable, right, righteous, rightful, rigid, scrupulous, strict, tried, true, trustworthy, unbiased, uncolored, upright, virtuous; SEE CONCEPTS 319,545

just [adj2] *accurate, precise*
cogent, correct, exact, faithful, good, justified, normal, proper, regular, right, sound, strict, true, undistorted, veracious, veridical, well-founded, well-grounded; SEE CONCEPTS 535,582

just [adj3] *suitable, appropriate*
apt, befitting, condign, deserved, due, felicitous, fit, fitting, happy, justified, legitimate, meet, merited, proper, reasonable, requisite, right, rightful, well-deserved; SEE CONCEPT 558

just [adv1] *definitely*
absolutely, accurately, completely, directly, entirely, exactly, expressly, perfectly, precisely, right, sharp, smack-dab*, square, squarely, unmistakably; SEE CONCEPT 535

just [adv2] *only now*
almost, a moment ago, approximately, at this moment, barely, by very little, hardly, just a while ago, just now, lately, nearly, now, presently, recently, right now, scarce, scarcely; SEE CONCEPTS 544,820

just [adv3] *merely*
at most, but, no more than, nothing but, only, plainly, simply, solely; SEE CONCEPT 557

just about [adv] *almost*
about, all but, approximately, around, as good as, close to, nearly, nigh, not quite, practically, well-nigh; SEE CONCEPTS 762,771,799

justice [n1] *lawfulness, fairness*
amends, appeal, authority, authorization, charter, code, compensation, consideration, constitutionality, correction, credo, creed, decree, due process, equity, evenness, fair play, fair treatment, hearing, honesty, impartiality, integrity, judicatory, judicature, justness, law, legality, legalization, legal process, legitimacy, litigation, penalty, reasonableness, recompense, rectitude, redress, reparation, review, right, rule, sanction, sentence, square deal*, truth; SEE CONCEPTS 376,645,691

justice [n2] *person who oversees court of law*
chancellor, court, judge, magistrate, umpire*; SEE CONCEPT 354

justifiable [adj] *reasonable, well-founded*
acceptable, admissible, allowable, condonable, defensible, excusable, fair, fit, forgivable, lawful, legit*, legitimate, licit, logical, pardonable, probable, proper, reasonable, remissible, right, right-

ful, sound, suitable, tenable, understandable, valid, vindicable, warrantable; SEE CONCEPTS 545,558

justification [n] *reason, excuse*
absolution, account, acquittal, advocacy, answer, apologia, apology, approval, argument, basis, confirmation, defense, exculpation, exoneration, explanation, extenuation, grounds, idea, mitigation, palliation, palliative, plea, pretext, raison d'être, rationale, rationalization, rebuttal, redemption, reply, response, salvation, sanctification, song and dance*, story, support, validation, vindication, warrant, whatfor*, wherefore*, whitewashing*, whole idea*, why and wherefore*; SEE CONCEPT 661

justify [v] *legitimize, substantiate*
absolve, acquit, advocate, alibi*, answer for, apologize for, approve, argue for, assert, be answerable for, bear out, brief, claim, clear, condone, confirm, contend, cop a plea*, countenance, crawl, defend, do justice to, establish, exculpate, excuse, exonerate, explain, favor, legalize, maintain, make allowances, make good*, palliate, pardon, plead, rationalize, rebut, show cause, speak in favor, square, stand up for, support, sustain, uphold, validate, verify, vindicate, warrant; SEE CONCEPTS 49,57

justly [adv] *fairly*
accurately, befittingly, beneficently, benevolently, benignly, candidly, charitably, correctly, decently, decorously, duly, duteously, dutifully, equally, equitably, evenhandedly, fitly, fittingly, frankly, helpfully, honestly, honorably, impartially, lawfully, legally, legitimately, moderately, nicely, piously, properly, reasonably, respectably, righteously, rightfully, rightly, straightforwardly, temperately, tolerantly, unreservedly, uprightly, virtuously, well; SEE CONCEPTS 544,545

jut [v] *extend*
beetle, bulge, elongate, impend, lengthen, overhang, poke, pop, pouch, project, protrude, proberate, stand out, stick out; SEE CONCEPT 201

juvenile [n] *young person*
adolescent, boy, child, girl, infant, kid*, minor, youngster, youth; SEE CONCEPT 424

juvenile [adj] *childish*
adolescent, babyish, beardless, blooming, boyish, budding, callow, childlike, developing, formative, fresh, girlish, green, growing, immature, inexperienced, infant, infantile, jejune, junior, kid stuff*, milk-fed*, naive, pubescent, puerile, teenage, tender, undeveloped, unfledged, unripe, unsophisticated, unweaned, vernal, young, younger, youthful; SEE CONCEPTS 401,578,797

K

keel over [v] *fall, faint*
black out, capsize, collapse, drop, founder, go down, overturn, pass out, pitch, plunge, slump, swoon, topple, tumble, upset; SEE CONCEPTS 152,181

keen [adj1] *enthusiastic*
agog, alert, animate, animated, anxious, appetent, ardent, athirst, avid, breathless, devoted, dying

to*, eager, earnest, ebullient, fervent, fervid, fierce, fond of, gung ho*, impassioned, impatient, intense, intent, interested, lively, perfervid, spirited, sprightly, thirsty, vehement, vivacious, warm, zealous; SEE CONCEPTS 401,403

keen [adj2] *sharp, piercing*
acid, acute, caustic, cutting, edged, extreme, fine, honed, incisive, intense, observant, penetrating, perceptive, pointed, quick-witted, razor-sharp*, sardonic, satirical, strong, tart, trenchant, un-blunted; SEE CONCEPT 267

keen [adj3] *intelligent*
astute, bright, brilliant, canny, clever, discerning, discriminating, Einstein*, know-it-all*, perceptive, perspicacious, quick, sagacious, sapient, sensitive, sharp, sharp as a tack*, shrewd, whiz, wise; SEE CONCEPT 402

keep [v1] *hold, maintain*
accumulate, amass, cache, care for, carry, conduct, conserve, control, deal in, deposit, detain, direct, enjoy, garner, grasp, grip, have, heap, hold back, manage, own, pile, place, possess, preserve, put, put up, reserve, retain, save, season, stack, stock, store, trade in, withhold; SEE CONCEPT 710

keep [v2] *tend; provide for*
administer, attend, board, care for, carry on, command, conduct, continue, defend, direct, endure, feed, foster, guard, look after, maintain, manage, mind, minister to, nourish, nurture, operate, ordain, protect, provision, run, safeguard, shelter, shield, subsidize, support, sustain, victual, watch over; SEE CONCEPTS 110,140

keep [v3] *prevent*
arrest, avert, block, check, constrain, control, curb, delay, detain, deter, hamper, hamstring, hinder, hold back, impede, inhibit, limit, obstruct, restrain, retard, shackle, stall, stop, withhold; SEE CONCEPT 121

keep [v4] *commemorate; pay attention to*
adhere to, bless, celebrate, comply with, consecrate, fulfill, hold, honor, laud, obey, observe, perform, praise, regard, respect, ritualize, sanctify, solemnize; SEE CONCEPT 377

keep at [v] *continue, endure*
be steadfast, carry on, complete, drudge, finish, grind, labor, last, maintain, persevere, persist, remain, slave, stay, stick, toil; SEE CONCEPTS 23,87

keepsake [n] *something precious*
emblem, favor, memento, memorial, relic, remembrance, reminder, souvenir, symbol, token, trophy; SEE CONCEPT 446

keep up [v] *maintain, sustain*
balance, compete, contend, continue, emulate, go on, hold on, keep pace, keep step, match, pace, persevere, preserve, rival, run with, vie; SEE CONCEPTS 23,87,363

keg [n] *barrel*
butt, cask, container, drum, firkin, hogshead, pipe, tub, tun, vat; SEE CONCEPT 494

kernel [n] *seed, essence*
atom, bit, center, core, crux, fruit, germ, gist, grain, heart, hub, keynote, marrow, matter, meat, morsel, nub, nubbin, nut, part, piece, pith, root, substance, upshot; SEE CONCEPTS 668,826

key [n1] *item that unlocks*
latchkey, opener, passkey, screw*, skeleton; SEE CONCEPT 499

key [n2] *answer, solution*
blueprint, brand, cipher, clue, code, core, crux,

cue, earmark, explanation, fulcrum, guide, hinge, index, indicator, interpretation, lead, lever, marker, means, nexus, nucleus, passport, password, pivot, pointer, root, sign, symptom, ticket, translation; SEE CONCEPTS 274,668

key [adj] *essential, important*
basic, chief, crucial, decisive, fundamental, indispensable, leading, main, major, material, pivotal, primary, principal, vital; SEE CONCEPT 568

keynote/keystone [n] *essence, theme*
basic idea, basis, center, core, cornerstone, criterion, crux, gist, heart, idea, kernel, linchpin, mainspring, marrow, measure, motive, nub, pith, principle, root, source, spring, standard, substance; SEE CONCEPTS 532,661,688

kick [n1] *thrill, enjoyment*
bang*, buzz*, excitement, fun, gratification, hoot*, joy, pleasure, refreshment, sensation, stimulation, wallop*; SEE CONCEPTS 388,410

kick [n2] *power, strength*
backlash, blow, boot*, force, intensity, jar, jolt, pep, punch, pungency, snap, sparkle, tang, verve, vitality, zest, zing*; SEE CONCEPTS 641,732

kick [v1] *hit with foot*
boot, calcitrate, dropkick, give the foot, jolt, punt; SEE CONCEPT 189

kick [v2] *complain*
anathematize, carp, combat, condemn, criticize, curse, damn, except, execrate, expostulate, fight, fuss, gripe, grumble, inveigh, mumble, object, oppose, protest, rebel, remonstrate, repine, resist, spurn, wail, whine, withstand; SEE CONCEPT 52

kick [v3] *quit a habit*
abandon, desist, give up, go cold turkey*, leave off, stop; SEE CONCEPT 234

kickback [n] *bribe*
cut, gift, graft, money under the table*, oil*, payment, payoff, payola, percentage, recompense, reward, share; SEE CONCEPTS 192,344

kick out [v] *get rid of*
ax, boot*, bounce*, can*, cashier*, chase, chuck, discharge, dismiss, drop, eject, evict, expel, extrude, fire, oust, out, reject, remove, sack*, throw out, toss out; SEE CONCEPTS 180,351,384

kid [n] *young person*
baby, bairn, boy, child, daughter, girl, infant, juvenile, lad, lass, little one*, son, teenager, tot, youngster, youth; SEE CONCEPTS 414,424

kid [v] *fool, ridicule*
bamboozle*, banter, beguile, bother, cozen, delude, dupe, flimflam*, fun*, gull, hoax, hoodwink, jape, jest, joke, jolly, josh, make fun of, make sport of, mock, pretend, rag*, razz, rib, roast, spoof, tease, trick; SEE CONCEPTS 59,273

kidnap [v] *abduct; hold for ransom*
bodysnatch*, bundle off, capture, carry away, carry off, coax, decoy, entice, grab, hijack, impress, inveigh, lay hands on, lure, make off with*, pirate, remove, run away with, seduce, seize, shanghai*, skyjack, snatch, spirit away*, steal, waylay; SEE CONCEPTS 90,139

kill [v1] *deprive of existence; destroy*
annihilate, asphyxiate, assassinate, crucify, dispatch, do away with*, do in*, drown, dump, electrocute, eradicate, erase*, execute, exterminate, extirpate, finish, garrote, get*, guillotine, hang, hit*, immolate, liquidate, lynch, massacre, murder, neutralize, obliterate, off*, poison, polish off*, put away*, put to death, rub out*, sacrifice, slaughter, slay, smother, snuff, strangle, suffo-

ju
ki

cate, waste*, wipe out*, X-out*, zap*; SEE CONCEPT 252

kill [v2] *turn off; cancel*
annul, cease, counteract, deaden, defeat, extinguish, forbid, halt, negative, neutralize, nix*, nullify, prohibit, quash, quell, recant, refuse, revoke, ruin, scotch*, shut off, smother, stifle, still, stop, suppress, turn out, veto; SEE CONCEPTS 121,239

kin [n] *blood relative*
affinity, blood, clan, connection, consanguinity, cousin, extraction, family, folk, house, kindred, kinsfolk, kinship, kinsperson, kith, lineage, member, people, race, relation, relationship, sibling, stock, tribe; SEE CONCEPTS 296,414,421

kind [n1] *class, species*
brand, breed, classification, family, genus, ilk, kin, order, race, set, sort, type, variety; SEE CONCEPT 378

kind [n2] *type, character*
breed, complexion, connection, denomination, description, designation, essence, fiber, gender, habit, ilk, likes, lot, manner, mold, nature, number, persuasion, set, sort, stamp, stripe, style, temperament, tendency, tribe, variety, way; SEE CONCEPTS 411,673

kind [adj] *generous, good*
affectionate, all heart*, altruistic, amiable, amicable, beneficent, benevolent, benign, big, bleeding-heart*, bounteous, charitable, clement, compassionate, congenial, considerate, cordial, courteous, eleemosynary, friendly, gentle, good-hearted, gracious, heart in right place*, humane, humanitarian, indulgent, kindhearted, kindly, lenient, loving, mild, neighborly, obliging, philanthropic, propitious, softhearted, soft touch, sympathetic, tenderhearted, thoughtful, tolerant, understanding; SEE CONCEPTS 401,404,542

kindhearted [adj] *compassionate, helpful*
altruistic, amiable, amicable, considerate, generous, good, good-natured, gracious, humane, kind, merciful, responsive, softhearted, sympathetic, tender, tenderhearted, warm, warmhearted; SEE CONCEPTS 404,542

kindle [v1] *start a fire*
blaze, burn, fire, flame, flare, glow, ignite, inflame, light, set alight, set fire; SEE CONCEPT 249

kindle [v2] *excite, incite*
agitate, animate, arouse, awaken, bestir, burn up*, challenge, egg on*, enkindle, exasperate, fire up*, foment, get smoking*, induce, inflame, inspire, key up*, provoke, rally, rouse, sharpen, stimulate, stir, thrill, turn on*, wake, waken, whet, work up*; SEE CONCEPTS 7,14,22,221

kindly [adj] *compassionate, helpful*
attentive, beneficial, benevolent, benign, benignant, cool, cordial, favorable, friendly, generous, genial, gentle, good, good-hearted, good-natured, gracious, hearty, humane, kind, kindhearted, mellow, merciful, mild, neighborly, pleasant, polite, sociable, sympathetic, thoughtful, warm; SEE CONCEPTS 404,542

kindly [adv] *with compassion*
affectionately, agreeably, benevolently, benignly, carefully, charitably, compassionately, considerately, cordially, courteously, delicately, generously, genially, good-naturedly, graciously, heedfully, helpfully, humanely, politely, solicitously, sympathetically, tenderly, thoughtfully, tolerantly, understandingly, well; SEE CONCEPTS 542,544

kindness [n1] *compassion, generosity*
affection, altruism, amiability, beneficence, benevolence, charity, clemency, consideration, cordiality, courtesy, decency, delicacy, fellow feeling, forbearance, gentleness, good intention, goodness, good will, grace, graciousness, heart, helpfulness, hospitality, humanity, indulgence, kindliness, magnanimity, mildness, patience, philanthropy, serviceability, solicitousness, solicitude, sweetness, sympathy, tact, tenderness, thoughtfulness, tolerance, understanding, unselfishness; SEE CONCEPTS 633,657

kindness [n2] *helping act; service*
accommodation, aid, alms, assistance, benediction, benefaction, benevolence, benison, blessing, boon, boost, bounty, charity, dispensation, favor, generosity, good deed, good turn, help, indulgence, lift, mercy, philanthropy, relief, succor; SEE CONCEPTS 110,657

kindred [n] *blood relative*
affinity, blood, clan, connection, consanguinity, cousin, family, flesh, folk, homefolk, house, kin, kinsfolk, kinsperson, lineage, race, relation, relationship, stock, tribe; SEE CONCEPTS 296,414,421

kindred [adj] *corresponding, matching*
affiliated, agnate, akin, alike, allied, analogous, cognate, congeneric, congenial, connate, connatural, consanguine, germane, homogeneous, incident, kin, likable, parallel, related, similar; SEE CONCEPT 563

kingdom [n] *historically, an area ruled by a monarch*
commonwealth, country, county, crown, division, domain, dominion, dynasty, empire, field, lands, monarchy, nation, possessions, principality, province, realm, reign, rule, scepter, sovereignty, sphere, state, suzerainty, sway, territory, throne, tract; SEE CONCEPTS 508,510

kink [n1] *bend, twist*
coil, corkscrew, crimp, crinkle, curl, curve, entanglement, frizz, knot, loop, tangle, wrinkle; SEE CONCEPT 436

kink [n2] *spasm of muscular tissue*
charley horse*, cramp, crick, knot, muscle spasm, pain, pang, pinch, stab, stitch, tweak, twinge; SEE CONCEPTS 185,728

kink [n3] *complication*
defect, difficulty, flaw, hitch, impediment, imperfection, knot, tangle; SEE CONCEPT 674

kink [n4] *person's idiosyncrasy*
eccentricity, fetish, foible, notion, peculiarity, quirk, singularity, vagary, whim; SEE CONCEPT 411

kinky [adj1] *twisted*
coiled, crimped, curled, curly, frizzled, frizzy, knotted, matted, matty, rolled, tangled; SEE CONCEPT 486

kinky [adj2] *bizarre, perverted*
degenerated, depraved, deviant, eccentric, far-out, licentious, odd, outlandish, outre, peculiar, queer, quirky, sick, strange, unconventional, unnatural, unusual, warped, weird; SEE CONCEPTS 372,542,580

kiss [n] *touching lips to another*
butterfly*, caress, embrace, endearment, osculation, peck, salutation, salute, smack*, smooch*; SEE CONCEPTS 185,375

kiss [v] *touch one's lips to another's*
blow, brush, butterfly*, French*, glance, graze, greet, lip*, make out*, mush*, neck*, osculate,

peck, pucker up*, salute, smack*, smooch*; SEE CONCEPTS 185,375

kit [n] *provisions, equipment*
accoutrements, apparatus, assortment, bag, collection, container, effects, gear, impedimenta, implements, material, outfit, pack, paraphernalia, rig, satchel, selection, set, stock, stuff, suitcase, supplies, tackle, things, tools, trappings, utensils; SEE CONCEPTS 494,496

kitchen [n] *room for cooking food*
canteen, cookery, cookhouse, cook's room, cuisine, eat-in, gallery, galley, kitchenette, mess, scullery; SEE CONCEPT 448

kittenish [adj] *frisky, playful*
childish, coquettish, coy, elvish, flirtatious, frolicsome, fun-loving, impish, jaunty, mischievous, sportive; SEE CONCEPT 401

knack [n] *ability, talent*
adroitness, aptitude, aptness, bent, capacity, command, dexterity, expertise, expertism, expertness, facility, faculty, flair, forte, genius, gift, handiness, hang of it*, head*, ingenuity, know-how, mastership, nose*, propensity, quickness, readiness, savvy*, set, skill, skillfulness, trick, turn; SEE CONCEPTS 409,630

knead [v] *mix by pressing*
aerate, alter, blend, form, manipulate, massage, mold, ply, press, push, rub, shape, squeeze, stroke, twist, work; SEE CONCEPTS 170,208

kneel [v] *get down on one's knees*
bow, bow down, curtsey, do obeisance, genuflect, kowtow, prostrate oneself, stoop; SEE CONCEPT 154

knickknack [n] *trinket; decorative piece*
bagatelle, bauble, bibelot, bric-a-brac, conversation piece, curio, curiosity, doodad, embellishment, flummery, frill, furbelow, gadget*, miniature, notion, novelty, objet d'art, ornament, plaything*, showpiece, souvenir, thingamajig*, toy, trapping, trifle, whatnot*, whimsy; SEE CONCEPTS 259,260,446

knife [n] *cutting tool*
bayonet, blade, bolo, cutlass, cutter, cutting edge, dagger, edge, lance, lancet, machete, point, ripper, sabre, scalpel, scimitar, scythe, shank, shiv, sickle, skewer, skiver, steel, stiletto, switchblade, sword, tickler; SEE CONCEPTS 495,499

knife [v] *stab with pointed tool*
brand, carve, chop down, clip, cut, hurt, impale, jag, kill, lacerate, lance, open up, pierce, shank, shiv, slash, slice, spit, stick, thrust, wound; SEE CONCEPTS 176,220,246

knit [v] *intertwine*
affiliate, affix, ally, bind, cable, connect, contract, crochet, fasten, heal, interlace, intermingle, join, link, loop, mend, net, purl, repair, secure, sew, spin, tie, unite, weave, web; SEE CONCEPTS 113,202,218

knob [n] *lump, handle*
bulge, bulk, bump, bunch, doorknob, hump, knot, knurl, latch, lever, nub, opener, projection, protrusion, protuberance, snag, stud, swell, swelling, trigger, tumor; SEE CONCEPTS 445,471

knock [n1] *pushing, striking*
beating, blow, box, clip, conk, cuff, hammering, hit, injury, lick, rap, slap, smack, swat, swipe, thump, whack; SEE CONCEPT 189

knock [n2] *strong criticism*
blame, censure, condemnation, defeat, failure,

flak, pan, rap, rebuff, rejection, reversal, setback, stricture, swipe; SEE CONCEPTS 52,278

knock [v1] *push over; strike*
abuse, bash, batter, beat, beat up, bob, bruise, buffet, clap, clout, cuff, damage, deck, drub*, fell, flatten, floor, hit, hurt, KO*, level, maltreat, manhandle, maul, mistreat, pound, punch, rap, roughhouse, slap, smack, tap, thrash, thump, thwack*, total, wallop, whack*, wound; SEE CONCEPT 189

knock [v2] *criticize harshly*
abuse, alive*, belittle, blame, carp, cavil, censure, condemn, denounce, denunciate, deprecate, disparage, find fault, lambaste, reprehend, reprobate, run down*, skin*, slam; SEE CONCEPT 52

knock about/knock around [v] *roam, wander*
drift, ramble, range, rove, traipse, travel, walk; SEE CONCEPTS 151,224

knock off [v1] *kill*
assassinate, do away with*, do in*, dust*, eliminate, execute, finish, liquidate, murder, rub out*, shoot, slay, stab, waste; SEE CONCEPT 252

knock off [v2] *steal*
filch, knock over, loot, pilfer, pinch, plunder, purloin, ransack, relieve, rifle, rip off*, rob, thieve; SEE CONCEPTS 139,192

knock off [v3] *stop action; accomplish*
achieve, cease, complete, conclude, desist, discontinue, eliminate, finish, give over, halt, leave off, quit, stop work, succeed, surcease, terminate; SEE CONCEPTS 119,234

knot [n1] *bow, loop*
bond, braid, bunch, coil, connection, contortion, entanglement, gnarl, helix, hitch, joint, kink, ligament, ligature, link, mat, nexus, perplexity, rosette, screw, snag, snarl, spiral, splice, tangle, tie, twirl, twist, vinculum, warp, whirl, whorl, yoke; SEE CONCEPTS 436,471

knot [n2] *lump; crowd*
aggregation, assemblage, assortment, band, bunch, circle, clique, clump, cluster, collection, company, crew, gang, gathering, group, heap, mass, mob, pack, pile, set, squad, swarm, tuft; SEE CONCEPT 432

knot [v] *weave, complicate*
bind, cord, entangle, knit, loop, secure, tat, tether, tie; SEE CONCEPTS 85,113,160

knotty [adj] *troublesome*
baffling, complex, complicated, difficult, effortful, elaborate, formidable, Gordian*, hard, intricate, involved, labyrinthine, mazy, mystifying, perplexing, problematical, puzzling, ramified, particular, rough, rugged, sophisticated, sticky*, terrible, thorny*, tough, tricky, uphill*; SEE CONCEPTS 529,565

know [v1] *understand information*
apperceive, appreciate, apprehend, be acquainted, be cognizant, be conversant in, be informed, be learned, be master of, be read, be schooled, be versed, cognize, comprehend, differentiate, discern, discriminate, distinguish, experience, fathom, feel certain, get the idea*, grasp, have, have down pat*, have information, have knowledge of, keep up on, ken, learn, notice, on top of*, perceive, prize, realize, recognize, see, undergo; SEE CONCEPTS 15,38

know [v2] *be familiar with*
associate, be acquainted with, be friends with, experience, feel, fraternize, get acquainted, have

dealings with, identify, savor, see, sustain, taste, undergo; SEE CONCEPT *384*

know-how [n] *skill, talent*
ability, adroitness, aptitude, art, background, capability, command, craft, cunning, dexterity, experience, expertise, expertness, faculty, flair, ingenuity, knack, knowledge, proficiency, savoir-faire, wisdom; SEE CONCEPTS *409,630*

knowing [adj] *experienced, aware*
alive, apprehensive, astute, awake, brainy, bright, brilliant, canny, clever, cognizant, competent, conscious, conversant, cool*, crack*, deliberate, discerning, expert, insightful, intelligent, intended, intentional, judicious, knowledgeable, observant, perceptive, percipient, qualified, quick, quick-witted, sagacious, sage, sensible, sentient, sharp, skillful, slick*, smart, sophic, sophisticated, tuned-in, vigilant, watchful, well-informed, wise, with-it, witting, worldly, worldly-wise; SEE CONCEPT *402*

knowledge [n] *person's understanding; information*
ability, accomplishments, acquaintance, apprehension, attainments, awareness, cognition, comprehension, consciousness, dirt*, discernment, doctrine, dogma, dope*, education, enlightenment, erudition, expertise, facts, familiarity, goods*, grasp, inside story*, insight, instruction, intelligence, judgment, know-how*, learning, light*, lore, observation, philosophy, picture, power*, principles, proficiency, recognition, scholarship, schooling, science, scoop*, substance, theory, tuition, wisdom; SEE CONCEPTS *274,409,529*

knowledgeable [adj] *aware, educated*
abreast, acquainted, alert, appreciative, apprised, au courant, au fait, brainy*, bright, brilliant, clever, cognizant, conscious, conversant, discerning, erudite, experienced, familiar, informed, insightful, intelligent, in the know, knowing, learned, lettered, omniscient, perceptive, plugged in*, posted, prescient, privy, quick-witted, sagacious, sage, savvy, scholarly, sensible, sharp, smart, sophic, sophisticated, tuned-in*, understanding, versed, well-informed, well-rounded, wise, with-it; SEE CONCEPT *402*

known [adj] *famous, popular*
accepted, acknowledged, admitted, avowed, celebrated, certified, common, confessed, conscious, down pat*, established, familiar, hackneyed, manifest, noted, notorious, obvious, patent, plain, proverbial, published, received, recognized, well-known; SEE CONCEPTS *529,567,576*

kook [n] *eccentric person*
crackpot, crank, crazy*, dingbat*, flake*, fruitcake*, lamebrain, lunatic, nut, screwball*, wacko*, weirdo; SEE CONCEPTS *412,423*

kowtow [v] *grovel*
bow, brownnose*, cave in*, court, cower, cringe, fawn, flatter, fold, genuflect, give in, go along with, kneel, knuckle under, lie down and roll over*, pander, prostrate, say uncle*, stoop, toe the mark*; SEE CONCEPT *384*

kudos [n] *praise, acclaim*
applause, credit, distinction, eminence, esteem, fame, flattery, glory, honor, illustriousness, laudation, notability, pat on the back*, plaudits, plum*, PR*, preeminence, prestige, prominence, puff*, pumping up*, raves*, regard, renown, repute, strokes*; SEE CONCEPTS *69,268*

L

label [n] *marker, description; brand*
characterization, classification, company, design, epithet, hallmark, identification, insignia, logo, mark, number, price mark, stamp, sticker, tag, tally, ticket, trademark; SEE CONCEPTS *268,270,284*

label [v] *mark, describe; brand*
call, characterize, class, classify, define, designate, identify, name, specify, stamp, sticker, tag, tally; SEE CONCEPTS *62,79*

labor [n1] *work, undertaking*
activity, chore, daily grind, diligence, drudgery, effort, employment, endeavor, energy, exercise, exertion, grind*, gruntwork*, industry, job, moonlight*, operation, pains*, pull, push, strain, stress, struggle, sweat, toil, travail; SEE CONCEPTS *87,100,351,360,362*

labor [n2] *person(s) performing service*
apprentice, blue collar, breadwinner, employee, hack*, hand*, hard hat*, help, helper, hireling, instrument, laborer, learner, operative, prentice, proletariat, rank and file*, toiler, worker, work force, working people; SEE CONCEPTS *325,348*

labor [n3] *childbirth process*
birth, birth pangs, childbearing, contractions, delivery, giving birth, pains, parturition, throes, travail; SEE CONCEPT *374*

labor [v] *work very hard*
bear down, cultivate, drive, drudge, endeavor, exert oneself, grind, plod, plug away*, pour it on*, slave, strain, strive, struggle, sweat, tend, toil, travail, work oneself to the bone*; SEE CONCEPTS *87,100*

labored [adj] *difficult to understand, unclear*
affected, arduous, awkward, clumsy, contrived, effortful, forced, hard, heavy, inept, maladroit, operose, overdone, overwrought, ponderous, stiff, strained, strenuous, studied, toilsome, unnatural, uphill*, weighty; SEE CONCEPT *538*

laborious [adj1] *hard, difficult*
arduous, backbreaking, burdensome, effortful, fatiguing, forced, heavy, herculean*, labored, onerous, operose, ponderous, rough go*, stiff, strained, strenuous, tiresome, toilsome, tough, tough job*, wearing, wearisome, wicked*; SEE CONCEPTS *538,565*

laborious [adj2] *hardworking*
active, assiduous, diligent, indefatigable, industrious, operose, painstaking, persevering, sedulous, tireless, unflagging; SEE CONCEPTS *538,550*

labyrinth [n] *maze, complexity*
coil, complication, convolution, entanglement, intricacy, jungle, knot, mesh, morass, perplexity, problem, puzzle, riddle, skein, snarl, tangle, web; SEE CONCEPTS *436,663,666*

lace [n1] *netted material*
appliqué, banding, border, crochet, edging, filigree, mesh, net, netting, openwork, ornament, tatting, threadwork, tissue, trim, trimming; SEE CONCEPT *473*

lace [n2] *string used to connect*
band, cord, rope, shoelace, thong, thread, tie; SEE CONCEPT *475*

lace [v] *fasten, intertwine*
add, attach, bind, close, do up, fortify, interlace,

interweave, mix, plat, spike, strap, thread, tie, twine; SEE CONCEPT 113

lacerate [v] *tear, cut; wound*
claw, gash, harm, hurt, injure, jag, lance, maim, mangle, mutilate, puncture, rend, rip, score, serrate, slash, stab, torment, torture; SEE CONCEPTS 137,176,214,220,246

lack [n] *deficiency, need*
abridgement, absence, curtailment, dearth, decrease, default, defect, deficit, depletion, deprivation, destitution, distress, exigency, exiguity, inadequacy, inferiority, insufficiency, insufficiency, loss, meagerness, miss, necessity, paucity, poverty, privation, reduction, retrenchment, scantiness, scarcity, shortage, shortcoming, shortfall, shortness, shrinkage, shrinking, slightness, stint, want; SEE CONCEPTS 707,709

lack [v] *do not have*
be deficient in, be short of, be without, have need of, hurting for*, minus, miss, need, not got* out, require, too little too late*, want; SEE CONCEPTS 20,646

lackadaisical [adj] *careless, indifferent*
abstracted, apathetic, daydreaming, disinterested, dreamy, dull, energyless, enervated, faineant, halfhearted, idle, inattentive, incurious, indolent, inert, laid-back, languid, languishing, languorous, lazy, lethargic, limp, listless, moony*, passive, romantic, sentimental, slothful, spiritless, spring fever*, unconcerned; SEE CONCEPTS 403,542,544

lacking [adj] *wanting, deficient*
can't cut it*, coming up short*, defective, deprived of, flawed, impaired, inadequate, incomplete, minus, missing, needed, needing, not hacking it*, not making it*, sans, short, without; SEE CONCEPTS 546,771

lackluster [adj] *dull, lifeless*
blah*, blind, boring, colorless, dark, dead, dim, drab, draggy*, dry, flat*, ho-hum*, laid-back*, leaden, lusterless, matte, muted, nothing*, obscure, pabulum*, prosaic, sombre, unimaginative, uninspired, vanilla*, vapid, zero*; SEE CONCEPTS 542,548,617

laconic [adj] *short, to the point*
breviloquent, brief, brusque, compact, compendiary, compendious, concise, crisp, curt, pithy, sententious, short and sweet*, succinct, terse; SEE CONCEPTS 267,773,798

lacy [adj] *delicate, netlike*
elegant, fancy, filigree, fine, frilly, gauzy, gossamer, lacelike, meshy, open, ornate, patterned, sheer, thin, transparent; SEE CONCEPT 606

lad [n] *young man*
boy, buddy, child, fellow, guy, half-pint*, juvenile, kid*, runt*, schoolboy, son, stripling, youngster, youth; SEE CONCEPTS 419,424

laden [adj] *loaded down*
burdened, charged, encumbered, fraught, full, hampered, oppressed, taxed, weighed down, weighted; SEE CONCEPTS 485,538

lag [v] *move slowly; delay*
be behind, dally, dawdle, decrease, dillydally*, diminish, drag, drag one's feet*, ebb, fail, fall off, falter, flag, get no place fast*, hang back, hobble, idle, inch, inch along*, jelly, limp, linger, loiter, lose strength, lounge, plod, poke, procrastinate, put off, retard, saunter, shuffle, slacken, slouch, slow, slow up, stagger, stay, straggle, tail, tarry, tool, trail, trudge, wane; SEE CONCEPTS 151,153

lair [n] *hideout, habitat*
burrow, cave, den, earth, form, hideaway, hole, nest, pen, refuge, resting place, retreat, sanctuary; SEE CONCEPT 515

laissez-faire [n] *free enterprise, for the most part unrestrained by law*
free trade, indifference, individualism, live and let live*, neutrality, nonintervention; SEE CONCEPTS 388,691

lake [n] *inland body of water*
basin, creek, inland sea, lagoon, lakelet, loch, mere, millpond,- mouth, pond, pool, reservoir, sluice, spring, tarn; SEE CONCEPT 514

lambaste [v] *punish, beat*
assail, attack, berate, blister, bludgeon, castigate, censure, criticize, cudgel, denounce, excoriate, flay, flog, hammer, hit, lash into*, pan, pelt, pound, pummel, rake over the coals*, read the riot act*, rebuke, reprimand, rip into, roast, scathe, scold, scorch, scourge, shellac, slam, slap, slash, smear, smother, strike, thrash, trim, upbraid, wallop, whip; SEE CONCEPTS 52,54,86

lame [adj1] *unable to walk properly*
bruised, deformed, disabled, game, gimp, gimpy, halt, handicapped, hobbling, limping, pained, raw, sidelined, sore, stiff; SEE CONCEPTS 314,489

lame [adj2] *feeble, weak*
faltering, faulty, flabby, flimsy, inadequate, ineffective, inefficient, insufficient, poor, thin, unconvincing, unpersuasive, unpleasing, unsatisfactory, unsuitable; SEE CONCEPTS 558,570

lament/lamentation [n] *grief, complaint*
complaining, dirge, elegy, grieving, jeremiad, keen, keening, lament, moan, moaning, mourning, plaint, requiem, sob, sobbing, sorrow, tears, threnody, ululation, wail, wailing, weeping; SEE CONCEPTS 29,278,410

lament [v] *to mourn or grieve deeply*
bawl, beat one's breast*, bemoan, bewail, bleed, cry, deplore, eat one's heart out*, howl, hurt, kick self*, moan, rain, regret, repine, rue, sing, sob, sorrow, take it hard*, wail, weep; SEE CONCEPTS 52,54

lamentable [adj] *upsetting, miserable*
afflictive, awful, bad, calamitous, deplorable, dire, dirty, distressing, doleful, dolorous, godawful, grievous, grim, heartbreaking, hurting, lousy, low, lugubrious, meager, mean, melancholy, mournful, pitiful, plaintive, poor, regretful, rotten, rueful, sad, sorrowful, stinking, tragic, unfavorable, unfortunate, unsatisfactory, woeful, wretched; SEE CONCEPTS 529,537

laminate [v] *cover with veneer*
coat, exfoliate, face, flake, foil, foliate, layer, overlayer, plate, separate, split, stratify, veneer; SEE CONCEPT 172

lampoon [n] *parody, satire*
burlesque, caricature, invective, pasquil, pasquinade, pastiche, ridicule, roast*, send-up*, skit, squib, takedown, takeoff*; SEE CONCEPTS 263,273

lampoon [v] *ridicule, make fun of*
burlesque, caricature, jape, mock, parody, pasquinade, put on*, rail, roast*, satirize, send up*, squib, take off*, travesty; SEE CONCEPT 273

land [n] *earth's surface; ownable property*
acreage, acres, area, beach, continent, country, countryside, dirt, district, earth, estate, expanse, extent, farming, farmland, field, ground, grounds, holding, home, homeland, loam, mainland,

kn
la

manor, nation, old sod, parcel, plot, province, purlieu, quarry, quinta, ranch, real estate, realty, region, shore, sod, soil, stretch, sweep, terra firma, terrain, territory, tillage, tract; SEE CONCEPTS *508,509,510,515*

land [*v1*] *arrive, come to rest on*
alight, berth, bring in, check in, come ashore, come down, come in, come to berth, debark, descend upon, disembark, ditch, dock, drop anchor, flatten out, get down, ground, level off, light on, make land, pilot, put down, put in, set down, set on deck, settle, sit down, splash down, steer, take down, thump, touch down; SEE CONCEPTS *159,181*

land [*v2*] *achieve, acquire*
annex, bring in, gain, get, have, obtain, pick up, procure, secure, win; SEE CONCEPTS *120,706*

landlord [*n*] *owner of property leased*
freeholder, hotelier, hotelkeeper, innkeeper, lessor, property owner, proprietor, saw, squire; SEE CONCEPT *347*

landmark [*n1*] *historical or notable sight*
battleground, benchmark, bend, blaze, feature, fragment, guide, hill, mark, marker, memorial, milepost, milestone, monument, mountain, museum, promontory, remnant, ruins, souvenir, specimen, stone, survival, trace, tree, vantage point, vestige, waypost; SEE CONCEPTS *198, 284,447*

landmark [*n2*] *turning point*
crisis, event, milepost, milestone, stage, watershed, waypost; SEE CONCEPTS *696,817*

landscape [*n*] *countryside; picture of countryside*
mural, outlook, painting, panorama, photograph, prospect, scene, scenery, sketch, view, vista; SEE CONCEPTS *259,509*

language [*n*] *system of words for communication*
accent, argot, articulation, brogue, cant, communication, conversation, dialect, diction, dictionary, discourse, doublespeak*, expression, gibberish, idiom, interchange, jargon, lexicon, lingua franca, palaver, parlance, patois, phraseology, prose, signal, slang, sound, speech, style, talk, terminology, tongue, utterance, verbalization, vernacular, vocabulary, vocalization, voice, word, wording; SEE CONCEPT *276*

languid [*adj*] *drooping, dull, listless*
apathetic, blah*, blahs*, comatose, dopey, easy, energyless, enervated, faint, feeble, heavy, impassive, inactive, indifferent, inert, infirm, lackadaisical, laid-back, languishing, languorous, lazy, leaden, leisurely, lethargic, limp, moony*, nebbish, phlegmatic, pining, sickly, sleepyhead*, slow, sluggish, snoozy*, spiritless, supine, torpid, unconcerned, unenthusiastic, unhurried, uninterested, weak, weary, wimpy*; SEE CONCEPTS *403,542,584*

languish [*v*] *droop; become dull, listless*
be disregarded, be neglected, brood, conk out*, decline, desire, despond, deteriorate, die on vine*, dwindle, ebb, fade, fag, fag out, fail, faint, fizzle out, flag, go soft*, go to pieces*, grieve, hanker, hunger, knock out, long, pine, repine, rot, sicken, sigh, snivel, sorrow, suffer, tucker, waste, waste away, weaken, wilt, wither, yearn; SEE CONCEPTS *20,105,469*

lanky [*adj*] *tall and thin*
angular, attenuated, beanpole*, beanstalk*, bony, broomstick*, extenuated, gangling, gangly, gaunt, lean, meager, rangy, rawboned, scraggy,

scrawny, slender, spare, spindling, spindly, stilt, stringy, twiggy*, weedy; SEE CONCEPTS *491,779*

lap [*n*] *orbit, circuit*
circle, course, distance, loop, round, tour; SEE CONCEPTS *364,436*

lap [*v1*] *slosh, wash against*
bathe, bubble, burble, drink, gurgle, lave, lick, lip, plash, purl, ripple, sip, slap, splash, sup, swish; SEE CONCEPT *144*

lap [*v2*] *overlap*
cover, enfold, envelop, fold, imbricate, overlie, override, ride, shingle, swaddle, swathe, turn, twist, wrap; SEE CONCEPTS *172,201*

lapse [*n1*] *mistake*
blunder, breach, bungle, crime, error, failing, failure, fault, flub, foible, frailty, gaff, goof, goof-up*, indiscretion, miscue, negligence, offense, omission, oversight, screw-up*, sin, slip, slip-up, transgression, trespass, trip*, vice, violation; SEE CONCEPTS *101,674*

lapse [*n2*] *break in action*
gap, intermission, interruption, interval, lacuna, lull, passage, pause; SEE CONCEPT *807*

lapse [*n3*] *backsliding*
decadence, declension, decline, degeneration, descent, deterioration, devolution, drop, fall, recession, regression, relapse, retrogradation, retrogression; SEE CONCEPTS *230,316,388*

lapse [*v*] *become void; fall back into previous pattern*
apostatize, backslide, become obsolete, cease, decline, degenerate, descend, deteriorate, die, elapse, end, expire, go by, pass, recede, recidivate, relapse, retrograde, return, revert, run out, slide, slip, subside, terminate, weaken; SEE CONCEPTS *119,698*

larceny [*n*] *theft*
burglary, crime, lift, misappropriation, pilfering, pinch, purloining, robbery, steal, stealing, thievery, thieving, touch*; SEE CONCEPTS *139,192*

large [*adj*] *big, abundant*
ample, barn door*, blimp*, booming, broad, bulky, capacious, colossal, comprehensive, considerable, copious, enormous, excessive, exorbitant, extensive, extravagant, full, generous, giant, gigantic, goodly, grand, grandiose, great, gross, hefty, huge, humongous*, immeasurable, immense, jumbo*, liberal, massive, monumental, mountainous, plentiful, populous, roomy, sizable, spacious, stupendous, substantial, super, sweeping, thumping, tidy, vast, voluminous, whopping*, wide; SEE CONCEPTS *773,781*

largely [*adv*] *to a great extent*
abundantly, as a rule, broadly, by and large, chiefly, commodiously, comprehensively, considerably, copiously, expansively, extensively, extravagantly, generally, generously, grandly, immoderately, imposingly, in a big way, in a grand manner, lavishly, liberally, magnificently, mainly, mostly, on a large scale, overall, predominantly, primarily, principally, prodigally, prodigiously, voluminously, widely; SEE CONCEPTS *544,772*

lascivious [*adj*] *sexually aroused; displaying excessive interest in sex*
bawdy, blue, bodily, carnal, coarse, crude, evil-minded, fast*, fleshly, gross*, hard-core*, hot*, immoral, incontinent, indecent, lecherous, lewd, libertine, libidinous, licentious, low-down*, lubricious, lustful, nasty, obscene, off-color*, of-

fensive, orgiastic, pornographic, prurient, randy, raunchy*, raw, ribald, rough, salacious, scurrilous, sensual, smutty*, soft-core*, steamy, suggestive, unchaste, voluptuous, vulgar, wanton, X-rated*; SEE CONCEPTS 372,403

lash [v1] *beat, whip*

baste, batter, buffet, chastise, dash, drum, flagellate, flay, flog, hammer, hide, hit, horsewhip, knock, lam, lather, pound, pummel, scourge, smack, strap, strike, thrash, wear out, whale*; SEE CONCEPT 189

lash [v2] *criticize harshly*

abuse, attack, baste, bawl out*, belabor, berate, blister, castigate, censure, chew out*, exprobate, flay, fulminate, jaw, lambaste, lampoon, ridicule, satirize, scold, tear into*, tell off*, tongue-lash*, upbraid; SEE CONCEPT 52

last [n] *end*

close, completion, conclusion, ending, finale, finis, finish, omega, termination; SEE CONCEPT 832

last [adj] *final; newest*

aftermost, antipodal, at the end, bitter end, climactic, closing, concluding, conclusive, crowning, curtains*, definitive, determinate, determinative, end, ending, eventual, extreme, far, far-off, farthest, finishing, furthest, hindmost, lag, latest, least, lowest, meanest, most recent, once and for all*, outermost, rearmost, remotest, supreme, swan song*, terminal, ulterior, ultimate, utmost, uttermost; SEE CONCEPTS 585,778,799

lasting [adj] *enduring, unending*

abiding, constant, continual, continuing, deep-rooted, durable, endless, eternal, everlasting, forever, incessant, indelible, indissoluble, inexhaustible, inexpungible, in for the long haul*, lifelong, long-standing, long-term, old, perdurable, perennial, permanent, perpetual, persisting, stable, till the cows come home*, unceasing, undying, unremitting; SEE CONCEPTS 551,798

lastly/last [adv] *in the end*

after, after all, all in all, at last, at the end, behind, bringing up rear*, finally, in conclusion, in the rear, to conclude, to sum up, ultimately; SEE CONCEPTS 585,799

latch [n] *lock*

bar, bolt, catch, clamp, fastening, hasp, hook, padlock; SEE CONCEPTS 445,499

latch [v] *fasten with lock*

bar, bolt, cinch, close, close up, lock, make fast, secure; SEE CONCEPTS 85,160

late [adj1] *not on time*

backward, behind, behindhand, behind time, belated, blown*, delayed, dilatory, eleventh-hour*, gone, held up, hung up*, in a bind*, in the lurch*, jammed*, lagging, last-minute, missed the boat*, out of luck*, overdue, postponed, put off, remiss, slow, strapped*, tardy, too late, unpunctual; SEE CONCEPTS 548,799

late [adj2] *new*

advanced, fresh, just out, modern, recent; SEE CONCEPTS 578,797

late [adj3] *dead*

asleep, bygone, cold, deceased, defunct, departed, erstwhile, ex-*, exanimate, extinct, former, inanimate, lifeless, old, once, onetime, past, preceding, previous, quondam, sometime; SEE CONCEPT 539

late [adv] *at the last minute*

backward, behind, behindhand, behind time, be-

latedly, dilatorily, slowly, tardily, unpunctual; SEE CONCEPT 799

lately [adv] *new, recently*

afresh, anew, a short time ago, in recent times, just now, latterly, newly, not long ago, of late; SEE CONCEPT 820

latent [adj] *dormant, hidden*

abeyant, between the lines, concealed, contained, covert, hidden, idle, immature, implied, in abeyance, inactive, inert, inferential, inferred, inherent, inoperative, intrinsic, invisible, involved, lurking, passive, possible, potential, quiescent, rudimentary, secret, sleeping, smoldering, suppressed, suspended, tacit, torpid, underdeveloped, underlying, undeveloped, unexposed, unexpressed, unrealized, unripe, unseen, veiled, vestigial; SEE CONCEPTS 404,576

later [adj] *coming after*

downstream, ensuing, following, more recent, next, posterior, postliminary, proximate, subsequent, subsequential, succeeding, ulterior; SEE CONCEPT 799

later [adv] *happening after*

after, afterward, again, at another time, behind, by and by*, come Sunday*, down the line*, down the road*, in a while, infra, in time, later on, latterly, more recent, next, subsequently, succeeding, thereafter; SEE CONCEPT 799

lateral [adj] *sideways*

crabwise, edgeways, flanking, oblique, side, side-by-side, sidelong, sideward, sidewise, skirting; SEE CONCEPTS 581,583

lather [n1] *bubbles*

cream, foam, froth, head, soap, soapsuds, spume, suds, yeast; SEE CONCEPTS 260,437

lather [n2] *commotion, fuss*

agitation, bustle, clamor, confusion, dither, fever, flap*, fluster, hassle, hoopla*, hubbub*, hullaba-loo*, state, stew*, storm*, sweat*, tizzy*, tumult, turbulence, turmoil, twitter*; SEE CONCEPTS 230,388

lather [v] *cause to bubble*

beat, foam, froth, scrub, soap, wash, whip; SEE CONCEPT 165

latitude [n] *freedom, room to move; scope*

breadth, compass, elbow room, extent, independence, indulgence, laxity, leeway, liberty, license, margin, play, range, reach, room, run, run of, space, span, spread, sweep, swing, unrestrictedness, width; SEE CONCEPTS 651,739,756,788

latter [adj] *latest, concluding*

closing, eventual, final, following, hindmost, lag, last, last-mentioned, later, modern, rearmost, recent, second, terminal; SEE CONCEPTS 585,799

lattice [n] *mesh, trellis*

filigree, frame, fretwork, grating, grid, grill, latticework, net, network, openwork, reticulation, screen, structure, tracery, web; SEE CONCEPT 259

laud [v] *acclaim, praise*

admire, adore, approve, bless, boost, build up, celebrate, commend, compliment, cry up, eulogize, extol, flatter, glorify, hand it to*, honor, hymn, magnify, panegyrize, pat on the back*, revere, reverence, sing the praises of*, stroke, venerate, worship; SEE CONCEPT 69

laudable [adj] *admirable*

commendable, creditable, deserving, estimable, excellent, mean, meritable, meritorious, of note, praisable, praiseworthy, stellar, terrific, thankworthy, worthy; SEE CONCEPT 574

la
la

laudatory [adj] complimentary

acclamatory, adulatory, approbative, approbatory, approving, commendatory, encomiastic, eulogistic, flattering, laudative, panegyrical, praiseful; SEE CONCEPT 267

laugh/laughter [n] audible expression of amusement

amusement, cachinnation, cackle, chortle, chuckle, chuckling, crack-up*, crow, fit, gesture, giggle, giggling, glee, guffaw, hilarity, howling, merriment, mirth, peal, rejoicing, roar, shout, shriek, snicker, snigger, snort, sound, titter, yuck*; SEE CONCEPTS 77,185

laugh [v] expressing amusement, happiness with sound

be convulsed*, be in stitches*, break up*, burst*, cachinnate, chortle, chuckle, crack up*, crow, die laughing*, fracture*, giggle, grin, guffaw, howl, roar, roll in the aisles*, scream, shriek, snicker, snort, split one's sides*, titter, whoop*; SEE CONCEPTS 77,185

laughable [adj] easily made fun of

absurd, amusing, asinine, bizarre, camp, campy, comic, comical, derisive, derisory, diverting, droll, eccentric, entertaining, facetious, fantastic, farcical, funny, gelastic, har-har*, hilarious, humorous, inane, jocose, jocular, jokey, joshing, ludicrous, mirthful, mocking, nonsensical, preposterous, rich, ridiculous, riot, risible, scream, unusual, witty; SEE CONCEPTS 267,550

laugh at [v] ridicule

belittle, deride, hoot, jeer, lampoon, make fun of, mock, scoff, taunt; SEE CONCEPT 54

launch [v1] send off

barrage, bombard, bung, cast, catapult, discharge, dispatch, drive, eject, fire, fling, heave, hurl, lance, pitch, project, propel, send forth, set afloat, set in motion, shoot, sling, throw, toss; SEE CONCEPTS 179,222

launch [v2] begin, initiate

bow, break the ice*, break the seal*, commence, embark upon, get show on road*, inaugurate, instigate, institute, introduce, jump, kick off*, open, originate, set going, start, start ball rolling*, usher in*; SEE CONCEPT 221

laurels [n] credit, praise

acclaim, accolade, award, badge, bays, blue ribbon, commendation, crown, decoration, distinction, fame, feather in cap*, glory, gold, gold star*, kudos, prestige, recognition, renown, reward; SEE CONCEPTS 69,278,337

lavish [adj] profuse; splendid

abundant, bountiful, copious, effusive, exaggerated, excessive, extravagant, exuberant, first-class, free, generous, gorgeous, grand, immoderate, impressive, improvident, inordinate, intemperate, liberal, lush, luxuriant, luxurious, munificent, openhanded, opulent, plentiful, plush, posh, prodigal, profligate, profusive, prolific, riotous, ritzy, sumptuous, swanky, thriftless, unreasonable, unrestrained, unsparing, unstinging, wasteful, wild; SEE CONCEPTS 334,589,781

lavish [v] pamper, shower

be generous, be wasteful, deluge, dissipate, expend, fritter, give, go through, heap, pour, run through*, scatter, spend, spend money like water*, squander, thrust upon, waste; SEE CONCEPTS 110,327,341

law [n1] rules of a government, society

act, assize, behest, bidding, bylaw, canon, case,

caveat, charge, charter, code, command, commandment, constitution, covenant, decision, decree, decretum, demand, dictate, divestiture, due process, edict, enactment, equity, garnishment, injunction, institute, instruction, jurisprudence, legislation, mandate, measure, notice, order, ordinance, precedent, precept, prescript, prescription, reg, regulation, requirement, ruling, statute, subpoena, summons, warrant, writ; SEE CONCEPT 318

law [n2] standard, principle of behavior

assumption, axiom, base, canon, cause, criterion, exigency, formula, foundation, fundamental, generalization, ground, guide, maxim, origin, postulate, precept, principium, proposal, proposition, reason, regulation, rule, source, theorem, truth, usage; SEE CONCEPT 688

lawful [adj] allowable, legitimate

authorized, bona fide, canonical, card-carrying*, commanded, condign, constitutional, decreed, due, enacted, enforced, enjoined, established, innocent, judged, judicial, jural, juridical, jurisprudent, just, justifiable, kosher*, legal, legalized, legislated, legit*, legitimatized, licit, mandated, official, of right, on the level*, on the up and up*, ordained, ordered, passed, permissible, proper, protected, rightful, ruled, statutory, valid, vested, warrantable, warranted; SEE CONCEPTS 319,545

lawless [adj] reckless, ungoverned

anarchic, anarchical, anarchistic, bad, barbarous, chaotic, contumacious, criminal, despotic, disobedient, disordered, disorderly, evil, fierce, heterodox, infringing, insubordinate, insurgent, mutinous, nihilistic, noncompliant, nonconformist, piratical, rebellious, recusant, revolutionary, riotous, savage, seditious, tempestuous, terrorizing, traitorous, turbulent, tyrannous, uncivilized, uncultivated, unorthodox, unpeaceful, unrestrained, unruly, untamed, violent, warlike, wild; SEE CONCEPTS 319,545

lawn [n] cultivated area of green grass

backyard, garden, grass, grassplot, green, park, plot, terrace, yard; SEE CONCEPTS 509,513,517

lawsuit [n] case brought to court

accusation, action, argument, arraignment, assumpsit, bill, cause, claim, contest, dispute, impeachment, indictment, litigation, presentment, proceedings, prosecution, replevin, suit, trial; SEE CONCEPT 318

lawyer [n] person who is trained to counsel or argue in cases of law

advocate, attorney, attorney-at-law, barrister, counsel, counsellor, counselor, defender, jurisprudent, jurist, legal adviser, legal eagle*, legist, member of the bar, mouthpiece*, pleader, practitioner, proctor, procurator, solicitor; SEE CONCEPT 355

lax [adj] slack, remiss

any way*, asleep on job*, behindhand, broad, careless, casual, delinquent, derelict, devil-may-care*, disregardful, easygoing, flaccid, forgetful, general, imprecise, inaccurate, indefinite, indifferent, inexact, lenient, neglectful, negligent, nonspecific, oblivious, overindulgent, paying no mind*, regardless, shapeless, slipshod, sloppy, soft, unmindful, vague, yielding; SEE CONCEPTS 401,542,557

lay [adj] amateur, not trained in a religious or other profession

inexpert, nonclerical, nonprofessional, nonspe-

lay [v1] *put, place*

arrange, deposit, dispose, establish, fix, leave, locate, order, organize, plant, posit, position, repose, rest, set, set down, set out, settle, spread, stick, systematize; SEE CONCEPTS 158,201

lay [v2] *produce, advance*

adduce, allege, bear, bring forth, bring forward, cite, deposit, generate, lodge, offer, present, put forward, submit, yield; SEE CONCEPTS 66,205

lay [v3] *credit, allocate*

accredit, address, aim, allot, apply, ascribe, assess, assign, attribute, burden, cast, charge, direct, encumber, impose, impute, incline, level, point, refer, saddle, tax, train, turn, zero in*; SEE CONCEPTS 49,50,88,187

lay [v4] *design, plan*

concoct, contrive, devise, hatch, plot, prepare, work out; SEE CONCEPT 36

lay [v5] *make smooth*

allay, alleviate, appease, assuage, calm, even, flatten, flush, iron, level, plane, press, quiet, relieve, steam, still, suppress; SEE CONCEPTS 235,250

lay [v6] *bet, wager*

gamble, game, give odds, hazard, play, risk, stake; SEE CONCEPT 363

layer [n] *coating, tier*

band, bed, blanket, coat, coping, couch, course, cover, covering, film, flag, flap, floor, fold, girdle, lamina, lamination, lap, mantle, overlap, overlay, panel, ply, row, seam, sheet, slab, story, stratum, stripe, substratum, thickness, zone; SEE CONCEPTS 744,835

lay into [v] *criticize, attack*

assail, battle, belabor, fire at*, invade, lambaste, let fly at*, set about; SEE CONCEPTS 52,86

layoff [n] *dismissal from job or responsibility*

cutback, discharge, early retirement, respite, unemployment; SEE CONCEPT 351

lay off [v1] *stop doing*

cease, desist, end, give a rest, give up, halt, leave alone, leave off, let up, lie by, quit, rest, spell; SEE CONCEPTS 119,234

lay off [v2] *relieve of responsibility*

discharge, dismiss, drop, fire, let go, oust, pay off, retire early; SEE CONCEPT 351

layout [n] *physical arrangement*

blueprint, chart, design, diagram, draft, formation, geography, map, organization, outline, plan, purpose; SEE CONCEPTS 625,660

lay out [v1] *spend money*

disburse, expend, give, invest, lend, outlay, pay, put out, put up, shell out*; SEE CONCEPTS 327,341

lay out [v2] *design, plan*

arrange, chart, diagram, display, exhibit, map, outline, set out, spread out; SEE CONCEPTS 36,158,174

layperson [n] *amateur person, not trained in religious or other profession*

believer, dilettante, follower, laic, member, neophyte, nonprofessional, novice, outsider, parishioner, proselyte, recruit, secular; SEE CONCEPTS 361,423

lay up/lay by [v] *set aside, store*

accumulate, amass, build up, bury, conserve, cumulate, garner, hide, hoard, keep, lay in, preserve, put away, roll up, salt away, save, spare, store up, treasure; SEE CONCEPTS 120,134

lay up [v2] *hurt, incapacitate*

beat up, confine, disable, harm, hospitalize, injure; SEE CONCEPT 246

laziness [n] *unwillingness to work, be active*

apathy, dilatoriness, do-nothingness, dormancy, dreaminess, drowsiness, dullness, faineance, faineancy, heaviness, idleness, inactivity, indolence, inertia, inertness, lackadaisicalness, languidness, languorousness, laxness, leadenness, leisureliness, lethargy, listlessness, neglectfulness, negligence, otioseness, otiosity, passivity, remissness, slackness, sleepiness, sloth, slothfulness, slowness, sluggishness, stolidity, supineness, tardiness, torpescence, torpidness, weariness; SEE CONCEPTS 411,633

lazy [adj] *inactive, sluggish*

apathetic, asleep on the job*, careless, comatose, dallying, dilatory, drowsy, dull, flagging, idle, inattentive, indifferent, indolent, inert, lackadaisical, laggard, lagging, languid, languorous, lethargic, lifeless, loafing, neglectful, out of it*, passive, procrastinating, remiss, shiftless, slack, sleepy, slothful, slow, slow-moving, snoozy*, somnolent, supine, tardy, tired, torpid, trifling, unconcerned, unenergetic, unindustrious, unpersevering, unready, weary; SEE CONCEPTS 401,404

lead [n1] *first place, supremacy*

advance, advantage, ahead, bulge, cutting edge*, direction, edge, example, facade, front rank, guidance, head, heavy, leadership, margin, model, over, pilot, point, precedence, primacy, principal, priority, protagonist, spark, star, start, title role, top, top spot, vanguard; SEE CONCEPTS 668,693,828

lead [n2] *clue*

evidence, guide, hint, indication, proof, sign, suggestion, tip, trace; SEE CONCEPTS 274,284

lead [v1] *guide physically*

accompany, attend, be responsible for, chaperone, coerce, compel, conduct, convey, convoy, direct, drive, escort, find a way, force, get, go along with, guard, impel, induce, manage, pass along, persuade, pilot, point out, point the way, precede, prevail, protect, quarterback*, route, safeguard, see, shepherd, show, show around, show in, show the way, span, squire, steer, traverse, usher, watch over; SEE CONCEPT 187

lead [v2] *guide mentally; influence*

affect, bring, bring on, call the shots*, cause, command, conduce, contribute, convert, direct, dispose, draw, get the jump on*, go out in front*, govern, head, helm, incline, induce, introduce, manage, motivate, move, persuade, preside over, prevail, produce, prompt, quarterback*, result in, run things*, serve, shepherd, spearhead*, spur, supervise, tend, trail-blaze*; SEE CONCEPTS 68,117,221

lead [v3] *surpass*

be ahead, blaze a trail*, come first*, exceed, excel, outdo, outstrip, precede, preface, transcend, usher; SEE CONCEPT 141

lead (a life) [v4] *experience*

have, live, pass, spend, undergo; SEE CONCEPT 678

leader [n] *person who guides*

boss, captain, chief, chieftain, commander, conductor, controller, counsellor, dean, dignitary, director, doyen, eminence, exec, forerunner,

la
le

general, governor, guide, harbinger, head, herald, lead, lion*, luminary, manager, mistress, notability, notable, officer, pacesetter, pilot, pioneer, precursor, president, principal, rector, ringleader, ruler, shepherd, skipper, superintendent, superior; SEE CONCEPTS 347,354

leadership [n] *guidance*
administration, authority, capacity, command, conduction, control, conveyance, direction, directorship, domination, foresight, hegemony, influence, initiative, management, pilotage, power, preeminence, primacy, skill, superintendency, superiority, supremacy, sway; SEE CONCEPTS 376,687

leading [adj] *chief, superior*
arch, banner, champion, dominant, dominating, famous, first, foremost, governing, greatest, headmost, highest, inaugural, initial, main, noted, notorious, number one*, outstanding, popular, preeminent, premier, primary, principal, prominent, ruling, stellar, top, well-known; SEE CONCEPTS 574,585

leaf [n1] *green foliage of plant*
blade, bract, flag, foliole, frond, leaflet, needle, pad, petal, petiole, scale, stalk, stipule; SEE CONCEPT 428

leaf [n2] *page of document*
folio, paper, sheet; SEE CONCEPT 270

leaf [v] *flip through*
browse, dip into, glance, riff, riffle, run through, scan, skim, thumb; SEE CONCEPTS 72,623

leafy [adj] *abundant in foliage*
abounding, abundant, covered, green, hidden, leafed, leaved, shaded, shady, umbrageous, verdant, wooded; SEE CONCEPTS 485,583

league [n1] *association, federation*
alliance, band, bunch, circle, circuit, club, coalition, combination, combine, compact, company, confederacy, confederation, conference, consortium, crew, gang, group, guild, loop, mob, order, organization, outfit, partnership, pool, ring, society, sodality, union, unit; SEE CONCEPTS 365,381,387

league [n2] *group of a certain ability*
category, circle, class, grade, grouping, level, pigeonhole*, rank, status, tier; SEE CONCEPTS 388,630

league [v] *associate*
ally, amalgamate, band, coadjute, collaborate, combine, concur, confederate, conjoin, consolidate, cooperate, federate, join forces, unite; SEE CONCEPTS 8,10,114

leak [n] *opening; seepage through opening*
aperture, chink, crack, crevice, decrease, destruction, detriment, drip, drop, escape, expenditure, exposure, fissure, flow, hole, leakage, leaking, loss, outgoing, percolation, pit, puncture, short circuit, slip; SEE CONCEPTS 116,513

leak [v] *seep; make known*
break, come out, discharge, disclose, divulge, drip, drool, escape, exude, get out, give away, let slip*, make public, ooze, out, pass, pass on, percolate, reveal, slip, spill, spill the beans, tell, transpire, trickle; SEE CONCEPTS 60,116,179

lean [adj] *bare, thin*
angular, anorexic, barren, beanpole*, bony, emaciated, gangling, gangly, gaunt, haggard, inadequate, infertile, lank, lanky, meager, no fat, pitiful, poor, rangy, rawboned, scanty, scraggy, scrawny, shadow*, sinewy, skinny, slender, slim,

spare, sparse, stick, stilt, stringy, svelte, sylphlike, twiggy*, unfruitful, unproductive, wasted, wiry, wizened, worn; SEE CONCEPTS 485,491

lean [v1] *bend, angle toward*
bear on, beetle, be off, be slanted, bow, cant, careen, cock, curve, decline, deflect, dip, divert, drift, droop, fasten on, hang on, heel, incline, jut, list, nod, overhang, pitch, place, prop, put weight on, recline, repose, rest, rest on, roll, sag, sheer, sink, slant, slope, tilt, tip, turn, twist, veer; SEE CONCEPTS 147,201,738

lean [v2] *be disposed*
be prone, be willing, favor, gravitate toward, have propensity, incline, look, not mind, prefer, tend; SEE CONCEPT 20

lean [v3] *count, depend on*
bank on*, believe in, bet bottom dollar*, bet on*, confide, gamble on*, have faith, hinge on*, lay money on*, put faith in, rely, trust; SEE CONCEPTS 12,26

leaning [n] *tendency, bias*
aptitude, bent*, cup of tea*, disposition, drift, favor, favoritism, inclination, inclining, liking, mindset, partiality, penchant, predilection, predisposition, proclivity, proneness, propensity, sentiment, taste, thing, weakness; SEE CONCEPTS 20,32,689

leap [n] *jump; increase*
bound, caper, escalation, frisk, hop, rise, skip, spring, surge, upsurge, upswing, vault; SEE CONCEPTS 194,780

leap [v] *jump, jump over; increase*
advance, arise, ascend, bounce, bound, caper, cavort, clear, escalate, frisk, hop, hurdle, lop, mount, rise, rocket, saltate, skip, soar, spring, surge, vault; SEE CONCEPTS 194,780

learn [v1] *acquire information*
apprentice, attain, become able, become versed, be taught, be trained, brush up on*, burn midnight oil*, commit to memory, con, crack the books*, cram*, determine, drink in*, enroll, gain, get, get down pat*, get the hang of*, get the knack of*, grasp, grind, imbibe, improve mind, lucubrate, major in, master, matriculate, memorize, minor in, peruse, pick up*, pore over, prepare, read, receive, review, soak up*, specialize in, study, take course*, take in, train in, wade through*; SEE CONCEPTS 31,33

learn [v2] *discover, find out*
ascertain, catch on, detect, determine, dig up*, discern, gain, gather, hear, see, smoke out*, stumble upon*, trip over, tumble, uncover, understand, unearth; SEE CONCEPTS 34,183

learned [adj] *well-informed*
abstruse, academic, accomplished, bookish, brainy*, conversant, cultivated, cultured, deep*, educated, erudite, esoteric, experienced, expert, grave, grounded, highbrow*, intellectual, in the know*, judicious, lettered, literary, literate, omniscient, pansophic, pedantic, philosophic, philosophical, polymath, posted, professorial, recondite, sage, sapient, scholarly, scientific, sharp, skilled, solemn, solid, sound, studied, studious, versed, well-educated, well-grounded, well-read, well-rounded; SEE CONCEPT 402

learner [n] *person who receives education*
abecedarian, apprentice, beginner, bookworm, catechumen, disciple, initiate, neophyte, novice, probationer, pupil, scholar, student, trainee; SEE CONCEPT 350

learning [n] *education, knowledge*
acquirements, attainments, culture, erudition, information, letters, literature, lore, research, scholarship, schooling, science, study, training, tuition, wisdom; SEE CONCEPTS 274,409

lease [v] *rent object, residence*
charter, hire, let, loan, rent out, sublease, sublet; SEE CONCEPTS 89,115

leash [n] *rein*
bridle, chain, check, control, cord, curb, deterrent, hold, lead, restraint, rope, strap, tether; SEE CONCEPT 475

leash [v] *rein, hold*
bridle, check, clog, control, curb, entrammel, fasten, fetter, hamper, hobble, hog-tie*, hold back, restrain, secure, shackle, suppress, tether, tie, tie up, trammel; SEE CONCEPT 191

least [adj] *slightest, smallest*
atomic, bottom, entry-level, feeblest, fewest, finical, first, gutter, infinitesimal, last, lowest, meanest, microcosmic, microscopic, minimal, minimum, minute, minutest, molecular, most trivial, nadir, next to nothing*, niggling*, piddling*, poorest, second, short-end*, third*, tiniest, trivial, unimportant; SEE CONCEPTS 585,789

leathery [adj] *hard, durable*
coriaceous, hardened, leatherlike, rough, rugged, strong, tough, wrinkled; SEE CONCEPTS 489,606

leave [n1] *permission*
allowance, assent, authorization, concession, consent, dispensation, freedom, go-ahead*, green light*, liberty, okay, permit, sanction, sufferance, tolerance; SEE CONCEPTS 376,685

leave [n2] *holiday, time off*
adieu, departure, farewell, furlough, goodbye, leave of absence, leave-taking, liberty, parting, retirement, sabbatical, vacation, withdrawal; SEE CONCEPTS 802,805

leave [v1] *depart, abandon physically*
abscond, beat it*, break away, clear out*, come away, cut out, decamp, defect, desert, disappear, ditch*, elope, embark, emigrate, escape, exit, flee, flit, fly, forsake, give the slip*, go, go away, go forth, head out*, issue, migrate, move, move out, part, pull out*, push off*, quit, relinquish, remove oneself, retire, ride off*, run along*, sally, say goodbye*, scram, set out, slip out, split*, start, step down, take a hike*, take leave, take off, vacate, vamoose*, vanish, walk out, withdraw; SEE CONCEPT 195

leave [v2] *abandon, renounce*
back out*, cease, cede, desert, desist, drop, drop out*, evacuate, forbear, forsake, give notice, give up*, hand over, knock off, maroon, quit, refrain, relinquish, resign, stop, surrender, terminate, waive, yield; SEE CONCEPT 234

leave [v3] *forget, neglect*
allow, drop, have, lay down, leave behind, let, let be, let continue, let go, let stay, mislay, omit, permit, suffer; SEE CONCEPTS 30,83

leave [v4] *give, especially after death*
allot, apportion, assign, bequeath, bequest, cede, commit, confide, consign, demise, devise, entrust, give over, hand down, leave behind, legate, refer, transmit, will; SEE CONCEPTS 108,317

leave off [v] *stop*
abstain, break off, cease, desist, discontinue, end, give over, give up, halt, knock off*, quit, refrain, surcease; SEE CONCEPT 234

lecherous [adj] *lustful, lewd*
carnal, concupiscent, corrupt, fast*, hot and heavy*, incontinent, lascivious, libertine, libidinous, licentious, low-down*, lubricous, prurient, raunchy*, salacious, satyric, sensual, unchaste, wanton; SEE CONCEPTS 372,401

lecture [n1] *lesson, speech*
address, allocution, chalk talk*, discourse, disquisition, harangue, instruction, oration, pep talk*, pitch*, soapbox*, spiel*, talk; SEE CONCEPTS 60,278

lecture [n2] *speech of criticism*
castigation, censure, chiding, dressing-down*, going-over*, harangue, moralism, preaching, preachment, rebuke, reprimand, reproof, scolding, sermon, talking-to*, telling off*; SEE CONCEPTS 52,54

lecture [v1] *give a lesson, speech*
address, declaim, deliver, discourse, expound, get on a soapbox*, give a talk, harangue, hold forth, orate, prelect, recite, speak, spiel*, spout, talk, teach; SEE CONCEPTS 60,266

lecture [v2] *criticize lengthily*
admonish, berate, chide, exprobate, flay, give going-over*, give piece of mind*, moralize, preach, rank on, rate, reprimand, reprove, scold, sermonize, tell off; SEE CONCEPT 52

ledge [n] *shelf*
bar, bench, berm, bracket, console, edge, jut, mantle, offset, path, projection, reef, ridge, rim, route, sill, step, strip, tier, track, trail, walk, way; SEE CONCEPTS 445,513

leer [n/v] *look at longingly*
eye, eyeball*, gloat, goggle*, ogle, smirk, sneer, squint, stare, wink; SEE CONCEPT 623

leery [adj] *suspicious*
careful, cautious, chary, distrustful, doubting, dubious, on one's guard*, shy, skeptical, uncertain, unsure, wary; SEE CONCEPT 529

leeway [n] *room to move, grow*
elbow room*, extent, headway, latitude, margin, play, scope, space; SEE CONCEPT 739

left [adj1] *on west side when facing north*
hard to left, larboard, near, nigh side, port, portside, sinister, sinistral, south; SEE CONCEPTS 581,583

left [adj2] *politically radical*
leftist, left-wing, liberal, progressive, revolutionary, socialist; SEE CONCEPT 529

left [adj3] *abandoned*
continuing, departed, extra, forsaken, gone out, leftover, marooned, over, remaining, residual, split, staying; SEE CONCEPT 577

leftover [n] *remainder, remains*
debris, leavings, legacy, oddments, odds and ends*, orts, remnants, residue, scraps, surplus, survivor, trash; SEE CONCEPTS 260,457

leftover [adj] *remaining, excess*
extra, residual, surplus, unconsumed, uneaten, untouched, unused, unwanted; SEE CONCEPTS 560,771

leg [n] *appendage used for support*
brace, column, lap, limb, member, part, pile, pole, portion, post, prop, section, segment, shank, stage, stake, stilt, stretch, stump, support, upright; SEE CONCEPTS 392,471,832

legacy [n] *inheritance, heritage*
bequest, birthright, devise, endowment, estate, gift, heirloom, throwback, tradition; SEE CONCEPTS 337,710

le
le

legal [adj] *allowable, permissible*
acknowledged, allowed, authorized, card-carrying*, chartered, clean*, condign, constitutional, contractual, decreed, due, enforced, enforcible, enjoined, fair, forensic, granted, innocent, judged, judicial, juridical, just, justifiable, justified, lawful, legalized, legit*, legitimate, licit, on the level*, on the up and up*, ordained, passed, precedented, prescribed, proper, protected, right, rightful, sanctioned, sound, statutory, straight, sure enough, valid, warranted, within the law; SEE CONCEPT *319*

legalize [v] *allow, validate*
approve, authorize, clean up, codify, constitute, decree, decriminalize, enact, formulate, launder, legislate, legitimate, legitimatize, license, ordain, permit, regulate, sanction; SEE CONCEPTS *298,317*

legend [n1] *story of the past, often fictitious*
fable, fiction, folklore, folk story, folk tale, lore, myth, mythology, mythos, narrative, saga, tale, tradition; SEE CONCEPT *282*

legend [n2] *brief description in document*
cipher, code, device, epigraph, epitaph, head, heading, inscription, key, motto, rubric, table, underline; SEE CONCEPTS *268,270*

legendary [adj1] *fictitious but well known*
allegorical, apocryphal, created, customary, doubtful, dubious, fabled, fabricated, fabulous, fanciful, figmental, handed-down, imaginary, imaginative, improbable, invented, mythical, mythological, related, romantic, storied, told, traditional, unhistoric, unhistorical, unreal, unverifiable; SEE CONCEPTS *267,552*

legendary [adj2] *famous*
celebrated, famed, illustrious, immortal, renowned, well-known; SEE CONCEPT *568*

legible [adj] *easy to read*
clear, coherent, decipherable, distinct, easily read, intelligible, lucid, neat, plain, readable, sharp, understandable; SEE CONCEPTS *267,535,576*

legion [n] *mass, force of people*
army, body, brigade, cloud, company, division, drove, flock, group, horde, host, multitude, myriad, number, phalanx, rout, scores, throng, troop; SEE CONCEPTS *322,387,417*

legion [adj] *numerous*
countless, many, multifarious, multitudinal, multitudinous, myriad, numberless, populous, several, sundry, various, very many, voluminous; SEE CONCEPTS *762,781*

legislation [n] *law of a government*
act, bill, charter, codification, constitution, enactment, lawmaking, measure, prescription, regulation, ruling, statute; SEE CONCEPT *318*

legislative [adj] *lawmaking*
congressional, decreeing, enacting, jurisdictive, lawgiving, legislational, legislatorial, ordaining, parliamentarian, parliamentary, senatorial, statute-making, synodical; SEE CONCEPT *319*

legislator [n] *person in government who makes laws*
administrator, aldermember, assemblymember, council member, deputy, lawgiver, lawmaker, leader, member, member of Congress, parliamentarian, representative, senator; SEE CONCEPT *354*

legislature [n] *governmental body, most often elected, that makes laws*
assembly, body, chamber, congress, council, diet, house, house of representatives, lawmakers, parliament, plenum, senate, voice of the people; SEE CONCEPT *299*

legitimate [adj] *authentic, valid, legal*
accepted, accredited, acknowledged, admissible, appropriate, authorized, canonical, certain, cogent, consistent, correct, customary, fair, genuine, innocent, just, justifiable, lawful, licit, logical, natural, normal, official, on the level, on the up and up, orthodox, probable, proper, real, reasonable, received, recognized, regular, reliable, rightful, sanctioned, sensible, sound, statutory, sure, true, typical, usual, verifiable, warranted, well-founded; SEE CONCEPTS *319,558,582*

leisure [n] *free time and its activities*
chance, convenience, ease, freedom, holiday, idle hours, intermission, leave of absence, liberty, one's own sweet time*, opportunity, pause, quiet, range, recess, recreation, relaxation, repose, requiescence, respite, rest, retirement, sabbatical, scope, spare moments*, spare time, time, time off*, unemployment, vacant hour*, vacation; SEE CONCEPTS *363,681,807*

leisurely [adj] *casual, unhurried*
comfortable, delayed, deliberate, dilatory, easy, free, gentle, laggard, laid-back*, languid, lax, lazy, relaxed, restful, slack, slackened, slow, slow-moving, unhasty; SEE CONCEPTS *550,584,799*

leisurely [adv] *casually, unhurriedly*
at one's convenience*, at one's leisure, calmly, comfortably, composedly, deliberately, dilatorily, easily, gradually, inactively, indolently, laggardly, langorously, languidly, lazily, lethargically, lingeringly, listlessly, slowly, sluggishly, taking one's time*, tardily, torpidly, with delay, without haste; SEE CONCEPTS *544,584,799*

lend [v] *loan, accommodate*
add, advance, afford, allow, bestow, confer, contribute, entrust, extend, furnish, give, grant, impart, lay on one, lend-lease, let, loan shark*, oblige, permit, present, provide, shark, stake, supply, trust; SEE CONCEPTS *115,140*

length [n] *extent of object, distance, time*
breadth, compass, continuance, diameter, dimension, duration, elongation, endlessness, expanse, expansion, extensiveness, height, interval, lastingness, lengthiness, limit, linearity, loftiness, longitude, longness, magnitude, measure, mileage, orbit, panorama, period, piece, portion, protractedness, purview, quantity, radius, range, ranginess, reach, realm, remoteness, season, section, segment, space, spaciousness, span, stretch, stride, tallness, term, unit, width, year; SEE CONCEPTS *651,721,743,788,804*

lengthen [v] *extend*
amplify, augment, continue, dilate, distend, drag out, draw, draw out*, elongate, expand, increase, let out, make longer, pad, proceed, prolong, prolongate, protract, reach, spin out*, stretch, string out*; SEE CONCEPTS *236,239,245*

lengthy [adj] *extended*
diffuse, dragging, drawn-out, elongate, elongated, interminable, lengthened, long, longish, long-winded, overlong, padded, prolix, prolonged, protracted, tedious, tiresome, very long, wearisome, windy, wordy; SEE CONCEPTS *267,482,782*

lenient [adj] *permissive*
allowing, amiable, assuaging, assuasive, being

big*, benign, benignant, charitable, clement, compassionate, complaisant, compliant, condoning, easy, easygoing, emollient, excusing, favoring, forbearing, forgiving, gentle, going easy on*, good-natured, humoring, indulgent, kind, kindly, letting, live with*, loving, merciful, mild, mollycoddling*, obliging, pampering, pardoning, permitting, soft, softhearted, soft-shell*, sparing, spoiling, sympathetic, tender, tolerant, yielding; SEE CONCEPTS 401,542

less [adj] *smaller, inferior*
beneath, declined, deficient, depressed, diminished, excepting, fewer, lacking, lesser, limited, lower, minor, minus, negative, not as great, reduced, secondary, shortened, shorter, slighter, subordinate, subtracting, unsubstantial, without; SEE CONCEPTS 574,762,789

less [adv] *little*
barely, in a lower degree, meagerly, to a smaller extent; SEE CONCEPTS 530,544

lessen [v] *lower, reduce*
abate, abridge, amputate, attenuate, become smaller, clip, close, contract, crop, curtail, cut, cut back, decline, decrease, de-escalate, degrade, die down, dilute, diminish, downsize, drain, dwindle, ease, erode, grow less, impair, lighten, minify, minimize, mitigate, moderate, narrow, roll back, shrink, slacken, slack up, slow down, soft-pedal*, take the bite out*, take the edge off*, take the sting out*, taper, taper off, thin, truncate, weaken, wind down; SEE CONCEPTS 247,698,776

lesser [adj] *inferior, secondary*
a notch under*, bottom, bush, bush-league*, dinky*, insignificant, less important, low, lower, minor, minor-league*, nether, second-fiddle*, second-string*, slighter, small, small-fry*, small-time*, subjacent, subordinate, third-string*, undersized; SEE CONCEPTS 575,793

lesson [n1] *information taught*
assignment, chalk talk*, class, coaching, education, exercise, homework, instruction, lecture, period, practice, quiz, reading, recitation, schooling, study, task, teaching, test, tutoring; SEE CONCEPTS 274,285,287

lesson [n2] *helpful example, communication*
admonition, censure, chiding, deterrent, exemplar, helpful word, message, model, moral, noble action, notice, precept, punishment, rebuke, reprimand, reproof, scolding, warning; SEE CONCEPTS 123,661,686

let [v1] *allow*
accredit, approve, authorize, be big*, cause, certify, commission, concede, enable, endorse, free up, give, give leave, give okay, give permission, grant, have, hear of, leave, license, live with, make, permit, sanction, sit still for*, suffer, tolerate, warrant; SEE CONCEPTS 50,83,88

let [v2] *rent out object, property*
charter, hire, lease, sublease, sublet; SEE CONCEPTS 89,115

letdown [n] *disappointment*
anticlimax, balk, bitter pill*, blow, chagrin, comedown, disgruntlement, disillusionment, frustration, setback, washout*; SEE CONCEPTS 410,728

let down [v] *disappoint*
abandon, depress, disenchant, disillusion, dissatisfy, fail, fall short, leave in lurch*, leave stranded*, lower, pull down, take down; SEE CONCEPTS 7,19

lethal [adj] *deadly*
baleful, dangerous, deathly, destructive, devastating, fatal, harmful, hurtful, malignant, mortal, mortiferous, mortuary, murderous, necrotic, noxious, pernicious, pestilent, pestilential, poisonous, virulent; SEE CONCEPT 537

lethargic [adj] *lazy, sluggish*
apathetic, blah*, comatose, debilitated, dilatory, dopey, dormant, draggy*, drowsy, dull, enervated, having spring fever*, heavy, idle, impassive, inactive, indifferent, inert, lackadaisical, laggard, laid-back*, languid, languorous, listless, moony*, nebbish, out of it*, passive, phlegmatic, sleepy, sleepyhead*, slothful, slow, slumberous, snoozy, somnolent, spiritless, stolid, stretchy, stupefied, supine, torpid, wimpy*; SEE CONCEPTS 401,403,584

lethargy [n] *laziness, sluggishness*
apathy, coma, disinterest, disregard, drowsiness, dullness, hebetude, heedlessness, idleness, impassivity, inaction, inactivity, inanition, indifference, indolence, inertia, inertness, insouciance, languor, lassitude, listlessness, passiveness, phlegm, sleep, sleepiness, sloth, slowness, slumber, stupor, supineness, torpidity, torpidness, torpor, unconcern, unmindfulness; SEE CONCEPTS 315,410,633,748

let off [v] *make not subject to punishment or action*
abandon, absolve, discharge, dispense, drop, excuse, exempt, exonerate, forgive, let go, pardon, privilege from, release, relieve, remove, spare; SEE CONCEPTS 50,83,88,317

let on [v] *acknowledge, admit*
allow, avow, betray, concede, confess, disclose, divulge, give away, grant, hint, imply, indicate, let out, make known, mouth*, own, own up*, reveal, say, spill*, suggest, tell, uncover, unveil; SEE CONCEPTS 57,60

letter [n1] *symbol of an alphabet*
ABCs*, alphabet, cap, capital, character, majuscule, minuscule, rune, sign, small letter, type, uncial; SEE CONCEPT 284

letter [n2] *written communication*
acknowledgment, answer, billet, dispatch, epistle, junk mail*, kite, line, memo, memorandum, message, missive, note, postcard, reply, report, thank you; SEE CONCEPTS 271,278

letup [n] *pause*
abatement, break, cessation, interval, lapse, lessening, lull, recess, remission, respite, slackening; SEE CONCEPT 807

let up [v] *pause*
abate, cease, decrease, die down, die out, diminish, ease, ease off, ease up, ebb, fall, moderate, release, relent, slacken, slow down, stop, subside, wane; SEE CONCEPTS 240,698

level [n1] *horizontal position or thing*
altitude, elevation, floor, height, layer, plain, plane, story, stratum, surface, zone; SEE CONCEPTS 738,744

level [n2] *rank, position*
achievement, degree, grade, stage, standard, standing, status; SEE CONCEPTS 286,388

level [adj] *smooth, balanced*
akin, aligned, alike, calm, commensurate, common, comparable, consistent, constant, continuous, equable, equivalent, even, exact, flat, flush, horizontal, identical, in line, leveled, like, lined up, matched, matching of, of same height, on a line, on a par, on one plane, parallel, plain, planate,

le
le

plane, planed, polished, precise, proportionate, regular, rolled, same, stable, steady, straight, trim, trimmed, unbroken, unfluctuating, uniform, uninterrupted; SEE CONCEPTS 401,490,566

level [v1] *make even*

equalize, equate, even, even off, even out, flatten, flush, grade, lay, make equal, make flat, mow, plane, press, roll, smooth, smoothen, straighten, surface; SEE CONCEPT 250

level [v2] *destroy, demolish*

bring down, bulldoze*, devastate, down*, drop, equalize, fell, flatten, floor, ground, knock down, knock over, lay low, mow*, pull down, raze, ruin, smooth, tear down, waste*, wreck; SEE CONCEPTS 208,252

level [v3] *be honest*

be above-board, be frank, be on the up and up*, be open, be straight, be straightforward, be upfront*, come clean*, come to terms*, keep nothing back*, talk straight*, tell the truth; SEE CONCEPT 49

level [v4] *aim, direct*

address, beam, cast, focus, incline, lay, point, slant, train, turn, zero in on; SEE CONCEPT 187

levelheaded [adj] *reasonable, calm*

all there*, balanced, collected, commonsensical, composed, cool, cool as cucumber*, coolheaded*, dependable, discreet, even-tempered, far-sighted, in one's right mind*, judicious, practical, prudent, rational, sane, self-possessed, sensible, steady, together, unflappable, wise, with all marbles*; SEE CONCEPTS 403,542

leverage [n] *influence*

advantage, ascendancy, authority, bargaining chip*, break, clout, drag, edge, grease*, jump on*, power, pull, rank, ropes*, suction, weight; SEE CONCEPTS 687,693

levity [n] *funniness, silliness*

absurdity, amusement, buoyancy, facetiousness, festivity, fickleness, flightiness, flippancy, folly, foolishness, frivolity, giddiness, happiness, high spirits, hilarity, jocularity, laughs, lightheartedness, mirth, picnic*, pleasantry, repartee, trifling, triviality, volatility, wit; SEE CONCEPTS 273,410

levy [n] *assessment, tax*

burden, collection, custom, duty, exaction, excise, fee, gathering, imposition, impost, muster, tariff, toll; SEE CONCEPT 329

levy [v] *assess, impose*

call, call up, charge, collect, demand, exact, extort, gather, lay on, place, put on, raise, set, summon, tax, wrest, wring; SEE CONCEPT 330

lewd [adj] *vulgar, indecent*

bawdy, blue, coarse, erotic, fast*, filthy*, foulmouthed, gross*, hard-core*, immodest, immoral, improper, impure, in bad taste, incontinent, indelicate, lascivious, lecherous, libertine, libidinous, licentious, loose*, lustful, naughty, obscene, off-color*, pornographic, profligate, questionable, racy*, rakish, ribald, risqué, salacious, scandalous, scurrilous, shameless, smutty*, suggestive, taboo, unchaste, unclean, unconventional, unvirtuous, vile, wanton, wicked, X-rated*; SEE CONCEPTS 372,542,545

lexicon [n] *collection of word meanings, usage*

dictionary, glossary, terminology, thesaurus, vocabulary, wordbook, wordlist, word stock; SEE CONCEPTS 276,280

liability [n1] *answerability, responsibility*

accountability, accountableness, amenability,

amenableness, arrearage, blame, burden, compulsion, culpability, debt, duty, indebtedness, obligation, onus, owing, subjection, susceptibility; SEE CONCEPT 645

liability [n2] *burden, debt*

account, arrear, arrearage, bad news*, baggage*, balance, bite*, chance, chit*, contingency, contract, damage, debit, disadvantage, drag*, drawback, due*, encumbrance, handicap, hindrance, impediment, inconvenience, indebtedness, indebtment, involvement, IOU*, lease, loan, millstone*, minus, misfortune, mortgage, nuisance, obligation, onus, pledge, possibility, remainder, responsibility, tab; SEE CONCEPTS 332,674

liability [n3] *chance, probability*

exposure, likelihood, openness, proneness, susceptibility, tendency, vulnerability, vulnerableness; SEE CONCEPTS 650,657

liable [adj1] *answerable, responsible*

accountable, amenable, bound, chargeable, obligated, subject, tied; SEE CONCEPT 545

liable [adj2] *open, likely*

apt, assailable, attackable, beatable, conquerable, disposed, exposed, given, inclined, in danger, penetrable, prone, sensitive, subject, susceptible, tending, verisimilar, vincible, vulnerable; SEE CONCEPTS 542,552

liaison [n1] *person who acts as go-between*

communication, connection, contact, fixer, hookup, in, interchange, interface, intermediary, link; SEE CONCEPTS 348,354,423

liaison [n2] *love affair*

amour, encounter, entanglement, fling, illicit romance, interlude, intrigue, romance; SEE CONCEPTS 32,388

liar [n] *person who tells falsehood*

cheat, con artist, deceiver, deluder, dissimulator, equivocator, fabler, fabricator, fabulist, false witness, falsifier, fibber, maligner, misleader, perjurer, phony, prevaricator, promoter, storyteller, trickster*; SEE CONCEPT 412

libel [n] *purposeful lie about someone, often malicious*

aspersion, calumny, defamation, denigration, lying, malicious, obloquy, smear, vituperation; SEE CONCEPTS 63,318

libel [v] *purposefully lie about someone*

asperse, bad-mouth*, blister, burlesque, calumniate, caricature, crack, defame, denigrate, derogate, drag name through mud*, give a black eye*, knock, malign, mark*, mark wrong, revile, roast, scandalize, scorch, sizzle, slur, smear, tear down, traduce, travesty, vilify; SEE CONCEPTS 63,192

libelous [adj] *derogatory*

aspersive, backbiting, calumniatory, calumnious, contumelious, debasing, defamatory, depreciative, detracting, detractory, disparaging, false, injurious, invidious, malevolent, malicious, maligning, opprobrious, pejorative, sarcastic, scurrilous, traducing, untrue, vilifying, vituperative; SEE CONCEPT 267

liberal [adj] *progressive*

advanced, avant-garde, broad, broad-minded, catholic, enlightened, flexible, free, general, high-minded, humanistic, humanitarian, indulgent, intelligent, interested, latitudinarian, left, lenient, libertarian, loose, magnanimous, permissive, radical, rational, reasonable, receiving, receptive, reformist, tolerant, unbiased, unbigoted, unconventional, understanding, unorthodox, un-prejudiced; SEE CONCEPTS *529,542*

liberal [adj2] *giving, generous*
altruistic, beneficent, benevolent, bighearted*, bounteous, bountiful, casual, charitable, eleemosynary, exuberant, free, free-and-easy, handsome, kind, lavish, loose, munificent, openhanded, openhearted, philanthropic, princely, prodigal, profuse, soft-touch, unselfish, unsparing, unstinging; SEE CONCEPTS *334,401,404*

liberal [adj3] *abundant, profuse*
ample, aplenty, bounteous, bountiful, copious, dime a dozen*, galore, generous, handsome, lavish, munificent, no end, plentiful, plenty, rich; SEE CONCEPT *771*

liberate [v] *give freedom*
bail one out*, deliver, detach, discharge, disembarrass, emancipate, free, free up*, get out from under*, let loose*, let out*, loose, loosen, manumit, redeem, release, rescue, save, save one's neck*, set free, unbind, unchain, unhook, unshackle; SEE CONCEPTS *83,110*

liberty [n] *freedom*
autarchy, authorization, autonomy, birthright, carte blanche, choice, convenience, decision, deliverance, delivery, dispensation, emancipation, enfranchisement, enlightenment, exemption, franchise, free speech, immunity, independence, leave, leisure, liberation, license, opportunity, permission, power of choice, prerogative, privilege, relaxation, release, rest, right, sanction, self-determination, self-government, sovereignty, suffrage, unconstraint; SEE CONCEPTS *388,691*

libidinous [adj] *lustful*
carnal, coarse, concupiscent, debauched, fast, hot*, impure, incontinent, lascivious, lecherous, libertine, loose*, obscene, passionate, prurient, salacious, satyric, sensual, unchaste, wanton, wicked; SEE CONCEPTS *372,545*

license [n1] *authority, permission*
authorization, carte blanche*, certificate, charter, consent, dispensation, entitlement, exemption, freedom, go-ahead*, grant, green light*, immunity, independence, latitude, leave, liberty, okay*, permit, privilege, right, self-determination, ticket, unconstraint, warrant; SEE CONCEPT *685*

license [n2] *abandon, indulgence*
anarchy, animalism, arrogance, audacity, boldness, complacency, debauchery, disorder, effrontery, excess, forwardness, gluttony, immoderation, impropriety, irresponsibility, lawlessness, laxity, looseness, presumptuousness, prodigality, profligacy, refractoriness, relaxation, relaxedness, sauciness*, self-indulgence, sensuality, slackness, temerity, unrestraint, unruliness, wantonness, wildness; SEE CONCEPTS *633,645*

license [v] *authorize*
accredit, allow, certify, commission, empower, enable, let, permit, privilege, sanction, suffer, warrant; SEE CONCEPTS *50,83,88*

licentious [adj] *immoral, uncontrolled*
abandoned, amoral, animal, carnal, corrupt, debauched, depraved, desirous, disorderly, dissolute, fast, fast and loose*, fleshly, impure, incontinent, in the fast lane*, lascivious, lax, lecherous, lewd, libertine, libidinous, lickerish, loose*, lubricious, lustful, oversexed, profligate, promiscuous, relaxed, reprobate, salacious, satyric, scabrous, sensual, swinging, unconstrained,

uncontrollable, uncurbed, unmoral, unprincipled, unruly, wanton; SEE CONCEPTS *372,401,545*

lick [n] *light touch; little amount*
bit, brush, cast, dab, dash, hint, sample, smack, speck, stroke, suggestion, taste, tinge, trace, whiff; SEE CONCEPTS *612,831*

lick [v1] *touch with tongue*
brush, calm, caress, fondle, glance, gloss, graze, lap, lap against, move over, osculate, pass over, play, quiet, ripple, rub, soothe, stroke, sweep, taste, tongue, touch, wash; SEE CONCEPTS *185,612*

lick [v2] *play over with fire*
blaze, burn, dart, flick, flicker, fluctuate, flutter, ignite, kindle, leap, palpitate, quiver, ripple, run over, shoot, touch, tremble, vacillate, vibrate, waver; SEE CONCEPTS *249,612*

lick [v3] *defeat, sometimes by hitting*
beat, best, clobber, conquer, down, excel, flog, hit, hurdle, lambaste, master, outdo, outstrip, overcome, overwhelm, rout, slap, smear, smother, spank, strike, surmount, surpass, thrash, throw, top, trim, trounce, vanquish, wallop, whip; SEE CONCEPTS *95,141,189*

lid [n] *top covering*
cap, cover, hood, roof, top; SEE CONCEPT *836*

lie [n] *untruth*
aspersion, backbiting, calumniation, calumny, deceit, deception, defamation, detraction, dishonesty, disinformation, distortion, evasion, fable, fabrication, falsehood, falseness, falsification, falsity, fib, fiction, forgery, fraudulence, guile, hyperbole, inaccuracy, invention, libel, mendacity, misrepresentation, misstatement, myth, obloquy, perjury, prevarication, revilement, reviling, slander, subterfuge, tale, tall story*, vilification, white lie*, whopper; SEE CONCEPTS *63,278*

lie [v1] *tell an untruth*
bear false witness, beguile, be untruthful, break promise, BS*, bull*, con, concoct, deceive, delude, dissemble, dissimulate, distort, dupe*, equivocate, exaggerate, fabricate, fake, falsify, fib, forswear, frame, fudge, go back on*, invent, make believe, misguide, misinform, misinstruct, mislead, misrepresent, misspeak, misstate, overdraw, palter, perjure, pervert, phony, plant*, prevaricate, promote, put on*, put up a front*, snow*, soft-soap*, string along*, victimize; SEE CONCEPT *63*

lie [v2] *be prostrate, flat*
be prone, be recumbent, be supine, couch, go to bed*, laze, lie down, loll, lounge, nap, recline, repose, rest, retire, siesta, sleep, sprawl, stretch out, turn in; SEE CONCEPTS *154,201*

lie [v3] *be situated*
be, be beside, be buried, be established, be even, be fixed, be found, be interred, be level, be located, belong, be on, be placed, be seated, beset, be smooth, exist, extend, have its seat in, occupy, prevail, reach, remain, spread, stretch; SEE CONCEPT *7*

life [n1] *animation, spirit*
activity, being, breath, brio, dash, élan*, élan vital*, energy, enthusiasm, entity, esprit, essence, excitement, get-up-and-go*, go*, growth, heart, high spirits, impulse, lifeblood, liveliness, oomph*, sentience, soul, sparkle, verve, viability, vigor, vitality, vivacity, zest*, zing*; SEE CONCEPT *411*

le
li

life [n2] *existence, duration*

being, career, continuance, course, cycle, days, endurance, epoch, era, expectancy, extent, generation, history, length, life span, lifetime, longevity, orbit, period, pilgrimage, record, season, span, survival, time; SEE CONCEPTS 816,817

life [n3] *being*

animal, animateness, animation, body, breath, consciousness, continuance, creature, endurance, entity, essence, existence, flesh, flesh and blood*, growth, human, human being, individual, living, living being, living thing, man, metabolism, mortal being, organism, person, personage, presence, soul, subsistence, substantiality, survival, symbiosis, viability, vitality, vital spark*, wildlife, woman; SEE CONCEPT 389

life [n4] *history, biography*

autobiography, bio, career, confession, curriculum vitae, journal, life story, memoir, memorial, story; SEE CONCEPT 271

life [n5] *person's experiences*

attainment, behavior, circumstances, conduct, development, enjoyment, enlightenment, growth, hand one is dealt*, happiness, human condition, journey, knowledge, lifestyle, participation, personality, realization, suffering, trials and tribulations*, vicissitudes, way of life*, world; SEE CONCEPT 678

lifeless [adj1] *not living, not containing living things*

asleep, bare, barren, brute, cold, comatose, dead, deceased, defunct, departed, desert, empty, examinate, extinct, faint, inanimate, inert, inorganic, insensate, insensible, late, out cold*, sterile, unconscious, uninhabited, waste; SEE CONCEPTS 485,539

lifeless [adj2] *dull, spiritless*

blah*, cold, colorless, drab, draggy*, flat, hollow, insipid, lackluster, lethargic, listless, lusterless, nothing*, pabulum*, passive, prosaic, prosy, slothful, slow*, sluggish, spent, static, stiff*, torpid, wooden*, zero*; SEE CONCEPTS 401,542,584

lifelong [adj] *lasting*

constant, continuing, deep-rooted, enduring, for life, inveterate, lifetime, livelong, long-lasting, long-lived, long-standing, old, perennial, permanent, persistent; SEE CONCEPT 798

lifetime [n] *span of animate being's existence*

all one's born days*, career, continuance, course, cradle to grave*, days, endurance, existence, life, life span, natural life, period, time; SEE CONCEPT 817

lifework [n] *person's calling*

business, career, interest, mission, occupation, profession, purpose, pursuit, vocation, work; SEE CONCEPTS 349,360

lift [n1] *transportation*

car ride, drive, journey, passage, ride, run, transport; SEE CONCEPT 155

lift [n2] *help, aid*

assist, assistance, boost, comfort, encouragement, hand, leg up*, pick-me-up*, reassurance, relief, secours, shot in the arm*, succor, support; SEE CONCEPTS 110,700

lift [v1] *move upwards; ascend*

arise, aspire, bear aloft, boost, bring up, build up, buoy up, climb, come up, disappear, disperse, dissipate, draw up, elevate, erect, goose*, heft, hike, hike up, hoist, jack up, jump up, mount, move up, pick up, put up, raise, raise high, rear,

rise, soar, take up, up, upheave, uphold, uplift, upraise, uprear, vanish; SEE CONCEPTS 196,200,236,245

lift [v2] *repeal, revoke*

annul, cancel, countermand, dismantle, end, recall, relax, remove, rescind, reverse, stop, terminate; SEE CONCEPTS 234,317

lift [v3] *steal*

abstract, appropriate, cop, copy, crib, filch, hook, nip, pilfer, pinch, pirate, plagiarize, pocket, purloin, snitch, swipe, take, thieve; SEE CONCEPTS 139,200

lift [v4] *promote, improve*

advance, ameliorate, boost, build up, dignify, elevate, enhance, exalt, hike, jack up, raise, support, upgrade; SEE CONCEPTS 110,244

ligature [n] *link*

band, bandage, binding, bond, connection, knot, ligament, nexus, rope, tie, yoke; SEE CONCEPTS 471,831

light [n1] *luminescence from sun or other source*

aurora, beacon, blaze, brightness, brilliance, brilliancy, bulb, candle, coruscation, dawn, daybreak, daylight, daytime, effulgence, emanation, flare, flash, fulgor, glare, gleam, glimmer, glint, glitter, glow, illumination, incandescence, irradiation, lambency, lamp, lantern, lighthouse, luminosity, luster, morn, morning, phosphorescence, radiance, radiation, ray, refulgence, scintillation, sheen, shine, sparkle, splendor, star, sun, sunbeam, sunrise, sunshine, taper, torch, window; SEE CONCEPTS 620,624,628,810

light [n2] *context, point of view; understanding*

angle, approach, aspect, attitude, awareness, comprehension, condition, education, elucidation, enlightenment, example, exemplar, explanation, illustration, information, insight, interpretation, knowledge, model, paragon, slant, standing, vantage point, viewpoint; SEE CONCEPTS 274, 409,682,686

light [adj1] *illuminated*

ablaze, aglow, bright, brilliant, burnished, clear, cloudless, flashing, fluorescent, glossy, glowing, lambent, lucent, luminous, lustrous, phosphorescent, polished, radiant, refulgent, resplendent, rich, scintillant, shining, shiny, sunny, unclouded, unobscured, vivid, well-lighted, well-lit; SEE CONCEPTS 617,618

light [adj2] *blond, fair*

bleached, faded, fair-skinned, light-hued, light-skinned, light-toned, pale, pastel, tow-headed; SEE CONCEPTS 406,618

light [adj3] *not heavy*

agile, airy, atmospheric, buoyant, crumbly, dainty, delicate, downy, easy, effervescent, ethereal, featherweight, feathery, filmy, flimsy, floatable, floating, fluffy, friable, frothy, gossamery, graceful, imponderous, inconsequential, insubstantial, light-footed, lightweight, lithe, little, loose, meager, nimble, petty, porous, portable, sandy, sheer, slender, slight, small, spongy, sprightly, sylphlike, thin, tissuelike, trifling, trivial, unheavy, unsubstantial, weightless; SEE CONCEPT 491

light [adj4] *small in amount, content*

casual, digestible, faint, fractional, fragmentary, frivolous, frugal, gentle, hardly any, hardly enough, inadequate, inconsequential, inconsiderable, indistinct, insignificant, insufficient, mild, minor, minuscule, minute, moderate, modest, not many, not much, not rich, puny, restricted, scanty, shoestring*, slight, soft, sparse, superficial, thin, tiny, trifling, trivial, unimportant, unsubstantial, weak, wee; SEE CONCEPTS 762,789

light [*adj5*] *simple, easy*
effortless, facile, manageable, moderate, smooth, undemanding, unexacting, untaxing, untroublesome; SEE CONCEPT 538

light [*adj6*] *funny, cheery*
airy, amusing, animated, blithe, carefree, cheerful, chipper*, chirpy, diverting, dizzy, entertaining, fickle, flighty, frivolous, gay, giddy, high, humorous, lighthearted, lively, merry, perky, pleasing, sunny, sunny-side up*, superficial, trifling, trivial, up, upbeat, witty; SEE CONCEPTS 401,542

light [*v1*] *illuminate*
animate, brighten, cast, fire, flood, floodlight, furnish with light, highlight, ignite, illume, illumine, inflame, irradiate, kindle, lighten, light up, limelight, make bright, make visible, put on, shine, spot, spotlight, switch on, turn on; SEE CONCEPTS 250,624

light [*v2*] *start on fire*
burn, enkindle, fire, flame, ignite, inflame, kindle, set fire to, set on fire, spark, strike a match; SEE CONCEPT 249

light [*v3*] *step down; land*
alight, arrive, come down, deplane, detrain, disembark, drop, fly down, get down, perch, rest, roost, set down, settle, settle down, sit, sit down, stop, touch down; SEE CONCEPTS 159,181

lighten [*v1*] *illuminate*
become light, brighten, flash, gleam, illume, irradiate, light, light up, make bright, shine; SEE CONCEPT 624

lighten [*v2*] *reduce weight, load*
allay, alleviate, ameliorate, assuage, attenuate, buoy, change, comfort, cut down, decrease, dilute, disburden, disencumber, ease, empty, eradicate, extenuate, facilitate, free, jettison, lessen, levitate, make less, make lighter, mitigate, mollify, pour out, put off, reduce, relieve, remove, shift, take, take a load off*, thin, throw out, unburden, unload, uplight, upraise; SEE CONCEPTS 110,244,250

lighten [*v3*] *cheer up; inspire*
brighten, buoy up, cheer, elate, encourage, gladden, hearten, lift, perk up, revive, take a load off; SEE CONCEPTS 7,22

light-headed [*adj*] *silly; feeling faint*
changeable, delirious, dizzy, empty, featherbrained*, fickle, flighty, flustered, foolish, frivolous, gaga*, giddy, harebrained*, hazy, punchy*, reeling, rocky, scatterbrained*, shallow, superficial, swimming, swimmy, tired, trifling, vertiginous, whirling, woozy*; SEE CONCEPTS 314,401

lighthearted [*adj*] *carefree, untroubled*
blithe, blithesome, bright, buoyant, cheerful, effervescent, expansive, feelgood*, frolicsome, gay, glad, gleeful, happy, happy-go-lucky*, high-spirited, insouciant, jocund, jolly, jovial, joyful, joyous, laid-back, lightsome, lively, merry, playful, resilient, spirited, sprightly, sunny, upbeat, vivacious, volatile; SEE CONCEPTS 404,542

lightly [*adv*] *gently, effortlessly*
agilely, airily, breezily, carelessly, casually, daintily, delicately, easily, ethereally, faintly, flippantly, freely, frivolously, gingerly, heedlessly, indifferently, leniently, mildly, moderately, nim-

bly, peacefully, quietly, readily, simply, slightingly, slightly, smoothly, softly, sparingly, sparsely, subtly, tenderly, tenuously, thinly, thoughtlessly, timidly, unsubstantially, well; SEE CONCEPTS 538,544,584

light out [*v*] *run away*
abscond, depart, escape, head, leave, make, make off, quit, set out, strike out, take a hike, take off; SEE CONCEPT 195

lightweight [*adj*] *inconsequential*
failing, featherweight, foolish, imponderous, incompetent, insignificant, of no account, paltry, petty, slight, trifling, trivial, unimportant, weightless, worthless; SEE CONCEPTS 491,575

likable [*adj*] *nice, pleasant*
agreeable, amiable, appealing, attractive, charismatic, charming, engaging, enjoyable, friendly, genial, good, good-natured, pleasing, preferable, relishable, sweet, sweet-natured, sympathetic, winning, winsome; SEE CONCEPT 404

like [*adj*] *similar*
according to, agnate, akin, alike, allied, allying, analogous, approximating, approximative, close, coextensive, cognate, commensurate, comparable, compatible, conforming, congeneric, congenerous, consistent, consonant, corresponding, double, equal, equaling, equivalent, homologous, identical, in the manner of, jibing, matching, much the same, near, not far from, not unlike, on the order of, parallel, related, relating, resembling, same, selfsame, such, twin, undifferentiated, uniform; SEE CONCEPTS 487,573

like [*v1*] *enjoy, be fond of*
admire, adore, appreciate, approve, be gratified by, be keen on, be partial to, be pleased by, be sweet on, care for, care to, cherish, delight in, derive pleasure from, dig*, dote on, esteem, exclaim, fancy, feast on, find appealing, get a kick out of*, go for*, hanker for, hold dear, indulge in, love, luxuriate in, prize, rejoice in, relish, revel in, savor, stuck on*, take an interest in, take delight in, take satisfaction in, take to; SEE CONCEPT 32

like [*v2*] *choose, feel inclined*
care to, desire, elect, fancy, feel disposed, feel like, have a preference for, incline toward, please, prefer, select, want, will, wish; SEE CONCEPTS 20,41

likelihood [*n*] *chance of something happening*
coin flip*, direction, even break, fair shake, fifty-fifty*, fighting chance*, good chance*, liability, likeliness, long shot*, outside chance*, plausibility, possibility, presumption, probability, prospect, reasonableness, shot at*, strong possibility, tendency, toss-up*, trend; SEE CONCEPT 650

likely [*adj*] *probable, apt, hopeful*
acceptable, achievable, anticipated, assuring, attainable, believable, conceivable, conjecturable, credible, destined, disposed, expected, fair, favorite, feasible, given to, imaginable, inclined, in favor of, inferable, in the cards*, in the habit of*, liable, odds-on*, on the verge of, ostensible, plausible, possible, practicable, predisposed, presumable, promising, prone, rational, reasonable, seeming, subject to, supposable, tending, thinkable, true, up-and-coming*, verisimilar, workable; SEE CONCEPT 552

likely [*adv*] *probably*
assumably, doubtless, doubtlessly, in all likelihood, in all probability, like as not, most likely,

no doubt, presumably, presumptively, prima facie, seemingly, to all appearances; SEE CONCEPT 552

likeness [n] *correspondence in appearance; something that corresponds*

affinity, agreement, alikeness, analogousness, analogy, appearance, carbon, clone, comparableness, comparison, conformity, copy, counterpart, dead ringer*, delineation, depiction, ditto*, double, effigy, equality, equivalence, facsimile, form, guise, identicalness, identity, image, knock-off*, lookalike*, model, parallelism, photocopy, photograph, picture, portrait, replica, representation, reproduction, resemblance, sameness, semblance, similarity, simile, similitude, study, uniformity, Xerox*; SEE CONCEPTS 664,670,716

likewise [adj] *also, similarly*

additionally, along, as well, besides, correspondingly, further, furthermore, in addition, in like manner, in the same way, more, moreover, so, too, withal; SEE CONCEPT 563

liking [n] *fondness, taste*

affection, affinity, appetite, appreciation, attachment, attraction, bent, bias, desire, devotion, fancy, favoritism, inclination, love, mind, palate, partiality, passion, penchant, pleasure, predilection, preference, proneness, propensity, relish, soft spot*, stomach, sympathy, tendency, tooth, velleity, weakness, will; SEE CONCEPTS 20,32,529

limb [n] *appendage*

arm, bough, branch, extension, extremity, fin, gam*, leg, lobe, member, offshoot, part, pin, pinion, process, projection, spray, sprig, spur, stem, switch, unit, wheel, wing; SEE CONCEPTS 392,428

limber [adj] *flexible*

agile, deft, elastic, graceful, lissome, lithe, lithesome, loose, nimble, plastic, pliable, pliant, resilient, springy, spry, supple; SEE CONCEPTS 406,488

limbo [n] *state of uncertainty*

demilitarized zone, left field*, nothingness, nowhere, oblivion, out there*, Siberia*; SEE CONCEPTS 679,705

limit [n1] *greatest extent*

absolute, bitter end*, border, bottom line*, bound, bourne, breaking point*, brim, brink, cap, ceiling, check, circumscription, conclusion, confinement, confines, curb, cutoff point*, deadline, destination, edge, end, end point, extremity, far out, farthest point, farthest reach, fence, finality, goal, limitation, margin, maximum, obstruction, restraint, restriction, rim, termination, the max*, the most*, tops*, ultimate, utmost, verge; SEE CONCEPTS 529,548,832

limit [n2] *physical boundary*

border, borderland, compass, confines, edge, end, extent, extreme, extremity, frontier, perimeter, periphery, precinct, purlieu; SEE CONCEPTS 513,745

limit [v] *confine, restrict*

appoint, assign, bar, bottle up, bound, cap, check, circumscribe, constrict, contract, cork, cramp, curb, define, delimit, delimitate, demarcate, draw the line, fix, hem in, hinder, inhibit, keep the lid on*, lessen, narrow, prescribe, ration, reduce, restrain, set, specify; SEE CONCEPTS 5,130

limitation [n] *restraint, disadvantage*

bar, block, check, circumspection, condition, con-

straint, control, cramp, curb, definition, drawback, impediment, inhibition, injunction, modification, obstruction, qualification, reservation, restriction, snag, stint, stricture, taboo; SEE CONCEPTS 666,674

limited [adj 1] *restricted, definite*

bound, bounded, checked, circumscribed, confined, constrained, controlled, curbed, defined, delimited, determinate, finite, fixed, hampered, hemmed in, local, modified, narrow, particular, precise, qualified, reserved, restrained, sectional, topical; SEE CONCEPTS 554,557

limited [adj 2] *inadequate, short*

cramped, diminished, faulty, ineffectual, insufficient, little, mean, minimal, narrow, paltry, poor, reduced, restricted, set, small, unsatisfactory; SEE CONCEPT 771

limitless [adj] *never-ending, infinite*

bottomless, boundless, countless, endless, illimitable, immeasurable, immense, incomprehensible, indefinite, inexhaustible, innumerable, measureless, no end of*, no end to*, no holds barred*, no strings*, numberless, unbounded, uncalculable, undefined, unending, unfathomable, unlimited, untold, vast, wide-open; SEE CONCEPTS 762, 771,798

limp [n] *faltering walk*

bad wheel, falter, flat wheel, floppy, gimp, halt, hitch, hobble, lameness; SEE CONCEPT 151

limp [adj] *not stiff; weak*

bending, debilitated, drooping, droopy, ductile, enervated, exhausted, feeble, flabby, flaccid, flexible, flexuous, flimsy, floppy, impressible, infirm, languid, languishing, lax, lethargic, limber, listless, loose, plastic, pliable, pliant, relaxed, slack, soft, spent, spiritless, supple, tired, unsubstantial, weakened, wearied, worn out, yielding; SEE CONCEPTS 490,604

limp [v] *walk with faltering step*

clump, dodder, falter, flag, gimp, halt, hitch, hobble, hop, lag, scuff, shamble, shuffle, stagger, stumble, teeter, totter, waddle, walk lamely; SEE CONCEPT 151

limpid [adj] *clear, comprehensible*

bright, comprehensible, crystal-clear, crystalline, definite, distinct, filmy, intelligible, lucid, luculent, obvious, pellucid, perspicuous, pure, seethrough, thin, translucent, transparent, transpicuous, unambiguous; SEE CONCEPT 535

line [n1] *mark, stroke; border*

band, bar, borderline, boundary, channel, configuration, contour, crease, dash, delineation, demarcation, edge, figuration, figure, frontier, furrow, groove, limit, lineament, lineation, outline, profile, rule, score, scratch, silhouette, streak, stripe, tracing, underline, wrinkle; SEE CONCEPTS 284, 436

line [n2] *row, succession; course*

arrangement, array, axis, band, block, border, catalogue, channel, column, concatenation, crack, direction, division, drain, echelon, file, fissure, formation, furrow, groove, group, lane, length, list, magazine, mark, order, path, progression, queue, rank, ridge, road, route, row, scar, seam, sequence, series, street, string, thread, tier, track, train, trajectory, trench, way; SEE CONCEPTS 501,727,738,744

line [n3] *cord, rope*

cable, filament, strand, string, thread, wire; SEE CONCEPT 475

line [n4] *belief, policy*
approach, avenue, course, course of action, ideology, method, polity, position, practice, principle, procedure, program, route, scheme, system; SEE CONCEPTS 688,689

line [n5] *person's calling, interest*
activity, area, business, department, employment, field, forte, job, occupation, profession, province, pursuit, racket*, specialization, trade, vocation, work; SEE CONCEPTS 349,360

line [n6] *ancestry*
breed, descent, family, heredity, lineage, pedigree, race, stock, strain, succession; SEE CONCEPT 296

line [n7] *written communication*
card, letter, message, note, postcard, report, word; SEE CONCEPT 271

line [n8] *hint; influential communication*
clue, indication, information, lead, patter, persuasion, pitch, prepared speech, song and dance*, spiel*; SEE CONCEPT 278

line [n9] *merchandise carried by store*
commodity, goods, involvement, materials, produce, trade, vendibles, wares; SEE CONCEPT 338

line [v1] *border, mark*
abut, adjoin, align, allineate, array, bound, butt against, communicate, crease, cut, delineate, draw, edge, fix, follow, fringe, furrow, group, inscribe, join, line up, march, marshal, neighbor, order, ordinate, outline, place, queue, range, rank, rim, rule, score, skirt, touch, trace, underline, verge; SEE CONCEPTS 79,84,753

line [v2] *put covering inside object*
bush, ceil, cover, encrust, face, fill, incrust, interline, overlay, panel, quilt, reinforce, sheath, stuff, wad, wainscot; SEE CONCEPTS 172,218

lineage [n] *ancestry*
birth, blood, breed, clan, descendants, descent, extraction, family, folk, forbears, genealogy, heredity, house, kin, kindred, line, offspring, origin, pedigree, progenitors, progeny, race, stirps, stock, succession, tribe; SEE CONCEPT 296

linger [v1] *loiter, delay*
amble, be dilatory, be long, be tardy, crawl, dally, dawdle, dillydally*, drift, falter, fool around*, fritter away*, goof off*, hang around*, hang out*, hesitate, hobble, idle, lag, loll, lumber, mope, mosey, plod, poke, procrastinate, put off, putter, remain, saunter, shuffle, sit around, slouch*, stagger, stay, stick around, stop, stroll, take one's time*, tarry, tool, totter, trail, traipse, trifle, trudge, vacillate, wait, wait around; SEE CONCEPTS 151,681

linger [v2] *continue, endure*
abide, bide, cling, hang on, last, persist, remain, stand, stay, stick around, survive, wait; SEE CONCEPTS 23,239

lingo [n] *dialect spoken by a group*
argot, cant, idiom, jargon, language, patois, patter, slang, speech, talk, tongue, vernacular, vocabulary; SEE CONCEPT 276

link [n] *component, connection*
articulation, association, attachment, bond, channel, connective, constituent, contact, copula, coupler, coupling, division, element, fastening, hitch, hookup, in, interconnection, interface, intersection, joining, joint, junction, knot, ligament, ligation, ligature, loop, member, network, nexus, part, piece, relationship, ring, seam, section,

splice, tie, tie-up, vinculum, weld, yoke; SEE CONCEPTS 471,835

link [v] *connect*
associate, attach, bind, bracket, combine, conjoin, conjugate, couple, fasten, group, hitch on, hook up, identify, incorporate, interface, join, meld with, network, plug into, relate, slap on, tack on, tag along, tag on, team up with, throw in with*, tie, tie in with, unite, yoke; SEE CONCEPTS 113,114,193

lip [n1] *edge, brink*
border, brim, chops, flange, flare, labium, labrum, margin, nozzle, overlap, portal, projection, rim, spout; SEE CONCEPTS 392,484,513

lip [n2] *insolence*
back talk, cheek*, effrontery, guff*, impertinence, jaw*, mouth*, rudeness, sass*, sauce*, sauciness*; SEE CONCEPTS 54,278

liquid [n] *fluid*
aqua, aqueous material, broth, elixir, extract, flow, flux, goo*, goop*, juice, liquor, melted material, nectar, sap, secretion, slop*, solution, swill*; SEE CONCEPT 467

liquid [adj1] *fluid, flowing, melting*
aqueous, damp, deliquescent, dissolvable, dissolved, dulcet, fluent, fluidic, fusible, ichorous, juicy, liquefied, liquescent, liquiform, luscious, mellifluent, mellifluous, mellow, meltable, melted, moist, molten, moving, pulpy, running, runny, sappy, serous, smooth, soft, solvent, splashing, succulent, thawed, thin, uncongealed, viscous, watery, wet; SEE CONCEPTS 485,584,603

liquid [adj2] *readily available*
convertible, fluid, free, marketable, negotiable, quick, ready, realizable, usable; SEE CONCEPT 334

liquidate [v1] *pay; change into cash*
cash, cash in, cash out, clear, convert, discharge, exchange, honor, pay off, quit, realize, reimburse, repay, satisfy, sell off, sell up, settle, square; SEE CONCEPT 330

liquidate [v2] *destroy, dissolve*
abolish, annihilate, annul, cancel, dispatch, do away with*, do in*, eliminate, exterminate, finish off*, get rid of*, kill, murder, purge, remove, rub out*, silence, terminate, vaporize, wipe out*; SEE CONCEPT 252

liquor [n] *drink; alcoholic beverage*
alcohol, aqua vitae, booze*, broth, decoction, drinkable, elixir, extract, firewater*, fluid, hard stuff*, inebriant, infusion, intoxicant, liquid, moonshine*, poison*, potable, sauce*, solvent, spirits, stock, the bottle*, whiskey; SEE CONCEPT 455

list [n] *record, tabulation*
account, agenda, archive, arrangement, ballot, bill, brief, bulletin, calendar, canon, catalog, catalogue, census, checklist, contents, dictionary, directory, docket, draft, enumeration, file, gazette, index, inventory, invoice, lexicon, lineup, listing, loop, manifest, memorandum, menu, outline, panel, poll, program, prospectus, register, roll, roll call, row, schedule, screed, scroll, series, slate, statistics, syllabus, table, tally, thesaurus, ticket, timetable, vocabulary; SEE CONCEPT 281

list [v] *keep a record; tabulate*
arrange, bill, book, button down, calender, catalogue, census, chart, chronicle, classify, detail, docket, enroll, enter, enumerate, file, index, inscribe, insert, inventory, invoice, itemize, keep

count, manifest, note, numerate, particularize, peg, place, poll, post, put down as, put down for, record, register, run down, schedule, set down, specialize, specify, spell out, tab, tally, tick off, write down; SEE CONCEPTS **79,125**

list [v2] *lean, slant*
cant, careen, heel, incline, pitch, recline, slope, tilt, tip; SEE CONCEPTS **154,201,738**

listen [v] *hear and pay attention*
accept, admit, adopt, attend, audit, auscult, auscultate, be all ears*, be attentive, catch, concentrate, eavesdrop, entertain, get, get a load of*, give an audience to, give attention, give heed to, hang on words*, hark, harken, hearken, hear out, hear tell, lend an ear*, mind, monitor, obey, observe, overhear, pick up on*, prick up ears*, receive, take advice*, take into consideration*, take notice, take under advisement*, tune in, tune in on*, welcome; SEE CONCEPT **596**

listless [adj] *spiritless, without energy*
absent, abstracted, apathetic, blah*, bored, careless, dormant, dreamy, drowsy, dull, easygoing, energyless, enervated, faint, heavy, heedless, impassive, inanimate, inattentive, indifferent, indolent, inert, insouciant, lackadaisical, lagging, laidback*, languid, languishing, languorous, leaden, lethargic, lifeless, limp, lukewarm, lymphatic, mopish, neutral, out of it*, passive, phlegmatic, slack, sleepy, slow, sluggish, stupid, supine, thoughtless, torpid, uninterested, vacant; SEE CONCEPTS **401,584**

litany [n] *recital of items, often part of religious services*
account, catalogue, enumeration, invocation, list, petition, prayer, recitation, refrain, repetition, supplication, tale; SEE CONCEPTS **278,368**

literacy [n] *ability to read*
articulacy, articulateness, background, cultivation, education, knowledge, learning, proficiency, refinement, scholarship; SEE CONCEPTS **409,630**

literal [adj] *word for word; exact, real*
accurate, actual, apparent, authentic, bona fide, close, critical, faithful, genuine, gospel, methodical, natural, not figurative, ordinary, plain, scrupulous, simple, strict, to the letter*, true, undeviating, unerring, unexaggerated, unvarnished, usual, veracious, verbal, verbatim, veritable, written; SEE CONCEPTS **267,557**

literally [adv] *word for word; exactly*
actually, completely, correctly, direct, directly, faithfully, indisputably, letter by letter*, literatim, not figuratively, plainly, precisely, really, rightly, rigorously, sic*, simply, straight, strictly, to the letter*, truly, undeviatingly, undisputably, unerringly, unmistakably, verbatim, veritably; SEE CONCEPTS **267,557**

literary [adj] *concerning books*
belletristic, bookish, classical, erudite, formal, learned, lettered, literate, scholarly, well-read; SEE CONCEPTS **267,536**

literature [n] *written matter, both fictional and nonfictional*
abstract, article, belles-lettres, biography, books, brochure, classics, comment, composition, critique, discourse, discussion, disquisition, dissertation, drama, essay, exposition, findings, history, humanities, information, leaflet, letters, lit*, literary works, lore, novel, observation, pamphlet, paper, poetry, precis, prose, report, research, story, summary, theme, thesis, tract, treatise,

treatment, writings, written work; SEE CONCEPT **280**

lithe [adj] *flexible, graceful and slender*
agile, lean, lightsome, limber, lissome, loose, nimble, pliable, pliant, slight, slim, spare, supple, thin; SEE CONCEPTS **488,491,584**

litigate [v] *bring matter before court of law*
appeal, contest, dispute, drag into court*, file suit, go to court, go to law, institute legal proceedings, press charges, prosecute, see one in court*, sue, take the law on*; SEE CONCEPT **317**

litigation [n] *matter coming before court of law*
action, case, cause, contention, dispute, lawsuit, process, prosecution, suit, trial; SEE CONCEPT **318**

litter [n1] *mess, debris*
clutter, collateral, confusion, detritus, disarray, disorder, garbage, hash, hodgepodge, jumble, jungle, junk, mishmash, muck, muddle, offal, rash, refuse, rubbish, rummage, scattering, scramble, shuffle, trash, untidiness, waste; SEE CONCEPTS **260,432**

litter [n2] *animal offspring*
brood, cubs, family, kittens, piglets, progeny, puppies, school, young; SEE CONCEPTS **394,397**

litter [v] *make a mess*
clutter, confuse, derange, dirty, disarrange, disarray, disorder, jumble, mess up, scatter, strew; SEE CONCEPT **254**

little [n] *small amount of something*
bit, dab, dash, fragment, hint, modicum, particle, pinch, snippet, soupçon, speck, spot, taste, touch, trace, trifle, whit; SEE CONCEPT **835**

little [adj1] *small in size, amount*
babyish, bantam, brief, cramped, diminutive, dinky, elfin, embryonic, fleeting, hardly any, hasty, immature, imperceptible, inappreciable, inconsiderable, infant, infinitesimal, insufficient, junior, light, Lilliputian*, limited, meager, microscopic, mini, miniature, minute, not big, not large, peanut*, petite, scant, short, short-lived, shrimpy*, shriveled, skimpy, slight, snub, sparse, stubby, stunted, teeny, tiny, toy, truncated, undersized, undeveloped, wee, wizened, young; SEE CONCEPTS **773,789**

little [adj2] *not important*
casual, inconsiderable, insignificant, light, minor, minute, negligible, paltry, petty, shoestring*, small, trifling, trivial, unimportant; SEE CONCEPT **575**

little [adj3] *narrow-minded*
base, bigoted, cheap, contemptible, hidebound, illiberal, ineffectual, limited, mean, narrow, paltry, petty, provincial, self-centered, selfish, set, small, small-minded, vulgar, wicked; SEE CONCEPT **404**

little [adv] *infrequently, not much*
a little, barely, hardly, hardly ever, not many, not often, not quite, only just, rarely, scarcely, seldom, somewhat; SEE CONCEPTS **530,544**

liturgy [n] *worship, ceremony*
celebration, ceremonial, form, formality, formula, observance, rite, ritual, sacrament, service, services; SEE CONCEPT **368**

livable [adj] *adequate, acceptable*
bearable, comfortable, cozy, endurable, fit, habitable, homey, inhabitable, lodgeable, passable, satisfactory, snug, sufferable, supportable, sustainable, tenantable, tolerable, worthwhile; SEE CONCEPTS **485,558**

live [adj1] *existent*
alive, animate, aware, breathing, conscious, living, vital; SEE CONCEPT *539*

live [adj2] *energetic, vigorous*
active, alert, brisk, burning, controversial, current, dynamic, earnest, effective, effectual, efficacious, efficient, functioning, hot*, lively, operative, pertinent, pressing, prevalent, running, topical, unsettled, vital, vivid, working; SEE CONCEPTS *542,560*

live [v1] *exist*
abide, be, be alive, breathe, continue, draw breath, endure, get along, get by, have life, last, lead, maintain, make it, move, pass, persist, prevail, remain, remain alive, subsist, survive; SEE CONCEPT *407*

live [v2] *inhabit a dwelling*
abide, bide, bunk*, crash*, dwell, hang one's hat*, hang out*, locate, lodge, nest, occupy, perch, reside, roost, settle; SEE CONCEPT *226*

live [v3] *enjoy being alive*
be happy, delight, experience, flourish, love, luxuriate, make the most of, prosper, relish, savor, take pleasure, thrive; SEE CONCEPT *678*

live [v4] *make money to support living*
acquire a livelihood, earn a living, earn money, fare, feed, get along*, get by*, maintain, make ends meet*, make it, profit, subsist, support; SEE CONCEPT *351*

livelihood [n] *occupation*
alimentation, art, bread and butter*, business, circumstances, craft, employment, game*, grind*, income, job, keep*, living, maintenance, means, nine-to-five*, profession, racket*, rat race*, resources, slot, source of income, subsistence, support, sustenance, thing*, trade, vocation, what one is into*, work; SEE CONCEPTS *349,351,360*

lively [adj] *energetic, active, busy*
agile, alert, animate, animated, astir, blithe, blithesome, bouncy, bright, brisk, buoyant, bustling, buzzing, cheerful, chipper*, chirpy*, complex, dashing, driving, effervescent, enjoyable, enterprising, entertaining, festive, frisky, frolicsome, full of pep*, gay, go-go*, happy, hyper*, industrious, involved, jocund, jumping, keen, merry, nimble, peppy*, perky, pert, provocative, quick, refreshing, rousing, snappy, sparkling, spirited, sprightly, spry, stimulating, stirring, vigorous, vivacious, zippy*; SEE CONCEPTS *401,542,548*

livid [adj1] *pale, ashen*
ashy, blanched, bloodless, colorless, discolored, dusky, gloomy, greyish, grisly, leaden, lurid, murky, pallid, pasty, wan, waxen; SEE CONCEPT *618*

livid [adj2] *bruised*
black-and-blue, contused, purple; SEE CONCEPT *618*

livid [adj3] *extremely angry*
beside oneself, black*, boiling, enraged, exasperated, flaming, fuming, furious, hot*, incensed, indignant, infuriated, mad, offended, outraged*; SEE CONCEPTS *403,542*

living [n] *lifestyle; source of income*
alimentation, bread and butter*, existence, income, job, keep*, livelihood, maintenance, means, mode, occupation, salt*, subsistence, support, sustainment, sustenance, sustentation, way, work; SEE CONCEPTS *335,351*

living [adj] *existing, active*
alert, alive, animated, around, awake, breathing, brisk, contemporary, continuing, current, developing, dynamic, existent, extant, in use, live, lively, ongoing, operative, persisting, strong, subsisting, ticking, vigorous, vital, warm; SEE CONCEPTS *539,560*

load [n1] *cargo, freight*
amount, bale, bundle, capacity, charge, consignment, contents, encumbrance, goods, haul, heft, hindrance, lading, mass, pack, parcel, part, payload, shipment, shot, weight; SEE CONCEPTS *338,432*

load [n2] *burden, pressure*
affliction, albatross, care, charge, cumber, deadweight*, drag, drain, duty, encumbrance, excess baggage*, incubus, liability, millstone*, obligation, onus, oppression, responsibility, task, tax, trouble, trust, weight, worry; SEE CONCEPT *674*

load [v1] *burden, saddle*
arrange, ballast, bear, carry, charge, chock, choke, containerize, cram, fill, flood, freight, glut, gorge, heap, heap up, jam*, lade, lumber, mass, oversupply, pack, pile, pile it on, pile up, place, pour in, put aboard, ram in, stack, store, stow, stuff, surfeit, swamp, top, top off, weigh, weigh down, weight; SEE CONCEPT *209*

load [v2] *overburden, pressure*
burden, charge, encumber, hamper, lade, oppress, saddle, task, tax, trouble, weigh down, weight, worry; SEE CONCEPT *14*

loaf [n] *block of something*
bun, cake, cube, dough, lump, mass, pastry, roll, slab, twist; SEE CONCEPTS *436,457,460,461*

loaf [v] *be idle, lazy*
be inactive, be indolent, be slothful, be unoccupied, bum*, bum around*, dally, dillydally*, dream, drift, evade, fool around*, fritter away*, goldbrick, hang out*, idle, kill time*, knock around*, laze, let down, lie, loiter, loll, lounge, lounge around, malinger, not lift a finger*, pass time, piddle, relax, saunter, shirk, sit around, slack, slow down, stall, stand around, stroll, take it easy, trifle, twiddle thumbs*, vegetate, waste time, while away hours*; SEE CONCEPTS *210,681*

loafer [n] *person who is idle, lazy*
beachcomber, deadbeat, do-nothing, good-for-nothing*, goof-off*, idler, lazybones*, lounger, malingerer, ne'er-do-well*, shirker, slacker, slouch, sluggard, sponger, wanderer, waster, wastrel; SEE CONCEPT *412*

loan [n] *money given temporarily*
accommodation, advance, allowance, credit, extension, floater, investment, mortgage, time payment, trust; SEE CONCEPT *332*

loan [v] *give money, possession temporarily*
accommodate, advance, allow, credit, lay on one, lend, let out, provide, score, scratch, stake, touch; SEE CONCEPT *115*

loath [adj] *against, averse*
afraid, counter, disinclined, hesitant, indisposed, opposed, reluctant, remiss, resisting, uneager, unwilling; SEE CONCEPTS *29,542*

loathe [v] *dislike strongly*
abhor, abominate, be allergic to*, be down on, decline, despise, detest, execrate, feel repugnance, find disgusting, hate, have aversion to, have no use for*, refuse, reject, repudiate, revolt, spurn; SEE CONCEPT *29*

li
lo

loathsome [adj] *hateful*

abhorrent, abominable, beastly, bitchy*, creepy, deplorable, detestable, disgusting, execrable, gross, hideous, horrible, invidious, lousy, nasty, nauseating, obnoxious, odious, offensive, pesky, pestiferous, repellent, repugnant, repulsive, revolting, sleazy*, slimy*, uncool*, vile; SEE CONCEPTS 485,529,570

lobby [n] *entrance hall*

antechamber, corridor, doorway, foyer, gateway, hall, hallway, passage, passageway, porch, vestibule, waiting room; SEE CONCEPTS 441,448

lobby [v] *press for political action*

advance, affect, alter, bill, billboard*, boost, bring pressure to bear*, build up, campaign for change, drum, exert influence, further, hard sell*, high pressure, hype*, induce, influence, make a pitch for*, modify, persuade, pitch, plug, politick, press, pressure, procure, promote, pull strings*, push, put pressure on, request, sell, sell on*, soft-sell*, soft-soap*, solicit, solicit votes, splash, spot, sway, sweet-talk*, thump, urge; SEE CONCEPTS 68,300

local [n] *person deeply rooted in community*

character, inhabitant, native, resident; SEE CONCEPTS 413,423

local [adj] *of a community, restricted to immediate area*

bounded, civic, confined, district, divisional, geographical, insular, legendary, limited, narrow, neighborhood, parish, parochial, provincial, regional, sectarian, sectional, small-town, territorial, town, vernacular; SEE CONCEPT 536

locale/locality [n] *physical setting*

area, bailiwick, belt, district, domain, haunt, hole, home, location, locus, neck of the woods*, neighborhood, place, position, region, scene, sector, site, sphere, spot, stage, stomping ground*, territory, theater, tract, turf, venue, vicinity, zone; SEE CONCEPT 198

locate [v1] *find*

come across, come upon, detect, determine, discover, establish, ferret out*, get at, happen upon, hit upon, hook*, lay one's hands on*, light upon*, meet with, pick up on, pin down, pinpoint, place, position, read, search out, smell out, smoke out*, spot, station, strike, stumble on, track down, trip over*, uncover, unearth, zero in on*; SEE CONCEPT 183

locate [v2] *settle*

dig in, dispose, dwell, establish, fix, hang one's hat*, inhabit, park, place, put, reside, seat, set, situate, squat, stand; SEE CONCEPT 226

location [n] *place of residence or activity*

area, bearings, district, fix*, hole, locale, locality, locus, neck of the woods*, neighborhood, part, point, position, post, region, scene, section, site, situation, spot, station, tract, turf, venue, whereabouts; SEE CONCEPT 198

lock [n] *device that fastens and bars free passage*

bar, bolt, bond, catch, clamp, clasp, clinch, connection, fastening, fixture, grapple, grip, hasp, hook, junction, latch, link, padlock; SEE CONCEPT 499

lock [v] *fasten, clasp*

bar, bolt, button, button up, clench, close, clutch, embrace, encircle, enclose, engage, entwine, grapple, grasp, hug, join, latch, link, mesh, press, seal, secure, shut, turn the key, unite; SEE CONCEPTS 85,160

lodge [n] *cabin; vacation residence*

abode, auberge, burrow, camp, chalet, cottage, couch, country house, den, dormitory, dwelling, gatehouse, haunt, home, hospice, hostel, hostelry, hotel, house, hut, inn, motel, public house, retreat, roadhouse, shack, shanty, shelter, stopover, tavern, villa; SEE CONCEPT 516

lodge [v1] *become fixed or wedged*

abide, catch, come to rest, embed, entrench, fix, imbed, implant, infix, ingrain, install, plant, remain, root, stay, stick; SEE CONCEPT 201

lodge [v2] *stay at temporary residence*

abide, accommodate, bestow, board, bunk, canton, crash, domicile, dwell, entertain, harbor, hole up*, hostel, house, locate, nest, park*, perch*, put up, quarter, rent, reside, room, roost*, shelter, sojourn, squat, station, stay, stay over, stop; SEE CONCEPT 226

lodging [n] *accommodation for rent*

abode, address, apartment, bed and breakfast, boarding house, camp, castle, chambers, cover, domicile, dorm, dwelling, habitation, harbor, home, hostel, hotel, inn, lodge, lodgment, motel, palace, pied-à-terre, place, port, protection, quarters, residence, resort, roof, room, room and board, rooming house, shelter; SEE CONCEPT 516

loft [n] *room on upper floor*

apartment, attic, dormer, garret, storage, studio; SEE CONCEPT 448

lofty [adj1] *high, elevated*

aerial, airy, high-rise, lifted, raised, sky-high, skyscraping, skyward, soaring, spiring, tall, towering; SEE CONCEPT 779

lofty [adj2] *grand, stately*

arresting, benevolent, big, chivalrous, commanding, considerate, dignified, distinguished, elevated, exalted, generous, great, illustrious, imposing, magnanimous, majestic, noble, renowned, striking, sublime, superb, superior, utopian, visionary; SEE CONCEPT 574

lofty [adj3] *arrogant, high and mighty*

ambitious, cavalier, condescending, disdainful, grandiose, haughty, high-minded, immodest, insolent, overbearing, patronizing, pretentious, proud, snooty, supercilious; SEE CONCEPT 401

log [n1] *stump of tree*

block, bole, chunk, length, piece, stick, timber, trunk, wood; SEE CONCEPTS 428,479

log [n2] *record*

account, book, chart, daybook, diary, journal, listing, logbook, register, tally; SEE CONCEPT 271

logic [n] *science of reasoning*

antithesis and synthesis, argumentation, coherence, connection, course of thought, deduction, dialectic, good sense, induction, inference, linkage, philosophy, ratiocination, rationale, relationship, sanity, sense, sound judgment, syllogism, syllogistics, thesis, train of thought; SEE CONCEPTS 37,349,689

logical [adj1] *probable, reasonable*

analytic, analytical, clear, cogent, coherent, commonsensical, compelling, congruent, consequent, consistent, convincing, deducible, discerning, discriminating, extensional, fair, germane, holding together, holding water*, inferential, intelligent, judicious, juridicious, justifiable, kosher*, legit*, legitimate, lucid, most likely, necessary, obvious, perceptive, perspicuous, pertinent, plausible, rational, relevant, sensible, sound, subtle, telling, valid, well-organized, wise; SEE CONCEPTS *402,529,552*

loiter [v] *hang around; stroll*
amble, dabble, dally*, dawdle, delay, diddle, drag, flag, fritter away, get no place fast*, halt, hover, idle, lag, linger, loaf, loll, lounge, pass time, pause, poke, procrastinate, put off, ramble, saunter, shamble, shuffle, slacken, slough, tarry, trail, traipse, wait, waste time; SEE CONCEPTS *151,210,681*

loll [v] *lay sprawled*
bum, dangle, dawdle, droop, drop, flap, flop, goof off, hang, hang loose, idle, lean, loaf, loiter, lounge, recline, relax, rest, sag, slouch, slump, sprawl; SEE CONCEPTS *154,210*

lone [adj] *by oneself; only*
abandoned, alone, deserted, forsaken, isolated, lonely, lonesome, one, onliest, particular, secluded, separate, separated, single, singular, sole, solitary, solo, stag, unaccompanied, unique; SEE CONCEPT *577*

lonely [adj] 1 *feeling friendless, forlorn*
abandoned, alone, apart, by oneself, comfortless, companionless, deserted, desolate, destitute, disconsolate, down, empty, estranged, forsaken, godforsaken, homeless, isolated, left, lone, lonesome, outcast, reclusive, rejected, renounced, secluded, single, solitary, troglodyte, unattended, unbefriended, uncherished, unsocial, withdrawn; SEE CONCEPTS *403,555*

lonely [adj] 2 *out-of-the-way*
alone, deserted, desolate, godforsaken, isolated, obscure, off the beaten track*, private, quiet, remote, removed, retired, secluded, secret, sequestered, solitary, unfrequented, uninhabited; SEE CONCEPT *583*

lonesome [adj] *forlorn, friendless*
alone, cheerless, companionless, deserted, desolate, dreary, gloomy, homesick, isolated, lone, lonely, solitary; SEE CONCEPTS *403,555*

long [adj] 1 *extended in space or time*
continued, deep, distant, drawn out, elongate, elongated, enduring, enlarged, expanded, extensive, faraway, far-off, far-reaching, gangling, great, high, lanky, lasting, lengthened, lengthy, lingering, lofty, longish, outstretched, prolonged, protracted, rangy, remote, running, spread out, spun out, stretch, stretched, stretching, stringy, sustained, tall, towering; SEE CONCEPTS *482,779,798*

long [adj] 2 *interminable, excessive in length*
boundless, delayed, diffuse, diffusive, dilatory, dragging, drawn-out, for ages*, forever and a day*, late, lengthy, limitless, lingering, long-drawn-out*, long-winded*, overlong, prolix, prolonged, protracted, slow, sustained, tardy, unending, verbose, without end, wordy; SEE CONCEPTS *544,798*

long [v] *desire, crave*
ache, aim, aspire, covet, dream of, hanker, have a yen for, hunger, itch, lust, miss, pine, sigh, spoil for, suspire, thirst, want, wish, yearn; SEE CONCEPT *20*

longing [n] *strong desire*
ambition, aspiration, coveting, craving, fire in the belly*, hankering, hunger, hungering, itch, pining, thirst, urge, wish, yearning, yen; SEE CONCEPTS *20,709*

longing [adj] *desirous*
anxious, ardent, avid, craving, eager, hungry, languishing, pining, ravenous, wishful, wistful, yearning; SEE CONCEPT *403*

look [n] 1 *visual examination*
attention, beholding, case, cast, contemplation, evil eye*, eye*, flash, gander, gaze, glance, glimpse, gun, inspection, introspection, keeping watch, leer, look-see*, marking, noticing, observation, once-over, peek, reconnaissance, regard, regarding, review, scrutiny, sight, slant, speculation, squint, stare, surveillance, survey, swivel, view, viewing; SEE CONCEPT *623*

look [n] 2 *characteristic, stylish appearance*
air, aspect, bearing, cast, complexion, countenance, demeanor, effect, expression, face, fashion, guise, manner, mien, mug*, physiognomy, presence, seeming, semblance, visage; SEE CONCEPTS *655,673,716*

look [v] *examine visually*
admire, attend, behold, beware, consider, contemplate, eye, feast one's eyes*, flash, focus, gape, gawk, gaze, get a load of, glance, glower, goggle, heed, inspect, mark, mind, note, notice, observe, ogle, peep, peer, pore over, read, regard, rubberneck*, scan, scout, scrutinize, see, spot, spy, stare, study, survey, take a gander*, take in the sights*, tend, view, watch; SEE CONCEPT *623*

look [v] 2 *appear, seem to be*
display, evidence, exhibit, express, indicate, look like, make clear, manifest, present, resemble, show, sound, strike as; SEE CONCEPTS *261,716*

look [v] 3 *expect, anticipate*
await, count on, divine, forecast, foretell, hope, hunt, reckon on, search, seek; SEE CONCEPT *26*

look [v] 4 *face*
front, front on, give onto, overlook; SEE CONCEPT *746*

look down on [v] *hold in contempt*
abhor, contemn, despise, disdain, scorn, scout, sneer, spurn, turn nose up at*; SEE CONCEPT *29*

look into [v] *check, research*
audit, check out, delve into, dig, examine, explore, follow up, go into, inquire, inspect, investigate, look over, make inquiry, probe, prospect, scrutinize, sift, study; SEE CONCEPT *103*

lookout [n] *guard; place from which to guard*
anchor, beacon, belvedere, case, catbird seat*, citadel, crow's nest*, cupola, eagle eye*, hawk, observance, observation, observatory, outlook, overlook, panorama, patrol, post, scene, scout, sentinel, sentry, spotter, station, surveillance, tip, tower, view, vigil, vigilance, ward, watch, watcher, watch person watchtower*, weather eye*; SEE CONCEPTS *198,358,623*

look out [v] *be wary*
be alert, be careful, be on guard, beware, check out, have a care, heads up*, hearken, keep an eye out*, keep tabs*, listen, mind, notice, pay attention, peg*, pick up on*, scope, shotgun*, size up, spot, spy, watch out; SEE CONCEPTS *35,623*

look up [v] 1 *research*
come upon, confirm, discover, find, hunt for, peruse, scan, search for, seek, seek out, track down; SEE CONCEPTS *72,216*

look up [v] 2 *improve*
advance, ameliorate, come along, convalesce, gain, get better, mend, perk up, pick up, progress, recuperate, shape up, show improvement; SEE CONCEPTS *303,700*

loom [v] *appear, often imposingly*
approach, await, be at hand*, become visible, be

lo
lo

coming, be forthcoming, be imminent, be in the cards*, be in the wind*, be near, break through, brew, bulk, come forth, come into view, come on, come on the scene*, dawn, dominate, emanate, emerge, figure, gather, hang over, hover, impend, impress, issue, lower, make up, menace, mount, near, overhang, overshadow, overtop, portend, rear, rise, seem huge, seem large, show, soar, stand out, take shape, threaten, top, tower; SEE CONCEPTS 118,159,261

loop [n] *circle, spiral*
bend, circuit, circumference, coil, convolution, curl, curve, eyelet, hoop, kink, knot, loophole, noose, ring, twirl, twist, whorl, wreath; SEE CONCEPT 436

loop [v] *circle, spiral*
arc, arch, begird, bend, bow, braid, coil, compass, connect, crook, curl, curve, curve around, encircle, encompass, fold, gird, girdle, join, knot, ring, roll, surround, tie together, turn, twist, wind around; SEE CONCEPTS 147,201,754

loose [adj1] *not tight; unconstrained*
apart, asunder, at large, baggy, clear, detached, disconnected, easy, escaped, flabby, flaccid, floating, free, hanging, insecure, lax, liberated, limp, loosened, movable, not fitting, relaxed, released, separate, slack, slackened, sloppy, unattached, unbolted, unbound, unbuttoned, uncaged, unclasped, unconfined, unconnected, undone, unfastened, unfettered, unhinged, unhooked, unlatched, unlocked, unpinned, unrestrained, unrestricted, unsecured, unshackled, untied, wobbly; SEE CONCEPT 485

loose [adj2] *indefinite, vague*
detached, diffuse, disconnected, disordered, ill-defined, imprecise, inaccurate, indistinct, negligent, obscure, rambling, random, remiss; SEE CONCEPTS 267,529

loose [adj3] *promiscuous*
abandoned, capricious, careless, corrupt, debauched, disreputable, dissipated, dissolute, easy, fast, heedless, high living*, immoral, imprudent, inconstant, lax, lewd, libertine, licentious, light, negligent, out of control*, playing, profligate, rash, reckless, speeding, swinging, thoughtless, unchaste, unmindful, unrestrained, wanton; SEE CONCEPTS 372,401,545

loose/loosen [v] *set free; unbind*
alleviate, become unfastened, break up, deliver, detach, discharge, disconnect, disengage, disenthrall, disjoin, ease, ease off, emancipate, extricate, free, let go, let out, liberate, manumit, mitigate, relax, release, separate, slacken, unbar, unbolt, unbuckle, unbutton, unchain, unclasp, undo, unfasten, unfix, unhitch, unhook, unlace, unlash, unlatch, unleash, unlock, unloose, unpin, unscrew, unsnap, unstick, unstrap, untie, untighten, work free, work loose; SEE CONCEPTS 127,250

loot [n] *stolen goods*
booty, dough*, graft, haul, hot goods*, lift*, make*, money, pickings*, pillage, plunder, plunderage, prize, seizure, spoils, squeeze, take*; SEE CONCEPTS 337,340

loot [v] *steal goods*
appropriate, boost, burglarize, despoil, grab, gut, liberate, lift, loft, make, moonlight requisition*, pillage, plunder, raid, ransack, ravage, relieve, requisition, rifle, rip off*, rob, sack, salvage,

smash and grab*, snatch, snitch*, stick up, swipe, take, thieve, tip over; SEE CONCEPTS 139,192

lopsided [adj] *leaning, falling to one side; larger on one side*
askew, asymmetrical, awry, cockeyed, crooked, disproportional, disproportionate, inclinatory, irregular, nonsymmetrical, off-balance, one-sided, out of shape, overbalanced, squint, tilting, top-heavy, unbalanced, unequal, uneven, unsteady, warped; SEE CONCEPT 480

loquacious [adj] *talkative*
babbling, chattering, chatty, fluent, gabby*, garrulous, gossipy, jabbering, long-winded*, loose-lipped*, motormouth*, multiloquent, prolix, verbose, voluble, wordy, yacking*; SEE CONCEPTS 267,401

lore [n] *myths, traditional wisdom*
adage, belief, custom, doctrine, enlightenment, erudition, experience, fable, folklore, information, knowledge, learning, legend, letters, mythology, mythos, saga, saw, saying, scholarship, science, superstition, tale, teaching, tradition; SEE CONCEPTS 274,282,287

lose [v1] *be deprived of; mislay*
be careless, become poorer, be impoverished, bereave, be reduced, capitulate, consume, default, deplete, disinherit, displace, dispossess, dissipate, divest, drain, drop, exhaust, expend, fail, fail to keep, fall short, forfeit, forget, give up, lavish, misplace, miss, misspend, oust, pass up, relinquish, rob, sacrifice, squander, suffer, suffer loss, surrender, use up, waste, yield; SEE CONCEPTS 116,156

lose [v2] *be defeated*
be humbled, be outdistanced, be sunk, be taken to cleaners*, be the loser, be worsted*, come up short, decline, drop, drop a bundle*, fall, kiss goodbye*, lose out, miss, succumb, suffer defeat, take a beating*, take the count*, take the heat*, yield; SEE CONCEPTS 384,674

lose [v3] *escape; avoid*
clear, dodge, duck, elude, evade, give the slip*, leave behind, outrun, rid, shake, shake off*, slip away, stray, throw off*, unburden, wander from; SEE CONCEPTS 30,102

loser [n] *person, thing that fails*
also-ran*, deadbeat*, defeated, disadvantaged, down-and-outer*, dud*, failure, flop*, flunkee*, has-been, underdog, underprivileged; SEE CONCEPTS 412,423,433

loss [n] *misfortune, deficit; something misplaced or lost*
accident, bad luck, bereavement, calamity, casualty, cataclysm, catastrophe, cost, damage, death, debit, debt, defeat, deficiency, depletion, deprivation, destitution, destruction, detriment, disadvantage, disappearance, disaster, dispossession, failure, fall, fatality, forfeiture, harm, hurt, impairment, injury, losing, misadventure, mishap, mislaying, misplacing, need, perdition, privation, retardation, ruin, sacrifice, shrinkage, squandering, trial, trouble, undoing, want, waste, wreckage; SEE CONCEPTS 407,674,707

lost [adj1] *missing, off-track*
absent, adrift, astray, at sea, cast away, disappeared, disoriented, down the drain*, fallen between cracks*, forfeit, forfeited, gone, gone astray, hidden, invisible, irrecoverable, irretrievable, irrevocable, kiss goodbye*, lacking, minus, mislaid, misplaced, missed, nowhere to be

found*, obscured, off-course, out the window*, strayed, unredeemed, vanished, wandering, wayward, without; SEE CONCEPT *576*

lost [adj2] *extinct, destroyed*
abolished, annihilated, bygone, consumed, dead, demolished, devastated, dissipated, eradicated, exterminated, forgotten, frittered, gone, lapsed, misspent, misused, obliterated, obsolete, out-of-date, past, perished, ruined, squandered, unremembered, wasted, wiped out*, wrecked*; SEE CONCEPTS *539,560*

lost [adj3] *distracted, dreaming*
absent, absentminded, absorbed, abstracted, bemused, bewildered, distrait, dreamy, engrossed, entranced, faraway, feeble, going in circles*, ignorant, inconscient, musing, perplexed, preoccupied, rapt, spellbound, taken in*, taken up*, unconscious, wasted; SEE CONCEPT *403*

lot [n1] *piece of property*
acreage, allotment, apportionment, area, block, clearing, division, field, frontage, parcel, part, patch, percentage, piece, plat, plot, plottage, portion, property, real estate, tract; SEE CONCEPTS *509,710*

lot [n2] *quantity, often large*
abundance, aggregate, aggregation, amplitude, assortment, barrel, batch, body, bunch, bundle, circle, clump, cluster, clutch, collection, conglomerate, conglomeration, consignment, crowd, great deal, group, heap, load, mass, mess*, much, multiplicity, number, ocean, oodles, order, pack, pile, plenitude, plenty, push, reams, requisition, scores, set, stack, stacks; SEE CONCEPTS *432,787*

lot [n3] *portion, share*
allotment, allowance, bite, cut, parcel, part, percentage, piece, quota, ration, slice, take; SEE CONCEPTS *710,835*

lot [n4] *fate, destiny*
accident, break, breaks, chance, circumstance, decree, doom, foreordination, fortune, hand one is dealt*, hazard, karma, kismet, Moirai, plight, portion, predestination, run of luck*, way cookie crumbles*, wheel of fortune*; SEE CONCEPT *679*

lotion [n] *creamy solution*
balm, cosmetic, cream, demulcent, embrocation, lenitive, liniment, medicine, ointment, palliative, preparation, salve, unguent, wash; SEE CONCEPTS *311,446,466*

loud [adj1] *blaring, noisy*
big, blatant, blustering, boisterous, booming, cacophonous, clamorous, crashing, deafening, deep, ear-piercing, ear-splitting, emphatic, full, full-mouthed, fulminating, heavy, high-sounding, intense, loud-voiced, lusty, obstreperous, pealing, piercing, powerful, rambunctious, raucous, resonant, resounding, ringing, roaring, rowdy, sonorous, stentorian, strident, strong, thundering, tumultuous, turbulent, turned up, uproarious, vehement, vociferous, wakes the dead*; SEE CONCEPTS *592,594*

loud [adj2] *offensive, gaudy*
brash, brassy, brazen, chintzy, coarse, crass, crude, flamboyant, flashy, garish, glaring, gross, lurid, meretricious, obnoxious, obtrusive, ostentatious, raucous, rude, showy, tasteless, tawdry, vulgar; SEE CONCEPTS *401,542,589*

lounge [n] *club, socializing place*
bar, barroom, club room, cocktail lounge, dive*, drinkery, hideaway, lobby, mezzanine, parlor,

pub, reception, saloon, spot, tap, taproom, watering hole*; SEE CONCEPTS *293,449*

lounge [v] *lie about, waste time*
bum*, dawdle, fritter away, goldbrick*, goof off*, idle, kill time*, laze, loaf, loiter, loll*, pass time, recline, relax, repose, saunter, sprawl, take it easy*; SEE CONCEPTS *154,210,681*

lousy [adj] *very bad*
awful, base, contemptible, despicable, dirty, disliked, execrable, faulty, harmful, hateful, horrible, inferior, low, mean, miserable, no good*, outrageous, poor, rotten, second-rate*, shoddy, slovenly, terrible, unpopular, unwelcome, vicious, vile; SEE CONCEPT *571*

lovable [adj] *very likable; endearing*
adorable, agreeable, alluring, amiable, angelic, appealing, attractive, bewitching, captivating, charming, cuddly, delightful, desirable, enchanting, engaging, enthralling, entrancing, fascinating, fetching, friendly, genial, lovely, lovesome, pleasing, ravishing, seductive, sweet, winning, winsome; SEE CONCEPT *404*

love [n1] *adoration; very strong liking*
adulation, affection, allegiance, amity, amorousness, amour, appreciation, ardency, ardor, attachment, case*, cherishing, crush, delight, devotedness, devotion, emotion, enchantment, enjoyment, fervor, fidelity, flame, fondness, friendship, hankering, idolatry, inclination, infatuation, involvement, like, lust, mad for, partiality, passion, piety, rapture, regard, relish, respect, sentiment, soft spot*, taste, tenderness, weakness, worship, yearning, zeal; SEE CONCEPT *32*

love [n2] *person who is loved by another*
admirer, angel, beau, beloved, boyfriend, courter, darling, dear, dearest, dear one, flame, girlfriend, honey, inamorata, inamorato, Juliet*, loved one, lover, paramour, passion, Romeo*, spark, suitor, swain, sweet, sweetheart, truelove, valentine; SEE CONCEPT *423*

love [v1] *adore, like very much*
admire, adulate, be attached to, be captivated by, be crazy about, be enamored of, be enchanted by, be fascinated with, be fond of, be in love with, canonize, care for, cherish, choose, deify, delight in, dote on, esteem, exalt, fall for, fancy, glorify, go for*, gone on*, have affection for, have it bad*, hold dear, hold high, idolize, long for, lose one's heart to*, prefer, prize, put on pedestal*, think the world of*, thrive with, treasure, venerate, wild for*, worship; SEE CONCEPT *32*

love [v2] *have sexual relations*
caress, clasp, cling, cosset, court, cuddle, draw close, embrace, feel, fondle, hold, hug, kiss, lick, look tenderly, make love, neck*, pet*, press, shine, soothe, stroke, take into one's arms, tryst, woo; SEE CONCEPTS *375,384*

love affair [n] *sexual relationship outside of marriage*
adultery, affair, amour, devotion, extracurricular activity*, flirtation, intrigue, liaison, love, menage à trois, passion, romance, thing, triangle; SEE CONCEPTS *375,388*

lovely [adj] *beautiful, charming; agreeable*
admirable, adorable, alluring, amiable, attractive, beauteous, bewitching, captivating, comely, dainty, delectable, delicate, delicious, delightful, enchanting, engaging, enjoyable, exquisite, fair, good-looking, gorgeous, graceful, gratifying, handsome, knockout, lovesome, nice, picture,

lo
lo

pleasant, pleasing, pretty, pulchritudinous, rare, scrumptious, splendid, stunning, sweet, winning; SEE CONCEPTS 537,579,589

lover [n] *person having sexual relationship*
admirer, beau, beloved, boyfriend, companion, courter, darling, dear, dearest, escort, fiancé, fiancée, flame, girlfriend, idolizer, inamorata, inamorato, infatuate, Juliet*, paramour, petitioner, Romeo*, significant other, solicitor, steady, suitor, suppliant, swain, sweetheart, truelove, valentine, wooer; SEE CONCEPT 423

loving [adj] *expressing adoration*
admiring, affectionate, amatory, amiable, amorous, anxious, appreciative, ardent, attached, attentive, benevolent, bound up, caring, concerned, considerate, cordial, dear, demonstrative, devoted, doting, earnest, enamored, erotic, expressive, faithful, fervent, fond, friendly, generous, idolatrous, impassioned, infatuated, kind, liking, loyal, passionate, respecting, reverent, reverential, romantic, sentimental, solicitous, tender, thoughtful, valuing, warm, warm-hearted, worshipful, zealous; SEE CONCEPTS 372,401,542

low [adj1] *close to the ground; short*
below, beneath, bottom, bottommost, crouched, decumbent, deep, depressed, flat, ground-level, inferior, junior, lesser, level, little, lowering, low-hanging, low-lying, low-set, minor, nether, not high, profound, prostrate, rock-bottom, shallow, small, squat, squatty, stunted, subjacent, subsided, sunken, under, unelevated; SEE CONCEPTS 583,779,782,793

low [adj2] *reduced; mediocre*
cheap, cut, cut-rate*, deficient, depleted, economical, inadequate, inexpensive, inferior, insignificant, little, low-grade, marked down, meager, moderate, modest, nominal, paltry, poor, puny, reasonable, scant, second-rate*, shoddy, slashed, small, sparse, substandard, trifling, uncostly, worthless; SEE CONCEPTS 334,574,789

low [adj3] *crude; vulgar*
abject, base, blue, coarse, common, contemptible, crass, crumby, dastardly, degraded, depraved, despicable, disgraceful, dishonorable, disreputable, gross*, ignoble, ill-bred, inelegant, mean, menial, miserable, nasty, obscene, off-color*, offensive, raw, rough, rude, scrubby, scruffy*, scurvy, servile, sordid, unbecoming, uncouth, undignified, unrefined, unworthy, vile, woebegone, woeful, wretched; SEE CONCEPT 404,542

low [adj4] *living in, coming from poor circumstances*
base, baseborn, humble, ignoble, lowborn, lowly, mean, meek, obscure, plain, plebeian, poor, simple, unpretentious, unwashed; SEE CONCEPT 549

low [adj5] *depressed*
bad, blue*, crestfallen, dejected, despondent, disheartened, down, down and out*, downcast, downhearted, down in the dumps*, down in the mouth*, dragged, fed up, forlorn, gloomy, glum, in the pits*, low-down*, miserable, moody, morose, sad, singing the blues*, spiritless, unhappy; SEE CONCEPT 403

low [adj6] *not feeling well*
ailing, debilitated, dizzy, dying, exhausted, faint, feeble, frail, ill, indisposed, poorly, prostrate, reduced, sick, sickly, sinking, stricken, unwell, weak; SEE CONCEPT 314

low [adj7] *not loud*
faint, gentle, hushed, muffled, muted, quiet, soft, subdued, whispered; SEE CONCEPT 594

lower [adj] *under; inferior*
bush-league*, curtailed, decreased, diminished, junior, lessened, lesser, low, lower rung, minor, nether, pared down, reduced, secondary, second-class, second-fiddle*, second-string*, smaller, subjacent, subordinate, under; SEE CONCEPTS 586,772

lower [v1] *let down; fall*
bring low, cast down, couch, demit, depress, descend, detrude, droop, drop, ground, let down, make lower, push down, reduce, set down, sink, submerge, take down; SEE CONCEPT 181

lower [v2] *reduce, minimize*
abate, clip, curtail, cut, cut back, cut down, decrease, decry, de-escalate, deflate, demote, depreciate, devaluate, devalue, diminish, downgrade, downsize, lessen, mark down, moderate, pare, prune, roll back, scale down, shave, slash, soften, tone down, undervalue, write off; SEE CONCEPTS 236,240,242

lower [v3] *belittle, disgrace*
abase, bemean, cast down, condescend, debase, degrade, deign, demean, depress, devalue, downgrade, humble, humiliate, stoop; SEE CONCEPTS 7,19

low-key [adj] *subdued*
easygoing, laid-back*, loose, low-pitched, muffled, muted, played down, quiet, relaxed, restrained, sober, softened, soft-sell*, subtle, toned down, understated; SEE CONCEPTS 542,544,548

lowly [adj] *inferior, plain*
average, base, baseborn, cast down, common, commonplace, docile, dutiful, everyday, gentle, humble, ignoble, low, lowborn, mean, meek, menial, mild, modest, mundane, obscure, obsequious, ordinary, plebeian, poor, proletarian, prosaic, retiring, reverential, servile, simple, submissive, subordinate, subjection, unassuming, unpretentious, withdrawing; SEE CONCEPTS 404,547,549

loyal [adj] *faithful, dependable*
allegiant, ardent, attached, behind one, believing, coming through, constant, devoted, dutiful, dyed-in-the-wool*, firm, on one's side*, patriotic, resolute, staunch, steadfast, steady, tried-and-true*, true, true-blue*, trustworthy, trusty, unfailing, unswerving, unwavering; SEE CONCEPTS 404,545

loyalty [n] *faithfulness, dependability*
adherence, allegiance, ardor, attachment, bond, conscientiousness, constancy, devotedness, devotion, duty, earnestness, faith, fealty, fidelity, homage, honesty, honor, incorruptibility, integrity, inviolability, obedience, patriotism, probity, reliability, resolution, scrupulousness, sincerity, single-mindedness, singleness, staunchness, steadfastness, subjection, submission, support, tie, troth, trueheartedness, trueness, trustiness, trustworthiness, truth, truthfulness, uprightness, zeal; SEE CONCEPTS 411,645

lubricate [v] *make slippery*
anoint, cream, grease, lard, lube, make, oil, oil the wheels*, slick, smear, smooth, tallow, wax; SEE CONCEPT 202

lucid [adj1] *evident, obvious*
apprehensible, clear, clear-cut, comprehendible, comprehensible, crystal clear, distinct, explicit, fathomable, graspable, intelligible, knowable, limpid, luminous, pellucid, plain, translucent,

transparent, transpicuous, unambiguous, unblurred, understandable; SEE CONCEPT *529*

lucid [*adj2*] *brilliant, shining*
beaming, bright, effulgent, gleaming, incandescent, lambent, luminous, lustrous, radiant, refulgent, resplendent; SEE CONCEPT *617*

lucid [*adj3*] *clear, transparent*
clear, crystalline, diaphanous, gauzy, glassy, limpid, obvious, pellucid, pure, sheer, translucent, transpicuous, unblurred; SEE CONCEPTS *606,619*

lucid [*adj4*] *clearheaded, sensible*
all there, compos mentis, cool, got head together*, in right mind, normal, rational, reasonable, right, sane, sober, sound, together; SEE CONCEPTS *402,403*

luck [*n1*] *good fortune*
advantage, big break*, blessing, break*, fluke*, fortunateness, godsend*, good luck, happiness, health, in the cards*, karma*, kismet*, luckiness, lucky break*, occasion, opportunity, profit, prosperity, run of luck*, serendipity, smile*, streak of luck, stroke, success, triumph, victory, weal, wealth, win, windfall; SEE CONCEPT *693*

luck [*n2*] *chance*
accident, break, destiny, fate, fifty-fifty*, fortuity, fortune, hap*, happenstance, hazard, occasion, occurrence, toss-up* unforeseen event; SEE CONCEPT *679*

luckily [*adv*] *happily*
by chance, favorably, fortuitously, fortunately, opportunely, propitiously, providentially; SEE CONCEPTS *544,572*

lucky [*adj*] *fortunate, opportune*
advantageous, adventitious, all systems go*, auspicious, beneficial, benign, blessed, charmed, coming up roses*, everything going*, favored, felicitous, fortuitous, getting a break*, golden, happy, hit it big*, holding aces*, hopeful, hot*, in the groove*, into something, on a roll*, on a streak, promising, propitious, prosperous, providential, serendipitous, striking it rich*, successful, timely, well; SEE CONCEPTS *537,572*

lucrative [*adj*] *productive, well-paid*
advantageous, beneficial, fatness, fruitful, gainful, good, high-income*, in the black*, money-making, paying, profitable, remunerative, sweet, worthwhile; SEE CONCEPT *334*

ludicrous [*adj*] *absurd, ridiculous*
antic, bizarre, burlesque, comic, comical, crazy, droll, fantastic, farcical, foolish, funny, gelastic, grotesque, incongruous, laughable, nonsensical, odd, outlandish, preposterous, risible, silly, zany; SEE CONCEPT *548*

lug [*v*] *drag something around*
bear, buck, carry, convey, draw, ferry, haul, heave, hump, jerk, lift, lurch, pack, pull, rake, schlepp*, snap, tote, tow, transport, trawl, tug, vellicate, yank; SEE CONCEPT *206*

luggage [*n*] *bag, suitcase*
baggage, carry-on, case, fortnighter, gear, impedimenta, paraphernalia, suit bag, things*, tote bag, trunk, valise; SEE CONCEPTS *446,494*

lukewarm [*adj1*] *slightly heated*
blood-warm, milk-warm, tepid, warm, warmish; SEE CONCEPT *605*

lukewarm [*adj2*] *indifferent, unenthusiastic*
apathetic, chilly, cold, cool, halfhearted, hesitant, indecisive, irresolute, phlegmatic, tepid, uncertain, uncommitted, unconcerned, undecided, un-

interested, unresolved, unresponsive, wishy-washy*; SEE CONCEPTS *403,542*

lull [*n*] *pause, calm*
abeyance, break, breather, breathing spell, calmness, coffee break, comma*, downtime*, hiatus, hush, layoff, letup, pausation, quiescence, quiet, respite, silence, stillness, stop, time-out*, tranquility; SEE CONCEPT *807*

lull [*v*] *calm, ease off*
abate, allay, balm, becalm, cease, chill out*, compose, cool*, cool off*, decrease, die down, diminish, dwindle, ebb, fall, hush, lay back, let up, lullaby, moderate, pacify, put a lid on*, qualify, quell, quiet, quiet down, settle, slacken, soft-pedal*, soothe, still, stroke, subdue, subside, take it easy*, take the edge off, take the sting out*, temper, tranquilize, wane; SEE CONCEPTS *7,22, 210,698*

lumber [*v1*] *walk heavily, clumsily*
barge, clump, galumph, lump, plod, shamble, shuffle, slog, stump, trudge, trundle, waddle; SEE CONCEPT *151*

lumber [*v2*] *burden*
charge, cumber, encumber, impose upon, lade, land, load, saddle, tax, weigh; SEE CONCEPT *14*

lumbering [*adj*] *clumsy, awkward*
blundering, bovine, bumbling, clodhopping*, clunking, elephantine, gauche, gawky, halting, heavy, heavy-footed, hulking, inept, klutzy*, lead-footed*, lumpish, maladroit, overgrown, ponderous, splay, two left feet*, ungainly, unhandy, unwieldy, wooden; SEE CONCEPTS *406,584*

luminary [*n*] *very important person*
big name*, celeb*, celebrity, dignitary, eminence, leader, lion*, name, notability, notable, personage, personality, somebody*, star, superstar, VIP*, worthy; SEE CONCEPTS *352,423*

luminescent [*adj*] *glowing, shining*
bright, effulgent, fluorescent, luminous, phosphorescent, radiant; SEE CONCEPT *617*

luminous [*adj1*] *bright, glowing*
beaming, brilliant, clear, crystal, effulgent, fulgent, illuminated, incandescent, lambent, lighted, lit, lucent, lucid, luminescent, lustrous, radiant, refulgent, resplendent, shining, translucent, transparent, vivid; SEE CONCEPT *617*

luminous [*adj2*] *obvious, understandable*
apprehensible, bright, brilliant, clear, comprehendible, comprehensible, evident, fathomable, graspable, intelligible, knowable, lucid, perspicacious, perspicuous; SEE CONCEPT *529*

lump [*n*] *clump, mass*
agglomeration, ball, bit, block, bulge, bulk, bump, bunch, cake, chip, chunk, cluster, crumb, dab, gob, group, growth, handful, hunk, knot, knurl, lot, morsel, mountain, much, nugget, part, peck, piece, pile, portion, protrusion, protuberance, scrap, section, solid, spot, swelling, tumescence, tumor, wad, wedge; SEE CONCEPTS *432,470,471*

lump [*v*] *tolerate, withstand*
abide, bear, brook, digest, endure, put up with, stand, stomach, suffer, swallow, take; SEE CONCEPT *23*

lunacy [*n*] *craziness, madness*
aberration, absurdity, alienation, asininity, dementia, derangement, distraction, fatuity, folly, foolhardiness, foolishness, idiocy, imbalance, imbecility, inanity, ineptitude, insanity, mania, psy-

chopathy, psychosis, senselessness, silliness, stupidity; SEE CONCEPTS 410,633

lunatic [n] *person who is crazy, mad*
crackpot*, crank, cuckoo*, demoniac, flake*, fruitcake*, kook*, lamebrain*, loon*, maniac, neurotic, nut*, paranoid, psycho*, psychopath, psychotic, scatterbrain, schizophrenic, sociopathic; SEE CONCEPTS 412,809

lunatic [adj] *crazy, mad*
absurd, baked*, balmy*, bananas*, bonkers*, cracked, crazed, daft, demented, deranged, dippy*, flaky*, flipped out*, foolish, freaked out*, fried*, idiotic, insane, irrational, kooky*, loco, maniac, maniacal, nonsensical, nutty*, preposterous, psyched out*, psychotic, schizoid*, screwy*, stupid, unsound, whacko*, zany; SEE CONCEPTS 401,403

lunge [n] *pounce*
charge, cut, jab, jump, pass, spring, stab, swing, swipe, thrust; SEE CONCEPTS 159,194

lunge [v] *pounce, dive for*
bound, burst, charge, cut, dash, drive, fall upon, hit, jab, jump, leap, lurch, pitch, plunge, poke, push, set upon, stab, strike, surge, thrust; SEE CONCEPTS 159,194

lurch [v] *move toward with jerk*
blunder, bumble, careen, dodge, duck, falter, flounder, heave, jerk, lean, list, move to the side, pitch, reel, rock, roll, seesaw, slide, slip, stagger, stumble, sway, swing, teeter, tilt, toss, totter, wallow, weave, wobble, yaw; SEE CONCEPTS 80,150,152,194

lure [n] *bait*
allurement, ambush, appeal, attraction, bribe, call, camouflage, carrot*, come-on*, con game*, decoy, delusion, draw, enticement, fake, gimmick, hook, illusion, incentive, inducement, inveiglement, invitation, magnet*, mousetrap*, pull, seducement, seduction, siren song*, sitting duck*, snare, sweetener*, temptation, tout, trap, trick; SEE CONCEPTS 32,529

lure [v] *attract, seduce*
allure, bag, bait, beckon, beguile, bewitch, cajole, captivate, capture, catch, charm, come on*, decoy, drag, draw, enchant, ensnare, entice, fascinate, grab, haul, hit on*, hook, inveigle, invite, lead on, pull, rope, steer, suck in*, sweep off one's feet*, tempt, train, turn on; SEE CONCEPT 11

lurid [adj] *shocking, gruesome*
ashen, bloody, deep, disgusting, distinct, exaggerated, extreme, fiery, ghastly, gory*, graphic, grim, grisly, hideous, horrible, horrid, horrifying, livid, low-down, macabre, melodramatic, obscene, off-color*, offensive, purple*, racy, raunchy, revolting, rough, salty, sanguine*, savage, sensational, sinister, startling, terrible, terrifying, violent, vivid, yellow*; SEE CONCEPTS 267,537

lurk [v] *hide; move stealthily*
conceal oneself, creep, crouch, go furtively, gumshoe, lie in wait, prowl, skulk, slide, slink, slip, snake, sneak, snoop, stay hidden, steal, wait; SEE CONCEPTS 151,188

luscious [adj] *delicious, delectable*
adorable, ambrosial, appetizing, choice, darling, delish, deluxe, distinctive, divine, exquisite, flamboyant, flavorsome, heavenly, honeyed, juicy, lush, luxurious, mellow, mouth-watering, nectarious, opulent, ornate, palatable, palatial, piquant, rare, rich, savory, scrumptious, succulent, sumptuous, sweet, toothsome, voluptuous, yummy*; SEE CONCEPTS 574,613

lush [adj] *profuse and delightful*
abundant, ambrosial, delectable, delicious, deluxe, dense, elaborate, extensive, extravagant, exuberant, flourishing, fresh, grand, green, heavenly, juicy, lavish, luscious, luxuriant, luxurious, opulent, ornate, overgrown, palatial, plush, prodigal, prolific, rank, rich, riotous, ripe, ritzy, scrumptious, sensuous, succulent, sumptuous, teeming, tender, verdant, voluptuous; SEE CONCEPTS 574,589,771

lust [n] *appetite, passion*
animalism, aphrodisia, appetence, appetition, avidity, carnality, concupiscence, covetousness, craving, cupidity, desire, eroticism, excitement, fervor, greed, hunger, itch, lasciviousness, lechery, lewdness, libido, licentiousness, longing, prurience, pruriency, salaciousness, salacity, sensualism, sensuality, thirst, urge, wantonness, weakness, yen; SEE CONCEPTS 20,709

lust [v] *desire strongly*
ache, be consumed with desire, be hot for*, covet, crave, hanker, hunger for, itch, long, need, pine, thirst, want, wish, yearn, yen; SEE CONCEPT 20

luster [n] *gloss, shine*
afterglow, brightness, brilliance, brilliancy, burnish, candescence, dazzle, effulgence, glaze, gleam, glint, glitter, glow, incandescence, iridescence, lambency, luminousness, opalescence, polish, radiance, refulgence, resplendence, sheen, shimmer, sparkle; SEE CONCEPT 620

lustrous [adj] *glossy, shining*
bright, burnished, dazzling, effulgent, fulgent, glacé, gleaming, glinting, glistening, glorious, glowing, incandescent, lambent, lucent, luminous, polished, radiant, refulgent, shimmering, shiny, sparkling, splendid, waxy; SEE CONCEPT 617

lusty [adj] *energetic, healthy*
brawny, dynamic, hale, hearty, potent, powerful, red-blooded, robust, rugged, stalwart, stout, strapping, strenuous, strong, sturdy, tough, vigorous, vital; SEE CONCEPTS 314,485,489

luxuriant [adj] *profuse, plush*
abundant, ample, copious, deluxe, dense, elaborate, excessive, extravagant, exuberant, fancy, fecund, fertile, flamboyant, flourishing, fruitful, lavish, luscious, lush, opulent, overflowing, palatial, plenteous, plentiful, prodigal, productive, profusive, prolific, rampant, rank, rich, riotous, sumptuous, superabundant, teeming, thriving; SEE CONCEPTS 574,589

luxuriate [adj] *indulge, prosper*
abound, bask, be in clover*, bloom, burgeon, delight, eat up*, enjoy, feast, flourish, grow, increase, live extravagantly, live high on hog*, live in luxury*, live it up*, love, overdo, relish, revel, riot, roll, rollick, take it easy*, thrive, wallow, wanton; SEE CONCEPTS 539,544,589

luxurious [adj] *affluent, indulgent*
comfortable, costly, deluxe, easy, elaborate, epicurean, expensive, extravagant, fancy, fit for a king/queen*, gorgeous, grand, grandiose, gratifying, hedonistic, immoderate, imposing, impressive, in the lap of luxury, lavish, luscious, lush, magnificent, majestic, opulent, ostentatious, palatial, pampered, pleasurable, pleasure-loving, plush, plushy, posh, pretentious, rich, ritzy*, self-indulgent, sensual, sensuous, splendid, stately,

sumptuous, sybaritic, upscale, voluptuous, well-appointed; SEE CONCEPTS 544,574,589

luxury [n] *great pleasure, indulgence*
affluence, bliss, comfort, delight, enjoyment, exorbitance, extravagance, frill, gratification, hedonism, high living, immoderation, intemperance, leisure, luxuriousness, opulence, rarity, richness, satisfaction, splendor, sumptuousness, treat, well-being; SEE CONCEPTS 337,388,712

lying [adj] *dishonest*
committing perjury, deceitful, deceptive, delusive, delusory, dissembling, dissimulating, double-crossing*, double-dealing*, equivocating, false, falsifying, fibbing, guileful, inventing, mendacious, misleading, misrepresenting, misstating, perfidious, prevaricating, shifty, treacherous, tricky, two-faced*, two-timing*, unreliable, untruthful, wrong; SEE CONCEPT 267

M

macabre [adj] *eerie; deathlike*
cadaverous, deathly, dreadful, frightening, frightful, ghastly, ghostly, ghoulish, grim, grisly, gruesome, hideous, horrible, horrid, lurid, morbid, offensive, scary, spookish, spooky, terrible, unearthly, weird; SEE CONCEPTS 537,547

machinate [v] *maneuver, plot*
cogitate, collude, come up with, connive, conspire, contrive, design, devise, engineer, finagle, hatch, intrigue, invent, plan, play games*, promote, pull strings*, scheme, trump up*, wangle; SEE CONCEPT 36

machination [n] *maneuver, plot*
artifice, cabal, conspiracy, design, device, dirty work*, dodge*, intrigue, monkey business*, on the make*, ploy, practice, ruse, scheme, sellout, skullduggery*, song and dance*, stratagem, trick; SEE CONCEPT 660

machine [n1] *device that performs a task*
apparatus, appliance, automaton, automobile, computer, contraption, contrivance, engine, gadget, implement, instrument, mechanism, motor, robot, thingamabob*, tool, vehicle, widget*; SEE CONCEPT 463

machine [n2] *well-run political organization*
agency, lineup, machinery, movement, party, ring, setup, structure, system; SEE CONCEPT 301

machine [n3] *person who acts automatically*
agent, automaton, clone, drudge, grind, laborer, mechanical, puppet, robot, zombie*; SEE CONCEPTS 348,423

machinery [n] *devices performing work*
accoutrement, agency, agent, apparatus, appliance, channel, contraption, contrivance, engine, equipment, gadget, gear, habiliments, implement, instrument, materiel, means, mechanism, medium, method, motor, organ, outfit, paraphernalia, shifts, structure, system, tackle, tool, utensil, vehicle, works; SEE CONCEPTS 463,770

mad [adj1] *crazy, insane*
aberrant, absurd, bananas*, batty, crazed, cuckoo*, daft, delirious, demented, deranged, distracted, fantastic, foolhardy, foolish, frantic, frenetic, frenzied, illogical, invalid, ir-

rational, kooky*, loony*, ludicrous, lunatic, mental, non compos mentis, nonsensical, nutty*, off one's rocker*, of unsound mind, out of one's mind*, preposterous, psychotic, rabid, raving, senseless, unbalanced, unhinged, unreasonable, unsafe, unsound, unstable, wacky*; SEE CONCEPTS 403,529

mad [adj2] *angry*
abandoned, agitated, berserk, distracted, distraught, enraged, exasperated, excited, frantic, frenetic, fuming, furious, incensed, infuriated, irritated, livid, provoked, raging, resentful, seeing red*, uncontrolled, very upset, wild, wrathful; SEE CONCEPT 403

mad [adj3] *enthusiastic; in love*
ardent, avid, crazy, daft, devoted, enamoured, enthused, fanatical, fond, hooked*, impassioned, infatuated, keen, nuts*, wild, zealous; SEE CONCEPTS 32,403

madcap [adj] *crazy, impulsive*
brash, foolhardy, foolish, frivolous, harebrained*, heedless, hotheaded, ill-advised, imprudent, incautious, inconsiderate, lively, rash, reckless, stupid, thoughtless, wild; SEE CONCEPT 548

madden [v] *make angry*
anger, annoy, bother, craze, derange, distract, drive crazy, drive insane, drive out of mind*, drive to distraction*, enrage, exasperate, frenzy, incense, inflame, infuriate, ire, irritate, make see red*, pester, possess, provoke, shatter, steam up*, umbrage, unbalance, unhinge*, upset, vex; SEE CONCEPTS 7,19

made-up [adj] *invented mentally*
fabricated, false, fictional, imaginary, make-believe, mythical, prepared, specious, trumped-up, unreal, untrue; SEE CONCEPT 582

madhouse [n] *place where mentally ill live; place full of commotion*
asylum, bedlam, chaos, insane asylum, loony bin*, mental hospital, mental institution, pandemonium, psychiatric hospital, sanitarium, turmoil, uproar; SEE CONCEPTS 312,449,516,674

madly [adv] *wildly, fiercely*
absurdly, crazily, deliriously, dementedly, desperately, devotedly, distractedly, energetically, exceedingly, excessively, excitedly, extremely, foolishly, frantically, frenziedly, furiously, hard, hastily, hurriedly, hysterically, insanely, intensely, irrationally, like mad, ludicrously, nonsensically, passionately, psychotically, quickly, rabidly, rapidly, rashly, recklessly, senselessly, something fierce, speedily, stormily, to distraction, tumultuously/tumultuously, turbulently, unreasonably, violently; SEE CONCEPTS 537,540,544

mad person [n] *person who is considered mentally ill*
bedlamite, crazy person, demented, deranged, idiot, imbecile, loon, lunatic, maniac, mental case*, patient, psycho*, psychopath, psychotic, raver*, schizophrenic, sociopath; SEE CONCEPTS 412,423

magazine [n1] *periodic publication*
annual, bimonthly, biweekly, booklet, broadside, brochure, circular, daily, digest, gazette, glossy, joint, journal, manual, monthly, newsletter, newspaper, organ, pamphlet, paper, periodical, pulp*, quarterly, rag*, review, semiweekly, sheet*, slick, throwaway*, weekly; SEE CONCEPT 280

magazine [n2] *arsenal of weapons*
ammunition dump, armory, cache, depository, de-

magic [*n*] *supernatural power; appearance of impossible feats by tricks*
abracadabra*, alchemy, allurement, astrology, augury, bewitchment, black art, conjuring, conjury, devilry, diabolism, divination, enchantment, exorcism, fascination, foreboding, fortune-telling, hocus-pocus*, horoscopy, illusion, incantation, legerdemain, magnetism, necromancy, occultism, power, prediction, presage, prestidigitation, prophecy, rune, sleight of hand, soothsaying, sorcery, sortilege, spell, superstition, taboo, thaumaturgy, trickery, voodoo, voodooism, witchcraft, wizardry; SEE CONCEPTS 370,689

magic/magical [*adj*] *bewitching, charming*
bewitched, charismatic, clairvoyant, conjuring, demoniac, diabolic, eerie, enchanted, enchanting, ensorcelled, entranced, entrancing, extraordinary, fascinating, fiendish, ghostly, haunted, imaginary, magnetic, marvelous, miraculous, mysterious, mystic, mythical, necromantic, occult, otherworldly, parapsychological, runic, sorcerous, spectral, spellbinding, spellbound, spiritualistic, spooky, telekinetic, thaumaturgic, tranced, uncanny, unusual, weird, witching, witchlike, wizardly, wonderful; SEE CONCEPTS 537,548,582

magician [*n*] *person who performs supernatural feats or tricks*
archimage, charmer, conjurer, diabolist, diviner, enchanter, enchantress, exorciser, exorcist, fortune-teller, genie, genius, illusionist, marvel, medicine person, medium, miracle worker, necromancer, prophet, satanist, seer, shaman, siren, soothsayer, sorcerer, spellbinder, thaumaturge, theurgist, trickster, virtuoso, voodoo, warlock, witch, witch doctor, wizard; SEE CONCEPTS 352,361

magnanimous [*adj*] *giving and kind*
all heart, altruistic, beneficent, benevolent, big, bighearted, bountiful, charitable, considerate, forgiving, free, generous, great, greathearted, handsome, has heart in right place*, high-minded, kindly, knightly, liberal, lofty, loose, munificent, noble, openhanded, Santa Claus*, selfless, soft*, soft-touch*, ungrudging, unselfish, unstinting; SEE CONCEPTS 404,542

magnate [*n*] *important person, usually in business*
aristocrat, bigwig*, businessperson, capitalist, captain of industry, chief, figure, financier, industrialist, leader, lion*, merchant, mogul, name, noble, notable, peer, personage, plutocrat, tycoon, VIP*; SEE CONCEPT 347

magnetic [*adj*] *drawing, attractive*
alluring, appealing, arresting, bewitching, captivating, charismatic, charming, enchanting, entrancing, fascinating, hypnotic, inviting, irresistible, mesmerizing, pulling, seductive; SEE CONCEPTS 404,537

magnetism [*n*] *charm, attractiveness*
allure, appeal, attraction, captivatingness, charisma, draw, drawing power, enchantment, fascination, glamour, hypnotism, influence, lure, magic, mesmerism, power, pull, seductiveness, spell, witchcraft, witchery; SEE CONCEPTS 411,676

magnificent [*adj*] *glorious, wonderful*
arresting, august, brilliant, chivalric, commanding, elegant, elevated, exalted, excellent, fine, glittering, gorgeous, grand, grandiose, high-minded, imperial, imposing, impressive, lavish, lofty, luxurious, magnanimous, magnific, majestic, noble, opulent, outstanding, palatial, plush, pompous, posh, proud, radiant, regal, resplendent, rich, royal, smashing, splendid, standout, stately, striking, sublime, sumptuous, superb, superior, superlative, swanky, towering, transcendent; SEE CONCEPTS 485,572

magnify [*v*] *enlarge, intensify*
aggrandize, aggravate, amplify, augment, bless, blow up, boost, build up, deepen, dignify, dilate, distend, enhance, ennoble, eulogize, exalt, expand, extend, glorify, heighten, hike, hike up, increase, inflate, intensate, jack up, jump up, mount, multiply, pad, pyramid, redouble, rise, rouse, run up, step up, sweeten, swell; SEE CONCEPTS 236,244,245

magnify [*v2*] *exaggerate, blow out of proportion*
aggravate, blow up*, boost, color, dramatize, embellish, embroider, enhance, fudge*, inflate, make mountain of molehill*, overcharge, overdo, overdraw, overemphasize, overestimate, overlay, overrate, overstate, overstress, pad*, puff up*, pyramid; SEE CONCEPTS 49,69,266

magnitude [*n1*] *importance*
consequence, degree, eminence, grandeur, greatness, import, mark, moment, momentousness, note, pith, significance, signification, weight, weightiness; SEE CONCEPT 668

magnitude [*n2*] *size*
admeasurement, amount, amplitude, bigness, breadth, bulk, capacity, compass, dimension, dimensions, enormity, enormousness, expanse, extent, greatness, hugeness, immensity, intensity, largeness, mass, measure, measurement, proportion, proportions, quantity, range, reach, sizableness, space, strength, tremendousness, vastness, volume; SEE CONCEPT 730

maiden [*adj*] *earliest*
beginning, first, fresh, inaugural, initial, initiatory, intact, introductory, new, original, pioneer, primary, prime, unbroached, untapped, untried, unused; SEE CONCEPTS 548,585

mail [*n*] *written correspondence; system for sending correspondence*
air mail, communication, junk mail, letter, package, parcel, post, postal service, postcard, post office; SEE CONCEPTS 271,770

mail [*v*] *send through the postal system*
dispatch, drop, express, forward, post, send by mail, transmit; SEE CONCEPT 217

maim [*v*] *cripple, put out of action*
batter, blemish, break, castrate, crush, damage, deface, disable, disfigure, dismember, disqualify, gimp*, hack, hamstring*, harm, hog-tie*, hurt, impair, incapacitate, injure, lame, mangle, mar, massacre, maul, mayhem, mutilate, spoil, truncate, warp, wound; SEE CONCEPT 246

main [*n*] *pipe for system*
cable, channel, conduit, duct, line, trough, trunk; SEE CONCEPT 494

main [*adj1*] *principal, predominant*
capital, cardinal, central, chief, controlling, critical, crucial, essential, foremost, fundamental, head, leading, major, necessary, outstanding, paramount, particular, preeminent, premier, prevailing, primary, prime, special, star, stellar, supreme, vital; SEE CONCEPTS 546,567,829

main [*adj2*] *absolute, utter*
brute, direct, downright, entire, mere, only, pure,

sheer, simple, undisguised, utmost; SEE CONCEPT 535

mainly [adv] for the most part
above all, chiefly, essentially, first and foremost, generally, in general, in the main, largely, mostly, most of all, on the whole, overall, predominantly, primarily, principally, substantially, to the greatest extent, usually; SEE CONCEPTS 530,544,772

mainstay [n] chief support
anchor, backbone, brace, bulwark, buttress, crutch*, good right arm*, linchpin*, maintainer, pillar, prop, right-hand person*, sinew, staff, standby, stay, strength, supporter, sustainer, upholder; SEE CONCEPTS 646,712

maintain [v1] care for, keep up
advance, carry on, conserve, continue, control, cultivate, finance, go on with, guard, keep, keep going, look after, manage, nurture, perpetuate, persevere, preserve, prolong, protect, provide, renew, repair, retain, save, supply, support, sustain, take care of, uphold; SEE CONCEPTS 134,140

maintain [v2] assert, claim; argue for
advocate, affirm, allege, asseverate, attest, aver, avow, back, champion, contend, correct, declare, defend, emphasize, fight for, hold, insist, justify, persist, plead for, profess, protest, rectify, report, right, say, stand by, state, stress, uphold, vindicate; SEE CONCEPTS 46,49,68

maintenance [n] perpetuation, support; sustenance
aliment, alimentation, alimony, allowance, bacon*, bread, bread and butter*, care, carrying, conservation, continuance, continuation, food, keep, keeping, livelihood, living, nurture, preservation, prolongation, provision, repairs, resources, retainment, salt*, subsistence, supply, sustaining, sustainment, sustention, upkeep, wherewithal; SEE CONCEPTS 134,340,457,712

majestic [adj] impressive, splendid
august, awesome, ceremonious, cool, courtly, dignified, elevated, exalted, fab*, grand, grandiose, imperial, imposing, lofty, magnific, magnificent, marvelous, mind-blowing*, monumental, noble, out of this world*, pompous, regal, royal, smashing, sovereign, stately, stunning, sublime, sumptuous, superb; SEE CONCEPTS 567,572,574

major [adj1] bigger
above, better, big, chief, considerable, dominant, elder, exceeding, extensive, extreme, greater, hefty, higher, large, larger, large-scale, leading, main, most, oversized, primary, senior, sizable, superior, supreme, ultra, upper, uppermost; SEE CONCEPTS 574,773

major [adj2] important
big, chief, critical, crucial, dangerous, grave, great, grievous, heavyweight, influential, life and death*, main, major-league, meaningful, notable, outstanding, overshadowing, preeminent, principal, radical, serious, significant, star, stellar, top, vital, weighty; SEE CONCEPT 568

majority [n1] plurality, most
best part*, bulk, greater number, greater part, larger part, lion's share*, mass, max*, more, more than half*, preponderance, superiority; SEE CONCEPTS 766,829,835

majority [n2] adulthood
age of consent, drinking age, estate, full age, legal maturity, manhood, maturity, prime, prime of life*, ripe age*, seniority, voting age, womanhood; SEE CONCEPTS 715,817

make [v1] create, build
accomplish, adjust, arrange, assemble, beget, brew, bring about, cause, compose, conceive, constitute, construct, cook, cook up*, dash off*, draw on, dream up, effect, engender, fabricate, fashion, forge, form, frame, generate, get ready, give rise to, hatch, initiate, invent, knock off*, lead to, manufacture, mold, occasion, originate, parent, prepare, procreate, produce, put together, secure, shape, spawn, synthesize, tear off, throw together*, whip, whip out*; SEE CONCEPTS 168,173,205,221

make [v2] induce, compel
bring about, cause, coerce, concuss, constrain, dragoon, drive, effect, force, horn in*, impel, impress, initiate, interfere, meddle, oblige, press, pressurize, prevail upon, require, secure, shotgun, start, tamper; SEE CONCEPTS 14,221

make [v3] designate, appoint
advance, assign, constitute, create, delegate, elect, finger, install, invest, name, nominate, ordain, proffer, select, tap, tender; SEE CONCEPTS 50,88

make [v4] enact, execute
act, carry on, carry out, carry through, conduct, declare, decree, do, draft, draw up, effect, engage in, establish, fix, form, formulate, frame, legislate, pass, perform, practice, prepare, prosecute, wage; SEE CONCEPTS 91,100,242

make [v5] add up to; constitute
amount to, come to, compose, compound, comprise, construct, embody, equal, fabricate, form, make up, mix, organize, put together, represent, structure, synthesize, texture; SEE CONCEPTS 664,667

make [v6] estimate, infer
calculate, collect, conclude, deduce, deduct, derive, dope out, draw, figure, gather, gauge, judge, reckon, suppose, think; SEE CONCEPTS 15,37

make [v7] earn, acquire
bring home bacon*, bring in, clean up*, clear, gain, get, harvest, hustle, net, obtain, pull, pull down*, rate, realize, reap, receive, secure, sock*, take in; SEE CONCEPTS 120,124,351

make [v8] arrive, aim at
advance, arrive at, arrive in time, attain, bear, break for, catch, get to, go, head, light out, meet, move, proceed, progress, reach, set out, strike out, take off; SEE CONCEPTS 159,224

make believe [v] pretend, dream
act as if, act as though, counterfeit, enact, fantasize, feign, fool, imagine, play, playact*, simulate; SEE CONCEPTS 12,59

make-believe [n] unreality
charade, disguise, dissimulation, dream, fairy tale, fakery, fantasy, imagination, pageant, playacting, pretense, pretension, pretentiousness, sham; SEE CONCEPTS 689,725

make-believe [adj] imagined, unreal
acted, dream, false, fantasized, fantasy, fictional, fraudulent, imaginary, made-up, mock, pretend, pretended, sham, simulated; SEE CONCEPTS 529,582

make off [v] flee, run away
abscond, bolt*, clear, cut and run, decamp, depart, escape, fly*, go, leave, make away, quit, retire, run, run for it, run off, scamper, scoot, skedaddle*, skip*, withdraw; SEE CONCEPTS 102,150,195

make out [v1] see, recognize
detect, discern, discover, distinguish, espy, notice, observe, perceive, remark; SEE CONCEPT 626

make out [v2] understand
accept, catch, collect, compass, comprehend, conclude, decipher, deduce, deduct, derive, dig, fathom, follow, gather, grasp, infer, judge, perceive, realize, recognize, see, take in, work out; SEE CONCEPTS 15,18

make out [v3] get by, succeed
accomplish, achieve, do, do well enough, do with, endure, fare, flourish, get along, get on, manage, muddle through, prosper, score, thrive; SEE CONCEPTS 23,91,140

makeshift [n] temporary help
expediency, expedient, last resort, pis aller, recourse, refuge, replacement, resort, resource, shift, stopgap, substitute; SEE CONCEPTS 658,712

makeshift [adj] temporary
alternative, Band-Aid*, expedient, hit-or-miss*, make-do*, provisional, quick-and-dirty*, slapdash*, stopgap, substitute, temp, throwaway*; SEE CONCEPTS 551,560

makeup [n1] cosmetics
blush, face*, foundation, greasepaint, lipstick, maquillage, paint, pancake, powder*; SEE CONCEPT 446

makeup [n2] structure, composition
architecture, arrangement, assembly, configuration, constitution, construction, content, contents, design, form, format, formation, layout, order, ordering, organization, plan, scheme, setup, shape, spread, style; SEE CONCEPT 757

makeup [n3] person's character
build, cast, complexion, constitution, disposition, fiber, figure, frame of mind, grain, humor, individualism, individuality, make, mold, nature, personality, stamp, stripe, temper, temperament, vein; SEE CONCEPT 411

make up [v1] create
ad-lib*, blend, coin, combine, compose, compound, concoct, construct, contrive, cook up*, devise, dream up, fabricate, fake it, fashion, fix, formulate, frame, fuse, hatch, improv*, improvise, invent, join, knock off, make, meld, merge, mingle, mix, originate, play by ear*, prepare, pretend, put together, ready, trump up, whip up*, wing it*, write; SEE CONCEPTS 173,202

make up [v2] comprise, constitute
complete, compose, consist, fill, form, furnish, include, make, meet, provide, supply; SEE CONCEPT 643

make up [v3] compensate, reconcile
accommodate, atone, balance, bury the hatchet*, come to terms, compose, conciliate, counterbalance, counterpoise, countervail, forgive and forget, make amends, make peace, mend, offset, outweigh, pacify, recompense, redeem, redress, requite, set off, settle, shake hands; SEE CONCEPTS 126,384

maladroit [adj1] awkward, clumsy
all thumbs*, blundering, bumbling, bungling, clunky, floundering, gauche, halting, heavy-handed, inept, inexpert, klutzy*, lumbering, stumbling, two left feet*, ungraceful, unhandy, unskillful; SEE CONCEPTS 401,584

maladroit [adj2] tactless
brash, gauche, impolitic, inconsiderate, inelegant, insensitive, thoughtless, undiplomatic, untactful, untoward; SEE CONCEPT 401

malaise [n] depression, sickness
angst, anxiety, debility, decrepitude, despair, discomfort, disquiet, distress, doldrums, enervation, feebleness, illness, infirmity, infirmness, lassitude, melancholy, pain, sickliness, unease, uneasiness, unhealthiness, weakness; SEE CONCEPTS 316,410

male [n] man
boy, brother, father, fellow, gent*, gentleman, grandfather, guy, he, husband, Mr., sir, son; SEE CONCEPT 419

male [adj] masculine
macho*, manful, manlike, manly, paternal, potent, virile; SEE CONCEPTS 371,408

malediction [n] curse
anathema, commination, curse word, cuss, cuss word, damn, damnation, damning, darn, denunciation, dirty name*, dirty word*, execration, expletive, four-letter word*, imprecation, jinx, no-no*, oath, swear word, whammy*; SEE CONCEPT 278

malevolent [adj] hateful
bad-natured, baleful, catty*, despiteful, dirty, evil, evil-minded, hellish, hostile, malicious, malign, malignant, murder, murderous, pernicious, poison, rancorous, rough, sinister, spiteful, tough, vengeful, vicious, vindictive, waspish, wicked; SEE CONCEPTS 401,542

malformed [adj] distorted
abnormal, contorted, crooked, deformed, grotesque, irregular, misshapen, twisted, warped; SEE CONCEPT 486

malfunction [n] breakdown, failure
bug*, defect, fault, flaw, glitch*, gremlin*, impairment, slip; SEE CONCEPTS 658,674

malice [n] hate, vengefulness
acerbity, animosity, antipathy, bad blood, bane, bile, bitterness, despite, despitefulness, dirt, dislike, down, enmity, evil, grudge, hatefulness, hatred, hostility, ill will, implacability, malevolence, maliciousness, malignance, malignity, meanness, mordacity, poison, rancor, repugnance, resentment, spite, spitefulness, spleen, umbrage, venom, viciousness, vindictiveness; SEE CONCEPT 29

malicious [adj] hateful
awful, bad-natured, baleful, beastly, bitter, catty*, cussed, deleterious, despiteful, detrimental, envious, evil, evil-minded, green*, green-eyed*, gross*, ill-disposed, injurious, jealous, low, malevolent, malign, malignant, mean, mischievous, nasty, noxious, ornery, pernicious, petty, poisonous, rancorous, resentful, spiteful, uncool*, vengeful, venomous, vicious, virulent, wicked; SEE CONCEPTS 267,401,542

malign [adj] hurtful, injurious
antagonistic, antipathetic, bad, baleful, baneful, deleterious, despiteful, destructive, detrimental, evil, harmful, hateful, hostile, inimical, malefic, maleficent, malevolent, malignant, noxious, pernicious, rancorous, sinister, spiteful, vicious, wicked; SEE CONCEPTS 267,537,542

malign [v] slander, defame
abuse, accuse, asperse, backbite*, bad-mouth*, befoul, besmirch, bespatter, blacken, calumniate, cast aspersion, curse, decry, defile, denigrate, depreciate, derogate, detract, dirty*, disparage, harm, injure, insult, misrepresent, mudsling, opprobriate, pollute, rap, revile, roast*, run down*, scandalize, slur, smear, soil, spatter*, speak ill of,

stain, sully, taint, take a swipe at*, tarnish, tear down, traduce, vilify, villainize, vituperate; SEE CONCEPTS *44,52,54,63*

malignant [*adj*] *diseased*
cancerous, deadly, destructive, fatal, internecine, lethal, mortal, pestilential, poisonous; SEE CONCEPT *314*

mall [*n*] *commercial complex with many individual retail stores*
commercial center, market, mart, mini-mart, plaza, shopping center, shopping mall; SEE CONCEPTS *325,439,449*

malleable [*adj*] *pliable*
adaptable, compliant, ductile, flexible, governable, go-with-the-flow*, impressionable, manageable, moldable, plastic, pliant, putty in hands*, rolls with punches*, soft, submissive, supple, tractable, tractile, transformable, workable, yielding; SEE CONCEPTS *403,485*

malodorous [*adj*] *foul-smelling*
bad, decayed, decomposed, fetid, foul, frowzy, funky*, fusty, gamy*, high*, infested, lousy, mephitic, musty, nasty, nauseating, noisome, noxious, off*, offensive, pestilential, poisonous, polluted, putrid, rancid, rank, reeking, rotten, smelly, stale, stenchful, stinking, strong, tainted, vile; SEE CONCEPT *598*

malpractice [*n*] *abuse, misconduct*
carelessness, dereliction, malefaction, misbehavior, misdeed, mismanagement, negligence, offense, transgression, violation; SEE CONCEPTS *101,156,310,324*

mammoth [*adj*] *huge*
behemothic, colossal, elephantine, enormous, gargantuan, giant, gigantic, high, immense, jumbo, large, leviathan, long, massive, mighty, monstrous, monumental, mountainous, prodigious, stupendous, titanic, vast; SEE CONCEPT *773*

man [*n2*] *male human*
beau, boyfriend, brother, father, fellow, gentleman, grandfather, guy, he, husband, Mr., nephew, papa, sir, son, spouse, swain*, uncle; SEE CONCEPT *419*

manage [*v1*] *be in charge, control*
administer, advocate, boss, call the shots*, call upon, captain, care for, carry on, command, concert, conduct, counsel, designate, direct, disburse, dominate, engage in, engineer, execute, govern, guide, handle, head, hold down*, influence, instruct, maintain, manipulate, minister, officiate, operate, oversee, pilot, ply, preside, regulate, request, rule, run, run the show, steer, superintend, supervise, take care of, take over, take the helm*, train, use, watch, watch over, wield; SEE CONCEPTS *94,117*

manage [*v2*] *accomplish*
achieve, arrange, bring about, bring off, carry out, con*, contrive, cook*, cope with, deal with, doctor*, effect, engineer, execute, finagle, fix, jockey*, plant*, play games*, pull strings*, push around, put one over*, rig*, scam*, succeed, swing, upstage, wangle, work; SEE CONCEPTS *91,706*

manage [*v3*] *survive, get by*
bear up, carry on, cope, endure, fare, get along*, get on*, make do*, make out*, muddle, scrape by*, shift, stagger; SEE CONCEPTS *23,407*

management [*n1*] *persons running an organization*
administration, authority, board, bosses, brass, directorate, directors, employers, execs*, executive, executives, executive suite, front office*, head, mainframe*, management, micro management*, person upstairs*, top brass*, upstairs*; SEE CONCEPT *325*

management [*n2*] *running an organization*
administration, care, charge, command, conduct, control, direction, governance, government, guidance, handling, intendance, manipulation, operation, oversight, rule, superintendence, superintendency, supervision; SEE CONCEPTS *117,324*

manager [*n*] *person who runs organization*
administrator, boss, comptroller, conductor, controller, director, exec*, executive, governor, handler, head, head person, officer, official, organizer, overseer, producer, proprietor, slave-driver*, straw boss*, superintendent, supervisor, zookeeper*; SEE CONCEPT *347*

mandate [*n*] *authority, order*
authorization, behest, bidding, blank check*, carte blanche*, charge, command, commission, decree, dictate, directive, edict, fiat, go-ahead*, green light*, imperative, injunction, instruction, okay*, precept, sanction, warrant, word*; SEE CONCEPTS *318,685*

mandatory [*adj*] *required, necessary*
binding, commanding, compelling, compulsatory, compulsory, de rigueur, essential, forced, imperative, imperious, indispensable, involuntary, irremissible, needful, obligatory, requisite; SEE CONCEPT *546*

maneuver [*n1*] *move, tactic*
action, angle, artifice, contrivance, curveball, demarche, device, dodge, fancy footwork*, feint, finesse, gambit, game, gimmick, intrigue, jig*, machination, manipulation, measure, movement, plan, play, plot, ploy, procedure, proceeding, ruse, scheme, shenanigans*, shuffle*, step, stratagem, stunt, subterfuge, trick; SEE CONCEPTS *6,660*

maneuver [*n2*] *military practice, operation*
battle, deployment, drill, evolution, exercise, measure, movement, parade, plan, procedure, proceeding, stratagem, tactics, war games; SEE CONCEPT *320*

maneuver [*v1*] *plan, scheme*
angle, beguile, cheat, come up with, con*, conspire, contrive, cook, design, devise, doctor, engineer, exploit, fence, finagle, finesse, go around, intrigue, jockey, leave holding the bag*, machinate, manage, manipulate, move, navigate, operate, play, play games*, plot, proceed, pull strings*, push around, put one over*, rig, scam, sham*, shift, trick, upstage, wangle, work; SEE CONCEPTS *36,59*

maneuver [*v2*] *direct physically*
deploy, dispense, drive, exercise, guide, handle, manipulate, move, navigate, negotiate, pilot, ply, steer, swing, wield; SEE CONCEPTS *187,225*

mangle [*v*] *mutilate, deform*
batter, break, bruise, butcher, carve, contort, crush, cut, damage, deface, destroy, disfigure, distort, flay, hack, hash, impair, injure, lacerate, maim, mar, maul, rend, ruin, separate, slash, slay, slice, slit, spoil, tear, wound, wreck; SEE CONCEPTS *176,246,252*

mangy [*adj*] *scruffy*
decrepit, dirty, impoverished, indigent, mean,

moth-eaten*, poor, ragtag*, shabby, shoddy, sick, sleazy*, squalid, tattered; SEE CONCEPTS 485,621

manhood/womanhood [n] *physical maturity and strength of adult male or female*
adulthood, coming of age*, fecundity, femininity, fertility, manfulness, manliness, masculinity, mettle, potency, virility, womanliness, womanness; SEE CONCEPTS 633,715

mania [n] *fixation, madness*
aberration, ax to grind*, bee*, bee in bonnet*, bug*, bug in ear*, compulsion, craving, craze, craziness, delirium, dementia, derangement, desire, disorder, enthusiasm, fad, fancy, fascination, fetish, fixed idea, frenzy, furor, grabber*, hangup*, idée fixe, infatuation, insanity, lunacy, monomania, obsession, on the brain*, partiality, passion, preoccupation, rage, thing, tiger*, tiger by the tail*; SEE CONCEPTS 20,32,410,529

maniac [n] *person who is crazy, overenthusiastic*
bedlamite, bigot, crackpot*, enthusiast, fan, fanatic, fiend, flake*, freak, fruitcake*, kook*, loon, loony*, lunatic, madperson, nut*, nutcase*, psycho*, psychopath, schizoid*, screwball*, Section 8*, zealot; SEE CONCEPT 412

manic/maniacal [adj] *overexcited, crazy*
berserk, crazed, demented, deranged, excited, flipped*, flipped out*, freaked out*, freaky*, frenzied, high*, insane, lunatic, mad, nutty*, psychotic, rabid, raving, turned-out, unbalanced, up*, wild; SEE CONCEPT 403

manifest [adj] *clear, obvious*
apparent, big as life*, bold, clear-cut*, conspicuous, crystal clear*, disclosed, distinct, divulged, evidenced, evident, evinced, glaring, noticeable, open, palpable, patent, plain, prominent, revealed, shown, straightforward, told, unambiguous, unmistakable, visible; SEE CONCEPTS 529,576

manifest [v] *exhibit, make plain*
confirm, declare, demonstrate, display, embody, establish, evidence, evince, expose, express, exteriorize, externalize, flash, illustrate, incarnate, let it all hang out*, mark, materialize, objectify, ostend, parade, personalize, personify, personize, proclaim, prove, reveal, set forth, show, show and tell*, showcase, signify, sport, strut, substantiate, suggest, utter, vent, voice, wave around*; SEE CONCEPTS 118,261

manifestation [n] *exhibition, proof*
appearance, demonstration, disclosure, display, explanation, exposure, expression, indication, instance, mark, materialization, meaning, phenomenon, revelation, show, sign, symptom, token; SEE CONCEPTS 642,672

manifold [adj] *abundant, many*
assorted, complex, copious, different, diverse, diversified, diversiform, multifarious, multifold, multiform, multiple, multiplied, multitudinous, multivarious, numerous, sundry, varied, various; SEE CONCEPTS 564,762,781

manipulate [v1] *maneuver, handle physically*
employ, feel, finger*, form, manage, mold, operate, ply, shape, swing, thumb*, use, wield, work; SEE CONCEPTS 225,612

manipulate [v2] *change to suit one's desire*
beguile, conduct, control, direct, engineer, exploit, finagle, finesse, guide, handle, influence, jockey, machinate, maneuver, massage, mold, negotiate, play, play games*, pull strings*, pull

wires*, push around, shape, steer, upstage, use; SEE CONCEPTS 14,234

manner [n1] *person's behavior, conduct*
address, affectation, affectedness, air, appearance, aspect, bearing, comportment, demeanor, deportment, idiosyncrasy, look, mannerism, mien, peculiarity, presence, style, tone, turn, way; SEE CONCEPTS 411,633,644

manner [n2] *method, approach*
consuetude, custom, fashion, form, genre, habit, habitude, line, means, mode, modus, practice, procedure, process, routine, style, system, tack, technique, tenor, tone, trick, usage, use, vein, way, wise, wont; SEE CONCEPTS 6,660

manner [n3] *class, category*
brand, breed, form, kind, nature, sort, type, variety; SEE CONCEPT 378

mannered [adj] *affected, put-on*
airish*, apish*, artificial, artsy, campy*, chichi*, conscious, gone Hollywood*, highfaluting*, posed, pretentious, self-conscious, stilted, stuck up*, unnatural; SEE CONCEPT 401

mannerism [n] *peculiarity of how someone behaves, acts*
affectation, air, characteristic, eccentricity, foible, habit, idiosyncrasy, oddness, pose, pretension, queerness, quirk, singularity, trait, trick; SEE CONCEPT 644

mannerly [adj] *polite, well-behaved*
charming, civil, civilized, considerate, courteous, decorous, genteel, gracious, polished, refined, respectful, well-bred, well-mannered; SEE CONCEPT 401

manners [n] *polite, refined social behavior*
amenities, bearing, behavior, breeding, carriage, ceremony, civilities, comportment, conduct, courtesy, culture, decorum, demeanor, deportment, dignity, elegance, etiquette, formalities, good breeding, good form, mien, mores, polish, politeness, politesse, propriety, protocol, p's and q's*, refinement, social graces, sophistication, taste, urbanity; SEE CONCEPT 633

mansion [n] *very large house*
abode, building, castle, chateau, dwelling, estate, habitation, hall, home, manor, palace, residence, seat, villa; SEE CONCEPTS 439,516

manslaughter [n] *killing without malicious forethought*
crime, foul play*, hit*, homicide, killing, murder; SEE CONCEPT 252

manual [n] *book giving instruction*
bible, compendium, cookbook, enchiridion, guide, guidebook, handbook, primer, reference book, schoolbook, text, textbook, workbook; SEE CONCEPT 280

manual [adj] *done by hand*
chiral, hand-operated, human, not automatic, physical, standard; SEE CONCEPT 544

manufacture/manufacturing [n] *production of processed goods*
accomplishment, assembling, assembly, casting, completion, composing, composition, construction, creation, doing, erection, fabrication, finishing, forging, formation, making, mass-production, preparing, produce, tooling; SEE CONCEPT 324

manufacture [v] *build, produce*
accomplish, assemble, carve, cast, cobble*, complete, compose, construct, create, execute, fabricate, fashion, forge, form, frame, fudge

together*, machine, make, make up, mass-produce, mill, mold, prefab, process, put together, shape, synthesize, throw together, tool, turn out; SEE CONCEPT 205

manufacture [v2] *concoct, invent*
contrive, cook up*, create, devise, fabricate, hatch, make up, produce, think up, trump up*; SEE CONCEPTS 35,36

many [n] *abundance; a lot*
gobs*, heaps*, horde, jillion*, large numbers, mass, multitude, oodles*, piles*, plenty, scads*, scores, thousands, throng, tons, umpteen*, whole slew*; SEE CONCEPTS 432,787

many [adj] *profuse, abundant*
abounding, alive with, bounteous, bountiful, copious, countless, divers, frequent, innumerable, legion, lousy with*, manifold, multifarious, multifold, multiplied, multitudinous, myriad, no end of*, numberless, numerous, plentiful, populous, prevalent, rife, several, sundry, teeming, umpteen, uncounted, varied, various; SEE CONCEPTS 762,771

map [n] *chart of geographic area*
atlas, delineation, design, diagram, draft, drawing, elevation, globe, graph, ground plan, outline, picture, plan, plat, portrayal, print, projection, sketch, topographical depiction, tracing; SEE CONCEPT 625

mar [v] *hurt, damage*
bend, blemish, blight, blot, break, bruise, deface, deform, detract, ding*, disfigure, foul up, harm, impair, injure, louse up, maim, mangle, mess up*, mutilate, queer*, rough up, ruin, scar, scratch, shake up, spoil, stain, sully, taint, tarnish, tweak, vitiate, warp, wreck; SEE CONCEPT 246

maraud [v] *pillage and plunder*
despoil, forage, foray, harass, harry, loot, raid, ransack, ravage, sack; SEE CONCEPTS 86,139

march [v] *walk with deliberation*
advance, boot, debouch, drill, file, forge ahead, go on, hoof it*, journey, mount, move, move out, pace, parade, patrol, pound, pound the pavement*, proceed, progress, promenade, range, space, stalk, step, step out, stomp, stride, strut, traipse, tramp, tread; SEE CONCEPT 150

margin [n] *border; room around something*
allowance, bound, boundary, brim, brink, compass, confine, edge, elbowroom*, extra, field, frame, hem, latitude, leeway, limit, lip, perimeter, periphery, play, rim, scope, selvage, shore, side, skirt, space, surplus, trimming, verge; SEE CONCEPTS 270,484,513

marginal [adj] *borderline; slight*
bordering, insignificant, low, minimal, minor, negligible, on the edge, peripheral, rimming, small, verging; SEE CONCEPTS 513,789

marine/maritime [adj] *concerning the sea*
abyssal, aquatic, coastal, deep-sea, hydrographic, littoral, maritime, natatorial, nautical, naval, navigational, Neptunian, oceangoing, oceanic, oceanographic, of the sea, pelagic, saltwater, sea, seafaring, seagoing, seashore, seaside, shore; SEE CONCEPT 536

mariner [n] *person who makes living on the sea*
bluejacket*, captain, crew, mate, navigator, sailor, salt*, sea dog*, seafarer, shipmate, swab*, yachtie*; SEE CONCEPTS 348,366

marital [adj] *concerning marriage*
conjugal, connubial, married, matrimonial, nuptial, spousal, wedded; SEE CONCEPT 555

mark [n1] *blemish; character*
autograph, blaze, blot, blotch, brand, brand name, bruise, check, cross, dent, dot, impression, imprint, ink, John Hancock*, John Henry*, label, line, logo, nick, pock, point, record, register, representation, scar, score, scratch, sign, signature, smudge, splotch, spot, stain, stamp, streak, stroke, symbol, tag, ticket, trace, trademark, underlining, X*; SEE CONCEPTS 79,284

mark [n2] *characteristic, symptom*
affection, attribute, badge, blaze, brand, character, device, distinction, earmark, emblem, evidence, feature, hallmark, idiosyncrasy, image, impression, incision, index, indication, indicia, label, marking, note, particularity, peculiarity, print, proof, property, quality, seal, sign, significant, stamp, symbol, token, trait, type, virtue; SEE CONCEPTS 411,644,716

mark [n3] *criterion, standard*
gauge, level, measure, norm, yardstick; SEE CONCEPTS 561,783

mark [n4] *goal, target*
aim, ambition, bull's eye*, duty, end, function, object, objective, prey, purpose, use; SEE CONCEPT 659

mark [n5] *importance*
consequence, dignity, distinction, effect, eminence, fame, influence, manifestation, notability, note, notice, prestige, quality, regard, result, standing, value; SEE CONCEPTS 346,668

mark [v1] *blemish, stain*
autograph, blaze, blot, blotch, brand, bruise, chalk, check, dent, dot, impress, imprint, initial, ink, inscribe, label, letter, nick, pinpoint, point, print, scar, score, scratch, seal, sign, smudge, splotch, stamp, streak, stroke, trace, underline, write, X*; SEE CONCEPTS 79,250

mark [v2] *characterize*
bespeak, betoken, brand, check off, demonstrate, denote, designate, distinguish, earmark, evidence, evince, exemplify, exhibit, feature, identify, illustrate, indicate, individualize, individuate, label, manifest, mark off, ostend, point out, point up*, proclaim, qualify, remark, set apart, show, show up, signalize, signify, singularize, stake out*, stamp; SEE CONCEPT 261

mark [v3] *see, notice*
attend, behold, chronicle, discern, distinguish, eye, hearken, mind, note, observe, pay attention, pay heed, perceive, regard, register, remark, take notice of, view, watch, write down; SEE CONCEPTS 38,626

marked [adj] *apparent, obvious*
arresting, clear, considerable, conspicuous, decided, distinct, evident, manifest, notable, noted, noticeable, outstanding, patent, pointed, prominent, pronounced, remarkable, salient, signal, striking; SEE CONCEPTS 485,535,589

markedly [adv] *distinctly*
clearly, considerably, conspicuously, decidedly, especially, evidently, greatly, manifestly, notably, noticeably, obviously, outstandingly, particularly, patently, remarkably, signally, strikingly, to a great extent; SEE CONCEPTS 535,544

market/mart [n] *place, venue for selling goods*
bazaar, bodega, booth, business, chain store, co-op, corner store, deli, delicatessen, department store, dimestore, drugstore, emporium, exchange, fair, general store, grocery store, mall, mart, outlet, shop, shopping mall, showroom, souk,

square, stall, stock exchange, store, supermarket, trading post, truck, variety store, warehouse; SEE CONCEPTS 323,333,449

market [v] *package and sell goods*
advertise, barter, display, exchange, merchandise, offer for sale, retail, vend, wholesale; SEE CONCEPTS 324,345

marketable [adj] *easily sold; in demand*
bankable, commercial, fit, for sale, good, hot*, merchandisable, merchantable, profitable, salable, sellable, selling, sought after, sound, trafficable, vendible, wanted; SEE CONCEPTS 334,546

maroon [v] *abandon*
beach, cast ashore, cast away, desert, forsake, isolate, leave, leave high and dry*, strand; SEE CONCEPTS 195,384

marriage [n] *legal joining of two people; a union*
alliance, amalgamation, association, confederation, conjugality, connubiality, consortium, coupling, espousal, holy matrimony, link, match, mating, matrimony, merger, monogamy, nuptials, pledging, sacrament, spousal, tie, tie that binds*, wedded bliss*, wedded state, wedding, wedding bells*, wedding ceremony, wedlock; SEE CONCEPTS 297,388

marrow [n] *heart, essence*
bottom, core, cream, essentiality, gist, kernel, meat, pith, quick, quintessence, quintessential, soul, spirit, stuff, substance, virtuality; SEE CONCEPT 826

marry [v] *become husband and wife in legal ceremony*
ally, associate, become one, bond, catch*, combine, conjoin, conjugate, contract, couple, drop anchor*, espouse, get hitched*, get married, join, knit, land*, lead to altar, link, match, mate, merge, one, pledge, plight one's troth, promise, relate, settle down*, take vows, tie, tie the knot*, unify, unite, walk down aisle*, wed, yoke; SEE CONCEPT 297

marsh [n] *swamp*
bog, estuary, everglade, fen, mire, morass, moss, quag, quagmire, slough, swampland, wetland; SEE CONCEPT 509

marshal [v] *organize, guide*
align, arrange, array, assemble, collect, conduct, deploy, direct, dispose, distribute, draw up, escort, gather, group, lead, line up, methodize, mobilize, muster, order, rally, rank, shepherd, space, systematize, usher; SEE CONCEPTS 84,117,187

martial [adj] *having to do with armed hostilities*
aggressive, bellicose, belligerent, combative, hostile, military, pugnacious, soldierly, warlike; SEE CONCEPT 401

martyrdom [n] *suffering endured for sake of a cause*
affliction, agonizing, agony, anguish, crucifixion, devotion, distress, mortification, ordeal, pain, persecution, sacrifice, self-immolation, self-sacrifice, torment, torture, unselfishness; SEE CONCEPTS 410,411

marvel [v] *wonder*
curiosity, genius, miracle, one for the books*, phenomenon, portent, prodigy, sensation, something else*, stunner, whiz; SEE CONCEPTS 529,671

marvel [v] *be amazed*
be awed, be surprised, feel surprise, gape, gaze, goggle, stand in awe, stare, wonder; SEE CONCEPT 17

marvelous [adj1] *hard to believe; amazing*
astonishing, astounding, awe-inspiring, awesome, awful, bewildering, breathtaking, confounding, difficult to believe, extraordinary, fabulous, fantastic, implausible, improbable, incomprehensible, inconceivable, incredible, miraculous, phenomenal, prodigious, remarkable, singular, spectacular, staggering, strange, striking, stunning, stupendous, supernatural, surprising, unbelievable, unimaginable, unlikely, unusual, wonderful, wondrous; SEE CONCEPTS 529,552

marvelous [adj2] *superb, great*
agreeable, astonishing, bad*, boss*, colossal, cool*, divine, dreamy*, enjoyable, excellent, fab*, fabulous, fantastic, glorious, greatest, groovy*, hot*, keen, magnificent, neat*, out of this world*, outrageous, peachy, pleasant, pleasurable, prime*, rewarding, satisfying, sensational, smashing, solid*, solid gold*, spectacular, splendid, stupendous, super, supreme, swell, terrific, wonderful; SEE CONCEPT 574

masculinity/masculine [n/adj] *manly*
andric, gender, macho*, male, manful, mannish, potent, virile; SEE CONCEPTS 371,372,408,648

mash [v] *smash, squash*
brew, bruise, chew, crush, decoct, grind, hash, infuse, macerate, masticate, mush up, pound, press, pulp, pulverize, push, reduce, scrunch, squeeze, squish, steep, triturate; SEE CONCEPTS 170,186,208

mask [n] *false face, cover*
affectation, air*, appearance, aspect, beard*, blind, camouflage, cloak*, concealment, cover-up, disguise, disguisement, dissembling, dissimulation, domino*, facade, fig leaf*, front, guise, hood, masquerade, pose, posture, pretense, pretext, put-on*, screen, semblance, show*, simulation, veil*, veneer, visage, visor, window dressing*; SEE CONCEPTS 450,716

mask [v] *disguise*
beard, camouflage, cloak, conceal, cover, cover up, defend, dissemble, dissimulate, dress up, front, guard, hide, obscure, protect, safeguard, screen, secrete, shield, veil; SEE CONCEPTS 172,188,384

masquerade [n] *disguise; social occasion for disguises*
carnival, circus, cloak, color, costume, costume ball, cover, cover-up, deception, dissimulation, domino*, facade, festivity, front, guise, impersonation, imposture, Mardi Gras*, mask, masked ball, masking, mummery, personation, pose, pretense, put-on, revel, screen, show, subterfuge, veil; SEE CONCEPTS 172,188,383,451

masquerade [v] *disguise*
attitudinize, dissemble, dissimulate, frolic, impersonate, mask, pass as, pass for, pass off, pose, posture, pretend, revel; SEE CONCEPT 59

mass [n1] *body of matter; considerable portion*
accumulation, aggregate, assemblage, band, batch, block, bunch, chunk, clot, coagulation, collection, combination, concretion, conglomeration, core, corpus, crowd, entirety, gob, great deal, greater part, group, heap, horde, host, hunk, knot, lion's share*, load, lot, lump, majority, mob, mound, mountain, much, number, object, peck, piece, pile, plurality, preponderance, pyramid, quantity, shock, stack, staple, stockpile, sum, sum total, throng, totality, troop, volume, wad, whole; SEE CONCEPTS 432,787,835

mass [n2] *bulk, measurement*
dimension, extent, greatness, magnitude, size, span, volume; SEE CONCEPT 792

massacre [n] *killing of many*
annihilation, assassination, bloodbath, bloodshed, butchery, carnage, decimation, extermination, genocide, internecion, murder, slaughter, slaying; SEE CONCEPT 252

massacre [v] *kill, often in great numbers*
annihilate, butcher, decimate, depopulate, exterminate, mass murder, murder, slaughter, slay; SEE CONCEPT 252

massage [n] *kneading of body parts*
back rub, beating, chirapsia, manipulation, rolfing*, rubbing, rubbing-down, stroking; SEE CONCEPTS 308,310

massage [v] *knead body parts*
caress, manipulate, pat, press, push, rolf*, rub, rub down, stimulate, stroke; SEE CONCEPTS 208,308,310

masses [n] *public, crowd*
commonalty, common people, great unwashed*, hoi polloi*, lower class, mob, multitude, proletariat, rabble, rank and file*, riffraff*; SEE CONCEPT 417

massive [adj] *large*
big, bulky, colossal, cracking, cumbersome, cumbrous, elephantine, enormous, extensive, gargantuan, gigantic, grand, great, gross, heavy, hefty, huge, hulking, immense, imposing, impressive, mammoth, mighty, monster, monumental, mountainous, ponderous, prodigious, solid, stately, substantial, titanic, towering, tremendous, unwieldy, vast, walloping, weighty, whopping*; SEE CONCEPTS 773,781

master [n1] *person in charge, female or male*
administrator, boss, captain, chief, chieftain, commandant, commander, commanding officer, conqueror, controller, director, employer, general, governor, guide, guru, head, head person, instructor, judge, lord, manager, matriarch, overlord, overseer, owner, patriarch, pedagogue, preceptor, principal, pro, ruler, schoolmaster/mistress, skipper, slave driver*, spiritual leader, superintendent, supervisor, swami*, taskmaster, teacher, top dog*, tutor, wheel*; SEE CONCEPTS 347,350,354

master [n2] *expert, skilled person, female or male*
ace*, adept, artist, artiste, authority, buff*, champion, connoisseur, conqueror, doctor, doyen, doyenne, genius, guru, maestro, maven, old hand*, old pro*, past master, prima donna*, pro, professional, proficient, pundit, real pro*, sage, savant, scientist, shark*, victor, virtuoso, whiz*, whizbang*, winner, wizard; SEE CONCEPTS 350,366,423

master [adj1] *expert*
ace*, adept, crack*, crackerjack*, experienced, masterly, proficient, skilled, skillful; SEE CONCEPT 527

master [adj2] *main*
ascendant, chief, controlling, foremost, grand, great, leading, major, original, overbearing, paramount, predominant, predominate, preponderant, prevalant, prime, principal, regnant, sovereign, supreme; SEE CONCEPT 568

master [v1] *learn; become proficient*
acquire, beat the game*, beat the system*, bone up*, bury yourself in*, comprehend, cram, excel in, gain mastery, get down cold*, get down pat*,
get hold of*, get the hang of*, get the knack of*, grasp, grind, hit the books*, learn the ropes*, megastudy*, pick up, study, swamp*, understand; SEE CONCEPTS 31,630

masterful [adj1] *expert, skilled*
adept, adroit, clever, consummate, crack, crackerjack*, deft, dexterous, excellent, exquisite, fine, finished, first-rate, master, masterly, preeminent, proficient, skillful, superior, superlative, supreme, transcendent; SEE CONCEPT 527

masterpiece [n] *respected work of art*
chef d'oeuvre, classic, cream*, cream of the crop*, flower, gem*, jewel*, magnum opus, masterstroke, master work, model, monument, perfection, pièce de résistance*, prize, showpiece, standard, tour de force*, treasure; SEE CONCEPT 259

mastery [n1] *command, expertise*
ability, acquirement, adeptness, adroitness, attainment, capacity, cleverness, comprehension, cunning, deftness, dexterity, expertism, expertness, familiarity, finesse, genius, grasp, grip, ken, knack, know-how, knowledge, mastership, power, proficiency, prowess, skill, understanding, virtuosity, wizardry; SEE CONCEPT 630

match [n1] *competition*
bout, contest, engagement, event, game, meet, race, rivalry, sport, test, trial; SEE CONCEPT 363

match [n2] *counterpart, equal*
adversary, analogue, antagonist, approximation, companion, competitor, complement, copy, correlate, countertype, dead ringer*, double, duplicate, equivalent, like, lookalike, mate, opponent, parallel, peer, replica, ringer*, rival, spitting image*, twin; SEE CONCEPTS 664,667,716

match [n3] *couple*
affiliation, alliance, combination, duet, espousal, marriage, mating, pair, pairing, partnership, union; SEE CONCEPTS 297,388

matching [adj] *corresponding, equal*
analogous, comparable, coordinating, double, duplicate, equivalent, identical, like, paired, parallel, same, twin; SEE CONCEPT 566

matchless [adj] *unequalled, unique*
alone, consummate, excellent, exquisite, incomparable, inimitable, nonpareil, only, peerless, perfect, superior, superlative, supreme, unapproached, unmatched, unparalleled, unrivaled; SEE CONCEPT 574

mate [n] *one of a pair; partner*
acquaintance, alter ego, analog, assistant, associate, bedmate, bride, buddy*, chum*, classmate, cohort, colleague, companion, compeer, complement, comrade, concomitant, consort, coordinate, counterpart, coworker, crony, double, duplicate, familiar, friend, groom, helper, helpmate, intimate, match, pal*, peer, playmate, reciprocal, roommate, schoolmate, sidekick*, spouse, twin; SEE CONCEPTS 296,423,664

mate [v] *marry and breed*
cohabit, copulate, couple, crossbreed, generate, join, land*, match, merge, pair, procreate, serve, tie, tie the knot*, wed, yoke; SEE CONCEPTS 297,375

material [n1] *matter, fabric*
being, body, bolt, cloth, component, constituent, crop, element, entity, equipment, gear, goods, habiliments, individual, ingredient, machinery, materiel, object, outfit, paraphernalia, staple, stock,

stuff, substance, supply, tackle, textile, thing; SEE CONCEPTS *475,523*

material [*n2*] *written matter*
data, evidence, facts, information, notes, reading, text, work; SEE CONCEPTS *271,274*

material [*adj1*] *bodily, tangible*
actual, animal, appreciable, carnal, concrete, corporeal, earthly, fleshly, incarnate, nonspiritual, objective, palpable, perceptible, phenomenal, physical, real, sensible, sensual, substantial, true, worldly; SEE CONCEPT *485*

material [*adj2*] *important, relevant*
ad rem, applicable, applicative, apposite, apropos, big, cardinal, consequential, considerable, essential, fundamental, germane, grave, indispensable, intrinsic, key, meaningful, momentous, pertinent, pointful, primary, serious, significant, substantial, vital, weighty; SEE CONCEPT *567*

materialistic [*adj*] *thinking mainly about physical things*
acquisitive, banausic, carnal, earthly-minded, earthy, greedy, material, mundane, object-oriented, possessive, profane, secular, sensual, temporal, terrestrial, unspiritual; SEE CONCEPT *542*

materialize [*v*] *come into being*
actualize, appear, become concrete, become real, become visual, be incarnate, be realized, coalesce, come about, come to pass, corporealize, develop, embody, emerge, entify, evolve, exteriorize, externalize, happen, hypostatize, make real, manifest, metamorphose, objectify, occur, personalize, personify, personize, pragmatize, realize, reify, substantialize, substantiate, symbolize, take form, take place, take shape, turn up, typify, unfold, visualize; SEE CONCEPTS *105,173,184,231,251*

maternity [*n*] *period of being pregnant with child*
gestation, maternology, motherhood, parenthood; SEE CONCEPTS *316,817*

mathematical [*adj*] *concerning manipulation of numbers*
algebraic, algorithmic, analytical, arithmetical, computative, geometrical, math, measurable, numerical, scientific, trigonometric; SEE CONCEPT *762*

matriculate [*v*] *begin, enroll*
enter, join, register, sign up for; SEE CONCEPTS *114,119*

matrimonial [*adj*] *married*
betrothed, conjugal, connubial, engaged, epithalamic, espoused, marital, nuptial, spousal, wedded, wedding; SEE CONCEPT *555*

matrimony [*n*] *being joined in marriage*
alliance, bells*, conjugality, connubiality, marital rites, marriage, match, nuptials, shotgun wedding*, union, wedding, wedding bells*, wedding ceremony, wedlock; SEE CONCEPT *297*

matrix [*n*] *something from which another originates*
cast, forge, form, grid, model, mold, origin, pattern, source, womb; SEE CONCEPT *648*

matted [*adj*] *tangled*
disordered, kinky, knotted, rumpled, snarled, tousled, twisted, uncombed; SEE CONCEPT *606*

matter [*n1*] *substance*
amount, being, body, constituents, corporeality, corporeity, element, entity, individual, material, materialness, object, phenomenon, physical world, protoplasm, quantity, stuff, substantiality, sum, thing; SEE CONCEPTS *407,433,470*

matter [*n2*] *concern, issue*
affair, bag, business, circumstance, episode, event, goings-on*, incident, job, lookout, nub, occurrence, proceeding, question, shooting match*, situation, subject, thing, topic, transaction, undertaking; SEE CONCEPTS *532,696*

matter [*n3*] *subject, thesis*
argument, context, focus, head, interest, motif, motive, point, purport, resolution, sense, subject matter, substance, text, theme, topic; SEE CONCEPTS *349,529*

matter [*n4*] *significance, meaning*
amount, body, burden, consequence, content, core, extent, gist*, import, importance, magnitude, meat, moment, neighborhood, note, order, pith, range, sense, substance, text, tune, upshot, vicinity, weight; SEE CONCEPTS *651,668*

matter [*n5*] *difficulty, problem*
circumstance, complication, distress, grievance, perplexity, predicament, to-do*, trouble, upset, worry; SEE CONCEPTS *666,674*

matter [*n6*] *secretion of a sore*
discharge, infection, maturation, purulence, pus, suppuration, ulceration; SEE CONCEPTS *311,467*

matter [*v*] *be of consequence, importance*
affect, be important, be of value, be substantive, carry weight, count, cut ice*, express, have influence, imply, import, involve, make a difference, mean, mean something, signify, value, weigh; SEE CONCEPTS *7,19,22,130,682*

matter-of-fact [*adj*] *realistic, unembellished*
apathetic, calm, cold, cold-blooded*, deadpan, down-to-earth*, dry, dull, earthy, emotionless, factual, feasible, flat, hard-boiled*, impassive, impersonal, lifeless, mundane, naked*, objective, phlegmatic, plain, practical, pragmatic, prosaic, prosy, serious, sober, stoic, stolid, unaffected, unidealistic, unimaginative, unimpassioned, unsentimental, unvarnished; SEE CONCEPTS *267,582*

mature [*adj*] *adult, grown-up*
complete, cultivated, cultured, developed, fit, full-blown, full-fledged, full-grown, fully grown, grown, in full bloom, in one's prime, matured, mellow, mellowed, of age, perfected, prepared, prime, ready, ripe, ripened, seasoned, settled, sophisticated; SEE CONCEPTS *485,578,797*

mature [*v*] *become adult, fully grown*
advance, age, arrive, attain majority, become experienced, become wise, bloom, blossom, come of age, culminate, develop, evolve, fill out, flower*, grow, grow up, maturate, mellow*, mushroom*, perfect, prime, progress, reach adulthood, reach majority, ripen, round, season, settle down*, shoot up*; SEE CONCEPT *704*

maturity [*n*] *adulthood, full growth*
ability, advancement, capability, civilization, completion, cultivation, development, experience, fitness, full bloom, fullness, majority, manhood, maturation, matureness, maturescence, mellowness, mentality, perfection, postpubescence, prime, prime of life, readiness, ripeness, sophistication, wisdom, womanhood; SEE CONCEPTS *678,715,720*

maudlin [*adj*] *teary, overemotional*
bathetic, befuddled, confused, cornball*, drippy*, gushing, insipid, lachrymose, mawkish, mushy*, romantic, schmaltzy*, sentimental, slush*, soap*, soapy*, soppy*, syrupy*, tearful, tear-jerking*, weak, weepy; SEE CONCEPTS *529,542*

maul [v] *mangle, abuse*
bang, bash, batter, beat, beat up, bludgeon, break face, buffet, claw, clean, drub, flagellate, flail, handle roughly, hit, hurt, ill-treat, knock about*, knock around*, lacerate, lash, lean on*, let have it*, maltreat, molest, mug, muscle, paste*, paw, pelt, pound, pummel, put in the hospital*, rough up, skin, take care of*, thrash, trample, wax, whip, work over*; SEE CONCEPTS 189,246

mauve [adj] *purplish color*
lavender, lilac, plum, violaceous, violet; SEE CONCEPT 618

maverick [n] *person who takes chances, departs from accepted course*
bohemian, dissenter, extremist, malcontent, nonconformist, radical; SEE CONCEPTS 348,423

mawkish [adj] *sentimental, emotional*
bathetic, cloying, feeble, gooey*, gushing, gushy*, lovey-dovey*, maudlin, mushy*, nauseating, romantic, sappy*, schmaltzy*, sickening, sloppy, tear-jerking*, teary; SEE CONCEPTS 401,542

maxim [n] *saying*
adage, aphorism, apophthegm, axiom, belief, brocard, byword, canon, commonplace, device, dictum, epithet, formula, law, moral, motto, platitude, precept, prescript, proverb, rule, saw, tenet, theorem, truism; SEE CONCEPTS 278,689

maximum [n] *upper limit, greatest amount*
apex, apogee, ceiling, climax, crest, culmination, extremity, height, max*, maxi*, most, nonpareil, peak, pinnacle, preeminence, record, summit, supremacy, the end*, top, utmost, uttermost, zenith; SEE CONCEPTS 706,766,836

maximum [adj] *highest, utmost*
best, biggest, greatest, largest, maximal, most, mostest, outside, paramount, superlative, supreme, top, topmost, ultimate; SEE CONCEPTS 574,762,781

maybe [adv] *possibly*
as it may be, can be, conceivable, conceivably, could be, credible, feasible, imaginably, it could be, might be, obtainable, perchance, perhaps, weather permitting; SEE CONCEPT 552

mayhem [n] *chaos, confusion*
anarchy, commotion, destruction, disorder, fracas, havoc, pandemonium, trouble, violence; SEE CONCEPTS 106,675

maze [n] *labyrinth; confusion*
bewilderment, convolution, entanglement, hodgepodge, imbroglio, intricacy, jungle, knot, meander, meandering, mesh, miscellany, morass, muddle, network, perplexity, puzzle, quandary, skein, snarl, tangle, torsion, twist, uncertainty, web, winding; SEE CONCEPTS 436,529,674

meadow [n] *grassy field*
bottoms*, carpet*, grassland, heath, lea, mead, pasturage, pasture, plain, prairie, rug*, steppe, veldt; SEE CONCEPT 509

meager [adj1] *small, inadequate; poor*
bare, barren, deficient, exiguous, flimsy, inappreciable, inconsiderable, infertile, insubstantial, insufficient, little, mere, minimum, miserable, paltry, puny, scant, scanty, scrimp, scrimpy, shabby, short, skimp, skimpy, slender, slight, spare, sparse, subtle, tenuous, too little too late*, unfinished, unfruitful, unproductive, wanting, weak; SEE CONCEPTS 546,789

meager [adj2] *very thin*
angular, bare, beanpole*, beanstalk*, bony,

broomstick*, emaciated, gangling, gangly, gaunt, hungry, lacking, lank, lanky, lean, lithe, little, narrow, rattleboned, rawboned, scraggy, scrawny, skin and bones*, skinny, slender, slim, spare, starved, stinted, stunted, tenuous, underfed, wanting, willowy, withered; SEE CONCEPT 491

meal [n] *food, often taken by several individuals together*
banquet, blue plate*, board, breakfast, brunch, carryout, chow*, chow time*, collation, cookout, dessert, din-din*, dinner, eats*, fare, feast, feed, grub*, lunch, luncheon, mess, munchies*, picnic, potluck, refection, refreshment, regalement, repast, snack, special*, spread, square meal*, supper, table, tea; SEE CONCEPT 459

mean [n] *average*
balance, center, compromise, happy medium, median, middle, middle course, midpoint, norm, par; SEE CONCEPTS 727,830

mean [adj1] *ungenerous*
close, greedy, mercenary, mingy, miserly, niggard, parsimonious, penny-pinching*, penurious, rapacious, scrimpy, selfish, stingy, tight, tightfisted*; SEE CONCEPT 334

mean [adj2] *hostile, rude*
bad-tempered, callous, cantankerous, churlish, contemptible, dangerous, despicable, difficult, dirty*, disagreeable, dishonorable, down*, evil, formidable, hard, hard-nosed*, ignoble, illtempered, infamous, knavish, liverish, lousy*, low-down and dirty*, malicious, malign, nasty, perfidious, pesky, rotten, rough, rugged, scurrilous, shameless, sinking, snide, sour, the lowest*, touch, treacherous, troublesome, ugly, unfriendly, unpleasant, unscrupulous, vexatious, vicious, vile; SEE CONCEPTS 267,401,542

mean [adj3] *poor; of or in inferior circumstances*
base, beggarly, common, contemptible, déclassé, down-at-heel*, hack, humble, ignoble, ineffectual, inferior, insignificant, limited, low, lowborn, lowly, mediocre, menial, miserable, modest, narrow, obscure, ordinary, paltry, petty, pitiful, plebeian, proletarian, run-down*, scruffy*, secondclass*, second-rate, seedy*, servile, shabby*, sordid, squalid, tawdry, undistinguished, unwashed, vulgar, wretched; SEE CONCEPTS 334,485,589

mean [adj4] *average*
common, conventional, halfway, intermediate, medial, median, mediocre, medium, middle, middling, normal, popular, standard, traditional; SEE CONCEPTS 547,585

mean [v1] *signify, convey*
add up, adumbrate, allude, allude to, argue, attest, augur, betoken, connote, denote, designate, determine, drive at*, express, foreshadow, foretell, herald, hint at, imply, import, indicate, intimate, involve, name, point to, portend, presage, promise, purport, represent, say, speak of, spell, stand for, suggest, symbolize, tell the meaning of, touch on; SEE CONCEPTS 55,73,682

mean [v2] *have in mind; intend*
aim, anticipate, aspire, contemplate, design, desire, destine, direct, expect, fate, fit, make, match, plan, predestine, preordain, propose, purpose, resolve, set out, suit, want, wish; SEE CONCEPTS 26,36

meander [v] *wander, zigzag*
be all over the map*, change, drift, extravagate, gallivant, get sidetracked, peregrinate, ramble,

range, recoil, roam, rove, snake, stray, stroll, traipse, turn, twine, twist, vagabond, wind; SEE CONCEPTS *151,738*

meaning [*n1*] *message, signification*
acceptance, allusion, bearing, bottom line*, connotation, content, context, definition, denotation, drift, effect, essence, explanation, force, gist, heart*, hint, implication, import, interpretation, intimation, meat, name of the game*, nature of beast*, nitty-gritty*, nuance, nuts and bolts*, pith, point, purport, sense, significance, spirit, stuff, subject, subject matter, substance, suggestion, symbolization, tenor, thrust, understanding, upshot, use, value, worth; SEE CONCEPTS *278,661,682*

meaning [*n2*] *intention, aim*
animus, design, end, goal, idea, intent, interest, object, plan, point, purpose, trend; SEE CONCEPT *659*

meaningful [*adj*] *significant*
allusive, big, clear, concise, consequential, considerable, deep, eloquent, essential, exact, explicit, expressive, heavy, important, indicative, intelligible, material, momentous, pointed, pregnant, purposeful, relevant, sententious, serious, substantial, succinct, suggestive, useful, valid, weighty, worthwhile; SEE CONCEPTS *267,567*

meaningless [*adj*] *without use, value, worth*
absurd, aimless, blank, doesn't cut it*, doublespeak*, double-talk*, empty, feckless, fustian, futile, good-for-nothing, hollow, hot air*, inane, inconsequential, insignificant, insubstantial, nonsensical, nothing, nugatory, pointless, purportless, purposeless, senseless, trifling, trivial, unimportant, unmeaning, unpurposed, useless, vacant, vague, vain, valueless, vapid, worthless; SEE CONCEPT *575*

means [*n1*] *way, method*
agency, agent, aid, apparatus, auspices, avenue, channel, course, dodge*, expedient, factor, fashion, gimmick*, instrument, instrumentality, instrumentation, intermediary, machinery, manner, measure, mechanism, medium, ministry, mode, modus operandi, organ, organization, paraphernalia, path, power, process, road, route, step, stepping-stone, system, tactic, technique, trick, vehicle, ways and means*; SEE CONCEPT *6*

means [*n2*] *wealth, resources*
ace in the hole*, affluence, assets, backing, bankroll, budget, bundle, capital, dough*, estate, finances, fortune, funds, holdings, income, intangibles, kitty*, money, nest egg*, nut*, pocket, possessions, property, purse, rainy day*, reserves, revenue, riches, savings, securities, sock*, stake, stuff, substance, ways and means*, wherewithal; SEE CONCEPTS *332,340*

meantime [*n/adv*] *in the intervening time*
at the same time, concurrently, for now, for the duration, for the moment, for then, interim, interregnum, interruption, interval, in the interim, in the interval, in the meanwhile, meanwhile, recess, simultaneously, while; SEE CONCEPTS *799,807*

meanwhile [*adv*] *at the same time*
ad interim, concurrently, during the interval, for now, for the duration, for the moment, for then, for the time being, in the interim, in the interval, in the intervening time, in the meantime, meantime, simultaneously, till, until, up to, when; SEE CONCEPT *799*

measly [*adj*] *skimpy*
beggarly, contemptible, insignificant, meager, mean, miserable, miserly, niggling*, paltry, pathetic, petty, picayune, piddling*, pitiful, poor, puny, scanty, stingy, trifling, trivial, ungenerous, unimportant, valueless, worthless; SEE CONCEPT *789*

measurable [*adj*] *determinable*
assessable, calculable, commensurate, computable, fathomable, gaugeable, material, mensurable, perceptible, quantifiable, quantitative, significant, surveyable, weighable; SEE CONCEPT *529*

measure [*n1*] *portion, scope*
admeasurement, admensuration, allotment, allowance, amount, amplification, amplitude, area, bang, breadth, bulk, capacity, degree, depth, dimension, distance, duration, extent, fix, frequency, height, hit, magnitude, mass, meed, mensuration, nip, part, pitch, proportion, quantity, quantum, quota, range, ratio, ration, reach, share, shot, size, slug, span, strength, sum, volume, weight; SEE CONCEPTS *787,792,835*

measure [*n2*] *standard, rule*
benchmark*, canon, criterion, example, gauge, meter, method, model, norm, pattern, scale, system, test, touchstone*, trial, type, yardstick; SEE CONCEPTS *686,688*

measure [*n3*] *preventive or institutive action*
act, action, agency, bounds, control, course, deed, device, effort, expedient, limit, limitation, makeshift, maneuver, means, moderation, move, procedure, proceeding, project, proposal, proposition, resort, resource, restraint, shift, step, stopgap*, strategem; SEE CONCEPT *5*

measure [*n4*] *bill, law*
act, enactment, project, proposal, proposition, resolution, statute; SEE CONCEPT *318*

measure [*n5*] *beat, rhythm*
accent, cadence, cadency, division, melody, meter, rhyme, step, stress, stroke, swing, tempo, throb, time, tune, verse, vibration; SEE CONCEPTS *65,262*

measure [*v*] *calculate, judge*
adapt, adjust, align, appraise, assess, average, beat, blend, bound, calibrate, caliper, check, check out, choose, compute, delimit, demarcate, determine, dope out*, estimate, evaluate, even, eye*, figure, fit, gauge, gradate, grade, graduate, level, limit, line, look over, mark, mark out, mete, pace off, peg*, plumb, portion, quantify, rank, rate, read, reckon, regulate, rhyme, rule, scale, shade, size, size up, sound, square, stroke, survey, tailor, take account, time, value, weigh; SEE CONCEPTS *103,197,764*

measurement [*n*] *calculation*
altitude, amount, amplitude, analysis, appraisal, area, assessment, calibration, capacity, computation, degree, density, depth, determination, dimension, distance, estimation, evaluation, extent, frequency, height, judgment, length, magnitude, mass, measure, mensuration, metage, pitch, quantification, quantity, range, reach, scope, size, survey, thickness, time, valuation, volume, weight, width; SEE CONCEPTS *730,792*

meat [*n1*] *flesh of animal consumed as food*
aliment, brawn, chow, comestible, eats*, edible, fare, food, foodstuff, grub*, muscle, nourishment, nutriment, provision, ration, subsistence, sustenance, victual; SEE CONCEPTS *399,457,460*

meat [n2] core, gist
burden, essence, heart, kernel, marrow, matter, nub, nucleus, pith, point, sense, short, substance, thrust, upshot; SEE CONCEPTS 682,826

meaty [adj] significant
compact, epigrammatic, factual, full of content, interesting, meaningful, pithy, pointed, profound, rich, substantial, weighty; SEE CONCEPT 267

mechanical [adj] done by machine; machinelike
automated, automatic, cold, cursory, emotionless, fixed, habitual, impersonal, instinctive, involuntary, laborsaving, lifeless, machine-driven, matter-of-fact, monotonous, perfunctory, programmed, routine, spiritless, standardized, stereotyped, unchanging, unconscious, unfeeling, unthinking, useful; SEE CONCEPT 544

mechanism [n1] machine, device
apparatus, appliance, black box*, components, contrivance, doohickey*, gadget, gears, gimmick, innards, instrument, machinery, motor, structure, system, tool, workings, works; SEE CONCEPT 463

mechanism [n2] means, method
agency, execution, functioning, medium, operation, performance, procedure, process, system, technique, workings; SEE CONCEPT 6

medal [n] decoration of honor
badge, commemoration, gold, hardware*, laurel, medallion, reward, ribbon, wreath; SEE CONCEPTS 337,476

meddle [v] intervene, interfere
abuse rights, advance, barge in, break in on, busybody*, butt in*, chime in, come uninvited, crash the gates*, dabble in, encroach, encumber, fool with, hinder, horn in*, impede, impose, infringe, inquire, interlope, intermeddle, interpose, intrude, invade, kibitz*, mess around*, mix in, molest, obtrude, pry, push in, put two cents in*, sidewalk-superintend*, snoop*, stick nose in*, tamper, trespass, worm in*; SEE CONCEPTS 14,384

meddlesome [adj] interfering
busy, busybody*, chiseling*, curious, encumbering, hindering, impeding, impertinent, intermeddling, interposing, interrupting, intruding, intrusive, kibitzing*, meddling, mischievous, nosy, obstructive, officious, prying, pushy, snooping*, snoopy*, tampering, troublesome; SEE CONCEPT 555

media [n] communication by publication or broadcast
announcement, announcing, cable, communications, correspondence, disclosure, expression, intelligence, news, publishing, radio, television; SEE CONCEPT 279

median [n/adj] middle
average, center, centermost, central, equidistant, halfway, intermediary, intermediate, mean, medial, mid, middlemost, midmost, midpoint, midway, par; SEE CONCEPTS 585,727,746,830

mediate [v] try to bring to an agreement
act as middle*, arbitrate, bring to terms, conciliate, deal, go fifty-fifty*, intercede, interfere, intermediate, interpose, intervene, make a deal, make peace, meet halfway*, moderate, negotiate, propitiate, reconcile, referee, resolve, restore harmony, settle, step in, strike happy medium*, trade off, umpire; SEE CONCEPTS 126,324,384

mediation [n] attempt to bring to agreement
arbitration, conciliation, intercession, interposition, intervention, negotiation, reconciliation; SEE CONCEPTS 126,324,384

mediator [n] person who negotiates agreement
advocate, arbiter, arbitrator, broker, conciliator, fixer, go-between*, interagent, interceder, intermediary, intermediator, judge, medium, middle person, moderator, negotiator, peacemaker, ref*, referee, rent-a-judge*, troubleshooter*, umpire; SEE CONCEPTS 348,423

medicine/medication [n] substance that helps cure, alleviate, or prevent illness
anesthetic, antibiotic, antidote, antiseptic, antitoxin, balm, biologic, capsule, cure, dose, drug, elixir, injection, inoculation, liniment, lotion, medicament, ointment, pharmaceutical, pharmacon, physic, pill, potion, prescription, remedy, salve, sedative, serum, tablet, tincture, tonic, vaccination, vaccine; SEE CONCEPT 307

medieval [adj] having to do with the Middle Ages; old
antediluvian, antiquated, antique, archaic, feudal, Gothic, old, old-fashioned, primitive, unenlightened; SEE CONCEPTS 549,578,797

mediocre [adj] average, commonplace
characterless, colorless, common, conventional, decent, dull, fair, fairish, fair to middling*, humdrum*, indifferent, inferior, insignificant, intermediate, mainstream, mean, medium, middling, moderate, no great shakes*, of poor quality, ordinary, passable, pedestrian, run-of-the-mill*, second-rate, so-so*, standard, tolerable, undistinguished, unexceptional, uninspired, vanilla*; SEE CONCEPTS 533,547

meditate [v] think deeply about
brood over, cogitate, consider, contemplate, deliberate, design, devise, dream, entertain idea*, figure, have in mind*, intend, moon*, mull over, muse, plan, ponder, purpose, put on thinking cap*, puzzle over, reflect, revolve, roll, ruminate, say to oneself, scheme, speculate, study, think, think over, track, view, weigh; SEE CONCEPT 17

medium [n1] means, mode
agency, agent, avenue, channel, clairvoyant, factor, form, instrument, instrumentality, intermediate, measure, mechanism, ministry, organ, psychic, seer, tool, vehicle, way; SEE CONCEPTS 658,712

medium [n2] atmosphere, setting
ambience, ambient, climate, conditions, element, habitat, influences, milieu, surroundings; SEE CONCEPTS 673,696

medium [n3] area of artistic expression
art, drama, interpretation, manifestation, mark, music, painting, revelation, sculpture, speech, writing; SEE CONCEPTS 259,263,293

medium [adj] midway, average
common, commonplace, fair, fairish, intermediate, mean, medial, median, mediocre, middle, middling, moderate, neutral, normal, ordinary, par, passable, popular, run-of-the-mill*, so-so*, standard, tolerable; SEE CONCEPTS 533,547

medley [n] miscellany
assortment, brew, collection, combo, composition, confusion, conglomeration, farrago, hodgepodge, jumble, mélange, melee, mingling, mishmash, mixed bag, mixture, pasticcio, pastiche, patchwork, potpourri, salmagundi, variety; SEE CONCEPTS 262,432

meek [adj] shy; compliant
acquiescent, deferential, docile, forbearing, gentle, humble, lenient, longanimous, long-suffering, lowly, manageable, mild, milquetoast*, modest,

nothing, orderly, pabulum*, passive, patient, peaceful, plain, resigned, serene, soft, spineless, spiritless, subdued, submissive, tame, timid, tolerant, unassuming, unpretentious, unresisting, weak, weak-kneed*, wishy-washy*, yielding, zero*; SEE CONCEPT 401

meet [n] *sporting event involving several participants*
athletic event, competition, conflict, contest, event, match, meeting, tournament, tourney; SEE CONCEPT 363

meet [adj] *fitting*
accommodated, applicable, appropriate, apt, conformed, equitable, expedient, fair, felicitous, fit, good, happy, just, proper, reconciled, right, suitable, timely; SEE CONCEPT 558

meet [v1] *happen on*
accost, affront, brush against, bump into, chance on, clash, collide, come across, come up against, confront, contact, cross, dig up*, encounter, engage, experience, face, fall in with*, find, front, get together, grapple, greet, hit, light, luck*, make a meet, meet face to face, rendezvous with, rub eyeballs*, run across, run into, run up against, salute, see, strike, stumble, touch shoulders*, tumble, tussle, wrestle; SEE CONCEPTS 183,384,626

meet [v2] *connect, join*
abut, adhere, adjoin, border, coincide, connect, converge, cross, intersect, link, link up, reach, touch, unite; SEE CONCEPTS 612,759

meet [v3] *perform, carry out*
answer, approach, come up to, comply, cope with, discharge, equal, execute, fit, fulfill, gratify, handle, match, measure up, rival, satisfy, suffice, tie, touch; SEE CONCEPT 91

meet [v4] *come together, convene*
appear, assemble, be introduced, be present, be presented, collect, congregate, converge, enter in, flock, foregather, gather, get together, get to know, join, make acquaintance, muster, open, rally, rendezvous, show, sit; SEE CONCEPTS 114,324

meeting [n1] *gathering, conference*
affair, assemblage, assembly, assignation, audience, bunch, call, cattle call*, company, competition, conclave, concourse, concursion, confab*, conflict, confrontation, congregation, congress, contest, convention, convocation, date, encounter, engagement, gang, get-together, huddle, introduction, meet, one on one*, parley, powwow*, rally, rendezvous, reunion, session, showdown, talk, tryst, turnout*; SEE CONCEPTS 324,363,384

meeting [n2] *convergence, intersection*
abutment, agreement, apposition, concourse, confluence, conjunction, connection, contact, crossing, joining, junction, juxtaposition, unification, union; SEE CONCEPTS 113,684

melancholy [n] *depression, sadness*
blahs*, blue devils*, blue funk*, blues*, boredom, bummer*, dejection, despair, desperation, despondency, dismals, dolefuls, dolor, downer*, down trip*, dumps, ennui, funk, gloom, gloominess, grief, letdown, low spirits, miserableness, misery, mopes*, mournfulness, pensiveness, sorrow, tedium, unhappiness, wistfulness, woe, wretchedness; SEE CONCEPT 410

melancholy [adj] *depressed, sad*
blue*, dejected, despondent, destroyed, disconsolate, dismal, dispirited, doleful, dolorous, down*,

down and out*, downbeat, downcast, downhearted, down in the dumps*, down in the mouth*, dragged, droopy, funereal, gloomy, glum, grim, heavyhearted, in blue funk*, joyless, lachrymose, low, low-spirited, lugubrious, mirthless, miserable, moody, moony*, mournful, pensive, saddened, saddening, somber, sorrowful, sorry*, torn up, trite, unhappy, wet blanket*, wistful, woebegone, woeful; SEE CONCEPT 403

mélange [n] *mixture*
assortment, combo, confusion, farrago, gallimaufry, hodgepodge, jumble, medley, miscellany, mishmash, mix, mixed bag, pasticcio, pastiche, patchwork, potpourri, salmagundi, soup, stew; SEE CONCEPT 432

meld [v] *blend, bring together*
amalgamate, associate, compound, dissolve, feather in, fuse, interblend, interface, interfuse, intermingle, marry, merge, mingle, mix, unite; SEE CONCEPTS 113,193

melee [n] *battle, fight*
affray, battle royal*, brawl, broil, brouhaha*, brush, clash, donnybrook*, fracas, fray, free-for-all*, knock-down-drag-out*, row, ruckus, ruction, rumpus, scrimmage, scuffle, set-to*, skirmish, to-do*, tussle, words; SEE CONCEPT 106

mellow [adj] *ripe, mature; softened*
aged, cultured, cured, delicate, developed, dulcet, flavorful, full, full-flavored, fully developed, juicy, matured, mellifluent, mellifluous, melodious, perfect, perfected, rich, ripened, rounded, sapid, savory, seasoned, smooth, soft, soothing, sweet, tuneful; SEE CONCEPTS 462,578,594,797

mellow [v] *ripen, mature*
age, arrive, develop, grow up, improve, maturate, milden, mollify, perfect, ripe, season, settle down, soften, sweeten; SEE CONCEPTS 678,704

melodious/melodic [adj] *harmonious, musical*
accordant, agreeable, assonant, canorous, clear, concordant, dulcet, euphonic, euphonious, harmonic, in tune, mellifluous, mellow, pleasing, resonant, silvery, soft, songful, sweet, sweet-sounding, symphonic, symphonious, tuned, tuneful, well-tuned; SEE CONCEPT 594

melodramatic [adj] *extravagant in speech, behavior*
artificial, blood-and-thunder*, cliff-hanging*, cloak-and-dagger*, exaggerated, ham*, hammy*, histrionic, hokey*, overdramatic, overemotional, sensational, spectacular, stagy, theatrical; SEE CONCEPT 542

melody [n] *harmony, tune*
air, aria, assonance, carillon, chant, chime, concord, consonance, descant, diapason, euphony, inflection, lay, lyric, measure, melodiousness, music, musicality, refrain, resonance, run, song, strain, theme, tunefulness, unison; SEE CONCEPTS 262,595

melt [v1] *liquefy; dissolve*
cook, deliquesce, diffuse, disappear, disintegrate, disperse, evanesce, evaporate, fade, flow, flux, fuse, go, heat, merge, pass away, render, run, smelt, soften, thaw, vanish, warm, waste away; SEE CONCEPTS 250,255

melt [v2] *give in, yield*
become lenient, disarm, forgive, mollify, relax, relent, show mercy, soften, touch; SEE CONCEPT 35

member [n1] *part of a group*
affiliate, associate, branch, chapter, component, comrade, constituent, cut, division, joiner, offshoot, parcel, piece, portion, post, representative, section, segment, unit; SEE CONCEPTS 417,834,835

member [n2] *appendage*
arm, component, constituent, element, extremity, feature, fragment, leg, limb, organ, part, portion, segment; SEE CONCEPT 392

membership [n] *belonging to organization; those belonging to a group*
associates, association, body, club, company, enrollment, fellows, group, members, participation, society; SEE CONCEPTS 381,417

membrane [n] *covering layer*
film, lamina, leaf, mucosa, sheath, sheet; SEE CONCEPT 484

memento [n] *souvenir*
keepsake, memorial, relic, remembrance, remembrancer, reminder, token, trace, trophy, vestige; SEE CONCEPTS 337,446 ,

memoir [n] *record of experiences*
account, anecdote, annal, autobiography, bio*, biography, chronicle, confessions, diary, discourse, dissertation, essay, journal, life, life story, memory, monograph, narrative, note, recollection, register, reminiscence, thesis, tractate, transactions, treatise, vita; SEE CONCEPTS 271,280,282

memorable [adj] *noteworthy, significant*
A-1*, big-league*, bodacious, catchy, celebrated, critical, crucial, decisive, distinguished, doozie*, enduring, eventful, extraordinary, famous, great, heavy*, heavyweight*, historic, hot*, illustrious, important, impressive, indelible, interesting, lasting, major-league, meaningful, mind-blowing*, momentous, monumental, notable, observable, red-letter*, remarkable, rememberable, rubric, serious, signal, something, standout, striking, super, surpassing, terrible, terrific, top-drawer, unforgettable; SEE CONCEPTS 529,548

memorandum/memo [n] *written note*
announcement, chit, diary, directive, dispatch, epistle, jotting, letter, message, minute, missive, notation, notice, record, reminder, tickler; SEE CONCEPTS 271,277,278

memorial [n] *monument, testimonial in honor, praise*
cairn, ceremony, column, headstone, inscription, keepsake, mausoleum, memento, monolith, obelisk, pillar, plaque, record, relic, remembrance, reminder, shaft, slab, souvenir, statue, stele, tablet, token, tombstone, trophy; SEE CONCEPTS 337,386

memorial [adj] *commemorative*
canonizing, celebrative, commemoratory, consecrating, consecrative, dedicatory, deifying, enshrining, in tribute, memorializing, monumental, remembering; SEE CONCEPT 537

memory [n1] *ability to hold in the mind*
anamnesis, awareness, camera-eye*, cognizance, consciousness, dead-eye*, flashback, memorization, mind, mindfulness, mind's eye*, recall, recapture, recognition, recollection, reflection, remembrance, reminiscence, retention, retentiveness, retrospection, subconsciousness, thought; SEE CONCEPT 409

memory [n2] *specific thing remembered*
concept, cue, fantasy, hint, image, jog, memo, memoir, mnemonic, picture, prod, prompt, re-

minder, representation, suggestion, thought, vision; SEE CONCEPTS 529,678

menace [n] *danger; pest*
annoyance, caution, commination, hazard, intimidation, jeopardy, nuisance, peril, plague, risk, scare, threat, thunder, trouble, troublemaker, warning; SEE CONCEPTS 412,675

menace [v] *bother, frighten*
alarm, bad-eye*, browbeat, bully, chill, compromise, endanger, hazard, impend, imperil, intimidate, jeopardize, lean on, loom, lower, overhang, peril, portend, push around, put heat on*, risk, scare, scare hell out of*, spook, terrorize, threaten, torment, whip around*; SEE CONCEPTS 7,19

menacing [adj] *intimidating, ominous*
alarming, approaching, dangerous, frightening, imminent, impending, intimidatory, looming, louring, lowering, minacious, minatory, overhanging, threatening; SEE CONCEPTS 401,537,548

mend [v] *correct, improve, fix*
aid, ameliorate, amend, better, condition, convalesce, cure, darn, doctor, emend, fiddle with, gain, get better, get well, heal, knit, look up, overhaul, patch, perk up, ready, rebuild, recondition, reconstruct, recover, rectify, recuperate, redress, refit, reform, refurbish, rejuvenate, remedy, renew, renovate, repair, restore, retouch, revamp, revise, right, service, sew; SEE CONCEPTS 126,244,303,700

mendacious [adj] *dishonest*
deceitful, deceptive, duplicitous, equivocating, erroneous, fallacious, false, fibbing, fraudulent, insincere, lying, paltering, perfidious, perjured, prevaricating, shifty, spurious, untrue, untruthful, wrong; SEE CONCEPT 267

menial [adj] *lowly, low-status*
abject, base, baseborn, boring, common, degrading, demeaning, dull, fawning, grovelling, humble, humdrum, ignoble, ignominious, low, mean, obeisant, obsequious, routine, servile, slavish, sorry, subservient, sycophantic, unskilled, vile; SEE CONCEPTS 574,575

men's movement [n] *men's attempt to redefine gender roles*
gender revisionism, men's liberation, male reform, men's studies; SEE CONCEPT 388

mental [adj1] *concerning the mind*
brainy*, cerebral, clairvoyant, deep, heavy, ideological, imaginative, immaterial, inner, intellective, intellectual, mysterious, phrenic, psychic, psychical, psychological, rational, reasoning, spiritual, subconscious, subjective, subliminal, telepathic, thinking, thoughtful, unreal; SEE CONCEPTS 402,403

mental [adj2] *insane*
deranged, disturbed, fruity, loco*, lunatic, mad, maniac, mentally ill, mindless, non compos mentis, nuts*, nutsy*, psychiatric, psychotic, unbalanced, unstable; SEE CONCEPTS 314,403

mentality [n] *state of mind; intelligence*
attitude, brainpower, brains, cast, character, comprehension, disposition, frame of mind*, headset*, intellect, intelligence quotient, IQ, makeup, mental age, mind, mindset*, outlook, personality, psychology, rationality, reasoning, routine, sense, turn of mind*, understanding, way of thinking*, wit; SEE CONCEPTS 409,411

mention [n] *referral, observation*
acknowledgment, allusion, citation, comment,

footnote, indication, naming, note, notice, notification, recognition, reference, remark, specifying, tribute, utterance; SEE CONCEPTS 73,278

mention [v] *refer to*
acknowledge, acquaint, adduce, advert, allude to, bring up, broach, call attention to, cite, communicate, declare, designate, detail, disclose, discuss, divulge, enumerate, hint at, impart, infer, instance, intimate, introduce, make known, name, notice, notify, observe, point out, point to, quote, recount, remark, report, reveal, speak about, speak of, specify, state, suggest, tell, throw out, touch on; SEE CONCEPT 73

mentor [n] *person who advises*
adviser, coach, counsellor, guide, instructor, teacher, trainer, tutor; SEE CONCEPT 350

menu [n] *list from which to choose, often to choose food*
bill of fare, card, carte, carte du jour, cuisine, food, spread, table; SEE CONCEPT 283

mercenary [n] *person who fights, kills for money*
hireling, legionnaire, merc, professional soldier, slave, soldier of fortune, warrior; SEE CONCEPTS 358,412

mercenary [adj] *greedy for money*
acquisitive, avaricious, bribable, corrupt, covetous, grabby, grasping, miserly, money-grubbing, selfish, sordid, stingy, unethical, unprincipled, unscrupulous, venal; SEE CONCEPT 401

merchandise [n] *goods for sale*
commodity, effects, job lot, line, material, number, produce, product, seconds, staple, stock, stuff, truck, vendible, wares; SEE CONCEPT 338

merchandise [v] *sell goods*
advertise, buy and sell, deal in, distribute, do business in, market, promote, publicize, retail, trade, traffic in, vend, wholesale; SEE CONCEPT 345

merchant [n] *person who sells goods*
broker, businessperson, consigner, dealer, exporter, handler, jobber, marketer, operator, retailer, salesperson, seller, sender, shipper, shopkeeper, storekeeper, trader, tradesperson, trafficker, tycoon, vendor, wholesaler; SEE CONCEPT 347

merciful [adj] *kind, sparing*
all heart*, beneficent, benign, benignant, bleeding heart*, charitable, clement, compassionate, condoning, easygoing, feeling, forbearing, forgiving, generous, gentle, gracious, heart in right place*, humane, humanitarian, indulgent, kindly, lenient, liberal, mild, pardoning, pitiful, pitying, soft*, softhearted*, sympathetic, tender, tenderhearted, tolerant; SEE CONCEPTS 401,542

merciless [adj] *mean, heartless*
barbarous, callous, compassionless, cruel, cutthroat, dog-eat-dog*, fierce, gratuitous, grim, hard, hardhearted, harsh, hatchet job*, having a killer instinct*, implacable, inexorable, inhumane, iron-fisted, mean machine*, mortal, pitiless, relentless, ruthless, severe, unappeasable, uncalled-for, unfeeling, unflinching, unforgiving, unmerciful, unpitying, unrelenting, unsparing, unsympathetic, unyielding, wanton; SEE CONCEPTS 401,542

mercurial [adj] *flighty, temperamental*
blowing hot and cold*, bubbleheaded*, buoyant, capricious, changeable, effervescent, elastic, erratic, expansive, fickle, flaky, flip*, fluctuating, gaga*, gay, impulsive, inconstant, irregular, irrepressible, lighthearted, lively, lubricious, mad,

mobile, movable, quicksilver, resilient, short-fuse*, spirited, sprightly, ticklish, unpredictable, unstable, up-and-down*, variable, volatile, yo-yo*; SEE CONCEPTS 401,404

mercy [n] *kindness, compassion*
benevolence, benignancy, blessing, boon, charity, clemency, commiseration, favor, forbearance, forgiveness, generosity, gentleness, godsend, goodwill, grace, humanity, kindliness, lenience, leniency, lenity, lifesaver, luck, mildness, pity, quarter, relief, ruth, softheartedness, sympathy, tenderness, tolerance; SEE CONCEPTS 32,633

mere [adj] *nothing more; absolute*
bald, bare, blunt, common, complete, entire, insignificant, little, minor, plain, poor, pure, pure and simple, sheer, simple, small, stark, unadorned, unadulterated, unmitigated, unmixed, utter, very; SEE CONCEPTS 535,589

meretricious [adj] *gaudy, flashy*
blatant, bogus, brazen, chintzy, counterfeit, garish, glaring, insincere, loud, misleading, ornate, phony, plastic*, put-on*, sham, showy, spurious, superficial, tawdry, tinsel, trashy; SEE CONCEPTS 542,589

merge [v] *bring or come together*
absorb, amalgamate, assimilate, become lost in, become partners, be swallowed up*, blend, cement, centralize, coalesce, combine, come aboard*, compound, conglomerate, consolidate, converge, deal one in, fuse, hitch on*, hook up*, immerge, incorporate, interface, intermingle, intermix, join, join up, line up, marry, meet, meld, melt into, mingle, mix, network, plug into, pool, slap on, submerge, synthesize, tack on*, tag, team up*, throw in together*, tie in, unite; SEE CONCEPTS 113,193,324

merger [n] *consolidation*
alliance, amalgamation, cahoots*, coadunation, coalition, combination, fusion, hookup, incorporation, lineup, melding, mergence, merging, organization, pool, takeover, tie-in, tie-up, unification, union; SEE CONCEPTS 323,324,703

meridian [n] *summit, climax*
acme, apex, apogee, crest, culmination, extremity, high noon, high-water mark, peak, pinnacle, zenith; SEE CONCEPTS 832,836

merit [n] *advantage*
arete, asset, benefit, caliber, credit, desert, dignity, excellence, excellency, good, goodness, honor, integrity, perfection, quality, stature, strong point, talent, value, virtue, worth, worthiness; SEE CONCEPT 693

merit [v] *be entitled to*
be in line for, be worthy, deserve, earn, get one's comeuppance*, get one's due*, get one's desserts*, get what is coming*, have a claim, have a right, have coming, incur, justify, rate, warrant; SEE CONCEPT 129

meritorious [adj] *honorable, commendable*
admirable, boss*, choice, creditable, deserving, estimable, excellent, exemplary, golden, good, laudable, meritable, noble, praisable, praiseworthy, right, righteous, thankworthy, top drawer*, virtuous, winner, world-beating*, worthy; SEE CONCEPTS 404,548,572

merriment/merrymaking [n] *enjoyment, amusement*
brawl, buffoonery, cheerfulness, conviviality, festivity, frolic, fun, fun and games*, gaiety, glee, happiness, hilarity, hoopla*, indulgence, jocular-

ity, jocundity, jollity, joviality, joy, laughs, laughter, levity, liveliness, mirth, picnic, recreation, revel, revelry, self-indulgence, shindig, sport, whoopee*, wingding*; SEE CONCEPTS **386,410**

merry [*adj*] *very happy; festive*
amusing, blithe, blithesome, boisterous, boon, carefree, cheerful, comic, comical, convivial, enjoyable, entertaining, facetious, frolicsome, fun-loving, funny, gay, glad, gleeful, grooving*, hilarious, humorous, jocund, jolly, joyful, joyous, jumping, larking, lighthearted, lively, mad, mirthful, perky, pleasant, riotous, rip-roaring*, rocking, rollicking, saturnalian, sportive, sunny, unconstrained, uproarious, vivacious, wild, winsome, zappy*, zingy*, zippy*; SEE CONCEPTS **403,548,572**

mesh [*n*] *netting, entanglement*
cobweb, jungle, knot, labyrinth, maze, morass, net, network, plexus, reticulation, screen, skein, snare, snarl, tangle, toils, tracery, trap, web; SEE CONCEPTS **611,733**

mesh [*v*] *entangle, connect*
agree, catch, coincide, combine, come together, coordinate, dovetail, engage, enmesh, ensnare, fit, fit together, harmonize, interlock, knit, net, snare, tangle, trap; SEE CONCEPTS **113,193**

mesmerize [*v*] *captivate*
catch up, control, deaden, drug, ensorcell, enthrall, entrance, fascinate, grip, hold spellbound, hypnotize, magnetize, numb, render unconscious, spellbind, stupefy; SEE CONCEPTS **11,14**

mess [*n1*] *disorder, litter*
botch, chaos, clutter, combination, compound, confusion, debris, dirtiness, disarray, discombobulation*, disorganization, every which way*, eyesore, fright, hash, hodgepodge, jumble, mayhem, mishmash, monstrosity, salmagundi, shambles, sight, turmoil, untidiness, wreck, wreckage; SEE CONCEPTS **230,260**

mess [*n2*] *difficulty, predicament*
dilemma, fix, imbroglio, jam, mix-up, muddle, perplexity, pickle*, plight, stew; SEE CONCEPT **674**

message [*n1*] *communication, often written*
bulletin, cannonball, communiqué, directive, dispatch, dope, earful, epistle, information, intelligence, intimation, letter, memo, memorandum, missive, news, note, notice, paper, report, tidings, wire, word; SEE CONCEPTS **271,274**

message [*n2*] *meaning, idea*
acceptation, import, intendment, moral, point, purport, sense, significance, significancy, signification, theme, understanding; SEE CONCEPTS **661,682**

mess around [*v*] *fiddle; goof off*
amuse oneself, dabble, dawdle, doodle, fool around, loiter, muck around*, play, play around, play the fool*, potter, puddle, putter, tinker, trifle; SEE CONCEPTS **87,363**

messenger [*n*] *person carrying information to another*
agent, ambassador, bearer, carrier, commissionaire, courier, crier, delegate, delivery person, detachment, detail, dispatcher, emissary, envoy, errand person*, flag-bearer, forerunner, go-between*, gofer*, harbinger, herald, intermediary, mediator, minister, post, precursor, prophet, runner, schlepper*; SEE CONCEPT **348**

mess up [*v*] *disorder, dirty*
befoul, besmirch, bobble, bollix*, botch, bungle, clutter, confuse, damage, derange, destroy, disarrange, discompose, dishevel, disorganize, disturb, foul, goof up*, gum up*, jumble, litter, louse up, muddle, pollute, ruin, rummage, scramble, screw up*, smear, soil, spoil, unsettle, upset; SEE CONCEPTS **158,252,254**

messy [*adj*] *cluttered, dirty*
blotchy*, careless, chaotic, confused, disheveled, disordered, disorganized, grimy, grubby*, littered, muddled, raunchy*, rumpled, slapdash*, slipshod*, sloppy, slovenly, unfastidious, unkempt, untidy; SEE CONCEPTS **485,621**

metal [*n*] *lustrous chemical element*
alloy, casting, deposit, foil, hardware, ingot, leaf, load, mail, mineral, native rock, ore, plate, solder, vein; SEE CONCEPT **476**

metamorphose [*v*] *convert, transform*
age, alter, be reborn, change, commute, develop, diverge, mature, mutate, remake, remodel, reshape, ripen, transfigure, translate, transmogrify, transmute, transubstantiate, vary; SEE CONCEPTS **469,697,701**

metamorphosis [*n*] *conversion, transformation*
alteration, change, changeover, evolution, mutation, rebirth, transfiguration, transfigurement, translation, transmogrification, transmutation, transubstantiation; SEE CONCEPTS **469,697,701**

metaphor [*n*] *figure of speech, implied comparison*
allegory, analogy, emblem, hope, image, metonymy, personification, similitude, symbol, trope; SEE CONCEPT **275**

metaphysical [*adj*] *not physical; without physical presence*
abstract, abstruse, bodiless, deep, difficult, discarnate, esoteric, eternal, fundamental, high-flown, ideal, immaterial, impalpable, incorporeal, insubstantial, intangible, intellectual, jesuitic, mystical, nonmaterial, nonphysical, numinous, oversubtle, philosophical, preternatural, profound, recondite, spiritual, superhuman, superior, supermundane, supernatural, suprahuman, supramundane, supranatural, theoretical, transcendental, unearthly, unfleshly, universal, unphysical, unreal, unsubstantial; SEE CONCEPTS **529,582**

mete [*v*] *administer, distribute*
admeasure, allocate, allot, allow, apportion, assign, deal, dispense, divide, dole, give, lot, measure, parcel, portion, ration, share; SEE CONCEPTS **98,108**

meteoric [*adj*] *brief, sudden*
dazzling, ephemeral, flashing, fleeting, momentary, overnight, rapid, spectacular, speedy, swift, transient; SEE CONCEPTS **548,798,799**

meter [*n*] *rhythm, beat*
cadence, cadency, feet, lilt, measure, mora, music, pattern, poetry, rhyme, structure, swing; SEE CONCEPTS **65,262**

method [*n1*] *means, procedure*
adjustment, approach, arrangement, channels, course, custom, design, disposal, disposition, fashion, form, formula, habit, line, manner, mechanism, method, mode, modus, modus operandi, nuts and bolts*, plan, practice, proceeding, process, program, receipt, recipe, red tape*, ritual, rote, routine, rubric, rule, rut, schema, scheme, shortcut, style, system, tack, tactics, technic, technique, tenor, the book*, usage, way,

ways and means*, wise, wrinkle*; SEE CONCEPTS
6,660

method [n2] *order, pattern*
arrangement, classification, design, form, orderliness, organization, plan, planning, purpose, regularity, structure, system; SEE CONCEPTS 727,770

methodical/methodic [adj] *organized, precise*
all together, analytical, businesslike, by the
book*, by the numbers, careful, cut-and-dried*,
deliberate, disciplined, efficient, exact, fixed,
framed, in a groove*, logical, methodized, meticulous, neat, ordered, orderly, painstaking,
planned, regular, scrupulous, set-up*, structured,
systematic, tidy, together, well-regulated; SEE
CONCEPTS 326,542,544,585

meticulous [adj] *detailed, perfectionist*
accurate, cautious, conscientious, conscionable,
crossing the t's*, dotting the i's*, exact, fastidious, fussy, heedful, microscopic, nitpicking*,
painstaking, particular, persnickety*, picky, precise, punctilious, punctual, scrupulous, stickling,
strict, thorough; SEE CONCEPTS 542,544,557

metropolitan [adj] *concerning a city*
city, cosmopolitan, modern, municipal, urban, urbane; SEE CONCEPT 536

mettle [n] *boldness, strength of character*
animation, ardor, backbone, bravery, caliber,
courage, daring, dauntlessness, disposition, energy, fire, force, fortitude, gallantry, gameness,
grit*, guts*, hardihood, heart*, indomitability,
kidney*, life*, makeup, moxie, nature, nerve,
pluck, quality, resolution, resolve, spirit, spunk,
stamina, stamp*, starch, temper, temperament,
valor, vigor, vitality; SEE CONCEPT 411

microbe [n] *bacteria*
bacillus, bacterium, bug*, crud, germ, microorganism, pathogen, plague, virus; SEE CONCEPT
306

microscopic [adj] *tiny, almost undetectable*
atomic, diminutive, imperceptible, infinitesimal,
invisible, little, minuscule, minute, negligible,
teeny*, wee*; SEE CONCEPTS 773,789

middle [n] *center*
core, deep, focus, halfway, halfway point, heart,
inside, marrow, mean, media, midpoint, midriff,
midsection, midst, thick, waist; SEE CONCEPTS
746,761,830,833

middle [adj] *central*
average, between, betwixt and between*, center,
centermost, equidistant, halfway, inner, inside,
intermediate, intervening, mainstream, mean, medial, median, medium, mezzo*, middlemost, middle of the road*, midmost, smack in the middle,
straddling the fence*; SEE CONCEPTS 547,583,830

middle person [n] *person who acts as intermediary*
agent, broker, connection, distributor, entrepreneur, fixer, go-between*, influence, interagent,
interceder, intercessor, intermediate, intermediator, jobber*, mediator, representative, salesperson, wholesaler; SEE CONCEPT 348

middling [adj] *adequate, okay*
all right, average, common, conventional, decent,
fair, fairish, good, indifferent, intermediate,
mean, mediocre, medium, moderate, modest,
okay, ordinary, passable, run-of-the-mill*, so-
so*, tolerable, traditional, unexceptional, unremarkable; SEE CONCEPT 547

midget [n] *small person*
bantam, gnome, homuncule, homunculus, Lilli

putian*, little person, manikin, midge, runt*; SEE
CONCEPT 424

midget [adj] *short, small*
baby, diminutive, knee-high*, Lilliputian, miniature, minikin, pocket, teensy*, teeny*, tiny; SEE
CONCEPTS 773,779

midst [n] *middle, core*
betwixt and between*, bosom, center, deep,
depths, halfway, heart, hub, interior, mean, medium, midpoint, nucleus, thick; SEE CONCEPT 830

mien [n] *person's presence, manner*
act, address, air, appearance, aspect, aura, bearing, carriage, countenance, demeanor, deportment, expression, front, image, look, mannerism,
port, set, style; SEE CONCEPTS 411,644

miff [v] *annoy*
aggrieve, bother, displease, hurt, irk, irritate, nettle, offend, pester, pique, provoke, put out, resent, upset, vex; SEE CONCEPTS 7,19

might [n] *ability, power*
adequacy, arm, authority, capability, capacity,
clout, command, competence, control, domination, efficacy, efficiency, energy, force, forcefulness, forcibleness, get-up-and-go*, jurisdiction,
lustiness, mastery, moxie*, muscle*, potency,
powerfulness, prowess, puissance, punch, qualification, qualifiedness, sinew*, steam, strength,
strenuousness, strong arm*, sway, valor, vigor,
vigorousness; SEE CONCEPTS 411,641,732

mightily [adv1] *very much, extremely*
decidedly, exceedingly, greatly, highly, hugely,
intensely, mighty, notably, surpassingly, very;
SEE CONCEPT 569

mightily [adv2] *forcefully*
arduously, energetically, forcibly, hard, hardly,
laboriously, lustily, might and main*, powerfully,
strenuously, strongly, vigorously, with all one's
strength; SEE CONCEPTS 540,544

mighty [adj1] *forceful, powerful*
boss*, doughty, hardy, indomitable, lusty, muscular, omnipotent, potent, powerhouse, puissant,
robust, stalwart, steamroller*, stout, strapping,
strengthy, strong, strong as ox*, sturdy, vigorous,
wieldy; SEE CONCEPTS 489,540

mighty [adj2] *gigantic, monumental*
august, bulky, colossal, considerable, dynamic,
eminent, enormous, extensive, extraordinary,
grand, great, heroic, high, huge, illustrious, immense, imposing, impressive, intense, irresistible,
large, magnificent, majestic, massive, moving,
notable, prodigious, renowned, stupendous, titanic, towering, tremendous, vast; SEE CONCEPTS
537,773,781

migrant [n] *person who moves to a foreign place*
departer, drifter, emigrant, evacuee, expatriate,
gypsy, immigrant, itinerant, migrator, mover, nomad, rover, tinker, transient, traveler, vagrant,
wanderer; SEE CONCEPT 413

migrant/migratory [adj] *moving, traveling*
casual, changing, drifting, emigrating, errant,
gypsy, immigrant, immigrating, impermanent,
itinerant, migrative, migratorial, mobile, nomad,
nomadic, on the move, passing over, passing
through, peripatetic, ranging, roving, seasonal,
shifting, temporary, tramp, transient, transmigratory, unsettled, vagabond, vagrant, wandering;
SEE CONCEPT 584

migrate [v] *move, travel to another place*
drift, emigrate, immigrate, journey, leave, no

madize, range, roam, rove, shift, transmigrate, trek, voyage, wander; SEE CONCEPTS *198,224*

mild [adj1] *gentle, temperate, nonirritating*
balmy, benign, benignant, blah*, bland, breezy, calm, choice, clear, clement, cool, dainty, delicate, demulcent, easy, emollient, exquisite, faint, fine, flat, genial, ho-hum*, lenient, lenitive, light, lukewarm, medium, mellow, moderate, mollifying, nothing, nothing much*, pabulum, pacific, peaceful, placid, smooth, soft, soothing, sunny, tempered, tepid, untroubled, vanilla*, warm, weak, wimpy*; SEE CONCEPTS *485,525,537*

mild [adj2] *easygoing, pleasant in personality*
amiable, balmy, bland, calm, clement, compassionate, complaisant, deferential, docile, dull, easy, equable, feeble, flat, forbearant, forbearing, forgiving, gentle, good-humored, good-natured, good-tempered, humane, indulgent, insipid, jejune, kind, lenient, meek, mellow, merciful, mild-mannered, moderate, obeisant, obliging, pacific, patient, peaceable, placid, serene, smooth, soft, spiritless, subdued, submissive, subservient, tame, temperate, tender, tranquil, unassuming, vapid, warm; SEE CONCEPTS *401,404*

mile [n] *5,280 feet/1.609 kilometers measured*
nautical, square, statute; SEE CONCEPTS *790,791*

milestone [n] *achievement*
anniversary, breakthrough, discovery, event, landmark, milepost, occasion, turning point, waypost; SEE CONCEPTS *2,706*

milieu [n] *environment, atmosphere*
ambience, ambient, background, bag, climate, element, locale, location, medium, mise-en-scène, nabe, neighborhood, place, scene, setting, space, sphere, surroundings, turf; SEE CONCEPT *673*

militant [n] *person who fights, is aggressive*
activist, belligerent, combatant, demonstrator, fighter, objector, partisan, protester, rioter, warrior; SEE CONCEPTS *358,359*

militant [adj] *aggressive, combative*
active, assertive, assertory, bellicose, belligerent, combating, contending, contentious, embattled, fighting, gladiatorial, in arms, martial, militaristic, military, offensive, pugnacious, pushy, quarrelsome, scrappy, self-assertive, truculent, up in arms, vigorous, warlike, warring; SEE CONCEPT *401*

military [n] *armed force*
air force, army, force, marines, navy, service, servicepeople, soldiery, troop; SEE CONCEPT *322*

military [adj] *soldierlike; concerning the armed forces*
aggressive, armed, army, combatant, combative, fighting, martial, militant, militaristic, noncivil, soldierly, warlike, warmongering; SEE CONCEPT *536*

milk [n] *liquid produced by mammals*
buttermilk, chalk*, condensed, cream, evaporated, formula, goat, half-and-half, homogenized, laiche, low fat, moo juice*, pasteurized, powdered, raw, skim, two-percent, whole; SEE CONCEPT *467*

milk [v] *tap; exploit*
bleed, drain, draw off, elicit, empty, evince, evoke, exhaust, express, extort, extract, fleece, impose on, let out, press, pump, siphon, suck, take advantage, take out, use, wring; SEE CONCEPTS *139,142,156,225*

milky [adj] *white, cloudy*
alabaster, clouded, frosted, lacteal, lacteous, lac-tescent, milk-white, opalescent, opaline, opaque, pearly, whitish; SEE CONCEPT *618*

mill [n] *factory*
foundry, manufactory, plant, shop, sweatshop, works; SEE CONCEPTS *439,449*

mill [v] *grind*
comminute, crush, granulate, grate, pound, powder, press, pulverize; SEE CONCEPT *186*

mimic [n] *person who imitates*
actor, caricaturist, comedian, copycat, imitator, impersonator, impressionist, mime, mummer, parodist, parrot, performer, playactor, player, thespian, trouper; SEE CONCEPT *352*

mimic [v] *imitate, mock*
act, ape, burlesque, caricature, copy, copycat, ditto*, do, do like*, echo, enact, fake, go like*, impersonate, look like*, make believe, make fun of, make like*, mime, mirror, pantomime, parody, parrot, perform, personate, play, resemble, ridicule, sham, simulate, take off*, travesty; SEE CONCEPTS *54,59,111,171*

mince [v1] *chop up*
chip, crumble, cut, dice, divide, grind, hack, hash, whack; SEE CONCEPT *176*

mince [v2] *pose, put on airs*
attitudinize, flounce, posture, prance, sashay, strut; SEE CONCEPT *59*

mince [v3] *euphemize, hold back in communication*
alleviate, decrease, diminish, extenuate, lessen, minimize, moderate, palliate, soften, spare, tone down, weaken; SEE CONCEPT *266*

mincing [adj] *affected, pretentious*
artificial, dainty, delicate, effeminate, fastidious, finical, finicky, fussy, genteel, insincere, la-di-da*, nice, particular, persnickety, precious, sissy, squeamish, stilted, too-too*, unnatural; SEE CONCEPTS *401,404*

mind [n1] *intelligence*
apperception, attention, brain*, brainpower, brains*, capacity, cognizance, conception, consciousness, creativity, faculty, function, genius, head, imagination, ingenuity, instinct, intellect, intellectual, intellectuality, intuition, judgment, lucidity, marbles*, mentality, observation, perception, percipience, power, psyche, ratiocination, reason, reasoning, regard, sanity, sense, soul, soundness, spirit, talent, thinker, thought, understanding, wisdom, wits; SEE CONCEPTS *393,409*

mind [n2] *memory*
attention, cognizance, concentration, head, mark, note, notice, observance, observation, recollection, regard, remark, remembrance, subconscious, thinking, thoughts; SEE CONCEPTS *409,630*

mind [n3] *inclination, tendency; belief*
attitude, bent, conviction, desire, determination, disposition, eye, fancy, feeling, humor, impulse, intention, judgment, leaning, liking, mood, notion, opinion, outlook, persuasion, pleasure, point of view, purpose, sentiment, strain, temper, temperament, thoughts, tone, urge, vein, view, way of thinking, will, wish; SEE CONCEPTS *20,657,689*

mind [v1] *be bothered; care*
be affronted, be opposed, complain, deplore, disapprove, dislike, look askance at, object, resent, take offense; SEE CONCEPT *21,29*

mind [v2] *comply, obey*
adhere to, attend, behave, do as told, follow, fol-

low orders, heed, keep, listen, mark, note, notice, observe, pay attention, pay heed, regard, respect, take heed, watch; SEE CONCEPTS 23,91

mind [v3] *attend, tend*
baby-sit, be attentive, behold, care for, discern, discipline, ensure, give heed to, govern, guard, have charge of, keep an eye on*, listen up, look, make certain, mark, mind the store*, note, notice, observe, oversee, perceive, regard, ride herd on*, see, sit, superintend, supervise, watch; SEE CONCEPTS 110,295,596,623

mind [v4] *be careful*
be cautious, be concerned, be on guard, be solicitous, be wary, have a care, mind one's p's and q's*, take care, tend, toe the line*, trouble, watch, watch one's step*, watch out*; SEE CONCEPT 34

mind [v5] *remember*
bethink, bring to mind, cite, recall, recollect, remind, reminisce, retain; SEE CONCEPT 40

mindful [adj] *attentive, aware*
alert, alive to, apprehensive, au courant, be up on*, cagey, careful, cautious, chary, cognizant, conscientious, conscious, conversant, heedful, in the know, know all the answers*, knowing, know ins and outs*, knowledgeable, observant, observative, observing, on one's toes*, on the ball*, on the job*, on to*, plugged in*, regardful, respectful, sensible, solicitous, thoughtful, tuned in*, vigilant, wary, watchful, with eyes peeled*; SEE CONCEPTS 402,403,542

mindless [adj] *oblivious, stupid; automatic*
asinine, brutish, careless, daydreaming, foolish, forgetful, gratuitous, heedless, idiotic, imbecilic, inattentive, mooning, moony, moronic, neglectful, negligent, nitwitted, obtuse, out, out of it*, rash, senseless, silly, simple, spaced-out*, thoughtless, unaware, unintelligent, unmindful, unthinking, witless; SEE CONCEPTS 403,538

mine [n] *deposit, supply*
abundance, bed, bonanza, ditch, excavation, field, fount, fountain, fund, gold mine, hoard, lode, pit, quarry, reserve, shaft, source, spring, stock, store, treasure trove, treasury, trench, vein, wealth, well, wellspring; SEE CONCEPTS 449,509,712

mine [v] *dig up*
burrow, delve, dig for, drill, excavate, extract, hew, pan, quarry, sap, scoop, shovel, unearth, work; SEE CONCEPT 178

mingle [v1] *physically join*
admix, alloy, blend, coalesce, commingle, compound, intermingle, intermix, interweave, make up, marry, meld, merge, mix, unite, wed; SEE CONCEPT 193

mingle [v2] *socialize*
associate, circulate, consort, fraternize, gang up*, hang out*, hobnob, mix, network, pool, rub shoulders*, tie in, work the room*; SEE CONCEPT 384

miniature [n] *tiny thing*
baby, insignificancy, midget, model, pocket edition, toy; SEE CONCEPT 730

miniature [adj] *tiny*
baby, diminutive, itsy-bitsy*, itty-bitty*, Lilliputian*, little, midget, mini, minikin, minuscule, minute, mite, model, petite, pint-sized, pocket, reduced, scaled-down, small, small-scale, teensy*, teeny*, toy, wee; SEE CONCEPTS 773,789

minimal [adj] *littlest, slightest*
basal, basic, essential, fundamental, least, least

possible, lowest, minimum, nominal, smallest, token; SEE CONCEPTS 762,773,789

minimize [v] *make smaller; underrate*
abbreviate, attenuate, belittle, cheapen, curtail, cut down to size, cut rate, decrease, decry, deprecate, depreciate, derogate, detract, diminish, discount, disparage, downplay*, dwarf*, knock*, knock down*, lessen, make light of*, make little of, miniaturize, pan, play down, pooh-pooh*, poor-mouth*, prune, put down, reduce, run down, shrink, underestimate, underplay; SEE CONCEPTS 54,240,247

minimum [n] *lowest amount*
atom, bottom, dab, depth, dot, gleam, grain, hair, iota, jot, least, lowest, margin, modicum, molecule, nadir, narrowest, particle, pittance, point, scintilla, scruple, shadow, slightest, smallest, smidgen, soupçon, spark, speck, trifle, whit; SEE CONCEPTS 787,831

minimum [adj] *least, lowest*
least possible, littlest, merest, minimal, slightest, smallest, tiniest; SEE CONCEPTS 762,789

minister [n1] *person in charge of church*
abbot, archbishop, archdeacon, bishop, chaplain, clergy, clergyperson, cleric, clerical, clerk, confessor, curate, deacon, dean, diocesan, divine, ecclesiastic, lecturer, missionary, monk, parson, pastor, preacher, prelate, priest, pulpiteer, rector, reverend, shepherd, vicar; SEE CONCEPT 361

minister [n2] *person high in government*
administrator, agent, aide, ambassador, assistant, cabinet member, consul, delegate, diplomat, envoy, executive, legate, liaison, lieutenant, officeholder, official, plenipotentiary, premier, prime minister, secretary; SEE CONCEPT 354

minister [v] *help, serve*
accommodate, administer, aid, answer, attend, be solicitous of, cater to, cure, doctor, do for, foster, heal, nurse, pander, pander to, remedy, succor, take care of, tend, treat, wait on, watch over; SEE CONCEPT 110

minor [n] *person under legal age of maturity*
adolescent, baby, boy, child, girl, infant, junior, juvenile, lad, little one, schoolboy, schoolgirl, teenager, underage, youngster, youth; SEE CONCEPT 424

minor [adj] *insignificant, small*
accessory, below the mark, bush-league*, casual, dependent, dinky*, inconsequential, inconsiderable, inferior, junior, lesser, light, low, minus, negligible, paltry, petty, piddling, secondary, second-string*, slight, smaller, small-fry*, small-time, subordinate, subsidiary, tacky, trifling, trivial, two-bit*, unimportant, younger; SEE CONCEPTS 575,773,789

mint [n] *a lot of money*
boodle, bundle, fortune, heap, million, packet, pile, pot, roll, wad; SEE CONCEPTS 340,787

mint [adj] *brand-new*
excellent, first-class, fresh, intact, original, perfect, spanking-new*, spick-and-span*, unblemished, undamaged, unmarred, untarnished, virgin; SEE CONCEPTS 574,578,797

mint [v] *create, coin*
cast, construct, devise, fabricate, fashion, forge, invent, issue, make, make up, mold, monetize, produce, provide, punch, stamp, strike, think up; SEE CONCEPTS 43,173,205,251

minute [n] *brief time period*
bat of an eye*, breath, breathing, crack, flash,

instant, jiffy*, min*, mo*, moment, nothing flat*, sec*, second, shake, short time*, sixtieth of hour, sixty seconds, split second, twinkling*; SEE CONCEPTS 803,807,821

minute [adj1] *very small*
atomic, diminutive, exact, exiguous, fine, inconsiderable, infinitesimal, insignificant, invisible, little, microbic, microscopic, miniature, minim, minimal, minuscule, molecular, peewee*, piddling, precise, puny, slender, teeny-weeny*, tiny, wee; SEE CONCEPTS 773,789

minute [adj2] *unimportant*
immaterial, inconsiderable, insignificant, light, little, minor, negligible, nonessential, paltry, petty, picayune, piddling, puny, slight, small, trifling, trivial; SEE CONCEPT 575

minute [adj3] *exact, precise*
blow-by-blow*, careful, circumstantial, clock-like, close, critical, detailed, elaborate, exhaustive, full, itemized, meticulous, painstaking, particular, particularized, punctilious, scrupulous, specialized, thorough; SEE CONCEPT 557

miracle [n] *wonderful, surprising event or thing*
marvel, phenomenon, portent, prodigy, rarity, revelation, sensation, stunner, supernatural occurrence, surprise, thaumaturgy, unusualness, wonder; SEE CONCEPTS 671,689,693

miraculous [adj] *surprisingly wonderful*
amazing, anomalous, astonishing, astounding, awesome, extraordinary, fabulous, freakish, heavy, incredible, inexplicable, magical, marvelous, monstrous, numinous, phenomenal, preternatural, prodigious, spectacular, staggering, strange, stupefying, stupendous, superhuman, superior, supermundane, supernatural, supranatural, thaumaturgic, the utmost, unaccountable, unbelievable, unearthly, unimaginable, unreal, underworking, wondrous; SEE CONCEPTS 529,548,572

mirage [n] *imaginary vision*
delusion, fantasy, hallucination, ignis fatuus, illusion, optical illusion, phantasm; SEE CONCEPTS 529,628

mire [n] *muck, morass*
bog, dirt, fen, glop*, goo*, gunk*, marsh, moss, mud, ooze*, quagmire, quicksand, slime*, swamp; SEE CONCEPTS 509,674

mire [v] *delay, catch up in*
bog down, cling, decelerate, detain, dirty, embroil, enmesh, ensnare, entangle, entrap, flounder, hang up, implicate, involve, retard, set back, sink, slow down, slow up, snare, soil, stick, tangle, trap; SEE CONCEPTS 112,121

mirror [n] *glass that reflects image*
cheval glass, gaper, hand glass, imager, looking glass, pier glass, polished metal, reflector, seeing glass, speculum; SEE CONCEPTS 443,470

mirror [v] *copy, reflect*
act like, depict, double, echo, embody, emulate, epitomize, exemplify, follow, glass, illustrate, image, imitate, make like*, mimic, personify, represent, show, simulate, symbolize, take off*, typify; SEE CONCEPTS 111,118,171

mirth [n] *great joy*
amusement, cheer, cheerfulness, convulsions, entertainment, festivity, frivolity, frolic, fun, gaiety, gladness, glee, happiness, hilarity, hysteria, hysterics, jocularity, jocundity, jollity, joviality, joyousness, kicks*, laughs, laughter, levity, lightheartedness, merriment, merrymaking, plea-

sure, rejoicing, revelry, sport, whoopee*; SEE CONCEPTS 388,410

misadventure [n] *bad luck, mishap*
accident, adversity, bad break*, blunder, calamity, casualty, cataclysm, catastrophe, debacle, disaster, error, failure, faux pas, ill fortune, lapse, mischance, misfortune, reverse, setback, slip, tragedy, woe; SEE CONCEPT 674

misanthrope [n] *person who hates others*
cynic, doubter, egoist, egotist, hater, isolate, loner, misanthropist, recluse, skeptic; SEE CONCEPT 412

misanthropic [adj] *unsociable, cynical*
antisocial, egoistic, egotistical, eremitic, hating, inhumane, malevolent, misanthropical, reclusive, reserved, sarcastic, selfish, solitary, standoffish, unfriendly; SEE CONCEPT 404

misapprehend [v] *get the wrong idea, impression*
blunder, confuse, err, misconceive, misconstrue, misinterpret, misread, miss, mistake, misunderstand; SEE CONCEPT 15

misappropriate [v] *use wrongly; steal*
abuse, appropriate, defalcate, embezzle, misapply, misspend, misuse, peculate, plunder, pocket, rob, swindle; SEE CONCEPTS 139,156,341

misbegotten [adj] *illegitimate, illicit*
baseborn, bastard, dishonest, disreputable, illegal, natural, poor, shady, spurious, stolen, supposititious, unlawful, unrespectable; SEE CONCEPTS 319,549

misbehave [v] *act in inappropriate manner*
act up, be at fault, be bad, be dissolute, be guilty, be immoral, be indecorous, be insubordinate, be mischievous, bend the law*, be out of line*, be out of order*, be reprehensible, carry on, cut up, deviate, do evil, do wrong, fail, fool around*, get into mischief, go astray, go wrong, make trouble, misconduct, offend, roughhouse*, sin, sow wild oats*, take a wrong turn*, transgress, trespass; SEE CONCEPTS 633,645

misbehavior [n] *naughty act, conduct*
acting up*, fault, immorality, impropriety, incivility, indiscipline, insubordination, mischief, misconduct, misdeed, misdemeanor, misdoing, monkey business*, naughtiness, rudeness, shenanigans*, transgression, wrongdoing; SEE CONCEPTS 633,645

miscalculate [v] *make a mistake*
blow*, blunder, discount, disregard, drop the ball*, err, get signals crossed*, get wrong, go wrong, mess up*, misconstrue, miscount, misinterpret, misjudge, misread, misreckon, miss by a mile*, misunderstand, mix up, overestimate, overlook, overrate, overvalue, slip up, stumble, underestimate, underrate, undervalue; SEE CONCEPT 101

miscarriage [n] *failure*
abortion, botch, breakdown, defeat, error, interruption, malfunction, misadventure, mischance, misfire, mishap, miss, mistake, nonsuccess, perversion, undoing; SEE CONCEPTS 230,699

miscellaneous [adj] *diversified, various*
assorted, confused, conglomerate, different, disordered, disparate, divergent, divers, diverse, heterogeneous, indiscriminate, jumbled, many, mingled, mixed, motley, muddled, multifarious, multiform, odd, promiscuous, scattered, scrambled, sundry, unmatched, unsorted, varied, variegated; SEE CONCEPT 564

478

miscellany [n] *varied collection*
accumulation, aggregation, anthology, assortment, brew, collectanea, combination, combo, compilation, conglomeration, cumulation, diversity, farrago, gallimaufry, garbage*, hash, hodgepodge, jumble, medley, mélange, melee, mess, mishmash, mix, mixed bag, mixture, muddle, odds and ends*, olio, pasticcio, pastiche, patchwork, potpourri, salad, salmagundi, smorgasbord, stew, variety; SEE CONCEPTS 432,665

mischief [n] *trouble, damage*
atrocity, catastrophe, devilment, devilry, dirty trick*, evil, fault, friskiness, frolicsomeness, funny business*, gag, harm, high jinks*, hurt, ill, impishness, injury, misbehavior, mischievousness, misconduct, misdoing, misfortune, monkey business*, naughtiness, outrage, playfulness, prank, rascality, roguery, roguishness, sabotage, shenanigans, sportiveness, transgression, vandalism, waggery, waggishness, waywardness, wrong, wrongdoing; SEE CONCEPTS 192,633,645

mischievous [adj] *devilish, wicked*
arch, artful, bad, bothersome, damaging, dangerous, deleterious, destructive, detrimental, dickens*, evil, exasperating, foxy*, frolicsome, harmful, hazardous, holy terror*, hurtful, ill, ill-behaved, impish, injurious, insidious, irksome, malicious, malignant, misbehaving, naughty, noxuous, perilous, pernicious, playful, precarious, puckish, rascal, rascally, risky, rude, sinful, sly, spiteful, sportive, teasing, tricky, troublesome, vexatious, vexing, vicious, wayward; SEE CONCEPTS 401,545

misconception [n] *wrong idea, impression*
delusion, error, fallacy, fault, misapprehension, misconstruction, misinterpretation, mistake, mistaken belief, misunderstanding; SEE CONCEPTS 409,689

misconduct [n] *bad or unethical behavior*
delinquency, dereliction, evil, immorality, impropriety, malfeasance, malpractice, malversation, misbehavior, mischief, misdemeanor, misdoing, mismanagement, naughtiness, offense, rudeness, transgression, wrongdoing; SEE CONCEPTS 192,633,645

misconstrue [v] *get a wrong or false impression*
distort, exaggerate, misapprehend, misconceive, misinterpret, misjudge, misread, mistake, mistranslate, misunderstand, pervert, take the wrong way; SEE CONCEPT 15

miscreant [n] *person who is very bad, immoral*
blackguard, black sheep*, bootlegger, bully, cad, caitiff, convict, criminal, culprit, delinquent, drunkard, evildoer, felon, fink*, heel*, hoodlum, jailbird, loafer, louse*, lowlife*, malefactor, outcast, outlaw, pickpocket, racketeer, rapscallion, rascal, rat*, reprobate, rowdy, ruffian, scalawag, scamp, scoundrel, scum*, sinner, sneak, vagabond, villain, wretch, wrongdoer; SEE CONCEPT 412

miscreant [adj] *evil, immoral*
corrupt, criminal, degenerate, depraved, flagitious, infamous, iniquitous, nefarious, perverse, rascally, reprehensible, reprobate, unhealthy, unprincipled, vicious, villainous, wicked; SEE CONCEPTS 401,545

misdeed/misdemeanor [n] *sin, crime*
breach of law, criminality, dirt*, dirty deed*, dirty pool*, fault, infringement, malefaction, misbehavior, misconduct, miscue, offense, peccadillo,

slipup, transgression, trespass, villainy, violation, wrong, wrongdoing; SEE CONCEPTS 192,633,645

miser [n] *person who hoards money, possessions*
cheapskate*, churl, harpy*, hoarder, moneygrubber*, penny-pincher*, pinchfist*, pinchpenny*, Scrooge*, stiff*, tightwad*; SEE CONCEPTS 348,412,423

miserable [adj1] *unhappy, depressed*
afflicted, agonized, ailing, anguished, brokenhearted, crestfallen, dejected, desolate, despairing, despondent, destroyed, disconsolate, discontented, distressed, doleful, dolorous, down, downcast, down in the mouth*, forlorn, gloomy, heartbroken, hopeless, hurt, hurting, ill, injured, in pain, melancholy, mournful, on a downer*, pained, pathetic, pitiable, racked, rueful, ruthful, sad, sick, sickly, sorrowful, strained, suffering, tormented, tortured, tragic, troubled, woebegone, wounded, wretched; SEE CONCEPT 403

miserable [adj2] *destitute, shabby*
abject, bad, contemptible, deplorable, despicable, detestable, disgraceful, godforsaken, impoverished, indigent, inferior, lamentable, low, meager, mean, needy, paltry, pathetic, penniless, piteous, pitiable, poor, poverty-stricken, sad, scanty, scurvy, shameful, sordid, sorry, squalid, tragic, vile, worthless, wretched; SEE CONCEPTS 485,570

miserly [adj] *greedy, stingy*
abject, avaricious, beggarly, cheapskate*, churlish, close, close-fisted, covetous, grasping, ignoble, illiberal, mean, parsimonious, pennypinching*, penurious, skinflint*, sordid, tightfisted*, ungenerous; SEE CONCEPTS 326,334, 401,404

misery [n1] *pain, mental or physical*
ache, agony, anguish, anvil chorus, bad news*, blues*, depression, desolation, despair, despondency, discomfort, distress, dolor, gloom, grief, hardship, headache, heartache, hurting, melancholy, pang, passion, sadness, sorrow, squalor, stitch, suffering, throe, torment, torture, twinge, unhappiness, woe, worriment, worry, wretchedness; SEE CONCEPT 728

misery [n2] *trouble, disaster*
adversity, affliction, anxiety, bitter pill*, burden, calamity, catastrophe, curse, destitution, difficulty, grief, indigence, load, misfortune, need, ordeal, penury, poverty, privation, problem, sordidness, sorrow, squalor, trial, tribulation, want, woe; SEE CONCEPTS 335,666,674

misfortune/mishap [n] *bad luck; disaster*
accident, adversity, affliction, annoyance, anxiety, bad break*, bad news*, blow*, burden, calamity, casualty, cataclysm, catastrophe, contretemps, cross, crunch, debacle, disadvantage, disappointment, discomfort, dole, failure, hard luck*, hardship, harm, inconvenience, infelicity, loss, misadventure, mischance, misery, nuisance, reverse, rotten luck, setback, stroke of bad luck*, tough luck*, tragedy, trial, tribulation, trouble, unpleasantness, visitation, worry; SEE CONCEPTS 674,679

misgiving [n] *uncertainty*
anxiety, apprehension, apprehensiveness, distrust, doubt, fear, foreboding, hesitation, mistrust, premonition, prenotion, presage, presentiment, qualm, reservation, scruple, suspicion, unbelief, unease, worry; SEE CONCEPTS 21,689,690

misguided [adj] ill-advised, deluded

bearded, bum-steer*, confused, deceived, disinformed, erroneous, faked-out*, foolish, imprudent, indiscreet, inexpedient, injudicious, led up the garden path*, misled, misplaced, mistaken, stonewalled*, uncalled for, unreasonable, unwarranted, unwise, wrong; SEE CONCEPTS *544, 548,520*

mishandle/mismanage [v] mess up

abuse, be incompetent, be inefficient, blow, blunder, botch*, bungle, confound, err, flub*, foul up, fumble, goof*, goof up*, gum up*, harm, make a hash of*, make a mess of*, maladminister, misapply, misconduct, misdirect, misemploy, misgovern, mistreat, misuse, muff*, overlook, pervert, prostitute, put foot in*, screw up*, shoot oneself in foot*; SEE CONCEPTS *101,156,384*

misinform [v] give wrong information intentionally

bait and switch*, cover up, deceive, disinform, doublespeak*, double-talk*, lead astray, lie, misdirect, misguide, mislead, misstate, mousetrap*, pervert, prevaricate, put on*, put on an act*, put on false front*, put up smoke screen*, signify, string along*, wrong steer*; SEE CONCEPT *63*

misjudge [v] get the wrong idea

bark up wrong tree*, be misled, be overcritical, be partial, be unfair, be wrong, come to hasty conclusion, dogmatize, drop the ball*, err, misapprehend, miscalculate, miscomprehend, misconceive, misconjecture, misconstrue, misdeem, misreckon, miss by a mile*, mistake, misthink, misunderstand, overestimate, overrate, prejudge, presume, presuppose, put foot in*, stumble, suppose, underestimate, underrate; SEE CONCEPTS *12,18,101*

mislead [v] give someone the wrong idea, information

bait, beguile, betray, bilk, bluff, bunk, cheat, cozen, deceive, defraud, delude, double-cross*, dupe, enmesh, ensnare, entangle, entice, fool, fudge*, gull, hoax, hoodwink*, hose*, illude, inveigle, juggle, lead astray, lead on*, lie, lure, misdirect, misguide, misinform, misrepresent, outwit, overreach, pervert, pull wool over eyes*, put on*, rip off*, rook, rope in*, scam, seduce, shaft, snow*, take in, tempt, trick, victimize; SEE CONCEPTS *59,63*

misleading [adj] deceptive, confusing

ambiguous, beguiling, bewildering, casuistical, catchy, confounding, deceitful, deceiving, deluding, delusive, delusory, demagogic, disingenuous, distracting, evasive, fallacious, false, inaccurate, perplexing, puzzling, sophistical, specious, spurious, tricky, wrong; SEE CONCEPTS *267,548*

misplace [v] lose; be unable to find

be unable to lay hands on*, confuse, disarrange, dishevel, disorder, disorganize, displace, disturb, forget whereabouts of, lose track of, misfile, mislay, miss, mix, muss, place unwisely, place wrongly, put in wrong place, remove, scatter, unsettle; SEE CONCEPTS *116,201*

misrepresent/misquote [v] lie, distort

adulterate, angle, beard*, belie, build up, cloak, color, con, confuse, cover up, disguise, distort, dress, embellish, embroider, equivocate, exaggerate, falsify, garble, give snow job*, mangle, mask, miscolor, misinterpret, misreport, misstate, overdraw, overstate, palter, pervert, phony up*, pirate*, prevaricate, promote, puff*, skew, slant,

snow*, spread it on*, stretch, take out of context*, throw a curve*, trump up*, twist, warp; SEE CONCEPT *63*

miss [n] failure

absence, blunder, default, defect, error, fault, loss, mishap, mistake, omission, oversight, slip, want; SEE CONCEPTS *101,699*

miss [v] fail, make a mistake

be late for, blow, blunder, botch, disregard, drop, drop the ball*, err, fall flat on face*, fall short, flub*, forget, fumble, ignore, jump, let go, let slip, lose, miscarry, misfire, mislay, misplace, muff*, neglect, omit, overlook, overshoot, pass over, pass up, skip, slight, slip, trip, trip up, undershoot; SEE CONCEPTS *101,699*

miss [v2] want; feel a loss

crave, desire, long, need, pine, wish, yearn; SEE CONCEPT *20*

missile [n] projectile weapon

ammunition, arrow, bar, bird*, bolt, bomb, bullet, cartridge, dart, MX*, pellet, projectile, rocket, shot, stealth, trajectic; SEE CONCEPT *500*

missing [adj] gone, absent

astray, away, AWOL*, disappeared, lacking, left behind, left out, lost, mislaid, misplaced, not present, nowhere to be found*, omitted, removed, short, unaccounted for, wanting; SEE CONCEPTS *539,576*

mission [n] person's task, responsibility

aim, assignment, business, calling, charge, commission, duty, end, errand, goal, job, lifework, object, objective, office, operation, profession, purpose, pursuit, quest, sortie, trade, trust, undertaking, vocation, work; SEE CONCEPTS *360,362,659*

missionary [n] person who aids, does religious work

apostle, clergy, clergyperson, converter, evangelist, herald, messenger, minister, missioner, pastor, preacher, promoter, propagandist, proselytizer, revivalist, teacher; SEE CONCEPTS *361,416*

missive [n] written communication

dispatch, epistle, letter, line, memo, memorandum, message, note, report, word; SEE CONCEPTS *271,278*

misspent [adj] wasted

blown*, dissipated, down the drain*, idle, imprudent, misapplied, prodigal, profitless, squandered, thrown away; SEE CONCEPTS *544,560,570*

misstep [n] mistake, wrong move

bad move*, blunder, bungle, error, failure, false step, faux pas, fluff*, gaffe, indiscretion, lapse, miscue, miss, slip, slipup*, stumble, trip; SEE CONCEPTS *101,674,699*

mist [n] film, vapor

brume, cloud, condensation, dew, drizzle, fog, ground clouds, haze, moisture, rain, smog, soup*, spray, steam, visibility zero*; SEE CONCEPT *524*

mist [v] cloud, steam up

becloud, befog, blur, dim, drizzle, film, fog, haze, mizzle, murk, obscure, overcast, overcloud, rain, shower, sprinkle, steam; SEE CONCEPT *526*

mistake [n] error, misunderstanding

aberration, blooper*, blunder, boo-boo*, bungle, confusion, delusion, erratum, false move, false step, fault, faux pas, flub*, fluff*, gaffe, illusion, inaccuracy, inadvertence, lapse, misapplication, misapprehension, miscalculation, misconception, misinterpretation, misjudgment, misprint, misstatement, misstep, muddle, neglect, omission, overestimation, oversight, slight, slip, slip of tongue*, slipup*, snafu*, solecism, trip*, typographical error, underestimation; SEE CONCEPTS 101,230,410

mistake [v] *mix up, misunderstand*

addle, be off the mark*, be wrong, blunder, botch*, bungle, confound, confuse, deceive oneself, err, fail, get wrong, goof*, have wrong impression, jumble, lapse, make a mess*, misapprehend, miscalculate, misconceive, misconstrue, miscount, misdeem, misinterpret, misjudge, misknow, misread, miss, miss the boat*, not know, omit, overestimate, overlook, put foot in*, slip*, slip up*, snarl, take for*, tangle, underestimate; SEE CONCEPTS 15,101

mistaken [adj] *wrong, incorrect*

all wet*, at fault, barking up wrong tree*, confounded, confused, confused with, deceived, deluded, duped, erroneous, fallacious, false, faulty, fooled, ill-advised, illogical, inaccurate, inappropriate, misconstrued, misguided, misinformed, misinterpreting, misjudging, misled, misunderstanding, off base*, off track*, tricked, unadvised, under wrong impression, unfounded, unreal, unsound, untrue, warranted, way off*, wide of mark*, wrongly identified, wrong number*; SEE CONCEPTS 402,529

mistreat [v] *treat badly or wrongly*

abuse, backbite, bash, brutalize, bung up*, chop, do wrong, dump on*, give black eye*, handle roughly, harm, injure, kick around, knock around, maltreat, maul, mess up, misuse, molest, outrage, push around, rip, roughhouse*, rough up, shake up, total*, trash*, wax*, wound, wrong; SEE CONCEPTS 14,156,246

mistrust [n] *doubtfulness*

apprehension, chariness, concern, distrust, doubt, dubiety, dubiosity, fear, foreboding, incertitude, misgiving, presentiment, scruple, skepticism, suspicion, uncertainty, wariness, wonder; SEE CONCEPTS 21,27,690

mistrust [v] *doubt*

apprehend, beware, be wary, challenge, disbelieve, dispute, distrust, fear, have doubts, question, scruple, suspect, suspicion; SEE CONCEPT 21

misty [adj] *filmy, obscure*

bleary, blurred, closed in, clouded, cloudy, dark, dewy, dim, enveloped, foggy, fuzzy, hazy, indistinct, murky, mushy, nebulous, opaque, overcast, shrouded, socked in, soupy*, unclear, vague, vaporous; SEE CONCEPTS 525,603,617

misunderstand [v] *get the wrong idea*

be at cross purposes*, be bewildered, be confused, be perplexed, confound, confuse, fail, get signals crossed*, get signals mixed*, get wrong, get wrong impression*, misapply, misapprehend, miscalculate, miscomprehend, misconceive, misconstrue, misinterpret, misjudge, misknow, misread, misreckon, miss*, miss the point*, mistake, not register*, take amiss, take wrongly; SEE CONCEPT 15

misunderstanding [n1] *instance of having the wrong idea*

confounding, confusion, delusion, error, false impression, misapprehension, misconception, misconstruction, misinterpretation, misjudgment, misreckoning, mistake, mix-up; SEE CONCEPT 409

misunderstanding [n2] *argument, fight*

bad vibes*, blowup*, breach, break, clash, conflict, crossed wires*, debate, difference, difficulty, disagreement, discord, dissension, falling-out*, feud, fuss, quarrel, rift, row, run-in*, rupture, set-to, sour note*, spat, squabble, tiff*, variance, words*; SEE CONCEPTS 46,106

misuse [n] *abuse; wrong application*

abusage, barbarism, catachresis, corruption, cruel treatment, desecration, dissipation, exploitation, harm, ill-treatment, injury, malapropism, maltreatment, misapplication, misemployment, mistreatment, misusage, perversion, profanation, prostitution, rough handling, solecism, squandering, waste; SEE CONCEPT 156

misuse [v] *abuse; apply wrongly*

blow*, brutalize, corrupt, cut up, desecrate, dissipate, exploit, go through, handle roughly, illtreat, maltreat, maul, mess up*, misapply, misemploy, mistreat, molest, outrage, pervert, profane, prostitute, run through*, shake up, squander, waste, wrong; SEE CONCEPT 156

mitigate [v] *check, diminish, lighten*

abate, allay, alleviate, appease, assuage, blunt, calm, come together, cool*, dull, ease, extenuate, lessen, meet halfway*, moderate, modify, mollify, pacify, palliate, placate, quiet, reduce, relieve, remit, soften, soothe, subdue, take the edge off*, temper, tone down, tranquilize, weaken; SEE CONCEPTS 233,240

mix/mixture [n] *assortment, combination*

admixture, adulteration, alloy, amalgam, amalgamation, assimilation, association, batter, blend, brew, combine, combo, commixture, composite, compound, concoction, confection, conglomeration, cross, crossing, dough, fusion, goulash, grab bag*, hodgepodge, hybrid, hybridization, incorporation, infiltration, interfusion, jumble, mash, medley, melange, mingling, miscellany, mishmash, mixed bag, mosaic, package, patchwork, potpourri, salmagundi, saturation, soup*, stew*, transfusion, union, variety; SEE CONCEPTS 260,432

mix [v1] *combine, join*

admix, adulterate, alloy, amalgamate, associate, blend, braid, coalesce, commingle, commix, compound, conjoin, cross, embody, fuse, hybridize, incorporate, infiltrate, infuse, instill, interbreed, intermingle, interweave, jumble, knead, link, lump, make up, merge, mingle, mix up, put together, saturate, stir, suffuse, synthesize, tangle, transfuse, unite, weave, work in; SEE CONCEPTS 113,193

mix [v2] *socialize*

associate, come together, consort, get along, hang out, hobnob, join, mingle; SEE CONCEPT 114

mixed [adj] *assorted, combined*

alloyed, amalgamated, assimilated, assorted, blended, brewed, composite, compound, conglomerate, crossbred, crossed, different, disordered, diverse, diversified, embodied, fused, heterogeneous, hybrid, hybridized, incorporated, infused, interbred, interdenominational, joint, kneaded, married, merged, mingled, miscellaneous, mongrel, motley, multifarious, tied, transfused, united, varied, woven; SEE CONCEPTS 485,564,772

mix up [v] *confuse*

addle, befuddle, bewilder, confound, derange, disorder, disorganize, disrupt, distract, disturb, dizzy, fluster, foul up*, jumble, mess up*, mistake, muddle, perplex, puzzle, snafu*, upset; SEE CONCEPTS 16,158

mix-up [n] *confusion, misunderstanding*
botch*, chaos, commotion, disorder, jumble, mess, mistake, muddle, shambles*, tangle, turmoil; SEE CONCEPTS 230,674

moan [n] *groan, complaint*
beef, cry, gripe, grouse, grumble, lament, lamentation, plaint, sigh, sob, wail, whine; SEE CONCEPTS 52,77

moan [v] *groan, complain*
bemoan, bewail, carp, deplore, grieve, gripe, grouse, grumble, keen, lament, mourn, sigh, sob, wail, whine; SEE CONCEPTS 52,77

mob [n] *large group of people*
assemblage, body, cabal, camp, canaille, cattle, circle, clan, class, clique, collection, commonality, company, coterie, crew, crowd, crush, drove, flock, gang, gathering, herd, horde, host, jam, lot, mass, masses, multitude, pack, populace, posse, press, proletariat, rabble, riffraff*, ring, riot, scum, set, swarm, throng, troop; SEE CONCEPTS 378,417,432

mob [v] *come upon by pushing; surround*
attack, cram, crowd, fill, hustle, jam, jostle, overrun, pack, riot, set upon, swarm, throng; SEE CONCEPTS 208,758

mobile [adj] *movable, travelling*
adaptable, ambulatory, changeable, fluid, free, itinerant, locomotive, loose, migrant, migratory, motile, motorized, moving, mutable, nomadic, peripatetic, portable, roaming, roving, unsettled, unstable, unstationary, unsteadfast, unsteady, versatile, wandering; SEE CONCEPTS 576,584

mobilize [v] *ready for action, movement*
activate, actuate, animate, assemble, call to arms, call up, catalyze, circulate, drive, gather, get ready, impel, make ready, marshal, muster, organize, prepare, propel, put in motion, rally, ready, set in motion, set off; SEE CONCEPTS 148,187,221,320

mock [adj] *artificial, fake*
apish*, bogus*, counterfeit, dummy, ersatz*, faked, false, feigned, forged, fraudulent, hokey*, imitation, imitative, make-believe, mimic, phony, pretended, pseudo*, put-on*, quasi*, sham*, simulated, so-called*, spurious, substitute, unreal; SEE CONCEPTS 566,582

mock [v1] *ridicule*
buffoon, burlesque, caricature, chaff, deride, flout, hoot, insult, jape, jeer, kid, laugh at, make fun of, needle, parody, poke fun at*, rally, rib*, scoff, scorn, show contempt, sneer, taunt, tease, thumb nose at*, travesty; SEE CONCEPTS 7,19,49

mock [v2] *mimic*
affect, ape, assume, burlesque, caricature, counterfeit, ditto*, do, fake, feign, hoke, imitate, lampoon, mime, mirror, parody, satirize, send up*, simulate, take off*, travesty; SEE CONCEPT 111

mock [v3] *deceive*
beguile, belie, betray, challenge, cheat, defeat, defy, delude, disappoint, double-cross*, dupe, elude, foil, fool, frustrate, juggle, let down*, mislead, sell out*, thwart; SEE CONCEPTS 59,63

mockery [n1] *joke, parody*
burlesque, butt*, caricature, deception, farce, imitation, jest, lampoon, laughingstock, mimicry,

mock, pretense, send-up*, sham*, spoof, sport*, take-off*, travesty; SEE CONCEPTS 111,278

mockery [n2] *insult, disrespect*
contempt, contumely, derision, disdain, disparagement, gibe, jeer, ridicule, scoffing, scorn, sport; SEE CONCEPTS 49,278

mode [n1] *manner, way*
approach, book, channels, condition, course, custom, fashion, form, mechanism, method, modus, nuts and bolts*, plan, posture, practice, procedure, process, quality, rule, situation, state, status, style, system, technique, tone, vein, wise; SEE CONCEPTS 6,644

mode [n2] *trend, fad*
chic, convention, craze, cry, dernier cri*, fashion, furor, last word*, latest thing*, latest wrinkle*, look, mainstream, now*, rage*, style, thing*, vogue; SEE CONCEPTS 529,655

model [n1] *imitation, replica*
cartoon, clone, copy, copycat, dead ringer*, ditto*, dummy, duplicate, effigy, engraving, facsimile, figure, figurine, game plan, illustration, image, knock-off, layout, look-alike, miniature, mock-up, painting, paste-up, photograph, picture, pocket, portrait, print, relief, representation, ringer*, setup, sketch, spitting image*, statue, statuette, tracing, visual; SEE CONCEPTS 259,625,628,667

model [n2] *example, standard*
apotheosis, archetype, beau ideal, criterion, design, emblem, embodiment, epitome, exemplar, gauge, hero, ideal, lodestar, mirror, mold, nonesuch, nonpareil, original, paradigm, paragon, pattern, prototype, quintessence, role model, saint, symbol, touchstone, type; SEE CONCEPTS 686,688

model [n3] *person, thing that poses*
dummy, manikin, mannequin, nude, sitter, subject; SEE CONCEPT 348

model [n4] *type, version*
configuration, design, form, kind, mark, mode, style, variety; SEE CONCEPTS 378,463,505,654

model [adj] *typical, ideal*
archetypal, classic, classical, commendable, copy, dummy, exemplary, facsimile, flawless, illustrative, imitation, miniature, paradigmatic, perfect, prototypical, quintessential, representative, standard, typical, very; SEE CONCEPTS 566,574

model [v1] *form, shape*
base, carve, cast, create, design, fashion, mold, pattern, plan, sculpt; SEE CONCEPT 184

model [v2] *display, pose*
parade, represent, set example, show off, sit, sport, wear; SEE CONCEPT 138

moderate [adj1] *calm, temperate*
abstinent, balanced, bearable, careful, cautious, compromising, conservative, considerate, considered, controlled, cool, deliberate, disciplined, dispassionate, equable, even, gentle, impartial, inconsiderable, inexpensive, judicious, limited, low-key, measured, middle-of-the-road*, midway, mild, modest, monotonous, neutral, nonpartisan, not excessive, pacific, peaceable, pleasant, reasonable, reserved, restrained, sober, soft, steady, straight, tame, tolerable, tolerant, tranquil, untroubled; SEE CONCEPTS 533,563

moderate [adj2] *fair, average, so-so*
bland, fairish*, fair to middling*, inconsequential, inconsiderable, indifferent, intermediate, mean, mediocre, medium, middling*, ordinary,

paltry, passable, piddling*, trifling, trivial, unexceptional; SEE CONCEPTS 547,575

moderate [v1] *restrain, control*

abate, allay, alleviate, appease, assuage, calm, chasten, check, constrain, cool*, cool out*, curb, decline, decrease, die down, diminish, ease off, fall, lessen, let up, meet halfway, mitigate, modify, modulate, mollify, pacify, play down, qualify, quiet, reduce, regulate, relent, relieve, repress, slacken, slow, soften, soft-pedal, subdue, subside, tame, temper, tone down, wane; SEE CONCEPTS 94,130,240

moderate [v2] *mediate, arbitrate*

chair, judge, make peace*, negotiate, preside, referee, take the chair*, umpire; SEE CONCEPTS 18,317

moderately [adv] *to a degree, to some extent*

a little, averagely, enough, fairly, gently, in moderation, in reason, kind of, more or less*, more than not*, not exactly, passably, pretty, quite, quite a bit, rather, reasonably, slightly, some, something, somewhat, sort of, so-so*, temperately, tolerable, tolerably, tolerantly, within limits*, within reason*; SEE CONCEPTS 544,772

moderation [n] *temperance*

balance, calmness, composure, constraint, coolness, dispassionateness, equanimity, fairness, forbearance, golden mean, judiciousness, justice, justness, lenity, measure, mildness, moderateness, patience, poise, quiet, reasonableness, restraint, sedateness, sedation, sobriety, steadiness, toleration; SEE CONCEPTS 633,657

modern [adj] *new, up-to-date*

avant-garde, coincident, concomitant, concurrent, contempo, contemporary, current, cutting-edge*, fresh, last word*, late, latest, latter-day*, leading-edge*, modernistic, modernized, modish, neoteric, newfangled*, new-fashioned, novel, now, present, present-day, prevailing, prevalent, recent, state-of-the-art*, stylish, today, twenty-first century*, up-to-the-minute, with-it*; SEE CONCEPTS 578,589,797

modernize [v] *bring up to date; remodel*

improve, refresh, regenerate, rejuvenate, remake, renew, renovate, restore, revamp, revive, update; SEE CONCEPTS 168,177,202

modest [adj1] *shy*

bashful, blushing, chaste, coy, demure, diffident, discreet, humble, lowly, meek, moderate, nice, proper, prudent, quiet, reserved, resigned, reticent, retiring, seemly, self-conscious, self-effacing, sheepish, silent, simple, temperate, timid, unassertive, unassuming, unassured, unboastful, unobtrusive, unpresuming, unpretending, unpretentious, withdrawing; SEE CONCEPTS 401,404

modest [adj2] *limited, ordinary*

average, cheap, discreet, dry, economical, fair, humble, inelaborate, inexpensive, middling, moderate, natural, plain, reasonable, simple, small, unadorned, unaffected, unembellished, unembroidered, unexceptional, unexcessive, unextravagant, unextreme, unobtrusive, unornamented, unostentatious, unpretentious, unradical, unstudied; SEE CONCEPTS 334,547,562

modesty [n] *shyness*

bashfulness, celibacy, chastity, constraint, coyness, decency, delicacy, demureness, diffidence, discreetness, humbleness, humility, inhibition, innocence, lack of pretension, meekness, propriety, prudery, purity, quietness, reserve, reticence, self-effacement, simplicity, timidity, unobtrusiveness, unostentatiousness, unpretentiousness, virtue; SEE CONCEPT 633

modicum [n] *bit, small amount*

atom, crumb, dash, drop, fraction, fragment, grain, inch, iota, jot, little, minim, mite, molecule, ounce, pinch, scrap, shred, smidge, speck, tinge, touch, trifle, whit; SEE CONCEPT 831

modify [v1] *alter, change*

adapt, adjust, become, convert, correct, customize, doctor, mutate, recast, redo, refashion, reform, remodel, reorganize, repair, reshape, revise, rework, shift gears*, switch over, transfigure, transform, transmogrify, transmute, turn, turn one around*, turn over new leaf*, turn the corner*, turn the tables*, tweak*, vary; SEE CONCEPT 232

modify [v2] *lessen, reduce*

abate, curb, decrease, limit, lower, mitigate, moderate, modulate, qualify, relax, remit, restrain, restrict, slacken, soften, temper, tone down; SEE CONCEPTS 236,240,247

modish [adj] *fashionable*

a la mode*, all the rage*, chic, contemporary, current, dashing, exclusive, faddy, fresh, happening, hip*, in*, in-thing*, last-word, latest, mod*, now*, smart, stylish, swank, swish*, trendy, up-to-date, up-to-the-minute, vogue, voguish, with-it*; SEE CONCEPTS 578,589,797

modulate [v] *adjust, harmonize*

attune, balance, fine-tune, inflect, regulate, restrain, revamp, switch, temper, tone, transmogrify, tune, tweak, vary; SEE CONCEPT 202

mogul [n] *person who has great power, many possessions*

executive, key player*, king, magnate, notable, personage, potentate, prince, princess queen, royalty, top brass*, tycoon, VIP*; SEE CONCEPTS 347,354

moist [adj] *wet, wettish*

clammy, damp, dampish, dank, dewy, dripping, drippy, drizzly, humid, irriguous, muggy, not dry, oozy*, rainy, soggy, teary, watery; SEE CONCEPT 603

moisten [v] *make wet, damp*

bathe, bedew, dampen, dip, drench, humidify, lick, mist, moisturize, rain on, rinse, saturate, shower, soak, sog, sop, splash, splatter, spray, sprinkle, squirt, steam, steep, wash, water, water down, waterlog, wet; SEE CONCEPT 256

moisture [n] *dampness; liquid*

damp, dankness, dew, drizzle, fog, humidity, mist, perspiration, precipitation, rain, sweat, water, wateriness, wet, wetness; SEE CONCEPTS 467,524

mold [n] *form, pattern*

cast, cavity, character, class, depression, description, design, die, frame, image, impression, kind, lot, matrix, model, nature, shape, sort, stamp, type, womb; SEE CONCEPTS 378,411,436

mold [v] *form, give shape*

build, construct, devise, erect, fashion, forge, form, frame, make, pat, plan, plant, plot, put together, round, scheme, sculpt, whittle; SEE CONCEPTS 173,175,184,251

molecule [n] *smallest part*

bit, fragment, iota, jot, minim, mite, modicum, mote, ounce, particle, ray, speck, unit; SEE CONCEPTS 393,831

molest [v1] *physically abuse*

accost, assail, attack, disorganize, displace, disturb, encroach, fondle, harm, hinder, hurt, illtreat, injure, interfere, intrude, maltreat, meddle, misuse, rape; SEE CONCEPTS 246,375

molest [v2] *bother, annoy*

abuse, afflict, badger, bait, bedevil, beset, break in, bug*, confuse, discommode, discompose, disquiet, disturb, encroach, frighten, harass, harry, heckle, hector, interrupt, intrude, irk, irritate, obtrude, persecute, perturb, pester, plague, pother, pursue, scare, tease, terrify, torment, trouble, upset, vex, worry; SEE CONCEPTS 7,14,19

mollify [v] *pacify, soothe*

abate, allay, alleviate, ameliorate, appease, assuage, blunt, calm, compose, conciliate, cool, cushion, decrease, diminish, dulcify, ease, fix up, lessen, lighten, lull, mellow, mitigate, moderate, modify, pacify, patch things up*, placate, propitiate, quell, quiet, reduce, relieve, soften, sweeten, take sting out*, temper, tranquilize; SEE CONCEPTS 7,22,244,698

moment [n1] *brief time period*

bit, breathing, crack, date, flash, hour, instant, jiff*, jiffy*, juncture, minute, nothing flat*, no time*, occasion, point, point in time, sec*, second, shake, split second*, stage, three winks*, tick*, time, trice*, twinkle*, twinkling*, while, wink*; SEE CONCEPTS 807,808

moment [n2] *importance*

advantage, avail, concern, consequence, gravity, import, magnitude, momentousness, note, pith, profit, seriousness, significance, signification, substance, use, value, weight, weightiness, worth; SEE CONCEPT 668

momentarily [adv] *for a short time*

briefly, for a little while, for a minute, for a moment, for an instant, for a second, for a short time, for a short while, immediately, instantly, now, right now, temporarily; SEE CONCEPT 820

momentary [adj] *brief, fleeting*

cursory, dreamlike, ephemeral, evanescent, flashing, flitting*, flying, fugacious, fugitive, gone in flash*, hasty, impermanent, impulsive, instantaneous, in wink of an eye*, like lightning, passing, quick, shifting, short, short-lived, spasmodic, summary, temporary, transient, transitory, vanishing, volatile; SEE CONCEPT 798

momentous [adj] *important; serious*

big, chips are down*, consequential, considerable, critical, crucial, decisive, earth-shaking, earth-shattering, epochal, eventful, far-reaching, fateful, grave, heavy, heavy number, historic, material, meaningful, memorable, notable, of moment, outstanding, pivotal, significant, substantial, vital, weighty; SEE CONCEPT 568

momentum [n] *impetus, push*

drive, energy, force, impulse, power, propulsion, strength, thrust; SEE CONCEPTS 641,712

monarch [n] *ruler*

autocrat, crowned head, despot, emperor, empress, king, majesty, potentate, prince, princess, queen, sovereign; SEE CONCEPTS 354,422

monastery [n] *place where monks live*

abbey, cloister, friary, house, lamasery, priory, religious community; SEE CONCEPTS 368,439,516

monetary [adj] *concerning money, finances*

budgetary, capital, cash, commercial, financial, fiscal, pecuniary, pocket; SEE CONCEPT 334

money [n] *currency accepted as exchange for goods, services*

almighty dollar*, banknote, bankroll, bill, bread*, bucks*, capital, cash, check, chips, coin, coinage, dough*, finances, fund, funds, gold, gravy*, greenback*, hard cash*, legal tender, loot*, medium of exchange, pay, payment, pesos*, property, resources, riches, roll, salary, silver, specie, treasure, wad*, wage, wealth, wherewithal*; SEE CONCEPT 340

moneyed [adj] *rich*

affluent, fat-cat*, flush*, leisure-class*, loaded*, opulent, prosperous, upper-class, upscale, uptown, wealthy, well-heeled*, well-off*, well-to-do*; SEE CONCEPT 334

moneymaking [adj] *producing profit*

advantageous, gainful, going, good, lucrative, paying, profitable, remunerative, successful, thriving, well-paying; SEE CONCEPT 334

mongrel [n] *animal of mixed background*

bastard, cross, crossbreed, cur, half-blood, half-breed, hybrid, mixed breed, mixture, mule, mutt; SEE CONCEPT 394

monitor [n] *person who watches, oversees*

adviser, auditor, counselor, director, eavesdropper, guide, informant, invigilator, listener, overseer, supervisor, watchdog; SEE CONCEPTS 348,350

monitor [v] *listen, watch carefully*

advise, audit, check, control, counsel, follow, keep an eye on*, keep track of*, observe, oversee, record, scan, supervise, survey, track; SEE CONCEPTS 117,596,623

monk [n] *man who devotes life to contemplation of god*

abbot, anchorite, ascetic, brother, cenobite, eremite, friar, hermit, monastic, priest, recluse, religious, solitary; SEE CONCEPT 361

monkey [n] *primate*

anthropoid, ape, baboon, chimpanzee, gorilla, imp, lemur, monk, orangutan, rascal, scamp, simian; SEE CONCEPT 394

monkey [v] *fiddle, tamper with*

busybody, butt in*, fool, fool around*, fool with*, horn in*, interfere, interlope, intermeddle, make*, meddle, mess, play, pry, tinker, trifle; SEE CONCEPTS 87,612

monologue [n] *speech by one person*

address, descant, discourse, disquisition, harangue, lecture, sermon, soliloquy, speech, stand-up bit*, talk; SEE CONCEPTS 266,278

monopolize [v] *dominate, control*

absorb, acquire, bogart, consume, copyright, corner, corner the market*, devour, employ, engross, exclude, exercise control, have, hog*, hold, keep to oneself, lock up*, manage, own, own exclusively, patent, possess, restrain, sew up*, sit on*, syndicate, take over, take up, use, utilize; SEE CONCEPTS 94,324,710

monopoly [n] *something held, owned exclusively*

cartel, consortium, copyright, corner, holding, oligopoly, ownership, patent, pool, possessorship, proprietorship, syndicate, trust; SEE CONCEPT 710

monotonous [adj] *all the same, remaining the same*

banausic, blah*, boring, colorless, dreary, droning, dull, dull as dishwater*, flat, flat as pancake*, ho-hum*, humdrum*, monotone, nothing, nothing pedestrian, plodding, prosaic, puts one to sleep*, recurrent, reiterated, repetitious, repetitive, samely, sing-song*, soporific, tedious, tiresome, toneless, treadmill, unchanged, unchanging, uniform, uninflected, uninteresting, unrelieved, unvaried, unvarying, wearisome, wearying; SEE CONCEPTS 529,534,544

monotony [n] *boredom; sameness*
colorlessness, continuance, continuity, dreariness, dryness, dullness, ennui, equability, evenness, flatness, humdrum*, identicalness, invariability, levelness, likeness, monotone, monotonousness, oneness, repetitiousness, repetitiveness, routine, same old thing*, similarity, tediousness, tedium, tiresomeness, unchangeableness, uniformity, wearisomeness; SEE CONCEPTS 410,637,673

monster [n] *giant animal; supernatural being*
abnormality, barbarian, beast, behemoth, brute, centaur, colossus, demon, devil, dragon, fiend, Frankenstein, freak, giant, hellion, horror, leviathan, lusus naturae, mammoth, miscreation, monstrosity, mutant, ogre, phoenix, savage, titan, villain, werewolf, whale; SEE CONCEPTS 370,394,412

monstrous [adj] *unnatural, shocking*
aberrant, abnormal, atrocious, cruel, desperate, devilish, diabolical, disgraceful, dreadful, egregious, evil, fiendish, flagitious, foul, freakish, frightful, grotesque, gruesome, heinous, hellish, hideous, horrendous, horrible, horrifying, infamous, inhuman, intolerable, loathsome, macabre, miscreated, morbid, obscene, odious, ominous, outrageous, preposterous, rank, satanic, scandalous, teratoid, terrible, uncanny, unusual, vicious, villainous; SEE CONCEPTS 537,564,582

monstrous [adj2] *very large*
colossal, cracking, elephantine, enormous, fantastic, gargantuan, giant, gigantic, grandiose, great, huge, immense, impressive, magnificent, mammoth, massive, monumental, prodigious, stupendous, titanic, towering, tremendous, vast, whopping; SEE CONCEPTS 773,781

monument [n] *memorial, remembrance*
cairn, cenotaph, column, commemoration, erection, footstone, gravestone, headstone, ledger, magnum opus, marker, masterpiece, mausoleum, memento, monolith, obelisk, pile, pillar, record, reminder, shrine, slab, statue, stele, stone, tablet, testament, token, tomb, tombstone, tower, tribute, witness; SEE CONCEPTS 259,271,305,470

monumental [adj] *impressive, overwhelming*
awe-inspiring, awesome, classic, enduring, enormous, fantastic, gigantic, grand, great, historic, huge, immense, immortal, important, lasting, lofty, majestic, mammoth, massive, memorable, mighty, mortal, mountainous, outstanding, prodigious, significant, stupendous, towering, tremendous, unforgettable, vast; SEE CONCEPTS 568,773

mood [n] *state of mind*
affection, air, atmosphere, attitude, aura, bent*, blues*, caprice, character, color*, condition, crotchet, cue, depression, desire, disposition, doldrums, dumps*, emotion, fancy, feel*, feeling, frame of mind*, high spirits, humor, inclination, individuality, low spirits, melancholy, mind, personality, pleasure, propensity, response, scene, semblance, soul, spirit, strain, temper, temperament, tendency, tenor, timbre, vagary, vein, whim, wish; SEE CONCEPTS 410,411,673

moody [adj] *crabby, temperamental*
angry, cantankerous, capricious, changeable, crabbed*, crestfallen, cross, dismal, doleful,

dour, downcast, down in the dumps*, down in the mouth*, erratic, fickle, fitful, flighty, frowning, gloomy, glum, huffy, ill-humored, ill-tempered, impulsive, in a huff*, in the doldrums, introspective, irascible, irritable, lugubrious, melancholy, mercurial, miserable, moping, morose, offended, out of sorts*, pensive, petulant, piqued, sad, saturnine, short-tempered, splenetic, sulky, sullen, testy, touchy; SEE CONCEPT 403

moon [n] *Earth's satellite*
celestial body, crescent, full moon, half-moon, heavenly body, new moon, old moon, orb of night*, planetoid, pumpkin*, quarter-moon, satellite; SEE CONCEPTS 511,809

moon [v] *dream about; desire*
daydream, idle, languish, mope, pine, waste time, yearn; SEE CONCEPT 20

moor [v] *anchor, fasten securely*
berth, catch, chain, dock, fix, lash, make fast, picket, secure, tether, tie, tie up; SEE CONCEPTS 85,160

moot [adj] *doubtful, arguable*
at issue, contestable, controversial, debatable, disputable, dubious, open, open to debate, problematic, questionable, suspect, uncertain, undecided, unresolved, unsettled; SEE CONCEPT 535

mop [n1] *tangle of material, often used to absorb liquid*
duster, sponge, squeegee, swab, sweeper, towel; SEE CONCEPTS 392,499

mop [n2] *thick mass of hair*
mane, shock, tangle, thatch, tresses; SEE CONCEPT 399

mop [v] *clean by using water and cloth*
dab, dust, pat, polish, rub, soak up, sponge, squeegee, swab, towel off, wash, wipe; SEE CONCEPT 165

mope [v] *pout, be dejected*
ache, be apathetic, be down in the mouth*, be gloomy, be in a funk*, bleed*, brood, chafe, despair, despond, droop, eat one's heart out, fret, grieve, grumble, grump, idle, lament, languish, lose heart, moon, pine, pine away*, regret, repine, sink, stew over*, sulk, sweat over*, waste time*, wear a long face*, yearn; SEE CONCEPTS 20,410

moral [n] *lesson, proverb*
adage, aphorism, apophthegm, axiom, dictum, epigram, gnome, maxim, meaning, message, moralism, motto, point, precept, rule, saw, saying, sermon, significance, truism; SEE CONCEPTS 278,283

moral [adj] *ethical, honest*
aboveboard, blameless, chaste, conscientious, correct, courteous, decent, decorous, dutiful, elevated, exemplary, good, high-minded, honorable, immaculate, incorruptible, innocent, just, kindly, kosher*, laudable, meet, meritorious, modest, moralistic, noble, praiseworthy, principled, proper, pure, respectable, right, righteous, saintly, salt of the earth*, scrupulous, seemly, square, straight, true-blue*, trustworthy, truthful, upright, upstanding, virtuous, worthy; SEE CONCEPT 545

morale [n] *confidence, self-esteem*
assurance, attitude, disposition, drive, esprit, esprit de corps, heart, humor, mettle, mood, outlook, resolve, self-confidence, self-possession, spirit, temper, temperament, turn, vigor; SEE CONCEPTS 410,411

morality [n] *ethics, honesty*
chastity, conduct, decency, ethicality, ethicalness, gentleness, godliness, good habits, goodness, honor, ideals, incorruptibility, incorruption, integrity, justice, manners, moral code, morals, mores, philosophy, principle, principles, probity, purity, rectitude, righteousness, rightness, saintliness, standards, uprightness, virtue, worthiness; SEE CONCEPT *645*

morals [n] *personal principles, standards*
behavior, beliefs, conduct, customs, dogmas, ethic, ethics, habits, ideals, integrity, manners, morality, mores, policies, scruples; SEE CONCEPTS *411,645,688*

morass [n] *bog; mess*
chaos, confusion, fen, jam, jungle, knot, labyrinth, marsh, maze, mesh, mix-up, muddle, quagmire, skein, snarl, swamp, tangle, web; SEE CONCEPTS *230,509*

morbid [adj] *gloomy, nasty, sickly*
aberrant, abnormal, ailing, brooding, dark, deadly, depressed, despondent, diseased, dreadful, frightful, ghastly, ghoulish, grim, grisly, gruesome, hideous, horrid, infected, irascible, macabre, malignant, melancholy, monstrous, moody, pessimistic, saturnine, sick, somber, sullen, unhealthy, unnatural, unsound, unusual, unwholesome; SEE CONCEPTS *314,403,537*

more [adj] *additional, greater*
added, aggrandized, also, amassed, and, another, augmented, besides, bounteous, deeper, else, enhanced, exceeding, expanded, extended, extra, farther, fresh, further, heavier, higher, in addition, increased, innumerable, larger, likewise, major, massed, more than that, new, numerous, other, over and above, spare, supplementary, too many, wider; SEE CONCEPTS *762,771*

more [adv] *to a greater extent*
additionally, along with, also, as well, besides, better, beyond, further, furthermore, in addition, likewise, longer, moreover, over, too, withal; SEE CONCEPTS *544,772*

moreover [adv] *additionally*
also, as well, besides, by the same token*, further, furthermore, in addition, likewise, more, to boot*, too, what is more*, withal, yet; SEE CONCEPTS *544,772*

morning [n] *first part of the day*
after midnight, AM, ante meridiem, aurora, before lunch, before noon, breakfast time*, break of day, cockcrow*, crack of dawn*, dawn, daybreak, daylight, dayspring, early bright*, first blush*, foreday, forenoon, morn*, morningtide, morrow, prime*, sunrise, sunup, wee hours*; SEE CONCEPTS *801,802,806,810*

moron [n] *stupid person*
addlepate, blockhead*, boob*, dimwit, dingbat*, dolt, dope*, dork*, dumbbell*, dummy*, dunce, fool, halfwit, idiot, ignoramus, imbecile, lamebrain*, loony*, loser*, mental defective*, nerd*, simpleton; SEE CONCEPT *423*

morose [adj] *depressed, pessimistic*
acrimonious, blue*, brusque, cantankerous, choleric, churlish, crabbed*, crabby*, cranky*, cross, dolorous, dour, down, down in the dumps*, down in the mouth*, frowning, gloomy, glum, grouchy, gruff, harsh, having blue devils*, having the blahs*, ill-humored, ill-tempered, in a bad mood*, in a blue funk*, irritable, low, melancholy, moody, moping, mournful, perverse, per-

versive, sad, saturnine, singing the blues*, snappish, sour, splenetic, sulky, sullen, surly, taciturn, testy, troubled, ugly; SEE CONCEPT *403*

morsel [n] *tiny piece*
bait, bit, bite, chunk, crumb, cut, delicacy, drop, fraction, fragment, grain, hunk, lump, mouthful, nibble, nosh, part, sample, scrap, segment, slice, snack, soupçon, taste, tidbit, treat; SEE CONCEPTS *457,458,831,835*

mortal [n] *human being*
animal, being, body, character, creature, earthling, human, individual, living soul, man, naked ape, party, person, personage, soul, woman; SEE CONCEPT *417*

mortal [adj1] *deadly*
bitter, death-dealing, deathly, destructive, dire, ending, extreme, fatal, grave, great, grievous, grim, intense, killing, last, lethal, malignant, merciless, monstrous, mortiferous, murderous, noxious, pestilent, pestilential, poisonous, relentless, remorseless, ruthless, severe, terminal, terrible, unrelenting; SEE CONCEPT *537*

mortal [adj2] *human*
animate, bipedal, corporeal, creatural, earthly, ecce homo, ephemeral, evanescent, fading, finite, frail, fugacious, impermanent, momentary, passing, perishable, precarious, sublunary, temporal, transient, weak, worldly; SEE CONCEPT *549*

mortality [n1] *death*
bloodshed, carnage, deadliness, destruction, dying, extinction, fatality, killing, lethality, loss of life; SEE CONCEPT *407*

mortality [n2] *humanness*
being, ephemerality, flesh, Homo sapiens, humanity, humankind, human race, impermanence, temporality, transience; SEE CONCEPTS *417,648*

mortify [v] *embarrass*
abase, abash, affront, annoy, belittle, chagrin, chasten, confound, control, crush, deflate, deny, disappoint, discipline, discomfit, disgrace, displease, get one's comeuppance*, harass, humble, humiliate, put to shame, ridicule, shame, subdue, take down a peg*, take the wind out*, vex, worry; SEE CONCEPTS *7,19,52,54*

most [adj] *best, greatest*
better, biggest, greater, highest, largest, lion's share*, max*, maximum, ultimate, utmost, uttermost; SEE CONCEPTS *771,772*

most [adv] *nearly all; extremely*
about, all but, almost, approximately, close, eminently, exceedingly, in the majority, mightily, much, nearly, nigh, practically, remarkably, super, surpassingly, too, very, well-nigh; SEE CONCEPTS *544,569,771*

mostly [adv] *generally, mainly*
above all, almost entirely, as a rule*, chiefly, customarily, essentially, for the most part*, frequently, in many instances*, largely, many times, most often, often, on the whole*, overall, particularly, predominantly, primarily, principally, regularly, usually; SEE CONCEPTS *544,548,772*

motel [n] *temporary, short-term residence, often for travelers*
cabin, court, hotel, inn, lodge, motor court, resort, roadhouse; SEE CONCEPTS *439,449,516*

mother [n] *female person who has borne children*
ancestor, child-bearer, creator, forebearer, mom*, mommy*, origin, parent, predecessor, procreator, progenitor, source; SEE CONCEPTS *394,400, 414,415,423*

motion [*n1*] *movement, action*

act, advance, agitation, ambulation, body English*, change, changing, direction, drift, dynamics, flow, fluctuation, flux, full swing*, gesticulation, gesture, high sign*, inclination, kinetics, locomotion, mobility, motility, move, oscillation, passage, passing, progress, sign, signal, stir, stirring, stream, sway, sweep, swing, tendency, travel, wave, wavering; SEE CONCEPT 145

motion [*n2*] *formal suggestion in a meeting*

plan, proposal, proposition, recommendation, submission; SEE CONCEPTS 75,278

motion [*v*] *gesture, direct*

beckon, flag, gesticulate, guide, invite, move, nod, sign, signal, signalize, wave; SEE CONCEPT 149

motionless [*adj*] *calm, not moving*

apoplectic, at a standstill, at rest, becalmed, dead, deadlocked, deathly, firm, fixed, frozen, halted, immobile, immotile, inanimate, inert, lifeless, numb, palsied, paralyzed, petrified, quiescent, quiet, spellbound, stable, stagnant, stalled, standing, static, stationary, steadfast, still, stock-still, torpid, transfixed, unmovable, unmoved, unmoving; SEE CONCEPTS 488,584

motivate [*v*] *stimulate, instigate*

actuate, arouse, bring, cause, dispose, draw, drive, egg on*, excite, fire, galvanize, give incentive, goad, goose*, impel, incite, incline, induce, innervate, innerve, inspire, inspirit, lead, move, persuade, pique, predetermine, predispose, prevail upon, prompt, propel, provoke, quicken, rouse, set afoot, set astir, sound, spark, spur, suggest, sway, touch off, trigger, whet; SEE CONCEPTS 14,68,242

motivation [*n*] *ambition, inspiration*

action, actuation, angle, catalyst, desire, disposition, drive, encouragement, fire, get up and go*, gimmick, goose*, hunger, impetus, impulse, impulsion, incentive, incitement, inclination, inducement, instigation, interest, kick*, motive, persuasion, predetermination, predisposition, provocation, push, reason, right stuff*, spur, stimulus, suggestion, wish; SEE CONCEPTS 20,411,689

motive [*n*] *reason, purpose*

aim, antecedent, basis, cause, consideration, design, determinant, drive, emotion, end, feeling, grounds, idea, impulse, incentive, incitement, inducement, influence, inspiration, intent, intention, mainspring, motivation, object, occasion, passion, rationale, root, spring, spur, stimulus, thinking; SEE CONCEPTS 20,661,689

motley [*adj*] *mixed, varied*

assorted, conglomerate, dappled, discrepant, disparate, dissimilar, diversified, heterogeneous, indiscriminate, kaleidoscopic, mingled, miscellaneous, mixed, mottled, multicolor, multicolored, multiform, multihued, polychromatic, prismatic, rainbow, unlike, varicolored, variegated, various, versicolor; SEE CONCEPTS 564, 618,772

mottled [*adj*] *speckled*

blotchy, checkered, dappled, flecked, freckled, maculate, marbled, motley, piebald, pied, skewbald, spotted, streaked, tabby, variegated; SEE CONCEPTS 606,618

motto [*n*] *saying, slogan*

adage, aphorism, apothegm, battle cry, byword, catchphrase, cry, epigram, formula, maxim, precept, proverb, rallying cry, rule, saw, sentiment, shibboleth, war cry, watchword, word; SEE CONCEPT 278

mound [*n*] *heap, hill*

anthill, bank, drift, dune, embankment, hillock, knoll, mass, molehill, mountain, pile, rise, shock, stack, tumulus; SEE CONCEPTS 432,509

mount [*v1*] *climb*

arise, ascend, back, bestride, clamber up, climb onto, climb up on, escalade, escalate, get astride, get up on, go up, jump on, lift, rise, scale, soar, tower up, vault; SEE CONCEPTS 149,154,166

mount [*v2*] *increase, grow*

accumulate, aggravate, augment, build, deepen, enhance, enlarge, escalate, expand, heighten, intensate, intensify, multiply, pile up, redouble, rise, rouse, swell, upsurge, wax; SEE CONCEPTS 704,780

mount [*v3*] *affix, frame*

emplace, exhibit, fit, install, place, position, prepare, produce, put in place, put on, set up, show, stage; SEE CONCEPTS 174,261

mountain [*n*] *very large hill*

abundance, alp, bank, bluff, butte, cliff, crag, dome, drift, elevation, eminence, glob, heap, height, hump, mass, mesa, mound, mount, palisade, peak, pike, pile, precipice, pyramid, range, ridge, shock, sierra, stack, ton, tor, volcano; SEE CONCEPTS 432,509

mourn [*v*] *be sad over loss*

ache, agonize, anguish, be brokenhearted*, bemoan, be sad, bewail, bleed, blubber, carry on, complain, cry, deplore, fret, grieve, hurt, keen, lament, languish, long for, miss, moan, pine, regret, repine, rue, sigh, sob, sorrow, suffer, take it hard*, wail, wear black*, weep, wring hands*, yearn; SEE CONCEPTS 23,410

mourning [*n*] *sadness, time of sadness*

aching, bereavement, blackness, crying, darkness, grief, grieving, keening, lamentation, lamenting, languishing, moaning, pining, repining, sorrowing, wailing, weeping, woe; SEE CONCEPTS 388,410

mousy [*adj*] *drab, quiet*

bashful, colorless, diffident, dull, indeterminate, ineffectual, pale, plain, self-effacing, shy, timid, timorous, unassertive, unassuming; SEE CONCEPTS 401,618

mouth [*n1*] *opening*

aperture, beak, box, cavity, chops*, clam, crevice, delta, door, embouchement, entrance, estuary, firth, fly trap, funnel, gate, gills, gob, harbor, inlet, jaws, kisser*, lips, mush*, orifice, portal, rim, trap*, yap*; SEE CONCEPTS 392,513

mouth [*n2*] *backtalk*

boasting, braggadocio, bragging, cheek, empty talk*, freshness, gas*, guff*, hot air*, idle talk, impudence, insolence, lip*, rudeness, sass*, sauce*; SEE CONCEPTS 54,278

movable [*adj*] *transportable*

adaptable, adjustable, ambulatory, conveyable, deployable, detachable, in parts, liftable, loose, mobile, motile, moving, not fastened, not fixed, on wheels, portable, portative, removable, separable, shiftable, transferable, turnable, unattached, unfastened, unstationary, unsteady; SEE CONCEPTS 488,584

move [*n*] *progress, deed*

act, action, alteration, change, maneuver, measure, modification, motion, movement, ploy, procedure, proceeding, shift, step, stir, stirring, stratagem, stroke, turn, variation; SEE CONCEPTS *2,660*

move [*v1*] *be in motion, put in motion*
actuate, advance, blow, budge, bustle, carry, change, climb, crawl, cross, depart, dislocate, disturb, drift, drive, exit, flow, fly, get away, get going, get off, glide, go, go away, head for, hurry, impel, jump, leap, locomote, march, migrate, off-load, position, proceed, progress, propel, pull out, push, quit, relocate, remove, roll, run, scram, shift, ship, shove, skip out, split, switch, take off, transfer, transport, transpose, travel, traverse, walk, withdraw; SEE CONCEPTS *147,149,198*

move [*v2*] *motivate, influence*
activate, actuate, advocate, affect, agitate, bring, bring up, budge, carry, cause, convert, draw up, drive, excite, get going, give rise to, impel, impress, incite, induce, inspire, inspirit, instigate, introduce, lead, operate, persuade, play on, prevail upon, prompt, propel, propose, push, put forward, quicken, recommend, rouse, shift, shove, start, stimulate, stir, strike, submit, suggest, sway, touch, tug at, turn, urge, work on; SEE CONCEPTS *7,19,22,75,242*

movement [*n1*] *motion, activity*
act, action, advance, agitation, alteration, change, changing, deed, development, displacement, dynamism, evolution, evolving, exercise, flight, flow, flux, gesture, journey, journeying, locomotion, maneuver, migration, mobility, motility, movableness, move, moving, operation, operativeness, passage, progress, progression, regression, roaming, shift, shifting, steps, stir, stirring, transferal, transit, translating, transplanting, undertaking, velocity, voyaging, wandering; SEE CONCEPTS *2,145,697*

movement [*n2*] *drive, campaign*
change, crusade, current, demonstration, displacement, drift, evolution, faction, flight, flow, front, group, grouping, march, mobilization, organization, party, patrol, shift, sweep, swing, tendency, transfer, transition, trend, unrest, withdrawal; SEE CONCEPTS *381,697*

movie [*n*] *presentation of action on continuous film*
cine, cinema, cinematics, cinematograph, feature, film, flick*, motion picture, moving picture, photoplay, picture, screenplay, show, silent*, silver screen*, talkie*, talking picture, videotape; SEE CONCEPTS *263,293*

moving [*adj1*] *affecting, exciting*
affective, arousing, awakening, breathless, dynamic, eloquent, emotional, emotive, expressive, facund, far-out*, felt in gut*, grabbed by*, gripping, hairy*, heartbreaking, heartrending, impelling, impressive, inspirational, inspiring, meaningful, mind-bending*, mind-blowing*, motivating, persuasive, poignant, propelling, provoking, quickening, rallying, rousing, sententious, significant, something*, stimulating, stimulative, stirring, stunning, touching, turned on by*; SEE CONCEPTS *529,537*

moving [*adj2*] *mobile*
advancing, changing, climbing, evolving, flying, going, jumping, motile, movable, nomadic, portable, progressing, roaming, roving, running, shifting, traversing, unfixed, unstable, unsteadfast, unsteady, walking; SEE CONCEPTS *488,584*

much [*n*] *a great deal*
abundance, all kinds of*, a lot*, amplitude, appreciable amount, barrel, breadth, completeness, copiousness, excess, exuberance, fullness, gobs*, great quantity, heaps*, loads*, lots*, lump, mass, mess*, mountain, multiplicity, oodles*, overage, oversupply, pack, peck, pile, plentifulness, plenty, plethora, profuseness, riches, scads*, sufficiency, superabundance, superfluity, thousands, tons*, very much, volume, wealth; SEE CONCEPT *771*

much [*adj*] *plenty*
abundant, adequate, a lot of*, ample, complete, considerable, copious, countless, endless, enough, everywhere, extravagant, full, galore, generous, great, heaps*, immeasurable, jam-packed*, lavish, loads*, lotsa*, many, mega*, mucho*, no end*, plenteous, plentiful, profuse, satisfying, scads*, sizable, substantial, sufficient, very many, voluminous; SEE CONCEPTS *772,781*

much [*adv*] *greatly, a lot*
again and again, a great deal*, considerably, decidedly, eminently, exceedingly, exceptionally, extremely, frequently, highly, hugely, indeed, notably, oft, often, over and over*, regularly, repeatedly, surpassingly, time and time again*, very; SEE CONCEPTS *530,544,548*

muddle [*n*] *confused state*
ataxia, awkwardness, botch, chaos, clutter, complexity, complication, confusion, daze, difficulty, dilemma, disarrangement, disarray, disorder, disorganization, emergency, encumbrance, fog, foul-up*, hash, haze, intricacy, involvement, jumble, mess, mess and a half*, mix-up*, muss*, perplexity, plight, predicament, quandary, rat's nest*, screw-up*, shambles*, snarl, struggle, tangle, trouble; SEE CONCEPTS *230,410,666*

muddle [*v*] *confuse, disorganize*
addle, befuddle, bewilder, blunder, botch, bungle, clutter, complicate, confound, daze, derange, disarrange, discombobulate*, disorder, disorient, disturb, entangle, fluster, foul, foul up*, jumble, louse up, make a mess of*, mess, misarrange, mix, mix up*, muck, mumble, murmur, nonplus, perplex, perturb, psych out*, rattle, ravel, ruffle, scramble, shuffle, snafu*, snarl, spoil, stir up, stumble, stupefy, tangle, throw, throw off, tumble; SEE CONCEPTS *16,84,242*

muddy [*adj*] *dark and cloudy*
addled, bemired, bespattered, black, blurred, boggy*, caked, confused, dingy, dirty, dull, filthy, flat, foul, fuzzy, gloomy, greasy, grimy, grubby*, gummy*, gunky*, hazy, impure, indistinct, marshy, miry, mucky*, obscure, opaque, roily, sloppy, slushy, smoky, sodden, soggy, soiled, subfuse, swampy, turbid, unclean, unclear; SEE CONCEPTS *485,606,618*

muffle [*v*] *suppress, make quiet*
conceal, cover, cushion, dampen, deaden, decrease, drown, dull, envelop, gag, hide, hush, mellow, mute, muzzle, put the lid on*, quieten, shut down, silence, sit down on*, smother, soften, soft-pedal*, squelch, stifle, subdue, tone down*, wrap*; SEE CONCEPTS *65,121,240*

muffled [*adj*] *quietened*
deadened, dim, dull, faint, flat, indistinct, mute, muted, obscure, silenced, stifled, strangled, subdued, suppressed; SEE CONCEPT *594*

muggy [*adj*] *humid*
clammy*, close, damp, dampish, dank, moist,

mucky*, oppressive, soggy, sticky, stuffy, sultry;
SEE CONCEPTS 525,603

mull [v] *think about seriously*
brood over, chaw, consider, contemplate, delay,
deliberate, examine, figure, hammer away at*,
linger, meditate, moon*, muse on, ponder, pore
over, procrastinate, rack one's brains*, reflect, review, revolve, ruminate, stew over*, study, sweat
over*, think over, turn over, weigh, woolgather*;
SEE CONCEPT 17

multicolored [adj] *having various hues*
checkered, dappled, flecked, kaleidoscopic, marbled, motley, mottled, multicolor, particolored,
piebald, pied, polychrome, prismatic, speckled,
spotted, streaked, varicolored, veined, versicolor;
SEE CONCEPT 618

multiculturalism [n] *doctrine acknowledging con-
tributions and interests of many cultures*
cross-culturalism, cultural diversity, diversity,
ethnic inclusiveness, ethnic mosaic, multiracial-
ism, pluralism; SEE CONCEPTS 665,689

multimedia [n] *combined use of several media*
interactive media, intermedia, mixed media; SEE
CONCEPT 274

multiple/multifarious [adj] *diversified, miscellaneous*
assorted, collective, conglomerate, different, diverse, diversiform, heterogeneous, indiscriminate, legion, manifold, many, mixed, motley,
multiform, multiplex, multitudinal, multitudinous, numerous, populous, several, sundry, varied, variegated, various, voluminous; SEE
CONCEPTS 564,762,772

multiply [v] *increase; reproduce*
accumulate, add, aggrandize, aggregate, augment,
boost, breed, build up, compound, cube, double,
enlarge, expand, extend, generate, heighten, magnify, manifold, mount, populate, procreate, produce, proliferate, propagate, raise, repeat, rise,
spread, square; SEE CONCEPTS 171,374

multitude [n] *large group*
aggregation, army, assemblage, assembly, collection, commonalty, concourse, congregation,
crowd, crush, drove, great number, heap, herd,
horde, host, infinitude, infinity, jam*, legion,
loads, lot, lots*, majority, mass, mob, much, myriad, number, numbers, ocean*, oodles*, people,
plenitude, plurality, populace, proletariat, public,
push*, quantity, scores*, sea, slew*, swarm,
throng, turnout; SEE CONCEPTS 417,432

multitudinous [adj] *many, considerable*
abounding, abundant, copious, countless, great,
heaps*, infinite, innumerable, innumerous, legion, manifold, multifarious, myriad, numberless,
numerous, populous, profuse, several, sundry,
teeming, uncountable, uncounted, unnumbered,
untold, various, voluminous; SEE CONCEPTS
762,781

mumble [v] *say low and inarticulately*
grumble, maunder, murmur, mutter, ramble, rumble, say to oneself, speak, stammer, stutter, swallow, talk, utter, verbalize, vocalize, voice,
whimper, whine, whisper; SEE CONCEPTS 47,77

munch [v] *chew, eat*
bite, break up, champ, chomp, crunch, crush,
grind, mash, masticate, press, reduce, ruminate,
scrunch, smash, soften; SEE CONCEPTS 169,185

mundane [adj] *ordinary*
banal, commonplace, day-to-day, earthly, everyday, humdrum*, lowly, normal, prosaic, routine,

workaday*, workday, worldly; SEE CONCEPT 547

municipal [adj] *concerning cities*
borough, burghal, city, civic, civil, community,
corporate, domestic, home, incorporated, internal,
local, metropolitan, native, public, town, urban;
SEE CONCEPT 536

munificent [adj] *giving, generous*
beneficent, benevolent, big, big-hearted, bounteous, bountiful, charitable, free, handsome, kind,
lavish, liberal, loose, magnanimous, openhanded,
philanthropic, rich, unsparing, unstinting; SEE
CONCEPTS 334,401

murder [n] *killing*
annihilation, assassination, blood, bloodshed,
butchery, carnage, crime, death, destruction, dispatching, felony, foul play*, hit*, homicide, knifing, liquidation, lynching, manslaughter,
massacre, off*, offing*, one-way ticket*, rub
out*, shooting, slaying, taking out*, terrorism,
the business*, the works*; SEE CONCEPTS
192,252

murder [v] *kill*
abolish, asphyxiate, assassinate, behead, blot
out*, bump off*, butcher, chill*, cool*, decapitate, defeat, destroy, dispatch, do in*, drub*, dust
off*, electrocute, eliminate, eradicate, execute,
exterminate, extinguish, finish, garotte, guillotine,
hang, hit*, knife, knock off*, liquidate, lynch,
mangle, mar, massacre, misuse, off*, put away*,
rub out*, ruin, shoot, slaughter, slay, smother,
snuff, spoil, strangle, take a life, take for a ride*,
take out*, thrash*, waste*; SEE CONCEPTS
192,252

murderer [n] *person who kills*
assassin, butcher, criminal, cutthroat, enforcer,
executioner, hit-and-run*, hit person*, homicide,
killer, manslaughterer, perpetrator, slaughterer,
slayer, soldier, trigger person*; SEE CONCEPT 412

murderous [adj] *difficult*
arduous, brutal, criminal, cruel, dangerous,
deadly, destroying, destructive, devastating, exhausting, fell, ferocious, harrowing, hellish, killing, lethal, ruinous, sapping, savage, strenuous,
unpleasant; SEE CONCEPTS 538,548,565

murky [adj] *gloomy, obscure*
black, caliginous, cheerless, cloudy, dark, darkened, dim, dingy, dirty, dismal, drab, dreary,
dull, dun*, dusk, dusky, filthy, foggy, foul, fuzzy,
glowering, gray, grubby*, impenetrable, lowering, misty, mucky, muddy, nasty, nebulous, ni-
bilous, overcast, roily, sad, smoky, somber,
squalid, stormy, tenebrous, turbid, unclean; SEE
CONCEPTS 617,618

murmur [n] *low, continuous sound*
babble, buzz, buzzing, drone, grumble, hum,
humming, mumble, murmuration, mutter, muttering, purr, rumble, rumor, undertone, whisper,
whispering; SEE CONCEPTS 65,595

murmur [v] *make low, continuous sound*
babble, burble, buzz, drip, drone, flow, growl,
gurgle, hum, meander, moan, mumble, mutter,
purl, purr, ripple, rumble, stage-whisper, stammer, stutter, susurrate, tinkle, trickle, utter, verbalize, vocalize, voice, whisper; SEE CONCEPTS
65,77

muscle [n1] *large fibers of animal body*
beef, brawn, flesh, meat, might, sinew, tendon,
thew, tissue; SEE CONCEPTS 393,420

muscle [n2] *power, influence*
brawn, clout, energy, force, forcefulness, might,

muscular [adj] powerfully built

able-bodied, athletic, brawny, bruising, burly, fibrous, hefty, Herculean*, hulky, husky, lusty, mighty, muscled, powerful, powerhouse*, pumped up*, ripped*, robust, ropy, sinewy, stalwart, stout, strapping, stringy, strong, sturdy, tiger*, tough, vigorous, well-built, wiry; SEE CONCEPTS 485,489

muse [v] think about, dream

be lost in thought*, brood, build castles in air*, chew over*, cogitate, consider, contemplate, deliberate, feel, meditate, moon*, mull over, percolate, ponder, puzzle over, reflect, revolve, roll, ruminate, speculate, think, think over, turn over, weigh; SEE CONCEPT 17

museum [n] place for viewing artifacts or exhibits

archive, building, depository, exhibition, foundation, gallery, hall, institution, library, menagerie, repository, salon, storehouse, treasury, vault; SEE CONCEPTS 439,449

mushroom [v] sprout; grow quickly

augment, blow up, boom, burgeon, burst, detonate, expand, explode, flourish, go off, grow, grow rapidly, increase, luxuriate, proliferate, shoot up, spread, spring up; SEE CONCEPTS 179,704

mushy [adj1] doughy, soft

gelatinous, jelled, mashy*, muddy, pap*, pastelike, pulpous, pulpy, quaggy, semiliquid, semisolid, slushy, spongy, squashy*, squishy*; SEE CONCEPTS 604,606

mushy [adj2] romantic, corny

bathetic, effusive, emotional, lovey-dovey*, maudlin, mawkish, saccharine, schmaltzy*, sentimental, sloppy*, slushy*, soppy*, sugary, syrupy, tear-jerking, weepy, wet; SEE CONCEPTS 267,542

music [n] sounds that are pleasant, harmonized

a cappella, acoustic, air, bebop, bop, chamber, classical, folk, fusion, hard rock, harmony, heavy metal, hymn, instrumental, jazz, measure, melody, modern, opera, piece, plainsong, popular, ragtime, rap, refrain, rock, rock and roll, singing, song, soul, strain, swing, tune; SEE CONCEPTS 263,595

musical [adj] harmonic, lyrical

agreeable, blending, chiming, choral, consonant, dulcet, euphonious, harmonious, lilting, mellow, melodic, melodious, operatic, orchestral, pleasing, rhythmic, silvery, songful, sweet, sweet-sounding, symphonic, symphonious, tuned, tuneful, vocal; SEE CONCEPT 594

musician [n] person who performs music

artist, artiste, composer, conductor, diva, entertainer, instrumentalist, performer, player, session player, soloist, virtuoso, vocalist; SEE CONCEPT 352

muss [n] disorder

chaos, confusion, disarrangement, hash, mess, mess-up, mix-up*, muddle, shambles, turmoil; SEE CONCEPTS 230,674

muss [v] dishevel, disorder

clutter, crumple, disarrange, disarray, disorganize, disrupt, disturb, jumble, mess up, mix up*, muddle, ruffle, rummage, rumple, tangle, tousle, upset, wrinkle; SEE CONCEPT 158

must [n] necessity, essential

charge, commitment, committal, condition, devoir, duty, fundamental, imperative, necessary, need, obligation, ought, precondition, prerequisite, requirement, requisite, right, sine qua non; SEE CONCEPTS 646,709

must [v] ought, should

be compelled, be destined, be directed, be doomed*, be driven*, be made, be necessitated, be obliged, be one's fate, be ordered, be required, got to, have, have got to*, have no choice, have to, must needs*, need, pushed to the wall*; SEE CONCEPT 650

muster [n] gathering

aggregation, assemblage, assembly, call-up*, collection, company, congeries, convocation, crowd, draft, group, head count*, meeting, mobilization, nose count*, rally, roll, roll call*, roster, round-up*; SEE CONCEPTS 417,432

muster [v] gather, come together

assemble, call together, call up, collect, congregate, congress, convene, convoke, enroll, enter, group, join up, marshal, meet, mobilize, organize, raise, rally, rendezvous, round up, sign on, sign up, summon; SEE CONCEPT 109

musty [adj1] stuffy, aged

airless, ancient, antediluvian, antique, crumbling, dank, decayed, decrepit, dirty, dried-out*, dry, fetid, filthy, frowzy*, malodorous, mildewed, mildewy, moldy, moth-eaten*, noisome, old, putrid, rotten, smelly, spoiled, squalid, stale, stuffy; SEE CONCEPTS 578,598,603,797

musty [adj2] worn-out, clichéd

ancient, antiquated, banal, common, commonplace, dull, hackneyed, hoary, obsolete, old-fashioned, old hat*, shopworn*, stale, stereotypical, threadbare, timeworn*, tired, trite, warmed-over*, worn; SEE CONCEPTS 267,530,578,797

mutation [n] metamorphosis

alteration, ancient, antediluvian, change, deviant, deviation, evolution, innovation, modification, mutant, novelty, permutation, transfiguration, transformation, variation, vicissitude; SEE CONCEPTS 665,697

mute [adj] unable to speak

aphasiac, aphasic, aphonic, muffled, mum, quiet, silenced, silent, speechless, tongueless, tongue-tied, unexpressed, unpronounced, unsounded, unspeaking, unspoken, voiceless, wordless; SEE CONCEPT 593

mute [v] muffle, tone down sound

benumb, bottle up*, cork up*, dampen, deaden, decrease the volume, drown, gag, hush, keep it down*, lower, moderate, muzzle, pipe down*, put damper on*, put the lid on*, reduce, silence, soften, soft-pedal*, subdue, turn down; SEE CONCEPTS 65,240

mutilate [v] maim, damage

adulterate, amputate, batter, bowdlerize, butcher, cripple, crush, cut to pieces, cut up, deface, disable, disfigure, dismember, distort, expurgate, hack*, hash up*, hurt, injure, lacerate, lame, mangle, mar, mess up*, ravage, scratch, spoil, weaken; SEE CONCEPTS 176,246

mutiny [n] defiance, resistance

disobedience, insubordination, insurrection, refusal to obey, revolt, revolution, riot, rising, strike, uprising; SEE CONCEPTS 300,388,633

mutiny [v] defy, revolt

be insubordinate, disobey, insurrect, kick over, rebel, refuse to obey, resist, rise against, rise up, strike; SEE CONCEPTS 300,384

mutter [v] *grumble, mumble*
complain, croak, groan, grouch*, grouse, growl, grunt, moan, muddle, murmur, rumble, snarl, sputter, swallow, whisper; SEE CONCEPTS *52,77*

mutual [adj] *shared, common*
associated, bilateral, collective, communal, conjoint, conjunct, connected, convertible, correlative, dependent, give-and-take*, given and taken*, interactive, interchangeable, interchanged, interdependent, intermutual, joint, partaken, participated, public, reciprocal, reciprocated, related, requited, respective, returned, two-sided*, united; SEE CONCEPTS *563,708*

mutually [adv] *together*
all at once, as a group, by agreement, by contract, commonly, conjointly, cooperatively, en masse, in collaboration, in combination, in conjunction, jointly, reciprocally, respectively; SEE CONCEPTS *544,577*

muzzle [n] *covering for control*
cage, cover, envelope, gag, guard, sheath, wrap; SEE CONCEPT *172*

muzzle [v] *gag, quiet*
bottle up*, censor, check, choke, clamp down on*, cork, crack down on*, curb, dry up*, dummy up*, hush, ice*, muffle, prevent, quieten, repress, restrain, restrict, shush, shut down, silence, squash, squelch, stifle, still, stop, suppress, tongue-tie*, trammel; SEE CONCEPTS *121,250*

myopic [adj] *able only to see things near at hand*
astigmatic, biased, blind, halfsighted, nearsighted, presbyopic, shortsighted; SEE CONCEPT *619*

myriad [n] *a lot*
army, flood, heap, horde, host, loads*, mint, mountain*, multitude, oodles*, scores, slew, stacks*, swarm, thousands*; SEE CONCEPT *787*

myriad [adj] *innumerable*
countless, endless, gobs*, heaping, immeasurable, incalculable, infinite, multiple, multitudinous, no end of*, numberless, thousand-and-one*, uncounted, untold, variable; SEE CONCEPTS *762,781*

mysterious [adj] *secret, concealed*
abstruse, alchemistic, arcane, astrological, baffling, cabalistic, covert, cryptic, curious, dark, difficult, enigmatic, enigmatical, equivocal, esoteric, furtive, hidden, impenetrable, incomprehensible, inexplicable, inscrutable, insoluble, magical, mystical, mystifying, necromantic, obscure, occult, oracular, perplexing, puzzling, recondite, secretive, sphinxlike, spiritual, strange, subjective, symbolic, transcendental, uncanny, unfathomable, unknowable, unknown, unnatural, veiled, weird; SEE CONCEPTS *529,576*

mystery [n] *puzzle, secret*
abstruseness, brainteaser*, braintwister*, charade, chiller, cliffhanger*, closed book*, conundrum, crux, cryptogram, difficulty, enigma, grabber, inscrutability, inscrutableness, mindboggler*, mystification, occult, oracle, perplexity, poser, problem, puzzlement, question, rebus, riddle, rune, secrecy, sixty-four-thousand-dollar question*, sphinx, stickler, stumper, subtlety, teaser, thriller, tough nut to crack*, twister, whodunit*, why?; SEE CONCEPTS *282,532,696*

mystic/mystical [adj] *secret, esoteric*
abstruse, anagogic, arcane, cabalistic, cryptic, enigmatical, hidden, imaginary, impenetrable, inscrutable, magic, magical, metaphysical, mysterial, mysterious, necromantic, nonrational, numinous, occult, otherworldly, paranormal, preternatural, quixotic, sorcerous, spiritual, supernatural, telestic, thaumaturgic, transcendental, unaccountable, unknowable, visionary, wizardly; SEE CONCEPTS *529,549,582*

mystify [v] *bewilder, confuse*
baffle, bamboozle*, beat*, befog*, buffalo*, confound, deceive, elude, escape, floor*, fog in*, hoodwink*, lick*, lie, perplex, puzzle, stump*, throw*, trick; SEE CONCEPT *16*

mystique [n] *person's strong impression*
attitude, awe, character, charisma, charm, complex, fascination, glamour, magic, nature, spell, temperament; SEE CONCEPT *411*

myth [n] *fictitious story, often ancient*
allegory, apologue, creation, delusion, fable, fabrication, fairy story, fancy, fantasy, fiction, figment, folk ballad, folk tale, illusion, imagination, invention, legend, lore, mythos, parable, saga, superstition, tale, tall story*, tradition; SEE CONCEPT *282*

mythical/mythological [adj] *make-believe, fairytale*
allegorical, chimerical, created, fabled, fabricated, fabulous, false, fanciful, fantasy, fictitious, fictive, folkloric, imaginary, invented, legendary, made-up, mythic, nonexistent, pretended, storied, supposititious, traditional, unreal, untrue, visionary, whimsical; SEE CONCEPTS *267,582*

mythology [n] *folklore*
belief, conviction, folk tales, legend, lore, mythicism, mythos, myths, stories, tradition; SEE CONCEPT *282*

N

nab [v] *seize*
apprehend, arrest, capture, catch, clutch, cop*, detain, grab, nail*, pick up*, run in*, snatch*, take*, take into custody; SEE CONCEPTS *90,317*

nag [v] *harass, bother*
annoy, badger, bait, berate, bug*, carp at, dog*, eat*, egg*, find fault, fuss, give a hard time*, goad, harry, heckle, hector, hound, importune, irk, irritate, needle, nudge*, pester, pick at, plague, prod, provoke, ride, scold, take it out on*, tease, torment, upbraid, urge, vex, work on*, worry; SEE CONCEPTS *7,19,52*

nail [v1] *fasten, fix with pointed object*
attach, beat, bind, drive, hammer, hit, hold, join, pin, pound, secure, sock*, spike, strike, tack, whack*; SEE CONCEPTS *85,160,189*

nail [v2] *capture, arrest*
apprehend, bag, catch, collar*, detain, get*, hook*, nab, pinch*, prehend, secure, seize, take*; SEE CONCEPTS *90,317*

naive [adj] *childlike, trusting*
aboveboard, artless, callow, candid, confiding, countrified, credulous, forthright, frank, fresh, green*, guileless, gullible, harmless, ignorant, impulsive, ingenuous, innocent, innocuous, instinctive, jejune, lamb*, like a babe in the woods*, natural, open, original, patsy*, plain, simple, simple-minded, sincere, spontaneous,

square, sucker*, unaffected, unjaded, unpretentious, unschooled, unsophisticated, unsuspecting, unsuspicious, untaught, unworldly, virgin, wide-eyed*; SEE CONCEPTS 401,542,678

naïveté [n] *innocence, gullibility*
artlessness, callowness, candor, childishness, credulity, frankness, guilelessness, inexperience, ingenuousness, naturalness, openness, simplicity; SEE CONCEPTS 633,657,678

naked [adj1] *without covering*
au naturel, bald, bare, bared, bare-skinned, barren, defenseless, denuded, disrobed, divested, exposed, helpless, in birthday suit*, in dishabille*, in the altogether*, in the buff*, in the raw*, leafless, natural, nude, open, peeled*, raw, stark-naked*, stripped, threadbare, unclad, unclothed, unconcealed, uncovered, undraped, undressed, unprotected, unveiled, vulnerable, without a stitch*; SEE CONCEPTS 485,589

naked [adj2] *manifest, evident*
artless, blatant, disclosed, discovered, dry, matter-of-fact, obvious, open, overt, palpable, patent, plain, pure, revealed, sheer, simple, stark, unadorned, undisguised, unexaggerated, unmistakable, unqualified, unvarnished; SEE CONCEPTS 267,529

name [n1] *title given to something, someone*
agname, agnomen, alias, appellation, autograph, autonym, brand, cognomen, compellation, denomination, designation, epithet, eponym, flag*, handle*, head, heading, label, matronymic, moniker, monogram, nickname, nom de guerre, nom de plume, nomen, patronymic, pen name, pet name, place name, prenomen, proper name, pseudonym, rubric, sign, signature, sobriquet, stage name, style, surname, tag, term, trade name; SEE CONCEPTS 268,683

name [n2] *fame, distinction*
character, credit, eminence, esteem, honor, note, praise, renown, rep*, report, reputation, repute; SEE CONCEPTS 388,668

name [n3] *celebrity*
big name*, celeb*, entertainer, headliner, hero, lion*, luminary, notability, notable, personality, somebody*, star, superstar; SEE CONCEPTS 352,366

name [v1] *give a title*
baptize, call, characterize, christen, classify, cognominate, define, denominate, designate, dub, entitle, give a handle*, identify, label, nickname, nomenclature, put tag on, style, tag, term, ticket, title; SEE CONCEPT 62

name [v2] *choose, designate*
announce, appoint, cite, classify, commission, connote, declare, delegate, denote, elect, identify, index, instance, list, make, mark, mention, nominate, peg*, pin down*, point to, put down for, put finger on*, recognize, refer to, remark, select, signify, single out, slot, specify, suggest, tab, tag, tap; SEE CONCEPTS 41,50,88

nameless [adj] *unknown, anonymous*
incognito, inconspicuous, innominate, obscure, pseudonymous, unacknowledged, uncelebrated, undesignated, undistinguished, unfamed, unheard-of, unnamed, unnoted, unsung, untitled, whatchamacallit*, X*; SEE CONCEPTS 267,576

namely [adv] *that is to say*
by way of explanation, especially, expressly, id est*, i.e., in other words, in plain English*, particularly, scilicet, specially, specifically, strictly

speaking, that is, to wit, videlicet, viz.; SEE CONCEPT 557

nap [n1] *short, light sleep*
break, catnap, doze, few z's*, forty winks*, interlude, intermission, microsleep*, nod, pause, respite, rest, shuteye*, siesta, snooze*, spot; SEE CONCEPT 315

nap [n2] *grain of material*
down, feel, fiber, grit, outside, pile, roughness, shag, smoothness, surface, tooth, wale, warp, weave, weft, woof; SEE CONCEPTS 473,611

nap [v] *take a short, light sleep*
catch forty winks*, catnap, doze, drop off*, drowse, get some shut-eye*, grab some z's*, nod, nod off, rack*, relax, rest, sleep, snooze, take a siesta*, take a snooze*; SEE CONCEPTS 210,315

narcissistic [adj] *concerned only with oneself*
conceited, egotistic, egotistical, self-centered, self-involved, self-loving, stuck-up*, vain, vainglorious; SEE CONCEPTS 401,404

narcotic [n] *powerful drug inducing anesthesia or sleep*
analgesic, anesthetic, anodyne, dope*, downer*, fix*, hard drug, hard stuff*, heroin, hypnotic, junk*, laudanum, lenitive, merchandise*, nepenthe, opiate, opium, painkiller, sedative, somnifacient, soporific, stuff*, stupefacient, tranquilizer; SEE CONCEPT 307

narcotic [adj] *dulling, painkilling*
analgesic, anesthetic, calming, deadening, hypnotic, numbing, opiate, sedative, somnifacient, somnific, somnolent, somnorific, soporiferous, soporific, stupefacient, stupefactive, stupefying; SEE CONCEPT 537

narrate [v] *describe, detail*
characterize, chronicle, delineate, depict, descant, disclose, discourse, enumerate, expatiate, give an account of, hold forth, make known, paint, picture, portray, proclaim, recite, recount, rehearse, relate, repeat, report, reveal, set forth, spin, state, tell, tell a story, unfold; SEE CONCEPTS 55,72

narration [n] *description, reading*
account, anecdote, explanation, narrative, recital, recountal, recounting, rehearsal, relation, report, story, storytelling, tale, telling, voice-over*, yarn*; SEE CONCEPTS 55,72,282

narrative [n] *story, tale*
account, anecdote, book, chronicle, chronology, description, detail, fiction, history, line, long and short of it*, narration, plot, potboiler*, recount, report, statement, version, yarn*; SEE CONCEPTS 271,282

narrative [adj] *storylike, chronological*
anecdotal, fictional, fictive, historical, narrated, recounted, reported, retold, sequential; SEE CONCEPT 267

narrow [adj1] *confined, restricted*
attenuated, circumscribed, close, compressed, confining, constricted, contracted, cramped, definite, determinate, exclusive, exiguous, fine, fixed, incapacious, limited, linear, meager, near, paltry, pent, pinched, precarious, precise, scant, scanty, select, set, shrunken, slender, slim, small, spare, strait, taper, tapered, tapering, thin, thread-like, tight; SEE CONCEPTS 554,773

narrow [adj2] *intolerant, small-minded*
biased, bigoted, conservative, conventional, dogmatic, hidebound, illiberal, inexorable, inflexible, narrow-minded, obdurate, parochial, partial, prejudiced, reactionary; SEE CONCEPTS 403,542

mu
na

narrow [adj3] *cheap, stingy*
avaricious, close, mean, mercenary, scrimpy*, tight*, ungenerous; SEE CONCEPT *334*

narrow [v] *reduce, simplify*
circumscribe, constrict, contract, diminish, limit, taper, tighten; SEE CONCEPTS *130,236,247*

narrowly [adv] *just, closely*
almost, barely, by a hair*, by a whisker*, by narrow margin, carefully, close, nearly, only just, painstakingly, scarcely, scrutinizingly; SEE CONCEPTS *544,799*

narrow-minded [adj] *biased, intolerant*
bigoted, conservative, conventional, hidebound, illiberal, insular, narrow, opinionated, parochial, petty, prejudiced, provincial, reactionary, short-sighted, small-minded, strait-laced, unenlarged; SEE CONCEPTS *403,542*

nasty [adj1] *disgusting, offensive*
awful, beastly, bum*, dirty, disagreeable, fierce, filthy, foul, gross, grubby, hellish, horrible, horrid, icky*, impure, loathsome, lousy, malodorous, mephitic, murderous*, nauseating, noisome, noxious, objectionable, obnoxious, obscene, odious, ornery, outrageous, poison, polluted, raunchy*, repellent, repugnant, repulsive, revolting, rough, sickening, soiled, squalid, stinking, tough, unappetizing, unclean, uncleanly, ungodly, unholy, unpleasant, vile, vulgar, yucky*; SEE CONCEPTS *485,548,571*

nasty [adj2] *indecent, smutty*
blue*, coarse, dirty, filthy, foul, gross, immodest, immoral, improper, impure, indecorous, indelicate, lascivious, lewd, licentious, obscene, pornographic, raunchy*, ribald, scatological, shameful, unseemly, vulgar, wicked, X-rated*; SEE CONCEPTS *372,545*

nasty [adj3] *bad-tempered, mean*
abusive, annoying, beastly, critical, cruel, despicable, disagreeable, distasteful, evil, fierce, hateful, malevolent, malicious, malign, malignant, ornery, ruthless, sarcastic, sordid, spiteful, squalid, unkind, unpleasant, vicious, vile, wicked; SEE CONCEPT *401*

nasty [adj4] *injurious, dangerous*
bad, critical, damaging, harmful, noxious, painful, poisonous, serious, severe, ugly; SEE CONCEPT *537*

nation [n] *country with its own government*
body politic, commonwealth, community, democracy, domain, dominion, empire, land, monarchy, people, populace, population, principality, public, race, realm, republic, society, sovereignty, state, tribe, union; SEE CONCEPT *510*

national [adj] *concerning a country with a government*
civic, civil, communal, countrywide, domestic, ethnic, federal, general, governmental, home, imperial, inland, internal, interstate, nationwide, native, politic, political, public, royal, social, societal, sovereign, state, sweeping, vernacular, widespread; SEE CONCEPT *536*

nationality [n] *place of birth*
allegiance, body politic, citizenship, community, country, ethnic group, nation, native land, origin, political home, race, society; SEE CONCEPTS *380,510*

native [n] *person born in the country in which he/she dwells*
aboriginal, aborigine, ancient, autochthon, citizen, dweller, home towner, indigene, inhabitant, local, national; SEE CONCEPT *413*

native [adj1] *innate, inherent*
built-in, congenital, connate, connatural, constitutional, endemic, essential, fundamental, genuine, hereditary, implanted, inborn, inbred, indigenous, ingrained, inherited, instinctive, intrinsic, inveterate, inwrought, natal, natural, original, real, unacquired, wild; SEE CONCEPTS *404,549*

native [adj2] *domestic, home*
aboriginal, autochthonous, belonging, endemic, from, homegrown, homemade, indigenous, inland, internal, local, municipal, national, original, primary, primeval, primitive, regional, related, vernacular; SEE CONCEPT *536*

natural [adj1] *normal, everyday*
accustomed, anticipated, characteristic, common, commonplace, congenital, connatural, consistent, constant, counted on, customary, essential, familiar, general, habitual, inborn, indigenous, ingenerate, inherent, innate, instinctive, intuitive, involuntary, legitimate, logical, looked for, matter-of-course, natal, native, ordinary, prevailing, prevalent, probable, reasonable, regular, relied on, spontaneous, typic, typical, unacquired, uncontrolled, uniform, universal, usual; SEE CONCEPTS *530,547*

natural [adj2] *open, unaffected*
artless, being oneself, candid, childlike, credulous, direct, easy, folksy, forthright, frank, genuine, homey*, ignorant, impulsive, unaffected, ingenuous, innocent, instinctive, laid-back*, naive, plain, primitive, provincial, real, rustic, simple, simplehearted, sincere, spontaneous, straightforward, trusting, unassumed, uncontrived, undesigning, unembarrassed, unfeigned, unforced, unlabored, unpolished, unpretentious, unschooled, unsophisticated, unstudied, unworldly, up-front*; SEE CONCEPTS *267,401,404*

natural [adj3] *organic, unrefined*
agrarian, agrestal, crude, native, plain, pure, raw, unbleached, uncultivated, undomesticated, unmixed, unpolished, unprocessed, whole, wild; SEE CONCEPTS *462,485*

naturally [adv] *as anticipated*
artlessly, but of course*, by birth, by nature, candidly, casually, characteristically, commonly, consistently, customarily, easily, freely, generally, genuinely, habitually, impulsively, informally, innocently, instinctively, normally, openly, ordinarily, readily, simply, spontaneously, typically, unaffectedly, uniformly, unpretentiously, usually; SEE CONCEPT *544*

nature [n1] *character, disposition*
attributes, being, bottom line*, complexion, constitution, description, drift, essence, essentiality, features, heart*, humor, individualism, individuality, like, makeup, meat*, mood, name of game*, name of tune*, nature of beast*, outlook, personality, point, quality, score, stuff, temper, temperament, texture, traits, type; SEE CONCEPTS *411,682*

nature [n2] *type, kind*
anatomy, brand, cast, category, character, color, conformation, description, figure, framework, ilk, shape, sort, species, stripe*, structure, style, variety, way; SEE CONCEPT *378*

nature [n3] *earth, creation*
cosmos, country, countryside, environment, for-

est, generation, landscape, macrocosm, megacosm, natural history, outdoors, scenery,
seascape, setting, universe, view, world; SEE
CONCEPTS 407,429,509,511

naughty [*adj1*] *bad, misbehaved*
annoying, badly behaved*, contrary, disobedient,
disorderly, evil, exasperating, fiendish, fractious,
froward, headstrong, impish, indecorous, insubordinate, intractable, mischievous, obstreperous,
perverse, playful, rascally, raunchy, recalcitrant,
refractory, rough, rowdy, sinful, teasing, tough,
ungovernable, unmanageable, unruly, wanton,
wayward, wicked, willful, worthless, wrong; SEE
CONCEPT *401*

naughty [*adj2*] *obscene, vulgar*
adult, bawdy, blue*, dirty*, hot*, improper, lascivious, lewd, loose*, off-color*, pornographic,
purple*, ribald, risqué, steamy*; SEE CONCEPTS
372,545

nausea [*n*] *sickness in stomach; revulsion*
abhorrence, aversion, biliousness, disgust, hatred,
loathing, offense, qualm, qualms, queasiness, re-
gurgitation, rejection, repugnance, retching,
squeamishness, vomiting; SEE CONCEPTS *316,410*

nauseate [*v*] *make sick; disgust*
bother, disturb, horrify, offend, reluct, repel, repulse, revolt, sicken; SEE CONCEPTS *14,308*

nauseous [*adj*] *disgusting*
abhorrent, brackish, detestable, distasteful, ill,
loathsome, nauseated, nauseating, offensive,
queasy, repugnant, repulsive, revolting, rocky*,
seasick, sick, sick as dog*, sickening, squeamish;
SEE CONCEPTS *314,529*

nautical/naval [*adj*] *concerning ships, sea*
abyssal, aquatic, boating, cruising, deep-sea, marine, maritime, navigating, navigational, oceangoing, oceanic, oceanographic, pelagic, rowing,
sailing, sailorly, salty, seafaring, seagoing, sea-
loving, thalassic, yachting; SEE CONCEPT *536*

navigate [*v*] *guide along route, often over water*
captain*, cross, cruise, direct, drive, handle, head
out for*, helm, journey, lay the course*, maneuver, operate, pilot, plan, pilot, ride out, sail, skipper*, steer, voyage; SEE CONCEPTS *148,187,224*

navigation [*n*] *traveling, guiding along route, often over water*
aeronautics, boating, cruising, exploration, flying,
helmsmanship, nautics, navigating, ocean travel,
pilotage, piloting, plotting a course, sailing, seafaring, seamanship, shipping, steerage, steering,
voyage, voyaging, yachting; SEE CONCEPTS
155,187,224

near [*adj1*] *close by physically*
abreast, abutting, adjacent, adjoining, alongside,
along toward, approximal, around, at close quarters, available, beside, bordering, burning, close,
close-at-hand, close-by, close shave*, conterminous, contiguous, convenient, hair's breadth*,
handy, immediate, in close proximity*, near-at-
hand*, nearby, neighboring, next door*, nigh*,
not remote, practically, proximal, proximate,
ready, side-by-side, touching, vincinal, warm*,
within stone's throw*; SEE CONCEPTS *586,778*

near [*adj2*] *close in time; forthcoming*
approaching, approximate, at hand, coming, comparative, expected, imminent, impending, in the
offing*, looming, near-at-hand*, next, relative;
SEE CONCEPTS *812,820*

near [*adj3*] *familiar*
affecting, akin*, allied, attached, close, con-

nected, dear, friendly, intimate, related, touching;
SEE CONCEPT *555*

nearby [*adj*] *adjoining*
adjacent, close, close-at-hand, close-by, contiguous, convenient, handy, immediate, neighboring,
proximate, ready; SEE CONCEPTS *586,778*

nearby [*adv*] *within reach*
about, at close quarters, close, close at hand, hard,
near, near-at-hand*, nigh*, not far away; SEE
CONCEPTS *586,778*

nearing [*adj*] *approaching*
advancing, approximating, coming, forthcoming,
imminent, impending, oncoming, threatening, upcoming; SEE CONCEPTS *548,820*

nearly [*adv*] *almost*
about, all but*, approaching, approximately, as
good as*, circa*, close but no cigar*, closely,
give or take a little*, in effect, in essence, in substance, in the ballpark*, in the neighborhood*,
just about, more or less, most, much, nearabout,
not quite, practically, pretty near, roughly, round,
roundly, some, somewhere, upwards of*, virtually, well-nigh*, within a little*; SEE CONCEPT
566

neat [*adj1*] *arranged well, uncluttered*
accurate, apple-pie order*, chic*, correct, dainty,
dapper, elegant, exact, fastidious, finical, finicky,
immaculate, in good order, in good shape, methodical, natty, neat as a pin*, nice, orderly, precise, prim, proper, regular, shipshape*, sleek,
slick, smart, spick-and-span*, spotless, spruce,
systematic, tidy, trim, well-groomed, well-kept;
SEE CONCEPTS *485,589,621*

neat [*adj2*] *clever, practiced*
able, adept, adroit, agile, apt, artful, deft, dexterous, efficient, effortless, elegant, expert, finished,
graceful, handy, nimble, precise, proficient,
quick, ready, skillful, speedy, stylish, well-
judged; SEE CONCEPTS *527,542*

nebulous [*adj*] *confused, obscure*
ambiguous, amorphous, cloudy, dark, dim, hazy,
imprecise, indefinite, indeterminate, indistinct,
misty, murky, shadowy, shapeless, uncertain, unclear, unformed, vague; SEE CONCEPTS *535,617*

necessarily [*adv*] *inevitably, certainly*
accordingly, as a matter of course*, automatically,
axiomatically, beyond one's control*, by definition, by its own nature*, cardinally, come what
may*, compulsorily, consequently, exigently,
from within*, fundamentally, incontrovertibly, indubitably, ineluctably, inescapably, inexorably,
irresistibly, naturally, no doubt, of course, of
necessity, perforce, positively, pressingly, significantly, undoubtedly, unpreventably, unquestionably, vitally, willy-nilly*, without fail*; SEE
CONCEPTS *535,544*

necessary [*adj1*] *essential*
all-important, basic, binding, bottom-line*, cardinal, chief, compelling, compulsory, crucial, decisive, de rigueur*, elementary, exigent, expedient,
fundamental, imperative, incumbent on, indispensable, mandatory, momentous, name of
game*, needed, needful, obligatory, paramount,
prerequisite, pressing, prime, principal, quintessential, required, requisite, significant, specified,
unavoidable, urgent, vital, wanted; SEE CON-
CEPTS *546,568*

necessary [*adj2*] *inevitable*
assured, certain, fated, imminent, ineluctable, ineludible, inerrant, inescapable, inevasible, inexo-

rable, infallible, returnless, unavoidable, undeniable, unescapable; SEE CONCEPTS *535,548*

necessitate [v] *call for, make necessary*

ask, behoove, cause, coerce, command, compel, constrain, crave, demand, drive, entail, force, impel, make, oblige, postulate, require, take; SEE CONCEPTS *53,242,646*

necessity [n] *need, essentiality*

call, cause, claim, compulsion, demand, desideratum, duress, essence, exaction, exigency, fundamental, godsend*, imperative, indispensability, inevitability, inexorableness, life or death*, must, necessary, needfulness, no alternative, no choice, obligation, pinch, precondition, prerequisite, privation, requirement, requisite, sine qua non, stress, undeniability, urgency, vital part, vitals, want; SEE CONCEPTS *646,709*

need [n1] *want, requirement*

charge, commitment, committal, compulsion, demand, desideratum, devoir, duty, essential, exigency, extremity, longing, must, obligation, occasion, ought, requisite, right, the urge, urgency, use, weakness, wish; SEE CONCEPTS *20,709*

need [n2] *poverty*

deprivation, destitution, distress, extremity, impecuniousness, impoverishment, inadequacy, indigence, insufficiency, lack, neediness, paucity, pennilessness, penury, poorness, privation, shortage, want; SEE CONCEPTS *335,709*

need [n3] *emergency; pressing lack*

deficiency, exigency, inadequacy, insufficiency, necessity, obligation, shortage, urgency, want; SEE CONCEPTS *646,709*

need [v] *want something*

be deficient, be deprived, be down and out*, be hard up*, be inadequate, be in need of, be in want, be needy, be poor, be short, be without, call for, claim, covet, crave, demand, desire, die for*, do without, drive for*, exact, feel a dearth of*, feel the necessity for, feel the pinch*, go hungry*, hanker, have occasion for, have occasion to, have use for*, hunger, hurt for, lack, long, lust, miss, necessitate, pine, require, suffer privation, thirst, wish, yearn, yen for; SEE CONCEPTS *20,646*

needle [v] *tease, annoy*

aggravate, badger, bait, bedevil, bother, examine, gnaw, goad, harass, hector, irk, irritate, nag, nettle, pester, plague, prick, prod, provoke, question, quiz, ride*, rile, ruffle, spur, sting, taunt, tweak*, worry; SEE CONCEPTS *7,19,54*

needless [adj] *unnecessary, groundless*

causeless, dispensable, excessive, expendable, gratuitous, inessential, nonessential, pointless, redundant, superfluous, uncalled-for, undesired, unrequired, unwanted, useless; SEE CONCEPTS *546,575*

needy [adj] *deprived, impoverished*

beggared, dead broke*, destitute, dirt poor*, disadvantaged, down-and-out*, down at heel*, down to last cent*, flat*, impecunious, indigent, necessitous, penniless, penurious, poor, poverty-stricken, underprivileged, unprosperous; SEE CONCEPT *334*

nefarious [adj] *bad, sinful*

abominable, atrocious, base, corrupt, criminal, degenerate, depraved, detestable, dreadful, evil, execrable, flagitious, flagrant, foul, glaring, gross, heinous, horrible, infamous, infernal, iniquitous, miscreant, monstrous, odious, opprobrious, out-rageous, perverse, putrid, rank, rotten, shameful, treacherous, vicious, vile, villainous, wicked; SEE CONCEPTS *401,545,548*

negate [v] *contradict, countermand*

abate, abolish, abrogate, annihilate, annul, belie, blackball*, break with*, cancel, cancel out, controvert, countercheck, cross*, deny, ding*, disaffirm, disallow, disprove, dump*, fly in the face of*, frustrate, gainsay, impugn, invalidate, kill, negative, neutralize, nullify, oppose, put down, quash*, rebut, redress, refute, repeal, rescind, retract, reverse, revoke, stonewall*, traverse, turn down, turn thumbs down*, undo, vitiate, void; SEE CONCEPTS *46,50,88,121*

negation [n] *contradiction, denial*

antithesis, antonym, blank, cancellation, contrary, converse, counterpart, disavowal, disclaimer, forget it*, gainsaying, inverse, negatory, neutralization, no, nonexistence, nothingness, nullification, nullity, opposite, opposition, proscription, refusal, rejection, renunciation, repudiation, reverse, vacuity, veto, void; SEE CONCEPTS *121,278,685*

negative [n] *contradiction*

denial, disavowal, nay, refusal, refutation; SEE CONCEPT *278*

negative [adj] *bad, contradictory*

abrogating, adverse, against, annulling, antagonistic, anti, balky, colorless, con, contrary, contravening, counteractive, cynical, denying, detrimental, disallowing, disavowing, dissentient, dissenting, gainsaying, gloomy, impugning, invalidating, jaundiced, naysaying, neutralizing, nugatory, nullifying, opposing, pessimistic, privative, recusant, refusing, rejecting, removed, repugnant, resisting, resistive, unaffirmative, unenthusiastic, unfavorable, uninterested, unwilling, weak; SEE CONCEPTS *267,403,570*

neglect [n1] *disregard*

carelessness, coolness, delinquency, disdain, disregardance, disrespect, heedlessness, inadvertence, inattention, inconsideration, indifference, laxity, laxness, oversight, scorn, slight, thoughtlessness, unconcern; SEE CONCEPTS *410,657*

neglect [n2] *failure, default*

carelessness, chaos, delay, delinquency, dereliction, dilapidation, forgetfulness, lapse, laxity, laxness, limbo, neglectfulness, negligence, omission, oversight, pretermission, remissness, slackness, slovenliness; SEE CONCEPTS *674,699*

neglect [v1] *be indifferent, leave alone*

affront, brush aside, brush off, condemn, depreciate, despise, detest, discount, disdain, dismiss, disregard, have nothing to do with*, ignore, keep at arm's length*, keep one's distance*, laugh off*, let go*, live with*, make light of*, not care for*, overlook, pass by, pass over, pass up, pay no attention to, pay no mind*, pretermit, rebuff, reject, scant, scorn, shrug off*, slight, slur, spurn, tune out*, underestimate; SEE CONCEPTS *30,681*

neglect [v2] *fail to do; forget*

be careless, be derelict, be irresponsible, be negligent, be remiss, bypass, defer, discard, dismiss, disregard, elide, evade, gloss over*, let pass*, let slide*, look the other way*, lose sight of*, miss, not trouble oneself*, omit, overleap, overlook, overpass, pass over, postpone, procrastinate, shirk, skimp, skip, suspend, think little of*, trifle; SEE CONCEPTS *101,699*

neglectful [*adj*] *careless, failing*

behindhand, delinquent, derelict, disregardful, heedless, inattentive, indifferent, lax, lazy, negligent, regardless, remiss, slack, thoughtless, uncaring, unmindful; SEE CONCEPTS **401,542**

negligent [*adj*] *careless, indifferent*

asleep at switch*, behindhand, cursory, delinquent, derelict, discinct, disregardful, forgetful, heedless, inadvertent, inattentive, inconsiderate, incurious, lax, neglectful, nonchalant, offhand, regardless, remiss, slack, slapdash*, slipshod*, sloppy*, slovenly, thoughtless, unconcerned, unheedful, unmindful, unthinking; SEE CONCEPTS **401,542**

negligible [*adj*] *insignificant*

imperceptible, inconsequential, minor, minute, off*, outside, petty, remote, slender, slight, slim, small, trifling, trivial, unimportant; SEE CONCEPTS **552,575,789**

negotiate [*v1*] *bargain, discuss*

accommodate, adjudicate, adjust, agree, arbitrate, arrange, bring to terms*, bury the hatchet*, come across with*, compose, concert, conciliate, confer, connect, consult, contract, covenant, cut a deal*, deal, debate, dicker*, haggle, hammer out a deal*, handle, horse trade*, intercede, make a deal, make peace*, make terms*, manage, mediate, moderate, network, parley*, referee, settle, step in*, stipulate, swap, transact, treat, umpire*, work out*, work out a deal; SEE CONCEPTS **8,56,68**

negotiate [*v2*] *traverse, cross*

clear, get around, get over, get past, hurdle, leap over, overleap, pass, pass through, surmount, vault; SEE CONCEPTS **149,224**

negotiation [*n*] *bargaining*

agreement, arbitration, colloquy, compromise, conference, consultation, debate, diplomacy, discussion, intervention, mediation, meeting, transaction; SEE CONCEPTS **56,68,684**

negotiator [*n*] *person who bargains, controls discussion*

adjudicator, ambassador, arbitrator, broker, delegate, diplomat, fixer*, go-between*, interagent, intermediary, intermedium, judge, mediator, middleperson, moderator; SEE CONCEPTS **348, 354,423**

neighbor [*n*] *person who lives close by*

acquaintance, bystander, friend, homebody*, nearby resident, next-door neighbor; SEE CONCEPT **423**

neighbor [*v*] *be next to*

abut, adjoin, be adjacent, be contiguous, be near, be nearby, border, butt against, communicate, connect, join, line, march, surround, touch, verge; SEE CONCEPT **759**

neighborhood [*n*] *community, surroundings*

adjacency, area, block, closeness, confines, contiguity, district, environs, ghetto, hood, jungle*, locale, locality, nearness, neck of the woods*, parish, part, precinct, propinquity, proximity, purlieus, quarter, region, section, slum, stomping ground*, street, suburb, territory, tract, turf, vicinage, vicinity, ward, zone, zoo*; SEE CONCEPTS **198,379,516**

neighborly [*adj*] *friendly*

amiable, civil, companionable, considerate, cooperative, cordial, genial, gracious, gregarious, harmonious, helpful, hospitable, kind, obliging, sociable, social, well-disposed; SEE CONCEPT **401**

neologism [*n*] *new word*

buzz word*, coinage, neology, new phrase, slang, synthetic word*, vogue word*; SEE CONCEPT **275**

nerve [*n*] *daring, boldness*

assumption, assurance, audacity, backbone, brass*, bravery, brazenness, cheek*, chutzpah*, confidence, coolness, courage, crust*, determination, effrontery, endurance, energy, face*, fearlessness, firmness, force, fortitude, gall*, gameness, grit*, guts*, hardihood, hardiness, heart*, impertinence, impudence, insolence, intestinal fortitude, intrepidity, mettle, might, moxie*, pluck*, presumption, resolution, sauce*, spirit, spunk*, starch*, steadfastness, stomach*, temerity, vigor, will; SEE CONCEPT **411**

nerve [*v*] *strengthen, hearten*

animate, brace, cheer, embolden, encourage, enhearten, fortify, inspirit, invigorate, steel; SEE CONCEPTS **7,14,22**

nerveless [*adj1*] *calm, cool*

collected, composed, controlled, impassive, imperturbable, intrepid, patient, self-possessed, tranquil, unemotional; SEE CONCEPT **542**

nerveless [*adj2*] *scared to death*

afraid, cowardly, debilitated, enervated, fearful, feeble, nervous, petrified, spineless*, timid, weak, yellow-bellied*; SEE CONCEPTS **401,403**

nerves [*n*] *extreme anxiety*

fretfulness, hysteria, imbalance, irritation, nervousness, neurasthenia, sleeplessness, strain, stress, tenseness, tension; SEE CONCEPT **410**

nervous [*adj*] *anxious, fearful*

afraid, agitated, annoyed, apprehensive, basket case*, bothered, concerned, distressed, disturbed, edgy, excitable, fidgety, fitful, flustered, fussy*, hesitant, high-strung*, hysterical, irritable, jittery*, jumpy*, nervy*, neurotic, on edge*, overwrought, querulous, restive, ruffled, sensitive, shaky*, shrinking, shy, skittish, snappish, solicitous, spooked*, taut, tense, timid, timorous, troubled, twitchy*, uneasy, unrestful, unstrung*, upset, uptight, volatile, weak, wired*, worried; SEE CONCEPTS **403,542**

nervousness [*n*] *anxious state*

agitation, all-overs*, anger, animation, butterflies*, cold sweat*, creeps*, delirium, discomfiture, disquiet, disquietude, dithers*, excitability, feverishness, fidgets*, flap*, fluster*, fuss*, impatience, jitters*, jumps*, moodiness, neurasthenia, neuroticism, perturbation, quivers, sensitivity, shakes, stage fright, stimulation, stress, tension, timidity, tizzy*, to-do*, touchiness, trembles*, tremulousness, turbulence, uneasiness, willies*, worry; SEE CONCEPTS **410,657**

nervy [*adj*] *bold, pushy*

cheeky*, crass, crude, forward, fresh*, impudent, inconsiderate, pert, plucky*, rude, sassy*, smart, smart-alecky*, wise; SEE CONCEPT **401**

nestle [*v*] *curl up*

bundle, burrow, cuddle, huddle, lie against, lie close, make snug*, move close, nuzzle, settle down, snug*, snuggle, take shelter; SEE CONCEPTS **154,612**

net [*n*] *mesh, web*

cloth, fabric, lace, lacework, lattice, netting, network, openwork, reticulum, screen, tracery; SEE CONCEPTS **473,770**

net [*adj*] *profiting*

after deductions, after taxes, clear, excluding, exclusive, final, irreducible, pure, remaining, take-home, undeductible; SEE CONCEPT *334*

net [*vl*] *capture*
bag*, catch, enmesh, ensnare, entangle, hook*, lasso*, nab*, trap; SEE CONCEPT *90*

net [*v2*] *gain after expenses*
accumulate, bring in, clean up, clear, earn, make, profit, realize, reap; SEE CONCEPT *330*

nettle [*v*] *provoke, upset*
annoy, chafe, disgust, disturb, exasperate, fret, get*, goad, harass, huff, incense, insult, irritate, miff, peeve*, pester, pet, pique, put out*, rile, roil, ruffle, snit*, stew*, sting*, tease, tiff*, vex; SEE CONCEPTS *7,14,19*

network [*n*] *system of connections*
arrangement, artery, chain, checkerboard*, circuitry, complex, convolution, crisscross*, fabric, fiber, grid, grill*, grillwork, hookup, interconnections, jungle, labyrinth, maze, mesh, net, netting, nexus, organization, patchwork*, plexus, reticulation, reticule, screening, structure, system, tessellation, tracks, wattle, weave, web, wiring; SEE CONCEPTS *381,388,770*

network [*v*] *to socialize for professional or personal gain*
associate, circulate, hobnob, make contacts, meet, meet and greet*, mingle, rub elbows*, schmooze*; SEE CONCEPT *384*

neurosis [*n*] *mental disturbance, disorder*
aberration, abnormality, affliction, breakdown, compulsion, crack-up*, derangement, deviation, hysteria, inhibition, insanity, instability, madness, maladjustment, mental illness, neurasthenia, obsession, personality disorder, phobia, psychological disorder, psychopathy; SEE CONCEPTS *316,410*

neurotic [*adj*] *mentally maladjusted*
aberrant, abnormal, anxious, basket case*, bundle of nerves*, choked*, clutched*, compulsive, deviant, disordered, disoriented, distraught, disturbed, erratic, hung up*, hysteric, inhibited, manic, nervous, nervous wreck*, obsessive, overwrought, psychoneurotic, unhealthy, unstable, upset, uptight, wired*; SEE CONCEPTS *314,403*

neuter [*v*] *remove sex organs*
alter, castrate, change, desexualize, doctor, dress, fix, geld, make barren, make impotent, make infertile, make sexless, mutilate, spay, sterilize, unsex; SEE CONCEPTS *157,250*

neutral [*adj1*] *impartial, noncommittal*
aloof, bystanding, calm, clinical, collected, cool, detached, disengaged, disinterested, dispassionate, easy, evenhanded, fair-minded, impersonal, inactive, indifferent, inert, middle-of-road*, nonaligned, nonbelligerent, nonchalant, noncombatant, nonparticipating, nonpartisan, on sidelines*, on the fence*, pacifistic, poker-faced*, relaxed, unaligned, unbiased, uncommitted, unconcerned, undecided, uninvolved, unprejudiced; SEE CONCEPTS *403,542*

neutral [*adj2*] *flat, dull to senses*
abstract, achromatic, colorless, drab, expressionless, indeterminate, indistinct, indistinguishable, intermediate, toneless, undefined, vague, vanilla*; SEE CONCEPTS *485,537,618*

neutralize [*v*] *counteract*
abrogate, annul, balance, cancel, compensate for, conquer, counteract, countercheck, counterpoise, countervail, defeat, frustrate, invalidate, negate, negative, nullify, offset, overcome, over-

ride, overrule, redress, subdue, undo; SEE CONCEPTS *121,232*

never [*adv*] *not at any time*
at no time, don't hold your breath*, forget it, nevermore, not at all, not ever, not in any way, not in the least, not on your life*, not under any condition, no way*; SEE CONCEPT *799*

never-ending [*adj*] *continual, unceasing*
amaranthine, boundless, ceaseless, constant, continuous, endless, eternal, everlasting, immortal, incessant, interminable, nonstop, perpetual, persistent, relentless, timeless, unbroken, unchanging, uninterrupted, unremitting; SEE CONCEPTS *482,798*

nevertheless [*adv*] *however*
after all, although, but, even so, even though, howbeit, nonetheless, not the less, notwithstanding, regardless, still, still and all, though, withal, yet; SEE CONCEPT *544*

new [*adj1*] *recent, fresh*
advanced, au courant, brand-new, contemporary, current, cutting-edge*, dewy, different, dissimilar, distinct, fashionable, inexperienced, just out*, late, latest, modern, modernistic, modish*, neoteric, newfangled*, novel, now*, original, recent, spick-and-span*, state-of-the-art, strange, topical, ultramodern, unaccustomed, uncontaminated, unfamiliar, unique, unknown, unlike, unseasoned, unskilled, unspoiled, untouched, untrained, untried, untrodden, unused, unusual, up-to-date, virgin, youthful; SEE CONCEPTS *564,578,797*

new [*adj2*] *additional*
added, another, else, extra, farther, fresh, further, increased, more, other, supplementary; SEE CONCEPTS *771,824*

new [*adj3*] *modernized, restored*
altered, changed, improved, redesigned, refreshed, regenerated, renewed, revived; SEE CONCEPT *589*

new [*adv*] *recently*
afresh, anew, freshly, lately, newly, of late; SEE CONCEPT *820*

new age [*adj*] *of a broad-ranging consciousness-raising movement*
Age of Aquarius*, alternative, astrological, balanced, crystal healing, holistic, mystic, occult, planetary, spiritual, supernaturalist; SEE CONCEPTS *403,529*

newcomer [*n*] *person who has just arrived in area*
alien, arrival, beginner, blow-in*, colt*, foreigner, greenhorn*, immigrant, incomer, Johnny-come-lately*, late arrival, latecomer, maverick, neophyte, new kid on the block*, novice, novitiate, outsider, rookie, settler, stranger, tenderfoot*; SEE CONCEPTS *413,423*

newfangled [*adj*] *quite recent*
contemporary, fashionable, fresh, gimmicky*, in vogue, modern, modernistic, neoteric, new, new-fashioned, novel, popular, unique; SEE CONCEPTS *578,589,797*

newly [*adv*] *recently*
anew, freshly, just, lately, latterly, of late; SEE CONCEPT *820*

news [*n*] *information, revelation*
account, advice, announcement, broadcast, bulletin, cable, cognizance, communication, communiqué, copy, data, description, disclosure, discovery, dispatch, enlightenment, exposé, eye-opener*, front-page news*, headlines, hearsay, intelligence, itemization, knowledge, leak, low-

down, message, narration, news flash, particularization, recital, recognition, release, report,
rumor, scandal, scoop*, specification, statement,
story, telecast, telegram, telling, the goods*, tidings*, word*; SEE CONCEPTS 268,274,293

newspaper [n] *regular, continuous publication
containing information*
biweekly, bulldog*, community, daily, extra, gazette, journal, magazine, metropolitan, organ, paper, periodical, press, rag*, record, review,
scandal sheet*, sheet, tabloid, trade, weekly; SEE
CONCEPTS 279,280

next [adj] *coming immediately after in space, time,
order*
abutting, adjacent, adjoining, after, alongside,
attached, back-to-back, beside, close, closest,
coming, consequent, co-terminous, ensuing, following, hard by*, later, meeting, nearest, neighboring, on the side, proximate, side-by-side,
subsequent, succeeding, touching; SEE CONCEPTS
585,586,799

next [adv] *immediately after in time, space, order*
after, afterward, afterwhile, behind, by and by,
closely, coming up, following, later, latterly, next
off, subsequently, thereafter; SEE CONCEPTS
585,586,799

nibble [n] *morsel, bite*
crumb, peck, snack, soupçon, taste, tidbit; SEE
CONCEPTS 458,831

nibble [v] *bite, pick at*
crop, eat, eat like a bird*, gnaw, munch, nip*,
nosh on*, peck*, snack; SEE CONCEPT 169

nice [adj] *likable, agreeable*
admirable, amiable, approved, attractive, becoming, charming, commendable, considerate, copacetic, cordial, courteous, decorous, delightful,
ducky, fair, favorable, fine and dandy*, friendly,
genial, gentle, good, gracious, helpful, ingratiating, inviting, kind, kindly, lovely, nifty*, obliging, okay*, peachy*, pleasant, pleasurable, polite,
prepossessing, seemly, simpatico, superior, swell,
unpresumptuous, welcome, well-mannered, winning, winsome; SEE CONCEPTS 404,548,572

nice [adj2] *precise, neat, refined*
accurate, becoming, befitting, careful, choosy,
conforming, correct, critical, cultured, dainty, decent, delicate, discerning, discriminating, distinguishing, exact, exacting, fastidious, fine,
finespun, finical, finicking, finicky*, fussy*, genteel, hairsplitting*, meticulous, minute, particular, persnickety*, picky*, proper, respectable,
right, rigorous, scrupulous, seemly, squeamish,
strict, subtle, tidy, trim, trivial*, virtuous, well-
bred; SEE CONCEPTS 542,557,558

niche [n] *place all one's own*
alcove, byplace, calling, compartment, corner,
cranny*, cubbyhole*, hole, hollow, indentation,
nook, opening, pigeonhole*, position, recess,
slot, vocation; SEE CONCEPTS 440,513,630

nick [n/v] *chip, scratch*
cut, damage, dent, dint, indent, jag, knock, mark,
mill, notch, scar, score, slit; SEE CONCEPTS
137,176,208

nickname [n] *informal title*
appellation, byname, byword, denomination, diminutive, epithet, familiar name, handle*, label,
moniker, pet name*, sobriquet, style, tag*; SEE
CONCEPTS 268,683

nifty [adj] *marvelous*
chic, clever, cool*, dandy, enjoyable, excellent,

groovy*, keen, neat, peachy*, pleasing, quick,
sharp, smart, spruce, stylish, super, swell, terrific;
SEE CONCEPT 572

night [n] *part of day after sundown and before
sunrise*
after dark, after hours*, bedtime, before dawn,
black*, blackness, dark, dark hours, darkness,
dead of night*, dim, duskiness, dusk to dawn,
evening, eventide, gloom, midnight, nightfall,
nighttide, nighttime, obscurity*, pitch dark, twilight, witching   hour*;   SEE   CONCEPTS
620,801,806,810

nightclub [n] *place for evening entertainment*
bar, bistro, cabaret, café, casino, disco*, disco-
theque, dive*, hideaway*, honky-tonk*, joint*,
nightery, night spot, nitery, restaurant, roadhouse,
saloon, speakeasy*, spot, supper club, tavern, theatre, watering hole*; SEE CONCEPTS 293,439,449

nightfall [n] *beginning of darkness*
black*, crepuscule, dim, dusk, eve, eventide, sundown, sunset, twilight, vespers; SEE CONCEPT
810

nightgown [n] *dress in which to sleep*
bedgown, lingerie, negligee, nightdress, nightie*,
nightrobe, nightshirt, pajamas, PJs*, sleeper*;
SEE CONCEPT 451

nightly [adj/adv] *each evening; after dark*
at night, by night, every night, in the night, night
after night, nights, nighttime, nocturnal, noctur-
nally; SEE CONCEPTS 541,799,801

nightmare [n] *bad dream or experience*
dream, fancy, fantasy, hallucination, horror, illusion, incubus, ordeal, phantasm, succubus, torment, trial, tribulation, vision; SEE CONCEPTS
315,674

nihilism [n] *refusal to believe*
abnegation, agnosticism, anarchy, atheism, denial, disbelief, disorder, lawlessness, mob rule*,
nonbelief, rejection, renunciation, repudiation,
skepticism, terrorism; SEE CONCEPT 689

nil [adj] *nonexistent*
naught, nihil, nix*, none, nothing, nought, zero;
SEE CONCEPTS 539,762,771

nimble [adj] *dexterous, smart*
active, adept, adroit, agile, alert, bright, brisk,
clever, deft, handy, light, lissome, lithe, lively,
proficient, prompt, quick, quick-witted, ready,
skillful, sprightly, spry, swift, vigilant, wide-
awake; SEE CONCEPTS 402,527,584

nip [n] *swallow, taste*
bite, catch, dram, drop, finger, jolt, morsel,
mouthful, nibble, pinch, portion, shot*, sip,
slug*, snifter, soupçon, toothful; SEE CONCEPTS
458,831

nip [v1] *bite; take small part*
catch, clip, compress, grip, munch, nab at*, nibble, pinch, sink teeth into*, snag, snap*, snip*,
squeeze*, take a chunk out of*, tweak, twinge,
twitch; SEE CONCEPTS 142,169,190

nip [v2] *stop, thwart*
arrest, balk, blight, check, dash, end, frustrate;
SEE CONCEPTS 121,234

nobility [n] *aristocracy; eminence*
dignity, elevation, elite, ennoblement, exaltation,
excellence, generosity, gentry, glorification, grandeur, greatness, high society, honor, illustriousness, incorruptibility, integrity, loftiness,
magnanimity, magnificence, majesty, nobleness,
patricians, peerage, royalty, ruling class, society,
stateliness, sublimity, superiority, upper class, up-

rightness, virtue, worthiness; SEE CONCEPTS 378,388,668

noble [n] *member of royal or important family*
archduchess, archduke, aristocrat, blue blood*, count, countess, duchess, duke, emperor, empress, gentleman, gentlewoman, lady, lord, patrician, peer, prince, princess, royalty, silk stocking*; SEE CONCEPTS 422,423

noble [adj1] *aristocratic*
gentle, highborn, imperial, kingly, nobiliary, patrician, queenly, titled, wellborn; SEE CONCEPTS 549,555

noble [adj2] *dignified, excellent*
august, beneficent, benevolent, benign, big, bounteous, brilliant, charitable, courtly, cultivated, dignified, distinguished, elevated, eminent, extraordinary, first-rate, generous, gracious, grand, great, great-hearted, high-minded, honorable, humane, imposing, impressive, liberal, lofty, magnanimous, magnificent, meritorious, preeminent, refined, remarkable, reputable, splendid, stately, sublime, supreme, sympathetic, tolerant, upright, virtuous, worthy; SEE CONCEPTS 401,404,572

nobody/nonentity [n] *person of little importance*
cipher, insignificancy, lightweight*, menial, nix*, nothing, parvenu*, small potato*, squirt*, upstart, wimp*, zero*, zip; SEE CONCEPT 423

nocturnal [adj] *happening at night*
after dark, late, night, night-loving, nightly, nighttime; SEE CONCEPTS 799,801

nod [n] *gesture of the head*
acceptance, acknowledgment, affirmative, beckon, bow, dip, greeting, inclination, indication, permission, salute, sign, signal, yes; SEE CONCEPTS 74,185,685

nod [v1] *gesture with head*
acknowledge, acquiesce, agree, approve, assent, beckon, bend, bow, concur, consent, curtsy, dip, duck, greet, indicate, recognize, respond, salute, say yes, sign, signal; SEE CONCEPTS 10,50,74,88,185

nod [v2] *fall asleep*
become inattentive, be sleepy, doze, drift, drift off, droop, drowse, nap, sleep, slump; SEE CONCEPTS 210,315,681

node/nodule [n] *knot, growth*
bud, bulge, bump, burl, clot, knob, lump, protuberance, swelling, tumor; SEE CONCEPTS 471,831

noise [n] *sound that is loud or not harmonious*
babble, babel, bang, bedlam, bellow, bewailing, blare, blast, boisterousness, boom, buzz, cacophony, caterwauling, clamor, clang, clatter, commotion, crash, cry, detonation, din, discord, disquiet, disquietude, drumming, eruption, explosion, fanfare, fireworks, fracas*, fuss*, hoo-ha*, hubbub*, hullabaloo*, jangle, lamentation, outcry, pandemonium, peal, racket, ring, roar, row, shot, shouting, sonance, squawk, stridency, talk, thud, tumult, turbulence, uproar, uproariousness, yelling, yelp; SEE CONCEPTS 521,595

noiseless [adj] *quiet*
hushed, hushful, inaudible, mute, muted, silent, soundless, speechless, still, voiceless, wordless; SEE CONCEPT 594

noisome [adj] *immoral, bad, offensive*
baneful, dangerous, deadly, deleterious, disgusting, fetid, foul, harmful, horrid, hurtful, injurious, insalubrious, insalutary, loathsome, malodorous, mephitic, mischievous, nauseating, noxious, pernicious, pestiferous, pestilential, poisonous, putrid, rank, reeking, repulsive, sickening, sickly, smelly, stinking, unhealthful, unhealthy, unwholesome, vile, yucky*; SEE CONCEPTS 537,571,598

noisy [adj] *very loud and unharmonious in sound*
blatant, blusterous, boisterous, booming, cacophonous, chattering, clamorous, clangorous, clattery, deafening, disorderly, ear-popping*, ear-splitting*, jumping, loudmouth, obstreperous, piercing, rackety, raising Cain*, raising the roof*, rambunctious, raspy, riotous, rowdy, screaming, strepitous, strident, tumultuous/tumultuous, turbulent, turned up, uproarious, vociferous; SEE CONCEPTS 592,594

nomad [n] *person who wanders from place to place*
hobo, itinerant, migrant, pilgrim, rambler, roamer, rover, vagabond, wanderer, wayfarer; SEE CONCEPT 413

nomadic [adj] *itinerant*
drifting, gypsy, itinerate, migrant, migratory, pastoral, perambulant, perambulatory, peripatetic, roaming, roving, traveling, vagabond, vagrant, wandering, wayfaring; SEE CONCEPTS 401,536,584

nomenclature [n] *vocabulary*
classification, codification, glossary, locution, phraseology, taxonomy, terminology; SEE CONCEPTS 275,276,683

nominal [adj1] *supposed, theoretical*
alleged, apparent, as advertised, formal, given, honorary, in effect only, in name only, mentioned, named, ostensible, pretended, professed, puppet, purported, seeming, self-styled, simple, so-called, stated, suggested, titular; SEE CONCEPT 582

nominal [adj2] *insignificant*
cheap, inconsiderable, inexpensive, low, low-priced, meaningless, minimal, small, symbolic, token, trifling, trivial, unnecessary; SEE CONCEPTS 334,575,789

nominate [v] *designate, select*
appoint, assign, call, choose, cognominate, commission, decide, denominate, draft, elect, elevate, empower, intend, make, mean, name, offer, present, proffer, propose, purpose, put down for, put up, recommend, slate, slot, specify, submit, suggest, tab, tag, tender, term; SEE CONCEPTS 41,50,75,88,300

nomination [n] *appointment for responsibility*
choice, designation, election, naming, proposal, recommendation, selection, suggestion; SEE CONCEPTS 41,50,75,88,300

nonchalant [adj] *easygoing, laid back*
airy, aloof, apathetic, blasé, calm, careless, casual, cold, collected, composed, cool, detached, disimpassioned, disinterested, dispassionate, easy, effortless, happy, impassive, imperturbable, incurious, indifferent, insouciant, lackadaisical, light, listless, loose, lukewarm, mellow, neglectful, negligent, neutral, offhand, placid, serene, smooth, trifling, uncaring, unconcerned, unemotional, unexcited, unfeeling, unflappable, unimpressible, unperturbed, unruffled, untroubled; SEE CONCEPTS 401,404,542

noncommittal [adj] *unwilling to decide*
ambiguous, buttoned up*, careful, cautious, circumspect, clammed up*, constrained, discreet, equivocal, evasive, even-steven*, guarded, hush-hush*, incommunicable, indefinite, judicious, middle-ground*, middle-of-the-road*, neutral, on-the-fence*, politic, reserved, restrained, tact-

ful, temporizing, tentative, unrevealing, vague, wary, zipped*; SEE CONCEPTS 267,403,542

noncompliant [adj] unwilling to go along with something

belligerent, contumacious, declinatory, declining, divergent, impatient, irregular, negative, objecting, rebellious, recalcitrant, refractory, refusing, restive, truculent; SEE CONCEPTS 401,542

nonconformist [n] person who goes against normal behavior, beliefs

beatnik*, bohemian*, demonstrator, different breed*, dissenter, dissentient, dissident, dropout, eccentric, fish out of water*, freak*, heretic, iconoclast, individualist, liberal, malcontent, maverick, misbeliever, night person, oddball, offbeat, original, protester, radical, rebel, sectary, separatist, swinger, weirdo*; SEE CONCEPTS 359,423

nonconformist [adj] unwilling to behave, believe as most do

beatnik*, bohemian*, dissident, freak*, heretical, heterodox, hippie*, iconoclastic, maverick, oddball, offbeat, original, rebel, schismatic*, sectarian, swinger, unorthodox, weird*; SEE CONCEPTS 401,542

nonconformity [n] belief, behavior different from most

bohemianism, breach, contumaciousness, denial, disaffection, disagreement, disapprobation, disapproval, discordance, disobedience, dissent, eccentricity, exception, heresy, heterodoxy, iconoclasm, insubordination, lawlessness, mutinousness, negation, nonacceptance, nonagreement, noncompliance, nonconsent, objection, opposition, originality, recalcitrance, recusance, recusancy, rejection, strangeness, transgressiveness, unconventionality, uniqueness, unorthodoxy, unruliness, veto, violation; SEE CONCEPTS 633,657,689

nondescript [adj] undistinguished, commonplace
characterless, colorless, common, dull, empty, featureless, garden*, indescribable, indeterminate, mousy*, ordinary, unclassifiable, unclassified, unexceptional, uninspiring, uninteresting, unmemorable, unremarkable, vague; SEE CONCEPTS 529,537,547

none [prep] not one thing
nil, nobody, no one, no one at all, no part, not a bit, not any, not anyone, not anything, not a soul, not a thing, nothing, not one, zero, zilch*; SEE CONCEPT 407

nonessential [adj] not needed or important
deadwood*, dispensable, excess baggage*, excessive, expendable, extraneous, inessential, insignificant, peripheral, petty, superfluous, trivial, unimportant, unnecessary; SEE CONCEPTS 546,575

nonexistent [adj] fictional, not real
absent, airy, baseless, blank, chimerical, dead, defunct, departed, dreamlike, dreamy, empty, ethereal, extinct, extinguished, fancied, flimsy, gone, gossamery, groundless, hallucinatory, hypothetical, illusory, imaginary, imagined, immaterial, imponderable, insubstantial, legendary, lost, missing, mythical, negative, null, null and void*, passed away, passed on, perished, shadowy, tenuous, ungrounded, unreal, unsubstantial, vacant, vague, vaporous, void, without foundation; SEE CONCEPTS 539,582

nonpartisan [adj] impartial; not political
detached, equitable, fair, free-wheeling*, independent, indifferent, just, middle-of-the-road*, neutral, nonaligned, nondiscriminatory, objective, on one's own*, on-the-fence*, playing it cool*, unaffected, unaffiliated, unbiased, unbigoted, uncolored, unimplicated, uninfluenced, uninvolved, unprejudiced; SEE CONCEPT 542

nonplus [v] confuse, perplex
astonish, astound, baffle, balk, beat, bewilder, boggle, buffalo*, confound, daze, discomfit, disconcert, discountenance, dismay, dumbfound, embarrass, faze, floor*, flurry, fluster, frustrate, get*, mess with one's head*, muddle, mystify, overcome, paralyze, puzzle, rattle, rattle one's cage*, stagger, stick, stump, stun, stymie*, take aback, throw*, throw into tizzy*, thwart; SEE CONCEPTS 14,16

nonsense [n] craziness, ridiculousness
absurdity, babble, balderdash*, baloney*, bananas*, bombast, bull*, bunk*, claptrap*, drivel, fatuity, flightiness, folly, foolishness, fun, gibberish, giddiness, hogwash*, hooey*, hot air*, imprudence, inanity, irrationality, jazz, jest, jive*, joke, ludicrousness, madness, mumbo jumbo*, palaver, poppycock*, prattle, pretense, ranting, rashness, rot, rubbish, scrawl, scribble, senselessness, silliness, soft soap*, stupidity, thoughtlessness, trash*, tripe*; SEE CONCEPTS 230,388,633

nonstop [adj] continuous, direct
ceaseless, constant, endless, incessant, interminable, relentless, round-the-clock*, steady, unbroken, unending, unfaltering, uninterrupted, unremitting; SEE CONCEPTS 482,584,798

nonviolent [adj] peaceful
irenic, nonbelligerent, pacifist, passive, peaceable, quiet, resistant, without violence; SEE CONCEPT 401

nook [n] corner, cubbyhole
alcove, byplace, cavity, compartment, cranny, crevice, den, hideout, hole, inglenook, niche, opening, quoin, recess, retreat; SEE CONCEPTS 440,513

noon [n] the middle of a day
apex, high noon, meridian, midday, noonday, noontide, noontime, twelve noon, twelve o'clock; SEE CONCEPTS 801,802,806

norm [n] average, standard
barometer, benchmark*, criterion, gauge, mean, measure, median, medium, model, par, pattern, rule, scale, touchstone*, type, yardstick; SEE CONCEPTS 647,686,688

normal [adj] common, usual
accustomed, acknowledged, average, commonplace, conventional, customary, general, habitual, mean, median, methodical, natural, orderly, ordinary, popular, prevalent, regular, routine, run-of-the-mill*, standard, traditional, typic, typical, unexceptional; SEE CONCEPT 547

normal [adj] sane, rational
all there*, compos mentis*, cool*, healthy, in good health, in one's right mind*, lucid, reasonable, right, right-minded, sound, together, well-adjusted, whole, wholesome; SEE CONCEPTS 314,403

normally [adv] usually
as a rule, commonly, habitually, in accordance with, ordinarily, regularly, typically; SEE CONCEPT 547

north [adj/adv] toward the top pole of the earth
arctic, boreal, cold, frozen, hyperborean, north-

no
no

bound, northerly, northern, northmost, northward, polar, septentrional, toward North Pole, tundra; SEE CONCEPTS *581,583*

nose [n] *smelling organ of animate being*
adenoids, beak*, bill*, horn*, muzzle*, nares, nostrils, olfactory nerves, proboscis, schnoz*, smeller*, sneezer*, sniffer*, snoot*, snout*, snuffer*, whiffer*; SEE CONCEPTS *392,601*

nose [v] *detect, search*
busybody*, examine, inspect, meddle, mouse*, pry, scent, smell, sniff, snoop*; SEE CONCEPTS *103,216*

nostalgia [n] *pleasant remembrances*
fond memories*, hearts and flowers*, homesickness, longing, pining, reminiscence, remorse, schmaltz*, sentimentality, tear-jerker*, wistfulness, yearning; SEE CONCEPTS *20,410*

nostalgic [adj] *longingly remembering*
cornball*, down memory lane*, drippy*, homesick, like yesterday*, lonesome, longing, mushy*, regretful, sappy*, sentimental, sloppy, syrupy*, wistful, yearning; SEE CONCEPTS *403,529*

nostrum [n] *cure-all, often ineffective*
catholicon, cure, drug, elixir, fix, formula, home remedy, medicine, panacea, patent medicine, potion, quack medicine*, quick fix*, remedy, treatment; SEE CONCEPTS *307,311*

nosy [adj] *curious; prying*
eavesdropping, inquisitive, inquisitorial, inquisitory, interested, interfering, intermeddling, intrusive, meddlesome, personal, searching, snooping, snoopy; SEE CONCEPT *401*

notable [n] *person who is famous, important*
big name*, big shot*, big-time operator*, big wheel*, celebrity, chief, dignitary, eminence, executive, figure*, heavyweight*, high-up, hotdog*, leader, lion*, luminary, magnate, mogul, name, notability, personage, personality, poohbah*, power, somebody*, star, superstar, VIP*, worthy; SEE CONCEPTS *347,352,423*

notable [adj] *important; famous*
big-league*, bodacious*, celebrated, celebrious, conspicuous, distingué, distinguished, eminent, eventful, evident, extraordinary, famed, great, heavy*, high-profile*, illustrious, major-league*, manifest, marked, memorable, momentous, nameable, noteworthy, noticeable, notorious, observable, outstanding, preeminent, prominent, pronounced, rare, red-letter*, remarkable, renowned, rubric, serious, something else*, striking, top-drawer*, uncommon, unusual, well-known; SEE CONCEPT *568*

notably [adv] *especially*
conspicuously, distinctly, exceedingly, exceptionally, extremely, greatly, highly, hugely, markedly, noticeably, outstandingly, particularly, prominently, remarkably, reputably, signally, strikingly, uncommonly, very; SEE CONCEPT *569*

notation [n] *written remarks*
characters, chit, code, documentation, figures, jotting, memo, memorandum, note, noting, record, representation, script, signs, symbols, system; SEE CONCEPTS *268,284*

notch [n1] *indentation*
cleft, cut, gap, gash, groove, incision, indent, indenture, mark, mill, nick, nock, rabbet, rut, score, scratch; SEE CONCEPT *513*

notch [n2] *level within classification*
cut, degree, grade, rung, stage, step; SEE CONCEPTS *388,744*

notch [v] *indent*
chisel, cleave, crenelate, crimp, cut, dent, gash, incise, jag, mark, mill, nick, scallop, score, scratch; SEE CONCEPTS *137,176,208*

note/notes [n1] *written communication*
agenda, annotation, calendar, comment, commentary, datum, definition, diary, dispatch, entry, epistle, gloss, inscription, jotting, journal, letter, line, marginalia, mark, memo, memorandum, message, minute, missive, obiter dictum, observation, record, remark, reminder, scratch, scrawl, scribble, summary, thank-you, word; SEE CONCEPT *271*

note [n2] *symbol, often used in reference to music*
character, degree, figure, flat, indication, interval, key, lick*, mark, natural, pitch, representation, scale, sharp, sign, step, token, tone; SEE CONCEPTS *262,284*

note [n3] *attention, heed*
cognizance, mark, mind, notice, observance, observation, regard, remark; SEE CONCEPT *529*

note [v] *observe, perceive*
catch, clock, denote, descry, designate, dig, discern, discover, distinguish, document, enter, get a load of*, get an eyeful*, heed, indicate, jot down, mark, mention, notice, pick up on*, put down, record, register, remark, see, set down, spot, take in*, transcribe, view, write, write down; SEE CONCEPTS *34,626*

noted [adj] *famous, eminent*
acclaimed, celeb, celebrated, conspicuous, distinguished, esteemed, illustrious, leading, name, notable, notorious, of note, popular, prominent, recognized, redoubted, renowned, somebody*, star, well-known; SEE CONCEPT *568*

noteworthy [adj] *important*
boss*, conspicuous, cool*, evident, exceptional, extraordinary, heavy*, high-profile*, hot*, major-league*, manifest, meaningful, memorable, mind-blowing*, murder, nameable, notable, noticeable, observable, outstanding, patent, prominent, red-letter*, remarkable, serious, significant, something else*, splash*, stand-out*, super, terrific, the end*, underlined*, unique, unusual, utmost; SEE CONCEPTS *567,568*

nothing/nothingness [n] *emptiness, nonexistence*
annihilation, aught, blank, cipher, extinction, fly speck*, insignificancy, naught, nihility, nobody, nonbeing, nonentity, not anything, nought, nullity, obliteration, oblivion, shutout*, trifle, void, wind*, zero*, zilch*, zip; SEE CONCEPTS *407,707*

nothingness [n2] *insignificance*
pettiness, smallness, unimportance, worthlessness; SEE CONCEPT *668*

notice [n1] *observation*
apprehension, attention, care, cognizance, concern, consideration, ear, grasp, heed, mark, mind, note, observance, regard, remark, respect, thought, understanding; SEE CONCEPTS *34,532*

notice [n2] *announcement, information*
admonition, advertisement, advice, caution, caveat, circular, clue, comment, comments, communication, criticism, critique, cue, declaration, directive, enlightenment, goods*, handbill, info*, instruction, intelligence, intimation, know*, lowdown*, manifesto, memo, memorandum, news, note, notification, order, picture, poster, proclamation, remark, review, score, sign, squib*, story, tip, warning, whole story*, write-up; SEE CONCEPTS *271,274,278*

notice [v] *observe, perceive*
acknowledge, advert, allude, catch, clock, descry, detect, dig*, discern, distinguish, espy, flash on*, get a load of*, heed, look at, make out*, mark, mind, note, pick up on, recognize, refer, regard, remark, see, spot, take in; SEE CONCEPTS 34,626

noticeable [adj] *conspicuous, evident*
apparent, appreciable, arresting, arrestive, big as life*, can't miss it*, clear, distinct, eye-catching, manifest, marked, notable, noteworthy, observable, obvious, open and shut*, outstanding, palpable, patent, perceptible, plain, pointed, prominent, remarkable, salient, sensational, signal, spectacular, striking, under one's nose*, unmistakable; SEE CONCEPTS 529,537,567

notify [v] *inform*
acquaint, advise, air, alert, announce, apprise, assert, blazon, brief, broadcast, cable, caution, circulate, clue in, convey, cue, debrief, declare, disclose, disseminate, divulge, enlighten, express, fill in, give, herald, hint, let in on, let know, make known, mention, pass out, post, proclaim, promulgate, publish, radio, report, reveal, send word, speak, spread, state, suggest, talk, teach, telephone, tell, tip off, vent, warn, wire, wise up*, write; SEE CONCEPTS 60,79

notion [n1] *belief, idea*
angle, apprehension, approach, assumption, awareness, clue, comprehension, conceit, concept, conception, consciousness, consideration, cue, discernment, flash, hint, image, imagination, impression, inclination, indication, inkling, insight, intellection, intimation, intuition, judgment, knowledge, opinion, penetration, perception, sentiment, slant, spark, suggestion, telltale, thought, twist, understanding, view, wind, wrinkle; SEE CONCEPTS 529,532,689

notion [n2] *whim, desire*
caprice, conceit, fancy, humor, imagination, impulse, inclination, wish; SEE CONCEPT 20

notoriety [n] *reputation*
ballyhoo*, celebrity, center stage*, dishonor, disrepute, éclat*, fame, flak*, infamy, ink*, name*, obloquy, opprobrium, renown, rep*, scandal, splash*, spotlight*, wise*; SEE CONCEPTS 388,411

notorious [adj] *known for a trait, often an unadmirable one*
belled, blatant, crying, dishonorable, disreputable, flagrant, glaring, ill-famed, infamous, leading, noted, obvious, open, opprobrious, overt, patent, popular, prominent, questionable, scandalous, shady, shameful, undisputed, wanted, well-known, wicked; SEE CONCEPT 404

notwithstanding [adv/prep] *although, however*
after all, against, at any rate, but, despite, for all that, however, in any case, in any event, in spite of, nevertheless, nonetheless, on the other hand, regardless of, though, to the contrary, withal, yet; SEE CONCEPT 544

nourish [v] *feed, care for*
attend, cherish, comfort, cultivate, encourage, foster, furnish, maintain, nurse, nurture, promote, provide, supply, support, sustain, tend; SEE CONCEPTS 140,295

nourishing [adj] *healthful*
alimentative, beneficial, health-giving, healthy, nutrient, nutrimental, nutritious, nutritive, wholesome; SEE CONCEPTS 462,537

nourishment [n] *food*
aliment, diet, feed, foodstuff, home cooking*, maintenance, nutriment, nutrition, pabulum, pap*, provender, support, sustenance, viands, victuals, vittles*; SEE CONCEPT 457

novel [n] *fictional book*
best-seller, cliff-hanger, fiction, narrative, novelette, novella, paperback, potboiler*, prose, romance, story, tale, yarn*; SEE CONCEPT 280

novel [adj] *new, original*
at cutting edge*, atypical, avant-garde, breaking new ground*, contemporary, different, far cry*, fresh, funky*, innovative, just out*, modernistic, neoteric, newfangled, new-fashioned, now*, odd, offbeat, peculiar, rare, recent, singular, strange, uncommon, unfamiliar, unique, unusual; SEE CONCEPTS 564,578,797

novelty [n1] *newness, originality*
change, crazy*, creation, dernier cri*, freshness, innovation, last word*, modernity, mutation, newfangled contraption, oddball, oddity, original, origination, permutation, recentness, sport*, strangeness, surprise, unfamiliarity, uniqueness, vicissitude, weird*; SEE CONCEPTS 665,697,715

novelty [n2] *trinket, gadget*
bagatelle*, bauble, bibelot*, conversation piece, curio, curiosity, gewgaw*, gimcrack*, gimmick, item, knick-knack, memento, objet d'art*, oddity, souvenir, trifle, whatnot*; SEE CONCEPTS 260,446

novice [n] *person just learning something*
amateur, apprentice, beginner, colt*, convert*, cub*, first of May*, fledgling, greenhorn, gremlin, know from nothing*, learner, mark*, neophyte, newcomer, new kid on the block*, novitiate, plebe, postulant, prentice, probationer, proselyte, punk*, pupil, recruit, rookie, starter, student, tenderfoot*, trainee; SEE CONCEPTS 348,350,423

now [adv] *presently*
any more, at once, at the moment, at this moment, at this time, away, directly, first off, forthwith, here and now, immediately, in a minute, in a moment, in nothing flat, instanter, instantly, just now, like now*, momentarily, nowadays, on the double*, PDQ*, promptly, pronto*, right away, right now, soon, straightaway, these days, this day, today; SEE CONCEPTS 812,820

noxious [adj] *deadly, injurious*
baneful, corrupting, dangerous, deleterious, destructive, detrimental, fetid, foul, harmful, hurtful, insalubrious, insalutary, noisome, pernicious, pestiferous, pestilent, pestilential, poisonous, putrid, sickly, spoiled, stinking, toxic, unhealthful, unhealthy, unwholesome, venomous, virulent; SEE CONCEPTS 485,537

nuance [n] *slight difference; shading*
dash, degree, distinction, gradation, hint, implication, nicety, refinement, shade, shadow, soupçon, subtlety, suggestion, suspicion, tinge, touch, trace; SEE CONCEPT 665

nub [n1] *core, gist*
basic, bottom line*, crux, essence, heart*, kernel, meat*, meat and potatoes*, nitty-gritty*, nubbin, nucleus, pith, point, short, substance, upshot; SEE CONCEPTS 661,682,826

nub [n2] *bump, knot*
bulge, knob, lump, node, protuberance, swelling; SEE CONCEPT 471

no
nu

nuclear weapon [n] *explosive driven by nuclear energy*
A-bomb, atomic bomb, atomic weapon, doomsday machine*, H-bomb, hydrogen bomb, mininuke*, mirv*, MX*, neutron bomb, nuke*; SEE CONCEPT *500*

nucleus [n] *core; basis for something's beginning*
bud, center, crux, embryo, focus, foundation, germ, heart, hub, kernel, matter, nub, pivot, premise, principle, seed, spark; SEE CONCEPTS *393,826,828*

nude [adj] *without clothes, covering*
au naturel*, bald, bare, bare-skinned, buck naked*, dishabille*, disrobed, exposed, garmentless, in birthday suit, in one's skin*, in the altogether*, naked, peeled*, raw, skin, stark, stark-naked*, stripped, unattired, unclad, unclothed, uncovered, undraped, undressed, wearing only a smile*, without a stitch*; SEE CONCEPT *485*

nudge [n/v] *bump, elbow*
dig, jab, jog, poke, prod, punch, push, shove, tap, touch; SEE CONCEPTS *208,612*

nugget [n] *lump, solid piece; often of metal ore*
asset, bullion, chunk, clod, clump, gold, hunk, ingot, mass, plum, rock, treasure, wad*; SEE CONCEPT *471*

nuisance [n] *annoyance; annoying person*
besetment, blister, bore, bother, botheration, botherment, bum*, creep, drag*, drip*, exasperation, frump, gadfly, headache*, inconvenience, infliction, insect*, irritant, irritation, louse, nag*, nudge*, offense, pain, pain in the neck*, pest, pester, pesterer, pill*, plague, poor excuse*, problem, terror, trouble, vexation; SEE CONCEPTS *412,674*

null [adj] *ineffectual, valueless*
absent, bad, barren, characterless, imaginary, ineffective, inefficacious, inoperative, invalid, negative, nonexistent, nothing, null and void*, powerless, unavailing, unreal, unsanctioned, useless, vain, void, worthless; SEE CONCEPTS *560,570*

nullify [v] *cancel, revoke*
abate, abolish, abrogate, annihilate, annul, ax, blue pencil*, bring to naught*, call all bets off*, compensate, confine, counteract, counterbalance, countervail, disannul, forget it*, invalidate, kill*, limit, negate, neutralize, nig*, offset, quash*, render null and void*, renege, renig*, repeal, rescind, restrict, scratch*, scrub*, squash*, stamp out*, take out*, torpedo*, trash*, undo, veto, vitiate, void, wash out*, wipe out*, zap*; SEE CONCEPTS *50,88,121,234*

numb [adj] *deadened, insensitive*
aloof, anesthetized, apathetic, asleep, benumbed, callous, casual, comatose, dazed, dead, detached, disinterested, frozen, immobilized, incurious, indifferent, insensate, insensible, insentient, lethargic, listless, numbed, paralyzed, phlegmatic, remote, senseless, stupefied, stuporous, torpid, unconcerned, unconscious, uncurious, unfeeling, uninterested; SEE CONCEPTS *403,609*

numb [v] *deaden*
anesthetize, benumb, blunt, chill, desensitize, dull, freeze, frost, immobilize, obtund, paralyze, stun, stupefy; SEE CONCEPTS *250,255*

number [n1] *unit of the mathematical system*
cardinal, character, chiffer, cipher, count, decimal, denominator, digit, emblem, figure, folio, fraction, googol, integer, numeral, numerator, ordinal, prime, representation, sign, statistic, sum, symbol, total, whole number; SEE CONCEPTS *765,784*

number [n2] *aggregate, bunch*
abundance, amount, caboodle*, collection, company, conglomeration, crowd, estimate, flock, horde, jillion*, lot, manifoldness, many, multitude, plenitude, plenty, product, quantity, slew*, sum, throng, total, totality, umpteen*, volume, whole, zillion*; SEE CONCEPTS *432,787*

number [v] *count, calculate*
account, add, add up, aggregate, amount, come, computer, count heads*, count noses*, count off, enumerate, estimate, figure in, figure out, include, keep tabs, numerate, reckon, run, run down, run into, run to, sum, take account of, tale, tally, tell, tick off*, total, tote*, tote up*; SEE CONCEPT *764*

numbered [adj] *limited in number*
categorized, checked, contained, counted, designated, doomed, enumerated, fated, fixed, included, indicated, marked, specified, told, totalled; SEE CONCEPT *554*

numberless [adj] *infinite*
countless, endless, heaps*, incalculable, innumerable, jillion, many, multitudinous, myriad, no end of*, no end to*, numerous, umpteen*, uncountable, uncounted, unnumbered, untold, zillion*; SEE CONCEPTS *482,762,781*

numeral [n] *symbol of mathematical system*
character, chiffer, cipher, digit, figure, integer, number; SEE CONCEPTS *284,784*

numeric/numerical [adj] *concerning mathematics*
algebraic, algorithmic, arithmetic, arithmetical, binary, differential, digital, exponent, exponential, fraction, fractional, integral, logarithm, logarithmic, mathematical, numeral, numerary, statistical; SEE CONCEPT *762*

numerous [adj] *many, abundant*
big, copious, diverse, great, infinite, large, legion, lousy with*, multifarious, multitudinal, multitudinous, plentiful, populous, profuse, rife, scads*, several, sundry, thick, umpteen*, various, voluminous, zillion*; SEE CONCEPTS *762,781*

nun [n] *woman in religious order*
abbess, anchorite, canoness, mother superior, postulant, prioress, religious woman, sister, vestal; SEE CONCEPT *361*

nuptial [adj] *concerning marriage*
bridal, conjugal, connubial, espousal, marital, married, matrimonial, spousal, wedded, wedding; SEE CONCEPT *555*

nuptials [n] *marriage ceremony*
bridal, espousal, marriage, matrimony, spousal, wedding; SEE CONCEPT *297*

nurse [n] *person who tends to sick, cares for someone*
assistant, attendant, baby sitter, caretaker, foster parent, medic, minder, nurse practitioner, practical nurse, registered nurse, RN, sitter, therapist, wet nurse; SEE CONCEPTS *357,414*

nurse [v] *care for, tend*
advance, aid, attend, baby-sit, cherish, cradle, cultivate, encourage, father, feed, forward, foster, further, harbor, humor, immunize, indulge, inoculate, irradiate, keep alive, keep an eye on*, keep tabs on*, look after, medicate, minister to, mother, nourish, nurture, pamper, preserve, promote, see to, serve, sit, succor, support, take care

of, take charge of, treat, vaccinate, wait on, watch out for, watch over; SEE CONCEPTS 110,140

nurse [v2] *give milk, usually from breast*
bottle-feed, breast-feed, cradle, dry-nurse, feed, give suck, lactate, nourish, nurture, suck, suckle, wet-nurse; SEE CONCEPTS 140,295

nurture [n] *development, nourishment*
breeding, care, diet, discipline, edibles, education, feed, food, instruction, nutriment, provender, provisions, rearing, subsistence, sustenance, training, upbringing, viands, victuals; SEE CONCEPTS 457,712

nurture [v] *feed, care for*
back, bolster, bring up, cherish, cultivate, develop, discipline, educate, foster, instruct, nourish, nurse, nursle, provide, raise, rear, school, support, sustain, tend, train, uphold; SEE CONCEPTS 110,140,295

nut [n1] *seed of fruit, vegetable*
achene, caryopsis, kernel, stone, utricle; SEE CONCEPT 428

nut [n2] *crazy, overenthusiastic person*
bedlamite, bigot, crackpot, crank, dement, eccentric, fanatic, fiend, freak, harebrain*, loony*, lunatic, maniac, non compos mentis, screwball*, zealot; SEE CONCEPTS 412,423

nutrition [n] *food*
diet, menu, nourishment, nutriment, subsistence, sustenance, victuals; SEE CONCEPT 457

nutritious [adj] *healthy*
alimental, alimentative, balanced, beneficial, good, healthful, health-giving, invigorating, nourishing, nutrient, nutrimental, nutritive, salubrious, salutary, strengthening, wholesome; SEE CONCEPT 462

nuts/nutty [adj] *mentally deranged*
absurd, batty*, bedlamite, cracked*, crazy, daffy, daft, demented, eccentric, enthusiastic, foolish, gung ho*, harebrained*, insane, irrational, keen, kooky, loony, lunatic, mad, out of one's mind*, ridiculous, touched, unusual, wacky*, warm, zealous; SEE CONCEPT 403

nuzzle [v] *cuddle*
bundle, burrow, caress, fondle, nestle, nudge, pet, snug, snuggle; SEE CONCEPTS 190,612

nymph [n] *female nature spirit*
dryad, fairy, goddess, mermaid, naiad, nymphet, spirit, sprite, sylph; SEE CONCEPTS 415,424

O

oaf [n] *person who is clumsy, stupid*
beast, blunderer, bruiser, brute, chump*, clod, clown, dolt, dumb ox*, dunce, fool, goon*, idiot, imbecile, klutz*, loser, lout*, moron, nincompoop*, ox*, sap*, simpleton; SEE CONCEPT 412

oasis [n] *refuge*
haven, resting place, retreat, sanctuary, sanctum, spot, tract; SEE CONCEPT 515

oath [n1] *promise*
adjuration, affidavit, affirmation, avowal, bond, contract, deposition, pledge, profession, sworn declaration, sworn statement, testimony, vow, word, word of honor; SEE CONCEPTS 71,278

oath [n2] *curse*
blasphemy, cuss*, cuss word*, dirty name*, dirty

word*, expletive, four-letter word*, imprecation, malediction, no-no*, profanity, strong language, swearword; SEE CONCEPTS 54,278

obdurate [adj] *pigheaded, stubborn*
adamant, bullhead*, callous, cold fish*, dogged, firm, fixed, hanging tough*, hard, hard-boiled*, hard-hearted*, hard-nosed*, harsh, heartless, immovable, implacable, indurate, inexorable, inflexible, iron*, mean, mulish*, obstinate, perverse, relentless, rigid, set in stone*, stiff-necked*, thick-skinned*, tough, tough nut to crack*, unbending, uncompassionate, uncompromising, uncooperative, unemotional, unfeeling, unimpressible, unrelenting, unshakable, unsympathetic, unyielding; SEE CONCEPTS 401,542

obedience [n] *good behavior; submissiveness*
accordance, acquiescence, agreement, compliance, conformability, conformity, deference, docility, duteousness, dutifulness, duty, manageability, meekness, observance, orderliness, quietness, respect, reverence, servility, submission, subservience, tameness, tractability, willingness; SEE CONCEPTS 411,633

obedient [adj] *well-behaved; submissive*
acquiescent, amenable, at one's beck and call*, attentive, biddable, complaisant, compliant, controllable, deferential, devoted, docile, docious, duteous, dutiful, faithful, governable, honoring, in one's clutches*, in one's pocket*, in one's power*, law-abiding, loyal, obsequent, obliging, observant, on a string*, pliant, regardful, resigned, respectful, reverential, sheeplike*, subservient, tame, tractable, under control, venerating, well-trained, willing, wrapped around finger*, yielding; SEE CONCEPTS 401,404

obeisance [n] *salutation*
allegiance, bending of the knee*, bow, curtsy, deference, fealty, genuflection, homage, honor, kowtow*, loyalty, praise, respect, reverence, salaam*; SEE CONCEPTS 154,384

obese [adj] *very overweight*
adipose, avoirdupois, corpulent, fat, fleshy*, gross*, heavy, outsize, paunchy, plump, porcine, portly, pudgy, rotund, stout; SEE CONCEPT 491

obey [v] *conform, give in*
abide by, accede, accept, accord, acquiesce, act upon, adhere to, agree, answer, assent, be loyal to, be ruled by, bow to*, carry out, comply, concur, discharge, do as one says, do one's bidding, do one's duty, do what is expected, do what one is told, embrace, execute, follow, fulfill, get in line*, give way*, heed, hold fast*, keep, knuckle under*, live by, mind, observe, perform, play second fiddle*, respond, serve, submit, surrender, take orders, toe the line*; SEE CONCEPTS 91,136

obituary [n] *notice of person's death*
announcement, death notice, eulogy, mortuary tribute, necrology, obit, register; SEE CONCEPTS 268,270

object [n1] *thing able to be seen/felt/perceived*
article, body, bulk, commodity, doodad*, doohickey*, entity, fact, gadget, gizmo*, item, mass, matter, phenomenon, reality, something, substance, thingamajig*, volume, whatchamacallit*, widget*; SEE CONCEPT 433

object [n2] *purpose, use*
aim, design, duty, end, end in view, end purpose, function, goal, idea, intent, intention, mark, mission, motive, objective, point, reason, target, view, wish; SEE CONCEPT 659

object [*n3*] *aim, recipient*
butt*, focus, ground zero*, receiver, target, victim, zero*; SEE CONCEPTS *124,532*

object [*v*] *disagree, argue against*
balk, be displeased, challenge, complain, crab*, criticize, cross, demur, deprecate, disapprove, disavow, discommend, discountenance, disesteem, dispute, dissent, except, expostulate, frown, go-one-on-one*, gripe, grouse, inveigh, kick*, make a stink*, mix it up with*, oppose, protest, rail, raise objection, rant, rave, remonstrate, sound off*, spurn, squawk*, storm, take exception, take on, tangle*; SEE CONCEPTS *12,21,46*

objection [*n*] *argument, disagreement*
cavil, censure, challenge, counter-argument, criticism, declination, demur, demurral, demurring, difficulty, disapprobation, disapproval, discontent, disesteem, disinclination, dislike, displeasure, dissatisfaction, doubt, exception, grievance, gripe, hesitation, kick, niggle*, odium, opposition, protest, protestation, question, rejection, reluctance, remonstrance, remonstration, repugnancy, revilement, scruple, shrinking, squawk*, stink*, unwillingness; SEE CONCEPTS *21,46,410,689*

objectionable [*adj*] *not nice; unpleasant*
abhorrent, censurable, deplorable, disagreeable, dislikable, displeasing, distasteful, exceptionable, ill-favored, inadmissible, indecorous, inexpedient, insufferable, intolerable, invidious, loathsome, lousy, murder, noxious, obnoxious, offensive, opprobrious, poison, regrettable, repellent, reprehensible, repugnant, repulsive, revolting, unacceptable, undesirable, unfit, unpalatable, unsatisfactory, unseemly, unsuitable, unwanted, unwelcome; SEE CONCEPTS *548,558,570*

objective [*n*] *aim, goal*
ambition, aspiration, design, end, end in view*, ground zero*, intention, mark, mission, object, purpose, target, zero*; SEE CONCEPT *659*

objective [*adj*] *fair, impartial*
cold, cool, detached, disinterested, dispassionate, equitable, evenhanded, impersonal, judicial, just, like it is*, nondiscriminatory, nonpartisan, open-minded*, straight, strictly business*, unbiased, uncolored, unemotional, uninvolved, unprejudiced, unprepossessed; SEE CONCEPTS *403,542*

objectively [*adv*] *impartially*
considerately, detachedly, disinterestedly, dispassionately, equitably, evenhandedly, indifferently, justly, neutrally, on the up and up*, openmindedly*, soberly, squarely, with an open mind*, with impartiality, with objectivity, without favor, without prejudice; SEE CONCEPTS *542,544*

obligate [*v*] *require*
astrict, bind, constrain, force, indebt, make indebted, oblige, restrain, restrict; SEE CONCEPTS *53,130,646*

obligation [*n*] *responsibility*
accountability, accountableness, agreement, bond, burden, business, call, cause, charge, chit*, commitment, committal, compulsion, conscience, constraint, contract, debit, debt, devoir, due bill, dues, duty, engagement, IOU*, liability, must, necessity, need, occasion, onus, ought, part, place, promise, requirement, restraint, right, trust, understanding; SEE CONCEPTS *329,335,388,645*

obligatory [*adj*] *essential, required*
binding, coercive, compulsatory, compulsory, de rigueur, enforced, imperative, imperious, mandatory, necessary, requisite, unavoidable; SEE CONCEPT *546*

oblige [*v1*] *require*
bind, coerce, command, compel, constrain, force, impel, make, necessitate, obligate, shotgun*; SEE CONCEPTS *14,242,646*

oblige [*v2*] *do a favor or kindness*
accommodate, aid, assist, avail, bend over backward*, benefit, come around, contribute, convenience, don't make waves*, favor, fill the bill*, fit in, go fifty-fifty*, gratify, grin and bear it*, help, indulge, make a deal*, make room*, meet halfway*, please, profit, put oneself out*, roll with it*, serve, swim with the tide*, take it*, toe the mark*; SEE CONCEPTS *110,136,384*

obliging [*adj*] *friendly, helpful*
accommodating, agreeable, amiable, cheerful, civil, complaisant, considerate, cooperative, courteous, eager to please, easy, easygoing, good-humored, good-natured, hospitable, kind, lenient, mild, polite, willing; SEE CONCEPTS *401,404*

oblique [*adj1*] *slanting; at an angle*
angled, askance, askew, aslant, asymmetrical, awry, bent, cater-cornered, crooked, diagonal, distorted, diverging, inclined, inclining, leaning, on the bias, pitched, pitching, sideways, skew, slanted, sloped, sloping, strained, tilted, tilting, tipped, tipping, turned, twisted; SEE CONCEPTS *485,490*

oblique [*adj2*] *indirect, evasive*
backhanded, circuitous, circular, circumlocutory, collateral, devious, implied, obliquitous, obscure, roundabout, sidelong, vague; SEE CONCEPT *267*

obliterate [*v*] *destroy*
annihilate, ax*, black out*, blot out*, blue pencil*, bog, cancel, cover, cut, defeat, delete, do in*, efface, eliminate, eradicate, erase, expunge, exterminate, extirpate, finish, finish off*, kill, knock off*, knock out*, KO*, level*, liquidate, mark out*, nix*, obscure, off, ravage, root out*, rub off*, rub out*, scratch, scrub, shoot down, sink, smash, squash, take apart, take out*, torpedo* total*, trash*, wash out*, waste, wipe off face of earth*, wipe out*, X-out*, zap*; SEE CONCEPT *252*

oblivion [*n1*] *mental blankness*
abeyance, amnesia, carelessness, disregard, forgetfulness, inadvertence, indifference, insensibility, insensibleness, Lethe*, neglect, nirvana*, obliviousness, unawareness, unconcern, unconsciousness, unmindfulness; SEE CONCEPTS *410,633*

oblivion [*n2*] *nothingness, obscurity*
blackness, darkness, eclipse, emptiness, extinction, limbo, nihility, nirvana*, nonexistence, nothing, nowhere*, nullity, out there*, void; SEE CONCEPTS *407,672,679*

oblivious [*adj*] *unaware, ignorant*
absent, absentminded, absorbed, abstracted, amnesic, blind*, blundering, careless, deaf*, disregardful, distracted, dreamy, forgetful, forgetting, gone, heedless, inattentive, incognizant, inconversant, insensible, neglectful, negligent, not all there*, out to lunch*, overlooking, preoccupied, regardless, spacey*, strung out*, unacquainted, unconcerned, unconscious, undiscerning, unfamiliar, uninformed, uninstructed, unknowing, un-

mindful, unnoticing, unobservant, unrecognizing, unwitting, zonked*; SEE CONCEPTS 402,403,542

oblong [adj] elongated and rounded
egg-shaped, ellipsoidal, elliptical, elongate, long, oval, ovaliform, ovaloid, ovate, ovated, ovoid, rectangular; SEE CONCEPT 486

obnoxious [adj] offensive, repulsive
abhorrent, abominable, annoying, awful, beastly*, big mouth*, detestable, disagreeable, disgusting, dislikable, displeasing, foul, gross*, hateable, hateful, heel, horrid, insufferable, invidious, loathsome, mean, nasty, nauseating, objectionable, odious, off-color*, ornery, pain in the neck*, pesky*, pestiferous, pill*, repellent, reprehensible, repugnant, revolting, rotten, sickening, stinking, unpleasant; SEE CONCEPTS 267,401,542

obscene [adj] indecent, offensive, immoral
atrocious, barnyard*, bawdy, blue*, coarse, crude, dirty*, disgusting, evil, filthy, foul, gross, heinous, hideous, horrible, immodest, improper, impure, lascivious, lewd, licentious, loathsome, loose*, lustful, nasty, noisome, outrageous, porno*, pornographic, profane, prurient, rank*, raunchy*, raw, repellent, repugnant, ribald, salacious, scabrous, scatological, scurrilous, shameless, shocking, sickening, smutty*, suggestive, unchaste, unclean, unwholesome, vile, wanton, wicked, X-rated*; SEE CONCEPTS 267,372,545

obscenity [n] indecency, immorality; vulgarism
abomination, affront, atrocity, bawdiness, blight, blueness*, coarseness, curse, dirtiness, dirty name*, dirty word*, evil, filthiness, foulness, four-letter word*, immodesty, impropriety, impurity, indecency, indelicacy, lewdness, licentiousness, lubricity, offense, outrage, porn*, pornography, profanity, prurience, salacity, scatology, scurrility, sleaze*, smut*, smuttiness, suggestiveness, swearword, vileness, vulgarity, wrong, X-rating*; SEE CONCEPTS 278,645

obscure [adj1] not easily understood
abstruse, ambiguous, arcane, clear as mud*, complicated, concealed, confusing, cryptic, dark, deep, dim, doubtful, enigmatic, enigmatical, esoteric, far-out, hazy, hidden, illegible, illogical, impenetrable, incomprehensible, inconceivable, incredible, indecisive, indefinite, indeterminate, indistinct, inexplicable, inscrutable, insoluble, intricate, involved, mysterious, occult, opaque, recondite, unaccountable, unbelievable, unclear, undefined, unfathomable, unintelligible, vague; SEE CONCEPT 529

obscure [adj2] cloudy, shadowy
blurred, caliginous, clouded, dark, dense, dim, dusk, dusky, faint, fuliginous, gloomy, indistinct, lightless, murky, obfuscated, shady, somber, tenebrous, umbrageous, unilluminated, unlit, veiled; SEE CONCEPT 617

obscure [adj3] out-of-the-way, little-known
abstruse, arcane, blind, cabalistic, close, covered, cryptic, dark, deep, devious, distant, enigmatic, esoteric, far, far-off, hidden, humble, inaccessible, inconspicuous, inglorious, invisible, irrelevant, lonesome, lowly, minor, mysterious, nameless, odd, oracular, orphic, rare, recondite, remote, removed, reticent, retired, secluded, secret, secretive, seldom seen, sequestered, solitary, undisclosed, undistinguished, unheard-of, unhonored, unimportant, unknown, unnoted, unseen, unsung; SEE CONCEPT 576

obscure [v] conceal, hide
adumbrate, becloud, bedim, befog, belie, blear, blind, block, block out, blur, camouflage, cloak, cloud, cloud the issue*, con, confuse, cover, cover up, darken, dim, disguise, double-talk*, eclipse, equivocate, falsify, fog, fuzz, gloom, gray, haze, mask, misrepresent, mist, muddy, muddy the waters*, murk, obfuscate, overcast, overcloud, overshadow, pettifog*, screen, shade, shadow, shroud, stonewall*, throw up smoke screen*, veil, wrap; SEE CONCEPTS 16,63,172,188

obsequious [adj] groveling, submissive
abject, beggarly, brownnosing*, complacent, compliable, compliant, cringing, crouching, deferential, enslaved, fawning, flattering, ingratiating, kowtowing*, menial, obeisant, oily*, parasitic, parasitical, prostrate, respectful, servile, slavish, sneaking, sniveling, spineless*, stipendiary, subject, submissive, subordinate, subservient, sycophantic, toadying*, unctuous; SEE CONCEPTS 401,404

observable [adj] apparent
appreciable, clear, detectable, discernible, discoverable, evident, noticeable, obvious, open, palpable, patent, perceivable, perceptible, recognizable, sensible, tangible, visible; SEE CONCEPTS 529,576

observance [n1] attention to, knowledge of something
acknowledgment, acquittal, acquittance, adherence, awareness, carrying out, celebration, cognizance, compliance, discharge, fidelity, fulfillment, heed, heeding, honoring, keeping, mark, mind, note, notice, obedience, observation, performance, regard, remark, satisfaction; SEE CONCEPTS 409,410,633

observance [n2] ceremony, rite
celebration, ceremonial, custom, fashion, form, formality, liturgy, performance, practice, ritual, rule, service, tradition; SEE CONCEPTS 377,384,688

observant [adj] alert, watchful
advertent, alive, attentive, bright, clear-sighted*, comprehending, considering, contemplating, correct, deducing, detecting, discerning, discovering, discriminating, eager, eagle-eyed*, heedful, intelligent, intentive, interested, keen, mindful, not missing a trick*, obedient, observative, on one's toes*, on the ball*, penetrating, perceptive, questioning, quick, regardful, searching, sensitive, sharp, sharp-eyed*, surveying, understanding, vigilant, wide-awake*; SEE CONCEPTS 402,403

observation [n1] attention, scrutiny
ascertainment, check, cognition, cognizance, conclusion, consideration, detection, estimation, examination, experience, heedfulness, information, inspection, investigation, knowledge, mark, measurement, mind, monitoring, note, notice, noticing, once-over*, overlook, perception, probe, recognizing, regard, remark, research, review, search, study, supervision, surveillance, view, watching; SEE CONCEPTS 409,410

observation [n2] comment on something scrutinized
annotation, catch phrase, comeback, commentary, crack*, finding, mention, mouthful*, note, obiter dictum, opinion, pronouncement, reflection, remark, saying, say so*, thought, utterance, wisecrack; SEE CONCEPTS 51,278

ob
ob

observe [v1] *see, notice*

beam, behold, catch, contemplate, detect, dig, discern, discover, distinguish, eagle-eye*, espy, examine, eyeball*, flash*, get a load of*, get an eyeful of*, inspect, keep one's eye on*, lamp*, look at, make out*, mark, mind, monitor, note, pay attention to, perceive, pick up on*, read, recognize, regard, scrutinize, spot, spy, study, survey, take in*, view, watch, witness; SEE CONCEPTS 24,34,103,265,626

observe [v2] *comment, remark*

animadvert, commentate, declare, mention, mouth off*, note, opine, say, state, wisecrack; SEE CONCEPT 51

observe [v3] *celebrate, commemorate*

dedicate, hold, honor, keep, remember, respect, revere, reverence, solemnize, venerate; SEE CONCEPT 377

observe [v4] *abide by, obey*

adhere, adopt, comply, comply with, conform, follow, fulfill, heed, honor, keep, mind, perform, respect; SEE CONCEPTS 91,384

obsessed [adj] *consumed, driven about belief, desire*

bedeviled, beset, bewitched, captivated, controlled, dogged*, dominated, eat sleep and breathe*, engrossed, fiendish, fixated, gripped, harassed, haunted, have on the brain*, held, hooked, hung up on*, immersed in, infatuated, into*, overpowered, plagued*, possessed, preoccupied, prepossessed, really into*, seized, taken over, tied up*, tormented, troubled, turned on, up to here in*, wound up with*, wrapped up in*; SEE CONCEPTS 403,404

obsession [n] *fixation; consumption with belief, desire*

attraction, ax to grind*, bug in ear*, case*, complex, compulsion, concrete idea, craze*, crush, delusion, enthusiasm, fancy, fascination, fetish, hang-up*, idée fixe, infatuation, mania, monkey*, must, neurosis, one-track mind*, passion, phantom, phobia, preoccupation, something on the brain*, thing*, tiger by the tail*; SEE CONCEPTS 20,410,529,689,690

obsolete [adj] *no longer in use, in vogue*

anachronistic, ancient, antediluvian, antiquated, antique, archaic, bygone, dated, dead, dead and gone*, dinosaur*, discarded, disused, done for*, dusty, extinct, fossil, gone, had it*, has-been*, horse and buggy*, kaput*, moldy*, moth-eaten*, old, old-fashioned, old-hat, old-school, out*, outmoded, out-of-date, out-of-fashion, outworn, passé, stale, superannuated, superseded, timeworn, unfashionable; SEE CONCEPTS 539,560,589

obstacle [n] *impediment, barrier*

bar, block, booby trap*, bump*, catch, Catch-22*, check, clog*, crimp*, difficulty, disincentive, encumbrance, hamper, handicap, hang-up*, hardship, hindrance, hitch*, hurdle, interference, interruption, joker*, monkey wrench*, mountain, obstruction, restriction, rub*, snag, stumbling block*, traverse, vicissitude; SEE CONCEPTS 470,532,666,674

obstinate [adj] *stubborn, determined*

adamant, cantankerous, contradictory, contrary, contumacious, convinced, dead set on*, dogged, dogmatic, firm, hardened, headstrong, heady, immovable, indomitable, inflexible, intractable, intransigent, locked in*, mulish*, obdurate, opinionated, opinionative, persistent, pertinacious, perverse, pigheaded*, recalcitrant, refractory, relentless, resolved, restive, self-willed, steadfast, strong-minded, tenacious, unalterable, unflinching, unmanageable, unyielding, willful; SEE CONCEPTS 401,542

obstruct [v] *prevent, restrict*

arrest, bar, barricade, block, check, choke, clog, close, congest, crab, curb, cut off, drag one's feet*, fill, foul up, frustrate, get in the way*, hamper, hamstring*, hang up*, hide, hinder, hold up, impede, inhibit, interfere, interrupt, mask, monkey with*, obscure, occlude, plug, restrain, retard, sandbag*, shield, shut off, slow down, stall, stonewall*, stop, stopper, stymie*, terminate, throttle, thwart, trammel, weigh down; SEE CONCEPTS 5,121,130

obstruction [n] *obstacle, impediment*

bar, barricade, barrier, block, blockage, blocking, booby trap*, check, checkmate*, circumvention, difficulty, gridlock*, hamper, hindrance, hurdle, interference, jam*, lock, monkey wrench*, mountain*, restraint, roadblock*, snag, stop, stoppage, stumbling block*, trammel, trouble, wall; SEE CONCEPTS 470,532,666,674

obtain [v] *get, acquire*

access, accomplish, achieve, annex, attain, beg borrow or steal*, capture, chalk up*, collect, come by, compass, cop*, corral, drum up*, earn, effect, fetch, gain, gather, get at, get hold of*, get one's hands on*, glean, gobble up*, grab, have, hoard, inherit, invade, lay up, make use of, nab*, occupy, pick up, pocket*, procure, purchase, reach, realize, reap, receive, recover, retrieve, salvage, save, score, scrape together, scrape up, secure, seize, snag, take, wangle, win; SEE CONCEPT 120

obtainable [adj] *achievable, available*

at hand*, attainable, derivable, duck soup*, gettable, in stock, no problem*, no sweat*, on deck*, on offer*, on tap*, piece of cake*, procurable, purchasable, pushover, ready, realizable, securable, there for the taking*, to be had*; SEE CONCEPTS 528,576

obtrusive [adj] *pushy, obvious*

bulging, busy, forward, impertinent, importunate, interfering, intrusive, jutting, meddlesome, meddling, nosy, noticeable, officious, presumptuous, projecting, prominent, protruding, protuberant, prying, sticking out; SEE CONCEPTS 401,542

obtuse [adj1] *slow to understand*

dense, dopey*, dull*, dumb, imperceptive, insensitive, opaque, slow on uptake*, stolid, thick, uncomprehending, unintelligent; SEE CONCEPT 402

obtuse [adj2] *blunt, not sharp*

round, rounded; SEE CONCEPTS 485,486

obviate [v] *make unnecessary*

anticipate, avert, block, counter, counteract, deter, do away with, forestall, forfend, hinder, interfere, interpose, intervene, preclude, prevent, remove, restrain, rule out, stave off, ward off; SEE CONCEPT 121

obvious [adj] *apparent, understandable*

accessible, barefaced, bright, clear, clear as a bell*, conclusive, conspicuous, discernible, distinct, distinguishable, evident, explicit, exposed, glaring, indisputable, in evidence, lucid, manifest, noticeable, observable, open, overt, palpable, patent, perceivable, perceptible, plain, precise, prominent, pronounced, public, recognizable, self-evident, self-explanatory, standing out,

straightforward, transparent, unconcealed, undeniable, undisguised, unmistakable, unsubtle, visible; SEE CONCEPTS *485,529*

occasion [n1] *chance*
break*, convenience, demand, excuse, incident,
instant, moment, need, occurrence, opening, opportunity, possibility, season, shot*, show, time,
use; SEE CONCEPT *693*

occasion [n2] *reason, cause*
antecedent, basis, call, circumstance, determinant, excuse, foundation, ground, grounds, incident, inducement, influence, justification,
motivation, motive, necessity, obligation, prompting, provocation, purpose, right, warrant; SEE
CONCEPT *661*

occasion [n3] *event, happening*
affair, celebration, circumstance, episode, experience, go*, goings-on*, happening, incident, instant, milepost*, milestone, moment, occurrence,
scene, thing*, time, while; SEE CONCEPTS *2,386*

occasion [v] *make happen, bring about*
breed, cause, create, do, effect, elicit, engender,
evoke, generate, give rise to, hatch, induce, influence, inspire, lead to, move, muster, originate,
persuade, produce, prompt, provoke, work up;
SEE CONCEPTS *68,242*

occasional [adj] *irregular, sporadic*
casual, desultory, especial, exceptional, exclusive, few, incidental, infrequent, intermittent, not
habitual, odd, off and on*, particular, random,
rare, scarce, seldom, semioccasional, special, specific, uncommon, unfrequent, unusual; SEE CON-
CEPTS *530,541*

occasionally [adv] *every now and then*
at intervals, at random, at times, every so often,
from time to time, hardly, infrequently, irregularly, now and again, once in a blue moon*, once
in a while, once or twice*, on occasion, periodically, seldom, sometimes, sporadically, uncommonly; SEE CONCEPTS *530,541*

occlude [v] *block, prevent*
choke, clog, close, close out, congest, curb, fill,
hinder, impede, leave out, lock out, obstruct,
plug, seal, shut, stopper, stop up, throttle; SEE
CONCEPTS *121,201*

occult [adj] *mysterious, secret; supernatural*
abstruse, acroamatic, arcane, cabalistic, concealed, deep, eerie, esoteric, hermetic, hidden,
invisible, magic, magical, mystic, mystical, obscure, orphic, preternatural, profound, psychic,
recondite, transmundane, unearthly, unknown,
unrevealed, veiled, weird; SEE CONCEPTS
576,582

occupancy [n] *residence of place*
control, deed, habitation, holding, inhabitance, inhabitancy, occupation, ownership, possession, retention, settlement, tenancy, tenure, term, title,
use; SEE CONCEPTS *518,710*

occupant [n] *person who resides in a place*
addressee, denizen, dweller, holder, householder,
incumbent, indweller, inhabitant, lessee, occupier, possessor, renter, resident, resider, tenant,
user; SEE CONCEPT *414*

occupation [n1] *profession, business*
activity, affair, calling, chosen work, craft, daily
grind*, day gig*, do, dodge*, employment,
game*, grindstone*, hang*, job, lick*, line, line
of work, métier, moonlight*, nine-to-five*, play*,
post, pursuit, racket*, rat race*, slot*, thing*,

trade, vocation, walk of life*, what one is into*,
work; SEE CONCEPTS *349,351,360*

occupation [n2] *control, possession*
habitation, holding, inhabitancy, inhabitation, occupancy, ownership, residence, settlement, tenancy, tenure, title, use; SEE CONCEPTS *518,710*

occupation [n3] *seizure, takeover*
attack, capture, conquest, entering, foreign rule,
invasion, subjugation; SEE CONCEPTS *86,90,320*

occupied [adj1] *busy*
active, clocked up*, employed, engaged, engrossed, head over heels*, tied up*, too much on
plate*, working; SEE CONCEPT *542*

occupied [adj2] *inhabited; in use*
busy, engaged, full, leased, lived-in*, peopled*,
populated, populous, rented, settled, taken, unavailable, utilized; SEE CONCEPT *560*

occupy [v1] *be busy with*
absorb, amuse, attend, be active with, be concerned with, busy, divert, employ, engage, engross, entertain, fill, hold attention, immerse,
interest, involve, keep busy, monopolize, preoccupy, soak, take up, tie up, utilize; SEE CONCEPTS
7,17,19,22

occupy [v2] *reside; use*
be established, be in command, be in residence,
cover, dwell, ensconce, establish, fill, hold, inhabit, involve, keep, live in, maintain, own, people, permeate, pervade, populate, possess,
remain, sit, stay, take up, tenant, utilize; SEE CON-
CEPTS *225,226*

occupy [v3] *seize, take over*
capture, conquer, garrison, hold, invade, keep,
obtain, overrun, take possession; SEE CONCEPTS
86,90,320

occur [v1] *take place, happen*
action, appear, arise, befall, be found, be present,
betide, chance, come about, come off*, come to
pass, cook*, crop up, develop, ensue, eventualize, eventuate, exist, follow, go, jell*, manifest,
materialize, obtain, present itself, result, shake*,
show, smoke*, take place, transpire, turn out, turn
up; SEE CONCEPTS *4,242*

occur [v2] *come to mind*
come to one*, cross one's mind*, dawn on*, expose, flash*, go through one's head*, hit, offer
itself, present itself, reveal, spring to mind*,
strike, suggest itself; SEE CONCEPTS *34,43*

occurrence [n] *happening, development*
accident, adventure, affair, appearance, circumstance, condition, contingency, emergency, episode, event, exigency, existence, incidence,
incident, instance, juncture, manifestation, materialization, occasion, pass, piece, proceeding, routine, scene, situation, state, thing*, transaction,
transpiration; SEE CONCEPTS *3,4,230,696*

ocean [n] *very large body of water*
blue*, bounding main*, brine, briny*, briny
deep*, Davy Jones's locker*, deep, drink*, high
seas*, main, pond, puddle, salt water, sea, sea-
way, Seven Seas, sink, tide; SEE CONCEPT *514*

odd/oddball [adj1] *unusual, abnormal*
atypical, avant-garde, bizarre, character, crazy,
curious, deviant, different, eccentric, erratic, exceptional, extraordinary, fantastic, flaky*, freak*,
freakish*, freaky*, funny, idiosyncratic, irregular, kinky*, kooky*, offbeat, off-the-wall*, outlandish, out of the ordinary, peculiar, quaint,
queer, rare, remarkable, singular, spacey*,
strange, uncanny, uncommon, unconventional,

ob
od

unique, way out*, weird, weirdo*, whimsical;
SEE CONCEPTS 404,542,564

odd [adj2] *miscellaneous, various*
accidental, casual, chance, contingent, different,
fluky*, fortuitous, fragmentary, incidental, irregular, occasional, odd-lot*, periodic, random, seasonal, sundry, varied; SEE CONCEPT 552

odd [adj3] *single, unmatched; uneven*
additional, alone, exceeding, individual, irregular, left, leftover, lone, lonely, over, over and
above, remaining, singular, sole, solitary, spare,
surplus, unconsumed, unitary, unpaired; SEE
CONCEPTS 480,577

oddity [n1] *abnormality*
anomaly, bizarreness, characteristic, conversation
piece, curiosity, eccentricity, extraordinariness,
freak, freakishness, idiosyncrasy, incongruity, irregularity, kink, oddness, outlandishness, peculiarity, phenomenon, queerness, quirk, rarity,
singularity, strangeness, unconventionality, unnaturalness; SEE CONCEPTS 260,411,665

oddity/oddball [n2] *person who is very different*
case*, character, duck*, eccentric, fish out of water*, maverick, misfit, odd bird*, original*, rara
avis, screwball*, weirdo*; SEE CONCEPT 423

odds [n1] *advantage*
allowance, benefit, bulge, difference, disparity,
dissimilarity, distinction, draw, edge, handicap,
head start, lead, overlay, start, superiority, vantage; SEE CONCEPT 693

odds [n2] *probability*
balance, chances, favor, likelihood, superiority,
toss-up; SEE CONCEPT 650

odds and ends [n] *miscellaneous paraphernalia*
assortment, bits, bits and pieces*, debris, etcet-
era*, hodgepodge, jumble, leavings, litter, medley, mélange, melee, miscellany, motley,
oddments, olio, particles, potpourri, remnants,
rest, rubbish, rummage, scraps, sundry items, this
and that*; SEE CONCEPTS 260,432,446

odious [adj] *hateful, horrible*
abhorrent, abominable, creepy*, detestable, disgusting, execrable, foul, hateable, horrid, loathsome, mean, obnoxious, offensive, ornery, pain
in the neck*, repellent, repugnant, repulsive, revolting, unpleasant, vile; SEE CONCEPTS 401,404

odium [n] *shame, dishonor*
abhorrence, antipathy, aversion, bar sinister*,
black eye*, blame, blot, blur, brand, censure, condemnation, detestation, disapproval, discredit,
disesteem, disfavor, disgrace, dislike, disproba-
tion, disrepute, enmity, execration, hate, hatred,
ignominy, infamy, malice, obloquy, onus, opprobrium, rebuke, reprobation, resentment, slur,
spot, stain, stigma; SEE CONCEPTS 29,388

odor [n] *scent*
air, aroma, bouquet, effluvium, efflux, emanation,
essence, exhalation, flavor, fragrance, musk, perfume, pungence, pungency, redolence, smell,
snuff, stench, stink, tang, tincture, trail, whiff;
SEE CONCEPT 599

odorless [adj] *without fragrance*
deodorant, deodorizing, flat, inodorous, odor-
free, unaromatic, unfragrant, unperfumed, un-
scented, unsmelling; SEE CONCEPT 598

odorous [adj] *having fragrance*
aromatic, balmy, dank, effluvious, fetid, flavorsome, flowery, foul, fragrant, heady, honeyed,
loud, malodorous, mephitic, miasmic, moldy,
musty, nauseous, odoriferant, odoriferous, offen-

sive, olfactive, olfactory, perfumatory, perfumed,
perfumy, pungent, putrid, redolent, reeking, rotten, savorous, savory, scented, scentful, scent-
laden, skunky*, smelly, spicy, stagnant, stale,
stinking, strong, sweet, sweet-scented, sweet-
smelling, tumaceous, unsavory, whiffy*; SEE
CONCEPT 598

of course [adv] *as expected*
by all means, certainly, definitely, indeed, indubitably, naturally, obviously, surely, undoubtedly,
without a doubt; SEE CONCEPT 544

off [adj1] *gone; remote*
absent, canceled, finished, inoperative, negligible,
not employed, not on duty, on vacation, outside,
postponed, slender, slight, slim, small, unavailable; SEE CONCEPT 552

off [adj2] *inferior; spoiled*
bad, decomposed, disappointing, disheartening,
displeasing, low-quality, mortifying, not up to
par*, not up to snuff*, poor, putrid, quiet, rancid,
rotten, slack, sour, substandard, turned, unrewarding, unsatisfactory; SEE CONCEPT 570

off [adv] *apart, away*
above, absent, afar, ahead, aside, away from, behind, below, beneath, beside, disappearing, divergent, elsewhere, far, farther away, gone away, in
the distance, not here, out, over, removed, to one
side, turning aside, up front, vanishing; SEE CON-
CEPTS 583,778

offbeat [adj] *strange, very different*
bizarre, bohemian*, eccentric, far-out, freaky,
fresh, idiosyncratic, novel, oddball, outré, uncommon, unconventional, unique, unorthodox, unusual, way-out*, weird; SEE CONCEPT 564

off-color [adj] *risqué*
blue*, indelicate, purple*, racy*, salty*, shady,
suggestive, vulgar, wicked; SEE CONCEPT 545

offend [v] *displease, insult*
affront, aggrieve, anger, annoy, antagonize, be
disagreeable, disgruntle, disgust, disoblige, distress, disturb, exasperate, fret, gall, horrify, hurt,
irritate, jar, miff, nauseate, nettle, outrage, pain,
pique, provoke, repel, repulse, rile, shock, sicken,
sin, slight, slur, snub, sting, transgress, trespass,
turn one off*, upset, vex, wound, zing*; SEE CON-
CEPTS 7,14,19

offense [n1] *violation, trespass*
breach, crime, delinquency, fault, infraction,
lapse, malfeasance, misdeed, misdemeanor, peccadillo, sin, transgression, wrong, wrongdoing;
SEE CONCEPTS 192,691

offense [n2] *insult, displeasure*
affront, aggression, assailment, assault, attack,
battery, black eye*, blitz*, blitzkrieg*, dig*, dirty
dig*, harm, hit*, hurt, indignation, indignity, injury, injustice, left-handed compliment*, mugging, offensive, onset, onslaught, outrage, push*,
put-down*, slam*, slap in the face*, slight, snub,
zinger*; SEE CONCEPTS 52,278

offense [n3] *anger, hard feelings*
annoyance, conniption*, displeasure, explosion,
fit, flare-up*, huff, indignation, ire, miff, needle*,
outburst, pique, resentment, scene, tantrum, tizzy*, umbrage, wounded feelings, wrath; SEE
CONCEPT 410

offensive [n] *attack*
aggression, assailment, assault, drive, invasion,
onset, onslaught, push; SEE CONCEPTS 86,320

offensive [adj1] *disrespectful, insulting; displeasing*

abhorrent, abusive, annoying, biting, cutting, detestable, disagreeable, discourteous, distasteful, dreadful, embarrassing, evil, foul, ghastly, grisly, gross, hideous, horrible, horrid, impertinent, insolent, invidious, irritating, nauseating, objectionable, obnoxious, odious, off-color*, offending, opprobrious, outrageous, repellent, reprehensible, repugnant, repulsive, revolting, rotten, rude, shocking, stinking*, terrible, uncivil, unmannerly; SEE CONCEPTS 267,529,537

offensive [adj2] *attacking*

aggressive, assailing, assaulting, belligerent, invading; SEE CONCEPT 548

offer [n] *proposal, suggestion*

action, attempt, bid, endeavor, essay, feeler*, hit*, overture, pass*, pitch*, presentation, proposition, propoundment, rendition, submission, tender; SEE CONCEPTS 66,67,278

offer [v1] *present, propose for acceptance*

accord, advance, afford, allow, award, be at service, bid, come forward, display, donate, exhibit, extend, furnish, give, grant, hold out, lay at one's feet*, make available, move, place at disposal*, ply, pose, press, proffer, propound, provide, put forth, put forward, put on the market, put up, put up for sale, sacrifice, show, submit, suggest, tender, volunteer; SEE CONCEPT 67

offer [v2] *propose*

adduce, advance, advise, allege, cite, make a motion, make a pitch*, present, proposition, submit, suggest; SEE CONCEPT 66

offer [v3] *try*

assay, attempt, endeavor, essay, seek, strive, struggle, undertake; SEE CONCEPT 87

offering [n] *donation*

alms, atonement, benefaction, beneficence, charity, contribution, expiation, gift, oblation, present, sacrifice, subscription; SEE CONCEPTS 337,340

offhand [adj1] *abrupt, careless*

aloof, breezy, brusque, casual, cavalier, cool*, curt, easygoing, folksy, glib, informal, laid-back, mellow, perfunctory, unceremonious, unconcerned, uninterested; SEE CONCEPTS 267,401,542

offhand [adj2/adv] *ad-lib, extemporaneous*

extemporary, extempore, impromptu, improvised, informal, off the cuff*, off the hip*, off the top of head*, spontaneous, spur-of-the-moment*, throwaway*, unpremeditated, unprepared, unrehearsed, unstudied, without preparation; SEE CONCEPT 267

office [n1] *business, responsibility*

appointment, berth, billet, capacity, charge, commission, connection, duty, employment, function, job, obligation, occupation, performance, place, post, province, responsibility, role, service, situation, spot, station, trust, work; SEE CONCEPTS 351,362,376

office [n2] *place of business*

agency, building, bureau, cave*, center, department, facility, factory, foundry, room, salt mines*, setup, shop, store, suite, warehouse, workstation; SEE CONCEPTS 312,439,441,448,449

officer [n1] *person who has high position in organization*

administrator, agent, appointee, bureaucrat, chief, civil servant, deputy, dignitary, director, executive, functionary, head, leader, magistrate, manager, officeholder, official, president, public servant, representative; SEE CONCEPT 347

officer [n2] *person in law enforcement*

arm*, badge*, black and white*, captain, cop*, deputy, detective, flatfoot*, mounty, police, police officer, sergeant, sheriff; SEE CONCEPTS 354,355,358

official [n] *person representing organization*

administrator, agent, big shot*, boss, brains*, brass*, bureaucrat, CEO*, chancellor, civil servant, commissioner, comptroller, dignitary, director, exec*, executive, front office*, functionary, governor, head person, higher-up*, incumbent, leader, magistrate, manager, marshal, mayor, minister, officeholder, officer, panjandrum, premier, president, representative, secretary, top*, top brass*, top dog*, top drawer*, treasurer; SEE CONCEPTS 347,354

official [adj] *authorized, legitimate*

accredited, approved, authentic, authenticated, authoritative, bona fide, canonical, cathedral, ceremonious, certified, cleared, conclusive, correct, customary, decided, decisive, definite, endorsed, established, ex cathedra, ex officio, fitting, formal, legitimate, licensed, okay*, ordered, orthodox, positive, precise, proper, real, recognized, rightful, sanctioned, suitable, true, valid; SEE CONCEPT 535

officiate [v] *oversee, manage*

act, boss, chair, command, conduct, direct, do the honors*, emcee, function, govern, handle, preside, run, serve, superintend, umpire; SEE CONCEPT 117

officious [adj] *self-important, dictatorial*

busy, forward, impertinent, inquisitive, interfering, intrusive, meddlesome, meddling, obtrusive, opinionated, overzealous, pragmatic, pushy, rude; SEE CONCEPT 404

off-key [adj] *not harmonious*

abnormal, anomalous, clinker*, deviant, discordant, dissonant, divergent, inharmonious, irregular, jarring, out of keeping*, out of tune*, sour*, sour note*, unnatural; SEE CONCEPT 594

offset [v] *counterbalance, compensate*

account, allow for, atone for, balance, be equivalent, cancel out, change, counteract, counterpoise, counterpose, countervail, equal, equalize, equipoise, make amends, make up for, negate, neutralize, outweigh, recompense, redeem, requite, set off; SEE CONCEPTS 126,232

offshoot [n] *development, product*

adjunct, appendage, branch, by-product, derivative, descendant, limb, outgrowth, spin-off, sprout; SEE CONCEPTS 260,824

offspring [n] *child, children*

baby, bambino*, brood, chip off old block*, cub, descendant, family, generation, heir, heredity, issue, kid*, lineage, offshoot, posterity, produce, progeniture, progeny, pup*, scion, seed, spawn, succession, successor, young; SEE CONCEPTS 296,414

often [adv] *frequently*

again and again, a number of times, generally, many a time, much, oftentimes, ofttimes, over and over, recurrently, regularly, repeatedly, time after time, time and again, usually; SEE CONCEPT 541

ogre [n] *nasty person*

demon, devil, fiend, giant, monster, monstrosity, specter, troll; SEE CONCEPT 412

oil [v] *lubricate*
anoint, coat, grease, lard, lube, pomade, slick, smear; SEE CONCEPTS *172,256*

oily [adj 1] *fatty, greasy*
adipose, buttery, creamy, lardy, lubricant, lubricative, lubricous, lustrous, oiled, oil-soaked, oleaginous, polished, rich, saponaceous, sleek, slippery, smeary, smooth, soapy, soothing, swimming, unctuous, waxy; SEE CONCEPTS *603,606*

oily [adj 2] *flattering*
bland*, cajoling, coaxing, compliant, fulsome, glib, gushing*, hypocritical, ingratiating, insinuating, obsequious, plausible, servile, slick, smarmy*, smooth, smooth-tongued*, suave, supple, unctuous; SEE CONCEPTS *267,401*

ointment [n] *cream for treatment*
balm, cerate, demulcent, dressing, embrocation, emollient, lenitive, liniment, lotion, medicine, salve, unguent; SEE CONCEPTS *311,466*

okay [n] *agreement*
acceptance, affirmation, approbation, approval, assent, authorization, benediction, blessing, consent, endorsement, favor, go-ahead*, green light*, permission, sanction, say-so*, seal of approval*, yes; SEE CONCEPT *684*

okay [adj] *acceptable, satisfactory*
accurate, adequate, all right, approved, convenient, correct, fair, fine, good, in order, middling, not bad, passable, permitted, so-so*, surely, tolerable; SEE CONCEPT *558*

okay [v] *agree to*
accept, accredit, approve, authorize, certify, condone, confirm, consent to, endorse, give one's consent, give the go-ahead*, give the green light*, notarize, pass, rubber-stamp*, sanction, say yes to; SEE CONCEPTS *10,50,88*

old [adj 1] *advanced in age*
aged, along in years*, ancient, broken down*, debilitated, decrepit, elderly, enfeebled, exhausted, experienced, fossil*, geriatric, getting on*, gray, gray-haired*, grizzled*, hoary*, impaired, inactive, infirm, mature, matured, not young, olden, oldish, over the hill*, past one's prime*, seasoned, senile, senior, skilled, superannuated, tired, venerable, versed, veteran, wasted*; SEE CONCEPTS *578,797*

old [adj 2] *obsolete, outdated*
aboriginal, age-old, antediluvian, antiquated, antique, archaic, bygone, cast-off, crumbling, dated, decayed, demode, done, early, erstwhile, former, hackneyed*, immemorial, late, moth-eaten*, of old, of yore, olden, oldfangled, old-fashioned, old-time, once, onetime, original, outmoded, out-of-date, passé, past, primeval, primitive, primordial, pristine, quondam, relic, remote, rusty, sometime, stale, superannuated, time-worn, traditional, unfashionable, unoriginal, venerable, worn-out*; SEE CONCEPTS *558,560,799*

old [adj 3] *traditional, long-established*
age-old, constant, continuing, enduring, established, experienced, familiar, firm, hardened, inveterate, lifelong, long-lasting, long-lived, of long standing, perennial, perpetual, practiced, skilled, solid, staying, steady, time-honored, versed, veteran, vintage; SEE CONCEPTS *482,530,798*

old age [n] *latter part of animate life*
advancing years*, age, agedness, autumn of life*, caducity, debility, declining years*, decrepitude, dotage, elderliness, evening of life*, feebleness, golden age*, golden years*, infirmity, second childhood*, senectitude, senescence, senility, years; SEE CONCEPTS *715,817*

older [adj] *most senior*
earlier, elder, eldest, first, first-born, former, lower, of a former period, of an earlier time, preceding, prior, senior; SEE CONCEPTS *578,585,797*

old-fashioned [adj] *outmoded, obsolete*
ancient, antiquated, antique, archaic, behind the times*, bygone, corny*, dated, dead*, demode, demoded, disapproved, dowdy*, extinct, grown old, moldy*, musty, neglected, not current, not modern, not with it*, obsolescent, odd*, of old, of olden days*, of the old school*, olden, old-fangled*, old-hat*, old-time, out*, outdated, out-of-date, out of it*, out-of-style, outworn, passé*, past, primitive, rococo*, superannuated, unfashionable, unstylish, vintage; SEE CONCEPTS *578,589,797,799*

old hand [n] *person experienced in something*
expert, longtimer, old guard*, old school*, old-timer*, pro*, vet*, veteran; SEE CONCEPT *423*

oligarchic [adj] *governed by small group*
cabalistic, cliquey*, elite, exclusive, select; SEE CONCEPTS *554,568*

omen [n] *sign of something to come*
augury, auspice, bodement, boding, foreboding, foretoken, harbinger, indication, portent, premonition, presage, prognostic, prognostication, prophecy, straw, warning, writing on the wall*; SEE CONCEPTS *74,278,689*

ominous [adj] *menacing, foreboding*
apocalyptic, augural, baleful, baneful, clouded, dangerous, dark, dire, direful, dismal, doomed, doomful, fateful, fearful, forbidding, gloomy, grim, haunting, hostile, ill-boding, ill-fated, impending, inauspicious, inhospitable, lowering, malefic, malificent, malign, minatory, perilous, portentous, precursive, premonitory, presaging, prescient, prophetic, sinister, suggestive, threatening, unfriendly, unlucky, unpromising, unpropitious; SEE CONCEPT *548*

omission [n] *something forgotten or excluded*
blank, breach, break, cancellation, carelessness, chasm, cutting out, default, disregard, disregardance, elimination, elision, excluding, exclusion, failing, failure, forgetfulness, gap, hiatus, ignoring, inadvertence, inadvertency, lack, lacuna, lapse, leaving out, missing, neglect, noninclusion, overlook, overlooking, oversight, passing over, preclusion, preterition, pretermission, prohibition, repudiation, skip, slighting, slip, withholding; SEE CONCEPTS *25,116,699*

omit [v] *exclude, forget*
bar, blink at*, bypass, cancel, cast aside, count out, cut, cut out, delete, discard, dismiss, disregard, drop, edit, eliminate, evade, except, fail, ignore, knock off, leave out, leave undone, let go, let slide*, miss, miss out, neglect, overlook, overpass, pass by, pass over, preclude, prohibit, reject, repudiate, skip, slight, snip, trim, void, withhold, X-out*; SEE CONCEPTS *25,121,211*

omnipotent [adj] *all-powerful*
almighty, divine, godlike, mighty, supreme, unlimited, unrestricted; SEE CONCEPT *574*

omniscient [adj] *all-knowing*
all-seeing, almighty, infinite, knowledgeable, pansophical, preeminent, wise; SEE CONCEPT *402*

on [adv] *in contact; ahead of*
about, above, adjacent, against, approaching, at, beside, close to, covering, forth, forward, held,

leaning on, near, next, on top of, onward, over, resting on, situated on, supported, touching, toward, upon, with; SEE CONCEPTS 585,586,750

once [*adj/adv*] *in the past; occurred one time only*
already, a single time, at one time, away back, back, back when, before, but once, bygone, earlier, erstwhile, formerly, heretofore, in the old days, in the olden days, in times gone by, in times past, late, long ago, old, once only, once upon a time, one, one time before, one time previously, only one time, on one occasion, previously, quondam, sometime, this time, time was, whilom; SEE CONCEPTS 799,820

oncoming [*adj*] *impending*
advancing, approaching, coming, expected, forthcoming, imminent, looming, nearing, onrushing, upcoming; SEE CONCEPTS 548,799

one [*adj*] *individual*
alone, definite, different, lone, odd, one and only, only, particular, peculiar, precise, separate, single, singular, sole, solitary, special, specific, uncommon, unique; SEE CONCEPTS 577,762,789

onerous [*adj*] *difficult; requiring hard labor*
arduous, austere, backbreaking, burdensome, crushing, cumbersome, demanding, difficult, distressing, embittering, exacting, excessive, exhausting, exigent, fatiguing, formidable, galling, grave, grinding, grueling, hard*, harsh, headache, heavy*, intolerable, irksome, laborious, merciless, oppressive, overpowering, overtaxing, painful, plodding, ponderous, pressing, responsible, rigorous, serious, severe, strenuous, taxing, tiresome, tiring, toilsome, troublesome, vexatious, weighty; SEE CONCEPTS 538,565

ongoing [*adj*] *continuous*
advancing, continuing, current, developing, evolving, extant, growing, heading, in process, in progress, marching, open-ended, progressing, successful, unfinished, unfolding; SEE CONCEPTS 482,798

onlooker [*n*] *person observing an event*
beholder, bystander, eyewitness, looker-on, observer, sightseer, spectator, viewer, watcher, witness; SEE CONCEPT 423

only [*adj*] *singular*
alone, apart, by oneself, exclusive, individual, isolated, lone, matchless, once in a lifetime, one, one and only, one shot, onliest, particular, peerless, single, sole, solitary, solo, unaccompanied, unequaled, unique, unparalleled, unrivaled; SEE CONCEPT 577

only [*adv*] *barely; exclusively*
alone, at most, but, entirely, hardly, just, merely, nothing but, particularly, plainly, purely, simply, solely, totally, uniquely, utterly, wholly; SEE CONCEPTS 535,772

onset [*n*] *beginning; attack*
access, aggression, assailment, assault, birth, charge, commencement, dawn, dawning, encounter, inception, incipience, kickoff*, offense, offensive, onfall, onrush, onslaught, opening, origin, outbreak, outset, outstart, rush, seizure, start; SEE CONCEPTS 86,221,832

onslaught [*n*] *attack*
aggression, assailment, assault, blitz, charge, incursion, invasion, offense, offensive, onfall, onrush, onset; SEE CONCEPT 86

onus [*n*] *burden*
bar sinister*, black eye*, blame, blot, blur, brand, charge, culpability, deadweight*, duty, encumbrance, fault, guilt, incubus, liability, load, millstone*, obligation, odium, oppression, responsibility, slur, spot, stain, stigma, task, tax, weight; SEE CONCEPTS 388,674

onward/onwards [*adv*] *ahead, beyond*
alee, along, forth, forward, in front, in front of, moving, on, on ahead; SEE CONCEPTS 585,778

ooze [*n*] *liquid emitted*
alluvium, fluid, glop*, goo*, gook*, gunk*, mire, muck*, mud, silt, slime*, sludge; SEE CONCEPTS 466,467

ooze [*v*] *emit liquid*
bleed, discharge, drain, dribble, drip, drop, escape, exude, filter, flow, issue, leach, leak, overflow, percolate, perspire, seep, spurt, strain, sweat, swelter, trickle, weep, well; SEE CONCEPT 179

opaque [*adj1*] *clouded, muddy*
blurred, cloudy, dark, darkened, dim, dirty, dull, dusky, filmy, foggy, frosty, fuliginous, gloomy, hazy, impenetrable, lusterless, misty, muddied, murky, nontranslucent, nontransparent, nebulous, obfuscated, shady, smoky, sooty, thick, turbid; SEE CONCEPTS 606,617,618

opaque [*adj2*] *hard to understand*
abstruse, amphibological, arcane, baffling, concealed, cryptic, difficult, enigmatic, equivocal, imperceptive, incomprehensible, nebulous, obscure, obtuse, perplexing, purblind, tenebrous, uncertain, unclear, unfathomable, unintelligible, vague; SEE CONCEPT 529

open [*adj1*] *unfastened, unclosed*
accessible, agape, airy, ajar, bare, clear, cleared, dehiscent, disclosed, emptied, expanded, expansive, exposed, extended, extensive, free, gaping, made passable, naked, navigable, passable, patent, patulous, peeled, removed, rent, revealed, ringent, rolling, spacious, spread out, stripped, susceptible, unbarred, unblocked, unbolted, unburdened, uncluttered, uncovered, unfolded, unfurled, unimpeded, unlocked, unobstructed, unplugged, unsealed, unshut, unstopped, vacated, wide, yawning; SEE CONCEPTS 485,576

open [*adj2*] *accessible; not forbidden*
admissible, agreeable, available, approachable, appropriate, attainable, available, employable, fit, free, general, getable*, nondiscriminatory, not posted, obtainable, on deck*, on tap*, open-door*, operative, permitted, practicable, proper, public, reachable, securable, suitable, to be had*, unconditional, unoccupied, unqualified, unrestricted, usable, vacant, welcoming, within reach; SEE CONCEPTS 560,576

open [*adj3*] *clear, obvious*
apparent, avowed, barefaced, blatant, conspicuous, downright, evident, flagrant, frank, manifest, noticeable, overt, plain, unconcealed, undisguised, visible, well-known; SEE CONCEPTS 267,535

open [*adj4*] *undecided*
ambiguous, arguable, controversial, debatable, doubtful, dubious, dubitable, equivocal, indecisive, in question, moot, problematic, questionable, uncertain, unresolved, unsettled, up for discussion*, up in the air*, yet to be decided*; SEE CONCEPTS 267,529

open [*adj5*] *honest, objective*
artless, candid, disinterested, fair, frank, free, guileless, impartial, ingenuous, innocent, lay it on the line*, mellow, natural, objective, on the lev-

oi
op

el*, open-and-shut*, openhearted*, plain, receptive, sincere, straightforward, talking turkey*, transparent, unbiased, uncommitted, unconcealed, undisguised, undissembled, unprejudiced, unreserved, up-front*; SEE CONCEPTS *267,542*

open [*v1*] *begin*
begin business, bow, commence, convene, embark, get things rolling*, inaugurate, initiate, jump, kick off, launch, meet, raise the curtain*, ring in*, set in motion, set up shop*, sit, start, start the ball rolling*; SEE CONCEPT *221*

open [*v2*] *clear, expose; spread*
bare, break in, break out, broach, burst, bust in, come apart, crack, disclose, display, disrupt, expand, fissure, free, gap, gape, hole, jimmy, kick in, lacerate, lance, penetrate, perforate, pierce, pop, puncture, release, reveal, rupture, separate, sever, slit, slot, split, tap, throw wide, unbar, unblock, unbolt, unclose, unclothe, uncork, uncover, undo, unfasten, unfold, unfurl, unlatch, unlock, unroll, unseal, unshut, unstop, untie, unwrap, vent, ventilate, yawn, yawp*; SEE CONCEPTS *135,250,469*

opening [*n1*] *gap, hole*
aperture, breach, break, cavity, chink, cleft, crack, cranny, crevice, cut, discontinuity, door, fissure, hatch, interstice, mouth, orifice, outlet, perforation, recess, rent, rift, rupture, scuttle, slit, slot, space, split, spout, tear, vent, window; SEE CONCEPT *513*

opening [*n2*] *chance*
availability, big break*, connection, cut*, fling*, go*, go-at*, in the running*, iron in the fire*, look-in*, occasion, opportunity, place, possibility, run, scope, shot*, show, squeak*, time, vacancy, whack*; SEE CONCEPT *693*

opening [*n3*] *beginning*
birth, coming out, commencement, curtain-raiser*, dawn, inauguration, inception, initiation, kickoff, launch, launching, onset, opener, outset, start; SEE CONCEPT *832*

openly [*adv*] *honestly*
aboveboard, artlessly, blatantly, brazenly, candidly, face to face, flagrantly, forthrightly, frankly, fully, honestly, in broad daylight, in full view, ingenuously, in public, in the open, naively, naturally, plainly, publicly, readily, shamelessly, simply, straight, unabashedly, unashamedly, under one's nose*, unhesitatingly, unreservedly, wantonly, warts and all*, willingly, without pretense, without reserve*; SEE CONCEPTS *267,544*

operate [*v1*] *perform, function*
accomplish, achieve, act, act on, advance, behave, be in action, bend, benefit, bring about, burn, carry on, click*, compel, complete, concern, conduct, contact, contrive, convey, cook*, determine, direct, do, enforce, engage, exert, finish, fulfill, get results, go, hit*, hum, influence, keep, lift, move, ordain, percolate, proceed, produce, produce a result, progress, promote, react, revolve, roll, run, serve, spin, take, tick, transport, turn, work; SEE CONCEPTS *91,680,706*

operate [*v2*] *manage, use*
administer, be in charge, be in driver's seat*, be in saddle*, call the play*, call the shots*, call the signals*, carry on, command, conduct, drive, handle, hold the reins*, keep, make go*, maneuver, manipulate, ordain, pilot, play, ply, pull the strings*, pull the wires*, run, run the show*, run

things*, sit on top of*, steer, wield, work; SEE CONCEPTS *94,117,148*

operate [*v3*] *perform surgery*
amputate, carve up, cut, excise, explore, open up, remove, set, transplant, treat; SEE CONCEPT *310*

operation [*n1*] *movement, working*
act, action, activity, affair, agency, application, ballgame*, bit, carrying on, conveyance, course, deal, deed, doing, effect, effort, employment, engagement, enterprise, exercise, exercising, exertion, exploitation, force, handiwork, happening, influence, instrumentality, labor, manipulation, motion, movement, performance, play, procedure, proceeding, process, progress, progression, scene, service, transaction, transference, trip, undertaking, use, work, workmanship; SEE CONCEPTS *658,680*

operation [*n2*] *business concern*
affair, deal, enterprise, proceeding, transaction, undertaking; SEE CONCEPTS *324,325*

operation [*n3*] *surgical procedure*
biopsy, excision, surgery; SEE CONCEPT *310*

operative [*adj*] *active, functioning; influential*
accessible, alive, crucial, current, dynamic, effective, efficient, employable, functional, important, indicative, in force, in operation, key, live, open, operational, practicable, relevant, running, serviceable, significant, standing, usable, workable, working; SEE CONCEPTS *560,567*

opinion [*n*] *belief*
assessment, assumption, attitude, conception, conclusion, conjecture, estimate, estimation, eye*, fancy, feeling, guess, hypothesis, idea, imagining, impression, inclination, inference, judgment, mind, notion, persuasion, point of view, postulate, presumption, presupposition, reaction, say-so*, sentiment, slant, speculation, supposition, surmise, suspicion, take*, theorem, theory, thesis, think*, thought, view, viewpoint; SEE CONCEPT *689*

opinionated [*adj*] *believing very strongly and conveying it*
adamant, arbitrary, assertive, biased, bigoted, bossy, bullheaded*, cocksure*, cocky*, conceited, dictatorial, doctrinaire, dogmatic, hard-line*, high-handed, inflexible, intransigent, locked in*, obdurate, obstinate, one-sided, oracular, overbearing, pigheaded*, positive, pragmatic, pragmatical, prejudiced, self-assertive, set in stone*, set-on, single-minded, stubborn, tilted, uncompromising, unyielding, weighted; SEE CONCEPTS *267,404*

opponent [*n*] *person with whom one competes*
adversary, antagonist, anti*, aspirant, assailant, bandit*, bidder, candidate, challenger, competitor, con, contestant, counteragent, dark horse*, disputant, dissentient, enemy, entrant, foe, litigant, match, opposer, opposition, oppugnant, player, rival; SEE CONCEPT *366*

opportune [*adj*] *advantageous, lucky*
appropriate, apt, auspicious, convenient, favorable, felicitous, fit, fitting, fortuitous, fortunate, happy, helpful, pat, proper, propitious, seasonable, suitable, timely, timeous, well-timed; SEE CONCEPTS *548,572*

opportunity [*n*] *lucky chance; favorable circumstances*
befalling, break*, connection, contingency, convenience, cut*, event, excuse, fair shake*, fighting chance*, fitness, fling*, fortuity, freedom,

go*, good fortune, good luck, happening, hope, hour, iron in the fire*, juncture, leisure, liberty, moment, occasion, one's move*, one's say*, one's turn*, opening, pass, prayer*, probability, relief, room, run, scope, shot*, show, space, spell, squeak, stab, the hunt*, the running*, time, turn, whack*; SEE CONCEPT 693

oppose [v1] *fight, obstruct*
argue, assail, assault, attack, bar, battle, bombard, call in question, check, combat, confront, contradict, controvert, counter, counterattack, cross, debate, defy, deny, disagree, disapprove, dispute, encounter, expose, face, face down*, fight, fly in the face of*, frown at, gainsay, hinder, neutralize, not countenance, prevent, protest, resist, reverse, run counter to, search out, speak against, stand up to, take a stand, take issue, take on, taunt, thwart, turn the tables*, withstand; SEE CONCEPTS *21,54,106*

oppose [v2] *compare, play off*
array, confront, contrast, counter, counterbalance, face, match, pit, set against, vie; SEE CONCEPTS *73,363*

opposed/opposing [adj] *antagonistic, against*
against the grain*, allergic*, anti*, antipathetic, antithetical, antonymous, at cross-purposes, at odds, averse, battling, clashing, combating, conflicting, confronting, contrary, controverting, counter, crossing, defending, defensive, denying, disagreeing, disputed, disputing, dissentient, enemy, exposing, facing, gainsaying, hostile, incompatible, inimical, in opposition, irreconcilable, objecting, obstructive, opposite, protesting, repelling, restrictive, rival, up against, warring; SEE CONCEPTS *403,542,564*

opposite [n] *something completely unlike another*
adverse, antilogy, antipode, antipole, antithesis, antonym, contra*, contradiction, contrary, contrast, converse, counterpart, foil, inverse, obverse, opposition, other extreme*, other side*, other side of coin*, paradox, reverse, vice versa; SEE CONCEPT *665*

opposite [adj] *unlike, conflicting; completely different*
adverse, antagonistic, antipodal, antipodean, antithetical, contradictory, contrapositive, contrary, contrasted, corresponding, counter, crosswise, diametric, diametrically opposed, different, differing, dissimilar, diverse, facing, flip-side*, fronting, hostile, inconsistent, independent, inimical, inverse, irreconcilable, obverse, opposed, ornery, paradoxical, polar, repugnant, retrograde, reverse, reversed, separate, unalike, unconnected, unrelated, unsimilar, violative, vis-à-vis; SEE CONCEPT *564*

opposition [n1] *obstruction, antagonism*
action, antinomy, antithesis, aversion, brush, civil disobedience, clash, combat, competition, con, conflict, confronting, contention, contest, contradistinction, contraposition, contrariety, counteraction, counterattack, defense, defiance, disapproval, duel, encounter, engagement, fray, grapple, hostility, negativism, obstructiveness, oppose, oppugnancy, prevention, repugnance, repulsion, resistance, rivalry, skirmish, strife, struggle, unfriendliness, violation, war, warfare; SEE CONCEPTS *29,92,106,665*

opposition [n2] *person, people competing*
adversary, antagonist, disputant, enemy, foe, iconoclast, opponent, other side, rebel, rival; SEE CONCEPTS *348,366*

oppress [v] *depress, subdue*
abuse, afflict, aggrieve, annoy, beat down*, burden, crush, despotize, dishearten, dispirit, distress, encumber, force, handicap, harass, harry, hound*, keep down, maltreat, outrage, overcome, overload, overpower, overthrow, overwhelm, persecute, pick on, plague, press, prey on, put down, put screws to*, put the squeeze on*, put upon, ride, rule, sadden, saddle*, smother, strain, subjugate, suppress, tax, torment, torture, trample, trouble, tyrannize, vex, weigh heavy upon, worry, wrong; SEE CONCEPTS *7,14,19,133*

oppression [n] *misery, hardship*
abuse, abusiveness, autocracy, brutality, calamity, coercion, compulsion, conquering, control, cruelty, despotism, dictatorship, domination, fascism, force, forcibleness, hardness, harshness, injury, injustice, iron hand*, maltreatment, martial law, overthrowing, persecution, severity, subduing, subjection, suffering, torment, tyranny; SEE CONCEPTS *14,320,674*

oppressive [adj1] *overwhelming, repressive*
backbreaking*, bleak, brutal, burdensome, confining, cruel, demanding, depressing, depressive, despotic, dictatorial, discouraging, disheartening, dismal, dispiriting, exacting, exigent, gloomy, grievous, grinding, harsh, headache*, heavy, heavy-handed*, hefty, inhuman, ironhanded*, mean, onerous, overbearing, rough going*, severe, somber, superincumbent, taxing, tough, troublesome, tyrannical, unjust, weighty; SEE CONCEPTS *537,548*

oppressive [adj2] *hot and humid*
airless, close, heavy, muggy, overpowering, steam bath*, steamy, sticky, stifling, stuffy, suffocating, sultry, sweat box*, torrid; SEE CONCEPT *525*

opprobrious [adj] *abusive, hateful*
abasing, calumniatory, contemptuous, contumelious, damaging, debasing, defamatory, defaming, denigrating, depreciative, derogative, despicable, despiteful, detractive, disgracing, dishonoring, disparaging, humiliating, hurting, injuring, injurious, insolent, insulting, invective, libeling, malevolent, malign, malignant, maligning, notorious, offending, offensive, pejorative, reproaching, reviling, scandalous, scurrilous, shaming, spiteful, truculent, vile, vitriolic, vituperative, vulgar; SEE CONCEPTS *267,404,542*

opt [v] *choose*
cull, decide, elect, exercise choice, go for*, make a selection, mark, pick, prefer, select, single out*, take; SEE CONCEPT *41*

optimism [n] *state of having positive beliefs*
anticipation, assurance, brightness, buoyancy, calmness, certainty, cheer, cheerfulness, confidence, easiness, elation, encouragement, enthusiasm, exhilaration, expectation, good cheer, happiness, hopefulness, idealism, looking on bright side*, positivism, rose-colored glasses*, sanguineness, sureness, trust; SEE CONCEPTS *410,689*

optimistic [adj] *believing positively*
assured, bright, buoyant, cheerful, cheering, confident, encouraged, expectant, happy, high, hopeful, hoping, idealistic, keeping the faith, merry, on cloud nine*, on top of world*, positive, promising, ray of sunshine*, rose-colored*, rosy, san-

op
op

guine, sunny*, trusting, upbeat, Utopian; SEE CONCEPTS 404,542

optimum [adj] best
24-carat*, A1*, ace, capital, choice, choicest, excellent, flawless, gilt-edge*, greatest, highest, ideal, matchless, maximum, most advantageous, most favorable, optimal, peak, peerless, perfect, select, solid gold*, superlative, world class*; SEE CONCEPT 574

option [n] alternative
advantage, benefit, choice, claim, dibs*, dilemma, discretion, druthers, election, flipside*, franchise, free will*, grant, license, opportunity, other side of coin*, pickup, preference, prerogative, privilege, right, selection, take it or leave it*; SEE CONCEPTS 376,712

optional [adj] possible; available as choice
alternative, arbitrary, discretional, discretionary, elective, extra, facultative, free, noncompulsory, nonobligatory, no strings attached*, not required, open, unforced, unrestricted, up to the individual, volitional, voluntary; SEE CONCEPTS 552,576

opulent [adj] rich, luxurious, profuse
abundant, affluent, copious, deluxe, extravagant, exuberant, fruitful*, lavish, luscious, luxuriant, moneyed, ostentatious, palatial, plentiful, plush, pretentious, prodigal, profusive, prolific, prosperous, rich, riotous, showy, sumptuous, swank, upholstered*, velvet*, wealthy, well-heeled*, well-off*, well-to-do*; SEE CONCEPTS 334,589,781

opus [n] great work of writing or music
composition, creation, magnum opus, music, oeuvre, piece, product, production; SEE CONCEPTS 263,271

oracle [n] prophecy
answer, apocalypse, augury, canon, commandment, divination, edict, fortune, law, prediction, prognostication, revelation, vision; SEE CONCEPTS 70,278,689

oracular [adj] prophetic
ambiguous, anticipating, apocalyptic, arcane, auguring, auspicious, authoritative, cabalistic, clairvoyant, cryptic, Delphian, discovering, divining, divulging, dogmatic, fatidic, foreboding, forecasting, foretelling, imperious, interpretive, mantic, mysterious, mystical, obscure, occult, ominous, peremptory, portending, portentous, positive, predicting, presaging, prescient, proclaiming, prognosticating, prophesying, sage, secret, sibylline, significant, soothsaying, vague, vatic, venerable, wise; SEE CONCEPT 267

oral [adj] spoken
articulate, ejaculatory, lingual, narrated, phonated, phonetic, phonic, recounted, related, said, sonant, sounded, told, unwritten, uttered, verbal, viva voce, vocal, voiced, word-of-mouth; SEE CONCEPT 267

orange [n/adj] combination of red and yellow
apricot, bittersweet, cantaloupe, carrot, coral, peach, red-yellow, salmon, tangerine, titian; SEE CONCEPTS 618,622

oration [n] speech
address, chalk talk*, declamation, discourse, harangue, homily, lecture, pep talk*, pitch*, sermon, soapbox*, spiel*; SEE CONCEPTS 266,278

orb [n] globe
ball, circle, eye*, lamp, ring, rondure, round, sphere; SEE CONCEPT 436

orbit [n1] circuit, revolution
apogee, circle, circumgyration, course, curve, cy-

cle, ellipse, lap, locus, path, pattern, perigee, rotation, round, track, trajectory; SEE CONCEPTS 436,738

orbit [n2] influence, domain
ambit, area, arena, boundary, bounds, career, circle, circumference, compass, course, department, dominion, extension, extent, field, jurisdiction, limit, pilgrimage, precinct, province, purview, radius, range, reach, realm, scope, sphere, sweep; SEE CONCEPTS 349,673,687

orchestrate [v] organize; cause to happen
arrange, blend, compose, concert, coordinate, harmonize, integrate, manage, present, put together, score, set up, symphonize, synthesize, unify; SEE CONCEPTS 117,242

ordain [v] establish, install
anoint, appoint, bless, call, commission, consecrate, constitute, deal, deal with, decree, delegate, destine, dictate, elect, enact, enjoin, fix, frock, impose, institute, invest, lay down the law*, legislate, nominate, order, prescribe, pronounce, put foot down*, rule, set, walk heavy*, will; SEE CONCEPTS 18,50,88,317

ordeal [n] trouble, suffering
affliction, agony, anguish, calamity, calvary, cross, crucible, difficulty, distress, nightmare, test, torment, torture, trial, tribulation, visitation; SEE CONCEPTS 674,728

order [n1] arrangement, organization
adjustment, aligning, array, assortment, cast, categorization, classification, codification, composition, computation, disposal, disposition, distribution, establishment, form, grouping, harmony, layout, line, lineup, management, method, neatness, ordering, orderliness, pattern, placement, plan, procedure, procession, progression, propriety, regularity, regulation, rule, scale, scheme, sequence, series, setup, standardization, structure, succession, symmetry, system, tidiness, uniformity; SEE CONCEPT 727

order [n2] lawfulness
calm, control, decorousness, decorum, discipline, goodness, integrity, law, law and order, niceness, orderliness, peace, peacefulness, probity, properness, propriety, quiet, rectitude, rightness, seemliness, suitability, tranquility, uprightness; SEE CONCEPTS 633,691

order [n3] class, status
bracket, branch, breed, cast, caste, degree, description, estate, family, feather, genre, genus, grade, hierarchy, ilk, kidney, kind, line, nature, pecking order*, pigeonhole*, place, position, rank, set, slot, sort, species, station, stripe, subclass, taxonomic group, type; SEE CONCEPT 378

order [n4] command
authorization, behest, bidding, charge, commandment, decree, dictate, direction, directive, injunction, instruction, law, mandate, ordinance, permission, precept, regulation, rule, say-so*, stipulation, ukase, word*; SEE CONCEPTS 53,278,685

order [n5] request; purchase agreement
amount, application, booking, bulk, commission, engagement, goods, materials, purchase, quantity, requisition, reservation, reserve, shipment, stipulation; SEE CONCEPTS 332,338,684

order [n6] organization
association, brotherhood, club, community, company, fraternity, guild, league, lodge, sect, sister-

order [*v1*] *command, authorize*

adjure, apply for, bid, book, buy, call for, call the shots*, call the signals*, charge, contract for, decree, dictate, direct, enact, engage, enjoin, hire, instruct, obtain, ordain, prescribe, pull strings*, request, require, reserve, rule the roost*, secure, send away for, tell, warn; SEE CONCEPTS 50,53,88,327

order [*v2*] *arrange, organize*

adapt, adjust, align, alphabetize, array, assign, catalogue, class, classify, conduct, control, control, dispose, distribute, establish, file, fix, formalize, furnish, group, index, lay out, line up, locate, manage, marshal, methodize, neaten, normalize, pattern, place, plan, put away, put to rights*, range, regiment, regularize, regulate, right, routine, set guidelines, set in order, settle, sort out, space, standardize, streamline, systematize, tabulate, tidy; SEE CONCEPTS 84,158

orderly [*adj1*] *methodical, organized*

alike, all together, arranged, businesslike, careful, clean, conventional, correct, exact, fixed, formal, framed, in apple-pie order*, in good shape, in order, in shape, methodic, neat, neat as button*, neat as pin*, precise, regular, regulated, scientific, set-up, shipshape*, slick, spick-and-span*, systematic, systematized, thorough, tidy, together, to rights*, trim, uncluttered, uniform; SEE CONCEPTS 326,485,585,589

orderly [*adj2*] *well-behaved*

at peace, calm, controlled, decorous, disciplined, docile, law-abiding, manageable, nonviolent, obedient, peaceable, quiet, restrained, submissive, tranquil, well-mannered; SEE CONCEPT 401

ordinance [*n*] *law, rule*

authorization, canon, code, command, decree, dictum, direction, edict, enactment, fiat, mandate, order, precept, prescript, reg, regulation, ruling, statute, ukase; SEE CONCEPT 318

ordinarily [*adv*] *usually*

as a rule, commonly, customarily, frequently, generally, habitually, in general, normally, regularly; SEE CONCEPT 530

ordinary [*adj1*] *common, regular*

accustomed, customary, established, everyday, familiar, frequent, general, habitual, humdrum*, natural, normal, popular, prevailing, public, quotidian, routine, run-of-the-mill*, settled, standard, stock, traditional, typical, usual, wonted; SEE CONCEPTS 533,547

ordinary [*adj2*] *average; not distinctive*

characterless, common, commonplace, conventional, dull, fair, familiar, garden*, garden variety*, generic, habitual, homespun, household, humble, indifferent, inferior, mean, mediocre, modest, no great shakes*, normal, pedestrian, plain, plastic, prosaic, quotidian, routine, run-of-the-mill*, second-rate, simple, so-so*, stereotyped, undistinguished, uneventful, unexceptional, uninspired, unmemorable, unnoteworthy, unpretentious, unremarkable, usual, vanilla*, white-bread*, workaday; SEE CONCEPTS 530,575

organ [*n*] *means, tool*

agency, agent, channel, device, element, forum, implement, instrument, journal, magazine, medium, member, ministry, mouthpiece, newspaper, paper, part, periodical, process, publication, re-

view, structure, unit, vehicle, voice, way; SEE CONCEPTS 280,499,712

organic [*adj*] *basic, natural*

amoebic, anatomical, animate, basal, biological, biotic, cellular, constitutional, elemental, essential, fundamental, inherent, innate, integral, live, living, necessary, nuclear, original, plasmic, primary, prime, primitive, principal, structural, vital; SEE CONCEPT 549

organism [*n*] *living thing*

animal, being, body, creature, entity, morphon, person, plant, structure; SEE CONCEPTS 389,429

organization [*n1*] *arrangement, arranging*

alignment, assembling, assembly, chemistry, composition, configuration, conformation, constitution, construction, coordination, design, disposal, format, formation, forming, formulation, framework, grouping, harmony, institution, make-up, making, management, method, methodology, organism, organizing, pattern, plan, planning, regulation, running, situation, standard, standardization, structure, structuring, symmetry, system, unity, whole; SEE CONCEPTS 84,117,727

organization [*n2*] *group bound by interest/work/goal*

affiliation, aggregation, alliance, association, band, body, business, cartel, circle, clique, club, coalition, combination, combine, company, concern, concord, confederation, consortium, cooperative, corporation, coterie, crew, establishment, federation, fraternity, guild, house, industry, institute, institution, league, lodge, machine, monopoly, order, outfit, party, profession, set, society, sodality, sorority, squad, syndicate, team, trade, troupe, trust, union; SEE CONCEPT 381

organize [*v*] *arrange, systematize*

adapt, adjust, be responsible for, catalogue, classify, codify, combine, compose, constitute, construct, coordinate, correlate, create, dispose, establish, fashion, fit, form, formulate, frame, get going*, get together, group, harmonize, lick into shape*, line up, look after, marshal, methodize, mold, pigeonhole*, put in order, put together, range, regulate, run, see to, settle, set up, shape, standardize, straighten, straighten out, tabulate, tailor, take care of, whip into shape*; SEE CONCEPTS 36,84,158

orgy [*n*] *celebration devoted to sensual enjoyment*

bacchanal, bacchanalia, bender*, binge*, blowout*, bout*, carousal, circus*, debauch, dissipation, excess, feast, fling*, indulgence, jag*, merrymaking, overindulgence, party, rampage*, revel, revelry, saturnalia, splurge, spree, surfeit, tear*; SEE CONCEPTS 377,383

orient [*v*] *familiarize*

acclimatize, adapt, adjust, align, conform, determine, direct, get one's bearings*, locate, orientate, turn; SEE CONCEPTS 35,202

orientation [*n*] *introduction, adjustment*

acclimatization, adaptation, assimilation, bearings, breaking in*, coordination, direction, familiarization, fix*, lay of the land*, location, position, sense of direction, settling in*; SEE CONCEPTS 31,832

origin [*n1*] *cause, basis*

agent, ancestor, ancestry, antecedent, author, base, causality, causation, connection, creator, derivation, determinant, egg*, element, embryo, fountain, generator, germ, horse's mouth*, impulse, inception, inducement, influence, inspiration, mainspring, motive, nucleus, occasion, parent, parentage, principle, producer, progenitor, provenance, provenience, root, roots, seed, source, spring, stock, well, wellspring; SEE CONCEPTS 229,648,661

origin [n2] *beginning, inception*
alpha, birth, blast off, commencement, creation, dawn, dawning, day one*, early stage, embarkation, emergence, entrance, entry, forging, foundation, genesis, git go*, inauguration, ingress, initiation, introduction, launch, nativity, opener, origination, outbreak, outset, rise, square one*, start, starting point*; SEE CONCEPT 832

origin [n3] *family, heritage*
ancestry, beginnings, birth, blood, descent, extraction, lineage, maternity, parentage, paternity, pedigree, stock; SEE CONCEPT 296

original [n1] *standard, prototype*
archetype, coinage, creation, exemplar, forerunner, invention, model, novelty, paradigm, pattern, precedent, precursor, type; SEE CONCEPTS 260,686

original [n2] *person who is eccentric*
anomaly, card*, case*, character, eccentric, nonconformist, oddball, oddity, queer, weirdo*; SEE CONCEPT 423

original [adj1] *earliest*
aboriginal, archetypal, authentic, autochthonous, beginning, commencing, early, elementary, embryonic, first, first-hand, genuine, inceptive, infant, initial, introductory, opening, pioneer, primary, prime, primeval, primitive, primordial, pristine, prototypal, rudimental, rudimentary, starting, underivative, underived; SEE CONCEPTS 549,585

original [adj2] *fresh, new*
avant garde, breaking new ground*, causal, causative, conceiving, creative, demiurgic, devising, envisioning, fertile, formative, generative, imaginative, ingenious, innovational, innovative, innovatory, inspiring, inventive, novel, originative, productive, quick, ready, resourceful, seminal, sensitive, unconventional, unprecedented, untried, unusual; SEE CONCEPTS 578,589,797

originality [n] *creativeness*
boldness, brilliance, cleverness, creative spirit, creativity, daring, freshness, imagination, imaginativeness, individuality, ingeniousness, ingenuity, innovation, innovativeness, invention, inventiveness, modernity, new idea, newness, nonconformity, novelty, resourcefulness, spirit, unconventionality, unorthodoxy; SEE CONCEPTS 409,410

originally [adv] *initially*
at first, at the outset, at the start, basically, by birth, by origin, first, formerly, incipiently, in the beginning, in the first place, primarily, primitively, to begin with; SEE CONCEPTS 578,585,797,799

originate [v1] *begin; spring*
arise, be born, birth, come, come from, come into existence, commence, dawn, derive, emanate, emerge, flow, hail from, issue, proceed, result, rise, start, stem; SEE CONCEPTS 105,221

originate [v2] *create, introduce*
break the ice*, bring about, cause, coin, come up with, compose, conceive, develop, discover, evolve, form, formulate, found, generate, give birth to, hatch, inaugurate, initiate, innovate, institute, invent, launch, make, open up, parent,

pioneer, procreate, produce, set in motion, set up, spark, spawn, start, think up, usher in; SEE CONCEPTS 43,173,251

ornament [n] *decoration*
accessory, adornment, art, bauble, beautification, design, doodad*, embellishment, embroidery, flower, frill, frou frou*, garnish, gewgaw*, gimcrack*, gingerbread*, honor, jewel, knickknack*, pride, treasure, trimming, trinket; SEE CONCEPTS 259,476

ornament [v] *decorate*
adorn, array, beautify, bedeck, bedizen, brighten, deck, dress, dress up*, embellish, embroider, enrich, festoon, fix up*, garnish, gild, grace, ornamentalize, polish, prank, prettify, primp, prink, smarten*, spruce up*, trim; SEE CONCEPTS 162,167,177

ornamental [adj] *decorative*
accessory, adorning, attractive, beautiful, beautifying, decking, decorating, delicate, dressy, elaborate, embellishing, enhancing, exquisite, fancy, festooned, florid, for show*, furbishing, garnishing, heightening, luxurious, ornate, setting off*, showy; SEE CONCEPTS 579,589

ornate [adj] *fancily decorated*
adorned, aureate, baroque, beautiful, bedecked, bright, brilliant, busy, colored, convoluted, dazzling, elaborate, elegant, embroidered, fancy, fine, flamboyant, flashy, flaunting, florid, flowery, fussy, gaudy, gilded, glamorous, glitzy, glossy, high-wrought, jeweled, lavish, luscious, magnificent, meretricious, opulent, ornamented, ostentatious, overdone, overelaborate, pretentious, resplendent, rich, rococo, showy, sparkling, splashy, sumptuous, superficial, tawdry, variegated; SEE CONCEPTS 579,589

orphan [n] *child without parents*
foundling, ragamuffin*, stray, waif; SEE CONCEPT 414

orthodox [adj] *accepted, traditional*
according to the book*, acknowledged, admitted, approved, authoritative, buttoned-down*, by the numbers*, canonical, conformist, conservative, conventional, correct, customary, devout, diehard, doctrinal, established, in line*, legitimate, official, old-line*, pious, proper, punctilious, reactionary, received, recognized, religious, right, rightful, sanctioned, sound, square, standard, straight, straight arrow, traditional, traditionalistic, true, well-established; SEE CONCEPTS 533,558

oscillate [v] *change back and forth*
be unsteady, dangle, fishtail, flicker, fluctuate, librate, lurch, palpitate, pendulate, pitch, pivot, reel, ripple, rock, roll, seesaw, stagger, sway, swing, switch, swivel, teeter, teeter-totter*, thrash, toss, totter, undulate, vacillate, vary, vibrate, waddle, wag, waggle, waltz, wave, waver, whirl, wiggle, wobble; SEE CONCEPTS 13,147,697

ossify [v] *become hard from aging*
congeal, fossilize, freeze, harden, indurate, petrify, solidify, stiffen, thicken, turn to bone; SEE CONCEPT 469

ostensible [adj] *alleged, supposed*
apparent, avowed, colorable, demonstrative, exhibited, illusive, illusory, likely, manifest, notable, outward, plausible, pretended, professed, purported, quasi, seeming, semblant, so-called*, specious, superficial; SEE CONCEPTS 552,582

ostensibly [*adv*] *apparently*
at first blush*, evidently, externally, for all intents and purposes*, for show*, officially, on the face*, on the surface*, outwardly, professedly, seemingly, sensibly, superficially, supposedly, to the eye*; SEE CONCEPT *582*

ostentation [*n*] *exhibitionism, flashiness*
affectation, array, boast, boasting, brag, braggadocio*, bragging, bravado, demonstration, display, exhibition, false front*, flamboyance, flash*, flaunting, flourish, fuss, garishness, grandstand play*, magnificence, pageant, pageantry, parade, parading, pomp, pomposity, pompousness, pretending, pretension, pretentiousness, put-on, shine*, show, showiness, showing off*, showoff*, spectacle, splendor, splurge, swagger*, swaggering, swank*, vainglory, vaunt, vaunting*, window-dressing; SEE CONCEPTS *633,655*

ostentatious [*adj*] *flashy, showy*
boastful, chichi*, classy, conspicuous, crass*, dashing, egotistic, exhibitionistic, extravagant, flamboyant, flatulent, flaunted, fussy, garish, gaudy, gay, glittery, grandiose, highfaluting*, jaunty, loud, obtrusive, peacocky, pompous, pretentious, spectacular, splashy, splurgy, sporty, swank, swanky*, theatrical, tinsel*, tony*, uptown*, vain, vulgar; SEE CONCEPTS *401,589*

ostracize [*v*] *exile, banish*
avoid, blackball*, blacklist*, boycott, cast out, cold-shoulder*, cut, deport, displace, drop, exclude, excommunicate, expatriate, expel, expulse, leave in the cold, oust, reject, shun, shut out, snub, throw out; SEE CONCEPTS *25,384*

other [*adj1*] *additional, added*
alternative, another, auxiliary, else, extra, farther, fresh, further, more, new, spare, supplementary; SEE CONCEPT *771*

other [*adj2*] *different*
contrasting, disparate, dissimilar, distant, distinct, divergent, diverse, opposite, otherwise, remaining, separate, unalike, unequal, unlike, unrelated, variant; SEE CONCEPT *564*

otherwise [*adv*] *in another way; alternatively*
any other way, contrarily, differently, diversely, elseways, if not, in different circumstances, on the other hand, or else, or then, under other conditions, variously; SEE CONCEPT *544*

ounce [*n*] *one-sixteenth of a pound/28.35 grams of weight*
avoirdupois, troy, uncia; SEE CONCEPT *795*

oust [*v*] *expel, get rid of*
banish, bereave, boot out*, bounce*, bundle off*, cast out, chase, depose, deprive, dethrone, discharge, disinherit, dislodge, displace, dispossess, divest, drive out, eject, evict, expulse, fire, force out, give the 1-2-3*, kick out, lay off, let go, lose, ostracize, pack off, pink slip*, relegate, remove, rob, sack, send packing*, show the door*, throw out, topple, transport, turn out, unseat; SEE CONCEPTS *25,211,351*

out [*adj*] *not possible; gone*
absent, antiquated, at an end, away, behind the times*, cold, dated, dead, demode, doused, ended, exhausted, expired, extinguished, finished, impossible, not allowed, not on, old-fashioned, old-hat*, outmoded, outside, passé, ruled out, unacceptable, unfashionable, used up; SEE CONCEPTS *539,552,576*

out [*adv*] *outside, outdoors*
out of doors, outward, without; SEE CONCEPT *583*

outbreak [*n*] *sudden happening*
beginning, blowup, brawl, break, breaking, burst, bursting, commencement, commotion, convulsion, crack, crash, dawn, detonation, discharge, disorder, disruption, ebullition, effervescence, epidemic, eruption, explosion, fit, flare-up, flash, fury, gush, gushing, insurrection, irruption, mutiny, onset, outburst, outpouring, paroxysm, plague, rebellion, rending, revolution, roar, sally, sortie, spasm, spurt, storm, sundering, surge, thunder, tumult, uprising, volley; SEE CONCEPTS *2,86,179,832*

outburst [*n*] *fit of temper*
access, attack, blow, burst, conniption*, discharge, eruption, explosion, flare, flare-up, frenzy, gush, gust, outbreak, outpouring, paroxysm, rapture, scene, spasm, storm, surge, tantrum, transport, upheaval; SEE CONCEPT *633*

outcast [*n*] *person who is unwanted, not accepted*
bum*, castaway, deportee, derelict, displaced person, exile, expatriate, fugitive, gypsy, hobo*, persona non grata*, rascal, refugee, reprobate, tramp, untouchable, vagabond, vagrant, wretch; SEE CONCEPT *423*

outcome [*n*] *consequence, effect*
aftereffect, aftermath, blowoff, causatum, chain reaction*, conclusion, end, end result*, event, fallout, issue, payback*, payoff*, reaction, result, score, sequel, upshot*; SEE CONCEPT *230*

outcry [*n*] *scream, exclamation*
clamor, commotion, complaint, convulsion, cry, ferment, flak*, how-ha*, howl, hubba-hubba*, hullabaloo*, noise, objection, outburst, protest, screech, tumult, uproar, upturn, yell; SEE CONCEPTS *77,278*

outdated/out-of-date [*adj*] *old-fashioned*
anachronous, antiquated, antique, archaic, back number*, behind the times*, dated, démodé, dusty, has-been*, moth-eaten*, musty, not with it*, obsolete, old, old-hat*, outmoded, out-of-style*, passé, square, tired, unfashionable, vintage; SEE CONCEPTS *578,589,797*

outdo [*v*] *better, overcome*
beat, best, blow out of water*, bulldoze*, bury*, cook*, cream*, defeat, do in*, down*, eclipse, exceed, excel, fake out*, go one better*, leave behind*, lick*, outclass, outdistance, outfox, outgun, outjockey, outmaneuver, outrival, outshine, outsmart, outstrip, pull a fast one*, shake off*, shoot ahead*, snow*, surpass, top, transcend, trash*; SEE CONCEPTS *95,141*

outdoor [*adj/adv*] *in the open air*
alfresco, casual, free, garden, healthful, hilltop, informal, in the open, invigorating, mountain, natural, nature-loving, out-of-doors, out of the house, outside, patio, picnic, rustic, unrestricted, woods, yard; SEE CONCEPT *583*

outdoors [*n*] *open air; nature*
bucolic surroundings, country, countryside, environment, fresh air, garden, green earth*, hill, mountain, open, out-of-doors, patio, without, woods, yard; SEE CONCEPT *198*

outer [*adj*] *external, exposed*
alien, beyond, exoteric, exterior, extraneous, extrinsic, outermost, outlying, outmost, outside, outward, over, peripheral, remote, superficial, surface, without; SEE CONCEPTS *484,583*

outfit [*n1*] *set of clothes or equipment*
accoutrements, apparatus, appliances, clothing, costume, ensemble, garb, gear, get-up*, guise,

or
ou

kit, machinery, materiel, outlay, paraphernalia, provisions, rig, rigging, suit, supplies, tackle, togs, trappings*, wardrobe; SEE CONCEPTS 451,496

outfit [n2] *large group; business*
band, clique, company, concern, corps, coterie, crew, enterprise, establishment, firm, house, organization, party, set, squad, team, troop, troupe, unit; SEE CONCEPTS 325,417

outfit [v] *clothe, equip*
accoutre, appoint, arm, deck out*, drape, fit out*, furnish, gear, prepare, provide, provision, rig up*, stock, suit, supply, tog*, turn out*; SEE CONCEPTS 167,182

outgoing [adj1] *demonstrative, extroverted*
approachable, civil, communicative, cordial, easy, expansive, extrovert, friendly, genial, gregarious, informal, kind, open, sociable, sympathetic, unconstrained, unreserved, unrestrained, warm; SEE CONCEPT 404

outgoing [adj2] *leaving*
departing, ex-*, former, last, migratory, outbound, outward-bound, past, retiring, withdrawing; SEE CONCEPTS 581,584

outgrowth [n1] *projection*
bulge, enlargement, excrescence, jut, node, offshoot, outcrop, process, prolongation, prominence, protuberance, shoot, sprout, swelling; SEE CONCEPTS 471,824

outgrowth [n2] *product, consequence*
aftereffect, branch, by-product*, derivative, descendant, development, effect, emergence, end, end result*, issue, member, offshoot, offspring, outcome, result, spin-off*, yield; SEE CONCEPTS 230,260

outing [n] *short trip*
airing, drive, excursion, expedition, jaunt, junket, long weekend, picnic, pleasure trip, roundabout, spin*, vacation, weekend; SEE CONCEPTS 224,386

outing [n2] *politically motivated exposure of another's secrets*
announcement, declaration, demystification, disclosure, proclamation, revealing, tossing, uncloseting, unmasking; SEE CONCEPT 60

outlandish [adj] *bizarre, strange*
alien, awkward, barbaric, barbarous, boorish, clumsy, curious, droll, eccentric, erratic, exotic, extravagant, fantastic, far-out*, foreign, freakish, gauche, graceless, grotesque, kinky*, odd, outrageous, outré, peculiar, preposterous, quaint, queer, ridiculous, rude, singular, tasteless, ultra, unconventional, uncouth, unheard-of*, unorthodox, unusual, weird, whimsical, wild; SEE CONCEPTS 401,548

outlast [v] *endure beyond another*
hang on, outlive, outstay, outwear, remain, survive; SEE CONCEPT 407

outlaw [n] *person who is running from the law*
bandit, brigand, con, criminal, crook, desperado, drifter, ex-con, fugitive, gangster, gunslinger*, hood*, hoodlum, hooligan*, jailbird, marauder, mobster, mug*, outcast, pariah, racketeer, robber, wrong number*; SEE CONCEPT 412

outlaw [v] *prohibit; make illegal*
ban, banish, bar, condemn, damn, disallow, embargo, enjoin, exclude, forbid, illegalize, inhibit, interdict, prevent, proscribe, stop, taboo; SEE CONCEPTS 121,317

outlay [n] *expenses*
bite*, bottom line*, charge, cost, damage, disbursement, expenditure, expense, highway robbery*, investment, price tag, score*, setback*, spending, tab*, throw*, tune*; SEE CONCEPT 344

outlet [n1] *place or means of escape, release*
aperture, avenue, break, channel, crack, duct, egress, escape, exit, hole, nozzle, opening, orifice, porthole, release, safety valve, spout, tear, vent, way out; SEE CONCEPTS 513,693

outlet [n2] *store that sells discounted items*
factory store, market, mill store, seconds store, shop, showroom; SEE CONCEPTS 439,448,449

outline [n1] *plan, sketch*
bare facts*, blueprint, diagram, draft, drawing, floor plan, frame, framework, ground plan, layout, main features, recapitulation, résumé, rough draft, rough idea, rundown, skeleton, summary, synopsis, thumbnail sketch*, tracing; SEE CONCEPT 268

outline [n2] *form, tracing of an object*
configuration, conformation, contour, delineation, figuration, figure, profile, shape, silhouette; SEE CONCEPTS 436,625

outline [v] *sketch out; plan*
adumbrate, block out, characterize, chart, delineate, describe, draft, lay out, paint, plot, recapitulate, rough out, sketch, skeletonize, summarize, tell about, trace; SEE CONCEPTS 36,55,174

outlook [n1] *point of view*
angle*, attitude, direction, frame of mind*, headset*, mind-set*, perspective, routine, scope, side, size of it*, slant*, standpoint, viewpoint, views, vision; SEE CONCEPTS 410,689

outlook [n2] *probable future*
appearances, chance, expectation, forecast, law of averages*, likelihood, normal course, opening, opportunity, possibility, probability, prospect, prospects, risk; SEE CONCEPT 679

outlook [n3] *scene, view*
aspect, lookout, panorama, perspective, prospect, scape, sight, vista; SEE CONCEPTS 509,628

outlying [adj] *in rural area; remote*
afar, backwoods, distant, external, faraway, far-flung*, far-off, off-lying, outer, out-of-the-way*, peripheral, provincial, removed; SEE CONCEPT 583

outmoded [adj] *obsolete, old-fashioned*
anachronistic, antediluvian, antiquated, antique, archaic, behind the times*, bent, bygone, dated, dead, démodé, dinosaur*, disused, extinct, fossilized, has-been*, horse and buggy*, moldy*, moth-eaten*, musty*, obsolescent, obsolete, olden, old-hat*, old-time, out, out-of-date, out-of-style, outworn, passé*, superannuated, superseded, tired, unfashionable, unstylish, unusable, vintage; SEE CONCEPTS 560,578,589,797

output [n] *something produced*
achievement, amount, crop, gain, harvest, making, manufacture, manufacturing, producing, product, production, productivity, profit, take, turnout, yield; SEE CONCEPTS 205,260

outrage [n1] *atrocity, evil*
abuse, affront, barbarism, damage, desecration, enormity, evildoing, harm, hurt, indignity, inhumanity, injury, insult, mischief, misdoing, offense, profanation, rape, rapine, ravishing, ruin, shock, violation, violence, wrongdoing; SEE CONCEPTS 192,645,674

outrage [n2] *anger*
blowup, flare-up*, fury, huff*, hurt, indignation, resentment, ruckus*, shock*, stew*, storm*, wrath; SEE CONCEPT 29

outrage [v] *wrong, offend, abuse*
affront, aggrieve, boil over*, burn up*, defile, deflower, desecrate, do violence to, fire up*, force, ill-treat, incense, infuriate, injure, insult, jar*, kick up a row*, madden, make hit the ceiling*, maltreat, mistreat, misuse, oppress, persecute, raise Cain*, rape, ravage, ravish, reach boiling point*, scandalize, shock, spoil, violate, whip up*; SEE CONCEPTS 7,19,29,246

outrageous [adj1] *very bad*
abominable, atrocious, barbaric, beastly, brazen, contemptible, contumelious, corrupt, criminal, debasing, debauching, degenerate, depraving, disgraceful, disgracing, egregious, flagitious, flagrant, gross, heinous, horrendous, horrible, ignoble, infamous, inhuman, iniquitous, malevolent, monstrous, nefarious, notorious, odious, opprobrious, scandalous, scurrilous, shameless, shaming, shocking, sinful, unbearable, ungodly, unspeakable, villainous, violent, wanton, wicked; SEE CONCEPT 571

outrageous [adj2] *beyond reasonable limits*
barbarous, crazy*, excessive, exorbitant, extortionate, extravagant, immoderate, inordinate, last straw*, offensive, out of bounds*, preposterous, scandalous, shocking, steep*, too much*, uncivilized, unconscionable, unreasonable; SEE CONCEPTS 569,771

outright [adj] *complete, unconditional*
absolute, all, arrant, consummate, definite, direct, downright, entire, flat, gross, out-and-out*, perfect, positive, pure, straightforward, thorough, thoroughgoing, total, undeniable, unequivocal, unmitigated, unqualified, utter, whole, wholesale*; SEE CONCEPTS 531,535

outside [n] *exterior; out-of-doors*
appearance, covering, facade, face, front, integument, open, open air, outdoors, seeming, sheath, skin, surface, topside, without; SEE CONCEPTS 198,484

outside [adj1] *external*
alfresco, alien, apart from, away from, exterior, extramural, extraneous, extreme, farther, farthest, foreign, furthest, open-air, out, outdoor, outer, outermost, outward, over, surface; SEE CONCEPTS 484,583

outside [adj2] *slight, slim*
distant, faint, far, marginal, negligible, off, remote, slender, small, unlikely; SEE CONCEPTS 552,789

outsider [n] *person who is foreign to something*
alien, floater*, foreigner, incomer*, interloper, intruder, newcomer, odd one out*, outlander, refugee, stranger; SEE CONCEPTS 413,423

outskirts [n] *edge of a geographic area*
bedroom community*, border, boundary, edge, environs, limit, outpost, periphery, purlieu, purlieus, sticks*, suburb, suburbia, vicinity; SEE CONCEPTS 508,513

outspoken [adj] *explicit, unreserved*
abrupt, artless, blunt, calling spade a spade*, candid, direct, forthright, frank, free, laying it on the line*, open, plain, plain-spoken, point-blank*, round, square, straightforward, strident, talking turkey*, unceremonious, unequivocal, unreticent, up front*, vocal; SEE CONCEPTS 267,404

outstanding [adj1] *superior, excellent*
ace*, A-number-1*, A-1*, bad*, boss*, capital*, celebrated, chief, cool*, crack*, distinguished, dominant, eminent, eventful, exceptional, famous, far-out*, great, greatest, hundred-proof*, important, impressive, magnificent, main, major, meritorious, momentous, mostest, number one*, out-of-sight*, out-of-this-world*, phenomenal, predominant, preeminent, primo*, principal, special, standout, star, steller, super, superior, superlative, tops*, well-known, world-class; SEE CONCEPTS 568,574

outstanding [adj2] *noticeable, striking*
arresting, arrestive, conspicuous, distinguished, eye-catching, important, leading, marked, memorable, notable, noteworthy, prominent, pronounced, remarkable, salient, signal; SEE CONCEPTS 485,537

outstanding [adj3] *referring to an unpaid debt*
due, mature, ongoing, open, overdue, owing, payable, pending, remaining, uncollected, unresolved, unsettled; SEE CONCEPT 334

outward [adj] *visible; for appearances*
apparent, evident, exterior, external, from within, noticeable, observable, obvious, on the surface, open, ostensible, out, outer, outside, over, perceptible, superficial, surface, to the eye, toward the edge; SEE CONCEPTS 576,581,583

outwardly [adv] *to all appearances*
apparently, as far as one can see, evidently, externally, for all intents and purposes*, in appearance, officially, on the face of it, on the surface, ostensibly, professedly, seemingly, superficially, to the eye; SEE CONCEPTS 544,576

outweigh [v] *override, dominate*
atone for, balance, cancel out, compensate, counterbalance, counterpoise, countervail, eclipse, exceed, excel, make up for, offset, outbalance, outrival, outrun, overcome, overshadow, predominate, preponderate, prevail, set off, surpass, take precedence, tip the scales; SEE CONCEPT 141

outwit/outsmart [v] *get the better of; figure out before arriving*
baffle, bamboozle*, beat*, bewilder, cap, cheat, circumvent, con*, confuse, deceive, defeat, defraud, dupe, end-run*, fake out*, finagle*, fox*, goose*, gull*, have*, hoax, hoodwink, lead astray*, make a fool of*, make a monkey of*, mislead, outdo, outfox, outgeneral, outguess, outjockey, outmaneuver, outthink, overreach, pull a fast one on*, put one over on*, run circles around*, swindle, take in*, top*, trick, worst*; SEE CONCEPTS 15,59

oval [adj] *long and rounded in shape*
egg-shaped, ellipsoidal, elliptic, elliptical, oblong, ooid, ovaloid, ovate, oviform, ovoid; SEE CONCEPT 486

ovation [n] *clapping and cheers*
acclaim, acclamation, applause, big hand*, bravos, cheering, hand, laudation, plaudits, praise, salvo, testimonial, tribute; SEE CONCEPTS 69,264

over [adj1] *accomplished*
ancient history, at an end, by, bygone, closed, completed, concluded, done, done with, ended, finished, gone, past, settled, up; SEE CONCEPTS 531,548

over [adj2/adv1] *in addition*
additionally, beyond, ever, excessively, extra, extremely, immensely, in excess, inordinately, left

ou
ov

over, more, over and above, overly, overmuch, remaining, superfluous, surplus, too, unduly, unused; SEE CONCEPTS 544,771

over [adv2] *above*
aloft, beyond, covering, farther up, higher than, in heaven, in the sky, off, on high, on top of, overhead, overtop, straight up, traversely, upstairs; SEE CONCEPTS 583,793

overabundance [n] *excess*
embarrassment of riches*, glut, nimiety, overflow, overkill, overmuch, oversupply, plethora, profusion, superabundance, superfluity, surfeit, surplus, surplusage, too much*; SEE CONCEPTS 767,787

overall [adj] *complete, general*
all-embracing, blanket, comprehensive, global, inclusive, long-range, long-term, sweeping, thorough, total, umbrella; SEE CONCEPT 772

overall [adv] *in general*
all over, chiefly, everyplace, everywhere, generally speaking, in the long run, largely, mainly, mostly, on the whole, predominantly, primarily, principally, throughout; SEE CONCEPTS 548,772

overbearing [adj] *arrogant, domineering*
ascendant, autocratic, bossy, cavalier, cocky*, despotic, dictatorial, disdainful, dogmatic, egotistic, haughty, high-and-mighty*, high-handed*, imperative, imperial, imperious, insolent, magisterial, officious, oppressive, overweening, paramount, peremptory, predominant, preponderant, prevalent, proud, regnant, sniffy*, snotty*, sovereign*, stuffy, supercilious, superior, tyrannical, uppity*; SEE CONCEPTS 401,404

overblown [adj] *excessive, too much*
aureate, bombastic, disproportionate, euphuistic, flowery, fulsome, grandiloquent, hyped up*, immoderate, inflated, magniloquent, oratorical, overdone, pompous, pretentious, profuse, rhetorical, sonorous, superfluous, turgid, undue, verbose, windy; SEE CONCEPTS 267,548

overcast [adj] *cloudy, darkened*
clouded, clouded over, dark, dismal, dreary, dull, gray, hazy, leaden, lowering, murky, nebulous, not clear, not fair, oppressive, somber, sunless, threatening; SEE CONCEPT 525

overcome [adj] *overwhelmed; visibly moved*
affected, at a loss for words, beaten, blown-away*, bowled-over*, buried*, conquered, defeated, overthrown, run-over*, speechless, swamped, swept off one's feet*, taken*, unable to continue; SEE CONCEPT 403

overcome [v] *beat, defeat*
best*, be victorious, come out on top*, conquer, crush, down*, drown, get around*, get the better of*, hurdle, knock over*, knock socks off*, lick*, master, outlive, overpower, overthrow, overwhelm, prevail, prostrate, reduce, render, rise above*, shock, stun, subdue, subjugate, surmount, survive, throw*, triumph over, vanquish, weather*, whelm*, win, worst*; SEE CONCEPT 95

overconfident [adj] *overly sure of oneself*
brash, careless, cocksure*, cocky*, foolhardy, heading for a fall*, heedless, hubristic, impudent, overweening, presuming, presumptuous, pushy*, rash, reckless, self-assertive; SEE CONCEPTS 401,542

overdo [v] *go to extremes; carry too far*
amplify, be intemperate, belabor, bite off too much*, do to death, drive oneself, exaggerate, fatigue, go overboard*, go too far*, hype, lay it

on*, magnify, make federal case*, not know when to stop*, overburden, overestimate, overindulge, overload, overplay, overrate, overreach, overstate, overtax, overtire, overuse, overvalue, overwork, pile on*, pressure, puff*, run into the ground*, run riot*, strain oneself, stretch, talk big*, wear down*, wear oneself out*; SEE CONCEPTS 87,112,156

overdue [adj] *late, behind schedule*
behindhand, behind time, belated, delinquent, due, held up*, hung up*, jammed*, long delayed, mature, not punctual, outstanding, owing, payable, tardy, unpaid, unpunctual, unsettled; SEE CONCEPTS 334,548,799

overflow [n] *flood, inundation*
advance, cataclysm, cataract, congestion, deluge, discharge, encroachment, enforcement, engorgement, excess, exuberance, flash flood, flooding, infringement, niagara, overabundance, overcrowding, overkill, overmuch, overproduction, plethora, pour, propulsion, push, redundancy, spate, spill, spillover, submergence, submersion, superfluity, surfeit, surplus, torrent; SEE CONCEPT 740

overflow [v] *pour out, flood*
brim, bubble over, cascade, cover, deluge, discharge, drain, drown, engulf, fall over, gush, inundate, irrupt, issue, jet, leak, overbrim, overrun, overtop, pour, run over, rush, shed, shower, slop, slosh, soak, spill, spill over, spout, spray, spurt, squirt, submerge, surge, swamp, water, wave, well, well over, wet, whelm; SEE CONCEPTS 179,256,740

overhang [v] *bulge, hang over*
beetle, be imminent, be suspended, cast a shadow, command, dangle over, droop over, endanger, extend, flap over, impend, jut, loom, menace, overtop, poke, portend, pouch, project, protrude, rise above, stand out, stick out, swing over, threaten, tower above; SEE CONCEPT 752

overhaul [v] *redo, restore*
check, debug, doctor*, do up*, examine, fiddle with*, fix, give facelift*, improve, inspect, mend, modernize, patch, rebuild, recondition, reconstruct, reexamine, renew, repair, retread, revamp, service, survey; SEE CONCEPTS 126,202,212

overhead [n] *general, continuing costs of operation*
budget, burden, cost, depreciation, expense, penses, insurance, outlay, rent, upkeep, utilities; SEE CONCEPTS 329,332

overhead [adj/adv] *up above*
above, aerial, aloft, atop, hanging, in the sky, on high, over, overhanging, roof, skyward, upper, upward; SEE CONCEPT 586

overjoyed [adj] *extremely happy*
charmed, delighted, deliriously happy, elated, euphoric, happy as a clam*, happy as a lark*, joyful, jubilant, on cloud nine*, only too happy*, over the moon*, rapturous, ravished, thrilled, tickled pink*, transported; SEE CONCEPT 403

overlap [v] *lie over something else*
extend along, flap, fold over, go beyond, imbricate, lap over, overhang, overlay, overlie, overrun, project, protrude, ride, run over, shingle; SEE CONCEPT 759

overlook [v] *disregard, neglect*
discount, disdain, fail to notice, forget, ignore, leave out, leave undone, let fall between the cracks*, let go, let slide*, make light of*, miss,

omit, overpass, pass, pass by, pay no attention, slight, slip up*; SEE CONCEPTS 30,101,699

overlook [v2] *make allowances for*
bear with*, blink at*, condone, disregard, excuse, forgive, go along with, grin and bear it*, handle, ignore, let bygones be bygones*, let go, let pass*, live with*, look the other way, pay no mind*, play past*, put up with*, roll with punches*, stand for, stomach, swim with the tide*, take, tune out*, turn blind eye to*, whitewash*, wink at*, wipe slate clean*; SEE CONCEPTS 10,83

overlook [v3] *have a view of something*
afford a view, command, command a view, dominate, front on, give on, give upon, have a prospect of, inspect, look down, look out, look out on, look over, mount, oversee, overtop, soar above, surmount, survey, top, tower over, watch over; SEE CONCEPT 752

overlook [v4] *supervise*
boss, chaperon, control, oversee, quarterback*, superintend, survey; SEE CONCEPTS 94,117

overly [adv] *excessively*
ever, exceedingly, extremely, immensely, immoderately, inordinately, over, overfull, overmuch, too, too much, too-too*, unduly, very much; SEE CONCEPT 544

overplay [v] *be dramatic*
accent, accentuate, blow out of proportion*, dramatize, exaggerate, get carried away*, ham it up*, hyperbolize, labor at, lay it on thick*, magnify, maximize, mug*, overact, overdo, overdraw, overemphasize, overstate, overstress, overuse, overwork, point up*, show off*, stretch; SEE CONCEPTS 59,87,292

overpower [v] *beat; get the upper hand*
bear down, beat down, blank, blow away*, bulldoze*, bury, clobber, conquer, cream*, crush, defeat, drown, drub*, immobilize, knock out*, lay one out*, murder*, overcome, overthrow, overwhelm, prostrate, put away*, quell, reduce, roll over*, rout, shellack*, shut off*, smash, subdue, subjugate, swamp*, take care of*, take out*, torpedo*, total*, trash*, trounce, vanquish, waste*, wax*, whelm*; SEE CONCEPTS 95,191

overrate [v] *assign too much value, importance*
assess too highly, build up, exaggerate, exceed, expect too much of, magnify, make too much of*, overassess, overesteem, overestimate, overpraise, overprize, overreckon, oversell, overvalue, rate too highly, think too highly of*, think too much of*; SEE CONCEPTS 12,49

override/overrule [v] *cancel, reverse a decision*
alter, annul, bend to one's will*, control, countermand, direct, disallow, disregard, dominate, govern, ignore, influence, invalidate, make null and void*, make void, not heed, nullify, outvote, outweigh, overturn, prevail over, quash, recall, repeal, rescind, revoke, ride roughshod*, rule against, set aside, supersede, sway, take no account of, thwart, trample, upset, vanquish, veto; SEE CONCEPTS 50,88,121,298,317

overriding [adj] *central, most important*
cardinal, compelling, determining, dominant, final, main, major, number one*, overruling, paramount, pivotal, predominant, prevailing, primary, prime, principal, ruling, supreme, ultimate; SEE CONCEPT 568

overrun [v1] *defeat, invade*
beat, clobber, drub*, foray, inroad, lambaste, lick*, massacre, occupy, overwhelm, put to flight,

raid, rout, swamp*, thrash, trim, whip; SEE CONCEPTS 86,95

overrun [v2] *infest, spread over; exceed*
beset, choke, deluge, go beyond, inundate, invade, overflow, overgrow, overshoot, overspread, overstep, overwhelm, permeate, ravage, run on, run over, spill, spread like wildfire*, surge, surpass, swarm, well over; SEE CONCEPTS 172,179,551

overseas [adj] *across an ocean*
abroad, across, away, foreign, in foreign land, transatlantic, transoceanic, transpacific; SEE CONCEPT 583

oversee [v] *manage, supervise*
baby-sit*, be in driver's seat*, boss, call the shots*, captain, chaperon, command, eye*, herd, inspect, keep one's eye on*, look after, overlook, quarterback*, ride herd on*, run the show*, shepherd, sit on top of*, skipper, superintend, survey, watch; SEE CONCEPT 117

overseer [n] *person who supervises others' work*
executive, head, head honcho*, manager, pit boss*, straw boss*, superintendent, supervisor; SEE CONCEPT 347

overshadow [v] *make obscure, dim, vague*
adumbrate, becloud, bedim, cloud, command, darken, dim, dominate, dwarf, eclipse, excel, govern, haze, leave in the shade*, obfuscate, outshine, outweigh, overcast, overcloud, overweigh, preponderate, rise above*, rule, shadow, steal spotlight*, surpass, take precedence, tower above*, veil; SEE CONCEPTS 620,668

oversight [n1] *failure, omission*
blank*, blunder, carelessness, chasm, default, delinquency, dereliction, disregard, error, fault, inattention, lapse, laxity, miscue, mistake, neglect, overlook, overlooking, preterition, pretermission, skip, slip, slipup*; SEE CONCEPT 101

oversight [n2] *care, supervision*
administration, aegis, charge, check, control, custody, direction, guard, guardianship, handling, inspection, intendance, keep, keeping, maintenance, management, superintendence, surveillance, tutelage; SEE CONCEPT 117

overt [adj] *obvious, unconcealed*
apparent, clear, definite, manifest, observable, open, patent, plain, public, undisguised, visible; SEE CONCEPT 535

overtake [v] *catch; pass*
beat, befall, better, catch up with, come upon, engulf, gain on, get past, get to, happen, hit, leave behind, outdistance, outdo, outstrip, overhaul, overwhelm, reach, strike, take by surprise; SEE CONCEPTS 95,141

overthrow [v] *defeat, destroy*
abolish, beat, bring down, bring to ruin, conquer, crush, demolish, depose, dethrone, do away with, eradicate, exterminate, knock down, knock over, level, liquidate, oust, overcome, overpower, overrun, overturn, overwhelm, purge, put an end to, raze, ruin, subdue, subjugate, subvert, terminate, tip, topple, tumble, unseat, upend, upset, vanquish; SEE CONCEPTS 95,252,320

overtone [n] *implication, hint*
association, connotation, flavor, inference, innuendo, intimation, meaning, nuance, sense, suggestion, tone, undercurrent, undertone; SEE CONCEPT 278

overture [n] *introduction, approach*
advance, bid, conciliatory move, exordium, fore-

word, invitation, offer, opening, preamble, preface, prelude, prelusion, presentation, proem, prologue, proposal, proposition, signal, suggestion, tender; SEE CONCEPTS *278,384,828,832*

overturn [v] *flip over*
annul, bring down, capsize, countermand, down, invalidate, invert, keel over, knock down, knock over, nullify, overbalance, prostrate, repeal, rescind, reverse, roll, set aside, spill, tip over, topple, tumble, turn over, turn upside down, upend, upset, upturn, void; SEE CONCEPTS *147,232*

overweight [adj] *heavier than average*
ample, bulky, corpulent, fat, fleshy, gross, heavy, hefty, huge, massive, obese, outsize, overfed, overstuffed, plump, portly, pudgy, rotund, stout, upholstered*, weighty; SEE CONCEPT *491*

overwhelm [v1] *flood, beat physically*
bury, conquer, crush, defeat, deluge, destroy, drown, drub*, engulf, inundate, massacre, overcome, overflow, overpower, overrun, overthrow, rout, smother, submerge, swamp, thrash, total*, whip*, win*; SEE CONCEPTS *86,95*

overwhelm [v2] *astonish, devastate*
bewilder, blow out of the water*, bowl over*, confound, confuse, demoralize, destroy, disturb, do in*, downgrade*, drown, dumbfound, floor*, kill*, overcome, overpower, prostrate, puzzle, render speechless*, run circles around, shatter, shock, stagger, steamroller*, stun, subordinate, surprise, swamp, upset, wreck; SEE CONCEPTS *16,42*

overwrought [adj] *exhausted and excited*
affected, agitated, all shook up*, beside oneself*, crazy, distracted, emotional, excitable, fired-up*, flipped out*, frantic, freaked-out*, high*, hot-and-bothered*, hot under collar*, hyper*, in a state*, keyed-up*, nervous, neurotic, on edge*, overexcited, overstrung, overworked, spent, steamed up*, stirred*, strung-out*, tense, tired, uneasy, unstrung*, uptight*, weary, wired, worked-up, worn, wound-up; SEE CONCEPTS *401,403,542*

owe [v] *have an obligation*
be beholden, be bound, be contracted, behind, be in arrears, be in debt, be indebted, be into one for, be obligated, be under obligation, feel bound, get on credit, have borrowed, incur, in hock*, lost, on the tab*, ought to, run up a bill*; SEE CONCEPT *335*

owing [adj] *unpaid*
attributable, comeuppance, due, in debt, mature, matured, outstanding, overdue, owed, payable, unsettled; SEE CONCEPT *334*

own [adj] *belonging to individual*
endemic, hers, his, individual, inherent, intrinsic, its, mine, owned, particular, peculiar, personal, private, resident, theirs, very own, yours; SEE CONCEPT *710*

own [v1] *possess; be responsible for*
be in possession of, be possessed of, boast, control, dominate, enjoy, fall heir to, have, have in hand, have rights, have title, hold, inherit, keep, occupy, reserve, retain; SEE CONCEPT *710*

own [v2] *acknowledge, admit*
allow, assent to, avow, come clean*, concede, confess, declare, disclose, grant, let on*, make clean breast of*, own up, recognize, tell the truth; SEE CONCEPT *57*

owner [n] *person who has possession of something*
buyer, governor, heir, heir-apparent, heiress, heritor, holder, keeper, landowner, legatee, partner, possessor, proprietor, purchaser, sharer, squire, titleholder; SEE CONCEPTS *343,347,414*

ownership [n] *possession of property*
buying, claim, control, cut, deed, dominion, end, hand, having, holding, occupancy, partnership, piece, possessorship, property, proprietary rights, proprietorship, purchase, purchasing, residence, slice, takeover, tenancy, tenure, title, use; SEE CONCEPT *710*

P

pace [n1] *steps in walking*
clip, footstep, gait, getalong, lick*, measure, step, stride, tread, walk; SEE CONCEPT *149*

pace [n2] *speed, tempo of motion*
beat, bounce, celerity, clip, downbeat, lick*, momentum, motion, movement, progress, quickness, rapidity, rapidness, rate, swiftness, time, velocity; SEE CONCEPTS *755,818*

pace [v1] *walk back and forth*
ambulate, canter, foot it*, gallop, hoof*, march, patrol, pound*, step, stride, traipse, tread, troop, trot, walk up and down; SEE CONCEPT *149*

pace [v2] *measure by footsteps*
count, determine, mark out, step, step off*; SEE CONCEPTS *291,764*

pacify [v] *make peaceful; appease*
allay, ameliorate, assuage, bury the hatchet*, butter up*, calm, chasten, compose, con, conciliate, cool, dulcify, fix up, grease*, kiss and make up*, lay back, lull, make peace, mitigate, moderate, mollify, pacificate, placate, propitiate, put the lid on*, qualify, quell, quiet, relieve, repress, silence, smooth over, soften, soft-pedal*, soothe, square, still, stroke, subdue, sweeten*, take the edge off*, tame, temper, tranquilize; SEE CONCEPTS *7,22,250*

pack [n1] *kit, package*
backpack, baggage, bale, bundle, burden, equipment, haversack, knapsack, load, luggage, outfit, parcel, rucksack, truss; SEE CONCEPTS *260,446,496*

pack [n2] *group, bunch*
assemblage, band, barrel, bundle, circle, collection, company, crew, crowd, deck, drove, flock, gang, great deal, heap, herd, horde, lot, lump, mess, mob, much, multiplicity, number, peck, pile, press, set, swarm, throng, troop; SEE CONCEPTS *397,417,432*

pack [v1] *make ready for transport*
batch, bind, brace, bunch, bundle, burden, collect, dispose, fasten, gather, get ready, load, package, put in order, store, stow, tie, warehouse; SEE CONCEPT *202*

pack [v2] *fill, compact*
arrange, bind, charge, chock, choke, compress, condense, contract, cram, crowd, drive in, heap, insert, jam, jam-pack*, lade, load, mob, pile, press, push, put away, ram, ram in*, sardine*, squeeze, stuff, tamp, throng, thrust in, top off, wedge; SEE CONCEPT *209*

pack [v3] *transport, carry*
bear, buck, convey, ferry, freight, gun, haul, heel,

hump, jag, journey, lug, piggyback*, ride, shlep*, shoulder, tote, trek, truck; SEE CONCEPTS *148,217*

package [*n*] *bundle; whole*
amalgamation, assortment, bag, baggage, bale, batch, biddle, bottle, box, bunch, burden, can, carton, combination, container, crate, entity, kit, load, lot, luggage, pack, packet, parcel, pile, sack, sheaf, stack, suitcase, tin, trunk, unit; SEE CONCEPTS *432,494*

packed [*adj*] *full*
arranged, awash, brimful, brimming, bundled, chock, chock-full*, compact, compressed, congested, consigned, crammed, crowded, filled, full to the gills*, jammed, jam-packed*, loaded, mobbed, overflowing, overloaded, packed like sardines*, seething, serried, stuffed, swarming, to the roof*, tumid, up to the hilt*, up to the rafters*, wall-to-wall*, wrapped; SEE CONCEPTS *481,483,740,774*

packet [*n*] *small, often flat, bundle*
bag, carton, container, envelope, file, folder, package, parcel, wrapper, wrapping; SEE CONCEPT *494*

pact [*n*] *agreement*
alliance, arrangement, bargain, bond, compact, concord, concordat, contract, convention, covenant, deal, league, paper, piece of paper, protocol, settlement, transaction, treaty, understanding; SEE CONCEPTS *271,684*

pad/padding [*n1*] *protection*
buffer, cushion, filling, packing, stuffing, wad, wadding, waste; SEE CONCEPTS *473,475*

pad [*n2*] *tablet of paper*
block, jotter, memorandum, notebook, notepad, paper, parchment, quire, ream, scratch, scratch pad, slips; SEE CONCEPTS *260,475*

pad [*v1*] *protect with cushioning*
cushion, fill, fill out, line, pack, protect, shape, stuff; SEE CONCEPTS *134,202*

pad [*v2*] *elaborate, amplify*
augment, bulk, embellish, embroider, enlarge, exaggerate, expand, fill out, flesh out*, fudge*, increase, inflate, lengthen, magnify, overdraw, overstate, protract, spin, stretch; SEE CONCEPTS *63,244*

pad [*v3*] *walk quietly; walk ploddingly*
creep, go barefoot, line, march, patter*, pitter-patter*, plod, pussyfoot*, sneak, steal, traipse, tramp, trek, trudge; SEE CONCEPT *149*

paddle [*n*] *item used for propelling object*
oar, paddlewheel, pole, propeller, pull, scull, sweep; SEE CONCEPTS *479,499*

paddle [*v*] *propel with arms or tool*
boat, cruise, cut water*, drift, drive, navigate, oar, pull, row, run rapids*, scull, sky an oar*, slop, splash, stir, sweep, thrash, wade; SEE CONCEPT *147*

pagan [*n*] *person who does not believe in an orthodox religion*
agnostic, atheist, doubter, freethinker, heathen, heretic, iconoclast, idolater, idolist, infidel, paganist, pantheist, polytheist, scoffer, skeptic, unbeliever; SEE CONCEPTS *361,423*

pagan [*adj*] *irreligious*
agnostic, atheistic, heathen, idolatrous, impious, infidel, polytheistic, profane; SEE CONCEPT *542*

page [*n1*] *sheet of paper*
folio, leaf, recto, side, signature, surface, verso; SEE CONCEPT *475*

page [*n2*] *person who serves others*
attendant, bellhop, equerry, errand runner, servant, youth; SEE CONCEPTS *348,354*

page [*v1*] *call for over communications system*
announce, beep, call, call out, call the name of, hunt for, preconize, seek, send for, summon; SEE CONCEPTS *74,78*

page [*v2*] *mark sheets of document*
check, count, foliate, number, paginate; SEE CONCEPTS *79,764*

pageant [*n*] *spectacle or contest*
celebration, charade, display, exhibition, exposition, extravaganza, fair, make-believe, motorcade, parade, pomp, procession, ritual, show, tableau; SEE CONCEPTS *292,377*

pain [*n1*] *physical suffering*
ache, affliction, agony, burn, catch, convulsion, cramp, crick, discomfort, distress, fever, gripe, hurt, illness, injury, irritation, laceration, malady, misery, pang, paroxysm, prick, sickness, smarting, soreness, spasm, sting, stitch, strain, tenderness, throb, throe, tingle, torment, torture, trouble, twinge, wound; SEE CONCEPTS *316,728*

pain [*n2*] *mental suffering*
affliction, agony, anguish, anxiety, bitterness, despondency, distress, grief, heartache, hurt, malaise, martyrdom, misery, rack, sadness, shock, suffering, torment, torture, travail, tribulation, woe, worry, wretchedness; SEE CONCEPTS *410,728*

pain [*n3*] *problem*
aggravation, annoyance, bore, bother, drag, effort, exertion, irritation, nuisance, pest, trouble, vexation; SEE CONCEPT *532*

pain [*v*] *bother, trouble*
ache, afflict, aggrieve, agonize, ail, anguish, annoy, bite, chafe, chasten, constrain, convulse, cut to the quick*, discomfort, disquiet, distress, exasperate, excruciate, gall, grieve, gripe, harass, harm, harrow, hit where one lives*, hurt, inflame, injure, irk, irritate, nick, prick, punish, rack, rile, sadden, smart, sting, strain, stress, suffer, throb, tingle, torment, torture, upset, vex, worry, wound; SEE CONCEPTS *7,19,246*

painful [*adj*] *physically or mentally agonizing*
aching, afflictive, agonizing, arduous, awful, biting, burning, caustic, conscionable, difficult, dire, disagreeable, distasteful, distressing, dreadful, excruciating, extreme, extremely bad, grievous, hard, harrowing, hurtful, hurting, inflamed, irritated, laborious, piercing, raw, saddening, sensitive, severe, sharp, smarting, sore, stinging, tedious, tender, terrible, throbbing, tormenting, troublesome, trying, uncomfortable, unpleasant, vexatious; SEE CONCEPTS *529,537*

painstaking [*adj*] *meticulous, thorough*
assiduous, by the book*, by the numbers*, careful, conscientious, conscionable, diligent, earnest, exact, exacting, finicky, fussbudget*, fussy, hardworking, heedful, industrious, particular, persevering, persnickety*, picky, punctilious, punctual, scrupulous, sedulous, stickler*, strenuous, thoroughgoing; SEE CONCEPTS *326,538*

paint [*n*] *tinted covering*
acrylic, chroma, color, coloring, cosmetic, dye, emulsion, enamel, flat, gloss, greasepaint, latex, makeup, oil, overlay, pigment, rouge, stain, tempera, varnish, veneer, wax; SEE CONCEPTS *467,475*

ov
pa

paint [v] *apply colored tint, often to make design*
brush, catch a likeness, coat, color, compose, cover, cover up, daub, decorate, delineate, depict, design, draft, draw, dye, figure, fresco, gloss over, limn, ornament, outline, picture, portray, put on coats*, represent, shade, sketch, slap on*, slather, stipple, swab, tint, touch up, wash; SEE CONCEPTS 172,174

pair [n] *two of something*
brace, combination, combine, combo, couple, deuce, doublet, duality, duo, dyad, match, mates, span, team, twins, two, two of a kind, twosome, yoke; SEE CONCEPTS 432,784

pair [v] *make, become a twosome*
balance, bracket, combine, couple, join, marry, match, match up, mate, pair off, put together, team, twin, unite, wed, yoke; SEE CONCEPT 113

pajamas [n] *sleeping clothes*
jamas*, jammies*, jams*, loungewear, lounging robe, nightdress, nightie*, nightshirt, nightwear, PJ's*, sleeper, sleeping suit; SEE CONCEPT 451

pal [n] *person's friend*
amiga, amigo, associate, boon companion*, bosom buddy*, bro*, brother, buddy, chum, companion, comrade, connate, crony, cuz, good buddy*, homeboy, homegirl, mate, sidekick, sis*, sister; SEE CONCEPT 423

palace [n] *royal or enormous home*
alcazar, castle, chateau, dwelling, hall, manor, mansion, official residence, royal residence; SEE CONCEPT 516

palatable [adj] *delicious, agreeable*
acceptable, A-OK*, aperitive, appetizing, attractive, cool, copacetic, delectable, delightful, divine, enjoyable, fair, flavorsome, good-tasting, heavenly, home-cooking*, luscious, mellow, mouthwatering, peachy, pleasant, relishing, sapid, saporific, saporous, satisfactory, savory, scrumptious, sugar-coated*, sweetened, tasteful, tasty, tempting, toothsome, toothy*, yummy*; SEE CONCEPTS 529,613

palatial [adj] *grand, opulent*
deluxe, grandiose, illustrious, imposing, impressive, lush, luxuriant, luxurious, magnificent, majestic, monumental, noble, plush, regal, rich, silken, spacious, splendid, stately, sumptuous, upholstered; SEE CONCEPTS 334,485,589

pale [adj] *light in color or effect*
anemic, ashen, ashy, blanched, bleached, bloodless, cadaverous, colorless, deathlike, dim, doughy, dull, faded, faint, feeble, ghastly, gray, haggard, inadequate, ineffective, ineffectual, insubstantial, livid, lurid, pallid, pasty, poor, sallow, sick, sickly, spectral, thin, unsubstantial, wan, washed-out, waxen, waxlike, weak, white, whitish; SEE CONCEPTS 537,618

pale [v] *become, make lighter or weakened*
blanch, decrease, dim, diminish, dull, fade, faint, go white, grow dull, lessen, lose color, lose luster, muddy, tarnish, whiten; SEE CONCEPTS 240,250

pall [n] *cloud, gloom*
cloak, cloth, covering, damp, damper, dismay, mantle, melancholy, shadow, shroud, veil; SEE CONCEPTS 620,674

pall [v] *bore, tire*
become dull, become tedious, cloy, disgust, fill, glut, gorge, jade, sate, satiate, sicken, surfeit, weary; SEE CONCEPTS 7,19

palliate [v] *gloss over; cover up*
abate, allay, alleviate, apologize for, assuage, camouflage, cloak, conceal, condone, cover, diminish, disguise, dissemble, ease, exculpate, excuse, extenuate, gloze, hide, hush up*, justify, lessen, lighten, make light of*, mask, minimize, mitigate, moderate, mollify, prettify, put on a Band-Aid*, qualify, quick fix*, relieve, screen, soften, soothe, sugarcoat*, temper, varnish, veil, veneer, vindicate, white, whiten, whitewash*; SEE CONCEPTS 57,59,172,188

palpable [adj1] *clear, obvious*
apparent, appreciable, arresting, believable, blatant, certain, colorable, conspicuous, credible, detectable, discernible, distinct, evident, manifest, noticeable, observable, open, ostensible, patent, perceivable, perceptible, plain, plausible, positive, remarkable, seeming, sensible, straightforward, striking, sure, tangible, unequivocal, unmistakable, visible; SEE CONCEPTS 529,535

palpable [adj2] *concrete, real*
material, sensible, solid, substantial, tactile, tangible, touchable; SEE CONCEPTS 485,582

palpitate [v] *beat at a rapid pace, like a heart*
flutter, pitpat*, pitter-patter*, pound, pulsate, pulse, quiver, shiver, throb, tremble, vibrate; SEE CONCEPTS 152,308

palsied [adj] *crippled*
arthritic, atonic, debilitated, disabled, diseased, helpless, neurasthenic, paralytic, paralyzed, rheumatic, sclerotic, shaking, shaky, sick, spastic, trembling, tremorous, weak; SEE CONCEPTS 314,485

paltry [adj] *poor; worthless*
base, beggarly, cheap, common, contemptible, derisory, despicable, inconsiderable, ineffectual, insignificant, limited, low, low-down*, meager, mean, measly, minor, miserable, narrow, petty, picayune, piddling, pitiful, puny, set, shabby, shoddy, sleazy*, slight, small, sorry*, trashy, trifling, trivial, unconsequential, unimportant, vile, wretched; SEE CONCEPTS 334,485

pamper [v] *serve one's every need, whim*
baby, caress, cater to, coddle, cosset, dandle*, fondle, gratify, humor, indulge, mollycoddle*, overindulge, pet, please, regale, satisfy, spare the rod*, spoil, spoil rotten*, tickle, yield; SEE CONCEPTS 136,295

pamphlet [n] *booklet*
announcement, broadside, brochure, bulletin, circular, compilation, flyer*, folder, handout, leaflet, throwaway*, tract, tractate; SEE CONCEPTS 271,280

pan [n] *container for cooking food*
bucket, casserole, double boiler, frying pan, kettle, pail, pannikin, pot, roaster, saucepan, sheet, skillet, vessel; SEE CONCEPTS 493,494

pan [v1] *look, search for over a wide area*
follow, move, scan, separate, sift, sweep, swing, track, traverse, wash; SEE CONCEPT 216

pan [v2] *criticize strongly*
blame, censure, condemn, cut up, denounce, denunciate, disparage, flay, hammer, jeer at, knock, rap, reprehend, review unfavorably, roast, slam; SEE CONCEPT 52

panacea [n] *cure-all*
catholicon, cure, elixir, nostrum, patent medicine, relief, remedy; SEE CONCEPTS 307,311

panache [n] *person's flamboyant spirit*
brio, charisma, dash, élan, flair, flamboyance,

flourish, style, swagger, verve, vigor; SEE CONCEPT 411

pancake [n] *flat, round breakfast cake*
batter cake, blanket*, cake, crepe, flapjack, griddlecake, hot cake, johnnycake, jonnycake, sourdough, waffle, wheat*, wheat cake; SEE CONCEPTS 457,461

pandemonium [n] *craziness, commotion*
anarchy, babel, bedlam, bluster, brouhaha*, chaos, clamor, clatter, confusion, din, hassle, hubbub*, hue and cry*, hullabaloo*, jangle, noise, racket, riot, ruckus*, rumpus, tumult, turbulence, turmoil, uproar; SEE CONCEPTS 388,674

pander [v] *cater to, indulge*
brownnose*, cajole, fall all over*, gratify, lay it on*, massage, play the game*, play up to*, please, politic, satisfy, snow*, soap*, soften up, stroke, suck up to*; SEE CONCEPTS 59,136,384

pang [n] *ache, twinge*
agony, anguish, bite, discomfort, distress, gripe, misery, pain, prick, spasm, stab, sting, stitch, throb, throw, wrench; SEE CONCEPT 728

panic [n1] *extreme fright*
agitation, alarm, cold feet*, confusion, consternation, crush, dismay, dread, fear, frenzy, horror, hysteria, jam, rush, scare, stampede, terror, trepidation; SEE CONCEPTS 27,410,690

panic [n2] *sudden drop in value in financial markets*
Black Monday*, bust, crash, depression, rainy day*, slump; SEE CONCEPT 335

panic [v] *become, make afraid or distressed*
alarm, become hysterical, be terror-stricken, chicken out*, clutch, come apart, freeze up*, go to pieces*, have a fit*, lose it*, lose nerve*, overreact, push panic button*, run scared*, scare, shake in boots*, stampede, startle, terrify, unnerve; SEE CONCEPTS 14,27

panorama [n] *scene, horizon*
bird's-eye view*, compass, dimension, diorama, extent, orbit, overview, perspective, picture, prospect, purview, radius, range, reach, scenery, scenic view, scope, spectacle, survey, sweep, view, vista; SEE CONCEPTS 529,628,651

pan out [v] *come to pass; succeed*
click*, come out*, culminate, eventuate, go, go over*, happen, net*, prove out, result, turn out, work out, yield; SEE CONCEPT 706

pant [v1] *gasp for air*
be out of breath, blow, breathe, chuff, gulp, heave, huff, palpitate, pour, snort, throb, wheeze, whiff, wind; SEE CONCEPT 163

pant [v2] *long for*
ache, aim, aspire, covet, crave, desire, hunger, lust, pine, sigh, thirst, want, wish, yearn; SEE CONCEPT 20

pants [n] *clothing for legs, lower half of body*
Bermudas*, bloomers, blue jeans, boxer shorts, breeches, briefs, britches*, chaps*, chinos, clam diggers*, cords*, corduroys, denims, drawers, dungarees, jeans, jodhpurs, knickers, overalls, pantaloons*, panties*, pedal pushers*, shorts, slacks, trousers, underpants; SEE CONCEPT 451

paper/papers [n1] *legal document*
affidavit, archive, bill, certificate, certification, citation, contract, credentials, data, deed, diaries, diploma, documentation, dossier, file, grant, ID*, identification papers, indictment, instrument, letter, letters, order, passport, plea, record, subpoena, summons, testimony, token, visa,

voucher, warrant, will, writ, writings; SEE CONCEPTS 271,318

paper [n2] *newspaper*
daily, gazette, journal, news, organ, rag*, weekly; SEE CONCEPT 280

paper [n3] *thesis, article*
analysis, assignment, composition, critique, dissertation, essay, examination, monograph, report, script, study, theme, treatise; SEE CONCEPTS 271,280

paper [n4] *material upon which one writes*
card, filing card, letterhead, newsprint, note, note card, note pad, onion skin, pad, papyrus, parchment, poster, rag, sheet, stationery, tissue, vellum; SEE CONCEPTS 260,475

paper [adj] *thin, flimsy*
cardboard, disposable, insubstantial, paper-thin, papery, wafer-thin; SEE CONCEPT 606

paper [v] *line with material*
cover, hang, paste up, plaster, wallpaper; SEE CONCEPTS 172,177

par [n] *average, equilibrium*
adequation, balance, coequality, criterion, equal footing, equality, equatability, equivalence, equivalency, level, mean, median, model, norm, parity, sameness, standard, usual; SEE CONCEPTS 636,667

parade [n] *pageant, display*
array, autocade, cavalcade, ceremony, column, demonstration, exhibition, fanfare, flaunting, line, march, ostentation, panoply, pomp, procession, review, ritual, shine, show, spectacle, train, vaunting; SEE CONCEPTS 377,386

parade [v] *show off; march*
advertise, air, boast, brag, brandish, declare, demonstrate, disclose, display, disport, divulge, exhibit, expose, flash, flaunt, march in review, prance, proclaim, publish, reveal, sport, strut, swagger, trot out*, vaunt; SEE CONCEPT 261

paradigm [n] *example*
archetype, beau ideal*, chart, criterion, ensample, exemplar, ideal, mirror, model, original, pattern, prototype, sample, standard; SEE CONCEPT 686

paradise [n] *land, feeling of great pleasure; absence of evil*
Arcadia*, ballpark, bliss, cloud nine*, delight, divine abode*, Eden*, felicity, happy hunting ground*, heaven, heavenly kingdom, kingdom come*, next world*, pearly gates*, promised land, Shangri-la*, Utopia*, wonderland, Zion*; SEE CONCEPTS 370,410,515

paradox [n] *contradiction, puzzle*
absurdity, ambiguity, anomaly, catch, Catch-22*, enigma, error, inconsistency, mistake, mystery, nonsense, oddity, opposite, reverse; SEE CONCEPT 532

paragon [n] *outstanding example*
apotheosis, archetype, beau ideal*, beauty, best, champ, champion, crackerjack*, cream*, criterion, cynosure, epitome, essence, exemplar, gem, ideal, jewel*, love, lovely, model, nonesuch, nonpareil, original, paradigm, pattern, peach*, perfection, pick, prototype, quintessence, standard, sublimation, tops*, trump*, ultimate; SEE CONCEPTS 671,686

parallel [n] *complement, correlation*
analogue, analogy, comparison, corollary, correlate, correspondence, correspondent, counterpart, countertype, double, duplicate, duplication, equal, equivalent, homologue, kin*, likeness,

match, parallelism, resemblance, similarity, twin; SEE CONCEPTS 667,670

parallel [adj1] *aligned, side-by-side*
alongside, coextending, coextensive, coordinate, equidistant, extending equally, in the same direction, lateral, laterally, never meeting, running alongside; SEE CONCEPTS 581,586

parallel [adj2] *akin, similar*
agnate, alike, analogous, comparable, complementary, conforming, consonant, correspondent, corresponding, equal, identical, like, matching, resembling, uniform; SEE CONCEPTS 487,573

parallel [v] *be alike*
agree, assimilate, collimate, collocate, compare, complement, conform, copy, correlate, correspond, equal, equate, imitate, keep pace, liken, match, paragon, parallelize; SEE CONCEPTS 111,171,667

paralytic [adj] *impaired in movement*
diplegic, disabled, immobile, immobilized, inactive, incapacitated, insensible, lame, numb, palsied, palsified, paralyzed, paraplegic, powerless, quadriplegic; SEE CONCEPTS 314,485

paralyze [v] *immobilize*
anesthetize, appall, arrest, astound, bemuse, benumb, bring to grinding halt*, close, daunt, daze, deaden, debilitate, demolish, destroy, disable, disarm, enfeeble, freeze, halt, incapacitate, knock out, lame, make inert, make nerveless, nonplus, numb, palsy, petrify, prostrate, shut down*, stop dead*, stun, stupefy, transfix, weaken; SEE CONCEPTS 14,121,246,252

parameter [n] *limit*
constant, criterion, framework, guideline, limitation, restriction, specification; SEE CONCEPT 688

paramount [adj] *principal, superior*
ascendant, capital, cardinal, chief, commanding, controlling, crowning, dominant, eminent, first, foremost, headmost, leading, main, outstanding, overbearing, predominant, predominate, preeminent, premier, preponderant, prevalent, primary, prime, regnant, sovereign, supreme; SEE CONCEPTS 568,574

paraphernalia [n] *equipment, belongings*
accoutrements, apparatus, appurtenances, baggage, effects, equipage, gear, habiliments, impedimenta, impediments, machinery, material, materiel, outfit, regalia, stuff, tackle, things, trappings; SEE CONCEPTS 446,496

paraphrase [n] *translation, interpretation*
digest, explanation, rehash, rendering, rendition, rephrasing, restatement, rewording, summary, version; SEE CONCEPTS 55,57,268

paraphrase [v] *interpret, translate*
express in other words, express in own words, recapitulate, rehash, render, rephrase, restate, reword, summarize, transcribe; SEE CONCEPTS 55,57

parasite [n] *something that exists by taking from or depending on another*
barnacle, bloodsucker*, bootlicker*, deadbeat*, dependent, flunky, freeloader*, groupie*, hanger-on*, idler, leech, scrounger, sponge*, stooge*, sucker*, sycophant, taker*; SEE CONCEPTS 394,412

parcel [n1] *container prepared to be sent*
bindle, bundle, carton, load, pack, package, packet; SEE CONCEPT 494

parcel [n2] *group, bunch*
array, band, batch, body, clot, clump, cluster,

clutch, collection, company, crew, crowd, gang, lot, pack; SEE CONCEPT 432

parcel [n3] *piece of land*
acreage, plat, plot, property, tract; SEE CONCEPTS 509,513

parcel [n4] *part, piece*
bite, chunk, cut, division, lion's share*, member, moiety, piece of the action*, portion, rake-off*, section, segment, slice; SEE CONCEPTS 829,835

parch [v] *dry, burn*
blister, brown, dehydrate, desiccate, dry up, evaporate, exsiccate, make thirsty, scorch, sear, shrivel, stale, wither; SEE CONCEPTS 249,255

parched [adj] *dry*
arid, burned, cotton-mouth*, dehydrated, dried out, dried up*, dry as dust*, scorched, shriveled, thirsty, waterless, withered; SEE CONCEPT 603

pardon [n] *forgiveness*
absolution, acquittal, allowance, amnesty, anchor, clemency, commute, conciliation, condonation, discharge, exculpation, excuse, exoneration, forbearance, freeing, grace, indemnification, indemnity, indulgence, justification, kindness, lifeboat*, lifesaver*, mercy, release, remission, reprieve, vindication; SEE CONCEPTS 10,318,685

pardon [v] *forgive*
absolve, accept, acquit, amnesty, blink at*, bury the hatchet*, clear, condone, discharge, exculpate, excuse, exonerate, free, give absolution, grant amnesty, justify, let off*, let off easy*, liberate, lifeboat*, overlook, release, remit, reprieve, rescue, spring*, suspend charges, tolerate, wink at*, wipe slate clean*, write off*; SEE CONCEPTS 10,50,88,317

pare [v] *peel, trim*
carve, clip, crop, cut, cut back, cut down, decorticate, decrease, dock, flay, knock off, lop, lower, mark down, prune, reduce, scalp, scrape, shave, shear, skin, skive, slash, strip, thin, uncover; SEE CONCEPTS 176,202,236,247

parent [n] *person, source of product*
ancestor, architect, author, begetter, cause, center, creator, father, folks, forerunner, fountainhead, guardian, mother, origin, originator, procreator, progenitor, prototype, root, source, wellspring; SEE CONCEPTS 414,648

parental [adj] *having the quality or nature of a parent*
affectionate, benevolent, benign, caring, comforting, devoted, fatherly, fond, forbearing, gentle, indulgent, kind, loving, maternal, matriarchal, motherly, paternal, patriarchal, protective, sheltering, supportive, tender, warm, watchful; SEE CONCEPTS 401,542

parenthetical [adj] *incidental*
bracketed, by the way, episodic, explanatory, extraneous, extrinsic, incidental, in parenthesis, inserted, intermediate, interposed, qualifying, related, subordinate; SEE CONCEPTS 544,577

parish [n] *congregation of a church*
archdiocese, bethel, church, churchgoers, community, flock*, fold*, parishioners, territory; SEE CONCEPT 369

parity [n] *equality, balance*
adequation, affinity, agreement, analogy, approximation, closeness, coequality, conformity, congruity, consistency, correspondence, equal terms, equivalence, equivalency, likeness, nearness, par, parallelism, paraphernalia, resemblance, same-

ness, similarity, similitude, uniformity, unity; SEE CONCEPTS 667,670

park [n] *land that is reserved for pleasure, recreation*
esplanade, estate, forest, garden, grass, green, grounds, lawn, lot, meadow, parkland, place, playground, plaza, pleasure garden, recreation area, square, tract, village green, woodland; SEE CONCEPTS 509,513

park [v] *place vehicle in a position*
deposit, leave, line up, maneuver, order, position, put, seat, stand, station, store; SEE CONCEPTS 148,201

parlor [n] *sitting room*
drawing room, front room, guest room, living room, lounge, reception, salon, waiting room; SEE CONCEPT 448

parochial [adj] *narrow-minded, restricted*
biased, bigoted, conservative, conventional, insular, inward-looking, limited, local, narrow, petty, prejudiced, provincial, regional, sectarian, sectional, shallow, small-minded, small-town; SEE CONCEPT 542

parody [n] *imitation, spoof*
apology, burlesque, caricature, cartoon, copy, derision, farce, irony, jest, joke, lampoon, mime, mimicry, misrepresentation, mockery, mock-heroic*, pastiche, play-on*, raillery, rib*, ridicule, roast*, satire, send-up*, skit, takeoff*, travesty; SEE CONCEPTS 59,273,292

parody [v] *imitate, spoof*
ape, burlesque, caricature, copy, deride, disparage, distort, do a takeoff of*, exaggerate, impersonate, jeer, jest, joke, lampoon, laugh at, mime, mimic, mock, poke fun at, put on*, ridicule, roast, satirize, send up, sheik*, take off*, travesty; SEE CONCEPTS 59,111,273

paroxysm [n] *seizure, spasm*
agitation, anger, attack, convulsion, eruption, excitement, explosion, fit, flare-up*, frenzy, frothing, fuming, furor, fury, hysterics, outbreak, outburst, passion, rage, violence; SEE CONCEPTS 308,316,410

parrot [v] *repeat*
ape, chant, copy, copycat, echo, imitate, mime, mimic, quote, recite, reiterate; SEE CONCEPTS 47,77,171

parry [v] *ward off, circumvent*
anticipate, avoid, block, bypass, deflect, dodge, duck*, elude, evade, fence*, fend off, forestall, hold at bay*, preclude, prevent, rebuff, rebuke, repel, repulse, resist, shirk, shun, sidestep, stave off; SEE CONCEPTS 25,30,121

parsimonious [adj] *penny-pinching*
avaricious, chintzy*, close, frugal, greedy, illiberal, mean, miserly, penurious, prudent, saving, scrimpy, selfish, skinflint*, sparing, stingy*, tight*, tightfisted*, tightwad*; SEE CONCEPTS 334,401

part [n1] *piece, portion of something*
allotment, any, apportionment, articulation, atom, bit, bite, branch, chip, chunk, component, constituent, cut, department, detail, division, element, extra, factor, fraction, fragment, helping, hunk, ingredient, installment, item, limb, lot, lump, measure, meed, member, module, moiety, molecule, organ, parcel, particle, partition, piece, quantum, quota, ration, scrap, section, sector, segment, share, side, slab, slice, sliver, splinter, subdivision, unit; SEE CONCEPT 834

part [n2] *person or group's interest, concern*
behalf, bit, business, capacity, cause, charge, duty, faction, function, involvement, office, party, place, responsibility, role, say, share, side, task, work; SEE CONCEPTS 362,532

part [n3] *theatrical role*
antagonist, bit, bit part, cameo, character, dialogue, hero, lead, leading role, lines, minor role, piece, principal character, protagonist, romantic lead, silent bit, stock character, straight part, supporting role, title role, villain, walk-on; SEE CONCEPT 263

part [v1] *break, disconnect*
articulate, break up, cleave, come apart, detach, dichotomize, disjoin, dismantle, dissever, disunite, divide, factor, itemize, particularize, partition, portion, rend, section, segment, separate, sever, slice, split, strip, subdivide, sunder, tear; SEE CONCEPTS 98,135

part [v2] *leave, go away from someone*
break, break off, break up, clear out*, cut and run*, dedomicile, depart, ease out, go, go separate ways*, hit the road*, leave flat*, part company, pull out*, push off, quit, quit the scene*, say goodbye, separate, ship out*, shove off*, split, split up*, take a hike*, take leave, take off, walk out on, withdraw; SEE CONCEPTS 195,297,384

partake [v] *eat, share*
be a party to, be in on, be into, consume, devour, divide, engage, enter into, feed, get in the act, have a finger in, ingest, participate, receive, sample, savor, sip, sit in, sit in on, take, take part, tune in; SEE CONCEPTS 169,225

partial [adj1] *incomplete*
fractional, fragmentary, half done, halfway, imperfect, limited, part, sectional, uncompleted, unfinished, unperformed; SEE CONCEPT 531

partial [adj2] *biased, prejudiced*
colored, discriminatory, disposed, favorably inclined, influenced, interested, jaundiced, minded, one-sided, partisan, predisposed, prepossessed, tendentious, unfair, unindifferent, unjust, warped; SEE CONCEPTS 403,542

partiality [n] *favoritism, fondness*
affinity, bias, cup of tea*, dish, druthers*, flash, inclination, inclining, leaning, liking, love, partisanship, penchant, predilection, predisposition, preference, prejudice, proclivity, propensity, taste, tendency, thing*, type, weakness; SEE CONCEPTS 32,709

partially [adv] *incompletely*
by degrees, by installments, fractionally, halfway, in part, in some measure, little by little, moderately, not wholly, partly, piece by piece, piecemeal, somewhat, to a certain degree, to a certain extent; SEE CONCEPTS 531,544

participant [n] *person who takes part in activity*
actor, aide, a party to, assistant, associate, attendant, colleague, contributor, helper, in, member, partaker, participator, partner, party, player, shareholder, sharer; SEE CONCEPTS 352,366,423

participate [v] *take part in activity*
aid, associate with, be a participant, be a party to, be into*, chip in*, come in, compete, concur, cooperate, engage, engage in, enter into, get in on*, get in on the act*, go into, have a hand in*, have to do with, join in, latch on*, lend a hand, partake, perform, play, share, sit in*, sit in on*,

strive, take an interest in, tune in*; SEE CONCEPT
100

particle [n] *atom, piece*
bit, crumb, dot, dribble, drop, fleck, fragment,
grain, hoot*, iota, jot, minim, mite, modicum,
molecule, morsel, mote, ounce, ray, scrap, scruple, seed, shred, smidgen, smithereen, speck,
spot, stitch, whit; SEE CONCEPT 831

particular [n] *detail*
ABC's*, article, bottom line*, brass tacks*, case,
chapter and verse*, circumstance, clue, cue, element, fact, facts of life, feature, gospel, item,
know*, lowdown*, nitty-gritty*, nuts and bolts*,
picture, point, rundown*, scoop*, score*, speciality, specific, specification, story, thing*, what's
what*, whole story*; SEE CONCEPTS 274,532,832

particular [adj1] *exact, specific*
accurate, appropriate, blow-by-blow*, circumstantial, clocklike, detailed, distinct, especial, express, full, individual, intrinsic, itemized, limited,
local, meticulous, minute, painstaking, particularized, peculiar, precise, scrupulous, selective, singular, special, thorough, topical; SEE CONCEPT
557

particular [adj2] *notable, uncommon*
especial, exceptional, exclusive, lone, marked,
noteworthy, odd, one, only, peculiar, personal,
remarkable, respective, separate, single, singular,
sole, solitary, unique, unusual; SEE CONCEPT 564

particular [adj3] *finicky, demanding*
careful, choicy, choosy, critical, dainty, discriminating, exacting, fastidious, finical, fussbudget*,
fussy, hard to please, meticulous, nice, nit-
picking*, persnickety*, picky*, rough, stickler*,
tough; SEE CONCEPTS 404,542

particularly [adv] *specifically*
decidedly, distinctly, especially, exceptionally,
explicitly, expressly, individually, in particular,
markedly, notably, outstandingly, peculiarly,
principally, singularly, specially, surprisingly, uncommonly, unusually; SEE CONCEPT 557

parting [n] *goodbye, separation*
adieu, bisection, break, breaking, breakup, crossroads*, departure, detachment, divergence, division, farewell, going, leave-taking, on the rocks*,
partition, rift, rupture, severance, split, split-up,
valediction; SEE CONCEPTS 195,297,384

parting [adj] *farewell*
departing, final, goodbye, last, valedictory; SEE
CONCEPT 267

partisan [n] *person devoted to another or cause*
accessory, adherent, backer, champion, cohort,
defender, devotee, disciple, follower, satellite,
stalwart, supporter, sycophant, sympathizer, upholder, votary, zealot; SEE CONCEPTS 359,423

partisan [adj] *interested, factional*
accessory, adhering, biased, bigoted, blind, cliquish, colored, conspiratorial, denominational, devoted, diehard*, exclusive, fanatic, jaundiced,
one-sided, overzealous, partial, prejudiced, prepossessed, sectarian, sympathetic, tendentious,
unjust, unreasoning, warped, zealous; SEE CON-
CEPTS 401,542,548

partition [n] *divider, division*
allotment, apportionment, barrier, detachment,
disconnection, dissolution, distribution, disunion,
dividing, hindrance, obstruction, parting, portion,
rationing, rupture, screen, segregation, separation, severance, share, splitting, wall; SEE CON-
CEPTS 98,440,443,470

partition [v] *divide, separate*
apportion, cut, cut in, cut into, cut up, deal, disburse, dispense, disperse, distribute, divvy up*,
dole out*, fence off*, measure out, parcel out,
portion, screen, section, segment, separate, share,
size into, slice, split, split up, subdivide, wall off*;
SEE CONCEPTS 98,135

partly [adv] *not completely*
at best, at least, at most, at worst, bit by bit, by
degrees, carelessly, halfway, inadequately, in a
general way, in bits and pieces*, incompletely, in
part, in some measure, in some ways, insufficiently, little by little, measurably, notably, not
entirely, not fully, noticeably, not strictly speaking, not wholly, partially, partly, piece by piece, piecemeal, relatively, slightly, so far as possible,
somewhat, to a certain degree, to a certain extent,
up to a certain point, within limits*; SEE CONCEPT
531

partner [n] *person who takes part with another*
accomplice, ally, assistant, associate, buddy,
chum*, cohort, collaborator, colleague, companion, comrade, confederate, consort, coworker,
crony*, date, friend, helper, helpmate, husband,
mate, pal*, participant, playmate, sidekick*,
spouse, teammate, wife; SEE CONCEPTS
348,414,423

partnership [n] *alliance; participation*
affiliation, assistance, association, band, body,
brotherhood, business, cahoots*, cartel, chummi-
ness, clique, club, combination, combine, community, companionship, company, conglomerate,
conjunction, connection, consociation, cooperation, cooperative, corporation, coterie, crew, faction, firm, fraternity, friendship, gang, help,
hookup, house, interest, joining, lodge, mob, organization, ownership, party, ring, sharing, sisterhood, society, sorority, tie-up, togetherness,
union; SEE CONCEPTS 325,381,388

party [n1] *social gathering*
affair, amusement, at-home*, ball, banquet, barbecue, bash*, blowout*, carousal, carousing*,
celebration, cocktails, coffee klatch, coming-out,
dinner, diversion*, do*, entertainment, feast, festive occasion, festivity, fete, fun, function, gala,
get-together, luncheon, movable feast*, orgy*,
prom, reception, riot, shindig*, social, soiree,
splurge*, spree*, tea; SEE CONCEPT 383

party [n2] *gang, group*
assembly, band, bevy, body, bunch, cluster, company, corps, covey, crew, crowd, detachment,
force, gathering, mob, multitude, outfit, squad,
team, troop, troupe, unit; SEE CONCEPTS 417,432

party [n3] *group supporting certain beliefs*
alliance, association, bloc, body, cabal, clique,
coalition, combination, combine, confederacy,
coterie, electorate, faction, grouping, junta,
league, ring, sect, set, side, union; SEE CONCEPTS
301,381

party [n4] *individual*
being, body, character, creature, human, man,
mortal, part, person, personage, somebody, someone, woman; SEE CONCEPT 417

party [n5] *person(s) involved in legal action*
actor, agent, cojuror, compurgator, confederate,
contractor, defendant, litigant, partaker, participant, participator, plaintiff, plotter, sharer; SEE
CONCEPT 355

pass [n1] *opening through solid*
canyon, cut, gap, gorge, passage, passageway, path, ravine; SEE CONCEPTS **509,513**

pass [n2] *authorization, permission*
admission, chit*, comp, free ride*, furlough, identification, license, order, paper, passport, permit, safe-conduct*, ticket, visa, warrant; SEE CONCEPTS **271,685**

pass [n3] *sexual proposition*
advance, approach, overture, play, suggestion; SEE CONCEPTS **375,384**

pass [n4] *predicament*
condition, contingency, crisis, crossroads*, emergency, exigency, juncture, pinch, plight, situation, stage, state, strait, turning point*, zero hour*; SEE CONCEPT **674**

pass [v1] *go by, elapse; move onward*
befall, blow past, catch, come off, come to pass, come up, crawl, cross, cruise, depart, develop, drag, fall out, fare, flow, fly, fly by, get ahead, give, glide, glide by, go, go past, happen, hie, journey, lapse, leave, linger, move, occur, pass away, pass by, proceed, progress, push on, reach, repair, rise, roll, run, run by, run out, slip away, take place, transpire, travel, wend; SEE CONCEPTS **2,149,242**

pass [v2] *surpass, beat*
exceed, excel, go beyond, go by, leave behind, outdistance, outdo, outgo, outrace, outshine, outstrip, shoot ahead of, surmount, top, transcend; SEE CONCEPT **141**

pass [v3] *succeed, graduate*
answer, do, get through, matriculate, pass muster, qualify, suffice, suit; SEE CONCEPT **706**

pass [v4] *give, transfer*
buck, convey, deliver, exchange, hand, hand over, kick, let have, reach, relinquish, send, shoot, throw, transmit; SEE CONCEPTS **108,217**

pass [v5] *cease*
blow over*, cash in*, close, decease, demise, depart, die, disappear, discontinue, dissolve, drop, dwindle, ebb, end, evaporate, expire, fade, go, melt away, pass away, perish, peter out*, stop, succumb, terminate, vanish, wane; SEE CONCEPTS **105,119**

pass [v6] *enact, legislate*
accept, adopt, approve, authorize, become law, become ratified, become valid, be established, be ordained, be sanctioned, carry, decree, engage, establish, ordain, pledge, promise, ratify, sanction, undertake, validate, vote in; SEE CONCEPTS **298,317**

pass [v7] *express formally*
claim, declare, deliver, pronounce, state, utter; SEE CONCEPTS **49,60**

pass [v8] *decide not to do*
decline, discount, disregard, fail, forget, ignore, miss, neglect, not heed, omit, overlook, pass on, pass up, refuse, skip, slight; SEE CONCEPTS **25,30**

pass [v9] *rid of waste*
defecate, discharge, eliminate, emit, empty, evacuate, excrete, expel, exude, give off, send forth, void; SEE CONCEPT **179**

passable [adj1] *acceptable, admissible*
adequate, allowable, all right, average, common, fair, fair enough, mediocre, middling, moderate, not too bad*, ordinary, presentable, respectable, so-so*, tolerable, unexceptional; SEE CONCEPT **558**

passable [adj2] *clear and able to be traveled*
accessible, attainable, beaten, broad, crossable, easy, fair, graded, motorable, navigable, open, penetrable, reachable, travelable, traveled, traversable, unblocked, unobstructed; SEE CONCEPTS **559,576**

passage/passageway [n1] *path for travel*
access, alley, alleyway, avenue, channel, corridor, course, doorway, entrance, entrance hall, exit, gap, hall, hallway, lane, line, lobby, opening, pathway, road, route, shaft, subway, thoroughfare, tunnel, vestibule, way; SEE CONCEPTS **440,501**

passage [n2] *excerpt from document*
clause, extract, paragraph, piece, portion, quotation, reading, section, sentence, text, transition, verse; SEE CONCEPT **270**

passage [n3] *travel*
advance, change, conversion, crossing, flow, journey, motion, movement, passing, progress, progression, tour, traject, transfer, transference, transit, transition, transmission, transmittal, transmittance, traverse, traversing, trek, trip, voyage; SEE CONCEPTS **145,217,224,704**

passage [n4] *authorization; enactment*
acceptance, allowance, establishment, freedom, legalization, legislation, passing, passport, permission, ratification, right, safe-conduct, visa, warrant; SEE CONCEPTS **318,685**

pass away [v] *die*
decease, demise, depart, drop, expire, pass on, perish, succumb; SEE CONCEPT **304**

pass by [v] *neglect, forget*
abandon, disregard, fail, ignore, leave, miss, not choose, omit, overlook, overpass, pass over; SEE CONCEPTS **25,30**

passé [adj] *old-fashioned*
antiquated, belated, dated, dead, démodé, disused, extinct, has-been*, obsolete, outdated, outmoded, out-of-date, outworn, superseded, unfashionable, yesterday; SEE CONCEPTS **578,589,797**

passenger [n] *person who rides in vehicle conducted by another*
commuter, customer, excursionist, fare*, hitchhiker, patron, pilgrim, rider, tourist, traveler, voyager, wanderer, wayfarer; SEE CONCEPT **423**

passing [n] *death*
decease, defunction, demise, dissolution, end, finish, loss, silence, sleep, termination; SEE CONCEPT **304**

passing [adj] *brief, casual*
cursory, ephemeral, evanescent, fleeting, fugacious, fugitive, glancing, hasty, impermanent, momentary, quick, shallow, short, short-lived, slight, superficial, temporary, transient, transitory; SEE CONCEPTS **551,798**

passion [n1] *strong emotion*
affection, affectivity, agony, anger, animation, ardor, dedication, devotion, distress, dolor, eagerness, ecstasy, excitement, feeling, fervor, fire, fit, flare-up, frenzy, fury, heat, hurrah, indignation, intensity, ire, joy, misery, outbreak, outburst, paroxysm, rage, rapture, resentment, sentiment, spirit, storm, suffering, temper, transport, vehemence, warmth, wrath, zeal, zest; SEE CONCEPT **410**

passion [n2] *adoration, love*
affection, amorousness, amour, appetite, ardor, attachment, concupiscence, craving, crush*, de-

sire, emoting, eroticism, excitement, fondness, infatuation, keenness, lust, prurience, urge, weakness, yen; SEE CONCEPTS *32,372*

passion [n3] *strong interest*
craving, craze, drive, enthusiasm, fad*, fancy, fascination, idol, infatuation, jazz*, mania, obsession; SEE CONCEPTS *349,532,690*

passionate [adj1] *sensual, desirous*
amorous, ardent, aroused, concupiscent, desirous, erotic, heavy*, hot*, lascivious, libidinous, loving, lustful, prurient, romantic, sexy, steamy*, stimulated, sultry, turned-on*, wanton, wistful; SEE CONCEPT *372*

passionate [adj2] *excited; enthusiastic*
affecting, animated, ardent, blazing, burning, deep, dramatic, eager, eloquent, emotional, expressive, fervent, fervid, fierce, fiery, flaming, forceful, frenzied, glowing, headlong, heartfelt, heated, high-powered, high-pressure, hot*, hot-blooded*, impassioned, impetuous, impulsive, inspiring, intense, melodramatic, moving, poignant, precipitate, quickened, spirited, steamed up*, stimulated, stirring, strong, thrilling, vehement, violent, warm, wild, zealous; SEE CONCEPTS *401,542*

passionate [adj3] *angry*
all shook up*, choleric, enraged, fiery, frantic, furious, hotheaded*, hottempered*, inflamed, irascible, irritable, mean, peppery, quick-tempered, shaken, steamed-up*, stormy, tempestuous, testy, touchy*, vehement, violent; SEE CONCEPTS *401,542*

passive [adj] *lifeless, inactive*
acquiescent, apathetic, asleep, bearing, compliant, cool, docile, enduring, flat, forbearing, going through motions*, hands off*, idle, indifferent, inert, laid-back*, latent, long-suffering, moony, motionless, nonresistant, nonviolent, patient, phlegmatic, poker-faced* quiescent, quiet, receptive, resigned, sleepy, static, stolid, submissive, tractable, unassertive, unflappable, uninvolved, unresisting, walking through it*, yielding; SEE CONCEPTS *542,584*

pass off [v] *give because one does not want it*
eject, foist, make a pretense of*, palm, palm off*, send forth, work off; SEE CONCEPT *108*

pass out [v] *become unconscious, usually from abusing a substance*
black out*, drop, faint, keel over*, lose consciousness, swoon; SEE CONCEPT *308*

pass over [v] *ignore, disregard*
dismiss, fail, forget, miss, neglect, not dwell on, omit, overlook, overpass, pass, pass by, skip, take no notice of*; SEE CONCEPTS *25,30*

passport [n] *identification of origin, country*
authorization, credentials, key, license, pass, permit, safe-conduct*, ticket, travel permit, visa, warrant; SEE CONCEPTS *271,685*

password [n] *secret word given for entry*
countersign, identification, key, key word, open sesame*, parole, phrase, signal, ticket, watchword, word; SEE CONCEPT *278*

past [n1] *time gone by*
antiquity, days bygone by*, former times, good old days*, history, long ago, olden days*, old lang syne, old times*, time immemorial*, times past*, years ago*, yesterday, yesteryear, yore; SEE CONCEPTS *807,811,816,818*

past [adj1] *preceding, done*
accomplished, ago, antecedent, anterior, com-

pleted, elapsed, ended, extinct, finished, foregoing, forgotten, former, gone, gone by, over, over and done, precedent, previous, prior, spent; SEE CONCEPTS *531,585*

past [adj2] *olden time, former*
ages ago*, ancient, ancient history*, back when*, behind one*, bygone, bypast, down memory lane*, earlier, early, erstwhile, ex-*, foregoing, gone-by*, good old days*, late, latter, latter-day, long-ago, old, olden days*, once, one-time, over, preceding, previous, prior, quondam, recent, retired, sometime, time was*, way back*, way back when*; SEE CONCEPT *820*

paste [n/v] *glue, adhesive*
cement, fasten, fix, gum, mucilage, patch, plaster, spit, stick, stickum*; SEE CONCEPTS *85,160,466*

pastel [adj] *muted in color*
delicate, light, pale, soft-hued, toned; SEE CONCEPT *618*

pastiche [n] *work of art formed from disparate sources*
assortment, collage, collection, compilation, copy, hodgepodge, imitation, mishmosh*, paste-up, patchwork, potpourri, reappropriation, reproduction, synthesis; SEE CONCEPT *260*

pastime [n] *leisure activity*
amusement, distraction, diversion, entertainment, fun, fun and games*, game, hobby, play, recreation, relaxation, sport; SEE CONCEPT *363*

pastor [n] *person who conducts church services*
cleric, divine, ecclesiastic, minister, parson, preacher, priest, rector, reverend, shepherd, vicar; SEE CONCEPT *361*

pastoral [adj] *peaceful, especially referring to the countryside*
agrarian, agrestic, Arcadian, bucolic, countrified, country, idyllic, outland, provincial, rural, rustic, simple, sylvan; SEE CONCEPT *583*

pastry [n] *baked product made with flour*
bread, cake, croissant, dainty, Danish, delicacy, doughnut, éclair, panettone, patisserie, phyllo, pie, strudel, sweet roll, tart, turnover; SEE CONCEPTS *457,461*

pasty [adj1] *sticky*
adhesive, doughy, gelatinous, gluelike, gluey, glutinous, gooey, mucilaginous, starchy; SEE CONCEPT *606*

pasty [adj2] *pale*
anemic, ashen, bloodless, dull, pallid, sallow, sickly, unhealthy, wan, waxen; SEE CONCEPT *618*

pat [n1/v] *tap, touch*
beat, caress, dab, fondle, form, hit, massage, mold, pet, punch, rub, slap, stroke, tip, whittle; SEE CONCEPTS *184,189,612*

pat [n2] *small slice or slab*
cake, dab, lump, piece, portion; SEE CONCEPTS *458,835*

pat [adj] *relevant, suitable*
apposite, apropos, apt, auspicious, felicitous, fitting, happy, neat, opportune, pertinent, propitious, rehearsed, timely, to the point; SEE CONCEPT *558*

pat [adv] *exactly, fittingly*
aptly, faultlessly, flawlessly, just right, opportunely, perfectly, plumb, precisely, relevantly, seasonably; SEE CONCEPTS *535,557*

patch [n1] *piece, spot, area*
bit, blob, chunk, fix, ground, hunk, land, lot, plat,

plot, scrap, shred, stretch, strip, tract; SEE CONCEPTS 452,471,513

patch [n2] *piece applied to cover a gap or lack*
application, appliqué, Band-Aid*, mend, reinforcement; SEE CONCEPTS 452,831

patch [v] *fix, mend*
cobble, cover, darn, do up, fiddle with, overhaul, rebuild, recondition, reconstruct, reinforce, repair, retread, revamp, sew; SEE CONCEPTS 212,218

patch up [v] *settle differences*
adjust, appease, bury the hatchet*, compensate, conciliate, make friends*, mediate, negotiate, placate, restore, settle*, smooth; SEE CONCEPT 384

patchwork [n] *mixture, hodgepodge*
check, confusion, disorder, hash*, jumble, medley, miscellany, mishmash, muddle, olio, pastiche, plaid, salad*, salmagundi, stew*, tartan; SEE CONCEPTS 260,432,475

patchy [adj] *spotty, not consistent*
erratic, fitful, irregular, random, sketchy, uneven, variable, varying; SEE CONCEPT 482

patent [n] *copyright on an invention*
charter, concession, control, franchise, license, limitation, privilege, protection; SEE CONCEPTS 271,318,685

patent [adj] *unconcealed, conspicuous*
apparent, barefaced*, blatant, clear, clear-cut, controlled, crystal clear*, distinct, downright, evident, exclusive, flagrant, glaring, gross*, indisputable, limited, manifest, obvious, open, open and shut*, palpable, plain, prominent, rank, straightforward, transparent, unequivocal, unmistakable; SEE CONCEPT 576

path [n] *course, way*
aisle, artery, avenue, beat, beaten path, boulevard, byway, crosscut, direction, drag, footpath, groove, highway, lane, line, pass, passage, pathway, procedure, rail, road, roadway, route, rut, shortcut, street, stroll, terrace, thoroughfare, track, trail, walk, walkway; SEE CONCEPTS 6,501

pathetic [adj] *sad, affecting*
commiserable, deplorable, distressing, feeble, heartbreaking, heartrending*, inadequate, lamentable, meager, melting, miserable, moving, paltry, petty, piteous, pitiable, pitiful, plaintive, poignant, poor, puny, rueful, sorry*, tender, touching, useless, woeful, worthless, wretched; SEE CONCEPTS 485,529

pathos [n] *deep sadness*
desolation, emotion, feeling, passion, pitiableness, pitifulness, plaintiveness, poignance, poignancy, sentiment; SEE CONCEPT 410

patience [n] *capacity, willingness to endure*
backbone*, bearing, calmness, composure, constancy, cool*, diligence, endurance, equanimity, even temper, forbearance, fortitude, grit*, guts*, gutsiness, heart, humility, imperturbability, intestinal fortitude*, legs*, leniency, longanimity, long-suffering, moderation, moxie*, nonresistance, passiveness, passivity, perseverance, persistence, poise, resignation, restraint, self-control, serenity, starch*, staying power*, stoicism, submission, sufferance, tolerance, toleration, yielding; SEE CONCEPTS 411,657

patient [n] *person being treated for medical problem*
case, convalescent, emergency, inmate, invalid, outpatient, shut-in, sick person, subject, sufferer, victim; SEE CONCEPT 357

patient [adj] *capable, willing to endure*
accommodating, calm, composed, easy-going, enduring, even-tempered, forbearing, forgiving, gentle, imperturbable, indulgent, lenient, long-suffering, meek, mild, mild-tempered, persevering, persistent, philosophic, philosophical, quiet, resigned, self-possessed, serene, stoical, submissive, tolerant, tranquil, uncomplaining, understanding, unruffled, untiring; SEE CONCEPTS 404,542

patrician [n] *person born to upper-class*
aristocrat, blue blood*, gentleperson, noble, nobleperson, peer, silk stocking*, upper cruster*; SEE CONCEPT 423

patrician [adj] *upper-class*
aristocratic, blue-blooded*, gentle, grand, high-born, high-class, noble, royal, well-born; SEE CONCEPTS 334,549

patriot [n] *person who loves his or her country*
flag-waver*, good citizen, jingoist*, loyalist, nationalist, partisan, patrioteer, statesperson, ultranationalist, volunteer; SEE CONCEPT 413

patrol [n] *guarding; guard*
convoying, defending, escorting, garrison, lookout, patroler, policing, protecting, protection, rounds, safeguarding, scouting, sentinel, spy, vigilance, watch, watching, watchperson; SEE CONCEPTS 134,354,358

patrol [v] *guard, protect*
cruise, inspect, keep guard, keep watch, make the rounds*, mount, police, pound, range, ride shotgun, safeguard, shotgun, walk the beat*, watch; SEE CONCEPTS 134,623

patron [n1] *person who supports a cause*
advocate, angel*, backer, benefactor, booster, champion, defender, encourager, fairy godparent*, fan, financer, friend, front*, guarantor, guardian, guide, head, helper, leader, partisan, patron saint*, philanthropist, protector, sponsor, supporter, surety, sympathizer, well-wisher; SEE CONCEPTS 348,359,423

patron [n2] *person who does business at establishment*
buyer, client, customer, frequenter, habitué, purchaser, shopper; SEE CONCEPT 348

patronage [n1] *support of a cause*
advocacy, aegis, aid, assistance, auspices, backing, benefaction, championship, encouragement, financing, grant, guardianship, help, promotion, protection, recommendation, sponsorship, subsidy, support; SEE CONCEPTS 110,332,341

patronage [n2] *business done at an establishment*
buying, clientage, clientele, commerce, custom, shopping, trade, trading, traffic; SEE CONCEPTS 323,324

patronage [n3] *condescension*
civility, cronyism, deference, deigning, disdain, insolence, patronization, patronizing, stooping, sufferance, toleration; SEE CONCEPTS 83,300

patronize [v1] *condescend*
be gracious to, be lofty, be overbearing, deign, favor, indulge, look down on*, pat on the back*, snub, stoop, talk down to*, toss a few crumbs*, treat as inferior, treat badly, treat like a child*; SEE CONCEPT 384

patronize [v2] *support a cause*
assist, back, befriend, foster, fund, help, maintain, promote, sponsor, subscribe to; SEE CONCEPTS 110,341

patronize [v3] *do business at an establishment*
be a client, be a customer, buy, buy from, deal with, frequent, give business to, habituate, purchase from, shop at, shop with, trade with; SEE CONCEPTS 324,327

patter [n1/v1] *light walk; soft beat*
chatter, pad, pat, pelt, pitapat*, pitter-patter*, rat-a-tat*, rattle, scurry, scuttle, skip, tap, tiptoe, trip; SEE CONCEPTS 65,149

patter [n2] *casual talk*
argot, cant, chatter, dialect, jabber*, jargon, jive*, line*, lingo, monologue, patois, pitch*, prattle*, slant*, spiel*, vernacular; SEE CONCEPTS 276,278

patter [v2] *gab, chatter*
babble, blab*, clack*, hold forth*, jabber, jaw*, prate, prattle, rattle, spiel*, spout, tattle, yak*, yakety-yak*; SEE CONCEPT 266

pattern [n1] *design, motif*
arrangement, decoration, device, diagram, figure, guide, impression, instruction, markings, mold, motive, original, ornament, patterning, plan, stencil, template, trim; SEE CONCEPTS 259,625

pattern [n2] *arrangement, order*
constellation, kind, method, orderliness, plan, sequence, shape, sort, style, system, type, variety; SEE CONCEPTS 6,727,770

pattern [n3] *model, example*
archetype, beau ideal*, copy, criterion, cynosure, ensample, exemplar, guide, mirror, norm, original, paradigm, paragon, prototype, sample, specimen, standard; SEE CONCEPT 686

pattern [v] *copy, imitate; decorate*
design, emulate, follow, form, model, mold, order, shape, style, trim; SEE CONCEPTS 111,171

paucity [n] *lack, scarcity*
absence, dearth, deficiency, famine, fewness, insufficiency, insufficiency, meagerness, paltriness, poverty, rarity, scantiness, scarceness, shortage, slenderness, slightness, smallness, sparseness, sparsity; SEE CONCEPTS 335,646,767

paunch [n] *large stomach*
abdomen, belly, bulge, epigastrium, fat, gut, potbelly*, spare tire*, tummy*; SEE CONCEPT 399

pauper [n] *person who is poor*
almsperson, bankrupt, beggar, bum, dependent, destitute, down-and-out*, have-not*, homeless person, indigent, insolvent, in the gutter*, lazarus*, mendicant, poor person, supplicant; SEE CONCEPT 423

pause [n] *wait, delay*
abeyance, break, break-off*, breathing space*, breathing spell*, caesura, cessation, coffee break*, comma, cutoff, deadlock, discontinuance, downtime*, freeze*, gap, gridlock*, halt, happy hour*, hesitancy, hesitation, hiatus, hitch*, hush*, interim, interlude, intermission, interregnum, interruption, interval, lacuna, lapse, layoff, letup*, lull, pausation, recess, respite, rest, rest period, stand, standstill, stay, stillness, stopover, stoppage, suspension, time out*; SEE CONCEPT 807

pause [v] *wait, delay*
break it up*, call time*, catch one's breath*, cease, come to standstill*, deliberate, desist, discontinue, drop, halt, hesitate, hold back, interrupt, put on hold, reflect, rest, shake, sideline, stop briefly, suspend, take a break*, take a breather*, take five*, take ten*, think twice*, waver; SEE CONCEPTS 119,121,234

pave [v] *cover with asphalt, concrete*
brick, cobblestone, flagstone, gravel, lay asphalt, lay concrete, macadamize, surface, tar, tile; SEE CONCEPTS 168,172

pavilion [n] *domed building or tent*
awning, canopy, cover, covering, dome, structure; SEE CONCEPT 439

paw [v] *touch roughly*
clap, claw, clutch, dig, feel, finger, fondle, grab, grate, grope, handle, hit, maul, molest, palpate, pat, rake, rasp, rub, scratch, search, slap, smite, stroke; SEE CONCEPTS 216,612

pawn [n1] *security for a loan*
assurance, bond, collateral, earnest, forfeit, gage, gambit, guarantee, guaranty, pledge, security, token, warrant; SEE CONCEPT 332

pawn [n2] *person who is a fool*
creature, dupe*, instrument, mark*, patsy*, pigeon*, puppet, stooge*, sucker*, tool, toy, victim; SEE CONCEPT 412

pawn [v] *give as security for a loan*
deposit, give in earnest, hazard, hock*, hook*, mortgage, pledge; SEE CONCEPTS 115,330

pay [n] *earnings from employment*
allowance, bacon*, bread*, commission, compensation, consideration, defrayment, emoluments, fee, hire*, honorarium, income, indemnity, meed, payment, perquisite, pittance, proceeds, profit, reckoning, recompensation, recompense, redress, reimbursement, remuneration, reparation, requital, return, reward, salary, satisfaction, scale, settlement, stipend, stipendium, take-home*, takings*, wage, wages; SEE CONCEPTS 329,332, 340,344

pay [v1] *give money for goods, services*
adjust, bear the cost, bear the expense, bequeath, bestow, chip in*, clear, come through, compensate, confer, cough up*, defray, dig up*, disburse, discharge, extend, foot*, foot the bill*, grant, handle, hand over*, honor, kick in*, liquidate, make payment, meet, offer, plunk down*, prepay, present, proffer, put up*, recompense, recoup, refund, reimburse, remit, remunerate, render, repay, requite, reward, satisfy, settle, stake, take care of*; SEE CONCEPTS 327,341,351

pay [v2] *be advantageous*
benefit, be worthwhile, repay, serve; SEE CONCEPT 700

pay [v3] *make amends*
answer, atone, be punished, compensate, get just desserts*, suffer, suffer consequences; SEE CONCEPT 23

pay [v4] *profit, yield*
be profitable, be remunerative, bring in, kick back*, make a return, make money, pay dividends, pay off*, pay out*, produce, provide a living, return, show gain, show profit, sweeten*, yield profit; SEE CONCEPT 330

pay [v5] *get revenge*
avenge oneself, get even, make up for, pay back*, pay one's dues*, punish, reciprocate, recompense, repay, requite, retaliate, settle a score*, square, square things*; SEE CONCEPT 122

payable [adj] *to be paid*
due, mature, maturing, obligatory, outstanding, overdue, owed, owing, receivable, unpaid, unsettled; SEE CONCEPT 334

payment [n] *fee; installment of fee*
acquittal, advance, alimony, amends, amortization, amount, annuity, award, bounty, cash, de-

frayal, defrayment, deposit, disbursement, discharge, down, fee, hire, indemnification, outlay, part, paying, pay-off, pension, portion, premium, quittance, reckoning, recompense, redress, refund, reimbursement, remittance, remuneration, reparation, repayment, requital, restitution, retaliation, return, reward, salary, settlement, subsidy, sum, support, wage; SEE CONCEPT 344

payoff [n] *conclusion, climax*

adjustment, clincher*, consequence, culmination, day of reckoning*, finale, final reckoning*, judgment, moment of truth*, outcome, pay, payment, punch line*, result, retribution, reward, settlement, upshot*; SEE CONCEPTS 230,679

peace [n1] *harmony, agreement*

accord, amity, armistice, cessation, conciliation, concord, friendship, love, neutrality, order, pacification, pacifism, reconciliation, treaty, truce, unanimity, union, unity; SEE CONCEPTS 388,691

peace [n2] *calm, serenity*

amity, calmness, composure, concord, congeniality, contentment, equanimity, harmony, hush, lull, peacefulness, placidity, quiet, quietude, relaxation, repose, reserve, rest, silence, stillness, sympathy, tranquility; SEE CONCEPTS 410,705, 720

peaceable [adj] *friendly, serene*

amiable, amicable, calm, complacent, conciliatory, gentle, irenic, mild, neighborly, nonviolent, pacific, pacificatory, pacifist, peaceful, peace-loving, placid, quiet, restful, still, tranquil; SEE CONCEPT 548

peaceful [adj] *friendly, serene*

all quiet, amicable, at peace, bloodless, calm, collected, composed, constant, easeful, equable, free from strife*, gentle, halcyon, harmonious, irenic, level, mellow, neutral, neutralist, nonbelligerent, nonviolent, on friendly terms*, on good terms*, pacifistic, peaceable, peace-loving, placatory, placid, quiet, restful, smooth, sociable, steady, still, tranquil, undisturbed, unruffled, untroubled, without hostility; SEE CONCEPTS 485,542.

peacemaker [n] *person who settles problem*

appeaser, arbitrator, conciliator, diplomat, makepeace, mediator, negotiator, pacificator, pacifier, pacifist, peacekeeper, peacemonger*, placater, statesperson; SEE CONCEPTS 354,416

peak [n1] *top of something*

aiguille, alp, apex, brow, bump, cope, crest, crown, hill, mount, mountain, pinnacle, point, roof, spike, summit, tip, vertex; SEE CONCEPTS 509,836

peak [n2] *maximum, zenith*

acme, apex, apogee, capstone, climax, crown, culmination, extreme, height, high point, meridian, ne plus ultra, pinnacle, summit, tip, top; SEE CONCEPTS 668,766,767,832

peak [v] *reach highest point*

be at height, climax, come to a head*, crest, culminate, reach the top, reach the zenith, top out*; SEE CONCEPTS 763,780

peaked [adj] *pale, sick*

ailing, bilious, emaciated, ill, in bad shape*, peaky, poorly, sickly, under the weather*, wan; SEE CONCEPTS 314,618

peal [n] *chime, clang*

blast, carillon, clamor, clap, crash, resounding, reverberation, ring, ringing, roar, rumble, sound, thunder, tintinnabulation*; SEE CONCEPT 595

peal [v] *chime, clang*

bell, bong, crack, crash, knell, resonate, resound, reverberate, ring, ring out, roar, roll, rumble, sound, strike, thunder, tintinnabulate*, toll; SEE CONCEPT 65

pearly [adj] *opalescent*

fair, frosted, iridescent, ivory, milky, nacreous, off-white, opaline, pearl, silver; SEE CONCEPT 618

peck [n/v] *bite*

beak, dig, hit, jab, kiss, mark, nibble, pick, pinch, poke, prick, rap, strike, tap; SEE CONCEPTS 169,189

peculiar [adj1] *characteristic, distinguishing*

appropriate, diacritic, diagnostic, distinct, distinctive, endemic, exclusive, idiosyncratic, individual, intrinsic, local, particular, personal, private, proper, restricted, special, specific, typical, unique; SEE CONCEPTS 404,557

peculiar [adj2] *bizarre, odd*

abnormal, bent*, creepy*, curious, eccentric, exceptional, extraordinary, flaky*, freakish, freaky, funny, idiosyncratic, kinky*, kooky*, oddball, offbeat, off-the-wall*, outlandish, quaint, queer, singular, strange, uncommon, unconventional, uncustomary, unusual, wacky*, way-out*, weird, wonderful; SEE CONCEPTS 404,564

peculiarity [n] *characteristic; oddity*

abnormality, affectation, attribute, bizarreness, character, distinctiveness, eccentricity, feature, foible, freakishness, gimmick, idiosyncrasy, kink*, mannerism, mark, odd trait, particularity, property, quality, queerness, quirk, savor, schtick*, singularity, slant*, specialty, trait, twist*, unusualness; SEE CONCEPTS 411,665

pedagogic [adj] *educational*

academic, dogmatic, instructive, learned, professorial, profound, scholastic, teaching; SEE CONCEPTS 529,536

pedantic [adj] *bookish, precise*

abstruse, academic, arid, didactic, doctrinaire, donnish, dry, dull, egotistic, erudite, formal, fussy, hairsplitting*, learned, nit-picking, ostentatious, overnice, particular, pedagogic, pompous, priggish*, punctilious, scholastic, schoolish, sententious, stilted; SEE CONCEPTS 401,529

peddle [v] *sell door to door*

canvas*, hawk*, huckster*, market, monger*, push, shove, solicit, trade, vend; SEE CONCEPT 345

pedestrian [n] *person traveling on foot*

ambler, hiker, jaywalker*, passerby, stroller, walker; SEE CONCEPT 366

pedestrian [adj] *everyday, dull*

banal, banausic, blah*, boring, commonplace, dim, dreary, flat, humdrum*, inane, jejune, mediocre, monotone, monotonous, mundane, ordinary, platitudinous, plodding, prosaic, run-of-the-mill*, stodgy, truistic, unimaginative, uninspired, uninteresting, wishy-washy*; SEE CONCEPTS 530,547

pedigree [n] *ancestry, heritage*

blood, breed, clan, derivation, descent, extraction, family, family tree, genealogy, heredity, line, lineage, origin, race, stirps, stock; SEE CONCEPT 296

pedigree [adj] *purebred*

full-blooded, pedigreed, pure-blood, thoroughbred; SEE CONCEPT 549

pa
pe

peek/peep [n] *sneaked look*
blink, gander*, glance, glimpse, look-see, sight; SEE CONCEPT 623

peek/peep [v] *sneak a look*
blink, glance, glimpse, have a gander*, peer, snatch, snoop, spy, squint, stare, take a look; SEE CONCEPT 623

peel [n] *skin, covering*
bark, cover, epicarp, exocarp, husk, peeling, pellicle, rind, shell, shuck; SEE CONCEPTS 428,484

peel [v] *take off outer covering*
decorticate, delaminate, desquamate, excorticate, exfoliate, flake, flay, pare, pull off, scale, shave, skin, strip, tear off, uncover; SEE CONCEPTS 142,176,211

peep [n2/v2] *chirp*
chatter, cheep, chirrup, chuck, churr, coo, cry, hoot, pipe, squeak, tweet, twitter; SEE CONCEPT 64

peep/peer [v3/v2] *appear briefly*
become visible, crop up, emerge, open to view, peep out, peer out, show partially; SEE CONCEPT 261

peer [n] *person who is another's equal*
associate, coequal, companion, compeer, like, match, rival; SEE CONCEPT 423

peer [v1] *scan, scrutinize*
bore, eagle eye*, eye*, eyeball*, focus, gape, gawk, gaze, get a load of, glare, glim, gloat, inspect, look, peep, pin*, pry, rubberneck*, snoop, spy, squint, stare; SEE CONCEPTS 103,623

peerless [adj] *having no equal; superior*
aces*, all-time, alone, best, beyond compare, champion, excellent, faultless, gilt-edge*, greatest, incomparable, matchless, most, nonpareil*, only, outstanding, perfect, second to none*, solid-gold*, super, superlative, supreme, tops*, unequaled, unexampled, unique, unmatched, unparagoned, unparalleled, unrivaled, unsurpassed, world class*; SEE CONCEPT 574

peeve [n] *something strongly disliked*
annoyance, bother, gripe, nuisance, pest, sore point*, vexation; SEE CONCEPTS 532,690

peeve [v] *bother, annoy*
aggravate, anger, bug*, bum*, burn*, disturb, drive up the wall*, exasperate, gall, get, get one's goat*, hack*, irk, irritate, miff*, nettle, pique, provoke, put out, rile, roil, rub the wrong way*, steam*, T-off*, vex; SEE CONCEPTS 7,19

peevish [adj] *irritable, testy*
acrimonious, angry, bad-tempered, cantankerous, captious, carping, caviling, childish, churlish, complaining, crabbed*, cranky, critical, cross, crotchety*, crusty*, cussed, fault-finding, fractious, fretful, fretting, grouchy, grousing, growling, grumpy, huffy, ill-natured, mean, morose, obstinate, ogre, ornery, out-of-sorts*, pertinacious, petulant, querulous, short-tempered, snappy, splenetic, sulky, sullen, surly, tetchy, touchy, ugly, waspish, waspy, whining; SEE CONCEPTS 401,542

peg [v] *attach*
clinch, fasten, fix, join, make fast, pin, secure, tighten; SEE CONCEPTS 85,160

pejorative [adj] *negative, belittling*
debasing, deprecatory, depreciatory, derisive, derogatory, detracting, detractive, detractory, disadvantageous, disparaging, irreverent, rude, slighting, uncomplimentary, unpleasant; SEE CONCEPT 267

pell-mell [n] *disorder*
anarchy, ataxia, chaos, clutter, confusion, disarray, ferment, helter-skelter, huddle, muddle, pandemonium, snarl, tumult, turmoil, upheaval; SEE CONCEPT 674

pell-mell [adj] *disordered*
chaotic, confused, disarrayed, disorganized, haphazard, muddled, tumultous/tumultuous; SEE CONCEPTS 562,585

pell-mell [adv] *hurriedly and carelessly*
foolishly, full tilt*, hastily, headlong, heedlessly, helter-skelter, impetuously, incontinently, indiscreetly, posthaste, precipitiously, rashly, recklessly, thoughtlessly; SEE CONCEPTS 544,799

pelt [n] *animal fur*
coat, epidermis, fell, hair, hide, jacket, skin, slough, wool; SEE CONCEPT 399

pelt [v] *beat; throw hard*
assail, batter, belabor, belt, bombard, career, cast, charge, dash, hammer, hurl, knock, lapidate, pepper, pound, pour, pummel, rain, rush, shoot, shower, sling, speed, stone, strike, swat, tear, thrash, wallop; SEE CONCEPTS 189,222

pen [n1] *enclosure*
cage, coop, corral, fence, fold, hedge, hutch, jail, penitentiary, prison, sty, wall*; SEE CONCEPTS 439,443

pen [n2] *writing instrument*
ball point, felt-tip, fountain pen, marker, nib, quill, reed, stick, stylograph; SEE CONCEPTS 277,499

pen [v1] *enclose*
box, cage, case, close in, confine, coop, corral, fence in, hedge, hem in, mew*, shut in; SEE CONCEPTS 191,758

pen [v2] *write*
autograph, commit to paper, compose, draft, draw up, engross, indict, jot down; SEE CONCEPT 79

penal [adj] *disciplinary*
chastening, corrective, penalizing, punishing, punitive, punitory, reformatory, retributive; SEE CONCEPTS 548,583

penalize [v] *punish*
amerce, castigate, chasten, chastise, condemn, correct, discipline, dock*, fine, handicap, hit with*, impose penalty, inflict handicap, judge, mulct, put at disadvantage, scold, slap with*, throw the book at*; SEE CONCEPT 122

penalty [n] *punishment*
amends, amercement, cost, damages, disadvantage, discipline, dues, fall, fine, forfeit, forfeiture, handicap, mortification, mulct, price, rap*, retribution; SEE CONCEPTS 344,679

penance [n] *reparation for wrong*
absolution, atonement, attrition, compensation, compunction, confession, contrition, expiation, forgiveness, hair shirt*, mortification, penalty, penitence, punishment, purgation, remorse, remorsefulness, repentance, retribution, rue, ruth, sackcloth and ashes*, self-flagellation*, shift, sorrow, suffering; SEE CONCEPTS 126,367, 384,410

penchant [n] *fondness, inclination*
affection, affinity, attachment, bias, disposition, druthers*, inclining, itch*, leaning, liking, partiality, predilection, predisposition, proclivity, proneness, propensity, taste, tendency, tilt*, turn*, weakness, yen; SEE CONCEPTS 20,32, 411,709

pending [*adj*] *about to happen*

awaiting, continuing, dependent, forthcoming, hanging, imminent, impending, indeterminate, in line*, in the balance*, in the offing*, in the works*, ominous, on board*, on line*, pensile, undecided, undetermined, unsettled, up in the air*; SEE CONCEPT 548

pendulous/pendent [*adj*] *hanging*

dangling, dependent, drooping, pending, pendulant, pensile, suspended, swinging; SEE CONCEPTS 485,584

penetrate [*v1*] *pierce; get through physically*

access, barge in, bayonet, blow in, bore, break in, breeze in, bust in, charge, come, crack, diffuse, drill, drive, eat through, encroach, enter, filter in, force, get in, gore, go through, impale, infiltrate, ingress, insert, insinuate, introduce, invade, jab, knife, make a hole, make an entrance, pass through, percolate, perforate, permeate, pervade, pop in, prick, probe, puncture, ream, run into, saturate, seep, sink into, spear, stab, stick into, suffuse, thrust, trespass; SEE CONCEPTS 159,179,220

penetrate [*v2*] *understand or be understood*

affect, become clear, come across*, comprehend, decipher, discern, fathom, figure out, get across*, get over*, get through*, get to the bottom*, grasp, impress, perceive, put over*, see through*, sink in*, soak in*, touch, unravel, work out; SEE CONCEPT 15

penetrating [*adj1*] *stinging, harsh*

biting, carrying, clear-cut, crisp, cutting, edged, entering, forcing, going through, infiltrating, ingoing, intrusive, passing through, penetrant, permeating, pervasive, piercing, pointed, puncturing, pungent, sharp, shrill, strong, trenchant; SEE CONCEPTS 267,537

penetrating [*adj2*] *intelligent*

acute, astute, critical, discerning, discriminating, incisive, keen, penetrative, perceptive, perspicacious, profound, quick, quick-witted, sagacious, searching, sharp, sharp-witted, shrewd; SEE CONCEPT 402

penitence [*n*] *shame, sorrow*

anguish, attrition, compunction, contriteness, contrition, debasement, degradation, distress, grief, humbling, humiliation, penance, qualm, regret, remorse, remorsefulness, repentance, rue, ruefulness, ruth, sadness, scruple, self-castigation, self-condemnation, self-flagellation, self-punishment, self-reproach; SEE CONCEPT 410

penitent [*adj*] *shamed, sorrowful*

abject, apologetic, atoning, attritional, compunctious, conscience-stricken, contrite, penitential, regretful, remorseful, repentant, rueful, sorry; SEE CONCEPTS 403,542

penitentiary [*n*] *jail*

big house*, campus, can*, college, cooler*, correctional institution, inside*, joint*, lockup*, pen*, penal institution, prison, reformatory, slammer*, stockade; SEE CONCEPTS 439,449,516

pennant [*n*] *flag, banner*

banderole, bunting, burgee, color, decoration, emblem, ensign, jack, pennon, screamer, standard, streamer; SEE CONCEPTS 260,473

penniless [*adj*] *without any money*

bankrupt, broke*, clean*, cleaned out*, dead broke*, destitute, dirt poor*, down to last penny*, flat*, flat broke*, impecunious, impoverished, indigent, in the gutter*, lacking, moneyless, neces-

sitous, needy, on last leg*, over a barrel*, penurious, poor, poverty-stricken, ruined, strapped*, tapped out*, without a dime*; SEE CONCEPT 334

pension [*n*] *benefits paid after retirement*

allowance, annuity, gift, grant, IRA*, payment, premium, retirement account, reward, social security, subsidy, subvention, superannuation, support; SEE CONCEPTS 332,344

pensive [*adj*] *meditative, solemn*

absorbed, abstracted, attentive, cogitative, contemplative, dreamy, grave, musing, pondering, preoccupied, reflecting, reflective, ruminating, ruminative, serious, sober, speculative, thinking, thoughtful, wistful, withdrawn; SEE CONCEPT 403

pent-up [*adj*] *held within*

bottled-up, bridled, checked, constrained, curbed, held-back, held in check, inhibited, repressed, restrained, restricted, smothered, stifled, suppressed; SEE CONCEPTS 401,403

people [*n*] *human beings*

bodies, body politic*, bourgeois, cats*, citizens, clan, commonality, common people, community, crowd, family, folk, folks, general public, heads*, herd, hoi polloi*, horde, humanity, humankind, human race, humans, inhabitants, John/Jane Q. Public*, kin, masses, mob, mortals, multitude, nation, nationality, person in the street*, persons, plebeians, populace, population, proletariat, public, rabble, race, rank and file*, riffraff*, society, tribe; SEE CONCEPTS 296,379,380,417

pep [*n*] *vim, vigor*

animation, bang, birr, energy, get-up-and-go*, go, gusto, hardihood, high spirits, life, liveliness, moxie*, potency, punch*, push, snap*, spirit, starch*, tuck*, verve, vitality, vivacity, zip*; SEE CONCEPTS 411,633

peppery [*adj1*] *highly seasoned*

fiery, hot, piquant, poignant, pungent, racy, snappy, spicy, zestful, zesty; SEE CONCEPT 613

peppery [*adj2*] *irritable; sarcastic*

acute, angry, astringent, biting, caustic, choleric, cranky, cross, fiery, hot-tempered, incisive, irascible, keen, lively, passionate, quick-tempered, sharp, sharp-tempered, snappish, spirited, spunky, stinging, testy, touchy, trenchant, waspish; SEE CONCEPTS 267,401,542

peppy [*adj*] *lively, vigorous*

active, alert, animate, animated, bright, gay, keen, perky, sparkling, spirited, sprightly, vivacious; SEE CONCEPTS 401,542

pep up [*v*] *invigorate, inspire*

animate, enliven, exhilarate, jazz up*, quicken, stimulate, vitalize, vivify; SEE CONCEPTS 7,22

perceive [*v1*] *notice, see*

apperceive, apprehend, be aware of, behold, descry, discern, discover, distinguish, divine, espy, feel, grasp, identify, look, make out, mark, mind, note, observe, realize, recognize, regard, remark, seize, sense, spot, spy, take; SEE CONCEPTS 38,626

perceive [*v2*] *understand*

appreciate, apprehend, comprehend, conclude, copy, deduce, distinguish, feature, feel, flash*, gather, get, get the message*, get the picture*, grasp, know, learn, pin*, read, realize, recognize, see, sense, track; SEE CONCEPT 15

percentage [*n*] *portion, allotment*

allowance, bite, bonus, chunk, commission, corner*, cut, discount, division, duty, fee, holdout,

pe
pe

interest, juice*, payoff, percent, piece, piece of the action*, points*, proportion, quota, rate, ratio, section, slice*, split*, taste*, winnings; SEE CONCEPTS 766,784,835

perceptible [adj] *noticeable, obvious*
apparent, appreciable, audible, clear, cognizable, conspicuous, detectable, discernible, discrete, distinguishable, evident, lucid, observable, palpable, perceivable, perspicuous, recognizable, sensible, signal, tangible, understandable, visible; SEE CONCEPTS 529,576

perception [n] *understanding, idea*
acumen, apprehending, apprehension, approach, attention, attitude, awareness, big idea*, brainchild*, brain wave*, conceit, concept, conception, consciousness, discernment, feeling, flash, grasp, image, impression, insight, intellection, judgment, knowledge, light, notion, observation, opinion, perspicacity, picture, plan, realizing, recognition, sagacity, sensation, sense, study, taste, thought, viewpoint; SEE CONCEPTS 409,410,689

perceptive [adj] *alert, sensitive*
acute, astute, awake, aware, brainy*, conscious, discerning, discreet, ear to the ground*, gnostic, incisive, insighted, insightful, intuitive, judicious, keen, knowing, knowledgeable, knows what's what*, observant, penetrating, penetrative, percipient, perspicacious, quick, rational, responsive, sagacious, sage, savvy*, sharp, sophic, tuned in*, wise, wise to*; SEE CONCEPTS 402,542

perch [n] *object placed high for sitting on*
branch, landing place, lounge, pole, post, resting place, roost, seat; SEE CONCEPTS 443,479

perch [v] *sit atop of*
alight, balance, land, light, rest, roost, set down, settle, sit on, squat, touch down; SEE CONCEPT 154

percolate [v] *seep, drip (liquid)*
bleed, bubble, charge, drain, exude, filter, filtrate, impregnate, leach, ooze, pass through, penetrate, perk, permeate, pervade, saturate, strain, sweat, transfuse, transude, weep; SEE CONCEPTS 179,181

peremptory [adj] *overbearing, authoritative*
absolute, arbitrary, assertive, autocratic, binding, bossy, categorical, certain, commanding, compelling, decided, decisive, dictatorial, dogmatic, domineering, final, finished, firm, fixed, high-handed, imperative, imperial, imperious, incontrovertible, intolerant, irrefutable, magisterial, obligatory, obstinate, positive, rigorous, severe, stringent, tyrannical, uncompromising, undeniable; SEE CONCEPTS 535,537,542

perennial [adj] *enduring, perpetual*
abiding, annual, ceaseless, chronic, constant, continual, continuing, deathless, durable, eternal, everlasting, immortal, imperishable, incessant, inveterate, lasting, lifelong, long-lasting, long-lived, long-standing, never-ending, old, perdurable, permanent, persistent, recurrent, seasonal, sustained, unceasing, unchanging, undying, unfailing, uninterrupted, yearlong, yearly; SEE CONCEPTS 539,798

perfect [adj1] *flawless, superlative*
absolute, accomplished, aces*, adept, A-OK*, beyond compare, blameless, classical, consummate, crowning, culminating, defectless, excellent, excelling, experienced, expert, faultless, finished, foolproof, ideal, immaculate, impeccable, indefectible, matchless, out-of-this-world*, paradis-

iac, paradisiacal, peerless, pure, skilled, skillful, sound, splendid, spotless, stainless, sublime, superb, supreme, ten*, unblemished, unequaled, unmarred, untainted, untarnished, utopian; SEE CONCEPT 574

perfect [adj2] *whole, intact*
absolute, choate, complete, completed, consummate, downright, entire, finished, flawless, full, gross, integral, out-and-out*, outright, positive, rank, sheer, simple, sound, unadulterated, unalloyed, unblemished, unbroken, undamaged, unimpaired, unmitigated, unmixed, unqualified, utter; SEE CONCEPTS 482,485

perfect [adj3] *accurate, correct*
appropriate, bull's-eye*, certain, close, dead-on*, definite, distinct, exact, express, faithful, fit, ideal, model, needed, on target*, on the button*, on the money*, precise, proper, required, requisite, right, sharp, strict, suitable, textbook, to a T*, to a turn*, true, unerring, very; SEE CONCEPTS 535,557,558

perfect [v] *polish; achieve*
accomplish, ameliorate, carry out, complete, consummate, crown, cultivate, develop, effect, elaborate, finish, fulfill, hone, idealize, improve, perform, put finishing touch on, realize, refine, round, slick, smooth; SEE CONCEPTS 91,244,706

perfection [n] *achievement, completeness*
accomplishment, achieving, acme, arete, completion, consummation, crown, ending, entireness, evolution, exactness, excellence, excellency, exquisiteness, faultlessness, finish, finishing, fulfillment, ideal, idealism, impeccability, integrity, maturity, merit, paragon, perfectness, phoenix, precision, purity, quality, realization, ripeness, sublimity, superiority, supremacy, transcendence, virtue, wholeness; SEE CONCEPTS 671,706

perfectly [adv1] *absolutely*
altogether, completely, consummately, entirely, fully, quite, thoroughly, totally, utterly, well, wholly; SEE CONCEPTS 531,544

perfectly [adv2] *without flaw*
admirably, correctly, excellently, exquisitely, faultlessly, fitly, flawlessly, ideally, impeccably, superbly, superlatively, supremely, to perfection, wonderfully; SEE CONCEPT 574

perforate [v] *make a hole in*
bore, drill, drive, hole, honeycomb*, penetrate, permeate, pierce, pit, poke full of holes*, probe, punch, puncture, shoot full of holes*, slit, stab; SEE CONCEPT 220

perform [v1] *carry out, accomplish*
achieve, act, be engaged in, behave, bring about, bring off, carry through, carry to completion, complete, comply, deliver the goods*, discharge, dispose of, do, do justice to*, do to a turn*, effect, end, enforce, execute, finish, fulfill, function, go that route*, implement, meet, move, observe, operate, percolate, perk, pull off*, put through, react, realize, run with the ball*, satisfy, take, take care of business*, tick, transact, wind up, work; SEE CONCEPTS 91,199

perform [v2] *act, depict as entertainment*
act out, appear as, be on, bring down the house*, discourse, display, do a number*, do a turn*, dramatize, emote, enact, execute, exhibit, give, go on, ham*, ham it up*, impersonate, offer, personate, play, playact, present, produce, put on, render, represent, show, stage, tread the boards*; SEE CONCEPT 292

performance [n1] *accomplishment*
achievement, act, administration, attainment, carrying out, completion, conduct, consummation, discharge, doing, enforcement, execution, exploit, feat, fruition, fulfillment, pursuance, realization, work; SEE CONCEPT 706

performance [n2] *acting, depiction*
act, appearance, ballet, behavior, burlesque, business, ceremony, concert, custom, dance, display, drama, exhibition, gig*, interpretation, matinee, offering, opera, pageant, play, portrayal, presentation, production, recital, rehearsal, representation, review, revue, rigmarole, rite, set, show, special, spectacle, stage show, stunt, to-do*; SEE CONCEPT 263

performance [n3] *efficiency*
action, conduct, effectiveness, efficacy, exercise, functioning, operation, practice, pursuit, running, working; SEE CONCEPT 630

perfume [n] *scent, often manufactured and packaged for personal use*
aroma, attar, balm, balminess, bouquet, cologne, eau de cologne, essence, fragrance, incense, odor, oil, redolence, sachet, smell, spice, sweetness; SEE CONCEPTS 599,600

perfunctory [adj] *automatic, unthinking*
apathetic, careless, cool, cursory, disinterested, going through the motions*, heedless, impersonal, inattentive, indifferent, involuntary, lackadaisical, laid-back*, mechanical, negligent, offhand, phoning it in*, routine, sketchy, slipshod*, slovenly, standard, stereotyped, stock, superficial, unaware, unconcerned, uninterested, usual, walking through it*, wooden*; SEE CONCEPTS 542,544

perhaps [adv] *possibly*
as it may be, as the case may be, conceivably, feasibly, for all one knows, imaginably, it may be, maybe, perchance, reasonably; SEE CONCEPT 552

peril [n] *danger, risk*
cause for alarm*, double trouble*, endangerment, exposure, hazard, insecurity, jeopardy, liability, menace, openness, pitfall, risky business*, uncertainty, vulnerability; SEE CONCEPT 675

perilous [adj] *dangerous*
chancy, delicate, dicey*, dynamite, exposed, hairy*, hazardous, insecure, loaded*, on thin ice*, playing with fire*, precarious, risky, rugged, Russian roulette*, shaky, threatening, ticklish, touch and go*, touchy, treacherous, uncertain, unhealthy, unsafe, unsound, unstable, unsteady, unsure, vulnerable, wicked*; SEE CONCEPTS 548,587

perimeter [n] *circumference, border*
ambit, borderline, boundary, bounds, brim, brink, circuit, compass, confines, edge, fringe, hem, limit, margin, outline, periphery, skirt, verge; SEE CONCEPTS 484,745,792

period [n1] *extent of time*
aeon, age, course, cycle, date, days, duration, epoch, era, generation, interval, measure, season, space, span, spell, stage, stretch, term, time, while, years; SEE CONCEPTS 807,822

period [n2] *ending*
cessation, close, closing, closure, conclusion, discontinuance, end, limit, stop, termination; SEE CONCEPT 832

periodic [adj] *at fixed intervals*
alternate, annual, at various times, centennial, cyclic, cyclical, daily, epochal, every once in a while, every so often, fluctuating, hourly, infrequent, intermittent, isochronal, isochronous, monthly, occasional, on-again-off-again*, on certain occasions, orbital, perennial, periodical, recurrent, recurring, regular, repeated, rhythmic, routine, seasonal, serial, spasmodic, sporadic, weekly, yearly; SEE CONCEPTS 541,799

periodical [n] *regular publication*
journal, mag*, magazine, monthly, newspaper, number, paper, quarterly, rag*, review, serial, sheet*, slick*, throwaway*, weekly; SEE CONCEPT 280

peripatetic [adj] *constantly traveling*
ambulant, itinerant, itinerate, migrant, mobile, nomadic, perambulant, roaming, roving, vagabond, vagrant, wandering, wayfaring; SEE CONCEPTS 401,584

peripheral [adj] *minor, outside*
beside the point, borderline, exterior, external, incidental, inessential, irrelevant, minor, outer, outermost, perimetric, secondary, superficial, surface, tangential, unimportant; SEE CONCEPTS 575,583,831

periphery [n] *outskirts, outer edge*
ambit, border, boundary, brim, brink, circuit, circumference, compass, covering, edge, fringe, hem, margin, outside, perimeter, rim, skirt, verge; SEE CONCEPTS 484,745

perish [v] *die, decline, decay*
be destroyed, be killed, be lost, bite the dust*, break down, buy the farm*, cease, check out*, collapse, corrupt, croak, crumble, decease, decompose, demise, depart, disappear, disintegrate, end, expire, fall, give up the ghost*, go, go under, kick the bucket*, lose life, OD*, pass, pass away, pass on, rot, succumb, vanish, waste*, wither; SEE CONCEPTS 13,105,304

perishable [adj] *liable to spoil, rot*
decaying, decomposable, destructible, easily spoiled, short-lived, unstable; SEE CONCEPTS 462,485

perjure [v] *give false testimony*
bear false witness*, commit perjury, deceive, delude, equivocate, falsify, forswear, lie, lie under oath, mislead, prevaricate, swear falsely, trick; SEE CONCEPTS 63,317

perk [n] *benefit*
advantage, bonus, dividend, extra, fringe benefit, gratuity, gravy*, lagniappe, largess, perquisite, plus, tip; SEE CONCEPT 344

perk up [v] *cheer*
ameliorate, be refreshed, brighten, buck up*, cheer up, convalesce, gain, improve, invigorate, liven up, look up, mend, pep up, rally, recover, recuperate, refresh, renew, revive, shake, take heart*; SEE CONCEPTS 7,22,244,308

perky [adj] *animated, happy*
active, alert, aware, bouncy, bright, bright-eyed and bushy-tailed*, brisk, bubbly, buoyant, cheerful, cheery, gay, in fine fettle*, jaunty, lively, spirited, sprightly, sunny, vivacious; SEE CONCEPTS 401,404

permanent [adj] *constant, lasting*
abiding, changeless, continual, diurnal, durable, enduring, everlasting, fixed, forever, forever and a day*, for keeps*, immutable, imperishable, indestructible, in for the long haul*, invariable, long-lasting, perdurable, perduring, perennial, perpetual, persistent, set, set in concrete*, set in

stone*, stable, steadfast, unchanging, unfading; SEE CONCEPTS 551,649,798

permeable [adj] absorbent, penetrable
absorptive, accessible, enterable, passable, pervious, porose, porous, spongelike, spongy; SEE CONCEPTS 576,604,606

permeate [v] filter, spread throughout
charge, diffuse, drench, fill, go through, imbue, impregnate, infiltrate, infuse, ingrain, interfuse, invade, pass through, penetrate, percolate, pervade, pierce, saturate, seep, soak, stab, stalk, steep, suffuse, transfuse; SEE CONCEPTS 159,179,256

permissible [adj] allowable, legal
acceptable, admissible, all right, approved, authorized, bearable, endorsed, kosher*, lawful, legalized, legit*, legitimate, licit, okay*, on the up and up*, permitted, proper, sanctioned, tolerable, tolerated, unforbidden, unprohibited; SEE CONCEPTS 319,548,554

permission [n] authorization, consent
acceptance, acknowledgment, acquiescence, admission, agreement, allowance, approbation, approval, assent, avowal, canonization, carte blanche*, concession, concurrence, condonance, condonation, dispensation, empowerment, endorsement, freedom, imprimatur, indulgence, leave, letting, liberty, license, okay, permit, privilege, promise, recognition, rubber stamp*, sanctification, sanction, stamp of approval*, sufferance, tolerance, toleration, verification, warrant; SEE CONCEPTS 50,83,88,376,685

permissive [adj] lenient
acquiescent, agreeable, allowing, approving, easy-going, forbearing, free, indulgent, latitudinarian, lax, liberal, open-minded, permitting, susceptible, tolerant; SEE CONCEPT 401

permit [n] authorization
admittance, allowance, charter, concession, consent, empowering, favor, franchise, go-ahead*, grant, green light*, indulgence, leave, legalization, liberty, license, pass, passport, patent, permission, privilege, safe-conduct, sufferance, toleration, visa, warrant; SEE CONCEPTS 271,376,685

permit [v] allow participation
abet, accede, accept, acquiesce, admit, agree, authorize, bless, blink at*, boost, buy, charter, concede, concur, condone, consent, empower, enable, endorse, endure, franchise, give leave, give permission, go for, grant, have, humor, indulge, leave, let, let pass, license, okay, pass, privilege, sanctify, sanction, say yes, shake on*, sign, sign off on*, suffer, take kindly to*, thumbs up*, tolerate, warrant, wink at*; SEE CONCEPTS 50,83,88

pernicious [adj] bad, hurtful
baleful, damaging, dangerous, deadly, deleterious, destructive, detrimental, devastating, evil, fatal, harmful, iniquitous, injurious, killing, lethal, maleficent, malevolent, malicious, malign, malignant, miasmatic, miasmic, mortal, nefarious, noisome, noxious, offensive, pestiferous, pestilent, pestilential, poisonous, prejudicial, ruinous, sinister, toxic, venomous, virulent, wicked; SEE CONCEPTS 537,548,571

perpendicular [adj] at right angles to
erect, horizontal, on end, plumb, sheer, standing, stand-up, steep, straight, straight-up, upright, vertical; SEE CONCEPTS 581,583

perpetrate [v] be responsible for
act, bring about, carry out, commit, do, effect, enact, execute, inflict, perform, pull, up and do*, wreak; SEE CONCEPT 91

perpetual [adj] continual, lasting
abiding, ceaseless, constant, continued, continuous, endless, enduring, eternal, everlasting, going on, immortal, imperishable, incessant, infinite, interminable, intermittent, never-ceasing, never-ending, perdurable, perennial, permanent, persistent, recurrent, recurring, reoccurring, repeated, repeating, repetitious, returning, sempiternal, unceasing, unchanging, undying, unending, unfailing, uninterrupted, unremitting, without end; SEE CONCEPTS 551,649,798,799

perpetuate [v] keep going
bolster, conserve, continue, eternalize, eternize, immortalize, keep, keep alive, keep in existence, keep up, maintain, preserve, support, sustain; SEE CONCEPT 239

perplex [v] confuse, mix up
astonish, astound, baffle, balk, befuddle, beset, bewilder, buffalo*, complicate, confound, discombobulate*, discompose, dumbfound, encumber, entangle, fog, get to*, involve, jumble, muck, muddle, muddy the waters*, mystify, nonplus, perturb, pose, puzzle, rattle, ravel, snarl up, stumble, stump, surprise, tangle, thicken, thwart; SEE CONCEPTS 16,84

per se [adv] essentially
alone, as such, by and of itself, by definition, by itself, by its very nature, fundamentally, independently, in essence, in itself, intrinsically, of itself, singularly, solely, virtually; SEE CONCEPTS 544,577

persecute [v] wrong, torment
afflict, aggrieve, annoy, badger, bait, beat, be on one's case*, bother, crucify, distress, dog*, dragoon, drive up the wall*, exile, expel, harass, hector, hound*, hunt, ill-treat, injure, maltreat, martyr, molest, oppress, outrage, pester, pick on, plague, pursue, tease, torture, tyrannize, vex, victimize, worry; SEE CONCEPTS 7,19,44,246

perseverance [n] diligence, hard work
backbone*, constancy, continuance, cool, dedication, determination, doggedness, drive, endurance, grit*, guts*, immovability, indefatigability, moxie*, persistence, pertinacity, pluck*, prolonging, purposefulness, pursuance, resolution, sedulity, spunk, stamina, steadfastness, stick-to-itiveness*, tenacity; SEE CONCEPTS 411,633

persevere [v] keep at; work hard
be determined, be resolved, be stubborn, carry on, continue, endure, go for broke*, go for it*, go on, hang in*, hang tough*, hold fast*, hold on, keep driving*, keep going, keep on, leave no stone unturned*, maintain, persist, plug away*, press on, proceed, pursue, remain, see it through*, stand firm*, stay the course*, stick with it*; SEE CONCEPTS 87,239

persist [v] carry on, carry through
abide, be resolute, be stubborn, continue, endure, follow through*, follow up*, go all the way*, go on, go the limit*, grind, hold on, insist, keep up*, last, leave no stone unturned*, linger, obtain, perdure, persevere, persevere, prevail, pursue, recur, remain, repeat, see through, stick it out*, stick to guns*, strive, tough it out*; SEE CONCEPTS 23,87,91,239

persistent [adj] determined; continuous
assiduous, bound, bound and determined*, bull-dogged*, constant, continual, dogged, endless, enduring, firm, fixed, immovable, incessant, indefatigable, in for long haul*, insistent, interminable, like bad penny*, never-ending, obdurate, obstinate, perpetual, perseverant, persevering, persisting, pertinacious, relentless, repeated, resolute, steadfast, steady, sticky*, stubborn, tenacious, tireless, unflagging, unrelenting, unremitting, unshakable; SEE CONCEPTS 326,401, 404,538

persnickety [n1] fussy, particular
careful, choosy, fastidious, finicky, nice, picky; SEE CONCEPT 404

person [n] human being
being, body, character, creature, customer, gal, guy, human, identity, individual, individuality, joker*, life, living soul, man, mortal, party, personage, personality, self, somebody, soul, specimen, spirit, unit*, woman; SEE CONCEPT 417

personable [adj] friendly, sociable
aces*, affable, agreeable, all heart*, all right*, amiable, attractive, charming, easygoing, good egg*, gregarious, likable, nice, okay, pleasant, pleasing, presentable, sweetheart*, white-hat*, winning; SEE CONCEPT 404

personage/personality [n/n2] celebrity, notable
big shot*, bigwig*, brass*, celeb*, chief, cynosure, dignitary, distinguished person, eminence, face*, hot shot*, individual, luminary, monster*, name*, public figure, somebody, star, superstar, top dog*, VIP*, worthy; SEE CONCEPTS 352,354,423

personal [adj] private, individual
claimed, exclusive, intimate, own, particular, peculiar, privy, retired, secluded, secret, special; SEE CONCEPT 536

personality [n1] person's character, traits
charisma, charm, complexion, disposition, dynamism, emotions, identity, individuality, likableness, magnetism, makeup, nature, psyche, self, selfdom, selfhood, singularity, temper, temperament; SEE CONCEPT 411

personally [adv] independently
alone, by oneself, directly, for oneself, for one's part, individualistically, individually, in one's own view, in person, in the flesh, narrowly, on one's own, privately, solely, specially, subjectively; SEE CONCEPTS 544,577

personify [v] represent some other being, character
act out, body forth, contain, copy, emblematize, embody, epitomize, exemplify, express, exteriorize, externalize, hominify, humanize, illustrate, image, imitate, impersonate, incarnate, live as, make human, manifest, materialize, mirror, objectify, personize, substantiate, symbolize, typify; SEE CONCEPTS 261,716

personnel [n] employees of business or other enterprise
cadre, corps, crew, faculty, group, helpers, human resources, members, men and women, office, organization, people, shop, staff, troop, troops, workers, work force; SEE CONCEPTS 325,417

perspective [n] view, outlook
angle, aspect, attitude, broad view, context, frame of reference*, headset*, landscape, mindset*, objectivity, overview, panorama, proportion, prospect, relation, relative importance, relativity,

scene, size of it*, viewpoint, vista, way of looking; SEE CONCEPTS 410,629,689

perspicacious [adj] observant, perceptive
acute, alert, astute, aware, clear-sighted, clever, discerning, heady*, judicious, keen, penetrating, percipient, sagacious, savvy*, sharp, sharp-witted, shrewd; SEE CONCEPT 402

perspicuous [adj] clear, obvious
apparent, clear-cut, comprehensible, crystal*, crystal-clear*, distinct, easily understood, explicit, intelligible, limpid, lucent, lucid, luminous, pellucid, plain, self-evident, straightforward, transparent, unambiguous, unblurred, understandable; SEE CONCEPT 529

perspire [v] become wet with sweat
be damp, be wet, break a sweat*, drip, exude, get in a lather*, glow, lather, pour, secrete, swelter; SEE CONCEPTS 185,469

persuade [v] cause to believe; convince to do
actuate, advise, affect, allure, argue into, assure, blandish, brainwash*, bring around, bring to senses, cajole, coax, convert, counsel, draw, enlist, entice, exhort, gain confidence of, get, impel, impress, incite, incline, induce, influence, inveigle, lead, lead to believe, lead to, move, prevail upon, prompt, propagandize, proselyte, proselytize, reason, satisfy, seduce, sell, stroke, sway, talk into, touch, turn on to, urge, wear down*, wheedle, win argument, win over, woo, work over; SEE CONCEPT 68

persuasion [n1] influencing to do, believe
alignment, alluring, arm-twist*, blandishment, brainwashing*, cajolery, cogency, con*, conversion, enticement, exhortation, force, goose*, hard sell*, hook*, inducement, inveiglement, persuasiveness, potency, power, promote, pull*, seduction, sell*, snow job*, soft soap*, squeeze*, sweet talk*, wheedling, winning over, working over; SEE CONCEPTS 68,687

persuasion [n2] belief, religion
bias, camp, certitude, church, communion, connection, conviction, credo, creed, cult, denomination, eye, faction, faith, feeling, mind*, opinion, partiality, party, predilection, prejudice, school, school of thought*, sect, sentiment, side, tenet, view; SEE CONCEPT 689

persuasive [adj] effective, influential
actuating, alluring, cogent, compelling, conclusive, convictive, convincing, credible, effectual, efficacious, efficient, eloquent, energetic, enticing, forceful, forcible, impelling, impressive, inducing, inspiring, inveigling, logical, luring, moving, plausible, pointed, potent, powerful, seductive, slick, smooth, sound, stimulating, stringent, strong, swaying, telling, touching, unctuous, valid, weighty, wheedling, winning; SEE CONCEPTS 267,537,542

pert [adj] lively, bold
animated, audacious, brash, brazen, breezy, bright, brisk, cheeky*, dapper, daring, dashing, disrespectful, flip*, flippant, forward, fresh, gay, impertinent, impudent, insolent, jaunty, keen, nervy, perky, presumptuous, sassy*, saucy*, smart, smart-alecky*, spirited, sprightly, vivacious, wise; SEE CONCEPTS 401,404

pertain [v] be relevant to
affect, appertain, apply, associate, be appropriate, bear on, befit, belong, be part of, be pertinent, combine, concern, connect, inhere in, join, refer, regard, relate, touch, vest; SEE CONCEPT 532

pe
pe

pertinent [adj] *relevant, suitable*

admissible, ad rem, applicable, apposite, appropriate, apropos, apt, connected, fit, fitting, germane, kosher*, legit*, material, on target*, on the button*, on the nose*, opportune, pat*, pertaining, proper, related, right on, to the point, to the purpose; SEE CONCEPT 558

perturb [v] *upset, unsettle*

agitate, alarm, annoy, bewilder, bother, bug*, confound, confuse, disarrange, discompose, disconcert, discountenance, dismay, disorder, disquiet, disturb, flurry, fluster, irritate, make a scene*, make waves*, muddle, needle, perplex, pester, ruffle, stir up*, trouble, vex, worry; SEE CONCEPTS 7,16,19

peruse [v] *check out; examine*

analyze, browse, glance over, inspect, look through, pore over, read, scan, scrutinize, skim, study; SEE CONCEPTS 72,103

pervade [v] *affect strongly; spread through*

charge, diffuse, extend, fill, imbue, impregnate, infuse, overspread, penetrate, percolate, permeate, suffuse, transfuse; SEE CONCEPTS 172,179

pervasive [adj] *extensive*

all over the place*, can't get away from*, common, general, inescapable, omnipresent, permeating, pervading, prevalent, rife, ubiquitous, universal, wall-to-wall*, widespread; SEE CONCEPT 772

perverse [adj] *mean, ornery; troublesome*

abnormal, bad-tempered, cantankerous, capricious, contradictory, contrary, contumacious, corrupt, crabby*, cross, degenerate, delinquent, depraved, deviant, disobedient, dogged*, erring, fractious, hard-nosed*, headstrong, intractable, intransigent, irritable, miscreant, mulish*, nefarious, obdurate, obstinate, petulant, pigheaded*, rebellious, refractory, rotten*, self-willed, spiteful, stubborn, unhealthy, unmanageable, unreasonable, unyielding, villainous, wayward, wicked, willful; SEE CONCEPTS 401,542,571

pervert [n] *person who lacks morals*

debauchee, degenerate, deviant, deviate, freak, weirdo*; SEE CONCEPT 412

pervert [v] *twist, turn away from what is acceptable or correct*

abuse, adulterate, alloy, animalize, brainwash, color, corrupt, cut*, debase, debauch, demoralize, deprave, desecrate, distort, divert, doctor, doctor up*, fake, falsify, fudge*, garble, misconstrue, misinterpret, misrepresent, misstate, mistreat, misuse, outrage, phony up*, prostitute, ruin, salt*, seduce, spike, vitiate, warp, water*; SEE CONCEPTS 14,63,156,252

perverted [adj] *immoral, evil*

abandoned, aberrant, abnormal, abused, contorted, corrupt, corrupted, debased, debauched, defiled, depraved, deviant, deviating, distorted, foreign, grotesque, impaired, kinky*, misguided, misused, monstrous, outraged, polluted, queer, sick, tainted, twisted, unhealthy, unnatural, vicious, vitiate, vitiated, warped, wicked; SEE CONCEPTS 485,545

pesky [adj] *bothersome*

annoying, disturbing, irksome, mean, nettlesome, peeving, provoking, troublesome, ugly, vexatious, vexing, wicked; SEE CONCEPTS 529,537

pessimism [n] *belief in bad outcome*

cynicism, dark side*, dejection, depression, despair, despondency, dim view*, distrust, dyspep-

sia, expectation of worst, gloom, gloominess, gloomy outlook, glumness, grief, hopelessness, low spirits, melancholy, sadness, unhappiness; SEE CONCEPTS 410,689

pessimist [n] *person who expects bad outcome*

complainer, crepehanger*, cynic, defeatist, depreciator, downer, gloomy, killjoy*, misanthrope, party pooper*, prophet of doom*, sourpuss*, wet blanket*, worrier, worrywart*; SEE CONCEPTS 412,423

pessimistic [adj] *expecting bad outcome*

bleak, cynical, dark, dejected, depressed, despairing, despondent, discouraged, distrustful, downhearted, fatalistic, foreboding, gloomy, glum, hopeless, melancholy, misanthropic, morbid, morose, resigned, sad, sullen, troubled, worried; SEE CONCEPTS 403,548

pest [n] *person or thing that presents problem*

annoyance, badgerer, bane, besetment, blight, blister, bore, bother, bothersome, bug*, contagion, crashing bore*, creep, curse, drag, drip, epidemic, exasperation, headache*, infection, irritant, irritation, nag, nudge, nuisance, pain*, pain in the neck*, pesterer, pestilence, pill*, plague*, scourge*, tease*, thorn in side*, tormentor, trial*, trouble, vexation, virus*; SEE CONCEPTS 306,398,412,694

pester [v] *bother, harass*

annoy, badger, be at, bedevil, beleaguer, bug*, disturb, dog*, drive crazy, drive up the wall*, fret, get at*, get in one's hair*, get on one's nerves*, get to*, harry, hassle, hector, hound, importune, insist, irk, mess with*, nag, nudge, pick at*, plague, provoke, remind, ride*, tantalize, tease, torment, work on*, worry; SEE CONCEPTS 7,19,48

pestilent/pestilential [adj] *dangerous, harmful*

baneful, contagious, contaminating, corrupting, deadly, deleterious, destructive, detrimental, diseased, evil, fatal, infectious, injurious, lethal, mortal, noxious, pernicious, pestiferous, ruinous, tainting, troublesome, vicious; SEE CONCEPTS 314,537

pet [n] *favorite thing, person*

apple of eye*, beloved, cat, darling, dear, dog, evergreen*, idol, jewel*, love, lover, persona grata*, treasure*; SEE CONCEPTS 394,416

pet [adj] *favorite*

affectionate, cherished, darling, dear, dearest, endearing, favored, loved, precious, preferred, special; SEE CONCEPTS 568,574

pet [v] *stroke, kiss*

baby, caress, cuddle, cosset, cuddle, dandle, embrace, fondle, grab, hug, love, make love, neck*, pamper, pat, smooch*, spoil, spoon*, touch; SEE CONCEPTS 375,612

peter out [v] *dwindle, decrease*

abate, come to nothing*, die out*, diminish, drain, ebb, evaporate, fade, fail, give out, lessen, pall, rebate, recede, run dry, run out, stop, taper off, wane; SEE CONCEPTS 105,698

petite [adj] *small*

baby, bantam, dainty, delicate, diminutive, elfin, little, miniature, minikin*, slight, smallish, tiny, wee*; SEE CONCEPTS 773,779,789

petition [n] *appeal, plea*

address, application, entreaty, imploration, imprecation, invocation, memorial, prayer, request, round robin, solicitation, suit, supplication; SEE CONCEPTS 271,662

petition [v] *plead, appeal for*
adjure, ask, beg, beseech, call upon, entreat, impetrate, implore, pray, press, put in for, request, seek, solicit, sue, supplicate, urge; SEE CONCEPTS 48,53

petrify [v1] *make hard*
calcify, clarify, fossilize, harden, lapidify, mineralize, set, solidify, turn to stone; SEE CONCEPT 250

petrify [v2] *frighten*
alarm, amaze, appall, astonish, astound, benumb, chill, confound, daze, dismay, dumbfound, horrify, immobilize, numb, paralyze, put chill on*, scare, scare silly*, scare stiff*, spook*, startle, stun, stupefy, terrify, transfix; SEE CONCEPTS 7,14,19,42

petty [adj] *trivial, insignificant*
base, casual, cheap, contemptible, frivolous, inconsequent, inconsiderable, inessential, inferior, irrelevant, junior, lesser, light, little, lower, measly, minor, narrow-minded, negligible, nickel-and-dime*, niggling*, paltry, peanut*, penny-ante*, pettifogging*, picayune, piddling*, scratch, secondary, shabby, shallow, shoestring*, slight, small, small-minded, subordinate, trifling, two-bit*, unimportant; SEE CONCEPTS 403,575

petulant [adj] *crabby, moody*
bad-tempered, captious, caviling, complaining, cranky*, cross, crybaby*, displeased, fault-finding, fractious, fretful, grouchy, grumbling, huffy, ill-humored, impatient, irritable, mean, peevish, perverse, pouting, querulous, snappish, sour, sulky, sullen, testy, touchy, ungracious, uptight*, waspish, whining, whiny; SEE CONCEPTS 401,542

phantom [n] *ghost; figment of the imagination*
apparition, chimera, daydream, delusion, dream, eidolon, figment, hallucination, haunt, ignis fatuus, illusion, mirage, nightmare, phantasm, revenant, shade, shadow, specter, spirit, spook, vision, wraith; SEE CONCEPTS 370,529

phase [n] *period in life of something*
appearance, aspect, chapter, condition, development, facet, juncture, point, position, posture, stage, state, step, time; SEE CONCEPTS 816,834

phenomenal [adj] *astounding, exceptional*
extraordinary, fantastic, marvelous, miraculous, outstanding, preternatural, prodigious, rare, remarkable, sensational, singular, substantial, uncommon, unique, unparalleled, unusual, unwonted, wondrous; SEE CONCEPTS 564,574

phenomenology [n] *study of subject and objects of a person's experience*
intentionality, life-world, lived experience, meaning-making; SEE CONCEPTS 282,349

phenomenon [n] *rare occurrence; wonder*
abnormality, actuality, anomaly, appearance, aspect, circumstance, curiosity, episode, event, exception, experience, fact, happening, incident, marvel, miracle, nonpareil, one for the books*, paradox, peculiarity, portent, prodigy, rara avis*, rarity, reality, sensation, sight, something else*, spectacle, stunner*, uniqueness; SEE CONCEPTS 230,529,678

philanderer [n] *person who has many love affairs*
adulterer, chaser, cruiser, dallier, debaucher, flirt, gallant, lover, operator*, swinger; SEE CONCEPT 423

philanthropic [adj] *charitable, giving*
altruistic, beneficent, benevolent, benignant, big-hearted, bountiful, contributing, donating, eleemosynary, generous, good, gracious, helpful, humane, humanitarian, kind, kindhearted, liberal, magnanimous, munificent, openhanded, patriotic, public-spirited; SEE CONCEPTS 404,542

philosophical/philosophic [adj1] *thinking deeply, rationally*
abstract, cogitative, deep, erudite, judicious, learned, logical, pensive, profound, rational, reflective, sagacious, sapient, theoretical, thoughtful, wise; SEE CONCEPT 402

philosophical/philosophic [adj2] *calm, serene*
collected, commonsensical, composed, cool*, cool as cucumber*, enduring, impassive, imperturbable, patient, resigned, stoical, tranquil, unagitated, unflappable, unmoved, unruffled; SEE CONCEPT 401

philosophy [n] *principles, knowledge*
aesthetics, attitude, axiom, beliefs, conception, convictions, doctrine, idea, ideology, logic, metaphysics, ontology, outlook, rationalism, reason, reasoning, system, tenet, theory, thinking, thought, truth, values, view, viewpoint, wisdom; SEE CONCEPTS 349,688,689

phobia [n] *fear*
anxiety, aversion, avoidance, awe, detestation, disgust, dislike, distaste, dread, fear, hang-up*, hatred, horror, irrationality, loathing, neurosis, obsession, repulsion, resentment, revulsion, terror, thing*, thing about*; SEE CONCEPTS 27,29,529

phony [adj] *fake, false*
affected, artificial, assumed, bogus, counterfeit, forged, imitation, pseudo, put-on*, sham*, spurious, trick*; SEE CONCEPT 582

photocopy [n/v] *mechanical image produced from a copier; making the image*
copy, duplicate, reproduce, stat, velox, Xerox; SEE CONCEPT 269

photograph [n] *a still picture taken with a camera*
blowup, close-up, image, Kodachrome*, Kodak*, likeness, microfilm, mug*, negative, photo, photostat, pic*, picture, pinup*, pix*, Polaroid*, portrait, positive, print, shot*, slide, snap, snapshot, transparency; SEE CONCEPT 265

photograph [v] *take a picture with a camera*
capture*, capture on film*, cinematize, close-up*, copy, film, get, get a likeness*, get a shot*, illustrate, lens*, make a picture*, microfilm, mug*, photo, photoengrave, photostat, picture, print, record, reproduce, roll, shoot, snap*, snapshot, take*, turn*, X-ray*; SEE CONCEPT 174

photographic [adj] *exact, retentive in detail*
accurate, cinematic, detailed, faithful, filmic, graphic, lifelike, minute, natural, pictorial, picturesque, precise, realistic, true-to-life*, visual, vivid; SEE CONCEPT 557

phrase [n] *group of words; way of speaking*
byword, catchphrase, catchword, diction, expression, idiom, locution, maxim, motto, parlance, phraseology, phrasing, remark, saying, shibboleth, slogan, styling, tag, terminology, utterance, verbalism, verbiage, watchword, wordage, wording; SEE CONCEPTS 275,278

phrase [v] *express in words carefully*
couch, formulate, frame, present, put, put into words, say, term, utter, voice, word; SEE CONCEPT 55

physical [adj1] *tangible, material*
concrete, corporeal, environmental, gross, mate-

pe
ph

rialistic, natural, objective, palpable, phenomenal, ponderable, real, sensible, solid, somatic, substantial, visible; SEE CONCEPT 582

physical [adj2] concerning the body
bodily, brute, carnal, corporal, corporeal, earthly, fleshly, incarnate, mortal, personal, somatic, unspiritual, visceral; SEE CONCEPT 485

physician [n] person trained in medical science
bones*, doc*, doctor, general practitioner, healer, intern, MD*, medic, medical practitioner, quack*, sawbones*, specialist, surgeon; SEE CONCEPT 357

physique [n] build of human body
anatomy, body, built, character, configuration, constitution, corpus, figure, form, frame, habit, habitus, makeup, muscles, nature, shape, structure, type; SEE CONCEPTS 405,757

pick [n] a chosen option, usually the choicest
aces, bag, best, choice, choosing, cream*, crème de la crème*, cup of tea*, decision, druthers*, elect, elite, flower*, preference, pride, prime, prize, select, selection, top, tops; SEE CONCEPTS 529,671

pick [v1] choose, select
cull, decide upon, elect, finger*, fix upon, go down the line*, hand-pick, mark, name, optate, opt for, pick and choose, pick out, prefer, say so, separate, settle on, sift out*, single out, slot, sort out, tab, tag, take, take it or leave it*, tap, winnow; SEE CONCEPT 41

pick [v2] gather, harvest
accumulate, choose, collect, cull, cut, draw, pluck, pull; SEE CONCEPTS 41,109,206

pick [v3] break into something closed, locked
break open, crack, dent, force, hit, indent, jimmy, open, pry, strike; SEE CONCEPT 192

pick at/pick on [v] nag, provoke
badger, bait, blame, bully, carp, cavil, criticize, find fault, foment, get at*, get to*, goad, hector, incite, instigate, quibble, start, tease, torment; SEE CONCEPTS 7,19,52

picket [n1] post of structure
pale, paling, palisade, panel, peg, pillar, rail, stake, stanchion, upright; SEE CONCEPTS 445,479

picket [n2] person who demonstrates for cause
demonstrator, picketer, protester, striker; SEE CONCEPTS 348,359

picket [n3] person acting as guard
guard, lookout, patrol, scout, sentinel, sentry, spotter, vedette, ward, watch, watchperson; SEE CONCEPT 348

picket [v] protest against, for cause
blockade, boycott, demonstrate, hit the bricks*, strike, walk out; SEE CONCEPTS 300,351

pickle [n] sticky situation
bind, box*, corner*, difficulty, dilemma, disorder, fix, hole*, hot water*, jam*, predicament, quandary, scrape, spot*, tight spot*; SEE CONCEPT 674

pickle [v] preserve fruit or vegetable
can, cure, keep, marinade, salt, souse, steep; SEE CONCEPT 170

pick up [v1] lift, raise
elevate, gather, grasp, hoist, rear, take up, uphold, uplift, upraise, uprear; SEE CONCEPT 196

pick up [v2] obtain, find
acquire, annex, buy, chalk up*, come across, compass, cull, extract, gain, garner, gather, get, get the hang of*, glean, happen upon*, have,

learn, procure, purchase, score, secure, take; SEE CONCEPTS 31,120,183

pick up [v3] improve
continue, gain, gain ground*, get better, get well, increase, make a comeback*, mend, perk up*, rally, recommence, recover, renew, reopen, restart, resume, swell, take up; SEE CONCEPTS 234,700

pick up [v4] call for socially
accompany, collect, drop in for*, get*, give a lift*, go for*, go to get*, invite, offer, proposition, stop for*; SEE CONCEPTS 224,384

pick up [v5] arrest for crime
apprehend, book*, bust*, collar*, detain, nab, pinch*, pull in*, run in*, take into custody; SEE CONCEPT 317

picky [adj] choosy, finicky
captious, critical, dainty, fastidious, fault-finding, fussy, nice, particular, persnickety; SEE CONCEPT 404

picnic [n1] outdoor meal
barbecue, clambake, cookout, dining alfresco, excursion, fish fry, outing, weiner roast; SEE CONCEPTS 386,459

picnic [n2] easy undertaking
breeze*, child's play*, cinch, duck soup*, kid stuff*, lark*, light work, no trouble, piece of cake*, pushover*, setup*, smooth sailing*, snap, sure thing, walkover*; SEE CONCEPTS 362,693

picture [n1] illustration, likeness of something
account, art, blueprint, canvas, cartoon, copy, delineation, depiction, description, doodle, double, draft, drawing, duplicate, effigy, engraving, figure, icon, image, impression, lookalike, outline, painting, panorama, photo, photograph, piece, portrait, portrayal, presentment, print, re-creation, replica, report, representation, ringer*, similitude, simulacrum, sketch, spectacle, spitting image*, statue, tableau, twin; SEE CONCEPTS 259,625

picture [n2] perfect example
archetype, embodiment, epitome, essence, idea, personification; SEE CONCEPT 686

picture [n3] entertainment film
cartoon, cinema, flick*, motion picture, movie, moving picture, photoplay, picture show, show; SEE CONCEPT 293

picture [v1] depict, describe
delineate, draw, illustrate, image, interpret, limn, paint, photograph, portray, render, represent, show, sketch; SEE CONCEPTS 79,174

picture [v2] form vision in one's mind
conceive of, create, daydream, dream, envision, fancy, fantasize, imagine, portray, see, see in the mind's eye*, visualize; SEE CONCEPTS 17,43

picturesque [adj] attractive, referring to scenery
arresting, artistic, beautiful, charming, colorful, graphic, photographic, pictorial, pleasant, pretty, quaint, scenic, striking, vivid; SEE CONCEPTS 579,589

piddling [adj] insignificant
derisory, little, measly*, niggling*, paltry, peanut*, pettifogging*, petty, picayune, puny, trifling, trivial, unimportant, useless, worthless; SEE CONCEPTS 575,789

piece [n1] part
allotment, bit, bite, chunk, cut, division, dole, end, example, fraction, fragment, gob, half, hunk, instance, interest, iota, item, length, lot, lump, member, moiety, morsel, parcel, percentage, portion, quantity, quota, sample, scrap, section, seg-

ment, share, shred, slice, smithereen*, specimen; SEE CONCEPTS 834,835

piece [n2] *work of art, music, writing*
arrangement, article, bit, composition, creation, discourse, dissertation, engraving, exposition, icon, item, lines, painting, paper, part, photograph, print, production, sketch, song, statue, study, theme, thesis, treatise, treatment, vignette, work; SEE CONCEPTS 259,262,263,271

piece [v] *put together*
assemble, combine, compose, create, fix, join, make, mend, patch, repair, restore, unite; SEE CONCEPTS 113,173,193,251

piecemeal [adj/adv] *bit by bit*
at intervals, by degrees, by fits and starts*, fitfully, fragmentary, gradual, gradually, intermittent, intermittently, interrupted, little by little*, partial, partially, patchy, spotty, step by step*; SEE CONCEPTS 531,544

pier [n] *support; place for boats*
berth, buttress, column, dam, dock, jetty, landing, levee, mole, pierage, pilaster, pile, piling, pillar, post, promenade, quay, slip, upright, wharf; SEE CONCEPTS 439,443,479

pierce [v] *cut, penetrate*
bore, break, break in, break through, cleave, crack, crack open, drill, enter, gash, incise, intrude, pass through, perforate, plow, prick, probe, puncture, run through, slash, slice, slit, spike, stab, stick into, transfix; SEE CONCEPTS 137,159,176,220

piercing [adj] *intense to the senses*
acute, agonizing, arctic, biting, bitter, blaring, cold, deafening, earsplitting, excruciating, exquisite, fierce, freezing, frosty, high, high-pitched, keen, knifelike, loud, numbing, painful, penetrating, powerful, racking, raw, roaring, severe, sharp, shattering, shooting, shrill, stabbing, stentorian, stentorious, thin, treble, wintry; SEE CONCEPTS 406,537,592,594

piety [n] *devotion, religiousness*
allegiance, application, ardor, belief, devoutness, docility, dutifulness, duty, faith, fealty, fervor, fidelity, godliness, grace, holiness, loyalty, obedience, passion, religion, religiosity, reverence, sanctity, veneration, zeal; SEE CONCEPTS 633,689

pig [n] *animal of swine family*
boar, cob roller*, hog, piggy*, piglet, porker*, porky, shoat, sow, swine; SEE CONCEPTS 394,400

pigheaded [adj] *stubborn*
bullheaded, contrary, dense*, forward, headstrong, inflexible, insistent, intractable, mulish*, obstinate, perverse, recalcitrant, self-willed, stiffnecked, stupid*, unyielding, willful; SEE CONCEPTS 404,542

pigment [n] *color, shade*
colorant, coloring, coloring matter, dye, dyestuff, oil, paint, stain, tincture, tint; SEE CONCEPTS 259,622

pile [n1] *heap, collection*
accumulation, aggregate, aggregation, amassment, assemblage, assortment, bank, barrel, buildup, chunk, conglomeration, drift, gob, great deal, hill, hoard, hunk, jumble, lump, mass, mound, mountain, much, ocean, oodles*, pack, peck, pyramid, quantity, shock, stack, stockpile; SEE CONCEPTS 432,787

pile [n2] *wealth*
affluence, boodle*, bundle*, dough*, fortune,

mint*, money, pot*, riches, wad*; SEE CONCEPTS 335,340

pile [v] *gather, pack; put up on top of another*
accumulate, amass, assemble, bank, bunch, collect, crowd, crush, fill, flock, heap, hill, hoard, jam, load, mass, mound, rush, stack, store; SEE CONCEPTS 84,109,201,750

pilfer [v] *steal, embezzle*
annex, appropriate, borrow, cop*, crib*, filch*, liberate*, lift*, moonlight*, palm*, pinch*, pluck*, purloin, requisition, rip off*, rob, scrounge, snare, snatch, swipe, take, thieve, walk off with*; SEE CONCEPTS 139,142,192

pilgrimage [n] *long journey*
crusade, excursion, expedition, mission, tour, travel, trip, wayfaring; SEE CONCEPT 224

pill [n1] *capsule of medicine*
bolus, dose, lozenge, medicine, pellet, pilule, tablet, troche; SEE CONCEPTS 307,470

pill [n2] *person who is annoying*
bore, drag*, nuisance, pain*, pain in the neck*, pest, trial*; SEE CONCEPTS 412,423

pillage [v] *plunder, destroy*
appropriate, arrogate, confiscate, depredate, desecrate, desolate, despoil, devastate, devour, gut, invade, lay waste*, lift*, loot, maraud, nab*, pilfer, pinch*, purloin, raid, ransack, ravage, rifle*, rob, ruin, sack, spoil, spoliate, steal, strip, thieve, trespass, waste; SEE CONCEPTS 86,139,252

pillar [n1] *column of building, or freestanding column*
colonnade, mast, obelisk, pedestal, pier, pilaster, piling, post, prop, shaft, stanchion, support, tower, upright; SEE CONCEPT 440

pillar [n2] *mainstay; source of strength*
backbone*, guider, leader, light*, rock*, sinew, supporter, tower of strength*, upholder, worthy; SEE CONCEPTS 423,712

pilot [n] *person who guides aircraft, ship, or other vehicle*
ace*, aerialist, aeronaut, aviator, bellwether*, captain, conductor, coxswain, dean, director, doyen/doyenne, eagle*, flier*, flyer, guide, helmsperson, jockey*, lead, leader, navigator, one at the controls, one at the wheel, scout*, steerer, steersperson, wheelperson; SEE CONCEPT 348

pimple [n] *small swelling on the skin*
abscess, acne, beauty spot, blackhead, blemish, blister, boil, bump, carbuncle, caruncle, excrescence, furuncle, hickey*, inflammation, lump, papula, papule, pustule, spot, whitehead, zit*; SEE CONCEPT 306

pin [v] *attach, hold in place*
affix, bind, clasp, close, fasten, fix, hold down, hold fast, immobilize, join, pinion, press, restrain, secure; SEE CONCEPTS 85,160,190

pinch [n1] *tight pressing*
compression, confinement, contraction, cramp, grasp, grasping, hurt, limitation, nip, nipping, pressure, squeeze, torment, tweak, twinge; SEE CONCEPT 728

pinch [n2] *small amount*
bit, dash, drop, jot, mite, small quantity, soupçon, speck, splash, splatter, taste; SEE CONCEPT 831

pinch [n3] *predicament*
box*, clutch, contingency, crisis, crunch*, difficulty, emergency, exigency, hardship, juncture, necessity, oppression, pass, plight, pressure,

ph
pi

strait, stress, tight spot*, tight squeeze*, turning point*, zero hour*; SEE CONCEPT 674

pinch [v1] *press tightly*
chafe, compress, confine, cramp, crush, grasp, hurt, nip, pain, squeeze, tweak, twinge, wrench, wrest, wring; SEE CONCEPTS 219,313

pinch [v2] *be stingy*
afflict, distress, economize, oppress, pinch pennies*, press, scrape, scrimp, skimp, spare, stint; SEE CONCEPT 330

pinch [v3] *steal*
cop*, crib*, filch*, knock off*, lift*, nab*, pilfer, purloin, rob, snatch, swipe, take; SEE CONCEPT 139

pinch [v4] *arrest*
apprehend, bust*, collar*, detain, hold, nab*, pick up*, pull in*, run in*, take into custody; SEE CONCEPTS 90,317

pine [v] *long for*
ache, agonize, brood, carry a torch*, covet, crave, desire, dream, fret, grieve, hanker, languish for, lust after, mope*, mourn, sigh, spoil for*, thirst for, want, wish, yearn, yen for; SEE CONCEPT 20

pink [n1/adj] *rose color*
blush, coral, flush, fuchsia, rose, roseate, salmon; SEE CONCEPT 622

pink [n2] *best condition*
acme*, best, bloom*, fitness, good health, height*, peak, perfection, prime, summit, trim*, verdure; SEE CONCEPTS 316,388

pink [v] *cut in zigzag*
incise, notch, perforate, prick, punch, scallop, score; SEE CONCEPT 176

pinnacle [n] *top, crest*
acme*, apex, apogee, climax, cone, crown, culmination, greatest, height, max*, most*, needle*, obelisk, peak, pyramid, spire, steeple, summit, tops, tower, vertex, zenith; SEE CONCEPTS 706,836

pinpoint [v] *define, locate*
determinate, diagnose, distinguish, finger*, get a fix on*, home in on*, identify, place, recognize, spot; SEE CONCEPTS 38,183

pioneer [n] *person who finds a new place, founds something*
colonist, colonizer, developer, explorer, founder, frontier settler, guide, homesteader, immigrant, innovator, leader, pathfinder, pilgrim, scout, settler, squatter, trailblazer; SEE CONCEPTS 348,413

pioneer [adj] *early, first*
avant-garde, brave, experimental, head, inaugural, initial, lead, original, primary, prime; SEE CONCEPT 585

pioneer [v] *invent; lay the groundwork*
begin, colonize, create, develop, discover, establish, explore, found, go out in front*, initiate, instigate, institute, launch, map out, open up, originate, prepare, show the way, spearhead*, start, take the lead, trailblaze*; SEE CONCEPTS 173,221,324

pious [adj] *dedicated, religious*
born-again*, clerical, devoted, devout, divine, ecclesiastical, godly, goody-goody*, orthodox, prayerful, priestly, reverent, righteous, sacred, saintly, sanctimonious, spiritual; SEE CONCEPT 401

pipe [n] *passage, tube*
aqueduct, canal, channel, conduit, conveyer, duct, hose, line, main, pipeline, sewer, spout, trough, vent, vessel; SEE CONCEPTS 475,499

pipe [v1] *conduct through tube, passage*
bring in, carry, channel, convey, funnel, siphon, supply, traject, transmit; SEE CONCEPT 217

pipe [v2] *make a sound; peep*
blubber*, boohoo*, cheep*, cry, play, say, shout, sing, sob, sound, speak, talk, toot*, trill, tweet, twitter, wail, warble, weep, whistle; SEE CONCEPTS 47,65,77

piquant [adj] *flavorful, biting*
highly-seasoned, interesting, lively, peppery, poignant, provocative, pungent, racy, savory, sharp, snappy, sparkling, spicy, spirited, stimulating, stinging, tangy, tart, well-flavored, with a kick*, zestful, zesty; SEE CONCEPTS 529,613

pique [n] *anger, irritation*
annoyance, blowup*, conniption*, dander*, displeasure, flare-up, grudge, huff, hurt, irk, miff*, offense, peeve, pet*, provocation, resentment, rise, ruckus*, slow burn*, snit, sore*, stew*, storm*, tiff*, umbrage, vexation; SEE CONCEPTS 29,410

pique [v] *offend, provoke*
absorb, affront, annoy, arouse, bother, bug*, displease, egg on*, exasperate, excite, fire up*, gall, galvanize, get*, get a rise out of*, get under skin*, give a hard time*, give the business*, goad, goose*, grab, ignite, incense, irk, irritate, kindle, make waves*, miff*, mortify, motivate, move, nettle, offend, peeve, prick, put out*, quicken, rile, rouse, spur, stimulate, sting*, stir, vex, whet, work up*, wound; SEE CONCEPTS 7,14,19,22

pit [n] *hole, cavity*
abyss, chasm, crater, dent, depression, dimple, excavation, grave, gulf, hell, hollow, indentation, mine, perforation, pockmark, pothole, puncture, shaft, tomb, trench, well; SEE CONCEPTS 509,513

pit [v] *oppose, play off*
contend, counter, match, put in opposition, set against, vie; SEE CONCEPTS 92,363

pitch [n1] *tilt*
angle, cant, degree, dip, gradient, height, incline, level, point, slant, slope, steepness; SEE CONCEPTS 692,738

pitch [n2] *tone of sound*
frequency, harmonic, modulation, rate, sound, timbre; SEE CONCEPT 65

pitch [n3] *talk to convince*
patter*, persuasion, sales talk, song and dance*, spiel*; SEE CONCEPTS 68,278

pitch [v1] *throw, hurl*
bung, cast, chuck*, fire, fling, gun, heave, launch, lob, peg, sling, toss, unseat; SEE CONCEPT 222

pitch [v2] *put up, erect*
fix, locate, place, plant, raise, settle, set up, station; SEE CONCEPT 168

pitch [v3] *dive, roll*
ascend, bend, bicker, careen, descend, dip, drive, drop, fall, flounder, go down, heave, lean, lunge, lurch, plunge, rise, rock, seesaw, slope, slump, stagger, tilt, topple, toss, tumble, vault, wallow, welter, yaw; SEE CONCEPTS 147,181,201

pitch in [v] *help; get busy*
aid, attack, begin, buckle down*, chip in*, come through, commence, contribute, cooperate, do, do one's bit*, fall to*, get cracking*, get going, go to it*, hop to it*, join in, jump in*, launch, lend a hand*, participate, plunge into*, set about, set to, subscribe, tackle, tee off*, volunteer, wade in; SEE CONCEPTS 100,110

piteous [adj] *miserable, pathetic*
beseeching, commiserable, deplorable, distressing, doleful, dolorous, entreating, grievous, heartbreaking, heart-rending, imploring, lamentable, melancholy, mournful, moving, pitiable, pitiful, plaintive, poignant, poor, rueful, ruined, sad, sorrowful, supplicating, woeful, wretched; SEE CONCEPTS 485,529

pitfall [n] *hazard, trap*
booby trap*, catch*, danger, deadfall*, difficulty, downfall, drawback, entanglement, hook*, mesh*, mousetrap*, peril, pit*, quicksand*, risk, setup*, snag*, snare, swindle*, toil, web; SEE CONCEPTS 674,679

pithy [adj] *brief, to the point*
cogent, compact, concise, crisp, curt, down to brass tacks*, effective, epigrammatic, expressive, honed, laconic, meaningful, meaty*, pointed, short, short-and-sweet*, significant, succinct, terse, trenchant; SEE CONCEPT 267

pitiful [adj] *in bad shape; poor*
abject, affecting, afflicted, arousing, base, beggarly, cheap, cheerless, comfortless, commiserative, compassionate, contemptible, deplorable, despicable, dismal, distressed, distressing, grievous, heartbreaking, heartrending, inadequate, insignificant, joyless, lamentable, low, mean, miserable, mournful, moving, paltry, pathetic, piteous, pitiable, sad, scurvy, shabby, sorrowful, sorry, stirring, suffering, tearful, touching, vile, woeful, worthless, wretched; SEE CONCEPTS 485,529

pitiless [adj] *without mercy or care*
austere, barbarous, brutal, callous, cold*, cold-blooded*, coldhearted*, cruel, cutthroat*, dog-eat-dog*, frigid, hardhearted*, harsh, hatchetjob*, heartless, implacable, indifferent, inexorable, inhuman, inhumane, insensible, killer instinct*, mean, merciless, obdurate, relentless, remorseless, ruthless, satanic, savage, soulless*, stony*; SEE CONCEPT 401

pittance [n] *small amount*
allowance, bit, chicken feed*, dribble*, drop*, drop in the bucket*, inadequacy, insufficiency, mite, modicum, peanuts*, pension, portion, ration, scrap*, slave wages*, smidgen, trace, trifle; SEE CONCEPTS 344,787

pity [n1] *feeling of mercy toward another*
benevolence, charity, clemency, comfort, commiseration, compassion, compunction, condolement, condolence, dejection, distress, empathy, favor, forbearance, goodness, grace, humanity, kindliness, kindness, lenity, melancholy, mercy, philanthropy, quarter, rue, ruth, sadness, solace, sorrow, sympathy, tenderness, understanding, warmth; SEE CONCEPTS 410,657

pity [n2] *sad situation*
bad luck, catastrophe, crime, crisis, crying shame*, disaster, mischance, misfortune, mishap, regret, shame, sin; SEE CONCEPT 674

pity [v] *feel sorry for; spare*
ache*, be sorry for, be sympathetic, bleed for*, comfort, commiserate, condole, console, feel for, feel with, forgive, give quarter*, grant amnesty, grieve with, have compassion, have mercy on, identify with, lament with, pardon, put out of one's misery*, relent, reprieve, show forgiveness*, show sympathy*, solace, soothe, sympathize, take pity on*, understand, weep for*; SEE CONCEPTS 10,34,83

pivot [n] *center point about which something revolves*
axis, axle, center, focal point, fulcrum, heart, hinge, hub, kingpin, shaft, spindle, swivel, turning point; SEE CONCEPTS 445,464,498,830

pivot [v] *revolve around center point*
be contingent, depend, hang, hinge, rely, rotate, sheer, spin, swivel, turn, twirl, veer, volte-face, wheel, whip, whirl; SEE CONCEPTS 147,532

pivotal [adj] *important*
cardinal, central, climactic, critical, crucial, decisive, determining, essential, focal, middle, momentous, overriding, overruling, principal, ruling, vital; SEE CONCEPT 568

placate [v] *soothe, pacify*
appease, assuage, calm, cheer, comfort, conciliate, humor, make peace*, make up*, mollify, pacify, play up to*, pour oil on*, propitiate, reconcile, satisfy, soft-pedal*, soothe, stroke*, sweeten, tranquilize, win over*; SEE CONCEPTS 7,22,126

place [n1] *location with purpose, function*
abode, accommodation, apartment, area, berth, city, community, compass, corner, country, distance, district, domicile, dwelling, field, habitat, hamlet, hangout, hole*, home, house, joint, latitude, lay, locale, locality, locus, longitude, neighborhood, niche, nook, pad*, part, plant, point, position, property, quarter, region, reservation, residence, room, seat, section, site, situation, spot, station, stead, suburb, town, venue, vicinity, village, volume, whereabouts, zone; SEE CONCEPTS 435,515

place [n2] *position, rank*
capacity, character, footing, grade, pecking order*, slot, standing, state, station, status; SEE CONCEPT 388

place [n3] *job, employment*
appointment, berth, connection, occupation, office, position, post, profession, situation, spot, trade; SEE CONCEPT 360

place [n4] *duty, role*
affair, charge, concern, function, prerogative, responsibility, right; SEE CONCEPT 532

place [v1] *locate, situate*
allocate, allot, assign, deposit, distribute, establish, finger, fix, install, lay, lodge, nail, park, peg, plant, position, put, quarter, repose, rest, set, settle, spot, stand, station, stick, store, stow; SEE CONCEPT 201

place [v2] *order, sort*
allocate, appoint, approximate, arrange, assign, call, charge, class, classify, commission, constitute, delegate, deputize, designate, entrust, estimate, fix, give, grade, group, judge, name, nominate, ordain, put, rank, reckon; SEE CONCEPTS 50,84,88,98

place [v3] *identify, recognize*
associate, determinate, determine, diagnose, distinguish, figure out*, finger*, indicate, know, nail*, peg*, pinpoint, put one's finger on*, remember, set in context, spot, tell; SEE CONCEPT 38

placid [adj] *calm, mild*
collected, composed, cool*, cool as a cucumber*, detached, easygoing, equable, even, even-tempered, gentle, halcyon, hushed, imperturbable, irenic, peaceful, poised, quiet, restful, self-possessed, serene, still, tranquil; SEE CONCEPTS 401,485

pi
pl

plagiarism [n] *copying of another's written work*
appropriation, borrowing, counterfeiting, cribbing, falsification, fraud, infringement, lifting, literary theft, piracy, stealing, theft; SEE CONCEPTS *139,192*

plague [n1] *disease that is widespread*
affliction, contagion, curse, epidemic, hydra, infection, infestation, influenza, invasion, outbreak, pandemic, pestilence, rash, ravage, scourge; SEE CONCEPT *306*

plague [n2] *annoyance, curse*
affliction, aggravation, bane, besetment, blast, blight, bother, botheration, calamity, cancer, evil, exasperation, hydra, irritant, nuisance, pain, pest, problem, scourge, thorn in side, torment, trial, vexation; SEE CONCEPTS *674,679*

plague [v] *annoy, disturb*
afflict, badger, bedevil, beleaguer, bother, chafe, fret, gall, gnaw, harass, harry, hassle, haunt, hector, hound, infest, irk, molest, pain, persecute, pester, pursue, ride, tease, torment, torture, trouble, vex, worry; SEE CONCEPTS *7,14,19*

plain [n] *level land*
champaign, expanse, field, flat, flatland, grassland, heath, level, meadow, moor, moorland, open country, plateau, prairie, steppe, tundra; SEE CONCEPT *509*

plain [adj1] *clear, obvious*
apparent, audible, big as life*, broad, comprehensible, definite, distinct, evident, legible, lucid, manifest, open, open-and-shut*, palpable, patent, talking turkey*, transparent, understandable, visible; SEE CONCEPTS *529,535,576*

plain [adj2] *straightforward in speech*
abrupt, artless, blunt, candid, direct, forthright, frank, guileless, honest, impolite, ingenuous, open, outspoken, rude, sincere; SEE CONCEPT *267*

plain [adj3] *normal, everyday*
average, common, commonplace, conventional, dull, homely, lowly, modest, ordinary, quotidian, routine, simple, traditional, usual, vanilla*, whitebread*, workaday; SEE CONCEPT *547*

plain [adj4] *unembellished, basic*
austere, bare, bare bones*, clean, discreet, dry, modest, muted, pure, restrained, severe, simple, spartan, stark, stripped down, unvarnished, vanilla*; SEE CONCEPTS *485,589*

plain [adj5] *ugly*
deformed, hard on the eyes*, homely, not beautiful, ordinary, plain-featured; SEE CONCEPT *579*

plaintive [adj] *pathetic, woebegone*
beefing*, bellyaching*, cantankerous, crabby*, cranky*, disconsolate, doleful, grief-stricken, grievous, grousing, grumpy*, heartrending, lamenting, lugubrious, melancholy, mournful, out of sorts*, pathetic, piteous, pitiful, rueful, sad, saddening, sorrowful, wailing, wistful, woeful; SEE CONCEPTS *401,529*

plan [n1] *scheme, design, way of doing things*
aim, angle, animus, arrangement, big picture*, contrivance, course of action, deal, device, disposition, expedient, game plan, gimmick, ground plan, idea, intent, intention, layout, machination, meaning, means, method, orderliness, outline, pattern, picture, platform, plot, policy, procedure, program, project, projection, proposal, proposition, purpose, scenario, stratagem, strategy, suggestion, system, tactics, treatment, trick, undertaking; SEE CONCEPT *660*

plan [n2] *written description; diagram*
agenda, agendum, blueprint, chart, delineation, draft, drawing, form, illustration, layout, map, projection, prospectus, representation, road map, rough draft, scale drawing, sketch, time line, view; SEE CONCEPTS *268,271,625*

plan [v1] *think out; prepare in advance*
arrange, bargain for, block out, blueprint, brainstorm*, calculate, concoct, conspire, contemplate, contrive, cook up*, craft, design, devise, draft, engineer, figure on, figure out, form, formulate, frame, hatch*, intrigue, invent, lay in provisions, line up*, make arrangements, map, meditate, organize, outline, plot, project, quarterback*, ready, reckon on, represent, rough in*, scheme, set out, shape, sketch, steer, trace, work out; SEE CONCEPT *36*

plan [v2] *intend, mean*
aim, bargain for*, contemplate, count on, design, envisage, foresee, have every intention*, mind, propose, purpose, reckon on*; SEE CONCEPTS *26,35*

plane [n1] *flat surface; level*
condition, degree, extension, face, facet, footing, grade, horizontal, obverse, position, sphere, stratum; SEE CONCEPTS *744,757*

plane [n2] *aircraft*
airbus, airplane, airship, bird*, craft, crate, jet, ship, twin-engine; SEE CONCEPT *504*

plane [adj] *level, horizontal*
even, flat, flush, plain, planate, regular, smooth, uniform; SEE CONCEPTS *490,581*

planet [n] *celestial body orbiting a star*
apple*, asteroid, earth, globe, heavenly body, luminous body, marble, orb*, planetoid, sphere, terrene, wandering star*, world; SEE CONCEPT *511*

plant [n1] *organism belonging to the vegetable kingdom*
annual, biennial, bush, creeper*, cutting*, flower, grass, greenery, herb, perennial, seedling, shoot, shrub, slip, sprout, tree, vine, weed; SEE CONCEPT *429*

plant [n2] *factory and its buildings, equipment*
apparatus, forge, foundry, gear, machinery, manufactory, mill, shop, works, yard; SEE CONCEPTS *439,449,463,496*

plant [v1] *put in the ground for growing*
bury, cover, farm, grow, implant, pitch, pot, raise, scatter, seed, seed down, set out, sow, start, stock, transplant; SEE CONCEPTS *178,253*

plant [v2] *establish, set*
deposit, fix, found, imbed, insert, install, institute, lodge, park, plank, plank down, plop, plunk, root, settle, station; SEE CONCEPTS *18,201,221*

plaster [n] *thick, gooey material that hardens*
adhesive, binding, cement, coat, dressing, glue, gum, gypsum, lime, mortar, mucilage, paste, plaster of Paris, stucco; SEE CONCEPTS *466,475*

plaster [v] *spread, smear*
adhere, bedaub, besmear, bind, cement, coat, cover, daub, glue, gum, overlay, paste, smudge; SEE CONCEPT *202*

plastic [adj1] *flexible, soft; made of manufactured, treated compounds*
bending, ductile, elastic, fictile, formable, moldable, molded, pliable, pliant, resilient, shapeable, supple, workable; SEE CONCEPT *604*

plastic [adj2] *easily influenced*
amenable, bending, compliant, docile, ductile, flexible, giving, impressionable, influenceable,

malleable, manageable, moldable, pliable, pliant, receptive, responsive, suggestible, supple, susceptible, tractable, yielding; SEE CONCEPT 542

plastic [adj] *artificial; made of manufactured compounds*

cast, chemical, ersatz, false, manufactured, phony, pseudo*, substitute, synthetic, unnatural; SEE CONCEPT 582

plate [n1] *dish or meal served*

bowl, casserole, course, helping, platter, portion, service, serving, trencher; SEE CONCEPTS 459,493

plate [n2] *sheet, panel*

coat, disc, foil, lamella, lamina, layer, leaf, plane, print, scale, slab, slice, spangle, stratum; SEE CONCEPT 475

plate [v] *coat with metallic material*

anodize, bronze, chrome, cover, electroplate, enamel, encrust, face, flake, foil, gild, laminate, layer, nickel, overlay, platinize, scale, silver, stratify; SEE CONCEPTS 172,202

plateau [n] *level; flat, often high, land*

elevation, highland, mesa, plain, stage, table, tableland, upland; SEE CONCEPTS 509,744

platform [n1] *stand or stage*

belvedere, dais, floor, podium, pulpit, rostrum, scaffold, scaffolding, staging, terrace; SEE CONCEPTS 440,443

platform [n2] *political stance, promises*

manifesto, objectives, party line*, plank, policy, principle, program, soapbox*, stump*, tenets; SEE CONCEPTS 278,689

platitude [n] *dull, overused saying*

banality, boiler plate*, bromide*, buzzword, chestnut*, cliché, commonplace, corn*, evenness, familiar tune*, flatness, hackneyed saying, high camp*, hokum*, inanity, insipidity, monotony, motto, old chestnut*, old story*, potboiler*, prosaicism, proverb, saw*, shibboleth, stereotype, tag*, triteness, trite remark, triviality, truism, vapidity, verbiage; SEE CONCEPTS 278,388

platonic [adj] *expressing nonphysical love*

ideal, idealistic, intellectual, quixotic, spiritual, transcendent, Utopian, visionary; SEE CONCEPTS 403,555

platoon [n] *group of military people*

army, array, batch, battery, bunch, clump, cluster, company, detachment, lot, outfit, parcel, patrol, set, squad, squadron, team, troop, unit; SEE CONCEPTS 322,417

plausible [adj] *reasonable, believable*

conceivable, credible, creditable, like enough*, likely, logical, persuasive, possible, presumable, probable, smooth, sound, supposable, tenable, valid, very likely; SEE CONCEPT 552

play [n1] *theater piece*

comedy, curtain-raiser*, drama, entertainment, farce, flop*, hit*, mask*, musical, one-act*, opera, performance, potboiler*, show, smash*, smash hit, stage show, theatrical, tragedy, turkey*; SEE CONCEPT 263

play [n2] *amusement, entertainment*

caper, dalliance, delight, disport, diversion, foolery, frisk, frolic, fun, gambol, game, gaming, happiness, humor, jest, joking, lark, match, pastime, pleasure, prank, recreation, relaxation, romp, sport, sportiveness, teasing; SEE CONCEPTS 292,363

play [n3] *latitude, range*

action, activity, elbowroom*, exercise, give, leeway, margin, motion, movement, operation,

room, scope, space, sweep, swing, working*; SEE CONCEPTS 651,745

play [v1] *have fun*

amuse oneself, be life of party*, caper, carouse, carry on, cavort, clown, cut capers, cut up*, dally, dance, disport, divert, entertain oneself, fool around, frisk, frolic, gambol, go on a spree*, horse around*, idle away, joke, jump, kibitz*, kick up heels*, let go*, let loose*, let one's hair down*, make merry, mess around*, rejoice, revel, romp, show off, skip, sport, toy, trifle; SEE CONCEPTS 292,384

play [v2] *compete in sport*

be on a team, challenge, contend, contest, disport, engage in, participate, recreate, rival, sport, take on, take part, vie; SEE CONCEPTS 92,363

play [v3] *act; take the part of*

act the part of, discourse, do*, enact, execute, ham*, ham it up*, impersonate, lay an egg*, perform, personate, playact, play a gig*, portray, present, read a part, represent, take the role of, tread the boards*; SEE CONCEPT 292

play [v4] *gamble, risk*

bet, chance, exploit, finesse, game, hazard, jockey*, lay money on*, maneuver, manipulate, put, set, speculate, stake, take, wager; SEE CONCEPTS 341,363

play [v5] *produce music*

blow, bow, drum, execute, fiddle, fidget, finger, operate, pedal, perform, render, tickle, work; SEE CONCEPT 65

play down [v] *pretend as if something were unimportant*

belittle, deemphasize, gloss over*, hold back*, make light of, make little of*, minimize, mute, restrain, soften, soft-pedal*, underplay, underrate; SEE CONCEPTS 49,59,63

player [n1] *person participating in sport*

amateur, athlete, champ, competitor, contestant, jock*, member, opponent, participant, pro, professional, rookie, sportsperson, superjock*, sweat*, team player; SEE CONCEPT 366

player [n2] *person who acts in performance*

actor, bit player, entertainer, extra, ham*, hambone*, impersonator, lead, mime, mimic, performer, playactor, scene stealer*, stand-in, star, thespian, trouper, understudy, walk-on; SEE CONCEPT 352

player [n3] *person who produces music*

artist, instrumentalist, musician, music maker, performer, rocker, soloist, virtuoso; SEE CONCEPT 352

playful [adj] *funny, fun-loving*

antic, blithe, cheerful, coltish*, comical, elvish*, feeling one's oats*, flirtatious, frisky, frolicsome, full of pep*, gamesome, gay, good-natured, impish, jaunty, jesting, jocund, joking, joyous, lighthearted, lively, merry, mirthful, mischievous, prankish, puckish, rollicking, snappy, spirited, sportive, sprightly, teasing, tongue-in-cheek*, vivacious, waggish, whimsical, zippy*; SEE CONCEPTS 401,542

plaything [n] *toy*

amusement, bauble, doll, gadget, game, gimcrack, pastime, trifle, trinket; SEE CONCEPT 446

play up [v] *emphasize*

accentuate, bring to the fore*, call attention to, feature, highlight, italicize*, magnify, make a production of*, point up, stress, turn spotlight on*, underline, underscore; SEE CONCEPT 49

pl
pl

playwright [n] *person who writes for the theater*
author, dramatist, dramaturge, dramaturgist, librettist, scenarist, scripter, tragedian, writer; SEE CONCEPT 348

plaza [n] *central location, spot*
common, court, green, park, square, village green; SEE CONCEPTS 509,513

plea [n1] *begging request*
appeal, application, entreaty, imploration, imprecation, intercession, orison, overture, petition, prayer, round robin*, solicitation, suit, supplication; SEE CONCEPT 662

plea [n2] *excuse, defense*
action, alibi, allegation, apology, argument, cause, claim, cop-out*, explanation, extenuation, fish tale*, justification, mitigation, out, palliation, pleading, pretext, rationalization, right, song and dance*, story, vindication, whitewash*; SEE CONCEPTS 57,278,318

plead [v1] *beg, request*
appeal, ask, beseech, cop a plea*, crave, crawl, entreat, entreaty, implore, importune, make up for, petition, pray, solicit, square things*, supplicate; SEE CONCEPT 48

plead [v2] *present a defense*
adduce, advocate, allege, answer charges, argue, assert, avouch, cite, cop a plea*, declare, give evidence, maintain, plea bargain, present, put forward, respond, use as excuse, vouch; SEE CONCEPTS 49,317

pleasant [adj] *acceptable; friendly*
affable, agreeable, amiable, amusing, bland, charming, cheerful, civil, civilized, congenial, convivial, cool*, copacetic, cordial, delectable, delightful, diplomatic, enchanting, engaging, enjoyable, fine, fine and dandy*, fun, genial, good-humored, gracious, gratifying, homey, jolly, jovial, kindly, likable, lovely, mild, mild-mannered, nice, obliging, pleasing, pleasurable, polite, refreshing, satisfying, social, soft, sweet, sympathetic, urbane, welcome; SEE CONCEPTS 542,548,572

pleasantry [n] *nice remark*
badinage, banter, bon mot*, humor, jest, joke, joking, levity, merriment, quip, quirk, repartee, sally*, squib*, wit, witticism; SEE CONCEPTS 273,278

please [v1] *delight, make happy*
amuse, charm, cheer, content, enchant, entertain, fill the bill*, gladden, go over big*, grab, gratify, hit the spot*, humor, indulge, kill*, make the grade*, overjoy, satisfy, score, suit, sweep off feet*, tickle*, tickle pink*, titillate, turn on*, wow*; SEE CONCEPTS 7,22

please [v2] *will, elect to do*
be inclined, choose, command, demand, desire, like, opt, prefer, see fit, want, wish; SEE CONCEPT 20

pleasing/pleasurable [adj] *welcome, nice*
agreeable, amiable, amusing, charming, congenial, delightful, enchanting, engaging, enjoyable, entertaining, favorable, good, grateful, gratifying, likable, luscious, musical, palatable, pleasant, polite, satisfactory, satisfying, savory, suitable, sweet, winning; SEE CONCEPTS 537,572

pleasure [n1] *delight, happiness*
amusement, bliss, buzz*, comfort, contentment, delectation, diversion, ease, enjoyment, entertainment, felicity, flash*, fruition, game, gladness, gluttony, gratification, gusto, hobby, indulgence,

joie de vivre, joy, joyride*, kick*, kicks*, luxury, primrose path*, recreation, relish, revelry, satisfaction, seasoning, self-indulgence, solace, spice, thrill, titillation, turn-on*, velvet*, zest; SEE CONCEPTS 388,410

pleasure [n2] *will, inclination*
choice, command, desire, fancy, liking, mind, option, preference, purpose, velleity, want, wish; SEE CONCEPTS 20,659

plebeian [n] *person of lower class*
commonalty, commoner, common people, peasant, person in the street*, pleb*, plebe*, proletarian, rank and file*; SEE CONCEPTS 413,423

plebeian [adj] *base, lower-class*
banal, coarse, common, conventional, humble, ignoble, low, lowborn, lowly, mean, ordinary, pedestrian, popular, proletarian, traditional, uncultivated, unrefined, unsophisticated, unwashed*, vulgar, working-class; SEE CONCEPT 549

pledge [n1] *word of honor*
agreement, assurance, covenant, guarantee, health, oath, promise, toast, undertaking, vow, warrant, word; SEE CONCEPTS 71,278

pledge [n2] *sign of good faith*
bail, bond, collateral, deposit, earnest, gage, guarantee, guaranty, pawn, security, surety, token, warrant, warranty; SEE CONCEPTS 318,332,446

pledge [v] *guarantee; give word of honor*
contract, covenant, engage, give word*, hock*, hook*, mortgage, pawn, plight, promise, sign for, soak*, swear, undertake, vouch, vow; SEE CONCEPT 71

plenary [adj] *entire, whole*
absolute, complete, full, general, inclusive, open, sweeping, thorough; SEE CONCEPT 531

plentiful/plenty [adj] *abundant, productive*
abounding, ample, bounteous, bountiful, bumper*, chock-full*, complete, copious, enough, excessive, extravagant, exuberant, fertile, flowing, flush*, fruitful, full, fulsome, generous, improvident, infinite, large, lavish, liberal, lousy with*, lush, luxuriant, overflowing, plenteous, prodigal, profuse, prolific, replete, rife, sufficient, superabundant, superfluous, swarming, swimming, teeming; SEE CONCEPTS 762,781

plenty [n] *much, abundance*
affluence, avalanche*, capacity, copiousness, cornucopia, deluge*, flood*, fruitfulness, full house*, fund, good deal*, great deal*, heaps*, loads*, lots, luxury, mass, masses*, mine*, mountains*, oodles*, opulence, peck*, piles*, plethora, profusion, prosperity, quantity, stacks*, store, sufficiency, torrent*, volume, wealth; SEE CONCEPTS 767,787

plethora [n] *excess*
deluge, flood, glut, many, much, overabundance, overflow, overkill, overmuch, plenty, profusion, superabundance, superfluity, surfeit, surplus; SEE CONCEPTS 767,787

pliable [adj] *bendable, adaptable*
compliant, docile, ductile, easily led, easy, flexible, impressionable, limber, lithe, malleable, manageable, manipulable, moldable, obedient, plastic, pliant, putty*, receptive, responsive, rolling with the punches*, spongy, submissive, supple, susceptible, tractable, yielding; SEE CONCEPTS 404,488

plight [n] *dilemma, difficulty; situation*
bad news*, circumstances, condition, corner*,

plod [v1] *walk heavily*
clump*, drag, flounder, hike, lumber*, plug, schlepp*, slog*, stamp, stomp, toil, tramp, trample, tread, tromp, trudge, wallow; SEE CONCEPT 151

plod [v2] *work slowly and under duress*
bear down*, buckle down*, drudge, grind, knuckle down*, labor, persevere, plough through*, plug away*, scratch*, slave, sweat*, toil; SEE CONCEPTS 87,677

plot [n1] *plan, scheme*
artifice, booby trap*, cabal, collusion, complicity, connivance, conniving, conspiracy, contrivance, covin, design, device, fix, frame, frame-up*, game, intrigue, little game*, machination, maneuver, practice, ruse, scam, setup, stratagem, trick; SEE CONCEPT 660

plot [n2] *story line*
action, design, development, enactment, events, incidents, movement, narrative, outline, picture, progress, scenario, scene, scheme, story, structure, subject, suspense, theme, thread, unfolding; SEE CONCEPTS 264,282

plot [n3] *tract of land*
acreage, allotment, area, division, ground, land, lot, parcel, patch, piece, plat, spread; SEE CONCEPTS 509,513

plot [v1] *plan, scheme*
angle, brew*, cabal, cogitate, collude, conceive, concoct, connive, conspire, contrive, cook up*, design, devise, draft, finagle, frame, hatch*, imagine, intrigue, lay*, machinate, maneuver, operate, outline, project, promote, rough out*, set up, sketch, wangle; SEE CONCEPT 36

plot [v2] *map out; draw*
calculate, chart, compute, draft, lay out, locate, mark, outline, put forward; SEE CONCEPTS 36,79,174

plow [v] *dig up ground for cultivation*
break, break ground, bulldoze, cultivate, farm, furrow, harrow, harvest, list, push, rake, reap, ridge, rush, shove, smash, till, trench, turn, turn over; SEE CONCEPT 178

ploy [n] *game, trick*
artifice, contrivance, device, dodge, feint, gambit, maneuver, move, play, ruse, scheme, stratagem, subterfuge, tactic, wile; SEE CONCEPT 59

pluck [n] *person's resolution; courage*
backbone*, boldness, bravery, dauntlessness, determination, grit, guts*, hardihood, heart*, intestinal fortitude*, intrepidity, mettle, moxie*, nerve, resolution, spirit, spunk; SEE CONCEPT 411

pluck [v] *grab, pull out; pick at*
catch, clutch, collect, cull, draw, finger, gather, harvest, jerk, plunk, pull at, snatch, strum, tug, tweak, yank; SEE CONCEPT 206

plug [n1] *stopper*
bung, connection, cork, filling, fitting, occlusion, river, spigot, stopple, tampon, wedge; SEE CONCEPTS 471,836

plug [n2] *publicity*
advertisement, blurb*, good word*, hype*, mention, push*, write-up; SEE CONCEPT 274

plug [v1] *stop up*
block, bung, choke, clog, close, congest, cork, cover, drive in, fill, obstruct, occlude, pack, ram,

seal, secure, stop, stopper, stopple, stuff; SEE CONCEPT 209

plug [v2] *publicize*
advertise, boost*, build up*, hype*, mention, promote, push*, write up; SEE CONCEPTS 49,60

plum [n] *reward, prize*
asset, bonus, carrot*, catch*, cream*, dividend, find, meed, nugget*, pick, premium, treasure; SEE CONCEPTS 337,712

plumb [adj] *vertical*
erect, perpendicular, sheer, straight, straight up, up and down, upright; SEE CONCEPT 581

plumb [v] *probe, go into*
delve, explore, fathom, gauge, get to the bottom of*, measure, penetrate, search, sound, take soundings, unravel; SEE CONCEPTS 181,216,291

plummet [v] *fall hard and fast*
collapse, crash, decline, decrease, descend, dip, dive, downturn, drop, drop down, dump, fall, nose-dive, plunge, precipitate, sink, skid, stoop, swoop, tumble; SEE CONCEPTS 181,698,763

plump [adj] *chubby, fat*
beefy*, burly, buxom, chunky*, corpulent, filled, fleshy, full, obese, portly, pudgy*, rotund, round, stout, tubby*; SEE CONCEPT 491

plunder [n] *something stolen*
booty, goods*, graft, hot goods*, loot, make*, pickings*, pillage, plunderage, prey, prize, quarry, rapine, raven, spoil, stuff*, take*, trappings*, winnings*; SEE CONCEPT 710

plunder [v] *ravage, steal*
appropriate, burn, depredate, despoil, devastate, fleece, forage, foray, grab, gut, kip, knock off*, knock over*, lay waste, liberate, lift, loft, loot, maraud, moonlight requisition*, pillage, prey, prowl, raid, ransack, relieve, requisition, rifle, rip off*, rob, sack, salvage, smash and grab*, snatch, spoil, stick up*, strip; SEE CONCEPTS 86,139,252

plunge [n] *quick dive; enthusiastic attempt*
belly flop*, descent, dive, duck, dunk, fall, high dive, immersion, investment, jump, nose-dive, spree, submergence, submersion, swoop, venture; SEE CONCEPTS 100,150,152,181,194

plunge [v] *dive or fall fast*
belly-flop*, career, cast, charge, dash, descend, dip, drive, drop, duck, fling, go down, go the limit, go whole hog*, hurtle, immerge, immerse, jump, keel, lunge, lurch, nose-dive, pitch, plummet, plunk, propel, rush, shoot the works*, sink, sound, submerge, submerse, swoop, take a flyer*, take a header*, tear, throw, throw oneself, thrust, topple, tumble; SEE CONCEPTS 100,150, 152,181,194

plurality [n] *large part of a group*
advantage, bulk, greater part, lead, majority, mass, most, multiplicity, nearly all, numerousness, preponderance, profusion, variety; SEE CONCEPTS 382,829

plus [n] *asset; something added*
advantage, benefit, bonus, extra, gain, good point, overage, overstock, oversupply, perk, surplus; SEE CONCEPT 693

plus [adj] *added, extra*
additional, augmented, boosted, enlarged, expanded, increased, positive, supplementary, surplus; SEE CONCEPTS 762,771

plush [adj] *luxurious, rich*
costly, deluxe, elegant, lavish, luscious, lush, luxury, opulent, palatial, ritzy, silken, sumptuous; SEE CONCEPTS 334,589

pl
pl

ply [v] *use, work at*
carry on, dispense, employ, exercise, exert, follow, function, handle, maneuver, manipulate, practice, pursue, put out, swing, throw, utilize, wield; SEE CONCEPTS 100,225

poach [v] *infringe upon; trespass*
appropriate, encroach, filch, fish illegally, hunt illegally, intrude, pilfer, plunder, rob, smuggle, steal; SEE CONCEPTS 139,192

pocket [n] *cavity, pouch*
bag, chamber, compartment, hole, hollow, opening, receptacle, sack, socket; SEE CONCEPTS 452,513

pocket [adj] *small, portable*
abridged, canned, capsule, compact, concise, condensed, diminutive, epitomized, itsy-bitsy*, little, midget, miniature, minute, peewee*, pint-sized*, potted, tiny, wee; SEE CONCEPT 773

pocket [v] *help oneself to something*
abstract, appropriate, conceal, enclose, filch, hide, lift, nab, pilfer, pinch, purloin, shoplift, steal, swipe, take; SEE CONCEPTS 139,142

pocketbook [n] *accessory for carrying personal items*
bag, clutch, frame, handbag, hide, leather, pouch, purse, reticule, suitcase, wallet; SEE CONCEPTS 446,450

pod [n/v] *encasement of vegetable seeds*
capsule, case, covering, hull, husk, sheath, sheathing, shell, shuck, skin, vessel; SEE CONCEPTS 428,484

podium [n] *structure from which speakers orate*
dais, platform, pulpit, rostrum, soapbox*, stage, stump*; SEE CONCEPT 443

poem [n] *highly expressive, rhythmical literary piece*
ballad, beat, blank verse, composition, creation, epic, free verse, haiku, limerick, lines, lyric, ode, poesy, poetry, quatrain, rhyme, rime, rune, sestina, song, sonnet, verse, villanelle, words, writing; SEE CONCEPTS 268,282

poet [n] *person who writes expressive, rhythmic verse*
artist, author, balladist, bard, dilettante, dramatist, librettist, lyricist, lyrist, maker, metrist, odist, parodist, poetaster, rhapsodist, rhymer, rimer, sonnetist, versifier, writer; SEE CONCEPTS 348,423

poetic [adj] *with rhythm and beauty; related to poetic composition*
anapestic, dactylic, dramatic, elegiac, epic, epical, epodic, iambic, idyllic, imaginative, lyric, lyrical, melodious, metrical, odic, rhythmical, romantic, songlike, tuneful; SEE CONCEPT 267

poetry [n] *expressive, rhythmic literary work*
balladry, doggerel, metrical composition, paean, poems, poesy, rhyme, rhyming, rime, rune, song, stanza, verse, versification; SEE CONCEPTS 268,282,349

poignant [adj1] *affecting, painful*
agitating, agonizing, bitter, distressing, disturbing, emotional, heartbreaking, heartrending, impressive, intense, moving, passionate, pathetic, perturbing, piteous, pitiful, sad, sentimental, sorrowful, touching, upsetting; SEE CONCEPTS 529,548

poignant [adj2] *sharp, bitter*
acrid, acute, biting, caustic, keen, penetrating, peppery, piercing, piquant, pointed, pungent, racy, sarcastic, severe, snappy, spicy, stinging, tangy, zesty; SEE CONCEPTS 267,613

point [n1] *speck*
bit, count, dot, fleck, flyspeck, full stop, iota, mark, minim, mite, mote, notch, particle, period, scrap, stop, tittle, trace; SEE CONCEPTS 79,831

point [n2] *specific location*
locality, locus, place, position, site, situation, spot, stage, station, where; SEE CONCEPT 198

point [n3] *sharp end, top, end of extension*
apex, awn, barb, beak, bill, cape, claw, cusp, dagger, foreland, head, headland, jag, nib, pin point, prick, prickler, promontory, prong, snag, spike, spine, spire, spur, sticker, stiletto, summit, sword, thorn, tine, tip, tooth; SEE CONCEPTS 827,836

point [n4] *circumstance, stage; limited time*
brink, condition, date, degree, duration, edge, extent, instant, juncture, limit, moment, period, point in time, position, threshold, time, verge, very minute; SEE CONCEPTS 696,815

point [n5] *goal, aim*
appeal, attraction, bottom line*, charm, cogency, design, effectiveness, end, fascination, intent, intention, interest, motive, name of the game*, nitty-gritty*, nub, nuts and bolts*, object, objective, punch*, purpose, reason, significance, use, usefulness, utility, validity, validness; SEE CONCEPT 659

point [n6] *meaning, essence*
argument, bottom line*, burden, core, crux, drift, force, gist, head, heart, idea, import, kicker*, main idea, marrow, matter, meat*, motif, motive, name of the game*, nitty-gritty*, nub, nuts and bolts*, pith, pointer, proposition, punch line*, question, score, stuff, subject, subject matter, text, theme, thrust, tip, tip-off*, topic; SEE CONCEPTS 274,682

point [n7] *aspect, characteristic*
attribute, case, circumstance, circumstantial, constituent, detail, element, facet, feature, instance, item, material, nicety, part, particular, peculiarity, property, quality, respect, side, thing*, trait; SEE CONCEPTS 274,411,654

point [n8] *scoring unit of sport competition*
count, mark, notch, score, tally; SEE CONCEPTS 364,784

point [v1] *show as probable; call attention*
bespeak, button down*, denote, designate, direct, finger*, hint, imply, indicate, lead, make*, name, offer, peg*, pin down*, put down for*, put finger on*, signify, suggest, tab*, tag*; SEE CONCEPTS 118,138

point [v2] *direct, lead*
aim, beam*, bring to bear, cast, face, guide, head, influence, lay, level, look, slant, steer, tend, train, turn, zero in*; SEE CONCEPTS 187,201,623

pointed [adj1] *having a sharp end or part*
acicular, aciculate, acuminate, acuminous, acute, barbed, cornered, cuspidate, edged, fine, keen, mucronate, peaked, piked, pointy, pronged, sharp, sharp-cornered, spiked; SEE CONCEPTS 490,606

pointed [adj2] *penetrating, biting*
accurate, acid, acute, barbed, boiled down, calling a spade a spade*, cutting, in a nutshell*, incisive, insinuating, keen, laid on the line*, legit, meaty*, on the button*, on the nose*, pertinent, pregnant, right-on*, right to it*, sarcastic, sharp,

short-and-sweet*, tart, telling, trenchant; SEE
CONCEPT 267

pointer [n1] *indicator*

arrow, dial, director, gauge, guide, hand, index,
mark, needle, register, rod, signal; SEE CONCEPTS
464,498

pointer [n2] *hint, suggestion*

advice, caution, clue, information, recommendation, steer, tip, tip-off, warning; SEE CONCEPTS
75,274

pointless [adj] *ridiculous, senseless*

absurd, aimless, around in circles*, fruitless, futile, going nowhere*, impotent, inane, inconsequential, ineffective, ineffectual, insignificant, in
vicious circle*, irrelevant, meaningless, needle in
haystack*, nongermane, nonsensical, not pertinent, on treadmill*, powerless, purportless,
remote, silly, stupid, trivial, unavailing, uninteresting, unnecessary, unproductive, unprofitable,
useless, vague, vain, worthless; SEE CONCEPTS
529,548

point out [v] *call attention to*

advert, allude, bring up, denote, designate, identify, indicate, mention, refer, remind, reveal,
show, specify; SEE CONCEPTS 49,73,261

poise [n] *self-composure, dignity*

address, aplomb, assurance, balance, bearing,
calmness, confidence, cool, coolness, delicatesse,
diplomacy, elegance, equability, equanimity,
equilibrium, grace, gravity, polish, presence,
presence of mind, sangfroid, savoir-faire, self-
assurance, self-possession, serenity, stasis, tact,
tactfulness, tranquility; SEE CONCEPTS 633,717

poise [v] *balance, suspend*

ballast, be ready, brood, float, hang, hold, hover,
position, stabilize, stand, steady, support, wait;
SEE CONCEPT 154

poison [n] *substance that causes harm, death*

adulteration, bacteria, bane, blight, cancer, contagion, contamination, corruption, germ, infection, malignancy, miasma, toxicant, toxin, toxoid,
venin, venom, virus; SEE CONCEPTS 307,475,
674,675

poison/poisonous [adj] *harmful*

bad, baleful, baneful, corrupt, corruptive, dangerous, deadly, deleterious, destructive, detrimental,
evil, fatal, hurtful, infective, lethal, malicious,
malignant, mephitic, miasmatic, morbid, mortal,
nocuous, noisome, noxious, peccant, pernicious,
pestiferous, pestilential, septic, toxic, toxicant,
toxiferous, venomous, vicious, viperous, virulent;
SEE CONCEPT 537

poison [v] *contaminate, pollute*

adulterate, corrupt, debase, defile, deprave, destroy, envenom, fester, harm, infect, injure, kill,
make ill, murder, pervert, stain, subvert, taint,
undermine, vitiate, warp; SEE CONCEPTS 14,246,
252

poke [n] *push, thrust*

blow, boost, bunt, butt, dig, hit, jab, nudge, prod,
punch, shove, stab; SEE CONCEPTS 189,208

poke [v1] *push at; thrust*

arouse, awaken, bulge, butt*, crowd, dig, el-
bow*, goose*, hit, jab, jostle, jut, nudge*, overhang, prod, project, protrude, provoke, punch,
ram, rouse, shoulder*, shove, stab, stand out,
stick, stick out, stimulate, stir; SEE CONCEPTS
189,208,723

poke [v2] *interfere, snoop*

busybody*, butt in*, intrude, meddle, nose*,
peek, pry, tamper; SEE CONCEPT 384

poke [v3] *move along slowly*

dally, dawdle, delay, drag, get no place fast*,
idle, lag, loiter, mosey*, procrastinate, put off*,
shlep along*, tarry, toddle*, trail; SEE CONCEPT
151

polar [adj1] *cold*

arctic, extreme, farthest, freezing, frigid, frozen,
glacial, icy, north, south, terminal; SEE CONCEPTS
583,605

polar [adj2] *opposite, opposed*

antagonistic, antipodal, antipodean, antithetical,
contradictory, contrary, converse, counter, diametric, reverse; SEE CONCEPT 564

pole [n] *bar, post*

beam, extremity, flagpole, flagstaff, leg, mast,
pile, plank, rod, shaft, spar, staff, stake, standard,
stave, stick, stilt, stud, terminus; SEE CONCEPTS
440,470,475,479

police/police officer [n] *person, people hired to
uphold the laws*

arm of the law*, badge*, bear*, beat cop, black
and white*, blue*, bluecoat*, bobby, constable,
constabulary, cop*, copper*, corps*, detective,
fed*, flatfoot*, force, gendarme, heat*, law, law
enforcement, narc*, patrol; SEE CONCEPTS
299,354

policy [n] *procedure, tactics*

action, administration, approach, arrangement,
behavior, channels, code, course, custom, design,
guideline, line, management, method, order, organization, plan, polity, practice, program, protocol, red tape*, rule, scheme, stratagem, strategy,
tenet, the book*, the numbers*, theory; SEE CON-
CEPTS 6,271,660,688

polish [n1] *shine, brightness*

brilliance, burnish, finish, glaze, glint, gloss, luster, sheen, smoothness, sparkle, varnish, veneer,
wax; SEE CONCEPTS 492,611,620

polish [n2] *cultivated look, performance*

breeding, class, cultivation, culture, elegance, finesse, finish, grace, politesse, refinement, style,
suavity, urbanity; SEE CONCEPTS 388,633,655

polish [v1] *shine, buff*

brighten, burnish, clean, finish, furbish, glaze,
gloss, rub, scour, scrub, sleek, slick, smooth,
wax; SEE CONCEPTS 202,215

polish [v2] *improve performance, look*

amend, better, brush up, correct, cultivate,
emend, enhance, finish, furbish, make improvement, mature, mend, perfect, refine, round, sleek,
slick, smooth, touch up; SEE CONCEPT 244

polish off [v] *finish using*

consume, devour, dispatch, dispose of, do away
with*, down*, eat, eat up, eliminate, get rid of*,
liquidate, put away*, swill*, use up, wolf*; SEE
CONCEPTS 169,225

polite [adj] *mannerly, civilized*

affable, amenable, amiable, attentive, bland, civil,
complaisant, concerned, conciliatory, condescending, considerate, cordial, courteous, courtly,
cultured, deferential, diplomatic, elegant,
friendly, genteel, gentle, good-natured, gracious,
mild, neighborly, nice, obliging, obsequious,
pleasant, polished, politic, punctilious, refined,
respectful, smooth, sociable, solicitous, sympathetic, thoughtful, urbane, well-behaved, well-
bred, well-mannered; SEE CONCEPT 401

**pl
po**

politic [adj] *wise, tactful*
adroit, advisable, canny*, cool, delicate, diplomatic, discreet, expedient, in one's best interests*, judicious, on the lookout*, perspicacious, prudent, sagacious, sensible, sharp, shrewd, smooth, tactical, tuned in*, urbane; SEE CONCEPT 401

politically correct [adj] *sensitive to all forms of oppression*
bias-free, dogmatic, gay/lesbian affirmative, gender-free, inclusive, liberal, multicultural, nondiscriminatory, nonsexist, nonracist, PC*, respectful, revisionary; SEE CONCEPTS 529,542

politician [n] *person pursuing or occupying elective office*
baby-kisser*, boss, chieftain, congressperson, democrat, grandstander*, handshaker*, lawmaker, leader, legislator, member of Congress, member of parliament, officeholder, office seeker, orator, partisan, party member, president, public servant, republican, senator, speaker, statesperson, whistle-stopper*; SEE CONCEPT 359

politics [n] *art and science of administration of government*
affairs of state; backroom*, campaigning, civics, domestic affairs, electioneering, foreign affairs, government, government policy, hat in the ring*, internal affairs, jungle*, legislature, matters of state, political science, polity, smoke-filled room*, statecraft, stateship, zoo*; SEE CONCEPTS 300,301

poll [n] *census; tally of answers to questions of opinion*
ballot, canvass, count, figures, opinion, returns, sampling, survey, vote, voting; SEE CONCEPTS 48,300

poll [v] *take census; question*
ballot, canvass, enroll, examine, interview, list, register, sample, send up a balloon*, survey, tally, test the waters*, vote; SEE CONCEPTS 48,300

pollute [v] *make dirty; corrupt*
adulterate, alloy, befoul, besmirch, contaminate, debase, debauch, defile, deprave, desecrate, dirty, dishonor, foul, infect, make filthy, mar, poison, profane, soil, spoil, stain, sully, taint, violate; SEE CONCEPTS 246,254

pollution [n] *dirtiness, contamination*
abuse, adulteration, besmearing, besmirching, blight, corruption, decomposition, defilement, desecration, deterioration, dirtying, fouling, foulness, impairment, impurity, infection, misuse, polluting, profanation, rottenness, soiling, spoliation, taint, tainting, uncleanness, vitiation; SEE CONCEPT 720

pomp [n] *pageantry, display*
affectation, array, ceremonial, ceremony, fanfare, flourish, formality, grandeur, grandiosity, magnificence, ostentation, pageant, panoply, parade, pomposity, ritual, shine, show, solemnity, splendor, state, vainglory; SEE CONCEPTS 335,377,655

pompous [adj] *arrogant, egotistic*
affected, bloated, boastful, bombastic, conceited, flatulent, flaunting, flowery, fustian, grandiloquent, grandiose, high and mighty*, highfaluting*, high-flown*, imperious, important, inflated, magisterial, magniloquent, narcissistic, orotund, ostentatious, overbearing, overblown, pontifical, portentous, presumptuous, pretentious, puffed up*, puffy*, rhetorical, self-centered, self-important, selfish, showy, sonorous, stuck-up*, supercilious, turgid, uppity*, vain, vainglorious, windy*; SEE CONCEPTS 267,401,542

pond [n] *small body of water*
basin, dew, duck pond, lagoon, lily pond, millpond, pool, puddle, small lake, splash; SEE CONCEPT 514

ponder [v] *think about seriously*
appraise, brood, build castles in air*, cerebrate, cogitate, consider, contemplate, daydream, debate, deliberate, dwell, evaluate, examine, excogitate, figure, give thought to, meditate, mind, moon*, mull, mull over, muse, noodle around*, perpend, pipe dream*, put on thinking cap*, puzzle over, reason, reflect, revolve, roll, ruminate, speculate, study, think out, think over, turn over, weigh, woolgather*; SEE CONCEPTS 17,24

ponderous [adj1] *heavy, cumbersome*
awkward, bulky, burdensome, clumsy, cumbrous, dull, elephantine, graceless, hefty, huge, laborious, lifeless*, lumbering, massive, onerous, oppressive, substantial, troublesome, unhandy, unwieldy, weighty; SEE CONCEPTS 491,565

ponderous [adj2] *dreary, tedious*
arid, barren, cardboard*, dry, dull, heavy, humdrum*, labored, lifeless, long-winded*, monotonous, pedantic, pedestrian, plodding, prolix, stiff*, stilted, stodgy, stuffy*, vapid, verbose, wooden*; SEE CONCEPTS 267,529,542

pool [n1] *collection of liquid*
basin, bath, lagoon, lake, mere, millpond, mud puddle, natatorium, pond, puddle, splash, swimming pool, tank, tarn; SEE CONCEPTS 364,514

pool [n2] *supply of money, goods*
bank, combine, conglomerate, equipment, funds, group, jackpot, kitty*, pot, provisions, stakes; SEE CONCEPTS 340,432

pool [v] *combine*
amalgamate, blend, join forces, league, merge, put together, share; SEE CONCEPTS 113,193

poor [adj1] *lacking sufficient money*
bad off*, bankrupt, beggared, beggarly, behind eight ball*, broke*, destitute, dirt poor*, down-and-out*, empty-handed*, flat*, flat broke*, fortuneless, hard up*, impecunious, impoverished, indigent, in need, insolvent, in want, low, meager, moneyless, necessitous, needy, pauperized, penniless, penurious, pinched*, poverty-stricken, reduced*, scanty*, stone broke*, strapped*, suffering, truly needy, underprivileged, unprosperous; SEE CONCEPT 334

poor [adj2] *deficient, inadequate*
base, below par, common, contemptible, crude, diminutive, dwarfed, exiguous, faulty, feeble, humble, imperfect, incomplete, inferior, insignificant, insufficient, lacking, low-grade, lowly, meager, mean, mediocre, miserable, modest, niggardly*, ordinary, paltry, pitiable, pitiful, plain, reduced, rotten, scanty, second-rate*, shabby, shoddy, skimpy, slight, sorry*, sparse, subnormal, subpar, substandard, trifling, trivial, unsatisfactory, valueless, weak, worthless; SEE CONCEPTS 570,574

poor [adj3] *weak, unfertile*
bare, barren, depleted, exhausted, feeble, fruitless, impaired, imperfect, impoverished, indisposed, infertile, infirm, puny, sick, sterile, unfruitful, unproductive, worthless; SEE CONCEPT 314

poor [adj4] *unfortunate, unhappy*
commiserable, hapless, ill-fated, luckless, miser-

able, pathetic, piteous, pitiable, pitiful, rueful, unlucky, wretched; SEE CONCEPTS *542,548*

poorly [*adj*] *not well*
ailing, below par, failing, ill, indisposed, low,
mean, out of sorts*, rotten*, sick, sickly, under
the weather*, unwell; SEE CONCEPT *314*

poorly [*adv*] *unsatisfactorily*
badly, crudely, defectively, inadequately, incompetently, inexpertly, inferiorly, insufficiently,
meanly, shabbily, unsuccessfully; SEE CONCEPTS
544,571,574

pop [*n*] *bang*
burst, crack, explosion, jump, leap, report, snap,
strike, thrust, whack; SEE CONCEPT *595*

pop [*v*] *jump, burst*
appear, bang, blow, crack, dart, explode, go, go
off, hit, insert, leap, protrude, push, put, report,
rise, shove, snap, sock, stick, strike, thrust,
whack; SEE CONCEPT *145*

popular [*adj1*] *well-known, favorite*
accepted, approved, attractive, beloved, caught
on*, celebrated, crowd-pleasing*, faddish*, famous, fashionable, favored, in*, in demand, in
favor, in the mainstream*, in vogue, leading, likable, liked, lovable, noted, notorious, now*,
okay*, pleasing, praised, preferred, prevailing,
prominent, promoted, right stuff*, run-after*,
selling, social, societal, sought, sought-after, stylish, suitable, the rage*, thing*, trendy, well-liked,
well-received; SEE CONCEPTS *555,589*

popular [*adj2*] *common, standard*
accepted, accessible, adopted, approved, conventional, current, demanded, embraced, familiar,
general, in demand, in use, ordinary, prevailing,
prevalent, proletarian, public, rampant, regnant,
rife, ruling, stock, ubiquitous, universal, widespread; SEE CONCEPT *530*

popularity [*n*] *recognition, celebrity*
acceptance, acclaim, adoration, approval, currency, demand, esteem, fame, fashion, fashionableness, favor, following, heyday, idolization,
lionization, prevalence, regard, renown, reputation, repute, universality, vogue; SEE CONCEPTS
388,655

popularize [*v*] *make widely popular, accessible*
catch on, contemplate, disseminate, familiarize,
give currency, make available, promote, restore,
resurrect, revive, simplify, spread, universalize;
SEE CONCEPTS *324,384*

population [*n*] *inhabitants of a place*
citizenry, community, culture, denizens, dwell-
ers, folk, natives, people, populace, public, residents, society, state; SEE CONCEPT *379*

populous [*adj*] *packed with inhabitants*
crawling, crowded, dense, heavily populated,
jammed, legion, many, multifarious, multitudinal,
multitudinous, numerous, occupied, overpopu-
lated, peopled, populated, settled, several, swarming, teeming, thick, thronged, various, voluminous; SEE CONCEPT *583*

pore [*n*] *small aperture in skin*
foramen, opening, orifice, outlet, stoma, sweat
gland, vesicle; SEE CONCEPT *418*

pore [*v*] *go over carefully*
brood, contemplate, dwell on, examine, look
over, muse, peruse, ponder, read, regard, scan,
scrutinize, study; SEE CONCEPTS *24,72,103*

pornographic [*adj*] *obscene*
adult, immoral, indecent, lewd, off-color, offensive, porn*, porno*, prurient, purple*, raunchy*,

rough, salacious, sexy, smutty*, steamy*,
X-rated*; SEE CONCEPTS *267,372,545*

porous [*adj*] *having holes; absorbent*
absorptive, penetrable, permeable, pervious,
spongelike, spongy; SEE CONCEPT *606*

port [*n*] *place for boat docking, traffic, and storage*
anchorage, boatyard, dockage, docks, dockyard,
gate, harbor, harborage, haven, landing, piers,
refuge, retreat, roads, roadstead, sanctuary, sea-
port, shelter, wharf; SEE CONCEPTS *449,509*

portable [*adj*] *easily transported*
carriageable, cartable, compact, convenient, conveyable, easily carried, handy, haulable, light,
lightweight, manageable, movable, portative,
transportable, wieldy; SEE CONCEPTS *491,584,
773*

portal [*n*] *hole or door in vessel*
doorway, entrance, entry, entryway, gate, gateway, ingress, opening, way in; SEE CONCEPT *502*

portend [*v*] *foreshadow, indicate*
adumbrate, augur, be in the cards*, bespeak, betoken, bode, call*, crystal-ball*, forebode, forecast, foreshow, foretell, foretoken, forewarn,
harbinger, have a hunch, hint, omen, point
to, predict, premonish, presage, prognosticate,
promise, prophesy, read, see coming*, threaten,
warn of; SEE CONCEPTS *71,78,261*

portent [*n1*] *indication, forewarning*
augury, bodement, boding, caution, clue, foreboding, foreshadowing, foretoken, funny feeling*, handwriting on the wall*, harbinger, hunch,
omen, premonition, presage, presentiment, prognostic, prognostication, sign, sinking feeling*,
threat, vibes*, warning; SEE CONCEPT *278*

portent [*n2*] *miracle*
marvel, phenomenon, prodigy, sensation, stunner,
wonder; SEE CONCEPTS *230,529*

porter [*n*] *person who serves as attendant, caretaker*
baggage carrier, bearer, bellhop, carrier, concierge, doorkeeper, doorperson, gatekeeper, janitor, red cap*, sky cap*, transporter; SEE CONCEPT
348

portfolio [*n*] *flat case for transporting papers*
attaché case, bag, brief bag, briefcase, case, container, envelope, folder, notebook, valise; SEE
CONCEPT *494*

portion [*n1*] *share, cut, ration*
allocation, allotment, allowance, apportionment,
bang, bit, chunk, division, divvy*, drag*, dram,
excerpt, extract, fix, fraction, fragment, gob,
helping, hit, hunk, lagniappe, lion's share*, lot,
lump, measure, meed, member, moiety, morsel,
parcel, part, piece, piece of action*, plum, quantity, quantum, quota, scrap, section, segment,
serving, shot*, slug*, smithereen*, taste; SEE
CONCEPT *835*

portion [*n2*] *fate, destiny*
circumstance, cup*, doom, fortune, kismet*, lot*,
luck; SEE CONCEPT *679*

portion [*v*] *divide into pieces*
administer, allocate, allot, apportion, assign, deal,
dispense, distribute, divvy up*, dole out*, mete
out*, parcel, part, partition, piece, prorate, quota,
ration, section, share, shift; SEE CONCEPTS
98,140

portly [*adv*] *bulky, fat*
ample, avoirdupois, beefy*, broad, burly, corpulent, fleshy, heavy, hefty, husky, large, obese,

overweight, plump, rotund, stout; SEE CONCEPT 491

portrait [n] drawn representation; description
account, characterization, depiction, figure, image, likeness, model, painting, photograph, picture, portraiture, portrayal, profile, silhouette, simulacrum, sketch, snapshot, spitting image*, vignette; SEE CONCEPTS 259,268,625

portray [v] represent, imitate
act like, characterize, copy, delineate, depict, describe, draw, duplicate, figure, illustrate, image, impersonate, interpret, limn, mimic, paint, parody, photograph, picture, render, reproduce, simulate, sketch; SEE CONCEPTS 55,174,265

pose [n] artificial position
act, affectation, air, attitude, attitudinizing, bearing, carriage, facade, fake, false show, front, guise, mannerism, masquerade, mien, posture, posture, posturing, pretense, pretension, role, stance, stand; SEE CONCEPTS 633,716

pose [v1] sit, stand in place
arrange, model, peacock, poise, position, posture, sit for, strike a pose, strut; SEE CONCEPTS 154,174

pose [v2] pretend, fake
act, affect, attitudinize, feign, grandstand*, impersonate, make believe, make out like*, masquerade, pass off*, peacock*, playact, posture, profess, purport, put on airs*, put up a front*, sham*, show off*, strike an attitude*, take off as*; SEE CONCEPTS 59,63,633

pose [v3] offer, put forward idea
advance, ask, extend, give, hold out, posit, prefer, present, proffer, propose, proposition, propound, put, query, question, set, state, submit, suggest, tender; SEE CONCEPTS 66,67,75

posh [adj] luxurious, upper-class
chic, classy, deluxe, elegant, exclusive, fashionable, grand, high-class, la-di-da*, luxury, modish*, opulent, rich, ritzy*, smart, swank, swanky*, swish*, trendy; SEE CONCEPTS 334,589

position [n1] physical place
area, bearings, district, environment, fix, geography, ground, locale, locality, location, locus, point, post, reference, region, scene, seat, setting, site, situation, space, spot, stand, station, surroundings, topography, tract, whereabouts*; SEE CONCEPT 198

position [n2] posture, stance
arrangement, attitude, ballgame*, bearing, carriage, circumstances, condition, deportment, disposition, form, habit, how things stack up*, like it is*, manner, mien, pass, plight, port, pose, predicament, situation, spot, stand, state, status, strait, the size of it*; SEE CONCEPT 696

position [n3] belief, point of view
angle, attitude, color, judgment, opinion, outlook, slant, stance, stand, standpoint, view, viewpoint; SEE CONCEPT 689

position [n4] class, stature
cachet, capacity, caste, character, consequence, dignity, footing, importance, place, prestige, rank, reputation, situation, sphere, standing, station, status; SEE CONCEPTS 378,388

position [n5] responsibility in business or other enterprise
berth, billet, capacity, connection, do*, duty, employment, function, job, nine-to-five*, occupation, office, place, profession, role, situation, slot*, spot*, trade; SEE CONCEPTS 324,349,360

position [v] place physically in location
arrange, array, dispose, fix, lay out, locate, put, set, settle, stand, stick; SEE CONCEPTS 158,201

positive [adj1] definite, certain
absolute, actual, affirmative, assured, categorical, clear, clear-cut, cocksure*, cold*, complete, conclusive, concrete, confident, consummate, convinced, decided, decisive, direct, downright, explicit, express, factual, firm, forceful, forcible, genuine, hard, inarguable, incontestable, incontrovertible, indisputable, indubitable, irrefutable, out-and-out*, outright, perfect, rank, real, specific, sure, thorough, thoroughgoing, unambiguous, undeniable, unequivocal, unmistakable, unmitigated; SEE CONCEPTS 535,582

positive [adj2] beneficial, helpful
affirmative, constructive, effective, efficacious, forward-looking, good, practical, productive, progressive, reasonable, sound, useful; SEE CONCEPT 572

positively [adv] absolutely, definitely
amen*, assuredly, categorically, certainly, doubtless, doubtlessly, easily, emphatically, firmly, flat*, flat out*, for a fact*, indubitably, no catch*, no holds barred*, no ifs ands or buts*, no kicker*, no strings attached*, on the money*, on the nose*, really truly*, right on*, sure, surely, the ticket*, to a tee*, undeniably, undoubtedly, unequivocally, unmistakably, unquestionably, with certainty, without qualification; SEE CONCEPTS 535,544,582

possess [v] have or obtain
acquire, bear, be blessed with, be born with, be endowed with, carry, control, corner*, corner the market*, dominate, enjoy, get hands on*, get hold of*, grab, have to name*, hog*, hold, latch on to, lock up, maintain, occupy, own, retain, seize, sit on, take over, take possession; SEE CONCEPTS 120,710

possessed [adj] bewitched; under a spell
bedeviled, berserk*, consumed, crazed*, cursed, demented, enchanted, enthralled, fiendish, frenetic, frenzied, gone*, haunted, hooked*, insane, into*, mad*, obsessed, raving*, taken over*, violent; SEE CONCEPT 401

possession [n1] control, ownership
custody, dominion, hold, occupancy, occupation, possessorship, proprietary, proprietary rights, proprietorship, retention, tenancy, tenure, title; SEE CONCEPTS 343,710

possession [n2] something owned; property
accessories, appointments, appurtenances, assets, baggage, belongings, chattels, effects, equipment, estate, fixtures, furnishings, furniture, goods, impedimenta, paraphernalia, province, real estate, settlement, tangibles, territory, things, trappings, tricks, wealth; SEE CONCEPTS 446,710

possibilities [n] potential
capabilities, potentiality, promise, prospects, talent; SEE CONCEPTS 411,650

possibility [n] feasibility, likelihood; chance
achievability, action, attainableness, break, circumstance, contingency, fair shake*, fifty-fifty*, fling*, fluke*, fortuity, happening, hazard, hope, incident, instance, liability, likeliness, occasion, occurrence, odds*, opportunity, outside chance*, plausibility, play*, potentiality, practicability, prayer*, probability, prospect, risk*, shot*, stab*, toss-up*, workableness; SEE CONCEPTS 650,693

possible [adj] *likely, attainable*
accessible, achievable, adventitious, advisable, available, breeze*, can do*, cinch, conceivable, credible, dependent, desirable, doable, dormant, duck soup*, easy as pie*, expedient, feasible, fortuitous, hopeful, hypothetical, imaginable, indeterminate, latent, no sweat*, piece of cake*, potential, practicable, probable, promising, pushover*, realizable, setup, simple as ABC*, snap, thinkable, uncertain, viable, welcome, within reach, workable; SEE CONCEPTS 528,552,576

possibly [adv] *by chance; in some way*
at all, by any chance, by any means, conceivably, could be, God willing*, if possible, in any way, likely, maybe, not impossibly, peradventure, perchance, perhaps, probably, within realm of possibility; SEE CONCEPTS 544,552

post [n1] *upright support*
column, doorpost, leg, mast, newel, pale, palisade, panel, pedestal, picket, pile, pillar, pole, prop, rail, shaft, stake, standard, stilt, stock, stud; SEE CONCEPTS 440,445,470,479

post [n2] *job, employment*
appointment, assignment, berth, billet, office, place, position, situation; SEE CONCEPTS 351,362

post [n3] *lookout, station*
beat, locus, place, position, whereabouts; SEE CONCEPTS 198,321,439

post [n4] *mail service*
collection, delivery, mail, PO*, postal service, post office; SEE CONCEPTS 299,770

post [v1] *situate, position*
assign, establish, locate, place, put, set, station; SEE CONCEPT 201

post [v2] *advise, inform*
acquaint, apprive, brief, clue, fill in, notify, put wise to, report, tell, warn, wise up; SEE CONCEPT 60

poster [n] *large paper advertisement*
affiche, announcement, banner, bill, billboard, broadside, handbill, notice, placard, public notice, sheet, sign, signboard, sticker; SEE CONCEPT 271

posterior [n] *behind of animate being*
back, backside, bottom, butt*, buttocks, can*, cheeks*, derriere, duff*, fanny*, hind part, keester*, moon*, rear, rear end, rump, seat, tail, tail end, tuchis*, tush*; SEE CONCEPT 392

posterior [adj1] *rear*
after, back, behind, dorsal, hind, hinder, hindmost, in back of, last, retral; SEE CONCEPTS 583,827

posterior [adj2] *subsequent*
after, coming after, ensuing, following, later, latter, next, postliminary, subsequential, succeeding; SEE CONCEPTS 585,799

posterity [n] *future generations*
breed, brood, children, descendants, family, heirs, issue, lineage, next generation, offspring, progeniture, progeny, scions, seed, stock, succeeding generations, successors, unborn; SEE CONCEPT 296

posthaste [adj/adv] *fast*
at once, breakneck*, directly, double-quick*, expeditious, flat-out*, fleet, fleetly, full tilt*, hastily, hasty, headlong, lickety-split*, pell-mell*, promptly, pronto, quick, quickly, rapid, rapidly, speedily, speedy, straightaway, swift, swiftly; SEE CONCEPTS 544,588,799

postmortem [n] *analysis after death*
autopsy, coroner's report, dissection, examination, necropsy, post*; SEE CONCEPTS 103,310

postmortem [adj] *following death*
future, later, posthumous, postmundane, postobit, post-obituary; SEE CONCEPT 799

postpone [v] *put off till later time*
adjourn, cool it*, defer, delay, give a rain check*, hang fire*, hold off, hold over, hold up, lay over, pigeonhole*, prorogue, put back, put on back burner*, put on hold, shelve, suspend, table; SEE CONCEPT 130

postulate [v] *suppose, figure*
advance, affirm, assert, assume, aver, estimate, guess, hypothesize, posit, predicate, premise, presuppose, propose, put forward, speculate, suppose, take for granted, theorize; SEE CONCEPTS 12,26

posture [n1] *stance, circumstance*
aspect, attitude, bearing, brace, carriage, condition, demeanor, deportment, disposition, mien, mode, phase, port, pose, position, positure, presence, set, situation, state; SEE CONCEPTS 657,723

posture [n2] *beliefs*
attitude, disposition, feeling, frame of mind, inclination, mood, outlook, point of view, sentiment, stance, standpoint; SEE CONCEPT 410

posture [v] *display an attitude*
affect, attitudinize, display, do a bit*, do for effect*, fake, fake it, make a show*, masquerade, pass for, pass off, playact, pose, put on airs*, put up a front*, show off*; SEE CONCEPTS 59,261

pot [n1] *container, cauldron*
basin, bowl, bucket, can, canister, crock, crucible, cup, jar, jug, kettle, mug, pan, pitcher, receptacle, saucepan, tankard, urn, vessel; SEE CONCEPT 494

pot [n2] *marijuana*
cannabis, grass*, hashish, maryjane*, weed*; SEE CONCEPT 307

potency [n] *effectiveness*
authority, birr, capability, capacity, command, control, dominion, efficacy, efficiency, energy, force, go*, hardihood, influence, juice*, kick*, might, moxie*, muscle*, pep, potential, power, puissance, punch, sinew*, snap, sock*, steam*, strength, sway, vigor, virtue, what it takes*, zap*, zing*, zip*; SEE CONCEPTS 411,676,732

potent [adj] *effective, powerful, forceful*
almighty, authoritative, ball of fire*, cogent, commanding, compelling, convincing, dominant, dynamic, efficacious, forcible, full-bodied, go-getter*, great, gutsy*, impressive, influential, lusty, mighty, persuasive, powerhouse, puissant, punchy, robust, spanking, stiff, strong, sturdy, telling, trenchant, useful, vigorous; SEE CONCEPTS 372,489,540

potential [n] *possibility for achievement*
ability, aptitude, capability, capacity, potentiality, power, the makings*, what it takes*, wherewithal; SEE CONCEPTS 650,706

potential [adj] *promising*
abeyant, budding, conceivable, dormant, embryonic, future, hidden, imaginable, implied, inherent, latent, likely, lurking, plausible, possible, prepatent, probable, quiescent, thinkable, undeveloped, unrealized, within realm of possibility; SEE CONCEPTS 528,552

po
po

potion [n] *concoction prepared for mental or physical effect*
aromatic, brew, cordial, cup, dose, draft, dram, draught, drink, elixir, libation, liquid, liquor, medicine, mixture, nip, philter, remedy, restorative, spirits, stimulant, tonic; SEE CONCEPTS 307,467

potpourri [n] *miscellany*
assortment, blend, collection, combination, combo, gallimaufry, goulash, hash, hodgepodge, medley, mélange, mishmash, mixed bag, mixture, motley, olio*, pastiche*, patchwork, salmagundi*, soup, stew; SEE CONCEPTS 260,432

pottery [n] *containers made from clay; clay art*
ceramics, crockery, earthenware, firing, glazing, porcelain, porcelainware, stoneware, terra cotta; SEE CONCEPTS 174,259,494

pouch [n] *soft container, often made of cloth or skin*
bag, pocket, poke, purse, receptacle, sac, sack; SEE CONCEPTS 446,450,494

pounce [n/v] *leap at; take by surprise*
ambush, attack, bound, dart, dash, dive, drop, fall upon, jump, snatch, spring, strike, surge, swoop, take unawares; SEE CONCEPTS 86,159,194

pound [n] *sixteen ounces/.454 kilograms of weight*
avoirdupois, pint, troy; SEE CONCEPT 795

pound [v1] *crush; beat rhythmically*
batter, belabor, bruise, buffet, clobber, comminute, drub, hammer, hit, malleate, palpitate, pelt, pestle, pound, pulsate, pulse, pulverize, pummel, stomp, strike, thrash, throb, thump, tramp, triturate, wallop; SEE CONCEPTS 150,186,189

pound [v2] *impress; make someone listen*
din, drive, drub, drum, grave, hammer, stamp; SEE CONCEPTS 14,49

pour [v] *be or make flowing*
cascade, cataract, course, crowd, decant, deluge, discharge, drain, drench, emit, flood, flow, give off, gush, inundate, issue, jet, let flow, proceed, rain, rill, roll, run, rush, sheet, shower, sluice, spew, spill, splash, spout, spring, stream, swarm, teem, throng; SEE CONCEPTS 146,179,209

pout [n] *sad face*
frown, glower, long face, moue, sullen look; SEE CONCEPT 716

pout [v] *make a sad face; be sad*
be cross, be in bad mood*, be moody, be petulant, be sullen, frown, grouch, grump*, make a long face*, make a moue, mope, stick one's lip out*, sulk; SEE CONCEPTS 261,410

poverty [n] *want; extreme need, often financial*
abjection, aridity, bankruptcy, barrenness, beggary, dearth, debt, deficiency, deficit, depletion, destitution, difficulty, distress, emptiness, exiguity, famine, hardship, impecuniousness, impoverishment, inadequacy, indigence, insolvency, insufficiency, lack, meagerness, necessitousness, necessity, pass, paucity, pauperism, pennilessness, penury, pinch, poorness, privation, reduction, scarcity, shortage, starvation, straits, underdevelopment, vacancy; SEE CONCEPTS 335,709

poverty-stricken [adj] *in great need; financially poor*
bad off*, bankrupt, beggared, beggarly, broke*, destitute, dirt poor*, distressed, down-and-out*, hard up*, impecunious, impoverished, indigent, in dire circumstances, in want, moneyless, necessitous, needful, needy, penniless, penurious, short*, stone broke*, stranded*, strapped*, unmoneyed, wanting; SEE CONCEPT 334

powder [n] *fine, loose grains made by crushing a solid*
crumb, dust, film, grain, grit, meal, particle, pounce, pulverulence, seed, talc; SEE CONCEPTS 471,831

powder [v] *crush into fine grains; sprinkle fine grains*
abrade, bray, comminute, cover, crumble, crunch, dredge, dust, file, flour, granulate, grate, grind, pestle, pound, pulverize, rasp, reduce, scatter, scrape, smash, strew, triturate; SEE CONCEPTS 186,222

powdery [adj] *consisting of fine, loose grains*
arenaceous, arenose, branny, chalky, crumbling, crumbly, dry, dusty, fine, floury, friable, grainy, granular, gravelly, gritty, impalpable, loose, mealy, pulverized, pulverulent, sandy; SEE CONCEPT 606

power [n1] *ability, competence*
aptitude, bent, capability, capacity, competency, dynamism, effectiveness, efficacy, endowment, faculty, function, gift, influence, potential, potentiality, qualification, skill, talent, turn, virtue; SEE CONCEPT 630

power [n2] *physical ability, capacity*
applied force, arm*, brawn, dynamism, energy, force, forcefulness, horsepower, intensity, mechanical energy, might, muscle*, omnipotence, potency, potential, puissance, sinew*, strength, vigor, vim, virtue, voltage, weight; SEE CONCEPTS 520,641,732

power [n3] *control, dominance*
ascendancy, authority, authorization, birthright, clout, command, connection, diadem, direction, domination, dominion, hegemony, imperium, influence, inside track*, jurisdiction, law, leadership, license, management, might, moxie*, omnipotence, paramountcy, predominance, prerogative, prestige, privilege, regency, right, rule, say-so*, sovereignty, steam, strength, strings*, superiority, supremacy, sway, warrant, weight*, wire*; SEE CONCEPTS 376,671

powerful [adj] *strong, effective*
able, all-powerful, almighty, authoritarian, authoritative, capable, cogent, commanding, compelling, competent, controlling, convincing, dominant, dynamic, effectual, efficacious, energetic, forceful, forcible, impressive, in control, influential, in the saddle*, mighty, omnipotent, overruling, paramount, persuasive, potent, preeminent, prevailing, puissant, robust, ruling, sovereign, stalwart, strapping*, strengthy, sturdy, supreme, telling, upper hand*, vigorous, weighty, wicked*, wieldy; SEE CONCEPTS 489,527, 540,574

powerfully [adv] *with energy, authority*
effectively, energetically, forcefully, forcibly, hard, intensely, mightily, severely, strongly, vigorously, with might and main; SEE CONCEPTS 540,544,569

powerless [adj] *weak; unable*
blank, chicken*, debilitated, defenseless, dependent, disabled, disenfranchised, etiolated, feeble, frail, gutless, helpless, impotent, incapable, incapacitated, ineffective, ineffectual, inert, infirm, out of gas*, paralyzed, passive, prostrate, subject, supine, tied, unarmed, unfit, vulnerable, wimp*, wishy-washy*; SEE CONCEPTS 489,527

powwow [n] *discussion*
confab*, confabulation, conference, consultation, council, get-together, huddle, meeting, palaver, parley, talk; SEE CONCEPTS 56,324,384

powwow [v] *discuss*
advise, confab*, confabulate, confer, consult, get together, go into a huddle*, huddle, meet, palaver, parley, talk, treat; SEE CONCEPT 56

practicable [adj] *within the realm of possibility*
accessible, achievable, applicable, attainable, doable, employable, feasible, functional, handy, open, operative, performable, possible, practical, serviceable, usable, useful, utile, utilizable, viable, workable; SEE CONCEPT 560

practical [adj1] *realistic, useful*
applied, both feet on the ground*, businesslike, commonsensical, constructive, doable, down-to-earth, efficient, empirical, experimental, factual, feasible, functional, handy, hard-boiled*, implicit, in action, in operation, matter-of-fact*, nuts and bolts*, operative, orderly, possible, practicable, pragmatic, rational, reasonable, sane, sensible, serviceable, sober, solid, sound, systematic, unidealistic, unromantic, usable, utile, utilitarian, virtual, workable, workaday, working; SEE CONCEPTS 533,542,560

practical [adj2] *experienced, proficient*
accomplished, cosmopolitan, effective, efficient, qualified, seasoned, skilled, sophisticated, trained, versed, vet*, veteran, working, worldly, worldly-wise; SEE CONCEPTS 326,527,528,678

practically [adj] *almost; nearly*
about, all but, approximately, as good as, as much as, basically, close to, essentially, for all intents and purposes*, fundamentally, in effect, in essence, morally, most, much, nearly, nigh, virtually, well-nigh; SEE CONCEPTS 531,772

practice [n1] *routine, usual procedure*
convenance, convention, custom, fashion, form, habit, habitude, manner, method, mode, praxis, proceeding, process, rule, system, tradition, trick, usage, use, usefulness, utility, way, wont; SEE CONCEPT 688

practice [n2] *exercise, application*
action, assignment, background, discipline, drill, drilling, effect, experience, homework, iteration, operation, preparation, prepping, recitation, recounting, rehearsal, relating, repetition, seasoning, study, training, tune-up, use, work-out; SEE CONCEPTS 87,100,658

practice [n3] *business; clientele of business*
career, clients, patients, profession, vocation, work; SEE CONCEPTS 325,417

practice [v1] *repeat action to improve*
become seasoned, build up, discipline, do again, dress, dress rehearse*, drill, dry run*, exercise, go over, habituate, hone, iterate, polish, prepare, recite, rehearse, run through, shake-down*, sharpen, study, train, try out, tune up, walk through, warm up, work, work out; SEE CONCEPTS 87,100

practice [v2] *carry out; undertake*
apply, carry on, do, engage in, execute, follow, fulfill, function, live up to, observe, perform, ply, pursue, put into effect, specialize in, work at; SEE CONCEPTS 91,310,317,324

pragmatic [adj] *sensible*
businesslike, commonsensical, down-to-earth, efficient, hard, hard-boiled*, hardheaded*, logical,

matter-of-fact, practical, realistic, sober, unidealistic; SEE CONCEPTS 401,542

praise [n] *congratulations; adoration*
acclaim, acclamation, accolade, applause, appreciation, approbation, approval, big hand*, boost, bravo, celebration, cheer, cheering, citation, commendation, compliment, cry, devotion, encomium, esteem, eulogy, exaltation, extolment, flattery, glorification, glory, good word*, homage, hurrah, hymn, kudos*, laudation, obeisance, ovation, panegyric, pat on the back*, plaudit, puff*, rave, recognition, recommendation, regard, sycophancy, thanks, tribute, worship; SEE CONCEPTS 69,278

praise [v] *congratulate; adore*
acclaim, admire, adulate, advocate, aggrandize, applaud, appreciate, approve, bless, boost, bow down*, build up*, cajole, celebrate, cheer, cite, clap, commend, compliment, cry up*, dignify, distinguish, elevate, endorse, ennoble, eulogize, exalt, extol, flatter, give thanks, glorify, hail, honor, laud, make much of*, panegyrize, pay homage, pay tribute, proclaim, puff*, rave over, recommend, resound, reverence, root*, sanction, sing the praises*, smile on*, stroke*, tout, worship; SEE CONCEPT 69

praiseworthy [adj] *deserving congratulations, adoration*
admirable, commendable, creditable, estimable, excellent, exemplary, fine, gnarly, gone, honorable, keen, laudable, meritable, meritorious, pillar, salt of earth*, select, slick, stellar, swell, thankworthy, tough, worthy; SEE CONCEPTS 568,574

prance [v] *cavort; show off*
bound, caper, dance, flounce, foot it*, frisk, gambol, hoof it*, jump, leap, mince, parade, romp, sashay, skip, spring, stalk, step, strut, swagger, sweep, tread; SEE CONCEPTS 150,292,384

prank [n] *practical joke; frivolity*
antic, caper, caprice, escapade, fancy, fooling, frolic, gag, gambol, high jinks*, horseplay*, hotfoot*, lark, levity, lightness, monkeyshines*, play, put-on, rib*, rollick, roughhouse*, roughhousing*, rowdiness, shenanigans, shine*, skylarking*, spoof, sport, tomfoolery, trick, whim; SEE CONCEPTS 59,384

pray [v] *plead; call upon for help, answer*
adjure, appeal, ask, beseech, brace, commune with, crave, cry for, entreat, implore, importune, invocate, invoke, petition, recite, request, say, solicit, sue, supplicate, urge; SEE CONCEPTS 48,367

prayer [n] *pleading, especially with a deity; request for help, answer*
adoration, appeal, application, begging, benediction, beseeching, communion, devotion, entreaty, grace, imploration, imploring, imprecation, invocation, litany, orison, petition, plea, pleading, request, rogation, service, suit, supplication, worship; SEE CONCEPTS 48,367,662

preach [v1] *speak publicly about beliefs*
address, deliver, deliver sermon, evangelize, exhort, give sermon, homilize, inform, minister, mission, missionary, orate, prophesy, pulpiteer, sermonize, talk, teach; SEE CONCEPTS 51,285,367

preach [v2] *lecture, moralize*
admonish, advocate, blow, exhort, get on a soapbox*, harangue, pile it on*, preachify, sermonize, talk big*, urge; SEE CONCEPTS 51,75

po
pr

preacher [n] *person who gives religious instruction*
clergy, cleric, clerical, divine, ecclesiastic, evangelist, evangelizer, minister, missionary, parson, pulpiter, reverend, revivalist, sermonizer; SEE CONCEPT 361

precarious [adj] *tricky, doubtful*
ambiguous, borderline, chancy, contingent, dangerous, delicate, dicey*, dubious, dynamite, equivocal, hairy*, hanging by a thread*, hazardous, iffy*, impugnable, indecisive, insecure, loaded, on thin ice*, open, out on a limb*, perilous, problematic, risky, rocky, rugged*, sensitive, shaky, slippery, ticklish, touch and go*, touchy, uncertain, unhealthy, unreliable, unsafe, unsettled, unstable, unsteady, unsure; SEE CONCEPTS 535,587

precaution [n] *carefulness; preventative measure*
anticipation, canniness, care, caution, circumspection, discreetness, discretion, foresight, forethought, insurance, protection, providence, provision, prudence, regard, safeguard, safety measure, wariness; SEE CONCEPTS 410,633,729

precede [v] *go ahead of in space, time, order*
announce, antecede, antedate, anticipate, be ahead of, come first, forerun, foreshadow, go before, go in advance, guide, harbinger, have a head start*, head, head up, herald, introduce, lead, light the way*, outrank, pace, pave the way*, pioneer, predate, pre-exist, preface, presage, rank, ring in*, run ahead, scout, take precedence, usher; SEE CONCEPTS 727,747,813,818

precedence [n] *highest in rank; first in order*
antecedence, anteposition, earliness, lead, precedency, precession, preeminence, preexistence, preference, prevenience, previousness, primary, priority, rank, seniority, superiority, supremacy; SEE CONCEPTS 671,727,747,818

precedent [n] *authoritative example*
antecedent, authority, criterion, exemplar, instance, model, paradigm; SEE CONCEPT 686

preceding [adj] *earlier, above*
above-mentioned, above-named, aforeknown, aforementioned, aforesaid, ahead of, antecedent, anterior, before, erstwhile, foregoing, forerunning, former, forward, front, head, heretofore, introductory, lead, leading, one time, other, past, pioneer, pioneering, precedent, precursive, precursory, preexistent, prefatory, preliminary, preparatory, prevenient, previous, prior, supra; SEE CONCEPTS 585,586,799,811,818

precept [n] *law, rule of behavior, action*
axiom, behest, bidding, byword, canon, command, commandment, decree, decretum, direction, doctrine, dogma, edict, formula, fundamental, guideline, injunction, instruction, law, mandate, maxim, motto, ordinance, prescript, principle, regulation, rule, saying, statute, tenet; SEE CONCEPTS 318,688

precious [adj1] *favorite, valued*
adored, beloved, cherished, darling, dear, dearest, idolized, inestimable, loved, pet, prized, treasured; SEE CONCEPTS 529,567

precious [adj2] *expensive; rare*
choice, costly, dear, exquisite, fine, high-priced, inestimable, invaluable, priceless, prizable, prized, recherché, rich, treasurable, valuable, worth a king's ransom*, worth eyeteeth*, worth one's weight in gold*; SEE CONCEPT 334

precious [adj3] *extremely sophisticated and picky*
affected, alembicated, artful, artificial, chichi*, choosy, dainty, delicate, fastidious, finicky, fragile, fussy, la-di-da*, nice, ostentatious, overnice, overrefined, particular, persnickety*, precieux, pretentious, refined, showy, stagy, studied; SEE CONCEPT 401

precipice [n] *face or brink of a rock, mountain*
bluff, cliff, crag, height, sheer drop, steep; SEE CONCEPTS 509,513

precipitate [v] *hurry, speed*
accelerate, advance, bring on, cast, discharge, dispatch, expedite, fling, further, hasten, hurl, launch, let fly, press, push forward, quicken, send forth, speed up, throw, trigger; SEE CONCEPTS 152,242,704

precipitation [n] *moisture in air or falling from sky*
cloudburst, condensation, drizzle, hail, hailstorm, heavy dew, precip*, rain, rainfall, rainstorm, sleet, snow, storm, wetness; SEE CONCEPTS 467,524,526

precipitous/precipitate [adj1] *fast, sudden; impulsive; initial*
abrupt, breakneck*, brief, frantic, gone off half-cocked*, harum-scarum*, hasty, headlong, heedless, hurried, ill-advised, impatient, impetuous, indiscreet, jump the gun*, madcap, off the hip*, off the top of head*, plunging, precipitant, quick, rapid, rash, reckless, refractory, rushing, subitaneous, swift, unanticipated, uncontrolled, unexpected, unforeseen, violent, willful, without warning; SEE CONCEPTS 229,401,542,588,799

precipitous [adj2] *steep, falling sharply*
abrupt, arduous, craggy, dizzy, dizzying, high, perpendicular, precipitate, sharp, sheer; SEE CONCEPTS 490,583,779

precis [n] *abridgment*
abstract, aperçu, compendium, condensation, digest, outline, pandect, résumé, rundown, sketch, summary, survey, syllabus, synopsis; SEE CONCEPT 283

precise [adj1] *exact, accurate*
absolute, actual, categorical, circumscribed, clear-cut, correct, decisive, definite, determinate, explicit, express, fixed, individual, limited, literal, narrow, nice, on the button*, on the money*, on the nose*, particular, proper, restricted, right, rigid, rigorous, specific, strict, stringent, unequivocal, very, well-defined; SEE CONCEPTS 535,557,653

precise [adj2] *meticulous, fastidious*
careful, ceremonious, choosy, exact, finicky, formal, fussy, genteel, inflexible, nice, particular, persnickety*, picky, priggish, prim, prissy, punctilious, rigid, scrupulous, stickling, stiff*, strict, stuffy, uncompromising; SEE CONCEPTS 401,542

precisely [adv] *exactly, just*
absolutely, accurately, as well, correctly, definitely, even, expressly, for a fact, for sure, just so, literally, no ifs ands or buts*, no mistake*, on the button*, on the money*, on the nose*, plumb, right, sharp, smack*, smack-dab*, specifically, square, squarely, strictly, sure, sure thing*, the ticket*, the very thing*, to a tee*; yes; SEE CONCEPTS 535,557

precision [n] *accuracy*
attention, care, carefulness, correctness, definiteness, definitiveness, definitude, exactitude, exactness, fidelity, heed, meticulousness, nicety,

particularity, preciseness, rigor, sureness; SEE CONCEPTS 638,654

preclude [v] *inhibit; make impossible*
avert, cease, check, debar, deter, discontinue, exclude, forestall, forfend, hinder, impede, interrupt, make impracticable, obviate, prevent, prohibit, put a stop to, quit, restrain, rule out, stave off, stop, ward; SEE CONCEPTS 121,234

precocious [adj] *exceptionally smart, ahead of age in understanding*
advanced, aggressive, ahead of time*, beforehand, bold, brassy*, bright, cheeky*, cocky*, developed, early, flip*, flippant, forward, fresh, intelligent, mature, nervy, premature, presumptuous, pushy, quick, sassy*, smart-alecky*; SEE CONCEPT 402

preconception [n] *idea formed before event occurs or facts are received*
assumption, bias, delusion, illusion, inclination, notion, preconceived idea, predisposition, prejudgment, prejudice, prepossession, presumption, presupposition; SEE CONCEPT 689

precursor [n1] *something that indicates outcome or event beforehand*
forerunner, harbinger, herald, messenger, outrider, usher, vanguard; SEE CONCEPTS 70,278

precursor [n2] *something that precedes another*
ancestor, antecedent, antecessor, forebear, foregoer, forerunner, original, originator, parent, pioneer, predecessor, prototype; SEE CONCEPTS 648,727,828

predatory [adj] *eating, destroying for sustenance or without conscience*
bloodthirsty, carnivorous, depredatory, despoiling, greedy, hungry, hunting, marauding, pillaging, plundering, predacious, predative, preying, rapacious, raptorial, ravaging, ravening, thieving, voracious, vulturine, vulturous, wolfish; SEE CONCEPTS 401,406

predecessor [n] *something, someone that comes before*
ancestor, antecedent, antecessor, forebear, foregoer, forerunner, former, precursor, previous, prior, prototype; SEE CONCEPTS 414,828

predetermined [adj] *decided in advance*
agreed, arranged, calculated, cut and dried*, deliberate, destined, determined, doomed, fated, fixed, foredestined, foreordained, forethought, planned, prearranged, precogitated, predestined, premeditated, preordained, preplanned, proposed, set, settled, set up; SEE CONCEPT 548

predicament [n] *difficult situation*
asperity, bad news*, bind*, Catch-22*, circumstance, clutch, condition, corner*, crisis, deadlock, deep water*, dilemma, drag*, emergency, exigency, fix*, hang-up*, hardship, hole, hot water*, imbroglio, impasse, jam*, juncture, large order*, lot, mess*, muddle, pass, perplexity, pickle*, pinch, plight, position, posture, puzzle, quagmire, quandary, rigor, rough go*, scrape*, soup*, spot*, state*, strait, tall order* ticklish spot* tight situation* trouble, vicissitude; SEE CONCEPTS 388,674

predict [v] *express an outcome in advance*
adumbrate, anticipate, augur, be afraid, call, call it, conclude, conjecture, croak, crystal-ball* divine, envision, figure, figure out, forebode, forecast, foresee, forespeak, foretell, gather, guess, have a hunch*, hazard a guess*, infer, judge, make book*, omen, portend, presage, presume,

prognosticate, prophesy, psych out*, read, see coming*, see handwriting on wall*, size up*, soothsay, suppose, surmise, telegraph*, think, vaticinate; SEE CONCEPT 70

predictable [adj] *easy to foretell*
anticipated, calculable, certain, expected, foreseeable, foreseen, likely, prepared, sure, sure-fire*; SEE CONCEPTS 404,542,548

prediction [n] *declaration made in advance of event*
anticipation, augury, cast, conjecture, crystal gazing*, divination, dope, forecast, forecasting, foresight, foretelling, fortune-telling, guess, horoscope, hunch*, indicator, omen, palmistry, presage, prevision, prognosis, prognostication, prophecy, soothsaying, surmising, tip, vaticination, zodiac; SEE CONCEPTS 70,278,689

predilection [n] *inclination, preference toward something*
bent*, bias, cup of tea*, dish*, druthers*, fancy, flash, fondness, groove, inclining, leaning, liking, love, mindset*, partiality, penchant, predisposition, proclivity, proneness, propensity, taste*, tendency, thing*, type, weakness; SEE CONCEPTS 20,32,709

predispose [v] *influence to believe something*
activate, affect, animate, bend*, bias, cultivate, dispose, govern, impress, incline, indoctrinate, induce, inspire, lead, make expectant, make of a mind to*, prejudice, prepare, prime, prompt, stimulate, strike, sway, teach, urge; SEE CONCEPTS 12,14,26,68

predisposed [adj] *willing, inclined*
agreeable, amenable, biased, eager, enthusiastic, fain, given to, liable, likely, minded, partial, prone, ready, subject, susceptible; SEE CONCEPT 403

predisposition [n] *willingness, inclination*
bent*, bias, choice, cup of tea*, dish*, disposition, druthers*, flash, groove, leaning, likelihood, liking, option, partiality, penchant, potentiality, predilection, preference, proclivity, proneness, propensity, susceptibility, tendency, thing*, type, weakness; SEE CONCEPTS 20,32,410,709

predominant [adj] *ruling; most important*
absolute, all-powerful, almighty, arbitrary, ascendant, authoritative, capital, chief, controlling, directing, dominant, dominating, effective, efficacious, governing, holding the reins*, imperious, influential, leading, main, mighty, official, omnipotent, overbearing, overpowering, paramount, potent, predominate, preponderant, prevailing, prevalent, primary, prime, principal, prominent, reigning, sovereign, superior, superlative, supervisory, supreme, surpassing, transcendent, weighty; SEE CONCEPTS 568,574

predominate [v] *be the most important, noticeable*
carry weight*, command, dominate, domineer, get the upper hand*, govern, hold sway*, manage, outweigh, overrule, overshadow, preponderate, prevail, reign, rule, tell; SEE CONCEPTS 94,117,141

preeminent [adj] *most important; superior*
capital, chief, consummate, distinguished, dominant, excellent, foremost, incomparable, main, major, matchless, number one*, outstanding, paramount, peerless, predominant, principal, renowned, stellar, supreme, surpassing, towering, transcendent, ultimate, unequalled, unmatchable,

unrivalled, unsurpassable, unsurpassed; SEE CONCEPTS 568,574

preempt [v] *take over in place of another*
accroach, acquire, annex, anticipate, appropriate, arrogate, assume, bump, commandeer, confiscate, expropriate, obtain, seize, sequester, take, usurp; SEE CONCEPTS 121,142,234

preface [n] *introduction*
beginning, exordium, explanation, foreword, overture, preamble, preliminary, prelude, prelusion, proem, prolegomenon, prologue; SEE CONCEPT 270

preface [v] *introduce*
begin, commence, launch, lead, lead up to, open, precede, prefix, usher; SEE CONCEPTS 57,221

prefer [v] *favor; single out*
adopt, advance, aggrandize, be partial to, be turned on to, choose, cull, desire, elect, elevate, fancy, finger, fix upon, go for, incline, like better, mark, optate, opt for, pick, place, pose, present, promote, propone, proposition, propound, put, put forward, raise, select, suggest, tag, take, tap, upgrade, wish, would rather*, would sooner*; SEE CONCEPTS 20,41

preference [n1] *first choice*
alternative, choice, cup of tea*, desire, druthers*, election, favorite, flash*, groove, inclination, option, partiality, pick, predilection, prepossession, propensity, say, say so*, selection, top, weakness; SEE CONCEPTS 20,529,709

preference [n2] *favorable treatment*
advancement, advantage, elevation, favoritism, first place, precedence, preferment, prelation, pride of place, priority, promotion, upgrading; SEE CONCEPT 693

preferred [adj] *favorite, chosen*
adopted, approved, culled, decided upon, elected, endorsed, fancied, favored, handpicked, liked, named, picked, popular, sanctioned, selected, set apart, settled upon, singled out, taken, well-liked; SEE CONCEPTS 555,574

pregnant [adj1] *carrying developing offspring within the body*
abundant, anticipating, carrying a child, enceinte, expectant, expecting*, fecund, fertile, fraught, fruitful, gestating, gravid, heavy, hopeful, in family way*, parous, parturient, preggers*, productive, prolific, replete, teeming, with child*; SEE CONCEPTS 406,485

pregnant [adj2] *significant, meaningful*
charged, cogent, consequential, creative, eloquent, expressive, fecund, imaginative, important, inventive, loaded, momentous, original, pointed, redolent, rich, seminal, sententious, suggestive, telling, weighty; SEE CONCEPTS 267,567

prejudice [n] *belief without basis, information; intolerance*
ageism, animosity, antipathy, apartheid, aversion, bad opinion, bias, bigotry, chauvinism, contemptuousness, detriment, discrimination, disgust, dislike, displeasure, disrelish, enmity, foregone conclusion, illiberality, injustice, jaundiced eye, mindset*, misjudgment, narrow-mindedness, onesidedness, partiality, pique, preconceived notion, preconception, prejudgment, prepossession, racism, repugnance, revulsion, sexism, slant, spleen, tilt, twist, umbrage, unfairness, warp, xenophobia; SEE CONCEPT 689

prejudice [v] *influence another's beliefs without basis, information*
angle*, bend*, bias, blemish*, color*, damage, dispose, distort, harm, hinder, hurt, impair, incline, indoctrinate, injure, jaundice, mar, poison*, predispose, prejudge, prepossess, skew*, slant*, spoil, sway*, twist*, undermine, vitiate, warp*; SEE CONCEPTS 7,14,19

prejudicial [adj] *harmful, undermining*
bad, biased, bigoted, counterproductive, damaging, deleterious, detrimental, differential, disadvantageous, discriminatory, evil, hurtful, inimical, injurious, mischievous, nocuous, unfavorable, unjust; SEE CONCEPTS 537,545,570

preliminary [n] *introductory event; beginning*
first round, foundation, groundwork, initiation, introduction, opening, preamble, preface, prelims*, prelude, preparation, start; SEE CONCEPTS 828,832

preliminary [adj] *introductory, initial*
basic, elemental, elementary, exploratory, first, fundamental, inductive, initiatory, opening, pilot, preceding, precursory, prefatory, preparatory, preparing, primal, primary, prior, qualifying, readying, test, trial; SEE CONCEPTS 549,585,799

prelude [n] *beginning of event*
commencement, curtain-raiser*, exordium, foreword, intro*, introduction, overture, preamble, preface, preliminary, prelusion, preparation, proem, prolegomenon, prologue, start; SEE CONCEPTS 264,832

premature [adj1] *earlier in occurrence than anticipated*
a bit previous, abortive, early on, embryonic, forward, green*, immature, incomplete, inopportune, overearly, oversoon, precipitate, predeveloped, previous, raw*, soon, unanticipated, undeveloped, unfledged, unripe, untimely; SEE CONCEPTS 485,549

premature [adj2] *rash, impulsive*
half-baked*, half-cocked*, hasty, ill-considered, inopportune, jumping the gun*, overhasty, precipitate, previous, too soon, untimely; SEE CONCEPTS 401,542

premeditated [adj] *planned, intended*
advised, aforethought, calculated, conscious, considered, contrived, deliberate, designed, fixed, framed up, intentional, laid-out*, prepense, purposed, rigged*, set-up*, sewn-up*, stacked deck*, studied, thought-out, willful; SEE CONCEPTS 542,548

premier [adj] *leading; original*
arch, beginning, champion, chief, earliest, first, foremost, head, highest, inaugural, initial, main, opening, primary, prime, principal; SEE CONCEPTS 568,585

premiere [n] *original production*
beginning, debut, first night, first performance, first showing, opening, opening night; SEE CONCEPTS 263,832

premise [n] *hypothesis, argument*
apriorism, assertion, assumption, basis, evidence, ground, posit, postulate, postulation, presumption, presupposition, proof, proposition, supposition, thesis; SEE CONCEPTS 529,689

premise [v] *hypothesize*
announce, assume, begin, commence, introduce, posit, postulate, predicate, presume, presuppose, start, state, suppose; SEE CONCEPTS 18,37

premises [n] *grounds and buildings*
bounds, campus, digs, establishment, fix, flat, hangout*, home, house, joint*, land, lay, layout, limits, neck of the woods*, office, pad, place, plant, property, real estate*, roof, scene, site, spot, terrace, turf, zone; SEE CONCEPTS 198,515

premium [n] *bonus, prize*
appreciation, boon, bounty, carrot*, dividend, extra, fee*, gravy*, guerdon, meed, percentage, perk*, perquisite, plum*, recompense, regard, remuneration, reward, spiff*, stock, store, value; SEE CONCEPTS 337,344

premium [adj] *excellent*
choice, exceptional, prime, select, selected, superior; SEE CONCEPT 574

premonition [n] *feeling that an event is about to occur*
apprehension, apprehensiveness, feeling, feeling in bones*, foreboding, forewarning, funny feeling, handwriting on wall*, hunch, idea, intuition, misgiving, omen, portent, prenotion, presage, presentiment, sign, sinking feeling, suspicion, vibes, vibrations, warning, wind change*, winds*, winds of change*, worriment; SEE CONCEPTS 410,529,689,690

preoccupied [adj] *busy; mentally caught up in something*
absent, absent-minded, absorbed, abstracted, airheaded*, asleep*, bemused, bugged*, daydreaming, deep*, distracted, distrait, engaged, engrossed, faraway, fascinated, forgetful, have on the brain*, heedless, hung up*, immersed, inconscient, intent, lost, lost in thought*, mooning*, moony*, oblivious, obsessed, rapt, removed, spellbound, spread out*, taken up, unaware, woolgathering*, wrapped-up*; SEE CONCEPT 403

preparation [n1] *development, readiness*
alertness, anticipation, arrangement, background, base, basis, build-up*, construction, dry run*, education, establishment, evolution, expectation, fitting, foresight, formation, foundation, gestation, getting ready, groundwork, homework, incubation, lead time*, making ready, manufacture, measure, plan, precaution, preparedness, preparing, provision, putting in order, qualification, readying, rehearsal, rundown, safeguard, schoolwork, study, substructure, training, tryout, workout; SEE CONCEPTS 35,202,285

preparation [n2] *something concocted, put together*
arrangement, blend, brew, composition, compound, concoction, confection, decoction, medicine, mixture, product, tincture; SEE CONCEPT 260

preparatory [adj] *introductory, basic*
before, elementary, in advance of, in anticipation of, inductive, opening, precautionary, prefatory, preliminary, prelusive, prep*, preparative, previous, primary, prior to; SEE CONCEPTS 546,585

prepare [v] *make or get ready*
adapt, adjust, anticipate, appoint, arrange, assemble, brace, build up, coach, concoct, construct, contrive, cook, develop, dispose, draw up, endow, equip, fabricate, fashion, fill in, fit, fit out, fix, form, formulate, fortify, furnish, gird, groom, lay the groundwork, make, make provision, make up, outfit, perfect, plan, practice, prime, produce, provide, put in order, put together, qualify, ready, settle, smooth the way*, steel*, strengthen, sup-

ply, train, turn out, warm up; SEE CONCEPTS 35,202

prepared [adj] *ready in body or mind*
able, adapted, adjusted, all bases covered*, all set*, all systems go*, arranged, available, disposed, fit, fixed, framed, gaffed, groomed, handy, inclined, in order, in readiness, minded, of a mind, on guard*, planned, predisposed, prepped, primed, processed, psyched-up*, put up, qualified, rehearsed, rigged*, set, set-up, sewed-up, stacked, up*, up on*, willing, wired; SEE CONCEPTS 403,485,560

preponderance [n] *great numbers; supremacy*
advantage, ascendancy, bigger half*, bulk, command, dominance, domination, dominion, extensiveness, greater part, lion's share*, mass, max*, mostest, power, predominance, prevalence, superiority, sway, weight; SEE CONCEPTS 671,687,767

prepossessed [adj] *made partial by initial impression*
biased, colored, inclined, jaundiced, one-sided, opinionated, partisan, predisposed, prejudiced, tendentious, unindifferent, warped; SEE CONCEPTS 403,542

prepossessing [adj] *attractive, handsome*
alluring, amiable, appealing, attracting, beautiful, bewitching, captivating, charming, drawing, enchanting, engaging, fair, fascinating, fetching, good-looking, inviting, likable, lovable, magnetic, pleasant, pleasing, striking, taking, winning; SEE CONCEPTS 404,537

preposterous [adj] *ridiculous, bizarre*
absurd, asinine, crazy, excessive, exorbitant, extravagant, extreme, fantastic, far-out*, foolish, harebrained*, impossible, incredible, insane, irrational, laughable, ludicrous, monstrous, nonsensical, out of the question*, outrageous, senseless, shocking, silly, stupid, taking the cake*, thick*, too much*, unbelievable, unreasonable, unthinkable, unusual, wacky*, wild; SEE CONCEPTS 529,548,552

prerequisite [n] *condition, necessity*
essential, imperative, must, need, postulate, precondition, qualification, requirement, requisite, sine qua non; SEE CONCEPTS 646,709

prerequisite [adj] *necessary*
called for, essential, expedient, imperative, important, indispensable, mandatory, necessitous, needful, obligatory, of the essence, required, requisite, vital; SEE CONCEPT 546

prerogative [n] *right, privilege*
advantage, appanage, authority, birthright, choice, claim, droit, due, exemption, immunity, liberty, perquisite, sanction, title; SEE CONCEPT 376

presage [n] *prediction, indication*
apprehension, apprehensiveness, augury, auspice, bodement, boding, forecast, foretoken, forewarning, harbinger, intimation, misgiving, omen, portent, premonition, prenotion, presentiment, prognostic, prognostication, prophecy, sign, warning; SEE CONCEPTS 410,529,689

presage [v] *predict or have a feeling*
adumbrate, announce, augur, betoken, bode, divine, feel, forebode, forecast, forerun, foresee, foreshadow, foreshow, foretell, foretoken, forewarn, harbinger, herald, intuit, omen, point to, portend, preindicate, prognosticate, promise,

prophesy, sense, signify, soothsay, vaticinate, warn; SEE CONCEPTS 34,70,118

prescribe [v] *stipulate action to be taken*
appoint, assign, choose, command, decide, decree, define, designate, determine, dictate, direct, enjoin, establish, fix, guide, impose, lay down, ordain, order, pick out, require, rule, select, set, settle, specify, write prescription; SEE CONCEPTS 50,60,61,88

prescription [n] *formula, medicine*
decree, direction, drug, edict, instruction, law, mixture, ordinance, preparation, prescript, recipe, regulation, remedy, rule; SEE CONCEPTS 274,307, 311,318

presence [n1] *occupancy, attendance*
being, companionship, company, existence, habitation, inhabitance, latency, occupation, omnipresence, potentiality, residence, subsistence, ubiety, ubiquity, whereabouts; SEE CONCEPTS 407,518,710

presence [n2] *appearance, demeanor*
address, air, aspect, aura, bearing, behavior, carriage, comportment, deportment, ease, look, mien, personality, poise, port, seeming, self-assurance, set; SEE CONCEPTS 411,673,716

presence [n3] *closeness, vicinity*
immediate circle, nearness, neighborhood, propinquity, proximity; SEE CONCEPT 747

presence [n4] *ghost*
apparition, manifestation, shade, specter, spirit, supernatural being, wraith; SEE CONCEPT 370

presence [n5] *composure of mind*
acumen, alertness, aplomb, calmness, cool, coolness, imperturbability, levelheadedness, quickness, sangfroid, self-assurance, self-command, self-composure, self-possession, sensibility, sobriety, watchfulness, wits; SEE CONCEPTS 410,657

present [n1] *existing time*
here and now, instant, nonce, now, present moment, the time being, this day, this time, today; SEE CONCEPTS 802,807,815

present [n2] *gift*
benefaction, benevolence, boon, bounty, compliment, donation, endowment, favor, gifting, giveaway, goodie*, grant, gratuity, handout, largess, lump, offering, stake, write-off; SEE CONCEPT 337

present [adj1] *existing; at this time*
ad hoc, already, at this moment, begun, being, coeval, commenced, contemporaneous, contemporary, current, even now, existent, extant, for the time being, going on, immediate, in duration, in process, instant, just now, modern, nowadays, present-day, prompt, started, today, topical, under consideration, up-to-date; SEE CONCEPT 820

present [adj2] *nearby, here*
accounted for, at hand, attendant, available, existent, in attendance, in view, made the scene*, near, on board, on deck, on hand, on-the-spot, ready, show up, there, there with bells on*, within reach; SEE CONCEPTS 539,583

present [v1] *introduce; demonstrate*
acquaint, adduce, advance, allege, cite, declare, display, do, do the honors, exhibit, expose, expound, extend, fix up, get together, give, give an introduction, hand, imply, infer, intimate, lay, make a pitch*, make known, manifest, mount, offer, open to view, perform, pitch, pose, produce, proffer, proposition, put forward, put on,

raise, recount, relate, roll out, show, stage, state, submit, suggest, tender, trot out; SEE CONCEPTS 66,261

present [v2] *give, hand over*
award, bestow, come up with, confer, devote, donate, entrust, furnish, gift, give away, grant, hand out, kick in*, lay on*, offer, proffer, put as disposal, put forth; SEE CONCEPTS 67,108

presentable [adj] *respectable; fit to be seen*
acceptable, attractive, becoming, decent, fit, good enough*, not bad*, okay*, passable, prepared, proper, satisfactory, suitable, tolerable; SEE CONCEPTS 558,579

presentation [n] *performance; something given, displayed*
act, appearance, arrangement, award, bestowal, coming out, conferral, debut, delivering, delivery, demonstration, display, dog and pony show*, donation, exhibition, exposition, giving, introduction, investiture, knockdown*, launch, launching, offering, overture, pitch, present, production, proposal, proposition, reception, remembrance, rendition, representation, sales pitch*, show, staging, submission; SEE CONCEPTS 261,263,337

presentiment [n] *anticipation, expectation*
apprehension, apprehensiveness, discomposure, disquietude, disturbance, fear, feeling, feeling in bones*, foreboding, forecast, forethought, funny feeling*, handwriting on wall*, hunch, intuition, misgiving, perturbation, premonition, prenotion, presage, sinking feeling, vibes*, worriment; SEE CONCEPTS 410,532,689

presently [adv] *in a short while*
anon, before long, before you know it, by and by, directly, down the line*, down the pike*, down the road*, immediately, in a minute, in a moment, in a short time, now, nowadays, pretty soon, shortly, soon, today, without delay; SEE CONCEPT 820

preservation [n] *maintenance, protection*
canning, care, conservancy, conservation, curing, defense, evaporation, freezing, guard, guardianship, keeping, perpetuation, pickling, preserval, refrigeration, safeguard, safeguarding, safekeeping, safety, salvation, saving, security, shield, storage, support, sustentation, tanning, upholding, ward; SEE CONCEPTS 134,170,202,257

preserve [v] *care for, maintain; continue*
bottle, can, conserve, cure, defend, evaporate, freeze, guard, keep, keep up, mothball*, mummify, perpetuate, pickle, process, protect, put up, refrigerate, retain, safeguard, save, season, secure, shelter, shield, store, sustain, uphold; SEE CONCEPTS 134,170,202

preserves [n] *thickened fruit prepared for storage and use as a condiment*
confection, confiture, conserve, extract, gelatin, jam, jell, jelly, marmalade, pectin, spread, sweet; SEE CONCEPTS 457,461

preside [v] *be in authority*
administer, advise, be at the head of*, be in driver's seat*, call the signals*, carry on, chair, conduct, control, direct, do the honors, govern, handle, head, head up, keep, lead, manage, officiate, operate, ordain, oversee, pull the strings*, run, run the show*, sit on top of*, supervise; SEE CONCEPTS 94,117

press [n1] *people or person working in communications*
columnist, correspondent, editor, fourth estate*,

interviewer, journalism, journalist, magazine, media, newspaper, newsperson, paper, periodical, photographer, publicist, publisher, reporter, writer; SEE CONCEPTS *280,349,356*

press [*n2*] *horde, large group*
bunch, crowd, crush, drove, flock, herd, host, mob, multitude, pack, push, swarm, throng; SEE CONCEPT *432*

press [*n3*] *strain, pressure*
bustle, confusion, demand, hassle, haste, hurry, rush, stress, urgency; SEE CONCEPTS *230,674*

press [*v1*] *push on with force*
bear down, bear heavily, bulldoze*, clasp, compress, condense, constrain, crowd, crush, cumber, depress, embrace, enfold, express, finish, flatten, force down, hold, hug, impel, iron, jam, level, mangle, mash, mass, move, pack, pile, pin down, ram, reduce, scrunch, shove, smooth, squash, squeeze, squish, steam, stuff, thrust, unwrinkle, weigh; SEE CONCEPTS *191,208*

press [*v2*] *pressure, trouble*
afflict, assail, beg, beset, besiege, buttonhole*, come at, compel, constrain, demand, depress, disquiet, enjoin, entreat, exhort, force, harass, implore, importune, insist on, lean on, oppress, petition, plague, plead, pressurize, push, railroad*, sadden, sell, squeeze, sue, supplicate, torment, urge, vex, weigh down, work on; worry; SEE CONCEPT *14*

pressing [*adj*] *important; urgent*
acute, burning, claiming, clamant, clamorous, compelling, constraining, critical, crucial, crying, demanding, dire, distressing, exacting, exigent, forcing, heat-on*, high-priority, hurry-up*, immediate, imperative, importunate, insistent, instant, life-and-death*, obliging, requiring, serious, vital; SEE CONCEPTS *548,568*

pressure [*n1*] *physical force, weight*
burden, compressing, compression, crushing, encumbrance, heaviness, load, mass, shear, squeeze, squeezing, strain, strength, stress, tension, thrust; SEE CONCEPTS *641,734*

pressure [*n2*] *demand, difficulty*
adversity, affliction, albatross*, burden, choke, clout, coercion, compulsion, confinement, constraint, crunch, discipline, distress, drag, duress, exigency, force, full court press*, hardship, hassle, heat, hurry, influence, inside track*, load, misfortune, necessity, obligation, persuasion, power, press, pressure cooker*, pull, requirement, strain, stress, sway, tension, trouble, unnaturalness, urgency, weight; SEE CONCEPTS *14,666,674,687*

pressure [*v*] *bother, urge*
come at, compel, constrain, drive, impel, insist, lean on*, politick, press, push, push around*, rush, sell, squeeze, twist arm*, work over*; SEE CONCEPTS *7,14,19,22*

prestige [*n*] *fame, influence*
authority, cachet, celebrity, consequence, control, credit, dignity, distinction, éclat*, eminence, esteem, fame, illustriousness, importance, kudos*, position, power, preeminence, prominence, prominency, rank, regard, renown, reputation, repute, standing, state, stature, status, sway, weight; SEE CONCEPTS *388,668*

prestigious [*adj*] *famous, influential*
celebrated, distinguished, eminent, esteemed, exalted, famed, great, illustrious, important, impos-

ing, impressive, notable, prominent, renowned, reputable, respected; SEE CONCEPTS *555,568*

presumably [*adv*] *likely, reasonably*
apparently, assumably, credible, doubtless, doubtlessly, hypothetically, in all likelihood, in all probability, indubitably, it would seem, most likely, on the face of it, presumptively, probably, seemingly, supposedly, surely, theoretically, unquestionably; SEE CONCEPTS *544,552*

presume [*v1*] *make assumption; believe*
assume, bank on*, be afraid, conclude, conjecture, consider, count on, depend, figure, gather, guess, infer, jump the gun*, posit, postulate, predicate, premise, presuppose, pretend, rely, speculate, suppose, surmise, take for granted, take it, think, trust; SEE CONCEPTS *12,26,28*

presume [*v2*] *dare; take the liberty*
go so far, have the audacity, impose, infringe, intrude, make bold, undertake, venture; SEE CONCEPT *87*

presumption [*n1*] *belief, hypothesis*
anticipation, apriorism, assumption, basis, chance, conjecture, grounds, guess, likelihood, opinion, plausibility, posit, postulate, postulation, premise, presupposition, probability, reason, shot, shot in the dark*, sneaking suspicion*, stab, supposition, surmise, suspicion, thesis; SEE CONCEPT *689*

presumption [*n2*] *forwardness, daring*
arrogance, assurance, audacity, boldness, brashness, brass, cheek*, chutzpah*, confidence, contumely, effrontery, gall, impudence, insolence, nerve, presumptuousness, rudeness, temerity; SEE CONCEPT *633*

presumptuous [*adj*] *self-confident*
arrogant, audacious, bold, cheeky*, conceited, confident, contumelious, egotistic, foolhardy, forward, fresh, insolent, overconfident, overfamiliar, overweening, pompous, presuming, pretentious, pushy, rash, rude, self-assertive, self-assured, self-satisfied, smug, supercilious, uppity*; SEE CONCEPTS *401,542*

pretend [*v1*] *fake, falsify*
act, affect, allege, assume, be deceitful, beguile, be hypocritical, bluff, cheat, claim, claim falsely, counterfeit, cozen, deceive, delude, dissemble, dissimulate, dupe, fake out*, feign, fish*, fool, fudge*, hoodwink*, impersonate, jazz*, jive*, lay claim*, let on*, make out*, malinger, masquerade, mislead, pass off*, pass oneself off as*, profess, purport, put on*, put up a front*, sham*, shuck and jive*, simulate, stonewall*, sucker*, whitewash*; SEE CONCEPTS *59,63*

pretend [*v2*] *play the part of*
act, assume the role, imagine, imitate, impersonate, make as if, make believe, make out like, make up, masquerade, mimic, play, playact, portray, pose, purport, put on a front*, put on airs*, put on an act*, represent, reproduce; SEE CONCEPTS *111,171,292,384*

pretended [*adj*] *alleged; imaginary*
affected, artificial, assumed, avowed, bluffing, bogus, charlatan, cheating, concealed, counterfeit, covered, dissimulated, factitious, fake, false, falsified, feigned, fictitious, impostrous, imposturous, lying, make-believe, masked, mock, ostensible, phony, pretend, professed, pseudo*, purported, put-on*, quack*, sham*, shammed*, simulated, so-called, spurious, supposed; SEE CONCEPTS *545,582*

pretense [n] *falsehood, affected show; cover*
act, acting, affectation, appearance, artifice, charade, claim, cloak, deceit, deception, display, dissimulation, double-dealing*, dumb act*, evasion, excuse, fabrication, facade, fakery, faking, falsification, feigning, gag, guise, insincerity, invention, make-believe, mask, masquerade, misrepresentation, misstatement, ostentation, posing, posturing, pretentiousness, pretext, routine, ruse, schtick*, semblance, sham*, shuffling, simulation, stall, stunt, subterfuge, trickery, veil, veneer, wile; SEE CONCEPTS 59,63,633,716

pretension [n1] *airs, snobbishness*
affectation, big talk*, charade, conceit, disguise, fake*, false front*, front, hypocrisy, ostentation, phony, pomposity, pretentiousness, put-on*, self-importance, show, showboat*, showiness, show-off, snobbery, splash*, vainglory, vanity; SEE CONCEPT 633

pretension [n2] *false claim, assertion of importance*
allegation, ambition, ambitiousness, aspiration, assumption, charade, declaration, demand, disguise, maintenance, make-believe, pageant, pretense, pretext, profession, title; SEE CONCEPTS 278,657

pretentious [adj] *snobbish, conceited*
affected, arty, assuming, aureate, big*, bombastic, chichi*, conspicuous, euphuistic, exaggerated, extravagant, feigned, flamboyant, flashy, flaunting, flowery, gaudy, grandiloquent, grandiose, highfaluting*, high-flown*, high-sounding*, hollow, imposing, inflated, jazzy*, la-di-da*, lofty, magniloquent, mincing, ornate, ostentatious, overambitious, overblown, pompous, puffed up*, put-on*, rhetorical, showy, specious, splashy, stilted, swank, too-too*, tumid, turgid, utopian, vainglorious; SEE CONCEPTS 401,542, 589

preternatural [adj] *unusual, abnormal*
aberrant, anomalous, atypical, deviant, deviative, extraordinary, ghostly, inexplicable, irregular, marvelous, miraculous, mysterious, odd, peculiar, strange, superhuman, superior, supermundane, supernatural, unaccountable, unearthly, unnatural, unrepresentative, untypical; SEE CONCEPT 564

pretext [n] *disguise; alleged reason*
affectation, alibi, appearance, bluff, cleanup, cloak, color*, coloring*, copout*, cover, cover story*, cover-up*, device, excuse, face, feint, fig leaf*, front, guise, mask, masquerade, plea, ploy, pretense, red herring*, routine, ruse, semblance, show, simulation, song and dance*, stall, stratagem, subterfuge, veil*; SEE CONCEPTS 59,661, 716

pretty [adj] *attractive*
appealing, beauteous, beautiful, boss*, charming, cheerful, cher*, comely, cute, dainty, darling, delicate, delightful, dishy*, dreamboat*, elegant, eyeful*, fair, fine, foxy*, good-looking, graceful, handsome, looker, lovely, neat, nice, picture, pleasant, pleasing, pulchritudinous, tasteful; SEE CONCEPT 579

pretty [adv] *considerable; somewhat*
a little, ample, fairly, kind of, large, moderately, more or less, much, notable, pretty much, quite, rather, reasonably, sizable, some, something, sort of, tolerably; SEE CONCEPTS 531,569

prevail [v] *dominate, control*
abound, beat, be common, be current, be prevalent, best, be usual, be victorious, be widespread, carry, come out on top*, command, conquer, domineer, exist generally, gain, get there, go great guns*, go places*, hit pay dirt*, luck out*, make it, make out, master, move out, obtain, overcome, overrule, predominate, preponderate, prove, reign, succeed, take off, triumph, win; SEE CONCEPTS 94,95,141

prevailing [adj] *general, dominant*
all-embracing, by the numbers*, catholic, common, comprehensive, current, customary, ecumenical, established, familiar, fashionable, influential, in style, in vogue, main, operative, ordinary, popular, predominant, predominating, preponderating, prevalent, principal, rampant, regnant, regular, rife, ruling, set, steady, sweeping, universal, usual, widespread, worldwide; SEE CONCEPT 530

prevail upon/prevail on [v] *persuade, influence*
affect, argue into, bring around, convince, crack, dispose, draw, get, get around, impress, incline, induce, promote, prompt, put across, ram down throat*, sell*, suck in*, sway, talk into, win over; SEE CONCEPT 68

prevalent [adj1] *accepted, widespread*
accustomed, common, commonplace, current, customary, established, everyday, extensive, faddy, frequent, general, habitual, in use, latest*, latest word*, leading edge*, natural, new, normal, now*, ongoing, popular, prevailing, rampant, regnant, regular, rife, run-of-the-mill*, state-of-the-art*, stylish, swinging, trendy, typic, typical, ubiquitous, universal, up-to-date, usual, with it*, wonted; SEE CONCEPTS 530,547,589

prevalent [adj2] *governing, superior*
ascendant, compelling, dominant, overbearing, paramount, powerful, predominant, predominate, preponderant, prevailing, regnant, ruling, sovereign, successful; SEE CONCEPTS 536,574

prevaricate [v] *deceive; stretch the truth*
beat around the bush*, beg the question*, belie, cavil, con, distort, dodge, equivocate, evade, exaggerate, fabricate, falsify, fib, garble, hedge, invent, jive*, lie*, misrepresent, misspeak, palter, phony up*, put on*, quibble, shift, shuffle, tergiversate; SEE CONCEPT 63

prevent [v] *keep from happening or continuing*
anticipate, arrest, avert, avoid, baffle, balk, bar, block, check, chill*, cool, cork, counter, counteract, dam, debar, defend against, foil, forbid, forestall, forfend, frustrate, halt, hamper, head off, hinder, hold back, hold off, impede, inhibit, intercept, interdict, interrupt, keep lid on*, limit, nip in the bud*, obstruct, obviate, preclude, prohibit, put an end to, put a stop to, repress, restrain, restrict, retard, rule out, shut out, stave off, stop, thwart, turn aside, ward off; SEE CONCEPT 121

preview [n] *preliminary showing*
examination, preliminary study, research, show, sneak, sneak peek*, survey, viewing; SEE CONCEPTS 263,292,832

previous [adj1] *former, prior*
antecedent, anterior, earlier, erstwhile, ex, foregoing, one-time, past, precedent, preceding, quondam, sometime; SEE CONCEPTS 585,811, 818,820

previous [adj2] *premature*
ahead of, early, inopportune, overearly, oversoon,

precipitate, soon, too early, too soon, unfounded, untimely, unwarranted; SEE CONCEPTS *558,799*

previously [*adv*] *earlier*
ahead, already, ante, antecedently, at one time, away back, a while ago, back, back when, before, beforehand, erstwhile, fore, formerly, forward, heretofore, hitherto, in advance, in anticipation, in days gone by, in the past, long ago, once, one-shot, precedently, then, time was, until now; SEE CONCEPT *820*

prey [*n*] *target of attack*
casualty, chased*, dupe*, game, kill, loot, mark, martyr, mug*, pillage, quarry, quest, raven, spoil, sufferer, underdog, victim; SEE CONCEPTS *394,423*

prey on [*v*] *attack, terrorize*
blackmail, bleed, bully, burden, consume, depredate, devour, distress, eat, exploit, feed on, fleece, haunt, hunt, intimidate, live off, load, oppress, plunder, raid, seize, take advantage of, tax, trouble, victimize, weigh, worry; SEE CONCEPTS *14,86,169*

price [*n1*] *financial value*
amount, appraisal, appraisement, asking price, assessment, barter, bill, bounty, ceiling, charge, compensation, consideration, cost, damage, demand, disbursement, discount, dues, estimate, exaction, expenditure, expense, face value, fare, fee, figure, hire, outlay, output, pay, payment, premium, price, quotation, ransom, rate, reckoning, retail, return, reward, score, sticker*, tab, tariff, ticket, toll, tune*, valuation, wages, wholesale, worth; SEE CONCEPT *329*

price [*n2*] *consequences of action*
cost, expense, penalty, sacrifice, toll; SEE CONCEPT *230*

price [*v*] *assess financial value*
appraise, cost, estimate, evaluate, fix, mark down, mark up, put a price on, rate, reduce, sticker, value; SEE CONCEPT *330*

priceless [*adj1*] *precious, irreplaceable*
beyond price, cherished, collectible, costly, dear, expensive, incalculable, incomparable, inestimable, invaluable, out-of-bounds*, out-of-sight*, prized, rare, rich, treasured, valuable, valued, without price, worth a king's ransom*, worth its weight in gold*; SEE CONCEPTS *334,568*

priceless [*adj2*] *extremely funny*
absurd, amusing, comic, droll, hilarious, humorous, killing, rib-tickling*, ridiculous, riotous, scream, sidesplitting; SEE CONCEPT *267*

prick [*n*] *small hole made by stab*
cut, gash, jab, jag, perforation, pinhole, prickle, puncture, stab, wound; SEE CONCEPT *309*

prick [*v*] *stab, perforate*
bore, cut, drill, enter, hurt, jab, lance, pierce, pink, punch, puncture, slash, slit, smart, spur, sting; SEE CONCEPT *220*

prickly [*adj1*] *thorny or difficult*
annoying, barbed, bothersome, brambly, briery, bristly, complicated, echinated, intricate, involved, knotty, nettlesome, pointed, sharp, spiny, stimulating, ticklish, tricky, troublesome, trying; SEE CONCEPTS *485,565*

prickly [*adj2*] *irritable, bad-tempered*
cantankerous, edgy, fractious, fretful, grumpy, irritable, peevish, petulant, snappish, touchy, waspish; SEE CONCEPT *401*

pride [*n1*] *self-esteem*
amour-propre, delight, dignity, ego, egoism, ego-

tism, ego trip, face, gratification, happiness, honor, joy, pleasure, pridefulness, repletion, satisfaction, self-admiration, self-confidence, self-glorification, self-love, self-regard, self-respect, self-satisfaction, self-sufficiency, self-trust, self-worth, sufficiency; SEE CONCEPT *411*

pride [*n2*] *arrogance, self-importance*
airs, assumption, big-headedness*, cockiness*, conceit, condescension, contumely, disdain, disdainfulness, egoism, egotism, haughtiness, hauteur, hubris, huff, immodesty, insolence, loftiness, narcissism, overconfidence, patronage, pragmatism, presumption, pretension, pretentiousness, proud flesh*, self-exaltation, self-love, smugness, snobbery, superbity, superciliousness, swagger, swelled head*, vainglory, vanity; SEE CONCEPT *633*

pride [*n3*] *treasure; best*
boast, choice, cream, elite, fat, flower*, gem*, glory, jewel*, pick, pride and joy*, prime, prize, top*; SEE CONCEPTS *446,668,688*

pride [*v*] *take pleasure in accomplishment*
be proud, boast, brag, congratulate, crow, exult, felicitate, flatter oneself, gasconade, glory in, hold head high, overbear, pique*, plume*, prance, preen, presume, puff up*, revel in, strut, swagger, swell, vaunt; SEE CONCEPTS *10,633*

priest [*n*] *man who is minister in Roman or Orthodox Catholic church*
clergyperson, cleric, curate, divine, ecclesiastic, elder, father, father confessor, friar, holy man, lama, man of God, man of the cloth*, monk, padre, pontiff, preacher, rector, vicar; SEE CONCEPT *361*

prim [*adj*] *particular, fussy*
blue-nose*, ceremonial, ceremonious, choosy, cleanly, conventional, correct, dapper*, decorous, demure, fastidious, formal, genteel, good, goody-goody*, nice, nit-picking*, orderly, overmodest, polite, precise, priggish, prissy, proper, prudish, puritanical, rigid, shipshape*, spic-and-span*, spruce, stickling, stiff, straight, strait-laced, stuffy*, tidy, uncluttered, upright, Victorian, well-groomed, wooden*; SEE CONCEPTS *401,404*

primarily [*adv1*] *generally; for the most part*
above all, basically, chiefly, especially, essentially, fundamentally, generally, largely, mainly, mostly, on the whole, overall, predominantly, principally; SEE CONCEPTS *531,544,772*

primarily [*adv2*] *in the beginning*
at first, at the start, first and foremost, from the start, initially, in the first place, originally, primitively; SEE CONCEPTS *548,799*

primary/prime [*adj1*] *best, principal*
capital, cardinal, chief, crackerjack*, dominant, excellent, fab*, first, first-class*, greatest, heavy, highest, hot*, leading, main, number one*, paramount, primo*, state-of-the-art*, stellar, top, top-of-the-line*, tough*, world-class*; SEE CONCEPTS *567,574*

primary/prime [*adj2*] *earliest*
aboriginal, beginning, direct, first, firsthand, immediate, initial, original, pioneer, primal, primeval, primitive, primordial, pristine; SEE CONCEPTS *585,799*

primary/prime [*adj3*] *basic, fundamental*
basal, beginning, bottom, central, elemental, elementary, essential, first, foundational, introductory, meat-and-potatoes*, original, primitive, principal, radical, rudimentary, simple, three

pr
pr

prime [n1] *best part of existence*
R's*, ultimate, underivative, underived, underlying; SEE CONCEPTS *549,585*

prime [n1] *best part of existence*
best, best days*, bloom, choice, cream*, elite, fat*, flower*, flowering*, height, heyday, maturity, peak, perfection, pink*, prize, spring, springtime, top, verdure, vitality, zenith; SEE CONCEPT *816*

prime [n2] *beginning; spring*
adolescence, aurora, dawn, daybreak, dew, greenness*, juvenility, morn*, morning, opening, puberty, pubescence, springtime, start, sunrise, sunup, tender years*, vitality, youth, youthfulness; SEE CONCEPTS *817,832*

prime [v] *get ready; prepare*
break in, brief, clue*, coach, cram, excite, fill in, fit, galvanize, groom, inform, innervate, make ready, motivate, move, notify, prep*, provoke, rehearse, stimulate, tell, train; SEE CONCEPTS *7,19,22,35,202*

primeval [adj] *ancient*
earliest, early, first, old, original, prehistoric, primal, primary, primitive, primordial, pristine; SEE CONCEPT *799*

primitive [adj1] *ancient, original*
archaic, basic, earliest, early, elementary, essential, first, fundamental, old, primal, primary, primeval, primordial, pristine, substratal, underivative, underived, underlying, undeveloped, unevolved; SEE CONCEPT *799*

primitive [adj2] *barbaric, crude*
animal, atavistic, austere, barbarian, barbarous, brutish, childlike, fierce, ignorant, naive, natural, nonliterate, preliterate, raw, rough, rude, rudimentary, savage, simple, uncivilized, uncultivated, uncultured, underdeveloped, undeveloped, undomesticated, unlearned, unrefined, unsophisticated, untamed, untaught, untrained, untutored, vestigial, wild; SEE CONCEPTS *406,485*

primordial [adj] *earliest*
basic, early, elemental, first, fundamental, original, prehistoric, primal, primary, prime, primeval, primitive, pristine, radical; SEE CONCEPT *799*

primp [v] *beautify and dress nicely*
deck out*, dress up, fix up, get dressed up, groom, gussy up*, preen, prepare, slick*, smarten, spiff, spruce, titivate; SEE CONCEPTS *162,167,202*

principal [n1] *person in charge of organization, often an educational one*
administrator, boss, chief, dean, director, exec*, head, key player*, lead, leader, preceptor, protagonist, rector, ruler, star, superintendent; SEE CONCEPTS *347,350*

principal [n2] *original amount of property either owned or owed*
assets, capital, capital funds, money; SEE CONCEPT *332*

principal [adj] *most important*
arch, capital, cardinal, champion, chief, controlling, crowning, dominant, essential, first, foremost, greatest, head, highest, incomparable, key, leading, main, mainline, major, matchless, maximum, outstanding, paramount, peerless, predominant, preeminent, premier, prevailing, primary, prime, prominent, second-to-none, sovereign, star, stellar, strongest, supereminent, superior, supreme, transcendent, unapproachable, unequaled, unparalleled, unrivaled; SEE CONCEPTS *568,574*

principally [adv] *mainly*
above all, basically, before anything else, cardi-nally, chiefly, dominantly, eminently, especially, essentially, first and foremost, first of all, for the most part, fundamentally, generally, importantly, in the first place, in the main, largely, materially, mostly, notably, particularly, peculiarly, predominantly, preeminently, prevailingly, prevalently, primarily, substantially, superlatively, supremely, to a great degree, universally, vitally; SEE CONCEPTS *531,544,772*

principle [n1] *law, standard*
assumption, axiom, basis, canon, convention, criterion, dictum, doctrine, dogma, ethic, form, formula, foundation, fundamental, golden rule*, ground, maxim, origin, postulate, precept, prescript, principium, proposition, regulation, rule, source, theorem, truth, usage, verity; SEE CONCEPTS *318,688*

principle/principles [n2] *belief, morality; morals*
attitude, character, code, conduct, conscience, credo, ethic, ethics, faith, ideals, integrity, opinion, policy, probity, rectitude, scruples, sense of duty, sense of honor, system, teaching, tenet, uprightness; SEE CONCEPTS *645,689*

print [n] *publication; something impressed*
black-and-white*, book, characters, composition, copy, edition, engraving, face, font, impress, impression, imprint, indentation, issue, lettering, letters, lithograph, magazine, newspaper, newsprint, periodical, photograph, printed matter, stamp, type, typeface, typescript, typesetting, writing; SEE CONCEPTS *259,265,280*

print [v] *produce writing, impression; reproduce publication*
calligraph, compose, disseminate, engrave, go to press, impress, imprint, issue, let roll, letter, mark, offset, publish, put to bed*, reissue, reprint, run off, set, set type, stamp, strike off; SEE CONCEPTS *174,203,205*

prior [adj] *earlier*
above-mentioned, aforementioned, ahead, antecedent, anterior, before, foregoing, former, forward, past, precedent, preceding, preexistent, preexisting, previous; SEE CONCEPTS *811,812, 818,820*

priority [n] *first concern*
antecedence, arrangement, crash project*, greatest importance, lead, order, precedence, preeminence, preference, prerogative, previousness, rank, right of way*, seniority, superiority, supremacy, transcendence; SEE CONCEPTS *532,668, 727*

prison [n] *residence for incarcerating criminals*
bastille, can*, clink*, confinement, cooler*, dungeon, G*, guardhouse, jail, keep, lockup, pen*, penal institution, penitentiary, reformatory, slammer*, statesville*, stockade, up the river*; SEE CONCEPTS *439,449,516*

prisoner [n] *person jailed for crime; person kept against their will*
captive, chain gang member, con, convict, culprit, detainee, hostage, internee, jailbird*, lag*, lifer*, loser*, tough*, yardbird*; SEE CONCEPT *412*

prissy [adj] *particular and fussy*
epicene, fastidious, finicky, genteel, goody-goody*, goody-two-shoes*, overnice, pansified, persnickety, picky, precious, prim, prim and proper*, prudish, puritanical, sissified, sissy, squeamish, stickling, strait-laced, stuffy*, tight-laced*, Victorian; SEE CONCEPTS *401,404*

privacy [n] *solitude, secrecy*
aloofness, clandestineness, concealment, confidentiality, isolation, one's space, penetralia, privateness, quiet, retirement, retreat, seclusion, separateness, separation, sequestration, solitude; SEE CONCEPTS 388,631,714

private [n] *lowest rank of person enlisted in armed service*
enlisted person, first-class*, GI, infantry, private soldier, sailor, second-class*, soldier; SEE CONCEPT 358

private [adj1] *personal, intimate*
behind the scenes*, clandestine, closet*, close to one's chest*, confidential, discreet, exclusive, hushed, hush-hush*, independent, individual, inside, nonpublic, not open, off the record*, own, particular, privy*, reserved, secret, separate, special, under one's hat*, unofficial; SEE CONCEPTS 267,406

private [adj2] *hidden, isolated*
concealed, discreet, quiet, removed, retired, secluded, secret, separate, sequestered, solitary, withdrawn; SEE CONCEPTS 576,583

privilege [n] *right, due*
advantage, allowance, appanage, appurtenance, authority, authorization, benefit, birthright, boon, chance, charter, claim, concession, entitlement, event, exemption, favor, franchise, freedom, grant, immunity, liberty, license, opportunity, perquisite, prerogative, right, sanction; SEE CONCEPT 376

privileged [adj1] *favored, elite*
advantaged, entitled, honored, indulged, powerful, ruling, special; SEE CONCEPTS 334,574

privileged [adj2] *allowed, exempt*
authorized, chartered, eligible, empowered, entitled, excused, franchised, free, furnished, granted, immune, kosher*, legit*, licensed, okay*, okayed*, palatine, qualified, sanctioned, special, vested; SEE CONCEPT 548

privileged [adj3] *confidential, secret*
exceptional, for eyes only*, inside, not for publication, off the record*, on the QT*, privy, special, top secret, under one's hat*; SEE CONCEPT 267

privy [adj1] *secret*
buried, concealed, confidential, covert, hidden, hush-hush*, obscured, off the record*, personal, private, separate, shrouded, ulterior; SEE CONCEPTS 267,576

privy [adj2] *aware*
acquainted, apprised, cognizant, conscious, informed, in on*, in the know*, private, privileged, wise; SEE CONCEPT 402

prize [n1] *award, winnings*
accolade, acquirement, acquisition, advantage, blue ribbon*, bonus, bounty, cake*, capture, carrot*, championship, citation, crown, decoration, dividend, feather in cap*, first place*, gold*, gold star*, gravy*, guerdon, haul, honor, inducement, jackpot, laurel, loot*, medal, meed, payoff, pickings*, pillage, plum*, plunder*, possession, premium, privilege, purse, recompense, requital, reward, scholarship, spoil, spoils, stakes, strokes*, swag*, title, trophy, windfall; SEE CONCEPTS 337,344,693,710

prize [n2] *goal; best*
aim, ambition, choice, conquest, cream*, desire, elite, fat, flower*, gain, gold*, hope, pick, pride, prime, top*; SEE CONCEPTS 659,709

prize [adj] *best*
award-winning, champion, choice, cream*, elite, fat*, first-class*, first-rate*, outstanding, pick, prime, top, topnotch, winning; SEE CONCEPT 574

prize [v] *value highly*
appreciate, apprize, cherish, count, enshrine, esteem, guard, hold dear, rate, regard highly, set store by*, treasure; SEE CONCEPTS 10,32

probability [n] *likelihood of something happening*
anticipation, chance, chances, conceivability, contingency, credibility, expectation, feasibility, hazard, liability, likeliness, odds, outside chance*, plausibility, possibility, practicability, prayer, presumption, promise, prospect, reasonableness, shot, snowball's chance*, toss-up*; SEE CONCEPT 650

probable [adj] *likely to happen*
apparent, believable, credible, earthly, feasible, illusory, in the cards*, mortal, most likely, odds-on*, ostensible, plausible, possible, presumable, presumed, rational, reasonable, seeming; SEE CONCEPT 552

probably [adv] *likely to happen*
apparently, as likely as not, assumably, as the case may be, believably, dollars to doughnuts*, doubtless, expediently, feasibly, imaginably, in all likelihood, in all probability, like enough, maybe, most likely, no doubt, one can assume, perchance, perhaps, plausibly, possibly, practicably, presumably, presumptively, reasonably, seemingly; SEE CONCEPT 552

probe [n] *investigation*
delving, detection, examination, exploration, fishing expedition*, inquest, inquiry, inquisition, legwork*, probing, quest, research, scrutiny, study, third degree*; SEE CONCEPTS 31,103,216,290

probe [v] *explore, investigate*
ask, catechize, check, check out, check over, check up, delve into, dig, examine, eye, feel around, feel out, go into, inquire, interrogate, look into, look-see, penetrate, pierce, poke, prod, prospect, put out a feeler*, query, quiz, scrutinize, search, sift, sound, sound out, study, test, test the waters*, verify; SEE CONCEPTS 31,103,216

probity [n] *fairness, honesty*
equity, fidelity, goodness, honor, integrity, justice, morality, rectitude, righteousness, rightness, sincerity, trustworthiness, truthfulness, uprightness, virtue, worth; SEE CONCEPTS 411,645

problem [n1] *difficulty; bad situation*
botheration, box*, bugaboo*, can of worms*, complication, count*, crunch*, dilemma, disagreement, dispute, disputed point, doubt, headache*, hitch*, hot water*, issue, mess*, obstacle, pickle*, point at issue*, predicament, quandary, question, scrape*, squeeze*, trouble, worriment; SEE CONCEPTS 666,674

problem [n2] *puzzle, question*
brainteaser*, bugaboo*, cliff-hanger*, conundrum, enigma, example, grabber*, illustration, intricacy, mind-boggler*, mystery, poser*, puzzle, query, riddle, sixty-four thousand dollar question*, stickler, stumper, teaser, twister; SEE CONCEPTS 529,532

problematic [adj] *open to doubt*
ambiguous, arguable, chancy, debatable, disputable, doubtful, dubious, dubitable, enigmatic, iffy*, indecisive, moot, open, precarious, problematical, puzzling, questionable, suspect,

pr
pr

tricky, uncertain, unsettled, up for grabs*; SEE CONCEPT 529

procedure [n] *process, system for accomplishing something*

action, agenda, agendum, channels, conduct, course, custom, daily grind*, fashion, form, formula, game plan*, gimmick, grind, idea, layout, line, maneuver, measure, method, mode, modus operandi, move, nuts and bolts*, operation, performance, plan, policy, polity, practice, proceeding, program, red tape*, routine, scheme, setup, step, strategy, style, the book*, the numbers*, transaction; SEE CONCEPT 6

proceed [v1] *physically or mentally carry on, carry out*

advance, continue, fare, get, get going, get on with, get under way*, go ahead, go on, hie, journey, make a start, march, move on, move out, pass, press on, progress, push on, repair, set in motion, travel, wend; SEE CONCEPTS 43,91

proceed [v2] *flow from; originate*

arise, come, derive, emanate, ensue, extend, follow, head, issue, pass, result, rise, spring, stem; SEE CONCEPTS 179,230,676

proceeding [n] *undertaking, course of action*

act, action, adventure, casualty, circumstance, come off, deed, exercise, experiment, go-down*, goings-on*, happening, incident, maneuver, measure, move, movement, occurrence, operation, performance, procedure, process, step, transaction, venture; SEE CONCEPTS 2,3

proceedings [n] *account, report of event*

affairs, annals, archives, business, dealings, documents, doings*, matters, minutes, records, transactions; SEE CONCEPT 271

proceeds [n] *earnings from business*

gain, gate, handle, income, interest, lucre, produce, product, profit, receipts, result, returns, revenue, reward, split, take, takings, till, yield; SEE CONCEPT 344

process [n] *method; series of actions to achieve result*

action, advance, case, channels*, course, course of action*, development, evolution, fashion, formation, growth, manner, means, measure, mechanism, mode, modus operandi, movement, operation, outgrowth, performance, practice, procedure, proceeding, progress, progression, red tape*, routine, rule, stage, step, suit, system, technique, transaction, trial, unfolding, way, wise, working; SEE CONCEPT 6

process [v] *subject to series of actions to achieve result*

alter, concoct, convert, deal with, dispose of, fulfill, handle, make ready, prepare, refine, take care of, transform, treat; SEE CONCEPT 204

procession [n] *parade, sequence*

advance, autocade, cavalcade, column, consecution, cortege, course, cycle, file, march, motorcade, movement, order, process, run, series, string, succession, train; SEE CONCEPTS 155,727

proclaim [v] *advertise, make known*

affirm, announce, annunciate, blast, blaze, blazon, broadcast, call, circulate, declare, demonstrate, disseminate, enunciate, evidence, evince, exhibit, expound, get on a soapbox*, give out, herald, illustrate, indicate, manifest, mark, ostend, pass the word*, profess, promulgate, publish, shoot off mouth*, shout out, show, sound off, spiel*, spout, spread it around*, stump*,

trumpet*, utter, vent, ventilate, voice; SEE CONCEPTS 49,60

proclamation [n] *advertisement, announcement*

broadcast, declaration, decree, edict, manifesto, notice, notification, promulgation, pronouncement, pronunciamento*, publication; SEE CONCEPTS 271,278

proclivity [n] *inclination, tendency*

bent*, bias, cup of tea*, disposition, druthers, facility, flash*, groove*, inclining, leaning, liableness, penchant, predilection, predisposition, proneness, propensity, thing for*, type, weakness; SEE CONCEPTS 20,32,411

procrastinate [v] *delay, put off doing*

adjourn, be dilatory, cool*, dally, dawdle, defer, drag, drag one's feet*, give the run around*, goldbrick*, hang fire*, hesitate, hold off, lag*, let slide, linger, loiter, pause, play a waiting game*, play for time*, poke*, postpone, prolong, protract, retard, shilly-shally*, stall, stay, suspend, tarry, temporize, wait; SEE CONCEPTS 121,237, 681

procreate [v] *reproduce*

beget, breed, conceive, create, engender, father, generate, get, give birth to, hatch, impregnate, make, mother, multiply, originate, parent, produce, progenerate, proliferate, propagate, sire, spawn; SEE CONCEPTS 173,251,374

procure [v] *acquire, obtain*

annex, appropriate, bring around, buy, buy out, buy up, come by, compass, cop*, corral, draw, earn, effect, find, gain, get, get hold of, grab, have, induce, land*, latch on to, lay hands on, make a haul*, manage to get*, persuade, pick up, prevail upon, promote, purchase, score, secure, solicit, wangle, win; SEE CONCEPTS 68,120,327

prod [v1] *poke at*

crowd, dig, drive, elbow, goose, jab, jog, nudge, press, prick, punch, push, shove; SEE CONCEPT 208

prod [v2] *urge, incite*

crowd*, egg on*, excite, exhort, goad, goose*, impel, instigate, jog memory, motivate, move, pique, prick, prompt, propel, provoke, push, remind, rouse, sic*, sound, spark, spur, stimulate, stir up, trigger, turn on; SEE CONCEPTS 7,19,22,242

prodigal [n] *person who spends a lot*

big spender*, compulsive shopper*, deep pockets*, dissipator, high roller*, profligate, spender, spendthrift, sport, squanderer, waster, wastrel; SEE CONCEPTS 348,412

prodigal [adj1] *wasteful*

dissipated, excessive, extravagant, immoderate, improvident, intemperate, lavish, profligate, reckless, spendthrift, squandering, wanton; SEE CONCEPTS 401,560

prodigal [adj2] *luxurious, profuse*

abundant, bounteous, bountiful, copious, exuberant, lavish, lush, luxuriant, moneyed, munificent, opulent, riotous, sumptuous, superabundant, teeming; SEE CONCEPTS 334,781

prodigious [adj] *huge, enormous*

big, colossal*, fantastic, giant, gigantic, gross, Herculean*, immeasurable, immense, inordinate, jumbo*, king-size*, large, mammoth, massive, mighty, monstrous, monumental, mortal, stupendous, towering, tremendous, vast; SEE CONCEPTS 773,781

prodigious [adj2] *extraordinary, fabulous*
abnormal, amazing, astonishing, astounding, bad, exceptional, fab*, fantastic, heavy, impressive, marvelous, miraculous, out-of-this-world*, phenomenal, preternatural, remarkable, spectacular, staggering, startling, state-of-the-art*, striking, stupendous, surprising, unreal, unusual, utmost, wonderful; SEE CONCEPTS 567,572,574

prodigy [n] *person or thing that is extraordinary*
brain*, child genius, curiosity, enormity, freak*, genius, intellect, marvel, mastermind, miracle, monster, natural, one in a million*, phenomenon, portent, rare bird*, rarity, sensation, spectacle, stunner, talent, whiz*, whiz kid*, wizard, wonder, wonder child, wunderkind; SEE CONCEPTS 416,671,706

produce [n] *fruit and vegetables*
crop, fruitage, goods, greengrocery, harvest, outcome, outgrowth, outturn, production, yield; SEE CONCEPTS 426,429,431,457,461

produce [v1] *generate, create*
afford, assemble, author, bear, beget, blossom, breed, bring forth, bring out, build, come through, compose, conceive, construct, contribute, cultivate, deliver, design, develop, devise, effectuate, engender, erect, fabricate, fetch, flower, form, frame, furnish, give, give birth, give forth, imagine, invent, make, manufacture, multiply, offer, originate, parent, present, procreate, propagate, provide, put together, render, reproduce, return, show fruit, supply, turn out, write, yield; SEE CONCEPTS 173,205,251,374

produce [v2] *cause, effect*
beget, breed, bring about, draw on, engender, generate, get up, give rise to, hatch, induce, make, make for*, muster, occasion, provoke, result in, secure, set off, work up; SEE CONCEPT 242

produce [v3] *demonstrate, show*
advance, bring forward, bring to light, display, exhibit, offer, present, put forward, set forth, unfold; SEE CONCEPT 261

produce [v4] *put on a public performance*
act, come through, direct, do, exhibit, make, mount, percolate, perform, perk, play, present, pull off*, show, stage; SEE CONCEPTS 292,324

product [n] *result or goods created*
aftermath, amount, artifact, blend, brand, brew, by-product, commodity, compound, concoction, confection, consequence, contrivance, creation, crop, decoction, device, effect, emolument, fabrication; fruit, gain, handiwork, invention, issue, legacy, line, manufacture, merchandise, offshoot, outcome, outgrowth, output, preparation, produce, production, profit, realization, result, returns, spinoff, stock, synthetic, upshot, work, yield; SEE CONCEPTS 230,338

production [n] *creating of goods, result*
assembly, authoring, bearing, blossoming, construction, creation, direction, elongation, engendering, extention, fabrication, formulation, fructification, generation, giving, lengthening, making, management, manufacture, manufacturing, origination, preparation, presentation, producing, prolongation, protraction, provision, rendering, reproduction, return, staging, yielding; SEE CONCEPT 205

productive [adj] *fruitful, creative*
advantageous, beneficial, constructive, dynamic, effective, energetic, fecund, fertile, gainful, generative, gratifying, inventive, plentiful, produc-ing, profitable, prolific, rewarding, rich, teeming, useful, valuable, vigorous, worthwhile; SEE CONCEPTS 537,542,560

productivity [n] *output, work rate*
abundance, capacity, fecundity, fertility, mass production, potency, production, productiveness, richness, yield; SEE CONCEPT 630

profane [adj] *immoral, crude, disrespectful of religion*
abusive, atheistic, blasphemous, coarse, dirty*, filthy*, foul, godless, heathen, idolatrous, impious, impure, indecent, infidel, irreligious, irreverent, irreverential, mundane, nasty, obscene, pagan, profanatory, raunchy, sacrilegious, sinful, smutty*, temporal, transient, transitory, unconsecrated, ungodly, unhallowed, unholy, unsanctified, vulgar, wicked, worldly; SEE CONCEPTS 267,401,545

profane [v] *defile, desecrate*
abuse, be evil, befoul, blaspheme, commit sacrilege, commit sin, contaminate, curse, cuss, damn, darn, debase, despoil, do wrong, flame, hoodoo*, misuse, mock, mudsling*, pervert, pollute, prostitute, put double whammy on*, revile, scorn, swear, talk dirty*, tar, trash, vice, violate, vitiate, voodoo*; SEE CONCEPTS 44,52,58,63

profanity [n] *foul language*
abuse, blasphemy, curse, cursing, cuss, cuss word, dirty language*, dirty name*, dirty word*, execration, four-letter word*, impiety, imprecation, irreverence, malediction, no-no*, obscenity, profaneness, sacrilege, swearing, swearword, taboo; SEE CONCEPTS 278,645

profess [v] *declare, assert*
acknowledge, act as if, admit, affirm, allege, announce, asseverate, aver, avouch, avow, blow hot air*, certify, claim, come out*, confess, confirm, constate, croon, cross heart*, depose, dissemble, fake, feign, get off chest*, get on soapbox*, maintain, make out, open up*, own, own up*, predicate, pretend, proclaim, purport, say so*, sing*, soapbox*, spiel*, spout*, state, stump*, swear on bible*, swear up and down*, talk big*, vouch; SEE CONCEPTS 49,63

profession [n1] *line of work requiring academic or practical preparation*
art, avocation, berth, billet, biz*, business, calling, career, chosen work, concern, craft, dodge*, employment, engagement, field, game*, handicraft, lifework, line*, line of work*, métier, occupation, office, position, post, pursuit, rat race*, role, service, situation, slot*, specialty, sphere, thing*, trade, undertaking, vocation, walk of life*; SEE CONCEPT 360

profession [n2] *declaration*
acknowledgment, affirmation, assertion, attestation, avowal, claim, confession, pretense, statement, testimony, vow; SEE CONCEPT 278

professional [n] *person prepared for work by extended study or practice*
adept, artist, artiste, authority, brain*, egghead*, expert, hotshot*, old hand*, old pro*, old warhorse*, phenom, powerhouse, pro, proficient, pundit, shark, specialist, star, superstar, virtuoso, whiz*, whiz kid*, wizard; SEE CONCEPTS 347,348

professional [adj] *skilled, trained*
able, ace, acknowledged, adept, competent, crackerjack*, efficient, experienced, expert, finished, knowing one's stuff*, known, learned, li-

pr
pr

censed, on the ball*, polished, practiced, proficient, qualified, sharp, skillful, slick*, there*, up to speed*, well-qualified; SEE CONCEPTS 326,402,527,528

professor [n] *person who teaches college courses*
assistant, brain*, educator, egghead*, faculty member, fellow, instructor, lecturer, pedagogue, principal, prof*, pundit, quant*, rocket scientist*, sage, savant, teacher, tutor; SEE CONCEPT 350

proffer [v] *suggest, offer*
extend, gift, give, hand, hit on, hold out, make a pitch*, pose, present, propose, proposition, propound, submit, tender, volunteer; SEE CONCEPTS 66,67,75

proficiency [n] *ability, skillfulness*
accomplishment, advance, advancement, aptitude, chops, competence, dexterity, efficiency, expertise, expertness, facility, formula, green thumb*, headway*, knack*, know-how*, knowledge, learning, makings, mastery, moxie*, oil*, progress, right stuff*, savvy*, skill, stuff, talent, what it takes*; SEE CONCEPTS 409,630,706

proficient [adj] *able, skilled*
accomplished, adept, apt, capable, clever, competent, consummate, conversant, crack*, crackerjack*, drilled, effective, effectual, efficient, exercised, experienced, expert, finished, gifted, on the beam*, phenom, pro, qualified, savvy*, sharp, skillful, slick*, talented, trained, up to speed*, versed, whiz*, with it*; SEE CONCEPTS 402,527,528

profile [n1] *drawing of outline*
contour, delineation, figuration, figure, form, likeness, line, lineament, lineation, portrait, shadow, shape, side view, silhouette, sketch; SEE CONCEPTS 259,625

profile [n2] *description, characterization*
analysis, biography, character sketch, chart, diagram, review, sketch, study, survey, thumbnail sketch, vignette, vita; SEE CONCEPTS 268,283

profit [n] *gain*
accumulation, acquisition, advancement, advantage, aggrandizement, augmentation, avail, benefit, bottom line*, cleanup, earnings, emoluments, gate*, goods*, gravy*, gross, harvest, income, interest, killing, lucre, net, output, outturn, percentage, proceeds, product, production, receipt, receipts, remuneration, return, revenue, saving, skim*, split*, surplus, take*, takings*, turnout, use, value, velvet*, winnings, yield; SEE CONCEPTS 332,344,693

profit [v] *gain; get or give an advantage*
aid, avail, benefit, be of advantage, better, capitalize on, cash in on, clear, contribute, earn, exploit, help, improve, learn from, make a haul*, make a killing*, make capital, make good use of*, make it big*, make money, make the most of*, pay, pay off, promote, prosper, put to good use*, realize, reap the benefit*, recover, score, serve*, stand in good stead*, take advantage of, thrive, turn to advantage, use, utilize, work for*; SEE CONCEPTS 110,124,330,693

profitable [adj] *advantageous; money-making*
assisting, beneficial, commercial, conducive, contributive, cost-effective, effective, effectual, favorable, fruitful, gainful, going*, good, instrumental, in the black*, lucrative, paid off, paying, paying well, practical, pragmatic, productive, remunerative, rewarding, self-sustaining, serviceable, successful, sustaining, sweet*, use-

ful, valuable, well-paying, worthwhile; SEE CONCEPTS 334,537,572

profligate [n] *person who is immoral*
debauchee, degenerate, dissipater, good-for-nothing*, lecher, libertine, nighthawk*, no-good*, old goat*, operator*, prodigal, rake, reprobate, roué, swinger, waster, wastrel; SEE CONCEPT 412

profligate [adj1] *immoral, corrupt*
abandoned, debauched, degenerate, depraved, dissipated, dissolute, iniquitous, lax, lewd, libertine, licentious, loose, promiscuous, reprobate, shameless, unprincipled, vicious, vitiated, wanton, wicked, wild; SEE CONCEPT 545

profligate [adj2] *wasteful*
extravagant, immoderate, improvident, lavish, prodigal, reckless, spendthrift, squandering; SEE CONCEPTS 334,401

profound [adj1] *intellectual, thoughtful*
abstruse, acroamatic, deep, difficult, discerning, enlightened, erudite, esoteric, heavy*, hermetic, informed, intellectual, intelligent, knowing, knowledgeable, learned, mysterious, occult, Orphic, penetrating, philosophical, recondite, reflective, sagacious, sage, scholarly, secret, serious, shrewd, skilled, subtle, thorough, weighty, wise; SEE CONCEPTS 402,529

profound [adj2] *bottomless*
abysmal, buried, cavernous, deep, fathomless, subterranean, yawning; SEE CONCEPT 777

profound [adj3] *intense; emotional*
abject, absolute, acute, consummate, deep, deeply felt, deep-seated, exhaustive, extensive, extreme, far-reaching, great, hard, heartfelt, heartrending, hearty, keen, out-and-out*, pronounced, sincere, thorough, total, utter; SEE CONCEPTS 403,531,569

profuse [adj] *abundant, excessive*
abounding, alive with*, ample, aplenty, bounteous, bountiful, copious, crawling with*, dime a dozen*, extravagant, extreme, exuberant, fulsome, galore, generous, immoderate, lavish, liberal, lush, luxuriant, no end*, openhanded, opulent, overflowing, plentiful, plenty, prodigal, profusive, prolific, riotous, sumptuous, superfluous, swarming, teeming, thick with*, unstinting; SEE CONCEPTS 762,781

progeny [n] *offspring*
begats, breed, children, descendants, family, get*, issue, kids*, lineage, posterity, progeniture, race, scions, seed, stock, young; SEE CONCEPTS 296,414

prognosis [n] *forecast*
cast, diagnosis, expectation, foretelling, guess, prediction, prevision, prognostication, projection, prophecy, speculation, surmise; SEE CONCEPTS 274,689

prognosticate [v] *predict, foretell*
adumbrate, augur, betoken, call it*, crystal-ball*, divine, forebode, forecast, foreshadow, harbinger, have a hunch*, herald, make book*, point to, portend, presage, prophesy, read, see coming*, soothsay, vaticinate; SEE CONCEPT 70

program [n1] *agenda, list*
affairs, appointments, arrangements, bill, bulletin, business, calendar, card, catalog, chores, curriculum, details, docket, happenings, index, lineup, listing, meetings, memoranda, necessary acts*, order of business*, order of events*, order of the day*, plan, plans, preparations, record,

schedule, series of events, slate, syllabus, things to do*, timetable; SEE CONCEPTS *281,283*

program [*n2*] *scheme, plan*
course, design, instructions, line, order, plan of action, policy, polity, procedure, project, sequence; SEE CONCEPTS *274,660*

program [*n3*] *performance in medium*
broadcast, presentation, production, show; SEE CONCEPT *263*

program [*v*] *plan out; supply instructions*
arrange, bill, book, budget, calculate, compile, compute, design, draft, edit, engage, enter, estimate, feed, figure, formulate, get on line*, itemize, lay on, lay out, line up, list, map out, pencil in*, poll, prearrange, prioritize, process, register, schedule, set, set up, slate, work out; SEE CONCEPTS *36,60,84,384*

progress [*n*] *advancement, gain*
advance, amelioration, anabasis, betterment, boost, break, breakthrough, buildup, course, dash, development, evolution, evolvement, expedition, flowering, growth, headway, hike, impetus, improvement, increase, journey, lunge, march, momentum, motion, movement, ongoing, pace, passage, process, procession, proficiency, progression, promotion, rate, rise, step forward, stride, tour, unfolding, voyage, way; SEE CONCEPTS *704,706*

progress [*v1*] *move forward*
advance, continue, cover ground*, dash, edge, forge ahead, gain ground, get along, get on, go forward, keep going, lunge, make headway*, make strides*, move on, proceed, shoot, speed, travel; SEE CONCEPTS *149,159*

progress [*v2*] *improve, advance*
ameliorate, become better, better, blossom, boost, develop, gain, grow, increase, make first rate, mature, shape up, straighten up, truck, turn over new leaf*, upgrade; SEE CONCEPT *700*

progressive [*adj*] *liberal; growing*
accelerating, advanced, advancing, avant-garde*, bleeding-heart*, broad, broad-minded, continuing, continuous, developing, dynamic, enlightened, enterprising, escalating, forward-looking, go-ahead*, gradual, graduated, increasing, intensifying, left*, left of center*, lenient, modern, ongoing, onward, open-minded, radical, reformist, revolutionary, tolerant, up-and-coming*, up-to-date, wide; SEE CONCEPTS *542,544*

prohibit [*v*] *make impossible; stop*
ban, block, bottle up*, box in*, bring to screeching halt*, constrain, cool*, cork*, debar, disallow, enjoin, forbid, forfend, freeze*, gridlock, halt, hamper, hang up*, hinder, hold up, impede, inhibit, interdict, jam up*, keep lid on*, kill, lock up, nix, obstruct, outlaw, pass on*, preclude, prevent, proscribe, put a lock on*, put a stopper in*, put chill on*, put down, put half nelson on*, restrain, restrict, rule out, shut out, spike*, stymie*, taboo*, throw cold water on*, tie up*, veto, zing*; SEE CONCEPTS *50,88,121,130,317*

prohibited [*adj*] *forbidden*
banned, barred, closed down, contraband, crooked*, illegal, illicit, no-no*, not allowed, not approved, off limits*, out of bounds*, out of line*, proscribed, refused, restricted, shady*, taboo, verboten, vetoed, wildcat*; SEE CONCEPTS *554,576*

prohibition [*n*] *ban, forbiddance*
bar, constraint, disallowance, don't*, embargo,

exclusion, injunction, interdict, interdiction, negation, no-no*, obstruction, off limits*, out of bounds*, prevention, proscription, refusal, repudiation, restriction, taboo, temperance, veto; SEE CONCEPTS *121,130,652,691*

prohibitive [*adj*] *restrictive; beyond one's financial means*
conditional, excessive, exorbitant, expensive, extortionate, forbidding, high-priced, limiting, preposterous, preventing, prohibiting, proscriptive, repressive, restraining, sky-high*, steep*, suppressive; SEE CONCEPTS *334,554*

project [*n*] *undertaking, work*
activity, adventure, affair, aim, assignment, baby*, blueprint*, business, concern, deal, design, enterprise, exploit, feat, game plan, intention, job, matter, occupation, outline, pet*, plan, program, proposal, proposition, scheme, setup, strategy, task, thing*, venture; SEE CONCEPTS *324,349,362*

project [*v1*] *plan*
arrange, blueprint, calculate, cast, chart, conceive, contemplate, contrive, delineate, design, devise, diagram, draft, envisage, envision, estimate, extrapolate, feature, forecast, frame, gauge, image, imagine, intend, map out, outline, predetermine, predict, propose, purpose, reckon, scheme, see, think, vision, visualize; SEE CONCEPTS *28,36,37,70*

project [*v2*] *bulge, hang out*
be conspicuous, beetle, be prominent, extend, hang over, jut, lengthen, overhang, poke, pop out, pout, prolong, protrude, protuberate, push out, stand out, stick out, stretch out, thrust out; SEE CONCEPT *747*

project [*v3*] *throw, discharge*
cast, fling, heave, hurl, launch, pitch, propel, shoot, transmit; SEE CONCEPTS *179,222*

projection [*n1*] *bulge, overhang*
bump, bunch, eaves, extension, hook, jut, knob, ledge, outthrust, point, prolongation, prominence, protrusion, protuberance, ridge, rim, shelf, sill, spine, spur, step, swelling; SEE CONCEPTS *471,509,513*

projection [*n2*] *prediction*
calculation, computation, estimate, estimation, extrapolation, forecast, guess, prognostication, reckoning; SEE CONCEPTS *28,278*

proliferate [*v*] *increase quickly*
breed, burgeon, engender, escalate, expand, generate, grow rapidly, multiply, mushroom*, procreate, propagate, reproduce, run riot*, snowball*; SEE CONCEPT *780*

prolific [*adj*] *fruitful, productive*
abounding, abundant, bountiful, breeding, copious, creative, fecund, fertile, generating, generative, luxuriant, profuse, proliferant, rank, reproducing, reproductive, rich, spawning, swarming, teeming, yielding; SEE CONCEPTS *485,542*

prolong [*v*] *extend, draw out*
carry on, continue, delay, drag one's feet*, drag out*, hold, hold up, increase, lengthen, let it ride*, make longer, pad*, perpetuate, protract, spin out*, stall, stretch, stretch out; SEE CONCEPTS *239,250*

prominence [*n*] *something that sticks out*
bulge, bump, cliff, conspicuousness, crag, crest, elevation, eminence, headland, height, high point, jutting, markedness, mound, pinnacle, projection,

pr
pr

promontory, protrusion, protuberance, rise, spur, swelling, tor; SEE CONCEPTS 513,836

prominence [n2] *distinction, outstandingness*
celebrity, eminence, fame, greatness, illustriousness, importance, influence, kudos*, name, notability, precedence, preeminence, prestige, rank, renown, reputation, salience, specialness, standing, top billing*, weight; SEE CONCEPT 668

prominent [adj1] *sticking out; conspicuous*
arresting, beetling, bulging, easily seen, embossed, extended, extrusive, eye-catching, flashy, hanging out, hilly, in the foreground, jutting, marked, noticeable, obtrusive, obvious, outstanding, projecting, pronounced, protruding, protrusive, protuberant, raised, relieved, remarkable, rough, rugged, salient, shooting out, signal, standing out, striking, to the fore, unmistakable; SEE CONCEPTS 485,583,619

prominent [adj2] *important; famous*
big-league*, big-name*, big-shot*, celebrated, chief, distinguished, eminent, famed, foremost, great, high-profile*, leading, main, notable, noted, notorious, outstanding, popular, preeminent, renowned, respected, top, underlined, VIP*, well-known, well-thought-of, world-class*; SEE CONCEPT 568

promiscuous [adj] *indiscriminately sexually active*
abandoned, debauched, dissipated, dissolute, easy*, fast*, immoral, indiscriminate, lax, libertine, licentious, loose*, of easy virtue, oversexed, profligate, pushover, unbridled, unchaste, undiscriminating, unrestricted, wanton, wild; SEE CONCEPTS 372,545

promise [n1] *one's word that something will be done*
affiance, affirmation, agreement, asseveration, assurance, avowal, betrothal, bond, commitment, compact, consent, contract, covenant, earnest, engagement, espousal, guarantee, insurance, marriage, oath, obligation, pact, parole, pawn, pledge, plight, profession, promissory note, sacred word, security, stipulation, swear, swearing, token, troth, undertaking, vow, warrant, warranty, word, word of honor; SEE CONCEPTS 71,278

promise [n2] *hope, possibility*
ability, aptitude, capability, capacity, encouragement, flair, good omen, outlook, potential, talent; SEE CONCEPTS 630,650

promise [v] *give word that something will be done*
accede, affiance, affirm, agree, answer for, assent, asseverate, assure, bargain, betroth, bind, commit, compact, consent, contract, covenant, cross heart*, declare, engage, ensure, espouse, guarantee, hock*, insure, live up to*, mortgage, obligate, pass, pawn*, pledge, plight, profess, say so*, secure, stipulate, string along*, subscribe, swear, swear on bible*, swear up and down*, take an oath, undertake, underwrite, vouch, vow, warrant; SEE CONCEPT 71

promise [v2] *bring hope, possibility*
augur, bespeak, betoken, bode, denote, encourage, forebode, foreshadow, foretoken, give hope, hint, hold out hope*, hold probability, indicate, lead to expect, like, look, omen, portend, presage, seem likely, show signs of*, suggest; SEE CONCEPTS 118,650

promising [adj] *hopeful*
able, assuring, auspicious, bright, encouraging, favorable, gifted, happy, likely, lucky, propitious,

reassuring, rising, roseate, rosy, talented, up-and-coming; SEE CONCEPTS 406,548

promote [v] *help, advance*
advertise, advocate, aid, assist, avail, back, befriend, benefit, bolster, boost, build up*, call attention to, champion, contribute, cooperate, cry*, develop, encourage, endorse, espouse, forward, foster, further, get behind, hype*, improve, nourish, nurture, patronize, plug*, popularize, propagandize, publicize, puff*, push, push for, recommend, sell, serve, speak for, speed, sponsor, stimulate, subsidize, succor, support, uphold, urge, work for; SEE CONCEPTS 49,110,324

promote [v2] *give a higher position in organization*
advance, aggrandize, ascend, better, dignify, elevate, ennoble, exalt, favor, graduate, honor, increase, kick upstairs*, magnify, move up, prefer, raise, skip, up*, upgrade; SEE CONCEPT 351

promotion [n1] *higher position in organization*
advance, advancement, advocacy, aggrandizement, backing, betterment, boost, break, breakthrough, buildup, bump, elevation, encouragement, ennoblement, exaltation, favoring, furtherance, go-ahead*, hike, honor, improvement, jump, jump up, lift, move up, preference, preferment, prelation, progress, raise, rise, step up, support, upgrade, upgrading; SEE CONCEPT 351

promotion [n2] *publicity*
advertising, advertising campaign, ballyhoo*, blurb*, buildup*, hard sell*, hoopla*, hype*, notice, pitch, pizzazz*, plug*, PR*, press*, press-agentry, promo*, propaganda, publicity, public relations, puff*, puffery*, pushing, squib*; SEE CONCEPTS 49,110,271,324

prompt [n] *hint*
cue, help, jog, jolt, mnemonic, prod, reminder, spur, stimulus, twit; SEE CONCEPT 274

prompt [adj] *early, responsive*
alert, apt, brisk, eager, efficient, expeditious, immediate, instant, instantaneous, on the ball*, on the button*, on the dot*, on the nose*, on time, precise, punctual, quick, rapid, ready, smart, speedy, swift, timely, unhesitating, vigilant, watchful, wide-awake, willing; SEE CONCEPTS 401,799

prompt [v] *incite, cue*
advise, aid, arouse, assist, bring up, call forth, cause, convince, draw, egg on*, elicit, evoke, exhort, get, give rise to, goad, help, help out, hint, impel, imply, indicate, induce, inspire, instigate, jog, mention, motivate, move, occasion, persuade, prick*, prod, propel, propose, provoke, refresh, remind, sic*, spur, stimulate, suggest, talk into, urge, win over; SEE CONCEPTS 68,242

promptly [adv] *immediately*
at once, directly, expeditiously, fast, flat-out*, fleetly, hastily, in nothing flat*, instantly, lickety-split*, like a shot*, now, on the dot*, on the double*, on time, PDQ*, posthaste, pronto, punctually, quickly, rapidly, right away, sharp, speedily, straightaway, swiftly, unhesitatingly; SEE CONCEPTS 544,799

promulgate [v] *make known*
advertise, announce, annunciate, broadcast, call, circulate, communicate, declare, decree, disseminate, drum, issue, make public, notify, pass the word*, proclaim, promote, publish, sound, spread, toot, trumpet; SEE CONCEPT 60

prone [adj1] *lying down*

decumbent, face down, flat, horizontal, level, procumbent, prostrate, reclining, recumbent, re-supine, supine; SEE CONCEPT *583*

prone [adj2] *liable, likely*

apt, bent, devoted, disposed, exposed, fain, given, inclined, minded, open, predisposed, ready, sensitive, subject, susceptible, tending, willing; SEE CONCEPTS *542,552*

pronounce [v1] *produce words vocally*

accent, articulate, enunciate, phonate, say, sound, speak, stress, utter, verbalize, vocalize, voice; SEE CONCEPT *47*

pronounce [v2] *announce, declare*

affirm, assert, blast, call, decree, deliver, drum, judge, mouth, proclaim, say, sound off, spread around, trumpet, verbalize; SEE CONCEPT *49*

pronounced [adj] *distinct, evident*

arresting, assured, broad, clear, clear-cut, con-spicuous, decided, definite, marked, notable, no-ticeable, obvious, outstanding, striking, strong, unmistakable; SEE CONCEPTS *535,576,619*

pronouncement [n] *declaration, statement*

advertisement, announcement, broadcast, decree, dictum, edict, judgment, manifesto, notification, proclamation, promulgation, pronunciamento*, publication, report, ukase; SEE CONCEPTS *271,274,278*

proof [n1] *evidence, authentication*

affidavit, argument, attestation, averment, case, certification, chapter and verse*, clincher*, clue, confirmation, corroboration, credentials, crite-rion, cue*, data, demonstration, deposition, docu-ments, establishment, exhibit, facts, goods*, grabber*, grounds, information, lowdown*, nitty-gritty*, paper trail*, picture, reason, reasons, record, scoop*, score*, skinny*, smoking gun*, straight stuff*, substantiation, testament, testi-mony, trace, validation, verification, warrant, wherefore*, why*, whyfor*, witness; SEE CON-CEPT *274*

proof [n2] *photographic print*

galley, galley proof, impression, page proof, pass, pull, repro, revise, slip, stereo, trial, trial print, trial proof; SEE CONCEPT *265*

prop [n] *support*

aid, assistance, brace, buttress, column, mainstay, post, shore, stanchion, stay, strengthener, strut, truss, underpinning; SEE CONCEPTS *440,470*

prop [v] *hold up or lean against*

bear up, bolster, brace, buoy, buttress, carry, maintain, rest, set, shore, stand, stay, strengthen, support, sustain, truss, underprop, uphold; SEE CONCEPTS *190,201*

propaganda [n] *information that is designed to mislead or persuade*

advertising, agitprop, announcement, brainwash-ing*, disinformation, doctrine, evangelism, hand-out, hogwash*, hype*, implantation, inculcation, indoctrination, newspeak, promotion, promulga-tion, proselytism, publication, publicity; SEE CONCEPT *278*

propagate [v1] *breed, reproduce*

bear, beget, engender, father, fecundate, fertilize, generate, grow, impregnate, increase, inseminate, make pregnant, mother, multiply, originate, pro-create, produce, proliferate, raise, sire; SEE CON-CEPT *374*

propagate [v2] *spread, make known*

broadcast, circulate, develop, diffuse, disperse,

disseminate, distribute, proclaim, promulgate, publicize, publish, radiate, scatter, strew, trans-mit; SEE CONCEPTS *60,222*

propel [v] *throw; release into air*

actuate, drive, force, impel, launch, mobilize, move, press, push, send, set going, set in motion, shoot, shove, start, thrust; SEE CONCEPTS *208,221,222*

propensity [n] *inclination, weakness*

ability, aptness, bent*, bias, capacity, compe-tence, disposition, flash, inclining, leaning, liabil-ity, partiality, penchant, predilection, predisposition, proclivity, proneness, susceptibil-ity, sweet tooth*, talent, tendency, thing*, tilt*, yen; SEE CONCEPTS *20,411,630,709*

proper [adj1] *suitable*

able, applicable, appropriate, apt, au fait, becom-ing, befitting, capable, competent, convenient, de-cent, desired, felicitous, fit, fitting, good, happy, just, legitimate, meet, qualified, right, suited, true, useful; SEE CONCEPT *558*

proper [adj2] *mannerly, decent*

becoming, befitting, by the book*, by the num-bers*, comely, comme il faut*, conforming, cor-rect, decorous, demure, de rigueur*, genteel, in line, kosher*, moral, nice, polite, precise, prig-gish, prim, prissy, prudish, punctilious, puritani-cal, refined, respectable, right, seemly, solid, square*, stone, straight*, strait-laced*, stuffy*; SEE CONCEPTS *401,404*

proper [adj3] *conventional, correct*

absolute, accepted, accurate, arrant, complete, consummate, customary, decorous, established, exact, formal, free of error, on target*, on the button*, on the nose*, on the right track*, ortho-dox, out-and-out*, precise, right, unmistaken, usual, utter; SEE CONCEPTS *326,533*

proper [adj4] *individual, personal*

characteristic, distinctive, idiosyncratic, own, par-ticular, peculiar, private, respective, special, spe-cific; SEE CONCEPTS *549,557*

property [n1] *possessions, real estate*

acreage, acres, assets, belongings, buildings, cap-ital, chattels, claim, dominion, effects, equity, es-tate, farm, freehold, goods, holdings, home, house, inheritance, land, means, ownership, plot, possessorship, premises, proprietary, proprietor-ship, realty, resources, riches, substance, title, tract, wealth, worth; SEE CONCEPTS *446,509,515,710*

property [n2] *characteristic, feature*

ability, affection, attribute, character, hallmark, idiosyncrasy, mark, peculiarity, quality, trait, vir-tue; SEE CONCEPTS *411,654*

prophecy [n] *prediction*

apocalypse, augury, cast, divination, forecast, foretelling, oracle, presage, prevision, prognosis, prognostication, revelation, second sight, sooth-saying, vision; SEE CONCEPTS *70,278,689*

prophesy [v] *predict, warn*

adumbrate, augur, call*, call the turn*, crystal-ball*, divine, forecast, foresee, foretell, forewarn, have a hunch*, make book*, portend, predict, presage, prognosticate, psych it out*, see com-ing*, soothsay, vaticinate; SEE CONCEPT *70*

prophet [n] *person, thing that predicts future*

astrologer, augur, auspex, bard, clairvoyant, di-viner, druid, evocator, forecaster, fortuneteller, haruspex, horoscopist, magus, medium, meteo-rologist, oracle, ovate, palmist, predictor, prognosticator, prophesier, reader, seer, seeress, sibyl, soothsayer, sorcerer, tea-leaf reader, witch, wizard; SEE CONCEPTS 361,423

prophetic [adj] telling of the future

apocalyptic, augural, Delphian*, divinatory, fatidic, foreshadowing, mantic, occult, oracular, predictive, presaging, prescient, prognostic, prophetical, pythonic, sibylline, vaticinal, veiled; SEE CONCEPT 267

propitious [adj1] full of promise; good, favorable

advantageous, auspicious, beneficial, benign, brave, bright, dexter, encouraging, favoring, fortunate, happy, hopeful, lucky, opportune, pat*, promising, prosperous, rosy, seasonable, timely, toward, useful, well-timed; SEE CONCEPTS 548,560,572

propitious [adj2] friendly

benevolent, benign, favorably inclined, gracious, kind, nice, well-disposed; SEE CONCEPT 401

proponent [n] person who advocates, supports cause

advocate, backer, champion, defender, enthusiast, exponent, expounder, friend, partisan, patron, protector, second, seconder, spokesperson, subscriber, supporter, upholder, vindicator; SEE CONCEPTS 355,359,423

proportion [n1] relative amount, size of part to whole

admeasurement, amplitude, apportionment, breadth, bulk, capacity, cut, degree, dimension, distribution, division, equation, expanse, extent, fraction, magnitude, measure, measurement, part, percentage, portion, quota, rate, ratio, relationship, scale, scope, segment, share, volume; SEE CONCEPTS 730,783

proportion [n2] balance between parts of whole

agreement, congruity, correspondence, harmony, symmetry; SEE CONCEPTS 664,717

proportionate/proportional [adj] balanced, corresponding

commensurable, commensurate, comparable, comparative, compatible, consistent, contingent, correlative, correspondent, corresponding, dependent, equal, equitable, equivalent, even, in proportion, just, reciprocal, relative, symmetrical, uniform; SEE CONCEPTS 480,563

proposal [n] suggestion, presentation for action

angle, bid, big idea*, brain child*, design, feeler*, game plan*, idea, layout, motion, offer, outline, overture, pass, picture, pitch, plan, proffer, program, project, proposition, recommendation, scenario, scheme, setup, tender, terms; SEE CONCEPTS 271,324,662

propose [v1] suggest, present for action

adduce, advance, advise, affirm, ask, assert, broach, come up with*, contend, counsel, hit on*, hold out, introduce, invite, kibitz*, lay before*, lay on the line*, make a motion, make a pitch*, move for, name, nominate, offer, pose, prefer, press, proffer, propone, proposition, propound, put forward, put to, put up, recommend, request, set forth, solicit, speak one's piece*, spitball*, state, submit, tender, urge, volunteer; SEE CONCEPTS 66,75

propose [v2] intend; have in mind

aim, contemplate, design, have every intention, mean, mind, plan, purpose, scheme; SEE CONCEPTS 26,36

propose [v3] ask for hand in marriage

ask in marriage, fire the question*, get down on one knee*, make a proposal, offer marriage, pop the question*, press one's suit*; SEE CONCEPTS 48,297

proposition [n] suggestion; scheme

hypothesis, invitation, motion, overture, plan, premise, presentation, proffer, program, project, proposal, recommendation; SEE CONCEPTS 384, 662

proposition [v] make suggestion, often improper

accost, approach, ask, pose, prefer, propose, propound, put, solicit, suggest; SEE CONCEPTS 48,375

proprietor [n] person who owns something

freeholder*, front office, holder, land owner, meal ticket*, owner, possessor, proprietary, titleholder; SEE CONCEPTS 343,347

propriety [n1] suitableness, appropriateness

accordance, advisability, agreeableness, appositeness, aptness, becomingness, compatibility, concord, congruity, consonance, convenience, correctness, correspondence, decorum, ethicality, expedience, fitness, harmony, justice, legitimacy, meetness, morality, order, pleasantness, properness, recommendability, rectitude, respectability, rightness, seemliness, suitability; SEE CONCEPT 656

propriety [n2] good manners

accepted conduct, amenities, breeding, civilities, correctness, courtesy, decency, decorum, delicacy, dignity, etiquette, good behavior, good form, modesty, mores*, niceties, politeness, politesse, protocol, punctilio, rectitude, refinement, respectability, rules of conduct, seemliness, social conventions, social grace, the done thing*; SEE CONCEPTS 633,644

prosaic [adj] unimaginative

actual, banal, blah*, boring, clean, colorless, common, commonplace, dead*, diddly*, drab, dry, dull, everyday, factual, flat*, garden-variety*, hackneyed, ho-hum*, humdrum*, irksome, lackluster, lifeless, literal, lowly, lusterless, matter-of-fact, monotonous, mundane, nothing, nowhere, ordinary, pabulum*, pedestrian, platitudinous, plebeian, practicable, practical, prose, prosy, routine, square, stale, tame, tedious, trite, uneventful, unexceptional, uninspiring, vanilla*, vapid, workaday, yawn*, zero*; SEE CONCEPTS 267,537,547

proscribe [v] condemn, exclude

ban, banish, blackball*, boycott, censure, damn, denounce, deport, doom*, embargo, excommunicate, exile, expatriate, expel, forbid, interdict, ostracize, outlaw, prohibit, reject, sentence; SEE CONCEPTS 25,121,317

prose [n] written, nonrhythmic literature

book, composition, essay, exposition, fiction, nonfiction, speech, story, talk, text, tongue*, writing; SEE CONCEPTS 268,271

prosecute [v1] bring action against in court

arraign, bring suit, bring to trial, contest, do, haul into court*, indict, involve in litigation, law, litigate, prefer charges, pull up, put away*, put on docket, put on trial, see in court*, seek redress, sue, summon, take to court, try, turn on the heat*; SEE CONCEPT 317

prosecute [v2] follow through, persevere

carry on, carry through, conduct, continue, direct, discharge, engage in, execute, follow up, manage, perform, persist, practice, pursue, put through, see through, wage, work at; SEE CONCEPT 91

prospect [n1] *outlook for future*
anticipation, calculation, chance, contemplation, expectancy, expectation, forecast, future, hope, in the cards*, irons in the fire*, likelihood, odds, opening, plan, possibility, presumption, probability, promise, proposal, thought; SEE CONCEPTS 689,693

prospect [n2] *landscape, vista*
aspect, lookout, outlook, overlook, panorama, perspective, scape, scene, sight, spectacle, view, vision; SEE CONCEPTS 509,628

prospect [v] *look for; seek*
delve, dig, explore, go after, go into, inquire, investigate, look, look into, probe, search, sift, survey; SEE CONCEPT 216

prospective [adj] *anticipated, potential*
about to be, approaching, awaited, coming, considered, destined, eventual, expected, forthcoming, future, hoped-for, imminent, impending, intended, likely, looked-for, planned, possible, promised, proposed, soon-to-be, to be*, to come; SEE CONCEPTS 548,552

prospectus [n] *details, outline of event*
announcement, catalogue, conspectus, design, list, plan, program, scheme, syllabus, synopsis; SEE CONCEPT 283

prosper [v] *be fortunate; succeed*
advance, arrive, augment, batten, bear, bear fruit, become rich, become wealthy, be enriched, benefit, bloom, blossom, catch on*, do well, do wonders*, fare well, fatten*, feather nest*, flourish, flower, gain, get on*, get there*, go places*, go to town*, grow rich, hit it big, hit the jackpot*, increase, make a killing*, make good*, make it*, make mark*, make money, make out*, multiply, produce, progress, rise, score*, strike it rich*, thrive, turn out well, yield; SEE CONCEPT 706

prosperity [n] *affluence, good fortune*
abundance, accomplishment, advantage, arrival, bed of roses*, benefit, boom, clover, do, ease*, easy street*, exorbitance, expansion, flying colors*, fortune, good, good times, gravy train*, growth, high on the hog*, increase, inflation, interest, life of luxury*, luxury, opulence, plenteousness, plenty, prosperousness, riches, success, successfulness, the good life*, thriving, velvet, victory, wealth, welfare, well-being; SEE CONCEPTS 335,706

prosperous [adj1] *successful, thriving*
affluent, blooming, booming, comfortable, doing well, easy, flourishing, fortunate, halcyon, in clover*, in the money*, lousy rich, lucky, mainline*, moneyed, money to burn*, on top of heap*, opulent, palmy, prospering, rich, roaring, robust, sitting pretty*, snug, substantial, upper-class*, uptown, wealthy, well, well-heeled*, well-off, well-to-do; SEE CONCEPTS 334,528

prosperous [adj2] *promising, advantageous*
appropriate, auspicious, bright, convenient, desirable, favorable, felicitous, fortunate, good, happy, lucky, opportune, profitable, propitious, seasonable, timely, well-timed; SEE CONCEPTS 548,572

prostitute [n] *person who sells own abilities, talent, or name for inferior purpose*
betrayer, cheater, deceiver, gigolo, hustler, seducer; SEE CONCEPT 412

prostitute [v] *to put one's talent to an unworthy use*
abuse, cheapen, corrupt, debase, debauch, degrade, demean, deprave, devalue, misapply, misemploy, misuse, pervert, profane, vitiate; SEE CONCEPTS 156,645

prostrate [adj1] *flat, horizontal*
abject, bowed low, procumbent, prone, reclining, recumbent, supine; SEE CONCEPT 583

prostrate [adj2] *helpless*
beaten, defenseless, disarmed, impotent, open, overcome, overpowered, overwhelmed, paralyzed, powerless, reduced, weak; SEE CONCEPT 542

prostrate [adj3] *tired, worn*
crippled, dejected, depressed, disarmed, drained, drowned, exhausted, fagged*, fallen, frazzled*, immobilized, incapacitated, inconsolable, knocked over*, obedient, overcome, paralyzed, pooped*, spent*, submissive, subservient, tuckered*, wearied, worn out; SEE CONCEPTS 406,485

prostrate [v1] *fall on knees; submit*
abase, bow, bow down, cast before, cringe, fall at feet, give in, grovel, kneel, kowtow*, obey, surrender; SEE CONCEPT 384

prostrate [v2] *overwhelm; wear out*
bring low, cripple, debilitate, defeat, destroy, disable, disarm, drain, drown, exhaust, fatigue, fell, floor, frazzle*, immobilize, impair, incapacitate, knock over, level, mow*, overcome, overpower, overthrow, overtire, overturn, paralyze, reduce, ruin, sap, tire, tucker out*, weary, whelm, wreck; SEE CONCEPTS 95,250,252

protagonist [n] *person who takes the lead; central figure of narrative*
advocate, central character, champion, combatant, exemplar, exponent, hero, idol, lead, lead character, leader, mainstay, prime mover, principal, standard-bearer, warrior; SEE CONCEPTS 352, 359,423

protect [v] *take care of; guard from harm*
assure, bulwark, care for, champion, chaperon, conserve, cover, cover all bases*, cover up, cushion, defend, fend, foster, give refuge, give sanctuary*, go to bat for*, harbor, hedge, insulate, keep, keep safe, look after, preserve, ride shotgun for*, safeguard, save, screen, secure, sentinel, shade, shelter, shield, shotgun*, stand guard, stonewall*, support, take under wing*, watch, watch over; SEE CONCEPTS 96,134

protection [n] *care, guardianship*
aegis, armament, armor, assurance, barrier, buffer, bulwark, camouflage, certainty, charge, conservation, cover, custody, defense, fix, guard, guarding, insurance, invulnerability, preservation, protecting, reassurance, refuge, safeguard, safekeeping, safety, salvation, screen, security, self-defense, shelter, shield, stability, strength, surety, tutelage, umbrella*, ward, wardship; SEE CONCEPTS 712,729

protective [adj] *guarding, securing*
careful, conservational, conservative, covering, custodial, defensive, emergency, guardian, insulating, jealous, possessive, preservative, protecting, safeguarding, sheltering, shielding, vigilant, warm, watchful; SEE CONCEPTS 542,550

protest [n] *complaint, disapproval*
bellyache*, big stink*, blackball*, challenge, clamor, declaration, demonstration, demur, demurral, difficulty, dissent, flak*, formal com-

pr
pr

plaint, grievance, gripe, grouse*, holler*, howl, kick*, knock*, march, moratorium, nix, objection, outcry, protestation, question, rally, remonstrance, remonstration, revolt, riot, stink*, tumult, turmoil; SEE CONCEPTS 52,54,300

protest [v] *complain, disapprove; argue against*
affirm, assert, asseverate, attest, avouch, avow, back-talk*, be against, be displeased by, blast*, buck, combat, constate, contend, cry out, declare, demonstrate, demur, disagree, except, expostulate, fight, holler, howl, insist, inveigh against, kick*, maintain, make a stink*, object, oppose, predicate, profess, put up a fight*, rebel, remonstrate, resist, revolt, say no*, sound off*, squawk*, take exception*, testify, thumbs down*; SEE CONCEPTS 46,52,54,300

protocol [n] *rules of conduct, behavior in certain situation*
agreement, code, compact, concordat, contract, conventions, courtesy, covenant, custom, decorum, etiquette, formalities, good form, manners, obligation, order, pact, politesse, propriety, p's and q's*, treaty; SEE CONCEPTS 684,688

prototype [n] *original, example*
ancestor, antecedent, antecessor, archetype, criterion, first, forerunner, ideal, mock-up*, model, norm, paradigm, pattern, precedent, precursor, predecessor, standard, type; SEE CONCEPT 686

protract [v] *extend, draw out*
continue, cool*, defer, delay, drag on*, drag out*, draw, elongate, hold off, hold up, keep going, lengthen, pad*, postpone, procrastinate, prolong, prolongate, put off, put on hold, spin out*, stall, stretch, stretch out; SEE CONCEPTS 237,239,250

protrude [v] *stick out*
beetle, bulge, butt out, come through, distend, extend, extrude, jut, jut out, obtrude, overhang, point, poke, pop, pouch, pout, project, shoot out, stand out, start, stick up, swell; SEE CONCEPTS 208,746

protuberance [n] *lump, outgrowth*
bulge, bump, excrescence, jut, jutting, knob, outthrust, process, projection, prominence, protrusion, swelling, tumor; SEE CONCEPTS 471,824

proud [adj1] *pleased, pleasing*
appreciative, august, content, contented, dignified, eminent, fiery, fine, glad, glorious, gorgeous, grand, gratified, gratifying, great, greathearted, honored, illustrious, imposing, impressive, magnificent, majestic, memorable, noble, red-letter*, rewarding, satisfied, satisfying, self-respecting, spirited, splendid, stately, sublime, superb, valiant, vigorous, well-pleased; SEE CONCEPTS 403,572,574

proud [adj2] *arrogant, self-important*
bloated, boastful, cavalier, cocky*, conceited, contemptuous, cool*, disdainful, dismissive, domineering, egotistic, egotistical, haughty, high-and-mighty*, high-handed*, huffy*, imperious, insolent, lofty, narcissistic, ostentatious, overbearing, pompous, presumptuous, pretentious, puffed up*, scornful, self-satisfied, sniffy*, snobbish, snooty*, stuck-up*, supercilious, superior, vain, vainglorious; SEE CONCEPTS 401,542

prove [v] *establish facts; put to a test*
add up, affirm, analyze, ascertain, assay, attest, authenticate, back, bear out, certify, check, confirm, convince, corroborate, declare, demonstrate, determine, document, end up, evidence, evince, examine, experiment, explain, find, fix, have a case*, justify, make evident, manifest, pan out*, result, settle, show, show clearly, show once and for all*, substantiate, sustain, test, testify, trial, try, turn out, uphold, validate, verify, warrant, witness; SEE CONCEPTS 57,118,138

proverb [n] *saying referring to common fact, knowledge*
adage, aphorism, apophthegm, axiom, byword, catch phrase, daffodil*, dictum, epigram, folk wisdom, gnome, maxim, moral, motto, platitude, precept, repartee, saw*, text, truism, witticism, word; SEE CONCEPTS 275,278

proverbial [adj] *conventional, traditional*
accepted, acknowledged, archetypal, axiomatic, current, customary, famed, familiar, famous, general, legendary, notorious, self-evident, time-honored, typical, unquestioned, well-known; SEE CONCEPT 530

provide [v1] *supply, support*
accommodate, add, administer, afford, arrange, bestow, bring, care, cater, contribute, dispense, equip, favor, feather*, feed, fit, fit out, fix up, fix up with, furnish, give, grant, hand over, heel*, impart, implement, indulge, keep, lend, line, look after, maintain, minister, outfit, prepare, present, procure, produce, proffer, provision, ration, ready, render, replenish, serve, stake, stock, stock up*, store, sustain, take care of, transfer, turn out, yield; SEE CONCEPTS 108,110,136,140

provide [v2] *determine, specify*
condition, lay down, postulate, require, state, stipulate; SEE CONCEPTS 18,646

provident [adj] *careful, frugal*
canny, cautious, discreet, economical, expedient, far-sighted, foresighted, judicious, penny-pinching*, politic, prepared, prudent, sagacious, saving, shrewd, sparing, thrifty, tight, unwasteful, vigilant, well-prepared, wise; SEE CONCEPTS 334,401

providing/provided [conj] *as long as; with the understanding*
contingent upon, given, if, if and only if, in case, in the case that, in the event, on condition, on the assumption, on these terms, subject to, supposing, with the proviso; SEE CONCEPTS 544,546

province [n] *area of rule, responsibility*
arena, bailiwick, business, calling, canton, capacity, champaign, charge, colony, concern, county, demesne, department, dependency, district, division, domain, dominion, duty, employment, field, function, jurisdiction, line, office, orbit, part, post, pursuit, realm, region, role, section, shire, sphere, terrain, territory, tract, walk, work, zone; SEE CONCEPTS 198,349,362,508,532

provincial [adj] *countrified; limited*
bigoted, bucolic, country, hidebound, home-grown, homespun, insular, inward-looking, local, narrow, narrow-minded, parochial, pastoral, petty, rude, rural, rustic, sectarian, small-minded, small-town, uninformed, unpolished, unsophisticated; SEE CONCEPTS 403,549,589

provision [n1] *supplies, supplying*
accouterment, arrangement, catering, emergency, equipping, fitting out, foundation, furnishing, groundwork, outline, plan, prearrangement, precaution, preparation, procurement, providing, stock, store, supplying; SEE CONCEPTS 140,712

provision/proviso [n2] *stipulation, condition of agreement*
agreement, catch*, Catch-22*, clause, demand,

fine print*, joker*, kicker*, limitation, prerequisite, qualification, requirement, reservation, restriction, rider, small print*, specification, stipulation, strings*; term, terms; SEE CONCEPTS *270,684,711*

provisional [adj] *contingent, tentative*
conditional, dependent, ephemeral, experimental, interim, limited, makeshift, passing, pro tem, provisionary, provisory, qualified, rough-and-ready*, stopgap*, temporary, test, transient, transitional; SEE CONCEPTS *546,554,711*

provocation [n] *incitement, stimulus*
affront, annoyance, bothering, brickbat*, casus belli, cause, challenge, dare, defy, grabber*, grievance, grounds, harassment, incentive, indignity, inducement, injury, instigation, insult, irking, justification, motivation, offense, provoking, reason, taunt, vexation, vexing; SEE CONCEPTS *14,240,532*

provocative [adj1] *aggravating*
annoying, challenging, disturbing, exciting, galling, goading, heady, incensing, inciting, influential, inspirational, insulting, intoxicating, offensive, outrageous, provoking, pushing, spurring, stimulant, stimulating; SEE CONCEPT *529*

provocative [adj2] *sexually stimulating*
alluring, arousing, enchanting, erotic, exciting, heady, interesting, intoxicating, intriguing, inviting, seductive, sexy, stimulating, suggestive, tantalizing, tempting; SEE CONCEPTS *372,537*

provoke [v1] *make angry*
abet, abrade, affront, aggravate, anger, annoy, bother, bug*, chafe, enrage, exasperate, exercise, foment, fret, gall*, get*, get on one's nerves*, get under one's skin*, grate, hit where one lives*, incense, incite, inflame, infuriate, insult, irk, irritate, madden, make blood boil*, make waves*, nag, offend, perturb, pique, put out, raise, rile, roil, ruffle, set*, set on*, try one's patience*, upset, vex, whip up*, work into lather*, work up*; SEE CONCEPTS *7,19*

provoke [v2] *start, evoke; stimulate*
animate, arouse, awaken, begin, bestir, bring about, bring down, bring on, bring to one's feet*, build up, call forth, cause, challenge, draw forth, electrify, elicit, enthuse, excite, fire, fire up*, galvanize, generate, give rise to, incite, induce, inflame, innervate, innerve, inspire, instigate, kindle, lead to, make, motivate, move, occasion, pique, precipitate, prime, produce, promote, prompt, quicken, rally, rouse, roust, stir, suscitate, thrill, titillate, titivate, waken, whet; SEE CONCEPTS *7,19,22,221,242*

prowess [n1] *ability, skill*
accomplishment, address, adeptness, adroitness, aptitude, attainment, command, deftness, dexterity, excellence, expertise, expertness, facility, genius, mastery, readiness, sleight, talent; SEE CONCEPT *630*

prowess [n2] *bravery*
backbone*, boldness, courage, daring, dauntlessness, fearlessness, gallantry, grit*, guts*, heart*, heroism, intrepidity, mettle, moxie*, nerve, pluck, right stuff*, spunk, starch*, stomach*, stuff*, true grit*, valiance, valiancy, valor, valorousness, what it takes*; SEE CONCEPTS *411,633*

prowl [v] *move stealthily*
cruise, hunt, lurk, nose around*, patrol, range, roam, rove, scavenge, skulk, slink, snake, sneak, stalk, steal, stroll, tramp; SEE CONCEPT *151*

proximity [n] *nearness to something*
adjacency, appropinquity, closeness, concurrence, contiguity, contiguousness, immediacy, juxtaposition, propinquity, togetherness; SEE CONCEPT *747*

prudent [adj] *wise, sensible in action and thought*
advisable, canny, careful, cautious, circumspect, discerning, discreet, economical, far-sighted, frugal, hedging one's bets*, judgmatic, judicious, leery, playing safe*, politic, provident, reasonable, sagacious, sage, sane, sapient, shrewd, sound, sparing, tactical, thinking twice*, thrifty, vigilant, wary; SEE CONCEPTS *401,542*

prudish [adj] *shy and strict in behavior*
affected, artificial, austere, bigoted, conventional, demure, fastidious, finicky*, genteel, illiberal, mincing, narrow, narrow-minded, offish, overexact, overmodest, overnice, precise, pretentious, priggish*, prim, prissy*, proper, puritanical, rigid, rigorous, scrupulous, severe, simpering, square, squeamish*, starchy*, stern, stiff*, stilted, strait-laced, stuffy, uptight*, Victorian*; SEE CONCEPT *401*

prune [v] *trim; cut short*
clip, cut back, dock, eliminate, exclude, gut, knock off, lop, pare down, reduce, shape, shave, shear, shorten, skive, snip, thin; SEE CONCEPTS *137,176,236,247*

pry [v1] *interfere in someone else's business*
be a busybody*, be all ears*, be curious, be inquisitive, be nosy, bug*, ferret out, gape, gaze, hunt, inquire, intrude, investigate, listen in, meddle, nose, peek, peep, peer, poke, poke nose into*, ransack, reconnoiter, rubberneck*, search, snoop, spy, stare, tap, tune in on*, wiretap; SEE CONCEPTS *216,384,623*

pry [v2] *force or break open*
disengage, disjoin, divide, elevate, elicit, extort, extract, heave, hoist, jimmy, lever, lift, move, pick up, press, prize, pull, push, raise, rear, separate, take up, tear, tilt, turn, turn out, twist, uplift, upraise, uprear, wrest, wring; SEE CONCEPTS *196,206,211*

psalm [n] *song of praise*
canticle, celebration, chant, chorale, eulogy, hymn, paean, shout, verse; SEE CONCEPT *595*

pseudo [adj] *artificial, fake*
bogus, counterfeit, ersatz, false, imitation, mock, not genuine, not kosher*, not legit*, not real, phony, pirate, pretend, pretended, quasi*, sham*, simulated, spurious, wrong; SEE CONCEPT *582*

pseudonym [n] *false name*
AKA*, alias, ananym, anonym, assumed name, handle*, incognito*, nickname, nom de guerre, nom de plume, pen name, professional name, stage name, summer name*; SEE CONCEPTS *268,683*

psyche [n] *innermost self; personality*
anima, animus, character, ego, élan vital, essential nature, individuality, inner child, inner self, mind, pneuma, self, soul, spirit, spirituality, subconscious, true being; SEE CONCEPTS *410,411*

psychedelic [adj] *affecting the mind so as to produce vivid visions*
consciousness-expanding, crazy*, experimental, freaky*, hallucinatory, hallucinogenic, kaleidoscopic, mind-bending*, mind-blowing*, mind-changing, mind-expanding*, multicolored*, psychoactive, psychotomimetic, psychotropic, trip*; SEE CONCEPTS *529,537*

pr
ps

psychiatrist [n] *person who treats mental disorders*
analyst, clinician, doctor, psychoanalyst, psychologist, psychotherapist, shrink*, therapist; SEE CONCEPT 357

psychic [adj] *extrasensory in perception*
analytic, cerebral, clairvoyant, immaterial, impressible, impressionable, intellective, intellectual, mental, metaphysical, mystic, occult, preternatural, psychal, psychical, psychogenic, psychological, responsive, sensible, sensile, sensitive, sentient, spiritual, supernatural, supersensible, supersensitive, supersensory, supersensual, susceptible, susceptive, telekinetic, telepathic, transmundane, unworldly; SEE CONCEPTS 402, 403

psychobabble [n] *rhetoric using psychological-terms*
argot, buzzword, jargon, patter, pop psych*, psychospeak, self-help; SEE CONCEPT 275

psychological [adj] *concerning the mind*
cerebral, cognitive, emotional, experimental, imaginary, intellective, intellectual, in the mind, mental, psychical, subconscious, subjective, unconscious; SEE CONCEPTS 403,536

psychology [n] *study of the mind; emotional and mental constitution*
attitude, behaviorism, medicine, mental make-up, mental processes, personality study, psych*, science of the mind, therapy, way of thinking*, where head is at*; SEE CONCEPTS 349,360,410

psychopath [n] *person who is mentally deranged, often prone to hurt others*
antisocial personality, insane person, lunatic, mad person, maniac, mental case*, nutcase*, psycho*, psychotic, schizoid*, sociopath, unstable personality; SEE CONCEPT 412

psychotic [adj] *mentally deranged*
certifiable*, crazy, demented, distracted, flipped-out*, insane, lunatic, mad, manic-depressive, mental, non compos mentis, nuts*, off one's rocker*, over the edge*, psycho*, psychopathic, schizophrenic, sick, unbalanced, unhinged*; SEE CONCEPT 403

pub [n] *business where liquor and food are served*
after-hours joint*, ale house*, bar, barroom, beer joint*, drinkery, drinking establishment, gin mill*, inn, joint*, lounge, public house, roadhouse, saloon, taproom, tavern; SEE CONCEPTS 439,448,449

puberty [n] *young adulthood*
adolescence, awkward stage*, boyhood, girlhood, greenness*, high-school years, juvenescence, juvenility, potency, preadolescence, pubescence, spring*, springtide*, springtime*, teenage years, teens, youth, youthfulness; SEE CONCEPT 817

public [n] *people of community; people interested in something*
audience, bodies*, buyers, citizens, clientele, commonalty, community, country, electorate, everyone, followers, following, heads, masses, men and women, mob, multitude, nation, patrons, people, populace, population, society, suite, supporters, voters; SEE CONCEPTS 379,417

public [adj1] *community, general*
accessible, city, civic, civil, common, communal, conjoint, conjunct, country, federal, free, free to all, government, governmental, intermutual, metropolitan, municipal, mutual, national, not private, open, open-door, popular, social, state, universal, unrestricted, urban, widespread, without charge; SEE CONCEPTS 536,576

public [adj2] *known, acknowledged*
exposed, general, in circulation, notorious, obvious, open, overt, patent, plain, popular, prevalent, published, recognized, social, societal, usual, vulgar, widespread; SEE CONCEPTS 267, 530

publication [n1] *printing of written or visual material*
advertisement, airing, announcement, appearance, broadcast, broadcasting, communication, declaration, disclosure, discovery, dissemination, divulgation, issuance, issuing, notification, proclamation, promulgation, pronunciamento, publicity, public relations, publishing, reporting, revelation, statement, ventilation, writing; SEE CONCEPTS 60,274,292

publication [n2] *something printed for reading*
annual, book, booklet, brochure, handbill, information, issue, leaflet, magazine, news, newsletter, newspaper, pamphlet, periodical; SEE CONCEPT 280

publicity [n] *promotion of something, someone*
advertising, announcement, announcing, attention, ballyhoo*, big noise*, billing, blurb*, boost*, broadcasting, build-up*, clout*, commercial, currency, distribution, fame, handout, hoopla*, hype*, ink*, limelight*, noise*, notoriety, pitch, plug*, PR*, press, press-agentry, promo*, promulgation, propaganda, public notice, public relations, puff*, puffery*, pushing, réclame, release, report, scratch*, spotlight*, spread, write-up; SEE CONCEPTS 274,280,293

publicize [v] *make widely known; promote*
advance, advertise, announce, bill, billboard, boost*, broadcast, build up*, cry, drum*, extol, hard sell*, headline, hype*, immortalize, make a pitch for, pitch, play up*, plug*, press-agent, promulgate, propagandize, puff*, push, put on the map*, skywrite*, soft-sell*, splash, spot*, spotlight*, spread, tout, trumpet*, write up; SEE CONCEPTS 60,292,324

pucker [n] *wrinkle*
crease, crinkle, crumple, fold, furrow, plait, ruck, ruckle; SEE CONCEPT 754

pucker [v] *draw together; wrinkle*
cockle, compress, condense, contract, crease, crinkle, crumple, fold, furrow, gather, knit, purse, ruckle, ruck up, ruffle, screw up, squeeze, tighten; SEE CONCEPTS 185,219

pudgy [adj] *slightly fat*
chubby*, hefty, plump, plumpish, rotund, round, stout, thick-bodied, tubby*; SEE CONCEPTS 491,773

puerile [adj] *childish*
babyish, babylike, callow, foolish, green*, immature, inane, inexperienced, infantile, irresponsible, jejune, juvenile, naive, petty, ridiculous, silly, trivial, unfledged, ungrown, weak, young; SEE CONCEPTS 401,578,797

puff [n1] *blast of air*
breath, draft, drag, draught, draw, emanation, flatus, flurry, gust, pull, smoke, waft, whiff, wind, wisp; SEE CONCEPTS 437,524

puff [n2] *advertisement*
advertising, blurb*, boost*, buildup*, commendation, favorable mention, good word, hype*, laudation, plug*, praise, press-agentry, promo*,

promotion, publicity, puffery*, push*, sales talk, write-up; SEE CONCEPTS 69,278,324

puff [v1] *inhale or exhale air*
blow, breathe, distend, drag, draw, enlarge, fill, gasp, gulp, heave, huff, huff and puff*, inflate, pant, pull at, pull on, smoke, suck, swell, wheeze, whiff; SEE CONCEPTS 163,185,526

puff [v2] *publicize*
admire, advertise, ballyhoo*, blow up*, build, commend, congratulate, cry*, flatter, hype*, overpraise, plug*, praise, press-agent*, promote, push; SEE CONCEPTS 49,69

puffy [adj] *swollen*
billowy, bloated, blown, bulgy, distended, distent, enlarged, expanded, full, increased, inflamed, inflated, puffed up; SEE CONCEPT 485

pugnacious [adj] *belligerent*
aggressive, antagonistic, argumentative, bellicose, brawling, cantankerous, chip on shoulder*, choleric, combative, contentious, defiant, disputatious, have a bone to pick*, hot-tempered, irascible, irritable, itching to fight*, militant, petulant, pushing, pushy*, quarrelsome, ready to fight, rebellious, salty*, scrappy*, self-assertive, truculent, warlike; SEE CONCEPTS 401,542

pull [v1] *drawing something with force*
cull, dislocate, drag, evolve, extract, gather, haul, heave, jerk, lug, paddle, pick, pluck, remove, rend, rip, row, schlepp*, sprain, strain, stretch, take out, tear, tow, trail, truck, tug, twitch, uproot, weed*, wrench, yank; SEE CONCEPT 206

pull [v2] *attract*
draw, entice, get, lure, magnetize, obtain, pick up, secure, win; SEE CONCEPT 11

pull down [v] *destroy; knock over*
annihilate, bulldoze, decimate, demolish, destruct, dismantle, let down, lower, raze, remove, ruin, take down, tear down, wreck; SEE CONCEPT 252

pull in [v1] *arrest*
apprehend, bust, collar, detain, nab, nail, pick up, pinch, run in, take into custody; SEE CONCEPTS 90,317

pull in [v2] *attract, obtain*
absorb, bring in, clear, draw, draw in, earn, gain, gross, make, net, pocket, suck, take home*; SEE CONCEPT 120

pull off [v] *accomplish*
achieve, bring off, carry out, manage, score, score a success, secure, succeed, win; SEE CONCEPTS 91,706

pull out [v] *quit*
abandon, depart, evacuate, exit, get off, go, leave, retire, retreat, shove off, stop, stop participating, take off, withdraw; SEE CONCEPTS 119,121,195

pull through [v] *recover*
come through, get better, get over, improve, rally, ride out*, survive, triumph, weather*; SEE CONCEPTS 303,700,706

pull up [v] *stop, halt*
arrive, brake, bring up, come to a halt, come to a stop, draw up, fetch up, get there, haul up, pause, reach a standstill; SEE CONCEPTS 119,121,159

pulp [n] *flesh of plant, animal*
batter, curd, dough, grume, jam, marrow, mash, mush, pap, paste, pomace, poultice, sarcocarp, semisolid, soft part, sponge, triturate; SEE CONCEPTS 399,428

pulp [adj] *cheap, vulgar, especially regarding reading material*
lurid, mushy, rubbish, sensational, trash, trashy; SEE CONCEPT 267

pulp [v] *mash, pulverize*
bruise, coagulate, crush, gelatinate, macerate, squash, triturate; SEE CONCEPTS 208,219

pulpit [n] *structure from which sermon is given*
desk, lectern, platform, podium, rostrum, soapbox*, stage, stump*; SEE CONCEPTS 368,443

pulsate/pulse [v] *quiver, beat*
drum, fluctuate, hammer, oscillate, palpitate, pound, pump, roar, throb, thrum, thud, thump, tick, vibrate; SEE CONCEPTS 147,185

pulse [n] *rhythm, beat*
beating, oscillation, pulsation, stroke, throb, throbbing, vibration; SEE CONCEPTS 147,185

pulverize [v1] *smash by beating, crushing*
abrade, atomize, beat, bray, break up, buck, comminute, contriturate, crumble, crunch, crush, flour, fragment, fragmentalize, fragmentize, granulate, grate, grind, levigate, micronize, mill, mull, pestle, pound, powder, shatter, splinter, triturate; SEE CONCEPTS 186,219

pulverize [v2] *destroy*
annihilate, crush, decimate, defeat, demolish, destruct, dynamite, flatten, rub out*, ruin, shatter, smash, tear down*, vanquish, vaporize, wax, wreck; SEE CONCEPT 252

pump [v1] *draw or push out*
bail out, blow up, dilate, distend, draft, drain, draw, draw off, drive, drive out, elevate, empty, force, force out, inflate, inject, pour, push, send, siphon, supply, swell, tap; SEE CONCEPTS 142,206,208

pump [v2] *question relentlessly*
cross-examine, draw out, give the third degree*, grill, interrogate, probe, query, question, quiz, worm out of*; SEE CONCEPTS 48,53

pun [n] *play on words*
ambiguity, calembour, conceit, double entendre, double meaning, equivoque, joke, paronomasia, quibble, quip, witticism; SEE CONCEPTS 273,278

punch [n1/v1] *hit*
bash, belt, biff, blow, bop, box, buffet, clip, clout, cuff, dig, jab, jog, knock, lollop, nudge, one-two*, plug, plunk*, poke, prod, pummel, rap, shot, slam, slap, slug, smack, smash, sock, strike, stroke, thrust, thump, wallop; SEE CONCEPT 189

punch [n2] *energy, vigor*
bite, cogency, drive, effectiveness, force, forcefulness, impact, point, validity, validness, verve; SEE CONCEPTS 676,682

punch [v2] *perforate, prick*
bore, cut, drill, jab, pierce, poke, puncture, stab, stamp; SEE CONCEPT 220

punctilious [adj] *careful, finicky*
ceremonious, conscientious, conscionable, conventional, exact, formal, formalistic, fussy, good eye*, heedful, meticulous, nice, observant, overconscientious, overscrupulous, painstaking, particular, persnickety, precise, proper, punctual, right on*, scrupulous, strict; SEE CONCEPTS 401,542,557

punctual [adj] *on time*
accurate, careful, conscientious, conscionable, constant, cyclic, dependable, early, exact, expeditious, fussy, heedful, in good time*, meticulous, on schedule, on the button*, on the dot*, on

ps
pu

the nose*, painstaking, particular, periodic, precise, prompt, punctilious, quick, ready, recurrent, regular, reliable, scrupulous, seasonable, steady, strict, timely, under the wire*; SEE CONCEPTS 544,550,799

punctuate [v] *lay stress on*
accent, accentuate, break, divide, emphasize, interject, interrupt, intersect, intersperse, mark, pepper*, point, point up*, separate, sprinkle, stress, underline; SEE CONCEPTS 49,79,98,266

puncture [n] *hole, rupture*
break, cut, damage, flat, flat tire*, jab, leak, nick, opening, perforation, prick, slit, stab; SEE CONCEPTS 309,513,674

puncture [v] *poke hole in*
bore, cut, cut through, deflate, drill, go down, go flat, knife, lacerate, lance, nick, open, penetrate, perforate, pierce, prick, punch, riddle, rupture; SEE CONCEPTS 137,220

puncture [v2] *deflate someone's idea, feelings*
blow sky high*, discourage, discredit, disillusion, disprove, explode, flatten*, humble, knock bottom out*, knock props from under*, poke full of holes*, shoot full of holes*, take down a peg*, take wind out of sails*; SEE CONCEPTS 7,19,54

pundit [n] *person who is authority*
auger, bookworm, brain*, buff, cereb*, cognoscenti, egghead*, expert, intellectual, learned one, philosopher, professor, savant, scholar, solon, teacher, thinker; SEE CONCEPTS 416,423

pungent [adj1] *highly flavored*
acid, acrid, aromatic, bitter, effluvious, hot, nosey*, odoriferous, peppery, piquant, poignant, racy, rich, salty, seasoned, sharp, snappy, sour, spicy, stinging, stinking*, strong, tangy, tart, whiffy*, zesty; SEE CONCEPT 613

pungent [adj2] *sharp, stinging in speech*
acrimonious, acute, barbed, biting, bitter, caustic, cutting, exciting, hot, incisive, keen, mordant, penetrating, peppery, piercing, poignant, pointed, provocative, racy, salt, salty, sarcastic, scathing, snappy, spicy, stimulating, stringent, total, trenchant, zesty; SEE CONCEPT 267

punish [v] *penalize for wrongdoing*
abuse, attend to, batter, beat, beat up, blacklist, castigate, chasten, chastise, correct, crack down on*, cuff, debar, defrock, discipline, dismiss, do in, execute, exile, expel, fine, flog, give a going over*, give the works*, harm, hurt, immure, incarcerate, injure, knock about, lash, lecture, maltreat, misuse, oppress, paddle, rap knuckles*, reprove, rough up, scourge, sentence, slap wrist, spank, switch, teach a lesson, throw the book at*, train, whip; SEE CONCEPT 122

punishment [n] *penalty*
abuse, amercement, beating, castigation, chastening, chastisement, comeuppance, confiscation, correction, deprivation, disciplinary action, discipline, forfeit, forfeiture, gallows, hard work, infliction, just desserts*, lumps, maltreatment, mortification, mulct, ostracism, pain, penance, proof, punitive measures, purgatory, reparation, retribution, rod, rough treatment, sanction, sequestration, short shrift*, slave labor*, suffering, torture, trial, unhappiness, victimization, what for*; SEE CONCEPT 123

punitive [adj] *concerning punishment*
castigating, correctional, disciplinary, in reprisal, in retaliation, penal, punishing, punitory, retaliative, retaliatory, revengeful, vindictive; SEE CONCEPT 319

puny [adj] *small, insignificant*
diminutive, feeble, fragile, frail, half-pint*, inconsequential, inferior, infirm, little, measly*, minor, niggling*, nothing, paltry, peanut*, peewee*, petty, picayune, piddling*, pint-sized*, runt, shrimp*, small-fry*, small time*, stunted, tiny, trifling, trivial, two-bit*, unconsequential, underfed, undersized, undeveloped, unsound, unsubstantial, weak, weakly, wee*, worthless, zero*, zilch*; SEE CONCEPTS 489,575,773

pupil [n] *person who is learning something*
adherent, attendant, beginner, bookworm*, brain*, catechumen, disciple, first-year student, follower, graduate student, junior, learner, neophyte, novice, satellite, scholar, schoolboy/girl, senior, sophomore, student, tenderfoot*, undergraduate; SEE CONCEPT 350

puppet [n] *person or toy manipulated by another*
creature, doll, dupe*, figurehead, figurine, instrument, jerk*, manikin, marionette, moppet, mouthpiece*, patsy*, pawn, pushover, schlemiel*, servant, soft touch*, stooge*, tool*, victim; SEE CONCEPTS 423,446

purchase [n] *possession obtained with money*
acquirement, acquisition, asset, bargain, booty*, buy, gain, investment, property, steal; SEE CONCEPTS 446,710

purchase [v] *buy, obtain*
achieve, acquire, attain, come by, cop*, deal in, earn, gain, get hold of, go shopping, invest, make a buy, make a purchase, market, patronize, pay for, pick up, procure, realize, redeem, secure, shop, shop for, take, take up, truck*, win; SEE CONCEPT 327

pure [adj1] *unmixed, genuine*
authentic, bright, classic, clear, complete, fair, flawless, kosher*, limpid, lucid, natural, neat, out-and-out*, pellucid, perfect, plain, plenary, pure and simple, real, simple, straight, total, transparent, true, twenty-four carat*, unadulterated, unalloyed, unclouded, undiluted, unmingled; SEE CONCEPT 485

pure [adj2] *clean, uncontaminated*
disinfected, germ-free, immaculate, intemerate, pasteurized, pristine, purified, refined, sanitary, snowy, spotless, stainless, sterile, sterilized, taintless, unadulterated, unblemished, undebased, unpolluted, unsoiled, unspotted, unstained, unsullied, untainted, untarnished, wholesome; SEE CONCEPT 621

pure [adj3] *virginal, chaste*
babe in woods*, blameless, celibate, clean, continent, decent, exemplary, fresh, good, guileless, honest, immaculate, inculpable, innocent, inviolate, irreproachable, kid, lily white*, maidenly, modest, pure as driven snow*, righteous, sinless, spotless, stainless, true, unblemished, unblighted, uncorrupted, undefiled, unprofaned, unspotted, unstained, unsullied, upright, virgin, virtuous, wet behind ears*, wide-eyed; SEE CONCEPT 372

pure [adj4] *absolute, utter*
blasted*, blessed*, complete, confounded, infernal*, mere, out-and-out*, sheer, thorough, unmitigated, unqualified; SEE CONCEPTS 531,535

pure [adj5] *theoretical*
abstract, academic, philosophical, speculative, tentative, unproved; SEE CONCEPT 529

purely [adv] simply, absolutely
all, all in all, altogether, barely, completely, entirely, essentially, exactly, exclusively, in toto*, just, merely, only, plainly, quite, solely, totally, utterly, wholly; SEE CONCEPTS 531,544

purge [n] elimination, removal
abolition, abstersion, catharsis, clarification, cleaning, cleanup, coup, crushing, disposal, disposition, ejection, eradication, evacuation, excretion, expulsion, expurgation, extermination, extirpation, liquidation, murder, purification, reign of terror*, suppression, witch hunt; SEE CONCEPTS 165,211,252

purge [v] rid of; clean out
abolish, absolve, clarify, cleanse, clear, depurate, disabuse, dismiss, dispose of, do away with*, eject, eradicate, erase, excrete, exonerate, expel, expiate, expunge, exterminate, forgive, kill, liquidate, oust, pardon, prevent, purify, remove, rout out, shake out*, sweep out, unload, wash, wipe off map*, wipe out; SEE CONCEPTS 165,211,252

purification [n] freeing, cleansing
ablution, absolution, atonement, baptism, bathing, catharsis, depuration, disinfection, distillation, expiation, expurgation, forgiveness, grace, lavation, laving, lustration, purgation, purge, purifying, rarefaction, rebirth, redemption, refinement, regeneration, salvation, sanctification, washing; SEE CONCEPTS 165,367

purify [v] free; make clean
absolve, aerate, aerify, atone, chasten, clarify, clean, cleanse, clear, decontaminate, deodorize, depurate, deterge, disinfect, edulcorate, elutriate, exculpate, exonerate, expiate, filter, fumigate, lustrate, oxygenate, purge, rarify, redeem, refine, remit, sanctify, sanitize, shrive, sublimate, wash; SEE CONCEPTS 165,367

purple [n/adj] blue and red colors mixed together
amaranthine, amethyst, bluish red, color, heliotrope, lavender, lilac, magenta, mauve, mulberry, orchid, perse, plum, pomegranate, reddish blue, violaceous, violet, wine; SEE CONCEPTS 618,622

purport [n] meaning, implication
acceptation, aim, bearing, burden, connotation, core, design, drift, gist, heart, idea, import, intendment, intent, intention, matter, meat, message, nub, object, objective, pith, plan, point, purpose, score, sense, significance, significancy, signification, spirit, stuff, substance, tendency, tenor, thrust, understanding, upshot; SEE CONCEPTS 20,659,660,689

purport [v] assert, mean
allege, betoken, claim, convey, declare, denote, express, imply, import, indicate, intend, maintain, point to, pose as, pretend, proclaim, profess, signify, suggest; SEE CONCEPTS 49,682

purpose [n1] intention, meaning, aim
ambition, animus, aspiration, big idea*, bourn, calculation, design, desire, destination, determination, direction, dream, drift, end, expectation, function, goal, hope, idea, intendment, intent, mecca, mission, object, objective, plan, point, premeditation, principle, project, proposal, proposition, prospect, reason, resolve, scheme, scope, target, ulterior motive, view, whatfor*, where one's headed*, whole idea*, why and wherefore*, whyfor*, will, wish; SEE CONCEPTS 20,659, 660,689

purpose [n2] persistence, resolve
confidence, constancy, determination, faith, firm-

ness, resolution, single-mindedness, steadfastness, tenacity, will; SEE CONCEPTS 633,644

purpose [n3] use
advantage, avail, benefit, duty, effect, function, gain, goal, good, mark, mission, object, objective, outcome, profit, result, return, target, utility; SEE CONCEPTS 658,694

purpose [v] intend, set sights on
aim, aspire, bid for, commit, conclude, consider, contemplate, decide, design, determine, have a mind to*, have in view, intend, make up one's mind*, mean, meditate, mind, plan, ponder, propose, pursue, resolve, think to, work for, work toward; SEE CONCEPTS 18,36,80

purposeful [adj] resolved to do something
bent, be out for blood*, bound, calculated, dead set on*, decided, deliberate, determined, firm, fixed, intense, intent, mean business*, obstinate, persistent, playing hard ball*, positive, purposive, resolute, settled, single-minded, stalwart, staunch, steadfast, steady, strong-willed, stubborn, teleological, tenacious, undeviating, unfaltering, unwavering; SEE CONCEPTS 326,403,542

purposeless [adj] useless, insignificant
aimless, designless, desultory, drifting, empty, feckless, floundering, fustian, goalless, good-for-nothing*, haphazard, hit-or-miss*, indiscriminate, irregular, meaningless, motiveless, needless, nonsensical, pointless, purportless, random, senseless, uncalled for, undirected, unhelpful, unnecessary, unplanned, unprofitable, unpurposed, vacuous, wanton, worthless; SEE CONCEPTS 544,560

purposely [adv] intentionally
advisedly, by design, calculatedly, consciously, deliberately, designedly, explicitly, expressly, knowingly, on purpose, prepensely, purposedly, willfully, with intent; SEE CONCEPTS 529,544

purse [n1] tote for carrying personal items
bag, billfold, bursa, carryall, clutch, frame, handbag, hide, leather, lizard, moneybag, pocket, pocketbook, poke, pouch, receptacle, reticule, sack, wallet; SEE CONCEPTS 339,446,450,494

purse [n2] award; winnings
coffers, exchequer, funds, gift, means, money, present, prize, resources, reward, stake, treasury, wealth, wherewithal; SEE CONCEPTS 337,344

purse [v] press together
close, cockle, contract, crease, knit, pucker, ruffle, tighten, wrinkle; SEE CONCEPTS 185,208

pursue [v1] chase, follow
accompany, attend, badger, bait, bird-dog*, bug, camp on the doorstep of*, chivy, dog*, fish*, give chase, go after, harass, harry, haunt, hound, hunt, hunt down, move behind, nose around*, oppress, persevere, persist, plague, play catch up*, poke around, prowl after, ride, run after, run down, scout out, search for, search high heaven*, search out, seek, shadow, stalk, tag, tail*, take out after*, trace, track, track down, trail; SEE CONCEPT 207

pursue [v2] have as one's goal
aim for, aspire to, attempt, desire, go in for, go out for, have a go at, purpose, seek, strive for, try for, work for, work toward; SEE CONCEPTS 20,36

pursue [v3] persist, persevere
adhere, apply oneself, carry on, conduct, continue, cultivate, engage in, hold to, keep on, maintain, perform, ply, practice, proceed, prosecute,

see through, tackle, wage, work at; SEE CONCEPTS 87,100,239

pursue [v4] *seek social alliance with*
address, call, chase, chase after, court, date, go after, go for, pay attention, pay court*, play up to, rush*, spark, sue, sweetheart*, woo; SEE CONCEPT 384

pursuit [n1] *chase, search*
following, going all out, hunt, hunting, inquiry, pursual, pursuance, pursuing, quest, reaching, seeking, stalk, tracking, trail, trailing; SEE CONCEPT 207

pursuit [n2] *occupation, interest of person*
accomplishing, accomplishment, activity, biz*, business, calling, career, do*, employment, game*, go*, hang*, hobby, job, line*, occupation, pastime, pleasure, racket, thing*, undertaking, venture, vocation, work; SEE CONCEPT 349

push [n1] *physical force*
advance, assault, attack, bearing, blow, butt, charge, drive, driving, effort, energy, exerting, exertion, forcing, impact, jolt, lean, mass, nudge, offensive, onset, poke, prod, propulsion, shove, shoving, straining, thrust, thrusting, weight; SEE CONCEPTS 200,208,641,724

push [n2] *mental determination*
ambition, drive, dynamism, energy, enterprise, get-up-and-go*, go*, gumption*, guts*, initiative, pep, punch, snap, spunk, starch, vigor, vitality; SEE CONCEPTS 410,411

push [v1] *thrust, press with force*
accelerate, bear down, budge, bulldoze*, bump, butt, crowd, crush against, depress, dig, drive, elbow, exert, force, gore, high pressure*, hustle, impel, jam, jostle, launch, lie on, make one's way*, move, muscle, nudge, poke, pour it on*, pressure, propel, push the arm on*, railroad*, ram*, rest on, shift, shoulder, shove, squash, squeeze, squish, steamroll*, stir, strain, strong-arm*; SEE CONCEPTS 200,208,243

push [v2] *incite, urge*
bear down, browbeat, bulldoze*, coerce, constrain, dragoon, egg on*, encourage, exert influence, expedite, fire up*, goad, goose*, go to town on*, hurry, impel, influence, inspire, jolly, key up*, kid, lean on*, motivate, oblige, overpress, persuade, pour it on*, press, pressure, prod, push around*, put the screws to*, put up to*, railroad*, sell on*, speed, speed up, spur, squeeze, steamroll*, strong-arm*, turn on*; SEE CONCEPTS 14,68,243

push [v3] *advertise, promote*
advance, boost, cry up*, hype*, make known, plug*, propagandize, publicize, puff*; SEE CONCEPTS 49,324

push off/push on [v] *leave; go to another place*
beat it*, continue, depart, exit, fare, get away, get lost*, go, go away, hie, hit the road*, journey, keep going, launch, light out, make oneself scarce*, make progress, pass, proceed, process, pull out, quit, repair, shove off, start, take off, travel, wend, withdraw; SEE CONCEPTS 195,704

pushover [n] *something or someone easily influenced*
breeze, child's play*, chump*, cinch, duck soup*, easy game*, easy mark*, easy pickings*, fool, kid stuff*, picnic*, piece of cake*, setup, snap, soft touch*, stooge*, sucker, victim, walkover; SEE CONCEPTS 423,693

pushy [adj] *aggressive, offensive*
ambitious, assertive, bold, brash, bumptious, forceful, loud, militant, obnoxious, obtrusive, officious, presumptuous, pushful, pushing, self-assertive; SEE CONCEPTS 401,404

pussyfoot [v] *walk or act carefully*
avoid, beat around the bush*, be noncommittal, creep, dodge, equivocate, evade, glide, hedge, hem and haw*, lurk, prevaricate, prowl, shuffle, sidestep, sit on the fence*, skulk, slide, slink, slip, sneak, steal, tergiversate, tergiverse, tiptoe, tread warily, weasel*; SEE CONCEPTS 151,410

put [v1] *position*
bring, concenter, concentrate, deposit, embed, establish, fasten, fix, fixate, focus, insert, install, invest, lay, nail, park, peg, place, plank, plank down, plant, plop, plunk, plunk down, quarter, repose, rest, rivet, seat, set, settle, situate, stick; SEE CONCEPT 201

put [v2] *propose; express in words*
advance, air, bring forward, couch, express, formulate, forward, give, offer, phrase, pose, posit, prefer, present, propone, proposition, propound, render, set, set before, state, submit, suggest, tender, translate, transpose, turn, utter, vent, ventilate, word; SEE CONCEPTS 47,66,67

put [v3] *commit, assign*
condemn, consign, constrain, doom, employ, enjoin, force, impose, induce, inflict, levy, make, oblige, require, set, subject, subject to; SEE CONCEPTS 14,242

putative [adj] *commonly believed*
accepted, alleged, assumed, conjectural, hypothetical, imputed, presumed, presumptive, reported, reputed, supposed, suppositional, suppositious; SEE CONCEPT 529

put away/put aside/put by [v1/v] *keep in reserve*
cache, deposit, keep, lay aside, lay away, lay by, lay in, put by, put out of the way, salt away*, save, set aside, squirrel away*, stockpile, store, store away*, stow away; SEE CONCEPTS 129,134

put away [v2] *incarcerate*
certify, commit, confine, institutionalize, jail, lock up; SEE CONCEPT 317

put away [v3] *consume*
devour, eat up, gobble*, gulp down, polish off*, punish, put down, shift, swill, wolf down*; SEE CONCEPT 169

put away [v4] *kill*
assassinate, bury, cool*, cut off, destroy, dispatch, do away with, do in*, dust off*, execute, finish, inter, knock off*, liquidate, murder, plant, put down*, put out of its misery*, put to sleep*, slay, tomb; SEE CONCEPT 252

put down [v1] *write into record*
enter, inscribe, jot down, log, record, set down, take down, transcribe, write down; SEE CONCEPT 79

put down [v2] *subdue*
annihilate, crush, defeat, dismiss, extinguish, quash, quell, reject, repress, silence, squash*, stamp out*, suppress; SEE CONCEPTS 95,252

put down [v3] *comment negatively*
belittle, condemn, crush, decry, deflate, derogate, discount, dismiss, disparage, downcry, humiliate, minimize, mortify, opprobriate, reject, run down, shame, slight, snub, write off; SEE CONCEPT 54

put-down [n] *nasty commentary*
cut*, dig*, disparagement, gibe*, humiliation, indignity, insult, jibe*, knock*, pan*, rebuff, sar-

casm, slight, sneer*, snub, suppression; SEE CONCEPTS 54,278

put off [v] *defer, delay*

adjourn, dally, dawdle, dillydally*, drag one's feet*, hold off, hold over, lag*, lay over, linger, loiter, poke*, postpone, prorogue, put back, reschedule, retard, shelve, stay, suspend, tarry, trail; SEE CONCEPTS 121,234

put on [v1] *pretend*

act, affect, assume, bluff, confound, confuse, counterfeit, deceive, don, fake, feign, make believe, masquerade, playact, pose, pull, put on a front, put on an act, sham, simulate, strike, take on, trick; SEE CONCEPT 59

put on [v2] *stage a performance*

do, mount, present, produce, show; SEE CONCEPT 292

put out [v1] *upset, irritate; inconvenience*

aggravate, anger, annoy, bother, burn, confound, discomfit, discommode, discompose, disconcert, discountenance, disoblige, displease, dissatisfy, disturb, embarrass, exasperate, gall, get*, grate, harass, impose upon, incommode, inflame, irk, nettle, perturb, provoke, put on the spot*, rile, roil, trouble, vex; SEE CONCEPTS 7,14,19

put out [v2] *extinguish fire*

blow out, douse, out, quench, smother, snuff out, stamp out; SEE CONCEPT 252

putrefy [v] *rot*

break down, corrupt, crumble, decay, decompose, deteriorate, disintegrate, go bad*, molder, putresce, spoil, stink, taint, turn; SEE CONCEPT 469

putrid [adj] *rotten, stinking*

bad, contaminated, corrupt, decayed, decomposed, fetid, foul, high, malodorous, moldered, nidorous, noisome, off, putrefied, rancid, rank, reeking, rotting, smelly, spoiled, strong, tainted, whiffy*; SEE CONCEPTS 485,598

putter [v] *dawdle*

doodle, fiddle, fritter, goof around*, loiter, mess, mess around*, niggle, poke*, potter*, puddle*, shuffle around, tinker*; SEE CONCEPTS 87,210

put up [v1] *accommodate guest*

bestow, billet, board, bunk, domicile, entertain, give lodging, harbor, house, lodge, make welcome, provide, quarter, take in; SEE CONCEPTS 324,384

put up [v2] *build, erect*

construct, fabricate, forge, make, put together, raise, rear, shape, uprear; SEE CONCEPT 168

puzzle [v] *baffle, confuse*

addle, amaze, bamboozle*, beat, befog, befuddle, bemuse, bewilder, buffalo*, complicate, confound, discombobulate*, disconcert, distract, disturb, dumbfound, flabbergast, floor*, flummox, foil, frustrate, get to*, mystify, nonplus, obscure, perplex, pose, profundiate, psych out*, put off, rattle, snow*, stir, stumble, stump, throw; SEE CONCEPT 16

puzzle [v2] *wonder about*

ask oneself, brood, cudgel, marvel, mull over, muse, ponder, rack one's brains*, study, think about, think hard; SEE CONCEPT 17

puzzled [adj] *confused*

at a loss*, at sea*, baffled, bewildered, bollixed, clueless, come apart, come unzipped*, discombobulated*, dopey*, doubtful, floored*, foggy, fouled up*, hung up*, in a fog*, lost, loused up*, messed up*, mind-blown*, mixed up*, mucked up*, mystified, nonplussed, perplexed, rattled,

screwed up*, shook, shook up, spaced out*, stuck, stumped, thrown, unglued*, without a clue; SEE CONCEPTS 403,690

puzzling [adj] *confusing*

abstruse, ambiguous, baffling, bewildering, beyond one, difficult, enigmatic, hard, incomprehensible, inexplicable, involved, knotty, labyrinthine, misleading, mystifying, obscure, perplexing, surprising, unaccountable, unclear, unfathomable; SEE CONCEPT 529

Q

quack [n] *person who pretends to be an expert*

actor, bum*, bunco artist, charlatan, cheat, con artist, counterfeiter, counterfeiter, fake, faker, flimflammer*, four-flusher*, fraud, hoser*, humbug, impostor, mountebank, phony, playactor, pretender, pseudo*, put-on*, quacksalver*, sham, shammer*, shark*, sharp*, simulator, slicker*, whip*; SEE CONCEPT 412

quack [adj] *counterfeit*

bum*, dishonest, dissembling, fake, false, fraudulent, phony, pretended, pretentious, pseudo*, sham*, simulated, unprincipled; SEE CONCEPT 582

quaff [v] *drink down*

down, gulp, guzzle, imbibe, ingurgitate, partake, sip, sup, swallow, swig, swill, toss; SEE CONCEPT 169

quagmire [n1] *bad situation*

box*, corner*, difficulty, dilemma, entanglement, fix, hole*, imbroglio, impasse, involvement, jam, mire, morass, muddle, pass, perplexity, pickle*, pinch*, plight, predicament, quandary, scrape, trouble; SEE CONCEPTS 666,674

quagmire [n2] *bog*

fen, marsh, marshland, mire, morass, moss, quag, quicksand, slough, swamp; SEE CONCEPT 509

quail [v] *cower, shrink*

blanch, blench, cringe, droop, faint, falter, flinch, have cold feet*, quake, recoil, shake, shudder, start, tremble, wince; SEE CONCEPTS 35,149,195

quaint [adj1] *strange, odd*

bizarre, curious, droll, eccentric, erratic, fanciful, fantastic, freakish, freaky*, funny, idiosyncratic, laughable, oddball, offbeat, off the beaten track*, original, outlandish, peculiar, queer, singular, special, unusual, weird*, whimsical; SEE CONCEPTS 564,589

quaint [adj2] *old-fashioned; nostalgically attractive*

affected, ancient, antiquated, antique, archaic, artful, baroque, captivating, charming, colonial, curious, cute, enchanting, fanciful, Gothic*, ingenious, old-world, picturesque, pleasing, Victorian*, whimsical; SEE CONCEPTS 578,589,797

quake [n] *earthquake*

aftershock, convulsion, quaker, seism, shake, shock, temblor, tremblor, tremor; SEE CONCEPT 526

quake [v] *shake, vibrate*

convulse, cower, fluctuate, jar, jitter, move, pulsate, quail, quiver, rock, shiver, shrink, shudder, throb, totter, tremble, tremor, twitter, waver, wobble; SEE CONCEPT 152

qualification [n1] *ability, aptitude*
accomplishment, adequacy, attainment, attribute, capability, capacity, competence, eligibility, endowment, experience, fitness, goods, makings, might, qualifiedness, quality, skill, stuff, suitability, suitableness, what it takes*; SEE CONCEPT 630

qualification [n2] *requirement, restriction*
allowance, caveat, condition, contingency, criterion, essential, exception, exemption, limitation, modification, need, objection, postulate, prerequisite, provision, proviso, requisite, reservation, stipulation; SEE CONCEPTS 646,652

qualified [adj1] *able, skillful*
accomplished, adept, adequate, all around, au fait, capable, catechized, certified, competent, disciplined, efficient, equipped, examined, experienced, expert, fit, fitted, good, instructed, knowledgeable, licensed, practiced, pro*, proficient, proper, proved, quizzed, talented, tested, trained, tried, up to snuff*, up to speed*, vet*, veteran, war-horse*, wicked; SEE CONCEPT 527

qualified [adj2] *limited, restricted*
bounded, circumscribed, conditional, confined, contingent, definite, determined, equivocal, fixed, guarded, modified, partial, provisional, reserved; SEE CONCEPT 554

qualify [v1] *make or become ready, prepared*
authorize, capacitate, certify, check out, come up to snuff*, commission, condition, cut it*, earn one's wings*, empower, enable, endow, entitle, equip, fill the bill*, fit, get by*, ground, hack it*, make it*, make the cut*, make the grade*, measure up, meet, pass, pass muster*, permit, ready, sanction, score, suffice, suit, train; SEE CONCEPTS 99,630

qualify [v2] *lessen, restrict*
abate, adapt, alter, assuage, change, circumscribe, diminish, ease, limit, mitigate, moderate, modify, modulate, reduce, regulate, restrain, soften, temper, vary, weaken; SEE CONCEPTS 240,698

qualify [v3] *characterize, distinguish*
ascribe, assign, attribute, describe, designate, impute, individualize, individuate, mark, name, predicate, signalize, singularize; SEE CONCEPT 411

quality [n1] *characteristic, feature*
affection, affirmation, aspect, attribute, character, condition, constitution, description, element, endowment, essence, factor, genius, individuality, kind, make, mark, name of tune*, nature, nature of beast*, parameter, peculiarity, predication, property, savor, sort, trait, virtue, way of it*; SEE CONCEPT 543

quality [n2] *value, status*
arete, caliber, capacity, character, class, condition, distinction, excellence, excellency, footing, grade, group, kind, merit, perfection, place, position, preeminence, rank, repute, standing, state, station, stature, step, superbness, superiority, variety, virtue, worth; SEE CONCEPTS 346,378,668

qualm [n] *nagging doubt*
agitation, anxiety, apprehension, compunction, conscience, demur, disquiet, foreboding, hesitation, indecision, insecurity, misdoubt, misgiving, mistrust, nervousness, objection, pang, perturbation, presentiment, regret, reluctance, remonstrance, remorse, scruple, suspicion, twinge, uncertainty, unease, uneasiness; SEE CONCEPTS 410,532

quandary [n] *delicate situation*
bewilderment, bind, Catch-22*, clutch, corner*, difficulty, dilemma, double trouble*, doubt, embarrassment, hang-up*, impasse, mire, perplexity, pickle*, plight, predicament, puzzle, spot*, strait, uncertainty, up a tree*; SEE CONCEPTS 532,674,690

quantity [n] *number or amount*
abundance, aggregate, allotment, amplitude, batch, body, budget, bulk, capacity, deal, expanse, extent, figure, greatness, length, load, lot, magnitude, mass, measure, multitude, part, pile, portion, profusion, quota, size, sum, total, variety, volume; SEE CONCEPT 787

quarrel [n] *disagreement*
affray, altercation, argument, battle royal*, beef*, bickering*, brannigan*, brawl, breach, broil*, catfight*, combat, commotion, complaint, contention, controversy, difference, difference of opinion, difficulty, disapproval, discord, disputation, dispute, dissension, dissidence, disturbance, dust*, falling-out*, feud, fight, fisticuffs*, fracas, fray, fuss, hassle, misunderstanding, objection, rhubarb*, row, ruckus*, run-in, scrap, set-to*, spat, squabble, strife, struggle, tiff, tumult, vendetta, wrangle; SEE CONCEPTS 46,106

quarrel [v] *disagree*
altercate, argue, battle, be at loggerheads*, bicker, brawl, break with, bump, carp, caterwaul, cavil, charge, clash, collide, complain, contend, contest, cross swords*, differ, disapprove, dispute, dissent, divide, embroil, fall out*, feud, fight, find fault, get tough with*, hassle, have it out*, have words*, lock horns*, mix it up*, object to, row, scrap, set to, spar, spat, squabble, strive, struggle, take exception, take on, tangle, vary, war, wrangle; SEE CONCEPTS 46,106

quarrelsome [adj] *being disagreeable*
argumentative, bad-tempered, bellicose, belligerent, brawling, cantankerous, cat-and-dog*, choleric, churlish, combative, contentious, crabby*, cross, disputatious, dissentious, excitable, fiery, fractious, gladiatorial, hasty, have chip on shoulder*, hotheaded*, huffy, impassioned, irascible, irritable, litigious, ornery, passionate, peevish, pettish, petulant, pugnacious, querulous, ructious, snappy, tempestuous, thin-skinned*, touchy, truculent, turbulent, unruly, violent, war; SEE CONCEPTS 401,542

quarry [n] *goal*
aim, chase, game, objective, prey, prize, quest, raven, victim; SEE CONCEPT 659

quarter [n1] *one of four equal parts*
division, farthing, fourth, one-fourth, part, portion, quad, quadrant, quartern, section, semester, span, term, two bits*; SEE CONCEPT 835

quarter [n2] *area, neighborhood*
barrio, bearing, direction, district, division, domain, ghetto, inner city, locality, location, neck of the woods*, old town, part, place, point, position, precinct, province, region, section, sector, side, skid row, slum, spot, station, stomping ground*, territory, turf, zone, zoo*; SEE CONCEPTS 508,512

quarter [n3] *forgiveness*
clemency, compassion, favor, grace, leniency, lenity, mercy, pity; SEE CONCEPTS 410,633

quarter [v1] *divide into four equal parts*
cleave, cut, cut up, dismember, fourth; SEE CONCEPT 98

quarter [v2] *provide lodging*
accommodate, billet, board, bunk, canton, domicile, domiciliate, entertain, establish, harbor, house, install, lodge, place, post, put up, settle, shelter, station; SEE CONCEPT *140*

quarters [n] *place to live or sleep*
abode, accommodation, apartment, barracks, billet, cabin, cantonment, chambers, condo, cottage, digs*, domicile, dorm, dwelling, flat, fraternity, habitat, habitation, home, house, lodge, lodging, place, post, ranch, residence, room, roost*, shelter, sorority, station, tent; SEE CONCEPT *516*

quash [v1] *destroy, defeat*
annihilate, beat, crush, extinguish, extirpate, overcome, overthrow, put down, quell, quench, repress, scrunch*, snow under*, squash*, squish*, subdue, suppress, trash; SEE CONCEPTS *95,252*

quash [v2] *nullify, cancel*
abrogate, annul, black out*, bottle up*, clamp down on, cork up*, crack down on*, declare null and void*, discharge, dissolve, hush up*, invalidate, kill, negate, overrule, overthrow, put damper on*, put the lid on*, repeal, rescind, reverse, revoke, set aside, shut down, squelch, undo, vacate, veto, vitiate, void, watergate*; SEE CONCEPTS *121,234,266*

quasi [adj] *almost; to a certain extent*
apparent, apparently, fake, mock, near, nominal, partly, pretended, pseudo-*, seeming, seemingly, semi-, sham*, so-called, supposedly, synthetic, virtual, would-be*; SEE CONCEPT *582*

queasy [adj] *not feeling well; not comfortable*
anxious, bilious, concerned, fidgety, green around gills*, groggy, ill, ill at ease, indisposed, nauseated, pukish, qualmish, queer, restless, rocky*, sick, sick as a dog*, sickly, squeamish, troubled, uncertain, uncomfortable, under the weather*, uneasy, unwell, upset, worried; SEE CONCEPTS *314,403*

queer [adj1] *odd; abnormal*
anomalous, atypical, bizarre, crazy, curious, demented, disquieting, doubtful, droll, dubious, eccentric, eerie, erratic, extraordinary, fishy*, flaky*, fly ball*, freaky*, funny, idiosyncratic, irrational, irregular, kinky*, kooky*, mad, mysterious, odd, off the wall*, outlandish, outré, peculiar, puzzling, quaint, questionable, remarkable, shady, singular, strange, suspicious, touched, unbalanced, uncanny, uncommon, unconventional, unhinged, unnatural, unorthodox, unusual, wacky*, weird; SEE CONCEPTS *404,548,564*

queer [adj2] *not feeling well*
dizzy, faint, giddy, green*, ill, lightheaded, pukish*, qualmish, qualmy*, queasy*, reeling, sick, squeamish*, uneasy; SEE CONCEPT *314*

quell [v1] *defeat, suppress*
annihilate, conquer, crush, extinguish, hush up*, kill, overcome, overpower, put down, put the lid on*, queer, quench, shut down, silence, sit on, stamp out*, stifle, stop, subdue, subjugate, vanquish; SEE CONCEPTS *95,121,234*

quell [v2] *alleviate, calm*
allay, appease, assuage, check, compose, deaden, dull, ease, mitigate, moderate, mollify, pacify, quiet, reduce, silence, soothe, still; SEE CONCEPTS *7,22,110*

quench [v1] *destroy, extinguish*
annihilate, check, choke, crush, dampen, decimate, demolish, destruct, dismantle, douse, end, kill, knock down, moisten, put down, put out, quash*, quell, raze, ruin, shatter, smother, snuff out*, stifle, suppress, wreck; SEE CONCEPTS *234,252*

quench [v2] *satisfy, especially thirst*
allay, alleviate, appease, assuage, content, cool*, glut, gorge, gratify, lighten, mitigate, moisten, relieve, sate, satiate, slake; SEE CONCEPTS *136,244*

querulous [adj] *grouchy, hard to please*
bearish, bemoaning, cantankerous, captious, carping, censorious, complaining, critical, cross, crying, deploring, discontented, dissatisfied, edgy, fault-finding, fretful, grousing, grumbling, grumbly, huffy* irascible, irritable, lamenting, out of sorts* peevish, petulant, plaintive, scrappy, snappy, sour, testy, thin-skinned* touchy, uptight, wailing, waspish, waspy, whimpering, whining, whiny; SEE CONCEPTS *401,542*

query [n] *demand for answers*
concern, doubt, dubiety, inquiry, interrogation, interrogatory, mistrust, objection, problem, question, questioning, reservation, skepticism, suspicion, uncertainty; SEE CONCEPTS *21,48,53,662*

query [v] *ask*
catechize, challenge, disbelieve, dispute, distrust, doubt, enquire, examine, hit up, impeach, impugn, inquire, interrogate, knock, mistrust, put out a feeler* question, quiz, suspect, test the waters*; SEE CONCEPTS *21,48,53*

quest [n] *search, exploration*
adventure, chase, crusade, delving, enterprise, examination, expedition, hunt, inquest, inquiry, inquisition, investigation, journey, mission, pilgrimmage, prey, probe, probing, pursual, pursuit, quarry, research, seeking, voyage; SEE CONCEPTS *48,103,216*

question [n1] *asking for answer*
catechism, examination, inquest, inquiring, inquiry, inquisition, interrogation, interrogatory, investigation, poll, Q and A*, query, questioning, third degree*, wringer*; SEE CONCEPTS *48,53*

question [n2] *controversy, doubt*
argument, challenge, confusion, contention, debate, demur, demurral, difficulty, dispute, dubiety, enigma, misgiving, mystery, objection, problem, protest, puzzle, query, remonstrance, remonstration, uncertainty; SEE CONCEPTS *666,674*

question [n3] *issue, point at issue*
discussion, motion, point, problem, proposal, proposition, subject, theme, topic; SEE CONCEPTS *532,690*

question [v1] *ask for answer*
ask about, catechize, challenge, cross-examine, enquire, examine, give the third degree*, go over, grill, hit*, hit up*, hold out for, inquire, interrogate, interview, investigate, knock*, make inquiry, petition, pick one's brains*, probe, pry, pump, put through the wringer*, put to the question*, query, quest, quiz, raise question, roast*, search, seek, show curiosity, solicit, sound out*, sweat it out of*, work over*; SEE CONCEPTS *48,53*

question [v2] *doubt*
call into question, cast doubt upon, challenge, controvert, disbelieve, dispute, distrust, hesitate, impeach, impugn, mistrust, oppose, puzzle over, query, suspect, suspicion, wonder about; SEE CONCEPT *21*

questionable [adj] *doubtful, uncertain*
ambiguous, apocryphal, arguable, contingent, controversial, controvertible, cryptic, debatable, disputable, dubious, dubitable, enigmatic, equivocal, fishy*, hard to believe, hypothetical, iffy*, indecisive, indefinite, indeterminate, moot, mysterious, obscure, occult, open to doubt, open to question, oracular, paradoxical, problematic, problematical, provisional, shady, suspect, suspicious, unconfirmed, undefined, under advisement, under examination, unproven, unreliable, unsettled, vague; SEE CONCEPTS *529,535*

queue [n] *sequence*
chain, concatenation, echelon, file, line, order, progression, rank, row, series, string, succession, tail, tier, train; SEE CONCEPTS *432,727*

quibble [n] *objection, complaint*
artifice, cavil, criticism, dodge, duplicity, equivocation, evasion, hair-splitter*, nicety, niggle*, nit-picker*, pretense, prevarication, protest, quiddity, quirk, shift, sophism, subterfuge, subtlety; SEE CONCEPTS *46,52*

quibble [v] *disagree over minor issues*
altercate, argue over, argufy, avoid, bicker, blow hot and cold*, carp, catch at straws*, cavil, chicane, criticize, dispute, equivocate, evade, fence*, flip-flop*, hassle, have at it*, hem and haw*, hypercriticize*, make a big thing about*, nit-pick*, paralogize, pettifog*, pretend, prevaricate, put up an argument, set to, shift, spar, split hairs*, squabble, talk back, waffle, wrangle; SEE CONCEPTS *46,52*

quick [adj] *fast, speedy*
abrupt, accelerated, active, agile, alert, a move on*, animated, ASAP*, breakneck*, brief, brisk, cursory, curt, double time*, energetic, expeditious, expeditive, express, fleet, flying, going, harefooted*, hasty, headlong, hurried, immediate, impatient, impetuous, instantaneous, keen, lively, mercurial, move it, nimble, on the double*, perfunctory, posthaste, prompt, pronto*, rapid, snappy, spirited, sprightly, spry, sudden, swift, the lead out*, winged*; SEE CONCEPTS *544,588*

quick [adj2] *smart*
able, active, acute, adept, adroit, all there, apt, astute, bright, canny, capable, clever, competent, deft, dexterous, discerning, effective, effectual, intelligent, keen, knowing, nimble-witted, on the ball*, perceptive, perspicacious, prompt, quick on the draw, quick on the trigger*, quick on the uptake*, quick-witted, ready, receptive, savvy*, sharp, sharp as a tack*, shrewd, skillful, slick, smart as a whip*, vigorous, whiz*, wired*, wise; SEE CONCEPT *402*

quicken [v] *make faster; invigorate*
accelerate, activate, actuate, animate, arouse, awaken, dispatch, energize, excite, expedite, galvanize, goad, grow, hasten, hurry, impel, incite, increase, innervate, innerve, inspire, kindle, liven, make haste, motivate, move, pique, precipitate, promote, refresh, revitalize, revive, rouse, shake up, speed, spring, spur, step up, stimulate, stir, strengthen, urge, vitalize, vivificate, vivify; SEE CONCEPTS *7,19,22,250*

quick-tempered [adj] *easily upset, angered*
choleric, cranky, cross, excitable, fiery, hot-tempered, impatient, impulsive, inflammable, irascible, irritable, passionate, peppery, petulant, quarrelsome, ratty, sensitive, short-tempered, shrewish, splenetic, temperamental, testy, waspish; SEE CONCEPTS *401,404*

quick-witted [adj] *smart*
acute, agile, alert, apt, astute, brainy, bright, brilliant, canny, clever, facetious, humorous, intelligent, keen, knowing, nimble-witted, on the ball*, penetrating, penetrative, perceptive, prompt, quick, quick on the draw*, quick on the uptake*, ready, savvy*, sharp, sharp as a tack*, sharp-sighted, sharp-witted, shrewd, slick*, whiz*, wired*, wise, witty; SEE CONCEPTS *267,402*

quiet [n] *calmness, silence*
calm, cessation, dead air*, ease, hush, lull, noiselessness, peace, quietness, quietude, relaxation, repose, rest, serenity, soundlessness, speechlessness, still, stillness, stop, termination, tranquillity; SEE CONCEPTS *65,315,592,673,705*

quiet [adj1] *without or with little sound*
buttoned up*, clammed up*, close, close-mouthed, could hear a pin drop*, dumb, hushed, hushful, inaudible, low, low-pitched, muffled, mute, muted, noiseless, not saying boo*, peaceful, quiescent, quieted, reserved, reticent, secretive, silent, soft, soundless, speechless, still, stilled, taciturn, tight-lipped*, uncommunicative, unexpressed, unspeaking, unuttered, whist; SEE CONCEPTS *592,594*

quiet [adj2] *calm, peaceful*
collected, contented, docile, fixed, gentle, halcyon, hushed, inactive, isolated, level, meek, mild, motionless, pacific, placid, private, remote, reserved, restful, retired, secluded, secret, sedate, sequestered, serene, shy, smooth, stable, stagnant, still, tranquil, unanxious, undisturbed, unexcited, unfrequented, unruffled, untroubled; SEE CONCEPTS *401,583,584,705*

quiet [adj3] *simple, unobtrusive*
conservative, homely, inobtrusive, modest, plain, restrained, sober, subdued, tasteful, unassuming, unpretentious; SEE CONCEPT *589*

quiet [v] *make silent, calm*
allay, ameliorate, appease, assuage, becalm, button one's lip*, calm down, can it, choke, clam up*, compose, console, cool it*, cool out*, dummy up*, fix up, gag, gratify, hold it down, hush, ice*, inactivate, lull, moderate, mollify, muffle, muzzle, pacify, palliate, patch things up*, please, quieten, reconcile, relax, satisfy, settle, shush, shut up, silence, slack, smooth, soften, soft-pedal*, soothe, square, squash, squelch, still, stroke, subdue, take the bite out of*, tranquilize; SEE CONCEPTS *126,244,266*

quilt [n] *thick bedcovering made of patches*
batt, bedspread, blanket, comforter, counterpane, cover, coverlet, down, duvet, eiderdown, pad, patchwork, pouf, puff; SEE CONCEPTS *445,451, 473*

quintessence [n] *essence, core*
apotheosis, bottom, distillation, epitome, essentiality, extract, gist, heart, kernel, last word, lifeblood, marrow, pith, quiddity, soul, spirit, stuff, substance, ultimate, virtuality; SEE CONCEPTS *682,826*

quip [n] *witty communication, often verbal*
badinage, banter, bon mot, crack, drollery, gag, gibe, insult, jeer, jest, joke, mockery, offense, pleasantry, pun, repartee, retort, riposte, sally, satire, spoof, wisecrack, witticism; SEE CONCEPTS *273,278*

quirk [n] *oddity of personality, way of doing something*

aberration, caprice, characteristic, conceit, crotchet, eccentricity, equivocation, fancy, fetish, foible, habit, humor, idée fixe, idiosyncrasy, irregularity, kink, knack, mannerism, peculiarity, quibble, singularity, subterfuge, trait, turn, twist, vagary, whim, whimsy; SEE CONCEPTS *411,644*

quit [v] *abandon, leave*

abdicate, blow*, book*, bow out, check out, cut out*, decamp, depart, desert, drop, drop out, evacuate, exit, forsake, get off, give up, go, go away from, hang it up*, leave flat*, leave hanging*, pull out, push off*, relinquish, renounce, resign, retire, run out on, surrender, take a walk*, take off, throw over*, vacate, walk out on, withdraw, yield; SEE CONCEPT *195*

quit [v2] *stop doing something*

abandon, break off, call it a day*, call it quits*, cease, conclude, cut it out*, desist, discontinue, drop, end, get on the wagon*, give notice, give over*, give up, halt, hang it up*, kick over*, kick the habit*, knock off*, leave, leave off*, pack in*, quit cold, resign, retire, secede, sew up*, surcease, suspend, take the cure*, terminate, wind up*, withdraw, wrap up*; SEE CONCEPTS *119,234*

quite [adv1] *completely*

absolutely, actually, all, all in all, all told, altogether, considerably, entirely, fully, in all respects, in fact, in reality, in toto, in truth, just, largely, perfectly, positively, precisely, purely, really, thoroughly, totally, truly, utterly, well, wholly, without reservation; SEE CONCEPTS *531,582*

quite [adv2] *to a certain extent*

considerably, fairly, far, moderately, more or less, pretty, rather, reasonably, relatively, significantly, somewhat, to some degree, very; SEE CONCEPTS *569,772*

quiver [n] *shaking, vibration*

convulsion, flash, glimmer, glitter, oscillation, palpitation, pulsation, shake, shimmer, shiver, shudder, sparkle, spasm, throb, tic, tremble, tremor, twinkle; SEE CONCEPT *152*

quiver [v] *shake, vibrate*

agitate, beat, convulse, dither, jitter, oscillate, palpitate, pulsate, pulse, quake, quaver, shiver, shudder, thrill, throb, tremble, tremor, twitter; SEE CONCEPT *152*

quiz [n] *questioning, often in an organized academic setting*

blue book*, check, exam, examination, investigation, query, shotgun*, test; SEE CONCEPT *290*

quiz [v] *question*

ask, catechize, check, cross-examine, examine, give the third degree*, grill*, inquire, interrogate, investigate, pick one's brains*, pump*, query, test; SEE CONCEPT *48*

quizzical [adj] *appearing confused or curious*

amusing, aporetic, arch, bantering, derisive, disbelieving, eccentric, incredulous, inquiring, inquisitive, mocking, odd, probing, quaint, queer, questioning, sardonic, searching, show-me*, skeptical, supercilious, suspicious, teasing, unbelieving, unusual; SEE CONCEPTS *267,485*

quota [n] *portion allotted to something*

allocation, allotment, allowance, apportionment, assignment, bite, chunk, cut, division, divvy*, end, lot, measure, meed, part, partage, percentage, piece, piece of action*, proportion, quantum, ration, share, slice, split; SEE CONCEPTS *768,835*

quotation/quote [n1] *repetition of something spoken or written by someone*

citation, citing, cutting, excerpt, extract, passage, quote, recitation, reference, saying, selection; SEE CONCEPTS *274,278*

quotation/quote [n2] *financial estimate*

bid, bid price, charge, cost, current price, figure, market price, price, price named, published price, quote, rate, stated price, tender; SEE CONCEPTS *274,332,784*

quote [v] *repeat something spoken, written by another*

adduce, attest, cite, detail, excerpt, extract, instance, name, paraphrase, parrot, proclaim, recall, recite, recollect, reference, refer to, retell; SEE CONCEPTS *79,171*

R

rabid [adj] *very angry; maniacal*

berserk, bigoted, bitten, corybantic, crazed*, crazy, delirious, deranged, enthusiastic, extreme, extremist, fanatical, fervent, flipped*, foaming at the mouth*, frantic, freaked out*, frenetic, frenzied, furious, hot*, infuriated, insane, intemperate, intolerant, irrational, keen, mad, mad-dog*, narrow-minded, nutty*, obsessed, overboard, poisoned, radical, raging, revolutionary, sick*, sizzling, smoking*, steamed up*, ultra, ultraist, violent, virulent, wild, zealous; SEE CONCEPT *403*

race [n1] *pursuit; running, speeding*

chase, clash, clip, competition, contention, contest, course, dash, engagement, event, go, marathon, match, meet, relay, rivalry, run, rush, scurry, sprint, spurt; SEE CONCEPT *363*

race [n2] *ethnic group*

blood, breed, clan, color, cultural group, culture, family, folk, house, issue, kin, kind, kindred, line, lineage, nation, nationality, offspring, people, progeny, seed, species, stock, strain, tribe, type, variety; SEE CONCEPT *380*

race [n3] *stream, river*

branch, brook, creek, duct, gill, raceway, rill, rindle, rivulet, run, runnel, sluice, tide; SEE CONCEPT *514*

race [v] *run, speed in competition*

boil, bolt, bustle, career, chase, compete, contest, course, dart, dash, fling, fly, gallop, haste, hasten, hie, hurry, hustle, lash, outstrip, plunge ahead, post, pursue, rush, scamper, scramble, scud, scuttle, shoot, skim, sprint, spurt, swoop, tear, whisk, wing; SEE CONCEPTS *150,363*

racial [adj] *ethnic*

ancestral, ethnological, folk, genealogical, genetic, hereditary, lineal, national, phyletic, phylogenetic, tribal; SEE CONCEPT *549*

racism [n] *prejudice against an ethnic group*

apartheid, bias, bigotry, discrimination, illiberality, one-sidedness, partiality, racialism, sectarianism, segregation, unfairness; SEE CONCEPT *689*

rack [n] *frame, framework*

arbor, bed, box, bracket, counter, furniture, holder, ledge, perch, receptacle, shelf, stand, structure, trestle; SEE CONCEPTS *443,479*

rack [v] *torture; strain*
afflict, agonize, crucify, distress, excruciate, force, harass, harrow, martyr, oppress, pain, persecute, pull, shake, stress, stretch, tear, torment, try, wrench, wring; SEE CONCEPTS *7,19,246*

racket [n1] *commotion; fight*
agitation, babel, battle, blare, brawl, clamor, clangor, clash, clatter, din, disturbance, fracas, free-for-all*, fuss, hoo-ha*, hubbub*, jangle, noise, outcry, pandemonium, riot, roar, row, ruction, rumpus*, shouting, shuffle, squabble, squall, stir, to-do*, tumult, turbulence, turmoil, uproar, vociferation, wrangle; SEE CONCEPTS *65,106,230*

racket [n2] *criminal activity*
cheating, confidence game, con game, conspiracy, corruption, crime, dirty pool*, dishonesty, dodge, extortion, fraud, game, graft, illegality, illicit scheme, intrigue, lawlessness, lay, plot, push, scheme, shakedown, squeeze*, swindle, swindling, theft, trick, underworld; SEE CONCEPT *192*

racy [adj1] *energetic, zestful*
animated, bright, buoyant, clever, distinctive, entertaining, exciting, exhilarating, fiery, forceful, forcible, gingery, heady, keen, lively, mettlesome, peppery, piquant, playful, poignant, pungent, rich, salty, saucy*, sharp, snappy, sparkling, spicy, spirited, sportive, sprightly, stimulating, strong, tangy, tart, tasty, vigorous, vivacious, witty, zesty; SEE CONCEPTS *401,613*

racy [adj2] *risqué, vulgar*
bawdy, blue*, broad, erotic, immodest, indecent, indelicate, lewd, lurid, naughty, off-color*, purple*, shady*, smutty*, spicy*, suggestive, wicked; SEE CONCEPTS *267,545*

radiance [n1] *brightness, luminescence*
brilliance, effulgence, glare, gleam, glitter, glow, incandescence, light, luminosity, luster, resplendence, shine; SEE CONCEPT *620*

radiance [n2] *happiness*
delight, gaiety, joy, pleasure, rapture, warmth; SEE CONCEPT *633*

radiant [adj1] *bright, luminous*
beaming, brilliant, effulgent, gleaming, glittering, glorious, glowing, incandescent, lambent, lucent, lustrous, radiating, refulgent, resplendent, shining, sparkling, sunny; SEE CONCEPT *617*

radiant [adj2] *happy in appearance*
beaming, beatific, blissful, bright, cheerful, cheery, delighted, ecstatic, gay, glad, glowing, joyful, joyous, rapturous; SEE CONCEPT *401*

radiate [v] *give off; scatter*
afford, beam, branch out, broadcast, circulate, diffuse, disseminate, distribute, diverge, emanate, emit, expand, give out, gleam, glitter, illumine, irradiate, issue, light up, pour, proliferate, propagate, ramble, ramify, send out, shed, shine, shoot out, spread, spread out, sprinkle, strew, throw out, transmit, yield; SEE CONCEPTS *118,217,620,716*

radical [n] *person who advocates significant, often extreme change*
agitator, anarchist, avant-garde, extremist, fanatic, firebrand, freethinker, iconoclast, insurgent, insurrectionist, leftist, left-winger, militant, mutineer, nihilist, nonconformist, objector, pacifist, progressive, rebel, reformer, renegade, revolter, revolutionary, rioter, secessionist, subversive, ultraist; SEE CONCEPT *359*

radical [adj1] *fundamental, basic*
basal, bottom, cardinal, constitutional, deep-seated, essential, foundational, inherent, innate, intrinsic, meat-and-potatoes*, native, natural, organic, original, primal, primary, primitive, profound, thoroughgoing, underlying, vital; SEE CONCEPTS *546,549*

radical [adj2] *deviating by extremes*
advanced, anarchistic, complete, entire, excessive, extremist, fanatical, far-out*, freethinking, iconoclastic, immoderate, insubordinate, insurgent, insurrectionary, intransigent, lawless, leftist, militant, mutinous, nihilistic, progressive, rabid, rebellious, recalcitrant, recusant, refractory, restive, revolutionary, riotous, seditious, severe, sweeping, thorough, ultra, ultraist, uncompromising, violent, way out*; SEE CONCEPTS *403,529,542*

radio [n] *communication by electronic air waves*
AM-FM, CB, Marconi, radionics, radiotelegraph, radiotelegraphy, radiotelephone, radio-telephonics, receiver, shortwave, telegraphy, telephony, transmission, Walkman, wireless; SEE CONCEPT *279*

radius [n] *range, sweep*
ambit, boundary, compass, expanse, extension, extent, interval, limit, orbit, purview, reach, semidiameter, space, span, spoke; SEE CONCEPT *651*

raffish [adj] *unmindful of social conventions*
bohemian*, careless, casual, coarse, dashing, devil-may-care*, disreputable, fast*, gay, jaunty, rakish, sporty, tasteless, tawdry, unconventional, uncouth, vulgar, wild; SEE CONCEPT *401*

raffle [n] *lottery for a prize*
bet, betting, disposition, draw, drawing, flier*, gambling, game of chance, gaming, long odds*, lots*, numbers*, numbers game*, pool, random shot, speculation, stake, sweep, sweepstake, tossup*, wager, wagering; SEE CONCEPTS *363,364*

ragamuffin [n] *person who is poor, tattered*
beggar, bum*, gamin, guttersnipe*, hobo, loafer, orphan, scarecrow, street person, tatterdemalion*, tramp, urchin, vagabond, vagrant, waif, wastrel; SEE CONCEPTS *412,423*

rage [n1] *extreme anger*
acerbity, acrimony, agitation, animosity, apoplexy, asperity, bitterness, blowup*, bluster, choler, convulsion, dander, eruption, exasperation, excitement, explosion, ferment, ferocity, fireworks, frenzy, furor, fury, gall, heat*, hemorrhage, huff*, hysterics, indignation, ire, irritation, madness, mania, obsession, outburst, paroxysm, passion, rampage, raving, resentment, spasm, spleen, squall, storm, tantrum, temper, umbrage, uproar, upset, vehemence, violence, wingding*, wrath; SEE CONCEPTS *410,657*

rage [n2] *something in vogue; popular notion*
caprice, chic, conceit, craze, crotchet, cry, dernier cri, enthusiasm, fad, fancy, fashion, freak, furor, happening, hot spot*, in*, in-spot*, in-thing*, last word*, latest*, latest thing*, latest wrinkle*, mania, mode, newest wrinkle*, now*, passion, style, thing*, up to the minute*, vagary, whim; SEE CONCEPTS *388,655*

rage [v] *be angry*
be beside oneself*, be furious, be uncontrollable, blow a fuse*, blow one's top*, blow up*, boil over*, bristle, chafe, champ at bit*, erupt, fly off the handle*, foam at the mouth*, fret, fulminate, fume, go berserk, have a fit, have a tantrum, let

off steam*, look daggers*, make a fuss over, overflow, rail at, rampage, rant, rant and rave*, rave, roar, scold, scream, seethe, snap at, splutter, steam, storm, surge, tear, throw a fit*, work oneself into sweat*, yell; SEE CONCEPTS 29,410

ragged [adj] worn-out; in shreds

badly dressed, badly worn, battered, broken, contemptible, crude, desultory, dilapidated, dingy, disorganized, down at the heel*, fragmented, frayed, frazzled, full of holes*, in holes*, in rags, in tatters*, irregular, jagged, mean, moth-eaten, notched, patched, poor, poorly made, rent, rough, rugged, scraggy, seedy, serrated, shabby, shaggy, shoddy, shredded, tacky*, tattered, tatty*, threadbare, torn, uneven, unfinished, unkempt, unpressed, worse for wear*; SEE CONCEPT 485

raging [adj] violent; mad

angry, at boiling point*, bent*, bent out of shape*, beside oneself*, blowing a gasket*, blowing one's top*, blustering, blustery, boiling mad*, boiling over*, enraged, fit to be tied*, frenzied, fuming, furious, going ape*, incensed, infuriated, irate, mad as a hornet*, on the warpath*, rabid*, ranting and raving*, raving, raving mad, rough, seeing red*, seething, stormy, tempestuous, throwing a fit, turbulent, wild; SEE CONCEPTS 403,542

raid [n] attack, seizure

arrest, assault, break-in, bust, capture, descent, foray, forced entrance, hit-and-run*, incursion, inroad, invasion, irruption, onset, onslaught, pull, reconnaissance, roundup, sally*, shootup*, sortie*, surprise attack, sweep, tipover*; SEE CONCEPTS 86,317

raid [v] attack, pillage

assail, assault, blockade, bomb, bombard, breach, break in, charge, descend on, despoil, devastate, fall upon, fire on, forage, foray, harass, harry, heat, inroad, invade, knock off*, knock over*, lean against, lean on, loot, maraud, march on, overrun, pirate, plunder, rake, ransack, rifle, rob, sack, sally, sally forth, shell, slough, spoliate, storm, strafe, strike, sweep, swoop, tip over*, torpedo, waste; SEE CONCEPT 86

rail/railing [n] post, pole along an edge

balustrade, banister, bar, barrier, fence, paling, rails, rest, siding; SEE CONCEPTS 443,479

rail [v] criticize harshly

abuse, attack, bawl out*, berate, blast, castigate, censure, chew out*, complain, fulminate, fume, inveigh, jaw, objurate, rant, rate, revile, scold, thunder, tongue-lash*, upbraid, vituperate, vociferate, whip; SEE CONCEPT 52

rain [n] downpour of water or other substance

cat-and-dog weather*, cloudburst, condensation, deluge, drencher, drizzle, fall, flood, flurry, hail, heavy dew, liquid sunshine*, mist, monsoon, pour, pouring, precip*, precipitation, raindrops, rainfall, rainstorm, sheets, shower, showers, sleet, spate, spit, sprinkle, sprinkling, stream, sun shower*, torrent, volley*, wet stuff*, window washer*; SEE CONCEPT 526

rain [v] drop water or other substance

bestow, bucket, come down in buckets*, deposit, drizzle, fall, hail, lavish, mist, patter, pour, shower, sleet, sprinkle, storm; SEE CONCEPT 526

raise [n] increase in salary or position

accession, accretion, addition, advance, augmentation, boost, bump, hike, hold-up*, increment, jump, jump-up*, leg*, leg-up*, move-up*, promotion, raising, rise, step-up*; SEE CONCEPTS 344,351,763

raise [v1] lift; build from the ground

boost, bring up, construct, elevate, erect, establish, exalt, heave, hoist, hold up, lever, lift, lift up, mount, move up, place up, promote, pry, pull up, put on its end, put up, rear, run up, set up, set upright, shove, stand up, take up, throw up, upcast, upheave, uplift, upraise, uprear; SEE CONCEPTS 168,196

raise [v2] increase, augment

advance, aggravate, amplify, assemble, boost, build up, collect, congregate, congress, dignify, enhance, enlarge, escalate, exaggerate, exalt, fetch up, forgather, form, gather, get, goose*, goose up*, heighten, hike, hike up*, honor, inflate, intensify, jack up, jump, jump up, levy, look up, magnify, mass, mobilize, mushroom*, muster, obtain, perk up, pile up, promote, put up, pyramid, rally, recruit, reinforce, rendezvous, run up*, send through the roof*, shoot up, snowball*, strengthen, up; SEE CONCEPTS 236,244,245

raise [v3] start up, motivate; introduce

abet, activate, advance, arouse, awaken, bring up, broach, cause, evoke, excite, foment, foster, incite, instigate, kindle, moot, motivate, provoke, put forward, resurrect, set, set on, stir up, suggest, whip up; SEE CONCEPTS 75,221

raise [v4] nurture, care for

breed, bring up, cultivate, develop, drag up, fetch up, foster, group, grow, nourish, nurse, plant, produce, propagate, provide, rear, sow, suckle, support, train, wean; SEE CONCEPTS 253,257,295

rake [v] scrape up, hoe

break up, clean up, clear, clear up, collect, comb, enfilade, examine, finecomb, fine-tooth-comb*, gather, grade, graze, grub, harrow, hunt, ransack, rasp, remove, rummage, scan, scour, scrape, scratch, scrutinize, search, smooth, sweep, weed; SEE CONCEPTS 109,165,178,216

rakish [adj] charming and immoral

abandoned, chic, dashing, debauched, depraved, devil-may-care*, dissipated, dissolute, fashionable, fast*, flashy, gay, jaunty, lecherous, licentious, loose*, natty, prodigal, profligate, raffish, saucy, sinful, smart, sporty, wanton, wild; SEE CONCEPTS 401,545

rally [n1] celebratory meeting

assemblage, assembly, celebration, clambake*, convention, convocation, get-together, mass meeting, meet, pep rally, pow-wow*, session; SEE CONCEPTS 377,386

rally [n2] turn for the better

comeback, improvement, recovery, recuperation, renewal, resurgence, revival, turning point; SEE CONCEPT 700

rally [v1] reorganize, unite

arouse, assemble, bestir, bond together, bring together, bring to order, call to arms*, challenge, charge, collect, come about, come together, come to order, convene, counterattack, encourage, fire, gather, get together, inspirit, kindle, marshal, mobilize, muster, organize, reassemble, redouble, reform, regroup, rejuvenate, renew, restore, resurrect, resuscitate, revive, round up, rouse, summon, surge, urge, wake, waken, whip, wreak havoc*; SEE CONCEPTS 7,22,117,320

rally [v2] revive; take a turn for the better

bounce back, brace up, come along, come around,

ra
ra

come from behind, enliven, get act together*, get back in shape*, get better, get second wind*, grow stronger, improve, invigorate, make a comeback, perk up, pick up, pull through, recover, recuperate, refresh, regain strength, shape up, snap out of it, surge, turn around, turn things around*; SEE CONCEPT 700

ram [v] *bang into; pack forcibly*
beat, butt, collide with, cram, crash, crowd, dash, dig, drive, drum, force, hammer, hit, hook, impact, jack, jam-pack, pack, plunge, poke, pound, run, run into, sink, slam, smash, stab, stick, strike, strike head-on, stuff, tamp, thrust, wedge; SEE CONCEPTS 189,208,209

ramble [n] *aimless walk*
constitutional, excursion, hike, perambulation, peregrination, roaming, roving, saunter, stroll, tour, traipse, trip, turn; SEE CONCEPTS 151,224

ramble [v1] *wander about; travel aimlessly*
amble, bat around*, be all over the map*, branch off, clamber, climb, cruise, depart, digress, divagate, diverge, drift, excurse, extend, fork, gad, gallivant, get sidetracked*, knock about*, knock around*, meander, perambulate, percolate, peregrinate, promenade, range, roam, rove, saunter, scramble, snake, sprangle, sprawl, spread, spread-eagle, straddle, straggle, stray, stroll, trail, traipse, turn, twist, walk, wind, zigzag; SEE CONCEPTS 151,154,581,692

ramble [v2] *talk aimlessly, endlessly*
amplify, babble, beat around bush*, be diffuse, blather, chatter, depart, descant, digress, divagate, diverge, drift, drivel, dwell on, enlarge, excurse, expatiate, get off the subject*, go astray, go off on tangent*, go on and on*, gossip, harp on, lose the thread*, maunder, meander, prose, protract, rant and rave*, rattle on*, stray, talk nonsense, talk off top of head*, talk randomly, wander; SEE CONCEPT 51

rambling [adj1] *disconnected, wordy*
circuitous, confused, desultory, diffuse, digressive, discursive, disjointed, incoherent, incongruous, irregular, long-winded, periphrastic, prolix; SEE CONCEPT 267

rambling [adj2] *sprawling, spread out*
at length, covering, gangling, here and there, irregular, random, scattered, spreading, straggling, strewn, trailing, unplanned; SEE CONCEPTS 485,772

rambunctious [adj] *loud, energetic*
boisterous, noisy, raucous, rough, rowdy, rude, termagant, tumultuous/tumultous, turbulent, unruly; SEE CONCEPT 542

ramification [n] *consequence, development*
bifurcation, branch, branching, breaking, complication, consequence, divarication, division, excrescence, extension, forking, offshoot, outgrowth, partition, radiation, result, sequel, subdividing, subdivision, upshot; SEE CONCEPTS 98,230,824

ramp [n] *incline*
access, adit, grade, gradient, hill, inclination, inclined plane, rise, slope; SEE CONCEPTS 443,757

rampage [n] *storm, violence*
binge, blowup, boiling point*, destruction, disturbance, ferment, fling, frenzy, fury, mad*, more heat than light*, orgy, rage, ruckus, splurge, spree, tear, tempest, tumult, turmoil, uproar, wingding; SEE CONCEPT 86

rampage [v] *go crazy; storm*
go berserk, rage, run amuck, run riot, run wild, tear; SEE CONCEPTS 86,384

rampant [adj] *uncontrolled, out of hand*
aggressive, blustering, boisterous, clamorous, dominant, epidemic, exceeding bounds, excessive, extravagant, exuberant, fanatical, flagrant, furious, growing, impetuous, impulsive, luxuriant, on the rampage, out of control, outrageous, pandemic, predominant, prevalent, profuse, raging, rampaging, rank, rife, riotous, spreading, tumultuous/tumultuous, turbulent, unbridled, unchecked, uncontrollable, ungovernable, unrestrained, unruly, vehement, violent, wanton, widespread, wild; SEE CONCEPTS 544,554,772

rampart [n] *fortification, stronghold*
barricade, barrier, bastion, breastwork, bulwark, defense, earthwork, elevation, embankment, fence, fort, guard, hill, mound, parapet, protection, ridge, security, support, vallation, wall; SEE CONCEPTS 321,439,509

ramshackle [adj] *falling apart; in poor condition*
broken-down, crumbling, decrepit, derelict, dilapidated, flimsy, jerry-built*, rickety, shabby, shaky, tottering, tumble-down, unfirm, unsafe, unsteady; SEE CONCEPTS 485,488

rancid [adj] *rotten, strong-smelling*
bad, carious, contaminated, curdled, decomposing, disagreeable, disgusting, evil-smelling, feculent, fetid, foul, frowzy, fusty, gamy, high, impure, loathsome, malodorous, moldy, musty, nasty, nidorous, noisomé, noxious, off, offensive, olid, polluted, putrefactive, putrefied, putrescent, putrid, rank, reeky, repulsive, sharp, smelly, sour, soured, stale, stinking, strong, tainted, turned, unhealthy, whiffy; SEE CONCEPTS 462,570,598,613

rancor [n] *bitterness, hatefulness*
acerbity, acrimony, animosity, animus, antagonism, antipathy, aversion, bad blood*, bile*, dudgeon, enmity, grudge, hardness of heart*, harshness, hate, hatred, hostility, ill feeling, ill will, malevolence, malice, malignity, mordacity, pique, resentfulness, resentment, retaliation, revengefulness, ruthlessness, spite, spitefulness, spleen, umbrage, uncharitableness, unfriendliness, variance, vengeance, vengefulness, venom, vindictiveness, virulence; SEE CONCEPTS 29,410, 633

random [adj] *haphazard, chance*
accidental, adventitious, aimless, arbitrary, casual, contingent, designless, desultory, driftless, fluky, fortuitous, hit-or-miss*, incidental, indiscriminate, irregular, objectless, odd, promiscuous, purposeless, slapdash*, spot, stray, unaimed, unconsidered, unplanned, unpremeditated; SEE CONCEPTS 535,548,557

range [n1] *sphere, distance, extent*
ambit, amplitude, area, bounds, circle, compass, confines, diapason, dimension, dimension, domain, earshot*, elbowroom*, expanse, extension, extensity, field, gamut, hearing, ken, latitude, leeway, length, limits, magnitude, matter, neighborhood, orbit, order, panorama, parameters, play, province, purview, radius, reach, realm, run, run of, scope, space, span, spectrum, sphere, spread, stretch, sweep, swing, territory, tune, vicinity, width; SEE CONCEPTS 651,743,745,756,761,788

range [n2] *order, series*
assortment, chain, class, collection, file, gamut,

kind, line, lot, rank, row, selection, sequence, sort, string, tier, variety; SEE CONCEPTS *727,769*

range [*v1*] *order, categorize*
align, allineate, arrange, array, assort, bias, bracket, catalogue, categorize, class, classify, dispose, draw up, file, grade, group, incline, line, line up, pigeonhole*, predispose, rank; SEE CONCEPTS *84,158*

range [*v2*] *wander, roam*
circumambulate, cover, cross, cruise, drift, encompass, explore, float, follow one's nose*, gallivant, globe-trot*, hit the road*, hit the trail*, make circuit, meander, pass over, ply, prowl, ramble, reach, reconnoiter, rove, scour, search, spread, straggle, stray, stroll, sweep, traipse, tramp, travel, traverse, trek; SEE CONCEPTS *151,224*

range [*v3*] *extend; change within limits*
differ, diverge from, fluctuate, go, reach, run, stretch, vary, vary between; SEE CONCEPT *697*

rangy [*adj*] *long and lean*
gangling, gangly, lanky, leggy, long-legged, long-limbed, reedy, skinny, spindling, spindly, thin, weedy; SEE CONCEPTS *491,779*

rank [*n1*] *standing in a system, often a social one*
ancestry, authority, birth, blood, cachet, capacity, caste, circumstance, class, classification, condition, consequence, degree, dignity, distinction, division, echelon, estate, esteem, family, footing, grade, hierarchy, level, nobility, note, order, paramountcy, parentage, pecking order, pedigree, place, position, primacy, privilege, quality, reputation, seniority, situation, slot, sort, sovereignty, sphere, state, station, stature, status, stock, stratum, supremacy, type; SEE CONCEPTS *296,378, 388,744*

rank [*n2*] *column, tier of individuals*
echelon, file, formation, group, hierarchy, line, queue, range, row, series, string; SEE CONCEPT *727*

rank [*adj1*] *stinking, foul*
bad, dank, disagreeable, disgusting, evil-smelling, feculent, fetid, funky*, fusty*, gamy*, graveolent, gross*, high, humid, loathsome, mephitic, moldy, musty, nasty, nauseating, noisome, noxious, obnoxious, off, offensive, olid, pungent, putrescent, putrid, rancid, reeking, repulsive, revolting, smelly, sour, stale, strong, strong-smelling, tainted, turned; SEE CONCEPT *598*

rank [*adj2*] *abundant, luxurious*
coarse, dense, excessive, extreme, exuberant, fertile, flourishing, fructiferous, grown, high-growing, junglelike, lavish, lush, luxuriant, overabundant, overgrown, productive, profuse, prolific, rampant, rich, semitropical, tropical, vigorous, wild; SEE CONCEPT *485*

rank [*adj3*] *utter, absolute*
arrant, blatant, capital, complete, conspicuous, consummate, downright, egregious, excessive, extravagant, flagrant, glaring, gross, noticeable, outright, outstanding, perfect, positive, rampant, sheer, thorough, total, undisguised, unmitigated; SEE CONCEPTS *531,535*

rank [*adj4*] *obscene, vulgar*
abusive, atrocious, coarse, crass, dirty, filthy, foul, gross, indecent, nasty, outrageous, raunchy, scurrilous, shocking, smutty, wicked; SEE CONCEPT *545*

rank [*v1*] *line up; classify in system*
align, arrange, array, assign, assort, button

down*, class, dispose, establish, estimate, evaluate, fix*, give precedence, grade, include, judge, list, locate, marshal, order, peg, pigeonhole*, place, place in formation, position, put, put away, put down as, put down for, put in line, range, rate, regard, settle, size up, sort, tab, typecast, valuate, value; SEE CONCEPTS *37,84,158*

rank [*v2*] *be worthwhile; have supremacy*
antecede, be classed, belong, be worth, come first, count among, forerun, go ahead of, go before, have the advantage, outrank, precede, stand, take the lead; SEE CONCEPTS *388,671*

rankle [*v*] *annoy, irritate*
aggravate, anger, bother, chafe, embitter, exasperate, fester, fret, gall, get one's goat*, harass, hurt, inflame, irk, irritate, mortify, nettle, obsess, pain, pester, plague, rile, torment, vex; SEE CONCEPTS *7,14,19*

ransack [*v*] *turn inside out in search; ravage*
appropriate, comb, despoil, explore, ferret, filch, go over with a fine-tooth-comb*, go through, gut*, hunt, investigate, lay waste, leave no stone unturned*, lift, look all over for*, look high and low*, look into, loot, make off with*, maraud, overhaul, peer, pilfer, pillage, pinch, plunder, poach, probe, pry, purloin, raid, rake, rape, ravish, rifle, rob, rummage, rustle, sack, scan, scour, scrutinize, search, seek, seize, shake down*, sound, spoil, spy, steal, strip, take away, thieve; SEE CONCEPTS *103,139,142,216*

ransom [*n*] *blackmail money paid for return of possession or person*
bribe, compensation, deliverance, expiation, liberation money, payment, payoff, price, redemption, release, rescue; SEE CONCEPT *344*

ransom [*v*] *pay blackmail money for return of possession or person*
buy freedom of, buy out, deliver, emancipate, extricate, free, liberate, manumit, obtain release of, pay for release of, recover, redeem, regain, release, reprise, repurchase, rescue, save, set free, unchain, unfetter; SEE CONCEPTS *127,131,341*

rant [*n*] *yelling, raving*
bluster, bombast, diatribe, fustian, harangue, oration, philippic, rhapsody, rhetoric, rodomontade, tirade, vociferation; SEE CONCEPTS *44,49,52*

rant [*v*] *yell, rave*
bellow, bloviate, blow one's top*, bluster, carry on, clamor, cry, declaim, fume, harangue, mouth, objurgate, orate, perorate, rage, rail, roar, scold, shout, sizzle*, soapbox*, sound off*, spiel*, spout*, storm*, stump*, take on*, vociferate; SEE CONCEPTS *44,49,52*

rap [*n1/v1*] *hit quickly and lightly*
beat, blow, conk, crack, knock, lick, pat, strike, swat, swipe, tap, whack; SEE CONCEPT *189*

rap [*n2*] *conversation*
causerie, chat, chin*, colloquy, confabulation, conference, deliberation, dialogue, discourse, discussion, prose, talk, ventilation, yarn; SEE CONCEPTS *56,266*

rap [*n3*] *blame; criticism*
admonishment, admonition, censure, chiding, flak, knock, pan*, punishment, rebuke, reprimand, reproach, reproof, responsibility, sentence, swipe; SEE CONCEPTS *52,123,317*

rap [*v2*] *talk casually; speak abruptly*
babble, bark, chat, chatter, chitchat, confabulate, converse, discourse, jabber, palaver, run off at the mouth*, spit, talk; SEE CONCEPTS *56,266*

ra
ra

rap [v3] *criticize*

blame, castigate, censure, condemn, denounce, denunciate, knock*, pan*, reprehend, reprimand, reprobate, scold, skin, tick off*; SEE CONCEPT 52

rape [n] *defilement; a forced sexual assault*

abduction, abuse, criminal attack, depredation, despoilment, despoliation, forcible violation, maltreatment, molestation, pillage, plunder, plundering, rapine, spoliation, statutory offense, violation; SEE CONCEPTS 192,375

rape [v] *sexual assault by force; act of plunder*

abuse, attack, betray, compromise, corrupt, deceive, despoil, force, loot, molest, pillage, plunder, ransack, ruin, sack, seize, spoliate, violate; SEE CONCEPTS 192,375

rapid [adj] *very quick*

accelerated, active, agile, breakneck, brisk, double time, expeditious, expeditive, express, fast, fleet, fleet of foot*, flying, hasty, hurried, in nothing flat*, light-footed*, like a house on fire*, lively, mercurial, nimble, on the double*, precipitate, prompt, quick as a wink*, quickened, ready, really rolling*, screaming*, speedy, spry, swift, winged; SEE CONCEPTS 541,588,799

rapidity [n] *quickness*

acceleration, alacrity, bat, briskness, celerity, dispatch, expedition, fleetness, gait, haste, hurry, pace, precipitateness, promptitude, promptness, rapidness, rush, speed, speediness, swiftness, velocity; SEE CONCEPTS 755,805

rapidly [adv] *very quickly*

at speed, briskly, expeditiously, fast, flat out*, full tilt*, hastily, hurriedly, immediately, in a hurry, in a rush, in haste, lickety-split*, like a shot*, posthaste, precipitately, promptly, speedily, swiftly, with dispatch; SEE CONCEPTS 544,588,799

rapport [n] *understanding between people*

affinity, agreement, bond, compatibility, concord, cotton, empathy, good vibes*, good vibrations, groove, harmony, hitting it off*, interrelationship, link, relationship, same wavelength*, simpatico*, soul, sympathy, the groove*, togetherness, unity; SEE CONCEPT 388

rapprochement [n] *restoration of harmony*

agreement, cordiality, detente, friendliness, friendship, harmonization, harmony, reconcile, reconciliation, reunion, softening; SEE CONCEPTS 384,388

rapt [adj] *absorbed, fascinated*

absent, absent-minded, abstracted, beguiled, bewitched, blissful, busy, captivated, carried away*, caught up in*, charmed, daydreaming, deep*, delighted, dreaming, ecstatic, employed, enamored, engaged, engrossed, enraptured, enthralled, entranced, gripped, happy, held, hung up*, hypnotized, immersed, inattentive, intent, involved, lost, oblivious, occupied, overwhelmed, preoccupied, rapturous, ravished, spellbound, taken*, transported, unconscious, wrapped*, wrapped up*; SEE CONCEPT 403

rapture [n] *extreme happiness and delight in something*

at-oneness*, beatitude, bliss, buoyancy, cheer, cloud nine*, communion, contentment, cool*, delectation, ecstasy, elation, elysium, enchantment, enjoyment, enthusiasm, euphoria, exaltation, exhilaration, felicity, gaiety, gladness, glory, good spirits, gratification, heaven, inspiration, joy, jubilation, nirvana, paradise, passion, pleasure, rav-

ishment, rhapsody, satisfaction, seventh heaven*, spell, transport, well-being; SEE CONCEPTS 32,410

rare [adj1] *exceptional, infrequent*

attenuate, attenuated, deficient, extraordinary, few, few and far between*, flimsy, inconceivable, isolated, light, limited, occasional, out of the ordinary, rarefied, recherché, scanty, scarce, scattered, seldom, semioccasional, short, singular, sparse, sporadic, strange, subtile, subtle, tenuous, thin, uncommon, unfrequent, unheard of, unimaginable, unique, unlikely, unthinkable, unusual, unwonted; SEE CONCEPTS 530,576

rare [adj2] *precious, excellent*

admirable, choice, dainty, delicate, elegant, exquisite, extreme, fine, great, incomparable, invaluable, matchless, peerless, priceless, recherché, rich, select, superb, superlative, unique; SEE CONCEPT 574

rare [adj3] *not fully cooked*

bloody, half-cooked, half-raw, moderately done, nearly raw, not done, rarely done, red, undercooked, underdone; SEE CONCEPT 462

rarely [adv] *not often; exceptionally*

almost never, barely, extra, extraordinarily, extremely, finely, hardly, hardly ever, infrequently, little, notably, now and then, once in a while, once in blue moon*, on rare occasions, remarkably, scarcely ever, seldom, singularly, uncommon, uncommonly, unfrequently, unoften, unusually; SEE CONCEPTS 530,542

rascal [n] *person who is unprincipled, does not work hard*

beggar, blackguard, black sheep*, bully, bum, cad, cardsharp*, charlatan, cheat, delinquent, devil, disgrace, felon, fraud, good-for-nothing*, grafter, hooligan*, hypocrite, idler, imp, liar, loafer, mischief-maker, miscreant, opportunist, pretender, prodigal, profligate, recreant, reprobate, robber, rowdy, ruffian, scamp, scoundrel, sinner, skunk*, sneak*, swindler, tough*, tramp, trickster, varmint*, villain, wastrel, wretch; SEE CONCEPT 412

rash [n] *outbreak of disease or condition*

breakout, epidemic, eruption, flood, hives, pandemic, plague, series, spate, succession, wave; SEE CONCEPTS 230,306

rash [adj] *careless, impulsive*

adventurous, audacious, bold, brash, daring, determined, devil-may-care*, fiery, foolhardy, frenzied, furious, harebrained, hasty, headlong, headstrong, heedless, hotheaded, ill-advised, illconsidered, immature, impetuous, imprudent, incautious, indiscreet, injudicious, insuppressible, irrational, jumping to conclusions*, madcap, overhasty, passionate, precipitant, precipitate, premature, reckless, thoughtless, unguarded, unthinking, unwary, venturesome, venturous, wild; SEE CONCEPT 401

rasp [v] *grind, rub*

abrade, bray, excoriate, file, grate, irk, irritate, jar, pound, raze, rub, sand, scour, scrape, scratch, vex, wear; SEE CONCEPTS 7,19,186,215

rate [n1] *ratio, proportion*

amount, comparison, degree, estimate, percentage, progression, quota, relation, relationship, relative, scale, standard, weight; SEE CONCEPT 768

rate [n2] *fee charged for service, privilege, goods*

allowance, charge, cost, dues, duty, estimate, fig-

rate [n3] *speed, pace*
clip, dash, flow, gait, gallop, hop, measure, motion, movement, pace, spurt, tempo, time, tread, velocity; SEE CONCEPT **755**

rate [v1] *judge, classify*
adjudge, admire, appraise, apprise, assay, assess, button down*, calculate, class, consider, count, deem, determine, esteem, estimate, evaluate, fix, grade, guess at, measure, peg, pigeonhole*, price, put away, put down as*, put down for*, rank, reckon, redline*, regard, relate to standard, respect, score, set at, size up*, stand in with, survey, tab*, tag, take one's measure, think highly of, typecast*, valuate, value, weigh; SEE CONCEPTS **12,37**

rate [v2] *be entitled to*
be accepted, be favorite, be welcome, be worthy, deserve, earn, merit, prosper, succeed, triumph; SEE CONCEPTS **129,376,388**

rather [adv1] *moderately*
a bit, a little, averagely, comparatively, enough, fairly, in a certain degree, kind of, more or less, passably, pretty, quite, ratherish, reasonably, relatively, slightly, some, something, somewhat, sort of, so-so*, tolerably, to some degree, to some extent; SEE CONCEPTS **544,548**

rather [adv2] *significantly*
a good bit, considerably, noticeably, quite, somewhat, very, well; SEE CONCEPTS **544,772**

rather [adv3] *preferably; instead*
alternately, alternatively, as a matter of choice, by choice, by preference, first, in lieu of, in preference, just as soon, more readily, more willingly, much sooner, sooner, willingly; SEE CONCEPT **529**

ratify [v] *affirm, authorize*
accredit, approve, authenticate, bear out, bind, bless, certify, commission, confirm, consent, corroborate, endorse, establish, give stamp of approval*, go for*, license, okay*, rubber stamp*, sanction, sign, substantiate, uphold, validate; SEE CONCEPTS **50,88**

ratio [n] *percentage, relation of part to whole*
arrangement, correlation, correspondence, equation, fraction, proportion, proportionality, quota, quotient, rate, relationship, scale; SEE CONCEPT **768**

ration [n] *allotment of limited supply*
allowance, apportionment, assignment, bit, consignment, cut, distribution, division, dole, drag, food, helping, measure, meed, part, piece of action*, portion, provender, provision, quantum, quota, share, store, supply; SEE CONCEPTS **457,835**

ration [v] *divide something into portions*
allocate, allot, apportion, assign, budget, conserve, control, deal, distribute, divvy*, divvy up*, dole, give out, issue, limit, measure out, mete, mete out, parcel, parcel out, proportion, prorate, quota, restrict, save, share; SEE CONCEPTS **98,140**

rational [adj] *realistic; of sound mind*
all there*, analytical, balanced, calm, cerebral, circumspect, cognitive, collected, cool*, deductive, deliberate, discerning, discriminating, enlightened, far-sighted, impartial, intellectual, intelligent, judicious, knowing, levelheaded, logical, lucid, normal, objective, perspicacious, philosophic, prudent, ratiocinative, reasonable,

reasoning, reflective, sagacious, sane, sensible, sober, sound, stable, synthetic, thinking, thoughtful, together, well-advised, wise; SEE CONCEPT **402**

rationale [n] *logic for belief, action*
account, excuse, explanation, exposition, grounds, hypothesis, justification, motivation, motive, philosophy, principle, raison d'être, rationalization, reason, reasons, song and dance*, sour grapes*, story*, the big idea*, theory, the whole idea*, whatfor*, why and wherefore*, whyfor*; SEE CONCEPT **661**

rationalize [v] *make excuse; justify*
account for, apply logic, cop a plea*, cop out*, deliberate, elucidate, excise, excuse, explain away, extenuate, give alibi*, intellectualize, justify, make allowance, reason, reason out, reconcile, resolve, think, think through, vindicate; SEE CONCEPT **57**

rattle [v1] *bang, jiggle*
bicker, bounce, clack, clatter, drum, jangle, jar, jolt, jounce, knock, shake, shatter, sound, vibrate; SEE CONCEPTS **65,152**

rattle [v2] *talk aimlessly, endlessly*
babble, cackle, chat, chatter, clack, gab, gabble, gush, jabber, jaw, list, prate, prattle, reel off, run on, run through, yak; SEE CONCEPT **51**

rattle [v3] *disconcert, upset someone*
abash, addle, bewilder, bother, confound, confuse, discombobulate, discomfit, discompose, discountenance, distract, disturb, embarrass, faze, flummox, frighten, get to*, muddle, nonplus, perplex, perturb, psych out*, put off, put out, put out of countenance, rattle one's cage*, scare, shake, throw, unnerve; SEE CONCEPT **16**

raucous [adj1] *noisy, rough*
absonant, acute, atonal, blaring, blatant, braying, brusque, cacophonous, discordant, dissonant, dry, ear-piercing, grating, grinding, gruff, harsh, hoarse, husky, inharmonious, jarring, loud, piercing, rasping, sharp, squawking, stertorous, strident, thick, unharmonious, unmusical; SEE CONCEPTS **592,594**

raucous [adj2] *rowdy*
boisterous, disorderly, intemperate, rambunctious, tumultuous/tumultuous, turbulent, unruly; SEE CONCEPT **401**

ravage [v] *destroy, ransack*
annihilate, break up, capture, consume, cream*, crush, damage, demolish, desecrate, desolate, despoil, devastate, dismantle, disorganize, disrupt, exterminate, extinguish, forage, foray, gut, harry, impair, lay waste, leave in ruins, loot, overrun, overthrow, overwhelm, pillage, pirate, plunder, prey, prostrate, pull down, raid, rape, raze, rob, ruin, sack, seize, shatter, sink, smash, spoil, spoliate, stamp out, strip, sweep away, total*, trample, trash, waste, wreak havoc, wreck, wrest; SEE CONCEPTS **86,252**

rave [v1] *talk endlessly*
babble, be delirious, bloviate, blow one's top*, carry on*, come unglued*, declaim, flip one's lid*, freak out*, fume, gabble, go ape*, go bananas*, go crazy, go mad, harangue, jabber, make a to-do*, mouth, orate, perorate, prate, prattle, rage, rail, rant, rattle on, roar, run amuck*, splutter, storm, talk wildly, thunder, wander; SEE CONCEPTS **51,54**

rave [v2] *be very enthusiastic*
be delighted, be excited, be mad about, be wild

about, bubble*, carry on about*, cry up*, effervesce, enthuse, fall all over*, go on about*, gush, make a to-do*, praise, rhapsodize; SEE CONCEPTS 49,410

ravel [v] *come apart; unwind*
disentangle, free, loosen, make plain, smooth out, unbraid, unravel, unsnarl, untangle, untwine, untwist, unweave, unwind, weave out; SEE CONCEPTS 250,469

ravenous [adj] *very hungry; desirous*
avaricious, could eat a horse*, covetous, devouring, edacious, empty, famished, ferocious, gluttonous, grasping, greedy, insatiable, insatiate, omnivorous, predatory, rapacious, ravening, starved, starved to death*, starving, voracious, wolfish; SEE CONCEPT 406

ravine [n] *gap in earth's surface*
abyss, arroyo, break, canyon, chasm, clove, coulee, crevasse, crevice, cut, defile, ditch, fissure, flume, gorge, gulch, gulf, gully, notch, pass, valley, wash; SEE CONCEPTS 509,513

ravish [v1] *enchant*
allure, attract, bewitch, captivate, charm, delight, draw, enrapture, enthrall, entrance, fascinate, hold, hypnotize, magnetize, mesmerize, overjoy, please, spellbind, trance, transport; SEE CONCEPT 11

ravish [v2] *sexually assault*
abduct, abuse, force, rape, violate; SEE CONCEPTS 192,375

raw [adj1] *not cooked, prepared*
basic, bloody, callow, coarse, crude, fibrous, fresh, green, hard, immature, impure, native, natural, organic, rough, roughhewn, rude, unbaked, uncooked, undercooked, underdone, undressed, unfashioned, unformed, unfried, ungraded, unpasteurized, unprepared, unprocessed, unrefined, unripe, unsorted, unstained, untreated; SEE CONCEPTS 462,485

raw [adj2] *exposed, tender, referring to skin*
abraded, au naturel, blistered, bruised, chafed, cut, dressed, galled, grazed, naked, nude, open, pared, peeled, scraped, scratched, sensitive, skinned, sore, unclad, unclothed, uncovered, wounded; SEE CONCEPTS 406,485

raw [adj3] *inexperienced*
callow, fresh, green*, ignorant, immature, inexperienced, new, unconversant, undisciplined, unpracticed, unseasoned, unskilled, untaught, untrained, untried, unversed, young; SEE CONCEPT 527

raw [adj4] *vulgar, nasty*
coarse, crass, crude, dirty, filthy, foul, gross, indecent, inelegant, low, mean, obscene, pornographic, rank, rough, rude, smutty, uncouth, unrefined, unscrupulous; SEE CONCEPTS 372,545

raw [adj5] *harsh, unpleasant, referring to weather*
biting, bitter, bleak, breezy, chill, chilly, cold, damp, freezing, piercing, wet, wind-swept, windy; SEE CONCEPT 525

ray [n] *beam; indication*
bar, blaze, blink, emanation, flash, flicker, gleam, glimmer, glint, glitter, hint, incandescence, irradiation, light, moonbeam, patch, pencil, radiance, radiation, scintilla, shaft, shine, spark, sparkle, streak, stream, sunbeam, trace, wave; SEE CONCEPTS 624,628

raze [v] *flatten, knock down; wipe out*
batter, blow down, bomb, break down, bulldoze, capsize, cast down, crash, decimate, delete, demolish, destroy, dynamite, efface, erase, expunge, extinguish, extirpate, fell, level, mow down, obliterate, overthrow, overturn, pull down, reduce, remove, rub out*, ruin, scatter, scratch out, smash, spill, strike out, subvert, tear down, tear up, throw down, topple, total, unbuild, undo, unmake, upset, wipe out, wrack, wreck, zap*; SEE CONCEPT 252

reach [n] *extent, range; stretch*
ability, ambit, capacity, command, compass, distance, extension, gamut, grasp, horizon, influence, jurisdiction, ken, latitude, magnitude, mastery, orbit, play, power, purview, radius, scope, spread, sweep, swing; SEE CONCEPTS 651,756

reach [v1] *arrive at*
arrive, attain, catch up to, check in, clock in*, come, come to, enter, gain on*, get as far as, get in, get to, hit, hit town*, land, make, make it, make the scene*, overtake, ring in*, roll in, show, show up, sign in, turn up, wind up at; SEE CONCEPT 159

reach [v2] *stretch to; touch*
approach, attain, buck, carry to, come at, come up to, contact, continue to, encompass, end, equal, extend to, feel for, get a hold of, get hold of, get to, go, go as far as, go on, go to, grasp, hand, hold out, join, lead, lunge, make, make contact with, overtake, pass, pass along, put out, roll on, seize, shake hands, shoot, span, spread, stand, strain, strike; SEE CONCEPTS 108,612,756

reach [v3] *attain; rise*
accomplish, achieve, amount to, arrive at, climb to, come to, drop, fall, gain, move, rack up*, realize, score, sink, win; SEE CONCEPTS 706, 763,780

reach [v4] *communicate with*
affect, approach, contact, get, get in touch, get through, get to, influence, keep in contact, keep in touch, maintain, move, sway, touch; SEE CONCEPTS 7,19,22,266

react [v] *respond; conduct oneself*
acknowledge, act, answer, answer back, backfire, be affected, behave, boomerang*, bounce back*, counter, echo, feel, get back at, give a snappy comeback*, give back, have a funny feeling*, have vibes*, operate, perform, proceed, rebound, reciprocate, recoil, recur, reply, return, revert, take, talk back, turn back, work; SEE CONCEPTS 45,633

reaction [n1] *response*
acknowledgment, answer, attitude, backfire, backlash, back talk*, boomerang*, comeback, compensation, counteraction, counterbalance, counterpoise, double-take*, echo, feedback, feeling, hit, kick, kickback, knee-jerk*, lip*, opinion, reagency, rebound, reception, receptivity, reciprocation, recoil, reflection, reflex, rejoinder, repercussion, reply, retort, return, reverberation, revulsion, sass*, snappy comeback*, take*, vibes*, wisecrack; SEE CONCEPTS 45,633

reaction [n2] *political conservatism*
backlash, backsliding, counterrevolution, obscurantism, regression, relapse, retreat, retrenchment, retrogression, right, right wing, status quo, Toryism, withdrawal; SEE CONCEPTS 300,689

reactionary [n] *person who is politically conservative*
bitter-ender*, counterrevolutionary, diehard*, hard hat*, intransigent, obscurantist, reactionist,

rightist*, right-winger, royalist, standpatter*, Tory*, traditionalist, ultraconservative; SEE CONCEPT 359

reactionary [adj] conservative
counterrevolutionary, die-hard*, obscurantist, old-line*, orthodox, regressive, retrogressive, right, rightist*, rigid, standpat*, tory*, traditional, traditionalistic; SEE CONCEPTS 529,542

read [v1] look at and understand written word
apprehend, bury oneself in*, comprehend, construe, decipher, dip into*, discover, flip through*, gather, glance, go over, go through, interpret, know, leaf through*, learn, make out*, perceive, peruse, pore over*, refer to, scan, scratch the surface*, see, skim, study, translate, unravel, view; SEE CONCEPT 72

read [v2] express, state
affirm, announce, assert, declaim, deliver, display, explain, expound, hold, indicate, mark, paraphrase, pronounce, recite, record, register, render, restate, say, show, speak, utter; SEE CONCEPT 266

readable [adj1] understandable, legible
clear, coherent, comprehensible, decipherable, distinct, explicit, flowing, fluent, graphic, intelligible, lucid, orderly, plain, precise, regular, simple, smooth, straightforward, tidy, unequivocal, unmistakable; SEE CONCEPTS 272,529

readable [adj2] pleasurable to peruse
absorbing, amusing, appealing, brilliant, clever, easy, eloquent, engaging, engrossing, enjoyable, entertaining, enthralling, exciting, fascinating, gratifying, gripping, ingenious, interesting, inviting, pleasant, pleasing, relaxing, rewarding, satisfying, smooth, stimulating, well-written, worthwhile; SEE CONCEPT 272

readily [adv] quickly; effortlessly
at once, at the drop of a hat*, cheerfully, eagerly, easily, facilely, freely, gladly, hands down*, immediately, in a jiffy*, in no time*, lightly, no sweat*, nothing to it*, piece of cake*, promptly, quick as a wink*, right away, slick as whistle*, smoothly, speedily, straight away, swimmingly, unhesitatingly, well, willingly, without delay, without demur, without difficulty, without hesitation; SEE CONCEPTS 544,820

readiness [n] skill; eagerness
address, adroitness, alacrity, aptness, deftness, dexterity, dispatch, ease, eloquence, expedience, expedition, facility, fitness, fluency, good will, handiness, inclination, keenness, maturity, preparation, preparedness, promptitude, promptness, prowess, quickness, rapidity, ripeness, sleight, volubility, willingness; SEE CONCEPTS 630,633, 678

reading [n] interpretation of written word
account, book-learning, commentary, conception, construction, edification, education, erudition, examination, grasp, impression, inspection, knowledge, learning, lesson, paraphrase, perusal, rendering, rendition, review, scholarship, scrutiny, study, translation, treatment, understanding, version; SEE CONCEPTS 72,271,274

ready [adj1] prepared; available
accessible, adjusted, all set, all systems go*, anticipating, apt, arranged, at beck and call*, at fingertips*, at hand, at the ready, champing at bit*, close to hand, completed, convenient, covered, equal to, equipped, expectant, fit, fixed for, handy, in line, in order, in place, in position, in

readiness, in the saddle*, near, on call, on hand, on tap*, on the brink*, open to, organized, primed, qualified, ripe, set, waiting, wired*; SEE CONCEPTS 560,576,799

ready [adj2] willing, inclined
agreeable, apt, ardent, disposed, eager, enthusiastic, fain, game, game for, glad, happy, keen, minded, predisposed, prompt, prone, psyched up*, wired*, zealous; SEE CONCEPTS 401,542

ready [adj3] skillful, intelligent
active, acute, adept, adroit, alert, apt, astute, bright, brilliant, clever, deft, dexterous, dynamic, expert, handy, keen, live, masterly, perceptive, proficient, prompt, quick, quick-witted, rapid, resourceful, sharp, skilled, smart; SEE CONCEPTS 402,527

ready [v] prepare
arrange, brace, brief, clear the decks*, equip, fill in, fit, fit out, fix, fortify, gear up*, get, get ready, get set, gird, keep posted*, let in on*, make, make ready, make up, order, organize, pave the way*, post, prep, provide, psych up*, put on to*, set, strengthen, warm up, wise up*; SEE CONCEPTS 35,60,202

real [adj] genuine in existence
absolute, actual, authentic, bodily, bona fide, certain, concrete, corporal, corporeal, de facto, embodied, essential, evident, existent, existing, factual, firm, heartfelt, honest, incarnate, indubitable, in the flesh*, intrinsic, irrefutable, legitimate, live, material, original, palpable, perceptible, physical, positive, present, right, rightful, sensible, sincere, solid, sound, stable, substantial, substantive, tangible, true, unaffected, undeniable, undoubted, unfeigned, valid, veritable; SEE CONCEPT 582

realistic [adj1] sensible, matter-of-fact
astute, businesslike, commonsense, down-to-earth, earthy, hard, hard-boiled*, levelheaded, practical, pragmatic, pragmatical, prudent, rational, real, reasonable, sane, sensible, shrewd, sober, sound, unfantastic, unidealistic, unromantic, unsentimental, utilitarian; SEE CONCEPTS 403, 542,548

realistic [adj2] genuine
authentic, faithful, graphic, lifelike, natural, original, representational, representative, true, true to life, truthful; SEE CONCEPT 582

reality [n] facts of existence
absoluteness, actuality, authenticity, being, bottom line*, brass tacks*, certainty, concreteness, corporeality, deed, entity, existence, genuineness, how things are*, like it is*, materiality, matter, name of the game*, nuts and bolts*, object, palpability, perceptibility, phenomenon, presence, realism, realness, real world*, sensibility, solidity, substance, substantiality, substantive, tangibility, truth, validity, verisimilitude, verity, way of it*, what's what*; SEE CONCEPTS 689,725

realize [v1] appreciate, become aware of
apprehend, be cognizant of, become conscious of, catch, catch on*, comprehend, conceive, discern, envisage, envision, fancy*, feature*, get, get it*, get the idea*, get the picture*, get through one's head*, grasp, image, imagine, know, pick up*, recognize, see daylight*, take in*, think, understand, vision, visualize; SEE CONCEPT 15

realize [v2] accomplish
actualize, bring about, bring off*, bring to fruition, carry out, carry through, complete, consum-

ra
re

mate, corporealize, do, effect, effectuate, fulfill, make concrete, make good*, make happen, materialize, perfect, perform, reify; SEE CONCEPT *91*

realize [*v3*] *gain, earn*

accomplish, achieve, acquire, attain, bring in, clear, get, go for*, make, make a profit, net, obtain, produce, rack up*, reach, receive, score*, sell for, take in, win; SEE CONCEPTS *120,124,330*

really [*adv*] *without a doubt*

absolutely, actually, admittedly, as a matter of fact, assuredly, authentically, beyond doubt, categorically, certainly, de facto, easily, for real*, genuinely, honestly, in actuality, indeed, indubitably, in effect, in fact, in point of fact, in reality, legitimately, literally, no ifs ands or buts*, nothing else but, of course, positively, precisely, surely, truly, undoubtedly, unmistakably, unquestionably, verily, well; SEE CONCEPTS *535,582*

realm [*n*] *area of responsibility or rule*

branch, compass, country, department, dimension, domain, dominion, empire, expanse, extent, field, ground, kingdom, land, monarchy, neck of the woods*, neighborhood, orbit, place, principality, province, purview, radius, range, reach, region, scope, sphere, state, stomping grounds*, sweep, territory, turf*, world, zone; SEE CONCEPTS *349,362,512,651*

reap [*v*] *collect, harvest*

acquire, bring in, come to have, crop, cull, cut, derive, draw, gain, garner, gather, get, get as a result, glean, ingather, mow, obtain, pick, pick up, pluck, procure, produce, profit, realize, receive, recover, retrieve, secure, strip, take in, win; SEE CONCEPTS *109,120,124,257*

rear [*n*] *back or end part*

afterpart, back, back door*, back end, back seat*, backside, behind, bottom, butt, buttocks, end, heel, hind, hind part, hindquarters, posterior, postern, rear end, rear guard, rearward, reverse, rump, seat, stern, tail, tail end, tailpiece, tush*; SEE CONCEPTS *825,827*

rear [*adj*] *back, end*

aft, after, astern, backward, behind, dorsal, following, hind, hinder, hindermost, hindmost, last, mizzen, posterior, postern, rearmost, rearward, retral, reverse, stern, tail; SEE CONCEPT *583*

rear [*v*] *raise young*

breed, bring up, care for, cultivate, educate, foster, grow, nurse, nurture, propagate, train; SEE CONCEPT *295*

rear [*v2*] *lift, rise*

bring up, elevate, hoist, hold up, jump, leap, loom, pick up, raise, set upright, soar, spring up, support, take up, tower, turn up, uphold, uplift, upraise; SEE CONCEPTS *194,196,741*

rear [*v3*] *build*

construct, erect, fabricate, put up, raise, set up, uprear; SEE CONCEPT *168*

reason [*n1*] *mental analysis*

acumen, apprehension, argumentation, bounds, brain*, brains*, comprehension, deduction, dialectics, discernment, generalization, induction, inference, intellect, intellection, judgment, limits, logic, lucidity, marbles*, mentality, mind, moderation, propriety, ratiocination, rationalism, rationality, rationalization, reasonableness, reasoning, saneness, sanity, sense, senses*, sensibleness, sound mind, soundness, speculation, understanding, wisdom, wit; SEE CONCEPTS *37,409*

reason [*n2*] *intention, aim*

antecedent, argument, basis, cause, consideration, design, determinant, end, goal, grounds, idea, impetus, incentive, inducement, motivation, motive, object, occasion, proof, purpose, rationale, root, spring, target, ulterior motive, warrant, wherefore*, why, why and wherefore*, whyfor*; SEE CONCEPT *659*

reason [*n3*] *explanation for an action*

account, apologia, apology, argument, case, cover, defense, excuse, exposition, ground, idea, justification, notion, proof, rationale, rationalization, song and dance*, sour grapes*, the whole idea*, vindication, whatfor*, wherefore*, why*, why and wherefore*, whyfor*; SEE CONCEPT *661*

reason [*v1*] *mentally analyze*

adduce, cerebrate, cogitate, conclude, contemplate, decide, deduce, deduct, deliberate, draw conclusion, draw from, examine, figure out, gather, generalize, infer, make out, philosophize, ratiocinate, rationalize, reflect, resolve, solve, speculate, study, suppose, syllogize, think, think through, thresh out, work out; SEE CONCEPT *37*

reason [*v2*] *argue, persuade*

bring around, contend, debate, demonstrate, discourse, discuss, dispute, dissuade, establish, expostulate, justify, move, point out, prevail upon, prove, remonstrate, show error of ways*, talk into, talk out of, urge, win over; SEE CONCEPTS *46,56,68*

reasonable [*adj1*] *moderate, tolerable*

acceptable, analytical, average, cheap, circumspect, conservative, controlled, discreet, equitable, fair, feasible, fit, honest, humane, impartial, inexpensive, judicious, just, justifiable, knowing, legit, legitimate, low-cost, low-priced, making sense, modest, objective, okay, plausible, politic, proper, prudent, rational, reflective, restrained, right, sane, sapient, sensible, sound, standing to reason*, temperate, understandable, unexcessive, unextreme, valid, within reason; SEE CONCEPTS *547,558*

reasonable [*adj2*] *intelligent, practical*

advisable, all there*, arguable, believeable, cerebral, clear-cut, cognitive, commonsensical, conscious, consequent, consistent, cool*, credible, in one's right mind*, judicious, justifiable, levelheaded, logical, perceiving, percipient, plausible, ratiocinative, rational, reasoned, reasoning, reflective, sane, sensible, sober, sound, tenable, thoughtful, thought-out, together*, tolerant, unbiased, unprejudiced, well-advised, wise; SEE CONCEPT *402*

reasoning [*n*] *logic, interpretation*

acumen, analysis, apriority, argument, case, cogitation, concluding, corollary, deduction, dialectics, exposition, generalization, hypothesis, illation, induction, inference, interpretation, logistics, premise, proof, proposition, ratiocination, rationale, rationalizing, reason, syllogism, syllogization, thinking, thought, train of thought; SEE CONCEPTS *37,529*

reassure [*v*] *restore confidence to*

assure, bolster, brace, buoy, cheer, comfort, console, convince, encourage, give a lift*, give confidence, guarantee, hearten, inspire, inspirit, perk up, put one's mind to rest*, relieve, snap one out of it*; SEE CONCEPTS *7,22*

rebate [*n*] *refund given to purchaser*

abatement, allowance, bonus, deduction, discount, kickback, payback, reduction, reimbursement, remission, repayment, subtraction; SEE CONCEPT 344

rebel [n] *person who does not obey*
agitator, anarchist, antagonist, apostate, demagogue, deserter, disectarian, dissenter, experientialist, experimenter, frondeur, guerrilla, heretic, iconoclast, independent, individualist, innovator, insurgent, insurrectionary, malcontent, mutineer, nihilist, nonconformist, opponent, overthrower, recreant, renegade, resistance, revolter, revolutionary, revolutionist, rioter, schismatic, secessionist, seditionist, separatist, subverter, traitor, turncoat; SEE CONCEPTS 359,412,423

rebel [adj] *not obeying*
insubordinate, insurgent, insurrectionary, mutinous, rebellious, revolutionary; SEE CONCEPT 401

rebel [v] *refuse to obey*
be insubordinate, boycott, break with*, censure, combat, come out against*, criticize, defy, denounce, disobey, dissent, drop out*, fight, get out of line*, insurrect, make waves*, mutiny, oppose, opt out*, overthrow, overturn, remonstrate, renounce, resist, revolt, riot, rise up*, rock the boat*, run amok*, secede, strike, take up arms, turn against, upset; SEE CONCEPTS 106,633

rebellion [n] *disobedience; revolt*
apostasy, defiance, disobedience, dissent, heresy, insubordination, insurgence, insurgency, insurrection, nonconformity, revolution, rising, schism, uprising; SEE CONCEPTS 106,300,320,633

rebellious [adj] *disobedient, unmanageable*
alienated, anarchical, attacking, bellicose, contumacious, defiant, difficult, disaffected, disloyal, disobedient, disorderly, dissident, factious, fractious, iconoclastic, incorrigible, individualistic, insurgent, insurrectionary, intractable, mutinous, obstinate, pugnacious, quarrelsome, radical, rebel, recalcitrant, refractory, resistant, restless, revolutionary, rioting, riotous, sabotaging, seditious, threatening, treasonable, turbulent, ungovernable, unruly, warring; SEE CONCEPTS 401, 529,542

rebuff [n] *turning away; ignoring*
brushoff*, check, cold shoulder*, cut, defeat, denial, discouragement, go-by*, hard time*, insult, kick in the teeth*, nix*, nothing doing*, opposition, rebuke, refusal, rejection, reprimand, repulse, slight, snub, thumbs down*, turndown; SEE CONCEPTS 30,278

rebuff [v] *turn away; give the cold shoulder**
beat off*, brush off, check, chide, cross, cut, decline, deny, disallow, discourage, dismiss, disregard, fend off, hold off, ignore, keep at a distance*, keep at arm's length*, keep at bay, lash out at, neglect, not hear of, oppose, pass up, push back, put in one's place*, put off, rebuke, refuse, reject, repel, reprove, repudiate, repulse, resist, send away, slight, snub, spurn, stave off, tell off*, turn down, ward off; SEE CONCEPTS 30,54

rebuke [n] *reprimand; harsh criticism*
admonishment, admonition, affliction, bawling-out*, berating, blame, castigation, censure, chewing-out*, chiding, comeuppance, condemnation, correction, disapproval, dressing-down*, earful*, expostulation, going-over*, hard time*, kick in the teeth*, lecture, lesson, objurgation, ostracism, punishment, put-down, rap*, rating, rebuff, refusal, remonstrance, reprehension, reproach, reproof, reproval, repulse, row, scolding,

slap in the face*, snub, talking-to*, telling-off*, tongue-lashing*, upbraiding; SEE CONCEPTS 44,52,278

rebuke [v] *reprimand; criticize harshly*
admonish, bawl out*, berate, blame, call on the carpet*, carp on, castigate, censure, chew out*, chide, climb all over*, dress down*, fry*, go after*, jawbone*, jump down one's throat*, jump on*, lay into*, lean on*, lecture, lesson, monish, oppose, pay, rake, read*, reprehend, reprimand, reproach, reprove, rip*, scold, sit on*, sound off*, take to task*, tear apart*, tell off*, tick off*, upbraid, zap*; SEE CONCEPTS 44,52

rebut [v] *argue against; prove wrong*
break, come back at, confound, confute, controvert, cross, defeat, deny, disconfirm, disprove, evert, fend off, get back at, hold off, invalidate, keep off, negate, negative, overturn, prove false, quash, refute, repel, repulse, stave off, take on, top, ward off; SEE CONCEPTS 46,54

recalcitrant [adj] *disobedient, uncontrollable*
contrary, contumacious, defiant, fractious, indomitable, insubmissive, insubordinate, intractable, obstinate, opposing, radical, rebellious, refractory, resistant, resisting, stubborn, undisciplinable, undisciplined, ungovernable, unmanageable, unruly, untoward, unwilling, wayward, wild, willful, withstanding; SEE CONCEPT 401

recall [n1] *remembrance*
anamnesis, memory, recollection, reminiscence; SEE CONCEPT 529

recall [n2] *request for return*
annulment, cancellation, nullification, recision, repeal, rescindment, rescission, retraction, revocation, withdrawal; SEE CONCEPTS 662,685

recall [v1] *remember*
arouse, awaken, bethink, bring to mind, call to mind, call up, cite, come to one, educe, elicit, evoke, extract, flash, flash on*, look back, mind, nail it down*, recollect, reestablish, reinstate, reintroduce, remind, reminisce, renew, retain, retrospect, revive, ring a bell*, rouse, stir, strike a note*, summon, think back*, think of, waken; SEE CONCEPT 40

recall [v2] *ask for return of offending thing*
abjure, annul, call back, call in, cancel, countermand, discharge, dismantle, dismiss, disqualify, forswear, lift, nullify, palinode, recant, repeal, rescind, retract, reverse, revoke, suspend, take back, unsay, withdraw; SEE CONCEPTS 50,88, 131,143

recant [v] *take back something said*
abjure, abnegate, abrogate, annul, apostatize, back down, back off, back out, backtrack*, call back, cancel, contradict, countermand, deny, dial back*, disavow, disclaim, disown, eat one's words*, forswear, go back on one's word*, nullify, recall, renege, renounce, repeal, repudiate, rescind, retract, revoke, take back, unsay, void, weasel out*, welsh*, withdraw, worm out of*; SEE CONCEPTS 25,266

recapitulate [v] *go over something again*
epitomize, go over same ground*, go the same round*, outline, paraphrase, recap*, recount, rehash, reiterate, repeat, rephrase, replay, restate, review, reword, run over*, run through again*, summarize, sum up; SEE CONCEPT 266

recede [v] *withdraw; diminish*
abate, back, close, decline, decrease, depart, die off, diminish, drain away, draw back, drop, dwin-

re
re

dle, ebb, fade, fall back, flow back, go away, go back, lessen, reduce, regress, retire, retract, retreat, retrocede, retrograde, retrogress, return, shrink, sink, subside, taper, wane; SEE CONCEPTS 195,698,776

receipt [n1] *acknowledgment of delivery*
cancellation, certificate, chit, counterfoil, declaration, discharge, letter, notice, proof of purchase, quittance, release, sales slip, slip, stub, voucher; SEE CONCEPTS 271,332

receipt [n2] *delivery of goods*
acceptance, accession, acquiring, acquisition, admission, admitting, arrival, getting, intaking, receiving, reception, recipience, taking; SEE CONCEPT 124

receipts [n] *money earned in business venture*
bottom line*, cash flow, comings in*, earnings, gain, gate, get*, gross, handle*, income, net, proceeds, profit, return, revenue, revenue stream, royalty, take*, take-in*, taking*; SEE CONCEPT 344

receive [v1] *accept delivery of something*
accept, acquire, admit, apprehend, appropriate, arrogate, assume, be given, be informed, be in receipt of, be told, catch, collect, come by, come into, cop*, corral*, derive, draw, earn, gain, gather, get, get from, get hands on*, get hold of*, grab, have, hold, inherit, latch on to*, make, obtain, perceive, pick up, pocket*, procure, pull, pull down*, reap, redeem, secure, seize, snag*, take, take in, take possession, win; SEE CONCEPT 124

receive [v2] *endure, sustain*
bear, be subjected to, encounter, experience, go through, meet with, suffer, undergo; SEE CONCEPT 23

receive [v3] *take in guest or member*
accept, accommodate, admit, allow entrance, bring in, entertain, greet, host, induct, initiate, install, introduce, invite, let in, let through, make comfortable, make welcome, meet, permit, roll out red carpet*, shake hands*, show in, take in, usher in, welcome; SEE CONCEPTS 50,83,88,140

recent [adj] *current*
contempo*, contemporary, fresh, hot off the fire*, hot off the press*, just out*, late, lately, latter-day, modern, modernistic, neoteric, new, newborn, newfangled, novel, present-day, the latest*, today, up-to-date, young; SEE CONCEPTS 578, 797,820

recently [adv] *currently*
afresh, anew, freshly, in recent past, in recent times, just a while ago, just now, lately, latterly, new, newly, not long ago, of late, short while ago, the other day; SEE CONCEPT 820

receptacle [n] *container for disposal, storage*
bowl, box, holder, hopper, repository, vessel, wastebasket; SEE CONCEPT 494

reception [n1] *acceptance; acknowledgment*
accession, acquisition, admission, disposition, encounter, gathering, greeting, induction, introduction, meeting, reaction, receipt, receiving, recipience, recognition, response, salutation, treatment, welcome; SEE CONCEPTS 83,124,384

reception [n2] *celebratory party*
buffet, dinner, do*, entertainment, function, gathering, levee, matinee, soiree, supper, tea; SEE CONCEPT 383

receptive [adj] *open to new ideas*
acceptant, acceptive, accessible, alert, amenable,

approachable, bright, favorable, friendly, hospitable, influenceable, interested, observant, open, open-minded, open to suggestions, perceptive, persuadable, pushover*, quick on the uptake*, ready, recipient, responsive, sensitive, suggestible, susceptible, swayable, sympathetic, welcoming, well-disposed; SEE CONCEPT 404

recess [n1] *niche, corner*
alcove, ambush, angle, apse, bay, break, carrel, cavity, cell, closet, cove, cranny, crutch, crypt, cubicle, dent, depression, depths, embrasure, fork, heart, hiding place, hole, hollow, indentation, mouth, nook, opening, oriel, penetralia, reaches, retreat, secret place, slot, socket; SEE CONCEPTS 440,513

recess [n2] *break, interval in action*
break-off, breather*, breathing spell*, cessation, closure, coffee break*, cutoff, downtime*, halt, happy hour*, hiatus, holiday, interlude, intermission, interregnum, layoff, letup, lull, pause, respite, rest, stop, suspension, ten*, time-out, vacation; SEE CONCEPT 807

recess [v] *stop action*
adjourn, break off*, break up*, call time*, dissolve, drop, drop it, pigeonhole*, prorogate, prorogue, put on hold, rise, shake, sideline*, take a break, take a breather*, take five*, take ten*, terminate; SEE CONCEPTS 119,121

recession [n] *reversal of action; reduction of business activity*
bad times*, bankruptcy, big trouble*, bottom-out*, bust, collapse, decline, deflation, depression, downturn, hard times*, inflation, rainy days*, shakeout*, slide, slump, stagnation, unemployment; SEE CONCEPT 335

recipe [n] *directions, formula*
compound, ingredients, instructions, method, modus operandi, prescription, procedure, process, program, receipt, technique; SEE CONCEPT 274

reciprocal [adj] *exchanged, alternate*
changeable, companion, complementary, convertible, coordinate, correlative, corresponding, dependent, double, duplicate, equivalent, exchangeable, fellow, give-and-take*, interchangeable, interdependent, matching, mutual, reciprocative, reciprocatory, twin; SEE CONCEPTS 566,577

reciprocate [v] *exchange, alternate; equal*
barter, be equivalent, correspond, equal, feel in return, interchange, make up for*, match, pay one's dues*, recompense, render, repay, reply, requite, respond, retaliate, retort, return, return the compliment*, scratch one's back*, serve out, share, square, swap, swing, tit for tat*, trade, vacillate; SEE CONCEPTS 45,104,384

recital [n] *narrative, rendering*
account, concert, description, detailing, enumeration, fable, musical, musicale, narration, narrative, performance, portrayal, presentation, reading, recapitulation, recitation, recountal, recounting, rehearsal, relation, repetition, report, statement, story, tale, telling; SEE CONCEPTS 263,264

recitation [n] *reading to audience*
address, appeal, declaiming, delivery, discourse, discoursing, discussion, exercise, holding forth, lecture, monologue, narrating, narration, oration, passage, performance, piece, playing, proclamation, recital, recounting, rehearsal, rendering, re-

port, selection, soliloquizing, speaking, talk, telling; SEE CONCEPTS 72,263,266

recite [v] *read out loud; narrate*
account for, address, answer, chant, communicate, convey, declaim, delineate, deliver, describe, detail, discourse, dramatize, enact, enlarge, enumerate, expatiate, explain, give an account, give a report, give verbal account, hold forth, impart, interpret, itemize, mention, narrate, parrot*, perform, picture, portray, quote, recapitulate, recount, reel off*, rehearse, relate, render, repeat, reply, report, retell, soliloquize, speak, state, tell, utter; SEE CONCEPTS 55,57,72,266

reckless [adj] *irresponsible in thought, deed*
adventuresome, adventurous, any which way*, audacious, brash, breakneck, carefree, careless, daredevil, daring, desperate, devil-may-care*, fast and loose*, feckless, foolhardy, harebrained, hasty, headlong, heedless, helter-skelter, hopeless, hotheaded*, ill-advised, imprudent, inattentive, incautious, inconsiderate, indiscreet, kooky*, madcap, mindless, negligent, overventuresome, playing with fire*, precipitate, rash, regardless, temerarious, thoughtless, uncareful, venturesome, venturous, wild; SEE CONCEPTS 401,542

reckon [v1] *add up; evaluate*
account, appraise, approximate, calculate, call, cast, cipher, compute, conjecture, consider, count, count heads*, count noses*, deem, enumerate, esteem, estimate, figure, figure out, foot, gauge, guess, hold, judge, keep tabs*, look, number, place, put, rate, regard, run down, square, sum, surmise, take account of, tally, think of, tick off*, tot, total, tote*, tote up*, tot up, view; SEE CONCEPTS 37,764

reckon [v2] *suppose, imagine*
assume, bank on, bargain for, believe, be of the opinion, build on, conjecture, count on, depend on, expect, fancy, gather, guess, plan on, rely on, surmise, suspect, take, think, trust in, understand; SEE CONCEPTS 12,26

reckoning [n] *computation, account*
adding, addition, arithmetic, bad news*, bill, calculation, charge, check, ciphering, cost, count, counting, debt, due, estimate, estimation, fee, figuring, grunt*, invoice, IOU*, score, settlement, statement, summation, tab, working; SEE CONCEPT 331

recline [v] *lie down*
be recumbent, cant, heel, lay down, lean, lie, list, loll, lounge, repose, rest, slant, slope, sprawl, stretch, stretch out, tilt, tip; SEE CONCEPTS 154,201

recluse [n] *person who does not want social contact*
anchorite, ascetic, cenobite, eremite, hermit, monk, nun, solitaire, solitary, troglodyte; SEE CONCEPT 423

recluse/reclusive [adj] *hermitlike, unsociable*
antisocial, ascetic, cloistered, eremetic, hermetic, isolated, misanthropic, monastic, reserved, retiring, secluded, secluse, seclusive, sequestered, solitary, standoffish, withdrawn; SEE CONCEPTS 404,555

recognition [n1] *identification, acknowledgment*
acceptance, acknowledging, admission, allowance, apperception, appreciation, apprehending, assimilation, avowal, awareness, cognizance, concession, confession, consciousness, detection,

discovery, double take*, high sign*, identifying, memory, notice, noticing, perceiving, perception, realization, recall, recalling, recognizance, recollection, recurrence, remembering, remembrance, respect, salute, sensibility, tumble*, understanding, verifying; SEE CONCEPT 38

recognition [n2] *appreciation given*
acceptance, acknowledgment, approval, attention, credit, esteem, gratitude, greeting, honor, notice, pat on back*, pat on head*, plum*, puff*, puffing up*, pumping up*, rave, regard, renown, salute, strokes*; SEE CONCEPTS 10,337,689

recognize [v1] *identify*
admit, be familiar, button down*, descry, determine, diagnose, diagnosticate, distinguish, espy, finger*, flash on*, know, know again, make*, make out, nail*, note, notice, observe, peg*, perceive, pinpoint, place, recall, recollect, remark, remember, ring a bell*, see, sight, spot, tab, tag, verify; SEE CONCEPT 38

recognize [v2] *acknowledge, understand; approve*
accept, admit, agree, allow, appreciate, assent, avow, be aware of, comprehend, concede, confess, grant, greet, honor, make own, perceive, realize, respect, salute, sanction, see; SEE CONCEPT 15

recoil [v] *shrink away*
backfire, balk, blanch, blench, blink, carom, cringe, demur, dodge, draw back, duck, falter, flinch, hesitate, jerk, kick, pull back, quail, quake, react, rebound, reel, resile, shake, shirk, shrink, shudder, shy away, spring, start, step back, stick, stickle, swerve, tremble, turn away, waver, wince, withdraw; SEE CONCEPTS 150,194,195

recollect [v] *remember*
arouse, awaken, bethink, bring to mind, call to mind, cite, come to one, flash, flash on*, look back on, mind, place, recall, recognize, remind, reminisce, retain, retrospect, revive, rouse, stir, summon, waken; SEE CONCEPT 40

recommend [v] *advise, approve*
acclaim, advance, advocate, applaud, back, be all for*, be satisfied with, celebrate, commend, compliment, confirm, counsel, endorse, enjoin, esteem, eulogize, exalt, exhort, extol, favor, front for*, glorify, go on record for*, hold up, justify, laud, magnify, plug*, praise, prescribe, prize, propose, put forward, put in a good word*, put on to*, sanction, second, speak highly of, speak well of, stand by, steer, suggest, think highly of, uphold, urge, value, vouch for; SEE CONCEPTS 10,75

recommendation [n] *advice, approval*
advocacy, approbation, blessing, certificate, character reference, charge, commendation, counsel, direction, endorsement, esteem, eulogy, favorable mention, good word*, guidance, injunction, instruction, judgment, letter of support, order, pass, plug*, praise, proposal, proposition, reference, sanction, steer*, suggestion, support, testimonial, tip, tribute, two cents' worth*, urging; SEE CONCEPTS 274,278

recompense [n] *something returned, paid back*
amends, atonement, bus fare*, compensation, cue, damages, emolument, expiation, gravy*, indemnification, indemnity, overcompensation, pay, payment, propitiation, quittance, recoupment, recovery, redemption, redress, remuneration, reparation, repayment, requital, restitution, retrieval, retrievement, return, reward, salvo, sat-

re
re

isfaction, solatium, sweetener*, tip, wages; SEE CONCEPTS 578

recompense [v] pay back, make restitution

ante up*, atone, atone for, balance, comp*, compensate, cough up*, counterbalance, counterpoise, counteravail, do business*, equalize, expiate, fix, give satisfaction, grease*, indemnify, make amends, make good*, make up for, offset, overcompensate, pay, pay for, propitiate, put out*, reciprocate, recoup, recover, redress, reimburse, remunerate, repay, requite, retaliate, retrieve, return, reward, satisfy, spring for, square*, sweeten the pot*, swing for*, take care of; SEE CONCEPTS 126,341

reconcile [v1] make peace; adjust

accommodate, accord, accustom, appease, arbitrate, arrange, assuage, attune, bring together, bring to terms, bury the hatchet*, come together, compose, conciliate, conform, cool*, coordinate, fit, fix up, get together on, harmonize, integrate, intercede, kiss and make up*, make matters up, make up, mediate, mitigate, pacify, patch things up*, patch up*, placate, propitiate, proportion, reconciliate, rectify, re-establish, regulate, resolve, restore harmony, reunite, settle, suit, tune, win over; SEE CONCEPTS 384,697

reconcile [v2] resign oneself to something

accept, accommodate, get used to*, make the best of*, put up with*, resign, submit, yield; SEE CONCEPT 23

recondite [adj] mysterious, obscure

abstruse, academic, acroamatic, arcane, cabalistic, concealed, cryptic, dark, deep, difficult, esoteric, hard, heavy*, hermetic, hidden, involved, little-known, mystic, mystical, occult, orphic, pedantic, profound, scholarly, secret; SEE CONCEPTS 529,576

reconsider [v] think about again

amend, change one's mind, consider again, correct, emend, go over, have second thoughts*, polish, rearrange, reassess, recheck, reevaluate, reexamine, rehash, replan, rethink, retrace, review, revise, reweigh, rework, run through, see in a new light*, sleep on, take another look, think better of*, think over, think twice*, work over; SEE CONCEPT 17

reconstruct [v] reorganize, build up

copy, deduce, doctor*, do up*, fix, fix up, make over, modernize, overhaul, patch, piece together, reassemble, rebuild, recast, recondition, reconstitute, recreate, reestablish, refashion, reform, regenerate, rehabilitate, rejuvenate, remake, remodel, remold, renovate, reorient, repair, replace, reproduce, reshuffle, restore, retool, revamp, rework; SEE CONCEPTS 84,168,171

record [n1] account of event or proceedings

almanac, annals, archive, archives, chronicle, comic book*, diary, directory, document, documentation, entry, evidence, file, history, inscription, jacket, journal, legend, log, manuscript, memo, memoir, memorandum, memorial, minutes, monument, note, paper trail*, register, registry, remembrance, report, script, scroll, story, swindle sheet*, testimony, trace, track record*, transcript, transcription, witness, writing, written material; SEE CONCEPTS 271,281

record [n2] background, experience

accomplishment, administration, career, case history, conduct, curriculum vitae, history, past be-

havior, performance, reign, studies, track record*, way of life*, work; SEE CONCEPT 678

record [n3] achievement

ceiling, maximum; SEE CONCEPT 706

record [v1] write down; store information

book, can*, catalog, chalk up*, chronicle, copy, cut, cut a track*, document, dub*, enroll, enter, enumerate, file, indite, inscribe, insert, jot down, keep account, lay down, list, log, make a recording, mark, mark down, matriculate, note, post, preserve, put down, put in writing, put on file*, put on paper*, put on tape*, register, report, set down, tabulate, take down, tape, tape-record, transcribe, video*, videotape, wax*, write in; SEE CONCEPT 125

record [v2] give evidence of

contain, designate, explain, indicate, mark, point out, point to, read, register, say, show; SEE CONCEPT 261

recount [v] tell a story

break a story*, convey, delineate, depict, describe, detail, echo, enumerate, give an account of, itemize, narrate, picture, play back, portray, recap*, recapitulate, recite, rehash, rehearse, relate, repeat, report, run by again*, run down*, run through*, say again, state, tell, track, unload, verbalize; SEE CONCEPTS 55,266

recoup [v] recover, make up for

compensate, get back, get out from under*, get well, make good, make redress for, make well, redeem, refund, regain, reimburse, remunerate, repay, repossess, requite, retrieve, satisfy, win back; SEE CONCEPTS 124,126,342,700

recourse [n] alternative

aid, appeal, choice, expediency, expedient, help, makeshift, option, refuge, remedy, resort, resource, shift, stand-by, stopgap, substitute, support, way out; SEE CONCEPTS 693,712

recover [v1] find again

balance, bring back, catch up, compensate, get back, make good, obtain again, offset, reacquire, recapture, reclaim, recoup, recruit, redeem, rediscover, regain, reoccupy, repair, replevin, replevy, repossess, rescue, restore, resume, retake, retrieve, salvage, take back, win back; SEE CONCEPTS 120,183

recover [v2] improve in health

be out of woods*, better, bounce back*, come around, convalesce, feel oneself again*, forge ahead, gain, get back on feet*, get better, get in shape, get out from under*, get over, get well, grow, heal, increase, make a comeback*, mend, overcome, perk up*, pick up, pull through, rally, rebound, recuperate, refresh, regain one's health, regain one's strength, rejuvenate, renew, restore, return to form, revive, snap back*, sober up*, start anew, take turn for better; SEE CONCEPTS 303,700

recreation [n] sports, games, special interests

amusement, avocation, ball*, disport, dissipation, distraction, diversion, divertissement, ease, enjoyment, entertainment, exercise, festivity, field day*, frolic, fun, fun and games*, game, hilarity, hobby, holiday, jollity, laughs*, leisure activity, mirth, pastime, picnic, play, playtime, pleasure, R and R*, rec, refreshment, relaxation, relief, repose, rollick, sport, vacation; SEE CONCEPTS 363,364

recruit [n] person beginning service

apprentice, beginner, convert, draftee, enlisted

person, fledgling, GI*, greenhorn*, helper, initiate, learner, neophyte, newcomer, new person, novice, novitiate, plebe*, proselyte, rookie, sailor, selectee, serviceperson, soldier, tenderfoot*, trainee, volunteer; SEE CONCEPTS 348,358

recruit [v] *gather resources*

augment, better, build up, call to arms, call up, deliver, draft, engage, enlist, enroll, fill up, find human resources, gain, impress, induct, levy, mobilize, muster, obtain, procure, proselytize, raise, reanimate, recoup, recover, recuperate, refresh, regain, reinforce, renew, repair, replenish, repossess, restore, retrieve, revive, round up, select, sign on, sign up, store up, strengthen, supply, take in, take on, win over; SEE CONCEPTS 41,109,120,320

rectify [v] *correct a situation; make something right*

adjust, amend, clean up, clean up act*, debug, dial back*, doctor, emend, fix, fix up, go over, improve, launder, make good*, make up for*, mend, pay one's dues*, pick up, put right, recalibrate, redress, reform, remedy, repair, revise, right, scrub, shape up, square, straighten out, straighten up, turn things around*; SEE CONCEPT 126

recuperate [v] *improve in health*

ameliorate, be on the mend*, be out of the woods*, bounce back*, convalesce, gain, get back on one's feet*, get better, get well, heal, look up, make a comeback*, mend, perk up*, pick up, pull out of it*, pull through, rally, recover, regain health, snap out of it*, turn the corner*; SEE CONCEPTS 303,700

recur [v] *happen again; repeat in one's mind*

be remembered, be repeated, come again, come and go, come back, crop up again*, haunt thoughts*, iterate, persist, reappear, recrudesce, reiterate, repeat, return, return to mind, revert, run through one's mind*, turn back; SEE CONCEPTS 3,242

recurrent [adj] *repeating*

alternate, chain, continued, cyclical, frequent, habitual, intermittent, isochronal, isochronous, periodic, periodical, recurring, regular, reoccurring, repeated, repetitive, rolling; SEE CONCEPTS 541,544

red [n/adj] *color of blood; shade resembling such a color*

bittersweet, bloodshot, blooming, blush, brick, burgundy, cardinal, carmine, cerise, cherry, chestnut, claret, copper, coral, crimson, dahlia, flaming, florid, flushed, fuchsia, garnet, geranium, glowing, healthy, inflamed, infrared, magenta, maroon, pink, puce, rose, roseate, rosy, rubicund, ruby, ruddy, rufescent, russet, rust, salmon, sanguine, scarlet, titian, vermilion, wine; SEE CONCEPTS 618,622

redden [v] *blush, make rosy*

bloody, color, crimson, dye, encarmine, encarnadine, flush, glow, go red, mantle, paint, pink, pinken, rose, rouge, rubify, rubric, rubricate, ruby, ruddle, ruddy, rust, suffuse, tint, turn red; SEE CONCEPTS 250,469

redeem [v1] *recover possession*

buy back, buy off, call in, cash, cash in, change, cover, defray, discharge, exchange, get back, make good, pay off, purchase, ransom, recapture, reclaim, recoup, regain, reinstate, repay, replevin, replevy, repossess, repurchase, restore, retrieve,

settle, take in, trade in, win back; SEE CONCEPTS 104,131,327

redeem [v2] *free; buy the freedom of*

deliver, disenthrall, disimprison, emancipate, extricate, liberate, loose, manumit, pay ransom, ransom, release, rescue, save, set free, unbind, unchain, unfetter; SEE CONCEPTS 127,327

redeem [v3] *atone for; compensate*

abide by, absolve, acquit, adhere to, balance, carry out, compensate, counterbalance, counterpoise, countervail, defray, discharge, fulfill, hold to, keep, keep the faith*, make amends, make good, make up for, meet, offset, outweigh, perform, redress, rehabilitate, reinstate, restore, satisfy, save, set off; SEE CONCEPTS 91,126

redress [n] *help, compensation*

aid, amendment, amends, assistance, atonement, balancing, change, conciliation, correction, cure, ease, indemnity, justice, offsetting, payment, quittance, recompense, rectification, reestablishment, reformation, rehabilitation, relief, remedy, remission, remodeling, renewal, repair, reparation, reprisal, requital, restitution, retribution, return, revision, reward, reworking, satisfaction, vengeance; SEE CONCEPTS 344,712

redress [v] *change, rectify*

adjust, amend, annul, balance, cancel, compensate, correct, counteract, countercheck, dial back*, ease, even out, frustrate, make amends, make reparation, make restitution, make up for, mend, negate, negative, neutralize, pay for, pay one's dues*, put right*, recalibrate, recompense, reform, regulate, relieve, remedy, repair, restore, revise, square, turn around, turn over new leaf*, turn things around*, vindicate; SEE CONCEPTS 126,697

reduce [v1] *make less; decrease*

abate, abridge, bankrupt, bant, break, cheapen, chop, clip, contract, curtail, cut, cut back, cut down, debase, deflate, depreciate, depress, diet, dilute, diminish, discount, drain, dwindle, go on a diet*, impair, impoverish, lessen, lose weight, lower, mark down, moderate, nutshell, pare, pauperize, rebate, recede, roll back, ruin, scale down, shave, shorten, slash, slim, slow down, step down, take off weight, taper, taper off, tone down, trim, truncate, turn down, weaken, wind down; SEE CONCEPTS 137,236,240,247,698

reduce [v2] *defeat*

bear down, beat down, break, bring, conquer, cripple, crush, disable, drive, enfeeble, force, master, overcome, overpower, ruin, subdue, subjugate, undermine, vanquish, weaken; SEE CONCEPT 95

reduce [v3] *humble, humiliate*

abase, break, bring low, bump*, bust*, declass, degrade, demerit, demote, disgrade, disrate, downgrade, lower, take down a peg*; SEE CONCEPTS 7,19,384

redundant [adj] *excessive; repetitious*

bombastic, de trop*, diffuse, extra, extravagant, inessential, inordinate, iterating, long-winded*, loquacious, oratorical, padded*, palaverous, periphrastic, pleonastic, prolix, reiterating, spare, supererogatory, superfluous, supernumerary, surplus, tautological, unnecessary, unwanted, verbose, wordy; SEE CONCEPTS 553,781

reef [n] *underwater or partially submerged ledge*

atoll, bank, bar, beach, cay, coral reef, ridge,

rock, rock barrier, sand bar, shoal, skerry; SEE CONCEPT 509

reek [n] *strong odor*
effluvium, fetor, mephitis, smell, stench, stink; SEE CONCEPT 600

reek [v] *smell of; be characterized by*
be permeated by, be redolent of, emit, fume, give off odor, have an odor, smell, smoke, steam, stench, stink; SEE CONCEPT 600

reel [v] *wobble; spin around*
bob, career, falter, feel giddy, go around, lurch, pitch, revolve, rock, roll, shake, stagger, stumble, sway, swim, swing, swirl, teeter, titubate, totter, turn, twirl, waver, weave, wheel, whirl; SEE CONCEPTS 151,153

refer [v1] *mention*
accredit, adduce, advert, allude, ascribe, assign, associate, attribute, bring up, charge, cite, credit, designate, direct attention, excerpt, exemplify, extract, give as example, glance, hint, impute, indicate, insert, instance, interpolate, introduce, invoke, lay, make allusion, make mention of, make reference, name, notice, point, point out, put down to, quote, speak about, speak of, specify, touch on; SEE CONCEPT 73

refer [v2] *direct, guide*
commit, consign, deliver, hand in, hand over, introduce, pass on, point, put in touch, recommend, relegate, send, submit, transfer, turn over; SEE CONCEPTS 143,187

refer [v3] *concern, apply*
answer, appertain, be about, be a matter of, bear upon, be directed to, belong, be relevant, connect, correspond with, cover, deal with, encompass, have a bearing on, have reference, have relation, have to do with, hold, include, incorporate, involve, pertain, point, regard, relate, take in, touch; SEE CONCEPT 532

refer [v4] *seek information*
advise, apply, commune, confer, consult, go, have recourse, look up, recur, repair, resort, run, turn, turn to; SEE CONCEPTS 72,216

referee [n] *person who mediates, judges*
adjudicator, arbiter, arbitrator, conciliator, judge, ref*, umpire; SEE CONCEPTS 348,366

referee [v] *judge, mediate*
adjudge, adjudicate, arbitrate, umpire; SEE CONCEPT 18

reference [n1] *remark, citation*
advertence, allusion, associating, attributing, bringing up, connecting, hint, implication, indicating, innuendo, insinuation, mention, mentioning, note, plug*, pointing out, quotation, relating, resource, source, stating; SEE CONCEPT 278

reference [n2] *testimonial of good character*
certificate, certification, character, credentials, endorsement, good word, recommendation, tribute; SEE CONCEPTS 69,274

reference [n3] *printed matter with information*
archives, cyclopedia, dictionary, encyclopedia, evidence, source, thesaurus, writing; SEE CONCEPTS 271,280

refine [v1] *purify*
clarify, cleanse, distill, filter, process, rarefy, strain; SEE CONCEPT 165

refine [v2] *perfect, polish*
better, civilize, clarify, cultivate, elevate, explain, hone, improve, make clear, round, sleek, slick, smooth, temper; SEE CONCEPT 244

refined [adj1] *cultured, civilized*
aesthetic, civil, classy*, courteous, courtly, cultivated, delicate, discerning, discriminating, elegant, enlightened, exact, fastidious, fine, finespun, genteel, gracious, high-brow*, high-minded, nice, plush, polished, polite, posh, precise, punctilious, restrained, ritzy*, sensitive, snazzy*, sophisticated, spiffy*, suave, sublime, subtle, swanky*, tasteful, urbane, well-bred, well-mannered; SEE CONCEPTS 401,555,589

refined [adj2] *cleaned of impurities*
aerated, boiled down, clarified, clean, cleansed, distilled, drained, expurgated, filtered, processed, pure, purified, rarefied, strained, washed; SEE CONCEPT 621

refinement [n1] *cleansing*
clarification, cleaning, depuration, detersion, distillation, draining, filtering, processing, purification, rarefaction, rectification; SEE CONCEPT 165

refinement [n2] *culture, civilization*
affability, civility, courtesy, courtliness, delicacy, dignity, discrimination, elegance, enlightenment, erudition, fastidiousness, fineness, fine point*, finesse, fine tuning*, finish, gentility, gentleness, good breeding, good manners, grace, graciousness, knowledge, lore, nicety, nuance, polish, politeness, politesse, precision, sophistication, style, suavity, subtlety, tact, taste, urbanity; SEE CONCEPTS 388,633,655

reflect [v1] *give back*
cast, catch, copy, echo, emulate, flash, follow, give forth, imitate, match, mirror, rebound, repeat, repercuss, reply, reproduce, resonate, resound, return, reverberate, reverse, revert, shine, take after, throw back; SEE CONCEPTS 65,171,624

reflect [v2] *think about*
cerebrate, chew*, cogitate, consider, contemplate, deliberate, meditate, mull over, muse, ponder, reason, ruminate, speculate, stew*, study, think, weigh, wonder; SEE CONCEPTS 17,24

reflect [v3] *demonstrate, indicate*
bear out, bespeak, communicate, display, evince, exhibit, express, indicate, manifest, reveal, show; SEE CONCEPT 261

reflection [n1] *thought, thinking*
absorption, brainwork, cerebration, cogitation, consideration, contemplation, deliberation, idea, imagination, impression, meditation, musing, observation, opinion, pensiveness, pondering, rumination, speculation, study, view; SEE CONCEPTS 17,24

reflection [n2] *mirror image*
appearance, counterpart, duplicate, echo, idea, image, impression, light, likeness, picture, representation, reproduction, shadow; SEE CONCEPT 628

reflection [n3] *criticism*
animadversion, aspersion, blame, censure, derogation, discredit, disesteem, imputation, obloquy, reproach, slam, slur, stricture; SEE CONCEPT 52

reflective [adj] *thoughtful*
cogitating, contemplative, deliberate, meditative, pensive, pondering, reasoning, ruminative, speculative, studious; SEE CONCEPT 403

reform [v] *correct, rectify*
ameliorate, amend, better, bring up to code*, change one's ways*, clean up, clean up one's act*, convert, correct, cure, emend, go straight*, improve, make amends, make over, mend, rearrange, rebuild, reclaim, reconstitute, reconstruct,

refrain [n] *chorus of musical piece*
burden, melody, music, song, strain, theme, tune, undersong; SEE CONCEPTS 264,595

refrain [v] *do without; keep from doing*
abstain, arrest, avoid, be temperate, cease, check, curb, desist, eschew, forbear, forgo, give up, go on the wagon*, halt, inhibit, interrupt, keep, leave off, not do, pass, pass up, quit, renounce, resist, restrain, sit out*, stop, take the cure*, take the pledge*, withhold; SEE CONCEPTS 121,681

refresh [v] *make like new; give new life*
brace, breathe new life into, bring around, brush up, cheer, cool, enliven, exhilarate, freshen, inspirit, jog, modernize, prod, prompt, quicken, reanimate, recreate, regain, reinvigorate, rejuvenate, renovate, repair, replenish, restore, resuscitate, revitalize, revive, revivify, stimulate, update, vivify; SEE CONCEPTS 202,697

refreshment [n] *small amount of food or drink*
bite, pick-me-up*, snack, spread, tidbit; SEE CONCEPT 457

refrigerate [v] *chill, usually in storage*
air-condition, air-cool, cool, freeze, ice, keep cold, make cold; SEE CONCEPTS 202,255

refuge [n] *place to hide, have privacy*
ambush, anchorage, asylum, cover, covert, den, escape, exit, expedient, fortress, harbor, harborage, haven, hideaway, hideout, hiding place, hole, home, immunity, ivory tower*, makeshift, opening, outlet, port, preserve, protection, recourse, resort, resource, retreat, safe place, sanctuary, security, shelter, shield, stopgap*, stronghold, way out*; SEE CONCEPTS 198,515

refugee [n] *person running from something, often oppression*
alien, bad person*, castaway, defector, derelict, deserter, displaced person, DP*, emigrant, émigré, escapee, evacuee, exile, expatriate, expellee, foreigner, foundling, fugitive, homeless person, leper, maroon, outcast, outlaw, prodigal, renegade, runaway, stateless person; SEE CONCEPTS 359,413

refund [n] *returned money*
acquittance, allowance, compensation, consolation, discharge, discount, give-back*, give-up*, kickback, money back, payment, rebate, reimbursement, remuneration, repayment, restitution, retribution, return, satisfaction, settlement; SEE CONCEPTS 340,344

refund [v] *return money; rebate*
adjust, balance, compensate, give back, honor a claim, indemnify, make amends, make good*, make repayment, make up for, pay back, recompense, recoup, redeem, redress, reimburse, relinquish, remit, remunerate, repay, restore, reward, settle; SEE CONCEPT 341

refurbish [v] *spruce up*
clean up, do up*, fix up, gussy up*, mend, modernize, overhaul, recondition, redo, reequip, refit, refresh, rehab, rehabilitate, rejuvenate, remodel, renew, renovate, repair, restore, retread, revamp, set to rights, spruce, update; SEE CONCEPTS 177,202

refusal [n] *denial of responsibility; unwillingness*
abnegation, ban, choice, cold shoulder*, declension, declination, defiance, disallowance, disapproval, disavowal, disclaimer, discountenancing, disfavor, dissent, enjoinment, exclusion, forbidding, interdiction, knockback*, negation, nix*, no, nonacceptance, noncompliance, nonconsent, option, pass*, prohibition, proscription, rebuff, refutation, regrets, rejection, renouncement, renunciation, repudiation, repulse, repulsion, reversal, thumbs down*, turndown, veto, withholding, writ; SEE CONCEPTS 278,633

refuse [n] *garbage*
debris, dregs, dross, dump, dust, hogwash*, junk, leavings, litter, muck, offal, rejectamenta*, remains, residue, rubbish, scraps, scum*, sediment, slop*, sweepings, swill, trash, waste, waste matter; SEE CONCEPT 260

refuse [v] *deny; say no*
beg off, brush off*, decline, demur, desist, disaccord, disallow, disapprove, dispense with, dissent, dodge, evade, give thumbs down to*, hold back, hold off, hold out, ignore, make excuses, nix*, not budge, not budget, not buy*, not care to*, pass up, protest, rebuff, refuse to receive, regret, reject, repel, reprobate, repudiate, send off*, send regrets*, set aside*, shun, spurn, turn away, turn deaf ear to*, turn down, turn from, turn one's back on*, withdraw, withhold; SEE CONCEPTS 30,49,266

refute [v] *prove false; discredit*
abnegate, argue against, blow sky high*, break, burn, burn down, cancel, cancel out, confute, contend, contradict, contravene, convict, counter, crush, debate, demolish, disclaim, disconfirm, dispose of, disprove, dispute, evert, explode, expose, gainsay, give the lie to*, give thumbs down to*, invalidate, negate, oppose, overthrow, parry, quash, rebut, reply to, repudiate, shoot down, shoot full of holes*, show up, silence, squelch, take a stand against, tear down*, top*; SEE CONCEPT 54

regain [v] *get back, get back to*
achieve, attain, compass, gain, get out from under, get well, make well, reach, reach again, reacquire, reattain, recapture, reclaim, recoup, recover, recruit, redeem, repossess, retake, retrieve, return to, save, take back, win back; SEE CONCEPTS 120,124,131

regal [adj] *fit for royalty*
august, glorious, imposing, kingly, magnificent, majestic, monarchal, monarchical, noble, proud, queenly, resplendent, royal, sovereign, splendid, stately, sublime; SEE CONCEPT 589

regale [v] *throw a party; have fun*
amuse, delight, divert, entertain, feast, fracture, give a party, grab, gratify, have a get-together, laugh it up, nurture, party, please, ply, refresh, satisfy, serve, toss a party; SEE CONCEPTS 292,384

regard [n1] *attention, look*
care, carefulness, cognizance, concern, consciousness, curiosity, gaze, glance, heed, interest, interestedness, mark, mind, note, notice, observance, observation, once-over*, remark, scrutiny, stare, view; SEE CONCEPTS 596,623,626,690

regard [n2] *affection, good opinion*
account, appreciation, approbation, approval, attachment, care, cherishing, concern, consideration, curiosity, deference, devotion, esteem,

estimation, favor, fondness, homage, honor, interest, interestedness, liking, love, note, opinion, prizing, reputation, repute, respect, reverence, satisfaction, store, sympathy, thought, value, valuing, veneration, worship; SEE CONCEPTS *10,532,689*

regard [n3] *feature, detail*
aspect, bearing, concern, connection, item, matter, particular, point, reference, relation, relevance, respect; SEE CONCEPTS *532,644*

regard [v1] *look at; listen to*
advertise, attend, beam, behold, contemplate, eye, eyeball*, flash, gaze, get a load of*, give attention, heed, look on, mark, mind, note, notice, observe, overlook, pay attention, pipe*, pore over*, read, remark, respect, scan, scrutinize, see, spy, stare at, take into consideration, take notice of, view, watch, witness; SEE CONCEPTS *596,623,626*

regard [v2] *believe, judge*
account, adjudge, admire, assay, assess, consider, deem, esteem, estimate, look upon, rate, reckon, respect, revere, see, suppose, surmise, think, treat, value, view; SEE CONCEPTS *10,12*

regard [v3] *have something to do with*
apply to, bear upon, be relevant to, concern, have a bearing on, have to do with*, interest, pertain to, refer to, relate to; SEE CONCEPT *532*

regardful [adj] *attentive, observant*
advertent, arrect, aware, careful, considerate, deferential, duteous, dutiful, heedful, intentive, mindful, observative, observing, respectful, thoughtful, watchful; SEE CONCEPT *401*

regardless [adj] *indifferent, unconcerned*
behindhand, blind, careless, coarse, crude, deaf, delinquent, derelict, disregarding, heedless, inadvertent, inattentive, inconsiderate, insensitive, lax, listless, mindless, neglectful, negligent, nonobservant, rash, reckless, remiss, rude, slack, unfeeling, unheeding, uninterested, unmindful; SEE CONCEPT *401*

regardless [adv] *despite everything*
against, although, anyway, aside from, at any cost, but, come what may, despite, distinct from, for all that, in any case, in spite of everything, leaving aside, nevertheless, no matter what, nonetheless, notwithstanding, without considering, without regard to; SEE CONCEPTS *544,548*

regards [n] *best wishes*
commendations, compliments, deference, devoirs, good wishes, greeting, love, love and kisses*, remembrances, respects, salutation, salutations; SEE CONCEPT *278*

regenerate [v] *breathe new life into*
change, exhilarate, inspirit, invigorate, produce, raise from the dead*, reanimate, reawaken, reconstruct, recreate, reestablish, refresh, reinvigorate, rejuvenate, renew, renovate, reproduce, restore, revive, revivify, uplift; SEE CONCEPTS *7,22,173,202,251*

regime [n] *leadership of organization*
administration, dynasty, establishment, government, incumbency, management, pecking order*, reign, rule, system, tenure; SEE CONCEPTS *299,325*

region [n] *area, domain; scope*
arena, bailiwick, belt, block, clearing, country, demesne, district, division, domain, dominion, environs, expanse, field, ghetto, ground, inner city, jungle, land, locale, locality, neck of

woods*, neighborhood, part, place, precinct, province, quarter, range, realm, scene, section, sector, shire, sphere, stomping ground*, suburb, terrain, territory, tract, turf*, vicinity, walk, ward, world, zone; SEE CONCEPTS *198,508,512*

register [n] *list, record*
annals, archives, book, catalog, catalogue, chronicle, diary, entry, file, ledger, log, memorandum, registry, roll, roll call, roster, schedule, scroll; SEE CONCEPT *281*

register [v1] *enter in list, record*
catalogue, check in, chronicle, enlist, enroll, file, inscribe, join, list, note, record, schedule, set down, sign on, sign up, sign up for, subscribe, take down, weigh in; SEE CONCEPTS *79,114,125*

register [v2] *indicate, reveal*
be shown, bespeak, betray, disclose, display, exhibit, express, manifest, mark, point out, point to, read, record, reflect, say, show; SEE CONCEPT *261*

register [v3] *make an impression*
come home to, dawn on, get through to, have an effect on, impress, sink in, tell; SEE CONCEPTS *7,19,22*

regress [v] *return to earlier way of doing things*
backslide, degenerate, deteriorate, ebb, fall away, fall back, fall off, go back, lapse, lose ground, recede, relapse, retreat, retrogress, revert, roll back, sink, throw back, turn back; SEE CONCEPTS *633,698*

regret [n] *upset over past action*
affliction, anguish, annoyance, apologies, apology, bitterness, care, compunction, concern, conscience, contrition, demur, disappointment, discomfort, dissatisfaction, dole, grief, heartache, heartbreak, lamentation, misgiving, nostalgia, pang, penitence, qualm, regretfulness, remorse, repentance, ruefulness, scruple, self-accusation, self-condemnation, self-disgust, self-reproach, sorrow, uneasiness, woe, worry; SEE CONCEPTS *21,410*

regret [v] *be upset about*
apologize, be disturbed, bemoan, be sorry for, bewail, cry over*, cry over spilled milk*, deplore, deprecate, disapprove, feel remorse, feel sorry, feel uneasy, grieve, have compunctions*, have qualms*, kick oneself*, lament, look back, miss, moan, mourn, repent, repine, rue, weep, weep over; SEE CONCEPTS *21,410*

regretful [adj] *sad, sorry*
apologetic, ashamed, attritional, compunctious, contrite, disappointed, mournful, penitent, remorseful, repentant, rueful, sorrowful; SEE CONCEPT *403*

regrettable [adj] *unfortunate, wrong*
afflictive, calamitous, deplorable, dire, disappointing, distressing, dreadful, grievous, heartbreaking, ill-advised, lamentable, pitiable, pitiful, sad, shameful, unfavorable, unhappy, woeful; SEE CONCEPTS *548,571*

regular [adj1] *normal, common*
approved, bona fide, classic, commonplace, correct, customary, daily, established, everyday, formal, general, habitual, lawful, legitimate, natural, normal, official, ordinary, orthodox, prevailing, prevalent, proper, routine, run-of-the-mill*, sanctioned, standard, time-honored, traditional, typic, typical, unexceptional, unvarying, usual; SEE CONCEPTS *530,533,547*

regular [adj2] *orderly, consistent, balanced*
accordant, alternating, arranged, automatic, clas-

sified, congruous, consonant, constant, cyclic, dependable, efficient, established, even, exact, expected, fixed, flat, formal, harmonious, in order, invariable, level, measured, mechanical, methodical, momentary, ordered, organized, patterned, periodic, precise, probable, punctual, rational, recurrent, regulated, rhythmic, routine, serial, set, smooth, standardized, stated, steady, straight, successive, symmetrical, systematic, uniform; SEE CONCEPTS 326,544,566,585

regulate [v] *manage, organize*
adapt, adjust, administer, allocate, arrange, balance, classify, conduct, control, coordinate, correct, determine, direct, dispose, fit, fix, govern, guide, handle, improve, legislate, measure, methodize, moderate, modulate, monitor, order, oversee, pull things together*, put in order, readjust, reconcile, rectify, rule, run, set, settle, shape up*, square, standardize, straighten up, superintend, supervise, systematize, temper, time, true, tune, tune up*; SEE CONCEPTS 94,117

regulation [n] *managing, organizing*
adjustment, administration, arrangement, classification, codification, control, coordination, direction, governance, governing, government, guidance, handling, management, moderation, modulation, reconciliation, regimentation, reorganization, settlement, standardization, superintendence, supervision, systematization, tuning; SEE CONCEPTS 94,117

regulation [n2] *rule, requirement*
bible, book, canon, chapter and verse*, code, commandment, decree, decretum, dictate, direction, edict, law, no-nos*, numbers, order, ordinance, precept, prescript, principle, procedure, reg*, statement, statute; SEE CONCEPTS 318,688

rehabilitate [v] *renovate, adjust*
change, clear, convert, fix up, furbish, improve, make good*, mend, rebuild, reclaim, recondition, reconstitute, reconstruct, recover, redeem, reestablish, reform, refurbish, rehab*, reinstate, reintegrate, reinvigorate, rejuvenate, renew, restitute, restore, save; SEE CONCEPTS 35,126,134,202

rehash [v] *talk over again*
change, discuss, reiterate, repeat, rephrase, restate, reuse, rework, rewrite, say again, state differently; SEE CONCEPT 56

rehearsal [n] *preparation for performance*
call, description, drill, dry run*, experiment, going-over, practice, practice session, prep*, reading, readying, recital, recitation, recounting, rehearsing, relation, retelling, run-through, shakedown*, test flight*, trial balloon*, trial performance, tryout, workout; SEE CONCEPTS 264,292,363

rehearse [v] *prepare for performance*
act, depict, describe, do over, drill, dry run*, experiment, go over, go through, hold a reading*, hone, iterate, learn one's part, narrate, practice, ready, recapitulate, recite, recount, reenact, reiterate, relate, repeat, review, run lines, run through, study, take from the top*, tell, test, train, try out, tune up, walk through*, warm up, work out; SEE CONCEPTS 266,292,363

reign [n] *rule, dominion*
administration, ascendancy, command, control, dynasty, empire, hegemony, incumbency, influence, monarchy, power, regime, sovereignty, supremacy, sway, tenure; SEE CONCEPTS 198,376

reign [v] *have power over; prevail*
administer, be in power, be in the driver's seat*, be supreme, boss, command, dominate, domineer, govern, head up, helm, hold power, hold sway*, influence, manage, obtain, occupy, overrule, predominate, preponderate, rule, rule the roost*, run the show*, run things*, sit, superabound, wear the crown*; SEE CONCEPTS 117,298

reimburse [v] *pay back something owed*
balance, compensate, indemnify, make reparations, make up for, offset, pay, recompense, recover, refund, remunerate, repay, requite, restore, return, square, square up; SEE CONCEPT 341

rein [n] *restraint, control*
bit, brake, bridle, check, curb, deterrent, governor, halter, harness, hold, line, restriction, strap; SEE CONCEPT 499

rein [v] *restrain, control*
bridle, check, collect, compose, cool, curb, halt, hold, hold back, limit, repress, restrict, simmer down, slow down, smother, suppress; SEE CONCEPT 130

reinforce [v] *strengthen, augment*
add fuel to fire*, add to, back up, beef up*, bolster, boost, build up, buttress, carry, emphasize, energize, enlarge, fortify, harden, heat up, hype, increase, lend a hand, multiply, pick up, pillar, prop, prop up, punch up, shore up, soup up*, stand up for, stiffen, stress, stroke, supplement, support, sustain, toughen, underline; SEE CONCEPTS 5,236,245,250

reinstate [v] *give back responsibility*
bring back, put back, put in power again, recall, redeem, reelect, reestablish, rehabilitate, rehire, reintroduce, reinvest, renew, replace, restore, return, revive; SEE CONCEPTS 351,384

reiterate [v] *say or do again*
come again, ditto*, double-check, echo, go over again, ingeminate, iterate, play back, recap*, recapitulate, recheck, rehash, renew, repeat, reprise, resay, restate, retell, reword, say again; SEE CONCEPTS 100,171,266

reject [v] *say no to*
burn*, cashier*, cast aside, cast off, cast out, chuck, decline, deny, despise, disallow, disbelieve, discard, discount, discredit, disdain, dismiss, eliminate, exclude*, give thumbs down to*, jettison, jilt, kill*, nix*, not buy*, pass by, pass on, pass up, put down, rebuff, refuse, renounce, repel, reprobate, repudiate, repulse, scoff, scorn, scout, scrap, second, shed, shoot down*, shun, slough, spurn, throw away, throw out, turn down, veto; SEE CONCEPTS 21,30,180

rejection [n] *denial, refusal*
bounce, brushoff*, cold shoulder*, disallowance, dismissal, elimination, exclusion, hard time*, kick in teeth*, nix*, no dice*, no go*, nothing doing*, no way*, pass*, rebuff, renunciation, repudiation, slap in the face*, thumbs down*, turndown, veto; SEE CONCEPTS 21,30,180

rejoice [v] *be very happy about something*
be glad, be overjoyed, celebrate, delight, enjoy, exult, feel happy, glory, joy, jump for joy, make merry, revel, triumph; SEE CONCEPT 410

rejuvenate [v] *make new again*
breathe new life into*, do, do up*, exhilarate, give face lift to*, give new life to, make young again, modernize, reanimate, reclaim, recondition, reconstruct, recover, refresh, refurbish, regenerate, rehab, reinvigorate, renew, renovate,

re
re

restitute, restore, retread, revitalize, revivify, spruce, spruce up*, update; SEE CONCEPTS 35,202

relapse [n] *deterioration, weakening*
backsliding, fall, fall from grace*, lapse, loss, recidivism, recurrence, regression, repetition, retrogression, return, reversion, setback, turn for the worse*, worsening; SEE CONCEPT 698

relapse [v] *deteriorate, weaken*
backslide, be overcome, be overtaken, degenerate, fade, fail, fall, fall back, lapse, recidivate, regress, retrogress, revert, sicken, sink, slide back, slip back, suffer, turn back, worsen; SEE CONCEPT 698

relate [v1] *give an account of*
break a story*, chronicle, clue one in*, depict, describe, detail, disclose, divulge, express, get off one's chest*, give the word*, impart, itemize, lay it on the line*, let one's hair down*, narrate, particularize, picture, present, recite, recount, rehearse, report, retell, reveal, run down, run through, set forth, shoot the breeze*, sling*, spill, spill the beans*, spin a yarn*, state, tell, track, verbalize; SEE CONCEPT 55

relate [v2] *correlate, pertain*
affect, ally, appertain, apply, ascribe, assign, associate, bear upon, be joined with, be relevant to, bracket, combine, compare, concern, conjoin, connect, consociate, coordinate, correspond to, couple, credit, have reference to, have to do with, identify with, impute, interconnect, interdepend, interrelate, join, link, orient, orientate, pertain, refer, tie in with, touch, unite, yoke; SEE CONCEPT 532

related [adj] *connected, accompanying*
affiliated, agnate, akin, alike, allied, analogous, associated, cognate, complementary, concomitant, connate, connatural, consanguine, convertible, correlated, correspondent, dependent, enmeshed, fraternal, germane, incident, interchangeable, interconnected, interdependent, interrelated, intertwined, interwoven, in the same category, in touch by blood, joint, knit together*, like, linked, mutual, of that ilk, parallel, pertinent, reciprocal, relevant, similar, tied up; SEE CONCEPTS 487,573,577

relation [n] *connection, family connection*
affiliation, affinity, alliance, association, consanguinity, kin, kindred, kinship, kinsperson, liaison, propinquity, relationship, relative, sibling, similarity; SEE CONCEPTS 296,414,421,714

relationship [n] *connection; friendship*
accord, affair, affiliation, affinity, alliance, analogy, appositeness, association, bond, communication, conjunction, consanguinity, consociation, contact, contingency, correlation, dependence, dependency, exchange, homogeneity, hookup, interconnection, interrelation, interrelationship, kinship, liaison, likeness, link, marriage, nearness, network, parallel, pertinence, pertinency, proportion, rapport, ratio, relation, relativity, relevance, similarity, tie, tie-in, tie-up; SEE CONCEPTS 388,714

relative [n] *member of a family*
agnate, aunt, blood, brother-in-law, clansperson, cognate, connection, cousin, father, father-in-law, folk, folks, grandparents, great-grandparents, in-laws, kinsperson, mother, mother-in-law, nephew, niece, relation, sib*, sibling, sister-in-law, stepbrother, stepparent, stepsister, uncle; SEE CONCEPT 414

relative [adj1] *comparative, respective*
about, allied, analogous, approximate, associated, concerning, conditional, connected, contingent, corresponding, dependent, in regard to, near, parallel, proportionate, reciprocal, referring, related, relating to, reliant, with respect to; SEE CONCEPT 563

relative [adj2] *pertinent, applicable*
apposite, appropriate, appurtenant, apropos, contingent, dependent, germane, pertaining, referring, related, relevant; SEE CONCEPT 558

relatively [adv] *in or by comparison*
almost, approximately, comparably, comparatively, nearly, proportionately, rather, somewhat, to some extent; SEE CONCEPTS 544,772

relax [v1] *be or feel at ease*
breathe easy*, calm, calm down*, collect oneself, compose oneself, cool off*, ease off, feel at home, hang loose*, knock off*, laze, let oneself go*, lie down, loosen up, make oneself at home*, put one's feet up*, recline, repose, rest, settle back, simmer down*, sit around, sit back, soften, stop work, take a break*, take a breather*, take it easy*, take one's time*, take ten*, take time out*, tranquilize, unbend, unlax*, unwind; SEE CONCEPT 210

relax [v2] *diminish, lessen*
abate, ease, ease off, ebb, lax, let up, loose, loosen, lose speed, lower, mitigate, moderate, modify, modulate, reduce, relieve, remit, slack, slacken, slow, slow down, untighten, weaken; SEE CONCEPTS 240,698

relaxation [n] *entertainment; resting or recovering*
alleviation, amusement, assuagement, diversion, enjoyment, fun, leisure, loosening, mitigation, pleasure, reclining, recreation, refreshment, relief, repose, requiescence, rest; SEE CONCEPTS 210,292,363

relay [v] *pass on, transmit*
broadcast, carry, communicate, deliver, hand down, hand on, hand over, send, send forth, spread, transfer, turn over; SEE CONCEPT 143

release [n1] *delivery; dispensation*
absolution, acquittal, acquittance, charge, clemency, commute, deliverance, discharge, dispensation, emancipation, exemption, exoneration, floater, freedom, freeing, let-off*, liberation, liberty, lifeboat, lifesaver, manumission, relief, spring, turnout, walkout; SEE CONCEPTS 127,685

release [n2] *publication*
announcement, flash*, handout, issue, leak, news, notice, offering, proclamation, propaganda, publicity, story; SEE CONCEPTS 271,280

release [v] *let go, let out*
absolve, acquit, bail out, cast loose, clear, commute, deliver, discharge, disengage, dispense, drop, emancipate, exculpate, excuse, exempt, exonerate, extricate, free, give off, give out, go easy on, issue, leak, let off, let off steam*, let up on*, liberate, loose, loosen, manumit, open up, set at large, set free, set loose, spring, surrender, take out, turn loose, turn out, unbind, unchain, undo, unfasten, unfetter, unleash, unloose, unshackle, untie, vent, wipe slate clean*; SEE CONCEPTS 50,60,88,127,143

relegate [v1] *assign, transfer*
accredit, charge, commend, commit, confide,

consign, credit, delegate, entrust, hand over, pass on, refer, turn over; SEE CONCEPTS *41,143*

relegate [v2] *banish, downgrade*
demote, deport, dismiss, displace, eject, exile, expatriate, expel, expulse, lag, ostracize, remove, throw out, transport; SEE CONCEPTS *30,121,211*

relent [v] *die down; let up*
acquiesce, be merciful, capitulate, cave in*, change one's mind, come around, comply, cool it*, cry uncle*, die away, drop, ease, ease off, ease up on*, ebb, fall, fold, forbear, give in, give quarter*, give some slack*, give up, give way, go along with, go easy on*, have mercy, have pity, lay back, let go, let it happen*, lighten up*, mellow out*, melt, moderate, quit, relax, say uncle*, show mercy, slacken, slow, soften, subside, wane, weaken, yield; SEE CONCEPTS *35,698,776*

relentless [adj1] *cruel, merciless*
adamant, bound, bound and determined, dead set on*, determined, dogged, ferocious, fierce, go for broke*, grim, hang in*, hang-tough*, hard, harsh, implacable, inexorable, inflexible, inhuman, mortal, obdurate, pitiless, remorseless, rigid, rigorous, ruthless, single-minded, stiff, stop at nothing, strict, stringent, unappeasable, unbending, uncompromising, undeviating, unflinching, unforgiving, unrelenting, unstoppable, unyielding, vindictive; SEE CONCEPT *401*

relentless [adj2] *continuous, neverending*
incessant, nonstop, persistent, pertinacious, punishing, sustained, tenacious, unabated, unbroken, unfaltering, unflagging, unrelenting, unrelieved, unremitting, unstoppable; SEE CONCEPTS *326,534,798*

relevant [adj] *appropriate; to the purpose*
accordant, admissible, ad rem, allowable, applicable, applicatory, apposite, appurtenant, apt, becoming, cognate, compatible, concerning, conformant, conforming, congruent, congruous, consistent, consonant, correlated, correspondent, fit, fitting, germane, harmonious, having direct bearing on, having to do with, important, material, on the button*, on the nose*, pat*, pertaining to, pertinent, pointful, proper, referring, related, relative, significant, suitable, suited to, to the point, weighty; SEE CONCEPT *558*

reliable [adj] *trustworthy*
candid, careful, certain, conscientious, constant, decent, decisive, definite, dependable, determined, devoted, faithful, firm, good, high-principled, honest, honorable, impeccable, incorrupt, loyal, okay, positive, predictable, proved, reputable, respectable, responsible, righteous, safe, sincere, solid, sound, stable, staunch, steadfast, steady, sterling, strong, sure, there, tried, tried-and-true*, true, true-blue*, true-hearted, trusty, unequivocal, unfailing, unimpeachable, upright, veracious; SEE CONCEPTS *535,542,544*

reliance [n] *confidence*
assurance, belief, credence, credit, dependence, faith, hope, interdependence, interdependency, stock, trust; SEE CONCEPT *689*

relic [n] *something saved from the past*
antique, antiquity, archaism, artifact, curio, curiosity, evidence, fragment, heirloom, keepsake, memento, memorial, monument, remains, remembrance, remembrancer, reminder, remnant, residue, ruins, scrap, souvenir, survival, testimo-

nial, token, trace, trophy, vestige; SEE CONCEPT *446*

relief [n] *remedy, aid; relaxation*
abatement, allayment, alleviation, amelioration, appeasement, assistance, assuagement, balm, break, breather, cheer, comfort, comforting, consolation, contentment, cure, deliverance, diversion, ease, easement, extrication, fix, hand, happiness, help, let-up, lift, lightening, load off one's mind*, maintenance, mitigation, mollification, palliative, quick fix*, refreshment, release, remedy, remission, reprieve, respite, rest, restfulness, satisfaction, softening, solace, succor, support, sustenance; SEE CONCEPTS *681,712*

relieve [v1] *make less painful; let up on*
abate, allay, alleviate, appease, assuage, break, brighten, calm, comfort, console, cure, decrease, diminish, divert, dull, ease, free, interrupt, lighten, mitigate, moderate, mollify, palliate, qualify, quiet, relax, salve, slacken, soften, solace, soothe, subdue, take load off one's chest*, take load off one's mind*, temper, vary; SEE CONCEPTS *244,700*

relieve [v2] *help; give assistance*
aid, assist, bring aid, give a break*, give a hand*, give a rest, spell, stand in for, substitute for, succor, support, sustain, take over from, take the place of; SEE CONCEPT *110*

relieve [v3] *remove blame, responsibility*
absolve, deliver, discharge, disembarrass, disencumber, dismiss, dispense, excuse, exempt, force to resign, free, let off, privilege, pull, release, spare, throw out, unburden, yank*; SEE CONCEPTS *50,88,351*

religion [n] *belief in divinity; system of beliefs*
church, communion, creed, cult, denomination, devotion, doctrine, higher power, morality, myth, mythology, observance, orthodoxy, pietism, piety, prayer, preference, religiosity, rites, ritual, sacrifice, sanctification, sect, spirituality, spiritual-mindedness, standards, superstition, theology, veneration; SEE CONCEPTS *368,689*

religious [adj1] *concerning belief in divinity*
believing, born-again*, canonical, churchgoing, churchly, clerical, deistic, devotional, devout, divine, doctrinal, ecclesiastical, god-fearing, godly, holy, ministerial, moral, orthodox, pietistic, pious, pontifical, prayerful, priestly, pure, reverent, righteous, sacerdotal, sacred, sacrosanct, saint-like, saintly, scriptural, sectarian, spiritual, supernatural, theistic, theological; SEE CONCEPTS *536,545*

religious [adj2] *conscientious, scrupulous*
exact, faithful, fastidious, meticulous, punctilious, rigid, rigorous, steadfast, unerring, unswerving; SEE CONCEPT *538*

relinquish [v] *give up, let go*
abandon, abdicate, abnegate, back down, cast, cast off, cede, cut loose*, desert, discard, ditch*, drop, drop like hot potato*, drop out, dump*, forbear, forgo, forsake, forswear, hand over, kick, kiss good-bye*, lay aside, leave, opt out, quit, quit cold turkey*, release, renounce, repudiate, resign, retire from, sacrifice, shed, stand down, surrender, swear off*, take the oath*, take the pledge*, vacate, waive, withdraw, yield; SEE CONCEPTS *119,127,234*

relish [n] *great appreciation of something*
appetite, bias, delectation, diversion, enjoying, enjoyment, fancy, flair, flavor, fondness, gusto,

heart, leaning, liking, love, loving, palate, partiality, penchant, pleasure, predilection, prejudice, propensity, sapidity, sapor, savor, smack, stomach, tang, taste, zest; SEE CONCEPTS 20,32

relish [v] *look forward to; appreciate*
admire, be fond of, cherish, delight in, dig*, enjoy, fancy, go, go for*, like, luxuriate in, mind, prefer, revel in, savor, taste; SEE CONCEPT 32

reluctant [adj] *unenthusiastic, unwilling*
afraid, averse, backward, calculating, cautious, chary, circumspect, demurring, diffident, discouraged, disheartened, disinclined, grudging, hanging back, hesitant, hesitating, indisposed, involuntary, laggard, loath, opposed, queasy, recalcitrant, remiss, shy, slack, slow, squeamish, tardy, uncertain, uneager, wary; SEE CONCEPT 401

rely [v] *have confidence in*
await, bank, be confident of, believe in, be sure of, bet, bet bottom dollar on*, build, calculate, commit, confide, count, depend, entrust, expect, gamble on, have faith in, hope, lay money on*, lean, look, reckon, ride on coattails*, swear by*, trust; SEE CONCEPTS 12,26

remain [v] *stay, wait*
abide, be left, bide, bivouac, bunk*, cling, continue, delay, dwell, endure, freeze, go on, halt, hang, hang out, hold over, hold the fort*, hover, inhabit, keep on, last, linger, live, lodge, make camp, nest, outlast, outlive, pause, perch, persist, prevail, put on hold, remain standing, reside, rest, roost, sit out, sit through, sit tight*, sojourn, squat, stand, stay behind, stay in, stay over, stay put, stick around, stop, survive, tarry, visit, wait; SEE CONCEPTS 23,239,681,804

remainder [n] *balance, residue*
bottom of barrel*, butt, carry-over, detritus, dregs, excess, fragment, garbage, hangover*, heel, junk, leavings, leftover, obverse, oddment, odds and ends*, overplus, refuse, relic, remains, remnant, residuum, rest, ruins, salvage, scrap, stump, surplus, trace, vestige, waste, wreck, wreckage; SEE CONCEPTS 260,835

remark [n] *comment, observation*
acknowledgment, annotation, assertion, attention, back talk, bon mot*, cognizance, comeback, commentary, conclusion, consideration, crack*, declaration, elucidation, exegesis, explanation, explication, exposition, expression, gloss, heed, illustration, interpretation, mention, mind, note, notice, obiter dictum, observance, observation, opinion, point, recognition, reflection, regard, saying, statement, talk, thought, two cents' worth*, utterance, wisecrack, witticism, word; SEE CONCEPTS 51,278

remark [v] *notice and comment*
animadvert, behold, catch, commentate, crack*, declare, descry, espy, heed, make out, mark, mention, mouth off*, note, observe, pass comment, perceive, pick up on, reflect, regard, say, see, speak, spot, state, take note, take notice, utter, wisecrack; SEE CONCEPTS 38,51,626

remarkable [adj] *extraordinary, unusual*
arresting, arrestive, conspicuous, curious, distinguished, exceptional, famous, gilt-edged*, greatest, important, impressive, marked, miraculous, momentous, notable, noteworthy, noticeable, odd, outstanding, peculiar, phenomenal, preeminent, primo*, prominent, rare, salient, signal, significant, singular, smashing, solid, splashy*,

strange, striking, super, surprising, uncommon, uncustomary, unique, unordinary, unwonted, weighty, wicked*, wonderful, world class*, zero cool*; SEE CONCEPT 574

remedial [adj] *healing, restorative*
alleviative, antidotal, antiseptic, corrective, curative, curing, healthful, health-giving, invigorating, medicating, medicinal, purifying, recuperative, reformative, remedying, repairing, restitutive, restorative, sanative, sanatory, solving, soothing, therapeutic, tonic, treating, vulnerary, wholesome; SEE CONCEPT 537

remedy [n] *cure, solution*
antidote, assistance, biologic, corrective, counteractant, counteraction, counteractive, counteragent, countermeasure, counterstep, cure-all*, drug, elixir, fix, improvement, medicament, medicant, medicine, panacea, pharmaceutical, pharmacon, physic, pill, quick fix*, redress, relief, restorative, support, therapy, treatment; SEE CONCEPTS 307,311,693,712

remedy [v] *fix, cure*
aid, alleviate, ameliorate, amend, assuage, attend, change, clean up, clean up one's act*, control, correct, debug*, doctor, ease, fiddle with, fix up, go over, heal, help, launder, make up for, mitigate, palliate, pick up, put right, recalibrate, rectify, redress, reform, relieve, renew, repair, restore, revise, right, scrub, set right, set to rights*, shape up, solve, soothe, square*, square up*, straighten out, treat, upgrade; SEE CONCEPTS 126,212,310

remember [v] *keep in mind; summon into mind*
bear in mind, bethink, brood over, call to mind, call up, cite, commemorate, conjure up, dig into the past*, dwell upon, educe, elicit, enshrine, extract, fix in the mind, flash on*, get, go back, have memories, hold dear*, keep forever, know by heart*, learn, look back, memorialize, memorize, mind, nail down*, recall, recognize, recollect, refresh memory, relive, remind, reminisce, retain, retrospect, revive, revoke, ring a bell*, strike a note*, summon up, think back, treasure; SEE CONCEPT 40

remembrance [n1] *memory, recollection*
afterthought, anamnesis, flash*, flashback*, hindsight*, mental image, mind, recall, recognition, reconstruction, regard, reminiscence, retrospect, thought; SEE CONCEPTS 40,529

remembrance [n2] *gift, testimonial*
commemoration, favor, keepsake, memento, memorial, monument, present, relic, remembrancer, reminder, reward, souvenir, token, trophy; SEE CONCEPT 337

remind [v] *awaken memories of something*
admonish, advise, bethink, bring back to, bring to mind, call attention, call to mind, call up, caution, cite, emphasize, give a cue*, hint, imply, intimate, jog one's memory*, make one remember, make one think, mention, note, point out, prod, prompt, put in mind, recall, recollect, refresh memory, remember, reminisce, retain, retrospect, revive, stir up, stress, suggest, warn; SEE CONCEPTS 7,19,22,40,78

reminder [n] *warning, notice; keepsake*
admonition, expression, gesture, hint, indication, intimation, memento, memo, memorandum, memorial, note, notice, relic, remembrance, remembrancer, sign, souvenir, suggestion, token, trinket, trophy; SEE CONCEPTS 271,278,529

reminisce [v] *go over in one's memory*
bethink, call up, cite, hark back, live in the past, look back, mind, muse over, recall, recollect, remember, remind, retain, retrospect, review, revive, think back; SEE CONCEPTS *17,40*

reminiscent [adj] *suggestive of something in the past*
bringing to mind, evocative, implicative, mnemonic, nostalgic, recollective, redolent, remindful, similar; SEE CONCEPT *529*

remiss [adj] *careless, thoughtless*
any old way*, any which way*, asleep at switch*, asleep on job*, behindhand, culpable, daydreaming, defaultant, delinquent, derelict, dilatory, disregardful, fainéant, forgetful, heedless, inattentive, indifferent, indolent, lackadaisical, lax, lazy, neglectful, negligent, regardless, slack, slapdash, slipshod, sloppy, slothful, slow, tardy, uninterested, unmindful, woolgathering*; SEE CONCEPT *401*

remission [n1] *acquittal, pardon*
absolution, amnesty, discharge, excuse, exemption, exoneration, forgiveness, indulgence, mercy, pardon, release, reprieve; SEE CONCEPT *685*

remission [n2] *pause; lessening*
abatement, abeyance, alleviation, amelioration, break, decrease, delay, diminution, ebb, interruption, let-up, lull, moderation, reduction, relaxation, release, respite, suspension; SEE CONCEPTS *303,698,807*

remit [v1] *send, transfer*
address, consign, dispatch, forward, mail, make payment, pay, post, route, settle, ship, square, transmit; SEE CONCEPTS *217,341*

remit [v2] *stop, postpone*
abate, absolve, alleviate, amnesty, cancel, condone, decrease, defer, delay, desist, diminish, dwindle, ease up, excuse, exonerate, fall away, forbear, forgive, halt, hold off, hold up, intermit, mitigate, moderate, modify, mollify, pardon, prorogue, put off, reduce, relax, release, repeal, reprieve, rescind, respite, shelve, sink, slack, slacken, soften, stay, suspend, wane, weaken; SEE CONCEPTS *234,698*

remnant [n] *leftover part*
balance, bit, dregs, dross, end, end piece, excess, fragment, hangover*, heel, leavings, lees, leftovers, odds and ends*, orts, part, particle, piece, portion, remainder, remains, residual, residue, residuum, rest, rump, scrap, shred, strip, surplus, survival, vestige; SEE CONCEPTS *260,835*

remonstrate [v] *argue against*
animadvert, blame, censure, challenge, combat, complain, criticize, decry, demur, deprecate, disapprove, disparage, dispute, dissent, except, expostulate, fight, find fault, frown upon, inveigh, kick*, nag, object, oppose, pick at, protest, rain, recriminate, resist, scold, sound off*, take exception, take issue, withstand; SEE CONCEPTS *46,52,54*

remorse [n] *guilty or bad conscience*
anguish, attrition, compassion, compunction, contriteness, contrition, grief, guilt, pangs of conscience*, penance, penitence, penitency, pity, regret, remorsefulness, repentance, rue, ruefulness, self-reproach, shame, sorrow; SEE CONCEPTS *410,728*

remorseful [adj] *guilty, ashamed*
apologetic, attritional, chastened, compunctious,

conscience-stricken, contrite, guilt-ridden, mournful, penitent, penitential, regretful, repentant, rueful, sad, self-reproachful, sorrowful, sorry; SEE CONCEPT *401*

remorseless [adj] *without guilt in spite of wrongdoing*
avaricious, barbarous, bloody, callous, cruel, fierce, forbidding, greedy, grim, hard, hard-bitten, hardened, hard-hearted, harsh, impenitent, implacable, inexorable, inhuman, inhumane, insensitive, intolerant, merciless, murderous, obdurate, pitiless, relentless, rigorous, ruthless, sanguinary, savage, shameless, sour, tough, tyrannical, uncompassionate, uncontrite, unforgiving, unmerciful, unregenerate, unrelenting, unremitting, unrepenting, unyielding, vindictive; SEE CONCEPT *401*

remote [adj1] *out-of-the-way; in the distance*
alien, back, backwoods, beyond, boondocks*, devious, distant, far, faraway, far-flung, far-off, foreign, frontier, godforsaken*, god-knows-where*, in a backwater*, inaccessible, isolated, lonely, lonesome, middle of nowhere*, obscure, off-lying, off the beaten path*, outlandish, outlying, private, removed, retired, secluded, secret, undiscovered, unknown, unsettled, wild; SEE CONCEPT *583*

remote [adj2] *irrelevant, unrelated*
abstracted, alien, alone, apart, detached, exclusive, extraneous, extrinsic, farfetched, foreign, immaterial, inappropriate, indirect, nongermane, obscure, outside, pointless, removed, strange, unconnected; SEE CONCEPTS *564,575*

remote [adj3] *unlikely, improbable*
doubtful, dubious, faint, implausible, inconsiderable, meager, negligible, off, outside, poor, slender, slight, slim, small; SEE CONCEPT *552*

remote [adj4] *cold, detached; unapproachable*
abstracted, aloof, casual, cool*, disinterested, distant, faraway, icy, incurious, indifferent, introspective, introverted, laid-back*, offish, putting on airs, removed, reserved, standoffish, stuck up, uncommunicative, unconcerned, uninterested, uninvolved, uppity, withdrawn; SEE CONCEPTS *401,404*

remove [v1] *lift or move object; take off, away*
abolish, abstract, amputate, carry away, carry off, cart off, clear away, cut out, delete, depose, detach, dethrone, dig out, discard, discharge, dislodge, dismiss, displace, disturb, do away with, doff, efface, eject, eliminate, erase, evacuate, expel, expunge, extract, get rid of, junk*, oust, pull out, purge, raise, relegate, rip out, separate, shed, ship, skim, strike out, take down, take out, tear out, throw out, transfer, transport, unload, unseat, uproot, wipe out*, withdraw; SEE CONCEPT *211*

remove [v2] *do away with; kill*
assassinate, blot out*, clear away, dispose of, do away with, do in*, drag, drag down, efface, eliminate, eradicate, erase, exclude, execute, expunge, exterminate, extirpate, get rid of, liquidate, murder, obliterate, purge, scratch, sterilize, take down, take out, waste*, wipe out*; SEE CONCEPTS *121,252*

remunerate [v] *compensate, reward*
accord, ante up*, award, dish out*, do business*, grant, guerdon, indemnify, pay, pay off, pay up, post, recompense, redress, reimburse, repay, requite, shell out*, spring for*, vouchsafe; SEE CONCEPT *341*

re
re

render [v1] contribute
cede, deliver, distribute, exchange, furnish, give, give back, give up, hand over, impart, make available, make restitution, minister, part with, pay, pay back, present, provide, relinquish, repay, restore, return, show, submit, supply, surrender, swap, tender, trade, turn over, yield; SEE CONCEPTS 108,140

render [v2] show; execute
act, administer, administrate, carry out, delineate, depict, display, do, evince, exhibit, govern, image, interpret, limn, manifest, perform, picture, play, portray, present, represent; SEE CONCEPTS 91,261

render [v3] translate, explain
construe, deliver, interpret, paraphrase, pass, put, reproduce, restate, reword, state, transcribe, transliterate, transpose, turn; SEE CONCEPTS 57,266

rendezvous [n1] get-together
affair, appointment, assignation, blind date, date, double date, engagement, heavy date*, matinee, meet, meeting, one night stand*, tête-à-tête, tryst; SEE CONCEPT 384

rendezvous [n2] place for get-together
gathering point, hangout*, haunt, love nest*, meeting place, purlieu, resort, spot, stomping ground*, venue, watering hole*; SEE CONCEPT 198

rendezvous [v] meet, often secretly
assemble, be closeted, be reunited, collect, come together, congregate, congress, converge, forgather, gather, get together, join up, meet behind closed doors*, meet privately, muster, raise, rally; SEE CONCEPT 384

rendition [n] explanation; interpretation
arrangement, construction, delivery, depiction, execution, interpretation, performance, portrayal, presentation, reading, rendering, transcription, translation, version; SEE CONCEPTS 263,278

renegade [n] person who is rebellious
abandoner, apostate, backslider, betrayer, defector, deserter, dissident, double-crosser*, escapee, exile, forsaker, fugitive, heretic, iconoclast, insurgent, mutineer, outlaw, rebel, recreant, refugee, runaway, schismatic, snake*, snake in the grass*, tergiversator, traitor, turnabout, turncoat; SEE CONCEPTS 359,412

renegade [adj] rebellious
apostate, backsliding, disloyal, dissident, heterodox, mutinous, outlaw, radical, reactionary, rebel, recreant, revolutionary, runaway, schismatic, traitorous, unfaithful, untraditional; SEE CONCEPTS 401,542

renew [v] start over; refurbish
begin again, brace, breathe new life into*, bring up to date*, continue, exhilarate, extend, fix up, freshen, gentrify, go over, mend, modernize, overhaul, prolong, reaffirm, reawaken, recommence, recondition, recreate, reestablish, refit, refresh, regenerate, rehabilitate, reinvigorate, rejuvenate, remodel, renovate, reopen, repair, repeat, replace, replenish, restate, restock, restore, resume, resuscitate, retread, revitalize, revive, spruce, stimulate, transform; SEE CONCEPTS 35,202,221

renounce [v] abandon, reject
abdicate, abjure, abnegate, abstain from, apostacize, arrogate, cast off, decline, defect, demit, deny, desert, disavow, discard, disclaim, disown, divorce oneself from*, drop out, dump*, eschew, forgo, forsake, forswear, give up, leave flat*, leave off, opt out, quit, rat*, recant, reject, relinquish, repudiate, resign, sell out*, spurn, swear off, take the pledge*, tergiversate, tergiverse, throw off, throw over, toss over, turn, waive, walk out on, wash hands of*; SEE CONCEPTS 30,54,195

renovate [v] fix up, modernize
clean, cleanse, do*, do up*, face-lift*, gussy up*, make over, overhaul, reactivate, recondition, reconstitute, recreate, refit, reform, refresh, refurbish, rehabilitate, rekindle, remake, remodel, renew, repair, restore, resurrect, resuscitate, retread, retrieve, revamp, revitalize, revive, revivify, spruce, spruce up*, update; SEE CONCEPTS 168,177,202

renown [adj] fame
acclaim, celebrity, distinction, éclat, eminence, glory, honor, illustriousness, kudos, luster, mark, note, notoriety, preeminence, prestige, prominence, prominency, rep*, reputation, repute, stardom; SEE CONCEPT 668

renowned [adj] famous
acclaimed, celebrated, celebrious, distinguished, eminent, esteemed, extolled, famed, great, illustrious, in the limelight*, lauded, monster*, name*, notable, noted, of note, outstanding, praised, prominent, redoubted, signal, splashy, star, superstar, well-known; SEE CONCEPTS 568,574

rent [n1] fee paid for use, service, or privilege
hire, lease, payment, rental, tariff; SEE CONCEPT 329

rent [n2] opening, split
breach, break, chink, cleavage, crack, discord, dissension, division, faction, fissure, flaw, fracture, gash, hole, perforation, rift, rip, rupture, schism, slash, slit, tatter, tear; SEE CONCEPTS 513,665

rent [v] pay or charge fee for use, service, or privilege
allow the use of, borrow, charter, contract, engage, hire, lease, lend, let, loan, make available, put on loan, sublet, take*; SEE CONCEPTS 89,115

renunciation [n] abandonment, rejection
abdication, abjuration, abnegation, abstention, cancellation, denial, disavowal, disclaimer, eschewal, eschewing, forbearing, forswearing, giving up, rebuff, refusal, relinquishment, remission, renouncement, repeal, repudiation, resignation, sacrifice, self-abnegation, self-denial, self-sacrifice, spurning, surrender, veto, waiver, yielding; SEE CONCEPTS 30,54,195

repair [n] restoration, fixing
adjustment, darn, improvement, mend, new part, overhaul, patch, reconstruction, reformation, rehabilitation, replacement, substitution; SEE CONCEPTS 513,700,824

repair [v1] fix, restore
compensate for, correct, darn, debug*, doctor*, do up*, emend, fiddle with, give a face-lift*, heal, improve, make good, make up for, mend, overhaul, patch, patch up, put back together, put in order, put right, rebuild, recondition, recover, rectify, redress, reform, refresh, refurbish, rejuvenate, remedy, renew, renovate, restore, retread, retrieve, revamp, revive, right, settle, sew, square*, touch up; SEE CONCEPT 212

repair [v2] leave; retire
apply, betake oneself, fare, go, head for, hie, journey, move, pass, proceed, process, push on, re-

cur, refer, remove, resort, run, set off for, travel, turn, wend, withdraw; SEE CONCEPT *195*

reparation [n] *compensation, amends*
adjustment, apology, atonement, damages, dues, emolument, expiation, indemnification, indemnity, making good, payment, penance, propitiation, quittance, recompense, redemption, redress, remuneration, renewal, repair, repayment, reprisal, requital, restitution, retribution, reward, satisfaction, settlement, squaring things*; SEE CONCEPTS *337,344,722*

repartee [n] *pleasant conversation*
answer, badinage, banter, bon mot*, comeback, humor, irony, persiflage, pleasantry, quip, raillery, rejoinder, reply, response, retort, riposte, sally, sarcasm, satire, wit, witticism, wittiness, wordplay; SEE CONCEPTS *45,56,266*

repay [v1] *give back money or possession*
accord, award, balance, compensate, indemnify, make amends, make restitution, make up for, offset, pay back, pay dues, rebate, recompense, refund, reimburse, remunerate, requite, restore, return, reward, settle up, square*; SEE CONCEPTS *131,341*

repay [v2] *get even; obtain restitution for past injustice*
avenge, even the score, get back at, get revenge, make reprisal, pay back, reciprocate, requite, retaliate, return, return the compliment*, revenge, settle the score*, square accounts*; SEE CONCEPTS *7,19,246,384*

repeal [n] *cancellation*
abolition, abrogation, annulment, invalidation, nullification, rescinding, rescindment, rescission, revocation, withdrawal; SEE CONCEPTS *121,318,685*

repeal [v] *declare null and void*
abolish, abrogate, annul, back out, backpedal*, blow, call off*, cancel, countermand, dismantle, invalidate, kill*, KO*, lift, nix*, nullify, opt out, recall, renig, rescind, reverse, revoke, scrub, set aside, shoot down, stand down, throw over, vacate, void, wash out, weasel out*, wipe out, withdraw, worm out*, X-out*, zap*; SEE CONCEPTS *50,88,121,317*

repeat [n] *something done over; duplicate*
echo, recapitulation, reiteration, repetition, replay, reproduction, rerun, reshowing; SEE CONCEPT *695*

repeat [v] *duplicate, do again*
chime, come again, din, ditto*, drum into*, duplicate, echo, go over again, hold over, imitate, ingeminate, iterate, make like*, occur again, play back, play over, quote, read back, reappear, recapitulate, recast, reciprocate, recite, reconstruct, recrudesce, recur, redo, refashion, reform, rehash*, rehearse, reissue, reiterate, relate, remake, renew, reoccur, replay, reprise, reproduce, rerun, resay, reshow, restate, retell, return, revert, revolve, rework*, run over, sing same old song*; SEE CONCEPTS *91,111,171*

repeatedly [adv] *over and over again*
again, again and again, frequently, many a time, many times, much, oft, often, oftentimes, ofttimes, regularly, time after time, time and again; SEE CONCEPT *553*

repel [v1] *push away; repulse*
beat back, beat off, brush off, buck, cast aside, chase away, check, confront, cool*, cut, decline, dismiss, disown, dispute, drive away, drive back,

drive off, duel, fend off, fight, force back, force off, give cold shoulder to*, hold back, hold off, keep at arm's length*, keep at bay*, keep off, kick, knock down, oppose, parry, push back, put down, put to flight, rebuff, rebut, refuse, reject, resist, stand up against, stave off, traverse, turn down, ward off, withstand; SEE CONCEPTS *30,208*

repel [v2] *induce aversion*
disgust, give a pain in neck*, make sick*, offend, put off*, reluct, repulse, revolt, sicken, turn off*, turn one's stomach*; SEE CONCEPTS *7,19,303*

repent [v] *ask forgiveness*
apologize, atone, be ashamed, be contrite, be sorry, bewail, deplore, feel remorse, have qualms, lament, reform, regret, relent, reproach oneself, rue, see error of ways*, show penitence, sorrow; SEE CONCEPTS *48,410*

repentance [n] *feeling bad for past action*
attrition, compunction, conscience, contriteness, contrition, grief, guilt, penitence, penitency, regret, remorse, rue, ruth, self-reproach, sorriness, sorrow; SEE CONCEPTS *410,728*

repercussion [n] *consequence*
backlash, chain reaction, echo, effect, fallout, feedback, flak*, follow-through*, follow-up, impact, imprint, influence, kickback*, mark, reaction, rebound, recoil, re-echo, result, reverberation, side effect, spinoff*, waves*; SEE CONCEPT *230*

repertory [n] *collection*
bit, cache, depot, list, range, rep*, repertoire, repository, routine, schtick*, stock, stockroom, store, storehouse, stunt*, supply; SEE CONCEPTS *263,432,712*

repetition [n] *duplication; doing again*
alliteration, broken record*, chant, chorus, copy, echo, encore, ingemination, iteracy, iterance, iteration, litany, paraphrase, periodicity, perseveration, practice, reappearance, recapitulation, recital, recurrence, redundancy, rehearsal, reiteration, relation, renewal, reoccurrence, repeat, repetitiousness, replication, report, reproduction, restatement, return, rhythm, rote, tautology; SEE CONCEPT *695*

repetitious [adj] *wordy, tedious*
alliterative, boring, dull, echoic, iterant, iterative, long-winded, plangent, pleonastic, prolix, recapitulatory, redundant, reiterative, repeating, repetitive, resonant, tautological, verbose, windy; SEE CONCEPT *553*

replace [v] *take the place of; put in place of*
alter, back up, change, compensate, displace, fill in, follow, front for*, give back, mend, oust, outplace, patch, pinch hit for*, put back, reconstitute, recoup, recover, redeem, redress, reestablish, refund, regain, reimburse, reinstate, repay, restitute, restore, retrieve, ring, ring in, shift, sit in, stand in, stand in lieu of, step into shoes of*, sub*, substitute, succeed, supersede, supplant, supply, swap places, take out, take over, take over from; SEE CONCEPTS *104,128,211,697*

replenish [v] *fill, stock*
furnish, make up, provide, provision, refill, refresh, reload, renew, replace, restock, restore, stock, top; SEE CONCEPTS *140,209*

replete [adj] *full, well-stocked*
abounding, abundant, alive, awash, brimful, brimming, charged, chock-full*, complete, crammed, crowded, filled, full up*, glutted, gorged, jammed, jam-packed, lavish, loaded, lux-

urious, overfed, overflowing, packed, plenteous, rife, sated, satiated, stuffed, swarming, teeming, thronged, well-provided; SEE CONCEPTS *483,740*

replica [n] *duplicate*

carbon, carbon copy, chip off old block*, clone, copy, ditto*, dupe*, facsimile, flimsy*, imitation, likeness, lookalike, mimeo, mimic, miniature, model, photocopy, reduplication, repeat, replication, repro, reproduction, stat, Xerox*; SEE CONCEPTS *260,670,686*

reply [n] *answer*

acknowledgment, antiphon, back talk*, comeback, counter, echo, feedback, knee-jerk reaction*, lip*, reaction, reciprocation, rejoinder, respond, response, retaliation, retort, return, riposte, sass*, snappy comeback*, vibes*, wisecrack; SEE CONCEPT *278*

reply [v] *answer*

acknowledge, be in touch*, come back*, counter, echo, feedback, field the question*, get back to, react, reciprocate, rejoin, respond, retaliate, retort, return, riposte, shoot back*, squelch*, top*, write back; SEE CONCEPT *45*

report [n1] *account, story*

address, announcement, article, blow by blow*, brief, broadcast, cable, chronicle, communication, communique, declaration, description, detail, digest, dispatch, handout, history, hot wire*, information, message, narration, narrative, news, note, opinion, outline, paper, picture, piece, precis, proclamation, pronouncement, recital, record, relation, release, résumé, rundown, scoop* statement, summary, tale, telegram, tidings, version, wire, word*, write-up; SEE CONCEPTS *274,282, 283*

report [n2] *gossip, talk*

advice, blow by blow*, buzz*, canard, chat, chatter, chitchat, comment, conversation, cry*, dirt*, earful, grapevine*, hash*, hearsay, intelligence, murmur, news, prating, rumble*, rumor, scandal, scuttlebutt*, small talk*, speech, tattle, the latest*, tidings, whispering, word*; SEE CONCEPTS *51,278*

report [n3] *loud noise*

bang, blast, boom, crack, crash, detonation, discharge, explosion, reverberation, sound; SEE CONCEPT *595*

report [n4] *reputation*

character, esteem, fame, name, regard, rep*, repute; SEE CONCEPT *388*

report [v1] *communicate information, knowledge*

account for, advise, air, announce, bring word, broadcast, cable, circulate, cover, declare, describe, detail, disclose, document, enunciate, give an account of, give the facts, impart, inform, inscribe, itemize, list, make known, make public, mention, narrate, note, notify, pass on, present, proclaim, promulgate, provide details, publish, recite, record, recount, rehearse, relate, relay, retail, reveal, set forth, spread, state, summarize, telephone, tell, trumpet, wire, write up; SEE CONCEPT *60*

report [v2] *present oneself*

appear, arrive, be at hand, be present, clock in*, come, get to, reach, show, show up, turn up*; SEE CONCEPT *159*

reporter [n] *person who informs*

anchor, anchorperson, announcer, columnist, correspondent, cub*, editor, ink slinger*, interviewer, journalist, legperson*, newscaster,

newshound*, newsperson, newswriter, press person, scribe, scrivener, stringer, writer; SEE CONCEPTS *348,356*

repose [n] *restfulness; calm*

ease, inaction, inactivity, leisure, peace, quiet, quietness, quietude, refreshment, relaxation, relaxing, renewal, requiescence, respite, rest, restoration, sleep, slumber, stillness, tranquillity; SEE CONCEPTS *410,681,720*

repose [v] *relax; recline*

deposit, lay down, lie, lie down, loaf, loll, lounge, place, rest, settle, settle down, slant, sleep, slumber, stretch, stretch out, take it easy, tilt; SEE CONCEPTS *154,210*

reprehensible [adj] *very bad; shameful*

amiss, blamable, blameworthy, censurable, condemnable, culpable, delinquent, demeritorious, discreditable, disgraceful, errant, erring, guilty, ignoble, objectionable, opprobrious, remiss, sinful, unholy, unworthy, wicked; SEE CONCEPT *571*

represent [v1] *present image of; symbolize*

act as, act as broker, act for, act in place of, appear as, assume the role of, be, be agent for, be attorney for, be proxy for, betoken, body, buy for, copy, correspond to, do business for, emblematize, embody, enact, epitomize, equal, equate, exemplify, exhibit, express, factor, hold office, imitate, impersonate, mean, perform, personify, play the part, produce, put on, reproduce, sell for, serve, serve as, show, speak for, stage, stand for, steward, substitute, symbolize, typify; SEE CONCEPTS *87,317,682,716*

represent [v2] *depict, show*

body forth, delineate, denote, describe, design, designate, display, draft, enact, evoke, exhibit, express, hint, illustrate, interpret, limn, mirror, narrate, outline, picture, portray, realize, relate, render, reproduce, run down, run through, sketch, suggest, track; SEE CONCEPTS *261*

representative [n1] *person who acts in the stead of another*

agent, assemblyperson, attorney, commissioner, congressperson, councilor, councilperson, counselor, delegate, deputy, lawyer, legislator, member, messenger, proxy, rep*, salesperson, senator, spokesperson; SEE CONCEPTS *348,354*

representative [n2] *typical example*

archetype, case, case history, embodiment, epitome, exemplar, illustration, instance, personification, sample, sampling, specimen, type; SEE CONCEPT *686*

representative [adj] *characteristic, typical*

adumbrative, archetypal, classic, classical, delineative, depictive, emblematic, evocative, exemplary, ideal, illustrative, model, presentational, prototypal, prototypical, quintessential, rep*, symbolic, symbolical; SEE CONCEPTS *487,573*

repress [v] *keep back, hold in*

black out*, bottle, chasten, check, collect, compose, control, cool*, cork*, crush, curb, gridlock*, hinder, hold back, inhibit, jam up, keep in, keep in check, keep under wraps*, kill*, lock, master, muffle, overcome, overpower, quash, quelch, quell, rein, restrain, shush, silence, simmer down*, smother, squelch, stifle, subdue, subjugate, suppress, swallow, throw cold water on*, tie up*; SEE CONCEPTS *121,130*

reprieve [n] *relief of blame, responsibility*

abatement, abeyance, absolution, acquittal, alleviation, amnesty, anchor*, clearance, clemency, commute, deferment, freeing, let-up*, lifeboat*, lifesaver*, mitigation, palliation, pardon, postponement, release, remission, respite, spring*, stay, suspension, truce; SEE CONCEPTS 318,685

reprieve [n] *relieve of blame, responsibility*
abate, absolve, allay, alleviate, amnesty, excuse, forgive, grant a stay, let go, let off, let off the hook*, let off this time*, let up on*, mitigate, palliate, pardon, postpone, remit, respite; SEE CONCEPTS 50,88,317

reprimand [n] *oral punishment*
admonishment, admonition, bawling out*, blame, calling down*, castigation, censure, chiding, comeuppance, dressing-down*, going over*, grooming, hard time*, lecture, piece of one's mind*, ragging*, rap*, rebuke, reprehension, reproof, scolding, slap on wrist*, talking-to, telling-off, tongue-lashing, what for*; SEE CONCEPTS 123,278

reprimand [v] *blame, scold*
admonish, call on the carpet*, castigate, censure, check, chew out*, chide, come down on*, criticize, denounce, dress down*, give piece of one's mind*, give the dickens*, lecture, lesson, light into*, lower the boom*, monish, rap, rebuke, reprehend, reproach, reprove, take to task*, tell off, tick off*, upbraid; SEE CONCEPTS 44,52

reprisal [n] *revenge*
avengement, avenging, counterblow, counterstroke, eye for an eye*, paying back, requital, retaliation, retribution, vengeance; SEE CONCEPT 384

reproach [n] *strong criticism; dishonor*
abuse, admonishment, admonition, blame, blemish, censure, chiding, condemnation, contempt, disapproval, discredit, disgrace, disrepute, ignominy, indignity, obloquy, odium, opprobrium, rap*, rebuke, reprehension, reprimand, reproof, scorn, shame, slight, slur, stain, stigma; SEE CONCEPTS 44,52,123,388

reproach [v] *find fault with*
abuse, admonish, blame, call down, call to task*, cavil, censure, chide, condemn, criticize, defame, discredit, disparage, give comeuppance*, give the devil*, jawbone*, lay on*, lesson, rake, ream, rebuke, reprehend, reprimand, reprove, scold, sit on*, take to task, trim, upbraid; SEE CONCEPTS 44,52

reproduce [v1] *make more copies of*
carbon*, clone, copy, do again, dupe*, duplicate, echo, emulate, engross, follow, imitate, knock off, manifold, match, mimeo*, mimeograph, mirror, parallel, photocopy, photograph, photostat, pirate, portray, print, reawaken, recount, recreate, redo, reduplicate, reenact, reflect, relive, remake, repeat, replicate, represent, reprint, restamp, revive, stereotype, transcribe, type, Xerox*; SEE CONCEPTS 111,171

reproduce [v2] *make something new; give birth*
bear, beget, breed, engender, father, fecundate, generate, hatch, impregnate, mother, multiply, procreate, produce young, progenerate, proliferate, propagate, repopulate, sire, spawn; SEE CONCEPTS 173,251,374

reproduction [n] *something duplicated; duplication*
breeding, carbon*, carbon copy, chip off old block*, clone, copy, ditto*, dupe*, facsimile, fake, flimsy, generation, imitation, increase, lookalike, mimeo*, mimeograph, mirror image*, mul-

tiplication, offprint, photocopy, photograph, Photostat, pic*, picture, portrayal, print, procreation, proliferation, propagation, recreation, reduplication, reenactment, renewal, replica, replication, reprinting, repro*, revival, stat, transcription, twin, Xerox*, X-ray*; SEE CONCEPTS 173,625,670,716

repudiate [v] *reject; turn one's back on*
abandon, abjure, apostatize, banish, be against, break with, cast, cast off, cut of, decline, default, defect, demur, deny, desert, disacknowledge, disapprove, disavow, discard, disclaim, dishonor, disinherit, dismiss, disown, dump, flush*, fly in the face of*, forsake, nix*, oust, rat*, recant, refuse, renounce, repeal, reprobate, rescind, retract, reverse, revoke, spurn, tergiversate, tergiverse, turn, turn down, wash one's hands of*; SEE CONCEPTS 13,21,30

repugnant [adj] *bad, obnoxious; hostile*
abhorrent, abominable, adverse, against, alien, antagonistic, antipathetic, averse, conflicting, contradictory, counter, creepy*, different, disagreeable, disgusting, distasteful, extraneous, extrinsic, foreign, foul, hateful, horrid, incompatible, inconsistent, inconsonant, inimical, in opposition, invidious, loathsome, nasty, nauseating, noisome, objectionable, odious, offensive, opposed, opposite, repellent, revolting, revulsive, sickening, unconformable, unfitted, unfriendly, vile; SEE CONCEPTS 401,564,571

repulse [n] *snub; rejection*
brush-off*, check, cold shoulder*, defeat, disappointment, failure, nix*, nothing doing*, rebuff, refusal, reverse, slap in the face*, spurning, thumbs down*, turndown; SEE CONCEPTS 388,674

repulse [v1] *push away*
beat off, brush off*, check, defeat, drive back, fend off, fight off, heave-ho*, hold off, keep off, kick in the teeth*, nix*, overthrow, push back, put down, rebuff, rebut, reject, repel, resist, set back, stave off, throw back, ward off; SEE CONCEPTS 96,208

repulse [v2] *make sick*
disdain, disgust, disregard, give a pain*, rebuff, refuse, reject, reluct, repel, revolt, sicken, snub, spurn, turn down, turn off*; SEE CONCEPTS 21,410

repulsion [n] *hatred, disgust*
abhorrence, abomination, antipathy, aversion, denial, detestation, disrelish, distaste, hate, horror, loathing, malice, rebuff, refusal, repugnance, repugnancy, resentment, revolt, revulsion, snub; SEE CONCEPT 29

repulsive [adj] *very disgusting, offensive*
abhorrent, abominable, animal*, creepy*, disagreeable, distasteful, forbidding, foul, gross, hateful, hideous, horrid, loathsome, nasty, nauseating, noisome, objectionable, obnoxious, odious, off-putting, pugnacious, repellent, revolting, sickening, sleazy*, ugly, undesirable, unpleasant, unsightly, vile; SEE CONCEPTS 529,571,579

reputable [adj] *worthy of respect*
acclaimed, celebrated, conscientious, constant, creditable, dependable, distinguished, eminent, esteemed, estimable, excellent, fair, faithful, famed, famous, favored, good, high-principled, high-ranking, honest, honorable, honored, illustrious, in high favor, just, legitimate, notable, of good repute, popular, prominent, redoubted, reliable, renowned, respectable, righteous, salt of the

re
re

earth*, sincere, straightforward, trustworthy, truthful, upright, well-known, well-thought-of; SEE CONCEPTS 545,567,574

reputation [n] *commonly held opinion of person's character*
acceptability, account, approval, authority, character, credit, dependability, distinction, éclat, eminence, esteem, estimation, fame, favor, honor, influence, mark*, name*, notoriety, opinion, position, prestige, privilege, prominence, rank, regard, reliability, renown, rep*, report, repute, respectability, standing, stature, trustworthiness, weight; SEE CONCEPTS 388,411,689

reputed [adj] *believed*
accounted, alleged, assumed, conjectural, considered, deemed, estimated, gossiped, held, hypothetical, ostensible, putative, reckoned, regarded, reported, rumored, said, seeming, supposed, suppositional, suppositious, supposititious, suppositive, supposititory; thought; SEE CONCEPT 529

request [n] *question or petition*
appeal, application, asking, begging, call, commercial, demand, desire, entreaty, inquiry, invitation, offer, prayer, recourse, requisition, solicitation, suit, supplication; SEE CONCEPT 662

request [v] *ask for*
appeal, apply, beg, beseech, bespeak, call for, demand, desire, entreat, hit, hit up for*, hold out for*, hustle*, inquire, petition, pray, promote, put in for*, requisition, seek, solicit, sponge*, sue, supplicate, touch; SEE CONCEPT 53

require [v1] *need, want*
crave, depend upon, desire, feel necessity for, have need, hurting for, lack, miss, stand in need, wish; SEE CONCEPTS 20,646

require [v2] *ask, demand; necessitate*
assert oneself, beg, beseech, bid, call for, call upon, cause, challenge, claim, command, compel, constrain, crave, demand, direct, enjoin, entail, exact, expect, insist upon, instruct, involve, look for, obligate, oblige, order, postulate, push for, request, requisition, solicit, take; SEE CONCEPTS 53,646

required/requisite [adj] *necessary*
appropriate, called for, compulsatory, compulsory, condign, demanded, deserved, due, enforced, essential, imperative, imperious, indispensable, just, mandatory, needed, needful, obligatory, prerequisite, prescribed, recommended, right, rightful, set, suitable, unavoidable, vital; SEE CONCEPT 546

requirement/requisite [n] *necessity, want*
claim, compulsion, concern, condition, demand, desideratum, element, engrossment, essential, exaction, exigency, extremity, fulfillment, fundamental, imperative, lack, must, need, obligation, obsession, pinch, precondition, preliminary, preoccupation, prepossession, prerequisite, prescription, provision, proviso, qualification, sine qua non, specification, stipulation, terms, urgency, vital part; SEE CONCEPTS 646,709

requisition [n] *demand; application for need*
appropriation, call, commandeering, demand, occupation, request, seizure, summons, takeover; SEE CONCEPT 662

requisition [v] *ask for; apply for something needed*
buy, call for, challenge, claim, demand, exact, order, postulate, put dibs on*, put in for, request, require, solicit; SEE CONCEPTS 48,53

requite [v] *compensate, give in return*
indemnify, make, make amends, make good, pay, pay off, quit, reciprocate, recompense, redeem, redress, reimburse, remunerate, repay, respond, restitution, retaliate, return, revenge, reward, satisfy, settle; SEE CONCEPTS 126,131,341,384

rescind [v] *declare null and void*
abolish, abrogate, annul, back out of, backpedal*, backwater*, call off, cancel, countermand, crawl out of*, dismantle, forget, invalidate, lift, nix*, overturn, pull the plug*, quash, recall, remove, renege, repeal, retract, reverse, revoke, scrub*, set aside, void, wangle out*, weasel out*, X-out*; SEE CONCEPTS 121,234,317

rescue [n] *saving from danger*
deliverance, delivery, disembarrassment, disentanglement, emancipation, exploit, extrication, feat, heroics, heroism, liberation, performance, ransom, reclaiming, reclamation, recovering, recovery, redemption, release, relief, salvage, salvation, saving; SEE CONCEPT 134

rescue [v] *save from danger*
bail one out*, conserve, deliver, disembarrass, disentangle, emancipate, extricate, free, get off the hook*, get out, get out of hock*, give a break, hold over, keep, liberate, manumit, preserve, protect, pull out of the fire*, ransom, recapture, recover, redeem, regain, release, retain, retrieve, safeguard, salvage, save life of, set free, spring*, unleash, unloose; SEE CONCEPT 134

research [n] *examination, study*
analysis, delving, experimentation, exploration, fact-finding, fishing expedition*, groundwork, inquest, inquiry, inquisition, investigation, legwork*, probe, probing, quest, R and D*, scrutiny; SEE CONCEPTS 349,362

research [v] *examine, study*
analyze, consult, do tests, experiment, explore, inquire, investigate, look into, look up, play around with*, probe, read up on, scrutinize; SEE CONCEPTS 31,103

resemblance [n] *correspondence, similarity*
affinity, alikeness, analogy, birds of a feather*, carbon*, carbon copy, clone, closeness, coincidence, comparability, comparison, conformity, counterpart, double, facsimile, image, kinship, likeness, like of, look-alike, parallel, parity, peas in a pod*, ringer*, sameness, semblance, simile, similitude, spitting image*, two of a kind*, Xerox*; SEE CONCEPTS 664,670,716

resemble [v] *look or be like*
appear like, approximate, bear resemblance to, be similar to, be the very picture of*, bring to mind, coincide, come close to, come near, correspond to, double, duplicate, echo, favor, feature, follow, have earmarks of*, have signs of, match, mirror, parallel, pass for, relate, remind one of, seem like, simulate, smack of*, sound like, take after; SEE CONCEPTS 664,670,716

resent [v] *be angry about*
bear a grudge, begrudge, be in a huff*, be insulted, be offended by, be put off by*, be rubbed wrong way*, be vexed, dislike, feel bitter, feel sore*, frown at, get nose out of joint*, grudge, harbor a grudge*, have hard feelings*, object to, take amiss, take as an insult, take exception, take offense, take umbrage; SEE CONCEPTS 29,410

resentment [n] *hate, anger*
acerbity, acrimony, animosity, animus, annoyance, antagonism, bad feeling, bitterness, choler,

cynicism, displeasure, dudgeon, exacerbation, exasperation, fog, fury, grudge, huff, hurt, ill feeling, ill will, indignation, ire, irritation, malice, malignity, miff, offense, outrage, passion, perturbation, pique, rage, rancor, rise, spite, umbrage, vehemence, vexation, wrath; SEE CONCEPTS 29,410

reservation [n1] *condition, stipulation*
catch, circumscription, demur, doubt, fine print*, grain of salt*, hesitancy, kicker*, provision, proviso, qualification, restriction, scruple, skepticism, string*, strings*, terms; SEE CONCEPTS 646,711

reservation [n2] *the act of holding something, or thing held for future use*
bespeaking, booking, exclusive possession, place, restriction, retaining, retainment, setting aside, withholding; SEE CONCEPT 710

reservation [n3] *habitat for large group*
enclave, homeland, preserve, reserve, sanctuary, territory, tract; SEE CONCEPTS 512,516

reserve [n1] *supply*
ace in hole*, assets, backlog, cache, capital, drop, emergency fund*, fund, hoard, insurance, inventory, nest egg*, plant, provisions, rainy day fund*, reservoir, resources, savings, stash*, stock, stockpile, store, wealth; SEE CONCEPTS 340,710,712

reserve [n2] *coolness of manner*
aloofness, backwardness, calmness, caution, coldness, constraint, coyness, demureness, diffidence, formality, inhibition, modesty, quietness, reluctance, repression, reservation, restraint, reticence, secretiveness, self-restraint, shyness, silence, suppression, taciturnity, uncommunicativeness, unresponsiveness; SEE CONCEPT 633

reserve [v1] *keep, hold back*
conserve, defer, delay, duck*, have, hoard, hold, keep back, keep out, lay up, maintain, plant, possess, postpone, preserve, put away, put by, put off, retain, save, set aside, squirrel*, squirrel away*, stash, stockpile, store, store up, stow away, withhold; SEE CONCEPT 129

reserve [v2] *hold for future use*
bespeak, book, contract, engage, prearrange, preengage, retain, schedule, secure; SEE CONCEPT 53

reserved [adj1] *silent, unsociable; constrained*
aloof, bashful, cautious, ceremonious, close, close-mouthed, cold*, collected, composed, conventional, cool, demure, diffident, distant, eremitic, formal, frigid, gentle, icy*, mild, misanthropic, modest, noncommittal, offish, peaceful, placid, prim, quiet, reclusive, restrained, reticent, retiring, secretive, sedate, self-contained, serene, shy, soft-spoken, solitary, standoffish, taciturn, unapproachable, uncommunicative, uncompanionable, undemonstrative, unresponsive, withdrawn; SEE CONCEPTS 401,404

reserved [adj2] *held for future use*
appropriated, arrogated, booked, claimed, engaged, kept, laid away, limited, preempted, private, qualified, restricted, retained, roped off, set apart, set aside, spoken for, taken; SEE CONCEPTS 576,710

reservoir [n] *accumulation, repository*
backlog, basin, cistern, container, fund, holder, lake, nest egg*, pond, pool, receptacle, reserve, source, spring, stock, stockpile, storage, store, supply, tank, tarn; SEE CONCEPTS 514,712

reside [v] *live or exist in*
abide, be intrinsic to, be vested, bide, consist, continue, crash*, dig*, dwell, endure, hang one's hat*, inhabit, inhere, lie, locate, lodge, nest, occupy, park*, people, perch, populate, remain, rest with, roost, settle, sojourn, squat, stay, take up residence, tenant; SEE CONCEPTS 226 407

residence [n] *place for living*
abode, address, apartment, condo, co-op, domicile, dwelling, habitation, hall, headquarters, hole, home, homeplate*, house, household, inhabitancy, inhabitation, living quarters, lodging, manor, mansion, occupancy, occupation, palace, rack*, roof*, roost*, seat, settlement, villa; SEE CONCEPT 516

resident [n] *person living in a particular place*
citizen, denizen, dweller, habitant, householder, indweller, inhabitant, inmate, liver, local, lodger, native, occupant, resider, squatter, suburbanite, tenant, urbanite; SEE CONCEPT 413

residual [adj] *leftover*
balance, continuing, enduring, extra, lingering, net, remaining, surplus, unconsumed, unused, vestigial; SEE CONCEPTS 560,771

residue [n] *leftover part*
balance, debris, dregs, dross, excess, extra, garbage, heel, junk, leavings, leftovers, orts, parings, remainder, remains, remnant, residual, residuum, rest, scourings, scraps, scum, sewage, shavings, silt, slag, surplus, trash; SEE CONCEPTS 260,432

resign [v] *give up responsibility*
abandon, abdicate, bail out, bow out, capitulate, cease work, cede, demit, divorce oneself from, drop, drop out, end service, fold, forgo, forsake, give notice, give up the ship*, hand in resignation, hand over, hang it up*, leave, quit, relinquish, renounce, retire, secede, separate oneself from, sign off, stand aside, stand down, step down, surrender, terminate, throw in the towel*, turn over, vacate, waive, walk out, wash hands of*, yield; SEE CONCEPTS 119,195,351

resignation [n1] *relinquishment of responsibility*
abandonment, abdication, departure, giving up, leaving, notice, quitting, renunciation, retirement, surrender, tendering, termination, vacating, withdrawal; SEE CONCEPTS 119,195,351

resignation [n2] *endurance, passivity*
acceptance, acquiescence, compliance, conformity, deference, docility, forbearing, fortitude, humbleness, humility, longanimity, lowliness, meekness, modesty, nonresistance, patience, patientness, resignedness, submission, submissiveness, sufferance; SEE CONCEPTS 410,657

resigned [adj] *enduring, passive*
accommodated, acquiescent, adapted, adjusted, agreeable, amenable, biddable, calm, compliant, cordial, deferential, docile, genial, gentle, long-suffering, manageable, nonresisting, obedient, patient, peaceable, philosophical, pliant, quiescent, quiet, ready, reconciled, relinquishing, renouncing, satisfied, stoical, subdued, submissive, subservient, tame, tolerant, tractable, unassertive, unprotesting, unresisting, well-disposed, willing, yielding; SEE CONCEPTS 401,542

resilient [adj] *bouncy, flexible*
airy, buoyant, effervescent, elastic, expansive, hardy, irrepressible, plastic, pliable, quick to recover, rebounding, rolling with punches*, rub-

re
re

bery, snapping back, springy, stretchy, strong, supple, tough, volatile; SEE CONCEPTS *488,489*

resist [v] *withstand, oppose*
abide, abstain from, antagonize, assail, assault, battle, bear, brook, buck, check, combat, confront, contend, continue, counteract, countervail, curb, defy, die hard, dispute, duel, endure, fight back, forbear, forgo, hinder, hold, hold off, hold out against, keep from, leave alone, maintain, persevere, persist, prevent, put up a fight, refrain, refuse, remain, remain firm, repel, stand up to, stay, stonewall*, struggle against, suffer, thwart, traverse, turn down, weather, withstand; SEE CONCEPTS *23,35,96,106*

resistance [n] *fighting, opposition*
battle, blocking, check, combat, contention, counteraction, cover, defiance, detention, fight, friction, halting, hindrance, holding, impedance, impediment, impeding, intransigence, obstruction, parrying, protecting, protection, rebuff, refusal, retardation, safeguard, screen, shield, stand, striking back, struggle, support, warding off, watch, withstanding; SEE CONCEPTS *23,96,106,410*

resolute [adj] *determined, strong-willed*
adamant, bold, constant, courageous, dead set on*, decided, dogged, faithful, firm, fixed, immutable, inflexible, intent upon, intrepid, loyal, meaning business*, obstinate, persevering, persistent, persisting, purposeful, relentless, resolved, serious, set, settled, staunch, steadfast, steady, strong, stubborn, tenacious, true, unbending, unchanging, uncompromising, undaunted, unfaltering, unflagging, unflinching, unshakable, unshaken, unwavering, unyielding, valiant; SEE CONCEPTS *403,542*

resolution [n1] *determination, strong will*
aim, boldness, constancy, courage, dauntlessness, decidedness, decision, declaration, dedication, determination, doggedness, earnestness, energy, firmness, fixed purpose, fortitude, guts*, heart*, immovability, intent, intention, judgment, mettle, moxie*, obstinacy, perseverance, pluck, purpose, purposefulness, purposiveness, relentlessness, resoluteness, resolve, settlement, sincerity, spirit, spunk, staunchness, staying power, steadfastness, stubbornness, tenacity, verdict, willpower; SEE CONCEPTS *410,657*

resolution [n2] *answer, judgment*
analysis, assertion, breakdown, call, conclusion, decision, declaration, determination, dissection, elucidation, end, exposition, finding, interpretation, motion, nod, outcome, pay dirt*, presentation, proposal, proposition, quick fix*, recitation, recommendation, resolve, settlement, solution, solving, sorting out, ticket*, unravelling, upshot, verdict, working out; SEE CONCEPTS *18,230,274*

resolve [n] *decision, determination*
boldness, conclusion, courage, decidedness, design, earnestness, firmness, fixed purpose, intention, objective, project, purpose, purposefulness, purposiveness, resoluteness, resolution, steadfastness, undertaking, will, willpower; SEE CONCEPTS *410,659,689*

resolve [v] *make up one's mind; find solution*
agree, analyze, anatomize, answer, break, break down, choose, clear up, clinch*, conclude, deal with, decide, decipher, decree, design, determine, dissect, dissolve, elect, elucidate, fathom, figure, fix, intend, iron out*, lick, make a point of, pan

out*, pass upon, propose, purpose, puzzle out, remain firm, rule, settle, solve, take a stand, undertake, unfold, unravel, untangle, unzip*, will, work, work out, work through; SEE CONCEPTS *15,18,24*

resonant [adj] *vibrant in sound*
beating, booming, clangorous, consonant, deep, deep-toned, earsplitting, echoing, electrifying, enhanced, full, heightened, intensified, loud, mellow, noisy, orotund, plangent, powerful, profound, pulsating, pulsing, resounding, reverberant, reverberating, rich, ringing, roaring, round, sonorant, sonorous, stentorian, strident, thrilling, throbbing, thundering, thunderous; SEE CONCEPT *594*

resort [n1] *vacation place*
camp, fat farm*, hangout, harbor, haunt, haven, hideaway, hideout, holiday spot, hotel, hot spring*, inn, lodge, mineral spring, motel, nest, park, purlieu, refuge, rendezvous, retreat, spa, spot, spring, stomping ground*, tourist center, tourist trap*; SEE CONCEPTS *198,516*

resort [n2] *alternative, recourse*
chance, course, device, expediency, expedient, hope, makeshift, opportunity, possibility, reference, refuge, relief, resource, shift, stopgap, substitute, surrogate; SEE CONCEPTS *693,712*

resort [v] *have recourse to; make use of*
address, affect, apply, avail oneself of, benefit by, bring into play, devote, direct, employ, exercise, fall back on, frequent, go, go to, haunt, head for, look to, make use of, put to use, recur, recur to, refer to, repair, run, take up, try, turn, turn to, use, utilize, visit; SEE CONCEPT *225*

resource [n] *supply drawn upon, either material or nonmaterial*
ability, appliance, artifice, assets, capability, capital, cleverness, contraption, contrivance, course, creation, device, expedient, fortune, hoard, ingenuity, initiative, inventiveness, makeshift, means, measure, method, mode, nest egg*, property, quick-wittedness, recourse, refuge, relief, reserve, resourcefulness, riches, shift, source, step, stock, stockpile, store, stratagem, substance, substitute, support, surrogate, system, talent, way, wealth, worth; SEE CONCEPTS *340,523,658,710,712*

resourceful [adj] *imaginative*
able, active, adventurous, aggressive, bright, capable, clever, creative, enterprising, ingenious, intelligent, inventive, original, quick-witted, sharp, talented, venturesome; SEE CONCEPT *402*

resources [n] *money, possessions, natural resources*
ace in hole*, assets, backing, bankroll, basics, belongings, budget, capital, collateral, effects, funds, holdings, income, kitty*, material goods, means, nest egg*, nut*, property, reserves, revenue, riches, savings, sock*, stuff, supplies, the goods*, ways and means*, wealth, wherewithal*; SEE CONCEPTS *340,446,523,710,712*

respect [n1] *admiration given by others*
account, adoration, appreciation, approbation, awe, consideration, courtesy, deference, dignity, esteem, estimation, favor, fear, homage, honor, obeisance, ovation, recognition, regard, repute, reverence, testimonial, tribute, veneration, worship; SEE CONCEPT *689*

respect [n2] *way, sense*
aspect, bearing, character, connection, detail,

facet, feature, matter, particular, point, reference, regard, relation; SEE CONCEPT *682*

respect [v] *admire; obey*
abide by, adhere to, adore, appreciate, attend, be awed by, be kind to, comply with, defer to, esteem, follow, have good opinion of, have high opinion, heed, honor, look up to, note, notice, observe of, pay attention, recognize, regard, revere, reverence, set store by, show consideration, show courtesy, spare, take into account, think highly of, uphold, value, venerate; SEE CONCEPTS *10,32*

respectable [adj1] *good, honest*
admirable, appropriate, august, becoming, befitting, comely, conforming, correct, creditable, decent, decorous, dignified, done, estimable, fair, honorable, mediocre, moderate, modest, nice, ordinary, passable, presentable, proper, redoubtable, redoubted, reputable, reputed, respected, satisfactory, seemly, sublime, suitable, tolerable, upright, venerable, virtuous, well-thought-of, worthy; SEE CONCEPT *572*

respectable [adj2] *substantial, ample*
appreciable, considerable, decent, fair, fairly good, good, goodly, presentable, reasonable, sensible, sizable, tidy, tolerable; SEE CONCEPT *771*

respectful [adj] *courteous, mannerly*
admiring, appreciative, civil, considerate, courtly, deferential, duteous, dutiful, gracious, humble, obedient, obeisant, polite, recognizing, regardful, regarding, reverent, reverential, self-effacing, solicitous, submissive, upholding, venerating, well-mannered; SEE CONCEPT *401*

respective [adj] *particular, specific*
corresponding, each, individual, own, personal, relevant, separate, several, singular, various; SEE CONCEPT *556*

respects [n] *good wishes*
best wishes, compliments, courtesies, deference, devoirs, greetings, kind wishes, regards, salaam*, salutations; SEE CONCEPT *278*

respite [n] *pause, suspension in activity*
acquittal, adjournment, break, breath*, breather*, breathing space*, cessation, coffee break*, deadlock, deferment, delay, deliverance, discharge, downtime*, ease, exculpation, five*, forgiveness, halt, hiatus, immunity, intermission, interregnum, interruption, interval, layoff, leisure, letup*, lull, moratorium, pardon, postponement, protraction, recess, relaxation, release, relief, reprieve, rest, stay, stop, ten*, time, time out*, truce; SEE CONCEPTS *121,681,807*

resplendent [adj] *bright, radiant*
beaming, blazing, brilliant, dazzling, effulgent, flaming, gleaming, glittering, glorious, glossy, glowing, gorgeous, irradiant, luminous, lustrous, magnificent, proud, refulgent, shining, shiny, splendid, splendiferous, splendorous, sublime, superb; SEE CONCEPTS *579,589,617*

respond [v] *act in answer to something*
acknowledge, act in response, answer, answer back, behave, be in touch with, come back, come back at, come in, counter, feedback, feel for, field the question*, get back to*, get in touch, react, reciprocate, rejoin, reply, retort, return, talk back; SEE CONCEPTS *45,384*

response [n] *answer, reaction*
acknowledgment, antiphon, back talk*, comeback, counter, double-take*, echo, feedback, hit, kickback*, knee-jerk reaction*, lip*, rejoinder, reply, respond, retort, return, reverberation, riposte, sass*, snappy comeback*, vibes*, wisecrack; SEE CONCEPT *278*

responsibility [n1] *accountability, blame*
albatross*, amenability, answerability, authority, boundness, burden, care, charge, constraint, contract, culpability, duty, encumbrance, engagement, fault, guilt, holding the bag*, importance, incubus, incumbency, liability, obligation, obligatoriness, onus, pledge, power, rap, restraint, subjection, trust; SEE CONCEPT *645*

responsibility [n2] *maturity, trustworthiness*
ability, capableness, capacity, competency, conscientiousness, dependability, dependableness, efficiency, faithfulness, firmness, honesty, levelheadedness, loyalty, rationality, reliability, sensibleness, soberness, stability, steadfastness, trustiness, uprightness; SEE CONCEPTS *411,633*

responsible [adj1] *accountable, in charge*
answerable, at fault, at the helm, authoritative, bonded, bound, bound to, carrying the load, censurable, chargeable, compelled, constrained, contracted, culpable, decision-making, devolving on, duty-bound, engaged, executive, exposed, fettered, guilty, hampered, held, high, important, in authority, in incumbent, liable, minding the store*, obligated, obliged, on the hook*, open, pledged, subject, susceptive, sworn to, tied, to blame, under contract, under obligation; SEE CONCEPT *545*

responsible [adj2] *trustworthy, mature*
able, adult, capable, competent, conscientious, dependable, dutiful, effective, efficient, faithful, firm, levelheaded, loyal, qualified, rational, reliable, self-reliant, sensible, sober, sound, stable, steadfast, steady, tried, trusty, upright; SEE CONCEPTS *401,404*

responsive [adj] *quick to react*
acknowledging, active, alive, answering, awake, aware, compassionate, conscious, forthcoming, impressionable, influenceable, kindhearted, open, passionate, perceptive, persuadable, reactive, receptive, replying, respondent, sensible, sensile, sensitive, sentient, sharp, softhearted, susceptible, susceptive, sympathetic, tender, warm, warmhearted; SEE CONCEPTS *401,542*

rest [n1] *inactivity*
break, breather*, breathing space*, calm, calmness, cessation, coffee break*, comfort, composure, cutoff, downtime*, doze, dreaminess, ease, forty winks*, halt, holiday, hush, idleness, interlude, intermission, interval, leisure, letup*, lull, motionlessness, nap, pause, peace, quiescence, quiet, quietude, recess, recreation, refreshment, relaxation, relief, repose, respite, siesta, silence, sleep, slumber, somnolence, standstill, stay, stillness, stop, time off, tranquillity, vacation; SEE CONCEPTS *315,681,807*

rest [n2] *remainder of something*
balance, bottom of barrel*, dregs, dross, excess, heel, leavings, leftovers, odds and ends*, orts, others, overplus, remains, remnant, residual, residue, residuum, rump, superfluity, surplus; SEE CONCEPTS *260,835*

rest [n3] *base, foundation*
basis, bed, bottom, footing, ground, groundwork, holder, pedestal, pediment, pillar, prop, seat, seating, shelf, stand, stay, support, trestle; SEE CONCEPTS *442,825*

re
re

rest [v1] *be calm; sleep*
be at ease, be comfortable, breathe, compose one-self, doze, dream, drowse, ease off, ease up, idle, laze, lean, let down, let up, lie by, lie down, lie still, loaf, loll, lounge, nap, nod, put feet up*, recline, refresh oneself, relax, repose, sit down, slack, slacken, slack off, sleep, slumber, snooze, spell, stretch out, take a break, take a nap, take five*, take it easy*, take life easy*, take ten*, take time out, unbend, unlax*, unwind, wind down; SEE CONCEPTS *210,315,681*

rest [v2] *lie, recline*
be quiet, be supported, lay, lean, lie still, loll, lounge, pause, prop, repose, roost, settle, sit, stand, stand still, stretch out; SEE CONCEPTS *154,681*

rest [v3] *depend, hinge*
base, be based, be contingent, be dependent, be founded, be seated on, be supported, be upheld, bottom, count, establish, found, ground, hang, lie, predicate, rely, reside, stay, turn; SEE CONCEPT *711*

restaurant [n] *business establishment serving food and drink*
bar, café, cafeteria, canteen, chophouse*, coffee shop, diner, dining room, dive*, doughnut shop, drive-in, eatery, eating house, eating place, fast-food place, greasy spoon*, grill, hamburger stand, hashery*, hideaway*, hotdog stand, inn, joint*, luncheonette, lunchroom, night club, outlet*, pizzeria, saloon, soda fountain, watering hole*; SEE CONCEPTS *439,448,449*

restitution [n] *compensation, repayment*
amends, dues, indemnification, indemnity, payment, quittance, rebate, recompense, redress, refund, reimbursement, remuneration, reparation, reprisal, requital, restoration, return, satisfaction, squaring things*; SEE CONCEPT *344*

restive [adj] *impatient, nervous*
agitated, balky, contrary, edgy, fidgety, fractious, fretful, froward, ill at ease, jittery, jumpy, nervy, obstinate, on edge, ornery*, perverse, recalcitrant, refractory, restless, stubborn, tense, uneasy, unruly, unyielding, uptight; SEE CONCEPTS *401,542*

restless [adj] *not content; moving about*
active, agitated, antsy*, anxious, bundle of nerves*, bustling, changeable, disturbed, edgy, fidgeting, fidgety, fitful, footloose*, fretful, hurried, ill at ease, inconstant, intermittent, irresolute, itchy*, jumpy, nervous, nomadic, on edge, perturbed, restive, roving, sleepless, spasmodic, strung out*, tossing and turning*, transient, troubled, turbulent, uneasy, unpeaceful, unquiet, unrestful, unruly, unsettled, unstable, unsteady, wandering, worried; SEE CONCEPTS *403,542,584*

restlessness [n] *constant motion; discontent*
activity, agitation, ailment, ants*, antsiness*, anxiety, bustle, disquiet, disquietude, disturbance, edginess, excitability, ferment, fitfulness, fretfulness, hurry, inconstancy, inquietude, insomnia, instability, jitters, jumpiness, movement, nervousness, restiveness, transience, turbulence, turmoil, uneasiness, unrest, unsettledness, worriedness; SEE CONCEPTS *410,657,748*

restore [v1] *fix, make new*
bring back, build up, cure, heal, improve, make healthy, make restitution, mend, modernize, reanimate, rebuild, recall, recondition, reconstitute, reconstruct, recover, redeem, reenforce, reerect, re-establish, refresh, refurbish, rehabilitate, reim-

pose, reinstate, reintroduce, rejuvenate, renew, renovate, repair, replace, rescue, retouch, revitalize, revive, revivify, set to rights, strengthen, touch up, update, win back; SEE CONCEPTS *126,212,244*

restore [v2] *give back*
hand back, put back, replace, return, send back; SEE CONCEPTS *131,232*

restrain [v] *keep under control; hold back*
arrest, bind, bottle up, box up, bridle, chain, check, choke back, circumscribe, confine, constrain, contain, control, cool*, cork*, crack down*, curb, curtail, debar, delimit, detain, deter, direct, fetter, gag, govern, guide, hamper, handicap, harness, hem in, hinder, hogtie*, hold, impound, imprison, inhibit, jail, keep, keep down, keep in line*, kill*, limit, lock up, manacle, muzzle, pinion, prevent, proscribe, pull back, repress, restrict, sit on, stay, subdue, suppress, tie down, tie up; SEE CONCEPTS *121,130,191*

restrained [adj] *calm, quiet*
bottled up, calm and collected, chilled, conservative, controlled, cool, corked up, discreet, in charge, in check, inobtrusive, laid-back*, mild, moderate, muted, on a leash*, plain, reasonable, reticent, retiring, self-controlled, shrinking, soft, steady, subdued, tasteful, temperate, unaffable, undemonstrative, under control, under wraps*, unexcessive, unexpansive, unextreme, unobtrusive, uptight, withdrawn; SEE CONCEPTS *401,542*

restraint [n1] *self-control*
abstemiousness, abstinence, caution, coercion, command, compulsion, confines, constraint, control, coolness, curtailment, economy, forbearance, grip, hindrance, hold, inhibition, limitation, moderation, prevention, repression, reserve, restriction, secretiveness, self-denial, self-discipline, self-government, self-possession, self-restraint, silence, suppression, unnaturalness, withholding; SEE CONCEPT *633*

restraint [n2] *limitation; something that holds*
abridgment, arrest, ban, bar, barrier, bondage, bridle, captivity, chains, check, command, confinement, constraint, cramp, curb, decrease, deprivation, detention, determent, deterrence, embargo, fetters, hindrance, impediment, imprisonment, instruction, interdict, limit, manacles, obstacle, obstruction, order, pinions, prohibition, reduction, rein, repression, restriction, rope, stop, stoppage, straitjacket, string*, taboo, weight; SEE CONCEPTS *5,666,674*

restrict [v] *confine, limit situation or ability to participate*
bind, bottle up, bound, chain, check, circumscribe, come down on, constrict, contain, contract, cool down, cramp, curb, decrease, define, delimit, delimitate, demarcate, demark, diminish, encircle, enclose, hamper, handicap, hang up, hem in, hold back, hold down, impede, inclose, inhibit, keep within bounds, keep within limits, moderate, modify, narrow, pin down, prelimit, put away, put on ice*, qualify, reduce, regulate, restrain, send up, shorten, shrink, shut in, surround, temper, tether, tie; SEE CONCEPT *130*

restriction [n] *limit*
ball and chain*, bounds, brake, catch, check, circumscription, condition, confinement, constraint, containment, contraction, control, cramp, curb, custody, demarcation, excess baggage*, fine print*, glitch*, grain of salt*, handicap, hang-

up*, inhibition, limitation, limits, lock*, no-no*, qualification, regulation, reservation, restraint, rule, small difficulty, stint, stipulation, stricture, string*, stumbling block*; SEE CONCEPTS 666,674

result [n] *effect brought about by something*
aftereffect, aftermath, arrangement, backwash*, by-product, close, completion, conclusion, consequence, consummation, corollary, creature, crop, decision, denouement, determination, development, emanation, end, ensual, event, eventuality, execution, finish, fruit*, fruition, harvest, issue, offshoot*, outcome, outcropping, outgrowth, pay-off, proceeds, product, production, reaction, repercussion, returns, sequel, sequence, settlement, termination, upshot; SEE CONCEPT 230

result [v] *happen, develop*
accrue, appear, arise, attend, become of, be due to, come about, come forth, come from, come of, come out, conclude, culminate, derive, effect, emanate, emerge, end, ensue, eventualize, ensure, eventuate, finish, flow, follow, fruit, germinate, grow, happen, issue, occur, originate, pan out, proceed, produce, rise, spring, stem, terminate, turn out, wind up, work out; SEE CONCEPTS 4,119,242

résumé [n] *outline of experience*
abstract, bio*, biography, curriculum vitae, CV*, digest, epitome, precis, recapitulation, review, rundown, sum, summary, summation, summing-up, synopsis, vita, work history; SEE CONCEPTS 271,283

resume [v] *begin again*
assume again, carry on, come back, continue, go on, go on with, keep on, keep up, occupy again, pick up, proceed, reassume, recapitulate, recommence, recoup, regain, reinstitute, reoccupy, reopen, repossess, restart, retake, return to, take back, take up; SEE CONCEPTS 221,239

retain [v1] *hold on to physically or mentally*
absorb, bear in mind, cling to, clutch, contain, detain, enjoy, grasp, hand onto, have, hold, hold fast, husband, keep, keep in mind, keep possession, maintain, memorize, mind, own, possess, preserve, put away, recall, recognize, recollect, remember, reminisce, reserve, restrain, retrospect, save, withhold; SEE CONCEPTS 40,190,710

retain [v2] *hire*
commission, contract, employ, engage, maintain, pay, reserve; SEE CONCEPT 351

retaliate [v] *get even with someone*
even the score*, exact retribution, get, get back at, give and take*, make reprisal, pay, pay back, reciprocate, recompense, repay, requite, retrospect, return, return the compliment, revenge, revive, settle, square accounts*, strike back, take an eye for an eye*, take revenge, turn the tables on*, turn upon, wreak vengeance; SEE CONCEPTS 126,384

retard [v] *hinder, obstruct*
arrest, back off, baffle, balk, bog, bog down, brake, bring to screeching halt*, check, choke, choke off, clog, close off, crimp, dawdle, decelerate, decrease, defer, delay, detain, down, encumber, falter, fetter, flag, hamper, handicap, hang up, hesitate, hold back, hold up, impede, lessen, let up, loaf, loiter, mire, obstruct, postpone, reduce, retardate, set back, shut down, shut off, slacken, slow down, slow up, stall, take down; SEE CONCEPTS 121,130,190,240

reticent [adj] *secretive, quiet*
bashful, clammed up*, close, close-mouthed, dried up*, dummied up*, hesitant, mum, reserved, restrained, shy, silent, taciturn, tight-lipped, uncommunicative, unforthcoming, unspeaking, uptight*; SEE CONCEPTS 267,401

retire [v] *leave a place or responsibility*
absent oneself, decamp, deny oneself, depart, draw back, ebb, exit, fall back, get away, get off, give ground, give up work, give way, go, go away, go to bed, go to one's room*, go to sleep, hand over, hit the sack*, leave service, make vacant, part, pull back, pull out, recede, regress, relinquish, remove, repeal, rescind, resign, retreat, revoke, run along, rusticate, secede, seclude oneself, separate, sever connections, stop working, surrender, take off, turn in, withdraw, yield; SEE CONCEPTS 195,234,351

retiring [adj] *shy, undemonstrative*
backward, bashful, coy, demure, diffident, humble, meek, modest, nongregarious, not forward, quiet, rabbity, recessive, reclusive, reserved, restrained, reticent, self-effacing, shrinking, timid, timorous, unaffable, unassertive, unassuming, unexpansive, unsociable, withdrawing, withdrawn; SEE CONCEPT 401

retort [n] *snappy answer*
antiphon, back answer, back talk, comeback, cooler, counter, crack*, gag*, jape, jest, joke, lip*, parting shot*, quip, rejoinder, repartee, reply, reprisal, respond, response, retaliation, return, revenge, riposte, sally, snappy comeback*, topper*, wisecrack, witticism; SEE CONCEPT 278

retort [v] *answer*
answer back, come back at*, counter, crack*, rebut, rejoin, repay, reply, requite, respond, retaliate, return, riposte, sass*, shoot back*, snap back*, squelch*, talk back, top*; SEE CONCEPT 45

retract [v] *take back; renege on*
abjure, back, back down, back off, back out of, call off, cancel, change one's mind, countermand, deny, disavow, disclaim, disown, draw in, eat one's words*, eliminate, exclude, fall back, forget it, forswear, go back on, have change of heart*, nig*, pull back, pull in, recall, recant, recede, reel in*, renege, renounce, repeal, repudiate, rescind, retreat, retrocede, retrograde, reverse, revoke, rule out, sheathe, suspend, take back, take in, unsay, welsh*, withdraw; SEE CONCEPTS 25,49,119,697

retreat [n1] *departure*
ebb, evacuation, flight, retirement, withdrawal; SEE CONCEPTS 30,195

retreat [n2] *place one goes for peace*
adytum, ark, asylum, cell, cloister, convent, cover, covert, defense, den, habitat, harbor, haunt, haven, hermitage, hideaway, hiding place, ivory tower*, port, privacy, refuge, resort, retirement, safe house, safe place, sanctuary, seclusion, security, shelter, solitude; SEE CONCEPT 516

retreat [v] *pull back, go away*
abandon, avoid, back, back away, back down, back off, back out, backtrack, beat it, cave in, decamp, depart, disengage, draw back, ebb, elude, escape, evacuate, evade, fall back, fold, give ground, go, go along with, go back, hand over, hide, keep aloof, keep apart, lay down, leave, move back, opt out*, pull out, quail, quit, recede, recoil, reel, regress, relinquish, resign, re-

tire, retrocede, retrograde, reverse, run, seclude oneself, sequester, shrink, start back, turn tail*, vacate, withdraw; SEE CONCEPTS *30,195*

retribution [n] *payback for another's action*
avengement, avenging, comeuppance, compensation, counterblow, eye for an eye*, just desserts*, justice, punishment, reckoning, recompense, redress, repayment, reprisal, requital, retaliation, revanche, revenge, reward, satisfaction, vengeance, what for*; SEE CONCEPTS *123,126,384*

retrieve [v] *get back*
bring back, fetch, get back, reacquire, recall, recapture, reclaim, recoup, recover, recruit, redeem, regain, repair, repossess, rescue, restore, salvage, save, win back; SEE CONCEPTS *120,124,131*

retrospect [n] *afterthought*
hindsight, recollection, reconsideration, reexamination, remembering, remembrance, reminiscence, retrospection, review, revision, survey; SEE CONCEPTS *17,40,410*

return [n1] *coming again*
acknowledgment, answer, appearance, arrival, coming, entrance, entry, homecoming, occurrence, reaction, reappearance, rebound, recoil, recoiling, recompense, recompensing, recovery, recrudescence, recurrence, reestablishment, reinstatement, rejoinder, reoccurrence, replacement, repossession, restitution, restoration, restoring, retreat, reversion, revisitation; SEE CONCEPTS *4,695*

return [n2] *earnings, benefit*
accrual, accruement, advantage, avail, compensation, gain, gate, income, interest, lucre, proceeds, profit, reciprocation, recompense, reimbursement, reparation, repayment, requital, results, retaliation, revenue, reward, take*, takings, yield; SEE CONCEPTS *340,710*

return [n3] *answer*
antiphon, comeback, rejoinder, reply, respond, response, retort, riposte; SEE CONCEPT *278*

return [n4] *summary*
account, form, list, record, report, statement, tabulation; SEE CONCEPTS *283,331*

return [v1] *go back, turn back*
back up, bounce back, circle back, come again, come back, double back, go again, hark back to, move back, react, reappear, rebound, recoil, reconsider, recrudesce, recur, reel back, reenter, reexamine, reoccur, repair, repeat, retire, retrace steps, retreat, revert, revisit, revolve, rotate, turn, turn back; SEE CONCEPTS *159,242*

return [v2] *give back, send back*
bestow, carry back, convey, give, hand back, make restitution, pay back, put back, react, rebate, reciprocate, recompense, reestablish, refund, reimburse, reinsert, reinstate, remit, render, repay, replace, requite, reseat, restitute, restore, retaliate, roll back, send, take back, thrust back, toss back, transmit; SEE CONCEPTS *108,131,217*

return [v3] *earn*
bring in, cash in on*, clean up*, clear*, make, make a killing*, net, pay, pay dividend, pay off, repay, score, show profit, yield; SEE CONCEPT *330*

return [v4] *answer*
announce, arrive at, bring in, come back, come in, come to, communicate, declare, deliver, pass, rejoin, render, reply, respond, retort, state, submit; SEE CONCEPT *45*

reveal [v1] *disclose, tell*
acknowledge, admit, affirm, announce, avow, be-

tray, break the news*, bring out into open*, bring to light*, broadcast, come out with, communicate, concede, confess, declare, divulge, explain, expose, get out of system*, give away, give out, give the low-down*, impart, inform, leak, let cat out of the bag*, let fall, let on, let out, let slip*, make known, make plain, make public, notify, proclaim, publish, put cards on table*, report, talk, tell, unfold, utter; SEE CONCEPT *60*

reveal [v2] *show, uncover*
bare, disclose, display, exhibit, expose, flash, lay bare, manifest, open, unclothe, unearth, unmask, unveil; SEE CONCEPT *138*

revel [n] *celebration, merrymaking*
bacchanal, carousal, carouse, debauch, festivity, frolic, gaiety, gala, high jinks*, jollification, jollity, merriment, party, reveling, revelment, saturnalia, skylarking*, spree, wassail, whoopee*; SEE CONCEPTS *292,377*

revel [v] *take pleasure; celebrate*
bask, blow off steam*, carouse, carry on, crow, cut loose*, delight, enjoy, fool around*, frolic, gloat, go on a spree*, indulge, kick up heels*, kid around*, lap up*, lark, let go*, let loose*, live it up*, luxuriate, make merry, paint the town*, rejoice, relish, riot, roister, roll, rollick, run around, savor, step out, thrive, wallow, whoop it up*; SEE CONCEPTS *292,377,384*

revelation [n] *disclosure, telling*
adumbration, announcement, apocalypse, betrayal, blow by blow*, break, broadcasting, clue, communication, cue, discovery, display, divination, divulgement, earful, exhibition, expose, exposition, exposure, eye-opener*, flash, foreshadowing, inspiration, leak, lightning bolt*, manifestation, news, oracle, proclamation, prophecy, publication, scoop*, showing, sign, the latest*, tip, uncovering, unearthing, unveiling, vision; SEE CONCEPTS *60,274*

revelry [n] *merrymaking*
carousal, carouse, celebration, debauch, debauchery, entertainment, festival, festivity, fun, gaiety, high jinks*, jollification, jollity, party, reveling, revelment, saturnalia, spree, whoop-de-do*, whoopla*; SEE CONCEPTS *377,384*

revenge [n] *retaliation for wrong, grievance*
animus, attack, avenging, avengment, counterblow, counterinsurgency, counterplay, eye for an eye*, fight, getting even*, ill will, implacability, malevolence, measure for measure, rancor, repayment, reprisal, requital, retribution, return, ruthlessness, satisfaction, sortie, spitefulness, tit for tat*, vengeance, vengefulness, vindictiveness; SEE CONCEPTS *86,122,384*

revenge [v] *retaliate for wrong, grievance*
avenge, be out for blood*, defend, even the score*, fight back, fix, fix one's wagon*, get, get back at, get even, give comeuppance, give just desserts*, hit back, justify, kick back, make reprisal, match, pay back, pay back in spades*, pay off, punish, reciprocate, redress, repay, requite, retort, return, return the compliment*, score, settle up, settle with, square, stick it to, take an eye for an eye*, turn the tables on*, venge, vindicate; SEE CONCEPTS *86,122,384*

revenue [n] *income, profit*
acquirement, annuity, bottom line*, cash flow, credit, dividend, earnings, emolument, fruits*, fund, gain, gate*, get*, gravy*, handle*, interest, means, net, pay, payoff, perquisite, proceeds, re-

ceipt, resources, return, reward, salary, split*, stock, strength, take*, takings*, wages, wealth, yield; SEE CONCEPTS *329,332,344*

reverberate [*v*] *vibrate in sound*
echo, react, rebound, recoil, redound, re-echo, resound, ring; SEE CONCEPT *65*

revere/reverence [*v*] *have a high opinion of*
admire, adore, apotheosize, appreciate, be in awe of, cherish, defer to, deify, enjoy, esteem, exalt, hold in awe, honor, look up to*, love, magnify, pay homage, prize, put on pedestal*, regard, respect, think highly of, treasure, value, venerate, worship; SEE CONCEPTS *10,32*

reverence [*n*] *high opinion of something*
admiration, adoration, apotheosis, approbation, approval, awe, bow, deference, deification, devotion, devoutness, esteem, fealty, fear, genuflection, high esteem, homage, honor, love, loyalty, obeisance, obsequiousness, piety, praise, prostration, religiousness, respect, veneration, worship; SEE CONCEPTS *10,32*

reverie [*n*] *daydream*
absent-mindedness, absorption, abstraction, castle-building*, castles in the air*, contemplation, detachment, dreaminess, dreaming, fantasy, fool's paradise*, head trip*, inattention, meditation, mind trip*, muse, musing, pensiveness, phantasy, pipe dream*, preoccupation, study, thought, trance, trip*, woolgathering*; SEE CONCEPTS *529,532*

reverse [*n1*] *opposite*
about-face, antipode, antipole, antithesis, back, bottom, change of mind, contra, contradiction, contradictory, contrary, converse, counter, counterpole, flip-flop*, flip side*, inverse, other side, overturning, rear, regression, retrogression, retroversion, reversal, reversion, switch, turn, turnabout, turn around, turning, underside, verso, volte-face, wrong side; SEE CONCEPTS *665,697,738*

reverse [*n2*] *bad luck; failure*
adversity, affliction, bath, blow, catastrophe, check, conquering, defeat, disappointment, hardship, misadventure, misfortune, mishap, repulse, reversal, setback, trial, turnabout, vanquishment, vicissitude; SEE CONCEPTS *674,679*

reverse [*v1*] *turn upside down or backwards*
about-face*, back, backpedal*, backtrack, back up, capsize, double backpack*, evaginate, evert, exchange, flip-flop*, go back, go backwards, interchange, inverse, invert, move backwards, overturn, rearrange, retreat, revert, shift, switch, transfer, transplace, transpose, turn around, turn back, turn over, upend, upset; SEE CONCEPTS *158,213,697*

reverse [*v2*] *cancel, change*
alter, annul, backpedal*, backtrack, convert, countermand, declare null and void*, dismantle, double back*, flip-flop*, invalidate, lift, modify, negate, nullify, overrule, overset, overthrow, overturn, quash, recall, renege, repeal, rescind, retract, revoke, set aside, turn around, turn the tables*, undo, upset; SEE CONCEPTS *13,234,697*

revert [*v*] *return to an earlier, less-developed condition*
about-face*, backslide, change, come back, decline, degenerate, deteriorate, fall off the wagon*, flip-flop*, go back, hark back, inverse, invert, lapse, react, recrudesce, recur, regress, relapse, resume, retrograde, retrogress, return, take up

where left off*, throw back, transpose, turn, turn back; SEE CONCEPTS *13,385,698*

review [*n1*] *examination, study*
analysis, another look*, audit, check, checkup, drill, file, fresh look*, inspection, march past*, once-over*, parade, procession, reassessment, recapitulation, reconsideration, reflection, report, rethink, retrospect, revision, scan, scrutiny, second look, second thought, survey, view; SEE CONCEPTS *24,103*

review [*n2*] *critique; summary*
abstract, analysis, appraisal, article, assessment, blurb, book review, canvass, column, comment, commentary, criticism, discourse, discussion, dissertation, essay, evaluation, exposition, inspection, investigation, journal, judgment, magazine, mention, monograph, notice, organ, outline, pan*, periodical, recapitulation, redraft, reviewal, revision, study, synopsis, theme, thesis, treatise, write-up; SEE CONCEPTS *280,283*

review [*v1*] *go over again*
analyze, brush up*, call to mind, check out, check thoroughly, debrief, go over, hash over*, look at again, look back on, polish up, reassess, recall, recap*, recapitulate, recollect, reconsider, reevaluate, reexamine, reflect on, rehash*, remember, rethink, revise, revisit, run over, run through, run up flagpole*, summon up, take another look, think over; SEE CONCEPT *103*

review [*v2*] *criticize, scrutinize*
assess, bad-mouth*, correct, discuss, evaluate, examine, give one's opinion, inspect, judge, knock*, pan*, put down*, rave, read through, re-edit, revise, rip, skin alive*, slam*, study, swipe at*, take down*, trash*, weigh, write a critique, zap*; SEE CONCEPTS *49,52*

revise [*v*] *correct, edit*
alter, amend, blue pencil*, change, clean up, compare, cut, debug, develop, emend, go over, improve, launder, look over, modify, overhaul, perfect, polish, recalibrate, recast, reconsider, redo, redraft, redraw, reexamine, rehash, reorganize, restyle, revamp, review, rework, rewrite, run through, scan, scrub, scrutinize, study, tighten, update, upgrade; SEE CONCEPTS *79,126,244*

revision [*n*] *change; rewriting*
afterlight, alteration, amendment, correction, editing, emendation, homework, improvement, modification, overhauling, polish, recension, reconsideration, rectification, rectifying, redaction, redraft, reediting, reexamination, rescript, restyling, retrospect, retrospection, review, revisal, revise, updating; SEE CONCEPTS *79,126,244,700*

revival [*n*] *rebirth, reawakening*
awakening, cheering, consolation, enkindling, freshening, invigoration, quickening, reanimation, recovery, recrudescence, regeneration, rejuvenation, renaissance, renascence, renewal, restoration, resurgence, resurrection, resuscitation, revitalization, revivification, risorgimento; SEE CONCEPTS *119,221*

revive [*v*] *start again; bring back to life*
animate, arouse, awaken, bounce back*, breathe new life into*, brighten, bring around*, bring to*, cheer, come around*, come to life, comfort, console, encourage, energize, enkindle, enliven, exhilarate, gladden, inspirit, invigorate, make whole*, overcome, please, quicken, rally, reanimate, recondition, recover, refresh, rejuvenate,

re
re

rekindle, relieve, renew, renovate, repair, restore, resurrect, resuscitate, revitalize, rouse, snap out of it*, solace, spring up*, strengthen, touch up*, wake up; SEE CONCEPTS *13,221,469,697*

revoke [v] *take back; cancel*
abjure, abolish, abrogate, annul, back out of, backpedal*, call back, call off, countermand, counterorder, declare null and void*, deny, disclaim, dismantle, dismiss, disown, erase, expunge, forswear, invalidate, lift, negate, nix*, nullify, obliterate, quash*, recall, recant, remove, renounce, repeal, repudiate, rescind, retract, reverse, rub out*, scrub*, set aside, vacate, void, wipe out*, withdraw; SEE CONCEPTS *50,88, 121,234*

revolt [n] *uprising*
defection, displeasure, insurgency, insurrection, mutiny, rebellion, revolution, rising, sedition; SEE CONCEPTS *106,300,320*

revolt [v1] *rebel, rise up against*
arise, boycott, break, defect, defy, drop out, get out of line*, insurrect, make waves*, mutiny, oppose, opt out, overthrow, overturn, rebel, renounce, resist, riot, rock the boat*, strike, take up arms, turn against; SEE CONCEPTS *106,300,320*

revolt [v2] *disgust, nauseate*
crawl*, gross out*, make flesh crawl*, make sick, offend, pain, reluct, repel, repulse, shock, sicken, turn off*, turn stomach*; SEE CONCEPTS *7,19*

revolting [adj] *disgusting, nauseating*
abhorrent, abominable, appalling, awful, distasteful, foul, gross, horrible, horrid, loathsome, nasty, nauseous, noisome, obnoxious, obscene, offensive, repellent, repugnant, repulsive, rotten, shocking, sickening, sleazy*, vile; SEE CONCEPT *529*

revolution [n1] *drastic action or change, often in politics*
anarchy, bloodshed, cabal, coup, coup d'état, crime, debacle, destruction, disorder, foment, golpe, guerrilla activity, innovation, insubordination, insurgency, metamorphosis, mutiny, outbreak, overthrow, overturn, plot, radical change, rebellion, reformation, reversal, revolt, rising, row, shake-up, shift, strife, strike, subversion, transformation, tumult, turbulence, turmoil, turnover, underground activity, unrest, upheaval, uprising, uproar, upset, violence; SEE CONCEPTS *106,300,320,697*

revolution [n2] *circuit around something*
circle, circumvolution, cycle, gyration, gyre, lap, orbit, pirouette, reel, revolve, revolving, roll, rotation, round, spin, swirl, turn, turning, twirl, wheel, whirl; SEE CONCEPTS *436,484,738,792*

revolve [v1] *turn, circle*
circumduct, go around, gyrate, gyre, orbit, roll, rotate, spin, turn around, twist, wheel, whirl; SEE CONCEPTS *147,738*

revolve [v2] *think about*
consider, deliberate, meditate, mull over, muse, ponder, reflect, roll, ruminate, study, think over, turn over in mind; SEE CONCEPT *17*

revulsion [n] *disgust, hatred*
abhorrence, abomination, aversion, detestation, dislike, distaste, hate, horror, loathing, recoil, repugnance, repulsion; SEE CONCEPT *29*

reward [n] *payment, prize*
accolade, award, benefit, bonus, bounty, carrot*, comeuppance, compensation, crown*, cue, dividend, feather in cap*, fringe benefit, gain, garland, goodies*, gravy*, grease*, guerdon, honor, just deserts*, meed, merit, perks*, plum*, premium, profit, punishment, recompense, remuneration, repayment, requital, retribution, return, salve, strokes*, sweetener*, tip, wages; SEE CONCEPTS *337,344*

reward [v] *pay; give prize*
compensate, honor, recompense, remunerate, repay, requite, stroke*, sugarcoat*, take care of*, tip; SEE CONCEPTS *108,132,341*

rewarding [adj] *beneficial, pleasing*
advantageous, edifying, fruitful, fulfilling, gainful, gratifying, productive, profitable, remunerative, satisfying, valuable, worthwhile; SEE CONCEPTS *548,572*

rhetoric [n] *wordiness; long speech*
address, balderdash*, big talk*, bombast, composition, discourse, elocution, eloquence, flowery language, fustian, grandiloquence, hot air*, hyperbole, magniloquence, oration, oratory, pomposity, rant, verbosity; SEE CONCEPTS *51,277,278*

rhetorical [adj] *wordy; flowery in speech*
articulate, aureate, bombastic, declamatory, eloquent, embellished, euphuistic, exaggerated, flamboyant, flashy*, florid, fluent, glib*, grand, grandiloquent, grandiose, high-flown, hyperbolic, imposing, inflated, magniloquent, mouthy, oratorical, ornate, ostentatious, overblown, overdone, overwrought, pompous, pretentious, showy, silver-tongued, sonorous, stilted, swollen, tumescent, tumid, turgid, verbose, vocal, voluble, windy*; SEE CONCEPT *267*

rhyme [n] *poetry in which lines end with like sounds*
alliteration, beat, cadence, couplet, doggerel, half-rhyme, harmony, iambic pentameter, measure, meter, nursery rhyme, ode, poem, poesy, poetry, rhythm, rune, slant rhyme, song, tune, verse, vowel-chime; SEE CONCEPTS *278,595*

rhythm [n] *beat, accent of sound, music*
bounce, cadence, cadency, downbeat, flow, lilt, measure, meter, metre, movement, pattern, periodicity, pulse, regularity, rhyme, rise and fall, swing, tempo, time, uniformity; SEE CONCEPT *595*

ribald [adj] *vulgar, obscene*
base, bawdy, blue*, coarse, devilish, earthy, fast*, filthy*, foul-mouthed, gross*, indecent, indecorous, juicy, lascivious, lewd, licentious, lowdown and dirty, naughty, off-color, out of line*, purple*, racy, rascally, raunchy, raw*, risqué*, rogue, rough, rude, salacious, salty, scabrous, scurrilous, sly, smutty, spicy*, unbecoming; SEE CONCEPTS *267,401*

rich [n] *wealthy people or institutions*
bountiful, haves*, landed, monied, nouveau riche, old money, upper class, upper crust*, well-to-do*; SEE CONCEPT *423*

rich [adj1] *having a lot of money*
affluent, bloated, comfortable, easy, fat, filthy rich*, flush, gilded, in clover*, independent, in the money*, loaded*, made of money*, moneyed, opulent, plush, propertied, prosperous, rolling in it*, swimming, upscale, uptown, wealthy, well-heeled*, well-off*, well provided for*, well-to-do*, worth a million*; SEE CONCEPT *334*

rich [adj2] *abundant, well-supplied*
abounding, ample, chic, classy, copious, costly, deluxe, elaborate, elegant, embellished, expensive, exquisite, extravagant, exuberant, fancy, fe-

cund, fertile, fine, fruitful, full, gorgeous, grand, high-class, lavish, lush, luxurious, magnificent, ornate, palatial, plenteous, plentiful, plush, posh, precious, palatial, productive, prolific, resplendent, ritzy*, smart, snazzy*, spiffy, splendid, stylish, sumptuous, superb, swank*, swanky*, swell*, valuable, well-endowed; SEE CONCEPTS 334,589,771

rich [*adj3*] *flavorful*
creamy, delicious, fatty, full-bodied, heavy, highly flavored, juicy, luscious, nourishing, nutritious, oily, satisfying, savory, spicy, succulent, sustaining, sweet, tasty; SEE CONCEPT 613

rich [*adj4*] *full in color or sound*
bright, canorous, deep, dulcet, eloquent, expressive, intense, mellifluous, mellow, resonant, rotund, significant, silvery, sonorous, strong, vibrant, vivid, warm; SEE CONCEPTS 406,594,618

rich [*adj5*] *very funny*
absurd, amusing, comical, diverting, droll, entertaining, farcical, foolish, hilarious, humorous, incongruous, laughable, ludicrous, odd, preposterous, queer, ridiculous, risible, side-splitting*, slaying*, splitting*, strange; SEE CONCEPTS 267,529

riches [*n*] *money and possessions*
abundance, affluence, assets, clover, fortune, gold, lap of luxury*, means, opulence, plenty, property, resources, richness, substance, treasure, wealth, worth; SEE CONCEPTS 335,340,446,710

rickety [*adj*] *unsound, broken-down*
broken, decrepit, derelict, dilapidated, feeble, flimsy, fragile, frail, imperfect, infirm, insecure, jerry-built*, precarious, ramshackle, rattletrap*, rocky, shaky, tottering, tottery, tumble-down, unsteady, wavering, weak, wobbly; SEE CONCEPT 488

rid [*v*] *do away with; free*
abolish, clear, deliver, disabuse, disburden, disembarrass, disencumber, dump*, eject, eliminate, eradicate, expel, exterminate, extinguish, extirpate, fire, give the brush*, heave-ho*, junk*, kiss goodbye*, liberate, make free, purge, release, relieve, remove, roust, scrap, send packing*, shake off, shed, throw away, throw out, toss out, unburden, unload, uproot; SEE CONCEPTS 180,211

riddle [*n*] *brain-teaser*
bewilderment, brain-twister*, charade, closed book*, complexity, complication, confusion, conundrum, cryptogram, dilemma, distraction, doubt, embarrassment, enigma, entanglement, intricacy, knotty question*, labyrinth, maze, mindboggler*, mystery, mystification, perplexity, plight, poser, predicament, problem, puzzle, puzzlement, quandary, question, rebus, sixty-four dollar question*, stickler*, strait, stumper*, teaser, tough nut to crack*, tough proposition, twister*; SEE CONCEPT 532

riddle [*v*] *perforate, permeate*
bore, corrupt, damage, honeycomb*, impair, infest, mar, pepper, pervade, pierce, pit, puncture, spoil; SEE CONCEPTS 156,220

ride [*n*] *journey, trip in vehicle*
airing, commute, drive, excursion, expedition, hitch, jaunt, joyride*, lift, outing, pick up*, run, spin, Sunday drive, tour, transportation, turn, whirl; SEE CONCEPT 224

ride [*v1*] *carry or be carried*
be supported, control, cruise, curb, direct, drift, drive, float, go, go with, guide, handle, hitch a ride*, hitchhike, journey, manage, motor, move, post, progress, restrain, roll, sit, sit on, thumb a ride*, tool around*, tour, travel; SEE CONCEPTS 94,148,224

ride [*v2*] *dominate, oppress*
afflict, annoy, badger, bait, be arbitrary, be autocratic, berate, disparage, domineer, enslave, grip, harass, harry, haunt, hector, hound, override, persecute, rate, reproach, revile, scold, torment, torture, tyrannize, upbraid; SEE CONCEPTS 7,14,19

ridge [*n*] *raised part of solid*
backbone, chine, corrugation, crease, crinkle, elevation, esker, fold, furrow, hill, hogback, moraine, parapet, plica, pole, range, rib, rim, rimple, rivel, ruck, seam, spine, upland, wrinkle; SEE CONCEPTS 471,509,513

ridicule [*n*] *contemptuous laughter at someone or something*
badinage, banter, buffoonery, burlesque, caricature, chaff, comeback, contempt, derision, dig*, disdain, disparagement, farce, foolery, gibe, irony, jab*, jeer, laughter, leer, mockery, mordancy, needling, parody, parting shot*, persiflage, putdown*, put-on*, raillery, rally, razz*, rib*, roast*, sarcasm, sardonicism, satire, scorn, slam*, sneer*, swipe*, taunt, taunting, travesty; SEE CONCEPTS 54,59

ridicule [*v*] *make contemptuous fun of something or someone*
banter, caricature, cartoon, chaff, deflate, deride, expose, fleer, gibe, haze, humiliate, jape, jeer, jive, jolly, josh*, kid, lampoon, laugh at, make a fool of*, make a game of*, make a laughingstock*, make fun of, mimic, mock, needle, pan*, parody, poke fun at*, pooh-pooh*, pull one's leg*, put down*, quiz, rag, rail at, rally, razz*, rib*, ride*, roast*, run down*, satirize, scoff, scorn, send up*, show up, sneer, takeoff, taunt, travesty, twit, unmask; SEE CONCEPTS 54,59

ridiculous [*adj*] *stupid, funny*
absurd, antic, bizarre, comic, comical, contemptible, daffy*, derisory, droll, fantastic, farcical, foolheaded*, foolish, gelastic, goofy*, grotesque, harebrained*, hilarious, impossible, incredible, jerky*, laughable, ludicrous, nonsensical, nutty*, outrageous, preposterous, risible, sappy*, silly, slaphappy*, unbelievable, wacky*; SEE CONCEPTS 529,548,552

rife [*adj*] *overflowing*
abounding, abundant, alive, common, current, epidemic, extensive, frequent, general, many, multitudinous, numerous, pandemic, plentiful, popular, prevailing, prevalent, profuse, raging, rampant, regnant, replete, ruling, swarming, teeming, thronged, ubiquitous, universal, widespread; SEE CONCEPTS 771,772

rifle [*v*] *ransack*
burglarize, burgle, despoil, go through, grab, gut, loot, pillage, plunder, rip, rip off*, rob, rummage, sack, smash and grab*, strip, take, tip over*, trash*, waste*; SEE CONCEPT 139

rift [*n1*] *break, crack*
breach, chink, cleavage, cleft, cranny, crevice, fault, fissure, flaw, fracture, gap, hiatus, interruption, interval, opening, parting, rent, rima, rime, space, split; SEE CONCEPT 513

rift [*n2*] *difference of opinion*
alienation, breach, break, clash, disagreement, division, estrangement, falling out*, misunderstand-

re
ri

ing, quarrel, rupture, schism, separation, split;
SEE CONCEPTS 46,106,388

rig [n] *equipment*
accouterments, apparatus, equipage, fittings, fixtures, gear, machinery, outfit, paraphernalia, tackle; SEE CONCEPT 496

rig [v] *outfit, supply*
accouter, appoint, arm, array, attire, clothe, costume, dress, equip, fit out, furnish, gear, kit, provision, set up, turn out; SEE CONCEPTS 140,167,182

rig [v2] *arrange for certain outcome*
doctor, engineer, fake, falsify, fiddle with*, fix, gerrymander*, juggle, manipulate, tamper with, trump up*; SEE CONCEPTS 202,697

right [n1] *privilege*
advantage, appanage, authority, benefit, birthright, business, claim, comeuppance, desert, deserving, due, exemption, favor, franchise, freedom, immunity, interest, liberty, license, merit, permission, perquisite, power, preference, prerogative, priority, title; SEE CONCEPT 376

right [n2] *justice, morality*
correctness, emancipation, enfranchisement, equity, freedom, good, goodness, honor, independence, integrity, lawfulness, legality, liberty, morality, properness, propriety, reason, rectitude, righteousness, rightness, straight, truth, uprightness, virtue; SEE CONCEPT 645

right [adj1] *fair, just*
appropriate, condign, conscientious, deserved, due, equitable, ethical, fitting, good, honest, honorable, justifiable, lawful, legal, legitimate, merited, moral, proper, requisite, righteous, rightful, scrupulous, stand-up*, suitable, true, upright, virtuous; SEE CONCEPT 545

right [adj2] *accurate, precise*
absolute, admissible, amen, authentic, bona fide, complete, correct, exact, factual, faithful, free of error, genuine, immaculate, indubitable, inerrant, infallible, just, nice, on the money*, on the nose*, out-and-out*, perfect, proper, punctilious, real, right as rain*, righteous, right on*, rigorous, satisfactory, solemn, sound, strict, sure, thoroughgoing, true, undistorted, undoubted, unerring, unmistaken, utter, valid, veracious, veridical, veritable, watertight*; SEE CONCEPTS 535,557,582

right [adj3] *appropriate, fitting*
acceptable, adequate, advantageous, all right, becoming, befitting, comely, comme il faut, common, condign, convenient, correct, decent, decorous, deserved, desirable, done*, due, favorable, felicitous, fit, good, happy, ideal, merited, nice, opportune, proper, propitious, requisite, rightful, satisfactory, seemly, sufficient, suitable, tolerable; SEE CONCEPTS 558,572

right [adj4] *sane, healthy*
all there, balanced, circumspect, compos mentis, discerning, discreet, enlightened, far-sighted, fine, fit, hale, in good health*, in the pink*, judicious, lucid, normal, penetrating, rational, reasonable, sound, unimpaired, up to par*, well, wise; SEE CONCEPTS 314,403

right [adj5] *conservative politically*
die-hard*, old-line*, orthodox, reactionary, right wing, traditionalistic; SEE CONCEPTS 529,689

right [adj6] *opposite of left*
clockwise, dexter, dextral, right-handed; SEE CONCEPT 581

right [v] *fix, correct*
adjust, amend, balance, clean up, compensate for, debug*, dial back*, doctor*, do justice, emend, fiddle with*, fix up, go straight, launder, make up for, mend, overhaul, patch, pick up, put in place, put right, recalibrate, recompense, recondition, reconstruct, rectify, redress, repair, restore, reward, scrub, set straight, settle, set upright, shape up, sort out, square, straighten, straighten out, turn around, vindicate; SEE CONCEPTS 126,212

right [adv1] *accurately, precisely*
absolutely, all the way, altogether, bang*, clear, completely, correctly, entirely, exactly, factually, fully, genuinely, just, perfectly, precisely, quite, sharp, slap, smack-dab*, square, squarely, thoroughly, totally, truly, utterly, well, wholly; SEE CONCEPTS 531,557,582

right [adv2] *appropriately, suitably*
acceptably, adequately, amply, aptly, becomingly, befittingly, fittingly, properly, satisfactorily, well; SEE CONCEPTS 558,572

right [adv3] *fairly, justly*
conscientiously, decently, dispassionately, equitably, ethically, evenly, honestly, honorably, impartially, lawfully, legitimately, morally, objectively, properly, reliably, righteously, sincerely, squarely, virtuously, without bias, without prejudice; SEE CONCEPT 545

right [adv4] *beneficially*
advantageous, exceedingly, extremely, favorably, for the better, fortunately, highly, notably, perfectly, remarkably, to advantage, very, well; SEE CONCEPTS 537,572

right [adv5] *directly, without delay*
at once, away, direct, due, first off, forthwith, immediately, instanter, instantly, now, promptly, quickly, right away, straight, straight away, straightly, undeviatingly; SEE CONCEPT 799

righteous [adj] *good, honest*
angelic, blameless, charitable, commendable, conscientious, creditable, deserving, devoted, devout, dutiful, equitable, ethical, exemplary, fair, faithful, godlike, guiltless, holy, honorable, impartial, innocent, irreproachable, just, laudable, law-abiding, matchless, meritorious, moral, noble, peerless, philanthropic, philanthropical, praiseworthy, punctilious, pure, reverent, right-minded, saintly, scrupulous, sinless, spiritual, sterling, trustworthy, upright, virtuous, worthy; SEE CONCEPT 545

rightful [adj] *legitimate*
applicable, appropriate, apt, authorized, befitting, bona fide, canonical, card-carrying*, condign, deserved, due, ethical, fair, fit, fitting, holding water, honest, just, kosher*, lawful, legal, legit*, merited, moral, moralistic, noble, official, on the level*, on the up and up*, orthodox, permitted, principled, proper, real, requisite, right, right-minded, suitable, true, twenty-four carat*, valid, virtuous; SEE CONCEPTS 545,558

rigid [adj] *stiff, strict, severe*
adamant, adamantine, austere, bullheaded, changeless, chiseled*, dead set*, definite, determined, exact, firm, fixed, hard, hard-line*, harsh, incompliant, inelastic, inexorable, inflexible, intransigent, invariable, locked in*, obdurate, rigorous, set, set in stone*, single-minded, solid, static, stern, strait-laced*, stringent, tough nut to crack*, unalterable, unbending, unbreakable, unchanging, uncompromising, undeviating, unmov-

ing, unpermissive, unrelenting, unyielding; SEE CONCEPTS 403,534,535

rigor [n] *strictness, exactness*

accuracy, affliction, asperity, austerity, conscientiousness, conventionality, difficulty, exactitude, firmness, hardness, hardship, harshness, inclemency, inflexibility, intolerance, meticulousness, obduracy, ordeal, preciseness, precision, privation, punctiliousness, rigidity, roughness, severity, sternness, stiffness, stringency, suffering, tenacity, thoroughness, traditionalism, trial, tribulation, vicissitude, visitation; SEE CONCEPTS 638,654,666

rigorous [adj] *severe; exact*

accurate, ascetic, austere, bitter, brutal, burdensome, correct, definite, dogmatic, exact, exacting, hard, harsh, inclement, inflexible, intemperate, ironhanded, meticulous, nice, onerous, oppressive, precise, proper, punctilious, right, rigid, rugged, scrupulous, stern, stiff, strict, stringent, uncompromising, unpermissive; SEE CONCEPTS 535,557,565

rile [v] *anger, upset*

acerbate, aggravate, annoy, bother, bug*, disturb, exasperate, gall, get one's goat*, get under skin*, grate, inflame, irk, irritate, nettle, peeve, pique, provoke, put out*, roil, rub one the wrong way*, try one's patience*, vex; SEE CONCEPTS 7,19

rim [n] *border; top edge*

band, brim, brink, brow, circumference, confine, curb, end, fringe, hem, ledge, limit, line, lip, margin, outline, perimeter, periphery, ring, skirt, strip, terminus, top, verge; SEE CONCEPTS 484,836

ring [n1] *circle; circular object*

arena, band, brim, circlet, circuit, circus, enclosure, eye, girdle, halo, hoop, loop, ringlet, rink, round; SEE CONCEPTS 436,446

ring [n2] *group participating together*

association, band, bloc, bunch, cabal, camp, cartel, cell, circle, clan, clique, coalition, combination, combine, corner, coterie, crew, crowd, faction, gang, in-group, junta, junto, knot, Mafia, mob, monopoly, organization, outfit, party, pool, push, racket, syndicate, troop, troupe, trust; SEE CONCEPTS 325,381

ring [n3] *chime, bell-like noise*

buzz, call, clangor, clank, jangle, jingle, knell, peal, reverberation, tinkle, toll, vibration; SEE CONCEPT 595

ring [v1] *encircle*

begird, belt, circle, circumscribe, compass, confine, enclose, encompass, gird, girdle, hem in, inclose, loop, move around, rim, round, seal off, surround; SEE CONCEPT 758

ring [v2] *chime; make bell-like noise*

bang, beat, bong, buzz, clang, clap, jangle, jingle, knell, peal, play, pull, punch, resonate, resound, reverberate, sound, strike, tinkle, tintinnabulate, toll, vibrate; SEE CONCEPT 65

rinse [v] *wash off, out*

bathe, clean, cleanse, dip, flush, soak, splash, wash, water, wet; SEE CONCEPTS 165,256

riot [n1] *uprising, disorder*

anarchism, anarchy, branigan*, brawl, burst, commotion, confusion, distemper, disturbance, flap, fray, free-for-all*, fuss, hassle, lawlessness, misrule, mix-up, mob violence, protest, quarrel, racket, row, ruckus, ruction, rumble, rumpus, run-in, scene, shivaree, shower, snarl, stir, storm,

street fighting, strife, to-do*, trouble, tumult, turbulence, turmoil, uproar, wingding*; SEE CONCEPTS 106,300

riot [n2] *very funny happening*

boisterousness, carousal, confusion, excess, extravaganza, festivity, flourish, frolic, high jinks*, howl*, jollification, lark, merrymaking, panic*, revelry, romp, scream*, sensation, show, sidesplitter*, skylark*, smash*, splash*, tumult, uproar, wow*; SEE CONCEPTS 384,386

riot [v] *protest; cause an uproar*

arise, debauch, dissipate, fight, go on rampage, racket, rampage, rebel, revolt, rise, run riot*, stir up trouble*, take to the streets*; SEE CONCEPTS 106,300

rip [n] *tear, cut*

cleavage, gash, hole, laceration, rent, slash, slit, split; SEE CONCEPTS 309,513

rip [v] *tear, cut*

burst, claw, cleave, fray, frazzle, gash, hack, lacerate, rend, rive, score, shred, slash, slit, split; SEE CONCEPT 214

ripe [adj1] *fully developed; experienced*

accomplished, adult, aged, completed, consummate, conditioned, enlightened, enriched, filled out, finished, fit, full, full-blown, full-fledged, fully grown, grown, grown-up, increased, informed, in readiness, judicious, learned, mature, matured, mellow, overdue, perfected, plump, prepared, prime, ready, ripened, sagacious, seasoned, skilled, skillful, sound, timely, usable, versed, well-timed, wise; SEE CONCEPTS 462,560,578,797

ripe [adj2] *favorable, ideal*

auspicious, opportune, right, suitable, timely; SEE CONCEPT 558

rip off [v] *rob; trick*

abuse, appropriate, bleed*, cheat, con*, cop*, defraud, dupe, exploit, filch*, fleece*, heist, impose on*, lift*, nab*, pilfer, pinch, plunder, ransack, relieve, rifle, skin*, soak*, stick*, swindle, swipe, thieve, use; SEE CONCEPTS 139,192

rip-off [n] *trick; robbery*

cheat, con*, exploitation, fraud, gyp*, larceny, lift*, pinch*, purloining, racket*, steal, stealing, swindle, theft, thievery, thieving; SEE CONCEPTS 139,192

rise [n1] *increase, improvement*

acceleration, accession, accretion, addition, advance, advancement, aggrandizement, ascent, augmentation, boost, breakthrough, climb, distention, doubling, enlargement, growth, heightening, hike, increment, inflation, intensification, intensifying, multiplication, piling up, progress, promotion, raise, stacking up, step-up, surge, swell, upgrade, upsurge, upswing, upturn, waxing; SEE CONCEPTS 700,780

rise [n2] *movement upward; upward slope*

acclivity, ascension, ascent, climb, elevation, eminence, highland, hillock, incline, lift, mount, rising, rising ground, soaring, surge, towering, upland, upsurge; SEE CONCEPTS 166,738,752

rise [v1] *get up; ascend*

arise, arouse, aspire, awake, be erect, be located, be situated, blast off*, bob up*, climb, come up, get out of bed, get steeper, get to one's feet*, go uphill, grow, have foundation, levitate, lift, mount, move up, pile out*, push up, reach up, rise and shine*, rise up, rocket, roll out*, rouse, scale, sit up, slope upwards, soar, sprout, stand

ri
ri

up, straighten up, surface, surge, surmount, sweep upward, tower, turn out, up*, upspring; SEE CONCEPTS 154,166,738

rise [v2] *increase, grow*
accelerate, add to, advance, aggravate, arise, ascend, augment, billow, build, bulge, climb, deepen, distend, double, enhance, enlarge, expand, go through the roof*, go up, heighten, improve, inflate, intensate, intensify, levitate, lift, magnify, mount, move up, multiply, perk up, pick up, pile up, raise, redouble, rouse, soar, speed up, spread, stack up, swell, take off, upsurge, wax; SEE CONCEPTS 700,780

rise [v3] *progress in business*
advance, be elevated, be promoted, better oneself, climb the ladder*, flourish, get on, get somewhere*, go places*, progress, prosper, succeed, thrive, work one's way up*; SEE CONCEPTS 351,704

rise [v4] *become apparent*
appear, arise, befall, begin, betide, chance, come, crop up, dawn, derive, develop, emanate, emerge, eventuate, fall out*, flare up, flow, go, happen, head, issue, loom, occur, originate, proceed, spring, stem, surface, transpire, turn up*; SEE CONCEPTS 4,716

rise [v5] *rebel*
insurrect, mount, mutiny, resist, revolt, riot, take up arms; SEE CONCEPT 106

risk [n] *chance taken*
accident, contingency, danger, exposedness, exposure, flyer*, fortuity, fortune, gamble, hazard, header, jeopardy, liability, liableness, luck, openness, opportunity, peril, plunge, possibility, prospect, shot in the dark*, speculation, stab*, uncertainty, venture, wager; SEE CONCEPTS 675,693

risk [v] *take a chance*
adventure, beard, be caught short*, brave, chance, compromise, confront, dare, defy, defy danger, encounter, endanger, expose to danger, face, gamble, go out of one's depth*, hang by a thread*, hazard, imperil, jeopardize, jeopardy, leap before looking*, leave to luck*, meet, menace, peril, play with fire*, plunge, put in jeopardy, run the chance, run the risk, skate on thin ice*, speculate, tackle, take a flyer*, take a header*, take a plunge*, take on*, take the liberty*, venture, wager; SEE CONCEPTS 87,100

risky [adj] *dangerous*
chancy, delicate, dicey*, endangered, fraught with danger*, going for broke*, hairy*, hanging by a thread*, hazardous, iffy*, insecure, jeopardous, long shot*, not a prayer*, off the deep end*, on slippery ground*, on the spot*, on thin ice*, out on a limb*, perilous, playing with fire*, precarious, rocky*, sensitive, speculative, ticklish, touch-and-go*, touchy, treacherous, tricky, uncertain, unhealthy, unsafe, unsound, venturesome, wicked, wide-open; SEE CONCEPT 548

risqué [adj] *improper, referring to sex*
amoral, bawdy*, blue*, breezy, crude, daring, dirty, earthy, erotic, filthy*, foul, gross*, hot*, immodest, immoral, indecent, indecorous, indelicate, indiscreet, inelegant, lewd, lurid, naughty, obscene, off-base*, off-color, offensive, out-of-line, provocative, purple*, racy, raw, ribald, salacious, salty, shady, sizzling, smart, smutty,

spicy*, suggestive, unrefined, vulgar, wanton, warm, wicked, X-rated*; SEE CONCEPTS 267,545,548

rite [n] *ceremony, tradition*
act, celebration, ceremonial, communion, custom, form, formality, liturgy, observance, occasion, ordinance, practice, procedure, ritual, sacrament, service, solemnity; SEE CONCEPTS 377,386

ritual [n] *ceremony, tradition*
act, ceremonial, communion, convention, custom, form, formality, habit, liturgy, observance, ordinance, practice, prescription, procedure, protocol, red tape*, rite, routine, sacrament, service, solemnity, stereotype, usage; SEE CONCEPTS 386,634,688

rival [n] *person who opposes in competition*
adversary, antagonist, bandit, buddy, challenger, competition, competitor, contender, contestant, emulator, entrant, equal, equivalent, match, opponent, opposite number, peer; SEE CONCEPTS 348,366,423

rival [adj] *opposing*
battling, combatant, combating, competing, competitive, conflicting, contending, contesting, cutthroat, disputing, emulating, emulous, equal, opposed, striving, vying; SEE CONCEPTS 542,564

rival [v] *oppose; be a match for*
amount, approach, approximate, bear comparison with*, come near to*, come up to*, compare with, compete, contend, contest, correspond, emulate, equal, go after, go for, jockey for position*, match, measure up to, meet, near, partake, resemble, rivalize, scramble for, seek to displace, tie, touch, vie with; SEE CONCEPTS 92,667

road [n] *path upon which travel occurs*
alley, artery, asphalt, avenue, back street, boulevard, byway, cobblestone, concrete, course, crossroad, direction, drag*, dragway, drive, expressway, highway, lane, line, main drag*, parking lot*, parkway, passage, pathway, pavement, pike, roadway, route, street, subway, terrace, thoroughfare, throughway, thruway, track, trail, turnpike, viaduct, way; SEE CONCEPT 501

roam [v] *wander about*
bum*, bum around*, drift, gad, gallivant, hike, hit the road*, knock around*, meander, peregrinate, prowl, ramble, range, rove, saunter, straggle, stray, stroll, struggle along, traipse, tramp, travel, traverse, trek, vagabond, walk; SEE CONCEPTS 151,224

roar [n1] *growl, howl*
barrage, bawl, bay, bellow, blast, bluster, boom, clamor, clash, crash, cry, detonation, din, drum, explosion, holler, outcry, reverberation, rumble, shout, thunder, uproar, yell; SEE CONCEPTS 77,595

roar [n2/v2] *laugh loudly*
belly laugh, guffaw, hoot, howl, scream; SEE CONCEPT 77

roar [v1] *growl, howl*
bark, bawl, bay, bellow, blast, bluster, boom, brawl, bray, clamor, crash, cry, detonate, din, drum, explode, holler, rebound, reecho, repercuss, resound, reverberate, roll, rout, rumble, shout, sound, thunder, trumpet, vociferate, yell; SEE CONCEPTS 64,77

rob [v] *steal, deprive*
abscond, appropriate, bereave, break into, burglarize, burgle, cheat, con, cop*, defalcate, defraud, despoil, disinherit, dispossess, divest, do

out of*, embezzle, filch*, heist, hijack, hold up*, hustle, liberate, lift*, loot, lose, mug, oust, peculate, pilfer, pillage, pinch, plunder, promote, purloin, raid, ransack, relieve, requisition, rifle, rip off*, roll*, sack*, scrounge, snitch*, stick up, strip, strong-arm*, swindle, swipe, take, thieve, withhold; SEE CONCEPTS *139,142,192*

robber [n] *person who steals*
bandit, brigand, buccaneer, burglar, cardsharper*, cat burglar, cattle thief*, cheat*, chiseler*, con artist, corsair, crook, desperado, despoiler, fence, forager, fraud, grafter, hijacker, holdup artist*, housebreaker, looter, marauder, mugger, operator, pickpocket, pilferer, pillager, pirate, plunderer, prowler, punk*, raider, rustler, safecracker, sandbagger*, second-story operator*, shoplifter, stealer, stickup, swindler, thief, thug; SEE CONCEPT *412*

robe [n] *gown, often for wearing at home*
bathrobe, cape, costume, covering, dress, dressing gown, frock, garment, habit, housecoat, kimono, mantle, muumuu, negligee, outfit, peignoir, vestment, wrapper; SEE CONCEPT *451*

robust [adj] *healthy, strong*
able-bodied, athletic, boisterous, booming, brawny, built, concentrated, fit, fit as fiddle*, flourishing, full-bodied, hale, hardy, hearty, hefty, husky, in fine fettle*, in good health, in good shape, in the pink*, live, lusty, muscular, peppy, potent, powerful, powerhouse, prospering, prosperous, roaring, rough, rugged, sinewy, snappy, sound, stout, strapping, sturdy, thriving, tiger*, tough, vigorous, well, wicked*, zappy*, zippy*; SEE CONCEPTS *314,489,613*

rock [n1] *stone*
bedrock, boulder, cobblestone, crag, crust, earth, gravel, lava, lodge, mass, metal, mineral, ore, pebble, promontory, quarry, reef, rubble, shelf, slab, slag; SEE CONCEPTS *470,474,477,478, 509,523*

rock [n2] *foundation*
anchor, bulwark, cornerstone, defense, mainstay, protection, Rock of Gibraltar*, strength, support; SEE CONCEPTS *442,712*

rock [v] *move back and forth*
agitate, billow, careen, concuss, convulse, falter, heave, jiggle, jog, jolt, jounce, lurch, move, oscillate, pitch, push and pull, quake, quaver, quiver, reel, roll, roll about, shake, shock, stagger, sway, swing, toss, totter, tremble, undulate, vibrate, wobble; SEE CONCEPTS *147,149*

rocky [adj1] *unyielding, inflexible*
bouldered, craggy, flinty, hard, inflexible, jagged, lapidarian, lithic, pebbly, petrified, petrous, rockbound, rock-ribbed, rough, solid, stonelike; SEE CONCEPTS *485,604*

rocky [adj2] *unyielding, inflexible*
adamant, bloodless, firm, flinty, hard, impassible, insensate, insensible, insensitive, obdurate, pitiless, rocklike, rough, rugged, solid, steady, tough; SEE CONCEPT *401*

rocky [adj3] *doubtful, undependable*
dizzy, ill, rickety, shaky, sick, sickly, staggering, ticklish, tottering, tricky, uncertain, unreliable, unstable, unsteady, unwell, weak, wobbly; SEE CONCEPTS *488,489*

rod [n] *bar, pole*
baton, billet, birch, cane, cylinder, dowel, ingot, mace, pin, rodule, scepter, sceptre, shaft, slab,

spike, staff, stave, stick, strip, switch, wand; SEE CONCEPTS *436,470,479*

rogue [n] *person who deceives, swindles*
bad egg*, bad news*, blackguard*, black sheep*, charlatan, cheat, cheater, con artist, criminal, crook, defrauder, devil, fraud, heel*, hooligan*, lowlife*, mischief, miscreant, monstrosity, ne'er-do-well*, outlaw, problem*, rapscallion, rascal, reprobate, scalawag, scamp, scoundrel, swindler, trickster, villain; SEE CONCEPT *412*

role [n1] *impersonation of a character*
act, acting, appearance, aspect, bit, character, clothing, execution, extra, guise, hero, ingenue, lead, look, part, performance, personification, piece, player, portrayal, presentation, representation, seeming, semblance, show, star, stint, super, title, walk-on; SEE CONCEPTS *263,716*

role [n2] *duty, function*
act, bit, business, capacity, execution, game*, guise, job, office, part, piece, pose, position, post, posture, province, stint, task, what one is into*; SEE CONCEPTS *362,694*

roll [n1] *revolving, turning*
cycle, gyration, reel, revolution, rotation, run, spin, trundling, turn, twirl, undulation, whirl; SEE CONCEPTS *147,201*

roll [n2] *cylindrical object*
ball, barrel, bobbin, cartouche, coil, cone, convolution, cornucopia, cylinder, fold, reel, rundle, scroll, shell, spiral, spool, trundle, volute, wheel, whorl; SEE CONCEPT *436*

roll [n3] *list, roster*
annals, catalog, census, chronicle, directory, head count, index, muster, nose count*, register, roll call, schedule, scroll, table; SEE CONCEPT *281*

roll [n4] *growl, reverberation*
barrage, boom, booming, clangor, drone, drumbeat, drumming, echoing, grumble, quaver, racket, rat-a-tat*, resonance, roar, rumble, rumbling, thunder; SEE CONCEPT *595*

roll [v1] *revolve, turn; proceed smoothly*
alternate, be in sequence, bowl, circle, circumduct, coil, curve, drape, drive, eddy, elapse, enfold, entwine, envelop, flow, fold, follow, furl, go around, go past, gyrate, gyre, impel, pass, pirouette, pivot, propel, reel, rock, rotate, run, spin, spiral, succeed, swaddle, swathe, swing around, swirl, swivel, trundle, twirl, twist, undulate, wheel, whirl, wind, wrap; SEE CONCEPTS *147,201*

roll [v2] *spread out*
even, flatten, grind, level, press, pulverize, smooth; SEE CONCEPTS *137,208,250*

roll [v3] *thunder, reverberate*
bombinate, boom, cannonade, drum, echo, growl, grumble, hum, pattern, quaver, rattle, re-echo, resound, roar, ruffle, rumble, rustle, sound, trill, whirr; SEE CONCEPT *65*

roll [v4] *rock, sway*
billow, drift, flow, glide, heave, incline, jibe, lean, lumber, lurch, pitch, ramble, range, reel, roam, rove, run, stagger, stray, surge, swagger, swing, toss, tumble, undulate, waddle, wallow, wave, welter, yaw; SEE CONCEPTS *147,149*

rollicking [adj] *fun-loving, lively*
antic, boisterous, carefree, cavorting, cheerful, devil-may-care*, exuberant, frisky, frolicsome, glad, happy, hearty, jaunty, jovial, joyful, joyous, lighthearted, merry, playful, rip-roaring*, romping, spirited, sportive, sprightly; SEE CONCEPTS *401,548*

ri
ro

romance [n1] *love affair*
affair, affair of the heart*, amour, attachment, courtship, enchantment, fascination, fling, flirtation, intrigue, liaison, love, love story, passion, relationship; SEE CONCEPTS 375,384

romance [n2] *fanciful story or narrative*
ballad, fairy tale, fantasy, fiction, idealization, idyll, legend, love story, lyric, melodrama, novel, story, tale, tear-jerker*; SEE CONCEPT 280

romance [n3] *adventure, flight of fancy*
charm, color, excitement, exoticness, fairy tale, fancy, fantasy, fascination, glamour, hazard, idealization, idyll, mystery, nostalgia, risk, sentiment, venture; SEE CONCEPT 673

romantic [adj] *sentimental, idealistic*
adventurous, amorous, bathetic, charming, chimerical, chivalrous, colorful, corny*, daring, dreamy, enchanting, erotic, exciting, exotic, extravagant, fairy-tale, fanciful, fantastic, fascinating, fond, glamorous, idyllic, impractical, lovey-dovey*, loving, maudlin, mushy*, mysterious, nostalgic, passionate, picturesque, poetic, quixotic, sloppy*, soppy*, starry-eyed, syrupy, tear-jerking*, tender, unrealistic, utopian, visionary, whimsical, wild; SEE CONCEPTS 403,542,548

romp [n] *fun; caper*
antic, cakewalk*, cavort, dance, escapade, frisk, frolic, gambol, hop, lark, leap, play, rollick, rout, skip, sport; SEE CONCEPTS 292,384

romp [v] *have fun, enjoy oneself*
caper, cavort, celebrate, cut capers*, cut up*, fool around*, frisk, frolic, gambol, go on the town*, kid around*, lark, let loose*, make merry, play, prance, revel, roister, rollic, skip, skylark, sport, whoop it up*; SEE CONCEPTS 292,384

room [n1] *space, range*
allowance, area, capacity, chance, clearance, compass, elbowroom, expanse, extent, latitude, leeway, license, margin, occasion, opening, opportunity, place, play, range, reach, rein, rope, scope, sway, sweep, territory, vastness, volume; SEE CONCEPTS 651,756

room [n2] *enclosed section of building designed for specific purpose*
accommodation, alcove, apartment, cabin, cave*, chamber, cubbyhole, cubicle, den, flat, flop*, joint*, lodging, niche, office, setup*, suite, turf, vault; SEE CONCEPT 448

roomy [adj] *having ample space*
ample, broad, capacious, commodious, extensive, generous, large, sizable, spacious, wide; SEE CONCEPT 583

root [n] *base, core*
basis, bedrock, beginnings, bottom, cause, center, crux, derivation, essence, essentiality, footing, foundation, fountain, fountainhead, fundamental, germ, ground, groundwork, heart, inception, infrastructure, mainspring, marrow, motive, nub, nucleus, occasion, origin, pith, provenance, provenience, quick, quintessence, radicle, radix, reason, rhizome, rock bottom*, seat, seed, soul, source, starting point, stem, stuff, substance, substratum, tuber, underpinning, well; SEE CONCEPTS 442,648,661,826,829

root [v] *dig and search*
burrow, delve, embed, ferret, forage, grub, grub up, hunt, ingrain, lodge, nose, place, poke, pry, rummage; SEE CONCEPT 178

rope [n] *cord, line*
braiding, cable, cordage, hawser, lace, lanyard,

lariat, lasso, strand, string, tape, thread, twine; SEE CONCEPT 475

roster [n] *list of items, names*
agenda, catalog, head count, index, inventory, listing, muster, nose count*, program, record, register, roll, roll call, rota, schedule, scroll, table; SEE CONCEPTS 281,283

rosy [adj1] *pink, reddish in color*
aflush, blooming, blushing, colored, coral, deep pink, fresh, glowing, healthy-looking, high-colored, incarnadine, pale red, peach, red, red-complexioned, red-faced, roseate, rose-colored, rubicund, ruddy; SEE CONCEPT 618

rosy [adj2] *cheerful, hopeful*
alluring, auspicious, bright, encouraging, favorable, glowing, likely, optimistic, pleasing, promising, reassuring, roseate, rose-colored, sunny; SEE CONCEPTS 529,548

rot [n1] *corrosion, disintegration*
blight, canker, corrosion, decay, decomposition, deterioration, mold, putrefaction, putrescence; SEE CONCEPTS 469,698

rot [n2] *garbage, nonsense*
balderdash, bilge, bunk, claptrap, drivel, foolishness, guff, hogwash, hooey*, moonshine*, poppycock, rubbish, silliness, stuff and nonsense*, tommyrot; SEE CONCEPTS 278,529

rot [v] *corrode, deteriorate*
break down, corrupt, crumble, debase, debauch, decay, decline, decompose, degenerate, demoralize, deprave, descend, disimprove, disintegrate, fester, go bad*, go downhill*, go to pot*, languish, molder, perish, pervert, putrefy, retrograde, sink, spoil, stain, taint, turn, warp, waste away, wither, worsen; SEE CONCEPTS 240,469,698

rotary [adj] *turning*
encircling, gyral, gyratory, revolving, rotating, rotational, rotatory, spinning, vertiginous, vorticular, whirligig, whirling; SEE CONCEPTS 581,584

rotate [v1] *go around in circle*
circle, circumduct, circumvolve, gyrate, gyre, move, pirouette, pivot, reel, revolve, roll, spin, swivel, troll, trundle, turn, twirl, twist, waltz, wheel, whirl, whirligig, whirr; SEE CONCEPTS 147,738

rotate [v2] *alternate*
bandy, ensue, exchange, follow, follow in sequence, interchange, relieve, spell, succeed, switch, take turns; SEE CONCEPTS 104,697

rotten [adj1] *decayed, decaying*
bad, bad-smelling, corroded, corrupt, crumbled, crumbling, decomposed, decomposing, disgusting, disintegrated, disintegrating, fecal, feculent, festering, fetid, foul, gross, infected, loathsome, loud, mephitic, moldering, moldy, noisome, noxious, offensive, overripe, perished, polluted, purulent, pustular, putrescent, putrid, putrified, rancid, rank, rotting, smelling, sour, spoiled, stale, stinking, strong, tainted, touched, unsound; SEE CONCEPTS 462,485

rotten [adj2] *dishonest, immoral*
bent, bribable, contaminated, corrupt, crooked, debauched, deceitful, defiled, degenerate, depraved, dirtied, dishonorable, disloyal, faithless, filthy, flagitious, impure, mercenary, nefarious, perfidious, perverse, polluted, soiled, sullied, tainted, treacherous, unclean, untrustworthy, venal, vicious, villainous, vitiated; SEE CONCEPTS 404,545

rotten [adj3] *despicable, inferior, bad*
amiss, base, below par*, bruised, bum*, contemptible, crummy*, defective, deplorable, dirty, disagreeable, disappointing, diseased, displeasing, dissatisfactory, filthy, impaired, inadequate, injured, lousy*, low-grade, mean, nasty, poor, punk*, regrettable, rough, scurrilous, shaky, sorry, sour, substandard, unacceptable, unfortunate, unhappy, unlucky, unpleasant, unsatisfactory, unsound, vile, wasted, wicked, withering, wrong; SEE CONCEPTS 570,571,574

rough [adj1] *uneven, irregular*
asperous, bearded, brambly, bristly, broken, bumpy, bushy, chapped, choppy, coarse, cragged, craggy, cross-grained, disheveled, fuzzy, hairy, harsh, jagged, knobby, knotty, nappy, nodular, not smooth, ridged, rocky, ruffled, rugged, scabrous, scraggy, shaggy, sharp, stony, tangled, tousled, tufted, unequal, uneven, unfinished, unlevel, unshaven, unshorn, woolly, wrinkled, wrinkly; SEE CONCEPTS 485,606

rough [adj2] *stormy; not quiet*
agitated, blustering, blustery, boisterous, buffeting, cacophonous, choppy, coarse, discordant, dry, furious, grating, gruff, harsh, hoarse, husky, inclement, inharmonious, jarring, raging, rasping, raucous, rugged, squally, stridulent, tempestuous, tumultous/tumultuous, turbulent, unmusical, wild; SEE CONCEPTS 525,592,594

rough [adj3] *rude, impolite*
bearish, bluff, blunt, boisterous, boorish, brief, brusque, churlish, coarse, crass, crude, cruel, crusty, curt, discourteous, drastic, extreme, gross*, hairy*, hard, harsh, ill-mannered, improper, inconsiderate, indecorous, indelicate, inelegant, loud, loutish, mean, nasty, raw, rowdy, severe, sharp, short, tough, unceremonious, uncivil, uncouth, uncultivated, uncultured, unfeeling, ungracious, unjust, unmannerly, unpleasant, unpolished, unrefined, untutored, violent, vulgar; SEE CONCEPTS 267,401

rough [adj4] *basic, incomplete*
austere, crude, cursory, formless, hard, imperfect, raw, rough-and-ready*, roughhewn, rudimentary, shapeless, sketchy, spartan, uncompleted, uncut, undressed, unfashioned, unfinished, unformed, unhewn, unpolished, unprocessed, unrefined, unwrought; SEE CONCEPT 531

rough [adj5] *approximate*
amorphous, estimated, foggy, general, hazy, imprecise, inexact, proximate, rude, sketchy, uncertain, unprecise, vague; SEE CONCEPT 557

rough out [v] *do preliminary draw*
adumbrate, block out, chalk, characterize, delineate, draft, outline, plan, skeleton, sketch, suggest; SEE CONCEPTS 36,79,174

rough up [v] *beat up*
bash, batter, hit, knock about, knock around, maltreat, mishandle, mistreat, roughhouse, slap around, thrash; SEE CONCEPTS 189,246

round [n1] *globe, ball; semicircular area*
arc, arch, band, bend, bow, circle, circlet, curvation, curvature, curve, disc, disk, equator, eye, gyre, hoop, loop, orb, orbit, ring, ringlet, sphere, wheel; SEE CONCEPT 436

round [n2] *cycle, stage*
ambit, beat, bout, circuit, circulation, circumvolution, compass, course, division, gyration, lap, level, performance, period, revolution, rotation, round trip, routine, schedule, sequence, series,

session, succession, tour, turn, wheel, whirl; SEE CONCEPTS 364,727,807

round [n3] *unit of ammunition*
bullet, cartridge, charge, discharge, load, shell, shot; SEE CONCEPTS 498,500

round [adj1] *ball-shaped; semicircular area*
annular, arced, arched, arciform, bent, bowed, bulbous, circular, coiled, curled, curved, curvilinear, cylindrical, discoid, disk-shaped, domical, egg-shaped, elliptical, globose, globular, looped, orbed, orbicular, orbiculate, oval, ringed, rotund, rounded, spherical, spheroid, spiral; SEE CONCEPT 486

round [adj2] *complete*
accomplished, done, entire, finished, full, rounded, solid, unbroken, undivided, whole; SEE CONCEPT 531

round [adj3] *full-bodied, ample in size*
chubby, expansive, fleshy, generous, large, plump, plumpish, pudgy*, roly-poly*, rotund, rounded, tubby; SEE CONCEPTS 491,773

round [adj4] *resonant, rich in sound*
consonant, full, mellifluous, orotund, plangent, resounding, ringing, rotund, sonorous, vibrant; SEE CONCEPT 594

round [adj5] *honest, direct*
blunt, candid, frank, free, outspoken, plain, straightforward, unmodified, vocal; SEE CONCEPT 267

round [v1] *turn; encircle*
begird, bypass, circle, circulate, circumnavigate, compass, encompass, flank, gird, girdle, go around, gyrate, hem, pivot, revolve, ring, roll, rotate, skirt, spin, surround, wheel, whirl; SEE CONCEPTS 147,149,187

round [v2] *make curved; remove angles*
arch, bend, bow, coil, convolute, crook, curl, curve, form, loop, mold, perfect, polish, recurve, refine, shape, sleek, slick, smooth, whorl; SEE CONCEPTS 184,202

round [adv1] *approximate*
about, all but, almost, around, as good as, close to, in the neighborhood of, just about, most, near, nearly, practically, roughly; SEE CONCEPT 762

roundabout [adj] *indirect*
ambiguous, circuitous, circular, circumlocutory, collateral, deviating, devious, discursive, evasive, meandering, oblique, obliquitous, periphrastic, taking the long way*, tortuous; SEE CONCEPTS 559,581,584

round off [v] *finish*
bring to a close, cap, climax, close, complete, conclude, crown, culminate, finish off, settle, top off; SEE CONCEPT 234

roundup [n] *collection, collation*
assembly, branding, gathering, herding, marshalling, muster, rally, summary, survey; SEE CONCEPTS 257,397

round up [v] *collect, gather*
assemble, bring in, bring together, cluster, drive, group, herd, marshal, muster, rally; SEE CONCEPTS 109,257

rouse [v1] *wake*
arouse, awake, awaken, call, get up, raise, rise, stir, wake up; SEE CONCEPT 250

rouse [v2] *stimulate, excite*
aggravate, agitate, anger, animate, arouse, ask for it*, awaken, bestir, bug*, challenge, craze, deepen, disturb, enhance, enliven, exhilarate, fire up*, foment, galvanize, get going, heighten, in-

cite, inflame, innervate, innerve, instigate, intensate, intensify, key up*, kindle, magnify, make waves*, mount, move, needle, pep up*, pique, provoke, quicken, rally, redouble, rile, rise, startle, steam up*, stir, trigger, urge, vivify, wake, waken, wake up, whet, whip up*, work up; SEE CONCEPTS 7,22,244

rout [n] *overwhelming defeat*
beating, clobbering*, comedown, confusion, debacle, disaster, drubbing*, embarrassment, flight, hiding, overthrow, retreat, romp, ruin, shambles, shutout, thrashing, trashing*, upset, vanquishment, walkover*, washout*, waxing*, whipping; SEE CONCEPTS 95,119,363

rout [v] *defeat overwhelmingly*
bash, beat, blow out of water*, bulldoze*, bury*, chase, clean up on*, clobber, conquer, cream*, crush, cut to pieces*, destroy, discomfit, dispel, drive off, expel, finish*, hunt, kill*, lambaste*, larrup*, murder*, outmaneuver, overpower, overthrow, put to flight*, repulse, scatter, scuttle, shut out*, skunk*, subdue, subjugate, swamp*, torpedo*, total*, trounce, vanquish, wallop, wax*, whip, wipe off map*, wipe out*, worst, zap*; SEE CONCEPT 95

route [n] *path over which someone or something travels*
avenue, beat, beeline, byway, circuit, course, detour, digression, direction, divergence, itinerary, journey, line, meandering, passage, pavement, pike, plot, program, rambling, range, road, round, rounds, run, short cut, tack, track, trail, wandering, way; SEE CONCEPTS 501,660

route [v] *send along a path*
address, conduct, consign, convey, direct, dispatch, escort, forward, guide, lead, pilot, remit, see, shepherd, ship, show, steer, transmit; SEE CONCEPTS 187,217

routine [n] *habitual activity*
act, beaten path*, bit, channels, custom, cycle, daily grind*, drill, formula, grind*, groove*, habit, line, method, order, pace, pattern, piece, practice, procedure, program, rat race*, rote, round, rut, schtick*, spiel*, system, tack, technique, treadmill, usage, way, wont; SEE CONCEPTS 6,362,770

routine [adj] *habitual*
accepted, accustomed, chronic, conventional, customary, everyday, familiar, general, methodical, normal, ordinary, periodic, plain, quotidian, regular, seasonal, standard, typical, unremarkable, usual, wonted, workaday; SEE CONCEPTS 530,547,548

row [n1] *sequence, series*
bank, chain, column, consecution, echelon, file, line, order, progression, queue, range, rank, string, succession, tier, train; SEE CONCEPTS 432,727,744

row [n2] *fight, ruckus*
affray, altercation, bickering, brawl, castigation, commotion, controversy, dispute, disturbance, falling-out*, fracas, fray, fuss, knock-down-dragout*, lecture, melee, noise, quarrel, racket, reprimand, reproof, riot, rumpus, run-in*, scrap*, set-to*, shouting match*, squabble, talking-to*, telling-off*, tiff, tongue-lashing*, trouble, tumult, uproar, words*, wrangle; SEE CONCEPTS 46,52,106

row [v1] *move boat with paddle*
drag, oar, paddle, pull, punt, sail, scud, scull, sky an oar, swim*; SEE CONCEPT 187

row [v2] *argue, fight*
bawl out, berate, bicker, brawl, call on the carpet*, dispute, jaw, quarrel, ream, scold, scrap, spat, squabble, tiff, tongue-lash*, wrangle; SEE CONCEPTS 46,106

rowdy [n] *person who is boisterous, noisy*
brawler, bully, hellion, hooligan, lout, punk, roughneck, ruffian, terror*, troublemaker; SEE CONCEPT 412

rowdy [adj] *boisterous, noisy*
disorderly, lawless, loud, loudmouthed, loutish, mischievous, obstreperous, rambunctious, raucous, rebellious, rough, roughhouse, rude, turbulent, unruly, uproarious, wild; SEE CONCEPT 401

royal [adj] *monarchical, grand*
aristocratic, august, authoritative, baronial, commanding, dignified, elevated, eminent, grandiose, high, high-born, honorable, illustrious, imperial, imposing, impressive, kingly, lofty, magnificent, majestic, noble, queenly, regal, regnant, reigning, renowned, resplendent, ruling, sovereign, splendid, stately, superb, superior, supreme, worthy; SEE CONCEPTS 549,574

rub [n1] *stroke, massage*
abrasion, attrition, brushing, caress, friction, grinding, kneading, pat, polish, rasping, scouring, scraping, shine, smear, smoothing, stroking, swab, swipe, wear, wipe; SEE CONCEPT 215

rub [n2] *difficulty, problem*
bar, catch, crimp, dilemma, drawback, hamper, hindrance, hitch, hurdle, impediment, obstacle, predicament, snag, stumbling block*, traverse, trouble; SEE CONCEPTS 666,674

rub [v] *stroke, massage*
abrade, anoint, apply, bark, brush, buff, burnish, caress, chafe, clean, coat, cover, curry, daub, erase, erode, excoriate, file, fray, fret, furbish, glance, glaze, gloss, grate, graze, grind, knead, mop, paint, pat, plaster, polish, put, rasp, scour, scrape, scrub, shine, slather, smear, smooth, spread, swab, triturate, wear, wear down, wipe; SEE CONCEPT 215

rubbish [n1] *garbage*
debris, dregs, dross, junk, litter, lumber, offal, refuse, rubble, rummage, scrap, sweepings, trash, waste; SEE CONCEPT 260

rubbish [n2] *nonsense*
balderdash, bilge*, bunkum, drivel, gibberish, hogwash, hooey*, poppycock, rot*, stuff and nonsense*, tommyrot; SEE CONCEPTS 230,278

ruddy [adj] *pinkish, blushing*
blooming, blowsy, bronzed, crimson, florid, flush, flushed, fresh, full-blooded, glowing, healthy, pink, red, red-complexioned, reddish, roseate, rosy, rubicund, ruby, sanguine, scarlet; SEE CONCEPT 618

rude [adj1] *disrespectful, rough*
abrupt, abusive, bad-mannered, barbarian, barbaric, barbarous, blunt, boorish, brusque, brutish, cheeky, churlish, coarse, crabbed, crude, curt, discourteous, graceless, gross, gruff, ignorant, illiterate, impertinent, impolite, impudent, inconsiderate, insolent, insulting, intrusive, loutish, low, obscene, offhand, peremptory, raw, savage, scurrilous, short, surly, uncivil, uncivilized, uncouth, uncultured, uneducated, ungracious, un-

mannerly, unpolished, unrefined, vulgar, wild;
SEE CONCEPTS 267,401

rude [adj2] *crude, primitive*
angular, artless, barbarous, callow, coarse, formless, fresh, green, ignorant, inartistic, inelegant,
inexperienced, inexpert, makeshift, primal, raw,
rough, roughhewn, roughly made, rudimental, rudimentary, shapeless, simple, uncivilized, unconversant, uncultivated, unfashioned, unfinished,
unformed, unhewn, unpolished, unprocessed, unrefined, wild; SEE CONCEPTS 490,531

rude [adj3] *sudden; approximate*
abrupt, guessed, harsh, imperfect, imprecise, inexact, in the ballpark*, proximate, rough, sharp,
startling, stormy, surmised, turbulent, unpleasant,
unprecise, violent; SEE CONCEPTS 557,799

rudimentary [adj] *basic, fundamental*
abecedarian, basal, beginning, early, elemental,
elementary, embryonic, immature, initial,
introductory, larval, nuts-and-bolts*, primary,
primitive, simple, simplest, uncompleted, undeveloped, vestigial; SEE CONCEPTS 546,549

ruffle [v1] *mess up*
cockle, confuse, crease, crinkle, crumple, crush,
derange, disarrange, discompose, dishevel, disorder, pucker, purse, rifle, rumple, tangle, tousle,
wrinkle; SEE CONCEPT 158

ruffle [v2] *upset, irritate*
abrade, agitate, anger, annoy, bluster, bother,
browbeat, bully, chafe, confuse, cow*, disconcert,
cert, disquiet, disturb, excite, floor*, flummox,
flurry, fluster, fret, fuddle, gall, get to*, harass,
intimidate, irk, nettle, peeve, perturb, provoke,
put off, put out, rattle, rattle one's cage*, shake
up*, stir, stump, throw into tizzy*, torment, trouble, unsettle, vex, wear, worry; SEE CONCEPTS
7,14,19

rugged [adj1] *bumpy, weathered*
asperous, broken, coarse, craggy, difficult, furrowed, harsh, hilly, irregular, jagged, leathery,
lumpy, mountainous, ragged, rocky, rough,
roughhewn, scabrous, scraggy, stark, uneven, unlevel, unpolished, unrefined, unsmooth, weather-
beaten, worn, wrinkled; SEE CONCEPTS 490,606

rugged [adj2] *severe, violent*
bitter, brutal, difficult, hard, harsh, inclement, intemperate, rigorous, rough, stormy, tempestuous,
turbulent; SEE CONCEPTS 525,537

rugged [adj3] *uncouth, crude*
barbarous, blunt, boorish, churlish, graceless, ill-
bred, loutish, rude, uncultured, unpolished, unrefined; SEE CONCEPT 401

rugged [adj4] *difficult, rigorous*
arduous, demanding, exacting, formidable,
hairy*, hard, harsh, heavy*, heavy sledding*,
knotty*, laborious, large order*, mean, murder*,
no picnic*, operose, rough, stern, strenuous, taxing, tough, trying, uncompromising, uphill*; SEE
CONCEPTS 538,565

rugged [adj5] *big, strong*
able-bodied, athletic, brawny, energetic, forceful,
hale, hardy, healthy, husky, indefatigable, lusty,
muscular, robust, sturdy, tough, unflagging, vigorous, well-built; SEE CONCEPTS 314,489

ruin [n] *situation of devastation*
atrophy, bane, bankruptcy, bath, breakdown, collapse, confusion, crackup, crash, crumbling, damage, decay, defeat, degeneracy, degeneration,
demolition, destitution, destruction, deterioration,
dilapidation, disintegration, disrepair, dissolution,

downfall, downgrade, extinction, failure, fall,
havoc, insolvency, loss, nemesis, overthrow, ruination, skids*, subversion, the end*, undoing,
waste, waterloo, wreck, wreckage; SEE CONCEPT
674

ruin [v] *devastate, destroy*
bankrupt, beggar, botch, break, bring down, bring
to ruin, bust, clean out, crush, decimate, deface,
defeat, defile, demolish, deplete, deplore, depredate, desecrate, despoil, devour, dilapidate, disfigure, do in*, drain, exhaust, fleece, impoverish,
injure, lay waste, maim, make a mess of, mangle,
mar, mutilate, overthrow, overturn, overwhelm,
pauperize, pillage, rape, ravish, raze, reduce,
sack, shatter, smash, spoil, despoil, total, use up,
wipe out*, wrack, wreak havoc on, wreck; SEE
CONCEPTS 234,246,252

ruinous [adj] *disastrous, devastating*
annihilative, baleful, baneful, calamitous, cataclysmic, catastrophic, crippling, damaging,
deadly, deleterious, depleting, dire, disastrous,
draining, exhausting, extravagant, fatal, fateful,
harmful, hurtful, immoderate, impoverishing, injurious, murderous, noxious, pernicious, shattering, suicidal, unfortunate, wasteful, withering,
wrackful; SEE CONCEPTS 537,548,570

ruins [n] *buildings that are dilapidated*
ashes, debris, destruction, detritus, foundation,
relics, remains, remnants, residue, rubble, traces,
vestiges, wreck, wreckage; SEE CONCEPTS
439,733

rule [n1] *standard, principle of behavior*
aphorism, apothegm, assize, axiom, basis, brocard, canon, chapter and verse*, command, commandment, criterion, decorum, decree, decretion,
dictum, direction, edict, etiquette, formula, fundamental, gnome, guide, guideline, keynote, keystone, law, maxim, model, moral, no-no's*,
order, ordinance, precedent, precept, prescription,
propriety, regimen, regulation, ruling, statute, tenet, test, the book*, the numbers*, truism; SEE
CONCEPT 688

rule [n2] *leadership of organization*
administration, ascendancy, authority, command,
control, direction, domination, dominion, empire,
government, influence, jurisdiction, power, regime, regnancy, reign, sovereignty, supremacy,
sway; SEE CONCEPTS 299,376

rule [n3] *method, way*
course, custom, formula, habit, normalcy, normality, order of things, policy, practice, procedure, routine; SEE CONCEPTS 6,647

rule [v1] *govern, manage*
administer, be in authority, be in driver's seat*, be
in power, bridle, command, conduct, control,
crack the whip*, curb, decree, dictate, direct,
dominate, domineer, guide, hold sway*, hold the
reins*, keep under one's thumb*, lay down the
law*, lead, order, overrule, predominate, preponderate, preside, prevail, regulate, reign, restrain,
rule the roost*, run, run the show*, sit on top of*,
sway, take over; SEE CONCEPTS 117,133,298

rule [v2] *judge, decide*
adjudge, adjudicate, conclude, decree, deduce,
determine, establish, figure, find, fix, gather,
hold, infer, lay down, pass upon, postulate, prescribe, pronounce, resolve, settle, theorize; SEE
CONCEPTS 18,81

rule out [v] *exclude, reject*
abolish, avert, ban, bate, cancel, count out, debar,

ro
ru

deter, dismiss, eliminate, except, forbid, forestall, forfend, leave out, not consider, obviate, preclude, prevent, prohibit, proscribe, recant, revoke, stave off, suspend, ward off; SEE CONCEPTS 25,121

ruler [n] *historically, person who ruled an area*
baron, baroness, caesar, caliph, contessa, count, countess, crowned head, czar, czarina, dame, duchess, duke, dynast, emperor, empress, gerent, imperator, kaiser, khan, king, lady, lord, magnate, maharajah, maharani, majesty, mikado, mogul, monarch, oligarch, overlord, pasha, potentate, prince, princess, queen, rajah, rani, rex, royal, shah, sovereign, sultan, sultana, tycoon; SEE CONCEPT 422

ruler [n2] *tool for measuring or calculating length*
folding rule, measure, measuring stick, rule, slide rule, straightedge, T-square, yardstick; SEE CONCEPT 499

ruling [n] *judgment, decree*
adjudication, decision, directive, edict, finding, judgment, law, order, precept, pronouncement, resolution, rule, ukase, verdict; SEE CONCEPT 318

ruling [adj] *dominant, governing*
cardinal, central, commanding, controlling, leading, overriding, overruling, pivotal, regnant, reigning, sovereign, supreme, upper; SEE CONCEPT 574

ruling [adj2] *prevailing, main*
chief, dominant, pivotal, popular, predominant, preeminent, preponderant, prevalent, principal, rampant, rife, widespread; SEE CONCEPT 568

rumble [v] *growl, thunder*
boom, grumble, resound, roar, roll; SEE CONCEPT 65

ruminate [v] *think about seriously*
brainstorm*, brood, chew over, cogitate, consider, contemplate, deliberate, excogitate, figure, meditate, mull over, muse, ponder, rack one's brains*, reflect, revolve, sense about*, think, turn over, use one's head*, weigh; SEE CONCEPT 24

rummage [v] *ransack, search*
beat the bushes*, comb, delve, dig out, disarrange, disarray, disorder, disorganize, disrupt, disturb, examine, explore, ferret out, fish, forage, grub, hunt, jumble, leave no stone unturned*, look high and low*, mess up, mix up, poke, rake, root, scour, search high heaven*, seek, shake, shake down, spy, toss, turn inside out*, turn upside down*; SEE CONCEPTS 158,216

rumor [n] *talk about supposed truth*
back-fence talk*, breeze*, bruit, canard, comment, cry, dispatch, earful*, fabrication, falsehood, fame, fiction, gossip, grapevine*, hearsay, hoax, innuendo, intelligence, invention, lie, news, notoriety, report, repute, rumble, scandal, scuttlebutt*, story, suggestion, supposition, tale, tattle, tidings, whisper, wire*, word; SEE CONCEPTS 274,277,278

rumor [v] *tell a supposed truth*
bruit, buzz*, circulate, gossip, noise about*, pass around, publish, report, say, talk, tattle, whisper; SEE CONCEPTS 44,54

rump [n] *bottom, posterior of animal or human*
back, backside, beam, behind, breech, bum*, butt, butt end, buttocks, can*, croup, derrière, duff*, fanny*, haunches, hind end, hindquarters, keister*, moon*, prat, rear, rear end, sacrum, seat, tail*, tail end, tush*; SEE CONCEPTS 392,825

rumple [v] *crush, wrinkle*
bedraggle, cockle, crease, crimp, crinkle, crumple, derange, dishevel, disorder, fold, mess up, muss up, pucker, ruck up, ruffle, screw up, scrunch, seam, tousle, wreathe; SEE CONCEPTS 137,219,250

run [n1] *fast moving on foot*
amble, bound, break, canter, dart, dash, drop, escape, fall, flight, gallop, jog, lope, pace, race, rush, scamper, scuttle, spring, sprint, spurt, tear, trot, whisk; SEE CONCEPTS 150,195

run [n2] *journey*
drive, excursion, jaunt, joy ride*, lift, outing, ride, round, spin, tour, travel, trip; SEE CONCEPT 224

run [n3] *sequence, course*
bearing, chain, continuance, continuation, continuity, current, cycle, drift, duration, endurance, field, flow, line, motion, movement, passage, path, period, persistence, progress, prolongation, round, route, season, series, spell, streak, stream, stretch, string, succession, swing, tendency, tenor, tide, trend, way; SEE CONCEPTS 721,727,738

run [v1] *move fast on foot*
abscond, amble, barrel, beat it*, bolt, bound, bustle, canter, career, clear out, course, cut and run*, dart, dash, decamp, depart, dog it*, escape, flee, flit, fly, gallop, go like lightning*, hasten, hie, hotfoot*, hurry, hustle, jog, leg it*, light out*, lope, make a break*, make off, make tracks*, pace, race, rush, scamper, scoot, scorch, scramble, scud, scurry, shag, shoot, skedaddle*, skip, skitter, smoke*, speed, spring, sprint, spurt, take flight, take off, tear, tear out, travel, trot, whisk; SEE CONCEPTS 150,195

run [v2] *move rapidly, flowingly*
bleed, cascade, course, deliquesce, diffuse, discharge, dissolve, drop, fall, flow, flux, fuse, glide, go, go soft, gush, issue, leak, leap, liquefy, melt, pass, pour, proceed, roll, sail, scud, skim, slide, spill, spin, spout, spread, stream, thaw, tumble, turn to liquid, whirl, whiz; SEE CONCEPT 146

run [v3] *operate, drive*
act, bear, carry, command, control, convey, go, govern, handle, manage, maneuver, move, perform, ply, propel, tick, transport, use, work; SEE CONCEPTS 225,680

run [v4] *manage, supervise*
administer, be in charge, be in driver's seat*, be in saddle*, boss, carry on, conduct, control, coordinate, direct, head, head up*, helm*, keep, lead, look after, operate, ordain, oversee, own, pull the strings*, regulate, ride herd on*, superintend, take care of*; SEE CONCEPT 117

run [v5] *continue, range*
be current, circulate, cover, encompass, extend, go, go around, go on, last, lie, move past, persevere, proceed, reach, spread, stretch, trail, vary; SEE CONCEPTS 651,721

run [v6] *attempt to be elected to public office*
be a candidate, challenge, compete, contend, contest, hit the campaign trail*, kiss babies*, oppose, politick, race, ring doorbells*, shake hands*, stand, stump, whistlestop*; SEE CONCEPT 300

run-around [n] *avoidance*
come-off, delay, detour, difficulty, diversion, elusion, escape, escaping, eschewal, evasion, inertia, postponement, roundabout, shunning; SEE CONCEPTS 30,121

runaway [n] *person who is trying to escape*
absconder, delinquent, deserter, escapee, escaper, fugitive, lawbreaker, maroon, offender, truant, wanted person; SEE CONCEPT *412*

runaway [adj] *out of control*
delinquent, disorderly, escaped, fleeing, fugitive, loose, out of hand*, running, uncontrolled, wild; SEE CONCEPT *401*

rundown [n] *summary*
briefing, outline, precis, recap*, recapitulation, report, résumé, review, run-through, sketch, synopsis; SEE CONCEPT *283*

run down [v] *ridicule*
belittle, criticize, decry, defame, denigrate, depreciate, derogate, detract, diminish, disparage, dispraise, downcry, knock*, make fun of, opprobriate, revile, speak ill of, vilify; SEE CONCEPTS *52,54*

run-down [adj] *shabby, in bad shape*
abandoned, beat-up, below par, broken-down, crumbling, debilitated, decrepit, derelict, deserted, desolate, dilapidated, dingy, dog-eared*, down-at-the-heel*, drained, enervated, exhausted, fatigued, forsaken, frowzy*, in a bad way*, neglected, old, out of condition, peaked, ramshackle, ratty*, rickety, seedy, shabby, tacky, tattered*, tired, tumble-down, uncared-for, under the weather*, unhealthy, untended, used up, weak, weary, worn-out; SEE CONCEPTS *314,485,570*

rung [n] *notch, step*
bar, board, crossbar, crosspiece, degree, grade, level, rod, round, rundle, stage, tread; SEE CONCEPTS *471,744*

run in [v] *arrest*
apprehend, bust, collar, cop*, detain, handcuff, jail, nab, pick up, pinch*, pull in, put the cuffs on*, take into custody, throw in jail*; SEE CONCEPTS *298,317*

run-in [n] *argument*
altercation, bickering, brush, confrontation, contretemps, dispute, encounter, falling-out*, fight, hassle, quarrel, row, set-to*, skirmish, tussle; SEE CONCEPTS *46,106*

running [n] *management of organization*
administration, care, charge, conduct, control, coordination, direction, functioning, handling, intendance, leadership, maintenance, operation, organization, oversight, performance, regulation, superintendence, supervision, working; SEE CONCEPT *117*

running [adj] *continuous, flowing, operating*
active, alive, constant, cursive, dynamic, easy, effortless, executing, fluent, functioning, going, in action, incessant, in operation, in succession, live, moving, operative, perpetual, proceeding, producing, smooth, together, unbroken, unceasing, uninterrupted, working; SEE CONCEPTS *538,560,581*

running [adv] *continually*
consecutively, continuously, night and day*, successively, together, unintermittedly, uninterruptedly; SEE CONCEPTS *482,798*

run out [v] *fail, be exhausted*
be cleaned out*, be out of, cease, close, come to a close, depart, disappear, dry up, end, exhaust, expire, finish, give out, go, have no more, have none left, lose, peter out*, stop, terminate, tire, waste, waste away, weaken, wear out; SEE CONCEPTS *105,699*

runt [n] *very small person*
half-pint*, homunculus, Lilliputian, midget, pee-wee*, punk*, shrimp*; SEE CONCEPT *424*

run through [v] *use up; waste*
blow, consume, dissipate, exhaust, expend, finish, fritter away, lose, spend, squander, throw away, wash up; SEE CONCEPT *156*

rupture [n1] *break, split*
breach, burst, cleavage, cleft, crack, division, fissure, fracture, hernia, herniation, parting, rent, schism, tear; SEE CONCEPTS *309,513*

rupture [n2] *disagreement, dissolution*
altercation, breach, break, break-up, bust-up*, clash, contention, detachment, disruption, disunion, division, divorce, divorcement, estrangement, falling-out, feud, hostility, misunderstanding, parting, partition, quarrel, rift, schism, separation, split, split-up*; SEE CONCEPTS *46, 388*

rupture [v1] *break open*
breach, burst, cleave, crack, disrupt, divide, erupt, fracture, hold, open, part, puncture, rend, rive, separate, sever, shatter, split, sunder, tear; SEE CONCEPTS *98,246,308*

rupture [v2] *disagree; dissolve union*
break off, break up, come between, disjoin, disrupt, dissect, dissever, disunite, divide, divorce, part, separate, split, split up, sunder; SEE CONCEPTS *297,384*

rural [adj] *country, not urban*
agrarian, agricultural, agronomic, Arcadian, backwoods, bucolic, countrified, farm, georgic, idyllic, natural, outland, pastoral, provincial, ranch, rustic, rustical, simple, sylvan, unsophisticated; SEE CONCEPT *583*

ruse [n] *trick, deception*
angle, artifice, blind, booby trap*, curveball*, deceit, device, dodge, feint, gambit, game, game plan*, gimmick, hoax, imposture, jig*, maneuver, ploy, scenario, sham, shenanigans*, shift, stratagem, stunt, subterfuge, switch*, twist*, wile; SEE CONCEPTS *59,674*

rush [n1] *hurry, speed*
blitz, charge, dash, dispatch, expedition, flood, flow, flux, haste, hastiness, hurriedness, precipitance, precipitancy, precipitation, race, scramble, stream, surge, swiftness, urgency; SEE CONCEPTS *145,748,818*

rush [n2] *attack*
assault, blitz, charge, onslaught, push, storm, surge, violence; SEE CONCEPT *86*

rush [v1] *hurry, speed*
accelerate, barrel, bolt, break, career, charge, chase, course, dart, dash, dispatch, expedite, fire up*, fleet, fling, flit, fly, get cracking*, get the lead out*, go like lightning*, haste, hasten, hotfoot*, hurry up, hustle, lose no time*, make haste, make short work of*, press, push, quicken, race, roll, run, scramble, scud, scurry, shake a leg*, shoot, speed up, sprint, step on gas*, streak, surge, tear, whiz*, zip*, zoom*; SEE CONCEPTS *91,150,152*

rush [v2] *charge, attack*
capture, overcome, storm, surge, take by storm*; SEE CONCEPT *86*

rust [n] *corrosion*
blight, corruption, decay, decomposition, dilapidation, mold, oxidation, rot, wear; SEE CONCEPTS *309,720*

ru
ru

rust [v] *corrode*
decay, decline, degenerate, deteriorate, oxidize, stale, tarnish, wither; SEE CONCEPT 469

rustic [n] *person from the country, with little experience*
backwoodsperson, boor, country cousin*, countryperson, farmer, hayseed*, hick*, hillbilly, mountaineer, peasant, provincial, redneck*, rural, yokel*; SEE CONCEPT 413

rustic [adj1] *country, rural*
agrarian, agricultural, Arcadian, artless, austere, bucolic, countrified, homely, homespun, homey, honest, natural, outland, pastoral, picturesque, plain, primitive, provincial, simple, sylvan, unaffected, unpolished, unrefined, unsophisticated, verdant; SEE CONCEPTS 583,589

rustic [adj2] *crude, uncouth*
awkward, boorish, churlish, clodhopping, clownish, coarse, countrified, dull, foolish, graceless, ignorant, inelegant, loutish, maladroit, rough, rude, stupid, uncultured, uneducated, ungainly, unmannerly, unpolished, unsophisticated; SEE CONCEPT 401

rustle [n] *whisper, swish*
crackle, crepitation, crinkling, friction, noise, patter, ripple, rustling, sound, stir; SEE CONCEPT 595

rustle [v] *swish, whisper*
crackle, crepitate, crinkle, hum, murmur, patter, sigh, stir, tap, whir, whish, whoosh; SEE CONCEPT 65

rusty [adj1] *corroded*
decayed, oxidized, rust-covered, rusted; SEE CONCEPT 485

rusty [adj2] *out of practice; inexperienced*
deficient, impaired, neglected, not what it was*, sluggish, soft, stale, unpracticed, unqualified, weak; SEE CONCEPT 527

rut [n1] *groove, indentation*
furrow, gouge, hollow, pothole, rabbet, score, track, trench, trough; SEE CONCEPT 513

rut [n2] *routine of daily life*
circle, circuit, course, custom, daily grind*, dead end*, grind*, groove, habit, humdrum*, pace, pattern, performance, practice, procedure, rote, round, system, treadmill, usage, wont; SEE CONCEPTS 6,647

ruthless [adj] *mean, heartless*
adamant, barbarous, brutal, callous, cold, coldblooded, cruel, cutthroat, dog-eat-dog*, feral, ferocious, fierce, grim, hard, hard-hearted, harsh, implacable, inexorable, inhuman, ironfisted, killer, malevolent, merciless, mortal, obdurate, pitiless, rancorous, relentless, remorseless, revengeful, sadistic, savage, severe, stern, stony, surly, unappeasable, unfeeling, unforgiving, unmerciful, unrelenting, unsympathetic, unyielding, vicious, vindictive, without pity; SEE CONCEPTS 401,404

S

sable [adj] *very dark in color*
black, dark, dusky, dusty, ebon, ebony, gloomy, inky, jet, jetty, murky, pitch-black, pitch-dark, raven, somber; SEE CONCEPT 618

sabotage [n] *damage*
demolition, destruction, disruption, impairment, injury, mischief, overthrow, subversion, subversiveness, treachery, treason, undermining, vandalism, wreckage, wrecking; SEE CONCEPTS 86,246,252

sabotage [v] *incapacitate, damage*
attack, block, bollix, break up, cripple, deep six*, destroy, disable, disrupt, do*, do in*, foul up*, frustrate, hamper, hinder, louse up*, mess up*, obstruct, put out of action, put out of commission*, screw up*, subvert, take out*, throw a monkey wrench into*, torpedo*, undermine, vandalize, wreck; SEE CONCEPTS 86,246,252

sack [v1] *remove from position of responsibility*
ax*, bounce*, can*, cashier, discharge, dismiss, drop, expel, fire, give a pink slip*, give marching orders*, give the boot*, kick out, send packing*, ship, terminate; SEE CONCEPT 351

sack [v2] *raid, plunder*
demolish, depredate, desecrate, desolate, despoil, destroy, devastate, devour, fleece, gut, lay waste, loot, maraud, pillage, ravage, rifle, rob, ruin, spoil, spoliate, strip, waste; SEE CONCEPTS 139,252

sacred [adj1] *holy, blessed*
angelic, cherished, consecrated, divine, enshrined, godly, hallowed, numinous, pious, pure, religious, revered, sacramental, saintly, sanctified, solemn, spiritual, unprofane, venerable; SEE CONCEPT 574

sacred [adj2] *protected*
dedicated, defended, guarded, immune, inviolable, inviolate, invulnerable, sacrosanct, secure, shielded, untouchable; SEE CONCEPT 587

sacrifice [v] *give up, let go*
cede, drop, endure, eschew, forfeit, forgo, immolate, kiss goodbye*, lose, offer, offer up, part with, renounce, resign oneself to, spare, suffer, surrender, waive, yield; SEE CONCEPTS 108,116

sacrilege [n] *irreverence*
blasphemy, crime, curse, desecration, heresy, impiety, mockery, offense, profanation, profaneness, profanity, sin, violation; SEE CONCEPT 645

sad [adj1] *unhappy, depressed*
bereaved, bitter, blue*, cheerless, dejected, despairing, despondent, disconsolate, dismal, distressed, doleful, down, downcast, down in dumps*, down in mouth*, forlorn, gloomy, glum, grief-stricken, grieved, heartbroken, heartsick, heavyhearted, hurting, in doldrums*, in grief, in the dumps*, languishing, low, low-spirited, lugubrious, melancholy, morbid, morose, mournful, out of sorts*, pensive, pessimistic, sick at heart*, somber, sorrowful, sorry, troubled, weeping, wistful, woebegone; SEE CONCEPT 403

sad [adj2] *unfortunate, distressing*
bad, calamitous, dark, dejecting, deplorable, depressing, disastrous, discomposing, discouraging, disheartening, dismal, dispiriting, dreary, funereal, grave, grievous, hapless, heart-rending, joyless, lachrymose, lamentable, lugubrious, melancholic, miserable, moving, oppressive, pathetic, pitiable, pitiful, poignant, regrettable, saddening, serious, shabby, sorry, tearful, tearjerking*, tragic, unhappy, unsatisfactory, upsetting, wretched; SEE CONCEPTS 529,548

sadden [v] *upset, depress*
break one's heart*, bring one down*, bum out*, cast down, dampen spirits, dash, deject, deplore,

desolate, discourage, dishearten, dispirit, distress, down, drag down*, grieve, make blue*, oppress, press, put a damper on*, put into a funk*, throw cold water on*, turn one off*, weigh down*; SEE CONCEPTS 7,19

sadistic [adj] *cruel, perverted*
barbarous, brutal, fiendish, perverse, ruthless, vicious; SEE CONCEPTS 542,545

sadness [n] *unhappiness, depression*
anguish, blahs*, bleakness, blue devils*, blue funk*, broken heart*, bummer, cheerlessness, dejection, despondency, disconsolateness, dismals*, dispiritedness, distress, dolefulness, dolor, downcastness, downer*, dysphoria, forlornness, funk, gloominess, grief, grieving, heartache, heartbreak, heavy heart*, hopelessness, letdown, listlessness, melancholy, misery, moodiness, mopes*, mournfulness, mourning, poignancy, sorrow, sorrowfulness, the blues*, the dumps*, tribulation, woe; SEE CONCEPT 410

safe [adj1] *free from harm*
buttoned up*, cherished, free from danger, guarded, home-free*, impervious, impregnable, in safety, intact, inviolable, invulnerable, maintained, okay*, out of danger, out of harm's way*, preserved, protected, safe and sound*, safeguarded, secure, sheltered, shielded, sitting pretty*, snug, tended, unassailable, undamaged, under lock and key*, under one's wing*, unharmed, unhurt, uninjured, unmolested, unscathed, unthreatened, vindicated, watched; SEE CONCEPT 587

safe [adj2] *not dangerous*
certain, checked, clear, competent, decontaminated, dependable, harmless, healthy, innocent, innocuous, innoxious, inoffensive, neutralized, nonpoisonous, nontoxic, pure, reliable, risk-free, riskless, secure, sound, tame, trustworthy, uninjurious, unpolluted, wholesome; SEE CONCEPTS 314,537,548

safe [adj3] *cautious, conservative*
calculating, careful, chary, circumspect, competent, considerate, dependable, discreet, gingerly, guarded, on safe side*, prudent, realistic, reliable, sure, tried and true*, trustworthy, unadventurous, wary; SEE CONCEPTS 401,542

safeguard [n] *protection*
aegis, armament, armor, buffer, bulwark, convoy, defense, escort, guard, screen, security, shield, surety, ward; SEE CONCEPT 712

safeguard [v] *protect*
assure, bulwark, conserve, cover, defend, ensure, fend, guard, insure, look after, preserve, ride shotgun*, save, screen, secure, shield, watch over; SEE CONCEPT 96

safety [n] *protection from harm*
assurance, asylum, cover, defense, freedom, immunity, impregnability, inviolability, invulnerability, refuge, safeness, sanctuary, security, shelter; SEE CONCEPT 729

safety net [n] *level of economic security guaranteed by government*
benefits, buffer, government aid, insurance, precaution, protective umbrella, safeguard, subsidy; SEE CONCEPT 344

sag [n] *drop, decline*
basin, cant, concavity, depression, dip, distortion, downslide*, downswing*, downtrend, downturn, droop, fall, fall-off, hollow, list, settling, sink,

sinkage, sinkhole, sinking, slant, slip, slump, tilt; SEE CONCEPTS 181,698,776

sag [v] *droop*
bag, bend, bow, bulge, cave in, curve, dangle, decline, dip, drop, drop off, fail, fall, fall away, fall off, flag, flap, flop, give way, hang, hang down, languish, lean, settle, sink, slide, slip, slump, swag, wilt; SEE CONCEPTS 181,698,776

saga [n] *story, often long*
adventure, chronicle, epic, legend, narrative, soap opera*, tale, yarn; SEE CONCEPT 282

sagacious [adj] *smart, judicious*
acute, apt, astucious, astute, cagey, canny, clear-sighted, clever, cool*, discerning, discriminating, far-sighted, foxy*, gnostic, heady, hip*, insightful, intelligent, keen, knowing, knowledgeable, perceptive, perspicacious, prudent, rational, sage, sapient, savvy*, sensible, sharp, shrewd, smooth, sophic, wise, witty; SEE CONCEPT 402

sail [v] *travel through water, air; glide*
boat, captain, cast anchor, cast off, cross, cruise, dart, drift, embark, flit, float, fly, get under way*, leave, make headway, motor, move, navigate, pilot, put to sea*, reach, run, scud, set sail, shoot, skim, skipper, skirr, soar, steer, sweep, tack, voyage, weigh anchor, wing; SEE CONCEPT 224

sailboat [n] *a boat propelled with wind by sailcloth*
bark, brig, brigantine, catamaran, craft, cutter, dory, gaff-rigged sailboat, galleon, galley, jack, ketch, pinnace, ragboat*, schooner, ship, skiff, sloop, Sunfish, tall ship, windjammer, wooden boat, yacht, yawl; SEE CONCEPT 506

sailor [n] *person who travels by sea*
able-bodied sailor, bluejacket*, boater, cadet, circumnavigator, deck hand, diver, hearty*, jack*, lascar*, marine, mariner, mate, middy, midshipman/woman, navigator, old salt*, pilot, pirate, salt*, sea dog*, seafarer, sea person, shellback*, shipmate, swab, swabber*, swabbie*, tar*, tarpaulin*, water dog*, windjammer*, yachter; SEE CONCEPTS 348,358,366

saintly [adj] *good, righteous*
angelic, beatific, blameless, blessed, devout, divine, god-fearing, godly, holy, pious, pure, religious, sainted, saintlike, seraph, sinless, upright, upstanding, virtuous, worthy; SEE CONCEPT 404

sake [n1] *benefit, gain*
account, advantage, behalf, consideration, good, interest, profit, regard, respect, welfare, well-being; SEE CONCEPT 693

sake [n2] *reason, objective*
aim, cause, consequence, end, final cause, motive, principle, purpose, score; SEE CONCEPTS 659,661

salary [n] *money paid for work done*
bacon*, bread*, earnings, emolument, fee, hire, income, pay, payroll, recompense, remuneration, scale, stipend, take, take-home*, wage, wages; SEE CONCEPT 344

sale [n] *exchange of object for money*
auction, barter, business, buying, clearance, closeout, commerce, consuming, deal, demand, disposal, dumping, enterprise, marketing, negotiation, purchase, purchasing, reduction, selling, trade, transaction, unloading, vending, vendition; SEE CONCEPTS 324,345

salient [adj] *noticeable, important*
arresting, arrestive, conspicuous, famous, impressive, intrusive, jutting, marked, moving, notable, obtrusive, obvious, outstanding, pertinent, pro-

ru
sa

jecting, prominent, pronounced, protruding, remarkable, signal, significant, striking, weighty; SEE CONCEPT 567

sallow [adj] pale, unhealthy
anemic, ashen, ashy, bilious, colorless, dull, greenish-yellow, jaundiced, muddy, pallid, pasty, wan, waxy, yellowish; SEE CONCEPT 618

saloon [n] business establishment that primarily serves liquor
alehouse, bar, barroom, beer joint*, cocktail lounge, dive*, drinkery, gin mill*, hangout*, joint*, night club, pub, public house, speakeasy, taproom, tavern, watering hole*; SEE CONCEPTS 439,448,449

salt away [v] save, store up
accumulate, amass, bank, cache, hide, hoard, invest, lay aside, lay away, put away, put by, put in the bank, save, save for rainy day*, set aside, spare, stash, stockpile; SEE CONCEPT 330

salty [adj1] flavored with sodium chloride
acrid, alkaline, brackish, briny, highly flavored, oversalted, pungent, saliferous, saline, salt, salted, saltish, sour; SEE CONCEPTS 462,613

salty [adj2] spicy, colorful
humorous, lively, piquant, pungent, racy, sharp, snappy, tangy, tart, witty, zestful; SEE CONCEPTS 401,589

salubrious [adj] health-giving
beneficial, good, healthful, healthy, hygienic, invigorating, salutary, sanitary, wholesome; SEE CONCEPTS 560,572

salute/salutation [n] greeting, recognition
address, bow, howdy*, kiss, obeisance, tribute, welcome; SEE CONCEPT 38

salute [v] greet; honor
accost, acknowledge, address, bow, call to, congratulate, hail, pay homage, pay respects, pay tribute, present arms, receive, recognize, snap to attention*, speak, take hat off to*, welcome; SEE CONCEPTS 38,69,320

salvage [v] save, rescue
deliver, get back, glean, ransom, reclaim, recover, redeem, regain, restore, retrieve, salve; SEE CONCEPT 134

salvation [n] rescue, saving
conservancy, conservation, deliverance, emancipation, escape, exemption, extrication, keeping, liberation, lifeline, pardon, preserval, preservation, redemption, release, reprieve, restoration, safekeeping, sustentation; SEE CONCEPT 134

salve [n] ointment for relief of pain or illness
aid, balm, cerate, counterirritant, cream, cure, dressing, emollient, help, liniment, lotion, lubricant, medication, medicine, remedy, unction, unguent; SEE CONCEPTS 311,466

same [adj1] alike, identical
aforementioned, aforesaid, carbon*, carbon-copy*, clone, coequal, comparable, compatible, corresponding, ditto*, double, dupe*, duplicate, equal, equivalent, indistinguishable, interchangeable, in the same manner, like, likewise, look-alike, related, same difference, selfsame, similar, similarly, synonymous, tantamount, twin, very, Xerox*; SEE CONCEPTS 487,566,573

same [adj2] unchanging
changeless, consistent, constant, invariable, perpetual, unaltered, unchanged, unfailing, uniform, unvarying; SEE CONCEPT 534

sameness [n] likeness, similarity
adequation, alikeness, analogy, equality, equiva-

lency, identicalness, identity, indistinguishability, monotony, no difference, oneness, par, parity, predictability, repetition, resemblance, selfsameness, standardization, tedium, uniformity, unison, unity, unvariedness; SEE CONCEPTS 667,670

sample [n] example, model
bit, bite, case, case history, constituent, cross section, element, exemplification, fragment, illustration, indication, individual, instance, morsel, part, pattern, piece, portion, representative, sampling, segment, sign, specimen, typification, unit; SEE CONCEPTS 686,835

sample [v] taste, try
examine, experience, experiment, inspect, partake, savor, sip, test; SEE CONCEPTS 103,616

sanctify [v] hold in highest esteem
absolve, anoint, bless, cleanse, consecrate, dedicate, deify, enshrine, glorify, hallow, purify, set apart, worship; SEE CONCEPTS 10,12

sanctimonious [adj] self-righteous
bigoted, canting, deceiving, false, goody-goody*, holier-than-thou*, hypocritical, insincere, pharisaical, pietistic, pious, preachy, self-satisfied, smug, stuffy, unctuous; SEE CONCEPTS 401,404

sanction [n1] authorization
acquiescence, allowance, approbation, approval, assent, authority, backing, confirmation, consent, countenance, encouragement, endorsement, fiat, go-ahead*, green light*, leave, nod, okay*, permission, permit, ratification, recommendation, seal of approval*, stamp of approval*, sufferance, support, word; SEE CONCEPT 685

sanction [n2] embargo, punishment
ban, boycott, coercive measure, command, decree, injunction, penalty, punitive measure, sentence, writ; SEE CONCEPT 123

sanction [v] authorize, confirm
accredit, allow, approve, back, bless, certify, commission, countenance, empower, endorse, get behind*, give the go-ahead*, give the green light*, give the nod*, go for*, license, okay*, permit, ratify, support, vouch for, warrant; SEE CONCEPTS 50,88

sanctuary [n1] church; holiest room or area in religious building
altar, chancel, holy place, sanctorium, sanctum, shrine, temple; SEE CONCEPTS 368,439,448

sanctuary [n2] place to hide, be safe
asylum, church, convent, cover, covert, defense, den, harbor, harborage, haven, hideaway, hideout, hole, hole-up*, ivory tower*, oasis, port, protection, refuge, resort, retreat, safe house, screen, shelter, shield; SEE CONCEPTS 515,516

sanctuary [n3] safe place for wildlife
asylum, conservation area, game refuge, harborage, national park, nature preserve, park, preserve, refuge, reserve, retreat, shelter; SEE CONCEPT 517

sane [adj] mentally sound; reasonable
all there*, balanced, both oars in water*, commonsensical, compos mentis, discerning, fair-minded, fit, having all marbles*, healthy, in one's right mind*, intelligent, judicious, levelheaded, logical, lucid, moderate, normal, of sound mind, oriented, playing with full deck*, prudent, rational, right, right-minded, sagacious, sage, sapient, self-possessed, sensible, sober, sound, steady, together*, well, wise; SEE CONCEPTS 314,402,403

sanguine [adj1] happy; optimistic
animated, assured, buoyant, cheerful, confident,

enthusiastic, expectant, hopeful, lively, positive, secure, self-assured, self-confident, spirited, undoubtful, upbeat; SEE CONCEPTS 403,542

sanguine [adj2] *reddish; flushed*
bloody, florid, flush, glowing, red, rubicund, ruddy, scarlet; SEE CONCEPT 618

sanitary [adj] *clean, germ-free*
healthful, healthy, hygienic, prophylactic, purified, salubrious, sanative, sterile, uncontaminated, uninfected, unpolluted, unsullied, wholesome; SEE CONCEPT 621

sanity [n] *mental health; soundness of judgment*
acumen, balance, clear mind, common sense, comprehension, good judgment, healthy mind, intelligence, judiciousness, levelheadedness, lucidity, lucidness, marbles*, normality, prudence, rationality, reason, reasonableness, right mind*, sagacity, saneness, sense, sound mind, soundness, stability, understanding, wit; SEE CONCEPTS 409,410

sap [n] *stupid person*
chump, dolt, dupe, fool, idiot, jerk, nitwit, patsy*, pigeon*, simpleton, sucker*, weakling; SEE CONCEPT 412

sap [v] *squeeze out; weaken*
attenuate, bleed, blunt, cripple, debilitate, deplete, destroy, devitalize, disable, drain, enervate, enfeeble, erode, exhaust, impair, prostrate, rob, ruin, subvert, undermine, vitiate, wear down, wreck; SEE CONCEPTS 142,156,240,246

sappy [adj] *foolish, sentimental*
absurd, balmy, bathetic, crazy*, drippy*, idiotic, illogical, insane, loony*, maudlin, mushy*, preposterous, silly, slushy*, soppy*, sticky*, stupid; SEE CONCEPTS 403,542

sarcasm [n] *mocking remark*
acrimony, aspersion, banter, bitterness, burlesque, causticness, censure, comeback, contempt, corrosiveness, criticism, cut*, cynicism, derision, dig*, disparagement, flouting, invective, irony, lampooning, mockery, mordancy, putdown*, raillery, rancor, ridicule, satire, scoffing, scorn, sharpness, sneering, superciliousness, wisecrack; SEE CONCEPTS 52,54,277,278

sarcastic [adj] *nasty, mocking in speech*
acerb, acerbic, acid, acrimonious, arrogant, austere, backhanded, biting, bitter, brusque, captious, carping, caustic, chaffing, contemptuous, contumelious, corrosive, cussed*, cutting, cynical, derisive, disillusioned, disparaging, disrespectful, evil, hostile, irascible, ironical, mean, mordant, needling, offensive, ornery*, salty, sardonic, satirical, saucy*, scorching, scornful, scurrilous, severe, sharp, smart-alecky*, snarling, sneering, taunting, trenchant, twitting, weisenheiming*; SEE CONCEPT 267

satiate [v] *stuff, satisfy completely or excessively*
cloy, content, feed to gills*, fill, glut, gorge, gratify, indulge, jade, nauseate, overdose, overfill, pall, sate, saturate, slake, surfeit; SEE CONCEPTS 169,740

satire [n] *ridicule intended to expose truth*
banter, burlesque, caricature, causticity, chaffing, irony, lampoon, lampoonery, mockery, parody, pasquinade, persiflage, play-on, put-on*, raillery, sarcasm, send-up*, skit, spoof, squib*, takeoff*, travesty, wit, witticism; SEE CONCEPTS 263,271,280

satirical/satiric [adj] *mocking*
abusive, bantering, biting, bitter, burlesque, caus-

tic, censorious, chaffing, cutting, cynical, farcical, incisive, ironical, lampooning, mordant, paradoxical, parodying, pungent, ridiculing, sarcastic, sardonic, spoofing, taunting; SEE CONCEPT 267

satisfaction [n] *giving or enjoying a state of comfort, content*
achievement, amends, amusement, atonement, bliss, cheerfulness, comfort, compensation, complacency, conciliation, contentedness, contentment, delight, ease, enjoyment, fulfillment, gladness, good fortune, gratification, happiness, indemnification, indulgence, joy, justice, peace of mind, pleasure, pride, propitiation, recompense, redress, refreshment, reimbursement, relief, reparation, repletion, resolution, reward, satiety, serenity, settlement, vindication, well-being; SEE CONCEPTS 344,410,720

satisfactory [adj] *acceptable, sufficient*
adequate, all right, ample, A-OK*, appeasing, assuaging, assuasive, average, cogent, comfortable, competent, cool*, decent, delighting, enough, fair, fulfilling, good, good enough, gratifying, groovy*, passable, peachy*, pleasing, satisfying, solid, sound, sufficing, suitable, tolerable, unexceptional, up to snuff*, valid; SEE CONCEPTS 529,558,560

satisfy [v1] *please, content*
amuse, animate, appease, assuage, befriend, brighten up, captivate, capture, cheer, cloy, comfort, conciliate, content, delight, do the trick*, elate, enliven, entertain, enthrall, exhilarate, fascinate, fill, fill the bill*, flatter, get by, gladden, glut, gorge, gratify, hit the spot*, humor, indulge, make merry, make the grade*, mollify, pacify, placate, propitiate, quench, rejoice, sate, satiate, score, sell, sell on, slake, suit, surfeit; SEE CONCEPTS 7,22

satisfy [v2] *answer, persuade*
accomplish, appease, assuage, assure, avail, be adequate, be enough, be sufficient, come up to, complete, comply with, conform to, convince, dispel doubt, do, equip, fill, fulfill, furnish, get by, induce, inveigle, keep promise, make good, make the grade*, meet, observe, pass muster*, perform, provide, put mind at ease*, qualify, quiet, reassure, score, sell, serve, serve the purpose*, suffice, tide over*, win over; SEE CONCEPTS 108,140,656

satisfy [v3] *pay, compensate*
answer, atone, clear up, disburse, discharge, indemnify, liquidate, make good*, make reparation, meet, pay off, quit, recompense, remunerate, repay, require, reward, settle, square*; SEE CONCEPTS 126,341

saturate [v] *drench, wet through*
bathe, douche, douse, imbue, immerse, impregnate, infuse, overfill, penetrate, percolate, permeate, pervade, sate, satiate, soak, sop, souse, steep, suffuse, surfeit, transfuse, wash, waterlog; SEE CONCEPT 256

saucy [adj] *disrespectful*
arch, audacious, bold, brash, brazen, cheeky*, combative, contumelious, flip*, flippant, forward, fresh, impertinent, impudent, insolent, intrusive, meddlesome, nervy, obtrusive, pert, presumptuous, rude, sassy, smart, smart-alecky*, smug, snippy*, volatile, weisenheiming*, wise; SEE CONCEPTS 267,401

sa
sa

saunter [n] *stroll*
airing, amble, constitutional, promenade, ramble, turn, walk; SEE CONCEPT 151

saunter [v] *stroll along*
amble, ankle, dally, drift, linger, loiter, meander, mope*, mosey*, ooze*, percolate, promenade, ramble, roam, rove, sashay, stump, tarry, toddle, traipse, trill, wander; SEE CONCEPT 151

savage [adj1] *wild, untamed*
aboriginal, ancient, archaic, barbarian, barbaric, bestial, brutal, brute, crude, earliest, feral, ferocious, fierce, first, fundamental, harsh, in a state of nature, lupine, native, natural, nonliterate, original, primary, primeval, primitive, primordial, pristine, rough, rude, rugged, rustic, simple, turbulent, unbroken, uncivilized, uncultivated, uncultured, undomesticated, unmodified, unrestrained, unspoiled, vicious; SEE CONCEPTS 401,485

savage [adj2] *cruel, vicious*
atrocious, barbarous, beastly, bestial, bloodthirsty, bloody, brutal, brutish, cold-blooded, crazed, demoniac, destructive, devilish, diabolical, fell, feral, ferine, ferocious, fierce, frantic, furious, grim, harsh, heartless, hellish, infernal, inhuman, inhumane, malevolent, malicious, merciless, murderous, pitiless, rabid, raging, rapacious, ravening, relentless, remorseless, ruthless, sadistic, truculent, unrelenting, violent, wolfish; SEE CONCEPTS 401,540,542

save [v1] *rescue*
bail out, come to rescue, defend, deliver, emancipate, extricate, free, get off the hook*, get out of hock*, give a break, liberate, pull out of fire*, ransom, recover, redeem, salvage, save one's neck*, set free, spring, unchain, unshackle; SEE CONCEPTS 127,134

save [v2] *economize; set money aside for later use*
amass, be frugal, be thrifty, cache, collect, conserve, cut corners*, deposit, economize, feather nest*, gather, hide away, hoard, hold, keep, lay aside, lay away, maintain, make ends meet*, manage, pile up, pinch pennies*, put by, reserve, retrench, roll back*, salt away*, save for rainy day*, scrimp, skimp, sock away*, spare, squirrel*, stash, stockpile, store, stow away, tighten belt*, treasure; SEE CONCEPTS 120,129,330

save [v3] *guard, protect*
conserve, defend, keep safe, keep up, look after, maintain, preserve, safeguard, screen, shield, sustain, take care of; SEE CONCEPTS 96,117

savings [n] *provision for future*
accumulation, ace in hole*, cache, fund, funds, gleanings, harvest, hoard, investment, kitty*, mattress full*, means, money in the bank, nest egg*, property, provision, provisions, rainy day fund*, reserve, reserves, resources, riches, sock, stake, stockpile, store; SEE CONCEPTS 335,340,446,710

savior [n] *person who redeems, aids in time of difficulty*
conservator, defender, deliverer, friend in need*, Good Samaritan*, guardian, guardian angel, hero, liberator, preserver, protector, rescuer, salvager, salvation; SEE CONCEPTS 370,416

savor [n1] *taste, flavor*
odor, piquancy, relish, salt, sapidity, sapor, scent, smack, smell, spice, tang, tinge, zest; SEE CONCEPT 614

savor [n2] *distinctive quality*
affection, attribute, character, characteristic, excitement, feature, flavor, interest, mark, property, salt, spice, trait, virtue, zest; SEE CONCEPTS 411,543

savor [v] *delight in, enjoy*
appreciate, experience, feel, gloat, know, like, luxuriate in, partake, relish, revel in, sample, sip, smack, smell, taste; SEE CONCEPTS 32,616

savory [adj] *pleasing, delicious in flavor*
agreeable, ambrosial, aperitive, appetizing, aromatic, dainty, decent, delectable, exquisite, fragrant, full-flavored, good, luscious, mellow, mouthwatering, palatable, perfumed, piquant, pungent, redolent, relishing, respectable, rich, sapid, savorous, scrumptious, spicy, sweet, tangy, tasty, tempting, toothsome, wholesome; SEE CONCEPT 613

say [v] *make declaration*
add, affirm, allege, announce, answer, assert, break silence*, claim, come out with, communicate, conjecture, convey, declare, deliver, disclose, divulge, do, estimate, express, flap*, gab*, give voice*, guess, imagine, imply, jaw, judge, lip*, maintain, make known, mention, opine, orate, perform, pronounce, put forth, put into words, rap*, read, recite, rehearse, relate, remark, render, repeat, reply, report, respond, reveal, rumor, speak, spiel*, state, suggest, tell, utter, verbalize, voice, yak*; SEE CONCEPTS 51,266

saying [n] *maxim, proverb*
adage, aphorism, apophthegm, axiom, byword, dictum, epigram, motto, precept, saw, statement, truism; SEE CONCEPT 278

scale [n1] *graduated system*
calibration, computation, degrees, extent, gamut, gradation, hierarchy, ladder, order, pecking order*, progression, proportion, range, ranking, rate, ratio, reach, register, rule, scope, sequence, series, spectrum, spread, steps, system, way; SEE CONCEPTS 651,744,770,788

scale [n2] *thin covering, skin*
film, flake, incrustation, lamina, layer, plate, scurf; SEE CONCEPTS 399,484

scale [v1] *ascend, climb*
clamber, escalade, escalate, go up, mount, surmount; SEE CONCEPT 166

scale [v2] *measure*
adjust, balance, calibrate, compare, compute, estimate, gauge, graduate, proportion, prorate, regulate, size; SEE CONCEPT 764

scamper [v] *run, dash*
bolt, dart, flee, fly, hasten, hie, hurry, light out, make off, race, romp, rush off, scoot, scurry, scuttle, shoot, skedaddle*, skip, speed, speed away, sprint, tear, trot, whip, zip*; SEE CONCEPT 150

scan [v] *look over, scrutinize lightly*
browse, check, consider, contemplate, dip into*, examine, flash*, flip through, give the once-over*, glance at, glance over, have a look-see*, inquire, investigate, leaf through*, look, look through, look up and down*, overlook, regard, riff, riffle, rumble, run over, run through, scour, search, size up, skim, study, survey, sweep, take a gander*, take stock of*, thumb through*; SEE CONCEPTS 103,623

scandal [n] *public embarrassment*
aspersion, backbiting, backstabbing, belittlement, calumny, crime, defamation, depreciation, detraction, dirty linen*, discredit, disgrace, dishonor,

disparagement, disrepute, dynamite, eavesdropping, gossip, hearsay, idle rumor, ignominy, infamy, mud, obloquy, opprobrium, reproach, rumor, scorcher, shame, sin, skeleton in closet*, slander, tale, talk, turpitude, wrongdoing; SEE CONCEPTS 278,645,674

scandalous [*adj*] *disreputable*
atrocious, backbiting, calumnious, crying, defamatory, desperate, detracting, detractive, disgraceful, gossiping, heinous, ignominious, infamous, libelous, maligning, monstrous, odious, opprobrious, outrageous, red hot*, scurrilous, shameful, shocking, slanderous, traducing, unseemly, untrue, vilifying; SEE CONCEPT 545

scant/scanty [*adj*] *inadequate*
bare, barely sufficient, close, deficient, exiguous, failing, insufficient, limited, little, meager, minimal, narrow, poor, rare, restricted, scrimpy, short, shy, skimpy, slender, spare, sparing, sparse, stingy, thin, tight, wanting; SEE CONCEPTS 766,767,789

scapegoat [*n*] *person who takes blame for another's action*
dupe, goat*, mark*, patsy*, sacrifice, substitute, sucker, target, victim; SEE CONCEPT 412

scar [*n*] *blemish from previous injury or illness*
blister, cacatrice, cicatrix, crater, defect, discoloration, disfigurement, flaw, hurt, mark, pockmark, scab, track, wound; SEE CONCEPT 580

scar [*v*] *mark, hurt*
beat, blemish, brand, cut, damage, deface, disfigure, flaw, injure, maim, mar, pinch, score, scratch, slash, stab, traumatize; SEE CONCEPTS 7,19,137,176,246

scarce [*adj*] *insufficient, infrequent*
at a premium, deficient, failing, few, few and far between*, in short supply, limited, occasional, rare, scant, scanty, seldom, seldom met with, semioccasional, short, shortened, shy, sparse, sporadic, truncated, uncommon, unusual, wanting; SEE CONCEPTS 541,789

scarcely [*adv*] *barely*
hardly, imperceptibly, infrequently, just, just barely, only just, rarely, scantily, seldom, slightly; SEE CONCEPTS 541,789

scare [*n*] *frightened state*
alarm, alert, fright, panic, shock, start, terror; SEE CONCEPTS 230,410

scare [*v*] *frighten someone*
affright, alarm, awe, chill, daunt, dismay, freeze, give a fright, give a turn*, intimidate, panic, paralyze, petrify, scare silly*, scare stiff*, scare the pants off*, shake up*, shock, spook, startle, strike terror in, terrify, terrorize; SEE CONCEPTS 7,19,42

scared [*adj*] *frightened*
afraid, aghast, anxious, fearful, having cold feet*, panicked, panicky, panic-stricken, petrified, shaken, startled, terrified, terror-stricken; SEE CONCEPT 403

scary [*adj*] *frightening, terrifying*
alarming, bloodcurdling, chilling, creepy, eerie, hair-raising, hairy*, horrendous, horrifying, intimidating, shocking, spine-chilling, spooky, unnerving; SEE CONCEPTS 529,548

scathing [*adj*] *nasty, critical in remarks*
belittling, biting, brutal, burning, caustic, cruel, cutting, harsh, mordacious, mordant, salty, sarcastic, scorching, scornful, searing, severe, sulphurous, trenchant, withering; SEE CONCEPT 267

scatter [*v*] *strew, disperse*
besprinkle, broadcast, cast, derange, diffuse, disband, discard, disject, dispel, disseminate, dissipate, distribute, disunite, diverge, divide, expend, fling, intersperse, litter, migrate, part, pour, put to flight*, run away, scramble, separate, set, set asunder, sever, shatter, shed, shower, sow, spend, split up, spray, spread, sprinkle, sunder, take off in all directions*, throw around, throw out; SEE CONCEPTS 179,217,222

scatterbrained [*adj*] *not thinking clearly*
birdbrained*, careless, dizzy, empty-headed*, featherbrained*, flighty, forgetful, frivolous, giddy, harebrained*, illogical, inattentive, irrational, irresponsible, madcap, silly, slaphappy*, stupid, thoughtless; SEE CONCEPT 402

scenario [*n*] *master plan; sequence of events*
book, outline, pages, plot, résumé, rundown, scheme, sides, sketch, story line, summary, synopsis; SEE CONCEPTS 282,283,660

scene [*n1*] *setting of a performance or event*
arena, backdrop, background, blackout, display, exhibition, flat, flats, landscape, locale, locality, location, mise en scène, outlook, pageant, picture, place, representation, scenery, seascape, set, setting, show, sight, site, spectacle, spot, stage, tableau, theater, view; SEE CONCEPTS 263,625,628

scene [*n2*] *part of a dramatic performance*
act, bit, episode, incident, part, piece, routine, schtick, spot; SEE CONCEPT 264

scene [*n3*] *display of emotion*
carrying-on*, commotion, confrontation, exhibition, fit, fuss, performance, row, tantrum, temper tantrum, to-do*, upset; SEE CONCEPT 633

scene [*n4*] *field of interest*
arena, business, compass, culture, environment, field, milieu, setting, sphere, world; SEE CONCEPT 349

scenery [*n*] *surroundings*
backdrop, decor, flat, flats, furnishings, furniture, landscape, mise en scène, neighborhood, properties, props, prospect, set, setting, spectacle, sphere, stage set, stage setting, terrain, view, vista; SEE CONCEPTS 263,628

scenic [*adj*] *beautiful, picturesque*
breathtaking, dramatic, grand, impressive, panoramic, spectacular, striking; SEE CONCEPTS 485,579

scent [*n*] *smell, aroma*
aura, balm, bouquet, essence, fragrance, incense, odor, perfume, redolence, spice, tang, track, trail, whiff; SEE CONCEPT 599

scent [*v*] *detect, smell*
be on the track of*, be on the trail of*, discern, get wind of*, nose, nose out*, recognize, sense, sniff; SEE CONCEPTS 601,602

schedule [*n*] *plan for one's time*
agenda, appointments, calendar, catalog, chart, diagram, docket, inventory, itinerary, lineup*, list, order of business, program, record, registry, roll, roster, sked*, table, timetable; SEE CONCEPTS 271,283,660

schedule [*v*] *plan one's time*
appoint, arrange, be due, book, card, catalog, engage, get on line*, line up*, list, note, organize, pencil in*, program, record, register, reserve, set, set up, sew up*, slate, time, write in one's book*; SEE CONCEPTS 36,125

sa
sc

scheme [n1] *course of action*
arrangement, blueprint, chart, codification, contrivance, design, device, diagram, disposition, draft, expedient, game plan, layout, order, ordering, outline, pattern, plan, presentation, program, project, proposal, proposition, purpose, schedule, schema, strategy, suggestion, system, tactics, theory; SEE CONCEPTS *271,625,660*

scheme [n2] *plot, maneuver to get result*
action, angle*, brainchild*, cabal, conspiracy, coven, dodge*, frame-up*, game, game plan*, gimmick, hookup*, hustle, hype*, intrigue, layout, machination, picture*, pitch, ploy, practice, proposition, put-up job*, ruse, scenario, scene, setup*, shift*, story, stratagem, subterfuge, tactics, trick*, twist*; SEE CONCEPTS *59,645,660*

scheming [adj] *deceitful, sly*
artful, calculating, conniving, crafty, cunning, designing, duplicitous, foxy, slippery, tricky, underhand, wily; SEE CONCEPT *542*

scholar [n] *person who is very involved in education and learning*
academic, augur, bookish person, bookworm*, brain*, critic, disciple, doctor, egghead*, gnome*, grind*, intellectual, learned person, learner, litterateur, person of letters, philosopher, professor, pupil, sage, savant, schoolchild, scientist, student, teacher, tool, wise person; SEE CONCEPT *350*

scholarly [adj] *academic*
bookish, cultured, educated, erudite, intellectual, learned, lettered, literate, longhair*, scholastic, schooled, studious, taught, trained, well-read; SEE CONCEPT *402*

school [n1] *place, system for educating*
academy, alma mater, blackboard*, college, department, discipline, establishment, faculty, hall, halls of ivy*, institute, institution, jail*, schoolhouse, seminary, university; SEE CONCEPTS *287,289*

school [n2] *persons receiving education*
academy, adherents, circle, class, clique, denomination, devotees, disciples, faction, followers, following, group, party, pupils, sect, set; SEE CONCEPTS *288,350*

school [n3] *body of philosophy on subject*
belief, creed, faith, outlook, persuasion, school of thought, stamp*, way, way of life; SEE CONCEPTS *349,689*

school [v] *teach*
advance, coach, control, cultivate, direct, discipline, drill, educate, guide, indoctrinate, inform, instruct, lead, manage, prepare, prime, show, train, tutor, verse; SEE CONCEPT *285*

science [n] *methodical study of part of material world*
art, body of knowledge, branch, discipline, education, erudition, information, learning, lore, scholarship, skill, system, technique, wisdom; SEE CONCEPTS *274,349,360*

scientific [adj] *systematic; discovered through experimentation*
accurate, clear, controlled, deductive, exact, experimental, logical, mathematical, methodical, objective, precise, sound; SEE CONCEPT *535*

scintillating [adj] *bright, stimulating*
animated, brilliant, clever, dazzling, ebullient, exciting, flashing, gleaming, glimmering, glinting, glittering, lively, shining, smart, sparkling,

sprightly, twinkling, witty; SEE CONCEPTS *401,529,617*

scion [n] *offshoot, descendant*
begotten, branch, brood, child, chip off old block*, graft, heir, heiress, issue, junior, offspring, progeny, seed, shoot, slip, sprout, successor, twig; SEE CONCEPTS *414,428*

scoff [v] *make fun of; despise*
belittle, boo*, contemn, deride, dig at*, disbelieve, discount, discredit, disdain, flout, gibe, jeer, knock*, laugh at, make light of*, mock, pan*, poke fun at, pooh-pooh*, rag*, rally, reject, revile, ride, ridicule, scorn, show contempt, sneer, tease; SEE CONCEPT *54*

scold [v] *find fault with*
abuse, admonish, asperse, berate, blame, castigate, cavil, censure, chasten, chide, criticize, denounce, disparage, dress down*, expostulate, give a talking-to*, jump on*, keep at*, lay down the law*, lecture, light into*, nag, objurate, preach, put down, rail, rake over the coals*, rate, ream, rebuke, recriminate, reprimand, reproach, reprobate, reprove, revail, take to task*, taunt, tell off*, upbraid, vilify, vituperate; SEE CONCEPTS *44,52,54*

scoop [n1] *utensil, tool for shovelling*
bail, dipper, ladle, shovel, spade, spoon, trowel; SEE CONCEPTS *493,499*

scoop [n2] *previously secret information that is suddenly public*
beat, exclusive, exposé, inside story*, news, revelation, sensation; SEE CONCEPT *274*

scoop [v] *dig up; shovel*
bail, clear away, dig, dig out, dip, empty, excavate, gather, gouge, grub, hollow, lade, ladle, lift, pick up, remove, scrape, spade, sweep away, sweep up, take up; SEE CONCEPT *178*

scope [n] *extent or range of something*
ambit, amplitude, area, breadth, capacity, compass, comprehensiveness, confines, elbow room*, extension, field, field of reference, freedom, fullness, latitude, leeway, liberty, margin, opportunity, orbit, outlook, play, purview, radius, reach, room, run, space, span, sphere, wideness; SEE CONCEPTS *651,739,788*

scorch [v] *burn*
bake, blacken, blister, broil, char, cook, melt, parch, roast, scald, sear, seethe, shrivel, simmer, singe, stale, stew, swelter, wither; SEE CONCEPTS *249,255*

score [n1] *total, points*
account, addition, aggregate, amount, average, count, final count, grade, mark, number, outcome, rate, reckoning, record, result, stock, sum, summary, summation, tab, tally; SEE CONCEPTS *364,784*

score/scores [n2] *large group; a great number*
army, cloud, crowd, drove, flock, host, hundred, legion, lot, mass, million, multitude, myriad, rout, swarm, throng, very many; SEE CONCEPT *432*

score [n3] *musical arrangement*
charts, composition, music, orchestration, transcript; SEE CONCEPT *262*

score [n4] *obligation; account payable*
account, amount due, bill, charge, debt, grievance, grudge, injury, injustice, invoice, reckoning, statement, tab, tally, total; SEE CONCEPTS *332,645*

score [v1] *achieve, succeed*

accomplish, amass, arrive, attain, chalk up*, connect, flourish, gain, gain advantage, get*, hit pay dirt*, impress, luck out*, make a killing*, make an impression*, make the grade*, notch, procure, prosper, pull off*, put over*, rack up*, reach, realize, secure, take the cake*, thrive, triumph, win; SEE CONCEPTS 704,706

score [v2] *keep count*

add, calculate, chalk up, count, enumerate, keep tally, reckon, record, register, tally, total; SEE CONCEPTS 125,764

score [v3] *cut, nick*

cleave, crosshatch, deface, furrow, gash, gouge, graze, groove, indent, line, mark, mill, notch, scrape, scratch, serrate, slash, slit; SEE CONCEPTS 137,176

score [v4] *write a musical arrangement*

adapt, arrange, compose, orchestrate, set; SEE CONCEPTS 79,292

scorn [n] *contempt toward something*

contemptuousness, contumely, derision, despisal, despisement, despite, disdain, disparagement, disregard, jeering, mockery, ridicule, sarcasm, scoffing, scornfulness, slight, sneer, sport, taunting, teasing; SEE CONCEPTS 29,54

scorn [v] *hold in contempt; look down on*

abhor, avoid, be above, confute, consider beneath one*, contemn, defy, deride, despise, disdain, disregard, flout, gibe, hate, ignore, make fun of, mock, put down, refuse, refute, reject, renounce, repudiate, ridicule, run down*, scoff at, shun, slight, sneer, spurn, taunt, trash*, turn back on*, turn nose up at*; SEE CONCEPTS 21,30,52,54

scoundrel [n] *person who is deceptive and uncaring of others*

bad egg*, bad news*, blackguard*, black sheep*, caitiff, cheat, creep, crook, dastard, good-for-nothing*, heel, imp, incorrigible, lowlife*, maggot*, mischiefmaker, miscreant, ne'er-do-well*, rascal, reprobate, scalawag, scamp, thief, vagabond, villain, wretch; SEE CONCEPT 412

scour [v1] *clean, polish thoroughly*

abrade, brush, buff, burnish, cleanse, flush, furbish, mop, pumice, purge, rub, sand, scrub, wash, whiten; SEE CONCEPT 165

scour [v2] *search thoroughly*

beat, comb, ferret out, find, forage, go over with a fine-tooth comb*, grub, hunt, inquire, leave no stone unturned*, look for, look high and low*, look up and down*, rake, ransack, rout, rummage, seek, track down, turn inside out*, turn upside-down*; SEE CONCEPT 216

scourge [n] *plague, torment*

affliction, bane, correction, curse, infliction, misfortune, penalty, pest, pestilence, punishment, terror, visitation; SEE CONCEPTS 674,675

scourge [v] *beat, punish, often physically*

afflict, belt, cane*, castigate, chastise, curse, discipline, excoriate, flail, flog, harass, hit, horsewhip*, lambaste*, lash, penalize, plague, scathe, scorch*, tan*, terrorize, thrash, torment, trounce, wallop*, whale*, whip; SEE CONCEPTS 14,52,122,189

scout [n] *person who is searching, investigating*

advance, adventurer, detective, escort, explorer, guard, lookout, outpost, outrider, patrol, picket, pioneer, precursor, reconnoiterer, recruiter, runner, sleuth, spotter, spy, vanguard; SEE CONCEPTS 348,358

scout [v] *investigate, check out*

case, examine, explore, ferret, have a look-see*, hunt, inspect, look for, observe, probe, reconnoiter, run reconnaissance, rustle up*, search, seek, set eyes on*, spot, spy, stake out, survey, take in, track down, watch; SEE CONCEPTS 103,216,623

scowl [n] *frown*

black look*, dirty look*, evil eye*, glower, grimace; SEE CONCEPTS 185,716

scowl [v] *frown*

disapprove, glare, gloom, glower, grimace, look daggers at*, lour, lower, make a face*; SEE CONCEPT 185

scram [v] *leave quickly*

beat it*, clear out*, decamp, depart, disappear, get lost*, go away, hightail*, make oneself scarce*, make tracks*, scoot*, skedaddle*, take off, vamoose*; SEE CONCEPT 195

scramble [n] *mix-up, confusion*

clutter, commotion, competition, conglomeration, free-for-all*, hash*, hassle, hustle, jumble, jungle, litter, melee, mishmash, muddle, race, rat race*, rush, shuffle, struggle, tumble, tussle; SEE CONCEPTS 230,388,432

scramble [v] *race; get into position clumsily*

clamber, climb, contend, crawl, hasten, jockey for position*, jostle, look alive*, make haste, move, push, run, rush, scrabble, scurry, scuttle, strive, struggle, swarm, trek, vie; SEE CONCEPTS 87,150

scrap [n1] *tiny bit of something*

atom, bite, bits and pieces*, butt, castoff, chip, chunk, crumb, cutting, discard, end, fragment, glob, gob, grain, hunk, iota, jot, junk, leaving, leftover*, lump, mite, modicum, morsel, mouthful, odds and ends*, orts, part, particle, piece, portion, remains, shred, slice, sliver, smithereen*, snatch, snippet, speck, stump, trace, waste; SEE CONCEPTS 831,835

scrap [n2] *argument, fight*

affray, battle, brawl, broil*, disagreement, dispute, fracas, fray, quarrel, row, scuffle, set-to*, squabble, tiff*, wrangle; SEE CONCEPTS 46,106

scrap [v1] *abandon; throw away*

abandon, break up, cast, chuck, consign to scrap heap*, demolish, discard, dismiss, dispense with, ditch, do away with*, drop, forsake, get rid of, jettison, junk, put out to pasture*, reject, retire, shed, slough, throw out, toss out, write off; SEE CONCEPTS 121,180

scrap [v2] *fight, argue*

battle, bicker, caterwaul, come to blows*, fall out, have shouting match*, have words*, quarrel, row, spat, squabble, tiff, wrangle; SEE CONCEPTS 46,106

scrape [n] *bad or embarrassing situation*

awkward situation, corner*, difficulty, dilemma, discomfiture, distress, embarrassment, fix*, hole*, jam*, mess*, pickle*, plight, predicament, tight spot*, trouble; SEE CONCEPT 674

scrape [v1] *scratch, remove outer layer*

abrade, bark, bray, chafe, clean, erase, file, grate, graze, grind, irritate, pare, peel, rasp, rub, scour, scuff, shave, skin, squeak, thin, triturate; SEE CONCEPTS 165,186,215

scrape [v2] *be very frugal*

cut it close*, get along, get by, pinch, save, scrimp, shave, skimp, stint, struggle; SEE CONCEPT 330

scratch [n] *small cut or mark*
blemish, claw mark, gash, graze, hurt, laceration, score, scrape; SEE CONCEPTS 309,513

scratch [v1] *cut; make a mark on*
claw, damage, etch, grate, graze, incise, lacerate, mark, prick, rasp, rub, scarify, score, scrape, scrawl, scribble; SEE CONCEPTS 79,176

scratch [v2] *cancel*
annul, delete, eliminate, erase, pull, pull out, strike, withdraw; SEE CONCEPT 121

scrawl [v] *write erratically*
doodle, inscribe, scrabble, scratch, scribble, squiggle; SEE CONCEPT 79

scrawny [adj] *unhealthily thin*
angular, bony, gaunt, lank, lanky, lean, raw-boned, scraggy, skeletal, skin-and-bones*, skinny, spare, undernourished, underweight; SEE CONCEPTS 490,491,773

scream [n1] *outcry*
cry, high-pitched shout, holler*, howl, screech, shriek, wail, yell, yelp; SEE CONCEPT 595

scream [n2] *person or thing that is very funny*
card*, character*, comedian, comedienne, comic, entertainer, guffaw*, hoot*, howl*, joker, laugh, panic*, riot, sensation, sidesplitter*, wit; SEE CONCEPTS 423,529

scream [v] *cry out*
bawl, bellow, blare, caterwaul, holler*, howl, jar, roar, screak, screech, shout, shriek, shrill, sing out, squeal, voice, wail, yell, yip, yowl; SEE CONCEPT 77

screen [n] *protection used in or as furniture, motion picture display*
awning, canopy, cloak, concealment, cover, covering, curtain, divider, envelope, guard, hedge, mantle, mask, net, partition, security, shade, shelter, shield, shroud, veil; SEE CONCEPTS 277,440,443,445,473

screen [v1] *hide, protect*
adumbrate, blind, block out, bulwark, bury, cache, camouflage, cloak, close, conceal, cover, cover up, defend, disguise, ensconce, fend, guard, mask, obscure, obstruct, safeguard, seclude, secrete, secure, separate, shade, shadow, shelter, shield, shroud, shut off, shut out, shutter, stash, umbrage, veil, wall off; SEE CONCEPTS 96,188

screen [v2] *examine and choose*
cull, eliminate, evaluate, extract, filter, gauge, grade, pick out, process, riddle, scan, select, separate, sieve, sift, sort, winnow; SEE CONCEPT 41

screw [v1] *twist in*
spiral, tighten, turn, twine, wind, work; SEE CONCEPTS 85,160

screw [v2] *twist, contort*
contract, crimp, crinkle, crumple, distort, pucker, rimple, ruck up, rumple, scrunch, wrinkle; SEE CONCEPT 219

screw [v3] *pressure*
bilk, bleed, cheat, chisel, coerce, constrain, defraud, do*, exact, extort, extract, force, hold a knife to*, oppress, pinch*, pressurize, put screws to*, ream*, shake down*, squeeze, wrench, wrest, wring; SEE CONCEPTS 14,192

screw up [v] *make a mess of*
blow, bobble, bollix*, botch, bungle, confuse, flub*, foul up, goof*, goof up*, louse, make hash of*, mess, mess up, mishandle, mismanage, muck up*, muddle, muff, queer, snafu*, spoil; SEE CONCEPT 101

script [n1] *handwriting*
calligraphy, characters, chirography, fist, hand, letters, longhand, penmanship, writing; SEE CONCEPTS 79,284

script [n2] *story for a performance*
article, book, copy, dialogue, libretto, lines, manuscript, playbook, scenario, text, typescript, words; SEE CONCEPTS 263,271

scrounge [v] *beg, forage for*
bum, freeload, hunt, sponge, wheedle; SEE CONCEPTS 48,216

scrub [v1] *clean with force*
abrade, brush, buff, cleanse, mop, polish, rub, scour, wash; SEE CONCEPT 165

scrub [v2] *cancel*
abandon, abolish, abort, call off, delete, discontinue, do away with, drop, forget about, give up; SEE CONCEPTS 121,234

scruffy [adj] *rough, bedraggled*
badly groomed, frowzy*, mangy*, messy, ragged, run-down, seedy, shabby, slovenly, tacky*, tattered, threadbare, ungroomed, unkempt, untidy; SEE CONCEPTS 485,589

scrumptious [adj] *delicious*
ambrosial, appetizing, delectable, delightful, exquisite, heavenly, inviting, luscious, lush, magnificent, mouthwatering, rich, succulent, tasty, yummy; SEE CONCEPTS 529,613

scruple [n] *misgiving, doubt*
anxiety, caution, censor, compunction, conscience, demur, difficulty, faltering, hesitancy, hesitation, pause, perplexity, qualm, reconsideration, reluctance, reluctancy, second thought*, squeamishness, supererogs, twinge, uneasiness; SEE CONCEPTS 532,690

scruple [v] *balk, have misgivings*
be loath, be reluctant, be unwilling, boggle, demur, doubt, falter, fret, gag, have qualms, hesitate, question, shy, stick, stickle, stumble, think twice about*, vacillate, waver, worry; SEE CONCEPT 21

scrupulous [adj] *extremely careful*
conscientious, conscionable, critical, exact, fastidious, fussy, heedful, honest, honorable, just, meticulous, minute, moral, nice, painstaking, particular, precise, principled, punctilious, punctual, right, rigorous, strict, thinking twice*, true, upright; SEE CONCEPTS 401,538,542

scrutinize [v] *examine closely*
analyze, burn up, candle, canvass, case, check, check out, check over, comb*, consider, contemplate, dig, dissect, explore, eyeball*, get a load of*, go over with a fine-tooth comb*, inquire into, inspect, investigate, look over, overlook, peg*, penetrate, perlustrate, peruse, pierce, pore over, probe, put under a microscope*, scan, scope, scrutinate, search, sift, smoke*, stare, study, survey, take the measure of, view, watch, weigh; SEE CONCEPTS 24,103,623

scrutiny [n] *close examination*
analysis, audit, close-up, eagle eye*, exploration, inquiry, inspection, investigation, long hard look*, perlustration, perusal, review, scan, search, sifting, study, surveillance, survey, tab*, the eye*, view; SEE CONCEPTS 24,103,623

scuffle [n] *fight*
affray, brawl, broil, commotion, disturbance, fracas, fray, fuss*, go*, jump, mix-up, row, ruckus, ruction, rumpus, scrap, set-to*, shuffle, strife, tussle, wrangle; SEE CONCEPT 106

scuffle [v] *fight*
clash, come to blows, contend, cuff, grapple, jostle, skirmish, struggle, tussle, wrestle; SEE CONCEPT 106

sculpture [v] *form a three-dimensional art object*
carve, cast, chisel, cut, engrave, fashion, hew, model, mold, sculp, sculpt, shape; SEE CONCEPTS 137,174,184

scum [n1] *superficial impurities, dirt*
algae, crust, dross, film, froth, residue, scruff, spume, waste; SEE CONCEPT 260

scum [n2] *people who are bad, despicable*
curs*, dregs, lowest, mass, mob, proletariat, rabble, riffraff, rubbish*, scum of the earth*, trash*, unwashed, vermin; SEE CONCEPT 412

scurrilous [adj] *foul-mouthed, vulgar*
abusive, coarse, contumelious, defamatory, dirty, filthy, foul, gross, indecent, infamous, insulting, invective, lewd, low, nasty, obscene, offending, offensive, opprobrious, outrageous, raunchy, ribald, salacious, scabrous, scandalous, shameless, slanderous, smutty*, truculent, vituperative, vituperatory, vituperous; SEE CONCEPTS 267,542,545

scurry [v] *move along swiftly*
barrel, bustle, dart, dash, dust, fly, hasten, hop along, hurry, race, rip, run, rush, scamper, scoot, scud, scutter, scuttle, shoot, skim, sprint, step along, tear, whirl, whisk, zip*; SEE CONCEPT 150

sea [n] *large body of water; large mass*
abundance, blue*, bounding main*, brine, briny*, briny deep*, Davy Jones's locker*, deep, drink*, expanse, lake, main, multitude, number, ocean, plethora, pond, profusion, sheet, splash*, surf, swell, waves; SEE CONCEPT 514

seal [n] *authentication; stamp*
allowance, assurance, attestation, authorization, cachet, confirmation, imprimatur, insignia, notification, permission, permit, ratification, signet, sticker, tape, tie; SEE CONCEPTS 284,685

seal [v1] *make airtight*
close, cork, enclose, fasten, gum, isolate, paste, plaster, plug, quarantine, secure, segregate, shut, stop, stopper, stop up, waterproof; SEE CONCEPTS 85,160

seal [v2] *ensure, finalize*
assure, attest, authenticate, clinch, conclude, confirm, consummate, establish, ratify, settle, shake hands on*, stamp, validate; SEE CONCEPTS 234,324

seam [n] *line where two objects are connected*
bond, closure, connection, coupling, gore, gusset, hem, joint, junction, juncture, pleat, stitching, suture, tuck, union; SEE CONCEPTS 452,471

seamy [adj] *corrupt, unwholesome*
bad, dark, degraded, disagreeable, disappointing, disreputable, disturbing, low, nasty, rough, sordid, squalid, unpleasant; SEE CONCEPT 545

sear [v] *dry, burn*
blight, brand, brown, burn up, cauterize, cook, dehydrate, desiccate, dry out, dry up, exsiccate, harden, parch, scorch, seal, shrivel, sizzle, tan, toast, wilt, wither; SEE CONCEPTS 170,249

search [n] *seeking to find something*
chase, examination, exploration, fishing expedition*, frisking*, going-over*, hunt, inquest, inquiry, inspection, investigation, legwork*, perquisition, pursual, pursuance, pursuing, pursuit, quest, research, rummage, scrutiny, shakedown*, wild-goose chase*, witch hunt*; SEE CONCEPT 216

search [v] *seek to find something*
beat, beat about, cast about, chase after, check, comb, examine, explore, ferret, forage, frisk, go in quest of, go over with a fine-tooth comb*, go through, grope, grub, gun for*, hunt, hunt for, inquire, inspect, investigate, leave no stone unturned*, look, look for, look high and low*, look over, poke into, probe, prospect, pry, quest, rake, ransack, rifle through, root, rummage, run down, scan, scour, scout, scrutinize, seek, shake down, sift, smell around, study, track down, turn inside out*, turn upside down*; SEE CONCEPT 216

season [n] *time of year governed by annual equinoxes*
autumn, division, fall, interval, juncture, occasion, opportunity, period, spell, spring, summer, term, time, while, winter; SEE CONCEPT 814

season [v1] *flavor food*
color, enliven, lace, leaven, pep, pepper, salt, spice; SEE CONCEPT 170

season [v2] *acclimatize, prepare*
acclimate, accustom, anneal, climatize, discipline, fit, habituate, harden, inure, mature, qualify, school, steel, temper, toughen, train; SEE CONCEPTS 35,202

seasonable [adj] *timely, appropriate*
apropos, apt, auspicious, convenient, favorable, fit, opportune, pertinent, propitious, prosperous, providential, relevant, seasonal, suitable, timeous, towardly, welcome, well-timed; SEE CONCEPT 558

seasoning [n] *flavoring for food*
condiment, dressing, gravy, herb, pepper, pungency, relish, salt, sauce, spice, zest; SEE CONCEPTS 457,461

seat [n1] *furniture for sitting, reclining*
bench, chair, chaise lounge, chesterfield, couch, davenport, lounge, loveseat, pew, recliner, settee, settle, stall, stool, wing chair; SEE CONCEPT 443

seat [n2] *central location of organization*
abode, axis, capital, center, cradle, focal point, fulcrum, headquarters, heart, house, hub, location, mansion, nerve center, place, polestar, post, residence, site, situation, source, spot, station; SEE CONCEPT 198

seat [n3] *base, foundation*
basement, basis, bed, bottom, cause, fitting, footing, ground, groundwork, rest, seating, support; SEE CONCEPT 442

seat [n4] *rear end of animate being*
backside, behind, bottom, breech, derrière, duff*, fanny*, fundament*, keister*, posterior, rear, rear end, rump, tush*; SEE CONCEPTS 392,825,827

seat [v] *place in furniture, position*
accommodate, deposit, establish, fix, hold, install, locate, lounge, nestle, perch, plant, put, roost, set, settle, sit, squat, take; SEE CONCEPTS 154,201,384

secede [v] *pull away; split from*
abdicate, apostatize, break with, disaffiliate, leave, quit, resign, retire, retract, retreat, separate, withdraw; SEE CONCEPTS 119,298,384

seclude [v] *isolate, hide*
blockade, boycott, cloister, closet, conceal, confine, cover, embargo, enclose, evict, immure, ostracize, quarantine, retire, screen, segregate, separate, sequester, shut off, withdraw; SEE CONCEPTS 121,135,188

secluded [adj] *isolated, sheltered*
abandoned, alone, aloof, beleaguered, blockaded,

sc
se

cloistered, close, closet, confidential, covert, cut off, deserted, hermetic, hidden, incommunicado, insular, isolate, lonely, lonesome, off the beaten track*, out-of-the-way*, personal, private, quarantined, quiet, reclusive, remote, removed, reserved, retired, screened, secluse, seclusive, secret, segregated, sequestered, shut off, shy, singular, solitary, tucked away*, unapproachable, unfrequented, uninhabited, unsociable, withdrawn; SEE CONCEPTS **401,576,583**

seclusion [n] *isolation*
aloneness, aloofness, beleaguerment, blockade, concealment, desolation, detachment, hiding, privacy, privateness, quarantine, reclusion, reclusiveness, remoteness, retirement, retreat, seclusiveness, separateness, separation, sequestration, shelter, solitude, withdrawal; SEE CONCEPTS **135,188,388,631**

second [n1] *shortest interval of time*
bat of an eye*, flash, instant, jiffy*, moment, nothing flat*, sec*, shake*, split second, twinkling*, wink; SEE CONCEPTS **803,821**

second [n2] *support; duplicate*
assistant, backer, double, exponent, helper, placer, proponent, reproduction, runner-up, supporter, twin; SEE CONCEPTS **423,670**

second [adj] *next; subordinate*
additional, alternative, another, double, duplicate, extra, following, further, inferior, lesser, lower, next, next in order, other, place, repeated, reproduction, runner-up, secondary, subsequent, succeeding, supporting, twin, unimportant; SEE CONCEPTS **575,585**

second [v] *support, advance a suggestion*
aid, approve, assist, back, back up, encourage, endorse, forward, further, give moral support, go along with, promote, stand by, uphold; SEE CONCEPTS **298,324,384**

secondary [adj1] *subordinate; less important*
accessory, alternate, auxiliary, backup, bush-league*, collateral, consequent, contingent, dependent, dinky*, extra, inconsiderable, inferior, insignificant, lesser, lower, minor, minor-league*, petty, relief, reserve, second, second-rate, small, small-fry*, small-time*, subject, subservient, subsidiary, substract, supporting, tributary, trivial, under, unimportant; SEE CONCEPTS **574,575**

secondary [adj2] *derivative*
auxiliary, borrowed, consequent, dependent, derivate, derivational, derived, developed, eventual, indirect, proximate, resultant, resulting, second-hand, subordinate, subsequent, subsidiary, vicarious; SEE CONCEPT **549**

second-rate/second-class [adj] *inferior, cheap*
cheap and dirty*, common, commonplace, déclassé, hack*, low-grade, low-quality, mean, mediocre, poor, shoddy*, substandard, tacky*, tawdry; SEE CONCEPTS **334,567,574**

secrecy [n] *concealment*
clandestineness, confidence, confidentiality, covertness, dark, darkness, furtiveness, hiding, hush, isolation, mystery, privacy, reticence, retirement, seclusion, secretiveness, secretness, silence, solitude, stealth, suppression, surreptitiousness; SEE CONCEPT **631**

secret [n] *something kept hidden, unrevealed*
cipher, classified information, code, confidence, confidential information, enigma, formula, key, magic number*, mystery, occult, oracle, pass-word, privileged information, puzzle, skeleton in cupboard*, unknown; SEE CONCEPTS **274,631**

secret [adj1] *hidden, unrevealed*
abstruse, ambiguous, arcane, backdoor, camouflaged, classified, cloak-and-dagger*, close, closet, clouded, conspiratorial, covered, covert, cryptic, dark, deep, disguised, enigmatical, esoteric, furtive, hush-hush*, mysterious, mystic, mystical, obscure, occult, on the QT*, out-of-the-way*, private, recondite, reticent, retired, secluded, shrouded, strange, undercover, underground, under wraps*, undisclosed, unenlightened, unfrequented, unintelligible, unknown, unpublished, unseen, veiled; SEE CONCEPTS **529,576**

secret [adj2] *underhand, clandestine*
backdoor, backstairs, camouflaged, classified, close, confidential, covert, cryptic, discreet, disguised, dissembled, dissimulated, furtive, hush-hush*, in ambush, incognito, inside, restricted, secretive, sly, sneak, sneaky, stealthy, sub-rosa, surreptitious, top secret, unacknowledged, under false pretense*, underhanded, under-the-table*; SEE CONCEPTS **545,576**

secrete [v1] *hide*
bury, cache, conceal, cover, cover up, deposit, disguise, ditch, ensconce, finesse, harbor, hide out, keep quiet, keep secret, keep to oneself, keep under wraps*, palm*, paper, plant, screen, seclude, secure, shroud, squirrel*, stash, stash away, stonewall*, stow, sweep under rug*, veil, whitewash*, withhold; SEE CONCEPTS **188,266**

secrete [v2] *give off, emit*
discharge, emanate, excrete, extravasate, extrude, exude, perspire, produce, sweat; SEE CONCEPTS **146,179**

secretive [adj] *uncommunicative*
backstairs*, buttoned up*, cagey, clammed up*, close, close-mouthed*, covert, cryptic, enigmatic, feline, furtive, hushed, in chambers*, in privacy*, in private, in the background*, in the dark*, on the QT*, reserved, reticent, silent, taciturn, tight-lipped*, undercover, unforthcoming, withdrawn, zipped*; SEE CONCEPTS **267,548**

secretly [adv] *in hidden manner*
behind closed doors*, behind someone's back*, by stealth, clandestinely, confidentially, covertly, furtively, hush-hush*, in camera*, in confidence, in holes and corners*, in secret, insidiously, in strict confidence*, intimately, obscurely, on the QT*, on the quiet*, on the sly*, personally, privately, privily, quietly, slyly, stealthily, sub rosa, surreptitiously, underhandedly, under the table*, unobserved; SEE CONCEPTS **267,548**

sect [n] *school of thought*
camp, church, communion, connection, creed, crew, cult, denomination, division, faction, faith, following, group, order, party, persuasion, religion, school, splinter group, team, wing; SEE CONCEPTS **381,382**

sectarian [n] *person who is narrow-minded*
adherent, bigot, cohort, disciple, dissenter, dissident, dogmatist, extremist, fanatic, heretic, maverick, misbeliever, nonconformist, partisan, radical, rebel, revolutionary, satellite, schismatic, separatist, supporter, true believer, zealot; SEE CONCEPTS **359,423**

sectarian [adj] *narrow-minded, exclusive*
bigoted, clannish, cliquish, dissident, doctrinaire, dogmatic, factional, fanatic, fanatical, hidebound,

insular, limited, local, nonconforming, nonconformist, parochial, partisan, provincial, rigid,
schismatic, skeptical, small-town*, splinter; SEE
CONCEPT 403

section [n] *division, portion*
area, belt, bite, branch, category, chunk, classification, component, cross section, cut, department,
district, drag, end, field, fraction, fragment, hunk,
installment, locality, lump, member, moiety, parcel, part, passage, piece, precinct, quarter, region,
sample, sector, segment, share, slice, slot, sphere,
split, subdivision, territory, tier, tract, vicinity,
zone; SEE CONCEPT 835

sectional [adj] *localized, divided*
exclusive, factional, local, narrow, partial, regional, selfish, separate, separatist; SEE CON-
CEPTS 557,785

sector [n] *area, subdivision*
category, district, division, part, precinct, quarter,
region, stratum, zone; SEE CONCEPTS 508,835

secular [adj] *not spiritual or religious*
civil, earthly, laic, laical, lay, material, materialistic, nonclerical, nonreligious, of this world*,
profane, temporal, unsacred, worldly; SEE CON-
CEPTS 529,549

secure [adj1] *safe*
defended, guarded, immune, impregnable, out of
harm's way, protected, riskless, safe, sheltered,
shielded, unassailable, undamaged, unharmed;
SEE CONCEPT 587

secure [adj2] *fastened, stable*
adjusted, anchored, bound, buttoned down*, fast,
firm, fixed, fortified, immovable, iron, locked,
nailed, safe and sound*, set, solid, solid as a
rock*, sound, staunch, steady, strong, sure, tenacious, tight; SEE CONCEPT 488

secure [adj3] *certain, definite*
able, absolute, assured, at ease, balanced, carefree, cinch, conclusive, confident, determined,
easy, established, firm, hopeful, in the bag*,
locked on*, nailed down*, on ice*, reassured, reliable, resolute, sanguine, self-assured, self-
confident, settled, shoo-in*, solid, sound, stable,
steadfast, steady, strong, sure, sure thing*, tried
and true*, unanxious, undoubtful, well-founded;
SEE CONCEPTS 403,535

secure [v1] *obtain*
access, achieve, acquire, annex, assure, bag*,
buy, capture, catch, chalk up*, cinch, come by,
ensure, gain, get, get hold of, grasp, guarantee,
have, hook, insure, land, lock, lock up, make
sure, pick up, procure, rack up*, take, win; SEE
CONCEPT 120

secure [v2] *attach, tie up*
adjust, anchor, batten down, bind, bolt, button,
button down, catch, cement, chain, clamp, clinch,
close, fasten, fix, hitch, hook on, lash, lock, lock
up, make fast, moor, nail, padlock, pinion, rivet,
settle, tie, tie down, tighten; SEE CONCEPTS
85,160

secure [v3] *protect, make safe*
assure, bulwark, cover, defend, ensure, fend,
guarantee, guard, insure, safeguard, screen,
shield; SEE CONCEPT 96

security [n1] *safety, protection*
aegis, agreement, armament, armor, asylum, bail,
bond, care, collateral, compact, contract, covenant, cover, custody, defense, earnest, freedom,
guarantee, guard, immunity, insurance, pact,
pawn, pledge, precaution, preservation, promise,

protection, redemption, refuge, retreat, safeguard,
safekeeping, safeness, safety, safety measure, salvation,
sanctuary, shelter, shield, surety, surveillance, token, ward, warrant; SEE CONCEPTS 712,729

security [n2] *peace of mind*
assurance, calm, certainty, confidence, conviction, ease, freedom, positiveness, reliance, soundness, sureness, surety; SEE CONCEPT 410

sedate [adj] *calm, collected*
cold sober*, composed, cool, cool as cucumber*,
decorous, deliberate, demure, dignified, dispassionate, earnest, grave, imperturbable, laid-back*,
no-nonsense, placid, proper, quiet, seemly, serene, serious, sober, solemn, somber, staid,
steady, tranquil, unflappable, unruffled; SEE CON-
CEPTS 404,542

sedative [n] *soothing agent, medicine*
analgesic, anodyne, barbiturate, calmant, calmative, depressant, dope*, downer, drug, hypnotic,
knockout pill, medication, narcotic, nerve medicine, opiate, pacifier, pain-killer, pain pill*, qui-
etive, sleeping pill, tranquillizer; SEE CONCEPT
307

sedative [adj] *soothing*
allaying, anodyne, calmative, calming, lenitive,
relaxing, sleep-inducing, soporific, tranquillizing;
SEE CONCEPT 537

sedentary [adj] *motionless, lazy*
desk, desk-bound, idle, inactive, seated, settled,
sitting, sluggish, stationary, torpid; SEE CON-
CEPTS 542,584

sediment [n] *solid residue from liquid solution*
debris, deposit, dregs, dross, gook*, grounds,
gunk*, lees, matter, powder, precipitate, precipitation, residuum, settling, silt, slag, solids, trash,
waste; SEE CONCEPT 260

seduce [v1] *tempt, ensnare*
bait, beguile, betray, bribe, coax, deceive, decoy,
delude, draw, entice, entrap, hook, induce, inveigle, invite, lead astray*, lead on*, lure, mislead,
mousetrap*, persuade, pull, rope in, steer, string
along*, sucker*, wheedle; SEE CONCEPT 11

seduce [v2] *entice sexually*
allure, attract, beguile, captivate, charm, come on
to*, enamour, entrance, sweep off one's feet*,
tempt; SEE CONCEPT 375

seductive [adj] *alluring, sexy*
attracting, attractive, beguiling, bewitching, captivating, charming, come-hither*, desirable,
drawing, enchanting, enticing, fascinating, flirtatious, inviting, irresistible, magnetic, provocative,
ravishing, siren, specious, tempting; SEE CON-
CEPTS 372,579

see [v1] *perceive with eyes*
beam, be apprised of, behold, catch a glimpse of,
catch sight of, clock*, contemplate, descry, detect, discern, distinguish, espy, examine, eye,
flash, gape, gawk, gaze, get a load of*, glare,
glimpse, heed, identify, inspect, lay eyes on*,
look, look at, make out, mark, mind, note, notice,
observe, pay attention to, peek, peep, peer, peg*,
penetrate, pierce, recognize, regard, remark, scan,
scope, scrutinize, sight, spot, spy, stare, survey,
take notice, view, watch, witness; SEE CONCEPTS
590,626

see [v2] *appreciate, comprehend*
appraise, ascertain, behold, catch, catch on, conceive, descry, determine, discern, discover, distinguish, envisage, envision, espy, experience,
fancy, fathom, feature, feel, find out, follow, get,

se
se

get the drift*, get the hang of*, grasp, have, hear, imagine, investigate, know, learn, make out, mark, mind, note, notice, observe, perceive, ponder, realize, recognize, remark, study, suffer, sustain, take in, think, tumble, undergo, understand, unearth, view, visualize, weigh; SEE CONCEPTS **15,31,43**

see [v3] *accompany, guide*
associate with, attend, bear company, call, come by, come over, conduct, consort with, date, direct, drop by, drop in, encounter, escort, go out with, go with, keep company with, lead, look up, meet, pilot, pop in, receive, route, run into, shepherd, show, speak to, steer, stop by, stop in, take out, usher, visit, walk; SEE CONCEPTS **187,227,384**

see [v4] *visualize*
anticipate, conceive, divine, envisage, envision, fancy, feature, foresee, foretell, imagine, picture, realize, think, vision; SEE CONCEPT **12**

seed [n1] *beginning, source*
berry, bud, cell, conceit, concept, conception, core, corn, ear, egg, embryo, germ, grain, image, impression, inkling, kernel, notion, nucleus, nut, ovule, ovum, particle, rudiment, semen, spark, sperm, spore, start, suspicion; SEE CONCEPTS **393,428,648**

seed [n2] *children*
brood, descendants, heirs, issue, offspring, posterity, progenitor, progeny, race, scions, spawn, successors; SEE CONCEPT **414**

seedy [adj] *run-down, dilapidated*
ailing, beat up, bedraggled, crummy*, decaying, decrepit, dingy, dog-eared*, down-at-the-heel*, drooping, droopy, faded, flagging, frowzy, gone to seed*, grubby, in a bad way*, mangy, messy, neglected, old, overgrown, poor, poorly, ragged, ratty, sagging, scruffy, shabby, sickly, sleazy*, slovenly, squalid, tacky, tattered, threadbare, tired, torn, unkempt, untidy, unwell, used up, wilted, wilting, worn; SEE CONCEPTS **485,570**

seek [v1] *look for*
be after, beat the bushes*, bird-dog*, bob for, cast about, chase, comb, delve, delve for, dig for, dragnet, explore, fan, ferret out, fish, fish for*, follow, go after, gun for*, hunt, inquire, investigate, leave no stone unturned*, look about, look around, look high and low*, mouse*, nose*, prowl, pursue, quest, ransack, root, run after, scout, scratch, search for, search out, sniff out*, track down; SEE CONCEPT **216**

seek [v2] *try, attempt*
aim, aspire to, assay, endeavor, essay, have a go at*, offer, pursue, strive, struggle, undertake; SEE CONCEPT **87**

seek [v3] *ask, inquire*
beg, entreat, find out, invite, petition, query, request, solicit; SEE CONCEPT **48**

seem [v] *appear; give the impression*
assume, be suggestive of, convey the impression, create the impression, give the feeling of*, give the idea of*, have the appearance of, have the aspects of, have the earmarks of*, have the features of, have the qualities of, hint, imply, insinuate, intimate, look, look as if, look like, look to be, make a show of, pretend, resemble, show, show every sign of, sound, sound like, strike one as being, suggest; SEE CONCEPT **543**

seeming [adj] *apparent*
appearing, illusive, illusory, ostensible, outward,

professed, quasi-, semblant, specious, surface; SEE CONCEPTS **487,573**

seemly [adj] *appropriate, suitable*
becoming, befitting, comme il faut, compatible, conforming, congenial, congruous, consistent, consonant, correct, decent, decorous, fit, fitting, in good taste, meet, nice, pleasing, proper, suited, timely; SEE CONCEPT **558**

seep [v] *leak*
bleed, drain, drip, exude, flow, ooze, percolate, permeate, soak, sweat, transude, trickle, weep, well; SEE CONCEPTS **146,179**

seethe [v] *be very angry*
be furious, be incensed, be livid, be mad, be on the warpath*, blow one's stack*, blow up*, boil, breathe fire*, bristle, burn, ferment, flare, flip, foam, foam at mouth*, froth, fume, hit the ceiling*, rage, see red*, simmer, smolder, spark, stew*, storm; SEE CONCEPTS **29,34**

segment [n] *part of something*
articulation, bit, compartment, cut, division, member, moiety, parcel, piece, portion, section, sector, slice, subdivision, wedge; SEE CONCEPT **835**

segregate [v] *discriminate and separate*
choose, close off, cut off, disconnect, dissociate, divide, insulate, island, isolate, quarantine, select, sequester, set apart, sever, single out, split up; SEE CONCEPTS **21,135,645**

seize [v1] *grab, take*
appropriate, catch, catch hold of, clasp, clench, clinch, clutch, compass, embrace, enclose, enfold, envelope, fasten, grapple, grasp, grip, hang onto, hold fast, lay hands on*, lay hold of*, pinch, pluck, snag, snatch, squeeze, take hold of; SEE CONCEPTS **142,164,190**

seize [v2] *abduct; take by force*
ambush, annex, apprehend, appropriate, arrest, arrogate, bag, bust, capture, carry off, catch, claw, clutch, commandeer, confiscate, conquer, exact, force, gain, get, grab, grasp, hijack, hook, impound, incorporate, kidnap, lift, nab, nail*, occupy, overcome, overpower, overrun, overwhelm, pick up, pounce, secure, snag, snare, spirit away*, subdue, take, take by storm*, take captive, take over, take possession of, throttle, trap, usurp, wrench; SEE CONCEPT **90**

seizure [n1] *convulsive attack*
access, breakdown, convulsion, fit, illness, paroxysm, spasm, spell, stroke, throe, turn; SEE CONCEPT **308**

seizure [n2] *capture, taking*
abduction, annexation, apprehension, arrest, bust*, collar*, commandeering, confiscation, drop, grab, grabbing, hook*, pinch*, seizing, snatch; SEE CONCEPT **90**

seldom [adv] *infrequently*
a few times, every now and then, from time to time, hardly, hardly ever, in a few cases, inhabitually, irregularly, little, not often, not very often, occasionally, on and off, once in a blue moon*, once in a while, rarely, scarcely, scarcely ever, semioccasionally, sometimes, sporadically, uncommonly, unoften, unusually, whimsically; SEE CONCEPT **541**

select [adj] *excellent, elite, preferable*
best, blue-chip*, boss*, choice, chosen, cool*, cream*, culled, delicate, discriminating, eclectic, elect, elegant, exclusive, exquisite, favored, first-class*, first-rate*, handpicked, limited, number

one*, pick, picked, posh, preferred, prime, privileged, rare, recherché, screened, selected, selective, special, superior, top, topnotch, tops*, weeded*, winner, winnowed, world-class*; SEE CONCEPTS 574,653

select [v] *pick out, prefer from among choices*
choose, cull, decide, elect, make, make a choice, make a selection, mark, name, opt, optate, opt for, peg*, pick, pin down, say so*, single out, slot*, sort out, tab*, tag*, take, tap*, winnow; SEE CONCEPT 41

selection [n] *preference from among choices*
alternative, choice, choosing, collection, culling, draft, druthers*, election, excerpt, option, pick, picking; SEE CONCEPT 529

selective [adj] *discriminating*
careful, choicy, choosy, discerning, discriminatory, eclectic, fussy, judicious, particular, persnickety*, picky, scrupulous, select; SEE CONCEPTS 404,542

self-centered [adj] *absorbed with oneself*
egocentric, egoistic, egomaniacal, egotistical, grandstanding, having a swelled head*, independent, inward-looking, know-it-all*, narcissistic, on an ego trip*, self-absorbed, self-indulgent, self-interested, self-involved, selfish, self-seeking, self-serving, self-sufficient, stuck on oneself*, wrapped up with oneself*; SEE CONCEPT 404

self-confident [adj] *secure with oneself*
assured, fearless, hotdog*, hotshot*, know-it-all*, poised, sanguine, self-assured, self-reliant, sure of oneself, undoubtful; SEE CONCEPT 404

self-conscious [adj] *insecure with oneself*
affected, anxious, artificial, awkward, bashful, diffident, discomfited, embarrassed, ill-at-ease, mannered, nervous, out of countenance, shamefaced, sheepish, shy, stiff, stilted, uncertain, uncomfortable, uneasy, unsure; SEE CONCEPTS 401,404

self-control [n] *willpower over one's actions*
abstemiousness, aplomb, balance, constraint, dignity, discipline, discretion, poise, repression, reserve, restraint, reticence, self-constraint, self-discipline, self-government, sobriety, stability, stoicism, strength of character; SEE CONCEPT 633

self-evident/self-explanatory [adj] *obvious*
apparent, axiomatic, clear, comprehensible, incontrovertible, inescapable, manifest, patently true, plain, prima facie, undeniable, understandable, unmistakable, unquestionable, visible; SEE CONCEPTS 529,548

selfish [adj] *thinking only of oneself*
egocentric, egoistic, egoistical, egomaniacal, egotistic, egotistical, greedy*, hoggish*, mean, mercenary, miserly, narcissistic, narrow, narrowminded, out for number one*, parsimonious, prejudiced, self-centered, self-indulgent, self-interested, self-seeking, stingy, ungenerous, wrapped up in oneself*; SEE CONCEPTS 404,542

self-respect/self-esteem [n] *pride in oneself*
amour-propre, conceit, confidence, dignity, egotism, faith in oneself, morale, narcissism, self-assurance, self-content, self-regard, self-satisfaction, vanity, worth; SEE CONCEPTS 411,689

self-righteous [adj] *smug*
affected, canting, complacent, egotistical, goody-goody*, holier-than-thou*, hypocritical, noble, pharisaic, pietistic, pious, preachy, sanctimonious, self-satisfied, superior; SEE CONCEPTS 401,542

self-satisfaction [n] *pride, contentment*
complacency, conceit, glow, peace of mind, self-approbation, self-approval, self-pleasure, smugness; SEE CONCEPTS 410,689

self-satisfied [adj] *proud, content*
complacent, conceited, egotistic, flushed, pleased, puffed up*, self-congratulatory, smug, vain; SEE CONCEPTS 404,542

self-sufficient [adj] *able to take care of oneself*
arrogant, closed, competent, conceited, confident, doing one's own thing*, efficient, egotistic, haughty, independent, individual, on one's own, out for number one*, self-confident, self-dependent, self-sufficing, self-supported, self-supporting, self-sustained, self-sustaining, smug, unit; SEE CONCEPTS 334,404

sell [v1] *exchange an object for money*
advertise, auction, bargain, barter, be in business*, boost, clinch the deal, close, close the deal, contract, deal in, dispose, drum, dump, exchange, handle, hawk, hustle, market, merchandise, move, peddle, persuade, pitch, plug, puff*, push, put across, put up for sale, retail, retain, snow, soft sell*, soft soap*, spiel*, stock, sweet talk*, trade, traffic, unload, vend, wholesale; SEE CONCEPT 345

sell/sell out [v2] *betray*
beguile, break faith, bunk, cross, deceive, deliver up, delude, disappoint, double-cross*, fail, four-flush*, give away, give up, mislead, play false, rat on*, sell down the river*, stab in the back*, surrender, take in, violate; SEE CONCEPTS 14,63

seller [n] *person who gives object in exchange for money*
agent, auctioneer, businessperson, dealer, marketer, merchant, peddler, representative, retailer, sales help, salesperson, shopkeeper, storekeeper, trader, tradesperson, vendor; SEE CONCEPTS 347,348

semblance [n] *aura, appearance*
affinity, air, alikeness, analogy, aspect, bearing, comparison, facade, face, false front*, feel, feeling, figure, form, front, guise, image, likeness, mask, mien, mood, pose, pretense, resemblance, seeming, show, showing, similarity, simile, similitude, simulacrum, veil, veneer; SEE CONCEPTS 673,716

semiotics [n] *study of signs as elements of communication*
langue, parole, pragmatics, semantics, sign systems, symbolism, syntactics; SEE CONCEPT 349

send [v1] *transmit, transfer through a system*
accelerate, address, advance, assign, broadcast, cast, circulate, commission, commit, communicate, consign, convey, delegate, deliver, detail, direct, dispatch, drop, emit, expedite, express, fire, fling, forward, freight, get under way, give off, grant, hasten, hurl, hurry off, impart, issue, let fly, mail, post, propel, put out, radiate, relay, remit, route, rush off, ship, shoot, televise, troll, wire; SEE CONCEPTS 217,223

send [v2] *please*
charm, delight, electrify, enrapture, enthrall, enthuse, excite, intoxicate, move, please, ravish, stir, thrill, titillate, turn on; SEE CONCEPTS 7,11,22

senile [adj] failing in physical and mental capabilities due to old age

aged, ancient, anile, decrepit, doddering, doting, enfeebled, feeble, imbecile, infirm, in second childhood*, old, senescent, shattered, sick, weak; SEE CONCEPTS 314,402,403

senior [n] older person

ancient, doyen, doyenne, elder, elderly person, first-born, golden-ager*, grandfather, grandmother, head, matriarch, old folk*, oldster*, old-timer*, patriarch, pensioner, retired person, senior citizen; SEE CONCEPTS 414,424

senior [adj] older or of higher rank

chief, elder, higher, leading, major, more advanced, next higher, superior; SEE CONCEPTS 574,578,585,797

seniority [n] rank in organization due to length of service

advantage, antiquity, eldership, precedence, preference, priority, rank, ranking, standing, station, superiority; SEE CONCEPTS 671,727

sensation [n1] feeling, perception

awareness, consciousness, emotion, gut reaction*, impression, passion, response, sense, sensitiveness, sensitivity, sentiment, susceptibility, thought, tingle, vibes*; SEE CONCEPTS 34,410,529

sensation [n2] something wonderful or awe-inspiring

agitation, bomb*, bombshell*, commotion, excitement, flash, furor, hit, marvel, miracle, phenomenon, portent, prodigy, scandal, stir, stunner, surprise, thrill, wonder, wow*; SEE CONCEPTS 293,529

sensational [adj1] startling, exaggerated

amazing, arresting, astounding, breathtaking, coarse, colored, conspicuous, dramatic, electrifying, emotional, excessive, exciting, extravagant, hair-raising, horrifying, juicy*, livid, lurid, marked, melodramatic, noticeable, outstanding, piquant, pointed, prominent, pungent, remarkable, revealing, rough, salient, scandalous, sensationalistic, shocking, signal, spectacular, staggering, stimulating, sultry, tabloid*, thrilling, vulgar, X-rated*; SEE CONCEPTS 267,537,545

sensational [adj2] excellent, superb

agitating, astonishing, breathtaking, cool*, dandy*, divine, dramatic, eloquent, exceptional, exciting, fabulous, first-class*, glorious, impressive, incredible, keen, marvelous, mind-blowing, most*, moving, out of this world*, smashing, spectacular, stirring, surprising, thrilling, zero cool*; SEE CONCEPT 574

sense [n1] feeling of animate being

faculty, feel, function, hearing, impression, kinesthesia, sensation, sensibility, sensitivity, sight, smell, taste, touch; SEE CONCEPT 405

sense [n2] awareness, perception

ability, appreciation, atmosphere, aura, brains, capacity, clear-headedness, cleverness, cognizance, common sense, consciousness, discernment, discrimination, feel, feeling, gumption*, imagination, impression, insight, intellect, intelligence, intuition, judgment, knowledge, mentality, mind, premonition, presentiment, prudence, quickness, reason, reasoning, recognition, sagacity, sanity, sentiment, sharpness, smarts*, soul, spirit, tact, thought, understanding, wisdom, wit; SEE CONCEPTS 33,409

sense [n3] point, meaning

acceptation, advantage, bottom line*, burden, core, definition, denotatiton, drift, gist, good, heart, implication, import, intendment, interpretation, logic, matter, meat*, meat and potatoes*, message, name of the game*, nature of the beast*, nitty-gritty*, nuance, nub, nuts and bolts*, punch line*, purport, purpose, reason, short, significance, significancy, signification, stuff, substance, thrust, understanding, upshot, use, value, worth; SEE CONCEPTS 668,682

sense [v] become aware of

anticipate, apperceive, appreciate, apprehend, believe, be with it, catch, catch on, catch the drift*, consider, credit, deem, dig*, discern, divine, feel, feel in bones*, feel in gut*, get the drift*, get the idea*, get the impression*, get the picture*, get vibes*, grasp, have a feeling*, have a hunch*, hold, know, notice, observe, perceive, pick up, read, realize, savvy*, suspect, take in, think, understand; SEE CONCEPT 34

senseless [adj] silly, meaningless

absurd, asinine, batty, crazy, daft, doublespeak*, double talk*, fatuous, flaky, foolish, idiotic, illogical, imbecilic, inane, incongruous, inconsistent, insignificant, irrational, ludicrous, mad, mindless, moronic, nonsensical, nutty, pointless, purportless, purposeless, ridiculous, simple, stupid, trivial, unimportant, unintelligent, unmeaning, unreasonable, unsound, unwise, wacky*, without rhyme or reason*; SEE CONCEPTS 548,558

sensibility [n] responsiveness; ability to feel

affection, appreciation, discernment, emotion, feeling, gut reaction*, heart*, insight, intuition, judgment, keenness, perceptiveness, rationale, sensation, sense, sensitiveness, sensitivity, sentiment, susceptibility, taste, vibes*; SEE CONCEPTS 409,410

sensible [adj] realistic, reasonable

all there*, astute, attentive, au courant, aware, canny, cognizant, commonsensical, conscious, consequent, conversant, cool*, discerning, discreet, discriminating, down-to-earth, far-sighted, having all one's marbles*, informed, in right mind, intelligent, judicious, knowing, logical, matter-of-fact, practical, prudent, rational, sagacious, sage, sane, sentient, shrewd, sober, sound, together, well-reasoned, well-thought-out, wise, witting; SEE CONCEPTS 402,542

sensitive [adj1] impressionable

acute, cognizant, conscious, delicate, easily affected, emotionable, emotional, feeling, fine, high-strung, hung up*, hypersensitive, impressible, irritable, keen, knowing, nervous, oversensitive, perceiving, perceptive, precarious, precise, psychic, reactive, receptive, responsive, seeing, sensatory, sensile, sensorial, sensory, sentient, supersensitive, susceptible, tense, ticklish, touchy, touchy feely*, tricky, tuned in*, turned on to*, umbrageous, understanding, unstable, wired*; SEE CONCEPT 403

sensitive [adj2] easily hurt

delicate, easily harmed, painful, sore, tender; SEE CONCEPT 406

sensitivity [n] responsiveness to stimuli

acuteness, affectibility, awareness, consciousness, delicacy, feeling, impressionability, nervousness, reactiveness, reactivity, receptiveness, sensation,

sense, sensitiveness, subtlety, susceptibility, sympathy; SEE CONCEPTS 405,410

sensory [adj] *affecting animate nerve organs*
acoustic, afferent, audible, audiovisual, auditory, aural, auricular, clear, discernible, distinct, gustative, gustatory, hearable, lingual, neural, neurological, ocular, olfactive, olfactory, ophthalmic, optic, perceptible, phonic, plain, receptive, sensational, sensatory, sensible, sensual, sonic, tactile, visual; SEE CONCEPT 406

sensual [adj] *physical, erotic*
animal, animalistic, arousing, bodily, carnal, debauched, delightful, epicurean, exciting, fleshly, heavy*, hedonic, hot*, lascivious, lecherous, lewd, libidinous, licentious, lustful, moving, pleasing, rough, sensuous, sexual, sexy, sharpened, steamy, stimulating, stirring, tactile, unchaste, unspiritual, voluptuous, X-rated*; SEE CONCEPTS 372,401

sensuous [adj] *gratifying to senses*
carnal, epicurean, exciting, fleshly, fleshy, hedonistic, luscious, lush, luxurious, passionate, physical, pleasurable, pleasure-loving, pleasure-seeking, primrose, rich, self-indulgent, sensory, sensual, sensualistic, sensuary, sumptuous, sybaritic, voluptuous; SEE CONCEPTS 372,537

sentence [n] *punishing decree*
book, censure, clock, condemnation, considered opinion, decision, determination, dictum, doom, edict, fall, getup*, hitch, jolt, judgment, knock, order, penalty, pronouncement, punishment, rap*, ruling, sending up the river*, sleep, stretch, term, time, trick, vacation, verdict; SEE CONCEPT 318

sentence [v] *decide punishment*
adjudge, adjudicate, blame, condemn, confine, convict, damn, denounce, devote, doom, impound, imprison, incarcerate, jail, judge, mete out, ordain, pass judgment, penalize, proscribe, punish, put away*, put on ice*, railroad*, rule, send to prison, send up the river*, settle, take the fall*, throw the book at*; SEE CONCEPTS 122,317

sentiment [n] *emotion, belief*
affect, affectivity, attitude, bias, conception, conviction, disposition, emotionalism, eye, feeling, hearts and flowers*, idea, inclination, inclining, judgment, leaning, mind, opinion, overemotionalism, partiality, passion, penchant, persuasion, position, posture, predilection, propensity, romanticism, sensibility, sentimentality, slant, softheartedness, tendency, tender feeling, tenderness, thought, view, way of thinking; SEE CONCEPTS 32,410,689

sentimental [adj] *emotional, romantic*
affected, affectionate, corny*, demonstrative, dewy-eyed, dreamy, effusive, gushing, gushy, idealistic, impressionable, inane, insipid, jejune, languishing, lovey-dovey*, loving, maudlin, moonstruck*, mushy*, nostalgic, overacted, overemotional, passionate, pathetic, rosewater*, saccharine*, sappy*, schmaltzy*, silly, simpering, sloppy*, slushy*, soapy*, soft, softhearted*, sugary*, sweet, syrupy*, tearful, tear-jerking*, tender, touching, vapid, visionary, weepy; SEE CONCEPTS 267,401,542

separate [adj] *disconnected*
abstracted, apart, apportioned, asunder, cut apart, cut in two, detached, disassociated, discrete, disembodied, disjointed, distant, distributed, disunited, divergent, divided, divorced, far between, free, independent, in halves, isolated, loose,

marked, parted, partitioned, put asunder, removed, scattered, set apart, set asunder, severed, sovereign, sundered, unattached, unconnected; SEE CONCEPT 577

separate [adj2] *alone, individual*
apart, autonomous, detached, different, discrete, distinct, distinctive, diverse, free, independent, lone, one, only, particular, peculiar, several, single, sole, solitary, unique, various; SEE CONCEPTS 557,564

separate [v1] *remove something from group; keep or set apart*
break, break off, cleave, come apart, come away, come between, detach, dichotomize, disconnect, disentangle, disjoin, disjoint, dissect, dissever, distribute, divide, divorce, intersect, part, rupture, sever, split, split up, sunder, uncombine, uncouple, undo; SEE CONCEPT 135

separate [v2] *isolate, segregate*
assign, break up, classify, close off, comb, compartment, compartmentalize, cut off, discriminate, distribute, draw apart, group, insulate, interval, intervene, island, order, put on one side, rope off, seclude, sequester, sift, single out, sort, space, split up, stand between, winnow; SEE CONCEPTS 158,201

separate [v3] *part company in a romantic relationship or marriage*
alienate, bifurcate, break it off*, break off, break up, dedomicile, depart, discontinue, disunify, disunite, diverge, divorce, drop, estrange, go away, go different ways*, go separate ways*, leave, part, pull out, split up, take leave, uncouple, unlink, untie the knot*; SEE CONCEPTS 297,384

separately [adv] *alone, individually*
apart, clearly, definitely, disjointly, distinctly, independently, one at a time, one by one, personally, severally, singly, solely; SEE CONCEPTS 544,577

separation [n] *being apart; break-up*
break, break-up, dedomiciling, departure, detachment, disconnection, disengagement, disjunction, disrelation, dissociation, dissolution, disunion, division, divorce, divorcement, embarkation, estrangement, farewell, gap, leave-taking*, parting, parting of the ways*, partition, pffft*, rift, rupture, segregation, severance, split, split-up*; SEE CONCEPTS 135,195,297,388

sequel [n] *follow-up*
aftereffect, aftermath, alternation, causatum, chain, close, closing, conclusion, consecution, consequence, continuation, development, effect, end, ending, epilogue, eventuality, finish, finishing, issue, order, outcome, part two*, payoff, progression, result, row, sequence, sequent, series, spin-off*, termination, train, upshot; SEE CONCEPTS 271,293,824,832

sequence [n] *series, order*
arrangement, array, catenation, chain, classification, concatenation, consecution, consecutiveness, continuance, continuity, continuousness, course, cycle, disposition, distribution, flow, graduation, grouping, ordering, pecking order*, perpetuity, placement, procession, progression, row, run, sequel, skein, streak, string, subsequence, succession, successiveness, track, train; SEE CONCEPTS 721,727

sequential [adj] *occurring in an order*
consecutive, constant, continuous, following, incessant, later, next, persistent, regular, sequent,

serial, steady, subsequent, subsequential, succedent, succeeding, successive; SEE CONCEPTS 482,548,585

sequester [v] *isolate, seclude*
cloister, close off, cut off, draw back, enisle, hide, insulate, island, secrete, segregate, separate, set apart, set off, withdraw; SEE CONCEPTS 90,188

serene [adj] *calm, undisturbed*
at peace, clear, collected, comfortable, composed, content, cool*, cool as a cucumber*, dispassionate, easy, easygoing, fair, halcyon, imperturbable, laid-back*, limpid, patient, peaceful, pellucid, phlegmatic, placid, poised, quiescent, quiet, reconciled, resting, satisfied, sedate, self-possessed, smooth, still, stoical, tranquil, undisturbed, unflappable, unruffled, untroubled; SEE CONCEPTS 401,485

serenity [n] *calm, peacefulness*
calmness, composure, cool, patience, peace, peace of mind, placidity, quietness, quietude, stillness, tranquillity; SEE CONCEPTS 633,673

serial [adj] *in continuing order*
consecutive, continual, continued, continuing, ensuing, following, going on, sequent, sequential, succedent, succeeding, successional, successive; SEE CONCEPTS 482,585

series [n] *order, succession*
alternation, arrangement, array, category, chain, classification, column, consecution, continuity, course, file, gradation, group, line, list, procession, progression, range, row, run, scale, sequel, sequence, set, skein, streak, string, suit, suite, tier, train; SEE CONCEPTS 721,727,769

serious [adj1] *somber, humorless*
austere, bound, bound and determined*, businesslike, cold sober*, contemplative, deadpan*, deliberate, determined, downbeat*, earnest, funereal, genuine, go for broke*, grave, grim, honest, intent, long-faced*, meditative, nononsense*, pensive, pokerfaced*, reflective, resolute, resolved, sedate, set, severe, sincere, sober, solemn, staid, steady, stern, thoughtful, unhumorous, unsmiling, weighty; SEE CONCEPTS 403,542

serious [adj2] *crucial, weighty*
arduous, dangerous, deep, difficult, far-reaching, fateful, fell, formidable, grave, grievous, grim, hard, heavy, important, laborious, major, meaning business*, meaningful, menacing, momentous, no joke*, no laughing matter*, of consequence, operose, out for blood*, playing hard ball*, pressing, severe, significant, smoking*, sobering, strenuous, strictly business*, threatening, tough, ugly, unamusing, unhumorous, urgent, worrying; SEE CONCEPTS 538,565,568

seriously [adv1] *not humorously*
actively, all joking aside*, cool it*, cut the comedy*, determinedly, down, earnestly, fervently, for real*, gravely, in all conscience, in all seriousness, in earnest, intently, passionately, purposefully, resolutely, sedately, simmer down*, sincerely, soberly, solemnly, sternly, straighten out, thoughtfully, vigorously, with a straight face*, with forethought, with sobriety, zealously; SEE CONCEPTS 535,542,544

seriously [adv2] *dangerously, critically*
acutely, badly, decidedly, deplorably, distressingly, gravely, grievously, harmfully, intensely, menacingly, perilously, precariously, quite, re-

grettably, severely, sorely, threateningly, very; SEE CONCEPTS 544,565,568

seriousness [n1] *humorlessness*
calmness, coolness, earnest, earnestness, gravity, intentness, sedateness, serious-mindedness, sincerity, sober-mindedness, sobriety, solemnity, staidness, sternness, thoughtfulness; SEE CONCEPTS 410,657

seriousness [n2] *danger; criticalness*
enormity, gravity, importance, moment, significance, urgency, weight; SEE CONCEPTS 668,675

sermon [n] *instructive speech with a moral*
address, advice, discourse, doctrine, exhortation, harangue, homily, lecture, lesson, moralism, pastoral, preach, preaching, preachment, tirade; SEE CONCEPTS 278,368

serrated [adj] *jagged*
denticulate, indented, notched, ragged, sawlike, sawtooth, saw-toothed, scored, serrate, serried, serriform, serrulate, toothed; SEE CONCEPT 486

servant [n] *person who waits on another*
assistant, attendant, cleaning person, dependent, domestic, drudge, help, helper, hireling, live-in, menial, minion, retainer, serf, server, slave; SEE CONCEPT 348

serve [v1] *aid, help; supply*
arrange, assist, attend to, be of assistance, be of use, care for, deal, deliver, dish up*, distribute, do for, give, handle, hit, minister to, nurse, oblige, play, present, provide, provision, set out, succor, wait on, work for; SEE CONCEPTS 110,136,140

serve [v2] *act, do*
accept, agree, attend, be employed by, carry on, complete, discharge, follow, fulfill, function, go through, hearken, labor, obey, observe, officiate, pass, perform, subserve, toil, work; SEE CONCEPT 91

serve [v3] *suffice; do the work of*
advantage, answer, answer the purpose, apply, avail, be acceptable, be adequate, be good enough, benefit, be of use, be useful, content, do, do duty as, fill the bill*, fit, function, make, profit, satisfy, service, suit, work, work for; SEE CONCEPTS 656,658

service [n1] *aid, help*
account, advantage, applicability, appropriateness, assistance, avail, benefit, business, check, courtesy, dispensation, duty, employ, employment, favor, fitness, indulgence, kindness, labor, maintenance, ministration, office, overhaul, relevance, serviceability, servicing, supply, use, usefulness, utility, value, work; SEE CONCEPTS 110,324,658

service [n2] *rite of a church*
ceremonial, ceremony, formality, function, liturgy, observance, ritual, sermon, worship; SEE CONCEPT 368

service [n3] *time in military operation*
action, active duty, combat, duty, fighting, sting; SEE CONCEPTS 320,321

serviceable [adj] *useful, functional*
advantageous, aiding, assistive, beneficial, convenient, dependable, durable, efficient, handy, hard-wearing, helpful, invaluable, operative, practical, profitable, usable, utile, utilitarian, valuable; SEE CONCEPT 560

servile [adj] *grovelling, subservient*
abject, base, beggarly, bootlicking, craven, cringing, despicable, eating crow*, eating humble pie*,

fawning, humble, ignoble, low, mean, obedient, obeisant, obsequious, passive, slavish, submissive, sycophantic, toadying, unctuous, unresisting; SEE CONCEPTS *401,404*

servitude [n] *slavery*
bondage, bonds, chains, confinement, enslavement, obedience, peonage, serfdom, serfhood, subjection, subjugation, thrall, thralldom, vassalage, yoke; SEE CONCEPTS *388,410*

session [n] *meeting, gathering*
affair, assembly, concourse, conference, discussion, get-together, hearing, huddle, jam session*, meet, period, showdown, sitting, term; SEE CONCEPTS *114,324*

set [n1] *physical bearing*
address, air, attitude, carriage, comportment, demeanor, deportment, fit, hang, inclination, mien, port, position, posture, presence, turn; SEE CONCEPT *757*

set [n2] *stage setting*
flats, mise en scène, scene, scenery, setting, stage set; SEE CONCEPT *263*

set [n3] *group, assortment*
array, assemblage, band, batch, body, bunch, bundle, camp, circle, clan, class, clique, clump, cluster, clutch, collection, company, compendium, coterie, crew, crowd, faction, gaggle, gang, kit, lot, mob, organization, outfit, pack, push, rat pack*, sect, series; SEE CONCEPTS *417,432,769*

set [adj1] *decided*
agreed, appointed, arranged, bent, certain, concluded, confirmed, customary, dead set on*, decisive, definite, determined, entrenched, established, firm, fixed, hanging tough*, immovable, intent, inveterate, ironclad, locked in*, obstinate, pat, pigheaded*, prearranged, predetermined, prescribed, regular, resolute, resolved, rigid, rooted, scheduled, set in stone*, settled, solid as a rock*, specified, stated, steadfast, stiff-necked, stipulated, stubborn, unflappable, usual, well-set; SEE CONCEPTS *535,542*

set [adj2] *firm, hardened; inflexible*
entrenched, fixed, hard and fast, hidebound, immovable, jelled, located, placed, positioned, rigid, settled, sited, situate, situated, solid, stable, stiff, strict, stubborn, unyielding; SEE CONCEPT *488*

set [v1] *position, place*
affix, aim, anchor, apply, arrange, bestow, cast, deposit, direct, embed, ensconce, establish, fasten, fix, head, insert, install, introduce, lay, level, locate, lock, lodge, make fast, make ready, mount, park, plank, plant, plop, plunk, point, post, prepare, put, rest, seat, settle, situate, spread, station, stick, train, turn, wedge, zero in*; SEE CONCEPTS *201,202*

set [v2] *decide upon*
agree upon, allocate, allot, appoint, arrange, assign, conclude, decree, designate, determine, dictate, direct, establish, estimate, fix, fix price, impose, instruct, lay down, make, name, ordain, prescribe, price, rate, regulate, resolve, schedule, settle, specify, stipulate, value; SEE CONCEPT *18*

set [v3] *harden*
become firm, cake, clot, coagulate, condense, congeal, crystallize, fix, gel, gelate, gelatinize, jell, jellify, jelly, solidify, stiffen, thicken; SEE CONCEPT *250*

set [v4] *decline*
descend, dip, disappear, drop, go down, sink, subside, vanish; SEE CONCEPT *181*

set [v5] *start, incite*
abet, begin, commence, foment, initiate, instigate, provoke, put in motion, raise, set on*, stir up*, whip up*; SEE CONCEPT *221*

setback [n] *disappointment*
about-face*, backset, bath*, blow, bottom, check, comedown, defeat, delay, difficulty, drawing board*, flip-flop*, hindrance, hitch*, hold-up, impediment, misfortune, obstacle, rebuff, regress, regression, reversal, reversal of fortune, reverse, slowdown, stumbling block*, trouble, upset, whole new ballgame*; SEE CONCEPTS *388,674,679*

set back [v] *delay, hinder*
bog down*, decelerate, defeat, detain, embog, hang up*, hold up, impede, mire, retard, reverse, slow, slow down, slow up; SEE CONCEPT *130*

setting [n] *scene, background*
ambience, backdrop, context, distance, environment, frame, framework, horizon, jungle, locale, location, mise en scène, mounting, perspective, set, shade, shadow, site, stage set, stage setting, surroundings; SEE CONCEPTS *198,263*

settle [v1] *straighten out, resolve*
achieve, adjudicate, adjust, appoint, arrange, call the shots*, choose, cinch, clean up, clear, clear up, clinch, come to a conclusion, come to a decision, come to an agreement, complete, concert, conclude, confirm, decide, determine, discharge, dispose, end, establish, figure, fix, form judgment, judge, make a decision, make certain, mediate, nail down*, negotiate, order, pay, put an end to, put into order, reconcile, regulate, rule, satisfy, seal, set to rights, square, verify, work out; SEE CONCEPTS *18,126,341*

settle [v2] *calm, relieve*
allay, assure, becalm, compose, lull, pacify, quell, quiet, quieten, reassure, relax, sedate, soothe, still, tranquilize; SEE CONCEPTS *7,22,469*

settle [v3] *come to rest; fall*
alight, bed down, decline, descend, flop, immerse, land, lay, light, lodge, perch, place, plop, plunge, put, repose, roost, seat, set down, settle down, sink, sit, submerge, submerse, subside, touch down; SEE CONCEPT *181*

settle [v4] *make one's home*
abide, colonize, dwell, establish, hang up one's hat*, inhabit, keep house, live, locate, lodge, move to, park, put down roots*, reside, set up home, squat, take root*, take up residence; SEE CONCEPT *226*

settlement [n1] *decision, conclusion*
adjustment, agreement, arrangement, clearance, compact, compensation, completion, conclusion, confirmation, contract, covenant, deal, defrayal, determination, discharge, disposition, establishment, happy medium*, liquidation, pay, payment, payoff, quietus, reimbursement, remuneration, resolution, satisfaction, showdown, termination, trade-off, working out; SEE CONCEPTS *230,684*

settlement [n2] *community*
colonization, colony, encampment, establishment, foundation, habitation, hamlet, inhabitancy, occupancy, occupation, outpost, plantation, principality, residence; SEE CONCEPTS *512,515*

set up [v] *start*
arrange, assemble, back, begin, build, build up,

se
se

compose, constitute, construct, create, elevate, erect, establish, excite, exhilarate, found, inaugurate, initiate, inspire, install, institute, introduce, launch, make provision for, open, organize, originate, prearrange, prepare, put together, put up, raise, rear, stimulate, strengthen, subsidize, usher in; SEE CONCEPT 221

sever [v1] *cut apart*
bisect, carve, cleave, cut, cut in two, detach, disconnect, disjoin, dissect, dissever, dissociate, disunite, divide, part, rend, rive, separate, slice, split, sunder; SEE CONCEPTS 98,176

sever [v2] *dissociate*
abandon, break off, disjoint, dissolve, divide, divorce, put an end to, separate, terminate; SEE CONCEPTS 297,384

several [adj] *assorted, various*
a few, a lot, any, certain, considerable, definite, different, disparate, distinct, divers, diverse, handful, hardly any, indefinite, individual, infrequent, manifold, many, not many, numerous, only a few, particular, personal, plural, proportionate, quite a few, rare, respective, scant, scanty, scarce, scarcely any, separate, single, small number, some, sparse, special, specific, sundry; SEE CONCEPTS 564,762

severe [adj1] *uncompromising, stern*
astringent, austere, biting, caustic, close, cold, cruel, cutting, disapproving, dour, earnest, firm, flinty, forbidding, grave, grim, hard, hard-nosed*, harsh, inconsiderate, inexorable, inflexible, iron-handed, obdurate, oppressive, peremptory, pitiless, relentless, resolute, resolved, rigid, satirical, scathing, serious, sober, stern, stiff*, strait-laced*, strict, tight-lipped*, unalterable, unbending, unchanging, unfeeling, unrelenting, unsmiling, unsparing; SEE CONCEPTS 401,534, 542

severe [adj2] *difficult, harsh*
acute, arduous, ascetic, austere, bitter, bleak, consequential, critical, dangerous, dear, demanding, despotic, distressing, domineering, drastic, effortful, exacting, extreme, fierce, forbidding, grave, grim, grinding, hard, heavy, hefty, implacable, inclement, intemperate, intense, mordant, oppressive, overbearing, pitiless, punishing, rigorous, rugged, serious, sharp, sore, strenuous, stringent, taxing, toilsome, tough, tyrannical, unpleasant, unrelenting, violent, weighty, wicked; SEE CONCEPTS 565,569

severely [adv] *harshly*
acutely, badly, critically, dangerously, extremely, firmly, gravely, hard, hardly, intensely, markedly, painfully, rigorously, roughly, seriously, sharply, sorely, sternly, strictly, with an iron hand; SEE CONCEPT 569

sew [v] *prepare fabric for clothing, covering*
baste, bind, embroider, fasten, piece, seam, stitch, tack, tailor, work; SEE CONCEPT 218

sex [n1] *male or female gender*
femininity, manhood, manliness, masculinity, sexuality, womanhood, womanliness; SEE CONCEPT 648

sex [n2] *intercourse between animate beings*
birds and the bees*, coition, coitus, copulation, facts of life*, fornication, generation, intimacy, lovemaking, magnetism, procreation, relations, reproduction, sensuality, sexuality; SEE CONCEPT 375

sexual [adj] *concerning reproduction, intercourse*
animal, animalistic, bestial, carnal, erotic, fleshly, generative, genital, genitive, intimate, loving, passionate, procreative, reproductive, sensual, sharing, venereal, voluptuous, wanton; SEE CONCEPT 372

sexy [adj] *being erotically attractive to another*
arousing, come-hither*, cuddly, flirtatious, hot*, inviting, kissable, libidinous, mature, provocative, provoking, racy, risqué, seductive, sensual, sensuous, slinky*, spicy*, steamy*, suggestive, titillating, voluptuous; SEE CONCEPT 372

shabby [adj1] *broken-down; in poor shape*
bare, bedraggled, crummy, decayed, decaying, decrepit, degenerated, desolate, deteriorated, deteriorating, dilapidated, dingy, disfigured, disreputable, dog-eared*, faded, frayed, gone to seed*, mangy, meager, mean, miserable, moth-eaten, neglected, pitiful, poor, poverty-stricken, ragged, ramshackle, ratty, rickety, ruined, ruinous, run-down, scrubby, scruffy, seedy, shoddy, sleazy, slipshod, squalid, tacky, tattered, threadbare, tired, worn, worn-out, worse for wear*, wretched; SEE CONCEPT 485

shabby [adj2] *despicable*
beggarly, cheap, contemptible, despisable, dirty, disgraceful, dishonorable, disreputable, ignoble, ignominious, inconsiderate, inglorious, low, low-down, mean, mercenary, miserly, rotten, scummy, selfish, shady, shameful, shoddy, sordid, sorry, stingy, thoughtless, unkind, unworthy; SEE CONCEPTS 401,404

shade [n1] *dimness*
adumbration, blackness, coolness, cover, darkness, dusk, gloominess, obscuration, obscurity, penumbra, screen, semidarkness, shadiness, shadow, shadows, umbra, umbrage; SEE CONCEPT 620

shade [n2] *blind, shield*
awning, canopy, cover, covering, curtain, screen, veil; SEE CONCEPT 445

shade [n3] *color, hue*
brilliance, cast, saturation, stain, tinge, tint, tone; SEE CONCEPTS 620,622

shade [n4] *slight difference*
amount, cast, dash, degree, distinction, gradation, hint, nuance, proposal, semblance, soupçon, spice, streak, suggestion, suspicion, tincture, tinge, trace, variation, variety; SEE CONCEPT 665

shade [n5] *ghost*
apparition, bogey, haunt, manes, phantasm, phantom, revenant, shadow, specter, spirit, umbra, wraith; SEE CONCEPT 370

shade [v] *shut out the light*
adumbrate, be overcast, blacken, cast a shadow, cloud, cloud over, cloud up, conceal, cover, darken, deepen, dim, eclipse, gray, hide, inumbrate, mute, obscure, overshadow, protect, screen, shadow, shelter, shield, shutter, tone down, umbrage, veil; SEE CONCEPTS 250,526

shadow [n1] *darkness*
adumbration, cover, dark, dimness, dusk, gloom, obscuration, obscurity, penumbra, protection, shade, shelter, umbra, umbrage; SEE CONCEPTS 620,622

shadow [n2] *hint, suggestion*
breath, intimation, memento, relic, smack, suspicion, tincture, tinge, touch, trace, vestige; SEE CONCEPT 278

shadow [v1] *make dark*
adumbrate, becloud, bedim, cast a shadow, cloud, darken, dim, gray, haze, inumbrate, obscure, overcast, overcloud, overhang, overshadow, screen, shade, shelter, shield, umbrage, veil; SEE CONCEPT 250

shadow [v2] *follow secretly*
dog, keep in sight, pursue, spy on, stalk, tag, tail, trail, watch; SEE CONCEPT 207

shady [adj1] *dark, covered*
adumbral, bosky, cloudy, cool, dim, dusky, indistinct, leafy, out of the sun*, screened, shaded, shadowed, shadowy, sheltered, umbrageous, umbrous, under a cloud, vague; SEE CONCEPTS 485,617

shady [adj2] *disreputable, suspicious*
crooked, disgraceful, dishonest, dishonorable, dubious, fishy, ignominious, infamous, inglorious, notorious, questionable, scandalous, shabby, shameful, shifty, shoddy, slippery, suspect, suspicious, underhanded, unethical, unrespectable, unscrupulous, untrustworthy; SEE CONCEPT 545

shaggy [adj] *hairy, unkempt*
furry, hirsute, long-haired, ragged, rough, ruffled, rugged, uncombed, unshorn; SEE CONCEPT 485

shake [v1] *quiver, tremble*
agitate, brandish, bump, chatter, churn, commove, concuss, convulse, discompose, disquiet, disturb, dither, dodder, flap, flicker, flit, flitter, flourish, fluctuate, flutter, jar, jerk, jog, joggle, jolt, jounce, move, oscillate, palpitate, perturb, quail, quake, quaver, rattle, reel, rock, roil, ruffle, set in motion, shimmer, shimmy, shiver, shudder, stagger, stir up, succuss, sway, swing, totter, tremble, tremor, twitter, upset, vibrate, waggle, water, wave, whip, wobble; SEE CONCEPTS 150,152

shake [v2] *upset deeply*
appall, bother, consternate, daunt, discompose, dismay, distress, disturb, frighten, horrify, impair, intimidate, jar, knock props out*, make waves*, move, rattle, throw, throw a curve*, undermine, unnerve, unsettle, unstring, upset, weaken, worry; SEE CONCEPTS 7,19

shake off [v] *lose by getting away*
clear, dislodge, drop, elude, get away from, get rid of, give the slip*, leave behind, remove, rid oneself of, throw off, unburden; SEE CONCEPTS 102,195

shake up [v] *upset, unsettle*
agitate, break with past*, cause revolution*, churn up*, clean out, clean up, clear out, disturb, liquidate, make a clean sweep*, mix, overturn, purge, remove, reorganize, rid, shock, stir up, turn upside down*; SEE CONCEPTS 14,324

shaky [adj1] *trembling*
all aquiver*, aquake, aquiver, ashake, faltering, fluctuant, infirm, insecure, jellylike, jerry-built*, jittery, nervous, not set, precarious, quaking, quivery, rattletrap, rickety, rocky, rootless, shaking, tottering, tottery, trembling, tremorous, tremulous, tumbledown, unfirm, unsettled, unsound, unstable, unsteady, unsure, vacillating, wavering, weak, wobbly, yielding; SEE CONCEPT 488

shaky [adj2] *doubtful*
dubious, indecisive, not dependable, not reliable, precarious, problematic, questionable, suspect, uncertain, unclear, undependable, unreliable, unsettled, unsound, unsteady, unsupported, unsure; SEE CONCEPT 535

shallow [adj1] *not deep*
cursory, depthless, empty, flat, hollow, inconsiderable, sand bar, shelf, shoal, slight, superficial, surface, trifling, trivial, unsound; SEE CONCEPTS 737,777

shallow [adj2] *unintelligent, ignorant*
cursory, empty, empty-headed, farcical, featherbrained, flighty, flimsy, foolish, frivolous, frothy, half-baked*, hollow, idle, inane, lightweight, meaningless, paltry, petty, piddling, puerile, simple, sketchy, skin-deep*, slight, superficial, surface, trifling, trivial, uncritical, unthinking, vain, wishy-washy*; SEE CONCEPT 402

sham [n] *hoax, trick*
burlesque, cant, caricature, cheat, counterfeit, cover-up, deceit, deception, facade, fake, fakery, false front, farce, feint, flimflam*, forgery, fraud, hypocrisy, hypocriticalness, imitation, impostor, imposture, jive*, mock, mockery, pharisaism, phoniness, pretend, pretense, pretext, pseudo*, put-on, sell, smoke*, snow job*, spoof, travesty, whitewash; SEE CONCEPTS 59,192

sham [adj] *artificial, counterfeit*
adulterated, affected, assumed, bogus*, dummy, ersatz*, fake, false, feigned, fictitious, forged, fraudulent, imitation, lying, make-believe, misleading, mock, phony, plaster*, pretend, pretended, pseudo*, simulated, so-called, spurious, substitute, synthetic, untrue; SEE CONCEPT 582

sham [v] *trick; pull a hoax*
act, affect, ape, assume, bluff, copy, counterfeit, create, do a number*, fake, fake it, feign, imitate, invent, lie, make like, mislead, mock, play possum*, pretend, put on, put up a front*, shuck and jive*, simulate, sucker*; SEE CONCEPTS 59,111, 171

shambles [n] *a mess*
anarchy, babel, bedlam, botch, chaos, confusion, disarray, disorder, disorganization, hash, havoc, hodge-podge, madhouse, maelstrom, mess-up, mix-up, muddle; SEE CONCEPTS 230,674

shame [n] *disgrace, embarrassment*
abashment, bad conscience*, blot, chagrin, compunction, confusion, contempt, contrition, degradation, derision, discomposure, discredit, disesteem, dishonor, disrepute, guilt, humiliation, ignominy, ill repute, infamy, irritation, loss of face*, mortification, obloquy, odium, opprobrium, pang, pudency, remorse, reproach, scandal, self-disgust, self-reproach, self-reproof, shamefacedness, skeleton in the cupboard*, smear, stigma, stupefaction, treachery; SEE CONCEPTS 388,410

shame [v] *disgrace, embarrass*
abash, blot, confound, cut down to size*, debase, defile, degrade, disconcert, discredit, dishonor, give a black eye*, humble, humiliate, mortify, reproach, ridicule, shoot down*, smear, stain, take down*, take down a peg*; SEE CONCEPTS 7,14,19

shameful [adj] *atrocious; disreputable*
base, carnal, contemptible, corrupt, dastardly, debauched, degrading, diabolical, disgraceful, dishonorable, drunken, embarrassing, flagrant, heinous, humiliating, ignominious, immodest, immoral, impure, indecent, infamous, intemperate, lewd, low, mean, mortifying, notorious, obscene, opprobrious, outrageous, profligate, reprehensible, reprobate, ribald, scandalous, shaming, shocking, sinful, unbecoming, unclean, unwor-

se
sh

thy, vile, villainous, vulgar, wicked; SEE CONCEPTS 401,545,571

shameless [adj] corrupt, indecent
abandoned, arrant, audacious, barefaced, bold, brash, brassy, brazen, cheeky*, depraved, dissolute, flagrant, forward, hardened, high-handed*, immodest, immoral, improper, impudent, incorrigible, insolent, lewd, outrageous, overbold, presumptuous, profligate, reprobate, rude, unabashed, unashamed, unblushing, unchaste, unprincipled, wanton; SEE CONCEPTS 401,545

shape [n1] form, structure
appearance, architecture, aspect, body, build, cast, chassis, circumscription, configuration, conformation, constitution, construction, contour, cut, embodiment, figure, format, frame, guise, likeness, lineation, lines, look, make, metamorphosis, model, mold, outline, pattern, profile, semblance, shadow, silhouette, simulacrum, stamp, symmetry; SEE CONCEPTS 436,754,757

shape [n2] condition, health
case, estate, fettle, fitness, kilter, order, repair, state, trim, whack*; SEE CONCEPTS 316,720

shape [v1] form, create
assemble, block out, bring together, build, carve, cast, chisel, construct, crystallize, cut, embody, fabricate, fashion, forge, frame, hew, knead, make, mint, model, mold, pat, pattern, produce, roughhew, sculpture, sketch, stamp, streamline, throw together*, trim, whittle; SEE CONCEPTS 137,184

shape [v2] devise, plan
accommodate, adapt, become, define, develop, form, frame, grow, guide, modify, prepare, regulate, remodel, tailor, take form, work up; SEE CONCEPT 36

shapeless [adj] formless
abnormal, amorphic, amorphous, anomalous, assymetrical, baggy, deformed, disfigured, embryonic, ill-formed, inchoate, indefinite, indeterminate, indistinct, invisible, irregular, malformed, misshapen, mutilated, nebulous, undeveloped, unformed, ungraceful, unmade, unshapely, unstructured, unsymmetrical, vague, without character, without form; SEE CONCEPTS 486,589

shapely [adj] well-proportioned
balanced, beautiful, built, comely, curvaceous, elegant, full-figured, graceful, neat, pleasing, proportioned, regular, rounded, sightly, statuesque, sylphlike, symmetrical, trim, well-formed, well-turned; SEE CONCEPTS 406,490

share [n] portion, allotment
allowance, apportionment, bite, chunk, claim, commission, contribution, cut, cut in, cut up, divide, dividend, division, divvy*, dose, drag*, due, end, fifty-fifty*, fraction, fragment, halver, helping, heritage, interest, lagniappe, lot, measure, meed, parcel, part, partage, percentage, piece, pittance, plum, points, proportion, quantum, quota, quotient, quotum, rake-off*, ration, segment, serving, slice, split, stake, taste, whack*; SEE CONCEPTS 710,835

share [v] use in common with others
accord, administer, allot, apportion, assign, be a party to, bestow, cut the pie*, deal, dispense, distribute, divide, divide with, divvy*, divvy up*, dole out, experience, give and take, give out, go Dutch*, go fifty-fifty*, go halves*, go in with, have a hand in, have a portion of, mete out, parcel out, part, partake, partition, pay half, piece up, prorate, quota, ration, receive, shift, slice, slice up, split, split up, take a part of, yield; SEE CONCEPTS 98,100,384

sharp [adj1] knifelike, cutting
aciculate, acuate, acuminate, acuminous, acute, apical, barbed, briery, cuspate, cuspidate, edged, fine, ground fine, honed, horned, jagged, keen, keen-edged, knife-edged, needlelike, needlepointed, peaked, pointed, pointy, prickly, pronged, razor-sharp, salient, serrated, sharpedged, sharpened, spiked, spiky, spiny, splintery, stinging, tapered, tapering, thorny, tined, tipped, unblunted, whetted; SEE CONCEPT 486

sharp [adj2] sudden
abrupt, distinct, extreme, intense, marked; SEE CONCEPTS 581,799

sharp [adj3] perceptive, quick-witted
acute, adroit, alert, apt, astute, brainy, bright, brilliant, canny, clever, critical, cute, discerning, discriminating, fast, foxy*, having smarts*, ingenious, intelligent, keen, knowing, nimble, nobody's fool*, not born yesterday*, observant, on the ball*, original, penetrating, penetrative, quick, quick on the trigger*, quick on the uptake*, ready, resourceful, savvy*, sensitive, slick, smart, smart as a tack*, subtle, wise; SEE CONCEPT 402

sharp [adj4] dishonest, deceitful
artful, bent, crafty, cunning, designing, ornery, salty, shady, shrewd, slick, slippery, sly, smart, snaky, two-faced*, underhand, unethical, unscrupulous, wily; SEE CONCEPT 545

sharp [adj5] severe, intense
acute, agonizing, biting, cutting, distinct, distressing, drilling, excruciating, fierce, keen, knifelike, painful, paralyzing, penetrating, piercing, shooting, smart, sore, stabbing, stinging, violent; SEE CONCEPTS 537,569

sharp [adj6] distinct, well-defined
audible, clear, clear-cut, crisp, definite, explicit, obvious, visible; SEE CONCEPT 535

sharp [adj7] stylish
chic, classy, dashing, distinctive, dressy, excellent, fashionable, fine, first-class*, fly*, in style, smart, snappy*, swank*, tony*, trendy; SEE CONCEPT 589

sharp [adj8] hurtful, bitter in speech
acrimonious, angry, barbed, biting, caustic, cutting, double-edged, harsh, incisive, inconsiderate, penetrating, peppery, piercing, pointed, pungent, sarcastic, sardonic, scathing, severe, short, stabbing, stinging, tart, thoughtless, trenchant, unceremonious, ungracious, virulent, vitriolic; SEE CONCEPT 267

sharp [adj9] having strong affect on animate senses
acerbic, acid, acrid, active, astringent, austere, bitter, brisk, burning, harsh, hot, lively, odorous, piquant, pungent, sour, strong-smelling, suffocating, tart, vigorous, vinegary; SEE CONCEPTS 537,598,613

sharp [adv] on time
abruptly, accurately, bang, exactly, just, on the button*, on the dot*, precisely, promptly, punctually, right, smack-dab*, square, squarely, suddenly; SEE CONCEPT 799

sharpen [v] make knifelike
acuminate, dress, edge, file, grind, hone, make acute, make sharp, put an edge on, put a point on, sharp, stroke, strop, taper, whet; SEE CONCEPTS 137,250

shatter [v1] *break into small pieces*
blast, blight, burst, crack, crash, crunch, crush, dash, demolish, destroy, disable, exhaust, explode, fracture, fragment, fragmentalize, fragmentize, impair, implode, overturn, pulverize, rend, rive, ruin, scrunch, shiver, smash, smash to smithereens*, smatter, snap, splinter, splinterize*, split, torpedo*, total*, wrack up*, wreck; SEE CONCEPTS 246,252

shatter [v2] *hurt someone badly*
break a heart*, crush, destroy, devastate, dumbfound, rattle, ruin, upset; SEE CONCEPTS 7,19

shave [v] *cut outer covering off*
barber, brush, clip, crop, cut, cut back, cut down, decorticate, graze, kiss, make bare, pare, peel, plane, prune, shear, shingle, shred, skim, skin, slash, slice thin, sliver, strip, touch, trim; SEE CONCEPTS 137,162,176,202

shed [v] *cast off*
afford, beam, cashier, cast, diffuse, disburden, discard, doff, drop, emit, exude, exuviate, give, give forth, jettison, junk, let fall, molt, pour forth, radiate, reject, scatter, scrap, send forth, shower, slip, slough, spill, sprinkle, take off, throw, throw away, throw out, yield; SEE CONCEPTS 179,180,181,211

sheen [n] *brightness, shine*
burnish, finish, glaze, gleam, glint, gloss, luster, patina, polish, shimmer, shininess, wax; SEE CONCEPT 620

sheepish [adj] *shy, embarrassed*
abashed, ashamed, chagrined, diffident, docile, foolish, guilty, mortified, retiring, self-conscious, shamefaced, silly, tame, timid, timorous, uncomfortable; SEE CONCEPT 401

sheer [adj1] *abrupt, steep*
arduous, erect, headlong, perpendicular, precipitate, precipitous, sideling, upright; SEE CONCEPTS 490,581

sheer [adj2] *utter, absolute*
altogether, arrant, blasted, blessed, complete, confounded, downright, gross, infernal, out-and-out*, outright, perfect, pure, quite, rank, simple, single, thoroughgoing, total, unadulterated, unalloyed, undiluted, unmitigated, unmixed, unqualified; SEE CONCEPTS 531,535,544

sheer [adj3] *see-through, thin*
airy, chiffon, clear, cobwebby, delicate, diaphanous, filmy, fine, flimsy, fragile, gauzy, gossamer, lacy, limpid, lucid, pellucid, pure, slight, smooth, soft, tiffany, translucent, transparent; SEE CONCEPT 606

sheet [n] *coating, covering; page*
area, blanket, coat, expanse, film, foil, folio, lamina, layer, leaf, membrane, overlay, pane, panel, piece, plate, ply, slab, stratum, stretch, surface, sweep, veneer; SEE CONCEPTS 172,270,475,484

shelf [n] *jutting, flat area or piece*
bank, bracket, console, counter, cupboard, ledge, mantelpiece, mantle, rack, reef, ridge, rock, shallow, shoal; SEE CONCEPTS 445,509,513

shell [n] *structure; covering*
carapace, case, chassis, crust, frame, framework, hull, husk, integument, nut, pericarp, plastron, pod, scale, shard, shuck, skeleton, skin; SEE CONCEPTS 399,428,484

shell out [v] *give*
ante up, disburse, expend, fork over*, hand over, lay out, outlay, pay, pay for, pay out, spend; SEE CONCEPT 341

shelter [n] *protection, habitat*
apartment, asylum, cave, condo, co-op, cover, covert, crib*, defense, den, digs*, dwelling, guard, guardian, harbor, harborage, haven, hermitage, hide, hideaway, hideout, hole in the wall*, home, homeplate*, house, housing, hut, joint*, lodging, pad*, pen, port, preserve, protector, quarterage, rack, refuge, retirement, retreat, roof, roof over head*, roost*, safety, sanctuary, screen, security, shack, shade, shadow, shed, shield, tent, tower, turf, umbrella; SEE CONCEPTS 515,712

shelter [v] *provide safety, cover*
chamber, conceal, cover, cover up, defend, enclose, guard, harbor, haven, hide, house, lodge, preserve, protect, roof, safeguard, screen, secure, shield, surround, take care of, take in, ward, watch over; SEE CONCEPTS 134,188

shelve [v] *defer, postpone*
delay, dismiss, drop, freeze*, give up, hang up, hold, hold off, hold over, hold up, lay aside, mothball*, pigeonhole*, prolong, prorogue, put aside, put off, put on back burner*, put on hold, put on ice*, scrub*, sideline, slow up, stay, suspend, table, tie up, waive; SEE CONCEPT 121

shield [n] *protection*
absorber, aegis, armament, armor, buckler, buffer, bulwark, bumper, cover, defense, escutcheon, guard, mail, rampart, safeguard, screen, security, shelter, ward; SEE CONCEPTS 712,729

shield [v] *protect*
bulwark, chamber, conceal, cover, cover all bases*, cover up, defend, fend, give cover, give shelter, go to bat for*, guard, harbor, haven, house, ride shotgun*, roof, safeguard, screen, secure, shelter, shotgun*, stonewall*, take under one's wing*, ward off; SEE CONCEPTS 96,134

shift [n1] *switch, fluctuation*
about-face*, alteration, bend, change, changeover, conversion, deflection, deviation, displacement, double, fault, modification, move, passage, permutation, rearrangement, removal, shifting, substitution, switch, tack, transfer, transference, transformation, transit, translocation, turn, variation, veering, yaw; SEE CONCEPTS 213,697

shift [n2] *trick, stratagem*
artifice, contrivance, craft, device, dodge, equivocation, evasion, expediency, expedient, gambit, hoax, makeshift, maneuver, move, ploy, recourse, refuge, resort, resource, ruse, stopgap*, strategy, substitute, subterfuge, wile; SEE CONCEPTS 59,660

shift [n3] *time served doing work*
bout, go, period, spell, stint, time, tour, trick, turn, working time; SEE CONCEPT 802

shift [v] *switch, fluctuate*
about-face*, alter, blow hot and cold*, bottom out*, budge, change, change gears, cook*, deviate, dial back*, dislocate, displace, disturb, do up*, drift, exchange, fault, flip-flop*, hem and haw*, move, move around, move over, rearrange, recalibrate, relocate, remove, replace, reposition, ship, shuffle, slip, stir, substitute, swap places, swerve, switch over, tack, transfer, transmogrify, transpose, turn, turn around, turn the corner*, turn the tables*, vacillate, vary, veer, waffle, yo-yo*; SEE CONCEPTS 213,232,697

shifty [adj] *deceitful, untrustworthy*
cagey, collusive, conniving, contriving, crafty, crooked, cunning, devious, dishonest, dodging, duplicitous, elusive, equivocating, evasive, fly-

sh
sh

by-night*, foxy, fraudulent, furtive, insidious, lying, mendacious, prevaricative, prevaricatory, roguish, scheming, shady, shrewd, shuffling, slick, slimy*, slippery, sly, sneaky, treacherous, tricky, underhand, unhonest, unprincipled, untruthful, wily; SEE CONCEPTS 401,404

shimmer [n] *gleam*
blinking, coruscation, diffused light, flash, glimmer, glint, glisten, glitter, gloss, glow, incandescence, iridescence, luster, phosphorescence, scintillation, sheen, spangle, spark, sparkle, twinkle; SEE CONCEPTS 620,624

shimmer [v] *glisten*
blaze, coruscate, dance, flare, flash, gleam, glint, glow, jiggle, phosphoresce, scintillate, shimmy, shine, sparkle, twinkle; SEE CONCEPT 624

shine [n] *brightness; polish*
flash, glare, glaze, gleam, glint, glitz, gloss, lambency, light, luminosity, luster, patina, polish, radiance, rub, sheen, shimmer, show, sparkle; SEE CONCEPT 620

shine [v1] *give off or reflect light*
beam, bedazzle, blaze, blink, burn, dazzle, deflect, emit light, flare, flash, flicker, give light, glare, gleam, glimmer, glisten, glitter, glow, illuminate, illumine, incandesce, irradiate, luminesce, mirror, radiate, scintillate, shimmer, sparkle, twinkle; SEE CONCEPT 624

shine [v2] *polish, burnish*
brush, buff, buff up, finish, furbish, give a sheen, glance, glaze, gloss, make brilliant, put a finish on, put a gloss on, rub, scour, sleek, wax; SEE CONCEPT 202

shiny [adj] *bright, glistening*
agleam, burnished, clear, gleaming, glossy, lustrous, polished, satiny, sheeny, slick, sparkling, sunny; SEE CONCEPT 617

ship [v] *send, transport*
address, consign, direct, dispatch, drop, embark, export, forward, freight, go aboard, haul, move, put on board, remit, route, shift, ship out, smuggle, transfer, transmit; SEE CONCEPTS 148,217

shirk [v] *avoid, get out of responsibility*
bypass, cheat, creep, dodge, dog*, duck, elude, eschew, evade, fence, get around, goldbrick*, lie down on job*, lurk, malinger, parry, pussyfoot*, quit, shuffle off, shun, sidestep, skulk, slack, slink, slip, slough off, snake, sneak, steal; SEE CONCEPTS 30,59,681

shiver [v1] *shake, tremble*
be cold, dither, flutter, freeze, have the quivers, have the shakes, palpitate, quake, quaver, quiver, shudder, tremor, twitter, vibrate, wave; SEE CONCEPTS 152,185

shiver [v2] *shatter; break into small pieces*
burst, crack, fragment, fragmentalize, pash, rive, smash, smash to smithereens*, smatter, splinter, splinterize*; SEE CONCEPTS 246,252

shock [n] *complete surprise; blow*
awe, bombshell*, breakdown, bump, clash, collapse, collision, concussion, confusion, consternation, crash, distress, disturbance, double whammy*, earthquake, encounter, excitement, eye-opener*, hysteria, impact, injury, jarring, jolt, percussion, prostration, ram, scare, start, stroke, stupefaction, stupor, trauma, traumatism, turn, upset, whammy*, wreck; SEE CONCEPTS 33,309,529

shock [v] *completely surprise*
abash, agitate, anger, antagonize, appall, astound,

awe, bowl over*, daze, disgust, dismay, displease, disquiet, disturb, electrify, flabbergast, flood, floor*, give a turn*, hit like ton of bricks*, horrify, insult, jar, jolt, knock out*, nauseate, numb, offend, outrage, overcome, overwhelm, paralyze, revolt, rock, scandalize, shake, shake up, sicken, stagger, startle, stun, stupefy, throw a curve*, traumatize, unsettle; SEE CONCEPT 42

shocking [adj] *outrageous; very surprising*
abominable, appalling, atrocious, awful, burning, crying, desperate, detestable, direful, disgraceful, disgusting, disquieting, distressing, dreadful, fearful, formidable, foul, frightful, ghastly, glaring, hateful, heinous, hideous, horrible, horrific, horrifying, loathsome, monstrous, nauseating, odious, offensive, repulsive, revolting, scandalous, shameful, sickening, stupefying, terrible, ugly, unspeakable; SEE CONCEPTS 548,571

shoddy [adj] *in bad shape*
base, broken-down, cheap, cheesy*, common, dilapidated, dingy, discreditable, disgraceful, dishonorable, disreputable, gaudy, ignominious, inferior, inglorious, junky, makeshift, mean, not up to snuff*, paltry, plastic, poor, pretentious, run-down, scruffy*, second-rate*, seedy, shabby, shady, shameful, sleazy*, slipshod, tacky*, tawdry, trashy, unrespectable; SEE CONCEPTS 485,571

shoot [v1] *discharge a projectile, often to injure or kill*
bag*, barrage, blast, bombard, bring down, catapult, dispatch, drop the hammer*, emit, execute, expel, explode, fire, fling, gun, hit, hurl, ignite, kill, launch, let fly, let go with, loose, murder, open fire*, open up*, pick off*, plug, pop*, project, propel, pull the trigger, pump*, set off, throw lead*, torpedo, trigger, zap*; SEE CONCEPTS 179,246,252

shoot [v2] *dash*
boil, bolt, charge, chase, dart, flash, fling, fly, gallop, hotfoot*, hurry, hurtle, lash, pass, race, reach, run, rush, scoot, skirr, speed, spring, spurt, streak, tear, whisk, whiz; SEE CONCEPTS 150,152

shop [n] *place of retail business*
boutique, chain, deli, department store, emporium, five-and-dime, market, mill, outlet, showroom, stand, store, supermarket; SEE CONCEPTS 439,441,448,449

shop [v] *look for merchandise to buy*
buy, go shopping, hunt for, look for, market, purchase, try to buy; SEE CONCEPTS 327,330

shore [n] *waterside*
bank, beach, border, brim, brink, coast, coastland, embankment, lakeshore, lakeside, littoral, margin, river bank, riverside, sand, sands, seaboard, seacoast, seashore, shingle, strand, waterfront; SEE CONCEPT 509

shore [v] *reinforce*
bear up, bolster, brace, bulwark, buttress, carry, hold, prop, strengthen, support, sustain, underpin, upbear, uphold; SEE CONCEPTS 110,190

short [adj] *abridged*
abbreviate, abbreviated, aphoristic, bare, boiled down, breviloquent, brief, compendiary, compendious, compressed, concise, condensed, curtailed, curtate, cut short, cut to the bone*, decreased, decurtate, diminished, epigrammatic, fleeting, in a nutshell*, laconic, lessened, little, momentary, not protracted, pithy, pointed, precise, sententious, short and sweet*, shortened, short-lived,

short-term, succinct, summarized, summary, terse, undersized, unprolonged, unsustained; SEE CONCEPTS 267,272,798

short [adj2] *not tall*
abbreviated, chunky, close to the ground, compact, diminutive, little, low, not long, petite, pint-sized*, pocket, pocket-sized*, runty, sawed-off*, skimpy, slight, small, squat, squatty, stocky, stubby, stunted, thick, thickset, tiny, undersized, wee; SEE CONCEPTS 773,779,782

short [adj3] *insufficient*
deficient, exiguous, failing, inadequate, lacking, limited, low on, meager, needing, niggardly, poor, scant, scanty, scarce, short-handed*, shy, skimpy, slender, slim, sparse, tight, wanting; SEE CONCEPTS 527,560,762

short [adj4] *abrupt, discourteous*
bad-tempered, blunt, breviloquent, brief, brusque, curt, direct, gruff, impolite, inconsiderate, irascible, offhand, rude, sharp, short-spoken, short-tempered, snappy*, snippety*, snippy*, straight, terse, testy, thoughtless, unceremonious, uncivil, ungracious; SEE CONCEPTS 267,401

short [adj5] *crumbly*
brittle, crisp, crunchy, delicate, fragile, friable; SEE CONCEPT 462

short [adv] *abruptly*
aback, by surprise, forthwith, sudden, suddenly, unanticipatedly, unaware, unawares, unexpectedly, without delay, without hesitation, without warning; SEE CONCEPT 799

shortage [n] *deficiency*
curtailment, dearth, defalcation, deficit, failure, inadequacy, insufficiency, lack, lapse, leanness, paucity, pinch, poverty, scantiness, scarcity, shortfall, tightness, underage, want, weakness; SEE CONCEPTS 646,709,767

shortcoming [n] *weak point*
bug*, catch*, defect, deficiency, demerit, drawback, failing, fault, flaw, frailty, imperfection, infirmity, lack, lapse, sin, weakness; SEE CONCEPTS 411,666,674,679

shorten [v] *diminish, decrease*
abbreviate, abridge, blue pencil*, bob, boil down*, chop, clip, compress, condense, contract, curtail, cut, cut back, cut down, cut to the bone*, dock, edit, elide, excerpt, lessen, lop, make a long story short*, minimize, put in a nutshell*, reduce, retrench, shrink, slash, snip, trim; SEE CONCEPTS 137,236,240,247

short-lived [adj] *temporary*
brief, ephemeral, evanescent, fleeting, fugacious, fugitive, impermanent, momentary, passing, short, short-haul*, short-run, short-term, transient, transitory; SEE CONCEPT 798

shortly [adv] *right away*
anon, any minute now, before long, by and by, in a little while, presently, proximately, quickly, soon; SEE CONCEPT 820

short-sighted [adj] *unmindful of future consequences*
astigmatic, blind, careless, foolish, headlong, ill-advised, ill-considered, imperceptive, impolitic, impractical, improvident, imprudent, injudicious, myopic, near-sighted, rash, stupid, unsagacious, unwary; SEE CONCEPTS 401,542

shot [n1] *try, chance*
attempt, break, conjecture, effort, endeavor, fling*, go*, guess, occasion, opening, opportu-

nity, pop*, show, slap*, stab*, surmise, time, turn, whack*, whirl*; SEE CONCEPT 693

shot [n2] *discharge; ammunition*
ball, buckshot, bullet, dart, lead, lob, missile, pellet, projectile, slug, throw; SEE CONCEPT 498

shoulder [v1] *be responsible for*
accept, assume, bear, carry, take on, take upon oneself; SEE CONCEPT 23

shoulder [v2] *push, jostle*
bulldoze*, elbow, hustle, nudge, press, push aside, shove, thrust; SEE CONCEPT 208

shout [n] *loud outcry*
bark, bawl, bellow, call, cheer, clamor, cry, howl, hue, roar, salvo, scream, screech, shriek, squall, squawk, tumult, vociferation, whoop*, yammer*, yap*, yawp*, yell; SEE CONCEPTS 77,595

shout [v] *cry out loudly*
bawl, bay, bellow, call out, cheer, clamor, exclaim, holler*, raise voice, roar, scream, screech, shriek, squall, squawk, vociferate, whoop*, yammer*, yap*, yawp*, yell; SEE CONCEPT 77

shove [v] *push without gentleness*
boost, buck, bulldoze*, cram, crowd, dig, drive, elbow, hustle, impel, jab, jam, jostle, nudge, poke, press, prod, propel, shoulder, thrust; SEE CONCEPT 208

shove off [v] *leave quickly*
blow, clear out, depart, exit, get off, go, go away, pull out, push off, quit, run along, start out, take off, vamoose*; SEE CONCEPT 195

show [n1] *demonstration, exhibition*
appearance, array, display, expo*, exposition, fair, fanfare, fireworks, grandstand, manifestation, occurrence, pageant, pageantry, panoply, parade, pomp, presentation, program, representation, shine*, showboat*, showing, sight, spectacle, splash*, view; SEE CONCEPT 261

show [n2] *entertainment event*
act, appearance, burlesque, carnival, cinema, comedy, drama, entertainment, film, flick*, motion picture, movie, pageant, picture, play, presentation, production, showing, spectacle; SEE CONCEPTS 263,293

show [n3] *false front; appearance given*
affectation, air, display, effect, face*, front, grandstand play*, guise, illusion, impression, likeness, make-believe*, ostentation, parade, pose, pretense, pretext, profession, seeming, semblance, sham, shine*, showboat*, showing, simulacrum, splash*; SEE CONCEPTS 633,716

show [v1] *actively exhibit something*
afford, air, arrive, attend, bare, blazon, brandish, deal in, demonstrate, display, disport, exhibit, expose, flash, flaunt, flourish, lay bare, lay out, mount, offer, parade, present, produce, proffer, put on, reveal, sell, set out, showcase, show off, sport, spread, stage, streak, submit, supply, trot out, unfold, unfurl, unveil, vaunt, wave; SEE CONCEPT 138

show [v2] *passively exhibit something*
appear, arrive, assert, be visible, blow in, clarify, come, demonstrate, determine, disclose, discover, display, divulge, elucidate, emerge, establish, evidence, evince, explain, get, get in, illustrate, indicate, instruct, lay out, loom, make known, make out, make the scene*, manifest, mark, materialize, note, ostend, point, present, proclaim, project, prove, put in appearance, reach, register, reveal, show one's face*, show up, teach, testify to, turn up, unveil; SEE CONCEPT 261

sh
sh

show [v3] *grant*
accord, act with, bestow, confer, dispense, give; SEE CONCEPT *108*

show [v4] *accompany*
attend, conduct, direct, escort, guide, lead, pilot, route, see, shepherd, steer; SEE CONCEPTS *187,384*

showdown [n] *confrontation*
breaking point, clash, climax, crisis, culmination, exposé, moment of truth, unfolding; SEE CONCEPTS *388,674*

showoff [n] *person who brags about him- or herself*
boaster, braggadocio, braggart, egotist, exhibitionist, swaggerer, vulgarian; SEE CONCEPT *412*

show off [v] *flaunt; brag*
advertise, boast, brandish, demonstrate, display, disport, exhibit, expose, flash*, hand a line*, make a spectacle of, parade, spread out, swagger, trot out*; SEE CONCEPTS *49,261*

show up [v1] *arrive, attend*
appear, be conspicuous, be visible, blow in*, come, get, get in, make an appearance, put in appearance, reach, show, stand out, turn up; SEE CONCEPT *159*

show up [v2] *expose, embarrass*
belittle, convict, debunk, defeat, discover, discredit, highlight, invalidate, lay bare, let down, mortify, pinpoint, put spotlight on*, put to shame*, reveal, shame, show in bad light*, uncloak, undress, unmask, unshroud, worst; SEE CONCEPTS *54,60*

showy [adj] *flamboyant, flashy*
classy, dashing, flash, garish, gaudy, glaring, histrionic, jazzy*, loud, luxurious, meretricious, opulent, ornate, ostentatious, overdone, overwrought, peacocky, pompous, pretentious, resplendent, screaming, sensational, snazzy*, splashy, splendiferous, sumptuous, swank*, tawdry, tinsel*, tony*; SEE CONCEPT *589*

shred [n] *tiny piece*
atom, bit, cantlet, crumb, fragment, grain, iota, jot, modicum, ounce, part, particle, rag, ray, ribbon, scintilla, scrap, shadow, sliver, smidgen, snippet, speck, stitch, tatter, trace, whit; SEE CONCEPT *831*

shred [v] *cut into ribbons*
cut, fray, frazzle, make ragged, reduce, shave, sliver, strip, tatter, tear; SEE CONCEPT *176*

shrewd [adj] *clever, intelligent*
acute, argute, artful, astucious, astute, brainy*, cagey, calculating, canny, crafty, cunning, cutting*, deep*, discerning, discriminating, farsighted, foxy*, heady*, ingenious, inside, in the know*, judicious, keen, knowing, on the inside*, on top of*, penetrating, perceptive, perspicacious, piercing, probing, profound, prudent, quickwitted, sagacious, savvy*, sensible, shark, sharp, slick*, slippery*, sly, smart, smooth, streetwise, tricky, underhand, up on*, wily, wise, wised up*; SEE CONCEPTS *401,402*

shriek [n/v] *high-pitched scream*
blare, cry, howl, screech, shout, shrill, squawk, squeal, wail, whoop, yell; SEE CONCEPTS *77,595*

shrill [adj] *high-pitched, harsh in sound*
acute, argute, blaring, blatant, cacophonous, clanging, clangorous, deafening, discordant, ear-piercing, ear-splitting, high, metallic, noisy, penetrating, piercing, piping, raucous, screeching, sharp, strident, thin, treble; SEE CONCEPTS *592,594*

shrine [n] *tribute to a god, idol, or spirit*
altar, chapel, church, enshrinement, grave, hallowed place, holy place, mausoleum, reliquary, sacred place, sanctorium, sanctuary, sanctum, sepulcher, temple; SEE CONCEPTS *368,439,448*

shrink [v1] *become smaller*
compress, concentrate, condense, constrict, contract, decrease, deflate, diminish, drop off, dwindle, fail, fall off, fall short, grow smaller, lessen, narrow, reduce, shorten, shrivel, wane, waste, waste away, weaken, wither, wrinkle; SEE CONCEPTS *137,698,776*

shrink [v2] *recoil, shy away*
blench, boggle, contract, cower, cringe, crouch, demur, draw back, flinch, hang back, huddle, quail, recede, refuse, retire, retreat, scruple, shudder, slink, wince, withdraw; SEE CONCEPTS *188,195*

shrivel [v] *dehydrate, dry up*
burn, contract, desiccate, dwindle, fossilize, mummify, mummy, parch, scorch, sear, shrink, stale, welter, wilt, wither, wizen, wrinkle; SEE CONCEPTS *137,250,255*

shudder [v] *shake, quiver*
convulse, dither, gyrate, jitter, quake, shimmy, shiver, tremble, tremor, twitter, wave; SEE CONCEPTS *34,150,152*

shuffle [v1] *move along lazily*
drag, limp, muddle, pad, scrape, scuff, scuffle, shamble, straggle, stumble, trail; SEE CONCEPT *151*

shuffle [v2] *rearrange, mix up*
break the deck*, change, change the order, confuse, disarrange, disarray, discompose, dislocate, disorder, disorganize, disrupt, disturb, intermix, jumble, mess up*, shift; SEE CONCEPTS *158,363*

shun [v] *avoid, ignore*
bilk, cold-shoulder*, cut, decline, despise, disdain, ditch*, dodge, double, duck, elude, escape, eschew, evade, get around, give a wide berth*, give the runaround*, have no part of*, have nothing to do with*, hide out, keep away from, keep clear of, neglect, palm off*, pass up, refuse, reject, scorn, shake, shake off, shy, snub, stall, stand aloof from, stay shy of, steer clear of*, turn back on*; SEE CONCEPTS *30,384*

shut [v] *close*
bar, batten down*, cage, close down, close up, confine, draw, drop the curtain*, enclose, exclude, fasten, fold, fold up, imprison, lock, push, put to, seal, secure, shut down, slam, wall off; SEE CONCEPTS *85,121,160,206,208,324*

shut off/shut out [v] *exclude; screen*
bar, beleaguer, blockade, block out, close, conceal, cover, debar, discontinue, evict, fence off, hide, keep out, lock out, mask, obstruct, ostracize, refuse, seclude, shroud, veil; SEE CONCEPTS *25,121,188*

shut up [v] *be or make quiet*
bottle up*, choke, dry up*, dummy up*, fall silent, gag, hold tongue*, hush, keep trap shut*, muzzle, pipe down*, quiet, quieten, quit chattering, shush*, silence, soft-pedal*, still, stop talking; SEE CONCEPT *77*

shy [adj1] *quiet and self-conscious*
afraid, apprehensive, averse, backward, bashful, cautious, chary, circumspect, conscious, coy, demure, diffident, disinclined, distrustful, fearful,

hesitant, humble, indisposed, introvert, introverted, loath, loner, modest, nervous, recessive, reluctant, reserved, reticent, retiring, selfeffacing, shamefaced, sheepish, shrinking, skittish, suspicious, timid, unassertive, unassured, uneager, uneffusive, unresponsive, unsocial, unwilling, wary; SEE CONCEPTS 401,404

shy [adj2] not lacking; failing
deficient, inadequate, insufficient, scant, scanty, scarce, short, unsufficient, wanting; SEE CONCEPTS 546,762,789

sick [adj1] not healthy
ailing, bedridden, broken down, confined, debilitated, declining, defective, delicate, diseased, disordered, down, feeble, feverish, frail, funny*, green*, hospitalized, ill, impaired, imperfect, in a bad way*, incurable, indisposed, infected, infirm, in poor health, invalid, laid-up, lousy, mean, nauseated, not so hot*, peaked, poorly, qualmish, queasy, rickety, rocky, rotten, run down, sick as a dog*, suffering, tottering, under medication, under the weather*, unhealthy, unwell, weak, wobbly; SEE CONCEPT 314

sick [adj2] morbid, gross
black, ghoulish, macabre, morose, sadistic, sickly; SEE CONCEPTS 537,571

sick [adj3] fed up, displeased
blasé, bored, disgusted, jaded, revolted, satiated, tired, up to here with*, weary; SEE CONCEPT 403

sicken [v] revolt, make ill
affect, afflict, derange, disgust, disorder, gross out*, nauseate, offend, reluct, repel, repulse, turn, turn one's stomach*, unhinge, unsettle, upset; SEE CONCEPTS 14,246

sickening [adj] disgusting, awful
diseased, distasteful, foul, gross*, icky*, loathsome, nasty, nauseating, nauseous, noisome, offensive, putrid, repugnant, repulsive, revolting, rotten, stinking, stomach-turning, tainted; SEE CONCEPTS 529,571

sickly [adj1] not healthy
ailing, below par, bilious, cranky, delicate, diseased, down, dragging, faint, feeble, indisposed, infirm, in poor health, lackluster, laid-low, languid, low, mean, off-color*, out of action*, out of shape*, pallid, peaked, peaky, pining, poorly, rocky, run-down, seedy, sickish, unhealthy, wan, weak; SEE CONCEPT 314

sickly [adj2] revolting
bilious, cloying, insalubrious, mawkish, morbid, morose, nauseating, noisome, noxious, sick, unwholesome; SEE CONCEPTS 537,571

sickness [n] ill or abnormal condition
affection, affliction, ailment, bug*, complaint, condition, disease, diseasedness, disorder, ill, ill health, illness, indisposition, infirmity, malady, nausea, queasiness, syndrome, unhealth, unhealthyfulness; SEE CONCEPT 306

side [n1] edge, exteriority of object
aspect, attitude, border, bottom, boundary, direction, disposition, division, elevation, face, facet, flank, front, hand, haunch, jamb, lee, limit, loin, margin, part, perimeter, periphery, posture, quarter, rear, rim, sector, stance, stand, surface, top, verge, view, wing; SEE CONCEPTS 513,835

side [n2] point of view
angle, appearance, aspect, belief, direction, facet, hand, light, opinion, outlook, phase, position, slant, stand, standpoint, viewpoint; SEE CONCEPT 689

side [n3] opposing person or view
behalf, belligerent, camp, cause, combatant, competition, contestant, crew, enemy, faction, foe, interest, part, party, rival, sect, team; SEE CONCEPTS 301,365

side [adj] minor; flanking
ancillary, incidental, indirect, lateral, lesser, marginal, not the main, oblique, off-center, postern, roundabout, secondary, sidelong, sideward, sideways, sidewise, skirting, subordinate, subsidiary, superficial; SEE CONCEPT 575

sideways [adv] to the edge, exteriority
alongside, aside, aslant, aslope, athwart, broadside, crabwise, edgeways, indirectly, laterally, obliquely, side by side, sidelong, sidewards, slanting, slantingly, slantwise, sloping, to the side; SEE CONCEPTS 581,583

sift [v] take out residue; remove impurities
analyze, clean, colander, comb, delve into, dig into, drain, evaluate, examine, explore, fathom, filter, go into, go through, grade, inquire, investigate, look into, pan, part, pore over, probe, prospect, purify, riddle, screen, scrutinize, search, separate, sieve, size, sort, strain, winnow; SEE CONCEPTS 103,165

sigh [v1] breathe out heavily
blow, complain, cry, exhale, gasp, grieve, groan, howl, lament, moan, murmur, pant, respire, roar, sob, sorrow, sough, suspire, wheeze, whine, whisper, whistle; SEE CONCEPT 163

sigh [v2] long for
ache, crave, dream, hanker, hunger, languish, lust, mourn, pine, suspire, thirst, yearn; SEE CONCEPT 20

sight [n1] ability to perceive with eyes
afterimage, appearance, apperception, apprehension, eye, eyes, eyeshot, eyesight, field of vision, ken, perception, range of vision, seeing, view, viewing, visibility, vision; SEE CONCEPT 629

sight [n2] spectacle
display, exhibit, exhibition, outlook, pageant, parade, point of interest, scene, show, view, vista; SEE CONCEPTS 261,293

sight [n3] horrifying person or thing
blot, eyesore, fright, mess, monstrosity, ogre, ogress, scarecrow, slob, spectacle, tramp; SEE CONCEPTS 412,513

sight [v] see
behold, discern, distinguish, eyeball*, make out*, observe, perceive, spot, view, witness; SEE CONCEPT 626

sign [n1] indication, evidence
assurance, augury, auspice, badge, beacon, bell, caution, clue, divination, flag, flash, foreboding, foreknowledge, foreshadowing, foretoken, forewarning, gesture, giveaway, handwriting on wall*, harbinger, herald, high sign*, hint, light, manifestation, mark, nod, note, omen, portent, precursor, prediction, premonition, presage, presentiment, prognostic, proof, signal, suggestion, symbol, symptom, token, trace, vestige, warning, wave, whistle, wink; SEE CONCEPTS 274,529,673,689

sign [n2] document with information; symbol
badge, board, character, cipher, crest, device, emblem, ensign, guidepost, insignia, logo, mark, notice, placard, proof, representation, signboard, signpost, symbolization, token, type, warning; SEE CONCEPTS 271,284

sh
si

sign [v1] *write name*
acknowledge, authorize, autograph, confirm, endorse, initial, ink, inscribe, put John Hancock on*, put John Henry on*, rubber-stamp*, set one's hand to*, signature, subscribe, witness; SEE CONCEPT 79

sign [v2] *motion to another*
beckon, express, flag, gesticulate, gesture, indicate, motion, signal, signalize, signify, use sign language, wave; SEE CONCEPT 74

signal [n] *indication; authorization*
alarm, alert, beacon, bleep, blinker, cue, flag, flare, gesture, go-ahead*, green light*, high sign*, indicator, mark, Mayday*, movement, nod, okay*, omen, sign, SOS*, tocsin, token, wink; SEE CONCEPTS 74,284,529,685

signal [adj] *extraordinary, outstanding*
arresting, arrestive, characteristic, conspicuous, distinctive, distinguished, eminent, exceptional, eye-catching, famous, illustrious, individual, marked, memorable, momentous, notable, noteworthy, noticeable, peculiar, prominent, pronounced, remarkable, renowned, salient, significant, striking; SEE CONCEPTS 568,574

signal [v] *indicate; give a sign to*
beckon, communicate, flag, flash, gesticulate, gesture, motion, nod, semaphore, sign, signalize, warn, wave, wink; SEE CONCEPT 74

significance [n1] *meaning*
acceptation, bottom line*, connotation, drift, force, heart, implication, import, intendment, kicker*, meat*, message, name of the game*, nature of the beast*, nitty-gritty*, nub, nuts and bolts*, point, punch line*, purport, score, sense, significancy, signification, stuff, understanding; SEE CONCEPT 682

significance [n2] *importance*
authority, consequence, consideration, credit, excellence, gravity, import, impressiveness, influence, magnitude, matter, merit, moment, momentousness, perfection, pith, prestige, relevance, signification, virtue, weight, weightiness; SEE CONCEPT 668

significant [adj1] *telling, meaningful*
cogent, compelling, convincing, denoting, eloquent, expressing, expressive, facund, forceful, heavy, important, indicative, knowing, meaning, momentous, powerful, pregnant, representative, rich, sententious, serious, sound, suggestive, symbolic, valid, weighty; SEE CONCEPTS 267,567

significant [adj2] *important, critical*
big, carrying a lot of weight*, consequential, considerable, heavy, material, meaningful, momentous, notable, noteworthy, serious, substantial, vital, weighty; SEE CONCEPT 568

signify [v1] *mean, indicate*
add up to, announce, bear, be a sign of, bespeak, betoken, carry, communicate, connote, convey, denote, disclose, evidence, evince, exhibit, express, flash, imply, import, insinuate, intend, intimate, manifest, matter, moment, proclaim, purport, represent, show, sign, spell, stand for, suggest, symbolize, talk, tell, wink; SEE CONCEPTS 55,266,682

signify [v2] *be of importance*
be of consequence, be of significance, carry weight, count, import, matter, mean, weigh; SEE CONCEPT 568

silence [n] *absence of sound, speech*
blackout, calm, censorship, dead air, death, dumbness, hush, hush-hush*, inarticulateness, iron curtain*, laconism, lull, muteness, noiselessness, peace, quiescence, quiet, quietness, quietude, quietus, reserve, reticence, saturninity, secrecy, sleep, speechlessness, still, stillness, sulk, sullenness, taciturnity, uncommunicativeness; SEE CONCEPT 65

silence [v] *make or be quiet*
choke off*, clam, clam up*, close up, cool it*, cut off, cut short, dampen, deaden, decrease the volume, dry up*, dull, dummy up*, extinguish, gag, hold one's tongue*, hush, hush-hush*, hush one's mouth*, keep it down*, lull, muffle, mute, muzzle, overawe, pipe down*, quash, quell, quiet, quiet down, quieten, say nothing, shush*, shut up, sit on*, soft-pedal*, squelch, stifle, still, strike dumb*, subdue, suppress, tongue-tie*; SEE CONCEPT 266

silent [adj1] *quiet; speechless*
bashful, buttoned up*, checked, clammed up*, close, closed up, closemouthed, curbed, dumb, dummied up*, faint, hush, hushed, iced*, inarticulate, incoherent, inconversable, indistinct, inhibited, laconic, mousy, mum, mute, muted, noiseless, nonvocal, not talkative, reserved, restrained, reticent, shy, silentious, sounding, still, struck dumb, taciturn, tongue-tied, unclear, uncommunicative, unheard, unsociable, unspeaking, voiceless, wordless, zipped*; SEE CONCEPT 594

silent [adj2] *understood, implied*
aphonic, implicit, indescribable, inexpressible, nameless, tacit, unexpressed, unpronounced, unspoken, unuttered, unvoiced, wordless; SEE CONCEPT 267

silhouette [n] *outline*
contour, delineation, etching, figuration, form, likeness, line, lineament, lineation, portrait, profile, shade, shadow, shape; SEE CONCEPTS 259,625

silky [adj] *very smooth; like satin*
cottony, delicate, glossy, like silk, luxurious, plush, satiny, silk, silken, sleek, soft, tender, velvety; SEE CONCEPT 606

silly [adj] *absurd, giddy, foolish*
asinine, balmy, brainless, childish, crazy, dippy*, dizzy*, empty, empty-headed*, fatuous, featherbrained*, flighty, foolhardy, frivolous, harebrained*, idiotic, ignorant, illogical, immature, imprudent, inane, inappropriate, inconsistent, irrational, irresponsible, ludicrous, meaningless, muddle-headed*, nitwitted, nonsensical, pointless, preposterous, puerile, ridiculous, senseless, sheepheaded*, simple, simple-minded, stupid, unintelligent, unreasonable, unwise, vacuous, witless; SEE CONCEPTS 401,403,542

silver [adj] *shiny gray in color*
argent, argentate, bright, lustrous, pale, pearly, plated, resplendent, silvered, silvery, sterling, white; SEE CONCEPT 618

similar [adj] *very much alike*
agnate, akin, allied, analogous, coincident, coincidental, coinciding, collateral, companion, comparable, complementary, congruent, congruous, consonant, consubstantial, correlative, corresponding, homogeneous, identical, in agreement, kin, kindred, like, matching, much the same, parallel, reciprocal, related, resembling, same, twin, uniform; SEE CONCEPTS 487,573

similarity [n] *likeness, correspondence*
affinity, agreement, alikeness, analogy, approxi-

mation, association, closeness, coincidence, collation, community, comparability, comparison, concordance, concurrence, conformity, congruence, congruity, connection, correlation, dead ringer*, harmony, homogeneity, identity, interrelation, kinship, likes of, look-alike, parallel, parallelism, parity, peas in a pod*, proportion, reciprocity, relation, relationship, resemblance, sameness, semblance, simile, similitude, synonymity, two of a kind*; SEE CONCEPT 670

simmer [v] *boil, smolder*
be agitated, be angry, be tense, be uptight*, bubble, burn, churn, cook, effervesce, ferment, fizz, fret, fricassee, fume, parboil, rage, seethe, smart, sparkle, stew, stir, warm; SEE CONCEPTS 35,170,410

simple [adj1] *clear, understandable; easy*
child's play*, cinch*, clean, easy as pie*, effortless, elementary, facile, incomplex, intelligible, light, lucid, manageable, mild, no problem*, no sweat*, not difficult, picnic*, piece of cake*, plain, quiet, self-explanatory, simple as ABC*, smooth, snap*, straightforward, transparent, uncomplicated, uninvolved, unmistakable, untroublesome, walkover*; SEE CONCEPTS 529,538

simple [adj2] *uncluttered, natural*
absolute, austere, classic, clean, discreet, elementary, folksy, homely, homey, humble, moderate, lowly, mere, modest, not complex, open and shut*, plain, pure, pure and simple*, rustic, sheer, single, Spartan, unadorned, unadulterated, unaffected, unalloyed, unblended, uncombined, uncomplicated, uncompounded, undecorated, unelaborate, unembellished, unfussy, unmitigated, unmixed, unornamented, unostentatious, unpretentious, unqualified, vanilla*; SEE CONCEPTS 562,589

simple [adj3] *childlike, innocent*
amateur, artless, bald, basic, childish, direct, frank, green, guileless, honest, ingenuous, naive, naked, natural, plain, sincere, square, stark, trusting, unaffected, unartificial, undeniable, unexperienced, unpretentious, unschooled, unsophisticated, unstudied, unvarnished*; SEE CONCEPTS 267,401,542

simple [adj4] *feeble-minded; not intelligent*
amateur, asinine, backward, brainless, credulous, dense, dimwitted, dull, dumb, fat, feeble, foolish, green*, gullible, half-witted, idiotic, ignorant, illiterate, imbecile, inane, inexperienced, inexpert, insensate, mindless, moronic, nitwitted, obtuse, senseless, shallow, silly, simple-minded, slow, soft, soft-headed*, stupid, thick, uneducated, unintelligent, witless; SEE CONCEPT 402

simplicity [n] *absence of complication, sophistication*
artlessness, candor, chastity, clarity, classicality, clean lines, clearness, directness, ease, easiness, elementariness, guilelessness, homogeneity, ingenuousness, innocence, integrity, lack of adornment, modesty, monotony, naïveté, naivety, naturalness, obviousness, openness, plainness, primitiveness, purity, restraint, severity, singleness, straightforwardness, uniformity, unity; SEE CONCEPTS 633,655,663

simplify [v] *make easy, intelligible*
abridge, analyze, boil down, break down, break it down, chasten, clarify, clean it up*, clean up, clear up, cut down, cut the frills*, decipher, disentangle, disinvolve, draw a picture*, elucidate,

explain, facilitate, get down to basics*, get to the meat*, hit the high spots*, interpret, lay out, let daylight in*, let sunlight in*, make clear, make perfectly clear, make plain, order, put in a nutshell*, put one straight*, reduce, shorten, spell out, streamline, unscramble; SEE CONCEPTS 57,110,261

simply [adv1] *plainly, clearly*
artlessly, candidly, commonly, directly, easily, frankly, guilelessly, honestly, ingenuously, intelligibly, matter-of-factly, modestly, naturally, openly, ordinarily, quietly, sincerely, straightforwardly, unaffectedly, unpretentiously, without any elaboration; SEE CONCEPTS 544,562

simply [adv2] *merely*
barely, but, just, only, purely, solely, utterly; SEE CONCEPTS 544,557

simply [adv3] *absolutely, completely*
altogether, in fact, really, totally, unreservedly, utterly, wholly; SEE CONCEPTS 531,535

simulate [v] *pretend, imitate*
act, act like, affect, ape, assume, bluff, borrow, cheat, concoct, copy, counterfeit, crib*, deceive, disguise, dissemble, do, do a take-off*, do like*, equivocate, exaggerate, fabricate, fake, favor, feature, feign, fence, gloss over, invent, knock off*, lie, lift, make believe, mimic, mirror, misrepresent, phony, pirate, play, playact, pose, prevaricate, put on*, put on an act*, replicate, reproduce, resemble, steal; SEE CONCEPTS 59,63,111,171

simultaneous [adj] *happening at about the same time*
accompanying, agreeing, at the same time, coetaneous, coeval, coexistent, coexisting, coincident, coinciding, concurrent, concurring, contemporaneous, contemporary, dead heat*, in sync*, synchronal, synchronic, synchronous, with the beat*; SEE CONCEPTS 548,799

sin [n] *illegal or immoral action*
anger, covetousness, crime, damnation, debt, deficiency, demerit, disobedience, envy, error, evil, evil-doing, fault, gluttony, guilt, immorality, imperfection, iniquity, lust, misdeed, offense, peccability, peccadillo, peccancy, pride, shortcoming, sinfulness, sloth, tort, transgression, trespass, ungodliness, unrighteousness, veniality, vice, violation, wickedness, wrong, wrongdoing, wrongness; SEE CONCEPTS 101,645

sin [v] *commit illegal or immoral action*
backslide*, break commandment, break law, cheat, commit crime, deviate, do wrong, err, fall, fall from grace*, go astray*, lapse, live in sin, misbehave, misconduct, offend, sow wild oats*, stray, take the primrose path*, transgress, trespass, wallow in the mire*, wander; SEE CONCEPTS 101,375,645

sincere [adj] *straightforward, honest*
aboveboard, actual, artless, bona fide, candid, dead-level*, dear, devout, earnest, faithful, forthright, frank, genuine, guileless, heartfelt, honest to God*, like it is*, meant, natural, no fooling*, no-nonsense*, on the level*, on the line*, on up and up*, open, outspoken, plain, pretensionless, real, regular, righteous, saintly, serious, square*, sure enough, true, true-blue*, trustworthy, twenty-four carat*, unaffected, undesigning, undissembled, unfeigned, unpretentious, up-front*, wholehearted; SEE CONCEPTS 267,401,542

sincerely [adv] *seriously, honestly*
aboveboard, candidly, deeply, earnestly, frankly, from bottom of heart, genuinely, in all conscience, in all sincerity, ingenuously, in good faith, naturally, profoundly, really, truly, truthfully, wholeheartedly, without equivocation; SEE CONCEPTS 267,582

sincerity [n] *straightforwardness, honesty*
artlessness, bona fides, candor, earnestness, frankness, genuineness, good faith, goodwill, guilelessness, heart, honor, impartiality, innocence, justice, openness, probity, reliability, seriousness, sincereness, singleness, trustworthiness, truth, truthfulness, veracity, wholeheartedness; SEE CONCEPTS 633,657

sinful [adj] *immoral, criminal*
amiss, bad, base, blamable, blameful, blameworthy, censurable, corrupt, culpable, damnable, demeritorious, depraved, disgraceful, erring, evil, guilty, iniquitous, irreligious, low, morally wrong, reprehensible, reprobate, shameful, ungodly, unholy, unregenerate, unrighteous, vicious, vile, wicked, wrong; SEE CONCEPTS 545,548

sing [v1] *carry a tune with one's voice*
belt out*, burst into song*, buzz*, canary*, cantillate, carol, chant, chirp, choir, croon, descant, duet, groan*, harmonize, hum, hymn, intone, lift up a voice*, line out*, lullaby, make melody*, mouth, pipe, purr*, resound, roar, serenade, shout, singsong, solo, trill, troll, tune, vocalize, wait, warble, whine, whistle, yodel; SEE CONCEPTS 47,77,292

sing [v2] *tattle on someone*
betray, blow the whistle*, fink*, inform, peach*, rat*, snitch*, spill the beans*, talk, turn in; SEE CONCEPTS 60,317

singer [n] *person who can carry a tune*
accompanist, artist, artiste, chanter, chanteuse, choralist, chorister, crooner, diva*, intoner, melodist, minstrel, musician, nightingale, serenader, soloist, songbird, songster, troubadour, vocalist, voice, warbler, yodeler; SEE CONCEPT 352

single [adj1] *alone, distinct*
distinct, distinguished, especial, exceptional, exclusive, individual, indivisible, isolated, lone, loner, not general, not public, odd, one, only, original, particular, peerless, personal, private, rare, restricted, secluded, separate, separated, simple, singled-out, singular, sole, solitary, special, specific, strange, unalloyed, unblended, uncommon, uncompounded, undivided, unique, unitary, unmixed, unrivaled, unshared, unusual, without equal; SEE CONCEPTS 564,577,762

single [adj2] *not married*
bachelor, companionless, divorced, eligible, free, living alone, loner, separated, sole, solo, spouseless, unattached, unfettered, unmarried, unwed; SEE CONCEPT 555

singly [adv] *individually*
apart, independently, one at a time, one by one, particularly, respectively, separately, severally, oneself; SEE CONCEPT 577

singular [adj1] *unique, odd*
atypical, avant-garde, bizarre, breaking new ground*, conspicuous, cool*, curious, eccentric, eminent, exceptional, extraordinary, loner, noteworthy, original, outlandish, out-of-the-way, outstanding, peculiar, prodigious, puzzling, queer, rare, remarkable, special, strange, uncommon,

unimaginable, unordinary, unparalleled, unprecedented, unthinkable, unusual, unwonted, weird; SEE CONCEPT 564

singular [adj2] *alone, separate*
certain, definite, discrete, exclusive, individual, one, only, particular, respective, single, sole, solitary, solo, unique, unrepeatable; SEE CONCEPT 577

sinister [adj] *nasty, menacing*
adverse, apocalyptic, bad, baleful, baneful, black-hearted, corrupt, deleterious, dire, disastrous, dishonest, disquieting, doomful, evil, foreboding, harmful, hurtful, ill-boding, inauspicious, injurious, lowering, malefic, malevolent, malign, malignant, menacing, mischievous, obnoxious, ominous, pernicious, perverse, poisonous, portentous, threatening, unfavorable, unfortunate, unlucky, unpropitious, woeful; SEE CONCEPTS 401,548,571

sink [v1] *fall in, go under*
bore, bring down, capsize, cast down, cave in, couch, decline, demit, depress, descend, dig, dip, disappear, drill, drive, droop, drop, drown, ebb, engulf, excavate, fall, flounder, force down, founder, go down, go to the bottom, immerse, lay, let down, lower, overturn, overwhelm, plummet, plunge, put down, ram, regress, run, sag, scuttle, set, settle, shipwreck, slope, slump, stab, stick, stoop, submerge, subside, swamp, thrust, tip over, touch bottom, wreck; SEE CONCEPTS 181,213

sink [v2] *fall, decrease*
abate, collapse, diminish, drop, lapse, lessen, relapse, retrogress, slip, slump, subside, wane; SEE CONCEPTS 698,776

sink [v3] *deteriorate*
decay, decline, decrease, degenerate, depreciate, descend, deteriorate, die, diminish, disimprove, disintegrate, dwindle, fade, fail, flag, go downhill*, lessen, retrograde, rot, spoil, waste, weaken, worsen; SEE CONCEPTS 469,698

sink [v4] *be humble or humbled*
abase, bemean, be reduced to, cast down, debase, degrade, demean, humiliate, lower, stoop, succumb; SEE CONCEPTS 7,19,35

sinuous [adj] *winding, twisting*
anfractuous, circuitous, coiling, convoluted, crooked, curved, curvy, deviative, devious, flexuous, indirect, meandering, meandrous, serpentine, snaky*, supple, tortuous, twisting and turning*, undulating, vagrant; SEE CONCEPT 581

sip [v] *drink slowly*
drink in, extract, imbibe, partake, quaff, sample, savor, sup, swallow, taste, toss; SEE CONCEPT 169

sister [n] *female sibling*
blood sister, kin, kinsperson, relation, relative, twin; SEE CONCEPTS 414,415

sit [v1] *rest on one's behind*
bear on, be seated, cover, ensconce, give feet a rest*, grab a chair*, have a place, have a seat, hunker*, install, lie, park*, perch*, plop down*, pose, posture, put it there*, relax, remain, rest, seat, seat oneself, settle, squat, take a load off*, take a place, take a seat; SEE CONCEPTS 154,201

sit [v2] *hold a meeting*
assemble, be in session, come together, convene, deliberate, hold an assembly, meet, officiate, open, preside; SEE CONCEPTS 324,384

site [n] *place of activity*
fix, ground, habitat, hangout, haunt, home, lay,

layout, locale, locality, location, locus, mise en scène, plot, point, position, post, range, scene, section, situation, slot, spot, station, wherever, X marks the spot*; SEE CONCEPT 198

situation [n1] *place of activity*

bearings, direction, footing, latitude, locale, locality, location, locus, longitude, position, post, seat, setting, site, spot, stage, station, where, whereabouts; SEE CONCEPT 198

situation [n2] *circumstances, status*

ballgame*, bargain, capacity, case, character, condition, footing*, how things stack up*, like it is*, mode, picture, place, plight, position, posture, rank, scene, size of it*, sphere, stage, standing, standpoint, state, state of affairs, station, status quo*; SEE CONCEPTS 388,696

situation [n3] *employment status*

appointment, berth, billet, capacity, connection, employment, engagement, hire, job, office, place, placement, position, post, profession, spot, trade; SEE CONCEPTS 351,360,668

sizable [adj] *considerable, large*

ample, big, burly, capacious, comprehensive, decent, decent-sized, extensive, good, goodly, great, gross, hefty, husky, jumbo*, largish, major, massive, ponderous, respectable, sensible, spacious, strapping, substantial, tidy, voluminous, whopping*; SEE CONCEPT 781

size [n] *extent or bulk of some dimension*

admeasurement, amount, amplitude, area, bigness, body, breadth, caliber, capaciousness, capacity, content, diameter, dimensions, enormity, extension, extent, greatness, height, highness, hugeness, immensity, intensity, largeness, length, magnitude, mass, measurement, proportion, proportions, range, scope, spread, stature, stretch, substance, substantiality, tonnage, vastness, volume, voluminosity, width; SEE CONCEPTS 730,792

sizzle [v] *hiss, fry*

broil, brown, buzz, cook, crackle, fizz, fizzle, frizzle, grill, roast, sear, sibilate, spit, sputter, swish, wheeze, whisper, whiz; SEE CONCEPTS 65,170

skeleton [n] *structure of bones in animate being or supports in an object*

bones, bony structure, cage, design, draft, frame, framework, osteology, outline, scaffolding, sketch, support; SEE CONCEPTS 393,733

skeptic [n] *person who is leery, unbelieving*

agnostic, apostate, atheist, cynic, disbeliever, dissenter, doubter, doubting Thomas*, freethinker, heathen, heretic, infidel, materialist, misanthrope, misbeliever, nihilist, pagan, pessimist, profaner, questioner, rationalist, scoffer, unbeliever; SEE CONCEPTS 361,423

skeptical [adj] *disbelieving, leery*

agnostic, aporetic, cynical, dissenting, doubtful, doubting, dubious, freethinking, hesitating, incredulous, mistrustful, questioning, quizzical, scoffing, show-me*, suspicious, unbelieving, unconvinced; SEE CONCEPT 403

sketch [n] *drawing, outline*

account, adumbration, aperçu, blueprint, cartoon, chart, compendium, configuration, copy, delineation, depiction, description, design, diagram, digest, doodle, draft, figuration, figure, form, illustration, likeness, monograph, painting, picture, piece, plan, portrayal, precis, report, representation, rough, shape, skeleton, summary,

survey, syllabus, version, vignette; SEE CONCEPTS 268,283,625

sketch [v] *draw, outline*

adumbrate, block out*, blueprint*, chalk, characterize, chart, delineate, depict, describe, design, detail, develop, diagram, doodle, draft, lay out*, line, map out, paint, plan, plot, portray, represent, rough out*, skeleton, skeletonize, trace; SEE CONCEPTS 36,174

sketchy [adj] *rough, incomplete*

coarse, crude, cursory, defective, depthless, faulty, imperfect, inadequate, insufficient, introductory, outline, perfunctory, preliminary, rough, scrappy, shallow, skimpy, slight, superficial, uncritical, unfinished, vague; SEE CONCEPT 531

skid [v] *slide against will*

drift, glide, go into skid, move, sheer, skew, slip, slue, swerve, veer; SEE CONCEPT 152

skill [n] *ability, talent to do something*

accomplishment, address, adroitness, aptitude, art, artistry, cleverness, clout, command, competence, craft, cunning, deftness, dexterity, dodge*, ease, experience, expertise, expertism, expertness, facility, finesse, goods*, handiness, ingenuity, intelligence, job, knack*, know-how*, line, makings, moxie*, one's thing*, profession, proficiency, prowess, quickness, readiness, right stuff*, savvy*, skillfulness, sleight, smarts*, stuff*, technique, trade, what it takes*; SEE CONCEPTS 409,630

skillful [adj] *able, talented*

accomplished, adept, adroit, a hand at*, apt, brainy, clever, competent, cool*, crack*, crackerjack*, dexterous, experienced, expert, good, handy, into*, learned, old*, on the ball*, practical, practiced, prepared, pretty, primed, pro*, professional, proficient, quick, ready, really into*, savvy*, seasoned, sharp, skilled, smart, smooth, there*, trained, tuned in*, versant, versed, vet*, veteran, well-versed, whiz, wicked*, wised up*; SEE CONCEPTS 402,527

skim [v1] *remove the top part*

brush, cream, dip, get the cream, glance, graze, ladle, ream, scoop, separate, shave, top; SEE CONCEPT 211

skim [v2] *glide over quickly, lightly*

brush, carom, coast, dart, float, fly, graze, kiss, ricochet, sail, scud, shoot, skate, skip, skirr, skitter, smooth along, soar, trip; SEE CONCEPTS 150,152

skim [v3] *look through cursorily*

browse, brush over, dip, examine, flip through, get the cream*, give the once-over*, glance, glance over, go once over lightly*, hit the high spots*, leaf through*, read, read swiftly, riff, riffle, run eye over*, scan, skip, thumb through*, turn the pages*; SEE CONCEPTS 72,103,623

skimp [v] *be cheap or frugal about*

be mean with, be sparing, cut corners*, make ends meet*, pinch, pinch pennies*, roll back, save, scamp, scant, scrape, screw, scrimp, slight, spare, stint, tighten one's belt*, withhold; SEE CONCEPT 330

skimpy [adj] *sparse, inadequate*

deficient, exiguous, failing, insufficient, meager, miserly, niggardly, poor, scant, scanty, scrimp, scrimpy, short, shy, spare, stingy, thin, tight, unsufficient, wanting; SEE CONCEPTS 334,762,789

skin [n] *outer covering, especially of animate being*
bark, carapace, case, casing, coating, crust, cutis, derma, dermis, epidermis, fell, film, fur, hide, hull, husk, integument, jacket, membrane, outside, parchment, peel, pelt, rind, sheath, sheathing, shell, shuck, slough, surface, tegument, vellum; SEE CONCEPTS *392,428,484*

skin [v] *remove outer covering*
abrade, bark, bark, cast, cut off, decorticate, excoriate, exuviate, flay, gall, graze, hull, husk, lay bare, pare, peel, pull off, remove, rind, scale, scalp, scrape, shave, shed, shuck, slough, strip, trim; SEE CONCEPTS *176,211*

skinny [adj] *very thin*
angular, bony, emaciated, gaunt, lank, lanky, lean, like a rail*, malnourished, rawboned, scraggy, scrawny, skeletal, skin-and-bone*, slender, spare, twiggy, undernourished, underweight; SEE CONCEPTS *490,491*

skip [v1] *bounce or jump over*
bob, bolt, bound, buck, canter, caper, carom, cavort, dance, flee, flit, fly, frisk, gambol, glance, graze, hippety-hop*, hop, leap, lope, make off, prance, ricochet, run, scamper, scoot, skedaddle*, skim, skirr, skitter, spring, step, tiptoe, trip; SEE CONCEPTS *150,194*

skip [v2] *avoid, miss*
cut, desert, disregard, escape, eschew, flee, leave out, miss out, neglect, omit, pass over, pass up, play hooky*, run away, skim over, split; SEE CONCEPTS *30,681*

skirt [n1] *border, edge*
brim, brink, fringe, hem, margin, outskirts, perimeter, periphery, purlieus, rim, skirting, verge; SEE CONCEPTS *484,825*

skirt [n2] *ladies' garment that hangs from waist*
culottes, dirndl, dress, hoop, kilt, midi, mini, pannier, petticoat, sarong, tutu; SEE CONCEPT *451*

skirt [v1] *border; be on the edge*
bound, define, edge, flank, fringe, hem, lie along, lie alongside, margin, rim, surround, verge; SEE CONCEPT *751*

skirt [v2] *avoid; get around*
burke, bypass, circumnavigate, circumvent, detour, dodge, duck, elude, equivocate, escape, evade, hedge, ignore, sidestep, skip, steer clear of; SEE CONCEPTS *30,102,147*

skittish [adj] *very nervous*
agitable, alarmable, capricious, changeable, combustible, dizzy*, edgy, excitable, excited, fearful, fickle, fidgety, flighty, frivolous, giddy, harebrained, high-strung*, irresponsible, jumpy, lightheaded, lively, peppy, playful, restive, scatterbrained*, sensitive, spirited, undependable, unreliable, volative, whimsical, zippy*; SEE CONCEPT *401*

sky [n] *Earth's atmosphere*
azure, celestial sphere, empyrean, firmament, heavens, lid*, the blue*, upper atmosphere, vault, vault of heaven*, welkin, wild blue yonder*; SEE CONCEPT *437*

slab [n] *chunk of solid object*
bar, billet, bit, board, boulder, chip, cut, cutting, hunk, ingot, lump, muck, piece, plate, portion, rod, slice, stave, stick, stone, strip, wedge; SEE CONCEPTS *471,835*

slack [n] *looseness, excess*
give, leeway, play, room, slackening, slowdown, slow-up; SEE CONCEPTS *513,807*

slack [adj1] *loose, baggy; inactive*
dull, easy, feeble, flabby, flaccid, flexible, flimsy, inert, infirm, laggard, lax, leisurely, limp, not taut, passive, quaggy, quiet, relaxed, sloppy, slow, slow-moving, sluggish, soft, supine, unsteady, weak; SEE CONCEPTS *485,584,589*

slack [adj2] *lazy, negligent*
asleep on the job*, behindhand, careless, delinquent, derelict, dilatory, disregardful, dormant, dull, easy-going, faineant, idle, inactive, inattentive, indolent, inert, lackadaisical, lax, lethargic, neglectful, not busy, permissive, quiescent, quiet, regardless, remiss, slothful, slow, slow-moving, sluggish, stagnant, tardy; SEE CONCEPT *538*

slack/slacken [v] *do little or nothing; loosen*
abate, decrease, diminish, dodge, drop off, dwindle, ease, ease off, featherbed*, flag, goldbrick*, goof off*, idle, lax, lay back, lessen, let up, lie down on job*, loose, moderate, neglect, reduce, relax, release, shirk, slack off, slow down, taper, tire, untighten, wane; SEE CONCEPTS *210,681,698*

slam [n1] *loud noise from impact*
bang, bash, blast, blow, boom, burst, clap, crack, crash, ding, pound, smack, smash, whack, wham; SEE CONCEPTS *189,595*

slam [n2] *harsh criticism*
animadversion, aspersion, jab, obloquy, potshot*, slap*, slur*, stricture, swipe*; SEE CONCEPTS *52,278*

slam [v1] *throw or push very hard*
bang, bat, batter, beat, belt, blast, clobber, close, crash, cudgel, dash, fling, hammer, hit, hurl, knock, pound, shut, slap, slug, smash, strike, swat, thump, thwack, wallop; SEE CONCEPTS *189,208,222*

slam [v2] *criticize very harshly*
attack, castigate, damn, excoriate, flay, lambaste*, lash into*, pan, scathe, scourge, shoot down, slap, slash, vilify; SEE CONCEPTS *52,54*

slander [n] *scandalous remark*
aspersion, backbiting*, backstabbing*, belittlement, black eye*, calumny, defamation, depreciation, detraction, dirt*, dirty linen*, disparagement, hit*, libel, lie, misrepresentation, muckraking, mud*, mud-slinging*, obloquy, rap*, scandal, slam*, slime*, smear*, tale; SEE CONCEPTS *54,192,278*

slander [v] *make a scandalous remark*
asperse, assail, attack, backbite*, bad-mouth*, belie, belittle, besmirch, blacken name*, blaspheme, blister, blot, calumniate, cast a slur on, curse, damage, decry, defame, defile, denigrate, depreciate, derogate, detract, dishonor, disparage, give a bad name*, hit*, hurt, injure, libel, malign, muckrake, pan*, plaster, revile, roast*, run smear campaign*, scandalize, scorch, slam*, sling mud*, slur, smear, smirch, sneer, strumpet, sully, tarnish, tear down, traduce, vilify; SEE CONCEPTS *54,192*

slang [n] *casual dialect*
argot, cant, colloquialism, informal speech, jargon, lingo, neologism, patois, patter, pidgin, shoptalk, slanguage* street talk, vernacular, vulgarism, vulgarity; SEE CONCEPT *276*

slant [n1] *angle, slope*
camber, cant, declination, diagonal, grade, gradient, inclination, incline, lean, leaning, pitch, rake, ramp, tilt; SEE CONCEPT *738*

slant [n2] *particular opinion*
angle, attitude, bias, direction, emphasis, judg-

ment, leaning, one-sidedness, outlook, point of view, predilection, predisposition, prejudice, prepossession, sentiment, side, standpoint, view, viewpoint; SEE CONCEPT 689

slant [v1] *angle off, slope*
aim, bank, beam, bend, bevel, cant, decline, descend, deviate, direct, diverge, grade, heel, incline, lean, level, lie obliquely, list, point, skew, splay, swerve, tilt, tip, train, veer; SEE CONCEPTS 201,738

slant [v2] *change to suit; distort*
aim, angle, bias, color, concentrate, direct, focus, influence, orient, point, prejudice, train, twist, warp, weight; SEE CONCEPTS 63,266

slap [n/v] *hard hit, often with hand*
bang, bash, blip, blow, box, buffet, bust, chop, clap, clout, crack, cuff, pat, percuss, poke, potch, punch, slam, smack, sock, spank, strike, swat, wallop, whack, wham; SEE CONCEPT 189

slash [v1] *cut*
carve, chop, gash, hack, incise, injure, lacerate, open up, pierce, rend, rip, score, sever, slice, slit, wound; SEE CONCEPTS 137,176

slash [v2] *reduce greatly*
abbreviate, abridge, clip, curtail, cut, cut back, cut down, drop, hack, lower, mark down, pare, retrench, shave, shorten; SEE CONCEPTS 236,240,247

slaughter [n] *killing*
annihilation, bloodbath, bloodshed, butchery, carnage, destruction, extermination, liquidation, massacre, murder, slaying; SEE CONCEPT 252

slaughter [v] *kill*
butcher, crush, decimate, defeat, destroy, do in*, exterminate, finish, liquidate, maim, mangle, massacre, murder, mutilate, overwhelm, rout, slay, stick, thrash, torture, total* trounce, vanquish, waste, wipe out*; SEE CONCEPT 252

slave [n] *person who serves, often under duress*
bondservant, captive, chattel, drudge, help, laborer, menial, peon, retainer, serf, servant, skivvy, subservient, thrall, toiler, vassal, victim, worker, workhorse; SEE CONCEPT 348

slave [v] *work very hard*
be servile, drudge, grind, grovel, grub, muck, plod, skivvy, slog, toil, work fingers to bone*; SEE CONCEPT 87

slavery [n] *state of working under duress or without freedom*
bondage, bullwork, captivity, chains* constraint, drudge, drudgery, enslavement, enthrallment, feudalism, grind, helotry, indenture, labor, menial labor, moil, peonage, restraint, serfdom, serfhood, servitude, subjection, subjugation, thrall, thralldom, toil, vassalage, work; SEE CONCEPTS 324,388

slay [v] *kill*
annihilate, assassinate, butcher, cut off, destroy, dispatch, do*, do away with, do in*, down*, eliminate, erase, execute, exterminate, finish, hit, knock off*, liquidate, massacre, murder, neutralize, put away*, rub out*, slaughter, snuff*, waste*; SEE CONCEPT 252

sleazy [adj] *disreputable*
base, broken-down, cheap, common, dilapidated, flimsy, limp, low, mean, paltry, poor, run-down, seedy, shabby, shoddy, sordid, squalid, tacky*, trashy, unsubstantial; SEE CONCEPTS 334,485,589

sleek [adj] *smooth, glossy*
glassy, glistening, lustrous, polished, satin, shiny, silken, silky; SEE CONCEPT 606

sleep [n] *suspension of consciousness*
bedtime, catnap, coma, dormancy, doze, dream, dullness, few z's*, forty winks*, hibernation, lethargy, nap, nod, repose, rest, sack time*, sandman*, shuteye*, siesta, slumber, slumberland*, snooze, torpidity, torpor, trance; SEE CONCEPT 315

sleep [v] *suspend consciousness*
bed down*, bunk*, catch a wink*, catch forty winks*, catnap, conk out*, cop some z's*, crash*, doze, dream, drop off*, drowse, fall asleep, fall out*, flop*, hibernate, hit the hay*, hit the sack*, languish, nap, nod, nod off, oversleep, relax, repose, rest, retire, sack out*, saw wood*, slumber, snooze, snore, take a nap, turn in*, yawn, zonk out*, zzz*; SEE CONCEPT 315

sleepy [adj] *tired, dull*
asleep, blah*, comatose, dopey*, dozy, draggy, drowsy, heavy, hypnotic, inactive, lethargic, listless, out*, out of it*, quiet, sleeping, sleepyhead*, slow, sluggish, slumberous, slumbersome, snoozy*, somnolent, soporific, torpid, yawning; SEE CONCEPTS 315,539

slender/slim [adj1] *thin, not heavy*
attenuate, beanpole*, beanstalk*, fine, insubstantial, lean, lithe, narrow, reedy, skeleton, skinny, slight, spare, stalky, stick, svelte, sylphlike, tenuous, threadlike, trim, twiggy, willowy; SEE CONCEPTS 490,491

slender/slim [adj2] *inadequate, flimsy*
bare, deficient, faint, feeble, fragile, inconsiderable, insufficient, little, meager, poor, remote, scant, scanty, scarce, short, shy, slight, small, spare, tenuous, thin, wanting, weak; SEE CONCEPTS 552,771

slice [n] *piece; share*
allotment, allowance, bite, chop, cut, helping, lot, part, piece of pie*, portion, quota, segment, sliver, thin piece, triangle, wedge; SEE CONCEPT 835

slice [v] *cut into portions, shares*
carve, chiv, cleave, dissect, dissever, divide, gash, hack, incise, pierce, segment, sever, shave, shred, slash, slit, split, strip, subdivide, sunder; SEE CONCEPTS 98,137,176

slick [adj1] *smooth, polished*
glossy, greasy, icy, lubricious, oily, oleaginous, shiny, sleek, sleeky, slippery, slithery, soapy; SEE CONCEPT 606

slick [adj2] *smart, clever*
adroit, cagey, canny, deft, dextrous, foxy, glib, knowing, meretricious, plausible, professional, quick, sharp, shrewd, skillful, sly, smooth, smooth-spoken, sophisticated, specious, streetwise*, unctuous, urbane, wise; SEE CONCEPTS 401,402

slide [v] *move smoothly; move down*
accelerate, coast, drift, drive, drop, fall, fall off, flow, glide, glissade, launch, move, move along, move over, propel, sag, scooch*, shift, shove, skate, skid, skim, slip, slither, slump, smooth along, spill, stream, thrust, toboggan, tumble, veer; SEE CONCEPTS 150,152

slight [n] *insult, disrespect*
affront, brush-off, call-down, cold shoulder*, contempt, cut, discourtesy, disdain, disregard, inattention, indifference, kick, neglect, put-down*,

sk
sl

rebuff, rejection, slap in the face*, snub; SEE CONCEPTS 30,384,529

slight [*adj1*] *insignificant, small*
fat, feeble, inconsiderable, insubstantial, meager, minor, modest, negligible, off, outside, paltry, petty, piddling, remote, scanty, slender, slim, sparse, superficial, trifling, trivial, unessential, unimportant, weak; SEE CONCEPTS 575,762,789

slight [*adj2*] *thin, small in build*
attenuate, broomstick*, dainty, delicate, feeble, flimsy, fragile, frail, light, reedy, shadow, skeleton, skinny, slender, slim, spare, stick, twiggy; SEE CONCEPTS 490,491

slight [*v*] *offend, insult*
affront, blink at, brush off, chill, contemn, cool*, cut*, despise, discount, disdain, disparage, disregard, fail, flout, forget, give the brush*, give the cold shoulder to*, ignore, make light of, neglect, not give time of day*, omit, overlook, poohpooh*, reject, scoff, scorn, show disrespect, shrug off, skip, slur, sneeze at*, snub, treat with contempt, turn deaf ear to*, upstage; SEE CONCEPTS 7,19,30,384

slightly [*adv*] *a little*
hardly, hardly at all, hardly noticeable, imperceptibly, inappreciably, inconsiderably, insignificantly, kind of, lightly, marginally, more or less, on a small scale, pretty, scarcely any, somewhat, to some degree, to some extent; SEE CONCEPTS 544,772

slim [*v*] *lose weight*
diet, reduce, slenderize; SEE CONCEPT 202

slime [*n*] *muck, gelled waste*
fungus, glop*, goo*, gunk*, mire, mucus, mud, ooze, scum, sludge; SEE CONCEPT 260

slimy [*adj*] *oozy, gooey*
clammy, glutinous, miry, mucky, mucous, muculent, muddy, scummy, viscous, yukky*; SEE CONCEPTS 485,621

sling [*v*] *throw or hang over*
bung, cast, catapult, chuck, dangle, fire, fling, heave, hoist, hurl, launch, lob, peg, pitch, raise, send, shoot, suspend, swing, toss, weight; SEE CONCEPTS 181,222

slink/slither [*v*] *creep by*
coast, cower, glide, glissade, go stealthily, gumshoe*, lurk, meander, pass quietly, prowl, pussyfoot*, shirk, sidle, slither, skulk, slick, slide, slip, snake, sneak, steal, undulate; SEE CONCEPT 151

slip [*n1*] *error, goof*
blooper*, blunder, bungle, failure, fault, flub*, fluff*, foul-up*, gaff, howler*, imprudence, indiscretion, lapse, misdeed, misstep, mistake, muff*, omission, oversight, screw-up*, slip of the tongue*, slip-up*, trip; SEE CONCEPT 101

slip [*n2*] *piece of paper*
label, leaf, page, sheet, sliver, strip, tag, ticket; SEE CONCEPTS 270,475

slip [*v1*] *fall; glide*
drop, glissade, lose balance, lose footing, lurch, move, shift, skate, skid, slick, slide, slither, smooth along, totter, trip; SEE CONCEPTS 150,152

slip [*v2*] *err*
blunder, drop the ball*, flub*, fluff*, goof*, go wrong, make a mistake, miscalculate, misjudge, mistake, muff*, put foot in mouth*, slip up, stumble, trip; SEE CONCEPT 101

slippery [*adj1*] *smooth, slick*
glace, glassy, glazed, glistening, greasy, icy, like a skating rink*, lubricious, lustrous, perilous, pol-

ished, satiny, silky, sleek, slimy, soapy, unctuous, unsafe, unstable, unsteady, waxy, wet; SEE CONCEPT 606

slippery [*adj2*] *uncertain, unreliable*
cagey, changeable, crafty, cunning, devious, dishonest, duplicitous, elusive, evasive, false, fly-by-night*, foxy, inconstant, insecure, mutable, shifty, slick, slithery, smooth, sneaky, treacherous, tricky, two-faced*, unpredictable, unsafe, unstable, unsteady, untrustworthy, variable; SEE CONCEPTS 401,534,535

slipshod [*adj*] *careless; not well done*
bedraggled, botched*, disheveled, faulty, fly-by-night*, fouled-up*, haphazard, imperfect, inaccurate, inexact, junky*, loose, messed-up, messy, neglected, negligent, raunchy, screwed-up*, scrubby*, scruffy*, shabby*, shoddy*, slapdash*, sloppy, slovenly, tacky*, tattered, threadbare, unkempt, unmeticulous, unsystematic, unthorough, untidy; SEE CONCEPTS 485,570,589

slit [*n*] *small opening, cut*
aperture, breach, cleavage, cleft, crack, crevice, fissure, gash, hole, incision, rent, split, tear; SEE CONCEPT 513

slit [*v*] *cut open*
gash, incise, knife, lance, pierce, rip, sever, slash, slice, slot, split open, tear; SEE CONCEPT 176

sliver [*n*] *tiny piece, usually of wood or metal*
bit, flake, fragment, paring, shaving, shred, slice, slip, snip, snippet, splinter, thorn; SEE CONCEPTS 471,831

slobber [*v*] *drool*
dribble, drip, drivel, froth, salivate, slabber, slaver, water at the mouth; SEE CONCEPT 185

slogan [*n*] *motto*
byword, catchphrase, catchword, expression, idiom, jingle, phrase, proverb, rallying cry*, saying, shibboleth*, trademark*, war cry*, watchword; SEE CONCEPT 278

slop [*v*] *splash; make a mess*
dash, drip, flounder, let run out, let run over, overflow, slosh, smear, smudge, spatter, spill, splatter, spray, wallow; SEE CONCEPT 250

slope [*n*] *slant, tilt*
abruptness, bank, bend, bevel, bias, cant, declination, declivity, deflection, descent, deviation, diagonal, downgrade, gradient, hill, inclination, incline, lean, leaning, obliqueness, obliquity, pitch, ramp, rise, rising ground, shelf, skew, steepness, swag, sway, tip; SEE CONCEPTS 738,757

slope [*v*] *slant, tilt*
angle, ascend, bank, bevel, cant, descend, dip, drop, drop away, fall, heel, incline, lean, list, pitch, rake, recline, rise, shelve, skew, splay, tip; SEE CONCEPTS 201,738

sloppy [*adj*] *messy*
awkward, bedraggled, botched, careless, clumsy, dingy, dirty, disheveled, inattentive, mediocre, muddy, not clean, poor, slapdash, slipshod, slovenly, sludgy*, slushy*, splashy*, tacky*, unkempt, unthorough, untidy, watery, wet; SEE CONCEPTS 531,603,621

slot [*n*] *opening, place*
aperture, channel, cut, groove, hole, niche, position, recess, slit, socket, space, time, vacancy; SEE CONCEPT 513

slouch [*v*] *slump over*
be lazy, bend, bow, crouch, droop, lean, loaf,

loll, lounge, sag, stoop, wilt; SEE CONCEPTS 154,201

slovenly [*adj*] *dirty, disordered*
bedraggled, botched, careless, dingy, disheveled, disorderly, dowdy, down-at-the-heel*, frowzy*, frumpy*, grody*, grubby, grungy*, heedless, icky*, loose, messed up*, messy, mussy, negligent, pigpen*, raunchy, seedy, slack, slapdash, sleazy*, slipshod, sloppy, tacky, topsy-turvy, unfastidious, unkempt, unthorough, untidy; SEE CONCEPTS 485,621

slow [*adj1*] *unhurried, lazy*
apathetic, crawling, creeping, dawdling, delaying, deliberate, dilatory, disinclined, dreamy, drowsy, easy, gradual, heavy, idle, imperceptible, inactive, indolent, inert, lackadaisical, laggard, lagging, leaden, leisurely, lethargic, listless, loitering, measured, moderate, negligent, passive, phlegmatic, plodding, ponderous, postponing, procrastinating, quiet, reluctant, remiss, slack, sleepy, slothful, slow-moving, sluggish, snaillike, stagnant, supine, tardy, torpid, tortoiselike; SEE CONCEPTS 538,584,588

slow [*adj2*] *behind, late*
backward, behindhand, belated, conservative, dead, delayed, detained, dilatory, down, draggy*, dull, gradual, hindered, impeded, inactive, lingering, long-delayed, long-drawn-out*, low, moderate, off, overdue, prolonged, protracted, reduced, slack, sleepy, sluggish, stagnant, stiff, tame, tardy, tedious, time-consuming, uneventful, unproductive, unprogressive, unpunctual; SEE CONCEPTS 529,537,548

slow [*adj3*] *unintelligent*
backward, dense, dim, dimwitted, dull, dumb, dunce, imbecile, limited, moronic, obtuse, simple, slow on the uptake*, stupid, thick, unresponsive; SEE CONCEPT 402

slow [*v*] *delay, restrict*
abate, anchor it, back-water*, bog down, brake, check, choke, curb, curtail, cut back, cut down, decelerate, decrease, detain, diminish, ease off, ease up, embog, handicap, hinder, hit the brakes*, hold back, hold up, impede, keep waiting, lag, lessen, let down flaps*, loiter, lose speed, lose steam*, mire, moderate, postpone, procrastinate, qualify, quiet, reduce, reduce speed, reef, regulate, rein in, relax, retard, retardate, set back, slacken, stall, stunt, temper, wind down; SEE CONCEPTS 130,234,250

slowdown [*n*] *slacking off; gradual decrease*
arrest, deceleration, decline, delay, downtrend, downturn, drop, drop-off, falloff, freeze, inactivity, retardation, slack, slackening, slow-up, stagnation, stoppage, strike; SEE CONCEPTS 121,130

sluggish [*adj*] *dull, slow-moving*
apathetic, blah*, comatose, dopey*, down, dragging, draggy*, drippy*, heavy, hebetudinous, inactive, indolent, inert, laid-back*, languid, languorous, leaden, lethargic, lifeless, listless, lumpish, mooney*, off, phlegmatic, pokey*, slack, sleepyheaded*, slothful, slow, sluggard, slumberous, stagnant, stiff, sullen, torpid, unresponsive; SEE CONCEPTS 401,584

slumber [*n*] *sleep*
coma, dormancy, doze, drowse, forty winks*, inactivity, languor, lethargy, nap, repose, rest, sack time*, shut-eye*, snooze, stupor, torpor; SEE CONCEPT 315

slump [*n*] *decline, failure*
bad period, bad times, blight, blue devils*, blue funk*, bottom, bust, collapse, crash, depreciation, depression, descent, dip, downer*, downslide*, downswing*, downtrend, downturn, drop, dumps*, fall, falling-off*, funk, hard times*, letdown*, low, rainy days*, recession, reverse, rut, sag, slide, slip, stagnation, the skids*, trough; SEE CONCEPTS 335,410,674

slump [*v*] *decline, sink*
bend, blight, cave in, collapse, crash, decay, deteriorate, droop, drop, fall, fall off*, go down, go downhill*, go to ruin*, hunch, keel over, loll, pitch, plummet, plunge, reach new low*, sag, slide, slip, slouch, topple, tumble; SEE CONCEPTS 181,698,699,763

slur [*n*] *insult*
accusation, affront, animadversion, aspersion, bar sinister*, black eye*, blemish, blot, blur, brand, brickbat*, calumny, dirty dig*, discredit, disgrace, dump, expose, hit, innuendo, insinuation, knock, obloquy, odium, onus, put-down*, rap*, reflection, reproach, slam, smear, stain, stigma, stricture, zinger*; SEE CONCEPTS 44,54,278

slur [*v1*] *insult*
blacken, blemish, blister, blot, blow off*, brand, calumniate, cap, chop*, cut to the quick*, cut up*, defame, denigrate, detract, discredit, disgrace, dump on*, give a black eye*, hit where one lives*, insinuate, kick in the teeth*, libel, malign, miff, offend, push, put down*, reproach, roast*, scorch*, skin alive*, slander, slap in the face*, slight, smear*, snub, spatter, stain, tear down, traduce, vilify, zing*; SEE CONCEPTS 7,19,44,54

slur [*v2*] *mumble words*
garble, mispronounce, miss, skip, stutter; SEE CONCEPT 47

sly [*adj*] *clever, devious*
arch, artful, astute, bluffing, cagey, calculating, canny, captious, conniving, covert, crafty, crooked, cunning, deceitful, deceptive, delusive, designing, dishonest, dishonorable, dissembling, double-dealing, elusive, foxy, furtive, guileful, illusory, impish, ingenious, insidious, intriguing, mean, mischievous, plotting, roguish, scheming, secret, sharp, shifty, shrewd, slick, smart, smooth, sneaking, stealthy, subtle, traitorous, treacherous, tricky, underhand, unscrupulous, wily; SEE CONCEPTS 401,542

smack [*n/v*] *strike, stun with hand*
bang, blip, blow, box, buffet, chop, clap, clout, crack, cuff, hit, pat, punch, slap, snap, sock, spank, tap; SEE CONCEPT 189

smack [*adv*] *directly, exactly*
accurately, bang*, clearly, just, plumb, point-blank*, precisely, right, sharp, square, squarely, straight; SEE CONCEPT 557

small [*adj1*] *tiny in size, quantity*
baby, bantam, bitty*, cramped, diminutive, humble, immature, inadequate, inconsequential, inconsiderable, insufficient, limited, little, meager, microscopic, mini*, miniature, minuscule, minute, modest, narrow, paltry, petite, petty, picayune, piddling*, pint-sized*, pitiful, pocket-sized*, poor, puny*, runty*, scanty, scrubby, short, shrimp*, slight, small-scale, stunted, teensy*, teeny, toy, trifling, trivial, undersized, unpretentious, wee*, young; SEE CONCEPTS 773,789

small [*adj2*] *unimportant*
bush-league*, inadequate, inconsiderable, ineffec-

sl
sm

tual, inferior, insignificant, lesser, light, limited, lower, mean, minor, minor-league*, minute, narrow, negligible, paltry, petty, secondary, set, small-fry*, small-time*, trifling, trivial, unessential; SEE CONCEPT 401

small [adj3] narrow-minded, nasty

base, grudging, ignoble, illiberal, limited, little, mean, narrow, petty, selfish, set, vulgar; SEE CONCEPT 401

smart [adj1] intelligent

acute, adept, agile, alert, apt, astute, bold, brainy*, bright, brilliant, brisk, canny, clever, crafty, effective, eggheaded*, fresh, genius, good, impertinent, ingenious, keen, knowing, long-haired*, nervy, nimble, on the ball*, pert, pointed, quick, quick-witted, ready, resourceful, sassy, sharp, shrewd, skull, slick*, whiz*, wise; SEE CONCEPT 402

smart [adj2] stylish, fashionable

chic, dapper, dashing, dressed to kill*, elegant, exclusive, fine, fly*, in fashion, last word*, latest thing*, modish, natty, neat, snappy, spruce, swank, trendy, trim, well turned-out, with it*; SEE CONCEPT 589

smart [adj3] brisk, lively

active, bold, brazen, cracking, energetic, forward, good, jaunty, nervy, pert, quick, saucy, scintillating, spanking, spirited, sprightly, vigorous; SEE CONCEPTS 401,542

smart [v] hurt, pain

ache, be painful, bite, burn, prick, prickle, sting, suffer, throb, tingle; SEE CONCEPTS 246,728

smash [n1] collision; defeat

accident, bang, bash, blast, blow, boom, breakdown, breaking, breakup, burst, clap, collapse, crack, crack-up, crash, debacle, destruction, disaster, downfall, failure, pile-up, ruin, shattering, slam, smash-up, sock, wallop, welt, whack, wham, wreck; SEE CONCEPTS 674,675

smash [n2] great success

hit, knockout, sensation, wow*; SEE CONCEPT 706

smash [v] break into pieces

bang, belt, blast, break to smithereens*, burst, clobber, collide, crack, crash, crush, demolish, disintegrate, fracture, fragment, hit, make mincemeat of*, pound, powder, pulverize, rive, scrunch, shatter, shiver, slam, slug, splinter, squash, squish, trash, wallop; SEE CONCEPTS 246,252

smash [v2] defeat, destroy

annihilate, break up, decimate, demolish, destruct, disrupt, lay in ruins*, lay waste*, overthrow, overturn, put out of action*, put out of commission*, raze, ruin, take down, tear down, topple, trash, tumble, wreck; SEE CONCEPTS 95,252

smear [v1] rub on, spread over

apply, bedaub, besmirch, blur, coat, cover, dab, daub, defile, dirty, discolor, overlay, overspread, patch, plaster, slop, smudge, soil, spatter, spray, sprinkle, stain, sully, taint, tar, tarnish; SEE CONCEPTS 172,202,215

smear [v2] tarnish a reputation

asperse, bad-mouth*, befoul, besmirch, blacken, blackguard*, blister, calumniate, defame, defile, denigrate, discolor, drag through mud*, give a black eye*, hit*, libel, malign, pan*, poormouth*, rap*, rip up*, scorch*, slam*, slander, sling mud*, slur, sully, taint, traduce, vilify; SEE CONCEPTS 54,63

smell [n] odor

aroma, bouquet, emanation, essence, flavor, fragrance, incense, perfume, redolence, savor, scent, spice, stench, stink, tang, trace, trail, whiff; SEE CONCEPTS 590,599

smell [v1] perceive with the nose

breathe, detect, discover, find, get a whiff*, identify, inhale, nose, scent, sniff, snuff; SEE CONCEPTS 590,601,602

smell [v2] have an odor

be malodorous, funk*, reek, smell to high heaven*, stench, stink, whiff; SEE CONCEPT 600

smelly [adj] having a bad odor

evil-smelling, fetid, foul, foul-smelling, funky*, high, malodorous, mephitic, noisome, olid, putrid, rancid, rank, reeking, stinking, strong, strong-smelling, whiffy*; SEE CONCEPT 598

smile [v] put on a happy expression

beam, be gracious, express friendliness, express tenderness, grin, laugh, look amused, look delighted, look happy, look pleased, simper, smirk; SEE CONCEPT 185

smirk [n] sly smile

beam, grin, leer, simper, smug look, sneer; SEE CONCEPT 185

smoky [adj] hazy, sooty

begrimed, black, burning, caliginous, dingy, fumy, gray, grimy, messy, murky, reeking, silvery, smoke-colored, smoldering, thick, vaporous; SEE CONCEPTS 485,618

smolder [v] burn, simmer

boil, bubble, churn, consume, erupt, explode, ferment, fester, fulminate, fume, seethe, smoke, steam, stir; SEE CONCEPTS 35,249

smooth [adj1] level, unwrinkled; flowing

bland, continuous, creamy, easy, effortless, equable, even, flat, fluent, fluid, flush, frictionless, gentle, glassy, glossy, hairless, horizontal, invariable, lustrous, mild, mirrorlike, monotonous, peaceful, plain, planate, plane, polished, quiet, regular, rhythmic, rippleless, serene, shaven, shiny, silky, sleek, soft, soothing, stable, steady, still, tranquil, unbroken, undeviating, undisturbed, uneventful, uniform, uninterrupted, unruffled, untroubled, unvarying, velvety; SEE CONCEPTS 406,480,606

smooth [adj2] suave in behavior

agreeable, bland, civilized, courteous, courtly, facile, genial, glib, ingratiating, mellow, mild, persuasive, pleasant, polite, slick, smarmy*, unctuous, urbane; SEE CONCEPT 401

smooth [v1] make level

burnish, clear, even, flatten, flush, glaze, gloss, grade, iron, lay, level, make uniform, perfect, plane, polish, press, refine, round, sand, sleek, slick, varnish; SEE CONCEPTS 137,250

smooth [v2] make peace

allay, alleviate, appease, assuage, calm, comfort, cool*, ease, extenuate, facilitate, iron out, mellow, mitigate, mollify, palliate, pat, pave the way*, soften, stroke, take the edge off*, take the sting out*; SEE CONCEPTS 7,22

smother [v] extinguish; cover, hide

asphyxiate, choke, collect, compose, conceal, control, cool, cork, douse, envelop, heap, hush up*, inundate, keep back, kill, muffle, overwhelm, quash, quell, quench, rein, repress, restrain, shower, shroud, simmer down, snuff,

squelch, stamp out, stifle, strangle, suffocate, suppress, surround, throttle; SEE CONCEPTS 130,172,188,234

smudge [n] *dirt smear*
blemish, blot, blur, macule, smut, smutch, soiled spot, spot; SEE CONCEPT 723

smudge [v] *smear, dirty*
begrime, blacken, blotch, blur, daub, defile, foul, grime, mark, plaster, slop, smirch, soil, spatter, sully, taint, tarnish; SEE CONCEPT 254

smug [adj] *pleased with oneself*
complacent, conceited, egoistic, egotistical, holier-than-thou*, hotshot*, pompous, priggish, puffed-up*, self-contented, self-righteous, self-satisfied, snobbish, stuck on oneself*, stuck-up*, stuffy, superior, vainglorious; SEE CONCEPTS 404,542

smuggle [v] *transfer illegal goods*
bootleg, deal, export, hide, moonshine*, pirate, push, run, run contraband*, run rum*, snake in*; SEE CONCEPT 192

smutty [adj] *obscene, vulgar*
bawdy, blue*, coarse, crude, dirty, filthy, foul, immoral, improper, indecent, indelicate, lewd, nasty, off-color, pornographic, prurient, racy, raunchy, raw, risqué, rough, salacious, salty, scatological, suggestive, X-rated*; SEE CONCEPTS 267,372,545

snack [n] *tiny meal*
bite, bite to eat*, break, eats*, goodies*, grub*, light meal, lunch, luncheon, midnight snack, morsel, munch*, nibble, nosh*, pickings, piece, refreshment, tea, tidbit; SEE CONCEPTS 457,459

snag [n] *complication in situation*
bar, barrier, blockade, brake, bug*, catch, Catch-22, clog, crimp, cropper, crunch, curb, difficulty, disadvantage, drag*, drawback, fix*, glitch, hamper, hitch, hold-up*, hole*, hurdle, impediment, inconvenience, knot, obstacle, obstruction, pickle*, problem, puzzler, scrape, spot, stumbling block, the rub*, tight spot*; SEE CONCEPTS 666,674

snag [v] *catch on something*
hole, nail, rip, run into, tear; SEE CONCEPT 214

snaky [adj1] *winding*
anfractuous, convoluted, entwined, flexuous, indirect, meandering, meandrous, serpentine, sinuous, tortuous, twisted, twisting, writhing, zigzag; SEE CONCEPT 581

snaky [adj2] *devious, sly*
crafty, insidious, lurking, perfidious, slinking, sneaky, subtle, treacherous, venomous, vipery, virulent; SEE CONCEPT 401

snap [n] *easy thing to accomplish*
breeze*, child's play*, cinch, duck soup*, ease, easy as pie*, kid stuff*, no problem, picnic*, pie*, smooth sailing*, soft touch*, walkover*; SEE CONCEPT 693

snap [v1] *separate, break*
click, come apart, crack, crackle, fracture, give way, pop; SEE CONCEPTS 98,246

snap [v2] *bite, seize*
bite at, catch, clutch, grab, grasp, grip, jerk, lurch, nip, snatch, twitch, yank; SEE CONCEPTS 90,191

snap [v3] *speak sharply*
bark, flare, flash, fly off the handle*, get angry, growl, grumble, grunt, jump down throat*, lash out, retort, roar, snarl, snort, take it out on*, vent, yell; SEE CONCEPTS 54,77

snappy [adj1] *nasty, irritable*
cross, disagreeable, edgy, fractious, hasty, huffy, petulant, quick-tempered, snappish, tart, testy, touchy, waspish; SEE CONCEPTS 267,401

snappy [adj2] *fashionable*
chic, classy, dapper, dashing, fly*, in good taste, modish, natty, sharp, smart, stylish, swank*, tony*, trendy, up-to-the-minute, with style; SEE CONCEPT 589

snappy [adj3] *fast*
abrupt, breakneck, expeditious, fleet, harefooted, hasty, immediate, instant, on-the-spot, quick, rapid, speedy, sudden, swift, unpremeditated; SEE CONCEPTS 588,799

snare [n] *trap*
allurement, bait, booby trap*, catch, come-on*, deception, decoy, enticement, entrapment, inveiglement, lure, net, noose, pitfall, quicksand, seducement, temptation, trick, wire*; SEE CONCEPTS 529,674

snare [v] *catch, trap*
arrest, bag*, corral, decoy, enmesh, entangle, entrap, get hands on*, involve, land, lure, net, pull in, round up, seduce, seize, tempt, wire*; SEE CONCEPTS 11,90

snarl [n] *complication, mess*
chaos, clutter, complexity, confusion, disarray, disorder, entanglement, intricacy, intricateness, jam, jungle, knot, labyrinth, maze, mishmash, morass, muddle, muss, skein, swarm, tangle, web; SEE CONCEPTS 663,666,674

snarl [v1] *grumble*
abuse, bark, bluster, bully, complain, fulminate, gnarl, gnash teeth, growl, mumble, murmur, mutter, quarrel, show teeth, snap, threaten, thunder, yelp; SEE CONCEPT 77

snarl [v2] *complicate, mess up*
confuse, embroil, enmesh, ensnarl, entangle, entwine, involve, muck, muddle, perplex, ravel, tangle; SEE CONCEPTS 16,158

snatch [n] *small part*
bit, fragment, piece, smattering, snippet, spell; SEE CONCEPTS 264,832

snatch [v] *grab away*
abduct, catch, clap hands on, clutch, collar*, gain, get fingers on*, grapple, grasp, grip, jerk, jump, kidnap, make off with, nab, nail*, pluck, pull, rescue, seize, snag, spirit away, steal, take, win, wrench, wrest, yank; SEE CONCEPTS 90,191

sneak [n] *person who is very dishonest*
cheater, con artist, coward, cur, dastard, heel*, informer, louse, rascal, reptile, scoundrel, skunk*, slink*, snake*, snake in grass*, toad*, weasel*, wretch; SEE CONCEPT 412

sneak [v] *move stealthily*
ambush, case, cheat, cower, crawl, creep, deceive, delude, evade, glide, gumshoe*, hide, lurk, mooch, move secretly, ooze, pad, pass, prowl, pussyfoot*, secrete, shirk, sidle, skulk, slide, slink, slip, slither, sly, smuggle, snake, snoop, spirit, steal, worm; SEE CONCEPTS 151,188

sneaky [adj] *underhanded, dishonest*
base, contemptible, cowardly, deceitful, devious, disingenuous, double-dealing*, duplicitous, furtive, guileful, indirect, low, malicious, mean, nasty, recreant, secretive, shifty, slippery, sly, sneaking, snide, stealthy, surreptitious, tricky, underhand, unreliable, unscrupulous, untrustworthy, yellow*; SEE CONCEPTS 267,401,542

sm
sn

sneer [v] *mock, condemn*
affront, belittle, burlesque, caricature, crack, curl one's lip at*, decry, deride, detract, disdain, disparage, dump, fleer, flout, gibe, gird, give Bronx cheer, grin, hold in contempt*, hold up to ridicule*, insult, jeer, jest, lampoon, laugh at, leer, look down on, put down, quip at, rally, rank out, ridicule, satirize, scoff, scorn, slam, slight, smile, sneeze at*, sniff at*, snigger, swipe, taunt, travesty, turn up one's nose*, twit, underrate; SEE CONCEPTS 30,52,54

snicker/snigger/sniggle [v] *laugh at mockingly*
chortle, chuckle, giggle, guffaw, hee-haw, smirk, sneer, teehee, titter; SEE CONCEPT 77

snide [adj] *hateful, nasty*
base, cynical, disparaging, hurtful, insinuating, malicious, mean, sarcastic, scornful, sneering, spiteful, unkind; SEE CONCEPT 401

sniff [v] *breathe in*
detect, inhale, inspire, nose, scent, smell, snift, snuff, snuffle; SEE CONCEPTS 601,602

snob [n] *person who looks down on others*
braggart, highbrow, name-dropper, parvenu, pretender, smarty pants*, stiff neck*, upstart; SEE CONCEPT 423

snobbish [adj] *stuck-up, conceited*
aloof, arrogant, condescending, egotistic, haughty, high-and-mighty*, high-flown*, high-hat*, ostentatious, overbearing, patronizing, persnickety*, pompous, pretentious, putting on airs*, remote, sniffy, snippy*, snooty*, snotty*, supercilious, superior, swanky, tony*, uppish, uppity*; SEE CONCEPT 401

snoop [n] *person who noses around*
busybody, butt-in*, detective, eavesdropper, ferret, gumshoe*, meddler, peeping Tom*, pragmatist, pry, pryer, quidnunc, rubberneck*, scout, sleuth, snooper; SEE CONCEPTS 348,423

snoop [v] *nose around*
busybody, interfere, intrude, meddle, mess with, mouse*, nose, peek, peep, peer, poke, poke nose in*, pry, snook, spy, stare; SEE CONCEPTS 216,384,623

snooze [n] *light sleep*
catnap, doze, forty winks*, nap, siesta, slumber; SEE CONCEPT 315

snooze [v] *sleep lightly*
catnap, doze, drop off, drowse, nap, nod off*, siesta, slumber, take forty winks*; SEE CONCEPTS 210,315

snore [v] *make sounds when sleeping*
breathe heavily, saw logs*, saw wood*, sleep, snort, snuffle, wheeze; SEE CONCEPTS 77,315

snub [v] *give someone the cold shoulder*
act cool*, boycott, brush off*, burr, censure, chill, cool, cut, cut dead*, disdain, disregard, duck, give the brush*, humble, humiliate, ice*, ice out*, ignore, look coldly upon, look right through*, mortify, neglect, not give time of day*, offend, ostracize, pass up, put down, rebuff, scold, scorn, scratch, shame, shun, slight, slur, snob, swank, upstage; SEE CONCEPTS 30,54,384

snug [adj] *cozy, warm*
close, comfortable, comfy, compact, convenient, cushy, easeful, easy, homelike, homely, intimate, neat, restful, sheltered, snug as a bug in a rug*, soft, substantial, tight, trim, well-off; SEE CONCEPT 485

snuggle [v] *cuddle*
bundle, burrow, curl up, grasp, huddle, hug, nestle, nuzzle, snug, spoon; SEE CONCEPTS 190,202

soak [v] *drench, wet*
absorb, assimilate, bathe, damp, dip, drink, drown, dunk, flood, imbrue, immerge, immerse, impregnate, infiltrate, infuse, macerate, marinate, merge, moisten, penetrate, percolate, permeate, pour into, pour on, saturate, seethe, soften, sop, souse, steep, submerge, take in, wash, water, waterlog; SEE CONCEPT 256

soar [v] *climb, fly*
arise, ascend, aspire, escalate, glide, lift, mount, rise, rocket, sail, shoot, shoot up, skyrocket, top, tower, up, uprear, wing; SEE CONCEPTS 148,150

sob [v] *cry hard*
bawl, blub, blubber, boohoo*, break down, cry a river*, cry convulsively, cry eyes out*, howl, lament, shed tears, snivel, turn on waterworks*, wail, weep, whimper; SEE CONCEPTS 185,410

sober [adj 1] *not partaking of alcohol*
abstaining, abstemious, abstinent, ascetic, calm, clear-headed, cold sober*, continent, controlled, dry, moderate, nonindulgent, not drunk, on the wagon*, restrained, sedate, self-possessed, serious, steady, temperate, took the pledge*; SEE CONCEPT 401

sober [adj 2] *calm, peaceful; dull*
abnegating, abstaining, calm, clear-headed, cold, collected, composed, constrained, cool, dark, disciplined, dispassionate, down-to-earth*, drab, earnest, eschewing, forgoing, grave, hard-boiled*, imperturbable, inhibited, levelheaded, low-key, lucid, no-nonsense, pacific, peaceful, plain, practical, quiet, rational, realistic, reasonable, reserved, restrained, sedate, serene, serious, severe, soft, solemn, somber, sound, staid, steady, subdued, toned down, unexcited, unimpassioned, unruffled; SEE CONCEPTS 401,542

so-called [adj] *supposed*
alleged, allegedly, commonly named, formal, nominal, ostensible, pretended, professed, purported, self-named, self-styled, soi-disant, supposed, titular, wrongly named; SEE CONCEPT 552

sociable [adj] *friendly, outgoing*
accessible, affable, approachable, close, clubby*, companionable, conversable, convivial, cordial, familiar, genial, good-natured, gregarious, intimate, neighborly, regular, social, warm; SEE CONCEPTS 401,555

social [adj] *public, friendly*
amusing, civil, collective, common, communal, communicative, community, companionable, convivial, cordial, diverting, entertaining, familiar, general, gracious, gregarious, group, hospitable, informative, mannerly, neighborly, nice, organized, pleasant, pleasurable, polished, polite, popular, public, sociable, societal; SEE CONCEPTS 536,555

socialize [v] *be friendly at gatherings*
associate, chum with*, club*, consort, entertain, fraternize, get about, get around, get together, go out, hang around with*, hang out, hobnob, join, keep company, league, make advances, make the rounds*, mingle, mix, pal around*, run with*, tie up with*; SEE CONCEPT 384

society [n 1] *humankind, people*
association, camaraderie, civilization, commonality, commonwealth, community, companionship, company, comradeship, culture, friendship, gen-

eral public, humanity, jungle*, nation, population, public, rat race*, social order, world, zoo*; SEE CONCEPTS 379,417

society [n2] *organization, institution*
alliance, association, circle, clan, clique, club, companionship, comradeship, corporation, coterie, gang, group, guild, hookup, institute, league, network, order, outfit, ring, sodality, syndicate, tie-in*, union; SEE CONCEPTS 381,387

society [n3] *upper class of people*
aristocracy, beau monde*, beautiful people*, country set*, elite, flower*, gentry, glitterati*, haut monde, high society, jet set*, main line, patriciate, polite society, quality, smart set*, top drawer*, upper crust*, who's who*; SEE CONCEPTS 387,388,417

sock [n/v] *hit hard*
beat, belt, bop, buffet, chop, clout, cuff, ding, nail, paste, punch, slap, smack, smash, soak, whack; SEE CONCEPT 189

soft [adj1] *cushioned, squishy*
bendable, comfortable, comfy, cottony, cozy, creamy, cushiony, cushy, delicate, doughy, downy, ductile, easeful, easy, elastic, feathery, fine, flabby, fleecy, fleshy, flexible, flimsy, flocculent, flowing, fluffy, fluid, formless, furry, gelatinous, impressible, limp, malleable, moldable, mushy, pappy, pithy, plastic, pliable, pulpy, quaggy, rounded, satiny, silken, silky, smooth, snug, spongy, squashy, supple, thin, velvety, yielding; SEE CONCEPTS 488,606

soft [adj2] *faint, temperate*
ashen, balmy, bland, caressing, comfortable, cool, cushy, delicate, diffuse, dim, dimmed, dulcet, dull, dusky, faint, gentle, hazy, lenient, light, low, low-key, mellifluous, mellow, melodious, mild, misty, murmured, muted, pale, pallid, pastel, pleasing, quiet, restful, shaded, smooth, sober, soothing, subdued, sweet, tinted, toned down, twilight, understated, wan, whispered; SEE CONCEPTS 525,537,592,618

soft [adj3] *compassionate*
affectionate, amiable, benign, courteous, easy, easy-going, effortless, gentle, gracious, indulgent, kind, kindly, lax, lenient, liberal, manageable, overindulgent, permissive, pitying, sensitive, sentimental, simple, spineless, sympathetic, tender, tender-hearted, undemanding, weak; SEE CONCEPT 401

soft [adj4] *out of condition*
doughy, fat, flabby, flaccid, fleshy, formless, gone to seed*, limp, out of shape*, overindulged, pampered, untrained, weak; SEE CONCEPTS 314,485

soft [adj5] *stupid*
daft, fatuous, feeble-minded, foolish, silly, simple, witless; SEE CONCEPT 402

soften [v] *calm, soothe*
abate, allay, alleviate, appease, assuage, become tender, bend, cushion, diminish, disintegrate, dissolve, ease, enfeeble, give, knead, lessen, lighten, lower, mash, mellow, melt, mitigate, moderate, modify, moisten, mollify, palliate, qualify, quell, relax, relent, still, subdue, temper, tenderize, thaw, tone down, turn down, weaken, yield; SEE CONCEPT 250

soggy [adj] *damp or soaking*
clammy, dank, dripping, heavy, humid, moist, mucky, muggy, mushy, pasty, pulpy, saturated,

soaked, sodden, soft, sopping, spongy, sticky, sultry, waterlogged; SEE CONCEPT 603

soil [n1] *earth, dirt*
clay, dry land, dust, grime, ground, land, loam, soot, terra firma; SEE CONCEPT 509

soil [n2] *land where one lives*
country, home, homeland, homestead, region, spread, terra firma; SEE CONCEPTS 198,510,511

soil [v] *make dirty*
bedraggle, befoul, begrime, besmirch, contaminate, crumb, debase, defile, degrade, dirty, discolor, disgrace, foul, grime, maculate, mess, mess up, muck*, muck up*, muddy, muss*, muss up*, pollute, shame, smear, smudge, spatter, spoil, spot, stain, sully, taint, tar, tarnish; SEE CONCEPT 254

sojourn [n] *brief travel; visit*
layover, residence, rest, stay, stop, stopover, tarriance, vacation; SEE CONCEPTS 224,226,227

sojourn [v] *travel briefly; visit*
abide, dwell, inhabit, linger, lodge, nest, perch, reside, rest, roost, squat, stay, stay over, stop, tarry, vacation; SEE CONCEPTS 224,226,227

solace [n] *comfort, peace*
alleviation, assuagement, condolement, condolence, consolation, pity, relief; SEE CONCEPTS 7,22,4100

solace [v] *give comfort, peace*
allay, alleviate, buck up, cheer, comfort, condole with, console, mitigate, soften, soothe, upraise; SEE CONCEPTS 7,22

soldier [n] *person serving in military*
airforce member, cadet, cavalryperson, commando, conscript, draftee, enlisted person, fighter, GI*, Green Beret, guard, guerrilla, gunner, infantry, infantryperson, marine, mercenary, military person, musketeer, officer, paratrooper, pilot, private, rank, recruit, scout, selectee, serviceperson, soldier, soldier-at-arms, trooper, veteran, volunteer, warmonger, warrior; SEE CONCEPT 358

sole [adj] *alone, singular*
ace, exclusive, individual, lone, one, one and only, onliest, only, only one, particular, remaining, separate, single, solitary, solo, unique, unshared; SEE CONCEPTS 555,564,577

solely [adv] *only, alone*
barely, but, completely, entirely, exclusively, individually, merely, onliest, purely, simply, single-handedly, singly, singularly, totally, undividedly, wholly; SEE CONCEPTS 544,577

solemn [adj1] *quiet, serious*
austere, brooding, cold sober*, deliberate, dignified, downbeat, earnest, funereal, glum, grave, heavy, intense, matter of life and death*, moody, no fooling*, no-nonsense*, pensive, portentous, reflective, sedate, sober, somber, staid, stern, thoughtful, weighty; SEE CONCEPTS 403,542

solemn [adj2] *impressive, sacred*
august, awe-inspiring, ceremonial, ceremonious, conventional, devotional, dignified, divine, formal, full, grand, grave, hallowed, holy, imposing, impressive, magnificent, majestic, momentous, ostentatious, overwhelming, plenary, religious, reverential, ritual, sanctified, stately, venerable; SEE CONCEPT 574

solicit [v] *plead for; try to sell*
accost, apply, approach, ask, beg, beseech, bespeak, bum, cadge, call, canvass, challenge, claim, come on to*, crave, demand, desire,

drum*, drum up*, entreat, exact, go, hawk, hit on*, hit up*, hustle, implore, importune, inquire, mooch, panhandle, pass the hat*, peddle, petition, postulate, pray, promote, proposition, query, question, refer, request, require, requisition, resort, seduce, seek, sponge, steer, sue for, supplicate, touch, tout, turn, whistle for*; SEE CONCEPTS 53,345

solicitous [adj] worried

anxious, appetent, apprehensive, ardent, athirst, attentive, avid, beside oneself, careful, caring, concerned, devoted, eager, earnest, heedful, impatient, keen, loving, mindful, raring, regardful, tender, thirsty, troubled, uneasy, worried sick*, worried stiff*; zealous; SEE CONCEPT 403

solicitude [n] worry, anxiety

attention, attentiveness, care, compunction, concern, concernment, considerateness, consideration, disquiet, disquietude, heed, presentiment, qualm, regard, scruple, tender loving care*, TLC*, unease, uneasiness, watchfulness; SEE CONCEPT 410

solid [adj1] hard, dimensional

brick wall*, close, compact, compacted, concentrated, concrete, consolidated, dense, firm, fixed, heavy, hefty, hulk, hunk, husky, massed, material, physical, rock, rocklike, rooted, secure, set, sound, stable, strong, sturdy, substantial, thick, tight, unshakable; SEE CONCEPTS 483,604

solid [adj2] continuous, complete

agreed, brick wall*, consecutive, consentient, continued, firm, like a rock, regular, set in stone*, stable, steady, unalloyed, unanimous, unbroken, undivided, uninterrupted, united, unmixed; SEE CONCEPTS 482,488,531

solid [adj3] dependable, reliable

cogent, constant, decent, estimable, genuine, good, law-abiding, levelheaded, pure, real, satisfactory, satisfying, sensible, serious, sober, sound, stalwart, steadfast, trustworthy, trusty, upright, upstanding, valid, worthy; SEE CONCEPTS 401,534

solitary [adj] alone, single; unsociable

aloof, antisocial, cloistered, companionless, deserted, desolate, distant, eremetic, forsaken, friendless, hermitical, hidden, individual, introverted, isolated, lone, lonely, lonesome, lorn, misanthropic, offish, only, out-of-the-way*, particular, reclusive, remote, reserved, retired, secluded, separate, sequestered, singular, sole, solo, stag, standoffish, unaccompanied, unapproachable, unattended, uncompanionable, unfrequented, unique, unsocial, withdrawn; SEE CONCEPTS 555,577,583

solitude [n] aloneness

confinement, desert, detachment, emptiness, isolation, loneliness, loneness, lonesomeness, peace and quiet*, privacy, quarantine, reclusiveness, retirement, seclusion, separateness, silence, solitariness, waste, wasteland, wilderness, withdrawal; SEE CONCEPTS 388,673,714

solution [n1] answer, resolution

Band-Aid*, clarification, elucidation, explanation, explication, key, pay dirt*, quick fix*, result, solving, the ticket*, unfolding, unraveling, unravelment; SEE CONCEPTS 230,661,712

solution [n2] mixture of liquid and another substance

blend, compound, dissolvent, elixir, emulsion,

extract, fluid, juice, mix, sap, solvent, suspension; SEE CONCEPTS 260,467

solve [v] answer, resolve

break*, clarify, clear up, construe, crack*, deal with, decide, decipher, decode, determine, disentangle, divine, do, elucidate, enlighten, explain, expound, fathom, figure out, find out, fix, get, get right, get to the bottom*, have, hit, hit upon*, illuminate, interpret, iron out*, lick*, make a dent*, make out*, pan out*, put two and two together*, puzzle, reason, settle, think out, unfold, unlock, unravel, unriddle, untangle, work, work out; SEE CONCEPTS 15,18,37

somber [adj] sad, depressing

black, bleak, blue*, caliginous, cloudy, dark, depressive, dim, dingy, dire, dismal, dispiriting, doleful, down, drab, dragged, dreary, dull, dusky, earnest, funereal, gloomy, grave, grim, hurting, joyless, lugubrious, melancholy, mournful, murky, no-nonsense, obscure, sad, sedate, sepulchral, serious, shadowy, shady, sober, solemn, sourpuss, staid, tenebrous, weighty; SEE CONCEPTS 403,485,529

somebody [n] person of fame, importance

celebrity, dignitary, heavyweight*, household name*, luminary, name*, notable, one, personage, person of note, public figure, so-and-so*, someone*, some person*, star, superstar, VIP*, whoever*; SEE CONCEPT 423

someday [adv] eventually

after a while, anytime, at a future time, finally, in a time to come, on a day, one day, one fine day*, one of these days, one time, one time or another, sometime, sooner or later, subsequently, ultimately, yet; SEE CONCEPTS 548,820

somehow [adv] by some means

after a fashion, anyhow, anyway, anywise, by hook or crook*, come what may*, in one way or another, in some such way, in some way, one way or another, somehow or another, somehow or other; SEE CONCEPT 544

something [n] entity

article, being, commodity, existence, existent, individual, object, substance, thing; SEE CONCEPT 433

sometimes [adv] every now and then

at intervals, at times, consistently, constantly, ever and again, every so often, frequently, from time to time, here and there, intermittently, now and again, now and then, occasionally, off and on, once in a blue moon*, once in a while, on occasion, periodically, recurrently; SEE CONCEPT 805

somewhat [adv] to some extent

adequately, a little, bearably, considerably, fairly, far, incompletely, in part, insignificantly, kind of, moderately, more or less, not much, partially, pretty, quite, rather, ratherish, significantly, slightly, some, something, sort of, to a degree, tolerably, well; SEE CONCEPTS 548,569,772

somewhere [adv] in, or at some place

about, any old place, around, around somewhere, elsewhere, here and there, in one place or another, kicking around*, parts unknown*, scattered, someplace, someplace or another, someplace or other, somewheres; SEE CONCEPT 583

song [n] melody sung or played with musical instrument

air, anthem, aria, ballad, canticle, carol, chant, chorale, chorus, ditty, expression, golden oldie*, hymn, lay, lullaby, lyric, melody, number, oldie*, opera, piece, poem, psalm, refrain, rock, rock and roll, round, shanty, strain, tune, verse, vocal; SEE CONCEPTS 262,293,595

soon [adv] in the near future

anon, any minute now, before long, betimes, by and by, coming down the pike*, directly, early, ere long, expeditiously, fast, fleetly, forthwith, hastily, in a little while, in a minute, in a second, in a short time, in due time, in short order, instantly, in time, lickety-split*, on time, posthaste, presently, promptly, pronto, quick, quickly, rapidly, short, shortly, speedily; SEE CONCEPTS 548,798,820

soothe [v] calm, ease

allay, alleviate, appease, assuage, balm, becalm, butter up*, calm down, cheer, compose, console, cool, cool off*, dulcify, help, hush, lighten, lull, make nice*, make up, mitigate, mollify, pacify, patch things up*, play up to*, pour oil on*, quiet, quieten, relieve, settle, smooth down, soften, square, still, stroke, subdue, take the edge off*, take the sting out*, tranquilize, unburden, untrouble; SEE CONCEPTS 7,22,110,384

sophisticated [adj1] cosmopolitan, cultured

adult, artificial, been around, blasé, bored, citified, cool*, couth, cultivated, cynical, disenchanted, disillusioned, experienced, in, in the know*, into*, jaded, jet-set*, knowing, laid-back*, mature, mondaine, on to*, practical, practiced, refined, schooled, seasoned, sharp, skeptical, smooth, stagy*, streetwise, studied, suave, svelte, switched on*, uptown*, urbane, well-bred, wised up*, wise to*, with it*, worldly, worldly wise, world-weary; SEE CONCEPTS 401,404,589

sophisticated [adj2] complex, advanced

complicated, delicate, elaborate, highly developed, intricate, involved, knotty, labyrinthine, modern, multifaceted, refined, subtle; SEE CONCEPT 562

sophistication [n] culture, style

composure, elegance, finesse, poise, refinement, savoir faire, savoir vivre, social grace, tact, urbanity, worldliness, worldly wisdom; SEE CONCEPTS 388,633,655

sophomoric [adj] inexperienced

brash, foolish, naive, reckless, young; SEE CONCEPT 401

soporific [adj] sleepy; sleep-inducing

anesthetic, balmy, calming, deadening, dozy*, drowsy, dull, hypnotic, mesmerizing, narcotic, nodding, numbing, opiate, quietening, sedative, slumberous, snoozy*, somniferous, somnolent, soothing, tranquilizing; SEE CONCEPTS 537,539

sorcery [n] black magic, witchcraft

abracadabra*, alchemy, bewitchment, black art, charm, conjuring, devilry, divination, enchantment, evil eye, hocus-pocus*, hoodoo* incantation, jinx, magic, mumbo-jumbo*, necromancy, spell, thaumaturgy, voodoo, witchery, witching, wizardry; SEE CONCEPTS 370,689

sordid [adj] dirty, bad, low

abject, avaricious, base, black, calculated, corrupt, covetous, debauched, degenerate, degraded, despicable, disreputable, dowdy, filthy, foul, grasping, grubby, ignoble, impure, low-down, mean, mercenary, miserable, miserly, nasty, poor, scurvy, seedy, selfish, self-seeking, servile, shabby, shameful, sleazy, slovenly, slum, slummy, small, small-minded, squalid, unclean,

uncleanly, ungenerous, venal, vicious, vile, wretched; SEE CONCEPTS 334,545,571

sore [adj1] hurt physically

abscessed, aching, acute, afflicted, annoying, bruised, burned, burning, chafed, critical, distressing, extreme, hurtful, hurting, inflamed, irritated, pained, painful, raw, reddened, sensitive, severe, sharp, smarting, tender, ulcerated, uncomfortable, unpleasant, vexatious; SEE CONCEPT 314

sore [adj2] angry; hurt mentally

afflicted, aggrieved, annoyed, annoying, critical, distressing, grieved, grieving, indignant, irked, irritated, pained, peeved, pressing, resentful, sensitive, smarting, stung, troubled, upset, urgent, vexed, weighty; SEE CONCEPT 403

sorrow [n] extreme upset, grief

affliction, agony, anguish, bad news*, big trouble*, blow, blues*, care, catastrophe, dejection, depression, distress, doom, grieving, hardship, heartache, heartbreak, lamenting, melancholy, misery, misfortune, mourning, pain, rain*, regret, remorse, repentence, rue, sadness, suffering, trial, tribulation, trouble, unhappiness, weeping, woe, worry, wretchedness; SEE CONCEPT 410

sorrow [v] be very upset, grieved

agonize, bemoan, be sad, bewail, carry on, cry a river*, deplore, eat heart out*, grieve, groan, hang crepe*, lament, moan, mourn, regret, sing the blues*, sob, take on*, weep; SEE CONCEPTS 34,410

sorrowful [adj] very upset; grieving

affecting, afflicted, dejected, depressed, disconsolate, distressing, doleful, dolent, full of sorrow, grievous, heartbroken, heartrending, heavy-hearted, hurting, in mourning, in pain, in sorrow, lamentable, lugubrious, melancholy, miserable, mournful, painful, piteous, plaintive, rueful, ruthful, sad, sick at heart*, singing the blues*, sorry, tearful, tear-jerking*, unhappy, woebegone, woeful, wretched; SEE CONCEPT 403

sorry [adj1] remorseful, regretful

apologetic, attritional, compunctious, conscience-stricken, contrite, guilt-ridden, melted, penitent, penitential, repentant, self-accusing, self-condemnatory, self-reproachful, shamefaced, softened, touched; SEE CONCEPTS 403,545

sorry [adj2] sad, heartbroken

bad, disconsolate, distressed, grieved, heavy-hearted, melancholy, mournful, pitiful, rueful, saddened, sorrowful, unhappy; SEE CONCEPT 403

sorry [adj3] despicable, pathetic

abject, base, beggarly, cheap, contemptible, deplorable, despisable, disgraceful, dismal, distressing, inadequate, insignificant, mean, miserable, paltry, piteous, pitiable, pitiful, poor, sad, scruffy*, scummy*, scurvy, shabby, shoddy, small, trifling, trivial, unimportant, vile, worthless, wretched; SEE CONCEPTS 485,529

sort [n] type, variety

array, batch, battery, body, brand, breed, category, character, class, clutch, denomination, description, family, genus, group, ilk, kind, likes, likes of*, lot, make, nature, number, order, parcel, quality, race, set, species, stamp, stripe, style, suite; SEE CONCEPT 378

sort [v] place in order

arrange, assort, button down*, catalogue, categorize, choose, class, classify, comb, cull, distribute, divide, file, grade, group, order, peg, pick, pigeonhole*, put down as, put down for, put in order, put in shape, put to rights*, rank, riddle, screen, select, separate, sift, size up, systematize, tab, typecast, winnow; SEE CONCEPTS 84,158

so-so [adj] *adequate, passable*
average, enough, fair, fairish, fair to middling*, indifferent, mediocre, medium, middling*, moderate, not bad*, okay*, ordinary, respectable, run-of-the-mill*, tolerable, undistinguished; SEE CONCEPTS 533,575

soul [n1] *psyche, inspiration, energy*
anima, animating principle, animation, animus, ardor, bosom, bottom, breast, breath of life, cause, conscience, courage, disposition, ego, elan vital, essence, feeling, fervor, force, genius, heart, individuality, intellect, intelligence, life, marrow, mind, nobility, noumenon, personality, pith, pneuma, principle, quintessence, reason, recesses of heart*, secret self*, spirit, spiritual being, stuff, substance, thought, vital force, vitality, vivacity; SEE CONCEPTS 409,410,411

soul [n2] *being*
body, character, creature, ghost, human being, individual, living soul*, man, mortal, person, personage, phantom, shadow, spirit, umbra, woman; SEE CONCEPT 389

sound [n] *something heard or audible*
accent, din, harmony, intonation, loudness, melody, modulation, music, noise, note, pitch, racket, report, resonance, reverberation, ringing, softness, sonance, sonancy, sonority, sonorousness, static, tenor, tonality, tone, vibration, voice; SEE CONCEPT 595

sound [adj1] *complete, healthy*
alive and kicking*, effectual, entire, firm, fit, flawless, hale, hearty, intact, in the pink*, perfect, right, right as rain*, robust, safe, sane, solid, stable, sturdy, substantial, thorough, total, unblemished, undamaged, undecayed, unhurt, unimpaired, uninjured, up to snuff*, vibrant, vigorous, vital, well, well-constructed, whole, wholesome, wrapped tight*; SEE CONCEPTS 314,488

sound [adj2] *logical, reasonable*
accurate, advisable, all there*, cogent, commonsensical, consequent, convincing, cool*, correct, deep, exact, fair, faultless, flawless, got it together*, impeccable, intellectual, judicious, just, levelheaded, orthodox, precise, profound, proper, prudent, rational, reliable, responsible, right, right-minded, right-thinking, satisfactory, satisfying, sensible, sober, solid, telling, thoughtful, together*, true, trustworthy, valid, well-advised, well-founded, well-grounded, wise; SEE CONCEPTS 403,529,558

sound [adj3] *accepted, established*
all there*, authoritative, canonical, dependable, fair, faithful, fly*, go*, hanging together*, holding together*, holding up*, holding up in wash*, holding water*, kosher*, legal, legit*, loyal, orthodox, proper, proven, received, recognized, reliable, reputable, safe, sanctioned, secure, significant, solid, solvent, stable, standing up*, tried-and-true*, true, valid, washing; SEE CONCEPTS 535,552,582

sound [v1] *produce noise*
babble, bang, bark, blare, blow, boom, burst, buzz, cackle, chatter, clack, clang, clank, clap, clatter, clink, crash, creak, detonate, echo, emit, explode, hum, jabber, jangle, jar, moan, murmur, patter, play, rattle, reflect, resonate, resound, reverberate, ring, roar, rumble, shout, shriek, shrill, sing, slam, smash, snort, squawk, thud, thump, thunder, toot, trumpet, vibrate, whine, whisper; SEE CONCEPT 65

sound [v2] *give the impression*
appear, appear to be, look, seem, strike as being; SEE CONCEPTS 543,716

sound bite [n] *very brief broadcast statement*
blurb*, buzzword, clip, excerpt, fifteen minutes of fame*, newsbreak, news item, one-liner, outtake, photo opportunity, piece, slogan, snippet, spot news; SEE CONCEPT 277

sour [adj1] *bad-tasting; gone bad*
acerb, acetic, acetose, acetous, acid, acidic, acidulated, acrid, astringent, bad, biting, bitter, briny, caustic, curdled, cutting, dry, fermented, green, keen, musty, peppery, piquant, pungent, rancid, salty, sharp, soured, sourish, stinging, tart, turned, unpleasant, unripe, unsavory, unwholesome, vinegary, with a kick*; SEE CONCEPTS 462,613

sour [adj2] *in a bad mood*
acid, acrid, acrimonious, bitter, churlish, crabby, cynical, disagreeable, discontented, displeasing, embittered, grouchy, grudging, ill-natured, ill-tempered, irritable, jaundiced, on edge*, peevish, rotten, tart, ungenerous, unhappy, unpleasant, waspish; SEE CONCEPTS 403,542

sour [v] *alienate*
acidify, curdle, disenchant, embitter, envenom, exacerbate, exasperate, make sour, spoil, turn, turn off; SEE CONCEPTS 14,250

source [n] *beginning; point of supply*
antecedent, author, authority, authorship, begetter, birthplace, cause, commencement, connection, dawn, dawning, derivation, determinant, expert, father, fount, fountain, fountainhead, horse's mouth*, inception, informant, maternity, mother, onset, opening, origin, origination, originator, parent, paternity, provenance, provenience, rise, rising, root, specialist, spring, start, starting point, wellspring; SEE CONCEPT 648

souse [v] *make very wet*
brine, deluge, dip, douse, drench, drown, duck, dunk, immerse, impregnate, marinate, pickle, preserve, seethe, soak, sop, steep, submerge, submerse, waterlog, wet; SEE CONCEPT 256

souvenir [n] *keepsake from event*
gift, memento, memorial, relic, remembrance, remembrancer, reminder, token, trophy; SEE CONCEPTS 337,446

sovereign [n] *supreme ruler*
autocrat, chief, czar, emperor, empress, king, leader, majesty, monarch, potentate, prince, princess, queen, ruler; SEE CONCEPT 354

sovereign [adj] *dominant, effective*
absolute, ascendant, autonomous, chief, commanding, directing, effectual, efficacious, excellent, guiding, highest, imperial, independent, lofty, majestic, monarchal, monarchial, overbearing, paramount, predominant, predominate, preponderant, prevalent, principal, regal, regnant, reigning, royal, ruling, self-governed, supreme, unlimited; SEE CONCEPTS 536,568

sovereignty [n] *domination*
ascendancy, ascendant, dominance, dominion, jurisdiction, preeminence, prepotence, prepotency, primacy, supremacy, supreme power, sway; SEE CONCEPT 299

sow [v] *plant*
broadcast, disject, disseminate, drill, fling, grow, implant, inseminate, lodge, pitch, propagate, put in, raise, scatter, seed, strew, toss; SEE CONCEPTS 253,257

space [n1] *room, scope*
amplitude, area, arena, blank, breadth, capacity, compass, distance, elbowroom, expanse, expansion, extension, extent, field, gap, headroom, headway, infinity, interval, lacuna, leeway, location, margin, omission, play, range, reach, slot, spaciousness, sphere, spot, spread, stretch, territory, tract, turf, volume, zone; SEE CONCEPTS 739,746,756

space [n2] *time interval*
bit, duration, period, season, span, spell, stretch, term, time, while; SEE CONCEPT 807

spacious [adj] *extensive, expansive*
ample, big, boundless, broad, capacious, cavernous, comfortable, commodious, endless, enormous, extended, generous, great, huge, immense, infinite, large, limitless, roomy, sizable, uncrowded, vast, voluminous, wide, widespread; SEE CONCEPTS 481,482,774

span [n] *distance, duration*
amount, compass, extent, interval, length, measure, period, reach, space, spell, spread, stretch, term, time; SEE CONCEPTS 756,807,822

span [v] *stretch over*
arch, bridge, connect, cover, cross, extend, ford, go across, link, pass over, range, reach, traverse, vault; SEE CONCEPT 756

spank [v] *slap, usually on bottom*
belt, blip, box, buffet, cane, chastise, clobber, clout, cuff, flax, flog, hide, larrup*, lash, lather*, leather*, lick, paddle, punch, punish, put over one's knee*, smack, sock, tan*, tan one's hide*, thrash, trim, wallop, welt, whip, whup*; SEE CONCEPT 189

spare [adj1] *extra, reserve*
additional, backup, de trop, emergency, free, in excess, in reserve, in store, lagniappe, leftover, more than enough*, odd, option, over, supererogatory, superfluous, supernumerary, surplus, unoccupied, unused, unwanted; SEE CONCEPTS 771,824

spare [adj2] *thin; sparse*
angular, bony, economical, exiguous, frugal, gaunt, lank, lanky, lean, meager, modest, poor, rangy, rawboned, scant, scanty, scraggy, scrawny, shadow, skimpy, skinny, slender, slight, slim, sparing, sparse, stick, stilt, stingy, wiry; SEE CONCEPTS 490,491,771

spare [v1] *do or manage without*
afford, allow, bestow, dispense with, give, grant, part with, pinch, provide, put by, relinquish, salt away*, save, scrape, scrimp, short, skimp, stint, supply; SEE CONCEPT 129

spare [v2] *forgive; have mercy upon*
absolve, bail out, be lenient, be merciful, discharge, dispense, excuse, exempt, forbear, get off the hook*, get out of hock* (of), give quarter to, go easy on*, leave, let go, let off*, pardon, pity, privilege from, pull out of the fire*, refrain from, relent, relieve from, save bacon*, save from, save neck*, spring; SEE CONCEPTS 50,88,134

sparing [adj] *careful, economical*
avaricious, canny, chary, close, cost-conscious, frugal, humane, mean, money-conscious, parsi-

monious, provident, prudent, saving, stewardly, stingy, thrifty, tight, tight-fisted, tolerant, ungiving, unwasteful, wary; SEE CONCEPTS 334,401

spark [n] *flash, trace*
atom, beam, fire, flare, flicker, gleam, glint, glitter, glow, hint, jot, nucleus, ray, scintilla, scintillation, scrap, sparkle, spit, vestige; SEE CONCEPTS 519,624,828,831

spark [v] *start, inspire*
animate, excite, kindle, precipitate, provoke, set in motion, set off, stimulate, stir, touch off, trigger; SEE CONCEPT 221

sparkle [n] *glitter, shine*
animation, brilliance, coruscation, dash, dazzle, élan, flash, flicker, gaiety, gleam, glimmer, glint, glitz, glow, life, panache, radiance, scintillation, shimmer, show, spark, spirit, twinkle, vim, vitality, vivacity, zap*, zip*; SEE CONCEPTS 411,624,628

sparkle [v] *glitter, shine*
beam, bubble, coruscate, dance, effervesce, fizz, fizzle, flash, flicker, gleam, glimmer, glint, glisten, glow, scintillate, shimmer, spark, twinkle, wink; SEE CONCEPT 624

sparse [adj] *very few and scattered*
dispersed, exiguous, few and far between, inadequate, infrequent, meager, occasional, poor, rare, scant, scanty, scarce, scrimpy, skimpy, spare, sporadic, thin, uncommon; SEE CONCEPTS 762,789

spasm [n] *twitch, fit*
access, attack, burst, contraction, convulsion, eruption, frenzy, jerk, outburst, pain, paroxysm, seizure, throe, yank; SEE CONCEPTS 185,728

spasmodic [adj] *twitching, erratic*
bits and pieces*, changeable, choppy, convulsive, desultory, fitful, fits and starts*, intermittent, irregular, jerky, on-again-off-again*, periodic, shaky, spastic, sporadic, spotty, spurtive, uncertain; SEE CONCEPTS 482,530,541

spatter [v] *splash, sprinkle*
bespatter, bestrew, broadcast, dash, daub, dirty, discharge, disperse, dot, douse, dribble, mottle, polka-dot, scatter, shower, slop, smudge, soil, spangle, speck, speckle, splutter, spot, spray, sputter, stipple, strew, swash, wet; SEE CONCEPTS 172,179,256

spawn [v] *produce*
bring forth, create, father, generate, give rise to, hatch, issue, make, mother, originate, parent, procreate, reproduce, sire; SEE CONCEPTS 173,251,374

speak [v1] *talk*
allege, articulate, assert, aver, blab*, break silence, chat, chew*, communicate, converse, convey, declare, deliver, descant, discourse, drawl, enunciate, expatiate, express, gab*, gas*, go*, jaw*, lip*, make known, make public, modulate, mouth, mumble, murmur, mutter, open one's mouth, perorate, pop off*, pronounce, put into words, rap*, say, shout, sound, speak one's piece*, spiel*, spill, state, tell, utter, verbalize, vocalize, voice, whisper, yak*, yakkety-yak*, yammer; SEE CONCEPTS 47,266

speak [v2] *address; give a lecture*
argue, declaim, descant, discourse, get across, harangue, hold forth, orate, pitch, plead, prelect, recite, sermonize, spiel*, spout*, stump, talk; SEE CONCEPTS 60,285

so
sp

speak out/speak up [v] *make one's position known*
assert, come out with, declare, have one's say*, insist, let voice be heard*, make oneself heard, make plain, say loud and clear*, sound off*, speak loudly, speak one's mind*, stand up for; SEE CONCEPTS **49,57**

special [adj] *distinguished, distinctive; important in own way*
appropriate, best, certain, characteristic, chief, choice, defined, definite, designated, determinate, different, earmarked, especial, exceptional, exclusive, express, extraordinary, festive, first, gala, individual, limited, main, major, marked, memorable, momentous, out of the ordinary, particular, peculiar, personal, primary, proper, rare, redletter*, reserved, restricted, select, set, significant, smashing*, sole, specialized, specific, uncommon, unique, unreal*, unusual; SEE CONCEPTS **557,564,567**

specialist [n] *person who is an expert in a field*
ace, adept, authority, connoisseur, consultant, devotee, doctor, guru*, old hand*, old pro*, pro*, professional, pundit, sage, savant, scholar, technician, veteran, virtuoso; SEE CONCEPTS **347,357**

specialize [v] *concentrate on specific area*
be into, develop oneself in, do one's thing*, go in for, have a weakness for*, limit oneself to, practice, practice exclusively, pursue, study intensively, train, work in; SEE CONCEPTS **91,324**

specially [adv] *particularly*
distinctively, especially, expressly, in specie, specifically, uniquely; SEE CONCEPT **557**

specialty [n] *distinctive feature; concentration*
career, claim to fame, cup of tea*, distinguishing feature, field of concentration, forte, game*, hobby, job, long suit*, magnum opus, major, masterpiece, minor, number, object of attention, object of study, occupation, pièce de résistance*, practice, profession, pursuit, racket*, special, speciality, special project, thing*, vocation, weakness, work; SEE CONCEPT **349**

species [n] *class, variety*
breed, category, collection, description, division, group, kind, likes*, lot, nature, number, order, sort, stripe*, type; SEE CONCEPT **378**

specific [adj] *particular, distinguishing*
bull's eye*, categorical, characteristic, clean-cut, clear-cut, cut fine*, dead on*, definite, definitive, different, distinct, downright, drawn fine, especial, exact, explicit, express, flat out*, hit nail on head*, individual, limited, on target, outright, peculiar, precise, reserved, restricted, right on, set, sole, special, specialized, straight-out, unambiguous, unequivocal, unique; SEE CONCEPTS **535,557,564**

specifically [adv] *expressly, particularly*
accurately, categorically, characteristically, clearly, concretely, correctly, definitely, distinctively, especially, exactly, explicitly, in detail, indicatively, individually, in specie, minutely, peculiarly, pointedly, precisely, respectively, specially; SEE CONCEPTS **557,564**

specification [n] *requirement, qualification*
blueprint, condition, designation, detail, item, particular, particularization, spec*, stipulation, term; SEE CONCEPTS **270,646**

specify [v] *designate; decide definitely*
be specific, blueprint*, button down*, cite, come to the point, condition, define, detail, determine, draw a picture*, enumerate, establish, finger*,

fix, get down to brass tacks*, get to the point*, go into detail, indicate, individualize, instance, inventory, itemize, lay out, limit, list, make, mention, name, particularize, peg, pin down, point out, precise, put down, put finger on*, set, settle, show clearly, slot, specialize, specificate, specificize, spell out, stipulate, tab, tag, tick off; SEE CONCEPTS **18,57**

specimen [n] *example, sample*
case, case history, copy, cross section, embodiment, exemplar, exemplification, exhibit, illustration, individual, instance, model, part, pattern, proof, representation, representative, sampling, sort, species, type, unit, variety; SEE CONCEPTS **686,831**

specious [adj] *misleading*
apparent, apparently right, beguiling, captious, casuistic, colorable, credible, deceptive, delusive, empty, erroneous, fallacious, false, flattering, hollow, idle, illogical, inaccurate, incorrect, likely, nugatory, ostensible, ostentatious, plausible, presumable, presumptive, pretentious, probable, seeming, sophistic, sophistical, sophisticated, spurious, unsound, untrue, vain, wrong; SEE CONCEPTS **552,582**

speck [n] *tiny bit*
atom, blemish, blot, crumb, defect, dot, fault, flaw, fleck, flyspeck, grain, iota, jot, mark, mite, modicum, molecule, mote, particle, point, shred, smidgen, speckle, splotch spot, stain, trace, whit; SEE CONCEPT **831**

speckled [adj] *dotted*
brindled, dappled, flaked, flecked, freckled, mosaic, motley, mottled, particolored, patchy, peppered, punctate, spotted, spotty, sprinkled, stippled, studded, variegated; SEE CONCEPTS **485,618**

spectacle [n] *something showy; exhibition*
comedy, curiosity, demonstration, display, drama, event, exposition, extravaganza, marvel, movie, pageant, parade, performance, phenomenon, play, production, representation, scene, show, sight, spectacular, tableau, view, wonder; SEE CONCEPTS **261,529**

spectacular [adj] *wonderful, impressive*
amazing, astonishing, astounding, breathtaking, daring, dazzling, dramatic, eye-catching, fabulous, fantastic, grand, histrionic, magnificent, marked, marvelous, miraculous, prodigious, razzle-dazzle*, remarkable, sensational, splendid, staggering, striking, stunning, stupendous, theatrical, thrilling, wondrous; SEE CONCEPTS **529,537,574**

spectator [n] *person who watches event*
beholder, bystander, clapper, eyewitness, fan, gaper*, gazer, kibitzer*, looker, looker-on, moviegoer, observer, onlooker, perceiver, playgoer, seer, showgoer, sports fan, standee, stander-by, theatergoer, viewer, watcher, witness; SEE CONCEPTS **366,423**

speculate [v] *think about deeply and theorize*
beat one's brains*, brainstorm*, build castles in air*, call it, call the turn, cerebrate, chew over*, cogitate, conjecture, consider, contemplate, deliberate, dope*, dope out*, excogitate, figure, figure out*, guess, guesstimate*, have a hunch*, hazard a guess, head trip*, hypothesize, kick around*, meditate, muse, pipe-dream*, psych out*, read, read between lines*, reason, reflect, review, ruminate, run it up flagpole*, scheme, size up,

study, suppose, surmise, suspect, weigh, wonder; SEE CONCEPTS *17,24,28,37*

speculate [*v2*] *gamble, risk*
dare, hazard, make book*, margin up*, play, play the market*, plunge, pour money into*, spec*, stick neck out*, take a chance, take a flier* take a fling*, venture, wildcat; SEE CONCEPTS *28,330,363*

speculation [*n1*] *theory, guess*
belief, brainwork*, cerebration, cogitation, conjecture, consideration, contemplation, deliberation, excogitation, guesstimate*, guesswork, hunch, hypothesis, meditation, opinion, reflection, review, shot, shot in the dark*, sneaking suspicion*, stab, stab in the dark*, studying, supposition, surmise, thinking, thought, weighing; SEE CONCEPTS *24,28,529,689*

speculation [*n2*] *risk, gamble*
backing, flier*, flutter, gambling, hazard, hunch, piece, plunge, risk, right money*, risky business*, risky venture, shot, shot in the dark*, smart money*, spec*, speculative enterprise, stab*, venture, wager; SEE CONCEPTS *192,330,363*

speech [*n1*] *talk*
accent, articulation, communication, conversation, dialect, dialogue, diction, discussion, doublespeak*, double talk*, elocution, enunciation, expressing, expression, idiom, intercourse, jargon, language, lingo, locution, mother tongue, native tongue, oral communication, palaver, parlance, prattle, pronunciation, prose, speaking, spiel, tone, tongue, utterance, verbalization, vernacular, vocal expression, vocalization, vocalizing, voice, voicing; SEE CONCEPTS *47,266,276*

speech [*n2*] *formal talk to audience*
address, allocution, appeal, bombast, chalk talk*, commentary, debate, declamation, diatribe, discourse, disquisition, dissertation, eulogy, exhortation, harangue, homily, invocation, keynote, lecture, opus, oration, oratory, panegyric, paper, parlance, parley, pep talk*, pitch, prelection, recitation, rhetoric, salutation, sermon, spiel*, stump*, tirade, valedictory; SEE CONCEPTS *60,285*

speechless [*adj*] *without ability to talk*
aghast, amazed, aphonic, astounded, buttoned up*, clammed up*, close-mouthed, cool*, cool as cucumber*, dazed, dumb, dumbfounded, dumbstruck, inarticulate, mum, mute, not saying boo*, reserved, shocked, silent, taciturn, thunderstruck*, tight-lipped*, tongue-tied*, uncommunicative, unflappable, voiceless, wordless; SEE CONCEPT *267*

speed [*n*] *rate of motion, often a high rate*
acceleration, activity, agility, alacrity, breeze, briskness, celerity, clip, dispatch, eagerness, expedition, fleetness, gait, haste, headway, hurry, hustle, legerity, lick, liveliness, momentum, pace, precipitancy, precipitation, promptitude, promptness, quickness, rapidity, rapidness, readiness, rush, rustle, snap, steam, swiftness, urgency, velocity; SEE CONCEPT *755*

speed [*v*] *move along quickly*
advance, aid, assist, barrel, belt, bomb, boost, bowl over, career, ched, cover ground*, cut along, dispatch, expedite, facilitate, flash, fly, further, gallop, gather momentum, gear up*, get a move on*, get moving, get under way, go all out*, go fast, go like the wind*, hasten, help, hightail*, hurry, impel, lose no time*, make haste, open up throt-

tle*, press on, promote, quicken, race, ride, run, rush, sail, spring, step on it*, tear, urge, whiz, zoom; SEE CONCEPTS *110,150,152*

speedy [*adj*] *fast, quick*
accelerated, agile, alacritous, breakneck, brisk, expeditious, express, fleet, harefooted, hasty, headlong, hurried, immediate, lissome, lively, nimble, precipitate, prompt, quick-fire, rapid, rapid-fire, ready, snappy, summary, supersonic, swift, ultrasonic, winged; SEE CONCEPTS *548,584,588*

spell [*n1*] *interval, period*
bit, bout, course, go, hitch, interlude, intermission, patch, relay, season, shift, space, stint, streak, stretch, term, time, tour, tour of duty, trick, turn, while; SEE CONCEPTS *807,817,822*

spell [*n2*] *magical aura over an entity*
abracadabra*, allure, amulet, bewitching, bewitchment, charm, conjuration, enchanting, enchantment, exorcism, fascination, glamour, hex, hexing, hocus-pocus*, incantation, jinx, magic, mumbo-jumbo*, rune, sorcery, talisman, trance, voodoo*, whack*, whammy*, witchery; SEE CONCEPTS *370,673,689*

spell [*n3*] *seizure*
access, attack, fit, illness, jag, paroxysm, spasm, stroke, throe, turn; SEE CONCEPTS *306,308*

spell [*v1*] *mean, imply*
add up to, amount to, augur, connote, denote, express, herald, import, indicate, intend, point to, portend, presage, promise, signify, suggest; SEE CONCEPTS *55,74,75*

spell [*v2*] *give rest, relief*
allow, breathe, free, lay off, lie by, release, relieve, stand in for, take over, take the place of; SEE CONCEPTS *83,110*

spellbound [*adj*] *enchanted, fascinated*
agape, amazed, bemused, bewildered, bewitched, breathless, captivated, caught up, charmed, enthralled, gripped, held, hooked, mesmerized, open-mouthed, petrified, possessed, rapt, transfixed, transported, under a spell; SEE CONCEPT *403*

spend [*v1*] *give, pay out*
absorb, allocate, ante up*, apply, bestow, blow*, cast away, come across, come through, concentrate, confer, consume, contribute, cough up*, defray, deplete, disburse, dispense, dissipate, donate, drain, drop, employ, empty, evote, exhaust, expend, foot the bill*, fritter, give, hand out, invest, lavish, lay out, liquidate, misspend, outlay, pay down, pay up, put in, run through, settle, shell out*, spring for*, squander, throw away, use, use up, waste; SEE CONCEPTS *156,169,225,341*

spend [*v2*] *use time; occupy*
consume, devote, drift, employ, fill, fool around*, fritter, go, idle, kill, laze, let pass, misuse, pass, put in, squander, waste, while away*; SEE CONCEPT *100*

spendthrift [*n*] *person careless with money*
big spender*, dissipater, high-roller*, improvident, imprudent, prodigal, profligate, spender, sport, squanderer, waster, wastrel; SEE CONCEPTS *348,353,423*

spent [*adj*] *used up, gone; tired out*
all in*, beat, blown, burnt-out*, bushed, consumed, dead*, debilitated, depleted, disbursed, dissipated, dog-tired*, done-in*, down the drain*, drained, effete, enervated, exhausted, expended,

spew [v] *spit out*
belch, bring up, cascade, disgorge, eject, eruct, erupt, expel, flood, gush, heave, irrupt, puke*, regurgitate, scatter, spit, spit up, spread, spritz, throw up, urp*, vomit; SEE CONCEPTS *179,308*

sphere [n1] *globular object*
apple*, ball, big blue marble*, circle, Earth, globe, globule, orb, pellet, pill, planet, rondure, round; SEE CONCEPTS *436,511*

sphere [n2] *domain of influence*
bailiwick, capacity, champaign, circle, class, compass, demesne, department, dominion, employment, field, function, ground, jungle, jurisdiction, level, neck of the woods*, orbit, pale, position, precinct, province, range, rank, realm, scope, station, stomping ground*, stratum, terrain, territory, turf*, walk of life, zone; SEE CONCEPTS *349,388,687*

spice [n] *flavor, zest*
aroma, color, excitement, fragrance, gusto, guts*, kick, pep, piquancy, pungency, relish, salt, savor, scent, seasoning, tang, zap*, zip*; SEE CONCEPTS *614,673*

spicy [adj1] *pungent, flavorful*
ambrosial, appetizing, aromal, aromatic, distinctive, fiery, flavorsome, fragrant, fresh, herbaceous, highly seasoned, hot, keen, odoriferous, peppery, perfumed, piquant, poignant, racy, redolent, savory, scented, seasoned, snappy, spirited, sweet, tangy, tasty, zesty, zippy*; SEE CONCEPT *613*

spicy [adj2] *off-color, vulgar*
breezy, broad, erotic, hot*, indelicate, racy, red hot*, ribald, risqué, salty*, scandalous, sensational, sophisticated, suggestive, titillating, unseemly, wicked, X-rated*; SEE CONCEPTS *267,372,545*

spike [v] *pierce*
fasten, impale, lance, make fast, nail, pin, prick, skewer, spear, spit, stick, transfix; SEE CONCEPT *220*

spill [v1] *slop, drop*
discharge, disgorge, dribble, drip, empty, flow, lose, overfill, overflow, overrun, overturn, pour, run, run out, run over, scatter, shed, spill over, splash, splatter, spray, sprinkle, spurt, squirt, stream, throw off, upset, well over; SEE CONCEPTS *179,181*

spill [v2] *reveal*
betray, blab, blow, disclose, divulge, give away, inform, let the cat out of the bag*, mouth, squeal, tattle, tell; SEE CONCEPT *60*

spin [n] *circular motion*
circuit, gyration, revolution, roll, rotation, spiral, turn, twist, whirl; SEE CONCEPT *748*

spin [v] *go around, make go around*
gyrate, gyre, oscillate, pendulate, pirouette, purl, reel, revolve, rotate, spiral, swim, turn, twirl, twist, wheel, whirl; SEE CONCEPTS *150,152,218*

spine [n] *backbone*
back, bone, chine, rachis, ridge, spinal column, vertebrae, vertebral column; SEE CONCEPTS *393,420*

spineless [adj] *cowardly*
amoebalike*, faint-hearted, fearful, feeble, forceless, frightened, gutless*, impotent, inadequate, ineffective, ineffectual, invertebrate, irresolute, lily-livered*, nerveless, pithless, soft, spiritless, squeamish, submissive, timid, vacillating, weak, weak-kneed, weak-willed, yellow*, yellow-bellied*; SEE CONCEPTS *401,542*

spiral [n] *curled shape*
coil, corkscrew, curlicue, flourish, gyration, gyre, helix, quirk, screw, volute, whorl; SEE CONCEPT *436*

spiral [adj] *curling, winding*
circling, circular, circumvoluted, cochlear, coiled, corkscrew, curled, helical, helicoid, radial, rolled, screw-shaped, scrolled, tendrillar, tortile, voluted, whorled, wound; SEE CONCEPT *486*

spirit [n1] *soul, attitude*
air, animation, ardor, backbone*, boldness, breath, character, complexion, courage, dauntlessness, disposition, earnestness, energy, enterprise, enthusiasm, essence, fire, force, frame of mind, gameness, grit*, guts*, heart, humor, jazz*, life, life force, liveliness, mettle, mood, morale, motivation, nerve, oomph*, outlook, psyche, quality, resolution, resolve, sparkle, spunk*, stoutheartedness, substance, temper, temperament, tenor, vigor, vitality, vital spark, warmth, will, willpower, zest; SEE CONCEPTS *407,411*

spirit [n2] *atmosphere, essence*
feeling, genius, gist, humor, intent, intention, meaning, purport, purpose, quality, sense, substance, temper, tenor, timbre, tone; SEE CONCEPTS *673,682*

spirit [n3] *ghost*
apparition, eidolon, phantasm, phantom, poltergeist, shade, shadow, soul, specter, spook, sprite, supernatural being, umbra, vision, wraith; SEE CONCEPT *370*

spirited [adj] *lively, vivacious*
active, alert, animate, animated, ardent, audacious, avid, bold, bouncy, brave, bright, burning, chirpy, courageous, dauntless, eager, effervescent, energetic, enthusiastic, fearless, fiery, full of life, game, gingery*, gritty, gutsy*, high-spirited, hot, hyper*, intrepid, jumping, keen, mettlesome, nervy, passionate, peppery, peppy, plucky, resolute, rocking, sharp, snappy, sparkling, sprightly, spunky, vigorous, zappy*, zealous, zesty, zingy*, zippy*; SEE CONCEPTS *404,542*

spiritless [adj] *depressed*
apathetic, blah*, blue*, broken, cast down, dejected, despondent, disconsolate, dispirited, dopey*, down, downcast, downhearted, down in the dumps*, down in the mouth*, draggy, drippy, droopy, dull, enervated, flat*, flat tire*, inanimate, indifferent, lackadaisical, lackluster, languid, languishing, languorous, lifeless, limp, listless, low, melancholic, melancholy, mopy, slothful, subdued, submissive, tame, torpid, unconcerned, unenthusiastic, unmoved, zero*; SEE CONCEPTS *403,542*

spiritual [adj] *religious, otherworldly*
airy, asomatous, devotional, discarnate, disembodied, divine, ethereal, extramundane, ghostly, holy, immaterial, incorporeal, intangible, metaphysical, nonmaterial, nonphysical, platonic, pure, rarefied, refined, sacred, supernal, unfleshly, unphysical; SEE CONCEPTS *536,582*

spit [n] *saliva*
discharge, dribble, drool, slaver, spittle, sputum, water; SEE CONCEPT 467

spit [v] *eject saliva or substance*
discharge, drool, expectorate, hawk, hiss, sibilate, sizz, slobber, spatter, spew, splutter, spritz, sputter, throw out; SEE CONCEPTS 179,185

spite [n] *hateful feeling*
animosity, antipathy, bad blood*, contempt, despite, enmity, gall, grudge, harsh feeling, hate, hatred, ill will, malevolence, malice, maliciousness, malignity, peeve, pique, rancor, resentment, revenge, spitefulness, spleen, umbrage, vengeance, vengefulness, venom, vindictiveness; SEE CONCEPT 29

spite [v] *offend, hurt*
annoy, begrudge, beset, crab*, cramp style*, discomfit, gall, get even*, grudge, hang up*, harass, harm, injure, louse up*, needle, nettle, persecute, pique, provoke, put out*, upset the apple cart*, vex; SEE CONCEPTS 7,19,121

spiteful [adj] *hurtful, nasty*
accidentally on purpose*, angry, barbed, catty*, cruel, cussed*, despiteful, dirty, evil, hateful, ill-disposed, ill-natured, malevolent, malicious, malign, malignant, mean, ornery*, rancorous, snide, spleenful, splenetic, venomous, vicious, vindictive, waspish, wicked; SEE CONCEPTS 401,542

splash [n] *spattering, impact*
burst, dash, display, effect, patch, sensation, splurge, stir, touch; SEE CONCEPT 676

splash [v] *throw liquid*
bathe, bespatter, broadcast, dabble, dash, douse, drench, drown, get wet, moisten, paddle, plash, plunge, shower, slop, slosh, soak, sop, spatter, splatter, spray, spread, sprinkle, squirt, strew, throw, wade, wallow, wet; SEE CONCEPTS 222,256

splendid [adj1] *luxurious, expensive*
baroque, beaming, beautiful, bright, brilliant, costly, dazzling, elegant, fab*, fat*, flamboyant, glittering, glowing, gorgeous, grand, grandiose, imposing, impressive, lavish, lustrous, mad*, magnificent, magnifico, marvelous, ornate, plush, posh, radiant, refulgent, resplendent, rich, solid gold*, splashy, splendiferous, splendrous, sumptuous, superb, swanky*; SEE CONCEPTS 334,485,589

splendid [adj2] *excellent, illustrious*
admirable, brilliant, celebrated, distinguished, divine, eminent, exceptional, exquisite, fantastic, fine, first-class, glorious, gorgeous, grand, great, heroic, impressive, magnificent, marvelous, matchless, outstanding, peerless, premium, proud, rare, remarkable, renowned, resplendent, royal, splendiferous, splendorous, sterling, sublime, superb, superlative, supreme, transcendent, unparalleled, unsurpassed, very good, wonderful; SEE CONCEPTS 568,574

splendor [n] *radiance, glory*
brightness, brilliance, ceremony, dazzle, display, effulgence, gorgeousness, grandeur, luster, magnificence, majesty, pageant, pomp, refulgence, renown, resplendence, richness, show, solemnity, spectacle, stateliness, sumptuousness; SEE CONCEPTS 620,655,673

splice [v] *join, interweave*
braid, entwine, graft, hitch, interlace, intertwine, intertwist, knit, marry, mate, mesh, plait, tie, unite, weave, wed, yoke; SEE CONCEPT 193

splinter [n] *thin piece of solid*
bit, chip, flake, fragment, needle, paring, shaving, sliver, wood; SEE CONCEPTS 471,479,831

splinter [v] *break into thin, small pieces*
break to smithereens*, burst, disintegrate, fracture, fragment, pash, rive, shatter, shiver, smash, split; SEE CONCEPT 246

split [n1] *opening*
breach, chasm, chink, cleavage, cleft, crack, damage, division, fissure, gap, rent, rift, rima, rimation, rime, rip, rupture, separation, slash, slit, tear; SEE CONCEPT 513

split [n2] *difference, disunion*
alienation, breach, break, break-up, discord, disruption, dissension, divergence, division, estrangement, fissure, fracture, partition, rent, rift, rupture, schism; SEE CONCEPTS 297,388

split [v1] *break up, pull apart*
bifurcate, branch, break, burst, cleave, come apart, come undone, crack, dichotomize, disband, disjoin, dissever, disunite, diverge, divide, divorce, give, give way, go separate ways, hack, isolate, open, part, part company, put asunder, rend, rip, rive, separate, sever, slash, slit, snap, splinter, sunder, tear, whack; SEE CONCEPTS 135,176,297

split [v2] *divide into parts*
allocate, allot, apportion, carve up, distribute, divide, divvy*, divvy up*, dole, go even-steven*, go fifty-fifty*, halve, mete out, parcel out, partition, share, slice, slice the pie*, slice up; SEE CONCEPT 98

splurge [v] *spend lavishly*
be extravagant, binge, celebrate, fling, give a party*, rampage, spread; SEE CONCEPTS 327,377

spoil [v1] *ruin, hurt*
blemish, damage, debase, deface, defile, demolish, depredate, desecrate, desolate, despoil, destroy, devastate, disfigure, disgrace, harm, impair, injure, make useless, mar, mess up*, muck up*, pillage, plunder, prejudice, ravage, sack, smash, spoliate, squash, take apart, tarnish, trash*, undo, upset, vitiate, waste, wreck; SEE CONCEPTS 246,252

spoil [v2] *baby, indulge*
accommodate, cater to, coddle, cosset, favor, humor, kill with kindness*, mollycoddle*, oblige, overindulge, pamper, spoon-feed*; SEE CONCEPTS 14,136

spoil [v3] *decay, turn bad*
addle, become tainted, become useless, break down, crumble, curdle, decompose, deteriorate, disintegrate, go bad, go off, mildew, molder, putrefy, rot, taint, turn; SEE CONCEPTS 456,469

spoils [n] *possessions stolen or gained*
booty*, cut*, gain, goods, graft, hot goods*, loot, make*, pickings, pillage, plunder, prey, prize, squeeze, swag, take; SEE CONCEPTS 337,710

spoken [adj] *by word of mouth*
announced, articulate, communicated, expressed, lingual, mentioned, oral, phonetic, phonic, put into words, said, sonant, told, traditional, unwritten, uttered, verbal, viva voce, voiced; SEE CONCEPT 267

spokesperson [n] *person who communicates for another*
agent, champion, delegate, deputy, mediator, mouth, mouthpiece*, prolocutor, prophet, protagonist, representative, speaker, stand-in, substitute, talker; SEE CONCEPTS 348,354,359

sp
sp

spongy [adj] cushioned, absorbent
absorptive, cushiony, elastic, light, mushy, pappy, porous, pulpous, pulpy, resilient, rubbery, soft, springy, squishy, yielding; SEE CONCEPT 606

sponsor [n] person who helps, promotes another
adherent, advocate, angel*, backer, benefactor, godparent, grubstaker, guarantor, mainstay, patron, promoter, supporter, surety, sustainer, underwriter; SEE CONCEPTS 348,423

sponsor [v] help, promote
answer for, back, bankroll, be responsible for, finance, fund, grubstake, guarantee, patronize, put up money, stake, subsidize, vouch for; SEE CONCEPTS 110,341

spontaneous [adj] impulsive, willing
ad-lib*, automatic, break loose, casual, down, extemporaneous, extempore, free, free spirited, from the hip*, impetuous, impromptu, improvised, inevitable, instinctive, involuntary, irresistible, natural, offhand, off the cuff*, off top of head*, simple, unartful, unavoidable, unbidden, uncompelled, unconscious, unconstrained, uncontrived, uncontrolled, unforced, unintentional, unplanned, unpremeditated, unprompted, unsophisticated, unstudied, up front, voluntary; SEE CONCEPTS 401,542,548

spoof [n] trick, mockery
bluff, bon mot, burlesque, caricature, cheat, deceit, deception, fake, flim-flam*, game, hoax, imposture, jest, joke, lampoon, parody, phony, prank, put-on, quip, satire, sell, send-up*, sham, take-off, travesty, trickery, wisecrack; SEE CONCEPTS 59,273

spooky [adj] frightening
chilling, creepy, eerie, ghostly, mysterious, ominous, scary, spine-chilling, supernatural, uncanny, unearthly, weird; SEE CONCEPTS 529,537

sporadic [adj] on and off
bits and pieces*, desultory, few, fitful, fits and starts*, hit-or-miss*, infrequent, intermittent, irregular, isolated, occasional, on-again-off-again*, random, rare, scarce, scattered, seldom, semioccasional, spasmodic, spotty, uncommon, unfrequent; SEE CONCEPT 541

sport [n1] recreational activity; entertainment
action, amusement, athletics, ball, disport, diversion, exercise, frolic, fun, fun and games*, gaiety, game, games, pastime, physical activity, picnic, play, pleasure, recreation; SEE CONCEPT 363

sport [n2] fun, joking
antics, badinage, banter, derision, drollery, escapade, frolic, horseplay, jest, jesting, joke, jollification, jollity, kidding, laughter, merriment, mirth, mockery, mummery, nonsense, pleasantry, practical joke, raillery, scorn, teasing, tomfoolery, trifling; SEE CONCEPTS 59,273

sport [n3] person who takes kidding
buffoon, butt, jestee, joke, laughingstock, mock, mockery, object of derision, object of ridicule, plaything, target; SEE CONCEPT 423

sport [v] display, wear
be dressed in, don, exhibit, have on, model, show off; SEE CONCEPTS 167,261

sporting/sportive [adj] playful and fair
antic, coltish, considerate, devil-may-care*, frisky, frolicsome, full of fun*, game, gamesome, gay, generous, impish, jaunty, joyous, larkish, lively, merry, mischievous, reasonable, roguish,

rollicking, sportspersonlike, sprightly, square, wild; SEE CONCEPT 401

spot [n1] mark, stain
atom, blemish, blot, blotch, daub, discoloration, dollop, dram, drop, flaw, iota, jot, little bit, mite, molecule, mote, nip, particle, pimple, pinch, shot, smidgen, smudge, snort, speck, taint, whit; SEE CONCEPTS 284,831

spot [n2] location
hangout*, hole*, joint*, layout, locality, locus, office, pad, place, plant, point, position, post, roof, scene, seat, section, sector, site, situation, slot, station, wherever*, X*, X marks the spot*; SEE CONCEPT 198

spot [n3] bad situation
box*, corner*, difficulty, dilemma, fix, hole*, jam, mess, pickle*, plight, predicament, quandary, scrape, trouble; SEE CONCEPTS 666,674

spot [n4] position in organization
appointment, berth, billet, connection, job, office, place, post, responsibility, situation, station, work; SEE CONCEPTS 351,362

spot [v1] mark, stain
besmirch, bespatter, blot, blotch, dapple, dirty, dot, fleck, maculate, marble, mottle, pepper, pimple, soil, spatter, speck, speckle, splash, splotch, stipple, streak, stripe, stud, sully, taint, tarnish; SEE CONCEPTS 79,179

spot [v2] see, recognize
catch, catch sight of, descry, detect, determinate, diagnose, discern, discover, distinguish, encounter, espy, ferret out, find, identify, locate, make out, meet with, observe, pick out, pinpoint, place, point out, sight, trace, track, turn up; SEE CONCEPTS 38,183,626

spotless [adj] very clean; innocent
above reproach, blameless, chaste, clean, decent, faultless, flawless, gleaming, hygienic, immaculate, irreproachable, modest, pure, sanitary, shining, snowy, stainless, unblemished, undefiled, unimpeachable, unsoiled, unstained, unsullied, untarnished; SEE CONCEPTS 404,621

spotlight [n] attention; bright beam of light
center stage, fame, flashlight, floodlight, interest, light, limelight, notoriety, public attention, public eye, publicity; SEE CONCEPTS 388,624,668

spotlight [v] focus attention on
accentuate, draw attention, feature, floodlight*, give prominence, highlight, illuminate, limelight*, point up, publicize, put on center stage*; SEE CONCEPTS 261,292

spotty [adj] blotchy, irregular
desultory, erratic, flickering, fluctuating, not uniform, on-again-off-again*, patchy, pimply, spasmodic, sporadic, unequal, uneven; SEE CONCEPT 534

spouse [n] one of a married couple
better half*, bride, companion, groom, helpmate, husband, man, mate, partner, roommate, wife, woman; SEE CONCEPT 414

spout [v1] spurt, emit
cascade, discharge, eject, erupt, expel, exude, gush, jet, pour, roll, shoot, spill, spray, squirt, stream, surge; SEE CONCEPT 179

spout [v2] talk forcefully
boast, brag, chatter, declaim, expatiate, go on, gush, harangue, hold forth, orate, pontificate, ramble, rant, sermonize, shoot off one's mouth*, speechify, spellbind, spiel, vapor, yell; SEE CONCEPTS 49,51

sprawl [v] *sit or lie spread out*
drape, extend, flop, lie, lie spread-eagle*, loll, lounge, ramble, recline, sit, slouch, slump, spread, straddle, straggle, stretch, trail; SEE CONCEPT 201

spray [n] *fine mist*
aerosol, atomizer, drizzle, droplets, duster, fog, froth, moisture, spindrift, splash, sprayer, sprinkler, vaporizer; SEE CONCEPTS 514,680

spray [v] *sprinkle, diffuse*
atomize, drizzle, dust, scatter, shoot, shower, smear, spatter, splash, spritz, squirt, throw around; SEE CONCEPTS 179,256

spread [n1] *expansion, development; extent*
advance, advancement, compass, diffusion, dispersion, dissemination, enlargement, escalation, expanse, extension, increase, period, profusion, proliferation, radiation, ramification, range, reach, scope, span, spreading, stretch, suffusion, sweep, term, transfusion, transmission; SEE CONCEPTS 651,704,721,788

spread [n2] *outlay of food, meal*
array, banquet, blowout, dinner, feast, lunch, regale, repast; SEE CONCEPT 459

spread [v1] *open or fan out*
arrange, array, be displayed, be distributed, bloat, branch off, broaden, cast, circulate, coat, cover, daub, develop, diffuse, dilate, disperse, diverge, enlarge, escalate, even out, expand, extend, flatten, flow, gloss, increase, lay, lengthen, level, lie, multiply, mushroom, open, outstretch, overlay, paint, pervade, prepare, proliferate, radiate, reach, roll out, set, settle, smear, sprawl, spray, stretch, strew, suffuse, swell, uncoil, unfold, unfurl, unroll, untwist, unwind, widen; SEE CONCEPTS 158,172,201

spread [v2] *publicize*
advertise, blazon, broadcast, cast, circulate, declare, diffuse, disseminate, distribute, make known, make public, proclaim, promulgate, propagate, publish, radiate, scatter, shed, sow, strew, transmit; SEE CONCEPT 60

spree [n] *wild activity*
bacchanalia, ball, bash, binge, caper, carousal, carouse, carousing, celebration, field day*, fling, frolic, high jinks*, high time*, jag, jamboree, junket, lark, merry-go-round*, orgy, party, rampage, revel, rip*, spending expedition, splurge, tear*; SEE CONCEPTS 327,377,384

sprightly [adj] *fun, vivacious*
active, agile, airy, alert, animate, animated, blithe, bouncy, breezy, bright, brisk, cheerful, cheery, chipper, chirpy, clever, dapper, dashing, energetic, fairylike, frolicsome, gay, good, grooving, hyper, jaunty, jolly, joyous, jumping, keen, keen-witted, light, lively, nimble, peppy, perky, playful, quick, quick-witted, saucy, scintillating, smart, snappy, spirited, sportive, spry, swinging, zappy*, zingy*, zippy*; SEE CONCEPTS 401,404,542

spring [n1] *jump, skip*
bounce, bounciness, bound, buck, buoyancy, elasticity, flexibility, give, hop, leap, recoil, resilience, saltation, springiness, vault; SEE CONCEPTS 194,731

spring [n2] *season following winter*
blackberry winter*, budding, budtime, flowering, prime, seedtime, springtide, springtime, vernal equinox, vernal season; SEE CONCEPT 814

spring [n3] *origin*
beginning, cause, consideration, fount, fountain, fountainhead, impetus, motive, root, source, stimulus, well, wellspring, whence; SEE CONCEPTS 648,661

spring [n4] *body of rushing waters*
artesian well, baths, fountain, geyser, hot spring, hydrolysate, spa, thermal spring, watering place, wells; SEE CONCEPT 514

spring [v1] *jump, skip*
bolt, bounce, bound, hippety hop*, hop, hurdle, leap, lop, lope, rebound, recoil, skitter, start, startle, trip, vault; SEE CONCEPT 194

spring [v2] *originate, emerge*
appear, arise, arrive, be derived, be descended, begin, birth, burgeon, come, come into being, come into existence, come out, commence, derive, descend, develop, emanate, flow, grow, hatch, head, issue, loom, mushroom, proceed, rise, shoot up, start, stem, upspring; SEE CONCEPTS 105,302,373

sprinkle [v] *scatter, disseminate*
baptize, christen, dampen, dot, dredge, dust, freckle, mist, moisten, pepper, powder, rain, shake, shower, smear, speck, speckle, spit, spot, spray, spritz, squirt, strew, stud; SEE CONCEPTS 179,222,256

sprinkling [n] *hint, dash*
admixture, dust, dusting, few, handful, lick, mixture, powdering, scattering, several, smattering, sprinkle, strain, taste, tinge, touch, trace; SEE CONCEPT 787

sprint [v] *run very fast*
dart, dash, go at top speed, hotfoot*, race, rush, scamper, scoot, scurry, shoot, tear, whiz; SEE CONCEPT 150

sprout [v] *develop*
bud, burgeon, germinate, grow, push, shoot, shoot up, spring, take root, vegetate; SEE CONCEPT 257

spruce [adj] *stylish, neat*
classy, clean, dainty, dapper, elegant, prim, smart, tidy, trim, well-groomed; SEE CONCEPT 589

spruce up [v] *make neat, well-groomed*
brush, deck out*, dress up, fix up, groom, prim, primp, sleek, slick, smarten, tidy, titivate, wash; SEE CONCEPTS 162,167,202

spry [adj] *active, vivacious*
agile, alert, brisk, energetic, fleet, full of pep, healthy, in full swing*, lithe, nimble, on the go*, prompt, quick, quick on the draw*, ready, robust, rocking, sound, spirited, sprightly, supple, vigorous; SEE CONCEPT 401

spunk [n] *courage, nerve*
backbone, determination, doggedness, fortitude, gameness, grit*, gumption*, guts*, intestinal fortitude*, mettle, moxie*, pluck, resolution, spirit, toughness, true grit*; SEE CONCEPTS 411,633

spur [n] *incitement, stimulus*
activation, actuation, catalyst, excitant, goad, goose*, impetus, impulse, incentive, incitation, inducement, motivation, motive, needle*, prick, stimulant, trigger, turn-on*, urge; SEE CONCEPT 661

spur [v] *incite, prompt*
animate, arouse, awaken, countenance, drive, egg on*, exhort, favor, fire up*, goad, goose*, impel, instigate, key up, press, prick, prod, propel, push, put up to*, rally, rouse, sic*, spark, stimulate, stir,

trigger, turn on, urge, work up; SEE CONCEPTS *14,68*

spurious [*adj*] *counterfeit, fake*
affected, apocryphal, artificial, assumed, bastard*, bent, bogus, bum, contrived, deceitful, deceptive, dummy*, ersatz, faked, false, feigned, forged, framed, illegitimate, imitation, make-believe, mock, phony, pirate, pretend, pretended, pseudo*, put-on*, sham*, simulated, specious, substitute, unauthentic, ungenuine, unreal; SEE CONCEPT *582*

spurn [*v*] *turn away; ignore*
air, contemn, cut, decline, despise, disapprove, disdain, dismiss, disregard, drop, dump, flout, flush*, give the cold shoulder*, hold in contempt, look down on*, nix*, not hear of*, pass by, rebuff, refuse, reject, reprobate, repudiate, repulse, scoff, scorn, slight, sneer, sneeze at*, snub, steer clear*, turn down, turn nose up at*; SEE CONCEPTS *21,30,384*

spurt [*n*] *burst of activity*
access, commotion, discharge, eruption, explosion, fit, jet, outburst, rush, spate, spritz, squirt, stream, surge; SEE CONCEPTS *1,119,179*

spurt [*v*] *erupt*
burst, emerge, flow, flow out, gush, issue, jet, ooze, pour out, shoot, spew, spout, spritz, squirt, stream, surge, well; SEE CONCEPT *179*

spy [*n*] *person who secretly finds out about another's business*
agent, detective, double agent, emissary, espionage agent, foreign agent, informer, inside agent, intelligencer, investigator, lookout, mole*, observer, operative, patrol, picket, plant*, scout, secret agent, secret service, sleeper, sleuth, snoop, spook, spotter, undercover agent, watcher; SEE CONCEPTS *348,412*

spy [*v*] *secretly follow, watch another's actions*
case, catch sight of, discover, examine, eyeball*, fish out*, get a load of*, glimpse, keep under surveillance, look for, meddle, notice, observe, peep, pry, recon*, reconnoiter, scout, scrutinize, search, set eyes on, shadow, sleuth, snoop, spot, stag, stake out, tail, take in, take note, trail, view, watch; SEE CONCEPTS *103,623*

squabble [*n*] *argument*
altercation, bickering, controversy, difference, difference of opinion, disagreement, dispute, feud, fight, flap*, fuss*, hassle, quarrel, row*, scene*, scrap*, set-to*, spat*, tiff*, words*, wrangle; SEE CONCEPT *46*

squabble [*v*] *argue*
argufy, bicker, brawl, clash, disagree, dispute, encounter, fall out*, fight, hassle, have words*, quarrel, quibble, row, scrap, spat, tiff*, wrangle; SEE CONCEPT *46*

squad [*n*] *team, crew*
band, battalion, company, division, force, gang, group, regiment, squadron, troop; SEE CONCEPTS *322,365,417*

squalid [*adj*] *poor, run-down*
abominable, base, broken-down, decayed, despicable, dingy, dirty, disgusting, disheveled, fetid, filthy, foul, grimy, gruesome, horrible, horrid, ignoble, impure, low, mean, miry, moldy, muddy, musty, nasty, odorous, offensive, poverty-stricken, ramshackle, reeking, repellent, repulsive, scurvy, seedy, shabby, shoddy, sloppy, slovenly, soiled, sordid, ugly, unclean, unkempt, vile, wretched; SEE CONCEPTS *334,485,570*

squander [*v*] *fritter away, use up*
be prodigal with, be wasteful, blow*, cash out*, consume, dissipate, expend, frivol, frivol away, go through, lavish, misspend, misuse, prodigalize, put out*, run through, scatter, spend, spend like water*, spring for*, throw away, throw money around*, trifle, waste; SEE CONCEPTS *156,225,327*

square [*n1*] *person who is old-fashioned, conventional*
antediluvian, conservative, diehard*, fuddy-duddy*, reactionary, stick-in-the-mud*, traditionalist; SEE CONCEPT *423*

square [*n2*] *municipal park*
area, center, circle, common, green, plaza, space, village green; SEE CONCEPT *509*

square [*adj1*] *honest, genuine*
aboveboard, decent, equal, equitable, ethical, even, fair, fair-and-square, impartial, impersonal, just, nonpartisan, objective, on-the-level, sporting, sportspersonlike, straight, straightforward, unbiased, unprejudiced, upright; SEE CONCEPTS *267,542*

square [*adj2*] *four-sided*
boxlike, boxy, equal-sided, equilateral, four-square, orthogonal, quadrate, quadratic, quadratical, rectangular, rectilinear, right-angled, squared, squarish; SEE CONCEPT *486*

square [*adj3*] *old-fashioned, conventional*
behind the times, bourgeois, button-down*, conservative, dated, orthodox, out-of-date, straight*, strait-laced*, stuffy*; SEE CONCEPTS *401,404*

square [*v1*] *correspond, agree*
accord, balance, check out, coincide, conform, dovetail*, fit, fit in, gee, harmonize, jibe, match, reconcile, tally; SEE CONCEPT *664*

square [*v2*] *pay off, satisfy*
balance, bribe, buy, buy off, clear, clear off, clear up, corrupt, discharge, fix, have, liquidate, make even, pay, pay up, quit, rig, settle, tamper with; SEE CONCEPT *341*

square [*v3*] *adapt, regulate*
accommodate, adjust, align, conform, even up, fit, level, quadrate, reconcile, suit, tailor, tailor-make*, true; SEE CONCEPTS *126,202*

squash [*v*] *compress*
annihilate, bear, bruise, crowd, crush, distort, extinguish, flatten, jam, kill, macerate, mash, pound, press, pulp, push, put down, quash, quell, scrunch, shut down, sit on, smash, squeeze, squish, stamp on, suppress, trample, triturate; SEE CONCEPTS *121,208,219*

squat [*adj*] *short and stocky*
broad, chunky, dumpy*, fat, heavy, heavyset, splay, thick, thick-bodied, thickset; SEE CONCEPTS *491,773,779*

squat [*v*] *lower body by bending knees*
bow, cower, crouch, hunch, hunker down, perch, roost, settle, sit, stoop; SEE CONCEPT *201*

squawk [*v1*] *make high-pitched, animal-like sound*
cackle, caw, crow, cry, hoot, screech, yap, yawp, yelp; SEE CONCEPTS *64,77*

squawk [*v2*] *gripe*
bellyache*, complain, kick up a fuss*, protest, raise Cain*, squeal, yammer; SEE CONCEPTS *52,54*

squeak [*v*] *make sharp, high-pitched sound*
cheep, creak, cry, grate, peep, pipe, scream, screech, scritch, shrill, sing, sound, squeal, talk, whine, yelp; SEE CONCEPTS *64,65*

squeal [n/vl] *yell in a loud and high-pitched manner*

bleat, cheep, creak, grate, howl, peep, rasp, scream, scream bloody murder*, screech, shout, shriek, shrill, squawk, wail, yelp, yip, yowl; SEE CONCEPTS 64,77

squeal [v2] *inform on*

betray, blab*, complain, protest, rat on*, sell down the river*, sing*, snitch*, squawk*, talk, tattle, tattletale*, tell; SEE CONCEPTS 54,60

squeamish [adj] *nauseated; finicky*

annoyed, captious, delicate, disgusted, dizzy, exacting, fastidious, fussy, hypercritical, mincing, particular, prim, prudish, puritanical, qualmish, queasy, queer, scrupulous, shaky, sick, sickly, sick to one's stomach*, strait-laced, unsettled, upset, vertiginous; SEE CONCEPTS 314,401,404

squeeze [n] *pressure, crushing*

clasp, clutch, congestion, crowd, crunch, crush, embrace, force, handclasp, hold, hug, influence, jam, press, restraint, squash; SEE CONCEPTS 219,674,687

squeeze [vl] *exert pressure on sides, parts of something*

bear, choke, clasp, clip, clutch, compress, contract, cram, crowd, crush, cuddle, embrace, enfold, force, grip, hold tight, hug, jam, jostle, nip, pack, pinch, press, quash, ram, scrunch, squash, squish, strangle, stuff, throttle, thrust, wedge, wring; SEE CONCEPT 219

squeeze [v2] *try to get money out of*

bleed*, bring pressure to bear, eke out, extort, extract, lean on*, milk*, oppress, pinch*, pressure, pressurize*, put screws to*, shake down*, wrench, wring; SEE CONCEPTS 53,192,342

squelch [v] *suppress, restrain*

black out, censure, crush, extinguish, kill, muffle, oppress, quelch, quench, repress, settle, shush, sit on, smother, squash, stifle, strangle, thwart; SEE CONCEPT 130

squint [v] *scrunch up eyes when viewing*

cock the eye, look, look askance, look cross-eyed, peek, peep, screw up eyes, squinch*; SEE CONCEPTS 185,623

squire [v] *accompany*

assist, attend, chaperon, companion, date, escort, serve; SEE CONCEPTS 384,714

squirm [v] *wiggle, fidget*

agonize, flounder, shift, skew, squiggle, toss, twist, wind, worm, wriggle, writhe; SEE CONCEPT 213

squirt [v] *squeeze out liquid*

eject, emit, flow, jet, pour, spatter, spit, splash, splur, spray, sprinkle, spritz, spurt, stream, surge; SEE CONCEPTS 179,256

stab [nl] *piercing cut*

ache, blow, gash, hurt, incision, jab, jag, pang, piercing, prick, puncture, rent, stick, thrust, transfixion, twinge, wound; SEE CONCEPT 309

stab [n2] *attempt*

attempt, crack*, endeavor, essay, fling*, go*, one's best*, shot*, try, venture, whack*, whirl*; SEE CONCEPT 87

stab [v] *puncture, pierce with sharp, pointed object*

bayonet, brand, carve, chop, cleave, clip, cut, drive, gore, hit, hurt, injure, jab, jag, knife, open up, penetrate, pierce, plow, plunge, prick, prong, punch, ram, run through, saber, shank, sink, slice,

spear, stick, thrust, transfix, wound; SEE CONCEPT 220

stability [n] *resistance of some degree*

adherence, aplomb, assurance, backbone, balance, cohesion, constancy, dependability, determination, durability, endurance, establishment, firmness, immobility, immovability, maturity, permanence, perseverance, resoluteness, security, solidity, solidness, soundness, stableness, steadfastness, steadiness, strength, substantiality, support, toughness; SEE CONCEPTS 411,731

stabilize [v] *make or keep in steady state; make resistant to change*

balance, ballast, bolt, brace, buttress, counterbalance, counterpoise, equalize, fasten, firm, firm up*, fix, freeze*, maintain, ossify, poise, preserve, prop, secure, set, settle, stabilitate, steady, stiffen, support, sustain, uphold; SEE CONCEPTS 110,250

stable [adj] *constant, fixed; resistant*

abiding, anchored, balanced, brick-wall*, calm, deep-rooted, durable, enduring, equable, established, even, fast, firm, immutable, invariable, lasting, nailed, perdurable, permanent, poised, reliable, resolute, safe, secure, set, set in stone*, solid, solid as a rock*, sound, stabile, stalwart, stationary, staunch, staying put, steadfast, steady, stout, strong, sturdy, substantial, sure, together, tough, unalterable, unchangeable, unfluctuating, uniform, unvarying, unwavering, well-built, well-founded; SEE CONCEPTS 404,488

stack [n] *pile*

assemblage, bank, bundle, cock, drift, heap, hill, hoard, load, mass, mound, mountain, pack, pyramid, sheaf; SEE CONCEPTS 432,440,509

stack [v] *pile up*

accumulate, amass, bank up, cock, drift, heap, hill, load, mound, pile, rick, stockpile; SEE CONCEPTS 109,158

stadium [n] *arena for recreation or spectating*

amphitheater, athletic field, bowl, coliseum, diamond, field, garden, gridiron, gymnasium, pit, ring, stade, strand; SEE CONCEPT 438

staff [nl] *employees of organization*

agents, assistants, cadre, cast, crew, deputies, faculty, force, help, officers, operatives, organization, personnel, servants, shop, teachers, team, workers, work force; SEE CONCEPT 325

staff [n2] *stick, usually for walking*

cane, club, pikestaff, pole, prop, rod, stave, walking stick, wand; SEE CONCEPTS 311,479

stage [nl] *level, period within structure or system*

date, degree, division, footing, grade, juncture, lap, leg, length, moment, node, notch, phase, plane, point, point in time, rung, standing, status, step; SEE CONCEPTS 727,744,816

stage [n2] *theater platform; theater life*

arena, boards*, Broadway, dais, drama, footlights, frame, legit*, limelight*, mise-en-scène, off-Broadway, play, scaffold, scaffolding, scene, scenery, set, setting, show biz*, show business, spotlight, stage set, staging, theater; SEE CONCEPTS 263,349,438,439,448

stage [v] *arrange, produce*

bring out, do, engineer, execute, give, mount, open, orchestrate, organize, perform, play, present, put on, show; SEE CONCEPTS 94,292

stagger [vl] *walk falteringly*

alternate, careen, dither, falter, halt, hesitate, lurch, overlap, pitch, reel, shake, stammer, step,

sp
st

sway, swing, teeter, titubate, topple, totter, vacillate, waver, wheel, whiffle, wobble, zigzag; SEE CONCEPT 151

stagger [v2] *astound, shock*
amaze, astonish, boggle, bowl over*, confound, consternate, devastate, dumbfound, flabbergast, floor*, give a shock, nonplus, overpower, overwhelm, paralyze, perplex, puzzle, shake, shatter, startle, strike dumb*, stump, stun, stupefy, surprise, take aback, take breath away*, throw off balance*; SEE CONCEPTS 7,19,42

stagnant [adj] *motionless, dirty*
brackish, dead, dormant, filthy, foul, idle, immobile, inactive, inert, lifeless, listless, passive, putrid, quiet, sluggish, stale, standing, static, stationary, still, unmoving; SEE CONCEPTS 584,621

stagnate [v] *deteriorate by lack of action*
constipate, decay, decline, fester, go to seed*, hibernate, idle, languish, lie fallow, not move, putrefy, rot, rust, stall, stand, stand still, stifle, stultify, trammel, vegetate; SEE CONCEPTS 698,748

staid [adj] *restrained, set*
calm, cold sober*, collected, composed, cool, decorous, demure, dignified, earnest, formal, grave, no-nonsense*, quiet, sedate, self-restrained, serious, settled, sober, solemn, somber, starchy, steady, stuffy, weighty; SEE CONCEPTS 401,404

stain [n] *spot of dirt, blot*
bar sinister*, black eye*, blemish, blot, blotch, blur, brand, color, discoloration, disgrace, dishonor, drip, dye, infamy, ink spot, mottle, odium, onus, reproach, shame, slur, smirch, smudge, spatter, speck, splotch, spot, stigma, tint; SEE CONCEPTS 230,622

stain [v] *dirty, taint*
animalize, bastardize, besmirch, bestialize, blacken, blemish, blot, brutalize, color, contaminate, corrupt, daub, debase, debauch, defile, demoralize, deprave, discolor, disgrace, drag through the mud*, dye, mark, pervert, smear, smudge, soil, spot, sully, tar, tarnish, tinge, tint; SEE CONCEPTS 54,250,254

stake [n1] *pole*
pale, paling, picket, post, rod, spike, stave, stick; SEE CONCEPTS 471,479

stake [n2] *bet, wager*
ante, chance, hazard, peril, pledge, pot, risk, venture; SEE CONCEPTS 329,363

stake [n3] *share, investment*
award, claim, concern, interest, involvement, prize, purse; SEE CONCEPTS 344,710,835

stake [v] *bet, wager*
back, bankroll*, capitalize, chance, finance, gamble, game, grubstake*, hazard, imperil, jeopardize, lay, play, pledge, put, put on, risk, set, stake down, venture; SEE CONCEPTS 330,363

stale [adj1] *old, decayed*
dried, dry, faded, fetid, flat, fusty, hard, insipid, malodorous, musty, noisome, parched, rank, reeking, smelly, sour, spoiled, stagnant, stenchy, stinking, tasteless, watery, weak, zestless; SEE CONCEPTS 462,485,598

stale [adj2] *overused, out-of-date*
antiquated, banal, bent, cliché, clichéd, cliché-ridden, common, commonplace, corny*, dead, drab, dull, dusty, effete, flat, fusty, hackneyed, insipid, like a dinosaur*, mawkish, moth-eaten*,

out*, passé, past, platitudinous, repetitious, shopworn, stereotyped, threadbare, timeworn, tired, trite, unoriginal, well-worn, worn-out, yesterday's*, zestless; SEE CONCEPTS 267,578,589,797

stalemate [n] *deadlock*
arrest, Catch-22*, check, delay, draw, gridlock, impasse, pause, standoff, standstill, tie; SEE CONCEPTS 230,807,832

stalk [n] *stem of plant*
axis, bent, helm, pedicel, pedicle, reed, shaft, spike, spire, support, trunk, twig, upright; SEE CONCEPT 428

stalk [v] *follow, creep up on*
ambush, approach, chase, drive, flush out, haunt, hunt, pace, pursue, shadow, striddle, stride, tail, track, trail, walk up to; SEE CONCEPTS 149,159,749

stall [v] *delay for own purposes*
arrest, avoid the issue*, beat around the bush*, brake, check, die, drag one's feet*, equivocate, fence, filibuster, halt, hamper, hedge, hinder, hold off, interrupt, not move, play for time*, postpone, prevaricate, put off, quibble, shut down, slow, slow down, stand, stand off, stand still, stay, still, stonewall*, stop, suspend, take one's time*, tarry, temporize; SEE CONCEPTS 121,234

stalwart [adj] *strong, valiant*
athletic, bold, bound, bound and determined*, brave, brawny, brick-wall*, courageous, daring, dauntless, dead set on*, dependable, fearless, forceful, gutsy*, hanging tough*, hefty, husky, indomitable, intrepid, lusty, muscular, nervy*, powerhouse*, redoubtable, robust, rugged, sinewy, solid, spunky*, staunch, steamroller*, stout, stouthearted, strapping, sturdy, substantial, tenacious, tough, unafraid, undaunted, valorous, vigorous; SEE CONCEPTS 404,489

stamina [n] *strength, vigor*
backbone*, endurance, energy, force, fortitude, grit*, guts*, gutsiness, heart, indefatigability, intestinal fortitude*, legs*, lustiness, moxie*, power, power of endurance, resilience, resistance, starch*, staying power, tolerance, toleration, vim, vitality, zip*; SEE CONCEPTS 411,732

stammer [v] *stutter in speech*
falter, halt, hammer, hem and haw*, hesitate, jabber, lurch, pause, repeat, splutter, sputter, stop, stumble, wobble; SEE CONCEPTS 47,266

stamp [n1] *impression, symbol, seal*
brand, cast, earmark, emblem, hallmark, impress, imprint, indentation, mark, mold, print, signature, sticker; SEE CONCEPTS 259,284

stamp [n2] *character*
breed, cast, cut, description, fashion, form, ilk, kind, lot, mold, sort, stripe, type; SEE CONCEPT 411

stamp [v1] *step on hard*
beat, clomp, clump, crush, stomp, stump, tramp, trample, tromp; SEE CONCEPT 149

stamp [v2] *imprint; press mark on*
brand, cast, drive, engrave, etch, fix, grave, hammer, impress, infix, inscribe, letter, mark, mold, offset, pound, print; SEE CONCEPTS 79,174

stampede [n] *rush of animals*
charge, chase, crash, dash, flight, fling, hurry, panic, rout, run, scattering, shoot, smash, tear; SEE CONCEPT 152

stance [n] *position, posture*
attitude, bearing, carriage, color, deportment,

posture, say-so*, slant, stand, standpoint, viewpoint; SEE CONCEPTS 689,757

stand [n1] *position, opinion*
angle, attitude, belief, carriage, determination, notion, poise, pose, sentiment, slant, sound, stance, standpoint, twist, two cents' worth*, view; SEE CONCEPT 689

stand [n2] *base, stage*
board, booth, bracket, counter, dais, frame, gantry, grandstand, place, platform, rack, rank, staging, stall, station, support, table; SEE CONCEPTS 442,443

stand [v1] *be or get upright*
be erect, be on feet, be vertical, cock, dispose, erect, jump up, locate, mount, place, poise, position, put, rank, rise, set, settle; SEE CONCEPT 201

stand/stand for [v2] *endure, bear*
abide, allow, bear with, brook, cope, countenance, experience, handle, hang on, hold, last, live with, put up with, resign oneself to, stay the course*, stomach*, submit, suffer, support, sustain, swallow, take, tolerate, undergo, wear, weather, withstand; SEE CONCEPT 23

stand [v3] *be in force, exist*
be located, belong, be situated, be valid, continue, endure, fill, halt, hold, last, obtain, occupy, pause, prevail, remain, rest, stay, stop, take up; SEE CONCEPT 407

standard [n1] *guideline, principle*
archetype, average, axiom, barometer, beau ideal, belief, benchmark, canon, code, criterion, ethics, example, exemplar, fundamental, gauge, grade, guide, guideline, ideal, ideals, law, mean, measure, median, mirror, model, morals, norm, par, paradigm, pattern, principle, requirement, rule, rule of thumb*, sample, specification, test, touchstone, type, yardstick; SEE CONCEPT 688

standard [n2] *flag*
banderole, banner, bannerol, color, colors, emblem, ensign, figure, insignia, jack, pennant, streamer, symbol; SEE CONCEPT 475

standard [adj] *regular, approved*
accepted, authoritative, average, basic, boilerplate*, canonical, classic, common, customary, definitive, established, everyday, garden variety*, general, normal, official, orthodox, popular, prevailing, recognized, regulation, run-of-the-mill*, set, staple, stock, typical, usual, vanilla*; SEE CONCEPT 533

standardize [v] *make regular, similar*
assimilate, bring into line, homogenize, institute, institutionalize, mass produce, normalize, order, regiment, stereotype, systematize; SEE CONCEPT 126

stand for [v] *signify, mean*
answer for, appear for, betoken, denote, exemplify, imply, indicate, represent, signify, suggest, symbol, symbolize; SEE CONCEPT 682

standing [n1] *position, rank*
cachet, capacity, character, condition, consequence, credit, dignity, eminence, estimation, footing, place, prestige, reputation, repute, scene, situation, slot, state, station, stature, status, term; SEE CONCEPTS 388,727

standing [adj] *permanent*
continuing, existing, fixed, perpetual, regular, repeated; SEE CONCEPT 551

standoffish [adj] *cold, distant*
aloof, antisocial, cool, distant, eremitic, haughty, indifferent, misanthropic, reclusive, remote, re-

served, solitary, unapproachable, uncompanionable, unsociable, withdrawn; SEE CONCEPTS 401,404

stand out [v] *be conspicuous, prominent*
attract attention, be distinct, beetle, be highlighted, be striking, bulge, bulk, catch the eye, emerge, jut, loom, overhang, poke, pouch, project, protrude, stick out; SEE CONCEPT 716

standstill [n] *stop*
arrest, cessation, check, checkmate, corner*, dead end*, deadlock, dead stop*, delay, gridlock, halt, hole, impasse, inaction, pause, stalemate, standoff, wait; SEE CONCEPTS 119,832

staple [adj] *necessary, basic*
chief, essential, fundamental, important, in demand, key, main, popular, predominant, primary, principal, standard; SEE CONCEPT 546

star [n] *person who is famous*
celebrity, draw*, favorite, headliner, hero, idol, lead, leading role, luminary, name, starlet, superstar, topliner*; SEE CONCEPTS 352,366

star [adj] *famous, illustrious*
brilliant, capital, celebrated, chief, dominant, leading, main, major, outstanding, paramount, predominant, preeminent, principal, prominent, talented, well-known; SEE CONCEPT 568

stare [v] *gape, watch*
beam*, bore*, eagle eye*, eye, eyeball*, fix, focus, gawk, gaze, glare, glim*, goggle*, lay eyes on*, look, look fixedly, ogle, peer, rivet, rubberneck*, take in; SEE CONCEPT 623

stark [adj1] *utter, absolute*
abrupt, arrant, bald, bare, blasted, blessed, blunt, complete, confounded, consummate, downright, entire, firm, flagrant, gross, infernal, out-and-out*, outright, palpable, patent, pure, rank, severe, sheer, simple, stiff, unalloyed, unmitigated; SEE CONCEPTS 531,569

stark [adj2] *bare, unadorned*
au naturel, austere, bald, barren, bleak, chaste, clear, cold, depressing, desolate, dreary, empty, forsaken, grim, harsh, naked, nude, plain, raw, severe, solitary, stripped, unclad, unclothed, uncovered, undraped, vacant, vacuous, void; SEE CONCEPT 485

start [n1] *beginning*
alpha*, birth, bow, commencement, countdown, dawn, dawning, day one*, derivation, embarkation, exit, first step, flying start*, foundation, inauguration, inception, initiation, jump-off, kickoff*, leaving, onset, opening, origin, outset, running start, setting out, source, spring, square one*, start-off, takeoff; SEE CONCEPTS 648,832

start [n2] *advantage*
allowance, backing, break, bulge, chance, draw, edge, handicap, head start, helping hand, introduction, lead, odds, opening, opportunity, sponsorship, vantage; SEE CONCEPT 693

start [n3] *flinch*
convulsion, jar, jump, scare, shock, spasm, turn, twitch; SEE CONCEPTS 150,194

start [v1] *begin; come into existence*
activate, appear, arise, arouse, come into being, commence, create, depart, embark, engender, enter upon, establish, found, get going, get under way*, go ahead, hit the road*, inaugurate, incite, initiate, instigate, institute, introduce, issue, launch, lay foundation, leave, light, make a beginning, open, originate, pioneer, rise, rouse, sally forth, see light, set in motion, set out, set up,

st
st

spring, take first step*, take the plunge*, turn on;
SEE CONCEPTS 221,241

start [v2] *frighten, surprise*
blanch, blench, bolt, bounce, bound, buck, dart,
draw back, jerk, jump, jump the gun*, leap, quail,
recoil, shrink, shy, spring, squinch, startle,
twitch, wince; SEE CONCEPTS 150,194

startle [v] *frighten, surprise*
affright, agitate, alarm, amaze, astonish, astound,
awe, bolt, consternate, floor, fright, give a turn*,
jump, make jump, rock, scare, scare to death*,
shake up, shock, spook, spring, spring something
on*, stagger, start, stun, take aback, terrify, terrorize; SEE CONCEPTS 7,19,42

starving/starved [adj] *deprived of food*
could eat a horse*, craving, dehydrated, drawn,
dying, emaciated, empty, faint, famished, haggard, hungering, hungry, malnourished, peaked,
peckish, perishing, pinched, ravenous, skinny,
thin, underfed, undernourished, weakened; SEE
CONCEPTS 406,546

state [n1] *condition or mode of being*
accompaniment, attitude, capacity, case, category, chances, character, circumstance, circumstances, contingency, element, environment,
essential, estate, event, eventuality, fix, footing,
form, frame of mind, humor, imperative, juncture, limitation, mood, nature, occasion, occurrence, outlook, pass, phase, plight, position,
posture, predicament, prerequisite, proviso, reputation, requirement, shape, situation, spirits,
stand, standing, state of affairs, station, status,
stipulation, time, welfare; SEE CONCEPTS
410,639,696,701,720

state [n2] *dignity, grandeur*
cachet, ceremony, consequence, display, glory,
majesty, pomp, position, prestige, rank, splendor,
standing, stature, status, style; SEE CONCEPT 388

state [n3] *government, country*
body politic, commonwealth, community, federation, land, nation, republic, sovereignty, territory, union; SEE CONCEPTS 508,510

state [v] *declare, assert*
affirm, air, articulate, asseverate, aver, bring out,
chime in*, come out with, deliver, describe, elucidate, enounce, enumerate, enunciate, explain,
expound, express, give, give blow-by-blow*, give
rundown*, interpret, narrate, pitch, present, pronounce, propound, recite, recount, rehearse,
relate, report, say, set forth, speak, specify,
spiel*, tell, throw out*, utter, vent, ventilate,
voice; SEE CONCEPTS 49,51,55

stately [adj] *dignified, impressive*
august, ceremonial, ceremonious, conventional,
courtly, deliberate, elegant, elevated, formal, gallant, gracious, grand, grandiose, haughty, high,
highfaluting*, high-minded*, imperial, imperious, imposing, kingly, large, lofty, luxurious,
magnificent, majestic, massive, measured, monumental, noble, opulent, palatial, pompous, portly,
proud, queenly, regal, royal, solemn, stiff, sumptuous, superb, towering; SEE CONCEPTS
401,574,589

statement [n1] *declaration, assertion*
ABCs*, account, acknowledgment, affidavit, affirmation, allegation, announcement, articulation,
aside, asseveration, assurance, averment, avowal,
blow-by-blow*, charge, comment, communication, communiqué, description, dictum, ejaculation, explanation, make*, manifesto, mention,

narrative, observation, picture, presentation, presentment, proclamation, profession, protestation,
recital, recitation, relation, remark, report, run-
down, testimony, utterance, ventilation, verbalization, vocalization, voice, word; SEE CONCEPTS
271,274,278

statement [n2] *account of finances*
affidavit, audit, bill, budget, charge, invoice,
reckoning, record, report, score, tab; SEE CON-
CEPT 331

static [adj] *motionless, changeless*
at a standstill, constant, deadlocked, fixed, format, gridlocked, immobile, immovable, inactive,
inert, latent, passive, rigid, stabile, stable, stagnant, stalled, standing still, stationary, sticky,
still, stopped, stuck, unchanging, unfluctuating,
unmoving, unvarying; SEE CONCEPTS 534,584

station [n1] *headquarters, base*
base of operations, depot, home office, house, location, locus, main office, place, position, post,
seat, site, situation, spot, stop, terminal, whereabouts; SEE CONCEPT 198

station [n2] *social or occupational status*
appointment, business, calling, capacity, caste,
character, class, duty, employment, estate, footing, grade, level, occupation, order, place, position, post, rank, service, situation, sphere,
standing, state, stratum; SEE CONCEPTS
349,376,388

station [v] *place at a location*
allot, appoint, assign, base, commission, establish, fix, garrison, install, lodge, park, plant, post,
put, set; SEE CONCEPTS 50,88,201,320,351

stationary [adj] *not moving; fixed*
anchored, at a standstill, immobile, inert, moored,
motionless, nailed*, nailed down*, parked*, pat*,
permanent, stable, stagnant, standing, static,
stock-still, unmoving; SEE CONCEPTS 488,551

statue [n] *trophy or memorial*
bronze, bust, cast, effigy, figure, icon, image,
ivory, likeness, marble, piece, representation,
sculpture, simulacrum, statuary, statuette, torso;
SEE CONCEPT 259

statuesque [adj] *tall and dignified*
beautiful, graceful, grand, imposing, majestic, regal, shapely, stately, trim, well-proportioned; SEE
CONCEPTS 579,589,779

stature [n] *importance*
ability, cachet, caliber, capacity, competence,
consequence, development, dignity, elevation,
eminence, growth, merit, position, prestige,
prominence, qualification, quality, rank, size,
standing, state, station, status, tallness, value, virtue, worth; SEE CONCEPTS 668,741

status [n] *rank*
cachet, caliber, capacity, character, condition,
consequence, degree, dignity, distinction, eminence, footing, grade, merit, mode, place, position, prestige, prominence, quality, rating,
renown, situation, stage, standing, state, station,
stature, worth; SEE CONCEPTS 388,668

statute [n] *rule, law*
act, assize, bill, canon, decree, decretum, edict,
enactment, measure, ordinance, precept, regulation; SEE CONCEPT 318

staunch [adj] *resolute, dependable*
allegiant, ardent, constant, faithful, fast, firm, inflexible, liege, loyal, reliable, secure, sound, stable, stalwart, steadfast, stiff, stout, strong, sure,

tough, tried-and-true, true, true-blue, trustworthy, trusty; SEE CONCEPTS *401,534,542*

stay [n1] *visit*
break, halt, holiday, sojourn, stop, stopover, vacation; SEE CONCEPT *227*

stay [n2] *hold, delay*
deferment, halt, pause, postponement, remission, reprieve, standstill, stop, stopping, suspension; SEE CONCEPTS *121,832*

stay [n3] *support, underpinning*
brace, buttress, column, hold, prop, reinforcement, shore, shoring, stanchion, truss, underpropping; SEE CONCEPTS *440,445*

stay [v1] *wait*
abide, bide, bunk, continue, dally, delay, endure, establish oneself, halt, hang, hang about, hang around, hang in, hang out, hold the fort*, hover, lag, last, linger, loiter, nest, outstay, pause, perch, procrastinate, put down roots*, remain, reprieve, reside, respite, roost*, settle, sit tight*, sojourn, squat, stand, stay out, stay put, stick around*, stop, sweat*, sweat it out*, tarry; SEE CONCEPTS *210,681*

stay [v2] *visit*
be accommodated, bide, dwell, live, lodge, put up, sojourn, stop, stop over, tarry; SEE CONCEPTS *226,227*

stay [v3] *hold in abeyance*
adjourn, arrest, check, curb, defer, delay, detain, discontinue, halt, hinder, hold, hold over, impede, intermit, interrupt, obstruct, postpone, prevent, prorogue, put off, shelve, stall, stop, suspend, ward off; SEE CONCEPT *121*

steadfast [adj] *loyal, steady*
abiding, adamant, allegiant, ardent, bound, changeless, constant, dedicated, dependable, enduring, established, faithful, fast, firm, fixed, immobile, immovable, inexorable, inflexible, intense, intent, liege, never-failing, obdurate, persevering, relentless, reliable, resolute, rigid, single-minded, stable, staunch, stubborn, sure, tried-and-true*, true, true-blue*, unbending, unfaltering, unflinching, unmovable, unqualified, unquestioning, unswerving, unwavering, unyielding, wholehearted; SEE CONCEPTS *401,534,542*

steady [adj1] *stable, fixed*
abiding, brick-wall*, certain, changeless, constant, durable, enduring, equable, even, firm, immovable, never-failing, patterned, regular, reliable, safe, set, set in stone*, solid, solid as a rock*, stabile, steadfast, steady-going, substantial, sure, unchangeable, unchanging, unfaltering, unfluctuating, uniform, unqualified, unquestioning, unshaken, unvarying, unwavering; SEE CONCEPTS *488,534*

steady [adj2] *continuing*
ceaseless, confirmed, consistent, constant, continuous, equable, eternal, even, faithful, habitual, incessant, never-ending, nonstop, persistent, regular, rhythmic, stabile, stable, steady-going, unbroken, unfaltering, unfluctuating, uniform, uninterrupted, unremitting, unvarying, unwavering; SEE CONCEPT *798*

steady [adj3] *balanced, faithful in mind*
allegiant, ardent, calm, constant, cool, dependable, equable, fast, imperturbable, intense, level-headed, liege, loyal, reliable, reserved, resolute, sedate, self-possessed, sensible, serene, serious-minded, settled, single-minded, sober, staid, staunch, steadfast, unswerving, unwavering, wholehearted; SEE CONCEPTS *403,542*

steal [v1] *take something without permission*
abduct, appropriate, blackmail, burglarize, carry off, cheat, cozen, defraud, despoil, divert, embezzle, heist, hold for ransom, hold up, housebreak*, keep, kidnap, lift*, loot, make off with*, misappropriate, peculate, pilfer, pillage, pinch*, pirate, plagiarize, plunder, poach, purloin, ransack, remove, rifle, rip off*, run off with*, sack*, shoplift, snitch*, spirit away*, stick up*, strip, swindle, swipe, take, take possession of, thieve, walk off with*, withdraw; SEE CONCEPT *139*

steal [v2] *sneak around*
creep, flit, glide, go stealthily, insinuate, lurk, pass quietly, skulk, slide, slink, slip, snake, tiptoe; SEE CONCEPTS *151,207*

stealthy [adj] *quiet and secretive*
catlike, catty*, clandestine, covert, crafty, cunning, enigmatic, feline, furtive, hush-hush*, noiseless, private, secret, shifty, silent, skulking, slinking, sly, sneak, sneaking, sneaky, sub-rosa*, surreptitious, undercover, underhand, under wraps*, wily; SEE CONCEPTS *401,576*

steam [n] *energy*
beef, force, might, muscle, potency, power, puissance, sinew, strength, vigor, vim; SEE CONCEPT *633*

steel [v] *prepare oneself*
animate, brace, buck up*, cheer, embolden, encourage, fortify, gird, grit teeth*, harden, hearten, inspirit, make up one's mind*, prepare, rally, ready, reinforce, strengthen; SEE CONCEPT *35*

steep [adj1] *extreme in direction, course*
abrupt, arduous, breakneck, declivitous, elevated, erect, headlong, high, hilly, lifted, lofty, perpendicular, precipitate, precipitous, prerupt, raised, sharp, sheer, straight-up; SEE CONCEPT *581*

steep [adj2] *very expensive*
dizzying, excessive, exorbitant, extortionate, extreme, high, immoderate, inordinate, overpriced, stiff, towering, uncalled-for, undue, unmeasurable, unreasonable; SEE CONCEPTS *334,762*

steep [v] *let soak*
bathe, damp, drench, fill, imbue, immerse, impregnate, infuse, ingrain, invest, macerate, marinate, moisten, permeate, pervade, saturate, soak, sodden, sop, souse, submerge, suffuse, waterlog; SEE CONCEPT *256*

steer [v] *guide, direct on a course*
beacon, be in the driver's seat*, captain, conduct, control, drive, escort, govern, head for, helm, herd, lead, pilot, point, route, run, run things, see, shepherd, show, skipper*, take over, take the helm, take the reins; SEE CONCEPTS *94,187*

stem [n] *stalk of plant*
axis, branch, pedicel, pedicle, peduncle, petiole, shoot, stock, trunk; SEE CONCEPT *428*

stem [v1] *come from*
arise, be bred, be brought about, be caused, be generated, derive, develop, emanate, flow, head, issue, originate, proceed, rise, spring; SEE CONCEPT *648*

stem [v2] *prevent, stop*
arrest, bring to a standstill, check, contain, control, curb, dam, hinder, hold back, oppose, resist, restrain, stay, withstand; SEE CONCEPT *121*

stench [n] *foul odor*
fetor, funk*, malodor, mephitis, noisomeness, redolence, smell, stink*; SEE CONCEPTS *599,600*

step [n1] *pace of feet in walking*
footfall, footprint, footstep, gait, impression, mark, print, spoor, stepping, stride, trace, track, trail, tread, vestige, walk; SEE CONCEPT *149*

step [n2] *action, move*
act, advance, advancement, deed, degree, expedient, gradation, grade, level, maneuver, means, measure, motion, notch, phase, point, procedure, proceeding, process, progression, rank, remove, rung, stage, start; SEE CONCEPTS *1,832*

step [n3] *one level of stairs*
doorstep, gradation, notch, rest, round, run, rung, stair, tread; SEE CONCEPTS *440,445*

step [v] *move foot to walk*
advance, ambulate, ascend, dance, descend, go backward, go down, go forward, go up, hoof, mince, move backward, move forward, pace, prance, skip, stride, tiptoe, traipse, tread, trip, troop, walk; SEE CONCEPT *149*

step in [v] *become involved*
arrive, be invited, chip in*, come, enter, intercede, interfere, intermediate, interpose, intervene, lend a hand*, mediate, negotiate, take action; SEE CONCEPTS *100,324,384*

step up [v] *accelerate*
augment, boost, escalate, hasten, hurry, improve, increase, intensify, lift, quicken, raise, shake up, speed, speed up, up; SEE CONCEPTS *236,244,245*

stereotype [n] *idea held as standard, example*
average, boilerplate*, convention, custom, fashion, formula, institution, mold, pattern, received idea; SEE CONCEPT *686*

stereotype [v] *categorize as being example, standard*
catalogue, conventionalize, define, dub, institutionalize, methodize, normalize, pigeonhole*, regulate, standardize, systematize, take to be, typecast*; SEE CONCEPTS *38,49*

stereotyped [adj] *standard, conventional*
banal, clichéd, cliché-ridden, commonplace, corny*, dull, hackneyed, mass-produced, ordinary, overused, platitudinous, played out*, stale, standardized, stock, threadbare*, tired*, trite, unoriginal, well-worn, worn-out, worn thin; SEE CONCEPT *530*

sterile [adj] *unproductive, clean*
antiseptic, arid, aseptic, bare, barren, bleak, dead, decontaminated, desert, desolate, disinfected, dry, effete, empty, fallow, fruitless, futile, gaunt, germ-free, hygienic, impotent, infecund, infertile, pasteurized, sanitary, septic, sterilized, unfruitful, uninfected, unprofitable, unprolific, vain, waste, without issue; SEE CONCEPTS *485,621*

sterilize [v] *make clean or unproductive*
alter, antisepticize, ascepticize, aseptify, autoclave, castrate, change, clean, decontaminate, desexualize, disinfect, emasculate, fix, fumigate, incapacitate, make sterile, neuter, pasteurize, purify, sanitize, spay; SEE CONCEPTS *231,250*

stern [adj] *serious, authoritarian*
ascetic, astringent, austere, bitter, bullheaded, by the book*, cruel, disciplinary, dyed-in-the-wool*, flinty, forbidding, frowning, grim, hang-tough*, hard, hard-boiled*, hard-core*, hardheaded*, hard-line*, hard-nosed*, hard-shell*, harsh, implacable, inexorable, inflexible, mortified, mulish, relentless, rigid, rigorous, rough, severe, steely, stiff-necked*, strict, stubborn, tough, unrelenting, unsparing, unyielding; SEE CONCEPTS *401,542*

stew [n1] *mixture, miscellany*
brew, goulash*, hash, jumble, medley, mélange, mishmash, mulligan*, olio*, pasticcio*, pie*, potpourri, salmagundi*, soup; SEE CONCEPTS *432,457,460,461*

stew [n2] *commotion; mental upset*
agitation, confusion, dither, flap, fretting, fuming, fuss, lather, pother, snit, sweat, tizzy, tumult, turbulence, turmoil, worry; SEE CONCEPT *410*

stew [v] *worry; steam*
boil, chafe, cook, fret, fume, fuss, pother, seethe, simmer; SEE CONCEPT *35*

stick [n] *pole, often wooden*
bar, bat, baton, billet, birch, bludgeon, board, branch, cane, club, cudgel, drumstick, ferrule, ingot, mast, rod, rule, ruler, shoot, slab, slat, staff, stake, stalk, stave, stem, strip, switch, timber, twig, wand, wedge; SEE CONCEPTS *470,479*

stick [v1] *adhere, affix*
attach, be bogged down, become embedded, become immobilized, bind, bond, braze, catch, cement, clasp, cleave, cling, cling like ivy*, clog, cohere, fasten, fix, freeze to, fuse, glue, hold, hold fast, hold on, hug, jam, join, linger, lodge, paste, persist, remain, snag, solder, stay, stay put, stick like barnacle*, stick together, unite, weld; SEE CONCEPTS *85,160*

stick [v2] *poke with pointed object*
dig, drive, gore, impale, insert, jab, penetrate, pierce, pin, plunge, prod, puncture, ram, run, sink, spear, stab, thrust, transfix; SEE CONCEPT *220*

stick [v3] *position, lay*
deposit, drop, establish, fix, install, place, plant, plonk, plunk, put, set, settle, store, stuff; SEE CONCEPT *201*

stick [v4] *endure*
abide, bear, bear up under, brook, get on with, go, grin and bear it*, last, persist, put up with, see through, stand, stay, stomach*, suffer, support, take, take it, tolerate, weather; SEE CONCEPT *23*

stick-in-the-mud [n] *person set in ways*
antediluvian, conservative, diehard*, fossil*, mossback*, old fogy*, reactionary; SEE CONCEPT *423*

stick out [v] *bulge*
beetle, come through, extend, extrude, jut, obtrude, outthrust, overhang, poke, pouch, pout, project, protend, protrude, push, show, stand out; SEE CONCEPT *751*

sticky [adj1] *gummy, adhesive*
agglutinative, clinging, gluey, glutinous, ropy, syrupy, tacky, tenacious, viscid, viscous; SEE CONCEPT *606*

sticky [adj2] *humid and hot*
clammy, close, dank, mucky, muggy, oppressive, soggy, sultry, sweltering; SEE CONCEPT *525*

sticky [adj3] *difficult, embarrassing*
awkward, delicate, discomforting, formidable, hairy*, hard, heavy*, knotty, laborious, nasty, operose, painful, rough, rugged, strenuous, thorny, tricky, unpleasant; SEE CONCEPT *565*

stiff [adj1] *hard, inflexible*
annealed, arthritic, benumbed, brittle, buckram, cemented, chilled, congealed, contracted, creaky, firm, fixed, frozen, graceless, hardened, immalleable, impliable, incompliant, indurate, inelastic, jelled, mechanical, numbed, ossified, petrified, refractory, resistant, rheumatic, rigid, set, solid, so-

lidified, starched, starchy, stark, steely, stiff as a board*, stony, taut, tense, thick, thickened, tight, unbending, unflexible, ungraceful, unsupple, unyielding, wooden; SEE CONCEPT **604**

stiff [adj2] formal, standoffish

angular, artificial, austere, ceremonious, cold, constrained, forced, hardheaded, headstrong, inflexible, intractable, labored, mannered, obstinate, pertinacious, pompous, priggish, prim, punctilious, relentless, starchy, stilted, strong, stubborn, uneasy, ungainly, ungraceful, unnatural, unrelaxed, unrelenting, wooden; SEE CONCEPT **401**

stiff [adj3] difficult

arduous, exacting, fatiguing, formidable, hard, laborious, tough, trying, uphill; SEE CONCEPT **565**

stiff [adj4] extreme, severe

austere, brisk, cruel, drastic, exact, excessive, exorbitant, extravagant, great, hard, harsh, heavy, immoderate, inexorable, inordinate, oppressive, pitiless, potent, powerful, rigorous, sharp, steep, strict, stringent, strong, towering, unconscionable, undue, vigorous; SEE CONCEPTS **540,569**

stiffen [v] make or become harder

anneal, benumb, brace, cake, candy, cement, chill, clot, coagulate, condense, congeal, crystallize, curdle, firm, fix, freeze, gel, harden, inflate, inspissate, jell, jelly, ossify, petrify, precipitate, prop, reinforce, set, solidify, stabilize, starch, steady, strengthen, tauten, tense, thicken; SEE CONCEPTS **137,250,469**

stifle [v] prevent, restrain

asphyxiate, black out, bring to screeching halt*, burke, check, choke, choke back, clamp down*, clam up*, constipate, cork, cover up, crack down*, curb, dry up*, extinguish, gag, hold it down, hush, hush up, kill*, muffle, muzzle, prevent, put the lid on*, repress, restrain, shut up, silence, sit on*, smother, spike, squash, squelch, stagnate, stop, strangle, stultify, suffocate, suppress, torpedo*, trammel; SEE CONCEPTS **121,130,191**

stigma [n] shame

bar sinister*, besmirchment, black mark*, blame, blemish, blot, brand, disfigurement, disgrace, dishonor, imputation, lost face*, mark, odium, onus, reproach, scar, slur, spot, stain, taint; SEE CONCEPTS **230,388,689**

still [n] quiet

hush, noiselessness, peace, quietness, quietude, silence, soundlessness, still, stillness, tranquillity; SEE CONCEPTS **65,748**

still [adj] calm, motionless, quiet

at rest, buttoned up*, clammed up*, closed, close-mouthed, deathlike, deathly, deathly quiet, deathly still, fixed, halcyon, hushed, hushful, inert, lifeless, noiseless, pacific, peaceful, placid, restful, sealed, serene, silent, smooth, soundless, stable, stagnant, stationary, stock-still, tranquil, undisturbed, unruffled, unstirring, untroubled, whist; SEE CONCEPTS **584,594**

still [v] make quiet, motionless, calm

allay, alleviate, appease, arrest, balm, becalm, calm, choke, compose, decrease volume, fix, gag, hush, lull, muffle, muzzle, pacify, quieten, settle, shush*, shut down, shut up, silence, slack, smooth, smooth over, soothe, squash, squelch, stall, stop, subdue, tranquilize; SEE CONCEPTS **7,22,65,121**

still [conj] however

after all, besides, but, even, for all that, furthermore, howbeit, nevertheless, nonetheless, notwithstanding, still and all, though, withal, yet; SEE CONCEPT **544**

stilted [adj] artificial, pretentious

affected, angular, aureate, bombastic, constrained, decorous, egotistic, euphuistic, flowery, forced, formal, genteel, grandiloquent, high-flown, high-sounding, inflated, labored, magniloquent, mincing, overblown, pedantic, pompous, prim, rhetorical, sonorous, stiff, unnatural, wooden; SEE CONCEPTS **267,401**

stimulant [n] substance that invigorates

analeptic, bracer, catalyst, drug, energizer, excitant, goad, impetus, impulse, incentive, incitation, incitement, motivation, motive, pick-me-up*, restorative, reviver, shot in the arm*, spark plug*, spur, stimulus, tonic, upper; SEE CONCEPTS **240,307,661**

stimulate [v] excite, provoke

activate, animate, arouse, build a fire under*, commove, dynamize, elate, encourage, energize, enliven, exhilarate, fan, fire, fire up*, foment, foster, galvanize, get one going*, get one started*, goad, grab, hook, impel, incite, inflame, innervate, innerve, inspire, instigate, jazz*, juice*, key up*, motivate, move, perk, pique, prod, prompt, quicken, rouse, send, set up, spark, spirit, spur, steam up*, stir up*, support, trigger, turn on*, urge, vitalize, vivify, wake up*, whet, work up*; SEE CONCEPTS **14,242**

stimulus [n] provocation

bang*, boost, catalyst, cause, charge, encouragement, eye-opener*, fillip, fireworks*, flash*, goad, impetus, impulse, incentive, incitation, incitement, inducement, instigation, invitation, kick*, motivation, nerve, piquing, propellant, provocation, push, shot in the arm*, spur, stimulant, stimulation, sting*, turn-on*, urging; SEE CONCEPTS **240,307,661**

sting [v] prick, pain

bite, burn, electrify, hurt, injure, inspire, needle, pique, poke, prickle, smart, tingle, wound; SEE CONCEPTS **220,246,313,728**

stingy [adj] penny-pinching, averse to spending money

acquisitive, avaricious, chary, cheap, chintzy*, churlish, close, close-fisted, costive, covetous, curmudgeonly, economical, extortionate, frugal, grasping, greedy, grudging, ignoble, illiberal, ironfisted, mean, miserly, narrow, near, parsimonious, pennywise*, penurious, petty, pinchpenny*, rapacious, saving, scrimping, scurvy, selfish, skimping, sordid, sparing, thrifty, tight-fisted, uncharitable, ungenerous, ungiving; SEE CONCEPTS **326,334,401**

stink [n] bad smell

fetor, foulness, foul odor, malodor, noisomeness, offensive smell, stench; SEE CONCEPTS **599,600**

stink [v1] smell badly

be offensive, be rotten, funk*, have an odor, offend, reek*, smell up, stink to high heaven*; SEE CONCEPT **600**

stink [v2] be lousy, bad

be abhorrent, be detestable, be held in disrepute, be no good, be offensive, be rotten, have a bad name*, smell; SEE CONCEPTS **230,388**

stint [n] period of responsibility

assignment, bit, chore, consignment, duty, job,

participation, quota, share, shift, spell, stretch, task, term, time, tour, turn, work; SEE CONCEPTS 362,807,822

stint [v] *economize; hold back*
be frugal, begrudge, be parsimonious, be sparing, be stingy, confine, cut corners*, define, go easy on, grudge, limit, make ends meet*, penny-pinch*, pinch, restrain, roll back*, save, save for rainy day*, scrape, scrimp, skimp on*, sock away*, spare, squirrel*, stash, tighten belt*, withhold; SEE CONCEPT 330

stipend [n] *payment for services*
allowance, award, consideration, emolument, fee, gratuity, hire, pay, pension, salary, take, wage; SEE CONCEPT 344

stipulate [v] *decide on conditions*
agree, arrange, bargain, condition, contract, covenant, designate, detail, engage, guarantee, impose, insist upon, lay down, lay finger on, make, make a point, name, particularize, pin down, pledge, postulate, promise, provide, put down for, require, settle, slot, specificate, specificize, specify, spell out, state; SEE CONCEPTS 8,18,60

stipulation [n] *condition of agreement*
agreement, arrangement, circumscription, clause, contract, designation, engagement, fine print*, limit, obligation, precondition, prerequisite, provision, proviso, qualification, requirement, reservation, restriction, settlement, sine qua non, small print*, specification, string attached*, term, terms; SEE CONCEPTS 270,318,684

stir [n] *commotion, excitement*
activity, ado, agitation, backwash*, bustle, din, disorder, disquiet, disturbance, ferment, flap*, flurry, furor, fuss, movement, pandemonium, pother, racket, row, scene, to-do*, tumult, turmoil, uproar, whirl, whirlwind; SEE CONCEPTS 230,388

stir [v1] *mix up, agitate*
beat, blend, disturb, flutter, mix, move, move about, quiver, rustle, shake, toss, tremble, whip, whisk; SEE CONCEPTS 158,170

stir [v2] *incite, stimulate*
abet, actuate, add fuel to fire*, addy*, affect, agitate, animate, arouse, awaken, bestir, challenge, craze, drive, electrify, energize, excite, feed the fire*, foment, galvanize, impel, inflame, inspire, kindle, make waves*, motivate, move, prompt, provoke, psych*, quicken, raise, rally, rile, rouse, roust, rout, set, spark, spook*, spur, stimulate, stir embers*, stir up, switch on, thrill, touch, trigger, urge, vitalize, wake, waken, whet, whip up*, work up*; SEE CONCEPTS 14,221

stir [v3] *get up and going*
awake, awaken, bestir, be up and about, budge, exert, get a move on*, get moving, hasten, look alive, make an effort, mill about, move, rouse, shake a leg*, wake, waken; SEE CONCEPT 149

stock [n1] *merchandise*
accumulation, array, articles, assets, assortment, backlog, cache, choice, commodities, fund, goods, hoard, inventory, nest egg*, produce, range, reserve, reservoir, selection, stockpile, store, supply, variety, wares; SEE CONCEPT 338

stock [n2] *animals raised on a farm*
animals, beasts, cattle, cows, domestic, farm animals, flock, fowl, herd, hogs, horses, livestock, pigs, sheep, swine; SEE CONCEPTS 394,397

stock [n3] *ancestry*
background, breed, clan, descent, extraction, fam-

ily, folk, forebears, house, kin, kindred, line, lineage, line of descent, parentage, pedigree, race, species, strain, tribe, type, variety; SEE CONCEPTS 296,378

stock [n4] *investment in company*
assets, blue chips, bonds, capital, convertible, funds, over-the-counter*, paper, property, share; SEE CONCEPT 332

stock [n5] *estimation, faith*
appraisal, appraisement, assessment, confidence, count, dependence, estimate, evaluation, figure, hope, inventory, judgment, reliance, review, trust; SEE CONCEPTS 37,689,764

stock [adj] *commonplace*
banal, basic, common, conventional, customary, dull, established, formal, hackneyed, normal, ordinary, overused, regular, routine, run-of-the-mill*, set, standard, staple, stereotyped, traditional, trite, typical, usual, worn-out; SEE CONCEPTS 530,547

stock [v] *supply with merchandise*
accumulate, amass, carry, deal in, equip, fill, furnish, gather, handle, have, hoard, keep, keep on hand, lay in, provide, provision, put away, reserve, save, sell, stockpile, store, stow away, trade in; SEE CONCEPTS 140,182,324

stocky [adj] *short and overweight; short and muscular*
chunky, corpulent, fat, heavyset, plump, solid, squat, stout, stubby, sturdy, thick, thickset; SEE CONCEPTS 491,773

stodgy [adj] *dull, stuffy*
banausic, boring, dim, dreary, formal, heavy, labored, monotonous, pedantic, pedestrian, plodding, ponderous, staid, tedious, turgid, unexciting, unimaginative, uninspired, uninteresting, weighty; SEE CONCEPTS 401,404

stoic/stoical [adj] *philosophic, calm*
aloof, apathetic, cool, cool as cucumber*, detached, dispassionate, dry, enduring, impassive, imperturbable, indifferent, indomitable, long-suffering, matter-of-fact, patient, phlegmatic, resigned, rolling with punches*, self-controlled, sober, stolid, unconcerned, unemotional, unflappable, unmoved; SEE CONCEPTS 401,404

stolid [adj] *apathetic, stupid*
blunt, bovine, dense, doltish, dry, dull, dumb, heavy, impassive, inactive, inert, lumpish, matter-of-fact, obtuse, passive, phlegmatic, slow, stoic, supine, unemotional, unexcitable, wooden; SEE CONCEPTS 401,402

stomach [n1] *digestive organ of animate being; exterior abdominal region*
abdomen, belly, below the belt*, breadbasket*, gut, inside, insides, maw*, paunch, pot*, potbelly*, solar plexus, spare tire*, tummy*; SEE CONCEPTS 393,420

stomach [n2] *appetite*
appetence, desire, inclination, mind, relish, taste, tooth; SEE CONCEPT 20

stomach [v] *endure, tolerate*
abide, bear, bear with, bite the bullet*, brook, digest, grin and bear it*, live with*, put up with, reconcile oneself, resign oneself, stand, submit to, suffer, swallow, sweat, take, tolerate; SEE CONCEPT 23

stone [n] *hard piece of earth's surface*
boulder, crag, crystal, gem, grain, gravel, jewel, metal, mineral, ore, pebble, rock; SEE CONCEPTS 474,477

stony [adj] hard, icy in appearance, response
adamant, blank, callous, chilly, cold, cold-blooded, coldhearted, cruel, expressionless, firm, frigid, hard-boiled*, hardened, heartless, hostile, indifferent, inexorable, inflexible, merciless, obdurate, pitiless, rough, tough, uncompassionate, unfeeling, unforgiving, unrelenting, unresponsive, unsympathetic; SEE CONCEPTS 401,485

stoop [n] slouched posture
droop, round shoulders, sag, slouch, slump; SEE CONCEPT 757

stoop [v1] bow down
be bowed, bend, be servile, bow, cringe, crouch, descend, dip, duck, hunch, incline, kneel, lean, relax, sink, slant, squat; SEE CONCEPTS 181,201

stoop [v2] condescend; lower oneself to another
accommodate, act beneath oneself, concede, debase oneself, deign, demean oneself, descend, favor, oblige, patronize, relax, resort, sink, thaw, unbend, vouchsafe; SEE CONCEPTS 35,384

stop [n1] end, halt; impediment
bar, barricade, blank wall*, block, blockade, break, break off, brick wall*, cease, cessation, check, close, closing, conclusion, control, cutoff, desistance, discontinuation, ending, fence, finish, freeze*, grinding halt*, hindrance, layoff, letup, lull, pause, plug, roadblock*, screeching halt*, standstill, stay, stoppage, termination, wall; SEE CONCEPTS 240,832

stop [n2] visit; place of rest
break, depot, destination, halt, rest, sojourn, stage, station, stay, stopover, termination, terminus; SEE CONCEPTS 198,227

stop [v1] bring or come to a halt or end
be over, blow off*, break, break off, call it a day*, cease, close, cold turkey*, come to a standstill*, conclude, cool it*, cut out*, cut short, desist, discontinue, draw up, drop, end, finish, halt, hang it up*, hold, kill, pause, pull up, put an end to, quit, quit cold*, refrain, run its course*, scrub*, shut down, sign off*, stall, stand, stay, tarry, terminate, wind up*, wrap up*; SEE CONCEPTS 119,234,237

stop [v2] prevent, hold back
arrest, avoid, bar, block, bottle, break, check, choke, choke off, clog, close, congest, cut off, disrupt, fill, fix, forestall, frustrate, gag, hinder, hush, impede, intercept, interrupt, muzzle, obstruct, occlude, plug, put a stop to, rein in, repress, restrain, seal, shut down, shut off, shut out, silence, stall, staunch, stay, stem, still, stopper, suspend, throw over, turn off, ward off; SEE CONCEPT 121

stopgap [n] temporary help
Band-Aid*, expediency, expedient, improvisation, makeshift, pis aller*, recourse, refuge, resort, resource, shift, substitute, temporary expedient; SEE CONCEPT 712

stopgap [adj] temporarily helping
Band-Aid*, emergency, expedient, impromptu, improvised, makeshift, practical, provisional, rough-and-ready*, rough-and-tumble*, substitute, temp, temporary, throwaway*; SEE CONCEPTS 551,560

stoppage [n] halt, curtailment
abeyance, arrest, blockage, check, close, closure, cutoff, deduction, discontinuance, down, downtime*, hindrance, interruption, layoff, lockout, obstruction, occlusion, shutdown, sit-down, standstill, stopping, walkout; SEE CONCEPT 832

store [n1] collection, supply
abundance, accumulation, backlog, cache, fount, fountain, fund, hoard, inventory, lode, lot, mine, nest egg*, plenty, plethora, provision, quantity, reserve, reservoir, savings, spring, stock, stockpile, treasure, wares, wealth, well; SEE CONCEPTS 432,710

store [n2] place for keeping supply
arsenal, bank, barn, box, cache, conservatory, depository, depot, magazine, pantry, repository, reservoir, stable, storehouse, storeroom, tank, treasury, vault, warehouse; SEE CONCEPTS 439,441,448,494

store [n3] business establishment that sells goods
boutique, chain store, convenience store, deli, department store, discount house, discount store, drugstore, emporium, five-and-dime*, five-and-ten*, grocery store, market, mart, outlet, repository, shop, shopping center, showroom, specialty shop, stand, storehouse, super*, superette*, supermarket; SEE CONCEPTS 325,439,448,449

store [v] collect and put aside
accumulate, amass, bank, bin, bottle, bury, cache, can, cumulate, deposit, freeze, garner, hide, hive, hoard, hutch, keep, keep in reserve, lay away, lay up*, lock away, lock up, mothball*, pack, pack away, park, plant, put, put away, put by, put in storage, reserve, roll up, salt away*, save, save for rainy day*, sock away*, squirrel*, stash, stock, stockpile, treasure, victual, warehouse; SEE CONCEPTS 109,129

storm [n1] strong weather
blast, blizzard, blow, cloudburst, cyclone, disturbance, downpour, gale, gust, hurricane, monsoon, precip*, precipitation, raining cats and dogs*, snowstorm, squall, tempest, tornado, twister, whirlwind, windstorm; SEE CONCEPT 526

storm [n2] commotion, turmoil
agitation, anger, annoyance, assault, attack, barrage, blitz, blitzkrieg, bluster, bomb, bombardment, broadside, burst, bustle, cannonade, clamor, clatter, convulsion, disturbance, drumfire, furor, fury, fusillade, hail, hassle, hysteria, offensive, onset, onslaught, outbreak, outburst, outcry, passion, perturbation, pother, rabidity, racket, rage, rampancy, roar, row, ruction, rumpus, rush, salvo, squall, stir, strife, temper, tumult, upheaval, violence, volley; SEE CONCEPTS 86,230,674

storm [v] attack, rush
aggress, assail, assault, beset, blow violently, bluster, breathe fire*, burn up, carry on*, charge, come at*, complain, drizzle, drop, fly, fume, go on, howl, pour, rage, rain, rant, rave, rip, roar, scold, set in, sizzle, sound off*, spit, squall, stalk, steam up*, stomp, strike, take by storm*, take on*, tear, thunder*; SEE CONCEPTS 52,86,150,526

stormy [adj] rough (referring to weather)
bitter, blowy, blustering, blustery, boisterous, cold, coming down*, damp, dirty, foul, frigid, furious, gusty, howling, menacing, murky, pouring, raging, raining cats and dogs*, rainy, riproaring*, roaring, savage, squally, stormful, storming, tempestuous, threatening, torrid, turbulent, violent, wet, wild, windy; SEE CONCEPT 525

story [n1] account, news
adventure, allegory, anecdote, apologue, article, autobiography, beat, biography, book, chronicle, cliffhanger*, comedy, conte, description, drama,

st
st

epic, fable, fairy tale, fantasy, feature, fiction, folktale, gag, history, information, legend, long and short of it*, memoir, myth, narration, narrative, news item, nonfiction, novel, old saw*, parable, potboiler*, recital, record, relation, report, romance, saga, scoop*, sequel, serial, spiel*, tale, tragedy, version, yarn*; SEE CONCEPTS 270,274,282

story [n2] *lie*
canard, cock-and-bull story*, fabrication, falsehood, falsity, fib, fiction, misrepresentation, prevarication, tale, untruism, untruth, white lie*; SEE CONCEPTS 278,282

stout [adj1] *overweight*
big, bulky, burly, corpulent, fat, fleshy, heavy, obese, plenitudinous, plump, porcine, portly, rotund, substantial, thick-bodied, tubby, upholstered, weighty, zaftig*; SEE CONCEPTS 491,773

stout [adj2] *strong, brawny*
able-bodied, athletic, hard, hardy, hulking, husky, indomitable, invincible, lusty, muscular, robust, stable, stalwart, staunch, strapping, sturdy, substantial, tenacious, tough, vigorous; SEE CONCEPTS 489,490

stout [adj3] *courageous*
bold, brave, dauntless, fearless, gallant, heroic, intrepid, lionhearted, plucky, resolute, stalwart, undaunted, valiant, valorous; SEE CONCEPTS 403,542

stow [v] *reserve, store*
bundle, deposit, load, pack, pack like sardines*, put away, secrete, stash, stuff, top off, tuck, warehouse*; SEE CONCEPT 209

straggle [v] *wander, stray*
be late, dawdle, drift, lag, loiter, maunder, meander, poke, poke around, ramble, range, roam, rove, scramble, spread, straddle, string out, tail, trail; SEE CONCEPT 151

straight [adj1] *aligned; not curved*
beeline*, collinear, consecutive, continuous, direct, erect, even, horizontal, in a line, in a row, inflexible, in line, invariable, level, like an arrow*, lineal, linear, near, nonstop, perpendicular, plumb, precipitous, rectilineal, rectilinear, right, running, sheer, short, smooth, solid, square, straightforward, successive, through, true, unbent, unbroken, uncurled, undeviating, undistorted, uninterrupted, unrelieved, unswerving, upright, vertical; SEE CONCEPTS 482,486,581

straight [adj2] *honest, fair*
aboveboard, accurate, authentic, bald, blunt, candid, categorical, decent, equitable, fair and square*, forthright, frank, good, honorable, just, law-abiding, moral, outright, plain, point-blank*, reliable, respectable, straightforward, summary, trustworthy, unqualified, upright; SEE CONCEPTS 267,542

straight [adj3] *orderly*
arranged, correct, exact, in order, neat, organized, put to rights, proper, shipshape*, sorted, tidy; SEE CONCEPTS 535,585

straight [adj4] *unmixed*
concentrated, neat, out-and-out*, plain, pure, strong, thoroughgoing, unadulterated, undiluted, unmodified, unqualified; SEE CONCEPTS 462,621

straight [adj5] *conventional, square*
bourgeois, buttoned-down*, conservative, orthodox, traditional; SEE CONCEPT 404

straight [adv1] *immediately, directly*
as the crow flies*, at once, away, dead*, direct,

due, exactly, first off, forthwith, in direct line, instanter, instantly, lineally, now, point-blank*, right, right away, straightaway, straightforwardly, straightly, undeviatingly; SEE CONCEPTS 581,820

straight [adv2] *honestly*
candidly, frankly, in plain English*, no holds barred*, no punches*, point-blank*; SEE CONCEPTS 267,544

straighten [v] *put in neat or aligned order*
align, arrange, compose, correct, even, level, make plumb, make straight, neaten, order, put in order, put perpendicular, put straight, put to rights, put upright, put vertical, rectify, set to rights, smarten up*, spruce up*, tidy, unbend, uncoil, uncurl, unfold, unravel, unsnarl, untwist; SEE CONCEPTS 158,202,231

straightforward [adj1] *honest*
aboveboard, barefaced*, candid, direct, forthright, frank, genuine, guileless, honorable, just, laid on the line*, level, like it is*, mellow*, open, outspoken, plain, plain-dealing*, pretenseless, right-on*, sincere, square-shooting*, straight, straight-arrow*, talking turkey*, truthful, unconcealed, undisguised, undissembled, undissembling, unequivocal, unvarnished, up front*, upright, upstanding, veracious; SEE CONCEPT 267

straightforward [adj2] *simple, easy*
apparent, clear, clear-cut, direct, distinct, elementary, evident, manifest, palpable, patent, plain, routine, straight, through, unambiguous, uncomplicated, undemanding, unequivocal, uninterrupted; SEE CONCEPTS 535,538

strain [n1] *pain, due to exertion*
ache, anxiety, bruise, brunt, burden, constriction, effort, endeavor, exertion, force, injury, jerk, pressure, pull, sprain, stress, stretch, struggle, tautness, tension, tensity, twist, wrench; SEE CONCEPT 728

strain [n2] *ancestry*
blood, breed, descent, extraction, family, lineage, pedigree, race, species, stock; SEE CONCEPTS 296,380

strain [n3] *suggestion, hint*
humor, manner, mind, shade, soupçon, spirit, streak, style, suspicion, temper, tendency, tinge, tone, touch, trace, trait, vein, way; SEE CONCEPTS 410,529,682

strain [n4] *melody*
air, descant, diapason, lay, measure, song, tune, warble; SEE CONCEPTS 262,595

strain [v1] *stretch, often to limit*
constrict, distend, distort, draw tight, drive, exert, extend, fatigue, injure, overexert, overtax, overwork, pull, push, push to the limit, rack, sprain, task, tauten, tax, tear, tighten, tire, twist, weaken, wrench; SEE CONCEPTS 156,206,208,313

strain [v2] *work very hard*
bear down, endeavor, exert, go all out*, go for broke*, grind, hammer, hustle, labor, moil, peg away*, plug, push, strive, struggle, sweat, toil, try; SEE CONCEPT 87

strain [v3] *filter*
exude, percolate, purify, refine, riddle, screen, seep, separate, sieve, sift; SEE CONCEPTS 135,202

strain [v4] *cause mental stress*
distress, harass, hassle, irk, pain, pick at, pain, stress, trouble, try; SEE CONCEPTS 7,19

strained [adj] *forced, pretended*
artificial, at end of rope*, awkward, choked, constrained, difficult, embarrassed, false, farfetched,

hard put*, in a state*, labored, nervous wreck*, put, self-conscious, stiff, strung out*, taut, tense, tight, uncomfortable, uneasy, unglued, unnatural, unrelaxed, uptight, wired*, wreck*; SEE CONCEPTS 267,401

strait [n1] *crisis, difficulty*
bewilderment, bind, bottleneck*, choke point*, contingency, crossroad, dilemma, distress, embarrassment, emergency, exigency, extremity, hardship, hole*, mess*, mystification, pass, perplexity, pinch*, plight, predicament, rigor, squeeze*, turning point*, vicissitude, zero hour*; SEE CONCEPT 674

strait [n2] *water channel*
inlet, narrows, sound; SEE CONCEPT 514

strand [n] *fine thread*
fiber, filament, length, lock, rope, string, tress; SEE CONCEPTS 392,452,475

stranded [adj] *marooned, abandoned*
aground, ashore, beached, cast away, godforsaken*, grounded, helpless, high and dry*, homeless, left at the altar*, left in the lurch*, on the rocks*, out in left field*, passed up, penniless, run aground, shipwrecked, sidelined, sidetracked*, wrecked; SEE CONCEPT 577

strange [adj1] *deviating, unfamiliar*
aberrant, abnormal, astonishing, astounding, atypical, bizarre, curious, different, eccentric, erratic, exceptional, extraordinary, fantastic, far-out*, funny, idiosyncratic, ignorant, inexperienced, irregular, marvelous, mystifying, new, newfangled*, odd, oddball*, off, offbeat*, outlandish, out-of-the-way*, peculiar, perplexing, quaint, queer, rare, remarkable, singular, unaccountable, unaccustomed, uncanny, uncommon, unheard of*, unseasoned, unusual, weird, wonderful; SEE CONCEPT 564

strange [adj2] *exotic, foreign*
alien, apart, awkward, detached, external, faraway, irrelevant, isolated, lost, new, novel, out of place, outside, remote, romanesque, romantic, unexplored, unfamiliar, unknown, unrelated, untried; SEE CONCEPTS 549,576

stranger [n] *person who is unfamiliar*
alien, drifter, foreign body, foreigner, guest, immigrant, incomer, interloper, intruder, itinerant person, migrant, migratory worker, new arrival, newcomer, outcomer, outlander, out-of-stater*, outsider, party crasher*, perfect stranger*, squatter*, transient, uninvited person, unknown, unknown person, visitor, wanderer; SEE CONCEPTS 413,423

strangle [v] *choke, stifle*
asphyxiate, gag, garrote/garrotte, inhibit, kill, muffle, quelch, repress, restrain, shush, smother, squelch, strangulate, subdue, suffocate, suppress, throttle; SEE CONCEPTS 130,191,252

strap [n] *long piece of material*
band, belt, harness, leash, strop, switch, thong, tie, whip; SEE CONCEPTS 471,475

strapped [adj] *destitute*
beggared, broke*, dirt poor*, flat*, fortuneless, impoverished, out of money, penniless, penurious, poor, stone-broke*; SEE CONCEPT 334

strapping [adj] *big and strong*
brawny, burly, hefty, hulk, hulking, hunk, husky, ox, powerful, powerhouse, robust, stalwart, stout, sturdy, tall, vigorous, well-built; SEE CONCEPTS 489,773

stratagem [n] *trick*
action, angle, artifice, bit*, booby trap*, brainchild*, con, deception, device, dodge, feint, gambit, game, game plan*, gimmick, grift, intrigue, layout, maneuver, method, pitch, plan, play, plot, ploy, pretext, proposition, racket, ruse, scenario, scene, scheme, setup, shift, slant, stall, story, subterfuge, switch, twist, wile; SEE CONCEPTS 59,660

strategic [adj1] *crucial*
cardinal, critical, decisive, imperative, important, key, vital; SEE CONCEPTS 546,567

strategic [adj2] *clever, calculated*
cunning, deliberate, diplomatic, dishonest, planned, politic, tricky; SEE CONCEPT 544

strategy [n] *plan of action*
action, angle, approach, artifice, blueprint*, brainchild*, craft, cunning, design, game, game plan*, gimmick, grand design, layout, maneuvering, method, plan, planning, policy, procedure, program, project, proposition, racket*, scenario, scene, scheme, setup, slant, story, subtlety, system, tactics; SEE CONCEPT 660

stray [adj] *abandoned, wandering*
devious, erratic, homeless, lost, roaming, roving, vagrant; SEE CONCEPT 583

stray [v1] *deviate, err*
circumlocute, depart, digress, divagate, diverge, do wrong, excurse, get off the subject*, get off the track*, get sidetracked*, go off on a tangent*, ramble, rove, straggle, swerve, traipse, turn, wander away, wander off; SEE CONCEPTS 101,266

stray [v2] *wander; get lost*
be abandoned, be lost, deviate, drift, err, gad*, gallivant, go all over the map*, go amiss, go astray, lose one's way, meander, ramble, range, roam, rove, straggle, swerve, traipse, turn, wander away, wander off; SEE CONCEPT 149

streak [n] *vein, line; small part*
band, bar, beam, dash, element, hint, intimation, layer, ray, ridge, rule, shade, slash, smear, strain, stream, strip, stripe, stroke, suggestion, suspicion, touch, trace; SEE CONCEPTS 436,628,657,727

streak [v] *make a line on*
band, dapple, daub, fleck, marble, slash, smear, spot, strake, striate, stripe, variegate, vein; SEE CONCEPT 250

stream [n] *small river*
beck, branch, brook, burn, course, creek, current, drift, flood, flow, freshet, race, rill, rindle, rivulet, run, runnel, rush, spate, spritz, surge, tide, torrent, tributary, watercourse; SEE CONCEPT 514

stream [v] *flow from*
cascade, continue, course, emerge, emit, flood, glide, gush, issue, move past, pour, roll, run, shed, sluice, spill, spout, spritz, spurt, surge; SEE CONCEPTS 146,179

street [n] *path upon which travel occurs*
artery, avenue, back alley*, boulevard, byway, court, dead end*, drag*, drive, highway, lane, parkway, passage, pavement, place, road, roadway, route, row, stroll, terrace, thoroughfare, track, trail, turf*, way; SEE CONCEPT 501

strength [n1] *stamina, mental or physical*
backbone, body, brawn, brawniness, brute force*, clout, courage, durability, energy, firmness, force, fortitude, hardiness, health, healthiness, lustiness, might, muscle, nerve, physique, pith, potency, pow*, power, powerhouse*, robustness, security, sinew, sock*, soundness, stability, stableness, stalwartness, steadiness, steamroller,

st
st

stoutness, strong arm*, sturdiness, substance, tenacity, toughness, verdure, vigor, vim, vitality, zip*; SEE CONCEPTS *410,732*

strength [n2] *intensity*

clout, cogency, concentration, depth, effectiveness, efficacy, energy, extremity, fervor, force, juice*, kick*, potency, power, resolution, spirit, vehemence, vigor, virtue; SEE CONCEPT *669*

strength [n3] *advantage, substance*

anchor, asset, body, burden, connection, core, gist, guts, in, intestinal fortitude, license, mainstay, meat, pith, purport, security, sense, strong point, succor, upper hand, weight, wire; SEE CONCEPTS *682,693*

strengthen [v1] *make more forceful, powerful*

add, add fuel to fire*, anneal, ascend, bolster, brace, build up, buttress, confirm, corroborate, empower, enhance, enlarge, establish, extend, fortify, harden, heighten, increase, intensify, invigorate, justify, make firm, mount, multiply, regenerate, reinforce, rejuvenate, renew, restore, rise, set up, sinew*, steel, step up, substantiate, support, sustain, temper, tone, tone up, toughen, wax*; SEE CONCEPTS *244,250*

strengthen [v2] *encourage, hearten*

animate, back, back up, bear out, bloom, brace, brace up, burgeon, carry weight, cheer, consolidate, embolden, enhearten, enliven, flourish, flower, fortify, gather resources, gird, give weight, harden, inspirit, invigorate, nerve, nourish, prepare, prosper, rally, ready, refresh, rejuvenate, restore, steel, substantiate, temper, thrive, toughen, uphold; SEE CONCEPTS *7,22,35*

strenuous [adj1] *difficult; requiring hard work*

arduous, demanding, effortful, energy-consuming, exhausting, hard, Herculean, laborious, mean, operose, taxing, toilful, toilsome, tough, tough going*, uphill*, wicked; SEE CONCEPT *538*

strenuous [adj2] *energetic, zealous*

active, aggressive, ardent, bold, determined, dynamic, eager, earnest, lusty, persistent, red-blooded, resolute, spirited, strong, tireless, vigorous, vital; SEE CONCEPTS *401,542*

stress [n1] *emphasis*

accent, accentuation, beat, force, import, importance, significance, urgency, weight; SEE CONCEPTS *65,668*

stress [n2] *physical or mental pressure*

affliction, agony, alarm, albatross*, anxiety, apprehensiveness, burden, clutch, crunch, disquiet, disquietude, distention, draw, dread, expectancy, extension, fear, fearfulness, ferment, flutter, force, hardship, hassle, heat, impatience, intensity, misgiving, mistrust, nervousness, nervous tension, oppression, overextension, passion, protraction, pull, restlessness, spring, strain, stretch, tautness, tenseness, tension, tensity, tightness, traction, trauma, trepidation, trial, urgency, worry; SEE CONCEPTS *410,720,728*

stress [v1] *accentuate, emphasize*

accent, belabor, dwell on, feature, harp on*, headline*, italicize*, lay emphasis on, make emphatic, play up, point up, repeat, rub in*, spot, spotlight*, underline*, underscore*; SEE CONCEPTS *49,68*

stress [v2] *put under physical or mental pressure*

afflict, burden, crunch, distend, force, fret, hassle, overdo, overextend, pull, put in traction*, put on trial*, spring, strain, stretch, tense, tense up*, traumatize, worry; SEE CONCEPTS *7,19,246,313*

stretch [n1] *expanse*

amplitude, area, branch, breadth, bridge, compass, dimension, distance, expansion, extension, extent, gamut, length, orbit, proliferation, purview, radius, range, reach, region, scope, space, span, spread, sweep, tract, wing; SEE CONCEPTS *651,721,746*

stretch [n2] *period of time*

bit, continuance, duration, extent, length, run, space, span, spell, stint, term, time, while; SEE CONCEPTS *807,822*

stretch [v] *extend, elongate*

amplify, branch out, bridge, burst forth, cover, crane, develop, distend, drag out, draw, draw out, expand, fill, go, grow, inflate, lengthen, lie out, magnify, make, make taut, make tense, open, overlap, pad, prolong, prolongate, protract, pull, pull out, pyramid, rack, range, reach, recline, repose, run, shoot up, span, spin out, spread, spread out, spring up, strain, string out, swell, tauten, tighten, unfold, unroll, widen; SEE CONCEPTS *137,250*

strict [adj1] *authoritarian*

austere, dead set*, disciplinary, dour, draconian*, exacting, firm, forbidding, grim, hard, hard-boiled*, harsh, iron-fisted*, no-nonsense*, oppressive, picky, prudish, punctilious, puritanical, rigid, rigorous, scrupulous, set, severe, square, stern, stickling, straight, strait-laced*, stringent, stuffy*, tough, unpermissive, unsparing, uptight*; SEE CONCEPTS *401,542*

strict [adj2] *accurate, absolute*

close, complete, exact, faithful, just, meticulous, particular, perfect, precise, religious, right, scrupulous, total, true, undistorted, utter, veracious, veridical; SEE CONCEPTS *535,557*

stride [v] *walk purposefully*

clump, drill, march, pace, parade, pound, stalk, stamp, stomp, striddle, stump, traipse, tramp, tromp; SEE CONCEPT *149*

strident [adj] *harsh, shrill*

blatant, boisterous, clamorous, clashing, discordant, grating, hoarse, jangling, jarring, loud, noisy, obstreperous, rasping, raucous, screeching, squawky, squeaky, stentorian, stertorous, stridulant, stridulous, unmusical, vociferant, vociferous; SEE CONCEPTS *592,594*

strife [n] *struggle, battle*

affray, altercation, animosity, argument, bickering, blowup, brawl, clash, combat, competition, conflict, contention, contest, controversy, difference, disagreement, discord, dispute, dissension, dissent, dissidence, disunity, emulation, faction, factionalism, fighting, friction, fuss, hassle, quarrel, rivalry, spat, squabble, squabbling, static, striving, tug of war*, variance, warfare, words*, wrangle, wrangling; SEE CONCEPTS *46,106,674*

strike [v] *hit hard*

bang, bash, beat, boff, bonk, box, buffet, bump into, chastise, clash, clobber, clout, collide, conk*, crash, cuff*, drive, force, hammer, impel, knock, percuss, plant*, pop*, pound, pummel, punch, punish, run into, slap, slug, smack, smash into, sock, swat, thrust, thump, touch, wallop, whop*; SEE CONCEPT *189*

strike [v2] *make an impact*

affect, be plausible, carry, come to mind*, dawn on*, get*, have semblance, hit*, impress, influence, inspire, look, move, occur to, reach, register*, seem, sway, touch; SEE CONCEPTS *7,19,22,716*

strike [v3] *find, discover*

achieve, arrive at, attain, catch, chance upon*, come across, come upon, dig up*, effect, encounter, happen upon*, hit upon*, lay bare*, light upon, open up, reach, seize, stumble across*, take, turn up*, uncover, unearth; SEE CONCEPTS *120,183*

strike [v4] *devastate, affect*

afflict, aggress, assail, assault, attack, beset, deal a blow, excruciate, fall upon, harrow, hit, invade, martyr, rack, set upon, smite, storm, torment, torture, try, wring; SEE CONCEPTS *7,19*

strike [v5] *walk out of job in protest*

arbitrate, be on strike, boycott, go on strike, hit the bricks*, hold out, mediate, mutiny, negotiate, picket, quit, refuse to work, resist, revolt, sit down*, sit in*, slow down, stick out, stop, tie up; SEE CONCEPT *351*

strike out [v] *leave to begin new venture*

bear, begin, get under way*, head, initiate, light out*, make, set out, start, start out, take off*; SEE CONCEPT *195*

striking [adj] *extraordinary; beautiful*

arresting, arrestive, astonishing, attractive, bizarre, charming, cogent, commanding, compelling, confounding, conspicuous, dazzling, distinguished, dynamite, electrifying, eye-catching, fascinating, forceful, forcible, handsome, impressive, jazzy*, lofty, marked, memorable, noteworthy, noticeable, out of the ordinary*, outstanding, powerful, prominent, remarkable, salient, showy, signal, singular, staggering, startling, stunning, surprising, telling, unusual, wonderful, wondrous; SEE CONCEPTS *574,579*

string [n1] *long fiber*

cord, rope, strand, twine, twist; SEE CONCEPT *475*

string [n2] *succession, series*

chain, consecution, echelon, file, line, order, procession, queue, rank, row, sequel, sequence, strand, tier, train; SEE CONCEPTS *727,769*

string along [v] *play with; keep dangling*

bluff, coquet, dally, deceive, dupe, flirt, fool, hoax, lead on*, put one over on*, take for a ride*, toy, trifle, wanton; SEE CONCEPT *59*

stringent [adj] *rigid, tight*

acrimonious, binding, brick-wall*, by the book*, by the numbers*, compelling, confining, convincing, dead set on*, demanding, draconian, drawing, dyed-in-the-wool*, exacting, forceful, hard, hard-nosed*, harsh, inflexible, ironclad, iron-fisted, picky, poignant, powerful, rigorous, rough, set, severe, stiff, strict, tough, unpermissive, valid; SEE CONCEPTS *401,535,569*

stringy [adj] *long, thin*

fibrous, gangling, gristly, lank, lanky, muscular, reedy, ropy, sinewy, spindling, spindly, thread-like, tough, wiry; SEE CONCEPT *490*

strip [n] *thin piece of material*

band, banding, bar, belt, billet, bit, fillet, ingot, layer, ribbon, rod, section, segment, shred, slab, slip, stick, stripe, swathe, tape, tongue; SEE CONCEPTS *471,834*

strip [v] *bare, uncover*

decorticate, denude, deprive, despoil, dismantle, displace, disrobe, divest, empty, excorticate, expose, gut, hull, husk, lay bare, lift, peel, pillage,

plunder, ransack, ravage, remove, rob, scale, shave, shed, shuck, skin, slip out of, spoil, take off, tear, unclothe, undress, withdraw; SEE CONCEPT *211*

stripe [n] *line, strip*

band, banding, bar, border, decoration, division, fillet, layer, ribbon, rule, streak, striation, stroke; SEE CONCEPTS *284,622*

strive [v] *try for, exert oneself*

aim, assay, attempt, bear down, bend over backward*, break one's neck*, compete, contend, do one's best*, do one's utmost*, drive, endeavor, essay, fight, go after, go all out*, go for broke*, go for the jugular*, go the limit*, hassle, jockey*, knock oneself out*, labor, leave no stone unturned*, make every effort, moil, offer, push, scramble, seek, shoot for*, strain, struggle, sweat, tackle, take on, toil, try hard, tug*, work; SEE CONCEPT *87*

stroke [n1] *accomplishment*

achievement, blow*, feat, flourish, hit*, move, movement; SEE CONCEPT *706*

stroke [n2] *seizure*

apoplexy, attack, collapse, convulsion, fit, shock; SEE CONCEPTS *33,308*

stroke [v] *pat lengthwise*

brush, caress, chuck, comfort, fondle, pet, rub, smooth, soothe, tickle; SEE CONCEPT *612*

stroll [n] *lazy walk*

airing, breath of fresh air*, constitutional, cruise, excursion, promenade, ramble, saunter, turn; SEE CONCEPT *151*

stroll [v] *walk along lazily*

amble, cruise, drift, gallivant, linger, make one's way*, mope*, mosey, promenade, ramble, roam, rove, sashay*, saunter, toddle, traipse, tramp, wander; SEE CONCEPT *151*

strong [adj1] *healthy, powerful*

able, able-bodied, active, athletic, big, capable, durable, enduring, energetic, firm, fixed, forceful, forcible, hale, hard as nails*, hardy, hearty, heavy, heavy-duty*, in fine feather*, mighty, muscular, reinforced, robust, rugged, secure, sinewy, solid, sound, stable, stalwart, stark, staunch, steady, stout, strapping, sturdy, substantial, tenacious, tough, unyielding, vigorous, well-built, well-founded, well-made; SEE CONCEPTS *314,489,540*

strong [adj2] *determined, resolute*

aggressive, brave, clear, cogent, courageous, dedicated, deep, eager, fervent, fervid, fierce, firm, forceful, gutsy*, handful*, hard-nosed*, independent, intelligent, intense, iron-willed, keen, mean, perceptive, plucky, potent, pushy, resilient, resourceful, sagacious, self-assertive, severe, staunch, steadfast, take charge*, tenacious, tough, unbending, uncompromising, unyielding, vehement, violent, wicked*, zealous; SEE CONCEPTS *403,542*

strong [adj3] *distinct, unmistakable*

clear, clear-cut, cogent, compelling, convincing, effective, fast, firm, forceful, formidable, great, hard, influential, marked, mighty, overpowering, persuasive, potent, powerful, redoubtable, secure, sharp, sound, stiff, stimulating, telling, trenchant, urgent, weighty, well-established, well-founded; SEE CONCEPTS *535,537*

strong [adj4] *extreme*

acute, draconian, drastic, forceful, intense, keen, severe, sharp, strict; SEE CONCEPT *569*

st
st

strong [adj5] *forceful on the senses*
biting, bold, bright, brilliant, concentrated, dazzling, effective, fetid, full-bodied, glaring, hard, heady, high, highly flavored, highly seasoned, hot, inebriating, intoxicating, loud, malodorous, noisome, piquant, potent, powerful, pungent, pure, rancid, rank, rich, robust, sharp, spicy, stark, stimulating, stinking, straight, strong-flavored, undiluted, unmixed; SEE CONCEPTS 462,598,618

stronghold [n] *refuge*
bastion, bulwark, castle, citadel, fastness, fort, fortification, fortress, garrison, keep, presidio, redoubt; SEE CONCEPTS 439,712

structure [n1] *makeup, form*
anatomy, architecture, arrangement, build, complex, configuration, conformation, construction, design, fabric, fabrication, format, formation, frame, framework, interrelation, make, morphology, network, order, organization, skeleton, system, texture; SEE CONCEPT 733

structure [n2] *building*
cage, construction, edifice, erection, fabric, house, pile, pile of bricks*, rockpile, skyscraper; SEE CONCEPT 439

struggle [n] *hard try; fight to win*
attempt, battle, brush, clash, combat, conflict, contest, effort, encounter, endeavor, essay, exertion, free-for-all*, grind, hassle, jam, jump, labor, long haul*, pains*, roughhouse*, row, scramble, set-to*, skirmish, strife, striving, toil, trial, tussle, undertaking, work, wrangle; SEE CONCEPTS 87,106,674

struggle [v1] *labor, work*
assay, attempt, bend over backwards*, break one's back*, break one's neck*, cope, dig, endeavor, exert oneself, give it one's best shot*, give the old college try*, go all out*, grind, hassle, have one's nose to grindstone*, hustle, make every effort*, offer, plug, plug away*, scratch, seek, slave, strain, strive, sweat, tackle, take a crack*, take a stab*, take on, toil, try, try one's hardest*, undertake, work like a dog*; SEE CONCEPT 87

struggle [v2] *fight, wrestle*
battle, brawl, buck, bump heads*, compete, contend, contest, cross swords*, go up against*, grapple, hassle, lock horns*, put up a fight*, romp, rough-house*, row, scrap, scuffle, shuffle, slug, smack, tangle; SEE CONCEPT 106

strut [v] *walk pompously*
flaunt, flounce, grandstand*, mince, parade, peacock*, play to audience, prance, put on airs*, sashay*, show off, stalk, stride, swagger, swank, sweep; SEE CONCEPTS 149,261

stub [n] *stumpy end*
butt, counterfoil, dock, remainder, remnant, root, short end*, snag, stump, tag, tail, tail end*; SEE CONCEPTS 825,827

stubborn [adj] *obstinate, unyielding*
adamant, balky, bullheaded, cantankerous, contumacious, cussed*, determined, dogged, firm, fixed, hardheaded, headstrong, inexorable, inflexible, insubordinate, intractable, mulish, obdurate, opinionated, ornery*, persevering, persistent, pertinacious, perverse, pigheaded*, rebellious, recalcitrant, refractory, relentless, rigid, self-willed, set in one's ways*, single-minded, steadfast, stiffnecked*, tenacious, tough, unbending, unman-

ageable, unreasonable, unshakable, untoward, willful; SEE CONCEPTS 401,404

stubby [adj] *short and thick*
fat, heavyset, squat, stocky, stout, stumpy, thick-bodied, thickset; SEE CONCEPTS 491,773,779

student [n] *person actively learning*
apprentice, disciple, docent, first-year student, grad, graduate, junior, learner, novice, observer, pupil, registrant, scholar, schoolchild, skill, sophomore, undergrad*, undergraduate; SEE CONCEPT 350

studied [adj] *intentional*
advised, affected, aforethought, calculated, conscious, considered, deliberate, designed, examined, gone into, investigated, planned, plotted, premeditated, prepared, prepense, purposeful, reviewed, studious, thought-about, thoughtful, thought-out, thought-through, voluntary, well-considered, willful, willing; SEE CONCEPTS 538,548

studious [adj] *scholarly, attentive*
academic, assiduous, bookish*, bookworm*, busy, careful, contemplative, diligent, eager, earnest, grubbing, hard-working, industrious, intellectual, learned, lettered, meditative, reflective, sedulous, serious, thoughtful, well-informed, well-read; SEE CONCEPTS 402,538

study [n] *learning, analysis*
abstraction, academic work, analyzing, application, attention, class, cogitation, comparison, concentration, consideration, contemplation, course, cramming, debate, deliberation, examination, exercise, inquiry, inspection, investigation, lesson, meditation, memorizing, muse, musing, pondering, questioning, reading, reasoning, reflection, research, reverie, review, rumination, schoolwork, scrutiny, subject, survey, thought, trance, weighing; SEE CONCEPTS 31,103

study [v1] *contemplate, learn*
apply oneself, bone up*, brood over, burn midnight oil*, bury oneself in*, coach, cogitate, consider, crack the books*, cram, dig*, dive into*, examine, excogitate, go into, go over, grind*, hit the books*, inquire, learn, learn the ropes*, lucubrate, meditate, mind, mull over, perpend, peruse, plug*, plunge, polish up*, ponder, pore over*, read, read up, refresh, think, think out, think over, tutor, weigh; SEE CONCEPT 31

study [v2] *examine, analyze*
brainstorm*, canvass, case, check out, check over, check up, compare, deliberate, do research, figure, give the eagle eye*, inspect, investigate, keep tabs*, look into, peruse, read, research, scope, scrutinize, sort out, survey, view; SEE CONCEPT 103

stuff [n1] *personal belongings*
being, effects, equipment, gear, goods, impedimenta, individual, junk*, kit, luggage, objects, paraphernalia, possessions, substance, tackle, things, trappings; SEE CONCEPTS 432,446

stuff [n2] *essence, substance*
bottom, bottom line*, essentiality, heart, marrow*, matter, meat*, nitty-gritty*, nuts and bolts*, pith, principle, quintessence, soul, staple, virtuality; SEE CONCEPTS 668,682

stuff [n3] *fabric*
cloth, material, raw material, textile, woven material; SEE CONCEPT 167

stuff [v] *load with*
choke up, clog up, compress, congest, cram,

crowd, fill, fill to overflowing, fill to the brim, force, glut, gobble, gorge, gormandize, guzzle, jam, jam-pack*, overfill, overindulge, overstuff, pack, pad, push, ram, sate, satiate, shove, squeeze, stow, wad, wedge; SEE CONCEPTS 169,209

stuffy [adj1] *close, oppressive*
airless, breathless, confined, fetid, heavy, humid, muggy, stagnant, stale, stifling, suffocating, sultry, thick, unventilated; SEE CONCEPT 525

stuffy [adj2] *old-fashioned, prim*
arrogant, bloated, conventional, dreary, dull, fusty, genteel, humorless, important, magisterial, musty, narrow-minded, pompous, priggish, prim and proper*, prissy, prudish, puffy, puritanical, self-important, staid, stilted, stodgy, straitlaced*, uninteresting, Victorian*; SEE CONCEPTS 401,404

stumble [v1] *slip, stagger*
blunder, bumble, careen, err, fall, fall down, falter, flounder, hesitate, limp, lose balance, lumber, lurch, muddle, pitch, reel, shuffle, stammer, swing, tilt, topple, totter, trip, wallow, waver, wobble; SEE CONCEPTS 101,181

stumble [v2] *happen upon*
blunder upon, bump, chance, chance upon*, come across, come up against, discover, encounter, fall upon, find, happen upon*, hit, light, light upon*, luck*, meet, run across, stub toe on*, tumble, turn up; SEE CONCEPTS 183,693

stump [n] *end piece*
butt, end, projection, stub, tail end, tip; SEE CONCEPTS 825,827

stump [v1] *confuse, bewilder*
baffle, bring up short, confound, dumbfound, foil, mystify, nonplus, outwit, perplex, puzzle, stagger, stick, stop, stymie; SEE CONCEPT 16

stump [v2] *walk with deliberation*
barge, clomp, clump, galumph, lumber, plod, stamp, stomp, stumble, trudge; SEE CONCEPT 149

stun/stupefy [v] *amaze, shock*
astonish, astound, bemuse, bewilder, blow away*, bowl over*, confound, confuse, daze, dumbfound, flabbergast, floor*, fog*, give a turn*, hit like ton of bricks*, knock out*, knock over*, knock unconscious, muddle, overcome, overpower, overwhelm, paralyze, petrify, rock*, shake up*, stagger, strike dumb*, surprise, take breath away*, throw a curve*; SEE CONCEPT 42

stunning [adj] *beautiful, marvelous*
beauteous, bonny, brilliant, comely, dazzling, devastating, excellent, fair, famous, fine, first-class*, first-rate*, gorgeous, great, handsome, heavenly, impressive, lovely, number one*, out of this world*, pretty, ravishing, remarkable, royal, sensational, smashing, spectacular, striking, superior, top, wonderful; SEE CONCEPTS 574,579

stunt [n] *deed, trick*
achievement, act, antic, caper, exploit, feat, feature, performance, sketch, skit, tour de force; SEE CONCEPTS 264,384

stunted [adj] *kept from growing*
bantam, diminutive, dwarf, dwarfed, dwarfish, half-pint*, little, measly, mite, peanut*, peewee*, pint-sized*, runted, runtish, runty, scrub, short, shot, shrimp*, small, small fry*, tiny, undergrown, undersized, wee*, yea big*, yea high*; SEE CONCEPTS 773,779

stupendous [adj] *wonderful, amazing*
astonishing, astounding, breathtaking, colossal,

dynamite, enormous, fab*, fabulous, fantastic, fat*, gigantic, great, huge, marvelous, mind-blowing*, mind-boggling*, miraculous, monster, monumental, overwhelming, phenomenal, prodigious, radical*, smashing, spectacular, staggering, stunning, super, superb, surprising, terrific, titantic, too much*, tremendous, unreal*, utmost*, vast, wonderful, wondrous; SEE CONCEPTS 574,781

stupid [adj] *not intelligent; irresponsible*
brainless, dazed, deficient, dense, dim, doltish, dopey*, dull, dumb, dummy*, foolish, futile, gullible, half-baked*, half-witted*, idiotic, ill-advised, imbecilic, inane, indiscreet, insensate, irrelevant, irresponsible, laughable, loser*, ludicrous, meaningless, mindless, moronic, naive, nonsensical, obtuse, out to lunch*, pointless, puerile, rash, senseless, shortsighted, simple, simpleminded, slow, sluggish, stolid, stupefied, thick, thick-headed*, trivial, unintelligent, unthinking, witless; SEE CONCEPTS 402,548

stupor [n] *daze, unconsciousness*
amazement, anaesthesia, apathy, asphyxia, bewilderment, coma, dullness, fainting, hebetude, hypnosis, inertia, inertness, insensibility, languor, lassitude, lethargy, narcosis, numbness, petrifaction, sleep, slumber, somnolence, sopor, stupefaction, suspended animation, swoon, swooning, torpor, trance; SEE CONCEPTS 315,316

sturdy [adj] *solid, durable*
athletic, built to last*, bulky, determined, durable, firm, flourishing, hardy, hearty, hefty, hulking, husky, lusty, muscular, powerful, powerhouse*, resolute, robust, rugged, secure, solid, sound, stalwart, staunch, steadfast, stiff, stout, stouthearted, strapping, strong, strong-arm*, substantial, tenacious, tough, unyielding, vigorous, well-built, well-made; SEE CONCEPTS 314,488,489

stutter [v] *speak haltingly*
dribble, falter, hesitate, splutter, sputter, stammer, stumble; SEE CONCEPT 77

style [n1] *fashion, manner*
appearance, approach, bearing, behavior, carriage, characteristic, cup of tea*, custom, cut*, description, design, druthers*, flash*, form, genre, groove*, habit, hand, idiosyncrasy, kind, method, mode, number, pattern, peculiarity, rage*, sort, spirit, strain, technique, tenor, thing*, tone, trait, trend, type, variety, vein, vogue, way; SEE CONCEPTS 411,655

style [n2] *fashionableness*
chichi*, comfort, cosmopolitanism, craze, dash, delicacy, dernier cri, dressiness, ease, élan, elegance, fad, flair, grace, grandeur, luxury, mode, panache, polish, rage, refinement, savoir-faire, smartness, sophistication, stylishness, taste, thing*, urbanity, vogue; SEE CONCEPTS 655,668

style [n3] *way of speaking, writing, expressing oneself*
diction, expression, mode of expression, phraseology, phrasing, treatment, turn of phrase*, vein, wording; SEE CONCEPT 276

style [v] *name, title*
address, baptize, call, christen, denominate, designate, dub, entitle, label, name, term; SEE CONCEPT 62

stylish [adj] *fashionable*
à la mode*, beautiful, chic, chichi*, classy, dap, dapper, dashing, dressed to kill*, dressed to the

st
st

teeth*, dressy, fly*, groovy*, high-class*, in, in fashion, in the mainstream*, in vogue, jazzy*, latest, mod*, modernistic, new, nifty, now*, ostentatious, polished, pretentious, rakish, ritzy, sassy*, sharp, showy, sleek, slick*, smart, snappy*, snazzy*, swank*, swell, tony*, trendy, upscale, up-to-date, uptown, urbane, voguish; SEE CONCEPTS 579,589

stymie [v] *frustrate, hinder*
balk, block, choke off, confound, corner, crab*, cramp, cramp one's style*, crimp, cut off, dead-end*, defeat, foil, give the run around*, hang fire*, hang up*, hold off, hold up, impede, mystify, nonplus, obstruct, pigeonhole*, prevent, put on back burner*, put on hold, puzzle, shelve, snooker*, stall, stonewall*, stump, throw a monkey wrench into*, thwart; SEE CONCEPTS 121,130

suave [adj] *charming, smooth*
affable, agreeable, bland, civilized, cordial, courteous, courtly, cultivated, cultured, diplomatic, distingué, fulsome, genial, glib, gracious, ingratiating, obliging, oily*, pleasant, pleasing, polished, polite, politic, refined, smooth-tongued*, sociable, soft*, soft-spoken, sophisticated, unctuous, urbane, well-bred, worldly; SEE CONCEPTS 401,404

subconscious [n] *inner thoughts*
essence, mind, psyche, soul, subconsciousness, subliminal, subliminal self, submerged mind, underconsciousness, undersense; SEE CONCEPT 410

subconscious [adj] *innermost in thought*
hidden, inmost, inner, intuitive, latent, mental, repressed, subliminal, suppressed, unconscious; SEE CONCEPT 529

subdivision [n] *smaller entity of whole*
class, community, development, group, lower group, minor group, subclass, subsidiary, tract; SEE CONCEPTS 513,835

subdue [v] *keep under control; moderate*
bear down, beat down, break, break in, check, conquer, control, crush, defeat, discipline, dominate, drop, extinguish, gentle, get the better of*, get the upper hand*, get under control, humble, mellow, overcome, overpower, overrun, put down, quash, quell, quench, quiet, quieten, reduce, repress, restrain, shut down, soften, squelch, subjugate, suppress, tame, temper, tone down, trample, triumph over, vanquish; SEE CONCEPTS 121,130,252

subdued [adj] *quiet, controlled*
chastened, crestfallen, dejected, dim, domestic, domesticated, downcast, down in the mouth*, grave, hushed, inobtrusive, low-key*, mellow*, moderated, muted, neutral, out of spirits*, repentant, repressed, restrained, sad, serious, shaded, sober, soft, softened, solemn, submissive, subtle, tasteful, tempered, toned down, unobtrusive; SEE CONCEPTS 401,403,594

subject [n1] *issue, matter*
affair, argument, business, case, chapter, class, core, course, discussion, field of reference, gist, head, idea, item, material, matter at hand, meat*, motif, motion, motive, object, point, principal object, problem, proposal, question, resolution, study, subject matter, substance, text, theme, theorem, thesis, thought, topic; SEE CONCEPTS 529,532,689

subject [n2] *one under authority or control of another*
case, client, customer, dependent, guinea pig*, liege, national, patient, serf, subordinate, vassal; SEE CONCEPTS 413,423

subject [adj] *at the mercy of; answerable*
accountable, apt, at one's feet*, bound by, captive, collateral, conditional, contingent, controlled, dependent, directed, disposed, enslaved, exposed, governed, in danger of, inferior, liable, likely, obedient, open, prone, provisional, ruled, satellite, secondary, sensitive, servile, slavish, sub*, subaltern, subjugated, submissive, subordinate, subservient, substract, susceptible, tentative, tributary, under, vulnerable; SEE CONCEPTS 552,575

subjective [adj] *emotional; based on inner experience rather than fact*
abstract, biased, fanciful, idiosyncratic, illusory, individual, instinctive, introspective, introverted, intuitive, nonobjective, nonrepresentative, personal, prejudiced, unobjective; SEE CONCEPTS 529,542

subjugate [v] *overpower, defeat*
bear down, beat down, bring to heel*, bring to knees*, coerce, compel, conquer, crush, enslave, enthrall, force, hold sway, keep under thumb*, kick around*, overcome, overthrow, put down, quell, reduce, reel back in*, rule, rule over, subdue, suppress, tame, triumph, vanquish; SEE CONCEPTS 95,117,133

sublime [adj] *great, magnificent*
abstract, august, divine, dynamite, elevated, eminent, exalted, glorious, gorgeous, grand, heavenly, high, holy, ideal, imposing, lofty, majestic, noble, outrageous, proud, resplendent, sacred, spiritual, splendiferous, splendorous, stately, super, superb, the most*, too much*, transcendent, transcendental; SEE CONCEPT 574

submerge [v] *dunk in liquid*
deluge, descend, dip, douse, drench, drown, duck, engulf, flood, go down, go under, immerse, impregnate, inundate, overflow, overwhelm, plunge, sink, sound, souse, submerse, subside, swamp, whelm; SEE CONCEPTS 181,256

submission [n] *compliance*
acquiescence, appeasement, assent, backing down, bowing, capitulation, cringing, defeatism, deference, docility, giving in, humbleness, humility, malleability, meekness, nonresistance, obedience, passivism, passivity, pliabilty, prostration, recreancy, resignation, servility, subjection, submissiveness, submitting, surrender, tractability, unassertiveness, yielding; SEE CONCEPT 633

submissive [adj] *compliant*
abject, accommodating, acquiescent, amenable, bowing down, comformable, complying, deferential, docile, domesticated, dutiful, giving-in*, humble, ingratiating, lowly, malleable, meek, menial, nonresistant, nonresisting, obedient, obeisant, obeying, obsequious, passive, patient, pliable, pliant, resigned, servile, slavish, subdued, tame, tractable, uncomplaining, unresisting, yes*, yielding; SEE CONCEPT 401

submit [v1] *comply, endure*
abide, accede, acknowledge, acquiesce, agree, appease, bend, be submissive, bow, buckle, capitulate, cave, cede, concede, defer, eat crow*, fold, give away, give ground, give in, give way, go with the flow*, grin and bear it*, humor, indulge, knuckle, knuckle under*, kowtow*, lay down arms, obey, put up with, quit, relent, relinquish, resign oneself, say uncle*, stoop, succumb, sur-

render, throw in the towel*, toe the line*, tolerate, truckle, withstand, yield; SEE CONCEPT *23*

submit [*v2*] *present, offer; argue for*
advance, advise, affirm, argue, assert, claim, commit, contend, hand in, make a pitch*, move, proffer, propose, proposition, propound, put, put forward, refer, state, suggest, table, tender, theorize, urge, volunteer; SEE CONCEPT *66*

subordinate [*n*] *person or thing that serves another*
aide, assistant, attendant, dependent, deputy, flunky*, gofer*, helper, inferior, junior, peon, poor relation*, scrub*, second, second fiddle*, second string*, serf, servant, slave, subaltern, third string*, underling; SEE CONCEPTS *348,423*

subordinate [*adj*] *lesser, supplementary*
accessory, adjuvant, ancillary, auxiliary, baser, below par, collateral, contributory, dependent, inferior, insignificant, junior, low, lower, minor, paltry, satellite, secondary, second-fiddle*, second-string*, smaller, sub, subaltern, subalternate, subject, submissive, subnormal, subservient, subsidiary, substract, tributary, under, underaverage, unequal; SEE CONCEPT *575*

subscribe [*v1*] *pay for use; contribute*
advocate, ante up*, buy, chip in*, come through*, consent, donate, do one's part*, endorse, enroll, give, grant, ink*, make a deal*, offer, pitch in*, pledge, promise, put up*, register, second, set, sign, signature, sign up*, support; SEE CONCEPTS *129,341*

subscribe [*v2*] *agree*
accede, acquiesce, advocate, approve, assent, autograph*, back, bless, boost, consent, cosign, countenance, ditto*, endorse, favor, get behind*, give stamp of approval* give the go-ahead*, go along with*, hold with*, ink*, obey, okay*, put John Hancock on*, rubber-stamp*, sanction, sign, signature, support, take, undersign, underwrite, yes*; SEE CONCEPTS *10,50,88*

subsequent [*adj*] *after*
consecutive, consequent, consequential, ensuing, following, later, next, posterior, postliminary, proximate, resultant, resulting, sequent, sequential, serial, subsequential, succeeding, successional, successive; SEE CONCEPTS *585,820*

subsequently [*adv*] *afterward*
after, afterwards, afterwhile, at a later date, behind, by and by, consequently, finally, infra, in the aftermath, in the end, later, latterly, next; SEE CONCEPTS *585,820*

subservient [*adj1*] *extremely compliant*
abject, acquiescent, a slave to*, at one's beck and call*, at one's mercy*, bootlicking, cowering, cringing, dancing, deferential, docile, fawning, ignoble, inferior, in one's clutches*, in one's pocket*, in one's power*, mean, menial, obeisant, obsequious, resigned, servile, slavish, subject, submissive, sycophantic, under one's thumb*; SEE CONCEPTS *401,404*

subservient [*adj2*] *secondary, useful*
accessory, adjuvant, ancillary, appurtenant, auxiliary, bush-league*, collateral, conducive, contributory, flunky, helpful, inferior, instrumental, minor, serviceable, subordinate, subsidiary, supplemental, supplementary; SEE CONCEPTS *560,575*

subside [*v*] *die down; decrease*
abate, cave in, collapse, decline, de-escalate, descend, die away, diminish, drop, dwindle, ease,

ease off, ebb, fall, let up, level off, lower, lull, melt, moderate, peter out*, quieten, recede, settle, sink, slacken, taper, wane; SEE CONCEPTS *181,698,776*

subsidiary [*adj*] *secondary, helpful*
accessory, adjuvant, aiding, ancillary, appurtenant, assistant, assisting, auxiliary, backup, branch, collateral, contributory, cooperative, lesser, minor, serviceable, subject, subordinate, subservient, supplemental, supplementary, tributory, useful; SEE CONCEPTS *560,575*

subsidize [*v*] *give money to get started*
angel*, back, bankroll*, contribute, endow, finance, fund, grubstake*, help, juice*, pick up the check*, pick up the tab*, prime the pump*, promote, put up the money for, sponsor, stake, support, underwrite; SEE CONCEPTS *110,341*

subsidy [*n*] *money given to help another*
aid, alimony, allowance, appropriation, assistance, bequest, bonus, bounty, contribution, endowment, fellowship, financial aid, gift, grant, gratuity, help, honorarium, indemnity, payment, pension, premium, reward, scholarship, subsidization, subvention, support, tribute; SEE CONCEPTS *337,344*

subsist [*v*] *keep going, living*
barely exist*, be, breathe, continue, eke out a living*, eke out an existence*, endure, exist, get along*, get by*, hang in*, hang on*, hang tough*, just make it*, last, live, make ends meet*, make it*, manage, move, remain, remain alive, ride out*, scrape by*, stay alive, stick it out*, stick with it*, survive, sustain; SEE CONCEPTS *23,330,407*

subsistence [*n*] *provisions for survival*
affluence, aliment, alimentation, bread*, bread and butter*, capital, circumstances, competence, earnings, existence, food, fortune, gratuity, income, independence, keep, legacy, livelihood, living, maintenance, means, money, necessities, nurture, pension, property, provision, ration, resources, riches, salary, salt*, substance, support, sustenance, upkeep, victuals, wages, wealth, wherewithal; SEE CONCEPTS *446,457,646,710*

substance [*n1*] *entity, element*
actuality, animal, being, body, bulk, concreteness, core, corpus, fabric, force, hunk, individual, item, mass, material, matter, object, person, phenomenon, reality, something, staple, stuff, texture, thing; SEE CONCEPTS *433,478,523*

substance [*n2*] *essence, meaning*
ABCs*, amount, basis, body, bottom, bottom line*, brass tacks*, burden, center, core, corpus, crux, drift, effect, essentiality, focus, general meaning, gist, gravamen, guts*, heart, import, innards, kernel, marrow, mass, matter, meat*, name of the game*, nitty-gritty*, nub, nuts and bolts*, pith, point, purport, quintessence, sense, significance, soul, staple, strength, stuff, subject, sum total*, tenor, theme, thrust, upshot, virtuality, way of it*; SEE CONCEPTS *682,689*

substance [*n3*] *wealth*
affluence, assets, estate, fortune, means, property, resources, riches, worth; SEE CONCEPT *335*

substantial [*adj1*] *important, ample*
abundant, big, big-deal*, bulky, consequential, considerable, durable, extraordinary, firm, generous, goodly, heavy, heavyweight, hefty, key, large, major-league*, massive, material, meaningful, momentous, plentiful, principal, serious, sig-

st
su

nificant, sizable, solid, sound, stable, steady, stout, strong, sturdy, superabundant, tidy, valuable, vast, weighty, well-built, worthwhile; SEE CONCEPTS 568,773,781

substantial [adj2] material, real
actual, card-carrying*, concrete, corporeal, existent, for real*, honest-to-god*, legit*, objective, phenomenal, physical, positive, righteous, sensible, solid, sure enough*, tangible, true, twenty-four-carat*, valid, visible, weighty; SEE CONCEPT 582

substantial [adj3] rich
affluent, comfortable, easy, opulent, prosperous, snug, solid, solvent, wealthy, well, well-heeled, well-off, well-to-do; SEE CONCEPT 334

substantially [adv] to a large extent
considerably, essentially, extensively, heavily, in essence, in fact, in reality, in substance, in the main, largely, mainly, materially, much, really; SEE CONCEPTS 569,772

substantiate [v] back up a statement, idea
actualize, affirm, approve, attest to, authenticate, bear out, check out, check up, complete, confirm, corroborate, debunk, demonstrate, establish, incarnate, justify, manifest, materialize, objectify, personify, prove, ratify, realize, reify, support, test, try, try on, try out, validate, verify; SEE CONCEPTS 49,138,317

substitute [n] someone or something that takes the place of another
agent, alternate, assistant, auxiliary, backup, changeling, delegate, deputy, dernier ressort*, double, dummy, equivalent, expediency, expedient, fill-in, ghost, ghost writer, locum, locum tenens, makeshift, pinch-hitter*, procurator, proxy, recourse, refuge, relay, relief, replacement, representative, reserve, resort, resource, stand-by, stand-in, stopgap*, sub*, succedaneum, successor, supplanter, supply, surrogate, symbol, temp*, temporary, temporary expedient, understudy, vicar; SEE CONCEPTS 423,712

substitute [adj] alternative
acting, additional, alternate, another, artificial, backup, counterfeit, dummy, ersatz*, experimental, false, imitation, makeshift, mock, near, other, provisional, proxy, pseudo*, replacement, representative, reserve, second, sham, simulated, spurious, stopgap*, substitutive, supplemental, supplementary, supposititious, surrogate, symbolic, temporary, tentative, vicarial, vicarious; SEE CONCEPTS 560,575

substitute [v] interchange, exchange
act for, alternate, answer for, back up, be in place of, change, commute, cover for, deputize, displace, do the work of, double for, fill in for, fill one's position, go as, proxy, relieve, replace, serve in one's stead, spell, stand for, stand in for, sub*, supersede, supplant, swap, swap places with*, switch, take another's place, take over; SEE CONCEPTS 87,104

subtle [adj1] nice, quiet, delicate
attenuate, attenuated, deep, discriminating, ethereal, exquisite, faint, fine, finespun, hairline, hairsplitting, illusive, implied, inconspicuous, indirect, indistinct, inferred, ingenious, insinuated, mental, penetrating, profound, refined, slight, sophisticated, suggestive, tenuous, thin, understated; SEE CONCEPTS 537,544

subtle [adj2] clever, cunning
analytic, analytical, artful, astute, complex, crafty, deep, designing, detailed, devious, dexterous, exacting, foxy, guileful, insidious, intriguing, keen, penetrating, perceptive, precise, ratiocinative, scheming, shrewd, skillful, sly, wily; SEE CONCEPT 402

subtract [v] take away
decrease, deduct, detract, diminish, discount, draw back, knock off, remove, take, take from, take off, take out, withdraw, withhold; SEE CONCEPTS 211,764

suburb [n] neighborhood outside of but reliant on nearby large city
bedroom community*, burb*, country, countryside, environs, fringe, hamlet, hinterland, outlying area, outpost, outskirts, precinct, purlieu, residential area, slub, suburbia, village; SEE CONCEPTS 508,512

subversive [adj] rebellious, destructive
incendiary, inflammatory, insurgent, insurrectionary, overthrowing, perversive, riotous, ruinous, seditious, treasonous, underground, undermining; SEE CONCEPT 401

subvert [v] rebel, destroy
capsize, contaminate, corrupt, debase, defeat, demolish, deprave, depress, extinguish, invalidate, invert, level, overthrow, overturn, pervert, poison, pull down, raze, reverse, ruin, sabotage, supersede, supplant, suppress, topple, tumble, undermine, upset, vitiate, wreck; SEE CONCEPTS 86,95,252

succeed [v1] attain good outcome
accomplish, achieve, acquire, arrive, avail, benefit, be successful, carry off*, come off*, conquer, distance, do all right*, do the trick*, earn, flourish, fulfill, gain, get, get to the top*, grow famous, hit*, make a fortune*, make good*, make it*, make out*, obtain, outdistance, outwit, overcome, possess, prevail, profit, prosper, pull off*, realize, reap, receive, recover, retrieve, score, secure, surmount, thrive, triumph, turn out*, vanquish, win, work, worst; SEE CONCEPTS 141,706

succeed [v2] come after; take the place of
accede, assume, be subsequent, come into, come into possession, come next, displace, ensue, enter upon, follow, follow after, follow in order, go next, inherit, postdate, replace, result, supersede, supervene, supplant, take over; SEE CONCEPTS 727,749,813

succeeding/successive [adj] following
alternating, consecutive, ensuing, following after, in a row, in line, next, next in line for, next in order, next off, next up, rotating, sequent, sequential, serial, seriate, subsequent, subsequential, succedent, successional; SEE CONCEPTS 585,811,812,818,820

success [n] favorable outcome
accomplishment, achievement, advance, arrival, ascendancy, attainment, bed of roses*, benefit, big hit*, boom*, clover*, consummation, do well, Easy Street*, éclat, eminence, fame, flying colors*, fortune, fruition, gain, good luck*, good times*, grand slam*, gravy train*, happiness, happy days*, hit, killing, lap of luxury*, laugher*, maturation, profit, progress, prosperity, realization, reward, savvy, sensation, snap, strike, successfulness, triumph, victory, walkaway*, walkover*, win; SEE CONCEPTS 693,706

successful [adj] favorable, profitable
acknowledged, advantageous, ahead of the game*, at the top*, at top of ladder*, auspicious,

bestselling, blooming, blossoming, booming, champion, crowned, efficacious, extraordinary, flourishing, fortuitous, fortunate, fruitful, happy, lucky, lucrative, moneymaking, notable, noteworthy, on track*, out in front*, outstanding, paying, prosperous, rewarding, rolling, strong, thriving, top, triumphant, unbeaten, undefeated, victorious, wealthy; SEE CONCEPT 528

succinct [adj] brief, to the point
blunt, boiled down*, breviloquent, brusque, compact, compendiary, compendious, concise, condensed, curt, cut to the bone*, in a nutshell*, in few words*, laconic, pithy, short, summary, terse; SEE CONCEPT 267

succulent [adj] juicy, delicious
divine, heavenly, luscious, lush, mellow, moist, mouthwatering, pulpy, rich, sappy, tasty, yummy*; SEE CONCEPTS 462,613

succumb [v] die or surrender
accede, bow, break down, buckle, capitulate, cave, cave in*, cease, collapse, croak, decease, defer, demise, depart, drop, eat crow*, expire, fall, fall victim to, flake out*, fold, give in, give into, give out, give up the ghost*, give way, go, go down, go under, knuckle, knuckle under*, meet waterloo*, pack it in*, pass, pass away, perish, quit, show white flag*, submit, take the count*, throw in the towel*, wilt, yield; SEE CONCEPTS 35,105,385

such [adj/conj] aforementioned, specific
aforesaid, akin, alike, analogous, comparable, corresponding, equivalent, like, parallel, said, similar, such a one, such a person, such a thing, suchlike, that, the like, this; SEE CONCEPT 557

sudden [adj] unexpected; happening quickly
abrupt, accelerated, acute, expeditious, fast, flash, fleet, hasty, headlong, hurried, immediate, impetuous, impromptu, impulsive, out of the blue*, precipitant, precipitate, precipitous, quick, quickened, rapid, rash, rushing, spasmodic, speeded, subito, swift, unforeseen, unusual; SEE CONCEPT 799

suddenly [adv] unexpectedly
aback, abruptly, all at once, all of a sudden, asudden, forthwith, on spur of moment*, quickly, short, sudden, swiftly, unanticipatedly, unaware, unawares, without warning; SEE CONCEPT 799

sue [v] bring legal charges against
accuse, appeal, beg, beseech, bring an action, charge, claim, claim damages, contest, demand, drag into court, enter a plea, entreat, file, file a claim, file suit, follow up, haul into court, have the law on, have up, indict, institute legal proceedings, litigate, petition, plead, prefer charges against, prosecute, pull up, put away, see in court, solicit, summon, supplicate, take out after, take to court; SEE CONCEPT 317

suffer [v1] be in pain
ache, agonize, ail, be affected, be at disadvantage, be convulsed, be handicapped, be impaired, be racked, be wounded, brave, complain of, deteriorate, droop, endure, experience, fall off, feel wretched, flag, get, go through, grieve, have a bad time*, hurt, languish, pain, sicken, smart, undergo, writhe; SEE CONCEPTS 308,313

suffer [v2] endure, permit
abide, accept, acquiesce, admit, allow, bear, bear with, bleed, bow, brave, brook, carry the torch*, concede, countenance, encounter, experience, feel, go through, have, hurt, indulge, know, let,

license, live with, put up with, receive, sanction, see, sit and take it, stand, stomach*, submit, support, sustain, swallow*, sweat*, take*, take it*, tolerate, undergo, wait out, yield; SEE CONCEPTS 23,83

suffering [n] pain, agony
adversity, affliction, anguish, difficulty, discomfort, distress, dolor, hardship, martyrdom, misery, misfortune, ordeal, passion, torment, torture; SEE CONCEPT 728

suffice [v] be adequate, enough
answer, avail, be good enough, be sufficient, be the ticket*, content, do, do the trick*, fill the bill*, get by, go over big*, hack it*, hit the spot*, make a hit*, make the grade*, meet, meet requirement, satisfy, serve, suit; SEE CONCEPT 713

sufficient [adj] enough, adequate
acceptable, agreeable, all right*, ample, aplenty, appreciate, comfortable, commensurable, commensurate, common, competent, copious, decent, due, galore, pleasing, plenteous, plentiful, plenty, proportionate, satisfactory, sufficing, tolerable, unexceptionable, unexceptional, unobjectionable; SEE CONCEPTS 558,560,771

suffocate [v] choke
asphyxiate, drown, smother, stifle, strangle; SEE CONCEPTS 163,246

suggest [v1] convey advice, plan, desire
advance, advise, advocate, broach, commend, conjecture, exhort, give a tip*, move, offer, plug*, pose, prefer, propone, propose, proposition, propound, put, put forward, put in two cents*, put on to something*, recommend, steer, submit, theorize, tip, tip off*, tout; SEE CONCEPT 75

suggest [v2] imply; bring to mind
adumbrate, advert, allude, be a sign of, connote, cross the mind, denote, evoke, hint, indicate, infer, insinuate, intimate, lead to believe, occur, point, point in direction of, promise, put in mind of, refer, represent, shadow, signify, symbolize, typify; SEE CONCEPTS 74,682

suggestion [n1] advice, plan
advancement, angle, approach, bid, big idea*, bit*, brainchild*, charge, commendation, exhortation, game plan*, gimmick, hot lead*, idea, injunction, instruction, invitation, lead, motion, opinion, outline, pitch, presentation, proffer, proposal, proposition, recommendation, reminder, resolution, scheme, setup, sneaking suspicion*, steer*, submission, telltale, tender, testimonial, thesis, tip, tip-off*; SEE CONCEPTS 278,689

suggestion [n2] hint, implication
allusion, association, autosuggestion, breath, clue, connotation, cue, indication, inkling, innuendo, insinuation, intimation, notion, overtone, reminder, self-suggestion, shade, signification, smack, soupçon, strain, suspicion, symbol, symbolism, symbolization, symbology, telltale, thought, tinge, trace, undertone, vein, whisper, wind; SEE CONCEPT 529

suggestive [adj1] signifying
evocative, evocatory, expressive, giving an inkling*, indicative, intriguing, pregnant, redolent, remindful, reminiscent, significative, symbolic, symptomatic; SEE CONCEPTS 267,529

suggestive [adj2] dirty, vulgar
bawdy, blue*, broad, erotic, immodest, improper, indecent, indelicate, obscene, off-color*, provocative, prurient, racy, ribald, risqué, rude, seduc-

tive, sexy, shady, tempting, titillating, unseemly, wicked; SEE CONCEPTS 372,545

suit [n1] *matching top and bottom clothing*
clothing, costume, dress, ensemble, getup*, gray flannel*, habit, livery, outfit, threads*, tuxedo, uniform, wardrobe; SEE CONCEPT 451

suit [n2] *legal action*
case, cause, lawsuit, litigation, proceeding, prosecution, trial; SEE CONCEPT 318

suit [n3] *appeal, request*
address, application, asking, attention, court, courtship, entreaty, imploration, imprecation, invocation, petition, plea, prayer, requesting, solicitation, soliciting, supplication, wooing; SEE CONCEPT 662

suit [v1] *be acceptable, appropriate*
accord, agree, answer, answer a need, become, befit, benefit, be proper for, beseem, be seemly, check, check out, conform, correspond, cut the mustard*, do, enhance, fill the bill*, fit, fit in, flatter, fulfill, get by, go, go together, go with, gratify, harmonize, make the grade*, match, pass muster*, please, satisfy, serve, square, suffice, tally; SEE CONCEPT 656

suit [v2] *adapt, tailor*
accommodate, adjust, amuse, change, conform, entertain, fashion, fill, fit, fit in, gratify, modify, please, proportion, quadrate, readjust, reconcile, revise, satisfy, tailor-make*, toe the mark*; SEE CONCEPTS 126,697

suitable [adj] *appropriate, acceptable*
advisable, applicable, apposite, apt, becoming, befitting, commodious, condign, convenient, co-pacetic, correct, cut out for*, deserved, due, expedient, felicitous, fit, fitting, good, good enough*, handy, happy, in character, in keeping*, just, kosher*, legit*, meet, merited, nice, okay*, opportune, peachy, pertinent, politic, presentable, proper, reasonable, relevant, requisite, right, righteous, rightful, satisfactory, seemly, sufficient, suited, swell, up to snuff*, useful, user friendly; SEE CONCEPT 558

suite [n1] *set of rooms or furniture*
apartment, array, batch, body, chambers, collection, flat, group, lodging, lot, parcel, rental, series, set, tenement; SEE CONCEPTS 441,516

suite [n2] *entourage of people*
array, attendants, batch, body, clutch, cortege, court, escort, faculty, followers, group, lot, retainers, retinue, servants, set, staff, train; SEE CONCEPT 417

suite [n3] *series*
chain, concatenation, consecution, line, order, progression, row, scale, sequel, sequence, string, succession, train; SEE CONCEPT 727

suitor [n] *person who desires another*
admirer, beau, boyfriend, cavalier*, courter, date, follower, girlfriend, lover, man, paramour, supplicant, swain, woman, wooer; SEE CONCEPT 423

sulk [v] *pout*
be down in the mouth*, be in a huff*, be morose, be out of sorts*, be silent, brood, frown, gloom, glower, gripe, grouse, grump*, look sullen, lower, moon*, mope*, scowl, take on; SEE CONCEPTS 35,52

sullen [adj] *brooding, upset*
bad-tempered, cheerless, churlish, crabbed*, crabby*, cross, cynical, dismal, dour, dull, fretful, frowning, gloomy, glowering, glum, gruff, grumpy*, heavy, hostile, ill-humored, inert, irri-table, malevolent, malicious, malign, mean, moody, morose, obstinate, ornery*, out of sorts*, peevish, perverse, pessimistic, petulant, pouting, pouty, querulous, saturnine, silent, somber, sour, sourpussed*, stubborn, sulking, sulky, surly, tenebrific, tenebrous, ugly, unsociable, uptight*; SEE CONCEPT 403

sultry [adj1] *hot and humid*
baking, broiling, burning, close, hot, mucky, muggy, oppressive, red-hot*, scorching, sizzling, smothering, soggy, sticky, stifling, stuffy, suffocating, sweltering, sweltry, torrid, wet; SEE CONCEPTS 525,605

sultry [adj2] *sensuous*
desirable, erotic, heavy*, hot*, lurid, passionate, provocative, seductive, sexy, steamy*, voluptuous, X-rated*; SEE CONCEPT 372

sum [n] *total*
aggregate, all, amount, body, bulk, entirety, entity, epitome, gross, integral, mass, quantity, reckoning, résumé, score, structure, summary, summation, sum total*, synopsis, system, tally, totality, value, whole, works*, worth; SEE CONCEPTS 432,784,787

summarily [adv] *without delay*
arbitrarily, at short notice, expeditiously, forthwith, immediately, on the spot, peremptorily, promptly, readily, speedily, swiftly, without waste; SEE CONCEPTS 544,799

summarize [v] *give a rundown*
abridge, abstract, boil down*, cipher, compile, condense, cut, cut back, cut down, digest, encapsulate, epitomize, get to meat*, give main points, inventory, outline, pare, precis, prune*, put in a nutshell*, recap*, recapitulate, rehash*, retrograde, review, run down*, run through*, shorten, skim, snip, sum, summate, sum up, synopsize, trim; SEE CONCEPTS 55,236,247

summary [n] *short statement of main points*
abbreviation, abridgment, abstract, analysis, apercu, brief, capitulation, case, compendium, condensation, conspectus, core, digest, epitome, essence, extract, inventory, long and short of it*, nutshell*, outline, pandect, precis, prospectus, recap*, recapitulation, reduction, rehash*, report, résumé, review, roundup, rundown, run-through, sense, skeleton*, sketch, sum and substance*, summing-up*, survey, syllabus, synopsis, version, wrap-up*; SEE CONCEPT 283

summary [adj] *concise, to the point*
arbitrary, boiled down*, breviloquent, brief, compact, compacted, compendiary, compendious, condensed, cursory, curt, hasty, in a nutshell*, laconic, perfunctory, pithy*, recapped, rehashed, run-down, run-through, short, short and sweet*, succinct, terse; SEE CONCEPTS 267,272

summer [n] *hot season of the year*
daylight savings time*, dog days*, heat, midsummer, picnic days*, riot time*, summer solstice, summertide, summertime, sunny season, vacation; SEE CONCEPT 814

summit [n] *top, crowning point*
acme, apex, apogee, capstone, climax, crest, crown, culmination, head, height, max, meridian, most, peak, pinnacle, roof, vertex, zenith; SEE CONCEPT 836

summon [v] *call to a place*
arouse, ask, assemble, beckon, beep, bid, call, call back, call for, call forth, call in, call into action, call together, call upon, charge, cite, com-

mand, conjure, convene, convoke, direct, draft, draw on, enjoin, gather, hail, invite, invoke, mobilize, motion, muster, order, petition, rally, recall, request, ring, rouse, send for, sign, signal, subpoena, toll; SEE CONCEPT 53

sumptuous [adj] *luxurious, splendid*
awe-inspiring, beautiful, costly, dear, deluxe, elegant, expensive, extravagant, gorgeous, grand, grandiose, imposing, impressive, lavish, luscious, luxuriant, magnificent, opulent, out of this world, palatial, plush, pompous, posh, prodigal, profuse, rich, ritzy*, splendiferous, superb, swank*, ultra*, upholstered; SEE CONCEPTS 334,485,574

sum up [v] *form an opinion of; summarize*
close, conclude, condense, digest, epitomize, estimate, examine, get the measure of, inventory, put in a nutshell*, recapitulate, review, size up, sum, synopsize, total; SEE CONCEPT 55

sundry [adj] *miscellaneous*
assorted, different, divers, manifold, many, quite a few, several, some, varied, various; SEE CONCEPTS 564,772

sunny [adj1] *bright, clear (referring to weather)*
brilliant, clarion, cloudless, fine, light, luminous, pleasant, radiant, rainless, shining, shiny, summery, sunlit, sunshiny, unclouded, undarkened; SEE CONCEPTS 525,617

sunny [adj2] *happy*
beaming, blithe, buoyant, cheerful, cheery, chirpy, genial, joyful, lighthearted, lightsome, optimistic, pleasant, smiling, sunbeamy; SEE CONCEPTS 401,542

sunrise [n] *rise of sun above horizon*
aurora, break of day*, bright, cockcrow*, dawn, dawning, daybreak, daylight, early bright*, light, morn, morning, sunup; SEE CONCEPT 810

sunset [n] *fall of sun below horizon*
close of day, crepuscular light, dusk, eve, evening, eventide, gloaming, nightfall, sundown, twilight; SEE CONCEPT 810

super [adj] *excellent*
cool*, divine, glorious, great, groovy*, hot*, incomparable, keen, magnificent, marvelous, matchless, neat, outstanding, peerless, sensational, smashing*, superb, terrific, topnotch, wonderful; SEE CONCEPT 574

superb [adj] *excellent, first-rate*
admirable, august, best, breathtaking, choice, elegant, elevated, exalted, exquisite, fine, glorious, gorgeous, grand, great, lofty, magnificent, majestic, marvelous, matchless, noble, optimal, optimum, outstanding, peerless, prime, proud, resplendent, solid, splendid, splendiferous, splendorous, standout, state-of-the-art*, stunning, sublime, super, superior, superlative, unrivaled, very best; SEE CONCEPT 574

supercilious [adj] *arrogant, stuck-up*
bossy, cavalier, cocky*, condescending, contemptuous, disdainful, egotistic, haughty, high-and-mighty*, imperious, insolent, lofty, nervy*, overbearing, patronizing, proud, putting on airs*, scornful, snobby, superior, uppity*, vainglorious; SEE CONCEPT 401

superficial [adj] *without depth, detail*
apparent, casual, cosmetic, cursory, depthless, desultory, empty, evident, exterior, external, flash, flimsy, frivolous, general, glib, half-baked*, hasty, hurried, ignorant, inattentive, lightweight, nodding, one-dimensional*, on the surface*, ostensible, outward, partial, passing,

perfunctory, peripheral, quick-fix*, seeming, shallow, shoal, silly, sketchy, skin-deep*, slapdash*, slight, smattery, summary, surface, tip of the iceberg*, trivial, uncritical, warped; SEE CONCEPTS 557,777

superficially [adv] *lightly; without care*
apparently, at first glance, carelessly, casually, externally, extraneously, flimsily, frivolously, hastily, ignorantly, not profoundly, not thoroughly, once over lightly*, on the surface*, ostensibly, outwardly, partially, skim, to the casual eye*; SEE CONCEPTS 531,544

superfluous [adj] *extra, unnecessary*
abounding, de trop, dispensable, excess, excessive, exorbitant, expendable, extravagant, extreme, gratuitous, inessential, in excess, inordinate, lavish, leftover, needless, nonessential, overflowing, overmuch, pleonastic, profuse, redundant, remaining, residuary, spare, superabundant, supererogatory, superfluent, supernumerary, surplus, unasked, uncalled-for, unneeded, unrequired, unwanted, useless; SEE CONCEPTS 546,560,824

superintendent [n] *person who oversees organization*
administrator, boss, caretaker, chief, conductor, controller, curator, custodian, director, foreperson, governor, head, head person, inspector, manager, overseer, sitter, slave driver*, straw boss*, super*, supervisor, zookeeper*; SEE CONCEPT 347

superior [n] *person higher or highest in rank*
boss, brass*, CEO*, chief, chieftain, director, elder, exec*, executive, head, head honcho*, heavyweight*, higher-up*, key player*, leader, manager, principal, ruler, senior, supervisor, VIP*; SEE CONCEPT 347

superior [adj1] *better, greater, higher; excellent*
above, a cut above*, admirable, capital, choice, dandy, deluxe, distinguished, exceeding, excellent, exceptional, expert, famous, fine, finer, first-class, first-rate, first-string*, five-star*, good, good quality, grander, high-caliber, high-class, major, more advanced, more skillful, noteworthy, of higher rank, over, overlying, paramount, predominant, preferable, preferred, premium, prevailing, primary, remarkable, senior, superhuman, supereminent, surpassing, unrivaled; SEE CONCEPT 574

superior [adj2] *arrogant, haughty*
airy, bossy, cavalier, cocky*, condescending, cool, disdainful, high-and-mighty*, high-hat*, insolent, lofty, overbearing, patronizing, pretentious, proud, snobbish, stuck-up*, supercilious, uppity*, upstage*, wiseguy*; SEE CONCEPT 401

superiority [n] *advantage, predominance*
ahead, ascendancy, authority, better, bulge, dominance, edge, eminence, excellence, influence, lead, meliority, nobility, perfection, position, power, predomination, preeminence, preponderance, prestige, prevalence, pull, rank, spark, supremacy, top, transcendence, upper hand*, vantage, victory, whip hand*; SEE CONCEPT 671

superlative [adj] *excellent, first-class*
accomplished, all-time*, A-1*, best, capital, consummate, crack, effusive, exaggerated, excessive, extreme, finished, gilt-edge*, greatest, highest, hundred-proof*, inflated, magnificent, matchless, of highest order*, optimum, outstanding, peerless, standout*, superb, supreme, surpassing, tops*,

transcendent, unexcelled, unparalleled, unrivaled, unsurpassed, winning, world-class*; SEE CONCEPT 574

supernatural [*adj*] *mysterious, not of this world*
abnormal, celestial, concealed, dark, fabulous, fairy, ghostly, heavenly, hidden, impenetrable, invisible, legendary, metaphysical, miraculous, mystic, mythical, mythological, numinous, obscure, occult, paranormal, phantom, phenomenal, preternatural, psychic, rare, secret, spectral, superhuman, superior, supermundane, superordinary, supranatural, transcendental, uncanny, uncomprehensible, unearthly, unfathomable, unintelligible, unknowable, unknown, unnatural, unrevealed, unusual; SEE CONCEPT 582

supersede [*v*] *take the place of; override*
abandon, annul, desert, discard, displace, forsake, oust, outmode, outplace, overrule, reject, remove, replace, repudiate, set aside, succeed, supplant, supplement, suspend, take over, usurp; SEE CONCEPTS 128,141

superstition [*n*] *belief in sign of things to come*
false belief, fear, irrationality, notion, shibboleth*, unfounded fear; SEE CONCEPT 689

supervise [*v*] *manage people, project*
administer, be in charge*, be in driver's seat*, be in the saddle, be on duty, be responsible for, boss, call the play*, call the shots*, chaperon, conduct, control, crack the whip*, deal with, direct, handle, inspect, keep an eye on*, look after, overlook, oversee, preside over, quarterback*, ride herd on*, run, run the show*, run things*, sit on top of*, superintend, survey, take care of; SEE CONCEPT 117

supervision [*n*] *management of people, project*
administration, auspices, care, charge, conduct, control, direction, guidance, handling, instruction, intendance, oversight, running, superintendence, superintendency, surveillance; SEE CONCEPT 117

supervisor [*n*] *person who manages people, project*
administrator, boss, brass hat*, caretaker, chief, curator, custodian, director, executive, foreperson, head, inspector, manager, overseer, slave driver*, straw boss*, super*, superintendent, zookeeper*; SEE CONCEPT 347

supplant [*v*] *displace, replace*
back up, bounce, cast out, crowd, cut out, eject, expel, fill in, force, force out, front for, oust, outplace, overthrow, remove, ring, ring in, sit in, stand in, substitute, succeed, supersede, swap places with, take out, take over, take the place of, transfer, undermine, unseat, usurp; SEE CONCEPT 128

supple [*adj*] *bendable*
adaptable, agile, bending, ductile, elastic, flexible, graceful, limber, lissome, lithe, lithesome, malleable, moldable, plastic, pliable, pliant, resilient, rubber, springy, stretch, stretchy, svelte, willowy, wiry, yielding; SEE CONCEPTS 488,604

supplement [*n*] *something added*
added feature*, addendum, addition, additive, appendix, bell*, bells and whistles*, codicil, complement, continuation, extra, insert, option, postscript, pullout, rider, sequel, spin-off*, subsidiary; SEE CONCEPTS 270,824

supplement [*v*] *add to*
add fuel to fire*, augment, beef up*, build up, buttress, complement, complete, enhance, enrich,

extend, fill out, fill up, fortify, heat up*, improve, increase, jazz up*, pad*, punch up*, reinforce, step up, strengthen, subsidize, supply, top; SEE CONCEPTS 236,244,245

supplies [*n*] *equipment, provisions*
food, foodstuffs, items, material, materials, necessities, provender, rations, raw materials, replenishments, stock, store, stores; SEE CONCEPTS 446,451,457

supply [*n*] *reserve of goods*
accumulation, amount, backlog, cache, fund, hoard, inventory, number, quantity, reservoir, source, stock, stockpile, store, surplus; SEE CONCEPT 712

supply [*v*] *furnish, provide, give a resource*
afford, cater, cater to, come across with*, come through*, come up with, contribute, deliver, dispense, drop, endow, equip, feed, fill, find, fix up, fulfill, give with, grant, hand, hand over, heel*, kick in*, minister, outfit, pony up*, produce, provide, provision, purvey, put out, put up, replenish, satisfy, slake, stock, store, transfer, turn over, victual, yield; SEE CONCEPTS 107,140

support [*n1*] *something that holds up structure*
abutment, agency, back, backing, base, bed, bedding, block, brace, buttress, collar, column, cornerstone, device, flotation, foothold, footing, foundation, fulcrum, groundwork, guide, hold, lining, means, medium, pillar, platform, pole, post, prop, rampart, reinforcement, rest, rib, rod, shore, stake, stanchion, stave, stay, stiffener, stilt, substratum, substructure, sustentation, timber, underpinning; SEE CONCEPTS 440,442,445,471

support [*n2*] *help, approval*
aid, assist, assistance, backing, blessing, championship, comfort, encouragement, friendship, furtherance, hand, lift, loyalty, moral support, patronage, protection, relief, succor, sustenance; SEE CONCEPTS 10,110,388,712

support [*n3*] *food, money, possessions for staying alive*
alimentation, alimony, allowance, care, keep, livelihood, living, maintenance, necessities, nutriment, payment, provision, relief, responsibility, stock, stores, subsidy, subsistence, sustenance, upkeep, victuals; SEE CONCEPTS 340,446,457,712

support/supporter [*n4/n*] *person who helps another*
adherent, advocate, ally, angel*, apologist, backbone, backer, benefactor, champion, cohort, comforter, confederate, coworker, defender, disciple, endorser, espouser, exponent, expounder, fan, follower, friend, helper, mainstay, maintainer, partisan, patron, pillar, preserver, prop, proponent, satellite*, second, sponsor, stalwart, stay, subscriber, supporter, sustainer, tower of strength*, upholder, well-wisher*; SEE CONCEPT 423

support [*v1*] *hold up*
base, be a foundation for, bear, bed, bolster, bottom, brace, buttress, carry, cradle, crutch, embed, found, ground, hold, keep from falling, keep up, mainstay, nurse, prop, reinforce, shore, shore up, shoulder, stand, stay, strut, sustain, undergird, upbear, uphold; SEE CONCEPT 190

support [*v2*] *take care of, provide for*
angel*, attend to, back, bankroll*, be a source of strength*, bring up, buoy up, care for, chaperon, cherish, earn one's keep, encourage, feed, fi-

nance, fortify, foster, fund, give a leg up*, guard, keep, keep an eye on*, look after, maintain, make a living, nourish, nurse, pay expenses of, pay for, pick up the check*, prop, put up money for*, raise, set up, sponsor, stake, stiffen, strengthen, stroke, subsidize, succor, sustain, underwrite, uphold; SEE CONCEPTS 7,19,22,140,295,341

support [v3] *defend, advocate belief*
abet, advance, agree with, aid, approve, assist, back, bear out, bolster, boost, boost morale, carry, champion, cheer, comfort, countenance, endorse, establish, forward, foster, get behind*, go along with, go to bat for*, help, hold, justify, keep up, maintain, plead for, promote, pull for, put forward, rally round, second, side with, stand behind, stand up for, stay, stick by*, stick up for*, substantiate, sustain, take one's side*, take the part of*, throw in one's lot with*, throw in with*, uphold, verify; SEE CONCEPTS 10,49,110

support [v4] *endure*
abide, bear, bear with, brook, carry on, continue, countenance, go, go through, handle, keep up, live with*, maintain, put up with*, stand, stand for*, stay the course*, stick it out*, stomach*, submit, suffer, swallow*, sweat out*, take, tolerate, undergo, wait out; SEE CONCEPT 23

suppose [v1] *assume, guess*
accept, admit, brainstorm, calculate, conjecture, cook up*, dare-say*, deem, divine, dream, estimate, expect, figure, go out on a limb*, grant, guess, guesstimate*, hazard a guess*, hypothesize, imagine, infer, judge, opine, posit, predicate, presume, presuppose, pretend, spark, speculate, surmise, suspect, take, take for granted, theorize, think, understand; SEE CONCEPT 28

suppose [v2] *believe*
assume, be afraid, conceive, conclude, conjecture, consider, deem, dream, expect, fancy, feel, gather, have a hunch*, have sneaking suspicion*, hypothesize, imagine, judge, postulate, reckon, regard, suspect, swear by, take, take as gospel truth*, take stock in*, think, understand, view; SEE CONCEPT 12

supposition [n] *guess, belief*
apriorism, assumption, condition, conjecture, doubt, guessing, guesstimate*, guesswork, hunch, hypothesis, idea, likelihood, notion, opinion, posit, postulate, postulation, premise, presumption, presupposition, rough guess*, shot in the dark*, sneaking suspicion*, speculation, stab in the dark*, suppose, surmise, suspicion, theory, thesis, view; SEE CONCEPT 689

suppress [v] *restrain, hold in check*
abolish, annihilate, beat down, bottle, bring to naught, burke, censor, check, clamp, conceal, conquer, contain, cover up, crack down on, crush, curb, cut off, extinguish, hold back, hold down, hold in, interrupt, keep in, keep secret, muffle, muzzle, overcome, overpower, overthrow, put an end to, put down, put kibosh on*, put lid on*, quash, quell, quench, repress, shush*, silence, sit on*, smother, snuff out*, spike, squash*, stamp out*, stifle, stop, subdue, trample, withhold; SEE CONCEPTS 121,130,252

supremacy [n] *total domination*
absolute rule, ascendancy, authority, command, control, dominance, dominion, driver's seat*, paramountcy, power, predominance, preeminence, preponderance, prepotence, primacy, principality,

sovereignty, superiority, supreme authority, sway, transcendence; SEE CONCEPTS 133,376

supreme [adj] *greatest, principal*
absolute, best, cardinal, chief, closing, crowning, culminating, excellent, extreme, final, first, foremost, head, highest, incomparable, last, leading, marvelous, matchless, maximum, paramount, peerless, perfect, predominant, preeminent, prevailing, prime, sovereign, superb, superlative, surpassing, terminal, top, top-drawer*, towering, transcendent, ultimate, unequaled, unmatched, unparalleled, unsurpassable, unsurpassed, utmost; SEE CONCEPTS 568,574

sure [adj1] *certain, definite*
abiding, assured, changeless, clear, confident, constant, convinced, convincing, decided, doubtless, enduring, firm, fixed, for a fact, free from doubt*, genuine, incontestable, incontrovertible, indisputable, indubitable, never-failing, persuaded, positive, real, satisfied, set, steadfast, steady, telling, unchangeable, unchanging, uncompromising, undeniable, unequivocal, unfailing, unfaltering, unqualified, unquestionable, unquestioning, unshakable, unshaken, unvarying, unwavering, valid; SEE CONCEPT 535

sure [adj2] *physically stable*
fast, firm, fixed, safe, secure, solid, staunch, steady, strong; SEE CONCEPT 488

sure [adj3] *inevitable*
assured, bound, certain, guaranteed, indisputable, ineluctable, inerrant, inescapable, infallible, irrevocable, surefire, unavoidable, unerring, unfailing; SEE CONCEPT 548

sure [adj4] *self-confident*
arrogant, assured, certain, composed, confident, decided, decisive, positive, self-assured, self-possessed; SEE CONCEPT 401

surely [adv] *without doubt*
absolutely, admittedly, assuredly, beyond doubt, beyond shadow of doubt*, certainly, clearly, come what may*, conclusively, decidedly, definitely, distinctly, doubtlessly, evidently, explicitly, fixedly, for certain, for real, indeed, indubitably, inevitably, inexorably, infallibly, irrefutably, manifestly, nothing else but, plainly, positively, rain or shine*, to be sure, undoubtedly, unequivocally, unerringly, unfailingly, unmistakably, unquestionably, unshakably, with certainty, without fail; SEE CONCEPT 535

surface [n] *external part of something*
area, cover, covering, expanse, exterior, exteriority, externality, facade, face, facet, level, obverse, outside, peel, periphery, plane, rind, side, skin, stretch, superficiality, superficies, top, veneer; SEE CONCEPT 484

surface [adj] *external*
apparent, covering, depthless, exterior, facial, outer, outside, outward, shallow, shoal, superficial, top; SEE CONCEPTS 485,583

surface [v] *come to the top of*
appear, arise, come to light, come up, crop up, emerge, flare up, materialize, rise, transpire; SEE CONCEPTS 166,716

surfeit [n] *excess*
bellyful*, excess, glut*, overabundance, overflow, overfullness, overindulgence, overkill, overmuch, overplus, plenitude, plethora, profusion, remainder, repletion, satiety, satisfaction, saturation, superabundance, superfluity, surplus, up to here*; SEE CONCEPT 740

surfeit [v] *overfill*

cloy, cram, eat, fill, glut, gorge, jade, overfeed, overindulge, pall, sate, satiate, satisfy, stuff; SEE CONCEPTS 209,740

surge [n] *rush, usually of liquid*

billow, breaker, deluge, efflux, flood, flow, growth, gush, intensification, outpouring, rise, roll, surf, swell, upsurge, wave; SEE CONCEPTS 432,467,787

surge [v] *rush, usually in liquid form*

arise, billow, climb, deluge, eddy, flow, grow, gush, heave, mount, pour, ripple, rise, roll, sluice, stream, swell, swirl, tower, undulate, well forth; SEE CONCEPTS 146,179

surly [adj] *gruff, bearish*

boorish, brusque, churlish, cross, crusty, curmudgeonly, discourteous, dour, fractious, glum, grouchy, ill-mannered, ill-natured, irritable, morose, perverse, rude, saturnine, sulky, sullen, testy, ugly, uncivil, ungracious; SEE CONCEPT 401

surmise [n] *guess, conclusion*

assumption, attempt, conjecture, deduction, guesstimate*, guesswork, hunch, hypothesis, idea, inference, notion, opinion, possibility, presumption, sneaking suspicion*, speculation, supposition, suspicion, theory, thought; SEE CONCEPTS 529,689

surmise [v] *come to a conclusion*

assume, conclude, conjecture, consider, deduce, fancy, guess, guesstimate*, hazard a guess*, hypothesize, imagine, infer, opine, presume, pretend, regard, risk assuming, speculate, suppose, suspect, take a shot*, take a stab*, theorize, think, venture a guess*; SEE CONCEPTS 18,28

surmount [v] *overcome, triumph over*

best, better, cap, clear, conquer, crest, crown, defeat, down, exceed, hurdle, leap, lick*, negotiate, outdo, outstrip, over, overpower, overtop, pass, prevail over, rise above, subdue, surpass, throw*, top*, vanquish, vault; SEE CONCEPTS 95,141

surpass [v] *outdo something or someone*

beat, best, better, cap, eclipse, exceed, excel, go beyond, go one better*, improve upon, outdistance, outgo, outmatch, outpace, outperform, outrank, outrival, outrun, outshine, outstep, outstrip, outweigh, override, overshadow, overstep, pass, put to shame*, rank*, surmount, top, tower, tower above*, transcend, trump*; SEE CONCEPT 141

surplus [n] *extra material*

balance, excess, overage, overflow, overkill, overmuch, overrun, overstock, oversupply, plethora, plus, remainder, residue, something extra, superabundance, superfluity, surfeit, surplusage, the limit, too much; SEE CONCEPTS 260,658,824

surplus [adj] *extra*

de trop, excess, in excess, leftover, odd*, over, remaining, spare, superfluent, superfluous, supernumerary, too much, unused; SEE CONCEPTS 560,781,824

surprise [n] *something amazing; state of amazement*

abruptness, amazement, astonishment, astoundment, attack, awe, bewilderment, bombshell*, consternation, curiosity, curveball*, disappointment, disillusion, eye-opener*, fortune, godsend*, incredulity, jolt*, kick*, marvel, miracle, miscalculation, phenomenon, portent, precipitance, precipitation, precipitousness, prodigy, rarity, revelation, shock, start, stupefaction,

suddenness, thunderbolt*, unexpected, unforeseen, whammy*, wonder, wonderment; SEE CONCEPTS 410,529

surprise [v1] *astonish; cause amazement*

amaze, astound, awe, bewilder, blow away*, bowl over*, cause wonder, confound, confuse, consternate, daze, dazzle, discomfit, disconcert, dismay, dumbfound, electrify, flabbergast, floor, jar, jolt, leave aghast, leave open-mouthed, nonplus, overwhelm, perplex, petrify, rattle, rock, shake up, shock, spring something on, stagger, startle, strike dumb*, strike with awe, stun, stupefy, take aback, take one's breath away*, throw a curve*, unsettle; SEE CONCEPT 42

surprise [v2] *sneak up on; catch*

ambush, burst in on, bushwhack*, capture, catch in the act*, catch off-balance*, catch off-guard*, catch red-handed*, catch unawares*, come down on, discover, drop in on, grab, grasp, lay for, lie in wait*, nab, seize, spring on, startle, take, take by surprise, waylay; SEE CONCEPTS 42,86

surrender [n] *giving up; resignation*

abandonment, abdication, acquiescence, appeasement, capitulation, cessation, dedition, delivery, giving way, relenting, relinquishment, renunciation, submission, succumbing, white flag*, yielding; SEE CONCEPTS 67,108,119,320

surrender [v] *give up; resign*

abandon, buckle under*, capitulate, cave in*, cede, commit, concede, consign, cry uncle*, deliver up, eat crow*, eat humble pie*, entrust, fall, fold, forego, give in, go along with, go down, go under, hand over, knuckle, knuckle under*, leave, let go, pack it in*, part with, play dead*, put up white flag*, quit, relinquish, renounce, roll over*, submit, succumb, throw in the towel*, toss it in*, waive, yield; SEE CONCEPTS 67,108,119,320

surreptitious [adj] *sneaky, secret*

clandestine, covert, fraudulent, furtive, hidden, hole-and-corner*, hush-hush*, on the QT*, on the sly*, private, skulking, slinking, sly, sneaking, stealthy, sub-rosa, unauthorized, undercover, underhand, under-the-table*, under wraps*, veiled; SEE CONCEPT 548

surrogate [n] *person or thing that acts as substitute*

agent, alternate, backup, delegate, deputy, expediency, expedient, fill-in, makeshift, pinch hitter*, proxy, recourse, refuge, replacement, representative, resort, resource, stand-in, stopgap*, sub*; SEE CONCEPTS 348,414,423

surround [v] *enclose, encircle something*

beleaguer, beset, besiege, blockade, border, bound, box in, circle, circumscribe, circumvent, close around, close in, close in on, compass, confine, edge, enclave, encompass, envelop, environ, fence in, fringe, gird, girdle, go around, hem in, inundate, invest, lay siege to, limit, loop, margin, outline, rim, ring, round, shut in, skirt, verge; SEE CONCEPT 758

surroundings [n] *environment*

ambience, atmosphere, background, climate, community, environs, home, location, medium, milieu, neighborhood, setting, vicinity; SEE CONCEPTS 198,673

surveillance [n] *close observation, following*

body mike*, bug*, bugging*, care, control, direction, eagle eye*, examination, eye, inspection, lookout, peeled eye*, scrutiny, spying, stakeout, superintendence, supervision, surveyance, tab*, tail*, tap*, track*, vigil, vigilance, watch, wire-tap; SEE CONCEPTS 103,298,749

survey [n] *scrutiny, examination*
analysis, aperçu, audit, check, compendium, critique, digest, inquiry, inspection, outline, overview, pandect, perlustration, perusal, precis, review, sample, scan, sketch, study, syllabus, view; SEE CONCEPTS 37,103,197,271,291

survey [v] *scrutinize, take stock of*
appraise, assay, assess, canvass, case, check, check out, check over, check up, contemplate, estimate, evaluate, examine, give the once over*, inspect, look over, look upon, measure, observe, overlook, oversee, plan, plot, prospect, rate, read, reconnoiter, research, review, scan, scope, scrutinize, set at, size, size up, stake out, study, summarize, superintend, supervise, take stock of*, test the waters*, valuate, value, view; SEE CONCEPTS 37,48,103,197,291

survive [v] *continue to live*
bear, be extant, be left, carry on, carry through, come through, cut it, endure, exist, get on, get through, go all the way*, go the limit*, handle, hold out, keep, keep afloat, last, live, live down, live on, live out, live through, make a comeback*, make the cut*, outlast, outlive, outwear, persevere, persist, pull out of it*, pull through, recover, remain, remain alive, revive, ride out*, see through, stand up, subsist, suffer, sustain, tough it out*, weather, withstand; SEE CONCEPTS 23,239,407

susceptible [adj] *exposed, naive*
affected, aroused, be taken in, disposed, easily moved, easy, fall for, given, gullible, impressed, impressible, impressionable, inclined, influenced, liable, mark, movable, nonresistant, obnoxious, open, out on a limb*, persuadable, predisposed, prone, pushover, ready, receptive, responsive, roused, sensible, sensile, sensitive, sentient, sitting duck*, soft, stirred, subject, sucker*, suggestible, susceptive, swallow, swayed, tender, touched, tumble for*, vulnerable, wide open; SEE CONCEPTS 403,542

suspect [adj] *doubtful*
doubtable, dubious, fishy*, incredible, open, problematic, pseudo*, questionable, ridiculous, shaky*, suspected, suspicious, thick*, thin*, unbelievable, uncertain, unclear, unlikely, unsure; SEE CONCEPTS 529,582

suspect [v] *distrust, guess*
assume, be afraid, believe, conceive, conclude, conjecture, consider, disbelieve, doubt, expect, feel, gather, harbor suspicion*, have a hunch*, have doubt, have sneaking suspicion*, hazard a guess*, hold, imagine, mistrust, presume, reckon, smell a rat*, speculate, suppose, surmise, think, think probable, understand, wonder; SEE CONCEPTS 21,28

suspend [v1] *hang from above*
append, attach, be pendent, dangle, depend, hang down, hang up, hook up, sling, swing, wave; SEE CONCEPTS 181,190

suspend [v2] *delay, hold off*
adjourn, arrest, bar, break up, can, cease, check, count out, cut short, debar, defer, discontinue, eject, eliminate, exclude, file, halt, hang, hang fire*, hang up, hold up, inactivate, intermit, interrupt, lay aside, lay off, lay on the table*, lay over, omit, pigeonhole*, pink-slip*, postpone, procrastinate, prorogue, protract, put an end to,

put a stop to, put off, put on back burner*, put on hold, put on ice*, put on the shelf*, reject, retard, rule out, shelve, stave off, stay, waive, withhold; SEE CONCEPTS 119,121,130,351

suspense [n] *anticipation*
anxiety, apprehension, chiller*, cliff-hanger*, cloak and dagger*, confusion, dilemma, doubt, eagerness, expectancy, expectation, grabber*, hesitancy, hesitation, impatience, indecision, indecisiveness, insecurity, irresolution, page-turner*, perplexity, potboiler*, tension, thriller*, uncertainty, wavering; SEE CONCEPTS 410,679

suspension [n] *delay*
abeyance, abeyancy, adjournment, break, breather*, breathing spell*, cessation, coffee break*, concluding, conclusion, cutoff, deferment, disbarment, discontinuation, discontinuing, doldrums, dormancy, downtime*, end, ending, finish, five*, freeze, halt, heave-ho*, intermission, interruption, latency, layoff, letup, moratorium, pause, period, postponement, quiescence, quiescency, remission, respite, stay, stoppage, suspense, ten*, termination, time-out; SEE CONCEPTS 119, 807,832

suspicion [n1] *doubt*
bad vibes*, chariness, conjecture, cynicism, distrust, dubiety, dubiosity, funny feeling*, guess, guesswork, gut feeling*, hunch, idea, impression, incertitude, incredulity, jealousy, lack of confidence, misgiving, mistrust, nonbelief, notion, qualm, skepticism, sneaking suspicion*, supposition, surmise, uncertainty, wariness, wonder; SEE CONCEPTS 532,689,690

suspicion [n2] *hint, trace*
cast, glimmer, intimation, shade, shadow, smell, soupçon, strain, streak, suggestion, tinge, touch, whiff; SEE CONCEPTS 529,831

suspicious [adj1] *distrustful*
apprehensive, cagey, careful, cautious, doubtful, green-eyed*, incredulous, in doubt, jealous, leery, mistrustful, not born yesterday* on the lookout*, questioning, quizzical, skeptical, suspect, suspecting, unbelieving, uptight*, wary, watchful, without belief, without faith, wondering; SEE CONCEPTS 403,542

suspicious [adj2] *doubtful, fishy*
borderline, debatable, different, disputable, doubtable, dubious, equivocal, farfetched, funny*, irregular, not kosher*, open, open to doubt, open to question, out of line*, overt, peculiar, phony, problematic, queer, questionable, reaching, rings untrue*, shady, shaky*, suspect, too much*, uncertain, uncommon, unsure, unusual, won't wash*; SEE CONCEPTS 529,564

sustain [v1] *keep up, maintain*
aid, approve, assist, back, bankroll, bear, befriend, bolster, brace, buoy, buttress, carry, comfort, confirm, continue, convey, defend, endorse, favor, feed, foster, go for, help, keep alive, keep from falling, keep going, lend a hand*, lug, nourish, nurse, nurture, pack, preserve, prolong, prop, protract, provide for, ratify, relieve, save, shore up, stand by, stick up for, supply, support, tote, transfer, transport, uphold, validate, verify; SEE CONCEPTS 110,140,190

sustain [v2] *endure, experience*
abide, bear, bear up under, bear with, brook, digest, encounter, feel, go, hang in, have, know, live with*, put up with*, see, stand*, stand up to,

stomach*, suffer, take it, tolerate, undergo, withstand; SEE CONCEPTS 23,678

sustenance [n] *necessities for existence*

aid, aliment, bacon*, bread*, bread and butter*, comestible, daily bread*, eatables, edibles, food, keep, livelihood, maintenance, nourishment, nutrition, pap*, provender, provision, ration, refreshment, salt*, subsistence, support, victual, wherewithal; SEE CONCEPTS 340,446,457,709

svelte [adj] *thin and well-built*

graceful, lean, lissom, lithe, slender, slinky, smooth, sylphlike, willowy; SEE CONCEPTS 490,491

swagger [v] *show off; walk pompously*

bluster, boast, brag, brandish, bully, cock, flourish, gasconade, gloat, grandstand*, hector, look big*, lord, parade, parade one's wares*, peacock*, play to the crowd*, pontificate, prance, put on, put on airs*, sashay*, saunter, strut, swank*, swashbuckle*, sway, sweep, swell; SEE CONCEPTS 49,149,716

swallow [v1] *consume*

absorb, belt*, bolt*, chugalug*, devour, dispatch, dispose, down, drink, drop, eat, gobble, gulp, imbibe, ingest, ingurgitate, inhale, put away, quaff, sip, slurp, swig, swill, take, toss, wash down*, wolf; SEE CONCEPT 169

swallow [v2] *believe without much thought*

accept, believe, buy, fall for; SEE CONCEPT 12

swamp [n] *wet land covered with vegetation*

bog, bottoms, everglade, fen, glade, holm, marsh, marshland, mire, moor, morass, mud, muskeg, peat bog, polder, quag, quagmire, slough, swale, swampland; SEE CONCEPT 509

swamp [v] *overwhelm, flood*

beset, besiege, crowd, drench, drown, engulf, inundate, overcrowd, overflow, overload, satiate, saturate, sink, snow*, submerge, submerse, surfeit, swallow up, upset, wash, waterlog, whelm; SEE CONCEPTS 146,179,641

swank/swanky [adj] *plush, stylish*

chichi*, classy, deluxe, exclusive, expensive, fancy, fashionable, flamboyant, flashy, glamorous, grand, lavish, luxurious, ostentatious, peacocky, plushy*, posh, pretentious, rich, ritzy*, sharp, showy, smart, snappy, splashy, sumptuous, tony*, trendy, with-it*; SEE CONCEPT 589

swap/swop [v] *exchange*

bandy, bargain, barter, change, interchange, substitute, switch, trade, traffic, truck; SEE CONCEPT 104

swarm [n] *large, moving group*

army, bevy, blowout, concourse, covey, crowd, crush, drove, flock, herd, horde, host, jam, mass, mob, multitude, myriad, pack, press, push, school, shoal, throng, troop, turnout; SEE CONCEPTS 397,417,432

swarm [v] *move forward as a group*

abound, be alive, be numerous, cluster, congregate, crawl, crowd, flock, flow, gather, gather like bees*, jam, mass, mob, move in a crowd, overrun, pullulate, rush together, stream, teem, throng; SEE CONCEPTS 113,114,159

swarthy [adj] *dark-complexioned*

black, brown, brunet, dark, dark-hued, darkish, dark-skinned, dusky, swart, tan, tawny; SEE CONCEPT 618

swat [v] *hit*

beat, belt, biff, box, buffet, clobber, clout, cuff,

ding, knock, slap, slug, smack, smash, sock, strike, wallop, whack; SEE CONCEPT 189

sway [n] *strong influence*

amplitude, authority, clout, command, control, dominion, empire, expanse, government, jurisdiction, mastery, might, power, predominance, range, reach, regime, reign, rule, run, scope, sovereignty, spread, stretch, sweep; SEE CONCEPTS 376,687

sway [v1] *move back and forth*

bend, blow hot and cold*, careen, fluctuate, hem and haw*, incline, lean, lurch, oscillate, pendulate, pulsate, rock, roll, stagger, swagger, swing, undulate, vibrate, wave, waver, weave, wobble, yo-yo*; SEE CONCEPTS 13,145,151

sway [v2] *influence, affect*

bias, brainwash, carry, conduct, control, crack*, direct, dispose, dominate, get*, govern, guide, hold sway over, hook, impact on, impress, incline, induce, inspire, lead by the nose*, manage, move, overrule, persuade, predispose, prevail on, put across, reign, rule, rule over, sell*, soften up*, strike, suck in*, touch, turn one's head*, twist one's arm*, whitewash*, win over, work on; SEE CONCEPTS 14,68,117

swear [v1] *declare under oath*

affirm, assert, attest, avow, covenant, cross one's heart*, depend on, depose, give one's word*, give witness, have confidence in, maintain, make an affidavit, pledge oneself, plight, promise, rely on, say so*, state, state under oath, swear by, swear to God*, swear up and down*, take an oath, testify, trust, vouch, vow, warrant; SEE CONCEPT 49

swear [v2] *speak profanely; be vulgar*

bedamn, be foul-mouthed, blaspheme, curse, cuss*, execrate, flame*, imprecate, take name in vain*, talk dirty*, use bad language*, utter profanity; SEE CONCEPTS 52,54

swearing [n] *foul language*

bad language*, blasphemy, cursing, cuss*, cussing*, dirty language*, dirty name*, dirty talk*, dirty word*, execration, expletives, four-letter word*, imprecation, malediction, no-no*, profanity, swearword; SEE CONCEPTS 54,276,278

sweat [n1] *body's perspiring*

diaphoresis, excretion, exudation, perspiration, steam, transudation; SEE CONCEPTS 185,467

sweat [n2] *hard work*

backbreaker*, chore, drudgery, effort, grind, labor, moil, slavery, task, toil, travail, work; SEE CONCEPTS 362,677

sweat [v1] *perspire*

break out in a sweat, drip, eject, exude, glow, ooze, secrete, seep, spout, swelter, transude, wilt; SEE CONCEPT 185

sweat [v2] *worry about; bear*

abide, agonize, be on pins and needles*, be on tenterhooks*, brook, chafe, endure, exert, fret, go, labor, lose sleep over*, stand, stay the course*, stick it out*, stomach*, suffer, take, toil, tolerate, torture, work hard; SEE CONCEPTS 23,35

sweaty [adj] *damp with perspiration*

bathed, clammy, covered with sweat, drenched, dripping, drippy, glowing, hot, moist, perspiring, perspiry, soaked, sticky, stinky, sweating, wet; SEE CONCEPT 406

sweep [n1] *range, extent*

ambit, breadth, compass, extension, latitude, length, orbit, purview, radius, reach, region, scope, span, stretch, vista; SEE CONCEPTS 651,756,788

sweep [n2] *movement*
arc, bend, course, curve, gesture, move, play, progress, stroke, swing; SEE CONCEPTS 145,748

sweep [v1] *brush off, away*
broom, brush, brush up, clean, clear, clear up, mop, ready, remove, scrub, tidy, vacuum; SEE CONCEPT 165

sweep [v2] *fly, glide*
career, fleet, flit, flounce, glance, hurtle, pass, sail, scud, skim, tear, wing, zoom; SEE CONCEPTS 150,152

sweeping [adj] *wide-ranging*
across-the-board, all-around, all-embracing, all-encompassing, all-inclusive, all-out, bird's-eye*, blanket, broad, complete, comprehensive, exaggerated, exhaustive, extensive, full, general, global, inclusive, indiscriminate, out-and-out*, overall, overdrawn, overstated, radical, thorough, thorough-going, unqualified, vast, wall-to-wall*, whole-hog*, wholesale*, wide; SEE CONCEPTS 531,772

sweet [n] *sugary food*
bonbon, candy, chocolate, confection, confectionery, confiture, delight, dessert, enjoyment, final course, gratification, joy, pleasure, pudding, snack, sugarplum, sweetmeat; SEE CONCEPTS 457,461

sweet [adj1] *sugary*
candied, candy-coated, cloying, delicious, honeyed, like candy, like honey, luscious, nectarous, saccharine, sugar-coated, sugared, sweetened, syrupy, toothsome; SEE CONCEPTS 462,613

sweet [adj2] *friendly, kind*
affectionate, agreeable, amiable, angelic, appealing, attractive, beautiful, beloved, charming, cherished, companionable, considerate, darling, dear, dearest, delectable, delicious, delightful, dulcet, engaging, fair, generous, gentle, good-humored, good-natured, heavenly, lovable, loving, luscious, mild, mushy, patient, pet, pleasant, pleasing, precious, reasonable, saccharine, sweet-tempered, sympathetic, taking, tender, thoughtful, treasured, unselfish, winning, winsome; SEE CONCEPTS 401,404,542

sweet [adj3] *nice-smelling*
ambrosial, aromal, aromatic, balmy, clean, fragrant, fresh, new, perfumed, perfumy, pure, redolent, savory, scented, spicy, sweet-smelling, wholesome; SEE CONCEPT 598

sweet [adj4] *nice-sounding*
dulcet, euphonic, euphonious, harmonious, mellifluous, mellow, melodic, melodious, musical, orotund, rich, rotund, silver-tongued, silvery, smooth, soft, sonorous, soothing, sweet-sounding, tuneful; SEE CONCEPT 594

sweeten [v1] *add sugar*
add sweetening, candy, candy-coat, honey, make sweet, make toothsome, mull, sugar, sugar-coat; SEE CONCEPT 170

sweeten [v2] *make happy; appease*
alleviate, assuage, conciliate, mollify, pacify, placate, propitiate, soften up, soothe; SEE CONCEPTS 7,22

sweetheart [n] *person whom another loves*
admirer, beau, beloved, boyfriend, companion, darling, dear, dear one, flame, girlfriend, heartthrob, honey*, inamorata, inamorato, love, lovebird*, lover, one and only*, paramour, pet,

significant other, steady*, suitor, swain, sweet, treasure*, truelove, valentine; SEE CONCEPTS 414,423

swell [n] *large increase, flow*
billow, crescendo, growth, ripple, rise, seat, surf, surge, undulation, uprise, wave; SEE CONCEPT 780

swell [adj] *wonderful*
awesome, cool*, dandy*, deluxe, desirable, excellent, exclusive, fashionable, fine, fly*, grand, groovy*, keen, marvelous, neat, nifty, plush, posh, ritzy*, smart, stylish, super, terrific; SEE CONCEPTS 548,574

swell [v] *become larger*
accumulate, add to, aggravate, amplify, augment, balloon, become bloated, become distended, become swollen, be inflated, belly, billow, blister, bloat, bulge, dilate, distend, enhance, enlarge, expand, extend, fatten, fill out, grow, grow larger, heighten, increase, intensity, mount, plump, pouch, pout, protrude, puff, puff up, rise, round out, surge, tumefy, uprise, well up; SEE CONCEPTS 236,245,780

swelling [n] *physical growth; lump*
abscess, blister, boil, bruise, bulge, bump, bunion, carbuncle, contusion, corn, dilation, distention, enlargement, hump, inflammation, injury, knob, knurl, node, nodule, pimple, pock, protuberance, puff, puffiness, pustule, ridge, sore, tumescence, tumor, wale, wart, weal, welt; SEE CONCEPTS 306,309

sweltering [adj] *very hot*
airless, baking, broiling, burning, close, fiery, humid, oppressive, perspiring, scorching, sizzling, stewing, sticky, stifling, stuffy, sultry, sweaty, sweltry, torrid; SEE CONCEPT 605

swerve [v] *turn aside, often to avoid collision*
bend, deflect, depart, depart from, deviate, dip, diverge, err, get off course, go off course, incline, lurch, move, sheer, sheer off, shift, sideslip, sidestep, skew, skid, slue, stray, swing, tack, train off, turn, veer, wander, waver, wind; SEE CONCEPTS 150,195,201

swift [adj] *very fast*
abrupt, alacritous, barrelling, breakneck, cracking*, double-quick*, expeditious, express, fleet, fleet-footed*, flying, hasty, headlong, hurried, in nothing flat*, like crazy*, like mad*, nimble, on the double*, precipitate, prompt, pronto, quick, rapid, ready, screaming, shaking a leg*, short, short-lived, snappy*, spanking*, speedball*, speedy, sudden, supersonic, unexpected, winged; SEE CONCEPTS 588,799

swiftly/swift [adv] *very fast*
apace, double-quick*, expeditiously, flat-out*, fleetly, full tilt*, hastily, hurriedly, in no time*, posthaste, promptly, quick, rapidly, rapidly, speedily, without losing time*, without warning*; SEE CONCEPTS 588,799

swim [v] *make way through water using arms, legs*
bathe, breast-stroke, crawl, dive, dog paddle, float, freestyle, glide, go for a swim, go swimming, go wading, high-dive, move, paddle, practice, race, skinny-dip*, slip, stroke, submerge, take a dip, wade; SEE CONCEPT 363

swimmingly [adv] *very well*
as planned, cosily, easily, effectively, effortlessly, favorably, fortunately, happily, like a dream*, like clockwork*, prosperously, quickly, satisfyingly, smoothly, successfully, well, with flying

colors*, with no trouble, without a hitch*; SEE CONCEPTS *528,544*

swindle [n] *cheating, stealing*
blackmail, cheat, con, crooked deal*, deceit, deception, dirty pool*, double-cross*, double-dealing*, extortion, fake, fast one*, fast shuffle*, frame-up, fraud, hoax, hustle, imposition, imposture, knavery, racket*, rip-off*, scam, sell, shady deal*, shakedown, sham, sharp practice*, shell game*, sting, trick, trickery; SEE CONCEPTS *59,139,192*

swindle [v] *cheat, steal*
bamboozle, beat*, bilk, clip*, con*, cozen, deceive, defraud, diddle*, do*, dupe, extort, fleece*, flimflam*, fool, frame*, fudge*, gouge*, gull*, hoodwink, overcharge, pluck, pull a fast one*, put one over on*, rip off*, rook, run a game on*, sandbag, scam, sell, shaft, stiff*, sting*, sucker, take for a ride*, take to the cleaners*, trick, trim*, victimize; SEE CONCEPTS *59,139,192*

swindler [n] *person who cheats another*
absconder, charlatan, cheat, cheater, chiseler, clip, con artist, confidence artist, counterfeiter, crook, deceiver, defrauder, dodger, double-dealer, falsifier, forger, four-flusher*, fraud, gouger, grifter, impostor, mechanic, mountebank, operator, rascal, rook, scammer, scoundrel, shark, sharp, sharper, slicker, thief, trickster; SEE CONCEPT *412*

swing [n] *moving back and forth*
beat, cadence, cadency, fluctuation, lilt, measure, meter, motion, oscillation, rhythm, stroke, sway, swaying, tempo, undulation, vibration; SEE CONCEPTS *65,748*

swing [v] *move back and forth; be suspended*
avert, away, be pendent, curve, dangle, deflect, divert, flap, fluctuate, hang, lurch, oscillate, palpitate, pendulate, pitch, pivot, reel, revolve, rock, roll, rotate, sheer, shunt, suspend, sway, swerve, swivel, turn, turn about, turn on an axis, twirl, undulate, vary, veer, vibrate, volte-face, wag, waggle, wave, wheel, whirl, wiggle, wobble; SEE CONCEPT *145*

swipe [n/v] *hit*
bash, blow, clip, clout, clump, cuff, knock, lash out, lick, rap, slap, smack, sock, strike, swat, wallop, wipe; SEE CONCEPT *189*

swipe [v2] *steal*
appropriate, cop, filch, heist, hook, lift, make off with, nab, nick, pilfer, pinch, purloin, sneak, snitch; SEE CONCEPT *139*

swirl [v] *spin around*
agitate, boil, churn, coil, crimp, crisp, curl, eddy, purl, roil, roll, snake, surge, swoosh*, twirl, whirl, whirlpool, whorl, wriggle; SEE CONCEPTS *145,738*

swish [adj] *fashionable, elegant*
classy, deluxe, exclusive, grand, in, plush, posh, ritzy*, smart, stylish, sumptuous, swank, swell, tony*, trendy, with-it*; SEE CONCEPT *589*

switch [n] *change, exchange*
about-face, alteration, change of direction, reversal, shift, substitution, swap, transformation; SEE CONCEPT *697*

switch [v] *change, exchange*
change course, convert, deflect, deviate, divert, interchange, rearrange, replace, shift, shunt, sidetrack, substitute, swap, trade, turn, turnabout, turn aside, veer; SEE CONCEPTS *104,232,697*

swivel [v] *spin around axis*
hinge, pirouette, pivot, revolve, rotate, swing around, turn, whirl; SEE CONCEPT *145*

swollen [adj] *enlarged*
bloated, bulgy, distended, distent, inflamed, inflated, puffed, puffy, tumescent, tumid; SEE CONCEPT *485*

swoop [v] *descend quickly*
dive, fall, plummet, plunge, pounce, rush, slide, stoop, sweep; SEE CONCEPTS *150,181*

sycophant [n] *person who caters to another*
adulator, backscratcher*, backslapper*, bootlicker*, brownnoser*, doormat*, fan, fawner, flatterer, flunky*, groupie*, groveler, handshaker*, hanger-on*, lackey, minion, parasite, politician, puppet, slave; SEE CONCEPT *423*

symbol [n] *letter, character, sign of written communication*
attribute, badge, denotation, design, device, emblem, figure, image, indication, logo, mark, motif, note, numeral, pattern, regalia, representation, stamp, token, type; SEE CONCEPT *284*

symbolic [adj] *representative*
allegorical, characteristic, denotative, emblematic, figurative, indicative, indicatory, significant, suggestive, symptomatic, token, typical; SEE CONCEPT *267*

symbolize [v] *represent; stand for*
betoken, body forth, connote, denote, emblematize, embody, epitomize, exemplify, express, illustrate, indicate, mean, mirror, personify, show, signify, suggest, symbol, typify; SEE CONCEPTS *74,138,682*

symmetrical [adj] *well-proportioned*
balanced, commensurable, commensurate, equal, in proportion, proportional, regular, shapely, well-formed; SEE CONCEPTS *480,485,579*

symmetry [n] *proportion*
agreement, arrangement, balance, centrality, conformity, correspondence, equality, equilibrium, equipoise, equivalence, evenness, finish, form, harmony, order, proportionality, regularity, rhythm, shapeliness, similarity; SEE CONCEPTS *716,717*

sympathetic [adj1] *concerned, feeling*
affectionate, all heart*, appreciating, benign, benignant, caring, commiserating, compassionate, comprehending, condoling, considerate, having heart in right place*, interested, kind, kindhearted, kindly, loving, pitying, responsive, sensitive, soft, softhearted, supportive, sympathizing, tender, thoughtful, understanding, vicarious, warm, warmhearted; SEE CONCEPT *542*

sympathetic [adj2] *agreeable, friendly*
amenable, appreciative, approving, companionable, compatible, congenial, congruous, consistent, consonant, cool, down, encouraging, favorably disposed, having a heart*, in sympathy with, like-minded, on same wavelength*, open, open-minded, pro*, receptive, responsive, simpatico, tuned in*, vicarious, well-disposed, well-intentioned; SEE CONCEPTS *401,542,563*

sympathize [v] *feel for, be compassionate*
ache, agree, appreciate, be in accord, be in sympathy, be kind to, be there for*, be understanding, bleed for*, comfort, commiserate, compassionate, comprehend, condole, emphathize, feel heart go out to*, go along with, grieve with, have compassion, identify with, love, offer consolation, pick up on, pity, relate to*, share another's sorrow,

show kindliness, show mercy, show tenderness, side with*, tune in*, understand; SEE CONCEPTS **34,110**

sympathy [n1] *shared feeling*
accord, affinity, agreement, alliance, attraction, benignancy, close relation, commiseration, compassion, concord, congeniality, connection, correspondence, empathy, feelings, fellow feeling, harmony, heart, kindliness, kindness, mutual attraction, mutual fondness, rapport, responsiveness, sensitivity, tenderness, understanding, union, unity, warmheartedness, warmth; SEE CONCEPTS **388,410,664**

sympathy [n2] *pity*
aid, cheer, comfort, commiseration, compassion, condolence, consolation, empathy, encouragement, reassurance, rue, ruth, solace, tenderness, thoughtfulness, understanding; SEE CONCEPTS **410,633**

symptom [n] *sign of illness or problem*
evidence, expression, index, indication, indicia, manifestation, mark, note, significant, syndrome, token, warning; SEE CONCEPTS **306,316**

syndicate [n] *group of business entities*
association, board, bunch, cabinet, cartel, chain, chamber, combine, committee, company, conglomerate, council, crew, gang, group, megacorp*, mob, multinational*, organization, outfit, partnership, pool, ring, trust, union; SEE CONCEPTS **323,325**

syndrome [n] *disease, condition*
affection, ailment, complaint, complex, diagnostics, disorder, infirmity, malady, problem, prognostics, sickness, sign, symptoms; SEE CONCEPTS **306,316,674**

synonymous [adj] *equivalent*
alike, apposite, coincident, compatible, convertible, correspondent, corresponding, equal, identical, identified, interchangeable, like, one and the same, same, similar, synonymic, tantamount; SEE CONCEPTS **487,573**

synopsis [n] *digest, summary*
abridgment, abstract, aperçu, breviary, brief, capsule, compendium, condensation, conspectus, epitome, outline, précis, recap*, résumé, review, rundown, run-through, sketch; SEE CONCEPT **283**

synthesis [n] *combining; combination*
amalgam, amalgamation, blend, building a whole, coalescence, composite, compound, constructing, construction, entirety, forming, fusion, integrating, integration, making one, organism, organization, structure, unification, union, unit, welding, whole; SEE CONCEPTS **113,837**

synthesize [v] *combine; make whole*
amalgamate, arrange, blend, harmonize, incorporate, integrate, manufacture, orchestrate, symphonize, unify; SEE CONCEPTS **113,205**

synthetic [adj] *artificial*
constructed, counterfeit, ersatz*, fabricated, factitious, fake, false, hokey*, made, makeshift, manufactured, mock, phony, plastic, unnatural; SEE CONCEPTS **485,582**

system [n1] *order, whole*
arrangement, classification, combination, complex, conformity, coordination, entity, fixed order, frame of reference, ideology, integral, integrate, logical order, orderliness, organization, philosophy, red tape*, regularity, rule, scheme, setup, structure, sum, theory, totality; SEE CONCEPTS **770,837**

system [n2] *method, plan*
arrangement, artifice, course of action, custom, definite plan, fashion, logical process, manner, methodicalness, methodology, mode, modus, modus operandi, operation, orderliness, orderly process, pattern, policy, practice, procedure, proceeding, process, regularity, routine, scheme, strategy, structure, systematic process, systematization, tactics, technique, theory, usage, way, wise; SEE CONCEPT **6**

systematic [adj] *orderly*
analytical, arranged, businesslike, complete, efficient, logical, methodic, methodical, ordered, organized, out-and-out*, precise, regular, standardized, systematized, thoroughgoing, well-ordered; SEE CONCEPTS **557,585**

systematize [v] *put in order*
arrange, array, contrive, design, devise, dispose, establish, frame, get act together, institute, make uniform, marshal, methodize, order, organize, plan, project, pull together, rationalize, regulate, schematize, shape up, standardize, straighten up, systemize, tighten up; SEE CONCEPTS **84,94**

T

tab [n1] *ticket, label*
bookmark, clip, flag, flap, holder, logo, loop, marker, slip, sticker, stop, strip, tag; SEE CONCEPTS **270,475**

tab [n2] *bill for service*
account, charge, check, cost, invoice, price, price tag, rate, reckoning, score, statement, tariff; SEE CONCEPT **329**

table [n1] *furniture upon which to work, eat*
bar, bench, board, buffet, bureau, console, counter, desk, dining table, dinner table, dresser, lectern, pulpit, sideboard, sink, slab, stand, wagon; SEE CONCEPT **443**

table [n2] *meal*
bill of fare, board, cuisine, diet, fare, food, meat and drink, menu, spread, victuals; SEE CONCEPT **459**

table [n3] *flatland*
flat, mesa, plain, plateau, tableland, upland; SEE CONCEPT **509**

table [n4] *diagram with columns of information*
agenda, appendix, canon, catalogue, chart, compendium, digest, graph, illustration, index, inventory, list, plan, record, register, roll, schedule, statistics, summary, synopsis, table of contents, tabulation; SEE CONCEPTS **283,625**

table [v] *postpone a proposition*
cool*, defer, delay, enter, hang*, hold off, hold up, move, pigeonhole*, propose, put aside, put forward, put off, put on back burner*, put on hold*, put on ice*, put on the shelf*, shelve, submit, suggest; SEE CONCEPTS **121,324**

tableau [n] *scene, often painted*
illustration, picture, representation, spectacle, view; SEE CONCEPTS **625,716**

tablet [n1] *sheaf of papers that are connected*
book, folder, memo pad, notebook, pad, quire, ream, scratch, scratch pad, sheets; SEE CONCEPT **475**

sw
ta

tablet [n2] *encapsulated medicine*
cake, capsule, dose, lozenge, medicine, pellet, pill, square, troche; SEE CONCEPT **307**

taboo [n] *something not allowed, permitted*
anathema, ban, disapproval, don't*, forbiddance, inhibition, interdict, law, limitation, no-no*, prohibition, proscription, regulation, religious convention, reservation, restraint, restriction, sanction, social convention, stricture, superstition, thou-shalt-not*; SEE CONCEPTS **532,688**

taboo [adj] *not allowed, permitted*
anathema, banned, beyond the pale*, disapproved, forbidden, frowned on*, illegal, off limits*, outlawed, out of bounds*, prohibited, proscribed, reserved, restricted, ruled out, unacceptable, unmentionable, unthinkable; SEE CONCEPT **548**

tabulate [v] *figure, classify*
alphabetize, arrange, catalogue, categorize, chart, codify, digest, enumerate, formulate, grade, index, list, methodize, order, range, register, systematize, tabularize; SEE CONCEPTS **84,764**

tacit [adj] *taken for granted; not said aloud*
alluded to, allusive, assumed, hinted at, implicit, implied, inarticulate, indirect, inferred, intimated, silent, suggested, undeclared, understood, unexpressed, unsaid, unspoken, unstated, unvoiced, wordless; SEE CONCEPTS **529,548**

taciturn [adj] *uncommunicative*
aloof, antisocial, brooding, clammed up*, close, close-mouthed*, cold, curt, distant, dour, dried-up*, dumb, laconic, mum, mute, quiet, reserved, reticent, sententious, silent, sparing, speechless, tight-lipped*, unexpressive, unforthcoming, withdrawn; SEE CONCEPTS **267,401**

tack [n1] *course of movement*
aim, alteration, approach, bearing, bend, deflection, deviation, digression, direction, double, echelon, heading, line, method, oblique course, path, plan, point of sail, procedure, set, shift, siding, sidling, sweep, swerve, switch, tactic, tangent, turn, variation, way, yaw, zigzag; SEE CONCEPTS **692,738**

tack [n2] *short pin for attaching*
brad, nail, point, pushpin, staple, thumbtack; SEE CONCEPT **475**

tack [v] *attach*
add, annex, append, baste, fasten, fix, hem, mount, nail, paste, pin, sew, staple, stitch, tag, tie; SEE CONCEPTS **85,160,218**

tackle [n] *equipment for activity*
accouterment, apparatus, appliance, gear, goods, habiliments, hook, impedimenta, implements, line, machinery, materiel, outfit, paraphernalia, rig, rigging, tools, trappings; SEE CONCEPT **496**

tackle [v1] *make an effort*
accept, apply oneself, attack, attempt, bang away at*, begin, come to grips with*, deal with, devote oneself to, embark upon, engage in, essay, give a try*, give a whirl*, go for it*, launch, make a run at*, pitch into, set about, square off*, start the ball rolling*, take a shot at*, take in hand*, take on, take up, try, try on for size*, turn one's hand to*, turn to, undertake, work on; SEE CONCEPTS **87,100**

tackle [v2] *jump on and grab*
attack, block, bring down, bring to the ground*, catch, challenge, clutch, confront, down, grapple, grasp, halt, intercept, nail, put the freeze on*,

sack, seize, smear, stop, take, take hold of, throw, throw down, upset; SEE CONCEPTS **90,164,191**

tacky [adj] *cheap, tasteless*
broken-down, crude, dilapidated, dingy, dowdy, down-at-heel*, faded, frumpy*, gaudy, inelegant, mangy*, messy, nasty*, outmoded, out-of-date, poky*, ratty, run-down, seedy, shabby, shoddy, sleazy*, sloppy*, slovenly, stodgy, threadbare, unbecoming, unkempt, unstylish, unsuitable, untidy, vulgar; SEE CONCEPTS **485,589**

tact [n] *finesse, thoughtfulness*
acumen, acuteness, address, adroitness, amenity, aptness, care, cautious, civil, common sense, consideration, control, courtesy, delicacy, delicatesse, diplomacy, discernment, discretion, discrimination, gallantry, good taste, head, horse sense*, intelligence, judgment, penetration, perception, perspicacity, poise, policy, politeness, presence, prudence, refinement, repose, savoir-faire, sensitivity, skill, smoothness, suavity, subtlety, tactfulness, understanding, urbanity; SEE CONCEPT **633**

tactful [adj] *thoughtful, careful*
adroit, aware, cautious, civil, considerate, courteous, deft, delicate, diplomatic, discreet, gentle, judicious, observant, perceptive, poised, polished, polite, politic, prudent, sensitive, skilled, skillful, suave, subtle, sympathetic, tactical, understanding, urbane, wise; SEE CONCEPT **401**

tactics [n] *strategy*
approach, campaign, channels, course, defense, device, disposition, generalship, line, maneuver, maneuvering, means, method, move, plan, plan of attack, ploy, policy, procedure, red tape*, scheme, stratagem, system, tack, technique, trick, way; SEE CONCEPT **660**

tactless [adj] *unthinking, careless*
awkward, blundering, boorish, brash, bungling, clumsy, crude, discourteous, gauche, gruff, harsh, hasty, impolite, impolitic, imprudent, inconsiderate, indelicate, indiscreet, inept, injudicious, insensitive, maladroit, misunderstanding, rash, rough, rude, sharp, stupid, thoughtless, uncivil, unconsiderate, undiplomatic, unfeeling, unkind, unperceptive, unpolished, unsubtle, unsympathetic, untactful, vulgar; SEE CONCEPT **401**

tag [n] *label, ticket*
badge, button, card, check, chip, docket, emblem, flap, ID*, identification, inscription, insignia, logo, mark, marker, motto, note, pin, slip, stamp, sticker, stub, tab, tally, trademark, voucher; SEE CONCEPTS **270,284,475**

tag [v1] *label; attach label*
add, adjoin, affix, annex, append, call, check, christen, designate, docket, dub, earmark, fasten, hold, identify, mark, name, nickname, style, tack, tally, tap, term, ticket, title, touch; SEE CONCEPTS **62,85,160**

tag [v2] *follow*
accompany, attend, bedog, chase, dog, heel, hunt, pursue, shadow, tail, trace, track, track down, trail; SEE CONCEPT **207**

tail [n] *end piece, part*
appendage, behind, butt*, buttocks, caudal appendage, conclusion, empennage, end, extremity, fag end*, hind end, hindmost part, hind part, last part, posterior, rear, rear end, reverse, rudder, rump*, stub, tag, tag end, tailpiece, train, tush*, wagger*; SEE CONCEPTS **392,825,827**

tail [v] *follow*
bedog, dog, eye*, hound, keep an eye on, pursue,

shadow, stalk, tag, track, trail; SEE CONCEPT *207*

tailor [*n*] *person who sews clothing*
clothier, costumier, couturier, dressmaker, garment maker, needle worker*, outfitter, suit maker; SEE CONCEPT *348*

tailor [*v*] *make to fit; adjust*
accommodate, adapt, alter, conform, convert, custom-make, cut, cut to fit, dovetail*, fashion, fit, make to order, modify, mold, quadrate, reconcile, shape, shape up, square, style, suit, tailor-make*; SEE CONCEPTS *126,202,218*

taint [*n*] *contamination, corruption*
black mark, blemish, blot, contagion, defect, disgrace, dishonor, fault, flaw, infection, pollution, shame, smear, spot, stain, stigma; SEE CONCEPTS *230,388*

taint [*v*] *dirty, contaminate; ruin*
adulterate, besmirch, blacken, blemish, blight, blot, blur, brand, break down, cast a slur, cloud, cook, corrupt, crud up*, crumble, cut, damage, debase, decay, decompose, defile, deprave, discolor, discredit, disgrace, dishonor, disintegrate, doctor, foul, give a bad name*, harm, hurt, infect, muddy, poison, pollute, putrefy, rot, shame, smear, soil, spike, spoil, stain, stigmatize, sully, tar, tarnish, trash*, turn, water, water down; SEE CONCEPTS *246,254,384*

take [*n*] *profit*
booty*, catch, catching, cut, gate, haul*, holding, part, proceeds, receipts, return, returns, revenue, share, takings, yield; SEE CONCEPT *344*

take [*v1*] *get; help oneself to*
abduct, accept, acquire, arrest, attain, capture, carry off, carve out, catch, clasp, clutch, collar*, collect, earn, ensnare, entrap, gain possession, gather up, get hold of, grab, grasp, grip, handle, haul in, have, hold, lay hold of, obtain, overtake, pick up, prehend, pull in, reach, reap, receive, secure, seize, snag, snatch, strike, take hold of, take in, win; SEE CONCEPTS *120,142*

take [*v2*] *steal*
abduct, abstract, accroach, annex, appropriate, arrogate, borrow, carry off, commandeer, confiscate, expropriate, filch*, haul in, liberate, lift*, misappropriate, nab*, nail*, nip*, pick up, pinch*, pluck, pocket*, preempt, pull in, purloin, rip off*, run off with*, salvage, seize, sequester, snag, snare, snatch*, snitch*, swipe*, take in; SEE CONCEPT *139*

take [*v3*] *buy; reserve*
book, borrow, charter, choose, cull, decide on, derive, draw, elect, engage, gain, get, hire, lease, mark, obtain, optate, opt for, pay for, pick, prefer, procure, purchase, rent, select, single out; SEE CONCEPTS *41,327*

take [*v4*] *endure*
abide, accept, accommodate, bear, bear with, brave, brook, contain, give access, go, go through, grin and bear it*, hack*, hang in*, hang on*, hang tough*, hold, let in, live with, put up with, receive, ride out*, stand, stand for, stick it out*, stomach, submit to, suffer, swallow, take it, take it lying down*, take it on the chin*, tolerate, undergo, weather, welcome, withstand; SEE CONCEPT *23*

take [*v5*] *consume*
devour, down, drink, eat, feed, feed on, imbibe, ingest, inhale, meal, partake of, swallow; SEE CONCEPT *169*

take [*v6*] *accept, adopt; use*
accommodate, admit, appropriate, assume, be aware of, behave, bring, deal with, delight in, do, effect, enjoy, enter upon, execute, exercise, exert, experience, function, give access, have, include, let in, like, luxuriate in, make, observe, operate, perform, play, practice, put in practice, react, receive, relish, sense, serve, take in, treat, undertake, utilize, welcome, work; SEE CONCEPTS *100,124,225*

take [*v7*] *understand*
accept, apprehend, assume, be aware of, believe, catch, compass, comprehend, consider, deem, expect, experience, feel, follow, gather, grasp, hold, imagine, interpret as, know, look upon, observe, perceive, presume, receive, reckon*, regard, see, see as, sense, suppose, suspect, take in, think, think of as; SEE CONCEPT *15*

take [*v8*] *win; be successful*
beat, be efficacious, do the trick, have effect, operate, prevail, succeed, triumph, work; SEE CONCEPT *706*

take [*v9*] *carry, transport; accompany*
attend, back, bear, bring, buck, cart, conduct, convey, convoy, drive, escort, ferry, fetch, go with, guide, gun, haul, heel, jag, journey, lead, lug, move, pack, piggyback*, pilot, ride, schlepp*, shoulder, steer, tote, tour, trek, truck, usher; SEE CONCEPTS *211,236,217*

take [*v10*] *captivate, enchant*
allure, attract, become popular, bewitch, charm, delight, draw, entertain, fascinate, magnetize, overwhelm, please, wile, win favor; SEE CONCEPT *11*

take [*v11*] *require*
ask, call for, crave, demand, necessitate, need; SEE CONCEPT *646*

take [*v12*] *subtract*
deduct, discount, draw back, eliminate, knock off, remove, subtract, take away, take off, take out; SEE CONCEPTS *211,236,247*

take [*v13*] *cheat, deceive*
bamboozle*, beat*, bilk, con, cozen, defraud, do*, dupe, fiddle, flimflam*, gull, hoodwink, pull a fast one*, swindle, take for a ride*, trick; SEE CONCEPTS *59,192*

take [*v14*] *contract, catch*
be seized, come down with*, derive, draw, get, sicken with, take sick with; SEE CONCEPT *308*

take down [*v1*] *write down*
inscribe, jot down, make a note of, minute, note, note down, put on record, record, set down, transcribe; SEE CONCEPT *125*

take down [*v2*] *humble*
deflate, humiliate, let down, lower, mortify, pull down, put down, take apart; SEE CONCEPTS *7,19,52*

take in [*v1*] *deceive, fool*
beguile, betray, bilk, bluff, cheat, con, defraud, delude, do*, double-cross*, dupe, flimflam*, four-flush*, gull, hoodwink, lie, mislead, pull wool over eyes*, swindle, trick; SEE CONCEPT *59*

take in [*v2*] *understand*
absorb, assimilate, comprehend, digest, get, grasp, perceive, receive, savvy, see, soak up, take; SEE CONCEPT *15*

takeoff [*n1*] *leaving*
ascent, climb, departure, hop, jump, launch, lift-off, rise, upward flight; SEE CONCEPTS *148,195,224*

ta
ta

takeoff [n2] *mockery, satire*
burlesque, caricature, cartoon, comedy, imitation, lampoon, mocking, parody, ridicule, send-up, spoof, travesty; SEE CONCEPTS *111,263,292*

take off [v1] *leave; leave the ground*
ascend, bear, beat it, become airborne, begone, blast off, blow*, clear out*, decamp, depart, disappear, exit, get off, get out, go, go away, head, hightail*, hit the road*, hit the trail*, lift off, light out*, make*, pull out, quit, scram*, set out*, shove off*, soar, split, take to the air*, vamoose*, withdraw; SEE CONCEPTS *148,195,224*

take off [v2] *mock, satirize*
ape, burlesque, caricature, imitate, lampoon, mimic, parody, ridicule, send up, spoof, travesty; SEE CONCEPTS *111,273,292*

take on [v1] *assume, accept*
acquire, add, address oneself to, adopt, agree to do, annex, append, attempt, become, begin, come to have, commence, develop, embrace, employ, endeavor, engage, enlist, enroll, espouse, handle, have a go at*, hire, launch, put on, retain, set about, tackle, take in hand*, take up, take upon oneself*, try, turn, undertake, venture; SEE CONCEPTS *87,221*

take on [v2] *compete*
attack, battle, contend, contest, encounter, engage, face, fight, match, meet, oppose, pit, vie; SEE CONCEPT *92*

take up [v] *begin or start again*
adopt, assume, become involved in, carry on, commence, continue, embrace, engage in, enter, espouse, follow through, get off, go on, initiate, kick off, open, pick up, proceed, recommence, renew, reopen, restart, resume, set to, start, tackle, take on, tee off, undertake; SEE CONCEPTS *221,239*

tale [n1] *story*
account, anecdote, fable, fairy tale, fiction, folk tale, legend, myth, narration, narrative, novel, relation, report, romance, saga, short story, yarn; SEE CONCEPT *282*

tale [n2] *made-up story*
canard, chestnut*, clothesline*, cock-and-bull story*, defamation, detraction, exaggeration, fabrication, falsehood, falsity, fib, fiction, lie, misrepresentation, prevarication, rigmarole*, rumor, scandal, slander, spiel*, tall story*, untruth, untruth, yarn*; SEE CONCEPTS *278,282*

talent [n] *ability*
aptitude, aptness, art, a way with*, bent*, capability, capacity, craft, endowment, expertise, facility, faculty, flair, forte, genius, gift, green thumb*, head*, inventiveness, knack*, knowhow*, nose*, power, savvy*, set, skill, smarts*, the formula*, the goods*, the right stuff*, thing*, turn*, what it takes*; SEE CONCEPT *630*

talk [n1] *speech, address to group*
allocution, chalk talk*, declamation, descant, discourse, disquisition, dissertation, epilogue, exhortation, expatiation, harangue, homily, lecture, monologue, oration, peroration, prelection, recitation, screed, sermon, spiel*; SEE CONCEPTS *60,285*

talk [n2] *gossip*
allusion, badinage, banter, blather*, bombast, bunk*, buzz*, cant, chat, chatter, chitchat, conversation, cry, gab, grapevine*, hearsay, hint, hot air*, idle talk, innuendo, insinuation, jaw*, jive*, lip*, noise, nonsense*, palaver, persiflage, prose,

racket*, raillery, report, rot*, rubbish*, rumble*, rumor, scuttlebutt*, small talk, tête-à-tête, trash*, yarn*; SEE CONCEPTS *51,278*

talk [n3] *discussion*
argument, colloquy, conclave, confabulation, conference, consultation, conversation, deliberation, dialogue, earful, encounter, eyeball-to-eyeball*, huddle*, interlocution, interview, meeting, negotiation, palaver, parlance, parley, powwow*, seminar, spiel*, straight talk, symposium, ventilation, visit; SEE CONCEPT *56*

talk [n4] *communication with language*
argot, chatter, dialect, discourse, jargon, lingo, locution, parlance, patois, slang, speaking, speech, utterance, verbalization, vocalization, words; SEE CONCEPTS *47,65*

talk [v1] *produce words; inform*
articulate, babble, broach, chant, chat, chatter, comment on, communicate, confess, converse, describe, divulge, drawl, drone, express, flap one's tongue*, gab, gabble*, give voice to, gossip, influence, intone, notify, palaver, parley, patter, persuade, prate, prattle, pronounce, reveal, rhapsodize, run on*, say, sing*, soliloquize, speak, spill the beans*, spout, squeak*, squeal*, talk one's leg off*, tell, tell all*, use, utter, ventriloquize, verbalize, voice, yak*; SEE CONCEPTS *60,266*

talk [v2] *discuss with another*
argue, be in contact, canvass, carry on conversation, chew*, collogue, commune, confabulate, confer, confide, consult, contact, deliberate, dialogue, engage in conversation, exchange, go into a huddle*, groupthink*, have a meet*, hold discussion, huddle*, interact, interface, interview, join in conversation, keep in touch*, negotiate, network*, palaver, parley, reach out, reason, relate, thrash out*, touch*, touch base*, vent, visit; SEE CONCEPT *56*

talk [v3] *address group*
accost, deliver a speech, discourse, give a talk, give speech, harangue, hold forth, induce, influence, lecture, orate, persuade, pitch, prelect, sermonize, speak, spiel*, spout*, stump*, sway*; SEE CONCEPTS *60,285*

talkative [adj] *excessively communicative*
articulate, big-mouthed*, chattering, chatty*, effusive, eloquent, fluent, full of hot air*, gabby*, garrulous, glib, gossipy, long-winded*, loose-lipped*, loquacious, loudmouthed*, mouthy*, multiloquent, prolix, rattling, slick*, smooth*, talky, verbal, verbose, vocal, voluble, windy*, wordy; SEE CONCEPT *267*

tall [adj1] *high in stature, length*
alpine, altitudinous, beanstalk*, big, elevated, giant, great, high-reaching, lank, lanky, lofty, rangy, sizable, sky-high, skyscraping, soaring, statuesque, towering; SEE CONCEPTS *779,782*

tall [adj2] *exaggerated, unreasonable*
absurd, demanding, difficult, embellished, exorbitant, farfetched, hard, implausible, impossible, outlandish, overblown, preposterous, steep, unbelievable; SEE CONCEPTS *529,565*

tally [n] *count, record*
account, mark, poll, reckoning, running total, score, summation, tab, total; SEE CONCEPTS *283,787*

tally [v] *add up; count, record*
catalog, compute, enumerate, inventory, itemize, keep score, mark, mark down, number, numerate,

reckon, register, sum, tale, tell, total, write down; SEE CONCEPTS *125,764*

tame [adj 1] *domesticated, compliant*
acclimatized, amenable, biddable, bridled, broken, busted, civilized, cultivated, disciplined, docile, domestic, fearless, gentle, gentle as a lamb*, habituated, harmless, harnessed, housebroken, kindly, manageable, meek, mild, muzzled, obedient, overcome, pliable, pliant, subdued, submissive, tractable, trained, unafraid, unresisting, yoked*; SEE CONCEPT *401*

tame [adj 2] *dull, uninteresting*
bland, bloodless, boiled down*, boring, conventional, diluted, feeble, flat*, halfhearted, humdrum*, insipid, lifeless, limp, mild, monotonous, prosaic, routine, spiritless, tedious, unexciting, uninspiring, vapid, weak, wearisome, whitebread*, without punch*; SEE CONCEPTS *529,542,548*

tame [v] *domesticate, make compliant*
break, break in, break the spirit*, bridle, bring to heel*, bust, check, conquer, curb, discipline, domesticate, domiciliate, enslave, gentle, housebreak, humble, humiliate, mitigate, mute, pacify, repress, restrain, soften, subdue, subjugate, suppress, temper, tone down, train, vanquish, water down*; SEE CONCEPTS *14,250*

tamper [v 1] *interfere, alter*
busybody*, butt in*, change, cook, cut, damage, destroy, diversify, doctor, fiddle with*, fool, horn in*, interfere, interlope, interpose, intrude, irrigate, manipulate, meddle, mess around with*, monkey around*, muck about*, phony up*, plant*, poke nose into*, spike*, tinker, vary, water*; SEE CONCEPT *232*

tamper [v 2] *bribe*
buy, buy off, corrupt, fix, get to, have, influence, lubricate, manipulate, reach, rig, square*; SEE CONCEPT *192*

tan [n/adj] *light brown*
beige, biscuit, bronze, brown, brownish, buff, cream, drab, ecru, gold, khaki, leather-colored, natural, olive, olive-brown, saddle, sand, suntan, tawny, umber, yellowish; SEE CONCEPTS *618,622*

tang [n] *biting taste or odor*
aroma, bite, flavor, guts*, kick*, nip, piquancy, pungency, reek, relish, sapidity, sapor, savor, scent, smack*, smell, spiciness, tanginess, thrill, twang, zest, zip*; SEE CONCEPTS *599,600,614*

tangible [adj] *real, concrete*
actual, appreciable, corporeal, definite, detectable, discernible, distinct, embodied, evident, factual, gross, incarnated, manifest, material, objective, observable, obvious, palpable, patent, perceivable, perceptible, phenomenal, physical, plain, positive, sensible, solid, stable, substantial, tactile, touchable, verifiable, visible, wellgrounded; SEE CONCEPTS *529,582*

tangle [n] *knot, confusion*
coil, complication, entanglement, jam, jungle, labyrinth, mass, mat, maze, mesh, mess, mix-up, morass, muddle, rummage, skein, snag, snarl, twist, web; SEE CONCEPTS *230,674,720*

tangle [v] *knot, complicate*
catch, coil, confuse, derange, discompose, disorganize, drag into, embroil, enmesh, ensnare, entangle, entrap, foul up*, hamper, implicate, interlace, interlock, intertwist, interweave, involve, jam, kink, make a party to*, mat, mesh, mess up*, mix up*, muck up*, obstruct, perplex, ravel, snarl, tie up, trap, twist, unbalance, upset; SEE CONCEPTS *112,190*

tantalize [v] *provoke, tease*
annoy, badger, baffle, bait, bedevil, beleaguer, charm, entice, fascinate, frustrate, gnaw, harass, harry, keep hanging*, lead on, make mouth water*, pester, plague, taunt, thwart, titillate, torment, torture, worry; SEE CONCEPTS *7,11,19,22*

tantamount [adj] *same*
alike, as good as, commensurate, duplicate, equal, equivalent, identical, indistinguishable, like, parallel, same as, selfsame, synonymous, uniform, very; SEE CONCEPTS *487,573*

tantrum [n] *fit*
anger, animosity, conniption, dander*, flare-up, hemorrhage*, huff*, hysterics, outburst, storm*, temper, temper tantrum, wax; SEE CONCEPTS *306,384*

tap [n] *faucet*
bibcock, cock, egress, hydrant, nozzle, petcock, spigot, spout, stopcock, valve; SEE CONCEPTS *445,464*

tap [v 1] *hit lightly*
beat, bob, dab, drum, knock, palpate, pat, percuss, rap, strike, tag, thud, thump, tip, touch; SEE CONCEPT *189*

tap [v 2] *pierce to drain*
bleed, bore, broach, draft, drain, draw; draw forth, draw off, draw out, drill, empty, lance, milk, mine, open, penetrate, perforate, pump, riddle, siphon, spear, spike, stab, unplug, unstopper, use, utilize; SEE CONCEPTS *142,220*

tape [n] *ribbon of material*
band, braid, edging, line, rope, strip; SEE CONCEPT *475*

tape [v 1] *stick together with material*
bandage, bind, bond, fasten, hold together, rope, seal, secure, support, swathe, tie, tie up, truss, wire, wrap; SEE CONCEPTS *85,160*

tape [v 2] *record sounds, sights*
audiotape, make a tape, register, tape-record, video, videotape; SEE CONCEPTS *125,292*

taper/taper off [v] *decrease to a point*
abate, bate, close, come to a point, die away, die out, diminish, drain, dwindle, fade, lessen, narrow, recede, reduce, rescind, subside, thin, thin out, wane, weaken, wind down; SEE CONCEPTS *137,698,776*

tardy [adj] *late*
backward, behindhand, belated, dawdling, delayed, delinquent, detained, dilatory, held up, hung up*, in a bind, jammed, laggard, loitering, not arrived, not done, overdue, procrastinating, retarded, slack, slow, sluggish, strapped for time*, too late, unpunctual; SEE CONCEPTS *542,548,799*

target [n 1] *aim, goal*
ambition, bull's-eye*, destination, duty, end, function, ground zero*, intention, mark, object, objective, point, purpose, spot, use; SEE CONCEPT *659*

target [n 2] *person as object of ridicule*
butt*, byword, game, mark*, pigeon*, prey, quarry, scapegoat*, scorn, sitting duck*, sport, victim; SEE CONCEPT *423*

tariff [n] *tax or fee*
assessment, charge, cost, duty, excise, impost, levy, price, price tag, rate, tab, tax, toll; SEE CONCEPT *329*

tarnish [v] *dirty, corrupt*
befoul, begrime, blacken, blemish, blot, contaminate, damage, darken, defame, defile, dim, discolor, disgrace, dull, embarrass, grime, harm, hurt, impair, injure, lose luster, lose shine, mar, muddy, pale, pollute, rust, slander, smear, smudge, soil, spoil, spot, stain, sully, taint, tar, vitiate; SEE CONCEPTS 246,254,469

tarry [v] *dawdle, delay*
abide, bide, dally, drag, drag one's feet*, dwell, filibuster, get no place fast*, goof around*, hang around*, hold the phone*, lag, linger, lodge, loiter, lose time, pause, poke, procrastinate, put off, remain, rest, sojourn, stall, stay, stick around, stop, stop over, tail, take one's time*, temporize, tool*, trail, visit, wait, warm a chair*; SEE CONCEPTS 35,151,210

tart [n] *pastry*
bun, Danish, eclair, fruit tart, pie, popover, roll, turnover; SEE CONCEPT 457

tart [adj] *bitter, sour in taste or effect*
acerb, acerbic, acetose, acid, acidulous, acrimonious, astringent, barbed, biting, caustic, cutting, dry, harsh, nasty, piquant, pungent, scathing, sharp, short, snappish, snappy, snippy, tangy, testy, trenchant, vinegary, wounding; SEE CONCEPTS 267,613

task [n] *job or chore, often assigned*
assignment, bother, burden, business, calling, charge, daily grind*, deadweight*, duty, effort, employment, enterprise, errand, exercise, fun and games*, function, gig*, grind*, grindstone*, headache*, job, labor, load, long row to hoe*, millstone*, mission, nuisance, occupation, office, onus, pain, project, province, responsibility, stint, strain, tax, toil, trouble, undertaking, vocation, work; SEE CONCEPTS 362,666

task [v] *assign, burden*
charge, encumber, entrust, exhaust, lade, load, oppress, overload, push, saddle, strain, tax, test, weary, weigh, weight; SEE CONCEPTS 14,112,666

taste [n1] *flavor of some quality*
aftertaste, aroma, bang*, bitter, drive, ginger, jolt, kick*, oomph*, palatableness, piquancy, punch*, relish, salt, sapidity, savor, savoriness, smack, sour, sting*, suggestion, sweet, tang*, wallop, zest, zing*, zip*; SEE CONCEPT 614

taste [n2] *tiny sample*
appetizer, bit, bite, canapé, chaw, dash, delicacy, drop, fragment, hint, hors d'oeuvre, morsel, mouthful, nip, sampling, sip, soupçon, spoonful, sprinkling, suggestion, swallow, tidbit, tincture, tinge, titbit, touch, trifle, whiff*, wink*; SEE CONCEPTS 458,835

taste [n3] *inclination, preference*
affection, appetence, appetite, attachment, bent*, comprehension, cup of tea*, desire, disposition, druthers*, fancy, fondness, gusto, heart, leaning, liking, palate, partiality, penchant, predilection, predisposition, prepossession, relish, soft spot*, stomach*, tendency, thing*, type, understanding, weakness, zest; SEE CONCEPTS 20,32,529,659

taste [n4] *capacity to sense flavor*
appetence, appetite, gout, gustation, palate, stomach, taste buds, tongue; SEE CONCEPTS 590,615

taste [n5] *judgment, propriety*
acumen, acuteness, aestheticism, appreciation, correctness, cultivation, culture, decorum, delicacy, discernment, discretion, discrimination, dis-

tinction, elegance, feeling, finesse, good taste, grace, nicety, penetration, perception, polish, politeness, refinement, restraint, style, susceptibility, tact, tactfulness, tastefulness; SEE CONCEPTS 388,411,655,689

taste [v1] *judge, try*
assay, bite, chew, criticize, differentiate, discern, distinguish, eat, enjoy, lick, nibble, partake, perceive, relish, sample, savor, sense, sip, test, touch, try, try the flavor of; SEE CONCEPTS 169,616

taste [v2] *experience*
appreciate, be exposed to, come up against, encounter, feel, have knowledge of, know, meet with, partake of, perceive, run up against, savor, undergo; SEE CONCEPT 678

tasteful [adj] *nice, refined*
aesthetically pleasing, artistic, beautiful, charming, chaste, classical, classy, cultivated, cultured, delectable, delicate, discriminating, elegant, esthetic, exquisite, fastidious, fine, graceful, gratifying, handsome, harmonious, in good taste, pleasing, plush, polished, posh, precise, pure, quiet, restrained, rich, savory, smart, snazzy*, spiffy*, splendiferous, stylish, subdued, swank*, tasty, unaffected, unobtrusive, uptown*; SEE CONCEPTS 529,574,589

tasteless [adj1] *without flavor*
big zero*, blah*, bland, boring, distasteful, dull, flat, flavorless, insipid, mild, nowhere*, pabulum*, plain, plain vanilla*, savorless, stale, tame, thin, unappetizing, uninspired, uninteresting, unpalatable, unpleasurable, unsavory, unseasoned, vanilla*, vapid, watered-down, watery, weak, without spice, zero*; SEE CONCEPT 613

tasteless [adj2] *cheap, vulgar*
artificial, barbaric, barbarous, coarse, crass, crude, flashy, foolish, garish, gaudy, graceless, hideous, impolite, improper, indecorous, indelicate, indiscreet, inelegant, loud, low, low-down, low-down-and-dirty*, makeshift*, off-color*, ornate, ostentatious, outlandish, pretentious, raunchy*, rough, rude, showy, stupid, tacky, tactless, tawdry, trivial, uncouth, unlovely, unpolished, unrefined, unseemly, unsightly, useless, wild; SEE CONCEPTS 401,570,589

tasty [adj] *delicious*
appetizing, delectable, delish*, divine, flavorful, flavorsome, flavory, full-flavored, good-tasting, heavenly, luscious, mellow, palatable, piquant, pungent, sapid, savory, scrumptious, spicy, sugarcoated, sweetened, tasteful, toothsome, toothy, yummy, zestful; SEE CONCEPT 613

tattle [v] *gossip; tell rumor*
babble, blab*, chat, chatter, give away, give the show away*, gossip, have a big mouth*, jabber, leak, noise, prate, prattle*, rumor, snitch, spill, spill the beans*, spread rumor*, squeal, talk, talk idly, tell on, tell tale*, yak*; SEE CONCEPTS 54,60

tattletale/tattler [n] *person who gossips, tells rumors*
bigmouth*, blabberer, blabbermouth*, busybody, canary*, fat mouth*, fink*, gossip, informer, rat*, rumormonger, scandalmonger, snitch*, squealer*, stool pigeon*, talebearer, taleteller, telltale*, tipster, troublemaker, whistleblower, windbag*; SEE CONCEPTS 412,423

taunt [n] *provocation; teasing*
backhanded compliment*, barb, brickbat*, censure, comeback, crack, cut, derision, dig, dirty

dig*, dump, gibe, insult, jab, jeer, mockery, outrage, parting shot*, put-down*, reproach, ridicule, sarcasm, slam*, slap*, snappy comeback*, swipe*; SEE CONCEPTS 7,19,266

taunt [v] *provoke, reproach; tease*
affront, bother, deride, dig*, disdain, dump on*, flout, insult, jab*, jeer, lout, mock, offend, outrage, put down, quiz, rally, revile, ridicule, scoff at, scorn, scout, slam*, slap*, sneer, swipe at, tantalize, torment, twitter, upbraid; SEE CONCEPTS 7,19,54

taut [adj] *rigid, tight*
close, firm, flexed, snug, stiff, strained, stressed, stretched, tense, tightly drawn, trim, unyielding; SEE CONCEPTS 488,604

tavern [n] *business establishment for serving drink, food*
alehouse, bar, barroom, beer joint*, dive*, drinkery, gin mill*, grog shop*, honky tonk*, hostelry, hotel, inn, joint*, lodge, lounge, night spot, nineteenth hole*, pub, public house, roadhouse, saloon, speakeasy*, suds*, taphouse*, taproom, watering hole*; SEE CONCEPTS 439,448,449

tawdry [adj] *cheap, tasteless*
blatant, brazen, chintzy*, common, crude, dirty, flaring, flashy, flaunting, garish, gaudy, gimcrack, glaring, glittering, glitzy, jazzy, junky*, loud, meretricious, obtrusive, offensive, plastic, poor, raffish, screaming, showy, sleazy*, sporty, tacky*, tinsel, vulgar; SEE CONCEPTS 334,589

tax [n1] *charge levied by government on property, income*
assessment, bite*, brokerage, capitation, contribution, cost, custom, dues, duty, excise, expense, fine, giveaway*, imposition, impost, levy, obligation, pork barrel*, price, rate, salvage, tariff, tithe, toll, towage, tribute; SEE CONCEPT 329

tax [n2] *burden*
albatross*, charge, deadweight*, demand, difficulty, drain, duty, imposition, load, millstone*, onus, pressure, strain, task, weight; SEE CONCEPTS 362,666

tax [v1] *levy charge on property, income*
assess, charge, charge duty, demand, demand toll, enact, exact, exact tribute, extract, impose, lay an impost, rate, require contribution, tithe; SEE CONCEPT 298

tax [v2] *burden*
charge, cumber, drain, encumber, enervate, exhaust, lade, load, make demands on, oppress, overburden, overtax, overuse, overwork, press hard on, pressure, prey on, push, put pressure on, saddle, sap, strain, stress, stretch, task, tire, try, weaken, wear out, weary, weigh, weigh down, weigh heavily on, weight; SEE CONCEPTS 14,208,240

tax [v3] *accuse*
arraign, blame, censure, charge, criminate, impeach, impugn, impute, incriminate, inculpate, indict, reproach, reprove; SEE CONCEPT 44

taxing [adj] *burdensome*
demanding, difficult, disturbing, enervating, exacting, exigent, grievous, heavy, onerous, oppressive, punishing, sapping, stressful, tedious, tiring, tough, troublesome, trying, wearing, wearisome, weighty; SEE CONCEPT 565

teach [v] *educate; instill knowledge*
advise, brainwash*, break in*, brief, catechize, coach, communicate, cram, demonstrate, develop, direct, discipline, drill, edify, enlighten,

exercise, explain, expound, fit, form, give instruction, give lessons, give the facts, ground, guide, illustrate, imbue, impart, implant, improve mind, inculcate, indoctrinate, inform, initiate, instruct, interpret, lecture, nurture, open eyes*, polish up*, pound into*, prepare, profess, rear, school, sharpen, show, show the ropes*, train, tutor; SEE CONCEPT 285

teacher [n] *person who educates*
abecedary, adviser, assistant, coach, disciplinarian, educator, faculty member, guide, instructor, lecturer, mentor, pedagogue, preceptor, professor, pundit, scholar, schoolteacher, supervisor, teach*, trainer, tutor; SEE CONCEPT 350

team [n] *group, crew*
aggregation, band, body, bunch, club, company, contingent, duo, faction, foursome, gang, lineup, organization, outfit, pair, partners, party, rig, sect, set, side, span, squad, stable, string, tandem, trio, troop, troupe, unit, workers, yoke; SEE CONCEPTS 365,397,417

tear [n1] *rip, cut*
breach, break, crack, damage, fissure, gash, hole, imperfection, laceration, mutilation, rent, run, rupture, scratch, split, tatter; SEE CONCEPT 513

tear/tears [n2] *droplets from eyes, often caused by emotion*
blubbering, crying, discharge, distress, drops, grieving, lachryma, lamentation, lamenting, moisture, mourning, pain, regret, sadness, sob, sob act*, sobbing, sorrow, teardrop, wailing, water, waterworks*, weep, weeping, weeps*, whimpering, woe; SEE CONCEPTS 185,467

tear [n3] *wild action*
bender, binge, bust, carousal, carouse, drunk, spree, wassail; SEE CONCEPTS 383,384

tear [v1] *cut, rip an object*
break, claw, cleave, crack, damage, divide, evulse, extract, fray, frazzle, gash, grab, impair, incise, injure, lacerate, mangle, mutilate, pluck, pull, pull apart, rend, ribbon, rift, rive, run, rupture, scratch, seize, separate, sever, shred, slash, slit, snatch, split, sunder, wrench, wrest, yank; SEE CONCEPTS 206,214

tear [v2] *move very fast*
boil, bolt, career, charge, chase, course, dart, dash, fling, fly, gallop, hurry, lash, race, run, rush, shoot, speed, spring, zoom; SEE CONCEPTS 150,152

tearful [adj] *crying, very upset*
bawling*, blubbering*, blubbery*, distressed, dolorous, in tears, lachrymose, lamentable, lamenting, moist, mournful, pathetic, pitiable, pitiful, poignant, sad, sniveling*, sobbing, sorrowful, teary, watery, weeping, weepy, wet, whimpering, woeful; SEE CONCEPTS 401,403

tease [v] *aggravate, provoke*
annoy, badger, bait, banter, be at, bedevil, beleaguer, bother, chaff, devil, disturb, dog*, gibe, give a hard time*, gnaw, goad, harass, harry, hector, importune, jive*, josh, lead on*, mock, needle*, nudge, pester, pick on*, plague, put down*, rag*, rally, razz*, rib*, ride, ridicule, roast*, send up*, slam, snap, sound, spoof, swipe at, tantalize, taunt, torment, vex, worry; SEE CONCEPTS 7,11,19,22

technical [adj] *concerning details, mechanics*
abstruse, high-tech*, industrial, mechanical, methodological, occupational, professional, re-

stricted, scholarly, scientific, special, specialized, technological, vocational; SEE CONCEPT 536

technique [n] *method*
address, approach, art, artistry, capability, capacity, course, craft, delivery, execution, facility, fashion, knack*, know-how*, manner, means, mode, modus, modus operandi, performance, procedure, proficiency, routine, skill, style, system, tactics, technic, touch, usage, way, wise; SEE CONCEPTS 6,630

tedious [adj] *dull, monotonous*
annoying, arid, banal, boring, bromidic, drab, dragging, draggy*, dreary, drudging, dry, dull as dishwater*, dusty*, endless, enervating, exhausting, fatiguing, ho-hum*, humdrum, insipid, irksome, laborious, lifeless, long-drawn-out*, mortal, pabulum*, poky*, prosaic, prosy, slow, snooze*, soporific, tiresome, tiring, unexciting, uninteresting, vapid, weariful, wearisome; SEE CONCEPTS 529,548

tedium [n] *dullness, monotony*
banality, boredom, deadness*, doldrums, drabness, dreariness, ennui, irksomeness, lack of interest, lifelessness, routine, sameness, tediousness, tiresomeness, wearisomeness, yawn*; SEE CONCEPTS 388,410,668

teem [v] *be abundant, full*
abound, bear, be crawling with, be full of, be numerous, be plentiful, be prolific, brim, bristle, burst, burst at seams*, bustle, crawl, crowd, flow, grow, jam, overflow, overrun, pack, pour, pour out, produce, prosper, pullulate, rain, roll in, shower, superabound, swarm, swell, swim in, wallow in; SEE CONCEPTS 146,179,740

teeming [adj] *abundant, full*
alive, brimful, brimming, bristling, bursting, chock-full, crammed, crawling, filled, fruitful, multitudinous, numerous, overflowing, packed, plentiful, populous, pregnant, replete, rife, swarming, thick, thronged; SEE CONCEPTS 481,483,774

teeny/teensy [adj] *very small*
diminutive, Lilliputian, microscopic, miniature, minuscule, minute, teensy-weensy*, teeny-weeny*, tiny, wee, weeny*; SEE CONCEPTS 773,789

teeter [v] *wobble back and forth*
balance, dangle, falter, flutter, lurch, pivot, quiver, reel, rock, seesaw, stagger, stammer, stumble, sway, teeter-totter*, topple, totter, tremble, tremble precariously, waver, weave, wiggle; SEE CONCEPT 145

telegram [n] *message sent by coded radio signals*
buzzer, cable, cablegram, call, coded message, flash, radiogram, report, signal, summons, telegraph, telegraphic message, teletype, telex, wire; SEE CONCEPTS 269,271

telepathy [n] *ability to know another's thoughts*
clairvoyance, ESP*, extrasensory perception, insight, mind-reading, parapsychology, premonition, presentiment, second sight*, sixth sense*, spiritualism, telepathic transmission, telesthesia, thought transference; SEE CONCEPTS 410,630

telephone [v] *communicate through telephone system*
buzz*, call, call up, contact, dial, get back to*, get on the horn*, get on the line*, give a call, give a jingle*, give a ring, make a call, phone, pick up*, put a call through*, ring, ring up, touch base with*; SEE CONCEPTS 225,266,269

television [n] *visual and audio entertainment transmitted via radio waves*
audio, baby-sitter*, boob tube*, box*, eye*, idiot box*, receiver, small screen, station, telly*, tube, TV, TV set, vid*, video; SEE CONCEPTS 277,279,293,463

tell [v1] *communicate*
acquaint, advise, announce, apprise, authorize, bid, break the news*, call upon, clue in*, command, confess, declare, direct, disclose, divulge, enjoin, explain, express, fill in*, give facts, give out, impart, inform, instruct, keep posted*, lay open*, leak, leave word, let in on*, let know, let slip*, level, make known, mention, notify, open up, order, proclaim, put before, recite, reel off*, report, represent, require, reveal, say, speak, spit it out*, state, summon, utter; SEE CONCEPT 266

tell [v2] *narrate, describe*
chronicle, depict, express, give an account of, portray, recount, rehearse, relate, report, set forth, speak, state; SEE CONCEPT 55

tell [v3] *understand, discern*
ascertain, be sure, clinch, comprehend, deduce, determine, differentiate, discover, discriminate, distinguish, divine, find out, identify, know, know for certain, learn, make out, perceive, recognize, see; SEE CONCEPT 15

tell [v4] *carry weight*
count, have effect, have force, make presence felt, make presence known, militate, register, take effect, take its toll*, weigh; SEE CONCEPT 676

tell [v5] *calculate*
compute, count, count one by one, enumerate, number, numerate, reckon, tale, tally; SEE CONCEPT 764

telling [adj] *effective, significant*
cogent, considerable, conspicuous, convincing, crucial, decisive, devastating, effectual, forceful, forcible, important, impressive, influential, marked, operative, potent, powerful, satisfactory, satisfying, solid, sound, striking, trenchant, valid, weighty; SEE CONCEPTS 537,567

tell off [v] *reprimand; criticize harshly*
berate, censure, chide, give piece of one's mind*, give tongue-lashing*, lecture, rail, rake over the coals*, rebuke, reproach, reprove, revile, scold, take to task*, tick off*, upbraid, vituperate; SEE CONCEPTS 44,52

temerity [n] *nerve, audacity*
assurance, boldness, brass*, carelessness, daring, effrontery, foolhardiness, forwardness, gall, hardihood, hastiness, heedlessness, impertinence, impetuosity, imprudence, impudence, impulsiveness, indiscretion, intrepidity, intrusiveness, nerve, overconfidence, pluck, precipitancy, precipitateness, precipitation, presumption, rashness, recklessness, rudeness, thoughtlessness, venturesomeness; SEE CONCEPTS 411,633

temper [n1] *state of mind*
atmosphere, attitude, attribute, aura, character, climate, complexion, condition, constitution, disposition, drift, frame of mind, humor, individualism, individuality, leaning, makeup, mind, mood, nature, orientation, outlook, peculiarity, personality, posture, property, quality, scene, soul, spirit, state, strain, style, temperament, tendency, tenor, thing*, timbre, tone, trend, type, vein, way; SEE CONCEPTS 410,411

temper [n2] *angriness; bad mood*
acerbity, anger, annoyance, bad-humor, cantan-

kerousness, crossness, dander*, excitability, fit, fretfulness, furor, fury, grouchiness, heat*, hot-headedness, huffiness, ill-humor, impatience, irascibility, ire, irritability, irritation, miff, outburst, passion, peevishness, petulance, pugnacity, rage, resentment, sensitivity, short fuse*, slow burn*, snit, sourness, stew*, sullenness, surliness, tantrum, tartness, tear*, tiff, tizzy*, touchiness, wax; SEE CONCEPTS 29,410

temper [n3] *calmness*
calm, composure, cool, coolness, equanimity, good humor, moderation, poise, self-control, tranquility; SEE CONCEPTS 32,410

temper [v1] *calm, moderate*
abate, adjust, admix, allay, alleviate, assuage, chill out*, cool, cool out*, curb, dilute, ease, fine tune, lessen, make reasonable, mitigate, modulate, mollify, monkey around with*, pacify, palliate, relieve, restrain, revamp, soften, soft-pedal*, soothe, switch, take the bite out of*, take the edge off*, take the sting out of*, tone down, transmogrify, weaken; SEE CONCEPTS 7,22, 110,126

temper [v2] *harden*
anneal, bake, braze, cement, chill, congeal, dry, indurate, mold, petrify, set, solidify, starch, steel, stiffen, strengthen, toughen, toughen up; SEE CONCEPTS 250,726

temperament [n] *disposition, personality*
attitude, bent, capacity, cast, character, complexion, constitution, distinctiveness, ego, emotions, frame of mind, humor, idiosyncrasy, inclination, individualism, individuality, inner nature, intellect, kind, makeup, mentality, mettle, mood, nature, outlook, peculiarity, quality, soul, spirit, stamp, structure, susceptibility, temperament, tendency, turn, type, way; SEE CONCEPTS 410,411

temperamental [adj] *angry most of the time; moody*
capricious, changeable, cussed*, easily upset, emotional, erratic, excitable, explosive, fickle, fiery, froward, headstrong, high-strung*, hot-headed*, hyper*, hypersensitive, impatient, in bad mood, inconsistent, irritable, mean, mercurial, neurotic, ornery, passionate, petulant, sensitive, thin-skinned*, ticklish, touchy, uncertain, undependable, unpredictable, unreliable, unstable, variable, volatile, willful; SEE CONCEPT 403

temperance [n] *self-restraint; abstinence*
abnegation, abstemiousness, asceticism, astringency, austerity, conservatism, constraint, continence, control, discretion, eschewal, forbearance, forgoing, frugality, golden mean*, happy medium*, measure, moderateness, moderation, moderatism, mortification, prohibition, prudence, reasonableness, refrainment, restraint, sacrifice, self-control, self-denial, self-deprivation, self-discipline, soberness, sobriety, stoicism, teetotalism, uninebriation, unintoxication; SEE CONCEPTS 410,633

temperate [adj1] *calm, moderate*
agreeable, balmy, checked, clement, collected, composed, conservative, constant, cool, curbed, discreet, dispassionate, equable, even, even-tempered, fair, gentle, levelheaded, medium, mild, modest, pleasant, reasonable, regulated, restrained, self-controlled, self-restrained, sensible, sober, soft, stable, steady, unexcessive, unextreme, unimpassioned, warm; SEE CONCEPTS 525,542,547

temperate [adj2] *controlled, sober*
abstemious, abstentious, abstinence, abstinent, continent, moderate, restrained, self-restraining; SEE CONCEPT 401

temperature [n] *hotness, coldness of some degree*
body heat, calefaction, climate, cold, condition, degrees, febricity, feverishness, heat, incalescence, pyrexia, thermal reading, warmth; SEE CONCEPT 610

tempest [n] *wild storm; commotion*
blizzard, bluster, chaos, convulsion, cyclone, disturbance, ferment, furor, gale, hurricane, squall, tornado, tumult, typhoon, upheaval, uproar, wildness, windstorm; SEE CONCEPTS 230,526

tempestuous [adj] *wild, stormy*
agitated, blustering, blustery, boisterous, breezy, coarse, emotional, excited, feverish, furious, gusty, heated, hysterical, impassioned, intense, passionate, raging, rough, rugged, squally, storming, tumultuous/tumultous, turbulent, unbridled, uncontrolled, unrestrained, violent, windy; SEE CONCEPTS 401,525,542

temple [n] *house of worship*
cathedral, chapel, church, holy place, house, house of God*, house of prayer*, mosque, pagoda, pantheon, place of worship, sanctuary, shrine, synagogue, tabernacle; SEE CONCEPTS 368,439

tempo [n] *beat, rhythm*
bounce, cadence, downbeat, measure, meter, momentum, pace, pulse, rate, speed, time, velocity; SEE CONCEPT 65

temporal [adj1] *material, worldly*
banausic, carnal, civil, earthly, earthy, fleshly, lay, materialistic, mortal, mundane, nonsacred, nonspiritual, physical, profane, secular, sensual, subcelestial, sublunary, terrestrial, unhallowed, unsacred, unsanctified, unspiritual; SEE CONCEPT 582

temporal [adj2] *momentary*
chronological, ephemeral, evanescent, fleeting, fugacious, fugitive, impermanent, momentary, of time, passing, short-lived, temporary, transient, transitory; SEE CONCEPT 799

temporary [adj] *lasting only a short while*
acting, ad hoc, ad interim, alternate, Band-Aid*, brief, changeable, ephemeral, evanescent, fleeting, for the time being*, fugacious, fugitive, impermanent, interim, limited, make-do*, makeshift*, momentary, mortal, overnight, passing, perishable, pro tem, pro tempore, provisional, provisory, shifting, short, short-lived, slapdash*, stopgap*, substitute, summary, supply, temp*, transient, transitory, unfixed, unstable, volatile; SEE CONCEPTS 551,798

tempt [v] *lure, entice*
allure, appeal to, attract, bait, butter up*, captivate, charm, coax, court, dare, decoy, draw, draw out, entrap, fascinate, honey*, hook*, incite, induce, influence, instigate, intrigue, inveigle, invite, lead on, make mouth water*, motivate, mousetrap*, move, oil, persuade, play up to, promote, provoke, risk, rouse, seduce, solicit, stimulate, tantalize, test, train, try, turn one's head*, wheedle, whet, woo*; SEE CONCEPTS 11,68

temptation [n] *lure, attraction*
allurement, appeal, attractiveness, bait, blandishment, coaxing, come-on*, decoy, draw, enticement, fancy, fascination, hankering, inducement, inveiglement, invitation, provocation, pull, se-

ducement, seduction, snare, tantalization, trap*, yen; SEE CONCEPTS **20,529,532,690,709**

tempting [adj] alluring, inviting
appetizing, attractive, charming, divine, enticing, fascinating, fetching, heavenly, intriguing, luring, magnetic, mouth-watering*, provoking, rousing, scrumptious, seductive, tantalizing, yummy*; SEE CONCEPTS **462,529**

tenable [adj] reasonable
arguable, believable, condonable, credible, defendable, defensible, excusable, impregnable, justifiable, maintainable, plausible, rational, reliable, secure, sound, strong, trustworthy, viable, vindicable, warrantable; SEE CONCEPTS **552,558**

tenacious [adj1] strong, unyielding
adamant, bound, clinging, cohering, cohesive, determined, dogged, fast, firm, forceful, inflexible, intransigent, iron, meaning business*, mulish, obdurate, obstinate, persevering, persistent, persisting, pertinacious, possessive, purposeful, relentless, resolute, retentive, set, solid, spunky, stalwart, staunch, steadfast, stout, strong-willed, stubborn, sturdy, sure, tight, tough, true, unforgetful, unshakable, unswerving; SEE CONCEPTS **326,401,489,542**

tenacious [adj2] sticky
adhesive, clinging, clingy, fast, firm, fixed, glutinous, gummy, inseparable, mucilaginous, resisting, retentive, secure, set, tacky, tight, viscid, viscose, viscous, waxy; SEE CONCEPTS **488,606**

tenacity [n] diligence, stubbornness
application, backbone, chutzpah*, clock*, courage, determination, doggedness, firmness, grit, guts*, gutsiness*, guttiness*, heart*, inflexibility, intestinal fortitude*, intransigence, moxie*, nerve, obduracy, obstinacy, perseverance, persistence, pertinacity, resoluteness, resolution, resolve, spunk, starch*, staunchness, steadfastness, stick-to-itiveness*, stomach*, strength of purpose, true grit*, what it takes*, willfulness; SEE CONCEPTS **411,657**

tenant [n] person who leases a place
addressee, boarder, dweller, holder, householder, indweller, inhabitant, leaseholder, lessee, lodger, occupant, occupier, possessor, renter, rent payer, resident, roomer; SEE CONCEPTS **348,423**

tend [v1] be apt, likely
aim, bear, be biased, be conducive, be disposed, be inclined, be in the habit of, be liable, bend, be predisposed, be prejudiced, conduce, contribute, dispose, drift, favor, go, gravitate, have an inclination, have a tendency, head, impel, incline, influence, lead, lean, look, make for, move, move toward, point, redound, result in, serve to, trend, turn, verge on; SEE CONCEPTS **411,650**

tend [v2] care for
accomplish, administer, attend, baby-sit, cater to, cherish, control, corral, cultivate, defend, direct, do, do for, feed, foster, guard, handle, keep, keep an eye on*, keep tabs on*, look after, maintain, manage, mind, minister to, nurse, nurture, oversee, perform, protect, ride herd on*, safeguard, see after, see to, serve, shepherd, shield, sit, superintend, supervise, take care of, take under wing*, wait on, watch, watch out for, watch over; SEE CONCEPTS **136,257,295**

tendency [n1] inclination to think or do in a certain way
addiction, affection, bent*, bias, current, custom, disposition, drift, habit, impulse, inclining, leaning, liability, mind, mindset*, partiality, penchant, predilection, predisposition, proclivity, proneness, propensity, readiness, run, set, shift, slant, susceptibility, temperament, thing*, trend, turn, type, usage, way*, weakness; SEE CONCEPT **657**

tendency [n2] direction of movement
aim, bearing, bent, bias, course, current, curve, drift, drive, heading, inclination, leaning, movement, purport, run, shift, tenor, trend, turn, turning, way; SEE CONCEPTS **692,738**

tender [adj1] fragile, soft
breakable, dainty, delicate, effete, feeble, frail, supple, weak; SEE CONCEPTS **604,606**

tender [adj2] young, inexperienced
callow, childish, childlike, green*, immature, impressionable, new, raw*, rookie*, sensitive, unripe, vernal, vulnerable, wet behind the ears*, youthful; SEE CONCEPTS **578,797**

tender [adj3] affectionate, loving
all heart*, amorous, benevolent, bleeding-heart*, caring, charitable, commiserative, compassionate, considerate, demonstrative, emotional, evocative, fond, forgiving, gentle, humane, kind, lenient, lovey-dovey*, merciful, mild, moving, mushy*, poignant, responsive, romantic, sensitive, sentimental, soft, softhearted, solicitous, sympathetic, tenderhearted, thoughtful, ticklish, tolerant, touching, touchy, warm, warmhearted, yielding; SEE CONCEPTS **401,542**

tender [adj4] painful, sore
aching, acute, bruised, delicate, hypersensitive, inflamed, irritated, oversensitive, raw, sensitive, smarting, thin-skinned, ticklish, touchy; SEE CONCEPTS **314,403,548**

tenebrous [adj] dark, ominous
ambiguous, amphibological, caliginous, dim, dingy, dusk, dusky, equivocal, gloomy, lightless, murky, obscure, shadowy, shady, somber, sunless, uncertain, unclear, unexplicit, unilluminated, unintelligible, unlit, vague; SEE CONCEPTS **535,617**

tenet [n] belief, principle
article of faith, assumption, canon, conception, conviction, credo, creed, doctrine, dogma, faith, impression, maxim, opinion, persuasion, position, precept, presumption, profession, rule, self-conviction, system, teaching, thesis, trust, view; SEE CONCEPTS **688,689**

tenor [n1] meaning, intent
aim, body, burden, core, course, course of thought, current, direction, drift, evolution, gist, inclination, meat, mood, path, pith, purport, purpose, run, sense, stuff, substance, tendency, theme, tone, trend, way; SEE CONCEPTS **529,682**

tenor [n2] high male voice
alto, countertenor, falsetto; SEE CONCEPT **65**

tense [adj1] tight, stretched
close, firm, rigid, stiff, strained, taut; SEE CONCEPTS **485,604**

tense [adj2] under stress, pressure
agitated, anxious, apprehensive, beside oneself*, bundle of nerves*, choked, clutched, concerned, edgy, excited, fidgety, fluttery, high-strung*, hung up*, hyper*, in a tizzy*, jittery, jumpy, keyed up*, moved, moving, nerve-racking, nervous, nervous wreck*, on edge, overanxious, overwrought, queasy, restive, restless, shaky, shot*, shot to pieces*, strained, stressful, strung out*, uneasy, unnerved, unquiet, up the wall*,

uptight*, white knuckled*, wired*, worried, worrying, wound up*, wreck*; SEE CONCEPTS *401,403,548*

tension [n1] *tightness*
astriction, balance, constriction, force, pressure, rigidity, stiffness, strain, straining, stress, stretching, tautness, tenseness, tensity; SEE CONCEPTS *723,726*

tension [n2] *mental stress*
agitation, antsiness*, ants in pants*, anxiety, apprehension, bad feeling*, brunt, concern, discomfort, disquiet, edginess, hostility, jitters*, jumps*, nail-biting*, nerves, nervousness, pins and needles*, pressure, restlessness, shakes*, strain, suspense, unease, uneasiness, worriment, worry; SEE CONCEPT *410*

tentative [adj1] *conditional, experimental*
acting, ad interim, conjectural, contingent, dependent, iffy*, indefinite, makeshift, not final, not settled, on trial, open for consideration, probationary, provisional, provisionary, provisory, speculative, subject to change, temporary, test, trial, unconfirmed, undecided, unsettled; SEE CONCEPTS *551,552*

tentative [adj2] *indefinite, uncertain*
backward, cautious, diffident, disinclined, doubtful, faltering, halting, hesitant, irresolute, reluctant, timid, undecided, unsure, vacillating, vacillatory, wobbly; SEE CONCEPTS *534,535,542*

tenuous [adj] *weak, thin*
aerial, airy, attenuate, attenuated, delicate, doubtful, dubious, ethereal, fine, flimsy, gossamer, insignificant, insubstantial, light, narrow, nebulous, questionable, rare, rarefied, reedy, shaky, sketchy, slender, slight, slim, subtle, twiggy; SEE CONCEPTS *489,491,575*

tenure [n] *time in position of responsibility*
administration, clamp, clasp, clench, clinch, clutch, dynasty, grasp, grip, hold, holding, incumbency, occupancy, occupation, ownership, possession, proprietorship, regime, reign, residence, security, tenancy; term; SEE CONCEPTS *287,816*

tepid [adj] *lukewarm*
apathetic, cool, disinterested, dull, halfhearted, indifferent, languid, lifeless, mild, milk-warm, moderate, slightly warm, spiritless, temperate, unenthusiastic, unlively, warm, warmish; SEE CONCEPTS *542,605*

term [n1] *description of a concept*
appellation, article, caption, denomination, designation, expression, head, indication, language, locution, moniker*, name, nomenclature, phrase, style, terminology, title, vocable, word; SEE CONCEPTS *275,683*

term [n2] *time period*
course, cycle, duration, go*, hitch*, interval, phase, quarter, season, semester, session, space, span, spell, standing, stretch, time, tour, turn, while; SEE CONCEPTS *807,822*

term [n3] *limit*
bound, boundary, close, conclusion, confine, confines, culmination, end, finish, fruition, limitation, terminus; SEE CONCEPTS *745,832*

term [v] *name something*
baptize, call, christen, denominate, describe, designate, dub, entitle, label, style, subtitle, tag, title; SEE CONCEPT *62*

terminal [n1] *end of road; limit*
boundary, depot, end, end of the line, extremity,

station, termination, terminus; SEE CONCEPTS *198,745*

terminal [n2] *computer screen, computer input/output device*
cathode ray tube, CRT*, display, input device, monitor, screen, VDT*, video display; SEE CONCEPT *463*

terminal [adj] *final, deadly*
bounding, check out*, closing, concluding, eventual, extreme, fatal, hindmost, incurable, killing, lag, last, latest, latter, lethal, limiting, mortal, on way out*, period, ultimate, utmost; SEE CONCEPTS *314,548*

terminate [v] *stop, finish*
abolish, abort, achieve, adjourn, annul, bounce, bound, bring to an end, cancel, cease, close, come to an end, complete, conclude, confine, cut off, define, desist, determine, discharge, discontinue, dismiss, dissolve, drop, eliminate, end, expire, extinguish, fire, halt, issue, lapse, limit, perfect, prorogate, prorogue, put an end to, recess, restrict, result, run out, sack, scratch, scrub*, tether, ultimate, wind down, wind up*, wrap*, wrap up*; SEE CONCEPTS *119,121,234*

termination [n] *end*
abortion, ballgame*, cease, cessation, close, completion, conclusion, consequence, curtains*, cutoff*, desistance, discontinuation, effect, ending, end of the line*, expiry, finale, finis, finish, issue, kiss-off*, outcome, payoff*, period, result, stop, terminus, windup*, wrap-up*; SEE CONCEPTS *119,832*

terms [n1] *conditions, agreement*
charge, circumstances, conclusion, condition, details, fee, fine print*, items, nitty-gritty*, particulars, payment, points, premise, premises, price, provision, provisions, proviso, provisos, qualifications, rate, reservation, size of it*, small print*, specifications, stipulation, stipulations, strings*, treaty, understanding, what it is*; SEE CONCEPTS *270,512,684*

terms [n2] *status of relationship*
balance, equality, equivalence, footing, par, parity, position, relations, relationship, standing; SEE CONCEPT *388*

terrain [n] *landscape*
area, bailiwick, contour, country, domain, dominion, field, form, ground, land, profile, province, region, shape, soil, sphere, territory, topography, turf; SEE CONCEPTS *508,509*

terrestrial [adj] *earthly*
earthbound, earthlike, earthy, global, mundane, physical, profane, prosaic, secular, sublunary, subsolar, telluric, temporal, terrene, uncelestial, unspiritual, worldly; SEE CONCEPT *536*

terrible [adj] *bad, horrible*
abhorrent, appalling, atrocious, awe-inspiring, awesome, awful, beastly, dangerous, desperate, dire, disastrous, disturbing, dread, dreaded, dreadful, extreme, fearful, frightful, ghastly, gruesome, harrowing, hateful, hideous, horrendous, horrible, horrid, horrifying, inconvenient, loathsome, monstrous, obnoxious, odious, offensive, petrifying, poor, repulsive, revolting, rotten, serious, severe, shocking, unfortunate, unnerving, unpleasant, unwelcome, vile; SEE CONCEPT *571*

terribly [adv] *very*
awfully, badly, decidedly, desperately, discouragingly, disturbingly, drastically, dreadfully, exceedingly, extremely, fearfully, frightfully,

te
te

gravely, greatly, highly, horribly, intensely, markedly, mightily, much, notoriously, remarkably, seriously, staggeringly, thoroughly, unbelievably, unfortunately, unhappily; SEE CONCEPTS 569,570

terrific [adj1] *intense*
agitating, appalling, awesome, awful, deafening, disquieting, dreadful, enormous, excessive, extreme, fearful, fierce, formidable, frightful, gigantic, great, harsh, horrible, horrific, huge, immense, large, monstrous, severe, shocking, terrible, terrorizing, thunderous, tremendous, upsetting; SEE CONCEPT 569

terrific [adj2] *wonderful*
ace*, amazing, breathtaking, divine, excellent, fabulous, fantastic, fine, glorious, great, groovy*, hot*, keen*, magnificent, marvelous, outstanding, sensational, smashing*, stupendous, super, superb, swell, very good; SEE CONCEPT 572

terrify [v] *scare*
alarm, appall, awe, chill, dismay, freeze, fright, frighten, horrify, intimidate, paralyze, petrify, scare stiff*, scare the pants off of*, scare to death*, shock, spook, startle, strike fear into*, stun, stupefy, terrorize; SEE CONCEPTS 7,19,42

territory [n] *domain, region*
area, belt, block, boundary, colony, commonwealth, country, district, dominion, empire, enclave, exclave, expanse, extent, field, land, mandate, nation, neck of the woods*, neighborhood, province, quarter, section, sector, sphere, state, stomping grounds*, street, terrain, terrene, township, tract, turf*, walk, zone; SEE CONCEPTS 198,349,508

terror [n] *intense fear*
alarm, anxiety, awe, consternation, dismay, dread, fearfulness, fright, horror, intimidation, panic, shock, trepidation, trepidity; SEE CONCEPTS 27,690

terrorize [v] *upset, threaten*
alarm, appall, awe, bludgeon, browbeat, bulldoze*, bully, coerce, cow, dismay, dragoon, fright, frighten, hector, horrify, intimidate, menace, oppress, petrify, scare, scare to death*, shock, spook, startle, strike terror into*, strongarm*, terrify; SEE CONCEPTS 7,14,19

terse [adj] *brief, short*
abrupt, aphoristic, boiled down*, breviloquent, brusque, clear-cut, clipped, close, compact, compendiary, compendious, concise, condensed, crisp, cryptic, curt, cut to the bone*, elliptical, epigrammatic, exact, gnomic, in a nutshell*, incisive, laconic, lean, neat, pithy, pointed, precise, sententious, short and sweet*, snappy, succinct, summary, taut, to the point, trenchant; SEE CONCEPTS 267,272

test [n] *examination, quiz*
analysis, approval, assessment, attempt, blue book*, catechism, check, comp*, confirmation, corroboration, countdown, criterion, dry run*, elimination, essay, evaluation, exam, experiment, final, fling*, go*, inquest, inquiry, inspection, investigation, lick*, oral*, ordeal, pop quiz, preliminary, probation, probing, proof, questionnaire, scrutiny, search, shibboleth, standard, substantiation, touchstone*, trial, trial and error*, trial run, try, tryout, verification, yardstick*; SEE CONCEPTS 5,290

test [v] *examine, quiz*
analyze, assay, assess, check, confirm, demonstrate, experiment, experimentalize, give a tryout, inquire, investigate, look into, make a trial run, match up, prove, prove out, put to the test*, question, run idea by someone*, run it up a flagpole*, see how it flies*, see how wind blows*, send up a balloon*, shake down*, stack up, substantiate, try, try on, try on for size*, try out, validate, verify; SEE CONCEPTS 5,103,291

testament [n] *tribute; last wishes*
attestation, colloquy, confirmation, covenant, demonstration, earnest, evidence, exemplification, instrument, proof, testimonial, testimony, will, witness; SEE CONCEPT 318

testify [v] *vouch for; give testimony*
affirm, announce, argue, assert, attest, bear witness, bespeak, betoken, certify, corroborate, cross one's heart*, declare, demonstrate, depone, depose, evince, give evidence, give facts, give one's word*, indicate, make evident, mount, point to, prove, say so*, show, sing*, stand up for, state, swear, swear to, swear up and down*, token, warrant, witness; SEE CONCEPTS 49,317

testimonial [n] *tribute*
affidavit, appreciation, attestation, certificate, character, commemoration, commendation, confirmation, credential, degree, endorsement, evidence, homage, honor, indication, manifestation, memorial, memorialization, monument, ovation, plug*, proof, recommendation, reference, remembrance, salute, salvo, say-so*, show, sign, symbol, testament, testimony, token, voucher, witness; SEE CONCEPTS 49,278,318

testimony [n] *declaration about truth; proof*
affidavit, affirmation, attestation, avowal, confirmation, corroboration, data, demonstration, deposition, documentation, evidence, facts, grounds, illustration, indication, information, manifestation, profession, statement, submission, substantiation, support, testament, verification, witness; SEE CONCEPTS 49,278,318

testy [adj] *irritable, touchy*
annoyed, bad-tempered, cantankerous, captious, choleric, crabbed, cranky*, cross, crotchety, edgy, exasperated, fretful, grouchy, grumpy*, impatient, irascible, mean, ornery*, out of sorts, peevish, peppery, petulant, quarrelsome, quicktempered, short-tempered, snappy*, splenetic, sullen, thin-skinned*, uptight*, waspish; SEE CONCEPTS 401,403,542

tether [n] *fastening*
binding, bond, chain, cord, fetter, halter, harness, lead, leash, picket, restraint, rope, shackle; SEE CONCEPT 475

tether [v] *fasten*
batten, bind, chain, fetter, leash, manacle, moor, picket, restrain, rope, secure, shackle, tie; SEE CONCEPTS 85,160

text [n1] *subject matter of document*
argument, body, consideration, content, contents, context, document, extract, fundamentals, head, idea, issue, line, lines, main body, matter, motify, motive, paragraph, passage, point, quotation, sentence, stanza, subject, theme, thesis, topic, verse, vocabulary, wording, words; SEE CONCEPTS 270,682

text [n2] *book used in education*
assignment, class book, course book, handbook, manual, reader, reference, reference book, required reading, schoolbook, source, syllabus, textbook, workbook; SEE CONCEPTS 280,287

texture [n] *characteristics of a surface*
arrangement, balance, being, character, coarseness, composition, consistency, constitution, disposition, essence, essentiality, fabric, feel, feeling, fiber, fineness, flexibility, form, framework, grain, intermixture, make, makeup, nap, nature, organization, pattern, quality, roughness, scheme, sense, smoothness, stiffness, strategy, structure, surface, taste, tissue, touch, warp, weave, web, woof; SEE CONCEPTS 611,673,682

thank [v] *express gratitude*
acknowledge, be grateful, be indebted, be obligated, be obliged, bless, bow down*, give thanks, kiss*, praise, say thank you, show appreciation, show courtesy, show gratitude, smile on*; SEE CONCEPTS 60,69,76

thankful [adj] *appreciative*
beholden, content, contented, grateful, gratified, indebted, much obliged, obliged, overwhelmed, pleased, relieved, satisfied; SEE CONCEPTS 401,403

thankless [adj1] *unappreciated*
barren, disagreeable, distasteful, fruitless, futile, miserable, not worth it*, ungrateful, unpleasant, unprofitable, unrecognized, unrequited, unreturned, unrewarding, useless, vain, wretched; SEE CONCEPTS 538,548

thankless [adj2] *unappreciative, inconsiderate (in behavior)*
careless, cruel, heedless, inappreciative, rude, self-centered, thoughtless, ungracious, ungrateful, unmindful, unthankful; SEE CONCEPT 401

thanks [n] *spoken or written appreciation*
acknowledgment, benediction, blessing, credit, grace, gramercy, gratefulness, gratitude, praise, recognition, thankfulness, thanksgiving, thank you note; SEE CONCEPTS 60,69,278

thaw [v] *unfreeze, warm*
become liquid, become soft, defrost, deliquesce, dissolve, flow, flux, fuse, liquefy, loosen, melt, mollify, open up, relax, relent, run, soften, unbend, warm up; SEE CONCEPTS 13,255,469

theater/theatre [n] *stage, building for performance*
amphitheater, arena, assembly hall, auditorium, barn, boards*, cinema, coliseum, concert hall, deck, drama, drive-in, footlights, hall, hippodrome, house, locale, movie, movie house, oak*, odeum, opera house, playhouse, room, scene, show hall, site; SEE CONCEPTS 263,293,439,448

theatrical [adj] *dramatic*
affected, amateur, artificial, campy*, ceremonious, comic, dramaturgic, exaggerated, ham*, hammy*, histrionic, legitimate, mannered, melodramatic, meretricious, operatic, ostentatious, pompous, schmaltzy*, show, showy, staged, stilted, superficial, theatric, thespian, tragic, unnatural, unreal, vaudeville; SEE CONCEPTS 401,536

theft [n] *stealing*
annexation, appropriation, break-in, burglary, caper, cheating, crime, defrauding, deprivation, embezzlement, extortion, filch, fleece*, fraud, grab*, heist, holdup, hustle*, job*, larceny, lift*, looting, mugging, peculation, pilferage, pilfering, pillage, pinch*, piracy, plunder, purloining, racket*, rapacity, rip-off*, robbery, robbing, score*, shoplifting, snatch*, snitch*, steal, stickup, swindle, swindling, swiping*, thievery, thieving, touch*, vandalism; SEE CONCEPTS 139,192

theme [n1] *idea, subject matter*
affair, argument, burden, business, case, head, keynote, leitmotif, line, matter, matter in hand, motif, motive, point, point at issue, problem, proposition, question, stuff, subject, text, thesis, thought, topic; SEE CONCEPTS 278,682,689

theme [n2] *written composition*
article, description, dissertation, essay, exercise, exposition, manuscript, paper, report, statement, thesis; SEE CONCEPT 271

then [adv1] *before; at another time*
again, all at once, anon, at that instant, at that moment, at that point, at that time, before long, formerly, later, next, on that occasion, soon after, suddenly, thereupon, when, years ago; SEE CONCEPT 799

then [adv2] *therefore*
accordingly, consequently, ergo, from that time, from then on, from there on, hence, so, thence, thenceforth, thereupon, thus, whence; SEE CONCEPT 548

theological [adj] *religious, concerning a god-centered philosophy*
apostolic, canonical, churchly, deistic, divine, doctrinal, ecclesiastical, metaphysical, scriptural, theistic; SEE CONCEPT 536

theorem [n] *explanation based on hypothesis and experiments*
assumption, axiom, belief, deduction, dictum, doctrine, formula, fundamental, law, postulate, principium, principle, proposition, rule, statement, theory, thesis; SEE CONCEPTS 529,688,689

theoretical [adj] *hypothetical*
abstract, academic, analytical, as a premise, assumed, codified, conjectural, contingent, formalistic, formalized, general, ideal, idealized, ideational, ideological, imaginative, impractical, instanced, intellectual, in the abstract, in theory, logical, metaphysical, notional, on paper*, pedantic, philosophical, postulated, presumed, problematical, pure, quixotic, speculative, suppositional, tentative, transcendent, transcendental, unearthly, unproved, unsubstantiated, vague; SEE CONCEPT 529

theorize [v] *hypothesize*
conjecture, formulate, guess, project, propound, speculate, submit, suggest, suppose, think; SEE CONCEPT 43

theory [n] *hypothesis, belief*
approach, argument, assumption, base, basis, belief, code, codification, concept, conditions, conjecture, doctrine, dogma, feeling, formularization, foundation, grounds, guess, guesswork, hunch, idea, ideology, impression, method, outlook, philosophy, plan, position, postulate, premise, presentiment, presumption, proposal, provision, rationale, scheme, shot*, speculation, stab*, supposal, suppose, supposition, surmise, suspicion, system, systemization, theorem, thesis, understanding; SEE CONCEPTS 529,689

therapeutic [adj] *healing*
ameliorative, analeptic, beneficial, corrective, curative, good, remedial, restorative, salubrious, salutary, sanative; SEE CONCEPT 537

therapy [n] *healing treatment*
analysis, cure, healing, medicine, remedial treatment, remedy, therapeutics; SEE CONCEPT 310

thereafter [adv] *from that time forward*
after that, consequently, following, forever after, from that day forward, from that day on, from

te
th

there on, hereafter, thenceforth, thenceforward; SEE CONCEPT 799

therefore [adv] *as a result; for that reason*
accordingly, and so, consequently, ergo, for, forasmuch as, for this reason, hence, inasmuch as, in consequence, in that event, on account of, on the grounds, since, so, then, thence, therefrom, thereupon, thus, to that end, whence, wherefore; SEE CONCEPTS 230,676

thesaurus [n] *dictionary of synonyms and antonyms*
glossary, language reference book, lexicon, onomasticon, reference book, sourcebook, storehouse of words, terminology, treasury of words, vocabulary, word list; SEE CONCEPT 280

thesis [n1] *belief, assumption to be tested*
apriorism, contention, contestation, hypothesis, idea, line, opinion, point, posit, position, postulate, postulation, premise, presumption, presupposition, principle, proposal, proposition, sentiment, statement, supposition, surmise, theory, view; SEE CONCEPTS 529,689

thesis [n2] *written dissertation*
argument, argumentation, composition, discourse, disquisition, essay, exposition, memoir, monograph, monography, paper, research, theme, tractate, treatise; SEE CONCEPTS 271,287

thick [adj1] *deep, bulky*
blubbery, broad, bulky, burly, chunky, compact, concrete, consolidated, fat, firm, hard, heavy, high, husky, massive, obese, pudgy, solid, squat, stocky, stubby, stumpy, substantial, thickset, wide; SEE CONCEPTS 491,773

thick [adj2] *concentrated, dense*
caked, clabbered, close, clotted, coagulated, compact, compressed, concrete, condensed, congealed, consolidated, crowded, curdled, deep, firm, fixed, gelatinous, gloppy*, gooey, gummous, gummy, gunky*, heavy, impenetrable, impervious, jelled, jellied, opaque, ossified, ropy, set, sloppy, solid, solidified, stiff, syrupy, thickened, turbid, viscid, viscous, vitrified; SEE CONCEPTS 483,606

thick [adj3] *crowded, packed*
abundant, brimming, bristling, bursting, chockfull*, close, compact, compressed, concentrated, condensed, considerable, covered, crammed, crawling with*, dense, frequent, full, great, heaped, impenetrable, impervious, inspissated, like sardines*, localized, multitudinous, numerous, populated, populous, profuse, rank, replete, several, solid, swarming, teeming, tight; SEE CONCEPT 771

thick [adj4] *stupid*
blockheaded, boneheaded, brainless, dense, dim-witted, doltish, dopey*, dull, dumb, ignorant, insensitive, moronic, numbskulled, obtuse, slow, slow-witted, thickheaded; SEE CONCEPT 402

thick [adj5] *dense (referring to weather)*
cloudy, dull, foggy, heavy, impenetrable, indistinct, muddy, obscure, soupy*, turbid; SEE CONCEPT 525

thick [adj6] *friendly*
chummy*, close, confidential, cordial, devoted, familiar, hand in glove*, inseparable, intimate, on good terms; SEE CONCEPT 555

thick [adj7] *unreasonable*
excessive, flimsy*, implausible, improbable, inconceivable, incredible, thin*, too much*, unbelievable, unconvincing, unfair, unjust, unsubstantial; SEE CONCEPTS 529,548

thicken [v] *set; make more dense*
add, buttress, cake, clabber, clot, coagulate, condense, congeal, curdle, deepen, enlarge, expand, freeze, gel, grow thick, harden, inspissate, jell, jelly, ossify, petrify, reinforce, solidify, stiffen, swell, widen; SEE CONCEPTS 137,250,469

thief [n] *person who steals*
bandit, burglar, cat burglar, cheat, clip*, criminal, crook, defalcator, embezzler, heister*, highway robber, hijacker, holdup artist, housebreaker, kleptomaniac, larcener, larcenist, lifter*, moonlighter*, mugger, owl*, pickpocket, pilferer, pirate, plunderer, porch climber*, prowler, punk*, purloiner, robber, scrounger, shoplifter, sniper, spider*, stealer, stickup artist*, swindler; SEE CONCEPT 412

thieving/thievish [adj] *criminal*
crooked, cunning, dishonest, fraudulent, furtive, kleptomaniacal*, larcenous, light-fingered*, pilfering, piratic*, plunderous, predatory, rapacious, secretive, sly, spoliative, stealthy, sticky-fingered*; SEE CONCEPT 401

thin [adj1] *fine, light, slender*
attenuate, attenuated, beanpole*, beanstalk*, bony*, cadaverous, delicate, emaciated, ethereal, featherweight, fragile, gangling, gangly, gaunt, haggard, lank, lanky, lean, lightweight, meager, narrow, peaked, pinched, pole*, puny*, rangy, rarefied, rawboned, reedy, rickety, scraggy*, scrawny, shadow, shriveled, skeletal, skinny, slight, slim, slinky, small, spare, spindly, stalky*, starved, stick*, stilt*, subtle, threadlike, twiggy*, twiglike, undernourished, underweight, wan, wasted, wizened; SEE CONCEPTS 491,773

thin [adj2] *transparent, fine*
attenuate, attenuated, delicate, diaphanous, filmy, flimsy, gossamer, paper-thin, permeable, rare, rarefied, refined, see-through, sheer, slight, slim, subtile, subtle, tenuous, translucent, unsubstantial, wafer-thin, wispy; SEE CONCEPT 606

thin [adj3] *deficient, weak*
diluted, feeble*, flat*, flimsy*, implausible, improbable, inadequate, inconceivable, incredible, insubstantial, insufficient, lame, meager, poor, questionable, scant, scanty, scarce, scattered, shallow, sketchy, skimpy*, slight, sparse, stretched, superficial, thick*, transparent, unbelievable, unconvincing, unpersuasive, unsubstantial, untenable, vapid, weak-kneed*; SEE CONCEPT 771

thin [adj4] *diluted*
diffuse, dilute, dispersed, fine, light, rarefied, refined, runny, subtle, watery, weak, wishy-washy*; SEE CONCEPT 485

thin [v] *make diluted or less dense*
attenuate, cook, cut, cut back, decrease, delete, diminish, disperse, doctor, edit, emaciate, expand, extenuate, irrigate, lace*, needle*, prune, rarefy, reduce, refine, shave, spike, trim, water, water down, weaken, weed out; SEE CONCEPTS 137,250

thing [n1] *something felt, seen, perceived*
affair, anything, apparatus, article, being, body, business, circumstance, commodity, concept, concern, configuration, contrivance, corporeality, creature, device, element, entity, everything, existence, existent, fact, figure, form, gadget, goods, implement, individual, information, instrument, item, machine, material, materiality, matter, means, mechanism, object, part, person,

phenomenon, piece, point, portion, shape, situation, stuff, subject, substance, tool, word; SEE CONCEPT 433

thing [n2] *act*
accomplishment, action, circumstance, deed, doing, duty, episode, event, eventuality, exploit, feat, happening, incident, job, movement, obligation, occasion, occurrence, phenomenon, proceeding, stunt, task, work; SEE CONCEPT 3

thing [n3] *aspect, characteristic*
article, attribute, detail, element, facet, factor, feature, item, particular, point, property, quality, statement, thought, trait; SEE CONCEPTS 411,657,834

thing/things [n4] *personal possessions*
apparel, attire, baggage, belongings, chattels, clothes, clothing, duds*, effects, equipment, gear, goods, habiliments, impedimenta, luggage, odds and ends*, paraphernalia, personal effects, personals*, property, raiment, stuff, trappings, tricks; SEE CONCEPTS 446,451

thing [n5] *idea, obsession*
attitude, bee in bonnet*, craze, fad, fetish, fixation, hang-up*, idée fixe, impression, mania, notion, opinion, phobia, preoccupation, quirk, style, thought; SEE CONCEPT 529

think [v1] *believe; anticipate*
assume, be convinced, comprehend, conceive, conclude, consider, credit, deem, determine, envisage, envision, esteem, estimate, expect, fancy, feature, feel, foresee, gather, guess, hold, image, imagine, judge, plan for, presume, project, realize, reckon, regard, see, sense, suppose, surmise, suspect, take, understand, vision, visualize; SEE CONCEPTS 12,26

think [v2] *contemplate*
analyze, appraise, appreciate, brood, cerebrate, cogitate, comprehend, conceive, consider, deduce, deliberate, estimate, evaluate, examine, figure out, have in mind, ideate, imagine, infer, intellectualize, judge, logicalize, meditate, mull, mull over, muse, ponder, rack one's brains*, rationalize, reason, reflect, resolve, revolve, ruminate, sort out, speculate, stew*, stop to consider, study, take under consideration, turn over, use one's head*, weigh; SEE CONCEPTS 17,33,43

think [v3] *remember*
call to mind, recall, recollect, reminisce; SEE CONCEPT 40

thinkable [adj] *believable, feasible*
cogitable, comprehendible, comprehensible, conceivable, convincing, imaginable, likely, possible, practicable, practical, presumable, reasonable, supposable, within realm of possibility*, within the limits; SEE CONCEPT 529

thirst [n] *craving (especially for liquid)*
appetite, aridity, desire, drought, dryness, eagerness, hankering, hunger, keenness, longing, lust, passion, thirstiness, yearning, yen; SEE CONCEPTS 20,709

thirsty [adj] *dry, desirous (especially for liquid)*
agog*, anxious, appetent, ardent, arid, athirst, avid, bone-dry*, breathless, burning, cotton-mouthed*, craving, crazy for*, dehydrated, droughty, dry as dust*, dying for*, eager, greedy, hankering, hungry, impatient, inclined, itching for*, juiceless, keen, longing, lusting, parched, partial to, sapless, thirsting, waterless, wild for*, yearning; SEE CONCEPTS 403,603

thorny [adj1] *sharp, pointed*
barbed, briery, bristling, bristly, prickly, spiked, spiky, spinous, spiny, stinging, thistly; SEE CONCEPT 485

thorny [adj2] *difficult, problematic*
awkward, baffling, bothersome, formidable, harassing, hard, irksome, nettlesome, perplexing, prickly, severe, sticky, ticklish, tough, tricky, troublesome, trying, unpleasant, upsetting, vexatious, worrying; SEE CONCEPT 565

thorough/thoroughgoing [adj1] *exhaustive*
absolute, all-embracing, all-inclusive, all-out*, all the way*, assiduous, blow-by-blow*, careful, circumstantial, clocklike, complete, comprehensive, conscientious, detailed, efficient, exact, from A to Z*, full, full-dress*, in-depth, intensive, itemized, meticulous, minute, painstaking, particular, particularized, plenty, royal, scrupulous, slam bang*, soup to nuts*, sweeping, tough, whole-hog*; SEE CONCEPTS 531,538

thorough/thoroughgoing [adj2] *absolute, utter*
arrant, complete, consummate, downright, entire, out-and-out*, outright, perfect, pure, rank, sheer, straight-out*, total, unmitigated, unqualified; SEE CONCEPTS 531,535,557

thoroughbred [adj] *pure, unmixed*
blood, full-blooded, graded, papered, pedigree, pedigreed, pure-blooded, purebred; SEE CONCEPT 549

thoroughly [adv1] *exhaustively*
all, assiduously, carefully, completely, comprehensively, conscientiously, earnestly, efficiently, exceedingly, exceptionally, extremely, flat out*, from A to Z*, from top to bottom*, fully, hard, highly, hugely, in and out*, in detail, inside out*, intensely, intensively, meticulously, notably, painstakingly, remarkably, scrupulously, strikingly, sweepingly, through and through*, throughout, unremittingly, up and down*, very, whole hog*, wholly; SEE CONCEPTS 531,538

thoroughly [adv2] *utterly*
absolutely, altogether, completely, downright, entirely, fully, perfectly, plumb, quite, totally, to the full, well, wholly, without reservation; SEE CONCEPTS 531,535,557

though [adv] *however*
after all, all the same, for all that, howbeit, nevertheless, nonetheless, notwithstanding, still, still and all, withal, yet; SEE CONCEPT 544

though [conj] *while*
albeit, allowing, although, but, despite, despite the fact, even if, even supposing, even though, granted, howbeit, if, much as, notwithstanding, when, whereas; SEE CONCEPT 544

thought [n1] *formation of mental objects*
anticipation, apprehending, attention, brainwork, cerebration, cogitation, cognition, concluding, consideration, considering, contemplation, deducing, deduction, deliberation, deriving, discerning, heed, hope, ideation, inducing, inferring, introspection, intuition, judging, knowing, logic, meditation, musing, perceiving, rationalization, rationalizing, realizing, reasoning, reflection, regard, rumination, scrutiny, seeing, speculation, study, theorization, thinking, understanding; SEE CONCEPTS 17,43,409,410

thought [n2] *idea, concept*
aim, anxiety, appreciation, aspiration, assessment, assumption, attentiveness, belief, brainchild*, brainstorm*, caring, compassion,

conception, concern, conclusion, conjecture, conviction, design, dream, drift, estimation, expectation, fancy, feeling, guess, hope, hypothesis, image, inference, intention, intuition, judgment, kindness, knowledge, notion, object, opinion, plan, premise, prospect, purpose, regard, reverie, solicitude, supposition, sympathy, theory, thinking, understanding, view, worry; SEE CONCEPT *529*

thoughtful [*adj1*] *caring, mindful*
anxious, astute, attentive, aware, benign, canny, careful, cautious, charitable, chivalrous, circumspect, civil, concerned, considerate, cooperative, courteous, deliberate, diplomatic, discreet, friendly, gallant, gracious, heedful, helpful, indulgent, kind, kindly, mindful, neighborly, obliging, observant, observative, observing, polite, prudent, regardful, responsive, sensitive, social, solicitous, tactful, unselfish, wary, well-bred, well thought-out; SEE CONCEPTS *401,555*

thoughtful [*adj2*] *contemplative, introspective*
absorbed, analytical, attentive, brainy*, calculating, cerebral, cogitative, deep, deliberative, discerning, earnest, engrossed, farsighted, grave, intellectual, intent, keen, levelheaded, logical, lost in thought*, meditative, melancholy, museful, musing, pensive, philosophic, pondering, preoccupied, rapt, rational, reasonable, reasoning, reflecting, reflective, retrospective, ruminative, serious, sober, studious, subjective, thinking, wise, wistful; SEE CONCEPTS *402,403,542*

thoughtless [*adj1*] *inconsiderate*
antisocial, apathetic, asocial, blind, boorish, brash, deaf, discourteous, egocentric, hasty, heedless, hot-headed, impolite, inattentive, incautious, indelicate, indifferent, indiscreet, insensitive, listless, madcap, neglectful, negligent, primitive, rash, reckless, rude, self-centered, selfish, sharp, short, tactless, uncaring, unceremonious, unconcerned, undiplomatic, ungracious, unheeding, unkind, unmindful, unrefined; SEE CONCEPTS *401,555*

thoughtless [*adj2*] *absent-minded, unobservant*
bovine, careless, confused, doltish, dull, empty-headed, flighty, foolish, heedless, ill-advised, ill-considered, imprudent, inadvertent, inane, inattentive, incomprehensible, inept, injudicious, irrational, irreflective, lamebrained*, loony*, mindless, neglectful, negligent, obtuse, puerile, rash, reckless, regardless, remiss, senseless, silly, stupid, undiscerning, unheeding, unmindful, unreasonable, unreasoning, unreflective, unthinking, vacuous, witless; SEE CONCEPTS *402,403,542*

thrash [*v*] *flail about; beat*
batter, beat up, belabor, belt, birch, buffet, bury, cane, chasten, chastise, clobber, crush, defeat, flagellate, flog, jerk, kill, lambaste*, lick, maul, murder, overwhelm, paste, pelt, pitch, pound, pummel, punish, rout, rush, scourge, seesaw, slaughter, spank, stir, strike, surge, tan, tan one's hide*, thresh, toss, toss and turn*, trash, trim, trounce, wallop, wax*, whip, work over*, writhe; SEE CONCEPTS *95,189*

threadbare [*adj1*] *worn, frayed*
beat up*, damaged, dilapidated, dingy, dog-eared, down-at-the-heel*, faded, frowzy*, impaired, injured, old, ragged, ratty*, run-down, scruffy, seedy, shabby, shopworn, tacky, tattered, timeworn, used, used-up, worn-out, worse for wear*; SEE CONCEPTS *485,606*

threadbare [*adj2*] *trite, corny*
banal, bathetic, cliché, clichéd, cliché-ridden, common, commonplace, conventional, dull, everyday, familiar, hackneyed, imitative, motheaten*, musty, overused, poor, set, stale, stereotyped, stock, tedious, tired, uncreative, well-worn, worn-out; SEE CONCEPT *267*

threat [*n*] *warning; danger*
blackmail, bluff, commination, fix, foreboding, foreshadowing, fulmination, hazard, impendence, intimidation, menace, omen, peril, portent, presage, risk, thunder, writing on the wall*; SEE CONCEPTS *278,675*

threaten [*v1*] *warn, pressure*
abuse, admonish, augur, blackmail, bluster, browbeat, bully, caution, comminate, cow, enforce, flex muscles*, forebode, forewarn, fulminate, growl, intimidate, look daggers*, make threat, menace, portend, presage, pressurize, push around*, scare, scowl, shake fist at*, snarl, spook, terrorize, torment, walk heavy*; SEE CONCEPTS *7,19,78*

threaten [*v2*] *endanger*
advance, approach, be dangerous, be gathering, be imminent, be in the air*, be in the offing*, be on the horizon*, brewing, come on, forebode, foreshadow, frighten, hang over*, impend, imperil, jeopardize, loom, overhang, portend, presage, put at risk, put in jeopardy, warn; SEE CONCEPTS *231,407*

threatening [*adj*] *menacing, ominous*
aggressive, alarming, apocalyptic, at hand, baleful, baneful, black, bullying, cautionary, close, comminatory, dangerous, dire, fateful, forthcoming, grim, ill-boding, imminent, impendent, impending, inauspicious, intimidatory, looming, loury, lowering, lowery, minacious, minatory, near, overhanging, portending, portentous, scowling, sinister, terrorizing, ugly, unlucky, unpropitious, unsafe, upcoming, warning; SEE CONCEPTS *525,548,570*

threshold [*n*] *opening; beginning*
brink, dawn, door, doorstep, doorway, edge, entrance, gate, inception, origin, outset, point, point of departure, sill, start, starting point, verge, vestibule; SEE CONCEPTS *440,513,648,832*

thrift [*n*] *economy*
austerity, carefulness, economizing, frugality, parsimony, providence, prudence, saving, stinginess, thriftiness; SEE CONCEPT *335*

thrifty [*adj*] *economical*
canny, careful, chary, cheap, chintzy*, close*, close-fisted, conserving, frugal, mean, parsimonious, penny-pinching, preserving, provident, prudent, saving, scrimpy*, sparing, steal, stingy*, tight*, unwasteful; SEE CONCEPTS *334,401*

thrill [*n*] *sudden excitement*
adventure, bang*, blast, charge*, circus, fireworks, flash*, flush*, fun, good feeling, inspiration, kicks*, lift*, pleasure, refreshment, response, sensation, stimulation, tingle*, titillation, turn-on*, twitter*, upper*, wallop*; SEE CONCEPTS *32,529*

thrill [*v*] *excite, stimulate*
animate, arouse, blow away*, delight, electrify, enchant, enthuse, fire up*, flush, flutter, galvanize, glow, go over big*, grab*, inspire, juice*, key up*, knock one's socks off*, move, palpitate, quicken, quiver, race one's motor*, rally, rouse, score, send, stir, stir up, tickle*, tingle*, titillate,

tremble, turn on*, wow*; SEE CONCEPTS **7,22**

thrilling [adj] *exciting*

blood-tingling*, boss*, breathtaking, electrifying, enchanting, exquisite, fab*, fabulous, frantic, gripping, hair-raising*, large, mad, magnificent, mind-bending*, mind-blowing*, miraculous, overwhelming, rip-roaring*, riveting, rousing, sensational, shivering, stimulating, stirring, swinging, trembling, wild, wondrous, zero cool*; SEE CONCEPTS *548,572*

thrive [v] *do well*

advance, arrive, batten, bear fruit, bloom, blossom, boom, burgeon, develop, flourish, get ahead*, get fat*, get on*, get places*, get there*, grow, grow rich, increase, make a go*, mushroom*, progress, prosper, radiate, rise, score*, shine, shoot up, succeed, turn out well, wax; SEE CONCEPTS *704,706*

thriving [adj] *successful*

advancing, arrived, blooming, booming, burgeoning, cooking*, developing, doing well, flourishing, going strong*, growing, have it made*, have the wherewithal*, healthy, home free*, on top of heap*, progressing, prolific, prospering, prosperous, rich, roaring, robust, rolling*, sitting pretty*, wealthy; SEE CONCEPTS *334,528*

throb [v] *pulsate, beat*

flutter, palpitate, pitpat, pound, pulse, resonate, thrill, thump, tingle, tremble, twitter, vibrate; SEE CONCEPTS *152,185*

throng [n] *large crowd*

assemblage, assembly, bunch, collection, concourse, congregation, crush, drove, everybody, flock, gathering, horde, host, jam, mass, mob, multitude, pack, press, push, sellout, swarm; SEE CONCEPTS *417,432*

throttle [v] *choke*

burke, control, gag, inhibit, silence, smother, stifle, strangle, strangulate, suppress; SEE CONCEPT *191*

through [adj] *done*

buttoned up*, complete, completed, concluded, ended, finis*, finished, in the bag*, over, terminated, wound up*, wrapped up*; SEE CONCEPTS *531,548*

through [adj2] *direct*

constant, free, nonstop, one-way, opened, rapid, regular, straight, straightforward, unbroken, unhindered, uninterrupted; SEE CONCEPTS *482,581*

through [prep1] *by way of*

as a consequence, as a result, at the hand of, because of, by, by dint of, by means of, by reason, by the agency of, by virtue of, for, in consequence of, in virtue of, per, through the medium of, using, via, with, with the help of; SEE CONCEPT *544*

through [prep2] *between, during*

about, by, clear, for the period, from beginning to end, in, in and out in, in the middle, into, past, round, straight, throughout, within; SEE CONCEPTS *583,798*

throughout [adj] *during the whole of*

all over, all the time, all through, around, at full length, completely, during, every bit, everyplace, everywhere, far and near, far and wide, for the duration, from beginning to end, from end to end, from one end to the other, from start to finish, from the start, from the word go*, high and low, in all respects, in every place, in everything, inside and out, on all accounts*, over, overall, right through, round, the whole time, through the whole

of, to the end, up and down; SEE CONCEPTS *482,531,798*

throw [v1] *propel something through the air*

bandy, barrage, bombard, buck, bunt, butt, cant, cast, catapult, chuck, dash, deliver, discharge, dislodge, drive, fell, fire, flick, fling, fling off, flip, floor, force, heave, hurl, impel, lapidate, launch, let fly*, let go, lift, lob, overturn, overwhelm, peg, pellet, pelt, pepper, pitch, precipitate, project, push, put, scatter, send, shove, shower, shy, sling, splatter, spray, sprinkle, start, stone, strew, thrust, toss, tumble, unhorse, unseat, upset, volley, waft; SEE CONCEPT *222*

throw [v2] *confuse*

addle, astonish, baffle, befuddle, bewilder, confound, disconcert, distract, disturb, dizzy, dumbfound, fluster, mix up*, throw off*, unsettle, upset; SEE CONCEPT *16*

throw away [v1] *dispose of*

abandon, cast, cast off, chase, clear, discard, dismiss, dispense with, ditch*, drop*, dump*, eject, eliminate, evict, extrude, free oneself of, get rid of, jettison, junk*, lose, refuse, reject, rid oneself of, scrap*, shake off*, shed, shuck, slip, throw off, throw out, turn down, unburden; SEE CONCEPT *180*

throw away [v2] *waste*

be wasteful, blow, consume, dissipate, fail to exploit, fritter, lose, refuse, reject, squander, trifle, turn down; SEE CONCEPT *156*

throw off [v] *elude, escape*

abuse, deceive, evade, get away from, give the slip*, leave behind, lose, outdistance, outrun, shake off, trick; SEE CONCEPT *102*

throw out [v] *comment*

bring forward, bring to light*, bring up, chime in*, come out with, declare, deliver, produce, reveal, say, state, suggest, tell, utter; SEE CONCEPT *51*

throw over [v] *abandon, leave*

break up with, break with, desert, discard, drop, eighty-six*, finish with, forsake, jilt*, quit, renounce, split up with, walk out on*; SEE CONCEPTS *195,384*

throw up [v1] *vomit, be nauseous*

be sick, bring up, disgorge, heave, puke*, regurgitate, retch, spew, spit up, upchuck*; SEE CONCEPTS *179,308*

throw up [v2] *build quickly*

build overnight*, jerrybuild*, knock together*, patch, put together, roughcast, roughhew, run up*, slap together*, throw together; SEE CONCEPT *168*

thrust [n1] *point of communication*

burden, core, effect, gist, meaning, meat*, pith*, purport, sense, short, substance, upshot; SEE CONCEPT *682*

thrust [n2] *forward movement*

advance, blitz, boost, drive, impetus, impulsion, jump, lunge, momentum, onset, onslaught, poke, pressure, prod, propulsion, punch, push, shove, stab, whack, wham; SEE CONCEPTS *208,222*

thrust [v] *push hard*

advance, assail, assault, attack, bear down, boost, buck, butt, chuck, chunk, clip, clout, crowd, cut, dig, drive, elbow*, embed, fire, force, heave, hump, impale, impel, interject, jab, jam, jostle, lob, lunge, nick, nudge, peg, pierce, pitch, plunge, poke, pour it on*, press, prod, propel, punch, push forward, put, railroad*, ram, run, shove, sink, sling, smack, stab*, stick, toss, transfix, urge, wham*; SEE CONCEPTS 208,222

thud/thump [n/v] *dull crash; dull sound*
bang, beat, blow, clonk, clout, clump, clunk, fall, flutter, hammer, hit, knock, plop, poke, pound, pounding, pulse, rap, slap, smack, strike, throb, thunk*, thwack*, wallop*, whack*; SEE CONCEPTS 65,181,189

thunder [n] *crashing sound*
barrage, blast, boom, booming, cannonade, clap, cracking, crash, crashing, detonation, discharge, drumfire, explosion, fulmination, outburst, peal, pealing, roar, rumble, rumbling, thunderbolt, thundercrack, uproar; SEE CONCEPTS 524,595

thunder [v1] *boom, crash*
blast, clamor, clap, crack, deafen, detonate, drum, explode, peal, resound, reverberate, roar, rumble, storm; SEE CONCEPTS 65,521,526

thunder [v2] *yell at*
bark, bellow, curse, declaim, denounce, fulminate, gnarl, growl, rail, roar, shout, snarl, threaten, utter threat; SEE CONCEPTS 52,54

thus [adv1] *in this manner*
along these lines, as follows, hence, in kind, in such a way, in this fashion, in this way, just like that, like so, like this, so, thus and so, thus and thus, thusly, to such a degree; SEE CONCEPT 544

thus [adv2] *accordingly*
consequently, ergo, for this reason, hence, on that account, so, then, therefore, thereupon; SEE CONCEPT 544

thwart [v] *stop, hinder*
baffle, balk, beat, bilk, check, circumvent, confuse, counter, crab*, cramp, crimp, cross, curb, dash, defeat, disappoint, ditch, dodge, doublecross*, duck, foil, foul up*, frustrate, give the slip*, hold up, impede, louse up*, match, obstruct, oppose, outwit, pit, play dirty*, prevent, queer*, restrain, ruin, scotch*, skin, snafu*, stymie, take down, take wind out of*, trammel, upset, upset one's apple cart*; SEE CONCEPTS 121,130

tic [n] *spasm*
contraction, fit, jerk, twitch; SEE CONCEPT 308

tick [n1] *clicking sound; one beat*
beat, blow, clack, click, clicking, flash, instant, metallic sound, minute, moment, pulsation, pulse, rap, second, shake, tag, tapping, throb, ticktock, twinkling, wink; SEE CONCEPTS 595,808,810

tick [n2] *checkmark*
check, cross, dash, flick, indication, line, mark, stroke, X*; SEE CONCEPT 284

tick [v] *click*
beat, clack, pulsate, tap, thump, ticktock; SEE CONCEPTS 65,189

ticket [n] *authorization on paper*
admission, badge, board, card, certificate, check, chit, coupon, credential, docket, document, invite, key, label, license, marker, note, notice, open sesame, paper, pass, passage, passport, password, permit, raincheck, receipt, record, slip, sticker, stub, tab, tag, token, voucher; SEE CONCEPTS 271,685

tickle [v] *make laugh*
amuse, brush, caress, convulse, delight, divert, enchant, entertain, excite, gratify, itch, pat, pet, please, stimulate, stroke, thrill, tingle, titillate, touch, vellicate; SEE CONCEPTS 7,22,612

ticklish [adj] *difficult, tricky*
awkward, capricious, chancy, changeable, critical, dangerous, delicate, fickle, inconstant, mercurial, nice, precarious, risky, rocky, sensitive, temperamental, thorny, touchy, trying, uncertain, unstable, unsteady, variable, volatile; SEE CONCEPTS 548,565

tidbit [n] *tiny portion*
bit, bite, delicacy, goody*, morsel, mouthful, snack, soupçon, titbit, treat; SEE CONCEPTS 458,835

tide [n] *flow, current*
course, direction, drag, drift, ebb, eddy, flood, flow, flux, movement, race, run, rush, sluice, spate, stream, tendency, torrent, trend, undercurrent, undertow, vortex, wave, whirlpool; SEE CONCEPT 514

tide over [v] *help along*
aid, assist, bridge the gap*, keep head above water*, keep one going, see through; SEE CONCEPT 110

tidings [n] *greetings, news*
advice, bulletin, communication, dirt, information, intelligence, message, report, word; SEE CONCEPT 274

tidy [adj] *clean, neat*
apple-pie order*, businesslike, chipper*, cleanly, in good shape, methodical, neat as a pin*, ordered, orderly, shipshape*, sleek, snug, spick-and-span*, spruce, systematic, to rights*, trim, uncluttered, well-groomed, well-kept, well-ordered; SEE CONCEPTS 485,585,621

tidy [adj2] *considerable*
ample, fair, generous, good, goodly, handsome, healthy, large, largish, respectable, sizable, substantial, vast; SEE CONCEPTS 762,781

tidy [v] *make neat and orderly*
clean, clear the decks*, fix up, frame*, get act together*, groom, neaten, order, police, pull together, put in good shape, put in order, put in shape, put to rights*, shape up, spruce, spruce up*, straighten, straighten up, tauten, whip into shape*; SEE CONCEPT 250

tie [n1] *fastening*
attachment, bandage, bond, brace, connection, cord, fastener, fetter, gag, hookup, joint, knot, ligament, ligature, link, network, nexus, outfit, rope, strap, string, tackle, tie-in, tie-up, yoke, zipper; SEE CONCEPT 680

tie [n2] *deadlock*
dead heat, draw, drawn battle*, equivalence, even game, level, photo finish*, push, stalemate, standoff; SEE CONCEPTS 364,667

tie [n3] *relationship*
affiliation, allegiance, association, bond, commitment, connection, duty, hookup, kinship, liaison, network, obligation, outfit, tie-in; SEE CONCEPT 388

tie [v1] *connect, interlace*
anchor, attach, band, bind, cinch, clinch, do up, fasten, gird, join, knot, lash, link, make a bow, make a hitch, make a knot, make fast, marry, moor, rivet, rope, secure, splice, tether, tie up, tighten, truss, unite, wed; SEE CONCEPTS 85,160,193

tie/tie up [v2] *hamper, hinder*
bind, clog, confine, curb, delay, entrammel, fetter, hog-tie*, hold, leash, limit, lock up, obstruct, restrain, restrict, shackle, stop, tie one's hands*, trammel; SEE CONCEPT 130

tie [v3] *equal*
balance, be even, be neck and neck*, be on a par,

break even*, deadlock*, draw, even up, keep up with, match, measure up, meet, parallel, rival, touch; SEE CONCEPTS *92,667*

tier [*n*] *level*
bank, category, class, course, echelon, file, grade, group, grouping, layer, league, line, order, pigeonhole*, queue, range, rank, row, series, story, stratum, string; SEE CONCEPTS *378,727,744*

tiff [*n*] *argument*
altercation, bad mood, bickering, difference, disagreement, dispute, falling-out*, fit, huff*, miff*, pet, quarrel, row*, run-in*, scrap, spat, squabble, sulk, tantrum, temper, words*, wrangle; SEE CONCEPTS *46,674*

tight [*adj1*] *close, snug*
bound, clasped, close-fitting, compact, constricted, contracted, cramped, crowded, dense, drawn, enduring, established, fast, firm, fixed, hidebound, inflexible, invulnerable, narrow, quick, rigid, secure, set, skintight, solid, stable, steady, stiff, strained, stretched, strong, sturdy, taut, tenacious, thick, tightened, unbending, unyielding; SEE CONCEPTS *483,485*

tight [*adj2*] *sealed*
airtight, blind, blocked, bolted, choking, clumped, cramping, crushing, cutting, fast, fastened, firm, fixed, hermetic, hermetically sealed, impenetrable, impermeable, impervious, locked, nailed, obstructed, padlocked, pinching, plugged, proof, sealed, secure, short, shrunken, shut, skintight, slammed, smothering, snapped, sound, stopped up, tied, tied up, uncomfortable, watertight; SEE CONCEPTS *489,576*

tight [*adj3*] *stingy*
cheap, close, grasping, mean, miserly, parsimonious, penny-pinching*, penurious, sparing, tightfisted; SEE CONCEPTS *334,401*

tight [*adj4*] *difficult, troublesome*
arduous, close, critical, dangerous, distressing, disturbing, exacting, hazardous, near, perilous, precarious, punishing, rough, sticky, tense, ticklish, tough, tricky, trying, upsetting, worrisome; SEE CONCEPTS *548,565*

tight [*adj5*] *intoxicated*
boozy*, buzzed*, drunk, drunken, high*, inebriated, loaded*, pickled*, plastered*, smashed*, stewed*, stoned*, tipsy, under the influence; SEE CONCEPTS *401,406*

tighten [*v*] *constrict*
bind, clench, close, compress, condense, congeal, contract, cramp, crush, fasten, fix, grip, harden, narrow, pinch, pressure, rigidify, screw, secure, squeeze, stiffen, strain, strangle, stretch, tauten, tense, toughen; SEE CONCEPTS *250,469,697*

till [*n*] *cash box*
box, cash drawer, cash register, kitty*, money box, safe, tray, treasury, vault; SEE CONCEPT *339*

till [*v*] *cultivate land*
dig, dress, farm, grow, harrow, hoe, labor, mulch, plant, plough, plow, prepare, raise crops, sow, tend, turn, turn over, work; SEE CONCEPTS *253,257*

tilt [*n1*] *lean, slope*
angle, cant, dip, drop, fall, grade, gradient, inclination, incline, leaning, list, pitch, rake, slant, slide; SEE CONCEPT *738*

tilt [*n2*] *fight*
attack, bout, clash, collision, combat, conflict, contest, duel, encounter, fracas, joust, meet, scrimmage, scuffle, set-to, skirmish, struggle,

tournament, tourney, tussle; SEE CONCEPT *106*

tilt [*v1*] *lean, slant*
bend, cant, careen, dip, heel, incline, list, lurch, pitch, rake, recline, seesaw, set at an angle, shift, slope, slouch, swag, sway, tip, turn, yaw; SEE CONCEPTS *147,149*

tilt [*v2*] *attack, fight*
break, charge, clash, combat, contend, cross swords*, duel, encounter, joust, overthrow, spar, thrust; SEE CONCEPT *106*

timber [*n*] *trees, wood*
balk, beam, board, boom, club, forest, frame, girder, grove, hardwood, log, mast, plank, pole, rafter, rib, stake, timberland, weald, woodland, wood lot, woods; SEE CONCEPTS *430,479*

time [*n1*] *temporal length of event or entity's existence, period*
age, allotment, bit, bout, chronology, clock, continuance, date, day, duration, epoch, era, eternity, extent, future, generation, go*, hour, infinity, instance, instant, interval, juncture, lastingness, life, life span, lifetime, many a moon*, moment, month, occasion, pace, past, point, present, season, second, shift, space, span, spell, stage, stint, stretch, tempo, term, tide, tour, turn, week, while, year; SEE CONCEPTS *801,806,809,819,823*

time [*n2*] *opportunity*
break, chance, heyday, look-in*, occasion, opening, peak, shot, show, squeak*; SEE CONCEPT *693*

timely [*adj*] *at the right time*
appropriate, auspicious, convenient, favorable, fit, fitting, in good time*, in the nick of time*, judicious, likely, meet, modern, now, opportune, pat, promising, prompt, proper, propitious, prosperous, punctual, seasonable, suitable, timeous, towardly, up-to-date, up-to-the-minute, well-timed, with it*; SEE CONCEPTS *558,799*

timid [*adj*] *shy*
afraid, ambivalent, apprehensive, badgered, bashful, browbeaten, bullied, capricious, cowardly, cowed, cowering, coy, daunted, demure, diffident, fainthearted, fearful, feeble, frightened, gentle, having cold feet*, humble, intimidated, irresolute, milquetoast, modest, mousy, nervous, pusillanimous, retiring, shaky, shrinking, shy, soft, spineless, spiritless, submissive, timid, timorous, trembling, unassertive, unassured, unnerved, vacillating, wavering, weak, yellow*; SEE CONCEPT *401*

tinge [*n1*] *color*
cast, colorant, coloration, coloring, dye, dyestuff, hue, pigment, shade, stain, tincture, tint, tone, wash; SEE CONCEPT *622*

tinge [*n2*] *hint*
bit, dash, drop, intimation, nib, pinch, shade, smack, smattering, soupçon, sprinkling, strain, streak, suggestion, tincture, touch, trace; SEE CONCEPTS *529,831*

tinge [*v*] *color*
complexion, dye, imbue, impregnate, infiltrate, saturate, shade, stain, streak, suffuse, tincture, tint; SEE CONCEPT *250*

tingle [*v*] *feel tickled, itchy*
creep, get excited, have goose bumps*, itch, prickle, shiver, sting, thrill, throb, tickle, twitter; SEE CONCEPT *612*

tinker [*v*] *fiddle with*
dabble, doodle*, fix, mess*, mess with*, monkey*, muck about*, niggle*, play, play with, pud-

th
ti

dle, putter, repair, take apart, toy, trifle with; SEE
CONCEPTS *87,212*

tinkle [v] *jingle, ring*
chime, chink, chinkle, clink, ding, jangle, make
bell sound, plink, sound, ting, tingle, tintinnabulate; SEE CONCEPT *65*

tint [n] *shade of color*
cast, chroma, color, coloration, complexion,
dash, dye, flush, glow, hint, hue, luminosity, pigmentation, rinse, stain, suggestion, taint, tinct,
tincture, tinge, tone, touch, trace, wash; SEE CON-
CEPT *622*

tint [v] *color with a certain shade*
affect, complexion, dye, influence, rinse, shade,
stain, taint, tincture, tinge, touch, wash; SEE CON-
CEPT *250*

tiny [adj] *very small*
bitsy*, bitty, diminutive, infinitesimal, insignificant, itsy-bitsy*, itty-bitty*, Lilliputian, little, microscopic, midget, mini*, miniature, minikin,
minimum, minuscular, minuscule, minute, negligible, pee-wee*, petite, pint-sized*, pocket,
pocket-size*, puny, slight, teensy*, teensy-
weensy*, teeny, trifling, wee, yea big*; SEE
CONCEPTS *762,773,789*

tip/tipoff [n1/n] *inside information*
bang*, bug*, buzz*, clue, cue, dope*, forecast,
hint, in*, information, inkling, inside wire,
knowledge, news, point, pointer, prediction,
prompt, secret information, steer*, suggestion,
two cents' worth*, warning, whisper, word, word
of advice, word to the wise*; SEE CONCEPT *274*

tip [n2] *very top*
apex, cap, crown, cusp, edge, end, extremity,
head, nip, peak, point, stub, summit, tiptop, vertex; SEE CONCEPT *836*

tip [n3] *gratuity paid*
compensation, cue, fee, gift, handout, lagniappe,
money, one-way*, perk, perquisite, pourboire, reward, small change, something*, sweetener; SEE
CONCEPT *344*

tip [v1] *knock over; cause to lean*
bend, cant, capsize, careen, dump, empty, heel,
incline, lean, list, overset, overturn, pour, recline,
shift, slant, slope, spill, tilt, topple, topple over,
turn over, unload, upend, upset, upturn; SEE CON-
CEPTS *189,201,208*

tip [v2] *give inside information*
advise, caution, clue, cue, forewarn, give a clue,
give a hint, give low-down*, hint, prompt,
steer, suggest, tip off, warn; SEE CONCEPT *60*

tipsy [adj] *inebriated*
addled, dazed, drunk, drunken, fuddled, happy,
high*, intoxicated, irrigated*, lit*, loaded*, mellow, merry, stewed*, tight, unsteady, woozy;
SEE CONCEPTS *401,406*

tirade [n] *abuse, outburst*
anger, berating, censure, condemnation, denunciation, diatribe, dispute, fulmination, harangue, invective, jeremiad*, lecture, malediction,
philippic*, ranting, revilement, screed, sermon,
tongue-lashing*, vituperation; SEE CONCEPTS
44,54,278

tire [v] *exhaust, weary*
annoy, bore, burn out*, bush*, collapse, crawl,
debilitate, deject, depress, disgust, dishearten,
dispirit, displease, distress, drain, droop, drop,
enervate, ennui, exasperate, fag, fail, faint, fatigue, flag, fold, give out, go stale, grow weary,
harass, irk, irritate, jade, nauseate, overburden,

overstrain, overtax, overwork, pain, pall, peter
out*, poop out*, prostrate, put to sleep, sap,
sicken, sink, strain, tax, vex, weaken, wear, wear
down, wear out, weary, wilt, worry, yawn*; SEE
CONCEPTS *13,14,469*

tired [adj] *exhausted, weary*
all in*, annoyed, asleep, beat*, bored, broken-
down, burned out*, collapsing, consumed, dead
on one's feet*, distressed, dog-tired*, done for*,
done in*, drained, drooping, droopy, drowsy,
empty, enervated, exasperated, fagged, faint, fatigued, fed up*, finished, flagging, haggard,
irked, irritated, jaded, narcoleptic, overtaxed,
overworked, petered out*, played out*, pooped*,
prostrated, run-down, sick of, sleepy, spent, stale,
tuckered out*, wasted, weary, worn, worn out;
SEE CONCEPTS *314,403,406*

tireless [adj] *determined*
active, ball of fire*, eager, energetic, enthusiastic,
grind, hard-working*, hyper*, incessant, indefatigable, industrious, jumping, on the go*, perky,
persevering, resolute, steadfast, strenuous, unflagging, untiring, unwearied, unwearying, vigorous;
SEE CONCEPTS *538,542*

tiresome [adj] *irritating, exasperating*
a bit much*, annoying, arduous, boresome, boring, burdensome, demanding, difficult, drag,
dragging, drudging, dull, enervative, exacting,
exhausting, fatiguing, flat, hard, heavy, hefty, ho-
hum*, humdrum, irksome, jading, laborious, monotonous, nowhere, onerous, oppressive,
strenuous, tedious, tired, tiring, too much*,
tough, trying, uncool*, uninteresting, unrelieved,
vexatious, wearing, wearisome, wearying, yawn*;
SEE CONCEPTS *529,537,538*

titillate [v] *excite, stimulate*
amuse, arouse, entertain, grab, grapple, hook, interest, palpate, provoke, switch on, tantalize,
tease, thrill, tickle, tickle pink*, turn on; SEE CON-
CEPTS *7,11,22*

title [n1] *heading, label*
appellation, banner, caption, close, description,
head, headline, inscription, legend, name, rubric,
salutation, sign, streamer, style, subtitle; SEE
CONCEPT *283*

title [n2] *name*
appellation, appellative, brand, cognomen, denomination, designation, epithet, handle*, honor-
ific, label, moniker*, nom de plume, nomen,
pseudonym, sobriquet, style, tab*, tag*, term;
SEE CONCEPT *683*

title [n3] *possession, laurel*
authority, championship, claim, commission,
crest, crown, decoration, deed, degree, desert,
dibs*, due, entitlement, holding, justification, license, medal, merit, ownership, power, prerogative, pretense, pretension, privilege, proof,
ribbon, right; SEE CONCEPTS *376,710*

title [v] *name*
baptize, call, christen, denominate, designate,
dub, entitle, label, style, term; SEE CONCEPT *62*

toast [n] *salutation when drinking alcohol*
acknowledgment, celebration, ceremony, commemoration, compliment, down, drink, health,
honor, pledge, proposal, salute, sentiment, shingle, thanksgiving, tribute; SEE CONCEPT *278*

toast [v] *brown with heat*
cook, crisp, dry, grill, heat, parch, roast, warm;
SEE CONCEPT *170*

to-do [n] *commotion, excitement*
agitation, bother, brouhaha*, bustle, clamor, disorder, disturbance, flap*, furor, fuss, hassle, hooha*, hoopla*, hubbub*, hurly-burly*, hurrah, performance, pother, quarrel, racket, ruction, rumpus, stir, tumult, turmoil, unrest, uproar, whirl; SEE CONCEPTS 230,674

together [adj] *composed*
calm, cool*, in sync*, stable, well-adjusted, well-balanced, well-organized; SEE CONCEPT 542

together [adv1] *as a group; all at once*
all together, as one, at one fell swoop*, closely, coincidentally, collectively, combined, commonly, concertedly, concomitantly, concurrently, conjointly, contemporaneously, en masse, hand in glove*, hand in hand*, in a body, in concert, in cooperation, in one breath*, in sync*, in unison, jointly, mutually, on the beat*, side by side, simultaneously, synchronically, unanimously, unitedly, with one accord, with one voice, with the beat; SEE CONCEPTS 538,544,548

together [adv2] *in a row*
consecutively, continually, continuously, in succession, night and day, one after the other, on end, running, successively, unintermittedly, without a break, without interruption; SEE CONCEPTS 482,585

toil [n] *hard work*
application, drudgery, effort, exertion, industry, labor, moil, nine-to-five*, occupation, pains*, sweat, travail; SEE CONCEPTS 100,362,677

toil [v] *work hard*
drive, drudge, grind, knock oneself out*, labor, moil, peg away*, plod, plug, push oneself, slave, strain, strive, struggle, sweat, tug, work, work like a dog*; SEE CONCEPTS 100,677

token [n] *indication, remembrance*
badge, clue, demonstration, earnest, evidence, expression, favor, gift, index, indicia, keepsake, manifestation, mark, memento, memorial, note, omen, pawn, pledge, presage, proof, relic, reminder, representation, sample, security, sign, significant, souvenir, symbol, symptom, trophy, warning, warrant; SEE CONCEPTS 284,337,529

tolerable [adj] *acceptable, average*
adequate, allowable, all right, average, bearable, better than nothing*, common, decent, endurable, fair, fairly good, fair to middling*, goodish*, indifferent, livable, mediocre, middling*, not bad*, okay*, ordinary, passable, presentable, respectable, run-of-the-mill*, satisfactory, so-so*, sufferable, sufficient, supportable, sustainable, tidy, unexceptionable, unexceptional, unimpeachable; SEE CONCEPTS 529,548

tolerance [n1] *open-mindedness*
altruism, benevolence, broad-mindedness, charity, clemency, compassion, concession, endurance, forbearance, freedom, good will, grace, humanity, indulgence, kindness, lenience, leniency, lenity, liberalism, liberality, liberalness, license, magnanimity, mercifulness, mercy, patience, permission, permissiveness, sensitivity, sufferance, sympathy, toleration, understanding; SEE CONCEPTS 410,657

tolerance [n2] *fortitude, grit*
endurance, guts*, hardiness, hardness, opposition, patience, resilience, resistance, stamina, staying power*, steadfastness, steadiness, strength, sufferance, toughness, vigor; SEE CONCEPT 732

tolerant [adj] *open-minded, easygoing*
advanced, benevolent, big, broad, broad-minded, catholic, charitable, clement, complaisant, condoning, easy on, easy with, excusing, fair, forbearing, forgiving, free and easy*, humane, indulgent, kindhearted*, lax, lenient, liberal, long-suffering*, magnanimous, merciful, patient, permissive, progressive, radical, receptive, soft, sophisticated, sympathetic, understanding, unprejudiced, wide; SEE CONCEPTS 403,542

tolerate [v] *allow, indulge*
abide, accept, admit, authorize, bear, bear with, blink at*, brook, condone, consent to, countenance, endure, go, go along with, have, hear, humor, live with, permit, pocket, put up with, receive, sanction, sit and take it*, sit still for*, stand, stand for, stay the course*, string along, submit to, suffer, sustain, swallow*, take, tough out*, undergo, wink at*; SEE CONCEPTS 23,83

toll [n1] *fee*
assessment, charge, cost, customs, demand, duty, exaction, expense, impost, levy, payment, price, rate, tariff, tax, tribute; SEE CONCEPT 329

toll [n2] *damage, deaths*
casualties, cost, expense, inroad, loss, losses, penalty, price; SEE CONCEPT 230

toll [v] *ring out*
announce, bell, bong, call, chime, clang, knell, peal, signal, sound, strike, summon, warn; SEE CONCEPT 65

tomb [n] *burial place*
box, burial, burial chamber, catacomb, coffin, crypt, grave, mausoleum, monument, pit, sepulcher, trough, vault; SEE CONCEPT 305

tome [n] *large, scholarly book*
classic, great work, magnum opus, novel, opus, publication, reference book, schoolbook, textbook, title, tradebook, volume, work, writing; SEE CONCEPT 280

tone [n1] *pitch, volume*
accent, emphasis, force, inflection, intonation, modulation, resonance, strength, stress, timbre, tonality; SEE CONCEPT 65

tone [n2] *attitude, spirit*
air, approach, aspect, character, condition, current, drift, effect, expression, fashion, feel, frame, grain, habit, humor, manner, mind, mode, mood, movement, nature, note, quality, state of things, strain, style, temper, tenor, trend, vein; SEE CONCEPTS 655,673,682

tone [n3] *color*
blend, cast, coloration, hue, shade, tinge, tint, value; SEE CONCEPT 622

tone [n4] *condition of the body*
elasticity, health, healthiness, resiliency, strength, tonicity, tonus, vigor; SEE CONCEPT 316

tone down [v] *moderate*
chill out*, cloud, dampen, darken, deepen, dim, mitigate, modulate, play down, reduce, restrain, shade, sober, soften, soft-pedal*, subdue, temper; SEE CONCEPT 240

tongue [n] *language*
argot, articulation, dialect, discourse, expression, idiom, language, lingo, parlance, patois, speech, talk, utterance, vernacular, voice; SEE CONCEPT 276

tonic [n] *restorative drink, medicine*
analeptic, boost, bracer, conditioner, cordial, drug, fillip, invigorator, livener, pick-me-up*,

pickup, refresher, restorative, roborant, shot in the arm*, stimulant, strengthener; SEE CONCEPT 307

too [adv1] *also*
additionally, along, as well, besides, further, furthermore, in addition, into the bargain, likewise, more, moreover, to boot, withal; SEE CONCEPTS 544,771

too [adv2] *excessively*
awfully, beyond, ever, exceptionally, exorbitantly, extremely, greatly, highly, immensely, immoderately, in excess, inordinately, notably, over, over and above, overly, overmuch, remarkably, strikingly, unconscionably, unduly, unreasonably, very; SEE CONCEPTS 569,772

tool [n1] *instrument used to shape, form, finish*
apparatus, appliance, contraption, contrivance, device, engine, gadget, gizmo*, implement, job, machine, means, mechanism, utensil, weapon, whatchamacallit*; SEE CONCEPT 499

tool [n2] *person who allows himself to be used*
accessory, accomplice, agent, auxiliary, chump*, creature, dupe, easy mark*, figurehead, flunky*, go-between, greenhorn*, hireling, idiot, intermediary, jackal, lackey, mark*, medium, messenger, minion, patsy*, pawn, peon, puppet, stooge, stool pigeon*, sucker*; SEE CONCEPTS 348,412,423

top [n1] *highest point*
acme, apex, apogee, cap, capital, ceiling, climax, cork, cover, crest, crown, culmination, cusp, face, fastigium, finial, head, height, high point, lid, limit, maximum, meridian, peak, pinnacle, point, roof, spire, stopper, summit, superficies, surface, tip, utmost, vertex, zenith; SEE CONCEPT 836

top [n2] *highest rank*
best, captain, chief, choice, cream, elite, first place, flower, head, lead, leader, pick, pride, prime, prize, utmost; SEE CONCEPT 668

top [adj] *best, most important; highest*
apical, capital, chief, crack, culminating, dominant, elite, excellent, fine, finest, first, first-class, first-rate, five-star*, foremost, greatest, head, lead, leading, loftiest, maximal, maximum, outside, paramount, preeminent, primary, prime, principal, ruling, sovereign, superior, supreme, tiptop*, top-drawer*, topmost, top-notch, upper, uppermost; SEE CONCEPTS 567,574,583

top [v1] *place on or reach highest part*
ascend, cap, climb, cloak, clothe, cover, crest, crown, face, finish, garnish, piggyback*, protect, reinforce, roof, scale, spread over, superimpose, surmount, tip; SEE CONCEPTS 172,201,750

top [v2] *surpass*
bash, beat, be first, best, better, blow away*, clobber*, eclipse, exceed, excel, fake out*, finagle*, fox*, go beyond, goose*, outdo, outfox, outshine, outstrip, overrun, run circles around*, shut out*, total*, transcend; SEE CONCEPTS 95,141

top [v3] *remove the upper part*
amputate, cream, crop, curtail, cut off, decapitate, detruncate, dock, file off, lop off, pare, pollard, prune, ream, scrape off, shave off, shear, shorten, skim, trim, truncate; SEE CONCEPT 211

topic [n] *subject matter*
affair, argument, business, case, division, field, head, issue, material, matter, matter in hand, moot point, motif, motion, motive, point, point in question, problem, proposition, question, resolution,

subject, text, theme, theorem, thesis; SEE CONCEPT 532

topical [adj1] *current*
contemporary, modern, newsworthy, nominal, popular, subjective, thematic, up-to-date; SEE CONCEPT 820

topical [adj2] *restricted, local*
confined, insular, limited, parochial, particular, regional, sectional; SEE CONCEPTS 557,583

topple [v] *fall or knock over; overthrow*
bring down, capsize, collapse, do a pratfall*, fall, falter, founder, go belly up*, go down, hit the dirt*, keel over, knock down, land, lose it*, lurch, nose-dive, oust, overbalance, overturn, pitch, plunge, slump, stagger, stumble, take a header*, teeter, tip over, totter, tumble, turn over, unhorse, unseat, upset; SEE CONCEPTS 95,147,181,208

topsy-turvy [adj] *mixed-up*
chaotic, cluttered, cockeyed, confused, disarranged, disheveled, disjointed, dislocated, disordered, disorderly, disorganized, downside-up*, inside-out, inverted, jumbled, littered, messy, muddled, overturned, pell-mell*, riotous, tangled, tumultuous/tumultuous, unhinged, untidy, upended, upside-down, upturned; SEE CONCEPTS 485,548,585

torment [n] *severe mental distress*
affliction, agony, anguish, annoyance, bane, bother, excruciation, harassment, hell, irritation, misery, nag, nagging, nuisance, pain, pain in the neck*, persecution, pest, plague, provocation, rack, scourge, suffering, torture, trouble, vexation, worry; SEE CONCEPTS 410,728

torment [v] *be or make very upset*
abuse, afflict, agonize, annoy, bait, bedevil, bone, bother, break, crucify, devil, distress, drive bananas*, drive up the wall*, excruciate, give a hard time*, harass, harrow, harry, heckle, hound, hurt, irritate, mistreat, molest, nag, pain, persecute, pester, plague, play cat and mouse*, provoke, punish, put through wringer*, rack, rub salt in wound*, smite, tease, torture, trouble, try, vex, worry, wring; SEE CONCEPTS 7,19,313

torn [adj1] *cut open*
broken, burst, cleaved, cracked, damaged, divided, fractured, gashed, impaired, lacerated, mangled, ragged, rent, ripped, ruptured, severed, shabby, slashed, sliced, slit, snapped, split, wrenched; SEE CONCEPT 485

torn [adj2] *undecided*
divided, irresolute, of two minds*, split, uncertain, unsure, vacillating, wavering; SEE CONCEPTS 403,542

torpid [adj] *lazy, slow*
apathetic, benumbed, comatose, dopey*, dormant, drowsy, dull, faineant, heavy, hebetudinous, idle, inactive, indifferent, indolent, inert, lackadaisical, languid, languorous, latent, leaden, lethargic, listless, lymphatic, motionless, numb, paralyzed, passive, slothful, slow-moving, sluggish, slumberous, sodden, somnolent, stagnant, static, stupid, stuporous; SEE CONCEPTS 401,538

torrent [n] *heavy flow*
cascade, cataclysm, cataract, cloudburst, deluge, downpour, effusion, flood, flooding, flux, gush, inundation, niagara, outburst, overflow, pour, rush, shower, spate, stream, tide, waterfall; SEE CONCEPTS 146,179,526

torrid [adj] *very hot*
arid, austral, blazing, blistering, boiling, broiling,

burning, dried, dry, fiery, heated, parched, parching, red-hot*, scalding, scorched, scorching, sizzling, stifling, sultry, sweltering, tropic, tropical; SEE CONCEPT 605

torrid [adj2] *sensuous*
ardent, blazing, burning, erotic, fervent, flaming, hot*, hot-blooded*, impassioned, intense, passionate, red-hot*, sexy, steamy*, sultry, white-hot*; SEE CONCEPT 372

tortuous [adj1] *very twisted*
anfractuous, bent, circuitous, convoluted, crooked, curved, flexuous, indirect, involute, labyrinthine, mazy, meandering, meandrous, roundabout, serpentine, sinuous, snaky, twisting, vermiculate, winding, zigzag; SEE CONCEPT 581

tortuous [adj2] *complicated*
ambiguous, convoluted, cunning, deceptive, devious, indirect, involute, involved, misleading, perverse, roundabout, tricky; SEE CONCEPT 562

torture [n] *severe mental or physical pain*
ache, affliction, agony, anguish, cruciation, crucifixion, distress, dolor, excruciation, impalement, laceration, martyrdom, misery, pang, persecution, rack, suffering, third degree*, torment, tribulation, twinge; SEE CONCEPTS 410,728

torture [v] *upset or hurt severely*
abuse, afflict, agonize, annoy, beat, bother, crucify, distress, disturb, excruciate, grill, harrow, impale, injure, irritate, lacerate, maim, mangle, martyr, martyrize, mistreat, mutilate, oppress, pain, persecute, rack, smite, torment, try, whip, wound, wring, wrong; SEE CONCEPTS 7,19,246,313

toss [n/v] *throw*
bung, cast, chuck, chunk, fire, fling, flip, heave, hurl, launch, lob, peg, pitch, project, propel, sling, twirl, wing; SEE CONCEPT 222

toss [v2] *move back and forth*
agitate, agonize, bob, buffet, disturb, flounder, heave, jiggle, joggle, jolt, labor, lurch, move restlessly, oscillate, pitch, rise and fall, rock, roll, seesaw, shake, squirm, stir, sway, swing, thrash, tumble, undulate, wallow, wave, wobble, wriggle, writhe; SEE CONCEPT 147

total [n] *whole*
aggregate, all, amount, body, budget, bulk, entirety, flat out*, full amount, gross, jackpot*, mass, quantity, quantum, result, sum, sum total*, tale, the works*, totality; SEE CONCEPTS 787,837

total [adj] *complete, thorough*
absolute, all-out, comprehensive, consummate, downright, entire, every, full, full-blown, full-scale, gross, inclusive, integral, out-and-out, outright, overall, perfect, plenary, positive, sheer, sweeping, thoroughgoing, totalitarian, unconditional, undisputed, undivided, unlimited, unmitigated, unqualified, unreserved, unrestricted, utter, whole; SEE CONCEPTS 531,762

total [v] *add up*
add, aggregate, amount to, calculate, cast, come, come to, comprise, consist of, equal, figure, foot, mount up to, number, pile up, reach, reckon, result in, ring up*, run into, run to, stack up, summate, sum up, totalize, tote*, yield; SEE CONCEPT 764

totalitarian [adj] *dictatorial*
absolute, authoritarian, autocratic, communist*, despotic, fascistic, monolithic, Nazi*, one-party, oppressive, total, totalistic, tyrannical, undemocratic; SEE CONCEPT 536

totally [adv] *completely*
absolutely, all, all in all, altogether, comprehensively, consummately, entirely, exactly, exclusively, flat out*, full blast*, fully, in toto*, just, perfectly, quite, thoroughly, top to bottom*, unconditionally, unmitigatedly, utterly, wholeheartedly, wholly; SEE CONCEPT 531

totter [v] *move falteringly*
blunder, careen, dodder, falter, flounder, hesitate, lurch, quake, quiver, reel, rock, roll, seesaw, shake, shimmy, slide, slip, stagger, stammer, stumble, sway, teeter, topple, tremble, trip, walk unsteadily, waver, weave, wheel, wobble, zigzag; SEE CONCEPT 151

touch [n1] *physical contact*
blow, brush, caress, collision, communication, contact, contingence, crash, cuddling, embrace, feel, feeling, fondling, graze, grope, handling, hit, hug, impact, junction, kiss, lick, manipulation, nudge, palpation, pat, peck, perception, percussion, petting, push, rub, rubbing, scratch, shock, stroke, stroking, tactility, taction, tap, taste, touching; SEE CONCEPTS 590,608,612

touch [n2] *tiny amount*
bit, dash, detail, drop, hint, inkling, intimation, jot, pinch, scent, shade, smack, small amount, smattering, soupçon, speck, spot, streak, suggestion, suspicion, taste, tincture, tinge, trace, whiff; SEE CONCEPTS 529,831,832

touch [n3] *manner, method*
ability, acquaintance, adeptness, adroitness, approach, art, artistry, awareness, characteristic, command, communication, contact, deftness, direction, effect, facility, faculty, familiarity, finish, flair, hand, handiwork, influence, knack, mastery, skill, style, talent, technique, trademark, understanding, virtuosity, way; SEE CONCEPTS 6,630,655

touch [v1] *make physical contact*
abut, adjoin, be in contact, border, brush, butt on, caress, come together, communicate, contact, converge, dab, examine, feel, feel up*, finger, fondle, frisk, glance, graze, grope, handle, hit, impinge upon, inspect, join, kiss, lay a finger on*, lick, line, manipulate, march, massage, meet, neighbor, osculate, palm, palpate, partake, pat, paw, percuss, pet, probe, push, reach, rub, scrutinize, sip, smooth, strike, stroke, suck, sweep, tag, tap, taste, thumb, tickle, tip, toy, verge; SEE CONCEPT 612

touch [v2] *have an effect on*
affect, arouse, carry, disturb, excite, feel out, get through to*, get to*, grab, impress, influence, inspire, make an impression*, mark, melt, move, quicken, soften, stimulate, stir, strike, strike a chord*, stroke, sway, tug at the heart*, upset; SEE CONCEPTS 7,19,22

touch [v3] *have to do with; regard*
affect, be a party to, bear on, bear upon, be associated with, belong to, center upon, concern, concern oneself with, consume, deal with, drink, eat, get involved in, handle, have to do with, interest, involve, partake of, pertain to, refer to, use, utilize; SEE CONCEPT 532

touch [v4] *make mention*
allude to, bring in, cover, deal with, discuss, go over, mention, note, refer to, speak of, treat; SEE CONCEPT 51

touch [v5] *compare with; correspond to*
amount, approach, be a match for*, be in the same

to
to

league*, be on a par*, come near, come to, come up to, equal, hold a candle to*, match, measure up, meet, parallel, partake of, rival, tie, verge on; SEE CONCEPT *561*

touched [*adj1*] *deeply moved emotionally*
affected, disturbed, grabbed*, impressed, melted*, softened, stirred, swayed, turned on by*, turned on to*, upset; SEE CONCEPTS *403,542*

touched [*adj2*] *crazy*
batty*, bizarre, bonkers*, cuckoo*, daft, eccentric, fanatic, flighty, insane, neurotic, not all there*, not right*, nuts*, nutty*, obsessed, out of one's mind*, peculiar, pixilated, queer, unhinged; SEE CONCEPTS *402,403*

touching [*adj1*] *affecting, moving emotionally*
compassionate, emotive, heartbreaking, heart-rending, impressive, melting, mind-blowing*, pathetic, piteous, pitiable, pitiful, poignant, responsive, sad, stirring, stunning, sympathetic, tear-jerking, tender, wistful; SEE CONCEPTS *529,537*

touch up [*v*] *fix up; improve*
amend, brush up, do up, enhance, finish off, give a face-lift*, gloss, make improvements, modify, patch up, perfect, polish, put finishing touches on*, remodel, renew, renovate, repair, retouch, revamp, rework, round off, tease*; SEE CONCEPTS *212,244*

touchy [*adj*] *easily offended*
bad-tempered, bundle of nerves*, cantankerous, captious, choleric, crabbed, cranky, cross, delicate, dicey*, grouchy, grumpy, hazardous, hypersensitive, irascible, irritable, jumpy*, mean, ornery*, oversensitive, peevish, perturbable, pettish, petulant, precarious, querulous, quick-tempered, risky, sensitive, splenetic, surly, temperamental, testy, thin-skinned*, ticklish*, tricky, unpredictable, unsafe, uptight*, volatile, wired up*, wound up*; SEE CONCEPTS *401,542,548*

tough [*n*] *person who is rowdy, mean*
bruiser, brute, bully, criminal, gangster, goon*, hood*, hoodlum, hooligan, punk*, rough*, roughneck, rowdy, ruffian, thug, villain; SEE CONCEPT *412*

tough [*adj1*] *sturdy, strong*
brawny, cohesive, conditioned, dense, durable, fibrous, firm, fit, flinty, hard, hard as nails*, hard-bitten*, hardened, hardy, healthy, indigestible, inflexible, leathery, lusty, mighty, molded, resilient, resistant, rigid, robust, rugged, seasoned, sinewy, solid, stalwart, steeled, stiff, stout, strapping, tenacious, tight, tough as nails*, unbreakable, unyielding, vigorous, withstanding; SEE CONCEPTS *314,489*

tough [*adj2*] *obstinate, rough*
adamant, arbitrary, callous, confirmed, cruel, desperate, drastic, exacting, ferocious, fierce, firm, fixed, hard, hard-bitten*, hard-boiled*, hard-line*, hard-nosed*, hard-shelled*, harsh, headstrong, immutable, inflexible, intractable, merciless, narrow, obdurate, pugnacious, refractory, resolute, ruffianly, ruthless, savage, severe, stern, stiff, strict, stubborn, taut, terrible, unalterable, unbending, uncompromising, uncontrollable, unforgiving, unmanageable, unyielding, vicious, violent; SEE CONCEPTS *403,542*

tough [*adj3*] *difficult, laborious*
arduous, backbreaking*, baffling, burdensome, demanding, effortful, exacting, exhausting, exigent, grievous, hairy*, handful*, hard, heavy, intractable, intricate, irksome, knotty*, labored, mean, no piece of cake*, onerous, oppressive, perplexing, puzzling, resisting, severe, stiff, strenuous, taxing, thorny, toilsome, troublesome, trying, unyielding, uphill*, weighty*, wicked; SEE CONCEPTS *538,565*

toughen [*v*] *harden*
acclimate, acclimatize, anneal, brutalize, climatize, develop, inure, make difficult, season, strengthen, temper; SEE CONCEPTS *202,250*

tour [*n*] *journey; stint*
bout*, circle tour*, circuit, course, cruise, excursion, expedition, getaway*, go*, hitch*, hop*, jaunt*, junket, outing, overnight*, peregrination, progress, road, round*, roundabout*, round trip, run, shift, spell, stretch, stump*, swing*, time, travel, trek, trick*, trip, turn, voyage, weekend, whistle-stop*; SEE CONCEPTS *81,224,807*

tour [*v*] *visit, journey*
barnstorm*, cruise, explore, globe-trot*, go on the road*, holiday*, hop*, jaunt, jet, junket, peregrinate, sightsee, stump*, swing*, take a trip, travel, vacation, voyage; SEE CONCEPTS *224,227*

tourist [*n*] *person who visits a place*
day-tripper, excursionist, globetrotter, jet-setter, journeyer, rubberneck*, sightseer, stranger, traveler, tripper*, vacationist, visitor, voyager, wayfarer; SEE CONCEPT *423*

tournament [*n*] *sporting competition*
clash, contest, duel, event, fight, games, joust, match, meet, meeting, series, sport, test, tilt, tourney; SEE CONCEPT *363*

tousled [*adj*] *disarrayed*
beat-up*, dirty, disarranged, disheveled, disordered, grubby*, messed-up*, messy, mussed-up*, ruffled, rumpled, sloppy, tangled, uncombed, unkempt; SEE CONCEPTS *485,589*

tout [*v*] *brag about, show off*
acclaim, ballyhoo*, boost, give a boost*, herald, laud, plug*, praise, proclaim, promote, publicize, push, steer, tip, tip off*, trumpet; SEE CONCEPTS *69,138*

tow [*v*] *pull along*
drag, draw, ferry, haul, lug, propel, push, trail, trawl, tug, yank; SEE CONCEPT *206*

toward/towards [*prep1*] *on the way to; near*
against, almost, approaching, close to, coming up, contra, en route, facing, for, fronting, headed for, in relation to, in the direction of, in the vicinity, just before, moving, nearing, nearly, not quite, on the road to, over against, pointing to, proceeding, shortly before, to, via, vis-à-vis; SEE CONCEPT *586*

toward/towards [*prep2*] *concerning*
about, against, anent, apropos, as for, as to, for, in re, re, regarding, with regard to, with respect to; SEE CONCEPT *532*

tower [*n*] *very high building or building part*
belfry, castle, citadel, cloud buster*, column, fort, fortification, fortress, high rise*, keep, lookout, mast, minaret, monolith, obelisk, pillar, refuge, skyscraper, spire, steeple, stronghold, turret; SEE CONCEPTS *439,440*

tower [*v*] *rise above*
ascend, be above, dominate, exceed, extend above, look down, look over, loom, mount, overlook, overtop, rear, soar, surmount, surpass, top, transcend; SEE CONCEPTS *141,752*

towering [*adj*] *huge, excessive*
   aerial, airy, colossal, elevated, extraordinary, extravagant, extreme, fantastic, gigantic, great, high, immoderate, imperial, imposing, impressive, inordinate, intense, lofty, magnificent, massive, mighty, monumental, outstanding, paramount, preeminent, prodigious, skyscraping, soaring, spiring, stately, stupendous, sublime, superior, supreme, surpassing, tall, towery, transcendent, tremendous, ultimate, undue, unmatchable, unmeasurable; SEE CONCEPTS *567,779*

town [*n*] *incorporated community*
   apple*, boondocks, borough, burg*, city, hamlet, metropolis, municipality, seat, sticks*, township, whistle-stop*; SEE CONCEPTS *507,508*

toxic [*adj*] *poisonous*
   baneful, deadly, harmful, lethal, mephitic, noxious, pernicious, pestilential, poison, septic, toxicant, venomous, virulent; SEE CONCEPT *537*

toy [*n*] *entertainment article*
   bauble, curio, doll, game, knickknack, novelty, plaything, trifle, trinket; SEE CONCEPT *446*

toy [*v*] *play with*
   amuse oneself, coquet, cosset, dally, dandle, fiddle, flirt, fool, fool around*, jest, lead on, mess around*, pet, play, play around, play games, sport, string along*, tease, trifle, wanton; SEE CONCEPT *384*

trace [*n*] *evidence; small bit*
   breath, crumb, dab, dash, drop, element, footmark, footprint, fragment, hint, indication, intimation, iota, jot, mark, memento, minimum, nib, nuance, particle, pinch, proof, record, relic, remains, remnant, scintilla, shade, shadow, shred, sign, slot, smell, smidgen, snippet, soupçon, speck, spoor, spot, sprinkling, strain, streak, suggestion, survival, suspicion, taste, tincture, tinge, tittle, token, touch, track, trail, tread, trifle, vestige, whiff, whisper; SEE CONCEPTS *529,831*

trace [*v1*] *seek, follow*
   ascertain, detect, determine, discern, discover, ferret out, find, hunt, perceive, pursue, run down, search for, shadow, smell out, spoor, spot, stalk, track, trail, unearth; SEE CONCEPTS *207,216*

trace [*v2*] *draw around*
   chart, copy, delineate, depict, duplicate, map, mark out, outline, record, reproduce, show, sketch; SEE CONCEPTS *79,174*

track [*n1*] *mark, print made by something*
   clue, footmark, footprint, footstep, groove, impress, impression, imprint, indication, memorial, monument, path, print, record, remains, remnant, rut, scent, sign, slot, spoor, step, symbol, token, trace, tract, trail, tread, vestige, wake; SEE CONCEPTS *513,628*

track [*n2*] *path, way*
   alley, artery, avenue, beaten path*, boulevard, clearing, course, cut*, drag*, footpath, highway, lane, line, orbit, passage, pathway, rail, rails, road, roadway, route, street, thoroughfare, track, trackway, trail, trajectory, walk; SEE CONCEPT *501*

track/track down [*v*] *follow, pursue*
   apprehend, beat the bushes*, be hot on the trail*, bird-dog*, bring to light*, capture, catch, chase, cover, dig up, discover, do, dog*, dog footsteps of*, draw an inference, expose, ferret out, find, go after, hunt, piece together, put together, run down, scout, shadow, smell out*, sniff out*,

stalk, stick to, tail, trace, trail, travel, traverse, unearth; SEE CONCEPTS *183,207,216*

tract [*n*] *area, lot*
   amplitude, belt, district, estate, expanse, extent, field, parcel, part, piece, plat, plot, portion, quarter, region, section, sector, spread, stretch, zone; SEE CONCEPTS *508,513*

tractable [*adj*] *manageable*
   acquiescent, amenable, biddable, complaisant, compliant, controllable, docile, ductile, facile, flexible, game, going along with*, governable, hanging loose*, malleable, meek, obedient, persuadable, plastic, pliable, pliant, putty in hands*, rolling with punches*, subdued, submissive, tame, tractile, willing, workable, yielding; SEE CONCEPTS *401,488,542*

traction [*n*] *physical resistance, friction*
   absorption, adherence, adhesion, constriction, contraction, drag, draught, drawing, grip, haulage, pull, pulling, purchase, resorption, strain, stress, stretch, suck, suction, towage; SEE CONCEPTS *731,748*

trade [*n1*] *buying and selling*
   barter, business, clientele, commerce, contract, custom, customers, deal, dealing, enterprise, exchange, industry, interchange, market, merchantry, patronage, public, sales, swap, traffic, transaction, truck; SEE CONCEPTS *324,327, 330,345*

trade [*n2*] *profession, work*
   art, avocation, business, calling, craft, employment, game, handicraft, job, line, line of work, métier, nine-to-five*, occupation, position, pursuit, skill, thing*, vocation; SEE CONCEPTS *349,360*

trademark [*n*] *logo, symbol*
   brand, brand name, identification, initials, label, logo, logotype, mark, stamp, tag; SEE CONCEPTS *259,284*

tradition [*n*] *established practice*
   attitude, belief, birthright, conclusion, convention, culture, custom, customs, ethic, ethics, fable, folklore, form, habit, heritage, idea, inheritance, institution, law, legend, lore, mores, myth, mythology, mythos, opinion, practice, praxis, ritual, unwritten law, usage, wisdom; SEE CONCEPT *688*

traditional [*adj*] *usual, established*
   acceptable, accustomed, acknowledged, ancestral, classic, classical, common, conventional, customary, doctrinal, fixed, folk, habitual, historic, immemorial, long-established, old, oral, popular, prescribed, regular, rooted, sanctioned, taken for granted, time-honored, transmitted, universal, unwritten, widely used, widespread; SEE CONCEPTS *530,533*

traffic [*n1*] *coming and going*
   cartage, flux, freight, gridlock, influx, jam, movement, parking lot*, passage, passengers, rush hour, service, shipment, transfer, transit, transport, transportation, travel, truckage, vehicles; SEE CONCEPTS *224,505,770*

traffic [*n2*] *buying and selling*
   barter, business, closeness, commerce, communication, communion, connection, custom, dealing, dealings*, doings*, exchange, familiarity, industry, interchange, intercourse, intimacy, merchantry, patronage, peddling, relations, relationship, soliciting, trade, transactions, truck*; SEE CONCEPTS *330,335*

to
tr

traffic [v] *buy and sell; do business*

bargain, barter, black-market*, bootleg*, connect with, contact, deal, deal in*, dicker, exchange, fence, handle, have dealings, have transaction, horse trade*, interact, interface, make a deal, market, moonshine*, negotiate, network, peddle, push, reach out, relate, shove, swap, touch, touch base*, trade, truck*, work out; SEE CONCEPTS *324,327,330,345*

tragedy [n] *disaster*

adversity, affliction, bad fortune, bad luck, blight, blow, calamity, cataclysm, catastrophe, contretemps, curse, curtains*, dole, dolor, doom, downer*, failure, hard knocks*, hardship, humiliation, lot, misadventure, mischance, misfortune, mishap, reverse, shock, struggle, the worst*, unluckiness, waterloo*, woe, wreck; SEE CONCEPTS *674,675*

tragic [adj] *catastrophic, very bad*

adverse, anguished, appalling, awful, calamitous, cataclysmic, crushing, deadly, deathly, deplorable, desolate, destructive, dire, disastrous, doleful, dreadful, fatal, fateful, forlorn, grievous, grim, hapless, harrowing, heartbreaking, heartrending, ill-fated, ill-starred, lamentable, miserable, mournful, painful, pathetic, pitiable, pitiful, ruinous, sad, shocking, sorrowful, terrible, unfortunate, unhappy, woeful, wretched; SEE CONCEPTS *548,571*

trail [n] *path, track*

aisle, beaten track*, byway, footpath, footprints, footsteps, groove*, mark, marks, pathway, road, route, rut, scent, spoor, stream, stroll, tail, trace, train, wake, way; SEE CONCEPT *501*

trail [v] *lag behind, follow*

bedog, bring up the rear*, chase, dally, dangle, dawdle, delay, dog*, drag, draggle, draw, droop, drop back, extend, fall back, fall behind, falter, flag, follow a scent*, halt, hang, hang back, hang down, haul, hunt, lag, linger, nose out*, plod, poke, poke along*, procrastinate, pull, pursue, shadow, shag, spook*, spoor, stalk, straggle, stream, string along*, tag along*, tail, take out after, tarry, tow, trace, track, traipse, trudge; SEE CONCEPTS *207,727,753*

train [n] *series*

alternation, appendage, caravan, chain, column, concatenation, consecution, convoy, cortege, course, court, entourage, file, following, gradation, line, order, procession, progression, retinue, row, run, scale, sequel, sequence, set, string, succession, suite, tail, thread, tier, track, trail, wake; SEE CONCEPTS *432,727*

train [v1] *prepare*

accustom, brainwash*, break in, care for, coach, cultivate, develop, discipline, drill, drum into, dry run*, educate, enlighten, equip, exercise, get a workout, get in shape, ground, grow strong, guide, habituate, harden, hone, improve, instruct, inure, make ready, mold, prime, qualify, rear, rehearse, run through, school, season, shape, sharpen, show the ropes*, study, tame, teach, tutor, update, warm up*, whip into shape*, wise up*, work out; SEE CONCEPTS *35,202,285*

train [v2] *aim at*

beam, bring to bear, cast, cock, direct, draw a bead*, focus, get in one's sights*, head, incline, lay, level, line up, point, slant, turn, zero in*; SEE CONCEPT *201*

training [n] *preparation*

background, basics, buildup, chalk talk*, coaching, cultivation, discipline, domestication, drill, education, exercise, foundation, grounding, groundwork, guidance, indoctrination, instruction, practice, preliminaries, preparation, principles, readying, schooling, seasoning, sharpening, teaching, tuition, tune-up*, tutelage, upbringing, warm-up*, workout*; SEE CONCEPTS *202,285, 678*

trait [n] *characteristic*

affection, attribute, birthmark, cast, character, custom, denominator, feature, habit, idiosyncrasy, lineament, manner, mannerism, mark, nature of the beast*, oddity, peculiarity, point, property, quality, quirk, savor, thing*, trick, virtue; SEE CONCEPTS *411,644,834*

traitor [n] *person who is disloyal*

apostate, backslider*, back-stabber*, Benedict Arnold*, betrayer, conspirator, deceiver, defector, deserter, double-crosser*, fink*, hypocrite, impostor, informer, intriguer, Judas*, miscreant, quisling, rebel, renegade, snake*, sneak*, snitch*, snitcher*, spy, squealer*, stool pigeon*, tattletale, traducer, treasonist, turncoat, two-timer*, whistle-blower*, wolf*; SEE CONCEPT *412*

tramp [n1] *person who is poor, desperate*

beggar, bum, derelict, down-and-out*, drifter, floater, hitchhiker, hobo, homeless person, loafer, outcast, panhandler, vagabond, vagrant, wanderer; SEE CONCEPT *412*

tramp [n2] *heavy walk*

cruise, excursion, expedition, footfall, footstep, hike, jaunt, march, ramble, saunter, slog, stomp, stroll, tour, traipse, tread, trek, turn, walking trip; SEE CONCEPTS *151,224*

tramp [v] *walk heavily*

crush, footslog, gallop, hike, hop, march, navigate, plod, pound, ramble, range, roam, rove, slog, stamp, stodge, stomp, stroll, stump, thud, toil, tour, traipse, trample, tread, trek, trip, tromp, trudge, walk over; SEE CONCEPTS *151,224*

trample [v] *walk forcibly over*

bruise, crush, encroach, flatten, grind, hurt, infringe, injure, override, overwhelm, pound, ride roughshod over*, run over, squash, stamp, step on, stomp, tramp, tread, tromp, violate; SEE CONCEPTS *137,208,246*

trance [n] *hypnotic state*

abstraction, coma, daze, dream, ecstasy, glaze, insensibility, muse, petrifaction, rapture, reverie, spell, study, stupor, transfixion, transfixture, unconsciousness; SEE CONCEPT *410*

tranquil [adj] *quiet, peaceful*

agreeable, amicable, at ease, at peace, balmy, calm, collected, comforting, composed, cool, easy, easygoing, even, even-tempered, gentle, halcyon, hushed, lenient, low, measured, mild, moderate, murmuring, pacific, paradisiacal, pastoral, patient, placid, pleasing, poised, possessed, quiet, reasonable, restful, sedate, sedative, serene, smooth, sober, soft, soothing, stable, still, tame, temperate, undisturbed, unexcitable, unexcited, unperturbed, unruffled, untroubled, whispering; SEE CONCEPTS *525,542,594*

tranquility [n] *peace, quiet*

ataraxia, calm, calmness, composure, coolness, equanimity, hush, imperturbability, imperturbation, law and order, order, peacefulness, placidity, quietness, quietude, repose, rest, restfulness, sedateness, serenity, stillness; SEE CONCEPTS 65,673

tranquilize [*v*] *make calm, quiet*
balm, calm, calm down, compose, hush, lull, pacify, put at rest, quell, quiet, quieten, relax, sedate, settle one's nerves*, soothe, still, subdue, unruffle; SEE CONCEPTS 7,22,310

transact [*v*] *do business, carry out*
accomplish, button down*, button up*, buy, carry on, clinch, close, conclude, conduct, discharge, do*, effectuate, enact, execute, finish, handle, jell, manage, move, negotiate, operate, perform, prosecute, pull off, run with the ball*, see to, sell, settle, sew up*, take care of, TCB*, work out a deal*, wrap up*; SEE CONCEPTS 91,223,324, 330,706

transaction [*n*] *business dealing; undertaking*
act, action, activity, affair, agreement, bargain, bond, business, buying, compact, contract, convention, coup, covenant, deal, deed, disposal, doings*, enterprise, event, execution, goings-on*, happening, intercourse, matter, negotiation, occurrence, pact, performance, play, proceeding, purchase, purchasing, sale, selling, step; SEE CONCEPTS 223,324,330,684

transcend [*v*] *go beyond; surpass*
beat, best, be superior, better, eclipse, exceed, excel, go above, leave behind, leave in the dust*, outdo, outrival, outshine, outstrip, outvie, overstep, overtop, rise above, top, transform; SEE CONCEPT 141

transcendent/transcendental [*adj*] *extraordinary, superior*
absolute, abstract, accomplished, beyond grasp, boundless, consummate, entire, eternal, exceeding, fantastic, finished, hypothetical, ideal, incomparable, infinite, innate, intact, intellectual, intuitive, matchless, obscure, original, otherworldly, peerless, perfect, preeminent, primordial, second to none*, sublime, supernatural, supreme, surpassing, theoretical, towering, transcending, transmundane, ultimate, unequalable, unequaled, unique, unparalleled, unrivaled, whole; SEE CONCEPT 574

transcribe [*v*] *transfer to another medium*
copy out, decipher, duplicate, engross, interpret, note, record, render, reprint, reproduce, rewrite, set out, take down, tape, tape-record, transfer, translate, transliterate, write out; SEE CONCEPTS 79,125,171

transfer [*n*] *change of possession*
alteration, assignment, conduction, convection, deportation, displacement, move, relegation, relocation, removal, shift, substitution, transference, translation, transmission, transmittal, transposition, variation; SEE CONCEPTS 108,143,217,223

transfer [*v*] *pass possession to*
assign, bear, bring, carry, cart, cede, change, consign, convert, convey, deed, delegate, deliver, dislocate, dispatch, dispense, displace, disturb, express, feed, ferry, find, forward, give, hand, hand over, haul, lug, mail, make over, metamorphose, move, pass on, pass the buck*, post, provide, relegate, relocate, remove, sell, send, shift, ship, shoulder, sign over, supply, taxi, tote, transfigure, translate, transmit, transmogrify, transmute, transplant, transport, transpose, turn over; SEE CONCEPTS 108,143,217,223,243

transfix [*v1*] *hold one's attention*
bewitch, captivate, enchant, engross, fascinate, hold, hypnotize, mesmerize, palsy, paralyze, petrify, rivet, root, spellbind, stop in one's tracks*, stop one dead*; stun; SEE CONCEPTS 11,14

transfix [*v2*] *pierce*
fix, impale, lance, nail down, penetrate, pin down, puncture, run through, skewer, skiver, spear, spike, spit, stick, transpierce; SEE CONCEPT 220

transform [*v*] *change completely*
alter, commute, convert, cook, denature, doctor, make over, metamorphose, mold, mutate, reconstruct, remodel, renew, revamp, revolutionize, shift gears*, sing different tune*, switch, switch over, transfer, transfigure, translate, transmogrify, transmute, transpose, turn around, turn over new leaf*, turn the corner*, turn the tables*; SEE CONCEPTS 232,697

transformation [*n*] *complete change*
about-face*, alteration, changeover, conversion, flip-flop*, metamorphosis, radical change, renewal, revolution, shift, switch, transfiguration, transmogrification, transmutation; SEE CONCEPT 697

transgression [*n*] *violation, misbehavior*
breach, breaking of the law, contravention, crime, defiance, disobedience, encroachment, erring, error, fault, infraction, infringement, iniquity, lapse, misdeed, misdemeanor, offense, overstepping, sin, slip, trespass, vice, wrong, wrongdoing; SEE CONCEPTS 101,192,645

transient/transitory [*adj*] *temporary, brief*
changeable, deciduous, emigrating, ephemeral, evanescent, flash, fleeting, flitting, fly-by-night*, flying, fugacious, fugitive, going by, impermanent, insubstantial, migrating, momentary, moving, passing, provisional, short, short-lived, short-term, temporal, transmigratory, unstable, vacating, volatile; SEE CONCEPT 798

transit [*n*] *transportation*
alteration, carriage, carrying, conveyance, crossing, infiltration, motion, movement, osmosis, passage, penetration, permeation, portage, shift, shipment, transfer, transference, transport, transporting, travel, traverse; SEE CONCEPTS 155,224

transition [*n*] *change, often major*
alteration, changeover, conversion, development, evolution, flux, growth, metamorphosis, metastasis, passage, passing, progress, progression, realignment, shift, transformation, transit, transmutation, turn, turning point, upheaval; SEE CONCEPT 697

translate [*v1*] *interpret, explain*
construe, convert, decipher, decode, do into, elucidate, explicate, gloss, make clear, metaphrase, paraphrase, put, render, reword, simplify, spell out, transcribe, transliterate, transpose, turn; SEE CONCEPTS 55,57

translate [*v2*] *change*
alter, commute, convert, metamorphose, transfigure, transform, transmogrify, transmute, transpose, turn; SEE CONCEPT 232

translation [*n*] *rewording; interpretation*
adaptation, construction, crib*, decoding, elucidation, explanation, gloss, key, metaphrase, paraphrase, reading, rendering, rendition, rephrasing, restatement, simplification, transcription, transliteration, version; SEE CONCEPTS 268,277,278

translucent [*adj*] *clear*
clear-cut, crystal, crystalline, diaphanous, glassy,

limpid, lucent, lucid, luminous, pellucid, see-through, semiopaque, semitransparent, translucent, unblurred; SEE CONCEPT 618

transmit [v] *communicate, send*
address, bear, bequeath, break, broadcast, carry, channel, conduct, consign, convey, diffuse, dispatch, disseminate, drop a line*, drop a note*, forward, funnel, give a call*, give a ring*, hand down, hand on, impart, instill, issue, mail, pass on, pipe, put on the air*, radio, relay, remit, route, send, send out, ship, siphon, spread, take, traject, transfer, transfuse, translate, transport; SEE CONCEPTS 217,266,292

transparent [adj1] *see-through*
cellophane, clear, crystal-clear, crystalline, diaphanous, filmy, gauzy, glassy, gossamer, hyaline, limpid, lucent, lucid, pellucid, permeable, plain, sheer, thin, tiffany, translucent, transpicuous, vitreous; SEE CONCEPTS 606,618

transparent [adj2] *obvious, understandable*
apparent, articulate, artless, candid, clear-cut, direct, distinct, distinguishable, easily seen, easy, evident, explicit, forthright, frank, guileless, honest, ingenuous, manifest, open, patent, perspicuous, plain, plain-spoken, recognizable, self-explanatory, sincere, straight, straightforward, unambiguous, undisguised, unequivocal, unmistakable, unsophisticated, visible; SEE CONCEPT 267

transpire [v1] *occur, happen*
arise, befall, betide, chance, come about, come to pass, develop, ensue, eventuate, fall out*, gel, go, occur, result, shake, take place, turn up; SEE CONCEPT 3

transpire [v2] *become known*
be disclosed, be discovered, be made public, break, come out, come to light, emerge, get out, leak; SEE CONCEPTS 261,266

transplant [v] *relocate*
displace, emigrate, graft, immigrate, move, readapt, recondition, remove, reorient, reset, resettle, revamp, shift, transfer, transpose, uproot; SEE CONCEPTS 213,310

transport [n1] *move, transfer*
carriage, carrier, carrying, carting, conveyance, conveying, conveyor, freightage, hauling, lift, movement, mover, moving, passage, removal, shipment, shipping, transference, transferring, transit, transportation, transporting, transshipment, truckage, vehicle; SEE CONCEPTS 155,503

transport [n2] *delight*
ardor, bliss, cloud nine*, ecstasy, enchantment, enthusiasm, euphoria, fervor, happiness, heaven, passion, rapture, ravishment, rhapsody, seventh heaven*; SEE CONCEPTS 32,410

transport [v1] *move, transfer*
back, bear, bring, carry, conduct, convey, ferry, fetch, haul, heel*, jag, lug, pack, piggyback*, remove, ride, run, schlepp*, ship, shoulder, take, tote, truck; SEE CONCEPTS 147,187,217

transport [v2] *exile*
banish, cast out, deport, displace, expel, expulse, oust, relegate, sentence; SEE CONCEPTS 211,317

transport [v3] *captivate, delight*
agitate, carry away, electrify, elevate, enchant, enrapture, entrance, excite, inflame, move, provoke, quicken, ravish, send, slay, spellbind, stimulate, stir, thrill, trance, uplight, wow; SEE CONCEPTS 7,22

transpose [v] *swap, switch*
alter, backtrack*, change, commute, convert, double back, exchange, flip-flop*, interchange, inverse, invert, metamorphose, move, put, rearrange, relocate, render, reorder, reverse, revert, shift, substitute, transfer, transfigure, transform, translate, transmogrify, transmute, turn, turn the tables*; SEE CONCEPTS 104,232,697

trap [n] *snare, trick*
allurement, ambuscade, ambush, artifice, bait, booby trap*, come-on*, conspiracy, deception, decoy, device, dragnet, enticement, feint, gambit, hook*, intrigue, inveiglement, lasso*, lure, machination, maneuver, net, noose, pitfall, plot, ploy, prank, quagmire, quicksand, ruse, seducement, snag*, stratagem, subterfuge, temptation, wile; SEE CONCEPT 674

trap [v] *catch, snare; trick*
ambuscade, ambush, beguile, box in*, circumvent, collar*, corner*, corral*, deceive, decoy, dupe, enmesh, ensnare, entangle, entrap, fool, grab, hook, inveigle, land*, mousetrap*, nab, nail*, net, overtake, rope in*, seduce, snag, suck in*, surprise, take, tangle, trammel, trip up*; SEE CONCEPTS 59,90

trappings [n] *paraphernalia, equipment*
accouterment, adornment, apparel, appointment, decoration, dress, embellishment, finery, fitting, fixture, furnishing, gear, livery, ornament, panoply, personal effects, raiment, rigging, things, trimming; SEE CONCEPTS 446,451,496

trash [n1] *garbage*
debris, dregs, droppings, dross, excess, filth, fragments, junk, leavings, litter, oddments, odds and ends*, offal, pieces, refuse, residue, rubbish, rubble, rummage, scourings, scrap, scraps, scum*, sediment, shavings, sweepings, waste; SEE CONCEPTS 260,834

trash [n3] *ridiculous communication*
balderdash, bilge*, drivel, foolish talk, hogwash, inanity, malarkey*, nonsense, rot, rubbish, tripe, twaddle; SEE CONCEPT 278

trauma [n] *severe mental or physical pain*
agony, anguish, blow, collapse, confusion, damage, derangement, disturbance, hurt, injury, jolt, ordeal, outburst, shock, strain, stress, suffering, torture, traumatization, upheaval, upset, wound; SEE CONCEPT 728

travel [n] *journey*
biking, commutation, cruising, drive, driving, excursion, expedition, flying, globe-trotting*, hop*, junket, movement, navigation, overnight*, passage, peregrination, ramble, ride, riding, sailing, seafaring, sightseeing, swing, tour, touring, transit, trek, trekking, trip, voyage, voyaging, walk, wandering, wanderlust, wayfaring, weekend; SEE CONCEPT 224

travel [v] *journey on a trip or tour*
adventure, carry, cover, cover ground, cross, cruise, drive, explore, fly, get through, go, go abroad, go camping, go into orbit*, go riding, hop*, jaunt, jet*, junket*, knock around, make a journey, make one's way, migrate, motor, move, overnight*, proceed, progress, ramble, roam, rove, sail, scour, set forth, set out, sightsee, take a boat, take a plane, take a train, take a trip, tour, transmit, traverse, trek, vacation, visit, voyage, walk, wander, weekend*, wend; SEE CONCEPT 224

traveler [n] *person who journeys*
adventurer, barnstormer*, bum*, commuter, displaced person, drifter, excursionist, expeditionist, explorer, floater, gadabout*, globetrotter, gypsy, haj, hiker, hobo, itinerant, jet-setter, journeyer, junketer, migrant, navigator, nomad, passenger, peddler, pilgrim, rambler, roamer, rover, sailor, seafarer, sightseer, tourist, tramp, transmigrant, trekker, tripper, trouper, truant, vagabond, vagrant, voyager, wanderer, wayfarer; SEE CONCEPTS 348,423

traverse [v1] *cross over; travel*
bisect, bridge, crisscross, cross, cut across, decussate, do, go across, go over, intersect, move over, negotiate, pace, pass over, pass through, perambulate, peregrinate, ply, quarter, range, roam, span, track, transverse, travel over, tread, walk, wander; SEE CONCEPTS 147,201,692,750

traverse [v2] *resist, contradict*
balk, buck, check, combat, contest, contravene, counter, counteract, cross, deny, disaffirm, dispute, duel, fight, frustrate, gainsay, go against, hinder, impede, impugn, negate, negative, obstruct, oppose, repel, thwart, withstand; SEE CONCEPTS 54,121

travesty [n] *spoof, ridicule*
burlesque, caricature, distortion, exaggeration, farce, lampoon, lampoonery, mimicry, mock, mockery, parody, perversion, play, put-on*, roast*, satire, send-up*, sham*, takeoff*; SEE CONCEPTS 273,292

travesty [v] *ridicule, spoof*
ape, burlesque, caricature, deride, distort, imitate, lampoon, make a mockery of, make fun of, mimic, mock, parody, pervert, play on*, put on*, satirize, send up*, sham*, take off*; SEE CONCEPTS 273,292

treacherous [adj1] *dishonest, disloyal*
betraying, catchy, deceitful, deceptive, double-crossing*, double-dealing*, duplicitous, faithless, false, false-hearted, fly-by-night*, insidious, misleading, perfidious, recreant, shifty*, slick*, slippery*, snake in the grass*, traitorous, treasonable, tricky, two-faced*, two-timing*, undependable, unfaithful, unloyal, unreliable, untrue, untrustworthy; SEE CONCEPTS 401,404

treacherous [adj2] *dangerous*
alarming, chancy, deceptive, difficult, dissembled, faulty, hairy*, hazardous, icy*, insecure, jeopardous, menacing, misleading, ominous, perilous, precarious, risky, shaky, slippery, ticklish, tricky, undependable, unhealthy, unreliable, unsafe, unsound, unstable, wicked; SEE CONCEPTS 565,587

treachery [n] *disloyalty, dishonesty*
betrayal, bunco, corruption, dirty dealing*, dirty pool*, dirty trick*, dirty work*, disaffection, dodge, double-cross*, double-dealing*, duplicity, faithlessness, fake, falseness, fast shuffle*, flim-flam*, grift, gyp*, infidelity, perfidiousness, perfidy, put-on*, racket*, recreancy, scam*, sellout, shell game*, skin game*, spoof, stab in the back*, sweet talk*, treacherousness, treason, two-timing*, whitewash*; SEE CONCEPTS 633,645

tread [n] *walk*
footstep, footsteps, gait, march, pace, step, stride, trace, track, tramp; SEE CONCEPTS 149,284

tread [v] *walk; bear down*
ambulate, crush, foot, hike, hoof, march, oppress, pace, plod, quell, repress, squash, stamp, stamp

on, step, step on, stride, subdue, subjugate, suppress, traipse, tramp, trample, troop, trudge; SEE CONCEPT 149

treason [n] *disloyalty*
breach of faith, crime, deceit, deceitfulness, deception, disaffection, dishonesty, duplicity, faithlessness, lèse majesté, mutiny, perfidy, revolt, revolutionary, sedition, seditious act, seditiousness, subversion, traitorousness, treachery; SEE CONCEPTS 192,645

treasure [n] *prized possession or entity*
abundance, apple of one's eye*, cache, capital, cash, catch*, darling, find, fortune, funds, gem, gold, hoard, jewel, money, nest egg*, nonpareil, paragon, pearl*, pile*, plum*, pride and joy*, prize, reserve, riches, richness, store, treasure trove, valuable, wealth; SEE CONCEPTS 332,337,446,710

treasure [v] *hold dear*
adore, appreciate, apprize, cherish, conserve, dote on, esteem, guard, idiolize, love, preserve, prize, revere, reverence, save, value, venerate, worship; SEE CONCEPT 32

treasury [n] *place where money, valuables are kept*
archive, bank, bursar, bursary, cache, chest, coffer, damper, depository, exchange, exchequer, Fort Knox*, gallery, hoard, museum, register, repository, safe, storage, store, storehouse, strongbox, treasure house, vault; SEE CONCEPTS 339,439,449

treat [n] *pleasing entity or occurrence*
amusement, banquet, celebration, dainty, delicacy, delight, enjoyment, entertainment, feast, fun, gift, goody*, gratification, joy, party, pleasure, refreshment, satisfaction, surprise, sweet, thrill, tidbit; SEE CONCEPTS 457,529,693

treat [v1] *act, behave towards*
account, act with regard to, appraise, conduct, conduct oneself toward, consider, deal with*, employ, estimate, evaluate, handle, have business with*, have recourse to*, have to do with*, hold, look upon, manage, negotiate, play, rate, react toward, regard, respect, serve, take, use, value, wield; SEE CONCEPT 633

treat [v2] *doctor, medicate*
administer, apply treatment, attend, care for, cure, dose, dress, heal, medicament, minister to, nurse, operate, prescribe; SEE CONCEPT 310

treat [v3] *pay the bill for someone else*
amuse, blow, buy for, divert, entertain, escort, feast, foot the bill*, give, indulge, pay for, pick up the check*, pick up the tab*, play host*, provide, regale, satisfy, set up, spring for*, stake, stand*, take out, wine and dine*; SEE CONCEPTS 327,384

treat [v4] *be concerned with; discuss*
advise, approach, arrange, comment, confabulate, confer, consider, consult, contain, criticize, deal with, deliberate, discourse on, discuss, enlarge upon, explain, go into, interpret, manipulate, reason, review, speak about, study, tackle, talk about, think, touch upon, weigh, write about; SEE CONCEPTS 17,56

treatise [n] *written study of a subject*
argument, book, commentary, composition, discourse, discussion, disquisition, dissertation, essay, exposition, memoir, monograph, pamphlet, paper, review, script, thesis, tract, tractate, work, writing; SEE CONCEPTS 271,280

tr
tr

treatment [n1] *medical care*
analysis, cure, diet, doctoring, healing, hospitalization, medication, medicine, operation, prescription, regimen, remedy, surgery, therapeutics, therapy; SEE CONCEPT 310

treatment [n2] *handling of entity, situation*
action towards, angle, approach, behavior towards, conduct, custom, dealing, employment, execution, habit, line, management, manipulation, manner, method, mode, modus operandi, practice, procedure, proceeding, processing, reception, strategy, usage, way; SEE CONCEPTS 117,633

treaty [n] *agreement, contract*
accord, alliance, arrangement, bargain, bond, cartel, charter, compact, concord, concordat, convention, covenant, deal, entente, league, negotiation, pact, reconciliation, sanction, settlement, understanding; SEE CONCEPTS 684,685

tree [n] *large plant enclosed in bark and shedding leaves*
forest, hardwood, pulp, sapling, seedling, shrub, softwood, stock, timber, wood, woods; SEE CONCEPT 430

trek [n] *long journey*
expedition, footslog, hegira, hike, long haul, march, odyssey, peregrination, slog, tramp, travel, trip; SEE CONCEPT 224

trek [v] *journey*
be on the move*, be on the trail*, foot, hike, hit the road*, march, migrate, plod, range, roam, rove, slog, traipse, tramp, travel, trudge, walk; SEE CONCEPT 224

tremble [v] *shake, vibrate*
flutter, have the shakes*, jar, jitter, oscillate, palpitate, quake, quaver, quiver, rock, shiver, shudder, teeter, throb, totter, tremor, wobble; SEE CONCEPT 152

tremendous [adj] *huge, overwhelming*
amazing, appalling, astounding, awesome, awful, blimp, colossal, cracking, deafening, dreadful, enormous, excellent, exceptional, extraordinary, fabulous, fantastic, fearful, formidable, frightful, gargantuan, gigantic, great, great big*, huge, humongous, immense, incredible, jumbo*, large, mammoth, marvelous, massive, mondo*, monstrous, monumental, prodigious, stupendous, super, terrible, terrific, titanic, towering, vast, whale*, whopper, whopping, wonderful; SEE CONCEPTS 574,773,781

tremor [n] *shaking, shock*
agitation, earthquake, flutter, quake, quaking, quaver, quiver, quivering, ripple, shake, shiver, shivering, tremble, trembling, trepidation, upheaval, vibration, wobble; SEE CONCEPTS 145,526

trench [n] *ditch, channel dug in earth*
arroyo, canal, cut, depression, dike, drain, drill, dugout, earthwork, entrenchment, excavation, fosse, foxhole, furrow, gorge, gulch, gully, gutter, hollow, main, moat, pit, rut, sink, trough, tube, waterway; SEE CONCEPTS 509,513

trenchant [adj] *sarcastic, scathing*
acerbic, acid, acidulous, acute, astringent, biting, caustic, clear, clear-cut, crisp, critical, crushing, cutting, distinct, driving, dynamic, effective, effectual, emphatic, energetic, explicit, forceful, forcible, graphic, hurtful, impressive, incisive, intense, keen, mordant, penetrating, piquant, pointed, potent, powerful, pungent, razor-sharp*,

salient, salty*, sardonic, sententious, severe, sharp, significant, strong, tart, to the point, unequivocal, unsparing, vigorous, weighty, well-defined; SEE CONCEPTS 267,537

trend [n1] *flow, current*
aim, bearing, bent, bias, course, direction, drift, inclination, leaning, movement, orientation, progression, run, swing, tendency, tenor, wind; SEE CONCEPTS 230,657,738

trend [n2] *style, fashion that is in favor*
craze, cry, fad, furor, in-thing*, latest thing*, look, mode, newest wrinkle*, rage, thing*, vogue; SEE CONCEPT 655

trendy [adj] *in fashion, style*
à la mode*, contemporary, fashionable, fly*, in, in vogue, latest, modish*, now*, popular, stylish, swank*, tony*, up-to-the-minute, voguish, with-it*; SEE CONCEPT 589

trepidation [n] *anxiety, worry*
agitation, alarm, apprehension, blue funk*, butterflies*, cold feet*, cold sweat*, consternation, creeps*, dismay, disquiet, disturbance, dread, emotion, excitement, fear, fright, goose bumps*, horror, jitters, nervousness, palpitation, panic, perturbation, shock, terror, trepidity, uneasiness, worriment; SEE CONCEPT 27

trespass [n] *invasion, offense*
breach, contravention, crime, delinquency, encroachment, entrenchment, error, evildoing, fault, infraction, infringement, iniquity, injury, intrusion, misbehavior, misconduct, misdeed, misdemeanor, obtrusion, poaching, sin, transgression, unlawful entry, violation, wrongdoing, wrongful entry; SEE CONCEPTS 101,192,645,691

trespass [v] *infringe, offend*
butt in*, chisel in*, crash, crash the gates*, deviate, displease, do wrong by, encroach, entrench, err, horn in*, interlope, intrude, invade, kibitz*, lapse, meddle, misbehave, mix in, muscle in*, nose in*, obtrude, overstep, penetrate, poach, poke, sin, stick nose in*, transgress, violate, wrong; SEE CONCEPTS 101,159,192,384

trial [n1] *test*
analysis, assay, attempt, audition, check, crack*, dry run*, effort, endeavor, essay, examination, experience, experiment, experimentation, fling*, go*, hassle*, investigation, lick*, probation, proof, R and D*, research and development, shakedown*, shot*, showcase*, stab*, striving, struggle, testing, test run, trial and error*, trial run, try, try on*, tryout, undertaking, venture, whack*, workout; SEE CONCEPTS 87,290,291

trial [n2] *legal proceeding*
action, arraignment, case, citation, claim, contest, counterclaim, court action, court martial, cross-examination, habeas corpus, hearing, impeachment, indictment, lawsuit, litigation, prosecution, rap*, seizure, suit, tribunal; SEE CONCEPTS 317,691

trial [n3] *trouble, big problem*
adversity, affliction, albatross*, anguish, annoyance, bane, blow, bother, burden, calvary, care, complication, cross to bear*, crucible*, difficulty, distress, drag*, grief, hardship, hard time*, hassle*, heartbreak, inconvenience, irritation, load, misery, misfortune, nightmare, nuisance, ordeal, pain, pain in the neck*, pest, plague, rigor, severe test, sorrow, suffering, thorn, tribulation, trying time*, unhappiness, vexation, vicissitude, visitation, woe, wretchedness; SEE CONCEPTS 674,728

trial [adj] experimental
balloon, exploratory, pilot, preliminary, proba-tionary, provisional, tentative, test, testing; SEE CONCEPTS 548,560

tribe [n] ethnic group; family
association, blood, caste, clan, class, division, dy-nasty, horde, house, ilk, kin, kind, kindred, lin-eage, people, race, seed, society, sort, stock, type; SEE CONCEPTS 296,380,421

tribulation [n] pain, unhappiness
adversity, affliction, albatross*, bad luck*, blow*, bummer*, burden, care, cross to bear*, crucible*, curse, difficulty, distress, double whammy*, downer*, drag*, grief, hard knock*, hard time*, headache*, heartache*, misery, misfortune, op-pression, ordeal, persecution, rainy day*, reverse, sorrow, suffering, trial, trouble, vexation, visita-tion, woe, worry, wretchedness, wronging; SEE CONCEPTS 666,728

tributary [adj] secondary; branch
accessory, dependent, feeding, minor, satellite, shoot, side, sub, subject, subordinate, under; SEE CONCEPT 560

tribute [n] testimonial, praise
accolade, acknowledgment, applause, apprecia-tion, citation, commendation, compliment, enco-mium, esteem, eulogy, gift, gratitude, honor, laudation, memorial, offering, panegyric, recog-nition, recommendation, respect, salutation, salvo; SEE CONCEPTS 69,278

trick [n1] deceit
ambush, artifice, blind, bluff, casuistry, cheat, chicanery, circumvention, con*, concealment, conspiracy, conundrum, cover, deception, decoy, delusion, device, disguise, distortion, dodge*, double-dealing, duplicity, equivocation, evasion, fabrication, fake, falsehood, feint, forgery, fraud, game, gimmick, hoax, illusion, imposition, im-posture, intrigue, invention, machination, maneu-ver, perjury, plot, ploy, ruse, snare, stratagem, subterfuge, swindle, trap, treachery, wile; SEE CONCEPTS 59,645

trick [n2] prank, joke
accomplishment, antic, caper, catch, device, es-capade, feat, frolic, funny business, gag*, gam-bol, jape, jest, lark, monkeyshine*, practical joke, put-on*, shenanigan*, sleight of hand, sport, stunt, tomfoolery; SEE CONCEPTS 59,273,384

trick [n3] expertise, know-how
ability, art, command, craft, device, facility, gift, hang, knack, method, secret, skill, swing, tech-nique; SEE CONCEPT 630

trick [n4] characteristic, habit
crotchet, custom, foible, habitude, idiosyncrasy, manner, mannerism, peculiarity, practice, praxis, quirk, trait, usage, use, way, wont; SEE CON-CEPTS 411,657

trick [v] fool; play joke on
bamboozle, catch*, cheat, con, deceive, defraud, delude, disinform, double deal*, dupe, fake, flim-flam*, fool, gull, hoax, hocus-pocus*, hoodwink, impose upon, jive*, mislead, outwit, play for a fool*, pull wool over*, put one over on*, rook*, screw*, set up*, swindle, take for a ride*, take in*, throw, trap, victimize; SEE CONCEPT 59

trickery [n] deception, joke
bait and switch*, cheat, cheating, chicane, chica-nery, con, deceit, dishonesty, dodge, double-cross*, double-dealing*, dupery*, fast shuffle*, flimflam*, fourberie, fraud, funny business*, guile, hoax, imposture, pretense, quackery, razzle-dazzle*, scam, sharp practice, shell game*, shenanigans*, snow job*, sting*, stunt, swin-dling, underhandedness; SEE CONCEPTS 59,645

trickle [v] run out
crawl, creep, distill, dribble, drip, drop, exude, flow, issue, leak, ooze, percolate, seep, stream, trill, weep; SEE CONCEPTS 146,179

tricky [adj1] complicated, difficult
catchy, complex, critical, delicate, intricate, in-volved, knotty*, perplexing, precarious, problem-atic, quirky, risky, rocky, sensitive, sticky, thorny, ticklish, touch-and-go*, touchy, unde-pendable, unstable; SEE CONCEPT 562

tricky [adj2] deceptive, sly
artful, astute, cagey, catchy, clever, crafty, cun-ning, deceitful, deep, delusive, delusory, devious, dishonest, foxy, greasy*, guileful, insidious, in-telligent, keen, misleading, scheming, shady, sharp, shifty, shrewd, slick*, slippery*, smooth, streetwise*, subtle, treacherous, wily, witted, wry; SEE CONCEPT 401

tried [adj] reliable
approved, certified, constant, demonstrated, de-pendable, faithful, proved, secure, staunch, stead-fast, tested, tried-and-true*, true-blue*, trustworthy, trusty, used; SEE CONCEPT 535

trifle [n1] novelty item
bagatelle, bauble, bibelot, curio, gewgaw*, knick-knack, nothing*, novelty, objet d'art, plaything, toy, trinket, triviality, whatnot*; SEE CONCEPT 446

trifle [n2] very small amount
bit, dash, diddly*, drop, eyelash*, fly speck*, fraction, hint, jot, little, no big deal*, particle, picayune*, pinch, shade, smack, soupçon*, speck, spice, spot, squat, suggestion, suspicion, touch, trace; SEE CONCEPTS 668,831

trifle [v] toy with; mess around
amuse oneself, be insincere, coquet, dabble, dally, dawdle, dilly-dally*, doodle, fidget, flirt, fool, fool around*, fool with*, fribble*, fritter, futz around*, horse around*, idle, indulge in, lead on, loiter, lollygag*, lounge, mess with*, misuse, monkey, monkey with*, palter, philander, play, play games with*, play with, potter, putter, squan-der, string along*, toy, twiddle, use up, wanton, waste, waste time, wink at*; SEE CONCEPTS 210,292,363

trifling [adj] insignificant, worthless
banal, dinky*, empty, forget it*, frivolous, hol-low, idle, idling, inane, inconsequential, incon-siderable, insipid, jejune, loitering, measly, minuscule, negligible, niggling*, no big deal*, no big thing*, nugatory, paltry, petty, picayune, pid-dling, puny, shallow, silly, slight, small, tiny, trivial, unimportant, vain, valueless, vapid; SEE CONCEPTS 575,789

trigger [v] cause to happen
activate, bring about, cause, elicit, generate, give rise to, produce, prompt, provoke, set in motion, set off, spark, start; SEE CONCEPT 242

trim [n1] decoration
adornment, border, edging, embellishment, frill, fringe, garnish, gingerbread*, ornamentation, pip-ing, trimming; SEE CONCEPTS 475,824

trim [n2] *condition, health*
commission, fettle*, fitness, form, kilter*, order, repair, shape, situation, state, whack*; SEE CONCEPT 316

trim [adj] *neat, orderly*
apple-pie order*, clean, clean-cut, compact, dapper, fit, in good shape, neat as a pin*, nice, shipshape*, slick, smart, snug, spick-and-span*, spruce, streamlined, symmetrical, tidy, to rights*, uncluttered, well-groomed; SEE CONCEPTS 485,621

trim [adj2] *shapely*
beautiful, clean, comely, fit, graceful, in fine fettle*, in good shape, sleek, slender, slick, slim, statuesque, streamlined, svelte, well-balanced, well-proportioned, willowy; SEE CONCEPTS 314,490,491

trim [v1] *cut shorter*
abbreviate, barber, blue pencil*, bob, boil down*, clip, crop, curtail, cut, cut back, cut down, dock, edit, even up, lop, mow, pare, pare down, plane, prune, put in a nutshell*, shave, shear, shorten, slice off, snip, tidy, truncate, whittle down*; SEE CONCEPTS 176,236,247

trim [v2] *decorate*
adorn, array, beautify, bedeck, beribbon, deck, dress, dress up, embellish, emblazon, embroider, garnish, ornament, prank, pretty up*, prink*, spangle, spruce up*; SEE CONCEPTS 162,177

trim [v3] *beat, defeat*
clobber, drub, lambaste, lick, smother, thrash, trounce, wax*, whip; SEE CONCEPT 95

trinket [n] *knickknack*
bagatelle, bauble, bead, bibelot, curio, doodad*, gadget, gewgaw*, gimcrack*, glass*, hardware, jewel, jewelry, junk, nothing*, novelty, objet d'art, ornament, plaything, rock*, sparkler*, stone, toy, trifle, whatnot*; SEE CONCEPT 446

trio/triple [n] *three of something*
leash, set of three, ternion, threesome, trey, triad, triangle, trilogy, trine, trinity, triplet, triplicate, triptych, triumvirate, triune, troika; SEE CONCEPTS 784,787

trip [n1] *journey, excursion*
cruise, errand, expedition, foray, hop*, jaunt, junket, outing, overnight, peregrination, ramble*, run, swing*, tour, travel, trek, voyage, weekend; SEE CONCEPT 224

trip [n2] *error, blunder*
bungle, fall, false move, false step, faux pas*, indiscretion, lapse, misstep, mistake, slip, stumble; SEE CONCEPTS 101,230

trip [v] *fall, err*
buck, canter, confuse, disconcert, fall, fall over, founder, frolic, go headlong*, go wrong, hop, lapse, lope, lose balance, lose footing, lurch, make a faux pas*, miscalculate, misstep, pitch, play, plunge, skip, slide, slip, slip on, slip up, sprawl, spring, stumble, throw off, topple, tumble, unsettle; SEE CONCEPTS 101,149

trite [adj] *silly, commonplace*
banal, bathetic, bromidic, chain, cliché, clichéd, common, cornball*, corny*, drained, dull, exhausted, familiar tune*, flat, hackneyed, hokey*, jejune, mildewed*, moth-eaten*, musty*, old hat*, ordinary, pedestrian, platitudinous, prosaic, ready-made, routine, run-of-the-mill*, set, shopworn, stale, stereotyped, stock, threadbare, timeworn, tired, uninspired, unoriginal, used-up,

vapid, warmed-over*, well-worn, worn, worn-out; SEE CONCEPTS 267,530

triumph [n1] *extreme happiness*
celebration, elation, exultance, exultation, festivity, joy, jubilance, jubilation, jubilee, merriment, pride, rejoicing, reveling; SEE CONCEPT 410

triumph [n2] *victory, achievement*
accomplishment, ascendancy, attainment, big hit*, big win*, cinch, clean sweep*, conquest, coup, feat, feather in cap*, gain, grand slam*, hit, hole in one*, homer*, pushover*, riot, score, sell, sensation, shoo-in*, smash-hit*, splash, success, sure bet*, sure thing*, surmounting, takeover, the gold*, tour de force*, vanquishing, vanquishment, walkover*, win; SEE CONCEPT 706

triumph [v1] *be very happy*
celebrate, crow, delight, exult, gloat, glory, jubilate, rejoice, revel, swagger; SEE CONCEPT 32

triumph [v2] *achieve, succeed*
beat the game*, beat the system*, best, blow away*, carry the day*, come out on top*, conquer, dominate, flourish, get last laugh*, overcome, overwhelm, prevail, prosper, sink, strike it big*, subdue, sweep, take it all*, take the cake*, thrive, trounce, vanquish, win, win hands down*, win out*; SEE CONCEPTS 95,141,706

triumphant [adj] *successful*
boastful, celebratory, champion, conquering, dominant, elated, exultant, glorious, happy, in the lead*, jubilant, looking good, lucky, on top, out front*, prizewinning, proud, rejoicing, swaggering, triumphal, unbeaten, undefeated, victorious, winning; SEE CONCEPT 528

trivia [n] *details*
fine points, memorabilia, minutiae, trifles, trivialities; SEE CONCEPTS 274,543

trivial [adj] *not important*
atomic, beside the point*, commonplace, diminutive, evanescent, everyday, flimsy, frivolous, immaterial, inappreciable, incidental, inconsequential, inconsiderable, insignificant, irrelevant, little, meager, mean, meaningless, microscopic, minor, minute, momentary, negligible, nonessential, nugatory, of no account, paltry, petty, piddling*, puny, scanty, skin-deep*, slight, small, superficial, trifling, trite, unimportant, valueless, vanishing, worthless; SEE CONCEPT 575

troop/troops [n] *group, often military*
armed forces, army, assemblage, assembly, band, body, bunch, collection, combatants, company, contingent, corps, crew, crowd, delegation, drove, fighting forces, flock, forces, gang, gathering, herd, horde, host, legion, military, multitude, number, outfit, pack, party, personnel, service personnel, soldiers, soldiery, squad, swarm, team, throng, troopers, troupe, unit; SEE CONCEPTS 322,417

trophy [n] *physical award*
blue ribbon*, booty, citation, crown, cup, decoration, gold*, gold star*, guerdon, keepsake, laurels, medal, memento, memorial, palm, prize, reminder, ribbon, souvenir, spoils*, token; SEE CONCEPT 337

tropical [adj] *warm and humid*
close, equatorial, hot, lush, steamy, sticky, stifling, sultry, sweaty, sweltering, torrid, tropic; SEE CONCEPTS 525,605

trot [v] *move along briskly*
amble, canter, go, hurry, jog, lope, pad, rack, ride, run, scamper, step lively; SEE CONCEPT 150

trot out [v] *bring forward*
brandish, bring up, come out with, display, disport, drag up, exhibit, expose, flash, flaunt, parade, recite, rehearse, reiterate, relate, repeat, represent, show, show off; SEE CONCEPT **138**

trouble [n1] *annoyance, worry*
agitation, anxiety, bad news*, bind, bother, commotion, concern, danger, difficulty, dilemma, dire straits, discontent, discord, disorder, disquiet, dissatisfaction, distress, disturbance, grief, hang-up*, heartache, hindrance, hot water*, inconvenience, irritation, mess, misfortune, nuisance, pain, pest, pickle*, predicament, problem, puzzle, row, scrape, sorrow, spot, strain, stress, strife, struggle, suffering, task, torment, tribulation, tumult, unrest, vexation, woe; SEE CONCEPTS **532,674,675,690,728**

trouble [n2] *something requiring great effort*
ado, attention, bother, bustle, care, concern, difficulty, effort, exertion, flurry, fuss, hardship, inconvenience, labor, pains, pother, rigor, strain, stress, struggle, thought, trial, while, work, worry; SEE CONCEPTS **666,677**

trouble [n3] *bad health*
affliction, ailment, complaint, curse, defect, disability, disease, disorder, failure, illness, malady, malfunction, upset; SEE CONCEPT **316**

trouble [v1] *bother, worry*
afflict, agitate, ail, annoy, bug*, burden, burn up*, concern, discommode, discompose, disconcert, disoblige, disquiet, distress, disturb, drive up the wall*, flip out*, fret, get to, give a bad time*, give a hard time*, grieve, harass, harry, impose on, inconvenience, irk, irritate, make a fuss*, make a scene*, make waves*, pain, perplex, perturb, pester, plague, psych*, put out*, sadden, spook*, stir up, strain, stress, torment, try, upset, vex; SEE CONCEPTS **7,19**

trouble [v2] *make an effort*
be concerned with, exert, go to the effort of, take pains*, take the time*; SEE CONCEPT **100**

troublemaker [n] *person who causes a problem*
agent provocateur, agitator, bad actor*, firebrand*, gremlin*, heel*, hellion, incendiary, inciter, inflamer, instigator, loose cannon*, meddler, mischief-maker, nuisance, phony*, punk*, rabble-rouser*, rascal, recreant, smart aleck*, snake*, stormy petrel*, weasel*; SEE CONCEPT **412**

troublesome [adj] *bothersome, worrisome*
alarming, annoying, arduous, burdensome, damaging, dangerous, demanding, difficult, disquieting, harassing, hard, heavy, importunate, inconvenient, infestive, intractable, irksome, irritating, laborious, mean, messy, murder, oppressive, painful, pesky, pestiferous, pestilential, problematic, refractory, repressive, rough, taxing, tiresome, tough, tricky, troublous, trying, ugly, ungovernable, unruly, uphill, upsetting, vexatious, vexing, wearisome, wicked, worrying; SEE CONCEPTS **529,565**

trough [n] *gutter, depression*
canal, channel, crib, cup, dike, dip, ditch, duct, flume, furrow, gully, hollow, manger, moat, trench, watercourse; SEE CONCEPTS **509,513**

trounce [v] *defeat overwhelmingly*
bash, beat, blank, bury, bust*, cap, clobber, conquer, cook one's goose*, crush, drub, dust*, fix one's wagon*, flog, hammer*, lambaste*, lather*, lick*, make mincemeat of*, murder, overcome, overwhelm, paste*, pommel*, put away*, rout, swamp, thrash*, total*, trash, walk over*, wallop*, waste*, wax*, whip, win, wipe off the mat*; SEE CONCEPT **95**

truce [n] *peaceful solution*
accord, agreement, amnesty, armistice, break, breather*, cease-fire, cessation, de-escalation, detente, halt, intermission, interval, letup, lull, moratorium, olive branch*, pause, peace, reconciliation, reprieve, respite, rest, stay, suspension, temporary peace, terms, treaty, white flag*, wind-down*; SEE CONCEPTS **230,298,684**

truck [n1] *commerce, merchandise*
barter, business, buying and selling, commercial goods, commodities, communication, communion, connection, contact, dealings, exchange, goods*, intercourse, relations, stock, stuff*, trade, traffic, wares*; SEE CONCEPTS **324,330,338**

truck [n2] *wheeled vehicle for hauling*
buggy*, car, carryall, crate*, dump, eighteen-wheeler*, four by eight*, four by four*, four-wheel drive*, freighter, jeep, lorry, pickup, rig*, semi*, van, wagon, wheels*; SEE CONCEPT **505**

truck [v] *buy and sell*
bargain, barter, deal, deal in*, do business, exchange, handle, have dealings, negotiate, peddle, retail, swap, trade, traffic, transact, wholesale*; SEE CONCEPTS **324,327,345**

truculent [adj] *belligerent, hateful*
abusive, aggressive, antagonistic, bad-tempered, barbarous, bellicose, browbeating, brutal, bullying, caustic, combative, contentious, contumelious, cowing, cross, defiant, ferocious, fierce, frightening, harsh, hostile, inhuman, inhumane, intimidating, invective, mean, militant, mordacious, mordant, obstreperous, opprobrious, ornery*, pugnacious, quarrelsome, rude, savage, scathing, scrappy, scurrilous, sharp, sullen, terrifying, terrorizing, trenchant, violent, vituperative, vituperous; SEE CONCEPTS **267,401**

trudge [v] *walk heavily*
clump, drag oneself*, footslog, hike, lumber, march, plod, plug along*, schlepp*, slog, step, stumble, stump, traipse, tramp, tread, trek, wade; SEE CONCEPT **151**

true [adj1] *real, valid; concordant with facts*
accurate, actual, appropriate, authentic, authoritative, bona fide, correct, dependable, direct, exact, factual, fitting, genuine, honest, indubitable, kosher*, lawful, legal, legitimate, natural, normal, on target*, perfect, precise, proper, pure, regular, right, rightful, sincere, straight, sure-enough*, trustworthy, truthful, typical, undeniable, undesigning, undoubted, unerring, unfaked, unfeigned, unquestionable, veracious, veridical, veritable, very, wash*; SEE CONCEPTS **267,535,582**

true [adj2] *loyal*
allegiant, ardent, confirmed, conscientious, constant, creditable, dedicated, dependable, devoted, dutiful, estimable, faithful, fast, firm, high-principled, honest, honorable, just, liege, no lie*, on the up and up*, pure, reliable, resolute, right, right-minded, scrupulous, sincere, square, staunch, steadfast, steady, straight, strict, sure, true-blue*, truehearted, trustworthy, trusty, unaffected, undistorted, unfeigned, unswerving, up front*, upright, veracious, veridical, wholehearted, worthy; SEE CONCEPTS **267,401,542**

tr
tr

true [adv] *honestly, accurately*
correctly, on target, perfectly, precisely, properly, rightly, truthfully, unerringly, veraciously, veritably; SEE CONCEPTS 267,535,544

truly [adv] *really, doubtlessly*
absolutely, accurately, actually, authentically, beyond doubt, beyond question, confirmedly, constantly, correctly, de facto, definitely, devotedly, exactly, factually, faithfully, firmly, genuinely, honestly, honorably, in actuality, in fact, in reality, in truth, legitimately, loyally, positively, precisely, reliably, righteously, rightly, sincerely, staunchly, steadily, surely, truthfully, unequivocally, veraciously, veritably, very, with all one's heart*, with devotion, without a doubt; SEE CONCEPTS 267,535,582

truncate [v] *shorten*
abbreviate, abridge, clip, crop, curtail, cut, cut off, cut short, lop, pare, prune, shear, top, trim; SEE CONCEPTS 137,236,247

trunk [n1] *body, core*
block, bole, butt, column, log, soma, stalk, stem, stock, thorax, torso; SEE CONCEPTS 392,428,826

trunk [n2] *long nose of animal*
beak, proboscis, prow, snoot*, snout; SEE CONCEPT 399

trunk [n3] *container, box*
bag, baggage, bin, case, chest, coffer, coffin, crate, foot locker, locker, luggage, portmanteau, suitcase, wardrobe; SEE CONCEPTS 494,502

trust [n1] *belief in something as true, trustworthy*
assurance, certainty, certitude, confidence, conviction, credence, credit, dependence, entrustment, expectation, faith, gospel truth*, hope, positiveness, reliance, stock, store, sureness; SEE CONCEPT 689

trust [n2] *responsibility, custody*
account, care, charge, duty, guard, guardianship, keeping, liability, moment, obligation, protection, safekeeping, trusteeship, ward; SEE CONCEPTS 376,645

trust [n3] *large company*
bunch, business, cartel, chain, combine, conglomerate, corporation, crew, crowd, gang, group, institution, megacorp*, mob, monopoly, multinational organization, outfit, pool, ring, syndicate; SEE CONCEPTS 323,325

trust [v1] *believe, place confidence in*
accredit, assume, bank on, be convinced, bet bottom dollar on*, bet on, build on, calculate on, confide in, count on, depend on, expect, gamble on, have faith in, hope, imagine, lay money on*, lean on, look to, place confidence in, place trust in, presume, reckon on, rely upon, suppose, surmise, swear by, take, take at face value*, think likely; SEE CONCEPT 12

trust [v2] *give to for safekeeping*
advance, aid, assign, command, commission, commit, confer, confide, consign, delegate, entrust, give over, grant, lend, let, let out, loan, make trustee, patronize, put into hands of, sign over, store, transfer, turn over; SEE CONCEPT 115

trustworthy/trusty [adj] *reliable, believable*
accurate, always there*, authentic, authoritative, convincing, credible, dependable, ethical, exact, honest, honorable, kosher*, levelheaded, mature, on the level*, on up and up*, open, plausible, principled, realistic, responsible, righteous, rock solid*, saintly, secure, sensible, solid, square, steadfast, straight, there*, to be trusted, tried,

tried-and-true*, true, true-blue*, trustable, truthful, unfailing, up-front*, upright, valid, veracious; SEE CONCEPTS 267,404,535

truth [n1] *reality, validity*
accuracy, actuality, authenticity, axiom, case, certainty, correctness, dope*, exactitude, exactness, fact, facts, factualism, factuality, factualness, genuineness, gospel*, gospel truth*, honest truth*, infallibility, inside track*, legitimacy, maxim, naked truth*, nitty-gritty*, perfection, picture, plain talk, precision, principle, rectitude, rightness, scoop, score, trueness, truism, truthfulness, unvarnished truth, veracity, verisimilitude, verity, whole story*; SEE CONCEPTS 278,638,725

truth [n2] *honesty, loyalty*
authenticity, candor, constancy, dedication, devotion, dutifulness, faith, faithfulness, fidelity, frankness, integrity, openness, realism, revelation, sincerity, uprightness, veridicality, verity; SEE CONCEPT 657

truthful [adj] *accurate, honest*
believable, candid, correct, exact, factual, faithful, forthright, frank, guileless, ingenuous, just, kosher*, legit*, like it is*, literal, on the level*, on the up and up*, open, outspoken, plainspoken, precise, real, realistic, reliable, righteous, scrupulous, sincere, square, straight, straightforward, true, true-blue*, trustworthy, truth-telling, unfeigned, unreserved, veracious, veritable; SEE CONCEPTS 267,542

try [n] *attempt*
all one's got*, best shot*, bid, crack*, dab, effort, endeavor, essay, fling*, go*, jab*, pop*, shot*, slap*, stab*, striving, struggle, trial, undertaking, whack*, whirl*; SEE CONCEPTS 87,677

try [v1] *attempt*
aim, aspire, attack, bear down, chip away at*, compete, contend, contest, do one's best*, drive for, endeavor, essay, exert oneself, go after, go all out*, go for, have a crack*, have a go*, have a shot*, have a stab*, have a whack*, knock oneself out*, labor, lift a finger*, make a bid, make an attempt, make an effort, make a pass at*, propose, put oneself out*, risk, seek, shoot for*, speculate, strive, struggle, tackle, undertake, venture, vie for, work, wrangle; SEE CONCEPT 87

try [v2] *experiment, test*
appraise, assay, check, check out, evaluate, examine, inspect, investigate, judge, prove, put to the proof*, put to the test*, sample, scrutinize, taste, try out, weigh; SEE CONCEPTS 103,291

try [v3] *bother, afflict*
agonize, annoy, crucify, distress, excruciate, harass, inconvenience, irk, irritate, martyr, pain, plague, rack, strain, stress, tax, tire, torment, torture, trouble, upset, vex, weary, wring; SEE CONCEPTS 7,19

try [v4] *bring before a judge*
adjudge, adjudicate, arbitrate, decide, examine, give a hearing, hear, judge, referee, sit in judgment; SEE CONCEPT 317

trying [adj] *difficult, bothersome*
aggravating, annoying, arduous, demanding, exacting, exasperating, exigent, fatiguing, hard, irksome, irritating, onerous, oppressive, pestilent, provocative, rough, severe, sticky, strenuous, stressful, taxing, tight, tiresome, tough, tricky, troublesome, upsetting, vexing, wearisome, weighty; SEE CONCEPTS 548,565

try on/try out [*v*] *evaluate, test*

appraise, audition, check out, demonstrate, experiment, fit, give a try, have a dry run*, have a fitting*, inspect, practice, probe, prove, put into practice, put to the test, sample, scrutinize, taste, try for size, wear; SEE CONCEPTS 103,167, 291,453

tryst [*n*] *meeting during a love affair*

appointment, assignation, date, engagement, meet, meeting, rendezvous, union; SEE CONCEPTS 375,384

tuck [*v*] *fold together*

constrict, contract, draw together, enfold, gather, hem, insert, make snug, pinch, plait, pleat, push, put in, seam, squeeze in, swaddle, wrap; SEE CONCEPTS 193,218

tuft [*n*] *clump of strands of something*

bunch, cluster, collection, cowlick, feathers, group, knot, plumage, ruff, shock, topknot, tussock; SEE CONCEPTS 392,432,471

tug [*n/v*] *quick pull*

drag, draw, haul, heave, jerk, lug, strain, toil, tow, traction, wrench, yank; SEE CONCEPT 206

tuition [*n*] *education; education costs*

charge, expenditure, fee, instruction, lessons, price, schooling, teaching, training, tutelage, tutoring; SEE CONCEPT 287

tumble [*v*] *fall or make fall awkwardly*

bowl down, bring down, descend, dip, disarrange, disarray, disorder, disturb, do a pratfall, down, drop, fall headlong*, flatten, floor, flop, go belly up*, go down, hit the dirt*, jumble, keel, keel over, knock down, knock over, level, lose footing, lose it*, mess up, nose-dive, pitch, plummet, plunge, roll, sag, skid, slip, slump, spill, stumble, take a header*, tip over, topple, toss, trip, unsettle, upset; SEE CONCEPTS 147,149,181

tumor [*n*] *abnormal growth in animate being*

bump, cancer, carcinoma, cyst, lump, neoplasm, sarcoma, swelling, tumefaction; SEE CONCEPT 316

tumult [*n*] *uproar, confusion*

ado, affray, agitation, altercation, babel, bedlam, brawl, clamor, commotion, convulsion, din, disorder, disturbance, dither, excitement, ferment, fight, fracas, fuss, hassle*, jangle, lather*, maelstrom, noise, outbreak, outcry, pandemonium, paroxysm, pother, quarrel, racket, riot, row, ruction, seething, stir, strife, turbulence, turmoil, unrest, unsettlement, upheaval, upturn, wildness; SEE CONCEPTS 230,674

tumultuous/tumultuous [*adj*] *confused; in an uproar*

agitated, boisterous, clamorous, disorderly, disturbed, excited, fierce, hectic, irregular, lawless, noisy, obstreperous, passionate, raging, rambunctious, raucous, restless, riotous, rowdy, rowdydowdy, rumbunctious, stormy, termagant, turbulent, unrestrained, unruly, uproarious, violent, vociferous, wild; SEE CONCEPT 548

tune [*n1*] *melody, harmony*

air, aria, carol, chorus, composition, concert, consonance, descant, diapason, ditty*, harmony, jingle, lay, measure, melodia, motif, number, piece, song, strain, theme, warble; SEE CONCEPTS 264,595

tune [*n2*] *agreement*

accord, chime, chorus, concert, concord, concordance, consonance, euphony, harmony, pitch, sympathy, unison; SEE CONCEPTS 670,714

tune/tune up [*v*] *bring into harmony*

accommodate, adapt, adjust, attune, conform, coordinate, dial, fix, harmonize, integrate, modulate, pitch, proportion, reconcile, regulate, set, string, tighten; SEE CONCEPTS 65,126

tunnel [*n*] *covered passageway*

adit, burrow, channel, crawl space, crawlway, crosscut, drift, hole, hole in the wall*, mine, passage, pit, shaft, subway, tube, underpass; SEE CONCEPTS 509,513

tunnel [*v*] *dig a passage through*

burrow, excavate, mine, penetrate, sap, scoop out, undermine; SEE CONCEPT 178

turbulent [*adj1*] *unsettled, raging (referring to weather)*

agitated, bitter, blustering, blustery, boiling, bumpy, choppy, coarse, confused, destructive, disordered, disturbed, fierce, foaming, furious, howling, inclement, moiling, noisy, restless, riotous, roaring, rough, ruffled, rugged, stirred up, stormful, storming, stormy, swirling, tempestuous, thunderous, tremulous, tumultuous/tumultuous, unstable, violent, wild; SEE CONCEPT 525

turbulent [*adj2*] *rebellious, unmanageable*

agitated, anarchic, angry, bitter, boisterous, chaotic, demonstrative, destructive, disorderly, excited, fierce, fiery, foaming, insubordinate, lawless, mutinous, obstreperous, passionate, perturbed, quarrelsome, rabid, rambunctious, rampant, raucous, refractory, riotous, rough, roughhouse*, rowdy, rude, seditious, shaking, stern, storming, termagant, tumultuous/tumultuous, unbridled, uncontrolled, undisciplined, ungovernable, unruly, untamed, uproarious, vehement, violent, vociferous, wild; SEE CONCEPT 401

turmoil [*n*] *chaos*

agitation, ailment, anxiety, anxiousness, bedlam, bustle, commotion, confusion, disorder, disquiet, disquietude, distress, disturbance, dither, ferment, flap*, flurry, free-for-all*, fuss, hassle*, hectic, hubbub*, lather*, mix-up, noise, pandemonium, pother, restiveness, restlessness, riot, row, ruckus, stir, strife, to-do*, topsy-turvy, trouble, tumult, turbulence, unrest, uproar, violence, whirl; SEE CONCEPTS 230,674

turn [*n1*] *revolution, curving*

about-face, angle, bend, bias, bow, branch, change, changeabout, circle, circuit, circulation, circumvolution, corner, curve, cycle, departure, detour, deviation, direction, drift, flection, flexure, fork, gyration, gyre, heading, hook, pirouette, pivot, quirk, retroversion, reversal, reverse, reversion, right-about, roll, rotation, round, shift, spin, spiral, swing, tack, tendency, trend, turnabout, turning, twist, twisting, wheel, whirl, wind, winding, yaw; SEE CONCEPTS 198,738,754

turn [*n2*] *sudden change*

alteration, bend, branch, crotch, deflection, departure, detour, deviation, digression, distortion, divarication, double, fork, modification, mutation, shift, tack, twist, variation, warp, yaw; SEE CONCEPT 697

turn [*n3*] *chance, opportunity*

accomplishment, act, action, bit, bout, crack*, deed, favor, fling*, gesture, go*, go around*, move, period, round, routine, say*, service, shift, shot*, spell, stint, succession, time, tour, trick, try; SEE CONCEPT 693

tr
tu

turn [n4] *walk, outing*
airing, circuit, constitutional, drive, excursion, jaunt, promenade, ramble, ride, saunter, spin, stroll; SEE CONCEPTS *147,224,363*

turn [n5] *aptitude, knack*
affinity, aptness, bent, bias, bump, disposition, faculty, flair, genius, gift, head, inclination, leaning, predisposition, propensity, talent; SEE CONCEPTS *411,630*

turn [n6] *scare*
attack, blow, fit, fright, jolt, seizure, shock, spell, start, surprise; SEE CONCEPTS *230,410*

turn [v1] *revolve, curve*
arc, bend, circle, circulate, circumduct, come around, corner, cut, eddy, go around, go round, ground, gyrate, gyre, hang a left*, hang a right*, incline, loop, make a left, make a right, move in a circle, negotiate, orbit, oscillate, pass, pass around, pirouette, pivot, revolve, roll, rotate, round, spin, sway, swing, swivel, take a bend*, twirl, twist, vibrate, weave, wheel, whirl, wind, yaw; SEE CONCEPTS *147,201,738,748*

turn [v2] *reverse; change course*
about-face, aim, alter, alternate, backslide, call off, capsize, change, change position, convert, curve, depart, detour, detract, deviate, digress, direct, diverge, double back, face about, go back, incline, inverse, invert, loop, move, pivot, rechannel, recoil, redirect, regress, relapse, retrace, return, revert, sheer, shift, shunt, shy away, sidetrack, subvert, sway, swerve, swing, switch, tack, transform, twist, upset, vary, veer, volte-face, wheel, whip, whirl, zigzag; SEE CONCEPTS *195,198,213*

turn [v3] *adapt, fit*
alter, become, change, change into, come, convert, divert, fashion, form, get, go, grow into, metamorphose, modify, mold, mutate, pass into, put, refashion, remake, remodel, render, run, shape, transfigure, transform, translate, transmute, transpose, vary, wax; SEE CONCEPTS *232,697*

turn [v4] *become sour or tainted*
acidify, become rancid, break down, crumble, curdle, decay, decompose, disintegrate, dull, ferment, go bad, molder, putrefy, rot, sour, spoil, taint; SEE CONCEPTS *456,469*

turn [v5] *use; resort to*
adapt, address, appeal, apply, approach, bend, be predisposed to, devote, direct, employ, favor, give, go, have recourse, incline, lend, look, prefer, recur, repair, run, tend, throw, turn one's energies to*, turn one's hand to*, undertake, utilize; SEE CONCEPTS *100,225*

turn [v6] *sicken*
derange, discompose, disgust, disorder, make one sick*, nauseate, revolt, unbalance, undo, unhinge*, unsettle, upset; SEE CONCEPTS *7,19,250*

turn [v7] *change one's mind; defect*
apostatize, bring round, change sides, desert, go over, influence, persuade, prejudice, prevail upon, rat*, renege, renounce, repudiate, retract, talk into, tergiversate, tergiverse; SEE CONCEPTS *21,41,54*

turn down [v] *reject*
decline, disapprove, dismiss, rebuff, refuse, reprobate, repudiate, say no, scorn, spurn, throw out; SEE CONCEPTS *18,54*

turn in [v] *go to bed*
bed, catch some z's*, flop*, go to sleep, hit the hay*, hit the sack*, lie down, nap, pile in, rest, retire, roll in; SEE CONCEPT *210*

turning point [n] *crucial occurrence*
axis, change, climacteric, climax, contingency, crisis, critical moment, critical period, crossing, crossroads, crux, culmination, decisive moment, development, emergency, exigency, hinge, juncture, moment of truth*, pass, peak, pinch, pivot, shift, strait, transition, twist, zero hour*; SEE CONCEPTS *679,832*

turn off [v1] *disgust*
alienate, bore, disenchant, disinterest, displease, irritate, lose one's interest, make one sick*, nauseate, offend, put off, repel, sicken; SEE CONCEPTS *7,19*

turn off [v2] *stop from operating*
close, cut, cut out, douse, extinguish, halt, hit the switch*, kill*, log off, put out, shut, shut down, shut off, switch off, turn out, unplug; SEE CONCEPTS *121,234*

turn on [v1] *excite, please*
arouse, attract, captivate, enchant, get started, initiate, introduce, show, stimulate, stir up, thrill, titillate, work up; SEE CONCEPT *11*

turn on [v2] *start the operation of*
activate, begin, energize, get started, ignite, initiate, introduce, log on, put in gear, put on, set in motion, start up, switch on; SEE CONCEPT *221*

turnout [n1] *group assembling for event*
assemblage, assembly, attendance, audience, congregation, crowd, gate, gathering, number, throng; SEE CONCEPT *417*

turnout [n2] *amount produced*
aggregate, output, outturn, product, production, productivity, quota, turnover, volume, yield; SEE CONCEPTS *338,787*

turn out [v1] *equip; produce*
accouter, appoint, arm, bear, bring out, build, clothe, dress, fabricate, finish, fit, fit out*, furnish, make, manufacture, outfit, process, put out, rig*, rig out*, yield; SEE CONCEPTS *167,205,234*

turn out [v2] *get out of bed*
appear, arise, come, emerge, get up, pile out*, rise, rise and shine*, roll out*, show up, uprise, wake, wake up; SEE CONCEPT *159*

turn over [v1] *give, transfer*
assign, come across with, commend, commit, confer, confide, consign, convey, delegate, deliver, entrust, feed, find, furnish, give over, give up, hand, hand over, pass on, provide, relegate, relinquish, render, supply, surrender, yield; SEE CONCEPTS *108,143*

turn over [v2] *think about seriously*
consider, contemplate, deliberate, give thought to, meditate, mull over, muse, ponder, reflect on, revolve, roll, ruminate, think over, wonder about; SEE CONCEPTS *17,24*

turn up [v1] *come, arrive*
appear, attend, blow in*, come, come in, enter, get, get in, make an appearance*, materialize, pop in*, punch in*, put in an appearance*, reach, roll in*, show, show up*, weigh in*; SEE CONCEPT *159*

turn up [v2] *discover or be discovered*
become known, be found, bring to light*, catch, come across, come to light*, come to pass, crop

up, descry, detect, dig up*, disclose, encounter, espy, expose, find, hit upon*, learn, meet, meet with*, pop up*, reveal, see, spot, track, track down*, transpire, uncover, unearth; SEE CONCEPTS 31,183

tutor [n] *person who teaches another privately*
coach, educator, governor, grind, guardian, guide, instructor, lecturer, mentor, preceptor, private teacher, prof*, teach*, teacher; SEE CONCEPT 350

tutor [v] *teach someone privately*
clue, coach, direct, discipline, drill, drum into*, edify, educate, guide, instruct, lay it out for*, lecture, let in on*, ready, school, train, update; SEE CONCEPT 285

twilight [n] *onset of darkness at end of day*
afterglow, afterlight, crepuscular light, decline, dimness, dusk, early evening, ebb, end, evening, eventide, gloaming, half-light, last phase*, late-afternoon, night, nightfall, sundown, sunset; SEE CONCEPTS 810,832

twin [n] *something exactly like another*
clone, companion, coordinate, corollary, counterpart, doppelgänger, double, duplicate, fraternal twin, identical twin, likeness, lookalike, match, mate, reciprocal, ringer*, Siamese twin; SEE CONCEPTS 414,664,670

twin [adj] *duplicate, similar*
accompanying, bifold, binary, copied, corresponding, coupled, double, dual, duplicating, geminate, identical, joint, like, matched, matching, paired, parallel, same, second, selfsame, twofold, very same; SEE CONCEPTS 487,563,573

twine [n] *rope, cord*
braid, brag, convolution, cordage, knot, snarl, string, tangle, thread, twist, whorl, yarn; SEE CONCEPT 475

twine [v] *coil, twist together*
bend, braid, corkscrew, curl, encircle, enmesh, entangle, entwine, interlace, interweave, knit, loop, meander, plait, spiral, splice, surround, tangle, twist, undulate, weave, wind, wrap, wreathe; SEE CONCEPTS 147,201,742

twinge [n] *sharp pain*
ache, bite, gripe, lancination, misery, pang, pinch, prick, shiver, smart, spasm, stab, stitch, throb, throe, tic, tweak, twist, twitch; SEE CONCEPT 728

twinkle [v] *glimmer, shine*
blink, coruscate, flash, flicker, gleam, glint, glisten, glitter, glow, illuminate, light, light up, scintillate, shimmer, sparkle, wink; SEE CONCEPT 624

twirl [v] *turn around circularly*
gyrate, gyre, pirouette, pivot, purl, revolve, rotate, spin, turn, twist, wheel, whirl, whirligig, wind; SEE CONCEPTS 150,152

twist [n1] *curl, spin*
arc, bend, braid, coil, convolution, curlicue, curve, flourish, hank, helix, jerk, meander, plug, ply, pull, roll, spiral, swivel, torsion, turn, twine, undulation, warp, wind, wrench, yank, zigzag; SEE CONCEPTS 738,754

twist [n1] *sudden development; oddity*
aberration, bent, change, characteristic, confusion, crotchet, eccentricity, entanglement, foible, idiosyncrasy, kink, knot, mess, mix-up, peculiarity, proclivity, quirk, revelation, screw up*, slant, snarl, surprise, tangle, trait, turn, variation; SEE CONCEPTS 411,832

twist [v1] *curl, spin*
coil, contort, corkscrew, encircle, entwine, intertwine, rick, screw, spiral, sprain, squirm, swivel, turn, turn around, twine, twirl, warp, weave, wiggle, wind, wrap, wrap around, wreathe, wrench, wriggle, wring, writhe, zigzag; SEE CONCEPTS 80,147,184,201,206,738

twist [v2] *misrepresent*
alter, belie, change, color, contort, distort, falsify, garble, misquote, misstate, pervert, warp; SEE CONCEPT 63

twitch [v] *have a spasm*
beat, blink, clasp, clutch, flutter, grab, grasp, grip, jerk, jiggle, jump, kick, lug, lurch, nip, pain, palpitate, pluck, pull, seize, shiver, shudder, snap, snatch, squirm, tic, tremble, tug, twinge, vellicate, yank; SEE CONCEPTS 185,206

tycoon [n] *person who has a lot of money, power*
administrator, big shot*, boss, business person, capitalist, captain of industry*, director, entrepreneur, executive, fat cat*, financier, industrialist, investor, magnate, mogul, wealthy person; SEE CONCEPT 347

type [n1] *class, kind*
blazon, brand, breed, cast, category, character, classification, cut, description, feather, form, genre, ilk, likes, lot, mold, nature, number, order, persuasion, rubric, sample, sort, species, specimen, stamp, standard, strain, subdivision, variety, way; SEE CONCEPTS 378,411

type [n2] *example, model*
archetype, epitome, essence, exemplar, original, paradigm, pattern, personification, prototype, quintessence, representative, sample, specimen, standard; SEE CONCEPT 686

type [n3] *printed characters*
case, emblem, face, figure, font, point size, print, printing, sign, symbol; SEE CONCEPTS 79,284

type [v1] *classify*
arrange, button down*, categorize, class, peg, pigeonhole*, put away, put down as, sort, standardize, stereotype, tab*, typecast; SEE CONCEPTS 18,84

type [v2] *hit keys on machine to print document*
copy, dash off*, enter data, hunt-and-peck*, teletype, touch, touch-type, transcribe, typewrite, write; SEE CONCEPTS 79,199,203

typical [adj] *usual, conventional*
archetypal, archetypical, average, characteristic, classic, classical, common, commonplace, emblematic, essential, everyday, exemplary, expected, general, habitual, ideal, illustrative, in character*, indicative, in keeping, matter-of-course*, model, natural, normal, old hat*, ordinary, orthodox, paradigmatic, patterned, prevalent, prototypal, prototypical, quintessential, regular, representative, standard, standardized, stock, suggestive, symbolic, typic, unexceptional; SEE CONCEPTS 530,533,547

typify [v] *represent, characterize*
body forth, characterize, describe, emblematize, embody, epitomize, exemplify, feature, illustrate, incarnate, mean, mirror, model, personify, stand for, sum up, symbolize; SEE CONCEPTS 55,261,682

tyranny [n] *dictatorship*
absolutism, authoritarianism, autocracy, coercion, cruelty, despotism, domination, fascism, high-handedness, imperiousness, monocracy, oligarchy, oppression, peremptoriness, reign of terror*,

tu
ty

severity, terrorism, totalitarianism, totality, unreasonableness; SEE CONCEPTS 299,301

tyrant [n] *person who dictates, oppresses*
absolute ruler, absolutist, authoritarian, autocrat, bully, despot, dictator, Hitler*, inquisitor, martinet, oppressor, slave driver*, Stalin*; SEE CONCEPTS 354,412

U

ubiquitous [adj] *ever-present*
all-over, everywhere, omnipresent, pervasive, ubiquitary, universal, wall-to-wall*; SEE CONCEPT 530

ugly [adj1] *unattractive*
animal, appalling, awful, bad-looking, beastly, deformed, disfigured, foul, frightful, grisly, gross, grotesque, hard-featured, hideous, homely, horrid, ill-favored, loathsome, misshapen, monstrous, not much to look at*, plain, repelling, repugnant, repulsive, revolting, unbeautiful, uncomely, uninviting, unlovely, unprepossessing, unseemly, unsightly; SEE CONCEPT 579

ugly [adj2] *unpleasant, disagreeable*
base, despicable, dirty, disgusting, distasteful, filthy, foul, frightful, hideous, horrid, ignoble, low, low-down, mean, messy, monstrous, nasty, nauseous, noisome, objectionable, odious, offensive, pesky, repellent, repugnant, repulsive, revolting, scandalous, servile, shocking, sickening, sordid, sorry, terrible, troublesome, troublous, vexatious, vile, wicked, wretched; SEE CONCEPTS 403,571

ugly [adj3] *dangerous, threatening*
angry, bellicose, black, cantankerous, crabbed, crabby, dark, disagreeable, dour, evil, fell, forbidding, formidable, gloomy, glum, grave, grievous, major, malevolent, menacing, morose, nasty, obnoxious, ominous, pugnacious, quarrelsome, rough, saturnine, scowling, serious, sinister, spiteful, sullen, surly, treacherous, truculent, vicious, violent, wicked; SEE CONCEPTS 401,548

ulterior [adj] *secret; pertaining to a hidden goal*
ambiguous, buried, concealed, covert, cryptic, dark, enigmatic, equivocal, guarded, hidden, implied, obscure, obscured, personal, privy, remote, secondary, selfish, shrouded, under cover, under wraps*, undisclosed, undivulged, unexpressed, unsaid; SEE CONCEPTS 544,576

ultimate [adj1] *last, final*
capping, chips down*, closing, concluding, conclusive, decisive, end, eventual, extreme, far out*, farthermost, farthest, final curtain*, furthermost, furthest, hindmost, latest, latter, lattermost, most distant, terminal; SEE CONCEPTS 799,820

ultimate [adj2] *best, greatest*
extreme, highest, incomparable, max*, maxi*, maximum, most, paramount, preeminent, significant, superlative, supreme, surpassing, the most, topmost, towering, transcendent, unequalable, unmatchable, unsurpassable, utmost; SEE CONCEPTS 568,574

ultimate [adj3] *fundamental*
absolute, basic, categorical, elemental, empyreal, empyrean, primary, radical, sublime, transcendental; SEE CONCEPTS 535,546

ultimately [adv] *eventually*
after all, after a while, as a conclusion, at last, at long last, at the close, basically, by and by, climactically, conclusively, finally, fundamentally, hereafter, in conclusion, in consummation, in due time, in future, in the end, in the sequel, presently, sequentially, someday, sometime, somewhere, sooner or later, yet; SEE CONCEPT 820

ultra [adj] *extreme*
all out*, drastic, excessive, extremist, fanatical, far-out*, gone*, immoderate, outlandish, out of bounds*, outré, rabid*, radical, revolutionary, too much*; SEE CONCEPTS 562,569

umbrage [n] *personal displeasure*
anger, annoyance, chagrin, exasperation, fury, grudge, high dudgeon*, huff, indignation, injury, ire, irking, irritation, miff*, nettling*, offense, pique, provoking, rage, resentment, sense of injury, vexation, wrath; SEE CONCEPTS 29,410

umpire [n] *person who settles dispute*
adjudicator, arbiter, arbitrator, assessor, compromiser, inspector, judge, justice, mediator, moderator, negotiator, peacemaker, proprietor, ref*, referee, settler, ump*; SEE CONCEPTS 348,366,423

unable [adj] *not having talent, skill*
can't cut it*, can't hack it*, can't make the grade*, clumsy, helpless, hog-tied*, impotent, impuissant, inadequate, incapable, incapacitated, incompetent, ineffectual, inefficacious, inefficient, inept, inoperative, no can do*, no good*, not able, not cut out for*, not equal to*, not up to*, out of commission*, powerless, sidelined*, unfit, unfitted, unqualified, unskilled, weak; SEE CONCEPT 527

unabridged [adj] *not shortened*
complete, entire, full-length, intact, total, unabbreviated, uncondensed, uncut, unexpurgated, unshortened, whole; SEE CONCEPTS 267,531

unacceptable [adj] *not suitable or satisfactory*
below par*, damaged, disagreeable, displeasing, distasteful, exceptionable, half-baked*, ill-favored, improper, inadmissible, insupportable, lousy*, not up to snuff*, objectionable, obnoxious, offensive, reject, repugnant, unappealing, undesirable, uninviting, unpleasant, unsatisfactory, unwanted, unwelcome, won't do*; SEE CONCEPTS 529,558

unaccompanied [adj] *alone*
abandoned, a cappella*, apart, by oneself, deserted, detached, hermit, individual, isolate, isolated, lone, loner, odd, on one's own, removed, single, solitary, solo, stag, traveling light*, unattended, unescorted; SEE CONCEPTS 555,577

unaccountable [adj] *not explainable; mysterious*
arcane, astonishing, baffling, extraordinary, impenetrable, incomprehensible, inexplicable, inscrutable, mystic, odd, peculiar, puzzling, strange, uncommon, unexplainable, unfathomable, unheard-of, unintelligible, unknowable, unusual, unwonted; SEE CONCEPTS 529,564

unaccustomed [adj1] *not prepared, ready; new to*
green*, ignorant, incompetent, inexperienced, newcome, not given to*, not used to, novice, unacquainted, unfamiliar with, uninformed, uninstructed, unpracticed, unseasoned, unskilled, untaught, untrained, unused to, unversed in; SEE CONCEPTS 527,678

unaccustomed [adj2] *new, strange*
alien, altered, bizarre, different, eccentric, excep-

tional, exotic, foreign, imported, novel, outlandish, out of the ordinary, quaint, remarkable, singular, special, surprising, uncommon, unconventional, uncustomary, unexpected, unfamiliar, unknown, unorthodox, unprecedented, unusual, unwonted, variant; SEE CONCEPTS 547,564

unadvised [adj] not smart; careless
brash, hasty, heedless, hot-headed, ignorant, ill-advised, imprudent, inadvisable, incautious, inconsiderate, indiscreet, injudicious, in the dark*, rash, reckless, thoughtless, unaware, unconsidered, uninformed, unknowing, unsuspecting, unwarned, unwary, unwise; SEE CONCEPTS 403,548

unaffected [adj1] honest, unsophisticated
artless, candid, direct, folksy*, forthright, frank, genuine, guileless, homey*, ingenuous, modest, naive, natural, plain, simple, sincere, single, spontaneous, straightforward, true, unartificial, unassuming, unpretentious, unschooled, unspoilt, unstudied, up front*; SEE CONCEPTS 401,404

unaffected [adj2] unchanged, unmoved
aloof, callous, calm, casual, cold fish*, cool, easy-going, hard-boiled*, hard-hearted*, impassive, impervious, laid-back*, not influenced, proof, steady, thick-skinned*, unaltered, unconcerned, unexcited, unimpressed, uninfluenced, unresponsive, unruffled, unstirred, untouched; SEE CONCEPTS 542,548

unanimous [adj] in agreement; uncontested
accepted, accordant, agreed, agreeing, as one, assenting, collective, combined, common, communal, concerted, concordant, concurrent, consensual, consentient, consistent, consonant, harmonious, homogeneous, in complete accord, like-minded, of one mind, popular, public, shared, single, solid, undisputed, undivided, unified, united, universal, unquestioned, with one voice*; SEE CONCEPTS 8,267,563

unappetizing [adj] distasteful
flat, flavorless, grody*, gross, icky*, insipid, savorless, stinky, tasteless, unappealing, unattractive, uninteresting, uninviting, unpalatable, unpleasant, unsavory, vapid, yucky*; SEE CONCEPTS 462,529

unapproachable [adj1] unfriendly
aloof, chilly*, cold, cool, distant, frigid, hesitant, inaccessible, remote, reserved, standoffish, uncommunicative, unsociable, withdrawn; SEE CONCEPTS 404,555

unapproachable [adj2] difficult to get to
inaccessible, out of reach, out-of-the-way, remote, unattainable, unobtainable, unreachable; SEE CONCEPT 576

unasked [adj] voluntary
arrogant, gratuitous, impudent, not asked, of one's own accord, overbearing, presumptuous, spontaneous, supererogatory, unbidden, uncalled-for, undemanded, undesired, uninvited, unprompted, unrequested, unsought, unwanted, unwelcome, voluntarily, willing, without prompting; SEE CONCEPTS 401,558

unassuming [adj] shy
backward, bashful, diffident, humble, lowly, meek, modest, mousy*, plain, prim, quiet, reserved, retiring, self-effacing, simple, unambitious, unassertive, unobtrusive, unostentatious, unpretending, unpretentious; SEE CONCEPTS 401,404

unauthorized [adj] not sanctioned, permitted
crooked*, dirty*, illegal, illegitimate, no-no*, off

base*, out of bounds*, out of line*, over the line*, pirated, shady*, unapproved, unconstitutional, under the table*, unjustified, unlawful, unofficial, unsanctioned, unwarranted, wildcat*, wrongful; SEE CONCEPTS 319,548

unavoidable [adj] bound to happen
certain, compulsory, fated, impending, ineluctable, ineludible, inescapable, inevasible, inevitable, inexorable, locked up*, necessary, obligatory, open and shut*, set, sure, unescapable; SEE CONCEPT 535

unaware [adj] ignorant
blind, careless, caught napping*, daydreaming, deaf, deaf to*, doped*, forgetful, heedless, ignorant, in a daze*, inattentive, incognizant, inconversant, insensible, mooning, negligent, nescient, not all there*, not cognizant, oblivious, out cold*, out of it*, out to lunch*, spacey*, unacquainted, unconcerned, unconscious, unenlightened, unfamiliar, uninformed, uninstructed, unknowing, unmindful, unsuspecting, unwitting; SEE CONCEPT 402

unawares [adv] without warning; suddenly
aback, abruptly, accidentally, by accident, by mistake, by surprise, carelessly, ignorantly, inadvertently, mistakenly, off guard, short, sudden, surprisingly, unconsciously, unexpectedly, unintentionally, unknowingly, unprepared, unready, unwittingly, without warning; SEE CONCEPTS 544,548,799

unbalanced [adj1] not even, stable
asymmetric, asymmetrical, disproportionate, irregular, lopsided, not balanced, off-balance, shaky, top-heavy, treacherous, unequal, uneven, unstable, unsteady, unsymmetrical, wobbly; SEE CONCEPT 480

unbalanced [adj2] crazy; mentally disturbed
batty*, daft, demented, deranged, eccentric, erratic, flaky*, freaky*, insane, irrational, kinky*, kooky*, lunatic, mad, nobody home*, non compos mentis*, not all there*, nutty*, out to lunch*, psychotic, touched, troubled, unglued*, unhinged*, unscrewed*, unsound, unstable; SEE CONCEPT 403

unbearable [adj] very bad; too much
a bit much*, enough, heavy-handed*, inadmissible, insufferable, insupportable, intolerable, last straw*, oppressive, unacceptable, unendurable, unsurpassable; SEE CONCEPTS 537,571

unbecoming [adj] improper, unsuitable
awkward, clumsy, discreditable, gauche, ill-suited, inappropriate, inapt, incongruous, indecent, indecorous, indelicate, inept, maladroit, malapropos, offensive, rough, salacious, tacky*, tasteless, unattractive, unbefitting, uncomely, undue, unfair, unfit, unfitting, unflattering, ungodly, unhandsome, unlovely, unseasonable, unseemly, unsightly, unsuited, untimely, untoward, unworthy; SEE CONCEPTS 558,579,589

unbelievable [adj] beyond the imagination
astonishing, beyond belief, cockamamie*, cockeyed*, doubtful, dubious, far-fetched, fishy*, flaky*, flimsy*, for the birds*, full of holes*, harebrained*, implausible, impossible, improbable, incogitable, inconceivable, incredible, kooky*, lamebrained*, open to doubt, outlandish, past belief, phony, preposterous, questionable, reaching, scatterbrained*, screwy*, staggering, suspect, thick*, thin*, too much*, unconvincing, unimaginable, unsubstantial, unthinkable, weak,

ty
un

won't hold water*, won't wash*; SEE CONCEPTS 529,548

unbending [adj] *rigid, tough*
aloof, crisp, distant, do or die*, dug in*, firm, formal, hard as nails*, hard-line*, hold one's ground*, hold the fort*, hold the line*, incompliant, inelastic, inexorable, inflexible, intractable, locked in*, obdurate, obstinate, relentless, reserved, resolute, set in stone*, severe, single-minded, standing one's ground*, standing pat*, sticking to one's guns*, stiff, strict, stubborn, uncompromising, unflexible, unrelenting, unswayable, unyielding, uptight; SEE CONCEPTS 401,534,604

unbiased [adj] *not prejudiced*
aloof, cold, disinterested, dispassionate, equal, equitable, even-handed, fair, honest, impartial, just, neutral, nondiscriminatory, nonpartisan, objective, on the fence*, open-minded, straight, unbigoted, uncolored, uninterested, unprejudiced; SEE CONCEPT 542

unblemished [adj] *not flawed*
chaste, clean, decent, faultless, flawless, immaculate, intact, modest, perfect, pure, sound, spotless, stainless, undamaged, undefiled, unflawed, unhurt, unimpaired, uninjured, unmarked, unmarred, unspotted, unstained, unsullied, untarnished, whole; SEE CONCEPTS 485,621

unbreakable [adj] *strong, tough*
adamantine, armored, brass-bound, durable, everlasting, firm, incorruptible, indestructible, infrangible, invulnerable, lasting, nonbreakable, perdurable, resistant, rugged, shatterproof, solid, tight, toughened, unshakable, unyielding; SEE CONCEPTS 488,489,798

unbroken [v] *continuous, whole*
ceaseless, constant, deep, endless, entire, even, fast, incessant, intact, perfect, perpetual, profound, progressive, regular, solid, sound, successive, total, undisturbed, unimpaired, uninterrupted, unremitting, unruffled, untroubled; SEE CONCEPTS 482,485,798

unburden [adj] *get rid of*
clear, confess, confide, disburden, discharge, disclose, disencumber, dispose of, divulge, dump, ease, empty, get off one's chest*, lay bare*, let hair down*, lighten, lose, out with it*, own, relieve, relinquish, reveal, shake, shake off*, tell all*, throw off, unbosom, unload; SEE CONCEPTS 60,211,244

uncanny [adj] *very strange, unusual*
astonishing, astounding, creepy, devilish, eerie, exceptional, extraordinary, fantastic, ghostly, ghoulish, incredible, inexplainable, inspired, magical, miraculous, mysterious, mystifying, preternatural, prodigious, queer, remarkable, scary, secret, singular, spooky, superhuman, supernatural, supernormal, supranormal, unearthly, unheard-of, unnatural, weird; SEE CONCEPTS 537,564

uncertain [adj] *doubtful, changeable*
ambiguous, ambivalent, chancy, conjectural, dubious, erratic, fitful, hanging by a thread*, hazy, hesitant, iffy*, incalculable, inconstant, indefinite, indeterminate, indistinct, insecure, irregular, irresolute, on thin ice*, precarious, questionable, risky, speculative, touch and go*, unclear, unconfirmed, undecided, undetermined, unfixed, unforeseeable, unpredictable, unreliable, unresolved, unsettled, unsure, up for grabs*, up in the air*, vacillating, vague, variable, wavering; SEE CONCEPTS 529,534,535

uncertainty [n] *doubt, changeableness*
ambiguity, ambivalence, anxiety, bewilderment, concern, confusion, conjecture, contingency, dilemma, disquiet, distrust, doubtfulness, dubiety, guesswork, hesitancy, hesitation, incertitude, inconclusiveness, indecision, irresolution, lack of confidence, misgiving, mistrust, mystification, oscillation, perplexity, puzzle, puzzlement, qualm, quandary, query, questionableness, reserve, scruple, skepticism, suspicion, trouble, uneasiness, unpredictability, vagueness, wonder, worry; SEE CONCEPTS 388,410,696

unchangeable [adj] *constant, steadfast*
changeless, continuing, firm, fixed, immovable, immutable, inalterable, inevitable, inflexible, invariable, irreversible, permanent, resolute, stable, strong, unalterable, unmodifiable, unmovable; SEE CONCEPT 534

unchanging [adj] *constant, permanent*
abiding, changeless, consistent, continuing, enduring, equable, eternal, even, fixed, immutable, imperishable, invariable, lasting, perpetual, rigid, same, stable, static, unchanged, unfading, unfailing, unfluctuating, uniform, unvarying; SEE CONCEPTS 534,551,649

uncivilized [adj] *wild, uncultured*
barbarian, barbaric, barbarous, boorish, brutish, churlish, coarse, crass, crude, discourteous, disrespectful, gross, ill-bred, impertinent, impolite, loutish, mannerless, outrageous, philistine, primitive, rude, rugged, savage, unconscionable, uncontrolled, uncouth, uncultivated, uneducated, ungodly, unholy, unmannered, unpolished, unrefined, unsophisticated, vulgar, wicked; SEE CONCEPT 401

unclean [adj] *dirty*
bedraggled, befouled, besmirched, black, blurred, common, contaminated, corrupt, decayed, defiled, desecrated, dusty, evil, feculent, fetid, filthy, foul, grimy, impure, messy, muddy, nasty, polluted, profaned, putrescent, putrid, rancid, rank, rotten, sloppy, slovenly, smeared, smudged, soiled, sooty, sordid, spotted, squalid, stable, stained, stall, stinking, sullied, tainted, tarnished, unhealthful, vile; SEE CONCEPT 621

uncomfortable [adj] *painful, rough*
afflictive, agonizing, annoying, awkward, bitter, cramped, difficult, disagreeable, distressing, dolorous, excruciating, galling, grievous, hard, harsh, ill-fitting, incommodious, irritating, thorny, torturing, troublesome, vexatious, wearisome; SEE CONCEPTS 529,537,583

uncomfortable [adj2] *distressed, upset*
aching, angry, anguished, annoyed, awkward, chafed, cheerless, comfortless, confused, discomfited, discomposed, disquieted, disturbed, embarrassed, exhausted, fatigued, galled, harsh, hurt, ill at ease, in pain, miserable, nervous, pained, restless, self-conscious, smarting, sore, stiff, strained, suffering, tired, troubled, uneasy, vexed, weary, worn, wracked, wretched; SEE CONCEPTS 403,485

uncommitted [adj] *free; not involved*
cut loose*, don't care*, fence-sitting*, floating, free-spirited, laid-back*, middle ground*, middle of the road*, neutral, nonaligned, nonpartisan, on the fence*, restrained, unaffiliated, unattached, uninvolved, unpledged; SEE CONCEPTS 403,542

uncommon [adj1] *very different*
aberrant, abnormal, anomalous, arcane, bizarre, curious, eccentric, egregious, exceptional, exotic, extraordinary, extreme, fantastic, few, freakish, infrequent, irregular, nondescript, noteworthy, novel, odd, original, out of the ordinary, out of the way*, outré, peculiar, prodigious, queer, rare, remarkable, scarce, seldom, singular, sporadic, startling, strange, surprising, unaccustomed, unconventional, uncustomary, unfamiliar, unheard of, unique, unorthodox, unusual, weird; SEE CONCEPT **564**

uncommon [adj2] *wonderful, exceptional*
distinctive, extraordinary, incomparable, inimitable, notable, noteworthy, outstanding, rare, remarkable, singular, special, superior, unimaginable, unique, unparalleled, unprecedented, unthinkable, unwonted; SEE CONCEPT **574**

uncommonly [adv] *infrequently*
exceptionally, extra, extremely, hardly ever, in few instances, irregularly, not often, now and then, occasionally, oddly, on occasion, particularly, peculiarly, rarely, remarkably, scarcely ever, seldom, sporadically, strangely, unusually, very; SEE CONCEPT **541**

uncommunicative [adj] *shy, silent*
aloof, buttoned up*, clammed up*, close, close-mouthed*, curt, distant, dried up*, evasive, guarded, hush-hush*, offish*, on the QT*, quiet, reserved, reticent, retiring, secretive, short, standoffish, taciturn, tight-lipped*, unapproachable, unresponsive, unsociable; SEE CONCEPT **267**

uncompromising [adj] *stubborn*
brick-wall*, decided, determined, firm, hardcore*, hard-line*, inexorable, inflexible, intransigent, locked, obdurate, obstinate, pigheaded*, relentless, resolute, rigid, set in stone*, single-minded, steadfast, stiff-necked*, strict, strong, tough, unbending; SEE CONCEPTS **401,542**

unconcerned [adj] *carefree; apathetic*
aloof, blind, blithe, callous, careless, cold, cool, deaf, detached, dispassionate, distant, easy, feckless, forgetful, hardened, hard-hearted, heedless, impassive, inattentive, incurious, indifferent, insensible, insensitive, insouciant, lackadaisical, lukewarm, negligent, neutral, nonchalant, oblivious, phlegmatic, relaxed, reserved, self-centered, serene, stony, supine, unbothered, uninterested, uninvolved, unmoved, unperturbed, unruffled, unsympathetic, untroubled, unworried; SEE CONCEPTS **403,542**

unconditional [adj] *absolute, total*
actual, all out, assured, categorical, certain, clear, complete, decisive, definite, determinate, downright, entire, explicit, final, flat out, full, genuine, indubitable, no catch*, no fine print*, no holds barred*, no ifs ands or buts*, no kicker*, no strings*, open, out-and-out*, outright, plenary, positive, straight out, thorough, thoroughgoing, unconstrained, unequivocal, unlimited, unmistakable, unmitigated, unqualified, unquestionable, unreserved, unrestricted, utter, whole, wide; SEE CONCEPTS **531,535,544**

unconscionable [adj] *immoral, immoderate*
amoral, barbarous, conscienceless, criminal, dishonest, excessive, exorbitant, extravagant, extreme, inordinate, knavish, outrageous, preposterous, sneaky, too much*, uncivilized, undue, unethical, unfair, ungodly, unholy, unjust,

unprincipled, unreasonable, unscrupulous, wanton, wicked; SEE CONCEPTS **545,569**

unconscious [adj1] *not awake; out cold*
benumbed, blacked out*, bombed*, cold*, comatose, dead to the world*, drowsy, entranced, feeling no pain*, flattened*, inanimate, in a trance, inert, insensate, insensible, knocked*, lethargic, numb, on the canvas*, out, out like a light*, palsied, paralyzed, passed out*, put away*, raving, senseless, stunned, stupefied, swooning, torpid, tranced, zonked*; SEE CONCEPTS **314,539**

unconscious [adj2] *ignorant; automatic*
accidental, gut*, ignorant, inadvertent, inattentive, inherent, innate, instinctive, involuntary, latent, lost, reflex, repressed, subconscious, subliminal, suppressed, unaware, uncalculated, undeliberate, unheeding, unintended, unintentional, unmindful, unpremeditated, unrealized, unwitting; SEE CONCEPTS **542,544**

uncontrollable [adj] *wild; carried away*
beside oneself, disorderly, excited, fractious, frantic, freaked, furious, headstrong, indocile, indomitable, insuppressible, insurgent, intractable, irrepressible, irresistible, lawless, like a loose cannon*, mad, obdurate, obstinate, recalcitrant, strong, stubborn, uncontainable, undisciplinable, undisciplined, ungovernable, unmanageable, unrestrainable, unruly, violent; SEE CONCEPT **401**

unconventional [adj] *very different; odd*
anarchistic, atypical, avant-garde, beat, bizarre, crazy, eccentric, far-out*, freakish, freaky, free and easy*, idiosyncratic, individual, individualistic, informal, irregular, kinky*, kooky*, nonconformist, oddball*, offbeat, off the beaten track*, off the wall*, original, out in left field*, out of the ordinary, unceremonious, uncommon, uncustomary, unique, unorthodox, unusual, way-out*, weirdo*; SEE CONCEPT **564**

uncouth [adj] *clumsy, uncultivated*
awkward, barbaric, boorish, cheap, clownish, clumsy, coarse, crass, crude, discourteous, disgracious, gawky, graceless, gross, heavy-handed, ill-bred, ill-mannered, impertinent, impolite, inelegant, loud, loud-mouthed, loutish, oafish, raunchy, raw, rough, rude, rustic, strange, tacky*, uncalled-for*, uncivil, uncivilized, uncultivated, ungainly, ungenteel, ungentlemanly, unpolished, unrefined, unseemly, vulgar; SEE CONCEPT **401**

uncover [v] *reveal, disclose*
bare, betray, break, bring to light*, crack, denude, dig up*, disclose, discover, display, divulge, expose, give away, hit upon, lay bare, lay open, leak, make known, open, open up, reveal, show, strike, strip, stumble on, subject, tap, tell, tip one's hand*, unclothe, unearth, unmask, unveil, unwrap; SEE CONCEPTS **60,183,261**

uncritical [adj] *casual, unfussy*
careless, cursory, easily pleased, imperceptive, imprecise, imprudent, inaccurate, indiscriminate, offhand, perfunctory, shallow, slipshod, superficial, undiscerning, undiscriminating, unexacting, uninformed, unperceptive, unselective, unthinking; SEE CONCEPT **542**

undaunted [adj] *brave, bold*
audacious, coming on strong*, courageous, dauntless, fearless, fire-eating*, gallant, icy*, indomitable, intrepid, not discouraged, not put off*, resolute, spunky, steadfast, unafraid, unalarmed, unapprehensive, undeterred, undiscouraged, un-

dismayed, unfaltering, unflinching, unshrinking, valiant, valorous; SEE CONCEPT *401*

undecided [*adj*] *not sure, not definite*
ambivalent, betwixt and between*, blowing hot and cold*, borderline, debatable, dithering*, doubtful, dubious, equivocal, hemming and hawing*, hesitant, iffy*, indecisive, indefinite, in the middle*, irresolute, moot, of two minds*, on the fence*, open, pending, pending, running hot and cold*, tentative, torn, uncertain, unclear, uncommitted, undetermined, unfinished, unsettled, unsure, up in the air*, vague, waffling, wavering, wishy-washy*; SEE CONCEPTS *403,529*

undeniable [*adj*] *definite, proven*
actual, beyond doubt, beyond question, binding, certain, clear, compulsory, evident, for sure*, inarguable, incontestable, incontrovertible, indisputable, indubitable, irrefutable, manifest, necessary, no ifs and or buts*, obligatory, obvious, open and shut*, patent, positive, real, sound, sure, sure thing*, true, unanswerable, unassailable, undoubted, unquestionable; SEE CONCEPT *535*

undependable [*adj*] *irresponsible*
bum, capricious, careless, changeable, dubious, erratic, fickle, fly-by-night*, inconsistent, inconstant, indefinite, indeterminate, loose*, no bargain*, no-good*, treacherous, trick, tricky, trustless, unassured, uncertain, unpredictable, unreliable, unsafe, unsound, unstable, unsure, untrustworthy, variable; SEE CONCEPTS *401,535*

under [*adv1/prep1*] *below*
beneath, bottom, concealed by, covered by, down, downward, held down, inferior, lower, nether, on the bottom, on the nether side, on the underside, pinned, pressed down, supporting, to the bottom, underneath; SEE CONCEPTS *586,735,793*

under [*adv2/prep2*] *secondary*
amenable, belonging, collateral, consequent, corollary, dependent, directed, following, governed, included, inferior, in the power of, junior, lesser, low, lower, obedient, obeying, reporting, sub, subject, subjugated, subordinate, subsequent, subservient, subsidiary, substract, subsumed; SEE CONCEPTS *560,575,577*

undercover [*adj*] *secret, spy*
clandestine, concealed, confidential, covert, creep, furtive, hidden, hole-and-corner*, hush-hush*, incognito*, intelligence, on the QT*, private, stealth, stealthy, sub-rosa*, surreptitious, underground, underhand, underneath, under wraps*; SEE CONCEPTS *544,576*

undercurrent [*n*] *drift, pull*
atmosphere, aura, crosscurrent, direction, eddy, feeling, flavor, hint, inclination, indication, insinuation, intimation, murmur, overtone, propensity, riptide, sense, suggestion, tendency, tenor, tinge, trace, trend, underflow, undertone, undertow, vibes*, vibrations; SEE CONCEPTS *673,738*

underdog [*n*] *unlikely winner in a contest or struggle*
bottom dog, dark horse, longshot, out-of-towner*; SEE CONCEPTS *366,423*

underestimate [*v*] *minimize; rate too low*
belittle, deprecate, depreciate, disesteem, disparage, make light of*, miscalculate, miscarry, not do justice*, put down*, sell short*, slight, think too little of*, underrate, undervalue; SEE CONCEPTS *12,54,764*

undergo [*v*] *be subjected to*
abide, bear, bear up, bow, defer, encounter, endure, experience, feel, go through, have, know, meet with, put up with, see, share, stand, submit to, suffer, support, sustain, tolerate, weather, withstand, yield; SEE CONCEPT *23*

underground [*adj1*] *below the surface*
below ground, buried, covered, in the recesses, subterranean, subterrestrial, sunken, underfoot; SEE CONCEPT *583*

underground [*adj2*] *secret, subversive*
alternative, avant-garde, clandestine, concealed, covert, experimental, hidden, hush-hush*, on the QT*, on the sly*, private, radical, resistant, resistive, revolutionary, surreptitious, unbowed, unconventional, undercover, under wraps*, unusual; SEE CONCEPTS *564,576*

underhand [*adj*] *deceitful*
clandestine, concealed, crafty, crooked, cunning, deceptive, devious, dirty-dealing*, dishonest, dishonorable, double-crossing*, duplicitous, fraudulent, furtive, guileful, hush-hush*, indirect, insidious, oblique, on the QT*, on the sly*, secret, secretive, shady, shifty, slippery*, sly*, sneaking, sneaky, stealthy, sub-rosa, surreptitious, treacherous, tricky, two-faced*, two-timing*, undercover, underhanded, under wraps*, unethical, unfair, unjust, unscrupulous, wily; SEE CONCEPTS *401,544*

underline [*v*] *emphasize; mark*
accentuate, bracket, call attention to, caption, check off, draw attention to, feature, give emphasis, highlight, indicate, interlineate, italicize, play up, point to, point up, rule, stress, underscore; SEE CONCEPTS *49,79*

underlying [*adj*] *fundamental, latent*
basal, basic, bottom, bottom-line*, cardinal, concealed, critical, crucial, elemental, elementary, essential, hidden, indispensable, intrinsic, lurking, necessary, needful, nitty-gritty*, nub, primary, prime, primitive, radical, root, substratal, veiled, vital; SEE CONCEPTS *546,549*

undermine [*v*] *weaken*
attenuate, blunt, clip one's wings*, corrode, cripple, debilitate, dig, dig out*, disable, eat away*, enfeeble, erode, excavate, foil, frustrate, hollow out, hurt, impair, knock the bottom out of*, mine, poke full of holes*, ruin, sabotage, sandbag*, sap, soften, subvert, threaten, thwart, torpedo*, tunnel, undercut, wear, whittle away, wreck; SEE CONCEPTS *14,240*

underneath [*adv/prep*] *below*
beneath, bottom, covered, lower, neath, nether, under; SEE CONCEPTS *586,735*

underprivileged [*adj*] *poor*
badly off*, depressed, deprived, destitute, disadvantaged, down and out*, handicapped, hapless, hard up*, have-not*, ill-fated, ill-starred, impoverished, indigent, in dire straits, in need, in want, needy, unfortunate, unlucky; SEE CONCEPT *334*

understand [*v1*] *appreciate, comprehend*
accept, apprehend, be aware, be conscious of, be with it*, catch, catch on, conceive, deduce, discern, distinguish, explain, fathom, figure out, find out, follow, get*, get the hang of*, get the idea*, get the picture*, get the point*, grasp, have knowledge of, identify with, infer, interpret, ken*, know, learn, make out*, make sense of, master, note, penetrate, perceive, possess, read, realize, recognize, register, savvy*, see, seize,

sense, sympathize, take in*, take meaning, tolerate; SEE CONCEPT *12*

understand [v2] *think, believe*
accept, assume, be informed, concede, conceive, conclude, conjecture, consider, count on, deduce, expect, fancy, feel for, gather, guess, hear, imagine, infer, learn, presume, reckon, suppose, surmise, suspect, take for granted, take it, think; SEE CONCEPT *12*

understanding [n1] *comprehension, appreciation*
acumen*, apperception, apprehension, assimilation, awareness, decipherment, discernment, discrimination, grasp, grip, insight, intellect, intelligence, intuition, judgment, ken, knowing, knowledge, mastery, penetration, perception, perceptiveness, perceptivity, percipience, perspicacity, prehension, realization, reason, recognition, savvy, sense, sharpness, wit; SEE CONCEPT *409*

understanding [n2] *belief*
acceptation, conception, conclusion, estimation, idea, import, impression, inkling, intendment, interpretation, judgment, knowledge, meaning, message, notion, opinion, perception, purport, sense, significance, significancy, signification, sympathy, view, viewpoint; SEE CONCEPTS *682,689*

understanding [n3] *informal agreement*
accord, common view, concord, deal, handshake*, harmony, meeting of minds*, pact; SEE CONCEPT *684*

understanding [adj] *accepting, tolerant*
compassionate, considerate, discerning, empathetic, forbearing, forgiving, generous, kind, kindly, patient, perceptive, responsive, sensitive, sympathetic; SEE CONCEPTS *401,542*

understood [adj] *assumed, implicit*
accepted, appreciated, axiomatic, down pat*, implied, inferential, inferred, known, on to*, pat, presumed, roger*, tacit, taken for granted, undeclared, unexpressed, unsaid, unspoken, unstated, wise to, wordless; SEE CONCEPT *529*

undertake [v] *attempt, engage in*
address oneself, agree, answer for, bargain, begin, commence, commit, commit oneself, contract, covenant, devote, embark, endeavor, enter upon, fall into, go about, go for, go in for, go into, guarantee, have a hand in*, have a try, hazard, initiate, launch, make a run at*, move, offer, pitch in, pledge, promise, set about, set in motion, set out, shoulder, stake, stipulate, tackle, take on, take the plunge*, take upon oneself, try, try out, venture, volunteer; SEE CONCEPTS *87,100*

undertaking [n] *endeavor, attempt*
adventure, affair, business, deal, effort, engagement, enterprise, essay, experiment, game, happening, hassle, hazard, job, move, operation, outfit, play, project, proposition, pursuit, shop, striving, struggle, task, thing*, trial, try, venture, what one is into*, work; SEE CONCEPTS *87,324,349,362*

undertone [n] *suggestion, whisper*
association, atmosphere, buzz, connotation, feeling, flavor, hint, hum, implication, low tone, mumble, murmur, mutter, overtone, rumor, tinge, touch, trace, undercurrent; SEE CONCEPTS *65,682*

underwear [n] *clothing worn under outerwear*
bikini, boxers*, boxer shorts, bra, briefs, BVDs*, corset, drawers*, intimate things, jockeys, jockey shorts, lingerie, long johns, panties, shorts, skivvies*, smallclothes, underclothes, underclothing,

undergarment, underpants, undershirt, underthings, undies; SEE CONCEPT *451*

underweight [adj] *thin*
angular, anorectic, bony, gangly, malnourished, puny, scrawny, shadow, skeleton*, skin and bones*, skinny, starved, stringbean*, undernourished, undersized; SEE CONCEPT *491*

underworld [n] *criminal activity, element*
abyss, Cosa Nostra, criminals, felony, gangland, gangsters, Mafia, mob*, organized crime, racket*, riffraff*, syndicate; SEE CONCEPTS *412,645*

underwrite [v] *endorse, insure*
accede, agree to, angel*, approve, back, bankroll*, collateral, consent, countersign, endow, finance, float, fund, guarantee, help, initial, okay*, pay, provide, provide financing, sanction, seal, secure, sign, sponsor, stake, subscribe, subsidize, support; SEE CONCEPTS *50,88,110,341*

undesirable [adj] *offensive, unacceptable*
abominable, annoying, bothersome, defective, disagreeable, disliked, displeasing, distasteful, dreaded, icky, inadmissible, incommodious, inconvenient, inexpedient, insufferable, loathed, loathsome, objectionable, obnoxious, offensive, outcast, out of place, rejected, repellent, repugnant, scorned, shunned, to be avoided, troublesome, unacceptable, unattractive, unlikable, unpleasing, unpopular, unsatisfactory, unsavory, unsought, unsuitable, unwanted, unwelcome, unwished for, useless; SEE CONCEPTS *529,570*

undeveloped [adj] *immature*
abortive, backward, behindhand, embryonic, halfbaked, ignored, inchoate, incipient, inexperienced, latent, potential, primitive, primordial, unactualized, underdeveloped, unevolved, unprogressive, untaught, untrained; SEE CONCEPTS *485,578,797*

undisputed/undisputable [adj] *positive, accepted*
acknowledged, admitted, arbitrary, assured, authoritative, beyond question, certain, conclusive, decided, dogmatic, final, incontestable, incontrovertible, indisputable, indubitable, irrefutable, not disputed, positive, recognized, sure, tyrannous, unchallenged, uncontested, undeniable, undoubted, unequivocal, unerring, unquestioned; SEE CONCEPT *535*

undivided [adj] *whole*
absorbed, circumspect, collective, combined, complete, concentrated, concerted, continued, deliberate, detailed, diligent, engrossed, entire, exclusive, fast, fixed, full, intense, intent, joined, lock stock and barrel*, minute, rigid, scrupulous, single, solid, steady, thorough, unanimous, unbroken, uncut, undistracted, unflagging, united, unswerving, vigilant, wholehearted; SEE CONCEPTS *482,531*

undo [v1] *open*
disengage, disentangle, free, loose, loosen, release, unbind, unblock, unbutton, unclose, unfasten, unfix, unlock, unloose, unloosen, unravel, unshut, unstop, untie, unwrap; SEE CONCEPT *135*

undo [v2] *nullify, invalidate*
abate, abolish, abrogate, annihilate, annul, break, bring down, bring to naught*, cancel, cramp*, craze, crimp*, decimate, defeat, demolish, destroy, have*, impoverish, injure, make waves*, mar, negate, neutralize, offset, outfox, outmaneuver, outsmart, overreach, overthrow, overturn, quash, queer*, raze, reverse, ruin, screw up*, shatter, skin*, smash, spoil, stymie*, subvert, un-

un
un

build, undermine, unsettle, upset, vitiate, wipe out*, wrack, wreck; SEE CONCEPTS 7,19,121,252

undoing [n] destruction, misfortune

accident, adversity, affliction, bad luck, bad omen, bane, blight, blow, blunder, calamity, casualty, catastrophe, collapse, curse, defeat, destroyer, difficulty, disgrace, doom, downfall, error, failure, fault, faux pas, flaw, fumble, grief, humiliation, last straw*, misadventure, miscalculation, mischance, mishap, misstep, omission, overthrow, overturn, reversal, reverse, ruin, ruination, shame, slip, smash, stumble, subversion, trial, trip, trouble, visitation, weakness, wreck; SEE CONCEPTS 230,674,679

undoubtedly [adv] certainly

assuredly, beyond question, beyond shadow of a doubt*, definitely, doubtless, easily, indeed, of course, really, surely, truly, undeniably, unmistakably, unquestionably, well, without doubt; SEE CONCEPT 535

undress [v] take off clothes

denude, disarray, dismantle, disrobe, divest oneself, doff, get off, get out of, husk, peel, shed, shock, slip off, slip out of, strip, unattire, uncloak, unclothe, unmask; SEE CONCEPTS 211,453

undue [adj] excessive, unnecessary

disproportionate, exceeding, exorbitant, extravagant, extreme, forbidden, illegal, ill-timed, immoderate, improper, inappropriate, inapt, indecorous, inept, inordinate, intemperate, needless, overmuch, sinister, too great, too much, unapt, uncalled-for, unconscionable, underhanded, undeserved, unfair, unfitting, unjust, unjustifiable, unjustified, unmeasurable, unreasonable, unseasonable, unseemly, unsuitable, untimely, unwarrantable, unwarranted; SEE CONCEPTS 546,558,569

unduly [adv] excessively

disproportionately, ever, extravagantly, extremely, illegally, immensely, immoderately, improperly, indecorously, inordinately, out of proportion, over, overfull, overly, overmuch, too, underhandedly, unfairly, unjustifiably, unjustly, unnecessarily, unreasonably; SEE CONCEPTS 544,546,569

undying [adj] never-ending

constant, continuing, deathless, eternal, everlasting, immortal, imperishable, indestructible, inextinguishable, infinite, interminable, perennial, permanent, perpetual, persistent, unceasing, undiminished, unended, unending, unfading; SEE CONCEPT 798

unearth [v] dig up

ascertain, bring to light*, catch on*, delve, determine, discover, disinter, dredge up, excavate, exhibit, exhume, expose, ferret, find, find out, hear, hit upon, learn, reveal, root, see, see the light, show, spark, spotlight*, strike, stumble on, turn up, unbury, uncover, uproot; SEE CONCEPTS 178,183

unearthly [adj] supernatural; very strange

abnormal, absurd, appalling, demoniac, devilish, eerie, ethereal, extraordinary, fiendish, frightening, funereal, ghastly, ghostly, ghoulish, hairraising, haunted, heavenly, hyperphysical, miraculous, nightmarish, not of this world, phantom, preternatural, ridiculous, scary, sepulchral, spectral, spooky*, sublime, superhuman, uncanny, ungodly, unholy, unreasonable, weird; SEE CONCEPTS 536,564,582

uneasy [adj] awkward, uncomfortable

afraid, agitated, alarmed, all nerves*, anguished, anxious, apprehensive, bothered, constrained, discomposed, dismayed, disquieted, disturbed, edgy, fearful, fidgety, fretful, harassed, ill at ease, impatient, insecure, in turmoil, irascible, irritable, jittery, jumpy, nervous, on edge, on the qui vive, palpitant, peevish, perplexed, perturbed, precarious, restive, restless, shaken, shaky, strained, suspicious, tense, tormented, troubled, unquiet, unsettled, unstable, upset, vexed, worried, wrung; SEE CONCEPTS 403,548,690

uneducated [adj] lacking knowledge

benighted, empty-headed, ignoramus, ignorant, illiterate, inerudite, know-nothing*, lowbrow*, uncultivated, uncultured, uninstructed, unlearned, unlettered, unread, unrefined, unschooled, untaught, untutored; SEE CONCEPT 402

unemotional [adj] not responsive

along for the ride*, apathetic, blah*, callous, chill*, cold, coldhearted*, cool, deadpan, dispassionate, emotionless, flat, frigid, glacial, going with the flow*, hard-boiled*, hard-hearted*, heartless, impassive, indifferent, insensitive, laidback*, listless, marble*, obdurate, passionless, phlegmatic, quiet, reserved, reticent, rolling with the punches*, thick-skinned*, uncompassionate, undemonstrative, unexcitable, unfeeling, unimpressionable, unresponsive, unsympathetic; SEE CONCEPTS 401,403

unemployed [adj] without a job

at liberty*, between jobs*, closed down*, disengaged, down, fired, free, idle, inactive, jobless, laid off, leisured, loafing*, on layoff, on the bench*, on the dole*, on the shelf*, out of action*, out of a job, out of work, resting, unapplied, underemployed, unengaged, unexercised, unoccupied, unused, without gainful employment, workless; SEE CONCEPT 538

unending [adj] continuing

amaranthine, ceaseless, constant, continual, continuous, endless, eternal, everlasting, immortal, incessant, infinite, interminable, never-ending, perpetual, steady, unceasing, uninterrupted, unremitting; SEE CONCEPTS 482,798

unequal [adj1] different

differing, disparate, dissimilar, distant, divergent, diverse, incommensurate, like night and day*, mismatched, not uniform, odd, poles apart*, unalike, unequivalent, uneven, unlike, unmatched, unsimilar, variable, various, varying, weird*; SEE CONCEPT 564

unequal [adj2] not balanced; lopsided

asymmetrical, disproportionate, ill-matched, inequitable, irregular, nonsymmetrical, off-balance, one-sided, overbalanced, unbalanced, uneven, unproportionate, unsymmetrical; SEE CONCEPT 480

unequaled [adj] supreme, pre-eminent

alone, beyond compare, incomparable, inimitable, matchless, nonpareil, only, paramount, peerless, second to none*, surpassing, towering, transcendent, ultimate, unique, unmatched, unparagoned, unparalleled, unrivaled, unsurpassed, without equal; SEE CONCEPT 574

unequivocal [adj] definite, positive

absolute, apparent, categorical, certain, clear, clear-cut, decided, decisive, direct, distinct, downright, evident, explicit, flat out*, incontestable, incontrovertible, indisputable, indubitable, manifest, no catch*, no fine print*, no holds barred*, no ifs ands or buts*, no strings attached*, obvious, open and shut*, palpable, patent, plain, straight, straightforward, straight out, unambiguous, uncontestable, undeniable, undisputable, univocal, unmistakable, unquestionable; SEE CONCEPT 535

unerring [adj] accurate
certain, errorless, exact, faultless, impeccable, inerrable, inerrant, infallible, invariable, just, perfect, reliable, sure, true, trustworthy, unfailing; SEE CONCEPTS 535,574

unethical [adj] dishonest, immoral
cheating, corrupt, crooked, dirty*, dirty-dealing*, dishonorable, disreputable, double-crossing*, fake, fishy*, flimflam*, fly-by-night*, illegal, improper, mercenary, scam*, shady*, sharp*, slick*, slippery*, sneaky*, two-faced*, two-timing*, underhand, unfair, unprincipled, unprofessional, unscrupulous, wrong; SEE CONCEPT 545

uneven [adj] not smooth or balanced
asperous, asymmetrical, broken, bumpy, changeable, craggy, differing, discrepant, disparate, disproportionate, fitful, fluctuating, harsh, illmatched, intermittent, irregular, jagged, jerky, leftover, lopsided, nonsymmetrical, notched, not flat, not level, not parallel, odd, off-balance, onesided, overbalanced, patchy, remaining, rough, rugged, scabrous, scraggy, serrate, spasmodic, spotty, unbalanced, unequal, unfair, unlevel, unsmooth, unsteady, unsymmetrical, variable; SEE CONCEPTS 480,566,606

uneventful [adj] monotonous, dull
boring, common, commonplace, humdrum, inconclusive, indecisive, ordinary, prosaic, quiet, routine, tedious, unexceptional, unexciting, unfateful, uninteresting, unmemorable, unnoteworthy, unremarkable, unvaried; SEE CONCEPT 548

unexpected [adj] surprising
abrupt, accidental, amazing, astonishing, chance, electrifying, eye-opening*, fortuitous, from left field*, impetuous, impulsive, instantaneous, not bargained for*, not in the cards*, out of the blue*, payback, prodigious, staggering, startling, stunning, sudden, swift, unanticipated, unforeseen, unheralded, unlooked-for, unpredictable, unpredicted, wonderful; SEE CONCEPTS 544,548

unfailing [adj] certain, unchanging
absolute, assiduous, bottomless, boundless, ceaseless, come-through*, consistent, constant, continual, continuing, continuous, counted on, delivering, dependable, diligent, dyed-in-thewool*, endless, eternal, faithful, inexhaustible, infallible, invariable, loyal, never-failing, persistent, reliable, rock solid*, same, solid, staunch, steadfast, straight, sure, surefire, there*, triedand-true*, true, trustworthy, unflagging, unlimited, unrelenting; SEE CONCEPTS 534,535,538

unfair [adj] prejudiced, wrongful
arbitrary, bad, base, biased, bigoted, blameworthy, cheating, criminal, crooked, cruel, culpable, discredited, discriminatory, dishonest, dishonorable, foul, grievous, illegal, immoral, improper, inequitable, inexcusable, iniquitous, injurious, low, mean, one-sided, partial, partisan, petty, shameful, shameless, uncalled-for, undue, unethical, unjust, unjustifiable, unlawful, unprincipled, unreasonable, unrightful, unscrupulous, unsporting, unwarranted, vicious, vile, wicked, wrong; SEE CONCEPTS 544,545,548

unfaithful [adj] disloyal, adulterous
adulterine, cheating, deceitful, double-crossing*, faithless, false, false-hearted, fickle, foresworn, inconstant, incontinent, moonlighting*, not true to, of bad faith, perfidious, philandering, recreant, shifty*, snaky*, sneaking, traitorous, treacherous, treasonable, two-faced*, two-timing*, unchaste, unreliable, untrue, untrustworthy, wicked; SEE CONCEPT 545

unfaltering [adj] steadfast
abiding, bent on, bound, bound and determined*, dead set on*, enduring, firm, going all the way*, indefatigable, meaning business*, mulish*, neverfailing, persevering, pigheaded, resolute, set, steady, stiff-necked*, stubborn, sure, tireless, unfailing, unflagging, unflappable, unflinching, unqualified, unquestioning, unswerving, untiring, unwavering, wholehearted; SEE CONCEPTS 403,535,538

unfamiliar [adj1] different, strange
alien, anomalous, bizarre, curious, exotic, extraordinary, fantastic, foreign, little known, new, novel, obscure, original, outlandish, out-of-theway*, peculiar, recondite, remarkable, remote, unaccustomed, uncommon, unexpected, unexplored, uninvestigated, unknown, unusual; SEE CONCEPT 564

unfamiliar [adj2] inexperienced; not knowing about
ignorant, incognizant, inconversant, not associated, not versed in, oblivious, out of contact, unaccustomed, unacquainted, unaware, unconversant, uninformed, uninitiated, uninstructed, unknowing, unknown, unpracticed, unskilled, unversed, unwitting; SEE CONCEPTS 402,678

unfathomable [adj1] bottomless
abysmal, boundless, deep, eternal, immeasurable, infinite, soundless, unending, unmeasured, unplumbed; SEE CONCEPTS 482,777

unfathomable [adj2] hard to believe; difficult to understand
abstruse, baffling, clear as mud*, deep, enigmatic, esoteric, heavy, impenetrable, incognizable, incomprehensible, indecipherable, inexplicable, obscure, profound, too deep*, uncomprehensible, ungraspable, unintelligible, unknowable; SEE CONCEPT 529

unfavorable [adj] very bad
adverse, antagonistic, calamitous, contrary, damaging, destructive, disadvantageous, discommodious, hostile, ill, ill-advised, improper, inadvisable, inauspicious, inconvenient, inexpedient, infelicitous, inopportune, late, low, malapropos, negative, objectionable, ominous, opposed, poor, regrettable, tardy, threatening, troublesome, unfit, unfortunate, unfriendly, unlucky, unpromising, unpropitious, unseasonable, unseemly, unsuited, untimely, untoward, wrong; SEE CONCEPTS 529,571

unfeeling [adj] hard-hearted, numb
anesthetized, apathetic, asleep, benumbed, brutal, callous, cantankerous, churlish, cold, coldblooded, cold fish*, cold-hearted, crotchety, cruel, deadened, exacting, feelingless, hard, hardened, heartless, icy, inanimate, inhuman, insensate, insensible, insensitive, iron-hearted, merciless, obdurate, pitiless, ruthless, sensationless, senseless, severe, stony, surly, thickskinned*, tough, unamiable, uncaring,

un
un

uncompassionate, uncordial, unemotional, unkind, unsympathetic; SEE CONCEPTS 314,403,542

unfinished [adj] *not completed*
amateurish, bare, crude, cut short, dabbling, defective, deficient, dilettante, faulty, formless, found wanting, fragmentary, half-baked*, half-done*, immature, imperfect, incomplete, in the making, in the rough*, lacking, natural, not done, plain, raw, rough, roughhewn, shapeless, sketchy, tentative, unaccomplished, unadorned, unassembled, uncompleted, unconcluded, under construction, undeveloped, undone, unexecuted, unfashioned, unfulfilled, unperfected, unpolished, unrefined, wanting; SEE CONCEPTS 485,531

unfit [adj1] *not appropriate or suited*
below par*, can't make the grade*, debilitated, decrepit, discordant, down, dragging, feeble, flimsy, ill-adapted, ill-equipped, ill-suited, improper, inadequate, inapplicable, inappropriate, incompatible, incongruous, incorrect, ineffective, inexpedient, infelicitous, inharmonious, laid low*, mistaken, not fit, out of element*, out of place, out of shape, poorly, rocky*, unbecoming, uncongenial, uncool, unhealthy, unlikely, unmeet, unpromising, unsuitable, unsuited, useless, valueless; SEE CONCEPT 558

unfit [adj2] *not ready*
amateur, awkward, blundering, bungling, bush league*, butter-fingered*, clumsy, debilitated, disqualified, feeble, heavy-handed, ill-equipped, impotent, inadequate, incapable, incapacitated, incompetent, ineffective, inefficient, ineligible, inept, inexperienced, inexpert, maladjusted, maladroit, no good*, not cut out for*, not equal to, not up to*, unable, unapt, unfitted, unhandy, unpracticed, unprepared, unproficient, unqualified, unskilled, unskillful, untrained, useless, weak; SEE CONCEPT 527

unflagging [adj] *persistent*
active, assiduous, constant, diligent, dynamic, energetic, fixed, indefatigable, inexhaustible, persevering, staunch, steady, tireless, unceasing, undeviating, unfailing, unfaltering, unrelenting, unremitting, unretiring, untiring, unwearied; SEE CONCEPTS 538,798

unflappable [adj] *cool and calm*
collected, composed, deliberate, disimpassioned, easy, impassive, imperturbable, level-headed, nonchalant, relaxed, self-possessed, unruffled; SEE CONCEPTS 401,542

unfold [v1] *spread out*
disentangle, display, expand, extend, fan, fan out, flatten, loosen, open, outspread, outstretch, reel out, release, shake out, spread, straighten, stretch out, unbend, uncoil, uncrease, uncurl, undo, unfurl, unravel, unroll, untwist, unwind, unwrap; SEE CONCEPT 201

unfold [v2] *make known*
announce, clarify, clear up, decipher, describe, disclose, discover, display, divulge, dope out, elucidate, explain, explicate, expose, figure out, illustrate, present, publish, resolve, reveal, show, solve, uncover, unravel; SEE CONCEPTS 55,261

unfold [v3] *develop*
bear fruit, demonstrate, elaborate, evidence, evince, evolve, expand, grow, manifest, mature; SEE CONCEPT 704

unforeseen [adj] *surprising*
abrupt, accidental, from left field*, not bargained for*, out of the blue*, startling, sudden, surprise,

unanticipated, uncalculated, unexpected, unlooked-for; SEE CONCEPTS 544,548

unfortunate [adj] *unlucky, bad*
adverse, afflicted, broken, burdened, calamitous, cursed, damaging, deplorable, desperate, destitute, disastrous, doomed, forsaken, hapless, hopeless, ill-fated, ill-starred, in a bad way*, inappropriate, infelicitous, inopportune, jinxed, lamentable, luckless, out of luck*, pained, poor, regrettable, ruined, ruinous, shattered, star-crossed*, stricken, troubled, unbecoming, unfavorable, unhappy, unpropitious, unprosperous, unsuccessful, unsuitable, untoward, wretched; SEE CONCEPTS 334,548,570

unfounded [adj] *not based on fact*
baseless, bottomless, deceptive, fabricated, fallacious, false, foundationless, gratuitous, groundless, idle, illogical, mendacious, misleading, off-base, spurious, trumped up*, uncalled-for, unjustified, unproven, unreal, unsubstantiated, untrue, untruthful, unwarranted, vain, without basis, without foundation; SEE CONCEPTS 267,582

unfriendly [adj] *nasty, hostile*
acrimonious, against, alien, aloof, antagonistic, antisocial, censorious, chilly, cold, combative, competitive, conflicting, contrary, disaffected, disagreeable, distant, estranged, grouchy, grudging, gruff, hateful, ill-disposed, inauspicious, inhospitable, inimical, malicious, malignant, misanthropic, not on speaking terms*, opposed, opposite, quarrelsome, sour, spiteful, surly, uncharitable, uncongenial, unfavorable, unneighborly, unpropitious, unsociable, vengeful, warlike; SEE CONCEPTS 401,548

ungodly [adj1] *not accepting a religious doctrine; impious*
atheistic, blasphemous, corrupt, depraved, godless, improper, indecent, indecorous, indelicate, irreligious, malevolent, profane, rough, sinful, undecorous, unhallowed, unholy, unseemly, vile, wicked; SEE CONCEPTS 542,545

ungodly [adj2] *outrageous*
atrocious, barbarous, dreadful, horrendous, horrid, intolerable, nasty, shocking, unbelievable, uncivilized, unconscionable, unearthly, unreasonable, unseemly; SEE CONCEPTS 529,548,570

ungrateful [adj] *not appreciative*
careless, demanding, candid, dissatisfied, faultfinding, forgetful, grasping, grumbling, heedless, ingrate, insensible, oblivious, self-centered, selfish, thankless, unappreciative, unmindful, unnatural, unthankful; SEE CONCEPT 401

unguarded [adj] *thoughtless; unwary*
accessible, artless, candid, careless, casual, direct, foolhardy, frank, headlong, heedless, honest, ill-considered, impolitic, imprudent, impulsive, incautious, indiscreet, ingenuous, naive, offhand, rash, spontaneous, straightforward, unalert, uncircumspect, unconscious, undiplomatic, unpremeditated, unreflective, unthinking, unvigilant, unwatchful, unwise, vulnerable, weak; SEE CONCEPT 401

unhappy [adj1] *sad*
bleak, bleeding*, blue*, bummed out*, cheerless, crestfallen, dejected, depressed, despondent, destroyed, disconsolate, dismal, dispirited, down*, down and out*, downbeat, downcast, down in the mouth*, dragged, dreary, gloomy, grim, heavy-hearted, hurting, in a blue funk*, in pain, in the dumps*, let-down*, long-faced, low, melancholy,

mirthless, miserable, mournful, oppressive, put away*, ripped*, sad, saddened, sorrowful, sorry, teary, troubled; SEE CONCEPT 403

unhappy [adj2] *unfortunate, unlucky*
afflicted, cursed, hapless, ill-fated, ill-starred, luckless, misfortunate, troubled, untoward, wretched; SEE CONCEPT 548

unhealthy [adj1] *sick*
ailing, below par, debilitated, delicate, diseased, down, dragging, feeble, frail, ill, in a decline, infirm, in ill health, in poor health, invalid, laid low*, out of action*, out of shape, peaked, poorly, run-down, shaky, sickly, unsound, unwell, weak; SEE CONCEPT 314

unhealthy [adj2] *very bad in effect on well-being*
baneful, chancy, corrupt, corrupting, dangerous, degenerate, degrading, deleterious, demoralizing, detrimental, harmful, hazardous, insalubrious, jeopardous, morbid, nefarious, negative, noisome, noxious, perilous, perverse, poisonous, risky, rotten, treacherous, undesirable, unhealthful, unsanitary, unsound, unwholesome, villainous, virulent, wicked; SEE CONCEPTS 537,571

unheard-of [adj] *unique, obscure*
exceptional, inconceivable, little-known, nameless, new, novel, outlandish, preposterous, rare, shocking, singular, unbelievable, undiscovered, unfamiliar, unknown, unlikely, unprecedented, unrenowned, unsung, unusual; SEE CONCEPTS 564,576

unholy [adj1] *sacreligious*
base, blameful, corrupt, culpable, depraved, dishonest, evil, godless, guilty, heinous, immoral, impious, iniquitous, irreligious, irreverent, irreverential, profane, sinful, ungodly, unhallowed, unsanctified, vile, wicked; SEE CONCEPTS 542,548

unholy [adj2] *outrageous*
appalling, awful, barbarous, dreadful, horrendous, shocking, uncivilized, unearthly, ungodly, unnatural, unreasonable; SEE CONCEPT 537

unidentified [adj] *secret*
anonymous, mysterious, nameless, not known, pseudonymous, unclassified, unfamiliar, unknown, unmarked, unnamed, unrecognized, unrevealed; SEE CONCEPT 576

unification [n] *joining together*
affinity, alliance, amalgamation, coalescence, coalition, combination, concurrence, confederation, connection, consolidation, coupling, federation, fusion, hookup, interlocking, linkage, melding, merger, merging, union, uniting; SEE CONCEPTS 230,388

uniform [n] *coordinated outfit*
attire, costume, dress, garb, gown, habit, khaki*, livery, monkey suit*, OD*, olive drab*, regalia, regimentals, robe, stripes*, suit; SEE CONCEPT 451

uniform [adj1] *consistent*
compatible, consonant, constant, equable, even, fated, fateful, fixed, habitual, homogeneous, immutable, incorrigible, inflexible, invariable, irreversible, level, methodical, monolithic, normal, of a piece*, ordered, orderly, ossified, plumb, regular, reliable, rigid, smooth, stable, static, steady, straight, symmetrical, systematic, true, unalterable, unbroken, unchanging, undeviating, undiversified, unfluctuating, unmodifiable, unvarying, well-balanced, well-proportioned; SEE CONCEPT 534

uniform [adj2] *alike*
agnate, akin, analogous, comparable, consistent, consonant, correspondent, ditto*, double, equal, identical, like, mated, monotonous, parallel, same, same difference*, self-same, similar, treadmill*, undifferentiated, unvaried; SEE CONCEPTS 487,573

unimaginable [adj] *mind-boggling*
beyond wildest dreams*, doubtful, exceptional, extraordinary, fantastic, impossible, improbable, inapprehensible, incogitable, incomprehensible, inconceivable, incredible, indescribable, ineffable, not understandable, rare, singular, unbelievable, uncommon, unheard-of, unique, unknowable, unordinary, unthinkable; SEE CONCEPTS 529,548

unimaginative [adj] *dull, predictable*
banal, barren, bromidic, common, commonplace, derivative, dime a dozen*, dry, dull as dishwater*, flat, hackneyed, ho hum*, lifeless, matter-of-fact, ordinary, pabulum, pedestrian, prosaic, routine, square*, tame, tedious, trite, uncreative, uninspired, unoriginal, unromantic, usual, vanilla*, well-worn, zero*; SEE CONCEPTS 542,547,548

unimportant [adj] *of no real worth, value*
beside the point*, casual, frivolous, frothy, immaterial, inconsequential, inconsiderable, indifferent, insignificant, irrelevant, little, low-ranking, meaningless, minor, minute, negligible, nonessential, nothing*, nugatory, null, of no account, of no consequence, paltry, petty, picayune, second-rate*, shoestring*, slight, trifling, trivial, unnecessary, useless, worthless, zero*, zilch*, zip*; SEE CONCEPT 575

uninhibited [adj] *free and easy; without restraint*
audacious, candid, cut loose*, expansive, fancy-free*, footloose*, frank, free, hanging out*, informal, instinctive, liberated, natural, no holds barred*, off the cuff*, open, relaxed, spontaneous, unbridled, unchecked, unconstrained, uncontrolled, uncurbed, ungoverned, unhampered, unrepressed, unreserved, unrestrained, unstricted, unself-conscious, unsuppressed; SEE CONCEPTS 267,401

uninspired [adj] *dull, unoriginal*
bromidic, commonplace, corny*, everyday, heavy-handed, humdrum, indifferent, old hat*, ordinary, phoned in*, ponderous, prosaic, stale, sterile, stock, uncreative, unexciting, unimaginative, unimpressed, uninspiring, uninteresting, uninventive, unmoved, yawn*; SEE CONCEPTS 542,547,548

unintelligible [adj] *not understandable*
ambiguous, equivocal, fathomless, Greek*, illegible, impenetrable, inarticulate, incognizable, incoherent, incomprehensible, indecipherable, indistinct, inexplicit, jumbled, meaningless, muddled, obscure, opaque, tenebrous, uncertain, unclear, unexplicit, unfathomable, ungraspable, unknowable, unreadable, vague; SEE CONCEPT 267

unintentional/unintended [adj] *not planned*
accidental, aimless, casual, chance, erratic, extemporaneous, fortuitous, haphazard, inadvertent, involuntary, purposeless, random, unconscious, undesigned, undevised, unexpected, unforeseen, unintended, unplanned, unpremeditated, unthinking, unthought, unwitting; SEE CONCEPTS 401,548

un
un

uninterested [adj] *oblivious to*
aloof, apathetic, blasé, bored, bored stiff*, casual, could care less*, detached, disinterested, distant, going through motions*, hard-hearted*, impassive, incurious, indifferent, listless, remote, thick-skinned*, turned off*, unconcerned, uncurious, uninvolved, unresponsive, weary, withdrawn; SEE CONCEPTS *401,403*

uninteresting [adj] *boring, uneventful*
arid, banal, big yawn*, bromidic, common, commonplace, depressing, dismal, drab, dreary, dry, dull, dusty*, fatiguing, flat, ho hum*, humdrum, insipid, irksome, jejune, monotonous, nothing*, nowhere*, pedestrian, prosaic, prosy, soporific, stale, stupid, tedious, tired, tiresome, trite, unenjoyable, unentertaining, unexciting, uninspiring, wearisome; SEE CONCEPTS *529,548*

uninterrupted [adj] *continuing; unbroken*
ceaseless, consecutive, constant, continual, continuous, direct, endless, interminable, nonstop, peaceful, perpetual, steady, straight, straightforward, sustained, through, unceasing, undistorted, unending, unremitting; SEE CONCEPTS *482,798*

union [n1] *merger, joining*
abutment, accord, agglutination, agreement, amalgam, amalgamation, blend, centralization, coadunation, combination, coming together, commixture, compound, concatenation, conciliation, concord, concurrence, confluence, congregation, conjunction, consolidation, correlation, coupling, fusion, harmony, hookup, incorporation, intercourse, joint, junction, juncture, meeting, melding, merging, mixture, seam, symbiosis, synthesis, tie-in, tie-up, unanimity, unification, unison, uniting, unity; SEE CONCEPTS *113,664,714*

union [n2] *group with shared interest, cause*
alliance, association, brotherhood, club, coalition, confederacy, confederation, congress, employees, federation, guild, labor union, league, local, order, sisterhood, society, sodality, syndicate, trade union; SEE CONCEPTS *325,381*

unique [adj1] *alone, singular*
different, exclusive, individual, lone, one, one and only*, onliest*, only, particular, rare, separate, single, solitary, solo, sui generis, uncommon, unexampled; SEE CONCEPTS *564,577*

unique [adj2] *one-of-a-kind; without equal*
anomalous, best, exceptional, extraordinary, far-out*, incomparable, inimitable, matchless, most, nonpareil, novel, only, peerless, primo*, rare, singular, something else*, special, standout, strange, uncommon, unequaled, unexampled, unimaginable, unmatched, unparagoned, unparalleled, unprecedented, unreal, unrivaled, utmost, weird*; SEE CONCEPTS *564,574*

unison [n] *harmony*
accord, accordance, agreement, alliance, community, concert, concord, concordance, conjunction, consent, consonance, cooperation, federation, league, reciprocity, sympathy, unanimity, union, unity; SEE CONCEPT *664*

unit [n1] *whole*
assemblage, assembly, bunch, complement, crew, crowd, detachment, entirety, entity, gang, group, mob, one, outfit, ring, section, system, total, totality; SEE CONCEPTS *432,837*

unit [n2] *part*
arm, block, component, constituent, detachment, detail, digit, element, factor, feature, fraction, ingredient, integer, item, joint, layer, length, link, member, module, piece, portion, section, segment, square, wing; SEE CONCEPT *834*

unite [v] *combine; join together*
affiliate, ally, amalgamate, associate, band, band together, become one, blend, close ranks*, coadjute, coalesce, commingle, concur, confederate, conjoin, connect, consolidate, cooperate, couple, embody, fuse, gather together, hang together*, harden, hook up with, incorporate, intertwine, join, join forces, keep together, league, link, marry, meet, merge, mix, pool, pull together, relate, solidify, stay together, stick together, strengthen, throw in with*, unify, wed; SEE CONCEPTS *113,193*

united [adj] *combined; in agreement*
affiliated, agreed, allied, amalgamated, assembled, associated, banded, coadunate, cognate, collective, concerted, concordant, confederated, congruent, conjoint, conjugate, conjunctive, consolidated, cooperative, corporate, federal, homogeneous, hooked up*, in accord, in cahoots*, incorporated, integrated, joined up, leagued, likeminded*, lined up*, linked, of one mind, of the same opinion, one, plugged in*, pooled, tied in, unanimous, undivided, unified, unitary; SEE CONCEPTS *563,577*

unity [n] *wholeness*
accord, agreement, alliance, coadunation, combination, concord, concurrence, confederation, consensus, consent, consonance, entity, federation, harmony, homogeneity, homogeneousness, identity, individuality, indivisibility, integral, integrality, integrity, interconnection, oneness, peace, rapport, sameness, singleness, singularity, soleness, solidarity, synthesis, totality, unanimity, undividedness, unification, uniformity, union, unison; SEE CONCEPTS *664,714,837*

universal [adj] *worldwide, entire*
accepted, all, all-embracing, all-inclusive, all-over, astronomical, broad, catholic, celestial, common, comprehensive, cosmic, cosmopolitan, customary, diffuse, ecumenical, empyrean, extensive, general, generic, global, multinational, mundane, omnipresent, planetary, prevalent, regular, stellar, sweeping, terrestrial, total, ubiquitous, undisputed, unlimited, unrestricted, usual, whole, widespread, worldly; SEE CONCEPTS *536,772*

universe [n] *everything in creation*
cosmos, everything, macrocosm, natural world, nature, world; SEE CONCEPTS *370,511*

unjust [adj] *not fair*
below the belt*, biased, fixed*, inequitable, influenced, low-down*, one-sided, partial, partisan, prejudiced, shabby*, underhand, undeserved, unfair, unforgivable, unjustified, unmerited, unrighteous, wrong, wrongful; SEE CONCEPT *545*

unkempt [adj] *shabby, sloppy*
bedraggled, coarse, crude, dilapidated, dirty, disarranged, disarrayed, disheveled, disordered, grubby*, grungy*, messed up*, messy, mussed up*, neglected, rough, rumpled, scruffy, shaggy, slipshod, slovenly, tousled, unclean, uncombed, unfastidious, ungroomed, unimproved, unneat, unpolished, untidy, vulgar; SEE CONCEPTS *485,621*

unkind [adj] *not nice*
barbarous, brutal, cold-blooded, coldhearted, cruel, hard-hearted, harsh, hateful, heartless, inconsiderate, inhuman, inhumane, insensitive, ma-

levolent, malicious, malignant, mean, nasty, sadistic, savage, spiteful, thoughtless, uncaring, uncharitable, unfeeling, unfriendly, unsympathetic; SEE CONCEPT 401

unknown [adj] *obscure, mysterious*

alien, anonymous, concealed, dark, desolate, distant, exotic, far, faraway, far-off, foreign,-hidden, humble, incog*, incognito, little known, nameless, new, remote, secret, so-and-so*, strange, such-and-such*, unapprehended, unascertained, uncelebrated, uncharted, undiscovered, undistinguished, unexplained, unexplored, unfamiliar, unheard-of, unidentified, unnamed, unnoted, unperceived, unrecognized, unrenowned, unrevealed, unsung, untold, X*; SEE CONCEPT 576

unlawful [adj] *against the law*

actionable, banned, bootleg*, criminal, flagitious, forbidden, illegal, illegitimate, illicit, improper, iniquitous, lawless, nefarious, outlawed, prohibited, taboo, unauthorized, under-the-counter*, unlicensed, wrongful; SEE CONCEPT 319

unlike [adj] *different*

apples and oranges*, clashing, conflicting, contradictory, contrary, contrasted, discordant, disharmonious, disparate, dissimilar, dissonant, distant, distinct, divergent, diverse, far cry from*, heterogeneous, hostile, incompatible, incongruous, inconsistent, mismatched, not alike, offbeat, opposed, opposite, poles apart*, separate, unalike, unequal, unrelated, variant, various, weird; SEE CONCEPT 564

unlikely [adj] *not probable*

absurd, contrary, doubtful, dubious, faint, implausible, improbable, inconceivable, incredible, not likely, out of the ordinary, outside chance, questionable, rare, remote, slight, strange, unbelievable, unconvincing, unheard-of, unimaginable, untoward; SEE CONCEPT 552

unlimited [adj] *extensive, complete*

absolute, all-encompassing, all-out*, boundless, countless, endless, full, full-blown*, full-out*, full-scale, great, illimitable, immeasurable, immense, incalculable, incomprehensible, indefinite, infinite, interminable, limitless, measureless, no end of*, no end to*, no strings*, numberless, total, totalitarian, unbounded, unconditional, unconfined, unconstrained, unfathomed, unfettered, universal, unqualified, unrestrained, unrestricted, untold, vast, wide open; SEE CONCEPT 772

unload [v] *take off; empty*

break bulk, cast, clear out, disburden, discharge, discommode, disencumber, disgorge, dump, get rid of, jettison, lighten, off-load, relieve, remove, rid, slough, take a load off, unburden, unlade, unpack, void; SEE CONCEPTS 180,211

unlucky [adj] *unfortunate, doomed*

afflicted, bad break*, behind eight ball*, black, calamitous, cataclysmic, catastrophic, cursed, dire, disastrous, down on luck*, hapless, hard luck, ill-fated, ill-starred, inauspicious, luckless, miserable, out of luck, star-crossed*, tough luck, tragic, unfavorable, unhappy, unsuccessful, untimely, untoward; SEE CONCEPTS 529,548

unmarried [adj] *not presently wed*

bachelor, eligible, husbandless, single, sole, spouseless, unattached, uncoupled, unwed, unwedded, widowed, wifeless; SEE CONCEPT 555

unmerciful [adj] *cruel*

bestial, bloodthirsty, brutal, coldhearted, hard,

heartless, hurtful, implacable, inhumane, merciless, monstrous, pitiless, relentless, remorseless, ruthless, tyrannous, uncaring, unfeeling, unpitying, unrelenting, unsparing, vengeful, vindictive; SEE CONCEPT 401

unmistakable [adj] *certain, definite*

apparent, clear, conspicuous, decided, distinct, evident, explicit, for certain, glaring, indisputable, manifest, no ifs and or buts*, obvious, open and shut*, palpable, patent, plain, positive, pronounced, self-explanatory, straightforward, sure, transparent, unambiguous, unequivocal, univocal; SEE CONCEPT 535

unmitigated [adj] *absolute, pure*

arrant, austere, clear-cut, complete, consummate, damned, downright, gross, intense, oppressive, out-and-out*, outright, perfect, persistent, rank, relentless, rigid, severe, sheer, simple, straightout*, thorough, thoroughgoing, unabated, unabridged, unadulterated, unalleviated, unbending, unbroken, undiluted, unmixed, unqualified, unrelieved, utter; SEE CONCEPTS 531,535,569

unnatural [adj] *not regular; artificial*

aberrant, abnormal, affected, anomalous, assumed, bizarre, concocted, contrary, contrived, ersatz*, extraordinary, fabricated, factitious, false, feigned, forced, freakish, freaky, imitation, incredible, insincere, irregular, labored, made-up*, make-believe*, odd, outlandish, outrageous, perverse, perverted, phony, preposterous, pseudo*, put-on*, queer, staged, stiff, stilted*, strained, strange, studied, supernatural, synthetic, theatrical, unaccountable, uncanny, unconforming, unorthodox, unusual; SEE CONCEPTS 564,582

unnecessary [adj] *not required*

accidental, additional, avoidable, beside the point*, casual, causeless, chance, dispensable, excess, exorbitant, expendable, extraneous, extrinsic, fortuitous, futile, gratuitous, haphazard, inessential, irrelevant, lavish, needless, noncompulsory, nonessential, optional, prodigal, profuse, random, redundant, supererogatory, superfluous, surplus, uncalled-for, uncritical, undesirable, unessential, unneeded, unrequired, useless, wanton, worthless; SEE CONCEPT 546

unnerve [v] *upset, intimidate*

agitate, bewilder, bowl over*, buffalo*, chill*, confound, daunt, demoralize, disarm, discombobulate, disconcert, discourage, dishearten, dismay, dispirit, distract, enervate, enfeeble, floor*, fluster, frighten, get to*, give a turn*, intimidate, needle*, perturb, psych out*, rattle, ride, sap*, shake, spook, throw, throw off*, uncalm, undermine, unhinge, unsettle, weaken; SEE CONCEPTS 7,14,19

unnoticed [adj] *ignored*

disregarded, glossed over, hidden, inconspicuous, neglected, overlooked, passed by, pushed aside, secret, unconsidered, undiscovered, unheeded, unobserved, unobtrusive, unperceived, unrecognized, unremarked, unremembered, unrespected, unseen, winked at; SEE CONCEPT 529

unobtrusive [adj] *keeping a low profile*

humble, inconspicuous, low-key, low-profile, meek, modest, quiet, reserved, restrained, retiring, self-effacing, soft-pedaled*, subdued, tasteful, unassuming, unnoticeable, unostentatious, unpretentious; SEE CONCEPTS 401,548

unorthodox [adj] *abnormal; other than accepted*

beatnik*, crazy*, different, dissident, eccentric,

un
un

far-out, flaky*, heretical, heterodox, irregular, kinky*, nonconformist, off the beaten path*, schismatic, sectarian, unconventional, uncustomary, unusual, unwonted, way-out*, weird*; SEE CONCEPT 564

unpaid [*adj1*] *free, voluntary*
contributed, donated, due, freewilled, gratuitous, honorary, unindemnified, unrewarded, unsalaried, volunteer; SEE CONCEPT 538

unpaid [*adj2*] *not settled; taken without remuneration*
delinquent, due, in arrears, mature, not discharged, outstanding, overdue, owing, past due, payable, undefrayed, unliquidated, unsettled; SEE CONCEPT 334

unparalleled [*adj*] *superlative*
all-time*, alone, beyond compare, champ*, champion, consummate, exceptional, greatest, incomparable, matchless, most, nonpareil, only, peerless, rare, single, singular, solid gold*, ten*, tops*, unequaled, unique, unmatched, unprecedented, unrivaled, unsurpassed, winner, without equal, world-class*; SEE CONCEPT 574

unpleasant [*adj*] *bad*
abhorrent, bad news*, bad scene*, disagreeable, displeasing, distasteful, fierce, grody*, gross, hard-time*, icky*, irksome, lousy, nasty, objectionable, obnoxious, poisonous, repulsive, rotten, sour, troublesome, unacceptable, unattractive, uncool*, undesirable, unhappy, unlikable, unlovely, unpalatable, yucky*; SEE CONCEPTS 529,570

unpopular [*adj*] *not liked or sought after*
abhorred, avoided, creepy*, despised, detested, disesteemed, disfavored, disliked, drip*, dumpy*, execrated, gross*, loathed, loser*, lousy, nerdy*, obnoxious, ostracized, out, out of favor, rejected, scorned, shunned, unaccepted, unattractive, uncared for, undesirable, unloved, unvalued, unwanted, unwelcome, weird, wimpy*; SEE CONCEPTS 529,555

unprecedented [*adj*] *exceptional, original*
aberrant, abnormal, anomalous, bizarre, eccentric, exotic, extraordinary, fantastic, freakish, idiosyncratic, marvelous, miraculous, modern, new, newfangled, novel, odd, outlandish, out-of-the-way*, outré, preternatural, prodigious, remarkable, signal, singular, sui generis, uncommon, unexampled, unheard-of, unique, unparalleled, unrivaled, unusual; SEE CONCEPTS 549,564,574

unpredictable [*adj*] *changeable*
capricious, chance, chancy, dicey*, doubtful, erratic, fickle, fluctuating, fluky*, from left field*, hanging by a thread*, iffy*, incalculable, inconstant, random, touch and go*, touchy, uncertain, unforeseeable, unreliable, unstable, up for grabs*, variable, whimsical; SEE CONCEPT 534

unprejudiced [*adj*] *fair*
balanced, dispassionate, equal, equitable, evenhanded, fair-minded, impartial, just, liberal, nondiscriminatory, nonpartisan, objective, open-minded, straight, unbiased, unbigoted, uncolored, uninfluenced; SEE CONCEPTS 319,401,542

unpretentious [*adj*] *simple, honest*
discreet, down, down home*, easy-going, folksy*, free-spirited, homey*, humble, inelaborate, laid-back*, lowly, modest, plain, prosaic, straightforward, unaffected, unambitious, unassuming, unbeautified, uncomplex, unembellished, unimposing, unobtrusive, unostentatious, unpresumptuous, unspoiled, up front; SEE CONCEPTS 401,404

unprincipled [*adj*] *corrupt*
abandoned, amoral, bent*, cheating, conscienceless, crooked, deceitful, devious, dirty-dealing*, dishonest, dissolute, double-crossing*, double-dealing*, immoral, licentious, mercenary, praetorian, profligate, reprobate, shady, sly, stop-at-nothing*, tricky, two-faced*, two-timing*, unconscionable, underhand, unethical, unprofessional, unscrupulous, venal, wanton; SEE CONCEPT 545

unprofessional [*adj*] *not done well or skillfully*
amateur, amateurish, ignorant, improper, inadequate, incompetent, inefficient, inexperienced, inexpert, lax, negligent, nonexpert, unethical, unfitting, unsuitable, untrained, unworthy; SEE CONCEPTS 527,538

unqualified [*adj1*] *not prepared, incompetent*
amateur, bush, bush-league*, disqualified, ill-equipped, inadequate, incapable, incompetent, ineligible, inexperienced, not equal to, not up to*, unequipped, unfit, unfitted, unprepared, unskilled; SEE CONCEPT 527

unqualified [*adj2*] *outright, absolute*
abiding, blasted, blessed, categorical, certain, clear, complete, confounded, consummate, downright, enduring, entire, explicit, express, firm, flat out*, infernal, never-failing, no catch*, no ifs ands or buts*, out-and-out*, perfect, positive, rank, sheer, simple, steadfast, steady, sure, thorough, thoroughgoing, total, unadulterated, unalloyed, unconditional, unfaltering, unlimited, unmitigated, unreserved, unrestrained, unrestricted, utter, wholehearted, without reservation; SEE CONCEPTS 531,535

unquestionable [*adj*] *definite; beyond doubt*
absolute, accurate, authentic, bona fide*, certain, clear, cold, conclusive, dependable, down pat*, downright, established, faultless, flat*, flawless, for certain, genuine, incontestable, incontrovertible, indisputable, indubitable, irrefutable, manifest, no ifs ands or buts*, obvious, pat, patent, perfect, positive, real, reliable, self-evident, superior, sure, sure-enough, true, undeniable, undisputable, undoubted, unequivocal, unimpeachable, unmistakable, veritable, well-founded, well-grounded; SEE CONCEPTS 529,535

unreal [*adj*] *fake, make-believe; hypothetical*
aerial, artificial, chimerical, delusive, dreamlike, fabled, fabulous, false, fanciful, fictitious, fictive, figmental, hallucinatory, ideal, illusory, imaginary, imagined, immaterial, impalpable, insincere, insubstantial, intangible, invented, legendary, misleading, mock, mythical, nebulous, nonexistent, notional, ostensible, phantasmagoric*, pretended, reachy, romantic, seeming, sham*, storybook*, suppositious, supposititious, theoretical, unbelievable, unsubstantial, visionary; SEE CONCEPT 582

unrealistic [*adj*] *not believable or practical*
blue sky*, floating, gone*, half-baked*, impossible, impracticable, impractical, improbable, ivory-tower*, nonrealistic, nonsensical, not applicable, not sensible, on cloud nine*, quixotic, reachy, romantic, silly, starry-eyed, theoretical, unreal, unworkable; SEE CONCEPTS 552,560

unreasonable [*adj1*] *not logical or sensible*
absurd, all wet*, arbitrary, biased, capricious, contradictory, erratic, fallacious, far-fetched,

foolish, full of hot air*, headstrong, illogical, incoherent, incongruous, inconsequential, inconsistent, invalid, irrational, loose, mad, nonsensical, off the wall*, opinionated, preposterous, quirky, reasonless, senseless, silly, stupid, thoughtless, unreasoned, vacant, wrong; SEE CONCEPTS 401,548

unreasonable [adj2] *extravagant; beyond normal limits*

absonant, arbitrary, costing an arm and a leg*, dear, excessive, exorbitant, extortionate, extreme, far-out*, illegitimate, immoderate, improper, inordinate, intemperate, out of bounds*, overkill*, overmuch, peremptory, posh, pricey*, senseless, steep*, stiff*, too great, too much, too-too*, uncalled-for*, unconscionable, undue, unfair, unjust, unjustifiable, unlawful, unrightful, unwarrantable, unwarranted, up to here*, way out*, wrongful; SEE CONCEPTS 334,762,771

unrelated [adj] *independent; different*

beside the point*, dissimilar, extraneous, inapplicable, inappropriate, irrelative, irrelevant, mismatched, nongermane, not germane, not kin, not kindred, not related, separate, unassociated, unattached, unconnected, unlike; SEE CONCEPTS 563,564

unrelenting [adj] *merciless*

bound, bound and determined, brick-wall*, ceaseless, constant, continual, continuous, cruel, dead set on*, endless, grim, hanging tough*, hardheaded*, implacable, incessant, inexorable, intransient, iron-fisted*, mortal, perpetual, persistent, pitiless, relentless, remorseless, rigid, ruthless, set, steady, stern, stiff, stiff-necked*, tenacious, tough, unabated, unbending, unbroken, unflinching, unremitting, unsparing, unwavering, unyielding; SEE CONCEPTS 401,548,798

unreliable [adj] *not trustworthy, not true*

capricious, deceitful, deceptive, delusive, disreputable, dubious, erroneous, fake, fallible, false, fickle, fly-by-night*, furtive, hallucinatory, hollow, implausible, inaccurate, inconstant, irresponsible, makeshift, meretricious, mistaken, pretended, pseudo*, questionable, sham, shifty, specious, treacherous, tricky, uncertain, unconvincing, undependable, underhand, underhanded, unfaithful, unsound, unstable, unsure, untrue, untrustworthy, vacillating, wavering, weak; SEE CONCEPTS 542,552,587

unresolved [adj] *uncertain; not settled*

betwixt and between*, changing, doubtful, faltering, hesitant, hesitating, hot and cold*, incomplete, indecisive, irresolute, moot, open to question*, pending, problematical, pussyfooting*, unanswered, unconcluded, undecided, undetermined, unfinished, unsettled, unsolved, up in the air*, vacillating, vague, waffling; SEE CONCEPTS 529,534

unrest [n] *state of agitation; disturbance*

altercation, anarchy, annoyance, anxiety, bickering, bother, chagrin, change, confusion, contention, controversy, crisis, debate, disaffection, discontent, discord, disease, disquiet, dissatisfaction, dissension, distress, dither*, ennui, grief, insurrection, irritation, malaise, moodiness, mortification, perplexity, perturbation, protest, quarrel, rebellion, restlessness, sedition, sorrow, strife, tension, tizzy*, trouble, tumult, turmoil, unease, uneasiness, uproar, upset, vexation, worry; SEE CONCEPTS 410,674

unruly [adj] *disobedient*

assertive, bawdy, disorderly, drunken, forward, fractious, headstrong, heedless, impervious, impetuous, imprudent, impulsive, incorrigible, inexorable, insubordinate, intemperate, intractable, lawless, mean, mutinous, obstreperous, opinionated, ornery, out of control, out of line*, perverse, quarrelsome, rash, rebellious, recalcitrant, reckless, refractory, restive, riotous, rowdy, turbulent, uncontrollable, ungovernable, unmanageable, unyielding, violent, wayward, wild, willful; SEE CONCEPT 401

unsafe [adj] *dangerous*

alarming, chancy, erratic, explosive, fearsome, hanging by a thread*, hazardous, insecure, on a limb*, on thin ice*, perilous, precarious, risky, shaky, slippery, threatening, ticklish*, touch and go*, touchy*, treacherous, uncertain, independable, unreliable, unsound, unstable, untrustworthy; SEE CONCEPT 587

unsaid [adj] *not expressed or partially expressed*

implicit, implied, inferred, left to the imagination*, silenced, tacit, undeclared, understood, unexpressed, unspoken, unstated, unuttered, unvoiced, wordless; SEE CONCEPT 267

unsatisfactory [adj] *insufficient, inadequate*

amiss, bad, damaged, deficient, disappointing, disconcerting, displeasing, disquieting, distressing, disturbing, for the birds*, junky*, lame, mediocre, no good, not good enough, not up to par*, offensive, poor, regrettable, rotten, schlocky*, second, thin, unacceptable, undesirable, unsuitable, unwelcome, unworthy, upsetting, vexing, weak, wrong; SEE CONCEPTS 529,558,570

unsavory [adj] *revolting, sickening*

acid, bitter, bland, disagreeable, distasteful, dull, flavorless, gross*, icky*, insipid, lousy, nasty, nauseating, no good*, objectionable, obnoxious, offensive, rancid, rank, raunchy*, repellent, repugnant, repulsive, rough, sad, shady, sharp, shifty, sour, stinking, tart, tasteless, tough, unappetizing, unpalatable, unpleasant, wrong; SEE CONCEPTS 462,571,613

unscathed [adj] *not hurt*

in one piece*, safe, sound, unharmed, unhurt, uninjured, unmarked, unscarred, unscratched, untouched, whole; SEE CONCEPT 314

unscrupulous [adj] *immoral*

arrant, base, casuistic, conscienceless, corrupt, crafty, crooked, deceitful, degraded, degrading, disgraceful, dishonest, dishonorable, exploitative, illegal, improper, low-down*, mercenary, perfidious, petty, questionable, recreant, ruthless, scandalous, scheming, selfish, self-seeking, shady, shameless, shifty, sinister, slippery, sly, two-faced*, unconscientious, unconscionable, underhand, underhanded, unethical, unfair, unprincipled, unworthy, venal, wicked, wrongful; SEE CONCEPTS 401,545

unseemly [adj] *improper; in bad taste*

cheap, coarse, crude, discreditable, disreputable, inappropriate, inapt, incorrect, indecent, indecorous, indelicate, inelegant, inept, in poor taste, malapropos, malodorous, out of keeping, out of place, poor, raffish, rough, rowdy, rude, ruffian, tawdry, unapt, unbecoming, unbefitting, undignified, ungodly, unrefined, unsuitable, untoward, vulgar, wrong; SEE CONCEPTS 401,558

unseen [adj] *hidden*

concealed, curtained, dark, imaginary, imagined,

impalpable, impenetrable, imperceptible, inconspicuous, invisible, lurking, not in sight, obscure, occult, out of sight, shrouded, undetected, undiscovered, unnoticed, unobserved, unobtrusive, unperceived, unsuspected, veiled; SEE CONCEPT 576

unselfish [adj] kind, giving
altruistic, benevolent, charitable, chivalrous, denying, devoted, disinterested, extroverted, generous, helpful, humanitarian, incorruptible, indulgent, liberal, loving, magnanimous, noble, open-handed, self-effacing, self-forgetting, selfless, self-sacrificing; SEE CONCEPTS 401,404

unsettle [v] bother, upset
agitate, confuse, dement, derange, disarrange, disarray, discommode, discompose, disconcert, disorder, disorganize, displace, disquiet, disrupt, disturb, down, flurry, fluster, fuddle, get to*, jumble, needle, perturb, psych out*, put off, rattle, ruffle, rummage, sicken, spook, throw, throw off*, trouble, turn, unbalance, unhinge*, unnerve; SEE CONCEPTS 7,19,242

unsettled [adj1] bothered, upset
active, agitated, antsy*, anxious, busy, changeable, changeful, changing, complex, complicated, confused, disorderly, disturbed, explosive, fidgety, fluid, flustered, inconstant, insecure, kinetic, mobile, mutable, on edge*, perilous, perturbed, precarious, rattled, restive, restless, shaken, shaky, shifting, shook up*, tense, thrown, ticklish, troubled, unbalanced, uncertain, uneasy, unnerved, unpeaceful, unpredictable, unquiet, unrestful, unstable, unsteady, variable, wavering, wobbling; SEE CONCEPTS 401,403

unsettled [adj2] not decided, taken care of
betwixt and between*, clouded*, debatable, doubtful, dubious, dubitable, due, immature, in arrears, moot, open, outstanding, overdue, owing, payable, pendent, pending, problematic, uncertain, unclear, undecided, undetermined, unfixed, unpaid, unresolved, up for grabs*, waffling; SEE CONCEPTS 334,535

unsightly [adj] not pretty
deformed, disagreeable, drab, dull, hideous, homely, horrid, lackluster, repulsive, revolting, ugly, unattractive, unpleasant, unprepossessing, unshapely; SEE CONCEPT 579

unsociable [adj] unfriendly
aloof, antagonistic, brooding, cold, cool, distant, easy-going, hostile, inaccessible, inhospitable, introverted, laid-back*, nongregarious, recessive, reclusive, reserved, retiring, secretive, sensitive, shy, standoffish*, stuck-up*, timid, unapproachable, unbending, uncommunicative, uncongenial, unforthcoming, unneighborly, unsocial, uppity*, withdrawn; SEE CONCEPTS 401,555

unsolicited [adj] unasked for
free, freewilled, gratis*, gratuitous, offered, spontaneous, uncalled-for*, undesirable, undesired, unforced, uninvited, unrequested, unsought, unwelcome, voluntary, volunteered; SEE CONCEPT 538

unsophisticated [adj] natural, simple
artless, authentic, bush-league*, callow, childlike, clean, cornball*, corny*, crude, folksy, genuine, green*, guileless, homey*, inexperienced, ingenuous, innocent, kid*, naive, plain, pure, raw, rookie, straightforward, unadulterated, unaffected, unartificial, uncomplicated, uninvolved,

unrefined, unschooled, unstudied, untutored, unworldly, wide-eyed*; SEE CONCEPTS 401,548, 562

unsound [adj] not well; flimsy
ailing, crazed, dangerous, decrepit, defective, delicate, demented, deranged, diseased, erroneous, fallacious, false, faulty, flawed, fragile, frail, ill, illogical, inaccurate, incongruous, incorrect, infirm, in poor health, insane, insecure, insubstantial, invalid, lunatic, mad, not solid, rickety, shaky, specious, tottering, unbacked, unbalanced, unhealthy, unhinged, unreliable, unsafe, unstable, unsteady, unsubstantial, unwell, weak, wobbly; SEE CONCEPTS 314,403,587

unspeakable [adj] very bad; beyond description
abominable, alarming, appalling, atrocious, awful, beastly, beyond words, calamitous, detestable, dire, disgusting, dreadful, evil, execrable, fearful, frightening, frightful, heinous, horrible, horrid, incommunicable, inconceivable, indefinable, indescribable, ineffable, inexpressible, inhuman, loathsome, monstrous, nameless, obnoxious, odious, offensive, outrageous, overwhelming, preternatural, repellent, repugnant, repulsive, revolting, shocking, unbelievable, unimaginable, unutterable; SEE CONCEPTS 548,571

unstable/unsteady [adj] doubtful, weak
ambiguous, borderline, capricious, changeable, dizzy, dubious, erratic, fickle, fitful, fluctuating, giddy, inconsistent, inconstant, insecure, irrational, lubricious, mercurial, mobile, movable, moving, mutable, not fixed, precarious, rickety, risky, rocky, sensitive, shaky, shifty, slippery, suspect, teetering, temperamental, ticklish, tricky, uncertain, unpredictable, unsettled, unsteady, untrustworthy, vacillating, variable, volatile, wavering, weaving, wiggly, wobbly; SEE CONCEPTS 488,534,542

unsuitable [adj] not proper, inappropriate
clashing, disagreeable, discordant, discrepant, disparate, disproportionate, dissident, dissonant, ill-suited, improper, inadequate, inadmissible, inapposite, inappropriate, inapt, incompatible, incongruous, inconsistent, ineligible, infelicitous, inharmonious, interfering, irrelevant, jarring, malapropos, out of character*, out of keeping, out of place, senseless, unacceptable, unbecoming, unbefitting, uncalled-for, undue, unfit, unfitting, unmatched, unseasonable, unseemly, unsuited; SEE CONCEPT 558

unsure [adj] doubtful, insecure
betwixt and between*, borderline, distrustful, dubious, fluctuant, fly-by-night*, hesitant, iffy*, in a quandary, indecisive, indeterminate, irresolute, lacking, mistrustful, open, problematic, rootless, shaky, skeptical, suspicious, touch and go*, unassured, uncertain, unclear, unconfident, unconvinced, undecided, undependable, unreliable, unstable, untrustworthy, untrusty, up for grabs*, vacillating, wavering, weak, wimpy*, wobbly; SEE CONCEPT 535

unsuspecting [adj] gullible
confiding, credulous, easy, inexperienced, ingenuous, innocent, naive, off guard*, simple, swallowing, taken in*, trustful, trusting, unconscious, undoubting, unsuspicious, unwarned, unwary; SEE CONCEPTS 401,404

unsympathetic [adj] without agreement in feeling
aloof, antipathetic, apathetic, aversive, callous,

cold, cold-blooded, cool, cruel, disinterested, frigid, halfhearted, hard, harsh, heartless, icy, indifferent, insensitive, lukewarm*, mean, nasty, obdurate, repellent, repugnant, stony, tough, uncompassionate, unconcerned, uncongenial, unemotional, unfeeling, unkind, unmoved, unpitying, unpleasant, unresponsive; SEE CONCEPTS *401,542*

untangle [v] *straighten out*
clear up, disembroil, disencumber, disentangle, explain, extricate, put in order, solve, unravel, unscramble, unsnarl, untwist, unweave; SEE CONCEPT *126*

unthinkable [adj] *incredible, unusual*
absurd, beyond belief, beyond possibility, exceptional, extraordinary, illogical, implausible, impossible, improbable, incogitable, inconceivable, insupportable, outlandish, out of the question*, preposterous, rare, singular, unbelievable, uncommon, unimaginable, unique, unlikely, unordinary, unreasonable; SEE CONCEPTS *564,582*

unthinking [adj] *careless*
blundering, brutish, feckless, foolish, heedless, impulsive, inadvertent, inconsiderate, indelicate, insensitive, instinctive, mechanical, napping, negligent, oblivious, outrageous, rash, rude, selfish, senseless, tactless, thoughtless, uncaring, unconscious, undiplomatic, unheeding, unintended, unmeant, unmindful, unpremeditated, unreasoning, untactful, unwise, vacant, witless; SEE CONCEPT *401*

untidy [adj] *dirty, disorderly*
bedraggled, careless, chaotic, cluttered, disarranged, disarrayed, disheveled, dowdy*, frowzy*, in disorder, jumbled, littered, mess, messy, mixed up*, muddled, rumpled, slapdash*, slipshod*, sloppy, slovenly, snarled, tacky*, tangled, topsy-turvy, tousled, uncombed, unfastidious, unkempt, unneat, unorderly, unsettled, upset; SEE CONCEPTS *589,621*

until [prep] *just before*
as far as, before, before the coming, continuously, down to, in advance of, in expectation, prior to, till, to, up till, up to; SEE CONCEPT *820*

untimely [adj] *inappropriate*
a bit previous*, abortive, anachronistic, awkward, badly timed, bright and early*, disagreeable, early, early bird*, early on, ill-timed, improper, inappropriate, inauspicious, inconvenient, inexpedient, inopportune, intrusive, malapropos, mistimed, out-of-date, overearly, oversoon, premature, previous, soon, too early, too late, undue, unfavorable, unfit, unfortunate, unlucky, unpropitious, unseasonable, unseemly, unsuitable, unsuited, wrong; SEE CONCEPTS *548,799*

untiring [adj] *determined, persevering*
constant, continued, continuing, dedicated, devoted, dogged, eager beaver*, fireball*, firm, go-go*, grind*, hyper*, incessant, indefatigable, indomitable, inexhaustible, jumping, patient, perky, persistent, pertinacious, plodding, plugging, resolute, staunch, steady, strong, tenacious, tireless, unceasing, undeterred, unfailing, unfaltering, unflagging, unflinching, unremitting, unstinted, unswerving, unwavering, unwearied; SEE CONCEPT *538*

untold [adj] *very many; enormous*
beyond measure, countless, gigantic, hidden, huge, immense, incalculable, indescribable, inexpressible, innumerable, innumerous, mammoth,

manifold, many, measureless, mighty, monstrous, multiple, multitudinous, myriad, numberless, private, prodigious, staggering, suppressed, titanic, uncountable, uncounted, undreamed of, unexpressed, unimaginable, unknown, unnumberable, unnumbered, unspeakable, unthinkable, vast; SEE CONCEPTS *529,762,781*

untouched [adj] *whole; not spoiled*
clear, entire, flawless, fresh, good, immaculate, incorrupt, indifferent, in good condition, intact, out of danger, perfect, pure, safe and sound*, sanitary, secure, shipshape, sound, spotless, unaffected, unblemished, unbroken, unconcerned, undamaged, unharmed, unhurt, unimpressed, uninjured, unmarred, unmoved, unscathed, unstained, unstirred, untried, virgin, virginal, without a scratch; SEE CONCEPTS *403,485,621*

untoward [adj1] *troublesome*
adverse, annoying, awkward, contrary, disastrous, disturbing, fractious, hapless, ill-starred, inauspicious, inconvenient, indocile, inimical, inopportune, intractable, irritating, luckless, misfortunate, perverse, recalcitrant, refractory, starcrossed, undisciplined, unfavorable, unfortunate, ungovernable, unhappy, unlucky, unmanageable, unpliable, unpropitious, unruly, untimely, unyielding, vexatious, wild; SEE CONCEPTS *542,548,570*

untoward [adj2] *improper; not suitable*
improprietous, inappropriate, indecent, indecorous, indelicate, malodorous, out of place*, rough*, unbecoming, uncouth, unfitting, ungodly*, unseemly; SEE CONCEPTS *401,558*

untroubled [adj] *calm, peaceful*
composed, cool, halcyon, hushed, placid, quiet, serene, steady, still, tranquil, unagitated, unconcerned, undisturbed, unflappable, unflustered, unperturbed, unruffled, unstirred, unworried; SEE CONCEPTS *403,548,594*

untrue [adj] *dishonest*
apocryphal, cheating, counterfactual, deceitful, deceptive, delusive, deviant, disloyal, dissembling, distorted, erroneous, faithless, fallacious, false, fictitious, forsworn, hollow, imprecise, inaccurate, inconstant, incorrect, inexact, lying, meretricious, misleading, mistaken, off*, out of line*, perfidious, perjured, prevaricating, recreant, sham*, specious, spurious, traitorous, treacherous, two-faced*, unfaithful, unloyal, unsound, untrustworthy, untruthful, wide, wrong; SEE CONCEPTS *267,545,582*

untrustworthy [adj] *not dependable, unfaithful*
capricious, conniving, crooked, deceitful, devious, dishonest, disloyal, dubious, fair-weather*, faithless, false, fickle, fink*, fly-by-night*, guileful, irresponsible, questionable, shady, sharp, shifty*, slippery, sneaky, treacherous, tricky, trustless, two-faced*, two-timing*, unassured, undependable, unfaithful, unreliable, unsafe, unsure, untrue, untrusty; SEE CONCEPTS *401,542,545*

unusual [adj] *different*
abnormal, amazing, astonishing, atypical, awe-inspiring, awesome, bizarre, conspicuous, curious, different, distinguished, eminent, exceptional, extraordinary, far-out*, inconceivable, incredible, memorable, noteworthy, odd, out of the ordinary*, outstanding, phenomenal, prodigious, prominent, queer, rare, refreshing, remarkable, significant, singular, something else*,

un
un

special, strange, surprising, uncommon, unconventional, unexpected, unfamiliar, unique, unparalleled, unwonted, weird*; SEE CONCEPT 564

unusually [adv] extremely
almighty*, awful*, awfully, curiously, especially, extra, extraordinarily, mighty, oddly, peculiarly, plenty, powerful, rarely, real, really, remarkably, right, so, so much, strangely, surprisingly, terribly, terrifically, too much, uncommon, uncommonly, very; SEE CONCEPTS 544,569

unvarnished [adj] plain, honest
bare, candid, clean, folksy*, for real*, frank, genuine, homey*, naked, open, open and shut*, pure, pure and simple*, simple, sincere, stark, straight, straightforward, unadorned, unconcealed, undisguised, undissembled, unembellished, vanilla*; SEE CONCEPTS 267,582

unveil [v] reveal
bare, betray, bring to light*, come out, disclose, discover, display, divulge, expose, give away, lay bare*, lay open*, let it all hang out*, make known, make public, open, open up, show, spring, tell, tip one's hand*, unbosom, uncover; SEE CONCEPTS 60,138

unwarranted [adj] not reasonable or right
baseless, bottomless, foundationless, gratuitous, groundless, indefensible, inexcusable, uncalled-for, unconscionable, undue, unfair, unfounded, ungrounded, unjust, unjustifiable, unjustified, unprovoked, unreasonable, unwarrantable, wrong; SEE CONCEPTS 545,548,558

unwary [adj] thoughtless, heedless
brash, careless, credulous, hasty, ignorant, ill-advised, impetuous, imprudent, incautious, inconsiderate, indiscreet, negligent, rash, reckless, unadvised, unalert, uncircumspect, unguarded, unprepared, unsuspecting, unsuspicious, unvigilant, unwatchful; SEE CONCEPTS 401,403

unwavering [adj] consistent, unchanging
abiding, brick-wall*, dead set on*, dedicated, determined, enduring, firm, fixed, intense, never-failing, pat, regular, resolute, set, set in stone*, single-minded, solid, staunch, steadfast, steady, sure, undeviating, unfaltering, unflagging, unflappable, unqualified, unshakable, unshaken, unswerving, untiring; SEE CONCEPTS 488,535,542

unwelcome [adj] not wanted, desired
blackballed*, disagreeable, displeasing, distasteful, exceptionable, excess baggage*, excluded, ill-favored, inadmissible, left out in cold*, lousy, not in the picture*, objectionable, obnoxious, rejected, repellent, shut out, thankless, unacceptable, unasked, undesirable, uninvited, unpleasant, unpopular, unsought, unwanted, unwished-for; SEE CONCEPTS 529,555,570

unwieldy [adj] awkward, bulky
burdensome, clumsy, cumbersome, cumbrous, encumbering, gross, hefty, inconvenient, lumbering, massive, onerous, ponderous, uncontrollable, ungainly, unhandy, unmanageable, weighty; SEE CONCEPTS 562,781

unwilling [adj] not in the mood
afraid, against, against the grain*, averse, backward, begrudging, compelled, contrary, demurring, disinclined, disobliging, evasive, forced, grudging, hesitating, indisposed, indocile, involuntary, laggard, loath, malcontent, opposed, recalcitrant, refractory, reluctant, remiss, resistant, shrinking, shy, slack, slow, unaccommodating, uncheerful, uncooperative, uneager, unenthusias-

tic, uninclined, unobliging, unready, unwishful, wayward; SEE CONCEPTS 401,542

unwind [v1] undo, untangle
disentangle, free, loose, loosen, ravel, separate, slacken, unbend, uncoil, unfurl, unravel, unreel, unroll, untwine, untwist, unwrap; SEE CONCEPT 158

unwind [v2] relax
calm down*, ease off*, loosen up*, quiet down*, quieten, recline, rest, sit back*, slow down*, take a break*, take it easy*, wind down*; SEE CONCEPT 210

unwise [adj] stupid, irresponsible
childish, foolhardy, foolish, ill-advised, ill-considered, immature, impolitic, improvident, imprudent, inadvisable, inane, inappropriate, indiscreet, inept, injudicious, misguided, naive, rash, reckless, senseless, short-sighted, silly, thoughtless, undesirable, unfortunate, unintelligent, unsound, witless; SEE CONCEPTS 401, 402,548

unwitting [adj] without fully realizing
accidental, aimless, chance, comatose, forgetful, haphazard, ignorant, inadvertent, incognizant, inconversant, innocent, involuntary, numb, oblivious, senseless, unacquainted, unaware, unconscious, undesigned, unfamiliar, uninformed, uninstructed, unintended, unintentional, unknowing, unmeant, unmindful, unplanned, unsuspecting, unthinking; SEE CONCEPTS 401, 544,548

unworldly [adj1] spiritual
abstract, astral, celestial, daydreaming, daydreamy, dreamy, ethereal, extraterrestrial, fantastic, incorporeal, metaphysical, nonmaterialistic, otherworldly, religious, supersensory, transcendental, unearthly, unreal, visionary; SEE CONCEPTS 536,582

unworldly [adj2] not sophisticated; inexperienced
artless, babe in woods*, clean, corn-fed*, country, folksy*, green*, idealistic, ingenuous, innocent, naive, natural, raw*, simple, trusting, unaffected, unartificial, uncool, unschooled, unsophisticated, unstudied, wide-eyed*; SEE CONCEPTS 401,555,589

unworthy [adj] not of value
base, beneath, blamable, contemptible, degrading, disgraceful, dishonorable, disreputable, good-for-nothing, ignoble, improper, inappropriate, ineligible, inexcusable, no-account*, no-good*, not deserving, not fit, not good enough, nothing, not worth, offensive, out of place*, recreant, reprehensible, shameful, unbecoming, unbefitting, undeserving, unfit, unmerited, unseemly, unsuitable, valueless, vile, wretched, wrong; SEE CONCEPTS 404,558,571

unwritten [adj] understood
accepted, conventional, customary, oral, spoken, tacit, traditional, unformulated, unrecorded, unsaid, verbal, vocal, word-of-mouth; SEE CONCEPTS 267,533

unyielding [adj] steadfast, resolute
adamant, dead set on*, determined, firm, fixed, hard, hard-core*, hardheaded, hard-line*, hard-nosed*, headstrong*, immalleable, immovable, implacable, impliable, inexorable, inflexible, intractable, locked in, merciless, mulish, obdurate, obstinate, pertinacious, pigheaded*, refractory, relentless, resolute, rigid, ruthless, single-minded, solid, staunch, stiff, stiff-necked, stubborn, tough,

unbending, uncompliant, uncompromising, unmovable, unrelenting, unswayable, unwavering; SEE CONCEPTS *401,542*

upbeat [*adj*] *cheerful*
buoyant, cheery, encouraging, favorable, fond, happy, heartening, hopeful, optimistic, positive, promising, rosy, sanguine; SEE CONCEPTS *403,572*

update [*v*] *bring up to date*
amend, modernize, refresh, refurbish, rejuvenate, renew, renovate, restore, revise; SEE CONCEPT *244*

upheaval [*n*] *major change*
about-face*, alteration, cataclysm, catastrophe, clamor, commotion, convulsion, disaster, disorder, disruption, disturbance, eruption, explosion, ferment, flip-flop*, new ball-game*, new deal*, outbreak, outburst, outcry, overthrow, revolution, shakeout*, stirring, switch, temblor, tremor, tumult, turmoil, turnaround, upturn; SEE CONCEPT *230*

uphill [*adj1*] *going up*
acclivous, ascending, climbing, mounting, rising, skyward, sloping upward, toward summit, up, uprising; SEE CONCEPT *581*

uphill [*adj2*] *difficult, laborious*
arduous, effortful, exhausting, grueling, hard, labored, operose, punishing, rugged, strenuous, taxing, toilsome, tough, wearisome; SEE CONCEPTS *538,565*

uphold [*v*] *maintain, support*
advocate, aid, assist, back, back up, bolster, boost, brace, buoy up, buttress, carry, champion, confirm, countenance, defend, elevate, encourage, endorse, help, hoist, hold to, hold up one's end*, justify, pick up, promote, prop, raise, rear, second, shore up, side with, stand by, stick by, stick up for*, sustain, take up, upbear, uplift, upraise, uprear, vindicate; SEE CONCEPT *110*

upkeep [*n*] *maintenance*
budget, conservation, costs, expenditure, expenses, keep, outlay, overhead, preservation, price, repair, running, subsistence, support, sustenance, sustentation; SEE CONCEPTS *117,344*

upper [*adj1*] *above*
high, higher, loftier, more elevated, overhead, top, topmost, uppermost, upward; SEE CONCEPT *583*

upper [*adj2*] *superior*
beautiful, elevated, elite, eminent, greater, important, more important; SEE CONCEPTS *555,567*

uppermost [*adj1*] *top*
apical, culminating, highest, loftiest, most elevated, topmost, upmost; SEE CONCEPT *583*

uppermost [*adj2*] *most important; chief*
best, big, boss, dominant, executive, foremost, greatest, high-up*, leading, main, paramount, predominant, preeminent, primary, principal, supreme, the most*, tops*, winner, world-class*; SEE CONCEPTS *568,632*

upright [*adj1*] *straight-up*
cocked, on end, on end up, erect, on end, perpendicular, plumb, raised, sheer, standing, stand-up, steep, straight, upended, upstanding, upward, vertical; SEE CONCEPTS *581,583*

upright [*adj2*] *honorable, honest*
aboveboard, blameless, circumspect, conscientious, correct, equitable, ethical, exemplary, fair, faithful, good, high-minded, impartial, incorruptible, just, kosher*, legit*, moral, noble, princi-

pled, punctilious, pure, right, righteous, square, straight, straightforward, true, true-blue*, trustworthy, unimpeachable, up front*, virtuous; SEE CONCEPTS *404,545*

uprising [*n*] *disturbance*
insurgence, insurrection, mutiny, outbreak, rebellion, revolt, revolution, riot, upheaval; SEE CONCEPTS *106,674*

uproar [*n*] *commotion, pandemonium*
ado, babble, babel, bedlam, bickering, big scene*, brawl, broil*, bustle, chaos, clamor, clangor, clatter, confusion, din, disorder, flap*, fracas*, free-for-all*, furor, fuss, hassle, jangle, mayhem, melee, noise, outcry, racket, riot, roughhouse*, row, ruction, shivaree*, stink*, stir, strife, to-do*, turbulence, turmoil, violence; SEE CONCEPTS *46,65,106,674*

uproot [*v*] *destroy; rip out of a place*
abate, abolish, annihilate, blot out, demolish, deracinate, dig up, displace, do away with*, eliminate, eradicate, excavate, exile, exterminate, extirpate, extract, move, overthrow, overturn, pull up, remove, root out, tear up, weed, weed out, wipe out; SEE CONCEPTS *147,178,211,252*

upset [*n*] *problem*
agitation, bother, complaint, defeat, destruction, disorder, disquiet, distress, disturbance, free-for-all*, goulash*, hassle, illness, malady, overthrow, queasiness, reverse, reversion, screw-up*, shakeup*, shock, sickness, stew*, subversion, surprise, tizzy*, trouble, turmoil, worry; SEE CONCEPT *674*

upset [*adj*] *disturbed, bothered*
agitated, all torn up*, amazed, antsy*, apprehensive, blue*, broken up*, bummed out*, capsized, chaotic, come apart*, confused, disconcerted, dismayed, disordered, disquieted, distressed, disturbed, dragged*, frantic, grieved, hurt, ill, in disarray, jittery, jumpy, low, muddled, overturned, overwrought, psyched out*, rattled, ruffled*, shocked, shook up*, sick, spilled, thrown, tipped over*, toppled, troubled, tumbled, unglued*, unsettled, unzipped*, upside-down, worried; SEE CONCEPTS *403,485,570*

upset [*v1*] *disorder; knock over*
capsize, change, derange, disarray, disorganize, disturb, invert, jumble, keel over, mess up*, mix up, muddle, overset, overturn, pitch, put out of order, reverse, rummage, spill, spoil, subvert, tilt, tip over, topple, tumble, turn, turn inside-out*, turn topsy-turvy*, turn upside-down*, unsettle, upend, upturn; SEE CONCEPTS *147,208,213*

upset [*v2*] *bother, trouble*
adjy*, afflict, agitate, ail, bewilder, bug*, confound, cramp, craze, debilitate, derange, discombobulate*, discompose, disconcert, dismay, disquiet, distract, distress, disturb, egg on*, fire up*, flip*, flip out*, floor*, flurry, fluster, get to*, give a hard time*, grieve, incapacitate, indispose, key up*, lay up, make a scene*, make waves*, perturb, pick on*, pother, psych*, rattle, rock the boat*, ruffle, sicken, spook, stir up, throw off balance*, turn, turn on, unhinge*, unnerve, unsettle; SEE CONCEPTS *7,19*

upset [*v3*] *defeat*
beat, be victorious, conquer, get the better of*, outplay, overcome, overpower, overthrow, overturn, topple, triumph over, win; SEE CONCEPT *95*

upshot [*n*] *end result*
aftereffect, aftermath, burden, climax, completion, conclusion, consequence, core, culmination,

un
up

denouement, development, effect, end, ending, event, eventuality, finale, finish, gist, issue, meaning, meat*, outcome, payoff, pith*, purport, result, sense, sequel, substance, termination, thrust; SEE CONCEPTS 230,682

upside-down [adj] overturned, inverted
backward, bottom-side up, bottom up, confused, disordered, downside-up*, haywire*, helter-skelter* in chaos, in disarray, jumbled, mixed-up, on head, reversed, tangled, topsy-turvy*, upended, wrong-side-up, wrong way; SEE CONCEPT 583

upstanding [adj] honorable
ethical, good, honest, incorruptible, moral, principled, straightforward, true, trustworthy, upright; SEE CONCEPT 545

uptight [adj] nervous
anxious, apprehensive, cautious, concerned, conventional, edgy, nervy, old-fashioned, on edge*, on the defensive*, restive, strict, tense, troubled, uneasy, withdrawn, worried; SEE CONCEPT 401

up-to-date [adj] current, modern
abreast, advanced, à la mode*, all the rage*, au courant, avant-garde, brand-new, contemporary, cutting edge*, dashing, expedient, faddish*, fashionable, fitting, hot*, in, in fashion, in-thing*, in vogue, modernistic, modish, neoteric, new, newest, newfangled, now*, opportune, popular, red-hot*, state-of-the-art*, stylish, suitable, timely, today*, trendy, up*, up-to-the-minute, with it*; SEE CONCEPTS 578,589,797,799

urban [adj] city
burghal, central, citified, civic, civil, downtown, inner-city, metropolitan, municipal, nonrural, oppidan, popular, public, town, village; SEE CONCEPT 536

urbane [adj] civilized
affable, balanced, bland, civil, cosmopolitan, courteous, cultivated, cultured, debonair, elegant, genteel, gracious, mannerly, metropolitan, obliging, poised, polished, polite, refined, smooth, sophisticated, suave, well-bred, well-mannered; SEE CONCEPT 401

urchin [n] mischievous youngster
brat*, cub, dickens*, gamin, imp, juvenile delinquent, punk*, pup*, ragamuffin, waif; SEE CONCEPT 423

urge [n] very strong desire
appetite, appetition, compulsion, craving, drive, druthers, fancy, fire in belly*, goad, impetus, impulse, incentive, itch*, longing, lust, motive, passion, pressure, stimulant, stimulus, sweet tooth*, weakness, wish, yearning, yen; SEE CONCEPTS 20,532

urge [v] beg, push for, encourage
adjure, advance, advise, advocate, appeal to, ask, attract, beseech, champion, charge, commend, compel, conjure, counsel, countenance, drive, egg on*, endorse, entreat, exhort, favor, fire up*, force, further, goad, hasten, impel, implore, incite, induce, influence, insist on, inspire, instigate, maneuver, move, plead, press, promote, prompt, propel, propose, push, put up to*, rationalize, recommend, request, sanction, solicit, speak for, spur, stimulate, support, tempt, wheedle; SEE CONCEPTS 68,75

urgent [adj] needing immediate attention
burning*, called-for, capital, chief, clamant, clamorous, compelling, critical, crucial, crying*, demanded, demanding, driving, essential, exi-

gent, foremost, heavy*, hurry-up, immediate, impelling, imperative, important, importunate, indispensable, insistent, instant, leading, life and death*, momentous, necessary, paramount, persuasive, pressing, primary, principal, required, salient, serious, top-priority, touch and go*, touchy*, vital, wanted, weighty*; SEE CONCEPTS 548,568

usable [adj] available, working
accessible, adaptable, advantageous, applicable, at disposal, at hand, beneficial, consumable, convenient, current, employable, exhaustible, expendable, exploitable, fit, functional, good, helpful, in order, instrumental, open, operative, practicable, practical, profitable, ready, running, serviceable, subservient, unused, useful, utile, utilizable, valid, valuable, wieldy; SEE CONCEPTS 560,576

usage [n] habit, custom
acceptance, control, convention, currency, form, formula, habitude, handling, management, matter of course, method, mode, operation, practice, praxis, procedure, regime, regulation, rote, routine, rule, running, tradition, treatment, trick, use, way, wont; SEE CONCEPTS 6,658

use [n] application; employment
account, adoption, advantage, appliance, applicability, appropriateness, avail, benefit, call, capitalization, cause, convenience, custom, end, exercise, exercising, exertion, fitness, good, habit, handling, help, helpfulness, mileage, mobilization, necessity, need, object, occasion, operation, point, practice, profit, purpose, reason, relevance, service, serviceability, treatment, usability, usage, usefulness, utility, value, way, wear and tear*, wont, worth; SEE CONCEPTS 225,658,709

use [v] work with; consume
accept, adopt, apply, avail oneself of, bestow, bring into play*, bring to bear*, capitalize, control, do with, draw on, employ, exercise, exert, exhaust, expend, exploit, find a use, govern, handle, make do with*, make the most of*, make use, manage, manipulate, operate, play on, ply, practice, press into service*, put forth*, put into action, put to use, put to work, regulate, relate, run, run through, set in motion, spend, take advantage of*, turn to account, utilize, waste, wield, work; SEE CONCEPTS 169,225

useful [adj] beneficial, valuable
advantageous, all-purpose, applied, appropriate, brave, commodious, convenient, effective, favorable, fit, fruitful, functional, good, handy, helpful, instrumental, meet, of assistance, of service, of use, practicable, practical, pragmatic, profitable, proper, propitious, purposive, salutary, serviceable, subsidiary, suitable, suited, toward, utile, utilitarian, workaday, worthwhile; SEE CONCEPT 560

useless [adj] not working; not valuable
abortive, bootless, counterproductive, disadvantageous, dysfunctional, expendable, feckless, fruitless, futile, good-for-nothing*, hopeless, idle, impracticable, impractical, incompetent, ineffective, ineffectual, inept, inoperative, inutile, meaningless, no good, nonfunctional, of no use, pointless, profitless, purposeless, scrap, stupid*, unavailable, unavailing, unfunctional, unproductive, unprofitable, unpurposed, unusuable, un-

workable, vain, valueless, waste, weak, worthless; SEE CONCEPT 560

user-friendly [adj] *easily operated*
accessible, adaptable, convenient, easy to use, feasible, foolproof, handy, manageable, practical, simple, straightforward, uncomplicated, useful, wieldy; SEE CONCEPTS 560,576

usher [n] *person who guides others to place*
attendant, conductor, doorkeeper, doorperson, escort, guide, herald, lead, leader, page, pilot, precursor; SEE CONCEPT 352

usher [v] *guide*
bring in, conduct, direct, escort, herald, inaugurate, initiate, institute, introduce, launch, lead, marshal, open the door, originate, pave the way*, pilot, precede, preface, receive, set up, show around, show in, show out, steer; SEE CONCEPTS 187,221

usual [adj] *common, typical*
accepted, accustomed, average, chronic, commonplace, constant, conventional, current, customary, cut-and-dried*, everyday, expected, familiar, fixed, frequent, garden variety*, general, grind, habitual, mainstream, matter-of-course, natural, normal, ordinary, plain, plastic, prevailing, prevalent, quotidian, regular, rife, routine, run-of-the-mill*, so-so*, standard, stock, typic, unremarkable, vanilla*, white-bread*, wonted, workaday; SEE CONCEPTS 530,547

usually [adv] *for the most part*
as a rule, as is the custom, as is usual, as usual, by and large, commonly, consistently, customarily, frequently, generally, habitually, in the main, mainly, more often than not, mostly, most often, normally, now and again, now and then, occasionally, once and again, on the whole, ordinarily, regularly, routinely, sometimes; SEE CONCEPTS 530,541

usurp [v] *take over*
accroach, annex, appropriate, arrogate, assume, barge in*, butt in*, clap hands on*, commandeer, cut out, displace, elbow in*, get hands on*, grab, grab hold of, highjack*, infringe upon, lay hold of, muscle in*, preempt, seize, squeeze in, supplant, swipe, take, work in, worm in*, wrest; SEE CONCEPTS 142,384

utensil [n] *tool, usually for eating*
apparatus, appliance, contrivance, convenience, device, equipment, fork, gadget, implement, instrument, knife, silverware, spoon, tableware, ware; SEE CONCEPTS 493,499

utilitarian [adj] *practical*
commonsensical, down-to-earth, effective, efficient, functional, hard, hardheaded, matter-of-fact, nuts and bolts*, pragmatic, pragmatical, realistic, sensible, serviceable, unidealistic, unromantic, useful; SEE CONCEPT 560

utility [n] *serviceableness*
account, adequacy, advantage, advantageousness, applicability, appropriateness, avail, benefit, convenience, efficacy, efficiency, expediency, favor, fitness, function, point, practicality, productiveness, profit, relevance, service, serviceability, use, usefulness; SEE CONCEPT 658

utilize [v] *make use of*
advance, apply, appropriate, avail oneself of, bestow, employ, exercise, exploit, forward, further, handle, have recourse to, profit by, promote, put to use, resort to, take advantage of, turn to account, use; SEE CONCEPT 225

utmost [adj] *extreme, maximum*
absolute, all-out*, chief, complete, entire, exhaustive, farthest, final, full, furthermost, greatest, highest, last, last straw*, maximal, most, most distant, outermost, out of bounds*, outside, paramount, plenary, preeminent, remotest, sheer, supreme, thorough, thoroughgoing, too much*, too-too*, top, topmost, total, ultimate, ultra*, unconditional, undiminished, unlimited, unmitigated, unqualified, unreserved, uttermost, whole, worst case*; SEE CONCEPTS 531,574,772

utopia [n] *ideal place and life*
Arcadia, bliss, dreamland, dreamworld, Eden, Elysian Fields*, Erehwon*, fairyland, Garden of Eden, heaven, land of milk and honey*, never-never land*, paradise, perfection, pie in the sky*, promised land*, seventh heaven*, Shangri-La*, wonderland; SEE CONCEPTS 370,689

utopian [adj] *imaginary, ideal*
abstract, airy, ambitious, arcadian, chimerical, dream, fanciful, fantasy, grandiose, hopeful, idealist, idealistic, ideological, illusory, impossible, impractical, lofty, otherworldly, perfect, pie-in-the-sky*, pretentious, quixotic, romantic, transcendental, unfeasible, visionary; SEE CONCEPTS 572,574,582

utter [adj] *outright, absolute*
all-fired*, arrant, blasted*, blessed*, blooming*, complete, confounded, consummate, downright, entire, flat-out*, infernal, out-and-out*, perfect, pure, sheer, stark, straight-out*, thorough, thoroughgoing, total, unmitigated, unqualified; SEE CONCEPTS 531,535

utter [v] *say, reveal*
affirm, air, announce, articulate, assert, asseverate, blurt, bring out, chime, chin*, come out with*, declaim, declare, deliver, disclose, divulge, ejaculate, enunciate, exclaim, express, give words to*, go, jaw*, lip*, make known, modulate, mouth*, mutter, proclaim, promulgate, pronounce, publish, put into words, recite, say, shout, speak, spiel*, state, talk, throw out, verbalize, vocalize, voice, whisper; SEE CONCEPTS 47,55

utterance [n] *revelation*
announcement, articulation, assertion, asseveration, declaration, delivery, discourse, ejaculation, expression, opinion, oration, peroration, pronouncement, rant, recitation, remark, reply, response, saying, sentence, speaking, speech, spiel, statement, talk, vent, verbalization, vocalization, vociferation, voice, word, words; SEE CONCEPTS 47,278

utterly [adv] *completely*
absolutely, all, all in all, altogether, entirely, exactly, extremely, fully, in toto, just, perfectly, plumb*, purely, quite, thoroughly, totally, to the core*, to the nth degree*, well, wholly; SEE CONCEPT 531

uttermost [adj] *extreme*
farthest, final, furthermost, furthest, last, outermost, outmost, remotest, utmost; SEE CONCEPTS 585,778

V

vacancy [n] *opening*
abstraction, blankness, desertedness, emptiness, gap, job, lack, opportunity, position, post, room,

situation, space, vacuity, vacuousness, vacuum, void, voidness; SEE CONCEPTS 513,516,693

vacant [*adj1*] *empty; unoccupied*
abandoned, available, bare, clear, deserted, devoid, disengaged, free, idle, not in use, stark, tenantless, to let, unemployed, unengaged, unfilled, uninhabited, unlived in, untaken, untenanted, unused, void, without contents; SEE CONCEPTS 481,560,740,774

vacant [*adj2*] *absent-minded; expressionless*
abstracted, blank, daydreaming, deadpan, dreaming, dreamy, empty-headed*, foolish, idle, inane, incurious, inexpressive, silly, stupid, thoughtless, unexpressive, unintelligent, unthinking, vacuous, vapid, witless; SEE CONCEPT 402

vacate [*v*] *leave empty*
abandon, abrogate, annul, clear, depart, discharge, dissolve, empty, evacuate, give up, go away, leave, move out, move out of, part with, quash, quit, relinquish, renounce, rescind, retract, reverse, revoke, void, withdraw; SEE CONCEPTS 195,234

vacation [*n*] *planned time spent not working*
break, breathing space*, day of rest, few days off*, fiesta, furlough, holiday, intermission, layoff, leave, leave of absence, liberty, long weekend*, R and R*, recess, recreation, respite, rest, sabbatical, spell, time off, two weeks with pay*; SEE CONCEPTS 363,807

vaccinate [*v*] *give a shot to treat or prevent disease*
immunize, inject, inoculate, mitigate, prevent, protect, treat, variolate; SEE CONCEPT 310

vacillate [*v*] *go back and forth*
alternate, be indecisive, be irresolute, change, change mind, dither, fence-straddle*, fluctuate, hedge, hem and haw*, hesitate, hover, oscillate, pause, pussyfoot around*, reel, rock, run hot and cold*, seesaw*, shilly-shally*, stagger, straddle, sway, swing, waffle, waver, whiffle*, yo-yo*; SEE CONCEPT 13

vacuous [*adj*] *empty; unintelligent*
airheaded*, birdbrained*, blank, drained, dull, dumb, emptied, foolish, half-baked*, inane, lamebrained*, minus*, shallow, silly*, stupid, superficial, uncomprehending, unreasoning, vacant, void; SEE CONCEPT 402

vacuum [*n*] *emptiness*
exhaustion, free space, gap, nothingness, rarefaction, space, vacuity, void; SEE CONCEPTS 513,740

vagabond [*n*] *person who leads an unsettled life; traveler*
explorer, gypsy, haji, pathfinder, pilgrim, pioneer, rambler, rover, tourist, trailblazer, trekker, wanderer, wayfarer; SEE CONCEPT 423

vagabond [*adj*] *unsettled; vagrant*
aimless, destitute, down-and-out*, drifting, errant, fancy-free*, fly-by-night*, footloose*, idle, itinerant, itinerate, journeying, mendicant, migratory, moving, nomadic, perambulant, perambulatory, peripatetic, prodigal, rambling, roaming, rootless, roving, sauntering, shifting, shiftless, straggling, stray, strolling, transient, travelling, unsettled, wandering, wayfaring, wayward; SEE CONCEPT 539

vagrant [*n*] *person with no permanent home and often with no means of support*
drifter, floater, homeless person, itinerant, rolling stone*, street person, transient, wanderer; SEE CONCEPT 423

vague [*adj*] *not definite or clear*
ambiguous, amorphous, amphibological, bewildering, bleary, blurred, cloudy, dark, dim, doubtful, dreamlike, dubious, enigmatic, equivocal, faint, fuzzy, generalized, hazy, ill-defined, impalpable, imprecise, indefinite, indeterminate, indistinct, inexplicable, lax, loose, misunderstood, muddy, nebulous, obscure, perplexing, problematic, puzzling, questionable, shadowy, superficial, tenebrous, uncertain, unclear, undetermined, unexplicit, unintelligible, unknown, unsettled, unspecified, unsure; SEE CONCEPTS 267,485,529

vain [*adj1*] *egotistical*
arrogant, big-headed*, boastful, cocky*, conceited, egocentric, egoistic, haughty, high-and-mighty*, inflated, narcissistic, ostentatious, overweening, pleased with oneself*, proud, puffed up*, self-important, stuck-up*, swaggering*, swollen-headed*, vainglorious; SEE CONCEPTS 401,404

vain [*adj2*] *futile, useless*
abortive, barren, bootless, delusive, delusory, empty, frivolous, fruitless, going nowhere*, hollow, idle, inefficacious, insignificant, in vicious circle*, misleading, not a prayer*, no-win*, nugatory, on a treadmill*, otiose, paltry, petty, pointless, profitless, puny, senseless, shuck, slight, sterile, time-wasting, trifling, trivial, unavailing, unimportant, unnotable, unproductive, unprofitable, valueless, void, worthless; SEE CONCEPTS 552,575

valedictory [*adj*] *farewell*
departing, final, goodbye, last, parting, terminal; SEE CONCEPT 267

valiant [*adj*] *brave*
adventurous, assertive, audacious, bold, brave, chivalrous, courageous, dauntless, fearless, fire-eating*, gallant, game, grand, great, gritty*, gutsy*, gutty*, heroic, high-spirited, indomitable, intrepid, lion-hearted, magnanimous, nervy*, noble, plucky*, powerful, puissant, redoubtable, self-reliant, spunky*, stalwart, steadfast, stout, stouthearted, strong-willed, unafraid, undaunted, undismayed, valorous, venturesome, venturous, vigorous, worthy; SEE CONCEPTS 401,404,538

valid [*adj*] *right, genuine*
accurate, attested, authentic, authoritative, binding, bona fide, cogent, compelling, conclusive, confirmed, convincing, credible, determinative, efficacious, efficient, good, in force, irrefutable, just, kosher*, lawful, legal, legit*, legitimate, logical, official, original, persuasive, potent, powerful, proven, pure, solid, sound, stringent, strong, substantial, telling, tested, true, trustworthy, ultimate, unadulterated, unanswerable, uncorrupted, weighty, well-founded, well-grounded; SEE CONCEPTS 319,545,582

validate [*v*] *ascertain the truth, authenticity of something*
approve, authenticate, authorize, bear out, certify, confirm, constitute, corroborate, endorse, give stamp of approval*, give the go-ahead*, give the green light*, give the nod*, John Hancock*, justify, legalize, legitimize, make binding*, make legal*, make stick*, okay*, ratify, rubber-stamp*, sanction, set seal on*, sign off on*, substantiate, verify; SEE CONCEPTS 50,88,317

validity [*n*] *genuineness, lawfulness*
authority, cogency, effectiveness, efficacy, force, foundation, gravity, grounds, legality, legitimacy,

persuasiveness, point, potency, power, punch, right, soundness, strength, substance, validness, weight; SEE CONCEPTS *645,691,725*

valley [n] *hollow in the land*
basin, bottom, canyon, channel, coulee, dale, dell, depression, dingle, glen, gorge, lowland, notch, plain, swale, trough, vale; SEE CONCEPTS *509,513*

valor [n] *bravery*
backbone*, boldness, courage, dash*, defiance, derring-do*, determination, fearlessness, fight, firmness, fortitude, gallantry, grit*, guts*, hardihood, heart, heroism, indomitableness, intestinal fortitude*, intrepidity, invincibility, mettle, moxie*, nerve, pluck, prowess, resolution, sand*, spirit, spunk, starch*, stomach*, tenacity, valiance, valiancy; SEE CONCEPTS *411,633*

valuable [n] *prized possession*
advantage, antique, asset, benefit, collectible, commodity, heirloom, nugget*, plum*, treasure; SEE CONCEPT *446*

valuable [adj] *very important; priceless*
admired, appreciated, beneficial, cherished, collectible, costly, dear, esteemed, estimable, expensive, heirloom, held dear, helpful, high-priced, hot*, hot property*, important, in demand, inestimable, invaluable, of value, precious, prized, profitable, relevant, respected, scarce, serviceable, treasured, useful, valued, worthwhile, worthy; SEE CONCEPTS *334,560,568*

value [n1] *financial worth*
amount, appraisal, assessment, charge, cost, equivalent, expense, market price, monetary worth, price, profit, rate; SEE CONCEPTS *335,336*

value [n2] *advantage, worth*
account, bearing, benefit, caliber, condition, connotation, consequence, content, denotation, desirability, distinction, drift, eminence, esteem, estimation, excellence, finish, force, goodness, grade, help, implication, import, importance, interpretation, mark, marketability, meaning, merit, power, preference, profit, purpose, quality, regard, repute, sense, serviceableness, significance, state, stature, substance, superiority, use, usefulness, utility, valuation; SEE CONCEPTS *346,658,668,682*

valve [n] *on-and-off device*
cock, faucet, flap, gate, hydrant, lid, pipe, plug, shutoff, spigot, stopper, tap; SEE CONCEPTS *445,464,499*

vandal [n] *person who defiles property*
defacer, despoiler, destroyer, hoodlum, looter, mischief-maker, pillager, pirate, plunderer, ravager, thief; SEE CONCEPT *412*

vanish [v] *disappear*
become invisible, be lost, clear, dematerialize, die, die out, dissolve, evanesce, evaporate, exit, fade, fade away, go away, melt; SEE CONCEPT *105*

vanity [n] *conceit, egotism*
affectation, airs, arrogance, big-headedness*, conceitedness, display, ego trip*, narcissism, ostentation, pretension, pride, self-admiration, self-love, self-worship, show*, showing off*, smugness, vainglory; SEE CONCEPT *410*

vanquish [v] *defeat soundly*
bear down, beat, conquer, crush, humble, overcome, overpower, overturn, overwhelm, put down, quell, reduce, repress, rout, subdue, subjugate, subvert, surmount, trample, triumph over; SEE CONCEPT *95*

vapid [adj] *flat, dull*
bland, boring, colorless, dead*, driveling, flat, flat tire*, flavorless, inane, innocuous, insipid, jejune, least, lifeless, limp, milk-and-water*, milquetoast*, nothing, nowhere, stale, tame, tasteless, tedious, tiresome, unimaginative, uninspiring, uninteresting, unpalatable, vacant, vacuous, watery, weak, wishy-washy*, zero*; SEE CONCEPTS *529,537,575*

vapor [n] *fumes, mist*
breath, condensation, dampness, dew, effluvium, exhalation, fog, gas, haze, miasma, moisture, reek, smog, smoke, steam; SEE CONCEPTS *437,524*

variable [adj] *changing, changeable*
capricious, changeful, fickle, fitful, flexible, fluctuating, fluid, iffy*, inconstant, irregular, mercurial, mobile, mutable, protean, shifting, shifty, slippery*, spasmodic, temperamental, ticklish, uncertain, unequable, unsettled, unstable, unsteady, vacillating, volatile, waffling, wavering, yo-yo*; SEE CONCEPT *534*

variance [n] *difference*
about-face*, argument, change, conflict, contention, deviation, difference of opinion, different strokes*, disaccord, disagreement, discord, discrepancy, dissension, dissent, dissidence, disunity, divergence, diversity, division, flip-flop*, fluctuation, incongruity, inconsistency, midcourse correction*, mutation, separation, severing, strife, sundering, switch, transmogrification, unharmoniousness, variation, variety; SEE CONCEPTS *388,665,697*

variant [n] *derived form*
alternative, branch, development, exception, irregularity, modification, result, spinoff, variation, version; SEE CONCEPT *665*

variant [adj] *different*
alternative, derived, differing, divergent, exceptional, modified, various, varying; SEE CONCEPT *564*

variation [n] *difference; alternative*
aberration, abnormality, adaptation, alteration, bend, break, change, contradistinction, contrast, curve, deflection, departure, departure from the norm*, deviation, digression, discrepancy, disparity, displacement, dissimilarity, dissimilitude, distinction, divergence, diversification, diversity, exception, fluctuation, inequality, innovation, modification, mutation, novelty, shift, swerve, turn, unconformity, variety; SEE CONCEPTS *665,697*

varied [adj] *different*
assorted, conglomerate, discrete, diverse, heterogeneous, indiscriminate, miscellaneous, mixed, motley, multifarious, separate, sundry, various; SEE CONCEPT *564*

variety [n1] *difference*
array, assortment, change, collection, combo*, conglomeration, cross section, departure, discrepancy, disparateness, divergency, diversification, diversity, fluctuation, heterogeneity, incongruity, intermixture, many-sidedness, medley, mélange, miscellany, mishmash, mixed bag*, mixture, modification, multifariousness, multiplicity, potpourri, range, shift, soup, stew, variance, variation; SEE CONCEPTS *432,665*

va
va

variety [n2] *type, sort*

assortment, brand, breed, category, character, class, classification, description, division, family, genus, grade, ilk, kidney, kind, make, nature, order, quality, race, rank, species, strain, stripe, tribe; SEE CONCEPT 378

various [adj] *miscellaneous, differing*

all manner of*, assorted, changeable, changing, different, discrete, disparate, distinct, distinctive, diverse, diversified, heterogeneous, individual, legion, manifold, many, many-sided, multifarious, multitudinal, multitudinous, numerous, omnifarious, peculiar, populous, separate, several, sundry, unalike, unequal, unlike, variant, varied, variegated; SEE CONCEPTS 564,771

varnish [v] *add a layer to; embellish*

adorn, coat, cover, decorate, enamel, finish, gild, glaze, gloss, japan, lacquer, luster, paint, polish, shellac, surface, veneer, wash, wax; SEE CONCEPTS 172,177

vary [v] *change*

alter, alternate, assort, be unlike, blow hot and cold*, convert, depart, deviate, differ, digress, disagree, displace, dissent, divaricate, diverge, diversify, divide, fluctuate, hem and haw*, inflect, interchange, modify, mutate, part, permutate, range, separate, shilly-shally*, swerve, take turns, transform, turn, variegate, yo-yo*; SEE CONCEPT 697

vast [adj] *very large; wide in range*

all-inclusive, ample, astronomical, big, boundless, broad, capacious, colossal, comprehensive, detailed, endless, enormous, eternal, expanded, extensive, far-flung, far-reaching, forever, giant, gigantic, great, huge, illimitable, immeasurable, immense, infinite, limitless, mammoth, massive, measureless, monstrous, monumental, never-ending, prodigious, prolonged, spacious, spread-out, stretched-out, sweeping, titanic, tremendous, unbounded, unlimited, voluminous, widespread; SEE CONCEPTS 772,773,781

vault [n] *depository*

basement, box, can, catacomb, cavern, cellar, crib*, crypt, dungeon, grave, mausoleum, pit, repository, safe, safe-deposit box, sepulcher, strong room, tomb; SEE CONCEPT 494

vault [v] *jump over; span*

arch, ascend, bend, bounce, bound, bow, clear, curve, hop, hurdle, leap, mount, negotiate, over, overleap, rise, soar, spring, surmount; SEE CONCEPTS 194,752

veer [v] *change direction*

angle off, avert, bear, be deflected, bend, change, change course, curve, cut, deflect, depart, deviate, digress, dip, divagate, diverge, divert, drift, get around, make a left*, make a right*, pivot, sheer, shift, skew, skid, swerve, swing, swivel, tack, train off, turn, twist, volte-face*, wheel, whip, whirl; SEE CONCEPTS 148,150,213

vegetable [n] *edible part of plant*

edible, green, greens, herb, herbaceous plant, legume, produce, root, salad, truck, yellow; SEE CONCEPT 431

vegetate [v1] *be very passive*

be inert, decay, deteriorate, exist, go to pot*, go to seed*, hibernate, idle, languish, loaf*, pass time, stagnate, weaken; SEE CONCEPTS 210,698

vegetate [v2] *grow, sprout*

bloom, blossom, bud, burgeon, germinate, shoot, spring, swell; SEE CONCEPTS 253,257

vehement [adj] *passionate, opinionated*

angry, ardent, concentrated, delirious, desperate, eager, earnest, emphatic, enthusiastic, exquisite, fervent, fervid, fierce, fiery, forceful, forcible, frantic, furious, hearty, heated, hopped up*, hot*, hyper*, impassioned, impetuous, inflamed, intense, lively, on the make*, potent, powerful, pronounced, rabid, strong, terrible, vicious, violent, wild, zealous; SEE CONCEPTS 401,542

vehicle [n1] *machine used for transportation*

agent, automobile, bicycle, boat, buggy, bus, cab, car, carrier, chariot, conveyance, crate*, jalopy*, jeep, mechanism, motorcycle, taxi, transport, truck, van, vector, wagon, wheels; SEE CONCEPT 503

vehicle [n2] *means of attaining end*

agency, agent, apparatus, channel, expedient, implement, instrument, instrumentality, intermediary, means of expression, mechanism, medium, ministry, organ, tool, vector, way, ways and means*; SEE CONCEPTS 6,277,278,694,712

veil [n] *disguise*

blind, cloak, coloring, cover, curtain, facade, false front, film, front, guise, mantilla, mask, screen, shade, shroud, veiling; SEE CONCEPTS 451,673

veil [v] *hide*

beard*, blanket, camouflage, cloak, conceal, cover, cover up, curtain*, dim, disguise, drape, enclose, enfold, enshroud, envelop, finesse, invest, launder, mantle, mask, obscure, put up a front*, screen, secrete, shield, shroud, stonewall*, whitewash*, wrap; SEE CONCEPT 172

vein [n1] *mood, tone*

attitude, bent, character, characteristic, complexion, dash, disposition, faculty, fashion, fettle, hint, humor, line, manner, mind, mode, nature, note, spice, spirit, strain, streak, style, suggestion, suspicion, tang, temper, temperament, tenor, tinge, touch, trace, turn, wave, way; SEE CONCEPTS 411,673,682

vein [n2] *blood vessel*

capillary, course, current, duct, follicle, hair, lode, nerve, seam, stratum, streak, stripe, thread, venation; SEE CONCEPTS 393,420

velocity [n] *speed*

acceleration, celerity, dispatch, expedition, fleetness, gait, haste, headway, hurry, impetus, momentum, pace, quickness, rapidity, rapidness, rate, swiftness, tempo; SEE CONCEPTS 755,792

vendor [n] *person who sells wares*

businessperson, dealer, hawker, huckster*, merchant, outcrier, peddler, pitcher, traveler, traveling salesperson; SEE CONCEPT 348

veneer [n] *pretense, front*

appearance, coating, cover, covering, disguise, exterior, facade, face, finish, gloss, guise, layer, leaf, mask, overlay, semblance, show, surface, window dressing*; SEE CONCEPTS 633,673,716

veneer [v] *cover, overlay*

blanch, coat, extenuate, face, finish, gloss, palliate, plate, shellac, sugarcoat, surface, varnish, whiten, whitewash; SEE CONCEPT 172

venerable [adj] *respected*

admirable, aged, august, dignified, esteemed, estimable, experienced, grand, grave, honorable, honored, imposing, matriarchal, noble, patriarchal, philosophical, revered, reverenced, reverend, sacred, sage, sedate, serious, stately, venerated, wise, worshipful, worshipped; SEE CONCEPT 574

vengeance [n] *retaliation for another's act*
avengement, avenging, counterblow, evening of score*, eye for an eye*, getting even*, repayment, reprisal, requital, retribution, return, revenge, settling of score*, tit for tat*, vengefulness, wrath; SEE CONCEPTS 29,384

vengeful [adj] *retaliating; hating*
antagonistic, avenging, hostile, implacable, inimical, punitive, rancorous, relentless, retaliatory, revengeful, spiteful, unforgiving, vindictive; SEE CONCEPTS 401,542

venom [n] *poison; hating*
acidity, acrimony, anger, bane, bitterness, contagion, gall, grudge, hate, hatred, ill will, infection, malevolence, malice, maliciousness, malignity, rancor, spite, spitefulness, spleen, taint, toxin, virulence, virus; SEE CONCEPTS 29,399

venomous [adj] *poisonous; hateful*
accidentally on purpose*, antagonistic, baleful, baneful, catty*, cussed*, deadly, destructive, dirty, evil, hostile, lethal, malefic, malevolent, malicious, malign, malignant, mean, mephitic, noxious, ornery*, poisonous, rancorous, savage, spiteful, toxic, toxicant, vicious, vindictive, viperish, viperous, virulent, waspish; SEE CONCEPTS 537,542,544

vent [n] *outlet*
aperture, avenue, chimney, drain, duct, exit, flue, hole, opening, orifice, pipe, split, spout, ventilator; SEE CONCEPTS 440,464

vent [v] *let out; express*
air, assert, come out with, declare, discharge, drive out, emit, empty, express, give, give off, give out, issue, loose, pour out, provide escape, put, release, state, take out on*, throw off*, unleash, utter, ventilate, verbalize, voice; SEE CONCEPTS 49,51,179

ventilate [v] *air out; make known*
advertise, air, bring into the open, bring up, broach, broadcast, circulate, debate, deliberate, discourse, discuss, examine, express, free, give, go into, introduce, moot, publish, put, scrutinize, sift, state, take up, talk about, talk of, talk over, thresh out, vent, verbalize; SEE CONCEPTS 51,60

venture [n] *gamble, attempt*
adventure, baby*, chance, deal, endeavor, enterprise, essay, experiment, exploit, feat*, hazard, header, investment, jeopardy, peril, pet project*, project, proposition, pursuit, risk, setup*, shot*, spec*, speculation, stab*, stake, test, thing*, trial, undertaking, wager; SEE CONCEPTS 87,675

venture [v] *take a chance*
advance, assay, attempt, bet, brave, challenge, chance, dare, dare say*, defy, endanger, essay, experiment, expose, feel, front*, gamble, get down*, go out on a limb*, grope, have a fling at*, hazard, imperil, jeopardize, lay open, make a stab at*, make bold, operate, play for, play the market*, presume, put in jeopardy*, put up*, risk, speculate, stake, stick one's neck out*, take a crack at*, take a flyer*, take a plunge*, try, try out, volunteer, wager; SEE CONCEPTS 87,330,363

venturesome [adj] *courageous*
adventurous, aggressive, audacious, bold, brave, daredevil, daring, enterprising, fearless, foolhardy, gutsy, intrepid, overbold, plucky, pushy, rash, reckless, resourceful, risky, spirited,

spunky, stalwart, stout, sturdy, temerarious, venturous; SEE CONCEPTS 401,548

veracious [adj] *true*
accurate, credible, dependable, direct, ethical, factual, faithful, frank, genuine, high-principled, honest, just, kosher*, legit*, like it is*, on the level*, on the line*, on the up and up*, open, reliable, right, righteous, straight-arrow*, straightforward, strict, true-blue*, trustworthy, truthful, undeceptive, up front*, valid, veridical; SEE CONCEPTS 267,545,582

veracity [n] *truth*
accuracy, actuality, authenticity, candor, correctness, credibility, exactitude, exactness, fact, fairness, fidelity, frankness, genuineness, gospel*, honest-to-god truth*, honesty, honor, impartiality, integrity, like it is*, openness, precision, probity, reality, real McCoy*, rectitude, rightness, sincerity, straight stuff*, trueness, truism, trustworthiness, truthfulness, uprightness, verisimilitude, verity, word*; SEE CONCEPTS 278,645

verbal [adj] *spoken*
exact, expressed, lingual, literal, oral, rhetorical, said, stated, told, unwritten, verbatim, word-for-word*, word-of-mouth*; SEE CONCEPT 267

verbatim [adj] *exactly*
accurately, direct, directly, literally, literatim, precisely, sic, to the letter*, word-for-word*; SEE CONCEPTS 267,535

verbiage [n] *repetition, wordiness*
circumlocution, expansiveness, floridity, long-windedness, loquacity, periphrase, periphrasis, pleonasm, prolixity, redundancy, tautology, verbosity; SEE CONCEPTS 278,695

verbose [adj] *wordy, long-winded*
bombastic, circumlocutory, diffuse, flowery, full of air*, fustian, gabby*, garrulous, grandiloquent, involved, loquacious, magniloquent, palaverous, periphrastic, pleonastic, prolix, redundant, repeating, repetitious, repetitive, rhetorical, talkative, talky*, tautological, tautologous, tedious, tortuous, windy*, yacking*; SEE CONCEPT 267

verdant [adj] *green, blooming*
flourishing, fresh, grassy, leafy, lush, verdurous; SEE CONCEPTS 485,618

verdict [n] *law judgment*
adjudication, answer, arbitrament, award, conclusion, decision, decree, deduction, determination, finding, opinion, ruling, sentence; SEE CONCEPT 318

verge [n] *extremity, limit*
border, borderline, boundary, brim, brink, edge, extreme, fringe, hem, lip, margin, point, rim, selvage, skirt, terminus, threshold; SEE CONCEPT 484

verge [v] *come near*
abut, adjoin, approach, be on the edge*, border, bound, brink on, butt on*, communicate, edge, end, fringe, gravitate toward, hem, incline, join, lean, line, march, margin, neighbor, outline, rim, skirt, surround, tend, touch, trench, trend; SEE CONCEPTS 657,749

verify [v] *confirm, validate*
add up*, attest, authenticate, bear out, certify, check, check out, check up, check up on*, confirm, corroborate, debunk, demonstrate, document, double-check, establish, eye*, eyeball*, find out, hold up, justify, make certain, make sure, pan out*, peg*, prove, settle, size*, size up*,

va
ve

stand up*, substantiate, support, test, try; SEE
CONCEPTS 291,317

verisimilitude [n] *authenticity*
color, credibility, genuineness, likeliness, likeness, plausibility, realism, resemblance, semblance, show, similarity, virtual reality; SEE
CONCEPT 725

veritable [adj] *authentic*
actual, bona fide, factual, for real*, genuine, indubitable, kosher*, legit*, real, true, undoubted,
unquestionable, very; SEE CONCEPT 582

vernacular [n] *native language*
argot, cant, dialect, idiom, jargon, jive talk*, language, lingo*, lingua franca, native tongue, parlance, patois, patter, phraseology, slang, speech,
street talk*, tongue; SEE CONCEPT 276

vernacular [adj] *native, colloquial*
common, dialectal, domesticated, idiomatic, indigenous, informal, ingrained, inherent, local,
natural, ordinary, plebian, popular, vulgar; SEE
CONCEPTS 267,549

versatile [adj] *adjustable, flexible*
able, accomplished, adaptable, adroit, all-around,
all-purpose, ambidextrous, conversant, dexterous,
elastic, facile, functional, gifted, handy, ingenious, many-sided, mobile, multifaceted, plastic,
pliable, protean, puttylike*, ready, resourceful,
skilled, skillful, talented, variable, varied; SEE
CONCEPTS 527,542

verse [n] *written composition*
ballad, epic, jingle, lay, lyric, ode, poem, poesy,
poetry, rhyme, rune, song, sonnet, stanza; SEE
CONCEPT 282

versed [adj] *experienced, informed*
abreast, accomplished, acquainted, au courant*,
au fait*, competent, conversant, familiar, in the
know*, knowledgeable, learned, practical, practiced, proficient, qualified, savvy, seasoned,
skilled, trained, tuned in*, up*, up on*, versant,
veteran, well-informed; SEE CONCEPTS 402,
403,527

version [n] *account of a happening*
adaptation, chronicle, clarification, condensation,
construction, exercise, form, history, interpretation, narrative, paraphrase, portrayal, reading, redaction, rendering, rendition, report, restatement,
rewording, side, simplification, sketch, statement,
story, tale, transcription, translation, variant; SEE
CONCEPT 282

vertex [n] *top*
acme, apex, apogee, cap, cope, crest, crown, culmination, extremity, fastigium, height, peak, pinnacle, roof, summit, tip, upper extremity, zenith;
SEE CONCEPT 836

vertical [adj] *upright*
bolt upright, cocked, erect, on end, perpendicular,
plumb, sheer, steep, straight-up, up-and-down,
upward; SEE CONCEPTS 581,583

very [adj] *real, exact*
actual, appropriate, authentic, bare, bona fide,
correct, especial, express, genuine, ideal, identical, indubitable, mere, model, perfect, plain, precise, pure, right, same, selfsame, sheer, simple,
special, sure-enough, true, undoubted, unqualified, unquestionable, veritable, very same; SEE
CONCEPTS 535,557

very [adv] *much, really; to a high degree*
absolutely, acutely, amply, astonishingly, awfully, certainly, considerably, dearly, decidedly,
deeply, eminently, emphatically, exaggeratedly,
exceedingly, excessively, extensively, extraordinarily, extremely, greatly, highly, incredibly, in-
dispensably, largely, notably, noticeably,
particularly, positively, powerfully, pressingly,
pretty, prodigiously, profoundly, remarkably,
substantially, superlatively, surpassingly, surprisingly, terribly, truly, uncommonly, unusually,
vastly, wonderfully; SEE CONCEPTS 544,569,772

vessel [n1] *ship*
barge, bark, bateau, boat, bottom, bucket*, can*,
craft, liner, ocean liner, steamer, tanker, tub*;
SEE CONCEPT 506

vessel [n2] *container, bowl*
basin, kettle, pitcher, pot, receptacle, urn, utensil;
SEE CONCEPT 494

vest [v] *authorize, entrust*
belong, bestow, confer, consign, empower, endow, furnish, invest, lodge, pertain, place, put in
the hands of*, settle; SEE CONCEPTS 50,88

vestibule [n] *small room for arrivals*
antechamber, anteroom, doorway, entrance, entrance hall, entry, entryway, foyer, gateway, hall,
hallway, lobby, narthex, porch, portal, portico;
SEE CONCEPT 448

vestige [n] *sign, indication*
evidence, glimmer, hint, memento, print, relic,
remainder, remains, remnant, residue, scrap,
shadow, suspicion, token, trace, track; SEE CON-
CEPTS 260,284,673

veteran [n] *person with much experience; particularly in war*
expert, GI*, old guard*, old hand*, old pro*, old
salt*, old soldier*, old-timer*, pro, shellback*,
sourdough*, trouper, vet*, warhorse*; SEE CON-
CEPTS 358,423

veteran [adj] *experienced, seasoned*
adept, battle-scarred*, been around*, disciplined,
exercised, expert, from way back*, hardened, inured, knows one's stuff*, long-serving, long-time,
not born yesterday*, of the old school*, old, old-
time, practical, practiced, pro*, proficient,
skilled, sophisticated, steady, trained, up to
speed*, versed, vet*, weathered, wise, wise to
ways*, worldly; SEE CONCEPTS 402,527,678

veto [n] *refusal of permission*
ban, blackball*, declination, denial, embargo, interdict, interdiction, negative, nonconsent, prohibition; SEE CONCEPTS 81,121,298,685

veto [v] *refuse permission*
ban, blackball*, burn, cut, decline, defeat, deny,
disallow, disapprove, discountenance, forbid,
give thumbs down*, interdict, kill, negate, negative, nix*, not go for*, pass, pass by, pass on,
prohibit, put down, refuse, reject, rule out*, shoot
down*, throw away*, throw out*, thumbs down*,
turn down; SEE CONCEPTS 50,81,88,121,298

vex [v] *distress, bother*
abrade, afflict, aggravate, agitate, anger, annoy,
be at, chafe, depress, displease, disquiet, disturb,
eat*, embarrass, exasperate, fret, gall*, get in
one's hair*, get under one's skin*, give a bad
time*, give a hard time*, grate on*, harass, harry,
hassle, infuriate, irk, irritate, molest, needle, nettle, offend, peeve, perplex, pester, pique, plague,
provoke, put out*, rasp, ride, rile, tease, tick off*,
torment, trouble, turn off*, upset, worry; SEE
CONCEPTS 7,19

vexatious [adj] *distressing, bothersome*
afflicting, aggravating, annoying, burdensome,
disagreeable, disappointing, disturbing, exasper-

ating, irksome, irritating, mean, nagging, pesky*, provoking, teasing, tormenting, troublesome, troublous, trying, ugly, unpleasant, upsetting, wicked, worrisome, worrying; SEE CONCEPTS 529,537

via [prep] by way of
along, as a means, by, by dint of, by means of, by this route, by virtue of, on the way, over, per, through, through the medium of, through this medium, with; SEE CONCEPT 544

viable [adj] reasonable, practicable
applicable, doable, feasible, operable, possible, usable, within possibility, workable; SEE CONCEPTS 552,560

vibrant [adj1] alive, colorful
active, animated, dynamic, electrifying, energetic, lively, peppy, responsive, sensitive, sound, sparkling, spirited, vigorous, virile, vital, vivacious, vivid, zesty*, zippy*; SEE CONCEPTS 401,618

vibrant [adj2] throbbing
aquiver, consonant, oscillating, palpitating, pulsating, pulsing, quaking, quivering, resonant, resounding, reverberant, ringing, sonorant, sonorous, trembling; SEE CONCEPT 584

vibrate [v] shake, quiver
beat, echo, fluctuate, flutter, jar, oscillate, palpitate, pulsate, pulse, quake, resonate, resound, reverberate, ripple, shiver, sway, swing, throb, tremble, tremor, undulate, wave, waver; SEE CONCEPTS 152,748

vibration [n] shaking, quivering
beating, fluctuation, judder, oscillation, pulsation, pulse, quake, quiver, resonance, reverberation, shake, shimmy, throb, throbbing, trembling, tremor, vacillation, wave, wavering; SEE CONCEPTS 152,748

vicarious [adj] done or felt for, or on behalf of, another
by proxy, commissioned, delegated, deputed, empathetic, eventual, imagined, indirect, pretended, secondary, substituted, substitutional, surrogate, sympathetic; SEE CONCEPTS 401,538

vice [n1] bad habit; sin
carnality, corruption, debasement, debauchery, decay, degeneracy, depravity, evil, evildoing, ill, immorality, indecency, iniquity, lechery, lewdness, libidinousness, licentiousness, looseness, lubricity, lust, maleficence, malignance, offense, perversion, profligacy, rot, sensuality, squalor, transgression, trespass, venality, wickedness, wrong; SEE CONCEPTS 372,645

vice [n2] weakness
blemish, defect, demerit, failing, fault, flaw, foible, frailty, imperfection, mar, shortcoming, weak point; SEE CONCEPTS 411,657,666

vice versa [adv] contrary, oppositely
about-face*, again, contra, contrariwise*, conversely, far from it*, in reverse, on the contrary, the other way around*, turn about; SEE CONCEPTS 544,564

vicinity [n] local area
around*, ballpark*, district, environment, environs, hood, locality, nearness, neck of the woods*, neighborhood, precinct, proximity, purlieus, range, region, surroundings, territory, turf*, vicinage; SEE CONCEPTS 198,747

vicious [adj1] corrupt, wrong
abandoned, abhorrent, atrocious, bad, barbarous, base, contaminated, cruel, dangerous, debased, degenerate, degraded, demoralized, depraved, diabolical, faulty, ferocious, fiendish, flagitious, foul, heinous, immoral, impious, impure, indecent, infamous, iniquitous, insubordinate, lewd, libidinous, licentious, miscreant, monstrous, nefarious, perverse, profligate, putrid, reprehensible, reprobate, rotten, savage, sinful, unprincipled, untamed, vile, villainous, violent, wicked, wild, worthless; SEE CONCEPTS 401,545,571

vicious [adj2] nasty, hateful
backbiting*, beastly, bloodthirsty, brutal, cruel, cussed*, defamatory, despiteful, dirty*, evil, fierce, frightful, furious, horrid, intense, lousy*, malevolent, malicious, malign, mean, murderous, ornery*, poisonous, rancorous, rough, savage, slanderous, spiteful, tough, vehement, venomous, vindictive, violent, wicked; SEE CONCEPTS 267,401,542

vicissitude [n] change
about-face*, alteration, alternation, diversity, flip-flop*, fluctuation, innovation, mid-course correction*, mutability, mutation, novelty, permutation, progression, reversal, revolution, shift, sport, switch, switchover, transposition, turnaround, uncertainty, ups and downs*, variation, variety; SEE CONCEPT 697

victim [n] someone or something sacrificed, preyed upon
babe in woods*, butt, casualty, clown, dupe, easy make*, easy mark*, fatality, fool, gambit, gopher*, gudgeon*, gull, hireling, hunted, immolation, injured party, innocent, mark, martyr, patsy, pawn, pigeon*, prey, pushover*, quarry, sacrifice, scapegoat, sitting duck*, sitting target*, soft touch*, stooge*, sucker*, sufferer, underdog, wretch; SEE CONCEPTS 423,659

victimize [v] cheat, fool
bamboozle*, burn*, canned*, chisel*, clip*, con, cozen, deceive, defraud, discriminate against, dupe, exploit, fleece, flimflam*, gull, have it in for*, hoax, hoodwink, immolate, persecute, pick on, pigeon*, prey on, rope in*, screw*, set up*, snow*, stack the deck*, stiff*, sting*, sucker*, swindle, take advantage of, trick, use; SEE CONCEPTS 14,59,192

victor [n] person who wins
champ, champion, conquering hero*, conqueror, defeater, first*, gold medalist, greatest, hero, king, medalist, prizewinner, queen, subjugator, title holder, top*, top dog*, vanquisher, winner; SEE CONCEPTS 366,416

victorious [adj] successful, winning
arrived, champion, conquering, on top, prizewinning, triumphant, vanquishing; SEE CONCEPT 528

victory [n] win, success
achievement, advantage, ascendancy, bull's-eye*, clean sweep*, conquest, control, defeat, defeating, destruction, dominion, feather in cap*, gain, grand slam*, hit, hole in one*, killing*, laurels, mission accomplished*, overthrow, prize, subjugation, superiority, supremacy, sweep, the gold*, triumph, upper hand*, upset, winning; SEE CONCEPTS 95,671,706,832

video [n/adj] related to the televised image
broadcast, canned*, music video, prerecorded, program, promotional film, recorded, taped, telegenic, television, TV; SEE CONCEPTS 277,293.

ve
vi

videocassette [n] *magnetic tape on which video image is recorded*
cartridge, flick*, movie, recording, rental, vid*, videotape; SEE CONCEPTS *277,293,464.*

vie [v] *compete*
be rivals, buck, challenge, contend, contest, counter, go for*, go for broke*, go for the gold*, go for the jugular*, jockey for position*, match, oppose, pit, play, play off, push, rival, scramble for, strive, struggle, sweat; SEE CONCEPTS *92,363*

view [n1] *something that is seen*
appearance, aspect, composition, contour, design, field of vision, glimpse, illustration, landscape, look, opening, outline, outlook, panorama, perspective, picture, prospect, range of vision, representation, scene, seascape, show, sight, spectacle, stretch, tableau, vision, vista, way; SEE CONCEPT *628*

view [n2] *examination*
analysis, audit, check, contemplation, display, eyeball*, flash*, gander*, inspection, lamp*, look, look-see, perlustration, review, scan, scrutiny, sight, slant, squint*, survey, viewing; SEE CONCEPTS *24,103*

view [n3] *belief*
attitude, belief, close-up, concept, conception, consideration, conviction, deduction, eye*, feeling, impression, inference, judgment, judgment call*, mind, notion, opinion, persuasion, point of view, say-so*, sentiment, slant*, thought, twist, two cents' worth*, value judgment*, way of thinking; SEE CONCEPT *689*

view [v1] *look at*
beam, behold, canvass, check out*, check over, consider, contemplate, descry, dig*, discern, distinguish, eagle eye*, espy, examine, explore, eye*, feast eyes on*, flash*, gaze, get a load of*, inspect, lay eyes on, mark, notice, observe, perceive, pipe*, read, regard, rubberneck*, scan, scope, scrutinize, see, set eyes on, spot, spy, stare, survey, take in*, watch, witness; SEE CONCEPTS *623,626*

view [v2] *believe*
account, consider, deem, judge, look on, reckon, regard, think about; SEE CONCEPT *12*

viewpoint [n] *way of thinking*
angle, aspect, attitude, direction, estimation, eye*, frame of reference, ground, light, long view, outlook, perspective, point of observation, point of view, position, posture, respect, side, slant, stance, stand, standpoint, twist, two cents' worth*, vantage point, view; SEE CONCEPT *689*

vigilance [n] *carefulness*
acuity, alertness, attention, attentiveness, caution, circumspection, diligence, lookout, observance, surveillance, vigil, watch, watchfulness; SEE CONCEPTS *644,657*

vigilant [adj] *careful, watchful*
acute, agog, alert, anxious, attentive, aware, cautious, circumspect, guarded, keen, looking for, looking to, observant, on alert, on guard, on the ball*, on the job*, on the lookout, on the qui vive, on toes*, open-eyed*, sharp, sleepless, unsleeping, waiting on, wakeful, wary, wide-awake, with eyes peeled*, with weather eye open*; SEE CONCEPTS *401,542,576*

vigor [n] *power, energy*
ability, action, activity, agility, alertness, bang*, birr, bounce, capability, capacity, dash, drive, dynamism, endurance, enterprise, exercise, fire, force, get-up-and-go*, go*, hardiness, healthiness, intensity, juice*, kick*, liveliness, lustiness, might, motion, moxie*, muscle*, nimbleness, pep*, pith, potency, puissance, punch*, push, quickness, snap*, sock, soundness, starch*, steam*, strength, tuck*, urgency, vehemence, vim, vitality, well-being, zing*, zip*; SEE CONCEPTS *316,411,732*

vigorous [adj] *energetic, powerful*
active, athletic, ball of fire*, bouncing, brisk, dashing, driving, dynamic, effective, efficient, enterprising, exuberant, flourishing, forceful, forcible, hale, hard-driving, hardy, healthy, hearty, intense, lively, lusty, mettlesome, peppy, persuasive, potent, red-blooded*, robust, rugged, snappy, sound, spanking, spirited, steamroller*, strapping, strenuous, strong, strong as an ox*, sturdy, take-charge*, take-over*, tough, vital, zealous, zippy*; SEE CONCEPTS *314,404,489*

vile [adj] *offensive, horrible*
abandoned, abject, appalling, bad, base, coarse, contemptible, corrupt, debased, degenerate, depraved, despicable, dirty, disgraceful, disgusting, evil, filthy, foul, horrid, humiliating, ignoble, immoral, impure, iniquitous, loathsome, low, mean, miserable, nasty, nauseating, nefarious, noxious, perverted, repellent, repugnant, repulsive, revolting, shocking, sickening, sinful, sleazy*, stinking*, ugly, vicious, vulgar, wicked, worthless, wretched; SEE CONCEPTS *529,545,571*

vilify [v] *criticize very harshly*
abuse, asperse, assail, attack, bad-mouth*, berate, blister, call down*, calumniate, censure, curse, cuss*, damn, debase, decry, defame, denigrate, denounce, dig*, disparage, dress down*, dump on*, give a black eye*, jinx, knock*, libel, malign, mistreat, mudsling*, pan*, put a whammy on*, put down*, rag on*, rap*, revile, rip up*, roast*, run down, scorch, skin alive*, slam*, slander, slur, smear*, speak ill of, tear down*, tear into*, traduce, vituperate, voodoo*; SEE CONCEPTS *44,52*

village [n] *small town*
center, crossroads, hamlet, suburb; SEE CONCEPT *507*

villain [n] *evil person*
antihero, blackguard*, brute, caitiff, creep*, criminal, devil, enfant terrible*, evildoer, heel, libertine, lowlife*, malefactor, mischief-maker*, miscreant, offender, profligate, rapscallion, rascal, reprobate, scoundrel, sinner, wretch; SEE CONCEPT *412*

vindicate [v] *prove one's innocence*
absolve, acquit, advocate, argue, assert, bear out, claim, clear, confute, contend, corroborate, defend, disculpate, disprove, do justice to, establish, exculpate, excuse, exonerate, free, free from blame, guard, justify, maintain, plead for, protect, prove, rationalize, refute, rehabilitate, second, shield, substantiate, support, uphold, warrant, whitewash*; SEE CONCEPTS *49,57,317*

vindictive [adj] *hateful, revengeful*
avenging, cruel, grim, grudging, implacable, malicious, malignant, merciless, rancorous, relentless, resentful, retaliatory, ruthless, spiteful, unforgiving, unrelenting, vengeful, venomous, wreakful; SEE CONCEPTS *401,542*

vintage [n] *crop, especially of wine*
collection, epoch, era, generation, grapes, harvest, origin, wine, year; SEE CONCEPT *429*

vintage [adj] superior

best, choice, classic, classical, excellent, mature, old, prime, rare, ripe, select, selected, venerable; SEE CONCEPTS 574,578,797

violate [v1] break a law, agreement

breach, contaminate, contravene, defy, disobey, disregard, disrupt, encroach, err, infract, infringe, meddle, offend, oppose, outrage, profane, resist, sacrilege, sin, tamper with, trample on, transgress, trespass, withstand; SEE CONCEPTS 101,192

violate [v2] rape, defile

abuse, assault, befoul, debauch, defile, desecrate, force, invade, outrage, pollute, profane, ravish, spoil; SEE CONCEPTS 246,375

violation [n1] breach; breaking of the law

abuse, break, breaking, contravention, encroachment, illegality, infraction, infringement, misbehavior, misdemeanor, negligence, nonobservance, offense, rupture, transgressing, transgression, trespass, trespassing, violating, wrong; SEE CONCEPTS 101,192

violation [n2] rape, defilement

assault, blasphemy, debasement, defacement, defacing, degradation, desecration, destruction, devastation, dishonor, invasion, mistreatment, outrage, pollution, profanation, rapine, ravishment, ruin, sacrilege, spoliation; SEE CONCEPTS 246,252,375

violence [n] extreme force, intensity

abandon, acuteness, assault, attack, bestiality, bloodshed, blowup, brutality, brute force, clash, coercion, compulsion, constraint, cruelty, destructiveness, disorder, disturbance, duress, ferocity, fervor, fierceness, fighting, flap, foul play, frenzy, fury, fuss, harshness, murderousness, onslaught, passion, power, raging, rampage, roughness, ruckus, rumble, savagery, severity, sharpness, storm, storminess, struggle, terrorism, tumult, turbulence, uproar, vehemence, wildness; SEE CONCEPTS 29,641,669,675

violent [adj1] destructive

agitated, aroused, berserk, bloodthirsty, brutal, coercive, crazy, cruel, demoniac, desperate, distraught, disturbed, enraged, fierce, fiery, forceful, forcible, frantic, fuming, furious, great, headstrong, homicidal, hotheaded*, hysterical, impassioned, impetuous, inflamed, intemperate, mad, maddened, maniacal, mighty, murderous, passionate, potent, powerful, raging, riotous, rough, savage, strong, uncontrollable, ungovernable, unrestrained, urgent, vehement, vicious, wild; SEE CONCEPTS 401,540,544

violent [adj2] severe, extreme

acute, agonizing, biting, blustery, coercive, concentrated, devastating, excruciating, exquisite, forceful, forcible, gale force*, great, harsh, immoderate, inordinate, intense, mighty, outrageous, painful, potent, powerful, raging, rough, ruinous, sharp, strong, tempestuous, terrible, tumultuous/tumultuous, turbulent, wild; SEE CONCEPTS 525,569

virgin/virginal [adj] brand-new, unused

first, fresh, idle, immaculate, initial, innocent, intact, modest, natural, new, original, primeval, pristine, pure, spotless, uncorrupted, undefiled, undisturbed, unmarred, unspoiled, unsullied, untapped, untested, untouched, untried, vestal; SEE CONCEPTS 372,560,578,797

virile [adj] potent, powerful

driving, energetic, forceful, generative, lusty, macho*, procreative, red-blooded*, reproductive, robust, sound, strong, vibrant, vigorous, vital; SEE CONCEPTS 372,401,404

virtual [adj] in essence

basic, constructive, essential, fundamental, implicit, implied, in all but name*, in conduct, indirect, in effect, in practice, potential, practical, pragmatic, tacit, unacknowledged; SEE CONCEPTS 487,537,544,573

virtually [adv] for all practical purposes

around, as good as, basically, effectually, essentially, for all intents and purposes*, fundamentally, give or take a little*, guesstimate*, implicitly, in all but name*, in effect, in essence, in substance, in the ballpark*, in the neighborhood*, morally, nearly, not absolutely, not actually, practically, something like*, upwards of*; SEE CONCEPTS 487,544,573

virtue [n] honor, integrity

advantage, asset, character, charity, chastity, consideration, credit, ethic, ethicality, ethicalness, excellence, faith, faithfulness, fineness, fortitude, generosity, goodness, good point*, high-mindedness, hope, ideal, incorruptibility, innocence, justice, kindness, love, merit, morality, plus*, probity, prudence, purity, quality, rectitude, respectability, righteousness, temper, temperance, trustworthiness, uprightness, value, worth, worthiness; SEE CONCEPTS 411,645

virtuoso [n] person who is an expert

ace, adept, artist, artiste, authority, big league*, brain*, celebrity, champ*, champion, crackerjack*, dilettante, egghead*, genius, hotshot*, hot stuff*, intelligent, magician, musician, natural*, no slouch*, old hand*, old pro*, performer, pro*, prodigy, professional, pundit, sharp*, star, superstar, whiz*, wizard; SEE CONCEPTS 348,352,416

virtuous [adj] good, ethical; innocent

blameless, celibate, chaste, clean-living, effective, effectual, efficient, excellent, exemplary, faithful, guiltless, high-principled, honest, honorable, incorruptible, inculpable, in the clear*, irreprehensible, kosher*, legit*, moral, moralistic, noble, on the level*, on the up and up*, praiseworthy, principled, pure, regular, righteous, right-minded, spotless, straight, true-blue*, unsullied, untainted, untarnished, up front*, upright, wholesome, without reproach, worthy; SEE CONCEPTS 401,545

virulent [adj1] poisonous, lethal

baneful, deadly, destructive, fatal, harmful, infective, injurious, malign, malignant, mephitic, pernicious, poison, septic, toxic, toxicant, unhealthy, unwholesome, venomous; SEE CONCEPTS 537,571

virulent [adj2] hostile

acrimonious, antagonistic, bitter, cutting, hateful, malevolent, malicious, rancorous, resentful, scathing, sharp, spiteful, splenetic, stabbing, unfriendly, venomous, vicious, vindictive, vitriolic; SEE CONCEPTS 267,542

viscous [adj] sticky, gummy

adhesive, clammy, gelatinous, gluey*, glutinous, gooey*, mucilaginous, ropy, slimy, stiff, syrupy, tenacious, thick, tough, viscid; SEE CONCEPT 606

visible [adj] apparent, seeable

arresting, big as life*, bold, clear, conspicuous, detectable, discernible, discoverable, distinguishable, evident, inescapable, in sight, in view, macroscopic, manifest, marked, not hidden, noticeable, observable, obtrusive, obvious, ocular, open, out in the open*, outstanding, palpable, patent, perceivable, perceptible, plain, pointed, pronounced, revealed, salient, seen, signal, striking, to be seen, unconcealed, under one's nose*, unhidden, unmistakable, viewable, visual; SEE CONCEPTS 529,576,619

vision [n1] *ability to perceive with eyes*
eyes*, eyesight, faculty, optics, perceiving, perception, range of view, seeing, sight, view; SEE CONCEPT 629

vision [n2] *mental image, concept*
angle, aspect, astuteness, breadth of view, castles in the air*, conception, daydream, discernment, divination, dream, facet, fancy, fantasy, farsightedness, foreknowledge, foresight, head trip*, idea, ideal, ideality, imagination, insight, intuition, keenness, mental picture, muse, nightmare, outlook, penetration, perspective, phantasm, pie in the sky*, pipe dream*, point of view, prescience, retrospect, slant, standpoint, trip, understanding, view; SEE CONCEPTS 529,532,689

vision [n3] *apparition*
apocalypse, chimera, delusion, ecstasy, fantasy, ghost, hallucination, haunt, illusion, mirage, nightmare, oracle, phantasm, phantom, phenomenon, presence, prophecy, revelation, specter, spirit, spook, trance, warlock, wraith; SEE CONCEPTS 370,529

vision [n4] *very beautiful thing or person*
angel*, dazzler, dream, eyeful*, feast for the eyes*, perfect picture*, picture, sight, sight for sore eyes*, spectacle, stunner*; SEE CONCEPTS 424,529

visionary [n] *person who dreams, is idealistic*
castle-builder*, daydreamer, Don Quixote*, dreamer, enthusiast, idealist, mystic, prophet, romancer, romantic, seer, stargazer, theorist, utopian, zealot; SEE CONCEPTS 361,416

visionary [adj] *idealized, romantic*
abstracted, ambitious, astral, chimerical, daydreaming, delusory, dreaming, dreamy, exalted, fanciful, fantastic, grandiose, ideal, idealist, idealistic, illusory, imaginary, impractical, in the clouds*, introspective, lofty, musing, noble, otherworldly, pretentious, prophetic, quixotic, radical, speculative, starry-eyed*, unreal, unrealistic, unworkable, unworldly, utopian; SEE CONCEPTS 529,560,582

visit [n] *social call upon another*
appointment, call, evening, holiday, interview, sojourn, stay, stop, stopover, talk, tarriance, vacation, visitation, weekend; SEE CONCEPTS 226,227

visit [v1] *be a guest of*
call, call on, chat, come around, come by, converse, crash, drop by, drop in, drop over, dwell, frequent, go over to*, go to see*, hit, inspect, look around, look in on, look up, pay a call*, pay a visit to, play, pop in*, reside, see, sojourn, stay at, stay with, step in, stop by*, stop off*, swing by*, take in, talk, tarry, tour; SEE CONCEPTS 226,227

visit [v2] *bother, haunt*
afflict, assail, attack, avenge, befall, bring down on, descend upon, force upon, impose, inflict, pain, punish, smite, trouble, wreak, wreck; SEE CONCEPTS 7,14,19

visitor [n] *person temporarily in a foreign location*
caller, company, foreigner, guest, habitué, inspector, invitee, out-of-towner, transient, visitant; SEE CONCEPT 417

visual [adj] *able to be seen with eyes*
beheld, discernible, imaged, observable, observed, ocular, optic, optical, perceptible, seeable, seen, viewable, viewed, visible, visional; SEE CONCEPTS 485,576,619

visualize [v] *make a picture of in the mind*
anticipate, apprehend, bring to mind, call to mind, call up, conceive of, conjure up, create, divine, dream up, envisage, envision, fancy, feature, foresee, get the picture*, image, imagine, object, picture, reflect, see, see in the mind's eye*, think, view, vision; SEE CONCEPTS 17,34

vital [adj1] *essential*
basic, bottom-line*, cardinal, coal-and-ice*, constitutive, critical, crucial, decisive, fundamental, heavy*, imperative, important, indispensable, integral, key, life-or-death*, meaningful, meat-and-potatoes*, name, name-of-the-game*, necessary, needed, nitty-gritty*, prerequisite, required, requisite, significant, underlined, urgent; SEE CONCEPTS 546,567

vital [adj2] *lively*
animated, dynamic, energetic, forceful, lusty, red-blooded, spirited, strenuous, vibrant, vigorous, vivacious, zestful; SEE CONCEPT 401

vital [adj3] *alive*
animate, animated, breathing, generative, invigorative, life-giving, live, living, quickening; SEE CONCEPT 539

vitality [n] *energy, spirit*
animation, ardor, audacity, bang, being, bloom, bounce, clout, continuity, drive, endurance, existence, exuberance, fervor, force, get-up-and-go*, go, guts*, intensity, life, liveliness, lustiness, pep, pizzazz*, power, pulse, punch, robustness, snap, sparkle, spunk*, stamina, starch*, steam, strength, stuff*, venturesomeness, verve, vigor, vim, vivaciousness, vivacity, zest, zing*, zip*; SEE CONCEPTS 407,411,633

vitiate [v1] *cancel*
abate, abolish, abrogate, annihilate, annul, delete, deny, invalidate, negate, nullify, quash, recant, revoke, undermine, undo; SEE CONCEPTS 121,317

vitiate [v2] *hurt, corrupt*
blemish, blight, brutalize, contaminate, damage, debase, debauch, defile, deprave, deteriorate, devalue, harm, impair, injure, mar, pervert, pollute, prejudice, spoil, sully, taint, tarnish, violate, warp, water down, weaken; SEE CONCEPTS 246,250

vituperate [v] *criticize harshly*
abuse, accuse, asperse, bark at*, bawl out*, berate, blame, calumniate, castigate, censure, chew out*, condemn, curse, denounce, find fault, growl, insult, lambaste*, lash, malign, rail, rate, reproach, revile, rip into*, run down*, scold, smear, tear into*, tongue-lash*, traduce, upbraid, vilify, yell at*; SEE CONCEPTS 44,52,54

vivacious [adj] *lively, spirited*
active, alert, animate, animated, bouncy, brash, breezy, bubbling, cheerful, ebullient, effervescent, exuberant, frolicsome, full of life*, gay, happy, high-spirited, jolly, jumping, keen, lighthearted, merry, playful, rocking, scintillating, sparkling, sportive, sprightly, swinging, upbeat, vibrant, vital, zesty; SEE CONCEPTS 401,404

vivid [*adj*] *intense, powerful*
active, animated, bright, brilliant, clear, colorful, definite, distinct, dramatic, dynamic, eloquent, energetic, expressive, flamboyant, gay, glowing, graphic, highly colored, lifelike, lively, lucid, meaningful, memorable, picturesque, realistic, resplendent, rich, sharp, shining, spirited, stirring, striking, strong, telling, theatrical, true-to-life, vigorous; SEE CONCEPTS 537,569,618

vocabulary [*n*] *language of a person or people*
cant, dictionary, glossary, jargon, lexicon, palaver, phraseology, terminology, thesaurus, wordbook, word-hoard*, words, word-stock*; SEE CONCEPTS 276,280

vocal [*adj1*] *spoken*
articulate, articulated, choral, expressed, intonated, lyric, modulated, operatic, oral, phonetic, phonic, pronounced, put into words*, said, singing, sonant, sung, uttered, verbal, viva voce, vocalic, vocalized, voiced, vowel; SEE CONCEPTS 267,594

vocal [*adj2*] *extroverted about opinion*
articulate, blunt, clamorous, eloquent, expressive, facile, fluent, forthright, frank, free, free-spoken, glib, noisy, outspoken, plain-spoken, round, smooth-spoken, stentorian, strident, venting, vociferous; SEE CONCEPTS 267,404

vocalize [*v*] *put into words or song*
belt out*, canary*, chant, chirp, communicate, convey, croon, emit, enunciate, express, give out*, groan, impart, let out*, moan, pronounce, say, shout, sing, sound, speak, talk, utter, vent, verbalize, voice, warble, yodel; SEE CONCEPT 77

vocation [*n*] *life's work*
art, business, calling, career, craft, do*, dodge*, duty, employment, field, game, handicraft, job, lifework, line*, line of business*, métier, mission, nine-to-five*, occupation, office, post, profession, pursuit, racket*, role, thing*, trade, undertaking; SEE CONCEPTS 349,360

vociferous [*adj*] *loud, insistent*
boisterous, clamant, clamorous, distracting, loudmouthed, noisy, obstreperous, ranting, shouting, shrill, strident, uproarious, vehement, vociferant; SEE CONCEPTS 267,592,594

vogue [*n*] *fashion; current practice*
chic, craze*, currency, custom, dernier cri, fad*, fashionableness, favor, in thing*, last word*, latest, mode, popularity, practice, prevalence, rage*, style, stylishness, thing*, trend, usage, use, way; SEE CONCEPT 655

vogue [*adj*] *fashionable*
faddy*, in*, latest, mod*, modish, now, popular, prevalent, rage*, state-of-the-art*, trendy, up-to-the-minute*, with it*; SEE CONCEPT 589

voice [*n1*] *expression, language*
articulation, call, cry, delivery, exclamation, inflection, intonation, modulation, murmur, mutter, roar, shout, song, sound, speech, statement, tone, tongue, utterance, vent, vocalization, vociferation, words, yell; SEE CONCEPTS 77,276

voice [*n2*] *opinion*
approval, choice, decision, expression, option, part, participation, preference, representation, right of free speech, say, say-so*, suffrage, vent, view, vote, vox populi, will, wish; SEE CONCEPTS 278,376

voice [*v*] *express opinion; put into words*
air, announce, articulate, assert, come out with*, cry, declare, divulge, emphasize, enunci-

ate, give expression, give utterance, inflect, intonate, modulate, present, proclaim, pronounce, put, recount, say, sound, speak, talk, tell, utter, vent, verbalize, vocalize; SEE CONCEPTS 49,51

void [*n*] *emptiness, want*
blank, blankness, cavity, gap, hole, hollow, lack, nihility, nothingness, nullity, opening, space, vacuity, vacuum; SEE CONCEPTS 513,646,709

void [*adj1*] *empty*
abandoned, bare, barren, bereft, clear, deprived, destitute, devoid, drained, emptied, free, lacking, scant, short, shy, tenantless, unfilled, unoccupied, vacant, vacuous, without; SEE CONCEPTS 481,583,740,774

void [*adj2*] *nullified, meaningless*
avoided, bad, dead, forceless, fruitless, ineffective, ineffectual, inoperative, invalid, negated, not viable, nugatory, null, null and void, set aside, sterile, unconfirmed, unenforceable, unfruitful, unratified, unsanctioned, unsuccessful, useless, vain, voided, worthless; SEE CONCEPT 560

void [*v1*] *get rid of; empty*
clear, deplete, discharge, dispose, drain, dump, eject, eliminate, emit, evacuate, flow, give off, go, pour, relieve, remove, throw out, vacate; SEE CONCEPTS 179,180

void [*v2*] *nullify, cancel*
abnegate, abrogate, annul, black out*, bleep*, blue pencil*, clean up, cut, declare null and void*, discharge, dissolve, drop*, gut*, invalidate, launder, rescind, sanitize, sterilize, take out, trim, vacate; SEE CONCEPTS 50,88,121,211

volatile [*adj*] *explosive, changeable*
airy, buoyant, capricious, effervescent, elastic, elusive, ephemeral, erratic, expansive, fickle, fleeting, flighty, flippant, frivolous, fugacious, fugitive, gaseous, gay, giddy, impermanent, imponderable, inconsistent, inconstant, light, lively, lubricious, mercurial, momentary, playful, resilient, short-lived, sprightly, subtle, temperamental, ticklish, transient, transitory, unsettled, unstable, unsteady, up-and-down, vaporous, variable, whimsical; SEE CONCEPTS 401,534

volition [*n*] *free will*
accord, choice, choosing, conation, desire, determination, discretion, election, option, preference, purpose, resolution, selection, will, willingness, wish; SEE CONCEPTS 20,41

volume [*n1*] *capacity, measure of capacity*
aggregate, amount, body, bulk, compass, content, contents, cubic measure, dimensions, extent, figure, mass, number, object, quantity, size, total; SEE CONCEPTS 719,740,794

volume [*n2*] *loudness of a sound*
amplification, degree, intensity, power, sonority, strength; SEE CONCEPTS 65,792

volume [*n3*] *book*
album, edition, publication, tome, treatise, version; SEE CONCEPT 280

voluminous [*adj*] *big, vast*
abundant, ample, billowing, bulky, capacious, cavernous, comprehensive, convoluted, copious, covering, expansive, extensive, full, great, large, legion, many, massive, multifarious, multitudinous, numerous, prolific, roomy, several, simple, spacious, sundry, swelling, various; SEE CONCEPTS 773,781

voluntarily [*adv*] *of one's own free will*
at one's discretion, by choice, by preference, deliberately, freely, intentionally, of one's own ac-

cord*, on one's own, on one's own initiative*, optionally, spontaneously, willingly, with all one's heart*, without being asked, without prompting; SEE CONCEPTS 538,544

voluntary [*adj*] *willing*
autonomous, chosen, deliberate, designful, discretional, elected, free, freely, free-willed, gratuitous, honorary, independent, intended, intentional, opted, optional, spontaneous, unasked, unbidden, uncompelled, unconstrained, unforced, unpaid, unprescribed, volitional, volunteer, willed, willful, wished, witting; SEE CONCEPTS 538,544

volunteer [*v*] *offer to do something*
advance, bring forward, chip in*, come forward, do on one's own volition*, enlist, go in*, let oneself in for*, offer services, present, proffer, propose, put at one's disposal*, put forward, sign up, speak up, stand up, step forward, submit oneself, suggest, take the bull by the horns*, take initiative*, take the plunge*, take upon oneself*, tender; SEE CONCEPTS 66,67

voluptuous [*adj*] *given to sensual pleasure; pleasurable to the senses*
appealing, attractive, delightful, desirable, enticing, erotic, fleshly, hedonist, hedonistic, indulgent, lubricious, luxurious, pleasing, salacious, self-indulgent, sensuous, sexy, sybaritic, wanton; SEE CONCEPTS 372,485

vomit [*v*] *disgorge*
be seasick*, be sick, bring up*, dry heave*, eject, emit, expel, gag*, heave*, hurl*, puke*, regurgitate, retch, ruminate, spew, spit up, throw up, upchuck*; SEE CONCEPTS 179,185,308

voracious [*adj*] *very hungry, greedy*
avid, covetous, devouring, dog-hungry*, edacious, empty, gluttonous, gorging, grasping, gross, insatiable, omnivorous, piggy*, prodigious, rapacious, ravening, ravenous, sating, starved, starved to death*, starving, uncontrolled, unquenchable; SEE CONCEPTS 20,401

vote [*n*] *decision or right to decide representation*
aye*, ballot, choice, franchise, majority, nay*, plebiscite, poll, referendum, secret ballot, show of hands*, suffrage, tally, ticket, will, wish, yea*, yes or no*; SEE CONCEPTS 300,376

vote [*v*] *decide on representation*
ballot, cast ballot, cast vote, choose, confer, declare, determine, effect, elect, enact, enfranchise, establish, go to the polls*, grant, judge, opt, pronounce, propose, put in office*, recommend, return, second, suggest; SEE CONCEPTS 41,300

vouch [*v*] *give assurance*
act as a witness, affirm, answer for, assert, asseverate, assure, attest to, avert, avow, back, bear testimony, be responsible for, certify, confirm, contend, corroborate, cosign, declare, get behind*, give an affidavit, guarantee, maintain, okay*, predicate, profess, prove, put forth, rubber-stamp*, say so*, sign for, sponsor, stand up for*, substantiate, support, swear to, swear up and down*, testify, uphold, verify, vow, warrant, witness; SEE CONCEPTS 49,71,317

vow [*n*] *promise*
affiance, assertion, asseveration, oath, pledge, profession, troth, word of honor; SEE CONCEPTS 278,689

vow [*v*] *make a solemn promise*
affirm, assure, consecrate, covenant, cross one's heart*, declare, dedicate, devote, give word of

honor*, pledge, plight, promise, swear, swear up and down*, testify, undertake solemnly*, vouch, warrant; SEE CONCEPTS 71,297

voyage [*n*] *journey, often by water*
boating, crossing, cruise, excursion, hop, jaunt, junket, overnight, passage, sail, swing, tour, travel, travels, trek, trip, weekend; SEE CONCEPTS 155,224

vulgar [*adj1*] *rude, offensive*
base, blue*, boorish, cheap, coarse, common, contemptible, crude, dirty, disgusting, dishonorable, filthy, fractious, gross*, hard-core*, ignoble, impolite, improper, indecent, indecorous, indelicate, inferior, low, malicious, nasty, naughty, obscene, odious, off-color, profane, raw, repulsive, ribald, risqué, rough, rude, scatological, slippery, smutty, sneaking, soft-core*, sordid, suggestive, tasteless, tawdry, uncouth, unmannerly, unrefined, unworthy, villainous, X-rated*; SEE CONCEPTS 267,372,545

vulgar [*adj2*] *common, general*
colloquial, conversational, dime a dozen*, everyday, familiar, garden variety*, low, native, ordinary, plastic, plebeian, popular, public, run-of-the-mill*, unrefined, vernacular; SEE CONCEPT 530

vulnerable [*adj*] *open to attack*
accessible, assailable, defenseless, exposed, liable, naked, on the line*, on the spot*, out on a limb*, ready, sensitive, sitting duck*, sucker*, susceptible, tender, thin-skinned*, unguarded, unprotected, unsafe, weak, wide open*; SEE CONCEPTS 403,587

W

wacky [*adj*] *acting crazy*
absurd, balmy, crazed, crazy, daft, demented, deranged, eccentric, erratic, foolish, hare-brained, insane, irrational, loony*, lunatic, mad, nuts*, nutty*, odd, preposterous, screwy*, silly, unpredictable, wild, zany*; SEE CONCEPTS 401,403

wad [*n*] *ball of something*
back, block, boodle, bunch, bundle, chunk, clump, cushion, fortune, gathering, heap, hunk, lining, lump, mass, mint, nugget, packet, pad, pile, plug, pot, ream, roll, slew, stuff, tuft, wadding; SEE CONCEPTS 432,436

waddle [*v*] *walk like a duck*
rock, shuffle, sway, toddle, totter, wiggle, wobble; SEE CONCEPT 151

wade [*v*] *plod, often through water*
attack, attempt, bathe, drudge, fall to, ford, get feet wet*, get stuck in*, go for, initiate, jump in, labor, launch, light into, paddle, pitch in, set about, set to, splash, start, stumble, tackle, tear into*, toil, trek, walk, work through; SEE CONCEPTS 87,151

waft [*v*] *carry*
bear, be carried, blow, carry, convey, drift, float, ride, transmit, transport; SEE CONCEPTS 147,217

wag [*n*] *person who is very funny*
a million laughs*, card*, clown, comedian, comic, cutup*, droll*, farceur*, funny person, funster*, humorist, jester*, joker, jokester,

kibitzer*, kidder, life of the party*, madcap*, prankster, punster, quipster, show-off*, trickster, wisecracker, wit, zany; SEE CONCEPTS 416,423

wag [v] *wiggle back and forth*
beat, bob, fish-tail*, flutter, lash, move side to side, nod, oscillate, quiver, rock, shake, shimmy, stir, sway, swing, switch, twitch, vibrate, waggle, wave; SEE CONCEPTS 150,152

wage/wages [n] *earnings for work*
allowance, bacon*, bacon and eggs*, bread*, compensation, cut, emolument, fee, hire, pay, payment, price, receipts, recompense, remuneration, return, returns, reward, salary, share, stipend, sugar*, take*, take-home*; SEE CONCEPT 344

wage [v] *carry on*
carry out, conduct, do, engage in, fulfill, make, practice, proceed with, prosecute, pursue, undertake; SEE CONCEPTS 91,100

wager [n] *money or something gambled*
action, ante*, bet, challenge, chunk, fifty-fifty*, fighting chance*, flyer*, gamble, handle, hazard, hedge, hunch, long shot*, odds on*, outside chance*, parlay, play, pledge, plunge, pot*, risk, stake, toss, venture; SEE CONCEPTS 329,363,364

wager [v] *bet money or something else in a gamble*
adventure, chance, gamble, game, hazard, hedge, hustle, lay, lay a wager, parlay, play, play the market*, pledge, plunge, put on*, put on the line*, put up, risk, set*, shoot*, shoot the works*, spec*, speculate, stake, take action, venture; SEE CONCEPTS 28,363

waif [n] *lost or unclaimed person or thing*
castaway, dogie, drop*, fetch*, flotsam, foundling, homeless one, jetsam, orphan, ragamuffin, stray, urchin; SEE CONCEPT 423

wail [v] *cry loudly*
bawl, bay, bemoan, bewail, carry on*, complain, cry the blues*, deplore, fuss, grieve, howl, jowl, keen, kick, lament, moan, mourn, repine, sob, squall, ululate, weep, whimper, whine; SEE CONCEPTS 77,185

wait [n] *pause, delay*
down, downtime*, halt, hold*, hold-up, interim, interval, on hold*, rest, stay, time wasted*; SEE CONCEPT 807

wait [v] *pause, rest*
abide, anticipate, await, bide, bide one's time*, cool it*, dally, delay, expect, fill time, foresee, hang*, hang around*, hang onto your hat*, hang out, hold back, hold everything*, hold on, hold the phone*, hole up*, keep shirt on*, lie in wait*, lie low*, linger, look for, look forward to, mark time*, put on hold*, remain, save it*, sit tight*, sit up for*, stall, stand by, stay, stay up for, stick around*, sweat it*, tarry, watch; SEE CONCEPTS 210,681

wait on [v] *serve*
arrange, attend, care for, deal, deliver, help, minister, nurse, portion, ready, set, tend; SEE CONCEPTS 136,324

waive [v] *give up; let go*
abandon, allow, cede, defer, delay, disclaim, disown, dispense with, forgo, grant, hand over, hold off, hold up, leave, neglect, postpone, prorogue, put off, refrain from, reject, relinquish, remit, remove, renege, renounce, reserve, resign, set aside, shelve, stay, surrender, suspend, table, turn over, yield; SEE CONCEPTS 121,234,317

waiver [n] *giving up; letting go*
abandonment, abdication, disclaimer, foregoing, postponement, refusal, rejection, relinquishment, remission, renunciation, reservation, resignation, setting aside, surrender, tabling; SEE CONCEPTS 121,318,685

wake [n1] *formal observance of a body before funeral*
deathwatch, funeral service, last rites, obsequies, rites, vigil, watch; SEE CONCEPTS 367,377

wake [n2] *trail behind something*
aftermath, backwash, furrow, path, track, train, wash, wave; SEE CONCEPTS 753,824

wake/waken [v1] *stop sleeping*
arise, awake, awaken, be roused, bestir, bring to life*, call, come to, get out of bed*, get up, nudge, open one's eyes*, prod, rise, rise and shine*, roll out, rouse, shake, stir, stretch, tumble out*, turn out, wake up; SEE CONCEPT 105

wake/waken [v2] *excite, stimulate*
activate, animate, arouse, awaken, challenge, enliven, fire, fire up*, freshen, galvanize, grasp, jazz up*, key up*, kindle, notice, pep up*, provoke, quicken, rally, renew, rouse, see, steam up*, stir up, switch on*, understand, whet, zip up*; SEE CONCEPTS 7,14,22

wakeful [adj] *alert, restless*
alive, astir, attentive, careful, heedful, insomniac, insomnious, observant, on guard, on the alert, on the lookout, on the qui vive, sleepless, unsleeping, vigilant, waking, wary, watchful, wideawake; SEE CONCEPTS 539,542

walk [n1] *brief period on foot*
airing, carriage, circuit, constitutional, gait, hike, jaunt, march, pace, parade, perambulation, peregrination, promenade, ramble, saunter, schlepp*, step, stretch, stride, stroll, tour, traipse, tramp, tread, turn; SEE CONCEPTS 149,224

walk [n2] *pathway*
aisle, alley, avenue, boardwalk, boulevard, bricks, bypath, byway, catwalk, cloister, course, court, crossing, esplanade, footpath, gangway, lane, mall, passage, path, pavement, pier, platform, promenade, road, sidewalk, street, track, trail; SEE CONCEPT 501

walk [n3] *discipline*
area, arena, bailiwick, calling, career, course, domain, dominion, field, line, metier, profession, province, sphere, terrain, territory, trade, vocation; SEE CONCEPTS 349,360

walk [v] *move along on foot*
advance, amble, ambulate, canter, escort, exercise, file, foot, go, go on foot*, hike, hit the road*, hoof it, knock about*, lead, leg*, locomote, lumber, march, meander, pace, pad, parade, patrol, perambulate, plod, prance, promenade, race, roam, rove, run, saunter, scuff, shamble, shuffle, slog, stalk, step, stride, stroll, strut, stump, take a walk, toddle, tour, traipse, tramp, travel on foot, traverse, tread, trek, troop, trudge, wander, wend one's way*; SEE CONCEPT 149

wall [n] *obstruction, divider*
bank, bar, barricade, barrier, block, blockade, bulwark, curb, dam, embankment, enclosure, facade, fence, fortification, hindrance, hurdle, impediment, levee, limitation, palisade, panel, paneling, parapet, partition, rampart, restriction, retainer, roadblock, screen, side, stockade, stop, surface; SEE CONCEPTS 440,666

wallop [*n*] *strong hit*
bash, belt, blow, bop, bump, clash, collision, crash, haymaker*, impact, jar, jolt, kick, percussion, punch, shock, slam, slug, smack, smash, thump, thwack*, whack; SEE CONCEPT *189*

wallop [*v1*] *beat, hit*
bam, bash, batter, belt, blast, boff, bop, buffet, bushwhack*, clobber*, drub*, hide, lambaste*, paste, pelt, plant one*, pound, pummel, punch, slam, slog, slug, smack, smash, sock, strike, swat, take out, tan*, thrash, thump, whack, wham, whomp, zap*; SEE CONCEPT *189*

wallop [*v2*] *defeat soundly*
beat, best, clobber*, crush*, drub*, lambaste*, lick*, rout, shellac*, thrash*, trim*, trounce, vanquish, whip*; SEE CONCEPT *95*

wallow [*v1*] *slosh around in*
bathe in, be immersed, blunder, flounder, get stuck, immerse, lie, loll, lurch, move around in, reel, roll, roll about, roll around in, splash around, sprawl, stagger, stumble, sway, toss, totter, tumble, wade, welter; SEE CONCEPTS *149,201*

wallow [*v2*] *become very involved in*
bask, delight, enjoy, glory, grovel, humor, indulge oneself, luxuriate, pamper, relish, revel, roll, rollick, spoil, take pleasure; SEE CONCEPT *384*

wan [*adj*] *colorless, weak*
anemic, ashen, ashy, bilious, blanched, bleached, bloodless, cadaverous, dim, discolored, faint, feeble, forceless, ghastly, haggard, ineffective, ineffectual, livid, pale, pallid, pasty, peaked, sickly, washed-out, waxen, white, worn; SEE CONCEPTS *314,618*

wand [*n*] *rod*
baton, caduceus, scepter, sprig, staff, stick, twig; SEE CONCEPTS *470,499*

wander [*v1*] *move about aimlessly*
aberrate, amble, circumambulate, circumlocute, circumnutate, cruise, deviate, divagate, diverge, drift, float, follow one's nose*, gad*, gallivant*, globe-trot, hike, hopscotch*, jaunt, maunder, meander, peregrinate, ramble, range, roam, roll, rove, straggle, stray, stroll, take to the road*, trail, traipse, tramp, trek, vagabond, walk the tracks*; SEE CONCEPTS *151,224*

wander [*v2*] *digress; get lost*
babble, depart, deviate, divagate, diverge, err, get off the track*, get sidetracked*, go astray*, go off on a tangent*, lose one's way, lose train of thought*, ramble, rave, shift, stray, swerve, talk nonsense*, veer; SEE CONCEPTS *101,266,665*

wanderer [*n*] *person who travels aimlessly*
adventurer, beachcomber, bum, drifter, explorer, floater, gad*, gadabout, gallivanter, globe-trotter, gypsy, itinerant, meanderer, nomad, pilgrim, rambler, ranger, roamer, rolling stone*, rover, straggler, stray, stroller, traveler, vagabond, vagrant, voyager; SEE CONCEPT *423*

wane [*v*] *diminish, lessen*
abate, atrophy, decline, decrease, die away, die down, die out, dim, draw to a close*, drop, dwindle, ease off, ebb, fade, fade away, fail, fall, fall short, let up, moderate, peter out*, relent, shrink, sink, slacken, slack off, subside, taper off, waste away, weaken, wind down*, wither; SEE CONCEPTS *698,776*

want [*n1*] *desire*
appetite, craving, demand, fancy, hankering, hunger, longing, necessity, need, requirement, thirst, wish, yearning, yen; SEE CONCEPT *20*

want [*n2*] *lack, need*
absence, dearth, default, defect, deficiency, destitution, exigency, exiguousness, famine, impecuniousness, impoverishment, inadequacy, indigence, insufficiency, meagerness, neediness, paucity, pauperism, penury, poorness, poverty, privation, scantiness, scarcity, shortage, skimpiness; SEE CONCEPTS *646,709*

want [*v1*] *desire*
ache, aspire, be greedy, choose, could do with*, covet, crave, desiderate, fancy, feel a need, hanker*, have ambition, have an urge for*, have a passion for*, have a yen for*, have eyes for*, hunger, incline toward*, itch for*, long, lust, need, pine, prefer, require, spoil for*, thirst, wish, yearn; SEE CONCEPT *20*

want [*v2*] *lack, need*
be deficient, be deprived of, be found wanting, be insufficient, be poor, be short of, be without, call for, demand, fall short in, have need of, miss, require, stand in need of, starve; SEE CONCEPT *646*

wanting [*adj*] *lacking, inadequate*
absent, away, bankrupt, bereft, burned out*, cooked*, cut off, defective, deficient, deprived, destitute, devoid, disappointing, empty, failing, faulty, gone, half-baked*, imperfect, incomplete, in default, inferior, less, minus, missing, needed, not good enough, not up to par*, omitted, out of gas*, patchy, poor, scant, scanty, scarce, short, shy, sketchy, substandard, too little too late*, unfulfilled, unsound; SEE CONCEPTS *531,546,560*

wanton [*n*] *profligate person*
debauchee, libertine, rake; SEE CONCEPTS *412,415,419*

wanton [*adj1*] *extravagant, lustful*
abandoned, fast*, lax, lewd, libertine, libidinous, licentious, outrageous, profligate, promiscuous, shameless, speedy*, unprincipled, unscrupulous, wayward, X-rated*; SEE CONCEPTS *372,401,545*

wanton [*adj2*] *cruel, malicious*
accidentally on purpose*, arbitrary, contrary, double-crossing*, evil, gratuitous, groundless, inconsiderate, malevolent, malicious, mean, merciless, motiveless, needless, ornery, perverse, senseless, spiteful, unasked, uncalled-for*, unfair, unjust, unjustifiable, unjustified, unprovoked, vicious, wayward, wicked, willful; SEE CONCEPT *401*

wanton [*adj3*] *careless*
capricious, changeable, devil-may-care*, extravagant, fanciful, fickle, fitful, fluctuating, free, frivolous, heedless, hot and cold*, immoderate, inconstant, intemperate, lavish, outrageous, prodigal, profuse, rash, reckless, spendthrift, spoiled, thriftless, unfettered, unreserved, unrestrained, up and down*, variable, volatile, wasteful, whimsical, wild; SEE CONCEPTS *534,542*

war [*n*] *armed conflict*
battle, bloodshed, cold war, combat, conflict, contention, contest, enmity, fighting, hostilities, hostility, police action, strife, strike, struggle, warfare; SEE CONCEPT *320*

war [*v*] *fight, battle*
attack, attempt, bombard, campaign against, challenge, clash, combat, contend, contest, differ, disagree, endeavor, engage in combat, go to war, kill, make war, march against, meet, murder, op-

pugn, shell, shoot, strive, struggle, take on, take the field against, take up arms, tug, wage war; SEE CONCEPTS *106,320*

ward [n1] *district*
area, canton, department, diocese, division, parish, precinct, quarter, territory, zone; SEE CONCEPTS *508,513*

ward [n2] *custody; person in one's custody*
adopted child, care, charge, child, client, dependent, foster child, godchild, guardianship, keeping, minor, orphan, protection, protégé, protégée, pupil, safekeeping, trust; SEE CONCEPTS *414,691*

ward/ward off [v] *defend, guard*
avert, avoid, beat off, block, check, deflect, deter, divert, fend, foil, forestall, frustrate, halt, hold off, interrupt, keep at arm's length*, keep at bay*, keep off, obviate, parry, preclude, prevent, rebuff, rebut, repel, repulse, rule out, stave off, stop, stymie*, thwart, turn, turn aside, turn away; SEE CONCEPTS *96,134*

warden [n] *person who guards and manages*
administrator, bodyguard, caretaker, curator, custodian, deacon, dogcatcher, gamekeeper, governor, guard, guardian, jailer/jailor, janitor, keeper, officer, overseer, prison head, ranger, skipper, superintendent, watchdog, watchkeeper; SEE CONCEPT *347*

wardrobe [n] *clothes or furniture for storing clothes*
apparel, attire, buffet, bureau, chest, chiffonier, closet, clothing, commode, costumes, cupboard, drapes*, dresser, dry goods, duds*, ensembles, garments, locker, outfits, rags*, suits, threads*, toggery, togs, trousseau, trunk, vestments, weeds*; SEE CONCEPTS *443,451*

warehouse [n] *storage place*
barn, bin, depository, depot, distribution center, establishment, repository, shed, stash house, stockpile, stockroom, store, storehouse; SEE CONCEPTS *439,449*

wares [n] *merchandise for sale*
articles, commodities, goods, line, lines, manufactures, material, produce, product, products, range, seconds, stock, stuff, vendibles; SEE CONCEPT *338*

warfare [n] *armed conflict*
armed struggle, arms, battle, blows, campaigning, clash, combat, competition, contest, counterinsurgency, discord, emulation, fighting, hostilities, military operation, passage of arms, rivalry, strategy, strife, striving, struggle, tug-of-war*, war; SEE CONCEPT *320*

warlike [adj] *hostile, battling*
aggressive, attacking, bellicose, belligerent, bloodthirsty, combative, contending, contentious, contrary, fighting, gladiatorial, hawkish, inimical, martial, militant, militaristic, military, offensive, pugnacious, quarrelsome, ructious, soldierly, truculent, unfriendly, warmongering, warring; SEE CONCEPTS *401,548*

warm [adj1] *moderately hot*
balmy, broiling, clement, close, flushed, glowing, heated, hot, lukewarm, melting, mild, perspiring, pleasant, roasting, scorching, sizzling, snug, summery, sunny, sweating, sweaty, sweltering, temperate, tepid, thermal, toasty, warmish; SEE CONCEPT *605*

warm [adj2] *friendly, kind*
affable, affectionate, amiable, amorous, ardent, cheerful, compassionate, cordial, empathetic, fervent, genial, gracious, happy, heartfelt, hearty, hospitable, kindhearted, kindly, loving, pleasant, responsive, sincere, softhearted, sympathetic, tender, warmhearted, wholehearted; SEE CONCEPTS *267,401,404*

warm [adj3] *enthusiastic*
amorous, angry, animated, ardent, earnest, effusive, emotional, excitable, excited, fervent, fervid, glowing, gung-ho*, heated, hot*, intense, irascible, keen, lively, nutty*, passionate, spirited, stormy, vehement, vigorous, violent, zealous; SEE CONCEPTS *401,542*

warm [v] *heat up*
bake, chafe, cook, fix, heat, melt, microwave, prepare, put on the fire, thaw, toast, warm over, warm up; SEE CONCEPTS *170,255*

warn [v] *give notice of possible occurrence*
acquaint, address, admonish, advise, advocate, alert, apprise, caution, clue in*, counsel, cry wolf*, deprecate, direct, dissuade, enjoin, exhort, fill in, forbid, forearm, forewarn, give fair warning, give the high sign*, give warning, guide, hint, inform, instruct, lay it out*, make aware, notify, order, post, predict, prepare, prescribe, prompt, put on guard, recommend, remind, remonstrate, reprove, signal, suggest, summon, tell, threaten, tip, tip off*, urge, wise up*; SEE CONCEPT *78*

warning [n] *notice of possible occurrence*
admonition, advice, alarm, alert, augury, caution, caveat, distress signal, example, exhortation, fore, foretoken, forewarning, guidance, handwriting on wall*, heads up*, hint, indication, information, injunction, intimation, lesson, look out*, Mayday*, notification, omen, portent, prediction, premonition, presage, recommendation, sign, signal, SOS*, suggestion, threat, tip, tip-off*, token, watch-it*, wink, word, word to the wise*; SEE CONCEPTS *78,274*

warning [adj] *cautionary*
admonishing, admonitory, cautioning, exemplary, exhortatory, monitorial, monitory, ominous, premonitory, threatening; SEE CONCEPT *267*

warp [v] *bend, distort*
bastardize*, brutalize, color, contort, corrupt, crook, curve, debase, debauch, deform, deprave, deviate, misrepresent, misshape, pervert, swerve, torture, turn, twist, vitiate, wind; SEE CONCEPTS *63,137,213,250*

warrant [n] *authorization*
accreditation, assurance, authentication, authority, basis, carte blanche, certificate, commission, credential, credentials, ducat, earnest, foundation, go-ahead*, green light*, guarantee, license, official document, okay*, pass, passport, pawn, permission, permit, pledge, right, sanction, security, shingle*, sticker, subpoena, summons, tag, testimonial, ticket, token, verification, warranty, word; SEE CONCEPTS *376,685*

warrant [v] *guarantee, justify, authorize*
affirm, answer for, approve, argue, assert, assure, attest, avouch, back, bear out, call for, certify, claim, commission, contend, declare, defend, delegate, demand, empower, endorse, ensure, entitle, excuse, explain, give grounds for, guarantee, guaranty, insure, license, maintain, necessitate, permit, pledge, privilege, promise, require, sanction, secure, sponsor, stand behind, state, stipulate, swear, take an oath*, undertake, underwrite,

wa
wa

uphold, vindicate, vouch for, vow; SEE CONCEPTS
50,57,71,88

warranty [n] *promise*
assurance, bail, bond, certificate, contract, covenant, guarantee, guaranty, pledge, security,
surety, written promise; SEE CONCEPTS 684,685

warrior [n] *person who fights in combat*
battler, champion, combatant, conscript, enlisted
person, fighter, fighting person, GI*, hero, serviceperson, soldier, trooper; SEE CONCEPT 358

wary [adj] *careful, cautious*
alert, attentive, cagey, calculating, canny, chary,
circumspect, considerate, discreet, distrustful,
doubting, frugal, gingerly, guarded, handling with
kid gloves*, heedful, keeping on one's toes*,
leery, on guard, on the lookout*, on the qui vive,
provident, prudent, safe, saving, sly, sparing, suspicious, thinking twice*, thrifty, unwasteful, vigilant, walking on eggs*, watchful, watching one's
step*, watching out, wide-awake; SEE CONCEPTS
401,403

wash [n1] *laundry, bath*
ablution, bathe, cleaning, cleansing, dirty clothes,
laundering, rinse, scrub, shampoo, shower, washing; SEE CONCEPTS 451,514

wash [n2] *wave; water movement*
ebb and flow, eddy, flow, gush, heave, lapping,
murmur, roll, rush, spurt, surge, surging, sweep,
swell, swirl, swishing, undulation; SEE CONCEPT
748

wash [n3] *coloring*
coat, coating, film, layer, overlay, rinse, stain,
suffusion, swab; SEE CONCEPT 475

wash [v1] *bathe, clean*
bath, brush up, bubble, cleanse, clean up, dip, do
the dishes*, do the laundry*, douse, drench, float,
freshen up*, fresh up*, hose, imbue, immerse,
lap, launder, lave, moisten, rinse, scour, scrub,
shampoo, shine, shower, slosh, soak, soap,
sponge, starch, swab, take a bath*, take a
shower*, tub, wash up*, wet, wipe; SEE CONCEPT
165

wash [v2] *be convincing*
be acceptable, bear scrutiny, be plausible, be reasonable, carry weight, convince, endure, hold up,
hold water*, stand up*, stick*; SEE CONCEPT 676

waste [n1] *spending, use without thought*
decay, desolation, destruction, devastation, dilapidation, dissipation, disuse, exhaustion, expenditure, extravagance, fritter*, havoc, improvidence,
lavishness, loss, lost opportunity*, misapplication, misuse, overdoing, prodigality, ravage, ruin,
squander, squandering, unthriftiness, wastage,
wastefulness; SEE CONCEPTS 156,252

waste [n2] *land that is uncultivated*
badlands, barren, bog, brush, brushland, bush,
desert, dust bowl, fen, jungle, marsh, marshland,
moor, quagmire, solitude, swamp, tundra, void,
wasteland, wild, wilderness, wilds; SEE CONCEPT
509

waste [n3] *garbage, refuse*
debris, dreck, dregs, dross, excess, hogwash*,
junk, leavings, leftovers, litter, offal, offscour-
ings, rubbish, rubble, ruins, rummage, scrap,
slop, sweepings, swill, trash; SEE CONCEPT 260

waste [v1] *spend or use without thought; dwindle*
atrophy, be of no avail*, blow, burn up, consume,
corrode, crumble, debilitate, decay, decline, decrease, deplete, disable, disappear, dissipate, divert, drain, droop, eat away, ebb, emaciate,

empty, enfeeble, exhaust, fade, fritter away*,
frivol away*, gamble away, gnaw, go to waste,
lavish, lose, misapply, misemploy, misuse, perish, pour down the drain*, run dry, run through*,
sap, sink, splurge, squander, thin, throw away,
trifle away, undermine, wane, wear, wear out,
wilt, wither; SEE CONCEPT 156

waste [v2] *ruin, destroy*
depredate, desecrate, desolate, despoil, devastate,
devour, lay waste, pillage, rape, ravage, raze, reduce, sack, spoil, spoliate, wreak havoc; SEE
CONCEPT 252

wasteful [adj] *not economical*
careless, cavalier, destructive, dissipative, extravagant, immoderate, improvident, incontinent, lavish, liberal, overdone, overgenerous, pound-
foolish*, prodigal, profligate, profuse, reckless,
ruinous, spendthrift, squandering, thriftless, uneconomical, unthrifty, wanton, wild; SEE CON-
CEPT 401

watch [n1] *clock worn on body*
analog watch, chronometer, digital watch, pocket
watch, stopwatch, ticker*, timepiece, timer,
wristwatch; SEE CONCEPT 463

watch [n2] *lookout*
alertness, attention, awareness, duty, eagle eye*,
eye*, gander, guard, hawk, heed, inspection, notice, observance, observation, patrol, picket, scrutiny, sentinel, sentry, supervision, surveillance,
tab, tout, vigil, vigilance, watchfulness, weather
eye*; SEE CONCEPTS 134,623

watch [v1] *look at*
attend, case, check out, concentrate, contemplate,
eagle-eye*, examine, eye*, eyeball*, focus, follow, gaze, get a load of*, give the once over*,
have a look-see*, inspect, keep an eye on*, keep
tabs on*, listen, look, mark, mind, note, observe,
pay attention, peer, pipe*, regard, rubberneck*,
scan, scope, scrutinize, see, spy, stare, take in,
take notice, view, wait; SEE CONCEPT 623

watch [v2] *guard, protect*
attend, be on alert*, be on the lookout*, be vigilant*, be wary, be watchful, care for, keep, keep
eyes open*, keep eyes peeled*, keep watch over,
look after, look out, mind, oversee, patrol, pick
up on, police, ride shotgun for*, superintend, take
care of, take heed*, tend, wait; SEE CONCEPTS
134,623

watchful [adj] *on the lookout*
alert, all ears*, attentive, careful, cautious, chary,
circumspect, glued*, guarded, heedful, hooked*,
keen, not missing a trick*, observant, on guard,
on one's toes*, on the ball*, on the job*, on the
qui vive, on the watch, open-eyed, prepared,
ready, see after, see to, suspicious, unsleeping,
vigilant, wakeful, wary, wide-awake, with eyes
peeled*; SEE CONCEPT 401

watchkeeper [n] *person who guards, is on lookout*
caretaker, curator, custodian, detective, flagger,
guard, keeper, lookout, observer, patrol, picket,
police officer, ranger, scout, security guard, security officer, sentinel, sentry, signaller, spotter,
spy, ward, warden, watch, watcher; SEE CONCEPT
348

water [n] *pure liquid hydrogen and oxygen*
Adam's ale*, aqua, aqua pura*, drink, H_2O, rain,
rainwater, saliva, tears; SEE CONCEPT 467

water [v] *dampen; put water in*
baptize, bathe, damp, dilute, doctor, douse,
drench, drool, flood, hose, imbue, inundate, irri-

gate, moisten, saturate, soak, sodden, souse, spatter, spray, sprinkle, steep, thin, wash, weaken, wet; SEE CONCEPT 256

watery [adj] liquid, diluted
adulterated, anemic, aqueous, bloodless, colorless, damp, dilute, doused, flavorless, fluid, humid, insipid, marshy, moist, pale, runny, serous, sodden, soggy, tasteless, thin, washed, watereddown, waterlike, water-logged, weak, wet; SEE CONCEPTS 485,603,618

wave [n] sea surf, current
bending, billow, breaker, coil, comber, convolution, corkscrew, crest, crush, curl, curlicue, drift, flood, foam, ground swell, gush, heave, influx, loop, movement, outbreak, rash, ridge, ripple, rippling, rocking, roll, roller, rush, scroll, sign, signal, stream, surge, sweep, swell, tendency, tide, tube, twirl, twist, undulation, unevenness, uprising, upsurge, whitecap, winding; SEE CONCEPTS 147,436,514

wave [v] move back and forth; gesture
beckon, billow, brandish, coil, curl, direct, falter, flap, flourish, flow, fluctuate, flutter, fly, gesticulate, indicate, motion, move to and fro, oscillate, palpitate, pulsate, pulse, quaver, quiver, reel, ripple, seesaw, shake, sign, signal, stir, stream, surge, sway, swell, swing, swirl, swish, switch, tremble, twirl, twist, undulate, vacillate, vibrate, wag, waggle, waver, whirl, wield, wigwag*, wobble; SEE CONCEPTS 74,147,149

waver [v] shift back and forth; be indecisive
be irresolute, be unable to decide*, blow hot and cold*, change, deliberate, dilly-dally*, dither, falter, flicker, fluctuate, halt, hedge, hem and haw*, hesitate, oscillate, palter, pause, pussyfoot around*, quiver, reel, run hot and cold*, seesaw*, shake, stagger, sway, teeter, totter, tremble, trim, undulate, vacillate, vary, waffle, wave, weave, whiffle, wobble, yo-yo*; SEE CONCEPTS 18,147,410

wax [v] become large, fuller
augment, become, build, come, develop, dilate, enlarge, expand, fill out, get bigger, get to, grow, grow full, heighten, increase, magnify, mount, multiply, rise, run, swell, turn, upsurge; SEE CONCEPTS 704,780

way [n1] method, technique
action, approach, contrivance, course, course of action, custom, design, expedient, fashion, form, groove*, habit, habitude, hang-up*, hook*, idea, instrument, kick, manner, means, measure, mode, modus, move, outline, plan, plot, policy, practice, procedure, process, scheme, shot, step, stroke, style, system, tack, thing*, usage, use, vehicle, wise, wont; SEE CONCEPT 6

way [n2] direction, route
access, admission, admittance, advance, alternative, approach, artery, avenue, bearing, boulevard, byway, channel, course, distance, door, drag*, elbowroom, entrance, entrée, entry, extent, forward motion, gate, gateway, headway, highway, ingress, journey, lane, length, line, march, movement, opening, orbit, passage, path, pathway, progress, progression, ride, road, room, row, space, stone's throw*, street, stretch, tendency, thataway*, thoroughfare, track, trail, trend, walk; SEE CONCEPTS 501,738,739

way [n3] characteristic, habit
aspect, behavior, circumstance, condition, conduct, consuetude, custom, detail, fashion, feature,

fettle, form, gait, groove, guise, habit, hook, idiosyncrasy, kick*, manner, nature, particular, personality, point, practice, praxis, respect, sense, shape, shot, situation, state, status, style, thing*, tone, trait, trick, usage, use, wont; SEE CONCEPT 411

wayfaring [adj] traveling
drifting, gadabout, globe-trotting, itinerant, itinerate, jet-setting*, journeying, nomadic, perambulant, perambulatory, peripatetic, rambling, roving, rubbernecking*, vagabond, vagrant, voyaging, walking, wandering; SEE CONCEPT 401

waylay [v] intercept, ambush
accost, ambuscade, assail, attack, box*, bushwhack*, catch, hold up, intercept, jump, lay for*, lie in wait, lurk, pounce on, prowl, set upon, skulk, slink, surprise, swoop down on*; SEE CONCEPTS 86,121

wayward [adj] contrary, unmanageable
aberrant, arbitrary, balky, capricious, changeable, contumacious, cross-grained, delinquent, disobedient, disorderly, errant, erratic, fickle, flighty, fractious, froward, headstrong, immoral, inconstant, incorrigible, insubordinate, intractable, mulish, obdurate, obstinate, ornery*, perverse, rebellious, recalcitrant, refractory, restive, self-indulgent, self-willed, stubborn, uncompliant, undependable, ungovernable, unpredictable, unruly, unstable, variable, whimsical, willful; SEE CONCEPT 401

weak [adj1] not strong
anemic, debilitated, decrepit, delicate, effete, enervated, exhausted, faint, feeble, flaccid, flimsy, forceless, fragile, frail, hesitant, impuissant, infirm, insubstantial, irresolute, lackadaisical*, languid, languorous, limp, makeshift, out of gas*, powerless, prostrate, puny, rickety, rocky*, rotten, senile, shaky, sickly, sluggish, spent, spindly, supine, tender, torpid, uncertain, undependable, unsound, unsteady, unsubstantial, wasted, wavering, weakened, weakly, wobbly; SEE CONCEPTS 314,488,489

weak [adj2] cowardly
faint-hearted, fluctuant, frightened, hesitant, impotent, indecisive, ineffectual, infirm, insecure, irresolute, laid-back*, nerveless, nervous, palsied, powerless, shaky, soft, spineless, tender, timorous, uncertain, undependable, unreliable, unstable, unsure, vacillating, wavering, weak-kneed*, wimpy, wishy-washy*, wobbly, zero*; SEE CONCEPTS 402,403,542

weak [adj3] faint, soft
bated, dim, distant, dull, feeble, gentle, imperceptible, inaudible, indistinct, low, muffled, pale, poor, quiet, reedy, slight, small, stifled, thin, unaccented, unstressed, whispered; SEE CONCEPT 594

weak [adj4] deficient, feeble
faulty, flabby, flimsy, forceless, green*, handicapped, hollow, immature, implausible, impotent, improbable, inadequate, incompetent, incomplete, inconceivable, inconclusive, incredible, ineffective, ineffectual, inept, invalid, lacking, lame, limited, pathetic, poor, raw, shaky, shallow, slight, slim, small, spineless, substandard, thick, thin, unbelievable, unconvincing, unprepared, unqualified, unsatisfactory, unsubstantial, unsure, untrained, wanting; SEE CONCEPTS 537,558,570

wa
we

weak [adj5] *exposed, vulnerable*
accessible, assailable, defenseless, helpless, indefensible, unguarded, unprotected, unsafe, untenable, wide-open*, woundable; SEE CONCEPTS 576,587

weak [adj6] *watered-down*
dilute, insipid, milk-and-water*, runny, tasteless, thin, washy, waterish, watery, wishy-washy*; SEE CONCEPTS 462,485

weaken [v] *reduce the strength of*
abate, adulterate, break up, cripple, crumble, cut, debase, debilitate, decline, decrease, depress, devitalize, dilute, diminish, droop, dwindle, ease up, enervate, exhaust, fade, fail, faint, flag, give way, halt, impair, impoverish, invalidate, languish, lessen, limp, lose, lose spirit, lower, minimize, mitigate, moderate, reduce, relapse, relax, sap, slow down, soften, temper, thin, thin out, tire, totter, tremble, undermine, vitiate, wane, water down, wilt; SEE CONCEPTS 240,698

weakling [n] *person who has no strength*
baby, chicken*, chicken heart*, coward, cream puff*, crybaby, dotard, invertebrate, jellyfish*, misfit, pushover, wimp*, yellow belly*; SEE CONCEPTS 412,423

weakness [n] *defect, proneness*
Achilles heel*, appetite*, blemish, chink in armor*, debility, decrepitude, deficiency, delicacy, enervation, failing, faintness, fault, feebleness, flaw, fondness, fragility, frailty, gap, impairment, imperfection, impotence, inclination, inconstancy, indecision, infirmity, instability, invalidity, irresolution, lack, languor, lapse, liking, passion, penchant, powerlessness, predilection, proclivity, prostration, senility, shortcoming, soft spot*, sore point*, taste*, vice, vitiation, vulnerability; SEE CONCEPTS 411,674,732

wealth [n] *money, resources*
abundance, affluence, assets, belongings, bounty, cache, capital, cash, clover*, commodities, copiousness, cornucopia, dough*, estate, fortune, funds, gold, goods, hoard, holdings, lap of luxury*, long green*, lucre, luxuriance, luxury, means, opulence, pelf, plenitude, plenty, possessions, profusion, property, prosperity, prosperousness, revenue, riches, richness, security, stocks and bonds, store, substance, substantiality, treasure, velvet*, worth; SEE CONCEPTS 340,710

wealthy [adj] *rich; having a lot of money*
affluent, booming, comfortable, having it made*, independent, in the money*, loaded, made of money*, moneyed, of independent means, opulent, pecunious, prosperous, rolling in it*, substantial, upscale, well-heeled*, well-off*, well-to-do*; SEE CONCEPT 334

wear [n] *use, corrosion*
abrasion, attrition, damage, depreciation, deterioration, dilapidation, diminution, disappearance, employment, erosion, friction, impairment, inroads, loss, mileage, service, usefulness, utility, waste, wear and tear; SEE CONCEPTS 658,698

wear [v1] *be clothed in*
array, attire, bear, be dressed in, carry, clothe oneself, cover, display, don, draw on, dress in, effect, exhibit, fit out, get into, get on, harness, have on, put on, show, slip on, sport, suit up*, turn out*, wrap; SEE CONCEPTS 167,453

wear [v2] *corrode, use*
abrade, become threadbare, become worn, be worthless, chafe, consume, crumble, cut down,

decay, decline, decrease, deteriorate, diminish, drain, dwindle, erode, exhaust, fade, fatigue, fray, gall, go to seed*, graze, grind, impair, jade, overuse, overwork, rub, scrape, scrape off, scuff, shrink, tax, tire, use up, wash away, waste, wear out, wear thin, weary, weather; SEE CONCEPTS 156,225,240,698

wear [v3] *bother, undermine*
annoy, drain, enervate, exasperate, exhaust, fatigue, get the better of, harass, irk, pester, reduce, tax, vex, weaken, wear down, weary; SEE CONCEPTS 7,19

wear [v4] *endure*
bear up, be durable, hold up, last, remain, stand, stand up; SEE CONCEPT 23

weary [adj] *tired*
all in*, beat*, bone-tired*, bored, burned out*, bushed, dead*, dead tired*, discontented, disgusted, dog-tired*, done in*, drained, drooping, drowsy, enervated, exhausted, fagged, fatigued, fed up, flagging, had it*, impatient, indifferent, jaded, knocked out, out of gas*, overworked, pooped*, punchy*, ready to drop*, sick, sick and tired*, sleepy, spent*, taxed, wearied, wearing, wiped out*, worn out, zonked*; SEE CONCEPTS 314,403,485

weary [v] *make tired*
annoy, bore, burden, cause ennui, cloy, debilitate, depress, disgust, dishearten, distress, drain, droop, drowse, enervate, enfeeble, exasperate, exhaust, fade, fag, fail, fall off, fatigue, flag, glut, grow tired, harass, have had enough*, irk, jade, leave one cold*, lose interest, make discontented, nauseate, oppress, overwork, pain, plague, sap, sicken, sink, strain, take it out of*, tax, tire, tire out, try the patience of*, tucker out*, vex, weaken, wear down, wear out, weigh; SEE CONCEPTS 13,250,303

weather [n] *atmospheric conditions*
climate, clime, elements; SEE CONCEPTS 522,524

weather [v] *endure*
acclimate, bear the brunt of*, bear up against*, become toughened, brave, come through, expose, get through, grow hardened, grow strong, harden, make it, overcome, pull through, resist, ride out*, rise above*, season, stand, stick it out*, suffer, surmount, survive, toughen, withstand; SEE CONCEPTS 23,35,202

weave [v] *blend, unite; contrive*
braid, build, careen, complect, complicate, compose, construct, create, criss-cross, crochet, cue, entwine, fabricate, fold, fuse, incorporate, interfold, interlace, interlink, intermingle, intertwine, introduce, knit, knot, loop, lurch, make, make up, manufacture, mat, merge, mesh, move in and out, net, piece together, plait, ply, put together, reticulate, sew, snake, spin, splice, twine, twist, twist and turn, whip through, wind, wreathe, writhe, zigzag; SEE CONCEPTS 147,158

web [n] *netting*
cobweb, complexity, entanglement, fabric, fiber, filigree, gossamer, interconnection, interlacing, involvement, labyrinth, lacework, lattice, mat, matting, maze, mesh, meshwork, morass, net, network, plait, reticulation, screen, skein, snarl, tangle, texture, tissue, toil, trellis, warp, weave, webbing, weft, wicker, woof; SEE CONCEPTS 260,473

wed [v1] *marry*
become husband and wife, be married, couple,

espouse, get hitched*, get married, join, lead to the altar, make one*, receive in marriage, say I do*, take in marriage, tie*, tie the knot*, unite; SEE CONCEPT 297

wed [v2] *join, unite*
ally, associate, blend, coalesce, cojoin, combine, commingle, connect, couple, dedicate, fuse, interweave, link, marry, merge, relate, unify, yoke; SEE CONCEPTS 113,193

wedding [n] *marriage rite*
bells*, bridal, espousal, hook, marriage, marriage ceremony, matrimony, nuptial rite, nuptials, spousal, union, wedlock; SEE CONCEPT 297

wedge [n] *solid piece, often triangular*
block, chock, chunk, cleat, cotter, cusp, keystone, lump, prong, quoin, shim, spire, taper; SEE CONCEPTS 471,499

weep [v] *cry*
bawl, bemoan, bewail, blubber*, boohoo*, break down*, burst into tears*, complain, deplore, drip, grieve, howl, keen, lament, let go*, let it out*, mewl, moan, mourn, shed tears, snivel, sob, squall, ululate, wail, whimper, yowl; SEE CONCEPTS 49,185

weigh [v1] *measure heaviness*
counterbalance, have a weight of, heft, measure, put in the balance, put on the scale, scale, tip the scales at; SEE CONCEPT 103

weigh [v2] *consider, contemplate*
analyze, appraise, balance, brainstorm*, deliberate, estimate, evaluate, examine, excogitate, give thought to, hash over*, meditate, mind, mull over, perpend, ponder, rate, reflect upon, rehash, sort out, study, sweat*, think about, think out, think over, track; SEE CONCEPT 24

weigh [v3] *have influence*
be heavy, be important, be influential, be something, burden, carry weight, charge, count, cumber, cut, cut some ice, import, impress, lade, matter, mean, militate, press, pull, register, saddle, show, signify, stack up against*, tax, tell; SEE CONCEPTS 7,19,22,237,682

weigh down [v] *depress*
bear down, burden, cumber, get down, hold down, oppress, overburden, overload, press, press down, prey on, pull down, sadden, task, trouble, weight, weigh down, worry; SEE CONCEPTS 7,19

weight [n1] *heaviness*
adiposity, avoirdupois, ballast, burden, density, G-factor*, gravity, gross, heft, heftiness, load, mass, measurement, net, ponderosity, ponderousness, poundage, pressure, substance, tonnage; SEE CONCEPT 795

weight [n2] *something used to measure heaviness*
anchor, ballast, bob, counterbalance, counterpoise, counterweight, mass, pendulum, plumb, plumb bob, poundage, pressure, rock, sandbag, sinker, stone; SEE CONCEPTS 290,470

weight [n3] *importance*
access, authority, clout, connection, consequence, consideration, credit, effectiveness, efficacy, emphasis, forcefulness, forcibleness, impact, import, influence, magnitude, moment, momentousness, persuasiveness, pith, potency, power, powerfulness, prestige, pull, significance, signification, substance, sway, value, weightiness; SEE CONCEPTS 668,682

weight [n4] *burden*
albatross*, ball and chain*, charge, cumber, cumbrance, deadweight*, duty, encumbrance, excess

baggage*, load, millstone*, onus, oppression, pressure, responsibility, strain, task, tax; SEE CONCEPTS 532,674,679,690

weighty [adj1] *heavy*
burdensome, cumbersome, cumbrous, dense, fat, fleshy, hefty, massive, obese, overweight, ponderous, porcine, portly, stout; SEE CONCEPT 491

weighty [adj2] *serious, important*
big, big deal*, consequential, considerable, critical, crucial, earnest, forcible, grave, heavy*, heavyweight, life and death*, material, meaningful, momentous, no-nonsense*, portentous, sedate, severe, significant, sober, solemn, somber, staid, substantial, underlined; SEE CONCEPTS 548,568

weighty [adj3] *troublesome, difficult*
backbreaking, burdensome, crushing, demanding, exacting, exigent, grievous, onerous, oppressive, superincumbent, taxing, tough, worrisome, worrying; SEE CONCEPTS 538,565

weird [adj] *odd, bizarre*
awe-inspiring, awful, creepy*, curious, dreadful, eccentric, eerie*, far-out*, fearful, flaky*, freaky*, funky*, ghastly, ghostly, grotesque, haunting, horrific, inscrutable, kinky*, kooky*, magical, mysterious, occult, oddball*, ominous, outlandish, peculiar, preternatural, queer, secret, singular, spooky*, strange, supernal, supernatural, uncanny, uncouth, unearthly, unnatural; SEE CONCEPTS 564,570

welcome [n] *greeting*
acceptance, entertainment, entrée, friendliness, handshake, hello, hospitality, howdy*, key to the city*, ovation, reception, red carpet*, rumble*, salutation, salute, tumble*; SEE CONCEPT 278

welcome [adj] *gladly received*
acceptable, accepted, agreeable, appreciated, cherished, congenial, contenting, cordial, delightful, desirable, desired, esteemed, favorable, genial, good, grateful, gratifying, honored, invited, nice, pleasant, pleasing, pleasurable, refreshing, satisfying, sympathetic, wanted; SEE CONCEPTS 555,572

welcome [v] *receive gladly*
accept, accept gladly, accost, admit, bid welcome, embrace, entertain, flag*, greet, hail, hug, meet, offer hospitality, receive, roll out red carpet*, salute, show in, take in, tumble*, usher in; SEE CONCEPTS 266,384

weld [v] *bind, connect*
bond, braze, cement, combine, fix, fuse, join, link, solder, unite; SEE CONCEPT 193

welfare/well-being [n] *health and prosperity*
abundance, advantage, benefit, contentment, ease, easy street*, euphoria, felicity, good, good fortune, happiness, interest, luck, profit, progress, satisfaction, success, thriving; SEE CONCEPTS 316,693,706

well [n] *water hole*
abyss, bore, chasm, depression, derivation, fount, fountain, fountainhead, geyser, hole, inception, mine, mouth, origin, pit, pool, repository, reservoir, root, shaft, source, spa, spout, spring, springs, watering place, wellspring; SEE CONCEPTS 509,513,514

well [adj1] *healthy*
able-bodied, alive and kicking*, blooming, bright-eyed*, bushy-tailed*, chipper*, fine, fit, flourishing, fresh, great, hale, hardy, hearty, husky, in good health, in the pink*, right, right as rain*,

we
we

robust, sane, solid as a rock*, sound, strong, strong as an ox*, together, trim, up to par*, vigorous, whole, wholesome, wrapped tight*; SEE CONCEPT 314

well [adj] *lucky, fortunate*
advisable, agreeable, bright, comfortable, fine, fitting, flourishing, good, happy, pleasing, profitable, proper, prosperous, providential, prudent, right, satisfactory, thriving, useful; SEE CONCEPTS 548,572

well [adv1] *happily, pleasantly; capably*
ably, accurately, adeptly, adequately, admirably, agreeably, attentively, capitally, carefully, closely, commendably, competently, completely, conscientiously, correctly, effectively, efficiently, excellently, expertly, famously, favorably, fully, in a satisfactory manner, irreproachably, nicely, proficiently, profoundly, properly, rightly, satisfactorily, skillfully, smoothly, soundly, splendidly, strongly, successfully, suitably, thoroughly, with skill; SEE CONCEPTS 527,528,544

well [adv2] *sufficiently*
abundantly, adequately, amply, appropriately, becomingly, by a wide margin, completely, considerably, easily, effortlessly, entirely, extremely, far, fittingly, freely, fully, greatly, heartily, highly, luxuriantly, plentifully, properly, quite, rather, readily, right, satisfactorily, smoothly, somewhat, substantially, suitably, thoroughly, very, wholly; SEE CONCEPTS 558,772

well-bred [adj] *mannerly*
aristocratic, blue-blooded*, civil, considerate, courteous, courtly, cultivated, cultured, gallant, genteel, gentle, noble, patrician, polished, polite, refined, taught, trained, upper-crust*, urbane, well-behaved, well-mannered; SEE CONCEPTS 334,401

well-known [adj] *familiar, famous*
acclaimed, big, big name*, celeb*, celebrated, common, conspicuous, eminent, illustrious, important, infamous, in the limelight*, in the public eye*, known, large, leading, name, notable, noted, notorious, outstanding, popular, prominent, public, recognized, renowned, reputable, somebody, splashy, star, superstar, VIP*, widely known, WK*; SEE CONCEPT 568

well-off [adj] *successful, wealthy*
affluent, comfortable, easy, flourishing, flush, fortunate, loaded, lucky, moneyed, prosperous, rich, snug, substantial, thriving, well, well-to-do; SEE CONCEPT 334

welt [n] *red mark*
bruise, contusion, injury, mouse, ridge, scar, streak, stripe, wale, weal, wheal, wound; SEE CONCEPT 309

wet [n] *dampness, moisture*
clamminess, condensation, damp, drizzle, humidity, liquid, rain, rains, water, wetness; SEE CONCEPT 607

wet [adj] *damp, moist*
aqueous, clammy, dank, dewy, drenched, dripping, drizzling, foggy, humid, misty, moistened, muggy, pouring, raining, rainy, saturate, saturated, showery, slimy, slippery, slushy, snowy, soaked, sodden, soggy, sopping, soppy, soused, stormy, teary, teeming, water-logged, watery, wringing-wet; SEE CONCEPT 603

wet [v] *cause to become damp, moist*
bathe, damp, dampen, deluge, dip, douse, drench, drown, hose, humidify, imbue, irrigate, moisten, rinse, saturate, soak, sop, souse, splash, spray, sprinkle, steep, wash, water; SEE CONCEPTS 161,256

whack [n1/v] *hit*
bang, bash, bat, beat, belt, biff, box, buffet, clobber, clout, crack, cuff, ding*, lambaste*, nail, rap, slap, slug, smack, smash, sock, strike, thrash, thump, thwack*, wallop, wham*; SEE CONCEPT 189

whack [n2] *try, attempt*
bash, crack, fling, go, pop, shot, slap, stab, turn, whirl; SEE CONCEPT 87

wharf [n] *boat storage*
berth, breakwater, dock, jetty, landing, landing stage, levee, pier, quay, slip; SEE CONCEPT 439

wheedle [v] *talk into*
banter, blandish, butter up*, cajole, charm, coax, con, court, draw, entice, finagle, flatter, inveigle, kowtow*, lay it on*, oil*, persuade, seduce, snow*, soap*, soften up*, soft-soap*, spread it on*, sweeten up*, sweet-talk*, work on*, worm*; SEE CONCEPT 68

wheel [n] *circle, revolution*
caster, circuit, circulation, circumvolution, cycle, disk, drum, gyration, gyre, hoop, pivot, pulley, ratchet, ring, roll, roller, rotation, round, spin, trolley, turn, twirl, whirl; SEE CONCEPTS 436,464,502

wheel [v] *turn, rotate*
circle, gyrate, orbit, pirouette, pivot, reel, revolve, roll, spin, swing, swivel, trundle, twirl, whirl; SEE CONCEPT 147

wheeze [v] *breathe roughly, heavily*
buzz, catch one's breath, cough, gasp, hiss, murmur, pant, puff, rasp, sibilate, snore, whisper, whistle; SEE CONCEPTS 163,308

when [conj] *though*
albeit, although, at, at the same time, during, howbeit, immediately upon, just after, just as, meanwhile, much as, whereas, while; SEE CONCEPT 799

where [n] *place*
location, locus, point, position, site, situation, spot, station; SEE CONCEPT 198

where/wherever [adv] *at which point*
anywhere, everywhere, in whatever place, in which, to what end, to which, whereabouts, whither; SEE CONCEPT 583

whet [v1] *make sharp*
edge, file, finish, grind, hone, sharpen, strop; SEE CONCEPTS 137,250

whet [v2] *arouse, excite*
animate, awaken, challenge, enhance, incite, increase, kindle, pique, provoke, quicken, rally, rouse, stimulate, stir, wake, waken; SEE CONCEPTS 7,11,22

whiff [n] *smell of an odor*
aroma, blast, breath, dash, draught, flatus, fume, gust, hint, inhalation, odor, puff, scent, shade, smack, sniff, snuff, soupçon, trace, trifle, waft; SEE CONCEPTS 599,601,602

while [n] *time interval*
bit, instant, interim, meantime, moment, occasion, period, space, spell, stretch, time; SEE CONCEPTS 807,822

while [conj1] *as long as*
although, at the same time, during, during the

time, in the time, throughout the time, whilst; SEE CONCEPT 799

while [*conj2*] *even though*
albeit, although, howbeit, much as, though, when, whereas; SEE CONCEPT 544

whim [*n*] *sudden idea*
caprice, conceit, craze, desire, disposition, dream, fad, fancy, fantasy, freak, humor, impulse, inclination, notion, passing thought, quirk, sport, thought, urge, vagary, vision, whimsy; SEE CONCEPTS 529,661

whimper [*v*] *cry softly*
bleat, blubber, complain, fuss, mewl, moan, object, pule, snivel, sob, weep, whine; SEE CONCEPTS 77,185

whimsical [*adj*] *playful, fanciful*
amusing, arbitrary, capricious, chancy, chimerical, comical, curious, dicey, droll, eccentric, erratic, fantastic, flaky*, freakish, funny, kinky*, mischievous, odd, peculiar, quaint, queer*, quizzical, singular, uncertain, unpredictable, unusual, waggish, wayward, weird*; SEE CONCEPTS 401,548

whine [*n*] *complaint, cry*
gripe, grouse, grumble, moan, plaintive cry, sob, wail, whimper; SEE CONCEPTS 54,77

whine [*v*] *complain, cry*
bellyache, carp, drone, fuss, gripe, grouse, grumble, howl, kick, mewl, moan, murmur, pule, repine, snivel, sob, wail, whimper; SEE CONCEPTS 54,77

whip [*n*] *length of material for hitting*
bat, belt, birch, bullwhip, cane, cat-o'-nine-tails, crop, goad, horsewhip, knout, lash, prod, push, rawhide, rod, ruler, scourge, strap, switch, thong; SEE CONCEPT 499

whip [*v1*] *hit repeatedly*
bash, beat, birch, bludgeon, cane, castigate, chastise, cudgel, drub, ferule, flagellate, flog, hide, larrup*, lash, lather*, punish, scourge, spank, strap, strike, switch, tan, thrash, trash, wallop, whale, whomp*; SEE CONCEPT 189

whip [*v2*] *defeat soundly*
beat, best, blast, clobber, conquer, drub, hammer*, kill*, lambaste, lick*, mop up*, outdo, overcome, overpower, overrun, overwhelm, put away*, rout, run circles around*, settle, steamroller*, subdue, take apart*, thrash, top, trim*, trounce, vanquish, wallop, wax*, whomp*, worst*; SEE CONCEPT 95

whip [*v3*] *dash, dart*
avert, deflect, dive, divert, flash, flit, fly, jerk, pivot, pull, rush, seize, sheer, shoot, snatch, surge, tear, turn, veer, wheel, whirl, whisk; SEE CONCEPTS 150,152

whip [*v4*] *agitate, stir up*
beat, blend, mix, whisk, work up; SEE CONCEPTS 152,170

whip up [*v*] *incite, excite*
abet, agitate, arouse, compel, disturb, drive, foment, goad, hound, inflame, instigate, kindle, prick, prod, provoke, push, raise, set, set on, spur, start, stir, stir up, urge, work up; SEE CONCEPTS 14,221

whirl [*n1*] *spin, revolution*
circle, circuit, circulation, circumvolution, flurry, gyration, gyre, pirouette, reel, roll, rotation, round, spin, surge, swirl, turn, twirl, twist, wheel, whir, whirlpool; SEE CONCEPTS 152,738

whirl [*n2*] *commotion, confusion*
ado*, agitation, bustle, clatter, daze, dither, ferment, flurry, fluster, flutter, furor, fuss, hubbub*, hurly-burly*, hurry, merry-go-round*, moil, pother, round, ruction, rush, series, spin, stir, storm, succession, tempest, tumult, turbulence, uproar, whirlwind; SEE CONCEPTS 230,388

whirl [*n3*] *attempt*
bash, crack, fling, go, pop, shot, slap, stab, try, whack*; SEE CONCEPT 87

whirl [*v*] *spin around*
circle, eddy, gyrate, gyre, pirouette, pivot, purl, reel, revolve, roll, rotate, swirl, swoosh, turn, turn around, twirl, twist, wheel, whir; SEE CONCEPT 152

whirlpool [*n*] *spinning water*
eddy, maelstrom, stir, undercurrent, undertow, vortex, whirl; SEE CONCEPT 514

whirlwind [*adj*] *very fast*
cyclonic, hasty, headlong, hurricane, impetuous, impulsive, lightning, quick, rapid, rash, short, speedy, swift, tornado; SEE CONCEPTS 588,798

whisk [*v*] *brush quickly; hasten*
barrel, bullet, dart, dash, flick, flit, flutter, fly, hurry, race, rush, shoot, speed, sweep, tear, whip, whiz, wipe, zip; SEE CONCEPT 152

whisper [*n1*] *rumor; information expressed in soft voice*
buzz*, confidence, disclosure, divulgence, gossip, hint, hum, hushed tone, innuendo, insinuation, low voice, mumble, murmur, mutter, report, secret, secret message, sigh, sighing, susurration, undertone, word; SEE CONCEPTS 274,278

whisper [*n2*] *trace, suggestion*
breath, dash, fraction, hint, shade, shadow, soupçon, suspicion, tinge, touch, whiff; SEE CONCEPTS 529,673,831

whisper [*v*] *speak softly*
breathe, buzz*, confide, gossip, hint, hiss, insinuate, intimate, mumble, murmur, mutter, say softly, say under one's breath*, sibilate, sigh, speak confidentially, spread rumor, susurrate, talk into someone's ear*, talk low, tell, tell a secret; SEE CONCEPTS 60,266

whistle [*v*] *make sharp, shrill sound*
blare, blast, fife, flute, hiss, pipe, shriek, signal, skirl, sound, toot, tootle, trill, warble, wheeze, whine, whiz*; SEE CONCEPTS 65,77

whit [*n*] *very tiny bit*
atom, crumb, dash, drop, fragment, grain, hoot*, iota, jot, little, mite, modicum, particle, piece, pinch, scrap, shred, speck, trace; SEE CONCEPTS 831,835

white [*adj*] *extremely pale; lacking color*
achromatic, achromic, alabaster, ashen, blanched, bleached, bloodless, chalky, clear, fair, frosted, ghastly, hoary, immaculate, ivory, light, milky, neutral, pallid, pasty, pearly, silver, silvery, snowy, transparent, wan, waxen; SEE CONCEPT 618

whiten [*v*] *make or become extremely pale*
blanch, bleach, blench, chalk, decolor, decolorize, dull, etiolate, fade, frost, grizzle, lighten, pale, silver, turn pale, white, whitewash; SEE CONCEPT 250

whitewash [*v*] *cover up the truth*
blanch, camouflage, conceal, exonerate, extenuate, gloss over, launder*, liberate, make light of*, paint, palliate, sugarcoat*, suppress, varnish, ve-

we
wh

neer, vindicate, white, whiten; SEE CONCEPTS *49,63*

whittle [v] *cut away at; reduce*
carve, chip, consume, decrease, diminish, eat away, erode, fashion, form, hew, lessen, model, mold, pare, sculpt, shape, shave, trim, undermine, wear away; SEE CONCEPTS *176,184,236,247*

whiz [n] *very intelligent person*
adept, expert, genius, gifted person, marvel, pro*, prodigy, professional, star, virtuoso, wonder; SEE CONCEPT *416*

whiz [v] *move quickly by*
bullet, buzz, dart, flit, fly, hiss, hum, hurry, hurtle, race, speed, swish, whir, whirl, whisk, whoosh*, zip; SEE CONCEPT *150*

whole [n] *total made up of parts*
aggregate, aggregation, all, amount, assemblage, assembly, being, big picture, body, bulk, coherence, collectivity, combination, complex, ensemble, entirety, entity, everything, fullness, gross, hook line and sinker*, integral, jackpot*, linkage, lock stock and barrel*, lot, lump, oneness, organism, organization, piece, quantity, quantum, result, sum, summation, sum total*, supply, system, the works*, totality, unit, unity, whole ball of wax*, whole enchilada*, whole nine yards*, whole shebang*; SEE CONCEPTS *432,635,837*

whole [adj1] *entire, complete*
accomplished, aggregate, all, choate, completed, concentrated, conclusive, consummate, every, exclusive, exhaustive, fixed, fulfilled, full, full-length, gross, inclusive, in one piece, integral, outright, perfect, plenary, rounded, total, unabbreviated, unabridged, uncut, undivided, unexpurgated, unqualified, utter; SEE CONCEPT *531*

whole [adj2] *unbroken, perfect*
complete, completed, developed, faultless, flawless, good, in good order*, in one piece*, intact, inviolate, mature, mint, plenary, preserved, replete, safe, ship-shape, solid, sound, thorough, together, undamaged, unharmed, unhurt, unimpaired, uninjured, unmarred, unmutilated, unscathed, untouched, without a scratch*; SEE CONCEPTS *485,574*

whole [adj3] *healthy*
able-bodied, better, cured, fit, hale, healed, hearty, in fine fettle, in good health, recovered, right, robust, sane, sound, strong, well, wholesome; SEE CONCEPT *314*

wholehearted/whole-hearted [adj] *enthusiastic, sincere*
abiding, ardent, authentic, bona fide, candid, committed, complete, dedicated, determined, devoted, earnest, emphatic, enduring, fervent, frank, genuine, heartfelt, hearty, impassioned, never-failing, passionate, real, serious, steadfast, steady, sure, true, unfaltering, unfeigned, unqualified, unquestioning, unreserved, unstinting, unwavering, warm, zealous; SEE CONCEPTS *542,548,582*

wholesale [adj] *all-inclusive*
broad, bulk, complete, comprehensive, extensive, far-reaching, general, in bulk, indiscriminate, in quantity, in the mass, large-scale, mass, overall, quantitative, sweeping, total, wide-ranging, widespread; SEE CONCEPTS *771,772*

wholesome [adj] *healthy, decent*
all there, beneficial, clean, edifying, ethical, exemplary, fit, good, hale, healthful, health-giving, helpful, honorable, hygienic, in fine feather*, innocent, in the pink*, invigorating, moral, nice, normal, nourishing, nutritious, nutritive, pure, respectable, restorative, right, righteous, safe, salubrious, salutary, sane, sanitary, sound, strengthening, together, virtuous, well, worthy; SEE CONCEPTS *314,462,537,545*

wholly [adv1] *completely, entirely*
all, all in all*, all the way*, altogether, comprehensively, from A to Z*, fully, heart and soul*, in every respect*, in toto, one hundred percent*, outright, perfectly, quite, roundly, thoroughly, top to bottom*, totally, utterly, well; SEE CONCEPTS *531,772*

wholly [adv2] *exclusively*
individually, just, only, purely, solely, specifically, without exception; SEE CONCEPT *557*

whoop [n/v] *hurrah*
bellow, boo, cheer, cry, cry out, holler, hoot, howl, jeer, scream, shout, shriek, squawk, yell; SEE CONCEPT *77*

whopping [adj] *enormous*
big, colossal, extraordinary, gargantuan, giant, gigantic, great, huge, immense, large, mammoth, massive, mighty, monstrous, mountainous, prodigious, tremendous; SEE CONCEPTS *773,781*

whorl [n] *spiral*
coil, corkscrew, curl, eddy, helix, swirl, twirl, twist, vortex, whirlpool; SEE CONCEPT *436*

wicked [adj1] *corrupt, bad*
abandoned, abominable, amoral, arch, atrocious, bad news*, base, contemptible, debased, degenerate, depraved, devilish, dissolute, egregious, evil, fiendish, flagitious, foul, gross, guilty, heartless, heinous, immoral, impious, impish, incorrigible, indecent, iniquitous, irreligious, low-down, mean, mischievous, nasty, naughty, nefarious, profane, reprobate, rotten, scandalous, shameful, shameless, sinful, unethical, unprincipled, unrighteous, vicious, vile, villainous, wayward, worthless; SEE CONCEPTS *401,545*

wicked [adj2] *destructive, troublesome*
acute, agonizing, awful, barbarous, bothersome, chancy, crashing, dangerous, difficult, distressing, dreadful, fearful, fierce, galling, harmful, hazardous, injurious, intense, mean, mighty, offensive, outrageous, painful, perilous, pesky, risky, severe, terrible, treacherous, troublous, trying, ugly, uncivilized, unconscionable, ungodly, unhealthy, unholy, unpleasant, unsound, vexatious; SEE CONCEPTS *537,565,571*

wicked [adj3] *expert*
able, adept, adroit, au fait, capable, clever, competent, deft, good, masterly, mighty, outstanding, powerful, pretty, qualified, skillful, strong; SEE CONCEPT *527*

wide [adj1] *expansive, roomy*
advanced, all-inclusive, ample, baggy, broad, capacious, catholic, commodious, comprehensive, deep, dilated, distended, encyclopedic, expanded, extensive, far-ranging, far-reaching, full, general, immense, inclusive, large, large-scale, liberal, loose, open, outspread, outstretched, progressive, radical, scopic, spacious, splay, squat, sweeping, tolerant, universal, vast, voluminous; SEE CONCEPTS *772,773,796*

wide [adj2] *off-course*
astray, away, distant, far, far-off, inaccurate, off, off-target, off the mark, remote; SEE CONCEPTS *581,583*

widen [v] *open up*
add to, augment, broaden, dilate, distend, enlarge, expand, extend, grow, grow larger, increase, multiply, open, open out, open wide, ream, spread, spread out, stretch, swell, unfold; SEE CONCEPTS 236,245,780

widespread [adj] *extensive*
across the board*, all over the place*, boundless, broad, common, comprehensive, current, diffuse, epidemic, far-flung, far-reaching, general, on a large scale, outspread, overall, pandemic, pervasive, popular, prevailing, prevalent, public, rampant, regnant, rife, ruling, sweeping, universal, unlimited, unrestricted, wall-to-wall*, wholesale; SEE CONCEPTS 530,536,772

width [n] *breadth, wideness of some amount*
amplitude, area, broadness, compass, cross measure, diameter, distance across, expanse, extent, girth, measure, range, reach, scope, span, squatness, stretch, thickness; SEE CONCEPTS 760,788,792

wield [v] *control, use*
apply, brandish, command, conduct, employ, exercise, exert, flourish, handle, have, have at one's disposal, hold, maintain, make use of, manage, maneuver, manipulate, operate, ply, possess, put to use, shake, swing, throw, utilize, wave, work; SEE CONCEPTS 94,147,225

wife [n] *married woman*
bride, companion, consort, helpmate, mate, monogamist, other half*, partner, roommate, spouse; SEE CONCEPTS 414,415

wiggle [n/v] *shake back and forth*
jerk, jiggle, shimmy, squirm, twist, twitch, wag, waggle, wave, worm, wriggle, writhe, zigzag; SEE CONCEPTS 80,150,152

wild [adj] *untamed*
agrarian, barbarian, barbaric, barbarous, dense, desert, deserted, desolate, escaped, feral, ferocious, fierce, free, indigenous, lush, luxuriant, native, natural, neglected, overgrown, overrun, primitive, rampant, rude, savage, unbroken, uncivilized, uncultivated, undomesticated, uninhabited, untouched, vicious, waste; SEE CONCEPTS 406,583

wild [adj2] *disorderly, rowdy*
avid, berserk, boisterous, chaotic, crazed, crazy, eager, enthusiastic, extravagant, flighty, foolhardy, foolish, giddy, hysterical, impetuous, impracticable, imprudent, incautious, irrational, lawless, licentious, mad, madcap, noisy, nuts, outrageous, preposterous, profligate, rabid, rash, raving, reckless, riotous, rough, self-willed, turbulent, unbridled, uncontrolled, undisciplined, unfettered, ungovernable, unmanageable, unrestrained, unruly, uproarious, violent, wayward; SEE CONCEPT 401

wild [adj3] *intense, stormy*
blustering, blustery, choppy, disturbed, furious, howling, inclement, raging, rough, storming, tempestuous, turbulent, violent; SEE CONCEPTS 525,569

wilderness/wilds [n] *uninhabited area*
back country, back of beyond*, badland, barrens, boondocks, bush, desert, forest, hinterland, jungle, middle of nowhere*, outback, primeval forest, sticks*, waste, wasteland, wild; SEE CONCEPT 517

wile [n] *cunning*
angle, artfulness, artifice, cheating, chicane, chicanery, con*, contrivance, craft, craftiness, deceit, deception, device, dishonesty, dissimulation, dodge, feint, flimflam*, fraud, gambit, game, gimmick, guile, hoax, horseplay, imposition, little game*, lure, maneuver, monkey business*, monkeyshines*, plot, ploy, racket*, ruse, scam*, scheming, setup*, shenanigans*, skullduggery*, slant, slyness, stratagem, stunt, subterfuge, switch, trick, trickery, twist; SEE CONCEPTS 59,63

will [n1] *personal choice*
aim, appetite, attitude, character, conviction, craving, decision, decisiveness, decree, design, desire, determination, discipline, discretion, disposition, fancy, feeling, hankering, heart's desire*, inclination, intention, liking, longing, mind, option, passion, pining, pleasure, power, preference, prerogative, purpose, resolution, resolve, self-control, self-discipline, self-restraint, temperament, urge, velleity, volition, willfulness, willpower, wish, wishes, yearning; SEE CONCEPTS 20,411,659

will [n2] *last wishes; command*
bequest, bestowal, declaration, decree, device, directions, dispensation, disposition, estate, heritage, inheritance, insistence, instructions, legacy, order, property, testament; SEE CONCEPT 318

will [v1] *cause*
authorize, bid, bring about, command, decide on, decree, demand, determine, direct, effect, enjoin, exert, insist, intend, ordain, order, request, resolve; SEE CONCEPT 242

will [v2] *choose*
be inclined, crave, desire, elect, have a mind to*, incline, like, opt, please, prefer, see fit*, want, wish; SEE CONCEPT 20

will [v3] *give, bequeath to another*
bequest, confer, cut off, devise, disherit, disinherit, leave, legate, pass on, probate, transfer; SEE CONCEPTS 108,317

willful [adj1] *stubborn, obstinate*
adamant, bullheaded, contumacious, determined, dogged, fractious, froward, headstrong, inflexible, intractable, intransigent, mulish, obdurate, persistent, pertinacious, perverse, pigheaded, refractory, resolved, self-willed, stiffnecked, uncompromising, unyielding; SEE CONCEPTS 401,542

willful [adj2] *voluntary*
conscious, contemplated, deliberate, designed, intended, intentional, planned, premeditated, purposeful, studied, unforced, volitional, willed, willing, witting; SEE CONCEPTS 401,535

willing [adj] *agreeable, ready*
accommodating, active, amenable, cheerful, compliant, consenting, content, deliberate, desirous, disposed, eager, energetic, enthusiastic, fair, favorable, feeling, forward, game, go along with, happy, in accord with, inclined in favor, intentional, in the mood, like-minded, obedient, one, pleased, predisposed, prepared, prompt, *prone, reliable, responsible, tractable, unasked, unbidden, unforced, voluntary, well-disposed, willful, witting, zealous; SEE CONCEPTS 401,403,576

willpower [n] *personal determination*
discipline, drive, firmness, fixity, force, grit, resolution, resolve, self-control, self-discipline, self-government, self-restraint, single-mindedness, strength, will; SEE CONCEPT 411

wilt [v] *sag, fail*
become limp, break down, cave in, collapse, di-

wh
wi

minish, droop, drop, dry up, dwindle, ebb, fade, faint, flag, give out, languish, melt, mummify, shrivel, sink, succumb, wane, waste, waste away, weaken, wither, wizen; SEE CONCEPTS 181,427,469,699

wily [adj] crafty, clever
arch, artful, astute, cagey, crazy like a fox*, crooked, cunning, deceitful, deceptive, deep, designing, foxy, greasy*, guileful, insidious, intriguing, knowing, sagacious, scheming, sharp, shifty, shrewd, slick*, slippery*, sly, smooth, sneaky, streetwise, tricky, underhanded; SEE CONCEPTS 401,545

win [n] victory
accomplishment, achievement, conquest, gain, gold*, gold star*, kill*, killing*, pay dirt*, score, slam, success, sweep, triumph; SEE CONCEPTS 95,141,832

win [v1] finish first; succeed
achieve, beat, be first, be victorious, carry the day*, come in first, conquer, edge, finish in front*, finish off, gain, gain victory, overcome, overwhelm, prevail, run circles around*, shut out*, sink*, take the prize, triumph, upset, walk away with*, walk off with*; SEE CONCEPTS 95,141,363

win [v2] achieve, obtain
accomplish, acquire, annex, approach, attain, bag*, bring in, catch, collect, come away with*, derive, earn, effect, gain, get, harvest, have, make, net, pick up, procure, rack up*, reach, realize, receive, score, secure; SEE CONCEPTS 120,706

win/win over [v3] influence, persuade
allure, argue into, attract, bring around, carry, charm, convert, convince, disarm, draw, get, induce, overcome, prevail upon, prompt, slay, sway, talk into, wow*; SEE CONCEPTS 11,68

wince [v] draw back
back off, blanch, blench, cower, cringe, dodge, duck, flinch, grimace, jib, make a face*, quail, recoil, shrink, shy, start, swerve, turn; SEE CONCEPTS 154,185

wind [n1] air currents
air, blast, blow, breath, breeze, chinook, cyclone, draft, draught, flurry, flutter, gale, gust, mistral, puff, tempest, typhoon, wafting, whiff, whirlwind, whisk, zephyr; SEE CONCEPT 524

wind [n2] warning, report
babble, clue, cue, gossip, hint, hot air*, idle talk, inkling, intimation, notice, rumor, suggestion, talk, tidings, whisper; SEE CONCEPT 278

wind [v] bend, turn
coil, convolute, corkscrew, cover, crook, curl, curve, deviate, distort, encircle, enclose, entwine, envelop, fold, furl, loop, meander, ramble, reel, roll, screw, slither, snake, spiral, swerve, twine, twist, weave, wrap, wreathe, wriggle, zigzag; SEE CONCEPTS 201,738

winding [adj] bending, turning
ambiguous, anfractuous, circuitous, convoluted, crooked, curving, devious, flexuous, gyrating, indirect, intricate, involved, labyrinthine, mazy, meandering, roundabout, serpentine, sinuous, snaky, spiraling, tortuous, twisting, wriggly, zigzag; SEE CONCEPTS 581,584

wind up [v] finish
be through with, bring to a close, clean up*, close, close down, come to the end, complete, conclude, determine, do, end, end up*, finalize, finish up,

halt, liquidate, settle, terminate, tie up loose ends*, wrap up*; SEE CONCEPT 234

windy [adj1] breezy
airy, blowing, blowy, blustering, blustery, boisterous, brisk, drafty, fresh, gusty, raw, squally, stormy, tempestuous, wild, windswept; SEE CONCEPT 525

windy [adj2] talkative; boastful
bombastic, diffuse, empty, garrulous, inflated, lengthy, long-winded, loquacious, meandering, palaverous, pompous, prolix, rambling, redundant, turgid, verbose, wordy; SEE CONCEPT 267

wing [n1] organ, device of flight
aileron, airfoil, appendage, feather, pennon, pinion; SEE CONCEPTS 399,502

wing [n2] section; extension
addition, adjunct, annex, arm, block, branch, bulge, circle, clique, coterie, detachment, division, ell, expansion, faction, group, part, projection, prolongation, protrusion, protuberance, section, segment, set, side, unit; SEE CONCEPTS 440,441,824,835

wink [n1/v] flutter, flick
bat, blink, flash, gleam, glimmer, glitter, nictate, nictitate, sparkle, squinch, squint, twinkle; SEE CONCEPTS 185,624

wink [n2] moment
flash*, instant, jiffy*, minute, second, shake*, split second*, twinkle*, twinkling*; SEE CONCEPTS 808,821

winner [n] someone or something that succeeds
champ, champion, conquering hero, conqueror, first, hero, medalist, medalwinner, number one*, prizewinner, title-holder, top dog*, vanquisher, victor; SEE CONCEPTS 366,416

winning/winsome [adj1] attractive, charming
acceptable, adorable, agreeable, alluring, amiable, bewitching, captivating, cute, delectable, delightful, disarming, enchanting, endearing, engaging, fascinating, fetching, gratifying, lovable, lovely, pleasing, prepossessing, sweet, taking; SEE CONCEPTS 401,404

winning [adj2] triumphant
champion, conquering, leading, successful, victorious; SEE CONCEPTS 528,632

winter [n] cold season of the year
chill, cold, frost, Jack Frost*, wintertide, wintertime; SEE CONCEPT 814

wintry [adj] cold, snowy
biting, bleak, brumal, chilly, cutting, desolate, dismal, freezing, frigid, frosty, frozen, harsh, hibernal, hiemal, icebox*, icy, raw, snappy, three-dog night*; SEE CONCEPTS 525,605

wipe [v] brush, swab
clean, clean off, clear, dry, dust, erase, mop, obliterate, remove, rub, sponge, take away, towel, wash; SEE CONCEPT 165

wipe out [v] destroy; get rid of
abate, abolish, annihilate, black out, blot out, cancel, decimate, delete, efface, eliminate, eradicate, erase, expunge, exterminate, extinguish, extirpate, kill, massacre, obliterate, remove, root out, slaughter, slay, uproot, X-out*; SEE CONCEPT 252

wiry [adj] thin and strong
agile, athletic, bristly, fibrous, lean, light, limber, muscular, ropy, sinewy, stiff, strapping, stringy, supple, tough; SEE CONCEPTS 490,491

wisdom [n] insight, common sense
acumen, astuteness, balance, brains*, caution, circumspection, clear thinking, comprehension, dis-

cernment, discrimination, enlightenment, erudition, experience, foresight, good judgment, gumption*, horse sense*, information, intelligence, judgment, judiciousness, knowledge, learning, pansophy, penetration, perspicacity, poise, practicality, prudence, reason, sagacity, sageness, sanity, sapience, savoir faire, savvy*, shrewdness, solidity, sophistication, stability, understanding; SEE CONCEPT 409

wise [adj] *intelligent, reasonable*
astute, aware, calculating, careful, clever, cogitative, contemplative, crafty, cunning, discerning, discreet, educated, enlightened, erudite, experienced, foresighted, grasping, informed, insightful, intuitive, judicious, keen, knowing, knowledgeable, perceptive, perspicacious, politic, prudent, rational, reflective, sagacious, sage, sane, sapient, scholarly, sensible, sensing, sharp, shrewd, smart, sophic, sound, tactful, taught, thoughtful, understanding, wary, well-informed, witty; SEE CONCEPT 402

wish [n] *desire*
ambition, aspiration, choice, disposition, hankering, hope, hunger, inclination, intention, invocation, itch, liking, longing, pleasure, prayer, preference, request, thirst, urge, want, whim, will, yearning, yen; SEE CONCEPTS 20,709

wish [v] *desire*
aspire, beg, choose, command, covet, crave, desiderate, elect, entreat, envy, expect, fancy, hanker*, hope, hunger, invoke, itch, like, long, look forward to*, need, order, please, pray for, prefer, request, set one's heart on*, sigh for, solicit, spoil for*, thirst, want, will, yearn, yen; SEE CONCEPT 20

wishy-washy [adj] *bland, dull*
banal, characterless, cowardly, enervated, feeble, flat, flavorless, indecisive, ineffective, ineffectual, insipid, irresolute, jejune, languid, listless, mediocre, namby-pamby*, sapless, spiritless, tasteless, thin, vacillating, vapid, watered-down, watery, wavering, weak, weak-kneed*; SEE CONCEPT 404

wisp [n] *strand*
bit, lock, piece, shock, shred, snippet, string, thread, tuft, twist; SEE CONCEPTS 392,831

wistful [adj] *daydreaming, longing*
contemplative, desirous, disconsolate, dreaming, dreamy, forlorn, hopeless, meditative, melancholy, mournful, musing, nostalgic, pensive, plaintive, reflective, sad, thoughtful, wishful, yearning; SEE CONCEPT 403

wit [n1] *humor*
aphorism, badinage, banter, bon mot, burlesque, drollery, facetiousness, fun, gag, jest, jocularity, joke, lark, levity, pleasantry, practical joke, prank, pun, quip, raillery, repartee, sally, satire, trick, whimsicality, wisecrack, wittiness, wordplay; SEE CONCEPTS 59,273,411

wit [n2] *person who is very funny*
a million laughs*, banterer, card, comedian, comic, cutup*, epigrammatist, farceur, funster, gag person, humorist, jester, joker, jokesmith, jokester, life of the party*, madcap, punster, quipster, trickster, wag, wisecracker; SEE CONCEPTS 352,416

wit/wits [n3] *judgment, intelligence*
acumen, acuteness, astucity, astuteness, awareness, balance, brainpower, brains*, cleverness, common sense, comprehension, depth of perception, discernment, discrimination, esprit, grasp,

ingenuity, insight, keenness, lucidity, marbles*, mentality, mind, perception, perspicacity, practicality, prudence, rationality, reason, sagaciousness, sagacity, sageness, saneness, sanity, sapience, sense, shrewdness, soundness, understanding, wisdom; SEE CONCEPT 409

witch [n] *person who casts spells over others*
conjurer, enchanter, magician, necromancer, occultist, sorcerer; SEE CONCEPTS 361,412,415

witchcraft [n] *spell-casting, magic*
abracadabra*, bewitchment, black art, black magic, charisma, conjuring, divination, enchantment, hocus-pocus*, hoodoo*, incantation, jinx, magnetism, mumbo-jumbo*, necromancy, occult, occultism, sorcery, spell, thaumaturgy, voodoo, voodooism, whammy*, witchery, witching, wizardry; SEE CONCEPTS 367,370,689

withdraw [v1] *remove something or someone from situation*
abjure, absent oneself, back out, bail out, blow, book, bow out, check out, depart, detach, disengage, draw away, draw back, drop out, ease out, eliminate, exfiltrate, exit, extract, fall back, get away, get lost, get off, give ground, give way, go, keep aloof, keep apart, leave, make oneself scarce*, phase out, pull back, pull out, quail, quit, recede, recoil, retire, retreat, run along, secede, seclude oneself, shrink, switch, take a hike*, take away, take leave, take off, take out, vacate; SEE CONCEPTS 195,211

withdraw [v2] *retract; declare void*
abjure, abolish, abrogate, annul, ban, bar, call off, disavow, disclaim, dissolve, forswear, invalidate, nullify, quash, recall, recant, renege, renig, repress, repudiate, rescind, retire, revoke, revolve, stamp out, suppress, take back, unsay; SEE CONCEPTS 50,88,121,697

withdrawal [n] *removal; retraction*
abandonment, abdication, abjuration, alienation, departure, disavowal, disclaimer, disengagement, egress, egression, exit, exiting, exodus, extraction, marooning, palinode, recall, recantation, relinquishment, repudiation, rescission, resignation, retirement, retreat, revocation, revulsion, secession; SEE CONCEPTS 195,211,685

withdrawn [adj1] *unsociable*
aloof, aseptic, casual, cool, detached, disinterested, distant, incurious, indifferent, introverted, nongregarious, offish, quiet, recluse, reclusive, remote, reserved, restrained, retired, retiring, retreated, shrinking, shy, silent, solitary, standoffish, taciturn, timorous, uncommunicative, uncompanionable, unconcerned, uncurious, undemonstrative, unforthcoming, uninterested; SEE CONCEPT 401

withdrawn [adj2] *hidden, remote*
cloistered, departed, isolated, out-of-the-way, private, recluse, removed, retreated, secluded, solitary, taken out; SEE CONCEPT 583

wither [v] *droop, decline*
atrophy, become stale, blast, blight, collapse, constrict, contract, decay, deflate, desiccate, deteriorate, die, disintegrate, dry, dry up, fade, fold, languish, perish, shrink, shrivel, wane, waste, waste away, wilt, wizen; SEE CONCEPTS 427,698

withhold [v] *keep back*
abstain, bridle, check, clam up*, conceal, constrain, curb, deduct, deny, detain, disallow, dummy up*, hide, hold, hold back, hold down, hold out, hold out on, inhibit, keep, keep secret,

wi
wi

keep to oneself*, keep under one's hat*, keep under wraps*, kill, refrain, refuse, repress, reserve, resist, restrain, retain, sit on, spike, stop oneself, suppress; SEE CONCEPTS *35,121,188*

within [*adv*] *inside*
in, in a period, indoors, inner, in reach, interior, inward, not beyond, not outside, not over; SEE CONCEPTS *586,772*

without [*adv*] *outside*
after, beyond, externally, left out, on the outside, out, outdoors, out-of-doors, outwardly, past; SEE CONCEPTS *586,772*

withstand [*v*] *endure, bear*
brace, brave, buck, combat, confront, contest, cope, cross, defy, dispute, duel, face, fight, fly in the face of*, grapple with, hang on*, hang tough*, hold off*, hold one's ground*, hold out*, oppose, prevail against, put up struggle*, put up with*, remain firm, repel, resist, ride out*, sit and take it*, stand, stand fast*, stand firm*, stand one's ground*, stand up against*, stand up to*, stick*, stick fast*, suffer, take, take it*, take on, thwart, tolerate, traverse, violate, weather, win out; SEE CONCEPTS *23,96*

witness [*n*] *person who observes an event*
attestant, attestor, beholder, bystander, corroborator, deponent, eyewitness, gawker, looker-on, observer, onlooker, proof, rubbernecker*, signatory, signer, spectator, testifier, testimony, viewer, watcher; SEE CONCEPTS *355,423*

witness [*v1*] *observe*
attend, be a witness, behold, be on hand*, be on the scene*, be present, eyeball*, flash on*, get a load of*, look on, mark, note, notice, perceive, pick up on, pipe*, read, see, sight, spot, spy, take in, view, watch; SEE CONCEPT *626*

witness [*v2*] *testify; authenticate*
affirm, announce, argue, attest, bear out, bear witness, be a witness, bespeak, betoken, certify, confirm, corroborate, countersign, depone, depose, endorse, give evidence, give testimony, indicate, say under oath, sign, stand for, subscribe, vouch for; SEE CONCEPTS *49,50,88,317*

witty [*adj*] *funny and clever*
amusing, bright, brilliant, campy*, crazy*, diverting, droll, entertaining, epigrammatic, facetious, fanciful, gay, humorous, ingenious, intelligent, jocose, jocular, joshing, keen, lively, original, penetrating, piercing, piquant, quick-witted, ridiculous, scintillating, screaming*, slapstick, sparkling, waggish, whimsical; SEE CONCEPTS *267,542*

wizard [*n1*] *person who can perform magic*
astrologer, augurer, clairvoyant, conjurer, diviner, enchanter, fortuneteller, hypnotist, magician, magus, medium, necromancer, occultist, palmist, seer, shaman, soothsayer, sorcerer, thaumaturge, warlock, witch; SEE CONCEPT *361*

wizard [*n2*] *person who is highly skilled*
ace*, adept, artist, authority, crackerjack*, expert, genius, hot shot*, pro*, prodigy, professional, proficient, shark*, star, virtuoso, whiz*, whiz kid*, wiz*; SEE CONCEPTS *348,423*

wizened [*adj*] *dried, shriveled up*
diminished, gnarled, lean, macerated, mummified, old, reduced, shrunk, shrunken, wilted, withered, worn, wrinkled; SEE CONCEPTS *485,603*

wobble [*v*] *stagger, quake*
be unsteady, careen, falter, flounder, lurch, oscillate, quiver, reel, rock, roll, seesaw, shake, shimmy, stumble, sway, swing, teeter, totter, tremble, vacillate, vibrate, waver, weave, wiggle; SEE CONCEPTS *150,152*

wobbly [*adj*] *shaky*
fluctuant, insecure, precarious, rattletrap, rickety, rocky, teetering, tottering, unbalanced, uneven, unsafe, unstable, unsteady, unsure, vacillating, wavering, wavy, weak, wiggling; SEE CONCEPT *488*

woe [*n*] *suffering*
adversity, affliction, agony, anguish, bemoaning, blues*, burden, calamity, care, cataclysm, catastrophe, curse, dejection, deploring, depression, disaster, distress, dole, drag, gloom, grief, grieving, hardship, headache*, heartache*, heartbreak, lamentation, melancholy, misadventure, misery, misfortune, pain, rain*, regret, rue, sadness, sorrow, tragedy, trial, tribulation, trouble, unhappiness, wretchedness; SEE CONCEPTS *410,532, 690,728*

woebegone [*adj*] *depressed, troubled*
black, bleak, blue*, bummed out*, chapfallen, cheerless, crestfallen, dejected, despondent, disconsolate, dismal, dispirited, doleful, down, downcast, downhearted, down-in-the-mouth*, dreary, forlorn, gloomy, grief-stricken, grim, hangdog*, hurting, in pain*, long-faced*, low, lugubrious, melancholy, miserable, mournful, sad, shot down*, sorrowful, unhappy, woeful, wretched; SEE CONCEPT *403*

woeful [*adj*] *terrible, sad*
afflicted, agonized, anguished, appalling, awful, bad, calamitous, catastrophic, cruel, deplorable, disappointing, disastrous, disconsolate, disgraceful, distressing, doleful, dreadful, feeble, gloomy, grieving, grievous, grim, heartbreaking, heartrending, heartsick, hopeless, inadequate, lamentable, lousy*, mean, miserable, mournful, paltry, pathetic, piteous, pitiable, pitiful, plaintive, poor, racked, rotten, shocking, sorrowful, sorry, tortured, tragic, unfortunate, unhappy, wretched; SEE CONCEPTS *548,571*

wolf [*v*] *consume sloppily and fast*
bolt, cram, devour, gobble, gorge, gulp, guzzle, ingurgitate, pack, slop, slosh, stuff, swallow; SEE CONCEPT *169*

woman [*n*] *female human*
aunt, daughter, gentlewoman, girl, girlfriend, grandmother, matron, mother, Ms./Miss/Mrs., niece, she, spouse, wife; SEE CONCEPTS *414,415*

wonder [*n1*] *amazement*
admiration, astonishment, awe, bewilderment, concern, confusion, consternation, curiosity, doubt, fascination, fear, incredulity, jar, jolt, marveling, perplexity, perturbation, puzzlement, reverence, shock, skepticism, start, stupefaction, stupor, surprise, suspicion, uncertainty, wondering, wonderment; SEE CONCEPTS *410,532,690*

wonder [*n2*] *something that is amazing*
act of God*, curiosity, cynosure, freak, marvel, miracle, nonpareil, oddity, phenomenon, portent, prodigy, rara avis, rarity, sensation, sight, spectacle, stunner*, wonderment; SEE CONCEPTS *529,687*

wonder [*v1*] *doubt; ponder*
ask oneself, be curious, be inquisitive, conjecture, disbelieve, inquire, meditate, puzzle, query, question, speculate, think; SEE CONCEPTS *17,21*

wonder [*v2*] *be amazed*
admire, be astonished, be awestruck, be con-

founded, be dumbstruck, be fascinated, be flabbergasted, be startled, be taken aback, boggle,
gape, gawk, look aghast, marvel, stare; SEE CON-
CEPT 34

wonderful [adj] great, extraordinary
admirable, amazing, astonishing, astounding,
awe-inspiring, awesome, brilliant, cool*, divine*,
dynamite*, enjoyable, excellent, fabulous, fantastic, fine, groovy*, incredible, magnificent, marvelous, miraculous, outstanding, peachy*,
phenomenal, pleasant, pleasing, prime, remarkable, sensational, something else*, staggering,
startling, strange, stupendous, super, superb, surprising, swell, terrific, too much*, tremendous,
unheard-of, wondrous; SEE CONCEPTS 529,574

wonk [n] excessive studier
bookworm, brain*, dweeb*, geek*, greasy
grind*, grind*, grub*, nerd, poindexter, swotter*;
SEE CONCEPT 350

woo [v] seek as romantic partner
address, aim for, beg, bill and coo*, butter up*,
caress, charm, chase, court, cultivate, curry favor*, date, entreat, go steady, importune, keep
company, make advances, make love, press one's
suit with*, propose, pursue, run after, rush, seek
in marriage*, seek the hand of*, set one's cap
for*, solicit, spark*, spoon*; SEE CONCEPTS
297,378,384

wood/woods [n] forest
copse, grove, lumber, thicket, timber, timberland,
trees, weald, woodland; SEE CONCEPTS
430,509,517

wooden [adj1] made of timber
board, clapboard, frame, ligneous, log, peg,
plant, slab, timber, timbered, woody; SEE CON-
CEPT 485

wooden [adj2] stiff, inflexible
awkward, bumbling, clumsy, gauche, gawky,
graceless, heavy, heavy-handed, inelegant, inept,
maladroit, obstinate, ponderous, rigid, stilted, unbending, ungainly, ungraceful, unhandy, unyielding, weighty; SEE CONCEPTS 488,542

word [n1] discussion
chat, chitchat*, colloquy, confab*, confabulation,
consultation, conversation, discussion, talk, tête-
à-tête; SEE CONCEPT 56

word [n2] statement
account, adage, advice, announcement, bulletin,
byword, comment, communication, communiqué,
declaration, directive, discourse, dispatch, expression, gossip, hearsay, information, intelligence,
intimation, introduction, message, news, notice,
pronouncement, proverb, remark, report, rumble,
rumor, saw, saying, scuttlebutt, speech, talk, tidings, utterance; SEE CONCEPTS 274,278

word [n3] unit of language
concept, designation, expression, idiom, lexeme,
locution, morpheme, name, phrase, sound, term,
usage, utterance, vocable; SEE CONCEPT 275

word [n4] command
behest, bidding, charge, commandment, decree,
dictate, edict, go-ahead*, green light*, injunction,
mandate, order, signal, ukase, will; SEE CONCEPT
685

word [n5] promise
affirmation, assertion, assurance, commitment,
declaration, engagement, guarantee, oath, parole,
pledge, plight, solemn oath*, solemn word*, vow,
warrant, word of honor; SEE CONCEPTS
71,278,689

word [n6] password
countersign, slogan, watchword; SEE CONCEPTS
684,685

wording [n] way of expressing a thought
choice of words, diction, language, locution, manner, mode, parlance, phraseology, phrasing, style,
terminology, turn of phrase, wordage, words; SEE
CONCEPTS 278,682

wordy [adj] talkative
bombastic, chatty*, diffuse, discursive, flatulent,
gabby*, garrulous, inflated, lengthy, long-
winded, loquacious, palaverous, pleonastic, prolix, rambling, redundant, rhetorical, tedious,
turgid, verbose, voluble, windy*; SEE CONCEPT
267

work [n1] labor, chore
assignment, attempt, commission, daily grind*,
drudge, drudgery, effort, elbow grease*, endeavor, exertion, functioning, grind, grindstone*,
industry, job, moil, muscle, obligation, pains*,
performance, production, push, salt mines*, servitude, slogging, stint, stress, striving, struggle,
sweat*, task, toil, travail, trial, trouble, undertaking; SEE CONCEPTS 87,362,677

work [n2] business, occupation
activity, art, calling, commitment, contract, craft,
do*, duty, employment, endeavor, gig*, grind*,
industry, job, line, line of business, livelihood,
métier, nine-to-five*, obligation, office, practice,
profession, pursuit, racket*, responsibility, skill,
slot*, specialization, stint, swindle, task, thing*,
trade, vocation, walk; SEE CONCEPTS 349,
351,360

work [n3] achievement
act, application, article, composition, creation,
deed, end product, function, handicraft, handiwork, oeuvre, opus, output, performance, piece,
product, production; SEE CONCEPTS 260,706

work [v1] be employed; exert oneself
apply oneself, be gainfully employed, buckle
down*, carry on, dig, do a job, do business, drive,
drudge, earn a living*, freelance, have a job, hold
a job, hustle*, knuckle down*, labor, manage,
manufacture, moil, moonlight*, nine-to-five it*,
peg away*, plug away*, ply, punch a clock*, pursue, report, scratch, slave, slog*, specialize,
strain, strive, sweat*, take on, toil, try; SEE CON-
CEPTS 100,351

work [v2] manipulate, operate
accomplish, achieve, act, behave, bring about,
carry out, cause, contrive, control, create, direct,
drive, effect, execute, force, function, go, handle,
implement, manage, maneuver, move, perform,
ply, progress, react, run, serve, take, tick, use,
wield; SEE CONCEPTS 94,117,199,204

work [v3] cultivate, form
care for, dig, dress, farm, fashion, handle, knead,
labor, make, manipulate, mold, process, shape,
tend, till; SEE CONCEPTS 173,184,257

workable [adj] feasible
applicable, breeze*, cinch*, doable, duck soup*,
easy, easy as pie*, exploitable, functional, no
sweat*, piece of cake*, possible, practicable,
practical, simple as ABC*, snap, usable, useful,
viable, working; SEE CONCEPTS 538,552,560

worker [n] person who is employed
artisan, blue collar*, breadwinner, company person, craftsperson, employee, hand, help, laborer,
nine-to-fiver*, operative, peasant, proletarian,
serf, slave, toiler, trader, tradesperson, wage

wi
wo

earner, white collar*, working person, working
stiff*; SEE CONCEPT 348

working [adj] active, occupied

alive, busy, dynamic, effective, employed, engaged, functioning, going, hot*, in a job, in force,
in full swing, in gear, in process, laboring, live,
moving, on fire*, on the job, on track*, operative,
practical, running, useful, viable; SEE CONCEPTS
538,560

workout [n] exercise, practice

conditioning, constitutional, drill, rehearsal, routine, session, test, training, tryout, warm-up,
work; SEE CONCEPTS 290,363

work out [v] solve; satisfy

accomplish, achieve, arrange, attain, be effective,
bring off, clear, come out, come to terms*, complete, compromise, construct, contrive, develop,
devise, elaborate, evolve, figure out, find out, finish, fix, form, formulate, get something done*,
go, go well, handle, happen, manipulate, pan
out*, plan, prosper, pull off*, put together, reach
agreement, resolve, result, succeed, swing*, turn
out, up, win; SEE CONCEPTS 706,713

work up [v] stimulate

agitate, animate, arouse, breed, cause, develop,
engender, excite, generate, get up, hatch, improve, incite, induce, inflame, instigate, move,
muster up, occasion, produce, rouse, spur, stir up;
SEE CONCEPTS 14,242

world [n1] planet, globe

cosmos, creation, earth, heavenly body, macrocosm, microcosm, nature, sphere, star, terrene,
universe; SEE CONCEPTS 511,770

world [n2] class of existing beings

class, division, everybody, everyone, group, humanity, humankind, human race, race, realm; SEE
CONCEPTS 378,391

world [n3] person's environment, experience

ambience, area, atmosphere, business, domain,
field, life, matters, memory, province, pursuits,
realm, sphere, system; SEE CONCEPT 678

worldly [adj1] material, nonreligious

carnal, earthly, earthy, fleshly, human, lay, materialistic, mundane, natural, physical, practical,
profane, secular, sublunary, telluric, temporal,
terrene, terrestrial, ungodly; SEE CONCEPTS
536,582

worldly [adj2] sophisticated, materialistic

avaricious, been around, blasé, callous, cool*,
cosmopolitan, covetous, disenchanted, grasping,
greedy, hardened, knowing, opportunistic, power-
loving, practical, self-centered, selfish, unprincipled, uptown*, urbane, worldly wise; SEE
CONCEPT 401

worldwide [adj] general

catholic, common, comprehensive, cosmic, ecumenical, extensive, global, international, multinational, omnipresent, pandemic, planetary,
ubiquitous, universal; SEE CONCEPT 536

worn/worn-out [adj] used, tired

beat, burned out*, bushed*, busted*, clichéd,
consumed, depleted, destroyed, deteriorated,
drained, drawn, effete, exhausted, fatigued,
frayed, gone, hackneyed, had it*, haggard, jaded,
kaput*, knocked out*, old, out of gas*, overused,
overworked, pinched, played out*, pooped*,
ragged, ruined, shabby, shot, spent, stale, tattered, the worse for wear*, threadbare, timeworn,
tired out, totaled*, used up, useless, wearied,

weary, well-worn, wiped out, worn down, wrung
out*; SEE CONCEPTS 485,560

worried [adj] anxious, troubled

afraid, apprehensive, beside oneself, bothered,
clutched, concerned, distracted, distraught, distressed, disturbed, fearful, fretful, frightened,
hung up*, ill-at-ease, nervous, on edge*, on pins
and needles*, overwrought, perturbed, solicitous,
tense, tormented, uneasy, upset, uptight, worried
stiff*; SEE CONCEPT 403

worry [n] anxiety, trouble

anguish, annoyance, apprehension, bad news*,
care, concern, disquiet, distress, disturbance,
doubt, fear, headache*, heartache*, irritation,
misery, misgiving, nag*, pain*, perplexity, pest,
plague, presentiment, problem, torment, torture,
trial, uncertainty, uneasiness, vexation, woe, worriment; SEE CONCEPTS 532,690

worry [v] be or make anxious, troubled

afflict, aggrieve, agonize, ail, annoy, attack, bedevil, beleaguer, beset, bite one's nails*, bother,
brood, bug*, chafe, concern oneself, depress, despair, disquiet, distress, disturb, dun, feel uneasy,
fret, gnaw at, goad, go for*, harass, harry, hassle,
have qualms, hector, importune, irritate, needle,
oppress, persecute, perturb, pester, plague, stew*,
sweat out*, take on, tantalize, tear, tease, test,
torment, torture, trouble, try, unsettle, upset, vex,
wince, writhe, wrong; SEE CONCEPTS
7,14,19,410

worsen [v] diminish, decay

aggravate, corrode, damage, decline, degenerate,
depress, descend, deteriorate, disintegrate, exacerbate, fall off, get worse, go downhill*, impair,
lower, retrograde, retrogress, rot, sink; SEE CON-
CEPTS 240,698

worship [n] honoring, glorification

adoration, adulation, awe, beatification, benediction, chapel, church service, deification, devotion,
exaltation, genuflection, glory, homage, honor,
idolatry, idolization, invocation, laudation, love,
offering, praise, prayer, prostration, regard, respect, reverence, rite, ritual, service, supplication,
veneration, vespers; SEE CONCEPTS 69,367

worship [v] honor, glorify

admire, adore, adulate, bow down to, canonize,
celebrate, chant, deify, dote on, esteem, exalt,
extol, idolize, laud, love, magnify, offer prayers
to, pay homage to, praise, pray to, put on a pedestal*, respect, revere, reverence, sanctify, sing,
sing praises to*, venerate; SEE CONCEPTS 69,367

worth [n] value, estimation associated with something

account, aid, assistance, avail, benefit, caliber,
class, consequence, cost, credit, desirability, dignity, equivalence, excellence, goodness, help, importance, mark, meaningfulness, merit, moment,
note, perfection, price, quality, rate, significance,
stature, use, usefulness, utility, valuation, virtue,
weight, worthiness; SEE CONCEPTS 335,346

worthless [adj] of no use; without value

abandoned, abject, barren, base, bogus, cheap,
contemptible, counterproductive, despicable,
empty, futile, good-for-nothing*, ignoble, inconsequential, ineffective, ineffectual, inferior, insignificant, inutile, meaningless, mediocre,
miserable, no-account*, no-good*, nothing, nugatory, paltry, pointless, poor, profitless, sterile,
trashy, trifling, trivial, unavailing, unessential,
unimportant, unproductive, unprofitable, unus-

able, useless, valueless, waste, wretched; SEE CONCEPTS *560,570,575*

worthwhile [*adj*] *helpful*

advantageous, beneficial, constructive, estimable, excellent, gainful, good, important, invaluable, justifiable, lucrative, meritorious, money-making, paying, priceless, productive, profitable, remunerative, rewarding, serviceable, useful, valuable, worthy; SEE CONCEPTS *560,567,572*

worthy [*adj*] *honorable, respectable*

aces*, admirable, A-1*, best, blameless, choice, commendable, creditable, decent, dependable, deserving, desirable, divine, estimable, ethical, excellent, exemplary, first-class*, first-rate*, good, honest, incorrupt, invaluable, laudable, meritorious, model, moral, noble, pleasing, praiseworthy, precious, priceless, pure, reliable, reputable, righteous, right-minded, salt of the earth*, satisfying, sterling, top-drawer*, top-notch*, true, trustworthy, upright, valuable, virtuous, winning, worthwhile; SEE CONCEPTS *545,567,572*

wound [*n*] *injury*

anguish, bruise, cut, damage, distress, gash, grief, harm, heartbreak, hurt, insult, laceration, lesion, pain, pang, shock, slash, torment, torture, trauma; SEE CONCEPT *309*

wound [*v1*] *cause bodily damage*

bruise, carve, clip*, contuse, cut, damage, ding*, gash, harm, hit, hurt, injure, irritate, lacerate, nick, open up, ouch*, pierce, rough up*, scrape, scratch, slash, slice, stick, total*; SEE CONCEPTS *137,246,313*

wound [*v2*] *cause mental hurt*

bother, cut to the quick*, distress, disturb, do in*, dump on* get*, grieve, hurt, hurt one's feelings, mortify, offend, outrage, pain, put down*, shake up*, sting, traumatize, trouble, upset; SEE CONCEPTS *7,14,19*

wrangle [*n*] *fight, argument*

altercation, battle royal*, bickering, blow-off*, blowup*, branigan*, brawl, brouhaha*, cash, contest, controversy, disagreement, dispute, exchange, falling-out*, flap*, fracas, knock-down drag-out*, quarrel, row, ruckus*, ruction, rumble, rumpus, scene, set-to*, squabble, tiff; SEE CONCEPTS *46,106*

wrangle [*v*] *fight, argue*

altercate, bicker, brawl, bump heads*, contend, cross swords*, disagree, dispute, fall out*, hassle, have at it*, have words*, lock horns*, pick a bone*, put up a fight, quarrel, quibble, row, scrap, spat, squabble, take on, tangle, tiff; SEE CONCEPTS *46,106*

wrap [*n*] *clothing that is worn over for warmth*

blanket, cape, cloak, coat, cover, fur, jacket, mantle, shawl, stole; SEE CONCEPT *451*

wrap [*v*] *surround with a covering*

absorb, bandage, bind, bundle, bundle up, camouflage, cloak, clothe, cover, drape, encase, encircle, enclose, enfold, envelop, fold, gift-wrap*, hide, immerse, invest, mask, muffle, pack, package, protect, roll up, sheathe, shelter, shroud, swaddle, swathe, twine, veil, wind; SEE CONCEPT *172*

wrap up [*v*] *finish*

bring to a close, close, complete, conclude, determine, end, halt, polish off, terminate, wind up; SEE CONCEPT *234*

wrath [*n*] *extreme anger*

acrimony, asperity, boiling point*, conniption*,

dander, displeasure, exasperation, flare-up, fury, hate, hatefulness, huff, indignation, ire, irritation, mad, madness, offense, passion, rage, resentment, rise, stew*, storm, temper, vengeance; SEE CONCEPTS *29,410*

wrathful [*adj*] *very angry*

beside oneself, displeased, enraged, furious, heated, incensed, indignant, infuriated, irate, ireful, mad, on the warpath*, raging, storming; SEE CONCEPT *403*

wreak [*v*] *force, cause*

bring about, carry out, create, effect, execute, exercise, force upon, inflict, unleash, vent, visit, work, wreck; SEE CONCEPT *242*

wreath [*n*] *circular decoration*

band, bay, bouquet, chaplet, circlet, coronal, coronet, crown, festoon, garland, laurel, lei, loop, ring, ringlet; SEE CONCEPTS *259,260,429*

wreck [*n*] *severe damage or severely damaged goods*

collapse, crash, crate, debacle, debris, derelict, destruction, devastation, disruption, fender bender*, heap*, hulk*, jalopy*, junk*, junker*, litter, mess, pile-up*, rear-ender*, relic, ruin, ruins, shipwreck, smashup*, total*, waste, wreckage; SEE CONCEPTS *260,674*

wreck [*v*] *ruin, destroy*

bash, batter, beach, break, capsize, crack up*, crash, cripple, dash, decimate, demolish, devastate, dilapidate, disable, do in*, efface, founder, impair, injure, mangle, mar, mess up*, pile up*, put out of commission*, ravage, raze, run aground, sabotage, scuttle, shatter, shipwreck, sink, smash, smash up, spoil, strand, subvert, take apart, take out, tear up, torpedo*, total*, trash*, undermine, vandalize, wrack*, wrack up*; SEE CONCEPT *252*

wrench [*v*] *jerk, force violently*

bend, coerce, compel, contort, dislocate, dislodge, distort, drag, exact, extract, pervert, pinch, pull, rend, rip, screw, sprain, squeeze, strain, tear, tug, tweak, twist, wrest, wring, yank; SEE CONCEPTS *80,206*

wrestle [*v*] *struggle physically or mentally with something*

battle, combat, contend, endeavor, essay, exert, fight, grapple, grunt, scuffle, strain, strive, tangle, tussle, work; SEE CONCEPTS *17,191,208*

wretched [*adj*] *terrible, very bad*

abject, afflicted, base, bummed, calamitous, cheap, contemptible, dejected, deplorable, depressed, despicable, disconsolate, distressed, dolorous, down, down-and-out*, downcast, faulty, flimsy, forlorn, gloomy, hapless, hopeless, hurting, inferior, in the pits*, low, low-down*, mean, melancholy, miserable, paltry, pathetic, pitiable, pitiful, poor, shabby, shameful, sordid, sorrowful, sorry, spiritless, tragic, unfortunate, unhappy, vile, weak, woebegone, woeful, worthless; SEE CONCEPTS *403,571*

wriggle [*v*] *maneuver out of; wiggle*

convulse, crawl, dodge, extricate oneself, glide, jerk, jiggle, ooze, skew, slink, slip, snake, sneak, squirm, turn, twist, twitch, wag, waggle, worm, writhe, zigzag; SEE CONCEPTS *30,149*

wring [*v*] *twist, contort*

choke, coerce, compress, draw out, exact, extort, extract, force, gouge, hurt, pain, pinch, pry, push, screw, shake down, squeeze, strain, strangle,

throttle, turn, wrench, wrest; SEE CONCEPTS
142,206,208

wrinkle [n] *crinkle, fold*
contraction, corrugation, crease, crow's-foot*,
crumple, depression, furrow, gather, line, pleat,
plica, pucker, ridge, rimple, rumple, tuck; SEE
CONCEPTS 418,513

wrinkle [v] *crinkle, fold*
compress, corrugate, crease, crimp, crisp, crumple, furrow, gather, line, prune up, pucker, purse,
rimple, ruck, rumple, screw up, scrunch, seam,
shrivel, twist; SEE CONCEPTS 185,201

writ [n] *court order*
command, decree, document, habeas corpus,
mandate, paper, prescript, process, replevin, subpoena, summons, warrant; SEE CONCEPT 318

write [v] *put language down on paper*
address, author, autograph, bang out*, chalk*,
commit, communicate, comp*, compose, copy,
correspond, create, dash off*, draft, draw up*,
drop a line*, drop a note*, engross, formulate,
ghost, indite, ink, inscribe, jot down, knock off*,
knock out*, letter, note, note down*, pen, pencil,
print, push a pencil*, put in writing, record, reproduce, rewrite, scrawl, scribble, scribe, scriven,
set down, set forth, sign, take down, tell, transcribe, turn out, typewrite, write down, write up;
SEE CONCEPTS 79,203

write off [v] *devalue; forget about*
cancel, cross out, decry, depreciate, disregard,
downgrade, give up, lower, mark down, shelve,
take a loss on, underrate, undervalue; SEE CON-
CEPT 54

writer [n] *person who composes with language*
author, biographer, columnist, contributor, correspondent, critic, dramatist, editor, essayist,
freelancer, ghostwriter, journalist, newspaper person, novelist, person of letters, poet, reporter,
screenwriter, scribbler, scribe, scripter, stenographer, stringer, wordsmith; SEE CONCEPTS
348,356

writhe [v] *contort; toss back and forth*
agonize, bend, distort, jerk, recoil, squirm, struggle, suffer, thrash, thresh, twist, wiggle, wince,
worm, wriggle; SEE CONCEPTS 80,150

writing [n1] *printing on paper*
autograph, calligraphy, chirography, cuneiform,
hand, handwriting, hieroglyphics, longhand,
manuscription, print, scrawl, scribble, script,
shorthand; SEE CONCEPTS 79,284

writing [n2] *printed composition*
article, belles-lettres, book, discourse, dissertation, document, editorial, essay, letter, literature,
manuscript, novel, ode, opus, pamphlet, paper,
piece, play, poem, prose, publication, record, review, signature, theme, thesis, tract, treatise,
work; SEE CONCEPT 271

wrong [n] *offense, sin*
abuse, bad deed, bias, blunder, crime, cruelty,
damage, delinquency, discourtesy, error, evil,
faux pas, favor, foul play, grievance, harm, hurt,
immorality, imposition, indecency, inequity, inhumanity, iniquity, injury, injustice, insult, libel,
malevolence, miscarriage, misdeed, misdemeanor, misdoing, mistake, oppression, persecution, prejudice, sinfulness, slander, slight, spite,
tort, transgression, trespass, turpitude, unfairness,
vice, villainy, violation, wickedness, wrongdoing;
SEE CONCEPT 645

wrong [adj1] *incorrect*
amiss, askew, astray, at fault, awry, bad, counterfactual, defective, erratic, erring, erroneous,
fallacious, false, faulty, fluffed, goofed*, inaccurate, in error, inexact, miscalculated, misconstrued, misfigured, misguided, mishandled,
mistaken, not precise, not right, not working, off-
target*, on the wrong track*, out, out of commission*, out of line*, out of order*, perverse,
rotten*, sophistical, specious, spurious, ungrounded, unsatisfactory, unsound, unsubstantial,
untrue, wide; SEE CONCEPTS 571,582

wrong [adj2] *immoral, dishonest*
amoral, bad, base, blamable, blameworthy, blasphemous, censurable, corrupt, criminal, crooked,
debauched, depraved, dishonorable, dissipated,
dissolute, evil, felonious, illegal, illicit, indecent,
iniquitous, naughty, profane, profligate, reprehensible, reprobate, risqué, sacrilegious, salacious,
shady, sinful, smutty, unethical, unfair, ungodly,
unholy, unjust, unlawful, unrighteous, vicious,
wanton, wicked, wrongful; SEE CONCEPT 545

wrong [adj3] *inappropriate, not suitable*
amiss, awkward, bad, disproportionate, funny,
gauche, ill-advised, improper, inapt, incongruous,
incorrect, indecorous, infelicitous, malapropos,
misplaced, not done*, off-balance, rotten*, unacceptable, unbecoming, unconventional, undesirable, unfit, unfitted, unfitting, unhappy,
unsatisfactory, unseemly, unsuitable; SEE CON-
CEPT 558

wrong [adj4] *reverse, opposite*
back, inside, inverse, obverse; SEE CONCEPT 586

wrong [v] *hurt, mistreat another*
abuse, aggrieve, cheat, damage, defame, discredit, dishonor, harm, hurt, ill-treat, impose
upon, injure, malign, maltreat, misrepresent, mistreat, offend, oppress, outrage, persecute, take advantage of; SEE CONCEPTS 7,19,246,313

wrong [adv] *astray*
afield, amiss, askew, badly, erroneously, inaccu-
rately, incorrectly, mistakenly, unfavorably,
wrongly; SEE CONCEPTS 544,548

wrongful [adj] *evil, illegal*
blameworthy, criminal, dishonest, dishonorable,
felonious, illegitimate, illicit, immoral, improper,
lawless, reprehensible, unethical, unfair, unjust,
unlawful, wicked; SEE CONCEPTS 319,545

wry [adj] *sarcastic, distorted*
askew, aslant, awry, contorted, crooked, cynical,
deformed, droll, dry, ironic, mocking, sardonic,
twisted, uneven, warped; SEE CONCEPTS 267,581

X

x-ray [n] *picture of inside a body*
actinism, cathode rays, encephalogram, fluoro-
scope, radioactivity, radiograph, refractometry,
Roentgen rays, ultraviolet rays; SEE CONCEPT 311

Y

yacht [n] *pleasure boat*
cabin cruiser, cruiser, ketch, racer, sailboat, sailing boat, sloop, yawl; SEE CONCEPT 506

yak/yap [n/v] *talk a lot*
babble, blather, chat, chatter, clack, confabulate, gab, gossip, jabber, jaw*, prate, prattle, run on*, tattle, yammer; SEE CONCEPTS *51,266*

yank [v] *pull hard and fast*
draw, evulse, extract, hitch, jerk, lug, snap, snatch, tear, tug, twitch, vellicate, wrench; SEE CONCEPT *206*

yard [n] *grassy area around a structure*
backyard, barnyard, clearing, close, corral, court, courtyard, enclosure, fold, garden, grass, lawn, lot, patch, patio, playground, quadrangle, terrace; SEE CONCEPT *509*

yarn [n1] *fiber for knitting*
cotton fiber, flaxen thread, fleece, spun wool, thread, twist, wool; SEE CONCEPT *473*

yarn [n2] *story, often long and made-up*
adventure, alibi, anecdote, fable, fabrication, fairy tale, lie, line, narrative, potboiler*, prose, sea story*, song*, song and dance*, string*, tale, tall story*, tall tale; SEE CONCEPT *282*

yawn [v] *open mouth wide, usually sign of fatigue*
catch flies*, divide, doze, drowse, expand, gap, gape, give, nap, part, sleep, snooze, spread, yaw, yawp*; SEE CONCEPTS *163,185*

yearly [adj] *every twelve months*
annual, annually, once a year, per annum, perennial, regularly, year by year, yearlong; SEE CONCEPTS *541,823*

yearn [v] *desire strongly*
ache, be desirous of, be eager for, be passionate, chafe, covet, crave, dream, hanker, have a crush on*, have a yen for, hunger, itch, languish, long, lust, pine, set one's heart on*, thirst, want, wish for; SEE CONCEPT *20*

years [n] *age; old age*
age, agedness, caducity, dotage, elderliness, generation, lifespan, lifetime, oldness, senescence, senility; SEE CONCEPT *715*

yell [n/v] *loud communication*
bawl, bellow, call, cheer, complain, cry, holler*, hoot, howl, lament, roar, scream, screech, shout, shriek, shrill, squawk, squeal, ululate, vociferate, wail, weep, whoop, yap, yelp, yip; SEE CONCEPTS *47,595*

yellow [n/adj1] *sunny color*
amber, bisque, blond, buff, chrome, cream, gold, ivory, lemon, saffron, sand, tawny; SEE CONCEPTS *618,622*

yellow [adj2] *cowardly*
chicken*, craven, deceitful, gutless, lily-livered*, low, offensive, pusillanimous, sneaking, treacherous, tricky, unethical, unprincipled; SEE CONCEPTS *267,401*

yelp [n/v] *short, high cry*
bark, hoot, howl, screech, yap, yip, yowl; SEE CONCEPT *64*

yen [n] *strong want*
craving, desire, hankering, hunger, itch, longing, lust, passion, thirst, urge, yearning; SEE CONCEPTS *20,709*

yes [adv] *agreed*
affirmative, all right*, amen, aye*, beyond a doubt, by all means, certainly, definitely, even so, exactly, fine, gladly, good, good enough, granted, indubitably, just so, most assuredly, naturally, of course, okay*, positively, precisely, surely, sure thing*, true, undoubtedly, unquestionably, very well, willingly, without fail, yea*, yep*; SEE CONCEPTS *535,572*

yesterday [n] *the day before today*
bygone, foretime, lang syne*, last day, not long ago, past, recently, the other day*; SEE CONCEPT *815*

yet [adv1] *up until now*
as yet, earlier, hitherto, prior to, so far, still, thus far, till, until now, up to now; SEE CONCEPT *820*

yet [adv2] *in spite of*
after all, although, at any rate, but, despite, even though, howbeit, however, nevertheless, nonetheless, notwithstanding, on the other hand, still, still and all, though, withal; SEE CONCEPT *544*

yet [adv3] *in addition*
additionally, along, also, as well, besides, further, furthermore, likewise, more, moreover, over and above*, still, still further, to boot*, too; SEE CONCEPT *548*

yet [adv4] *in the future*
after a while, at some future time, beyond this, even, eventually, finally, in due course, in the course of time, someday, sometime, sooner or later, ultimately; SEE CONCEPT *799*

yield [n] *production of labor*
crop, earnings, harvest, income, output, outturn, produce, profit, return, revenue, takings, turnout; SEE CONCEPTS *260,338*

yield [v1] *produce*
accrue, admit, afford, allow, beam, bear, blossom, bring forth, bring in, discharge, earn, furnish, generate, give, give off, hold out, net, offer, pay, proffer, provide, return, sell for, supply, tender, turn out; SEE CONCEPT *205*

yield [v2] *give in, surrender*
abandon, abdicate, admit defeat, back down, bend, bow, break, buy, call it quits*, capitulate, cave in, cede, collapse, come to terms*, crumple, defer, fold, fold up, give oneself over, give up, give way*, go, hand over, knuckle, knuckle under*, lay down arms*, leave, let go*, part with, relax, relent, relinquish, resign, sag, submit, succumb, suffer defeat, surrender, throw in the towel*; SEE CONCEPTS *14,18,35*

yield [v3] *grant, allow*
accede, accept, acknowledge, acquiesce, admit, agree, assent, bow, break, comply, concede, concur, consent, defer, fail, fit in, go along with*, go with the flow*, permit, play the game*, surrender, toe the line*, toe the mark*, waive; SEE CONCEPT *8*

yielding [adj1] *accommodating*
acquiescent, biddable, compliant, docile, easy, flexible, humble, nonresistant, obedient, passive, pliable, pliant, putty in one's hands, resigned, submissive, tractable; SEE CONCEPTS *401,404*

yielding [adj2] *soft, flexible*
elastic, malleable, mushy, pappy, plastic, pliable, pulpy, quaggy, resilient, spongy, springy, squishy, supple, tractable, tractile, unresisting; SEE CONCEPTS *488,606*

yoke [n] *bondage, bond*
burden, chain, coupling, enslavement, helotry, knot, ligament, ligature, link, nexus, oppression, peonage, serfdom, service, servility, servitude, slavery, tie; SEE CONCEPTS *513,677*

yoke [v] *bond together; join*
associate, attach, bracket, buckle, combine, conjoin, conjugate, connect, couple, fasten, fix, harness, hitch, link, secure, splice, strap, tack, tie, unite, wed; SEE CONCEPTS *85,160,193*

wr
yo

yokel [n] *person who is mired in local custom*
backwoods person, boor*, country cousin*, country person, hayseed*, peasant, rustic; SEE CONCEPT 413

yonder [adv] *faraway*
away, beyond, distant, farther, further, remote, yon; SEE CONCEPTS 586,778

young [n] *animate beings that are not mature*
babies, baby, brood, family, infants, issue, litter, little ones*, offspring, progeny; SEE CONCEPTS 394,414,424

young [adj] *immature*
adolescent, blooming, blossoming, boyish, boy-like, budding, burgeoning, callow, childish, childlike, crude, developing, early, fledgling, fresh, girlish, girllike, green*, growing, half-grown, ignorant, inexperienced, infant, inferior, junior, juvenile, little, modern, new, newborn, newish, not aged, pubescent, puerile, punk, raw, recent, tender, tenderfoot*, undeveloped, undisciplined, unfinished, unfledged, unlearned, unpracticed, unripe, unseasoned, untried, unversed, vernal, youthful; SEE CONCEPTS 578,678,715,797

youngster/youth [n/n] *person before the age of maturity*
boy, chick*, cub*, fledgling, girl, junior, juvenile, juvenile delinquent*, kid*, lad, lass, pup, pupil, student, teenager, young person; SEE CONCEPTS 414,424

youth [n2] *early period in life of animate being*
adolescence, awkward age, bloom, boyhood, childhood, girlhood, greenness, ignorance, immaturity, inexperience, innocence, juvenescence, minority, prime, puberty, salad days*, springtide, springtime of life, teens, tender age*, youthfulness; SEE CONCEPT 817

youthful [adj] *new, immature*
active, adolescent, boyish, budding, buoyant, callow, childish, childlike, enthusiastic, fresh, full of life, girlish, green*, inexperienced, infant, juvenile, keen, pubescent, puerile, tender, underage, vernal, vigorous, young; SEE CONCEPTS 542,578,797

yowl [n/v] *long, loud animate sound*
bawl, bay, caterwaul, cry, holler*, howl, mewl, scream, screech, squall, squeal, ululate, wail, whine, yell, yelp, yip; SEE CONCEPT 77

yuppie [n] *young upwardly mobile professional*
button-down, clone, conspicuous consumer, suit, three-piecer, urban professional, white-collar worker; SEE CONCEPT 348

Z

zany [n] *person who is wildly funny*
buffoon, card*, clown, comedian, comic, cutup*, farceur, funny person, gag person, humorist, idiot, jester, joker, madcap*, moron, nut*, practical joker, prankster, screwball*, show-off, simpleton*, wag*, wisecracker*; SEE CONCEPTS 352,423

zany [adj] *crazy, funny*
camp*, campy*, clownish, comical, dumb, eccentric, fool, foolish, goofy, hare-brained*, humorous, joshing, kooky*, loony*, madcap*, nutty*, sappy*, wacky*, witty; SEE CONCEPTS 267,401

zeal [n] *enthusiasm*
alacrity, ardor, bustle, determination, devotion, diligence, dispatch, drive, eagerness, earnestness, enterprise, fanaticism, fervor, fierceness, fire, gusto, hustle, inclination, initiative, intensity, intentness, keenness, mania, passion, perseverance, push, readiness, sincerity, spirit, stick-to-itiveness*, urgency, vehemence, verve, warmth, what-it-takes*, yen, zest; SEE CONCEPTS 32,410, 411

zealous [adj] *enthusiastic*
afire, antsy*, ardent, avid, burning, coming on strong*, dedicated, devoted, eager, earnest, fanatic, fanatical, fervent, fervid, fireball*, fired, frenetic, gung-ho*, hot*, impassioned, itchy*, keen, obsessed, passionate, possessed, pushy*, rabid, ripe, self-starting, spirited, wild-eyed*; SEE CONCEPTS 326,401,404

zenith [n] *top*
acme, altitude, apex, apogee, cap, capper, capstone, climax, crest, crown, culmination, elevation, eminence, height, high noon*, high point, meridian, payoff*, peak, pinnacle, roof, summit, tiptop*, topper*, vertex; SEE CONCEPTS 706,832, 836

zero [n] *nothing*
aught, blank, bottom, cipher, insignificancy, love*, lowest point, nada*, nadir, naught, nil*, nix*, nobody*, nonentity, nought, nullity, oblivion, ought, rock bottom*, scratch, shutout, void, zilch*, zip*, zot*; SEE CONCEPTS 407,784

zero hour [n] *vital moment*
appointed hour*, climax, contingency, countdown, crisis, crossroad, D-day*, emergency, exigency, jumping-off point*, juncture, moment of truth*, pinch, strait, target, the time*, turning point*; SEE CONCEPTS 668,815,832

zest [n] *taste, flavor*
bite, body, charm, flavoring, ginger, guts*, interest, kick*, nip, piquancy, punch*, pungency, relish, salt, savor, seasoning, smack*, snap*, spice, tang, zap*, zip*; SEE CONCEPT 614

zest [n2] *energy, gusto*
appetite, ardor, bliss, bounce, cheer, delectation, delight, eagerness, ecstasy, elation, enjoyment, enthusiasm, fervor, guts*, happiness, keenness, moxie*, passion, pep*, pleasure, relish*, satisfaction, zeal, zing*; SEE CONCEPTS 410,411

zigzag [adj] *moving side to side*
askew, awry, bent, crinkled, crooked, devious, diagonal, erratic, fluctuating, inclined, indirect, irregular, jagged, meandering, oblique, oscillating, rambling, serrated, sinuous, sloping, snaking, tortuous, transverse, twisted, twisting, undulating, waggling, winding; SEE CONCEPT 581

zip [n] *enthusiasm, energy*
brio, drive, get-up-and-go*, go*, gusto, life, liveliness, oomph*, pep, pizzazz*, punch, sparkle, spirit, verve, vigor, vim, vitality, zest, zing*; SEE CONCEPTS 411,633

zip [v] *move about quickly*
bustle, dash, flash, fly, hasten, hurry, run, rush, shoot, speed, tear, waltz, whisk, whiz, zoom; SEE CONCEPT 150

zone [n] *district*
area, band, belt, circuit, ground, realm, region, section, sector, segment, sphere, territory, tract; SEE CONCEPTS 508,513

zoom [v] *move very quickly*
buzz, dart, dash, dive, flash, fly, hum, hurtle, outstrip, rip, rocket, rush, shoot, shoot up, sky- rocket, speed, streak, surge, tear, whirl, whiz, zip*; SEE CONCEPT *150*

ROGET'S 21ST CENTURY CONCEPT INDEX

HOW TO USE THE CONCEPT INDEX

Simply put, a thesaurus is a collection of words grouped according to idea. 17,000 words appear in the A to Z listings of *Roget's 21st Century Thesaurus* with over 450,000 synonyms to choose from. This selection alone would seem generous enough to satisfy the lexicographer's expectation of what a thesaurus should contain. But a wealth of new alternatives is created when we begin to think about the higher connections that can be made between words and ideas in the language. This is the purpose of *Roget's 21st Century's* Concept Index.

The Concept Index not only helps writers and thinkers to *organize* their ideas but leads them from those very ideas to the words that can best express them. It is a semantic hierarchy of the most common concepts we use in American English, as it is spoken and written today. 837 concepts are classified according to their subject and usage, and are grouped under ten general categories of interest: Actions, Causes, Fields of Human Activity, Life Forms, Objects, the Planet, Qualities, Senses, States, and Weights and Measures.

Each of *Roget's 21st Century Thesaurus*'s 17,000 main entries is cross-referenced to any concept(s) to which it can be related. For example, when you look up the entry for ''knowledgeable'' in the A to Z listing, it is referenced to concept #402. Turning in the index to concept #402, ''attribute of intelligence,'' you will see over 100 other main entries that are also related to this concept:

MAIN ENTRY

with synonym list as it appears in the A to Z listing

> **knowledgeable** [*adj*] *aware, educated*·,
> abreast, acquainted, alert, appreciative, apprised,
> au courant, au fait, brainy, bright, brilliant, clever,
> cognizant, conscious, conversant, discerning, eru-
> dite, experienced, familiar, informed, insightful,
> intelligent, in the know, knowing, learned, lettered,
> omniscient, perceptive, plugged in*, posted, pre-
> scient, privy, quick-witted, sagacious, sage, savvy,
> scholarly, sensible, sharp, smart, sophic, sophisti-
> cated, tuned-in*, understanding, versed, well-
> informed, well-rounded, wise, with-it;   SEE
> CONCEPT *402*

CONCEPT

with collection of main entry words referenced to it in the index

> **402 attribute of intelligence:** able, abreast, ab-
> struse, academic, acute, adept, alert, amena-
> ble, analytic/analytical, appreciative, apt,
> astute, awake, aware, backward, bewildered,
> blank, blind, bright, brilliant, calculable,

canny, childish, clairvoyant, clear, clever,
clumsy, cognizant, coherent, common-sense,
complex, comprehensible, conscious, considered, contemplative, conversant, creative,
cunning, dark, deducible, deep, delirious,
dense, designedly, dexterous, dim, discerning, dizzy, dopey, down-to-earth, dull,
dumb, educated, efficient, elevated, empty,
empty-headed, enlightened, erudite, experienced, expert, familiar, farsighted, fatuous,
forgotten, frivolous, gifted, gullible, harebrained, hazy, idiotic, ignorant, illiterate, imbecile, impressionable, incisive,
incomprehensible, inefficient, ineligible, inept, inexperienced, informed, ingenious, inquiring, inquisitive, insipid, intellectual,
intelligent, intuitive, inventive, irrational, judicious, keen, knowing, knowledgeable,
learned, logical, lucid, mental, mindful, mistaken, nimble, oblivious, observant, obtuse,
omniscient, penetrating, perceptive, perspicacious, philosophical/philosophic, precocious,
privy, professional, proficient, profound, psychic, quick, quick-witted, rational, ready,
reasonable, resourceful, retarded, sagacious,
sane, scatterbrained, scholarly, senile, sensible, shallow, sharp, shrewd, simple, skillful,
slick, slow, smart, soft, stolid, studious, stupid, subtle, thick, thoughtful, thoughtless,
touched, unaware, uneducated, unfamiliar,
unwise, vacant, vacuous, versed, veteran,
weak, wise

Any of these main entry words appearing together as attributes of intelligence in the Concept Index—from "astute" to "ingenious" to "perspicacious" to "veteran"—
may be the one perfect word you are looking for. Or,
intrigued by the associations the word "veteran" brings to
mind, you could return to the A to Z listing to explore its
synonyms:

veteran [*adj*] *experienced, seasoned*
adept, battle-scarred*, been around*, disciplined,
exercised, expert, from way back*, hardened, inured, knows one's stuff*, long-serving, long-time,
not born yesterday*, of the old school*, old, old-
time, practical, practiced, pro, proficient, skilled,
sophisticated, steady, trained, up to speed*, versed,
vet*, weathered, wise, wise to ways*, worldly; SEE
CONCEPTS 402,527,678

Even further possibilities exist, when you realize that "veteran" is referenced to two additional concepts: #527, the
quality of "ability" and #678, the state of "experience."
Main entries are often referenced to as many as three or four
different concepts.

Simple to use, the Concept Index becomes invaluable in the effort to turn an idea into a specific word. By linking together the main entries that share similar concepts, but may not be direct synonyms, the index makes possible creative semantic connections between words in our language, stimulating thought and broadening vocabulary.

Whether you begin by browsing through the Concept Index for ideas, or in the A to Z listing with a particular word in mind, you will find that *Roget's 21st Century Thesaurus* goes beyond traditional thesauri and synonym-finders to offer thousands of word choices through access to its unique Concept Index.

QUICK REFERENCE GUIDE TO CONCEPTS

Actions

CLASS OF

1 action: act, action, activity, behave, feat, spurt, step

2 event: affair, anything, be, event, eventuate, experience, fact, incident, milestone, move, movement, occasion, outbreak, pass, proceeding

3 occurrence: development, episode, occurrence, proceeding, recur, thing, transpire

4 occurrence with one participant: act, befall, behave, break, chance, coincidence, come, come off, deed, episode, fall out, fluke, go, happen, happening, intervene, occur, occurrence, result, return, rise

5 occurrence with two participants: boundary, limit, measure, obstruct, reinforce, restraint, test

6 series of related actions: channel, commit, disposition, elapse, form, instrument, maneuver, manner, means, mechanism, method, mode, path, pattern, policy, procedure, process, routine, rule, rut, system, technique, touch, usage, vehicle, way

COGNITIVE

7 affect: abandon, abase, affect, afflict, affront, aggravate, agitate, agonize, alarm, alienate, allay, alleviate, allure, anger, annoy, antagonize, appall/appal, appeal, appease, appeasement, arouse, arrest, assuage, attract, awaken, awe, baffle, bait, beckon, bedazzle, befuddle, beguile, beleaguer, bemuse, beset, besiege, bewitch, bias, bombard, bore, bother, brighten, bring down, bug, buoy (up), burden, captivate, chafe, chagrin, charm, cheer, chill, clear, cloud, comfort, complicate, compose, concern, console, content, cow, craze, cross, crucify, crush, dampen, dash, daunt, debase, deceive, deception, defame, deflate, degrade, delight, demean, demoralize, deprecate, depreciate, depress, disaffect, disappoint, disarm, discomfit, discomfort, discommode, discompose, disconcert, discountenance, disgust, dishearten, dismay, disoblige, disparage, displease, disquiet, distress, disturb, divert, double-cross, downgrade, draw, dwarf, electrify, elevate, embarrass, embitter, embroil, enamor, enchant, encourage, encouragement, encroach, endear, energize, enliven, enrage, enrapture, enthrall, entice, enticement, entrance, estrange, exacerbate, exasperate, excite, exercise, exhilarate, fail, fascinate, faze, ferment, flurry, fluster, fortify, freak, fret, frustrate, fulfill, gall, galling, galvanize, get, govern, grate, gratify, grieve, grip, gripe, harass, harm, harry, hearten, horrify, hound, hurt, impress, inflame, ingratiate, inspire, instigate, interest, intimidate, intrigue, invigorate, irk, irritate, jar, kindle, let down, lighten, lower, lull, madden, matter, menace, miff, mock, molest, mollify, mortify, move,

nag, needle, nerve, nettle, occupy, offend, oppress, outrage, pacify, pain, pall, peeve, pep up, perk up, persecute, perturb, pester, petrify, pick at/pick on, pique, placate, plague, please, prejudice, pressure, prime, prod, provoke, puncture, put out, quell, quicken, rack, rally, rankle, rasp, reach, reassure, reduce, regenerate, register, remind, repay, repel, revolt, ride, rile, rouse, ruffle, sadden, satisfy, scar, scare, send, settle, shake, shame, shatter, sink, slight, slur, smooth, solace, soothe, spite, stagger, startle, still, strain, strengthen, stress, strike, support, sweeten, tantalize, taunt, tease, temper, terrify, terrorize, threaten, thrill, tickle, titillate, torment, torture, touch, tranquilize, transport, trouble, try, turn, turn off, undo, unnerve, unsettle, upset, vex, visit, wake/waken, wear, weigh, weigh down, whet, worry, wound, wrong

8 agree: accede, accept, acceptance, accession, accord, acknowledge, acknowledgment, acquiesce, acquiescence, agree, align, assent, back, bear, cleave, cohere, comply, compromise, concur, consent, conspire, contract, covenant, draft, encourage, enlist, follow, give in/give up, go, go along/go along with, go by, grant, league, negotiate, stipulate, unanimous, yield

9 amuse: amuse, bait, divert, entertain, humor

10 approve: acquiesce, acquiescence, advocate, agree, applaud, appreciate, approbation, approval, approve, authorize, blessing, champion, concur, condone, countenance, defend, deference, endorse, envy, espouse, exalt, exculpate, excuse, exonerate, favor, go for, honor, idolize, league, nod, okay, overlook, pardon, pity, pride, prize, recognition, recommend, regard, respect, revere/reverence, reverence, sanctify, subscribe, support

11 attract: attract, fascinate, grip, interest, intrigue, inveigle, lure, mesmerize, pull, ravish, seduce, send, snare, take, tantalize, tease, tempt, titillate, transfix, turn on, whet, win/win over

12 believe: accept, acceptance, acknowledge, appreciate, appreciation, assume, authenticate, bank on, bear, believe, bleed, consider, convert, count on/count upon, credit, deem, disagree, embrace, esteem, expect, feel, forgive, glorify, glory, hold, imagine, infer, lean, make believe, misjudge, object, overrate, postulate, predispose, presume, rate, reckon, regard, rely, sanctify, see, suppose, swallow, think, trust, underestimate, understand, view

13 change conception: ache, alternate, awakening, caprice, catharsis, concession, conformity, crack, crack up, fit, flare, fluctuate, give, go back/go back on, oscillate, perish, repudiate, reverse, revert, revive, sway, thaw, tire, vacillate, weary

14 compel: abet, alarm, attraction, badger, bait, bewilder, bind, brainwash, browbeat, brutality, bulldoze, bully, burden, coerce, coercion, come between, compel, confusion, conjure, constrain, constraint, convert, corrupt, dare, debauch, defeat, demoralize, deprave, discourage, disgrace, dispel, distract, domineer, duress, embitter, engross, enrage, enslave, entrance, excite, fan, fire, foment, force, freeze, frighten, galvanize, get back at, goad, grate, grind, harass, harassment, hassle, haunt, horrify, humble, humiliate, hurt, impel, impinge, imposition, incense, incite, inconvenience, inculcate, indoctrinate, induce, infest, inflame, infuriate, instill, interject, intimidate, intrude, inveigle, invigorate, jinx, jog, kindle, load, lumber, make, manipulate, meddle, mesmerize, mistreat, molest, motivate, nauseate, nerve, nettle, nonplus, oblige, offend, oppress, oppression, panic, paralyze, pervert, petrify, pique, plague, poison, pound, predispose, prejudice, press, pressure, prey on, provocation, push, put, put out, rankle, ride, ruffle, scourge, screw, sell/sell out, shake up, shame, sicken, sour, spoil, spur, stimulate, stir, sway, tame, task, tax, terrorize, tire, transfix, undermine, unnerve, victimize, visit, wake/waken, whip up, work up, worry, wound, yield

15 **comprehend:** appreciate, appreciation, apprehend, assimilate, catch, comprehend, conceive, decipher, deduce, deduction, derive, determine, differentiate, dig, digest, discern, discriminate, distinguish, do, draw, embrace, familiarize, fathom, feel, figure, follow, gather, get, grasp, hear, identify with, infer, know, make, make out, misapprehend, misconstrue, mistake, misunderstand, outwit/outsmart, penetrate, perceive, realize, recognize, resolve, see, solve, take, take in, tell, understand

16 **confuse:** confound, confuse, daze, dazzle, decoy, derange, disconcert, disrupt, distract, dumbfound, floor, fluster, foul up, get, hassle, humble, jumble, mix up, muddle, mystify, nonplus, obscure, overwhelm, perplex, perturb, puzzle, rattle, snarl, stump, throw

17 **consider:** absorb, ache, balance, begrudge, bleed, brood, buckle down, cogitate, commune, concentrate, consider, consult, contemplate, cook up, cram, daydream, deliberate, deliberation, devote, dream, dream up, dwell on/dwell upon, engross, entertain, envisage/envision, excogitate, eye, fancy, fantasize, focus, gnaw, grieve, harbor, heed, hide, immerse, marvel, meditate, mull, muse, occupy, picture, ponder, puzzle, reconsider, reflect, reflection, reminisce, retrospect, revolve, speculate, think, thought, treat, turn over, visualize, wonder, wrestle

18 **decide:** abnegation, adjudicate, adopt, adoption, appraisal, appraise, cancel, circumscribe, classification, classify, conclude, convict, count, credit, date, decide, dedicate, define, derive, destine, determine, disapprove, disavow, dispose of, distinguish, evaluate, falter, figure, fix, go along/go along with, go by, ground, group, hedge, impose, influence, intend, judge, make out, misjudge, moderate, ordain, plant, premise, provide, purpose, referee, resolution, resolve, rule, set, settle, solve, specify, stipulate, surmise, turn down, type, waver, yield

19 **depress:** abandon, abase, affect, afflict, affront, aggravate, agitate, agonize, alarm, alienate, anger, annoy, antagonize, appall/appal, appeal, arouse, arrest, awaken, awe, baffle, bait, befuddle, beguile, beleaguer, bemuse, beset, besiege, bias, bombard, bore, bother, bring down, bug, burden, chafe, chagrin, chill, cloud, complicate, concern, cow, craze, cross, crucify, crush, dampen, dash, daunt, debase, deceive, deception, deflate, degrade, demean, demoralize, deprecate, depreciate, depress, disaffect, disappoint, disarm, discomfit, discomfort, discommode, discompose, disconcert, discountenance, disgust, dishearten, dismay, disoblige, disparage, displease, disquiet, distress, disturb, divert, double-cross, downgrade, draw, dwarf, embarrass, embitter, embroil, encroach, enrage, enthrall, entice, enticement, estrange, exacerbate, exasperate, excite, exercise, fail, faze, ferment, flurry, fluster, freak, fret, frustrate, gall, galling, get, govern, grate, grieve, gripe, harass, harm, harry, horrify, hound, hurt, impress, inflame, instigate, intimidate, irk, irritate, jar, let down, lower, madden, matter, menace, miff, mock, molest, mortify, move, nag, needle, nettle, occupy, offend, oppress, outrage, pain, pall, peeve, persecute, perturb, pester, petrify, pick at/pick on, pique, plague, prejudice, pressure, prime, prod, provoke, puncture, put out, quicken, rack, rankle, rasp, reach, reduce, register, remind, repay, repel, revolt, ride, rile, ruffle, sadden, scar, scare, shake, shame, shatter, sink, slight, slur, spite, stagger, startle, strain, stress, strike, support, take down, tantalize, taunt, tease, terrify, terrorize, threaten, torment, torture, touch, trouble, try, turn, turn off, undo, unnerve, unsettle, upset, vex, visit, wear, weigh, weigh down, worry, wound, wrong

20 **desire:** addiction, advance(s), affinity, aim, ambition, angle for, appetite, aspiration, aspire, avid, behest, burn, care, covet, crave, craving, crush, cupidity, curiosity, dependence/dependency, desire, drool, eagerness, envy, expect, famished, fancy, fantasy, fascination, fish for, free will, goad, greed, hanker after/hanker for, hankering, hope, hunger, hungry, impulse, inclination, indulge, insatiable, interest, itch, lack, languish, lean, leaning, like, liking, long, longing, lust, mania, mind, miss, moon, mope, motivation, motive, need, nostalgia, notion, obsession, pant, penchant, pine, please, pleasure, predilection, predisposition, prefer, preference, proclivity, propensity, purport, purpose, pursue, relish, require, sigh, stomach, taste, temptation, thirst, urge, volition, voracious, want, will, wish, yearn, yen

21 **doubt:** begrudge, controvert, deplore, despair, disallow, disapprove, disbelief, disbelieve, discount, discountenance, discredit, dissent, distrust, doubt, frown, fume, grudge, hesitate, hesitation, mind, misgiving, mistrust, object, objection, oppose, query, question, regret, reject, rejection, repudiate, repulse, scorn, scruple, segregate, spurn, suspect, turn, wonder

22 **elated:** affect, allay, alleviate, allure, appeal, appease, appeasement, arouse, arrest, as-

suage, attract, awaken, awe, beckon, bedazzle, beguile, bemuse, bewitch, brighten, buoy (up), captivate, charm, cheer, clear, comfort, compose, concern, console, content, delight, disarm, divert, draw, elated, electrify, elevate, enamor, enchant, encourage, encouragement, endear, energize, enliven, enrapture, enthrall, entice, enticement, entrance, excite, exhilarate, fascinate, ferment, fortify, fulfill, galvanize, get, govern, gratify, grip, hearten, impress, inflame, ingratiate, inspire, instigate, interest, intrigue, invigorate, kindle, lighten, lull, matter, mollify, move, nerve, occupy, pacify, pep up, perk up, pique, placate, please, pressure, prime, prod, provoke, quell, quicken, rally, reach, reassure, regenerate, register, remind, rouse, satisfy, send, settle, smooth, solace, soothe, still, strengthen, strike, support, sweeten, tantalize, tease, temper, thrill, tickle, titillate, touch, tranquilize, transport, wake/waken, weigh, whet

23 endure: abide, accept, accommodate, acquiesce, bear, bear with, bow, brave, brook, come in for, come through, condone, cope, descend, digest, do without, endure, face, go, go through, hang on, have, keep at, keep up, linger, lump, make out, manage, mind, mourn, pay, persist, receive, reconcile, remain, resist, resistance, shoulder, stand/stand for, stick, stomach, submit, subsist, suffer, support, survive, sustain, sweat, take, tolerate, undergo, wear, weather, withstand

24 examine: analysis, analyze, assay, assess, assessment, bury, canvass, check, chew, cogitate, compare, comparison, consider, consideration, debate, decompose, deduce, deduction, deliberate, deliberation, dissect, dissection, evaluate, evaluation, examine, excogitate, experiment, go into, go over, inquire, inquiry, introspection, observe, ponder, pore, reflect, reflection, resolve, review, ruminate, scrutinize, scrutiny, speculate, speculation, turn over, view, weigh

25 exclude: abnegation, abstain, blacklist, boycott, count out, disallow, disavow, disinherit, except, exception, exclude, exclusion, jump, omission, omit, ostracize, oust, parry, pass, pass by, pass over, proscribe, recant, retract, rule out, shut off/shut out

26 expect: anticipate, anticipation, assume, await, bargain for, calculate, count, count on/count upon, demand, depend, expect, foresee, imagine, lean, look, mean, plan, postulate, predispose, presume, propose, reckon, rely, think

27 fear: apprehension, blanch, dismay, dread, fear, funk, horror, mistrust, panic, phobia, terror, trepidation

28 guess: believe, bet, calculation, call, conjecture, deem, divine, estimate, estimation, forecast, gamble, guess, hazard, implication, presume, project, projection, speculate, speculation, suppose, surmise, suspect, wager

29 hate: abhor, abominable, abomination, aggression, anarchy, anger, animosity, antagonism, antipathy, atrocity, aversion, blow up, boil, burn, contempt, deplore, despise, detest, discrimination, disdain, disfavor, disinclination, dislike, disrespect, dissatisfaction,

dissent, distaste, enmity, exasperation, execrate, execration, frown, fume, fury, grudge, hate, hatred, horror, ill will, indignation, lament/lamentation, loath, loathe, look down on, malice, mind, odium, opposition, outrage, phobia, pique, rage, rancor, repulsion, resent, resentment, revulsion, scorn, seethe, spite, temper, umbrage, vengeance, venom, violence, wrath

30 ignore: blink, brush aside/brush off, bypass, disallow, discount, disdain, disobey, dispense with, disregard, drop, eliminate, elude, eschew, evade, except, exception, exclude, exclusion, fence, forget, forsake, hedge, ignore, leave, lose, neglect, overlook, parry, pass, pass by, pass over, rebuff, refuse, reject, rejection, relegate, renounce, renunciation, repel, repudiate, retreat, run-around, scorn, shirk, shun, skip, skirt, slight, sneer, snub, spurn, wriggle

31 learn: absorb, acquaint, ascertain, catch, decipher, determine, dig, discover, discovery, edification, find out, get, glean, hear, learn, master, orientation, pick up, probe, research, see, study, turn up

32 love: acceptance, activity, admiration, admire, adoration, adore, adulation, affair, affection, affinity, amour, appetite, appreciate, appreciation, approval, attachment, attention, bag, bask, bewitched, bliss, canonize, care, charity, cherish, consideration, consolation, constancy, court, delight in, devotion, dig, discriminate, discrimination, dote on/dote upon, empathy, enamored, endear, enjoy, enjoyment, esteem, exaltation, exult, exultation, fall for, fancy, fascinated, fascination, favor, fidelity, flame, flirtation, fond, fondness, go for, gratitude, homage, idolize, infatuated, leaning, liaison, like, liking, love, lure, mad, mania, mercy, partiality, passion, penchant, predilection, predisposition, prize, proclivity, rapture, relish, respect, revere/reverence, reverence, savor, sentiment, taste, temper, thrill, transport, treasure, triumph, zeal

33 mental event: learn, sense, shock, stroke, think

34 mental perception: ascertain, attend, behold, beware, burn, come at, feel, gnaw, gravitate, grope, hallucinate, learn, mind, note, notice, observe, occur, pity, presage, seethe, sensation, sense, shudder, sorrow, sympathize, visualize, wonder

35 mental preparation: abide, adjust, bottle up, capitulate, center, centralize, comply, concede, conceive, condition, convert, cope, crawl, dare, deign, descend, design, determine, dismiss, dispel, face, forbear, get over, habituate, harden, look out, manufacture, melt, orient, plan, preparation, prepare, prime, quail, ready, reform, refresh, rehabilitate, rejuvenate, relent, renew, resist, season, simmer, sink, smolder, stew, stoop, strengthen, succumb, sulk, sweat, tarry, train, weather, withhold, yield

36 plan: arrange, assure, base, block out, book, brew, budget, calculate, chart, coin, concoct, connive, conspire, contemplate, contrive, cook up, coordinate, daydream, design, devise, draft, dream up, engineer, fabricate, finesse, fix, formulate, frame, hatch, intend, intrigue, invent, lay, lay out, machinate, maneuver, manufacture, mean, organize, outline, plan, plot, program, project, propose, purpose, pursue, rough out, schedule, shape, sketch

37 **reason:** analyze, cipher, clear up, conclude, construe, crack, criticize, date, decipher, dialectic, do, educe, equate, estimate, figure, forecast, gauge, generalize, induction, infer, judgment, logic, make, premise, project, rank, rate, reason, reasoning, reckon, solve, speculate, stock, survey

38 **recognize:** acknowledge, ascertain, come across, conjure up, crack, cut, detect, detection, diagnose, differentiate, discern, discriminate, distinguish, elude, encounter, familiarize, fathom, feel, identify, know, mark, perceive, pinpoint, place, recognition, recognize, remark, salute/salutation, salute, spot, stereotype

39 **relate:** ascribe, associate, association, categorize, class, classification, classify, codify, compare, comparison, contrast, correlate, equate, identify with, implication

40 **remember:** block out, forget, mind, recall, recollect, remember, remembrance, remind, reminisce, retain, retrospect, think

41 **select:** aim, allocate, allot, allow, appoint, appointment, assign, assignment, cast, choice, choose, cull, designate, designation, elect, election, excerpt, favoritism, finger, like, name, nominate, nomination, opt, pick, prefer, recruit, relegate, screen, select, take, turn, volition, vote

42 **surprise:** alarm, amaze, appall/appal, astonish, astound, awe, backfire, baffle, bedazzle, befuddle, bewilder, confound, daze, dazzle, deluge, dumbfound, electrify, flabbergast, frighten, jolt, overwhelm, petrify, scare, shock, stagger, startle, stun/stupefy, surprise, terrify

43 **think:** count, design, devise, envisage/envision, fancy, imagine, mint, occur, originate, picture, proceed, see, theorize, think, thought

COMMUNICATIVE

44 **accuse:** accuse, affront, arraign, bastardize, betray, betrayal, blame, blow up, charge, condemn, condemnation, decry, denounce, discredit, forswear, gripe, groan, grumble, heckle, humble, humiliate, impeach, implicate, impute, indict, indictment, invective, inveigh, malign, persecute, profane, rant, rebuke, reprimand, reproach, scold, slur, tax, tell off, tirade, vilify, vituperate

45 **answer:** acknowledge, agree, answer, counter, decline, denial, fill in, give in/give up, react, reaction, reciprocate, repartee, reply, respond, retort, return

46 **argue:** agitate, altercation, argue, argument, back talk, battle, beard, bicker, brawl, clash, conflict, confront, confrontation, confute, contend, contention, contest, contradict, contradiction, contravene, controversy, controvert, demur, deny, dicker, differ, difference, difficulty, disagree, disagreement, dispute, dissension, dissent, diverge, divide, encoun-

ter, expostulate, fall out, feud, fight, fracas, friction, fuss, haggle, hassle, imbroglio, maintain, misunderstanding, negate, object, objection, protest, quarrel, quibble, reason, rebut, remonstrate, rift, row, run-in, rupture, scrap, squabble, strife, tiff, uproar, wrangle

47 **articulate:** articulate, call, cry, delivery, diction, elocution, enunciate, exclaim, expression, hail, heckle, mumble, parrot, pipe, pronounce, put, sing, slur, speak, speech, stammer, talk, utter, utterance, yell

48 **ask:** accost, apologize, apology, appeal, application, apply, approach, ask, beg, beseech, canvass, catechize, charter, conjure, consult, consultation, crave, crawl, cross-examine, desire, entreat, examine, grill, hearing, implore, inquest, inquire, inquiry, interrogate, interview, investigate, investigation, invitation, invite, invocation, invoke, pester, petition, plead, poll, pray, prayer, propose, proposition, pump, query, quest, question, quiz, repent, requisition, scrounge, seek, survey

49 **assert:** accredit, acknowledge, advance, advocate, affirm, affirmation, allegation, allege, announce, announcement, ascribe, assert, assertion, attest, avow, bemoan, blow up, bluster, boast, brag, bravado, color, come clean, corroborate, crow, debunk, declaim, declaration, declare, defend, deny, dramatize, drum into, embellish, emphasize, establish, exclaim, exclamation, exult, generalize, gloat, glory, gloss, gush, impress, impute, insinuate, insist, intimate, justify, lay, level, magnify, maintain, mock, mockery, overrate, pass, play down, play up, plead, plug, point out, pound, proclaim, profess, promote, promotion, pronounce, puff, punctuate, purport, push, rant, rave, refuse, retract, review, rumor, show off, speak out/speak up, spout, state, stereotype, stress, substantiate, support, swagger, swear, testify, testimonial, testimony, underline, vent, vindicate, voice, vouch, weep, whitewash, witness

50 **authorize:** accede, accord, accredit, acknowledge, acknowledgment, acquit, affirm, aggrandize, appoint, appointment, approve, arm, assign, authorize, back, ban, bar, bear out, bless, blessing, certify, charter, commission, concession, consent, constitute, contract, countenance, countermand, crown, decree, dedicate, delegate, delegation, detail, disown, empower, enable, enact, endorse, enforce, enjoin, entitle, entrust, establish, exempt, fire, forgive, grant, induct, inflict, invest, invoke, lay, let, let off, license, make, name, negate, nod, nominate, nomination, nullify, okay, ordain, order, override/override, pardon, permission, permit, place, prescribe, prohibit, ratify, recall, receive, release, relieve, repeal, reprieve, revoke, sanction, spare, station, subscribe, underwrite, validate, vest, veto, void, warrant, withdraw, witness

51 **comment:** accost, acknowledge, add, air, annotate, aside, babble, badger, bemoan, brag, bravado, bring up, broach, circumlocution, comment, commentary, congratulate, conjecture, couch, critique, declaim, decline, deliver, discourse, enunciate, express, extem-

porize, greet, greeting, harangue, hearsay, interject, interrupt, jabber, jaw, observation, observe, preach, ramble, rattle, rave, remark, report, rhetoric, say, spout, state, talk, throw out, touch, vent, ventilate, voice, yak/yap

52 criticize: abuse, admonish, air, aspersion, assail, assault, attack, barb, baste, beef, belittle, berate, blast, browbeat, carp, castigate, censure, chasten, chastise, chew out, chide, come down on, complain, complaint, condemn, condemnation, confront, correct, cow, criticism, criticize, critique, crucify, cut, cut up, damn, debase, decry, denigrate, denounce, denunciation, deny, deprecate, depreciate, deride, derision, detract, detraction, diatribe, disapprove, disparage, disparagement, dress down, excoriate, flak, fulminate, fulmination, gainsay, gibe, gird, grievance, gripe, groan, grouch, grumble, hiss, humble, humiliate, impeach, impugn, insult, invective, inveigh, jaw, kick, knock, lambaste, lament, lash, lay into, lecture, malign, moan, mortify, mutter, nag, offense, pan, pick at/pick on, profane, protest, quibble, rail, rant, rap, rebuke, reflection, remonstrate, reprimand, reproach, review, row, run down, sarcasm, scold, scorn, scourge, slam, sneer, squawk, storm, sulk, swear, take down, tell off, thunder, vilify, vituperate

53 demand: ask, beckon, beg, behest, bid, bidding, bribe, call, challenge, charge, claim, command, countermand, crave, cross-examine, dare, decree, demand, dictate, direct, enjoin, entreat, exact, extort, extortion, grill, importune, impose, inflict, insist, instruct, interrogate, necessitate, obligate, order, petition, pump, query, question, request, require, requisition, reserve, solicit, squeeze, summon

54 deny: abuse, accusation, affront, aspersion, attack, backbiting, barb, belie, belittle, blacken, blame, blemish, casuistry, confront, contradict, curse, damn, debase, defamation, defame, defile, demean, demur, denial, denigrate, deride, detract, detraction, dig, diminish, disclaim, discountenance, discredit, disgrace, dishonor, disown, disparage, disparagement, downgrade, embarrass, explode, flout, forswear, fulminate, fulmination, gainsay, gibe, gird, insult, invective, inveigh, jeer, lambaste, lament, laugh at, lecture, lip, malign, mimic, minimize, mortify, mouth, needle, oath, oppose, protest, puncture, put down, put-down, rave, rebuff, rebut, refute, remonstrate, renounce, renunciation, ridicule, rumor, run down, sarcasm, scoff, scold, scorn, show up, slam, slander, slur, smear, snap, sneer, snub, squawk, squeal, stain, swear, swearing, tattle, taunt, thunder, tirade, traverse, turn, turn down, underestimate, vituperate, whine, write off

55 describe: articulate, articulation, blab, define, denote, describe, detail, mean, narrate, narration, outline, paraphrase, phrase, portray, recite, recount, relate, signify, spell, state, summarize, sum up, tell, translate, typify, unfold, utter

56 discuss: argue, bargain, canvass, communicate, confer, conference, consult, debate, deliberate, deliberation, dialogue/dialog, discourse, discuss, discussion, gossip, huddle, intercede, interchange, jabber, jaw, negotiate, negotiation, powwow, rap, reason, rehash, repartee, talk, treat, word

57 explain: account for, admission, admit, annotate, cite, clarification, clarify, clear up, come clean, comment, concede, confide, confirm, construe, corroborate, declare, defense, define, demonstrate, detail, dilate, elaborate, elucidate, emphasize, enlighten, enumerate, evidence, excuse, expand, explain, explicate, expound, gloss, illuminate, illustrate, interpret, itemize, justify, let on, own, palliate, paraphrase, plea, preface, prove, rationalize, recite, render, simplify, speak out/speak up, specify, translate, vindicate, warrant

58 fabricate: aspersion, backbiting, belie, bluff, disprove, embroider, fabricate, impugn, profane

59 fool: affect, artifice, assume, bamboozle, banter, beguile, bilk, blow up, bluff, burn, cajole, charade, cheat, chicanery, circumvent, color, con, copy, corner, counterfeit, cross, deceit, deceive, deception, decoy, default, defraud, delude, disguise, dishonesty, dissemble, dissimulate, do, dodge, do out of, double-cross, double-dealing, dramatize, dupe, duplicity, elude, enmesh, ensnare, entangle, entrap, evasion, excuse, extort, fake, feign, fence, finesse, flatter, flattery, fleece, fool, fooling, forge, forgery, fraud, frolic, fudge, gag, game, garble, gimmick, hanky-panky, have, hoax, hocus-pocus, impersonate, imposition, imposture, inveigle, invent, juggle, kid, make believe, maneuver, masquerade, mimic, mince, mislead, mock, outwit/outsmart, overplay, palliate, pander, parody, play down, ploy, pose, posture, prank, pretend, pretense, pretext, put on, ridicule, ruse, scheme, sham, shift, shirk, simulate, spoof, sport, strategem, string along, swindle, take, take in, trap, trick, trickery, victimize, wile, wit

60 inform: acknowledge, acquaint, address, advance, advertise, advise, allow, allude, allusion, announce, avow, bare, betray, betrayal, bill, blab, break, breathe, brief, briefing, broadcast, buzz, chronicle, circulate, clue, come out, come out with, confess, confession, convene, convey, cover, debunk, declare, define, deliver, detail, develop, dictate, disclose, divulge, enlighten, expose, exposure, feature, furnish, get across, give, give away, gossip, herald, hint, impart, inform, instruct, intimate, introduce, issue, leak, lecture, let on, notify, outing, pass, plug, post, prescribe, proclaim, program, promulgate, propagate, publication, publicize, ready, release, report, reveal, revelation, show up, sing, speak, speech, spill, spread, squeal, stipulate, talk, tattle, thank, thanks, tip, unburden, uncover, unveil, ventilate, whisper

61 instruct: bar, direct, educate, instruct, prescribe

62 label: attach, call, christen, define, designate, dub, entitle, identify, label, name, style, tag, term, title

63 lie: backbiting, belie, bunk, cant, casuistry, color, default, detraction, distort, distortion, duplicity, embroider, equivocate, equivocation, evasion, exaggerate, exaggeration, fabricate, fabrication, falsehood, falsify, feign, fib, fiction, fudge, garble, gloss, hoax, hypocrisy, invent, invention, juggle, libel, lie, malign, misinform, mislead, misrepresent/misquote, mock, obscure, pad, perjure, pervert, play down, pose, pretend, pretense, prevaricate, profane, profess, sell/sell out, simulate, slant, smear, twist, warp, whitewash, wile

64 noise, animal: bark, bay, call, cheep, chirp, howl, peep, roar, squawk, squeak, squeal, yelp

65 noise-making: bang, blare, blast, blow, boom, buzz, cadence, chant, chime, clank, clash, clatter, click, clink, clump, cough, crash, creak, crinkle, drone, drum, grumble, gurgle, harmony, hum, hush, inflection, jangle, jar, jingle, measure, meter, muffle, murmur, mute, patter, peal, pipe, pitch, play, quiet, racket, rattle, reflect, reverberate, ring, roll, rumble, rustle, silence, sizzle, sound, squeak, still, stress, swing, talk, tempo, tenor, thud/thump, thunder, tick, tinkle, toll, tone, tranquility, tune/tune up, undertone, uproar, volume, whistle

66 offer: allude, extend, lay, offer, pose, present, proffer, propose, put, submit, volunteer

67 offer to give: amends, apologize, apology, bid, bidding, come forward, concession, expiate, extend, furnish, offer, pose, present, proffer, put, surrender, volunteer

68 persuade: advance, argue, argument, assure, bend, bring around, budge, cajole, carry, coax, coerce, coercion, convince, disarm, discourage, dissuade, draw, drive, drum up, egg on, elicit, eloquence, entice, enticement, forward, get, goad, hammer away/hammer into, impel, induce, inducement, influence, ingratiate, invite, lead, lobby, maintain, motivate, negotiate, negotiation, occasion, persuade, persuasion, pitch, predispose, prevail upon/prevail on, procure, prompt, push, reason, spur, stress, sway, tempt, urge, wheedle, win/win over

69 praise: accent, acclaim, acclamation, accolade, accredit, adulation, aggrandize, applaud, applause, approbation, benediction, blarney, bless, champion, cheer, citation, commemorate, commend, commendation, compliment, congratulate, congratulations, consecrate, credit, crown, dedicate, dedication, deify, distinguish, elevate, elevation, endorse, enshrine, eulogize, eulogy, exalt, exaltation, extol, felicitate, flatter, flattery, further, glorify, hail, homage, kudos, laud, laurels, magnify, ovation, praise, puff, reference, salute, thank, thanks, tout, tribute, worship

70 predict: announce, anticipate, astrology, augur, augury, call, forebode, forecast, foreordain, foresee, foreshadow, foretell, oracle, precursor, predict, prediction, presage, prognosticate, project, prophecy, prophesy

71 promise: assurance, assure, avow, commitment, covenant, go back/go back on, guarantee, oath, pledge, portend, promise, vouch, vow, warrant, word

72 read: leaf, look up, narrate, narration, peruse, pore, read, reading, recitation, recite, refer, skim

73 refer: attach, attribute, drive at, instance, intend, mean, mention, oppose, point out, refer

74 signal: beckon, call, flag, gesture, gesture/gesticulate, hail, harbinger, hint, indicate, indication, nod, omen, page, sign, signal, spell, suggest, symbolize, wave

75 suggest: advice, advise, advocate, approach, ask, cajole, come up with, commend, connote, counsel, drum into, enlighten, exhort, exhortation, fish for, foreshadow, get at, guidance, guide, hint, imply, innuendo, insinuate, intimate, motion, move, nominate, nomination, pointer, pose, preach, proffer, propose, raise, recommend, spell, suggest, urge

76 thank: appreciate, gratitude, thank

77 vocalize: accent, air, bark, bawl, bellow, blare, cackle, caterwaul, chant, cheer, chortle, chuckle, clamor, croak, cry, drawl, drone, exclamation, giggle, groan, growl, grumble, hail, harmonize, hiss, howl, hum, laugh/laughter, laugh, moan, mumble, murmur, mutter, outcry, parrot, pipe, roar, scream, shout, shriek, shut up, sing, snap, snarl, snicker/snigger/sniggle, snore, squawk, squeal, stutter, vocalize, voice, wail, whimper, whine, whistle, whoop, yowl

78 warn: admonish, alert, bluster, caution, caveat, charge, defy, dissuade, enjoin, exhort, exhortation, forebode, foreboding, forecast, foretell, forewarn, page, portend, remind, threaten, warn, warning

79 write: abstract, address, annotate, autograph, chronicle, compile, compose, correspond, correspondence, cover, depict, dot, draft, draw, draw up, edit, endorse, engrave, engraving, enroll, extract, fill in, fleck, hand, inscribe, label, line, list, mark, notify, page, pen, picture, plot, point, punctuate, put down, quote, register, revise, revision, rough out, score, scratch, scrawl, script, sign, spot, stamp, trace, transcribe, type, underline, write, writing

GENERAL

80 act abstractly: freak, jerk, lurch, twist, wiggle, wrench, writhe

81 act over an area: decree, rule, tour, veto

82 admit: accede, accept, acquiesce, admit, allow, concede, concur, grant

83 allow: absolve, accord, acquit, admission, admit, allow, approve, authorize, capitulate, capitulation, contribute, defer, enable, entitle, excuse, exempt, grant, leave, leave, let, let off, liberate, license, overlook, patronage, permission, permit, pity, receive, reception, spell, suffer, tolerate

84 arrange: adjust, alphabetize, antedate, arrange, arrangement, array, center, centralize, codify, collate, collocate, compile, concentrate, coordinate, derange, dispose, disrupt, distribute, disturb, divide, file, graduate, group, index, jumble, line, marshal, muddle, order, organization, organize, perplex, pile, place, program, range, rank, reconstruct, sort, systematize, tabulate, type

85 **attach:** adhere, adjoin, affix, anchor, annex, append, attach, batten, bind, bond, cement, chain, clamp, clasp, cling, cohere, connect, engage, fasten, fix, hitch, knot, latch, lock, moor, nail, paste, peg, pin, screw, seal, secure, shut, stick, tack, tag, tape, tether, tie, yoke

86 **attack:** aggression, ambush, assail, assault, attack, bashing, besiege, blast, blitz, bomb, bombard, brutality, burst, charge, combat, come at, coup d'état, descent, embroil, encounter, engage, fire, fix, foray, fray, go for, incursion, infest, inroad, insurrection, invade, invasion, lambaste, lay into, maraud, occupation, occupy, offensive, onset, onslaught, outbreak, overrun, overwhelm, pillage, plunder, pounce, prey on, raid, rampage, ravage, revenge, rush, sabotage, storm, subvert, surprise, waylay

87 **attempt:** adhere, angle for, answer, apply, assume, attempt, bid, bother, buckle down, campaign, chance, commit, counteract, counterbalance, crack, dabble, dare, defy, delve, dip into, direct, drill, drive, drudge, effort, emulate, endeavor, engage, enterprise, essay, exercise, exert, exertion, experiment, fiddle, function, further, go, hammer away/hammer into, hazard, hush, imitate, keep at, keep up, labor, mess around, monkey, offer, overdo, overplay, persevere, persist, plod, practice, presume, pursue, putter, represent, risk, scramble, seek, slave, stab, strain, strive, struggle, substitute, tackle, take on, tinker, trial, try, undertake, undertaking, venture, wade, whack, whirl, work

88 **authorize:** accede, accord, accredit, acknowledge, acknowledgment, acquit, affirm, aggrandize, appoint, appointment, approve, arm, assign, authorize, back, ban, bar, bear out, bless, blessing, certify, charter, commission, concession, consent, constitute, contract, countenance, countermand, crown, decree, dedicate, delegate, delegation, detail, disown, empower, enable, enact, endorse, enforce, enjoin, entitle, entrust, establish, exempt, fire, forgive, grant, induct, inflict, invest, invoke, lay, let, let off, license, make, name, negate, nod, nominate, nomination, nullify, okay, ordain, order, override/overrule, pardon, permission, permit, place, prescribe, prohibit, ratify, recall, receive, release, relieve, repeal, reprieve, revoke, sanction, spare, station, subscribe, underwrite, validate, vest, veto, void, warrant, withdraw, witness

89 **borrow:** borrow, charter, lease, let, rent

90 **capture:** apprehend, apprehension, arrest, bag, besiege, capture, catch, collar, commandeer, confinement, conquer, corner, coup d'état, custody, enslave, ensnare, entangle, entrap, expropriate, fetch, foray, get, grab, grasp, imprison, incarcerate, kidnap, nab, nail, net, occupation, occupy, pinch, pull in, seize, seizure, sequester, snap, snare, snatch, tackle, trap

91 **carry out:** accomplish, action, application, assure, avail, complement, complete, comply, conclude, contrive, discharge, do, duplicate, echo, effect, enact, execute, execution, fill, finalize, finish, follow, follow through,

fulfill, hammer out, handle, hustle, implement, make, make out, manage, meet, mind, obey, observe, operate, perfect, perform, perpetrate, persist, practice, proceed, prosecute, pull off, realize, redeem, render, repeat, rush, serve, specialize, transact, wage

92 **compete:** bout, boxing, compete, competition, contend, contention, contest, opposition, pit, play, rival, take on, tie, vie

93 **contract:** catch, come down with, contract, get, incur

94 **control:** auspices, contain, contrive, deal/deal with, determine, deregulate, direct, discipline, dominate, domineer, harness, manage, moderate, monopolize, operate, overlook, predominate, preside, prevail, regulate, regulation, ride, stage, steer, systematize, wield, work

95 **defeat:** beat, best, confute, conquer, conquest, coup de grâce, crush, defeat, discomfit, edge, extinguish, finish, floor, lick, outdo, overcome, overpower, overrun, overtake, overthrow, overwhelm, prevail, prostrate, put down, quash, quell, reduce, rout, smash, subjugate, subvert, surmount, thrash, top, topple, trim, triumph, trounce, upset, vanquish, victory, wallop, whip, win

96 **defend:** beard, bulwark, convoy, counteract, counterbalance, cover, defend, ensure, fend, fend off, fight back/fight off, guard, protect, repulse, resist, resistance, safeguard, save, screen, secure, shield, ward/ward off, withstand

97 **demonstrate:** advertising, bear out, demonstrate, establish, evidence, exemplify, give, illustrate, imply

98 **divide:** allocate, apportion, bestow, bisect, cleave, disconnect, dismember, disrupt, dissect, distribute, distribution, divide, division, fork, fragment, halve, mete, part, partition, place, portion, punctuate, quarter, ramification, ration, rupture, sever, share, slice, snap, split

99 **enable:** allow, enable, implement, qualify

100 **engage in:** address, anticipate, apply, collaborate, dig in, drudge, embark on, exist, fall to, fare, fend for, fight, give, go about, go into, go on, grub, immerse, labor, make, participate, pitch in, plunge, ply, practice, pursue, reiterate, risk, share, spend, step in, tackle, take, toil, trouble, turn, undertake, wage, work

101 **err:** blunder, botch, bungle, butcher, compromise, err, error, fault, faux pas, flounder, frailty, fumble, gaffe, guilt, impropriety, inaccuracy, indiscretion, lapse, malpractice, miscalculate, mishandle/mismanage, misjudge, miss, misstep, mistake, neglect, overlook, oversight, screw up, sin, slip, stray, stumble, transgression, trespass, trip, violate, violation, wander

102 **escape:** abscond, avoid, avoidance, bail out, break, break out, bypass, circumvent, disappear, disappearance, dodge, duck, elude, equivocate, escape, eschew, evade, evasion, extricate, flee, flight, flinch, fly, getaway, get out, lose, make off, shake off, skirt, throw off

103 **examine:** analysis, analyze, assay, audit, authenticate, autopsy, case, check, compare, confirm, criticize, decompose, delve, dig,

evaluate, evaluation, examination, examine, experiment, explore, follow up, go into, go over, go through, grade, graduate, hearing, inspect, inspection, investigate, investigation, judgment, look into, measure, nose, observe, peer, peruse, pore, postmortem, probe, quest, ransack, research, review, sample, scan, scout, scrutinize, scrutiny, sift, skim, spy, study, surveillance, survey, test, try, try on/try out, view, weigh

104 exchange: alternate, amends, barter, commute, exchange, interchange, reciprocate, redeem, replace, rotate, substitute, swap/swop, switch, transpose

105 existential change: age, arise, awaken, awakening, begin, come from, date, demise, disappear, disappearance, dissipate, dissolution, dissolve, emerge, fade, form, go, go out, languish, materialize, originate, pass, perish, peter out, run out, spring, succumb, vanish, wake/waken

106 fight: altercation, battle, bout, box, brawl, brush, clamor, clash, combat, conflict, confrontation, contend, contention, contest, contravene, dispute, encounter, engage, engagement, faction, ferment, feud, fight, fight back/fight off, fighting, fracas, fray, free-for-all, friction, fuss, grapple, hassle, imbroglio, mayhem, melee, misunderstanding, oppose, opposition, quarrel, racket, rebel, rebellion, resist, resistance, revolt, revolution, rift, riot, rise, row, run-in, scrap, scuffle, strife, struggle, tilt, uprising, uproar, war, wrangle

107 fuel: charge, feed, fill, fuel, supply

108 give: administer, afford, allocate, allot, allow, apportion, atone, bear, bequeath, bestow, cast, cede, commend, commit, compensate, confide, consign, consignment, contribute, deal, deliver, delivery, descend, devote, disburse, disseminate, dole out, donate, drop off, emit, endow, entrust, finance, furnish, give, give away, hand out, hand over, impart, leave, mete, pass, pass off, present, provide, reach, render, return, reward, sacrifice, satisfy, show, surrender, transfer, turn over, will

109 group: aggregate, alloy, amass, bank, blend, bunch, cluster, collect, collection, commingle, compilation, compile, compound, concentrate, confluence, congregate, consolidate, consolidation, cull, distribution, flock, garner, gather, get together, group, heap, herd, muster, pick, pile, rake, reap, recruit, round up, stack, store

110 help: abet, aid, alleviate, assist, assistance, attend, baby, backing, bail out, befriend, benefit, bolster, boost, break, care, chip in, coddle, commiserate, contribute, convoy, cooperate, cooperation, cover, cultivate, cultivation, cure, defend, dispense, doctor, do for, ease, encourage, encouragement, facilitate, favor, fawn, forward, foster, free, further, furtherance, guarantee, guide, hand, help, hold, indulge, intercede, intervene, invigorate, keep, kindness, lavish, liberate, lift, lighten, limb, minister, nurse, nurture, oblige, patronage, patronize, pitch in, profit, promote, promotion, provide, quell, reform, relieve, serve, service, shore, simplify,

soothe, speed, spell, sponsor, stabilize, subsidize, support, sustain, sympathize, temper, tide over, underwrite, uphold

111 imitate: ape, imitate, mimic, mirror, mock, mockery, parallel, parody, pattern, pretend, repeat, reproduce, sham, simulate, takeoff, take off

112 involve: attack, coalesce, confuse, contain, cooperate, cooperation, count, devote, embody, embrace, enclose, encompass, enmesh, entangle, entrap, figure in, implicate, include, incorporate, interpolate, introduce, involve, mire, overdo, tangle, task

113 join: accompany, add, adhere, adjoin, affiliate, affix, alloy, amalgamate, annex, annexation, append, articulate, articulation, assemble, assembly, attach, band, bridge, butt, cleave, close, coalesce, cohere, combine, compound, connect, converge, couple, dovetail, embody, engage, fasten, fix, fuse, fusion, get together, graft, hitch, incorporate, integrate, intermingle, intersect, intertwine/interweave, introduce, join, knit, knot, lace, link, meeting, meld, merge, mesh, mix, pair, piece, pool, swarm, synthesis, synthesize, union, unite, wed

114 join socially: affiliate, align, assemble, associate, attach, attend, band, belong, bump into, call, cavort, chaperon, collect, collusion, confluence, congregate, consort, consultation, convene, convention, converge, convocation, couple, dalliance, dally/dally with, date, enroll, enter, escort, gather, group, hang about/hang around/hang out, huddle, integrate, intermingle, intertwine/interweave, join, league, link, matriculate, meet, mix, register, session, swarm, take

115 lend: finance, fund, invest, lease, lend, let, loan, pawn, rent, trust

116 lose: deliver, fall, forfeit, forget, leak, lose, misplace, omission, sacrifice

117 manage: adjust, administer, administration, boss, carry on, charge, compose, conduct, control, custody, deal/deal with, deregulate, direct, dispense, dispose, dominate, drill, economy, face, fare, farm, farming, fend for, get along, get by, get on, guide, handle, handling, head, lead, manage, management, marshal, monitor, officiate, operate, orchestrate, organization, overlook, oversee, oversight, predominate, preside, rally, regulate, regulation, reign, rule, run, running, save, subjugate, supervise, supervision, sway, treatment, upkeep, work

118 manifest: agree, comprehend, connote, embodiment, embody, emerge, exemplify, exude, give, indicate, loom, manifest, mirror, point, presage, promise, prove, radiate

119 modify an event: abide, advent, balk, birth, cancellation, cessation, close, closure, come on, come out, come up, coming, commence, complement, completion, conception, conclude, conclusion, culminate, dawn, desist, develop, discontinuance, disposal, embargo, end, ending, end up, ensue, entrance, expiration, expire, fall, finish, genesis, give in/give up, halt, knock off, lapse, lay off, matriculate, pass, pause, pull out, pull up, quit, recess, relinquish, resign, resignation, result, retract, revival, rout, secede, spurt, standstill, stop, surrender, suspend, suspension, terminate, termination

120 **obtain:** acquire, acquisition, amass, attain, capitalize, earn, gain, get, get at, get back, land, lay up/lay by, make, obtain, pick up, possess, procure, pull in, realize, reap, recover, recruit, regain, retrieve, save, secure, strike, take, win

121 **prevent:** abolish, abolition, abort, abrogate, abstain, adjourn, adjournment, anticipate, arrest, asphyxiate, avert, avoid, avoidance, baffle, balk, ban, banish, bar, birth control, block, bog down, brake, break, bridle, censor, cheat, check, choke, circumvent, clog, close, confine, constrain, constraint, contravene, cop out, counter, cripple, cross, curb, cut short, dash, defeat, defer, deferment/deferral, delay, deprivation, deprive, deter, discharge, discontinue, discourage, disqualify, dissolve, drop, drop out, encumber, exclude, exclusion, foil, forbear, forbid, forgo, freeze, frustrate, gag, halt, hesitate, hesitation, hinder, hold back/hold off, hold up, impede, incapacitate, inhibit, intercept, interfere, interference, interrupt, invalidate, jam, keep, kill, mire, muffle, muzzle, negate, negation, neutralize, nip, nullify, obstruct, obviate, occlude, omit, outlaw, override/overrule, paralyze, parry, pause, preclude, preempt, prevent, procrastinate, prohibit, prohibition, proscribe, pull out, pull up, put off, quash, quell, recess, refrain, relegate, remove, repeal, repress, rescind, respite, restrain, retard, revoke, rule out, run-around, scrap, scratch, scrub, seclude, shelve, shut, shut off/shut out, slowdown, spite, squash, stall, stay, stem, stifle, still, stop, stymie, subdue, suppress, suspend, table, terminate, thwart, traverse, turn off, undo, veto, vitiate, void, waive, waiver, waylay, withdraw, withhold

122 **punish:** avenge, chasten, chastise, correct, correction, discipline, evict, exile, expel, fine, pay, penalize, punish, revenge, scourge, sentence

123 **punishment:** blackmail, damage(s), discipline, eviction, fine, forfeit, lesson, punishment, rap, reprimand, reproach, retribution, sanction

124 **receive:** accept, acceptance, acquire, acquisition, bring in, come by, come in for, fetch, find, gain, have, inherit, make, object, profit, realize, reap, receive, reception, recoup, regain, retrieve, take

125 **record:** enroll, enter, enumerate, itemize, list, record, register, schedule, score, take down, tally, tape, transcribe

126 **rectify:** accommodate, amend, appease, appeasement, arbitrate, arbitration, atone, atonement, avenge, compensate, conclude, correct, correction, counteract, counterbalance, cover, cure, do up, edit, emend, equalize, expiate, fix, iron out, make up, mediate, mediation, mend, offset, overhaul, penance, placate, quiet, recompense, recoup, rectify, redeem, redress, reform, rehabilitate, remedy, requite, restore, retaliate, retribution, revise, revision, right, satisfy, settle, square, standardize, suit, tailor, temper, tune/tune up, untangle

127 **release:** acquittal, cede, clear, deliver, delivery, discharge, disentangle, dismiss, dismissal, emancipate, exculpate, exempt, exonerate, extricate, free, loose/loosen, ransom, redeem, release, relinquish, save

128 **replace:** change, fill in, follow, replace, supersede, supplant

129 **reserve:** allocate, assign, assignment, assumption, claim, clear, come by, deserts, deserve, designate, earmark, engage, enroll, entitle, gain, intend, merit, put away/put aside/put by, rate, reserve, save, spare, store, subscribe

130 **restrict:** bar, barricade, bind, block, bound, boycott, brake, check, circumscribe, clog, cocoon, confine, constrain, constraint, constrict, constriction, control, cramp, curb, curtail, dam, deaden, defer, deferment/deferral, delay, disable, embargo, encumber, enjoin, enslave, expatriate, expel, expulsion, fetter, fetters, foil, forbear, forgo, gag, govern, grind, ground, hamper, handicap, harness, hem/hem in, hinder, hobble, hold back/hold off, hold up, impair, impede, imposition, inhibit, limit, matter, moderate, narrow, obligate, obstruct, postpone, prohibit, prohibition, rein, repress, restrain, restrict, retard, set back, slow, slowdown, smother, squelch, stifle, strangle, stymie, subdue, suppress, suspend, thwart, tie/tie up

131 **return:** deliver, fetch, hand over, ransom, recall, redeem, regain, repay, requite, restore, retrieve, return

132 **reward:** award, commend, confer, decorate,

133 **rule:** abdicate, accession, command, depose, deposition, dictatorship, displace, enforce, enforcement, govern, impose, oppress, rule, subjugate, supremacy

134 **save:** cocoon, conservation, conserve, deposit, guard, harbor, lay up/lay by, maintain, maintenance, pad, patrol, preservation, preserve, protect, put away/put aside/put by, rehabilitate, rescue, salvage, salvation, save, shelter, shield, spare, ward/ward off, watch

135 **separate:** abstract, analyze, appropriate, appropriation, assign, class, classification, classify, dedicate, detach, disaffect, disconnect, disengage, disentangle, dislocate, dismantle, dismember, disperse, disrupt, dissociate, divide, division, filter, fragment, gape, garner, glean, hoard, open, part, partition, seclude, seclusion, segregate, separate, separation, split, strain, undo

136 **serve:** accommodate, administer, board, bondage, cater, obey, oblige, pamper, pander, provide, quench, serve, spoil, tend, wait on

137 **shape change:** beat, bisect, bruise, carve, chip, chisel, cleave, clip, compact, crimp, crinkle, cut, desiccate, disfigure, disguise, distort, disturb, divide, do in, edge, elongate, enlarge, fatigue, file, flatten, fragment, gash, hack, lacerate, nick, notch, pierce, prune, puncture, reduce, roll, rumple, scar, score, sculpture, shape, sharpen, shave, shorten, shrink, shrivel, slash, slice, smooth, stiffen, stretch, taper/taper off, thicken, thin, trample, truncate, warp, whet, wound

138 show: advertising, bare, circulate, model, point, prove, represent, reveal, show, substantiate, symbolize, tout, trot out, unveil

139 steal: abduct, appropriate, appropriation, assume, bilk, break in, burglary, cheat, confiscate, copy, divest, do out of, embezzle, embezzlement, extort, extortion, filch, fleece, hold up, kidnap, knock off, larceny, lift, loot, maraud, milk, misappropriate, pilfer, pillage, pinch, plagiarism, plunder, poach, pocket, ransack, rifle, rip off, rip-off, rob, sack, steal, swindle, swipe, take, theft

140 supply: appoint, contribute, deal, deluge, dish out, dispensation, dispense, disseminate, distribute, distribution, divide, dole out, equip, feed, foster, fuel, furnish, glut, hand out, infuse, issue, keep, lend, maintain, make out, nourish, nurse, nurture, portion, provide, provision, quarter, ration, receive, render, replenish, rig, satisfy, serve, stock, supply, support, sustain

141 surpass: abound, beat, better, break, cap, conquer, eclipse, exceed, excel, flourish, get ahead, go by, lead, lick, outdo, outweigh, overtake, pass, predominate, prevail, succeed, supersede, surmount, surpass, top, tower, transcend, triumph, win

142 take: acquire, acquisition, arrogate, assume, assumption, broach, burn, commandeer, compass, confiscate, cull, deplete, deprivation, deprive, disarm, disarmament, divest, drain, draw, educe, elicit, exact, excerpt, expropriate, extract, filch, harvest, have, milk, nip, peel, pilfer, pocket, preempt, pump, ransack, rob, sap, seize, take, tap, usurp, wring

143 transfer abstractly: afford, bear, bring, commit, consign, consignment, conveyance, delegate, delegation, infect, recall, refer, relay, release, relegate, transfer, turn over

MOTION

144 be moved: earthquake, elapse, flop, hang, lap

145 change of place: flicker, motion, movement, passage, pop, rush, sway, sweep, swing, swirl, swivel, teeter, tremor

146 flow: flow, pour, run, secrete, seep, stream, surge, swamp, teem, torrent, trickle

147 move: bob, budge, careen, churn, circulate, circulation, contort, cruise, curl, curve, dandle, deflect, descend, descent, dislocate, dislodge, displace, dive, drift, drive, entwine, falter, fidget, flex, flourish, gyrate, haul, lean, loop, move, oscillate, overturn, paddle, pitch, pivot, pulsate/pulse, pulse, revolve, rock, roll, rotate, round, skirt, tilt, topple, toss, transport, traverse, tumble, turn, twine, twist, uproot, upset, waft, wave, waver, weave, wheel, wield

148 move mechanically: aviation, bank, carriage, carry, cart, drive, fly, haul, mobilize, navigate, operate, pack, park, ride, ship, soar, takeoff, take off, veer

149 move oneself: ascend, ascension, bend, constitutional, flap, flex, flounce, gad, gait, gallivant, gambol, go ahead, go for, gyrate, hike, jerk, motion, mount, move, negotiate, pace, pad, pass, patter, progress, quail, rock,

roll, round, stalk, stamp, step, stir, stray, stride, strut, stump, swagger, tilt, tread, trip, tumble, walk, wallow, wave, wriggle

150 move oneself quickly: barge in/barge into, beat, bolt, bounce, bustle, capsize, coast, course, dart, dash, flash, flee, flinch, flit, flutter, fly, gallop, glide, hasten, hurry, hurtle, hustle, jerk, jiggle, lurch, make off, march, plunge, pound, prance, race, recoil, run, rush, scamper, scramble, scurry, shake, shoot, shudder, skim, skip, slide, slip, soar, speed, spin, sprint, start, storm, sweep, swerve, swoop, tear, trot, twirl, veer, wag, whip, whiz, wiggle, wobble, writhe, zip, zoom

151 move oneself slowly: amble, crawl, creep, cruise, dalliance, dally, decline, drag, hobble, jog, knock about/knock around, lag, limp, linger, loiter, lumber, lurk, meander, plod, poke, prowl, pussyfoot, ramble, range, reel, roam, saunter, shuffle, slink/slither, sneak, stagger, steal, straggle, stroll, sway, tarry, totter, tramp, trudge, waddle, wade, wander

152 move quickly: advance, advancement, agitate, capsize, convulsion, course, discharge, dispatch, fall, flicker, flourish, flutter, hasten, jerk, jiggle, jostle, keel over, lurch, palpitate, plunge, precipitate, quake, quiver, rattle, rush, shake, shiver, shoot, shudder, skid, skim, slide, slip, speed, spin, stampede, sweep, tear, throb, tremble, twirl, vibrate, vibration, wag, whip, whirl, whisk, wiggle, wobble

153 move slowly: dangle, float, lag, reel

154 position oneself: arise, bow, cant, duck, get down, get off, get up, hover, huddle, hunch, kneel, lie, list, loll, lounge, mount, nestle, obeisance, perch, poise, pose, ramble, recline, repose, rest, rise, seat, sit, slouch, wince

155 travelling: lift, navigation, procession, transit, transport, voyage

PHYSICAL

156 abuse: abuse, charge, consumption, cop out, corrode, defile, dissipate, dope, enervate, exploit, force, frazzle, fritter, impinge, lose, malpractice, milk, misappropriate, mishandle/mismanage, mistreat, misuse, overdo, pervert, prostitute, riddle, run through, sap, spend, squander, strain, throw away, waste, wear

157 anatomical change: distend, flake, neuter

158 arrange: align, arrange, bundle, collate, coordinate, crease, deploy, dispose, file, group, indent, lay, lay out, mess up, mix up, muss, order, organize, position, range, rank, reverse, ruffle, rummage, separate, shuffle, snarl, sort, spread, stack, stir, straighten, unwind, weave

159 arrive: admission, advent, appear, appearance, approach, arrival, arrive, billow, board, come, come in, coming, cross, cruise, disembark, dock, embark, encroach, enter, entrance, foray, get, get back, get in, get on, go, go ahead, gravitate, immigrate, infiltrate, influx, insinuate, intrude, invade, invasion,

constitute, contort, crumple, curl, curve, fold, form, materialize, model, mold, pat, round, sculpture, shape, twist, whittle, work

185 gesture: bawl, beam, beat, belch, bite, bleed, blink, blow, chew, clap, drag, dribble, drivel, drool, excrete, expire, frown, gesture, gnaw, grimace, grin, gulp, itch, kink, kiss, laugh/laughter, laugh, lick, munch, nod, perspire, pucker, puff, pulsate/pulse, pulse, purse, scowl, shiver, slobber, smile, smirk, sob, spasm, spit, squint, sweat, tear/tears, throb, twitch, vomit, wail, weep, whimper, wince, wink, wrinkle, yawn

186 grind: abrasion, corrode, creak, crunch, file, frazzle, granulate, grate, grind, mash, mill, pound, powder, pulverize, rasp, scrape

187 guide: aviation, channel, conduct, convey, direct, divert, drive, ease, ferry, funnel, guide, infuse, inject, lay, lead, level, maneuver, marshal, mobilize, navigate, navigation, point, refer, round, route, row, see, show, steer, take, transport, usher

188 hide: ambush, balk, bury, cache, camouflage, cloak, conceal, concealment, cover, cower, cringe, cut, disguise, dissemble, dissimulate, eavesdrop, embed, ensconce, envelop, harbor, hide, isolate, lurk, mask, masquerade, obscure, palliate, screen, seclude, seclusion, secrete, sequester, shelter, shrink, shut off/shut out, smother, sneak, withhold

189 hit: applaud, applause, bang, baste, bat, batter, battery, beat, belt, blow, boot, box, buffet, bump, bunt, butt, chip, clap, clash, clatter, clip, clobber, club, collide, collision, concussion, crack, crash, crown, cuff, dash, deflect, dent, drive, drum, flog, glance, hail, hammer, hand, hit, impact, jab, jar, jostle, kick, knock, lash, lick, maul, nail, pat, peck, pelt, poke, pound, punch, ram, rap, rough up, scourge, slam, slap, smack, sock, spank, strike, swat, swipe, tap, thrash, thud/thump, tick, tip, wallop, whack, whip

190 hold: anchor, cling, clog, clutch, cradle, cuddle, dandle, dangle, embrace, fondle, grab, hold, hook, hug, nip, nuzzle, pin, prop, retain, seize, shore, snuggle, support, suspend, sustain, tangle

191 hold forcefully: apprehend, brace, cage, captivity, clasp, clench, clinch, clutch, confinement, constrict, constriction, contain, cramp, dam, detain, detention, embrace, enfold, enslave, fetter, fetters, grapple, grasp, grip, gripe, harness, hold, imprison, incarcerate, leash, overpower, pen, press, restrain, snap, snatch, stifle, strangle, tackle, throttle, wrestle

192 illegal behavior: blackmail, bleed, breach, break, break in, bribe, bug, buy, cheat, conspire, contraband, contravene, crime, delinquency, depredation, disobey, entrench, extortion, fault, fix, fraud, graft, have, holdup, hold up, imposture, infraction, infringe, injustice, intrigue, jinx, kickback, knock off, larceny, libel, loot, mischief, misconduct, misdeed/misdemeanor, murder, offense, outrage, pick, pilfer, plagiarism, poach, racket, rape, ravish, rip off, rip-off, rob, screw, sham, slander, smuggle, specu-

lation, squeeze, swindle, take, tamper, theft, transgression, treason, trespass, victimize, violate, violation

193 join physically: link, meld, merge, mesh, mingle, mix, piece, pool, splice, tie, tuck, unite, wed, weld, yoke

194 jump: bounce, bound, clear, deflect, dive, flip, gallop, gambol, hop, hurdle, jump, leap, lunge, lurch, plunge, pounce, rear, recoil, skip, spring, start, vault

195 leave: abandon, abscond, back, blow, board, bolt, break, break out, clear out, cringe, dart, defection, depart, departure, desert, desertion, deviate, diaspora, digress, disappear, disappearance, dismount, distance, diverge, draw back, drop, ebb, egress, embark, evacuate, exit, exodus, fall back, farewell, flee, flight, fly, forsake, get along, get off, get out, go, goodbye, go off, go out, jaunt, jilt, leave, light out, make off, maroon, part, parting, pull out, push off/push on, quail, quit, recede, recoil, renounce, renunciation, repair, resign, resignation, retire, retreat, run, scram, separation, shake off, shove off, shrink, strike out, swerve, takeoff, take off, throw over, turn, vacate, withdraw, withdrawal

196 lift: boost, dip, elevate, heave, hoist, lift, pick up, pry, raise, rear

197 measure: balance, figure, measure, survey

198 move living quarters: anyplace, anywhere, approach, arena, battlefield, camp, colonization, cover, defect, defection, deport, deportation, destination, dominion, element, emigrate, empire, evict, eviction, exile, expatriate, expel, jurisdiction, landmark, locale/locality, location, lookout, migrate, move, neighborhood, outdoors, outside, point, position, post, premises, province, refuge, region, reign, rendezvous, resort, seat, setting, site, situation, soil, spot, station, stop, surroundings, terminal, territory, turn, vicinity, where

199 perform: fan, hit, perform, type, work

200 physical action: application, apply, drop, hit, hold, lift, push

201 position: aim, barricade, bow, cant, close, cock, coil, deposit, dial, dip, direct, disseminate, ensconce, entwine, fix, hang, indent, insert, install, installation, interpolate, intersperse, isolate, jut, lap, lay, lean, lie, list, lodge, loop, misplace, occlude, park, pile, pitch, place, plant, point, position, post, prop, put, recline, roll, seat, separate, set, sit, slant, slope, slouch, snuggle, sprawl, spread, squat, stand, station, stick, stoop, swerve, tip, top, train, traverse, turn, twine, twist, unfold, wallow, wind, wrinkle

202 prepare physically: acclimate, adjust, braid, brush, brush up, buff, bundle, burnish, coat, condition, disguise, doll up, domesticate, do up, dress, embalm, face, finish, fix up, formulate, fortify, gear, get, gild, glaze, gloss, grace, groom, habituate, housework, knit, lubricate, make up, modernize, modulate, orient, overhaul, pack, pad, pare, plaster, plate, polish, preparation, prepare, preservation, preserve, prime, primp, ready, reform, refresh, refrigerate, refurbish, regenerate, rehabilitate, rejuvenate, renew, renovate, rig, round, season, set, shave, shine, slim, smear,

Causes

ABSTRACT

228 affect: affect, cause, change, evoke

229 event that causes another: account, beginning, cause, origin, precipitous/precipitate

230 state of causation: adaptation, aftermath, amazement, anticlimax, armistice, astonishment, awe, backlash, backwash, bang, bedlam, bereavement, bind, blessing, bliss, blot, blunder, boom, bottom line, break, buildup, catharsis, certainty, change, chaos, check, coincidence, collapse, collision, comfort, complication, compromise, congestion, consequence, consternation, contamination, corollary, culmination, decay, deception, decomposition, decoy, degeneracy, degradation, descent, destruction, deterioration, disadvantage, disappointment, disarray, disorder, disposal, disrepair, dissipation, dissolution, effect, end, ending, error, event, eventuality, fall, flap, flurry, frailty, frenzy, fruit, fulfillment, furor, gaffe, headway, hubbub, huddle, impact, imperfection, impression, improvement, inaccuracy, infection, irony, issue; jinx, jitters, lapse, lather, mess, miscarriage, mistake, mix-up, morass, muddle, muss, nonsense, occurrence, outcome, outgrowth, payoff, phenomenon, portent, press, price, proceed, product, racket, ramification, rash, repercussion, resolution, result, rubbish, scare, scramble, settlement, shambles, solution, stain, stalemate, stigma, stink, stir, storm, taint, tangle, tempest, therefore, to-do, toll, trend, trip, truce, tumult, turmoil, turn, undoing, unification, upheaval, upshot, whirl

231 to be: alienate, animate, antagonize, awake, awaken, awakening, calm, cause, compound, energize, even, materialize, sterilize, straighten, threaten

232 to change: adapt, adjust, alter, alternate, assimilate, attune, cancel, change, commute, conversion, convert, co-opt, differentiate, distort, diversify, double back, equalize, expurgate, fashion, fit, fix, invert, modify, neutralize, offset, overturn, restore, shift, switch, tamper, transform, translate, transpose, turn

233 to change abstractly: demote, intensify, mitigate

234 to change an event: abbreviate, accelerate, acceleration, activate, actuate, adjourn, approach, arrest, bed, begin, break off, break up, build, cancel, cease, close, commence, complement, conclude, consummate, continue, crown, cut in, cut off, cut short, desist, determine, discontinue, dispatch, dispose of, disrupt, dissolve, end, enter, finish, foul up, graduate, halt, hurry, intervene, invalidate, kick, knock off, lay off, leave, leave off, lift, manipulate, nip, nullify, pause, pick up, preclude, preempt, put off, quash, quell, quench, quit, relinquish, remit, rescind, retire, reverse, revoke, round off, ruin, scrub, seal, slow, smother, stall, stop, terminate, turn off, turn out, vacate, waive, wind up, wrap up

235 to change cognitively: agree, change, concede, harden, lay

236 to change number or quantity: abbreviate, abridge, abstract, accumulate, add, addition, advance, aggrandize, alleviate, amplification, amplify, augment, blow up, boost, build, build up, commute, compress, condense, contract, curtail, cut, cut back, deduct, deepen, deflate, detract, digest, dilate, discount, double, downsize, draw out, enlarge, escalate, evolve, expand, extend, extension, fatten, hike, imbue, increase, inflate, jump, lengthen, lift, lower, magnify, modify, narrow, pare, prune, raise, reduce, reinforce, shorten, slash, step up, summarize, supplement, swell, take, trim, truncate, whittle, widen

237 to change or affect an event: delay, procrastinate, protract, stop, weigh

238 to change state of being: dispatch, do for

239 to continue: abide, bear, broaden, carry on, come, come back, continue, create, drag on/drag out, draw, drawl, draw out, dwell on/dwell upon, eke out, elongate, endure, extend, go, go on, hammer away/hammer into, hang on, hold, kill, lengthen, linger, perpetuate, persevere, persist, prolong, protract, pursue, remain, resume, survive, take up

240 to diminish: abate, adulterate, aggravate, aggravation, alloy, attenuate, blot, blunt, break, canker, cheapen, compound, compromise, cool, corrupt, cut, deaden, debase, debauch, debilitate, decay, decline, decrease, degrade, depress, disorder, doctor, downgrade, downsize, emasculate, enfeeble, fatigue, impair, imperil, let up, lower, minimize, mitigate, moderate, modify, muffle, mute, pale, provocation, qualify, reduce, relax, retard, rot, sap, shorten, slash, stimulant, stimulus, stop, tax, tone down, undermine, weaken, wear, worsen

241 to function: animate, begin, cause, start

242 to happen: accelerate, boomerang, breathe, bring, copy, engender, ensue, entail, eventuate, evoke, expedite, expedition, facilitate, follow, impel, incite, inconvenience, induce, inflict, influence, inspire, instigate, institute, intervene, make, motivate, move, muddle, necessitate, oblige, occasion, occur, orchestrate, pass, precipitate, prod, produce, prompt, provoke, put, recur, result, return, stimulate, trigger, unsettle, will, work up, wreak

243 to have: accent, give, push, transfer

244 to improve: advance, allay, ameliorate, amend, assuage, augment, augmentation, become, benefit, better, betterment, boost, brighten, bring about, brush up, civilize, confirm, contribute, cultivate, cure, dignify, enhance, enrich, freshen, garnish, help, improve, lift, lighten, magnify, mend, mollify, pad, perfect, perk up, polish, quench, quiet, raise, refine, relieve, restore, revise, revision, rouse, step up, strengthen, supplement, touch up, unburden, update

245 to increase quantity: accumulate, add, addition, advance, aggrandize, amplification, amplify, augment, augmentation, blow up, boost, build, build up, deepen, dilate, double, draw out, enlarge, escalate, evolve, expand, extend, extension, fatten, hike, imbue, increase, inflate, jump, lengthen, lift, magnify, raise, reinforce, step up, supplement, swell, widen

246 to injure: abuse, afflict, asphyxiate, batter, battery, beat, blemish, bruise, chip, cost, cripple, damage, debilitate, decay, deface, defile, deform, dent, desecrate, desecration, devastate, disable, disagree, discomfort, disfigure, endanger, expose, fragment, get back at, gripe, handicap, harm, hurt, impair, incapacitate, infect, injure, irritate, knife, lacerate, lay up, maim, mangle, mar, maul, mistreat, molest, mutilate, outrage, pain, paralyze, persecute, poison, pollute, rack, repay, rough up, ruin, rupture, sabotage, sap, scar, shatter, shiver, shoot, sicken, smart, smash, snap, splinter, spoil, sting, stress, suffocate, taint, tarnish, torture, trample, turn, violate, violation, vitiate, wound, wrong

247 to reduce quantity: abbreviate, abridge, abstract, alleviate, commute, compress, condense, contract, curtail, cut, cut back, deduct, deflate, detract, digest, discount, downsize, lessen, lower, minimize, modify, narrow, pare, prune, reduce, shorten, slash, summarize, take, trim, truncate, whittle

PHYSICAL

248 to break: collide, crack, crash, crumble, dash

249 to burn: arson, blaze, burn, char, conflagration, fire, flame, flare, glow, ignite, inflame, kindle, lick, light, parch, scorch, sear, smolder

250 to change physically: awake, bite, blacken, black out, bleach, blush, brighten, bruise, buttress, chip, color, compact, confirm, congeal, consolidate, corrode, crimp, crinkle, cross, darken, daub, debase, deepen, deform, dehydrate, desiccate, dilute, dim, discolor, disfigure, disorder, disorganize, distort, disturb, do in, douse, dry, dye, eclipse, edge, elongate, emasculate, enervate, exhaust, fade, fatigue, fatten, ferment, file, flatten, flush, fog, foul, gird, harden, hypnotize, intensify, jell, lay, level, light, lighten, loose/loosen, mark, melt, muzzle, neuter, numb, open, pacify, pale, petrify, prolong, prostrate, protract, quicken,

ravel, redden, reinforce, roll, rouse, rumple, set, shade, shadow, sharpen, shrivel, slop, slow, smooth, soften, sour, stabilize, stain, sterilize, stiffen, streak, strengthen, stretch, tame, temper, thicken, thin, tidy, tighten, tinge, tint, toughen, turn, vitiate, warp, weary, whet, whiten

251 to create: bear, beget, breed, conceive, concoct, constitute, construct, create, engineer, establish, fabricate, forge, form, generate, hatch, materialize, mint, mold, originate, piece, procreate, produce, regenerate, reproduce, spawn

252 to destroy: abolish, abolition, annihilate, annul, assassinate, batter, blight, bomb, break, bring down, bulldoze, burst, bust, butcher, carnage, clobber, collapse, consume, consumption, contaminate, coup de grâce, crucify, crumple, crush, cut down, damage, deface, demolish, demolition, depredation, desecrate, desecration, desolate, despoil, destroy, destruction, devastate, disintegrate, dismantle, disorganize, dispatch, dissolve, do away with, do for, do in, drown, end, endanger, enfeeble, eradicate, erode, erosion, execute, execution, expunge, exterminate, extinguish, extirpate, finish, hang, homicide, hunt, kill, knock off, level, liquidate, mangle, manslaughter, massacre, mess up, murder, obliterate, overthrow, paralyze, pervert, pillage, plunder, poison, prostrate, pull down, pulverize, purge, put away, put down, put out, quash, quench, ravage, raze, remove, ruin, sabotage, sack, shatter, shiver, shoot, slaughter, slay, smash, spoil, strangle, subdue, subvert, suppress, undo, uproot, violation, waste, wipe out, wreck

253 to grow: cultivate, develop, farm, farming, flower, plant, raise, sow, till, vegetate

254 to make dirty: adulterate, blur, clutter, contaminate, dirty, litter, mess up, pollute, smudge, soil, stain, taint, tarnish

255 to make hot or cold: air, boil, chill, cool, freeze, heat, melt, numb, parch, refrigerate, scorch, shrivel, thaw, warm

256 to make wet: absorb, absorption, dampen, deluge, dip, douse, drench, drivel, drool, drown, dunk, engulf, extinguish, immerse, moisten, oil, overflow, permeate, rinse, saturate, soak, souse, spatter, splash, spray, sprinkle, squirt, steep, submerge, water, wet

Fields of human activity

AGRICULTURE

257 action: agriculture, bed, bury, conservation, cross, cultivate, cultivation, culture, erosion, fertilize, gather, graft, harvest, preservation, raise, reap, roundup, round up, sow, sprout, tend, till, vegetate, work

258 organization: farm, grange

THE ARTS

259 art object: antique, antiquity, canvas, classic, coat, collage, composition, creation, decoration, depiction, design, dye, emblem, embroidery, enamel, etching, exhibit, figure, flourish, glaze, handicraft, illustration, image, insignia, knickknack, landscape, lattice, masterpiece, medium, model, monument, ornament, pattern, picture, piece, pigment, portrait, pottery, print, profile, silhouette, stamp, statue, trademark, wreath

260 created object: alloy, amulet, apparatus, ash(es), badge, brew, camouflage, capsule, card, change, cinder, composite, composition, compound, concoction, contrivance, creation, curiosity, debris, decoration, derivative, dip, discovery, embers, enamel, essence, fabrication, fake, fence, fertilizer, filth, foam, folder, formation, froth, fusion, fuzz, garbage, garland, gimmick, glass, grime, grit, grounds, half-breed, hash, hodgepodge, hook, huddle, hybrid, imitation, innovation, invention, junk, knickknack, lather, leftover, litter, mess, mix/mixture, novelty, oddity, odds and ends, offshoot, original, outgrowth, output, pack, pad, paper, pastiche, patchwork, pennant, potpourri, preparation, refuse, remainder, remnant, replica, residue, rest, rubbish, scum, sediment, slime, solution, surplus, trash, vestige, waste, web, work, wreath, wreck, yield

261 exhibition: appear, appearance, boast, brandish, demonstrate, demonstration, develop, display, exhibit, exhibition, expose, exposure, flash, flaunt, foreshadow, impress, look, loom, manifest, mark, mount, parade, peep/peer, personify, point out, portend, posture, pout, present, presentation, produce, record, reflect, register, render, represent, show, show off, sight, simplify, spectacle, sport, spotlight, strut, transpire, typify, uncover, unfold

262 musical instrument: accompaniment, arrangement, baton, bugle, compact disc, harmony, hymn, measure, medley, melody, meter, note, piece, score, song, strain

263 performance: anthem, aria, ballet, broadcasting, burlesque, carol, chant, character, comedy, composition, concert, drama, enactment, event, extravaganza, farce, impression, lampoon, medium, movie, music, opus, part, performance, piece, play, premiere, presentation, preview, program, recital, recitation, rendition, repertory, role, satire, scene, scenery, script, set, setting, show, stage, takeoff, theater/theatre

264 performance part: act, chorus, encore, epilogue, ovation, plot, prelude, recital, refrain, rehearsal, scene, snatch, stunt, tune

265 photograph: observe, photograph, portray, print, proof

COMMUNICATIONS

266 communication: address, ad-lib, answer, arrogate, audience, babble, back down, bewail, bid, build up, call, carry, censor, chat, chatter, circumlocution, colloquy, commune, communicate, communication, contact, conversation, converse, correspond, digress, discourse, divide, drivel, effusion, emit, exult, falter, gab, get, give, hush up, improvise, indicate, interact, intercourse, interplay, intervene, intrude, lecture, magnify, mince, monologue, oration, patter, punctuate, quash, quiet, rap, reach, read, recant, recapitulate, recitation, recite, recount, refuse, rehearse, reiterate, render, repartee, say, secrete, signify, silence, slant, speak, speech, stammer, stray, talk, taunt, telephone, tell, transmit, transpire, wander, welcome, whisper, yak/yap

267 communicative quality: abusive, acerbity, acid, acidulous, acrid, acrimonious, ad-lib, ambiguous, amusing, apologetic, articulate, artless, biting, bitter, bluff, blunt, boastful, bombastic, brazen, brief, broken, brusque, candid, captious, caustic, censorious, chatty, close, closemouthed, colloquial, communicative, complimentary, confidential, confidentially, convincing, courteous, crisp, critical, crude, cryptic, curt, cutting, cynical, debatable, defamatory, demonstrative, derisive, derogatory, descriptive, destructive, diffuse, direct, directly, disconnected, dishonest, disjointed, disrespectful, doctrinaire, dogmatic, droll, dry, effusive, eloquent, emphatic, encyclopedic, erroneous, et cetera, evasive, even, exaggerated, expansive, explanatory, explicit, expository, expressive, extemporaneous/extempory, facetious, fallacious, false, falsely, farcical, feeble, fictitious, figurative, filthy, firm, firsthand, flaming, flatulent, flimsy, florid, flowery, fluent, forceful, forcible, foreign, forensic, forthright, foul, fractious, frank, frankly, fresh, fulsome, funny, gabby, garrulous, genuine, glib, glowing, grandiloquent, graphic, gross, grouchy, groundless, gruff, guileless, hackneyed, harsh, hateful, heartfelt, heated, hollow, honest, humorous, hypocritical, idle, illogical, illustrative, imperative, imperious, implicit, implied, importunate, impromptu, improvised, imprudent, inarticulate, incisive, incoherent, indescribable, indicative, ineffable, inelegant, inexplicable, inflated, informative, ingenuous, inoffensive, insincere, insistent, insolent, ironic/ironical, jocular/jocose/jocund, jolly, keen, laconic, laudatory, laughable, legendary, legible, lengthy, libelous, literal, literally, literary, loose, loquacious, lurid, lying, malicious, malign, matter-of-fact, mean, meaningful, meaty, mendacious, misleading, mushy, musty, mythical/mythological, naked, nameless, narrative, natural, negative, noncommittal, oblique, obnoxious, obscene, offensive, offhand, oily, open, openly, opinionated, opprobrious, oracular, oral, outspoken, overblown, parting, pejorative, penetrating, peppery, persuasive, pithy, plain, poetic, poignant, pointed, pompous, ponderous, pornographic, pregnant, priceless, private, privileged, privy, profane, prophetic, prosaic, public, pulp, pungent, quickwitted, quizzical, racy, rambling, reticent, rhetorical, ribald, rich, risqué, rough, round, rude, sarcastic, satirical/satiric, saucy, scathing, scurrilous, secretive, secretly, sensational, sentimental, sharp, short, significant, silent, simple, sincere, sincerely, smutty, snappy, sneaky, speechless, spicy, spoken, square, stale, stilted, straight, straightforward, strained, succinct, suggestive, summary, symbolic, taciturn, talkative, tart, terse, threadbare, transparent, trenchant, trite, truculent, true, truly, trustworthy/trusty, truthful, unabridged, unanimous, uncommunicative, unfounded, uninhibited, unintelligible, unsaid, untrue, unvarnished, unwritten, vague, valedictory, veracious, verbal, verbatim, verbose, vernacular, vicious, virulent, vocal, vociferous, vulgar, warm, warning, windy, witty, wordy, wry, yellow, zany

268 **description:** deconstructionist, denotation, depiction, description, design, exposition, expression, formula, gloss, hermeneutical, history, hyperbole, identification, illustration, kudos, label, legend, name, news, nickname, notation, obituary, outline, paraphrase, plan, poem, obituary, passage, portrait, profile, prose, pseudonym, sketch, translation

269 **devices used for:** alarm, computer, copy, downlink, photocopy, telegram, telephone

270 **document, part:** addendum, advertisement, amendment, appendix, article, banner, body, chapter, clause, codicil, condition, entry, epilogue, excerpt, extract, feature, foreword, introduction, item, label, leaf, legend, margin, obituary, passage, preface, provision/proviso, sheet, slip, specification, stipulation, story, supplement, tab, tag, terms, text

271 **document, physical object:** act, affidavit, agreement, album, analysis, annal(s), annual, archive, article, balance sheet, bill, book, bulletin, card, caricature, catalog/catalogue, certificate, chronicle, circular, commitment, compact, composition, concord, constitution, contract, convention, corpus, credentials, criticism, critique, declaration, deed, deposition, digest, diploma, direction(s), directive, dispatch, dissertation, docket, document, draft, drama, enclosure, epistle, essay, explanation, exposition, facsimile, fiction, file, form, guarantee, history, identification, injunction, journal, letter, life, line, log, mail, material, memoir, memorandum/memo, message, missive, monument, narrative, note/notes, notice, opus, pact, pamphlet, paper/papers, paper, pass, passport, patent, permit, petition, piece, plan, policy, poster, proceedings, proclamation, promotion, pronouncement, proposal, prose, reading, receipt, record, reference, release, reminder, résumé, satire, schedule, scheme, script, sequel, sign, statement, survey, telegram, theme, thesis, ticket, treatise, writing

272 **document quality:** readable, short, summary, terse

273 **humorous tale:** banter, chaff, crack, jest, joke, kid, lampoon, levity, parody, pleasantry, pun, quip, spoof, sport, take off, travesty, trick, wit

274 **information:** advice, allusion, analysis, annotation, announcement, answer, broadcast, bulletin, buzz, calendar, caution, caveat, charge, clarification, clue, command, commitment, communication, confession, conjecture, construction, counsel, cybernetics, data, declaration, definition, dictate, direction(s), directive, disclosure, dope, evidence, excerpt, exhortation, explanation, exposé, fact, facts, gossip, grounds, groundwork, guidance, guide, herald, hint, hypermedia, illumination, information, instruction, intelligence, intimation, key, knowledge, lead, learning, lesson, light, lore, material, message, multimedia, news, notice, particular, plug, point, pointer, prescription, prognosis, program, prompt, pronouncement, proof, publication, publicity, quotation/quote, reading, recipe, recommendation, reference, report, resolution, revelation, rumor, science, scoop, secret, sign, statement, story, tidings, tip/tipoff, trivia, warning, whisper, word

275 **integral language parts:** adjective, adverb, antonym, aphorism, banality, barbarism, buzzword, byword, cant, catchword, clause, cliché, euphemism, expletive, figure of speech, grammar, idiom, jargon, metaphor, neologism, nomenclature, phrase, proverb, psychobabble, term, word

276 **language:** adage, adieu, alphabet, code, dialect, diction, expression, grammar, jargon, language, lexicon, lingo, nomenclature, patter, slang, speech, style, swearing, tongue, vernacular, vocabulary, voice

277 **media:** advertisement, banner, correspondence, criticism, desktop publishing, dispatch, infomercial, memorandum/memo, pen, rhetoric, rumor, sarcasm, screen, sound bite, television, translation, vehicle, video, videocassette

278 **object used in:** address, advertisement, alert, analogy, anathema, answer, aphorism, approach, assertion, assurance, axiom, babble, back talk, banner, banter, breath, bunk, call, cant, catchword, chat, chatter, claim, cliché, comeback, comment, commentary, commonplace, compliment, congratulations, contact, contention, contradiction, controversy, correspondence, criticism, cry, cue, curse, decision, declaration, defense, definition, derision, dialogue/dialog, dictum, digression, disapproval, dispatch, disputation, dispute, dissension, dissidence, dissonance, double entendre, double-talk, drivel, edict, eloquence, embellishment, epigram, epilogue, epitaph, equivocation, eulogy, euphemism, exaggeration, exaltation, fabrication, falsehood, falsity, farewell, fib, figure of speech, flak, fulmination, gab, gibberish, gibe, goodbye, gossip, grace, gratitude, grievance, gripe, groan, guidance, harangue, hearsay, hiss, hocus-pocus, hogwash, honor, implication, impropriety, indication, indignity, innuendo, instruction, insult, invective, invention, invocation, irony, issue, knock, lament/lamentation, laurels, lecture, letter, lie, line, lip, litany, malediction, maxim, meaning, memorandum/memo, mention, missive, mockery, monologue, moral, motion, motto, mouth, negation, negative, notice, oath, obscenity, observation, offense, offer, omen, oracle, oration, order, outcry, overtone, overture, password, patter, phrase, pitch, platform, platitude, plea, pleasantry, pledge, portent, praise, precursor, prediction, pretension, proclamation, profanity, profession, projection, promise, pronouncement, propaganda, prophecy, proverb, puff, pun, put-down, quip, quotation/quote, rebuff, rebuke, recommendation, reference, refusal, regards, remark, reminder, rendition, report, reprimand, respects, response, retort, return, rhetoric, rhyme, rot, rubbish, rumor, sarcasm, saying, scandal, sermon, shadow,

slam, slander, slogan, slur, statement, story, suggestion, swearing, tale, talk, testimonial, testimony, thanks, theme, threat, tirade, toast, translation, trash, tribute, truth, utterance, vehicle, veracity, verbiage, voice, vow, welcome, whisper, wind, word, wording

279 organization: media, newspaper, radio, television

280 publication: advertisement, almanac, anthology, article, authority, autobiography, bible, bill, biography, book, brochure, canon, cartoon, catalog/catalogue, dictionary, directory, edition, fiction, handbook, issue, journal, lexicon, literature, magazine, manual, memoir, newspaper, novel, organ, pamphlet, paper, periodical, press, print, publication, publicity, reference, release, review, romance, satire, text, thesaurus, tome, treatise, vocabulary, volume

281 record: annal(s), archive, calendar, itinerary, list, program, record, register, roll, roster

282 story: account, allegory, anecdote, biography, chronicle, epic, fable, fib, fiction, folklore, legend, lore, memoir, mystery, myth, mythology, narration, narrative, phenomenology, plot, poem, poetry, report, saga, scenario, story, tale, verse, version, yarn

283 summary: abbreviation, abridgement, abstract, agenda, annotation, bill, breakdown, brief, caption, citation, compendium, condensation, diagnosis, diary, directory, epitome, inventory, menu, moral, precis, profile, program, prospectus, report, résumé, return, review, roster, rundown, scenario, schedule, sketch, summary, synopsis, table, tally, title

284 symbol: arms, augury, autograph, badge, brand, capital, character, charm, check, code, crest, cue, device, dot, emblem, exponent, flag, fleck, flourish, hallmark, handwriting, harbinger, herald, impression, imprint, index, indication, insignia, label, landmark, lead, letter, line, mark, notation, note, numeral, script, seal, sign, signal, spot, stamp, stripe, symbol, tag, tick, token, trademark, tread, type, vestige, writing

EDUCATION

285 educate: address, break in, breed, care, catechize, coach, domesticate, drill, educate, education, form, groom, ground, illuminate, inculcate, indoctrinate, initiate, instill, instruct, instruction, lesson, preach, preparation, school, speak, speech, talk, teach, train, training, tutor

286 education level: class, grade, level

287 objects used in: class, college, course, dissertation, edification, education, erudition, lesson, lore, school, tenure, text, thesis, tuition

288 organization: academy, alma mater, class, college, enrollment, faculty, institute/institution, school

289 place of: academy, alma mater, class, college, school

290 test: assay, audition, criterion, dissection, drill, examination, exercise, experiment, index, inquest, inquiry, inspection, investiga-

tion, probe, quiz, test, trial, weight, workout

291 testing: fiddle, grade, pace, plumb, survey, test, trial, try, try on/try out, verify

ENTERTAINMENT

292 action: act, acting, amuse, amusement, antic, appear, arrange, bet, bill, broadcast, cruise, dance, diversion, dramatize, enact, enactment, entertain, featuring, feign, game, host, hype, impersonate, interpret, issue, overplay, pageant, parody, perform, play, prance, pretend, preview, produce, publication, publicize, put on, regale, rehearsal, rehearse, relaxation, revel, romp, score, sing, spotlight, stage, takeoff, take off, tape, transmit, travesty, trifle

293 object: auditorium, balloon, bet, broadcast, broadcasting, cinema, circus, comedy, distraction, drama, extravaganza, farce, film, fireworks, humor, lounge, medium, movie, news, nightclub, picture, publicity, sensation, sequel, show, sight, song, television, theater/theatre, video, videocassette

294 organization: band, cast, chorus, corps, ensemble, following, gallery

FAMILY

295 child raising: baby, baby-sit, breed, bring up, care, coddle, cradle, cultivate, form, foster, mind, nourish, nurse, nurture, pamper, raise, rear, support, tend

296 family: aristocracy, birth, blood, bride, bridegroom, brood, clan, class, consanguinity, court, descendant, descent, extraction, family, folk, genealogy, heritage, house, household, issue, kin, kindred, line, lineage, mate, offspring, origin, pedigree, people, posterity, progeny, rank, relation, stock, strain, tribe

297 marriage: annul, annulment, betroth, betrothal, couple, desert, desertion, divorce, elope, engage, engagement, espouse, estrange, estrangement, jilt, marriage, marry, match, mate, matrimony, nuptials, part, parting, propose, rupture, separate, separation, sever, split, vow, wed, wedding, woo

GOVERNMENT AND POLITICS

298 government action: abdicate, abolish, abolition, accession, administer, administration, amnesty, bust, colonization, command, depose, deposition, dethrone, displace, dominate, enact, enforce, enforcement, exile, expulsion, filibuster, legalize, override/overrule, pass, reign, rule, run in, secede, second, surveillance, tax, truce, veto

299 government organization: administration, ally, cabinet, capitalism, capitol, chamber, confederacy, congress, council, court, delegation, democracy, deregulation, dictatorship, direction, empire, fascism, government, house, jury, legislature, police/police officer, post, regime, rule, sovereignty, tyranny

300 political action: amnesty, arbitrate, arbitration, ballot, campaign, canvass, crusade, demonstrate, demonstration, displace, drive, drum up, elect, election, endorse, lobby, mutiny, nominate, nomination, patronage, picket, politics, poll, protest, reaction, rebellion, revolt, revolution, riot, run, vote

301 political organization: alliance, ballot, caucus, commonwealth, communism, confederacy, delegation, faction, fascism, machine, party, politics, side, tyranny

HEALTH

302 birth: bear, birth, breed, childbirth, conception, delivery, spring

303 change in: ache, black out, come down with, faint, fit, look up, mend, pull through, recover, recuperate, remission, repel, weary

304 death: abort, abortion, death, decease, demise, die, dissolution, end, expiration, expire, fatality, pass away, passing, perish

305 deathplace: cemetery, crypt, grave, graveyard, monument, tomb

306 disease: affliction, bacteria, blight, bug, cancer, canker, complaint, condition, contagion, contamination, cyst, disease, disorder, epidemic, germ, growth, illness, indigestion, infection, infirmity, microbe, pest, pimple, plague, rash, sickness, spell, swelling, symptom, syndrome, tantrum

307 drug: analgesic, anesthetic/anaesthetic, antidote, antiseptic, antitoxin, balm, capsule, contraceptive, cure, dope, dose, drug, medicine/medication, narcotic, nostrum, panacea, pill, poison, pot, potion, prescription, remedy, sedative, stimulant, stimulus, tablet, tonic

308 event: abort, abortion, ache, attack, catch, contract, convulsion, cough, cramp, crick, faint, gag, gargle, heal, massage, nauseate, palpitate, paroxysm, pass out, perk up, rupture, seizure, spell, spew, stroke, suffer, take, throw up, tic, vomit, wheeze

309 injury: abrasion, affliction, bite, blister, boil, bruise, concussion, contusion, cut, damage, defect, detriment, disability, disadvantage, disservice, fracture, gash, harm, injury, prick, puncture, rip, rupture, rust, scratch, shock, stab, swelling, welt, wound

310 medical action: alter, analyze, autopsy, bandage, castrate, cure, diagnose, dissection, doctor, dope, dress, drug, ease, examination, heal, inject, malpractice, massage, operate, operation, postmortem, practice, remedy, therapy, tranquilize, transplant, treat, treatment, vaccinate

311 medical instruments: bandage, cure, injection, lotion, matter, nostrum, ointment, panacea, prescription, remedy, salve, staff, x-ray

312 medical organization: asylum, clinic, hospital, madhouse, office

313 pain: ache, afflict, anesthesia/anaesthesia, discomfort, distress, gripe, harassment, harm, hurt, itch, pinch, sting, strain, stress, suffer, torment, torture, wound, wrong

314 quality of: able-bodied, ailing, anemic, bad, benign, better, burning, catching, clean, communicable, congenital, contagious, convalescent, crippled, curable, curative, delicate, disabled, diseased, dizzy, doddering, done in, drugged, drunk, dysfunctional, epidemic, excruciating, faint, febrile, fit, game, genetic, giddy, gory, groggy, haggard, hale, hardy, healthy, hearty, high, hurt, ill, immune, indisposed, inebriated, infectious, infirm, insane, invalid, irreparable, lame, light-headed, low, lusty, malignant, mental, morbid, nauseous, neurotic, normal, palsied, paralytic, peaked, pestilent/pestilential, poor, poorly, queasy, queer, right, robust, rocky, rugged, run-down, safe, sane, senile, sick, sickly, soft, sore, sound, spent, squeamish, strong, sturdy, tender, terminal, tired, tough, trim, unconscious, unfeeling, unhealthy, unscathed, unsound, vigorous, wan, weak, weary, well, whole, wholesome

315 sleep: anesthesia/anaesthesia, asleep, awake, coma, doze, drop off, hibernate, insomnia, lethargy, nap, nightmare, nod, quiet, rest, sleep, sleepy, slumber, snooze, snore, stupor

316 state of: ache, addiction, ailment, apoplexy, beat, collapse, complaint, condition, couple, debility, disability, dislocation, eating disorder, epidemic, faint, fatigue, fitness, form, gestation, hangover, health, hurt, hygiene, ill, immunity, insanity, lapse, malaise, maternity, nausea, neurosis, pain, paroxysm, pink, shape, stupor, symptom, syndrome, tone, trim, trouble, tumor, vigor, welfare/well-being

LEGAL

317 legal action: absolve, acquit, acquittal, action, adjudicate, adopt, adoption, annul, annulment, apprehend, apprehension, arraign, arrest, bequeath, book, bring, bust, charge, cite, collar, commute, condemn, condemnation, convict, conviction, counsel, covenant, cross-examine, cut off, decree, detail, detention, disinherit, enact, enforce, enforcement, evidence, excommunicate, exculpate, exonerate, extradite, hearing, impeach, imprison, incarcerate, indict, indictment, inherit, insure, jail, judge, leave, legalize, let off, lift, litigate, moderate, nab, nail, ordain, outlaw, override/overrule, pardon, pass, perjure, pick up, pinch, plead, practice, prohibit, proscribe, prosecute, pull in, put away, raid, rap, repeal, represent, reprieve, rescind, run in, sentence, sing, substantiate, sue, testify, transport, trial, try, validate, verify, vindicate, vitiate, vouch, waive, will, witness

318 objects used in legal practice: acquittal, act, affidavit, article, bail, bar, bench, bequest, bill, bond, brief, canon, case, claim, code, constitution, court, decree, deed, deposition, dictate, enactment, entreaty, evidence, indictment, injunction, inquest, institute, insurance, jury, law, lawsuit, legislation, libel, litigation, mandate, measure, ordinance, paper/papers, pardon, passage, patent, plea, pledge, precept, prescription, principle, regulation, repeal, reprieve, ruling, sentence, statute, stipulation, suit, terms, testament, testimonial, testimony, verdict, waiver, will, writ

319 quality of law: administrative, authoritarian, authoritative, autocratic, canonical, clear, constitutional, contraband, democratic, effectual, exempt, forensic, free, illegal, illegitimate, illicit, inadmissible, judicial, just, lawful, lawless, legal, legislative, legitimate, misbegotten, permissible, punitive, unauthorized, unlawful, unprejudiced, valid, wrongful

MILITARY

320 military action: action, aggression, barrage, blitz, blow up, campaign, conflict, contest, coup d'état, defeat, deploy, depose, deposition, descent, dethrone, disarm, disarmament, draft, engage, engagement, enlist, explode, explosion, fire, incursion, induct, induction, insurrection, invade, invasion, maneuver, mobilize, occupation, occupy, offensive, oppression, overthrow, rally, rebellion, recruit, revolt, revolution, salute, service, station, surrender, war, warfare

321 object used by military: armory, barracks, battery, battlefield, citadel, defense, draft, fort/fortress, magazine, post, rampart, service

322 organization: ally, army, artillery, battalion, brigade, cavalry, corps, defense, detachment, detail, enemy, fleet, force, legion, military, platoon, squad, troop/troops

MONETARY AND FINANCIAL AFFAIRS

323 association: association, board, cartel, conglomerate, establishment, federation, firm, industry, market/mart, merger, patronage, syndicate, trust

324 business action: advertise, advertising, annexation, appear, appointment, auction, aviation, cashier, commercialize, commission, conclave, conference, consultation, convene, convention, cry, deal, dealings, deficit spending, depression, dictate, discharge, dismiss, drudge, enterprise, exchange, export, farm, farming, fold, gathering, hold, hype, incorporate, intercourse, malpractice, management, manufacture/manufacturing, market, mediate, mediation, meet, meeting, merge, merger, monopolize, operation, patronage, patronize, pioneer, popularize, position, powwow, practice, produce, project, promote, promotion, proposal, publicize, puff, push, put up, sale, seal, second, service, session, shake up, shut, sit, slavery, specialize, step in, stock, table, trade, traffic, transact, transaction, truck, undertaking, wait on

325 business organization: agency, airport, association, bakery, bar, branch, bureau, bureaucracy, business, cartel, clientele, commerce, company, concern, conglomerate, corporation, council, direction, dispensation, enterprise, establishment, exchange, field, firm, house, industry, labor, mall, management, operation, outfit, partnership, personnel, practice, regime, ring, staff, store, syndicate, trust, union

326 business quality: accomplished, ambitious, businesslike, busy, careful, concentrated, diligent, discipline, eager, earnest, enterprising, grasping, greedy, methodical/methodic, miserly, orderly, painstaking, persistent, practical, professional, proper, purposeful, regular, relentless, stingy, tenacious, zealous

327 buying: buy, charge, lavish, lay out, order, patronize, pay, procure, purchase, redeem, shop, splurge, spree, squander, take, trade, traffic, treat, truck

328 cost: appraisal, cost, expense

329 fee: amount, bet, bill, bribe, charge, commission, damage(s), debt, duty, excise, expense, fare, fee, levy, obligation, overhead, pay, price, rate, rent, revenue, stake, tab, tariff, tax, toll, wager

330 financial action: assess, audit, bank, bargain, bet, bid, bidding, bill, bring, bring in, budget, bust, cash, charge, deduct, default, deficit spending, deposit, depress, depression, devalue, dicker, discount, earn, economize, economy, endorse, fail, frugality, gross, insure, invest, investment, levy, liquidate, net, pawn, pay, pinch, price, profit, realize, return, salt away, save, scrape, shop, skimp, speculate, speculation, stake, stint, subsist, trade, traffic, transact, transaction, truck, venture

331 financial document: account, agreement, book, coupon, reckoning, return, statement

332 financial object: account, adjustment, arrears, assessment, asset(s), backing, bail, balance, balance sheet, bargain, bill, budget, capital, cheap, draft, equity, fund, insurance, interest, investment, liability, loan, means, order, overhead, patronage, pawn, pay, pension, pledge, principal, profit, quotation/quote, receipt, revenue, score, stock, treasure

333 financial organization: bank, board, market/mart

334 financial quality: affluent, balanced, bankrupt, behind, broke, charitable, cheap, close, comfortable, commercial, complimentary, costly, dear, depressed, destitute, disadvantageous, down-and-out, due, economic, economical, exorbitant, expensive, extravagant, fat, financial, finished, fiscal, flush, free, frugal, gainful, generous, good, grasping, gratis, gratuitous, high, humble, impecunious, impoverished, improvident, indebted, indigent, inexpensive, insolvent, invaluable, lavish, liberal, liquid, low, lucrative, marketable, mean, miserly, modest, monetary, moneyed, moneymaking, munificent, narrow, needy, net, nominal, opulent, outstanding, overdue, owing, palatial, paltry, parsimonious, patrician, payable, penniless, plush, poor, posh, poverty-stricken, precious, priceless, privileged, prodigal, profitable, profligate, prohibitive, prosperous, provident, rich, second-rate/second-class, self-sufficient, skimpy, sleazy, sordid, sparing, splendid, squalid, steep, stingy, strapped, substantial, sumptuous, tawdry, thrifty, thriving, tight, underprivileged, unfortunate, unpaid, unreasonable, unsettled, valuable, wealthy, well-bred, well-off

335 financial state: afford, arrears, avarice, bankruptcy, boom, bring, circumstances, credit, cutback, default, deficit, depression, devalue, discount, economy, extravagance, fail, fortune, frugality, hyperinflation, inadequacy, inflation, living, misery, need, obligation, owe, panic, paucity, pile, pomp, poverty, prosperity, recession, riches, savings, slump, substance, thrift, traffic, value, worth

336 financial value state: cost, decline, expense, value

337 gift: acquisition, allowance, arrival, atonement, award, balm, benefit, bequest, bonus, boon, bounty, charity, citation, comfort, commendation, compensation, contribution, courtesy, decoration, diploma, dispensation, dividend, dole, donation, due, endowment, extravagance, find, fruit, gain, gem, gift, godsend, good, grant, gratuity, haul, heirloom, honor, indulgence, inheritance, laurels, legacy, loot, luxury, medal, memento, memorial, offering, plum, premium, present, presentation, prize, purse, recognition, remembrance, reparation, reward, souvenir, spoils, subsidy, token, treasure, trophy

338 merchandise: bargain, cargo, commodity, consignment, contraband, fabrication, freight, goods, hardware, harvest, haul, inventory, line, load, merchandise, order, product, stock, truck, turnout, wares, yield

339 monetary container: bag, bank, purse, till, treasury

340 money: advance, allowance, appropriation, asset(s), bill, bread, cash, change, chips, coin, contribution, currency, deposit, dollar, donation, endowment, estate, finances, financing, fund, funds, income, investment, loot, maintenance, means, mint, money, offering, pay, pile, pool, recompense, refund, reserve, resource, resources, return, riches, savings, support, sustenance, wealth

341 money giving: advance, blow, buy, compensate, disburse, discharge, endow, expend, finance, fritter, fund, invest, lavish, lay out, misappropriate, patronage, patronize, pay, play, ransom, recompense, refund, reimburse, remit, remunerate, repay, requite, reward, satisfy, settle, shell out, spend, sponsor, square, subscribe, subsidize, support, underwrite

342 money taking: bill, blackmail, bleed, clear, collect, extort, extortion, fine, fleece, recoup, squeeze

343 ownership part: hold, owner, possession, proprietor

344 payment: advance, alimony, bounty, collateral, commission, compensation, consideration, cut, deal, debt, deficit spending, deposit, disbursement, discharge, dividend, dole, draft, dues, earnings, equity, expenditure, expense, fee, financing, gain, graft, grant, gratuity, gross, income, installment, interest, kickback, outlay, pay, payment, penalty, pension, perk, pittance, premium, prize, proceeds, profit, purse, raise, ransom, rebate, receipts, recompense, redress, refund, reparation, restitution, revenue, reward, safety net, salary, satisfaction, stake, stipend, subsidy, take, tip, upkeep, wage/wages

345 selling: auction, bazaar, charge, handle, market, merchandise, peddle, sale, sell, solicit, trade, traffic, truck

346 value state: appreciation, benefit, decline, import, importance, mark, quality, value, worth

PROFESSIONS

347 business manager: administrator, banker, boss, businessperson, capitalist, captain, chief, commander, dealer, director, employer, entrepreneur, establishment, executive, farmer, financier, founder, head, landlord, leader, magnate, manager, master, merchant, mogul, notable, officer, official, overseer, owner, principal, professional, proprietor, seller, specialist, superintendent, superior, supervisor, tycoon, warden

348 businessperson: accountant, adjutant, adviser/advisor, agent, aid/aide, analyst, announcer, applicant, apprentice, arbitrator, archaeologist, architect, assistant, associate, astronaut, attendant, auditor, author, authority, aviator, baker, banker, barber, bearer, broker, builder, businessperson, butcher, buyer, caretaker, carpenter, cartoonist, cashier, chair, chairperson, clerk, client, collaborator, colleague, commuter, connection, consumer, cook, correspondent, courier, court, craftsperson, creator, critic, custodian, customer, dabbler, deputy, detective, drudge, emissary, employee, engineer, envoy, expert, farmer, fellow, financier, flyer, fortune-teller, fountainhead, friend, go-between, gourmet, groom, guard, guide, hack, hand, help, inferior, informant/informer, intermediary, inventor, investigator, janitor, journalist, labor, liaison, machine, mariner, maverick, mediator, messenger, middle person, miser, model, monitor, negotiator, novice, opposition, page, partner, patron, picket, pilot, pioneer, playwright, poet, porter, prodigal, professional, recruit, referee, reporter, representative, rival, sailor, scout, seller, servant, slave, snoop, spendthrift, spokesperson, sponsor, spy, subordinate, surrogate, tailor, tenant, tool, traveler, umpire, vendor, virtuoso, watchkeeper, wizard, worker, writer, yuppie

349 discipline: affair, anatomy, anthropology, appointment, archaeology, architecture, arithmetic, art, astronomy, botany, career, cinema, communications, cybernetics, department, discipline, domain, employment, ergonomics, field, geography, hermeneutics, lifework, line, livelihood, logic, matter, occupation, orbit, passion, phenomenology, philosophy, poetry, position, press, project, province, psychology, pursuit, realm, research, scene, school, science, semiotics, specialty, sphere, stage, station, territory, trade, undertaking, vocation, walk, work

350 educator: academic, adviser/advisor, alumnus/alumna, brain, coach, college student, dean, disciplinarian, expert, faculty, fountainhead, genius, graduate, guru, instructor, intellectual, inventor, learner, master, mastermind, mentor, monitor, novice, principal, professor, pupil, scholar, school, student, teacher, tutor, wonk

351 **employment:** ax/axe, bounce, can, collaborate, commission, demote, discharge, dismiss, dismissal, earn, elevate, elevation, employ, employment, engage, fire, gross, hire, interview, job, kick out, labor, layoff, lay off, live, livelihood, living, make, occupation, office, oust, pay, picket, post, promote, promotion, raise, reinstate, relieve, resign, resignation, retain, retire, rise, sack, situation, spot, station, strike, suspend, work

352 **entertainer:** acrobat, actor, artist, ballet dancer, buff, character, comedian, comic, connoisseur, creator, director, fan, fanatic, fledgling, follower, freak, hero/heroine, host, idol, joker, luminary, magician, mimic, musician, name, notable, participant, personage/personality, player, protagonist, singer, star, usher, virtuoso, wit, zany

353 **financier:** accountant, banker, bearer, broker, financier, spendthrift

354 **government officer:** administrator, ally, ambassador, arbiter, authoritarian, authority, autocracy, conqueror, consul, delegate, deputy, despot, dictator, diplomat, disciplinarian, envoy, establishment, executive, exile, expatriate, figure, figurehead, governor, informant/informer, inhabitant, intermediary, justice, leader, legislator, liaison, master, minister, mogul, monarch, negotiator, officer, official, page, patrol, peacemaker, personage/personality, police/police officer, representative, sovereign, spokesperson, tyrant

355 **legal practitioner:** attorney, bench, beneficiary, consul, counsel, counselor, heir, investigator, judge, lawyer, officer, party, proponent, witness

356 **media person:** commentator, journalist, press, reporter, writer

357 **medical practitioner:** analyst, doctor, nurse, patient, physician, psychiatrist, specialist

358 **military person:** commander, conqueror, deserter, fighter, lookout, mercenary, militant, officer, patrol, private, recruit, sailor, scout, soldier, veteran, warrior

359 **politician:** advocate, ally, anarchist, apostate, apostle, applicant, arbitrator, backer, bigot, candidate, conservative, demagogue, diehard, diplomat, dissident, donor, extremist, fanatic, hostage, idealist, insurgent, militant, nonconformist, partisan, patron, picket, politician, proponent, protagonist, radical, reactionary, rebel, refugee, renegade, sectarian, spokesperson

360 **profession:** business, calling, career, craft, employment, finance, hacker, job, labor, lifework, line, livelihood, mission, occupation, place, position, profession, psychology, science, situation, trade, vocation, walk, work

361 **religious person:** acolyte, agnostic, angel, apostle, believer, chaplain, clergyperson, convert, creator, cynic, disciple, doubter, father, hermit, layperson, magician, minister, missionary, monk, nun, pagan, pastor, preacher, priest, prophet, skeptic, visionary, witch, wizard

362 **task:** affair, assignment, bee, berth, chore, commission, concern, drudgery, duty, effort, enterprise, errand, exercise, exertion, function, grind, groove, job, labor, mission, office, part, picnic, post, project, province,

realm, research, role, routine, spot, stint, sweat, task, tax, toil, undertaking, work

RECREATION

363 **action:** aerobics/aerobic, angle, athletics, boating, bowl, boxing, bunt, chance, coach, competition, contest, cruise, dance, deal, defeat, dissipation, diversion, engage, event, exercise, fish, gamble, gambol, game, gymnastics, hike, hobby, hunt, keep up, lay, leisure, match, meet, meeting, mess around, oppose, pastime, pit, play, race, raffle, recreation, rehearsal, rehearse, relaxation, rout, shuffle, speculate, speculation, sport, stake, swim, tournament, trifle, turn, vacation, venture, vie, wager, win, workout

364 **objects used in:** amusement, avocation, bicycle, club, equipment, field, game, gymnasium, hobby, holiday, lap, point, pool, raffle, recreation, round, score, tie, wager

365 **organization:** conference, field, league, side, squad, team

366 **participants:** amateur, athlete, aviator, champion, coach, competitor, contestant, dabbler, entrant, entry, fan, fanatic, fighter, fledgling, follower, freak, hacker, mariner, master, name, opponent, opposition, participant, pedestrian, player, referee, rival, sailor, spectator, star, umpire, underdog, victor, winner

RELIGIOUS

367 **action:** anoint, baptism, baptize, bless, blessing, burial, bury, canonize, christen, communion, consecrate, dedicate, dedication, defect, defection, deify, enshrine, excommunicate, inter, penance, pray, prayer, preach, purification, purify, wake, witchcraft, worship

368 **objects used in:** abbey, beads, bible, casket, cathedral, cemetery, church, cloister, coffin, convent, deity, denomination, divinity, faith, grace, holiness, invocation, litany, liturgy, monastery, pulpit, religion, sanctuary, sermon, service, shrine, temple

369 **organization:** church, clergy, congregation, cult, parish

370 **supernatural:** angel, apparition, black magic, deity, demon, devil, divinity, elf, eternity, fairy, ghost, god, heaven, hell, hereafter, incantation, magic, monster, paradise, phantom, presence, savior, shade, sorcery, spell, spirit, universe, utopia, vision, witchcraft

SEX AND REPRODUCTION

371 **attribute of gender:** female, femininity/feminine, male, masculinity/masculine

372 **attribute of sexuality:** adulterous, amatory, amorous, aphrodisiac, bisexual, carnal, celibate, chaste, close, desirable, erotic, femininity/feminine, fertile, fertility, fleshly, gay,

homosexual, hot, kinky, lascivious, lecherous, lewd, libidinous, licentious, loose, loving, masculinity/masculine, nasty, naughty, obscene, passion, passionate, pornographic, potent, promiscuous, provocative, pure, raw, seductive, sensual, sensuous, sexual, sexy, smutty, suggestive, sultry, torrid, vice, virgin/virginal, virile, voluptuous, vulgar, wanton

373 birth: bear, birth, breed, childbirth, conception, delivery, spring

374 child bearing: beget, deliver, delivery, fertilize, generate, generation, get, have, labor, multiply, procreate, produce, propagate, reproduce, spawn

375 sex act: affair, alter, assignation, birth control, caress, climax, cohabit, conception, copulate, coquet, couple, cuddle, dalliance, dally/dally with, debauch, deflower, enamor, fertilize, flirt, flirtation, fondle, hug, impregnate, intercourse, kiss, love, love affair, mate, molest, pass, paw, pet, proposition, rape, ravish, romance, seduce, sex, sin, tryst, violate, violation, woo

SOCIAL INTERACTIONS

376 authority: agency, agent, ascendancy/ascendency, auspices, authority, carte blanche, censorship, chair, chairperson, chief, choice, claim, clearance, cogency, command, connoisseur, control, curb, custody, dominance, domination, dominion, duty, ease, empire, franchise, immunity, impunity, independence, jurisdiction, justice, leadership, leave, office, option, permission, permit, power, prerogative, privilege, rate, reign, right, rule, station, supremacy, sway, title, trust, voice, vote, warrant

377 celebration: acclamation, affair, banquet, baptism, carnival, celebrate, celebration, commemorate, commemoration, commencement, entertain, fair, fanfare, feast, festival, festivity, fete, fiesta, gaiety, gala, keep, observance, observe, orgy, pageant, parade, pomp, rally, revel, revelry, rite, splurge, spree, wake

378 class: branch, brand, breed, caste, category, class, classification, cut, denomination, description, division, echelon, estate, family, form, genre/genus, gradation, grade, kind, manner, mob, model, mold, nature, nobility, order, position, quality, rank, sort, species, stock, tier, type, variety, world

379 community: colony, commune, community, constituency, country, folk, neighborhood, people, population, public, society

380 ethnic group: nationality, people, race, strain, tribe

381 organization: affiliate, affiliation, agency, apparatus, assembly, bar, brigade, coalition, combination, commission, committee, council, crew, crowd, department, federation, foundation, guild, institute/institution, league, membership, movement, network, organization, partnership, party, ring, sect, society, union

382 part of a group: chapter, division, plurality, sect

383 party: affair, blowout, dance, entertainment, festivity, gala, masquerade, orgy, party, reception, tear

384 social action: abuse, accept, advance(s), adventure, amends, amuse, appeal, appointment, associate, befriend, betray, bite, blooper, bounce, caper, carouse, cavort, cohabit, collaborate, commemorate, compel, conclave, conduct, consort, cool, coquet, court, cower, cultivate, cut up, disaffect, discriminate, disgrace, disobey, disorganize, dissociate, encounter, endanger, engagement, enjoy, entertain, entertainment, escapade, escort, estrange, excursion, faux pas, fawn, fete, fight, flirt, flirtation, flock, forsake, frequent, frisk, frolic, go together/go with, grovel, hanky-panky, haunt, hold, host, hubbub, induct, induction, infringe, insinuate, interfere, interference, interrupt, introduce, invitation, invite, jilt, kick out, know, kowtow, lose, love, make up, maroon, mask, meddle, mediate, mediation, meet, meeting, mingle, mishandle/mismanage, mutiny, network, obeisance, oblige, observance, observe, ostracize, overture, pander, part, parting, pass, patch up, patronize, penance, pick up, play, poke, popularize, powwow, prance, prank, pretend, program, proposition, prostrate, pry, pursue, put up, rampage, rapprochement, reception, reciprocate, reconcile, reduce, regale, reinstate, rendezvous, repay, reprisal, requite, respond, retaliate, retribution, revel, revelry, revenge, riot, romance, romp, rupture, seat, secede, second, see, separate, sever, share, show, shun, sit, slight, snoop, snub, socialize, soothe, spree, spurn, squire, step in, stoop, stunt, tantrum, tear, throw over, toy, treat, trespass, trick, tryst, usurp, vengeance, wallow, welcome, woo

385 social change: breakup, civilize, give in/give up, revert, succumb

386 social event: adventure, assignation, ball, bee, benefit, binge, blast, bustle, caper, caricature, carnival, ceremony, clamor, clown, come between, conference, date, debut, display, dissipation, diversion, entertainment, escapade, exhibition, exposition, fair, feature, fiesta, fling, frolic, fun, function, funeral, gathering, inauguration, initiation, memorial, merriment/merrymaking, occasion, outing, parade, picnic, rally, riot, rite, ritual

387 social organization: association, band, circle, clan, class, clique, club, congregation, congress, crowd, cult, elite, entourage, faction, fellowship, following, gang, guild, league, legion, order, society

388 social state: amity, association, attendance, awkwardness, behind, belong, belonging, bigotry, bond, brawl, breach, break, breeding, calm, camaraderie, care, caste, celebrity, celibacy, censorship, ceremony, circumstances, civilization, class, clutches, coherence, commotion, companionship, compatibility, complicity, concert, concord, conflict, conjunction, connection, consanguinity, consequence, contact, contempt, cooperation, correlation, courtesy, courtship, credit, crunch, culture, dalliance, degree, detachment, difference, dignity, diplomacy, disaffection, disagreement, discord, disfavor, disgrace, disharmony, dishonor, disorder, dissociation, dissolution, distinction, disturbance, division, duty, ease, echelon, elite, eminence, enrollment, entertainment, entrée, entry, equality, estate, estrangement, excitement, face, fame, familiarity, favoritism, fellowship, feud, fidelity, footing, friendliness, friendship, frivolity, fun, furor, fuss, gaiety, genre/genus, gentility, get along, get on, glory, harmony, height, hospitality, housing, hubbub, humiliation, immunity, importance, infidelity, intimacy, intrigue, juncture, kick, laissez-faire, lapse, lather, league, level, liai-

son, liberty, love affair, luxury, marriage, match, men's movement, mirth, mourning, mutiny, name, network, nobility, nonsense, notch, notoriety, obligation, odium, onus, pandemonium, partnership, peace, pink, place, platitude, pleasure, polish, popularity, position, predicament, prestige, privacy, rage, rank, rapport, rapprochement, rate, refinement, relationship, report, reproach, repulse, reputation, rift, rupture, scramble, seclusion, separation, servitude, setback, shame, showdown, situation, slavery, society, solitude, sophistication, sphere, split, spotlight, standing, state, station, status, stigma, stink, stir, support, sympathy, taint, taste, tedium, terms, tie, uncertainty, unification, variance, whirl

Life forms

BEINGS

389 **beings:** being, body, cell, creation, creature, cur, egg, form, individual, life, organism, soul
390 **former beings:** body, cadaver, carcass/carcase, corpse
391 **group of beings:** band, flock, group, world
392 **limb or appendage of:** ankle, arm, back, backside, beak, behind, branch, bust, butt/buttocks, calf, chest, claw, digit, egg, extremity, eye, fiber, finger, flank, flesh, foot, freckle, germ, hair, hand, head, jaw, leg, limb, lip, member, mop, mouth, nose, posterior, rump, seat, skin, strand, tail, trunk, tuft, wisp
393 **organ:** abdomen, abdominal, bacteria, belly, blood, bone, bowels, brain, gut, heart, joint, mind, molecule, muscle, nucleus, seed, skeleton, spine, stomach, vein

BEINGS, ANIMAL

394 **animal:** adult, animal, beast, brute, buck, calf, cat, cattle, chicken, clam, cock, colt, cur, father, fawn, frog, game, goat, halfbreed, hound, hybrid, litter, mongrel, monkey, monster, mother, parasite, pet, pig, prey, stock, young
395 **bird:** bird, chicken
396 **fish:** aquarium, aquatic
397 **group of animals:** drove, family, herd, horde, litter, pack, roundup, stock, swarm, team
398 **insect:** bee, bug, grub, pest
399 **limb or appendage of:** bill, chin, coat, crest, feather, fertilizer, fur, meat, mop, paunch, pelt, pulp, scale, shell, trunk, venom, wing
400 **mammal:** cat, dog, donkey, father, fawn, goat, hound, mother, pig

GENERAL CHARACTERISTICS

401 **attribute of behavior:** abstemious, acerbity, acid, acrid, acrimonious, active, adamant, ad-

olescent, affable, affected, affectionate, agreeable, agreeably, aimless, alive, aloof, amiable, amuck, animate, animated, anxious, apathetic, arbitrary, arch, ardent, argumentative, arrogant, artificial, assured, attentive, audacious, austere, authoritarian, avid, babyish, backward, bad, balky, barbarian, barbaric, barbarous, barefaced, beaming, beastly, belligerent, benevolent, big, bland, blindly, boisterous, bold, brash, brassy, brave, brazen, brittle, brusque, brutal, calculating, calm, cantankerous, capricious, carnivorous, casual, cautious, cavalier, chary, childish, chill, chivalrous, chummy, civil, clumsy, coarse, cocky/cocksure, collected, combative, comic/comical, common, compassionate, complacent, complaisant, composed, compulsive, concerned, conciliatory, condescending, considerate, constructive, contemptuous, contrary, contumacious, convivial, cool, cordial, correct, corrupt, country, courageous, courteous, courtly, covetous, cowardly, coy, crabby/crabbed, crafty, cranky, crass, craven, cross, crotchety, crude, cruel, crusty, cunning, daring, dark, dauntless, deaf, debonair, deceitful, decent, deceptive, decided, decorous, defensive, deferential, defiant, deliberate, deliberately, delicate, delightful, delinquent, delirious, demonstrative, demure, desperate, detached, devious, diffident, diplomatic, disagreeable, disarming, discourteous, discreet, disdainful, disgruntled, disingenuous, disinterested, disloyal, disobedient, disobliging, disorderly, dispassionate, disputatious, disrespectful, disruptive, dissipated, dissolute, distant, distraught, docile, doctrinaire, dogged, dolorous, domineering, doting, doubledealing, dour, eager, earnest, easy, ebullient, edgy, effeminate, effervescent, emotionless, enthusiastic, envious, epicurean, equable, equal, evasive, even, exacting, excitable, excited, exuberant, faithful, faithless, fake, false, falsely, fanatical, favorable, favorably, fawning, fearful, fearless, feigned, ferocious, fervent/fervid, feverish, fickle, fidgety, fiery, fighting, finicky, flagrant, flamboyant, flexible, flighty, flippant, flirtatious, flushed, fool-hardy, foolish, foolishly, forceful, formal, forward, foxy, fractious, free, freely, fresh, fretful, frisky, frivolous, fulsome, fussy, genial, genteel, giddy, glacial, glowing, good, graceless, gracious, grandiose, grave, gritty, grouchy, gruff, grumpy, halfhearted, hard, hardhearted, haughty, headstrong, heartless, hearty, heedless, helpless, heroic, high-strung, hostile, hot, huffy, humane, humble, hypocritical, icy, idle, ill at ease, ill-mannered, ill-natured, impatient, impersonal, impertinent, impish, impolite, impolitic, importunate, impossible, impudent, impulsive, inactive, inclement, inconsiderate, inexorable, ingratiating, inhospitable, inhuman/inhumane, inimical, innocuous, insensitive, insidious, insolent, insubordinate, insurgent, intractable/intransigent, intrepid, invidious, irascible, irreconcilable, irrepressible, irreverent, irritable, jaded, jaundiced, jaunty, jovial, jubilant, jumpy, juvenile, keen, kind, kittenish, lax, lazy, lecherous, lenient, lethargic, level, liberal, licentious, lifeless, light, light-headed, listless, lively, lofty, loose, loquacious, loud, loving, lunatic, maladroit, malevolent, malicious, mannered, mannerly, martial, mawkish, mean, meek, menacing, mercenary, merciful, merciless, mercurial, mild, militant, mincing, mischievous, miscreant, miserly, modest, mousy, munificent, naive, narcissistic, nasty, natural, naughty, nefarious, neglectful, negligent, neighborly, nerveless, nervy, noble, nomadic, nonchalant, noncompliant, nonconformist, nonviolent, nosy, obdurate, obedient, obliging, obnoxious, obsequious, obstinate, obtrusive, odious, offhand, oily, orderly, ostentatious, outlandish, overbearing, overconfident, overwrought, parental, parsimonious, partisan, passionate, pedantic, peevish, pent-up, peppery, peppy, peripatetic, perky, permissive, persistent, pert, perverse, petulant, philosophical/philosophic, pious, pitiless, placid, plaintive, playful, polite, politic, pompous, possessed, pragmatic, precious, precipitous/precipitate, precise, predatory, premature, presumptuous, pretentious, prickly, prim, prissy, prodigal, profane, profligate, prompt, proper, propitious, proud, provident, prudent, prudish, puerile, pugnacious, punctilious, pushy, quarrelsome, querulous, quick-tempered, quiet, racy, radiant, raffish, rakish, rash, raucous, ready, rebel, rebellious, recalcitrant, reckless, refined, regardful, regardless, relentless, reluctant, remiss, remorseful, remorseless, remote, renegade, repugnant, reserved, resigned, respectful, responsible, responsive, restive, restrained, reticent, retiring, ribald, rocky, rollicking, rough, rowdy, rude, rugged, runaway, rustic, ruthless, safe, salty, sanctimonious, saucy, savage, scintillating, scrupulous, secluded, self-conscious, self-righteous, sensual, sentimental, serene, servile, severe, shabby, shameful, shameless, sheepish, shifty, short, short-sighted, shrewd, shy, silly, simple, sincere, sinister, skittish, slick, slippery, sluggish, sly, small, smart, smooth, snaky, snappy, sneaky, snide, snobbish, sober, so-ciable, soft, solid, sophisticated, sophomoric, sparing, spineless, spiteful, spontaneous, sporting/sportive, sprightly, spry, square, squeamish, staid, standoffish, stately, staunch, steadfast, stealthy, stern, stiff, stilted, stingy, stodgy, stoic/stoical, stolid, stony, strained, strenuous, strict, stringent, stubborn, stuffy, suave, subdued, submissive, subservient, subversive, sunny, supercilious, superior, sure, surly, sweet, sympathetic, taciturn, tactful, tactless, tame, tasteless, tearful, temperate, tempestuous, tenacious, tender, tense, testy, thankful, thankless, theatrical, thieving/thievish, thoughtful, thoughtless, thrifty, tight, timid, tipsy, torpid, touchy, tractable, treacherous, tricky, truculent, true, turbulent, ugly, unaffected, unasked, unassuming, unbending, uncivilized, uncompromising, uncontrollable, uncouth, undaunted, undependable, underhand, understanding, unemotional, unflappable, unfriendly, ungrateful, unguarded, uninhibited, unintentional/unintended, uninterested, unkind, unmerciful, unobtrusive, unprejudiced, unpretentious, unreasonable, unrelenting, unruly, unscrupulous, unseemly, unselfish, unsettled, unsociable, unsophisticated, unsuspecting, unsympathetic, unthinking, untoward, untrustworthy, unwary, unwilling, unwise, unwitting, unworldly, unyielding, uptight, urbane, vain, valiant, vehement, vengeful, venturesome, vibrant, vicarious, vicious, vigilant, vindictive, violent, virile, virtuous, vital, vivacious, volatile, voracious, wacky, wanton, warlike, warm, wary, wasteful, watchful, wayfaring, wayward, well-bred, whimsical, wicked, wild, willful, willing, wily, winning/winsome, withdrawn, worldly, yellow, yielding, zany, zealous

402 attribute of intelligence: able, abreast, abstruse, academic, acute, adept, alert, amenable, analytic/analytical, appreciative, apt, astute, awake, aware, backward, bewildered, blank, blind, bright, brilliant, calculable, canny, childish, clairvoyant, clear, clever, clumsy, cognizant, coherent, common-sense, complex, comprehensible, conscious, considered, contemplative, conversant, creative, cunning, dark, deducible, deep, delirious, dense, designedly, dexterous, dim, discerning, dizzy, dopey, down-to-earth, dull, dumb, educated, efficient, elevated, empty, empty-headed, enlightened, erudite, experienced, expert, familiar, far-sighted, fatuous, forgotten, frivolous, gifted, gullible, hare-brained, hazy, idiotic, ignorant, illiterate, imbecile, impressionable, incisive, incomprehensible, inefficient, ineligible, inept, inexperienced, informed, ingenious, inquiring, inquisitive, insipid, intellectual, intelligent, intuitive, inventive, irrational, judicious, keen, knowing, knowledgeable, learned, logical, lucid, mental, mindful, mistaken, nimble, oblivious, observant, obtuse, omniscient, penetrating, perceptive, perspicacious, philosophical/philosophic, precocious, privy, professional, proficient, profound, psychic, quick, quick-witted, rational, ready, reasonable, resourceful, sagacious, sane, scatterbrained, scholarly, senile, sensible, shallow, sharp, shrewd, simple, skillful, slick, slow, smart, soft, stolid, studious, stupid, subtle, thick, thoughtful, thoughtless, touched, unaware, uneducated, unfamiliar, unwise, vacant, vacuous, versed, veteran, weak, wise

403 attribute of mentality: abashed, absentee, absent-minded, absorbed, absorbing, accustomed, addled, affected, affectionate, afraid, aggrieved, aghast, agonizing, alert, amatory, amorous, angry, anxious, apathetic, appreciative, apprehensive, aspiring, assumed, attentive, automatic, averse, avid, bad, balmy, beaten, beholden, believable, bent, bewildered, bewitched, bigoted, black, bleak, blissful, blue, boiling, breathless, broad, broad-minded, broken, brokenhearted, buoyant, burning, calculating, captive, carnal, cautious, certain, cheerful, cheerless, chipper, circumspect, clairvoyant, clear, compassionate, complacent, concerned, confident, confused, conscious, contemplative, content, contented, contrite, crabby/crabbed, cranky, crazy, crestfallen, cross, crotchety, curious, cynical, daft, dearly, decided, dejected, delighted, delirious, demented, depressed, deranged, desolate, despairing, desperately, despondent, disaffected, disappointed, disbelieving, disconcerted, disconsolate, discontented/discontent, discouraged, discouraging, disenchanted, disgruntled, disgusted, disillusioned, disinclined, disinterested, disoriented, dispirited, dissatisfied, dissident, distraught, distressed, distrustful, doleful, dolorous, doubtful, down, downcast, downhearted, dumbfounded, ecstatic, elated, emotional, emotionless, enamored, engrossed, envious, excited, expectant, exultant, fascinated, fed up, festive, firm, flaming, flushed, foggy, forgetful, forgotten, forlorn, frantic, frenetic, fretful, frightened, frustrated, fulfilled, funereal, furious, gay, glad, gladly, gleeful, gloomy, grateful, greedy, grumpy, gut, half-baked, happily, happy, hard, headstrong, healthy, heavy, high, hopeful, hot, huffy, hurt, hysterical, ill at ease, impartial, impassioned, impressionable, inattentive, incensed, inconsolable, incredulous, indifferent, indignant, indiscriminate, infatuated, insane, insatiable, insecure, insular, intent, intently, interested, intolerant, intoxicated, invidious, irate, irrational, irresolute, irritable, jaundiced, jealous, jovial, joyful/joyous, joyless, jubilant, judicious, keen, lackadaisical, languid, lascivious, lethargic, levelheaded, livid, lonely, lonesome, longing, lost, low, lucid, lukewarm, lunatic, mad, malleable, manic/maniacal, melancholy, mental, merry, mindful, mindless, miserable, moody, morbid, morose, narrow, narrow-minded, negative, nerveless, nervous, neurotic, neutral, new age, noncommittal, normal, nostalgic, numb, nuts/nutty, objective, oblivious, observant, obsessed, opposed/opposing, overcome, overjoyed, overwrought, partial, penitent, pensive, pent-up, pessimistic, petty, platonic, predisposed, preoccupied, prepared, prepossessed, profound, proud, provincial, psychic, psychological, psychotic, purposeful, puzzled, queasy, rabid, radical, raging, rapt, realistic, reflective,

regretful, resolute, restless, right, rigid, romantic, sad, sane, sanguine, sappy, scared, sectarian, secure, senile, sensitive, serious, sick, silly, skeptical, solemn, solicitous, somber, sore, sorrowful, sorry, sound, sour, spellbound, spiritless, steady, stout, strong, subdued, sullen, susceptible, suspicious, tearful, temperamental, tender, tense, testy, thankful, thirsty, thoughtful, thoughtless, tired, tolerant, torn, touched, tough, ugly, unadvised, unbalanced, uncomfortable, uncommitted, unconcerned, undecided, uneasy, unemotional, unfaltering, unfeeling, unhappy, uninterested, unsettled, unsound, untouched, untroubled, unwary, upbeat, upset, versed, vulnerable, wacky, wary, weak, weary, willing, wistful, woebegone, worried, wrathful, wretched

404 attribute of personality: aboveboard, abrasive, adventurous, aggressive, airy, altruistic, amenable, amorphous, approachable, ardent, arrogant, artful, assertive, assuming, assured, audacious, august, bashful, belligerent, big, bitter, blasé, blessed, blithe, bloodless, boastful, bold, boorish, brash, bright, buoyant, busy, callous, calm, captious, carefree, catty, charitable, charming, chaste, cheerful, childlike, chill, chilly, choosy, churlish, clean, clear, clement, clinical, close, cocky/cocksure, co-dependent, cold, colorful, colorless, combative, conceited, confident, convivial, cool, courageous, coy, credulous, culpable, cursed, cute, dainty, dashing, decent, dedicated, deep, delicate, delightful, demonic/demoniac/demoniacal, demure, dependent, deserving, despicable, detached, determined, devious, die-hard, difficult, dignified, discriminating, dispassionate, disreputable, distant, docile, dynamic, easy, easygoing, effeminate, egocentric, egotistic/egoistic, elastic, enchanting, energetic, engaging, enterprising, exacting, exalted, excitable, exemplary, feckless, finicky, finished, flatulent, flirtatious, forbearing, fortunate, forward, foxy, free, fresh, frigid, fussy, gallant, game, garrulous, gauche, generous, genial, genteel, gentle, glacial, glib, good, good-humored, good-natured, green, gregarious, gritty, gutless, gutsy, happy-go-lucky, hardened, hard-hearted, hard-nosed/hardheaded, hateful, heroic, high-strung, humble, icy, ill-natured, immaculate, immovable, impassive, imperturbable, impetuous, individual, indomitable, indulgent, inexperienced, infamous, inflexible, inherent, inhibited, innocent, insipid, insouciant, intolerant, intrinsic, inveterate, inviting, irresponsible, jaunty, kind, kindhearted, kindly, latent, lazy, liberal, lighthearted, likable, little, lovable, low, lowly, loyal, magnanimous, magnetic, mercurial, meritorious, mild, mincing, misanthropic, miserly, modest, narcissistic, native, natural, nice, noble, nonchalant, notorious, obedient, obliging, obsequious, obsessed, odd/oddball, odious, officious, opinionated, opprobrious, optimistic, outgoing, outspoken, overbearing, particular, patient, peculiar, peppy, perky, persistent, persnickety, personable, pert, philanthropic, picky, pigheaded, pliable, predictable, prepossessing, prim, prissy, proper, pushy, queer, quick-tempered, receptive, recluse/reclusive, remote, reserved, responsible, rotten, ruthless, saintly, sanctimonious, sedate, selective, self-centered, self-confident, self-conscious, selfish, self-satisfied, self-sufficient, servile, shabby, shifty, shy, smug, sophisticated, spirited, spotless, sprightly, square, squeamish, stable, staid, stalwart, standoffish, stodgy, stoic/stoical, straight, stubborn, stuffy, suave, subservient, sweet, treacherous, trustworthy/trusty, unaffected, unapproachable, unassuming, unpretentious, unselfish, unsuspecting, unworthy, upright, vain, valiant, vigorous, virile, vivacious, vocal, warm, winning/winsome, wishy-washy, yielding, zealous

405 essential property of life forms: awkwardness, body, complexion, dotage, fatigue, hygiene, physique, sense, sensitivity

406 essential quality of life forms: adult, alimentary, animal, athletic, awake, awkward, barefoot, bearded, blank, bodily, breathless, brunette/brunet, bushy, buxom, cadaverous, corpulent, curly, curvaceous, dark, decrepit, drowsy, empty, exhausted, expectant, expressionless, fair, famished, fleshy, florid, full, gaunt, glassy, haggard, hairless, hairy, high, human, hungry, imperceptible, inborn/inbred, infertile, innate, insensitive, intestinal/intestine, intoxicated, intrinsic, jaded, light, limber, lumbering, piercing, predatory, pregnant, primitive, private, promising, prostrate, ravenous, raw, rich, sensitive, sensory, shapely, smooth, starving/starved, sweaty, tight, tipsy, tired, wild

407 existential state: be, being, casualty, coexistence, endure, exist, existence, flesh, gone, live, loss, manage, matter, mortality, nature, none, nothing/nothingness, oblivion, outlast, presence, reside, spirit, stand, subsist, survive, threaten, vitality, zero

408 gender: female, femininity/feminine, gender, male, masculinity/masculine

409 intelligence: acquaintance, acumen, anticipation, appreciation, apprehension, aptitude, attention, awareness, bent, brain, capacity, clairvoyance, clarity, cleverness, cognizance/cognition, common sense, comprehension, conception, consciousness, craft, dark, darkness, delusion, depth, dexterity, education, efficiency, empathy, enlightenment, erudition, experience, expertise/expertness, familiarity, fancy, feeling, finesse, foresight, forte, genius, gift, grasp, grip, head, idiocy, ignorance, illumination, imagination, innocence, insight, intellect, intelligence, intuition, invention, judgment, knack, know-how, knowledge, learning, light, literacy, memory, mentality, mind, misconception, misunderstanding, observation, originality, perception, proficiency, reason, sanity, sense, sensibility, skill, soul, thought, understanding, wisdom, wit/wits

410 mentality: absorption, abstraction, accession, ache, aggravation, agility, agonize, agony, alarm, alienation, alter ego, amazement, anger, anguish, anticipation, anxiety, apathy, application, assurance, astonishment, attention, attitude, attrition, avarice, awe, behalf,

belief, belonging, bigotry, bitterness, blues, boast, boredom, bosom, breakdown, breast, bristle, buoyancy/buoyance, capitulation, caprice, care, caution, censure, chagrin, cheer, clairvoyance, clemency, cogitation, collapse, comfort, compassion, complex, composure, compulsion, compunction, conception, concern, confusion, conquest, consideration, consolation, constancy, contemplation, content, contentment, contrition, conviction, corollary, credit, cult, curiosity, dark, darkness, daze, decision, defeat, deference, degradation, delight, delight in, delirium, delusion, dependence/dependency, depression, design, desolation, despair, desperation, difficulty, disability, disaffection, disappointment, discipline, discomfiture, discomfort, discontent, discouragement, discrimination, disgust, disinclination, dismay, disorder, displeasure, disquiet, dissatisfaction, distraction, distress, disturbance, doldrums, dolor, doubt, ease, ecstasy, elation, embarrassment, emotion, encouragement, enjoyment, ennui, envy, equanimity, euphoria, exaltation, exasperation, excitement, exhaustion, exhilaration, expectancy, expectation, exultation, fallacy, feeling, fever, firmness, fluster, fog, folly, forbearance, force, foresight, forethought, forgetfulness, fortitude, frazzle, free will, frenzy, fret, fright, frustration, fume, funk, furor, fury, gladness, glee, gloom, gratification, gratitude, grief, grieve, happiness, health, heart, heartbreak, heat, heaven, hesitation, hope, huff, humiliation, humor, hysteria, idiocy, imagination, impulse, indifference, indignity, insanity, insight, instability, introspection, ire, jitters, joy, kick, lament/lamentation, letdown, lethargy, levity, lunacy, malaise, mania, martyrdom, melancholy, merriment/merrymaking, mirth, mistake, monotony, mood, mope, morale, mourn, mourning, muddle, nausea, neglect, nerves, nervousness, neurosis, nostalgia, objection, oblivion, observance, observation, obsession, offense, optimism, originality, outlook, pain, panic, paradise, paroxysm, passion, pathos, peace, penance, penitence, perception, perspective, pessimism, pique, pity, pleasure, posture, pout, precaution, predisposition, premonition, presage, presence, presentiment, psyche, psychology, push, pussyfoot, qualm, quarter, rage, rancor, rapture, rave, regret, rejoice, remorse, repent, repentance, repose, repulse, resent, resentment, resignation, resistance, resolution, resolve, restlessness, retrospect, sadness, sanity, satisfaction, scare, security, self-satisfaction, sensation, sensibility, sensitivity, sentiment, seriousness, servitude, shame, simmer, slump, sob, solace, solicitude, sorrow, soul, state, stew, strain, strength, stress, subconscious, surprise, suspense, sympathy, tedium, telepathy, temper, temperament, temperance, tension, thought, tolerance, torment, torture, trance, transport, triumph, turn, umbrage, uncertainty, unrest, vanity, waver, woe, wonder, worry, wrath, zeal, zest

411 personality: aggression, ardor, arrogance, art, artifice, assumption, atrocity, attribute, audacity, backbone, bearing, being, best, bounce, bravery, buoyancy/buoyance, caliber, calm, candor, character, characteristic, charisma, charity, charm, complexion, compliance, conceit, confidence, constraint, courage, cultivation, dash, decision, dedication, demeanor, determination, dignity, disposition, disrepute, distinction, drive, effrontery, ego, egoism/egotism, élan, empathy, endowment, endurance, energy, enterprise, entity, essence, eye, failing, fiber, fight, fire, foible, forte, fortitude, frailty, gall, gallantry, generosity, geniality, gentility, go, goodness, good will/goodwill, greatness, grit, gumption, gusto, guts, heart, heroism, honor, humor, identity, idiosyncrasy, inclination, individuality, infamy, inhibition, initiative, innocence; integrity, kind, kink, laziness, life, loyalty, magnetism, makeup, manner, mark, martyrdom, mentality, mettle, mien, might, mold, mood, morale, morals, motivation, mystique, nature, nerve, notoriety, obedience, oddity, panache, patience, peculiarity, penchant, pep, perseverance, personality, pluck, point, possibilities, potency, presence, pride, probity, proclivity, propensity, property, prowess, psyche, push, qualify, quirk, reputation, responsibility, savor, self-respect/self-esteem, shortcoming, soul, sparkle, spirit, spunk, stability, stamina, stamp, style, taste, temerity, temper, temperament, tenacity, tend, thing, trait, trick, turn, twist, type, valor, vein, vice, vigor, virtue, vitality, way, weakness, will, willpower, wit, zeal, zest, zip

HUMANS

412 **bad person:** accessory, accomplice, addict, adversary, agitator, anarchist, antagonist, apostate, ass, assailant, assassin, authoritarian, bandit, barbarian, beggar, braggart, bum, bungler, burglar, cad, cannibal, captive, character, cheat, clod, clown, confederate, convict, criminal, critic, crook, culprit, cur, delinquent, demagogue, demon, derelict, deserter, desperado, despot, devil, dolt, dope, drone, dumbbell, dummy, dunce, enemy, exile, expatriate, failure, fake, felon, fiend, fighter, foe, fool, fraud, fugitive, gangster, glutton, good-for-nothing, gossip, grouch, hypocrite, idiot, imbecile, imp, impostor, incendiary, insurgent, interloper, intruder, joke, kook, liar, loafer, loser, lunatic, mad person, maniac, menace, mercenary, misanthrope, miscreant, miser, monster, murderer, nuisance, nut, oaf, ogre, outlaw, parasite, pawn, pervert, pessimist, pest, pill, prisoner, prodigal, profligate, prostitute, psychopath, quack, ragamuffin, rascal, rebel, renegade, robber, rogue, rowdy, runaway, sap, scapegoat, scoundrel, scum, showoff, sight, sneak, spy, swindler, tattletale/tattler, thief, tool, tough, traitor, tramp, troublemaker, tyrant, underworld, vandal, villain, wanton, weakling, witch

413 **community group member:** citizen, denizen, emigrant, foreigner, immigrant, inhabitant, local, migrant, native, newcomer, nomad, outsider, patriot, pioneer, plebeian, refugee, resident, rustic, stranger, subject, yokel

414 **family member:** ancestor, ancestry, antecedent(s), babe, baby, brother, child, descendant, domestic partner, father, fiancé/fiancée, forebearer, forerunner, guardian, heir, husband, hybrid, infant, issue, kid, kin, kindred, man, mother, nurse, occupant, offspring, orphan, owner, parent, partner, predecessor, progeny, relation, relative, scion, seed, senior, sister, spouse, surrogate, sweetheart, twin, ward, woman, young, youngster/youth

415 **female:** bachelor, bride, female, girl, girlfriend, mother, nymph, sister, wanton, wife, woman

416 **good person:** ace, angel, benefactor, expert, genius, hero/heroine, humanitarian, idealist, intellect, intellectual, intimate, missionary, peacemaker, pet, prodigy, pundit, savior, victor, virtuoso, visionary, wag, whiz, winner, wit

417 **group of people:** anybody, anyone, army, assemblage, attendance, audience, band, board, body, cadre, caucus, circle, civilization, class, clientele, clique, cloud, company, congregation, contingent, convention, corps, corpse, crew, crowd, crush, elite, enrollment, entourage, everybody/everyone, expedition, federation, field, flesh, following, force, gallery, gathering, horde, host, huddle, human, humankind, legion, masses, member, membership, mob, mortal, mortality, multitude, muster, outfit, pack, party, people, person, personnel, platoon, practice, public, set, society, squad, suite, swarm, team, throng, troop/troops, turnout

418 **limb or appendage:** ankle, beard, bosom, bottom, braid, breast, bristle, brow, can, cheek, coiffure, curl, elbow, features, pore, wrinkle

419 **male:** bachelor, boy, boyfriend, bridegroom, brother, escort, father, groom, husband, lad, male, man, wanton

420 **organ:** backbone, blood, bone, brain, heart, muscle, spine, stomach, vein

421 **racial group member:** kin, kindred, relation, tribe

422 **royalty:** crown, monarch, noble

423 **social group member:** acquaintance, addict, admirer, adventurer, advocate, alien, alliance, alter ego, another, apprentice, aristocracy, aristocrat, arrival, assistant, associate, augur, auxiliary, bachelor, beatnik, beau, beggar, beginner, believer, beloved, benefactor, beneficiary, bigot, boor, bore, boyfriend, braggart, brute, buddy, buff, buffoon, bully, bum, bungler, busybody, butt, bystander, captive, casualty, celebrity, chaperon, character, chicken, chum, churl, civilian, clairvoyant, clod, clown, cohort, collaborator, colleague, comedian, comic, companion, company, competitor, comrade, confidant, connection, conquest, consort, convoy, correspondent, couch potato, coward, craven, crony, cynic, darling, date, dear, derelict, deserter, devotee, diehard, dilettante, disciple, disciplinarian, dissident, dolt, donor, dope, doubter, driver, drunk/drunkard, dumbbell, dummy, dunce, dupe, eccentric, emigrant, emissary, enthusiast, entrant, epicurean,

equal, escort, exception, exile, expatriate, exponent, extremist, extrovert, eyewitness, failure, fan, father, favorite, fellow, fiancé/fiancée, fiend, figure, figurehead, flame, flirt, follower, fool, forerunner, fortune-teller, founder, freak, friend, gentleperson, girlfriend, go-between, gourmet, greenhorn, grouch, guardian, guest, guide, hanger-on, hedonist, herald, hermit, hostage, humanitarian, idealist, idol, inferior, informant/informer, interloper, intimate, introvert, intruder, jerk, jester, joke, joker, kook, layperson, liaison, local, loser, love, lover, luminary, machine, mad person, master, mate, maverick, mediator, miser, moron, mother, negotiator, neighbor, newcomer, noble, nobody/nonentity, nonconformist, notable, novice, nut, oddity/oddball, old hand, onlooker, original, outcast, outsider, pagan, pal, participant, partisan, partner, passenger, patrician, patron, pauper, peer, personage/personality, pessimist, philanderer, pill, pillar, plebeian, poet, prey, prophet, proponent, protagonist, pundit, puppet, pushover, ragamuffin, rebel, recluse, rich, rival, scream, second, sectarian, skeptic, snob, snoop, somebody, spectator, spendthrift, sponsor, sport, square, stick-in-the-mud, stranger, subject, subordinate, substitute, suitor, support/supporter, surrogate, sweetheart, sycophant, target, tattletale/

tattler, tenant, tool, tourist, traveler, umpire, underdog, urchin, vagabond, vagrant, veteran, victim, visitor, wag, waif, wanderer, weakling, witness, wizard, zany

424 traits: adolescent, adult, babe, baby, beauty, beginner, boy, brat, child, childish, dwarf, elder, eyeful, fledgling, freak, giant, girl, gnome, grown-up, infant, invalid, juvenile, kid, lad, midget, minor, nymph, runt, senior, vision, young, youngster/youth

PLANTS

425 flower: bloom, blossom, bouquet, flower

426 fruit: berry, fruit, produce

427 growth or death of: bloom, blossom, bud, develop, germinate, grow, growth, wilt, wither

428 part: bark, bough, branch, bud, fiber, flavoring, flower, foliage, fruit, grain, husk, juice, leaf, limb, log, nut, peel, pod, pulp, scion, seed, shell, skin, stalk, stem, trunk

429 plant: algae, bouquet, bramble, brush, bush, creation, crop, fertilizer, fossil, garland, grove, harvest, hedge, hybrid, nature, organism, plant, produce, vintage, wreath

430 tree: timber, tree, wood/woods

431 vegetable: produce, vegetable

Objects

ARTICLES. PHYSICAL

432 group of: accumulation, aggregate, amalgam, anthology, archive, armada, array, arsenal, assembly, assortment, backlog, bale, batch, battery, bevy, blend, body, bolt, bunch, bundle, cadre, canon, caravan, cavalcade, chain, clot, cloud, clump, cluster, clutter, collection, column, combination, compilation, complex, composite, compound, concentration, concoction, concourse, congestion, conglomeration, couple, crush, deluge, deposit, drift, drove, ensemble, everything, fleet, flock, fusion, group, hash, heap, herd, hodgepodge, host, huddle, jumble, junk, knot, litter, load, lot, lump, many, mass, medley, mélange, miscellany, mix/mixture, mob, mound, mountain, multitude, muster, number, odds and ends, pack, package, pair, parcel, party, patchwork, pile, pool, potpourri, press, queue, repertory, residue, row, score/scores, scramble, set, stack, stew, store, stuff, sum, surge, swarm, throng, train, tuft, unit, variety, wad, whole

433 object: anything, article, entity, fact, individual, loser, matter, object, something, substance, thing

434 part of: aspect, barb, carcass/carcase, compartment

435 place: asylum, barrier, base, center, depository, depot, dynasty, haunt, haven, heaven, hell, place

436 shape: angle, arc, arch, ball, bead, bend, bulb, bulge, check, circle, coil, cone, contortion, contour, convolution, corner, crescent, curl, curve, disk, dummy, effigy, elbow, globe, kink, knot, labyrinth, lap, line, loaf, loop, maze, mold, orb, orbit, outline, revolution, ring, rod, roll, round, shape, sphere, spiral, streak, wad, wave, wheel, whorl

ATMOSPHERE

437 air: air, atmosphere, billow, blast, breath, breeze, bubble, cloud, draft, dust, effervescence, firmament, fumes, lather, puff, sky, vapor

BUILDINGS. FURNISHINGS. POSSESSIONS

438 arena: aquarium, arena, bazaar, center, coliseum, dump, field, gymnasium, hall, stadium, stage

439 building: abbey, airport, architecture, archives, armory, arsenal, asylum, auditorium, bakery, bank, bar, barn, booth, building, cathedral, clinic, club, conservatory, construction, consulate, court, dock, domicile, edifice, embassy, enclosure, factory, food court, fort/fortress, fortification, framework, garage, gymnasium, hall, hangout, harbor, hospital, hotel, house, inn, installation, institute/institution, jail, joint, mall, mansion, mill, monastery, motel, museum, nightclub, office, outlet, pavilion, pen, penitentiary, pier, plant, post, prison, pub, rampart, restaurant, ruins, saloon, sanctuary, shop, shrine, stage, store, stronghold, structure, tavern, temple, theater/theatre, tower, treasury, warehouse, wharf

440 building part: aisle, alcove, annex, archway, attic, awning, balcony, basement, bay, belfry, bleachers, booth, buttress, canopy, ceiling, cellar, chimney, chute, closet, column, concourse, corner, corridor, cranny, den, department, dome, door, egress, entrance, entry, exit, fireplace, floor, foyer, gallery, gate, gutter, hall, niche, nook, partition, passage/passageway, pillar, platform, pole, post, prop, recess, screen, stack, stay, step, support, threshold, tower, vent, wall, wing

441 business place: agency, annex, building, bureau, factory, foyer, hall, lobby, office, shop, store, suite, wing

442 foundation: backbone, base, basis, bed, bottom, core, foot, footing, foundation, frame, groundwork, rest, rock, root, seat, stand, support

443 furniture: altar, antique, banister, bed, bench, bleachers, booth, buffet, bunk, bureau, cabinet, can, chair, cot, couch, cradle, crib, cupboard, fireplace, furniture, mirror, partition, pen, perch, pier, platform, podium, pulpit, rack, rail/railing, ramp, screen, seat, stand, table, wardrobe

444 furniture accessory: bedding, bedspread, candlestick, canopy, chandelier, curtain, cushion

445 furniture part: gate, handle, knob, latch, ledge, picket, pivot, post, quilt, screen, shade, shelf, stay, step, support, tap, valve

446 personal item: adornment, album, amulet, backpack, beads, belongings, bracelet, briefcase, brooch, cache, cargo, chain, charm, contraceptive, curio, disguise, doll, equipment, favorite, fetish, gem, glasses, goods, handbag, jewel, jewelry, keepsake, knickknack, lotion, luggage, makeup, memento, novelty, odds and ends, pack, paraphernalia, plaything, pledge, pocketbook, possession, pouch, pride, property, puppet, purchase, purse, relic, resources, riches, ring, savings, souvenir, stuff, subsistence, supplies, support, sustenance, thing/things, toy, trappings, treasure, trifle, trinket, valuable

447 recreation area: cabaret, casino, hangout, landmark

448 room: alcove, apartment, attic, auditorium, bath, bathroom, bedroom, cell, cellar, chamber, den, enclosure, food court, foyer, gallery, hall, kitchen, lobby, loft, office, outlet, parlor, pub, restaurant, room, saloon, sanctuary, shop, shrine, stage, store, tavern, theater/theatre, vestibule

449 workplace: bakery, base, bazaar, brothel, bureau, business, cabaret, café, canteen, capitol, church, clinic, conservatory, consulate, dairy, depot, diner, dive, dump, embassy, emporium, establishment, exchange, factory, farm, field, food court, gallery, garage, hangout, hospital, hotel, inn, jail, joint, lounge, madhouse, mall, market/mart, mill, mine, motel, museum, nightclub, office, outlet, penitentiary, plant, port, prison, pub, restaurant, saloon, shop, store, tavern, treasury, warehouse

CLOTHING

450 accessory: bag, bandanna, belt, boot, buckle, cap, collar, mask, pocketbook, pouch, purse

451 clothing: apparel, armor, array, attire, bathing suit, blouse, cape, cloak, clothes/clothing, coat, costume, disguise, dress, ensemble, finery, frock, garb, garment, gear, glove, gown, habit, hat, jacket, masquerade, nightgown, outfit, pajamas, pants, quilt, robe, skirt, suit, supplies, thing/things, trappings, underwear, uniform, veil, wardrobe, wash, wrap

452 part: collar, crease, crown, patch, pocket, seam, strand

453 state of dress: bareness, try on/try out, undress, wear

FOOD AND DRINK

454 beverage: alcohol, ale, beverage, brew, coffee, draft, drink

455 beverage, alcoholic: beer, liquor

456 change in: curdle, spoil, turn

457 food: appetizer, batter, bite, bread, brew, broth, bun, candy, casserole, confection, cracker, delicacy, diet, dish, doughnut, fare, food, frankfurter, game, grub, hamburger, helping, leftover, loaf, maintenance, meat, morsel, nourishment, nurture, nutrition, pancake, pastry, preserves, produce, ration, refreshment, seasoning, snack, stew, subsistence, supplies, support, sustenance, sweet, tart, treat

458 food part: morsel, nibble, nip, pat, taste, tidbit

459 meal: banquet, barbecue, bite, board, buffet, diet, dinner, fare, feast, meal, picnic, plate, snack, spread, table

460 produced from animal: dish, food, frankfurter, game, grub, hamburger, loaf, meat, stew

461 produced from plant: dish, doughnut, food, loaf, pancake, pastry, preserves, produce, seasoning, stew, sweet

462 quality of: acerbity, alcoholic, baked, crusty, done, eatable, edible, effervescent, mellow, natural, nourishing, nutritious, perishable, rancid, rare, raw, ripe, rotten, salty, short, sour, stale, straight, strong, succulent, sweet, tempting, unappetizing, unsavory, weak, wholesome

MACHINES

463 machine: alarm, apparatus, appliance, brake, catapult, clock, computer, contrivance, device, engine, fan, furnace, gadget, installation, instrument, jet, machine, machinery, mechanism, model, plant, television, terminal, watch

464 **machine part:** anchor, antenna, axle, bank, cog, cushion, engine, gear, pivot, pointer, tap, valve, vent, videocassette, wheel

MATTER. CONDITIONS OF

465 **gas:** gas, jet

466 **gel:** balm, batter, clot, cream, dip, gum, lotion, ointment, ooze, paste, plaster, salve

467 **liquid:** alcohol, broth, cream, drop, enamel, eruption, essence, flow, fluid, froth, fuel, gush, jet, juice, liquid, matter, milk, moisture, ooze, paint, potion, precipitation, solution, spit, surge, sweat, tear/tears, water

468 **liquid part:** cream, drop, froth

469 **physical change:** attrition, bubble, clot, cloud, coagulate, coagulation, collapse, color, congeal, consolidation, contraction, crack, crumble, cry, darken, decay, decompose, degeneracy, degenerate, dehydrate, die, discolor, disintegrate, dissipate, dissolution, dissolve, distend, dry, eat, erode, evaporate, evaporation, exhaust, fade, fester, fizz, flake, flare, flatten, fluctuate, flush, foam, foul, fragment, give, glow, go out, grow, growth, harden, heat, jell, languish, metamorphose, metamorphosis, open, ossify, perspire, putrefy, ravel, redden, revive, rot, rust, settle, sink, spoil, stiffen, tarnish, thaw, thicken, tighten, tire, turn, wilt

470 **solid:** band, bar, barricade, barrier, baton, block, blockade, bolt, brace, bulge, cake, cast, clot, club, clump, cord, dam, deposit, fossil, glass, hedge, hunk, hurdle, ice, jump, lump, matter, mirror, monument, obstacle, obstruction, partition, pill, pole, post, prop, rock, rod, stick, wand, weight

471 **solid part:** arm, attachment, back, bar, beam, block, bolt, branch, chunk, chute, closure, corner, deposit, flap, hinge, hump, hunk, knob, knot, leg, ligature, link, lump, node/nodule, nub, nugget, outgrowth, patch, plug, powder, projection, protuberance, ridge, rung, seam, slab, sliver, splinter, stake, strap, strip, support, tuft, wedge

MATTER. DIVISIONS OF

472 **chemical:** alkali, alkaline, ammonia, antiseptic

473 **fabric:** apparel, awning, bedding, blanket, canvas, carpet, cloth, fabric, flag, lace, nap, net, pad/padding, pennant, quilt, screen, web, yarn

474 **gem:** gem, jewel, rock, stone

475 **material:** appointment, binding, blanket, brace, cast, cement, cloak, coat, coating, glaze, glue, lace, leash, line, material, pad/padding, pad, page, paint, paper, patchwork, pipe, plaster, plate, poison, pole, rope, sheet, slip, standard, strand, strap, string, tab, tablet, tack, tag, tape, tether, trim, twine, wash

476 **metallic:** alloy, armor, badge, can, chain, fence, iron, medal, metal, ornament

477 **mineral:** rock, stone

478 **natural element:** blaze, carbohydrate, cell, conflagration, embers, ferment, film, fire, flame, jewel, rock, substance

479 **wood:** beam, board, cane, coffin, fence, framework, log, paddle, perch, picket, pier, pole, post, rack, rail/railing, rod, splinter, staff, stake, stick, timber

MATTER, QUALITIES OF

480 **balance:** awkward, dizzy, even, lopsided, odd, proportionate/proportional, smooth, symmetrical, unbalanced, unequal, uneven

481 **capacity:** brimming/brimful, capacious, capacity, close, compact, congested, crowded, empty, full, packed, spacious, teeming, vacant, void

482 **continuity:** broken, connected, continuous, direct, disconnected, discontinuous, disjointed, dragging, durable, endless, entire, episodic, eternal, fitful, flowing, indelible, intermittent, lengthy, long, never-ending, nonstop, numberless, old, ongoing, patchy, perfect, running, sequential, serial, solid, spacious, spasmodic, straight, through, throughout, together, unbroken, undivided, unending, unfathomable, uninterrupted

483 **density:** airtight, anemic, close, compact, concentrated, congested, cramped, crowded, dense, devoid, fraught, full, hollow, impenetrable, packed, replete, solid, teeming, thick, tight

484 **exteriority:** adjunct, adornment, annex, border, bound/bounds, boundary, brink, buffer, circuit, circumference, compass, confines, corner, cover, crust, cushion, edge, exterior, extreme, extremity, face, fringe, hem, horizon, hull, husk, jacket, lip, margin, membrane, outer, outside, peel, perimeter, periphery, pod, revolution, rim, scale, sheet, shell, skin, skirt, surface, verge

485 **physical:** ablaze, acid, acute, adulterated, aesthetic/esthetic, agile, alimentary, antiseptic, atomic, austere, bad, bald, bare, barren, bearded, beautiful, bland, blank, bloody, blunt, brawny, broken, burning, caustic, clean, combustible, comfortable, corrugated, corrupt, cozy, crippled, crumbly, cuddly, curable, damaged, decayed, decrepit, deformed, deserted, desolate, devoid, dilapidated, diluted/dilute, dingy, dirty, disgusting, disheveled, disordered, disorderly, disorganized, disrepair, done in, drained, drawn, droopy, dusty, effervescent, enervated, erect, exhausted, expectant, exposed, failing, faint, fallow, fat, fatigued, fatty, fertile, filthy, fireproof, fit, flaccid, flaming, flammable, flexible, foamy, forked, formless, foul, fragile, frail, free, fresh, frothy, game, gaping, ghastly, ghostly, gnarled, good, green, grimy, grubby, gruesome, hardy, immature, impaired, impalpable, impervious, impotent, inchoate, inconspicuous, incorruptible, incurable, indistinct, infirm, inflammable, insubstantial, intact, invisible, irreparable, laden, leafy, lean, lifeless, liquid, livable, loathsome, loose, lusty, magnificent, malleable, mangy, marked, material, mature, mean,

messy, mild, miserable, mixed, muddy, muscular, naked, nasty, natural, neat, neutral, noxious, nude, oblique, obtuse, obvious, open, orderly, outstanding, palatial, palpable, palsied, paltry, paralytic, pathetic, peaceful, pendulous/pendent, perfect, perishable, perverted, physical, piteous, pitiful, placid, plain, pregnant, premature, prepared, prickly, primitive, prolific, prominent, prostrate, puffy, pure, putrid, quizzical, ragged, rambling, ramshackle, rank, raw, rocky, rotten, rough, run-down, rusty, savage, scenic, scruffy, seedy, serene, shabby, shady, shaggy, shoddy, slack, sleazy, slimy, slipshod, slovenly, smoky, snug, soft, somber, sorry, speckled, splendid, squalid, stale, stark, sterile, stony, sumptuous, surface, swollen, symmetrical, synthetic, tacky, tense, thin, thorny, threadbare, tidy, tight, topsy-turvy, torn, tousled, trim, unblemished, unbroken, uncomfortable, undeveloped, unfinished, unkempt, untouched, upset, vague, verdant, visual, voluptuous, watery, weak, weary, whole, wizened, wooden, worn/worn-out

486 **shape:** angular, baggy, beaten, bent, billowy, blunt, checkered, circular, concave, conical/conic, convex, crescent, crooked, curly, curved, deformed, dull, elliptical, flabby, flat, flush, gnarled, grotesque, kinky, mal-formed, oblong, obtuse, oval, round, serrated, shapeless, sharp, spiral, square, straight

487 **similarity:** akin, alike, analogous, approximate, closely, cognate, comparable, comparative, conformable, different, equal, equivalent, faithful, homogenous, identical, interchangeable, like, parallel, related, representative, same, seeming, similar, synonymous, tantamount, twin, uniform, virtual, virtually

488 **stability:** adhesive, adrift, brittle, choppy, doddering, ductile, durable, fast, firm, firmly, fixed, flexible, hard, immobile, immovable, insecure, limber, lithe, motionless, movable, moving, pliable, ramshackle, resilient, rickety, rocky, secure, set, shaky, soft, solid, sound, stable, stationary, steady, sturdy, supple, sure, taut, tenacious, tractable, unbreakable, unstable/unsteady, unwavering, weak, wobbly, wooden, yielding

489 **strength:** able-bodied, athletic, brawny, breakable, brute, durable, failing, feeble, firmly, flimsy, fragile, frail, full-bodied, hale, hardy, indestructible, indomitable, infirm, invincible, lame, leathery, lusty, mighty, muscular, potent, powerful, powerless, puny, resilient, robust, rocky, rugged, stalwart, stout, strapping, strong, sturdy, tenacious, tenuous, tight, tough, unbreakable, vigorous, weak

490 **structure:** airtight, airy, amorphous, bare, beaten, bleak, blind, budding, cavernous, clean-cut, clear, cleft, composite, conglomerate, craggy, crooked, curvaceous, curved, dainty, delicate, depressed, detached, diaphanous, ductile, elastic, emaciated, even, flabby, flat, flush, gaping, gaunt, hollow, incarnate, irregular, jagged, level, limp, oblique, plane, pointed, precipitous, rude,

rugged, scrawny, shapely, sheer, skinny, slender/slim, spare, stout, stringy, svelte, trim, wiry

491 **weight:** bantam, beaten, buoyant, cadaverous, chubby, chunky, corpulent, dainty, emaciated, ethereal, fat, fine, fleshy, gargantuan, gaunt, giant, gigantic, haggard, heavy, hefty, lanky, lean, light, lightweight, lithe, meager, obese, overweight, plump, ponderous, portable, portly, pudgy, rangy, round, scrawny, skinny, slender/slim, slight, spare, squat, stocky, stout, stubby, svelte, tenuous, thick, thin, trim, underweight, weighty, wiry

TOOLS

492 **cleaner:** antiseptic, cleanser, deodorant, polish

493 **cooking:** barbecue, bowl, china, pan, plate, scoop, utensil

494 **container:** bag, baggage, barrel, basin, basket, bottle, bowl, box, briefcase, bucket, cabinet, cage, can, canteen, carton, case, cask, casket, cell, chamber, chest, coffer, coffin, container, crate, cup, dish, envelope, flask, glass, hamper, jar, jug, keg, kit, luggage, main, package, packet, pan, parcel, portfolio, pot, pottery, pouch, purse, receptacle, store, trunk, vault, vessel

495 **cutting:** blade, chisel, knife

496 **equipment:** equipment, gear, harness, installation, kit, outfit, pack, paraphernalia, plant, rig, tackle, trappings

497 **grasping:** bond, bridle, catch, clasp, curb

498 **part:** ammunition, hinge, hook, pivot, pointer, round, shot

499 **tool:** apparatus, ax/axe, blade, brace, broom, brush, cart, chain, chisel, clamp, club, conduit, connection, contrivance, device, drill, gadget, hardware, implement, instrument, key, knife, latch, lock, mop, organ, paddle, pen, pipe, rein, ruler, scoop, tool, utensil, valve, wand, wedge, whip

500 **weapon:** ammunition, armament(s), arms, artillery, atom bomb, baton, battery, bomb, bullet, catapult, cudgel, defense, explosive, fetters, gun, magazine, missile, nuclear weapon, round

TRANSPORTATION

501 **object used for:** access, alley, approach, artery, avenue, boulevard, bridge, career, channel, circuit, concourse, conduit, conveyance, course, crossing, detour, diversion, drain, duct, expressway, highway, intersection, line, passage/passageway, path, road, route, street, track, trail, walk, way

502 **part, vehicle:** anchor, bow, fender, handle, portal, trunk, wheel, wing

503 **vehicle:** caravan, conveyance, jet, transport, vehicle

504 **vehicle, air:** airplane, armada, balloon, craft, plane

505 **vehicle, land:** ambulance, automobile, bicycle, cab, car, cart, coach, hack, model, traffic, truck

506 **vehicle, water:** armada, barge, boat, canoe, craft, ferry, fleet, sailboat, vessel, yacht

The Planet

GEOGRAPHY

507 **city:** capital, center, city, town, village
508 **geographic division:** area, country, county, department, desert, district, dynasty, grounds, kingdom, land, outskirts, province, quarter, region, sector, state, suburb, terrain, territory, town, tract, ward, zone
509 **land:** abyss, avalanche, backwoods, bank, basin, bay, beach, bed, bluff, bog, canyon, cape, cave, cavern, clay, cliff, coast, compost, court, cove, crevice/crevasse, culvert, dirt, ditch, downgrade, drop, earth, elevation, eminence, excavation, expanse, farm, field, forest, fossil, frontier, garden, geography, glacier, glen, gorge, green, ground, gulf, gully, harbor, hill, horizon, inlet, island, land, landscape, lawn, lot, marsh, meadow, mine, mire, morass, mound, mountain, nature, outlook, parcel, park, pass, peak, pit, plain, plateau, plaza, plot, port, precipice, projection, property, prospect, quagmire, rampart, ravine, reef, ridge, rock, shelf, shore, soil, square, stack, swamp, table, terrain, trench, trough, tunnel, valley, waste, well, wood/woods, yard
510 **nation:** country, home, kingdom, land, nation, nationality, soil, state
511 **planet:** cosmos, Earth, environment, globe, moon, nature, planet, soil, sphere, universe, world
512 **region:** capital, colony, commonwealth, community, quarter, realm, region, reservation, settlement, suburb
513 **section:** aisle, alcove, backyard, barrier, beat, bed, belt, berth, blank, border, breach, brink, canyon, cavity, cell, chasm, clearance, clearing, cleavage, cleft, corner, country, county, court, crack, cranny, crevice/crevasse, crossing, den, depression, dip, ditch, edge, enclosure, excavation, expanse, fracture, frontier, furrow, gap, green, groove, gulf, gully, gutter, hem, hole, hump, interstice, lawn, leak, ledge, limit, lip, margin, marginal, mouth, niche, nook, notch, opening, outlet, outskirts, parcel, park, pass, patch, pit, plaza, plot, pocket, precipice, projection, prominence, puncture, ravine, recess, rent, repair, ridge, rift, rip, rupture, rut, scratch, shelf, side, sight, slack, slit, slot, split, subdivision, tear, threshold, track, tract, trench, trough, tunnel, vacancy, vacuum, valley, void, ward, well, wrinkle, yoke, zone
514 **water:** abyss, aquarium, aqueduct, arm, basin, bay, beach, billow, brine, brook, canal, cape, cascade, channel, coast, condensation, course, creek, current, deep, fountain, gulf, harbor, ice, inlet, lake, ocean, pond, pool, race, reservoir, sea, spray, spring, strait, stream, tide, wash, wave, well, whirlpool

HABITATS

515 **habitat:** abode, asylum, environment, habitat/habitation, harbor, haven, home, lair, land, oasis, paradise, place, premises, property, refuge, sanctuary, settlement, shelter
516 **habitat, human:** accommodations, address, apartment, asylum, barracks, berth, cabin, camp, castle, cloister, condominium, convent, cottage, domicile, dwelling, element, embassy, environs, estate, flat, grange, grounds, haunt, home, hotel, house, household, housing, hovel, hut, inn, jail, lodge, lodging, madhouse, mansion, monastery, motel, neighborhood, palace, penitentiary, prison, quarters, reservation, residence, resort, retreat, sanctuary, suite, vacancy
517 **habitat, rural:** barn, belt, burrow, cobweb, conservatory, dairy, desert, desolation, farm, field, forest, garden, grange, grove, jungle, lawn, sanctuary, wilderness/wilds, wood/woods
518 **state of:** domain, eco-rich, entrench, occupancy, occupation, presence

NATURAL RESOURCES

519 **electricity:** beam, current, spark
520 **energy:** electricity, energy, fuel, power
521 **expression of energy:** blast, blaze, boom, chill, combustion, concussion, crash, discharge, explosion, fire, flame, flash, freeze, noise, thunder
522 **natural event:** eclipse, effervescence, weather
523 **resources:** fuel, material, resource, resources, rock, substance

WEATHER

524 **object connected with:** avalanche, blast, breeze, chill, climate, cloud, cold, deluge, drift, film, flood, flurry, fog, frost, gale, gust, hail, haze, humidity, hurricane, mist, moisture, precipitation, puff, thunder, vapor, weather, wind
525 **quality of:** breezy, bright, clear, clement, close, cloudy, crisp, dirty, dismal, dreary, fair, fierce, fiercely, filmy, fine, foggy, furious, gentle, gloomy, gusty, hazy, heavy, humid, inclement, mild, misty, muggy, oppressive, overcast, raw, rough, rugged, soft, sticky, stormy, stuffy, sultry, sunny, temperate, tempestuous, thick, threatening, tranquil, tropical, turbulent, violent, wild, windy, wintry
526 **type of:** blizzard, blow, cloud, downpour, drizzle, earthquake, fog, gale, hail, hurricane, mist, precipitation, puff, quake, rain, shade, storm, tempest, thunder, torrent, tremor

Qualities

ABSTRACT

527 ability: able, accountable, adept, adroit, agile, artistic, awkward, barren, capable, commendable, competent, deft, dexterous, dilettante, disabled, effete, efficient, eligible, executive, experienced, expert, facile, feeble, gifted, good, great, handy, inapt, incapable, incompetent, inefficient, inept, inexperienced, master, masterful, neat, nimble, powerful, powerless, practical, professional, proficient, qualified, raw, ready, rusty, short, skillful, unable, unaccustomed, unfit, unprofessional, unqualified, versatile, versed, veteran, well, wicked

528 achievement: able, abortive, accomplished, ace, artful, attainable, complete, consummate, crack, defensible, done, effectual, efficacious, feasible, fine, finished, flourishing, forward, fruitful, fruitless, futile, gifted, great, obtainable, possible, potential, practical, professional, proficient, prosperous, successful, swimmingly, thriving, triumphant, victorious, well, winning

529 cognitive: academic, affective, afraid, afterthought, alternative, amicable, anathema, appalling, attractive, axiomatic, bad, bag, balm, bane, bearable, belief, black, boring, bothersome, breast, breathtaking, burdensome, cheering, chimera, comforting, comic/comical, comparison, complex, comprehensible, conceivable, considered, considering, corollary, crazy, daydream, deducible, deep, demonstrable, deplorable, depressing, derivable, desirous, detestable, dialectic, difficult, discouraging, disputable, disquieting, distasteful, doleful, doubtful, dream, dry, dull, elusive, enchanting, engrossing, enigmatic/enigmatical, equivocal, esoteric, evident, exalted, exciting, exhilarating, explicit, fabulous, fanciful, fantasy, far-fetched, fascinating, favored, favorite, fearful, fetish, figment, flat, fleshly, forerunner, forgotten, foul, frightful/frightening, frightful, funny, ghastly, glad, golden, good, grating, half-baked, hallucination, harbinger, hard, harebrained, harrowing, hazy, heady, heartbreaking, heinous, heretical, hilarious, hopeless, horizon, horrible/horrendous/horrid, humorous, hypnotic, hypothetical, idea, ideal, idyllic, illogical, illusory/illusive, image, imaginable, imaginary, imaginative, impalpable, impenetrable, impression, inadvisable, incomprehensible, inconceivable, incredible, incredulous, indelible, inexplicable, inner, innovation, innovative, inscrutable, inside, insoluble, inspiration, instinct, insufferable, intelligible, interesting, intimate, intolerable, inviting, inward, irrational, irrefutable, irresistible, itch, jocular/jocose/jocund, joy, knotty, knowledge, known, lamentable, leery, left, liberal, liking, limit, loathsome, logical, loose, lucid, luminous, lure, mad, make-believe, mania, manifest, marvel, marvelous, matter, maudlin, maze, measurable, memorable, memory, metaphysical, miraculous, mirage, mistaken, mode, monotonous, moving, mysterious, mystic/mystical, naked, nauseous, new age, nondescript, nostalgic, note, noticeable, notion, obscure, observable, obsession, obvious, offensive, opaque, open, painful, palatable, palpable, panorama, pathetic, pedagogic, pedantic, perceptible, perspicuous, pesky, phantom, phenomenon, phobia, pick, piquant, piteous, pitiful, plain, plaintive, poignant, pointless, politically correct, ponderous, portent, precious, preference, premise, premonition, preposterous, presage, problem, problematic, profound, provocative, psychedelic, pure, purposely, putative, puzzling, questionable, radical, rather, reactionary, readable, reasoning, rebellious, recall, recondite, remembrance, reminder, reminiscent, repulsive, reputed, reverie, revolting, rich, ridiculous, right, rosy, rot, sad, satisfactory, scary, scintillating, scream, scrumptious, secret, secular, selection, self-evident/self-explanatory, sensation, shock, sickening, sign, signal, simple, slight, slow, snare, somber, sorry, sound, spectacle, spectacular, speculation, spooky, strain, subconscious, subject, subjective, suggestion, suggestive, surmise, surprise, suspect, suspicion, suspicious, tacit, tall, tame, tangible, taste, tasteful, tedious, temptation, tempting, tenor, theorem, theoretical, theory, thesis, thick, thing, thinkable, thought, thrill, tinge, tiresome, token, tolerable, touch, touching, trace, treat, troublesome, unacceptable, unaccountable, unappetizing, unbelievable, uncertain, uncomfortable, undecided, understood, undesirable, unfathomable, unfavorable, ungodly, unimaginable, uninteresting, unlucky, unnoticed, unpleasant, unpopular, unquestionable, unresolved, unsatisfactory, untold, unwelcome, vague, vapid, vexatious, vile, visible, vision, visionary, whim, whisper, wonder, wonderful

530 commonality: accidental, antiquated, antique, automatic, banal, bourgeois, common, commonly, commonplace, conventional, current, customarily, customary, diffuse, dogmatic, dull, everyday, fair, familiar, frequent, frequently, general, generally, generic, habitual, hackneyed, infrequent, lay, less, little, mainly, much, musty, natural, occasional, occasionally, old, ordinarily, ordinary, pedestrian, popular, prevailing, prevalent, proverbial, public, rare, rarely, regular, routine, spasmodic, stereotyped, stock, traditional, trite, typical, ubiquitous, usual, usually, vulgar, widespread

531 completeness: absolutely, all-out, almost, altogether, blank, bodily, capsule, clean, complete, completely, comprehensive, conscientious, crowning, dead, deeply, deficient, definitive, demonstrative, done, downright, entire, entirely, every, exhaustive, fatal, final, finished, fulfilled, full, full-scale, fully, halfway, incomplete, inseparable, intact, integral, intensive, outright, over, partial, partially, partly, past, perfectly, piecemeal, plenary, practically, pretty, primarily, principally, profound, pure, purely, quite, rank, right, rough, round, rude, sheer, simply, sketchy, sloppy, solid, stark, superficially, sweeping, thorough/thoroughgoing, thoroughly, through, throughout, total, totally, unabridged, unconditional, undivided, unfinished, unmitigated, unqualified, utmost, utter, utterly, wanting, whole, wholly

532 concerned with: about, anxiety, appertain, apply, apropos, barrier, bear on/bear upon, beat, behalf, behind, belong, bother, bug, burden, business, care, challenge, charge, compulsion, concept, concern, consideration, conundrum, craze, debate, difficulty, discovery, disputation, disquiet, distraction, distress, ear, enigma, fancy, fascination, feeling, fixation, focus, guilt, hallucination, hang-up, heed, horror, include, interest, issue, keynote/keystone, matter, mystery, notice, notion, object, obstacle, obstruction, pain, paradox, part, particular, passion, peeve, pertain, pivot, place, presentiment, priority, problem, province, provocation, qualm, quandary, question, refer, regard, relate, reverie, riddle, scruple, subject, suspicion, taboo, temptation, topic, touch, toward/towards, trouble, urge, vision, weight, woe, wonder, worry

533 conformity: acceptable, adequate, admissible, befitting, classic, decent, formal, ideal, mediocre, medium, moderate, ordinary, orthodox, practical, proper, regular, so-so, standard, traditional, typical, unwritten

534 constancy: ambivalent, arbitrary, borderline, changeable, chronic, consistent, constant, continual, fickle, firmly, fitful, fluid, forever, formative, frozen, grim, halting, hesitant, immovable, immutable, impervious, incessant, inconsistent, indecisive, indestructible, indomitable, inexorable, insistent, intermittent, intractable/intransigent, invariable, inveterate, iron, irregular, irrevocable, monotonous, relentless, rigid, same, severe, slippery, solid, spotty, static, staunch, steadfast, steady, tentative, unbending, uncertain, unchangeable, unchanging, unfailing, uniform, unpredictable, unresolved, unstable/unsteady, variable, volatile, wanton

535 definiteness: absolute, absolutely, accurate, aimless, airtight, ambiguous, apparent, apparently, assured, automatic, canonical, categorical, certain, certainly, clean, clean-cut, clear-cut, clearly, close, complete, conclusive, concrete, conscious, controversial, debatable, decided, decidedly, decisive, definite, definitely, definitive, demonstrable, designedly, dicey, discernible, disordered, disorderly, disputable, distinct, doubtful, doubtless, dubious, easily, elective, emphatic, entirely, equivocal, erratic, especial, especially, evident, evidently, exact, exactly, experimental, explicit, express, expressly, factual, final, finally, finite, fixed, flat, formless, graphic, gross, guaranteed, haphazard, hard, hard-core, hesitant, illegible, impeccable, implicit, implied, inalienable, incalculable, incontrovertible, indecisive, indeed,

indefinite, indeterminate, indisputable, indistinct, inevitable, infallible, ingrained, intangible, irrefutable, irresolute, just, legible, limpid, main, marked, markedly, mere, moot, nebulous, necessarily, necessary, official, only, open, outright, overt, palpable, pat, peremptory, perfect, plain, positive, positively, precarious, precise, precisely, pronounced, pure, questionable, random, rank, really, reliable, right, rigid, rigorous, scientific, secure, seriously, set, shaky, sharp, sheer, simply, slippery, sound, specific, straight, straightforward, strict, stringent, strong, sure, surely, tenebrous, tentative, thorough/thoroughgoing, thoroughly, tried, true, truly, trustworthy/trusty, ultimate, unavoidable, uncertain, unconditional, undeniable, undependable, undisputed/undisputable, undoubtedly, unequivocal, unerring, unfailing, unfaltering, unmistakable, unmitigated, unqualified, unquestionable, unsettled, unsure, unwavering, utter, verbatim, very, willful, yes

536 domain: absolute, academic, administrative, agrarian, agricultural, aquatic, athletic, authoritative, autocratic, blessed, bridal, captive, celestial, chemical, city, civic, civil, classical, clerical, commanding, commercial, communal, confederate, constituent, country, democratic, dismal, domestic, drab, earthly, economic, fleshly, foreign, free, global, home, household, industrial, infernal, internal, international, itinerary, literary, local, marine/maritime, metropolitan, military, municipal, national, native, nautical/naval, nomadic, pedagogic, personal, prevalent, psychological, public, religious, social, sovereign, spiritual, technical, terrestrial, theatrical, theological, totalitarian, unearthly, universal, unworldly, urban, widespread, worldly, worldwide

537 effects: advisory, aphrodisiac, awesome, awry, bad, baleful, baneful, beastly, benign, bitter, bleak, bracing, bright, burning, calamitous, cogent, combustible, coming, consequent, convincing, corrective, corrosive, costly, cultural, curative, damaging, deadly, deathly, deep, defamatory, deleterious, demonstrative, desperate, destined, destructive, detrimental, dire, direful, disadvantageous, disagreeable, disastrous, disruptive, done by, doomed, dramatic, drastic, dread, dreadful, eclectic, ecumenical, eerie, effective, effectual, efficacious, embarrassing, emergent, entertaining, epidemic, exigent, expressive, extenuating, faint, fatal, fateful, favorable, favorably, fearful, fecund, fetching, fierce, fiercely, flat, fooled, forbidding, forcible, foreign, formative, formidable, fortunately, foul, fresh, frightful/frightening, fruitful, fruitless, fun, funereal, funny, furious, general, gentle, ghastly, ghostly, gloomy, good, gory, grateful, grave, greatly, grievous, grisly, gross, grotesque, harmful, harmless, harsh, healthful/healthy, heartbreaking, heavenly, helpful, hideous, highly, horrible/horrendous/horrid, hurtful, hypnotic, ill, ill-fated/ill-starred, imperceptible, imposing, incendiary, inconclusive, inconvenient, ineffective/ineffectual, inflammatory, influential, inimical, injurious, insipid, insufferable, intoxicating, invigorating, inviting, jazzy, juicy, lamentable, lethal, lovely, lucky, lurid, macabre, madly, magic/magical, magnetic, malign, memorial, menacing, mighty, mild, monstrous, morbid, mortal, moving, narcotic, nasty, neutral, noisome, nondescript, noticeable, nourishing, noxious, offensive, oppressive, outstanding, painful, pale, penetrating, peremptory, pernicious, persuasive, pesky, pestilent/pestilential, piercing, pleasing/pleasurable, poison/poisonous, prejudicial, prepossessing, productive, profitable, prosaic, provocative, psychedelic, remedial, right, rugged, ruinous, safe, sedative, sensational, sensuous, sharp, sick, sickly, slow, soft, soporific, spectacular, spooky, strong, subtle, telling, therapeutic, tiresome, touching, toxic, trenchant, unbearable, uncanny, uncomfortable, unhealthy, unholy, vapid, venomous, vexatious, virtual, virulent, vivid, weak, wholesome, wicked

538 efforts: ambitious, applied, assiduous, automated, automatic, concerted, conscientious, cooperative, difficult, diligent, employed, gladly, go-ahead, hard, heavy, idle, indolent, industrious, labored, laborious, laden, light, lightly, mindless, murderous, onerous, painstaking, persistent, religious, rugged, running, scrupulous, serious, simple, slack, slow, straightforward, strenuous, studied, studious, thankless, thorough/thoroughgoing, thoroughly, tireless, tiresome, together, torpid, tough, unemployed, unfailing, unfaltering, unflagging, unpaid, unprofessional, unsolicited, untiring, uphill, valiant, vicarious, voluntarily, voluntary, weighty, workable, working

539 existential: alive, almighty, animate, comatose, conscious, consist, dead, deadly, deceased, defunct, dormant, drowsy, dying, extant, extinct, fallen, fatal, immaterial, immortal, inanimate, incarnate, late, lifeless, live, living, lost, luxuriate, missing, nil, nonexistent, obsolete, out, perennial, present, sleepy, soporific, unconscious, vagabond, vital, wakeful

540 forcefulness: almighty, bang, blatant, bloody, brute, cumulative, desperate, driving, dynamic, effective, electric/electrical, fierce, fiercely, hard, insistent, invincible, madly, mightily, mighty, potent, powerful, powerfully, savage, stiff, strong, violent

541 frequency: annual, annually, casual, commonly, daily, hardly, nightly, occasional, occasionally, often, periodic, rapid, rarely, recurrent, scarce, scarcely, seldom, spasmodic, sporadic, uncommonly, usually, yearly

542 inclination: abrupt, accommodating, acquisitive, active, addicted, adrift, adventurous, affirmative, aggressive, agreeable, alive, aloof, ambitious, amicable, anxious, apt, arbitrary, arid, assiduous, base, beastly, benign, blindly, brisk, busy, careful, carefully, careless, casual, characteristic, charitable, cheap, co-dependent, cold-blooded, competitive, conducive, confirmed, conflicting, conservative, conspicuous, constant, contradictory, corporal, corporeal, correct,

crack, creditable, curious, decent, dedicated, deep, deliberate, deliberately, delicate, delicately, demanding, dependable, derelict, designing, determined, detestable, devoted, devout, dictatorial, die-hard, difficult, dilatory, diligent, dim, diplomatic, dirty, discriminating, disinclined, disingenuous, disposed, disputatious, distrustful, dogged, dogmatic, domestic, doubtful, dour, downtrodden, dull, dutiful, dynamic, eager, earnest, earthy, easy, economical, effervescent, effusive, elusive, emotional, emotionless, energetic, engaged, engrossed, enterprising, enthusiastic, equable, equal, equitable, errant, erratic, evasive, even, exact, exaggerated, exciting, execrable, exigent, exotic, expeditious, explosive, factious, fair, fairly, fallible, farcical, fast, fastidious, feckless, ferocious, fervent/fervid, fiery, firm, firmly, flexible, fluid, fly-by-night, fond, foolish, foolishly, forbearing, forced, fortunate, frantic, free, frenzied, fresh, frisky, frolicsome, funereal, gaily, gallant, gay, generous, gentle, genuine, gingerly, given to, gladly, go-ahead, godless, godly, good, gracious, grandiose, grasping, gratuitous, greedy, gross, guarded, guileless, gullible, gutless, gutsy, half-hearted, happily, happy-go-lucky, hard, hardcore, hardened, hard-nosed/hardheaded, harsh, hasty, headlong, heartless, hearty, helpless, hesitant, hospitable, hostile, humane, humanitarian, hurtful, hypocritical, hysterical, idle, ignoble, ignorant, imaginative, immersed, impartial, impassive, impatient, impersonal, impetuous, implacable, improper, improvident, imprudent, impulsive, inadvertent, inane, inattentive, incautious, indefatigable, indifferent, indignant, indiscriminate, indisposed, indolent, indulgent, inelegant, inert, infant/infantile, inflammatory, ingenuous, inhibited, innocent, inoffensive, inquiring, insecure, insidious, insincere, insouciant, intent, intolerant, intractable/intransigent, inventive, involved, irate, jaundiced, jealous, jolly, joyful/joyous, joyless, judicious, kind, kindhearted, kindly, kinky, lackadaisical, lackluster, languid, lax, lenient, levelheaded, lewd, liable, liberal, lifeless, light, lighthearted, live, lively, livid, loath, loud, loving, low, low-key, lukewarm, magnanimous, malevolent, malicious, malign, materialistic, maudlin, mawkish, mean, melodramatic, merciful, merciless, meretricious, methodical/methodic, meticulous, mindful, mushy, naive, narrow, narrow-minded, neat, neglectful, negligent, nerveless, nervous, neutral, nonchalant, noncommittal, noncompliant, nonconformist, nonpartisan, obdurate, objective, objectively, oblivious, obnoxious, obstinate, obtrusive, occupied, odd/oddball, offhand, open, opposed/opposing, opprobrious, optimistic, overconfident, overwrought, pagan, parental, parochial, partial, particular, partisan, passionate, passive, patient, peaceful, peevish, penitent, peppery, perceptive, peremptory, perfunctory, persuasive, perverse, petulant, philanthropic, pigheaded, plastic, playful, pleasant, politically correct, pompous, ponderous, poor, practical, pragmatic, precipitous/precipitate, precise, predictable, premature, premeditated, prepossessed, presumptuous, pretentious, productive, progressive, prolific, prone, prostrate, protective, proud, prudent, pugnacious, punctilious, purposeful, quarrelsome, querulous, radical, raging, rambunctious, reactionary, ready, realistic, rebellious, reckless, reliable, renegade, resigned, resolute, responsive, restive, restless, restrained, rival, romantic, sadistic, safe, sanguine, sappy, savage, scheming, scrupulous, scurrilous, sedate, sedentary, selective, selfish, self-righteous, self-satisfied, sensible, sentimental, serious, seriously, set, severe, short-sighted, silly, simple, sincere, sly, smart, smug, sneaky, sober, solemn, sour, spineless, spirited, spiritless, spiteful, spontaneous, sprightly, square, staunch, steadfast, steady, stern, stout, straight, strenuous, strict, strong, subjective, sunny, susceptible, suspicious, sweet, sympathetic, tame, tardy, temperate, tempestuous, tenacious, tender, tentative, tepid, testy, thoughtful, thoughtless, tireless, together, tolerant, torn, touched, touchy, tough, tractable, tranquil, true, truthful, unaffected, unbiased, uncommitted, uncompromising, unconcerned, unconscious, uncritical, understanding, unfeeling, unflappable, ungodly, unholy, unimaginative, uninspired, unprejudiced, unreliable, unstable/unsteady, unsympathetic, untoward, untrustworthy, unwavering, unwilling, unyielding, vehement, vengeful, venomous, versatile, vicious, vigilant, vindictive, virulent, wakeful, wanton, warm, weak, wholehearted/whole-hearted, willful, witty, wooden, youthful

543　is an attribute of: appear, appearance, belong, quality, savor, seem, sound, trivia

544　manner: abominable, absurd, advisedly, aimless, although, anyhow, anyway, as, beautifully, blah, blind, breezy, broken, brutal, brutally, busily, businesslike, busy, by, calm, camp, casual, catchy, circuitous, circumspect, counter, covert, covertly, cumbersome, delicately, despite, dreary, easy, equable, ergo, even, foolish, foolishly, for, forcibly, forthwith, fortunately, freely, frenzied, frequently, gradual, gradually, grievous, grim, grisly, hastily, helter-skelter, how, however, ill-advised, immediately, immoderate, impersonal, impolitic, inadvertent, incautious, incidentally, indelicate, indirect, intentional, intently, involuntary, irregularly, irresponsible, just, justly, kindly, lackadaisical, largely, leisurely, less, lightly, little, long, low-key, luckily, luxuriate, luxurious, madly, mainly, manual, markedly, mechanical, methodical/methodic, meticulous, mightily, misguided, misspent, moderately, monotonous, more, moreover, most, mostly, much, mutually, narrowly, naturally, necessarily, nevertheless, notwithstanding, objectively, of course, openly, otherwise, outwardly, over, overly, parenthetical, partially, pell-mell, perfectly, perfunctory, per se, personally, piecemeal, poorly, positively, possibly, posthaste, powerfully, presumably, primarily, principally, progressive, promptly,

providing/provided, punctual, purely, purposeless, purposely, quick, rampant, rapidly, rather, readily, recurrent, regardless, regular, relatively, reliable, separately, seriously, sheer, simply, slightly, solely, somehow, still, straight, strategic, subtle, summarily, superficially, swimmingly, though, through, thus, together, too, true, ulterior, unawares, unconditional, unconscious, undercover, underhand, unduly, unexpected, unfair, unforeseen, unusually, unwitting, venomous, very, via, vice versa, violent, virtual, virtually, voluntarily, voluntary, well, while, wrong, yet

545　morality: abandoned, answerable, astray, atrocious, bad, badly, bawdy, black, blasphemous, blue, broad, coarse, common, conscientious, contraband, corrupt, criminal, crooked, culpable, cunning, damnable, damned, dark, debauched, decadent, degenerate, demonic/demoniac/demoniacal, depraved, devilish, diabolic, dirty, disorderly, dissipated, dissolute, drunk, egregious, elevated, equitable, erotic, errant, ethical, evil, faithful, faithless, fast, faultless, fickle, filthy, flagrant, fleshly, fraudulent, frightful, good, gross, guileless, guiltless, guilty, heathen, heretical, holy, honest, ignoble, ill, illegal, illicit, immaculate, immoral, impious, improper, impure, incorruptible, indecent, indefensible, indelicate, inexcusable, infamous, infernal, inhuman/inhumane, innocent, insidious, insincere, involved, irreproachable, just, justifiable, justly, lawful, lawless, lewd, liable, libidinous, licentious, loose, loyal, mischievous, miscreant, moral, nasty, naughty, nefarious, obscene, off-color, perverted, profane, profligate, promiscuous, racy, rakish, rank, raw, religious, reputable, responsible, right, righteous, rightful, risqué, rotten, sadistic, scandalous, scurrilous, seamy, secret, sensational, shady, shameful, shameless, sharp, sinful, smutty, sordid, sorry, spicy, suggestive, unconscionable, unethical, unfair, unfaithful, ungodly, unjust, unprincipled, unscrupulous, untrue, untrustworthy, unwarranted, upright, upstanding, valid, veracious, vicious, vile, virtuous, vulgar, wanton, wholesome, wicked, wily, worthy, wrong, wrongful

546　necessity: absent, applied, auxiliary, bereft, binding, capital, chosen, collateral, component, compulsory, controversial, deciding, dependent, dire, discretionary, dispensable, elementary, enough, essential, expendable, extra, extraneous, famished, fresh, fundamental, gratuitous, imperative, inadequate, inapplicable, indebted, indispensable, insatiable, insufficient, integral, intrinsic, introductory, lacking, main, mandatory, marketable, meager, necessary, needless, nonessential, obligatory, preparatory, prerequisite, providing/provided, provisional, radical, required/requisite, rudimentary, shy, staple, starving/starved, strategic, superfluous, ultimate, underlying, undue, unduly, unnecessary, vital, wanting

547　normality: aberrant, abnormal, accepted, accustomed, all right, anomalous, astonishing, atypical, average, bizarre, characteristic, classic, common, conventional, curious, customarily, customary, disguised, eccentric, everyday, exorbitant, extreme, familiar, formal, general, generally, habitual, incidental, incongruous, irregular, lowly, macabre, mean, mediocre, medium, middle, middling, moderate, modest, mundane, natural, nondescript, normal, normally, ordinary, pedestrian, plain, prevalent, prosaic, reasonable, regular, routine, stock, temperate, typical, unaccustomed, unimaginative, uninspired, usual

548 occurrence: amusing, atrocious, ceremonial, ceremonious, chaotic, chronological, closed, coincident, coincidental, consequent, covert, covertly, crowning, cumulative, cursed, dangerous, dangerously, dark, desperate, didactic, dire, disagreeable, disastrous, disgusting, dismal, dramatic, droll, dull, egregious, embarrassing, empirical/empiric, endurable, enjoyable, ensuing, eventful, exciting, excruciating, exhilarating, exigent, exposed, express, festive, forbidden, forced, forcibly, forthcoming, fortuitous, foul, furious, furtive, futile, gala, gloomy, grateful, grave, grievous, gruesome, hairy, half-baked, hapless, happily, harrowing, hazardous, heavy, hectic, heinous, historic, historical, hopeful, hopeless, humdrum, hurried, ill-advised, ill-fated/ill-starred, ill-timed, imminent, impending, inane, inauspicious, incidental, inconclusive, inconvenient, incurable, indefensible, informal, insane, ironic/ironical, irregularly, jolly, joyful/joyous, joyless, juicy, lackluster, late, limit, lively, low-key, ludicrous, madcap, magic/magical, maiden, memorable, menacing, meritorious, merry, meteoric, miraculous, misguided, misleading, mostly, much, murderous, nasty, nearing, necessary, nefarious, nice, objectionable, offensive, ominous, oncoming, opportune, oppressive, outlandish, over, overall, overblown, overdue, partisan, peaceable, penal, pending, perilous, permissible, pernicious, pessimistic, pleasant, poignant, pointless, poor, predetermined, predictable, premeditated, preposterous, pressing, primarily, privileged, promising, propitious, prospective, prosperous, queer, random, rather, realistic, regardless, regrettable, rewarding, ridiculous, risky, risqué, rollicking, romantic, rosy, routine, ruinous, sad, safe, scary, secretive, secretly, self-evident/self-explanatory, senseless, sequential, shocking, simultaneous, sinful, sinister, slow, someday, somewhat, soon, speedy, spontaneous, studied, stupid, sure, surreptitious, swell, taboo, tacit, tame, tardy, tedious, tender, tense, terminal, thankless, then, thick, threatening, thrilling, through, ticklish, tight, together, tolerable, topsy-turvy, touchy, tragic, trial, trying, tumultous/tumultuous, ugly, unadvised, unaffected, unauthorized, unawares, unbelievable, uneasy, uneventful, unexpected, unfair, unforeseen, unfortunate, unfriendly, ungodly, unhappy, unholy, unimaginable, unimaginative, uninspired, unintentional/unintended, uninteresting, unlucky, unobtrusive, unreasonable, unrelenting, unsophisticated, unspeakable, untimely,

untoward, untroubled, unwarranted, unwise, unwitting, urgent, venturesome, warlike, weighty, well, whimsical, wholehearted/whole-hearted, woeful, wrong, yet

549 original: aboriginal, ancestral, automated, automatic, bastard, born, built-in, classical, colonial, congenital, constitutional, counterfeit, derivative, domestic, essential, ethereal, ethnic, exotic, extraneous, extrinsic, foreign, from, genetic, hereditary, human, humble, ignoble, illegitimate, implicit, imported, inborn/inbred, indigenous, ingrained, inherent, innate, intimate, low, lowly, medieval, misbegotten, mortal, mystic/mystical, native, noble, organic, original, patrician, pedigree, plebeian, preliminary, premature, primary/prime, proper, provincial, racial, radical, royal, rudimentary, secondary, secular, strange, thoroughbred, underlying, unprecedented, vernacular

550 peculiarity: ablaze, adaptable, aggressive, airy, ashamed, austere, authoritative, babyish, born, characteristic, clement, closed, contemptible, continent, conventional, corny, craven, cultured, dead, defensive, dreadful, fastidious, forbidding, forceful, forgetful, gawky, gingerly, halting, laborious, laughable, leisurely, protective, punctual

551 permanency: abiding, always, chronic, endless, fixed, fleeting, fly-by-night, forever, fugitive, invincible, irrevocable, lasting, makeshift, passing, permanent, perpetual, standing, stationary, stopgap, temporary, tentative, unchanging

552 probability: absurd, accidental, alleged, apparent, apparently, attainable, chance, chancy, clearly, conceivable, contingent, convincing, credible, definitely, dicey, disposed, doubtless, dubious, earthly, easily, eventual, eventually, far-fetched, feasible, fishy, fluky, fortuitous, funny, groundless, hardly, hypothetical, ideal, iffy, illusory/illusive, imaginable, immune, implausible, impossible, impractical/impracticable, improbable, inconceivable, incredible, inevitable, insurmountable, intended, invalid, legendary, liable, likely, logical, marvelous, maybe, negligible, odd, off, optional, ostensible, out, outside, perhaps, plausible, possible, possibly, potential, preposterous, presumably, probable, probably, prone, prospective, remote, ridiculous, slender/slim, so-called, sound, specious, subject, tenable, tentative, unlikely, unrealistic, unreliable, vain, viable, workable

553 repetition: again, alternate, away, redundant, repeatedly, repetitious

554 restrictiveness: absolute, all, autonomous, beyond, binding, bound, bounded, boundless, captive, cloistered, concentrated, conditional, confined, exclusive, exclusively, exclusive of, exempt, finite, fixed, independent, independently, limited, narrow, numbered, oligarchic, permissible, prohibited, prohibitive, provisional, qualified, rampant

555 social: accommodating, allied, amorous, antisocial, aristocratic, awkward, bigoted, blameless, brotherly, burlesque, busy, chummy, civilian, clandestine, clannish, close, commemorative, companionable, compatible, congenial, conjugal, connubial, cooperative, cultural, dear, defenseless, depressed, difficult, dignified, disadvantageous, disaffected, disgraceful, dishonorable, elite, eminent, engaged, fallen, familiar, forsaken, friendless, friendly, frisky, gentle, homeless, hospitable, hot, important, inelegant, intimate, lonely, lonesome, marital, matrimonial, meddlesome, near, noble, nuptial, platonic, popular, preferred, prestigious, recluse/reclusive, refined, single, sociable, social, sole, solitary, thick, thoughtful, thoughtless, unaccompanied, unapproachable, unmarried, unpopular, unsociable, unwelcome, unworldly, upper, welcome

556 specialization: alone, circumstantial, express, expressly, finicky, respective

557 specificity: accurate, all right, approximate, careless, catholic, certain, closely, correct, definite, descriptive, detailed, exact, exactly, extra, fine, general, just, lax, limited, literal, literally, meticulous, minute, namely, nice, particular, particularly, pat, peculiar, perfect, photographic, precise, precisely, proper, punctilious, random, right, rigorous, rough, rude, sectional, separate, simply, smack, special, specially, specific, specifically, strict, such, superficial, systematic, thorough/thoroughgoing, thoroughly, topical, very, wholly

558 suitability: absurd, acceptable, accepted, accordingly, adequate, adequately, agreeable, all right, ample, amply, applicable, appropriate, apropos, apt, awkward, becoming, befitting, best, conformable, congruous, correct, correctly, cut out for, decent, decorous, de rigueur, discordant, done, down-to-earth, due, duly, eligible, enough, excusable, exorbitant, expedient, extreme, favorable, favorably, feasible, felicitous, fit, fitted, fitting, fullgrown/full-fledged, fully, germane, good, granted, happy, improper, inadmissible, inadvisable, inapplicable, inappropriate, inapt, incongruous, incorrect, ineligible, inept, inopportune, just, justifiable, lame, legitimate, livable, meet, nice, objectionable, okay, old, orthodox, passable, pat, perfect, pertinent, presentable, previous, proper, reasonable, relative, relevant, right, rightful, ripe, satisfactory, seasonable, seemly, senseless, sound, sufficient, suitable, tenable, timely, unacceptable, unasked, unbecoming, undue, unfit, unsatisfactory, unseemly, unsuitable, untoward, unwarranted, unworthy, weak, well, wrong

559 transmission: infectious, passable, roundabout

560 usefulness: acting, adequately, barren, broken, convenient, damaged, dead, defective, defunct, dependable, derelict, desert, desirable, desolate, dilapidated, dissipated, drained, effective, effete, efficient, employed, enervated, excessive, exhausted, expedient, extravagant, faded, fallow, faulty, finished, fitted, fixed, fruitful, fruitless, functional, futile, good, handy, helpful, hollow, idle, impaired, impoverished, inactive, ineffective/ineffectual, inefficient, infallible, infertile, instead, instrumental, interim, invalid, irrelevant, leftover, live, living, lost, makeshift, misspent, null, obsolete, occupied, old,

open, operative, outmoded, practicable, practical, prepared, prodigal, productive, propitious, purposeless, ready, residual, ripe, running, salubrious, satisfactory, serviceable, short, spent, stopgap, subservient, subsidiary, substitute, sufficient, superfluous, surplus, trial, tributary, under, unrealistic, usable, useful, useless, user-friendly, utilitarian, vacant, valuable, viable, virgin/virginal, visionary, void, wanting, workable, working, worn/worn-out, worthless, worthwhile

COMPARATIVE

561 compared with: contrast, mark, touch

562 complexity: abstruse, artless, backward, bare, baroque, bilateral, blank, clarion, clear, complex, complicated, crude, cursory, elaborate, elementary, exaggerated, fancy, graphic, intricate, involved, modest, pell-mell, simple, simply, sophisticated, tortuous, tricky, ultra, unsophisticated, unwieldy

563 correspondence: akin, allied, applicable, close, commensurate, concurrent, conformable, congruent, congruous, consistent, consonant, duplicate, harmonious, kindred, likewise, moderate, mutual, proportionate/proportional, relative, sympathetic, twin, unanimous, united, unrelated

564 difference: alien, altered, alternative, ambivalent, another, assorted, atypical, avant-garde, averse, bizarre, converse, curious, deviant, diametric/diametrical, different, differently, discordant, discrepant, discrete, disparate, disproportionate, dissimilar, dissonant, distinct, distinctive, divergent, diverse, eccentric, especial, especially, exceptional, extraordinary, fantastic, freakish, funny, heterogeneous, incompatible, inconsistent, individual, inverse, irreconcilable, manifold, miscellaneous, mixed, monstrous, motley, multiple/multifarious, new, novel, odd/oddball, offbeat, opposed/opposing, opposite, other, particular, peculiar, phenomenal, polar, preternatural, quaint, queer, remote, repugnant, rival, separate, several, single, singular, sole, special, specific, specifically, strange, sundry, suspicious, unaccountable, unaccustomed, uncanny, uncommon, unconventional, underground, unearthly, unequal, unfamiliar, unheard-of, unique, unlike, unnatural, unorthodox, unprecedented, unrelated, unthinkable, unusual, variant, varied, various, vice versa, weird

565 difficulty: agonizing, arduous, awkward, complicated, defective, deficient, delicate, demanding, easily, easy, effortless, facile, formidable, grueling, hard, heavy, inaccurate, insurmountable, knotty, laborious, murderous, onerous, ponderous, prickly, rigorous, rugged, serious, seriously, severe, sticky, stiff, tall, taxing, thorny, ticklish, tight, tough, treacherous, troublesome, trying, uphill, weighty, wicked

566 equivalence: alike, alternate, approximately, balanced, commensurate, comparable, comparative, coordinate, corresponding, disproportionate, duplicate, equal, equivalent, even, identical, indistinguishable, level, matching, mock, model, nearly, reciprocal, regular, same, uneven

567 importance: above, august, below, beneath, beneficial, central, chiefly, chosen, climacteric/climacteric, collateral, component, conspicuous, costly, dear, dogmatic, elevated, essential, estimable, exclusive, front, fundamental, grave, high, holy, immediate, important, inferior, known, main, majestic, material, meaningful, noteworthy, noticeable, operative, precious, pregnant, primary/prime, prodigious, reputable, salient, second-rate/second-class, significant, special, strategic, telling, top, towering, upper, vital, worthwhile, worthy

568 importance, extreme: acute, basic, basically, beloved, best, better, big, blessed, bright, brilliant, burning, capital, cardinal, celebrated, chief, consequential, considerable, critical, crucial, deciding, dire, divine, dominant, earnest, eminent, exigent, fabled, famous, fatal, fateful, favored, favorite, first, foremost, glorious, grand, great, hallowed, head, historic, illustrious, immortal, influential, invaluable, key, legendary, major, master, momentous, monumental, necessary, notable, noted, noteworthy, oligarchic, outstanding, overriding, paramount, pet, pivotal, praiseworthy, predominant, preeminent, premier, pressing, prestigious, priceless, principal, prominent, renowned, ruling, serious, seriously, signal, significant, sovereign, splendid, star, substantial, supreme, ultimate, uppermost, urgent, valuable, weighty, well-known

569 intensity: acute, almighty, awfully, bad, badly, biting, blatant, bloody, concentrated, considerably, desperate, desperately, drastic, exceedingly, exquisite, extra, extreme, extremely, greatly, harsh, heavy, high, highly, immoderate, insanely, intense, mightily, most, notably, outrageous, powerfully, pretty, profound, quite, severe, severely, sharp, somewhat, stark, stiff, stringent, strong, substantially, terribly, terrific, too, ultra, unconscionable, undue, unduly, unmitigated, unusually, very, violent, vivid, wild

570 negative: adverse, affected, amiss, apocryphal, awful, awfully, bad, baleful, baneful, base, black, conflicting, creepy, cruel, damnable, damned, defiled, degenerate, deleterious, delinquent, deplorable, derogatory, despicable, detrimental, dire, direful, done for, egregious, empty, erroneous, evil, fallacious, false, faulty, fearful, filthy, grim, grisly, heinous, icky, ill, imperfect, inadequate, inauspicious, incendiary, incorrect, incorrigible, inexcusable, infamous, injurious, inordinate, insecure, lame, loathsome, miserable, misguided, misspent, negative, null, objectionable, off, poor, prejudicial, rancid, rotten, ruinous, run-down, seedy, slipshod, squalid, tasteless, terribly, threatening, undesirable, unfortunate, ungodly, unpleasant, unsatisfactory, untoward, unwelcome, upset, weak, weird, worthless

571 negative, extreme: abject, abominable, atrocious, awful, awfully, bad, badly, cursed, lousy, nasty, noisome, outrageous, pernicious, perverse, poorly, regrettable, reprehensible, repugnant, repulsive, rotten, shameful, shocking, shoddy, sick, sickening, sickly, sinister, sordid, terrible, tragic, ugly, unbearable, unfavorable, unhealthy, unsavory, unspeakable, unworthy, vicious, vile, virulent, wicked, woeful, wretched, wrong

572 positive: admirable, affirmative, agreeable, agreeably, all right, angelic, astonishing, auspicious, awesome, beloved, beneficial, benign, best, better, boss, comfort, comfortable, commendable, consummate, cool, decent, delicious, desirable, estimable, exceptional, exemplary, extraordinary, fabulous, fanciful, fantastic, faultless, favorable, favorably, fortunate, fortunately, fun, good, grateful, heavenly, idyllic, incredible, innocuous, interesting, luckily, lucky, magnificent, majestic, meritorious, merry, miraculous, nice, nifty, noble, opportune, pleasant, pleasing/pleasurable, positive, prodigious, profitable, propitious, prosperous, proud, respectable, rewarding, right, salubrious, terrific, thrilling, upbeat, utopian, welcome, well, worthwhile, worthy, yes

573 similarity: akin, alike, analogous, approximate, closely, cognate, comparable, comparative, conformable, different, equal, equivalent, faithful, homogenous, identical, interchangeable, like, parallel, related, representative, same, seeming, similar, synonymous, tantamount, twin, uniform, virtual, virtually

574 superiority: absolute, admirable, advanced, advantage, advisable, all right, all-time, arch, capital, cardinal, champion, chief, choice, chosen, classic/classical, coarse, commanding, correct, crack, dandy, definitive, delectable, delicate, deluxe, dependent, deplorable, dignified, distinctive, distinguished, divine, dominant, elegant, elite, eminently, enviable, especial, especially, excellent, exceptional, exemplary, exquisite, fantastic, fine, first-class/first-rate, flawless, glorious, golden, grand, great, head, holy, ideal, impeccable, imperative, imperfect, imperious, important, imposing, impressive, incomparable, ineffable, infallible, inferior, inimitable, irreproachable, irresistible, junior, laudable, leading, less, lofty, low, luscious, lush, luxuriant, luxurious, majestic, major, marvelous, matchless, maximum, menial, mint, model, omnipotent, optimum, outstanding, paramount, peerless, perfect, perfectly, pet, phenomenal, poor, poorly, powerful, praiseworthy, predominant, preeminent, preferred, premium, prevalent, primary/prime, principal, privileged, prize, prodigious, proud, rare, remarkable, renowned, reputable, rotten, royal, ruling, sacred, secondary, second-rate/second-class, select, senior, sensational, signal, solemn, spectacular, splendid, stately, striking, stunning, stupendous, sublime, sumptuous, super, superb, superior, superlative, supreme, swell, tasteful, top, transcendent/transcendental, tremendous, ultimate, uncommon, unequaled, unerring, unique, unparalleled, unprecedented, utmost, utopian, venerable, vintage, whole, wonderful

575 unimportance: empty, expendable, frivolous, immaterial, inconsequential/inconsiderable, insignificant, irrelevant, lesser, lightweight, little, meaningless, menial, minor, minute, moderate, needless, negligible, nominal, nonessential, ordinary, peripheral, petty, piddling, puny, remote, second, secondary, side, slight, small, so-so, subject, subordinate, subservient, subsidiary, substitute, tenuous, trifling, trivial, under, unimportant, vain, vapid, worthless

PHYSICAL

576 accessibility: accessible, adaptable, approachable, arcane, available, bereft, blind, broad, clandestine, close, closed, concealed, confidential, confidentially, cryptic, dark, defenseless, depleted, discernible, dissipated, distant, dubious, engaged, enigmatic/enigmatical, esoteric, exposed, flagrant, furtive, glaring, graphic, hidden, hush-hush, illegible, impenetrable, inaccessible, incognito, inconspicuous, inner, inscrutable, inside, insoluble, known, latent, legible, lost, manifest, missing, mobile, mysterious, nameless, obscure, observable, obtainable, occult, open, optional, out, outward, outwardly, passable, patent, perceptible, permeable, plain, possible, privy, prohibited, pronounced, public, rare, ready, recondite, reserved, secluded, secret, stealthy, strange, tight, ulterior, unapproachable, undercover, underground, unheard-of, unidentified, unknown, unseen, usable, user-friendly, vigilant, visible, visual, weak, willing

577 accompaniment: abandoned, again, alone, along, also, and, attendant, complementary, concomitant, connected, deserted, each, en masse, en route, ensemble, et cetera, except, furthermore, incidental, including, isolated, joint, jointly, left, lone, mutually, odd, one, only, parenthetical, per se, personally, reciprocal, related, separate, separately, single, singly, singular, sole, solely, solitary, stranded, unaccompanied, under, unique, united

578 age: adolescent, advanced, afresh, aged, ancient, antediluvian, antiquarian, antiquated, antique, archaic, big, callow, childish, contemporary, crude, doddering, elder, elderly, fresh, full-grown/full-fledged, green, immature, immemorial, inchoate, infant/infantile, innovative, junior, juvenile, late, mature, medieval, mellow, mint, modern, modish, musty, new, newfangled, novel, old, older, old-fashioned, original, originally, outdated/out-of-date, outmoded, passé, puerile, quaint, recent, ripe, senior, stale, tender, undeveloped, up-to-date, vintage, young, youthful

579 appearance: adorable, aesthetic/esthetic, artistic, attractive, beautiful, becoming, comely, cosmetic, crisp, cute, dapper, deathly, decorative, delectable, desirable, disheveled, dressy, elegant, exquisite, fair, fancy, fashionable, fetching, fine, flawless, glamorous, glorious, good-looking, gorgeous, graceful, grotesque, handsome, hideous, homely, imperfect, irresistible, lovely, ornamental, ornate, picturesque, plain, presentable, pretty, repulsive, resplendent, scenic, seductive, statuesque, striking, stunning, stylish, symmetrical, ugly, unbecoming, unsightly

580 deformity: blemish, blot, blotch, chip, contortion, defect, deformity, dent, distortion, fault, flaw, frailty, freak, scar

581 direction: about, across, adrift, along, around, astern, astray, at, away, awry, backward, below, centrifugal, circuitous, counter, crooked, crosswise/crossways, devious, diagonal, diagonally, direct, directly, due, erect, errant, erratic, forked, forth, forward, haphazard, horizontal, indirect, inward, lateral, left, north, outgoing, outward, parallel, perpendicular, plane, plumb, ramble, right, rotary, roundabout, sharp, sheer, sideways, sinuous, snaky, steep, straight, through, tortuous, uphill, upright, vertical, wide, winding, wry, zigzag

582 genuineness: abstract, actual, actually, airy, alias, allegorical, apocryphal, apparent, apparently, artificial, arty, assumed, authentic, authoritative, baseless, believable, bogus, certain, circumstantial, colored, concrete, conjectural, counterfeit, credible, dark, deceptive, de facto, delusive, dogmatic, dreamy, effective, empirical/empiric, enigmatic/enigmatical, erroneous, ersatz, esoteric, ethereal, extant, factual, fake, fallacious, false, fantastic, far-fetched, feigned, fictitious, figurative, frank, fraudulent, genuine, good, groundless, hard, heartfelt, historical, hypothetical, illusory/illusive, imaginary, imitative, inaccurate, indisputable, intangible, invisible, irrefutable, just, legitimate, make-up, magic/magical, make-believe, matter-of-fact, metaphysical, mock, monstrous, mystic/mystical, mythical/mythological, nominal, nonexistent, occult, ostensible, ostensibly, palpable, phony, physical, plastic, positive, positively, pretended, pseudo, quack, quasi, quite, real, realistic, really, right, sham, sincerely, sound, specious, spiritual, spurious, substantial, supernatural, suspect, synthetic, tangible, temporal, true, truly, unearthly, unfounded, unnatural, unreal, unthinkable, untrue, unvarnished, unworldly, utopian, valid, veracious, veritable, visionary, wholehearted/wholehearted, worldly, wrong

583 location: aboard, about, abroad, absent, absentee, advance, aerial, agricultural, aground, airy, alone, ashore, astride, at, beached, center, central, civic, civil, cloistered, coastal, diffuse, down, everywhere, exterior, external, fixed, forward, from, front, here, horizontal, inside, insular, interior, isolated, lateral, leafy, left, lonely, low, middle, north, off, out, outdoor, outer, outlying, outside, outward, over, overseas, pastoral, penal, peripheral, perpendicular, polar, populous, posterior, precipitous, present, private, prominent, prone, prostrate, quiet, rear, remote, roomy, rural, rustic, secluded, sideways, solitary, somewhere, stray, surface, through, top, topical, uncomfortable, underground, upper, uppermost, upright, upside-down, vertical, void, where/wherever, wide, wild, withdrawn

584 **movement:** ambulatory, billowy, brisk, centrifugal, clumsy, destined, fleet, flowing, fluent, flying, frozen, fugitive, gawky, graceful, graceless, heavy, immobile, inactive, indolent, inert, itinerant, languid, leisurely, lethargic, lifeless, lightly, liquid, listless, lithe, lumbering, maladroit, migrant/migratory, mobile, motionless, movable, moving, nimble, nomadic, nonstop, outgoing, passive, pendulous/pendent, peripatetic, portable, quiet, restless, rotary, roundabout, running, sedentary, slack, slow, sluggish, speedy, stagnant, static, still, vibrant, winding

585 **order:** advance, advanced, alphabetical, avant-garde, bottom, center, chronological, collective, confused, consecutive, direct, disjointed, disorganized, first, following, fore, foregoing, foremost, former, formerly, forward, front, immediate, incipient, indiscriminate, initial, intermediate, internal, introductory, last, lastly/last, latter, leading, least, maiden, mean, median, methodical/methodic, next, older, on, onward/onwards, orderly, original, originally, past, pell-mell, pioneer, posterior, preceding, preliminary, premier, preparatory, previous, primary/prime, regular, second, senior, sequential, serial, straight, subsequent, subsequently, succeeding/successive, systematic, tidy, together, topsy-turvy, uttermost

586 **relative placement:** about, abreast, adjacent, adjoining, after, ahead, ajar, almost, along, alongside, amid/amidst, among, apart, approximate, around, aside, askew, behind, below, beneath, beside, between, bottom, by, close, cockeyed, contiguous, convenient, direct, down, elsewhere, en route, far, faraway, farther, farthest, furthest, gone, halfway, handy, hard, immediate, lower, near, nearby, next, on, overhead, parallel, preceding, to-

ward/towards, under, underneath, within, without, wrong, yonder

587 **safety:** chancy, chary, perilous, precarious, sacred, safe, secure, treacherous, unreliable, unsafe, unsound, vulnerable, weak

588 **speed:** agile, cursory, expeditious, express, fast, fleet, gradual, gradually, hastily, hasty, headlong, hurried, instant, instantly, posthaste, precipitous/precipitate, quick, rapid, rapidly, slow, snappy, speedy, swift, swiftly/swift, whirlwind

589 **style:** adorable, bald, baroque, beautiful, becoming, bedraggled, black, bland, bold, bourgeois, brassy, casual, cheap, chic, class, classical, classy, conglomerate, contemporary, cosmopolitan, country, crude, cultural, cursory, dashing, distasteful, dowdy, dressy, elegant, exquisite, fashionable, fitted, flamboyant, flashy, floral, florid, flowery, formless, gaily, garish, gaudy, gay, generous, glamorous, glaring, gorgeous, graceful, grand, grandiose, graphic, homely, hot, humble, improvised, incognito, informal, ingenuous, innovative, jazzy, kinky, lavish, loud, lovely, lush, luxuriate, luxurious, marked, mean, mere, meretricious, modern, modish, naked, neat, new, newfangled, obsolete, old-fashioned, opulent, orderly, original, ornamental, ornate, ostentatious, outdated/out-of-date, outmoded, palatial, passé, picturesque, plain, plush, popular, posh, pretentious, prevalent, provincial, quaint, quiet, refined, regal, resplendent, rich, rustic, salty, scruffy, shapeless, sharp, showy, simple, slack, sleazy, slipshod, smart, snappy, sophisticated, splendid, spruce, stale, stately, statuesque, stylish, swank/swanky, swish, tacky, tasteful, tasteless, tawdry, tousled, trendy, unbecoming, untidy, unworldly, up-to-date, vogue

Senses

ASPECTS OF PERCEPTION

590 **physical:** burn, caress, hear, see, smell, taste, touch

AUDITORY

591 **attribute of hearing:** audible, deaf, distinct
592 **attribute of noise:** blatant, brassy, cacophonous, clarion, discordant, dissonant, grating, loud, noisy, piercing, quiet, raucous, rough, shrill, soft, strident, vociferous
593 **attribute of noise-making:** dumb, mute
594 **attribute of sound:** aloud, audible, blatant, brassy, cacophonous, clarion, deep, discordant, dissonant, dull, faint, full, gentle, grating, gruff, guttural, high, hoarse, hollow, husky, loud, low, mellow, melodious/melodic, muffled, musical, noiseless, noisy, off-key, piercing, quiet, raucous, resonant, rich, rough, round, shrill, silent, still, strident, sub-

dued, sweet, tranquil, untroubled, vocal, vociferous, weak

595 **audible object:** acknowledgment, air, alert, anthem, aria, arrangement, ballad, bang, bell, blast, boom, buzz, carillon, carol, chant, clamor, clank, clap, clatter, click, clink, clump, crack, crash, delivery, din, dirge, discord, dissonance, drone, echo, gasp, groan, growl, gurgle, harmony, hiss, howl, hymn, inflection, jangle, melody, murmur, music, noise, peal, pop, psalm, refrain, report, rhyme, rhythm, ring, roar, roll, rustle, scream, shout, shriek, slam, song, sound, strain, thunder, tick, tune, yell

596 **hearing:** attend, bug, commiserate, eavesdrop, hear, listen, mind, monitor, regard
597 **sound perception:** hearing

OLFACTORY

598 **attribute of odor:** aromatic, astringent, fetid, fragrant, high, malodorous, musty, noisome, odorless, odorous, putrid, rancid, rank, sharp, smelly, stale, strong, sweet

599 object that can be smelled: aroma, bouquet, breath, incense, odor, perfume, scent, smell, stench, stink, tang, whiff

600 odor: fragrance, fumes, incense, perfume, reek, smell, stench, stink, tang

601 olfactory perception: breathe, inhale, nose, scent, smell, sniff, whiff

602 smelling: scent, smell, sniff, whiff

TACTILE

603 attribute of dryness: absorbent, arid, balmy, clammy, damp, dank, dry, filmy, fluid, humid, juicy, liquid, misty, moist, muggy, musty, oily, parched, sloppy, soggy, thirsty, watery, wet, wizened

604 attribute of hardness: adamant, concrete, downy, erect, firm, firmly, flaccid, hard, impenetrable, impervious, inflexible, iron, limp, mushy, permeable, plastic, rocky, solid, stiff, supple, taut, tender, tense, unbending

605 attribute of temperature: ablaze, arctic, balmy, benign, biting, bland, boiling, bracing, brisk, broiling, burning, chill, chilly, close, cold, cool, cozy, crisp, febrile, feverish, fiery, freezing, frigid, frosty, frozen, glacial, heated, hot, icy, lukewarm, polar, sultry, sweltering, tepid, torrid, tropical, warm, wintry

606 attribute of texture: abrasive, adhesive, beaten, bias, breakable, brittle, bushy, coarse, corrugated, cozy, craggy, creamy, crisp, crumbly, crusty, dainty, delicate, diaphanous, diluted/dilute, downy, elastic, ethereal, fibrous, filmy, fine, firm, fleecy, flimsy, fluffy, fuzzy, gauzy, gelatinous, glassy, glossy, gooey, gossamer, greasy, gritty, icy, irregular, jagged, lacy, leathery, lucid, matted, mottled, muddy, mushy, oily, opaque, paper, pasty, permeable, pointed, porous, powdery, rough, rugged, sheer, silky, sleek, slick, slippery, smooth, soft, spongy, sticky, tenacious, tender, thick, thin, threadbare, transparent, uneven, viscous, yielding

607 dryness: drought, evaporation, humidity, wet

608 tactile perception: feeling, itch, touch

609 tactile quality: excruciating, numb

610 temperature: cold, fever, frost, glow, heat, temperature

611 texture: consistency, delicacy, feel, fiber, finish, gloss, grain, mesh, nap, polish, texture

612 touching: brush, caress, dab, feel, finger, graze, grope, handle, itch, lick, manipulate, meet, monkey, nestle, nudge, nuzzle, pat, paw, pet, reach, stroke, tickle, tingle, touch

TASTING

613 attribute of taste: acerbity, acid, acidulous, acrid, appetizing, astringent, bad, bitter, bland, corrupt, delectable, delicious, distasteful, done, eatable, edible, full-bodied, hot, insipid, luscious, palatable, peppery, piquant, poignant, pungent, racy, rancid, rich, robust, salty, savory, scrumptious, sharp, sour, spicy, succulent, sweet, tart, tasteless, tasty, unsavory

614 taste: bite, bitterness, flavor, savor, spice, tang, taste, zest

615 taste perception: taste

616 tasting: bite, gargle, sample, savor, taste

VISUAL

617 attribute of brightness: ablaze, beaming, bold, bright, brilliant, clear, colorful, crystal, dark, dim, dingy, drab, dull, dusky, effulgent, faded, faint, glaring, gloomy, glossy, glowing, incandescent, lackluster, light, lucid, luminescent, luminous, lustrous, misty, murky, nebulous, obscure, opaque, radiant, resplendent, scintillating, shady, shiny, sunny, tenebrous

618 attribute of color: amber, anemic, beige, black, blond/blonde, bloodless, blue, bold, bright, bronze, brown, brunette/brunet, buff, cadaverous, cherry, clear, colored, colorful, colorless, crystal, dappled, dark, deathly, deep, drab, dusky, faded, fair, florid, flushed, gaudy, gay, gloomy, glowing, gold/golden, gray/grey, green, iridescent, jet, light, livid, mauve, milky, motley, mottled, mousy, muddy, multicolored, murky, neutral, opaque, orange, pale, pastel, pasty, peaked, pearly, purple, red, rich, rosy, ruddy, sable, sallow, sanguine, silver, smoky, soft, speckled, strong, swarthy, tan, translucent, transparent, verdant, vibrant, vivid, wan, watery, white, yellow

619 attribute of vision: appreciable, blind, clear, concealed, conspicuous, discernible, disguised, distinct, fuzzy, glaring, glassy, graphic, impalpable, invisible, lucid, myopic, prominent, pronounced, visible, visual

620 brightness: dark, darkness, gleam, glitter, gloom, gloss, glow, illumination, light, luster, night, overshadow, pall, polish, radiance, radiate, shade, shadow, sheen, shimmer, shine, splendor

621 clean: grimy, grubby, hygienic, immaculate, impeccable, impure, mangy, messy, neat, pure, refined, sanitary, slimy, sloppy, slovenly, spotless, stagnant, sterile, straight, tidy, trim, unblemished, unclean, unkempt, untidy, untouched

622 color: auburn, beige, blush, cast, color, complexion, decor, fade, flush, gloom, glare, hue, orange, pigment, pink, purple, red, shade, shadow, stain, stripe, tan, tinge, tint, tone, yellow

623 looking: attend, avert, browse, contemplate, contemplation, dip into, eye, face, fix, focus, gape, gawk, gaze, glance, glare, glimpse, glower, heed, inspect, leaf, leer, look, look out, look out, mind, monitor, patrol, peek/peep, peer, point, pry, regard, scan, scout, scrutinize, scrutiny, skim, snoop, spy, squint, stare, view, watch

624 occurrence of light: beam, blink, bolt, cast, eclipse, flash, flicker, glance, glare, gleam, glimmer, glisten, glitter, glow, halo, illuminate, illumination, light, lighten, ray, reflect, shimmer, shine, spark, sparkle, spotlight, twinkle, wink

625 picture: arms, caricature, cartoon, chart, design, diagram, drawing, emblem, engraving, facsimile, figure, handwriting, impression, imprint, layout, map, model, outline, pattern, picture, plan, portrait, profile, reproduction, scene, scheme, silhouette, sketch, table, tableau

626 seeing: behold, distinguish, eye, gaze, make out, mark, meet, note, notice, observe, perceive, regard, remark, see, sight, spot, view, witness

627 visibility change: blur, clear, dim, fog

628 visible object: acknowledgment, alert, aspect, beacon, beam, blaze, buoy, cue, glance, glare, hallmark, halo, handwriting, light, mirage, model, outlook, panorama, prospect, ray, reflection, scene, scenery, sparkle, streak, track, view

629 visual perception: blindness, perspective, sight, vision

States

ABSTRACT

630 ability: ability, agility, artifice, artistry, awkwardness, bent, can, capability, capacity, competence, dexterity, disqualification, ease, efficiency, eloquence, endowment, expertise/expertness, facility, faculty, feebleness, flair, gift, hand, handicraft, head, inability, inclination, knack, know-how, league, literacy, master, mastery, mind, niche, performance, power, productivity, proficiency, promise, propensity, prowess, qualification, qualify, readiness, skill, talent, technique, telepathy, touch, trick, turn

631 accessibility: access, circulation, concealment, privacy, seclusion, secrecy, secret

632 be ahead: ahead, first, front, uppermost, winning

633 behavior: abandon, abstinence, acquit, acrimony, act, adultery, affectation, airs, alacrity, amenity, antithesis, apathy, arrogance, asperity, audacity, austerity, balance, barbarism, barbarity, bearing, behave, behavior, benevolence, betrayal, bitterness, bluster, brass, bravery, carriage, carry on, chastity, cheek, chivalry, coarseness, compassion, complaisance, condescend, condescension, condolence, conduct, cordiality, correctness, corruption, countenance, courage, courtesy, cruelty, culture, custom, cut, debauchery, deceit, decency, decorum, deference, defiance, demeanor, deportment, desperation, detachment, diffidence, diplomacy, dishonesty, disloyalty, disobedience, disregard, disrespect, dissidence, dissipation, distance, do, eagerness, earnestness, ebullience, effervescence, effrontery, endurance, enthusiasm, equanimity, equilibrium, etiquette, excess, excitement, exuberance, face, faithfulness, faithlessness, fanaticism, feint, fervor, firmness, flightiness, flippancy, folly, foolishness, forbearance, formality, freedom, frivolity, fuss, gall, geniality, grace, grit, grovel, haughtiness, heroism, honesty, honor, hostility, humility, hypocrisy, impatience, impertinence, indecency, indiscretion, insolence, irreverence, kindness, laziness, lethargy, license, lunacy, manhood/womanhood, manner, manners, mercy, misbehave, misbehavior, mischief, misconduct, misdeed/misdemeanor, moderation, modesty, mutiny, naïveté, nonconformity, nonsense, obedience, oblivion, observance, order, ostentation, outburst, pep, perseverance, piety, poise, polish, pose, precaution, presumption, pretense, pretension, pride, propriety, prowess, purpose, quarter, radiance, rancor, react, reaction, readiness, rebel, rebellion, refinement, refusal, regress, reserve, responsibility, restraint, scene, self-control, serenity, show, simplicity, sincerity, sophistication, spunk, steam, submission, sympathy, tact, temerity, temperance, treachery, treat, treatment, valor, veneer, vitality, zip

634 commonality: diffusion, frequency, ritual

635 completeness: bulk, complement, culmination, deficiency, entirety, finality, fullness, integrity, whole

636 conformity: adequacy, adhere, archetype, cohere, fidelity, par

637 constancy: consistency, constancy, continuance, instability, monotony

638 definiteness: accuracy, ambiguity, certainty, clarity, correctness, exactness, finality, precision, rigor, truth

639 exist in a condition: blame, condition, existence, state

640 extension: addition, continuation

641 forcefulness: clasp, clutches, dictatorship, efficacy, force, gravity, impact, impetus, impulse, intensity, kick, might, momentum, muscle, power, pressure, push, swamp, violence

642 made of: compose, have, inclusion, manifestation

643 make up: accompany, comprise, consist of, cover, form, include, make up

644 mannerism: air, attention(s), austerity, characterize, clemency, courtesy, custom, earmark, entity, fashion, foible, forgetfulness, habit, idiosyncrasy, manner, mannerism, mark, mien, mode, propriety, purpose, quirk, regard, trait, vigilance

645 morality: abandon, atrocity, blasphemy, coarseness, conscience, corruption, craft, debauchery, decadence, degeneracy, delinquency, depravity, dirt, disservice, enormity, environment, equality, equity, ethics/ethic, evil, excess, fairness, faithfulness, faithlessness, falsity, favoritism, fraud, good, goodness, good will/goodwill, greatness, guile, guilt, guise, holiness, honesty, honor, ideals, imposition, imposture, indecency, infamy, infidelity, infraction, iniquity, injustice, innocence, justice, liability, license, loyalty, misbehave, misbehavior, mischief, misconduct, misdeed/misdemeanor, morality, morals, obligation, obscenity, outrage, principle/principles, probity, profanity, prostitute, responsibility, right, sacrilege, scandal, scheme, score, segregate, sin, transgression, treachery, treason, trespass, trick, trickery, trust, underworld, validity, veracity, vice, virtue, wrong

646 necessity: absence, behoove, call for, dearth, defect, deficit, demand, do, do without, drought, enough, entail, essential, exigency/exigence, go without, have, lack, mainstay, must, necessitate, necessity, need, obligate, oblige, paucity, prerequisite, provide, qualification, require, requirement/requisite, reservation, shortage, specification, subsistence, take, void, want

647 normality: aberration, abnormality, anomaly, average, eccentricity, gauge, norm, rule, rut

648 origin: ancestry, birth, bottom, counterfeit, cradle, derivation, derive from, emanate, emanation, extraction, femininity/feminine, fountain, frill, germ, hail, head, heredity, heritage, home, inception, issue, masculinity/masculine, matrix, mortality, origin, parent, precursor, root, seed, sex, source, spring, start, stem, threshold

649 permanency: constant, fixed, forever, permanent, perpetual, unchanging

650 probability: absurdity, chance, contingency, credibility, eventuality, liability, likelihood, must, odds, possibilities, possibility, potential, probability, promise, tend

651 range: area, breadth, circulation, compass, continuation, degree, diffusion, dissemination, dissipation, distance, diversity, expanse, extent, gamut, go, jurisdiction, latitude, length, matter, overrun, panorama, play, radius, range, reach, realm, room, run, scale, scope, spread, stretch, sweep

652 restrictiveness: abbreviation, abridgment, autonomy, bar, block, blockade, bondage, captivity, constraint, curb, exemption, flexibility, prohibition, qualification

653 specialization: alone, circumstantial, express, precise, select

654 specificity: accuracy, correctness, exactness, model, point, precision, property, rigor

655 style: appeal, approach, artistry, behavior, clash, classic, classicism, cultivation, cut, dash, discrimination, elegance, fad, fashion, finish, frill, frippery, genre/genus, glamour, glitter, grace, look, mode, ostentation, polish, pomp, popularity, rage, refinement, simplicity, sophistication, splendor, style, taste, tone, touch, trend, vogue

656 suitability: absurdity, adequacy, agree, awkwardness, blend, consistency, correctness, do, expediency/expedience, fitness, propriety, satisfy, serve, suit

657 tendency: acrimony, alacrity, animation, aptitude, atrocity, care, charity, cultivation, dedication, defiance, determination, devotion, diligence, direction, discretion, dishonesty, disinclination, eagerness, earnestness, effervescence, enterprise, enthusiasm, equity, face, fairness, fashion, fervor, finesse, gallantry, generosity, grace, guile, gusto, guts, heat, hospitality, hostility, humility, hurry, hypocrisy, idleness, impatience, incline, indifference, indignation, indulgence, inertia, inhibition, initiative, kindness, liability,

mind, moderation, naïveté, neglect, nervousness, nonconformity, patience, pity, posture, presence, pretension, rage, resignation, resolution, restlessness, seriousness, sincerity, streak, tenacity, tendency, thing, tolerance, trend, trick, truth, verge, vice, vigilance

658 usefulness: agency, agent, convenience, efficiency, employment, expediency/expedience, good, help, makeshift, malfunction, medium, operation, practice, purpose, resource, serve, service, surplus, usage, use, utility, value, wear

COGNITIVE

659 goal: aim, ambition, aspiration, destination, dream, end, function, goal, intent/intention, mark, meaning, mission, object, objective, pleasure, point, prize, purpose, purpose, quarry, reason, resolve, sake, target, taste, victim, will

660 plan: angle, approach, architecture, calculation, channel, chart, chicanery, complication, complicity, concoction, conspiracy, contrivance, craft, deceit, design, device, diagram, diet, dispensation, disposition, dodge, draft, expediency/expedience, expedient, feint, form, gambit, game, gimmick, groundwork, idea, innovation, intrigue, invention, itinerary, layout, machination, maneuver, manner, method, move, plan, plot, policy, program, purport, purpose, route, scenario, schedule, scheme, shift, strategem, strategy, tactics

661 reason: alibi, angle, asset, basis, benefit, blame, boon, cause, confirmation, essence, essential, excuse, explanation, footing, fuel, goad, grounds, groundwork, hypothesis, idea, impetus, incentive, inducement, inspiration, justification, keynote/keystone, lesson, meaning, message, motive, nub, occasion, origin, pretext, rationale, reason, root, sake, solution, spring, spur, stimulant, stimulus, whim

662 request: command, demand, desire, directive, edict, entreaty, petition, plea, prayer, proposal, proposition, query, recall, request, requisition, suit

COMPARATIVE

663 complexity: complexity, exaggeration, labyrinth, simplicity, snarl

664 correspondence: accord, answer, approximate, balance, clash, community, conform, conformity, connection, consonance, consort, correspond, correspondence, double, dovetail, duplicate, fit, flatter, go, go together/go with, harmonize, harmony, identity, jibe, likeness, make, match, mate, proportion, resemblance, resemble, square, sympathy, twin, union, unison, unity

665 difference: aberration, antithesis, assortment, contradict, contradiction, contrast, controversy, converse, depart, departure, deviate, deviation, differ, difference, digression, disagree, disagreement, discrepancy, disharmony, disparity, disproportion, dissension, dissent, dissimilarity, dissonance, distinction, diverge, divergence, diversity, eccentricity, exception, foil, gap, gradation, grade, inequality, innovation, miscellany, multiculturalism, mutation, novelty, nuance, oddity, opposite, opposition, peculiarity, rent, reverse, shade, variance, variant, variation, variety, wander

666 difficulty: abomination, awkwardness, conundrum, deficiency, delay, disadvantage(s), downside, drawback, enormity, entanglement, facility, handicap, hindrance, hitch, impediment, labyrinth, limitation, matter, misery, muddle, obstacle, obstruction, plight, pressure, problem, quagmire, question, restraint, restriction, rigor, rub, shortcoming, snag, snarl, spot, task, tax, tribulation, trouble, vice, wall

667 equivalence: alternate, amount, balance, border on, cancel, cohere, coincide, coincidence, come up to, copy, correlation, counterpart, disproportion, duplicate, equal, equality, equate, equivalence, equivalent, image, make, match, model, par, parallel, parity, rival, sameness, tie

668 importance: accent, aspect, bearing, beauty, berth, best, celebrity, character, cipher, consequence, core, count, cream, crux, dignity, dominance, element, elevation, eminence, emphasis, essence, flower, forefront/foreground, fundamental, glory, grandeur, gravity, greatness, height, honor, import, importance, kernel, key, lead, magnitude, mark, matter, moment, name, nobility, nothingness, overshadow, peak, prestige, pride, priority, prominence, quality, renown, sense, seriousness, significance, signify, situation, spotlight, stature, status, stress, stuff, style, tedium, top, trifle, value, weight, zero hour

669 intensity: intensity, strength, violence

670 similarity: affinity, agree, analogy, community, consistency, equivalence, equivalent, identity, likeness, parallel, parity, replica, reproduction, resemblance, resemble, sameness, second, similarity, tune, twin

671 superiority: ascendancy/ascendency, distinction, elegance, eminence, excel, excellence, ideal, imperfection, importance, jewel, marvel, miracle, paragon, perfection, pick, power, precedence, preponderance, prodigy, rank, seniority, superiority, victory

OF BEING

672 abstraction: manifestation, oblivion

673 aura: air, allure, ambience, appeal, appearance, aspect, atmosphere, attribute, aura, background, being, blaze, celestial, charm, chorus, climate, cultivation, dash, dump, ease, environment, feel, feeling, flavor, glory, glow, kind, look, medium, milieu, monotony, mood, orbit, presence, quiet, romance, semblance, serenity, sign, solitude, spell, spice, spirit, splendor, surroundings, texture, tone, tranquility, undercurrent, veil, vein, veneer, vestige, whisper

674 bad situation: abortion, accident, adversity, affliction, anarchy, anticlimax, atrophy, backwash, bane, beaten, bedlam, bereavement, bind, blight, blooper, blow, brunt, calamity, casualty, cataclysm, catastrophe,

catch, chagrin, chaos, clamor, clog, clutter, cobweb, collapse, collision, comedown, commotion, complication, conflict, contamination, contempt, corner, crisis, crunch, curse, damage, deadlock, dearth, debacle, decay, decline, decomposition, deficiency, descent, detriment, devastation, difficulty, dilemma, disadvantage(s), disappointment, disaster, discomfiture, discouragement, disorganization, disrepair, disservice, distress, disturbance, downfall, downside, drag, drama, drawback, dud, duress, embarrassment, emergency, entanglement, error, exigency/exigence, eyesore, failing, fall, famine, ferment, fiasco, filth, fix, flap, flaw, flop, frenzy, friction, frustration, handicap, hang-up, hardship, harm, hassle, havoc, hell, hindrance, hitch, holdup, hole, hurdle, ill, impasse, imposture, impropriety, inadequacy, inconvenience, indiscretion, infirmity, injustice, jam, jump, kink, lapse, liability, limitation, load, lose, loss, madhouse, malfunction, matter, maze, mess, mire, misadventure, misery, misfortune/mishap, misstep, mix-up, muss, neglect, nightmare, nuisance, obstacle, obstruction, onus, oppression, ordeal, outrage, pall, pandemonium, pass, pell-mell, pest, pickle, pinch, pitfall, pity, plague, plight, poison, predicament, press, pressure, problem, puncture, quagmire, quandary, question, repulse, restraint, restriction, reverse, rub, ruin, rupture, scandal, scourge, scrape, setback, shambles, shortcoming, showdown, slump, smash, snag, snare, snarl, spot, squeeze, storm, strait, strife, struggle, syndrome, tangle, tiff, to-do, tragedy, trap, trial, trouble, tumult, turmoil, undoing, unrest, uprising, uproar, upset, weakness, weight, wreck

675 danger: calamity, cataclysm, corner, crunch, curse, danger, dilemma, disaster, emergency, fatality, hardship, hazard, ill, jeopardy, mayhem, menace, peril, poison, risk, scourge, seriousness, smash, threat, tragedy, trouble, venture, violence

676 effect: amount, attraction, because, cogency, combustion, cost, culmination, effectiveness, efficacy, feebleness, magnetism, potency, proceed, punch, splash, tell, therefore, wash

677 effort: concentration, cooperation, difficulty, diligence, direct, effort, exertion, force, go, groove, idleness, industry, plod, sweat, toil, trouble, try, work, yoke

678 experience: background, callow, career, culture, heritage, history, ignorance, lead (a life), life, live, maturity, mellow, memory, naive, naïveté, phenomenon, practical, readiness, record, sustain, taste, training, unaccustomed, unfamiliar, veteran, world, young

679 fate: accident, blessing, break, catch, chaff, chance, contingency, cost, demise, destiny, disadvantage, doom, downfall, dues, duty, fate, fluke, fortune, freak, future, godsend, good, jinx, judgment, limbo, lot, luck, misfortune/mishap, oblivion, outlook, payoff, penalty, pitfall, plague, portion, reverse, setback, shortcoming, suspense, turning point, undoing, weight

680 function: application, avail, bar, begin, bolt, cloak, closure, cord, cushion, decoy, deterrent, disguise, dump, gauge, operate, operation, run, spray, tie

681 inaction: abeyance, abide, asleep, bide, dalliance, dally, dawdle, doze, drag, fool around, forbear, forgo, hang, hesitate, hesitation, idleness, inertia, leisure, linger, loaf, loiter, lounge, neglect, nod, procrastinate, refrain, relief, remain, repose, respite, rest, shirk, skip, slack/slacken, stay, wait

682 meaning: ambiguity, connotation, content, context, cryptic, denotation, denote, double entendre, drift, drive at, emphasis, express, fiber, gist, imply, import, importance, light, matter, mean, meaning, meat, message, nature, nub, point, punch, purport, quintessence, represent, respect, sense, significance, signify, spirit, stand for, strain, strength, stuff, substance, suggest, symbolize, tenor, text, texture, theme, thrust, tone, typify, understanding, undertone, upshot, value, vein, weigh, weight, wording

683 name: alias, anonymous, denomination, designation, epithet, handle, name, nickname, nomenclature, pseudonym, term, title

684 of agreement: accord, agreement, alliance, armistice, arrangement, assent, bargain, bond, charter, chorus, coherence, coincidence, communion, compact, compliance, compromise, concert, concord, consensus, consent, contract, convention, covenant, deal, faction, meeting, negotiation, okay, order, pact, protocol, provision/proviso, settlement, stipulation, terms, transaction, treaty, truce, understanding, warranty, word

685 of authorization: approval, authority, certificate, charter, confirmation, consent, credentials, decree, delegation, determination, dispensation, enactment, endorsement, enforcement, entrée, entry, exemption, fiat, finding, forgiveness, go-ahead, grace, guarantee, induction, leave, license, mandate, negation, nod, order, pardon, pass, passage, passport, patent, permission, permit, recall, release, remission, repeal, reprieve, sanction, seal, signal, ticket, treaty, veto, waiver, warrant, warranty, withdrawal, word

687 of being an influence: bolt, contact, effect, effectiveness, fetish, gush, influence, instrument, leadership, leverage, muscle, orbit, persuasion, preponderance, pressure, sphere, squeeze, sway, wonder

688 of being a rule: authority, axiom, ban, basis, benchmark, canon, code, condition, convention, creed, criterion, custom, democracy, dictate, doctrine, dogma, edict, essence, ethics/ethic, fact, form, formality, formula, fundamental, gauge, generality, ideology, institute, keynote/keystone, law, line, measure, model, morals, norm, observance, parameter, philosophy, policy, practice, precept, principle, protocol, regulation, ritual, rule, standard, taboo, tenet, theorem, tradition

686 of being an example: archetype, case, classic, embodiment, epitome, example, exemplar, exponent, guide, ideal, illustration, instance, lesson, light, measure, model, norm, original, paradigm, paragon, pattern, picture, precedent, prototype, replica, representative, sample, specimen, stereotype, type

689 of belief: advocacy, ageism, allegiance, anticipation, aphorism, apparition, assumed, assumption, atheism, attitude, attrition, axiom, basis, belief, bias, black magic, capitalism, cause, chauvinism, church, commonplace, complaint, concept, conception, conclusion, confidence, conformity, conjecture, connotation, conscience, consensus, contention, conviction, credence, creed, cult, culture, decision, deduction, definition, delusion, democracy, denomination, dependence/dependency, derision, determination, diagnosis, dictum, disapproval, disbelief, discrimination, dissent, dissidence, dissonance, distrust, divinity, doctrine, dogma, doubt, estimate, estimation, ethics/ethic, evaluation, expectancy, expectation, eye, faith, faithfulness, fallacy, fanaticism, fantasy, fascism, fatalism, favor, feeling, fetish, foreboding, forgiveness, generality, gospel, grievance, guess, heresy, honor, hunch, hypothesis, idea, ideals, ideology, illusion, image, impression, incantation, induction, inkling, instinct, intimation, intuition, judgment, leaning, line, logic, magic, make-believe, maxim, mind, miracle, misconception, misgiving, motivation, motive, multiculturalism, nihilism, nonconformity, notion, objection, obsession, omen, opinion, optimism, oracle, outlook, perception, perspective, persuasion, pessimism, philosophy, piety, platform, position, preconception, prediction, prejudice, premise, premonition, presage, presentiment, presumption, pride, principle/principles, prognosis, prophecy, prospect, purport, purpose, racism, reaction, reality, recognition, regard, reliance, religion, resolve, respect, right, school, self-respect/self-esteem, self-satisfaction, sentiment, side, sign, slant, sorcery, speculation, spell, stance, stand, stigma, stock, subject, substance, suggestion, superstition, supposition, surmise, suspicion, taste, tenet, theme, theorem, theory, thesis, trust, understanding, utopia, view, viewpoint, vision, vow, witchcraft, word

690 of concern: afraid, aghast, alarm, anxiety, anxious, apprehension, burden, concern, conundrum, craze, difficulty, dismay, disquiet, distraction, distraught, distress, doubt, fascination, feeling, fixation, foreboding, frightened, guilt, hallucination, hang-up, horror, interest, jitters, jumpy, misgiving, mistrust, obsession, panic, passion, peeve, premonition, puzzled, quandary, question, regard, scruple, suspicion, temptation, terror, trouble, uneasy, weight, woe, wonder, worry

691 of law: abomination, annulment, autocracy, custody, exemption, freedom, independence, justice, laissez-faire, liberty, offense, order, peace, prohibition, trespass, trial, validity, ward

692 on a course: career, pitch, ramble, tack, tendency, traverse

693 opportunity: contingency, facility, fluke, freedom, handicap, hazard, hearing, interest, juncture, lead, leverage, luck, merit, miracle, occasion, odds, opening, opportunity, outlet, picnic, plus, possibility, preference, prize, profit, prospect, pushover, recourse, remedy, resort, risk, sake, shot, snap, start, strength, stumble, success, time, treat, turn, vacancy, welfare/well-being

694 purpose: application, employment, help, purpose, role, vehicle

695 repetition: boomerang, echo, repeat, repetition, return, verbiage

696 situation: case, circumstance, condition, context, environment, experience, instance, landmark, matter, medium, mystery, occurrence, point, position, situation, state, uncertainty

OF CHANGE

697 abstract: about-face, accommodation, adapt, adaptation, adjust, adjustment, back down, balance, deepen, depart, departure, deviate, deviation, digress, digression, dip, diversify, fluctuate, flux, get, interchange, metamorphose, metamorphosis, movement, mutation, novelty, oscillate, range, reconcile, redress, refresh, replace, retract, reverse, revive, revolution, rig, rotate, shift, suit, switch, tighten, transform, transformation, transition, transpose, turn, variance, variation, vary, vicissitude, withdraw

698 diminish: abate, atrophy, come down, cut, decline, decrease, degenerate, depreciate, deteriorate, deterioration, die, diminish, diminution, drain, drop, drop off, dwarf, dwindle, ebb, erosion, evaporate, evaporation, fade, fester, flag, go, go down, lapse, lessen, let up, lull, mollify, peter out, plummet, qualify, recede, reduce, regress, relapse, relax, relent, remission, remit, revert, rot, sag, shrink, sink, slack/slacken, slump, stagnate, subside, taper/taper off, vegetate, wane, weaken, wear, wither, worsen

699 fail: blow, bomb, comedown, decline, default, disappoint, disqualify, downfall, droop, error, fail, failure, fall, fault, fizzle, flag, flop, flounder, fold, founder, go, go down, go under, miscarriage, miss, misstep, neglect, omission, overlook, run out, slump, wilt

700 improve: accession, advance, advancement, amendment, boom, boost, clear up, come along, correction, develop, development, dignify, edification, elevate, embellish, embellishment, energize, expansion, furbish, grace, improve, improvement, lift, look up, mend, pay, pick up, progress, pull through, rally, recoup, recover, recuperate, relieve, repair, revision, rise

701 of state: acclimate, aging, alteration, alternate, approach, assimilate, backfire, become, break out, change, come, come about, conversion, convert, co-opt, metamorphose, metamorphosis, state

702 of structure: buckle, collapse, degenerate, dissolve, flatten

703 organizational: adjournment, dissolution, growth, merger

704 progress: advance, advancement, batten, boom, breakthrough, breeze, bring off, buildup, click, climax, coast, come on, consummate, course, develop, development, evolution, evolve, expansion, fare, flourish,

flower, form, fruition, furtherance, gestation, get along, get on, go, go ahead, go far, grow, growth, headway, inroad, jump, mature, mellow, mount, mushroom, passage, precipitate, progress, push off/push on, rise, score, spread, thrive, unfold, wax

705 unchanged: abeyance, calm, limbo, peace, quiet

OF NEED OR ACHIEVEMENT

706 achievement: ability, accomplish, accomplishment, achieve, achievement, acme, action, apex, arrive, art, attain, attainment, background, bloom, blossom, bring about, bring off, carry, carry out, climax, clinch, come at, comeback, come through, compass, completion, conquer, conquest, consummate, consummation, coup, craft, crown, deed, degree, discharge, distinction, doing, draw, drive, effect, efficacy, excel, execute, execution, exercise, exploit, extreme, extremity, failure, feat, find, finish, flair, flourish, fruition, fulfill, fulfillment, gain, get, get ahead, gift, go far, go over, hammer out, hit, land, manage, maximum, milestone, operate, pan out, pass, perfect, perfection, performance, pinnacle, potential, prodigy, proficiency, progress, prosper, prosperity, pull off, pull through, reach, record, score, smash, stroke, succeed, success, take, thrive, transact, triumph, victory, welfare/well-being, win, work, work out, zenith

707 lack: lack, loss, nothing/nothingness

708 mutual possession: communal, joint, mutual

709 need: addiction, affinity, bait, call, charge, claim, craving, cupidity, dearth, default, dependence/dependency, deprivation, desire, exigency/exigence, famine, hankering, hope, hunger, inadequacy, lack, longing, lust, must, necessity, need, partiality, penchant, poverty, predilection, predisposition, preference, prerequisite, prize, propensity, requirement/requisite, shortage, sustenance, temptation, thirst, use, void, want, wish, yen

710 possession: abundance, acquisition, asset(s), belongings, boast, buy, cache, capital, cash, clutches, commodity, custody, deserts, desolation, division, domain, dominion, due, dynasty, enjoy, enjoyment, entrench, estate, exuberance, finances, fortune, fund, funds, gain, get, grasp, have, hoard, hold, keep, legacy, lot, monopolize, monopoly, occupancy, occupation, own, ownership, plunder, possess, possession, presence, prize, property, purchase, reservation, reserve, reserved, resource, resources, retain, return, riches, savings, share, spoils, stake, store, subsistence, title, treasure, wealth

711 requirement: depend, hinge, provision/proviso, provisional, reservation, rest

712 resource: amenity, arrival, ballast, bastion, catalyst, comfort, convenience, edge, expediency/expedience, expedient, facility, find, guard, hoard, indulgence, luxury, mainstay, maintenance, makeshift, medium, mine, momentum, nurture, option, organ, pillar, plum, protection, provision, recourse, redress, relief, remedy, reparation, repertory, reserve, reservoir, resort, resource, resources, rock, safeguard, security, shelter, shield, solution, stopgap, stronghold, substitute, supply, support, vehicle

713 satisfaction: afford, suffice, work out

PHYSICAL

714 accompaniment: attend, both, chaperon, coincide, coincidence, conjunction, escort, friendship, go, privacy, relation, relationship, solitude, squire, tune, union, unity

715 age: antiquity, dotage, freshness, majority, manhood/womanhood, maturity, novelty, old age, years, young

716 appearance: appear, appearance, beard, blind, braid, cast, color, copy, countenance, decay, dissemble, double, dummy, duplicate, echo, expression, eyesore, facade, face, facsimile, favor, forgery, front, glare, grimace, grin, guise, illusion, image, imitation, likeness, look, mark, mask, match, personify, pose, pout, presence, pretense, pretext, radiate, represent, reproduction, resemblance, resemble, rise, role, scowl, semblance, show, sound, stand out, strike, surface, swagger, symmetry, tableau, veneer

717 balance: awkwardness, poise, proportion, symmetry

718 beauty: beauty, coiffure, countenance, elegance, embellishment, fright, glamour, glory, grace, hairstyle, imperfection

719 capacity: content, fill, hold, volume

720 condition: allure, apoplexy, beat, calm, carriage, comfort, connection, disability, disgust, dislocation, dissipation, distress, disturbance, emptiness, exhaustion, form, frazzle, health, maturity, peace, pollution, repose, rust, satisfaction, shape, state, stress, tangle

721 continuity: bridge, concatenation, continuity, durability, halt, length, run, sequence, series, spread, stretch

722 density: consistency, density, firmness

723 essential: austerity, brawn, corruption, decor, fat, fertility, fitness, poke, posture, smudge, tension

724 force: combustion, effort, force, push

725 genuineness: actuality, appear, certainty, counterfeit, credibility, fact, fallacy, falsity, feint, make-believe, reality, truth, validity, verisimilitude

726 hardness: firmness, temper, tension

727 order: arrangement, chain, column, concatenation, confusion, cosmos, course, disarray, dislocation, disorganization, distribution, file, form, gradation, grade, head, introduction, line, mean, median, method, order, organization, pattern, precede, precedence, precursor, priority, procession, queue, range, rank, round, row, run, seniority, sequence, series, stage, standing, streak, string, succeed, suite, tier, trail, train

728 pain: ache, affliction, agony, anesthesia/anaesthesia, cramp, crick, discomfort, distress, grief, harm, heartbreak, hurt, injury, itch, kink, letdown, misery, ordeal, pain, pang,

pinch, remorse, repentance, smart, spasm, sting, strain, stress, suffering, torment, torture, trauma, trial, tribulation, trouble, twinge, woe

729 safety: buffer, bulwark, fortification, precaution, protection, safety, security, shield

730 size: brevity, bulk, caliber, condensation, dimensions/dimension, enormity, extent, fullness, greatness, infinity, magnitude, measurement, miniature, proportion, size

731 stability: anchor, durability, equilibrium, firmness, flexibility, instability, spring, stability, traction

732 strength: brawn, durability, feebleness, firmness, infirmity, kick, might, potency, power, stamina, strength, tolerance, vigor, weakness

733 structure: anatomy, architecture, composition, delicacy, emptiness, fabric, figure, frame, framework, mesh, ruins, skeleton, structure

734 weight: buoyancy/buoyance, fat, fatness, pressure

SPATIAL

735 below: below, bottom, down, under, underneath

736 containment: capacity, contain, fill

737 depth: deep, depth, shallow

738 direction: ascent, circulation, crook, cross, current, curve, decline, descent, deviation, dip, direction, diverge, divergence, diversion, downgrade, fork, grade, gradient, inclination, incline, intersect, lean, level, line, list, meander, orbit, pitch, reverse, revolution, revolve, rise, rotate, run, slant, slope, swirl, tack, tendency, tilt, trend, turn, twist, undercurrent, way, whirl, wind

739 distance: altitude, bearing/bearings, distance, latitude, leeway, scope, space, way

740 fill: brim, charge, cloy, content, cram, crowd, flood, glut, hollow, overflow, packed, replete, satiate, surfeit, teem, vacant, vacuum, void, volume

741 height: dominate, dwarf, elevation, eminence, height, rear, stature

742 inside: contain, have, hold, interior, twine

743 length: extent, height, length, range

744 level: gradation, grade, layer, level, line, notch, plane, plateau, rank, row, rung, scale, stage, tier

745 limits, physical: boundary, confines, curb, demarcation, end, extent, extreme, extremity, frontier, limit, perimeter, periphery, play, range, term, terminal

746 location: absence, absenteeism, bearing/bearings, dissemination, front, hang, junction/juncture, lie, look, median, middle, protrude, space, stretch

747 location, relative: adjoin, border, butt, contact, cross, detachment, face, join, precede, precedence, presence, project, proximity, vicinity

748 motion: activity, agility, convulsion, discharge, hurry, lethargy, restlessness, rush, spin, stagnate, still, sweep, swing, traction, turn, vibrate, vibration, wash

749 nearness: abut, border on, intersect, stalk, succeed, surveillance, verge

750 **on:** cover, on, pile, top, traverse
751 **outside:** band, edge, skirt, stick out
752 **over:** above, altitude, dominate, overhang, overlook, rise, tower, vault
753 **sequential:** line, trail, wake
754 **shape:** bag, conformation, curvature, cut, entwine, figure, fold, form, hollow, loop, pucker, shape, turn, twist
755 **speed:** celerity, dispatch, expedition, haste, hurry, pace, rapidity, rate, speed, velocity
756 **spread:** balloon, branch off/branch out, breadth, bridge, go, latitude, range, reach, room, space, span, sweep
757 **structure:** aperture, ascent, attitude, bag,

beef, break, build, composition, condition, conformation, constitution, construction, crease, curvature, even, fabric, figure, fluid, form, frame, grade, gradient, makeup, physique, plane, ramp, set, shape, slope, stance, stoop
758 **surrounding:** circle, coil, compass, define, edge, encircle, enclose, encompass, fence, frame, gird, hedge, hem/hem in, mob, pen, ring, surround
759 **touching:** meet, neighbor, overlap
760 **width:** breadth, diameter, width
761 **within a group:** middle, range

Weights and measures

MATHEMATICS

762 **attribute of a number:** any, apiece, average, calculable, countless, dual, infinite, innumerable, just about, legion, less, light, limitless, manifold, many, mathematical, maximum, minimal, minimum, more, multiple/multifarious, multitudinous, myriad, nil, numberless, numeric/numerical, numerous, one, plentiful/plenty, plus, profuse, round, several, short, shy, single, skimpy, slight, sparse, steep, tidy, tiny, total, unreasonable, untold
763 **change in number:** accrue, appreciate, appreciation, deduction, discount, increase, increment, inflation, jump, peak, plummet, raise, reach, slump
764 **mathematic reasoning:** add, addition, appraise, arithmetic, average, balance, calculate, calculation, cast, computation, compute, count, enumerate, estimate, figure, gauge, measure, number, pace, page, reckon, scale, score, stock, subtract, tabulate, tally, tell, total, underestimate
765 **numeric symbol:** digit, fraction, number
766 **numeric value:** appraisal, count, couple, majority, maximum, peak, percentage, rate, scant/scanty
767 **quantity:** abundance, copiousness, enough, exuberance, greatness, overabundance, paucity, peak, plenty, plethora, preponderance, scant/scanty, shortage
768 **ratio:** quota, rate, ratio
769 **series:** array, chain, range, series, set, string
770 **system:** apparatus, automation, bureaucracy, business, capitalism, channel, circuit, commerce, communications, complex, cosmos, dispensation, file, finance, grammar, machinery, mail, method, net, network, pattern, post, routine, scale, system, traffic, world

QUANTIFIERS

771 **attribute of quantity:** about, additional, affluent, all, altogether, amply, below, best, better, big, bountiful, brimming/brimful, co-

pious, depleted, disproportionate, double, dual, enough, excessive, exhausted, exiguous, extra, extravagant, extreme, extremely, few, flush, fraught, further, good, hardly, huge, inadequate, insufficient, just about, lacking, leftover, liberal, limited, limitless, lush, luxuriant, many, more, most, much, new, nil, other, outrageous, over, plus, residual, respectable, rich, rife, slender/slim, spare, spent, sufficient, thick, thin, too, unreasonable, various, wholesale
772 **attribute of range:** abysmal, all, all-out, barely, besides, beyond, blanket, bodily, bounded, boundless, broad, capacious, catholic, chiefly, comprehensive, cosmic, dead, dearly, deeply, different, diffuse, diverse, eclectic, ecumenical, encyclopedic, exhaustive, expansive, extended, extensive, far, far-reaching, full-scale, fully, general, generally, global, greatly, inclusive, increasingly, indiscriminate, international, largely, lower, mainly, mixed, moderately, more, moreover, most, mostly, motley, much, multiple/multifarious, only, overall, pervasive, primarily, principally, quite, rambling, rampant, rather, relatively, rife, slightly, somewhat, substantially, sundry, sweeping, too, universal, unlimited, utmost, vast, very, well, wholesale, wholly, wide, widespread, within, without
773 **attribute of size:** angular, atomic, baby, bantam, better, big, brief, broad, burly, capacious, capsule, cavernous, chubby, chunky, commodious, compact, compendious, concise, corpulent, cramped, cumbersome, dwarf, enormous, extensive, fleshy, full, gargantuan, giant, gigantic, grand, great, gross, hearty, hefty, huge, husky, immeasurable, immense, imposing, impressive, incalculable, infinitesimal, inflated, laconic, large, little, major, mammoth, massive, microscopic, midget, mighty, miniature, minimal, minor, minute, monstrous, monumental, narrow, petite, pocket, portable, prodigious, pudgy, puny, round, scrawny, short, small, squat, stocky, stout, strapping, stubby, stunted, substantial, teeny/teensy, thick, thin, tiny, tremendous, vast, voluminous, whopping, wide

TIME

prime, primeval, primitive, primordial, prompt, promptly, punctual, rapid, rapidly, ready, right, rude, sharp, short, simultaneous, snappy, sudden, suddenly, summarily, swift, swiftly/swift, tardy, temporal, then, thereafter, timely, ultimate, unawares, untimely, up-to-date, when, while, yet

800 date: anniversary, date

801 day: afternoon, almanac, anniversary, daily, date, day, ephemeral, evening, journal, morning, night, nightly, nocturnal, noon, time

802 definite period: date, day, holiday, instant, leave, morning, noon, present, shift

803 division of: day, minute, second

804 duration: brevity, continuance, continuation, course, duration, endurance, endure, eternity, extent, go, halt, length, remain

805 frequency: rapidity, sometimes

806 hour: afternoon, evening, morning, night, noon, time

807 indefinite period: age, antiquity, anytime, bit, bout, break, breath, continuance, convenience, downtime, era, future, generation, hiatus, history, infinity, interim, interlude, intermission, interruption, interval, lapse, leave, leisure, letup, lull, meantime, minute, moment, past, pause, period, present, recess, remission, respite, rest, round, slack, space, span, spell, stalemate, stint, stretch, suspension, term, tour, trick, vacation, wait, while

808 minute: flash, instant, jiffy, moment, tick, wink

809 month: almanac, calendar, gestation, lunatic, moon, time

810 part of a day: afternoon, dark, dawn, day, daybreak, daylight, dusk, evening, gloom, light, morning, night, nightfall, sunrise, sunset, tick, twilight

811 past or future: following, future, past, preceding, previous, prior, succeeding/successive

812 proximity: immediate, near, now, prior, succeeding/successive

813 relative order: follow, precede, succeed

814 season: autumn, season, spring, summer, winter

815 specific: anniversary, beginning, date, dawn, daybreak, instance, juncture, point, present, yesterday, zero hour

816 stage of existence: administration, age, childhood, cycle, day, era, generation, life, past, phase, prime, stage, tenure

817 stage of life form: adolescence, age, babyhood, childhood, cradle, cycle, landmark, life, lifetime, majority, maternity, old age, prime, puberty, spell, youth

818 temporal association: anachronism, clockwork, dispatch, elapse, eternity, fly, following, future, haste, pace, past, precede, precedence, preceding, previous, prior, rush, succeeding/successive

819 temporal object: anytime, clock, time

820 time relative to present: abrupt, after, ago, ahead, amid/amidst, anew, antecedent, back, before, beforehand, behind, belated, between, bygone, circa, coincident, contemporary, current, deferred, destined, directly, during, early, ensuing, erstwhile, eventual, eventually, final, first, following, fore, fore-going, former, formerly, forthwith, future, historical, immediate, immediately, imminent, impending, infant/infantile, instantaneous, just, lately, momentarily, near, nearing, new, newly, now, once, past, present, presently, previous, previously, prior, readily, recent, recently, shortly, someday, soon, straight, subsequent, subsequently, succeeding/successive, topical, ultimate, ultimately, until, yet

821 unit of time measure: day, flash, minute, second, wink

822 within a time period: interim, interval, period, span, spell, stint, stretch, term, while

823 year: almanac, anniversary, annual, annually, time, yearly

WHOLENESS OR DIVISION

824 added part: arm, attachment, auxiliary, complement, complementary, excess, extension, extra, fitting, flap, fresh, frill, frippery, furthermore, garnish, new, offshoot, outgrowth, protuberance, ramification, repair, sequel, spare, superfluous, supplement, surplus, trim, wake, wing

825 bottom part: fringe, rear, rest, rump, seat, skirt, stub, stump, tail

826 core part: base, bosom, bottom, constituent, core, crux, element, essential, filling/filler, focus, foundation, fundamental, germ, heart, hub, inner, interior, internal, kernel, marrow, meat, nub, nucleus, quintessence, root, trunk

827 end part: addendum, back, border, butt, end, point, posterior, rear, seat, stub, tail

828 first part: appetizer, early, initial, introduction, lead, nucleus, overture, precursor, predecessor, preliminary, spark

829 main part: body, bulk, capital, chief, element, feature, flower, focus, fundamental, hulk, hull, main, majority, parcel, plurality, root

830 middle part: aisle, axis, axle, bowels, center, central, filling/filler, inside, inside, interior, intermediate, internal, joint, junction/juncture, mean, median, middle, midst, pivot

831 minor part: atom, bit, breath, chip, collateral, component, crumb, dash, detail, dot, drop, factor, feature, fiber, flake, fleck, flicker, glimmer, grain, grit, handle, iota, item, joint, lick, ligature, minimum, modicum, molecule, morsel, nibble, nip, node/nodule, particle, patch, peripheral, pinch, point, powder, scrap, shred, sliver, spark, specimen, speck, splinter, spot, sprinkling, suspicion, tinge, touch, trace, trifle, whisper, whit, wisp

832 of an event: chapter, close, conclusion, dawn, end, ending, finale, finality, finish, genesis, germ, head, height, highlight, inception, installation, interruption, last, leg, limit, meridian, onset, opening, orientation, origin, outbreak, overture, particular, peak, period, preliminary, prelude, premiere, preview, prime, sequel, snatch, stalemate, standstill,